Committee for Public Counsel Serv.

Training Manual for Criminal Defense

2010 EDITION

Jane Larmon White

MCLE
NEW ENGLAND™
Keep raising the bar.®

2100466B06

This publication should be cited: Jane Larmon White, *CPCS Training Manual for Criminal Defense* (CPCS/MCLE, Inc. 2010).

Library of Congress Card Number: 2010925476
ISBN: 1-57589-601-X

Massachusetts Continuing Legal Education, Inc.'s programs and publications are offered as an aid to maintaining professional competence with the understanding that neither the publisher nor the authors are rendering legal, tax, accounting or other professional advice. The statements contained in MCLE's products do not reflect a position of MCLE or its trustees, officers, or sponsors.

IRS CIRCULAR 230 NOTICE: Any U.S. tax advice found to be included in this publication is not intended or written to be used, and cannot be used, for the purpose of avoiding U.S. tax penalties or for promoting, marketing, or recommending to another party any tax-related matter addressed herein.

Due to the rapidly changing nature of the law, the information in MCLE products may become outdated. Therefore, attorneys using MCLE products should also research original and current sources of authority. Nonattorneys using MCLE products and having legal questions are encouraged to seek the legal advice of a qualified Massachusetts attorney.

Massachusetts Continuing Legal Education, Inc.
Ten Winter Place, Boston, MA 02108-4751
800-966-6253 | Fax 617-482-9498 | www.mcle.org

PREFACE

In 1997, Andrew Silverman (then CPCS training director) asked that I rewrite the *CPCS Training Manual for Criminal Defense*.

The first edition of the manual was the work of Brownlow Speer (now chief of the Public Defender Appeals Unit), and the written materials which Browny disseminated during "new lawyer training" at the Massachusetts Defenders Committee. By 1989, the Massachusetts Defenders Committee had become the "public counsel" or "public defender" division of the Committee for Public Counsel Services, which by statute was charged with the responsibility of oversight and training of not only full-time public defenders, but of the many hundreds of private attorneys accepting appointments to represent indigent criminal defendants. *See* G.L. c. 211D, §§ 9–10. The first CPCS Training Director was Martin Rosenthal, who served in that capacity until 1990. The first edition of the *Training Manual*, published by MCLE in 1989, was his work. That volume was "primarily intended for teaching and learning defense advocacy," and attempted "to provide a basic foundation for defense of indigents, primarily in the District Court Department of the Massachusetts Trial Court."

Case law in the area of criminal defense has been very rapidly expanding and developing during at least the past thirty years. In 1994, MCLE published a volume to supplement the initially published edition of the *Training Manual*. This supplement was admirably authored by Michael Schneider, then a CPCS staff attorney in the training unit, whose experience included trial and appellate work in two states. The Schneider supplement was most notably appreciated for its new chapter, devoted to jury issues.

Before and after accepting the "manual rewrite" assignment in 1997, I was guided both by my own prior usage of the manual and by defense practitioners who appreciated (as I did) that it had been the best-tailored source for certain authorities in our line of work. I heard also, however, that many attorneys had failed to break its unusual code of abbreviations and organizational structure, and were put off by its billing as [only] a "beginner's guide."

The manual now is intended to be used by all criminal defense attorneys, not just district court practitioners and "new" lawyers. I hope that its citations will well serve the most experienced attorneys as well as those just beginning the practice of criminal defense advocacy. Because I am myself an appellate attorney, I have attempted to make the book useful to others in this specialty. While I have tried to be thorough, you should always read the text of a cited case yourself before declaring it "on point" and controlling in a case of your own; it should go without saying that shepardizing is essential as well.

If you find errors in citations, I would appreciate the opportunity to correct them in subsequent editions. Please let me know (J. L. White, CPCS, 44 Bromfield Street, Boston, MA 02108).

Jane Larmon White
August 2010

ABOUT THE AUTHOR

JANE LARMON WHITE is a staff attorney in the public defender division of Committee for Public Counsel Services, and has worked in the appeals and training units and, briefly, in the trial unit. She is a graduate of Wellesley College (B.A., 1975) and Georgetown University Law Center (J.D., 1978), and was an associate at a small firm in Washington, D.C., before joining the appeals unit of the Massachusetts Defenders Committee in 1981.

ABOUT CPCS

The Committee for Public Counsel Services (CPCS) was created in 1984 pursuant to, and governed by, G.L. c. 211D, and is the Massachusetts agency responsible for assigning attorneys to represent indigent persons in all criminal cases and certain civil proceedings. CPCS's responsibilities include providing training, performance guidelines, and quality control procedures for all assigned counsel. A large majority of criminal cases in Massachusetts are assigned by CPCS to its more than 200 public defender division attorneys and approximately 2,000 private attorneys.

CITATIONS

Correct and complete citation form has been abandoned. Readers are urged, first, to read every item of interest; second, to shepardize all cases; and, third, to use authoritative citation references, e.g., *The Bluebook: A Uniform System of Citation.* Correct citations should include almost no abbreviated names, e.g., "Comm.," "D.Ct.," etc. Among the principal exceptions are reports, e.g., "Mass.," "Mass. App. Ct.," and "U.S." Typical citations used in this manual, compared with the correct citation forms, are:

CITATION ABBREVIATIONS

c 211D § 29 = G.L. c. 211D, § 29

***C v Lovett* 374 M 394 (78)** = *Commonwealth v. Lovett,* 374 Mass. 394 (1978), *habeas corpus granted sub. nom. Lovett v. Butterworth,* 610 F.2d 1002 (1st Cir. 1979), cert. denied, 447 U.S. 935 (1980)

***C v Xiarhos* 2 MAC 225 (74)** = *Commonwealth v. Xiarhos,* 2 Mass. App. Ct. 225 (1974)

CPCS P/G = CPCS Performance Guidelines Governing Representation of Indigents in Criminal Cases

---

CONTENTS

Chapter 1
OVERVIEW OF MASSACHUSETTS CRIMINAL JUSTICE

1-A. COMMITTEE FOR PUBLIC COUNSEL SERVICES AND RIGHT TO COUNSEL

See also Chapter 2, Standards and Ethics and Chapter 4, Arraignment;

G.L. c. 211D—CPCS created by statute in 1984; 15 members; Public Defender and Private Counsel Divisions; etc.;

C v Sheeran **370 M 82 (76)**—public defender attorney = OK; public defender provides competent & experienced criminal lawyers;

U.S. Constitution 6th Amendment—right to counsel;

Mass. Declaration of Rights, Article 12—right to counsel;

C v Hurley **391 M 76 (84)**, *C v Upton* **394 M 363 (85)**, etc.—Declaration of Rights (MA Constitution) = independent of (& in some situations more protective than) U.S. Constitution;

G.L. c. 263, § 5—person accused of crime has right to be heard by counsel (& rights to defend self, produce witnesses & proofs, & meet witnesses face-to-face);

C v Beauchamp **424 M 682, 690–91 (97)**; *Doyle v Ohio* **426 US 610 (76)**—protects D's request for attorney because **right to counsel = encompassed within Miranda warnings, & claim of right can't carry ad-**verse consequences, i.e., can't convey inference of guilt *(See also Chapter 11-G for more);*

SJC Rule 3:10, Assignment of Counsel—appoint CPCS if right to counsel & "indigent" or "indigent but able to contribute"; must advise re: right to counsel; any counsel-waiver must be "knowing," certified by party & judge; §§ 4, 7, 8—determinations & re-determinations of indigency; assignment of counsel; "stand-by" counsel option; § 3—waiver of counsel (waiver form mandated);

M.R.Sup.Ct. Rule 53: Assignment of Counsel—judge shall follow procedures in SJC Rule 3:10; clerk notifies CPCS Chief Counsel of murder case;

District/Municipal Court Rules of Crim.P. 3(e)—"arraignment," noting appointed counsel option;

Betts v Brady **316 US 455 (42)**—no right (yet) to appointed counsel;

Pugliese v Commonwealth **335 M 471 (57)**—**Mass. right to counsel for serious felony**;

Brown v Commonwealth **335 M 476 (57)**—(same);

See Chapter 4-B, Counsel Assignment;

Mocks v Commonwealth **426 M 1018 (98)**—no right to a **particular** court-appointed attorney; [but different if D is paying: *US v Gonzalez-Lopez* **548 US 140 (2006)**—

reversal for denying D his counsel of choice (out-of-state counsel's pro hac vice motion was rejected on ground that counsel had, in some other case, "supposedly violated . . . a . . . Rule of professional conduct," and trial court refused to even allow D to consult with this attorney during trial, where there was local counsel of record); refusing to attempt to apply "harmless error" analysis];

C v Wolf **34 MAC 949 (93)**—no right to "lay" rather than "legal" counsel, e.g., D here requested that ordained minister and theological professor be allowed to represent him;

Gideon v Wainwright **372 US 335 (63)—states must appoint counsel;** right to counsel at trial;

Argersinger v Hamlin **407 US 25 (72)—right to counsel for misdemeanor;**

Scott v Illinois **440 US 367 (79)**—no jail, no right (*See Chapter 4-A, Arraignment);*

Alabama v Shelton **535 U.S. 654 (2002)**—if declined to appoint counsel for indigent, can't later incarcerate for violating terms of probation;

Lavalee v Justices **442 M 228 (2004)**—state's failure to fund counsel for indigent criminal defendants: remedies for defendants for whom no attorney has appeared;

G.L. c. 211D, § 2A—judge may deny appointed counsel to indigent D charged with misdemeanors or minor offenses if judge promises no incarceration (and this must be noted on docket); judge may later appoint counsel for "good cause," but D then entitled to continuance; NOTE: use of uncounseled convictions (pursuant to **this** statute) & facial validity under state constitution open to challenge;

Gilday v Commonwealth **355 M 799 (69)**—no record of prior conviction can be used to impeach credibility unless witness thus attacked "can be shown to have had or waived counsel in the proceedings certified by the record";

C v Proctor **403 M 146 (88)**—same;

C v Saunders **50 MAC 865 (2001)**—conviction on which D not represented by counsel can't be used to revive otherwise stale "counseled" conviction for purposes of impeachment;

Coleman v Alabama **399 US 1 (70)**—because state's "preliminary hearing" = critical stage, right to counsel;

C v Faulkner **418 M 352 (94)**—right to counsel at probation surrender hearing in MA (*See Chapter 14-J, Sentencing, Probation Surrender Hearing);*

Quegan v Mass. Parole Board **423 M 834 (96)**—parole board lacks standing to seek removal of CPCS as counsel; public defender division may represent indigent defendants in all appeals & related post-conviction remedies, even if representation is not "required" by law or court rule, but representation before parole board by public defender OK only if there's a pending criminal proceeding & representation is appropriate in order to protect D's in-

terests in pending matter; private counsel division may be assigned to represent persons in such proceedings (other than those required by law or rules) as CPCS chief counsel determines counsel to be necessary;

C v Woods **427 M 169 (98)**—(dicta) post conviction probationary evaluation ("sex offender" evaluation) is neither "criminal proceeding" nor "critical stage" entitling D to counsel; distinguished from "classification" of sex offenders;

C v Sargent **449 M 576 (2007)**—no right to counsel at interview with "qualified examiner" under G.L. c. 123A ("sexually dangerous person" evaluation); though counsel had given advance notice to Commonwealth and treatment center that he wished to be present at all examinations of D, one qualified examiner had been unable to reach defense counsel because he was on vacation; D personally consented to go forward without counsel after explanations (including that examiner would prepare report even without D's participation); claim that D was entitled to advice of counsel regarding decision to participate in the evaluation suffered from lack of evidence "demonstrating that he did not have access to his attorney in the period leading up to the interviews . . . or that he asked [QE] to reschedule . . . so that he could consult with his attorney"; D here had already participated in evaluation with one QE five days earlier (with counsel present);

C v Trapp **423 M 356, 358, 668, cert. denied, 519 US 1045 (96)**—decision to undergo psychiatric evaluation = critical stage, but interview itself is not; decision whether to permit counsel to be present during psychiatric examination = discretionary with judge;

C v Baldwin **426 M 105, 110 (97)**—same;

US v Wade **388 US 218 (67)**—postindictment lineup = critical stage;

C v Donovan **392 M 647 (84)**—right to counsel at probable cause hearing;

Osborne v Commonwealth **378 M 104 (79)**—right to counsel at sentencing; and *Petition of Croteau* **353 M 736 (68)** & at sentence appeal;

C v Conceicao **388 M 255 (83)**—no constitutional right to assistance of appointed counsel in preparing/ presenting post-conviction motion for new trial; decision to appoint counsel in these circumstances = discretionary with judge;

Parker v Commonwealth **448 M 1021 (2007)**—single justice did not order CPCS to appoint counsel for D's post-conviction motion for new trial, but instead referred the case to CPCS "for evaluation only, that is, so that CPCS could determine whether [D's] case warranted an assignment of counsel"; subsequent decision not to assign counsel was not basis for CPCS to be held in contempt of court order;

1-B. COURT HIERARCHY

1-B.1. Administration/Powers

G.L. c. 211B, § 2—judges: 158 District Court + 30 BMC + 41 Juvenile Court Dept.; 82 Superior Court (14 counties) (per St. 2003, c. 26, § 449); *(See Chapter 7-M, Miscellaneous Issues, Recusal of Judges);*

K. Smith, *Criminal Practice & Procedure*, §§ 27–33 (2d ed. 1983 & Supp.)—jurisdiction of various courts;

***DA for Norfolk District v Quincy Division of District Court Dep't* 444 M 176 (2005)**—a warrantless arrest constitutes a finding of probable cause initially by arresting officer, & issuance of complaint thereafter by either clerk-magistrate or judge "is essentially a ministerial act," which is mandatory;

***O'Coins, Inc. v Treasurer of Worcester* 362 M 507 (72)**—judge may spend $ with SJC OK; courts have "inherent power to do whatever may be done under the general principles of jurisprudence to insure to the citizen a fair trial, whenever his life, liberty, property or character is at stake";

***Police Comm'r of Boston v Mun. Court of Dorchester District* 374 M 640 (78)**—courts' inherent powers ancillary to their statutory and common law jurisdiction;

G.L. c. 218, §§ 42A–43B—District Court Administrative Justice makes rules of practice & superintends District Court divisions;

***C v Brown* 395 M 604 (85)**—court rules have force of law, aren't just guidelines;

G.L. c. 211B, §§ 10–10A—trial court Chief Administrative Justice investigates non-compliance with orders of an administrative justice;

G.L. c. 218, § 26A, 27A—(restructuring District/Municipal Courts, abolishing "trial de novo" system, effective 1/94)—trial by jury required for all offenses within concurrent jurisdiction of District Courts unless D files written waiver after pretrial conference & compliance with discovery motions; discovery rights enumerated; direct review of District Court trials by Appeals Court;

G.L. c. 263, § 6—in District/Municipal Court, court can't deny D's jury waiver if there are no co-Ds and if waiver "is filed before case is transferred for jury trial to the appropriate jury session";

***C v Armand* 411 M 167 (91)** under one-trial system, D cannot be required to decide on jury waiver until judge rejects proposed disposition; judge not required to allow D to rescind an already-filed waiver once proposed disposition has been rejected; NB: form may be amended to make waiver contingent on judge's acceptance of D's sentence recommendation;

G.L. c. 278, § 18—in District/Municipal/juvenile courts, if D & DA cannot agree on joint recommendation, D allowed to tender plea (or admission) plus "dispositional request" which may be withdrawn if judge rejects specified disposition; pretrial motions already heard & decided in bench session before D makes decision on whether to waive jury will not be reheard in jury session, unless "substantial justice requires";

G.L. c. 218, § 27A procedures in jury of six session;

Opinion of the Justices 360 M 877 (71)—six jurors = OK;

G.L. c. 119, § 56—juveniles get 12 jurors if it's Superior Court jurisdiction, otherwise jury of six;

***C v Juvenile* 384 M 390 (81)**—juvenile's right to 12 jurors is important; (under repealed system of two-tier trials (& de novo) in District Court);

***C v McGovern* 397 M 863 (86)**—DA can indict though D elects first instance jury trial (see post, indictment supercedes District Court proceedings short of trial/dispo, subject to subject matter jurisdiction and double jeopardy bar);

***US v Goodwin* 457 US 368 (82)**—(same)

1-B.2. Subject Matter Jurisdiction: District Court v Superior Court

G.L. c. 218, § 26—District Court has concurrent jurisdiction over 5 year felonies, **except also**: assault & battery by means of dangerous weapon, indecent A&B, most breakings & enterings, burglar tools, deriving support, escape, forge/utter, larceny motor vehicle, malicious destruction of property, distribution Class A&B *(See Chapter 21-CC, Controlled Substances)*, etc.;

K. Smith, *Criminal Practice & Procedure*, § 32 (2d ed. 1983 & Supp.)—overview of District Court jurisdiction—District Court Standards for of Judicial Practice, Sentencing & Other Dispositions (1984), § 7:01 comment (84): District Court list, but **caution**: frequent amendments;

***C v Graham* 388 M 115 (83)**—derive support = District Court jurisdiction because 5 year maximum (though no house of correction alternative);

G.L. c. 274, § 1—"felony" if there is possibility of state prison penalty . . . ;

***Jones v Robbins* 7 M 329 (1857)**— . . . but no state prison without grand jury *(See Chapter 1-C, Grand Jury)*;

***C v Woolford* 108 M 483 (1871)**—District Court jurisdiction goes by maximum sentence, not minimum;

***C v Stoico* 45 MAC 559, 566 (98)**—maximum sentence for drug conspiracy depends on crime which was object of conspiracy (G.L. c. 94C, § 40), and maximum sentence for conspiracy to distribute marijuana is two years (G.L. c. 94C, § 32C(a)); since this is "not more than five years," see G.L. c. 218, § 26, District Court has jurisdiction;

***C v Sheeran* 370 M 82, 88 (76)**—still "felony," though District Court takes it;

***C v Drohan* 210 M 445 (12)**—but District Court can't give state prison sentence . . . ;

***Brown v Comm'r of Correction* 394 M 89 (85)**— . . . & Dept. of Correction can't transfer District Court prisoner to state prison;

C v Zawatsky **41 MAC 392 (96)**—G.L. c. 265, § 37 (interfering, by force, with rights secured under constitution or laws of U.S. or MA) not within District Court jurisdiction because, if bodily injury results, sentence may be 10 yrs (i.e. state prison); though Commonwealth argued that prosecution here was not relying on 'bodily injury' sentence enhancement under § 37, this was not true; conduct at issue here now punishable in District Court under G.L. c. 265, § 39 (1996 amendment);

G.L. c. 212, § 6—Superior Court has original jurisdiction over all crimes;

G.L. c. 277, § 47A—(subject matter) jurisdiction not waivable; can raise anytime (or judge should sua sponte); *(See Chapter 5-E, Jurisdictional Defects);*

1-B.3. Judge Declining Jurisdiction in District Court—"Concurrent" Felonies (& Double Jeopardy Issues)

CPCS P/G 3.1:"Declination Hearing"—strenuously argue D's interest re: whether proceed as District Court trial or as probable cause hearing;

K. Smith, *Criminal Practice & Procedure,* **§§ 670–73 (2d ed. 1983 & Supp.)**—"declination hearing";

G.L. c. 218, § 30—**shall** bind over if D appears guilty & no jurisdiction; **may** bind over . . . if within jurisdiction;

C v Zannino **17 MAC 73 (83)**—declination decision = judge's (not DA's);

C v Rice **216 M 480 (14)**—decline = judge's discretion; (timing = overruled by *Corey* **364 M 137 (73)**);

C v Norman **27 MAC 82, 91 (89), 406 M 1001 (89)**—DA could've asked judge to decline jurisdiction, reject plea, if Commonwealth was in process of procuring indictment (for enhanced charge & harsher sentencing option in Superior Court);

Corey v Commonwealth **364 M 137 (73)**—if decline jurisdiction, "probable cause" standard (*Myers v Commonwealth* **363 M 843 (73)**); n.7—must announce at outset after hearing (& maybe recuse self (**K Smith,** *Criminal Practice & Procedure* **(2d ed. 1983 & Supplement)** § 671));

C v Clemmons **370 M 288 (76)**—Superior Court barred by double jeopardy because District Court proceeding seemed "trial";

C v Crosby **6 MAC 679 (78)**—"probable cause" hearing not announced , so infer "trial," so double jeopardy;

C v Mesrobian **10 MAC 355 (80)**—(same); double jeopardy prohibition bars retrial;

C v Maloney **385 M 87 (82)**—(same);

C v Friend **393 M 310 (84)**—but if judge "reserves ruling," maybe a probable cause hearing;

C v DeFuria **400 M 485 (87)**—no "jeopardy" when D agreed to admit to sufficient facts & DA read facts; judge can bind over;

Stokes v Commonwealth **368 M 754 (75)**—juvenile transfer probable cause hearing = non-adjudicatory; later trial OK;

C v Ludwig **370 M 31 (76)**—jury-waived trial = "jeopardy" if evidence is taken;

Burks v US **437 US 1 (78)**—double jeopardy bars retrial after reversal for insufficient evidence; but . . . *Lydon v Commonwealth* **381 M 356 (80)**, habeas corpus relief denied, 466 US 294 (84): Burks inapplicable to de novo retrials;

See also Chapter 19, Double Jeopardy;

1-B.4. Probable Cause Hearing (because (Occasionally) DA Wants One, or Because D Successfully Pushes for One Prior to Indictment)—Goals, Strategies, & Post-bindover Issues

See Chapter 6, Discovery & Chapter 7, Preparing for Probable Cause Hearing (can admit at trial "prior recorded testimony"(e.g., probable cause hearing transcript) of unavailable witness); (GOAL = "no probable cause"? retain jurisdiction & guilt only of lesser-included? and/or discovery?);

CPCS P/G 3.2—usually seek probable cause hearing; prepare, investigate; motions, sequester; screening/discovery; want lesser included? *(See Chapter 5.1 & 5.2, Plea/Admitting Sufficient Facts, Negotiations, Client to Decide*); 3.2(g) order audiotape of proceedings; arrange for transcription of tape;

K. Smith, *Criminal Practice & Procedure,* **§§ 661–82 (2d ed. 1983 & Supp.)**—probable cause hearings;

G.L. c. 277, § 15—**"DISCHARGE" from custody if not indicted after 2 grand jury SITTINGS**; see G.L. c. 212, § 14A—sittings of Superior Court are set by Chief Justice of Superior Court Dept. ("sittings" have traditionally commenced on first Monday of each month);

G.L. c. 276, § 38—shall examine witnesses (for both) as soon as possible re: any material matter;

G.L. c. 218, § 30—shall "bind over" if D appears guilty;

G.L. c. 276, §§ 41–42—hold (or commit to bail) for trial if crime & probable cause re: D; otherwise "discharge";

C v Allain **36 MAC 595 (94)**—"no probable cause" resulting from successful suppression motion at probable cause hearing did not bar grand jury indictment, and did not bar hearing in Superior Court on motion to suppress (suppression there denied);

Gerstein v Pugh **420 US 103 (75)**—4th Amendment: need neutral determination of probable cause to hold D;

Coleman v Alabama **399 US 1 (70)**—Alabama's "preliminary hearing" = critical stage, so right to counsel, e.g., for discovery *(See Chapters 2 & 4, Appointment & Replacement of Counsel);*

Myers v Commonwealth **363 M 843 (73)**—cross-exam & evidentiary rules like trial (n.6); "screening" burden of proof = required finding of not guilty standard under G.L. c. 276, § 38; also discovery; but see *C v Latimore* **378 M 671 (79)** required finding of not guilty standard =

more than "some record evidence"; need sufficient "credible" evidence for jury to find guilt beyond reasonable doubt each element;

C v Silva **10 MAC 784 (80)**—probable cause hearing case dismissed partly because discovery orders were ignored (& also speedy trial right violated);

Lataille v District Court of East Hampden **366 M 525 (74)**—discovery & impeachment = "ancillary" to screening, not independent rights;

C v Look **379 M 893 (80)**—DA can call witness at Superior Court though D wasn't allowed to at probable cause hearing because not "exculpatory" (& D had excellent investigation); probable cause hearing discovery = ancillary; but see *C v St. Germain* **381 M 256, n.10 (80)** minor discrepancies in prior statements = "exculpatory" *(See Chapter 6, Discovery)*; ("Breakdown"—retain jurisdiction (& find guilty?) on lesser included offense? *(See Chapter 1-B, Ante)*; *(See Chapter 13, Plea Bargaining)* (e.g., admit to sufficient facts for lesser included offense, counsel's role if D denies) & P/G's 5.1–5.6);

Commesso v Commonwealth **369 M 368 (75)**— complete G.L. c. 278, § 58 bail review process; District Court can't increase bail just because bound over to grand jury, unless changed circumstances;

G.L. c. 218, § 30—after bind-over to grand jury, bail jurisdiction in Superior Court (new bail amount possible: warn client, & prepare arguments);

G.L. c. 248, § 21—District Court or Superior Court judge can issue habeas for bail hearing;

Superior Court Standing Order 2-86; "Case Management"—pretrial conference, etc.;

District/Municipal Court Special Rule 211— audiotapes: counsel responsible for parties & witnesses' use; destroyed in 2½ years for trial, evidentiary hearing, G plea or admission to suff. facts in crim. or delinquency case at which a judge presides; 1 year for almost everything else (so order as soon as possible, in case default & to prepare!); *(See Chapter 7-J, Tape or Transcript of Probable Cause Hearing (danger) making testimony of future "unavailable" witness available against D)*;

G.L. c. 278, § 23—inadmissible at Superior Court that D didn't offer evidence below *(See Chapter 10, Presenting Defense Evidence)*;

M.R.Crim.P. 3(e)—D can waive indictment, but DA still can indict;

Connaughton v District Court **371 M 301 (76)**—no SJC relief for denial of probable cause hearing stenographer because Superior Court has remedies—dismiss or remand;

C v Tanso **411 M 640 (92)**—District Court retains jurisdiction over case until D indicted, even after case bound over or probable cause hearing waived;

C v Matthews **406 M 380 (90)**—criminal responsibility is issue for trial, not (juvenile) probable cause hearing;

1-B.5. Prosecutorial Discretion to Indict, Depriving District Court of Jurisdiction (but Limited by D's Rights to Speedy Trial, and Against Double Jeopardy)

See also Chapter 14-B, Disposition: Dismissal & Chapter 7-O, Prepare Trial: Speedy & Chapter 19-E, Double Jeopardy;

District Court Standards of Judicial Practice, Trial & Probable Cause Hearing (1981), 3:04—don't dismiss complaint until D is arraigned in Superior Court;

Lataille v District Court of East Hampden **366 M 525 (74)**—can (usually) indict while probable cause hearing is pending; ((n.6): & maybe even if already started);

US v Goodwin **457 US 368 (82)**—felony indictment OK when D refuses to plead to pending misdemeanor bench trial;

C v McGovern **397 M 863 (86)**—DA can indict after D chooses first-instance jury trial;

C v Gallo **2 MAC 636 (74)**—concurrent felony indicted = OK without objection;

C v Allain **36 MAC 595 (94)**—despite successful suppression motion during probable cause hearing and resulting finding of no probable cause, indictment not barred: rulings on "admission of evidence" at probable cause hearing do not have preclusive effect in Superior Court;

C v Xiarhos **2 MAC 225 (74)**—indict after continuance (over objection) = no speedy trial denial; & no agreement shown (or violated); (see *Benton* **356 M 447 (69)**; *Silva* **10 MAC 784 (80)** etc.);

C v Spann **383 M 142 (81)**—can indict after case was continued, because no contrary agreement;

C v Zannino **17 MAC 73 (83)**—no "reliance" on promised bench trial;

Hadfield v Commonwealth **387 M 252 (82)**—(in theory) limit = "effrontery, obstruction, waste";

C v Raposa **386 M 666 (82)**—can nol pros & indict on trial date (while discovery pending), but dictum disfavors "deliberate obstruction & waste"; *(See also Chapter 14-C, Disposition: Nolle Prosequi & Hinterleitner 391 M 679 (84) no bad faith, so can nol pros & indict next day after continuance denied)* **BUT SEE** *C v Thomas* **353 M 429, 432 (67) ADA frustrated judge's ruling denying continuance by nol pros'ing complaints and obtaining indictments; dismissal proper;**

C v Reddy **74 MAC 304 (2009)**—on 4 District Court charges, D wanted only cc sentences to run with sentence in unrelated case on which he was being held on parole violation detainer; DA wanted 2½ years H.C.; judge told D he couldn't order "cc" on parole violation case because sentence had not yet been imposed on it; D wanted continuance to accomplish that, and judge scheduled for change of plea, to be "within 30 days," which did not happen; DA indicted D as habitual offender (exposed to mandatory 20-year sentence): appeals court reversed judge's dismissal of indictments: DA had made no promise on which D reasonably could rely (& judge here made factual finding that there was no evidence of "vindictiveness" or "bad faith" of Commonwealth), superceded by S.C. 457 M 1002 (2010) (still reversing dismissal order);

Illinois v Vitale **447 US 410 (80)**—double jeopardy usually bars prosecution for greater after guilty of lesser included offense (unless new evidence) *(See Chapter 19, Double Jeopardy)*;

C v McCan **277 M 199 (31)**—though usually can't charge greater after jeopardy on lesser included offense, can indict for rape after guilty of A&B, because District Court has no jurisdiction over rape: THIS IS NO LONGER THE LAW: UNCONSTITUTIONAL PER *WALLER v FLORIDA* **397 US 387, 394–95 (70)** AND *BROWN v OHIO* **432 US 161, 169 (77)**; see *C v Norman* **406 M 1001 (89)**, aff'g S.C. 27 MAC 82 (89);

C v Mahoney **331 M 510 (54)**—can indict robbery after "no probable cause" & G (& sentence) larceny from person & A&B; Mahoney = NO LONGER VALID RE: "jurisdictional" limitations of 1st court: see *C v Norman* **406 M 1001 (89)** (double jeopardy violation);

C v Gonzalez **388 M 865 (83)**—"reduction" was still probable cause hearing; (fn. 9: *Brown v Ohio* **432 US 161 (77)**) here inapplicable, because no "trial" occurred below)

Brown v Ohio **432 US 161 (77)**—double jeopardy bars larceny of motor vehicle indictment after conviction of lesser included offense (use without authority); but see *US v Goodwin* **457 US 368 (82)** felony indictment OK when D refuses to plead to pending misdemeanor bench trial; and *C v Johnson* **406 M 533 (90)** D's G plea to B&E in District Court no bar to vindictive continuing prosecution in Superior Court to possessing burglar's tools (because latter not strictly lesser included offense of former, & DA always intended to pursue case in Superior Court rather than District Court);

C v Norman **27 MAC 82 (89)**, affirmed, **406 M 1001 (89)**—District Court conviction for larceny barred subsequent Superior Court prosecution for armed robbery under *Brown v Ohio* **432 US 161 (77)**, even though District Court didn't have jurisdiction over greater offense;

Burke v Commonwealth **373 M 157 (77)**—can indict (or 2d probable cause hearing) after "no probable cause" finding, because no jeopardy attached;

Juvenile v Commonwealth **375 M 104 (78)**—2d probable cause hearing OK after "no probable cause," especially if new evidence;

Blackledge v Perry **417 US 21 (74)**—due process bars assault with intent to murder indictment after G & appeal on assault by means of dangerous weapon because appears vindictive & chills appeals;

Lovett v Butterworth **610 F.2d 1002 (1st Cir. '79)**—can't indict burglary (10–20 MCI-Cedar Junction) after G/appeal B&E because "semblance vindictiveness" & chills right to appeal;

C v Benton **356 M 447 (69)**—indictment barred by District Court plea bargain (& reliance);

C v Manning **373 M 438 (77)**—prophylactic dismissal for FBI misconduct;

C v Hine **393 M 564 (84)**—not egregious enough to dismiss; *(See Chapter 14-B, Sentencing . . . Dispositions: Dismissal)*;

C v Silva **10 MAC 784 (80)**—can't indict after dismissal for speedy trial violation & discovery non-compliance;

C v Thomas **353 M 429 (67)**—"speedy trial" dismissal of indictment because flouted 10-day rule; (See G.L. c. 276, § 35—ten-day rule in Chapter 4, Arraignment, but "10"-day rule was changed to "30" day rule by St. 1996, c. 211);

C v Ludwig **370 M 31 (76)**—continuance for over 10 days & dismissed "with prejudice" = speedy trial basis, so bars indictment; (but see *Zannino* **17 MAC 73 (83)** no "reliance" on promised bench trial);

C v Fields **371 M 274 (76)**—"speedy"-based dismissal bars indictment;

C v Balliro **385 M 618 (82)**—(same);

C v Amaral **16 MAC 230 (83)**—dismissal (because witness absent) wasn't for "speedy";

C v Bailey **13 MAC 1019 (82)**—dismissal wasn't for speedy or misconduct;

ABA Standards for Criminal Justice, Speedy Trial (2d ed. 1980) 12-1.3, Comment—continuance rules should cover non-trial proceedings having same impact, e.g., nol pros, with order allowing leave to re-charge;

Klopfer v North Carolina **386 US 213 (67)**—nol pros with leave to refile violates speedy trial right;

C v Pomerleau **13 MAC 530 (82)**—dismissal "without prejudice" is no bar to indictment;

C v Zannino **17 MAC 73 (83)**—"with prejudice" no bar either because unmerited or no breach of promise by D.A.;

C v Hinterleitner **391 M 679 (84)**—no bad faith, so can nol pros & indict next day after continuance denied; (see *Raposa* **386 M 666 (82)** can nol pros & indict on trial date (while discovery pending), but dictum disfavors "deliberate obstruction & waste";)

C v Mandile **15 MAC 83 (83)**—judge may take timely motion to reconsider dismissal, but 87 days not timely without special circumstances;

See Chapter 19 for cases on double jeopardy;

See Chapter 5-D for cases on lesser included offenses;

Monahan v Commonwealth **414 M 1001 (93)**—2d complaint after dismissal "with prejudice" at continuance request is improper; DA must appeal, not ignore and refile;

1-C. GRAND JURY—RIGHT, PROCEDURES, AND WAIVER ISSUES

G.L. c. 263, § 4; (also M.R.Crim.P. 3(b))—right to grand jury if punishable by state prison, unless concurrent jurisdiction & District Court retains;

C v Edwards **444 M 526 (2005)**—SJC adopts "forfeiture by wrongdoing" doctrine, which allowed introduction of "out of court statements" [here, grand jury testimony] of "unavailable" witness against Ds who intimidated, threatened, or murdered witness, or even "colluded" in making the witness unavailable/unwilling to testify at trial; "causal link necessary" may be established when D puts forward to witness the idea to avoid testifying by threats, coercion, persuasion, or pressure (BUT MERELY INFORMING WITNESS OF RIGHT TO REMAIN SILENT IS NOT SUFFICIENT TO CONSTITUTE FORFEITURE, n.23) or when D actively facilitates the carrying out of witness's independent intent not to testify; Commonwealth must prove by "preponderance of the evidence" that D procured witness's unavailability; parties must be given opportunity to present evidence, including live testimony, at evidentiary hearing outside jury's presence, prior to determination of forfeiture, BUT hearsay evidence, including unavailable witness's out-of-court statements, may be considered;

In the Matter of a Grand Jury Subpoena **447 M 88 (2006)**—spousal privilege (G.L. c. 233, § 20, Second) applies only to "TRIAL," so subject's wife couldn't claim it to avoid testifying before grand jury;

C v Barbosa **421 M 547 (95)**—motion to dismiss for "duplicity" lies when grand jury hears evidence of 2 alleged crimes but returns single count: no way of insuring that petit jury is convicting for same alleged crime as to which grand jury returned indictment; motion for bill of particulars not necessary;

C v Muniz **456 M 166 (2010)**—*C v Barbosa* error found when grand jury indictment referred to single instance of marijuana possession and trial evidence was that marijuana was seized on 2 separate occasions, albeit on the same day (conviction reversed);

Campagna v Commonwealth **454 M 1006 (2009)**—no *Barbosa* error found when grand jury returned 7 indictments for conspiracy but trial judge found that there was only one conspiracy "overarching" all the dates: here, "no confusion about the conduct underlying the indictments," and instead simply ruling of law that what was before the grand jury established at most one ongoing conspiracy: no change in substance to the grand jury's work;

C v Roman **74 MAC 251 (2009)**—D, driver of car holding 2 other co-Ds, was charged (as were others) with possessing >14 grams of cocaine: because there were 3 discrete amounts (console = 13,66 grams; single baggie = point 53 gram; in jacket of rear passenger/co-D = 27.89 grams), D argued that grand jury must not have found probable cause to charge him with jacket amount and that his conviction was invalid because based in part on that

amount, but appeals court rejected: grand jurors were not told of the greater (>28 grams) crime option, so no cache was omitted from their consideration; further, special verdict slip said G of each cache;

C v Clayton **63 MAC 608 (2005)**—Commonwealth needn't present to grand jury evidence of each theory under which D may be found G at trial; no requirement of "an exact match between the evidence presented at trial and that presented to the grand jury";

C v Berry **63 MAC 910, 912 (2005)**—same rationale, concerning multiple containers of cocaine supporting "intent to distribute";

C v Porro **74 MAC 676, further app. review allowed 455 M 1106 (2009)**—in responding to deliberating jury's question whether D could be convicted on "lesser" offense of assault by means of dangerous weapon on indictment charging assault and battery by means of dangerous weapon, judge said yes, but committed reversible error in failing to limit jury's consideration on lesser charge to the single act on which grand jury relied; MAC permitted retrial on lesser included offense of assault by means of dangerous weapon under "attempted battery theory" (noting at n.4 that "it is less clear" that "threatened battery theory" of assault by means of dangerous weapon is a lesser included of ABDW);

Jones v Robbins **74 M 329 342–50 (1857)**—"law of the land" = grand jury for state prison;

Brown v Comm'r **394 M 89 (85)**—can't transfer District Court prisoner to state prison;

K. Smith, *Criminal Practice & Procedure,* **§§ 761–22 (2d ed. 1983 & Supp.) Grand Jury**—see also G.L. c. 277, § 14A;

M.R.Crim.P. 5 & Reporter's Notes—23 jurors; 12 indict; secrecy; counsel right, but not appointed ("no witness may refuse to appear because of unavailability of counsel for that witness"); counsel may be present but not object;

In the Matter of a John Doe Grand Jury Investigation **415 M 727 (93)**—SJC vacates Superior Court judge's order allowing a TV station access to videotape of a lineup conducted at request of grand jury; disclosure "disserve(s) . . . important public interests";

G.L. c. 277, § 5—oath taken by grand jurors;

M.R.Sup.Ct. 63—stenographer sworn & takes all testimony;

A.G. v Pelletier **240 M 264, 307 (22)**—grand jury functions & activity; D.A. instructs re: law, but can't "attempt to influence";

C v Kelcourse **404 M 466 (89)**—DA can advise re: law if appropriate, but can't express opinion or overly influence;

C v Noble **429 M 44, 47–48 (99)**—SJC rejects D's argument that indictment was invalid because Commonwealth failed to inform grand jurors of elements of 1st and

2d degree murder; if grand jurors had asked for instructions about degrees of murder, they should have been given;

C v DePace **442 M 739 (2004)**—indictment for "murder" charges first, rather than second, degree murder, and needn't allege each theory of murder which the grand jury determined to be supported by probable cause; no relief, either, on argument that first trial jury's G was only under extreme atrocity or cruelty (and not deliberate premeditation), and no way of knowing whether this was a ground found by grand jury beforehand;

C v Carpenter **22 MAC 911 (86)**—no dismissal for R. 63 violation by DA going "off record" because no relevant evidence was presented & no injustice;

ABA Standards for Criminal Justice, Prosecution Function & Defense Function (3d ed. 1993) 3-3.5—prosecutor may explain law, but don't impermissibly influence, i.e., if statement/argument impermissible at trial before petit jury, improper here; communicate on the record; 3-3.6: present only admissible evidence, but can present witness to summarize admissible evidence; disclose exculpatory; should tell jurors they have right to hear any available witnesses; recommend no bill if not warranted;

C v Pezzano **387 M 69 (82)**—dismissal because unauthorized person present at grand jury;

C v Smith **414 M 437 (93)**—prosecuting attorney's presence during grand jurors' deliberations & voting, per their request (M.R.Crim.P. 5(g)), not violative of Article 12 or any federal constitutional provision;

C v Conefrey **410 M 1 (91)**—silent presence of victim-witness assistant near young sex assault complainant in grand jury room not improper;

Bank Nova Scotia v US **487 US 250 (88)**—harmless grand jury abuses *(See Chapter14-B)*;

C v McCravy **430 M 758 (2000)**—presentation of same evidence to 2d grand jury after 1st grand jury refused to indict didn't entitle D to dismissal, BUT pointed refusal to hold "that repeated submissions of the same evidence to multiple grand juries would withstand scrutiny"; states restricting resubmission of criminal charges to 2d grand jury are governed by specific legislation rather than judicial decision;

C v Wilcox **437 M 33 (2002)**—no requirement that the (at least) twelve grand jurors voting to indict must have heard all the evidence presented as to given case, despite possibility that some such jurors wouldn't have been present for some of the evidence (i.e., exculpatory, possibly erroneous identification) given over an intermittent six days in a three-month period; D's motion for discovery of attendance records of grand jurors denied;

G.L. c. 277, § 14A—witness's right to consult, have present, counsel (but can't talk); presumably indigent witness has right to appointed counsel—see *C v Gilliard* **36 MAC 183,186 (94)**;

C v Griffin **404 M 372 (89)**—right to counsel at grand jury = effective, no conflict; (no re-indict if dismissal for irremediable harm;

CPCS P/G 4.7(d)—consider motion to dismiss for insufficient grand jury evidence or impaired integrity of hearing;

C v Gilliard **36 MAC 183 (94)**—no right, under federal constitution, for grand jury witness to be warned s/he is a target; Court did not decide whether Article 12 gives such a right (fact findings here that witness/D was advised of rights not to testify & to counsel), but if there is such right, remedy for violation is not dismissal of indictment, but instead suppression of testimony (Query: but what if grand jury evidence was inadequate without that testimony?);

C v Gibson **368 M 518 (75)**—hearsay (usually) OK . . . ;

US v Dionisio **410 US 1 (73)**— . . . even tips & rumors . . . ;

C v St. Pierre **377 M 650 (79)**— . . . but can't sell grand jury "shoddy merchandise"; maybe dismissal if hearsay = really bad;

C v Leitzsey **421 M 694 (96)**—prosecutor reads witness's prior statement to grand jury, asks witness if s/he wants to add or delete anything; SJC refuses to find error;

C v Martinez **420 M 622 (95)**—no dismissal for leading questions here, or in any prior reported case, but SJC could "hypothesize" necessity of dismissal, e.g., if leading questions used "consciously and prejudicially to avoid the disclosure of exculpatory evidence";

Gerstein v Pugh **420 US 103 (75)**—can't detain without judicial probable cause finding;

C v McCarthy **385 M 160 (82)**—**dismissal for no probable cause at grand jury;**

C v Truong Vo Tam **49 MAC 31 (2000)**—indictments should have been dismissed for lack of sufficient evidence before grand jury; cop's testimony there was contradicted by grand jury exhibit (booking sheets);

C v Murphy **68 MAC 152 (2007)**—dismiss indictment for operating vehicle after suspension of license for OUI, because D had been issued a license: although it was "hardship license" and restricted hours he could drive, and D was arrested while driving outside permitted hours, plain meaning of statute ("prior to . . . issuance to him of a new license to operate") barred prosecution;

C v Alves **70 MAC 908 (2007)**—enough to indict D that in a "crate" in trunk of car belonging to D's mother (D alone, as driver) there was small gray nylon bag with cocaine and a duffel bag containing men's clothing (though not enough for constructive possession/guilt under *C v Garcia* 409 M 675, 680 [91]);

C v Rodriguez **75 MAC 235 (2009)**—after grand jury testimony that D was arrested at "1380" Main Street, prosecutor proceeded to inquire as to how close "1381" Main Street was to named school: even if this wasn't "transcription" error, grand jurors could have inferred that witness was referring to 1380 rather than 1381 when he answered question (no dismissal/relief);

C v Reveron **75 MAC 354 (2009)**—affirming dismissal of indictment for, inter alia, first degree murder: though D introduced victim to suppliers of large quantity of drugs, victim and suppliers left in car to make transaction; no evidence that D knew suppliers intended to assault and rob victim; even if D knew supplier was armed (presumed nexus between guns & drugs), impermissible to choose inference of robbery rather than mutually agreed drug deal; purported consciousness of guilt evidence (false statements to police, D not as friendly as usual) not determinative as wariness possibly concerned 15-year drug crime;

C v Moran **453 M 880 (2009)**—grand jury evidence subject to quibble (armed assault with intent to murder indictment) because threat was "contingent" or because of sequence (after D abandoned gun he threatened to kill), but SJC reversed dismissal of indictment;

C v DiRenzo **44 MAC 95, 101 n.9 (97)**—Appeals Court declined to address sufficiency of grand jury evidence because no transcript of grand jury proceedings was provided; **trial counsel must attach grand jury minutes to** *McCarthy* **motion, or have them admitted as exhibit on the motion;**

Connor v Commonwealth **363 M 572 (73)**—grand jury indicted "John Doe," so dismissal because they had no probable cause it's D;

C v Pellegrini **414 M 402 (93)**—error to dismiss indictment for "possession of cocaine" based on evidence from urine of D's newborn infant, from which mother's ingestion of cocaine while fetus was in-utero could be inferred;

C v Francil **15 MAC 35 (82)**—enough probable cause here; integrity not impaired;

C v Badgett **38 MAC 624 (95)**—evidence sufficient before grand jury if it merely establishes probable cause to arrest; bindover standard in probable cause hearing is more stringent (see *Myers* **363 M 843, 850 (73)**);

C v Riley **73 MAC 721 (2009)**—reversing judge's dismissal of so much of first degree murder indictment as charged first or second prong malice; sufficiency of evidence reviewed "according to the objective standard of probable cause to arrest"; for first degree indictment, evidence must establish one of the aggravating forms specified in G.L. c. 265, § 1;

C v McJunkin **11 MAC 609 (81)**—no duty (yet) to present exculpatory evidence;

C v Connor **392 M 838, 854 (84)**—almost dismissed for hiding exculpatory evidence;

C v O'Dell **392 M 445 (84)**—**dismissal for withholding exculpatory evidence**; McCarthy standard = probable cause to arrest, not required finding of not guilty standard;

C v Baran **74 MAC 256, 299 (2009)**—only a composite videotape, containing edited versions of interviews of child sexual assault complainants, was shown to grand jury, "a somewhat distorted portrayal of the children's allegations," which "omit[ed] significant exculpatory content," including explicit denials that D had done anything to them and statements accusing other persons of abuse, and statements that other people witnessed alleged acts

(which counsel could have use to challenge veracity of allegations);

C v Youngworth **48 MAC 249 (99)**—**McCarthy standard = significantly less rigorous than required finding of not guilty standard;**

C v Mayfield **398 M 615 (86)**—Commonwealth's reckless disregard of truth, leading to false/deceptive evidence presented to grand jury can also warrant dismissal of indictment (but evidence had to be material to probable cause question and D must establish that the false/deceptive testimony probably made a difference in decision to indict);

C v Wermers **61 MAC 182 (2004)**—no dismissal for failure to introduce booking form arguably limiting "tattoos" to "upper" arm of defendant, when robbery victim said culprit had tattoos on forearms (three IDs of defendant by same victim, and form's susceptibility to different interpretation relevant to holding);

C v Westbrook **58 MAC 692 (2003)**—rape complainant told police that she did not remember whether D penetrated her, but police testified to grand jury that she said D *HAD* penetrated (& at trial she so testified): "if" there was grand jury error, conviction of only lesser crime (assault with intent to rape) meant "no prejudice" to D;

C v Silva **455 M 503 (2009)**—detective's "no" answer to grand jury question whether there was anything that would justify D's shooting two men was "legal opinion" inadmissible at trial, but Commonwealth wasn't required to present evidence of "so-called defenses"; further, grand jury heard evidence that D believed self-defense;

C v Garrity **43 MAC 349 (97)**—evidence argued to be 'exculpatory' said not to be; trial defense based on same evidence did not prompt reasonable doubt; *C v O'Laughlin* **446 M 188 (2006)**—evidence pointing to 3rd party culprit needn't have been introduced to grand jury; it wasn't sufficient to create reasonable doubt for trial jury, so can't be said that it would have affected significantly the grand jury's result;

C v Ortiz **53 MAC 168 (2001)**—that a witness, sometime after testifying before grand jury & after indictment was returned, recanted identification of D as shooter was not a basis on which to dismiss indictments & failure of trial counsel to so move wasn't ineffective assistance; motion judge "found" that ADA didn't know that grand jury testimony was false;

C v McGahee **393 M 743 (85)**—did withheld evidence distort the identification?;

C v Donnelly **33 MAC 189 (92)**—prosecution not required to present views of witnesses contrary to its theory of case, so long as a witness's statements not distorted or misrepresented;

C v Clemmey **447 M 121 (2006)**—in presenting evidence to grand jury of illegal filling of wetlands, prosecutor wasn't required to introduce D's claim that he thought he could clear & fill the wetlands under "agricultural" exemption because prosecutor could rely on regulations & straightforward evidence that the land had not been used for agriculture for more than ten years, making claimed exemption inapplicable; that the applicability of the claimed exemption "may appropriately reemerge at trial" and/or could have changed vote of grand jurors to indict, this = "insufficient basis on which to set aside the indictment";

C v Lay **63 MAC 27 (2005)**—that prosecutor cut off witness's answer, which was about to veer into assertion that victim and companions were gang members, was not a basis for dismissing indictment, though D claimed on appeal that this concealed info unfavorable to Commonwealth; FURTHER, **failure to file motion to dismiss on this basis = waiver**; rejects argument that trial judge "should have dismissed sua sponte";

C v Fort **33 MAC 181 (92)**—officer's testimony that five eyewitnesses had previously identified D before recanting, was enough to withstand McCarthy motion to dismiss, where corroborated by other circumstantial evidence; presentation of recantations fulfilled duty to alert grand jury to existing "impeachment" of evidence presented;

C v Rice **441 M 291, 309 (2004)**—evidence to grand jury that D did not voluntarily surrender clothing for DNA testing probably did not impair integrity of proceedings;

US v Williams **504 US 36 (92)**—federal prosecutors not required to present exculpatory evidence to grand jury because grand jury "functionally independen(t)" from judiciary; NB: Mass. law to contrary, see *C v Mayfield* **398 M 615 (86)** & *C v O'Dell* **392 M 445 (84)**;

C v Roman **414 M 642 (93)**—no dismissal here for withholding evidence that D claimed drugs were for personal use (but other portion of D's statement would have made him G anyway);

C v Miranda **415 M 1 (93)**—prompted by motion to dismiss 2-count indictment due to false testimony before grand jury, Commonwealth obtained new "curative" indictment, and filed nolle prosequi on first indictment; Commonwealth could not thereafter vacate nolle prosequi as to one count of the original indictment and move for trial;

C v Salman **387 M 160 (82)**—can dismiss for false testimony at grand jury;

C v Richardson **37 MAC 482 (94)**—if Commonwealth knew false or acted with reckless disregard, & if testimony influenced decision to indict, dismiss;

C v Clarke **44 MAC 502 (98)**—for dismissal, not enough to show 'false'; must also show that return of indictment was influenced by the false testimony;

C v Leitzsey **421 M 694, 698 (96)**—SJC finds sufficient evidence apart from false (and, besides, maybe steno made mistake in transcribing!);

C v Gant **51 MAC 314 (2001)**—cop's testimony to grand jury couldn't be "chalked up to a 'mistake'," but no relief because (1) even the true account would have provided probable cause to indict, and (2) D failed to raise issue by way of motion to dismiss;

C v Edgerly **13 MAC 562, 577–80 (82)**—perjury = bad, but OK here;

C v Collado **426 M 675 (98)**—allegedly false testimony said to be witness's reasonable inference from

statement of co-D; another statement **was** false & recklessly made, but could not have influenced decision to indict;

C v Bray **19 MAC 751 (85)**—open question re: bad faith overcharging;

C v Gagliardi **21 MAC 439 (86)**—new trial, in part because DA overcharged (first degree murder though D's drunk) hoping for compromise verdict (G 2d degree); but see . . . . ;

SJC Rule 3:07, 3.8(a)—DA shall refrain from pressing charges without probable cause;

SJC Rule 3:07, 3.8(f)—DA shall not subpoena attorney re: client unless DA reasonably believes info sought isn't privileged, and that evidence sought = essential to complete investigation, and that there is no other way to get the info; **AND after these prerequisites = satisfied, must obtain prior judicial approval after opportunity for adversarial proceeding;**

US v Klubock **832 F.2d 664 (1st Cir. '87)**—3-3 split upholds (PF-15, the previous designation of SJC Rule 3:07, 3.8(f), forbidding prosecutors from summonsing defense counsel to grand jury absent judicial approval);

In Matter of Grand Jury Investigation **407 M 916 (90)**—PF-15, which requires judicial approval for prosecutorial summons of defense counsel, extends to defense investigators;

M.R.Crim.P. 13(c)—motions to dismiss (Note: can probably re-indict) (*See Chapter 19, Dismissal Double Jeopardy, Chapter 5, Complaints,* & *Griffin* **404 M 372 (89)** right to counsel at grand jury = effective, no conflict; (no re-indict if dismissal for irremediable harm);

Chambers v Commonwealth **421 M 49 (95)**—indictment charging D with sexual assault on V "on diverse dates between" 2 dates would not be dismissed for lack of specificity/notice, but SJC warns prosecutors of the ways in which defendants may benefit by such sloppy charging (see, e.g., *Hrycenko* **417 M 309, 315–18 (94)**);

G.L. c. 263, § 4A—right to waive indictment (but DA can still indict);

C v Perry P. **418 M 808 (94)**—juvenile D, under G.L. c. 119, § 61 had right to indictment; not permissible to infer waiver of this right, though can be waived "upon advice of counsel";

DeGolyer v Commonwealth **314 M 626 (43)**—waiver of indictment;

M.R.Crim.P. 3(b),(c), (e)—(same);

C v Baran **74 MAC 256 (2009)**—counsel's failure to protect D by not demanding but instead waiving indictment as to certain charges was ineffective assistance of counsel;

C v Peterson **445 M 782 (2006)**—D's waiver of right to indictment, consenting instead to new complaints which remedied defects in the language of preexisting indictments, to include specific reference to acts done in furtherance of the charged "attempts," didn't have to be in writing, notwithstanding language of Superior Court Rule 59 (2005) and M.R.Crim.P. 3, when record colloquy established voluntariness; grand jury had heard evidence of the "acts done" and quicker procedure of waiver was desirable to D, who had been held on bail pre-trial;

G.L. c. 276, § 38—with prior version of M.R.Crim.P. 3(a) in mind? attempts to force "election" between probable cause hearing and grand jury (but authorities agree it did not accomplish this, and prior rule language now (2004) deleted);

C v Cote **407 M 827 (90)**—prosecutor may not use power of grand jury subpoena to gather for trial evidence prosecutor doesn't intend to present to grand jury, but reversal required only where grand jury process is "seriously impaired";

C v Doe **408 M 764 (90)**—grand jury may not order person to appear in a lineup without articulable justification under *Terry v Ohio* **392 US 1 (68)**;

C v Downey **407 M 472 (90)**—grand jury may detain & compel blood tests for unindicted D so long as it has evidence sufficient to indict or arrest; D must be given opportunity to oppose order;

In the Matter of Grand Jury Investigation **427 M 221, 225 (98)**—procedure of prosecutor seeking from judge, on behalf of grand jury, order to compel submission to taking of blood sample = reasonable search & seizure, & "provides greater protection" to individual than would ex parte application for search warrant;

C v Williams **439 M 678 (2003)**—pre-indictment order from grand jury compelling D to produce hair, blood, and saliva samples need only be based on reasonable basis for believing that samples would provide test results that would significantly aid investigation; NOT necessary for grand jury to show probable cause to believe D committed the crime as prerequisite to such order;

In re Lavigne **418 M 831 (94)**—circumstances under which judge may order blood extracted from person not charged with crime and not the subject of a grand jury investigation: notice and opportunity for D to be heard, Commonwealth must show probable cause to believe D committed crime & that identity of source of blood found at crime scene would aid investigation;

C v Powell **450 M 229 (2007)**—rejects D's argument that grand jury petition for blood sample from D was erroneously allowed: D argued that knowing D's own blood was on, e.g., hammer (purportedly used to kill V) was useless, but "overlook[ed] the utility in the investigation of excluding him as the source of blood found on his person and clothing"; D waived, by failing to object to, requirements that petition be signed by foreperson under oath and/or having supporting affidavit from DA or grand juror; judge's failure to include in order the findings mandated by *C v Williams* **439 M 678 (2003)**, immaterial because order was preceded by adversary hearing and record supported order authorizing extraction of D's blood;

In Matter of Proceedings Before a Special Grand Jury **27 MAC 693 (89)**—witness justified in invoking 5th Amendment where not "perfectly clear" that testimony could not "possibly" incriminate him;

In the Matter of a Grand Jury Subpoena **442 M 1029 (2004)**—petitioner received no relief (on appeal to full bench from single justice's refusal on G.L. c. 211, § 3 petition to quash order of Superior Court judge that he testify before grand jury): "if prosecutor strays into a potentially protected area, petitioner may then exercise his privilege on a question by question basis"; USUAL WAY OF CHALLENGING SUCH ORDERS TO TESTIFY = disobey them, & appeal from subsequent contempt order;

C v Freeman **407 M 279 (90)**—references before grand jury to D's prior record undesirable though not cause for reversal; *C v Clemmey* **447 M 121 (2006)**—similar, re D's bad acts (no relief);

C v Saya **14 MAC 509 (82)**—tell grand jury D's record = bad, but OK here;

C v Jenks **426 M 582 (98)**—told grand jury of D's arrests not fatal; D's own statement (read to grand jurors) contained similar info; omitting **portion** of witness's statement (with opinion D acted in self-defense) not fatal (**opinion** irrelevant; other info probative of self-defense issue was before grand jury);

C v Olsen **35 MAC 929 (93)**—intentional presentation of "propensity" evidence called "needless but dangerous overkill"; no relief because not likely to have made a difference in decision to indict;

C v Vinnie **428 M 161, 174–75 (98)**—intentional presentation of unrelated criminal activity by D was clearly "improper," but D received no relief because couldn't show that the evidence "probably made a difference" in decision to indict;

C v Good **409 M 612 (91)**—showing "wanted" poster to grand jury risked reversal;

C v Mathews **450 M 874 (2008)**—cop testifying to grand jury that D invoked right to counsel implicates integrity of grand jury proceedings (citing cases) but no prejudice established (here, did not make a difference);

In the Matter of a John Doe Grand Jury Investigation **418 M 549, 555 (94)**—left open = question whether grand jury subpoena = enough to compel production of corporate records or whether warrant necessary (or probable cause to believe records contained evidence of the commission of a crime) (per Wilkins, J., cc); sole shareholders & directors of a corporation could not refuse to turn over to grand jury, corporate records, because "could not extend their individual rights against self-incrimination" to the corporation (dissenting opinion says this = contrary to *C v Doe* **405 M 676 (89)**); concurring opinion notes that majority's order that alternate keeper of corporate records be appointed may be futile, since witnesses had no obligation to identify the records for the alternate "keeper";

C v Rodriguez **58 MAC 610 (2003)**—reserving decision (because reversing on different ground) whether defendant may offer against Commonwealth the testimony of witness who testified before grand jury but claimed Fifth Amendment privilege at trial;

1-D. JUVENILE COURT—DISTRICT COURT LACKS JURISDICTION OVER THE PERSON

K. Smith, *Criminal Practice & Procedure*, § 33 & §§ 2631–701 (2d ed. 1983 & Supp.);

Nolan & Sartorio, *Criminal Law*, §§ 701–09 (3d ed. 2001)—"Juvenile Matters," including juvenile offenses generally, as well as care & protection issues, child in need of services matters (CHINS), child abandonment, truancy (& parent's criminal responsibility), and juvenile court rules;

G.L. c. 218, § 57—territorial jurisdiction of various juvenile court sessions specified;

M.R.Crim.P. 2(b)(10)—"Juvenile Court" defined; Comment ("It is in keeping with the policy of these rules to secure simplicity and uniformity in procedure to make the Juvenile Court Department subject to these rules, insofar as they are consistent with juvenile practice."); see also District Court Special Rule 204—"pertinent" District Court rules shall be applicable in proceedings against children between age 7 & 17, except as otherwise expressly provided;

Roper v Simmons 125 S.Ct. 1183 (2005)—imposing capital punishment upon juveniles under age 18 at time of offense violates Eighth Amendment's prohibition of cruel & unusual punishment;

C v Ogden O., a Juvenile, 448 M 798 (2007)—rejecting argument that ten-year-old did not have capacity to form specific intent necessary to commit mayhem: juvenile sprayed victim with dry gas, then threw lighted piece of paper on him, and laughed as victim tried to extinguish fire; underpinnings of juvenile justice system are already based on principle that juveniles frequently lack capacity to appreciate consequences of actions and should be afforded greater protections than adults;

C v Juvenile 27 MAC 78 (89)—DA need not prove D's age unless D raises it;

C v Ramos 47 MAC 792, 796–97 (99)—though D argued that it was only speculative whether alleged sexual assaults (reported almost 3 years after they allegedly stopped) occurred after D reached the age of seventeen (and Superior Court prosecution was thus barred by G.L. c. 119, § 74), Court held that jurors were made aware that it was "of critical significance" that the alleged crimes occurred on or after particular date, and that evidence was sufficient to make such a finding beyond a reasonable doubt;

G.L. c. 276, § 100B—shall SEAL after 3 years if asked & no more G.'s *(See Chapter 14-U, Sentencing: Sealing & Expunging Records)*;

Police Comm'r of Boston v Municipal Court of Dorchester District 374 M 640 (78)—Juvenile Court's broad mandate for welfare of kids, e.g., to order expunging of arrest records;

Victor V. v Commonwealth 423 M 793 (96)—preventive detention statute (G.L. c. 276, § 58A) applies to juveniles;

C v Thomas 359 M 386 (71)—statutory jury right;

Application of Gault 387 US 1 (67)—juvenile gets due process (rights to counsel, notice, confrontation, etc., & against self-incrimination);

ABA Model Code of Professional Responsibility (1969) Ethical Considerations 7-11—responsibilities may vary with client's intelligence, mental condition, or age; 7-12 additional responsibilities if client is "incapable of making considered judgment" *(See Chapter 2, Standards & Ethics)*;

SJC Rule 3:07, 1.14—Client Under A Disability: lawyer shall, as far as possible, maintain a normal client-lawyer relationship with client; if lawyer believes client has become incompetent or that normal client relationship "cannot be maintained . . . because client lacks sufficient capacity to communicate or to make adequately considered decisions" re: representation, & if lawyer believes client at risk of substantial harm, physical, mental, financial, or otherwise, lawyer "MAY" consult family members, adult protective agencies, or other individuals or entities that have authority to protect client AND, if appears necessary, lawyer may seek appointment of guardian ad litem, conservator, or guardian; lawyer may disclose confidential info ONLY to extent necessary to protect client's interests;

ABA Informal Op. 1160 (1971)—duty to seek N.G. though think D needs help;

C v Juvenile 389 M 128 (83)—special Miranda rules for kids; *(See Chapter 20-C for collected cases)*;

G.L. c. 231, § 85G (86)—parents civilly liable for $5,000 damages by kid 7-17;

Johnny Doe v Attorney General 425 M 210 (97)—sex offender act, & "registry" provisions therein, override confidentiality provision in G.L. c. 119, § 60A, 1st paragraph;

C v Bembury 406 M 552 (90)—witness's juvenile record, which had no rational tendency to show bias, was properly excludable;

Quinones v Commonwealth 423 M 1015 (96)—interstate compact on juveniles = effective in MA;

C v Matthews 406 M 380 (90)—criminal responsibility is issue for trial, not probable cause hearing;

C v A Juvenile 413 M 148 (92)—retroactive application of amendment to G.L. c. 119, § 61 allowing prosecutors to indict rather than bind over juvenile murder cases violated Article 24 ex post facto clause because of reduced evidentiary burdens for prosecutors;

C v Perry P. 418 M 808 (94)—juvenile had right to indictment (murder) under G.L. c. 119, § 61 & implied waiver of this right not permitted;

C v Thad T. 59 MAC 497, 510 (2003)—when juvenile is found delinquent, G.L. c. 119, § 58 allows judge either to place case on file OR place child on probation with conditions OR commit child to DYS; judge could not, as here, BOTH commit child to DYS and impose condition that he be banished from town of Groton until age 18 (constitutional arguments as to "banishment" avoided because child was over age 18 by time of decision, but see *C v Pike* 428 M 393 [98], re "banishment");

1-D.1. G.L. c. 119—Protection, Care of and Proceedings Against Children

("Transfer" law repealed, St. 1996, ch. 200)

G.L. c. 119, §§ 52–84—Delinquency/Youthful Offender § 52—ages 7–17

G.L. c. 119, § 53—"liberally construed"; not treated as "criminals";

G.L. c. 119, § 55A—right to jury trial, discovery in writing, appointment of stenographer;

G.L. c. 119, § 55B—plea, pre-trial motion not filed or filed without a decision prior to waiver of jury trial may be filed no later than 21 days after entry of jury waiver;

G.L. c. 119, § 56—hearings within 15 days, (e) jury sessions, six-person on delinquency complaint, 12-person on youthful offender indictment, (h) motion for stenographer in writing no later than 48 hours prior to trial;

G.L. c. 119, § 57—investigation by probation officer;

G.L. c. 119, § 58—can get continuance without a finding after trial, can get probation to age 18 or age 19 if case is disposed after 18th birthday on delinquency complaint;

G.L. c. 119, §§ 55B & 58—can't get continuance without a finding or have case 'filed' for indecent A&B on child, or rape of child;

G.L. c. 119, § 59—probation officer can arrest without warrant or court may issue warrant to child placed in care of probation prior to disposition;

G.L. c. 119, § 60—juvenile record may be used for impeachment purposes, same as adult convictions;

G.L. c. 119, § 60A—delinquency records not open to public, except with judge's consent, BUT name of child available to public by probation officer in certain circumstances, & youthful offender proceedings open to public inspection to same extent as adult criminal proceedings;

G.L. c. 119, § 62—child can be ordered to pay restitution;

G.L. c. 119, § 63—contributing to delinquency of minor = "exclusively" within juvenile court jurisdiction; but see *C v Lender* 47 MAC 164, 165–66 (99) juvenile court has jurisdiction over charge of contributing to delinquency of minor only if it's charged against an adult by complaint; if it's charged by indictment, must be prosecuted in Superior Court; language of c. 119, § 63 parsed;

C v Garcia 48 MAC 201, 205 (99)—after D's acquittal in District Court on receiving stolen property charge, collateral estoppel barred trial in juvenile court for contributing to delinquency;

G.L. c. 119, § 65—juvenile sessions shall be separate from other criminal business, general public is excluded; only those with "direct interest" in case allowed in session; if case is indicted, it's open to public;

G.L. c. 119, § 67—parent/guardian & probation get notice of child's arrest; detention facility at police station to be approved by DYS; detained children held separate from adults;

G.L. c. 119, § 68—care of children held pre-trial; 15 day limit between court appearances; child 14 or older charged with 1st or 2d degree murder held in custody of sheriff of county where court is;

G.L. c. 119, § 68A—court may refer child for 'diagnostic study' inpatient or outpatient, with consent of parent/guardian; report to be forwarded to court with recommendations;

G.L. c. 119, § 68B—DYS may maintain special foster homes for detained children;

G.L. c. 119, § 68C—DYS to maintain and provide diagnostic services for evaluations under § 68A;

G.L. c. 119, § 69—superintendent of public schools and any person in charge of private schools shall provide court upon request with attendance, conduct, and standing records of children with pending case or under supervision of the court (but compare *C v Buccella* 434 M 473 (2001) re: privacy right of student and relevant provisions, 603 CMR, e.g., § 23.02);

G.L. c. 119, § 72B—Superior Court has jurisdiction of child between ages 14 & 17 charged with first and second degree murder; after sentence, child is held in unit separate from adults until 17th birthday, then to state prison; if found guilty of lesser offense of murder, Superior Court to sentence in accord with § 58;

G.L. c. 119, § 74—juvenile court does not have jurisdiction over child between 14 & 17 charged with first or second degree murder;

1-D.2. Youthful Offender

("Transfer" law, G.L. c. 119, § 61, repealed in 1996, St. 1996, ch.200)

G.L. c. 119, § 52: definition of "Youthful Offender"—child between ages 14 & 17 charged with a felony, **and** has been previously committed to DYS **or** "has committed an offense which involves the infliction or threat of serious bodily harm," **or** is charged with specified firearms offenses; to prosecute a juvenile as a "youthful offender," Commonwealth must proceed by indictment;

G.L. c. 119, § 58—if found to be a youthful offender can get one of the following sentences: (1) an adult sentence, or (2) a "combination" sentence, i.e., commitment to DYS to age 21, with adult sentence (house of correction or state prison) suspended during the term of probation, which shall include successful completion of DYS commitment, or (3) commitment to DYS until age 21. Court shall conduct sentencing hearing; judge shall make written findings re: which sentence would protect present and long-term public safety; probation dept. to file presentence investigation report no less than 7 days prior to sentencing; prior to 17th birthday, child who receives adult sentence shall be held separate from adults, but with adults as of age 17;

C v Lucret **58 MAC 624 (2003)**—D was indicted at age sixteen, and at age 17, tendered G plea for disposition of DYS commitment until age 21, and two-year house of correction sentence, from and after, all to be suspended for two years; D's violation of terms of probation warranted imposition of the statutorily contemplated "combination" sentence of both DYS commitment and from and after house of correction incarceration; failure to acknowledge that this sentence did not comport with statutory require-ment that adult sentence be suspended, with any subse-quent adult committed sentence being dependent upon lack of success during DYS "commitment";

C v Clint C **420 M 217 (99)**—statutory rape (non-forcible) qualifies here (age difference, position of author-ity, vulnerability of complainant) as crime involving threat of serious bodily harm, so "youthful offender" prosecution ok; G.L. c. 119, § 54 "makes no provision for review of a prosecutor's decision to try the juvenile as an adult"; but see Ireland, J., dissenting;

C v Ulysses H **52 MAC 497, 501–02 (2001)**—juvenile D was charged with both A&B and ABDW, to wit, "shod foot"; because A&B = punishable only by not more than 2½ years in house of correction (or a fine), it could not be basis of 'youthful offender' indictment (con-viction & sentence vacated, & indictment dismissed); in future, when both indictable and nonindictable offenses arise out of same criminal conduct, Commonwealth should join the complaint with the indictment, "and proceed to trial before a twelve-person jury on all charges"; if D = 17 years old, can't be prosecuted as youthful offender, but court declined to adopt "common law" rule of age, i.e., that individual attains his "next age on the day **before** the anniversary of his birth," so this D was two hours less than age 17 at time of incident;

C v Quincy Q **434 M 859 (2001)**—grand jury lacked sufficient evidence to indict D as a youthful offender under G.L. c. 119, § 54, because no evidence had been presented of "the infliction or threat of serious bodily harm," one of the statutory prerequisites of a youthful offender indict-ment; any facts, including the requirements for youthful offender status, that would increase the penalty for such juveniles must be proved to a jury beyond a reasonable doubt (see *Apprendi v New Jersey* **530 US 466 (2000)**), & so, if Commonwealth determines to proceed against a ju-venile by indictment, it must present at the grand jury stage not only sufficient evidence of the underlying offense to warrant a finding of probable cause that the underlying crime has been committed, but also sufficient evidence that the requirements set forth in G.L. c. 119, § 54, have been met; likewise, at ensuing trial of "youthful offender" indictment, judge must instruct the jury that they must determine first whether the Commonwealth has proved beyond a reasonable doubt the elements of the underlying offense, and, if they so conclude, they must also determine whether the Commonwealth has proved beyond a reason-

able doubt the requirements of G.L. c. 119, § 54. (Some components = matter of law, i.e., status of underlying crime as a felony, and, in some cases, as one of the enu-merated firearms violations, & judge should not instruct the jury regarding such components); parties may stipulate to, e.g., D's age (& no instruction then necessary as to such an established fact); practically, usually only issue of infliction or threat of serious bodily harm will be for the jury to find, or not, beyond a reasonable doubt;

C v Hoshi H **72 MAC 18 (2008)**—youthful offender indictment properly dismissed as violent acts of principal could not be imputed to juvenile, charged as being acces-sory *after* fact for facilitating principal's escape and avoid-ance of arrest (principal was juvenile's boyfriend, who allegedly shot another man during a fight; juvenile called cab and lied to police); accessory *"before"* fact/joint ven-ture liability *would* involve requisite threat/infliction of serious bodily harm;

C v Hampton **64 MAC 27 (2005)**—citing *Schriro v Summerlin* 124 S.Ct. 2519 (2004), jury trial rights recog-nized in *Quincy Q* 434 M 859, 864–67, based on *Apprendi v New Jersey*, aren't "applied retroactively" to this D whose direct appeals were concluded before the *Quincy Q* decision;

C v Lamont L. **438 M 842 (2003)**—Commonwealth improperly joined an indictment for misdemeanor charge of assault and battery with an indictment of D as youthful offender on a charge of assault and battery by means of a dangerous weapon; when D was convicted only of the lesser charge, proper remedy was entry of a delinquency finding on the misdemeanor;

C v Dale D. **431 M 757 (2000)**—grand jury's refusal to indict D, a juvenile, on charges of forcible rape of child and indecent A&B on person fourteen or older, did not bar prosecution of D in juvenile court on complaints for same actions, but meant only that Commonwealth couldn't prosecute as "youthful offender" & impose harsher penalty upon juvenile;

1-D.3. Children Over Age 17

G.L. c. 119, § 72(a)—juvenile court retains jurisdic-tion over child who reaches age 18 pending final adjudica-tion, including all remands and retrials following appeals, continuances, or probation; child cannot be committed to DYS after turns age 19 unless indicted as a youthful of-fender; if child commits crime prior to age 17 but is not apprehended until between age 17 & 18, juvenile court retains jurisdiction over case; **(b)** if child is indicted, juve-nile court retains jurisdiction over child who reaches age 18 while case is pending final adjudication, including all remands and retrials following appeals, any determinations under § 58, and continuances or probation; child can't be committed to DYS after reaches age 21;

G.L. c. 120, §§ 17–19—juvenile's commitment to DYS prior to 18th birthday may be continued for addi-tional three years if DYS has "opinion" that youth "would be physically dangerous to the public"; after DYS issues extended commitment order, must request affirmation of order from Juvenile Court Dep't and must provide written statement of facts on which DYS bases its opinion; order "shall [not] . . . be discharged, merely because of its form or an asserted insufficiency of its allegations"; statute held unconstitutional in ***Kenniston v Dep't of Youth Services*** **453 M 179 (2009)**—statute fails to require any link between youth's alleged dangerousness and a mental condition or defect making youth incapable of controlling his behavior, and fails to provide any standard for what is "dangerousness", depriving youth of substantive due process, with impermissibly vague term; *Foucha v Louisiana* 504 US 71 (92) cited, requiring both mental illness and dangerousness to maintain involuntary commitment;

Santiago v Commonwealth **428 M 39 (98)**—amendment of § 72 by St. 1998, extending juvenile court jurisdiction beyond previous age limit, didn't violate "ex post facto" prohibition; juvenile who turned age 19 did not "age out" of juvenile court jurisdiction; compare (concerning old law) *C v Kelley* **411 M 212 (91)** retroactive application of amendment allowing extension of DYS commitments to age 21 upon showing of dangerousness, even if not product of "mental or physical deficiency," violated ex post facto clauses of Article 24 & Article 1, § 9 of US Constitution;

C v Rosenberg **410 M 347 (91)**—constitutional challenges to previous DYS extension procedures rejected;

G.L. c. 119, § 72A—if child commits crime prior to 17th birthday but isn't apprehended until after 18th birth day, juvenile court shall conduct hearing to determine whether probable cause exists to believe that juvenile committed the crime; court can either order person discharged if this is "consistent with the protection of the public," or can dismiss delinquency complaint and cause criminal complaint to be issued in adult court;

C v Bousquet **407 M 854 (90)**—transfer of 18-year-old D who was 16 at time of offense but not apprehended until over 18 requires only showing of probable cause & that transfer in public interest; G.L. c. 119, § 72A;

Fitzpatrick v Commonwealth **453 M 1014 (2009)**—G,L, c. 211, § 3 can't be used to "circumvent" SJC Rule 2:21, and isn't available for review of attempt to overturn juvenile court judge's finding probable cause and public interest in juvenile being charged as adult, leading to indictments (offenses allegedly committed < age 17, but arrest > age 18);

Jake J. v Commonwealth **433 M 20 (2000)**—juvenile court judge had authority to release juvenile on pre-trial probation with his consent, even though judge didn't specifically say such release was pursuant to G.L. c. 276, § 87; judge may surrender & hold child in DYS custody if s/he violates terms of release;

C v Connor C. **432 M 635 (2000)**—delinquency adjudication under G.L. c. 269, § 10(a) constitutes a prior conviction, such that juvenile could be indicted for "2d offense gun charge" under G.L. c. 269, § 10(d);

C v Furr **58 MAC 155 (2003)**—D's prior adjudication as youthful offender on charges of armed carjacking, armed robbery, etc., qualifies as predicate conviction to warrant enhanced sentences in G.L. c. 269, § 10(g);

C v Foreman **63 MAC 801 (2005)**—D, an adult, could be prosecuted as armed career criminal with predicate convictions being juvenile adjudications (Furr, supra, had still been a juvenile when indicted as armed career criminal, and so predicate convictions had necessarily been juvenile adjudications); predicate armed robbery conviction here had knife rather than gun, but still legitimate as "violent crime" in G.L. c. 140, § 121;

G.L. c. 119, § 29A—parents of unemancipated minor are liable for reasonable legal fees & expenses, not exceeding $300, of attorney, other than attorney supplied by CPCS or assigned by court; doesn't apply to parent who, as result of court decree, doesn't have custody of minor;

C v Florence F. **429 M 523, 526–27, 529 (99)**—after adjudication that juvenile was a child in need of services, juvenile court judge issued order permitting child to remain in custody of mother on condition child attend school; child's failure to attend school thereafter could NOT be punished in proceeding alleging delinquency by reason of criminal contempt: CHINS ("child in need of services") shall not be committed to institution operated for delinquents, and CHINS proceedings shall not be criminal proceedings (G.L. c. 119, §§ 39G & E); legislation requested to give juvenile court "the authority it needs" . . . "for more effective methods of enforcement" in CHINS cases "to prevent (subsequent criminal offenses and) delinquency";

News Group Boston, Inc. v Commonwealth **409 M 627 (91)** judge retains discretion to close proceedings or to bar electronic media where privileges in issue;

1-E. TERRITORIAL "JURISDICTION" (VENUE)

G.L. c. 218, §§ 1–3—various District Courts & venues;

U.S. Constitution, Sixth Amendment—"trial in district wherein crime committed";

Mass. Constitution, Declaration of Rights, Article 13—"verification of facts in vicinity where they (***allegedly***) happen is one of the greatest securities of liberty";

C v Brogan **415 M 169 (93)**—charge of violating, in Suffolk, Norfolk & Bristol counties, preliminary injunction issued in Middlesex Superior Court was not required to be tried in Suffolk, Norfolk and/or Bristol County; trial in Middlesex OK (**3 judges dissented**);

C v Faust **423 M 298 (96)**—D's escape from "community release center" run by Middlesex County Sheriff's

Dep't. in Suffolk County was properly prosecuted in Middlesex County (D had been sentenced to Middlesex Co. house of correction);

CPCS P/G 1.3(k)—within rules, should seek best forum, e.g. change venue;

C v Bonomi **335 M 327 (57)**—rarely change venue because of publicity;

K. Smith, *Criminal Practice & Procedure,* **§§ 25–26 (2d ed. 1983 & Supp.)**—overview;

C v Rankins **429 M 470, 476 (99)**—after D moved for change of venue to escape pretrial publicity in Hampshire and Hampden Counties & case was moved to Franklin Co. for trial, no relief when, 10 days later (7 days before trial), D unsuccessfully moved for reconsideration because minority population of Franklin County was smaller than that of Hampshire County; D should have thought of this issue before, and could have sought to limit counties to which case might be transferred BUT had "no State constitutional right to a transfer only to a county that had at least as great a minority population";

M.R.Crim.P. 37—raise it or waive it; motion must be made prior to trial; *C v Dineen* **70 MAC 1, 3 n.3 (2007)**—same, citing cases (D here challenged by pretrial motion to dismiss AND by motion for required finding of not guilty during trial);

C v Fafone **416 M 329 (93)**—Florida drug supplier, whose wares were transported by train to Connecticut, could not be prosecuted in MA: failure to prove that D intended or knew his acts to have any effect in MA ("failure of proof of territorial jurisdiction");

In re Vasquez **428 M 842, 846–50 (99)**—petitioner was divorced in 1985 from wife, and was ordered to make weekly child support payments for two children (he didn't); wife and children moved to Oregon in 1987, and thereafter Oregon officials obtained an indictment against D for criminal non-support; SJC held that Oregon could exercise jurisdiction over D on two rationales: (1) "effects" doctrine provides that acts done outside a jurisdiction, but intended to produce and producing detrimental effects within it, justify a State in punishing the cause of the harm as if D had been present at the effect, and (2) "crime involving a failure to act is committed at the place where the act is required to be performed"; context of this adjudication was D's arrest on a Mass. Governor's warrant after Oregon requested D's extradition, and D's petition for writ of habeas corpus (and temporary restraining order prohibiting extradition until the habeas action was adjudicated);

C v Armstrong **73 MAC 245 (2008)**—refusing to apply "effects" doctrine to find jurisdiction in MA over sexual assaults occurring outside MA during a trip beginning and ending in MA;

G.L. c. 277, § 62—mortal wound or poison in MA gives MA jurisdiction of homicide even if death occurs outside MA;

G.L. c. 277, § 57A—if prosecution notifies judge of "doubt" re: exact location, court can allow case to proceed;

G.L. c. 277, § 57—at sea if within one league of shore; within 50 rods of district or 100 rods of county;

G.L. c. 277, §§ 58–62—special rules (larceny, receiving stolen property, embezzlement, larceny by false pretenses, homicide);

C v Price **72 MAC 280 (2008)**—G.L. c. 277, § 59 (venue for 'larceny by false pretenses') allows prosecution in county where false pretense was made, or in or through which any of the property obtained was carried, sent, transported or received by D; where D in Suffolk County telephoned victims in Norfolk County inducing them to part with money based on false representation that victims' relatives were in distress ($ to ameliorate such distress), venue in Norfolk County upheld, even if delivery of $ was in Suffolk County: telephone communications produced detrimental effects within Norfolk;

G.L. c. 265, § 24A—dual venue where evidence proves act of conveyance of victim from "origin" county to "destination" county "in connection with" specified crimes: *C v Dineen* **70 MAC 1 (2007)**—needn't prove that conveyance was undertaken with plan to commit rape in destination county (here, simple fact that noncustodial father had daughter visit him in adjoining county = enough for dual venue, despite absence of showing that conveyance was done with intent to facilitate commission of the crime);

G.L. c. 277, § 20—caption alleges venue—see M.R. Crim.P.4;

G.L. c. 277, § 62A—alleged violations of G.L. c. 209A orders can be tried in jurisdiction of alleged violation or where original order was entered;

C v Clancy **261 M 345 (27)**—need not allege venue in complaint's text;

C v Adelson **40 MAC 585 (96)**—D not entitled (here) to have jury decide alleged lack of territorial jurisdiction; D's sending of bad checks from Middlesex County to Arizona established Middlesex jurisdiction (territorial) but see *C v Gilbert* **366 M 18, 28 (74)** may be jury question;

C v Frank **51 MAC 19 (2001)**—when indictment charged rapes of child "on divers dates and times between" two dates, & some of time period preceded family's living in MA, no relief: "in the end," Commonwealth had to establish that D committed crimes within MA, but assaults occurring elsewhere = admissible to prove "commission of crimes within the State";

C v Armstrong **73 MAC 245 (2008)**—no MA jurisdiction to try sexual assaults occurring during a trip beginning and ending in MA, but outside MA and "on the way to" Oregon; if applied as argued by Commonwealth here, "effects" doctrine (acts done outside jurisdiction but intended to produce and producing detrimental effects within jurisdiction) would "stretch . . . criminal law jurisdiction into . . . unrecognized realm";

C v Travis **408 M 1 (90)**—pursuant to G.L. c. 277, §§ 57A & 62, court had jurisdiction over murder case where victim's body was found in Rhode Island because violence or injury could have occurred during kidnapping in Massachusetts;

C v Robinson **48 MAC 329 (99)**—kidnapping which resulted in V's death began in Norfolk County, but body was found in Suffolk County, and unknown where death occurred; G.L. c. 277, § 57A permits prosecutor to petition court of either county for permission to proceed, but hearing should be held before petition is allowed; D's failure to object to lack of hearing/disposition of petition = waiver;

C v Lent **420 M 764 (95)**—for MA jurisdiction, must be causal "connection between" MA "violence or injury" and out-of-state death; found here in D's statement that unsuccessful anal intercourse (in MA) convinced D that V had to die (in NY);

Valentin v Commonwealth **411 M 608 (92)**—sending D to adjoining county for jury session trials barred by previous version of G.L. c. 218, § 27A, unless D waives rights; statute amended thereafter (so designated jury sessions have jurisdiction to hear cases from adjoining counties);

Smith v Commonwealth **420 M 291 (95)**—trial of Chelsea case in Middlesex rather than Suffolk County (due to crumbling Chelsea courthouse) not OK given non-white D's motion for change of venue & proffer that Suffolk population was 34% non-white and Middlesex population was only 8% non-white; but *C v Siciliano* **420 M 303 (95)** it's a "doubtful proposition to rely (merely) on geographical groups, such as residents of Chelsea or Revere, as basis of a 6th Amendment claim";

Related concept, "vicinage," area from which jurors are chosen—see *Valentin* **411 M 608 (92)** ("the record shows that arrangements have been made to use jurors from Plymouth County in the trial of Brockton cases in Stoughton."); *Smith* **420 M 291 (95)** (article 12 right to a trial by jury = "right to have issues of fact determined by the composite judgment of a fairly numerous and representative body of impartial residents of the county"); *Siciliano* **420 M 303 (95)** ("doubtful proposition to rely (merely) on geographical groups, such as residents of Chelsea or Revere, as basis of a 6th Amendment claim").

Chapter 2
STANDARDS AND ETHICS FOR DEFENSE COUNSEL

2-A. ADVERSARY SYSTEM AND DEFENSE OF LIBERTY/HUMAN DIGNITY

U.S. Constitution, Preamble—We the people . . . to establish Justice . . . and secure the Blessings of Liberty . . . ; 6th Amendment: right to assistance of counsel;

Mass. Declaration of Rights, Article 12—right to be fully heard . . . by self, or by counsel;

Universal Declaration of Human Rights (U.N. 1948)—human rights protected by rule of law, e.g., fair hearing, presume innocent, and necessary guarantees;

***C v Urena* 417 M 692 (94)**—Article 12 guarantees at **least** as much as 6th Amendment; if Article 12 is met, 6th Amendment is satisfied;

***Tehan v US ex rel. Shott* 382 US 406, 416 (66)**—5th Amendment's respect for individual/privacy conflicts with pursuit of truth;

***C v Bergstrom* 402 M 534(88)**—constitutional system means can't take shortcuts to liberty or dissolve protections for innocents because of societal pressures;

ABA Standards for Criminal Justice, Prosecution Function & Defense Function (3d ed. 1993), 4-1.2 (b)—defense counsel to advocate with courage & devotion; accompanying Commentary: "Advocacy is not for the timid, the meek, or the retiring. Our system of justice is inherently contentious, albeit bounded by the rules of professional ethics and decorum, and it demands that the lawyer be inclined toward vigorous advocacy";

***Guiney v Police Comm'r of Boston* 411 M 328, 333–34 (91)**—"Constitutional safeguards should not be abandoned simply because there is a drug problem in this country. Article 14 of the Declaration of Rights should not be a casualty in the war on drugs. It is at times when pressures on constitutional rights are greatest that courts must be especially vigilant in the protection of those rights";

***C v Cheek* 413 M 492, 497 (92)**—"The problems that may face the Grove Hall section of Roxbury or any other similar 'high crime area' will not be resolved any more readily by excluding the individuals who live there from the protections afforded by our Constitution"; cf. Shakespeare, *Henry VI* (II.4.2): Cade (the rebel): "When I'm king we'll (cause chaos)" . . . Dick (his ally): "The 1st thing we do, let's kill all the lawyers.";

***Sacher v US* 343 US 1, 38 (52)**—Frankfurter, J., dissenting: history of liberty = history of procedural protections; law itself, not just D's liberty, on trial in a criminal case;

J. Adams—English law = it's more beneficial that many guilty persons should escape unpunished than one innocent person should suffer;

I. Mather—"Cases of Conscience" (1692): better that 10 suspected witches escape than condemn 1 innocent; *(See Chapter 16, Presumption of Innocence)*;

Churchill—The mood & temper of the public in regards to treatment of crime and criminals is one of the most unfailing tests of civilization of a country;

T. Paine—Those who expect to reap the benefits of freedom must undergo the fatigue of supporting it;

L. Hand—Liberty lies in hearts & minds of men & women. When it dies there, no constitution, no law, no court can save it . . . or even do much to help;

C.E. Hughes—Supreme Court & courts of appeal will take care of themselves. Look after courts of the poor, who are most in need of justice;

***Herring v NY* 422 US 853, 857 (75)**—constitution depends on adversary system, so can't unduly restrict counsel (from arguing);

***Sacher v US* 343 US 1, 13–14 (52)**—Supreme Court "make(s) clear that . . . if its aid be needed, will unhesitatingly protect counsel in fearless, vigorous and effective performance of every duty pertaining to the office of the advocate on behalf of any person whatsoever . . . (b)ut will not equate contempt with courage or insults with independence";

***US v Gonzalez-Lopez* 548 US 140 (2006)**—reversal for denying D his counsel of choice (out-of-state counsel's pro hac vice motion was rejected on ground that counsel had, in some other case, "supposedly violated . . . a . . . Rule of professional conduct", and trial court refused to even allow D to consult with this attorney during trial, where there was local counsel of record); refusing to attempt to apply "harmless error" analysis;

***C v Manning* 373 M 438 (77)**—dismissal because federal agents impugned counsel *(See Chapter 2-G)*;

***C v Mullen* 72 MAC 136 (2008)**—D's waiver of counsel at trial was not "knowing and intelligent"; given no record colloquy re: decision to proceed pro se, proof lacking that D was adequately aware of seriousness of charges, magnitude of pro se undertaking, availability of advisory counsel, and disadvantages of self-representation; D's signature on waiver form insufficient, particularly where form had no certification (SJC Rule 3:10) by judge that she has informed D in accord with Rule and G.L. c. 211D § 5, and that D has knowingly elected to proceed without lawyer; while D's background, experience and conduct may be considered re: "knowing/intelligent," this source did not here establish requisite understanding; quality of a D's attempt at self-representation would have to rise beyond basic level of "appropriate" to establish legitimate waiver (motion for new trial allowed);

2-B. RULES, STANDARDS AND NORMS

See also Chapter 2-E, Defense Counsel: Competent/ Effective;

ABA Model Code of Professional Responsibility Preamble & Prelim. Statement (1969)—Canons (axiomatic norms); Disciplinary Rules ("DR") = mandatory minimum conduct; Ethical Considerations ("EC") = aspi-

rational & guidance; must understand reasons for standards, i.e., nature of office; ultimate incentive = desire for respect & confidence of peers & society;

***C v Goldman* 395 M 495, 503, n.9 (85)**—ABA Code's "Ethical Considerations" help interpret its "Disciplinary Rules";—after Model Code ('69), ABA Committee set forth new/revised "restatement format" of black letter rules & accompanying comments; this version, in '82, won over a format using the old "ethical considerations" and "disciplinary rules," and it was adopted in '83 & called "ABA Model Rules of Professional Conduct"; in Massachusetts, Rules of Professional Conduct (promulgated as SJC Rule 3:07) were adopted in 1997, effective 1/1/98. They are NOT the same as the ABA's Model Rules, but replaced rules which were based on, but not identical to, the former ABA Model Code of Professional Responsibility.

ABA Standards for Criminal Justice, Prosecution Function and Defense Function (3d ed. 1993)—guidelines long adhered to by best advocates; 4-1.2 attorney = professional representative, not client's "alter ego";

In re Bergeron **220 M 472, 477 (15)**—regulate attorneys because "officers of court";

Cammer v US **350 US 399 (56)**—attorney not officer of court like clerk/bailiff;

SJC Rule 3:07—R. 8 maintaining integrity of the profession; SJC Rule 3:09 (Code of Judicial Conduct), Canon 3(B)(3): judge shall report unprofessional conduct; SJC Rule 4:01, bar discipline (for each act or omission which violates any rule of professional conduct), Board of Bar Overseers, Bar Counsel;

SJC Rule 3:07, 8.3(a)—SHALL report others' violations if substantial question re: honesty/fitness;

CPCS Performance Guidelines—for evaluating, supervising & training; 1.1 know & adhere to all ethical opinions, standards, & rules; if in doubt, get guidance; resolve good faith ambiguities towards D's interests;

CPCS DISCIPLINARY RULES—for complaints against attorneys, e.g., Performance Guideline breaches;

CPCS Rules & Regs ('84)—full-time job; outside job, especially elected, needs permission; suggested process for referrals to outside attorneys;

G.L. c. 268A: Public Employees' Conduct—§ 4 no compensation, except from state; § 10 advisory opinions from Ethics Committee; § 23 no outside, incompatible employment, & no use of job to get special privileges;

G.L. c. 55, §§ 13–14—public employee can't (even "indirectly") solicit money for political purpose on state property;

G.L. c. 221, § 40—disbarment for deceit, malpractice, gross misconduct;

Wagenmann v Adams **829 F.2d 196 (1st Cir. '87)**—assigned counsel malpractice for not contesting commitment to Bridgewater State Hospital;

G.L. c. 258: Mass. Tort Claim Act—public employees immune for negligence; Attorney General represents, & state = liable; BUT employee may be liable for some intentional torts & civil rights claims, (but state may indemnify);

Tower v Glover **467 US 914 (84)**—public defender not § 1983 "state action"; but maybe state action for § 1983 conspiracy; no (absolute?) public defender immunity;

C v Senior **433 M 453 (2001)**—fact that hospital personnel perform blood alcohol test of D at request of D counsel doesn't mean that results are 'privileged', since hospital didn't agree to "agency" relationship;

SJC Rule 3:07, 8.4(a)—shall not circumvent rules through acts of others; 3:07, 5.3 must see that staff keeps confidences;

ABA Model Rules of Professional Conduct (1983)—5.2 no violation if get reasonable/arguable advice from superior; 5.1 supervisor must ensure ethics of others; 5.3 lawyers must ensure ethics by non-lawyer staff; 8.4 can't violate rule through another;

ABA Standards for Criminal Justice, Prosecution Function & Defense Function (3d ed. 1993) 4-1.5—need advisory councils to give prompt & confidential guidance re: standards;

ABA/MBA/MACDL Advisory Opinions—reference materials and source of advice (see CPCS P/G 1.1); Board of Bar Overseers, telephone 617-720-0700, informal advice; maybe logged in;

Burkoff, "Criminal Defense Ethics" (West Group, revised ed. 9/2001)—excellent resource: appendix contains ABA Model Code of Professional Responsibility; ABA Model Rules of Professional Conduct, as amended; the American Lawyer's Code of Conduct (American Trial Lawyers Foundation); and the ABA Standards for Criminal Justice (3d ed.) chapter 4, The Defense Function; Burkoff treatise's "primary value . . . is helping people to realize that many significant issues involving criminal defense ethics simply don't have 'obvious' resolutions", id., author's Introduction at vii;

Glenn v Aiken **409 M 699 (91)**—criminal defense counsel's liability for malpractice requires proof of D's actual innocence;

Labovitz v Feinberg **47 MAC 306, 312 (99)**—malpractice claimant is precluded from proclaiming his innocence and his lawyer's negligence in a malpractice action unless he has succeeded previously in withdrawing or vacating his guilty plea on direct appeal or through postconviction proceedings; only if guilty plea is vacated on some ground (inter alia, ineffective assistance of counsel) may D pursue malpractice action, subject to innocence requirement of *Glenn v Aiken* **409 M 699 (91)**;

2-C. ZEALOUSNESS (EVEN FOR THE GUILTY)

Lord Brougham: Queen Caroline's Defense—sacred duty to save client by all expedient means, at all hazards & costs, & reckless of consequences to country;

US v Wade **388 US 218, 258 (67)**—(White, J.) defend & cross-examine regardless of personal opinion; duty may require conduct unrelated to search for truth;

ABA Formal Op. 90 (1932)—can't condition employment on belief in innocence;

Samuel Johnson (to Boswell)—if argument convinces judge, but not yourself, judge is right & you are wrong;

ABA Standards for Criminal Justice, Prosecution Function & Defense Function (3d ed. 1993) 4-1.2—D-attorney's basic duty to system = advocate with courage, devotion, within law; 4-7.6(b) cross-examine truthful witness = appropriate;

SJC Rule 3:07, 1.4—duty to keep client informed; 3:07, 1.2 & 1.3 zealous & pursue client's lawful objectives & don't prejudice, damage client—except permitted waivers, unlawful acts, fraud (see D & G, below);

ABA Code of Professional Responsibility (1969), Ethical Considerations: ("ECs")—2-30 decline case if intense feelings may impair effectiveness; 2-26 lawyers should take unattractive cases; 2-27 belief in guilt or repugnance of case not reason to withdraw; 7-2 bounds of law often doubtful, uncertain, conflicting; 7-3 resolve towards client any doubts re: bounds of law; 7-6 (same) re: state of mind; 7-4 legal argument's permissible if "good faith" extension of law; 5-1 personal or other clients' interests can't compromise loyalty; 4-1—"fiduciary relationship" (re: preserving secrets);

CPCS P/G 1.1—resolve good faith rule-ambiguities in favor of client; but see id., 1.3 (a) "If personal reactions

make it impossible for counsel to fulfill the duty of zealous representation, he or she has a duty to refrain from representing the client";

C v Tabor 376 M 811, 817 n.10 (78)—zeal; decide conflicts in client's favor;

C v Mitchell 438 M 535 (2003)—Mass. R. Professional Conduct 3.3(e) (98) governs conduct of lawyer who learns that D intends to commit perjury (must try to dissuade, may not ask questions which would elicit perjury if D testifies, and may not argue probative value of false testimony in closing, **_BUT_** lawyer can't invoke this rule just because D has told inconsistent stories re: event, or because lawyer thinks D may be lying because of the Commonwealth's proof; lawyer must have firm basis in objective fact to believe D intends to commit perjury; SJC held that such basis here existed, and that it was acceptable procedure for D-counsel to raise matter at bench conference with ADA and judge (maybe error to not have D present, but purportedly no prejudice shown!), and thereafter to merely have D testify in narrative form and not argue testimony content to jury; "discretionary" with trial judge whether to have colloquy with D;

Pollock v Marshall 391 M 543, 555 (84)—duty = "unflinching fidelity" to client;

Hendrickson v Sears 365 M 83, 90 (74)—"highly fiduciary" relationship;

2-D. CONTROL, DIRECTION, AND CLIENT'S OBJECTIVES

SJC Rule 3:07, 1.2—(attorney shall seek lawful objectives of client through means permitted by law & ethical rules; client to decide what plea to enter, whether to waive jury trial, whether client will testify; attorney's representation of client isn't endorsement of client's view or activities, attorney may limit objectives of representation if client consents, attorney shan't counsel or assist in criminal/fraudulent conduct), 1.3 (attorney to represent client zealously within bounds of law, & with reasonable promptness & diligence), 1.4 (attorney to keep client informed, & must explain matters to permit client to make informed decisions re: representation);

ABA Standards for Criminal Justice, Prosecution Function & Defense Function (3d ed. 1993) 4-1.2—professional representative, not "alter ego"; "mouthpiece" image = unethical & harms usefulness (which depends on reputation for integrity/veracity); 4-3.8 keep client informed of all developments; 4-5.2 client decides plea (& whether to change upon plea agreement), jury-waiver, whether to testify, whether to appeal, but most others = strategic decisions for counsel (after full consultation); if disagreement on significant matters of tactics arises, counsel should make record of circumstances, counsel's advice, conclusion, but should protect confidentiality of lawyer-client relationship;

CPCS P/G 1.3(f)—(similar), & client must also decide whether to waive speedy trial;

ABA Model Code of Professional Responsibility (1969) Ethical Considerations 7-7—client decides areas affecting merits or substantially prejudicing rights, e.g. plea & appeal; 7-8 can emphasize morality & harsh consequences, but it's client's decision re: foregoing legally available objectives or methods; 7-11 responsibilities may vary with client's intelligence, mental condition, or age; 7-12 additional responsibilities if client's incapable of considered judgment;

SJC Rule 3:07, Rule 1.14—Client Under A Disability: lawyer shall, as far as possible, maintain a normal client-lawyer relationship with client; if lawyer believes client has become incompetent or that normal client relationship "cannot be maintained . . . because client lacks sufficient capacity to communicate or to make adequately considered decisions" re: representation, & if lawyer believes client at risk of substantial harm, physical, mental, financial, or otherwise, lawyer "MAY" consult family members, adult protective agencies, or other individuals or entities that have authority to protect client AND, if appears necessary, lawyer may seek appointment of guardian ad litem, conservator, or guardian; lawyer may disclose confidential info ONLY to extent necessary to protect client's interests;

C v Simpson 428 M 646 (99)—despite D's explicit direction to appellate counsel not to argue D's incompetency at trial, SJC says counsel "had the right, if not the duty, to advise the relevant courts of his or her concern about a client's competency to stand trial" & no appointment of guardian ad litem to authorize such argument was necessary;

***Godinez v Moran* 509 US 389 (93)**—competency standard for pleading G & waiving right to counsel = same as competency for standing trial despite compelling facts otherwise; cf. *C v Sanchez* 423 M 591 (96) D should have physical ability to communicate with attorney during trial (though court here found that seating arrangement did not infringe on this objective); **(cf. *C v Moore* 379 M 106 (79) D should not be required to sit in dock unless judge rules on record that extraordinary security measures required; *Walker v Butterworth* 599 F.2d 1074 (1st Cir. '79) seating D in prisoner's dock before jury dilutes presumption of innocence);**

C v Robidoux 450 M 144 (2007)—it is not error "for counsel to heed a competent D's informed refusal to pursue an insanity defense";

C v A.B. 72 MAC 10, 14 n 6 (2008)—reversing denial of motion for new trial on ground of ineffective assistance of counsel for failure to request competency determination *by the judge* "reasonably contemporaneous with the trial," but "troubled" by counsel's failure to pursue insanity defense on ground simply that D said he did not want insanity defense: D's competency being in question, his purported "directive" required "more analysis . . . by both counsel and the trial judge";

C v Rodgers 448 M 538 (2007)—extremely lengthy delays, purportedly for Commonwealth's testing of DNA, eventually prompted D's motion to dismiss appointed counsel, and there was "no justification . . . for the clerk's failure to docket the motion or bring it to the judge's attention"; while other types of pro se motions by Ds who are represented by counsel might permissibly be ignored, a motion to dismiss counsel does require "judicial action";

Jones v Barnes 463 US 745 (83)—while D has right to make fundamental decisions re: pleading G or NG, waiving jury, testifying in own behalf, or taking an appeal, D has no constitutional right to compel appointed appellate counsel to press nonfrivolous points requested by the client; counsel's own professional judgment as to best means of prosecuting appeal;

Indiana v Edwards 128 S Ct 2379 (2008)—Constitution forbids trial of accused lacking rational and factual understanding of proceedings and sufficient ability to consult with counsel with reasonable degree of rational understanding, BUT Constitution doesn't forbid states from insisting upon representation by counsel for accused who is "competent" to stand trial but who suffers from severe mental illness so not competent to represent himself;

C v McMahon 443 M 409 (2005)—that D belatedly made a poor strategic decision not to testify & thus undermined defense position given in great detail in counsel's opening statement was not a ground for mistrial (so counsel not ineffective in not having requested mistrial);

C v Moffett 383 M 201 (81)—appellate attorney's responsibilities on arguably "frivolous" appeal, including direction to present contentions of insistent client "succinctly in the brief in a way that will do the least harm to the defendant's cause"; withdrawal from representation is NOT an option;

C v Alvarez 69 MAC 438 (2007)—notwithstanding fact that D himself signed affidavit consenting to withdrawal of direct appeal, defense counsel asserting lack of meritorious issues was inadequate by itself to "discharge his constitutional obligations" (*Moffett* [383 M 201 (81)] brief said to be required), citing *Penson v Ohio* 488 US 75 (88); D's attempt to have appeal reinstated asserted that his previous consent was based on misinformation from appellate counsel; if true, consent = involuntary; D's claim of involuntariness is supported by affidavit AND by procedural history of case ("irregularities" noted);

See also Chapter 7-D, Pretrial Preparation: Competency/Responsibility Issues;

Maldonado v Denno 348 F.2d 12 (2d Cir. '65)—our respect for individual autonomy means D can go to jail under his own banner;

Faretta v California 422 US 806, 848 (75)—(Burger/Rehnquist dissenting dictum) against D's wish or without good consultation strategy, can't waive a constitutional right;

C v Means 454 M 81 (2009)—though a defendant by extraordinary misconduct may "forfeit" right to appointed counsel, this is an extreme sanction (invoked without prior warning to D of consequences of behavior) may be applied only in extraordinary circumstances (usually when D has had more than one appointed counsel, almost never to deny representation during trial, perhaps limited to threats or acts of violence against defense counsel or others, as "a last resort in response to the most grave and deliberate misconduct") after hearing at which D has full and fair opportunity to offer evidence as to all relevant circumstances; "waiver", in contrast, may be express and voluntary, or CAN be by conduct, but "waiver" may be found only after explicit warning has been given to D about threatened consequence of D's behavior and the consequences of proceeding without counsel ("waiver" being a "voluntary," "informed and intentional relinquishment of a known right");

Wainright v Sykes 433 US 72 (77)—(Burger) no federal habeas because lack of motion to suppress = attorney's tactical choice; (but see ***Kimmelman v Morrison* 477 US 365 (86)**, *C v Pena* 31 MAC 201 (91) ineffective assistance of counsel in failing to file motion to suppress)

C v Bernier 359 M 13 (71)—OK on facts not to go insanity; attorney is not D's tool & need not present the defense asked by D;

C v Federici 427 M 740, 744–45 (98)—the choice "not to label himself as 'criminally insane'" is the defendant's, and not defense counsel's or judge's, so long as D has been found competent and has been advised of consequences of his actions by both D counsel and judge; D here had been examined and found competent four times during proceedings, the last such time being when D declined judge's offer to instruct jury on criminal responsibility; "knowing, voluntary, and intelligent" was the standard here used by trial judge to find waiver (& this = a "higher degree of competence"), but SJC reserved issue whether this standard was required;

C v Simpson **428 M 646 (99)**—though D adamantly refused to allow defense counsel to raise issue of competency, it was nonetheless "appropriate" for counsel to bring good faith doubt about a client's competency to the attention of the courts, and "(t)o do so in general terms violates no rule of professional conduct"; appointment of "guardian ad litem" for purpose of authorizing counsel to raise competency issue thus unnecessary; unclear whether it's mandatory for attorney to flag possible incompetency ("obligation **may** exist even when" lawyer believes it's not in D's best interests to raise);

C v Jordan **49 MAC 802 (2000)—when counsel and court believe counsel to have conflict of interest pre-cluding representation of D, court is not required to accept D's insistent waiver of conflict-free counsel;**

C v Downey **65 MAC 547 (2006)**—when D's trial counsel wore concealed microphones without clients' consent pursuant to recording agreement with film company, there was actual conflict of interest; confidential info could be and was disclosed;

C v Finstein **426 M 200 (97)**—choice *not* to argue, simultaneously, "not culprit" and "diminished mental capacity" was strategic choice reasonably made, and D had concurred at the time;

C v Crowder **49 MAC 720, 722 (2000)**—failure to seek individual voir dire (interracial sex case) was tactical, wouldn't be "assumed" to be manifestly unreasonable; side-step of issue, clearly presented, re: whether decision to forego should be D's or counsel's, because motion judge rejected claim that counsel failed to inform D of right;

See also Chapter 2-E, post, re: failure to assert various client wishes;

2-E. COMPETENT AND EFFECTIVE

CPCS P/G 1.2—don't take case if too serious or complex; if appropriate, consult with others; (P/G's, generally, = step-by-step checklist); 1.3 "duty" NOT to represent D if "personal reactions make it impossible for counsel to fulfill the duty of zealous representation";

SJC Rule 3:07, 1.1—competence & adequate preparation; don't handle case alone if need help; don't neglect case; 5.2, don't let employer compromise your professional judgment; SJC Rule 4:01, bar discipline for each act or omission;

ABA Model Code of Professional Responsibility (1969), Ethical Considerations 6-1—become & remain proficient; 6-2 keep abreast, go to continuing legal education programs, participate in bar activities to improve profession; 6-5 obligation = pride, not just fear of sanctions;

ABA Standards for Criminal Justice, Prosecution & Defense Function (3d ed. 1993) 4-1.2—Commentary—seek up-to-date knowledge & adequate training, including "art of advocacy";

Padilla v Kentucky **130 S Ct 1473 (2010)**—Sixth Amendment requires defense counsel to provide *affirmative* (i.e., not just silence) competent advice to a noncitizen D regarding immigration consequences of a guilty plea (& absent such advice, noncitizen may raise claim of ineffective assistance of counsel); there is duty to inquire about citizenship/immigration status initially;

US v Wendy **575 F.2d 1025 (2d Cir. '78)**—admitted to bar doesn't mean competent for all cases;

C v Nwachukwu **65 MAC 112 (2005)**—though counsel had been admitted to practice for more than ten years, he was sufficiently inexperienced in criminal cases that he believed that a witness sequestration order applied to D, and told him to wait outside courtroom (where he missed the first fifteen minutes of trial); ineffectiveness found on this and other ground;

C v Melo **67 MAC 71 (2006)**—that (Rhode Island) trial attorney wasn't admitted to practice in Mass. generally, or specifically for this case wasn't per se ineffective assistance (no automatic reversal);

US v Cronic **466 US 648 (84)**—inexperienced, but not "ineffective"; fact of little time to prepare for trial doesn't automatically mean ineffective assistance (must instead show specific errors made by trial counsel); "per se" ineffective assistance of counsel should be found ONLY (1) where there is "complete denial of counsel" at critical stage of D's trial; (2) where counsel entirely fails to subject prosecution's case to meaningful adversarial testing; and (3) where, "although counsel is available to assist the accused during trial, the likelihood that any lawyer, even a fully competent one, could provide effective assistance is so small that a presumption of prejudice is appropriate";

Bell v Cone **535 US 685 (2002)**—must demonstrate specific prejudice for finding of ineffective assistance UNLESS "counsel ENTIRELY fails to subject prosecution's case to meaningful adversarial testing";

C v Harris **11 MAC 165 (81)**—9 months' experience enough for rape case because District Court experience & association with veterans;

C v Bernier **359 M 13 (71)**—same standards for retained attorney, public defender, & assigned counsel; not "ineffective" for tactics & judgments;

G.L. c. 211D, § 9(a)—CPCS Standards to include continuous/vertical representation, participation by attorneys in training programs;

Moore v US **432 F.2d 730 (3d Cir. '70)**—public defender office without continuous vertical representation may be ineffective counsel;

Chambers v Maroney **399 US 42 (70)**—early counsel appointment best, but not ineffective counsel if new public defender takes over on trial's eve;

Morris v Slappy **461 US 1 (83)**—deny continuance (asked by D, not attorney) & not ineffective counsel where senior public defender replaced ill public defender six days pre-trial; no right to counsel of choice or "meaningful relationship," & #2 was prepared;

Mocks v Commonwealth **426 M 1018 (98)**—no constitutional right to any **particular** court-appointed attorney; but: *C v Brennick* **14 MAC 952 (82)** public defenders aren't fungible;

ABA Standards for Criminal Justice, Providing Defense Services (3d ed. 1992) 5-6.2—"vertical" representation should be provided; "stage"/"horizontal" attorneys (different public defenders representing D at different stages of proceedings) disrupt D's relationship & trust; cf *US ex rel Thomas v Zelker* **332 F.Supp 595 (DSNY '71)** (in considering ineffective assistance of counsel claim, court noted D was represented by at least 4 public defenders before trial & wasn't aware of who was his attorney at any given time);

C v Vickers **60 MAC 24 (2003)**—defense counsel's response to judge's going forward with trial when D apparently defaulted after jury empanelment was a refusal to participate for more than a day as Commonwealth presented its case: this deprived D of representation for portion of trial (testimony went untested by objection or cross-examination; jury possibly left with impression of counsel's hostility to her own client);

C v Baran **74 MAC 256, 290–92 (2009)**—counsel's waiver of right to indictment = ineffective assistance;

C v Saferian **366 M 89 (74)**—test for ineffective assistance of counsel = conduct falling measurably below ordinary fallible attorney **AND** deprived D of otherwise available, substantial defense;

Strickland v Washington **466 US 668 (84)**—federal "ineffective" standard = reasonable competence, including at sentencing; must show prejudice to tip;

Boby v Hook **130 S Ct 13 (2009)**—to determine whether representation falls below objective standard of reasonableness in light of prevailing professional norms, can't use ABA Guidelines which were not announced until 18 years after D's trial;

Wong v Belmontes **130 S Ct 383 (2009)**—judicial scrutiny of counsel's performance must be deferential; burden is on D, not the state, to show reasonable probability that result would have been different but for counsel's deficient performance; reviewing court must consider both the good and the bad evidence when evaluating prejudice;

C v Richard **398 M 392, 394 n.2 (86)**—ineffective counsel per Article 12, Declaration of Rights may need less prejudice than Strickland;

C v Sargent **449 M 576 (2007)**—even assuming that Saferian standard applies to SDP proceedings (G.L. c. 123A), claim of "ineffective assistance" in counsel's advice not to testify at SDP trial failed, because D can't point to any advantage to be obtained from his own testimony concerning certain evidence as opposed to introduction of such evidence by other means (here purportedly accomplished);

Loe v Sex Offender Registry Board **73 MAC 673 (2009)**—leaving open question whether Saferian applies to claims of ineffective assistance before Board because "has not established and entitlement to relief" even under that standard (despite acknowledging he didn't advise client of right to submit letters from family & friends, was unfamiliar with facts, attempted to cross-examine Board's attorney "under the impression that he was a witness for the board," allowed client to testify without any preparation, didn't timely request client's sex offender treatment records, was unaware of 24 factors codified as indicia of risk of reoffense, waived closing argument, didn't file proposed findings and conclusions, etc., "conflict[ing] with numerous performance standards promulgated by [CPCS]";

C v Drew **447 M 635 (2006)**—can't measure 1980 work by CPCS standards promulgated in 1999, and even current violation of CPCS standards doesn't establish current ineffective assistance (but may be admissible as evidence of attorney negligence);

C v Conley **43 MAC 385, 391 (97)**—**calling action 'tactic' doesn't insulate it from scrutiny** in ineffective assistance claim; must be reasonable given all circumstances;

C v Lykus **406 M 135 (89)**—same;

C v Silva **431 M 401, 407–08 (2000) (Lynch, J., dissenting) though majority ignored merit of points, defense "strategy" here was inexcusable because it was no defense at all given the explicit language of the protective order D was charged with violating (unacknowledged by all was that "defense" was actually jury nullification; that trial judge instructed jury in a way which made the defense viable did not make "strategy" reasonable when it was undertaken, i.e., before the instructions constituting law of the case);**

C v Perreira **38 MAC 901 (95)**—strategy sufficiently flawed—relief;

Pineda v Craven **424 F.2d 369 (9th Cir. '70)**—ignorance not strategic/tactical;

2-E.1. Pro Se Defendant ((In)effective Assistance)

C v Jackson **419 M 716 (95)**—D waived right to effective assistance of counsel when he refused appointed counsel and stand-by counsel;

Indiana v Edwards **128 S Ct 2379 (2008)**—Constitution forbids trial of accused lacking rational and factual understanding of proceedings and sufficient ability to consult with counsel with reasonable degree of rational understanding, BUT Constitution doesn't forbid states from insisting upon representation by counsel for accused who is "competent" to stand trial but who suffers from severe mental illness so not competent to represent himself;

C v Kulesa **455 M 447 (2009)**—D was entitled to counsel at trial of "subsequent offender" portion of proceedings regarding G.L. c. 278, § 11A (criminal harassment, subsequent offender), and D's waiver of counsel for trial of substantive offense did NOT operate as waiver of counsel for second part of bifurcated proceeding (though judge COULD conduct colloquy prior to trial of substantive offense which clearly covered both portions, this didn't occur here);

2-E.2.   (Probable) Necessity of Motion for New Trial to Make 'Ineffective Assistance' Claim

C v Brookins **416 M 97 (93)**—without evidentiary hearing & findings of fact, appellate court not in position to know whether ineffective counsel existed;

C v McKinnon **35 MAC 398, 406 (93)**—similar;

C v McCormick **48 MAC 106, 107 (99)**—similar, plus appellate counsel faulted for failing to reconstruct record of inaudibly recorded bench conferences (appellate court "ha(d) no way of knowing whether the issues regarding the putative fresh complaint evidence did in fact arise during trial");

C v Hurley **455 M 53 (2009)**—raising ineffective counsel claim on direct appeal = "strongly disfavor[ed]"; SJC discerns several reasons/benefits in counsel's introducing recordings of conversations between D and girlfriend/alleged victim; trial judge questioned D on record as to his agreement with introducing info "that could be viewed as prejudicial to him"; that in hindsight it may have been "poor strategic decision" doesn't mean "manifestly unreasonable";

C v Duran **435 M 97 (2001)**—though breach of counsel's dramatic opening statement promise by counsel, that D would take stand and explain where he had been at time of crime, gave SJC some pause, refusal to reverse convictions for this (despite other enunciated failings presented on motion for new trial) because matter was not raised in motion for new trial; Court would require evidence why counsel initially believed D would testify & why this belief changed; but see *C v Simmarano* **50 MAC 312 (2000)** trial counsel's failure to request jury instruction re: defense, & failure to offer justification for evidence critical to that defense held to be ineffective assistance on direct appeal rather than via R. 30 motion; "ineffective" analysis used instead of more usual "substantial risk of miscarriage of justice" analysis (because trial counsel failed to object/preserve for appeal these same issues); *C v Livington* **70 MAC 745 (2007)**—failure to request jury instruction on "necessity" defense cognizable as ineffective assistance on direct appeal;

C v Stone **70 MAC 800 (2007)**—refusal to address on direct appeal D's claims of ineffective assistance: "trial counsel's decisions not to act on certain jury instructions or potentially prejudicial testimony could have been reasonable strategy," because, inter alia, objection could have resulted in emphasizing the testimony; motion for new trial accompanied by affidavits with potential for evidentiary hearing and findings = recommended course;

C v Saunders **75 MAC 505 (2009)**—claim that trial counsel ineffective because he brought out much damaging testimony during cross-examination of complainant not reached because factual basis/issue of [un]reasonable strategy not indisputably apparent on trial record;

C v Ramos **66 MAC 548 (2006)**—failure to call witness mentioned in opening statement alleged to have been ineffective assistance, but appellate court wouldn't conclude on present record that there was "no competent strategic reason" for this mention (prior to a critical ruling by trial judge as to what "bad act" evidence might be introduced by Commonwealth if witness were called);

C v Gaskins **419 M 809 (95)**—record on direct appeal (i.e., without R.30 motion and record which might thereby be made) did not support factual allegations made, and did not establish that 'better work would have accomplished something material for' D;

C v Elmes **43 MAC 903 (97)**—"ineffective" claims must usually be made by way of motion for new trial since direct appeal record will be silent as to relevant factors; but see exceptions, e.g., *C v Rossi* **19 MAC 257 (85)**—statutory inadmissibility of particular prior convictions for impeachment purposes probably apparent without motion for new trial (though motion for new trial was pursued, & ineffective counsel was found because defense counsel failed to note that the priors didn't qualify as 'impeachment' under statute, & after losing standard motion in limine, introduced them himself), *C v Grissett* **66 MAC 454, 459 n.11 (2006)** (ineffectiveness found on trial record when defense counsel opened the door to predictable and devastating impeachment of D); *C v Melo* **67 MAC 71, 75 (2006)** (factual basis of claim said to appear indisputably on trial record, BUT subsequently, at 78–79, court held that counsel's reasoning may have been strategic, & no affidavit provided insight); *C v Lester* **70 MAC 55, 60 n.9 (2007)**—failure to object to extremely damaging "totem pole" hearsay cognizable as ineffective assistance on direct appeal; cf. *C v Egardo* **426 M 48 (97)** (issue apparent on direct appeal, but held later not to have been waived then because appellate counsel was same as trial counsel) failure to object to Commonwealth's use against D of his post-**Miranda** silence = ineffective counsel (Commonwealth argued that silence then was inconsistent with "duress" defense offered at trial); *C v DeJesus* **71 MAC 799 (2008)**—record sufficient on direct appeal to consider ineffective assistance claim (failure to object to police testimony about source of photos in array, i.e., "arrested" obviously for other prior crime[s]);

C v Chase **433 M 293 (2001)**—ineffective counsel issue held, in context of R.30 motion, to have been waived by failure to argue it earlier, on "direct" appeal from conviction (issue was apparent on record of trial, i.e., trial counsel asked that jury NOT be instructed on lesser included offense of involuntary manslaughter);

C v Zinser **446 M 807 (2006)**—failure to argue ineffective assistance of counsel in direct appeal WAS NOT A WAIVER OF ISSUE, & judge's contrary holding in refusing to hear motion for new trial was error; "our courts strongly disfavor raising claims of ineffective assistance on direct appeal" & exception, i.e., when factual basis appears indisputably on trial record, "is narrow"; allegation here required consideration of new facts/evidence (trial counsel's failure to explore/present mental impairment defense resulting from D's brain injuries over a decade earlier; affidavit from forensic psychologist accompanied motion for new trial);

C v Collins **36 MAC 25 (94)**—no ineffective counsel shown in failure to call specified witnesses: no affidavits from witnesses to show what testimony would have been, so no showing it would have made a difference;

C v Ellerbe **430 M 769, 777–78 (2000)**—counsel's filing of two affidavits supporting D's motion to dismiss which contradicted each other (& provided basis for impeaching defense at trial) held not ineffective in circumstances;

C v Pena **455 M 1 (2009)**—counsel's apparent failure to provide discovery to Commonwealth (copies of records) led to judge's striking of some defense expert testimony & seemingly, exclusion of records, but SJC says struck/excluded matter was cumulative of other admitted evidence;

C v Stephens **44 MAC 940 (98)**—counsel's forgetting to impeach witness with prior convictions and pending criminal cases (and judge refused to allow him to reopen cross to do so) not found to be ineffective; no ineffective counsel shown by other D, who failed to file affidavits from two allegedly available defense witnesses not called by his trial attorney (and purported content of their testimony, described in D's own affidavit, said to be decidedly inconsistent with his theory at trial);

C v Baker **440 M 519 (2003)**—after judge allowed motion for funds for expert concerning hair embedded and indentation made in wall, judge revoked allowance upon DA's assertion that prosecution would not claim that baby's head was smashed against wall; when prosecution at trial made exactly this claim, defense counsel ineffective in failing to renew request for funds and move for continuance; SJC reversed order denying motion for new trial (accompanied by expert affidavits that hair was not from dead baby and indentation not made by baby's head);

C v Pagan **35 MAC 788, 791 n.1 (94)**—when ineffective counsel is alleged in motion for new trial, testimony of trial counsel is "highly useful" (and might be required), i.e., for analysis of reasonableness of tactic in circumstances known to counsel;

C v Garuti **454 M 48 (2009)**—though post-conviction counsel drafted affidavit and sent to trial counsel concerning D's claim of ineffective assistance, trial counsel replied that he could not help by signing because affidavit contents were inaccurate, and he did not respond to follow-up request that he change or re-write affidavit to make it accurate; SJC refused to hold that trial counsel has duty to provide such affidavit (though appellate counsel cited ethical and constitutional authorities), reasoning that refusal to be more specific "reasonably can be seen as fulfilling a duty to" D;

C v Silva **455 M 503 (2009)**—D having alleged that trial counsel was ineffective for telling him he had to testify and for failing to prepare him for direct and cross-examination, D's motion to strike counsel's responsive affidavit was properly denied: attorney-client privilege "must be deemed waived, in part, to permit counsel to disclose only those confidences necessary and relevant to the defense of the charge of ineffective assistance of counsel"; motion judge's review found affidavit disclosed no more than was necessary to the issue;

C v Beaz **69 MAC 500 (2007)**—refusing on direct appeal to rule on claim of ineffective assistance in failing to challenge for cause juror whose answers signaled partiality;

2-E.3. Opportunity to Prepare

US ex rel. Williams v Twomey **510 F.2d 634 (7th Cir. '75)**—bad trial on-the-fly; ineffective to proceed unprepared though D wanted it;

C v Johnson **424 M 338 (97)**—when "standby" counsel (for pro se D) was converted to full "lead" counsel on day of trial and requested continuance, OK to force D to proceed pro se & deny continuance;

Hawk v Olson **326 US 271 (45)**—ineffective assistance for no continuance; "D needs counsel & counsel needs time";

C v Alvarez **62 MAC 866 (2005)**—refusal to find ineffective assistance of counsel (per se) simply because trial of first degree murder charge occurred just ten days after counsel's first appearance in the case: post-conviction counsel failed to file affidavits of trial counsel or of any potential witnesses setting forth testimony they would have given if interviewed; see also cases cited id. at 871, including *Avery v Alabama* **308 US 444, 446 (40)** ("the Constitution nowhere specifies any period which must intervene between the required appointment of counsel and trial");

C v Philyaw **55 MAC 730 (2002)**—no error in denying continuance on day of trial, despite D-counsel's assertion that she was "totally unprepared," had learned only one day earlier that case was on for trial, and she had not spoken to crucial medical witnesses in nearly a year, because there had been many continuances, case was "relatively simple," counsel hadn't been diligent re: witnesses; proffers re: testimony, etc. may have helped;

C v Brennick **14 MAC 952 (82)**—public defenders not fungible; can't make 2d public defender fill in at jury session default-sentencing, so reverse for ineffective assistance; but see *US v Lespier* **558 F.2d 624 (1st Cir. '77)** contempt for attorney #2 (who did pre-trial hearings) not to fill in when #1 didn't show up (without excuse); *(See SJC Rule 3:07, 1.1, Competence: requires not only legal knowledge, skill, thoroughness, but such "preparation (as) reasonably necessary for the representation"; & SJC Rule 4:01, above; & Chapter 2-I, Counsel: Contempt & Sanctions, & Chapter 2-J, Counsel: Conflicts, Withdrawal, Removal)*;

C v Faulkner **418 M 352 (94)**—there is right to counsel at probation surrender hearing., & newly-appointed counsel must have opportunity to prepare, so error to deny continuance; D's alleged failure to appear at earlier scheduled hearing did not operate as waiver of right to counsel; (see also *Lindsey v Commonwealth* **331 M 1, 5 (54)** "denial of a continuance led to the petitioner being tried then and there for two serious offences with only the assistance of a lawyer who could know almost nothing about the cases and who had had no reasonable opportunity to prepare them");

C v Saferian **366 M 89 (74)**—improvised (though virtuosic) cross-examination = inadvisable; preparation, precision, & focus outweigh bludgeoning, allusive & florid; test = measurably below ordinary fallible att'y & deprived D of otherwise available, substantial ground of defense;

C v Alvarez **433 M 93 (2000)**—review of just the 5-page hospital discharge summary ineffective assistance of counsel given what voluminous medical records revealed to post-conviction counsel;

2-E.4. Conflict of Interests

SJC Rule 3:07, 1.7—(general rule), 1.8 (prohibited transactions), 1.9 (former client), 1.11(successive government & private employment), 1.12 (former judge or arbitrator)

C v Hurley **391 M 76 (84)**—Mass. Constitution Declaration of Rights, Article 12 standard = better than U.S. re: conflict; if conflict, no prejudice need be shown for ineffective assistance of counsel;

C v Downey **65 MAC 547 (2006)**—when D's trial counsel wore concealed microphones without clients' consent pursuant to recording agreement with film company, there was actual conflict of interest; confidential info could be and was disclosed;

C v Perkins **450 M 834 (2008)**—actual conflict of interest created: counsel's duty to give undivided loyalty to client vs. counsel wearing wireless microphone and giving third parties seemingly unfettered access to his confidential relationship with D; though D was not required to show actual prejudice (for art. 12 violation), judge made finding of fact that D had consented to the conflict; though "best practice" is for judges to be vigilant about conflicts

of interest and to initiate colloquy with counsel where appropriate, such action "not constitutionally mandatory";

C v Rondeau **378 M 408, 413 (79)**—failure to withdraw as counsel, so that attorney could testify in support of D's alibi defense = ineffective assistance; viewed as "conflict" between attorney's interest in not being a witness and client's interest in having alibi witness not impeachable with prior convictions & friendship with D;

Guzman v Commonwealth **74 MAC 466 (2009)**—(context = D's civil suit for monetary compensation for wrongful conviction)—trial counsel had refused to call two important witnesses, and moved in limine to prevent Commonwealth from calling one of them (despite knowing that one would be helpful to D) because counsel had represented witness in recently completed case and had assisted counsel in a pending case of witness, and believed it necessary to withdraw from representing D if these witnesses testified;

C v Jordan **49 MAC 802, 807 (2000)**—D has no absolute right to waive "conflict-free" counsel; court has discretion to disqualify conflicted attorney to protect fair & proper administration of justice; court rejects Commonwealth argument that waiver irrelevant since attorney was court-appointed and D had no right to choose own counsel;

C v Stote **456 M 213 (2010)**—appellate defense counsel, during the time of his representation of D, had intimate year-long personal relationship with an appellate ADA who did not participate in any aspect of D's case and who did not speak of it with work colleagues or defense counsel; SJC says no "actual" conflict, but "potential" one, so D not entitled to relief because did not show material prejudice resulting from potential conflict; REMINDER to attorneys to disclose any intimate personal relationship that might impair ability to provide "untrammeled and unimpaired assistance of counsel"; disclosure need not include name of third person, but client's *informed* consent should be sought to preclude later disputes; defense counsel's intimate relationship with the actual trial prosecutor had ended seventeen years before D's trial, and any potential conflict in that regard was disproved by defense counsel's lambasting ADA for trial transgressions;

C v Griffin **404 M 372 (89)**—dismissal for counsel conflict at grand jury = final if irremediable harm;

C v Miller **435 M 274, 280–82 (2001)**—while Miller was being represented by a (trial) public defender in Springfield, Thompson was being represented on appeal by public defender in Boston office &, after seeking advice from Bar Counsel & obtaining waiver of conflict from Thompson, Thompson's appellate counsel pressed inference from trial record (Thompson there represented by private counsel) that real killer was Miller; Miller's trial attorney was not advised of any possible conflict & continued to represent Miller; no 'actual' conflict of interest, held SJC;

2-E.5.　Failures in Jury Empanelment

C v Koonce **418 M 367, 376 (94)**—failure to seek individual voir dire re: racial bias not ineffective assistance because such voir dire may be "counter-productiv(e)," i.e., stirring up such bias without eliminating it;

C v DiRusso **60 MAC 235 (2003)**—rejecting appellate claim that trial counsel ineffective in failing to request individual voir dire re: child sex abuse, because maybe it was trial counsel's valid tactical judgment that inquiry itself would activate latent prejudice: need affidavit asserting not tactical reasoning;

C v Crowder **49 MAC 720, 722 (2000)**—failure to seek individual voir dire (interracial sex case) was tactical, wouldn't be "assumed" to be manifestly unreasonable; side-step of issue, clearly presented, re: whether decision to forego should be D's or counsel's, because motion judge rejected claim that counsel failed to inform D of right;

C v Ortiz **50 MAC 304 (2000)**—failure to peremptorily challenge police officer not ineffective assistance, but one justice dissented;

C v Torres **453 M 722 (2009)**—failure of counsel to peremptorily strike police relative not 'ineffective assistance';

C v Beaz **69 MAC 500 (2007)**—refusing on direct appeal to rule on claim of ineffective assistance in failing to challenge for cause juror whose answers signaled partiality; "the potential input from the attorney on a motion for new trial on any tactical reasons for his failure to challenge the juror seems to us to be potentially and particularly helpful";

2-E.6.　Discovery Failings

Chappee v Vose **843 F.2d 25 (1st Cir. '88)**—not ineffective assistance for expert witness being excluded because counsel failed to disclose pre-trial (reasoned stratagem, though stupid/unethical); but see (better state law?) *C v Conley* **43 MAC 385, 391 (97)**—calling action 'tactic' doesn't insulate it from scrutiny in ineffective assistance of counsel claim; must be reasonable given all circumstances;

C v Lykus **406 M 135 (89)**—same; AND PARTICULARLY

C v Sena **429 M 590, 594–96 (99)**—ineffective assistance for failure to obtain/familiarize self with defense investigative reports in advance of trial (reports in possession of prior counsel) and for failure to obey discovery orders requiring their disclosure to Commonwealth (which here resulted in judge's sanction of precluding use of important report);

C v Juzba **46 MAC 319 (99)**—though defense testimony excluded because of counsel's failure to obey discovery orders, no ineffective assistance found: appellate court believed that better work wouldn't have accomplished something material for defense, given its view of strength of prosecution case;

C v Bourgeois **68 MAC 433 (2007)**—failure to move to obtain rape complainant's counseling records NOT ineffective assistance, as D didn't establish how trial counsel "could have satisfied the stringent Bishop-Fuller criteria based on information contained in the materials that were properly in the defendant's possession prior to trial";

C v Hudson **446 M 709 (2006)**—counsel's failure to give notice of alibi witness (required by signed pretrial conference report), resulting in exclusion of her testimony, was conduct measurably below that of ordinary fallible lawyer, BUT D's failure to elucidate "the precise contours of [witness's] testimony", plus fact that witness was D's girlfriend and impeachable for bias, plus fact that D didn't name her to counsel until just before SECOND trial for murder (strongly impeachable for delay), meant her testimony would have been "virtually useless";

C v Alvarez **433 M 93 (2000)**—failure to obtain/familiarize self with D's medical records prior to trial = ineffective assistance; competent counsel would have investigated full extent of medical history which could have contributed to D's underlying mental disease or defect;

C v Baran **74 MAC 256 (2009)**—failure to obtain UN-EDITED videotaped interviews of child sexual assault complainants (showing, inter alia, denials of abuse by D, allegations of abuse by others), and failure to file any discovery motions = two of many grounds of ineffective assistance;

2-E.7.　Failure to File Motions

C v Tanner **417 M 1 (94)**—failure to move for speedy trial not ineffective assistance (no prejudice shown, and not conduct falling below that of reasonably competent attorney);

C v A.B. **72 MAC 10 (2008)**—failure to request competency determination by the judge close to time of trial was ineffective assistance;

C v Barrett **418 M 788 (94)**—ineffective assistance in failing to seek dismissal of 12 charges beyond statute of limitations;

C v Gillette **33 MAC 427 (92)**—failure to file motion in limine to exclude inadmissible evidence of D's predisposition to rape was ineffective assistance;

C v Diaz **448 M 286 (2007)**—failure to prevent jury view of "memorials to the victim erected at the murder scene" not ineffective assistance as counsel cited to jury certain names on the memorials to show bias of potential prosecution witnesses, a "strategic decision . . . not manifestly unreasonable" (and besides, co-D's counsel's objection had been overruled);

C v Hernandez **63 MAC 426 (2005)**—failure to consult client concerning issue of joinder of indictments not ineffective, & was instead here a valid tactical judgment;

C v Masonoff **70 MAC 162 (2007)**—failure to file motion to sever trial from co-D's trial held to have been illegitimate basis for judge to have found ineffective assistance and order new trial; ineffectiveness based on failure to file motion requires a D to show motion would likely have been granted, *C v Diaz* **448 M 286 (2007)**—failure to file severance motion not ineffective assistance because D could not show that motion "would likely have been granted";

C v Pagels **69 MAC 607 (2007)**—no ineffectiveness in failure to object to joinder of charges: assault and battery on girlfriend properly joined with intimidation of witness (the girlfriend): phone calls constituting proof of the latter would have been admissible as consciousness of guilt of former (and element of "witness" in latter concerned the former); D's claim that counsel's advising him to "assist" witness with her recantation affidavit was ineffective because it placed him in "dangerous situation" opening him to prosecution for witness intimidation also rejected (profanity-laced, threatening telephone calls from D to witness were tape-recorded from jail);

***Kimmelman v Morrison* 477 US 365 (86)**—ineffective assistance of counsel for no motion to suppress (because got no discovery, because relied on DA to turn over evidence & complaining witness to drop case);

C v Pena **31 MAC 201 (91)**—ineffective assistance in failure to file motion to suppress;

C v DiGeronimo **38 MAC 714 (95)**—ineffective counsel in failure to file suppression motion;

C v Comita **441 M 86 (2004)**—to prevail on motion for new trial on ground of ineffective assistance of counsel in failing to file motion to suppress evidence obtained by warrantless stop, D had burden to prove that Commonwealth could not have established legality of stop;

C v Clemente **452 M 295 (2008)**—not ineffective assistance to fail to file motions having minimal chance of success: statements would not have been suppressed because, according to SJC, D not in custody when questioned so no need of Miranda warnings (D was questioned in "neutral location, a room in a court house" and "voluntarily agreed" to speak with detective, and was allowed to leave to attend son's arraignment, not arrested until after that arraignment), and SJC believed no question of voluntariness either; failure to challenge photo ID not ineffective as ID not an issue at trial, D not disputing presence in restaurant or that he shot victims;

C v Hernandez **448 M 711 (2007)**—reasonable suspicion (D pacing in area of high incidence of drug trafficking, giving other man item hidden in his shoe, but no "exchange") apparently became probable cause simply because D fled from cop who approached him; this disposition allows SJC to reject D's claim of ineffective assistance in failing to file motion to suppress;

***Robinson v Commonwealth* 445 M 280 (2005)**—judge has discretion to deem D's voluntary absence (found, after hearing) from hearing on motion to suppress a waiver of D's right to be present, but such waiver is NOT a waiver of D's right to the suppression hearing or D's right to effective assistance of counsel at such hearing;

C v Crespo **59 MAC 926 (2003)**—appellate court here able to use trial record to resolve (& reject on merits)

ineffective assistance claim (for failure to file motion to suppress);

C v Johnston **60 MAC 13, 21–22 (2003)**—trial counsel's failure to specify in suppression motion that Miranda warnings omitted info that D had right to have attorney present during questioning meant that this particular issue wasn't preserved for appeal: failure might be ineffective assistance of counsel, but Rule 30 motion necessary;

C v Bennett **414 M 269 (93)**—no ineffective assistance in failing to file motion to suppress unless counsel reasonably should have known affiant for search warrant lied;

C v Jones **42 MAC 378 (97)**—though counsel failed to file motion to suppress very damaging statements by D (which motion would/should have been allowed), no ineffective assistance found because evidence of guilt so strong even without statements;

C v Tevlin **433 M 305 (2001)**—failure to file motion to suppress ID not ineffective assistance where record showed D & counsel considered issue for months & had legitimate strategic reason for not doing so; D's personal waiver of issue & concurrence with counsel's judgment on record here;

C v Wei H. Ye **52 MAC 390 (2001)**—no ineffective assistance in failure to file motion to suppress, because evidence at trial showed D had no expectation of privacy as to some evidence; as to others, record on direct appeal inadequate to establish whether or not D had any reasonable expectation of privacy (so motion for new trial would be necessary to press the claim);

C v Hunt **50 MAC 565 (2000)**—failure to file motion to suppress statements for purported lack of Miranda warnings (record silent on point, so warnings may have been given) not ineffective assistance since obvious tactical benefit was to allow introduction of D's "innocent" explanation for possession of stolen property, without having to testify at trial;

C v Cutts **444 M 821, 830–31 (2005)**—similar rationale in murder case for strategy of not filing suppression motion;

C v Segovia **53 MAC 184 (2001)**—ineffective assistance of counsel found in failure to file motion to suppress D's videotaped custodial interrogation where D had viable claim that cop ignored D's request for translator & paralegal before continuing the questioning, and where fruit of the interrogation was prosecution's discovery of a witness who provided damaging trial testimony;

C v Constantino **443 M 521, 523 n.1 (2005)**—failure to file motion to dismiss duplicative indictments argued to be "ineffective assistance of counsel", but SJC didn't rule on issue & decided, instead, substantial risk of a miscarriage of justice;

C v Delarosa **50 MAC 623, 632 (2000)**—failure to move for mistrial when cop-witness twice noted that D 'refused to cooperate'; judge sua sponte gave strong "strike" instruction & scathing denunciation of cop for so testifying ("If anything, you should look on it negatively that for some reason the witness felt the need to offer it to you. If there is any negative inference to be drawn, it's to the one stating it, not towards the defendant"), & counsel could well have concluded (given defense of police failures & inept investigation) that instructions did more for defense than another trial without either offending testimony or judge's critical comments;

C v Baker **440 M 519 (2003)**—after judge allowed motion for funds for expert concerning hair embedded and indentation made in wall, judge revoked allowance upon DA's assertion that prosecution would not claim that baby's head was smashed against wall; when prosecution at trial made exactly this claim, defense counsel ineffective in failing to renew request for funds and move for continuance; SJC reversed order denying motion for new trial (accompanied by expert affidavits that hair was not from dead baby and indentation not made by baby's head);

C v Watson **455 M 246 (2009)**—failure to move for funds for expert witness on ID not ineffective: until shortly before trial, D (who had retained counsel) said he had $ for expert, and even after, counsel did not believe D indigent; counsel presented vigorous ID defense in other respects; admissibility of expert testimony re: ID is not matter of right, but within judge's discretion;

C v Bell **455 M 408 (2009)**—failure to move for required finding when one should have been allowed = substantial risk of miscarriage of justice, so "we need not address this particular ineffective assistance . . . claim";

Roe v Flores-Ortega **528 US 470 (2000)**—failure to file notice of appeal after D has instructed counsel to do so = ineffective assistance; there is constitutionally-imposed duty to consult with client re: whether to appeal, when a rational D would want to appeal and when this particular D, regardless of merits, "reasonably demonstrated" to counsel that he was interested in appealing; to show prejudice from ineffective assistance here = demonstrate reasonable probability that D would have timely appealed but for counsel's deficient performance; need not show that appeal would have afforded relief; prejudice is "the forfeiture of a proceeding itself";

2-E.8. Failure to Investigate, Failure to Proffer Evidence

C v Barans **74 MAC 256 (2009)**—wholesale failures to obtain discovery, investigate case, file motions in limine, interview witnesses, call expert witnesses + waiving right to indictment and D's right to be present at competency hearing of child witnesses, inter alia = allowance of motion for new trial decades after conviction; at 276: "failure to involve at expert manifestly disadvantaged [D]";

C v Haggerty **400 M 437 (87)**—ineffective assistance for not investigating cause of death;

C v Martin **427 M 816, 821 & n.5 (98)**—failure to understand/utilize available evidence that prosecution's testimony concerning presence of LSD (cause of death)

relied merely on "screening" test, that false positives are common (error rates exceeding 60%), that confirmatory test was necessary to substantiate conclusion, was ineffective assistance;

C v Phinney **446 M 155 (2006)**—failure to present third-party culprit evidence was ineffective assistance of counsel (trial court judge's allowance of motion for new trial in murder case upheld by SJC after allowance of Commonwealth's "gatekeeper" petition);

C v Garcia **66 MAC 167 (2006)**—failure to note significance of information in discovery documents, with consequent failure to call witness who would impeach child sex complainant, was ineffective assistance; counsel's usual practice of never speaking to witnesses before trial = unreasonable on its face; can't make "tactical decision" without obtaining relevant facts; strategic choices made after less than complete investigation are reasonable only to extent that reasonable professional judgments support the limitations on investigation (citing *Wiggins v Smith* 539 US 510, 533 [2003]);

C v Naylor **73 MAC 518 (2009)**—judge abused discretion in denying evidentiary hearing on Rule 30 motion alleging ineffective assistance of trial counsel in failing to support misidentification defense with photo of D taken close in time to shooting, showing he had shoulder-length braids and mustache and beard; trial counsel elicited testimony that shooter had no facial hair but nothing about hairstyle, and failed to direct jury's attention to dramatic difference between D's appearance at trial and photo selected from array (affidavit submitted with new trial motion asserted D wore long braids and facial hair on date of offense as well as at trial);

C v Drumgold **423 M 230 (96)**—no ineffective assistance in counsel showing witness single photo of D pretrial **though this created a positive ID which did not otherwise exist** with this witness; same re: having D attend jury "view", counsel also afforded same witness opportunity for another admissible out-of-court ID;

C v Messere **14 MAC 1 (82)**—(harmless) failure to interview witness;

C v Gonzalez **443 M 799, 810 n.11 (2005)**—because witness's grand jury testimony = favorable to D, counsel not ineffective in calling her at trial, where her testimony = "significantly different" BUT "better practice" = to have "interviewed her";

C v Roberio **428 M 278 (98)**—counsel's failure to investigate and advance defense of lack of criminal responsibility = ineffective assistance; counsel's testimony in justification (that he asked D questions in order to determine that D could "focus on the situation") concerned competence, NOT criminal responsibility; although judge on motion for new trial concluded that testimony and report of a clinical psychologist were not "credible" (diseases/defects found were ADHD, traumatic brain injuries, language learning disability, oppositional defiant disorder, and substance abuse mood disorder (pathological intoxication, or personality change when drinking)), and denied motion for new trial on this basis, SJC reversed: once expert's individual qualifications were ratified and his area of expertise found to be scientifically legitimate, it's "error for judge to deny motion for new trial based on his assessment of the expert's credibility"; credibility is issue for jury, not judge; fact that expert was weakened by cross-examination is "not relevant in deciding the new trial question";

C v Milton **49 MAC 552 (2000)**—failure to obtain psych evaluation of D = ineffective assistance; failure of judge below to recognize, after evidentiary hearing ordered by appeals court on remand, what had been clear on record to him during guilty plea (i.e., that there was something "wrong" with D) was "critical error";

C v A.B. **72 MAC 10 (2008)**—counsel's failure to seek from the judge, reasonably contemporaneously with trial, a determination as to D's competency = ineffective assistance of counsel; court also "troubled" by trial counsel's eschewing insanity defense simply because (probably incompetent) D said "no" when asked if he wished to raise insanity defense (more analysis "appears to be required by both counsel and the trial judge" in this circumstance);

C v Candelario **446 M 847 (2006)**—counsel did obtain psych evaluation of D, and decision to forego presentation of psych evidence was appropriate tactical decision, given "weakness" of D's own expert evidence and strong contrary evidence that D was feigning any mental illness or impairment; no hearing on motion for new trial required when hearing wouldn't appreciably add to written material & submission didn't cast doubt on counsel's competence;

C v Hensley **454 M 721 (2009)**—with expert and medical records, motion for new trial argued statements' involuntariness & D's inability to waive Miranda due to combined effects of carbon monoxide poisoning (attempted suicide), ingestion of sleeping pills, cognitive impairments due to depression, and stress of interrogation, plus major depression, but SJC refuses relief; also, decision not to call particular expert at trial was not manifestly unreasonable for specified reasons, including probable admission of expert's opinion that D did not lack criminal responsibility;

Montgomery v Peterson **846 F.2d 407, 413 (7th Cir. '88)**—ineffective assistance for failure to investigate "timed receipt" document potentially dispositive re: alibi (& not cumulative);

C v Conley **43 MAC 385 (97)**—ineffective assistance in failing to have evidence tested as urged by D to corroborate D's version & refute prosecution witnesses;

C v Alvarez **433 M 93 (2000)**—failure to obtain/ familiarize self with D's medical records prior to trial = ineffective assistance; competent counsel would have investigated full extent of medical history which could have contributed to D's underlying mental disease or defect, & would have corroborated D's claim of head injury in vehicle accident;

C v Johnson **435 M 113 (2001)**—no ineffective assistance from presentation of inconsistent defenses: D himself insisted upon "hopeless" misidentification defense,

and explicitly concurred with presentation of mental impairment evidence after evaluation of prosecution's case-in-chief at trial, and counsel informed him that latter would negate the purportedly "primary" ID defense;

C v McCready **50 MAC 521 (2000)**—failure to obtain, prior to trial, a missing page from counsel's copy of D's hospital record, ensured that its mid-trial delivery and admission into evidence would be without benefit of reasoned and researched arguments against such introduction (but ineffective assistance not argued);

C v Squailia **429 M 101, 103–04 (99)**—no ineffective assistance in failing to examine contents of briefcase when briefcase was admitted as evidence (despite highly prejudicial documents inside), because contents purportedly not relevant to "jury's consideration of the key issue of intent";

C v Sarmanian **426 M 405, 407 (98)**—no ineffective assistance in failing to call additional witnesses re: D's intoxication because cumulative (but cf. *Bryer* **398 M 9, 12–13 (86)** though cumulative, evidence can be critically important because it **corroborates**; *C v Rondeau* **378 M 408, 413 (79)** similar, + failure to withdraw as counsel, so that attorney could testify in support of D's alibi defense = ineffective assistance);

C v Cepulonis **9 MAC 302 (80)**—(harmless) error from not investigating alibi & giving bad parole advice for plea;

C v Caban **48 MAC 179 (99)**—failure to investigate/ interview witness (employer + records) supporting D's alibi maybe ineffective assistance; error (abuse of discretion) in failing to hold hearing on motion for new trial because "substantial issue" of ineffective assistance found; "failure to investigate the only defense (D) has, if facts known to or with minimal diligence accessible to counsel support that defense, falls beneath" competency expected, EVEN THOUGH D failed to keep appointments with counsel; failure to request continuance to fully interview/ prepare alibi witness maybe ineffective assistance (despite fact that need for continuance was due to poor preparation by D-counsel);

C v Delp **41 MAC 435, 441 (96)**—failure to utilize sex assault complainant's school records indicating "impaired reality testing" might be ineffective assistance;

C v Oliveira **431 M 609 (2000)**—ineffective assistance in not obtaining, prior to trial, mental health treatment records of sex assault complainant could be shown only if contents of records were such that D was deprived of substantial ground of defense; post-conviction counsel here made sufficient proffer to obtain in camera review of records, and judge was to make available to counsel relevant portions so counsel could argue substantiality;

C v Finstein **426 M 200 (97)**—reasonable to forego "diminished capacity" because inconsistent with principal defense that D didn't commit the murder (no ineffective assistance);

C v Tolan **453 M 634 (2009)**—failure to introduce evidence of implied offers of leniency during D's interrogation not ineffective assistance because theory of defense was accident, and D's police statement as given was used to corroborate; focus on [in]voluntariness "would have been a distraction" offering little/no benefit to D;

C v Aviles **40 MAC 440 (96)**—failure (1) to introduce unimpeachable witnesses re: D's medical incapacity to commit crime (D on crutches at time), & (2) to argue alibi, was ineffective assistance;

C v Morales **453 M 40 (2009)**—failure to call specified alibi witnesses not ineffective as counsel reasonably judged testimony weak or not credible and likely to dilute defense that witnesses with "cooperation" agreements were lying; failure to pursue issue of D's voluntary intoxication not unreasonable as it would embrace witness about lack of sobriety but disbelieve him about crime details; "intoxication" defense would have been inconsistent with defense because implicitly conceding D's participation in murder;

C v Nwachukwu **65 MAC 112 (2005)**—failure to introduce work record of complainant that directly contradicted her testimony was ineffective assistance;

C v Ly **454 M 223 (2009)**—failure to obtain telephone records prior to rape complainant's testimony, to show that she repeatedly telephoned D after sex was ineffective assistance: D claimed that sex was consensual and that complainant made allegation because of parental ire, and carried through because D rejected her request that he take her away with him out of state; "centrality of the telephone calls to the only issue in the case is apparent"; that attorney was unprepared because he did not believe she would testify falsely (n.5) not justification;

C v Delacruz **61 MAC 445 (2004)**—hearing on motion for new trial should have been held, because maybe ineffective assistance to have failed to call one of perhaps three (but maybe only two) culprits in armed robbery, who had pled G, because he proffered that D was not involved; second culprit had plea-bargained and was chief witness against D; fact that he was impeachable as felon not dispositive;

C v Williams **450 M 879, 892 (2008)**—D's recorded statement was edited, defense wanting omission of references to D's incarceration, drug use, gang membership, & possession of guns, and DA wanting redaction of D's comments re: victim's reputation for violence and intimidation: because self-defense was at issue, victim's reputation was relevant and admissible (and defense counsel was perhaps ineffective in agreeing to this redaction, albeit as a 'quid pro quo' for other redactions: issue of 'tactic'/reasonableness would not be decided without hearing on motion for new trial);

C v Hudson **446 M 709 (2006)**—no ineffective assistance in failure to impeach prior recorded testimony of identifying witness with his signed affidavit recanting such testimony BECAUSE it would have been met by evidence that the affidavit was obtained from him under duress, i.e., by inmates visiting his cell; also not ineffective to have failed to call particular witnesses whose affidavits asserted that they would have impeached prosecution witnesses

with inconsistent statements, because counsel could have viewed the affidavits (from D's fellow inmates) as fabrications resulting from concerted efforts;

C v Hill **432 M 704, 717–19 (2000)**—affirming allowance of motion for new trial on ground, inter alia, that trial attorney didn't call eyewitness to arrival & departure of probable murderers at crime scene, despite Commonwealth's claim that testimony could have hurt D ("few witnesses are totally helpful");

C v Grissett **66 MAC 454 (2006)**—"grave error for counsel to call [D] to testify and then pose questions on direct . . . which left [D] vulnerable to a predictably devastating cross-examination", i.e., after direct elicited that D had never purchased or used cocaine, prosecutor received permission to impeach D with prior conviction for possession with intent to distribute cocaine; counsel should have been aware of prior conviction & avoided questioning which opened the door; ineffective assistance found;

C v O'Neil **51 MAC 170 (2001)**—failure to utilize evidence of reward to chief prosecution witness, failure to object to prosecutor's misconduct related to such reward/evidence, failure to make proffer and legal argument to judge re: evidentiary point of impeachment for motive = ineffective assistance;

C v Frank **433 M 185 (2001)**—failure to use expert testimony re: D's alcoholism & intoxication as negating specific intent & premeditation, as well as plausibility of D's memory failures (ridiculed by Commonwealth) not ineffective assistance, accepting trial attorney's claim that cross-examination of expert could be potentially damaging; expert testimony not necessary to raise mental impairment;

C v Egardo **426 M 48 (97)**—failure to object to Commonwealth's use against D of his post-**Miranda** silence = ineffective assistance (Commonwealth argued that silence then was inconsistent with "duress" defense offered at trial);

C v Epsom **422 M 1002, 661 NE2d 1337 (96)**—failure to call witness suggesting self-defense may have been ineffective assistance; and appellate counsel in murder-one case may have been similarly deficient for not pursuing motion for new trial prior to direct appeal;

C v Smith **49 MAC 127 (2000)**—not ineffective assistance to fail to call as defense witness the principal in crime, though principal's affidavit filed with motion for new trial asserted he committed crime alone without D's prior knowledge/assistance; affidavit from trial counsel asserted full review of all statements of principal prior to decision, & consultation & agreement with D that testimony "would do more damage than good"; appellate court thinks assertions by co-D "the weakest sort of evidence";

C v Barnette **45 MAC 486 (98)**—not ineffective assistance to fail to introduce in trial for "hate crime" against "Mexican" persons, evidence that D's niece (for whom he was baby-sitting at the time of incident) was "partially of Puerto Rican descent," despite argument that this negated "discriminatory animus element";

C v Donahue **430 M 710, 715–16 (2000)**—not ineffective assistance to introduce psychiatric testimony containing D's statements (with evidence of premeditation and extreme atrocity/cruelty, & D's clear memory, inconsistent with "dissociative disorder" proffered by defense at trial) because counsel "had little with which to work";

C v Kirkpatrick **423 M 436, 448 n.9 (96)**—maybe ineffective assistance in failing to obtain expert witness, held to be prerequisite to admitting medical records of D and sexual assault complainant, because records were not self-explanatory and were beyond expertise of lay jurors;

C v Baker **440 M 519 (2003)**—after judge allowed motion for funds for expert concerning hair embedded and indentation made in wall, judge revoked allowance upon DA's assertion that prosecution would not claim that baby's head was smashed against wall; when prosecution at trial made exactly this claim, defense counsel ineffective in failing to renew request for funds and move for continuance; SJC reversed order denying motion for new trial (accompanied by expert affidavits that hair was not from dead baby and indentation not made by baby's head);

C v McQuade **46 MAC 827 (99)**—D-counsel's introduction of D's criminal history, prior bad acts, incarceration said to be reasonable strategy of "defusing its impact," assuming (questionably) that Commonwealth would have been permitted to cross-examine D on the subjects; counsel's failure to introduce particular scientific evidence, a prerequisite to admissibility of D's expert's testimony, called an "oversight," and excused (record showed counsel had "educated himself" about the subjects and was able to cross-examine and present some evidence to raise questions about adequacy of Commonwealth's testing);

2-E.9. Failure to Cite Correct Legal Authority

C v Juzba **46 MAC 319 (99)**—counsel's failure to cite statute making admissible state police chemist's report concerning absence of sperm cells/seminal fluid was behavior falling below that of ordinary fallible lawyer, but no ineffective assistance found (because court believed nothing material for defense was lost as result);

C v Scheffer **43 MAC 398, 399–400 (97)**—failure to cite *Ruffen* **399 M 811 (87)** as basis for admissibility of proffered evidence = ineffective assistance (convictions rev'd);

C v Owen **57 MAC 529 (2003)**—D entitled to evidentiary hearing on motion for new trial based on ineffective assistance of trial and appellate counsel for purported failure to show that young sex assault complainant could have known about sex in some way other than abuse by D: DSS/police reports showed that complainant had seen mother and partner engaged in sex & had thereafter played with dolls in sexual manner, that adolescent cousin had sexually abused her, & that another adolescent had fondled her chest; trial counsel had abandoned the inquiry after judge deferred ruling on D's motion to question complain-

ant about past sex abuse (initially at a voir dire examination);

C v Simmarano **50 MAC 312 (2000)**—trial counsel's failure to request jury instruction re: defense, & failure to offer justification for evidence critical to that defense ("state of mind" exception to hearsay objection, plus admissible for impeachment (inconsistent statement) of alleged victim) held to be ineffective assistance on direct appeal rather than via R. 30 motion;

2-E.10. Effective Assistance, Opening Statements

C v DeCicco **44 MAC 111, 122 (98)**—error to state to jury that D might testify when counsel has not discussed possibility with D or prepared D to testify (here harmless);

C v Dahl **430 M 813 (2000)**—no ineffective assistance found though D argued that counsel hadn't advised that defendant's testimony was necessary/crucial for various proffered defenses, and though trial counsel told judge, on trial record, that he wasn't adequately representing D due to lack of sleep and travel to Florida on weekends, and pressure of having two clients on trial simultaneously in different states, here for 1st degree murder without death penalty, and there in a capital (death penalty) murder trial; SJC refused to find "genuine conflict of interest" in circumstances;

C v Duran **435 M 97, 109 (2001)**—despite counsel's failure to deliver on his opening statement promise that D would testify as to where he was at time of crime (D didn't testify), SJC would require, prior to finding ineffective assistance of counsel, explanation why counsel "initially believed (if he did)" that D would testify, and why this seeming belief changed, i.e., evidence during a motion for new trial required;

C v Ramos **66 MAC 548 (2006)**—though counsel promised in opening that jurors would hear from psychologist about D's state of mind & his suffering as a child & posttraumatic stress syndrome, counsel decided not to call the promised witness because PERHAPS ADA would be allowed to introduce a prior bad act/similar crime by D in cross-exam of psychologist: to arguments that statement shouldn't have been made prior to decision on calling witness, and that counsel should have taken up judge on offer of voir dire of witness (& probable early/pre-trial ruling on the admissibility of the bad act), appeals court said claim required better record than direct appeal;

C v McMahon **443 M 409 (2005)**—that D belatedly and contrary to all prior preparation made poor strategic decision not to testify & thus undermined defense position given in great detail in counsel's opening statement was not a ground for mistrial (so counsel not ineffective in not having requested mistrial);

Ouber v Guarino **293 F.3d 19 (1st Cir. 2002)**—ineffective assistance of counsel in repeatedly, stringently promising that D would testify, & thereafter not calling her: "error attributed to counsel consists of two inextricably intertwined events: the attorney's initial decision to present the petitioner's testimony as the centerpiece of the defense (and his serial announcement of that fact to the jury in his opening statement) in conjunction with his subsequent decision to advise the petitioner against testifying. Taken alone, each of these decisions may have fallen within the broad universe of acceptable professional judgments. Taken together, however, they are indefensible";

C v Wilson **443 M 122, 138 (2004)**—counsel's reference to alibi witness didn't amount to promising to call that witness [here];

C v Scott **430 M 351, 357 (99)**—failure to make opening statement not ineffective assistance here, and probably impossible to show that such failure influenced jury verdict anyway; *C v Williams* **450 M 879 (2008)**—same; waiving opening = reasonable tactic if. e.g., counsel not sure whether D will testify or where defense not offering witnesses;

Anderson v Butler **858 F.2d 16 (1st Cir. '88)**—broken opening promise = ineffective assistance;

C v Carney **34 MAC 922 (93)**—but in circumstances here, no prejudice from broken opening promise, so ineffective assistance not established;

C v Underwood **36 MAC 906 (94)**—failure to call witness mentioned in opening statement found to be legitimate, tactically, because D's trial testimony was inconsistent with that of potential witness and prosecution introduced evidence that D sought, from another person, false testimony supportive of self-defense;

C v Swan **38 MAC 539 (95)** after opening statement re: defense, counsel abandoned it altogether when judge sustained DA's objection to a question; counsel made no proffer concerning relevance and did not have marked for ID a copy of AG's regulations (critical/essential to defense); ineffective assistance found;

2-E.11. Issues Surrounding Plea Recommendations

McAleney v US **539 F.2d 282 (1st Cir. '76)**—mistake re: DA's G-plea recommendation = ineffective assistance & question re: attorney's fitness;

Turner v State of Tennessee **664 F.Supp 1113 (D. Tenn. '87)**—not urging G - plea & 2 years' sentence (D got 70) = ineffective assistance;

C v Mahar **442 M 11 (2004)**—a criminal defendant may challenge sentence on ground of ineffective assistance of counsel re: decision to reject plea bargain offer (but no ineffectiveness shown here);

2-E.12. Failure to Request Jury Instructions

C v Gilliard **36 MAC 183, 191–92 (94)**—failure to request lesser included offense jury instruction may be ineffective assistance; *S.C.* **46 MAC 348 (99)** allowance of motion for new trial affirmed on appeal: trial counsel "never considered" asking jury for lesser included offense

(though there was evid. basis for convicting D only of A&B (liability only as joint venturer intending to beat V with fists, with no intent to use or knowledge of, knife) instead of second degree murder); "never considering" was ineffective assistance, but it also would've been ineffective assistance if counsel considered and rejected option of requesting instruction on lesser offense; court didn't reach issue whether failure to consult D about gambling to forego lesser offense instruction is "misconduct which itself would warrant the allowance of a new trial" (but noted that Commonwealth's Brief acknowledged that counsel "unquestionably should have consulted" D);

C v Pagan **35 MAC 788 (94)**—failure to request lesser included offense not ineffective assistance here because would have detracted from defense of "didn't do it";

C v Gelpi **416 M 729 (94)**—failure to request instruction on defense of "honest & reasonable mistake of fact" (armed robbery case) = ineffective assistance;

C v Simmarano **50 MAC 312 (2000)**—trial counsel's failure to request jury instruction re: defense to home invasion, i.e., D's 'permission to enter through "cumulative practice" & failure to offer justification for evidence critical to that defense = ineffective assistance;

C v Livington **70 MAC 745 (2007)**—failure to request jury instruction on "necessity" defense = ineffective assistance (cognizable on direct appeal);

C v Acevedo **446 M 435 (2006)**—where evidence supports it, D is entitled to correct instructions on both provocation and self-defense; jury must have opportunity to consider voluntary manslaughter on both theories; correct instruction on self-defense doesn't cure erroneous instruction on provocation or eliminate prejudice from failure to instruct at all on provocation as theory of voluntary manslaughter; trial counsel's failure to request "provocation" instruction deprived D of an available defense;

C v Peloquin **52 MAC 480, 483–84**—further appellate review allowed (2001) ineffective assistance = failure to request instruction that D had no duty to retreat if victim was in D's dwelling unlawfully & D used reasonable means to defend 'self or others, & acted in reasonable belief that V was about to inflict great bodily injury or death upon D or another lawful occupant: see "castle law," G.L. c. 278, § 8A; on further review, 437 M 204 (2002), SJC affirmed denial of new trial, finding no ineffective assistance;

C v Scott **430 M 351, 356–57 (99)**—failure to request instruction on lack of criminal responsibility not ineffective assistance (and not entitled to one on this evidence anyway?); reasonable to ask instead for 2d degree murder based on diminished capacity due to substance abuse;

C v Evans **42 MAC 618 (97)**—failure to request model ID charge not ineffective assistance, given circumstances here;

2-E.13. Failure to Object/Request Limiting Instructions

C v Baran **74 MAC 256 (2009)**—failure to protect D's right to public trial (during testimony of child complainants, courtroom was closed) = ineffective assistance by trial counsel, and appellate counsel ineffective in failing to raise issue on direct appeal;

C v Gillette **33 MAC 427 (92)**—failure to file motion in limine to exclude inadmissible evidence of D's predisposition to rape was ineffective assistance;

C v Dwyer **448 M 122, 127 (2006)**—counsel's acquiescence to admission of unredacted medical records which included inadmissible hearsay was ineffective assistance;

C v Medeiros **456 M 52 (2010)**—distinguishes *Dwyer*; medical record naming D as perpetrator was consistent with defense that complainant had fabricated story of rape (but would have told same story to nurse); though doctor's 'clinical impression' of 'sexual assault' would have been redacted if requested, D not seriously prejudiced by this; though counsel perhaps should have objected to complainant's self-corroboration by non-first complaint testimony (i.e., she told police), testimony was consistent with and used by defense (strategy);

C v Cook **380 M 314 (80)**—ineffective assistance not to object to co-D taking stand & 5th Amendment;

C v DeJesus **71 MAC 799 (2008)**—failure to object to police testimony that array was compiled from database of those with prior arrest history, failure to seek or accept offered immediate curative instruction, failure to object to inadequacy of instruction eventually given in final charge were apparently missteps falling below normal competence, but did not deprive D of otherwise available substantial ground of defense given trial evidence here;

C v Brazie **66 MAC 315 (2006)**—when one child sexual assault complainant became too distraught, during direct examination, to continue testimony and was never cross-examined (resulting in withdrawal of indictments concerning her from jury consideration), ineffective assistance to (1) fail to move to strike testimony and (2) fail to object to judge's response to jury question that the testimony could be considered in resolving allegations of second complainant;

C v Frisino **21 MAC 551 (86)**—ineffective assistance for no objection or ask limiting instructions when hearsay was used for substantive purpose to defeat required finding of not guilty; *C v Boothby* **64 MAC 582 (2005)**—same: failure to object to admission of hearsay corroborating D's out-of-court admission was ineffective assistance, since without the corroborative evidence that D was driver of car, finding of not guilty was required;

C v Scullin **44 MAC 9 (97)**—ineffective assistance for no objection to bad 'fresh' complaint;

C v Sugrue **34 MAC 172 (93)**—same;

C v Perreira **38 MAC 901 (95)**—similar;

C v McCormick **48 MAC 106 (99)**—failure to request limiting instructions re: fresh complaint excused as tactical decision (no ineffective assistance);

C v Fanara **47 MAC 560 (99)**—failure to object to bad fresh complaint and intro of similar testimony excused as "well within the realm of reasonable trial strategy" because used as prior inconsistent statements and to further defense that complainants had conspired against D;

C v Carmona **428 M 268, 274–76 (98)**—failure to object to hearsay tying D to murder weapon not ineffective assistance: "reasoned tactical judgment" because it provided D with a benefit (impeachment of very damaging witness re: different matter); failure to use criminal records of Commonwealth witnesses for impeachment not ineffective assistance (testimony made it clear that main witnesses and D all had prior records); failure to cross-examine government witness for bias due to pending case irrelevant because witness purportedly ID'd D before such case arose (and remained consistent in such ID);

C v Lester **70 MAC 55, 60 n.9 (2007)**—failure to object to extremely damaging "totem pole" hearsay cognizable as ineffective assistance on direct appeal;

C v McLeod **39 MAC 461 (95)**—failure to object to horrific "bad acts" evidence not "ineffective" assistance because "tactical"; showed motive for complainants to want to get even with D by making false allegations;

C v Tolan **453 M 634 (2009)**—failure to move to strike evidence about D's sexual practices not ineffective in circumstances;

C v Baran **74 MAC 256, 284-289 (2009)**—failure to object/exclude evidence that chid complainant had gonorrhea of the throat, and that D was homosexual = ineffective assistance; though Commonwealth claimed not that it was relevant but that it was reasonable "strategy", any such strategy was manifestly unreasonable (& question was "not a close one"), particularly in light of DA's "devastating closing remarks" claiming that D's negative test for gonorrhea didn't mean that he had not had it "when he raped these children"; in 1984, homosexuality was routinely linked with criminality, indecency, pathology, moral turpitude, HIV, and pedophilia; failure to object to fresh complaint evidence = ineffective assistance, as was appellate counsel's failure to raise issue on appeal;

C v Delarosa **50 MAC 623, 632 (2000)**—failure to move for mistrial when cop-witness twice noted that D 'refused to cooperate' not ineffective assistance; judge sua sponte gave strong "strike" instruction & a scathing denunciation of cop for so testifying ("If anything, you should look on it negatively that for some reason the witness felt the need to offer it to you. If there is any negative inference to be drawn, it's to the one stating it, not towards the defendant"), & counsel could well have concluded (given defense of police failures & inept investigation) that instructions did more for defense than another trial without either offending testimony or judge's critical comments

C v White **48 MAC 658, 660 n.5 (2000)**—D-counsel has duty to request limiting instructions; judges ordinarily aren't required to instruct sua sponte "as to the purposes for which evidence is offered at trial"; though appellate counsel argued that failure to limit use of hearsay evidence made it useable substantively and decisively against D, Appeals Court held counsel used it effectively (no ineffective assistance);

C v Payton 35 MAC 586 (93)—in circumstances, failure to object to introduction of array of mugshots not ineffective assistance;

C v Hernandez 63 MAC 426 (2005)—failure to move for mistrial or request replacement juror, after judge questioned juror who appeared to be sleeping, wasn't ineffective assistance (judge was satisfied with juror's claim that he wasn't sleeping);

Lockhart v Fretwell 506 U.S. 364 (93)—counsel's failure to object under law which was valid then but later overruled, not prejudicial under federal analysis of 6th Amendment, and Strickland;

C v Perreira 38 MAC 901 (95)—reversal, on basis of "substantial risk of miscarriage of justice," though failure to object to inadmissible evidence was a matter of (ill-conceived) strategy;

C v Hardy 426 M 725 (98)—standard of appellate review under G.L. c. 278, § 33E (first degree murder convictions) provides more protection to D than constitutional ineffective assistance of counsel standard for failure to object, i.e., issue "unpreserved" for appeal;

C v Parker 420 M 242, 245 n.4 (95)—same; issue is whether error by counsel "was likely to have influenced the jury's conclusion";

C v Painten 429 M 536, 549–50 (99)—same, context of G.L. c. 278, § 33E review of 1st degree murder conviction; standard of review, including evaluation of trial counsel's performance, is more favorable to D than the ineffective assistance test set forth in *Saferian* 366 M 89, 96 (74);

C v Wright 411 M 678, 682 (92)—failure to object & preserve issue for appeal will not succeed as ineffective assistance claim if it does not succeed on parallel standard (for "unpreserved" error) of "substantial risk of miscarriage of justice";

C v Barnoski 418 M 523, 541 (94)—same;

C v Baran 74 MAC 256, 284 (2009)—failure to object to DA's grossly improper closing argument (appeals to sympathy, vouching for complainants' credibility, etc.) deprived D of possibly "curative" instruction or, at minimum, preservation of issue for appeal, resulting in substantial risk of miscarriage of justice;

2-E.14. Failures at Closing Argument

C v Sarvela 16 MAC 934 (83)—ineffective assistance to shift gears at argument, undermine D's case, & become juror (not advocate);

Johns v Smyth 176 F.Supp 949 (E.D. Va. '59)—lack of argument suggested counsel disbelieved D;

C v Westmoreland 388 M 269 (83)—abandon insanity defense at argument = ineffective assistance;

C v Street 388 M 281 (83)—same; D was left "denuded of a defense";

C v Urrea 443 M 530 (2005)—counsel's argument did not abandon a defense to extreme atrocity & cruelty theory of first degree murder, but instead asserted that D could not understand the extent of what he was doing and the harm he was inflicting; concession of disproportionate force in fact wasn't abandonment of defense re: D's mental state;

C v Doane 428 M 631 (99)—not ineffective assistance to "grasp at only straw at hand" for closing argument (i.e., that though D intentionally killed, mitigating factors negated inferences of deliberate premeditation or extreme atrocity or cruelty, so guilty of 2d degree murder rather than 1st degree);

C v Baran 74 MAC 256, 284 (2009)—failure to object to DA's closing argument = ineffective assistance;

2-E.15. Ineffective Assistance at Sentencing

Osborne v Commonwealth 378 M 104 (79)—no reason to try insanity; but bad sentencing pitch (misdirected, didn't ask alternatives, & neglected D's history);

C v Montanez 410 M 290 (91)—barebones sentencing pitch with minimal mention of D's background plus failure to request that sentences run concurrently was ineffective assistance;

C v Cameron 31 MAC 928 (91)—failure to make any argument for D at sentencing was ineffective assistance;

C v Moreau 30 MAC 677 (91), cert. denied, 502 US 1049 (92)—joining in recommendation which exceeded sentencing guidelines, failure to offer mitigating evidence until after joint recommendation was submitted, & possible failure to inform D of terms of joint recommendation may have been ineffective assistance;

Schriro v Landrigan 127 S Ct 1933 (2007)—no abuse of discretion in refusing to grant death penalty D an evidentiary hearing on claim of ineffective assistance for failure to offer mitigation evidence at sentencing: record showed that D had barred ex-wife and mother from testifying and D interrupted to prevent counsel from offering other evidence, saying "bring it on" (death penalty);

C v Monzon 51 MAC 245, 255–56 (2001)—**avoiding decision on issue that trial defense counsel provided ineffective assistance in failing to request continuance for pre-sentence investigation & report, failing to present mitigating factors, and failing to request sentences be served concurrently, by ordering re-sentencing because judge adopted DA's sentencing recommendation, & DA said recommendation based in part upon D's alleged perjury during trial testimony;**

C v Pagels 69 MAC 607 (2007)—conclusory and uncorroborated claims of counsel's ineffectiveness at sentence appeal (Appellate Division of Superior Court), though a cognizable constitutional claim, were permissibly rejected without a hearing: D failed to include written and oral record of proceedings in Appellate Division and omitted any explanatory affidavits from attorneys;

C v Hampton **64 MAC 27, 35 (2005)**—though D-counsel hadn't seen DYS records until five minutes before sentencing hearing and had not gone to DYS to examine D's file beforehand (though he should have known that judge was "required" to consider juvenile D's prior record on question of sentencing), no ineffectiveness found: documents revealed little more than was readily apparent from review of record provided by probation and summarized in pre-sentence report, and D showed no prejudice from lack of time to review documents;

C v Fenton F. **442 M 31 (2004)**—no ineffective assistance of counsel shown, so no basis for waiving 60-day window for filing R. 29 motion; not "ineffective" to advise after negotiated G plea & agreed-upon sentence that "as a practical matter" D was "stuck" with bargain, since one can't file motion to revoke & revise without stating grounds on which it's based;

2-E.16. Effective Assistance Re: Claim/Prosecution of Appeal

C v Moffett **383 M 201 (81)**—rules if client wants appeal which is, in counsel's opinion, "frivolous";

C v Frank **425 M 182 (97)**—failure to file appellate brief is ineffective assistance;

Breese v Commonwealth **415 M 249 (93)**—notwithstanding fact that D had no right to appointed counsel on appeal of M.R.Crim.P. 30 (motion for new trial) denial, such counsel as he did have had to provide effective assistance; (but cf. *Pennsylvania v Finley* **481 US 551 (87)** Supreme Court's ruling in *Anders v California* (as to steps appointed counsel must take (rather than merely withdrawing) when believes criminal defendant's direct appeal is frivolous) doesn't apply to postconviction proceedings in which D doesn't have a previously-established right to counsel;

C v Coral **72 MAC 222, further rev. denied 452 M 1107 (2008), cert. denied 129 S Ct 1633 (2009)**—avoiding D's claim of right to counsel on Rule 30 motion to withdraw guilty plea (is "the only method for challenging a guilty plea a "direct" appeal? a "collateral" attack? a "hybrid"?), D citing *Halbert v Michigan* **545 US 605 (2005)**, by ruling that this D's delay (three years after guilty plea) would "militate against" treating motion as analogous to direct appeal, and instead as a collateral challenge not requiring appointment of counsel;

Pires v Commonwealth **373 M 829 (77)**—must tell D of right to appeal *(See Chapter 15, Post-Conviction Remedies)*;

C v Trussell **68 MAC 452 (2007)**—if counsel fails to file timely (within one year of the conviction, or sentence, with permission of appellate court if beyond the 30+30 day period) the notice of appeal desired by D, finding of excusable neglect or good cause (M.R.App.P. 14(b) and 4(c)) is warranted if judge finds that "lack of timely appeal

resulted from act or omission of counsel, whether or not amounting to ineffective assistance, to which the D did not knowingly assent" (rejecting Commonwealth argument that mere omission isn't excusable neglect or good cause, so that D should be relegated to R.30 for any relief);

Roe v Flores-Ortega **528 US 470 (2000)**—defense counsel obligated to advise D about appeal rights; constitutionally-imposed duty to consult with D about appeal when there's reason to think either (1) rational D would want to appeal; or (2) this particular D demonstrated to counsel that he was interested in appealing;

C v Pagels **69 MAC 607 (2007)**—conclusory and uncorroborated claims of counsel's ineffectiveness at sentence appeal (Appellate Division of Superior Court), though a cognizable constitutional claim, were permissibly rejected without a hearing: D failed to include written and oral record of proceedings in Appellate Division and omitted any explanatory affidavits from attorneys; D claimed no one told him of right to withdraw sentence appeal, no one told him of possibility of increased sentence, counsel had failed to adequately respond to misrepresentation of his criminal record, and D was unpleasantly surprised to see trial counsel rather than appellate attorney at the proceeding;

Breese v Commonwealth **415 M 249 (93)**—no ineffective assistance by appellate counsel's failure to raise ineffective assistance of trial attorney unless D shows that such claim, if made, would have succeeded;

C v Lao **450 M 215 (2007)**—in reversing trial judge's denial of motion for new trial in a first degree murder case after direct appellate review (including G.L. c. 278, § 33E), SJC finds ineffective assistance to have permeated D's direct appeal: appellate counsel didn't make *Crawford v Washington* constitutional claim that victim's hearsay statements (admitted as spontaneous utterances) were inadmissible; *Crawford* decision = published 3/8/04, & D's appellate brief was filed on 4/13/04, SJC issuing decision on direct appeal on 3/31/05;

C v Kegler **65 MAC 907 (2006)**—appellate counsel's cavalier disregard of briefing deadlines caused dismissal of appeal ("blatant disregard of the rules of appellate procedure is conduct demonstrably below what is to be expected of reasonably competent counsel"); appellate court considered issues presented in months-late brief, after dismissal of appeal, to discern whether counsel's conduct deprived D of "available substantial ground of defense" (it didn't, so order denying motion to reinstate appeal was affirmed);

C v Alvarez **69 MAC 438 (2007)**—notwithstanding fact that D himself signed affidavit consenting to withdrawal of direct appeal, defense counsel asserting lack of meritorious issues was inadequate by itself to "discharge his constitutional obligations" (*Moffett* [383 M 201 (81)] brief said to be required), citing *Penson v Ohio* **488 US 75 (88)**; D's attempt to have appeal reinstated asserted that his previous consent was based on misinformation from appellate counsel; if true, consent = involuntary; D's claim of involuntariness is supported by affidavit AND by procedural history of case ("irregularities" noted);

C v Goewey **452 M 399 (2008)**—on Commonwealth's interlocutory appeal of allowance of D's motion to suppress, defense counsel failed to file any brief, after requesting and receiving extensions of time; MAC should not have held oral argument and decided the case in absence of advocacy on behalf of D; court's "unilateral review of the transcript" was not an adequate substitute for D's right to effective assistance of counsel, and it was not proper for court to determine without benefit of brief or argument from D that D was not prejudiced by absence of counsel; Commonwealth has misinterpreted the significance of *Kegler* 65 MAC 907; *Alvarez*, 69 MAC 438, 443 (2007) reiterates *Frank* 425 M 182(97): due process requires that D who has been denied right to counsel on appeal (actually or constructively) must be placed in same position he would have occupied were he presenting direct appellate claims in ordinary course;

C v Baran **74 MAC 256 (2009)**—failure to brief unpreserved issues which were later found (on motion for new trial) to have given rise to substantial risk of miscarriage of justice;

2-E.17. Lies to Client

C v Chetwynde **31 MAC 8 (91)**—counsel's material misrepresentation to D that a suppression motion had been heard & denied was ineffective assistance & violation of disciplinary rules;

C v Walker **443 M 867, 871 (2005)**—if D's plea counsel gives plainly incorrect advice & D relies on it in tendering G plea, it's ineffective assistance; "constitutional infirmity would create a substantial risk of a miscarriage of justice"; advice here, i.e., that judge's denial of suppression motion presented no appellate issue, wasn't ineffective assistance of counsel because it wasn't "patently wrong" at the time;

C v Conley **43 MAC 385 (97)**—reversal because counsel told D, falsely, that he moved to have evidence tested (for blood), and that motion was denied; but see *C v DiPietro* **35 MAC 638 (93)** could withdraw G plea as involuntary after attorney lied (that motion to suppress was filed & denied) only if showed **both** lie **and** that motion to suppress would have been allowed;

C v Berrios **447 M 701 (2006)**—though Appeals Court had ruled that ineffective assistance of counsel in failing to learn of witness's changed testimony in co-D's trial made D's guilty plea involuntary, 64 MAC at 547, SJC overruled this, and held guilty plea not involuntary simply because D felt that he had no choice but to so plead; consideration of the gravity of charges and possible sentences is "endemic to any system which asks a person to forgo certain rights in order to be spared certain penal-

ties"; that D chose to forgo a "viable defense" did not make situation unique and redressable;

C v Alvarez **69 MAC 438 (2007)**—if D consented to withdrawal/dismissal of appeal based on "misinformation" from appellate counsel, consent was involuntary;

2-E.18. Advice Re: Giving Statement or Testifying

US v Frappier **615 F.Supp 51 (D Mass. '85)**—advice to D to testify at bail/detention hearing was ineffective assistance given circumstances; see also *Escobedo v State of Illinois* **378 US 478 (64)** any lawyer worth his salt will tell client not to talk to police;

C v Moreau **30 MAC 677 (91), cert. denied, 502 US 1049 915 (92)**—counsel's advice that D give pre-arraignment confession may have been ineffective assistance, and R. 30 motion shouldn't have been denied without hearing; *People v Wilson* **133 A.D.2d 179, 180–81 (NY '87)** & *Frappier* **(615 F.Supp 51)**, inter alia, cited;

C v Smiley **431 M 477, 480 (2000)**—motion judge's findings of fact on D's motion to suppress statement adopted counsel's version of facts (i.e., despite counsel's advice not to, and explanation that one could be guilty even if didn't "pull trigger," D insisted upon making statement) rather than D's claim that attorney failed to adequately advise on consequences of making statement;

C v Freeman **29 MAC 635 (90)**—advising D not to testify on legally erroneous basis that juvenile delinquencies were admissible to impeach D's credibility violated D's right to testify & might have been ineffective assistance;

C v Kelly **57 MAC 201 (2003)**—though D claimed that counsel misadvised D that statement suppressed under Miranda couldn't be used against him if he testified, & trial counsel at hearing on motion for new trial agreed, judge could disbelieve counsel's testimony (so no ineffective assistance of counsel);

C v Stewart **422 M 385 (96)**—advice not to testify which included erroneous advice as to admissibility of 1 of 5 prior convictions not ineffective assistance (because here harmless beyond a reasonable doubt);

C v Grissett **66 MAC 454 (2006)**—"grave error for counsel to call [D] to testify and then pose questions on direct . . . which left [D] vulnerable to a predictably devastating cross-examination", i.e., after direct elicited that D had never purchased or used cocaine, prosecutor received permission to impeach D with prior conviction for possession with intent to distribute cocaine; counsel should have been aware of prior conviction & avoided questioning which opened the door; ineffective assistance found;

In the matter of Steven M. Foley **439 M 324 (2003)**—suspension from the practice of law for three years as result of attorney's embrace of undercover FBI agent's suggestion of perjury as defense to criminal charges;

2-F. CONFIDENCES, SECRETS AND PRIVILEGE (EXCEPT . . .)

See also Chapter 11-J, Privileges, Chapter 7-H, 5th Amendment & Article 12 privileges, & Chapter 2-L, Post, Criminal Offender Record Information, Chapter 20, Suppression Issues re: interference with right to counsel, confidentiality, etc.;

(**Anonymous**)—"A poor man's only privilege is perjury;"

SJC Rule 3:07, 1.6—shall not reveal . . . confidential info re: representation unless client consents, except for disclosures impliedly authorized to carry out representation, EXCEPT, "MAY" reveal (and to extent required by R. 3.3, 4.1(b) or 8.3, MUST REVEAL) to prevent crime or fraud that lawyer believes likely to result in death, substantial bodily harm, or substantial injury to financial interests or property of another, or to prevent wrongful execution or incarceration of another (1.6(b)(1)), to defend oneself vs. accusation by client or against criminal charge or civil claim against lawyer based upon conduct in which client was involved (1.6(b) (2)), to rectify client fraud in which lawyer's services have been used (1.6(b)(3)), if permitted by rules (below) or required by law/court order (1.6(b)(4)); EVEN WHEN INFO GAINED IN THE REPRESENTATION IS A MATTER OF PUBLIC RECORD, COUNSEL MAY NOT USE THE INFO (E.G., even by sharing pleadings with other counsel, so redact accordingly):

SJC Rule 3:07, 1.6—can't reveal confidential info re: representation unless client consents after consultation, except for disclosures impliedly authorized to carry out representation. Luke, Kenneth W., "Client secrets: going public with 'public' information," MBA Lawyers Journal (May 2002) ("unless disclosure is specifically required or permitted by one of the ethical rules, a lawyer should not reveal or use any confidential information without the client's consent regardless of whether the information is a matter of public record"); see also id., citing fact of private reprimand of lawyer for providing court with copies of correspondence that client sent to the media, because such correspondence was likely to be embarrassing or detrimental to the client if revealed;

***Purcell v D.A. for Suffolk District* 424 M 109 (97)**—crime-fraud exception to attorney-client privilege applies **only** to communications in which lawyer's advice is sought in furtherance of a crime or to obtain assistance with respect to criminal activity; **in camera** review may occur, in cautious exercise of discretion, but to warrant such review, opponent of attorney-client privilege must make showing of factual basis adequate to support reasonable belief that review may show the exception to apply;

***In the Matter of a Grand Jury Investigation* 453 M 453 (2009)**—client's communications to lawyer threatening harm = privileged UNLESS 'crime-fraud exception' applies; client, a father in care & protection case in Juvenile Court, left six messages on attorney's answering machine, indicating he knew where judge lived, that she had

two children, and that "some people need to be exterminated with prejudice"; attorney disclosed to judge; subsequent subpoenas to attorney for grand jury and District Court detention hearing should have been quashed; communications = expressions of frustration with legal system & its participants, & privilege served salutary purposes (dissuading conduct, with option of making limited disclosure to protect likely targets, as done here);

***C v Tennison* 440 M 553 (2003)**—attorney moved to withdraw upon info from D that D had been in contact with juror throughout trial; upon threat of contempt, attorney disclosed name of juror; conflict of interest apparent ("testimony" or not, disclosure was detrimental to D);

SJC Rule 3:07, 3.3(a)(4)—if lawyer has offered material evidence and lawyer comes to know of its falsity, lawyer "shall take reasonable remedial measures, EXCEPT 3.3(e)—in criminal case, must discourage client from testifying falsely; if know this intention before accepting representation, don't accept representation; if discover intent before trial, seek to withdraw, & disclose info "only to extent necessary to effect withdrawal" (apply to withdraw ex parte to judge other than trial judge, seek in camera hearing, and record of proceeding to be impounded); if unable to get permission to withdraw, can't stop client from testifying; IF TRIAL ALREADY UNDERWAY when learn of intent to falsely testify, need not file motion to withdraw if reasonably believe that seeking to withdraw will prejudice client; after false testimony, call upon client to rectify," but if client refuses, lawyer shall not reveal false testimony to tribunal; lawyer can't "examine the client in such a manner as to elicit" testimony known to be false, and can't argue probative value of false testimony in closing argument or any other proceeding, including appeals; *(But see Chapter 2-E, Effective Assistance re: e.g., "Closing Argument," above)*

***C v Sarvela* 16 MAC 934 (83)**—ineffective assistance to shift gears at argument, undermine D's case, & become juror (not advocate);

***Johns v Smyth* 176 F.Supp 949 (ED Va. '59)**—lack of argument suggested counsel disbelieved D;

***C v Westmoreland* 388 M 269 (83)**—abandon insanity defense at argument = ineffective assistance;

***C v Street* 388 M 281 (83)**—same; D was left "denuded of a defense")

SJC Rule 3:07, 4.1(b)—lawyer can't "fail to disclose" material fact to 3d person when disclosure necessary to avoid assisting criminal or fraudulent act by client, "unless disclosure is prohibited by Rule 1.6'";

SJC Rule 3:07, 8.3—(a)lawyer must inform Board of Bar Overseers of another lawyer's violations of Rules of Professional Conduct "that raises a substantial question as to that lawyer's honesty", and (b) must inform Commission on Judicial Conduct if know judge has violated rules of judicial conduct in way "that raises a substantial question as to the judge's fitness for office", BUT (c) not if info is protected by 1.6 or was gained while lawyer served as member of lawyer assistance program; see also website of the Board of Bar Overseers, **www.state.ma.us/obcbbo**, for answers to frequently-asked questions, articles;

C v Sullivan **435 M 722 (2002)—DEFENSE COUNSEL MAY CALL AS A WITNESS a prosecution witness's ATTORNEY, to inquire into attorney's conversations with prosecution regarding immunity: no violation of witness's attorney-client privilege;**

Garner v US **424 US 648, 655 (76)**—5th Amendment preserves adversary system;

Hatton v Robinson **31 M 416, 421–22 (1833)**—attorney's mouth forever sealed;

SJC Rule 3:07, 5.3—employees/associates = attorney's duty to prevent disclosures;

Prop.M.R.Evid. 502(a)(4)—privilege includes attorney's assistants;

Foster v Hall **29 M 89 (1831)**—privilege covers communications to agents & employees;

C v Senior **433 M 453 (2001)—though defense attorney took client to hospital for blood alcohol testing, with thought that it might be used in defense, results were incriminating; prosecution could obtain them and introduce them against D, notwithstanding D's argument that hospital/personnel were "agents" of defense counsel; purported 'agent' of defense counsel (or anyone else) has to agree to such role;**

Wigmore, *Evidence* **(McNauaghton rev. 1961) §§ 2290–329**—attorney "oath & honor"; later = client's trust; benefits = indirect/speculatives; & obstructs truth-seeking; related to 5th Amendment;

Brodin, M. and Avery, M., *Handbook of Massachusetts Evidence* **(8th ed. 2007)**—evidentiary privilege = consult as client re: legal business, communicate, in confidence; = D's option;

Prop.M.R.Evid. 502—Lawyer-Client privilege—client has privilege to refuse to disclose & prevent any other person from disclosing confidential communications made to facilitate rendition of legal services (1) between client or his representative and his lawyer or lawyer's representative; (2) between lawyer & lawyer's representative; (3) by him or his representative or his lawyer or lawyer's representative to lawyer or representative of lawyer representing another party in pending action; ETC.; privilege may be claimed by client, his guardian, personal representative of deceased, etc.;

Young, Pollets & Poreda, *Evidence,* **§§ 503.1–503.7 (2d ed. 1998)**—(overview); 503.5 communications/acts not within scope of client's privilege;

MBA Ethics Op. 76-11—client's ID (if attorney saw the crime) not "secret";

In re: Grand Jury Subpoena **615 F.Supp 958 (D.Mass. '85)**—quash subpoenas to attorneys because not shown they participated in crime/fraud;

In re: Grand Jury Matters **751 F.2d 13 (1st Cir. '84)**—unreasonable subpoenas to attorneys;

SJC Rule 3:07, 3.7—when lawyer can testify; 3.8(f) - when prosecutor can subpoena the attorney of investigation's target (RESTRICTIONS! can't do this unless prosecutor reasonably believes info sought isn't protected by privilege, info sought is essential to ongoing investigation/ prosecution AND there's no other way to get info, **AND prosecutor obtains prior judicial approval after opportunity for adversarial proceeding**);

US v Klubock **832 F.2d 664 (1st Cir. '87)**—3:3 split upholds (the formerly-numbered) SJC Rule 3:08, PF-15 (now denominated SJC Rule 3:07, 3.8(f));

In Matter of Grand Jury Investigation **407 M 916 (90)**—PF-15, which requires judicial ok for prosecutorial summons of defense counsel, also applies to defense investigators;

See also, Chapter 2-G, Counsel: Crimes, Frauds, & Bounds of Law, & Court Orders, re: eavesdropping in attorney-client talks;

See Chapter 2-L, Counsel: Files & Records, re: waiver of privilege when D alleges attorney misconduct;

Fisher v US **425 US 391 (76)**—D's won't confide if info = disclosable; but no privilege for (D's accountant's) documents because not within Fifth Amendment;

UpJohn Co. v US **449 US 383 (81)**—purpose of privilege = full & frank communication with attorney & promote public interest; work product = broader;

C v Noxon **319 M 495 (46)**—no "privilege" re: counsel talks with (expert) witness;

See also Chapter 6-D & 6-M, Pretrial . . . Motions, Discovery, Reciprocal/Work Product;

C v Goldman **395 M 495 (85)**—no waiver by witness by testifying re: events discussed with attorney (but waive if testify re: conversation); interest of justice may override privilege; limine (in camera) hearing re: privilege/conflict; n.2 no comment re: such un-consented disclosure of privileged communication;

Darius v City of Boston **433 M 274, 279 (2001)**—SJC rejects civil defendants' attempts to discover info conveyed by counsel to plaintiffs, argued to have been put in issue and attorney-client privilege thus waived by claim (in response to motion to dismiss) that plaintiffs were unaware of their cause of action against particular defendants until meeting with counsel on specific date; "at issue" waiver of attorney-client privilege will be found only when info is unavailable from any other source and when request is much more particularized/circumscribed; counsel's ethical obligations to avoid use of/take remedial measure against false affidavits, discovery responses, testimony;

US v Bump **605 F.2d 548 (10th Cir. '79)**—DA can cross-examine D about evidence promised by defense counsel in plea bargaining because disclosure waived privilege;

C v Michel **367 M 454 (75)**—can cross-examine witness re: plea discussions (but not advice) because told to 3d persons (DA & co-counsel);

See also Chapter 13-A, Plea Bargaining: Defense Counsel's Role;

In re: John Doe Grand Jury **408 M 480 (90)**—privileges survive death (re: crime-fraud exceptions);

Swidler & Berlin v US **524 US 399 (98)**—attorney-client privilege survives client's death; Office of Independent Counsel/grand jury barred from obtaining notes taken by attorney during consultation with client nine days before client committed suicide; "testamentary" exception to attorney-client privilege, whereby privileged communications are revealed to further client's intent, not reasonably applicable; refusal to hold that attorney-client privilege operates differently in criminal and civil cases; refusal to make exception for "information of substantial importance" in particular criminal cases;

2-G. CRIMES, FRAUDS, AND BOUNDS OF LAW AND COURT ORDERS

See also Chapter 2-I, re: Contempt & Sanctions;

SJC Rule 3:07, 1.2(a), 1.3—shan't prejudice/damage D; 1.2(d) can't counsel/assist known crime/fraud; 3.3(a)(2) shall reveal fraud unless "privileged" *(See Chapter 2-F)*; 8.4(c) no dishonesty, fraud, deceit, misrepresentation; 3.4(a) & (c) can't obstruct access to evidence; 1.16(a)(1) shall withdraw if know you'll violate a DR;

SJC Rule 3:07, 1.6(b)(1)—*(See Chapter 2-F)* must tell if know of (any) future crime if not privileged;

See Chapter 2-C, above, re: resolving ethical doubts/ conflicts in client's favor; See also Chapter 4-C, Arraignment & Bail Advocacy, re: "My client has no record"; Chapter 10-D, Defense Evidence, re: client perjury

ABA Model Rules of Professional Conduct (1983) 1.6—may reveal info re: representation of client to prevent substantial bodily harm;

ABA Standards for Criminal Justice, Prosecution Function & Defense Function (3d ed. 1993) 4-3.7(d)—may tell intended crime if reasonably believe necessary to prevent client from committing criminal act likely to result in "imminent death or substantial bodily harm"; 4-1.2(f) no intentional misrepresenting fact/law; & (g) should disclose legal authority "in the controlling jurisdiction" known to be directly adverse to D's position and not disclosed by prosecutor; 4-4.1(b) defense counsel shouldn't seek to acquire possession of physical evidence personally or via investigator where defense counsel's sole purpose is to obstruct access to such evidence; 4-4.6 if defense counsel receives item of physical evidence under circumstances implicating D, shouldn't disclose/deliver it to prosecution unless required by law or court order OR if contraband, may advise D to destroy IF no current case or investigation re: item is ongoing and destruction doesn't violate criminal statute; if destruction not permitted by statute or if retention is hazardous physically, counsel should disclose location or deliver to law enforcement authorities but should do so in manner best protecting D's interests;

Wigmore, *Evidence* **(McNaughton rev. 1961) § 2298**—(future) crime-fraud exception to privilege;

Purcell v D.A. for Suffolk District **424 M 109 (97)**—crime-fraud exception to attorney-client privilege applies **only** to communications in which lawyer's advice is sought in furtherance of a crime or to obtain assistance with respect to criminal activity; **in camera** review may occur, in cautious exercise of discretion, but to warrant such review, opponent of attorney-client privilege must make showing of factual basis adequate to support reasonable belief that review may show the exception to apply; tenant being evicted enunciating to attorney a threat to burn down apartment not shown to be within exception;

C v Dyer **243 M 472 (23)**—proposed (future) crime not privileged; D's intent, not attorney's, controls;

Higbee v Dresser **103 M 523 (1870)**—mere "general suggestion" still privileged;

US v Dyer **722 F.2d 174 (5th Cir. '83)**—no privilege for continuing or future crime;

US v Friedman **445 F.2d 1076 (9th Cir. '71)**—(same) for "present, continuing" crime;

C v Tennison **440 M 553 (2003)**—attorney moved to withdraw upon info from D that D had been in contact with juror throughout trial; upon threat of contempt, attorney disclosed name of juror; conflict of interest apparent ("testimony" or not, disclosure was detrimental to D);

C v Vickers **60 MAC 24 (2003)**—though D-counsel "chafed at going forward" with trial in absence of D, "it was a serious lapse in judgment to refuse to participate for more than a day as the Commonwealth proceeded with its case"; that counsel "deliberately declined to perform any defense functions" resulted in reversal of D's convictions; BUT **"this should not be misunderstood as a reward for deliberately unprofessional behavior"**;

In re Ryder **263 F.Supp 360 (E.D.Va. '67), aff'd 381 F.2d. 713 (4th Cir. '67)**—hide gun & money = intent to help crime, because fruits/instruments, not "mere evidence";

People v Belge **372 NYS2d 798 (Superior Court), aff'd 376 NYS2d.771 (75)**—OK (constitutional) zeal not to tell where (uncharged) murder bodies are; (dictum: but case harder if charged with obstructing justice *(See Chapter 2-H)*);

C v Stenhach **514 A.2d 114, 121 (Pa.Super. '86)**—majority rule = duty to give physical evidence (& hide source from jury); but too confusing to convict attorney of obstruction of justice;

C v Hughes **380 M 583 (80)**—no contempt for not surrendering gun because of 5th Amendment;

ABA Model Code of Professional Responsibility (1969) Comments, 4-101(C)(a)—discusses Belge/Ryder dilemmas; no disclosure unless future crime = beyond reasonable doubt;

McCormick, *Evidence* **(5th ed. 1999) § 89, particularly n.12**—Ryder & physical evidence issues;" § 95 crime/fraud exception to privilege;

SJC Rule 3:07, 1.6(b)(4)—may reveal when required by law or court order; 3.3 shall not fail to disclose material facts; 3.4(a) can't obstruct access to evidence; 3.4(c) shall not disobey obligation under rules "except for an open refusal based on an assertion that no valid obligation exists"; 1.2(a) treat with courtesy, fulfill professional commitments; 1.3 (comment) advise client of possibility of appeal; see also *Roe v Flores-Ortega* **528 US 470 (2000)** defense counsel obligated to advise D about appeal rights; constitutionally-imposed duty to consult with D about appeal when there's reason to think either (1) rational D would want to appeal; or (2) this particular D demonstrated to counsel that he was interested in appealing;

ABA Standards for Criminal Justice, Prosecution Function & Defense Function 4-7.1(d)—comply promptly with court orders, but make record & ask reconsideration;

ABA Model Rule of Professional Conduct (1983) 1.6, Comment—must invoke privilege, but must then comply with court order to give info.;

*See also Chapter 2-H & 2-I re: court orders (**Maness 419 US 449 (75)** and **Walker 388 US 307 (67)** etc.)*

G.L. c. 272, § 99—electronic eavesdropping *(See Chapter 20, Suppression Issues)*;

C v King **400 M 283 (87)**—no per se dismissal from co-D's eavesdropping in attorney-client talks, but no harm here;

C v Fontaine **402 M 491 (88)**—(same) re: jail cell videotape; dismiss 1 charge;

US v Mastroianni **749 F.2d 900 (1st Cir. '84)**—co-D fink can attend attorney-client meeting to not blow cover; wrong for government to de-brief, but no harm; **BUT SEE SUPPRESSION ISSUES, CHAPTER 20, RE: VIOLATION OF RIGHT TO COUNSEL, PARTICULARLY, E.G.,** *MAINE v MOULTON* **474 US 159 (85)** post-arraignment talk to co-D (police agent, but no questions or custody) violated 6th Amendment;

McCormick, *Evidence* **(5th ed. 1999) § 91 n.5**—eavesdropping vs. attorney-client privilege;

See also Chapter 14-B, Sentencing/Disposition: Dismissal (for DA misconduct), Chapter 20, (suppression of evidence);

SJC Rule 3:07, 3.1 & Comment—can't knowingly advance legally unwarranted claim, but can challenge law; criminal defense lawyer or respondent in proceeding that can result in incarceration, "may nevertheless so defend the proceeding as to require that every element of the case be established"; 3.3(a)(3) before court, shall disclose known, directly adverse law in controlling jurisdiction; 3.1 good faith (e.g., extend, modify law) vs. "frivolous"; Comment can use any arguable good faith construction of law; 3.2 make reasonable efforts to "expedite litigation

consistent with the interests of the client"; 3.3(a) (1) (2) & (3) no false statements of material fact or law; can't fail to disclose material fact when disclosure necessary to avoid assisting criminal or fraudulent act by client; must disclose any adverse legal authority "in the controlling jurisdiction";

ABA Model Rule of Professional Conduct (1983) 3.3: "Candor Towards Tribunal"—no knowingly false statements of fact or law; 3.1 no defense or assertion without good faith, non-frivolous basis—but criminal case can put prosecution to its proof;

Darius v City of Boston **433 M 274, 279 (2001)**—context of civil plaintiff-clients' affidavits supporting opposition to defendants' motion to dismiss: plaintiffs' attorney has ethical obligation to avoid use of false evidence by way of affidavit, discovery responses, or testimony (citing Mass Rule of Professional Conduct 3.3(a)(c), 3.4(a), and 8.4(c) (h)); SJC rejected defendants' attempts to obtain privileged attorney-client communications argued to have been put in issue by assertion that plaintiffs didn't know of cause of action against particular defendants until a meeting with counsel on specific date;

In the matter of Steven M. Foley **439 M 324 (2003)**—suspension from the practice of law for three years as result of attorney's embrace of undercover FBI agent's suggestion of perjury as defense to criminal charges;

C v Hill **432 M 704 (2000)**—affirming allowance of motion for new trial in murder case, in part because trial prosecutor did not press for correction of prosecution witness's testimony denying promise of reward for testimony ("Regardless whether the government has encouraged the false evidence of one of its witnesses, the prosecutor must advise the court of such false testimony");

ABA Standards for Criminal Justice, Prosecution Function & Defense Function (3d ed. 1993) 4-1.2, Comment—fundamental to be scrupulously candid & truthful; effectiveness depends on veracity reputation; "duty to disclose directly to court adverse legal authority in the controlling jurisdiction that has not been disclosed by the opposing party";

*See also **Moffett 383 M 201 (81)** in Chapter 2-E, Counsel: Effective Assistance, & Chapter 15, Post-Conviction Remedies, re: frivolous appeals;*

In Matter of Neitlich **413 M 416 (92)**—in civil context where client has no constitutional rights to counsel & against self-incrimination, counsel's withholding of material information in face of court order was fraudulent misrepresentation warranting bar discipline;

In Matter of Orfanello **411 M 551 (92)**—attorney's ex parte communication with judge to influence outcome of pending case violates DR 1-102-(A) (5) & (6);

SJC Rule 3:07, 3.4(i)—no racial, sex, religious, etc. bias (unless it is an issue in the case);

2-H. OBSTRUCT JUSTICE OR INFLUENCE WITNESS

C v Perkins **225 M 80 (16)**—common-law crime of conspiring to "obstruct justice" by procuring absence of a witness;

Dolan v Commonwealth **304 M 325 (39)**—conspire to obstruct justice by influencing jurors = contempt;

C v Gallarelli **372 M 573 (77)**—contempt complaint for bribing juror & obstructing justice; not duplicitous with G.L. c. 268, § 13B;

G.L. c. 268, § 36—take money, knowing of, & to conceal or compound a felony;

18 USC § 1503—corruptly or by threats, endeavor to influence, obstruct, or impede the due administration of justice (in FEDERAL case?—see *US v Regina* **504 F.Supp 629 (D.Md. 1980)** (probably));

US v Cintolo **818 F.2d 980 (1st Cir. '87)**—obstruction of justice to advise 5th Amendment at grand jury because D immunized & corrupt intent (to protect others), not traditional advocacy; line = case-by-case; law degree not sorcerer's amulet to immunize attorney;

P v Belge, etc. **372 NYS 2d 798 (Superior Court)**—*(Chapter 2-G, above)* custody of physical evidence;

ABA Model Rule of Professional Conduct (1983) 3.4—can't obstruct opponent's access to evidence;

G.L. c. 268, § 13B—felony for "indirectly . . . endeavors . . . by promise, misrepresentation, intimidation . . . to influence, obstruct, or interfere with witness, juror, or person furnishing information to . . . investigators . . . ";

C v Rondeau **27 MAC 55 (89)**—13B's "endeavor" = less close to success than attempt; (notes, but doesn't discuss, it may conflict with "accord and satisfaction");

C v Henderson **434 M 155 (2001)**—rejecting, on evidence, attempted defense of "accord & satisfaction" (G.L. c. 276, § 55) at trial for G.L. c. 268, § 13B crime (D sent letters promising financial compensation and marriage if girlfriend would extricate D from confinement and pending criminal charges);

SJC Rule 3:07, 3.4(f)—can't request non-relative or non-agent not to give info; 4.2, 4.3(b) can't communicate with person who has counsel without counsel's consent & can't give advice other than to get counsel if interests conflict; 3.4(g) can't pay witness contingent upon testimony or outcome; no fees (except expenses or experts);

G.L. c. 258B, § 3(m)—(prosecution) witness has the right "to be informed of the right to submit to or decline an interview by defense counsel or anyone acting on the defendant's behalf, except when responding to lawful process, and, if the . . . witness decides to submit to an interview, the right to impose reasonable conditions on the conduct of the interview"; BUT ONE CANNOT CONSTITUTION-ALLY DIFFERENTIATE BETWEEN "PROSECUTION" WITNESSES & "DEFENSE" WITNESSES, CAN ONE?? Either both sides have this right, or neither has this right; cf also *C v Brown* **11 MAC 288 (81)** one foundational requirement for impeachment of defense witness with failure to 'go to police' to give exculpatory information is that witness NOT have been requested by defense counsel to omit such revelations;

C v Boyer **52 MAC 590 (2001)**—affirming convictions of criminal defense attorney and his assistant for bribery (G.L. c. 268A, § 2(c) & interfering with witnesses (G.L. c. 268, § 13B);

In the matter of Steven M. Foley **439 M 324 (2003)**—suspension from the practice of law for three years as result of attorney's embrace of undercover FBI agent's suggestion of perjury as defense to criminal charges;

G.L. c. 268A, § 3—no $ for witness, except travel, time, or expert time;

ABA Standards for Criminal Justice, Prosecution Function & Defense Function (3d ed. 1993) 4-4.2, Comment—lawyer's special responsibility to see that agents act legally; 4-4.3 (c) & Comment need not warn witness of 5th Amendment because duty = to client; Comment says improper for either prosecution or defense to suggest to witness that witness not submit to an interview by opposing counsel, BUT may tell a witness who asks whether "proper to submit to an interview by opposing counsel or whether it is obligatory", that there is no legal obligation; proper for defense counsel to tell witness that s/he may contact counsel prior to talking to prosecutor, & counsel may request opportunity to be present (but can't demand as condition of interview); proper to counsel witness to exercise care in signing written statement prepared by someone else;

McNeal v Hollowell **481 F.2d 1145 (5th Cir. '73)**—OK to convince co-D (thru counsel) to take 5th Amendment (mid-trial); *(See Chapter 7-H, 5th Amendment)*;

Nolan & Sartorio, *Criminal Law* **(3d ed. 2001) §§ 611–18**—crimes against public justice, including perjury, bribery of judicial officers, obstruction of justice, bail crimes, escapes, contempt, "crimes related to attorneys and the practice of law," and "compounding a felony";

SJC Rule 3:07, 3.5(d)—after jury discharged, lawyer may not initiate communication with juror without leave of court for good cause shown; if juror initiates, lawyer may respond but may not ask questions or make comments intended only to harass, embarrass or influence future jury service & may not inquire into deliberation processes;

2-I. CONTEMPT AND SANCTIONS V. PROMPTNESS AND PROPER DECORUM

See also Chapter 2-G, Counsel: Crimes, Frauds, & Bounds of Law;

Allen v Snow **635 F.2d 12 (1st Cir. '80)**—"trying a case is not a parlor game"; judge may overreact; attorney may have to take chance & rely on appeal ("disapproval" of juror investigation wasn't an "order" to desist, so no error)

US Constitution, Amendments 5, 6, & 14—rights to due process & counsel;

Mass. Declaration of Rights 12—(due process), law of land, rights to defense & counsel;

Anonymous—"One who represents oneself has a fool for a lawyer"; COUNSEL to those giving the right to counsel: CPCS interventions when sanctions were threatened—Bar Advocate & Regional CPCS telephone #'s—(consult local listing); CPCS Boston #: 1-800-882-2095;

MACDL (Mass. Association of Criminal Defense Lawyers)—"strike force" for assisting criminal defense lawyers;

M.R.Crim.P. 31—stay of sentence (fines/costs shall be stayed pending appeal, imprisonment may be stayed, by sentencing judge, or Appeals Court or SJC judge (with bail, security considerations); M.R.Crim.P. 43(c) appeal summary contempt "only" appeal = to Appeals Court (**K. Smith, *Criminal Practice & Procedure*, § 2496 (2d ed. 1983 & Supp.**), saying SJC can take the case); Stay—ask trial judge first!

M.R.App.P. 6—stay must be sought first in lower court;

***Petition of Crystal* 330 M 583 (53)**—habeas petition springs D from contempt which is bad because no hearing; stated intention to disobey court order isn't summary contempt;

*(Re: comply with court orders, see Chapter 2-G & **Walker v City of Birmingham 388 US 307 (67) and Maness v Myers 419 US 449 (75)**, etc., below;)*

***C v Brogan* 415 M 169 (93)**—D charged with having violated, in Suffolk, Norfolk & Bristol Counties, terms of preliminary injunction issued in Middlesex County; Commonwealth not obligated to try D in the other 3 counties, rather than Middlesex;

***Chappee v Commonwealth* 659 F.Supp 1220, 1226–27 n.9 (D.Ma. '87)**—trial court costs = $1,500–$3,000/day; BUT CF. ***C v Gomes* 407 M 206 (90) "costs" must be only those actually calculable as resulting directly from D's willful default; cannot merely assign some amount, without evidence, as "reasonable" for "fair value of the waste of the (court's) time and resources" ("Court personnel are not paid on a piece-work basis, and defendants may not be charged as if they were"); M.R.Crim.P. 6(d)(1) and Reporter's Notes cited;**

***Beit v Probate and Family Court Dept.* 385 M 854 (82)**—attorney no-show (& no continuance) permits costs, but right to hearing; duty = punctual/present; generally no interlocutory appeal if delays case; 385 M at 860 n.11, court power over attorney = more than over D, penalize attorney (not D) for neglect, e.g., refer to Board of Bar Overseers;

***C v Rogers* 46 MAC 109 (99)**—after judge, irritated at the lack of speed in resolving the list, "announced in open court that all counsel were to remain in the court room until their cases were called and a disposition reached," judge assessed counsel $50 fine for being absent (because she was speaking to client in custody in effort to resolve the case); in general, such "costs" assessment is within a judge's power, though there should be "fair notice and a reasonable opportunity to be heard" re: costs; summary contempt here inappropriately invoked because counsel's violation of judge's order didn't "directly and materially disrupt the court's business," AND counsel's disobeying the order was not "violation of a warning constituting an independent ground supporting a judgment of summary contempt"; to be such a warning, it must be clear that specified conduct is impermissible "AND that specified sanctions may be imposed for its repetition";

***Florida Bar v Jackson* 494 So.2d 206 (Fla. 86)**—suspend for disobeying order to appear on religious holiday, because late notice to court & no good faith test;

SJC Rule 3:07, 1.2(a)—punctuality, courtesy, & consideration don't violate client's objectives;

CPCS P/G 1.3(m)—be prompt for court & appointments; or if need delay, minimize others' inconvenience;

ABA Standards for Criminal Justice, Prosecution Function & Defense Function (3d ed. 1993) 4-1.3—avoid unnecessary delays & be punctual; should not accept employment for purpose of delaying trial, shouldn't intentionally misrepresent facts or otherwise mislead court to obtain continuance;

M.R.Crim.P. 10—continuances only if necessary; if schedule conflict, must give 24-hour/reasonable notice; costs for unnecessary expenses; sanctions, e.g., contempt/costs/refer to BBO for rule/order violation;

See also Chapter 7-N re continuance requests

ABA Model Rules of Professional Conduct (1983) 1.3—promptness; 3.2 shall make reasonable efforts to expedite litigation consistent with client's interests;

***In re Lamson* 468 F.2d 551 (1st Cir. '72)**—not summary contempt for being 12 minutes late after recess (because elevator delays = acts not in court's presence);

***C v Dundon* 3 MAC 200 (75)**—admonish for demeanor (chewing gum);

***Jensen v S.Ct.* 201 Cal.Rptr. 275, 280 (Ct.App. 84)**—"as money-changers may be driven from temple," court can require appropriate dress, but turban = OK;

ABA Standards for Criminal Justice, Prosecution Function & Defense Function (3d ed. 1993) 4-1.2, Comment—"advocacy is not for the timid, meek, or retiring," justice system here is "inherently contentious"; 4-7.1 & Comment, decorum: support dignity of courtroom, authority of court, follow rules of decorum, respect others, don't purposefully irritate/annoy, avoid vituperation, personality conflicts, & donnybrooks; "Nonetheless, it is also important to the proper functioning of our adversary system that no artificial standards of courtroom conduct impede lawyers from rendering vigorous advocacy on behalf of their clients"; "judges must maintain scrupulously neutral and fair attitudes;

K. Smith, *Criminal Practice & Procedure* **(2d ed. 1983 & Supp.)**—Chs. 53 (Summary Contempt Proceedings) & 54 (Contempt) – overview Rules 43 & 44; § 2496 – SJC can take appeal (though it's to Appeals Court); "civil" = remedial, "criminal" = punitive;

G.L. c. 268, § 13C—willful disruption of court = 1 year maximum OR not more than $1,000 fine & can still be contempt; cf. **ABA Model Rule of Professional Conduct (1983) 3.5(c)**—no conduct intended to disrupt court;

M.R.Crim.P. 43—summary contempt: if necessary to maintain order, seen by judge, judgment immediate: maximum = 3 months or $500; summary hearing; can defer sentence to post-trial; appeal = to Appeals Court (see K. Smith, above);

Reporter's Notes—give due process unless overriding necessity; summary contempt = disfavored, unfair, only for willful/flagrant; R. 44 contempt (non-summary contempt, "indirect contempt") = all others; criminal complaint & right to jury; another judge if impartiality of 1st likely affected;

Bloom v Illinois **391 US 194 (68)**—federal/jury right only if six-month sentence;

Sussman v Commonwealth **374 M 692 (78)**—reverse summary contempt for 2d (excluded & re-phrased) cross-examination question because not flagrant; insufficient warnings (re: act & sanction); no need for immediate punishment to restore decorum/prevent demoralizing court authority; insufficient hearing (especially re: intent to disobey); no contemptuous act or intent (must not chill vigorous advocacy with summary contempt);

C v Segal **401 M 95 (87)**—not contempt for pressing objection; can't chill vigorous but respectful advocacy; & R.43 summary contempt procedures weren't followed;

C v Brennick **14 MAC 952 (82)**—public defender #2 objected, then complied with order to fill in for public defender #1 when default-sentence imposed; tipped for ineffective assistance;

S v Gasen **356 NE2d 505 (Ohio '76)**—can't force attorney to (handle probable cause hearing &) choose between ineffective assistance or contempt; Disciplinary Rules mandated that attorney decline to represent;

US v Wendy **575 F.2d 1025 (2d Cir. '78)**—new attorney's compliance with order to try (partner's) case might've violated Disciplinary Rules; so no "meaningful ability to comply because "Hobson's choice"—*(See also Chapter 2-E, Competent/Effective)*;

Maness v Meyers **419 US 449 (75)**—no contempt for good faith advice to D to take 5th Amendment; generally must comply with court order & tell D to, unless stay, & probably contempt even if order invalid, if court had jurisdiction; but order to reveal info permits precompliance review (& D risks contempt, but not attorney); See also *Walker v Birmingham, etc.*, **388 US 307 (67)**;

Sacher v US **343 US 1 (52)**—right to press claim though far-fetched, untenable; but can't resist/insult judge; can only preserve appeal; summary contempt OK though await (9 month) trial's end (avoiding disruption) & not

sent to 2d judge; some judges sometimes vain & arrogant, but most respect lawyering; (dissent: summary contempt = from Star Chamber, valid only to enforce court orders/decrees);

In re Watts **190 US 1 (03)**—no contempt for good faith (& wrong) advice that 2d court, not 1st, had jurisdiction & to obey its order, not 1st court's;

Shaw v Commonwealth **354 M 583 (68)**—no (reporter) contempt without clear, unequivocal command & equally clear disobedience;

C v Wiencis **48 MAC 688 (2000)**—summary contempt finding (ten-day sentence) against criminal D upheld: he screamed at jurors who returned G verdict, and again after they returned after being removed temporarily so he could be reprimanded and calmed, and continued diatribe after jurors were dismissed; failure of judge to include recital of facts upon which adjudication of guilt was based (or to sign such recital and enter it on record) "pardonable in the circumstances" & no prejudice to D from such failure;

C v Brunnell **65 MAC 423 (2006)**—summary contempt upheld: when judge denied motion to lower bail, D responded "fuck you, judge; fuck you," and after judge directed court officers to take D out, D continued, "you can suck my fuckin' dick"; "warning is not a condition precedent to criminal contempt in all cases"; conduct was sufficiently flagrant to undermine authority of court, so summary procedure for criminal contempt (& sentence of 60 days from and after) = okay; further response of increasing bail from 25K to 50K was "reconsidered" and set back to 25K six weeks later (and isn't addressed/analyzed in opinion, id. at 426 n.2);

Furtado v Furtado **380 M 137 (80)**—willful disobey clear (support) order = "criminal" contempt because punishment for obstructing administration of justice;

Nolan & Sartorio, *Criminal Law* **(3d ed. 2001) § 616**—line's blurred, but civil = remedial, to compel compliance; "criminal" = punitive, vindicates court's authority because obstructed it;

WA & HA Root v MacDonald **260 M 344 (27)**—line between civil & "criminal" = in "shadow"; if mixed criminal & civil, it's criminal, & due process, 5th Amendment rights apply;

NYCR v Ayer **253 M 122 (25)**—contempt = sui generis, not strictly criminal or civil;

US v Wendy **575 F.2d 1025 (2d Cir. '78)**—"civil" = conditional for disobey order; "criminal = unconditional, retrospective, vindicate court's authority for doing the prohibited;

Birchall, petitioner **454 M 837 (2009)**—henceforth, civil contempt finding must be supported by clear and convincing evidence of disobedience of clear and unequivocal command; petitioner held for years because of default judgment of over $2 million and his failure to "purge" 'self of contempt by paying judgment he contends he is not able to pay; judge may sentence judgment debtor to 30 days in contempt for failure to pay with proviso for release if he pays in full with interest and costs; if still failure, further hearings necessary to impose consecutive 30-day terms; judgment creditor has burden to prove contemnor's ability to pay;

C v Hughes **380 M 583 (80)**—no contempt (stayed & jointly appealed) for D's refusal to surrender gun, can't use contempt to compel 5th Amendment violation;

Miaskiewicz v Commonwealth **380 M 153 (80)**—perjury alone not contempt; but 11-day frivolous trial was obstruction of court, so contempt OK; But cf. *C v Phetsaya* **40 MAC 293 (96) double jeopardy prohibition barred 2d trial after judge declared mistrial because *he* thought case should not have been tried and D-counsel had no "presence before the jury" or strategy appreciated by the judge (no manifest necessity for mistrial)**;

Fay v Commonwealth **379 M 498 (80)**—restitution nonpayment = contempt because "conduct tending to interfere, obstruct" proper administration of justice;

Holt v Virginia **381 US 131 (65)**—no attorney contempt for false charges in recusal motion because doing his job & language was OK;

C v Diamond **46 MAC 103 (99)**—summary contempt (M.R.Crim.P 43) inappropriately invoked ($500 fine, refusal of request to be represented by counsel) against attorney who said to opposing counsel in a too-loud whisper that he would now get "discovery up the ass"; behavior didn't "immediately imperil ( ) the administration of justice"; options for future such "incivility by an attorney" that does not require immediate redress to preserve order: (1) initiation of contempt proceeding by complaint or indictment under M.R.Crim.P. 44; (2) referral to Board of Bar Overseers for disciplinary action when alleged conduct violates Rules of Professional Conduct; (3) "deliver(y of) a public or private admonition, combined in the judge's discretion with a warning, cautioning that repetition would be grounds for contempt proceedings";

In re McConnell **370 US 230 (62)**—can be strenuous/persistent without obstructing court, stated intent to persist/defy order not contempt unless carried out;

Craig v Harney **331 US 367 (47)—no contempt (for reporter) who criticized judge because contempt not for protection of judges sensitive to winds of public opinion; judges should be "men of fortitude, able to thrive in a hardy climate"**;

Eaton v City of Tulsa **415 US 697 (74)**—witness' single use of "street vernacular" ("chicken shit") not contempt;

Blankenburg v Commonwealth **260 M 369 (27)**—criminal contempt = punishment for act tending to obstruct or degrade administration of justice − to vindicate majesty of law;

C v Contach **47 MAC 247 (99)**—female (who had sought issuance of c. 209A protective order) made no response to judge's query "Did you have alcohol this morning?" (though the boyfriend responded that he had not) and as she was leaving the courtroom (restraining order having been denied), displayed her middle finger in a gesture to the boyfriend (Appeals Court: "nothing more than a short burst of temper—an emotion, we add, we have excused judges on various occasions when they have displayed it"); judge ordered her placed in custody, plus breathalyzer (.13 reading); hearing later that day resulted in finding of criminal contempt (and 10 day sentence), but Appeals Court reversed: D had not "lied" about alcohol, had apologized twice and explained "nervous" about coming to court (so drank); isolated gesture (not directed at judge, but instead at the person she claimed beat and threatened her) was not proper basis for criminal contempt (at 252), and there was "not even a hint of a threat to order in the courtroom from the D's consumption of alcohol"; judge chastised for not being more "sensitive"; "provisions of M.R.Crim.P. 44, 378 Mass. 920 (1979), . . . govern( ) "all criminal (i.e., 'summary') contempts not adjudicated pursuant to rule 43"; "Rule 43 . . . permits the summary punishment of a criminal contempt only if 'summary punishment is necessary to maintain order in the courtroom' (citation omitted); "summary contempt should be used only when the contemptuous behavior constitutes a threat that immediately imperils the administration of justice" (citation omitted); judge "could have employed M.R.Crim. P. 44 which has more procedural safeguards";

Fisher v Pace **336 US 155 (49)**—persist in argument = contempt because must abide by rulings (& appeal) even if error, otherwise mockery of orderly administration of justice; even provocation by judge doesn't justify contempt (see *Wilson* **421 US 309 (75)**);

M.R.Crim.P. 22: Objections—". . . If a party objects to a ruling or order of the court, he **may** state the precise legal grounds of his objection, but he **shall not argue or further discuss such grounds unless the court calls upon him** for such argument or discussion"; *(See Chapter 12-M & Chapter 15, prerequisites to appellate preservation)*;

Brown v US **356 US 148 (58)**—courts must not confuse offenses to sensibilities with obstruction of justice, but refusal to answer question can be contempt;

In re Little **404 US 553 (72)**—pro se D's vehement argument (about court's prejudice) not contempt because not "boisterous" & didn't disrupt;

Albano v Commonwealth **315 M 531 (44)**—contempt because bad manner/tone, falsity re: need for continuance trifled with court dignity, & unreasonable (20 minute) delay = disruptive; no excuse that he didn't intend contempt (cf. *Sussman* **374 M 692 (78)**);

US v Wilson **421 US 309 (75)**—"silence" = summary contempt though "respectful" because defiance of clear order (to testify), "affront" & "breakdown" of proceedings (see *Fisher* **336 US 155 (49)**), so need vindicate authority;

Walker v Birmingham **388 US 307 (67)**—violate court order (though maybe unconstitutional) = contempt because court had jurisdiction & no "collateral" challenge because D didn't contest it; "civilizing hand of law" = can't judge your own case; (dissent: magic transformation of abusive state act) (see *Ryan* **402 US 530 n.4**: Walker case was based on "earlier availability of review");

US v Ryan **402 US 530 (71)**—no appeal from denial of motion to quash subpoena; either comply, or refuse & risk contempt (& then appeal that);

In the Matter of a Grand Jury Subpoena **442 M 1029 (2004)**—petitioner received no relief (on appeal to full bench from single justice's refusal on G.L. c. 211, § 3 petition to quash order of Superior Court judge that he testify before grand jury): "if prosecutor strays into a potentially protected area, petitioner may then exercise his privilege on a question by question basis"; USUAL WAY OF CHALLENGING SUCH ORDERS TO TESTIFY = disobey them, & appeal from subsequent contempt order;

In re Providence Journal Co. **820 F.2d 1342 & 1353 (1st Cir. '87)**—bedrock rule: comply with court order, though unconstitutional, until amended/vacated — "collateral bar BAR Rule"; BUT OK to disobey "transparently invalid" (because of 1st Amendment) order if good faith effort at interlocutory relief;

City of Fitchburg v. 707 Main Corp. **707 369 M 748 (76)**—not contempt for violating court order because it's void within 1st Amendment, like Walker's (388 US 307) "transparent invalidity" rule;

Jordan v Sinsheimer **403 M 586 (88)**—no DA discretion to ignore court order (to return suppressed evidence) without appealing (so no civil immunity);

See also Chapter 2-G, & Maness **419 US 449 (75)** *no contempt for good faith advice to D to take 5th Amendment; generally must comply with court order & tell D to, unless stay, & probably contempt even if order invalid, if court had jurisdiction; but order to reveal info permits precompliance review (& D risks contempt, but not attorney) Petition of Crystal* **330 M 583 (53)** *habeas petition springs D from contempt which is bad because no hearing; stated intention to disobey court order isn't summary contempt;*

Cooke v US **267 US 517 (25)**—letter to judge = contempt, but not "flagrant defiance" & not summary contempt (only to prevent demoralization of court's authority); if personal attack, & not impractical, may have 2d judge hear it, especially on remand;

In re Oliver **333 US 257 (48)**—(same) can't sacrifice due process under guise of "demoralization of court";

Harris v US **382 US 162 (65)**—not summary contempt without open, serious threat to order;

Codispoti v Pennsylvania **418 US 506 (74)**—not summary contempt without "overriding necessity for instant action to preserve order"; aggregate from & after sentences entitled jury trial;

C v Malley **42 MAC 804 (97)**—OK summary contempt for D who boisterously & profanely "refused" on trial date to go forward with "this" attorney (who allegedly failed to get D's witnesses) and refused to waive counsel; Appeals Court held sufficient 'prior warning' and, implicitly, that D's action threatened immediate damage to administration of justice (M.R.Crim.P. 43(a)), and did not care that no one addressed D's complaint re: counsel's alleged failings; obvious denial of conflict-free counsel to

represent D in Superior Court proceeding excused/ignored; (but see *C v Moran* **17 MAC 200 (83)** if complete/irreconcilable "breakdown in communication," D can have new attorney (though here, request found to be dilatory tactic); judge must allow D to state reasons for dissatisfaction);

Taylor v Hayes **418 US 488 (74)**—less necessity for summary contempt if await trial's end; should be 2d judge because personal feelings expressed;

Mayberry v Pennsylvania **400 US 455 (71)**—personal/vicious/direct remarks to judge, so best to let 2d judge hear (post-trial) contempt case (& 11–22 year sentence);

C v Carr **38 MAC 179 (95)**—no summary contempt for 2 witnesses' failure to appear after judge ordered them to return to Court next day (trial was previously cut short for G plea); witnesses had not been warned & "time was not of the essence"; M.R.Crim.P. 43 here inapposite; R.44 was instead proper **if** there had been warning of 'contempt' as consequence for failure to appear;

C v Nicholas **74 MAC 164 (2009)**—no summary contempt 8 days after prosecution witness made hand gesture to D's father and brother as he left courtroom (like a gun, & saying "pop pop") causing altercation requiring police officers' presence and necessitating excusing two jurors in murder trial: **judge didn't witness gesture**, only ensuing fracas, and judge's actual observation of the contemptuous conduct = "bright line" rule for "summary" contempt; matter should have been pursued under M.R.Crim.P. 44 ("contempt") rather than R 43 ("summary" contempt);

Garabedian v Commonwealth **336 M 119 (57)**—no summary contempt for alleged perjury because depends on some facts out of judge's view;

C v Viera **41 MAC 206 (96)**—no summary contempt for alleged lie by D that his cousin, rather than D, was person arrested for (& perhaps G of) charge, though D's name was used (judge undertook investigation, compared signatures, pressed D to state whether he would persist in previous (arraignment) claim of misidentification; furthermore, perjury alone is not enough to support charge of nonsummary criminal contempt; must be further element of obstruction of court in performance of its duty;

US v Bryan **339 US 323 (50)**—inability to comply = complete defense (to no production of documents), but not refusal without good faith; see *Wendy* **575 F.2d 1025 (2d Cir. '78)**;

Panico v US **375 US 29 (63)**—must prove intent (for insane D) (but see *Sussman* **374 M 692**; *Albano* **315 M 531 (44)**)

Matter of Scott **377 M 364 (79)**—(stipulations 15–20): contempt abuses;

Shillitani v US **384 US 364 (66)**—though called "criminal," witness's "purge" option meant it's civil; must release on grand jury's end when compliance impossible;

Dolan v Commonwealth **304 M 325 (39)**—no right to purge (by disavowing);

Doe v Commonwealth **396 M 421 (85)**—any court (e.g. Superior) can hold juvenile in contempt;

C v Florence F., a juvenile **429 M 523 (99)**—cannot prosecute child in need of services (CHINS) for criminal contempt based on failure to comply with order concerning condition of custody (remain in mother's custody on condition she attend school); CHINS proceedings can't be "criminal," and charging CHINS juvenile with criminal contempt "is a remedy that directly contradicts . . . statutory provisions";

2-J. CONFLICTS, WITHDRAWAL, REMOVAL, ATTORNEY AS PROSPECTIVE WITNESS

Matthew 6:24—no man can serve two masters;

CPCS P/G 1.3(e)—be alert to & avoid all potential/actual conflicts;

SJC Rule 3:07, Rule 8: Maintain Integrity of Profession—R. 1.2 shall seek lawful objectives of client; 1.7, 1.10(a) decline case or withdraw if likely conflict between clients or between client and lawyer's own interests, or between client and another person to/for whom lawyer has "responsibilities," & if so, partner/associate disqualified; 1.7(a)(2) & (b)(2) if each potentially affected client consents, may represent; 1.3 (comment) "implicit in . . . rule" = shan't prejudice/damage client during professional relationship; 8.4(a) can't circumvent rules through acts of another)

Cuyler v Sullivan **446 US 335 (80)**—6th Amendment violated if attorney has actual conflict of interest and conflict had adverse effect on attorney's representation of D;

Holloway v Arkansas **435 US 475 (78)**—D counsel representing 3 co-Ds with "divergent interests" himself claimed, in timely motion for appointment of separate counsel, that he had disabling conflict; denial of such timely motion now = automatic reversal;

Mickens v Taylor **535 U.S. 162 (2002)**—to demonstrate 6th Amendment violation where trial court fails to inquire into potential conflict of interest about which it knew or reasonably should have known, D must show that conflict adversely affected counsel's performance; here, appointed counsel in capital case had been appointed to represent deceased victim in matter pending at time of death, & had met with client-victim at least once; appointed counsel did not inform court or co-counsel or D of this fact;

C v Fogarty **419 M 456 (95)**—under Article 12, Declaration of Rights, constitutional violation shown merely upon proof of actual conflict (without showing actual prejudice or adverse effect); if conflict was only "potential," conviction won't be reversed without showing actual prejudice to D;

ABA Standards for Criminal Justice, Prosecution Function & Defense Function (3d ed. 1993) 4-3.5 Comment—must put present case first & not be influenced by demands/interests of possible future case or future dealings with judge or prosecutor; Comment: co-D conflicts in great majority of cases, e.g., privilege, plea bargains, trial & sentencing, & joint representation "normally" shouldn't occur; but see ABA Model Rules of Professional Conduct (1983 & revisions) 1.7 decline case if "directly adverse" to 2d client (because loyalty's essential), but OK for unrelated matters only generally adverse;

1.9 former client, can't later handle 2d client in related matter, & can't use confidence ("info. relating to case") to harm 2d client (unless info's "generally known"); 1.10 imputed disqualification of associates (& "firm" includes legal services organization);

MBA Ethics Op. 84-3—still privilege for past client though info's notorious; SJC Rule 3:07 Rule 1.9, Conflict of Interest: Former Client—omits ABA Model Rules' exception from confidentiality info 'generally known'; if attorney contemplates representing new client "in same or substantially related matter" as attorney or his present or former firm represented former client & prospective client's interests are "materially adverse" to those of former client, attorney must have former client's consent; can't represent if lawyer acquired 'protected information' material to the matter from former client, unless former client consents; can't reveal confidential information relating to the representation (except Rules 1.6 or Rule 3.3);

See also Chapter 2-F, Confidences/Secrets

C v Davis **376 M 777 (78)**—Rule = colloquy re: co-D's aware of risks of joint representation, including "domination or martyrdom";

US v Donahue **560 F.2d 1039 (1st Cir. '77)**—(same);

C v Jordan **49 MAC 802, 811 n.10 (2000)**—prior to accepting any waiver by D of conflict-free counsel, "advisab(le)" to have independent counsel advise/consult D;

C v Bolduc **375 M 530 (78)**—bad joint representation at sentencing;

C v Michel **381 M 447 (80)**—conflict because co-D's attorney = associate of D's attorney, so D lost "undivided loyalty of counsel";

***C v Miller* 435 M 274, 280–82 (2001)—while Miller was being represented by a (trial) public defender in Springfield, Thompson was being represented on appeal by public defender in Boston office &, after seeking advice from Bar Counsel & obtaining waiver of conflict from Thompson, Thompson's appellate counsel pressed inference from trial record (Thompson there represented by private counsel) that real killer was Miller, who was neither a co-D nor a witness in Thompson case; Miller's trial attorney was not advised of any possible conflict & continued to represent Miller; no 'actual' conflict of interest, held SJC;**

Wheat v US **486 US 153 (88)**—discretion to override presumptive counsel choice if serious potential for conflict;

C v Jordan **49 MAC 802 (2000)**—court can override D's insistent waiver of conflict-free counsel; court not "required to tolerate an inadequate representation of a defendant," (result might be different if disqualification were sought by someone other than counsel himself, who had consulted authoritative sources beforehand, id. at 809–10);

G.L. c. 211D, § 6—CPCS Public Defender Division shan't represent co-D's in "any matter before any court"; & not assigned if conflict with another client; § 9 CPCS standards shall include vertical/continuous representation;

See Chapter 2-E, I, re: replacement attorney & meaningful relationship

C v Moran **17 MAC 200 (83)**—if complete/irreconcilable "breakdown in communication," D can have new attorney; not shown here (= dilatory tactic); judge must allow D to state reasons for dissatisfaction;

C v Tuitt **393 M 801 (85)**—(same); no right to "meaningful relationship";

C v Chavis **415 M 703, 710 (93)**—same; but see *C v Jordan* **49 MAC 802 (2000)** fact that D has no right to a particular appointed attorney doesn't mean he has no cognizable interest in continued representation by appointed attorney with whom he has developed good relationship;

C v Carsetti **53 MAC 558, 560 & n.2 (2002)**—**while D has no right to counsel change on the date of trial if counsel is prepared, DEFENSE COUNSEL HIMSELF SHOULD HAVE BROUGHT FORWARD THE CASE PRIOR TO TRIAL DATE; his telling D to 'come before this court prior to trial date' to raise the point WAS IMPROPER; obligation to inform trial judge of need for continuance rests on attorney, not D;**

C v Rodgers **448 M 538 (2007)**—extremely lengthy delays, purportedly for Commonwealth's testing of DNA, eventually prompted D's motion to dismiss appointed counsel, and there was "no justification . . . for the clerk's failure to docket the motion or bring it to the judge's attention"; while other types of pro se motions by Ds who are represented by counsel might permissibly be ignored, a motion to dismiss counsel does require "judicial action";

C v Vickers **60 MAC 24 (2003)**—disapproving judge's response to D's request for new counsel on date of trial, i.e., agreement to find new attorney, but threat to increase bail: appellate court couldn't "be confident that [D's] sudden change of heart [to keep present counsel & proceed to trial that day] was free of coercion and consistent with her right to counsel";

Brown v Craven **424 F.2d 1166 (9th Cir. '70)**—right to hearing re: "irreconcilable conflict" (& maybe new counsel);

Mack v Clerk of the Appeals Court **427 M 1011 (98)**—after Appeals Court allowed motions of two successively appointed counsel to withdraw from representing D, Court deemed D to be proceeding pro se (CPCS had informed D that no further counsel would be assigned if D couldn't work with second attorney); no abuse of discretion in single justice's refusal to either order past attorney to resume representation or order CPCS to appoint new counsel for appeal; 1st attorney's affidavit recounted that D twice spat in his face and cursed him when he appeared to represent D at appellate division of Superior Court, and 2d attorney cited D's "extreme and profane" behavior, D's

written request that he withdraw, and total breakdown of attorney-client relationship;

C v Gilliard **36 MAC 183, 191–92 (94)**—Appeals Court, sua sponte, directs appointment of new counsel because trial counsel also represented D on appeal, and did not raise any issue about failure to request/obtain instruction on lesser included offense (couldn't argue own ineffectiveness); **S.C. 46 MAC 348 (99)**—allowance of motion for new trial affirmed on appeal: trial counsel "never considered" asking jury for lesser included offense (though there was evidentiary basis for convicting D only of A&B (liability only as joint venturer intending to beat V with fists, with no intent to use or knowledge of, knife) instead of second degree murder); "never considering" was ineffective assistance, but it also would've been ineffective assistance if counsel considered and rejected option of requesting instruction on lesser offense; court didn't reach issue whether failure to consult D about gambling to forego lesser offense instruction is "misconduct which itself would warrant the allowance of a new trial" (but noted that Commonwealth's Brief acknowledged that counsel "unquestionably should have consulted" D);

C v Egardo **426 M 48 (97)**—D did not waive issue of ineffective assistance on direct appeal because his appellate attorney was an ineligible proponent (appellate attorney and trial counsel both public defenders);

C v DiBenedetto **427 M 414, 424 (98)**—though appellate counsel argued ineffective assistance of trial counsel, issue wasn't reached, and conviction was reversed on another ground; at D's insistence and with eventual permission of SJC, 1st trial attorney represented D at 2d trial; on appeal of that 2d conviction, though D argued that trial counsel had disabling conflict of interest at 2d trial, SJC said "no evidence of an actual conflict at the time of trial," so "the argument fails";

ABA Op. 342 (75)—disqualify whole firm = too harsh re: government agency (especially re: DR 9-101(B)); can screen confidences & individual attorney's participation;

US v Judge **625 F.Supp 901 (D.Haw. '86)**—ABA Op. 342 = "Chinese Wall Defense" & DA can't get public defender #2 removed because public defender #1's client will be witness; BUT SEE *C v Jordan* **49 MAC 802 (2000)** public defender had disabling conflict when another defender (& supervisee of PD#1) represented wife of individual who, at last minute, proffered testimony against murder client of PD#1, in exchange for dropping charges against the wife;

C v Geraway **364 M 168 (73)**—reverse though D's attorney unaware partner represents DA witness (in unrelated case); necessity of cross-checks!;

C v Smith **362 M 782 (73)**—attorney's prior (to D's trial) representation of prosecution witness on unrelated case = OK because no continuing duty/loyalty & no inhibition of cross-examination (e.g., by confidences);

C v Banister **428 M 211, 215–16 (98)**—attorney's representation of prosecution witness in unrelated case, ending a year before attorney began representing D, not ground for relief; "nothing . . . suggest(ed) that counsel owed or felt any continuing duty of loyalty to the witness at the time of trial . . . or that he continued at that time to be under any ethical, economic or social constraint arising out of his prior representation of the witness";

C v Murphy **442 M 485 (2004)**—attorney's representation, in a civil matter settled one year before D's trial, of potential prosecution witness not ground for relief: counsel told D and sought and obtained hearing on issue, and D there knowingly agreed to continue with attorney;

C v Hurley **391 M 76 (84)**—"genuine" conflict from attorney's prior representation of DA witness, so reverse without showing prejudice;

C v Baran **74 MAC 256, 272–73 n.24 (2009)**— appellate counsel's firm had previously represented alleged victim and her family in civil suit predicated upon D's alleged acts; testimony before judge on motion for new trial would have permitted finding of either actual conflict or potential conflict;

C v Cobb **379 M 456 (80)**—reverse for conflict because D's attorney represents DA's witness on unrelated matter;

C v Boateng **438 M 498 (2003)**—D-counsel represented medical examiner in unrelated civil case, D and trial judge were so informed, & judge conducted colloquy with D: conflict of interest held to have been only "potential," and not "actual," because medical examiner's testimony wasn't critical to defense (since defense was insanity);

C v Martinez **425 M 382 (97)—reversal of first degree murder conviction because defense counsel represented prosecution witness in unrelated case**, despite judge's obvious record attempt to have D waive any objection;

C v Agbanyo **69 MAC 841, further appellate review allowed, 450 M 1104 (2007)**—on morning of jury-waived trial, D learned that his attorney had accepted offer of future employment with DA's office prosecuting D's case; colloquy to assure D's consent failed to cover important matter, but Appeals Court holds conflict to have been only "potential," rather than "actual"; no relief because he failed to show that the potential conflict "materially prejudiced his defense"; counsel secured NG on most serious charge;

C v Hodge **386 M 165 (82)**—attorney's partner represents DA witness in unrelated civil case = conflict; no need to show prejudice;

C v Milley **67 MAC 685 (2006)**—that appointed attorney was involved in a scheme whereby his choice of particular individual as investigator would assure his continued appointments to represent indigent defendants did not establish actual conflict in D's case because representation of D occurred about two and a half years before the manipulation of the "appointment system"; even if potential conflict could be shown to exist, D hasn't shown prejudice from inadequate investigation (apart from claim of ineffective assistance of counsel);

C v Croken **432 M 266 (2000)**—on further review of 48 MAC 32 (99) motion for new trial remanded for evi-

dentiary hearing: D's attorney perhaps was in "intimate relationship" with an assistant DA employed by the office prosecuting D (though she had no "connection or involvement" in the particular prosecution); if intimate relationship existed, **disclosure to D was required; potential for conflict apparent, though "actual" not shown on papers; study SJC Rule 3:07, Rules 1.8(i) and 1.7(b) (re: when DISCLOSURE TO CLIENT REQUIRED); <u>S.C., after remand:</u> 59 MAC 921 (2003)**—accepts (as not "clearly erroneous") motion judge's findings, satisfied that potential conflict created by attorney's "intimate relationship with a member of the district attorney's office did not cause any material prejudice to the defendant";

C v Walter **19 MAC 82 (84)**—no actual conflict because attorney withdrew from 2d client-witness as soon as possible & no prejudice (e.g., restricted cross-examination because of confidences); proper investigation might've obviated problem; no rule re: which client to withdraw from, except practicalities (D's on trial);

C v Wooldridge **19 MAC 162 (85)**—prior representation of DA's witness (on related matter) doesn't "forever quarantine" attorney from cross-examining witness, & D signed waiver, so no conflict; absence of "contemporaneous file notes of conversations with D" about conflict problem, so SJC review difficult;

C v Clements **36 MAC 205 (94)**—when attorney was appointed to represent D (child sexual assault), attorney was representing Morton in a divorce case; 13 months later, Morton was charged with sex assault of same children: this was only "potential" conflict, and since no material prejudice shown, no relief;

C v Goldman **395 M 495 (85)**—attorney, representing the defendant at a criminal trial, to whom a witness for the Commonwealth previously had made confidential communications, was required to withdraw because of the conflict of interest which would be inherent in his continued representation of the defendant, unless the witness would waive his attorney-client privilege, or the defendant would waive his right to be represented by counsel who bears him undivided loyalty; but see *Martinez* **425 M 382 (97)** no waiver despite trial judge's attempts to so insulate issue in this manner; see also *C v Jordan* **49 MAC 802 (2000)** advisable to have independent counsel consult with D before accepting waiver;

C v Adams **374 M 722 (78)**—risky, but OK that attorney represented co-D and (potential, now missing) witness;

C v Soffen **377 M 433 (79)**—OK because attorney's relationship with deceased victim ended pre-trial; & OK though attorney had handled co-Ds at probable cause hearing;

MBA Ethics Ops. 76-12 & 77-1—OK to sue former client unless substantial relationship to current case or violate confidences/secrets; BUT SEE contra (violating confidences/secrets irrelevant to permissive breach of confidentiality in certain cases) SJC Rule 3:07, Rule 1.6(b) lawyer may reveal confidential info "to the extent the lawyer reasonably believes necessary to establish a claim or defense on behalf of the lawyer in a controversy between the lawyer and the client" (or to establish a defense to a criminal charge or civil claim against the lawyer based upon conduct in which the client was involved or to respond to allegations in any proceeding concerning the lawyer's representation of the client);

MBA Op. 75-7—bad employment as adversary to former client if he'd reasonably fear violation of privilege because "appearance of impropriety";

C v Edward 34 MAC 521 (93)—D's attorney's "acknowledged friendship" with fresh complaint witness, absent showing of actual prejudice to D, yielded no relief;

C v Bonefont 35 MAC 54 (93)—robbery D's attorney simultaneously represented V's parents in an unrelated guardianship proceeding in Probate Court concerning V's brother: given only "tenuous" or "potential" conflict, no relief absent showing of prejudice, i.e., that vigor of counsel's cross-examination of V "was sapped because of his involvement" in probate case;

C v McGuire 421 M 236 (95)—there was only potential for conflict from impending suspension of attorney's license to practice, but no evidence that D's G plea or DA's sentencing recommendation was affected by it; SJC refused to adopt **per se** ineffective assistance in these circumstances (attorney told D, gave D option of getting new attorney or pleading G);

SJC Rule 3:07, 1.16(a)(1–3)—WITHDRAWAL, SHALL try to withdraw if representation will result in violating rules of conduct or other law, or if lawyer's mental or physical condition impairs ability to represent, or if lawyer is discharged; 1.16(b) MAY if D insists on course of action which is criminal or fraudulent involving lawyer's services, or if client's objective is "repugnant or imprudent" in lawyer's judgment, or if D doesn't "fulfill an obligation to the lawyer, or if "other good cause"; 1.16(d) if granted, shall minimize PREJUDICE to D;

C v Tennison 440 M 553 (2003)—attorney moved to withdraw upon info from D that D had been in contact with juror throughout trial; upon threat of contempt, attorney disclosed name of juror; conflict of interest apparent ("testimony" or not, disclosure was detrimental to D); court unsympathetic to D's appellate argument that he was deprived of counsel during period before new attorney was appointed ("dilemma" created by D's own actions);

M.R.Crim.P. 7(b)(2)—no withdrawal in Superior Court without leave of court, unless it's within 14 days "after return day" & different attorney files notice of appearance simultaneously;

Special Rules of Boston Municipal Court Sitting for Criminal Business, Rule 10—attorney must file appearance slip; no attorney who has filed appearance may withdraw without consent of trial judge;

D.Ct.Supp.Crim.R. 8 (4)—attorney appointed = personally responsible at every stage of District Court; if new attorney appointed, first attorney shall cooperate;

ABA Model Code of Professional Responsibility (1969) Ethical Consideration #s 2-29—assigned attorney shouldn't seek withdraw without compelling reasons (not repugnance of case or belief in D's guilt); 2-30 & 5-2 decline case if personal feelings may hinder *(See Chapter 2-C)*;

CPCS P/G 1.3(h)—obligation to D until 2d attorney assigned, then fully cooperate;

SJC Rule 3:07, 3.7—attorney shall not be witness for D, except uncontested issue or "substantial hardship"; attorney may be advocate for D if attorney's associate is witness unless precluded by 1.7 or 1.9 (regarding conflicts of interest);

Superior Ct.R.12—if representing party at trial, can't be witness for client without "special leave of court";

C v White 367 M 280 (75)—attorney (DA) can cross-examine/impeach witness re: conversations with attorney, so long as "good faith";

ABA Model Rule of Professional Conduct (1983) 3.7—can't be both advocate & witness, unless exceptional case & manifestly unfair otherwise; no disqualification if associate's a witness; Comment, attorney-witness can prejudice opponent & be conflict for attorney, but balancing test;

C v Rondeau 378 M 408, 413 (79)—failure to withdraw as counsel, so that attorney could testify in support of D's alibi defense = ethical infraction & ineffective assistance; viewed as "conflict" between attorney's interest in not being a witness and client's interest in having alibi witness not impeachable with prior convictions & friendship with D; if attorney = witness, credibility suffers, so withdrawal maybe necessary;

Kendall v Atkins 374 M 320 (78)—attorney = competent as witness; maybe duty to testify for client, & court's discretion to permit; can even call opposing counsel, though best to give notice & withdrawal less likely;

Borman v Borman 378 M 775 (79)—disqualify attorney because opponent will call = "harsh," merits interlocutory hearing, & bad unless "participation taints system or trial"; unnecessary removal fosters public disrespect; rules self-executing & attorney decides if "ought" testify, or withdraw or get advice;

C v Goldman 395 M 495 (85)—if attorney = witness, credibility suffers, withdrawal maybe necessary;

C v Patterson 432 M 767, 777 (2000)—defense counsel obligated to withdraw as soon as apparent that cop would claim that D's interview statement included assertion which counsel (present during interview) knew was not made; decision to remain as counsel and forego testifying can't be justified as strategic choice (murder conviction reversed);

ABA Standards for Criminal Justice, Prosecution Function & Defense Function 4-4.3 & Comment—unless prepared to forego impeachment of witness by counsel's own testimony re: what witness said during interview, or to seek leave to withdraw from representation in the case in order to present impeaching testimony, don't interview witness without third person being present (because "normally" inappropriate to take stand (to impeach) & remain counsel); *(See also Chapter 7-A, Prepare Trial: Investigation)*;

ABA Op. 339 (75)—"substantial hardship" factors, e.g., long preparation, unanticipated need, extensive relationship/familiarity;

***C v Gatewood* 293 A.2d.80 (Pa.S.Ct. '72)**—right to present impeachment testimony isn't affected by fact that it's attorney's testimony;

***State v Lee* 28 S.E.2d.402 (SC '43)**—constitutional right to call prosecutor as witness;

***In re Conduct of Lathen* 654 P.2d.1110 (Or. '82)**—no attorney sanction because didn't know pre-trial that prosecutor = witness & court ordered proceed when moved to withdraw;

MBA Op. 74-2—need not (though best to) withdraw if no intent to call associate, if believe opponent would only call associate as removal device, or if think withdrawal = "substantial hardship because distinctive value" (see also 76-22);

MBA Op. 75-2—no substantial hardship/distinctive value re: real estate sale, so attorney-witness must withdraw (discusses factors); (cf. MBA Op. 75-4 need not withdraw as prospective witness until trial)

***C v Shraiar* 397 M 16 (86)**—stipulation = common/appropriate way to avoid conflict dilemma (especially letting opponent force removal) for uncontested fact;

SJC Rule 3:07, 3.8(f)—(Special Responsibilities of a Prosecutor) prior judicial approval (& opportunity for adversarial hearing) for subpoena to counsel re: "past or present client"; must reasonably believe info sought **isn't protected by any privilege**, is "essential to the successful completion of an ongoing investigation or prosecution," and no other feasible alternative to obtain the info *(See Chapter 2-F, Counsel: Confidences, Secrets & Privileges)*;

***Smith v Superior Court of Los Angeles* 440 P.2d 65 (Ca. '68)**—no involuntary removal of appointed counsel (for subjective "incompetence") because attorney-client relationship = inviolable, threat to independence of bar, & discriminates against indigents; cf. ***C v Phetsaya* 40 MAC 293 (96) double jeopardy prohibition barred 2d trial after judge declared mistrial because *he* thought case should not have been tried and D-counsel had no "presence before the jury" and no strategy appreciated by the judge (there was no "manifest necessity" for mistrial);**

***Quegan v Mass. Parole Board* 423 M 834 (96)**—parole board had no standing to move to disqualify CPCS from representing D on the ground stated;

***McKinnon v S* 526 P.2d 18 (Alas. '74)**—deprived of 6th Amendment right to "counsel of choice" to remove public defender & thrust unfamiliar/unwelcome counsel on D; can't blame attorney for sins of his overloaded/dilatory public defender office; but see ***C v Jordan* 49 MAC 802 (2000)** court's refusal to accept D's waiver of conflict-free attorney (public defender) not error; maybe different if counsel himself hadn't sought withdrawal after ethical consultations;

***Cannon v Commission on Judicial Qualifications* 537 P.2d.898 (Ca. '75)**—removal of public defenders & appointment of substitute counsel = "willful misconduct" for removal of judge; can't violate attorney-client sanctity of young public defenders and indigent clients—see also ***Judge* 625 F.Supp 901 (D.Haw. '86)**;

***Roswall v Municipal Court* 152 Cal.R.337 (79)**—no removal (without D's consent) for D's non-indigency;

***C v Desfonds* 32 MAC 311 (92)**—conflict due to counsel's contemporaneous civil representation of key Commonwealth witness as well as prior representation of complainant was validly waived; judge should elicit narrative rather than 'yes' or 'no' answers;

***C v Jiminez* 27 MAC 1165 (89)**—counsel retained by mother of sex abuse victim for husband D was not conflict of interest requiring vacating of guilty plea where wife's interests were in harmony with D's & where counsel properly pressed for leniency at sentencing;

***C v Dahl* 430 M 813 (2000)**—no ineffective assistance found though D argued that counsel hadn't advised that defendant's testimony was necessary/crucial for various proffered defenses, and **though trial counsel told judge, on trial record, that he wasn't adequately representing D due to lack of sleep and travel to Florida on weekends, and pressure of having two clients on trial simultaneously in different states, here for 1st degree murder without death penalty, and there in a capital murder trial**; SJC refused to find "genuine conflict of interest" in circumstances;

2-K. PUBLIC, PRESS, AND MEDIA COMMENTS

See Chapter 2-F, Confidences/Secrets;

Rule 3:07, 3.6—can't make statement reasonably expected to be disseminated "by means of public communication" if reasonably apparent that it will have 'substantial likelihood of materially prejudicing an adjudicative proceeding in the matter,'" except can state 'claim, offense, or defense involved, and except when prohibited by law, the identity of the persons involved,' & info in public record, & that investigation is in progress, & what is result or next scheduled step in litigation, & warning of danger if there's harm to public or an individual; in criminal case can state

ID, residence, occupation & family status of D, info necessary to aid in arresting D, facts re: arrest & ID of investigating/arresting officers/agencies; id., Comments no public statement by lawyer (& try to prevent employees/associates) re: D's or witness's character, credibility, or criminal record, or re: possible G plea or existence/contents of alleged confession, or D's failure to make statement, or re: nature of physical evidence to be presented, including results of any examination/test, or opinion re guilt; but can quote public record or protect D from prejudice from publicity/other party's public statements (this Rule is almost exactly ABA Model Rule of Professional Conduct (1983) 3.6);

ABA Model Code of Professional Responsibility (1969), Ethical Consideration 7-33—goals = impartial tribunal, jury (or judge) not influenced by publicity; Comments, based in part on *Sheppard v Maxwell* **384 US 333 (66)**;

Sheppard v Maxwell **384 US 333 (66)**—unfair trial because publicity (judge should've controlled);

ABA Standards for Criminal Justice, Fair Trial & Free Press (3d ed. 1992) 8-1.1—revision of standard made it comport almost exactly with ABA Model Rule of Professional Conduct 3.6 (1983); 8-1.2 unless substance of standard 8-1.1 is adopted by statute or via "supervisory authority of the highest court in the jurisdiction," courts should adopt it as rule governing attorney conduct; 8-2.1 similar rules for law enforcement agencies; 8-2.2 court personnel shouldn't disclose to "unauthorized person" info re: pending criminal case which isn't part of public record & may be prejudicial to prosecution or defense right to fair trial; see also G.L. c. 268, § 6A execution or "publishing" of any false written report by Commonwealth employee in the course of his official duties, when employee knows same to be materially false punishable by fine of $1,000 or less AND/OR one year's imprisonment;

Chicago Council of Lawyers v Bauer **522 F.2d 242 (7th Cir. '75)**—Disciplinary Rule (ABA Model Code of Professional Responsibility (1969)) # 7-107 is overbroad without limit to "serious/imminent" threat to administration of justice; attorneys = check to expose government abuse; scales imbalanced against defendants & rules don't help;

Hirschkop v Snead **594 F.2d 356 (4th Cir. '79)**—attorneys have 1st Amendment rights; 7-107's too broad because covers bench trials; judges can separate wheat/chaff;

Craig v Harney **331 US 367 (47)**—reporter not in contempt for criticizing judge unless "clear/present danger to administration of justice" because judges have fortitude;

SJC Rule 3:07 Preamble—lawyers should assist in improving the law & administration of justice;

Stern, *Right of Accused to Public Defense,* **Harvard Civil Rights/Civil Liberties Law Review, Winter '83**—curbs on defense comment = inequitable & cause miscarriages of justice; defenders' avoidance of media causes imbalanced coverage & harm to clients (present & future); how-to's re: media relations

SJC Rule 3:07, 8.2—no knowingly false statement or reckless disregard for truth/falsity accusations against a judge or magistrate or re: candidate for appointment to judicial or legal office;

Gentile v State Bar of Nevada **501 US 1030 (91)**—post-indictment press conference by defense counsel was protected political speech as there was "no substantial likelihood of materially prejudicing" proceedings;

2-L. FILES AND RECORDS—THOROUGH AND CURRENT

CPCS P/G's 1.3(d)—must maintain thorough/organized/current file for each case; 1.3(h) duty to "fully cooperate" if 2d attorney takes over, including "upon request, promptly provid(ing) successor counsel with the client's entire case file, including work product";

C v Wooldridge **19 MAC 162, 168 (85)**—took attorney's word re: D waiving the conflict though. document = "far from adequate" & attorney was "shy of any contemporaneous file notes" of talks with client;

SJC Rule 4:01, § 3—bar discipline − must respond to BBO requests for info.

SJC Rule 3:07, 1.6(b)(2)—may reveal confidences to defend 'self vs. accusation;

Laughner v US **373 F.2d. 326 (5th Cir. '67)**—privilege deemed waived when D charges ineffective, & counsel can be called as witness;

Prop.M.R.Evid. 502(d)(3)—no privilege re: anything relevant to issue of breach of duty by attorney;

C v Woodberry **26 MAC 636 (88)**—(same), e.g., motion to withdraw coerced plea;

SJC Rule 3:07, 1.16—no withdrawal without reasonable steps to avoid prejudice to D, e.g., deliver to D all "papers" to which D's "entitled"; may require client to pay for copying unless client has already paid; may withhold such 'work product' which client has not paid for, but "a lawyer may not refuse, on grounds of nonpayment, to make available materials in the client's file when retention would prejudice the client unfairly"; 1.15 must keep complete records of funds & other property of client; must give client all property (s)he is "entitled" to; "work product" defined as "documents & tangible things prepared in the course of the representation of the client by the lawyer or at the lawyer's direction by his or her employee, agent, or consultant, and **which are not** pleadings or papers filed in court **and are not** investigatory or discovery documents for which client has paid lawyer's out-of-pocket costs;

MBA Ethics Op. 78-6—duty of competence & proper care includes keeping "dead" files "reasonable" time;

G.L. c. 6, §§ 171–72 (Criminal Offender Record Information)—can't disseminate CORI (info. re: criminal justice proceedings) or "evaluative info." (re: mental, physical condition); individual has right to inspect/copy own CORI (including evaluative info);

803 CMR 2.04—agencies shall let individual inspect/copy/challenge evaluative information;

See also Chapter 2-F, Confidences, Secrets . . . , and Chapter 6-D, 6-M, Reciprocal Discovery; Work Product;

G.L. c. 111, § 70F—confidentiality of HIV/AIDS test results required absent specific written informed consent; HIV status should not be revealed in open court.

Chapter 3
DEFENDANT'S ENTRY INTO CRIMINAL JUSTICE SYSTEM

3-A. ARREST, GENERALLY

See Chapter 20, Post Arrest, Probable Cause, etc., Chapter 20-J for cases on arrest (& search warrants), including technical requirements, particularity & nexus requirements, nighttime entries, knock & announce requirement, Chapters 20-F through 20-K for cases on searches & seizures, including Chapter 20-H for cases on searches incident to arrest & inventory searches, and Chapter 20-M for cases on investigative stops & frisks for weapons;

U.S. Constitution, Fourth Amendment—"seizure" includes arrest/stop—see *Florida v Royer* **460 US 491 (83)**, etc.;

Kenneth Smith, *Criminal Practice & Procedure,* **Chapter 3 (2d ed. 1983 and Supplement)**—overview of arrest;

C v Gorman **288 M 294 (34)**—no dismissal for bad arrest; see also *U.S. v Alvarez-Machain* **504 US 655 (92)** forcible foreign kidnap does not bar prosecution in U.S. courts;

DA for Norfolk District v Quincy Division of District Court Dept. **444 M 176 (2005)**—a warrantless arrest con- stitutes a finding of probable cause initially by arresting officer, & issuance of complaint thereafter by either clerk- magistrate or judge "is essentially a ministerial act", which is mandatory;

Rothgery v Gillespie County, Texas **128 S Ct 2578 (2008)**—right to counsel attaches at first appearance be- fore judicial officer at which D is told of formal accusation against him and restrictions are imposed on liberty; that public prosecutor (as opposed to police officer) be aware of initial proceeding or involved in its conduct is NOT required; D's arrest without warrant as purported "felon" in possession of firearm was followed by appearance be- fore a "magistrate judge" for proceeding which combined a finding of probable cause with setting of bail; D's oral and written requests for counsel were unheeded until in- dictment and further delay more than six months later (and counsel promptly learned that arrest as "felon" was prem- ised on an erroneous record);

Atwater v City of Lago Vista **532 US 318 (2001)**— officer may arrest even for most minor of offenses without violating 4th Amendment as long as there is probable cause to believe that person committed such criminal offense in officer's presence; only if arrest is made "in an extraordinary manner, unusually harmful to (individual's) privacy or even physical interests" is arrest unreasonable and thus actionable under civil rights statute, 42 USC § 1983; arrest, separation from children, handcuffing, mug shots, removal of shoes, eyeglasses, etc., placed in cell, for driving without seat belt and not securing children in seatbelts not extraordinary, just normal "humiliation," embarrassment, & inconvenience;

3-B. ARREST WARRANTS

K. Smith, Criminal *Practice & Procedure,* Chapter 16 (2d ed. 1983 & Supp.)—(analyzing M.R.Crim.P. 6);

M.R.Crim.P. 6—summons, not arrest warrant, unless reason to believe D won't appear;

G.L. c. 276, § 24—(same); *(See also Chapter 3-F, re issuance of complaint)*;

G.L. c. 276, §§ 21–22: G.L. c. 218, §§ 33 & 35—judge, clerk, or ass't clerk issues; if judge issues, disqualified from trial if D objects;

G.L. c. 276, § 22—examine complaining witness under oath & issue process "if it appears a crime has been committed (by D)";

G.L. c. 218, § 35A: & *C v Baldassini* 357 M 670, 675 (70)—complaint (& arrest warrant) = OK under G.L. c. 276, § 22 & Declaration of Rights, Article 14, because had probable cause;

M.R.Crim.P. 6(b)(1)—issuer signs; must contain D's name or identifying info; substance of crime;

C v Morris Crotty & Others **92 M 403 (1865)**—void without identifying info;

M.R.Crim.P. 6(c)—served by "officers authorized to serve criminal process" (G.L. c. 218, § 3—deputy sheriffs, court officers, probation officers, etc.); if have it, show D; if not, inform of offense & show as soon as possible;

Payton v New York **445 US 573 (80)**—arrest warrant founded on probable cause carries limited authority to enter subject's residence "when there is reason to believe he is within";

C v Cundriff **382 M 137 (80)**—dwelling: "knock & announce" unless exigent circumstances;

C v Scalise **387 M 413 (82)**—(same) re: search warrant *(See Chapter 20)*;

C v Manni **398 M 741 (86)**—cops knew no-knock facts when got search warrant, & no new exigent facts to justify open-door entry before announcing presence;

G.L. c. 268, §§ 22–23—cop liable for delay/refusal to serve arrest warrant;

C v Hecox **35 MAC 277 (93)**—forceful arrest of D on mistaken belief that he was the subject of an outstanding arrest warrant resulted in suppression of cocaine; held that 4th Amendment 'good faith' exception to exclusionary rule did not apply;

C v Gomes **408 M 43 (90)**—factors for determining whether to suppress evidence after no knock violation; battering of door with sledgehammer required suppression;

C v Roviaro **32 MAC 956 (92)**—54-day delay in issuing OUI-to-cause serious injury citation required dismissal;

C v Cameron **34 MAC 44 (93)**—cop's delay in issuing operating to endanger citation 2 days after completing investigation did not fall within statutory exception to immediate citation rule allowing additional time "reasonably necessary to determine the nature of the violation or the identity of the violator," where cop was off duty for those 2 days; dismissal justified *(See Chapter 21-DD(3), post, re timely citation requirement in motor vehicle cases)*;

3-C. ARREST WITHOUT WARRANT

See also Chapter 20G, Probable Cause, Chapter 20H, Arrest, etc. suppression issues;

G.L. c. 41, §§ 94–99—appointment & duties of police;

Joyce v Parkhurst **150 M 243 (1889)**—"special" police officers (local by-laws);

G.L. c. 218, § 34—need no arrest warrant to arrest, but cop "shall endorse on complaint a statement of his doings";

C v Gorman **288 M 294 (34)**—complaint valid without "return";

Gerstein v Pugh **420 US 103 (75)**—4th Amendment requires neutral finding of "probable cause" to hold D; objective standard;

County of Riverside v McLaughlin **500 US 44 (91)**—judicial determination of probable cause under **Gerstein** must be held within 48 hours of arrest; no exception for weekends or holidays;

Jenkins v Chief Justice of District Court Dept. **416 M 221 (93)**—under Article 14, Declaration of Rights, probable cause determination by neutral magistrate must occur "no later than reasonably necessary" after arrest if D is being held, with outer limit of 24 hours "in the usual circumstances"; probable cause determination may occur at ex parte hearing at which D has no right to counsel; probable cause proffer may be oral or written, but must be under oath; probable cause determination need not be reviewed at arraignment;

DA for Norfolk District v Quincy Division of District Court Dept. **444 M 176 (2005)**—a warrantless arrest constitutes a finding of probable cause initially by arresting officer, & issuance of complaint thereafter by either clerk-magistrate or judge "is essentially a ministerial act", which is mandatory;

C v Viverito **422 M 228 (96)**—**Jenkins** violation does not warrant dismissal when there is no "prejudice"; "civil sanctions can protect the right without the adverse consequences of a dismissal with prejudice";

K. Smith, *Criminal Practice & Procedure*, **§ 96 (2d ed. 1983 & Supp.)**—warrantless arrest for felony standard = (objective) probable cause;

C v Snow **363 M 778 (73)**—probable cause = info reasonably permitting conclusion D probably committed felony; hearsay OK;

C v Holmes **344 M 524 (62)**—(same);

C v Jacobsen **419 M 269 (95)**—warrantless arrest of D for threat to commit crime, "to wit: domestic violence, in violation of G.L. c. 275, § 2" = illegal; no "threats" complaint under G.L. c. 275, §§ 2–3 may issue without examination of complainant under oath and if there is then "just fear," arrest warrant shall issue; dismissal of complaint (here) = too drastic a remedy; instead, suppress any evidence gained as fruit of seizure;

C v Charros **443 M 752 (2005)**—under Fourth Amendment, police had no authority, under warrant to search home, to seize subject & his wife one mile from their home, or to return & detain them in the home while search took place; reserving question whether Article 14 affords greater protection than Fourth Amendment re: off-premises seizures of occupants incident to execution of search warrant; informant's info in warrant application, however, gave probable cause for warrantless arrest of subject (for committing felony of selling cocaine to informant);

C v Thibeau **384 M 762 (81)**—officer must have reasonable suspicion to stop person for threshold inquiry;

C v Silva **366 M 402 (74)**—need specific & articulable facts, not hunch;

C v Swanson **56 MAC 459 (2002)**—when police passed D's room (on their way to arrest person in different room in rooming house), they observed razor blade and plate on bed and that room was smoky; order to D not to leave room was a seizure without even reasonable suspicion of crime (subsequent police observation of D throwing something into closet was product of illegal seizure and couldn't justify entry and search);

C v Gullick **386 M 278 (82)**—radio & collective knowledge = OK . . .

C v Hawkins **361 M 384 (72)**— . . . if cooperative effort;

C v Forde **367 M 798 (75)**—need warrant for dwelling unless exigent circumstances exist;

Payton v New York **445 US 573 (80)**—(same); *(See Chapter 20-L, re exigencies, homes)*;

Welsh v Wisconsin **466 US 740 (84)**—minor motor vehicle charge, and warrantless entry of home;

C v Pietrass **392 M 892 (84)**—violent crime, but no exigent circumstances;

C v Huffman **385 M 122 (82)**—DA's burden of proof to show exigent circumstances existed justifying warrantless entry;

C v Bradshaw **385 M 244 (82)**—induced D out;

C v Ramos **430 M 545 (2000)**—police telling D they'd wait outside until she came out of apartment and threatening they'd have fire department break down door if she didn't come out was not a mere "ruse" making her appearance voluntary; there was a "seizure," and photo of D & ID by witness from it ordered suppressed as fruits of illegal seizure;

C v Scalise **387 M 413 (82)** & *C v Cundriff* **382 M 137 (80)**—"knock & announce";

C v Conway **2 MAC 547 (74)**—warrantless arrest for misdemeanor: need either (1) statutory exception or (2) within police officer's presence or view, still continuing at arrest, & "breach of peace" (here, use without authority was hearsay to cop, so invalid arrest);

McDermott v W.T. Grant Co. **313 M 736 (43)**—misdemeanor must be in cop's presence;

G.L. c. 209A, § 6—if law officer has reason to believe that family or household member has been abused or is in danger of being abused, officer shall use all reasonable means to prevent further abuse, and shall . . . arrest any person a law officer "witnesses or has probable cause to believe has violated a temporary or permanent vacate, restraining, or no-contact order", & even if there are no such orders in effect, arrest = "the preferred response" whenever officer witnesses or has probable cause to believe that person has committed a felony, or has committed a misdemeanor involving "abuse" as defined in G.L. c. 209A, § 1, or has committed A&B (G.L. c. 265, § 13A);

Richardson v City of Boston **53 MAC 201 (2001)**—warrantless arrest of plaintiff proper because plaintiff's girlfriend came to station & claimed had just been assaulted/battered by him, her appearance corroborated this, she stated fear of life/safety, told of assault two days earlier (corroborated by police report as to that incident, which identified a witness to some of the violence); police sergeant had also assisted woman in getting restraining order against plaintiff about four months earlier (though no order then in effect); G.L. c. 209A, § 6(7) expanded authority of police to make warrantless arrests for misdemeanors in context of domestic abuse;

C v Howe **405 M 332 (89)**—deputy sheriff's power to arrest without warrant limited to situations involving breach of peace;

C v Gorman **288 M 294 (34)**—operating motor vehicle under influence = "breach of peace," because such intoxicated operation likely to make operator a public menace;

C v Baez **42 MAC 565, 570 (97)**—"breach of peace" = "often perceived as elastic concept," but act must at least "threaten to have some disturbing effect on the public"; operating vehicle after license revocation is **not** breach of peace;

C v Cavanaugh **366 M 277, 280–81 (74)**—high speed chase through city streets would constitute breach of peace;

C v Twombly **435 M 440 (2001)**—D drove too fast & passed improperly at time of 'moderate' traffic; G.L. c. 37, § 13 authorized extraterritorial stop to preserve the peace, protect public; police in town into which cop followed D authorized cop to make the stop, & statute allows such request/authorization for, inter alia, aid in preserving the peace (keeping safe from injury, harm, or destruction) here applicable; OVERRULING/VACATING *C v Twombly* **50 MAC 667 (2001)** pursuit and stop outside police jurisdiction for speeding and illegal passing required suppression (civil offenses); the cop radioed 2d town and was told to make the stop, mere mention of existing "mutual aid agreement" pursuant to G.L. c. 40, § 8G insufficient to justify (i.e., no evidence as to relevant terms of agreement, particularly what is required from personnel of one town in order to authorize action by the other); refusal also to justify stop under G.L. c. 37, § 13 (authorizing officer to request aid in criminal case, in preservation of the peace, or in apprehending/securing person for breach of peace): speeding and improper passing in manner here described not a breach of peace;

C v Nicholson **56 MAC 921 (2002)**—police officer who had been sworn in as special police officer in adjoining town had authority to stop D in that adjoining town; cop here had been so sworn, pursuant to G.L. c. 41, § 99 (town's authority to specially designate police officers from other cities/towns & give them same immunities and privileges as they have in their own cities/towns);

C v Mullins **31 MAC 954, 955 (91)**—breach of peace found when D screamed obscenities & blared music from window, because "good citizens" were disturbed;

C v Kiser **48 MAC 647 (2000)**—complaint of loud party prompted cops to knock on apartment door, but after D opened door and responded "yeah, okay" to request to turn down music, cops couldn't push on through (because they knew him to be a gang member, because an un-ID'd person ran across the room behind him, and because D pushed them back when they tried to lean into room for better view); D entitled to use reasonable force against intrusion if cop is attempting illegal entry (but *C v Montes* **49 MAC 789 (2000)**, citing *C v Moreira* **388 M 596, 601 (83)** common law right "to resist unlawful arrest" was abolished); *Welsh v Wisconsin* **466 US 740 (84)** (re: minor motor vehicle charge), cited as constitutional limitation upon reach of G.L. c. 41, § 98 (home entry to quell "riot" or breach of peace); cases upholding this statute as basis for warrantless home entry have involved "violent fighting, with . . . fear that someone inside was in physical danger";

C v Gomes **59 MAC 332 (2003)**—absent use of excessive/unnecessary force upon individual's person, he may not forcibly resist even an unlawful entry into his residence by one he knows or has good reason to believe is a police officer engaged in the performance of his duties;

C v Urkiel **63 MAC 445 (2005)**—while warrantless entry of D's home was unconstitutional (no exigent circumstances) & arrest was thus "bad," and *Gomes* 59 MAC 332 (2003) establishes that such unlawful entry isn't a defense to charge of resisting arrest, D had legitimate **self-defense** claim on facts here, & judge erred in assuming it inapplicable;

C v Mekalian **346 M 496 (63)**—bookmaking not "breach of peace";

Statutory Exceptions for misdemeanors (numerous), e.g.—

G.L. c. 276, § 28—stealing; known warrant; probable cause of spouse abuse or violation of restraining or no-contact order; but see *C v Urkiel* **63 MAC 445, 453 n.12 (2005)**—under G.L. c. 276, §§ 28 & 209A, § 6(7), power to arrest without warrant for misdemeanor of "abuse prevention" applies only when officer has reason to believe that family or household member has been abused or is in danger of being abused," not applicable on allegations here;

G.L. c. 272, § 59—local by-laws for obscene accosting & public drinking;

G.L. c. 270, § 15—spit on sidewalk (if name's unknown to cop);

G.L. c. 231, § 94B—probable cause shoplifting = defense to civil suit for false arrest;

G.L. c. 90, § 21—vehicle offenses (probable cause, operating under influence; use without authority, operating after suspension); see *C v Baez* **42 MAC at 569 n.6 (97)** (list of statutes);

Conway **2 MAC 547, 552 n.4 (74)**, & *Gorman* **288 M 294, 298 (34)**—lists of what misdemeanors are not breaches of the peace;

3-C.1. Extraterritorial Arrest

G.L. c. 41, § 98A—"fresh & continued pursuit" = OK for extraterritorial police;

C v Zorrilla **38 MAC 77 (95)**—though statute gave Brookline cop power to exercise, within 500 yards into Boston, his authority to arrest, cop had no "authority to arrest," even in Brookline, for a broken taillight (nonarrestable civil offense); cocaine here suppressed;

C v Magazu **48 MAC 466 (2000)**—cop may be "pursuing" even if he hasn't activated lights and siren in attempt to overtake/stop D; cop here was following D based on observing arrestable offense of operating under influence;

U.S. v Santana **427 US 38 (76)**—was hot pursuit (into house) though "not extended hue & cry in streets"; *(See Chapter 20-L, suppression/exigent circumstances)*;

C v Harris **11 MAC 165 (81)**—in state, if not hot pursuit, extraterritorial cop = citizen;

C v Mottola **10 MAC 775 (80)**—MBTA cop goes onto school grounds;

C v Grise **398 M 247 (86)**—warrant power = statewide; if no warrant, extraterritorial arrest only if hot pursuit from crime in his presence, or same as civilian (i.e., felony): Ludlow cops can't arrest after seeing D operating under influence in Springfield;

C v Owens **414 M 595 (93)**—Quincy police officer, by radio request for info, was told that owner of car had outstanding warrant for serious felony, so cop followed car into Boston, and arrested D: arrest/stop OK because cop "had reason to believe" that suspect had committed an arrestable offense when he began his pursuit; SJC didn't care that D was **not** the subject of warrant, but was instead subject's father (charged with guns & ammunition found in car);

C v Gullick **386 M 278 (82)**—out-of-state, depends on that state's law;

C v Callahan **428 M 335 (98)**—pursuant to G.L. c. 41, § 99, Mass. town appointed bordering N.H. town police officer to be "special police officer" in Mass. town; that cop began following speeding car in N.H. and car stopped in the Mass. town; under § 99, power is broad (and not, like G.L. c. 276, § 10A, limiting fresh pursuit into MA for chase of "felons"); stop OK (town here had followed SJC's suggestion in *C v Grise* **398 M 247, 252–53 n.6 (86)** re: appointing special police officers);

C v Nicholson **56 MAC 921 (2002)**—police officer who had been sworn in as special police officer in adjoining town had authority to stop D in that adjoining town; cop here had been so sworn, pursuant to G.L. c. 41, § 99 (town's authority to specially designate police officers from other cities/towns & give them same immunities and privileges as they have in their own cities/towns);

C v Savage **430 M 341 (99)**—Vermont state trooper couldn't cross into MA after receiving info from civilian that car was being driven "all over the road" & at high speed southbound on I-91, & fruits of stop suppressed in operating under influence prosecution; this wasn't fresh pursuit arrest authorized by G.L. c. 276, § 10A because neither trooper nor any other **officer** had observed illegal conduct IN VERMONT (and also OUI is misdemeanor rather than felony); *C v Morrissey* **422 M 1 (96)** distinguished; Vermont troopers could be sworn in as "special officers" in Mass. border towns (*See Grise* **398 M 247, 252–53 n.6 (86)**);

C v Mullen **40 MAC 404 (96)**—campus police officer's status as a "special State police officer" did not give him authority to stop motorist for civil infraction (G.L. c. 90C, §§ 1–3); fruits of stop (observations supporting operating under influence) suppressed;

C v Sawyer **389 M 686 (83)**—Maine arrest OK under Uniform Rendition Act;

C v LeBlanc **407 M 70 (90)**—unauthorized pursuit & stop for nonarrestable offense outside police jurisdiction required suppression of evidence;

C v Dise **31 MAC 701 (91)**—extraterritorial arrest made by cop valid because he had probable cause to believe D had committed felony and was in fresh and continuous pursuit of D (*see* G.L. c. 41, § 98A);

C v Coburn **62 MAC 314 (2004)**—pursuit of D in Concord for speeding made him stop (& fail sobriety test) just short of sign indicating town line of Lincoln; that defense counsel later found a stone marker with an "L" on one side and a "C" on opposite side, and that this was about 30 feet before the prominent sign, didn't result in suppression: lack of knowledge neither unreasonable nor based on police misconduct (citing *C v Wilkerson* **436 M 137, 141 (2002)**);

C v O'Hara **30 MAC 608 (91)**—car's crossing lines & wavering speed warranted belief that driver committing operating under influence or other "arrestable offense" justified "fresh pursuit" to make extraterritorial arrest under G.L. c. 41, § 98A;

C v Zirpolo **37 MAC 307 (94)**—officer observing operating under influence, reckless driving, & "hit and run" (albeit only a parked car was "hit") unsuccessfully ordered "stop" & radioed nearby patrol officer, who pursued car & stopped it just over town line: stop OK as first cop observed arrestable offense and 2d cop was acting "with" 1st cop, under "collective knowledge doctrine";

C v Whelan **408 M 29 (90)**—MDC police have jurisdiction over "metropolitan parks district";

C v Maher **408 M 34 (90)**—MDC police have jurisdiction over Mass. Water Resources Authority property;

See also Chapter 20;

3-C.2. Forceful Arrest

Julian v Randazzo **380 M 391 n.1 (80)**—"reasonable" force; "deadly" force is reasonable if (1) arrest is for felony by deadly force or threat, or there is risk of deadly force or threat of same without arrest; & (2) no risk to bystanders;

C v Klein **372 M 823 (77)**—(same), adopting Model Penal Code rule, etc.; not for property crime;

Tennessee v Garner **471 US 1 (85)**—U.S. Supreme Court adopts rule like MA;

Atwater v City of Lago Vista **532 US 318 (2001)**—officer may arrest even for most minor of offenses without violating 4th Amendment as long as there is probable cause to believe that person committed such criminal offense in officer's presence; only if arrest is made "in an extraordinary manner, unusually harmful to (individual's) privacy or even physical interests" is arrest unreasonable (& civilly actionable);

3-C.3. Protective Custody

G.L. c. 111B, § 8—non-criminal "protective custody" of "incapacitated person"; BUT can use force/frisk; treatment facility if "available," or hold (12 hour maximum);

C v Marler **11 MAC 1014 (81)**—reasonable" force to effectuate protective custody;

C v Ierardi **17 MAC 297 (83)**—each incident to protective custody;

C v Tomeo **400 M 23 (87)**—OK protective custody, then pat-down;

C v St. Hilaire **43 MAC 743 (97)**—fact that D was handcuffed did not negate "protective custody"; evidence supported implicit finding that D was "incapacitated" (G.L. c. 111B, § 3), overriding his right to refuse all treatment; though protective custody = "seizure in the constitutional sense, it was not an arrest", medical doctor, not police, ordered blood test "only for medical reasons," & cops holding D down didn't alter this conclusion;

C v O'Connor **406 M 112 (89)**—invalid protective custody search harmless because discovery inevitable during booking inventory; standards for inevitable discovery established;

C v McCaffery **49 MAC 713 (2000)**—upon reasonable belief that D was incapacitated within the meaning of G.L. c. 111B, § 3 (protective custody), cop could ask D to perform field sobriety test; that D was walking in middle of road at 3 a.m., apparently intoxicated, provided reasonable belief that he was "likely to suffer . . . physical harm" as covered by statute; during test, wallet from burglary was seen, & that cops' motive may have been desire to unearth evidence of burglary rather than protect D = irrelevant; but cf. *C v Lubiejewski* **49 MAC 212 (2000)** un-ID'd motorist telephoned state police to report pickup truck with specific plate # was traveling on wrong side of Rt. 195 in vicinity of Rt. 140, but called back again to say truck crossed grassy median & proceeded on right side of road before turning south on Rt. 240 in Fairhaven; trooper stopped the truck, not for any observed violation, but for tipster's report; odor of alcohol & failure of sobriety tests = suppressed; no corroboration of anything but obvious details = insufficient to compensate for unknown reliability of informant;

3-C.4. Citizen's (i.e., by Civilian) Arrest

C v Lussier **333 M 83 (55)**—civilian may arrest if D = "in fact committed" felony standard, not just probable cause (see also **Harris 11 MAC 165 (81)**);

C v Klein **372 M 823 (77)**—(same) (n.10); citizen must be assisting (cops); no deadly force unless . . . adopting Model Penal Code rule, etc.; not for property crime;

McDermott v W.T. Grant Co. **313 Mass 736 (43)**—must be in civilian's presence;

C v Vaidulas **433 M 247 (2001)**—cop's failure to complete course of study (G.L. c. 41, § 96B), though statute required as consequence of failure the "removal" of

such an appointed police officer, did not invalidate car stop made by cop (or subsequent probable cause to arrest for operating under influence of alcohol);

C v Dise **31 MAC 701 (91)**—extraterritorial arrest made by cop valid because probable cause to believe D had committed felony, and fresh and continuous pursuit of D (*see* G.L. c. 41, § 98A);

3-C.5. Detentions for Evidence Collection

Davis v Mississippi **394 US 721 (69)**—"to argue that the Fourth Amendment does not apply to the investigatory stage is fundamentally to misconceive the purposes of the Fourth Amendment"; dragnet seizures of "Negro youths" for fingerprinting at the police station (to match up prints left on window sill by rapist) unconstitutional, finger and palm prints suppressed;

C v Downey **407 M 472 (90)**—grand jury may compel detention for blood tests on unindicted D so long as there is probable cause to indict or arrest; D must be given opportunity to oppose order; see also *Matter of Lavigne* **418 M 831 (94)** person not yet charged & not subject of grand jury investigation may be compelled to submit blood sample only after hearing, & probable cause to believe D guilty and showing that blood = relevant to investigation; *C v. Williams* **439 M 678 (2003)**—pre-indictment order to produce blood, etc. need be based only on reasonable basis to believe samples would provide test results that would significantly aid prosecution (not necessary for grand jury to show probably cause that D committed the crime);

Rodriques v Furtado **410 M 878 (91)**—body cavity searches require warrant issued by judge based on "a strong showing of particularized need supported by a high degree of probable cause";

See Chapter 20-L for cases on warrantless home arrests (& searches), protective sweeps, exigent circumstances, emergency searches for missing persons, & Chapter 20-K for cases on consent;

3-D. INTERSTATE RENDITION

G.L. c. 276, §§ 11–20R—steps, time limits, Superior Court habeas, waiver, etc.;

District Court Standards for Sentencing and Other Dispositions (1984) 9:07—general discussion;

Michigan v Doran **439 US 282, 289 (78)**—after governor of 'asylum' state orders extradition, judge considering habeas relief/release can only decide (a) whether the extradition documents on their face are in order; (b) whether the petitioner has been charged with a crime in the demanding state; (c) whether the petitioner is the person named in the request for extradition; and (d) whether the petitioner is a fugitive;

In re Consalvi **376 M 699 (78)**—only questions = (1) papers; (2) identity (e.g., D wasn't in demanding state); (3) whether probable cause was found by neutral magistrate (& here, (3) not established);

In re Doucette **42 MAC 310 (97)**—(same); probable cause finding implicit in papers given relevant Florida statute;

In re Hinnant **424 M 900 (97)**—notwithstanding limited issues, **incompetent** D may not be rendited; D had right to counsel re: rendition, and such right is meaningless if D = so incompetent that he doesn't understand what is occurring and is unable to assist counsel

Petition of Upton **387 M 359 (82)**—G.L. c. 276, § 20D permits bail;

Juvenile, petitioner **396 M 116 (85)**—Uniform Crim. Extradition Act covers these petitioners, because they were adults under requesting state's law (Maryland); identify by name & sight corroboration;

Quinones v Commonwealth **423 M 1015 (96)**—demanding state had already found probable cause, & no probable cause had to be established in Mass; interstate compact on juveniles= in effect in MA; NOTE: if D's going, advise D & COPS re: 5th Amendment, invocation of right to silence and right to counsel! (see CPCS P/G 2.2(e))

In re Gay **406 M 471 (90)**—D still a "fugitive" subject to rendition despite receiving state's failure to abide by interstate detainer compact; rendition & detainers distinguished;

C v Beauchamp **413 M 60 (92)**—escaped lifer not to receive jail credit for time in another jurisdiction fighting extradition to MA;

C v Araujo **41 MAC 928 (96)**—(same)

New York v Hill **528 US 110 (2000)**—D-counsel agreeing to trial date beyond time limits set by Interstate Agreement on Detainers barred D from seeking dismissal for violation of time limits;

3-E. POLICE STATION

G.L. c. 263, § 1—inform of charges;

G.L. c. 127, § 3—sheriff & assistants keep records of all prisoners' property;

C v Benoit **382 M 210 (81)**—inventory search (vs. "mere pretext" *(See Chapter 20-H))*;

G.L. c. 276, § 33—examine everyone; report required if D's injured *(See Chapter 6-D, Discovery, re: booking report, police report, videotape, etc.)*;

G.L. c. 263, § 5A—operating under influence case = right to independent medical exam;

C v Andrade **389 M 874 (83)**—dismissal if no notice of G.L. c. 263, § 5A right *(See Chapter 21-DD, operating under influence)*;

G.L. c. 263, § 1A—fingerprints mandatory for felony, & photo = optional; (both = optional for misdemeanor); copies to be sent to state police 'within reasonable time'; but see Bos.Police Rules #318(1)—print & photo all crimes; ink prints for all serious crimes;

C v Dubois **353 M 223 (67)**—prints not arrest "fruit" because can get otherwise; but see *Davis v Mississippi* **394 US 721 (69)** fact that could get otherwise irrelevant to necessity of suppressing particular prints here (dragnet detention, for fingerprinting, of at least 24 black youths);

Hayes v Florida **470 US 811 (85)**—suppress print because arrest without probable cause *(See Chapter 20)*;

M.R.Crim.P. 7(a)—parents of juveniles must be notified of arrest;

G.L. c. 221, § 92A—hearing-impaired D gets interpreter—or suppress evidence (see, e.g., *C v Kelley* **404 M 459 (89)**);

3-E.1. Telephone Call

See Chapter 20, Suppression;

G.L. c. 276, § 33A—inform forthwith & let use phone within 1 hour;

C v Jones **362 M 497 (72)**—identification suppressed because G.L. c. 276, § 33 violated; vs . . .

C v McGaffigan **352 M 332 (67)**—no harm from denial of right;

C v Maylott **43 MAC 516 (97)**—relief only for "intentional" denial of right, and relief is suppression of evidence obtained as result of denial, rather than dismissal of charge; here, D's belligerence, refusal to answer booking questions resulted in magistrate's refusal to set bail: no relief;

C v Alicea **55 MAC 505 (2002)**—suppression of D's incriminatory statement made shortly after intentional violation of D's right to telephone (G.L. c. 276, § 33A) AND later incriminatory statement, because latter was fruit of poisonous tree;

C v Carey **26 MAC 339 (88)**—can video D before let call (within 1 hour), especially to family, not attorney; videotaping not violative of 5th Amendment;

C v Brazelton **404 M 783 (89)**—no right to call attorney before decide about breathalyzer;

K. Smith, *Criminal Practice & Procedure*, §§ 396–97 (2d ed. & Supp.)—telephone right; *(See also Chapter 20-B, post)*

C v Garcia **409 M 675 (91)**—D has no expectation of privacy in stationhouse phone conversation while cops are standing nearby;

C v Johnson **422 M 420 (96)**—D, handcuffed to station wall awaiting arrival of local and state police and arresting officers prior to booking, not informed "forthwith" upon arrival at station of telephone call right (G.L. c. 276, § 33A), but after more than an hour, D volunteered to passing officer that he (D) thought he (D) had "screwed up," and wanted to talk: no suppression, though suppression would be required if violation of statute had been "intentional" or "designed to gain inculpatory info";

C v White **422 M 487 (96)**—record of the telephone number which D called could be introduced against him at trial ("policy" of G.L. c. 276, § 33A not frustrated, & Miranda not required (not fruit of custodial interrogation));

C v Silanskas **433 M 678, 684 n.7 (2001)**—noting that trial court suppressed statements D made to counsel during telephone conversation from police station, overheard by zealous cop;

3-E.2. Counsel Right, Request

See Chapter 20, Suppression;

C v Sherman **389 M 287 (83)**—suppress statement because cops ignored request to confer by D's public defender (from another case);

Escobedo v State of Illinois **378 US 478 (64)**—any lawyer worth his salt will tell client NOT to talk to police; *(See Chapter 4-I & Chapter 7-H re: 5th Amendment)*;

C v Fontaine **402 M 491 (88)**—dismissal (of only one charge) for eavesdropping on attorney-client talks over audio-visual monitors;

Minnick v Mississippi **498 US 146 (90)**—once arrestee asserts (5th Amendment) right to counsel, interrogation forbidden unless: 1. counsel present or 2. D initiates further conversation & clearly waives counsel;

C v Perez **411 M 249 (91)** & *C v Galford* **413 M 364 (92)**—police-initiated interrogation after break in questioning where D is/isn't released in interim;

C v DiMuro **28 MAC 223 (90)**—even ambiguous assertion by D of right to counsel bars further police questioning;

C v Mencoboni **28 MAC 504 (90)**—cops' refusal to allow D to privately confer with attorney at stationhouse about taking breathalyzer was improper, but didn't require dismissal;

Rothgery v Gillespie County, Texas **128 S Ct 2578 (2008)**—right to counsel attaches at first appearance before judicial officer at which D is told of formal accusation against him and restrictions are imposed on liberty; that public prosecutor (as opposed to police officer) be aware of initial proceeding or involved in its conduct is NOT required; D's arrest without warrant as purported "felon" in possession of firearm was followed by appearance before a "magistrate judge" for proceeding which combined a finding of probable cause with setting of bail; D's oral and written requests for counsel were unheeded until indictment and further delay more than six months later (and counsel promptly learned that arrest as "felon" was premised on an erroneous record);

See Chapter 20-C for cases on custodial interrogation, 6th Amendment rights, including special rules for juveniles;

3-E.3. Bail Hearing, Right to

C v Whitcomb **37 MAC 929, 930 (94)**—D not entitled to bail hearing until after booking is completed & here it was suspended, legitimately, because D "refused to answer" any booking questions but didn't avail himself of right to telephone, to attorney, to breathalyzer, to independent medical exam;

C v Mahoney **400 M 524 (87)**—no 5th or 6th Amendment rights before booking, BUT SEE, re: booking questions (below): *Pennsylvania v Muniz* **496 US 582 (90)**, & *C v Guerrero* **32 MAC 263 (92)**;

G.L. c. 262, § 24—maximum bail commissioner's fee now $40 for misdemeanor or felony regardless of number of offenses; if extraterritorial recognizance, then additional $5 per charge up to $50 "total fee" maximum;

K. Smith, *Criminal Practice & Procedure,* **§§ 481–529 (2d ed. 1983 & Supp.)**—overview, including Superior Court Rules for Persons Authorized to Take Bail;

M.R.Crim.P. 7(a)—take unbailed D to court same day if court is in session;

C v Perito **417 M 674 (94)**—D has right to be **present** at bail hearing; here bail was set for hospitalized D (D injured in police chase) in D's absence; error not to take him from hospital to court immediately, or if court not open, at "next session" (D instead committed to Bridgewater for maximum of 30 days); remedy of dismissal appropriate only if D demonstrates actual prejudice and that Commonwealth intended delay to get tactical advantage or acted with reckless disregard for D's right to mount a defense;

C v Mason **453 M 873 (2009)**—egregious police misconduct in retaliating against D for his clash with police chief: bail commissioner on call set bail for five times expected amount after phone call from cop, without any opportunity for D's participation, AND thereafter intentional withholding of information led jail officials to believe that D had "no bail" status, depriving him of release between Saturday afternoon and Monday at court; dismissal held to have been too severe a sanction, there having been no "prejudice" affecting right to fair trial;

C v Maylott **43 MAC 516 (97)**—dismissal denied OUI 2d offense defendant who was refused bail opportunity at jail due to "loud"/argumentative refusal to answer booking questions;

C v Falco **43 MAC 253 (97)**—if a D is confined longer than this one (6½ hours), refusal of bail clerk to hold hearing as matter of "policy" (because jailer says D = intoxicated & D refuses breathalyzer) might be denial of statutory right to prompt hearing; it is "much . . . preferred" that decision to delay bail hearing be made case-by-case and "after 1st hand observation";

Rules Governing Persons Authorized to Take Bail, Rule 17—no person authorized shall delegate the setting or taking of bail or release on personal recognizance to a cop, jail official, bondsman, or anyone else; Rule 15 shan't respond to calls from professional bondsman, & instead only to D or his family or attorney, or jailer;

C v Hampe **419 M 514 (95)**—police decision that D needed to "sleep off" intoxication, despite his expressed interest in bail and obtaining independent test for intoxication, violated D's right to independent test (G.L. c. 263, § 5A; see G.L. c. 276, § 58); remedy of dismissal maybe inappropriate if there's overwhelming evidence of guilt apart from breathalyzer and police observations after denial of rights; suppression of breathalyzer and police testimony re: events/observations after denial of bail access, plus jury instruction (that police did wrong), may cure prejudice;

3-E.4. Bail/Right to Independent Medical Test (Breathalyzer)

C v Ames **410 M 603 (91)**—taking D to hospital where police offered blood alcohol test by "neutral" health care provider satisfied statutory requirements, despite subsequent failure to notify D of rights under G.L. c. 263, § 5A;

C v Rosewarne **410 M 53 (91)**—cops may not deprive D of reasonable opportunity to obtain independent blood alcohol test but need not "assist" him by driving him to hospital;

C v Lively **30 MAC 970 (91)**—directing D's attention to posted rights plus access to telephone was sufficient;

See Chapter 21-DD, Motor Vehicle Offenses;

3-E.5. Booking Questions

Pennsylvania v Muniz **496 US 582 (90)**—police booking questions calling upon OUI-D to calculate date of 6th birthday were improperly designed to elicit information for "investigatory purposes," not "biographical data necessary to complete booking or pretrial services";

C v Guerrero **32 MAC 263 (92)**—questions about employment status should be "scrubbed" from booking procedure in absence of **Miranda** warnings;

C v Acosta **416 M 279, 284 (93)**—(as amended) booking question as to address gave prosecution evidence that D lived in apartment where cocaine was found; SJC disingenuously claimed no prejudice because Commonwealth didn't "have to" prove D lived there (?!), Article 12 issue left open;

C v Woods **419 M 366 (95)**—but if "booking" question (e.g., about employment status) may produce incriminating statement, police must give **Miranda** warnings beforehand;

C v Dayes **49 MAC 419, 421 (2000)**—though booking response as to unemployment was introduced against D at trial, court claimed that **Miranda** warnings had been given at scene of arrest and there was no significant lapse of time between then and booking procedure at station, so no relief; court claimed that in Guerrero and Woods, defendants had not received **Miranda** warnings either at booking or at arrest; (disingenuous to assert carryover value of warnings given at arrest, because D wouldn't understand he had any right to refuse to answer such "administrative" questions as booking; cf. *C v Maylott* **43 MAC 516 (97)**, *C v Whitcomb* **37 MAC 929 (94)**, *C v Mahoney* **400 M 524 (87)** (appellate courts give no relief to Ds whose failure to cooperate with booking resulted in police withholding opportunity for release on bail));

See Chapter 20, Suppression;

C v Quinn **61 MAC 332, 336 n.3 (2004)**—though unremarked by parties, Appeals Court alarmed to see that booking videotape, admitted at trial, depicted D's refusal to take breathalyzer exam;

3-F. HEARING RE: ISSUANCE OF COMPLAINT

See also Chapter 5, Contents of Complaints;

G.L. c. 263, § 4—either indictment or complaint to charge a crime;

G.L. c. 276, § 22—complaint to a judge; swear & hear witnesses; writes complaint & complaining witness signs if it "appears a crime was committed"; summons or warrant issues;

G.L. c. 218, § 33—clerk, assistant, receive complaint, swear complaining witness, issue process;

C v Hanley **12 MAC 501, 503 n.3 (81)**—G.L. c. 276, § 22 applies to clerks, too;

Shadwick v Tampa **407 US 345 (72)**—clerk = OK because "neutral & detached" & can evaluate probable cause;

City of Tampa Attorney General v Lyons **220 M 536 (15)**—(mandamus) can compel court to "receive complaints";

DA for Norfolk District v Quincy Division of District Court Dept. **444 M 176 (2005)**—a warrantless arrest constitutes a finding of probable cause initially by arresting officer, & issuance of complaint thereafter by either clerk-magistrate or judge "is essentially a ministerial act", which is mandatory;

M.R.Crim.P. 4(b)—anyone can sign application; Reporter's Notes: single cop signing all = "sound administrative practice";

C v Haddad **364 M 795 (74)**—anyone can complain; but see *Taylor v Newton Division of District Court Department* **416 M 1006 (93)** clerk's refusal to provide forms for application for criminal complaint did not result in abridgement of plaintiff's substantive rights because no private citizen has a "judicially cognizable interest in the prosecution of another";

Carroll, petitioner **453 M 1006 (2009)**—sexual assault complainant applied for criminal complaint, which was issued by magistrate after hearing where neither alleged miscreant or his attorney appeared; alleged miscreant was summonsed for arraignment, but before that date, district attorney nol prossed case; private party had no right to keep criminal case alive, no requirement that nol pros occur only after arraignment;

G.L. c. 90C, § 4—persons other than cops may apply for complaint for a criminal auto violation;

C v Steadward **43 MAC 271 (97)**—citizen-initiated motor vehicle complaints, like cop-initiated, are subject to dismissal for G.L. c. 90C § 2 failure to give citation to alleged violator at time & place of the violation;

District Court Complaint Standards 2:03, 3:23—complaining witness need not be eyewitness, but must sign;

C v Cote **15 MAC 229 (83)**—anyone can subscribe; OK "oath";

C v Daly **12 MAC 338 (81)**—anyone can subscribe, even for threats;

C v Hanley **12 MAC 501 (81)**—OK (here) though complaining witness signed blank form; even assistant district attorney can sign;

C v Barhight **9 Gray 113 (1857)**—sign blank complaint = bad; "looseness & carelessness in instituting criminal process not to be encouraged";

K. Smith, *Criminal Practice & Procedure,* **§§ 629–32 (2d ed. 1983 & Supp.)**—show-cause hearing

District Court Standards of Judicial Practice Complaint Procedure (1975) 2:01, 2:02, 3:04–3:20; 3:10—suggests show cause hearing for all civilian complaints; Comment: suggests show cause hearing for most non-custody police (felony) complaints, but less necessary because "presumption of regularity in police work" (though probable cause still needed);

G.L. c. 218, § 35A—right to show cause hearing for non-custody misdemeanor, **unless** threat of imminent injury, crime or flight;

C v Tripolone **44 MAC 23 (97)**—administrative justice's policy of deeming any person being alleged to have violated G.L. c. 209A order to be such a threat (G.L. c. 218, § 35A - threat of imminent injury or crime) and thereby withholding right to show cause hearing is illegitimate; dismissal of complaint upheld;

C v Irick **58 MAC 129 (2003)**—show cause hearing is not constitutionally mandated, and statute provides no remedy for unjustified denial of hearing, though D should have been given notice of rights under G.L. c. 218, § 35A; *Tripolone* 44 MAC 23 (97) distinguished: there, magistrate deliberately disregarded/overrode statute;

C v Clerk of Boston Division of the Juvenile Court Dept. **432 M 693 (2000)**—magistrate must either grant or deny request for issuance of process; to instead merely leave "open" the matter "until year's end" while imposing conditions upon the juvenile was judicial usurpation of prosecutorial discretion;

Gordon v Fay **382 M 64 (80)**—G.L. c. 218, § 35A process; *(See also Chapter 3-G, re cross-complaints)*;

C v Cote **15 MAC 229 (83)**—no right to show cause hearing for felony, even if with misdemeanor;

C v Clerk-Magistrate of the West Roxbury Division of the District Court Department **439 M 352 (2003)**—magistrate has no authority to conduct show-cause hearing before acting on application for FELONY complaint; it's not a matter of discretion under Standard 3:10 of District Court Standards of Judicial Practice, because "Standard" doesn't override unambiguous statute (c. 218, § 35 limited clerk's authority to conduct slow-cause hearings to misdemeanors, BUT statute was rewritten in 2004, and the prior restriction no longer exists);

G.L. c. 218, § 35A—"opportunity to be heard" at show cause hearing; for misdemeanor, discretionary for felony, unless there's imminent threat of (a) bodily injury (b) commission of a crime, or (c) flight from Commonwealth; counsel (but silent re: indigent Ds);

C v Riley **333 M 414 (56)**—no show cause hearing right to cross-examination; but . . . ;

K. Smith, *Criminal Practice & Procedure,* **§ 632 (2d ed. 1983 & Supp.)**—brief/basic questions often allowed (see, e.g., *Hanley* 12 MAC 501, 502 (81));

G.L. c. 221, § 91B—right to stenographer (or tape?) at own expense at show cause hearing;

District Court Standards of Judicial Practice, Complaint Procedure (1975) 3:00, 3:08—broad discre-

tion for "screening, mediation, dispute settlement" (see also *Gordon v Fay* 382 M 64 (80));

G.L. c. 218, § 37—court can summons witnesses to show cause hearing;

C v Vitale **44 MAC 908 (97)**—for purpose of statute of limitations, date of complaint itself is relevant fact; prior dates of application for complaint, or of show cause hearing, not relevant;

Kenyon v City of Chicopee **320 M 528 (46)**—very rare, but can enjoin complaint if it is patently void, harasses, or rights irremediably threatened;

K. Smith, *Criminal Practice & Procedure,* **§ 625 (2d ed. 1983 & Supp.):** *C v Balliro* 385 M 618 (82): **& District Court Standards of Judicial Practice, Complaint Procedure (1975) 1.01**—bare-bones "Application for Complaint" (vs. Rule 4(6) "application for issuance of process")

CPCS P/G 2.5—consider motion to dismiss charge/element without probable cause;

G.L. c. 276, § 22: G.L. c. 218, § 35A—standard = probable cause;

District Court Standards of Judicial Practice, Complaint Procedure (1975) 3:17—standard = probable cause; suggests "avoid informal trial" & D must "completely undercut complaining witness's story . . . (to deny complaint)"; (see also 3:10 above); 2:00 & 2:04 & Comment - suggests "no denials of applications against persons under arrest";

K. Smith, *Criminal Practice & Procedure,* **§§ 625–26 (2d ed. 1983 & Supp.);**

C v Balliro **385 M 618 fn.2 (82)**—clerk/judge as 'rubber stamp'?; but see *C v Crowell* **403 M 381 (88)**—operating motor vehicle under influence per se license suspension = OK in part because complaint means probable cause has been found; & . . . ;

Gerstein v Pugh **420 US 103 (75)**—can't detain long without judicial probable cause finding;

C v Baldassini **357 M 670, 675 (70)**—complaint (& arrest warrant) = OK under G.L. c. 276, § 22 & Declaration of Rights Article 14 because had probable cause;

C v Cote **15 MAC 229, 237–38 (83)**—complaint = OK because had probable cause;

Whiteley v Warden, Wyoming State Penitentiary **401 US 560 (71)**—bad affidavit (for arrest warrant) because conclusory;

C v Hanley **12 MAC 501, 504 (81)**—would dismiss if complaint deviates from application or testimony;

District Court Standards of Judicial Practice, Complaint Procedure (1975) 2:00, Commentary—make *Gerstein v Pugh* (420 US 103 (75)) judicial probable cause determinations at arraignment (& "will be addressed in the Arraignment Standards") . . . ; but see **District Court Standards of Judicial Practice, Arraignment (1977) 6:00 & 6:02** - dismissal (on motion) maybe appropriate at Arraignment; (but no mention of probable cause issue); Hearing before judge if complaint denied? Yes, see. . . ;

Bradford v Knights **427 M 748 (98)**—fight between Bradford and Knights resulted in Knights's arrest for ABDW (later acquitted by jury); Knights applied to assistant clerk magistrate in Boston Municipal Court for issuance of criminal complaint against Bradford, but after hearing, clerk declined to issue complaint, saying no probable cause; Knights requested hearing before judge, but Bradford tried to stop it by G.L. c. 211, § 3 petition (saying no lawful basis for 2d determination after application for complaint was already denied); HELD: "judges of the BMC have inherent authority to rehear **denials** of applications for criminal complaints by clerks of that court"; see also Standard 3.21 of the District Court Standards of Judicial Practice, Complaint Procedure (1975);

C v DiBennadetto **436 M 310 (2002)**—but if application for complaint has been allowed, & complaint has issued after show cause hearing, judge may not conduct new evidentiary hearing to review finding of probable cause to issue process; instead, remedy = motion to dismiss, for failure to present sufficient evidence to clerk-magistrate (or judge), for "violation of the integrity of the proceeding" (e.g., 'unreasonable restrictions' on D's opportunity to present evidence would be denial of right to hearing created by G.L. c. 218, § 35A), "or for any other challenge to the validity of the complaint"; though cross-examination of witnesses proffered in support of the complaint goes to credibility of the complainant, there is no "right to cross-examine witnesses at hearing on issuance of process on complaint";

Carroll, petitioner **453 M 1006 (2009)**—sexual assault complainant applied for criminal complaint, which was issued by magistrate after hearing where neither alleged miscreant or his attorney appeared; alleged miscreant was summonsed for arraignment, but before that date, district attorney nol prossed case; private party had no right to keep criminal case alive, no requirement that nol pros occur only after arraignment;

G.L. c. 218, § 35—keep application one year (so no harassment), then destroy;

C v Balliro **385 M 618 (82)**—issuance denied on speedy trial grounds (DA played games); *(See Chapter 7-O, Speedy Trial & Chapter 14-B, Dismissal);*

M.R.Crim.P. 6(a): G.L. c. 276, §§ 24, 26—summons D, unless "reason to believe" (e.g., DA says) D won't appear; if no response, re-summons or arrest warrant, & punishable as contempt of court with fine up to $20;

G.L. c. 276, § 27—if D appears on summons, no bail "without special order";

M.R.Crim.P. 7(a)(2)—summonsed D can retain counsel & not attend if counsel enters appearance before return day and requests date for pretrial hearing or other proceeding;

C v Avola **28 MAC 988 (90)**—non-eyewitness cops may be designated under G.L. c. 90C, § 3(B) to sign operating under influence complaint as "complainants"; pretrial motion to dismiss generally required to preserve challenge to facial invalidity of complaint;

3-G. CROSS-COMPLAINTS

CPCS P/G 2.5(b)—where appropriate, consider (dis)advantages of cross-complaints;

C v Ahearn **370 M 283 (76)**—D's cross complaint application admissible later (to show cop's bias);

C v Herman **253 M 516 (25)**—attorney can assist DA, but not prosecute unless special prosecutor;

Whitely v Commonwealth **369 M 961 (75)**—no citizen's right to complaint; (open question re: public defender representing D as cross-complainant);

C v Belmonte **4 MAC 506 (76)**—(same); if issued, D.A. can delay prosecuting it;

District Court Standards of Judicial Practice, Complaint Procedure (1975) 2:01, Commentary—cops should not get special privileges; 3:07—Clerks shouldn't refer complaining witnesses to cops unless investigation's needed;

See Chapter 3-F, above, re: show cause hearing (for felony? cross-examination?);

G.L. c. 276, § 22—"upon a complaint to a justice . . . (s)he shall examine on oath the complainant & witnesses . . .";

Complaint Standard 3:21—complaining witness with "serious dissatisfaction" gets prompt re-hearing with judge; cf. Trial Ct.Mag.R.2(c): appeal to a judge magistrate's rulings on motions *(See Chapter 14B, Sentencing & Dispositions: dismissal re: coerced civil release by D)*

Bradford v Knights **427 M 748 (98)**—right to be heard by/appeal to judge if clerk denies issuance of complaint;

Chapter 4
ARRAIGNMENT AND BAIL ADVOCACY

4-A. D IS HAULED INTO THE HALLS OF, AND BEFORE A, JUSTICE

M.R.Crim.P. 7—D brought to court if in session; if not, next session;

District Court Standards of Judicial Practice, Complaint Procedure (1975) 2:01—efficient/orderly processing of complaint; could be delaying "release of an innocent"; (see **Gerstein v Pugh 420 US 103 (75) 4th Amendment requires neutral finding of "probable cause" to hold D; objective standard;** *(See Chapter 4-D below, Statement of Facts & Chapter 3-F, Hearings re: Issuance of Complaints)*;

C v Rosario **422 M 48 (96)**—otherwise admissible statement not to be excluded on basis of arraignment delay if statement is made within six hours of arrest; though right to prompt arraignment (no longer than six-hour delay) may be waived, waiver "form" should include notice to arrestee of right to probable cause determination by neutral magistrate and notice of "the time at which the defendant could next be taken to court";

McNabb v US **318 US 332 (43)** and *Mallory v US* **354 US 449 (57)**—arrested person's confession is inadmissible if given after unreasonable delay in bringing him before a judge;

Corley v US **129 S Ct 1558 (2009)**—holding that 18 USC § 3501 (enacted in response to *Miranda v Arizona*

384 US 436 and to the application of *McNabb/Mallory* in some courts) did not eliminate *McNabb/Mallory* rule; suppression judge must find whether D confessed within six hours of arrest (unless longer delay was reasonable considering means of transportation and distance to nearest available magistrate) and if it did and was voluntary, it's admissible; if confession occurred beyond six hours and before presentment, judge must decide whether delay was unreasonable or unnecessary under *McNabb/Mallory* cases, and if so, must suppress;

C v Obershaw **435 M 794 (2002)**—six-hour rule not violated because court finds that actual "arrest" of D occurred more than seven hours after police first "encountered" D, who offered to 'voluntarily stay & cooperate'; response ("can I talk to a lawyer first?") made to question whether he would take police to victim's body wasn't invocation of right to counsel: D was told to use the telephone, but declined & said he wanted to go outside and spend time with his dogs; after doing so, he initiated conversation with cop, who told him that if he wanted a lawyer, he could use the telephone & further conversation wasn't permissible if he wanted counsel (D declined again); *(See also Chapter 20, Suppression Issues)*;

CPCS Performance Guidelines 2.1(c)&(d)—no significant waivers at arraignment, including matters pertaining to competency/criminal responsibility examinations; 6.3 jury vs. jury-waived trial = D's decision after counsel's complete advice *(See Chapter 4-B, Question of Counsel, CPCS assignment, & Chapter 4-H Competency, Criminal Responsibility, Mental Health Issues)*;

Reporter's Notes, M.R.Crim.P. 7(a)—must give "time for consultation" at arraignment & don't "inadvertently foreclose the rights of uninformed D's";

Foley v Commonwealth **429 M 496, 497 (99)**—use of Plymouth County correctional facility as courtroom for arraignments and bail hearings upheld against constitutional challenges, given the state of the record, BUT essential prerequisites were listed (signs to guide public to location and assurance of free access by public, proper notice at respective District Court houses stating what specific arraignments are to be held at the facility and at what time, physical layout of facility and its accessibility will be examined to assure "properly public"; evidentiary hearings or trials present additional considerations not here addressed (approval of facility's use limited to arraignment sessions);

C v Butler **423 M 517, 520 n.5 (96)**—court's policy of refusing to arraign arrestees unless they're present in courthouse by 1 p.m. = improper: if courthouse is open, arraignments should occur;

C v DuBois **353 M 223 (67)**—hold overnight = OK;

C v Cote **386 M 354, 360–62 & n.11 (82)**—hold 9:00 a.m. to 1:00 p.m. = OK; but might suppress evidence if there's "purposeful" violation of M.R.Crim.P. 7;

C v Banuchi **335 M 649 (57)**—3-day delay not "unreasonable" (pre-Rule 7);

C v Hunter **426 M 715 (98)**—after D's arrest on unrelated charge, (pre-*Rosario*) delayed arraignment on new charge was excused (and incriminating statements not suppressed) because judge "found" that purpose of delay was "not to apply improper pressure on" D;

C v Barnes **40 MAC 666 (96)**—evidence supported motion judge's finding that police did not interfere with D's right to consult attorney, though CPCS made efforts to have attorney waiting/present in court long before D was brought there;

G.L. c. 276, § 27—D in on summons, no surety required "at any stage of the prosecution" without "special order"; *(re: D in on summons, see Chapter 3-F, Hearing re: Issuance of Complaint)*;

4-A.1. Probation Officer Interviews D

District Court Standards of Judicial Practice, Arraignment (1977) 2:00 & 2:01—"thorough inquiry"; see "Intake Form"—signed by D under pains & penalties of perjury; c) G.L. c. 276, § 85—probation officer duties: check D's criminal record; can include dismissals, but not 'not guilties'; notify authorities if D's on probation or parole;

US v Melanson **691 F.2d 579 (1st Cir. '81)**—5th & 6th Amendments permit later use of D's (counsel-less) blurted-out bail hearing statement *(See also Chapter 20B, Suppression, Alleged Statements)*;

Minnesota v Murphy **465 US 420 (84)**—non-custodial statements to supervising probation officer not involuntary & OK under 5th Amendment; (cf. *Estelle v Smith* **451 US 454 (81)** *(Chapter 7-D, Examination of D for Competency & Responsibility)* 6th and 5th Amendment rights to counsel/warnings for D before competency examination, or statements will be inadmissible later);

C v Bandy **38 MAC 329 (95)**—D's statement to probation officer (admission of wrongdoing) during indigency determination admissible absent showing that officer deliberately elicited the incriminating remarks;

SJC Rule 3:10 § 4:"Indigency" calculations—"indigent but able to contribute" (some $ to court); judge decides after written report & interrogating; § 1(b)—defining "available funds": if under age 17, includes funds of parents/guardian, unless they have "adverse interest" in the matter; if over age 16, but "substantially supported" by parent/guardian or if claimed as dependent for taxes, includes funds of parent/guardian, unless have adverse interest in the matter; § 9—inadmissibility of info obtained from D during indigency determination, except in prosecution for perjury or contempt committed in providing such info; § 7—judge may order reexamination of indigency determination at any time before end of proceeding;

C v Bandy **38 MAC 329 (95)**—D's **statement to probation officer** (admission of wrongdoing) **during indigency determination** admissible absent showing that officer deliberately elicited the incriminating remarks; BUT SEE SJC Rule 3:10, Assignment of Counsel:

See Chapter 7C, Prepare for Trial, Money for Experts, etc.;

District Court Standards of Judicial Practice, Arraignment (1977) 5:02—discourage appointments for convenience; 5:04—suggests withdrawal if D's not indigent;

SJC R.3:07, 1.6(b)(3), 3.3(e)—need not rectify D's (past) fraud if learned through privilege; *(See Chapter 2, Ethics: Withdrawal, Fraud, Bounds of Law)*;

***Roswall v Municipal Court* 152 Cal.R. 337 (79)**—no removal for indigency change; BUT see, contra, SJC R.3:10—judge may at any time order re-examination of indigency question;

G.L. c. 211D, § 2A—judge may refuse to appoint to indigent D charged with misdemeanors or minor offenses if judge notifies D that incarceration will not result; D may later receive appointed counsel for "good cause" but D entitled to continuance; NB: use of uncounseled convictions & facial validity under state constitution open to challenge; legal counsel fee increases periodically, with amendments (in 2002, it's $100), but judge may waive;

***C v Cote* 74 MAC 709 (2009)**—BUT judge's advice that D won't be incarcerated and thus D can't have appointed counsel did not make D's pro se appearance a valid waiver of the right to hire counsel, no explanation or colloquy having occurred re: perils of self-representation; "negligent operation" conviction reversed;

***Alabama v Shelton* 535 US 654 (2002)**—if charge results in even a suspended sentence (here, of 30 days), right to have counsel appointed;

***Cameron v Justice of Taunton District Court*, No. 92-203 (SJC for Suffolk County) (O'Connor, J.)**—appointed counsel shall not be removed because of D's failure to pay counsel fee;

***Fullan v Comm'r of Corrections of State of NY* 891 F.2d 1007 (2d Cir. '89), cert. denied 496 US 942 (90)**—assets of D's family & friends cannot be considered in determining D's indigency where D has no control over assets; amount D paid trial counsel irrelevant to D's indigency on appeal;

***C v Godwin* 60 MAC 605 (2004)**—D bears burden of demonstrating indigency; indigence determined through M.R.Crim.P. 8 and SJC Rule 3:10, § 4(a); "cf. G.L. c 261, § 27C(3)";

***FTC v Superior Court Trial Lawyers Ass'n* 493 US 411 (90)**—agreement amongst lawyers to refuse indigent appointments until compensation increased was federal antitrust violation;

SJC R.3:07, 1.6(b)(3)—shall reveal D's (past) fraud unless learned through privilege; 1.2(d)—can't counsel or assist illegal or fraudulent conduct; 1.6(b)(1) may (or must, in specified circumstances) reveal future crime; *(See Chapter 2, Ethics: Withdrawal, Fraud, Bounds of Law)*;

***Moore v Illinois* 434 US 220 (77)**—counsel right at arraignment, e.g., to prevent ID;

M.R.Crim.P. 7(a)(1)—assign CPCS, then arraign; Reporter's Note: appoint counsel promptly to consult re: "vital rights"; 7(c) read charges (D may waive) & enter plea = "Arraignment";

M.R.Crim.P. 12—Pleas = guilty, not guilty, (or, with judge's consent, nolo contendere); R.12(a)(2), in District Court, admission to sufficient facts; R.12(a)(1): D must personally make 'guilty' or 'nolo' plea, & also personally plead not guilty, except where D's appearance = excused (M.R.Crim.P. 7(c)(2)) and the court enters the plea on his behalf;

District Court Standards for Judicial Practice, Arraignment (1977) 3:00—read charge(s), including "pertinent language";

CPCS P/G 2.1—don't waive significant rights at arraignment; G.Plea/admission to sufficient facts inadvisable except . . . ; *(See Chapter 13, Plea Bargains & Chapter 2, Defense Counsel Standards/Ethics)*;

ABA Standards for Criminal Justice, Prosecution Function & Defense Function (3d ed. 1993) 4-3.6—D-counsel to take prompt action to protect D's rights;

***County of Riverside v McLaughlin* 500 US 44 (91)**—judicial determination of probable cause under ***Gerstein v Pugh* 420 US 103 (75)** must be held within 48 hours of arrest; no exception for weekends or holidays;

***Jenkins v Chief Justice of District Court Dept.* 416 M 221 (93)**—under Article 14 of Declaration of Rights, probable cause determination by neutral magistrate must occur within 24 hours at most, or "no later than reasonably necessary" after arrest *if* D is being held;

C v Viverito* 422 M 228 (96)**—dismissal not required for ***Jenkins violation;

4-B. QUESTION OF COUNSEL AND CPCS ASSIGNMENT

(See also Chapter 1-A, CPCS & Right to Counsel)
See Chapter 7-P re: right to interpreter;

SJC Rule 3:10—If law/rules give right to counsel, court shall advise, make findings, assign CPCS; *(See Chapter 4A, below re: indigency & D's statements)*;

M.R.Crim.P. 8—if crime "for which imprisonment may be imposed" (shall follow G.L. c. 211D & Rule 3:10 to assign counsel);

***C v Cote* 74 MAC 709 (2009)**—judge's advice that D won't be incarcerated and thus D can't have appointed

counsel did not make D's pro se appearance a valid waiver of the right to ***hire*** counsel, no explanation or colloquy having occurred re: perils of self-representation; "negligent operation" conviction reversed;

District Court Standards of Judicial Practice, Arraignment (1977) 5:00— . . . when the crime charged "includes a possible sanction of imprisonment"; *(See Chapter 1A)*;

***Rothgery v Gillespie County, Texas* 128 S Ct 2578 (2008)**—right to counsel attaches at first appearance before judicial officer at which D is told of formal accusation against him and restrictions are imposed on liberty; that public prosecutor (as opposed to police officer) be aware of initial proceeding or involved in its conduct is NOT required; D's arrest without warrant as purported "felon" in possession of firearm was followed by appearance before a "magistrate judge" for proceeding which combined a finding of probable cause with setting of bail; D's oral and written requests for counsel were unheeded until indictment and further delay more than six months later (and counsel promptly learned that arrest as "felon" was premised on an erroneous record);

Williams v Commonwealth **350 M 732 (66)**—based on then-existing R.10 of the "General Rules," D has right to counsel at probation revocation hearing;

Baldassari v Commonwealth **352 M 616 (67)**—counsel right for violation of terms of probation hearing;

C v Faulkner **418 M 352 (94)**—despite fact that Rule 10 no longer exists, reasoning of *Williams* **350 M 732 (66)**, remains valid, and there is right to counsel at probation revocation hearing; it is "a point in the sentencing process," and there is right to counsel at sentencing; fn. 9: even if D received notice of probation surrender hearing previously scheduled and failed to appear then, this alone can't be deemed a waiver of counsel at subsequent hearing;

Mulcahy v Commonwealth **352 M 613 (67)**—judge must advise re: counsel, not probation officer;

M.R.Crim.P. 7(b)(1)—appearance slips personally or by mail;

C v Lasher **428 M 202 (98)**—after arraignment attorney notified court and DA that he did not represent D, and that counsel should be appointed, it was not D's responsibility to "go to the probation office" to obtain counsel (though prior counsel had told him to do so); only the court had the power to appoint counsel, and probation dept merely determines whether person is eligible for appointed counsel; result here was that case was dismissed pursuant to M.R.Crim.P. 36 ("speedy"/case management), since uncounseled D (who hadn't waived counsel) would not be required to press his case or object to delays;

C v Vickers **60 MAC 24 (2003)**—can't link [threaten] increase in bail to D's request for change of allegedly unprepared counsel;

C v Means **454 M 81 (2009)**—though a defendant by extraordinary misconduct may "forfeit" right to appointed counsel, this is an extreme sanction (invoked without prior warning to D of consequences of behavior) may be applied only in extraordinary circumstances (usually when D has had more than one appointed counsel, almost never to deny representation during trial, perhaps limited to threats or acts of violence against defense counsel or others, as "a last resort in response to the most grave and deliberate misconduct") after hearing at which D has full and fair opportunity to offer evidence as to all relevant circumstances; "waiver", in contrast, may be express and voluntary, or CAN be by conduct, but "waiver" may be found only after explicit warning has been given to D about

threatened consequence of D's behavior and the consequences of proceeding without counsel ("waiver" being a "voluntary," "informed and intentional relinquishment of a known right"); judge here erred in imposing this consequence (resulting in pro se representation at trial and subsequent 'habitual offender' trial) without a hearing; D had asked for new counsel, and had sent letter to counsel threatening serious harm to him and his family if he did not withdraw from representation; fn.5: specific inquiry should have been made about D's precise complaints against counsel; mental illness impairing ability to control actions probable here;

C v Sparks **431 M 299 (2000)**—CPCS-appointed counsel can't do part of appeal work and sub-contract remainder to private counsel with compensation sought pursuant to M.R.Crim.P. 15(d);

4-B.1.   Pro Se Issues

Faretta v California **422 US 806 (75)**—Sixth Amendment right to act as own attorney;

Indiana v Edwards **128 S Ct 2379 (2008)**—Constitution forbids trial of accused lacking rational and factual understanding of proceedings and sufficient ability to consult with counsel with reasonable degree of rational understanding, BUT Constitution doesn't forbid states from insisting upon representation by counsel for accused who is "competent" to stand trial but who suffers from severe mental illness so not competent to represent himself;

SJC Rule 3:10, § 3—waiver of counsel (in writing);

C v Cavanaugh **371 M 46 (76)**—colloquy;

C v Martin **425 M 718 (97)**—D did not, here, prevail on argument that he had not made knowing & intelligent waiver of counsel; after valid waiver of counsel, D not entitled to reversal "based on his . . . lack of skill" **pro se**;

District Court Standards of Judicial Practice, Arraignment (1977) 5:01—D told to retain own counsel should be told to seek pre-trial hearing if unsuccessful;

Mocks v Commonwealth **426 M 1018 (98)**—"under no circumstances" does D have right to a **particular** court-appointed attorney;

C v Hurst **39 MAC 603 (96)**—unless D files written waiver of counsel, DA should **not** undertake plea negotiations with him;

Jordan v Superior Court **426 M 1019 (98)**—dicta: 'we have never held . . . that indigent defendants are automatically entitled to the assistance of counsel on motions to revise or revoke. Not all postconviction motions require the assistance of counsel';

C v Lee **394 M 209 (85)**—OK "waiver" (D asked for another lawyer);

C v Babb **416 M 732 (94)**—similar; refusal "without cause" to proceed with appointed counsel constituted "abandonment" of right to counsel; *C v Pamplona* **58 MAC 239 (2003)**—similar; absence of written waiver of right to counsel doesn't matter; extensive advice by judge re:

re: hazards of self-representation = reasonable approach to assure that choice is knowledgeable; SEE

C V Means **454 M 81 (2009)**—don't confuse "waiver" of counsel with "forfeiture" (fn 14): waiver by conduct require prior warning to D against misconduct, and "forfeiture" does not; forfeiture is 'typically' applied when D has had more than one appointed counsel, and is "rarely" applied to deny representation during trial; while forfeiture MAY be appropriate to D's threat or acts of violence against defense counsel or others, should be "a last resort in response to the most grave and deliberate misconduct" (D's mental illness likely impaired ability to control actions here); "waiver" only when there is voluntary, informed and intentional relinquishment of known right;

C v Kulesa **455 M 447 (2009)**—D was entitled to counsel at trial of "subsequent offender" portion of proceedings regarding G.L. c. 278, § 11A (criminal harassment, subsequent offender), and D's waiver of counsel for trial of substantive offense did NOT operate as waiver of counsel for second part of bifurcated proceeding (though judge could conduct colloquy prior to trial of substantive offense which clearly covered both portions, this didn't occur here);

Mack v Clerk of the Appeals Court **427 M 1011 (98)**—after Appeals Court allowed motions of two successively-appointed attorneys to withdraw from representation of D, Court could deem D to be proceeding pro se, and didn't have to order either that CPCS provide new counsel or that prior attorney resume representation; D had been informed by CPCS that no further counsel would be assigned if he couldn't work with 2d attorney (1st attorney's affidavit recounted D spitting in his face and cursing him; 2d attorney cited D's "extreme and profane" behavior, total breakdown of attorney-client relationship, and D's written request that he withdraw);

C v Britto **433 M 596 (2001)**—D who refuses without good cause to proceed with appointed counsel may be forced to choose between continued representation by same attorney or acting pro se;

4-B.2. Stand-by Counsel

SJC Rule 3:10 § 6—may assign to assist a pro se D (even though D doesn't want);

McKaskle v Wiggins **465 US 168 (84)**—rejecting contention on record here that stand-by counsel violated D's pro se right; guidelines for future: (1) pro se D = entitled to preserve actual control case presented to jury; (2) participation by standby counsel without D's consent can't destroy the jury's perception that the defendant is representing himself.

C v Molino **411 M 149, 152–55 (91)**—judge forbade "stand-by" counsel from speaking to D unless D asked for advice, e.g., counsel not allowed to prompt D to object, to

talk at sidebar conferences, to draft pleadings; SJC understands *McKaskle v Wiggins* **465 US 168 (84)** (one's Sixth Amendment rights were not violated when a trial judge appointed standby counsel to relieve the judge of the need to explain and enforce basic rules of courtroom protocol or help with overcoming routine obstacles) to mean trial judge had discretion to prohibit unsolicited participation by standby counsel, and like discretion to allow such participation; BUT "there is limited utility in assigning standby counsel who can advise a defendant only when the defendant requests such advice (because) (m)ost defendants will not know what questions to ask and will gain only a fraction of the advice that counsel could offer"; "may be appropriate, in the future, for a trial judge who appoints standby counsel to allow" counsel to give D unsolicited advice if D so desires;

C v Johnson **424 M 338 (97)**—when 'standby' counsel was converted to "lead" counsel on day of trial & requested continuance because not prepared, judge forced D to proceed pro se, given his prior "unequivocal" **pro se** desire; no relief on appeal;

C v Brown **378 M 165 (79)**—no "hybrid representation"; D not "co-counsel";

ABA Standards for Criminal Justice (2d ed. 1980) (Trial Judge) § 6-3.7—judge to consider standby to assist pro se D "when called upon" & to point things out to judge; Comment: not examine witnesses unless D wants, but "limited independent role";

4-B.3. Attorneys Not "Fungible"

C v Brennick **14 MAC 952 (82)**—public defenders not fungible; reversible error to make 2d public defender fill in & handle (disposition of de novo default);

C v Faulkner **418 M 352 (94)**—appointed counsel who had just received notice of probation surrender was not capable of assistance of counsel to which D was entitled, notwithstanding Commonwealth's argument that by failing to appear for previously-scheduled probation violation hearing D waived right to such counsel; refusal of continuance request made D's right to defend with counsel an "empty formality" (SJC rejected Commonwealth's argument that issue should be analyzed in terms of whether D received "effective assistance" of counsel, requiring D to show how prepared counsel would have made a difference);

US v Lespier **558 F.2d 624 (1st Cir. '77)**—contempt for attorney #2 (who did pre-trial hearings) not to fill in for other (absent without excuse) attorney;

Lindsey v Commonwealth **331 M 1 (54)**—violated due process to force 2d public defender to fill in & try attorney #1's case;

See Chapter 2, Ethics: Effectiveness/Court Orders/ Sanctions/Contempt;

4-C. PREPARATION FOR, AND CONDUCT OF, BAIL HEARING

US v Frappier **615 F.Supp 51 (D.Mass. '85)**—ineffective to put D on stand at bail hearing;

See Chapter 21-DD, Delay in Release on Bail After Arrest for Operating Under the Influence;

CPCS P/G 2.1-2.2—verify all info.; insist on adequate interview/investigation before bail hearing; etc.;

In re Troy **364 M 15, 26–39 (73)**—bail & arraignment abuses; hearing on bail "not satisfied by setting bail & having hearing later";

Matter of Scott **377 M 364, 373-81 (79)**—more "rough justice" re: bail;

G.L. c. 276, § 58—bail law & criteria; presume personal recognizance; take into account circumstances of offense charged, potential penalty, family ties, financial resources, employment record, history of mental illness, reputation, length of residence in the community, record of convictions, if any, any illegal drug distribution or present drug dependency, any defaults or uses of false identification/aliases; whether on bail with other pending charge(s), whether current charge = abuse (G.L. c. 209A, etc.), whether history of protective orders;

C v Torres **441 M 499 (2004)**—as a "general rule," a Superior Court judge may conduct a bail hearing for a D found incompetent to stand trial;

Leo v Commonwealth **442 M 1025 (2004)**—bail review judge refused to reduce bail on sole basis that D posed a suicide risk, "and thus presented a flight risk": whether this is true continues to be open question in Massachusetts, fn.1; thereafter D petitioned for reduction on basis that successful treatment for depression while in custody meant no longer risk of suicide, but because D failed to demonstrate that treatment and medication "could realistically be continued on the outside," or that judge could be assured that D would continue to follow his treatment regimen if released, no error of law or abuse of discretion in refusing to reduce bail;

Querubin v Commonwealth **440 M 108, 111 (2003)**—G.L. c. 276, § 57 = "applicable to the setting of bail in the Superior Court," "rather than G.L. c. 276, § 58"; no substantive or procedural due process deprivation in § 57; bail proceeding isn't "mini-trial," but judge has discretion to hold evidentiary hearing; standard of proof re: assuring D's presence/risk of flight = preponderance; OK to deny bail because of flight risk (instead of "danger");

Paquette v Commonwealth **440 M 121 (2003)**—D's arrest & arraignment on new charges = valid basis for revocation of bail on prior cases pursuant to G.L. c. 276, § 58, if judge also finds that release of D will seriously endanger any person or the community; but "notwithstanding ... § 58 & any inquiry into dangerousness," there's "inherent power" to revoke bail for breach of any condition of release; "probable cause to arrest" standard (rather than "directed verdict"/"bindover" standard) = sufficient for bail revocation; determinations of probable cause and

dangerousness for bail revocation can be made "without a full-blown evidentiary hearing," and evidentiary rules don't apply; judge has discretion to "reopen" hearing OR NOT, but proffered testimony going "only" to the merits of new case (rather than mere probable cause) doesn't require reopening; **Commonwealth may not "reserve" right to bail hearing on new charge until some future date, banking on continued confinement due to revocation on prior charge**, *Paquette v Commonwealth* 440 M at 135;

C v Pagan **445 M 315 (2005)**—arraignment judge on new charge not barred from revoking bail set by different judge in different court (even); to revoke bail pursuant to G.L. c. 276, § 58, judge must find probable cause that new offense was committed by D **during the period of D's release on the prior bail** and that release will "seriously" endanger someone or "the community" and that detention is necessary to assure safety; judge has discretion not to revoke even when probable cause and dangerousness are found; revocation is for **60 days**; no District Court judge may reinstate bail sooner than 60 days unless new charge or prior charge has been adjudicated, or revoking judge reconsiders and finds "manifest injustice"; D entitled to counsel and hearing prior to revocation; on sixtieth day after revocation, D must be returned to the court with jurisdiction over the charges to which bail revocation order relates, for new bail hearing on them; see companion cases *Cargill* **445 M 329 (2005)** and *Hall* **445 M 1016 (2005)**;

Sheriff of Suffolk County v Pires **438 M 96 (2002)**—habeas corpus petition can only be used when person is entitled to immediate release; it isn't substitute for appeal where appellate remedies exist; habeas isn't correct way to contest bail revocation order (G.L. c. 211, § 3 was instead the proper method of appealing revocation of bail, and "immediate release" wasn't in the cards, as D was held on $25,000 bail on new charges, bail having been revoked on prior charges due to new arrest/probable cause);

G.L. c. 276, § 27—no surety for D in on summons without "special order";

Jenkins v Chief Justice District Court **416 M 221 (93)**—unless D is held without bail after arrest, no right to probable cause determination by neutral magistrate within 24 hours;

C v Perito **417 M 674 (94)**—when D was hospitalized due to police chase & bail was set in his absence, D should have been taken immediately from hospital to court for in-person bail hearing (**not** from house of correction to Bridgewater for G.L. c. 123, § 18(a) evaluation not to exceed 30 days);

District Court Standards of Judicial Practice, Pretrial Release (1977) 1:01—"records should be available for D to inspect"; but M.R.Crim.P. 28 & G.L. c. 276, § 85—show counsel D's criminal record re: disposition; (silent re: bail hearing);

G.L. c. 6, § 172–CORI ("criminal offender record information").; (CPCS = approved "criminal justice agency");

G.L. c. 276, §§ 42, 57, 58—right to reasonably prompt bail hearing;

G.L. c. 221, § 62C—designated magistrate can . . . set arraignment bail during normal court day when judge not available as allowed by Rule approved by SJC;

C v Chistolini **422 M 854 (96)**—operating under influence arrestee not afforded bail determination, after 2 a.m. arrest, until after 6 a.m., because of police department policy that bail commissioner would only be called at 4-hour intervals during the night: **no relief** (dismissal requested);

C v Rosario **422 M 48 (96)**—6-hour "safe harbor" delay may be tolled by arrestee's intoxication (because arrestee must be able to understand "nature of bail" & release conditions);

C v King **429 M 169 (99)**—bail magistrate's policy of refusing to come to police barracks and hold bail hearing if OUI arrestee refused breathalyzer was unlawful; purported considerations of "safety of the public" or "avoidance of personal liability for actions of" D after release were not valid under G.L. c. 276, § 58; no evidence here that D so intoxicated he couldn't understand bail proceedings;

C v Finelli **422 M 860 (96)**—operating under influence arrestee (.14 breathalyzer) not seen by bail magistrate, who directed, by telephone, that D "sleep it off" for 5½ hours; determination of intoxicated state **should** be made after "firsthand observation," but no error here in relying on "credible police statement" including breathalyzer result;

US v Edson **487 F.2d 370 (1st Cir. '73)**—reduce bail because judge ignored presumption of personal recognizance;

C v Baker **343 M 162 (61)**—**discretionary bail for murder;**

Magraw v Commonwealth **429 M 1004 (99)**—though D had been free on bail prior to murder trial, no error when neither trial court judge nor SJC single justice allowed him to be free on bail pending retrial after appellate reversal of murder conviction; matter of "discretion";

US Constitution, 5th & 14th Amendments: due process clause—"beyond a reasonable doubt" burden of proof "provides concrete substance for the presumption of innocence—that bedrock 'axiomatic and elementary' principle whose "enforcement lies at the foundation of the administration of our criminal law" (*In re Winship* **397 US 358 (70)**));

Universal Declaration of Human Rights (48)—right to be presumed innocent;

Mass. Declaration of Rights, Article 26—no "excessive" bail;

U.S. Constitution, Amendment 8—(same);

K. Smith, *Criminal Practice & Procedure***, Chapter 8 (2d ed. 1983 & Supp.)**—various bail matters, including what may be used for bail (§§ 502–07);

G.L. c. 276, § 61B: Sureties/professional bondsmen—(see also "S.Ct. Rules Governing Bondsmen," reproduced in K. Smith, *Criminal Practice & Procedure,* § 501 (2d ed. 1983 & Supp); & District Court Standards of Judicial Practice, Pretrial Release (1977) 1:05–1.06),

C v Stuyvesant Ins. **366 M 611 (75)**—bondsman's liability re: default & forfeiture ends if default is removed & D is jailed; surety can surrender D if reason to believe D intends to jump bail;

G.L. c. 276, §§ 57 & 79:"Cash in lieu of surety"—District Court Pretrial Release Standards. 1:06 & 1:07 (full amount in cash, bankbook, or bonds); "% cash deposit" – Pretrial Rel.Std. 1:07 recommends it because incentive to return (& suggests 10%);

C v Ray **435 M 249, 258 (2001)**—construing G.L. c. 276, § 58's "equivalent amount" term: surety bond set at an amount ten times the amount of a cash bail is equal in effect to that cash bail;

Real Estate—K. Smith, *Criminal Practice & Procedure,* §§ 502 & 507 (2d ed. 1983 & Supp.); Std. 1:06 – rare & discouraged (see also G.L. c. 276, § 61A, misdemeanor for disposing of realty that's bail)

G.L. c. 276, § 63—no judge, except special judge of District Court, to get any fee for approving bail, & no one authorized to admit to bail in criminal cases shall receive anything of value in excess of the statutory fees therefore. No person shall act as attorney in any case in which he has admitted a prisoner or witness to bail.

Superior Court Rule 11—no attorney shall become bail or surety in any criminal proceeding in which he is employed;

G.L. c. 276, § 29—before releasing or admitting to bail any person brought before court, check for warrants; if any warrant outstanding, court is to determine bail on outstanding warrant(s); if court releases person on bail or recognizance, D shall be ordered to appear in court issuing warrant on particular date; if person not released, shall be transported to warrant-issuing court immediately, or to jail in the county of issuing court & thereafter, to next regular sitting of the warrant-issuing court; person arrested on default warrant for a felony or a misdemeanor punishable by >100 days may be released on bail or recognizance only by **judge** in place of arrest or judge of warrant-issuing court; anyone authorized to admit an accused to bail must check for warrants before setting bail/releasing; if it's for lesser crime, non-judge can release/set bail, but must notify warrant-issuing court;

G.L. c. 276, § 42A—"domestic abuse—related cases" can have special conditions;

G.L. c. 276, § 87—special conditions on pretrial release ok **when D consents** and is placed on probation;

K. Smith, *Criminal Practice & Procedure,* **§ 521 (2d ed. 1983 & Supp.)**—(changing/revoking bail);

Matter of King **409 M 590 (91)**—improper to confiscate bail posted by third parties for nondefaulting D to satisfy court costs & other obligations;

4-C.1. Preventive Detention/Conditional Release: "Dangerousness"

G.L. c. 276,   §§ 58–58A—preventive detention amendments to bail statute allowing bail to be set if D's "release will endanger any other person or the community," even if no risk of flight; whether acts alleged involve domestic abuse or restraining order violations, whether D has history of restraining order violations, plus nature & seriousness of danger added as new factors in setting bail; dangerousness hearings; predicate = charged offense must be felony that has as element of offense the use, attempted use, or threatened use of physical force against another person, "or any other felony that by its nature involves a substantial risk that physical force against the person of another may result," including crimes of burglary and arson . . . ;

C v Young **453 M 707 (2009)**—unlicensed possession of firearm is not a charge on which preventive detention may be sought; "threshold question in every case is whether the defendant has committed a predicate offense under § 58A"; *Alabi v Commonwealth* **453 M 1023 (2009)**—same, even when charged offense includes element of prior conviction of unlicensed firearm possession;

Schall v Martin **467 US 253 (84)**—detention of high risk juveniles;

US v Salerno **481 US 739 (87)**—adult preventive detention OK (if . . .)

Aime v Commonwealth **414 M 667 (93)**—1992 preventive detention amendments to bail statute adding dangerousness as new purpose & factor for bail struck down as violative of 14th Amendment due process clause; state constitutional questions left open; BUT, LATER:

Mendonza v Commonwealth **423 M 771 (96)**—preventive detention (for 90 days) statute, G.L. c. 276, § 58A, upheld despite "substantive due process" attacks; detention to be ordered only upon finding by clear & convincing evidence that no conditions of release will reasonably assure safety of other persons . . . rejects challenges to "reliable" hearsay allowance & to use of "facts" not involved in charged offense; court upholds three-day continuance for "dangerousness" hearing under § 58A: Commonwealth need show only probable cause for arrest and "good cause" for the continuance;

C v Lester L **445 M 250 (2005)**—while dangerousness hearing is to be held "immediately upon the person's first appearance before the court", a continuance is to be allowed on Commonwealth request "only if" Commonwealth shows good cause for same, as well as probable cause to arrest; "probable cause" is established upon "properly issued complaint", and if complaint hasn't been "properly issued," probable cause may be shown by reading or summarizing police report; decision to continue dangerousness hearing implicates due process procedural rights, but these rights are only right to counsel and the opportunity to make representations and arguments, but not right to present evidence or cross-examine witnesses;

continuance isn't to exceed 3 business days without "good cause"; **statute does not give judge discretion to release D pending dangerousness hearing once there is a determination that probable cause to arrest existed and there is good cause to continue the hearing;**

C v Hurley **455 M 53 (2009)**—while refusing to declare a "general rule" that witness's testimony from dangerousness hearing is always admissible at trial if witness becomes unavailable. HERE SJC finds that there was both opportunity for and exercise of cross-examination and that particular tactics at dangerousness hearing *were* same as for trial, i.e., attack on credibility in many ways (not drunkenness alone);

Victor V. v Commonwealth **423 M 793 (96)**—preventive detention statute (c. 276, § 58A) applies to juveniles;

Abbott A v Commonwealth **455 M 1005 (2009)**—juvenile found incompetent for trial was to be subjected to § 58A hearing, but counsel argued juvenile to be incompetent to assist attorney in § 58A hearing and petitioned pursuant to G.L. c. 211, § 3; SJC held petition untimely, and would be entertained only upon adverse ruling after 58A hearing (review then would include issue of whether it was appropriate to have held 58A hearing at all);

C v Murchison **428 M 303 (98)**—after determination in District Court that D is "dangerous" and is being held pursuant to G.L. c. 276, § 58A, D is entitled to new hearing in Superior Court after indictment: Commonwealth may not simply ask that District Court detention order remain in effect (but Commonwealth may submit transcript and record of District Court proceedings without supplementation, and judge may give these "whatever weight (s/he) deems appropriate," though D has right to present new info; judge must make "own independent determination of the facts based on the record as presented to him");

C v Dodge **428 M 860, 864 (99)**—judge's ordering as condition of release on bail under general bail statute (G.L. c. 276, § 58), in OUI case, that D undergo drug and alcohol screening and participate in any outpatient counseling (including Alcoholics Anonymous and Narc. Anonymous), both as determined by Department of Probation, was not permissible; notwithstanding illegality, SJC refused to vacate "contempt" conviction for D's refusal (D should have appealed the denial of his motion to dismiss contempt charge, rather than merely ignore the underlying (illegitimate, without statutory authority) orders; such conditions may be set under G.L. c. 276, §§ 42A, 87, or 58A;

G.L. c. 276, § 58, as amended by St. 2006, c. 48, § 8—sentence added to end of first paragraph: "If the justice or clerk or assistant clerk of the District Court, the bail commissioner or master in chancery determines it to be necessary, the defendant may be ordered to abide by specified restrictions on personal associations or conduct including, but not limited to, avoiding all contact with an alleged victim of the crime and any potential witness or witnesses who may testify concerning the offense, as a condition of release";

C v Carrara **58 MAC 86 (2003)**—after D was found incompetent to stand trial, he was committed to state hospital, and recommitted pursuant to G.L. c. 123, § 16(c); judge had no authority, in order of recommitment, to restrict D's unsupervised access to hospital grounds; authority to impose restriction rested with hospital (G.L. c. 123, § 16(e));

Jake J. v Commonwealth **433 M 70 (2000)**—given holding of *Dodge* **428 M 860**, SJC held what occurred here was "pretrial probation" with conditions (G.L. c. 276, § 87), rejecting argument that § 87 is primarily/exclusively a "dispositional" device; despite fact that § 87 provides no "enforcement" mechanism, judge permissibly adapted § 58B procedures for revocation of bail (& ordering juvenile into custody) under § 87; juvenile and his mother here signed "agreement with the probation department," with references to juvenile being "on probation"; in future, record should be clearer that release on bail or personal recognizance is via G.L. c. 276, § 58, that any "agreed-on conditions of probation" pre-trial is being accomplished via G.L. c. 276, § 87, and that violation of "conditions of release" will have consequences which are explained on record; see 2006 amendment to G.L. c. 276, § 58 (last sentence, 1st paragraph): even without D's consent, a defendant "may be ordered to abide by specified restrictions on personal associations or conduct including, but not limited to, avoiding all contact with an alleged victim of the crime and any potential witness or witnesses who may testify concerning the offense, as a condition of release".

SJC Standards on Substance Abuse (approved 1998)—see Policy Statement and Standards I, V, and XIII with Commentaries, for support when requesting substance abuse treatment in lieu of bail;

4-C.2. New Crimes while on Pretrial Release

G.L. c. 276, § 58—explicit condition of release for anyone under §§ 57 or 58 = on-record advice that if charged with new crime, bail can be revoked; if D is thereafter charged w/new offense, that arraignment court may hold D, if after hearing at D's 1st appearance before 2d court shows probable cause to believe D committed new crime & court determines D's release will seriously endanger any person or the community & detention is necessary to assure safety, court may revoke bail on the prior charge and may order D held without bail for up to 60 days pending adjudication of prior charge; continuance of hearing may be allowed only if "witness or document is not immediately available"; continuance may be only for 7 days if D requests, and only for 3 business days if Commonwealth requests;

C v Pagan **445 M 315 (2005)**—arraignment judge on new charge (even if in different court) may revoke bail set on prior charge pursuant to G.L. c. 276, § 58; must find probable cause that D committed new offense during period of release on prior bail, that D's release will seriously endanger a person or the community, and that detention is necessary to assure safety; judge has discretion **not** to revoke even if finds probable cause and dangerousness; revocation is **for 60 days**; no District Court judge may reinstate bail sooner than 60 days unless new or prior charge has been adjudicated or revoking judge reconsiders/ finds "manifest injustice"; D has right to counsel and hearing; see also *C v Cargill* **445 M 329 (2005)**—D, on bail in Superior Court case, was arraigned in District Court on new complaints, and District Court judge revoked bail set in connection with the Superior Court indictments (pursuant to G.L. c. 276, § 58, 3rd paragraph), ordering D to be held without bail for period not to exceed 60 days; ONLY Superior Court judge had authority to reinstate D's bail on Superior Court indictments; and *Hall* **445 M 1016 (2005)**;

Sheriff of Suffolk County v Pires **438 M 96 (2002)**— G.L. c. 211, § 3, is proper method of appealing revocation of bail (and not a state "habeas" petition); "immediate release" wasn't in the cards, as D was held on $25,000 bail on new charges when bail was revoked on prior charges due to new arrest/probable cause;

G.L. c. 279, § 8B—if D is on bail/personal recognizance for pending cases and commits new crimes, sentence for new crimes "shall run consecutively to the earlier sentence for the crime for which he was on release";

C v Hickey **429 M 1027 (99)—but if D is sentenced first for the later crime, G.L. c. 279, § 8B is no bar to a "forthwith" sentence on the first-occurring crime;**

C v Yancey **46 MAC 924 (99)—no error in denying motion to withdraw G plea on basis that sentence was ordered to run from & after sentence for crime for which D was on (money) bail at time of new crime; rejects argument that 'from & after' requirement = only re: new crimes while on "personal recognizance";**

4-C.3. "No Prior Record, Your Honor" (and Ethical Issues)

SJC Rule 3:07, 1.3—"zealous"; shall not prejudice or damage client;

Rule 3:07, 1.6—preserve confidences/"secrets"; may reveal future crime;

Rule 3:07, 3.3(a), 8.4(c)—don't knowingly misrepresent facts; don't fail to disclose material fact to tribunal when disclosure necessary "to avoid assisting a criminal or fraudulent act BY THE CLIENT";

Rule 3:07, 1.6, 3.3(e)—reveal fraud; including D's, unless privileged;

Rule 3:07, 3.4(e)—no personal fact knowledge or justness opinion;

ABA Standards for Criminal Justice, Prosecution Function & Defense Function (3d ed. 1993) 4-8.1, Comment—(at sentencing) can't "suggest" no record if know it exists;

Dunbrack v Commonwealth **398 M 502 (86)**—trial judge can change sentence when learned D hid prior record; trial judge said "silent fraud" by D, but no SJC opinion—fn.4;

See also Chapter 2, Standards/Ethics;

4-D. STATEMENT OF FACTS (HEARSAY, MOTION TO DISMISS?)

G.L. c. 276, § 58—re: bail, take into account "circumstances of offense," potential penalty faced, family ties, financial resources, employment record and history of mental illness, length of residence in the community, prior convictions, drug use, any prior defaults, use of aliases, whether on bail for prior charge, whether abuse or restraining orders presently or in past;

District Court Standards of Judicial Practice, Arraignment (1977) 7:04—(suggests that) cop rarely needed at **arraignment;**

CPCS P/G 2.3(a)—be alert to all opportunities for arraignment discovery;

Snow v Commonwealth **404 M 1007 (89)**—can use DA's hearsay to increase bail; (maybe rules should require an affidavit);

Prop.M.R.Evid. 1101—*(See Chapter 11, evidentiary rules don't apply to bail hearing)*;

See Chapter 3-C, Arrest without a Warrant, re: Gerstein v Pugh 420 US 103 (75) & motion to dismiss complaints without probable cause;

M.R.Crim.P. 7(a)(1): Reporter's Notes—counsel at arraignment. because motion to dismiss is possible;

District Court Standards of Judicial Practice, Arraignment (1977) 1:00, 6:00, 6:02—Dismissal = option at arraignment *(see Chapter 3)*; 6:01—If complaining witness or D.A. wants to "drop" charge(s), judge should: a) find out if "voluntary"; *(See also Chapter 14, Dismissal);* b) avoid criminal court for debt collection; *(See Chapter 21, re larceny)*; c) if D.A. won't proceed or nol pros, & not dismissal, "duty to enter 'not guilty'"

Snow v Commonwealth **404 M 1007 (89)**—judge had discretion to raise D's bail based on prosecutor's double hearsay about threats by D, although written statements of witness preferable;

Delaney v Commonwealth **415 M 490 (93)**—OK to raise bail on allegation of harassment of D's former wife (alleged victim in pending case) and OK to revoke bail altogether at subsequent court date, after testimony and fact-findings that D's continued release would seriously endanger her safety; no right to appeal to Superior Court when bail is revoked;

4-E. DEFAULT AND DEFAULT REMOVAL; CHANGE IN BAIL

G.L. c. 276, § 36—on reappearance, CAN remove default for good cause;

G.L. c. 276, § 82A—fail to appear: if for misdemeanor, fine of up to $10,000 and/or 1 year; if for felony, $50,000 and/or up to five years state prison or 2½ years house of correction;

G.L. c. 276, § 26—if D summonsed instead of arrested, failure to appear without reasonable cause = considered to be contempt; $20 fine;

Crosby v US **506 US 255 (93)**—federal rules prohibit trial in absentia where D not present at commencement of trial; midtrial flight distinguished; *(See Chapter 12-A(3), Presence of Defendant)*;

Sclamo v Commonwealth **352 M 576 (67)**—failure to appear = complaint, arraignment, due process (vs. contempt);

C v Sitko **372 M 305, 313 (77)**—when D failed to appear as ordered after 1-week stay of execution of sentence, judge increased sentence because D, inter alia, "took it upon himself to flee the jurisdiction"; but record silent re: reasons for failure to appear & even assuming "voluntary" absence, judge can't summarily punish for failure to appear;

C v Love **26 MAC 541 (88)**—"without lawful excuse" not vague; D's burden of production to shift burden of proof to DA; fear of unfair trial, etc. aren't excuses;

M.R.Crim.P. 6(d)—can impose costs and/or deposition if witness's "hardship";

District Court Standards of Judicial Practice, Pretrial Release (1977) 3:01-03—if DEFAULT, urge immediate forfeit, flight to avoid prosecution complaint, & maybe costs; 3:04—REMOVE & release, or maintain it (& new terms?);

C v Gomes **407 M 206 (90)**—tho M.R.Crim.P. 6(d)(1) allows "costs" assessment for expenses incurred as result of D's default, Reporter's Notes say "discretionary" and to be done only upon wilful default, and only as to costs which directly result therefrom; costs' assessment without hearing on "wilful"= improper, and also improper if don't reflect actual expenses: $50 here assessed, argued to "reflect( ) . . . fair value of (wasted) Dist. Ct. time," REJECTED: "Court personnel are not paid on a piecework basis, and defendants may not be charged as if they were"; D has right to counsel at hearing on wilfulness of default for nonpayment of fine where incarceration might result;

Matter of Scott **377 M 364 (79)**—(stip.#22): held D on default warrant though old case & complainant (wife) wants to drop charge;

C v Stuyvesant **366 M 611 (75)**—default removal & reinstatement of bail; (re: forfeiture of bail, see G.L. c. 276, §§ 71–78; & K. Smith, *Criminal Practice & Procedure,*

§§ 524-29 (2d ed. 1983 & Supp.)); *(See Chapter 2-E, re: confidentiality vs. revealing location of fugitive client)*;

***Commesso v Commonwealth* 369 M 368 (75)—can't change** bail **after probable cause hearing** without "changed circumstances";

***Magraw v Commonwealth* 429 M 1004 (99)**—rejecting D's argument that, **post-appellate reversal** of murder conviction, he was entitled to bail because he had been free on bail pre-trial; matter of discretion;

***Delaney v Commonwealth* 415 M 490 (93)**—OK to increase bail upon allegation that D harassed wife (subject of 'violating terms protective order' charge) while on personal recognizance, and OK to revoke bail after evidentiary hearing & finding that D would seriously endanger her safety: there is **no Superior Court review of bail revocation** and no requirement that Commonwealth initiate any additional criminal proceeding as a prerequisite to revocation;

D.Ct.P/R Stds. 2:01—don't EVER increase without changed circumstances; 2:02 nothing prohibits reduction if necessary; see also Snow 404 M 1007(89) can use DA's hearsay to increase bail; (maybe rules should require an affidavit);

4-F. BAIL APPEAL

G.L. c. 276, § 58—same day unless court determines not "practical"; any officer can transport D & papers to Superior Court; (See District Court form, "Statement of Reasons for Bail")

District Court Standards of Judicial Practice, Pre-trial Release (1977) 2:00—judges should resolve procedural problems re: bail appeals;

***Commesso v Commonwealth* 369 M 368 (75)**—heard de novo in Superior Court; (appellate procedures); under

G.L. c. 211 § 3 SJC single justice may review bail determinations under G.L. c. 276, § 58 AND the "full court" (SJC) has jurisdiction to review, on exceptions, report, or appeal, questions of law arising in a bail determination by a single justice;

G.L. c. 248, § 21—District Court or Superior Court judge can issue habeas for bail hearing;

G.L. c. 218, § 30—after District Court bound over to grand jury, Superior Court has bail jurisdiction;

4-G. SET HEARING DATE FOR TRIAL OR PROBABLE CAUSE HEARING

(See also Speedy Trial & Continuances in Chapter 7-N &7-O, Prepare Trial); CONSIDER motions to preserve specified evidence (but consider also whether such preservation will be harmful to D), e.g., turret tapes, diagrams, photos, rough notes & diagrams by police officers, IDs of witnesses not listed in official police reports, physical evidence which might be destroyed by certain forensic testing;

G.L. c. 276, § 35—if D "remains committed" pending trial, no continuance for more than thirty days if D objects (caselaw concerning § 35 utilizes pre-amendment limit of 10, rather than the now-applicable 30, days);

M.R.Crim.P. 46—don't count day of act (e.g., arraignment) or last day (unless Sat., Sun., holiday);

CPCS P/G 2.1(c)(2)—seek hearing within 30 days if D may be held; sanction for (previously applicable 10-day, now 30-day) violation = dismissal? (see ***Silva* 10 MAC 784 (80)**, ***Thomas* 353 M 429 (67)**);

***C v Ludwig* 370 M 31 (76)**—continued over 10 days & dismissed "with prejudice" = speedy trial basis, so bars indictment; 10-day violation (now "30", given revision of G.L. c. 276, § 35) = "presumptive prejudice" re: speedy (n.1);

***Ayala v Commonwealth* (SJC #85-298, 9/20/85, Wilkins)**—G.L. c. 211, § 3 relief where judge went beyond 10 days;

(See Chapter 21-CC re: drug analysis (delays); & Chapter 1 re: delays after probable cause hearings)

G.L. c. 211D, § 2A—new counsel entitled to continuance if judge initially denied D appointed counsel;

4-H. COMPETENCY, RESPONSIBILITY AND MENTAL HEALTH ISSUES

***C v Lyons* 426 M 466 (98)**—competency to stand trial: (1) present ability to consult with lawyer with reasonable degree of rational understanding **and** (2) rational as well as factual understanding of proceedings against him*(See Chapter 7-D& 7-G, competency of defendant, of witnesses)*;

CPCS P/G 2.1(d)—protect D's statutory/constitutional rights re: competency evaluation;

***Vuthy Seng v Commonwealth* 445 M 536 (2005)**—judge had discretion to allow Commonwealth's motion that D submit to second competency exam by expert cho-

sen by Commonwealth (after court-appointed expert said D not competent to stand trial), BUT SJC stresses at great length the protections required to prevent Fifth Amendment/Article 12 violations (e.g., "judge should order that evidence offered by the expert WILL NOT INCLUDE any incriminating statements, and any written report will be redacted, either by the expert or by the judge, before it is made available to the Commonwealth"); at n.12, SJC doesn't address "hypothetical point" argued by Commonwealth re: introduction by D of expert testimony based on exam other than Bridgewater State Hospital exam as being a waiver of any privilege;

G.L. c. 123, § 15(a)—D examined anytime when judge "doubts" competency or responsibility; (**BUT, despite statute's lumping of 'competency' with 'responsibility,' RESIST "responsibility" examinations, since that is matter of defense, not for judge**);

C v Brown **75 MAC 361 (2009)**—apparently purely because D counsel almost immediately questioned D's competency and asked court psychologist for competency screening, judge ordered § 15(b) exam for competency AND CRIMINAL RESPONSIBILITY; defense counsel "came into possession" of the latter report and "voluntarily supplied it to the Commonwealth" in plea negotiations; when subsequently D gave notice of defense of lack of criminal responsibility, Commonwealth then had right to examination by expert of its choosing, and could use the exam previously conducted;

C v Conaghan **433 M 105 (2000)**—G.L. c. 123, § 15(a) may be invoked "at any time" by a court of competent jurisdiction, and was here invoked by SJC in reviewing denial of a M.R.Crim.P. 30 motion to withdraw a guilty plea; allegations raised issue as to whether D, as "battered woman" was, at time of plea, capable of rationally consulting with lawyer & making voluntary decision; effect was to bypass rule barring indigent the funds to gather evidence in support of R.30 motion; case remanded to Superior Court for competency examination;

C v Hill **375 M 50 (78)**—competency hearing if substantial doubt; *(See Chapter 7-D)*;

C v Burkett **5 MAC 901 (77)**—not enough doubt for (D's) request for c. 123, § 15(a) examination;

Wagenmann v Adams **829 F.2d 196 (1st Cir. '87)**—upholds malpractice judgment of $50,000 (post-remittitur) against assigned counsel for improper Bridgewater State Hospital commitment under § 15(e);

C v Carrara **58 MAC 86 (2003)**—after D was found incompetent to stand trial, he was committed to state hospital, and recommitted pursuant to G.L. c. 123, § 16(c); judge had no authority, in order of recommitment, to restrict D's unsupervised access to hospital grounds; authority to impose restriction rested with hospital (G.L. c. 123, § 16(e));

Oliveira v Commonwealth **425 M 1004 (97)**—determination as to competency can be reviewed in normal appellate course, so no relief under G.L. c. 211, § 3;

C v DelVerde **398 M 288 (86)**—*(See Chapter 7-D)* no G. plea by incompetent D, even through guardian;

In re Hinnant **424 M 900 (97)**—if D = incompetent, he cannot (even) be rendited to other state on fugitive from justice warrant notwithstanding Commonwealth argument that only issues before court were whether papers were in order & D had been charged with crime;

C v Simpson **428 M 646 (99)**, *citing C v Hill* **375 M 50 (78)**—conviction of a guilty but incompetent D is a miscarriage of justice & violates due process (*Drope v Missouri* **420 US 162, 171-172 (75)**); discussion of pro-

ceedings when trial competency issue is first raised on appeal;

C v Goodreau **58 MAC 552 (2003)**—error to deny evidentiary hearing on motion for new trial five years after guilty plea when motion and affidavits alleged D's incompetence at time of G plea: supporting records disclosed bipolar disorder and major depression, possible underlying organic condition caused by alcohol or chemical toxicity (either job-related exposure or long-term alcoholism), suicide attempt before G plea;

District Court Standards of Judicial Practice, Arraignment (1977) 7:01—no hospital commitment without counsel representation; but see *Comm'r of Boston v. Commonwealth* **383 M 625 (81)** no *Blaisdell* **372 M 753 (77)** counsel right for G.L. c. 123, § 15 hearing; but see M.R.CrimP. 7(a), Reporter's Notes: need adequate opportunity to confer with counsel re: examination for competence;

Blaisdell v Commonwealth **372 M 753 (77)**—because of 5th Amendment, D's statements to criminal responsibility examiner = privileged, not to be given to DA; cf. Rule 14(b)(2)(B)(iii)—5th Amendment protections for criminal responsibility examination; G.L. c. 233, § 23B: §§ 15, 16 statements not admissible except on mental condition; cf. *Estelle v Smith* **451 US 454 (81)** *(Chapter 7-D)* 6th and 5th Amendment rights to counsel/warnings for D before competency examination—or statements will be inadmissible later;

C v Lamb **365 M 265 (74)**—G.L. c. 233, § 20B statements to psychotherapist can't be revealed for SDP commitment purposes unless patient was told that any communication made was NOT privileged;

C v Benoit **410 M 506, 517–20 (91)**—psychiatrist who conducted court-ordered competency examination permitted to testify at trial to rebut inaccuracies in testimony of D's psychiatrist, at least where D failed to assert psychiatrist-patient privilege;

C v Williams **30 MAC 543 (91)**—D's statements during court-ordered psychiatric examination were admissible at trial where D waived privilege by testifying about his mental state;

C v Delaney **404 M 1004 (89)**—judge had discretion to permit D to videotape psychiatric examination;

G.L. c. 123, § 15(b)—20 days (+20 extendable (routine at Bridgewater State Hospital)) if "reason to believe necessary"; Bridgewater State Hospital if male & if need maximum security; § 17(c) incompetent D may be released with or without bail; § 17(a) if incompetent D is determined after hearing to be competent, shall be returned to the custody of the court, but if D requests continued care/treatment during pendency of criminal proceedings &e superintendent or medical director agrees, court may order the further hospitalization of such person at the facility or Bridgewater State Hospital;

C v Sheriff **425 M 186 (97)**—**judge's mid-trial instruction, that D had been at Bridgewater State Hospital** voluntarily, was both untrue and strongly implied that D was there only to pad his "insanity" defense: reversal;

Bradley v Comm'r of Mental Health **386 M 363 (82)**—maximum security not justified;

Jackson v Indiana **406 US 715 (72)**—hospitalize only reasonable time to see if competent in near future; if not, need civil commitment;

G.L. c. 123, § 8—proceedings to commit dangerous persons; notice, hearing; G.L. c. 123, § 18(a) jailer (sheriff/superintendent) asks judge to hospitalize D;

G.L. c. 123, § 18(b)—D voluntarily admitted to hospital from jail;

G.L. c. 123, § 5(b)—if D asks, can stay & await trial for continued care;

G.L. c. 123, § 17(b)—allows counsel for incompetent D to obtain hearing before a judge with evidence & confrontation rights, so dismissal of criminal charges may be ordered if there is "lack of substantial evidence to support a conviction"; exempted from this option = defense of lack of criminal responsibility, and *Spero v Commonwealth* **424 M 1017 (97)** says no equal protection or confrontation violation on this basis;

G.L. c. 123, § 16(f)—court shall dismiss charges against incompetent D on day he would have been eligible for parole if given maximum sentence;

G.L. c. 123, § 9(b)—anyone petitions Superior Court for discharge of D from state hospital;

M.R.Crim.P. 10(c)—(judge may order as condition of granting continuance that testimony of a witness then present be taken & preserved for future use), M.R. Crim.P. 35—depositions for "exceptional circumstances" (e.g., to preserve helpful testimony during prolonged incompetence of D (D could later waive any objection to its occurring during his incompetence));

G.L. c. 123, § 12(e)—warrant of apprehension—District Court judge may commit up to 4 days if D shown to be mentally ill and to pose likelihood of serious harm;

4-I. MISCELLANEOUS ARRAIGNMENT AND BAIL PROBLEMS

4-I.1. Identification Issues

(Counsel's role & prophylactic measures)—*see Chapter 18* (CPCS P/G 2.2(b) (prevent I.D. opportunities), & *Moore v Illinois* **434 US 220 (77)** right to counsel at arraignment, e.g., to prevent ID;

4-I.2. Alcohol/Drug Offenses/Problems

See *C v Finnelli* **422 M 860 (96)** and *C v Chistolini* **422 M 854 (96)** permissible time between arrest & bail hearing tolled by intoxication (D must be capable of understanding bail proceeding and release conditions);

G.L. c. 111E—re: drug rehabilitation, stay, treatment, dismissal for drug "dependent";

District Court Standards of Judicial Practice, Arraignment (1977) 7:00—includes OUI; (in theory) request examination within 5 days;

Crimmins v Commonwealth **391 M 1004 (84)**—no G.L. c. 211, § 3 relief for denied G.L. c. 111E treatment;

(See Chapter 21, Common Crimes: Drugs; & Chapter 14, Dispositions);

4-I.3. "Alcoholic" Commitments

G.L. c. 123, § 35—30 days to approved facility (& voluntarily renewable) if hearing & find likelihood of serious harm; cop, doctor, relative, guardian, court official can petition.

4-I.4. Place of Confinement

G.L. c. 276, § 52A—pre-trial detainees transferred to other jails if DA approves OR Superior Court judge orders; if prior state time, can go to state prison;

MacDougall v Commonwealth **447 M 505 (2006)**—pretrial detainee's transfer from county jail to state correctional institution (including Cedar Junction or Souza-Baranowski) doesn't require judicial proceeding/court order if DA and commissioner of correction agree, and there is no provision in G.L. c. 276, § 52A for transfer to state institution by order of judge; if conditions of pretrial detention don't meet constitutional standards (no punishment prior to adjudication of guilt: *Brown v Commissioner* 394 M 89 [85]), remedy is to bring civil action against commissioner; N.B.: access to counsel for trial prep. cannot be abridged despite max. security confinement! 447 M at 512 n.12.

(See Chapter 14, Disposition: executed sentence (re: other transfers));

G.L. c. 127, § 117A—jail doctor's certificate gets D to hospital if needed;

CPCS P/G 2.3(f)—alert court to client's special needs, e.g., medical problems, & request court to order appropriate measures;

4-I.5. Pretrial Diversion

G.L. c. 276A & District Court Standards of Judicial Practice, Arraignment (1977) 7:02—technical "diversion" for D (17-22, no prior record, & would benefit from program); process (stay . . . dismissal);

CPCS P/G 2.1(c)(1)—admission to sufficient facts inadvisable at arraignment except rare case where adequate consultation & dispo (like dismissal) uniquely available;

(See Chapter 14-F, Dispositions: Continuances Without a Finding & Pre-trial Probation);

4-I.6. Mediation

G.L. c. 233, § 23C—statements to mediator = confidential;

(See Chapter 14-E, Dispositions: Pre-Trial Diversion & Mediation);

4-I.7. Civil Release for Cops

Civil Release for Cops in return for dismissal? *(See Chapter 14-B, Dismissal);*

4-I.8. Preserve Testimony

M.R.Crim.P. 10(c)—(Deposition) (judge may order as condition of granting continuance that testimony of a witness then present be taken & preserved for future use), M.R.Crim.P. 35—depositions for "exceptional circumstances";

(See Chapter 7, Continuance & Chapter 9, Cross-examination);

Probable Cause Hearing, i.e., prior statements— order cassette tape of probable cause hearing;

4-I.9. Begin Preparation

A.—copy court papers & seek police report (CPCS P/G 2.4);

B.—make appointment & exchange phone numbers (P/G 1.3(b)) with D;

C.—advise D re: 5th Amendment: *CPCS P/G 2.2(e): explain D's rights including 5th Amendment & Declaration of Rights, Article 12; **& tell D not to discuss case (OR ANY OTHER CASE OR CRIMINAL INVESTIGATION**: because see *C v Rainwater* **425 M 540 (97)** no relief from police interrogation of D, who had invoked right to counsel at arraignment, because **Miranda** said to be validly waived, & fruits of interrogation were used against D for crimes with which he had not yet been charged (tho such crimes were arguably overwhelmingly "related" to crime on which 6th Amendment right to counsel had been invoked); *Texas v Cobb* **532 US 162 (2001)** 6th Amendment invocation at arraignment doesn't bar police interrogation, without notice to counsel, about any crime which is not, on the "elements" test of *Blockburger v US* **284 US 229 (32)**, the "same" crime for which D has invoked counsel);

Watts v Indiana **338 US 49, 59 (49) (Jackson, J)**—any lawyer worth his salt will tell client not to talk (to police);

Weatherford v Bursey **429 US 545 (77)**—no violation of 6th Amendment for informant co-D to meet with D & D's counsel; BUT SEE *Maine v Moulton* **474 US 159 (85)** co-D = state "agent" & can't take info from D; state must use counsel as "medium"; *US v Henry* **447 US 264 (80)** (same); *(See Chapter 7-H, 5th Amendment & Chapter 20, Suppress);*

C v Manning **373 M 438 (77)**—dismissal for interfering with counsel right; v . . . ;

US v Mastroianni **749 F.2d 900 (1st Cir. '84)**— harmless & unintentional intrusion by co-D informant;

C v Mavredakis **430 M 848 (2000)**—police can't bar attorney from contact with suspect being interrogated; duty to inform suspect of attorney's efforts to render assistance is necessary to "actualize the abstract rights listed in Miranda v Arizona"; **Article 12 mandates broader protection from self-incrimination than does 5th Amendment under** *Moran v Burbine* **475 US 412 (86);**

ABA Standards for Criminal Justice, Prosecution Function & Defense Function (3d ed. 1993) 4-3.6— prompt advice about rights & actions to vindicate;

D.—advise re: witnesses *(See Chapter 10-C, Impeach D's Witnesses; Chapter 9-G, silence = prior inconsistent statement);* 1. avoid complaining witness *(see Chapter 2-H, Obstruct Justice or Influence Witness);* 2. ABA Standards for Criminal Justice, Prosecution Function & Defense Function (3d ed. 1993) 4-5.1(c) tell D to avoid communication with witnesses, except with approval of lawyer, & to avoid reality & appearance of any other improper activity; 3. SJC 3:07, 3.4(f): attorney can't discourage communication between witnesses & prosecution; 4. but cf., contra, *C v Brown* **11 MAC 288, 296 (81)**— (dictum) witnesses may have been told by counsel not to discuss case; otherwise impeachable by silence *(See Chapter 9-G);* e. document injuries (P/G 2.4): *such instruction by counsel as contemplated in Brown is prohibited: see C v Hart* **455 M 230 (2009),** *eliminating 4th "foundational" requirement of C v Brown;*

4-I.10. AIDS

G.L. c. 111, § 70E—right to confidentiality, "to the extent provided by law," of hospital records;

G.L. c. 111, § 70F—no testing for AIDS without written informed consent of patient (see *Langton v Comm'r of Correction* **34 MAC 564 (93));** no physician or health care provider shall disclose results of AIDS test or identify subject of such tests to anyone other than patient w/o written informed consent;

C v Maxwell **441 M 773 (2004)**—AIDS data = not immune from discovery under *Bishop-Fuller* (or other) protocol;

Globe Newspaper Co. v Chief Medical Examiner **404 Mass 132 (89)**—strong public policy favors confidentiality as to medical data about a person's body;

C v Martin **424 M 301 (97)**—"widespread ignorance about the nature of this disease (HIV/AIDS) and the accompanying prejudices against persons suffering from it or, as here, merely alleged to suffer from it, pose dangers to the accuracy and fairness of the legal process in many ways. See Court Management Issues and Guidelines, in AIDS and the Courts 189 (1990); National Judicial College & ABA AIDS Benchbook (1991)"; no relief afforded this D on basis of related issues at trial, however, in part due to lack of objection/request for instructions; judges are to be "alert to these dangers and take appropriate measures to guard against them";

Chapter 5
CONTENTS OF COMPLAINTS AND INDICTMENTS

See also Chapter 3-G, Hearings re: Issuance of Complaints; Chapter 1-G, Grand Jury (re: process & right to screening/finding elements); Chapter 14, Dispositions: Dismissals; & Chapter 6, Prepare Trial: Motions

---

5-A. IN GENERAL; FORMS

U.S. Constitution, Fifth Amendment -right to due process; Sixth Amendment—right to be informed of nature and cause of the accusation;

Mass. Constitution Declaration of Rights, Article 12—not answerable for crime unless fully/substantially/ plainly described;

CPCS P/G 2.4—get copy & carefully examine all court papers & police reports; seek preservation and discovery of evidence likely to become unavailable unless special measures are taken; where appropriate, e.g., turret tape ("911") recordings; 4.7(c) motion to dismiss for insufficient complaint/indictment;

G.L. c. 277, § 79—pleadings/forms re: indictments apply to complaints; forms = sufficient where apply, & similar ones OK for others if case & law allow; but see, e.g., *C v Lombard* **321 M 294 (47)**: disorderly statute amended (but form not amended);

C v Munoz **11 MAC 30 (80)**—OK complaint though not statutory form;

G.L. c. 277, §§ 18–39, 41–45—rules, definitions, etc. (e.g., larceny, receiving stolen property, drugs); § 37 EXCEPTION must be negative only if in law's enacting clause (see K. Smith, *Criminal Practice & Procedure*, § 726 (2d ed. 1983 & Supp.));

K. Smith, *Criminal Practice & Procedure*, **§§ 701 et seq. (2d ed. 1983 & Supp.)**—Form & Contents of Complaints/Indictments, Amendments,);

M.R.Crim.P. 4—indictment/complaint has caption & plain, concise description of the act constituting the crime or appropriate legal description;

See Chapter 5-G, re crimes which are vaguely charged because two or more statutes, with different penalty provisions, govern the charged conduct;

C v Fernandes **430 M 517 (99)**—indictment of two pages, with 1st page "count" charging new drug offense and 2d page "count" simply alleging a prior conviction: "count" 2 not a separate crime, but simply notifies D of sentence enhancement (& sufficient notice given by words "having been previously convicted of a similar offense," though better practice = specify date of prior offense and date and court in which prior conviction was obtained);

Bynum v Commonwealth **429 M 705 (99): G.L. c. 94C, § 32A(d)**—does not create an independent crime (having been convicted of a like drug offense previously), but is instead a sentencing enhancement provision;

Apprendi v New Jersey **530 US 466 (2000)**—after D's conviction by jury for shooting into someone's home, prosecutor asked for enhanced sentence because offense was "committed with a biased purpose," as described in applicable statute; D reserved right to challenge any 'hate crime sentence enhancement on the ground that it violates the U.S. Constitution"; though judge held evidentiary hearing on issue of "purpose" in shooting (& D testified), judge found by preponderance of evidence that D did act with racial bias motivation, so applied sentence enhancement; Supreme Court HELD that motivation factor NOT just sentencing issue, but was element of the crime, had to be included in charging document, proved beyond reasonable doubt, and be subject of jury trial unless D waived right; "it is unconstitutional for a legislature to remove from the jury the assessment of facts that increase the pre-scribed range of penalties to which a criminal defendant is exposed"; fact that state legislature placed its hate crime sentence 'enhancer 'within the sentencing provisions' of the criminal code' does not mean that the finding of a bi-ased purpose to intimidate is not an essential element of the offense; (BUT cf *C v Bruno* **432 M 489, 500 (2000)** legislature's statements in act's "preamble" to effect that sexually dangerous persons were to be committed for "care, custody, treatment and rehabilitation" and that pur-pose was "to protect . . . vulnerable members of commu-nity" cited as support for rejecting argument that act was "punitive" and thus, as to certain targets, was a prohibited "ex post facto" law);

G.L. c. 276, § 22—upon complaint to judge (clerk) he shall reduce to writing *(See Chapter 3-G)*;

C v Barhight **9 Gray 113 (1857)**—sign blank com-plaint = bad; "looseness & carelessness in instituting crim-inal process not to be encouraged";

C v Murphy **415 M 161 (93)**—statute allowed convic-tion on proof of any 1 of 3 intents, but indictment alleged all 3 intents (by careless use of "and" rather than "or"); no error in allowing "amendment" to clarify the theory of guilt relied upon at trial; Cf. *C v Brogan* **415 M 169 (93)** injunction forbidding doing X & Y is violated by doing either X or Y;

C v McLoon **5 Gray 91 (1855)**—forms & technical rules oughtn't be "lightly disregarded or negligently re-laxed";

C v Walters **12 MAC 389 (81)**—undesirable to in-clude alias unless necessary element or to identify D;

C v Sheline **391 M 279 (84)**—& should delete (hear-say) alias in drug certificate;

US v Grayson **166 F.2d 863, 867 (2d Cir. '48)**—alias "can serve no purpose but to arouse suspicion that the ac-cused is a person who has found it useful or necessary to conceal his identity";

C v Fetzer **19 MAC 1024, 1025 (85)**—for false name to be admissible as evidence of consciousness of guilt, its use must follow rather than precede the crime;

C v Barbosa **421 M 547 (95)**—indictment defective for "duplicity," the charging of separate offenses in a sin-gle count; must be assured that petit jury G is for precise transaction on which grand jury voted to indict;

C v Crowder **49 MAC 720 (2000)**—grand jury heard evidence of four separate acts of forcible penetration, but returned only one indictment for aggravated rape; *Barbosa* **421 M 547** ground for relief said to be inapplicable given nature of crime of rape;

C v Dingle **73 MAC 274 (2008)**—indictments charg-ing D with violating G.L. c. 272, § 29B by either distribut-ing or possessing with intent to distribute visual material containing representation of state of nudity OR act that depicts/represents sexual conduct of a child under age eighteen held to present no "Barbosa" error, rationale be-ing that the proscribed acts are not "separate crimes," but are instead "different means of committing the same of-fense";

C v Spencer **53 MAC 45 (2001)**—grand jury heard evidence of two drug sales by D, but returned indictments as to only one sale (distribution, & same sale, school zone); appellate court held that precise testimony & refer-ence to distance of sale from a school (for enhanced school zone charge) made it clear that indictment was based upon sale to cop rather than sale to prostitute;

See Chapter 1-C for cases on substantive defects in presentation before grand jury;

See Chapter 3-F for cases on formal defects in com-plaints;

5-B. FAILURE TO ALLEGE AN OFFENSE OR STATE A CRIME

C v Palladino **358 M 28 (70)**—sentencing on indict-ment charging no crime violates due process; must allege all elements directly or by implication, even judicially-required ones (like scienter re: obscene material);

G.L. c. 277, § 37—if exception/excuse not in statute or form, its absence need not be alleged; if form doesn't have exception/excuse, it's not necessary;

C v Sokorelis **254 M 454 (26)**—unrelated = element of accessory (though a negative); NG because not proven;

C v Cooper **264 Mass 378 (28)**—arson indictment worthless without "wilful/malicious";

C v Lombard **321 M 294 (47)**—"accosting" com-plaint saying "offensive" = inadequate because statute amended to read "and disorderly";

C v Bacon **374 M 358 (78)**—though knowledge = element of carry firearm, need not allege it; unlike *Pal-ladino* **358 M 28**, because gun's obvious (but see statute);

C v Sepulveda **6 MAC 868 (78)**—"unlawful" (posses-sion with intent to distribute) alleged "knowing";

Sullivan v Ward **304 M 614 (39)**—statutory exception part of definition; party pleadings must allege and prove inapplicable;

C v Donoghue **23 MAC 103 (86)**—need not allege exact words of statute; may set forth by implication; may-hem indictment OK because alleged knife slashed face, so implied (the element of) actual disfigurement/serious injury;

C v Green **399 M 565 (87)**—some common law terms, e.g., assault, battery, larceny, murder are short-hand for distinct elements, & common law terms OK without precise elements; indecent A&B complaint OK without element lack of consent because implicit in definitions of indecent A&B;

C v Soule **6 MAC 973 (79)**—conspiracy/drug laws need not say which (though penalty depends on it); solu-tion = bill of particulars;

C v Senior **454 M 12 (2009)**—D's claim that indictment for "attempted subornation of perjury" was defective because it failed to allege an "overt act" was considered on appeal (though not raised below) because "whether an indictment fails to allege a fact necessary to constitute an offense is a matter of jurisdiction";

G.L. c. 277, § 20—need not allege time/place unless essential; caption's alleged time means before indictment, after it's a crime, & within statue of limitations;

C v King **387 M 464 (82)**—date/time not essential; "divers dates" = OK and no harm because no bill of particulars sought *(See Chapter 5-C, Bill of Particulars (& Vague Complaints/Indictments))*; but *C v Pillal* **445 M 175 (2005)**—even though bill of particulars WAS sought and returned and D had prepared/presented evidence to refute claim of assault on particularized date, no relief for "discrepancy"/change in complainant's testimony;

C v O'Connell **432 M 657, 660–61 (2000)**—indictment for posing child in state of nudity (G.L. c. 272, § 29A) needn't name child; absent showing of prejudice, no relief; D here had grand jury minutes naming child, and D-opening statement referred to child by name, so no surprise;

C v Hrycenko **417 M 309 (94)**—no error in denying motion to dismiss four identically—worded indictments charging child sex assault **on ground of inadequate notice**, citing G.L. c. 277, § 47A and failure to move for bill of particulars; convictions reversed on related double jeopardy ground, however;

C v Clancy **261 M 345 (27)**—location not essential, & caption alleges venue *(See Chapter 1)*; *(see C v Tolliver 74 M 386 (1857), OK to prove Chelsea assault though complaint said Boston because same county & not essential element: see Chapter 5-D, Variance & Lesser-Included Offenses)*;

See also Chapters 5-C, Bill of Particulars & Chapter 5-F, Amendments re: time/date;

Garvey v Commonwealth **8 Gray 382 (1857)**—must allege '2nd or subsequent' (G.L. c. 278, § 11A); but see *C v Crocker* **384 M 353 (81)** need not allege common/notorious thief; see also *C v Fernandes* **430 M 517 (99)** & *Bynum v Commonwealth* **429 M 705 (99)**, at *(Chapter 5-A, Complaints/Indictments, In General)*, above;

5-C. BILL OF PARTICULARS (AND VAGUE COMPLAINTS/INDICTMENTS)

G.L. c. 277, § 34—no dismissal if indictment/complaint lets D understand charge & prepare defense, or if lacks information obtainable with bill of particulars;

K. Smith, *Criminal Practice & Procedure,* **§§ 1289–98 (2d ed. 1983 & Supp.)**—purpose of bill of particulars isn't like "interrogatories"; file within Rule 13 deadlines; read to jury, so move to strike them if irrelevant & prejudicial;

C v Snyder **282 M 401 (33)**—bill of particulars can be read to jury;

C v Deagle **10 MAC 563 (80)**—denial of bill of particulars (because late-filed) confused trial, sentencing (& appeal);

C v Sinclair **195 M 100 (07)**—(since G.L. c. 277, § 34,) remedy for lack of notice (of alleged abortion instrument) = bill of particulars, not dismissal; constitutional right to bill of particulars re: expected proof though D knows evidence & though grand jury needn't specify it;

C v Baker **368 M 58 (75)**—constitutional right; liberal rule, but no straightjacket; no harm here because discovery warned of evidence (of various larcenies);

C v Brien **67 MAC 309 (2006)**—citation in complaint only to the statutory section with **penalty** provisions would have violated art. 12, BUT adequate notice was given by language, "knowingly and willfully" and "defendant was given several payments to start a sun-room and never did, contrary to . . . G.L. c. 142A";

C v DePace **442 M 739 (2004)**—indictment for "murder" charges first-degree, rather than second-degree, murder, and needn't allege each theory of murder which the grand jury determined to be supported by probable cause;

no relief, either, on argument that first trial jury's G was only under extreme atrocity or cruelty (and not deliberate premeditation), and no way of knowing whether this was a ground found by grand jury beforehand;

C v Garner **59 MAC 350 (2003)**—Commonwealth not required to specify in bill of particulars "the type of murder it intends to prove nor theory under which it intends to proceed"; pretrial record here purportedly doesn't indicate deliberate misleading/subterfuge, but instead that "prosecution's case . . . remained open and in evidentiary development";

Russell v US **369 US 749 (62)**—contempt indictment too vague without particulars (re: Congress's questions which D wouldn't answer); bill of particulars no cure because grand jury must define crime;

C v Barbosa **421 M 547 (95)**—indictment defective for "duplicity," the charging of separate offenses in a single count; must be assured that petit jury 'guilty' is for precise transaction on which grand jury voted to indict; motion for bill of particulars wouldn't have solved; preserved here by motion to dismiss alleging, inter alia, "duplicity";

C v Smiley **431 M 477 (2000)**—there was only one indictment for armed assault in dwelling, but there were two occupants (& this crime is properly measured by # of assaults); Commonwealth wasn't required to bring 2 indictments or charge in separate counts; Barbosa ground for relief = wholly ignored; *C v Crowder* **49 MAC 720 (2000)** grand jury heard evidence of four separate acts of forcible penetration, but returned only one indictment for agg.

rape; Barbosa ground for relief said to be inapplicable given nature of crime of rape;

C v Leavitt **17 MAC 585 (84)**—bill of particulars advised D of charge (contempt/obstruct grand jury by withholding evidence), in part because no variance between bill of particulars & grand jury evidence; but fatal variance between bill of particulars & broader instructions by judge to jury; cf. *Connor v Commonwealth* **363 M 572 (73)** DA can't amend "John Doe" indictment (though law permits) because grand jury didn't indict D (though maybe heard evidence against D) *(See Chapter 5-F, Amendments to Complaints/Indictments)*;

M.R.Crim.P. 13 (b)—pretrial motion for bill of particulars = discretionary; "necessary & reasonable" notice of "the crime charged", e.g., time, place, manner, or means; DA can amend if material variance & justice requires;

C v Benjamin **3 MAC 604 (75)**—if inadequate bill of particulars, file motion for further particulars; if immaterial/prejudicial, move to strike (judge's discretion) because "particulars" are read to jury;

Note well: *C v Freitas* **59 MAC 903 (2003)**—*failure of indictment to specify dates of alleged crimes (i.e., on "divers dates") did not excuse D's failure to give notice of "alibi" witness* (whose testimony, that he habitually saw D at a bakery early in the morning at a time when D could not have been elsewhere committing assaults, was struck, permissibly, as sanction for reciprocal discovery violation);

C v Soule **6 MAC 973 (79)**—should've sought further particulars; (see also Deagle 10 MAC 563 (80));

C v Hrycenko **417 M 309 (94)**—should have sought bill of particulars to better understand six identically worded indictments charging child sex assaults; see also *C v Daughtry* **417 M 136 (94)** failure to press for further bill of particulars when bill stated murder was by any/all means by which it could be committed; Commonwealth relied at trial on the alternative theory that D was joint venturer rather than principal who fired shot; no relief;

C v Santiago **50 MAC 762, 764 (2001)**—at retrial after appellate reversal, given explicit direction by SJC, no error/relief from Comm's "expanded" culpability theory at retrial, i.e., not necessarily that D fired shot killing innocent bystander, but that D's engaging in shootout on street w/other man made both shooters responsible for death, regardless of who fired fatal shot;

C v Gichel **48 MAC 206 (99)**—indictment charged 6 rapes, but no one noticed that bill of particulars described particular type of sex act charged in only 5 of them; jury during deliberations questioned this, were told to "rely on their collective memories" re what was charged in 6th indictment; appellate court gave no relief, cited *C v Kirkpatrick* **423 M 436, 439–44 (96)** (when child testifies to continuous/repetitive pattern of differing types of sex abuse but "otherwise sp(eaks) in generalities," no requirement that Commonwealth "specify the exact acts on which each count rest(s)"), & found jurors aware of unanimity requirement;

C v Apalakis **396 M 292 (85)**—judge narrowed bill of particulars (like required finding of not guilty) before gave to jury;

C v Ries **337 M 565 (58)**—bill of particulars can't enlarge indictment scope to new offense;

C v Burns **8 MAC 194 (79)**—bill of particulars no cure for complaint without essential element; *(See Chapter 5-D)*;

C v Cantres **405 M 238 (89)**—indictment for conspiracy to violate controlled substances act need not specify provision violated, although D is entitled to bill of particulars as to substantive violation alleged; bill of particulars can't save defective indictment;

C v Whitehead **379 M 640 (80)**—if grand jury evidence differs from bill of particulars, it's waived unless D raises; no variance here because "intercourse" included cunnilingus & bill of particulars included "dual theory" of joint venture with male;

C v Burke **339 M 521 (59)**—must state charge with as much certainty as known circumstances permit;

C v Kozlowsky **238 M 379 (21)**—dicta: D entitled to (larceny of motor vehicle) owner's name, but OK because got it by bill of particulars;

C v O'Connell **432 M 657, 660–61 (2000)**—indictment for posing child in state of nudity (G.L. c. 272, § 29A) needn't name child; absent showing of prejudice, no relief; D here had grand jury minutes naming child, and D-opening statement referred to child by name, so no surprise;

C v Wainio **1 MAC 866 (74)**—B&E need not specify the felony; no harm if bill of particulars not asked (see *Hobbs* **385 M 863 (82)** G though indictment said B&E/larceny and instruction said 'any felony'; specification was surplusage, and harmless);

Regan v Commonwealth **415 M 376 (93)**—no error in refusing bill of particulars to specify what misdemeanor in B&E with intent to commit misdemeanor;

C v Iannello **344 M 723 (62)**—bill of particulars binds DA; but doesn't junk an OK indictment;

C v Benjamin **358 M 672 (71)**—OK indictment not dismissed for variance from bill of particulars;

C v Lussier **333 M 83 (55)**—because filed by DA, bill of particular amendments = more liberal; OK if not enlarging indictment's scope (especially without timely objection);

C v Jervis **368 M 638 (75)**—DA can amend (larceny of motor vehicle to 3 weeks earlier) because time not essential (to grand jury) and no harm because D didn't seek continuance or clarification of bill of partics (sought for both charges, but answered only for companion charge (having different date));

C v King **387 M 464 (82)**—no harm from "divers dates" indictment because no bill of particulars sought;

C v American News **333 M 74 (55)**—required finding of not guilty because no proof offense (in time period) as alleged in bill of particulars; could've amended, but didn't;

C v Dineen **70 MAC 1, 10–11 (2007)**—three abuse prevention order violations upheld by reference to inferences and "common knowledge" that Father's Day falls in mid-June;

See also Chapter 5-B & Chapters 5-D & 5-F, re: date/time;

C v Edelin **371 M 497 (76)**—bill of particulars like indictment & DA must prove; variance issue = "prejudice", 3 judges say "yes" & 3 "no" re: instructions different from bill of partics. (re: alleged time of abortion death) (see also *Leavitt* **17 MAC 585 (84)**, above);

C v Montanino **409 M 500 (91)**—open question whether due process ever requires that bill of particulars specify precise dates of child sexual assaults;

C v Erazo **63 MAC 624 (2005)**—reverses dismissal of complaint for sexual assaults upon complainant for failure to provide, in bill of particulars, precise dates of such assaults over a three-month period (complaint was issued on 11/26/02, and offenses allegedly occurred between 7/15/02 and 10/15/02);

C v Pillal **445 M 175 (2005)**—even though bill of particulars WAS sought and returned and D had prepared/presented evidence to refute claim of assault on particularized date, no relief for "discrepancy"/change in complainant's testimony;

C v LaCaprucia **429 M 440 (99)**—43 indictments charging sexual assaults on children, but required findings of not guilty were allowed on 22 indictments and judge then "reordered the indictment numbers to insulate the defendant from any prejudicial inference that the jury might draw from nonsequential indictment numbers"; such "reordering" became "source of the almost impenetrable confusion that followed"; jurors questioned how they could distinguish among the identically worded indictments and verdict slips, and were told to make notations on each verdict slip to "assist the court in knowing exactly what incident it was that you were voting on"; despite these factors AND reversal of convictions resulting from 1st trial, SJC purported to find basis on which to avoid *Hrycenko* **417 M 309, 316–17 (94)** dismissal, i.e., inability to determine which incidents were the ones on which first jury returned not guilty verdicts, so double jeopardy prohibition prevented retrial on any of the charges after the convictions which resulted from the 1st trial were reversed on appeal;

Chambers v Commonwealth **421 M 49 (95)**—providing no relief on interlocutory appeal of denial of pretrial motion to dismiss, but warning prosecutors of hazards of failing to be more specific than "on diverse dates";

5-D. VARIANCE AND LESSER-INCLUDED OFFENSES (LIOS)

See also Chapter 19, Double Jeopardy, and Chapter 12-G, Motion for Required Finding of Not Guilty

K. Smith, *Criminal Practice & Procedure*, **Chapter 14E(1), §§ 735–42 (overview) (2d ed. 1983 & Supp.);**

G.L. c. 277, § 35—not NG for variance if essential elements proven & no prejudice (e.g., immaterial mistake describing property or owner);

Cole v State of Arkansas **333 US 196 (48)**—due process violation if proof of different law from indictment; can't imprison on charge not made;

C v Murphy **415 M 161 (93)**—indictment properly asserted all 3 ways ("and" rather than "or") statutory crime could be committed; no error in 'amending' by specifying the one such way proved at trial;

C v Watkins **33 MAC 7 (92)**—D not entitled to dismissal of rape conviction simply because he was acquitted on separate identically worded indictment (same date, same victim, several penetrations); D should have moved for bill of particulars;

C v Snow **269 M 598 (30)**—similar tests for amend *(Chapter 5-F, Amendments, Chapter 19, variance, & double jeopardy)*;

G.L. c. 277 § 20—need not allege time & place unless "essential" element;

C v Manooshian **326 M 514 (50)**—guilty (though sale (of booze) = months before date specified) because within 6 years (statute of limitations) of complaint;

C v Bougas **59 MAC 368 (2003)**—statute of limitations is affirmative defense which must be raised or will be deemed waived; purporting therefore to reserve question whether, when particular crime charged is made within the statute of limitations, but the lesser crime of which D was convicted after trial, would have been barred by statute of limitations, relief (required finding of not guilty?) is necessary; QUERY: HOW CAN THIS ISSUE BE RAISED PRIOR TO TRIAL? It can't/won't because D isn't likely to want to relinquish option of lesser included offense at trial; *but see C v Bougas* **59 MAC at 372** (danger of DA overcharging to avoid statute of limitations on appropriate charge);

C v Megna **59 MAC 511 (2003)**—though indictment said extortion (obtaining money by threats of harm) re: one victim was between January 1991 and March 1991, proof [and jury instruction] was for timeframe of January 1988 to April 1991: no relief because date not essential element, notwithstanding D's argument that it was a "continuing offense" for which specified time period was essential; "continuing offense" is "an indivisible unlawful general practice that exists throughout the time span alleged," and doesn't refer to a discrete criminal act occurring between two dates; D knew before trial what proof was (bill of particulars), and can't claim prejudice;

C v Tivnon **8 Gray 375 (1857)**—date not essential; can prove any date before indictment (if within statute of limitations) though one's alleged;

C v Day **387 M 915 (83)**—same; 2 day uncertainty immaterial & no prejudice because no alibi and D admits presence; Cf *C v Ramos* **47 MAC 792, 796–97 (99)** though D argued that it was only speculative whether alleged sexual assaults (reported almost 3 years after they allegedly stopped) occurred after D reached the age of seventeen (and Superior Court prosecution was thus barred by G.L. c. 119, § 74, juvenile court instead necessary), Court held that jurors were made aware that it was "of critical significance" that the alleged crimes occurred on or after particular date, and that evidence was sufficient to make such a finding beyond a reasonable doubt;

C v Runge **231 M 598 (19)**—date essential for "continuing offense" (phony doctor), so fatal variance for proof outside allegations;

C v Ramirez **69 MAC 9 (2007)**—in prosecution for "knowingly failing to register" as sex offender, Commonwealth can't meet burden merely by establishing that knowledge was available to D (e.g., if he had happened to look in newspapers); if Commonwealth had relied on theory that after receiving notice (by arrest) that he was required to register, result could have been different IF complaint listed a range of dates instead of only the date of arrest; furthermore, there was no evidence that on day of arrest, D received notice of registration requirement, and complaint didn't issue until day following arrest;

C v Woods **382 M 1 (80)**—new trial because D in jail on "likely" date of rape (no discussion of time/date issue);

See also Chapter 5-B & 5-F, re: time/date;

C v Stone **300 M 160 (38)**—fatal variance to allege abortion by "instrument" but only prove "by unknown means";

C v Azer **308 M 153 (41)**—same; variance NG where D sold booze to X, but complaint said to Y; can re-try, however, for selling to X;

C v Ohanian **373 M 839 (77)**—NG because bad checks drawn on different bank from indictment because different offence & D prejudiced; but can re-indict;

C v Mandile **403 M 93 (88)**—took object (beer/soda can) not proof of robbery taking 'money';

C v Tolliver **74 M 386 (1857)**—OK to prove Chelsea assault though complaint said Boston because same county & not essential element; (see *Clancy* **261 M 345 (27)** location not essential and caption alleges venue);

C v Daughtry **417 M 136 (94)**—OK to rely, as alternative to D firing fatal shot, on theory of D being joint venturer with another person firing shot; indictment form for murder = sufficient to charge by whatever means and bill of particulars said "by any and all manner & means by which . . . crime( ) could be committed";

C v Santiago **50 MAC 762, 764 (2001)**—at retrial after appellate reversal, given explicit direction by SJC, no error/relief from Comm's "expanded" culpability theory at retrial, i.e., not necessarily that D fired shot killing innocent bystander, but that D's engaging in shootout on street w/other man made both shooters responsible for death, regardless of who fired fatal shot;

C v Kalinowski **360 M 682 (71)**—need not prove owner alleged in B & E charge so long as proof D's not the owner; (cf. G.L. c. 278, § 9);

C v Souza **397 M 236 (86)**—alleged (larceny) owner immaterial/unessential; so G though not proven (but maybe NG if different owner proven);

C v Armenia **4 MAC 33 (76)**—though not necessary to allege what crime's intended with burglary tool, once alleged (to steal from car) it must be proven; NG because facts look like car theft was intended; but cf. *C v Aldrich* **23 MAC 157 (86)** G though instruction (burglarious tool if intend any crime) incorrect (because charge said larceny); no prejudice because evidence only showed intent to commit larceny;

C v Collardo **13 MAC 1013 (82)**—NG because burglar's tool indictment didn't allege master key part of statute or intent/steal car (vs. from it) as proven;

C v Hobbs **385 M 863 (82)**—G though indictment alleged B & E/larceny & instruction said "any felony" because harmless & surplusage (see *Wainio* **1 MAC 866 (74)**);

C v Randolph **415 M 364 (93)**—same; indictment charged B&E, intent to murder and instruction said B&E, intent to murder or commit A&B, dangerous weapon; cf. *Rogan v Commonwealth* **415 M 376 (93)**—no error in refusing bill of particulars re what misdemeanor in B&E, intent to commit misdemeanor;

C v Rider **8 MAC 775 (79)**—NG for carrying firearm in vehicle because (arrested) D = in cruiser involuntarily & not charged with carrying on person (statute since amended);

G.L. c. 278, § 12—can be NG on part of felony & G of residue if "substantially charged"; *(See also Chapter 19-B, re: lesser-included offenses)*;

C v Gosselin **365 M 116 (74)**—though attempt = "lesser" offense to indictment for completed (escape), it's not included because essential element (overt act other than completion) not alleged, so required finding of NG; though G.L. c. 278, § 12 = felony, common-law permits lesser included offenses for misdemeanor; no jeopardy, so new complaint OK;

C v Burns **8 MAC 194 (79)**—(same); bill of particulars can't cure missing essential element;

C v Senior **454 M 12 (2009)**—D's claim that indictment for "attempted subornation of perjury" was defective because it failed to allege an "overt act" was considered on appeal (though not raised below) because "whether an indictment fails to allege a fact necessary to constitute an offense is a matter of jurisdiction"; relevant statute, however, G.L. c. 268, § 3 is type of attempt crime where crime itself and overt act are one and the same, so no relief (if D wanted more info, should have requested particulars);

C v Dean **109 M 349 (1872)**—D entitled to instruction that can't convict of lesser included offense (assault vs. rape) unless factually connected to rape indictment;

C v Dellinger **383 M 780 (81)**—QUERY: find G. of conspiracy: larceny over $100 on indictment for conspire: rob because it's lesser included offense??;

C v Saia **18 MAC 762 (84)**—conspiracy to commit unarmed robbery = lesser included offense of conspiracy to armed robbery;

C v Tilley **327 M 540 (51)**—G. of accessory: larceny = OK on indictment alleging accessory: B&E with intent to commit larceny because it's lesser included offense;

C v Bynoe **49 MAC 687 (2000)**—no relief though D was convicted of "lesser" crime which was not a lesser included offense (use without authority isn't lesser included of receiving stolen motor vehicle); D was expressly invited to challenge the instruction and seemed to be aware that it wasn't lesser included, but didn't object;

C v Robinson **26 MAC 441 (88)**—if not charged, can't instruct & convict on greater offense; but no harm resentencing on the lesser included offense originally charged;

C v Williams **73 MAC 833 (2009)**—following jury-waived trial (misdemeanor motor vehicle homicide by operating while under the influence; operating to endanger), judge said NG of motor vehicle homicide by operating under influence and G of operating to endanger but also "guilty of vehicular homicide by negligent operation"; later, the judge ordered that – instead of recording a new count on the complaint - the homicide crime was to be recorded as an amendment "of form" to operating to endanger complaint: error, as it was amendment of substance AND could not have been found within vehicle homicide complaint either; though same statute set forth both homicide by OUI and by negligent operation, text of complaint charged ONLY the OUI form; bill of particulars could not expand essential elements not charged in complaint, allegation of 'no prejudice' rejected;

C v Porro **74 MAC 676, further app. review allowed 455 M 1106 (2009)**—in responding to deliberating jury's question whether D could be convicted on "lesser" offense of assault by means of dangerous weapon on indictment charging assault and battery by means of dangerous weapon, judge said yes, but committed reversible error in failing to limit jury's consideration on lesser charge to the single act on which grand jury relied; MAC permitted retrial on lesser included offense of assault by means of dangerous weapon under "attempted battery theory" (noting at n.4 that "it is less clear" that "threatened battery theory" of assault by means of dangerous weapon is a lesser included of ABDW);

C v Johnson **75 MAC 903 (2009)**—D was convicted of both "trafficking" and possession with intent to distribute, the latter being enhanced for sentencing because it was a "second or subsequent", D receiving 3–5 sentence on trafficking, but 5 to 5& a day on possession with intent; convictions were duplicative; ordinarily, result would be to dismiss "lesser" offense, but here "lesser" carried the longer sentence (lesser included offense = one with fewer elements, and "having been previously convicted" is NOT an "element" but is instead a sentencing enhancement); HERE, remand for trial judge to decide which to vacate & which judgment to "affirm";

See Chapter 5-B, re: variance from bill of particulars;

See Chapter 19-A & 19-B for cases on double jeopardy, duplicity & related remedies;

C v Martin **425 M 718 (97)**—ABDW **is** lesser included offense of "2d branch" of mayhem (G.L. c. 265, § 14) though **not** of 1st branch;

C v Pizzotti **27 MAC 376 (89)**—judge may instruct on lesser included over D's objection if evidence gives basis for convicting D only of lesser offense;

C v Matos **36 MAC 958 (94)**—(same);

C v Woodward **427 M 659 (98)**—where evidence permits finding lesser included offense, judge **must**, upon request by either side, so instruct; D has no "veto" power re: this;

C v Vasquez **27 MAC 655 (89)**—Commonwealth not entitled to lesser included instruction over D's objection unless element distinguishing lesser from greater crime is in dispute;

C v Henry **37 MAC 429 (94)**—lesser offense of simple rape proper where cross-examination of complainant in aggravated rape called into question presence of dangerous weapon;

C v Connolly **49 MAC 424 (2000)**—very fact that jury had to determine, in circumstances, whether shod foot was dangerous weapon (in ABDW prosecution) meant that D was entitled to lesser included offense of simple A&B, so ABDW conviction was reversed; D was also charged with A&B (presumably, for "punching" during same fracas), but failure of judge to charge that convictions on both had to be based on separate acts meant that D couldn't be retried (on remand after reversal of the ABDW) for A&B; (D could, however, be sentenced for the A&B conviction already obtained, but placed on file);

C v Nardone **406 M 123 (89)**—in assault to murder trial, instruction on lesser of assault to kill was error where there was no evidence of mitigation;

***Ariel A. v Commonwealth* 420 M 281 (95)**—voluntary manslaughter not lesser included offense of murder because not **necessarily** included within; manslaughter finding depends on evidence establishing additional factor, i.e., reasonable provocation sufficient in law to mitigate an unlawful killing;

C v Clark **432 M 1, 21 (2000)**—here, no evidence justifying charge on lesser offense of manslaughter during first degree murder prosecution;

C v Dixon **34 MAC 653 (93)**—A&B not, in law, lesser included offense of attempted murder by strangulation, but Court allowed instead G of simple assault;

C v Donovan **422 M 349 (96)**—A&B not, in law, lesser-included of felony murder; A&B **is** lesser-included of 2d degree murder, but no substantial risk of miscarriage of justice on this evidence in omitting instruction on lesser-included offense;

C v Selby **426 M 168 (97)**—involuntary manslaughter not lesser included offense of felony murder; word "accidental" is of no consequence if felony is inherently dangerous to life;

C v Thayer **418 M 130 (94)**—statutory rape is lesser included offense of forcible rape of child;

C v LeFave **407 M 927 (90)**—indecent A&B on child is not lesser of child rape because lack of consent = element of former (BUT G.L. c. 265, § 113B was amended in 1986 to provide that child under 14 is legally incapable of consent to indecent A&B);

C v Traynor **40 MAC 527 (96)**—neither indecent A& B of person 14 or older nor simple A&B is lesser included offense of indecent A&B on person under 14; former crimes have as element lack of consent;

C v Walker **426 M 301 (97)**—where there is no dispute that V is under 14, indecent A&B under 14 is lesser included offense of forcible rape under 16;

C v Foskette **30 MAC 384 (91)**—indecent A&B over 14 was lesser included of aggravated rape, but not of child rape;

C v Ruggiero **32 MAC 964 (92)**—D not entitled to charge on lesser included of simple drug possession where she had been indicted only for separate sale; possession with intent to distribute dismissed because duplicitous with distribution;

C v Ahart **37 MAC 565 (94)**—D not entitled to lesser offense instruction re: larceny from person on unarmed robbery indictment involving purse snatch ("snatching of a purse necessarily involves the use of force");

C v Lopez **31 MAC 547 (91)**—conviction for duplicitous lesser included cannot be placed on file or given concurrent sentence; must instead be dismissed;

C v Schuchardt **408 M 347 (90)**—wanton destruction of property is not lesser included of malicious destruction;

C v Cowan **40 MAC 939 (96)**—since 1990 amendment of G.L. c. 269, § 10, firearm "possession" under § 10(h) not lesser included offense of § 10(a) when D is outside his residence or place of business;

C v Vinnicombe **28 MAC 934 (90)**—trespass is not lesser included of burglary;

C v Sanna **424 M 92 (97)**—killing without malice **not** "automatically involuntary manslaughter", though recognizing subtlety of lesser scope of risk distinguishing involuntary manslaughter from 3d prong malice;

C v Gordon **410 M 498 (91)**—judge cannot accept guilty plea to lesser included offense over prosecutor's objection;

C v Greaves **27 MAC 590 (89)**—judge cannot accept guilty plea to lesser included offense after guilty verdict over prosecutor's objection, but has discretion under M.R.Crim.P. 25(b)(2) to reduce charge;

5-E. JURISDICTIONAL DEFECTS (E.G., FAIL TO STATE CRIME)

G.L. c. 277, § 47A—motion to dismiss for fail to charge crime or show court's jurisdiction = make-able & notice-able ANY TIME . . . ;

C v Boone **394 M 851 (85)**— . . . and may be first raised on appeal;

C v Andler **247 M 580 (24)**—same; no sentence for non-crime; court must see sua sponte; *(See also Chapter 19, Double Jeopardy)*;

See Chapter 14-B, Sentencing, Dispositions: Dismissal;

C v Spear **43 MAC 583 (97)**—a double jeopardy "plea" to bar 2d trial must be asserted prior to trial or will be deemed waived (so isn't a "jurisdictional" defect);

C v Black **403 M 675 (89)**—motion to dismiss for failure to state crime heard as *Brandano* **359 Mass 332 (71)** motion;

C v Hill **49 MAC 58, 61 (2000)**—because D lacked standing to press motion to suppress drugs, she pressed same constitutional issues via motion to dismiss: dismissal is NOT "an alternative remedy when there is no 'fruit' of a Fourth Amendment violation," and illegal arrest, without more, isn't bar to subsequent prosecution;

Illinois v Somerville **410 US 458 (73)**—manifest necessity for mistrial for incurably defective indictment because trial futile; retrial OK *(See Chapter 19, Double Jeopardy)*;

G.L. c. 278, § 34—"No motion in arrest of judgment shall be allowed for a cause existing before verdict, unless it affects the jurisdiction of the court."

C v Cox **7 Allen 577 (1863)**—motion in arrest of judgment;

C v Hinds **101 M 209 (1869)**—motion in arrest of judgment after G. plea because no crime was charged;

C v Cooper **264 M 378 (28)**—grant post-trial motion arrest/judgment for mid-trial amendment adding "wilful/ malicious" to arson indictment because it didn't state an offense (was waste paper) & violated right to grand jury;

C v Bracy **313 M 121 (43)**—arrest/judgment after G because judge deleted part of 'derive support' indictment, so didn't state crime & no jurisdiction;

C v Clancy **261 M 345 (27)**—dismiss because amendment to use without authority complaint deleted "public way," so invalidated OK complaint; could've amended just the location (because surplusage);

C v Barbosa **421 M 547 (95)**—dismiss for "duplicity" (the charging of separate offenses in a single count), because no assurance that alleged transaction as to which petit jury found guilt was same transaction as to which grand jury returned indictment: 2 drug sales on 1 day purportedly observed by cops, but single indictment charged 3 counts (cocaine distribution, school zone cocaine distribution, and poss. with intent to distribute) with no specification of time or name of buyer;

See also Chapter 5-G, re: Unconstitutional Laws;

5-F. AMENDMENTS OR CHANGES IN INDICTMENTS/COMPLAINTS

K. Smith, *Criminal Practice & Procedure*, §§ 740–42 (2d ed. 1983 & Supp.);

M.R.Crim.P. 4(d)—on own or on party's motion, judge can amend form or if neither side prejudiced; Reporter's Note: "expands" prior law, & easier to amend complaint because no issue re: right to grand jury;

C v Rodriguez **11 MAC 379 (81)**—though no objection, reverse 'being present' where heroin is because not lesser included offense to possession & not alleged, so instruction on it = bad;

C v Bynoe **49 MAC 687 (2000)**—contra Rodriguez, no relief for conviction on charge not made (use without authority is not lesser included of receiving stolen motor vehicle, BUT D didn't object though was seemingly aware that it wasn't lesser included and was expressly invited to veto the instruction);

C v Morse **12 MAC 426 (81)**—can't amend firearm complaint (in de novo jury session after bench trial G) from possess to carry because changed "substance"; need not show prejudice;

C v Souza **42 MAC 186 (97)**—can't amend carrying dangerous weapon to wit handgun, in viol. of c. 269, § 10(b) to knowingly possessing firearm, c. 269, § 10(a);

C v Baker **10 MAC 852 (80)**—can amend carry firearm to "without license" because not essential element (see G.L. c. 278, § 7);

C v Sitko **372 M 305 (77)**—can amend B&E/ nighttime to daytime because lesser included offense;

C v Jones **12 MAC 489 (81)**—can amend (without objection, after arguments) from robbery by assault/fear to robbery by force/violence because "surplusage";

C v Rumkin **55 MAC 635 (2002)**—can amend assault by means of dangerous weapon to include "shod foot" specification, because surplusage;

C v Ruidiaz **65 MAC 426 (2006)**—cannot "amend" indictment for armed assault with intent to rob to charge armed assault with intent to rob person over sixty years of age;

C v Snow **269 M 598 (30)**—can't (over objection) amend extortion of complaining witness from threat injure complaining witness to threat to injure complaining witness's child because different offense; though need not name alleged victim, grand jury did so & it's "substance," not "form"; alternative test = would double jeopardy bar reprosecution? *(See Chapter 19, Double Jeopardy);*

C v Clemmons **370 M 288 (76)**—(if D objects) can't suspend District Court trial to amend to possession with intent to distribute & bind over *(See Chapter 19, Double Jeopardy);*

C v Balliro **385 M 618 (82)**—can't amend operating under influence (booze to drugs) because substance; *(See also Cooper 264 M 378 (28), Clancy 261 M 345 (27), & Bracy 313 M 121 (43), Chapter 5-E, Jurisdictional Defects);*

C v McGilvery **74 MAC 508, further review allowed 455 M 1101 (2009)**—can't amend possession of Class A ("heroin") to possession of Class B (Oxycodone) because amendment is of "substance," not "form"; facts that range of criminal sanctions after amendment was less severe and that D was not surprised, but appeared to have lain in wait for jeopardy to attach (at "required finding of not guilty" point) irrelevant; new complaint and trial upon proper charge are not barred;

C v Williams **73 MAC 833 (2009)**—following jury-waived trial (misdemeanor motor vehicle homicide by operating while under the influence; operating to endanger), judge said NG of motor vehicle homicide by operating under influence and G of operating to endanger but also "guilty of vehicular homicide by negligent operation"; later, the judge ordered that—instead of recording a new count on the complaint—the homicide crime was to be recorded as an amendment "of form" to operating to endanger complaint: error, as it was amendment of substance AND could not have been found within vehicle homicide complaint either; though same statute set forth both homicide by OUI and by negligent operation, text of complaint charged ONLY the OUI form; bill of particulars could not expand essential elements not charged in complaint, allegation of 'no prejudice' rejected;

C v Miranda **441 M 783 (2004)**—though D was indicted for "possession with intent to distribute heroin, with a second count alleging it as a second/subsequent offense," he was also indicted for distribution of heroin, and Commonwealth elected to proceed to trial first on the indictment for "distribution of heroin"; after conviction, judge permissibly "amended" the indictment just tried to engraft upon it the repeat-offender portion which was attached to the indictment NOT tried; per *Bynum v Commonwealth* 429 M 705 (99) (repeat-offender components of indictments don't describe independent crimes which may be charged apart from the substantive crimes whose penalties they enhance), this was non-substantive amendment;

Ross v Commonwealth **420 M 1001 (95)**—during discovery period after complaint for firearm violation, G.L. c. 269, § 10(e), ADA obtained new complaint for more serious G.L. c. 269, § 10(a): no error;

C v Dunnington **390 M 472 (83)**—amend (pre-trial) date because not element;

C v Jervis **368 M 638 (75)**—*(See Chapter 5-C, Bill of Particulars)*—amend date;

C v Knight **437 M 487 (2002)**—amendment of indictment to change date of murder by two days = one of form, not substance, even though undermined alibi defense (which hadn't yet been disclosed to prosecution); here, didn't undermine work of grand jury;

C v Hosmer **49 MAC 188 (2000)**—when, during testimony of 1st witness, ADA became aware that date of offense was 9/21 (11:40 p.m.) rather than 9/22 and moved to amend complaint, judge erred in denying motion and implicitly dismissing complaint on ground of fatal variance; no amendment need even have been sought, date was not material (unless D was prejudiced in his defense, and here he couldn't have been in doubt as to occasion of OUI charge);

C v Gallo **2 MAC 636 (74)**—amend date because not substantive and no prejudice;

C v LaFrennie **13 MAC 977 (82)**—(same) after question from alert (deliberating) jury;

C v Swain **36 MAC 433 (94)**—at close of prosecution evidence of sexual assault on child, amend indictments to specify ending date 3–4 years after ending dates in indictments: no prejudice to D;

C v Miranda **415 M 1 (93)**—following nolle pros of 2-count (2 dates) indictment and return of new indictment with only one count (of the dates) error to allow DA to revive other, nolle pros'd, count by motion to vacate nolle pros of that count;

C v DiStasio **294 M 273 (36)**—can amend indictment for murder of John Doe when learn V's name—unless grand jury evidence shows different person; but see ***Connor v Commonwealth*** **363 M 572 (73)** DA can't amend "John Doe" indictment (though law permits) because grand jury didn't indict D (though maybe heard evidence against D);

C v Murphy **415 M 161 (93)**—can amend, mid-trial, indictment charging all 3 "intents" by which guilt of statutory crime could be established, to specify the one theory/intent presented at trial; where crime can be committed in any 1 of several ways, indictment properly charges it's commission in all those ways, using conjunction "and";

C v Santiago **50 MAC 762, 764 (2001)**—no due process violation for Commonwealth's expanded theory of D's culpability at retrial following appellate reversal, since SJC had directed that D could be convicted whether he fired fatal shot to innocent bystander, or whether his adversary in shootout fired it;

See also Chapter 1-C, Grand Jury;

5-G. UNCONSTITUTIONAL STATUTES (E.G., VAGUE, OVERBROAD, PRIVACY, EQUAL PROTECTION)

US Constitution Amendment 14—Due Process;

Mass. Constitution Declaration of Rights, Articles 11 & 12—due process, etc.;

K. Smith, *Criminal Practice & Procedure*, § 6 overview (2d ed. 1983 & Supp.);

US v Morrison **529 US 598 (2000)**—neither Commerce Clause nor 14th Amendment, section 5, gave Congress authority to give victims of "gender-motivated violence" a federal civil remedy, so federal legislation was struck down;

C v Clemmey **447 M 121 (2006)**—SJC considers (& rejects, here) D's claim that, under Article 30 (separation of powers clause), legislature impermissibly delegated to Department of Environmental Protection the responsibility to define criminal conduct;

C v Guzman **446 M 344 (2006)**—accord and satisfaction statute (G.L. c. 276, § 55) upheld against DA's challenge that it violated "separation of powers" clause (Art. 30);

C v Oakes **401 M 602 (88)**—kiddie porno law = overbroad, but because statute had been amended to be constitutional (& because "overbreadth" challenges as to potential unconstitutionality when applied to others are sparingly entertained), *U.S. Supreme Court vacated & remanded,* **491 US 576 (90)**;

C v Kenney **449 M 840 (2007)**—rejecting First Amendment challenge to G.L. c. 272, § 29C (possession of child pornography) as overbroad, distinguishing *Ashcroft v Free Speech Coalition* **535 US 234 (2002)**; "depiction by computer" would be read to exclude images created without use of real children ("virtual" child pornography); legislature's choice not to provide "exemption for artistic or scientific materials does not invalidate the statute", though any overbreadth "should be cured through case-by-case analysis"; as to "scienter" requirement (D knows or should know person is underage), Commonwealth "must prove that no reasonable person would not have known that the child subject was under the age of eighteen";

C v Weston W. **455 M 24 (2009)**—Declaration of Rights protects "a fundamental right of free movement," and criminal processes and punishments in Lowell's "Youth Protection Curfew for Minors" held not to be least restrictive means of accomplishing ordinance's purposes, and not sufficiently tailored to survive "strict scrutiny" standard; civil enforcement provisions held okay;

C v Welch **444 M 80 (2005)**—at least three incidents are required to prove criminal harassment's element of "pattern" of conduct or "series" of actions (G.L. c. 265, § 43A); required finding of NG here because evidence established only two qualifying incidents after statute's effective date; "harassing" speech is within criminal harassment statute; statute not violative of First Amendment because intended to reach primarily what would be considered "fighting words", but challenges may be made on an "as applied" basis, & SJC will "ensure its application only to speech that is accorded no constitutional protection";

C v A. Juvenile **368 M 580 (75)**—must narrow disorderly definition from Model Penal Code;

C v Abramms **66 MAC 576 (2006)**—D (having protested the war, in assembly with other persons) convicted of "refusing or failing to obey order to disperse from unlawful assembly" (G.L. c. 269, §§ 1–2) presented on appeal only a "facial" challenge to the statute (as violative of First Amendment and arts. 16 & 19 of Declaration of

Rights): court construed "unlawful assembly" under § 2 to be further defined as members being "engage[d] in a common cause to be accomplished with violence and in a tumultuous manner" or "through force and violence", [or] where there is an "imminent danger of violence"; D provided neither trial transcript nor reliable record of jury instructions, risking too much on solely a "facial" challenge to statute, so his conviction was upheld; dissent asserted that opinion's "newly formulated definition of an unlawful assembly . . . is not tenable as a matter of statutory construction";

C v Marcavage **76 MAC 34 (2009)**—D, disobeying police order to stop using megaphone (being used within a foot of people's faces on Halloween night in Salem), attracted crowd, resisted arrest, and "engendered hostility toward police and disrespect for their authority among" large and raucous crowd, sufficient for conviction; that underlying conduct (dissemination of religious message) enjoyed First Amendment protection did not allow disregard of police commands "reasonably calculated at ensuring public safety";

C v Braica **68 MAC 244 (2007)**—that D made many complaints to government officials about neighbor (digging in wetlands, unleashed dog, smoke from furnace, debris on premises), several complaints leading to enforcement actions, could not support conviction for criminal harassment; complaints to government officials "directly implicate constitutionally protected speech";

C v Gagnon **387 M 567 (82)**—sell heroin law had vague penalty;

C v Cahill **442 M 127 (2004)**—ambiguity in statutes concerning necessary length of license suspension following OUI, second offense (when prior occurred more than ten years earlier) = lenity, in favor of suspension for not more than 90 days;

C v Zapata **455 M 530 (2009)**—language of current G.L. c. 265, § 18C omits language prohibiting probationary sentence (while stating punishment as "life" or any term not less than twenty years), and when read in context of amendments, rendered ambiguous proposition that sentence of "probation" was illegal (sentence of five years' probation upheld against Commonwealth challenge);

C v Wilkinson **415 M 402 (93)**—if judicial construction of statute is 'unexpected' and indefensible per previously expressed references, new construction can't be given retroactive effect;

C v Turner **59 MAC 825, 830–31 (2003)**—re: statute criminalizing possession of dangerous weapon by person being arrested on a warrant, there must be actual use, as a weapon, of any instrument which is not, per se, a dangerous weapon (because otherwise simple possession of, e.g., a wrench, would be criminalized by execution of an arrest warrant, violating due process requirement of fair notice of proscribed conduct);

C v Balthazar **366 M 298 (74)**—limit "unnatural act" to non-consensual/non-private;

C v Jasmin **396 M 653 (86)**—Mass. Constitution vagueness not (yet?) stricter than U.S.;

See Chapter 16, Defenses, re: Selective Prosecution;

C v Oakes **407 M 92 (90)**—motion for required finding (or request for limiting jury instructions) required to preserve for appeal as-applied challenge to constitutionality of statute; pretrial motion to dismiss did not preserve this issue;

C v Rosa **62 MAC 622 (2004)**—inserting finger or thumb into mouth of 11-year-old girl, with question, "Do you know how to suck on it?", held sufficient for G of "indecent assault & battery," with other evidence, including D's admission to police that he was referring to penis; because every person should know that "attempting to entice a young girl into playing a game of pseudo-fellatio" is "immoral & improper," statute not unconstitutionally vague as applied;

Carmell v Texas **529 US 513 (2000)**—amendment of state statutes couldn't be applied to D in trial for offenses committed before amendment's effective date because prohibited by US Constitution's bar of "ex post facto" laws; law at issue here "alter(ed) legal rules of evidence, and (required) less, or different testimony, than the law required at the time of the commission of the offence, in order to convict the offender";

C v Cory **454 M 559 (2009)**—G.L. c. 265, § 47 (requiring person placed on probation after conviction of designated sex offense to wear GPS tracking device) applied to D, BUT because it was punitive and was enacted after date of D's particular sex offense, it violated prohibition against ex post facto provisions of US and MA Constitutions;

Garner v Jones **529 US 244 (2000)**—amendment making less frequent the requirement of parole consideration could be applied to inmate without violating "ex post facto" laws' prohibition;

Rogers v Tennessee **532 US 451 (2001)**—application to D of rule abolishing common law "year and a day" rule in homicide prosecutions (death of V had to come within that time after D's action, or D not criminally liable) NOT violative of ex post facto clause because judicial interpretation of criminal statute was neither unexpected nor indefensible by reference to law as expressed prior to conduct in issue;

Gordon v Registry of Motor Vehicles **75 MAC 47 (2009)**—statute enacted requiring persons with two or more prior convictions of operating under influence who seek new license or reinstatement of license to install ignition interlock device (preventing ignition of engine if D's breath is over preset limit of blood alcohol concentration) upheld against challenge that it's an ex post facto penalty (US Constitution, art. I, § 10; Mass. Constitution, art. 24);

C v Kwiatkowski **418 M 543 (94)**—"stalking" (G.L. c. 265, § 43) unconstitutional as facially vague; for future, court supplied definitions of "harassing" and "pattern";

C v Martinez **43 MAC 408 (97)**—"repeatedly" following means more than 2 times, fixing vague stalking statute, G.L. c. 265, § 43;

C v Wotan **422 M 740 (96)**—"repeated" telephone calls solely to harass (G.L. c. 269, § 14A) is ambiguous; court construed it to mean at least three times & applied this definition to D;

C v Thetonia **27 MAC 783 (89)**—literal construction of "pimping" statute which would have led to "absurd" consequences rejected as contrary to due process;

C v Kelly **69 MAC 751 (2007)**—prosecution for making false written report under penalty of perjury to police officer about theft of vehicle (G.L. c. 268, § 39): D signed blank form when cop told her he'd complete it later in accord with her oral statement, and thereafter argued unsuccessfully that her signature alone wasn't "false written report": evidence was that D repeatedly orally pursued the false charges of motor vehicle theft (she had given permission for its use) despite opportunities to withdraw them, and her signature was immediately below notice that statements made were punishable under penalty of perjury; alternate statute (G.L. c. 269, § 13A) criminalizes knowingly making false report of crime, but its penalty is much less;

C v Pagan **445 M 161 (2005)**—standard and burden of proof ambiguous as to imposition of lifetime community parole in some cases, and so unconstitutional as to those; complaint or indictment must allege that D is repeat offender (if such is essential to imposition of LCP given the crime charged); warning that Supreme Court case law (*Apprendi v New Jersey* **530 US 466 (2000)**, etc.) dictates that this enhanced sentence cannot be based on factual findings made by judge rather than jury;

C v Kneram **63 MAC 371 (2005)**—literal construction of statute regarding "whoever" furnishes liquor to person under age twenty-one enforced, making nineteen-year-old college freshman criminally liable (for giving beer to nineteen-year-old friend, who subsequently drove into two pedestrians, killing one); no ambiguity found; "whoever" is term commonly used in criminal statutes; statute doesn't apply merely to liquor licensees;

R.A.V. v City of St. Paul Minn. **505 US 377 (92)**—St. Paul ordinance criminalizing placing on property of burning crosses etc. in order to arouse anger, alarm, or resentment on basis of race, religion or gender, violated 1st Amendment because content-based;

C v Fondakowski **62 MAC 939 (2005)**—"free speech" no defense to prosecution for filing a false registration as sex offender/"failing to register": D (erroneously) wrote that he was "homeless," that his state was "intoxication," his work city was "streets," etc.

C v Arment **412 M 55 (92)**—statutory amendment's failure to apply new stringent provisions to SDP commitments after certain date was equal protection violation;

Rushworth v Registrar of Motor Vehicles **413 M 265 (92)**—due process, equal protection, double jeopardy chal-

lenges to statute requiring license suspension for up to 5 years for drug convictions rejected;

C v Parzyck **44 MAC 655 (98)**—no equal protection violation in harsher statutory penalties for failures to return from furloughs than for failures to return from work release;

C v Alvarez **413 M 224 (92)**; *C v Santaliz* **413 M 238 (92)**; *C v Taylor* **413 M 243 (92)**—rejecting due process, equal protection, double jeopardy challenges to drug crimes "school zone" statute;

C v A Juvenile **413 M 148 (92)**—retroactive application of law allowing prosecutors to indict rather than bind over certain juveniles violated Article 24 ex post facto clause & required dismissal;

C v Corbett **422 M 391 (96)**—no ex post facto bar to statutorily mandated enhanced operating under influence sentence based in part on 8-year-old conviction (enhancing provision was made law in interim); *C v Maloney* **447 M 577 (2006)**—similar, re "Melanie's Law"; further, no bar to applying new statute to D, even though the prosecution was begun before passage of new "enhancement" provisions; court record of prior convictions, accompanied by other documentation, may be prima facie evidence of prior convictions; **N.B.:** *C v Koney* [**421 M 295, 302**] holding must be read into even this new statute (mere identity of name isn't enough to establish even prima facie case);

C v Schafer **32 MAC 682, 687 (92)**—facial overbreadth challenges limited to 1st Amendment claims;

C v Casey **42 MAC 512 (97)**—same; ordinance prohibiting possession of open alcoholic container in public **not** unconstitutionally vague, applicable to unsealed, though "capped," bottle of liquor within easy reach of vehicle's driver;

C v Disler **451 M 216 (2008)**—criminal "enticement" statute, G.L. c. 265, § 26C, may be proved by mere "words" (without 'overt act') when accompanied by proof of requisite intent to commit one of enumerated statutory crimes; state does not ban communication with adults or minors about sexual topics, even through indecent language, "contrasting *Ashcroft v American Civil Liberties Union* **542 US 656, 663, 670–71 (2004)** (statute criminalizing indecent Internet speech enacted to protect children was unconstitutionally overbroad, reaching protected speech between adults);

Opinion of Justices **406 M 1201 (89)**—child victim's refusal to testify at trial not proper basis for legislative definition of "unavailability" under Article 12;

Opinion of the Justices **412 M 1201, 1211 (92)**—article 12 of Declaration of Rights forbids instruction allowing adverse inference from D's refusal to take breathalyzer (supporting the argument that Article 12 forbids use of "missing witness" inference against a criminal defendant);

C v Zevitas **418 M 677, 683–684 (94)**—jury instructions per dictates of G.L. c. 90, § 24(1)(e) had same effect as admission of "refusal" evidence considered in *Opinion of the Justices* **412 M 1201 (92)**, i.e., implying that D's blood alcohol level had not been tested, & that reason for no test was D's refusal to submit to such a procedure;

C v Cedeno **404 M 190 (89)** rejecting vagueness challenge to G.L. c. 94C, § 32A(a) and § 32A(c), despite fact that they prescribe inconsistent penalties for possession of cocaine with intent to distribute (latter prescribes mandatory minimum one-yr. sentence);

C v Zwickert **37 MAC 364 (94)**—D argued on rule of lenity/vagueness that only the lesser penalty statute of 2 prescribing punishment for repeat offender distributing Class B drugs could apply; court rejected, saying harsher penalty was to apply to repeat distributors of 2 particular drugs within class B;

C v Ortiz **39 MAC 70 (95)**—failure to specify in body of indictment which statutory prohibition of cocaine distribution was charged did not entitle D to the more lenient sentencing option: "caption" of indictment had specified G.L. c. 94C, § 32A(c) (rather than G.L. c. 94C, § 32A(a));

Chapter 6
PRETRIAL CONFERENCE, MOTIONS AND DISCOVERY

6-A. GENERAL AND STRATEGY

Mass. Constitution Declaration of Rights, Article 12—right to produce all favorable proofs, to be fully heard in defense, to meet witnesses against him face-to-face

CPCS P/G's 3.2(e)—maximize probable cause hearing discovery; 4.3 file appropriate motions, but caution re: adverse impact; 4.5 partial discovery checklist; 4.10 seek prompt compliance and/or sanctions; 4.11 consider interlocutory relief *(See Chapter 15)*; 6.6(e) if surprise prosecution evidence, ask time to review &/or sanction;

ABA Standards for Criminal Justice, Prosecution Function & Defense Function (3d ed. 1993) 4-3.6—prompt action to vindicate all rights; consider all reason-

able motions and procedural steps; 4-5.2 strategic and tactical decisions = counsel's after consulting client; But see *C v Federici* **427 M 740, 744–45 (98)** decision to forego lack of criminal responsibility defense is defendant's, not counsel's;

M.R.Crim.P. 2 & Comment—Rules are to secure fairness; not intended to be inflexible *(See also Chapter 6-D, and R-1, Reporter's Notes)*;

Aldoupolis v Commonwealth **386 M 260, 269 (82)**—Reporter's Notes to M.R.Crim.P. not binding;

C v Clegg **61 MAC 197 (2004)**—judge abused discretion in denying Commonwealth request for continuance when sole witness (cop) on motion to suppress failed to appear and thereby allowing suppression and, effectively, dismissal;

Kimmelman v Morrison **477 US 365 (86)**—ineffective assistance of counsel in not moving to suppress [because no discovery motion (because expected DA to volunteer info & complainant to drop case)];

US v Frappier **615 F.Supp 51 (D.Mass. '85)**—finding ineffective assistance of counsel in advising D to testify at detention hearing, & allowing motion to suppress statements there made;

C v Soucy **17 MAC 471 (84)**—higher standard on appeal (must create reasonable doubt) for undisclosed witness's statement because no discovery motion was filed (because relied on "practice" of DA's volunteering info);

C v Leavitt **21 MAC 84, 88 n.5 (85)**—informal letter from counsel not "diligent effort"; treat (on appeal) as general/non-request; *(See Chapter 6-F, below)*;

C v Sullivan **17 MAC 981 (84)**—DA can impeach D with statement judge had suppressed [because of late (trial day) disclosure];

M.R.Crim.P. 13(a)(1)—pretrial motion written & signed within time given in 13(d);

See Chapter 10, Preparing/Presenting Defense Evidence;

G.L. c. 218, §§ 26A, 27A—(District Court trial de novo abolished): decision on jury-waiver to be made only after pretrial conference & compliance with discovery orders; discovery rights listed (judge "shall issue an order of discovery requiring any information to which the defendant is entitled" plus requiring that D "be permitted to discover, inspect, and copy any material and relevant evidence, documents, statements of persons, or reports of physical or mental examinations of any person or of scientific tests or experiments, within the possession, custody, or control of the prosecutor or persons under his direction and control': if D so moves, judge shall order Commonwealth to reveal names & addresses of prospective witnesses & probation department to produce record of prior convictions of same);

G.L. c. 278, § 18—pretrial motions heard & decided in primary session before decision on jury-waiver will not be reheard unless "substantial justice" requires;

Appellate Remedies—Take steps to have disputed discovery material designated/impounded cf. *C v O'Brien* **419 M 470, 477–78 (95)** error found in ADA's withholding from D counsel a document used to "refresh" witness on stand, but no relief for D because document not made part of record; "prejudice" showing couldn't be made. See also *C v Hall* **369 M 715 (76)** D may deserve cop's report, but didn't press/renew motion or get reports marked & preserved for appeal; *C v Esteves* **429 M 636, 642 (99)** error for Commonwealth to make and trial judge to allow motion for destruction of "Bishop" records withheld from defendant after holding that they were not relevant; D had right to review of this determination on direct appeal of conviction, and no destruction could occur until after direct appeal and any further proceedings thereby ordered; Interlocutory relief will NOT BE LIKELY: *See Chapter 15-C.4*, re: G.L. c. 211, § 3, e.g., *Lombard v Commonwealth* **427 M 1001 (98)** discovery denial not usually addressed by G.L. c. 211 § 3 petition/power; here, SJC suggested motion for reconsideration in trial court, with citation to recent SJC opinion;

EDITOR'S NOTE—meaningful appellate review of discovery orders possible (i.e., to show prejudice from withholding discovery) only if withheld material is available to appellate judges (i.e., identified, marked, impounded if necessary); but see *C v Liang* **434 M 131, 133–34 (2001)** G.L. c. 211, § 3 relief for Commonwealth from discovery order requiring disclosure of "victim witness advocate" notes;

6-B. PRETRIAL CONFERENCE—MANDATORY IN SUPERIOR COURT AND DISTRICT COURT

M.R.Crim.P. 11—"Among Issues to be Discussed" = witness availability, motions, plea bargain, trial date, jury or judge, stipulations, nature of defense; file report (& sanctions if not);

M.R.Crim.P. 13(d)—no motion unless can't agree on it at pretrial conference; CONSIDER, HOWEVER, adding supplemental pages to "form" pretrial conference report to define more specifically what parties have agreed to (e.g., instead of just police report for "details of identification," assert that you expect to know who else was present at ID, what was said, by whom, whether D was viewed by other witnesses, etc.); to foreclose dispute re what D counsel has received, list items delivered by Commonwealth on PTC form & otherwise memorialize (later, by letter); report should accurately & completely reflect parties' discovery agreements & disagreements so appropriate motions can be pressed about contested matters; motions to preserve specific materials (unless such requests will hurt D); Example: turret tape (911 call)—see *C v Allen* **22 MAC 413 (86)** omissions in complainant's statements there impeached ID of D [reversal for exclusion of tape];

CPCS P/G 4.4—carefully scrutinize/amend any pretrial conference form for fairness, case law, & D's needs;

K. Smith, *Criminal Practice & Procedure*, Chapter 21 (2d ed. 1983 & Supp.)—general discussion;

Superior Court Standing Order 2-86, Criminal Case Management—probation gives D's record & DA gives mandatory discovery at arraignment ["package" = "at least" copies of all police reports reasonably available to prosecutor, written statements of D & witnesses available to prosecutor, scientific tests, ballistics reports, fingerprint reports, & other documentary evidence available to the prosecutor, grand jury minutes, and opportunity to examine all photos or real evidence available to prosecutor; counsel reviews with D before pretrial conference; at pretrial conference, DA gives recommendation, probation tells if D's suitable, & judge fosters (constitutional) negotiations; "all" of pretrial conference agenda discussed & motion-filing rules strictly enforced;

C v Lopes **25 MAC 988 (88)**—surprise DA witness OK because no pretrial conference notice agreement;

C v Delaney **11 MAC 398 n.3 (81)**—agreements = equivalent of judge's order, & sanctions possible for failure to comply;

C v Pope **19 MAC 627, 630 n.3 (85)**—(same);

C v Scalley **17 MAC 224 (83)**—(same); but harmless late disclosure;

Chappee v Vose **843 F2d 25 (1st Cir. '88)**—exclude (D's) expert witness because cross-examination preparation & rebuttal foreclosed by not giving notice promised in pretrial conference report (upholding *C v Chappee* **397 M 508 (86)**);

C v Gliniewicz **398 M 744 (86)**—reverse because DA violated pretrial conference agreement (for inspection of physical evidence) by letting blood expert alter/destroy (D's boots);

C v Gallarelli **399 M 17 (87)**—new trial for suppressed lab report (showing no blood) because PTC report promised exculpatory & scientific; *(See Chapter 6-F, Exculpatory/Mitigating Evidence)*;

C v Chase **42 MAC 749 (97)**—no relief for disposal/sale of truck (homicide 'weapon'/means) despite PTC that D would be permitted inspection of all physical evidence upon 24-hour notice; no showing of materiality to defense, & had access to photos, & at worst "negligence" by Commonwealth;

C v Durning **406 M 485 (90)**—judge has discretion to prevent D from calling witness not listed in PTC report;

C v Freiberg **405 M 282 (89)**—testing & destruction by police of blood stains not improper where done before PTC report (& in absence of timely motion to preserve);

C v Capparelli **29 MAC 926 (90)**—D's failure to make specific PTC requests meant Commonwealth obligated only to disclose evidence "obviously supportive of" D's innocence; even if nondisclosed material (rewards to informant, who didn't testify, but whose info was crucial to case) fit this definition, D showed no prejudice because evidence of guilt was overwhelming;

C v Madigan **449 M 702 (2007)**—trial court judge correctly ordered Commonwealth to disclose info concerning promises, rewards, inducements to confidential informant where info was material to defense of entrapment, on which D made adequate pretrial showing;

C v Mello **453 M 760 (2009)**—though undercover cop was agent regarding whom D's affidavit effectively raised entrapment, D's motion to compel Commonwealth to say whether or not person who introduced D to him was government agent was denied: D's affidavit did not allege that this person induced D to commit crimes or that she participated in cop's inducement of those crimes; that Commonwealth failed to charge D with crime related to date on which this person was present perhaps to avoid disclosure of agency didn't matter (fn.5);

C v Brennick **14 MAC 952 (82): Counsel At Pretrial Conference**—see public defenders not fungible; D entitled to the presence and assistance of his own attorney at hearing re: whether to impose bench trial sentence; cf. *C v Faulkner* **418 M 352, 364–66 (94)** aid of attorney who could know nothing about case, having been appointed minutes before, was not the assistance of counsel to which D was entitled (at a probation surrender hearing);

6-C. MOTIONS, IN GENERAL

See Chapter 14-B, including for statute of limitations dismissal; see also Chapter 14-B, Motions to Dismiss; Chapter 20-A, Suppression, Motions, Filing; Chapter 18, I.D. Issues; Chapter 11-B, Evidence: Motions in Limine;

CPCS P/G 4.3—*(See Chapter 6-A)* caution re: affidavits (rules, 5th Amendment)

M.R.Crim.P. 13—filing "pre-trial" motion: time limits; must list all separate grounds; detailed affidavit on "personal knowledge" of all facts; waivers imputed; memorandum for M. to Dismiss or M. to Suppress (except for warrantless search), or if judge wants (see also Superior Court Rule 9); District Court hearing = any mutually convenient time; if denied, can renew if substantial justice;

Superior Court Rule 9—need not hear motion, or opposition thereto, unless affidavit verifies its facts; motion to dismiss & motion to suppress fruits of search by warrant must be accompanied at filing by memorandum of law "except when otherwise ordered by court";

K. Smith, *Criminal Practice & Procedure*, **Chapter 23 (2d ed. 1983 & Supp.)**—overview; "strict" affidavit rule; 1275: "all" motions if "pre-trial"; [But NOTE: no definition of "pre-trial"—Query re: sequestration (R-21), continue (R-10), sever (R-9), summons (R-17), voir dire (cf. §§ 1709 & 1714), limine, etc.];

C v Dubois **451 M 20, 29 (2008)**—failure of judge to rule on motion "is treated as an implicit denial"; implicit denial of motion assumed to indicate that judge did not find affidavit credible;

C v Yelle **390 M 678 (84)**—D's rape-shield motion = "not a motion under M.R.Crim.P." so no interlocutory appeal for DA under M.R.Crim.P. 15; rape shield issue = "trial motion"

C v Ruffen **399 M 811 (87)**—voir dire of child sexual assault complainant to learn of prior sex abuse and her knowledge beyond her years;

C v Walker **426 M 301 (97)**—complainant's knowledge about sexuality based on info from 'secondary source' might be relevant enough, in another case, to require voir dire on motion;

C v Lewin (III) **408 M 147 (90)**—defense questioning about seized items at evidentiary hearing gave prosecutor sufficient notice of items sought to be suppressed, despite lack of mention in suppression motion;

6-C.1. Timeliness

G.L. c. 277, § 47A—affirmative defenses to be raised by pretrial motion (but lack of jurisdiction can be noticed anytime);

C v Senior **454 M 12 (2009)**—D's claim that indictment for "attempted subornation of perjury" was defective because it failed to allege an "overt act" was considered on appeal (though not raised below) because "whether an indictment fails to allege a fact necessary to constitute an offense is a matter of jurisdiction";

C v Spear **43 MAC 583 (97)**—failure to assert double jeopardy bar by motion to dismiss prior to the trial which constituted "second" jeopardy = waiver of issue (despite fact that D was acting pro se);

C v Mazzantini **74 MAC 915, further app. review denied 454 M 1111 (2009)**—by pleading guilty to both possession of heroin and being present where same heroin was kept, D waived claim that convictions were duplicative (and conceded they aren't 'same' under elements-based analysis); D should have made argument that legislature did not intend both crimes be punished by pretrial motion to dismiss;

C v Scullin **44 MAC 9, 14 (97)**—while judge may be entitled to defer ruling on admissibility of particular evidence until during trial, judge must ensure that jury in not exposed to the evidence until after admissibility issue is decided;

C v Riveiro **393 M 224 (84)**—voir dire re: admissibility of D's statement (here, whether Miranda warnings were given) must take place outside presence of jury; here, failure to establish that warnings were given & consequent refusal to admit what occurred thereafter would have led jury to speculate that something detrimental to D was being kept from them;

C v White **44 MAC 168 (98)**—judge could properly find no 'good cause' to allow hearing on motion to suppress filed day before trial and 7 years after indictment, though based on allegation that only after interview of bar owner was there a basis for it (he said he did not supply info arguably attributed to him by cop, on which reasonable suspicion for stop was based); appellate court nonetheless held motion to suppress would have been denied, properly (NB: absence of record which might have been made, in hearing on motion to suppress, is glaring);

C v Stephens **44 MAC 940 (98)**—motions seeking records from ambulance service, hospital, and drug rehab program, filed on day scheduled for trial (six months after pretrial conference report) not timely under former M.R. Crim.P. 13(d)(2) (motions to be filed within 7 days after PTC report, or other date allowed by judge); furthermore, no abuse of discretion in denying because no apparent connection between alleged drug use in May '93 and events occurring in October '92;

6-C.2. Affidavit Requirements

Superior Court Rule 9—need not hear motion, or opposition thereto, unless affidavit verifies its facts, (PLUS memo must accompany filing of motion to dismiss and motion to suppress evidence seized in search by warrant "except when otherwise ordered by court");

C v Clegg **61 MAC 197 (2004)**—counsel's failure to file any affidavit with motion to suppress would have warranted DENIAL of motion without any hearing or, "at the very least," insistence upon affidavit before scheduling hearing; absent affidavit setting forth factual basis for expectation of privacy in seized bag, there was no legal basis for finding "search in the constitutional sense";

C v Zavala **52 MAC 770 (2001)**—late-filed affidavit contained only general "laundry list" of possible grounds of suppression, in violation of M.R.Crim.P. 13(a)(2) and requirement of affiant with personal knowledge, justifying judge in refusing to hear motion;

C v Smallwood **379 M 878 (80)**—affidavit needs personal knowledge;

C v Lampron **441 M 265, 271 (2004)**—"relaxation of personal knowledge requirement" for affidavit supporting motion under M.R.Crim.P. 17(a) (summons for production of documentary evidence/objects); can use hearsay, but must identify source and show reliability; this "relaxation . . . does NOT extend to any other pretrial motion";

C v Rebello **450 M 118 (2007)**—(concerning M.R.Crim.P. 30 motion for new trial) judge was entitled "to ignore the hearsay statement of trial counsel contained in appellate counsel's affidavit";

C v Luce **34 MAC 105 (93)**—failure to file affidavit supporting motion to suppress statements may be "dispositive of the . . . motion";

C v Ceria **13 MAC 230 (82)**—deny lineup without timely written motion and affidavit;

C v LaPierre **10 MAC 641 (80)**—need not hear late polygraph motion without affidavit;

C v Prater **431 M 86, 91 (2000)**—submitting "copy" rather than original of signed affidavit fatal; info said to be "not properly before" judge;

C v Roberts **433 M 45 (2000)**—unsigned affidavit "put no evidence whatsoever before the judge";

C v Parker **412 M 353 (92)**—counsel's affidavit citing conclusions of expert did not meet Rule 13 requirement that affiant have personal knowledge;

C v Fudge **20 MAC 382 (85)**—affidavit gets hearing re: search warrant because apprised court of grounds & enough for D's burden of proof; don't need memo if it's not D's burden of proof [see below], e.g., search & seizure beyond search warrant's scope;

C v Santosuosso **23 MAC 310 (86)**—affidavit must have facts satisfying D's burden of proof; District Court transcript would suffice, & if unavailable counsel's affidavit (re: testimony) OK because unlikely cop will sign for D;

C v Shaughessy **455 M 346 (2009)**—re: motion to discover confidential informant, judge could consider affidavit submitted ex parte (to be permitted in "exceptional circumstances"), BUT had to permit Commonwealth response, e.g., giving redacted or summary version of affidavit content; before presentation of affidavit from defendant himself after judge's demand (after concern for D's "exposure" should he sign affidavit), defense counsel had first submitted no affidavit at all, and on demand, counsel's affidavit outlining info obtained about informant from police reports, grand jury testimony, and cop testimony at suppression hearing (both deemed by judge inadequate);

C v Chase **14 MAC 1032 (82)**—affidavit asserting "info. & belief ID's suggestive & maybe unreliable" = inadequate & may not merit hearing; (cite *C v Dougan* **377 M 303 (79)** due process right to ID procedures meeting basic standard of fairness would mean little without right to be informed of the details of any out-of-court ID; get info per Dougan, then have grounds to assert, if possible, suggestive & unreliable);

C v Ramirez **416 M 41 (93)**—absence of affidavit excused because allegations didn't lend themselves to presentation by affidavits; instead, copious other material & "extensive written analysis of" same sufficed;

C v McNulty **42 MAC 955 (97)**—D's "assertion" in handwritten motion (for revision of sentence pursuant to M.R.Crim.P. 29), is insufficient: affidavit[s] must support it;

C v Francis **432 M 353, 372 n.16 (2000)**—[context of motion for new trial] "affidavits" bad, because only contained phrase "I swear," and "not verified by an oath before a magistrate or a notary public," & did not affirm that maker signed under pains and penalties of perjury;

C v Rivera **44 MAC 452 (98)**—D faulted for not providing "medical **affidavit**" with proffered medical records on R.30 motion for new trial;

C v Silva **371 M 819 (77)**—late motion (without affidavit) for shrink;

C v Santiago **30 MAC 207 (91)**—judge's denial of suppression motion without hearing because of technical defects in affidavits (e.g., affidavit by counsel rather than D) was abuse of discretion where affidavits gave judge & prosecutor sufficient notice, "in a form . . . not readily subject to change by the affiant" (here, trial testimony showed that cops were lying at m.supp. hearing held for 1 of the 3 co-Ds);

C v Stote **433 M 19 (2000)**—include, in expert's postconviction affidavit, assertion that s/he would have testified to the affidavit assertions if s/he had been called at trial;

6-C.3. Reconsideration of Motions

C v Cronk **396 M 194, 197 (85)**—availability of appellate review doesn't preclude reconsideration by judge if reconsideration request is made within reasonable time;

C v Downs **31 MAC 467 (91)**—motion for reconsideration of final orders of trial judge limited to 30 days; non-dispositive order limited to reasonable time during pendency of case; affidavit is desirable but not required; hearing is desirable if motion contains "fresh material" or if judge will "alter substantially" original disposition; explanation of change should be put on record;

C v Cryer **426 M 562 (98)**—motion for rehearing of previously denied motion may be denied without hearing unless it raises new issues or unless relevant law has changed; judge here (as both 1st motion & trial judge) entitled to reject D's factual assertions as to which he had knowledge from previously presiding;

C v Lugo **64 MAC 12 (2005)**—reconsideration is "permitted" when "substantial justice requires," and this isn't limited to instances "where there are allegations of new or additional grounds that could not have been reasonably known when the original motion was filed";

C v Pagan **73 MAC 369 (2008)**—reconsideration of suppression motion may occur when "substantial justice requires," and is not limited to instances of newly discovered evidence, BUT even when judge stated he would "assume" truth of new affidavits, he wasn't required to hold new hearing or reverse suppression order: "allowing 'do-overs' . . . undermines the integrity of the process and threatens the efficacy of the sequestration orders";

C v Baker **440 M 519 (2003)**—after judge allowed motion for funds for expert concerning hair embedded and indentation made in wall, judge revoked allowance upon DA's assertion that prosecution would not claim that baby's head was smashed against wall; when prosecution at trial made exactly this claim, defense counsel ineffective in failing to renew request for funds and move for continuance; Supreme Judicial Court reversed order denying motion for new trial (accompanied by expert affidavits that hair was not from dead baby and indentation not made by baby's head);

C v Mandile **15 MAC 83 (83)**—dismissal OK as discovery sanction; reconsideration also OK, but 87 days later not "timely";

C v Balboni **419 M 42 (94)**—**motion to reconsider "final"/dispositive order should be filed within 30 days (same as time for filing notice of appeal)**; *but see C v Haskell* **438 M 790 (2003)**—within judge's discretion to allow reconsideration of denial of suppression motion five years later (D had been on default during that time);

C v Montanez **410 M 290, 294 n.4 (91)**—motion to reconsider must be filed within 30 days (re: denial of motion for new trial);

C v Haskell **438 M 790 (2003)**—reconsideration of motion OK when "substantial justice requires." M.R.Crim. P. 13(a)(5), not limited to when there are new-and-not-reasonably-known-earlier grounds; judge's power to reconsider = firmly rooted in common law, and R. 13 doesn't change this; "judges are not condemned to abstain from entertaining second thoughts that may be better ones"); five-year gap between initial ruling on suppression motion and allowance of motion for reconsideration was due to D's default, but "within judge's discretion to reconsider" despite long delay;

Monahan v Commonwealth **414 M 1001 (93)**—trial judge's revival of complaint that had been dismissed with prejudice was improper where no motion for reconsideration was timely filed & where Commonwealth failed to file interlocutory appeal of original dismissal;

6-C.4. Appellate Preservation

C v Hall **369 M 715 (76)**—D may deserve cop's report, but didn't press/renew motion or get reports marked & preserved for appeal;

C v O'Brien **419 M 470 (95)**—failure to have contested document marked for appeal prevents D from establishing prejudice from its illegitimate withholding by DA;

C v Mercado **452 M 662, 669 n.11 (2008)**—motion in limine was discussed and ruled upon in an unrecorded conference: "We are impeded in our analysis of the case by the absence of the discussion that occurred in the unrecorded conference, and we emphasize again the importance of recording all conferences";

C v Kater (III) **409 M 433 (91)**—failure to raise claim in initial *O'Dell* **392 M 445 (84)** motion to dismiss (grand jury issue) before 1st trial & appeal barred D from later raising claim on appeal from 2d trial;

C v Stote **433 M 19 (2000)**—late disclosure by Commonwealth (5 days before trial) of chemist's report = no relief, but study to see what proffers are necessary for different result (request continuance, say what tasks should be performed as consequence of new info, what investigation for contrary evidence, including experts, should be undertaken, etc.);

6-C.5. Interlocutory Relief

C v Beausoleil **397 M 206, 208 n.2 (86)**—may merit interlocutory relief for some "pre-trial motions (e.g., limine); (*See Chapter 15*); see G.L. c. 211, § 3 (*See Chapter 15 post*); see also CPCS P/G 4.11 (consider seeking interlocutory relief re: adverse pretrial ruling) & *Yelle* **390 M 678 (84)** (re: Commonwealth's attempt to overturn trial judge's ruling on 'rape-shield' matter, G.L. c. 211, § 3 avenue "is not a means for second-guessing a trial judge's evidentiary rulings. Whether evidence is legally relevant is a decision generally left to the trial judge"); & K. Smith, *Criminal Practice & Procedure*, Chapter 25 (2d ed. 1983 & Supp.); double jeopardy bar = adjudicated by G.L. c. 211, § 3 (*See Chapter 19, post*);

C v Boncore **412 M 1013 (92)**—Commonwealth cannot appeal single justice's denial of leave for interlocutory appeal of allowance of suppression motion, G.L. c. 211, § 3, petition is available;

M.R.Crim.P. 34—Pre-Trial Report of law question: "If, prior to trial, or, with the consent of the defendant, after conviction of the defendant, a question of law arises which the trial judge determines is so important or doubtful as to require the decision of the Appeals Court, the judge may report the case so far as necessary to present the question of law arising therein. If the case is reported prior to trial, the case shall be continued for trial to await the decision of the Appeals Court."

M.R.Crim.P. 15(a)(1)—interlocutory appeal: DA may appeal allowance of motion to dismiss or "for appropriate relief," under M.R.Crim.P. 15(a)(2), D or DA may apply to SJC single justice for leave to appeal ruling on motion to suppress; under M.R.Crim.P. 15(a)(4), there is to be no appeal or report of issue[s] in probable cause hearing;

SJC Standing Order re: M.R.Crim.P. 15—NOTWITHSTANDING THE LANGUAGE OF RULE 15(b)(1) (allowing 10 days within which to file application for leave to appeal decisions on motions to suppress), application for leave to appeal must be filed within 7 days of order being appealed; opposition to be filed within 7 days after application's filing (or such shorter time as single justice orders); contents of application prescribed; usually decided without hearing;

C v Vaidulas **433 M 247, 251 (2001)**—Rule 15(c) inapplicable for review of trial judge's action, after jury's G, allowing D's pretrial motion in limine (on which he previously deferred ruling) and thus striking essential proof, resulting in required finding of not guilty: Rule 15 appeal is of a determination on a motion "decided by judge before D is placed in jeopardy"; SJC instead held appeal cognizable because judge's action below was, in effect, M.R. Crim.P. 30(c);

6-D. DISCOVERY, IN GENERAL, AND SANCTIONS

See also, Chapter 6-M, Reciprocal Discovery;

See also Chapter 5-C, Bill of Particulars, Chapter 11-H, re: sexual assault cases & Chapter 11-J, Privileges; & Chapter 7–B, Subpoena;

CONSIDER, ALSO, Freedom of Information Act (Mass. Public Records law) requests: consult G.L. c. 66, § 10, and G.L. c. 4, § 7, Twenty-sixth, as well as 950 Code of Mass. Regs. 32.01 through 32.09; CONSIDER, ALSO, using M.R.Crim.P. 17(a)(2) [e.g., *C v Wanis* **426 M 639 (98)** & *C v Rodriguez* **426 M 647 (98)** obtaining police internal affairs department's reports/interviews; *C v Neumyer* **432 M 23 (2000)** judge may order, via M.R. Crim.P 17(a)(2), rape counseling center to produce particular records (no statutory or other privilege applying to the particular info sought here)];

***Kettenbach v Board of Bar Overseers* 448 M 1019 (2007)**—public records law, according to "regulations implementing" it, applies only to the Executive branch of State government (not judicial or legislative) (see 950 CMR § 32.03);

***Montefusco v Commonwealth* 452 M 1015 (2008)**—D's petition for "mandamus" relief to force DA's office to produce file and discovery from his previously-concluded criminal case (presumably preparatory to filing motion for new trial) rejected: M.R.Crim.P. 30(c)(4) allows judge to authorize such discovery by specified procedure, and mandamus relief inappropriate when alternative means exist to obtain documents requested (including, presumably, obtaining documents from prior counsel); DA has no "clear cut duty to produce case file or other discovery" in these circumstances;

C v Bernardo B* 453 M 158 (2009)**—upholding pretrial discovery order that Commonwealth provide information to allow investigation of D's claim that he was being selectively prosecuted because of his gender: D was 14-year-old boy charged with statutory rape of 12-year-old girls, and his attempts to have those girls charged with raping ***him "in connection with the same alleged incidents" had been unsuccessful; cite to recent cases "enunciating standards governing the production of evidence concerning claims of selective prosecution," ***C v Thomas* 451 M 451 (2008) & *C v Lora* 451 M 425 (2008) & *C v Betances* 451 M 457 (2008)** (vital statistical evidence showing disparate treatment "may be relevant and material" under M.R.Crim.P. 14(a)(2)), but request must be "properly supported" and "not impose *undue* burdens on the Commonwealth");

***C v Thomas* 451 M 451 (2008)**—to extent D's discovery motion was for materials and data within control of a colonel of State Police and the registry of motor vehicles, it should have been denied, SJC rejecting argument that all Commonwealth agencies are part of "prosecution team";

***C v Lampron* 441 M 265, 268 (2004)**—"pursuit of documents and records in the possession of a nonparty must be considered and analyzed under rule 17(a)(2)"; D must make factual showing that items are relevant and have evidentiary value to defense (conclusory statements insufficient); affidavit must show that the documentary evidence sought has a rational tendency to prove or disprove an issue in the case; after privilege is asserted and pending application of "Bishop-Fuller" protocol, keeper of records should await further order of court rather than deliver records to court;

***C v Odgren* 455 M 171 (2009)**—pre-trial, DA issued subpoena to jail's record keeper directing production (by mail to DA's office) of books, papers, visitor log, taped phone calls, and pin list" concerning D held on bail prior to murder trial, and this was ILLEGITIMATE; a party must first obtain judicial approval under M.R.Crim.P.

17(a)(2) (& ***C v Lampron* 441 M 265 [2004]**) for production of records from third party before trial or evidentiary hearing; violation of that procedure did not itself require suppression of the telephone conversations; suppression motion had included constitutional claim (re: failure to establish probable cause prior to turning records over to Commonwealth) which was not yet decided by motion judge, but could now be considered by motion judge; see, however, ***In the Matter of a Grand Jury Subpoena* 454 M 685 (2009)**—(4:3 opinion) when all parties have notice that all calls are subject to monitoring and recording, neither a pretrial detainee nor an inmate has reasonable expectation of privacy;

***C v Oliveira* 438 M 325, 329 n.15 (2002)**—rule 17(a)(2) permits D to summons objects from a third party, but can't be unreasonable or oppressive;

***C v Matis* 446 M 632 (2006)**—judge may order pretrial access for defense counsel & investigators to inspect, measure, photograph crime scene, a third party's home (authority now under R. 14, but previously under rule 17(a)(2)) but notice and opportunity to be heard must be given Commonwealth and the third party, before issuance of any order & order "must be carefully tailored to protect legitimate privacy interests"; D must show: relevance, not otherwise accessible in advance of trial, can't properly prepare for trial without access & failure to obtain advance access may delay trial, & motion is in good faith and not fishing expedition;

***Jansen, petitioner* 444 M 112 (2005)**—upheld allowance of D's pretrial motion for order for "buccal swab" of a third party for DNA sample (D had made very substantial showing that such a sample with pristine chain of custody would show 3rd party rather than D to be source of sperm); order doesn't "implicate . . . rights under" 4th Amendment or Article 14;

***C v Draheim* 447 M 113 (2006)**—Commonwealth wanted "buccal swabs" from female D's two children and from rape complainants because prosecution alleged that the children were products of D's statutory rapes of teen-aged boys; notwithstanding quashing judge's rationale protective of the relationship between child and D's ex-husband (held irrelevant by SJC), burden was only to establish that the DNA evidence will probably provide evidence relevant to D's guilt; judge should consider seriousness of crime, importance of evidence, and [un]availability of less intrusive means of obtaining the evidence, factors relevant re: prosecution attempts to obtain physical samples from person's body;

***Lenardis v Commonwealth* 452 M 1001 (2008)**—nonparty directed to provide evidence (buccal swab) can challenge order by refusing to comply and appealing from any order of contempt that results; this petitioner instead sought relief from SJC single justice ("county court") via G.L. c. 211, § 3 petition, which was denied without hearing; appeal to full bench = moot because petitioner complied with order AND single justice's ruling would not be disturbed because party should have suffered contempt and appealed from contempt order;

C v Reed **444 M 803 (2005)**—when Commonwealth claimed that pelvic exam's finding of "erythema" (redness in vagina) corroborated complainant's claim of sexual assault, record of pelvic exam performed six weeks earlier was relevant, notwithstanding Commonwealth arguments to the contrary: earlier record would give fairer picture of the significance of the latter pelvic exam;

C v Lam **444 M 224 (2005)**—Commonwealth has standing to object to D's motion for summonses under rule 17; Commonwealth should not simply "oppose[ ] every one of the defendant's requests," depriving judge of opportunity for meaningful evaluation . . . prosecutor's obligations demand a more reasoned and constructive approach"; even when motion is unopposed, judge must ensure that *Lampron,* **441 M 265**, procedure "is not abused"; SJC affirms portions of orders for summonses to middle school for reports re: sex abuse allegations by complainant, to complainant's father for copies of journal entries, to DSS, etc.;

C v Mitchell **444 M 786 (2005)**—curtailing avenue of ex parte application by D for Rule 17 summonses: ex parte procedure to be used "only in exceptional circumstances," e.g., when D seeks to summons documents and can't make the showing required by *Lampron* without revealing info that may prove incriminating, or when advance notice of request for summons "would likely result in the destruction or alteration of the documents themselves"; if ex parte motion is never permitted, this "could require [D] to uncover, knowingly or unknowingly, evidence that is incriminating and will be used by the prosecution," a result seemingly disapproved at 795–96; **"The Commonwealth has no absolute pretrial right of access to a criminal defendant's investigation"**, at 796; while under *Lam*, Commonwealth has "interest in being heard on the relevancy issue" & role in ensuring no "harassment" of witnesses or "fishing expedition," judge "is perfectly capable of making the relevancy and other determinations without the input of the Commonwealth," at 796; ex parte application can't be justified on mere ground that disclosure would reveal trial strategy or work product or "might disclose client confidences"; judge should USUALLY seal D's motion & affidavit for ex parte process in whole or part, & then allow Commonwealth to be heard on "ex parte" nature of request; judge should have stenographic record made of all proceedings for ex parte summons; even after ex parte proceedings & summons, Commonwealth may learn of summons from recipient or by other means & might then "be entitled . . . to receive submissions requesting the documents & to make an appropriate response"; after documents are summonsed by ex parte Rule 17 motion, neither side may inspect "until after a full consideration of any privileges, privacy concerns, or other legitimate interests brought to the judge's attention," and then judge has discretion to permit Commonwealth's right of access; at 801, directs judge to determine whether or not

D "has made a sufficient showing of a compelling need for secrecy and relevancy of the document sought" to warrant ex parte procedure;

C v Shaughessy **455 M 346 (2009)**—allowing D's ex parte affidavit to support motion for disclosure of confidential informant in exceptional circumstances BUT before relying on it for decision, judge is required to reveal enough for Commonwealth to oppose (judge to seal/impound "only" what's necessary to protect D's interests); if Commonwealth wants to respond ex parte, Commonwealth must "make the case for it with the judge";

C v Caceres **63 MAC 747 (2005)**—defense counsel's affidavit in support of Rule 17 motion identified the hearsay sources of his knowledge (i.e., discovery provided by DSS, a named clinician, etc.), facts asserted in affidavit were "in the personal knowledge of counsel's sources", & relevance of requested documents was "identified with specificity"; the document holder can't object to summons until after it has been issued (i.e., there's no right to hearing before the issuance of the summons); document holder can challenge by way of motion to quash or assertion of a privilege (i.e., rejecting document holder's claim that "it should be permitted to object by way of an 'opposition memorandum'" instead); that defense counsel erroneously styled motion as one under Rule 14(a)(1)(C) instead of Rule 17 didn't matter (fn.3 at 748); civil contempt judgment against document holder affirmed;

G.L. c. 127, § 3—sheriff & assistants must keep record of all prisoners' property;

Information from relevant police departments, e.g., Boston Police website containing crime statistics for greater Boston: www.ci.boston.ma.us/police/ore.asp; state police website: www.state.ma.us/msp/cru/SPRESRCH.HTM;

Rule 14 & Reporter's Notes—mandatory vs. discretionary (anything material & relevant); reciprocal rules; alibi/insanity/license; sanctions; continuing duty;

C v Lewinski **367 M 889 (75)**—SJC's holding "provisional" until Rules adopted; but see

C v Lapka **13 MAC 24 (82)**—case law (e.g., Lewinski) = broader than rules; DA should follow broadest interpretation, e.g., D's [alleged] oral statements; new trial if prejudiced by late disclosure;

C v Giontzis **47 MAC 450 (99)**—DA's failure to give name, vita, of expert witness, perhaps on rationale that DA would not call until "rebuttal" (and then only if D expert stumbled convincingly into DA's set-up), severely criticized; SO, move for discovery of prospective expert testimony & forensic tests, "whether or not the Commonwealth intends to use same at trial either in its case in chief or in possible rebuttal"; move also that prosecutor be ordered to inquire re: existence of scientific tests, at least those conducted by Commonwealth's own crime laboratory, see *C v Martin* **427 M 816, 822 (98)**;

C v Reynolds **429 M 388 (99)**—defense was obligated to turn over statement of Commonwealth witness which defense intended to use for impeachment at trial, to prevent "sucker punch";

C v Vaughn **32 MAC 435, 440 (92)**—Commonwealth commits "sucker punch" by introducing at trial evidence not previously disclosed which was flatly contrary to pretrial discovery (3 sets of footprints rather than 2); though undisclosed evidence was inculpatory rather than exculpatory, distinction "is not significant where the issue is delayed disclosure, as opposed to failure to disclose"; "standards for the application of sanctions for delayed disclosure of the two types of evidence are similar"; reversal required;

C v Bockman **442 M 757 (2004)**—discovery revealed that particular state trooper would testify to collection & preservation of fingerprint evidence and its delivery to FBI, AND that a bloody print was made by finger with blood on it (rather than finger that touched blood already present on the door by other means); FBI agent was to testify regarding match of bloody print to D's thumb; when cross-examination of trooper assumed that trooper hadn't made the match and/or hadn't had that match confirmed by five others in the state police lab, but instead obtained a devastatingly contrary answer before the jury, no "abuse of discretion" by trial judge in denying mistrial and finding no breach of discovery obligation: it was not exculpatory and Commonwealth did not intend to present it at trial;

K. Smith, *Criminal Practice & Procedure***, Chapter 24 (2d ed. 1983 & Supp.)**—overview; "discretionary's" purpose is not to limit full disclosure, but to encourage reciprocal from D (below); *(NOTE: K.S. sometimes takes narrow view of rules vs. cases see Chapter 6-H & 6-I, below)*;

ABA Standards for Criminal Justice (2d ed. 1980) Discovery, 11-1.1—"full & free"; "open file" for fairness, informed plea bargains, less surprise/inequities/delays; 11-2.1(d) DA's obligation extends to staff and investigators under DA's "control"; counsel, not judge, should determine what's relevant; 11-4.1-2, Comments: delayed disclosure = obstruction; hurts D's preparation & strategy; may violate Due Process;

C v St. Germain **381 M 256, 261 n.8 (80)**—police = part of prosecution, so DA's duty extends to police info; (see K. Smith, *Criminal Practice & Procedure*, § 1379 (2d ed. 1983 & Supp.) & ABA Standards, above);

C v Baldwin **385 M 165 n.12 (82)**—ADA responsible for what cops know;

C v Eneh **76 MAC 672 (2010)**—same; having been forewarned that defense would be entrapment, prosecutor should have reviewed evidence anew with cops, which would have produced the "overlooked" bank records and assure timely disclosure to defense;

C v Martin **427 M 816, 824 (98)**—prosecutor's obligations extend to info in possession of any person who has participated in the investigation or evaluation of the case "and has reported to the prosecutor's office concerning the case" (here, info re: five inconclusive or failed confirmatory tests was in possession of perhaps only one chemist in state police lab, but prosecution had duty to inquire and could not satisfy the production order "simply by turning over test information that it had in its files");

Kyles v Whitley **514 US 419 (95)**—material possessed by police investigators and other agents of police or prosecutor = within prosecutor's control for purposes of discovery compliance; prosecutor "has a duty to learn of any favorable evidence known to the others acting on the government's behalf in the case, including the police";

C v Beal **429 M 530 (99)**—though D sought and obtained a court order that Commonwealth interview complainant and obtain from her info on mental health treatment and whether any prior sexual assault claims had been made by her, Commonwealth appealed; SJC held that info known to an "independent witness, but unknown to the prosecution, is not within the possession or control of the prosecution unless that witness has acted, in some capacity, as an agent of the government in the investigation and prosecution of the crime" and that prosecutor's "duty to disclose" doesn't apply to info which witness has but prosecutor doesn't; prosecutor has "serious" ethical duty not to keep himself willfully ignorant of potentially exculpatory info; D counsel should seek hearing to have "no contact" order amended to allow defense counsel/reps to inquire directly (but no pretense that complainant is required to answer);

C v Dexter **50 MAC 30 (2000)**—similar; complainant's refusal to provide to D name of treating physician "does not justify requiring prosecution to act as a conduit for the defense";

C v Garrey **436 M 422, 442 n.12 (2002)**—"The prosecutor has an affirmative obligation diligently to search for and preserve materials that are discoverable in every criminal case. A lackadaisical attitude with regard to this responsibility is unacceptable in any criminal prosecution, and most emphatically so in a prosecution of murder";

C v Zekirias **443 M 27 (2004)**—DA has "duty to ensure" that copies of police reports were provided to defense counsel in timely manner; "good faith assumption that discovery had been timely provided falls FAR SHORT OF FULFILLING THIS DUTY AND CANNOT BE CONDONED"; "pressure of work" and "busy caseloads" can't excuse nonperformance as to mandatory items of discovery actually in the case file;

C v Eneh **76 MAC 672 (2010)**—after defense counsel's opening statement (homeless impoverished heroin addict, only when in severe withdrawal, succumbed to undercover agent's repeated entreaties for heroin with intent to 'take some off the top' for his own addiction and that of his girlfriend) ADA presented defense counsel with bank account statement taken from D at arrest (D had more than $14,000) which cops had only then given to ADA: convictions reversed; that ADA did not use record in his "case in chief" was irrelevant, that ADA did not personally know of it earlier = irrelevant; that "late disclosure relates to [D's] OWN BANK ACCOUNT" = irrelevant because "obligations imposed on the prosecution to ensure that a criminal defendant receives a fair trial do not, and cannot, depend on something as unpredictable as the facts a criminal defendant chooses to disclose to his or her attorney";

C v Ira I. **439 M 805 (2003)**—written statements taken by school's assistant principal (re: after-school beating) were in his possession, and he wasn't acting as agent of police; error in dismissing charges on ground that DA failed to comply with discovery orders because he didn't provide these statements;

C v Niels N **73 MAC 689 (2009)**—electronic recording of multidisciplinary teams interview of sexual assault complainants is good practice, but SJC has not required that such recordings be made (citations) and D has not shown "any cognizable harm from the absence of a recording"; here D received in discovery copies of several participants' "notes";

C v Gilbert **377 M 887 (79)**—"penumbral effect" of "continuing duty" = DA must give witness's oral inconsistent statement to avoid misleading;

C v Daniels **445 M 392 (2005)**—trial judge abused discretion in denying **post-trial** discovery, given motion alleging newly discovered info that Commonwealth had withheld exculpatory info which had been specifically requested, and which cast doubt on credibility of ID made by sole eyewitness;

Dennis v US **384 US 855 (66)**—discovery promotes administration of justice & unlocks doors to truth; DA shouldn't have exclusive access to facts; judge (unlike advocates) can't tell impeachment value;

C v Allen **40 MAC 458 (96)**—move to require Commonwealth to videotape/record interviews with child sex complainants (repetitive & otherwise suggestive interviewing techniques create tainted and unreliable testimony which should be excluded);

C v Woodward **427 M 659 (98)**—move to allow D expert to be present at autopsy ("no reason why a judge may not order an opportunity for autopsy participation by [representative of] person charged in a homicide"); no error in refusal of second autopsy, since victim's family had rights to the body AND D FAILED TO ARTICULATE A SPECIFIC NEED (and second one "impracticable" because the procedure is "inherently destructive");

C v Conley **43 MAC 385 (97)**—ineffective assistance of counsel not to have moved for access to, and independent testing of, alleged victim's knife: evidence of D's and other victim's blood on it would have corroborated D's version of events and refuted Commonwealth's evidence, and D had repeatedly urged counsel to do this;

Williams v Florida **399 US 78 (70)**—adversary system isn't an end itself & not a "poker game," (so reciprocal discovery = OK);

Jencks v US **353 US 657 (57)**—FBI statement critical for confrontation; only defense can tell what's needed (then judge can rule);

C v White **47 MAC 430 (99)**—discovery conducted while first appeal was pending led to strong support for defense that cops added huge amount of dilutant to make

drugs weigh > 200 grams; though D counsel notified Commonwealth of intent to conduct independent analysis, drugs were destroyed; remedy = no conviction for drugs in amount requiring > 5 years minimum mandatory sentence;

C v Johnson **365 M 534 (74)**—sanction for unintentional failure to comply with discovery order (along with other grounds) = new trial;

C v Ellison **376 M 1, 3 (78)**—mistrial/new trial for (exculpatory) nondisclosure; inconsistent statements by prosecution witnesses = exculpatory for D;

Kyles v Whitley **514 US 419 (95)**—nondisclosure of crucial informant's inconsistent statements = reversal of capital case; prosecutor "has a duty to learn of any favorable evidence known to the others acting on the government's behalf in the case, including the police";

C v Silva **10 MAC 784 (80)**—dismissal for DA discovery refusal (+ speedy, 10-day violation); DA can't bypass sanction by indicting;

C v Gagliardi **21 MAC 439 (86)**—new trial because late (at trial) exculpatory discovery;

C v Molina **454 M 232 (2009)**—on fourth day of trial, ADA revealed that chief prosecution witness had been providing info unrelated to this case to state police drug unit before and after this murder: judge allowed defense interview of witness's state police contact and when witness declined to speak to defense counsel, judge held voir dire so that witness could be examined re: past and present relationship with police (before cross-exam with jury); this was adequate remedy; re: failure to disclose that trooper had amended log of findings concerning fingerprints found at scene (causing defense embarrassment on cross-exam), sufficient redress = Commonwealth's embarrassment via questions showing duty to have disclosed, failure to have done so;

C v Healy **438 M 672 (2003)**—[context of appeal of denial of R. 30 motion post-direct appeal] failure to disclose postmortem report noting absence of semen in deceased's mouth or rectum, or other "signs of recent sexual activity" was improper when Commonwealth claimed at trial that homicide occurred during homosexual encounter; no answer that D could have obtained info from another source, when he justifiably relied on DA's fulfillment of discovery obligations; *catalog of law re: nondisclosure of exculpatory evidence*;

C v Cronk **396 M 194 (85)**—dismissal sanction too severe because not irremediable or egregious; judge can reconsider before appeal's entry;

C v Steinmeyer **43 MAC 185 (97)**—sanction of striking defense witness's testimony too severe here; before imposing this severe a sanction, court must balance certain factors against right to present defense: prevention of surprise, bad faith or not, prejudice to other side, effectiveness of less severe sanction, materiality of testimony to case outcome;

C v Sena **429 M 590 (99)**—trial defense counsel was at fault ("ineffective") in failing to disclose to prosecution statements of witnesses as required by court order, but preclusion sanction was too draconian and continuance would have been adequate to protect Commonwealth interests; murder conviction reversed; trial judge "could have sanctioned defense counsel personally for violating the order, either by using her inherent powers or by referring him to the Board of Bar Overseers";

C v Juzba **46 MAC 319, 324 (99)**—trial defense counsel's default in discovery obligation caused judge to preclude testimony of defense witness, but appellate court says no "ineffective assistance" on this ground because better work wouldn't have accomplished something material for defense;

C v Dranka **46 MAC 38 (98)**—D counsel told prosecutor only just before jury impanelment that because of vasectomy, D incapable of being source of sperm; prosecutor voiced no objection to late disclosure of this fact (and physician witness) until two days later but the evidence was then excluded; reversal because judge failed to consider less drastic remedial measures, and anticipated testimony was "not the kind of sophisticated [evidence] that would appear to warrant extensive preparation time";

C v Lopez **433 M 406 (2001)**—when D was given notice of late-discovered Commonwealth witness only the day before murder trial began (when witness became known to Commonwealth), judge barred Commonwealth from calling witness in its case in chief five days later, but indicated might allow in rebuttal, after D had opportunity to investigate; no error in allowing such testimony in rebuttal nine days later, & no error in excluding "surrebuttal" of such witness, because proffered evidence was collateral or irrelevant;

C v Reynolds **429 M 388 (99)**—barring D's use of impeachment statements of Commonwealth witness was too severe a sanction for not disclosing them to Commonwealth; before sanction of preclusion, judge must make explicit findings regarding 5 factors outlined in *C v Durning* **406 M 485, 496 (90)**, "especially his consideration of alternative sanctions": prevention of surprise; evidence of bad faith in violation of pretrial conference report; [unfair] prejudice to other party caused by the testimony; effectiveness of less severe sanctions; materiality of the statements to outcome of case;

C v Cutty **47 MAC 671 (99)**—D himself cannot be precluded from testifying as sanction for failure to give notice of alibi (M.R.Crim.P. 14(b)(1)(D)) AND judge cannot bar counsel from using D's testimony in closing argument;

C v Freitas **59 MAC 903 (2003)**—though defense counsel claimed witness wasn't "alibi" witness, because "it's impossible to present an alibi witness to an indictment that says on divers dates over a seventeen month period", judge permissibly struck witness's testimony that he saw D regularly at a time when alleged assaults were occurring elsewhere;

C v McGann **20 MAC 59 (85)**—no harm from lateness because time to investigate & to use for cross-examination; *(See also Chapter 6-F below)*;

C v Soares **51 MAC 273 (2001)**—no harm from late addition (witness list) of daughter in household, in addition to mom (owner of ransacked jewelry boxes) & son (who discovered D in home), because cumulative, though D also argued that jurors hadn't been questioned at empanelment whether they knew such daughter; question to venire had been whether they knew named witnesses or 'any member of their immediate family';

C v Janvrin **44 MAC 917 (98)**—no harm from mid-trial production of ballistician's report, given defense of necessity presented at trial;

C v Shellenberger **64 MAC 70 (2005)**—midtrial on charge of motor vehicle homicide by negligent operation, DA switched from "speeding" theory to "under the influence of amphetamines", causing reversal: at minimum, there had to be evidence as to amount or concentration of the drug in D's system, and expert testimony indicating that the concentration would impair D's ability to operate a motor vehicle; that medical record recited that D had tested "pos" for amphetamines wasn't enough;

C v DeMaria **46 MAC 114 (99)**—when both prosecution and defense first learned on first day of trial that sexual assault complainant had tested positive for sexually transmitted disease and defense successfully moved for both funds for expert and short continuance, no relief for judge's refusal of three-day continuance because desired expert was on vacation; given absence of showing of bad faith or carelessness by prosecution, D required to show "material prejudice," here lacking (defense "adroitly" argued absence of evidence that defendant had contracted the disease);

C v Saunders **75 MAC 505 (2009)**—relying on discovery/police reports provided, D called police detective to show police had done nothing to verify complainant's allegations concerning hotel visits she purportedly made with D while she was underage, but detective cited portion of a report where he recorded interview with hotel clerk who recognized complainant's photo: judge struck testimony & appellate court said mistrial not required; voir dire revealed that "prosecution" was never given detective's entire report, and instead "some portions of it" were incorporated into a "final report" which was "provided to both the prosecution and the defense"; **NOTE WELL: THE "PROSECUTION"** *IS, AND INCLUDES, THE POLICE;* see *C v St. Germain* **381 M 256, 261 n.8 (80)**; *C v Baldwin* **385 M 165 n.12 (82)**—ADA responsible for what cops know; *C v Martin* **427 M 816, 824 (98)**—prosecutor's obligations extend to info in possession of any person who has participated in the investigation or evaluation of the case "and has reported to the prosecutor's office concerning the case"; *Kyles v Whitley* **514 US 419 (95)**—material possessed by police investigators and other agents of police or prosecutor = within prosecutor's control for purposes of discovery compliance; *C v Eneh* **76 MAC 672, 677 (2010)**—that prosecutor himself did not know of critical mandatory discovery material (D's bank account containing >$14,000, a document taken from D by police at arrest) until after defense opening statement portraying D as homeless and destitute heroin addict entrapped into selling drug in order to skim some off top for his own addiction was no excuse: reversal of convictions; delayed disclosure eviscerated ("crippled") the prepared defense, and it didn't matter that ADA did not introduce the record in prosecution's 'case in chief'; neither did it matter that the material withheld from D-counsel concerned info which D himself had to know (and also withheld from counsel, id. at 678: discovery obligations imposed on prosecution do not depend on "something as unpredictable as the facts [D] chooses to disclose to" counsel;

C v Lam Hue To **391 M 301 (84)**—dismissal with prejudice maybe OK because late disclosure (of exculpatory) hurt investigation, strategy, & opening; DA responsible for cops, "bungling";

C v Hardy **431 M 387 (2000)**—only days before homicide trial began, Commonwealth disclosed that a Commonwealth witness would attribute to D a statement revealing "motive"; though statement was very damaging, that's not the measure of prejudice; instead, it's consequence of delay which is relevant in determining any remedy, not the likely impact of the late-disclosed evidence; no suggestion that trial tactics would/should have changed if D had been aware of evidence earlier;

C v Hunter **426 M 715 (98)**—cop destroyed notes of witness statements viewable as self-incriminating (& thus exculpatory of D) but no relief because other cop kept his notes, they were in evidence, & D-counsel cross examined both cops re: witness's statements;

C v Mandile **15 MAC 83 (83)**—dismissal OK as discovery sanction; reconsideration also OK, but 87 days later not "timely";

C v Barnes-Miller **59 MAC 832 (2003)**—alleged victim of annoying telephone calls was purportedly the "other woman" prompting D's divorce; "victim's" claim of 5th Amendment privilege at deposition in divorce action held legitimate, and judge erred in dismissing, over Commonwealth objection, the criminal case (at which alleged victim remained committed to testifying); though G.L. c. 258B, § 3(m) gives victim/witness right to decline interview by defense "except when responding to lawful process," it is a legitimate response to lawful process to invoke constitutional privilege when legitimate (& privilege could be waived later, at criminal trial);

Chappee v Vose **843 F.2d 25 (1st Cir. 1988)**—may exclude (D's) witness because late (promised) disclosure to DA; *(See Chapter 6-M);*

Taylor v Illinois **484 US 400 (88)**—(same); adversary system depends on discovery rules;

C v Stote **433 M 19 (2000)**—chemist's report disclosed by Commonwealth only 5 days before trial, but no relief, study to see what proffers are necessary for different result;

C v Sullivan **17 MAC 981 (84)**—evidence excluded (for nondisclosure) may be used to impeach;

US v Carrigan **804 F2d 599 (10th Cir. '86)**—inherent sanction power includes ordering deposition;

C v Fossa **40 MAC 563 (96)**—assignment session judge and/or trial judge should have granted continuance sua sponte when defense counsel discovered, immediately prior to trial, that Commonwealth had failed to disclose lengthy police report re: interviews with 2 Commonwealth witnesses, a "glaring procedural foul";

C v Gordon **422 M 816 (96)**—short continuance, rather than mistrial, OK when Commonwealth expert testified not only to blood-type testing (as to which defense had received discovery), but also to "directionality" of blood stain (no prior notice in discovery); mistrial necessary only if undisclosed evidence was "virtually destructive of" D's case;

C v Marrero **436 M 488 (2002)**—DA's "inadvertent" late disclosure of Commonwealth witness only four days before trial adequately remedied by judge offering to require the witness to submit to a voir dire hearing or to an interview by defense counsel or defense investigator, or both;

C v Light **394 M 112 (85)**—police standard same as DA (re: exculpatory evidence); but withheld in bench court not intentional/egregious, so just remand from jury session, not dismiss; (see also *C v Cameron* **25 MAC 538 (88)**) D need not accept without question totem-pole hearsay that requested videotape of booking was "blank"; Commonwealth argument/conclusion on available record that tape had no exculpatory potential "could rest only on an arbitrary preference for the officers' testimony over that of the defendant" (OUI prosecution); rejecting argument that D had burden to summons persons to court concerning the missing videotape; despite repeated pretrial requests, cavalier lack of response (& lack of inquiry to relevant police) by serially-assigned prosecutors, re: videotape of booking not "bad faith," but still, obvious & redressable negligence: reversal of conviction, & D free at any retrial to question & comment about fact of videotape and its loss or withholding by Commonwealth (without permitting response that tape was "blank" or machine "malfunctioned")];

C v Monteiro **396 M 123 (85)**—DA responsible for cops' withholding;

C v Soucy **17 MAC 471 (84)**—DA's duty extends to special police officer's reports though not in DA's possession; see also *Lam Hue To* **391 M 301 (84)**;

C v Bing Sial Liang **434 M 131 (2001)**—DA must ask "victim witness advocates" for info, particularly re: any oral statements of witnesses, for possible inconsistencies;

C v Matthews **10 MAC 888 (80)**—(rescript) DA not responsible for insurance company private eye who destroyed evidence (of dubious value); but cf. *C v Harwood* **432 M 290 (2000)** loss of item by "insurance fraud bureau," which works closely with office of Attorney General = sanctionable conduct;

C v Gallarelli **399 M 17 n.4 (87)**—cop's having lab report tantamount to DA's having it;

C v Leibman **379 M 671 (80)**—D gets exculpatory federal grand jury minutes;

C v Lykus **451 M 310 (2008)**—where investigation was "joint" by Federal and State authorities (no less than 19 FBI agents testified at D's state trial), FBI's failure to disclose to D (or to ADA prior to trial, so ADA could disclose to D) voice-print laboratory report = properly imputed to Commonwealth;

C v Dew **443 M 620 (2005)**—D had no right to introduce evidence of murder two days earlier in same building, also involving crack cocaine, because he didn't "provide a basis for a conclusion that he was not the perpetrator of that crime" as well; **judge didn't err in limiting D's access to grand jury minutes re: that crime**, because disclosure could have adversely affected that investigation;

C v Donahue **396 M 590 n.11 (86)**—because DA has easier access, (s)he must get for D exculpatory info. from FBI under some circumstances; D could rely on this DA's "apparent cooperation" & not file motion;

C v Delp **41 MAC 435 (96)**—Appeals Court excuses DA's failure to turn over exculpatory evidence in records held by DSS; but cf.

C v Wanis **426 M 639 (98)** & *C v Rodriguez* **426 M 647 (98)**—use M.R.Crim.P. 17(a)(2) to obtain police internal affairs department's reports/interviews;

C v Neumyer **432 M 23 (2000)**—judge may order, via M.R.Crim.P 17(a)(2), rape counseling center to produce records;

US v Pollock **417 F.Supp 1332 (D.Mass. 1976)**—dismissal for Drug Enforcement Agency (DEA) bad faith destruction of notes of D's (alleged) confession;

Kent Smith, *Criminal Practice & Procedure*, **§ 1814 (2d ed. 1983 & Supp.)**—divided opinion re: destroyed FBI interview notes;

See Chapter 7-L, Lost or Destroyed Evidence in Preparing for Trial;

C v Charles **397 M 1, 14 (86)**—approving "balancing test" of *US v Bryant* **439 F.2d 642, 653 (DC Cir. 1971)** re: loss or destruction of evidence (i.e., culpability of government, materiality of the evidence, potential prejudice to D);

C v Tucceri **412 M 401 (92)**—prosecutor's failure to disclose exculpatory evidence requires new trial if disclosure "might have accomplished something material for defense"; judges should be "sensitive" to D's specific requests for "exculpatory" evidence;

C v Brown **57 MAC 852 (2003)**—Commonwealth not at fault for failing to provide police inventory report because D's request for "police reports" wasn't specific enough to give notice that it was sought; despite fact that it corroborated D's testimony and showed cops to be lying, court claimed D hadn't shown risk that jury would have reached different conclusion if it had been admitted at trial;

C v Schand **420 M 783 (95)**—on M.R.Crim.P. 30 motion alleging failure to disclose exculpatory out-of-court ID procedures, D required to show both "exculpatory" and "material," i.e., "a substantial basis for claiming prejudice from the nondisclosure";

C v Henderson **411 M 309 (91)**—loss of victim's contemporaneous written description of assailant, which was "potentially exculpatory," justified dismissal; neither actual prejudice nor bad faith by government required; federal rule of *Arizona v Youngblood* **488 US 51 (88)**, rejected;

C v Harwood **432 M 290 (2000)**—loss of original letter, without which defendant's expert couldn't evaluate signature [copy inadequate for purpose], justified sanction of preclusion of testimony from prosecution witness saying that the signature wasn't his (Commonwealth contended D forged signature); action (losing letter) of insurance fraud bureau, funded by insurance companies, but having "close & coordinated relationship" with Attorney General, was imputable to Commonwealth; rationale: D had lost opportunity to effectively cross-examine the witness;

C v Phoenix **409 M 408 (91)**—police destruction of evidence during forensic testing subjected to balancing test for appropriate relief;

C v Troy **405 M 253 (89)**—judge properly restricted prosecution theories of 1st degree murder because of government's careless destruction of blood sample;

C v White **47 MAC 430 (99)**—sanction: government's careless destruction of drugs resulted in appellate court's reducing sentencing culpability to trafficking in amount punishable by only mandatory minimum five years;

C v Lydon **413 M 309 (92)**—loss of car, papers & latent print from murder weapon did not require dismissal where loss not shown to be intentional or grossly negligent, no prejudice shown, & where defense did not move to preserve items;

C v Chase **42 MAC 749 (97)**—loss of truck driven by D in motor vehicle homicide did not require dismissal: no prejudice shown & at most negligence by Commonwealth;

C v Narea **454 M 1003 (2009)**—SJC on Commonwealth's 211/3 vacated trial judge's sanction for destroying purported "buy money" (i.e., precluding testimony at trial concerning it), saying D had to have "concrete evidence" that evidence was exculpatory/would have created reasonable doubt;

C v Buckley **410 M 209 (91)**—prosecutor's mid-trial disclosure of handwriting exemplar of person whom D claimed was true perpetrator should not have surprised D where D had given his own exemplar;

C v Gagliardi **29 MAC 392 (90)**—prosecutor's failure to disclose evidence until trial was neither deliberate nor prejudicial;

C v Giontzis **47 MAC 450 (99)**—prosecutor's failure to disclose expert witness called in rebuttal was deliberate and sleazy but appellate court believed jury verdict here was best D could ever get anyway;

C v Clements **36 MAC 205 (94)**—mid-trial disclosure of videotaped interview of witnesses not cause for mistrial when judge ordered its production and allowed D to use it and recall any witnesses (DA did not know of it, made by complainant's "treatment clinician");

C v Nester **32 MAC 983 (92)**—D should have been given 1-day mid-trial continuance to call rebuttal expert where Commonwealth expert gave unexpected testimony about possible presence of seminal fluid despite lab report results indicating absence of sperm;

C v Hamilton **426 M 67 (97)**—DA's disclosure, on 1st day of trial, that D's fingerprints were found inside car driven away from homicide by assailants, did not require 2 week continuance requested by D (who had prepared ID defense); if D counsel had not answered 'ready' after 2-day continuance or had insisted, on the record, with a proffer of facts, that mental impairment defense was now crucial, abuse of discretion might have been found;

C v Sullivan **410 M 521 (91)**—misplaced reliance by defense in opening statements on inaccurate pretrial discovery cured by judge's instruction blaming prosecutor; contrast *C v Eneh* **76 MAC 672 (2010)**—after defense opening, ADA disclosed info (which was within mandatory pretrial discovery obligations) which "crippled" the prepared defense of entrapment;

Pennsylvania v Ritchie **480 US 39 (87)**—constitutional due process right to in camera review of state agency's confidential investigative files & subsequent release of material info to defendant;

Jaffee v Redmond **518 US 1 (96)**—confidential communications between psychotherapist and patient = protected from compelled disclosure under Rule 501 of the Federal Rules of Evidence; see dissent by Scalia, J;

C v Stockhammer **409 M 867 (91)**—[NOTE WELL: STOCKHAMMER HOLDING WHOLLY ALTERED BY BISHOP, FULLER, **AND NOW C v DWYER 448 M 122 (2006)** ETC., POST] defense counsel in sexual assault cases must be given direct access to privileged psychiatric & social work records of complainant to ferret out bias, prejudice, motive to lie, or mental impairment under Article 12 (but later overruled/modified, huge procedural hurdles set: see *C v Fuller* **423 M 216 (96)**, though perhaps future revision, more favorably inclined to due process for D, signaled possible in *C v Sheehan* **435 M 183 (2001)**, concurring opinion by Sosman, J.);

C v Arthur **31 MAC 178 (91)**—Stockhammer extended to 51A & 51B DSS records;

C v Hrycenko **31 MAC 425 (91)**—Stockhammer applied to Dept. of Mental Health records; D entitled to in camera hearing if he seeks to introduce records into evidence;

C v Figueroa **413 M 193 (92)**—rule extended to Dept. of Mental Retardation records & other records relating to complainant's mental impairment; applied retroactively to cases pending on appeal where issue was preserved;

C v Gauthier **32 MAC 130 (92)**—Stockhammer extended to special education records;

C v Bishop **416 M 169 (93)**—IF a privilege is asserted when D seeks arguably privileged counseling/treatment records of sexual assault complainant, (1) judge must make written findings as to whether privilege applies; (2) if privileged records are sought, counsel must make written submission outlining theories under which the records are likely to be relevant to an issue in the case, and if proffer satisfies the judge, judge is to examine records in camera, separating relevant from irrelevant materials; (3) judge supplies relevant records to counsel, subject to protective orders if necessary, so that counsel may determine whether to seek disclosure/use of records at trial ("necessary to provide the defendant a fair trial"); (4) judge must rule on counsel's written motion for trial disclosure; (5) final determination as to admissibility of the records is made by trial judge, "subject to any other statutes or rules of evidence that may apply; **but now see *C v Dwyer* 448 M 122 (2006)**;

C v Fuller **423 M 216 (96)**—regarding G.L. c. 233, § 20J (records of "sexual assault counselors"), D must demonstrate good faith, specific, & reasonable basis for believing that records will contain exculpatory evidence relevant to D's guilt before in camera inspection by judge can be undertaken, but now see *C v Dwyer* **448 M 122 (2006)**;

C v Dwyer **448 M 122 (2006)**—protocols established by *C v Bishop* and *C v Fuller* are reconsidered, and now changed, as follows: (1) before judge determines whether summons for records may issue to any person or institution, the custodian of records and person who is subject of records shall be given notice and opportunity to be heard re: whether records are relevant or covered by statutory privilege (but privilege will be presumed, and won't be deemed waived even if subject fails to assert statutory privilege, & there's no requirement that judge determine at this stage whether or not the records are in fact privileged); (2) if judge orders issuance of Rule 17(a)(2) summons, all presumptively privileged records so summonsed are retained in court under seal, to be inspected only by counsel of record for D; (3) before inspecting such records, counsel shall sign and file protective order containing stringent nondisclosure provisions [i.e., inter alia, can't copy, disclose, disseminate contents to any person, INCLUDING THE DEFENDANT], and can't disclose to anyone unless and until judge "allows a motion for specific, need-based written modification of the protective order"; this decision is "informed by art. 12 of the Declaration of Rights" but isn't "constitutionally compelled," and thus applies only to cases tried after issuance of rescript in this opinion;

Rodriguez v Commonwealth **449 M 1029 (2007)**—G.L. c. 211, § 3 petition to force judge to mark for ID records whose production he had denied D under *Dwyer* [448 M 122] protocol, so that in normal course of appeal if convicted, appellate court could evaluate "prejudice", but SJC denies, saying that later appeal, if successful, would result in order that documents be produced and examined "to determine whether" D entitled to new trial;

Martin v Commonwealth **451 M 113 (2008)**—notwithstanding trial court judge's refusal to apply procedures for possible pretrial disclosure to D on ground that DSS records concerning complainant contained information about purportedly "absolutely protected" subjects of child custody and adoption placement, SJC held that

Dwyer protocol = applicable to ALL criminal cases; records privileged pursuant to G.L. c. 112, § 135B, G.L. c. 233, § 20B "or any other statute . . . are subject to the Dwyer protocol, regardless of their subject matter"; 3rd parties other than complainant need not be permitted to be heard on issues of privilege and relevancy even though records might divulge personal info about others;

C v Tripolone **425 M 487 (97)**—regarding "domestic violence counselor" records (G.L. c. 233, § 20K) D must demonstrate good faith, specific, & reasonable basis for believing that records will contain exculpatory evidence relevant to D's guilt before in camera inspection by judge can be undertaken;

C v Oliveira **431 M 609, 616 (2000)**—Fuller/Tripolone standard for obtaining in camera inspection extended to records of psychotherapist, privileged under G.L. c. 233, § 20B; trial counsel's failure to seek access to mental health treatment records of sex assault complainant might be ineffective assistance of counsel; post-conviction counsel's proffer of relevance needed to be [only] that standard which was in effect prior to trial (D shouldn't be prejudiced by applying more stringent standard which later came into being), and was here sufficient to obtain in camera review; counsel to submit another motion for new trial after obtaining access, to argue how records would have been useful at trial (standard: deprive of substantial ground of defense);

C v Maxwell **441 M 773 (2004)**—hospital/medical records containing info regarding infection with HIV (human immunodeficiency virus, "AIDS" status) not "absolutely" privileged (despite G.L c. 111, § 70F); Bishop-Fuller protocol applies;

C v Sosnowski **43 MAC 367 (97)**—insufficient proffer on motion for disclosure of privileged records ("based on my knowledge . . . , all requested discovery is relevant to the case . . . ");

C v Pare **427 M 427 (98)**—fact that privilege has been "asserted" does not mean that it applies in the circumstances; revised fn 4 makes clear that showing required of defense counsel in Tripolone/Fuller applies only when the records sought are privileged under G.L. c. 233, §§ 20J or 20K; trial judge may refuse to "revisit" motion for disclosure of the records and review them in camera unless there are changed circumstances;

C v Oliveira **438 M 325 (2002)**—judge can't bypass initial privilege analysis; non-privileged records summonsed under Bishop should be turned over to D counsel without any determination of relevancy by motion judge; social worker and psychotherapist privileges MUST BE ASSERTED BY PATIENT (unlike rape counselor privilege);

C v Pelosi **441 M 257 (2004)**—judge erred in bypassing stage of determining whether any privilege applied and whether it had been asserted; proffer sufficient when it sought to discern whether accusations were product of coaching or leading questions and/or appeared to change over time;

C v McCoy **443 M 1015 (2005)**—no relief for the Commonwealth pursuant to G.L. c. 211, § 3, although trial court judge "has not adhered to the precise steps and sequence of the Bishop-Fuller protocol," because these "technical errors do not amount here to a substantial claim of violation of substantive rights";

C v Narea **454 M 1003 (2009)**—SJC on Commonwealth's 211/3 vacated trial judge's sanction for destroying purported "buy money" (i.e., precluding testimony at trial concerning it), saying D had to have "concrete evidence" that evidence was exculpatory/would have created reasonable doubt;

C v Lampron **441 M 265 (2004)**—first step toward obtaining records from nonparty is to move under M.R. Crim.P. 17(a) for issuance of summons to produce; affidavit in support may contain hearsay, but must identify source of hearsay and show reliability; affidavit must show, specifically, relevance of documents requested; this step is PRE-"Bishop": if summons issues and nonparty either moves to quash based on claimed privilege, or asserts a privilege and refuses to produce the records, judge must then determine whether records are privileged and, if so, then move to the 'stage-two,' Bishop/Fuller [differently defined], 'relevance' determination);

C v Neumyer **48 MAC 154 (99), S.C. 432 M 23 (2000)**—fact that complainant contacted rape crisis center and date and time of call are not privileged; M.R.Crim.P. 17(a)(2) is proper tool for summonsing 3d party records into court; proffer sufficient under *Fuller* (conversations with counselor[s] sought for evidence of bias and prejudice, for evidence confirming theory that complainant had motive to fabricate); (see also *C v Wanis* **426 M 639 (98)** & *C v Rodriguez* **426 M 647 (98)** use M.R.Crim.P. 17(a)(2) to obtain police dept internal affairs reports/interviews;) see also *C v Beal* **429 M 530 (99)** info known to an "independent witness, but unknown to the prosecution, is not within the possession or control of the prosecution unless that witness has acted, in some capacity, as an agent of the government in the investigation and prosecution of the crime" and that prosecutor's "duty to disclose" doesn't apply to info which witness has but prosecutor doesn't; prosecutor has "serious" ethical duty not to keep himself wilfully ignorant of potentially exculpatory info; see also *C v Bing Sial Liang* **434 M 131 (2001)** DA must ask "victim witness advocates" for info, particularly re: any oral statements of witnesses, for possible inconsistencies;

Kyles v Whitley **514 US 419 (95)**—prosecutor "has a duty to learn of any favorable evidence known to the others acting on the government's behalf in the case, including the police"; "any argument for excusing a prosecutor from disclosing what he does not happen to know about boils down to a plea to substitute the police for the prosecutor, and even for the courts themselves, as the final arbiters of the government's obligation to ensure fair trials"; "Unless, indeed, the adversary system of prosecution is to descend to a gladiatorial level unmitigated by any prosecutorial obligation for the sake of truth, the government simply cannot avoid responsibility for knowing when the suppression of evidence has come to portend such an effect on a trial's outcome as to destroy confidence in its result"; goal = "preserve the criminal trial, as distinct from the prosecutor's private deliberations, as the chosen forum for ascertaining the truth about criminal accusations";

C v Fayerweather **406 M 78 (89)**—reversal for exclusion of evidence from privileged record that complainant claimed to hear voice of defendant telling her to do things;

C v Baxter **36 MAC 45, 51–52 (94)**—reversal for exclusion of evidence that complainant had been victimized previously &, that she was suffering from psychiatric problems as result, & that because of those problems & remarkable similarities between that trauma & present incident, complainant perhaps unable to distinguish between the two;

C v Pratt **42 MAC 695 (97)**—DSS social worker records indicated that complainant had failed to tell social worker about alleged sex assaults when it would have been natural to do so, & further, that social worker specifically asked complainant had been improperly touched & received negative response; reversal for exclusion of this evidence;

C v Sheehan **48 MAC 916 (2000), S.C., 435 M 183 (2001)**—reversal for failure to allow introduction of evidence that complainant had difficulty distinguishing fantasy from reality & that he fantasized to escape anxiety-provoking situations; concurring opinion (Sosman, J.) at 193–200 signals that *C v Bishop/C v Fuller* may be hugely revised, being criticized as a "failed experiment," id. at 199, and as "both unduly cumbersome and constitutionally flawed," id. at 194; higher priority must be given to D's constitutional right to a fair trial than to legislatively created privilege, id. at 196; Bishop procedures "ultimately fail to protect a defendant's right to a fair trial," id. at 197; "[i]t is always difficult, and often impossible, to demonstrate what important exculpatory evidence is in documents that one has not seen"; a D who is a stranger to a sex assault complainant "will never be able to meet the Fuller test," id. at 199;

C v Feliciano **442 M 728 (2004)**—single justice is empowered to act on 211/3 petition alleging foul play/

abuse by an interlocutory order of a panel of the Appeals Court considering a direct appeal from D's conviction; subject order merely directed delivery to Appeals Court of records held in Superior Court after finding/ruling by trial court judge that they contained nothing discoverable under Bishop-Fuller protocol, a matter as to which D sought review in direct appeal (SJC holds that if D's original proffer made plausible showing of relevance, the judge's in camera decision that records provide nothing or relevance IS SUBJECT TO APPELLATE REVIEW, and court must have access to the records; **at 735 n.5—trial judge has continuing obligation to release information from records as it may become material/important as proceedings progress, though "revisiting the prior judge's determination of relevance is not to be done sua sponte," and thus requires request by party;**

C v Seabrooks **433 M 439 (2001)**—patient (here D) may not claim the protection of G.L. c. 233, § 20B (psychotherapist-patient privilege), if s/he introduces mental/emotional condition as element of claim or defense, & judge finds "justice" from disclosure more important than protecting privilege, see G.L. c. 233, § 20B(c);

C v Callahan **440 M 436 (2003)**—Commonwealth cannot obtain D's old psychiatric records for use by "qualified examiners to determine alleged sexual dangerousness; G.L. c. 123A, § 13(b) did not abrogate existing privileges;

C v Fitzgerald **412 M 516 (92)**—prosecution's introduction of complainant's statements to rape crisis counselor opened door to D's introduction of counselor's notes relevant to complainant's motive to fabricate;

C v Reed **417 M 558 (94)**—claim that witness's psych treatment records should have been disclosed, because would enable defense expert to testify on witness's "veracity," unsuccessful: no witness may offer opinion as to another's credibility;

C v Esteves **429 M 636 (99)**—D had right to seek appellate review of relevance of documents withheld; Commonwealth may not move for their destruction until after appeal and any further proceedings thereby ordered;

6-E. ACCESS TO (AND KNOWLEDGE OF) WITNESS(ES)

See Chapter 6-L, Disclose Informant, & Chapter 11-H, Evidence, Sex Offenses;

M.R.Crim.P. 14—per 2004 revisions, mandatory discovery is expanded, *Smith v Illinois* **390 US 129 (67)**, summarized below: right to info for cross-examination (& purpose of discovery is to enable parties to be ready to try case at trial, without delays for investigation made possible only by belated disclosures); and see specifically G.L. c. 218 § 26A—in District Court/BMC, if D so moves, judge "shall order" Commonwealth to reveal names &

addresses of prospective witnesses & probation department to produce record of prior convictions of same);

Kent Smith, *Criminal Practice & Procedure*, §§ 1402 (2d ed. 1983 & Supp.)—(same); if give, can be protective order (e.g., tell only counsel, not D); § 202: informant disclosed if relevant & helpful;

Ray v Commonwealth **447 M 1008 (2006)**—no 211/3 relief for defense counsel pre-trial from order barring him from disclosing to D the identities of "civilian" witnesses against him, revealed in discovery materials given to counsel;

C v Holliday **450 M 794 (2008)**—protective order barring disclosure to defendants of addresses of witnesses, etc. upheld; though Commonwealth must show witness safety would be put at risk if info is made available to D without protective order, showing need not be "specific" when "danger to witness safety is inherent in the situation" (citing *Francis* 432 M 353 [2000], *Cobb* 379 M 456 [80], *Johnson* 365 M 534 [74]); order under review prohibited giving copies of witness statements to defendants BUT as implemented here defendants were given redacted copies of statements by agreement of Commonwealth; post-conviction hearing evidence supported findings by judge that counsel effectively prepared and communicated with clients within order's constraints as implemented so no prejudice shown;

ABA Standards for Criminal Justice (2d ed. 1980) Discovery 11-2.1—DA shall disclose W's names/addresses; ABA Standards, id., Prosecution Function & Defense Function (3d ed. 1993) 4-4.1: duty to promptly investigate all avenues to facts, including those known to law enforcement; 4-4.3 avoid interviewing witness alone *(See Chapter 2, Ethics: Lawyer as Witness)*; id., Comment, defense need not [i.e., but can] warn witness re: 5th Amendment;

C v Edwards **444 M 526 (2005)—if D is responsible or involved in procuring unavailability of a witness, witness's out of court statements (here, grand jury testimony) may be admitted against D; doctrine of "forfeiture by wrongdoing"**;

McNeal v Hollowell **481 F.2d 1145 (5th Cir. '73)**—OK to convince co-D (thru counsel) to take 5th Amendment;

SJC Rule 3:07, 3.4(f)—can't discourage/obstruct communication between witness & opposing counsel unless person is relative/employee/agent of client AND lawyer reasonably believes person's interests won't be adversely affected by refraining from giving such info; 4.3(b) can't . . . advise unrepresented person if interests conflict with D; 4.3(a) if lawyer reasonably should know that unrepresented person misunderstands the lawyer's role, lawyer shall correct misunderstanding;

(See also Chapter 14, Dismissal re: ethics of D's offers to "settle"; & Chapter 7-A, Investigation; & Chapter 2, Ethics: Bounds of Law, etc.)

C v Balliro **349 M 505, 516 (65)**—"witnesses belong to neither side"; D's right to interview jailed witness;

C v Curcio **26 MAC 738 (89)**—*(Chapter 6-L, Disclose Informant)* important witness under DA's control (not here) must be produced;

C v Dias **451 M 463 (2008)**—Commonwealth argued that informant needn't be disclosed because if judge would conduct in camera hearing, judge might determine that informant did not have info helpful to D, and would learn that informant would invoke 5th Amendment privilege; no in camera hearing necessary on facts here, because "clear from the record" that informant possessed relevant info helpful to defense (statements and actions attributed to informant by search warrant affiant identified only a female as the drug dealer, but although she had been charged, she was now to be the prosecution's star witness, claiming that D was instead the drug dealer); while informant did not waive 5th Amendment privilege by talking to police, privilege was properly determined if and when informant is called to testify;

C v Wanis **426 M 639 (98)**—police internal affairs records may be subpoenaed via M.R.Crim.P. 17(a)(2); here, Internal Affairs Division ordered to deliver to D statements received by it from percipient witnesses (including police officers) to events occurring at time of alleged crimes and defendant's arrest;

C v Rodriguez **426 M 647 (98) R.17(a)(2)**—approved as vehicle for discovery of police department Internal Affairs Division records; in order to obtain statements re D's "detention and arraignment," 1 & 3 days after arrest, D required to make showing (by affidavit) that there is specific reason for believing info relevant to a material issue in criminal case and "could be of real benefit to" D;

C v Neumyer **432 M 23, 34 (2000)**—judge could order rape counseling center to produce privileged records under M.R.Crim.P. 17(a)(2);

US v Bailey **834 F.2d 218 (1st Cir. '87)**—constitutional right to (at least supervised) access to witness who may be helpful, even just for cross-examination (& attorney duty to investigate);

US v Sclamo **578 F.2d 888 n.1 (1st Cir. '78)**—though not required by law, for fairness/efficiency government should reassess routine non-disclosure policy;

C v Adams **374 M 722 (78)**—D gets names of DA witnesses & their records *(See Chapter 6-H, Probation Records)*;

C v Figueroa **74 MAC 784 (2009)**—on day of trial, Commonwealth substituted one "drug expert" state trooper for the one previously listed: no relief since testimony likely not different from that anticipated, but "decision . . . should not be read as an invitation to a cavalier disregard of discovery rules";

M.R.Crim.P. 14(b) & Reporter's Notes—reciprocal discovery of alibi & insanity expert so DA can research & prepare; *(See Chapter 6-M re: disclosure of defense witnesses)*;

C v Ennis **1 MAC 499 (73)**—without disclosure of witness/informant, D was denied his rights to interview, summons, cross-examine; *(Chapter 6-L, Disclose Informants)* (particularly, e.g., *C v Choice* **47 MAC 907 (99)** during cop's testimony at trial, D counsel first learned of important witness, and cop should have been required to answer question as to his identity);

C v St. Pierre **377 M 650, 657–58 (79)**—if DA tells witness not to talk, ask judge to instruct witness and to provide access to neutral ground; but cf. G.L. c. 258B § 3(m) (complainant has "right" to be informed of "right" to submit to or to decline interview by D-counsel or anyone acting for D & "right" to impose "reasonable conditions");

US v Carrigan **804 F.2d 599 (10th Cir. '86)**—deposition ordered because DA told witness not to talk;

C v Flynn **362 M 455 (72)**—right to interview witnesses separately & privately;

C v Benoit **389 M 411 (83)**—(same), i.e., recess; not required to question witness on stand without interview (after DA summonsed witness for D); but see *C v Rivera* **424 M 266 (97)** Commonwealth's keeping "secret" for "security reasons" addresses of 3 witnesses, & allowing telephone contact by D counsel & investigator from DA's office; no relief for D when DA interrupted & told witness that he preferred to be present rather than let witness by interviewed in private by defense; choice was that of witness, after *Carita* **356 M132 (69)** colloquy between judge and witness;

C v Carita **356 M 132 (69)**—witness in custody of Commonwealth should be brought to court, instructed on right to consent to or refuse D-interview; record of advice should be kept; but see *C v McMiller* **29 MAC 392 (90)** Brown, J., concurring) suggesting violation of D's right to counsel in tactic of prosecutor insisting on listening on extension telephone as D counsel spoke to witness, access to whom was otherwise frustrated by Commonwealth;

C v Giacobbe **56 MAC 144 (2002)**—D, charged with sex assaults of ex-wife, sought to interview couple's children who were very belatedly added to Commonwealth's witness list; DA arranged interview at DA's office, but ex-wife insisted that D not be present and that victim witness advocate be present; trial judge refused any other accommodation upon D's motion to exclude testimony if these restrictions prevailed, and refused to bar "advocate" from discussing interviews with DA; no relief on appeal, since it was "victim" rather than DA who was setting the conditions; ON THE RECORD (i.e., not in lobby) D should have asked for neutral third party rather than "advocate" to attend interview, and should have requested Carita (356 M 132) procedure;

McGrath v VinZant **364 M 243 (73), 528 F.2d. 681 (1st Cir. '76)**—D can ask witness's address on cross-examination, but DA can get voir dire re: safety threat [fns. 5 (SJC) & 3 (1st Cir.) maybe private disclosure to counsel)];

C v Cobb **379 M 456 (80)**—(same);

C v Francis **432 M 353 (2000)**—judge permissibly excluded questions, after balancing D's need against witness safety;

C v Righini **64 MAC 19 (2005)**—Commonwealth's refusal to provide dates of birth of police witnesses was not a valid basis for dismissing complaint; Commonwealth claimed that this info, "in conjunction with a social security number" "could potentially reveal the home address" of the officer and endanger him/her; G.L. c. 218, § 26A allows D to obtain names, addresses, and record of prior convictions, but court essentially held that "address" of police witness was satisfied by "department or agency addresses"; *see* **M.R.Crim.P. 14(a) (automatic discovery of names, addresses, and dates of birth of Commonwealth witnesses "other than law enforcement witnesses")**;

Smith v Illinois **390 US 129 (67)**—right to cross-examination about (informant's) address for bias/truth/investigation; "[w]hen the credibility of a witness is in issue, the very starting point in 'exposing falsehood and bringing out the truth' . . . through cross-examination must necessarily be to ask the witness who he is and where he lives. The witness's name and address open countless avenues of in-court examination and out-of-court investigation. To forbid this most rudimentary inquiry at the threshold is effectively to emasculate the right of cross-examination itself";

Alford v US **282 US 687 (31)**—(same) to identify witness with his/her environment;

C v Francis **432 M 353, 357–58 (2000)**—cooperating witness in "gang" shooting could be shielded from cross-examination about current residence and employment addresses after judge concluded safety would be threatened by such disclosure;

C v Johnson **365 M 534 (74)**—witness (on cross-examination) can't hide identity of another witness;

C v Choice **47 MAC 907 (99)**—during cop's testimony at trial, D counsel first learned of important witness, & cop should have been required to answer question as to identity of same;

C v Hanger **377 M 503 (79)**—D's alibi disclosure maybe conditional on DA's timely disclosure of rebuttal witnesses so D can investigate;

C v Donovan **395 M 20 (85)**—no bad faith and no harm from 2 surprise witnesses not on DA's list;

C v Scalley **17 MAC 224 (83)**—same;

C v Monteiro **396 M 123 (85)**—because D did not request disclosure of witnesses' and informants' names or info received from them, prosecution's duty to disclose was limited to evidence in its possession "obviously supportive of D's innocence";

C v Lewin (I) **405 M 566 (89)**—prosecutorial & police misconduct involving either delayed disclosure or fabrication of informant by police didn't justify dismissal where irremediable prejudice to D not established; D entitled to voir dire hearing on potentially exculpatory evidence from putative informant & to elicit at trial government misconduct without rebuttal by prosecutor; motion judge's finding that informant existed was clearly erroneous where there was equally compelling evidence that informant was fabricated;

C v McMiller **29 MAC 392 (90)**—prosecutor's threat to prosecute government agent if she supported D's claim of entrapment was improper & required reversal;

C v Penta **423 M 546 (96)**—informant, testifying for D at motion to suppress hearing/reconsideration, inconsistently with prior testimony, was told by judge at DA's prompting that inconsistent testimony could result in perjury prosecution, and did not thereafter appear at trial: SJC found no error, contrasting *C v Turner* **37 MAC 385 (94)** [prosecutor's threats to defense witness ("you better not show up in court", "I'll tear you apart", "put you away too") caused new trial even though this may have been only part of reason witness failed to appear to testify for D]; and *U.S. v Morrison* **535 F2d 223 (3d Cir '76)** prosecutor summonsed defense witness to office and in presence of 3 officers, told her of dangers of testifying;

C v Snook **28 MAC 955 (90)**—prosecutor's possible intimidation of defense witness was harmless;

US v Osorio **929 F.2d 753 (1st Cir. '91)**—prosecution witness's prior drug activity was exculpatory evidence for which prosecution had duty to search;

C v McMiller **29 MAC 392 (90)**—ADA can't ignore disclosure order; "Nor can we accept the distinction urged by the Commonwealth between an informer who participates in the crime and one who is merely a witness"; either way, disclosure of identity is important to a fair determination of the case;

US v Formanczyk **949 F.2d 526 (1st Cir. '91)** prosecution's continuing obligations required disclosure that informant re-entered country;

6-F. EXCULPATORY (AND MITIGATING) EVIDENCE, E.G., PRIOR INCONSISTENT STATEMENTS OR PROMISES

See also Chapter 7-L, Evidence Lost by Police; & Chapter 6-H, Probation Records;

SJC Rule 3:07, 3.8(d)—DA shall make "timely" disclosure of evidence tending to negate or mitigate guilt; 3.8(j) and prosecutor shall not intentionally avoid pursuing adverse evidence; 3.3(a)(4) shall not offer evidence known false; 8.4(c) unprofessional to engage in conduct involving fraud, dishonesty, deceit, misrepresentation;

Brady v Maryland **373 US 83 (63)**—DA must disclose exculpatory evidence if asked;

C v Ellison **376 M 1, 22 n.9 (78)**—though not proof of innocence, it's "exculpatory" if tends to negate guilt, calls into question a material point of prosecution case, or challenges credibility of important prosecution witness;

US v Agurs **427 US 97 (76)**—if specific request, DA must give or ask judge; if not, still must disclose if obvious exculpatory; should err towards disclosure;

US v Bagley **473 US 667 (85)**—no difference between "exculpatory" and "impeachment" evidence for purposes of *Brady v Maryland* obligation; distinction between "specific" and "general or no" request by defense for pretrial discovery abandoned; regardless of request, favorable evidence is material, & its suppression = constitutional error, if there's reasonable probability that result of proceeding would have been different if evidence had been disclosed to D; "a 'reasonable probability' is a probability sufficient to undermine confidence in the outcome";

Youngblood v West Virginia **547 US 867 (2006)**— note which fully supported D's defense of consent and impeached sex assault complainants' credibility had been shown to cop before trial, but after reading it he refused to take possession of it and directed person holding it to destroy it; D's post-trial petition on this basis "clearly presented a federal constitutional Brady claim"; showing of materiality doesn't require D to prove that the suppressed evidence would have resulted in D's acquittal; trial court's distinction between "exculpatory" and "only impeachment" = bad, as was excuse that since cop failed to show note to prosecutor, state couldn't be faulted for failing to disclose to defense counsel;

Kyles v Whitley **514 US 419 (95)**—withholding of inconsistent statements by informant who fingered D = Brady violation; capital conviction reversed; after "constitutional error" found under *Bagley* **473 US 667** standard, "harmless error" can't be found;

C v Gagliardi **21 MAC 439 (86)**—new trial because exculpatory evidence disclosed too late; *(See also Chapter 6-B, 6-D, re: sanctions (e.g., Lam Hue To 391 M 301 (84))*;

C v Gallarelli **399 M 17 (87)**—new trial for suppressed lab report regardless of likelihood of changing result;

C v Merry **453 M 653 (2009)**—opinion of Commonwealth expert about cause of damage to vehicle windshield and that there was no evidence that D was sitting up at time of vehicle crash (D theory = suffered seizure, collapsed, body rigid, foot stuck on accelerator) not disclosed until after conviction: material and exculpatory, new trial required;

C v Laguer **448 M 585, 594 (2007)**—same standards noted; MA retains Agurs's different standards to be applied when specific request has been made (undisclosed evidence "might have affected the outcome of the trial") as opposed to when no request or "only a general request" has been made (undisclosed evidence must create reasonable doubt which did not otherwise exist), i.e., doesn't follow *Bagley* **473 US 667 (85)**; holding that withheld report of FOUR or more fingerprints on telephone whose cord was used to bind victim, none matching D's, didn't require new trial, because D already had, and used, fact that NO fingerprints or other forensic evidence from apartment linked D to the crime, and fact that telephone had yielded "one" unmatching print; SJC claims it's "speculative" to assume that prints belonged to actual culprit rather than to victim, her daughter, or police; trial counsel's affidavit failed to assert that he would have attempted to identify these prints had he known of them, and eschewing such investigation would not have been unreasonable; also, assertion that for prints to be "probative" there had to be evidence establishing when the prints were placed on the phone;

C v Martin **427 M 816, 824 (98)**—prosecutor did not himself have, so failed to turn over, state police lab report re: five inconclusive or failed confirmatory tests for presence of LSD in victim (allegedly the cause of death); Commonwealth had duty to inquire; obligations extended to info in possession of any person who "participated in the investigation or evaluation of the case and . . . reported to the prosecutor's office concerning the case"; conviction reversed on related issue;

C v Spann **383 M 142 (81)**—no prejudice from late disclosure of info omitted in witness's statement;

K. Smith, *Criminal Practice & Procedure,* **§§ 1382–98 (2d ed. 1983 & Supp.)**—overview; if late disclosure, D should ask continuance, maybe mistrial or dismissal;

C v Wilson **381 M 90, 109, n.39 (80)**—general (or no) request, & DA gives only "material" evidence (creates reasonable doubt); if specific (interest in particular piece of evidence), greater duty & easier to reverse on appeal;

See *Soucy* **17 MAC 471 (84)** & *Leavitt* **21 MAC 84, 88 n.5 (85)**—*(Chapter 6–A);*

US v Keough **391 F2d 138 (2d Cir. 1968)**—new trial, though no bad faith by DA, because specific request & non-disclosure;

C v Roberts **362 M 357, 362 n.3 (72)**—because no request, no due process violation for unintentional non-disclosure of witness's non-D identification;

Napue v Illinois **360 US 264 (59)**—DA can't knowingly use false testimony; due process violation not to correct it;

C v Nelson **3 MAC 90, 100 (75)**—reverse for DA's silence re: unsolicited false testimony (re: case against witness being dropped);

C v Hill **432 M 704 (2000)**—failure to disclose agreement for "consideration" on drug trafficking charge in exchange for testimony for Commonwealth in murder prosecution = constitutional due process violation; evidence impeaching credibility of key prosecution witness = clearly exculpatory; SJC "emphasize[s]" that any communication suggesting preferential treatment to a key government witness in return for testimony MUST BE DISCLOSED to defense; fact that the terms of the agreement are not clearly delineated ["imperfect in . . . clarity"] does not insulate the arrangement from disclosure; witness had testified, denying consideration, and DA failed to correct;

C v Rebello **450 M 118, 127 n.10 (2007)**—noting that Hampden DA's office repeatedly uses "same cooperation agreement" described (at 126) as "unquestionably vague" ("your cooperation will be taken into consideration . . . complete and truthful testimony will benefit you upon disposition of your case. It is our intention to treat you fairly"); finding of fact by motion judge = conclusive that there was no further undisclosed agreement prior to witness's testimony (though murder charge against witness was dismissed on witness's motion only five weeks after D's conviction);

C v Collins **386 M 1, 12 (82)**—"We do not think it necessary, as the motion judge concluded, that such an 'arrangement' be limited to situations where the favorable recommendation is explicitly hinged on receipt of favorable testimony"; must disclose "any material arrangement," e.g., plea offer (though not a quid pro quo for testimony);

C v Gilday **382 M 166 (80)**—affirm though DA didn't have (and didn't reveal to D) exculpatory FBI reports; DA must reveal "reward" to/understanding with witness's lawyer (though witness himself unaware) re: bias;

C v Pasciuti **12 MAC 833 (81)**—DA should've told sooner that witness in protective custody, but lateness = harmless;

C v O'Neil **51 MAC 170 (2001)**—ineffective assistance of defense counsel found in failing to introduce existence of plea agreement between prosecution witness & Commonwealth (when witness denied such on stand), in failing to make sufficient. proffer to judge, in failing to call as witness either witness's attorney or the prosecutor whose letter notified defense counsel of agreement, in not objecting to "disingenuous" questioning/false testimony of witness in redirect by prosecutor; perhaps independent ground for reversal for all these transgressions would be prosecutorial misconduct in misleading judge when describing pertinent document, in questioning, and in closing argument lauding witness as unimpeachable/"selfless and inherently credible";

C v DeCicco **51 MAC 159 (2001)**—Brown, J., dissenting: "It may never be known whether or to what extent the prosecutor had hinted to [witness/co-venturer in murder] . . . that helpful testimony would be rewarded. The temptation for the prosecutor to engage in such conduct with indicted but untried witness is plain: witness has every incentive to 'go all out' in efforts to please prosecutor, while government is permitted to enhance witness's credibility by touting the lack of a plea agreement . . . ultimate disposition of [witness's] case provides sufficient basis to infer secret existence of at least a tacit plea arrangement at time of trial"; 2 of 3 judges believed that prosecutor's misconduct in argument that witness would not "get[ ] a deal from this DA's office" & was unimpeachable for interest did not give rise to substantial risk of miscarriage of justice; all 3 judges faulted D counsel for failing to raise issue on direct appeal rather than in motion for new trial, even though it came to counsel's notice only in Commonwealth's brief on direct appeal that witness had received "deal" some ten months after D's convictions which were the subject of the direct appeal;

Giglio v US **405 US 150 (72)**—new trial if witness's uncorrected falsity might have affected jury; DA's negligence isn't excuse re: unauthorized promise by ex-DA (unknown to trial DA) to witness;

C v Daigle **379 M 541 (80)**—no new trial because neither DA nor witness knew testimony (re: witness's prior plea and sentence) was false;

C v St. Germain **381 M 256 n.8 & n.10 (80)**—exculpatory = anything "tending" to negate guilt; "minor discrepancies in prior statements" = exculpatory; DA's duty extends to police info *(See Chapter 6-D, Discovery in General);*

C v Donahue **396 M 590 (86)**—DA (here) obligated to get & give witness's prior (exculpatory) statement to FBI;

C v Baran **74 MAC 256 (2009)**—defense counsel received in discovery only "edited" videotapes of interviews of child sexual assault complainants; twenty years later, different D counsel obtained the unedited ones, which contained both denials that D abused them and allegations that others had, and "vividly demonstrate" that children had been "coached"; further, DA failed to produce "various police reports and other materials" supporting inference that complainants had been sexually abused by someone else (& this would have been useful for impeachment or to rebut allegations of age-inappropriate sexual knowledge); "a rule . . . declaring 'prosecutor may hide, defendant must seek,' is not tenable in a system constitutionally bound to accord defendants due process" (citation omitted); record did not settle question whether withholding was "deliberate", but transcript indications "consistent with that contention"; videotape shown to grand jury contained "edited versions" of interviews of children, revealing "somewhat distorted portrayal of . . . allegations";

Bartholomew v Wood **34 F3d 870 (9th Cir '94) rev. 516 US 1 (95)**—*Brady v Maryland* - due process violation in failure to disclose that main government witness failed polygraph even though D made no specific request and even though results not admissible under state law;

C v Allen **40 MAC 458 (96)**—D complaining of repetitive & suggestive interviewing practices by Commonwealth of child sex complainants, but foundation insufficient here for excluding testimony as tainted & unreliable; videotaping or otherwise recording the interviews should occur;

C v Vieira **401 M 828, 832 n.5 (88)** & *C v Vaughn* **32 MAC 435, 440 (92)** quoting *C v Ellison* **376 M 1, 22 (78)**—statement which was more incriminating than statements of witness given to defense earlier "was exculpatory in the sense that the variance with the previous statements permitted 'challenge[ ] [to] the credibility of a key prosecution witness'"; cf. *C v Villella* **39 MAC 426, 431 (95)** if chemist signing certificate of analysis had previously tampered with evidence or given an erroneous analysis, might be exculpatory (merely omitting to report some of the substances contained in a sample is not the same thing);

C v Simmons **417 M 60 (94)**—"notice of alibi" in co-D/chief prosecution witness's file, though signed by counsel, was prior inconsistent statement of witness & **exculpatory,** but because D had not made specific enough request ("Statements" of co-D), appellate review = whether substantial risk of miscarriage of justice;

C v Delp **41 MAC 435 (96)**—records indicating that sexual assault complainant suffered from "impaired reality testing" = exculpatory if expert testimony established that this diagnosis could establish a doubt that witness was able accurately to perceive and recollect incident in question (could be basis for motion for new trial on ground of ineffective assistance of trial counsel if counsel had access to records and didn't use, or for motion for new trial on ground of newly discovered evidence);

C v Leibman **388 M 483 (83)**—prior inconsistent statements at federal grand jury = impeachment material, so exculpatory;

C v Baldwin **385 M 165 (82)**—timely disclosure of even minor (exculpatory) discrepancies of key witness;

(late or) non-disclosure, & judge can continue, mistrial, or exclude witness; DA responsible for cops' knowledge;

C v Connor **392 M 838, 850–52 (84)**—DA must disclose prior statement contradicting trial testimony; & disclose false impression given re: bias/promises (though truth as witness knew it);

C v Gilbert **377 M 887 (79)**—oral prior inconsistent statement = exculpatory; DA cannot subvert obligations by not writing things down;

C v Hunter **426 M 715 (98)**—cop destroyed notes re statements of witness which could be interpreted as incriminating of the witness (& exculpatory of D): no relief, since no prejudice; other cop did have notes (in evidence) & both cops were cross examined re witness's statements;

C v Johnson **365 M 534 (74)**—reverse for denial of cross-examination re: other eyewitnesses plus (good faith) non-disclosure of their statements;

C v Dechristoforo **371 M 26 (76)**—no prejudice (not reasonable doubt) from non-disclosed grand jury prior inconsistent statement;

C v Gregory **401 M 437 (88)**—no remedy for midtrial disclosure of impeaching witness (because not shown to be available);

US v Pollock **417 F.Supp 1332 (D.Mass 76)**—*(Chapter 6-D)* destroyed FBI notes, lost evidence, etc.

C v Schand **420 M 783 (95)**—on R.30 motion alleging failure to disclose "exculpatory," D bears burden of showing exculpatory and "materiality" ("a substantial basis for claiming prejudice from the nondisclosure");

See Chapter 6–D, above, re counseling/treatment records of complaining witnesses, e.g.,;

C v Fuller **423 M 216 (96)**—re sexual assault counselor records G.L. c. 233, § 20J, and *C v Sheehan* **435 M 183 (2001)** reversal for failure to allow introduction of evidence that complainant had difficulty distinguishing fantasy from reality & that he fantasized to escape anxiety-provoking situations; concurring opinion at 193–200 signals that *C v Bishop/C v Fuller* may be hugely revised, being criticized as a "failed experiment," id. at 199;

M.R.Crim.P. 11(a)(1)(D)(iv)—at pretrial conference, discuss "availability of witnesses," etc.;

ABA Ethics Op. 1169 (70)—absolutely must disclose civil client's death, otherwise grave injustice;

Fambo v Smith **433 F.Supp 590 (WDNY '77)**—must disclose that alleged gunpowder was replaced with sawdust;

People v Rice **513 NYS 2d 108 (CANY '87)**—misleading defense that dead witness is available = serious & reprehensible (but harmless here); but see *People v Jones* **44 NY2d 76 (78)** guilty plea stands though DA hid fact that complainant had died;

Virzi v Grand Trunk **571 F.Supp 507 (EDMich '83)**—must disclose that client died;

G.L. c. 262, § 29—witness fee = $6/day + $.10/mile; to see DA & "assist investigation"; D's witness gets fee afterwards;

G.L. c. 233, § 3—if summonsed, get fee, unless summonsed for indigent D in criminal case; M.R.Crim.P.,

Reporter's Notes- witness summonsed (by court) via Rule 17 gets G.L. c. 262, § 29 fee;

See also Chapter 8-C, cross-examination re: bias, pending cases, impairment, etc.; & Chapter 7-G re: competency & psych. history of witness; & Chapter 11-H re: evidence in sex cases;

C v Tucceri **412 M 401 (92)**—Commonwealth's failure to produce exculpatory booking photos required rever-

sal despite D's failure to make specific request; judges should be "sensitive" re: motions for specific evidence claimed by D to be exculpatory;

C v Delaney **404 M 1004 (89)**: *C v Baldwin* **426 M 105 (97)**—judge may order audio/videotaping of Commonwealth's psychiatric expert's interview with D;

6-G. STATEMENTS OF COMMONWEALTH WITNESS (FOR DISCOVERY AND IMPEACHMENT)

See also Chapter 6-D re: DA's responsibility for ("control over") police; & Reciprocal Discovery, Chapter 6-M re: Work Product;

C v Lewinski **367 M 889 (75)**—(citing ABA) without showing need, unless work product or special circumstances (& hearing & preserve for appeal), preferably PRE-trial, & maybe reciprocally, D gets "written statement"-approved, transcribed, substantially verbatim, or "a report consisting of a statement by witness"; ("provisional" practice, "may be superceded" by '79 Rules) *(See Chapter 6-D, ++Discovery in General);* - "work product" per M.R.Crim.P. 14 (a)(5) = portions of records, reports, memos, correspondence, etc. "which are **only** the legal research, opinions, theories, or conclusions of" a party or the party's attorney and legal staff (i.e., not witness interview notes); But See *C v Bing Sial Liang* **434 M 131, 138 (2001)** requiring attorney to produce notes and memos of witnesses' oral statements = "particularly disfavored because it tends to reveal the attorney's mental processes" (citations omitted);

M.R.Crim.P. 14(a)(2) & (d)—giving pre-trial = "discretionary," i.e., triggers reciprocal; "statement" = signed, adopted, approved, or substantially verbatim recording/transcription; Reporter's Notes: derived from 18 U.S.C. § 3500(e) & *C v Lewinski* **367 M 889 (75)**;

M.R.Crim.P. 23—after witness testifies, statement given if relevant (or else in camera inspect, protective order, etc.); to facilitate, can give sooner; includes "portion of report consisting of verbatim declarations of witness";

K. Smith, *Criminal Practice & Procedure,* **§§ 1406 n.1, 1803–14 (2d ed. 1983 & Supp.)**—Rules "derived from" Lewinski (which permits discovery of oral statements); R-23 broader than R-14; *(See Chapter 6-D);*

ABA Standards for Criminal Justice (2d ed. 1980) Discovery. 11-2.1—routinely disclose witness's statements to prepare trial; pressure of mid-trial disclosure may deny effective assistance of counsel; Comment: may include rough notes;

C v Simmons **417 M 60 (94)**—chief witness & co-D's notice of alibi, because signed by co-D's attorney, not technically W's "statement," so no relief from failure to disclose (even though it was exculpatory because inconsistent with W's testimony against D) because D's discovery request not specific enough;

In re Roche **381 M 624 (80)**—statement (possible prior inconsistent statement) to reporter = critical to judge defending himself before Judicial Conduct Commission;

C v Gilbert **377 M 887, 89–96 (79)**—DA's continuing duty; may include oral statement, because can't mislead & circumvent by choosing not to write stuff;

Palermo v US **360 US 343 (59)**—18 U.S.C. §3500 must be witness's own words, but not necessarily an automatic word-for-word; does not include a selective, memorized summary with impressions & interpretations;

Campbell v US **373 US 487 (63)**—witness approved & "adopted" agent's recitation; experienced agent expected to be accurate;

C v McGann **20 MAC 59 (85)**—list or sketch can be "statement";

C v Campbell **378 M 680, 700ff (79)**—in camera inspection (& preserve for appeal) disputed material;

C v Esteves **429 M 636 (99)**—material ("Bishop" records) deemed by trial court judge to be irrelevant must be preserved until after direct appeal and any further proceedings thereby ordered, notwithstanding Commonwealth's belief that they were insignificant (here, Commonwealth moved for records' destruction);

Jencks v US **353 M 657 (57)**—*(Chapter 6-D)* federal statement rule;

C v Vaughn **32 MAC 435 (92)**—detective's change in oral statements from 3 to 2 sets of footprints was material & exculpatory; prosecutor's failure to disclose it required reversal, even though change was more incriminating;

C v Wanis **426 M 639 (98)** and *C v Rodriguez* **426 M 647 (98)**—D may subpoena via M.R.Crim.P. 17(a)(2), police internal affairs division records re D's arrest; here, D entitled to statements obtained by Internal Affairs Division from percipient witnesses, including police officers, to events occurring around time of alleged crimes and D's arrest;

C v Reynolds **429 M 388 (99)**—D held to have been required to disclose statements of Commonwealth witness which he intended to use for impeachment (though SJC held that sanction of barring their use was too severe); tip: agree, explicitly, in pretrial conference report to disclose only statements of witnesses D intends to call at trial.

6-H. PROBATION RECORDS OF COMMONWEALTH WITNESSES

G.L. c. 218, § 26A—in District Court/BMC, judge shall order probation department to produce if D requests;

See Chapter 9, Impeachment by prior record (G.L. c. 233, § 21) & pending cases (motive to please prosecution)];

Mass. Constitution Declaration of Rights, Article 12—right to produce all favorable proofs, to be fully heard in defense, to meet witnesses face-to-face;

C v Devlin **365 M 149, 164 n.13 (74)**—"emphasize the desirability" in many cases of making probation record available; but up to counsel to investigate them (& ask continuance if needed);

C v Adams **374 M 722, 732 (78)**—D "entitled" to (names of DA witnesses & their) probation records; but not DA's obligation to collect, & no showing of harm here;

but see M.R.Crim.P. 14(a)(2) "discretionary" to order Probation Department to give record of prior convictions of witness;

K. Smith, *Criminal Practice & Procedure*, § 1405 (2d ed. 1983 & Supp.)—asserts there's "no general right" to probation records (ed.: this is no longer valid per amendment (in 2004) of M.R.Crim.P. 14(a)(1)(D));

C v Donahue **396 M 590 (86)**—DA to give FBI rap sheet because DA (not D) has access;

Bellin v Kelley **435 M 261 (2001) reversing 48 MAC 573**—which had held that police could be liable civilly for violating confidentiality of criminal offender record information by telling D's employer, the victim of larceny under investigation, of D's prior criminality);

6-I. ALLEGED STATEMENTS OF DEFENDANT AND CO-DEFENDANT

See Chapter 20, Suppress D's Alleged Statements;

M.R.Crim.P. 13(d)—filing requirements for motion to suppress; *(See Chapter 8, Severance (for co-D's alleged statements or antagonistic defenses) & M.R.Crim.P. 9, (pretrial) motion for relief from joinder);*

See Chapter 10, Preparing Defense Evidence re: Impeachment of D by prior inconsistent statement;

CPCS P/G 4.5(b)—discover (alleged) oral/written statements of D;

ABA Standards for Criminal Justice (2d ed. 1980) Discovery 11-2.1—shall disclose substance of (alleged) oral statements of D & co-D—necessary for both preparation & orderly pre-trial litigation;

C v Lewinski **367 M 889, 903 (75)**—[pre-Rules] written & substance or oral (alleged) statement of D & co-D to be provided pre-trial;

C v Lapka **13 MAC 24 (82)**—case law discovery maybe more than Rules & Reporter's Notes; DA should follow broadest reading of cases & routinely disclose substance of D's oral (alleged) statements; cops shouldn't frustrate by not writing "high cards of investigation & cornerstone of DA's case," so should be in police reports; vs … but see M.R.Crim.P. 14—D's written (alleged) statements & recorded statements = mandatory; (thus implying that D's oral & all of co-D's (alleged) statements = "discretionary");

K. Smith, *Criminal Practice & Procedure*, § 1380 (2d ed. 1983 & Supplement)—suggests that, in contrast with Fed.R.Crim.P. 16(a)(1) & SJC cases decided before M.R.Crim.P., Rule 14 changes position of Court & doesn't require disclosure of D's (alleged) oral statements; but see K. Smith, § 1416- continue or sanctions for delayed disclosure of D's statement & …

C v Janard **16 MAC 931 (83)**—(rescript) DA bound to disclose D's (alleged) oral statement (citing "Lewinski rule", *Gilbert* **377 M 887 (79)**, *Lapka* **13 MAC 24 (82)**, &

"compare Rule 14"); DA can't get wind, feign ignorance, & withhold; but no harm because no objection or request for continuance, voir dire, or impeachment for prior inconsistent statement (omission in report);

C v Gilbert **377 M 887, 893–96 (79)**—can't subvert rules by choosing not to write;

C v Lopes **25 MAC 988 (88)**—should give statements though not written;

C v Santiago **30 MAC 207, 222 n.5 (91)**—(dictum) police should write down "general thrust" of conversations with D & substance or absence of any exculpatory statements;

C v Cundriff **382 M 137 (80)**—continuance and cross-examination, so no harm by unintentional late disclosure;

C v Blaikie **375 M 601 (78)**—mistrial granted for unintentional non-disclosure of D's (alleged) statement; (but DA can use it in 2d trial);

C v Kent K, a juvenile **427 M 754 (98)**—2-page report re: D's statement disclosed to defense counsel only during jury trial (which followed many discovery requests and a bench trial): "there should be no room in the criminal justice system for such carelessness—if that is what it was"; no relief/no prejudice; rebuffing claim that prejudice lay in inability of defense to argue in opening that D willingly spoke with police after the shooting;

C v Howard **8 MAC 318 (79)**—after motion allowed, continuing duty through trial; prejudicial nondisclosure = 1 reason to reverse;

C v Delaney **404 M 1004 (89)**—judge had discretion to order taping of Commonwealth expert's psych. interview of D; SJC had no need to decide reported question of whether such was required by D's constitutional right to effective assistance of counsel;

C v Baldwin **426 M 105 (97)**—judge may order audio/videotaping of Commonwealth's psychiatric expert's interview of defendant, but no constitutional right to such recording;

C v Stockwell **426 M 17 (97)**—on hearing conducted, no relief for judge's refusal to order psychiatric interview's taping;

US v Lewis **511 F.2d 798 (DC Cir. '75)**—error to use D's alleged statement if DA promised not to; alleged statement of D should be disclosed if asked;

US v Padrone **406 F.2d 560 (2d Cir. 69)**—late (post-direct) disclosure of D's (alleged) statement & serious prejudice, so new trial (though DA = unintentional);

US v Pollack **417 F.Supp 1332 (D.Mass. 1976)**—dismissal for FBI's bad faith destruction of notes of talk with D;

C v Gonzalez **443 M 799 (2005)**—trial witness's testimony concerning what coventurers did in "reenacting" fatal fight implicated hearsay concerns despite lack of testimony concerning anything "said" out of court; "conduct can serve as a substitute for words, and to the extent it communicates a message, hearsay considerations apply"; evidence that defendant was present during the reenactment, however, made it admissible as adoptive admission of defendant;

C v Reed **444 M 803 (2005)**—evidence of out-of-court accusation of D made in D's presence shouldn't have been admitted (there was unequivocal denial, so no adoptive admission by silence), but no objection/strike motion here; thereafter, judge should have allowed evidence of D's denial (curative admissibility);

See Chapter 6-B, Motions, Chapter 6-D, Discovery & Sanctions, & Chapter 7-L, Lost Evidence;

6-J. POLICE REPORTS

See also Chapter 6-F & 6-G, Exculpatory Evidence & Witness Statements; Chapter 11-H, re sexual assault complainant's identity;

M.R.Crim.P. 14—"discretion" re: any material & relevant documents possessed by anyone under direction & control of DA; Reporter's Notes: though SJC suggests police reports are discoverable, Rule intends generally NO unless "statement" within R-14 or R-23;

K. Smith, Criminal Practice & Procedure, § 1410 (2d ed. 1983 & Supp.)—excise & give statements by D, but otherwise pre-trial access = discretionary under case law;

C v Cobb **379 M 456 (80)**—(same); but see *C v Wanis* **426 M 639 (98)** and *C v Rodriguez* **426 M 647 (98)** D may subpoena, via M.R.Crim.P. 17(a)(2), records of (even) police internal affairs division; here, D entitled to get statements therein of percipient witnesses, including police officers, to events at the time of crimes and D's arrest;

Jencks v US **353 US 657 (57)**—*(Chapter 6-D, above)* witness's FBI statement critical for cross-examination; only counsel, not DA or judge, can tell what's relevant to defense;

C v Campbell **378 M 680 (79)**—(for new trial motion) defense should see & evaluate report & tell how it would've helped try or prepare;

G.L. c. 66, § 10—"public records";

G.L. c. 4, § 7(26)(f)—public record exemption for investigatory materials if disclosure would prejudice effective law enforcement;

Antell v Attorney General **52 MAC 244 (2001)**—materials privileged as work product under M.R.Civ.P. 26(b)(3) aren't protected from disclosure under public records statute, G.L. c. 66, § 10, & there is "no blanket exemption for police records or investigation materials"; at issue were documents re: witness interviews; court re-manded to permit appropriate redactions to preserve anonymity of voluntary witnesses in special circumstances here present;

Reinstein v Comm'r **378 M 281 (79)**—firearm discharge reports not automatically exempt from G.L. c. 4, § 7; case-by-case question whether ongoing investigation or "privacy";

Bougas v Chief **371 M 59 (76)** even if exempt under G.L. c. 4, § 7 from disclosure (as "investigatory materials"), report maybe discoverable within *Lewinski* **367 M 889, 903 (75)**;

Julian v Randazzo **380 M 391 (80)**—police report admissible as "business record," but not opinions or totem-pole hearsay *(See Chapter 11, Evidence)*;

C v Burns **43 MAC 263 (97)**—"absent meaningful argument to the contrary," court refused relief when cop prepared and disclosed only "summary" of his investigative notes, originally written on, e.g., scrap paper & napkins; discovery order did not say "original investigatory notes" were to be disclosed;

C v Tucceri **412 M 401 (92)**—prosecutor's failure to disclose exculpatory police booking photo required new trial;

C v Santiago **30 MAC 207, 222 n.5 (91)**—(dictum) police should write down "general thrust" of conversations with D & substance or absence of any exculpatory statements;

C v Scott **408 M 812 (90)**—D's failure to press for discovery of police reports re: purportedly similar attack by another person prevented appellate relief for judge's refusal to order "access" to that attack victim, and prevented counsel from making an adequate proffer at trial as to the relevance of the other crime (i.e., that it was distinctively similar so as to suggest strongly that the same person, not D, committed both that crime and the one being tried);

6-K. IDENTIFICATION—PROCEDURES AND PHOTOS

See Chapter 18, Identification issues; Chapter 6-C re: Motions; & Chapter 20, Suppression, re: deadlines & affidavit requirements for motions to suppress.

See also Chapter 7-B, Subpoenas (e.g., "911" tape, mugshot(s), videotape, etc.];

CPCS P/G 4.5(a)—seek details of ID procedures; 4.7(a) consider Motion for Nonsuggestive ID;

C v Jones **362 M 497, 501 (72)**—up to counsel to seek non-suggestive ID;

C v Dougan **377 M 303 (79)**—due process right to ID procedures meeting basic standard of fairness "would mean little if it did not carry with it the right to be informed of the details of any out-of-court identification, even if it were not used at trial; before any retrial here, should be "voir dire hearing at which all the circumstances surrounding the pretrial identification . . . can be developed"; due process right to fair ID procedures;

C v Dickerson **372 M 783 (77) abrogated by** *C v Paulding* **438 M 1 (2002)**—must give D complete voir dire because great & tragic dangers of mistake;

C v Farnkoff **16 MAC 433, 438–39 (83)**—judge should've given a voir dire (but no harm because no pretrial conference request & no suggestiveness);

C v Riley **17 MAC 950 (83)**—(rescript) discretion to deny voir dire re: suggestiveness;

Watkins v Sowders **449 US 341 (81)**—no (federal) due process right to voir dire without jury re: suggestiveness;

K. Smith, *Criminal Practice & Procedure,* **§ 1401 (2d. ed. 1983 & Supp.)**—D entitled to know at trial if photo was in group shown to witness, but not entitled to see entire array; [notwithstanding Judge Smith's apparent opinion, this is an indefensible assertion: see, e.g., *C v Dougan* **377 M 303, 316 (79)**, above, & *C v Tucceri* **412 M 401 (92)** Commonwealth's failure to produce exculpatory booking photos showing D with mustache, contradicting prosecution testimony that attacker was clean shaven, required reversal despite D's failure to make specific request]

C v Walker **14 MAC 544 (82)** no harm in failing to segregate & preserve photo complaining witness said "resembles" culprit;

6-L. DISCLOSE INFORMANT

See also Chapter 6-E, Access to Witnesses;

C v Ennis **1 MAC 499 (73)**—though state's privilege to withhold, need for truthful verdict compels disclose material witness; refusal denied rights to interview, compulsory process, & cross-examination *(See Chapters 9, 10)*;

C v Taliceo **13 MAC 925 (82)**—(rescript) (same); eyewitness maybe relevant/helpful;

Roviaro v US **353 US 53 (57)**—disclosure if ID = relevant or helpful to defense or essential to fair determination;

US v Bailey **834 F.2d 218 (1st Cir. 87)**—*Roviaro* **353 US 53 (57)** is a constitutional right;

C v Madigan **449 M 702, 711 (2007)**—even though D knows identity of person Commonwealth is calling "confidential informant," confirmation of D's "susp[icion]" implicates confidentiality/public policy concerns (but here, nonetheless required revelation of inducements/rewards to the informant, as material to defense and potentially exculpatory);

US v Valenzuela **458 US 858 (82)**—how to show relevance without prior access;

C v Dias **451 M 463 (2008)**—judge may hold in camera hearing to help determine whether disclosure of informant would provide material info to D when issue is not otherwise clear from record, but here, affidavit of police detective submitted in support of search warrant made clear that informant's info was relevant and helpful to D, and no such hearing warranted; further claim that in camera hearing could defeat D's disclosure motion because informant could indicate intention to invoke 5th Amendment privilege also rejected; while informant did not waive 5th Amendment privilege by talking to police, privilege would be properly determined if and when informant was called to *testify*; even if informant would not testify at trial, informant's identity would be of use to D in investigation and cross-examination of individual named by informant as his consistent and repeated drug source (who had been charged but would now be star prosecution witness claiming that instead D was the drug seller);

C v Collins **11 MAC 126 (81)**—if in doubt, judge must hold in camera hearing; but see *C v Clancy* **402 M 664 (88)** Declaration of Rights may require counsel's participation in camera review (of rape counselor privilege); & see . . .

C v Lugo **23 MAC 494 (87)**—same rules for surveillance location privilege; very hard for judge to be surrogate advocate in camera;

C v Grace **43 MAC 905 (97)**—surveillance location privilege may be overcome upon proffer as to how info is relevant and helpful to defense, or is essential to a fair determination;

C v Shaughessy **455 M 346 (2009)**—re: motion to discover confidential informant, judge could consider affidavit submitted ex parte (to be permitted in "exceptional circumstances"), BUT had to permit Commonwealth enough info for response, e.g., giving redacted or summary version of affidavit content; informant's lack of physical presence at point of drug activity for which D was indicted "is not determinative" of disclosure order; "ordinarily" protective order should be entered (if disclosure ordered) so identity will not be used beyond reason for disclosure;

C v Figueroa **74 MAC 784 (2009)**—(upholding refusal to disclose identity) that informant gave tip and made two controlled buys did not make him "a percipient witness to the incidents forming the basis of the indictments" purportedly because *prosecution's* case would rely only on evidence found in apartment later pursuant to search warrant; decision failed to comprehend that if informant would testify to having dealt [only] with different person, its value would be **exculpatory**, even if not conclusive of innocence (D cited *Brady v MD* 373 US 83 [63]), buttressing defense that he was NOT one of the 3 men involved in drug sales; disturbing burden shift in "analysis", i.e., "evidence that others were selling cocaine from the apartment in which he was found would not have negated the inference that the defendant was also involved in such sales";

US v Williams **496 F.2d 378 (1st Cir. '74)**—DA must give correct info &/or use reasonable diligence to locate informant;

C v Curcio **26 MAC 738 (89)**—varying DA duty to produce informant; OK here;

Franks v Del **438 US 154 (78)**—if substantial showing search warrant or arrest warrant affidavit's intentionally or recklessly false, hearing re: suppression;

C v Reynolds **374 M 142 (77)**—(same); *(See Chapter 20-J, Suppression: Arrest & Search Warrants)*;

C v Abdelnour **11 MAC 531 (81)**—no disclosure without substantial preliminary showing (intentionally or recklessly false & crucial to probable cause finding); D's burden of proof by affidavit or offer/proof that police were unreasonable;

C v Douzanis **384 M 434 (81)**—mandatory in camera hearing if preliminary showing made; otherwise, hearing's discretionary;

C v Nelson **26 MAC 794 (89)**—trial court judge ordering disclosure of informant identity because informant testimony could establish that (1) none of the defendants is the "Willie" whom the informant observed in the apartment, and (2) none of the defendants was seen by the informant during his observations of cocaine dealing in the apartment; remand to see if stipulation possible to solve informant question;

US Dept of Justice v Landano **508 US 165 (93)**—F0IA (Freedom of Information Act) exemption 7(D) (disclosure not compelled when info could reasonably be expected to disclose ID of confidential source) may not be invoked by FBI automatically whenever **any** individual or institutional source supplies info during criminal investigation: FBI must particularize any claim of confidentiality; implied assurance of confidentiality may be found from character of particular crime or source's relation to the crime, and paid informants normally **do** expect confidentiality;

Antell v Attorney General **52 MAC 244 (2001)**—materials privileged as work product under M.R.Civ.P. 26(b)(3) aren't protected from disclosure under public records statute, G.L. c. 66, § 10, & there is "no blanket exemption for police records or investigation materials"; at issue were documents re: witness interviews; court remanded to permit appropriate redactions to preserve anonymity of voluntary witnesses in special circumstances here present;

K. Smith, *Criminal Practice & Procedure*, §§ 186–92 & 202–7 (2d ed. 1983 & Supp.)—overview;

See Chapter 20-J, re veracity challenges to search warrant applications;

C v McMiller **29 MAC 392 (90)**—improper for prosecutor not to comply with court order to disclose informant's identity on ground that D "knows" who informant is;

C v Healis **31 MAC 527 (91)**—D entitled to name, address, & record of informant who was active participant in deal & whom D genuinely planned to call at trial; actual prejudice not required;

C v Connolly **454 M 808 (2009)**—only during trial did undercover cop reveal she had been introduced to D by an informant prior to controlled purchases allegedly made from D; judge responded by ordering ADA either to disclose identity or not to question witness regarding the earlier meeting; ADA chose latter option, and voir dire by D counsel did not provide argument that identity would be relevant/helpful to D;

C v Choice **47 MAC 907 (99)**—reversal because judge refused to order trial witness-cop to answer question as to identity of man who allegedly hooked cop up with D, allegedly drug seller (even though not apparent that the man knew he was cooperating with [undercover] police); not necessary that defense be able to show exactly how the info might have helped defense; sufficient that the man "was placed by the prosecution in a central role in the case";

C v Clarke **44 MAC 502, 511 (98)**—Commonwealth not required to disclose identity of informant who is not active participant in crime charged (unless prejudice can be shown in circumstances); but see *C v McMiller* **29 MAC 392 (90)** Court refused to accept distinction urged by Commonwealth between "participant" and "mere witness," the latter argued to be not discoverable;

C v Mello **453 M 760 (2009)**—though undercover cop was agent regarding whom D's affidavit effectively raised entrapment, D's motion to compel Commonwealth to say whether or not person who introduced D to him was government agent was denied: D's affidavit did not allege that this person induced D to commit crimes or that she participated in cop's inducement of those crimes; that Commonwealth failed to charge D with crime related to date on which this person was present perhaps to avoid disclosure of agency didn't matter (fn.5);

C v Madigan **449 M 702 (2007)**—trial court judge correctly ordered Commonwealth to disclose info concerning promises, rewards, inducements to confidential informant where info was material to defense of entrapment, on which D made adequate pretrial showing; Commonwealth's argument that entrapment not viable defense not cognizable as basis, pretrial, for refusing discovery;

C v Shaughessy **455 M 346 (2009)**—after considering D's ex parte affidavit documenting "importuning" by informant sufficient to meet D's burden of showing informant identity as material to entrapment defense, judge ordered Commonwealth to confirm or deny that named individual was confidential informant and if confirmed, to reveal promises, rewards, inducements; SJC held Commonwealth entitled to learn enough from ex parte affidavit to formulate opposition;

C v Manrique **31 MAC 597 (91)**—counsel's supposed failure to accept prosecutor's offer of informant's last known address construed as deliberate effort to pursue missing witness strategy;

C v Lugo **406 M 565 (90)**—right to cross-examination requires disclosure of surveillance location necessary to fair trial; right to disclosure greater at trial than at pretrial hearings;

C v Beauchemin **410 M 181 (91)**—cop's surveillance location for observing should have been disclosed;

Clairmont v Commonwealth **425 M 1025 (97)**—denial of motion to disclose identity of informant would not be reviewed by G.L. c. 211, § 3; normal course of appellate review after conviction would suffice;

C v Rios **412 M 208 (92)**—exclusion of D from courtroom during testimony about surveillance location violated Article 12;

C v Hernandez **421 M 272 (95)**—to obtain surveillance location, D need only make preliminary showing that disclosure would provide material evidence needed for fair presentation to jury: sufficient that defense needs basis for determining what cop/witness could see; sanction of dismissal with prejudice for refusal to reveal = too harsh; suppression of cop's testimony or dismissal without prejudice = OK (as to latter, should not re-charge & thereby avoid discovery order: cf. *Thomas* **353 M 429, 432 (67)** act of effrontery by DA in attempting to avoid judicial order);

C v Amral **407 M 511 (90)**—judge must hold in camera hearing where defense affidavits make "substantial preliminary showing" that affiant intentionally or recklessly made false statements; counsel not entitled to be present but may submit questions; judge may allow prosecutor to be present & may question informant as well as affiant; detailed procedures discussed; but see *C v Crawford* **410 M 75 (91)** where credibility of cop's assertion that informant's prior tip led to arrests & drug seizure necessary to justify warrantless search, D entitled to in camera hearing to demand names of arrestees; counsel may not be excluded at hearing to determine sufficiency of tip;

See Chapter 20-J.2 for Franks-Amral line of cases regarded false or perjurious affidavits in support of warrants;

C v Lewin (I) **405 M 566 (89)**—prosecutorial & police misconduct involving either delayed disclosure or fabrication of informant by police didn't justify dismissal where irremediable prejudice to D not established; D entitled to voir dire hearing on potentially exculpatory evidence from putative informant & to elicit at trial government misconduct without rebuttal by prosecutor; motion judge's finding that informant existed was clearly erroneous where there was equally compelling evidence that informant was fabricated;

C v Penta **423 M 546 (96)**—Commonwealth obligated to provide D with last known address of informant & to refrain from "obstructing access" to him; no relief for D when prosecutor's warning that inconsistent testimony in 2 judicial proceedings could prompt perjury prosecution resulted in informant's failure to appear & testify at trial; but see *McMiller* **29 MAC 392 (90)**; *Turner* **37 MAC 385 (94)**;

6-M. RECIPROCAL DISCOVERY—ALIBI, INSANITY, LICENSE, ETC.

See also Chapter 10-B, 10-C, preparing/presenting defense evidence, Chapter 7--H, Fifth Amendment & Article 12, Chapter 2-F, attorney-client privilege; see also Chapter 6-D (re: Sanctions for Discovery Violations, which include those for reciprocal discovery violations, e.g., failure to give notice of alibi witnesses)

M.R.Crim.P. 11—pretrial conference discussion to include "nature of defense", including alibi, insanity, license, or "claim of authority" *(See Chapter 6-B)*;

M.R.Crim.P. 14(a)(1)(B)—reciprocal discovery mandatory (after Commonwealth delivers discovery data);

C v Paiva **71 MAC 411 (2008)**—whether or not there is a pretrial conference report agreeing to reciprocal discovery, M.R.Crim.P. 14(a)(1) provides for automatic exchange of discovery regarding intended expert opinion evidence;

C v Durham **446 M 212 (2006)—in interpreting a version of Rule 14 which has since been changed, see id. at 244 footnote 10, SJC held that,** on motion of Commonwealth, D may (or may not, if motion judge so decides) be required to turn over to prosecution Commonwealth witnesses' statements which he intends to use at trial, including those intended for impeachment use, & including statements made to third parties unconnected to D's case, & Commonwealth may be permitted to disclose to the witnesses the substance of this discovery (in trial preparation); split SJC decision (4:3) rejects D's arguments that this is barred by work product exception to Rule 14, makes cross-examination ineffectual, exceeds scope of Rule 14(a)(3), & is unworkable; "contrary to the Federal doctrine, our work product doctrine favors liberal discovery"; dissenting opinions set forth significant policy considerations ("there is a world of difference between eliminating surprise defenses and eliminating surprise cross-examinations designed to test the credibility of the witnesses") and note, id. at 244 n.10, that new rule's scope of permissible (not "required") reciprocal discovery awaits further decision;

C v Morales **453 M 40 (2009)**—reciprocal discovery of recorded telephone conversation establishing that Commonwealth witness was lying to obtain benefits in "cooperation agreement" caused Commonwealth not to call that witness (and thus deprived D of ammunition as to D's contention that other cooperating witnesses were similarly motivated and lying); D could not call witness, either, as his attorney told counsel he would now invoke Fifth Amendment privilege; SJC nonetheless refuses to overrule *Durham* 446 M 212 as to reciprocal discovery of Commonwealth witnesses' statements useful in impeachment, claims ADA had other reasons for not calling witness AND that witness's invocation of Fifth Amendment was speculative (it was never claimed and judge had not thus had opportunity to discern its validity);

M.R.Crim.P. 14(b)(1)—on DA's motion, judge may require alibi notice (time, date, place, & witnesses); DA must give notice of rebuttal witnesses; sanction maybe exclude alibi; withdrawn alibi = inadmissible;

C v Freitas **59 MAC 903 (2003)**—though defense counsel claimed witness wasn't "alibi" witness, because "it's impossible to present an alibi witness to an indictment that says on divers dates over a seventeen month period", judge permissibly struck witness's testimony that he saw D regularly at a time when alleged assaults were occurring elsewhere; *see also Chapter 6—D, Discovery, . . . Sanctions;*

M.R.Crim.P. 14(b)(2)—special rules re: insanity defense; notice within motion deadline; court-ordered examination, 5th Amendment protections; sanctions if D refuses examination; *(See Chapter 7-E, Preparing for Trial, Defense of Lack of Criminal Responsibility);*

M.R.Crim.P. 14(b)(3)—within pre-trial motion deadline, notice of license, "claim of authority," ownership, or exemption; Reporter's Notes -definitions ("claim of authority" = lawful grant of express or implied right); nature of defense, but not "details";

M.R.Crim.P. 14(c)—sanctions = discretionary; can even exclude evidence (except D's testimony); Reporter's Notes: exclude only if "deliberate & prejudicial";

C v Hanger **377 M 503 (79)**—harmless error to order late & non-reciprocal discovery of alibi witnesses [pre R-14];

ABA Standards for Criminal Justice (2d ed. 1980) Discovery 11-3.2—D who's gotten discovery should, if asked, disclose photos or expert reports if intend to use (unless work product or privilege); Comment: "intent to use", i.e., not inculpatory, rule because government's burden of proof, D presumed innocent, & maybe required by 6th Amendment; 11-3.3, alibi & insanity, but not "nature of ANY defense"—Comments: prior standard was "ANY defense," but now limited to the 2 requiring special DA preparation;

SJC Rule 3:07, 3.4(f)—shall not request that person not give relevant info (unless person is client or relative/ employee "or other agent of a client" & lawyer believes person's interests won't be adversely affected by refraining from giving such information;

C v Gilbert **377 M 887, 893–96 (79)**—(DA) can't subvert rules by refusing to write;

See Chapter 6-G, re: definition of "statement";

C v Haggerty **400 M 437 (87)**—DA can't get extra discovery (of D's expert) just because D had to use Motion for Funds *(See Chapter 7-C)*; defense not required to disclose names of potential witnesses until decision that they will be called at trial; NOTE WELL: TO DISCLOSE TO PROSECUTION NAMES OF ALL POTENTIAL WITNESSES, WITHOUT HAVING INTERVIEWED THEM, MAY RESULT IN COMMONWEALTH INTERVIEWING THEM AND PRESENTING THEM IN PROSECUTION CASE; WITHOUT INTERVIEWING WITNESS, NO WAY TO KNOW WHETHER HELPFUL OR HARMFUL TO DEFENSE. PUBLIC REPRIMAND BY BOARD OF BAR OVERSEERS HAS OCCURRED FOR THIS "NEGLECT AND INADEQUATE PREPARATION IN VIOLATION OF [THEN DR 6-101(A)(2-3)]"; see BBO No. 98-5, Order of Public Reprimand, 26 *Mass. Lawyers Weekly* 2796 (August 3, 1998).

C v Trapp **423 M 356 (96)**—reciprocal discovery of D's psych. tests ordered despite D not using them at trial; Commonwealth used them in rebuttal; SJC **assumed,** but did not "decide," that this was error (see ***Haggerty* 400 M 437, 441 (87)** rationale, supporting "assumption"); no prejudice & no relief in **Trapp**; but see *C v Dupree* **16 MAC 600 (83)** (re: opening statement) D may not know what evidence, if any, to present until (s)he's heard DA's case;

C v Callahan **440 M 436 (2003)**—Commonwealth cannot obtain D's old psychiatric records for use by "qualified examiners" to determine alleged sexual dangerousness; G.L. c. 123A, § 13(b) did not abrogate existing privileges;

6-M.1. Fifth Amendment/Article 12 Issues; Attorney-Client Privilege (Sixth Amendment/ Article 12)

Wardius v Oregon **412 US 470 (73)**—reciprocal OK if D gets discovery;

C v Edgerly **372 M 337 (77)**—disclosure of alibi = constitutional because DA's reciprocal obligation; exclusion sanction only if extreme prejudice to DA;

C v Cutty **47 MAC 671 (99)**—D himself cannot be precluded from testifying as sanction for failure to give notice of alibi (M.R.Crim.P. 14(b)(1)(D)) AND judge cannot bar counsel from using D's testimony in closing argument;

C v McGann **20 MAC 59 (85)**—no harm from lateness because time to investigate & to use for cross-examination;

C v Hughes **380 M 583 (80)**—error for trial court to allow prosecution discovery request ordering D to produce his gun for independent ballistics tests by Commonwealth; this effectively compelled implicit statements as to existence, location, & control of gun in violation of 5th Amendment rights;

In Matter of Grand Jury Investigation 407 M 916 (90)—prosecution may not subpoena defense investigator (or other members of defense team) into grand jury without prior judicial approval; 'power to profit from defense attorney's investigative efforts by subpoenaing that attorney's investigator carries with it power to control & limit preparation of [D's] case'; (use language to contest any order requiring production of investigator's reports in advance of trial & before D-counsel decides to use them); [but see *C v Reynolds* **429 M 388 (99)** D held to have been required to disclose statements of Commonwealth witness which he intended to use for impeachment (though SJC held that sanction of barring their use was too severe); tip: agree, explicitly, in pretrial conference report to disclose only statements of witnesses D intends to **call** at trial]

C v Cote **407 M 827 (90)**—prosecutor may not use grand jury subpoena pretextually to gather evidence for trial;

C v Beauchemin **410 M 181 (91)**—judge's voir dire of defense witnesses improperly gave prosecutor "untoward discovery";

C v Trapp **396 M 202 (85)**—no 5th Amendment re: D's CAT-scan because non-testimonial; psychiatric reports discoverable with Rule 14 protections;

See also Chapter 2, Ethics: Attorney-Client Privilege; & Chapter 7-H, Fifth Amendment;

6-M.2. Criminal Responsibility Issue/ Discovery

Blaisdell v Commonwealth **372 M 753 (77)**—if D asserts lack of criminal responsibility & intends to intro. expert testimony which relies on his statements, D may be ordered to undergo psychiatric examination by prosecution expert;

C v Diaz **431 M 822, 830 (2000)**—orders allowing Commonwealth experts to conduct psychiatric examinations are not limited to cases in which defense is lack of criminal responsibility, but instead may be made whenever D places his statements and mental state in issue, e.g., when he alleges inability to premeditate or form a specific intent;

C v Ostrander **441 M 344 (2004)**—judge may order that Commonwealth expert be permitted to interview D if D places in issue his capacity to waive Miranda warnings (i.e., D is placing "mental state" in issue, even though it's not at time of crime);

C v Contos **435 M 19 (2001)**—same; & rejecting D-counsel's argument that he hadn't been notified of Commonwealth witness interview: judge had ordered it, over defense objection, & counsel had to know it would occur very soon due to imminent trial date;

C v Delaney **404 M 1004 (89)**—judge may allow D to videotape Commonwealth expert's psychiatric examination of D;

C v Trapp **423 M 356 (96)**—ordering videotaping of **Blaisdell** interview "might be a sound idea"; judge has discretion to allow D counsel to be present;

C v Baldwin **426 M 105 (97)**—judge **may** require audio/videotape of Blaisdell interview or permit D counsel to be present, & even if interview is not recorded, judge "may . . . exclude all or a portion of the expert's testimony if it is found to be unreliable," but no constitutional right to such recording;

C v Lo **428 M 45 (98)**—same; cross-examination is "appropriate antidote" to potential mischaracterization or overreaching by Commonwealth experts;

C v Guadalupe **401 M 372 (87)**—don't need expert for not guilty by reason of insanity (lack of criminal responsibility) defense; exclusion sanction for reciprocal discovery violation = only for expert, and only if D refuses examination *(See Chapter 7-E, Defense of Lack of Criminal Responsibility)*;

C v Hunter **416 M 831 (94)**—absent another court order, D had right to refuse to submit to **second** interview desired by Commonwealth shrink; error to allow shrink to testify for adverse inference from this valid claim of right to silence; **if** D-counsel had sought to impeach shrink for paucity of interview, refusal would be admissible to rehabilitate;

C v Brown **75 MAC 361 (2009)**—apparently purely because D counsel almost immediately questioned D's competency and asked court psychologist for competency screening, judge ordered § 15(b) exam for competency AND CRIMINAL RESPONSIBILITY; defense counsel "came into possession" of the latter report and "voluntarily supplied it to the Commonwealth" in plea negotiations; when subsequently D gave notice of defense of lack of criminal responsibility, Commonwealth then had right to examination by expert of its choosing, and could use the exam previously conducted;

6-M.3. Sanctions for Violating Reciprocal Discovery Orders

C v Steinmeyer **43 MAC 185 (97)** (citing *Michigan v Lucas* **500 US 145, 152 (91)**—sanctions other than evidence preclusion recommended in most cases) defense counsel's failure to give witness's self-generated typed statement to DA before trial did not justify striking witness's testimony: counsel had **told** DA what witness would say, statement was consistent with witness's trial testimony, and lunch recess would have provided ample opportunity for DA to study; nothing in it "reasonably would require further investigation" (conviction here reversed);

C v Dranka **46 MAC 38 (98)**—D counsel told prosecutor only just before jury empanelment that because of vasectomy, D incapable of being source of sperm (D counsel claimed that notice of sperm's presence was given to him by prosecution only ten days before trial, but Commonwealth disputed this); prosecutor voiced no objection to late disclosure of this fact (and doctor-witness) until two days later but then evidence was excluded; REVERSAL: judge failed to consider less drastic remedial measures, and anticipated testimony was "not the kind of sophisticated [evidence] that would appear to warrant extensive preparation time";

C v Paiva **71 MAC 411 (2008)**—whether or not there is a pretrial conference report agreeing to reciprocal discovery, M.R.Crim.P. 14(a)(1) provides for automatic exchange of discovery regarding intended expert opinion evidence; judge barred testimony from defense witness ("expert" sort of opinion by gun buff that gun at issue not likely capable of firing bullet) for failure to disclose to DA prior to trial, but this held to be abuse of discretion requiring reversal of conviction; in deciding sanctions, should assess prevention of surprise, evidence of bad faith, prejudice to other party, effectiveness of less sever sanctions, materiality of testimony to outcome of case (citations); Commonwealth arguments on appeal that exclusion was "harmless" because prosecution case purportedly strong misses point: issues of guilt/reasonable doubt should "be decided by juries, not by assumptions at the appellate level"; defense counsel should have articulated reasons for admitting despite violation, and suggestions for less serious sanction, but judge here rebuffed his efforts (at n.2);

C v Sena **429 M 590 (99)**—trial counsel was at fault ("ineffective") in failing to disclose to prosecution statements of witnesses as required by court order, but preclusion sanction was too draconian and continuance would have been adequate to protect Commonwealth interests; murder conviction reversed; trial judge "could have sanctioned defense counsel personally for violating the order, either by using her inherent powers or by referring him to the Board of Bar Overseers";

C v Pena **455 M 1 (2009)**—okay to strike defense expert's testimony based on report not disclosed to prosecutor (ineffective assistance of counsel urged on appeal);

C v Reynolds **429 M 388 (99)**—given language of pretrial conference report, D held to have been required to disclose statements of Commonwealth witness which he planned to use for impeachment, but preclusion sanction held too severe [TIP: agree in pretrial conference to disclose only statements of witnesses which D intends to call at trial];

Taylor v Illinois **484 US 400 (88)**—may exclude D's experts because not disclosed to DA as promised in pretrial conference report, but only if omission = "willful," motivated by desire to obtain tactical advantage minimizing effectiveness of cross-examination and ability to adduce rebuttal evidence; even so, exclusion sanction should be limited to only the most extreme cases; fn.20 acknowledges perhaps legitimate reasons for wanting to keep witness secret, but must clear with court by arguing "in advance of trial in response to the discovery request";

Chappee v Vose **843 F2d 25 (1st Cir. 1988)**—attributing to *Taylor v Illinois* **484 US 400 (88)** criteria relevant to "exclusion" sanction: weigh D's right to compulsory process against "countervailing public interests,"

i.e., integrity of the adversary process, fair & efficient administration of justice, potential prejudice to the truth-determining function of the trial process, plus consider D's explanation for failure to disclose, whether "willful" or not, "the relative simplicity of compliance, and whether or not some unfair tactical advantage has been sought";

C v Durning **406 M 485 (90)**—judge had discretion to prevent D from calling witness not listed in pretrial conference report whose testimony was cumulative or collateral;

C v Dotson **402 M 185 (88)**—don't exclude (shrink) unless no alternative;

C v Delaney **11 MAC 398 (81)**—non-disclosure of DA's rebuttal witnesses OK because unintentional & time for D to interview them *(See Chapter 6-D & 6-E)*; contrast *C v Giontzis* **47 MAC 450 (99)** prosecutor plotted "rebuttal" ambush with expert witness, failing to disclose name/ vita of same and setting defense expert up for devastation;

C v LaFrennie **13 MAC 977 (82)**—(rescript) exclude alibi because not disclosed (& poor offer of proof);

C v Porcher **26 MAC 517 (88)**—exclude D's late alibi witness because no excuse or offer of proof (showing why witness = "vital");

C v Cutty **47 MAC 671 (99)**—D himself cannot be precluded from testifying as sanction for failure to give notice of alibi (M.R.Crim.P. 14 (b)(1)(D)) AND judge cannot bar counsel from using D's testimony in closing argument;

6-M.4. "Work Product" Exception

ABA Standards for Criminal Justice (2d ed. 1980) Discovery—work product = opinion, theory, conclusion of attorney or staff;

M.R.Crim.P. 14(a)(5)—"Work Product" exception = D's statements & portions of documents which are legal research, opinions, theories, conclusions;

McCormick, *Evidence*, § 96 (5th ed. 1999)—work product, & attorney-client privilege;

K. Smith, *Criminal Practice & Procedure*, § 1417 (2d ed. 1983 & Supp.)—work product;

Hickman v Taylor **329 US 495 (47)**—though not attorney/client privilege, work product protects memos; privacy of counsel's work = essential to system;

US v Nobles **422 US 225, 238 n.11 (75)**—work product broader than attorney-client privilege; but judge can order disclosure of portions of report by investigator (who took stand) that are statements of other witnesses because "testimonial" use (vs. internal use) by D "waives" work product;

Goldberg v US **425 US 94, 105f (76)**—give witness's statement to DA (& excise the work product), at least where witness "adopted" it;

Upjohn v US **449 US 383 (81)**—strong public policy shelters counsel's mental process, including notes & memos of witness's oral statements;

C v Paszko **391 M 164 (84)**—D got similar reports from DA & should've given reports by ballistician &

investigator; M.R.Crim.P. 14 exception preserves the work product "core" mental processes, but narrower than federal (see above); & witnesses' written "statements" must be given; BUT cf. *C v Bing Sial Liang* **434 M 131, 138–40 (2001)** "work product" of prosecutors said to include the files of victim-witness advocates, & reasoning, with copious federal case law citations, that "[r]equiring an attorney to produce 'notes and memoranda of witnesses' oral statements is particularly disfavored because it tends to reveal *the attorney's* mental processes"; liberal notion of prosecutor's work product logically must be extended to defense counsel's work product, contrary to *Paszko* **391 M 164, 186–87 & n.27 (84)** (which rejected federal precedents embraced in **Bing Sial Liang**);

C v O'Brien **419 M 470, 477 & n.4 (95)**—assumed for purpose of discussion that prosecutor's notes taken during witness interview were work product; BUT if use "privileged" material (attorney work product) to refresh recollection of witness on stand, privilege = waived & opposing counsel may view; *** reserved question = whether privilege waived when witness is so refreshed prior to taking stand;

Antell v Attorney General **52 MAC 244 (2001)**—materials privileged as work product under M.R.Civ.P. 26(b)(3) aren't protected from disclosure under public records statute, G.L. c. 66, § 10, & there is "no blanket exemption for police records or investigation materials"; at issue were documents re: witness interviews; court remanded to permit appropriate redactions to preserve anonymity of voluntary witnesses in special circumstances here present;

Chapter 7
MISCELLANEOUS ISSUES IN PREPARING TRIAL AND PROBABLE CAUSE HEARING

See also Chapter 14-B, Motions to Dismiss; Chapter 11-B, Motions in Limine; Chapter 4-E, Default;

M.R.Crim.P. 1-2 & Reporter's Notes—rules not inflexible, but to secure fairness;

Aldoupolis v Commonwealth **386 M 260 (82)**—Reporter's Notes to M.R.Crim.P. not binding;

Moore v US **432 F.2d 730 (3d Cir. '70)**—courtroom skill not enough if don't prepare & investigate;

See Chapter 2-E, Standards/Ethics: Competent & Effective;

7-A. INVESTIGATION, INCLUDING VIEW OF SCENE

See also Chapter 6-E, Access to & Knowledge of Commonwealth Witnesses;

CPCS P/G 4.1—investigate all avenues leading to relevant facts, including info of police & DA's witnesses; 6.1 complete investigation to develop/refine most viable defense theory;

ABA Standards for Criminal Justice, Prosecution Function & Defense Function (3d ed. 1993) 4-4.1—duty to promptly & independently investigate all avenues to facts, including those known to law enforcement, & even if D admits G.; Comment: ingenuity & persistence, view scene, failure maybe ineffective (e.g., re: preparing cross-examination); 4-4.3 avoid interviewing alone, because tough to impeach; not "necessary" for defense counsel or defense investigator to caution witness concerning possible self-incrimination & need for counsel [but implicitly, certainly may do so, & see Comment re "proper for defense counsel to tell a witness that s/he may contact counsel prior to talking to" prosecutor, & tell need to exercise care in subscribing to statement prepared by another person];

See also Chapter 2, Ethics: Lawyer-Witness, Bounds of Law, Obstruct Justice, Influence Witness, Competent/Effective Assistance; File-Keeping;

C v Cepulonis **9 MAC 302 (80)**—failure to investigate plausible alibi = dangerous (but harmless here);

C v Aviles **31 MAC 244 (91)**—counsel's failure to investigate D's medical incapacity to commit crime might have been ineffective assistance; *S.C.* **40 MAC 440 (96)**

failure to utilize D's chiropractor with medical records and other neutral/non-family witness **was** ineffective assistance;

C v Alvarez **433 M 93 (2000)**—reviewing only 5-page hospital discharge summary = ineffective assistance of counsel, given what voluminous medical records revealed to post-conviction counsel;

C v Sena **429 M 590, 594–96 (99)**—ineffective assistance for failure to obtain/familiarize self with defense investigative reports in advance of trial (reports in possession of prior counsel) and for failure to obey discovery orders requiring their disclosure to Commonwealth (which here resulted in judge's sanction of precluding use of important report);

US v Bailey **834 F.2d 218 (1st Cir. '87)**—*(See Chapter 6-E)* duty to investigate all sources of evidence, even if "long shots" (so D gets access to DA's witnesses);

SJC Rule 3:07, 3.7—lawyer at trial can't be witness, except re: uncontested issue, or if relates to nature & value of legal services rendered in the case, or if disqualification would work substantial hardship on the client; lawyer in same firm can be witness unless run afoul of Rule 1.7 or 1.9 [conflicts of interest]; 3.4 can't unlawfully obstruct another party's access to evidence or unlawfully conceal document or other material having potential evidentiary value, or counsel other person to do any such act; can't request person other than client to refrain from voluntarily giving relevant info to another party unless the person is relative or employee or other agent of client & lawyer reasonably believes person's interests will not be adversely affected by refraining from giving such info; 4.2 can't communicate with person who has lawyer in matter without attorney's consent; 4.3 can't imply to person not represented by counsel that lawyer is disinterested, & must correct person's misunderstanding, if any, about attorney's role in the communication; can't give advice to person unrepresented by counsel, other than advice to get counsel, if interests of person are or have reasonable possibility of being in conflict with attorney's client;

G.L. c. 268, § 13B—"endeavor to influence witness" = up to 2½ yrs. house of correction or 10 years state prison plus $1,000–$5,000 fine;

See also Chapter 14-B re: ethics of negotiating restitution or accord/satisfaction;

C v Guzman **446 M 344 (2006)**—accord and satisfaction statute (G.L. c. 276, § 55) upheld against DA's challenge that it violated "separation of powers" clause (Art. 30);

G.L. c. 272, § 99—no electronic eavesdropping/recording without consent of **all parties** (or court warrant) [violate = felony AND punitive damages];

C v White **367 M 280 (75)**—can cross-examine re: statement witness made to attorney, if good faith basis;

C v Drumgold **423 M 230 (96)**—counsel's pretrial interviews of witness, during which he showed her a single photo of D, produced for the prosecution an ID witness (who had previously been unable to ID D as gunman);

counsel's having D attend the jury view of scene likewise enabled nearby resident witness to make another out-of-court ID;

C v Paszko **391 M 164 (84)**—D's investigator's report may be discoverable;

See Chapter 6-M, Reciprocal Discovery" but also see 'work product' topic;

C v Haggerty **400 M 437 (87)**—ineffective not to investigate cause of death with expert; & prosecution can't take advantage of motion for funds to get more reciprocal discovery than rules give;

C v Conley **43 MAC 385 (97)**—ineffective assistance of counsel not to have alleged victim's knife tested for D's and other V's blood, since D had repeatedly urged this and it would have corroborated D's version of events;

C v Lawson **425 M 528 (97)**—when, after Commonwealth witness testified to physical layout of a building rooftop and defense investigator made videotape to introduce as impeachment, no error in barring its admission because of failure to proffer it "as a fair and accurate representation of premises **at the relevant** time," i.e., about 18 months earlier; *(See Chapter 11-A &D, Evidence, Relevance, etc.);*

SJC Rule 3:07, 1.1—lawyer shall provide competent representation, i.e., legal knowledge, skill, thoroughness, & preparation reasonably necessary for the representation;

7-B. SUMMONSING WITNESSES—(AND "SUBPOENAS")

See also Chapter 1, probable cause hearing for discovery;

U.S. Constitution, Sixth & Fourteenth Amendments—compulsory process, confront witnesses; equal protection;

Mass. Constitution Declaration of Rights, Article 12—right to produce all proofs that may be favorable & to meet witnesses against him face-to-face;

Washington v Texas **388 US 14 (67)**—compulsory process;

US v Nixon **418 US 683 (74)**—integrity of system depends on full disclosure of facts & compulsory process;

Blazo v Superior Court **366 M 141 (74)**— indigent's constitutional right to get ex parte process so no explanation to adversary [pre-Rule 17]; *(Chapter 7-C, motion for funds/experts);*

M.R.Crim.P. 17 & Reporter's Notes—summons issued by anyone authorized to issue; to attend/testify; &/or produce object/document (may order inspect & copy prior to trial); ex parte application "necessary" to indigent D; expenses (travel & attend) paid after; service by anyone authorized, e.g., last/usual abode (or even mail); maybe warrant if "actual notice";

G.L. c. 233, § 1—Clerk, justice of the peace, or notary issues; § 2 service by any disinterested person; Rule

17, Reporter's Notes - appears to permit counsel to serve, but dubious . . .

See Chapter 7-A, Investigation, & Chapter 2, Lawyers as Witnesses;

G.L. c. 277, § 66—life felonies = right to summons for "necessary" witnesses; § 68 DA & AG's "subpoenas" to testify;

G.L. c. 233, §§ 5 & 6: M.R.Crim.P. 17(e)—sanctions for failure to comply = warrant or contempt ($200 &/or 1 month jail); if person served with summons fails to appear & court determines person received actual notice, warrant may issue to bring person before court;

G.L. c. 262, § 29—witness fee = $6/day + $.10/mile; to see DA & "assist investigation"; D's witness gets fee afterwards [see R-17 above, only for "testimony");

G.L. c. 233, § 3—if summonsed, get fee, unless summonsed for indigent D in criminal case; Rule 17, Reporter's Notes - witness summonsed (by court) via Rule 17 gets G.L. c. 262, § 29 fee; [omitted in revision of SJC Rule 3:07, 3.8, Responsibilities of a Prosecutor = prior SJC Rule 3:08 PF-3(c) summons for interview = unprofessional unethical; but see, nonetheless, ABA Standards for Criminal Justice, Prosecution Function & Defense Function (3d ed. 1993) 3-3.1—"prosecutor should not secure the attendance of persons for interviews by use of any communication which has the appearance or color of a subpoena or similar judicial process unless the prosecutor is authorized by law to do so"];

C v Smallwood **379 M 878 (80)**—DA can't summons for interview on non-trial day (but no dismissal);

C v Liebman **379 M 671 (80)**—no grand jury summons just to prepare DA's case;

M.R.Crim.P. 17, Reporter's Notes—prior inspection of documents not for discovery, but to avoid delay;

K. Smith, *Criminal Practice & Procedure***, Chapter 27 (overview) (2d ed. 1983 & Supp.)**—§ 1559—Rule 17 silent re: discretion for prior inspection; advisable if to prepare (vs. fishing) & delay if not;

C v McCready **50 MAC 521 (2000)**—failure to obtain, prior to trial, a missing (and prejudicial) page from counsel's copy of D's hospital record ensured that its midtrial delivery and admission into evidence would be without benefit of reasoned and researched arguments against such introduction (but ineffective assistance not argued);

C v Drew **397 M 65 (86)**—can deny summons for unnecessary hearsay witness;

G.L. c. 111, § 70—medical records = confidential without patient consent or court order;

M.R.Crim.P. 17(d) & G.L. c. 233, §§ 13A–D—process for out-of-state witness;

Barber v Page **390 US 719 (68)**—right to out-of-state witness;

C v Bryer **398 M 9 (86)**—motion for out-state witness = too late;

Mancusi v Stubbs **408 US 204 (72)**—dubious for foreign witness;

C v Wanis **426 M 639 (98):** *C v Rodriguez* **426 M 647 (98)**—use M.R.Crim.P. 17(a)(2) to get police internal affairs division records of witness statements, etc., in **discovery**;

SJC Rule 3:07, 3.4(f)—can't ask person other than client to refrain from voluntarily giving info to another party unless person is relative, employee, or agent of client and attorney reasonably believes that person's interests won't be adversely affected by refraining to give such info; 3.4(g) no fee except expenses or expert;

C v Balliro **349 M 505, 516 (65)**—"witnesses belong neither to the Commonwealth nor to the defense" (D's right to interview jailed witness);

C v Carita **356 M 132 (1969)**—right to interview prospective witness held in Commonwealth custody isn't satisfied by indirect communication to counsel that witness didn't wish to see them; defense counsel should file motion, witness should be brought to court & instructed re: rights to consent, or not, to interview; record to be kept of proceedings; within discretion of judge to make transcript of interview;

C v Adkinson **442 M 410 (2004)**—DYS, acting in loco parentis (temporary custody under G.L. c. 119, § 26(2)), had power to control visits to child by any third party, and could bar defense counsel's access to child for interview concerning alleged abuse of child by D, child's parent; neither child nor child's guardian ad litem needed

to hear "Carita" colloquy; purportedly here no indication that DYS was acting as "agent of the prosecution" such that denial of access constituted "impermissible interference with" D's rights;

C v St. Pierre **377 M 650, 657–58 (79)**—if DA tells witness not to talk, ask judge to instruct witness and to provide access to neutral ground; but cf. G.L. c. 258B, § 3(m) (complainant, i.e., prosecution's witness, has "right" to be informed of "right" to submit to or to decline interview by D-counsel or anyone acting for D & "right" to impose "reasonable conditions"); cite "equal protection" for similar rights of witness who will be called by defense (*Balliro* **349 M at 516** - witnesses "belong to neither to the Commonwealth nor to the defense"); compare/contrast SJC Rule 3:07, 3.4(f) lawyer [& DAs are lawyers] can't request person to refrain from voluntarily giving relevant info to another party;

C v Turner **37 MAC 385 (94)**—prosecutor's threats to prospective D witnesses (he'd "tear [them] apart" & "put[ting] [them] away too") compelled new trial when threats caused refusal to testify;

C v Koonce **418 M 367 (94)**—threat by DA made prosecution witness's testimony involuntary;

C v Rosa **412 M 147 (92)**—if prosecutorial misconduct/threats cause waiver of spousal privilege, ensuing testimony involuntary;

C v Brookins **33 MAC 626 (92)**—counsel's failure to move for continuance or capias to secure properly summonsed exculpatory alibi witness was ineffective assistance; but on further appellate review, **S.C. 416 M 97, 104 (93)**, SJC held that evidentiary hearing would be required before such an order could be made;

C v Adderley **36 MAC 918 (94)**—reversal for judge's refusal to issue bench warrant for properly subpoenaed witness; claim that testimony was "cumulative" ignored facts that opening statement had promised this witness **and** this witness not impeachable as friend of D (though others were);

C v Aviles **40 MAC 440 (96)**—counsel ineffective for failure to present D's chiropractor (with medical records) civil attorney, insurance agent to testify concerning D's injuries from motor vehicle accident, supporting defense of misidentification/physical incapacity in serious assault occurring 8 days later; D's family members as witnesses required interpreter's service & were impeached for familial bias;

In Matter of Grand Jury Investigation **407 M 916 (90)**—prosecutors may not summons defense investigators under PF-15 without prior judicial approval; see now SJC Rule 3:07, 3.8(f), for codification of restriction upon prosecutors;

C v Cote **407 M 827 (90)**—prosecutor may not summons evidence to grand jury simply to prepare case for trial;

C v White **28 MAC 417 (90)**—reversed on other grounds, 409 M 266 (91) prosecutor's summonsing of D's telephone service messages was not an invasion of privacy;

C v Feodoroff **43 MAC 725 (97)**—D had no reasonable expectation of privacy in her telephone billing records (G.L. c. 271, § 17B gave DA right to obtain records) as against AG or ADAs; "taps", used to record conversations, & "pen registers," used to record numbers dialed from a particular line, & "cross frame traps," recording numbers of incoming calls, distinguished;

Nivica v US **887 F.2d 1110 (1st Cir. '89), cert. denied, 494 US 1005 (90)**—defense summons requested late in trial for unnecessary witness was properly denied;

C v Degrenier **40 MAC 212 (96)**—when D counsel notified DA before trial that D witness was inmate in county jail and that he should be delivered to testify, it was error to deny mid-trial motion to produce witness when D was told, belatedly, that witness had been transferred to jail in remote part of state; D had informed judge of testimony substance;

Commissioner of Revenue v Demoulas Super Markets, Inc. **412 M 181 (92)**—assumed without deciding that summons by administrative agency unenforceable if solely in furtherance of criminal investigation; enforced here because no decision made whether to prosecute;

7-C. MONEY FOR EXPERTS AND OTHER EXPENSES

See Chapter 11-I, Opinions; Chapter 6, Pretrial Conference, Discovery (of DA witnesses' opinions, motions, filing rules, & reciprocal discovery (of witnesses' statements); & Chapter 12-F, Reasonable Doubt from Failure to Test;

CPCS P/G's 4.6(h)—consider motion for expert $; 4.4(g) discover DA witnesses' opinions; 6.1(a) get expert re: opinions & physical evidence; 6.7(d) expert to rebut DA's; 7.1(e) expert for sentencing;

U.S. Constitution, Fourteenth Amendment—equal protection of law;

Mass. Constitution, Declaration of Rights, Article 1—all persons born free & equal;

G.L. c. 261, § 27D—(per 2004 amendment) appeals from denial of relief from costs and fees: appeal is to single justice of Appeals Court if denial is in Superior, Land, Probate, or Housing Ct. departments; appeal is to Superior Court if denial is in juvenile court; appeal is to appellate division if denial is in District Court or Boston Municipal Court;

C v Matranga **455 M 45 (2009)**—judge has no authority to order CPCS to withhold funds from expert (here, judge so ordered as sanction, in annoyance that expert's double commitments postponed ongoing trial): although judge is to determine whether request for funds is reasonably necessary under G.L. c. 261, § 27C, judge lacks authority to enter order affecting CPCS's disbursement of funds; SJC does not here decide "whether (and in what circumstances) a judge may reduce the amount of money that had earlier been authorized to compensate" expert for time/effort when funds have not been approved for payment by CPCS, id. n.10;

C v De'Amicis **450 M 271 (2007)**—in context of D's appeal (and fee for entry into appellate court) of a finding that he was a sexually dangerous person, SJC rejects applicability of G.L. c. 261, § 29 (enacted in amendment to indigency schema with purpose of "deterring frivolous prisoner litigation by instituting economic costs for prisoners wishing to file civil claims"); D didn't file appeal of single justice's ruling within seven days (G.L. c. 261, § 27D), so appeal = dismissed;

Ake v Oklahoma **470 US 68 (85)**—due process right to shrink if sanity/danger = issue; also to prepare for cross-examination of DA's expert [check Rehnquist's dissent];

ABA Standards for Criminal Justice, Prosecution Function & Defense Function (3d ed. 1993) 4-4.4—don't try to dictate expert's opinion;

K. Smith, *Criminal Practice & Procedure*, § 1005 & § 2443 et seq (2d ed. 1983 & Supp.)—overview; G.L. c. 261 indigency standard differs from counsel appointment indigency standard [see below]

C v Chappee **397 M 508 (86)**—bad faith non-disclosure of (D's) experts prevented (DA's) cross-examination preparation, so exclude them because no time (for DA) to master subject, investigate witnesses, & obtain rebuttal;

SJC Rule 3:07, 3.4(g)—no fee except expenses or expert; otherwise no $ for witness;

G.L. c. 261, §§ 27A–G—Costs for Indigents - factors re: "indigent" (gets welfare, income under 125% poverty, or "unable to pay . . . 3"); affidavit of indigency; hearing & shall grant "extra" fees if "reasonably necessary" for a defense like a non-indigent; written reasons if deny & interlocutory appeal; court can provide alternative; counsel must submit bill & voucher;

C v Carter **429 M 266 (99), cited in *C v Dubois* 451 M 20, 33 (2008)**—G.L. c. 261, § 27C does not cover costs associated with motion for new trial; under M.R.Crim.P. 30(c)(5), judge has discretion to allow D "costs associated with" preparation and presentation of Rule 30 (post-conviction) motion;

Spencer v Beacon Hill Hotel **448 M 1017 n.1 (2007)**—statutory requirement of G.L. c. 261, § 27D that denial of request for waiver of court costs must be appealed within seven days would not be overridden by Appeals Court single justice;

Donald v Commonwealth **452 M 1029 (2008)**—D moved in Superior Court for free copy of transcript (albeit of Appellate Division proceedings); when motion was denied, he should have filed notice of appeal in Superior Court and judge should/would have made written findings (G.L. c. 261, § 27D), which clerk would forward with other relevant documents to Appeals Court clerk; G.L. c. 211, § 3 was not appropriate avenue for relief;

C v Phinney **448 M 621 (2007)**—upholding award of attorney fees (M.R.Crim.P. 30(c)(9)) to defense counsel who had to defend judge's grant of new trial motion in "capital case" on Commonwealth's appeal of same; see also M.R.Crim.P. 15(d) applies in context of interlocutory Commonwealth appeals from suppression ruling, R. 25(c)(2) where Commonwealth appeals from required finding of not guilty or reduction of verdict; R. 30(c)(8) where Commonwealth appeals from order granting new trial in other than "capital case"; if Administrative Office of Trial Court doesn't have funds for this expense, "then prosecutors must bear these costs," quoting *C v Murphy* **423 M 1010, 1011 (96)**; see also *C v Gonsalves*, **441 M 1007–08 (2004)**, and **432 M 613, 617–18 & n.5 (2000)**; rejects Commonwealth argument that D should have served motion on the AOTC, but at n.5 says AOTC should be served with request for fees and be given opportunity to respond in cases where AOTC is "clearly obligated by the budget provisions to pay" portion of fee, e.g., in R. 15(d) and R. 30(c)(8) cases; defense attorney here was not court appointed, and "[i]t is widely recognized and accepted that the rates set by the Legislature for the representation of indigent defendants do not equal the rates that privately retained counsel can and do reasonably charge for their representation";

M.R.Crim.P. 41—judge may "appoint" expert if justice requires (& determine reasonable compensation);

Superior Court Rule 54—no expert $ without notifying DA, hearing, & order naming; **But See Contra** (& cite constitutional equal protection grounds):

M.R.Crim.P. 17—summons on ex parte application; and

Blazo v Superior Court **366 M 141 (74)**—indigent gets summons ex parte so need not explain to opponent; if affidavit info doesn't show need, judge can ask for more; Fed.RCrim.P17: subpoena for indigent on ex parte application showing need; (but *see Chapter 6-D*, e.g., *C v Mitchell* **444 M 786 (2005)**—ex parte applications curtailed);

Thompson v Commonwealth **386 M 811 (82)**—D's psych. expert = aid to indigent D, not to court, like wealthy D; results are private unless used;

C v Dotson **402 M 185 (88)**—no role for DA on D's motion unless asked by judge;

C v Haggerty **400 M 437 (87)**—DA can't use motion for funds to get name of D's expert not being called as witness, & judge can issue protective order [so counsel ineffective not to get a medical expert for D];

US v Meriwether **486 F.2d 498 (5th Cir. '73)**—purpose of R-17 & ex parte procedure = not only to foreclose DA from opposing D's summons, but to hide theory of defense;

C v Noxon **319 M 495, 544 (46)**—no privilege re: attorney statements to expert;

C v Paszko **391 M 164 (84)**—D's ballistician's report and D's investigator's report (containing, inter alia, statements of witnesses) not "work product"; but cf *C v Bing Sial Liang* **434 M 131, 138–40 (2001)** "work product" of prosecutors said to include the files of victim-witness advocates, & reasoning, with copious federal court citations, that "[r]equiring an attorney to produce 'notes and memoranda of witnesses' oral statements is particularly disfavored because it tends to reveal *the attorney's* mental processes"; liberal notion of prosecutor's work product logically must be extended to defense counsel's work product, contrary to *C v Paszko* **391 M 164, 186–87 & n.27 (84)** (which rejected federal precedents embraced in Bing Sial Liang when **D** wanted to shield specified defense investigator's work concerning witnesses);

C v Silva **371 M 819 (77)**—motion for psych. expert late & no affidavit (factual predicate);

C v LaPierre **10 MAC 641 (80)**—polygraph motion too late & no affidavit;

C v Pope **392 M 493 (84)**—bad affidavit *(See Chapter 6-C, re: motions)*;

C v DeWolfe **389 M 120 (83)**—normally D can pick own expert, but inadequate reason was given to switch;

C v Lockley **381 M 156 (80)**—interlocutory appeal within 7 days (G.L. c. 261, § 27D) = exclusive remedy; test = "reasonably necessary to prevent . . . disadvantage in preparing or presenting case";

C v Souza **397 M 236 (86): G.L. c. 261, § 27D**—appeal maybe exclusive; can deny polygraph because flunk harm would far outweigh benefit, so not "reasonably necessary";

Im v Commonwealth **432 M 1018 (2000)**—after Superior Court judge denied motion for funds and appellate court single justice (in appellate avenue prescribed in G.L. c. 261, § 27D) affirmed denial, no relief by G.L. c. 211, § 3 petition: no showing that issue couldn't be raised in any direct appeal after a conviction, and case law and statute establish that single justice's decision on funds motion = "final";

C v Zimmerman **441 M 146 (2004)**—must appeal denial of funds interlocutorily, or issue is waived; addressed here, however, because motion judge didn't advise D of right to interlocutory appeal, as required (GL c. 261, § 27D); judge erred in considering only the cost and potential admissibility of expert testimony (here, re: capacity of eyewitnesses to make ID), and not also the "desirability or necessity" of the testimony to D's case;

C v Clarke **418 M 207 (94)**—can deny $1700 for presentencing psych. evaluation for D convicted of 1st-degree murder, because sentence is mandatory life without parole; a D could move for court ordered evaluation pursuant to G.L. c. 123, § 15(e), i.e., evaluation to "aid the court in sentencing"; [D can't then withhold adverse report];

C v McDonald **21 MAC 368 (86)**—question = prevent disadvantage?; not "conceivably" help or would rich D pay it?; consider cost/use; if deny, tell about appeal right;

C v Fitzpatrick **16 MAC 99 (83)**—no stenographer under G.L. c. 218, § 27A(h), even though "mandatory" because no funds available;

O'Coin's v Treasurer of Worcester County **362 M 507 (72)**—court can order expenses (SJC Rule 1:05)

C v Bart B. **424 M 911 (97)**—failure of juvenile delinquent-by-reason of murder counsel to request stenographer resulted in lack of record of any sidebar conference and thus no appellate issue which would be deemed "preserved," and ineffective assistance couldn't be proved in this regard because new counsel could not demonstrate that the sidebar conferences would have yielded winning issue;

C v Stirk **16 MAC 280 (83)**—D should've offered expert re: effect of prior homosexual assault on D's state of mind;

C v Bolduc **383 M 744 (81)**—possible expert re: gunpowder residue;

C v Francis **390 M 89 (83)**—Appeals Court judge gave $ for eyewitness ID expert on voir dire; but OK for trial judge to exclude testimony;

C v Charles **397 M 1 (86)**—expert re: cross-racial ID? *(See Chapter 18, Identification)*;

C v Zimmerman **441 M 146, 154–56 (2004) (concurring opinion)**—"own-race bias" ("performance deficit of one ethnic group in recognizing faces of another ethnic group compared with faces of one's own group") exists, and "the unreliability of cross-racial identification IS a subject 'beyond the ordinary experience and knowledge of the average juror'", and "expert testimony . . . should be admissible";

C v Smythe **23 MAC 348 (87)**—can't exclude testimony of D's breathalyzer expert unless unqualified; *(See Chapter 11-I, Opinions/Experts)*;

C v Gliniewicz **398 M 744 (86)**—suppress blood test results because DA violated pretrial conference agreement by letting expert destroy evidence without having D's expert present to observe *(See also Chapter 7-L, Lost Evidence)*;

C v Baker **440 M 519 (2003)**—after judge allowed motion for funds for expert concerning hair embedded and indentation made in wall, judge revoked allowance upon DA's assertion that prosecution would not claim that baby's head was smashed against wall; when prosecution at trial made exactly this claim, defense counsel ineffective in failing to renew request for funds and move for continuance; Supreme Judicial Court reversed order denying motion for new trial (accompanied by expert affidavits that hair was not from dead baby and indentation not made by baby's head);

US v Vachon **869 F.2d 653 (1st Cir. '89)**—D not entitled to 2d psychiatrist where government had only 1 & counsel conceded 1 was enough;

C v Rivera **424 M 1007 (97)**—indigent given very late notice of denial of motion for transcript of guilty plea colloquy, so did not file notice of appeal within 7 days & when he did attempt, clerk refused to accept; D should file motion in Superior Court to compel clerk to accept notice of appeal (not G.L. c. 211, § 3 matter);

M.R.Crim.P. 30(c)(5)—revision, effective 10/2001, gives judge considering R.30 motion discretion to allow costs associated with presentation of R.30 motion; prior to such revision, the following cases were controlling:

C v Davis **410 M 680 (91)**—indigents moving for new trial whose direct appeals have already been decided are not entitled to funds for scientific testing under G.L. c. 261, § 27C(4), until after R.30 motion granted; **but now see R.30(c)(5)**

C v Carter **429 M 266 (99)**—indigent moved for new trial and funds for investigator BEFORE direct appeal, but fared no better than Davis, above; "funds for an investigation to gather evidence in support of a new trial motion" generally may not be obtained under § 27C" and § 27C "does not authorize a judge to allow costs in connection with the presentation of a new trial motion based on a claim of ineffective assistance of counsel" **(but now see R.30(c)(5))** BUT D here had not made argument "that he was entitled CONSTITUTIONALLY to funds for an investigator" (equal protection, state [article 1] and federal [Fourteenth Amendment] constitutions; right to counsel under Sixth and Fourteenth Amendments and article 12);

C v Gould **413 M 707 (92)**—prior to briefing on direct appeal, D convicted of murder-one denied funds for psychiatrist to determine if that might have helped his defense; D faulted for not making "some showing that a basis for his claim exists"; **but now see R.30(c)(5)**

C v Swist **38 MAC 907 (95)**—indigent funds not allowed for purpose of filing new trial motion; funds for transcripts "traditionally" sought via G.L. c. 211, § 3; **but now see R.30(c)(5)**

C v Conaghan **433 M 105 (2000)**—SJC bypasses *Davis/Carter*, etc. holding **(but now see R.30(c)(5))** by ordering competency examination under G.L. c. 123, § 15(a), for D on Rule 30 motion to withdraw guilty plea, thereby allowing funds for examination of D to determine whether, at time of G plea, she was "battered woman" and plea was thus involuntary; see criticism in dissenting opinion, id. at 112–13;

C v Lynch **439 M 532 (2003)**—denial of funds for investigation to support postconviction claims not abuse of discretion; D must establish "prima facie case for relief," supported by affidavits, and D's and appellate counsel's affidavits here did not do so;

7-D. EXAMINATION OF D FOR COMPETENCY (AND RESPONSIBILITY)

See also Chapter 7-E, Responsibility, & Chapter 4-H, Arraignment;
G.L. c. 221, § 34E—Mental Health Legal Advisors;

G.L. c. 123, § 15(a)—examination at court (or jail) any time judge is "uncertain" of competence &/or responsibility; § 15(b) if further examination necessary, then 20 days (+ 20 if doctor asks, or longer if D asks) state hospital, or Bridgewater State Hospital if male & need "maximum security"; § 15(c) & (d) written report & hearing re: competence (preponderance of evidence); if so, trial's stayed until competent or dismissed; § 16(a) & (b) hospital for D found incompetent or not guilty by reason of insanity (50 days total, counting § 15), DA or superintendent can petition for civil commitment; § 16(f) if person incompetent for trial, shall dismiss charges at 'parole eligibility' [calculation method set forth in statute] OR "may" dismiss sooner in interest of justice; § 17 periodic review, return for trial if competent (but D can stay voluntarily), incompetent D can have motion to dismiss for "lack of substantial evidence" if has defense other than NGI, (lack of criminal responsibility) & regardless of incompetence, can have bail, or personal recognizance; § 36A competency reports = private, except judge's discretion and D, attorney, or DA can see;

G.L. c. 123, § 9(b)—anyone can petition Superior Court for discharge of person from state hospital or Bridgewater;

G.L. c. 123, § 16(f)—if D incompetent to stand trial, court shall dismiss charges as of date of parole eligibility, calculated as if convicted of most serious offense charged and receiving maximum sentence on that charge;

See also Chapter 4-H Arraignment, re: 15(b) commitments;

G.L. c. 123A, § 1—(definition of sexually dangerous person includes persons found incompetent to stand trial if charged with "sexual offense" & suffering from mental abnormality or personality disorder) & 15 (hearing re: guilt of offense beyond reasonable doubt is to judge, not jury, if D is not competent, AND if judge decides D's guilty, SDP proceedings may continue);

Foss v Commonwealth **437 M 584 (2002)**—charges against incompetent criminal D must be dismissed on final date of maximum sentence allowable on the SINGLE most serious crime charged (& not final date based on consecutive maximum sentences for each crime charged);

Chubbuck v Commonwealth **453 M 1018 (2009)**—D being held, incompetent, on two complaints lodged six months apart though arising out of same incident, and wanted dismissal of first on basis of c. 123, § 16(f) [and D didn't claim entitlement to dismissal of second]: no G.L. c. 211, § 3 relief as D wasn't being held unlawfully and could not show absence of avenue of relief (direct appeal) if later found competent, tried, & convicted on first complaint;

C v DelVerde **398 M 288 (86)**—no G. plea (through guardian) by incompetent D; no factual basis, especially re: responsibility; not "permanent limbo" (though likely permanent incompetence) because can fight commitment; maybe committable though retarded;

C v Conaghan **433 M 105 (2000)**—SJC orders use of c. 123, § 15(a) in remanding case after trial court's denial of R.30 motion to withdraw guilty plea, thereby affording expert assistance/funds; "[n]othing in the statute limits the

time within which" examination for competency may be done, and SJC, a "court of competent jurisdiction" had doubt as to D's competency at time she pled guilty (because plea may have been involuntary as product of 'battered woman syndrome');

Jackson v Indiana **406 US 715 (72)**—at hospital only for amount of "reasonable" time to see if competent in foreseeable future; if not, must try civil commitment;

Indiana v Edwards **128 S Ct 2379 (2008)**—Constitution forbids trial of accused lacking rational and factual understanding of proceedings and sufficient ability to consult with counsel with reasonable degree of rational understanding, BUT Constitution doesn't forbid states from insisting upon representation by counsel for accused who is "competent" to stand trial but who suffers from severe mental illness so not competent to represent himself;

Estelle v Smith **451 US 454 (81)**—D's statements to competency shrink can't be used (re: dangerousness) without notice to counsel & waiver (of 5th Amendment) by D;

G.L. c. 233, § 20B—communications with shrink for diagnosis = privileged; if D "waives," statements admissible (only on issue of mental condition);

C v Lamb **365 M 265 (74)**—unless D's warned about waiver, statements to shrink are within patient's G.L. c. 233, § 20B privilege;

Department of Youth Services v A Juvenile **398 M 516 (86)**—Lamb warnings re: extending DYS commitment;

Sheridan, petitioner **412 M 599 (92)**—legislature can't condition discharge from SDP confinement on requirement that D submit to examination & waive § 20B privilege;

G.L. c. 233, § 23B—statements given in §§ 15, 16 examinations inadmissible against D "in the trial" except on issue of mental condition;

C v Martin **393 M 781(85)**—(same); no objection, but miscarriage of justice requires reversal;

C v Callahan **386 M 784 (82)**—reversal of murder conviction because of use of D's statements obtained in court-ordered psychiatric examination (applying G.L. c. 233, § 23B);

C v O'Connor **7 MAC 314 (79)**—no harm from letting in D's admissions to § 15 shrink (because D's shrink said same, & D took stand & admitted);

C v Brown **75 MAC 361 (2009)**—no relief from Commonwealth expert's introducing D's inculpatory statement from § 15 exam (violating 233, 23B) because evidence wasn't "palpably different from" that of defendant's expert;

Blaisdell v Commonwealth **372 M 753 (77): G.L. c. 233, § 23B**—also precludes trial use of "fruits" of D's examination; beyond § 23B, D has 5th Amendment privilege, but partial waiver if offers insanity defense with examination by own shrink; D's statements not given to DA until & unless needed to cross-examine; [dictum: competency examination under G.L. c. 123, § 15 "ordinarily" won't have same problems];

C v Diaz **431 M 822, 830 (2000)**—judge may order that Commonwealth expert be permitted to interview D if D places in issue his statements and mental state, even if it's not for a defense of lack of criminal responsibility (e.g., alleged inability to premeditate or form specific intent);

C v Ostrander **441 M 344 (2004)**—judge may order that Commonwealth expert be permitted to interview D if D places in issue his capacity to waive Miranda warnings;

C v Hunter **416 M 831 (94)**—absent another court order, D had right to refuse to submit to **second** interview desired by Commonwealth shrink; error to allow shrink to testify for adverse inference from this valid claim of right to silence; **if** D-counsel had sought to impeach shrink for paucity of interview, refusal would be admissible to rehabilitate;

M.R.Crim.P. 14(b)(2)—(Blaisdell) protections, *(See Chapter 7-E)*;

C v Clifford C **415 M 38, 46 (93)**—juvenile at transfer hearing introducing expert evidence "reflecting his statements to an expert" can be compelled to submit to an examination by an expert designated by the Commonwealth;

K. Smith, *Criminal Practice & Procedure* (2d ed. 1983 & Supplement) § 1432—suggests (based on Blaisdell dictum) that Rule 14 protections not necessary for competency issues; but contra:

CPCS P/G 2.1—protect statutory/constitutional rights re: competency exams

C v Chubbuck **384 M 746 (81)**—"competence": sufficient ability to consult with attorney with reasonable amount of rational understanding, & rational/factual understanding of proceedings;

Dusky v US **362 US 402 (60)**—(same);

C v Lyons **426 M 466 (98)**—same; fact that judge relied in part on testimony of D's expert did not require him to reach expert's conclusion;

C v Goodreau **442 M 341 (2004)**—current mental illness and/or brain injury doesn't equal incompetence; medications prescribed to ameliorate adverse effects of mental illness don't equal inability to work with attorney; "rational"/competent D may be depressed and even suicidal when faced with overwhelming proof of guilt of murder and life imprisonment;

US v Timmins **301 F.3d 974 (9th Cir. 2002)**—D's refusal to accept/consider plea bargain with prison term of 12½ years when faced with overwhelming evidence & possible 30-year sentence meant he wasn't able "to assist properly in his defense," the 2d requirement of federal statute defining competency, 18 USC 4241(a); couldn't "give rational nondelusional consideration to an offer of a favorable plea agreement"; inability to make choice of plea "in rational terms fundamentally impairs the ability to assist properly in one's defense. In fact, that decision represents the very essence of a proper defense—whether to defend oneself at all";

C v Benoit **410 M 506, 517–20 (91)**—testimony by examining psychiatrist about court-ordered competency examination was admissible to rebut inaccuracies in testimony of D's psychiatrist, at least where D failed to assert privilege at trial;

Medina v California **505 US 437 (92)**—states may place burden of proving incompetence on D; (NB. Mass. rule places burden [to show competency] on Commonwealth: *C v Crowley* **393 M 393 (84)**—DA's burden of proof to prove competence by preponderance;

Godinez v Moran **509 US 389 (93)**—competency standard for pleading G or waiving right to counsel = same as competency to stand trial (NOT competency to actually represent self), BUT waiver of counsel must also be knowing, voluntary, and intelligent (see *C v Simpson* **428 M 646, 652 n.5 (99)**)

Pate v Robinson **383 US 375 (66)**—due process right; incompetent D can't waive right to have Court determine competency; see also *DelVerde* **398 M 288 (66)**;

C v Hill **375 M 50 (78)**—hearing mandatory, even sua sponte, if "substantial doubt," because trial competence = due process right;

C v Simpson **428 M 646 (99)**—though D adamantly refused to allow defense counsel to raise issue of competency, it was nonetheless "appropriate" for counsel to bring good faith doubt about a client's competency to the attention of the courts, and "[t]o do so in general terms violates no rule of professional conduct"; appointment of "guardian ad litem" for purpose of authorizing counsel to raise competency issue thus unnecessary; unclear whether it's mandatory for attorney to flag possible incompetency ("obligation may exist even when" lawyer believes it's not in D's best interests to raise);

C v A.B. **72 MAC 10 (2008)**—failure to request competency determination by the judge close to time of trial was ineffective assistance; court also troubled by failure of trial counsel to conduct further analysis/inquiry regarding insanity defense simply because (probably incompetent) D said "no" when asked if he wanted insanity defense;

C v Lombardi **378 M 612 (79)**—not incompetent (here) just because amnesia; but if true, trial maybe unfair;

C v Martin **35 MAC 96 (93)**—no waiver of competency from counsel's failure to file written motion requesting examination (instead **sua sponte** obligation on part of judge) but here D's proffer was only "amnesia" which by itself doesn't render incompetent;

C v Rise **7 MAC 106 (79)**—reverse because no hearing re: drug addict's competence;

C v Burkett **5 MAC 901 (77)** without past history, no substantial question re: D who removed shirt, crawled in dock, vomited & accused correctional officers of poisoning;

C v Hall **15 MAC 1 (82)**—no substantial question, so no hearing;

C v L'Abbe **421 M 262 (95)**—judge's factual finding that D was not "unable" but instead "unwilling" to discuss details of crime with counsel & psychiatrists doomed appellate claim of incompetency to stand trial; Supreme Court has held that competency to stand trial assures competency to plead G or to waive counsel (*Godinez v Moran*

509 US 389 (93)) SJC says same competency allows waiver of right to be present at trial;

C v Russin **420 M 309 (95)**—D not incompetent because he had limited education, difficult childhood, drug abuse in past, allegedly attempted suicide (factual finding that wounds were superficial, designed to gain attention), & pled to life without parole: no plea withdrawal 12 years later; competency hearing occurred day before G plea;

C v Laurore **437 M 65, 78–79 (2002)**—though suicidal D screamed and cried uncontrollably in cell, no error in judge proceeding with trial on the following day, after colloquy;

C v DeMinico **408 M 230 (90)**—D competent despite expert opinion that he suffered psychotic episode during trial;

C v McMahon **43 M 409, 421 (2005)**—that D had extreme emotional outburst, sobbing uncontrollably and expressing fear for family's safety, did not mean that he was incompetent (despite post-conviction expert opinion that D was incompetent at this point, negating his decision not to testify); no ineffective assistance in failure of trial counsel to tell judge and request competency hearing (because it's "mere speculation" that prompt inquiry into competency would have resulted in different finding);

C v Wentworth **53 MAC 82, 85–86 (2001)**—despite even prosecution expert's opinion that mentally retarded D would be seriously taxed to comprehend trial due to his limited capacity to "attend and concentrate", court refused to find abuse of discretion in trial judge's determination of competency; trial judge obtained defense expert's agreement to sit with D & attempt to help him maintain his focus, and embraced steps recommended by Commonwealth expert to ameliorate D's deficits (use simple words, break complex sentences, speak slowly, remind D to concentrate, frequently ask D questions about his understanding requiring something other than 'yes'/'no' responses);

ABA Standards for Criminal Justice, Prosecution Function & Defense Function (3d ed. 1993) 4-5.2—D decides whether to take stand, waive jury, what plea, & whether to appeal; all other tactics/strategy questions = counsel's (after consulting D); ABA Standards, id., Mental Health issues (2d ed. 1986) 7-4.2—attorney should seek evaluation if good faith doubt (even if D objects) because, though maybe not D's "pragmatic" interest, incompetent D can't make decisions, waive rights, so trial violates due process; in making motion for evaluation, or in making known to court info raising good faith doubt re: competence, defense counsel shouldn't divulge confidential communications or communications protected by attorney-client privilege;

SJC Rule 3:07, 1.2(a)—must seek client's lawful objectives; in criminal case, it's client's decision re: plea to enter, whether to waive jury trial, & whether to testify;

C v Federici **427 M 740 (98)**—choice to forego "lack of criminal responsibility" defense is D's, NOT DEFENSE COUNSEL'S OR JUDGE'S, so long as D has been found competent and been fully advised of consequences of his actions by both defense counsel and judge; not necessary to decide whether "higher degree of competence should be required before" D can validly waive insanity defense, since here the "higher" standard ("knowing, voluntary, and intelligent" waiver) was met; D here was evaluated four times for competency and found competent each time (last time was when D declined judge's offer to instruct on criminal responsibility);

C v Robidoux **450 M 144 (2007)**—that D rejected option of defense of lack of criminal responsibility (in exercise of his "protected autonomy" to make such decisions) did not establish his lack of competence to stand trial, or even raise substantial question of possible doubt about his competency, such that competency hearing would have been required; distinguishes *C v Hill* 375 M 50 (78); trial judge, who denied motion for new trial was in position to observe and determine competence;

See Chapter 2-D, Ethics: Control, Direction, & D's Objectives & CPCS P/G 1.3;

C v Simpson **428 M 646 (99)**—trial, conviction, or sentencing of a legally incompetent person violates that person's constitutional right to due process; appellate courts have jurisdiction to consider, sua sponte, whether this has occurred; though Appeals Court reversed convictions on ground that competency hearing should have been held mid-trial, on judge's own motion (44 MAC 154 (98)-"a person is not fit to manage the machinery of a trial, either to stand trial or to conduct a defense, if the world that person inhabits is distorted by irrationality"), SJC aff'd convictions but ordered defense counsel to file motion for new trial alleging D's incompetence at time of trial;

C v Delaney **404 M 1004 (89)**—judge had discretion to permit D to videotape psychiatric examination;

C v Trapp **423 M 356 (96)**—ordering videotape of Commonwealth's psych's interview of D "might be a sound idea"; judge has discretion to allow D-counsel to be present;

C v Baldwin **426 M 105 (97)**—judge **may** require audio/videotape of **Blaisdell** interviews, or permit D-counsel to be present, & even if interview is not recorded, judge "may . . . exclude all or a portion of the expert's testimony if it is found to be unreliable" BUT D has no constitutional right to such recording;

C v Lo **428 M 45 (98)**—same; cross-examination = "appropriate antidote" to potential mischaracterization, bias, or overreaching by Commonwealth experts;

7-E. DEFENSE OF LACK OF CRIMINAL RESPONSIBILITY (NGI)

C v Seguin **421 M 243 n.1 (95)**—"[though 'insanity defense' is] a shorthand way of referring to the lack of criminal responsibility . . . , the] burden is on the Commonwealth to prove that a defendant was criminally responsible, and thus the use of the word 'defense' is not strictly accurate"; SEE SUBSEQUENT CASES, POST, IN "BURDEN OF PROOF," re: volatility of topic;

See Chapter 7-D re: examination, experts, reports, evidence privilege, ethics/strategy;

C v McLaughlin **431 M 506 (2000)**—no relief for inconsistent verdicts: NGI as to two homicides, but third (at a site slightly removed in time and place) was G, involuntary manslaughter; mere inconsistency not ground for relief, and besides, maybe (via tortured analysis) not inconsistent;

7-E.1. Duty to Investigate/Present NGI Defense

C v Companonio **420 M 1003 (95)**—failure to investigate mental impairment could be ineffective assistance of counsel, but hearing required to establish (1) that D did suffer such impairment at time of murder & (2) that failure to pursue was neither reasonable tactic nor D's expressed desire;

C v Roberio **428 M 278 (98)**—ineffective assistance of counsel found in failure to investigate and advance defense of lack of criminal responsibility; that D could "focus on the situation" went to competence, not responsibility, and without expert assistance, counsel "could not have made an accurate assessment" of mental state at time of crime; traumatic brain injuries caused by two falls, attention deficit hyperactivity disorder (ADHD), language learning disability, oppositional defiant disorder, "substance abuse mood disorder" (pathological intoxication) AND alcohol (which D unable to resist as a result of mental defects) compounded the impairments were points made by D expert on motion for new trial; once expert's individual qualifications were ratified and his area of expertise found to be scientifically legitimate, motion judge could not deny new trial "based on his assessment of the expert's credibility," since credibility is issue for jury and not judge;

C v Westmoreland **388 M 269 (83)**—ineffective counsel to drop NGI defense at closing;

C v Street **388 M 281 (83)**—(same);

See Chapter 7-D, re: client's strategy choices;

Osborne v Commonwealth **378 M 104 (79)**—no reason to try NGI defense, so not ineffective;

C v A.B. **72 MAC 10 (2008)**—failure to request competency determination by the judge close to time of trial was ineffective assistance; court also troubled by failure of trial counsel to conduct further analysis/inquiry regarding insanity defense simply because (probably incompetent) D said "no" when asked if he wanted insanity defense;

C v Milton **49 MAC 552 (2000)**—ineffective assistance of counsel for failure to request psych evaluation of D; judge on motion for new trial made "critical error" in failure to acknowledge what was apparent to him, on record, at guilty plea hearing: something was "wrong" with D;

C v Matthews **406 M 380 (90)**—criminal responsibility is issue for trial, not (juvenile) probable cause hearing;

7-E.2. Psychiatric Exams

C v Silva **371 M 819 (77)**—*(Chapter 7-C, Funds for Experts)* deny motion for shrink funds because no "factual predicate";

M.R.Crim.P. 14(b)(2)—within motion's time limit (or longer if court allows) give notice of intent to go NGI, whether expert (& name, address), & whether relying on D's statements; if so, may order examination of D; report = sealed, not available to either side unless no privileged material, D moves to release, or during trial (needed to rebut, cross-examine);

C v Brown **75 MAC 361 (2009)**—apparently purely because D counsel almost immediately questioned D's competency and asked court psychologist for competency screening, judge ordered § 15(b) exam for competency AND CRIMINAL RESPONSIBILITY; defense counsel "came into possession" of the latter report and "voluntarily supplied it to the Commonwealth" in plea negotiations; when subsequently D gave notice of defense of lack of criminal responsibility, Commonwealth then had right to examination by expert of its choosing, and could use the exam previously conducted;

Blaisdell v Commonwealth **372 M 753 (77)**—if D going NGI, must take DA's examination, but 5th Amendment protections re: D's statements until needed for cross-examination *(Chapter 7-D, see Exams for Competency/Responsibility);*

C v Diaz **431 M 822 (2000)**—even if D's not going NGI, must take DA's examination if he's using psych. expert based on his statements & court orders;

C v Wayne W. **414 M 218 (93)**—juveniles presenting psychiatric expert at Part B transfer hearing may be required to submit to examination by Commonwealth psychiatrist;

C v Clifford C. **415 M 38 (93)**—judge relied solely on court clinic psychiatrist: refusal to hear experts retained by juvenile and refusal to compel juvenile to submit to examination by Commonwealth expert [because juvenile's experts relied on juvenile's statements to them] were errors;

Gilday v Commonwealth **360 M 170 (71)**—must notify DA of NGI intent; constitutionally OK;

C v Guadalupe **401 M 372 (87)**—don't need expert for NGI; exclusion for reciprocal violation = only for expert, & only if D refuses examination; see *C v Hunter* **416 M 831 (94)** judge ordered an examination by Commonwealth shrink, but D could legitimately refuse to submit to 2d interview because not ordered;

C v Contos **435 M 19, 22 (2001)**—though D introduced psych. testimony to place before the jury D's out-of-court statements re: D's state of mind when he killed girlfriend & two children, judge properly instructed that statements were not admitted for probative value & couldn't be used as evidence of the truth of their contents (& this meant that there was no evidence to support voluntary manslaughter instructions, since "provocation" inference available only from such statements);

C v Colleran **452 M 417 (2008)**—because D's drug use was "important" to defense expert, extent of D's drug use was purportedly relevant to shake foundation of defense expert's opinion and not inadmissible "prior bad act" evidence suggesting criminal propensity;

C v Buck **64 MAC 760 (2005)**—Commonwealth reprimanded for attempting to use D's alleged confession during a court-ordered psych exam (G.L. c. 123, § 15(b)), which was not a part of the record, to justify denying motion for new trial on unrelated grounds (of newly discovered evidence): "protestations to the contrary notwithstanding," Commonwealth was trying to use the statements as confession of guilt, which is "not permitted under the statute";

7-E.3. "Bifurcated" Trial ("Factual" Guilt, Then Criminal Responsibility Issues)

C v Haas **373 M 545 (77)**—can deny bifurcated trial (i.e., guilt, then responsibility issue);

C v Siegfriedt **402 M 424 (88)**—within discretion of judge to deny/grant bifurcation;

C v O'Connor **7 MAC 314 (79)**—OK to deny bifurcated; can instruct jury on practical consequences of not guilty by reason of insanity (*C v Mutina* **366 M 810 (75)** MUST instruct on consequences if D requests);

7-E.4. Evidence Necessary to Raise

C v Trapp **396 M 202 (85)**—can be "disease" though not "psychotic";

C v Fuller **421 M 400, 411 (95)**—SJC declines to define "mental disease/defect" because complex/obscure & definition is likely to mislead & confuse;

C v Smith **357 M 168, 180 (70)**—defining term would risk undermining jury's role as "sole judge";

C v Sheehan **376 M 765, 769 (78)**—"mental disease or defect" isn't "matter of medical terminology," but is instead term of art to help "resolve a specific set of legal problems";

C v Mulica **401 M 812, 817–20 (88)**—reversing conviction because judge instructed jury to determine whether D suffered from specific mental illness suggested in evidence (post-traumatic stress disorder) & this impermissibly reduced Commonwealth's burden of proving absence of "mental disease or defect"; (see G.L. c. 123, § 2 re: Dept of Mental Health Regulations);

C v Goulet **402 M 299 (88)**—"personality disorder" enough though not "major mental illness";

C v Torres **437 M 460 (2002)**—in murder case where defense was lack of criminal responsibility and cross-examination of defense expert by DA elicited info about "antisocial personality disorder," D counsel in redirect elicited that expert had not diagnosed D with this disorder, (expert clarifying that he had merely noted some "antisocial tendencies" from this case & "criminal history"); this opened the door to DA in recross-examination eliciting D's "long history of trouble with the law";

C v Roman **414 M 235 (93)**—judge's instruction that "law . . . [does not] parcel [out] criminal accountability among the various inhabitants of the mind" did not improperly prevent jury from acquitting based on multiple personality disorder defense; D's expert acknowledges that he found no evidence that, at time of crimes, D couldn't conform to laws and didn't know wrongfulness of conduct;

C v Roberio **428 M 278 (98)**—attention deficit hyperactivity disorder (ADHD), traumatic brain injuries, and a language learning disability: effect of these impairments was compounded by effects of alcohol (which D unable to resist due to mental defects), & D also afflicted with oppositional defiant disorder (ODD) and "substance abuse mood disorder"; failure to discern & present this evidence = forfeiture of substantial ground of defense (counsel held ineffective);

C v Lunde **390 M 42 (83)**—lay evidence re: D supports G.; (but see *Mutina* **366 M 810 (75)** bad conviction if D has 2 experts & DA has no affirmative evidence);

C v Cole **380 M 30 (80)**—(same) though 3 experts; (& because no psych. history); but see *C v Guiliana* **390 M 464 (83)**—(same); BUT new trial in SJC's G.L. c. 278, § 33E first degree murder review because "weight" of evidence = insane;

C v Robidoux **450 M 144 (2007)**—D obeyed what he believed to be a religious "leading," which led to his toddler's starvation, but no relief on G.L. c. 278, § 33E review, SJC citing evidence that he had in past altered course when "leadings" appeared to guide him astray, and substantial efforts to conceal body implied consciousness of guilt, germane to determination of whether D could appreciate wrongfulness of conduct;

C v Guadalupe **401 M 372 (87)**—don't need expert for NGI;

C v Johnson **422 M 420 (96)**—although don't need expert for NGI, evidence that D attempted suicide, that he acted illogically because he should have known he'd be 1st suspect & that he was "totally different" on night of murder because he'd never been violent to a witness before = insufficient to warrant NGI instruction;

C v Scott **430 M 351 (99)**—trial counsel not ineffective in failing to ask insanity instruction based on fact D repeatedly attempted suicide during the 10 days before murder; this not enough to support insanity instruction here;

G.L. c. 123B, § 1—not mentally ill solely because "retarded;

C v Sheehan **376 M 765 (78)**—drugs/booze addict not "mental disease";

C v Shelley **381 M 340 (80)**—(same); but see *C v Angelone* **413 M 82 (92)** judge must instruct that voluntary alcohol consumption is factor in determining criminal responsibility where D has latent mental disease or defect which might have been triggered by alcohol;

C v Herd **413 M 834 (92)**—McHoul could be satisfied on proof of hallucinations & delusions, though they were cocaine-induced paranoid psychosis features: Court "unwilling, in order to justify a homicide conviction, to permit the moral fault inherent in the unlawful consumption of drugs to substitute for the moral fault that is absent in one who lacks criminal responsibility";

C v Brennan **399 M 358 (87)**—when voluntary consumption of drug activates latent mental disease/defect which satisfies McHoul standard, lack of criminal responsibility would be established unless D knew or had reason to know [*** strike 'reason to know,' per *Ruddock* **428 M 288 (98)**], that the drugs would activate the illness];

C v Ruddock **428 M 288 (98)**—in light of *Herd* **413 M 834 (92)**, *C v Brennan's* **399 M 358 (87)** approval of "reason to know" is arguably erroneous; use [only] the "subjective" standard of what D knew, though given evidence in Ruddock, language not significant;

C v Sanna **424 M 92 (97)**—where only 'mental' evidence was that D voluntarily ingested crack cocaine (& this, according to D's statement, caused him to bludgeon & stab his great uncle), no NGI instruction warranted;

C v Cutts **444 M 821 (2005)**—trial counsel not ineffective for failing to present insanity defense (i.e., that D's conduct was result of unanticipated cocaine-induced psychotic episode), despite post-conviction counsel's presentation of affidavits from two addiction experts; trial counsel had retained expert who concluded that D wasn't suffering from any psychosis, and trial counsel pursued "diminished capacity" defense, based on "homosexual panic" in conjunction with paranoia heightened by cocaine use;

C v Gould **380 M 672 (80)**—"diminished capacity" [sic] for first degree murder; *(See Chapter 16, Defenses)*;

C v Mulica **401 M 812 (88)**—facts, not terms, matter; can consider compulsive gambling along with post-traumatic stress;

C v Mills **400 M 626 (87)**—facts & D's testimony merit NGI charge without expert;

C v LaPlante **416 M 433 (93)**—heinous nature of crimes alone doesn't support NGI;

C v Seabrooks **425 M 507 (97)**—evidence that D stabbed estranged girlfriend 50 times, killing her & son, that he then attempted suicide, and that, to his father, he "looked very incoherent" did not warrant NGI instruction;

C v Schulze **389 M 735 (83)**—general practitioner M.D. can tell observations & diagnosis of D around time of acts, but not opinion re: responsibility;

C v Monico **396 M 793 (86)**—psychologist maybe "expert" to give opinion; layperson can give facts; M.D. can give medical diagnosis & treatment;

C v Goudreau **422 M 731 (96)**—not error to exclude from trial certain evidence from psych who did compe-tency examination day after homicide, SJC apparently finding particular evidence irrelevant to criminal responsibility &, as "competency" material, possibly confusing to jury;

C v DeWolfe **389 M 120 (83)**—mental condition awaiting trial may be relevant/admissible, but not the finding of incompetence;

District Court Standards of Judicial Practice, Trials & Probable Cause Hearings (1981) 3:03—(opines that) NGI not appropriate for probable cause hearing because presume sane, so find "probable cause" *(See Chapter 1, probable cause hearings)*;

7-E.5. Burden of Proof; "Inference" of Sanity

C v Smith **357 M 168 (70)**—though all experts say insane, can infer sanity from common knowledge most are sane, so no required finding of not guilty;

C v Brown **387 M 220 (82)**—(same); but judge can't call it "presumption";

C v Kostka **370 M 516 (76)**—if issue's raised, DA's burden of proof on sanity, beyond reasonable doubt;

C v Kappler **416 M 574 (93)**—"presumption" of sanity has enough evidentiary weight to meet Commonwealth's burden, i.e., beyond a reasonable doubt; but see O'Connor, J., dissenting (fact that a great majority of people are sane says nothing about whether D in this case, with long history of mental illness & auditory hallucinations, was sane at time of completely inexplicable crime);

C v Krohn **36 MAC 905 (94)**: *C v Lapointe* **36 MAC 909 (94)**—no error found in instruction that jury could take into account that most people are same "and that there is a resulting probability that any particular person, including the defendant, was sane" (but see *Kappler* dissent by O'Connor, J., above);

C v Casey **428 M 867 (99)**—in protesting *C v Kappler* **416 M 574 (93)** holding, appellate counsel announced preference for burden shift to D, by preponderance, on lack of criminal responsibility, rather than the "presumption of sanity" instruction condoned in *Kappler*; point "deserves serious consideration," albeit for prospective application only. but see: *C v Keita* **429 M 843 (99)** SJC, after consideration, makes no change in allocation of burden of proof re: criminal responsibility; dissent believed that burden should be on D to prove lack of criminal responsibility by preponderance (rather than on Commonwealth to prove beyond reasonable doubt that D did not lack criminal responsibility), BECAUSE instruction that Commonwealth must prove criminal responsibility beyond a reasonable doubt, combined in this context with instruction that the burden is satisfied by virtue of a "presumption" of sanity, diminishes concept of reasonable doubt standard and makes likely the application of a lower standard of proof as to other elements of the crime;

C v McLaughlin **431 M 506 (2000)**—(Spina, J., concurring) support for change in allocation of burden of proof picks up another vote (now three SJC judges want it changed; in *Keita*, above, only 2 judges wanted change);

C v Cook **438 M 766 (2003)**—every expert who evaluated D testified that D was mentally ill; all evidence showed extreme mental illness, & diagnosis of paranoid schizophrenia predated the charged homicide of cop; Commonwealth produced NO witness to opine that D was criminally responsible, but SJC affirmed first degree murder conviction; contrast *C v Giuliana* 390 M 464 (83);

C v Rasmusen **444 M 657 (2005)**—despite facts that (1) D presented experts saying D not criminally responsible, and Commonwealth presented no experts on the issue, and (2) Commonwealth didn't ask for instruction on presumption of sanity, D could be found G (& criminally responsible); jury had "ample basis" for "rejecting" D's insanity defense; evidence of sanity was "compelling";

Clark v Arizona **548 US 735 (2006)**—no particular formulation of insanity defense is part of Constitutionally guaranteed "due process," and "insanity" rules are open to state choice; presumption of sanity is presumption that D has capacity to form requisite criminal mens rea; state may place upon D burden to prove insanity, whether by a preponderance of evidence, or to some greater degree (Arizona requires "clear and convincing", and this doesn't violate due process); Arizona has declined to adopt "diminished capacity" defense, and this policy would be undercut if evidence of incapacity could be considered for whatever a jury might think sufficient to raise reasonable doubt about mens rea;

C v Brown **449 M 747, 763–64 (2007)**—no error in prosecutor's question to cop concerning cop's conversation with D about Miranda rights because relevant that D apparently comprehended what cop said, so "relevant to the question of his sanity," distinguishing *C v Mahdi*, 388 M 679 (83) (which sought inference of sanity from exercise of right to silence);

C v Brown **75 MAC 361 (2009)**—though D argued unfair restriction on cross-exam of Commonwealth expert, who opined D = criminally responsible, defense counsel did elicit from his own expert the same facts, i.e., that Commonwealth's expert's opinion was flawed in that she found him not criminally responsible for a different act (resisting arrest) that occurred "seconds" after crime of carrying firearm;

7-E.6.   Jury Instructions (Definitions, Consequences of NGI Verdict)

Superior Court Criminal Practice Jury Instructions §§ 2.9, 3.1, 3.2—re Lack of Criminal Responsibility, including 3.2.1(a), consequences of NGI verdict, and 3.2.1(b), effect of alcohol and/or drugs on insanity; District Court Model Jury Instruction #6.03, "insanity", and 6.031, mental impairment short of insanity;

C v McHoul **352 M 544 (67)**—when did act, NGI if, because of mental disease/defect, lacked substantial capacity to appreciate criminality or conform to law;

C v Urrea **443 M 530 (2005)**—notwithstanding specific language in *C v McHoul* 352 M at 554 n.10, no error in DA's question of expert, did D appreciate difference between "right and wrong" at time of murder;

C v Goudreau **422 M 731, 735–36 (96)**—prosecution had to prove BOTH that D had substantial capacity to appreciate the wrongfulness of his conduct AND that D had the substantial capacity to conform his conduct to the requirements of the law (jury instruction here erroneously instead used "or"); extremely detailed "proper instruction on criminal responsibility" published in appendix, id. at 737–39;

C v Callahan **380 M 821 (80)**—instruct without D asking = OK (if no objection); see also *C v Seguin* **421 M 243 (95)** prospective ruling: when D requests, judge to conduct individual voir dire of prospective jurors re: ability to return NGI if Commonwealth fails in its burden to prove D criminally responsible;

C v Brennan **399 M 358 (87)**—when voluntary consumption of drug activates latent mental disease/defect which satisfies McHoul standard, lack of criminal responsibility would be established unless D knew or had reason to know that the drugs would activate the illness; criticized/altered by *C v Ruddock* **428 M 288 (98)** in light of *Herd* **413 M 834 (92)**, "reason to know" is arguably erroneous; use [only] the "subjective" standard of what D knew (given the evidence in Ruddock, error didn't result in relief);

C v Mutina **366 M 810 (75)**—if D asks, jury must be instructed on consequences of NGI verdict;

C v Ward **412 M 395 (92)**—D entitled to instruction on consequences of NGI verdict;

C v Robbins **422 M 305 (96)**—embellishment of **Mutina** instruction effectively told jury that if they cared about protecting community they should reject NGI, since prosecutor might not be able to keep D locked up later, given burden of proof; failure to object = no relief;

C v Biancardi **421 M 251 (95)**—refusal to instruct on consequences of NGI = reversal;

C v Loring **14 MAC 655 (82)**—instruction explains G.L. c. 123 - observation, commitment, & judicial supervision later;

C v Contos **435 M 19, 22 (2001)**—though D placed before the jury D's out-of-court statements to psychiatrist because he wanted them used to discern D's state of mind when he killed girlfriend & two children, judge properly instructed that statements were not admitted for probative value & couldn't be used as evidence of the truth of their contents (& this meant that there was no evidence to support voluntary manslaughter instructions, since "provocation" inference available only from such statements);

7-E.7.   Result of NGI Verdict May Be Commitment

G.L. c. 123, § 16—if NGI, court MAY order more observation; DA or Superintendent. of facility MAY petition for § 8 CIVIL COMMITMENT [6 months + 1 year renewals]; DA notified of later hearings; court can restrict D's movement at hospital]; cf. *Jones v US* 463 US 354 (83) (misdemeanor) indefinite NGI commitment OK;

Bradley v Commissioner of Mental Health 386 M 363 (82)—can commit this (NGI) D to DMH hospital, but not Bridgewater because doesn't need "maximum security"; *(See also Chapter 4-H, Competency, Mental Health Issues, in Chapter 4-H)*;

G.L. c. 276, § 87—PROBATION = before trial or after "finding or G. verdict" [Query: forced OUT-patient treatment after NGI??] *(See Chapter 7-F, Civil Commitment)*;

Foucha v Louisiana 504 US 71 (92)—NGI D's who later become sane may not be detained simply because they remain "dangerous";

7-E.8. Right to Be Tried Without Being Medicated

C v Louraine 390 M 28 (83)—right to be unmedicated for trial so jury can see demeanor; but may waive right to be competent for trial (n. 13);

Riggins v Nevada 504 US 127 (92)—forcible administration of antipsychotic medications to D during trial offends due process absent "overriding justification";

C v Colleran 452 M 417 (2008)—D, prior to trial and connected to determination of competency after hearing, had been ordered to continue treatment and medication; over 3 months later D gave notice of lack of criminal responsibility defense; six months later, trial began and question of right to be tried in unmedicated state was never presented to judge; no relief despite arguments of trial counsel's ineffectiveness of this ground and that right was 'fundamental'/'personal' and not subject to waiver by counsel: jurors were made well aware that demeanor at trial was not as appeared on date of homicide; trial/new trial motion judge made relevant findings;

C v Gurney 413 M 97 (92)—D had right to have expert explain that D's calm trial demeanor was due to antipsychotic medications;

7-F. CIVIL COMMITMENT

See also Chapter 7-D, Examination of D for Competency, Criminal Responsibility,

G.L. c. 221, § 34E—Mental Health Legal Advisors (617-338-2345; 800-342-9092

G.L. c. 123, §§ 5–8—rights to counsel, maybe independent examination & testimony, notice & speedy hearing (unless waived after consult counsel); question = likelihood of serious harm because mental illness? (see § 1); Bridgewater if need strict security; decided within 10 days, BUT, if write reasons, administrative justice of District Court Department may extend time; 6 mos. + 1 yr. extensions; § 9—appeal to Appellate Division of District Court (on law) or Superior Court (DISCHARGE petition); § 16 procedures after NGI;

G.L. c. 123, § 9(b)—any person can apply in writing to a Superior Court justice, any time & in any county, alleging that person named in application is being held in mental health facility or Bridgewater, but shouldn't be held any longer, or is subject of a medical treatment order issued by district/juvenile court, but shouldn't be so treated; names of "all persons interested in [subject's] confinement or medical treatment" should be listed, with request for discharge or other relief;

Hashimi v Kalil 388 M 607 (83)—procedural defenses, (e.g. . . . .);

Bradley v Commissioner of Mental Health 386 M 363 (82)—not Bridgewater unless need maximum security;

Thompson v Commonwealth 386 M 811 (82)—Commonwealth's burden of proof at § 8 annual review; but D's burden of proof on D's § 9(b) discharge petition;

C v Nassar 380 M 908 (80)—to fulfill purposes of G.L. c. 123, administrators should strive to find least burdensome/least oppressive controls over individual;

Rogers v Commissioner of Dept of Mental Health 390 M 489 (83)—committed person can make own treatment decisions (e.g., drugs) unless found incompetent;

See also DelVerde 398 M 288 (86), Chapter 7-D, Examination for Competency;

Kansas v Hendricks 521 US 346 (97)—upholding involuntary commitment of individual on basis of "mental abnormality," here pedophilia; fractured court inviting further challenges; cc opinion, **id.** at 371, noting that precedent would **not** support civil confinement as "mechanism for retribution or general deterrence";

See Chapter 7-E, re: "mental illness";

G.L. c. 123A, §§ 1, 15—if D is charged with sexual offense and is incompetent to stand trial, SDP proceedings may nonetheless be undertaken after "hearing" at which judge (not jury) decides beyond a reasonable doubt that D is guilty of the sexual offense;

7-G. COMPETENCY AND/OR EXAMINATION OF WITNESS

See Chapter 9-B, cross-examination, witness's mental impairment;

See Chapters 11-H & 11-J, Evidence: Rape/Privileges; Chapter 7-B, Summons; & Chapter 6-H, discover witness records;

G.L. c. 233, § 20—anyone "of sufficient understanding" may testify, (except . . .);

G.L. c. 233, § 81—out of court statement of child under age ten re: act of sexual contact = substantively admissible IF child "unavailable" for any of many reasons, including incompetency to testify! (§ 81(b)(6));

C v Colin C. **419 M 54 (94)**—child sexual assault complainant found incompetent, such that per G.L. c. 233, § 81, her out-of-court statements will be introduced because she is "unavailable": decision on facial invalidity of statute reserved; SJC requires (1) prior notice to D; (2) proof beyond reasonable doubt that hearsay necessary to avoid "severe & long-lasting trauma" to child; (3) statements must be found reliable, after a hearing & specific findings; (4) D & counsel must have opportunity to be present, unless "severe emotional trauma" to child would be caused; (5) if unavailability finding was based on inability to understand/tell "truth", reliability may well be called into question; (6) other admissible evidence must corroborate hearsay, as **additional** guarantee of trustworthiness; a "reliability" finding cannot be premised on expert testimony that child = credible, such testimony being incompetent and inadmissible;

Young, Pollets & Poreda, *Evidence* **(2d ed. 1998) §§ 601.1 et seq.**

Brodin, M. and Avery, M., *Handbook of Massachusetts Evidence* **(8th ed. 2007);**

C v Echavarria **428 M 593, 596 (98)**—the "not very stringent test of competence" would certainly have been met if D-counsel had moved for competency hearing re: 2 witnesses, so failure to so move was not "ineffective assistance"; this true even though one (adult) witness spoke no English, had been in US very short time, was illiterate, could not tell time, did not know what city he was in, did not know what year it was, and had difficulty estimating distances in feet;

C v Tatisos **238 M 322 (21)**—competence of child = can tell truth from falsehood, duty re: former & wickedness/punishment re: latter;

C v Monzon **51 MAC 245 (2001)**—though judge managed to cajole 6-year-old into adequate answer that she knew difference between 'truth' and 'lie', child responded to the contrary upon identical question during cross-examination; reversal because judge failed to question witness again to assure competency (& jury shouldn't have been allowed to consider witness's testimony); two parts of competency determination = ability to perceive, remember, recount AND duty to tell "truth"; colloquy here re: 1st part inadequate [judge asked 1 witness only her age, & other only 3 questions], but appellate court review of witnesses' trial testimony satisfied it that witnesses had ability to observe, remember, & tell;

C v Murphy **48 MAC 143 (99)**—error to buttress credibility/competence of ten year old witness by DA questioning her whether she believed in God, been taken to catechism, studied about God there, and realized it

"very serious" when she swears "to God to tell the truth" but no prejudice

C v Caine **366 M 366 (74)**—mental impairment or drug/booze habit = OK for impeachment re: competence, credibility, & testimonial faculties (capacity to perceive, remember, & articulate correctly); but hospitalization alone not shown relevant;

See also Chapter 9, Cross-Examination;

C v Sylvia **35 MAC 310 (93)**—appellate argument that alleged victim was incompetent because at time of alleged crimes she was severely intoxicated & by time of trial had suffered nervous breakdown & was being treated with heavy medications might have been more successful if made before trial judge; competency finding upheld because judge could "well" have found she understood duty to tell truth;

C v Corbett **26 MAC 773 (89)**—OK to find kid incompetent, but maybe continue a short time to teach about truth *(see Chapter 7-O, speedy trial/dismissal, e.g., Cordeiro 401 M 843 (88) (DA gets long continuance for "unavailable"/incompetent kid witness)*;

G.L. c. 123, § 19—judge's discretion for Dep't. Mental Health examination of witness/party's mental condition;

C v Despres **70 MAC 645 (2007)**—it was learned by defendant after conviction that indecent assault and battery complainant (mentally retarded and having "behavioral issues") had made unreliable reports about being mistreated or having his rights violated at "respite facility"; facility employees' averments about his "significant tendency to misperceive events, exaggerate and fabricate . . . in order to draw attention to himself" = insufficient basis for requiring new trial, so no "abuse of discretion" by trial judge in denying same; "character" evidence being "used to suggest that a mentally impaired witness is inherently untruthful" was "troubling" to Appeals Court; judge was within his discretion in concluding that the witnesses' qualifications were inadequate because they lacked advanced degrees in psychology or psychiatry;

C v Gamache **35 MAC 805 (94)**—competency finding OK for 5 year old to testify re: assaults allegedly committed when she was between 22 & 33 months old; let jury discount if appropriate;

C v Lamontagne **42 MAC 213 (97)**—judge has no sua sponte obligation to conduct voir dire on competency of 4 year old sexual assault complainant (age 3 at time of alleged offenses); refusal to adopt rule mandating voir dire competency determinations & presumption of incompetence of witnesses under age 7; HINT: request competency voir dire, object to leading questions; consider moving to strike entire testimony if internally bizarre/inconsistent [but maybe better in some circumstances (i.e., can't get required NG) to keep for argument to fact-finder that evidence = incredible];

C v Allen **40 MAC 458 (96)**—what proffer necessary to obtain hearing on suggestiveness of interview of child, preparatory to exclusion of testimony as incompetent; see

State v Michaels **136 NJ 299 (94)** suggestive techniques contaminating later testimony;

C v Gibbons **378 M 766 (79)**—examiner picked by Dept. of Mental Health; no G.L. c. 123, § 19 examination without hearing re: need; competency = only question for examination [(n.9) includes "impeach" re: capacity to perceive, remember, & articulate correctly];

C v Santos **402 M 775 (88)**—judge should have ordered G.L. c. 123, § 19 examination for witness with Down's Syndrome; testimony of expert on its symptoms = OK, but not as a substitute for impartial expert assigned by DMH per G.L. c. 123, § 19; expert testimony not to be used for assessing witness's "credibility"; cf. *Widrick* **392 M 884 (84)**) (judge can't order "psychiatric" examination re "credibility", for use by D to impeach a witness);

C v Aitahmedlamara **63 MAC 76 (2005)**—mentally retarded person may be competent to testify (here, complainant in indecent A&B on mentally retarded person, G.L. c. 265, § 13F); judge holds "broad discretion", conducted "thorough voir dire examination";

C v Hiotes **58 MAC 255 (2003)**—judge didn't abuse discretion in denying D's motion for psychiatric examination of elderly rape complainant, despite facts that her memory was demonstrably quite impaired and she talked about and spoke with "space people"; court cites "tendency . . . to let the witness testify [and let jury discount it or not]";

C v Gamache **35 MAC 805 (94)**—exclusion of D-counsel from G.L. c. 123, § 19 competency examination not error (but counsel here did not object and this might influence?);

C v Massey **402 M 453 (88)**—if voir dire, judge can question or else let both counsel;

C v Trowbridge **419 M 750 (95)**—if judge applies correct legal standard, competency determination = discretionary; legal standard = whether witness has general ability or capacity to observe, remember & give expression to what she has experienced/seen; (2) whether W understands

difference between truth & falsehood, obligation & duty to tell truth, & belief that failure will result in punishment; use or not of psych. expert to aid in competency determination = discretionary;

Cargill v Commonwealth **430 M 1006 (99)**—competency ruling not subject to interlocutory review; any error can be adequately remedied thru usual appellate process;

Kentucky v Stincer **482 US 730 (87)**—no "confrontation" right violation to exclude D & forbid cross-examination of witnesses at in camera competency hearing (but see *Colin C.* **419 M 54 (94)** [D & counsel must have opportunity to be present at competency hearing re: child, unless "severe emotional trauma" to child would be caused]);

C v Perreault **13 MAC 1072 (82)**—witness's hospitalization alone not relevant unless affects competence or credibility;

C v DiBenedetto **427 M 414, 424 (98)**—no error in denying D's motions (1) to suppress testimony of chief prosecution witness on ground it "unreliable," and (2) for a psychiatric examination to determine witness's competency; expert opinion "in effect commenting on [witness's] credibility would be inadmissible";

C v Carter **383 M 873 (81)**—(DA's) doctor can give opinion of kid's "reality testing," i.e., ability to differentiate what is real from what isn't real;

C v Mendrala **20 MAC 398 (85)**—can exclude (D's) expert re: effect of booze & marijuana on witness's ability to perceive, recollect, communicate, because impinges on decision as to what testimony to believe, and effects of alcohol are "common knowledge" *(see, however, Chapter 10, Defense Evidence, Right to Present)*; Court distinguishes (fn. 10) cases re: intoxication and criminal intent of D *(expert testimony admissible/[required?]: no, not required per cases in Chapter 16-C, Defenses: Intent)*;

7-H. FIFTH AMENDMENT AND MASSACHUSETTS DECLARATION OF RIGHTS ARTICLE 12 PRIVILEGE

See also Chapter 11, Evidence: Motion to Strike (cross-examination rights re: witness taking 5th; & Chapter 2, Ethics: Contempt, Bounds of Law (& court orders - re: order to attorney & client to produce, etc.), & attorney-client privilege;

Doyle v Ohio **426 US 610 (76)**—fundamentally unfair to use arrested person's silence to impeach explanation offered at trial, and silence can't be used as evidence of guilt;

C v Johnson **60 MAC 243, 247 (2003)**—introduction & comment upon facts that D said nothing, was "stone faced" to be avoided at retrial;

C v Cobb **374 M 514 (78)**—reversal for use against D of his statement ("what can I say"), in response to questions re: where gun is and who accomplices were, after he was arrested and given Miranda warnings;

C v Dupont **75 MAC 605 (2009)**, citing *C v Nawn* **394 M 1 (85)**, *C v Cancel* **394 M 567 (85)**, *C v Machado* **339 M 713 (59)**—D's denial of accusation of guilt isn't admissible unless some other hearsay exception applies, BUT if D responds to accusation in "equivocal, evasive or irresponsive way," D's statement IS admissible; cop's assertion to D that cop "knew he was involved in a drug transaction and believed that there was cocaine in his vehicle" was answered: "there is no cocaine in my vehicle or one me"; D's statement held admissible as "oddly specific" (not unequivocal);

C v Irwin **72 MAC 643 (2008)**—reversal (despite no objection) for prosecutor's use in case in chief, in cross-examination, and in closing argument) of D's failure to reach out to police and delay in speaking to police about allegation of sexual assault, citing *Thompson* 431 M 108, 117 (2000) and *Nickerson* 386 M 54 (82) (impeachment of D with fact of pre-arrest silence should be approached with caution, is of "extremely limited probative worth");

See Chapters 12-E.6; 10-A.3; 11—G.4 (Post-Arrest Silence Inadmissible) for more cases and distinctions, e.g.,

C v Guy **441 M 96 (2004)**—no *Doyle v Ohio* violation to impeach D's trial testimony with content of his post-Miranda conversations with nurse, security guard, and police officer and with answer to booking question re: injuries;

Ohio v Reiner **532 US 17 (2001)**—a witness's assertion of innocence doesn't deprive her of 5th Amendment privilege against self-incrimination (context of D's alternate suspect in homicide, i.e., the babysitter, being granted immunity to testify that she had nothing to do with injuries);

C v Barnes-Miller **59 MAC 832 (2003)**—alleged victim of annoying telephone calls was purportedly the "other woman" prompting D's divorce; "victim's" claim of 5th Amendment privilege at deposition in divorce action held legitimate, and not a cause for dismissal of the criminal case (at which she remained committed to testifying);

In the Matter of Proceedings Before a Grand Jury **55 MAC 17 (2002)**—facts that witness claimed innocence, that Commonwealth claimed that she wasn't target of investigation, and that witness was only wanted to testify consistently with her police interview didn't matter: witness's proximity to crime & potential for her to be implicated as alternative perpetrator or joint venturer or accessory made her invocation of privilege legitimate; judgment of contempt reversed;

C v Morganti **455 M 388 (2009)**—SJC holds D has no standing to challenge ruling of judge that witness had no valid privilege against self-incrimination; on basis of witness's answer as to when he established domicile out of MA, judge had held that statute of limitations as to witness's possible liability as accessory after fact of murder had run; though appointed counsel for witness subsequently told judge that witness had been mistaken about date and that limitations statute thus didn't bar prosecution, judge rejected "proffer" and ordered witness to testify, refusing further opportunity to consult with counsel and rejecting witness's claim of privilege with threat of "contempt" holding;

C v Clemente **452 M 295 (2008)**—judge refused to find that witness had privilege at grand jury, so witness testified; at trial, same judge found that witness DID have privilege against self-incrimination but also barred D from introducing the prior recorded testimony of the now unavailable witness: SJC held here that D failed to establish that Commonwealth had opportunity and similar motive to develop fully the witness's testimony at grand jury, so was not entitled to introduce it at trial; SJC rejected D's argument that he should have had access to transcript of hearing attended by prosecutor and witness's attorney which resulted in ruling that witness did NOT have privilege (SJC disingenuously separating latter holding/discussion from former);

In the Matter of a Grand Jury Subpoena **442 M 1029 (2004)**—petitioner received no relief (on appeal to full bench from single justice's refusal on G.L. c. 211, § 3 petition to quash order of Superior Court judge that he testify before grand jury): "if prosecutor strays into a potentially protected area [Article 12 / Fifth Amendment], petitioner may then exercise his privilege on a question by question basis"; USUAL WAY OF CHALLENGING SUCH ORDERS TO TESTIFY = disobey them, & appeal from subsequent contempt order;

US v Balsys **524 US 666 (98)**—though D refused to answer Justice Department questions about his alleged Nazi-related past (which could result in deportation under US immigration [non-criminal] statutes & could subject him to criminal prosecution in several foreign countries, though not here), Supreme Court said no 5th Amendment privilege; any criminal prosecution for false immigration statements was barred by statute of limitations;

[see *Padilla v Kentucky* **130 S Ct 1473 (2010)**—Sixth Amendment requires defense counsel to provide *affirmative* (i.e., not just silence) competent advice to a noncitizen D regarding immigration consequences of a guilty plea (& absent such advice, noncitizen may raise claim of ineffective assistance of counsel); there is duty to inquire about citizenship/immigration status initially]

McKune v Lile **536 U.S. 24 (2002)**—requiring inmates to complete & sign "admission of responsibility" form, accepting responsibility for crimes for which they have been sentenced, & to complete "sexual history form," detailing all prior sex activities, regardless of whether they're criminal (& have or haven't been prosecuted), as condition of participation in Kansas's "Sexual Abuse Treatment Program" doesn't amount to compelled self-incrimination despite loss/reduction of privileges for failure to participate; OBJECT TO ANY SUCH CONDITIONS/PROCEDURE UNDER ARTICLE 12, DECLARATION OF RIGHTS, STATE CONSTITUTION;

C v Mahoney **400 M 524 (87)**—Mass. Declaration of Rights, article 12, like 5th Amendment, covers only testimonial/communicative evidence (not booking video); [*BUT see evolution of concepts under article 12*, post, e.g., *C v Conkey* 430 M 139 (99) conduct offered to show D's state of mind is "testimonial";

C v Maylott **43 MAC 516 (97)**—videotape of D at booking not suppressed (showed lack of cooperation and manner suggestive of alcohol consumption);

C v Delaney **442 M 604 (2004)**—can introduce evidence that, after D was told of warrant authorizing police to take D to station to be examined by physician, he asked if he were under arrest (no), and then began to walk away from officers: evidence of resistance to warrant/court order doesn't violate Article 12; cases which don't involve refusal to comply with warrant or court order, & in which D has legitimate "choice" not to participate, distinguished;

C v Farley **431 M 306, 310 (2000)**—murder conviction reversed for DA's cross-examination of D about her failure to provide certain information to police during a statement she made after being advised of Miranda rights; distinguishes *C v Thompson* **431 M 108, 118 (2000)**, in which D never invoked right to silence or asked to stop questioning but instead gave a lengthy statement AND there, failure of D to inquire about his child was an omission logically inconsistent with innocence;

C v Peixoto **430 M 654 (2000)**—cross-examination of D asserting that, after Miranda rights, he said "I don't know if I should talk to you or not," held not an invocation of Miranda BUT testimony nonetheless inadmissible under state law, due process, article 12 of Declaration of Rights; D who has received Miranda warnings may inquire about them/think out loud about them without being subjected to unfair cross-examination;

C v Clarke **48 MAC 482, 486 (2000)**—statement by D, during his responses to police questioning, that he had nothing to say about why/how complainant would know D's address and its interior, admissible so as not to leave wonderment why questioning ended so abruptly BUT its use by prosecutor was impermissible, i.e., "against" D, arguing that D realized he was caught in lie & would have to change story, implying that innocent D would have kept answering (violation of *Doyle v Ohio* **426 US 610 (74)**);

See Chapter 11-G, Admissions By Defendant, Chapter 11-J, Privileges;

CPCS P/G 2.4—protect D's rights re: evidence sought by DA; *(See Chapter 4-I, Miscellaneous Arraignment Problems)*;

Brodin, M. and Avery, M., *Handbook of Massachusetts Evidence* **(8th ed. 2007)**;

Young, Pollets & Poreda, *Evidence,* **§ 502.1 et seq. (2d ed. 1998)**—(Privilege Against Self-Incrimination);

C v Francis **375 M 211 (78)**—though D pled guilty, still has 5th Amendment privilege (re: co-D's case) because liable for conspiracy; [see *C v Ianelli* **17 MAC 1011 (84)** & *C v Benson* **389 M 473 (83)** - conspiracy & underlying crime not "same"];

C v Somers **44 MAC 920 (98)**—introduction of signed **Miranda** form, in which D claimed right to silence, could suggest to jury that guilt could be inferred from failure to offer explanation for gun's presence in car;

C v DePace **433 M 379 (2001)**—DA displaying, by overhead projector, enlarged Miranda form, invoking right to counsel = reversal of murder conviction;

C v Isabelle **444 M 416 (2005)**—4:3 decision that DA's eliciting evidence re: D's request for attorney didn't warrant reversal (because purportedly "beyond a reasonable doubt" it didn't contribute to jury's verdict);

C v Martinez **34 MAC 131 (93)**—cross-examination, assailing D for not turning over evidence and otherwise "assisting" police, required reversal despite absence of consistent objections;

C v Rivera **62 MAC 859 (2005)**—error to allow cop to testify that D, in initial statement to police, did not tell them about any eyewitnesses to the physical confrontation between D and complainant; this was not a "statement" inconsistent with defense at trial; see also *C v Haas* **373 M 545, 559 (77)**; also error for ADA to argue that witness's testimony should be discounted because she did not call police at the time of the confrontation (no evidence introduced as to whether or not witness had called police);

C v Andujar **57 MAC 529 (2003)**—notwithstanding cross-examination of cop seeking to create inference that $375 found in D's pocket could have been from social security check rather than drug sales, ERROR for DA to ask cop on redirect whether D, at arrest, offered any explanation of the cash;

C v Vermette **43 MAC 789 (97)**—error to allow cop testify that D refused permission to search his car & photo his sneakers;

C v Egardo **426 M 48 (97)**—failure to object to testimony & arguments impeaching D for post-arrest silence = ineffective assistance of counsel;

Attorney General v Colleton **387 M 790 (82)**—Declaration of Rights Article 12 = more protective than 5th Amendment *(See Chapter 7–I, Immunity)*;

C v Powers **387 M 563 (82)**—5th Amendment applies if answer = "link in chain" to prosecute, unless clearly no possibility it'll tend to incriminate;

US v Hubbell **530 US 27 (2000)**—D was granted immunity & forced to turn over documents; "the Independent Counsel" then used the documents' contents to procure indictments of D, & claimed no 5th Amendment violation because didn't intend to use at trial D's "act of production"; Supreme Court held otherwise (government made "derivative use" of the testimonial aspect of the compelled production, because it was 1st step in chain of evidence leading to prosecution, & government had been unable to even describe the documents with reasonable particularity prior to their production);

Murphy v Commonwealth **354 M 81 (68)**—5th Amendment re: presence at scene because possible link in chain, so no grand jury contempt;

C v Dagenais **437 M 832 (2002)**—prospective defense witness, a fellow inmate, had legitimate 5th Amendment claim because witness intended to assert a lack of criminal responsibility in his own upcoming trial for murder; witness's testimony "would have given the Commonwealth an opportunity to inquire about (and demonstrate) his mental and perceptive abilities"; *possible defense use of this case: protective orders against even the most routine questioning of any D (e.g., medical history interviews, booking questions);*

C v Voisine **414 M 772 (93)**—5th Amendment claim of witness called by D in murder trial not defeated by fact of his G pleas earlier to crimes related to the murder; while voluntary testimony would waive, Court wouldn't equate G pleas with testimony by which waiver would be conclusively proved;

C v Francis **375 M 211 (78)**—co-D who pled G still has 5th re: conspiracy; witness's 5th Amendment prevails over D's 6th Amendment (compulsory process); [see also *C v Ianelli* **17 MAC 1011 (84)** & *C v Benson* **389 M 473 (83)**];

C v Freeman **442 M 779 (2004)**—defense witness, expected to testify that D's co-D confessed to witness that he rather than D was principal/shooter, instead claimed 5th Amendment privilege; no error since testimony could serve to incriminate on, e.g., conspiracy to commit perjury, obstruction of justice, etc.; though assertion of right shouldn't be accepted in "blanket" fashion, judge here determined that witness would not answer any questions regarding the "area" of his purported conversation with the D's co-D;

C v Rosario **444 M 550 (2005)**—after D summonsed person counsel believed to be true culprit in sale of drugs (for which D was on trial instead) & witness invoked privilege against self-incrimination, D had right to display the individual and his physical features before the jury; SJC rejects rationale that this was impermissibly "parading" witness to communicate to jury that he was invoking privilege; for appellate preservation, D-counsel adequately expressed to judge that middleman in sale to undercover cop would ID the witness as middleman's supplier (at 558 n.2);

C v Lucien **440 M 658 (2004)**—although not stating reason on record, judge legitimately allowed witness's claim of privilege against self-incrimination because, although witness had already pleaded guilty to a firearm offense, his prospective testimony subjected him to prosecution for possession of a second firearm and for "trading of firearms";

C v Holmes **34 MAC 916 (93)**—DA's request at hearing of motion to suppress that D-witness be interrupted & warned of 5th Amendment resulted in 5th A claim; no waiver because no knowing intelligent waiver by beginning to testify;

C v Farley **443 M 740 (2005)**—after trial judge ruled that witness had voluntarily waived 5th Amendment privilege by testifying at first trial, he was compelled to testify at second trial; allowing him to assert 5th Amendment privilege in response to several questions didn't here violate D's right to confrontation; BUT privilege against self-incrimination was held to be waived concerning question about a fact "related to but not necessarily mentioned in" the testimony given at the first trial;

C v Tracey **416 M 528 (93)** D claiming entrapment & that civilian middleman was used by cops in entrapment, had no right to compel middleman's testimony, he having legitimate 5th Amendment privilege since not clear on record that he knew cop was cop;

C v Joyce **326 M 751 (51)**—no 5th Amendment problem in leaving the scene charge because no real danger name/address will incriminate; & . . .

Cabot v Corcoran **332 M 44 (54)**—MA can't immunize from federal prosecution; cf. *C v Jordan* **439 M 47 (2003)**—federal authorities' letter of immunity for cooperating drug informant didn't cover Mass. detectives investigating murder (who told D they couldn't offer inducements or make any promises);

C v John **442 M 329 (2004)**—finding of fact, that federal "immunity" notice promised immunity ONLY if D testified against former gang cohorts, wouldn't be overturned; D's confession to murder was admissible; D's goal was to avoid testifying, & when threatened that he could/would be made to testify by filing of immunity notice (eliminating 5th Amendment privilege), he attained his goal by confessing murder (knowing that prosecutor would not use confessed murderer as witness);

C v Slaney **345 M 135 (62)**—though D = cross-examining, commendable for judge to warn witness re: 5th, but parties can't require it;

C v Phetsaya **40 MAC 293 (96)**—judge should not have presumed that D witness would incriminate 'self: should have asked DA why he expected this & made ruling rather than tell D counsel that witness could not be called without his parents' advice on 5th Amendment waiver (effectively barring presentation of defense witness);

C v Koonce **418 M 367 (94)**—witness called by D at 2d trial had testified for Commonwealth at 1st trial, but at 2d trial claimed 5th Amendment & judge "found" that 1st trial waiver had been involuntary because of DA's threats to prosecute witness;

C v McMiller **29 MAC 392 (90)**—government agent's 5th Amendment claim should be probed in view of prosecutor's threat to prosecute her if she testified for D; her testimony at co-D's trial was not waiver as to D's trial;

Webb v Texas **409 US 95 (72)**—error for judge to scare off D's witness by perjury threat;

Luna v Superior Court **407 M 747 (90)**—D waived 5th Amendment privilege by giving affidavit in pretrial proceeding on D's motion to dismiss;

C v Fisher **433 M 340 (2001)**—after taking stand, prosecution witness belatedly refused to answer questions; not ineffective assistance to fail to proffer witness's probable cause hearing testimony because (1) it wasn't substantially helpful & (2) SJC might have held that witness wasn't actually unavailable because assertion of privilege was not "valid" (but was instead because witness was now incarcerated & didn't want to be a Commonwealth witness because of feared retribution);

C v Hammond **50 MAC 171 (2000)**—witness gave affidavit recanting testimony adverse to D at trial, but prior to testimony at hearing on motion for new trial, ADA wanted judge to inform witness about risk of perjury prosecution, & thereafter witness was allowed to invoke privilege not to testify; appellate court distinguished *Luna* **407 M 747 (90)** on basis that this affiant, unlike Luna, "did not . . . meet with counsel before signing the affidavit";

C v Colantonio **31 MAC 299 (91)**—evidence insufficient that defense witness took 5th because prosecutor improperly postponed witness's sentencing;

Taylor v Commonwealth **369 M 183 (75)**—warn witness if "danger" in answer; no contempt because maybe link; no waiver re: trial testimony from D's statement to police;

C v Dormady **423 M 190 (96)**—waiver by testimony = limited to proceeding in which given; unsworn statements to police in criminal investigation do not operate as waiver;

C v Funches **379 M 283 (79)**—DA can object & witness has 5th (though testified to some facts); but D was denied cross-examination, so grant motion to strike *(See Chapter 11-C, Evidence: Objections, Motions to Strike, Offers of Proof, Record Protection)*;

C v Borans **379 M 117 (79)**—grand jury testimony = perjury & D not "trapped" because could've taken 5th Amendment; accord/compare: *Brogan v US* **522 US 398 (98)** D's simple denial of guilt during interview with federal investigative agents subjects him to liability for making false statement (18 USC § 1001); Supreme Court refuses to recognize "exculpatory no" exception and asserts that 5th Amendment doesn't confer "privilege to lie";

C v Viera **41 MAC 206 (96)**—judge's "press[ing] the defendant to indicate whether he persisted in his defense" of misidentification implicated 5th Amendment rights;

C v Woods **427 M 169 (98)**—probation condition = sex offender evaluation, but D argued 5th Amendment right not to talk; issue not reached **but** Court said no right to counsel there [*if judgment not final (& this G **was** reversed on appeal), statements might be used against D on retrial]; see also *Petition of Sheridan* **412 M 599 (92)** legislature can't condition SDP discharge on requirement that D submit to examination & waive privilege;

C v Rivera **37 MAC 244 (94)**—had no standing to raise 5th Amendment claim of witness who sought to avoid testifying at trial on ground that grand jury testimony was perjurious (but see *C v Rosa* **412 M 147 (92)** implicitly recognizing D's standing re witness's "involuntary" testimony, context of spousal privilege);

C v Tiexeira **29 MAC 200 (90)**—has no standing to object to judge's refusal to let witness take 5th Amendment as it is personal right of witness;

C v Molina **454 M 232 (2009)**—same; and because witness testified that he refused to take up D's offer to get into car with a "guy" (to earn "three and a half"), he could not incriminate himself; record supported judge's finding that witness's repeated statement that he did not want to testify was result of fear for family and not privilege; judge may remind witness of duty to tell truth;

Carney v City of Springfield **403 M 604 (88)**—transactional immunity when D's public employer coerces statements by threat of job loss or other disciplinary sanction;

C v Dormady **423 M 190 (96)**—same;

C v Borans **388 M 453 (83)**—waiver by testimony" (& full cross-examination) limited to that hearing; testimony at own trial (& grand jury) doesn't waive re: co-D's later trial;

C v Fallon **38 MAC 366 (95)**—'s testimony in civil suit = waiver, so that his deposition & hearing testimony could be introduced in criminal trial, *S.C.* **423 M 92, 98 (96)** agreeing with Appeals Court's reasoning;

C v Curtis **388 M 637 (83)**—to testify on own motion to immunize witness, D must waive 5th Amendment; (no choice between rights because no defense right to immunize a witness *(See Chapter 7-I, Immunity)*;

Simmons v US **390 US 377 (68)**—testimony of D on his motion to suppress inadmissible at trial re: guilt;

Prop.M.R.Evid. 104(d)—D's testimony on preliminary matter doesn't open him/her up to cross-examination on other issues;

C v Brusgulis **41 MAC 386 (96)**—D's testimony at 1st trial admitted against him at 2d trial, despite his claim that erroneous admission of prior bad acts had caused him to take stand at 1st trial;

Harrison v US **392 US 219 (68)**—introduction of coerced confession "coerced" D to take stand at 1st trial; government would not be allowed to exploit error by introducing against D at 2d trial the testimony prompted by wrongly-introduced confession;

C v Luna **418 M 749 (94)**—affidavit of cop re false statements made in warrant application & in murder case proceedings, though ordered by Superior Court judge, was voluntary (D had consulted with counsel);

Brown v US **356 US 148 (58)**—can be summary contempt for refusal to answer cross-examination questions (because of 5th Amendment);

C v Hughes **380 M 583 (80)**—no contempt for failure to produce gun because surrender itself is self-incriminating;

See Chapter 2-F & 2-G, Ethics;

ABA Standards for Criminal Justice (2d ed. 1986) Discovery 11-3.1—no 5th Amendment re: D's person because non-testimonial (writing, prints, voice, etc.); [see "refusal" cases below, however, e.g., *C v McGrail* **419 M 774 (95)**]

Fisher v US **425 US 391 (76)** forced surrender of documents if non-testimonial & possession/location are not issues; BUT SEE *US v Hubbell* **530 US 27 (2000)** D was granted immunity & forced to turn over documents; the "Independent Counsel" then used the documents' contents to procure indictments of D, & claimed no 5th Amendment violation because didn't intend to use at trial D's "act of production"; Supreme Court held otherwise (government made "derivative use" of the testimonial aspect of the compelled production, because it was 1st step in chain of evidence leading to prosecution, & government had been unable to even describe the documents with reasonable particularity prior to their production);

Schmerber v California **384 US 757 (66)** forced blood test of arrestee OK under 4th & 5th Amendments if consent or probable cause *(See Chapter 20)*;

C v Trigones **397 M 633 (86)**—no post-indictment blood sample without probable cause shown at adversary hearing;

C v Downey **407 M 472 (90)**—grand jury may compel blood tests for unindicted D so long as it has evidence sufficient to indict or arrest; D must be given opportunity to oppose order;

Matter of Lavigne **418 M 831 (94)**—procedure by which Comm may obtain blood sample from person NOT charged with crime nor the subject of grand jury investigation: Commonwealth must show probable cause that person committed the crime AND subject gets hearing at which judge makes findings as to degree of intrusion vs. need for the evidence; Commonwealth must show that identity of a source of blood would aid in the investigation;

Matter of Grand Jury Investigation **427 M 221 (98)**—upholding procedure/granting motion by prosecutor for order from Superior Court judge to compel blood sample from autistic rape victim's father & brother on basis of mere "reasonable belief" that one or the other caused V's pregnancy;

C v Sasu **404 M 596 (89)**—D need not file motor vehicle accident report after complaint;

US v Campbell **732 F.2d 1017 (1st Cir. '84)**—can't force D to write from dictation (because spelling's testimonial);

Pennsylvania v Muniz **496 US 582 (90)**—during booking, asking D to calculate date of 6th birthday improper because not designed to elicit necessary (identification) info, but rather information for "investigatory purposes";

See Chapter 20-C & 20-D for cases involving motions to suppress statements on Miranda & voluntariness grounds;

C v Gilliard **36 MAC 183 (94)**—leaving open the issue whether, under Article 12, D had right to be told before her grand jury testimony that she was a potential D; even if there is such a right, remedy is not dismissal, but instead suppression of testimony;

Opinion of the Justices to the Senate **412 M 1201 (92)**—proposed statute making refusal to take breathalyzer test admissible violates Article 12 (because it's equivalent to 'I know that I won't pass it');

C v Zevitas **418 M 677 (94)**—legislatively mandated instruction concerning absence of blood alcohol testing violated Article 12;

C v D'Agostino **421 M 281 (95)**—same;

C v Seymour **39 MAC 672 (96)**—prosecutor asking D in cross-examination whether she had refused to submit to breathalyzer = reversible error, here compounded by DA's argument (refusal = consciousness of guilt);

C v Quinn **61 MAC 332, 336 n.3 (2004)**—though unremarked by parties, Appeals Court alarmed to see that booking videotape, admitted at trial, depicted D's refusal to take breathalyzer exam;

C v McGrail **419 M 774 (95)**—evidence of refusal to perform field sobriety tests violates Article 12;

C v Grenier **45 MAC 58 (98)**—similar;

C v Hinckley **422 M 261 (96)**—error to allow testimony that D refused police request to relinquish his shoes for determination of whether they matched footprint left by B&E culprit;

C v Conkey **430 M 139 (99)**—can't introduce evidence that D first agreed to provide fingerprints, but then did not do so (violative of article 12); conduct offered to show D's state of mind is "testimonial";

C v Lydon **413 M 309 (92)**—D's refusal to submit to gunpowder residue test not admissible because equivalent to "I know test will show I recently fired gun" & because "compelled" under Article 12; reversal of murder 1 required;

See also Chapter 12-J, re: "missing witness" inference;

C v Conroy **396 M 266 (85)**—"inadvertent" testimony that D had been given opportunity to take breathalyzer, plus absence of any test results, did not require reversal when there was no argument or stress on the point;

C v Scott **359 M 407 (71)**—distinguished;

C v Hunter **416 M 831 (94)**—error to allow adverse inference from D's refusal to submit to a 2d examination/interview by Commonwealth shrink when only one was ordered per *Blaisdell* **372 M 753 (77)**;

Matter of Proceedings Before a Special Grand Jury **27 MAC 693 (89)**—witness justified in invoking 5th Amendment where not "perfectly clear" that testimony could not "possibly" incriminate him;

US v Pratt **913 F.2d 982 (1st Cir. '90), cert. denied, 498 US 1028 (91)**—government agent's 5th Amendment claim based on his exposure to state prosecution was valid, despite role in purported entrapment scheme;

C v Gagnon **408 M 185 (90)**—D has no right to call witness to stand to invoke 5th Amendment in front of jury;

C v Fisher **433 M 340 (2001)**—if witness possibly will invoke 5th, should have voir dire, without jury;

C v Oliveira **74 MAC 49 (2009)**—witness, the boyfriend of alleged A&B victim, testified that he had chosen to take stand despite 5th Amendment privilege; D argued this = error; no objection below, but dicta/rationale of 2/3 judges here = permissible "rehabilitative" evidence pre-emptively because given relationship, bias apparent; Lenk, J., said improper self-vouching for good character;

C v Doe **405 M 676 (90)**—corporate official may refuse to turn over corporate records under Article 12 if act might be personally incriminating;

Matter of John Doe Grand Jury Investigation **418 M 549 (94)**—requiring corporate official to appoint an alternate keeper of records, to sidestep *Doe* **405 M 676 (89)**, cc opinion of Wilkins, J., noted that targets could not be required to identify records to "alternate", noting that open question = whether warrant rather than subpoena was required;

In re the Enforcement of Subpoena **435 M 1 (2001)**—member of Commission on Judicial Conduct was required to comply with subpoena: whatever he had done violated only "internal confidentiality policy," & this wasn't a "crime"; though crime of "conspiracy" is broad, court rejects argument that petitioner was in jeopardy of such prosecution here;

C v Martin **423 M 496, 501 (96)**—"testimony before a grand jury should not be considered waiver of witness's privilege against self-incrimination for purpose of offering testimony at subsequent trial on indictment returned by that grand jury," though this proposition had been thrown into doubt as a result of *Luna,* **above, 407 M at 751**; witness may not rely on "bald assertion of" privilege if circumstances do not clearly indicate possibility of self-incrimination; AND witness must assert privilege with respect to particular questions rather than make "blanket assertion"; to make informed determination as to whether privilege invocation is proper, judge may question witness in camera, with only counsel for witness present, THOUGH THIS IS TO OCCUR ONLY when circumstances allow judge to conclude that witness had not established sufficient foundation for privilege invocation, and permissible scope of inquiry at hearing is "narrow" ("judge is simply providing the most favorable setting possible for the witness to 'open the door a crack' where there is no other way for the witness to verify his claim");

C v Sanders **451 M 290 (2008)**—D wanted out-of-State witness process (proposed witness in Texas prison), but judge denied motion after "nonevidentiary hearing" and telephone conference call with proposed witness's attorney, who said witness would claim 5th Amendment if called and would not testify unless granted immunity (same representation by attorney was made in affidavit), and judge was "aware that the Commonwealth would not grant" immunity; SJC rejects argument that judge erred in finding privilege and its invocation without the proposed witness appearing in person in court, said to be within "discretion" to accept attorney's assertion of claim of privilege; witness's anticipated testimony, according to D, was that he had "been a conduit in paying" for a murder;

Pixley v Commonwealth **453 M 827 (2009)**—D called witness, who claimed 5th A. and article 12 privileges, and judge held in camera Martin (423 M 496) hearing, finding privilege; on appeal after conviction, D could argue error in privilege determination, but would not be allowed access to "sealed"/impounded transcript of in camera hearing;

C v Slonka **42 MAC 760, 769 (97)**—if witness who claimed privilege at trial had given signed statement to defense counsel prior to trial "freely and voluntarily," then privilege against self-incrimination had been waived (conviction reversed here on other grounds, and this topic to be explored, if necessary, at retrial);

C v Pring-Wilson **448 M 718 (2007)**—(same); affidavit may be signed "freely and voluntarily" despite not having had "advice of counsel";

C v Penta **32 MAC 36 (92)**—government agent waived 5th Amendment privilege by giving testimony at 2 prior hearings in case, notwithstanding valid concern re: perjury;

C v Wayne W. **414 M 218 (93)**—when juvenile chooses to present expert testimony at transfer hearing part B which relies on D's own statements, D may be ordered to submit to examination by Commonwealth expert;

C v Clifford C **415 M 38, 46 (93)**—same. Accord, *Blaisdell v Commonwealth* **372 M 753 (77)**—re: D's experts on criminal responsibility;

C v Gagliardi **29 MAC 225 (90)**—witness's assertion of 5th Amendment at prior proceeding was not inconsistent with trial testimony & did not tend to show recent contrivance;

C v Barnoski **418 M 523 (94)**—prosecutor could cross-examine D re: failure to call ambulance or police, since if D's trial testimony were true, he would have done so to help friend (allegedly shot by someone else);

Petition of Sheridan **412 M 599 (92)**—legislature cannot condition discharge from SDP confinement on requirement that D submit to examination & waive G.L. c. 233, § 20B (patient-psychotherapist) privilege;

7-I. IMMUNITY

G.L. c. 233, §§ 20C–I—transactional immunity; SJC, Appeals Court, or Superior Court justice shall grant immunity at request of AG or DA, if (1) case (before grand jury, or in SJC, Appeals Court, or Superior Court) involves offense in 20D [but see *In Matter of John Doe Grand Jury Investigation* **405 M 125 (89)** witness may be given immunity for any crime, not just those listed in G.L. c. 233, § 20D] , and (2) witness validly refuses or is likely to refuse to testify or produce evidence on self-incrimination grounds; witness entitled to counsel at hearing on request, and hearing is not open to public; application for immunity stays criminal proceedings, but not grand jury proceedings; at least three days before hearing, AG or DA shall mail (certified) or deliver copy of application for immunity to all other DAs/AG (and all have right to be heard at hearing); § 20I–D not to be convicted solely on testimony of witness granted immunity;

C v St. John **173 M 566 (1899)**—no immunity merely from police detective or "city marshal" promise/deal (causing D to confess & turn state's evidence); instead, authority only in court re: just disposition, or in DA, who could nol pros *(See Chapter 13, Plea Bargain)*;

C v Russ R., a juvenile **433 M 515 (2001)**—Juvenile Court justices (& District Court judges) can't grant immunity under current law's plain meaning, even though G.L. c. 119, § 56(d) says that Juvenile Court judge has all powers/duties as a Superior Court justice has in trial & dispo of criminal cases; cc. opinion urges legislature to redress immediately;

C v Austin A **450 M 665 (2008)**—witness (to alleged crime committed by two juveniles and two adults) had been granted immunity by Superior Court judge, and Commonwealth moved in limine to have Juvenile Court honor this order to prevent witness from asserting privilege against self-incrimination and compel him to testify regarding same matters in separate Juvenile Court proceedings: SJC reverses order which refused to honor and apply in Juvenile Court the immunity ordered by Superior Court judge: achievement of statutory purpose requires that immunity be enforced so witness is protected from prosecution in *any* court;

Ohio v Reiner **532 US 17 (2001)**—a witness's assertion of innocence doesn't deprive her of 5th Amendment privilege against self-incrimination (context of D's alternate suspect in homicide, i.e., the babysitter, being granted immunity to testify that she had nothing to do with injuries);

Smith v Commonwealth **386 M 345 (82)**—no standing for D to object to witness's immunity;

C v Figueroa **451 M 566 (2008)**—same, rejecting D's argument that trial counsel was ineffective because failed to move to revoke immunity granted to witness or, alternatively, that judge erred in granting immunity because he knew that witness's testimony claiming lack of memory was lie;

US v Boylan **898 F.2d 230 (1st Cir. 1990), cert. denied, 498 US 849 ('90)**—D has right to cross-examine witness about terms of immunity as to veracity & bias;

C v Sullivan **435 M 722 (2002)**—DEFENSE COUNSEL MAY CALL AS A WITNESS a prosecution witness's ATTORNEY, to inquire into attorney's conversations with prosecution regarding immunity: no violation of witness's attorney-client privilege;

C v John **442 M 329 (2004)**—finding of fact, that federal "immunity" notice promised immunity ONLY if D testified against former gang cohorts, wouldn't be overturned; D's confession to murder was admissible;

Lindegren v Commonwealth **427 M 696, 698 (98)**—application for immunity may be signed by assistant AG or DA instead of chief (no bar to such delegation by "the" AG and DA);

C v Dalrymple **428 M 1014 (98)**—SJC rejects Commonwealth request to hold IN THIS CASE that prosecutor has inherent authority under common law to grant immunity in some context not addressed by immunity statute (issue need not be reached, since new broader statutory provisions held to apply, and to cover Commonwealth's needs);

7-I.1. No Conviction Solely upon Testimony of Immunized Witness (G.L. c. 233, § 20I)

C v Jacobs **6 MAC 618 (78)**—corroboration on any element = OK; no need to connect D to crime;

See Chapter 12-G, *Required Finding of Not Guilty* (e.g., *corroboration of confession*);

C v Knowlton **50 MAC 266 (2000): G.L. c. 233, § 20I**—(necessity of corroboration) refers to case in which there's a formally immunized witness, not a witness or two who have been promised that they won't be prosecuted;

C v Thomas **439 M 362 (2003)**—same; SJC declines to require, for conviction, that testimony of an informally

immunized witness must be corroborated (and here, there was evidence corroborating several elements of the offense; GL c. 233, § 20I requires corroboration only of one element of charged crime);

7-I.2. Scope of Immunity to Be Commensurate with Constitutional Privileges

AG v Colleton **387 M 790 (82)**—Mass. Const. Declaration of Rights, Article 12 requires transactional immunity;

Baglioni v Chief of Police of Salem **421 M 229 (95)**—public employee can't be compelled to testify after purported immunity grant by town counsel or police chief because neither has authority to grant transactional immunity; DA's letter "purport[ing] to grant transactional immunity" could **at most** cover his district (i.e., not another county's DA, or the AG or US Attorney); at time of this case, only statutory guidance re immunity involved single justice of SJC (G.L. c. 233, §§ 20C–I (subsequently revised, significantly, by St. 1998, c. 188);

US v Hubbell **530 US 27 (2000)**—after D was granted immunity & forced to turn over documents, "the Independent Counsel" used documents' contents to procure indictments of D, & claimed no 5th Amendment violation because didn't intend to use at trial D's "act of production"; Supreme Court held otherwise (government made "derivative use" of the testimonial aspect of the compelled production, because it was 1st step in chain of evidence leading to prosecution, & government had been unable to even describe the documents with reasonable particularity prior to their production);

C v Steinberg **404 M 602 (89)**—immunized witness's fear of perjury charge & out-of-state prosecution did not justify contemptuous refusal to testify before grand jury; witness had no standing to challenge statute of limitations for crime grand jury was investigating;

7-I.3. Immunity for Defense Witnesses?

C v Curtis **388 M 637 (83)**—no constitutional right to immunity for defense witness; due process may require limited immunity in "unique" case;

C v Wooden **70 MAC 185 (2007)**—no error in judge's refusal to subpoena witness desired by armed robbery D, since pretrial hearing, with witness and his attorney participating, established that witness had and would assert privilege against self-incrimination concerning the pertinent gun, seized from witness's home; **N.B.:** D didn't seek immunity for witness either from Commonwealth (G.L. c. 233, §§ 20C–20E) "or from the judge" (see *C v Curtis* 388 M 637, 646 [83]); D's argument about impropriety of "blanket" assertion of privilege wasn't made below;

C v Drew **447 M 635 (2006)**—judicial immunity not available if witness is actual or potential target of prosecution, or if proffered testimony is ambiguous, not clearly exculpatory, cumulative or "relates only to the credibility of the government witnesses" (quoting *C v Doherty* 394 M 341, 345 [85]); claim that trial attorney was ineffective in failing to seek immunity failed since request for immunity probably wouldn't have succeeded;

C v Cash 64 MAC 812 (2005)—when, at hearing on motion for new trial, recanting trial witness was appointed counsel to advise of rights and thereafter asserted privilege against self-incrimination, D wasn't denied due process by judge's "failure" to give witness immunity; affidavit's recantation version was "equivocal" as to D's actual guilt, so testimony was of "marginal" value anyway; no showing that prosecutor deliberately withheld immunity "for the purpose of hiding exculpatory evidence";

C v Grimshaw 412 M 505 (92)—murder D had no due process right to immunity for defense witness in absence of "unique circumstances";

C v Upton 390 M 562 (83)—not (yet) immunity for D's witness on these facts; but see ***Government of Virgin Islands v Smith* 615 F.2d 964 (3d Cir. 1980)**—immunity for exculpatory defense witness;

US v Angiulo 897 F.2d 1169, cert. denied, 498 US 845 (90)—withholding immunity from defense witness might be due process violation if testimony is necessary to an "effective defense" or if "prosecutorial misconduct" distorts fact-finding process; imprimatur of prosecutorial authorities for the grant of immunity in such circumstances is not required (though that is what Mass. "immunity" statutes contemplate, see G.L. c. 233, § 20E);

cf. ***C v Clemente* 452 M 295 (2008)**—judge refused to find that witness had privilege at grand jury, so witness testified; at trial, same judge found that witness DID have privilege against self-incrimination but also barred D from introducing the prior recorded testimony of the now unavailable witness: though D argued on appeal that he was denied right to present a defense, SJC held here that D failed to establish that Commonwealth had opportunity and similar motive to develop fully the witness's testimony at grand jury, so was not entitled to introduce it at trial; SJC (disingenuously separating the arguments/discussions) subsequently rejected D's argument that he should have had access to transcript of pretrial hearing (attended by prosecutor and witness's attorney) where judge ruled that witness did NOT have Fifth Amendment privilege);

C v Reynolds 429 M 388, 400 (99)—rejecting argument that trial judge should have granted "judicial immunity" to two prospective defense witnesses: proffered testimony said to be "not clearly exculpatory and the witnesses were potential targets of other prosecutions";

K. Smith, Criminal Practice & Procedure, §§ 810–22 (2d ed. 1983 & Supplement)—overview; no constitutional right to immunity for D's witnesses (§ 818) (but appeal denial by G.L. c. 211, § 3, & see cases, ante, including ***Angiulo* 897 F.2d 1169, cert. denied, 498 US 845 (90)**);

See also Chapter 10, Presenting Defense;

7-J. TAPE OR TRANSCRIPT OF TRIAL OR PROBABLE CAUSE HEARING

See Chapter 9, Cross-Examination re: prior inconsistent statement; Chapter 1-B, Probable Cause Hearing for discovery;

G.L. c. 221, § 91B—right to stenographer at any proceeding (at own expense);

G.L. c. 233, § 80—certified transcript by stenographer "duly appointed for the purpose and sworn" = admissible if competent [relevant/material] evidence;

Special Rules of District Courts of Mass., Rule 211—in all divisions of District Court Dept. & in BMC, all courtroom proceedings, including criminal & delinquency arraignments, shall be recorded electronically ("subject to availability & functioning of appropriate recording devices") except may but need not record call of list, proceedings being recorded by a court reporter, & proceedings before magistrate other than a judge; clerk to announce clearly name and docket of case, and to note on case papers or in separate log, the # of tape reel and index #s for beginning & end points; counsel responsible for assisting in creating audible record, including requesting judge to instruct proper use of microphones; preserve for at least 2½ years the original recording of any trial, evidentiary hearing, guilty plea, or admission to sufficient facts in criminal or juvenile delinquency case presided over by judge and any trial or evidentiary hearing in care & protection matter presided

over by judge (all other recordings to be preserved for at least 1 year); party to proceeding is responsible for bringing motion to obtain order for longer preservation for purpose of appeal, ex parte OK; access to cassette copies regulated here; covert recording forbidden, but may seek permission to record electronically if proceeding isn't being recorded by court reporter or by court's own sound recording device; recording by news media governed by SJC Rule 3:09, Canon 3(A)(7); see also Special Rules of the Boston Municipal Court Dept., Rule 308—same;

Matter of Scott 377 M 364 (79)—(stipulation #6) judge prevented taping of probation violation hearing = 1 of many misconduct charges;

CPCS P/G's 3.2(g)—after probable cause hearing, request tape; 6.1(a) obtain transcript; 6.1(e) try to get stenographer, not just tape of District Court trial (see G.L. c. 218, § 27(A)(h)), BECAUSE "TAPE" FAILS TO RECORD MUCH OF WHAT IS ESSENTIAL TO RIGHT OF APPEAL, AND BECAUSE THE ABSENCE OF A CONTEMPORANEOUS AND TRUE RECORD REQUIRES THE DEFENDANT TO DELEGATE THE RESPONSIBILITY OF RECONSTRUCTING WHAT HAPPENED TO THE VERY PARTIES RESPONSIBLE FOR ANY ERROR WHICH MIGHT HAVE OCCURRED;

G.L. c. 218, § 27A(h) & § 26A—invoke, timely, to obtain stenographer for District Court proceedings: request, in writing, addressed to clerk of court, at least 48 hours before stenographer is needed [NOTE: practice in some courts requires counsel to re-request for any continuance date[s] ordered]; hearing is to occur re: D's indigency (& D obligated to file affidavit of indigency and request for payment) & whether court reporter "reasonably necessary" under G.L. c. 261, §§ 27A–G; District Court "shall" appoint stenographer unless D indigent (equal protection issue***); District Court tape admissible if competent & certified, or if stipulated; if court "unable" to provide stenographer, proceeding may be recorded by electronic means;

C v Shea **356 M 358 (69)**—error to prohibit D's stenographer;

C v Britt **362 M 325 (72)**—abuse to prohibit D's taping;

Blazo v Superior Court **366 M 141 (74)**—indigent gets trial stenographer (*See Chapter 7-C, Money for 'Expenses'*);

Connaughton v District Court of Chelsea **371 M 301 (76)**—juvenile right to stenographer at probable cause hearing;

C v A Juvenile **361 M 214 (72)**—juvenile court transcript to impeach at [de novo] trial; [cf. G.L. c. 119, § 60 concerning impeachment use of delinquency adjudications & limitations on other use];

C v Fitzpatrick **16 MAC 99 (83)**—no G.L. c. 218, § 27A(h) stenographer if no $ available;

C v Bart B **424 M 911 (97)**—delinquent-by-reason-of murder juvenile unable to establish that any appellate issue had been "preserved," due to failure of electronic taping system to record **any** side bar conference; counsel had failed to request steno;

C v Swist **38 MAC 907 (95)**—D contemplating R.30 motion to withdraw G plea could not obtain transcript of proceedings via G.L. c. 261 §§ 27A–G; appropriate route = G.L. c. 211, § 3;

C v Coward **7 MAC 867 (79)**—judge can deny time to prepare probable cause hearing transcript because dilatory & could use tape;

C v Gordon **389 M 351 (83)**—tape to impeach (cumbersome!): authenticate!; clarify & verbal completeness for opponent; stipulation re: voices; judge can order editing &/or transcript; must have equipment;

C v Allen **22 MAC 413 (86)**—OK, even though tape defects, if value for jury (who decide weight);

C v Favorito **9 MAC 138 (80)**—testimony must be "substantially reproduced in all material aspects"; can't use unauthenticated notebooks; admissible portion of transcript/tape must be severable; BUT cf. *C v Cyr* **425 M 89 (97)** 3 friends of homicide victim allowed to testify at murder trial to their recollection of testimony given at probate court custody proceedings concerning the child whose mother was homicide V & whose father was charged with the killing;

District Court. Special Rule 211(A)(3)—Counsel's responsible for assisting in the creation of an audible record (i.e., speak with clarity and close to microphones, ask judge to tell others to do so); (A)(4) if case is being appealed, may make motion (can be brought ex parte) to preserve original recording for a longer period; originals of trials, evidentiary hearings, G pleas or admissions to sufficient facts, and hearings in care and protection cases, are to be preserved for at least two and one-half yrs without such motion, other matters preserved for at least one year;

Hardy v US **375 US 277, 288, 290 (64)**—(Goldberg, J, concurring) "most basic & fundamental tool" of effective appellate advocate is "the complete trial transcript"; availability of a "complete" transcript shouldn't be made to depend on the facts of the case; appointed counsel needs complete transcript to discharge his responsibility; "a lawyer appointed to represent the interests of a defendant should not be required to delegate his responsibility of determining whether error occurred at trial to participants at that trial whose conduct may have formed the very basis for the errors"; the right to notice plain errors or defects "is illusory if no transcript is available at least to one whose lawyer on appeal enters the case after the trial is ended;

Mayer v City of Chicago **404 US 189, 195 (71)**—where grounds of appeal make out colorable need for complete transcript, burden is on State to show that only a portion of the transcript or an "alternative" will suffice for effective appeal on those grounds;

C v Harris **376 M 74 (78)**—where transcript of criminal case is not available for appeal "through no fault of the parties," new trial not constitutionally required IF trial proceedings can be sufficiently reconstructed;

Parrott v US **314 F.2d 46 (10th Cir. '63)**—unavailability of full transcript made it impossible for appellate court to determine whether errors were harmless, so conviction reversed;

Charpentier v Commonwealth **376 M 80 (78)**—indigent defendant entitled to a complete transcript on appeal;

C v Shea **356 M 358, 361 (69)**—"record" created other than by independent contemporaneous recording opens door to conflicting versions of what occurred at trial, & "the failure to settle these questions satisfactorily might often result in a miscarriage of justice"; "It is conceivable that the defendant in fact suffered no prejudice by the lack of a stenographic record, but as to that we can only speculate.... We prefer to resolve any doubts on this score in favor of the defendant[,]" so new trial ordered;

M.R.Crim.P. 6(d)(2)—(if defense counsel is present on court date when D defaults, and a witness is present in court who would have hardship in appearing later (because of age, infirmity, profession, or other sufficient reason), judge may order testimony to be taken then, and preserved for use at trial or other proceeding), 10(c) (when granting a continuance, a judge may order as a condition that the testimony of a witness who is then present in court be taken & preserved for subsequent use); M.R.Crim.P. 35

(after showing of materiality & relevance, in "exceptional circumstances," when found to be in interests of justice that testimony of a witness be taken and preserved, judge may order witness's testimony to be taken by deposition; also for production of any unprivileged material);

See Chapter 7-K, Prior Reported Testimony as Substantive Evidence;

7-K. PRIOR REPORTED TESTIMONY AS SUBSTANTIVE EVIDENCE

See also Chapter 11-B, motions in limine; Chapter 9, Cross-Examination; & Chapter 1, Probable Cause Hearings;

U.S. Constitution, Sixth Amendment—right to be confronted by witnesses;

Mass. Constitution, Declaration of Rights, Article 12—rights to meet witnesses "face-to-face" [& G.L. c. 263, § 5] & to produce all proofs that MAY be favorable;

Young, Pollets & Poreda, *Evidence,* §§ 804.1–804.2 (2d ed. 1998);

Brodin, M. and Avery, M., *Handbook of Massachusetts Evidence* (8th ed. 2007);

C v Edwards 444 M 526 (2005)—SJC adopts "forfeiture by wrongdoing" doctrine, which allowed introduction of "out of court statements" (here, grand jury testimony) of "unavailable" witness against Ds who intimidated, threatened, or murdered witness, or even "colluded" in making the witness unavailable/unwilling to testify at trial; "causal link necessary" may be established when D puts forward to witness the idea to avoid testifying by threats, coercion, persuasion, or pressure (BUT MERELY INFORMING WITNESS OF RIGHT TO REMAIN SILENT IS NOT SUFFICIENT TO CONSTITUTE FORFEITURE, n.23) or when D actively facilitates the carrying out of witness's independent intent not to testify; Commonwealth must prove by "preponderance of the evidence" that D procured witness's unavailability; parties must be given opportunity to present evidence, including live testimony, at evidentiary hearing outside jury's presence, prior to determination of forfeiture, BUT hearsay evidence, including unavailable witness's out-of-court statements, may be considered;

C v Cyr **425 M 89 (97)**—3 friends of homicide victim allowed to testify at murder trial to their recollection of testimony given at probate court custody proceedings concerning the child whose mother was homicide V & whose father was charged with the killing;

7-K.1. Witness Unavailable at Trial, "Similar Motivation" to Question

Barber v Page **390 US 719 (68)**—cross-examination (& demeanor) essential to confrontation; prior recorded testimony = error without diligent effort to get witness to trial;

Ohio v Roberts **448 US 56 (80)**—prior recorded testimony OK because witness (called at probable cause hearing by D, but gave no help) now unavailable & D had "equivalent of cross-examination" at probable cause hearing;

Prop.M.R.Evid. 804(a)(5)—must show "industriously" tried to produce witness

Prop.M.R.Evid. 804(a)(2)—not yet adopted, says *C v Fisher* **433 M 340, 355–56 (2001)**, and suggesting (but not deciding) that witness isn't "unavailable" when merely refuses to testify, i.e., refusal perhaps instead must be based on "valid privilege" in order to admit prior recorded testimony;

C v Mustone **353 M 490 (68)**—though no probable cause hearing cross-examination, D had opportunity, so admissible later when kidnap complaining witness dies;

See Chapter 1 & CPCS P/G 3.2 re: discovery strategy at probable cause hearings;

C v DiPietro **373 M 369 (77)**—probable cause hearing transcript admissible because witness now "unavailable" (because marital disqualification);

C v Stewart **454 M 527 (2009)**—Commonwealth brought witness to court (incarcerated for unrelated matter), & informed judge he would claim privilege; appointed attorney determined witness had no such privilege & judge so informed witness; in jury's presence witness ignored clerk's recitation of oath; outside jury's presence, judge ordered witness to testify but he refused; because he was serving life sentence, judge stated it was futile to hold him in contempt, and allowed ADA to treat him as hostile witness; still without being sworn, witness took stand & to most of DA's leading questions (containing prosecution's entire theory of murder, & apparently relying on witness's statement to police and grand jury testimony) answered "no comment": REVERSAL of first degree murder conviction because all testimony should have been barred; judge was not permitted to waive requirement of oath, and leading questions "were effectively transformed into evidence" without opportunity for cross-examination;

C v DaSilva **66 MAC 556 (2006)**—no error in excluding from suppression hearing a witness's testimony given at probation surrender hearing because judge found it not relevant; issue of similarity of proceedings not reached;

C v Bohannon **385 M 733 (82)**—requirements: same parties, under oath, similar issue, opportunity to cross-examine, & unavailable (after good faith, diligent effort - not because 14 months ago Florida judge said "hardship"); Mass. law maybe stricter than federal;

C v Gallo **275 M 320 (31)**—diligent search by DA, so "unavailable";

C v Furtick **386 M 477 (82)**—DA's good faith effort to get witness in;

C v Perez **65 MAC 259 (2005)**—extreme efforts to get witness detailed, such that admission of prior testimony was allowed, despite DA's failing to take witness into custody when he was present and a capias had issued for that purpose; "failure to act on the capias was regrettable and unwise";

C v Pittman **60 MAC 161 (2003)**—judge erred in refusing to allow D to introduce defense witness's testimony from previous trial (ending in mistrial on some charges), and in basing ruling upon lack of proof of witness's attempts to be present at trial rather than upon counsel's "unchallenged representations concerning all his reasonable efforts to secure her presence" (timely subpoena, proof of service of subpoena, advice that despite summons she had traveled to funeral out-of-state, and had assured counsel she would be in court on specific date, witness's family members had told counsel of her "inability to return" as promised); defense counsel had first requested continuance of several days mid-trial, which judge denied;

C v Easterling **12 MAC 226 (81)**—witness "unavailable" because claimed 5th Amendment;

C v Koonce **418 M 367 (94)**—witness unavailable to testify for D at 2d trial because took 5th Amendment & judge found witness didn't waive by testifying for Commonwealth at first trial, since that waiver was involuntary, coerced by DA's threat to prosecute; first trial transcript thus introduced against D!

C v Ortiz **393 M 523 (84)**—can use prior recorded testimony from juvenile probable cause hearing;

C v DiBenedetto **414 M 37 (92)**—same, but not if judge limited D's cross to protect witness from self-incrimination;

C v Hurley **455 M 53 (2009)**—while refusing to declare a "general rule" that witness's testimony from pretrial detention/dangerousness hearing is always admissible at trial if witness becomes unavailable. HERE SJC finds that there was both opportunity for and exercise of cross-examination and that particular tactics at dangerousness hearing *were* same as for trial, i.e., attack on credibility in many ways (not drunkenness alone); fn.9: specific acknowledgment that in a different case, motive to cross-examine at pretrial detention hearing may differ from motive to cross-examine at trial, e.g., when at detention hearing counsel focuses solely on challenging D's dangerousness and doesn't challenge declarant's accuracy or credibility;

C v Negron **441 M 685 (2004)**—claim of spousal privilege made D's wife "unavailable" (in context of probation revocation hearing, so that cop's testimony re: wife's allegations, if substantial indicia of reliability, admissible at the hearing);

C v Cook **12 MAC 920 (81)**—mere refusal to enter & testify is NOT "unavailable";

Ibanez v Wilson **222 M 129 (15)**—not unavailable just because last address = Spain;

C v Ross **426 M 555 (98)**—not unavailable just because witness was studying abroad in Israel, even though when pressed at trial for recent info, prosecutor inquired & reported that she was on spring break in Rome and not expected to return to U.S. for ten weeks: Commonwealth never tried to see if she would have been willing to return to testify & never offered to pay her plane fare;

C v Childs **413 M 252 (92)**—Commonwealth made sufficiently "diligent" search for unavailable witness;

C v Roberio **440 M 245 (2003)**—one witness unavailable, though arrested in Florida during trial, because given steps necessary under Uniform Act to Secure the Attendance of Witnesses from Without a State in Criminal Proceedings (G.L. c. 233, §§ 13A–D), it was within judge's discretion to say "impractical" for jury to wait days/weeks to produce witness; emergency surgery during trial for a different witness, with doctor's letter saying she would be unable to attend court until date which was a week after close of evidence was "classic case of unavailability"; though counsel who cross-examined witness at first trial had been held "ineffective" in other ways, SJC found no deficiency in cross-examination, so prior testimony = "reliable" enough; SJC rejects argument that, per se, failure to present a certain defense as basis for reversal of first conviction means first trial's cross-examinations (which didn't include reference to such defense) were ineffective;

C v Hunt **38 MAC 291 (95)**—that witness = foreign citizen doesn't excuse lack of diligence, sincere effort to obtain witness's presence;

C v Sena **441 M 822 (2004)**—needn't begin efforts to locate witness until shortly before trial; fact that subsequent trial involves additional evidence against D doesn't mean that opportunity for cross-examination at earlier trial is inadequate to satisfy confrontation clause [here];

C v Arrington **455 M 437 (2009)**—no error in excluding prior recorded testimony of prosecution witness (deceased by time of trial) given at pretrial detention hearing: it was "unreliable" because of her medical condition at time (heavily medicated, in hospice care for terminal cancer, necessitating leading questions by prosecutor), which also meant lack of "reasonable opportunity" for effective cross-exam earlier;

C v Robinson **69 MAC 576 (2007)**—"due diligence implies more than partial notice and last minute activities"; Commonwealth's motion and affidavit blatantly failed to specify dates, precise number of visits to two locations, number of summonses and letters, date of tracking witness's brother's court cases, failures to use "many potential and significant sources of information"; Appeals Court vacates trial judge's finding of good faith effort to locate and produce witness, saying evidence insufficient to support judge's findings and ruling (admission of probable cause hearing testimony = error), **BUT ON FURTHER REVIEW, 451 M 672 (2008), SJC overrules**, finding prior recorded statements properly admitted; Commonwealth not required to "exhaust every lead to meet its burden," just "reasonable due diligence"; out of court ID statements by the missing witness permissibly introduced through cop, SJC rejecting D's Confrontation Clause argument, witness having "spontaneously" asserted, "that's the two guys";

Vigoda v Barton **348 M 478 (65)**—72 years old & ill, not unavailable;

A.T. Stearns Lumber Co. v Howlett **239 M 59 (21)**—no recollection (but not insane), not unavailable; [see "impeaching own witness" (Chapter 10B)];

M.R.Crim.P. 35—depositions in exceptional circumstances, after motion, notice, & summons; evidence later IF admissible & witness = "unavailable";

C v Ross **426 M 555 (98)**—R.35 does not trump trial confrontation right; Commonwealth has burden on "unavailability" & "must exercise substantial diligence";

US v Salerno **505 US 317 (92)**—exculpatory grand jury testimony of unavailable defense witness will be admissible if determined that prosecution had "similar motive" in questioning witness before grand jury as at trial;

C v Rodriguez **58 MAC 610 (2003)**—reserving decision (because reversing on different ground) whether defendant may offer against Commonwealth the testimony of witness who testified before grand jury but claimed Fifth Amendment privilege at trial;

C v Clemente **452 M 295 (2008)**—judge refused to find that witness had privilege at grand jury, so witness testified; at trial, same judge found that witness DID have privilege against self-incrimination but also barred D from introducing the prior recorded testimony of the now unavailable witness: SJC held here that D failed to establish that Commonwealth had opportunity and similar motive to develop fully the witness's testimony at grand jury, so was not entitled to introduce it at trial; if D can establish Commonwealth's opportunity and motive to develop fully grand jury witness's testimony, earlier testimony would be admissible, but this is "likely to be very difficult" test for D to meet (id. at 315);

C v Labelle **67 MAC 698 (2006)**—D cannot introduce his own grand jury testimony at trial, avoiding cross-examination by claiming Fifth Amendment privilege; D can't "create his own unavailability" in this manner;

C v Steven **29 MAC 978 (90)**—co-D's exculpatory suppression hearing testimony was not admissible as prosecution had different motive in cross-examining co-D;

C v Florek **48 MAC 414 (2000)**—though ID witness's testimony at hearing on motion to suppress ID deemed "reliable" because issue there and at trial (& focus of questioning) sufficiently similar, witness not "unavailable" because prosecution didn't make diligent enough effort to locate and produce witness at trial;

C v Tanso **411 M 640 (92)**—(decided on federal constitutional grounds) court-ordered deposition testimony of unavailable prosecution witness was not admissible where D didn't validly waive right to cross-examination in District Court;

C v DiBenedetto **414 M 37 (92)**—(decided on federal constitutional grounds) erroneous admission of prior recorded deposition testimony (not cross-examined and no valid waiver of same) can be harmless beyond a reasonable doubt, but wasn't here (only the deposition witness provided motive and ID'd D as an actual shooter); id. at 39

n.4—Article 12 not here construed; open to argue that harmlessness test shouldn't be adopted under Article 12 because it substitutes judgment of appellate court for that of jurors; cf. *Galvin v Welsh Mfg. Co.* **382 M 340, 345 (81)** (appellate court shouldn't speculate as to "whether the jury result necessarily would have been different. No one can tell.")

Delaware v Van Arsdall **475 US 673, 682 (86)**—no automatic reversal for denial of opportunity to cross-examine adverse witness; see also *Harrington v California* **395 US 250 (69)**;.

C v Burbank **27 MAC 97 (89)**—prior trial testimony of unavailable prosecution witness was admissible;

Opinion of the Justices to the Senate **406 M 1201 (89)**—child victim's refusal to testify at trial not proper basis for legislative definition of "unavailability";

C v Fisher **433 M 340 (2001)**—after taking stand, prosecution witness belatedly refused to answer questions; not ineffective assistance to fail to proffer witness's probable cause hearing testimony because (1) it wasn't substantially helpful & (2) appellate court might have held that witness wasn't actually unavailable because assertion of privilege was not "valid" (but was instead because witness was now incarcerated & didn't want to be a Commonwealth witness because of feared retribution);

7-K.2. Absence of 'Demeanor' Not Fatal to Consideration

C v Kater **412 M 800, 805 (92)**—judge hearing motion based on transcript may appraise credibility;

C v Cyr **433 M 617, 627 n.14 (2001)**—rejecting D's claim that testimony of D from 1st murder trial (admitted at 2d trial) would have been ignored given DA's arguing references to "uncontradicted" testimony & judge's instruction to determine credibility by 'how' witness said testimony, i.e., 'demeanor on the witness stand';

7-K.3. Admissions by Defendant in Prior Testimony

C v Hanlon **44 MAC 810, 823 (98)**—admissions in testimony given by D at 1st trial may be read to jury at 2d trial (called a "typed statement" of D), but D not entitled to introduce portions of the prior testimony which were unrelated to the admissions (instead, only those which would tend to "explain" the admissions);

C v Beauchamp **49 MAC 591 (2000)**—same, even though D claimed now that his testimony at 1st trial had been perjurious and "virtually coerced" such that it should be suppressed; court distinguished facts of *Harrison v US* **392 US 219, 222 (68)**, in which 1st trial testimony couldn't be used because it was essentially fruit of introduction of confession held on appeal to have been illegally obtained;

7-K.4. Witness Available, but Prior Testimony Used Substantively

C v Daye **393 M 55 (84)**—substantive use of grand jury testimony (contrary to trial testimony) re: identification under some circumstances *(See Chapter 9-F, Cross-Examination, Prior Inconsistent Statement)*;

C v Berrio **407 M 37 (90)**—sexual assault complainant's grand jury testimony, which was inconsistent with her recantation at trial, was substantively admissible;

Daye **393 M 55 (84)**—rule not limited to identification;

C v Donnelly **33 MAC 189 (92)**—diagram used by cop at grand jury substantively admissible under *Daye* **393 M 55 (84)**, despite cop's claim that diagram not fair & accurate;

C v Fort **33 MAC 181 (92)**—witness's inconsistent probable cause hearing testimony was substantively admissible under *Daye* **393 M 55 (84)**;

C v Noble **417 M 341 (94)**—substantive use of grand jury testimony, called false by the witness at trial, allowed to supply element critical to D's murder conviction, i.e., his knowledge that principal planned to shoot V, SJC adopting *US v Orrico* **599 F2d 113, 118, 119 (6th Cir. '79)**, which, however, supposedly bars such use when grand jury statements "are the only source of support for the central allegations of the charge";

C v Sineiro **432 M 735 (2000)**—similar to & worse than *Noble* **417 M 341 (94)**;

C v Clements **51 MAC 508**—(divided court), further appellate review allowed **434 M 1106 (2001)** worst yet conviction by hearsay testimony, uncorroborated;

S.C., 436 M 190 (2002)—revises/alters previous "Daye" formulations: for admissibility of prior testimony for its substantive value, (1) the present witness can be effectively cross-examined at trial regarding the accuracy of his prior statement & (2) the prior statement wasn't coerced and was more than a "mere confirmation or denial of an allegation by the interrogator," i.e., the statement must be that of the witness and not of the interrogator. IF that evidence "concerns an element of the crime, there is a separate requirement that the Commonwealth must meet to sustain its burden on the element: there must be other corroborating evidence on the issue" (though the additional

evidence "need not be sufficient in itself to establish a factual basis for each element of the crime"); SJC disavows prior statements to the contrary in, e.g., *C v Johnson* **435 M 113, 134 (2001)**; *C v Sineiro* **432 M 735, 741 (2000)**; *C v Noble* **417 M 341, 344 (94)**; *C v Berrio* **407 M 37, 45 (90)**;

C v Rivera **37 MAC 244 (94)**—witnesses' inconsistent grand jury testimony substantively admissible (despite their claim that it was perjurious, a claim relinquished eventually by one witness);

C v Martin **417 M 187 (94)**—D prevented from introducing complainant's probable cause hearing testimony re assailant's clothing because she claimed "not sure" it had been her testimony then;

C v Martinez **384 M 377 (81)**—D might use grand jury testimony of unavailable witness if clearly relevant, unambiguous, & DA had motive to develop as offered at trial;

7-K.5. Impeachment, Now, of Testimony Given Previously

C v Siegfriedt **402 M 424 (88)**—admit transcript though D has new info for cross-examination (true name/job) of now-absent witness; BUT SEE, LATER: *C v Pina* **430 M 66 (99)** when D introduced evidence that V's boyfriend confessed to the murder (admission against penal interest exception to hearsay), Commonwealth could introduce for impeachment the boyfriend's denial to cop; Prop.M.R.Evid. 806 adopted, at least for these circumstances;

C v Mahar **430 M 643, 648–50 (2000)**—after intro of "spontaneous utterance" of non-testifying witness (D's girlfriend), D entitled to introduce girlfriend's later contradictory statements to impeach the hearsay testimony; Prop.M.R.Evid. 806 adopted;

Ayers v Ratshesky **213 M 589 (13)**—absent witness statement impeached by prior conviction;

C v Brown **389 M 382 (83)**—if probable cause hearing prior reported testimony used, D can use co-D's cross-examination from such probable cause hearing;

C v Key **381 M 19 (80)**—definitely can impeach dying declarant's hearsay;

7-L. EVIDENCE LOST BY POLICE/D.A.

Arizona v Youngblood **488 US 51 (88)**—complaining witness's clothes (& semen stains) destroyed = OK because cops, good faith & not shown evidence = exculpatory;

C v Henderson **411 M 309 (91)**—loss of victim's contemporaneous written description of assailant, which was "potentially exculpatory," justified dismissal; actual prejudice, bad faith not required; (contrast *Arizona v Youngblood* **488 US 51 (88)**);

C v Willie **400 M 427 (87)**—balancing test: culpability, materiality, & prejudice; D must show reasonable possibility, based on concrete evidence rather than fertile im-

imagination, that access to material would have produced favorable evidence;

C v O'Day **440 M 296 (2003)**—police destruction of "grenade simulator" purportedly altered by attaching shrapnel justified by need to render it safe; no bad faith found; since D made specific request for item, D need only show a "reasonable possibility" that evidence was exculpatory/"might have affected the verdict" (but could not);

C v Kee **449 M 550 (2007)**—Commonwealth failed to preserve or make record of purportedly "marked" bill used to purchase drugs, claimed to have been found on D's person, so D sought (a) exclusion of testimony about it, or (b) jury instruction allowing adverse inference from its absence: SJC asserts that, despite money's materiality, D couldn't show that bill was exculpatory, and accepts explanation that bill had to be used for further "buys"; D at trial focused near-exclusively on absence of bill; in future, where evidence lost or destroyed, "it may be appropriate to instruct the jury that they may, but need not, draw an inference against the Commonwealth", after D's showing that access to the evidence "would have produced evidence favorable to his cause" (query: how to so prove? Presumption of innocence isn't enough? Simple claim by cop that the evidence was inculpatory defeats confrontation and permissible other conclusion?);

C v Olszewski **401 M 749 (88)**—"negligence" is culpable; suppress evidence re: some lost items & remand re: others;

C v Simmarano **50 MAC 312, 317–18 (2000)**—audiotapes of 911 calls & videotape of D's booking were destroyed after 90 days; no relief in circumstances (because no showing of reasonable possibility of potentially exculpatory evidence), BUT warning that such speedy destruction risks dismissal or other sanctions, & DA = "well advised" to ensure that "all pertinent physical evidence in hands of police (or other agents of the executive branch) is preserved pending trial"; destruction of electronic recordings unnecessary given current "information storage technology";

C v Mitchell **38 MAC 184 (95)**—at best, only misunderstanding as to what D-counsel wanted tested by FBI; D's theory of another culprit lacking evidentiary support;

ABA Standards for Criminal Justice (2d ed. 1986) Discovery 11-2.1(b)—DA shall inform D if intends to test & consume subject, or to dispose of relevant object;

C v Walker **14 MAC 544 (82)**—if D asks, DA should preserve; if lost, weigh government culpability, materiality, & prejudice; none shown from failure to take prints & losing beer can, nor in commingling (i.e., losing) the photo witness said "resembled" culprit;

C v Cintron **438 M 779 (2003)**—[computerized] "automated fingerprint filing & identification system" (AFIS) primer, reliability or lack thereof; D here shows no prejudice from loss of original fingerprint since photo of it formed basis for ID, D's own expert indicated photo of print was "qualitatively excellent," & Commonwealth used only the same evidence;

7-L.1. Defense Negligent/Disinterested (or too belatedly interested)

C v Lopez **433 M 406 (2001)**—D counsel had full knowledge of & possible access to truck for 1½ yrs before destruction, but didn't examine; all truck samples/examination reports/photos made available to D: no relief;

C v McIntyre **430 M 529 (99)**—police authorization of destruction of D's car, alleged site of murder, given only after D's family members didn't want it and a month before D-counsel moved for access to car, no ground for dismissal of indictment because D showed no reasonable possibility that exculpatory evidence was destroyed;

C v Fredette **56 MAC 253 (2002)**—twenty-year-old police reports, including one containing sexual assault complainant's initial denial of such abuse, were lost, but D bore some responsibility for moving to Canada, requiring that he be extradited after cases were reopened;

7-L.2. Prejudice Not Shown

C v Simmarano **50 MAC 312, 317–18 (2000)**—audiotapes of 911 calls & videotape of D's booking were destroyed after 90 days; no relief in circumstances (because no showing of reasonable possibility of potentially exculpatory evidence);

C v Burns **43 MAC 263 (97)**—no prejudice shown from destruction of 3 latent fingerprints taken from drive-by shooting car; Ds were ID'd as driver & shooter & car was owned by one D; merely suggesting something fishy about destruction isn't enough;

C v Noonan **48 MAC 356 (99)**—police discarding hat found at break scene, ID'd by witness as being the kind D wore, didn't require dismissal or exclusion of evidence about it, because D showed no reasonable possibility that hat loss deprived him of favorable evidence (hat was tested for hair, unsuccessfully);

C v McIntyre **430 M 529 (99)**—police authorization of destruction of D's car, alleged site of murder, given only after D's family members didn't want it and a month before D-counsel moved for access to car, no ground for dismissal of indictment because D showed no reasonable possibility that exculpatory evidence was destroyed; but see *C v Henderson* **411 M 309 (91)** loss by police of notes of eyewitness's description of perpetrator significant because reasonable possibility that notes could have been used to impeach ID witness, though impossible to determine "material & exculpatory";

C v Lopez **433 M 406 (2001)**—despite "retain as evidence" order by state police, after 1½ years, Dept. of Public Works destroyed truck in which murdered child was found at salvage yard; all truck samples/examination reports/photos made available to D: no relief;

C v North **52 MAC 603 (2001)**—D said he fled country while on bail was not because of consciousness of guilt, but because of fear for his & family's safety; audiotapes of threatening telephone calls to him were in police custody but were lost; D & police witness were allowed to testify about then, including D describing intonation, volume, & quality of taped voice, as well as its effect on D; no further remedy necessary (& not necessary that judge instruct jury that they could make adverse inference against prosecution because of the loss); tape "only marginally relevant" re flight, because call was made before June, '93, but D didn't flee until Sept. '94;

C v Neal **392 M 1 (84)**—destroy breathalyzer ampule OK because D had opportunity for independent test;

See Chapter 21, OUI;

***California v Trombetta* 467 US 479 (84)**—can discard breath ampule;

***C v Perito* 417 M 674 (94)**—"fuzzy" videotape of convenience store robber, returned to store before D became a suspect, and later destroyed by store: no culpability, useless, no prejudice;

***C v Chase* 42 MAC 749 (97)**—no prejudice shown from police release/sale of truck (the means of motor vehicle homicide/2d degree felony murder);

***C v Woodward* 427 M 659 (98)**—no error in the refusal of a second autopsy on 8-month old baby; baby's family had "statutory, as well as common-law and constitutional, rights to the body," and D failed to articulate a specific need; first autopsy "inherently destructive," so second one probably "impracticable";

See also Chapter 6, Discovery, & Chapter 6-D for cases on sanctions for noncompliance with discovery orders; & Chapter 7-C, Expert for D;

***C v Martinez* 420 M 622 (95)**—loss of co-D's wallet containing ticket stub (proof that Ds had arrived in city only day before execution of search warrant) but it would have provided only "slight support" to contention they did not know of drugs; could have been away only briefly & stubs had no bearing on violent crimes attending warrant execution;

***C v Hunter* 426 M 715 (98)**—one cop lost notes of witness statement which could have been interpreted as self-incriminatory, and thus exculpatory of D; but no prejudice since other cop had some notes, they were in evidence & both cops were cross-examined re: interview;

***C v McKay* 67 MAC 396 (2006)**—failure to preserve answering machine message from D, charged with violation of "no contact" order didn't require reversal: D testified to what he claimed it said (& cop gave contrary version); D should have attempted to obtain/record & preserve the message "at the time of his arrest" in anticipation of trial (even though it was on answering machine of ex-fiancee, alleged victim);

***C v Olszewski* 416 M 707 (93)**—witness's first statement, exculpatory of D, was destroyed by witness, with police acquiescence, when witness changed his story; because contents were known, generally, & there was extensive cross-examination, no prejudice;

7-L.3.   Control by Others, or Not

***C v Wilder* 18 MAC 782 (84)**—DA absolved if hospital destroys rape kit evidence;

***C v Richardson* 49 MAC 82 (2000)**—D's 14-year-old daughter alleged rape, declined to press charges, but changed mind 4 years later; D not entitled to dismissal on basis that complainant's diary, clothing, pertinent bed sheets, 2 notes allegedly written by D afterwards, & rape kit prepared by examining physician hadn't been preserved: none of items was ever in control of Commonwealth; court doesn't rule out possibility of dismissal upon

private person's destruction of evidence if it so taints possibility of fair trial that due process would be violated;

***C v Callahan* 386 M 784 (82)**—witness at retrial can tell observations about evidence lost by clerk without DA's fault;

***C v Harwood* 432 M 290 (2000)**—loss of original letter, without which defendant's expert couldn't evaluate signature [copy inadequate for purpose], justified sanction of preclusion of testimony from prosecution witness saying that the signature wasn't his (Commonwealth contended D forged signature); SJC rejected claim of Commonwealth that action (losing letter) of insurance fraud bureau, funded by insurance companies, but having "close & coordinated relationship" with Attorney General, wasn't imputable to Commonwealth; rationale = D had lost opportunity to effectively cross-examine witness;

***C v Sasville* 35 MAC 15 (93)**—DA authorized doctor to destroy aborted fetus; rape indictment dismissed since testing might have excluded D as father; "remedy" of suppressing evidence about the pregnancy was not adequate; cf *Doe v Senechal* 431 M 78, 85 (2000) physical examination (buccal swab paternity test) of alleged father in tort action meets "standard of reasonableness" IF 4th Amendment were applicable to private litigants' civil actions;

***C v Charles* 397 M 1 (86)**—government culpability = factor;

7-L.4.   Remedies

***C v White* 47 MAC 430 (99)**—evidence destroyed due to police negligence (failure to learn conviction reversed on appeal), and this prevented D from pursuing defense (which had some support already) of "stretching," i.e., that cocaine had been altered after seizure with a dilutant to make the weight much higher: remedy = reduction of conviction from trafficking in amount greater than 200 grams (15-year mandatory) to trafficking in amount less than 100 grams (5-year mandatory); absence of bad faith doesn't necessarily absolve government; unfair trial may result when police or prosecutor lose evidence despite good faith (no federal due process violation occurs from lost evidence absent bad faith, but Mass. Constitution offers better protection);

***C v Cameron* 25 MAC 538 (88)**—no dismissal, but reversal of conviction, & D free at any retrial to question & comment about fact of videotape and its loss or withholding by Commonwealth (without permitting response that tape was "blank" or machine "malfunctioned"); Commonwealth argument/conclusion on available record that tape had no exculpatory potential "could rest only on an arbitrary preference for the officers' testimony over that of the defendant" (OUI prosecution); rejecting argument that D had burden to summons persons to court concerning the missing videotape;

***C v Lewin* 405 M 566 (89)**—prosecutorial & police misconduct involving either delayed disclosure or fabrication of informant by police didn't justify dismissal where irremediable prejudice to D not established; D entitled to voir dire hearing on potentially exculpatory evidence from putative informant & to elicit at trial government misconduct without rebuttal by prosecutor;

C v Rodriguez 50 MAC 405 (2000)—when exhibits at rape trial were lost while in possession of clerk of Superior Court between 1st trial and 2d trial, & defense was identification, jurors were instructed that "if there is a dispute as to the description or any other physical characteristic of that missing physical evidence, and if your collective inability actually to look at that evidence raises in your mind a doubt about the actual description . . . or . . . a doubt as to any other physical attribute or characteristic of that evidence, then you must resolve that doubt in favor of the Defendant"; dismissal of charges not required (because evidence had been available to D previously, & was analyzed, with opportunity for D to engage own experts & cross-examine Commonwealth experts at 1st trial);

C v Gliniewicz 398 M 744 (86)—reverse because pretrial conference promise broken by expert altering D's boots; *(See also Chapter 12–F, Reasonable Doubt from What's Missing)*; testing of boots effective destroyed them; lack of notice to D prevented any D-expert from being present to observe and potentially refute "subjective aspects" of testing;

US v Pollock 417 F.Supp 1332 (D.Mass. '76)—FBI destroy notes of talk with D = dismiss;

US v Bryant 439 F.2d 642 (D.C.Cir. '71)—maybe sanctions for intentional destruction of tape of alleged drug deal unless DA shows took all reasonable steps to preserve exculpatory evidence;

C v Phoenix 409 M 408 (91)—police destruction of evidence during forensic testing subjected to balancing test to determine whether any remedy necessary;

C v Troy 405 M 253 (89)—judge properly restricted prosecution theories of 1st degree murder because of government's "careless" destruction of blood sample; dismissal re: felony murder theory not required as felony was general intent crime;

C v Holman 27 MAC 830 (89)—inadvertent erasure of videotaped booking did not require dismissal of OUI;

7-M. RECUSAL, MISCONDUCT, AND/OR DISCIPLINE OF JUDGES

See also Chapters 12-D, Overbearing Judge; 2-I, Contempt, Court Orders; 1, Venue; 22, re: jury impanelment & biases there inferable;

CPCS P/G 1.3(k)—consistent with rules, should seek best forum for D;

SJC Rule 3:07, 3.5—no ex parte communications by counsel with judge 'except as permitted by law'; 8.2 lawyer having knowledge that judge has committed violation of rules of judicial conduct "that raises a substantial question as to the judge's fitness for office" shall inform Commission on Judicial Conduct;

SJC Rule 3:09, Code of Judicial Conduct: Canon 3—judge to be faithful to law, unswayed by public clamor, or fear of criticism, courteous, patient; "should not permit private interviews, arguments or communications designed to influence his judicial action, where interests to be affected thereby are not represented before him, except in cases where provision is made by law for ex parte application"; disqualify 'self if impartiality reasonably questionable (e.g., bias, know disputed fact) but waivable if financial or family relationship;

Lena v Commonwealth 369 M 571 (76)—when judge's capacity to rule fairly is questioned, judge must first search own conscience/emotions, and if passes that test, must question as well whether this is a proceeding in which his impartiality might reasonably be questioned;

ABA Standards for Criminal Justice (2d ed. 1986) Trial Judge 6-1.1—professional respect to counsel, but must raise matters promoting justice; 6-1.2: adhere to canons & codes for judiciary & for legal profession; 6-1.7: recusal whenever impartiality can be reasonably questioned; D should get a peremptory challenge of judge;

Mass. Constitution, Declaration of Rights, Article 29—judges to be as free, impartial, & independent as the lot of humanity will admit;

District Court Standards of Judicial Practice, Trials and Probable Cause Hearings ((1981) 1:05—recusal: search conscience for internal bias; if none, objective standard [see SJC Rule 3:09, Canon 3(C), Disqualification];

M.R.Crim.P. 44(c)—non-summary contempt to be heard by another judge if alleged acts likely to affect judge's partiality *(See Chapter 2, Contempt)*;

G.L. c. 211C: Commission on Judicial Conduct—investigate complaint of "anyone" re: misconduct, willful/persistent failure of duty, habitual intemperance, conduct prejudicial to administration of justice, bring bench to disrepute, breach Canons of Judicial Ethics or Code of Professional Responsibility;

Matter of Scott 377 M 364 (79)—Appendix Document E (Stipulation of Facts) a catalog of the outrageous;

G.L. c. 211B, §§ 10–11—power to discipline a judge for not following an order of chief administrative judge;

G.L. c. 218, §§ 42A–43B—District Court Administrative Judge shall make rules/superintend all divisions of Dept. (i.e., not BMC/Juvenile Depts.); *(See Chapter 1-B & G.L. c. 211, § 3 (SJC has "general superintendence powers" over all lower courts), see Chapter 15)*;

C v O'Brien 432 M 578 (2000)—SJC has supervisory authority under G.L. c. 211, § 3 to intervene in interest of justice to order reassignment of case (& did so in prior proceedings here, "to eliminate any controversies and unnecessary issues in further proceedings and in any appeal); but see *Ewing v Commonwealth* 451 M 1005 (2008)—if D seeks review of judge's refusal to recuse (judge had presided over D's first trial, which had resulted in reversal, and was presently sitting in session in which retrial was to occur,), no 211/3 because could not establish that review could not be adequately obtained on appeal from possible conviction;

In Matter of Orfanello **411 M 551 (92)**—ex parte communication by an attorney with a judge to obtain courteous treatment for another lawyer in pending case was improper;

C v Quispe **433 M 508 (2001)**—G.L. c. 211, § 3 proper means by which to correct trial judge's actions violative of separation of powers; judge's view of particular legislation didn't afford authority to ignore it, so as to override both legislature & prosecutor re: charge & dispo in criminal case;

C v Clerk of Boston Division of the Juvenile Court Dept. **432 M 693 (2000)**—magistrate must either grant or deny request for issuance of process; to instead merely leave "open" the matter "until year's end" while imposing conditions upon the juvenile was judicial usurpation of prosecutorial discretion;

C v Blake **454 M 267 (2009)**—judge MUST render decision in jury-waived SDP trial (G.L. c. 123A, § 14) within thirty days of the end of trial "absent extraordinary circumstances" (lapse here of 13 months prompted holding);

C v Cheney **440 M 568 (2003)**—no (Brandano-type) pretrial probation and dismissal in Superior Court (rape of child, G.L. c. 265, § 23) over the objection of prosecutor (violates constitutional separation of powers);

C v Tim T. **437 M 592 (2002)**—indictment for rape of child (c. 265, § 23) brought in Juvenile Court can't be disposed of by (Brandano-type) pretrial probation and dismissal if DA objects; CAN accomplish "Brandano" pretrial probation & possible dismissal disposition under c. 278, § 18 (after tender of guilty plea or admission to sufficient facts) IF continuance without a finding isn't "prohibited by law" (but continuance without a finding (CWOF) is prohibited in rape of child case);

C v Barnes-Miller **59 MAC 832 (2003)**—alleged victim of annoying telephone calls was purportedly the "other woman" prompting D's divorce; "victim's" claim of 5th Amendment privilege at deposition in divorce action held legitimate, and judge erred in dismissing, over Commonwealth objection, the criminal case (at which alleged victim remained committed to testifying);

In re Troy **364 M 15 (73)**—remove (& disbar) in part for bail hearing abuses & failure to comply with District Court chief judge's directives;

Matter of King **409 M 590 (91)**—judge disciplined for improperly confiscating bail of nondefaulting D posted by 3d parties to satisfy D's other obligations, amongst other things;

C v Vickers **60 MAC 24 (2003)**—can't link [threaten] increase in bail to D's request for change of allegedly unprepared counsel;

C v Henriquez **440 M 1015 (2003), affirming 56 MAC 775 (2002)**—judge's comments at sentencing indicated probability that he was sentencing not merely for convictions but for uncharged conduct; *resentencing BEFORE DIFFERENT JUDGE necessary* to restore appearance of justice, distinguishing *C v White* 436 M 340 (2002) (no need for reassignment where judge mistakenly believed she was precluded from considering certain info but otherwise "conducted herself properly and considered only appropriate factors in" sentencing;

Bracy v Gramley **520 US 899 (97)**—habeas corpus petitioner alleged that state trial judge was accepting bribes from criminal defendants at time of D's capital trial, and that this induced a "compensatory bias" against Ds who didn't bribe him, since he didn't want to appear "soft" on criminal Ds generally; "no question that, if it could be proved, such compensatory, camouflaging bias on [the judge's] part in petitioner's own case would violate the Due Process Clause of the Fourteenth Amendment";

Mass. Constitution, Part II, c.3, article 1—"mandatory" retirement of judges at 70;

C v Loretta **386 M 794 (82)**—no en banc recusal of SJC hearing validity of judges' re-call (G.L. c. 32, § 35G); & D has no standing to object;

Opinion of Justices **362 M 895 (72)**—re-call after "retirement" = OK;

7-M.1. Prior Oversight of Case

Miaskiewicz v Commonwealth **380 M 153 (80)**—no recusal where contempt unlikely to affect judge's impartiality;

Mayberry v Pennsylvania **400 US 455 (71)**—due process requires 2d judge to hear non-summary contempt for direct, vicious, personal insults to 1st judge;

Fay v Commonwealth **379 M 498 (80)**—judge who decided restitution amount & said D's affidavit = "insult" can then conduct hearing re: violation of terms of probation (+ contempt for false affidavit);

G.L. c. 218, § 35—judge issued warrant/complaint, disqualified if D timely objects;

C v Williams **8 MAC 283 (79)**—no jury trial recusal though issued wiretap warrant;

G.L. c. 218, § 27A(d)—Jury of Six Judge can't preside over case if sat on, took part in, previously;

C v Adams **389 M 265 (83)**—judge who denied (at 1st instance jury) D's motion to dismiss, can hear case jury-waived;

Corey v Commonwealth **364 M 137 (73)**—if District Court judge heard "declination" question (i.e., whether to keep concurrent jurisdiction charge/case), may need to recuse 'self for trial; see also Chapter 1, ante];

M.R.Crim.P. 30, Reporter's Notes—on new trial motion, should grant recusal "liberally" (actual practice and appellate sentiment on this point suggests that Reporter's Notes = strongly rejected);

Matter of Scott **377 M 364 (79)**—(stipulation #27) charges include hearing juvenile transfer hearing after expressing opinion on merits;

King v Grace **293 M 244 (36)**—no automatic disqualification for prior expression of opinion about case;

William v Robinson **60 Mass. 333 (1850)**—may recuse for bias/prejudice/knowledge;

C v Campbell **5 MAC 571 (77)**—[overview]; no disqualification for knowledge gained in official duty (e.g., comments re: D or sat on D's prior cases);

Furtado v Furtado **380 M 137 (80)**—impact of judge's pre-trial contact varies;

C v Simpson **6 MAC 856 (78)**—can preside though (2 years ago) prior case with D;

Ewing v Commonwealth **451 M 1005 (2008)**—D didn't want judge who presided over first rape trial which resulted in conviction reversed on appeal to preside at retrial though same judge happened to be then sitting in the pertinent trial session: SJC refused pre-trial relief via G.L. c. 211, § 3 petition on basis of available review of issue after any conviction and direct appeal;

C v Dane Entertainment Services, Inc. **18 MAC 446 (84)**—no motion/recuse (& no miscarriage) where judge had prior case with D & criticized D's repeated trials;

C v Williams **364 M 145 (73)**—can preside over jury trial though heard motion to suppress;

C v Adkinson **442 M 410 (2004)**—can preside over jury-waived trial even though denied motion to suppress on the basis of finding defendant's testimony noncredible; colloquy in jury-waiver did not use "recusal" term, but inferentially referred to issue;

C v Valliere **366 M 479 (74)**—read inquest report, no (jury trial) disqualification;

C v Clark **379 M 623 (80)**—no recusal (& no motion) for judge who expressed opinion re: seriousness & possible bind-over;

C v Coleman **390 M 797 (84)**—OK here, but judge shouldn't pre-judge case until hears D's evidence;

C v Gogan **389 M 255 (83)**—no recusal (from jury trial) for judge's prior representation of policeman-witness;

C v Eddington **71 MAC 138 (2008)**—after judge took guilty plea from co-D (D's wife and joint venture in physical abuse of their children), ADA suggested in "abundance of caution" that he recuse himself from D's jury-waived trial, but D-counsel opposed recusal and specifically wanted this judge, who nonetheless recessed for almost three hours to consider recusal: recusal not required (judge ultimately heard co-D testify, with rigorous cross-exam);

US v Cowden **545 F.2d 257 (1st Cir. '76)**—no recusal for judge presiding over (severed) co-D's trial;

C v Kope **30 MAC 944 (91)**—judge's rejection of probation recommendation after plea discussions did not require recusal;

C v Taylor **69 MAC 526 (2007)**—judge had no sua sponte obligation to inform D of right to revoke jury waiver or proceed to trial before different judge, after this judge heard change of plea colloquy, including D's affirmative response to whether prosecutor's recitation of evidence was what had happened, before D "balked" in response to question whether she wanted to enter admission to sufficient facts; no relief from immediately succeeding conviction after trial by same judge;

C v Carter **50 MAC 902 (2000)**—judge's coercion of G plea (if D pled G, sentence would be six years, but if G after trial, sentence would be 18–20) made plea involuntary; this wasn't merely "informing the [D] of his options";

See also Chapter 14-A, Sentencing, Permissible/ Impermissible Factors; Chapter 13, Guilty Pleas;

7-M.2. Apparent/Actual Bias against Defendant/Defense Position

C v Senbatu **38 MAC 904 (95)**—judge saying to D-counsel in jury's presence during trafficking trial that "there was no evidence at all that [D] was a user" was "perilously close to" interfering with jury's fact finding function;

C v Ortiz **39 MAC 70 (95)**—by refusing D's requested instruction on prior inconsistent statements and instead instructing that "this is not a case on whether or not good police reports are being made" and "[the officer] is not being tried for what he puts or doesn't put in his police report," judge suggested what inferences should be drawn from the evidence: reversal;

C v Martelli **38 MAC 669 (95)**—judge not "want[ing] to hear" D's closing argument in jury-waived trial, with admonition "don't do this to yourself, please," violated right to closing argument, "never . . . harmless error";

C v Auguste **414 M 51 (92)**—error for judge to suggest/coerce, by ridicule and badgering, facially satisfactory assertions of impartiality; judge should instead conduct meaningful inquiry into acknowledged biases and should not suggest or "require" what jurors' answers must be;

C v Mills **51 MAC 366 (2001)**—resentencing ordered: here, judge alluded to public corruption inuring from a clerk-magistrate's alleged conduct, though there were no charges of this D based on such magistrate's alleged conduct, PLUS unfavorable comment on D's failure to admit wrongdoing, compared to judge's "childhood experience with priests listening to confession in church": "It should go without saying that a judge should not make references to his own personal religious views";

Elder v Commonwealth **385 M 128 (82)**—judge said unaffected, so no manifest necessity for mistrial though DA criticized (jury-waived) judge;

C v Phetsaya **40 MAC 293 (96)**—judge should not have presumed that D witness would incriminate 'self: should have asked DA why he expected this & made ruling rather than tell D counsel that witness could not be called without his parents' advice on 5th Amendment waiver (effectively barring presentation of defense witness); error for judge to decry counsel's performance & fact that case was being tried at all; no manifest necessity for mistrial: double jeopardy prohibition barred retrial;

C v Sneed **376 M 867 (78)**—jury probably aware that judge did not believe witness, and this severely eroded credibility;

C v Molina **454 M 232 (2009)**—judge could remind witness of duty to tell truth, penalty for perjury, where it apparent that he had already lied in denying testifying before grand jury;

C v Cote **5 MAC 365, 369 (77)**—partisan comments = "usurpation of the factfinding function of the jury";

C v Borges **2 MAC 869 (74)**—charge that "[y]ou don't go around paying somebody else's doctor's bills if you didn't cause the reason for it," was "instruction as to the inference which the jury should draw from the victim's testimony" and violated G.L. c. 231, § 81;

Cahalane v Poust **333 Mass. 689, 693–94 (56)**—judge conveyed "his own conclusions about the case";

C v Sylvester **388 M 749, 752 (83)**—jury could have concluded from judge's remark "that the defendant's testimony was not worthy of belief";

C v Sheriff **425 M 186 (97)**—judge's mid-trial instruction, that D had been at Bridgewater State Hospital voluntarily, was both untrue and strongly implied that D was there only to pad his "insanity" defense: reversal;

Blunt v US **244 F2d 355, 366 (DC Cir. '57)**—prejudice caused by judge's partisanship NOT CURED by standard instruction that it was for jury to find the facts;

C v Whitney **63 MAC 351 (2005)**—court rejects D's claim that judge's instruction about "common sense", made at beginning of fourth day of deliberations, had coercive effect on jury ("person could have twenty Ph.D.s . . . and not have an ounce of it," D implying without basis that one such degreed juror was a "hold out" for acquittal);

US v Fernandez **480 F.2d 726, 737 (2d Cir. '73)**—"impression of some sort of partnership between the prosecution and the judge";

Jackson v US **329 F.2d 893 (DC Cir. '64)**—that judge able to examine witnesses more skillfully than prosecutor doesn't justify participation; it's not judge's function;

US v Sheldon **544 F.2d 213, 219 (5th Cir. '76)**—judge must not appear to be partisan for prosecution or exhibit "a prosecutor's zeal," nor may he "add to the evidence adduced by either side";

Caperton v A.T. Massey Coal Co., Inc. **129 S Ct 2252 (2009)**—due process clause incorporates common law rule requiring recusal when judge has direct, personal, substantial, pecuniary interest in case, but S Ct has added to circumstances in which recusal is necessary, i.e., probability of actual bias is too high to be constitutionally tolerable; cite to *In re Murchison* 349 US 133 (D in criminal contempt proceeding must be tried before judge other than the one reviled by D); consider psychological tendencies and human weaknesses to discern risk of actual bias or prejudgment; here, recusal required under Constitution when

appellate judge had received $3 million in judicial campaign contributions from company's chairman and principal officer (and repeatedly refused to recuse 'self, was part of panel reversing $50 million verdict against company);

C v Watkins **63 MAC 69 (2005)**—in jury-waived trial, judge questioned police witness re: his identification of culprit, to elicit the degree of his certainty (which doesn't correlate with accuracy, *see C v Santoli* **424 M 837 (97)**), but court says it was for "source" of certainty, that questions were OK, and that D had obligation to object (so review was for "substantial risk of miscarriage of justice," not found);

S v Barron **465 S.W.2d 523 (Mo. '71)**—wrong for judge to shake head, etc. during defense evidence;

S v Larmond **244 N.W.2d 233 (Iowa '76)**—(same) . . . & nodding, smiling at DA evidence;

C v Moore **52 MAC 120 (2001)**—trial judge "finds" on motion for new trial that he didn't use voice tone during jury instructions to disparage defense position; appellate court suggests that counsel could seek instruction that jurors "were not to listen to the judge's voice inflections with the purpose of trying to ascertain the judge's thoughts as to a possible verdict"; [but see *C v Martin* **424 M 301 (97)** attempted curative/limiting instruction may have effect of "children, don't put beans up your nose" admonition]

C v Hassey **40 MAC 806 (96)**—judge's partisan "cross" examination of defense witness compelled reversal; cf. *C v Haley* **413 M 770 (92)** SJC offended that judge's written decision on D's motion for new trial was "taken virtually verbatim from" D's memo, thus purportedly lacking "substantive personal analysis";

C v Viera **41 MAC 206 (96)**—judge, apparently disbelieving of & offended by D's claim that he was not the person arrested but it was instead a cousin who had used D's car & name, undertook (as D was elsewhere in court building) to gather documents & compare signatures & profess satisfaction that D was the person who had signed the recognizance form after arrest: pronouncement of G of summary contempt & jailing forthwith for 40 days = IMPROPER; summary contempt appropriate when boisterous/offensive behavior disrupts court dignity; judge is not investigator/prosecutor; "press[ing] [D] to indicate whether he persisted in his defense" of mis-ID implicated 5th Amendment rights;

C v Webster **391 M 271 (84)**—judge intimidating juror holding up G verdict, causing her to call in "sick" the next court day;

Fogarty v Commonwealth **406 M 103 (89)**—bias or prejudice requiring recusal must stem from matters learned outside judge's participation in case;

7-N. JUDICIAL/PROSECUTORIAL IMMUNITY

Pierson v Ray **386 US 547 (67)**—judicial absolute immunity if acting within jurisdiction even if malicious or corrupt;

Temple v Marlborough Div of District Court **395 M 117 (85)**—(same) for discretionary acts; Clerk, too, if carrying out judge's order;

Matter of King **409 M 590 (91)**—Dept. judge censured & permanently enjoined from sitting in particular court for improperly confiscating bail of nondefaulting D (posted by 3d parties) to satisfy D's other obligations, & for obscene & derogatory remarks;

C v O'Neil **418 M 760 (94)**—clerk magistrate might be entitled to judicial immunity if acting at judge's direction, but clerk who punched & kicked court officer was acting to frustrate judge's order; court noted no precedent that judicial immunity extends to criminal conduct;

Bracy v Gramley **520 US 899 (97)**—habeas corpus petitioner alleged that state trial judge was accepting bribes from criminal defendants at time of D's capital trial, and that this induced a "compensatory bias" against Ds who didn't bribe him, since he didn't want to appear "soft" on criminal Ds generally; "no question that, if it could be proved, such compensatory, camouflaging bias on [the judge's] part in petitioner's own case would violate the Due Process Clause of the Fourteenth Amendment";

Imbler v Pachtman **424 US 409 (76)**—prosecutor has absolute immunity for initiating prosecutions and presenting state's evidence;

Kalina v Fletcher **522 US 118 (97)**—prosecutor was acting as a complaining witness rather than a lawyer when she executed certification "under penalty of perjury"; susceptible to civil lawsuit under 42 USC § 1983;

Chicopee Lions Club v DA of Hampden District **396 M 244 (85)**—DA's absolute federal & state immunity for quasi-judicial & official acts (e.g., investigation, gather evidence) even if malicious; remedies = electoral, bar discipline;

Andersen v Bishop **304 M 396 (39)**—DA immune (for nol pros decision);

Jordan v Sinsheimer **403 M 586 (88)**—DA has no discretion, so no immunity to disobey clear court order (to return suppressed evidence) not appealed;

7-O. CONTINUANCES

US Constitution, Amendments 6, 14—compulsory process, assistance of counsel, & due process;

Mass. Declaration of Rights, Article 12—produce all proofs; fully heard by counsel; law of land;

CPCS P/G 1.3(j)—seek any reasonably necessary continuance (& minimize others' inconvenience); 1.3(f) CLIENT decides whether to waive speedy rights; 6.6(e) if surprise DA evidence, ask time to review &/or sanctions on DA; 2.1(b) waive no significant rights at arraignment;

C v Sanchez **74 MAC 31 (2009)**—D's failure to object to order scheduling trial date beyond statutory deadline = waiver of right to trial within statutorily-set period for SDP trial; assertion that "the Commonwealth" has neither "sole responsibility" nor "sole power" to bring D to trial, because "court ultimately sets trial dates";

Powell v State of Alabama **287 US 45, 57 (32)**—thorough pretrial investigation/preparation = critical to right to counsel;

U.S. ex rel. Williams v Twomey **510 F.2d 634 (7th Cir. '75)**—ineffective not to seek continuance (even though D wanted trial) when D's witnesses don't appear;

ABA Standards for Criminal Justice, Prosecution Function & Defense Function (3d ed. 1993) 4–1.3 & Comment—avoid unnecessary delay, but seek continuance if need time to prepare; shouldn't accept employment for the purpose of delaying trial; 4-4.1 duty to investigate, explore all avenues, etc.;

ABA Standards for Criminal Justice (2d ed. 1986) Speedy Trial 12-1.3—continue only if good cause & necessary (including public interest), not just lack diligent preparation;

SJC Rule 3:07, 3.2—lawyer to make reasonable efforts to expedite litigation "consistent with the interests of the client"; 3.3 lawyer shall not knowingly make false statement of material fact or law to tribunal;

See Chapter 2, Standards (Contempt, Sanctions, Promptness, Competent/Effective);

M.R.Crim.P. 10—continuance only for cause & necessary in interest of justice; factors; notice or discretionary costs; possible "preservation of testimony" (& "right of cross-examination"); Reporter's Notes- 6th Amendment = right to "prepared" counsel; preserve testimony (like R.35) only in exceptional circumstances;

M.R.Crim.P. 35—deposition to preserve testimony in exceptional circumstances & interest of justice; after motion, notice, & summons [see Performance Guidelines above];

G.L. c. 278, § 6A—larceny of motor vehicle, receiving stolen motor vehicle; court shall order owner's testimony preserved at arraignment if DA shows "need" (& after "time for counsel to consult D"); if continued, court "shall" order preserve testimony & costs;

K. Smith, *Criminal Practice & Procedure*, Chapter 20 (2d ed. 1983 & Supp.)— overview; no time limit, but continuance motion must be timely; suggests need for affidavit; factors, including right to counsel & need to prepare; no costs if notice given (or if it's impossible);

Superior Court Rule 4—for continuance for want of material testimony can require affidavit (with witness names, nature of testimony, efforts to locate witnesses, etc.);

Superior Court Standing Order 2-86—no continuance in trial session & none without motion & affidavit (filed without delay) & good cause;

Rule 13(d)(1)—motions (e.g., continuance) heard any time mutually convenient; [ask clerk to mark up];

C v Clegg **61 MAC 197 (2004)**—judge abused discretion in denying Commonwealth request for continuance when sole witness (cop) on motion to suppress failed to appear and thereby allowing suppression and, effectively, dismissal;

C v Lucero **450 M 1032 (2008)**—G.L. c. 211, § 3 relief for Commonwealth after trial court judge's entry of "required finding of not guilty" when case was called for trial, but no opening statements were made or evidence presented: sexual assault complainant had not yet appeared at courtroom & DA said couldn't prove case without her; when DA subsequently learned that she had been present but in wrong courtroom, trial court judge had denied motion for reconsideration;

C v James **424 M 770 (97)**—no continuance for massive pretrial publicity here (continuance requested as possible alternative to venue change) because individual voir dire was conducted & all seated jurors said impartial & Ds not convicted of **all** charges (proving ability to "sift through the evidence");

C v Souza **397 M 236 (86)**—deny continuance because polygraph & transcript not necessary;

US v Zannino **895 F.2d 1 (1st Cir. 90), cert. denied, 494 US 1082 (90)**—continuances for medical reasons discussed; see *C v Rivera* **44 MAC 452 (98)**, summarized below (medical affidavit/records maybe essential);

7-O.1. Mid-Trial Continuance Requests, Other than for Belated Discovery

C v Rivera **44 MAC 452 (98)**—D's non-appearance on 2d day of trial did not justify mid-trial continuance despite counsel's assertion that D had been in car accident & had received pain medication causing drowsiness/oversleeping, when cops were told by D's mother that he was not home, where he did not return his own attorney's telephone call, & when he did not ever thereafter appear voluntarily (instead arrested several months later); further, counsel faulted for not providing **"medical affidavit"** with medical records on motion for new trial per R.30;

C v Puleio **394 M 101 (85)**—no continuance (suspend trial) to get witness's record;

Collins v Commonwealth **412 M 349 (92)**— (prosecutor's family emergency [death of relative] prompted defense counsel's request for continuance RATHER THAN MISTRIAL) judge's refusal to meaningfully consider mid-trial continuance of 1 week before declaring mistrial required dismissal on double jeopardy grounds;

7-O.2. Continuances Due to Desired Change of Counsel; Counsel's Busy Schedule; Counsel's Recent Entry into Case

G.L. c. 211D, § 2AD—entitled to continuance where court appoints counsel for misdemeanors etc. after having originally refused; *(See Chapter 1-A)*;

Lindsey v Commonwealth **331 M 1, 5 (54)**—"denial of a continuance led to the petitioner being tried then and there for two serious offences with only the assistance of a lawyer who could know almost nothing about the cases

and who had had no reasonable opportunity to prepare them";

C v Faulkner **418 M 352 (94)**—mere presence of counsel is not effective assistance, & counsel, just appointed, had no opportunity to prepare for probation surrender proceeding; denial of continuance made D's right to defend with counsel an "empty formality"; rejects Commonwealth argument that alleged willful default by D on prior surrender hearing date constituted waiver of right to [prepared] counsel;

C v Cavanaugh **371 M 46 (76)**—abuse to deny continuance where counsel unprepared & no inconvenience to DA;

C v Dunne **394 M 10 (85)**—defense counsel prepared & no communication breakdown; can deny pre-empanelment continuance to retain attorney;

C v McPherson **74 MAC 125 (2009)**—freedom to change counsel is legitimately restricted on day of trial;

C v Chavis **415 M 703 (93)**—even if breakdown, can deny continuance/counsel change on day of trial;

C v Carsetti **53 MAC 558, 560 & n.2 (2002)**—same, BUT DEFENSE COUNSEL HIMSELF SHOULD HAVE BROUGHT FORWARD THE CASE PRIOR TO TRIAL DATE; his telling D to 'come before this court prior to trial date' to raise the point WAS IMPROPER; obligation to inform trial judge of need for continuance rests on attorney, not D;

US v Poulack **556 F.2d 83 (1st Cir. '77)**—can deny 2d continuance (for counsel being on trial elsewhere) & appoint new counsel *(See Chapter 2-I & 2-J)*;

C v O'Brien **380 M 719 (80)**—lack of diligence in seeking court's assistance; new counsel was prepared enough;

C v Caban **48 MAC 179, 182–83 (99)**—finding of ineffective assistance of counsel might have been prevented if trial counsel had requested & received short continuance to fully interview & prepare a defense witness whom he decided, mid-trial, to call to support D's alibi;

Matter of Scott **377 M 364 (79)**—(stip. #13) - judicial misconduct/error to deny continuance after only 3 days to prepare, no interview of D, possible motion to suppress suggested by police reports, D-counsel told cops previously that she'd request continuance;

C v Richardson **37 MAC 482 (94)**—no abuse of discretion in Friday ordering of trial counsel to trial on Monday, when D had defaulted on scheduled trial date 4 months earlier and was arrested 10 days before trial;

7-O.3. Witnesses Currently Unavailable?

C v Chase **14 MAC 1032 (82)**—no continuance for 2 cops (expected, but not summonsed) because inadequate affidavit or offer of proof;

C v Holmes **34 MAC 916 (93)**—no continuance on day of trial although witnesses, unbeknownst to counsel, had gone out of state for 10 days, particularly since one witness had previously invoked 5th Amendment and defense had received continuance of trial date;

C v Bryer **398 M 9 (86)**—deny continuance because motion to summons non–Mass. witness = too late; but see *C v Cordeiro* **401 M 843 (88)** *(Chapter 7-O)* DA's continuance to await witness becoming competent;

C v Andrews **34 MAC 324 (93)**—no continuance on day of trial since counsel had had ample time to perform task & he couldn't proffer that task would produce material info;

C v Silva **6 MAC 866 (78)**—abuse to deny continuance where witness unavailable, D ready 3 times, & no prejudice to DA (who assented);

C v Clark **454 M 1001 (2009)**—abuse of discretion to deny Commonwealth continuance when victim who had moved out of state was not available on this date, but was committed to case and would be available for trial on any date in a given month except for "10th through 13th"; judge incorrectly attributed "age" of case to Commonwealth (D had discharged counsel and filed 112 motions, 41 of which were still outstanding) and was "improperly influenced" by her views that any sentence was insignificant in light of sentences D was already serving and that, given D's witness list, trial would consume "significant judicial resources";

C v Degrenier **40 MAC 212 (96)**—continuance/ motion to produce witness necessary because DA failed to deliver defense witness, inmate at county jail, transferred days earlier to remote part of state;

C v Brookins **33 MAC 626 (92)**—counsel's failure to move for continuance or capias to secure properly summonsed exculpatory alibi witness was ineffective assistance; *S.C.* **416 M 97 (93)**—(decided on different issue, but also involving continuance) because cross-examination of D implied that he'd contrived his testimony only after perusing discovery and learning how to address what Commonwealth witnesses would say, error to deny continuance for presence of court psychiatrist, to give testimony that D gave him, on day after events at issue, statement consistent with D's trial testimony;

US v Burns **898 F.2d 819 (1st Cir. '90)**—continuance should have been granted where co-D became unavailable after severance had allowed for D to obtain co-D's exculpatory testimony;

7-O.4. Belatedly-Disclosed Evidence?

C v DeMaria **46 MAC 114, 119 (99)**—on 1st day of trial, both prosecution and defense learned that rape complainant had tested positive for chlamydia; D-counsel noted she planned to intro this, plus argue "not guilty" from absence from Commonwealth case that D contracted disease; when Commonwealth introduced expert evidence that test result was probably "false positive," D counsel successfully moved for funds and to obtain "responsive medical testimony"; after early adjournment on a Thursday, and when desired expert was found to be on vacation, judge refused further continuance after Monday (denying 3-day continuance then): this was within sound discretion

of judge; when ground for continuance is late disclosure by Commonwealth WITHOUT ANY SHOWING OF BAD FAITH OR CARELESSNESS BY PROSECUTION, D "is required to show material prejudice from the disclosure before a new trial can be considered"; here, D "adroitly" stressed absence of evidence that D had caught disease;

C v Jervis **368 M 638 (75)**—if unprepared because of amendment, should ask continuance;

C v Small **10 MAC 606 (80)**—discretion to balance D's need vs. prejudice to DA; 2 days enough to pursue info learned at motion to suppress;

C v Grieco **5 MAC 350 (77)**—can deny continuance by giving D opportunity to interview witnesses disclosed on trial date;

C v Hamilton **426 M 67 (97)**—2 day continuance on trial date sufficient although DA only then 1st revealed (ID) D's fingerprint found in getaway car, when D counsel answered ready for trial & **did not request more time** after 2 days (though initially asked 2 weeks to reconsider different defense);

C v Fossa **40 MAC 563 (96)**—day-of-trial disclosure of lengthy police report/interview of/existence of 2 witnesses should have prompted sua sponte short continuance (but no relief for this D, who failed, post-conviction, to assert what particularly would have made a difference);

C v Gagliardi **21 MAC 439 (86)**—new trial because DA's disclosure of exculpatory evidence = too late for D to exploit; *(See Chapter 6, Discovery, including sanctions, reciprocal, etc.)*;

C v Nester **32 MAC 983 (92)**—D should have been given 1-day mid-trial continuance to counter unexpected expert testimony;

C v Gordon **422 M 816 (96)**—time to locate expert to counter unexpected expert testimony was appropriate; mistrial not necessary;

7-O.5. Re: Commonwealth's Request for Continuance/Refusal to Go Forward with Trial

C v Super **431 M 492 (2000)**—despite fact that prosecutor didn't want to "move for trial" and wanted a continuance (which was denied), JUDGE, NOT COMMONWEALTH, controls docket of court; no relief here from judge's impaneling jury and proceeding without Commonwealth's participation, and jeopardy attached, such that no further "trial" was permitted; but see, e.g., *C v Borders* **73 MAC 911 (2009)**—after continuances for several reasons (including unavailability of cop-witness at suppression hearing) Commonwealth's continuance motion on first set trial date (because same cop witness not available) should have been allowed; dismissal with prejudice vacated;

C v Jenkins **431 M 501 (2000)**—judge "dismissed the indictment" when Commonwealth answered "not ready for trial"; petition for relief under G.L. c. 211, § 3 was correctly denied because Commonwealth could obtain new indictment or could have appealed dismissal under M.R.Crim.P. 15 and G.L. c. 278, § 28E; judge nonetheless has inherent authority to dismiss indictment sua sponte, a "necessary corollary of the judge's authority to process criminal cases";

7-P. SPEEDY TRIAL AND/OR DISMISSAL FOR "WANT OF PROSECUTION"; STATUTE OF LIMITATIONS

U.S. Constitution, Sixth Amendment—right to speedy trial;

Mass. Constitution Declaration of Rights 11—right & justice . . . without delay;

M.R.Crim.P. 36 & Reporter's Notes—"Case Management": dismissal if untried within 1 year of "return day" [R-2(b)(15)] minus "excluded" days; shall dismiss sooner if unreasonable & prejudicial delay; dismissal includes "related" charges; detainer rules; *Barry v Commonwealth* **390 M 285 (83)**—on appeal, appellate court is normally "in as good a position as the judge below" to decide whether time limits have run, although appellate court must accord deference to motion judge if there has been an evidentiary hearing and concomitant assessments of "credibility";

ABA Standards for Criminal Justice (2d ed. 1986) Speedy Trial—overview; DA's obligations, e.g., with detainers; if shorter time limit for custody case, remedy = release; dismissal (on speedy grounds) bars reprosecution;

CPCS P/G 1.3(f)—client's decision whether to waive speedy rights;

C v Blake **454 M 267 (2009)**—judge MUST render decision in jury-waived SDP trial (G.L. c. 123A, § 14) within thirty days of end of trial "absent extraordinary circumstances" (13-month lapse here prompted holding);

C v McCants **20 MAC 294 (85)**—counsel's acquiescence to continuance = waiver (without D's explicit acquiescence);

C v Sanchez **74 MAC 31 (2009)**—D's failure to object to order scheduling trial date beyond statutory deadline = waiver of right to trial within statutorily-set period for SDP trial; assertion that "the Commonwealth" has neither "sole responsibility" nor "sole power" to bring D to trial, because "court ultimately sets trial dates";

G.L. c. 218, § 38—can adjourn District Court sitting or continue a case;

G.L. c. 276, § 35—if D remains committed, case shan't be adjourned for more than 30 days if D objects [prior version of § 35 set a 10-day limit] - *(See Chapter 4)*;

C v Plantier **22 MAC 314 (86)**—District Court "speedy" dismissal bars reprosecution;

C v Ludwig **370 M 31 (76)**—[previously 10-day] G.L. c. 276, § 35 objection satisfies *Barker v Wingo* (below) re: length & assertion; dismissal bars later prosecution;

C v Silva **10 MAC 784 (80): G.L. c. 276, § 35**—(& discovery) violation justifies dismissal with prejudice (though not specified);

C v Conant **12 MAC 287 (81): G.L. c. 276, § 35**—[then 10-day] violation not presumptive prejudice;

C v Balliro **385 M 618 (82)**—can dismiss application for complaint where earlier complaint nol pros'd on trial date (because of variance DA should've spotted);

Klopfer v State of NC **386 US 213 (67)**—speedy trial = fundamental right; can't nol pros with indefinite leave to reinstate;

Smith v Hooey **393 US 374 (69)**—even sentenced prisoners have right to speedy trial on outstanding charges; see M.R.Crim.P. 36(d);

C v Butler **68 MAC 658 (2007)**—prisoner applied for speedy trial on outstanding case, but delay of ten years and eight months between date of original complaint until commencement of trial didn't result in relief: D argued only Rule 36, and NOT any state or federal constitutional right to speedy trial (id. at 659 n.2); prosecution not responsible for District Court's failures/delays (D "must bear some . . . responsibility because he failed to" inquire as to status of request for speedy trial); D failed to show prejudice (in rejecting argument that D missed out on concurrent sentence on plea, perhaps available if disposition occurred during incarceration, opinion says that trial judge imposed sentence substantially less than Commonwealth requested [though such disposition occurred after he wrapped up prior sentence]);

C v Miranda **415 M 1 (93)**—following nol pros of a two-count indictment due to false testimony before grand jury, Commonwealth obtained (cured) new indictment charging only one count; error to allow, at time of trial, Commonwealth's motion to vacate the nol pros as to the count omitted from 2d indictment; both convictions were reversed because trial on the revived count made conviction more likely on the other, in which D's alleged involvement was "more peripheral";

C v Latimore **423 M 129 (96)**—after 1976 murder conviction, collateral post-conviction proceedings resulted in 1992 grant of new trial; motion to dismiss on speedy trial grounds **then** = rejected, post-conviction proceedings being irrelevant to speedy trial; delayed re-trial compromises no interest promoted by speedy trial guarantee;

Cousins v Commonwealth **442 M 1046 (2004)**—no relief under G.L. c. 211, § 3 for D demanding severance from co-D because co-D's change of counsel caused delay and D wanted a speedier trial (issue = denial of speedy trial urged by D to be irremediable years later, on direct appeal);

Barker v Wingo **407 US 514 (72)**—factors re: constitutional speedy trial right = length of delay, reason, D's assertion of right, & prejudice;

Turner v Commonwealth **423 M 1013 (96):** G.L. c. 211, § 3—will not be used to redress denials of motion to dismiss on R.36/speedy trial grounds;

C v Lutoff **14 MAC 434 (82)**—4 year delay + D's persistence − presumptive prejudice & dismissal;

C v Carlton **43 MAC 702 (97)**—no ineffective assistance in failing to move for speedy trial for 3 years after arraignment; no prejudice shown; mere death of one witness not proof (he may have died before an earlier trial, since no date of death was proffered, and no proffer as to how his testimony would have helped D); though delay made out prima facie R.36 violation, Comm met burden of justification merely by showing absence of record objection by D;

C v Tanner **417 M 1 (94)**—no ineffective assistance in failing to move for speedy trial; no prejudice shown (1st degree murder,16 months between arraignment & trial);

Matter of Scott **377 M 364 (79)**—(stip. #5) several Commonwealth continuances & complaining witness never appeared; judge wrongly required D to pay $50 costs for dismissal (Superior Court vacated 'pay' order);

C v Cordeiro **401 M 843 (88)**—DA gets (long) continuance for unavailable (incompetent kid) witness;

Burton v Commonwealth **432 M 1008 (2000)**—though D was arraigned on charge arising from a shooting death within four months of offense, complaint dismissed because witnesses refused to cooperate with prosecution; no right to dismissal six years later when indictment was brought (upon now agreeable witness's testimony); claim of 'general deterioration of ability to prepare defense' isn't a showing of 'actual prejudice,' as required under 'due process' analysis (requiring both prejudice and a showing that delay was intentionally undertaken for tactical advantage or was incurred in reckless disregard of known risks to D's ability to mount a defense);

C v Corbett **26 MAC 773 (89)**—dismissal after 4 months for "want of prosecution" wasn't speedy trial determination; if no harm, can reprosecute later when witness = competent, so strike judge's "with prejudice" order;

State Realty Co. of Boston v MacNeil Bros. Co. **358 M 374 (70)**—court's inherent power to dismiss for "want of prosecution";

C v Whittier **378 M 19 (79)**—after allowed D's speedy trial motion, ordered no further continuances, & DA didn't put case on list; can dismiss for speedy trial denial;

C v Sheridan **40 MAC 700 (96)**—after "NFC" [no further continuances] order (on D's proffer that his witnesses would be moving), DA's neglect to summons witnesses, & dismissal without prejudice, new complaint could be dismissed when Commonwealth wouldn't agree to pay for witness costs to return & wouldn't offer other remedial suggestions;

C v Carrunchio **20 MAC 943 (85)**—dismissal too draconian [though "no further continuances" order & DA not ready (because cop's vacation)]; D had had 2 continuances;

C v Marchionda **385 M 238 (82)**—dismissal motion was for "want of prosecution," not speedy trial, so can reprosecute after it's allowed; but see

C v Monahan **414 M 1001 (93)**—dismissal with prejudice when Commonwealth sought 2d continuance of trial date could not be frustrated by refiling same complaints 6 weeks later; Commonwealth could have appealed 1st dismissal. See also *C v Thomas* **353 M 429, 432 (96)** ADA frustrated judge's ruling denying continuance by nol pros'ing complaints and obtaining indictments; dismissal proper;

King v Commonwealth **430 M 1002 (99)**—dismissal for lack of prosecution, without prejudice, was followed by 2d complaint, and a motion to dismiss (denied), and petition under G.L. c. 211, § 3 for relief in SJC for Suffolk County: petitioner failed to show review of trial court decision could not adequately be obtained on appeal from conviction;

C v Ortiz **425 M 1011 (97)**—dismissal with prejudice **not** warranted on ground that complaining witness had failed previously to appear/Commonwealth couldn't locate, when DA told court that witness had been served with summons in-hand the night before trial date & DA requested continuance & capias issuance because witness's presence could not be otherwise secured; no speedy trial mention; no threat of prejudice to D shown, D not in custody;

C v Hrycenko **61 MAC 378 (2004)**—dismissal (without prejudice) for want of prosecution (witness didn't appear; Commonwealth hadn't summonsed her) could be undone by motion to vacate; *C v Steadward* **43 MAC 272 (97)** distinguished (dismissal there based on failure to comply with "no-fix" statute, G.L. c. 90C, § 2, re: motor vehicle violations, & Commonwealth didn't seek relief by way of appeal or trial court motion, and instead simply obtained new complaint); if D could show "misconduct" by Commonwealth or prejudice from reinstatement of charges, reinstatement may be improper);

C v Super **431 M 492 (2000)**—despite fact that prosecutor didn't want to "move for trial" and wanted a continuance (which was denied), JUDGE, NOT COMMONWEALTH, controls docket of court; no relief here from judge's impaneling jury and proceeding without Comm's participation, and jeopardy attached, such that no further "trial" was permitted;

C v Jenkins **431 M 501 (2000)**—judge "dismissed the indictment" when Commonwealth answered "not ready for trial"; petition for relief under G.L. c. 211, § 3 was correctly denied because Commonwealth could obtain new indictment or could have appealed dismissal under M.R.Crim.P. 15 and G.L. c. 278, § 28E; judge nonetheless has inherent authority to dismiss indictment sua sponte, a "necessary corollary of the judge's authority to process criminal cases";

C v Zannino **17 MAC 73 (83)**—can reprosecute after unmerited dismissal, though purportedly "with prejudice" (not speedy trial ground);

C v Borders **73 MAC 911 (2009)**—after continuances for several reasons (including unavailability of cop-witness at suppression hearing) Commonwealth's continuance motion on first set trial date (because same cop witness not available) should have been allowed; dismissal with prejudice vacated; separation of powers cited (judge usurped prosecutorial authority);

C v Pomerleau **13 MAC 530 (82)**—dismissal "without prejudice" wasn't for speedy denial, so no bar to indictment;

G.L. c. 212, § 29—if no criminal session, Superior Court (non-life) prisoner can petition civil session (if co-Ds join) . . . [for speedy trial];

C v Shea **35 MAC 717 (94)**—in federal custody for parole violation based on new state charges, D was hauled in for District Court bench trial and appealed for jury trial; failure of state to secure his presence for jury trial until 3 years later (some time after release from federal custody) entitled him to dismissal upon showing of prejudice from the delay; failure to file speedy trial motion no bar to relief here;

K. Smith, *Criminal Practice & Procedure*, Chapter 46 (2d ed. 1983 & Supplement)—overview, including detainers (§§ 2306–22);

G.L. c. 276, Appendix—Interstate Detainer Agreement - 120 or 180 days to try D unless "good cause" to extend;

C v Dickson **386 M 230 (82)**—extend Interstate Detainer Agreement's 120 days because "good cause";

New York v Hill **528 US 110 (2000)**—D-counsel's agreeing to trial date beyond time limits set by Interstate Agreement on Detainers barred D from seeking dismissal; speedy trial rights under the Agreement aren't among those "basic rights" that attorney can't waive without fully informed and publicly acknowledged consent of D; D bound by acts of "lawyer-agent";

Vermont v Brillon **129 S Ct 1283 (2009)**—between D's arrest and trial at least six different attorneys were appointed to represent him (D fired one, and threatened life of another), but Vermont court erred in ranking assigned counsel as "state actors" in system for speedy trial purposes; delays sought by assigned counsel are ordinarily attributable to D, though state may be charged with time lost if trial court failed to timely appoint replacement counsel, or if there is a "breakdown in the public defender system";

C v Copson **444 M 609 (2005)**—D's pro se motion for speedy trial here insufficient to initiate running of the 180-day period of Article III of IAD because under federal case law, the 180-day time limitation begins not when D gives request to custodian, but instead when prosecutor & court in receiving state actually receive the request for disposition, along with custodian's certificate (even if custodian is negligent or malicious in delaying forwarding D's request); D must send notice & request to custodial official in "sending State" (& such official is responsible for forwarding D's written notice & request to appropriate prose-

cuting official / court in "receiving State", together with "certificate of inmate status" (including info required per Article III(a), i.e., term of commitment under which D is being held, time already served & time remaining to be served, amount of "good time" earned, time of parole eligibility, & any decisions of state parole agency regarding D);

C v Malone **65 MAC 285 (2005)**—D's own "letter" to the Boston Police Department and District and Superior Courts, stating he was incarcerated and requesting final dispo of all complaints/indictments and speedy trial, did NOT serve to trigger dismissal provision because Massachusetts did not by this letter receive the required information (which would, under the IAD, have been supplied by D's jailer if D had instead (as envisioned by IAD) given warden written "notice" & "request", triggering warden's duties to forward written notice/request to appropriate prosecuting official with "certificate of inmate status"); Massachusetts did not receive any certificate of status, so 180-day deadline was not triggered; while constitutional speedy trial right was "far more viable claim" for D here, because Commonwealth knew where to find D for at least four years, if not nine years, and D had made attempt to assert right to trial: issue remanded for findings re: constitutional right and M.R.Crim.P. 36 rights;

Barry v Commonwealth **390 M 285 (83)**—R.36 is "management tool," not constitutional or statutory; exclude time if D agrees, acquiesces, or doesn't object;

C v Farris **390 M 300 (83)**—exclude acquiesced time [& see *McCants* **20 MAC 294 (85)**];

C v McDonald **21 MAC 368 (86)**—exclude time from filing (non-Rule 36) motion to dismiss until D's ready & it's heard;

C v Sigman **41 MAC 574 (96)**—continuances "by agreement" excludable when delay was for Comm to obtain complainant's counseling records, benefiting D;

C v Willis **21 MAC 963 (86)**—no Rule 36(c) "prejudicial delay," though DA not diligent, because no "prejudice";

C v Moore **20 MAC 1 (85)**—D need not press for trial after motion to dismiss denied; DA responsible for trial list (though not notified motion to dismiss was denied);

C v Amidon **44 MAC 338 (98)**—DA's complete control of list (see G.L. c. 278, § 1) prevented Ds from obtaining hearing on motion; unnecessary to show specific intent to delay trial; **BUT, ON FURTHER APPELLATE REVIEW**, dismissals reversed in major part (Ds' failure to object to 9-month delay, and agreement upon lengthy continuance date for filing pretrial motions = "disinterested attitude" which "can permit a finding of acquiescence"), **428 M 1005, 1007 (98)**; but see id. at 1010, concurring with Appeals Court's disapproval of Commonwealth's frustrating Ds' efforts to obtain hearings;

C v Marable **427 M 504 (98)**—Court excludes time from Sept 1 to December 13, period in which case was on trial list and not reached, because D did not "object, bring a motion for a speedy trial, or move to dismiss"; exclusion of another month because D had agreed to a date for pretrial motions' filing, and after that date, case "couldn't" be placed on trial list (unless D requested it!) because the next month's trial list had already been "set" by DA; periods of time in which court, by its own practice, does not sit for criminal sessions, or when "overcrowding or logistical problems" purportedly prevent hearings of criminal matters, are NOT EXCLUDED UNDER R.36;

C v Rodgers **448 M 538 (2007)**—when D, in pretrial conference report, "agrees" to a particular time for filing of pretrial motions, this period of "delay" is excluded in R. 36 calculation; rule would otherwise allow only exclusion of 7 days after pretrial conference report for filing of motions; docket and clerk's notes reflected D's agreement to lengthy continuances (239 days' delay) for DNA testing of fetal remains, and D didn't "refute" this prima facie evidence; that Commonwealth didn't succeed in getting the testing didn't negate D's assent; **although at some point D filed pro se motion to dismiss for delay**, D had not "expressed dissatisfaction" with counsel, and court could ignore pro se filings at that time since D-counsel was counsel of record (and was assenting to continuances); at the point at which D filed pro se motion to dismiss appointed counsel (citing, inter alia, delays), however, counsel's assents could no longer bind D, and there was "no justification . . . for clerk's failure to docket the motion or to bring it to the judge's attention"; "Hindsight claims that a D benefited from delay should not override his express statement that he does not agree to such delay";

C v Stevenson **22 MAC 963 (86)**—exclude time for DA's interlocutory appeal after motion to suppress was granted;

C v Lanigan **419 M 15 (94)**—no dismissal despite 53-month lapse between arraignment & trial largely attributable to interlocutory appeal on DNA admissibility; judge made findings under R.36(b)(2)(F) re ends of justice served by continuance outweighing interests of D & public in speedy trial;

C v Lasher **428 M 202 (98)**—when D has no counsel because appointed arraignment attorney will not represent (and D has not waived counsel), D is not chargeable with delays; split court upholds dismissal of drug charges; uncounseled D not required to "press his case" or object; Commonwealth should have put case on list to get counsel appointed (rejecting argument that D should have gone to probation department at courthouse sometime to "obtain counsel"); it's statutory duty of Commonwealth (G.L. c. 278, § 1) to manage list;

C v Campbell **401 M 698 (88)**—when DA promised (unconditionally) not to oppose G to only manslaughter & to recommend time served, D's assumption that she wouldn't be tried was reasonable, & her acquiescence to delay wasn't "voluntary"; time D relied on plea bargain = thus includable in R.36 delay;

US v Lovasco **431 US 783 (77)**—18 month pre-indictment delay OK; [cf. *Corbett* **26 MAC 773 (89)** even though OK to dismiss charge on ground of child-complainant's incompetency, "with prejudice" portion of order vacated; only four months elapsed between charge &

dismissal, so no 'speedy trial' right involved, and statute of limitations & "due process" arguments open to D in event of prejudice to him between alleged date of offense & any eventual later formal charge];

US v MacDonald **456 US 1 (82)**—(same) 5 years; no speedy trial right until charged;

G.L. c. 277, § 63—statute of limitations = none for murder; 15 years for rape, forcible rape of child under sixteen, [statutory] rape of child under sixteen, assault with intent to rape, assault on child under sixteen with intent to rape, and conspiracy or accessory toward any of these; 10 years for armed robbery, unarmed robbery, assault with intent to rob or murder, while armed, confining/putting in fear/injuring/threatening for purposes of stealing, and for incest, and for conspiracy or accessory toward any of these; 6 years for all other crimes; exclude any time D was living outside the Commonwealth; if alleged victim was under age 16, begin limitations period only when becomes age 16, or when 1st report to law enforcement, whichever occurs earlier;

C v McLaughlin **431 M 241, 250 (2000)**—conspiracy to commit murder had 6-year statute of limitations by plain reading of G.L. c. 277, § 63;

K. Smith, *Criminal Practice & Procedure*, §§ 1321–24 (2d ed. 1983 & Supplement)—(overview); § 707 - "continuing offenses";

C v Ciesla **380 M 346 (80)**—no statute of limitations because receiving stolen property = "continuing" offense;

C v Vitale **44 MAC 908 (97)**—statute of limitations barred prosecution even though application for complaint was filed 4 days before limitations period expired; "show cause" hearing did not occur until weeks after limitation period, & complaint issued still later;

Ackerman v Commonwealth **445 M 1025 (2006)**—refusing to address substantively on G.L. c. 211, § 3 petition (because issue could be presented in course of direct appeal, later) D's argument that statute of limitations barred indictment (despite fact that District Court complaint ["often functions as 'the portal of entry to the Superior Court'"]) as to same crime WAS issued before limitations period expired;

C v Valchuis **40 MAC 556 (96)**—5 years & 11 months after motor vehicle crimes, D was issued citation, hearing occurred 2 months later & complaint issued 10 days after hearing: statute of limitations (6 years) barred the prosecution; "leaving scene of accident" is **not** a "continuing offense" so as to moot statute of limitations issue;

C v Rocheleau **404 M 129 (89)**—change in statute of limitations for child rape from 6 to 10 years cannot be used retroactively to extend D's liability where it had lapsed under old statute;

C v Cogswell **31 MAC 691 (91)**—same; child rape amendment did not amend period for indecent A&B on child from 6 to 10 years;

C v Purinton **32 MAC 640 (92)**—statute of limitations is affirmative defense which must be raised by D;

C v Steinberg **404 M 602 (89)**—same; immunized grand jury witness had no standing to challenge statute of limitations for crime grand jury was investigating;

C v Bougas **59 MAC 368 (2003)**—statute of limitations is affirmative defense which must be raised or will be deemed waived; purporting therefore to reserve question whether, when particular crime charged is made within the statute of limitations, but the lesser crime of which D was convicted after trial, would have been barred by statute of limitations, relief (required finding of not guilty?) is necessary; QUERY: HOW CAN THIS ISSUE BE RAISED PRIOR TO TRIAL? It can't/won't because D isn't likely to want to relinquish option of lesser included offense at trial. *But see C v Bougas* 59 MAC at 372 (faced with time bar applicable to given offense, DA might "overcharge for the purpose of obtaining a form of relief from the statute of limitations that the Legislature never intended");

C v Jackson **27 MAC 521 (89)**—error to dismiss, with or without prejudice, when DA requested continuance for witness-cop's unavailability: maybe cop never got summons or thought DA would learn of his scheduled absence for National Guard duty; fact that D answered 'ready' and had 5 witnesses ready to testify was not alone enough to show 'prejudice' justifying dismissal;

C v Barrett **418 M 788 (94)**—ineffective assistance of counsel in failure to assert statute of limitations bar;

C v George **430 M 276 (99) re: G.L. c. 277, § 63**— provision tolling statute of limitations when D is not "usually and publicly resident within the Commonwealth," Court holds no violation of constitutional "right to travel," and that tolling provision applies even to Ds who did not leave the state for purpose of avoiding prosecution; due process relief might be available on showing of "prejudice", plus governmental "fault" (though reserve judgment whether prejudice alone should be sufficient to show due process violation when pre-indictment delay is substantial and delay is caused by failure of complainant to come forward, id. at 281 n.6);

C v Casanova **429 M 293 (99)**—though death (allegedly from shooting by D) did not occur until six years after the shooting, D was prosecuted for murder and moved to dismiss for violation of right to speedy trial and due process; no relief: no statute of limitations for murder (and thus no deprivation of "substantive due process"), and prior case (*C v Lewis* **381 M 411 (80), cert denied 450 US 929 (81)**) abolished common law "year and a day" rule limiting murder prosecutions to those in which death occurred within that period of time after infliction of injury; SJC would not replace it with some other period of limitation concerning causation, though legislature could do so;

See also Chapter 14-B, Dispositions: Dismissal (with & without prejudice); Chapter 1, Overview: Indictment after Dismissal, & Chapter 19, Double Jeopardy;

Doggett v US **505 US 647 (92)**—8½ year delay between indictment & arrest was 6th Amendment violation where 6 years was due to government's negligent failure to look for D; D not required to prove particularized prejudice;

C v McColgan **31 MAC 932 (91)**—9½ year preindictment delay because of D's flight from jurisdiction was not due process violation where D unable to show particularized prejudice;

C v Ridge **455 M 307 (2009)**—murders occurred in 1987, but no indictments until 2002: D argued that prosecution used "strategy of delay" for tactical advantage, but judge credited DA's affidavit that prosecution was awaiting particular witness's cooperation (which didn't happen until 2001) and didn't believe could convict without it; further, judge found no identified specific prejudice to D;

C v Adorno **407 M 428 (90)**—speedy trial claim must be raised before trial to preserve appellate rights;

C v Baker **36 MAC 901 (94)**—valid G plea = waiver of speedy trial issue;

C v Spaulding **411 M 503 (92)**—so long as D's speedy trial claim is properly preserved, period prior to D's first objection may be subject to speedy trial analysis; dismissal required after detailed Rule 36 computations;

C v Mattos **404 M 672 (89)**—trial judge's reliance upon prosecutor's factual assertions about reasons for pretrial delay was justified where D failed to file affidavit & memo of law;

C v Wysocki **28 MAC 45 (89)**—evidentiary hearing to settle factual conflict in affidavits required; failure to set trial date attributable to Commonwealth; changes of counsel attributable to D because they benefited him;

C v Rosado **408 M 561 (90)**—13-month delay due to interlocutory appeal was excludable under Rule 36;

C v Conefrey **410 M 1 (91)**—D's written waiver of speedy trial/continuance request based on "court congestion" was acquiescence making period attributable to D;

C v Lauria **411 M 63 (91)**—D's failure to express dissatisfaction with administrative delay & to assert prejudice was acquiescence making period attributable to D;

But see C v Bourdon **68 MAC 526 (2007)**—quoting *Spaulding*, 411 M 503, 506 (92): "we have never held that rule 36 time does not begin to run until the D first makes an objection. Such a holding would upset the balance of obligations envisioned by the rule"; though R. 36 clock was tolled when D filed motion to dismiss (on R. 36 grounds), "because a hearing promptly followed the filing," the ***subsequent*** delay (except for thirty days after the hearing of the motion) required dismissal: the judge did not decide the motion until about seventeen months after the hearing; if Commonwealth had tried to advance case during that time, it might have been tolled, or if judge had stated on record reasons for finding ends of justice served by grating continuance outweigh best interests of public and D in speedy trial; that D below didn't argue about this seventeen-month delay was irrelevant: "unwarranted delay caused by the judge's failure to dispose of the motion could not have been effectively remedied by the parties"; **BUT THIS WAS REVERSED/REMANDED BY SJC, 449 M 1109 (2007), and subsequently, 71 MAC 420 (2008), Appeals Court blamed D for acquiescing in delays, denying dismissal; even though parties had formulated** statement of agreed facts, "allowed and accepted by the District Court judge," establishing that for 17 months, three times per month, defense counsel contacted clerk magistrate about status of motion under advisement and objected to further delay, such objections were "casual," "over the back fence" [sic], and apparently devoid of import, "palpably inadequate", because *not placed on the record, filed with the court, or even sent directly to the judge"*, id. at 428;

U.S. v Scott 270 F.3d 30, 53–58 (1st Cir. 2001), cert. denied 535 US 1007 (2002)—statute allowed exclusion of only thirty days of the period of 134 days during which judge had suppression motion under advisement, so dis-

missal was required under Federal Speedy Trial Act, 18 USC §§ 3161(h)(1)(J) (2000);

C v Fleenor **39 MAC 25 (95)**—D's objections to court congestion continuances, allegedly made orally to the courtroom session clerk, were insufficient; official data said acquiescence (court docket, minutes of clerk, transcript of proceedings = relevant record);

C v Fling **67 MAC 232 (2006)**—judge could grant Commonwealth motion to "correct docket" with evidence from ass't. clerk-magistrate and trial prosecutor's file documents & affidavit, thereby defeating D's Rule 36 issue on appeal; "trial judge's correction is essentially conclusive";

7-Q. (FOREIGN) LANGUAGE INTERPRETER

CPCS P/G 1.3(1)—take steps, e.g., expert help, to ensure communication with, & understanding by, client; *(See also Chapter 7-C, above)*;

M.R.Crim.P. 41—District Court or Superior Court shall appoint (& pay reasonable $ to) "interpreter or expert" if justice requires;

G.L. c. 218, §§ 67 & 68—District Court can appoint interpreter;

G.L. c. 221, § 92—Superior Court appoints official interpreter; § 92A: interpreter for hearing impaired;

K. Smith, *Criminal Practice & Procedure*, §§ 2433–42 (2d ed. 1983 & Supp.)—id. at § 2441 questions are to witness, not to interpreter; no extraneous conversation;

B.M.C. Standing Order 2-83—counsel must give 48 hours' notice for interpreter, AND if hearing/trial is continued, litigants obligated to renew request in same manner;

C v Brito **402 M 761 (88)**—use impartial interpreter, not inmate, to interview D;

C v Garcia **379 M 422 n.6 (80)**—no right to bilingual attorney, if interpreter available;

C v Kozec **21 MAC 355 (85)**—must be "disinterested", not complaining witness's relative;

C v Festa **369 M 419 (76)**—questions are to witness, translate verbatim, no private talk;

US v Carrion **488 F.2d 12 (1st Cir. '73)**—right to interpreter for indigent D, but judge's discretion re: need;

US ex rel. Negron v State of NY **434 F.2d 386 (2d Cir. '70)**—6th Amendment violation by bad interpreter;

C v Colon **408 M 419 (90)**—admission of bilingual cop's stationhouse translation of D's confession did not pose miscarriage of justice despite D's claims of inaccuracy & lack of authentication;

C v Kelley **404 M 459 (89)**—possible suppression if no interpreters;

C v Esteves **46 MAC 339, 345, S.C. (reversing on other ground) 429 M 636 (99)**—Appeals Court found no error in interpreter, translating English testimony into Portuguese for D, being pressed into service to translate Portuguese-speaking witnesses' testimony into English for benefit of jurors and everyone else (D claimed that since only the English translation is evidence, the latter process prevented him from hearing the "actual evidence"); SJC did not address interpreter and other issues, saying they were "unlikely to arise at retrial";

C v Seng **436 M 537 (2002)**—inaccurate Khmer translation of Miranda warnings = suppression;

7-R. PRETRIAL PUBLICITY

C v James **424 M 770 (97)**—individual voir dire held to have accomplished in impartial jury (no venue change or continuance of trial date required, despite march to protest violence, held 2 days before trial, in which V's photo & name were featured);

C v Morales **440 M 536 (2003)**—in determining whether change of venue should be ordered, "public interest" in having trial occur where beloved officer was killed was NOT an appropriate factor for consideration; noting continuance of trial date to reduce effect of media attention on anniversary of death;

C v Rankins **429 M 470, 476 (99)**—after D successfully moved for change of venue to escape pretrial public-

ity, no relief when, 10 days later (7 days before trial), D unsuccessfully moved for reconsideration because minority population of new county was smaller than that of first county; D should have thought of this issue before, and could have sought to limit counties to which case might be transferred;

C v Druce **453 M 686 (2009)**—newspaper obtained videotape (made at prison medical unit of D allegedly reenacting victim's killing as it occurred in prison) and published article in which it was described in detail (videotape never seen by defense counsel during two years postkilling and pre-trial), but SJC held that voir dire of prospective jurors was sufficient to assure no prejudice to D;

7-S. PRESS COVERAGE/OPEN COURTROOM

George W. Prescott Publishing Co. v Stoughton Division of the District Court Dept **428 M 309 (98)**—judge's order, in contributing to delinquency of minor case, which prohibited newspaper from revealing name/address of any child who testified during proceedings, or any child allegedly engaging in any delinquency in connection with the proceedings, and from photographing any such child, was unlawful prior restraint on press, implicitly rejecting as inadequate the findings of judge (citing legislative interest in affording delinquent children protection from public exposure) to clearly establish and support a compelling state interest to protect against a serious and identified threat of harm; any prior restraint also had to be no greater than is necessary to protect the compelling state interest;

C v Clark **432 M 1 (2000)**—prior to trial, news media obtained relief from a single justice pursuant to G.L. c. 211, § 3 with regard to judge's order barring recording and broadcasting of most of trial, and broadcasting oc-curred; on appeal of murder conviction, D argued that single justice erred, but no relief: trial counsel's particular complaints were resolved when made (cameraman ordered not to point camera toward D and counsel, and equipment moved so as not to inhibit counsel's view of exhibits), and judge hadn't made/couldn't make findings justifying exclusion of electronic media as required by SJC Rule 3:09, Canon 3(A)(7) (coverage creates substantial likelihood of harm to any person or other serious harmful consequence) and case law accommodating US Constitution First Amendment (party seeking closure must advance "overriding interest" likely to be prejudiced; closure must be no broader than necessary to protect such interest; judge must consider alternatives to closure; judge must make particularized findings supported by record sufficient to support closure);

See also Chapter 12-A, issues arising immediately prior to trial, re: public trial, etc.

Chapter 8
SEVERANCE AND JOINDER

8-A. SEVERANCE OF CHARGES AGAINST A SINGLE DEFENDANT

U.S. Constitution, Fifth & Fourteenth Amendments—due process;

Mass. Declaration of Rights, Article 12—due process;

M.R.Crim.P. 9(a)—offenses "related" if based on same conduct/episode, course of conduct, series of connected episodes, or parts of 1 scheme/plan; if related, may charge as separate counts in same complaint; either party may ask join relateds; judge shall join unless "not in interests of justice"; D may consent to join unrelateds; 9(d) relief from joinder (*Chapter 8-C, post*); 9(e) unless D asks, conspiracy not to be tried with substantive offense;

C v Piper **426 M 8 (97) R. 9(e)**—no bar to joinder for trial of indictments for (1) murder of D's mother & (2) conspiracy to murder D's father because indictments involved different victims;

M.R.Crim.P. 37—transfer cases in different courts for joint trial;

C v Medina **64 MAC 708 (2005)**—Commonwealth must approve joinder of indictments pending in each of two or more counties if request for joinder is made by D (citing M.R.Crim.P. 37); M.R.Crim.P. 9 allows joinder of offenses for a single trial if in "best interests of justice"; denial of joinder here was understood as premised upon finding "not best interests of justice", particularly since one trial was scheduled to begin the next day;

K. Smith, *Criminal Practice and Procedure*, **§§ 1037–39, 1042–44, 1048–59 (2d ed. 1983)**—severance of offenses against single D;

Blumenson, Fisher, & Kanstroom, *Massachusetts* **Criminal Practice (Lexis Law Publishing 1998),** § 22.1—discussion of tactical & strategic issues;

G.L. c. 278, § 11A—separate trial on question of whether 2d or subsequent (*See Chapters 5 & 14-N*);

ABA Standards for Criminal Justice (2d ed. 1986) Join & Sever 13-3.1—both sides' right to sever "unrelated" offenses; shall sever "related" (see Standard 13-1.2: "related" if based on "same conduct," "single criminal episode," or "upon a common plan") crimes if necessary for fairness, even mid-trial (if D's consent or manifest necessity *(See Chapter 19, Double Jeopardy)*; factors, e.g., will finder be able to distinguish evidence & apply law intelligently?; Comment: lower standard pre-trial; factors, etc.;

See Chapter 11-E, "common plan" caselaw in, "bad acts/other crimes" evidence, admissibility of;

C v Blow **362 M 196 (72)**—sever = judge's discretion; factors = "1 chain of circumstances," substantially same evidence, single line of conduct, essentially 1 transaction; can't join this robbery with breaking & entering because jury likely influenced by accumulating evidence of separate offenses;

C v Sullivan **436 M 799 (2002)**—disavows *C v Blow* as continuing precedent, since it was decided before M.R.Crim.P. were adopted; joinder now governed now by G.L. c. 277, § 46, but by M.R.Crim.P. 9; no abuse of discretion here in joinder of various crimes related to theft or purportedly intended theft of jewelry (either by robbery or by B&E of retail stores) to fence for cash; episodes occurred in same general geographic region, and "no more than two weeks ever passed between" planning or execution of a crime; one crime was a fatal shooting without any theft;

C v Walker **442 M 185 (2004)**—can join three separate incidents over 17-month period for trial, each concerning woman brought to his home and being drugged with a drink containing sleeping medication, followed by sexual assaults; no relief, either, for introduction of evidence concerning another woman, though no indictments were brought re: her;

C v Auguste **414 M 51, 60 (92)**—OK to join indictments concerning 2 incidents six days apart: both occurred at same address & involved robbery of card game participants & assault used same tactics & types of weapons;

C v Souza **39 MAC 103 (95)**—OK to join indictments for sexual assaults upon numerous children & no error in joining the 2 Ds (grandmother & grandfather of complainants);

C v Williams **18 MAC 945 (84)**—can join 2 breaking & entering/assaults because closely related in time, location, method, & evidence of either admissible at trial of other re: common scheme, method; if "convincing showing" that D would testify on 1 & that he'd take 5th Amendment on the other, may sever;

Baker v US **401 F.2d 958 (D.C. Cir. '68)**—(same); need "convincing showing";

C v Cappellano **392 M 676 (84)**—in motion to sever, D didn't assert as basis inconsistent defenses (lack of criminal responsibility vs. identification), which would have been more compelling than just "better chance to win some" if severed;

C v Jervis **368 M 638 (75)**—can join if evidence of either (larceny, assault) admissible at separate trial of other;

C v Kegler **65 MAC 907 (2006)**—can join robbery (& assault and battery) with drug indictment for trial because D's drug dependency provided apparent motive for robbery;

C v Montez **45 MAC 802 (98)**—notwithstanding D's offer to plead guilty to open/gross lewdness, judge ruled that evidence of it would be admissible in B&E/sexual assault trial: no error;

C v Gallison **383 M 659 (81)**—test: evidence admissible in separate trial?; D's burden of proof on joinder prejudice & inadequacy of limiting instructions; prejudice not simply from better chances for not guilty at separate trial;

C v Pagels **69 MAC 607 (2007)**—assault and battery on girlfriend properly joined with intimidation of witness (the girlfriend): phone calls constituting proof of the latter would have been admissible as consciousness of guilt of former (and "witness" status concerned the former); claim of ineffective assistance for failure to object to joinder rejected;

C v Gaynor **443 M 245 (2005)**—aggravated rape and murder indictments concerning four victims permissibly joined (all occurring in same area, within 3½-month period, victims having history of cocaine use, and strangulation occurring after sexual assault, each victim found in state of undress, death occurring at about same time as sexual intercourse with D): that judge did not find similarities in cases sufficiently strong to establish "a signature mark to prove the identity of the killer" didn't make joinder inappropriate; rejects argument that joinder impermissible because D wanted to testify re: one charge (& alibi thereto) but judge denied D's motion to limit DA's cross-exam to only that charge (denial not shown to be "abuse of discretion");

C v Torres **442 M 554 (2004)**—no error in joining for trial indictments for fatal beating of baby (first degree murder by extreme atrocity/cruelty) and for ongoing non-fatal "simultaneously . . . perpetrated" abuse of two older siblings in household;

C v Wilson **427 M 336 (98)**—can join for trial indictments arising out of 6/14 standoff with police with 6/13 murder & firearm possession & 6/14 stalking indictments: "standoff" evidence would have been admissible at murder trial because of statements then made & because implied consciousness of guilt;

C v McCants **25 MAC 735 (88)**—can join 2 assaults closely related in time (2 hours), location, method (ID was main trial issue);

C v Mahar **21 MAC 307 (85)**—can join 2 assaults closely related, admissible as common scheme (& to show ID);

C v McGann **20 MAC 59 (85)**—can join 5 receiving stolen property charges; "business" modus operandi;

C v Todd **394 M 791 (85)**—joinder maybe bad if shows "criminal propensity"; can join murder, assault by dangerous weapon charges where latter = consciousness of guilt on former and it's series of connected episodes;

C v Hoppin **387 M 25 (82)**—should sever if "wholly unrelated"; joinder bad if same effect as inadmissible "criminal propensity" evidence;

C v Washington **39 MAC 195 (95)**—Court said (even if error) no prejudice from joinder of (1) Worcester cocaine trafficking and (2) W. Brookfield possession of crack cocaine with intent to distribute 4 months apart in time because required finding of not guilty ordered as to (2);

See also Blumenson, Fisher, & Kanstroom, *Massachusetts Criminal Practice*, above, § 22.4—("centerpiece" of analysis re: proper joinder = whether evidence as to one victim would be admissible in separate trial as to other victim); BUT SEE:

C v Sylvester **388 M 749 (83)**—admissibility of evidence of 1 offense at trial of 2d is not dispositive; must decide whether prejudice to D outweighs judicial economy; no special rule for joining sex cases; [O'Connor concurs: often best to sever multiple complaining witnesses & incidents];

C v Goetzendanner **42 MAC 637 (97)**—no ineffective assistance of counsel from failure to move to sever trial of intimidation of witnesses from trial of kidnap, rape & assault indictments; former evidence would have been admissible at rape/kidnap/assault trial as consciousness of guilt and to explain why complainant had recanted allegations once before reaffirming her original story (complainant = D's estranged girlfriend);

C v Cruz **424 M 207 (97)**—OK to join armed assault & stalking indictments with murder indictment; evidence re: former was relevant to malice & intent (same victim);

C v Anolik **27 MAC 701 (89)**—joinder of larceny & arson not improper where all evidence would have been admissible at separate trial; D's affidavit failed to make "convincing showing" of prejudice that joinder prevented him from testifying on key charges;

C v Marquetty **28 MAC 690 (90)**—joinder of 4th assault to other 3 not improper despite victim's failure to make identification, where other assaults would have been admissible at separate trial;

C v Mamay **407 M 412 (90)**—evidence of common scheme & method justified joinder of 6 sex assaults over 8-month period;

C v Pillal **445 M 175 (2005)**—no abuse of discretion in allowing joinder for trial of charges of indecent assault and battery of person under 14 on two different complainants, both of whom were friends of D's daughter, visiting the home for sleepovers, 4–5 months apart; D failed to meet burden of demonstrating "compelling prejudice" arising from joinder;

C v Ferraro **424 M 87 (97)**—judge erred in not allowing joinder of all 7 indictments charging sexual assault against young boys: all occurred within 4 miles of D's home, all involved assailant in hooded sweatshirt & bandanna or mask who knocked boy down, asked about money, then sexually assaulted & 5 of 7 V's received telephone calls from assailant after incident (judge had denied joinder of 2 of the 7 saying "geographical dissimilarities");

C v Montanez **410 M 290 (91)**—evidence of common scheme justified joinder of distribution & trafficking charges, despite 4-month interval between dates of offenses;

C v Auguste **414 M 51 (92)**—joinder of 2 armed robberies of card games at same address 6 days apart was justified where same tactics type of weapons used & where D's identity as robber based on more than circumstantial evidence;

See Chapter 11-E re "bad acts" evidence, admissibility of;

8-B. SEVERANCE AMONG CO-DEFENDANTS

Cohen v Commonwealth **448 M 1005 (2007)**—SJC denied G.L. c. 211, § 3 relief from trial court's refusal to sever co-Ds (review can adequately be obtained on appeal from any eventual conviction);

"Bruton" statements of nontestifying co-Ds, prejudice from *Bruton v US* **391 US 123 (68)** sever if co-D statement inculpates D, because can't expect jury to follow limiting instruction not to use it against D; confrontation right violated;

US Constitution, Sixth Amendment—confrontation right *(See Chapter 9, Cross-Examination)*;

Mass. Declaration of Rights, Article12—meet witnesses "face to face";

C v Moran **387 M 644 (82)**—OK if co-D takes stand & is cross-examined by D's counsel;

Nelson v O'Neil **402 US 622 (71)**—(same), even if co-D denies saying it;

C v Caillot **454 M 245 (2009)**—incoherent analysis of co-D's out-of-court statement by which ADA could argue motive for murder (that D's cousin had been murdered and that D had just been shot by that murderer, where Commonwealth argued instead that D and co-D had just fatally shot either that man or his companion), purportedly not hearsay because not offered for truth of matter (but instead for its falsity and consciousness of guilt), purportedly harmless (a puzzling result as it supplied motive which Commonwealth stressed in closing);

C v Martinez **37 MAC 948 (94)**—prosecution promised not to introduce co-D's statement that co-D was merely present and D was the seller of cocaine to undercover cop, so D relied & made no motion to sever; motion to sever made at trial, when co-D took stand to say same thing, came too late; mid-trial motion to sever must be on ground not previously known or reasonably anticipated;

Richardson v Marsh **481 US 200 (87)**—OK to admit co-D's confession with limiting instruction if redacted to ignore D, regardless of inculpatory context; query re: replacing D's name with neutral symbol (n.5);

C v Wilson **46 MAC 292 (99)**—no Richardson error, and no relief; introduction of statement by one co-D to a witness that "we stabbed [someone] last night . . . on Top-

liff Street" merely conveyed "that one or more persons, unnamed, anonymous, were with the speaker and in some relation to the stabbing";

Gray v Maryland **523 US 185 (98)**—when redaction consisted of erasing references to B and leaving blanks instead which, when testified to, were each rendered with the word "deleted" or "deletion", this powerfully incriminated B, "by a simple kind of inference from other evidence," and pushed the Richardson holding too far; reversal, severance should have occurred;

Cruz v NY **481 US 186 (87)**—Bruton applies even though D's own confession's admitted; more harm if more interlock between 2 confessions; [N.B., *Cruz* overrules plurality in *Parker v Randolph* **442 US 62 (79)** allowing joint trial if 2 confessions interlocked]; see intervening *Lee v Illinois* **476 US 530 (86)** DA may still offer co-D confession if co-D's unavailable & "sufficient indicia of "reliability" (e.g., D made one which interlocked)];

C v Best **381 M 472 (80)**—redaction of references to D in co-D's statement in lieu of severance;

C v Bacigalupo **455 M 485 (2009)**—reversal for Bruton error (admission of nontestifying co-D's accusation of a "friend"); that D's nickname surfaced during cross-examination by co-D's attorney didn't reduce prejudicial effect on D;

C v Keevan **400 M 557 (87)**—SJC might still consider contextual prejudice in assessing Bruton question, & might reject *Richardson* **481 US 200 (87)** under Mass. Constitution;

C v Moran **387 M 644 (82) at 653, n.4**—redaction criticized where statement said "we" & gave inculpatory inference;

C v Libran **405 M 634 (89)**: *Moran* **387 M 644 (82)**—not violated; any Bruton error was harmless;

C v Santiago **30 MAC 207 (91)**—co-D's stationhouse statement "We are all fucked" not sufficiently inculpatory as to require severance;

C v Johnson **412 M 318 (92)**—co-D's statement, despite redaction of D's name, nonetheless inculpated D;

ABA Standards for Criminal Justice (2d ed. 1986) Joinder & Severance 13-3.2—sever co-Ds if Bruton statement, DA will use, & can't redact without prejudice; or if joinder precludes fair trial; factors, e.g., trier can't distinguish evidence or apply law well "as to each offense and as to each defendant"; COMMENT: solution to Bruton problem = DA's choice; redaction maybe useless; not recommending "interlocking" exception;

K. Smith, *Criminal Practice & Procedure,* **§ 1073 (2d ed. 1983 & Supp.)**— no severance if adverse effect of co-D's statement only indirect/incidental; § 1074—if D's name not mentioned, "general rule" = no need to sever, but see § 1075, recognizing exception for "inculpatory connection"; § 1076—if co-D's statement = hearsay exception re: D, not barred; § 1077—if D & co-D have different charges, no Bruton problem [N.B., compare/contrast logic of *Cruz v NY* 481 US 186 (87)];

DeLuna v US **308 F.2d 140 (5th Cir. '62)**—sever if only one D testifies & will argue co-D's silence; see also *US v Johnson* **713 F.2d 633 (11th Cir. '83)** (comment on co-D's silence if defenses antagonistic); *C v Hassan* **235 M 26, 32–33 (20)** (co-D comment on D's failure to present evidence in lower court; statutory prohibition against such comment governs only prosecutor); but see *US v McClure* **734 F.2d 484 (10th Cir. '84)** (no court has followed De-Luna);

C v Vallejo **455 M 72 (2009)**—co-D's counsel stressing co-D's cooperation, full statement to cops, unobjected to by D, did not impinge upon D's right to silence; see also *C v Russo* 49 MAC 579 (2000); closing argument of co-D did not make defenses mutually antagonistic, requiring severance of defendants;

C v Adams **416 M 55 (93)**—reversible Bruton error to introduce at joint trial each D's statements blaming the other D when neither D took stand;

US v Johnson **478 F.2d 1129 (5th Cir. '73)**—sever when one D denies crime involvement but coD places D at scene;

C v McAfee **430 M 483 (99)**—non-testifying co-D's statement merely said co-D had seen D in a restaurant before the shooting at issue; this didn't sufficiently conflict with defense that D was mis-ID'd as shooter to require severance;

C v Blake **428 M 57 (98)**—though no D testified at trial, one's statement to police, and other two's grand jury testimony, were introduced at trial: no relief because either didn't expressly implicate others or not "sufficiently" inculpatory;

C v Bienvenu **63 MAC 632 (2005)**—oral motions to sever were made about half an hour before trial, and could be denied solely on procedural ground of failing to comply with Mass. R. Crim. P. 9(d)(2) (motion for relief from prejudicial joinder shall be in writing and made before trial and shall be supported by affidavit setting forth grounds upon which any alleged prejudice rests); further, while co-D's attempted to raise reasonable doubt re: individual guilt about possession of cocaine found in car, they "did not affirmatively point fingers at one another; no abuse of discretion substantively in denying severance;

C v Sinnott **399 M 863 (87)**—Bruton error where nontestifying co-D's inculpated each other, but statements merely "cumulative" of other substantial DA evidence (4 eyewitnesses), so harmless;

C v Horton **376 M 380 (78)**—deny severance where each D made highly incriminating statements;

Tennessee v Street **471 US 409 (85)**—can admit co-D's confession (with limiting instruction) to disprove D's claim that his confession's a coerced imitation of co-D's;

C v Corradino **368 M 411 (75)**—statements must inculpate & substantially prejudice D to trigger Bruton;

C v James **424 M 770 (97)**—James's statement (that he drank at his home with friends, including co-D, before going to home of girlfriend & spending night) did not require severance: James's girlfriend denied seeing him, & co-D's witnesses said co-D was with them all evening, studying for a test; SJC said statement not inconsistent with D's alibi & did no more than establish an association between the 2 Ds; this was not contextual incrimination requiring **Bruton** severance;

C v Flynn **362 M 455 (72)**—trial testimony of former co-D now as DA witness OK under Bruton;

C v DiCato **19 MAC 40 (84)**—no severance if co-D statement during/furthering joint venture with D, so admissible against D even if tried separately;

C v Clarke **418 M 207 (94)**—same; statements were that victim "was in the wrong place at the wrong time" and "we" are going to "get rid of [guns] because they're going to get us caught and in trouble";

C v Collado **426 M 675, 681 (98)**—same—enough evidence apart from statements to show joint venture existed; not necessary that such evidence be sufficient before coD's statements are introduced, because can move to strike;

C v Braley **449 M 316 (2007)**—statements of joint venturer admissible if Commonwealth establishes by "preponderance of the evidence" an "adequate probability of the existence of a common venture, including participation by the given defendant"; evidence to be viewed in light most favorable to Commonwealth;

C v Hardy **431 M 387, 394 n.3 (2000)**—though Commonwealth had agreed at hearing on motion to sever that co-D's statements created Bruton problem & wouldn't be admissible against D if the 2 were tried together, no error found in introducing the statements: despite "concession", no evidence that Commonwealth intended it to be "binding" regarding the admissibility of the statement or that D understood it to be so, and properly instructed jury could find that the joint venture was continuing at time statements were made (re: getting rid of gun and locating a place to go shortly after murder);

C v Adams **416 M 55, 59 n.4 (93)**—co-D's statements resulting from custodial interrogations cannot be "in furtherance of joint venture";

C v White **370 M 703 (76)**—confession after conspiracy not admissible against co-D;

C v Fernandes **427 M 90, 94–95 (98)**—alleged joint venturer's statements that he was going to "get" V & V's cousin admissible against D, despite fact statement was made before inception of joint venture; offered to prove declarant's state of mind (that he carried out his intent), statement was relevant to the purpose of joint venture;

C v Pontes **402 M 311 (88)**—can deny severance though DA used co-D's flight; even if communicative, it didn't inculpate D, so limiting instruction sufficient;

C v Bonnoyer **25 MAC 444 (88)**—after picking D's photo, witness expressed doubt, but cop said co-D confessed & fingered D: suppression of out-of-court AND in-court ID required because D couldn't cross-examine re: doubts without showing co-D's confession;

C v Dias **405 M 131 (89)**—admission of co-D's videotaped statement was Bruton error requiring reversal, even though D failed to move for severance; discussion of *Cruz v NY* **481 US 186 (87)**;

C v Hawkesworth **405 M 664 (89)** admission of co-D's unredacted statement was Bruton violation requiring reversal;

8-B.1. Prejudice from Irreconcilable/ Conflicting Defenses

C v Moran **387 M 644 (82)**—mutually antagonistic & irreconcilable defenses require severance (e.g., each blames other) if request made when necessity's firmly shown (and this can be anytime, renewed) [even though each can cross-examine the other];

C v Burr **33 MAC 637 (92)**—necessity for severance must be firmly established at time severance motion made; severance on Moran grounds not required because D's it-didn't-happen defense not irreconcilable with co-D's entrapment defense as co-D could have been involved in drug deal without D; no prejudice to D shown where co-D fled on 2d day of trial & didn't give entrapment testimony;

K. Smith, *Criminal Practice & Procedure*, §§ 1064–67 (2d ed. 1983 & Supp.)—sever for antagonistic defenses only if jury can't find 1 NG without G on other; in complicated, multiple D case may need severance for cumulative grounds; conspiracy issues;

C v Vieira **401 M 828 (88)**—no severance merely for inconsistent strategies or because 1 co-D has better chance alone;

C v Souza **39 MAC 103 (95)**—no severance of husband & wife for trial of indictments charging sexual assaults of their grandchildren;

C v Clarke **418 M 207 (94)**—one D argued "merely present, but not a participant" at shooting; other D defended on ground that Commonwealth witnesses were not credible: not mutually antagonistic & irreconcilable per *Moran* **387 M 644 (82)**;

C v Stephens **44 MAC 940 (98)**—one D argued 'merely present, but not participant at robbery'; other D defended on mis-ID; severance not required (neither D made statements implicating the other);

C v McAfee **430 M 483 (99)** & *C v Elliot* **430 M 498 (99)**—one D argued mis-ID; other D argued not a joint-venturer in shooting by other culprit or, alternatively, self-defense; severance not required purportedly because each D attacked credibility of chief Commonwealth witness, sharing "common approach to raising a reasonable doubt"; perhaps different result if co-D had vigorously attacked the "mis-ID" defendant, saying allegedly mis-identified D was shooter, and solely responsible;

C v Burr **33 MAC 637 (92)**—must firmly establish irreconcilability (might not be apparent at time request is made): drug deal "didn't happen" not necessarily inconsistent with entrapment defense because latter could have been involved in drug sale without other D's involvement;

C v DeCastro **24 MAC 937 (87)**—D's entrapment not antagonistic to co-D's denying any involvement in the drug sales at issue;

Zafiro v US **506 US 534 (93)**—federal rules don't automatically require severance of co-Ds with mutually antagonistic defenses, even where actual prejudice shown because "less drastic" remedies ordinarily sufficient;

C v Sinnott **399 M 863 (87)**—no motion by D, 4 eyewitnesses, & jury could've believed neither D, so OK not to sever;

C v Cordeiro **401 M 843 (88)**—no severance where one D says complainant consented with both & co-D said "mere presence";

C v Masonoff **70 MAC 162 (2007)**—failure to file motion to sever trial from co-D's trial held to have been illegitimate basis for judge to have found ineffective assistance and order new trial; Appeals Court holds defenses not irreconcilable and that severance isn't required if jury had option of disbelieving both Ds and finding guilt based on testimony from other witnesses; Court claims motion judge misapprehended degree of prejudice which must be shown to warrant separate trials; admissibility of co-D's statement turned on whether co-D testified, but he did;

C v Giannopoulos **34 MAC 937 (93)**—"antagonistic defenses require severance only when the defenses are so inconsistent that the jury would have to blame one D at the expense of the other"; although co-D here said she was duped by D, D herself acknowledged criminal acts but said coerced by husband (thus no "expense" to D from co-D's defense);

C v Cunningham **405 M 646 (89)**—severance on Moran grounds (387 M 644 (82) irreconcilable defenses) not required where D's defense was insanity & co-D's was mere presence; however, spillover from interlocking statements of nontestifying co-D's in violation of Bruton may have had effect on verdict & thus not harmless;

C v Smith **418 M 120 (94)**—though D argued that severance should have been granted due to co-D's successful objection to D's cross-examination of cop, court found no prejudice because desired evidence was cumulative;

8-B.2. Co-D as Witness for D, and Other Issues

C v Greene **400 M 144 (87)**—D's right to District Court bench trial though co-D claimed first instance jury trial; can't make D go first instance jury [re: now-abandoned system of jury trial de novo after G in "bench" trial];

Cousins v Commonwealth **442 M 1046 (2004)**—no relief under G.L. c. 211, § 3 for D demanding severance from co-D because co-D's change of counsel caused delay and D wanted a speedier trial (issue = denial of speedy trial urged by D to be irremediable years later, on direct appeal);

C v Weaver **21 MAC 524 n.1 (86)**—maybe sever for "judicial economy" D's carrying firearm from co-D's murder case, BUT SJC, on further review, **400 M 612 (87)**, held joinder perfectly OK on facts here;

C v Foley **7 MAC 608 (79)**—co-D's polygraph failure may require severance for D if co-D will testify at trial [NOTE: this was before SJC held that polygraph = inadmissible; see *C v Mendes* **406 M 201 (89)** all uses of polygraph evidence at trial barred because not "generally accepted by relevant scientific community"];

C v Bourgeois **391 M 869 (84)**—can deny mid-trial severance though jury heard nontestifying D tell co-D's attorney "we're in this together";

US v Echeles **352 F.2d 892 (7th Cir. '65)**—sever so D can procure co-D's testimony (co-D had testified 3 times that D hadn't suborned his perjury);

US v Shuford **454 F.2d 772 (4th Cir. '71)**—co-D would testify for D, not at own trial, because poor demeanor & wanted stay off stand, so D gets severance;

US v Burns **898 F.2d 819 (1st Cir. '90)**—D's showing of bona fide need for co-D's testimony & that co-D would testify after his trial required severance;

C v Barrett **6 MAC 952 (78)**—co-D testimony must exculpate D to sever - not merely denying guilt;

C v Hogg **365 M 290 (74)**—unelaborated assertion D wants to call co-D = too speculative to sever;

US v Mazza **792 F.2d 1210 (1st Cir. '86)**—generalized averment co-Ds will help doesn't require severance;

C v Flowers **5 MAC 557 (77)**—(Brown, concur) when pro se co-D disrupts trial, "much healthier" to sever or declare mistrial;

Jones v Commonwealth **379 M 607 (80)**—if co-D (or counsel) misbehavior provokes mistrial, judge should consider severing & continuing with D's trial; after jeopardy, less discretion;

Barton v Commonwealth **385 M 517 (82)**—if mistrial = over D's objection, because juror feared co-D, should've considered severance; if complex case/many co-Ds, severance less appropriate;

K. Smith, *Criminal Practice & Procedure*, **§ 1068 (2d ed. 1983 & Supp.)**—severance instead of mistrial option;

ABA Standards for Criminal Justice (2d ed. 1986) 13-3.3(d)(e)—double jeopardy and severance; *(See Chapter 19, Double Jeopardy)*;

8-C. MOTIONS FOR RELIEF FROM PREJUDICIAL JOINDER (I.E., TO SEVER)

M.R.Crim.P. 9(d)—motion for relief from prejudicial joinder: in writing, before trial *(N.B. not "pre-trial" within Rule 13? See Chapter 6-C)*, & supported by affidavit with grounds & prejudice; except can be before or at close of evidence if ground not previously known;

C v Corradino **368 M 411, n.8 (75)**—should renew motion to sever at trial;

C v Moran **387 M 644, 659–61 (82)**—premature request for severance, not renewed when necessity to sever has been established, is not sufficient;

C v Cordeiro **401 M 843 (88)**—failing to renew motion to sever when objectionable evidence (co-D on stand) introduced may waive it;

C v Dicato **19 MAC 40 (84)**—fail to move to sever pre-trial, where basis known = ground to deny when moved at trial;

C v Martinez **37 MAC 948 (94)**—same; co-D's pre-trial statement had been that D was seller of cocaine & co-D was merely present; when D moved to sever at trial because coD took stand to say this, motion was untimely;

ABA Standards for Criminal Justice (2d ed. 1986) Joinder & Severance 13-3.3—"Timeliness of motion; waiver, double jeopardy"; severance waived if don't renew motion before, or at close of, evidence; DA may have to disclose evidence (maybe in camera) to assist Court's decision; mid-trial sever on D's motion/consent permits 2d trial [*See Chapter 19, Double Jeopardy*]; COMMENT: D must renew motion during trial because prejudice maybe not apparent until then; see also *C v Burr* **33 MAC 637 (92)** necessity for severance must be "firmly established" at time request is made; pretrial anticipated defenses of "didn't happen" and "entrapment" not necessarily irreconcilable, since latter D could have been involved in drug sale without other D's involvement (entrapment D here fled on trial day 2 so no entrapment evidence was offered);

C v Steven **29 MAC 978 (90)**—co-D's midtrial flight did not require severance;

Chapter 9
CROSS-EXAMINATION— PREPARE AND EXECUTE

9-A. GENERAL; THEORY OF DEFENSE

*See Chapter 11 re: DA cross-examination of D's witnesses (& **Ward 15 MAC 400 (83)** (DA) can't ask witnesses if others are lying) & right to exculpatory evidence;*

U.S. Constitution, Amendment 6—D's right to be confronted with witnesses against him;

Mass. Constitution, Declaration of Rights, Article 12—right to meet accusers "face to face";

Presence of Defendant (as corollary)—"meet witnesses . . . face to face," confrontation

See also Chapter 12-A(2), Trial Issues: Witness Seating, Defendant Seating;

C v Rios **412 M 208 (92)**—exclusion of D from courtroom during testimony about surveillance location violated Article 12;

C v Caldwell **45 MAC 42 (98)**—D's constitutional right to be present at trial is one which attorney can't waive "without the fully informed and publicly acknowledged consent of" D, but harmless beyond reasonable doubt (given D's failure to reconstruct record of hearing, anyway) for attorney to have waived D's presence during colloquy/hearing at which a deliberating juror was dismissed and replaced;

C v Harrison **429 M 866 (99)**—holding probation revocation hearing in absence of D = federal constitutional violation; error not harmless beyond reasonable doubt (but SJC notes that Supreme Court has never held that such error is subject to "harmlessness" principle);

Coy v Iowa **487 US 1012 (88)**—screen between complaining witness & D violates confrontation;

C v Bergstrom **402 M 534 (88)**—Article 12 face-to-face forbids G.L. c. 278, § 16D (child sex complainant) video-testimony *(See Chapter 11-H, Evidence: Rape (& Other Sex Offenses) Charges)*;

C v Brown **451 M 200 (2008)**—no substantial risk of miscarriage of justice (no objection) from alleged victim's making "nonverbal responses" to cross-examination, record implying that when nervous, witness stuttered and avoided by nodding or shaking head; defense used these difficulties to advantage, and jury acquitted D of several charges;

C v Ramirez **49 MAC 257, 267–68 (2000)**—no relief from judge's order excluding D from hearing pursuant to *Franks v Delaware* (to question whether affidavit supporting search warrant contained material falsehoods) at which confidential informant and police detective testified, and barring defense counsel from discussing witnesses' testimony with D; *Ray v Commonwealth* **447 M 1008 (2006)**—no 211/3 relief for defense counsel pre-trial from order barring him from disclosing to D the identities of "civilian" witnesses against him, revealed in discovery materials given to counsel; but see *C v Lugo* **406 M 565 (90)**, *C v Hernandez* **421 M 272 (95)**;

C v Edwards **444 M 526 (2005)**—SJC adopts "forfeiture by wrongdoing" doctrine, which allowed introduction of "out of court statements" (here, grand jury testimony) of "unavailable" witness against Ds who intimidated, threatened, or murdered witness, or even "colluded" in making the witness unavailable/unwilling to testify at trial; "causal link necessary" may be established when D puts forward to witness the idea to avoid testifying by threats, coercion, persuasion, or pressure (BUT MERELY INFORMING WITNESS OF RIGHT TO REMAIN SILENT IS NOT SUFFICIENT TO CONSTITUTE FORFEITURE, n.23) or when D actively facilitates the carrying out of witness's independent intent not to testify; Commonwealth must prove by "preponderance of the evidence" that D procured witness's unavailability; parties must be given opportunity to present evidence, including live testimony, at evidentiary hearing outside jury's presence, prior to determination of forfeiture, BUT hearsay evidence, including unavailable witness's out-of-court statements, may be considered;

5 Wigmore, *Evidence*, **§ 1367 (Chadbourn rev. 1974)**—cross-examination = "beyond any doubt the greatest legal engine ever invented for the discovery of truth";

Davis v Alaska **415 US 308 (74)**—direct, personal cross-examination & immediate answer;

Pointer v Texas **380 US 400 (65)**—cross-examination = confrontation;

Douglas v Alabama **380 US 415 (65)**—(same); right was denied where DA used co-D confession after co-D took 5th Amendment *(See Chapter 11-C, motion to strike)*;

C v Almeida **452 M 601 (2008)**—though prosecution witness answered "I don't remember" 125 times, SJC rejected argument that D was denied "meaningful cross-examination": witness was asked "almost 1,000 questions on cross-examination that day"; "reasonable" for witness to have no memory of some info sought; testimony "did not sink to the levels that have been held to deny the right of cross-examination";

C v Brazie **66 MAC 315 (2006)**—when one child sexual assault complainant became too distraught, during direct examination, to continue testimony and was never cross-examined (resulting in withdrawal of indictments concerning her from jury consideration), ineffective assistance to (1) fail to move to strike testimony and (2) fail to object to judge's response to jury question that the testimony could be considered in resolving allegations of second complainant;

C v Lugo **406 M 565 (90)**—right to cross-examination requires disclosure of surveillance location necessary to fair trial;

C v Hernandez **421 M 272 (95)**—same, but remedy of dismissal with prejudice was too harsh; suppression of cop's testimony cited as one appropriate remedy;

See Chapter 11-F re: confrontation rights/hearsay issues;

C v Michel **367 M 454 (75)**—reasonable cross-examination re: bias maybe constitutional right; e.g., expect favors from Commonwealth;

CPCS P/G 6.1, 6.6—anticipate DA weaknesses & evidentiary issues; develop theory of case & closing's framework & integrate with cross-examination; decide whether to cross; prepare & be alert to surprises/omissions; etc.;

Young, Pollets, & Poreda, *Evidence*, **§ 611.2 (2d ed. 1998)**,—unlike federal rule, MA has unrestricted cross-examination;

Brodin, M. and Avery, M., *Handbook of Massachusetts Evidence* **(8th ed. 2007)**—great cross-examination latitude; not limited to scope of direct;

Younger, "Credibility & Cross-Examination," Chapter 4 **[N.P.I., '81]**—prepare with the zeal of a fanatic, plan closing argument first; 10 COMMANDMENTS: Brief, Short, Lead, Know Answer (or Don't Care), Don't Quarrel, Don't Repeat Direct, Don't Permit Explanations, Listen, Stop, Save Argument for Later;

Superior Court Rule 69—stand to examine witness (unless permission not to);

SJC Rule 3:07, 3.4(c)—can't intentionally violate rules, or 3.4(e) allude to fact without reasonable belief relevant & will be admitted; 4.4 can't use means with no purpose but to embarrass 3d party; Insinuations without support (e.g., introduction of hearsay during cross)

C v Dixon **425 M 223 (97)**—prosecutor allowed to cross critical D witness with insinuations that she was accessory after fact of crime (murder) since had "good faith basis" for questions (said to be "anonymous tip" [!!%#] and "unreliable witness" [!&$^%] who said witness had helped D flee and had aided in disposal of weapon); but *C v Pearce* **427 M 642 (98)** unless D had independent evidence re: person and time at which pregnant rape complainant had sex with someone else, D not allowed to cross-examine her as to this issue; presumption of innocence apparently inconsequential as "good faith basis" ("rape shield" statute invoked);

US v Oshatz **912 F.2d 534 (2d Cir. '90), cert. denied, 500 US 910 (91)**—prosecutor's posing to lay character witnesses of hypothetical questions assuming guilt is improper;

C v Fordham **417 M 10 (94)**—prosecutor's cross of D improper because attempted to communicate impressions by innuendo (since he could have had no reasonable hope that D would answer affirmatively), but no objection, no reversal;

C v Wynter **55 MAC 337 (2002)**—reversal for DA's leading questions, none of which had evidentiary or good faith basis, & elicited only "no" responses, but implied (without proof) a motive that Commonwealth's evidence otherwise lacked; equally improper was question, "you are aware that [named woman] gave a statement in this case?', since it conveyed to jury that the woman's hearsay statement had been the basis for the DA's questions;

C v Francis **432 M 353 (2000)**—error to allow ADA to cross-examine D (at trial for accessory before fact) concerning self-incriminating claims attributed to him in out-of-court statements to police by alleged principal: good faith basis to believe D made such statements couldn't be supplied by the statements, because they had been excluded from evidence (though improperly preserved & SJC held no prejudice in circumstances);

C v Delrio **22 MAC 712, 721 (86)**—where cross suggests new facts in an effort to impeach a witness, the examiner should be required to represent that he has a reasonable basis for the suggestion, and also be prepared with proof if the witness does not acquiesce in the suggestion by giving a self-impeaching answer. "Without such assurances, the questioning of the witness is improper, for it would amount to allowing the examiner to smear the witness by insinuation, and unfairly to cast on the other side (here the defendant-witness) a burden somehow to fend against it. See, e.g., Burger, J., concurring in *Jackson v United States* **297 F.2d 195, 198 (D.C. Cir. 1961)**; *Lee Won Sing v United States*, **215 F.2d 680 (D.C. Cir. 1954)**; *Pinkney v United States*, **363 F.2d 696, 698 n.4 (D.C. Cir. 1966)**. See also *Reichert v United States*, **359 F.2d 278, 281–82 (D.C. Cir. 1966)**";

C v Christian **430 M 552, 559–64 (2000)**—long series of questions, each answered "no" by D, was IMPROPER ('you told Obershaw . . . , didn't you?, etc., etc.), particularly since D counsel had told judge that Obershaw was an inmate involved in scheme to fabricate info in other inmates' pending cases to obtain favorable disposition of his own charges; when D denied making statement, judge should have barred further questions after first negative answer, ordered voir dire of Obershaw, or sought assurance from DA that she would call Obershaw to testify; this permitted DA to smear D by extrajudicial statements made by Obershaw while denying D opportunity to impeach Obershaw's credibility; cited with approval in *C v Christian* **430 M at 564**: *US v Hall* **989 F.2d 711, 716–17 (4th Cir. '93)** (improper "under the guise of 'artful cross-examination' to tell the jury the substance of inadmissible evidence") and *US v Sanchez* **176 F.3d 1214, 1221–22 (9th Cir. '99)** (reversing conviction because prosecutor cross-examined defendant about inadmissible statements) (these federal cases also cited in *C v Wynter* **55 MAC 337, 342 (2002)**);

C v Howell **49 MAC 42 (2000)**—ERROR for prosecutor to ask defense witness (D's father) whether his and D's brother's purpose in visiting robbery victim was to influence V in his identification ("no"), and then to ask witness for his and D's brother's heights and weights (objection overruled), and then to ask whether witness had asked victim "how much it would take for [the victim] to go away"; judge should have immediately stopped line of questioning and asked DA basis for questions, particularly since Commonwealth had not ever questioned victim (dur-ing V's own testimony, completed) about any such confrontation;

C v Alvarado **50 MAC 419 (2000)**—prosecutor's attempt to use hearsay to impeach D's alibi testimony = "particularly inappropriate";

C v Thompson **431 M 108, 119 (2000)**—DA in cross-examination implying the truth of a proposition which he KNEW to be false (i.e., that stains looked like blood, although stains had previously tested negative for blood) "skirted the bounds of" proper cross-examination;

C v Johnson **441 M 1 (2004)**—no relief on appeal for DA's "question" of D, "isn't it true you were mad at [victim] for what he said about the way you treated your two older daughters?", because DA wasn't asked to make known his basis for the questioning, D objected only to one such question, & objection was sustained; other "question" = "would it surprise you to know that the videotape of your booking shows no string on your pants?" said only to be improper as to "form" (witness's state of mind regarding the matter was irrelevant); failure to appreciate that DA was effectively testifying to content of booking video, & it was DA's burden to introduce *evidence* of absence of string, *C v Johnson* **441 M 1 at 7 n.9**; compare *C v DeMars* **42 MAC 788, 792–93 (97)**;

C v White **367 M 280, 284 (75)** "attempt to communicate impressions by innuendo through questions which are answered in the negative, . . . when the questioner has no evidence to support the innuendo, is an improper tactic which has often been condemned by the courts"; DA can cross-examine own witness re: prior inconsistent statement made to him, though DA couldn't take stand & prove it, IF good faith basis, not innuendo;

C v LaFaille **430 M 44, 54 (99)**—no "bad faith" found in prosecutor's questions to two witnesses because good faith basis: another (nontestifying) witness had told a cop that D and another individual were cousins; also jury instruction that there was no evidence of relationship "whatsoever," and jurors were to "totally disregard any references to that";

C v Murchison **418 M 58 (94)**—D can argue that police witness has reason to want to convict a D who was arrested by witness or who was target of witness's evidence-gathering (overruling Appeals Court's disapproval of D's opening and closing, see *S.C.,* **35 MAC 269 (93)**);

ABA Standards for Criminal Justice, Prosecution Function & Defense Function (3d ed. 1993) 4-7.6—dignified cross-examination without intimidation; can cross-examine though think W's truthful, but sometimes show restraint; § 4-5.2 strategy & questions (how to conduct cross) = counsel's choice (after consulting with D) *(See Chapter 2, Ethics, Control of Case);*

SJC Rule 3:07, 3.1—lawyer can't defend a proceeding, or controvert issue therein 'unless there is a basis for doing so'; criminal defense lawyer, or lawyer for anyone in proceeding that can result in incarceration "may nevertheless so defend the proceeding as to require that every element of the case be established";

C v Luna **46 MAC 90, 96 (98)**—cross-examination (here, of D) not unfairly severe "merely because the witness's story is badly shaken by it";

C v Kennedy **3 MAC 218 (75)**—OK to exclude cross-examination questions for 'form' defects; & D counsel chargeable then with abandoning the issue "voluntarily, although in frustration";

Sussman v C **374 M 692 (78)**—improper summary contempt for 2d (excluded & re-phrased) cross-examination question;

C v Saferian **366 M 89 (74)**—improvised cross-examination, even if virtuosic, maybe "ineffective"; preparation, precision, & focus preferable to impromptu, bludgeoning, allusive, older florid style;

C v Urena **417 M 692 (94)**—judge-initiated process of jurors questioning witnesses: fraught with potential for error, but not here barred outright; no oral questions; written questions must be discussed by judge with counsel outside hearing of jury; jurors must be given specific instructions about procedure, including that rules of evidence may forbid some questions; parties to be given opportunity for further examination of any witness after juror questions have been answered;

C v Bowden **379 M 472 (80)**—failure to test or produce evidence (prints on gun) = grounds for reasonable doubt defense; charge to ignore it = error; *(for other cases like this: see Chapter 12-F: reasonable doubt from investigation omissions);*

Smith v Illinois **390 US 129 (68)**—right to cross-examination about (informant's) address for bias/truth/investigation; "[w]hen the credibility of a witness is in issue, the very starting point in 'exposing falsehood and bringing out the truth' . . . through cross-examination must necessarily be to ask the witness who he is and where he lives. The witness's name and address open countless avenues of in-court examination and out-of-court investigation. To forbid this most rudimentary inquiry at the threshold is effectively to emasculate the right of cross-examination itself";

Alford v US **282 US 687 (31)**—(same) to identify witness with his/her environment; cross-examination is "exploratory" & may not know answer/purpose;

C v Johnson **365 M 534 (74)**—full & fair cross-examination = "absolute right"; e.g., can ask names of other witnesses at scene; "necessarily exploratory";

US v Bailey **834 F.2d 218 (1st Cir. '87)**—access to potential witnesses re: complaining witness's character & veracity for cross-examination; but see . . . .;

C v McGrath **364 M 243 (73)**—can ask complaining witness's address for background, but may need to give reason; excludable to balance witness's safety (fn. 5 suggests bench/lobby conference); *(see also Johnson* **365 M 534 (74))**; [DANGER: unfair implication of D's dangerousness, predilection for threats, intimidation, violence]

McGrath v Vinzant **528 F.2d. 681 (1st Cir. '76)**—can exclude questions to complaining witness re: address;

C v Rooney **365 M 484 (74)**—discredit = OK, but limits; "disinterested witnesses" shouldn't suffer grueling, bruising, & abrasive cross-examination with baseless insinuations & innuendos; [see DR 7-106 above];

C v Nassar **351 M 37 (66)**—discretion to limit cross-examination; test accuracy, veracity, credibility; lifestyle, infirmities, memory, discernment powers maybe relevant;

C v Ahearn **370 M 283 (76)**—ordinarily no offer of proof required for cross-examination if DA's objection sustained, but judge may ask how questions are relevant (see *McGrath,* **above, 364 M 243 (73)** re W's address);

C v Piedra **20 MAC 155 (85)**—(same); exculpatory evidence from lips of DA's witness more believable than from D; *(See also Chapter 9-C, Bias, below);*

C v Britland **300 M 492 (38)**—(same); but see *C v Cheek* **374 M 613 (78)** & . . .

Cheek v Bates **615 F.2d 559 (1st Cir. '80)**—can exclude cross-examination question because purpose (bias) unclear & possibly it's inadmissible; Mass. rule: counsel must tell question's purpose;

C v Martin **434 M 1016, 1017 20 (01)**—allowing D to introduce prior inconsistent statements is no substitute for evidence showing bias/motive; evidence of bias is what provides explanation for inconsistencies, inference of fabrication;

C v DeJesus **44 MAC 349, 353 n.5 (98)**—can exclude cross-examination of V concerning his job history & sources of income; proffer of relevance was deemed insufficient by trial judge;

C v Franklin **366 M 284 (74)**—retracted ID of co-D = collateral, but related to case & must be admitted;

C v Mosby **11 MAC 1 (80)**—relevant relationship = OK, but not specific sex acts without rape - shield steps *(See Chapter 21-L, Rape, and Chapter 11-H, Evidence: sex offenses);*

C v Nicholas **15 MAC 354 (83)**—bias from coaching child witness;

C v Russ **232 M 58 (19)**—judge's discretion not to limit witness to "yes or no" (i.e., to permit explanation);

Perry v Leeke **488 US 272 (89)**—can delay recess or forbid witness talking to (counsel) while still on stand, to prevent coaching or just regain poise; cross-examination needs to "punch holes at just the right time, in just the right way"; *(re: "missing witness" inference: see Chapter 12-J, Argument)*

C v Monahan **349 M 139, 162 (65)**—can cross-examine hostile witness called by self, but discretionary *(See Chapter 10-B, Direct Examination, including impeaching own witness);* repetitious questions OK because nonresponsive answers;

C v Haraldstad **16 MAC 565 (83)**—OK to deny cross-examination of co-D because "friendly";

C v Ward **15 MAC 400 (83) (DA)**—can't ask witness if others are lying;

C v Dickinson **394 M 702 (85)**—(same); and can't ask witness to assess credibility of others; but can ask to explain own inconsistencies;

C v Long **17 MAC 707 (84)**—too many questions re: testimony of other witnesses;

C v Triplett **398 M 561 (86)**—risk of miscarriage of justice from questions re: W (D's mother)'s credibility;

C v Pagano **47 MAC 55, 59–60 (99)**—improper to ask D why complaining witness would come into court and lie;

See also Chapter 10, Character Evidence by Reputation, & Young, Pollets &Poreda, Evidence, § 608 (2d ed. 1998) attacking witness's character; § 404 character evidence generally;

See Chapter 11-F for cases on hearsay & confrontation rights and Chapter 8-B for cases on confrontation necessitating severance of co-D's trials; Chapter 11-C, Evidence: Motions to Strike; 11-J, Privileges; Chapter 7-H, Pretrial Preparation: 5th Amendment; Chapter 6-E re Discovery of Witnesses; Chapter 7-C, Costs/Fees for Indigents;

C v Farley **443 M 740 (2005)**—after trial judge ruled that witness had voluntarily waived 5th Amendment privilege by testifying at first trial, he was compelled to testify at second trial; allowing him to assert 5th Amendment privilege in response to several questions didn't here violate D's right to confrontation; BUT privilege against self-incrimination was held to be waived concerning question about a fact "related to but not necessarily mentioned in" the testimony given at the first trial;

9-A.1. Child Witnesses, Attempts at "Protection" of; Abrogation of Face-to-Face Confrontation Rights

Idaho v Wright **497 US 805 (90)**—hearsay responses by 2½-year-old sexual assault complainant to pediatrician's leading questions were unreliable & violated 6th Amendment right to confrontation;

White v Illinois **502 US 346 (92)**—unavailability of child witness not required by 6th Amendment as prerequisite to admission of hearsay statement falling within "firmly rooted" exceptions to hearsay rule;

Maryland v Craig **497 US 836 (90)**—alternatives to face-to-face encounter at trial, such as closed circuit TV, do not violate 6th Amendment if necessary for public policy & reliable;

But see Mass. Declaration of Rights, Article 12 & Bergstrom 402 M 534 (88)—Article 12 violated by broad statute allowing child witnesses to testify other than face-to-face;

G.L. c. 233, §§ 81–83—strict conditions on substantive use of hearsay by children under 10 in sexual abuse & certain noncriminal proceedings;

C v Kirouac **405 M 557 (89)**—child sexual assault complainant's refusal to answer questions violated D's state & federal constitutional right of confrontation; *C v Brazie* **66 MAC 315 (2006)**—when one child sexual assault complainant became too distraught, during direct examination, to continue testimony and was never cross-examined (resulting in withdrawal of indictments concern-

ing her from jury consideration), ineffective assistance to (1) fail to move to strike testimony and (2) fail to object to judge's response to jury question that the testimony could be considered in resolving allegations of second complainant;

C v Amirault **404 M 221 (89)**—child sexual assault complainant's responses that she didn't remember was not a refusal to cooperate & did not violate D's right of confrontation;

C v Tufts **405 M 610 (89)**—eye contact between D & child rape complainant in videotaping room outside jury's presence satisfied Bergstrom & Article 12; quality of videotapes was adequate;

C v Dockham **405 M 618 (89)**—same; child rape complainant's observed behavior established beyond reasonable doubt that videotaping was necessary to avoid trauma & satisfied Bergstrom despite absence of expert testimony;

C v Conefrey **410 M 1 (91)**—seating of child sexual assault complainant at 45-degree angle from D did not prevent jury from observing witness's demeanor or cause jury to draw inference of guilt;

C v Kater (III) **409 M 433 (91)**—witness not required by confrontation clause to look at D, unless ability to make identification is in issue;

C v Johnson **417 M 498 (94)**—child witness required to be seated so as to allow D to see face, per Article 12, Declaration of Rights;

C v Souza **44 MAC 238 (98)**—*Johnson* issue waived since counsel should have known of objectionability since **Bergstrom 402 M 534 (88)**;

C v Amirault **424 M 618 (97)**—face-to-face issue deemed waived because counsel on direct appeal did not raise (M.R.Crim.P. 30 success thus barred);

C v Sanchez **423 M 591 (98)**—child sexual assault complainant testifying while seated at a table with both counsel and D seated 20 ft away not shown to have abridged confrontation (D argued that jury would not have been able to focus upon "interaction" between D & witness);

9-A.2. Hazard of Cross: "Opening the Door"

C v Watson **377 M 814, 831 (79)**—doctrine of "opening the door" is application of principle of "completeness";

C v Hearn **31 MAC 707, 710 (91)**—doctrine of verbal completeness "is a limited one";

C v Keyes **11 Gray 323, 325 (1858)**—additional matter must have tendency to illustrate, vary, or explain statement;

C v Crowe **21 MAC 456, 479 (86)**—additional portion must qualify or explain matter already introduced;

US v Winston **447 F.2d 1236, 1240 (D.C. Cir. '71)**—"Opening the door is one thing. But what comes through the door is another. Everything cannot come through the door";

C v Roderick **429 M 271 (99)**—although homicide D's motion in limine was allowed (so prior firearm conviction wouldn't be introduced) and D took stand, ADA asked

D on cross, over unsuccessful objection, "so you're saying that this is the first time you've ever carried a gun?": D's "yes" answer allowed ADA to intro. prior conviction; BUT ADA "should not ask a question that will inevitably lead to the introduction of" evidence which judge has excluded;

C v Fitzgerald **412 M 516 (92)**—prosecution's introduction of complainant's statements to rape crisis counselor opened door to D's introduction of counselor's notes relevant to her motive to fabricate;

C v Martinez **431 M 168, 174 (2000)**—despite fact that prosecution witness was distressed during her testimony (on direct), purported fact that she had been threatened by D's niece was more prejudicial than probative;

C v Moure **428 M 313, 319 (98)**—cross by D opened door to prosecutor rehabilitating witness with evidence which included prior bad acts of gang members (associated with D) toward witness;

C v Holliday **450 M 794 (2008)**—after defense counsel properly tried to discredit witnesses who only recently came forward, suggesting rewards from recent cooperation with prosecution or who did not initially inculpate D, witnesses in redirect permissibly explained their fear of retaliation;

C v Young **73 MAC 479 (2009)**—after defense impeached ID witness, introducing two letters he wrote, recanting his identification of D, witness on re-direct could explain recantation (he was incarcerated and did not want to be perceived by fellow inmates as "rat"); judge "reminded" jurors there was no evidence D was connected to any threats of assault on witness made by other inmates;

C v Bockman **442 M 757 (2004)**—discovery revealed that particular state trooper would testify to collection & preservation of fingerprint evidence and its delivery to FBI, AND that a bloody print was made by finger with blood on it (rather than finger that touched blood already present on the door by other means); FBI agent was to testify regarding match of bloody print to D's thumb; when cross-examination of trooper assumed that trooper hadn't made the match and/or hadn't had that match confirmed by five others in the state police lab, but instead obtained a devastatingly contrary answer before the jury, no "abuse of discretion" by trial judge in denying mistrial and finding no breach of discovery obligation: it was not exculpatory and Commonwealth did not intend to present it at trial;

C v Graham **62 MAC 642, 647–48 (2004)**—was within discretion of judge to find that D's testimony on direct (that he attempted to gain entry into apartment building because he was fleeing from police, having suffered serious injury in prior altercation with police a year earlier) opened door to cross-exam re: circumstances surrounding prior incident, "which included his convictions related to the altercation", OR given instructions and lack of mention in closing and strong evidence of guilt, "any error in permitting the inquiry was rendered harmless";

See Chapter 10-E for cases on rehabilitation of witnesses during redirect examination;

See Chapter 11-D for 'relevance' calculation in context of particular other testimony, e.g., **Roderick 429 M 271 (99); Saunders 45 MAC 340 (98); Maimoni 41 MAC 321 (96);**

9-A.3.   Prior Recorded Testimony

See specifically Chapters 7-K, Prior Reported Testimony as Substantive Evidence, and 11-F, Hearsay & Confrontation Rights;

C v Tanso **411 M 640 (92)**—deposition testimony of unavailable prosecution witness was not admissible because D didn't validly waive right to cross-examination;

C v Ross **426 M 555 (98)**—deposition testimony of prosecution witness not admissible because Commonwealth didn't make reasonably diligent effort to secure witness (fact that she was out of country for ten weeks not enough; no inquiry re: willingness to return nor offer to pay for return flight);

C v DiBenedetto **414 M 37 (92)**—witness's probable cause (transfer) hearing testimony not admissible against D at trial where judge had barred counsel from cross-examining witness about areas beyond scope of immunity promised by prosecutor;

C v Childs **413 M 252 (92)**—testimony from 1st trial admissible against D at 2d trial where Commonwealth made diligent search for unavailable witness & where prior counsel's ineffective assistance didn't mar cross-examination of this witness;

9-B. WITNESS'S MENTAL IMPAIRMENT

See Chapter 7-G, Competency/Examination of Witness & Chapter 11-J, Privileges;

Young Pollets & Poreda, *Evidence,* **§ 601 (2d ed. 1998)**—competency of witnesses; § 610, atheism, (cf. G.L. c. 233, §§ 19 [how to swear persons other than Christians; evidence of disbelief in God not to be received to affect credibility]), et seq.;

C v Caine **366 M 366 (74)**—impeach re: mental impairment or drug/booze habit-competence, credibility, & testimonial faculties (capacity to perceive, remember, & articulate correctly); but hospitalization alone not shown relevant;

C v Simmons **8 MAC 713 (79)**—judge's discretion re: complaining witness's emotional condition & veracity, accuracy, credibility;

C v Adkinson **442 M 410 (2004)**—judge denied D's motion for voir dire re: coercive interviews by prosecutors: children initially accused mother's ex-husband of abuse, & after coercion accused instead D (father); exploration of subject instead at trial here OK (excused?) because trial was jury-waived; "no need for the judge to conduct a separate competency hearing";

C v Courtney 7 MAC 4 (79)—identification witness's alcohol consumption obviously relevant to perception;

C v Bennett 13 MAC 954 (82)—booze & drugs re: ability to perceive;

C v Bianco 388 M 358 (83)—questions re: drug use must have basis, not innuendo;

C v Arce 426 M 601 (98)—question of D, on direct, re a prosecution witness's "drug problems" in the year of the crime permissibly excluded; if question instead cut to the chase and directly asked D for his observations of effect of drug consumption on witness's perception and memory, result may have been different;

C v Perreault 13 MAC 1072 (82)—mental impairment irrelevant unless affects credibility or ability to perceive & articulate;

C v Delp 41 MAC 435, 441 (96)—post-conviction defense discovery of sexual assault complainant's school & medical records indicating she suffered from "impaired reality testing" triggered invitation to file motion for new trial;

C v Fayerweather 406 M 78 (89)—exclusion of psychiatric report that rape complainant heard voices weeks before incident violated D's right of confrontation, notwithstanding psychotherapist privilege; expert testimony not required;

C v Slonka 42 MAC 760 (97)—when Commonwealth was permitted to intro hospital record saying complaining witness's "remote & recent memory seem intact," fairness demanded D be allowed to intro privileged communication from another record page, i.e., complaining witness saying she had "memory problems";

C v McIntyre 430 M 529, 538 (99)—OK to impeach hearsay (see Prop.M.R.Evid. 806) dying declaration with testimony of nurse that victim's consciousness was minimal and that nurse's impression was that victim "really didn't know" what nurse was saying to her; held not to be expert or other "opinion on credibility" [& *C v Mahar* 430 M 643 (2000) SJC adopts Prop.M.R.Evid. 806];

C v Stockhammer 409 M 867 (91)—privileged records of sexual assault complaints are discoverable in order to ferret out evidence of mental impairment etc., (*But see Chapters 6-D, Discovery, & 11-J, Evidence: Privileges, For Subsequent Many Hurdles & Restrictions*);

C v Allen 40 MAC 458 (96)—concerning child witnesses subjected to possibly suggestive/coercive interviewing techniques; research cited; call for taping of such interviews;

C v Perkins 39 MAC 577 (95)—expert testimony as to suggestibility of children, effect of repetitive questioning, etc. admitted;

C v Baxter 36 MAC 45 (94)—evidence of distinct sexual abuse of complainant relevant because she suffered "flashbacks" and auditory hallucinations, and her current allegations concerned similar place and a man with similar name;

C v Hynes 40 MAC 927 (96)—no mental impairment shown by fact that complaining witness had been sexually abused before; Baxter distinguished;

9-C. BIAS/MOTIVES, INCLUDING PENDING CASES, PROBATION, ETC.

See also Chapter 6, Discovery: Exculpatory Evidence & Promises;

Young Pollets & Poreda, *Evidence,* §§ 613 (2d ed. 1998)—(prior statements of witnesses), 801.2 prior consistent statement *(to rebut bias/motive, but see Chapter 11-F [Prior Consistent = Hearsay, unless prerequisites are met),* 806 (attacking credibility);

Brodin, M. and Avery, M., *Handbook of Massachusetts Evidence* (8th ed. 2007)—impeachment by proving bias/motive to lie [overview];

C v Haraldstad 16 MAC 565, 571 (83)—because "whiff of bias" is inherent for another suspect, D can show severed co-D (called by D) has no case pending;

C v Moore 50 MAC 730 (2001)—reversal for failure to allow impeachment of alleged victim with fact of pending criminal charges, alleging that she had committed much more serious crimes against D approximately 45 minutes after D's alleged criminal acts (motive to accuse him falsely of provocation);

See Chapter 6-F, Discovery: Exculpatory Evidence, e.g., C v O'Neil 51 MAC 170 (2001) *defense counsel ineffective in failing to introduce existence of plea agreement* between prosecution witness & Commonwealth, when witness denied such on stand;

C v Sullivan 435 M 722 (2002)—defense counsel may call as a witness the witness's attorney, to inquire into attorney's conversations with prosecution regarding immunity: no violation of witness's attorney-client privilege;

C v Smith 26 MAC 673 (88)—usually no bias from pending case for defense witness;

C v Sholley 48 MAC 495, S.C. 432 M 721, 728 (2000)—OK cross of D (for bias against government) re: prior conviction of A&B and that he was subject of a 209A order issued on behalf of his ex-wife and daughter, because D (a "father's rights activist") was on trial for threatening prosecutor and being disorderly person at the trial of another man accused of violating a 209A order (though it was "close" question whether probative value was outweighed by unfair prejudice); merely showing a testifying D's "general anti-government bias" not likely to be sufficiently probative to justify admitting past or pending criminal charges;

C v Supplee 45 MAC 265, 269 (98)—D not entitled to introduce fact of pending criminal cases against witness when witness is called not by Commonwealth but by co-D, since it's only a "government" witness who "may be moved to shade testimony to curry favor with" the government;

C v Castro **438 M 163 (2002)**—judge has discretion to exclude pending federal charges where there is no evidence that witness will get, or expects to get, break on federal charges as result of state court testimony; prosecutor asserted that there had been no communication between prosecution and federal authorities;

C v Marcellino **271 M 325 (30)**—complaining witness's lawsuit vs. D = relevant re: bias; cf G.L. c. 258B, § 3(u)—"victims" have right to be informed that they may have right to pursue civil action for damages, regardless of whether court has ordered D to make restitution to them [and id., § 3(o) "victims'" right to request that restitution be part of disposition of criminal case];

C v Elliot **393 M 824 (85)**—bias from $ motive—complaining witness suing landlord (D's boss) for bad security in building.;

C v Tabor **376 M 811 (78)**—dictum: D could have cross-examined re: G.L. c. 258A (G.L. c. 258A = repealed, but see, in its place, G.L. c. 258B–C, money opportunities for "victims");

G.L. c. 151A: (amendments approved 8/2001)—persons who 'lose their jobs' due to domestic violence against themselves or their dependent child[ren] are eligible for unemployment benefits;

G.L. c. 262, § 29—witness who "assists" DA gets fee for going to DA's office;

C v Barboza **54 MAC 99 (2002)**—error to exclude cross-examination of alleged rape victim & V's mother re: consulting civil lawyer (i.e., to sue D for money damages), but harmless given "overwhelming" evidence of G;

C v Graziano **368 M 325 (75)**—reasonable cross-examination re: bias = right; maybe constitutional;

C v Michel **367 M 454 (75)**—reasonable cross-examination re: bias maybe constitutional right; e.g., expect favors from Commonwealth;

C v Hogan **7 MAC 236, 241–42 (79)**—judge may not entirely preclude inquiry simply because **he** doesn't believe bias is inferable; D entitled to present bias theory to **jury**;

C v Ricardo **26 MAC 345 (88)**—bias from complaining witness's "you divorced me and you're going to pay";

C v Campbell **37 MAC 960 (94)**—after D's wife testified that D with her at time of shooting; proper to allow victim to testify in rebuttal that the wife approached V before trial and said that a lot of people would be angry if V showed up in court and D was sent to jail (BUT improper totem pole hearsay to admit V's testimony that D's wife said D said that he was sorry [reversal ordered]);

C v Piedra **20 MAC 155 (85)**—right to show (even remote) possibility of bias/motive to lie, e.g., affair with witness's wife; (see also *Haraldstad* **16 MAC 565 (83)**, *Hogan* **379 M 190 (79)**);

C v Aguiar **400 M 508 (87)**—(same) re: D's threat to turn in witness & (dead) V for drug dealing; entire relationship = admissible by right; [overview];

C v Redmond **357 M 333, 338 (70)**—D's right to show his entire relationship with witness;

C v Martin **50 MAC 877, 879 (2001)**—while acknowledging that cross for bias/motive (here, alleged victim had been charged with A&B upon D approximately 1 month before her allegations vs. D) has been held 'matter of right,' affirmed conviction anyway, asserting that cop's testimony (supporting version of alleged victim) was tiebreaker, so no error or no prejudice: **this rationale/result overruled on further appellate review, 434 M 1018 (2001):** cross for motive continues to be 'matter of right,' regardless of witness "corroborating" alleged victim & regardless of D's ability to otherwise impeach (with inconsistencies);

C v Morin **52 MAC 780 (2001)**—reversal for exclusion of cross-examination re: alleged victim's relationship with abusive boyfriend, arguably a motive for her to claim that D's presence in her apartment was nonconsensual;

See Chapter 11-H, Evidence: Rape & other sex charges, for e.g., C v Bohannon **376 M 90 (78)**; *C v Nichols* **37 MAC 382 (94)** *complaining witness's extraneous false allegations of sexual assault probative of her motive to lie in present case;*

C v Mosby **11 MAC 1 (80)**—prior relationship [vs. rape shield restrictions *(Chapter 11–H, Evidence: Rape)*];

C v Civello **39 MAC 373 (95)**—error to exclude questions to show that sex assault complainant knew, from prior experience, that accusing D of sex assault would result in D's removal from home (D = complainant's stepfather);

C v Herrick **39 MAC 291 (95)**—no relief from barred cross concerning complaining witness's motive to accuse D of rape, i.e., defense investigator alleged that friend of witness said witness told her she feared mother forcing medical examination re: her virginity (but witness, friend, and witness's mother denied each component on voir dire);

C v McNickles **22 MAC 114 (86)**—complaining witness's child custody fears = motive to lie;

C v Sugrue **34 MAC 172 (93)**—D's wife's child custody fear = motive to fabricate claim D raped son, and right to present this evidence overrode "marital communications" "disqualification/privilege (D made custody threats to wife for specific reasons);

Olden v Kentucky **488 US 227 (88)**—can't exclude complainant's cohabitation (re: bias);

C v Ahearn **370 M 283 (76)**—cross-examination (of purported victim of A&B on police officer) re: D's cross-complaint;

C v Nicholas **15 MAC 354 (83)**—bias shown by coaching of child witness; can cross-examine without foundation (i.e., without first proving bias); vs . . . .;

C v Cheek **374 M 613 (78)**—D must show why "bias" (offer/proof);

C v Armstrong **54 MAC 594 (2002)**—exclusion of questioning of cop about his "use of force" report not error: D didn't tell trial judge that questioning was to reveal motive to inflate the danger from D, on trial for assault with intent to murder;

C v Johnson **431 M 535 (2000)**—no error in excluding cross re: racial bias, because proffer inadequate to substantiate possible bias, i.e., witness had asked someone "whether or not she dated black men";

***Chipman v Mercer* 628 F.2d 528 (9th Cir. '80)**—distinguished;

C v Moorer **431 M 544 (2000)**—reversal for exclusion of cross-examination re: racial bias, e.g., growing up under apartheid system in former Rhodesia (+ judge's order, in presence of jury, "get off the racial card here. There is no racial card in this case"), given witness's testimony that [black] assailant's face "did not fit" with MIT cap he was wearing, that his facial features were "normal to negroid shape," and that he was "a black African";

C v Omonira **59 MAC 200 (2003)**—no error in cross-examination of D's wife concerning her knowledge of possible deportation consequences upon D's conviction (& D had already introduced D's national origin/ethnicity);

C v Howell **49 MAC 42, 48 (2000)**—error to impeach D's father with fact that he failed or refused to cooperate with police (no legal or moral obligation to do so); bias toward son already shown otherwise;

C v Bui **419 M 392 (95)**—D counsel sought to cross prosecution witnesses to show retribution - motivated fabrication, purportedly because D refused to be drug courier for W's father, but at voir dire witness had no memory of such a request & did not recall whether her father had even been present when/where request allegedly occurred & no other/further witness voir dire was requested : absent some plausible showing, particular bias theory "too tenuous" for pursuit entitlement;

Davis v Alaska **415 US 308 (74)**—juvenile record relevant re: bias;

C v Ferrara **368 M 182 (75)**—juvenile record & probation = bias; *(See also Chapter 9-D (Impeach Credibility by Prior Conviction)*, G.L. c. 119, § 60 (Juvenile Court "evidence" & delinquency adjudication, & "disposition" = inadmissible "AGAINST" former juvenile D for any purpose in any court, except in subsequent delinquency or criminal proceedings against the same person and further, adjudication of delinquency may be used for impeachment purposes in subsequent delinquency or criminal proceedings in the same manner and to the same extent as prior criminal convictions);

C v Santos **376 M 920 (78)**—juvenile record impeachment if witness on probation, is suspect, or has motive to please; sealed record can't impeach unless bears directly on bias/motive;

C v Carty **8 MAC 793 (79)**—complaining witness's juvenile probation = bias, reason to lie;

C v Lewis **12 MAC 562 (81)**—pending juvenile case = bias;

C v Hogan **379 M 190 (79)**—cross-examination re: pending case if bias at all possible;

C v Connor **392 M 838 (84)**—pending case = motive to cooperate, hope for lenity, fear of punishment; recent favorable disposition prompting favorable-to-Commonwealth testimony out of gratitude;

C v Traylor **43 MAC 239 (97)**—same, but no relief for excluding specifics (underlying probation = a 9–12 year suspended sentence); but cf *C v Piedra* **20 MAC 155, 157–58 (86)** - general acknowledgment is not equal to specific particulars in context of 'bias/motive' impeachment;

C v Evans **439 M 184 (2003)**—revealing nature of unresolved charges pending against witness = best, so jurors may gauge extent of motivation to curry favor (but no abuse of discretion here in allowing description "serious felony charges" instead of 'aggravated rape' and 'kidnapping';

C v Martinez **384 M 377 (81)**—pending de novo appeals show bias, possible agreement with Commonwealth;

C v Pina **430 M 266, 271 (99)**—no error in barring cross concerning witness's pending motion to revise and revoke sentence (M.R.Crim.P. 29) because postsentencing behavior cannot be considered on revise and revoke motion;

C v Joyce **382 M 222 (81)**—prior prostitution arrest & dismissal = bias (to avoid reprosecution);

C v Knight **10 MAC 597 (80)**—threat/promise to suspect-witness (but see *Haraldstad* **16 MAC 565 (83)**);

C v Haywood **377 M 755 (79)**—no cross-examination re: witness's arrest because it was after D's arrest & W's first statement (because W's statement adverse to D was made before alleged motive to lie [pending case] arose);

C v Purcell **423 M 880 (96)**—same; but see *C v Hamilton* **426 M 67 (97)** Haywood exception to "as-of-right" cross re pending cases is very limited and if it is to be invoked **at all**, voir dire should be held to establish factual basis for "sound exercise of [judge's] discretion in keeping with the narrow exception permitted by the **Haywood** case"; fact that Commonwealth hasn't actually promised witness anything doesn't foreclose cross-examination suggesting bias (see *C v Hill* **432 M 704, 711 (2000)** although the terms of the agreement may be "imperfect in . . . clarity," a "material arrangement" will be recognized & should be disclosed in discovery; see also *C v Collins* **386 M 1, 10 (82)** there can be "arrangement" which should be disclosed even if such isn't "explicitly hinged on receipt of favorable testimony";

C v Carmona **428 M 268 (98)**—failure of trial counsel to cross-examine Commonwealth witness for bias due to pending cases not ineffective assistance of counsel, since witness called police immediately and his ID of D as shooter was consistent from the time he first made the ID up through his trial testimony; Cf. *C v Lareau* **37 MAC 679 (94)** prior consistent statement inadmissible after intro of prior inconsistent, because motive to lie existed at time "consistent" statement was given;

See Chapter 9-F, Prior Inconsistent Statement or Conduct;

C v Zukoski **370 M 23 (76)**—prior consistent statements are not admissible simply because witness has been impeached with prior inconsistent statements; *(see topic in Chapter 11-F, Evidence: Hearsay);*

C v Henson **394 M 584 (85)**—can cross-examine re: charges against W arising after first statement because trial testimony has changed from earlier statement;

C v Diaz **422 M 269, 274–75 (96)**—prosecution witness impeached with pending charges and motive (non-incarceration dispo could mean regaining custody of children), but Commonwealth allowed to introduce testimony of W's lawyer re circumstances of her first statements to rebut inference of "recent" fabrication;

C v Rodwell **394 M 694 (85)**—bias from past deals in other counties; . . . ;

C v Gilday **382 M 166 (80)**—& from promise to attorney, though not told to witness;

C v Joyce **18 MAC 417 (84)**—DA impeaches own witness by bias, etc. *(See Chapter 10-B, Direct Examination, Including Impeaching Own Witness);*

C v Jenkins **34 MAC 135 (93), S.C., 416 M 736 (94)**—DA allowed to question witness (whose testimony at probable cause hearing was more adverse to D than was her testimony at trial) about statements made to her by people who did not want her to testify (response included that "something had been done to her house"); need not show that D played any role in alleged intimidation;

C v Martinez **431 M 168 (2000)**—abuse of discretion to allow witness to testify that D's niece threatened her (trial testimony was not more favorable/less adverse to D as result);

C v Auguste **418 M 643 (94)**—Commonwealth witnesses allowed, in judge's discretion, to testify that **fear** caused them to tell police initially less than they truly knew: relevant to explain prior omissions or silence, and to forestall request for missing witness instruction re one witness. Instruction here given = "There is no evidence whatsoever that D intimidated anyone in connection with this case. The fact that one or more witnesses may have expressed fear or concern about testifying in this case has no bearing on this D's guilt or innocence of these charges";

C v Stockhammer **409 M 867 (91)**—D had right to cross-examine rape complainant about parents' knowledge of her sexual activity with boyfriend to show bias, notwithstanding privileges or rape shield;

C v Fitzgerald **412 M 516 (92)**—prosecution's introduction of complainant's statements to rape crisis counselor opened door to D's introduction of counselor's notes relevant to her motive to fabricate;

C v Figueroa **422 M 72 (96)**—D entitled to investigate (and SHOULD HAVE investigated) Dep't of Mental Retardation record asserting that complainant's mother said complainant "may have fantasized" an allegation of sexual touching by a person other than D prior to alleging assault by D, "to determine whether such material is admissible in evidence or could lead to admissible evidence" (while acknowledging that the record assertion itself was inadmissible hearsay, not admissible even as "impeachment" if the mother denied making the statement);

C v Koulouris **406 M 281 (89)**—drug D had right to cross-examine federal agent about interest & involvement in forfeiture proceeding;

C v Hall **50 MAC 208 (2000)**—police witnesses' prolonged & violent beating of D at arrest went to their bias: reversal for refusal to allow independent witnesses' testimony regarding beating;

US v Boylan **898 F.2d 230 (1st Cir.), cert. denied, 489 US 849 (90)**—D had right to cross-examine witness about terms of immunity; (see also G.L. c. 233, § 20I—D can't be convicted solely on testimony of immunized witness; *Rivera* **430 M 91, 96–97 (99)** seek instruction that "government does not know whether the witness is telling the truth";

C v Meuse **423 M 831 (96)**—witness's plea agreement to produce a "prosecutable case" against D not violative of fundamental fairness as would be a plea agreement contingent upon obtaining a conviction; still, "better left out of a plea agreement";

C v Ciampa **406 M 257, 261–62 n.5 (89)**—plea agreement with witness contingent upon truthful testimony has effect of prosecutor vouching W credibility;

See also Chapter 12-K re jury instructions concerning plea agreements;

C v Colon **408 M 419 (90)**—plea agreements with cooperating witnesses should not require conformity with their prior statements but rather with truth; safeguards in *C v Ciampa* **406 M 257 (89)** must be followed;

C v Rivera **430 M 91, 96–97 (99)**—ADA may not ask cooperating witness on direct examination about the nature of his plea agreement obligations ("truth," etc.), even though D counsel's opening statement has attacked witness's credibility; ADA's "rehabilitation" must wait until after D's cross-examination of cooperating witness, per Ciampa; no objection here, no excessive repetition of "truth" obligation, and two instructions that ADA didn't know what "truth" was = no relief on appeal;

C v Taylor **455 M 372 (2009)**—cooperating co-D received favorable plea bargain & testified against D; OK to exclude cross-exam re: witness not testifying in trial of a separate co-D, witness's cousin, because cooperation agreement/terms weren't in record & without it, inference of witness's "bias" as reason not available;

C v LaVelle **414 M 146 (93)**—informant's prior unrelated false allegations of assault were properly excludable, despite similar allegations against D, because they neither showed bias (Haywood exception invoked) nor fell within *Bohannon* **376 M 90 (78)** exception;

C v Cruz **442 M 299 (2004)**—rejecting argument that testimony obtained by plea agreement must be excluded as "irretrievably unreliable";

9-D. IMPEACH CREDIBILITY BY PRIOR CONVICTION

See Chapter 11, Evidence: Bad Acts, Motions in Limine (& Record Protection);

G.L. c. 233, § 21   may impeach by "record" of prior convictions, except misdemeanors after 5 years, or felony after 10 years (without subsequent G.);

C v Burnett **417 M 740 (94)**—G.L. c. 233, § 21 Fourth, concerning "traffic violation, " does include operating to endanger (rejecting D's argument that this crime too serious to be called "traffic violation");

C v Johnson **431 M 535 (2000)**—error to allow introduction, for impeachment, of conviction for operating an uninsured motor vehicle (only a fine was imposed) because D hadn't been convicted of another crime within 5 years of time he testified, but no relief (proper basis for objection not stated, and unlikely that so "trivial" an offense would prejudice D with jurors);

C v Ioannides **41 MAC 904 (96)**—error, in absence of specific request by D, to "mask" nature of D's prior conviction by calling it "felony" (this is more likely to affect D unfairly than naming specific crime);

C v Eugene **438 M 343 (2003)**—fact of conviction and nature of crime committed are only facts which should be introduced when witness is impeached by prior conviction; sentence shouldn't be read except maybe if witness denies or equivocates on whether he was convicted;

C v Kalhauser **52 MAC 339, 345 (2001)**—*impeachment by prior conviction may NOT include the length of the sentence*; impeachment procedure = limited to establishing identity of the witness as the person named in the criminal record; details of the conviction, including victim's name and surrounding circumstances "may not be mentioned"; only if witness attempts to deny/equivocate about the existence of the conviction may examiner use facts contained in the record of conviction, including the length of sentence to establish the identity of the witness as the person named in the conviction;

C v Thomas **439 M 362 (2003)**—no error in refusing to admit certified copies of witness's convictions; impeachment = complete upon reading the records & identifying witness as person there named;

Substantive Effect/Use of Convictions: *Flood v Southland Corp* **416 M 62 (93)**—(plaintiff suing civilly for damages sustained in stabbing by defendant Darcy outside convenience store operated by defendant Southland Corp.) accepting/adopting Prop.M.R.Evid. 803 (22), i.e., the hearsay rule does not exclude "evidence of a final judgment, entered . . . upon a plea of guilty . . . adjudging a person guilty of a crime punishable by . . . confinement in excess of one year, to prove any fact essential to sustain the judgment . . ."; the guilty plea of one Darcy would thus be admissible against plaintiff and co-D Darcy, but was not "binding", even on Darcy (i.e., not conclusive);

C v Supplee **45 MAC 265, 268 (98)**—D sought unsuccessfully to impeach a Commonwealth witness, who testified that she saw X wielding a club but did not see X strike V, by introducing X's guilty plea to manslaughter; Appeals Court held judge had discretion to exclude because D didn't offer the evidence while the witness to be impeached was still on the stand; judge can permit "use of someone else's conviction in cross-examination to test the accuracy of a witness's perception";]

Brodin, M. and Avery, M., *Handbook of Massachusetts Evidence* **(8th ed. 2007)**—good overview;

Prop.M.R.Evid. 609—liberalized methods of proof, etc.;

C v Childs **23 MAC 33 (86)**—can't use if stale or pardoned;

C v DiGiambattista **59 MAC 190, 199 (2003), S.C. 442 M 423 (2004)**—fact that conviction with which D was impeached at trial was subsequently vacated (when D moved to withdraw its underlying guilty plea) did not mean there was reversible error, citing *C v Bartos* 57 MAC 751, 754–56 (2003) (discussing cases holding that guilty plea = conviction);

C v Pierce **66 MAC 283 (2006)**—no abuse of discretion by judge in excluding from D's use in impeaching prosecution witness convictions for indecent A&B on child and A&B dangerous weapon, and a third conviction because its docket was illegible: judge allowed use of seven other convictions, including larceny and giving false name to police officer; no relief for D on ground that witness lied in denying some convictions, because ADA recalled him to correct testimony and offer explanation (he didn't understand that "conviction" included charges on which he pled guilty) and D hadn't moved to strike his testimony; there was no basis for judge's allowing D's motion for required finding of not guilty simply because witness "lied" initially about the convictions;

C v Gore **20 MAC 960 (85)**—discretion to exclude D's impeachment of complaining witness because only misdemeanor of slight relevance;

C v Spare **353 M 263 (67)**—no prior bad acts without conviction; *(See Chapter 11-E, Evidence: Prior Bad Acts, Other Crimes (not admissible for 'propensity'));*

C v Parker **12 MAC 955 (81)**—fired for stealing = inadmissible without conviction;

C v Whitehead **379 M 640 (80)**—right to limiting instruction, but waive if not asked;

C v Roberts **378 M 116 (79)**—by tie to other questions, DA suggested criminal propensity/bad acts character, not just credibility;

C v Felton **16 MAC 63 (83)**—(same); & worse because DA promised not to use, so D took stand; (see EXCLUDE, below)

C v Diaz **49 MAC 587, 589–90 (2000)**—"plain error" for judge to allow jury to consider prior convictions of drug distribution and possession with intent to distribute to determine D's "intent" in case being tried; despite no objection, there would have been reversal BUT NOT HERE because D's testimony conceded distribution (despite D's apparent belief that merely going with informant to seller and happening to touch/transfer both drugs and money, with no personal gain of either, did not establish guilt);

C v Houston **430 M 616 (2000)**—SJC splits 3:3 over whether rape shield statute (G.L. c. 233, § 21A) trumps impeachment by priors statute (G.L. c. 233, § 21), so as to prevent D from impeaching credibility of rape complainant with her prior convictions for prostitution; because judge exercised the discretion he has under G.L. c. 233, § 21 to exclude, no error anyway; issue still open as to whether judge has discretion to allow impeachment of rape complainant with a prostitution conviction; see also *C v Joyce* **382 M 222 (81)** prostitution evidence admissible because relevant to motive to lie, and D's constitutional confrontation rights override rape-shield statute; [& see also *Washington v Texas* **388 US 14, 19 (67)** Sixth Amendment may override state-created evidentiary rules in favor of defendants' rights to present a defense; *Chambers v Mississippi* **410 US 284 (73)** state's application of "evidentiary" rules to prevent D from introducing evidence of another person's confessions to the crime violated Sixth Amendment]; **SJC ANSWERS QUESTION LEFT OPEN IN HOUSTON:**

C v Harris **443 M 714 (2005)**—judge has discretion to allow introduction, for impeachment of rape complainant under G.L. c. 233, § 21B, of prior convictions as common nightwalker;

C v Lavoie **47 MAC 1, 3 n.4 (99)**—conviction for malicious destruction of property (ex-wife's door, during course of domestic quarrel) inadmissible under G.L. c. 233, § 21 because it occurred thirteen years before trial and there had been no subsequent conviction; Court rejects claim that conviction was admissible for substantive purposes unlimited by the statute (because during D's direct testimony he denied ever physically abusing his ex-wife);

C v Roderick **429 M 271 (99)**—although homicide D's motion in limine was allowed (so prior firearm conviction wouldn't be introduced) and D took stand, ADA asked D on cross, over unsuccessful objection, "so you're saying that this is the first time you've ever carried a gun?": D's "yes" answer allowed ADA to introduce prior conviction; BUT ADA "should not ask a question that will inevitably lead to the introduction of" evidence which judge has excluded;

C v Powell **40 MAC 430, 435–37 (96)**—reversing because judge invited substantive use of witness's (formerly co-D) guilty plea to armed robbery against D on issue of whether gun was used;

C v Worcester **44 MAC 258 (98)**—reversal for prosecutor's closing argument making substantive use of witnesses' prior convictions to impeach D's character generally (D has "everything in common" with witnesses; "everybody has got criminal records");

C v Roberts **378 M 116 (79)**—by tie to other questions, DA "overreached," erroneously suggested criminal propensity/bad acts character, not just credibility;

C v Felton **16 MAC 63 (83)**—(same); & worse because DA promised not to use, so D took stand (reversal);

C v Velasquez **48 MAC 147 (99)**—drug distribution D took stand, was impeached with prior convictions, including two for possession with intent to distribute; on cross, D was permissibly asked about the substance of those convictions because those cases involved, as here, police raids at residences which D had shared with same persons involved in present case, in which stash was kept in basement and dealing occurring from apt. (probative of method of operation, D with same accomplices working in same style), relevant to rebut D's claim of mere presence;

C v Young **22 MAC 237 (86)**—juvenile (Superior Court) DYS commitment not "conviction";

C v Juvenile **384 M 390 (81)**—juvenile delinquency not "conviction";

G.L. c. 119, § 60—delinquency inadmissible except against D;

*See Chapter 9-C, ante, re impeaching by BIAS (**Davis 415 US 308 (74)**/**Ferrara 368 M 182 (75)**/**Santos 376 M 920 (78)**) above;*

C v Carmona **428 M 268, 274–75 (98)**—failure to use prior convictions to impeach Commonwealth witnesses not ineffective assistance of counsel because testimony/subject matter at trial made it clear that principal Commonwealth witnesses and D were involved in drug dealing and had prior records

Forcier v Hopkins **329 M 668 (53)**—G and suspended sentence = "conviction";

C v Stewart **422 M 385 (96)**—'probation' does not equal sentence, and eventual driver's license revocation as result of violation of terms of probation "probably" didn't qualify as sentence/"conviction";

C v Jackson **45 MAC 666, 668–70 (98)**—despite defense witness's own ignorance as to precise disposition terminology, his recent case for drug possession was DISMISSED after continuance without a finding for 6 months (a kind of "pretrial diversion" per G.L. c. 278, § 18); it was not therefore a "conviction" which revived (G.L. c. 233, § 21, second paragraph) the otherwise too-stale convictions (larceny, possessing burglar's tools, malicious destruction) which ADA introduced against witness for impeachment: conviction reversed;

C v Devlin **365 M 149 (74)**—misdemeanor needs sentence; felony needs only G. finding;

C v Rossi **19 MAC 257 (85)**—misdemeanor resulting in "filing" or probation is not "conviction";

C v Ortiz **47 MAC 777, 781 (99)**—trial judge erred in ruling that misdemeanor convictions inadmissible under statute because only fine was levied;

C v Gallarelli **372 M 573 (77)**—impeach with contempt *(See Chapter 2-I, Contempt & Sanctions)* = conviction;

C v Cook **371 M 832 (77)**—must show conviction had counsel;

C v Delorey **369 M 323 (75)**—(same), or valid waiver;

C v Deeran **364 M 193 (73)**—counsel name on complaint may not suffice;

C v Stewart **422 M 385 (96)**—docket entry saying that counsel was appointed = sufficient in absence of contrary evidence;

C v Saunders **435 M 691, 695–96 (2002)**—while in present case allows no "presumption" that counsel had or legitimately waived counsel, "The rule henceforth will presume that the counsel requirement was fulfilled, and the Commonwealth will not have to come forward with proof on the point unless the defendant first makes a showing that the conviction in issue was obtained without representation by, or waiver of, counsel";

Carey v Zayre **367 M 125 (75)**—counsel right on prior misdemeanor though only a fine;

C v Napier **417 M 32 (94)**—reserved judgment on whether witness, **not D**, can be impeached with prior conviction without showing representation by counsel or counsel waiver; Court held that, absent contrary evidence, documents entitled "Notice of Assignment of Counsel" sufficiently proved convictions were counseled;

Loper v Beto **405 US 473, 483–84 (72)**—absence of counsel impairs **reliability** of prior convictions (cf: so all priors should be shown to have been counseled);

C v Atkins **386 M 593 (82)**—must have actual record or certified copy (with G. finding) of complaint and appearance/waiver of counsel;

C v Puleio **394 M 101 (85)**—no right to continuance to get certified copy of prior convictions;

C v Walsh **196 M 369 (07)**—proof requires record; can't cross-examine without record or certified copy in court;

C v Connolly **356 M 617 (70)**—"record" = entire document (rape reduced to assault & battery);

C v Gagliardi **29 MAC 225 (90)**—if D's prior conviction was on lesser included of original charge, better practice for prosecutor is to mention only the lesser offense;

C v Rondoni **333 M 384 (55)**—jury can take it into jury room (even though 2 most serious counts on paper were nol pros'd: judge gave limiting instruction); but see *C v Ford* **397 M 298 (86)** sanitize extraneous stuff (default/warrant/violating terms of probation) or exclude document altogether; impeached witness can't explain;

C v St. Pierre **377 M 650 (79)**—need not introduce written record;

C v Kowalski **33 MAC 49 (92)**—unobjected-to admission of "unexpurgated records" showing defaults, warrants & probation violations required reversal where D's credibility was key issue;

C v Rondoni **333 M 384 (55)**—can ask witness if "same person" charged/convicted;

Ayers v Ratshesky **213 M 589 (13)**—complaint's identical name not enough ID to impeach, but can infer it here; *(NOTE: impeachment here of an ABSENT witness - see Chapter 7-K, Prior Recorded Testimony);* cf. *C v Zavala* **52 MAC 770 (2001)** mere identity of name wasn't enough to prove beyond reasonable doubt that D was the individual who had been previously convicted (context of enhanced crime/sentence for "second or subsequent" offense);

C v McGeoghean **412 M 839 (92)**—when witness impeached by prior convictions, party calling witness not ordinarily entitled to explain circumstances on redirect, unless door has been opened on cross;

C v Cameron **31 MAC 928 (91)**—same; D not entitled to rehabilitate D by eliciting that prior conviction was by plea rather than trial, because in that case, unlike instant case, D was guilty;

C v Riccard **410 M 718, 723–24 (91)**—instruction that jury could not consider witness's prior convictions on issue of credibility was improper & required reversal;

C v Hurley **32 MAC 620 (92)**—although D would have been entitled to instruction limiting use of D's prior convictions to impeachment if requested, D's failure to request instruction seemed like "tactical choice";

C v Garcia **443 M 824, 835 (2005)**—OK for DA to elicit that prosecution witness had been convicted of being accessory after fact of victim's murder (for which D was being tried) & had received probation, to minimize impact it would have had if instead introduced initially by defense;

9-E. MOTION (AND DISCRETION) TO EXCLUDE PRIOR CONVICTION(S)

See Chapter 11-B and 11-E, Evidence: Motions in Limine & Prior Bad Acts;

C v Crouse **447 M 558, 564 (2006)**—to preserve for appeal issue of judge allowing Commonwealth motion to impeach D with prior convictions, D must "renew his motion [in limine] during trial" [WHEN? D DIDN'T TESTIFY, SO UNCLEAR WHEN HE IS SUPPOSED TO HAVE "RENEWED" IT];

C v Gore **20 MAC 960 (85)**—discretion to exclude D's impeachment of complaining witness because only misdemeanor of slight relevance;

C v DiMarzo **364 M 669, 678 (74)**—(Hennessey concurs) danger of prejudice to D when D's prior is similar;

violent priors have little credibility value; limiting instructions = little value;

C v Chase **372 M 736 (77)**—judge's discretion to exclude unfair priors;

C v Maguire **392 M 466 (84)**—judge's decision = reviewable; can trade (exclude priors both of D's and DA's witnesses);

C v Reed **397 M 440, n.5 (86)**—can exclude DA's witnesses' records as trade-off;

G.L. c. 233, § 21—(*See Chapter 9-D, above*); & . . . but see Prop.M.R.Evid. 609: discretion to exclude D's record, but nobody else's; R. 609 NOT ADOPTED: see . . .

C v Burnett **417 M 740, 743 n.1 (94)**—to D's argument that R. 609 should be applied (allowing D as of right to use a prior against a prosecution witness), SJC noted it had "not adopted the proposed rules"; cf *C v Houston* **430 M 616 (2000)** while split 3:3 on whether rape shield statute overrides statute allowing use of prior convictions (here, prostitution) for impeachment of rape complainant (so as to NEVER allow such use of prostitution convictions), SJC finds no error in judge's ruling not allowing same, because he exercised his discretion and excluded; answering issue left open in Houston, = *C v Harris* **443 M 714 (2005)**—judge has discretion to allow introduction, for impeachment of rape complainant under G.L. c. 233, § 21B, of prior convictions as common nightwalker;

C v Bembury **406 M 552 (90)**—witness's juvenile record, which had no rational tendency to show bias, was properly excludable;

C v Dion **30 MAC 406 (91)**—admission of D's prior convictions required reversal where close rape case hinged on credibility contest;

C v Bly **444 M 640 (2005)**—DA in murder prosecution cross-examined D on prior murder conviction: no motion to exclude was made: there's no per se rule of exclusion of a prior conviction of similar crime for which D is on trial, & here, purportedly no "substantial likelihood of miscarriage of justice" from the evidence;

C v Crouse **447 M 558 (2006)**—despite fact that prior rape convictions (which judge would have allowed Commonwealth to use to impeach D if D had testified) were substantially similar to the murder as the prosecution alleged it occurred in case being tried, no abuse of discretion found (though court was using standard of review for unpreserved error, id. at 564);

C v Manning **47 MAC 923 (99)**—judge erred in ruling that DA was "entitled" to impeach D's alibi witness (i.e., believing he had no discretion to exclude prior conviction unless D was the witness at issue); "duty of the judge to exercise discretion, and it is error as a matter of law to refuse to exercise it";

C v Edgerly **13 MAC 562 (82)**—judge must exercise discretion one way or other;

C v McFarland **15 MAC 948 (83)**—reverse because judge thought no discretion;

C v Guilfoyle **396 M 1003 (85)**—reverse when judge admitted prior convictions because of similarity (wrong goal, i.e., propensity); *(see also C v Roberts 378 M 116 (79) & C v Felton 16 MAC 63 (83) ADA erroneously suggesting criminal propensity from prior convictions admitted for impeachment)*;

C v Diaz **49 MAC 587 (2000)**—trial judge denied D's motion in limine re prior convictions & ruled that priors could be admitted "but only 'to prove intent to distribute'", i.e., for propensity; though this was obvious error, court said "waived" because D failed to object at time priors were introduced and to the instruction given;

C v Little **453 M 766 (2009)**—judge's ruling on motion in limine was that priors for drug distribution would be admitted to impeach D (in drug distribution trial), and this caused reversal, despite fact that D failed to preserve issue by objecting at trial; D did not have to testify in order to raise on appeal;

C v Ruiz **400 M 214 (87)**—reverse for fail to weigh prejudice vs. probative value; (See also *C v Ruiz* **22 MAC 297** - factors; other ways to "soften prejudice");

C v Diaz **383 M 73 (81)**—5 factors re: prejudice vs. probative—crime of credibility, similarity to crime on trial, D's history since, need for D's testimony, importance of D's credibility;

C v Chartier **43 MAC 758 (97)**—though a D's prior convictions were for virtually same crimes as those being tried (violation of protective order, annoying telephone calls) & concerned same ex-girlfriend/victim, no reversal for their admission: they were D's **only** priors and so judge did not have option of admitting prior conviction for "unlike" crime while excluding similar crime;

C v Whitman **416 M 90 (93)**—at murder trial with evidence of actual or attempted sexual assault, prior conviction of D for assault with intent to rape admitted to impeach credibility: no abuse of discretion in large part because no other convictions existed to be used and prosecutor didn't mention it in argument;

C v Elliot **393 M 824 (85)**—admission of prior rape conviction may be abuse of discretion though limiting instruction given;

C v White **27 MAC 789 (89)**—D's priors must be at least sanitized;

C v Roucoulet **22 MAC 603 (86)**—prior drug crime not admissible on theory it's similar & repeat offender faces more time; but compare *C v Velasquez* **48 MAC 147 (99)** drug distribution D took stand, was impeached with prior convictions, including two for possession with intent to distribute; on cross, D was permissibly asked about the substance of those convictions because those cases involved, as here, police raids at residences which D had shared with same persons involved in present case, in which stash was kept in basement and dealing occurring from apt. (probative of method of operation, D with same accomplices working in same style), relevant to rebut D's claim of mere presence;

C v Ioannides **41 MAC 904 (96)**—error, in absence of specific request by D, to "mask" nature of D's prior conviction by calling it "felony" (this is more likely to affect D unfairly than naming specific crime);

C v Carter **429 M 266 (99)**—SJC declines invitation to adopt rule that only prior convictions which involve crimes of dishonesty, false statements, or moral turpitude may be admitted to impeach credibility (G.L. c. 233, § 21 has no such limitation);

C v Cavanaugh **7 MAC 33 (79)**—motion in limine (re: excluding prior convictions) should have offer of proof re: anticipated testimony on both sides; *(See Chapter 11-B, motions in limine)*;

C v Barber **14 MAC 1008 (82)**—offer of proof = important;

C v White **48 MAC 658, 661 (2000)**—no relief from ruling that (if D testified) 23 priors could be used to impeach D, at least where D didn't testify and no proffer was made as to what evidence he'd give; even if court willing to agree that some convictions shouldn't have been ruled admissible, "speculati[ve] to assume" D then would have chosen to testify; D didn't argue that particular convictions = too similar to charge being tried, or that particular convictions weren't really germane to honesty/credibility;

C v Leftwich **430 M 865, 869–70 and n.1 (2000)**—ruling that old armed burglary conviction (just few days from being time-barred under G.L. c. 233, § 21) could be admitted for impeaching murder D upheld, despite arguments that it was old and was of minimal probative value re: truthfulness; judge had barred use of 2 convictions from same date (assault to murder and assault to rape);

C v Brown **451 M 200 (2008)**—on further review of Appeals Court's reversal of D's convictions, SJC holds no abuse of discretion in admission of fourteen prior convictions of D, including 7 for larceny, four for malicious destruction of property, and one of resisting arrest, despite D's argument that trial issues (allegedly breaking down door and forcing victim to part with money) would be tainted with priors' implication of "propensity"; "convictions admitted here are not substantially similar to the charged offenses [armed home invasion, B&E felonious intent, receiving stolen property] in any way that we have heretofore recognized";

Luce v US **469 US 38 (84)**—D must (in federal court) take stand to preserve issue;

C v Crouse **447 M 558, 564 (2006)**—SJC declines to adopt the "Luce" rule requiring D to take stand to preserve issue concerning order allowing impeachment of D with prior convictions, BUT **D must renew his motion in limine during trial in order to have standard of review for "preserved" error;**

C v Cordeiro **401 M 843 (88)**—assume (without deciding) Luce preservation unnecessary;

C v Feroli **407 M 405 (90)**—assumed without deciding that motion in limine to preclude impeachment of D by prior convictions sufficient to preserve issue for appeal even if D doesn't testify (contra *Luce v US* **469 US 38 (1984)**);

C v Coviello **378 M 530 (79)**—judge's discretion re: D introducing own convictions as anticipatory/defusing tactic;

C v Johnson **21 MAC 28, 39 (85)**—"common practice" to ask on direct about priors; but compare *C v Cad-*

well **374 M 308, 312 (78)** DA could impeach own witness (conviction related to the case); neither side has right to be the proponent, with

C v McTigue **384 M 814 (81)**—D can't introduce own witness's conviction merely to impeach credibility (vs. anticipatory tactic);

C v Blodgett **377 M 495 (79)**—reason for allowing party to bring out criminal record of his own witness = avoid having jury draw inference that party calling the witness had misled/deceived jury as to witness's background;

C v Bly **444 M 640, 655–56 (2005)**—allowing party to bring out criminal record of his own witness IS NOT A BASIS for allowing cross-examiner to explore underlying details of prior convictions; prosecutor improperly elicited info in cross about identity of victim of prior murder conviction (a prosecutor), but no relief here ("forceful" intervention/instructions by judge, strong evidence, etc.);

C v Rossi **19 MAC 257 (85)**—when defense counsel introduced misdemeanor in direct, so as to remove anticipated sting on cross, he provided ineffective assistance because misdemeanor resulting in "filing" or probation is not "conviction" [& was inadmissible];

Ohler v US **529 US 753 (2000)**—FEDERAL LAW: D could not raise, on appeal, judge's denial of his motion in limine to exclude priors because D's own attorney had introduced the priors during direct examination of D, "preemptively," to remove their sting; majority claimed this was "common sense," & application of "general principle" that party introducing evidence can't complain on appeal that it was erroneously admitted (issue waived);

TIPS OVERALL, for appellate preservation—file motion in limine to exclude prior convictions & object if it's denied; if D or other witness doesn't testify because judge refused to exclude priors, make detailed proffer of what testimony would have been; if D or other witness does testify, OBJECT when convictions are introduced (i.e., motion in limine alone can be held NOT to have preserved the issue); if introducing the convictions preemptively in direct examination, at sidebar beforehand reiterate request/motion for exclusion and/or place on record that you still object to their admissibility, but wish to act pursuant to 'common practice' of 'defusing' recognized in *C v Johnson* **21 MAC 28, 39 (85)** [cf. *C v Coviello* **378 M 530 (79)** judge's discretion re: D introducing own convictions as anticipatory/defusing tactic]

9-F. PRIOR INCONSISTENT STATEMENT OR CONDUCT

See also chapter 9-G, Omissions/Silence.

See also Chapter 7-J, Tape Recording & Prior Testimony in Preparing for Trial, Chapter 6-F & 6-G, Discovery, Exculpatory Evidence & Witnesses' Statements, Chapter 2, Ethics: Attorney-Client Privilege;

Young, Pollets & Poreda, *Evidence,* **§ 613.1 (2d ed. 1998)**—acts, statements, or omissions tending to qualify testimony; wide variety of priors; includes OPINIONS; more leeway than current "failure of memory" on direct; § 613.2 - extrinsic evidence to prove;

G.L. c. 269, § 13A—1 year and/or $100–$500 fine for false report of crime

See also Chapter 10-B, "Impeach Own Witness" in direct examination;

Brodin, M. and Avery, M., *Handbook of Massachusetts Evidence* (8th ed. 2007)—Contradiction by Prior Inconsistent Statement; id. at f. "mechanics of impeachment/extrinsic proof" - witness may be examined re: prior statement without showing it to him or disclosing its contents, but upon request, it must be shown to opposing counsel; witness's prior inconsistent statement CAN be put into evidence by 'extrinsic proof' (e.g., testimony of another witness) without giving notice to impeached witness & opportunity to explain (see, e.g., *Sirk v Emery* **184 M 22, 25 (03)** UNLESS counsel is impeaching own witness: then, G.L. c. 233, § 3 requires counsel to designate to witness the prior occasion/statement, ask witness if s/he made such statement, and if yes, give opportunity to explain (see, e.g., *C v Champagne* **399 M 80, 88 (87)**);

Prop.M.R.Evid. 613—need not show/disclose prior inconsistent statement to witness, but show opposing counsel if asked;

C v Mahar **430 M 643 (2000)**—the credibility of a hearsay declarant may be attacked by any evidence which would be admissible for such purpose if declarant had testified as a witness (adopting Prop.M.R.Evid. 806); here, Commonwealth introduced D's girlfriend's alleged "spontaneous utterance" when she retracted her original inculpatory story and didn't testify at trial; judge erred in excluding girlfriend's later contradictory statements to impeach the hearsay testimony;

C v McIntyre **430 M 529, 538 (99)**—OK to impeach hearsay dying declaration with testimony of nurse that victim's consciousness was minimal and that nurse's impression was that victim didn't know what nurse was asking her;

CPCS P/G 6.1—have prior statements of DA witnesses accessible & organized for trial;

Langan v Pianowski **307 M 149 (40)**—need only "tend in a different direction"; witness can't escape by saying "I don't recall the [prior inconsistent statement]";

C v Hesketh **386 M 153 (82)**—discretionary if not "plainly contradictory";

C v Moore **50 MAC 730, 737 (2001)**—error to bar testimony that alleged victim told D's brother that she had loaned vehicle to D and wanted it back; this contradicted claim at trial that D's use of vehicle was unauthorized;

C v Munafo **45 MAC 597, 603 (98)**—no relief for exclusion of evidence that alleged domestic abuse victim had left her children with D for caretaking (for impeachment of her claim that she feared D) because of considerable other evidence of her ambivalent feelings about D and of cop testimony impeaching her version of events;

C v West **312 M 438 (42)**—must let in that W said "Sorry, but it's you or me";

C v Ricardo **26 MAC 345 (88)**—"accident or not, you'll pay" = inconsistent with complaining witness's testimony (that no accident);

C v Chin Kee **283 M 248 (33)**—failure of memory not inconsistent with having past memory—at least on direct examination of own witness;

C v Reddick **372 M 460 (77)**—(same); *(but see Langan above 307 M 149 (40))*;

C v Johnson **49 MAC 273, 278 (2000)**—though DA introduced, during examination of D's girlfriend, the affidavit she'd executed to obtain restraining order against D, she had testified that she had no memory of the events it recited and had not written it (though her signature appeared on the document), there's no inconsistency between present failure of memory and past existence of memory, & document shouldn't have been admitted as substantive evidence; reliance upon Prop.M.R.Evid. 801(d)(1)(A) misplaced (because no "inconsistency");

C v Martin **417 M 187, 196–97 (94)**—witness not recalling clothing of her assailant could not be impeached with probable cause hearing testimony that he had worn jeans: no inconsistency between present failure of memory & past existence of memory; reserved question "whether, when circumstances indicate that witness is falsifying lack of memory, judge may admit the statement as 'inconsistent' with the claim of lack of memory"; [as to SUBSTANTIVE use, even, of prior recorded testimony, see, e.g., *C v Noble* **417 M 341 (94)** & *C v Clements* **436 M 190 (2002)**, summarized below];

C v Santos **440 M 281 (2003)**—lack of memory at trial is not inconsistent with past existence of memory, i.e., at time of witness's grand jury testimony (so such testimony wasn't "inconsistent" statement);

C v Cobb **379 M 456 (80)**—DA can impeach own witness with prior inconsistent statement because witness denies statement (not just failure of memory);

C v Pimental **5 MAC 463 (77)**—only inconsistency was that W saw ANYTHING; DA can't bring out details of (own) W's prior inconsistent statement—especially if it's whole case;

C v Niels N **73 MAC 689 (2009)**—no 'abuse of discretion' in excluding portions of medical record in which nurse recorded that child sexual assault complainant was unsure whether there was penetration, whether D had ejaculated, whether she had bled, or whether others were present during attack: since child did not testify at trial concerning any of these "matters," there was no inconsistency;

C v Benoit **32 MAC 111 (92)**—prosecutor's calling of witness who would not give testimony desired by prosecutor was "mere subterfuge" to introduce witness's prior inconsistent statement which contained inadmissible confession by D: reversal;

C v Carter **38 MAC 952 (95)**—like *Benoit*, error to call witness to have her declared hostile, so as to introduce prior inconsistent statement (which contradicted D's first alibi), but here no prejudice because D had himself disclaimed first alibi;

C v Rosa **412 M 147 (92)**—prosecutor's use of witness's prior inconsistent statements as pretext to introduce inadmissible substantive evidence on identification & alibi required reversal, notwithstanding curative instructions; maybe forestall such prosecutorial tactics by citing *C v Benoit* **32 MAC 111 (92)**;

C v Hailey **62 MAC 250 (2004)**—distinguishes *Benoit* on ground that Commonwealth witness did have current memory of events and gave probative evidence, so no error in allowing prosecution to introduce witness's grand jury testimony in direct contradiction to trial testimony that he hadn't seen D on top of victim, choking him;

C v McAfee **430 M 483, 489–92 (99)**, *C v Elliot* **430 M 498, 502–3 (99)**—D can't call witness for sole purpose of impeaching her current version of events by a prior inconsistent statement, though G.L. c. 233, § 23 allows party to impeach own witness with prior inconsistency; party can't be permitted to evade principle of hearsay exclusion in this manner;

Model Jury Instructions for Use in the District Court 1.03 (rev. 1989)—"... if a witness's earlier statement is not consistent with that witness's present testimony, you may take that into account when you determine how much belief to give that witness's present testimony from the witness stand. The prior statement is relevant only as to the witness's credibility, and you may not take it as proof of any fact contained in it";

C v Juvenile **361 M 214 (72)**—can't exclude prior inconsistent statement re: main issue; G.L. c. 119, § 60 doesn't bar use of Juvenile Court testimony to later impeach same witness;

C v McGregor **39 MAC 919 (95)**—rape shield statute doesn't bar use of witness's statements to impeach him; W's prior statement that W = bisexual and this was a way to make money was inconsistent with trial testimony that W was "religious" and for this reason would not/could not perform fellatio on D consensually;

C v Haynes **45 MAC 192 (98)**—though DSS record (not found at trial) purportedly attributed to complainant the statement that her step-grandfather had inserted a carrot into her vagina, complainant on voir dire testified that she had no memory of such a carrot incident, but had been told by her mother and D that it had happened, and so believed it for awhile, but not now; D did not argue at trial admissibility as prior inconsistent statement: no substantial risk of miscarriage of justice found; alleged statement in DSS record not really that of complainant, said Appeals Court, in ruling on legal issue under *Bohannon* **376 M 90 (78)** (prior false allegations of rape by current complainant);

C v Pratt **42 MAC 695 (97)**—sexual assault complainant's assertions (in G.L. c. 119, §§ 51A–B reports) that she was safe and happy in household, and denial of being "touched" by anyone, admissible to impeach her; social worker/client privilege (G.L. c. 112, § 35A) "must

yield to D's constitutional right to use privileged communications in his own defense";

C v Denson **16 MAC 678 (83)**—admissible without showing that prior inconsistent statement = lie;

C v Clemons **12 MAC 580 (81)**—though excluded prior inconsistent statement was "collateral" (motive/state of mind), reverse because credibility was main issue;

C v Allen **22 MAC 413 (86)**—ambiguity (whether it's a prior inconsistent statement or the listener's interpretation) goes to weight;

C v Ortiz **39 MAC 70 (95)**—convictions reversed because judge's instruction implied that omissions of important info from police officer's report had no evidentiary value & couldn't be considered as impeachment;

C v Clayton **52 MAC 198, 207 (2001)**—at retrial, judge must specifically instruct on omissions as prior "inconsistencies";

C v Jones **42 MAC 378 (97)**—discretionary to bar D's prior attorney from testifying about alleged inconsistencies between trial testimony and two larceny victims' descriptions of assailant's skin tone during prior hearing (attorney's testimony re: relative skin color of the defendant and unidentified man in hearing courtroom said to be merely attorney's "opinion" conflicting with that of witness); [But cf. *C v Cyr* **425 M 89 (97)** 3 friends of homicide victim allowed to testify at murder trial to their recollection of testimony given at probate court custody proceedings concerning the child whose mother was homicide V & whose father was charged with the killing;]

C v Sherry **386 M 682 (82)**—exclude because collateral;

C v Thayer **20 MAC 234 (85)**—must admit inconsistent statement or conduct re: main issue—e.g., complaining witness socializing with D after alleged rape;

C v Neumyer **432 M 23, 32 (2000)**—fact that rape complainant spent night in D's bedroom less than one week after reporting that he had raped her "must call into question the validity of the report of rape" (emphasis in original);

C v Hunter **427 M 651 (98)**—Commonwealth allowed to introduce expert opinion that D's sitting quietly in courtroom while video of Vietnam combat played was inconsistent with defense that D suffered post-traumatic stress disorder as result of combat;

C v Baldwin **426 M 105, 113 (97)**—evidence of Commonwealth's witness's reluctance to be monitored = useful to impeach witness credibility (psychiatrist didn't want his interview with D taped, and didn't want D counsel to be present);

C v Basch **386 M 620 (82)**—prior inconsistent statement is impeachment, not hearsay; can't exclude if material; need only "tend in different direction";

C v Bookman **386 M 657 (82)**—limiting instruction appropriate;

C v Martin **19 MAC 117 (84)**—(same);

C v Cogswell **31 MAC 691 (91)**—D had right to introduce rape complainant's diary as to her credibility even though she disavowed key diary entries;

C v Pina **430 M 66, 75–76 (99)**—when murder D introduced victim's boyfriend's statement against penal interest (hearsay exception) that he had killed V, Commonwealth entitled to introduce boyfriend's out-of-court statement to cop that D "did this"; cop's testimony was prior inconsistent statement impeaching credibility of statement against penal interest, not admissible for truth of matter; "in the circumstances of this case," SJC adopts proposed M.R.Evid. 806 ("credibility of the declarant of a hearsay statement may be impeached by any evidence that would have been admissible if the declarant had testified, even if the declarant has no opportunity to deny or explain any inconsistent statement or behavior");

C v O'Brien **419 M 470 (95)**—when, on redirect, prosecution elicited that prior inconsistent statement was not accurate because given day after W's child's funeral, D counsel was barred (in judge's "discretion") from eliciting on recross that same inconsistent statement was also given much **later**, when W not so distraught; majority of SJC said D counsel should have introduced **all prior inconsistent statements** during initial cross (anticipating some such rehabilitation during redirect);

C v Scott **408 M 811 (90)**—prosecutor entitled to impeach own witness's recantation of identification where proper foundation laid;

C v Cong Duc Le **444 M at 432**—prior identification admissible substantively if witness testifies and is subject to cross-examination about prior ID;

C v White **367 M 280 (75)**—DA can cross-examine own witness re: prior inconsistent statement made to him, though DA couldn't take stand & prove it, IF good faith basis, not innuendo;

C v Ragland **72 MAC 815 (2008)**—after trial in which witnesses recanted their grand jury testimony, jury sent question, "what is the punishment for perjury?", judge with agreement of all parties responded that jurors were not to concern themselves with any punishment for any crime; particularly because D was not entitled to original instruction that recantation was adverse to witnesses' penal interest (because the evidence supporting witness's awareness of such adversity was objected to, and objection was sustained, & evidence thus stricken), no error because no basis for jury to consider what penal consequences might be; even if initial instruction was proper, it required no amplification, no substantial risk of miscarriage of justice;

C v Johnson **412 M 318 (92)**—prosecutor's mention of own recollection of prior interview with witness should not have been injected into foundation for impeaching own witness under G.L. c. 233, § 23;

See also Chapter 2, Ethics, re: counsel taking stand (or calling DA);

9-F.1. Proof of the Prior Inconsistent Statement (Tape Recordings, Transcripts, etc.)

C v Rodriguez **378 M 296 (79)**—extrinsic evidence (stenographer) OK to prove probable cause hearing prior inconsistent statement; *(See also Chapter 7-J, Tapes/Transcripts)*;

C v Campbell **394 M 77 (85)**—if D/DA's probable cause hearing transcripts vary, can admit both;

C v Allen **22 MAC 413 (86)**—can't exclude "911 call" transcript (just because incomplete) if it's a prior inconsistent statement; *(See Chapter 7-J, Tape or Transcript)*; but *C v Jerome* **36 MAC 59, 62 (94)** tape **can** be "so incomplete as to be untrustworthy, creating risk that jury will be misled" (upholding, nonetheless, therapist's audiotape of [only] a portion of his session[s] with sexual assault complainant, as fresh complaint, when therapist was a witness & cross examined);

G.L. c. 218, § 27A—TAPE of District Court trial, or certified transcript, admissible if competent *(See Chapter 7-J)*;

C v Gordon **389 M 351 (83)**—rules to impeach with tape recording - must index!;

C v Thames **6 MAC 849 (78)**—can use tape recording, but no delay to monitor;

C v Supplee **45 MAC 265, 266 (98)**—error to bar use of audiotaped witness statement (admitting instead transcript of same), since former **could** convey hesitance or other manner worthy of scrutiny; here, harmless (to Appeals Court's ears);

District Court Special Rule 211(A)(3)—counsel's responsible for assisting in the creation of an audible record (i.e., speak w/clarity and close to microphones, ask judge to tell others to do so); (A)(4) if case is being appealed, may make motion (can be brought ex parte) to preserve original recording for a longer period; originals of trials, evidentiary hearings, G pleas or admissions to sufficient facts, and hearings in care and protection cases, are to be preserved for at least two and one-half yrs without such motion; (B)(1) covert recordings forbidden;

9-F.2. Prior Consistent Statement Generally Inadmissible

See Chapter 11-F-3, 11-F-4, post.

C v Almeida **42 MAC 607 (97)**—admission of rape complainant's non-fresh complaint could not be justified on appeal by calling it a prior consistent statement when trial judge had not considered the appropriate factors or exercised discretion in that regard;

C v Poor **18 MAC 490 (84)**—prior consistent statement must be "substantially contemporaneous" (e.g., 3 days later) to prior inconsistent statement;

C v Jiles **428 M 66 (98)**—ONLY those portions of prior statement which were consistent with witness's trial testimony were properly admissible to rehabilitate him;

but counsel failed to object to excess on hearsay/constitutional confrontation ground (admitted here was assertion, in witness's written statement that "Mack Brown told me that he and [D] did the shooting but that [D] was the one that killed [victim]. [Brown] said that [D] shot [V] in the head"); "beyond the scope of permissible rehabilitation" was not a good enough objection for the SJC here;

Young, Pollets & Poreda, *Evidence,* **§ 611.3 (2d ed. 1998)**—rehabilitating on redirect/recross; § 801.2: prior consistent statement to rebut recent contrivance *(but see Chapter 11F, Hearsay,—MOST prior consistent statements are hearsay, & inadmissible)*;

C v Taylor **33 MAC 655 (92)**—whether or not complainant's statements to DSS worker made 11 months plus after incident were sufficiently fresh, they were admissible as prior consistent statements where D had used some of statements to discredit complainant; but see, e.g., *C v Zukoski* **370 M 23, 27 (76)** mere admission of prior inconsistent statement doesn't justify conclusion that claim of "recent" contrivance is inherent in circumstances; *C v Retkovitz* **222 M 245, 249–50 (1915)** ("mere fact that a witness has made statements on other occasions at variance with testimony given in court does not warrant the introducing of confirmatory evidence to the effect that he has given an account of the transaction at still other times in harmony with his sworn testimony"); *C v Tucker* **189 M 457, 483 (1905)** (admission of "simple contradictory statement" doesn't justify admission of prior statement consistent with witness's trial testimony);

C v Rivera **430 M 91, 99 (99)**—prior consistent statement admitted without objection; on appeal, SJC upheld, disagreeing with D as to when witness motive to fabricate arose;

C v Brookins **416 M 97 (93)**—after prosecutor's cross of D implied that he had tailored his testimony to answer everything he had learned in discovery, error to bar prior consistent statement (D's story to court clinic psychiatrist day after alleged crimes): prior consistent statement necessary to rebut implication of recent contrivance;

C v Caine **366 M 366 (74)**—redirect rehabilitation after prior inconsistent statement &/or prior consistent to rebut inference of recent contrivance; *(See Chapter 10-E, Redirect Examination)*; if rule not strictly applied, HEARSAY VIOLATION *(See Chapter 11-F)*;

C v Martinez **425 M 382 (97)**—intro of prior consistent statement on direct excused since, in SJC's view, it was "inevitable" that recent contrivance claim would be made on cross; prior consistent statement purportedly not for "truth of the matter," but only to rebut claim of recent fabrication;

C v Binienda **20 MAC 756 (85)**—prior consistent statement must be before motive to lie; decline to extend "fresh complaint" beyond sex cases;

C v Raymond **424 M 382 (97)**—written statement of co-D-turned Commonwealth witness was prior consistent statement but no objection & no prejudice here;

C v Lareau **37 MAC 679 (94)**—prior consistent statement inadmissible because made after motive to lie arose;

C v DiLego **387 M 394 (82)**—can't rehabilitate with subsequent consistent;

C v Avila **454 M 744 (2009)**—repetition of statement by witness ordinarily doesn't make it more trustworthy, so prior consistent statement usually inadmissible; crucial prosecution witness gave three statements to police, and cop took notes; doctrine of verbal completeness doesn't permit Commonwealth to ask witness (direct exam) questions about statement that itself would be inadmissible and then get entire "notes" admitted by claiming that cross-examiner chose to ask other equally selective questions about the statement;

9-F.3. Substantive Use of Prior (Sworn Testimony) Inconsistent Statements

C v Daye **393 M 55 (84)**—prior inconsistent statement admitted substantively where it's (1) prior identification statement acknowledged by witness, (2) grand jury testimony, (3) witness not led or coerced, & (4) witness recalls underlying facts;

C v Fryar **414 M 732 (93)**—grand jury testimony not admitted;

C v Rivera **37 MAC 244 (94)**—grand jury testimony of 2 witnesses, identifying D as firing fatal shots, admitted substantively even though one witness at trial continued to disclaim truth of grand jury testimony (other one acknowledged truth at grand jury); reserved decision on whether Article 12 is violated by *Daye* (meet witnesses "face-to-face");

C v Noble **417 M 341 (94)**—substantive use of grand jury testimony, called false by the witness at trial, allowed to supply element critical to D's murder conviction, i.e., his knowledge that principal planned to shoot V, SJC adopting *US v Orrico* **599 F2d 113, 118, 119 (6th Cir. '79)**, which, however, supposedly bars such use when grand jury statements "are the only source of support for the central allegations of the charge";

C v Sineiro **432 M 735 (2000)**—similar to & worse than *Noble* **417 M 341 (94)**; if judge finds witness's lack of memory at trial to be "feigned", prior sworn testimony (with opportunity for cross-examination) admissible substantively

C v Clements **51 MAC 508**—(divided court), further appellate review allowed **434 M 1106 (2001)** worst yet conviction by hearsay testimony, uncorroborated; *S.C.,* **436 M 190 (2002)** revises/alters previous "*Daye*" formulations: for admissibility of prior testimony for its substantive value, (1) the present witness can be effectively cross-examined at trial regarding the accuracy of his prior statement & (2) the prior statement wasn't coerced and was more than a "mere confirmation or denial of an allegation by the interrogator," i.e., the statement must be that of the witness and not of the interrogator. IF that evidence "concerns an element of the crime, there is a separate requirement that the Commonwealth must meet to sustain its burden on the element: there must be other corroborating evidence on the issue" (though the additional evidence "need not be sufficient in itself to establish a factual basis for each element of the crime"); SJC disavows prior statements to the contrary in, e.g., *C v Johnson* 435 M 113, 134 (2001); *C v Sineiro* 432 M 735, 741 (2000); *C v Noble* 417 M 341, 344 (94); *C v Berrio* 407 M 37, 45 (90); [*Daye* history: *C v Gore* 20 MAC 960 (85) won't extend *Daye* to probable cause hearing testimony; *C v Fort* 33 MAC 181 (92) witness's inconsistent probable cause hearing testimony was substantively admissible under *Daye*; *C v Weaver* 395 M 307 (85) won't extend *Daye* beyond grand jury prior inconsistent statement (& I.D.?);

C v Frisino 21 MAC 551 (86)—(same); counsel = ineffective for permitting substantive use; *C v Berrio* 407 M 37 (90) prior grand jury testimony of trial witness is substantively admissible; *Daye* rule not limited to identification issue; *C v Donnelly* 33 MAC 189 (92) D had right to introduce diagram used by cop at grand jury as prior inconsistent statement to impeach & as substantive evidence under *Daye* rule, despite cop's claim that diagram not fair & accurate];

C v Hailey 62 MAC 250 (2004)—no error under *C v Daye* 393 M at 73–75 in allowing prosecution to introduce witness's grand jury testimony in direct contradiction to trial testimony that he hadn't seen D on top of victim, choking him;

9-G. SILENCE OR OMISSION AS PRIOR INCONSISTENT "STATEMENT"

See also Chapter 10-C, Impeach by District Court Silence; & Chapter 11-G, Admissions by D; Chapter 12-J - "missing witness" inference;

C v Homer 235 M 526 (20)—extrinsic evidence to show witness omitted the gun in grand jury testimony;

C v Gurney 13 MAC 391 (82)—grand jury omission = prior inconsistent statement (if asked at grand jury);

C v Charles 47 MAC 191 (99)—though DA entitled to elicit from homicide D that she had omitted from her statement to police the portions of events on which she relied at trial to best establish self-defense, error to strike redirect testimony that D had omitted the facts in her statement to police because cop had assured her that "it just sounded like an argument that had got out of control and that everything was going to be all right"; D would then have believed, reasonably, that she had no need to exculpate herself, and so her failure to do so was not "inconsistent" with her trial testimony;

C v Ortiz 39 MAC 70 (95)—convictions reversed because judge's instruction implied that omissions of important info from police officer's report had no evidentiary value & couldn't be considered as impeachment;

C v Clayton 52 MAC 198, 207 (2001)—at retrial, judge must specifically instruct on omissions as prior "inconsistencies";

C v Kessler 442 M 770 (2004)—judge's refusal to give "prior inconsistent statements" instruction error when failure to mention something in earlier statement is inconsistent with a later statement of fact "when it would have been natural to include the fact in the initial statement";

C v Morrison 1 MAC 632 (73)—no inference from D's post-arrest silence;

C v Bennett 2 MAC 575 (74)—(same); but see *C v Habarek* 402 M 105 (88) for context, DA can prove D's entire statement, including decision to stop; but can't use to show guilt or impeach;

C v Clarke 48 MAC 482 (2000)—though invocation of right to be silent admissible to explain abrupt end of questioning, reversal because ADA argued that silence meant D had been caught in a lie and would have to change story;

C v Peixoto 430 M 654 (2000)—violation of due process safeguards of state constitution and article 12 to cross-examine D that, after receiving Miranda rights, he said that he didn't know whether he should talk to them or not, or whether he should have an attorney present; "unfair" to penalize D for inquiring about the rights, engaging them "tentatively," or "think[ing] out loud about" them;

C v Nickerson 386 M 54 (82)—though PRE-arrest, D's silence was understandable, so inadmissible;

C v Farley 431 M 306, 310 (2000) citing *Doyle* 426 US 610 (76)—cross of D re: why she'd failed to provide certain of the info to police during a statement she made after being advised of Miranda rights = reversible error;

C v Thompson 431 M 108, 1181 (2000)—distinguished (there, D never invoked right to silence or asked to stop interrogation);

C v Azar 32 MAC 290 (92)—prosecutor entitled to impeach D's explanation that baby was accidentally dropped from kitchen counter with his failure to explain accident to wife on day of incident, because D would have naturally been expected to have offered an explanation;

C v Barnoski 418 M 523 (94)—D's testimony properly impeached by his failure to call police or ambulance because if testimony were true, D would have so contacted to get help for his friend, who had purportedly been shot by some other person & lay critically wounded (D professing great concern for friend);

C v McClary 33 MAC 678 (92)—when D didn't invoke right to silence at arrest, but instead talked, a different story at trial may be impeached by D's failure to tell it originally;

C v Gagliardi 29 MAC 225 (90)—witness's assertion of 5th Amendment at prior proceeding inadmissible because not inconsistent with trial testimony & did not tend to show recent contrivance;

C v Auguste 418 M 643 (94)—Commonwealth witnesses allowed, in judge's discretion, to testify that **fear** caused them to tell police initially less than they truly knew: relevant to explain prior omissions or silence, and to forestall request for missing witness instruction re one witness; instruction here given: "There is no evidence whatsoever that D intimidated anyone in connection with this case. The fact that one or more witnesses may have expressed fear or concern about testifying in this case has no bearing on this D's guilt or innocence of these charges";

See Chapter 11-G.4 (Post-Arrest Silence Inadmissible) for more cases and distinctions, e.g.,

C v Guy **441 M 96 (2004)**—no *Doyle v Ohio* violation to impeach D's trial testimony with content of his post-Miranda conversations with nurse, security guard, and police officer and with answer to booking question re: injuries;

Griffin v California **380 US 609 (65)**—invitation to adverse inference from D's failure to testify/offer explanation violates Fifth Amendment;

US v Robinson **485 US 25 (88)**—after D-counsel argued to jury that government had not ever [reasonable interpretation being either before or during trial] allowed him to explain/tell his side of story, not error to allow prosecutor to argue that D could have taken the stand at trial (fair comment/response to D); "It is one thing to hold, as we did in *Griffin* **380 US 609 (65)**, that the prosecutor may not treat a defendant's exercise of his right to remain silent at trial as substantive evidence of guilt; it is quite another to urge, as defendant does here, that the same reasoning would forbid the prosecutor from fairly responding to an argument of the defendant by adverting to that silence";

Portuondo v Agard **529 US 61 (2000)**—U.S. Supreme Court refuses habeas relief for prosecutor's argument that D had "big advantage" of listening to all testimony before he testified; terms holding refusal to "extend" rationale of *Griffin v California* **380 US 609 (65)**—(involving comment upon D's refusal to testify);

C v Martinez **431 M 168, 176–77 (2000)**—post-*Portuondo v Agard* (though without mention of it), SJC reiterates that "questioning the defendant as to the fact that the defendant sat through the Commonwealth's case" = improper; "[t]o use against [D] his strategy to wait until after the prosecution had made its case before revealing his story would disparage the constitutional rights which allowed him that strategy," citing *C v Beauchamp* **424 M 682, 690–91 (97)**; see also *C v Person* **400 M 136 (87)** bad argument that D listened & "tailored" testimony; cf. *C v Brookins* **416 M 97 (93)** import of DA's cross-examination of D = suggestion that D tailored story (reversal for judge's failure to allow testimony re: D's prior consistent statement);

C v Jones **45 MAC 254 (98)**—reversal for DA's argument conveying that D had had a year to obtain discovery and falsely tailor his testimony to meet the Commonwealth's evidence, and that cop-witness (not having been told D's story earlier) did not anticipate that corroboration of cop testimony would be necessary; violations of D's

right to remain silent at arrest, right to be present at trial, right to confront witnesses, right to testify; *C v Ewing* **67 MAC 531 (2006), and SJC on further appellate review agrees, 449 M 1035 (2007)**—reversal for DA's cross-examination and argument "impeaching" D's testimony on grounds that he had advantage of pre-trial discovery to tailor his testimony and had not sought out police between charge and trial to report his exculpatory version of events;

CPCS P/G 6.7(f)—prepare D's witnesses for all foreseeable cross-examination, e.g., including failure to report info to police/prosecutor;

C v Brown **11 MAC 288 (81)**—DA must lay foundation: "natural" for witnesses to have spoken to police, otherwise their silence is inadmissible; foundation required = (1) witness knew of pending charges in sufficient detail to realize that he possessed exculpatory info; (2) witness had reason to make info available; (3) witness was familiar with means of reporting it to proper authorities; (4) D or his attorney did not ask witness to refrain from reporting; 4th requirement eliminated in *C v Hart* **455 M 230 (2009)**—prosecutor would face "ethical dilemma" because while required to ask the question to establish requisite foundation, he couldn't have good faith basis to believe that D or attorney DID ask witness not to speak to police, and further, SJC Rule 3:07, R.Prof.C. 3.4(f), attorney is barred from requesting person other than client, client's relative, client's employee, or client's agent to refrain from giving relevant info to another party; **IF DEFENSE WITNESS *HAS* BEEN REQUESTED BY D OR D-COUNSEL NOT TO PROVIDE LAW ENFORCEMENT AGENTS WITH THE EXCULPATORY INFO, DEFENSE COUNSEL MAY/SHOULD ATTEMPT TO PRECLUDE THE *BROWN* INFERENCE BY INFORMING JUDGE PRIOR TO WITNESS'S TESTIMONY "SO THAT THE MATTER MAY BE EXPLORED AT A BENCH CONFERENCE";** *note well:* at 238, decision acknowledges that it would not be natural for witness to provide police with exculpatory info "when she thinks that her information will not affect the decision to prosecute", and in such an instance silence should not be a basis for impeachment;

C v Berth **385 M 784 (82)**—foundation: knew exculpatory, knew how to report, not asked by D or counsel to be quiet [4th foundational requirement ("not asked by D/counsel to be quiet") is eliminated in *C v Hart* **455 M 230 (2009)**;

C v Ruidiaz **65 MAC 462 (2006)**—no abuse of discretion in allowing DA to question co-D's alibi witness re: failure to come forward, including foundation questions of whether co-D or his attorney told witness not to come forward, rejecting argument that this elicited hearsay and "invaded work product";

C v Rivera **62 MAC 859 (2005)**—error to allow cop to testify that D, in initial statement to police, did not tell them about any eyewitnesses to the physical confrontation between D and complainant; this was not a "statement" inconsistent with defense at trial; see also *C v Haas* **373 M**

545, 559 (77); also error for ADA to argue that witness's testimony should be discounted because she did not call police at the time of the confrontation (no evidence introduced as to whether or not witness had called police);

SJC Rule 3:07, 3.4(a)—shan't "unlawfully" obstruct another party's access to evidence, or conceal material having potential evidentiary value; Rule 3.4(f) shan't request a person other than client to refrain from voluntarily giving relevant info to another party, UNLESS person is relative, employee, or other agent of client AND lawyer reasonably believes person's interests won't be adversely affected by so refraining from giving info; BUT CF G.L. c. 258B, § 3 (m), Rights of "Victims [sic]" and Witnesses [defined in G.L. c. 258B, § 1 to refer only to those witnesses giving testimony supporting the prosecution, but most certainly can't be so restricted (equal protection, due process for D: must apply as well to witnesses whose testimony supports the defense)]: right for victims and witnesses "to be informed of the right to submit to or decline an interview by defense counsel or anyone acting on the defendant's behalf, except when responding to lawful process, and, if the victim or witness decides to submit to an interview, the right to impose reasonable conditions on the conduct of the interview"; in light of this ethical rule, SJC in *C v Hart* **455 M 230 (2009)** eliminated 4th foundational requirement under *C v Brown* **11 MAC 288 (81)**;

C v Passley **428 M 832, 839–40 (99)**—says *C v Gregory* **401 M 437, 444–45 (88)** approved Appeals Court holding in *C v Brown* **11 MAC 288 (81)**;

C v Roberts **433 M 45, 50 (2000)**—though upholding impeachment of alibi testimony by D's grandmother for her failure to tell cops, some discomfiture apparent ("even were we to conclude that the question intruded into the area of pretrial silence," there was only one such question, topic wasn't mentioned in closing argument, evidence of guilt was strong, & jury would discount testimony anyway because of witness's familial relationship to D);

C v Egerton 2 **396 M 499 (86)**—impeachment OK because witness's concern for D was reason to tell cops exculpatory info;

C v Adderley **36 MAC 918 (94)**—error to bar witness's explanation why he failed to report exculpatory information to the police;

C v Hassey **40 MAC 806, 809 (96)**—judge's partisan questioning of defense witness as to his failure to tell police of rape complainant's threat to "get" D = reversible error;

C v Rivers **21 MAC 645 (86)**—can't impeach because silence maybe from witness's reasonable fear of prosecution;

C v Hesketh **386 M 153 (82)**—proper "foundation" to impeach with silence;

C v Mahan **18 MAC 738 (84)**—"natural" for alibi W to go to cops, so impeachment OK;

C v Lopes **34 MAC 179 (93)**—OK impeachment because natural for defense W to go to cops (W was friend of both D & V, was with V when police arrived, no one told him not to contact cops, was a "law enforcement" student; he testified that fleeing assailant was darker & shorter than D);

C v Bassett **21 MAC 713 (86)**—no foundation for impeachment, improper (reverse without objection);

C v Senior **454 M 12 (2009)**—D's mother testified that prosecution witness had sought money in exchange for testifying in way helpful to D, & ADA asked in cross whether she had reported this to police (no); judge instructed jury that witness had no obligation to report crime to police, so no risk of miscarriage of justice;

C v Liberty **27 MAC 1 (89)**—inadequate foundation, but harmless error;

C v Brissett **56 MAC 862 (2002)**—reversal for DA's cross-examination of both D and alibi witness re: failure to report this to authorities; further, NO DISCRETION to allow questions of **_D_** re: this when portion of alleged "silence" occurred after D received notice of complaint against her, and entered not-guilty plea;

C v Passley **428 M 832, 840 (99)**—SJC finds that ADA's cross-examination was not impeachment for failure to come forward sooner, but was instead pointing out that the alibi witnesses had only recently been asked to testify and that they had had "an opportunity to formulate a common narrative";

C v Richardson **425 M 765 (97)**—no error in judge's refusal to instruct jury that witness had no obligation to go to police (requested after DA made contrary closing argument, without prior warning); *Brown* criteria (**11 MAC 288, 296–97 (81)**) were "largely met";

C v Cefalo **381 M 319 (80)**—can cross-examine re: witness's not talking to DA at probable cause hearing; OK under G.L. c. 278, § 23 *(See Chapter 10-C, Silence During Prior Proceedings Inadmissible)*;

C v Bly **29 MAC 911 (90)**—prosecutor's questioning of defense witness about failure to testify at prior hearing was improper; see G.L. c. 278, § 23;

9-H. PRESENT RECOLLECTION REVIVED (REFRESHED)

Young, Pollets & Poreda, *Evidence,* § 612.1 (2d ed. 1998)—witness can't read to or show jury; counsel can't refer aloud to recitals in the writing;

Brodin, M. and Avery, M., *Handbook of Massachusetts Evidence* (8th ed. 2007)—leading questions to re-

fresh memory of friendly witness; § 6.20 Present Recollection Revived;

C v Hartford **346 M 482 (63)**—discretion to permit leading questions on direct examination to refresh (or for hostile witness) *(See Chapter 10-B)*; (but see *Parotta* **316 M 307 (44)**, *Amado* **387 M 179 (82)**);

C v Fiore **364 M 819 (74)**—(same); or any document/object; if witness adopts prior statement, it becomes affirmative evidence;

C v Melchionno **29 MAC 939 (90)**—prosecutor permitted to use leading questions about prior testimony to refresh recollection of own child witness;

C v Quincy Q **434 M 859, 871 (2001)**—impermissible to allow party to refresh witness's recollection outside presence of jury, though this was done here by the prosecutor with a child sexual assault complainant (purportedly because child couldn't yet read & thus refresh herself in jury's presence); "possibility that the prosecutor, inadvertently or not, suggested to the child the desired substance of her testimony during the break and that the complainant tried to accommodate the prosecutor when she returned to the stand is too great for us to sanction such a process";

US v Riccardi **174 F.2d 883 (3d Cir. '49)**—can use a song, a scent, an allusion, even a past, false statement; BUT

C v Parrotta **316 M 307 (44)**—can't introduce (by questions) the content of document [not the witness's (revived) recollection];

Bendett v Bendett **315 M 59 (43)**—(same); but opponent can offer document to show it couldn't have refreshed;

C v Amado **387 M 179, n.8 (82)**—excessive use of inadmissible document to refresh; maybe confrontation issue;

See Chapter 9-A, above, insinuations without support (e.g., introduction of hearsay during cross);

C v O'Brien **419 M 470 (95)**—if use "privileged" material (purported attorney work product) to refresh during testimony, privilege = waived & opposing counsel may see it; reserved question = whether privilege waived when W uses such document to refresh *prior to* testimony;

See also Chapter 18, "Hypnosis," Identification;

9-I. PAST RECOLLECTION RECORDED

Brodin, M. and Avery, M., *Handbook of Massachusetts Evidence* **(8th ed. 2007)**—(Present Recollection Revived: may use leading questions, or use item that revives witness's recollection, or if witness's memory can't be revived, may admit document embodying witness's forgotten knowledge, i.e., 'past recollection recorded' exception to hearsay prohibition), 8.17 (Past Recollection Recorded);

Young, Pollets & Poreda, *Evidence,* **§ 803.5 (2d ed. 1998)**—(see also Prop.M.R.Evid. 803(5));

C v Bookman **386 M 657 (82)**—though now no memory, substantive evidence in judge's discretion if adopted as true when made & made when memory's fresh;

C v Greene **9 MAC 688 (80)**—(same);

C v Daye **393 M 55 (84)**—*(more complete summaries in Chapter 9-F, Prior Inconsistent Statements or Conduct)* not past recollection recorded because witness now denies it's true & denies first-hand knowledge when made;

C v Galvin **27 MAC 150 (89)**—police report = past recollection recorded re: D's license number though not "best evidence" (because cop lost notes of witness telling the number);

See Chapter 11-F, re hearsay issues concerning recordings generally;

C v Colon **408 M 419 (90)**—memo properly qualified as past recollection recorded admissible in toto or through testimony of declarant;

C v Cyr **425 M 89, 97 (97)**—persons who heard testimony at probate court proceedings allowed to testify to their memory of that testimony, SJC denominating this "prior recorded testimony" of now unavailable witness (i.e., the murder victim);

C v Fryar **414 M 732 (93)**—trial witness testifying no memory of street brawl; her grand jury testimony not admissible as past recollection recorded because she did not see or adopt the grand jury testimony "at or about the time of" events per *Bookman* **386 M at 664**; instead, witness did not see the transcript until one year after giving testimony, and statement that testimony was "true at the time she gave it" = too belated an adoption;

Catania v Emerson Cleaners, Inc. **362 M 388 (72)**—though signed statement of witness was given eight months after accident, it was admissible both for impeachment and as past recollection recorded (because trial was four YEARS after accident at issue, and 8-month memory logically was certainly as good, if not better).

Chapter 10
PREPARING AND PRESENTING DEFENSE EVIDENCE

10-A. GENERAL—RIGHT, STRATEGY, AND PREPARATION; THEORY OF DEFENSE

See also Chapter 9, Cross-Examination (including impeachment); Chapter 11, Evidence, & Chapter 2E, Ineffective Assistance of Counsel (failures to present evidence, failures to object to illegitimate impeachment of defense;

CPCS P/G 1.3—D decides whether to testify, counsel decides witnesses/evidence; 6.1(a) develop most viable defense theory; 6.7 sensible overall strategy (e.g., whether to put on any defense); what corroborates & what's missing?; check witnesses' prior convictions; careful preparation, etc. CAUTION re: reciprocal discovery of witnesses' statements *(See Chapter 6-M, Reciprocal Discovery)*; cf. *C*

v Dupree **16 MAC 600 (83)** (re: opening statement) D may not know what evidence, if any, to present until (s)he's heard Commonwealth case; but see *C v Federici* **427 M 740 (98)** D gets to decide whether or not to defend on basis of lack of criminal responsibility **if he is competent**;

C v Street **388 M 281 (83)**—ineffective assistance of counsel in abandoning insanity defense;

C v Westmoreland **388 M 269 (83)**—(same);

See Chapter 12-J, Closing Argument;

SJC Rule 3:07, 3.4(e)—counsel shall not allude to matter without reasonable belief it's relevant & will be admitted, & shall not assert own opinion, or 3.4(c), intentionally violate rule of evidence;

U.S. Constitution, Fifth and Sixth Amendments—can't compel witness against 'self; compulsory process for D's witnesses; Fourteenth Amendment, Due Process;

Mass. Constitution, Declaration of Rights, Article 12—can't compel giving evidence against oneself; right to all proofs that may be favorable & to be fully heard in defense;

***Chambers v Mississippi* 410 US 284, 302 (73)**—fundamental right to present witnesses/evidence;

***C v Jewett* 392 M 558 (84)**—*(See Chapter 18-C, Right to Show Mistaken ID)* D can introduce evidence that another person recently committed similar crime by similar methods, but similarity must be particularly distinguishing;

***C v Keizer* 377 M 264 (79)**—same;

***C v Conkey* 443 M 60 (2004)**—reversal of murder conviction for exclusion of third-party culprit's pattern of sexually aggressive acts against women (he was victim's landlord, & victim had declined his requests to date); strict "similarity" and actual "crime" not required;

***Holmes v South Carolina* 547 US 319 (2006)**—authority of state and federal evidentiary rules is subject to limitations commanded in Constitution; D has right to introduce evidence of 3rd party's culpability for crime, though there must be such proof of connection "as tends clearly to point out such other person as the guilty party"; can't exclude defense evidence simply because prosecution claims evidence of D's guilt is compelling;

***C v Alammani* 439 M 605 (2003)**—D (father) sought to blame mother of shaken baby for the death, but no error in exclusion of her statements that she hadn't "bonded" with victim, and, to D, that she was "sorry": statements were too ambiguous to be probative of alleged consciousness of guilt;

***C v Charros* 443 M 752, 768 (2005)**—rejects D's claim of error in exclusion of statements by man claimed by D to be owner of drugs (apologizing for leaving D to take the blame, but saying he had to solve his own problems with police): declarant wasn't called to testify & unavailability (due to possibility of claim of privilege against self-incrimination) won't be presumed; statements didn't qualify as "against penal interest";

***C v O'Laughlin* 446 M 188 (2006)**—no error in exclusion of handwritten note found in victim's bedroom, though D claimed that it implied that V's husband was hostile and motivated to attack V because of her extramarital ongoing affair; V denied that it was in her writing and did not recall writing the note; though expert testimony wasn't required and jurors could have compared this writing to a writing admittedly written by victim, content of note didn't reveal who speaker was and who was subject of speaker's venom;

***C v Peppicelli* 70 MAC 87 (2007)**—judge had discretion to exclude testimony of expert called by defense to testify generally "about the reasonableness of the use of firearms by civilians for self-defense in various situations"; judge determined that jury didn't need expert assistance in this determination;

***C v Rosario* 444 M 550 (2005)**—after D summonsed person counsel believed to be true culprit in sale of drugs (for which D was on trial instead) & witness invoked privilege against self-incrimination, D had right to display the individual and his physical features before the jury; SJC rejects rationale that this was impermissibly "parading" witness to communicate to jury that he was invoking privilege; for appellate preservation, D-counsel adequately expressed to judge that middleman in sale to undercover cop would ID the witness as middleman's supplier (at 558 n.2);

***C v Adjutant* 443 M 649 (2005)**—judge has discretion to admit "specific incidents of violence that the victim is reasonably alleged to have initiated" when D asserts self-defense and identity of first aggressor is in dispute; D needn't have known of such incidents at time of alleged crime;

***C v Benoit* 452 M 212 (2008)**—although "self-defense" instruction was legitimately refused (because D could have retreated), judge did instruct on voluntary manslaughter: D argued logical extension of *Adjutant*, i.e., prior violent acts by deceased argued to be admissible in context of whether he initiated sudden and violent combat which would cause reasonable person to be provoked to heat of passion; because of newness of *Adjutant* rule and lack of opportunity to examine its impact, SJC "not prepared to extend the rule *at this time*", but reversed conviction on different ground; Ireland, J., believed "court should have undertaken a full analysis of the merits of extending the *Adjutant* rule to this case, instead of dismissing it as premature":

***Jansen, petitioner* 444 M 112 (2005)**—upheld judge's allowing D's pretrial motion for order for "buccal swab" of a third party for DNA sample (D had made very substantial showing that such a sample with pristine chain of custody would show third party rather than D to be source of sperm); cites ***C v Conkey* 443 M 60, 66 (2004)** (D has constitutional right to present evidence at trial that some other individual may have committed the particular crime of which D has been accused);

***C v Poggi* 53 MAC 685 (2002)**—**reversal for failure to allow D to proffer his tattooed arm to the jury, where five witnesses to robbery testified that culprit wore short sleeved shirt, but no witness professed to have seen tattoos; display would have been "demonstrative," rather than "testimonial," so not properly barred because D wasn't taking stand/wasn't submitting to cross-examination; enough "foundation" because both a defense witness and medical records provided evidence that the tattoos pre-dated robbery; D = "entitled to a reasonable opportunity to make his best case,** including the proposition that his tattoos were so obvious that, had he been the robber, at least one of the witnesses would have observed them";

***C v DePace* 442 M 739 (2004)**—no error in excluding from evidence before jury the fact that D's conviction had been reversed following first trial, notwithstanding defense theory that alternate suspect's "finding" possible murder weapon only after that reversal was of impeachment value concerning that individual's testimony; court distinguished *C v Vardinski* **438 M 444 (2003)**—conviction reversed for judge's refusal to allow defense to cross-examine ID witness with exact version of mugshot used to ID D before trial, without redaction of prior bad act (pending firearms charge): D wanted to argue that witness's ID was impermissibly reinforced by this derogatory info;

C v DaSilva **66 MAC 556 (2006)**—no error in excluding from suppression hearing a witness's testimony given at probation surrender hearing because judge found it not relevant; issue of similarity of proceedings not reached;

10-A.1. Right to Subpoena, Bench Warrant

C v Adderley **36 MAC 918 (94)**—error to refuse to issue bench warrant for subpoenaed witness who did not appear; evidence not cumulative (& error not harmless) because missing witness was not impeachable as were others; *(See Chapter 7-B, Summonsing Witnesses, Subpoenas)*;

C v McCready **50 MAC 521 (2000)**—when page was missing from hospital records & D counsel in OUI case obtained (belatedly, only) by summonsing the record to court at trial, unpleasantly surprised to find that missing page contained intake note from nurse "Strong ETOH [meaning alcohol] on breath"; **OBTAIN RECORDS/DO INVESTIGATION** *BEFORE* **trial;**

See also BBO No. 98-5, Order of Public Reprimand, 26 Mass. Lawyers Weekly 2796 (August 3, 1998)—disclosing to adversary 'potential' evidence, without having evaluated it yourself for harm/help may result in facilitating your own client's conviction. This is "neglect and inadequate preparation in violation of [then-applicable disciplinary rules, DR 6-101(A)(2-3)]";

C v Wooden **70 MAC 185 (2007)**—no error in judge's refusal to subpoena witness desired by armed robbery D, since pretrial hearing, with witness and his attorney participating, established that witness had and would assert privilege against self-incrimination concerning the pertinent gun, seized from witness's home; **N.B.:** D didn't seek immunity for witness either from Commonwealth (G.L. c. 233, §§ 20C–20E) "or from the judge" (see *C v Curtis* 388 M 637, 646 [1983]); D's argument about impropriety of "blanket" assertion of privilege wasn't made below;

10-A.2. Decision Re: Defendant Testifying

ABA Standards for Criminal Justice, Prosecution Function & Defense Function (3d ed. 1993) 4-5.2— (counsel's advice, but) **D's decision** whether to testify; other witnesses = counsel's decision after consult with D;

C v Hennessey **23 MAC 384 (87)**—too complex & risky, so no colloquy needed re: D's waiver of testimony right;

C v Glacken **451 M 163 (2008)**—trial judge could decline to credit D's affidavit, seven years after trial, claiming that counsel did not advise him of right to testify and instead told him he would not; judge needn't engage in trial colloquy to determine that D has knowingly waived right to testify (here, relied on counsel's representations **at trial** that he had advised D of right to testify);

C v Grissett **66 MAC 454 (2006)**—"grave error for counsel to call [D] to testify and then pose questions on direct . . . which left [D] vulnerable to a predictably devastating cross-examination", i.e., after direct elicited that D had never purchased or used cocaine, prosecutor received permission to impeach D with prior conviction for possession with intent to distribute cocaine; counsel should have been aware of prior conviction & avoided questioning which opened the door; ineffective assistance found;

C v Siciliano **19 MAC 918 (84)**—don't need voir dire, but must show that D waived right to testify & inquiry to counsel or D maybe helpful;

C v Mitchell **438 M 535 (2003)**—Mass. R. Prof. C. 3.3(e) (98) governs conduct of lawyer who learns that D intends to commit perjury (must try to dissuade, may not ask questions which would elicit perjury if D testifies, and may not argue probative value of false testimony in closing, _**BUT**_ lawyer can't invoke this rule just because D has told inconsistent stories re: event, or because lawyer thinks D may be lying because of the Commonwealth's proof; lawyer must have firm basis in objective fact to believe D intends to commit perjury; SJC held that such basis here existed, and that it was acceptable procedure for D-counsel to raise matter at bench conference with ADA and judge (maybe error to not have D present, but purportedly no prejudice shown!), and thereafter to merely have D testify in narrative form and not argue testimony content to jury; "discretionary" with trial judge whether to have colloquy with D;

C v Dahl **430 M 813 (2000)**—no ineffective assistance found though D argued that counsel hadn't advised that defendant's testimony was necessary/crucial for various proffered defenses;

C v McMahon **443 M 409 (2005)**—that D belatedly made a poor strategic decision not to testify & thus undermined defense position given in great detail in counsel's opening statement was not a ground for mistrial (so counsel not ineffective in not having requested mistrial);

C v Medina **64 MAC 708 (2005)**—trial judge not required to engage in colloquy with D to determine whether D is "knowingly, voluntarily, and intelligently" electing to forego right to testify; judge's findings on motion for new trial alleging ineffective assistance of counsel for refusing to "honor [D's] request to testify" were that D himself had made the decision not to testify, after consultation with and advice from counsel (which was not manifestly unreasonable);

C v Sharpe **454 M 135 (2009)**—in motion for new trial, D claimed he didn't knowingly waive right not to testify and that trial counsel placed undue pressure upon him to testify; after evidentiary hearing, judge found that he had engaged D in colloquy prior to D's testifying (court stenographer didn't record it, but judge "settled the matter and corrected the record" under MRAppP 8(e)), that D made knowing & voluntary decision to testify after conferring with counsel and family, and that counsel wasn't ineffective (reasonable strategy);

C v Garuti **454 M 48 (2009)**—record, including contemporaneously recorded colloquy, supported judge's finding on motion for new trial that D's decision not to testify was knowing/voluntary, made after adequate consultation;

10-A.3. Impeachment of Defendant, What's OK and Not

Young, Pollets, & Poreda, *Evidence,* § 611.2 (2d ed. 1998)—D takes stand = subject to wide-open cross-examination;

C v Murphy **57 MAC 586 (2003)**—cross-examination of D, on trial for rape of seven-year-old son of D's fiancée, included "How did it feel when you were sucking your son's penis?" & was improper, sought merely to "degrade"; how D "felt" had no bearing on guilt, & no reasonable DA could have expected this "question" to produce an answer helpful to prosecution; "Trials are a search for truth, not socialized stonings"; *see also C v DeMars* **42 MAC 788 (97), S.C., 426 M 1008 (98)**—reverse for cumulative effect of DA's many transgressions in taunting cross-examination of D and in argument;

Anderson v Charles **447 US 404 (80)**—can impeach D by prior inconsistent statement; but . . . ;

C v Mosby **11 MAC 1 (80)**—can't even hint re: post-arrest silence;

C v Irwin **72 MAC 643 (2008)**—reversal (despite no objection) for prosecutor's use in case in chief, in cross-examination, and in closing argument) of D's failure to reach out to police and delay in speaking to police about allegation of sexual assault, citing *Thompson* 431 M 108, 117 (2000) and *Nickerson* 386 M 54 (82) (impeachment of D with fact of prearrest silence should be approached with caution, is of "extremely limited probative worth");

See Chapter 11-G.4 (Post-Arrest Silence Inadmissible) and Chapter 9-G (Silence as Prior Inconsistent Statement) for more cases and distinctions, and Chapter 7-H (Fifth Amendment and Massachusetts Declaration of Rights Article 12 Privilege), e.g.,

C v Guy **441 M 96 (2004)**—no *Doyle v Ohio* violation to impeach D's trial testimony with content of his post-Miranda conversations with nurse, security guard, and police officer and with answer to booking question re: injuries;

C v Ewing **67 MAC 531 (2006), and SJC on further appellate review agrees, 449 M 1035 (2007)**—reversal for DA's cross-examination and argument "impeaching" D's testimony on grounds that he had advantage of pretrial discovery to tailor his testimony and had not sought out police between charge and trial to report his exculpatory version of events;

C v Caldron **383 M 86 (81)**—"self-serving" not a valid objection to D's testimony;

C v Fatalo **345 M 85 (62)**—"self-serving" not valid basis for exclusion (it's to be expected that evidence proffered by a party is "self"-serving); really a hearsay issue; maybe a hearsay exception, e.g., state of mind;

C v Dupont **75 MAC 605 (2009)**, citing *C v Nawn* **394 M 1 (85)**, *C v Cancel* **394 M 567 (85)**, *C v Machado* **339 M 713 (59)**—D's denial of accusation of guilt isn't admissible unless some other hearsay exception applies, BUT if D responds to accusation in "equivocal, evasive or irresponsive way," D's statement IS admissible; cop's assertion to D that cop "knew he was involved in a drug transaction and believed that there was cocaine in his vehicle" was answered: "there is no cocaine in my vehicle or one me"; D's statement held admissible as "oddly specific" (not unequivocal);

C v Noxon **319 M 495, 544 (46)**—no privilege, so cross-examination of D's expert re: counsel's conversations = OK; *(See Chapter 6-M, Reciprocal Discovery)*; BUT cf *In Matter of Grand Jury Investigation* **407 M 916 (90)** PF-15, which requires judicial ok for prosecutorial summons of defense counsel, also applies to defense investigators; rationale for the rule;

C v Harris **364 M 236 (73)**—DA can impeach D with prior inconsistent statement although promised (at probable cause hearing) not to use and although suppressible pursuant to Miranda *(See Chapter 20, "impeachment exception" to 4th Amendment suppression, e.g., Harris v NY* **401 US 222 (71)**, *Walder v US* **347 US 62, 65 (54))**;

US v Havens **446 US 620 (80)**—suppressed evidence can impeach testifying D;

C v Graham **62 MAC 642, 647–48 (2004)**—was within discretion of judge to find that D's testimony on direct (that he attempted to gain entry into apartment building because he was fleeing from police, having suffered serious injury in prior altercation with police a year earlier) opened door to cross-exam re: circumstances surrounding prior incident, "which included his convictions related to the altercation", OR given instructions and lack of mention in closing and strong evidence of guilt, "any error in permitting the inquiry was rendered harmless";

Williams v Twomey **510 F.2d 634 (1st Cir. '75)**—ineffective (in part) because didn't warn D (who took stand) about impeachment by prior record; cf *C v Rossi* **19 MAC 257 (85)** ineffective for introducing prior record during direct examination upon mistaken belief that it would be admissible under G.L. c. 233, § 21 during cross;

C v Freeman **29 MAC 635 (90)**—counsel's erroneous advice that D's juvenile delinquencies were admissible to impeach violated D's right to testify;

C v Papadinis **402 M 73 (88)**—D must be permitted to testify on his state of mind or knowledge where it is "a factor" in proof of crime;

C v Graham **62 MAC 642, 648-649 (2004)**—OK to exclude witness who would corroborate D's testimony as to state of mind because "cumulative" of hospital records and purportedly on question only "indirectly linked to an element of the crime";

C v Chase **26 MAC 578 (88)**—D has unqualified right to explain why he lied to police, but must make offer of proof; (unless he's barred from making such offer—cf *C v Adderley* **36 MAC 918 (94)**);

C v Frank **433 M 185, 193 (2001)—offer of proof needed when judge sustains prosecutor's objection to question asked of D on direct examination;**

C v Alvarado **50 MAC 419 (2000)**—prosecutor's attempt to use hearsay to impeach D's alibi testimony = "particularly inappropriate";

10-A.4. Incompetent Defendant? Resolve Case Anyway?

G.L. c. 123, § 17(b)—on behalf of incompetent D, right to present a defense (other than lack of criminal responsibility) to a judge at a hearing, with possible result of dismissal;

10-A.5. Statutes/Rules Barring Evidence vs. Constitutional Right to Present Defense

Washington v Texas **388 US 14, 19 (67)**—Sixth Amendment overrides state-created evidentiary "disqualifications" in favor of D's right to present a defense;

Chambers v Mississippi **410 US 284 (73)**—as applied to this D, state's hearsay rule denied him Sixth Amendment right (& was unconstitutional);

Rock v Arkansas **483 US 44, 55 (87)**—state may not apply rule of evidence which permits witness to take stand but "arbitrarily excludes material portions of his testimony";

C v Grey **399 M 469, 471 n.3 (87)**—absent a strong state interest in ignoring such evidence, a rule which requires a jury to disregard evidence bearing directly on [D's] guilt would be a violation of due process of law and [D's] state and federal constitutional right to present a defense;

C v Joyce **382 M 222 (81)**—D's right to show bias, constitutional in nature, overrides "rape-shield" statute;

C v Thevenin **33 MAC 588 (92)**—D's right to present defense overrode purported applicability of rape-shield statute;

C v Sugrue **34 MAC 172 (93)**—despite "marital communications" exclusion (G.L. c. 233, § 20), D had constitutional right to introduce evidence of his wife's motive to falsely accuse him of child abuse, i.e., his intention, stated to her, to obtain custody of children after impending divorce;

C v Stockhammer **409 M 867 (91)**—statutory privileges of rape complainant must yield to D's Article 12 right to produce all favorable proofs;

C v Sheehan **435 M 183 (2001)—mental health records of sexual assault complainant erroneously withheld, indicated she had tendency to engage in fantasy, become "dissociated," etc.; at least three members of SJC now willing to abandon the convoluted "Bishop-Fuller" procedure for obtaining access to records: it** doesn't "belittle" the privileges at stake to say that D's "right to a fair trial is of greater weight" (Sosman, J., concurring opinion);

US v Scheffer **523 US 303 (98)**—blanket ban on admission of polygraph evidence (by M.R.Evid. 707(a)) not violative of 6th Amendment because evidence unreliable under *Daubert* **509 US 579 (93)** (right to present evidence presupposes materiality and threshold reliability of evidence);

10-A.6. Judge's Right to Exclude as Irrelevant/Unfairly Prejudicial/ Unsound/Cumulative; Procedural Default as Waiver

C v Pallotta **36 MAC 669 (94)**—simply because judge was gatekeeper on "expert" evidence, he could not claim superior expertise so as to bar defense evidence;

C v Roberio **428 M 278 (98)**—although judge on motion for new trial concluded that testimony and report of a clinical psychologist were not "credible", and denied motion for new trial on this basis, SJC reversed: once expert's individual qualifications were ratified and his area of expertise found to be scientifically legitimate, it's "error for judge to deny motion for new trial based on his assessment of the expert's credibility"; credibility is issue for jury, not judge; fact that expert was weakened by cross-examination is "not relevant in deciding the new trial question";

C v Hogan **7 MAC 236, 241–42 (79)**—D entitled to present defense theory to jury regardless of whether **judge** is moved by it;

C v Saunders **45 MAC 340, 342–43 (98)**— "collateral"/cumulative defense evidence may be excluded;

C v Carleton **36 MAC 137: S.C., 418 M 773 (94)**— no error in excluding defense evidence on bases of irrelevance and probative value being outweighed by "inflammatory nature";

C v Paiva **71 MAC 411 (2008)**—witness proffered by D was NOT an expert in use of drugs, but instead a percipient witness to D's own drug habit (including amounts), relevant to dispute "intent to distribute"; error to exclude, as observations not remote in time;

C v Silva-Santiago **453 M 782 (2009)**—defense counsel sought to question cop about info received from named person that another named person was the murderer (not D); proffered as "3rd party culprit information" and "to impeach the investigation," i.e., a "Bowden" defense; former basis was infirm, as it was hearsay (offered for truth); same info more likely admissible as part of Bowden defense (and judge erred in ruling that exclusion on former basis required exclusion on latter rationale); voir dire should have occurred, but counsel's proffer defective;

C v Doyle **67 MAC 846 (2006)**—facts indicate that rewards to informant for setting up D with undercover officer were admitted, relevant and material (though court refused to find error in exclusion of "cumulative" but overridingly prejudicial hearsay evidence that informant began working for police after a gun he had owned was implicated in a murder, an allegation "vigorously disputed" by prosecutor" (id. at 863 n.22));

C v Carroll **439 M 547 (2003)**—co-defendant, who had pled guilty, testified that D wasn't guilty of ABDW, and indeed had intervened to stop co-D's beating of victim; no error in excluding testimony concerning co-D's motive in the beating (victim had previously stolen co-D's property), because collateral: there's no requirement that joint venturers share a motive for success of the joint venture;

C v Moran **439 M 482 (2003)**—error to exclude medical record of rape complainant, who testified that she wouldn't have consented to sex because she had had recent laparoscopy, and that she had taken pain killer because of this surgery; record revealed an entirely different medical procedure, involving a different bodily entry point; no privilege applied, & no basis for invoking "Bishop-Fuller" protocol;

C v Murchison **418 M 58 (94)**—defense may be that police are lying (but see caveats);

C v Pearce **427 M 642, 646, 649 n.3 (98)**—defense cannot argue that rape complainant's pregnancy resulted from sex with someone other than D unless there is specific evidence that complainant engaged in sex with a specific someone else at a time consistent with pregnancy (a noteworthy holding given that constitutional values are supposed to be preeminent: presumption of innocence, see *In re Winship* **397 US 358 (70),** and Constitutionally-mandated burden of proof upon prosecution, see *Mullaney v Wilbur* **421 US 684 (75)**;

C v Small **10 MAC 606 (80)**—no abused (here) discretion to not let D reopen evidence after jury question because D had ample chance to offer it before *(See Chapter 12-H, re: rebuttal/reopening)*;

10-A.7. Absolute Right to Impeach Witnesses/Evidence

(See cases in Chapter 9-C & 9-D, Impeachment for Bias, & by Prior Convictions), e.g., **Davis v Alaska 415 US 308 (74) juvenile record relevant re: bias, & constitution guarantees right to impeach for bias/motive to lie;** *C v Ferrara* **368 M 182 (75) similar;** *C v Hogan* **7 MAC 236, 241–42 (79) D entitled to present to jury the defense theory** (of motive to lie) regardless of whether judge is moved by it;

Crane v Kentucky 476 US 683 (86) due process & 6th Amendment right to show confession's unreliability (after denial of motion to suppress);

Prop.M.R.Evid. 806—credibility of a declarant of a hearsay statement may be impeached by any evidence that would have been admissible if the declarant had testified, even if the declarant has had no opportunity to deny or explain the impeaching evidence;

C v Mahar **430 M 643, 648–50 (2000)**—SJC ADOPTS Proposed MR Evidence 806: "if a live witness's substantive testimony can be properly impeached by prior

inconsistent statements or other evidence, the same testimony admitted through an exception to the hearsay rule ought to be subject to the same impeachment. Otherwise, the fact finder is given a distorted and incomplete view of the evidence in a case where hearsay testimony that could be, but is not, impeached, is admitted. There is no reason to put a proponent of an absent witness in a better position than a proponent of a live witness" *(See Chapter 7-K, Prior Reported Testimony as Substantive Evidence)*;

10-A.8. Commonwealth's Motions in Limine

See Chapter 11-B, Motions in Limine;

C v Hood **389 M 581 (83)**—best not to exclude D's entire defense (on DA's motion in limine);

C v O'Malley **14 MAC 314, 325 (82)**—trial by jury not to be converted to trial by motion in limine, with effect of directing a verdict against a criminal D; see also Liacos, C.J., concurring in *C v Brogan* **415 M 169, 179 (93)**;

C v Conley **34 MAC 50, 59 (93)**—sua sponte requiring offer of proof on each witness wrong (and strongly disapproved), but here harmless;

C v Lora **43 MAC 136 (97)**—error to exclude, on Commonwealth's motion in limine, medical records substantiating D's chronic illness (necessity defense re driving without license, to pharmacy for prescriptions);

C v Ramos **66 MAC 548 (2006)**—though defense counsel in opening statement promised testimony of psychologist (post-traumatic stress syndrome a factor in stabbing of school counselor), possibility of Commonwealth cross-examining psychologist about his knowledge of other stabbing by D led counsel **not** to call the promised witness: though court declined to find ineffective assistance of counsel on this record, counsel could have omitted reference to the witness and could have followed up on judge's offer of voir dire to determine whether Commonwealth would be allowed to question about the extraneous bad act;

10-A.9. Exclusion of Evidence as Discovery Sanction

Chappee v Vose **843 F.2d 25 (1st Cir. '88)** exclude W for reciprocal discovery violation: *(BUT SEE Chapter 6-D, Discovery, & Sanctions)*, cases reversing for use of this sanction in particular circumstances [e.g., **C v Steinmeyer 43 MAC 185 (97) sanction of striking defense witness's testimony too severe here; before imposing this severe a sanction, court must balance certain factors against right to present defense: prevention of surprise, bad faith or not, prejudice to other side, effectiveness of less severe sanction, materiality of testimony to case outcome; C v Cutty 47 MAC 671 (99) D himself cannot be precluded from testifying as sanction for failure to give notice of alibi (M.R.Crim.P. 14(b)(1)(D))];**

10-A.10. Inconsistent Defenses?

Mathews v US **485 US 58 (88)**—hurts credibility of defense, but inconsistent defenses (entrap, no act/intent) = OK *(See Chapters 12-I & 12-K, 7-E, bifurcated trial in 'lack of criminal responsibility' setting);*

See Chapter 2-E, Ineffective Assistance of Counsel, & Chapter 7-D & 7-E, insanity re: control of case;

10-A.11. Prepare Witnesses

CPCS P/G 6.7(f)—prepare D's witnesses for all foreseeable cross-examination;

C v Benoit **32 MAC 111 (92)**—error to put in D's confession to brother as prior inconsistent statement of brother where brother now denies it;

C v Rosa **412 M 147 (92)**—(same) re: prior inconsistent by D to D's wife who now takes spousal privilege;

10-A.12. Witnesses' Privileges, Waivers

James v Illinois **493 US 307 (90)**—D's statement, which had been suppressed on 4th Amendment grounds, should not have been used by prosecutor to impeach defense witness where D didn't testify; "impeachment exception" to 4th Amendment suppression *Harris v NY* **401 US 222 (71)**, *Walder v US* **347 US 62, 65 (54)**;

See also Chapter 7-H (Fifth Amendment & Declaration of Rights Article 12 privilege); Chapter 12-J, Argument (Missing Witnesses, D's failure to testify); Chapter 6-I (discovery of D's alleged statements); Chapter 6-M (reciprocal discovery); Chapter 9-D&E (impeachment & excluding prior record); Chapter 11-B (motions in limine); Chapter 11 D&E ("character"/propensity evidence); Chapter 11-G (admissions of D by conduct/silence); Chapter 12-J, Missing Witness Inference; Chapter 11-I (opinion evidence); Chapter 7-A &7-B (investigation, summonses); etc.

C v Negron **441 M 685 (2004)**—claim of spousal privilege made D's wife "unavailable" at probation revocation hearing, so that cop's testimony re: wife's allegations, if substantial indicia of reliability, admissible;

C v Gagnon **408 M 185 (90)**—D not entitled under state or federal constitutions to call witness to stand to invoke 5th Amendment privilege;

C v Nadile **10 MAC 913 (80)**—if witness expected to take 5th Amendment, best not to call him/her before the jury; *(See Chapter 11-C, Move/Strike & Chapter 7-H, 5th Amendment Privilege Against Self-Incrimination);*

C v Freeman **442 M 779 (2004)**—defense witness, expected to testify that D's co-D confessed to witness that he rather than D was principal/shooter, instead claimed 5th Amendment privilege; no error since testimony could serve to incriminate on, e.g., conspiracy to commit perjury, obstruction of justice, etc.; though assertion of right shouldn't be accepted in "blanket" fashion, judge here determined that witness would not answer any questions regarding the "area" of his purported conversation with the D's co-D;

C v Penta **32 MAC 36 (92)**—government agent who waived right against self-incrimination by testifying at pretrial proceedings should have been required to testify for D despite validity of 5th Amendment-Article 12 claims re: perjury; **but see** *S.C., C v Penta* **423 M 546 (96)** no relief for D when witness failed to appear & testify at trial after DA asked judge, in open court, to tell witness at a prior hearing (for reconsideration of motion to suppress) that witness's inconsistent testimony could result in perjury prosecution: Commonwealth was only obligated to give D last known address of, & not obstruct access to, witness; but see *C v Turner* **37 MAC 385 (94)** threats, rather than fear of self-incrimination, were reason for witnesses' refusal to testify: "judge never considered the link between the threat by the prosecutor and the witness's fear of prosecution";

C v Lucien **440 M 658 (2004)**—although not stating reason on record, judge legitimately allowed witness's claim of privilege against self-incrimination because, although witness had already pleaded guilty to a firearm offense, his prospective testimony subjected him to prosecution for possession of a second firearm and for "trading of firearms";

US v Morrison **535 F.2d 223 (3d Cir. '76)**—prosecutor subpoenaed D-witness to prosecutor's office & in presence of "law enforcement officers," told her of dangers of testifying;

C v Rosa **412 M 147, 160–63 (92)**—if Commonwealth's misconduct re: threatened incarceration of D's wife (preventing her from caring for disabled child) coerced her waiver of spousal privilege, waiver was involuntary & testimony couldn't be introduced at 2d trial;

10-A.13. Prosecutorial/Judicial Threats against Defense Witnesses

Webb v Texas **409 US 95 (72)**—error to scare off D's witness by perjury threat;

C v McMiller **29 MAC 392 (90)**—prosecutor's threat to prosecute government agent if she testified in support of D's claim of entrapment was improper & required reversal;

C v Colantonio **31 MAC 299 (91)**—evidence that defense witness asserted 5th Amendment because prosecutor improperly postponed witness's sentencing was insufficient;

C v Koonce **418 M 367 (94)**—because of DA threats & other reasons, prosecution witness's waiver of 5th Amendment rights at 1st trial was held to be involuntary, so it would not act as waiver enabling D to call witness at retrial, **but** this testimony was read to jury at 2d trial; appellate counsel argued unsuccessfully that witness should have been required to testify;

C v Turner **37 MAC 385 (94)**—threats, rather than fear of self-incrimination, were reason for witnesses' refusal to testify: "judge never considered the link between the threat by the prosecutor and the witness's fear of prosecution";

US v Morrison **535 F.2d 223 (3d Cir. '76)**— prosecutor subpoenaed D-witness to prosecutor's office & in presence of "law enforcement officers," told her of dangers of testifying;

C v Rosa **412 M 147, 160–63 (92)**—prosecutorial misconduct coercing waiver by D's wife of her spousal privilege;

Buie v Sullivan **923 F.2d 10 (2d Cir. '90)**—government's arrest of exculpatory defense witness did not violate D's right to present defense where bad faith not shown;

C v Ranieri **65 MAC 366 (2006)**—refusing to find error in judge's deferral of decision on D's motion in limine until after D's expert testified, though deferral caused D-counsel to forego calling expert because adverse ruling on motion in limine would entail introduction of evidence of D's prior like crimes, through the expert's "notes"; court refused to treat issue as one of "excluding" D's evidence, instead calling choice to forego witness a "reasonable tactical decision" in light of possible adverse consequence;

10-B. DIRECT EXAMINATION (INCLUDING IMPEACHING OWN WITNESS)

C v Beauchemin **410 M 181 (91)**—judge's voir dire of proper defense witnesses improperly gave prosecutor "untoward discovery";

See also Chapter 9-D, Impeach by Priors, Chapter 11-C, Offers of Proof, etc.;

CPCS P/G 6.7—consider order of witnesses; prepare for cross-examination; protect against improper cross-examination; make offers/proof & re-phrase questions *(See Chapter 11, Evidence)*;

Superior Court Rule 69—stand up to examine witness (unless permission not to);

Young, Pollets & Poreda, *Evidence,* **§ 607.1 (2d ed.1998)**—(impeaching own witness); 608.1 (judge's discretion re: foundation); 611.4 (may lead only if witness is "hostile to your cause," with exception for preliminary questions, and judicial discretion to allow leading if witness = immature, obviously disconcerted, etc.); discovery of impeaching, i.e., inconsistent, statements = critical:

See Chapter 6-D, Discovery in General, Chapter 6-G, Statements of Commonwealth Witnesses;

C v Johnson **199 M 55 (08)**—exceptional, but sometimes narrative needed;

Brodin, M. and Avery, M., *Handbook of Massachusetts Evidence* **(8th ed. 2007)**—generally no leading, misleading, repetitious, or argumentative (e.g., assumes fact not in evidence) questions;

C v Ridge **455 M 307 (2009)**—decision to allow leading questions mostly left to judge's discretion; not improper to allow where witness's testimony is evasive, ambiguous, or inconsistent;

C v Phillips **162 M 504 (1895)**—DA's cross-examination question assumed fact in issue ["Did (complaining witness) tell you what D had done to her?"];

C v McHugh **17 MAC 1016 (84)**—(same);

US v Oshatz **912 F.2d 534 (2d Cir. '90), cert. denied, 500 US 910 (91)**—prosecutor's posing of hypothetical questions assuming D's guilt to lay character witnesses is improper;

10-B.1. Impeaching Own Witness

G.L. c. 233, § 23—can't impeach own witness by bad character; can contradict with prior inconsistent statement, but first let witness explain it;

Brodin, M. and Avery, M., *Handbook of Massachusetts Evidence* **(8th ed. 2007);**

See also Chapter 9, impeachment in general;

C v White **367 M 280 (75)**—can use own witness's prior inconsistent statement made to counsel if good faith, not just innuendo;

C v Cobb **379 M 456 (80)**—DA can use own witness's prior inconsistent statement though witness denies statement;

C v Reddick **372 M 460 (77)**—can't impeach mere "failure to remember";

C v Chin Kee **283 M 248(33)**—(same);

See Chapter 9, Cross-Examination & Young, Pollets & Poreda, Evidence, § 613 (2d ed. 1998), Prior Statements of Witnesses;

C v Pimental **5 MAC 463 (77)**—(DA) can only admit inconsistent portions of prior statement *(See Chapter 11F, Hearsay—Prior Consistent Statements)*;

C v McAfee **430 M 483, 489–92 (99)** & *C v Elliot* **430 M 498, 502–03 (99)**—though witness had earlier told D-counsel that she saw gun in V's hand (thus supporting self-defense), witness denied this during mid-trial voir dire hearing; D couldn't call witness for sole purpose of impeaching her with prior inconsistent statements [see *C v Benoit* **32 MAC 111 (92)** error to put in D's confession to brother as prior inconsistent statement of brother where brother now denies it]; **BUT CF.** *C v Sineiro* **432 M 735 (2000) prior grand jury testimony may be used substantively even though witness at trial disavows it (jury may conclude, from observing witness on stand, that what he said before is the truth rather than what he says now);**

C v Johnson **412 M 318 (92)**—prosecutor's mention of own recollection of prior interview with witness should not have been injected into foundation for impeaching own witness under c. 233, § 23;

C v Scott **408 M 811 (90)**—prosecutor entitled to impeach own witness's recantation of identification where proper foundation laid;

10-B.2. Leading Questions

C v Fiore **364 M 819 (74)**—can lead to refresh own witness' memory; [witness can answer "I think" or "I believe"];

C v LaFrance **361 M 53 (72)**—(fed. review other ground) cross-examination of own hostile witness; impeach by 1st letting witness explain;

Moody v Rowell **17 Pick. 490 (1835)**—discretion re: leading a child witness;

C v Baran **21 MAC 989 (86)**—(same);

C v Melchionno **29 MAC 939 (90)**—prosecutor permitted to use leading questions about prior testimony to refresh recollection of own child witness;

C v Lewis **346 M 373 (63)**—leading questions to refresh;

See Chapter 9-H, Present Recollection Refreshed;

C v Hartford **346 M 482 (63)**—leading to refresh or for hostile witness;

C v Monahan **349 M 139 (65)**—discretion re: "hostile";

C v Haraldstad **16 MAC 565 (83)**—co-D = "friendly," so no leading; Wigmore § 774 lead if witness = hostile, biased, or unwilling;

Prop.M.R.Evid. 611—lead hostile witness or witness "identified with an adverse party"; NOTES—this (Fed.R. Evid. 611) is broader than M.R.Civ.P. 43, which is unduly narrow;

10-C. IMPEACH BY FAILURE TO TESTIFY (SILENCE) IN EARLIER PROCEEDINGS

See also Chapter 9-G, Silence as Prior Inconsistent Statement; & Chapter 11-G, Admissions by Silence;

G.L. c. 278, § 23—at criminal trial in superior or District Court, fact that D didn't testify, or that he "waived examination," or did not offer any evidence, at any preliminary hearing, "shall not be used as evidence against him, nor be referred to or commented upon by the prosecuting officer";

C v Sherick **23 MAC 338 (87) [aff'd 401 M 302]**—G.L. c. 278, § 23 = related to, & overtaken by, 5th Amendment rights; (fn. 5) passed to overcome *Goldstein* **180 M 374**; argument OK here;

10-C.1. Treatment of Defendant

C v Harrington **152 M 488 (1890)**—can cross-examine D re: prior testimony if (s)he took stand (at earlier trial);

C v Rivera **425 M 633 (2000)**—if D does make statement, including in a pretrial affidavit, omissions from it/inconsistencies with his later statements or testimony are admissible for impeachment;

C v Lopez **447 M 625 (2006)**—rejecting D's appellate argument that his multi-day jury trial was essentially a guilty plea requiring plea colloquy, given that he was very adversely impacted at trial by his acknowledged confessions to police and his testimony at codefendants' trials; "it is axiomatic that, if [D] does not plead guilty and . . . waive these rights, the judge need not conduct a plea colloquy";

10-C.2. Treatment of Defense Witnesses

C v Palmarin **378 M 474 (79)**—statute was violated by DA's cross-examination of D's 5 witnesses;

C v Morrison **1 MAC 632 (73)**—same: improper to allow cross of defense witnesses that they had been present at probable cause hearing but hadn't testified then & hadn't told judge of their info; also improper reference to D's post-arrest silence;

C v Cefalo **381 M 319 (80)**—but DA can show D's witnesses were at probable cause hearing & could've told

police, for inference of recent contrivance *(See Chapter 9-G, Impeach by Prior Silence)*;

C v Egerton **396 M 499 (86)**—no violation from cross-examination re: failure to testify at probable cause hearing; no (explicit) reference to D's "failure" to introduce evidence; *** proper inquiry = *C v Brown* **11 MAC 288, 295–97 (81)** *(See Chapter 9G, Silence or Omissions as Prior Inconsistent Statement)* cross-examination of defense witnesses re: failure to come forward to police requires foundation, i.e., that witness knew of pending charges in sufficient detail to realize he possessed exculpatory info, that witness had reason to make the info available, that he was familiar with means of reporting it to proper authorities, and that D or D-counsel did not ask witness to refrain from doing so; because jury may be "misled" by such prosecutorial efforts at impeachment, judge has discretion to bar its introduction before the jury;

C v Hart* **455 M 230 (2009)—eliminated 4th foundational requirement in *C v Brown (that D or D-counsel didn't ask witness not to speak to law enforcement); prosecutor would face "ethical dilemma" because while required to ask the question to establish requisite foundation, he couldn't have good faith basis to believe that D or attorney DID ask witness not to speak to police, and further, SJC Rule 3:07, R.Prof.C. 3.4(f), attorney is barred from requesting person other than client, client's relative, client's employee, or client's agent to refrain from giving relevant info to another party; **IF DEFENSE WITNESS *HAS* BEEN REQUESTED BY D OR D-COUNSEL NOT TO PROVIDE LAW ENFORCEMENT AGENTS WITH THE EXCULPATORY INFO, DEFENSE COUNSEL MAY/ SHOULD ATTEMPT TO PRECLUDE THE *BROWN* INFERENCE BY INFORMING JUDGE PRIOR TO WITNESS'S TESTIMONY "SO THAT THE MATTER MAY BE EXPLORED AT A BENCH CONFERENCE"**; *note well:* at 238, decision acknowledges that it would not be natural for witness to provide police with exculpatory info "when she thinks that her information will not affect the decision to prosecute", and in such an instance silence should not be a basis for impeachment;

C v Passley **428 M 832, 839–40 (99)**—says SJC approved Appeals Court .'s *C v Brown* holding in *C v Gregory* **401 M 437, 444–45 (88)**;

C v Senior **454 M 12 (2009)**—same; judge here instructed jury that witness had no obligation to report crime to police, so no risk of miscarriage of justice;

C v Rivera **62 MAC 859 (2005)**—error to allow cop to testify that D, in initial statement to police, did not tell them about any eyewitnesses to the physical confrontation between D and complainant; this was not a "statement" inconsistent with defense at trial; see also *C v Haas* **373 M 545, 559 (77)**; also error for ADA to argue that witness's testimony should be discounted because she did not call police at the time of the confrontation (no evidence introduced as to whether or not witness had called police);

SJC Rule 3:07, 3.4 (a)—shall not "unlawfully" obstruct another party's access to evidence, or conceal material having potential evidentiary value; 3.4 (f) shan't request a person other than client to refrain from voluntarily giving relevant info to another party, UNLESS person is relative, employee, or other agent of client AND lawyer reasonably believes person's interests won't be adversely affected by so refraining from giving info; BUT CF G.L. c. 258B, § 3(m), Rights of "Victims" and Witnesses [defined in G.L. c. 258B, § 1 to refer only to those witnesses giving testimony supporting the prosecution, but most certainly can't be so restricted (equal protection, due process for D: must apply as well to witnesses whose testimony supports the defense)]: right for victims and witnesses "to be informed of the right to submit to or decline an interview by defense counsel or anyone acting on the defendant's behalf, except when responding to lawful process, and, if the victim or witness decides to submit to an interview, the right to impose reasonable conditions on the conduct of the interview";

10-C.3. Juvenile Court Evidence

G.L. c. 119, § 60—Juvenile Court "evidence" & delinquency adjudication, & "disposition" = inadmissible "AGAINST" former juvenile D for any purpose in any court, **except** in subsequent delinquency or criminal proceedings against the same person and further, adjudication of delinquency may be used for impeachment purposes in subsequent delinquency or criminal proceedings in the same manner and to the same extent as prior criminal convictions;

Davis v Alaska **415 US 308 (79)**—D should have been permitted to expose to jury facts suggestive of bias/motive on part of the witness, despite statute excluding such evidence (juvenile record);

C v Ferrara **368 M 182, 186–90 (75)**—despite G.L. c. 119, § 60 (since amended), D has constitutional right to use juvenile court records to impeach witness against him (motive to lie);

C v Franklin **366 M 284 (74)**—if objection, can't permit cross-examination of juvenile defendant's witness re: bench trial testimony; vs. . . . ;

C v Juvenile **361 M 214 (72)**—on appeal D can impeach Commonwealth witness with Juvenile Court testimony; & witness can use transcript to refresh memory;

See Chapter 9-F, Prior Inconsistent Statement or Conduct, Chapter 9-H, Present Recollection Refreshed;

10-D. (CLIENT) PERJURY—ETHICAL & LEGAL OBLIGATIONS

See Chapter 2, Ethics;

CPCS P/G 1.1—if ethics doubt, get advice, but give D benefit of doubt

SJC 3:07, 1.6(a)—can't knowingly reveal confidential info relating to representation without consent; 1.6(b)(1) MAY reveal client's intent to commit crime & info necessary to prevent *(See Chapter 2)*;

SJC 3:07, 1.3—(Zealous within Bounds of Law); 1.2(a) shall seek client's lawful objectives; 1.6(b)(3) if receive info clearly establishing fraud, must get D to rectify, or must reveal unless privileged; 3.3(a)(4) shall not knowingly use perjured testimony & if learn of it late, must take reasonable remedial measures; 3.3(e) if client intends to testify falsely, strongly discourage, advise unlawful, etc; don't accept representation if know this in advance, seek to withdraw from representation if discover it before trial; if discovery only during trial, needn't move to withdraw if reasonably believe D will be prejudiced, but call upon D to rectify; if D refuses, lawyer shall not reveal false testimony to tribunal; lawyer NOT to examine D in such a manner as to elicit testimony lawyer knows to be false & lawyer not to argue probative value of the false testimony thereafter, e.g., in closing or on appeal; 8.4 (c-d) no dishonesty, deceit, misrepresent, conduct prejudicial to administration of justice;

G.L. c. 268, §§ 1–3—perjury: "suborn" & "procure";

C v Kelly **33 MAC 934 (92)**—lying re: price of car not material;

Nix v Whiteside **475 US 157 (86)**—not "ineffective" to threaten withdraw or disclose intended, **"known" D perjury**; ethical standards = up to each state, but even Code mandates disclosure [but see concurrers];

C v Mitchell **438 M 535 (2003)**—Mass. R. Professional Conduct 3.3(e) (98) governs conduct of lawyer who learns that D intends to commit perjury (must try to dissuade, may not ask questions which would elicit perjury if D testifies, and may not argue probative value of false testimony in closing, ***BUT*** lawyer can't invoke this rule just because D has told inconsistent stories re: event, or because lawyer thinks D may be lying because of the

Commonwealth's proof; lawyer must have firm basis in objective fact to believe D intends to commit perjury; SJC held that such basis here existed, and that it was acceptable procedure for D-counsel to raise matter at bench conference with ADA and judge (maybe error to not have D present, but purportedly no prejudice shown!), and thereafter to merely have D testify in narrative form and not argue testimony content to jury; "discretionary" with trial judge whether to have colloquy with D;

In Matter of Neitlich **413 M 416, 423 (92)**—attorney must be truthful to court & opposing counsel, & where this duty "is in seeming conflict with the client's interest in zealous representation, the latter's interest must yield";

C v John Doe—[SJC #85-302 (Wilkins 10/3/85)] permit counsel who knows of intended perjury to withdraw; if not possible, normal direct examination probably necessary; but dubious re: argue it??; *(See Chapter 2, Standards/Ethics)*; see now SJC Rule 3:07, 3.3(e) lawyer "shall not" argue in closing or other proceedings, including appeals, the probative value of client testimony known to be false;

C v Wilson **381 M 90 n.59 (80)**—"ethics" difficulty of client's false testimony discussed without solution;

Johns v Smyth **176 F.Supp 949 (E.D.Va. '59)**—failure to argue D's case suggested counsel disbelieved it;

Lowery v Cardwell **575 F.2d 727 (9th Cir. '78)**—withdrawal motion after testimony violates due process because suggests disbelief to judge in jury-waived trial; see also id., Hufstedler, J., concurring ("No matter how commendable may have been counsel's motives, his interest in saving himself from potential violation of the canons was adverse to his client, and the end product was his abandonment of a diligent defense");

C v Sarvela **16 MAC 934 (83)**—D counsel's argument implied disbelief of D's testimony; counsel became juror, not advocate, and opposed client; conviction reversed (citing *Lowery*);

C v Cutty **47 MAC 671 (99)**—when (as sanction for reciprocal discovery violation) judge barred D counsel from arguing D's alibi (testified to by D at trial), jury would have inferred that counsel didn't believe D: reversal (citing Sarvela);

10-E. REDIRECT EXAMINATION

See Chapter 12-H, re: Reopening/Rebuttal;

CPCS P/G 6.7(k)—should conduct redirect as appropriate;

Brodin, M. and Avery, M., *Handbook of Massachusetts Evidence* **(8th ed. 2007)**—though scope of redirect = within discretion of judge, redirect examination to explain testimony on cross is "treated as a matter of right," citing, inter alia, *C v Helfant* **398 M 214, 222 (86)** (D had right to explain why he lied to police) & *C v Smith* **329 M 477 (52)** (refusal of judge to permit alibi witness to explain apparently contradictory statements made during direct and cross-examination prejudicial error); judge has discretion to allow redirect re: matters not addressed in cross-examination;

Young, Pollets & Poreda, *Evidence,* **§ 611.3 (2d ed. 1998)** to explain, modify, correct cross-examination; but judge's discretion; § 244, rehabilitate, including character for veracity; § 801.2 prior consistent statement to rebut recent contrivance *(See Chapter 9-F, Chapter 11-F)*;

C v Klosek **262 M 416 (28)**—to explain, modify, correct cross-examination answers;

C v Caine **366 M 366 (74)**—e.g., rehabilitate with prior consistent; but judge has discretion to permit beyond scope of cross-examination;

C v Charles **47 MAC 191, 192–93 (99)**—after DA's cross insinuated that D was lying because she had omitted from her statement to police the purported facts most supportive of her self-defense claim, she was entitled to explain on redirect that she had omitted the matter because cop's statement to her had led her to believe that she had had no need to exculpate herself (so her failure to do so was not "inconsistent" with her trial testimony);

C v Emence **47 MAC 299 (99)**—even before DA sought to cast doubt on defense witness's memory, defense was entitled (on direct) to elicit that witness remembered event because he had been required to stay at work four hours after shift ended in order to finish repairs to alleged victim's vehicle; though admissibility wasn't dependent upon the DA's attack on the witness's credibility, such an attack on cross subsequently was "fundamentally unfair" as a manipulation of the absence of evidence the DA had succeeded in excluding during direct; evidence was all the more relevant and "independently admissible" for purpose of rehabilitation during redirect;

C v Fatalo **345 M 85 (62)**—proper to explain cross-examination, e.g., unavailability of witnesses;

C v Sylvester **388 M 749 (83)**—(same) & limiting instruction later no substitute;

C v Holliday **450 M 794 (2008)**—after defense counsel properly tried to discredit witnesses who only recently came forward, suggesting rewards from recent cooperation with prosecution or who did not initially inculpate D, witnesses in redirect permissibly explained their fear of retaliation;

C v Mandeville **386 M 393 (82)**—can use previously excluded hearsay to explain motives that were questioned on cross-examination;

C v Haraldstad **16 MAC 565 (83)**—D could've clarified confusion from direct though not cross-examined on it by DA;

C v Rodriguez **75 MAC 235 (2009)**—carelessness/ "oversight" caused ADA to omit from cop's direct examination the requisite "school zone" measurement evidence, but no bar to eliciting on redirect examination of witness;

citing *C v Hoffer* 375 M 369 (78)—redirect exam may exceed scope of cross, trial judge having discretion to permit or limit questioning;

C v Hanlon 44 MAC 810, 823 (98)—after Commonwealth introduced "typed statement" of D (portions of D's testimony given at his first trial, read to jury by a trooper), D was not entitled to introduce rest of testimony; could only intro portions of statement which related to and explained sections read by trooper (none identified, no error);

Geders v US 425 US 80 (76)—can't bar D-attorney consult during post-direct overnight recess; other ways to prevent coaching, e.g., delay a recess;

Perry v Leeke 488 US 272 (89)—BUT can forbid consultation in 15-minute recess after D's direct testimony (no violation of 6th Amendment right to counsel);

10-F. CHARACTER EVIDENCE BY REPUTATION

See Prior Bad Acts in Chapter 11-E; & Chapter 16-D, Self-Defense;

CPCS P/G; 6.7(d)—consider use, preparation (especially for cross-examination), & risks of character witnesses;

G.L. c. 233, § 21A—evidence of reputation in work/ business community (as well as home) = admissible;

Brodin, M. and Avery, M., *Handbook of Massachusetts Evidence* **(8th ed. 2007)**—composite opinion of those likely to have assimilated a representative sample of D's conduct;

C v Edgerly 13 MAC 562 (82)—prove character by reputation, not opinion;

C v Walker 442 M 185, 197–99 (2004)—declining to adopt Proposed Mass. R. Evid. 405(a), which would have permitted character witnesses to testify not only about D's reputation in community, but also about their own opinions of D's character;

C v United Food 374 M 765 (78)—reputation, not event/statement/opinion; "Have you heard general reputation . . . ?" better than "Do you know reputation . . . ?";

Wetherbee v Norris 103 M 565 (1870)—must ask "Do you know X's reputation . . . ?" before "What is X's reputation . . . ?"; (see *Belton* 352 M 263 (67), *Montanino* 27 MAC 130 (89), post];

C v Gomes 11 MAC 933 (81)—5 anonymous talkers without context not "community";

C v LaPierre 10 MAC 871 (80)—cook and 2 waitresses not "community";

C v Belton 352 M 263 (67)—one talk with 3 of D's co-workers not "general reputation"; "Do you know reputation . . . ?" not enough foundation;

Edgington v US 164 US 361 (1896)—D's truth & veracity admissible re: guilt (for filing false claim);

C v Beal 314 M 210 (43)—"honesty & integrity," but not "truth & veracity," admissible re: guilt;

C v Leonard 140 M 473 (1886)—e.g., "honesty" re: receiving stolen property case; weight's up to jury, but character evidence can be reasonable doubt *(See Chapter 12-I, requests for instructions)*;

C v Sheline 391 M 279 (84)—truth character not material unless attacked; D's prior inconsistent not enough (but see concurrers at 298, footnotes);

C v Schmukler 22 MAC 432 (86)—after cross-examination of D, truth & veracity reputation admissible if foundation; jury instruction, too;

C v Simmons 383 M 40 (81)—judge's discretion re: instructing jury; & on complaining witness's reputation for violence, too;

C v Dilone 385 M 281 (82)—alleged victim's violent reputation re: self-defense; *(See Chapter 16, Defenses, but chiefly C v Adjutant* 443 M 649 (2005)—**specific incidents of "victim's" violent aggression admissible, in judge's discretion, regardless of whether D knew of them**);

C v Benoit 452 M 212 (2008)—although "self-defense" instruction was legitimately refused (because D could have retreated), judge did instruct on voluntary manslaughter: D argued logical extension of *Adjutant*, i.e., prior violent acts by deceased argued to be admissible in context of whether he initiated sudden and violent combat which would cause reasonable person to be provoked to heat of passion; because of newness of *Adjutant* rule and lack of opportunity to examine its impact, SJC "not prepared to extend the rule *at this time*", but reversed conviction on different ground; Ireland, J., believed "court should have undertaken a full analysis of the merits of extending the *Adjutant* rule to this case, instead of dismissing it as premature":

C v Marler 11 MAC 1014 (81)—complaining witness's reputation inadmissible unless D knew it; limits to cross-examination of D's character witness re: D's unrelated bad acts;

Michelson v US 335 US 469 (48)—DA can't use D's bad character in case chief; but can rebut or cross-examine D's character witness re: impact on his opinion of D's 27-year-old arrest (without conviction);

C v Montanino 27 MAC 130 (89)—MA permits cross-examination of D's character witnesses (re: D not type to molest boys) on rumors, other acts contradicting them; close question;

BUT see cases, Chapter 11-A (Evidence & Objections, General), e.g., *C v Christian* 430 M 552, 559–64 (2000)—**ERROR to ask long series of "questions", each answered in the negative, asserting that witness (here, D) "told" 3d party various things; while one such question OK if cross-examiner has basis in fact for asking,** good faith basis probably lacking here, since D-counsel alerted all that 3d party was an inmate fabricating info in several pending cases, presumably to obtain a favorable disposition of his own charges; judge should bar additional questions, order voir dire of 3d party, or seek assurance from prosecutor that 3d party would testify; "[t]o do otherwise would permit [DA] to smear [D] by extrajudicial statements made by [3d party] while denying [D] opportunity to impeach [3d party's] credibility";

C v Brown **411 M 115 (91):** *Montanino (I)* **27 MAC 130, approved**—prosecutor had right to cross-examine character witness on D's reputation for unrelated falsehoods;

C v Arthur **31 MAC 178 (91)**—D had right to show that sexual assault complainant had reputation for lying & exaggerating in school community;

C v Avalos **454 M 1 (2009)**—that complainant wrote in a diary, among other things, that she "needed to forgive herself for keeping so many secrets, and lying" was not admissible to impeach her credibility concerning D's alleged sexual abuse of her; evidence of particular bad acts of untruthfulness is inadmissible for impeachment;

Young, Pollets & Poreda, *Evidence,* **§ 404.2 (2d ed. 1998)**—no Mass. cases (yet) on extent of cross-examination of character witness; judge should prevent misuse, random shots, innuendo;

McCormick, *Evidence,* **§ 191 (5th ed. 1999)**—cross-examination of character witness replete with possibilities for prejudice; judge must weigh probative vs. prejudice; voir dire = advisable;

C v O'Brien **119 M 342 (1876)**—though can cross-examine character witness re: knowledge of facts testing credibility, no independent evidence of unrelated bad acts is admissible;

C v Piedra **20 MAC 155 (85)**—caution re: cross-examination about knowing 11-year-old bad act;

C v Kamishlian **21 MAC 931 (85)**—bad cross-examination (of veracity witness) re: unrelated violence; but no reversal because objections sustained;

G.L. c. 233, § 21B—"rape shield" law: complaining witness's reputation (prior sex) inadmissible in sex case *(See Chapter 11-H, Evidence: Sex Offense Charges)*;

Chapter 11
EVIDENCE AND OBJECTIONS

11-A. GENERAL

See also, Chapter 9, Cross-Examination; Chapter 10, Defense Evidence; Chapter 2, Standards & Ethics: Zeal, Contempt, etc.; & Trial; Chapter 12, The Overbearing Judge;

U.S. Constitution, Sixth Amendment; Mass. Declaration of Rights, Articles 11 & 12;

Washington v Texas **388 US 14 (67)**—constitutional right to compulsory process;

US v Nixon **418 US 683 (74)**—integrity of system depends on full disclosure of facts *(Chapter 6-D)* & compulsory process *(Chapter 7-B)*;

Chambers v Mississippi **410 US 284 (73)**—don't defeat ends of justice with mechanistic rules; [3d party confession = admissible though hearsay] *(Chapter 11-F)*;

Holmes v South Carolina **547 US 319 (2006)**—authority

of state and federal evidentiary rules is subject to limitations commanded in Constitution; D has right to introduce evidence of 3rd party's culpability for crime, though there must be such proof of connection "as tends clearly to point out such other person as the guilty party"; can't exclude defense evidence simply because prosecution claims evidence of D's guilt is compelling;

C v Joyce **382 M 222 (81)**—if relevant to "bias," "rape shield" statute does not preclude evidence of prior sexual conduct;

C v Bohannon **376 M 90 (78)**—complaining witness's prior false rape claim relevant to credibility];

C v 2 Juveniles **397 M 261 (86)**—D must show "legitimate need" to see confidential communication under

G.L. c. 233, § 20J before judge must review (in camera); Constitutional rights override rules and statutes;

C v Sugrue **35 MAC 172, 175–78 (93), citing, e.g.,** *Davis v Alaska* **415 US 308 (74)**—constitutional rights override evidentiary statutes/privileges/"disqualifications";

CPCS P/G's 6.1(c)—be fully informed of evidentiary rules & anticipate/prepare issues; (d) if helpful, seek advance rulings & prepare motions/memos.; (e) alert & preserve issues [objections/proffers/recordation]; 6.6 (b) analyze all potential DA evidence for problems; 6.7(g)–(j) same for your evidence, direct follows rules, re-phrase or offer/proof if excluded, guard vs. improper cross-examination;

Sussman v C **374 M 692 (78)**—not summary contempt for 2d (excluded/rephrased) cross-examination question because not flagrant, insufficient warnings, no contemptuous intent, & can't chill vigorous advocacy;

C v Segal **401 M 95 (87)**—not contempt for pressing objection; can't chill vigorous but respectful advocacy; *(See Chapter 2, Ethics)*;

Allen v Snow **635 F.2d 12 (1st Cir. '80)**—"trying a case is not a parlor game"; attorney may have to take chance & rely on appeal; [judge's "disapproval" of juror investigations wasn't order to desist, so no error];

ABA Standards for Criminal Justice, Prosecution Function & Defense Function (3d ed. 1993) 4-1.2, Commentary—"advocacy isn't for the timid/meek/retiring"; "our system of justice is inherently contentious, . . . and it demands that the lawyer be inclined toward vigorous advocacy. Nor can a lawyer be half-hearted in the application of his or her energies to a case"; *(See Chapter 11-C, Record Protection; Chapter, 12-D, Overbearing Judges)*;

C v Kennedy **3 MAC 218 (75)**—can exclude cross-examination questions because of form; & anyway, counsel abandoned the questions "voluntarily, though in frustration";

C v Britto **433 M 596 (2001)**—juror questioning of witnesses upheld, despite chaos, lack of legislative study/approval; recommended procedures set forth;

C v Cook **380 M 314 (80)**—ineffective not to object (co-D took stand & claimed 5th Amendment privilege);

C v Frisino **21 MAC 551 (86)**—ineffective counsel (didn't object, ask limiting instruction);

Wainwright v Sykes **433 US 72 (77)**—no timely objection (re: suppress statement), so no federal habeas relief;

C v Squailia **429 M 101, 103–4 (99)**—never fail to examine exhibits (here, briefcase contained personal papers extremely prejudicial to D and probative of nothing at issue);

See Chapter 9-A & Chapter 11-F re: questions assuming fact not in evidence, e.g., C v LaFaille 430 M 44 (99) DA asked if witness knew that D and another were cousins (no), and they were not, in fact: no relief because DA had reasonable basis for asking the question (no bad faith) & jury instruction ("no evidence of that whatsoever");

C v Francis **432 M 353 (2000)**—error to allow ADA to cross-examine D (at trial for accessory before fact) concerning self-incriminating claims attributed to him in out-of-court statements to police by alleged principal: good faith basis to believe D made such statements couldn't be supplied by the statements, because they had been excluded from evidence (though improperly preserved & SJC held no prejudice in circumstances);

C v Christian **430 M 552, 559–64 (2000)**—ERROR to ask long series of "questions", each answered in the negative, asserting that witness (here, D) "told" 3d party various things; while one such question OK if cross-examiner has basis in fact for asking, good faith basis probably lacking here, since D-counsel alerted all that 3d party was an inmate fabricating info in several pending cases, presumably to obtain a favorable disposition of his own charges; judge should bar additional questions, order voir dire of 3d party, or seek assurance from prosecutor that 3d party would testify; "[t]o do otherwise would permit [DA] to smear [D] by extrajudicial statements made by [3d party] while denying [D] opportunity to impeach [3d party's] credibility";

C v Wynter **55 MAC 337 (2002)**—reversal for cross-examination insinuations without evidence;

C v Ridge **455 M 307 (2009)**—prosecutor's leading questions containing witness's grand jury testimony as purported fact were not endorsed by witness, but no error because trial judge believed prosecutor's affidavit that he did not know that witness intended to claim no memory of prior testimony or that she intended to claim that the grand jury testimony was the result of "prompting by the police rather than her independent memory";

C v Supplee **45 MAC 265, 268 (98)**—D sought unsuccessfully to impeach a Commonwealth witness, who testified that she saw X wielding a club but did not see X strike V, by introducing X's guilty plea to manslaughter; Appeals Court held judge had discretion to exclude because D didn't offer the evidence while the witness to be impeached was still on the stand; judge can permit "use of someone else's conviction in cross-examination to test the accuracy of a witness's perception";]

C v Benoit **32 MAC 111 (92)**—though DA asserted that D's brother had previously told others that D confessed to him, DA also advised that the brother would testify now that he never had any conversation with D; ERROR to introduce this testimony (in effect, that witness had no evidence to offer) for sole purpose of "impeaching" it (with info that would undoubtedly be used substantively, despite "limiting" instruction that there was thus no testimony before jury);

C v Butler **445 M 568 (2005)**—when alleged victim was called to testify despite Commonwealth's advance knowledge that she would deny that D had hurt her & say she had lied to police when she alleged he had, evidence of D's prior bad acts/restraining orders against him were admissible to show "hostile nature of the relationship between" D and alleged victim, even though such evidence was purportedly inadmissible "to show a pattern or course of conduct by the defendant";

C v McAfee **430 M 483 (99)**—embracing logic and holding of *Benoit* **32 MAC 111 (92)**;

C v Raposa **440 M 684, 692–93 (2004)**—though witness had told police that he had seen victim after alleged time of death, witness at trial voir dire said he hadn't; D not allowed to call witness, who could offer no relevant testimony, solely for purpose of being impeached by prior inconsistent statement that was otherwise inadmissible;

C v Kane **388 M 128 (83)**—DA can call priest who said he'd keep privilege because reasonable to assume he'd cave in to judge;

C v Stewart **454 M 527 (2009)**—Commonwealth brought witness to court (incarcerated for unrelated matter), & informed judge he would claim privilege; appointed attorney determined witness had no such privilege & judge so informed witness; in jury's presence witness ignored clerk's recitation of oath; outside jury's presence, judge ordered witness to testify but he refused; because he was serving life sentence, judge stated it was futile to hold him in contempt, and allowed ADA to treat him as hostile witness; still without being sworn, witness took stand & to most of DA's leading questions (containing prosecution's entire theory of murder) answered "no comment": REVERSAL of first degree murder conviction because all testimony should have been barred; judge was not permitted to waive requirement of oath, and leading questions "were effectively transformed into evidence" without opportunity for cross-examination;

C v Melo **67 MAC 71 (2006)**—though pretrial filing by D suggested that witness would recant statement that D was driving car at relevant time, witness had other testimony useful to Commonwealth's case (that she owned car, and that she was D's sister); "Benoit rule applies where the Commonwealth knows its witness will provide nothing of value"; when witness testified that D wasn't driving car, Commonwealth could introduce her prior inconsistent statement for impeachment;

Douglas v Alabama **380 US 415 (65)**—denied confrontation to call co-D who took 5th Amendment, & then read his confession implicating D;

C v Cook **380 M 314 (80)**—ineffective not to object to co-D taking stand and invoking 5th Amendment;

C v Hesketh **386 M 153 (82)**—witness taking 5th Amendment shouldn't be before jury, but discretionary where no big harm;

C v Nadile **10 MAC 913 (80)**—same;

C v DiPietro **373 M 369 (77)**—DA can call wife expecting marital disqualification (i.e., unavailable) before using prior testimony; (& this is a cheap shot, circumventing the rule)

See Chapter 11-J, Privileges;

SJC Rule 3:07, 3.4—shan't knowingly violate a rule of the tribunal, or allude to matter without reasonable belief relevant/admitted; 3.8 prosecutor in criminal case shall make timely disclosure to defense of all evidence/info tending to negate or mitigate guilt; shall refrain from making extrajudicial comments having likelihood of "heightening public condemnation of" D; shan't assert personal knowledge of facts in issue, except if testifying as witness,

shan't assert personal opinion as to justness of cause, credibility of a witness, or guilt/innocence of D; shan't intentionally avoid pursuit of evidence because believe will damage prosecution case or aid D;

Young, Pollets & Poreda, *Evidence* **(2d ed. 1998), and Young, Pollets & Poreda,** *Massachusetts Evidentiary Standards: 2002 Edition, A Courtroom Reference* **(West 2002)**—both in format of the Prop.M.R.Evid.;

Brodin, M. and Avery, M., *Handbook of Massachusetts Evidence* **(8th ed. 2007)**—handy & authoritative, admirable "state court" focus, historically recognized as "the Bible" of MA. evidence, prior to and during the late Justice Liacos's tenure as Chief Justice, Supreme Judicial Court;

Prop.M.R.Evid. (1980)—not adopted as a body by SJC, but citation/reference invited [see Liacos, preface to '85 supplement]; 101: rules apply to all proceedings, EXCEPT grand jury, sentencing, probation, bail, & R-104; 104: preliminary questions on admissibility not bound by rules, EXCEPT privilege, conspiracy, & motions to suppress; Wigmore on Evidence (vols. 1–9, various current dates): **excellent** detailed theoretical & historical discussions; McCormick, Evidence (5th ed. 1999), two volume treatise + 2001 cumulative supplement - good overviews;

Imwinkelried, EJ & Blinka, DD, *Criminal Evidentiary Foundations* **(Lexis 1997);**

Burns v Commonwealth **430 M 444, 450–51 (99)**—"prima facie evidence" explained: it "compels" conclusion that evidence is true "until its effect is overcome by other evidence"; when evidence is introduced that contradicts prima facie evidence the prima facie evidence "loses its artificial force and a factual issue arises; *C v Maloney* **447 M 577 (2006)**—"Melanie's Law," concerning OUI prosecutions, allows court record of prior convictions, accompanied by other documentation, to be prima facie evidence of prior convictions; *C v Koney* [421 M 295, 302] holding must be read into even this new statute (mere identity of name isn't enough to establish even prima facie case);

C v Kappler **416 M 574, 591 (93)**—(O'Connor, J., dissenting opinion) collected cases: jury's non-acceptance of uncontroverted testimony does not warrant finding that opposite of testimony is true; if Commonwealth has burden & presents no evidence & D presents evidence favorable to D, prosecution can't prevail;

C v Miller **435 M 274 (2001)**—felony murder (aggravated rape, death by stabbing) conviction upheld, rejecting D's argument that mere disbelief of his statement that intercourse was consensual not proof to the contrary; evidence included testimony from murder V's neighbor that she heard woman crying out "Don't, don't, no", followed by a loud bang & silence + significant injuries to V's head, neck, anal, vaginal & groin areas;

Prop.M.R.Evid. 602—"witness may not testify to a matter unless evidence is introduced sufficient to support a finding that he has personal knowledge of the matter";

C v Almeida **433 M 717, 719 (2001)**—"sleep talk" of sexual assault complainant inadmissible; "common sense dictates that while asleep, one cannot distinguish between reality and fiction, a touchstone of admissibility";

C v Wilson **49 MAC 429, 433 (2000)**—error to allow witness to testify "why" her mother, the alleged victim, returned to the marital residence after allegedly being battered there by D; explanation was different from that of alleged victim (didn't "corroborate"), & no personal knowledge anyway;

C v Solomonsen **50 MAC 122 (2000)**—though witness can't say what another individual "meant" by words, here witness couldn't remember "exact words," & didn't understand judge's direction to him to testify to their "substance," so direction to "tell us what the meaning of what [D] said was . . . if you don't remember the exact words" was OK; judge didn't "use the word 'meaning' in the sense of interpretation";

C v DiFonzo **31 MAC 921 (91)**—judge has considerable discretion as to degree to which chalks can be used, even though jury generally permitted to considered exhibits formally admitted into evidence;

C v Manning **47 MAC 923 (99)**—when judge has discretion to admit/exclude evidence, it's reversible error not to exercise it, in belief that there is no discretion;

C v McFarland **15 MAC 948 (83)**—same;

Welch v Keene Corp. **31 MAC 157 (91)**—charts summarizing voluminous evidence admissible if accurately reflective of underlying documents & useful as demonstrative aid; judge properly instructed that charts not in evidence; video of experiments admissible within judge's discretion so long as experimental conditions substantially similar to conditions giving rise to litigation;

C v Lawson **425 M 528 (97)**—when, after Commonwealth witness testified to physical layout of a building rooftop and defense investigator made videotape to introduce as impeachment, no error in barring its admission because of failure to proffer it as fair and accurate representation of premises **at the relevant** time," i.e., about 18 months earlier;

C v Poggi **53 MAC 685 (2002)**—reversal for failure to allow D to proffer his tattooed arm to the jury, where five witnesses to robbery testified that culprit wore short sleeved shirt, but no witness professed to have seen tattoos; display would have been "demonstrative," rather than "testimonial," so not properly barred because D wasn't taking stand/wasn't submitting to cross-examination; enough "foundation" because both a defense witness and medical records provided evidence that the tattoos pre-

dated robbery; at a minimum, judge should have held voir dire to determine adequacy of the foundation;

C v Colon **33 MAC 304 (92)**—weak links in chain of custody go to weight not admissibility;

C v Penta **423 M 546 (96)**—same;

C v Jordan **50 MAC 369 (2000)**—on appeal, but not at trial, D argued failure of authentication of bullet [only inferably] taken from D's chest during elective surgery six months after criminal incident at issue, i.e., cop went to hospital when called, & a nurse on the operating floor gave him the bullet; any question went to weight of evidence; failure to object thought to be 'tactical,' because D's closing argued only 'speculative' that bullet came from D's chest (& if he'd objected at trial, prosecution could easily summon doctor or nurse nearby to supply the connection);

US v Ladd **885 F.2d 954 (1st Cir. '89)**—blood sample inadmissible because of unexplained 1-digit discrepancy in identification number;

C v Lenahan **50 MAC 180 (2000)**—in trial of D for soliciting "hit man" [undercover cop] to murder his wife, Commonwealth introduced photocopy of a restaurant's paper place mat on which D had written description of wife, her place of work, car, and alleged boyfriend, but D objected because not "best evidence," i.e., original mat; because it wasn't the "contents of the documents" which was to be proved here [but instead the fact that D had made the writings], "best evidence" didn't apply, & anyway good reason was shown for absence of original (simply that it "could not be found" after it had been introduced at a hearing on bail prior to trial);

C v McKay **67 MAC 396 (2006)**—testimony concerning content of taped voice mail message (not preserved for trial) was not barred by "best evidence" rule, which doesn't apply to tape recordings;

11-A.1. Judicial Notice

C v O'Brien **423 M 841 (96)**—judge who presided at earlier bail hearing could not rely on testimony given there to determine, at later transfer hearing, that juvenile was amenable to rehabilitation; testimony was not proper subject for judicial notice; reliance on non-record evidence "implicates fundamental fairness";

C v Rushin **56 MAC 515 (2002)**—judge can't take judicial notice of a city ordinance in the trial of a case, but can do so at hearing of motion to suppress, so that witness's testimony about it (purportedly city ordinance against public drinking) sufficed in lieu of introduction of actual ordinance itself;

11-B. MOTIONS IN LIMINE

K. Smith, *Criminal Practice & Procedure*, § 1454 (2d ed. 1983 & 2002 Supp.)—seek early ruling; either side may move in limine; not for DA to choke off defense OR as discovery device;

C v Mercado **452 M 662, 669 n. 11 (2008)**—motion in limine was discussed and ruled upon in an unrecorded conference: "We are impeded in our analysis of the case by the absence of the discussion that occurred in the unrecorded conference, and we emphasize again the importance of recording all conferences";

C v Ranieri **65 MAC 366 (2006)**—refusing to find error in judge's deferral of decision on D's motion in limine until after D's expert testified, though deferral caused D-counsel to forego calling expert because adverse ruling on motion in limine would entail introduction of evidence of D's prior like crimes, through the expert's "notes"; court refused to treat issue as one of "excluding" D's evidence, instead calling choice to forego witness a "reasonable tactical decision" in light of possible adverse consequence;

G.L. c. 233, § 23B—sample motion in limine; *See also Chapter 6, Pretrial Motions;*

C v Beauchemin **410 M 181 (91)**—judge's voir dire of proper defense witnesses improperly gave prosecutor "untoward discovery";

C v O'Malley **14 MAC 314 (82)**—shouldn't use pretrial DA's motion in limine to test sufficiency of D's evidence to raise (necessity) defense; motion in limine needs narrow focus on particular evidence; not a device for DA to get extra discovery; [comments, without specifics, that DA's motion didn't comply with Rule 13(a)]

C v Lopez **383 M 497, n.2 (81)**—motion in limine prevents irrelevant, inadmissible & prejudicial from being admitted; judge's discretion re: DA's motion in limine excluding evidence of D's prior 3 NG's on related complaints;

C v Diaz **383 M 73, 81 (81)**—prefer early ruling on D's motion in limine re: impeachment by prior conviction(s); *See Chapter 10, Defense Evidence;*

C v Barber **14 MAC 1008 (82)**—though prefer early ruling, not required, especially if motion in limine = midtrial & raises novel issues likely affected by later testimony;

C v Gonzalez **22 MAC 274, n.9 (86)**—prefer early ruling, but judge needs enough info for meaningful discretion; judge's discretion to alter previous motion in limine ruling if no prejudice;

C v Scullin **44 MAC 9, 14–15 (97)**—while motion in limine ruling might be deferred properly, judge must keep jury from being exposed to the questionable evidence before a decision on admissibility is made; failure to do so "might well" be basis for reversal;

C v Lavin **42 MAC 711 (97)**—motion in limine withdrawn by D when DA agreed not to introduce certain evidence; conviction reversed when DA/cop witness violated agreement;

C v Felton **16 MAC 63 (83)**—reverse because D.A. breached promise not to impeach D with prior conviction; but contrast *C v Saunders* **45 MAC 340 (98)** D counsel did not file motion in limine because DA agreed only not to intro certain evidence in case in chief (and said that he would advise court before attempting intro at all), but defense witness opened door for cross-examination; no relief despite failure to advise court beforehand BUT no argument that defense would not have called witness had it known evidence would be introduced;

C v Goldman **395 M 495 (85)**—motion in limine & in camera hearing re: counsel's conflict & attorney-client privilege (re: witness who's a past client);

C v Silva **455 M 503 (2009)**—D having alleged that trial counsel was ineffective for telling him he had to testify and for failing to prepare him for direct and cross-examination, D's motion to strike counsel's responsive affidavit was properly denied: attorney-client privilege "must be deemed waived, in part, to permit counsel to disclose only those confidences necessary and relevant to the defense of the charge of ineffective assistance of counsel"; motion judge's review found affidavit disclosed no more than was necessary to the issue;

C v Hood **389 M 581 (83)**—best await D's case before ruling on sufficiency of evidence to raise defense; no harm here from judge's pretrial ruling that D didn't raise competing harms defense because insufficient evidence;

C v Lloyd **45 MAC 931 (98)**—when D was prohibited from questioning complainant re: Prozac use (because no relevance without foundation that it affected perception or memory), no error in also refusing voir dire of witness (since expert testimony necessary for foundation): "incautious use of the voir dire" leads to "problems" and the grant of "untoward discovery" to one party;

C v Brogan **415 M 169 (93)**—(Liacos, CJ, concurring) similar (noting **jury** trial right, and concept of jury nullification);

C v Shea **401 M 731, 740 (88)**—"filing motion in limine doesn't by itself preserve [appellate] rights";

C v Oeun Lam **420 M 615, 617 n.5 (95)**—(same);

C v Walker **401 M 338 (87)**—trial objection after motion in limine denied, so review standard = abuse discretion, not miscarriage of justice; but see *C v Kozec* **21 MAC 355, 362 n.4 (86), S.C., 399 M 514 (87)** denial of D's pretrial motion in limine (re: evidence of D's jello wrestling) & D's objection (then) saved D's rights though evidence admitted later without 2d objection; [SJC reversed conviction for bad DA closing,, but didn't discuss motion in limine (399 M at 525)]; cf. 1 Wigmore, Evidence (Tillers rev. 1983) § 18, at pp. 801–07: judge's discretion whether to entertain motion in limine; if motion in limine denied, may have to reiterate objection at trial;

C v Spencer **53 MAC 45, 51 (2001)**—D's motion in limine inadequate to preserve issue of admissibility of what prostitute purportedly said to cops about D being heroin dealer she could "deliver" to them if they would not arrest her for prostitution;

C v Lonardo **74 MAC 566 (2009)**—D's motion in limine to bar "expert" testimony that everyone "on the street" who dealt with "runners" knew that vehicle 'accident' cases they brought to attorneys were "staged"/fraudulent did not preserve issue without "contemporaneous objection to the testimony";

C v Beausoleil **397 M 206, n.2 (86)**—motion in limine may merit interlocutory appeal (G.L. c. 211, § 3?);

C v Yelle **390 M 678 (84)**—no interlocutory for DA on evidentiary rulings *(See Chapter 15)*;

C v Gabbidon **398 M 1, 7 (86)**; *C v Boyer* **400 M 52, 57 (87)**—though motion in limine filed and denied, IF D DOESN'T OBJECT WHEN DA INTRODUCES EVIDENCE, D WAIVES right to appellate review;

C v Good **409 M 612 at n.6 (92)**—to preserve issue for appeal, D must object after admission of evidence, even though motion in limine had been pressed & denied;

C v Maylott **43 MAC 516 (97)**—same;

C v Ortiz-Soto **49 MAC 645, 647 (2000)**—same (re: evidence of D's presence in drug apartment 10 days before transaction at issue);

C v Diaz **49 MAC 587, 588 & n.2 (2000)**—failure to object to admission of D's prior convictions and/or to the instruction concerning their use (erroneous, independently, in that it allowed use "to prove intent to distribute" rather than just 'lack of credibility'), though motion in limine had been pressed and denied = waiver of the issue;

C v Roberts **433 Mass. 45 (2000)**—if motion in limine is denied, D should not only object when the evidence is later admitted at trial, BUT SHOULD ALSO THEN REQUEST INSTRUCTION LIMITING ITS USE, IF NECESSARY (charge conference request for limiting instruction comes too late, because offering party will have relied on its use for all purposes);

C v Gillette **33 MAC 427 (92)**—counsel's failure to move in limine to exclude inadmissible evidence of D's predisposition to rape was ineffective assistance;

C v Scullin **44 MAC 9 (97)**—ineffective counsel in failure to object to inadmissible "fresh complaint" concerning extraneous bad act (assault);

11-C. OBJECTION, MOTION TO STRIKE, OFFER OF PROOF, AND RECORD PROTECTION

See also Chapter 19, Mistrials & Chapters 5-E, 12-M, & 15 re: preserving/waiving issues;

CPCS P/G 6.7(i)—rephrase q. or make offer/proof if appropriate; 6.1(e) preserve all evidentiary issues;

District Court Special Rule 211(A)(3)—COUNSEL's responsible for assisting in the creation of an audible record (i.e., speak w/clarity and close to microphones, ask judge to tell others to do so);(A)(4) if case is being appealed, may make motion (can be brought ex parte) to preserve original recording for a longer period; originals of trials, evidentiary hearings, guilty pleas or admissions to sufficient facts, and hearings in care and protection cases, are to be preserved for at least two and one-half years without such motion; (B)(1) covert recordings forbidden;

C v Whyte **43 MAC 920 (97)**—failure to object to inadmissible hearsay (whose exclusion would have resulted in required finding of not guilty) was ineffective assistance of counsel;

Nadworny v Fair **685 F.Supp 20 (D.Mass. '88)**—no exhaustion for federal relief unless federal law cited "squarely" *(See Chapter 15)*;

M.R.Crim.P. 22—OBJECTIONS; no more "exceptions"; make known action desired or objected to; "**may state precise legal grounds of objection, but shall not argue or further discuss grounds unless court [asks]**";

K. Smith, *Criminal Practice and Procedure*, **§ 1778 (2d ed. 1983 & Supp.)**—re: Rule 22;

Superior Court Rule 8—(same as M.R.Crim.P. 22); contrast Prop.M.R.Evid. 103 - objections; offers of proof: error in evidentiary rulings not preserved for appellate review unless there's objection or motion to strike, **with specific ground of objection**, plus, if evidence was excluded, substance of evidence had to be made known to court by offer or be apparent from questions' context; in criminal cases, error may be noticed without preservation if 'substantial risk of a miscarriage of justice'; e.g., *Estelle v Williams* **425 US 501(76)** OK to try D in jail garb if no objection;

SJC Rule 3:07, 3.3—attorney can't knowingly make false statement of law to tribunal , or fail to disclose material fact to tribunal *(See Chapter 2, Standards)*;

Brodin, M. and Avery, M., *Handbook of Massachusetts Evidence* **(8th ed. 2007)**—timing/form of objection; preserving appellate rights;

1 Wigmore, *Evidence*, **§ 18 (Tillers rev. 1983)**—timing; form; general vs. specific tenor; waiver; burden of proving admissibility;

ABA Standards for Criminal Justice (2d ed. 1986) Trial Judge 6-1.6—judge "has duty to see that reporter makes true, complete, & accurate record of all proceedings"; judge "shouldn't change transcript without notice to both sides & hearing"; 6-2.4: should "respect obligation of counsel to present objections"; should permit counsel's succinct grounds of objection, but control length/manner;

C v Long **419 M 798, 805 (95)**—factual assertion by one attorney not contradicted/corrected by other, accepted by appellate court as accurate statement;

C v Sherman **389 M 287, 290 n.2 (83)**—pretrial motion to suppress wholly preserves issue for appellate review; trial objection not needed;

C v Jacobs **346 M 300, 310–11 (63)**—same;

C v Mitchell **350 M 458, 464 (66)**—(same);

C v Dirring **354 M 523, 530 n.4 (68)**—(same); but see *C v Acosta* **416 M 279 (93)** objection to denial of motion to suppress seemingly required to preserve issue for appeal;

C v Hill **38 MAC 982 (95)**—even though fully-argued motion to suppress ID was denied pretrial, failure to object at trial caused review on standard for unpreserved error,

DEFINITIVE WORD? *C v Whelton* **428 M 24 (98)**—"the denial of a motion to suppress evidence on constitutional grounds . . . is reviewable without further objection at trial"; BUT CONTRAST appellate preservation requirements concerning motions in limine, *C v Gabbidon* **398 M 1, 7 (86)**;

C v Robicheau **421 M 176, 184 n.7 (95)**—criminal D, as appealing party, bears burden of producing adequate record & when transcript (from tape) has inaudible segments and gaps, court will **not** assume proper objection was made;

C v Beauchamp **49 MAC 591, 604 n.17 (2000)**—party not permitted to raise issue before trial judge on a specific theory and then present issue to appellate court on different theory, so D here held to have waived issue;

C v Liotti **49 MAC 641, 643 n.3 (2000)**—appellate court criticized Commonwealth's attempt to shift position on appeal as to theory of culpability; "we will not disregard the theory of law in which the parties proceeded at trial"; but see *C v Dubois* **44 MAC 294, 297 n.3 (98)** (re appeal from denial of motion to suppress: "We ordinarily do not address an issue raised for the first time on appeal. We do so in this case, however, because the prevailing party, the Commonwealth, is 'entitled to argue on appeal that the judge was right for the wrong reason, even relying on a principle of law not argued below'");

C v Riveiro **393 M 224 (84)**—should voir dire cop (re: admissibility of D's statement) outside jury's presence; inculpatory value will be assumed by jury even as its use may be barred, so prevent jury's knowledge that there was any statement;

C v Nawn **394 M 1, n.2 (85)**—"better practice" for judge to allow counsel to make offers of proof at bench;

C v Adderley **36 MAC 918 (94)**—when judge denied D-counsel's request for bench warrant for alibi witness under subpoena but not in court, & refused to allow an offer of proof, appellate court assumed for purpose of decision that the witness's testimony would have supported D's alibi & that witness would be able to recall salient matters;

C v Johnson **431 M 535, 536 (2000)**—judge permissibly asked for offer of proof before allowing cross-examination re: racial bias, and proffer wasn't adequate (i.e., potential witness could testify that witness on stand once asked her whether or not she dated black men), so no error in exclusion; given inflammatory nature of suggestion of racial bias, "legitimate interest in excluding from the trial of cases references to matters without support in the evidence, or for which no legitimate basis is offered";

Chipman v Mercer **628 F.2d 528 (9th Cir. 1980)**—cited by D, distinguished for its "highly detailed" and "extensive" offer of proof supporting cross for racial bias; (on merits, rather than 'proffer' point, see also *C v Moorer* **431 M 544, 546–47 (2000)** error found in exclusion of cross for racial bias);

C v Frank **433 M 185, 193 (2001)**—offer of proof needed when judge sustains prosecutor's objection to question asked of D on direct;

McGrath v Vinzant **528 F.2d 681 (1st Cir. '76)**—usually no need for offer of proof re: cross-examination, but exception for witness's address because possible danger; fn. 3—suggest bench/lobby conference; *(See Chapter 9-A)*;

ABA Standards for Criminal Justice (2d ed. 1986) Jury Trial 15-3.9—frequent bench conferences distract jury; try to await recess unless necessary to avoid prejudice;

C v Gagnon **16 MAC 110 (83)**—[rev'd other grounds, 391M869] D's unsuccessful objection to testimony (that D's were in photos) not waived by D's later calling a witness (saying that D's were not in photos);

Brodin, M. and Avery, M., *Handbook of Massachusetts Evidence* **(8th ed. 2007)**—OK to overrule if objection's overbroad & includes OK stuff; or if general objection & evidence admissible for ANY purpose; or if incorrect, specific objection (though there's a valid ground to exclude);

C v Cancel **394 M 567 (85)**—general objection not enough here because reason unclear where answer not yet given; must renew objection after answer;

C v Martin **417 M 187, 191 (94)**—despite Commonwealth argument that objection came one question too late, SJC held objection sufficient because made when it was "apparent that any response would be inadmissible";

C v Johnson **431 M 535, 541 (2000)**—timely objection to DA's use of prior conviction in impeaching D held INSUFFICIENT TO PRESERVE precise issue (i.e., the 'prior' was for a traffic violation for which only a fine was imposed, so impermissible under statute); D didn't "state the proper basis for the objection" (but see, contra, M.R.Crim.P. 22's language saying party "may" state ground, not "shall"/"must");

C v McDuffee **379 M 353 (79)**—review ruling without objection because rule of law used by judge "so firmly established" that judge wouldn't have modified ruling;

C v Barrows **391 M 781 (84)**—not repeating objection next day (after judge had said she'd consider overnight D's request re: empanelment) = no objection;

C v Spence **38 MAC 88, 89–90 (95)**—withdrawing objection to obtain benefit from objectionable testimony = no appellate preservation but cf *C v Perreira* **38 MAC 901 (95)** - "strategy" pursued may be so flawed that appellate court will redress, either by standard of "substantial risk of miscarriage of justice" or ineffective counsel;

C v Kennedy **3 MAC 218 (75)**—OK to exclude cross-examination questions for 'form' defects; & D counsel chargeable then with abandoning the issue "voluntarily, although in frustration";

Sussman v C **374 M 692 (78)**—improper summary contempt for 2d (excluded & rephrased) cross-examination question;

C v White **48 MAC 658, 660 n.5 (2000)**—D-counsel has duty to request limiting instructions; judges ordinarily aren't required to instruct sua sponte "as to the purposes for which evidence is offered at trial"; though appellate counsel argued that failure to limit use of hearsay evidence made it useable substantively and decisively against D, appellate court held counsel used it effectively (no ineffectiveness of counsel);

C v Roberts **433 M 45, 48 (2000)**—D's motion to exclude evidence of his drug-dealing denied (because relevant to motive in homicide prosecution), & evidence was admitted; charge conference request for limiting instruction as to use of this evidence = TOO LATE, because party offering it would have relied on it being admitted for all purposes, and it was too late for that party to offer other evidence if it were needed;

C v Jackson **23 MAC 975 (87)**—objection (to charge) on multiple grounds "collectively" (though imprecisely) alerted judge & preserved issue;

See Chapter 12 re: Request Instructions & Chapter 11-B re: Motions in Limine;

Brodin, M. and Avery, M., *Handbook of Massachusetts Evidence* **(8th ed. 2007)**—need for specific motion to STRIKE indicating what's objectionable; if answer is admissible, but not strictly responsive to the question, striking is discretionary (§§ 3.8.1–2); counsel has burden to move to strike evidence admitted de bene [when foundation not subsequently laid] (§ 3.11);

Young, Pollets & Poreda, *Evidence,* **§§ 611.1 et seq. (2d ed. 1998)**—mode & order of interrogation and presentation; hazard of "narrative" testimony; evidence admitted conditionally may be subjected to motion to strike, etc.

D. Ct. Jury T/M, § 2.44—admitting evidence de bene "is not recommended";

US v Breedlove **576 F.2d 57 (5th Cir. '78)**—judge tried "hopelessly tardy" to "unring bell, put cat back in bag, deodorize jury of skunk's presence, unsing song";

See Chapter 19, Double Jeopardy: Mistrials," including strategy/legal choices;

C v Gagliardi **21 MAC 439 (86)**—new trial, in part, because DA ordered to "amend" misleading opening; then judge finds "tones less ardent" than first opening;

Peterson, Petitioner **354 M 110 (68)**—if evidence admitted de bene, must later move to strike or earlier objection's waived;

Newman v Newman **211 M 508 (12)**—jury-waived judge shouldn't admit evidence de bene & later exclude; fact-finder should hear only what law permits;

C v Riveiro **393 M 224 (84)**—similar: voir dire of cop should not occur in jury's presence;

C v Cardaleen **26 MAC 979 (88)**—if jury-waived, still must move to strike; but MAY relax rule, especially if objection = clear/prompt, & testimony = very harmful;

C v Simmonds **386 M 234 (82)**—can deny mistrial motion because no motion to strike or request for curative instruction (re: other crimes evidence);

C v Martin **424 M 301 (97)**—"limiting" instruction may **focus** attention rather than deflect improper use (likened to a "children, don't put beans up your nose" instruction);

C v Kamishlian **21 MAC 931 (85)**—affirm though bad cross-examination of D's character witness because objection sustained & no request for mistrial, curative instruction;

C v Geisler **14 MAC 268 (82)**—no right to strike equivocal testimony; if witness disavows direct testimony, motion to strike appropriate;

C v McCreary **12 MAC 690 (81)**—can strike unresponsive answer, but discretion if competent/relevant; must give precise reason in offer/proof re: excluded evidence, not "vague protestations," or no appellate review;

C v Bishop **5 MAC 738 (77)**—need not strike unresponsive but relevant answer; motion to strike must be specific as to part of answer unresponsive;

C v Dwyer **10 MAC 707 (80)**—refusal of witness on cross-examination to answer questions about collateral matters is not ground for striking the witness's testimony; but see *C v Kirouac* **405 M 557 (89)** child sex complainant's refusal to answer denied meaningful cross-examination;

C v Almeida **452 M 601 (2008)**—though prosecution witness answered "I don't remember" 125 times, SJC rejected argument that D was denied "meaningful cross-examination": witness was asked "almost 1,000 questions on cross-examination that day"; "reasonable" for witness to have no memory of some info sought; testimony "did not sink to the levels that have been held to deny the right of cross-examination"; further, memory problems "assisted [D] in his attempt to discredit" witness, so not "ineffective" for failing to move to strike;

Brodin, M. and Avery, M., *Handbook of Massachusetts Evidence* **(8th ed. 2007)**—Chapter 13, "Privileges and Disqualifications"; *(See post, Chapter 11-J);*

C v Stockhammer **409 M 867 (91)**—counsel's repeated efforts to make offer of proof preserved error;

C v Swan **38 MAC 539 (95)**—counsel abandoned defense, premised on AG's regulations on auto repair charges, after one objection was sustained: ineffective assistance found (counsel failed to proffer how relevant, and failed to have regulations marked for ID);

C v Lara **39 MAC 546 (95)**—after D counsel's objections to evidence were overruled, no waiver in either failure to persist or in undertaking questioning on the evidence (damage control);

C v Semedo **422 M 716 (98)**—D doesn't waive objection to admission of evidence by cooperating on redaction IF he objects to admission of statements after redaction;

Ohler v US **529 US 753 (2000)**—under federal law, D held to have waived objection to denial of motion in limine to exclude prior convictions for impeachment when she introduced them "preemptively" during direct examination so as to remove 'sting' on cross (5:4 decision); though dissent's more rational, majority says "common sense" = "general principle" that party introducing evidence can't complain that it was erroneously admitted;

C v Blake **409 M 146 (91);** *C v Allen* **29 MAC 373 (90);** *C v Chase* **26 MAC 578 (88)**—counsel's failure to make offer of proof justified exclusion of evidence;

C v O'Brien **419 M 470 (95)**—though it was error not to allow D counsel to see document used by DA to "refresh" witness, failure to have document **marked** prevented appellate court from any finding that error was prejudicial (no relief for D on appeal);

C v Best **50 MAC 722, 728 (2001)**—appellate issue of police report (exhibit)'s purportedly "prejudicial hearsay" not addressed because counsel failed to include in record appendix a copy of the report;

C v Carlton **43 MAC 702 (97)**—D's "speedy trial" issue failed due to lack of proffers as to **when** potential witness died and as to how testimony would have benefited D;

C v Conley **34 MAC 50 (93)**—judge's ordering defense counsel to make sidebar proffer of "area" of each defense witness's anticipated testimony "strongly disapproved"; judge's refusal to allow defense counsel to record objections resulted in treatment of issues on appeal as if properly preserved;

C v MacKenzie **413 M 498 (92)**—counsel's objection, which conceded admissibility of evidence to which he was objecting, did not preserve issue for appeal;

C v Foster **411 M 762, 768 (91)**—issue not preserved for appeal where objection made after witness answers objectionable question [i.e., also move to "strike"];

C v Almeida **34 MAC 901, 902 n.2 (93)**—['If you do that, judge'], "the dough may get shot in my face" deemed an objection;

C v Fleenor **39 MAC 25, 28 n.4 (95)**—counsel's reliance on "local practice" of recording objection by merely stating it to session clerk **misplaced**; file it in writing, unless actually see it written on clerk's log/docket sheet;

C v Almon **30 MAC 721 (91)**—substantial risk of miscarriage of justice standard for unpreserved errors requires genuine question of guilt, plausible that result might have been otherwise but for error & likely apparent that failure to object not reasonable tactical decision;

11-D. RELEVANCE AND MATERIALITY; AND BALANCING AGAINST PREJUDICE

SJC Rule 3:07, 3.4(e)—lawyer at trial shall not allude to any matter that the lawyer does not reasonably believe is relevant or that will not be supported by admissible evidence, assert personal knowledge of facts in issue except when testifying as a witness, or state a personal opinion as to the justness of a cause, the credibility of a witness, the culpability of a civil litigant, or the guilt or innocence of an accused; Rule 4.4—lawyer shall not use means that have no substantial purpose other than to embarrass, delay, or burden a third person, or use methods of obtaining evidence that violate the legal rights of such a person;

Prop.M.R.Evid. 401—"relevant" = having any tendency to make the existence of any fact of consequence to the determination of the action more or less probable than it would be w/o the evidence; 403, prejudice vs. probative value, character, bad acts; 405, proof of character; 406, habit, routine, practice; 410, plea (offer); 611, judge's reasonable control over mode/order of evidence, & can admit on condition relevancy will be established;

Brodin, M. and Avery, M., *Handbook of Massachusetts Evidence* **(8th ed. 2007)**—Chapter 4: relevance = "rational tendency to prove an issue in the case," i.e., two "components": tendency to prove a particular fact, and such fact must be "material to an issue in the case"; evidence may be admitted even if issue is conceded; evidence needn't be "conclusive" on the issue; enough that it, in connection with other evidence, "helps a little"; McCormick above, "a brick is not a wall";

Young, Pollets & Poreda, *Evidence*, **§§ 401–3 (2d ed. 1998)**—general theory of relevance; §§ 404–6: evidentiary value (or lack thereof) of character, habit, & customary practice;

2 Wigmore, *Evidence,* **§§ 24–43 (Tillers rev. 1983)**;

C v Fayerweather **406 M 78, 83 (89)**—2 components to relevancy concept: (a) evidence must have some tendency to prove or disprove particular fact, and (b) that particular fact must be material to an issue in the case;

C v O'Laughlin **446 M 188 (2006)**—evidence isn't "prejudicial" or inadmissible simply because it is "inconclusive"; jury is to determine probative value to be accorded relevant evidence (DNA test results of material sample indicated that D and V, as well as 50% of population, could have contributed to it);

C v Grinkley **75 MAC 798 (2009)**—because "mixed" sample from victim did not contain D's "entire" DNA profile, expert's testimony that only one in 320 billion African-Americans were possible contributors to the mixture found on the sample was "irrelevant" and "misleading"; "[w]hat the Commonwealth submitted here, ostensibly product rule statistics for a mixed sample without an identified primary contributor, was not permissible for reasons which should have been obvious";

C v Arana **453 M 214 (2009)**—lengthy presentation of medical testimony concerning examination and collection of "swabs" from complainants' bodies, and concomitant testimony from laboratory chemists, all of which resulted in bottom line of "no physical evidence" showing sexual assaults took place, but with dedicated testimony asserting that such evidence would be nearly impossible to find after five days' time (as here) criticized; suggestion (fn.25) of stipulation to 'no evidence of' assault, and then expert (preferably NOT one who examined subject complainants) testimony concerning general circumstances which could explain absence of physical evidence, countered if desired by defense expert;

C v Francis **432 M 353, 359 (2000)**—error to allow DA to question D about his alleged unlawful firearm possession: "its relevance to the charges against the defendant was tenuous and was substantially outweighed by its potential to suggest the defendant's criminal propensity";

C v Silva **455 M 503 (2009)**—three "manuals" (over 850 pages) written to assist persons taking examinations to become police officers had NO RELEVANCE, and were inadmissible; prosecutor failed to identify where in them jury could find evidence of D's purported competence to handle firearms, but no finding of prejudice;

C v Bonds **445 M 821 (2006)**—testimony by rape complainant's mother that complainant was overly trusting was admissible, because it "gave the jury a clear picture of who the victim was" & served to explain her limited mental capacity; criticism that "relevance" objection didn't serve to preserve appellate argument as to impermissible "character" testimony;

C v Adjutant **443 M 649 (2005)**—judge has discretion to admit "specific incidents of violence that the victim is reasonably alleged to have initiated" when D asserts self-defense and identity of first aggressor is in dispute; D needn't have known of such incidents at time of alleged crime;

C v Pring-Wilson **448 M 718 (2007)**—trial judge permissibly granted new trial because "Adjutant" evidence (history of violence by alleged victims) was proffered and excluded at trial, after which SJC decided *C v Adjutant* 443 M 649 (2005); judge may admit evidence of victim's "specific acts of prior violent conduct but may not admit evidence of his general reputation for violence", and **also** specific acts of violence by person assisting victim in the subject fight (judge must determine whether in light of evidence most favorable to D, the third party was acting in concert with or to assist victim); prior to trial, D is to give notice of specific evidence, and Commonwealth shall provide court and D notice of rebuttal evidence it intends to offer, judge then able to exercise "sound discretion" whether to admit;

C v Benoit **452 M 212 (2008)**—although "self-defense" instruction was legitimately refused (because D could have retreated), judge did instruct on voluntary manslaughter: D argued logical extension of Adjutant, i.e., prior violent acts by deceased argued to be admissible in context of whether he initiated sudden and violent combat which would cause reasonable person to be provoked to heat of passion; because of newness of Adjutant rule and lack of opportunity to examine its impact, SJC "not prepared to extend the rule *at this time*", but reversed conviction on different ground; Ireland, J., believed "court should have undertaken a full analysis of the merits of extending the *Adjutant* rule to this case, instead of dismissing it as premature":

C v Clemente **452 M 295 (2008)**—case tried long before Adjutant (2005 decision), but subsequent motion for new trial relied upon Adjutant: SJC declined to apply Adjutant ("a new common-law rule of evidence") retrospectively "in this case"; trial judge had allowed D to present substantial evidence of specific acts of violence by victims (unlike in *Adjutant* and *Pring-Wilson*), and during trial it was admitted without limitation; though final jury charge, (requested by D) told jurors they could consider only specific acts of violence by victims which were known to D, this purported limitation caused no prejudice, because D knew of the many specific acts of violence by victims;

C v Gaynor **73 MAC 71, further review allowed 452 M 1110 (2008)**—no error in excluding prior violent behavior by victim when identity of first aggressor was not in dispute (it was victim), and no live issue whether D was precluded from asserting self-defense on ground that it was he who had started fight; even if *Adjutant* evidence theoretically admissible, judge could exercise discretion to exclude proffered evidence as different in nature (domestic violence) from "street fight" being tried and as remote (four years earlier); DA's closing argument did not exploit absence of Adjutant evidence, instead arguing that fight was over, D didn't fear imminent harm, and had opportunity to retreat;

C v Williams **450 M 879, 892 (2008)**—D's recorded statement was edited, defense wanting omission of references to D's incarceration, drug use, gang membership, & possession of guns, and DA wanting redaction of D's comments re: victim's reputation for violence and intimidation: because self-defense was at issue, victim's reputation was relevant and admissible (and defense counsel was perhaps ineffective in agreeing to this redaction, albeit as a 'quid pro quo' for other redactions: issue of 'tactic'/ reasonableness would not be decided without hearing on motion for new trial);

C v McCoy **59 MAC 284 (2003)**—error to allow DA to question D about his knowledge (or not) that woman with D at time of arrest had criminal record for heroin distribution; FURTHER, judge's "inexplicable overruling of" D's objection "may have been seen by the jury as judicial endorsement of the improper questioning and innuendo";

Poirier v Plymouth **374 M 206, 210 (78)**—"Evidence is relevant if it renders the desired inference more probable than it would be without the evidence. . . . Evidence may be sufficiently relevant to be admitted if it "tends to establish the issue" or "constitutes a link in the chain of proof";

C v Prashaw **57 MAC 19 (2003)**—reversal for abuse of discretion in admitting provocative photo of nude D, whose minimal (or nonexistent) probative value was outweighed by prejudicial effect; though Commonwealth claimed relevance because photo was in bedroom in which drugs were found, D had acknowledged that bedroom was hers (but she'd been away for five days before search & named other person who perhaps had access);

C v Crouse **447 M 558 (2006)**—admission of bathing suit top was error (but no relief) because inadequate proof of link to victim, though it was found at crime scene (& Commonwealth claimed it bolstered theory of rape);

C v Murphy **48 MAC 143 (99)**—error to elicit from witness (10-year-old) that she believed in God, had been taken to catechism, studied about God there (and knows very serious to "swear to God to tell truth," as now);

C v Dahl **430 M 813, 822–23 (2000)**—testimony by prosecution witness as to her religious beliefs (might become a nun) shouldn't have been admitted; witness shouldn't have been allowed to testify holding rosary beads; disapproval of DA's citation of witness's religious beliefs as foreclosing doubt as to her credibility;

C v Rodriguez **57 MAC 368 (2003)**—DA's argument (not objected to) that complainant was simple & sincere person unlikely to have fabricated accusation cited witness's practice of placing a Bible in every window; despite Proposed Mass.R.Evid. 610 (evidence of religious beliefs/ opinions not admissible for purpose of showing one's credibility is impaired or enhanced), no relief, court professing that fact was cited to show how "simpleminded" the witness was;

C v Lawson **425 M 528 (97)**—no error in excluding D's proffered videotape of rooftop in issue because failed to proffer that it fairly/accurately represented premises at the relevant time, 18 months before tape was made;

C v Chipman **418 M 262 (94)**—though videotape of view from sniper's location was made ten months after crime, tape admissible because of testimony that only difference was that foliage was denser on video than it would have been during January shooting;

C v Clark **432 M 1, 17 (2000)**—no error in judge's allowing jury "view" of roadside scene at which state trooper was fatally shot, despite facts (a) a memorial erected there to trooper was inflammatory (judge ordered it covered with a cloth before jurors arrived), and (b) road construction had altered the site;

C v Best **50 MAC 722 (2001)**—no "abuse of discretion" in excluding 2 p.m. photos of area where 6 p.m. exchange of currency for glassine bag occurred;

Everson v Casualty Co. of America **208 M 214, 219–20 (11)**—general rule respecting the admission of photographs, plans and models = discretion of judge, who determines whether there is sufficient similarity between what is offered and the original which is the subject of inquiry to make it of any assistance to jurors;

C v Leneski **66 MAC 291 (2006)**—digital images stored in computer hard drive & transferred to a compact disc = subject to same rules of evidence as videotapes; no abuse of discretion in admission of store surveillance CD, though D argued it was more prejudicial than probative because incomplete in time and view;

C v Stewart **398 M 535, 542 (86)**—OK to admit into evidence weapon "identical in shape, size, configuration, and appearance to the missing murder weapon," though no contention it was the actual weapon used;

C v Kalhauser **52 MAC 339, 347 (2001)**—OK for Commonwealth to show witnesses/jury a .25 caliber-type handgun "similar" to one witnesses said was carried by D several times before date of shooting at issue; expert testified that shooting at issue was accomplished with a .25 caliber weapon; jurors were instructed that the "prototype" was illustrative only, and relevant to prove that D's gun had barrel of less than 16 inches (element of carrying firearm charge, G.L. c. 269, § 10[a]);

C v Carleton **36 MAC 137, S.C. 418 M 773 (94)**—no error in barring D, charged with violating order prohibiting blocking access to abortion clinic, from introducing (a) his own testimony that his actions were "inspired by German resistors to the Holocaust" (irrelevant) & (b) info about abortions scheduled on day of his arrest (more inflammatory than probative);

C v Howell **49 MAC 42 (2000)**—error to admit evidence that D's father (trial witness) refused or failed to "cooperate" with police in bringing in D for questioning: witness acknowledged "bias" toward son, and was under no "obligation, legal or otherwise, to honor" police "request";

C v Foley **12 MAC 983 (81)**—should delete "victim," "suspect," "rape" from hospital because prejudicial, but harmless here; [but cf G.L. c. 265, § 24C name of victim in 'arrest, investigation or complaint for rape or assault with intent to rape to be deleted from records of courts and police departments];

C v McNickles **22 MAC 114 (86)**—should warn witness: don't say "rape," "assault";

C v Jewett **442 M 356 (2004)**—testimony by medical examiners that V had been "sexually assaulted" = error, but no substantial risk of miscarriage of justice;

C v McCants **25 MAC 735 (88)**—can call complaining witness "victim" (here) because no issue of consent/didn't happen;

C v Phillips **162 M 504 (1895)**—DA's cross-examination questions assumed fact in issue ["Did (C/W) tell you what D had done to her?"];

C v Fernandes **46 MAC 455 (99)**—appearance of D's name on certificate of drug analysis "did not lend itself to an inference about what" D had to do with the drugs; jury already knew he was charged with them;

See also Chapter 16, Defenses: Presume Innocent; & Chapter 11-I, post, Opinion;

C v Ward **15 MAC 400 (83)**—whether witness believes another's testimony was truth or lie is irrelevant; [see also *C v Triplett* **398 M 561 (86)**]; *C v DeMars* **42 MAC 788 (97), aff'd, 426 M 1008 (98)** asking D whether cop witness was lying - improper, extremely prejudicial;

C v Powers **36 MAC 65 (94)**—fresh complaint witnesses' belief that complainant was telling truth = substantial risk of miscarriage of justice (reversal);

C v Bohannon **376 M 90 (78)**—complaining witness's prior false rape claim relevant to credibility;

C v Martin **417 M 187 (94)**—that D's former girlfriend had "instincts" and "suspicion" that D had something sexually to do with female houseguest = inadmissible, as was her disbelief of his denial;

C v McIntyre **430 M 529, 540 (99)**—similar, i.e., witness's testimony as to "bad vibes";

C v Ellison **376 M 1, n.17 (78)**—D's other assets can show no motive to rob;

C v Ward **14 MAC 37 (82)**—D's finances relevant in arson case; [see also Nolan and Sartorio, Criminal Law (2001) § 107—DA can introduce evidence of motive, even when not essential element of crime]; see also *Saunders*

45 MAC 340 (98) after defense witness testified to good finances, so no motive for arson, OK to cross re: IRS liens/debt;

C v Finn **362 M 206 (72)**—D's sudden wealth after robbery = relevant;

C v Snow **58 MAC 917 (2003)**—error to admit evidence that D was heroin addict, despite claim that it was relevant to show why he needed money (prosecution for breaking and entering and larceny): "[e]veryone needs money," & addiction was merely "bad character" evidence;

C v Scanlan **9 MAC 173 (80)**—testimony as to lack of entry on police roster admissible to show defendant hadn't worked particular shift;

C v Valliere **366 M 479 (74)**—evidence that D had NO money before robbery and that he both spent and deposited large sums immediately after robbery = relevant; exclusion of evidence that he, "some time" after crime, didn't have $500 to pay attorney not error (too remote for relevance);

C v Paiva **71 MAC 411 (2008)**—witness proffered by D was NOT an expert in use of drugs, but instead a percipient witness to D's own drug habit (including amounts), relevant to dispute "intent to distribute"; error to exclude, as observations not remote in time;

C v Carroll **439 M 547 (2003)**—co-defendant, who had pled guilty, testified that D wasn't guilty of ABDW, and indeed had intervened to stop co-D's beating of victim; no error in excluding testimony concerning co-D's motive in the beating (victim had previously stolen co-D's property), because collateral: there's no requirement that joint venturers share a motive for success of the joint venture;

C v Benitez **37 MAC 722 (94)**—900 packets of heroin found in co-D's apartment inadmissible against D in severed trial in which both were charged with possession with intent to distribute: D not charged as joint venturer and prosecution did not contend D owned or possessed the 900 packets; evidence suggested that D had purchased heroin from co-D, but "show[ing] entire sequence of events" insufficient basis for tarring D with 900 packets (though D and co-D had emerged from apartment together);

C v Griffin **45 MAC 396 (98)**—evidence of other drugs and paraphernalia seized at apartment, where D was searched as a "person present," admitted at D's trial without objection, though he not charged with their possession; no abuse of discretion found in implicit determination that probative value outweighed undue prejudicial effect;

C v Galluzzo **25 MAC 568 (88)**—other driver's drunk shows D not negligent;

C v Benjamin **430 M 673 (2000)**—evidence of deceased's violent character admissible only when known to D and D posits self-defense; refusal to expand admissibility to show D's state of mind when alleged murder is committed with extreme atrocity-cruelty; but cf *C v Fortini* **44 MAC 562 (98)** victim's out-of-court declaration ('I will kill them all . . . I'm the baddest motherfucker in town') even though not known to D, is probative of declarant's purpose in approaching/harassing D (though here exclu-

sion not error because cumulative, **etc.**); **NOW, see *C v Adjutant* 443 M 649 (2005) judge has discretion to admit prior specific acts of violence by "victim" on issue of who was first aggressor in altercation involving D (and D need not have known of such prior acts);**

C v Clemente **452 M 295 (2008)**—case tried long before *Adjutant* (2005 decision), but subsequent motion for new trial relied upon Adjutant: SJC declined to apply *Adjutant* ("a new common-law rule of evidence") retrospectively "in this case"; trial judge had allowed D to present substantial evidence of specific acts of violence by victims, and during trial it was admitted without limitation; though final jury charge (requested by D), told jurors they could consider only specific acts of violence by victims which were known to D, D knew of the many specific acts of violence so final "limiting" instruction caused no prejudice;

C v Hunter **426 M 715 (98)**—other person's bad act (strangling) not shown to be sufficiently distinctive to be (modus operandi) in this crime (bad acts as relevant to ID of perpetrator);

C v Rise **50 MAC 836, 844 (2001)**—that others had motive to kill V not admissible absent evidence suggesting that one or more of them actually did so;

C v Ridge **455 M 307 (2009)**—D was charged with execution-style shooting (in head) of male and female on 6/25, duct tape used over mouth, the male having been a drug dealer; on 6/26 local police received "national broadcast" from Florida police asking for contact from any agency having info on execution-style murder within past week involving two persons, possible male and female, tied to chairs & learned that the head shots and use of silver duct tape was "trademark of Columbians in the Florida drug world"; D didn't appeal trial judge's ruling that this "unknown third-party culprits" evidence was too speculative and remote for admission, but did argue that he should have been allowed to cross-examine police to argue failure to investigate (not hearsay because purportedly not "for truth of matter" that victims were killed by Columbian drug dealers); though there should have been a voir dire, no relief because probative value not shown to have outweighed "risk of unfair prejudice";

C v Easterling **12 MAC 226 (81)**—"robber whore" modus operandi evidence relevant to joint venture & background for jury to understand bizarre events;

C v Carter **39 MAC 439 (95) aff'd 424 M 409, 412 n.5 (97)**—D's statement to a friend that she should not use cocaine held irrelevant at his trial for possession with intent to distribute cocaine;

C v Wood **384 M 641(81)**—D's statements 3 weeks pre-murder re: being available to "waste" someone & how he'd dispose of a body = relevant;

C v Avila **454 M 744 (2009)**—telephone caller (reasonably inferred to be D) to murder victim's landlady warned her not to let victim into house anymore because a very dangerous person was looking to kill him because he didn't pay for something given to him: relevant as indicative of intent to kill, and any "ambiguity" went only to weight, not admissibility;

C v Anderson **448 M 548 (2007)**—D's statements (about ten years after homicide) describing the killing and burying of a woman on Cape Cod and, on another occasion, his boast of skill with a knife, cutting people up "pretty bad", including a woman on the South Shore were relevant, and admissible as admissions (they were not evidence of merely extraneous and prejudicial "bad acts");

C v Magraw **426 M 580 (98)**—[only] because D claimed he was at estranged wife's house at her invitation and that they got along well, evidence that she said she'd never willingly be alone with him, and that she perceived his leaving a gun on her bed as a threat = relevant & admissible in his trial for murder (hearsay exception: her state of mind); see also *C v Sharpe* **454 M 135 (2009)**—victim told others that she was getting a new apartment without D (& that D wasn't faithful, lied, & didn't contribute financially to household): because D knew this (he asked friend for help in finding apartment because of problems with girlfriend), relevant to his motive for killing her; part re: "infidelity is somewhat more problematic," but no objection;

C v Carlson **448 M 501 (2007)**—though D argued that testimony as to his calm demeanor ("wasn't crying" "wasn't an emotional wreck") was irrelevant while seeking to demonize him (indifferent to death of roommate-girlfriend), SJC held it relevant to refute D's claim of loss of control because deprived of his medications; also relevant re: voluntariness of D's statements and waiver of Miranda rights;

C v Richardson **59 MAC 94 (2003)**—"state of mind" was illegitimate basis on which to admit evidence that witness was told by a third person that D had threatened to kill third person and others; if witness had heard the threats, perhaps admissible (in judge's discretion) if relevant to D's motive;

C v Williams **46 MAC 700 (99)**—Vs' fear of D relevant to rebut D's self-defense claim that they pulled him into their apartment to fight;

C v Chasson **383 M 183 (81)**—discretion whether to exclude testimony of complaining witness' mother because slight materiality & great prejudice [but see *C v Bonds* 445 M 821 [2006] testimony of mother admissible to explain complainant's mental limitations/overly "trusting" nature];

C v Kirkpatrick **423 M 436 (96)**—without expert testimony, particular medical records lacked probative value for rape D;

C v Barresi **46 MAC 907 (99)**—similar; without such foundation, appellate court refused to hold abuse of discretion in excluding evidence proffered by D;

C v Lloyd **45 MAC 931 (98)**—absent expert testimony that Prozac use affected perception or memory, not relevant; no error in excluding cross concerning alleged use;

C v Stephens **44 MAC 940 (98)**—possible drug use in May '93 not relevant to ability to perceive or testify to events occurring in October '92;

C v Arce **426 M 601 (98)**—government witness's "drug problems" in the year of the crime irrelevant absent nexus to actual date and ability to perceive/recollect;

C v Roberts **433 M 45, 51–52 (2000)**—D's giving of a Massachusetts address as well as a NY address when stopped by a NY state trooper admissible because relevant to rebut defense that D didn't live in MA at time of fatal shooting; facts that narcotics were found as result of stop, that D gave false name to trooper, & that he was arrested & convicted of drug possession WERE ALL EXCLUDED because prejudicial & irrelevant;

Maillet v ATF-Davidson **407 M 185 (90)**—D's prior unrelated consumption of beer at work was inadmissible because not relevant to show he did so on day of accident;

C v Walker **69 MAC 137 (2007)**—no abuse of discretion in admitting D's statement to mother upon his arrest for "rape," "You know how girls are when you break up with them", although D argued he believed the arrest concerned complainant who had gone to high school with D rather than this trial complainant (a stranger to him); or even if it shouldn't have been admitted, DNA evidence made error harmless;

C v Phong Thu Ly **19 MAC 901 (84)**—D's possession of rubber gloves relevant to intent/rob though no evidence gloves used & D's fingerprints found at scene;

C v Darby **37 MAC 650 (94)**—photos of (a) child sexual assault complainant nude, in bathtub and (b) fully clothed D, sitting on sofa, with penis exposed and erect irrelevant; D's ability to achieve erection not an issue, given his simple denial; fact that trial was jury-waived did not excuse admission of inflammatory photos; conviction reversed;

C v LaSota **29 MAC 15 (90)**—pamphlet on incest found in D's home was inadmissible to show D's interest in incest because more prejudicial than probative; but see *C v Guy* **454 M 440 (2009)**—OK to admit testimony about D's interest in/books on serial killings (books seized 4 years after [single] murder), purportedly "relevant to issue of intent and motive" and not temporally remote;

C v Petrillo **50 MAC 104 (2000)**—pornographic movies had no rational tendency to prove issue in case because issue was whether D's sex with complainant was consensual, not whether they had had sex or watched the movies together (D admitted this); rationale that they "showed the whole transaction" or gave jury "the complete picture" is inapplicable when circumstances of alleged crime "are intelligible without viewing the offending material";

C v Jaundoo **64 MAC 56 (2005)**—reversal for admitting vast quantity of pornographic material, notwithstanding some relevance in that a sexually explicit videotape and other items corroborated child complainant's testimony that D showed her these materials;

C v Wallace **70 MAC 757 (2007)**—though dissent says *Jaundoo* should bar admission of lubricants, duct tape knife, & rope found in D's car, court holds no error in admitting either those or photos of clothed young girls at play, photos of nude adults in sex activity, and pornographic magazines; sole issue at trial was whether 12-year-old girl had "misconstrued" what was at most an accidental touching of her breast;

C v Bastarache **382 M 86 (80)**—grisly PHOTOS of body (altered by autopsy) admitted in discretion if important to resolve contested fact; compare *C v Richmond* **371 M 563 (76)** reversal due to grisly photo of murder V whose face was torn by dogs after death;

C v Haith **452 M 409 (2008)**—photo showing part of V's skull (shaved for autopsy) with a bent screwdriver inserted into a puncture wound was admissible in judge's discretion because evidence was that D stabbed V with screwdriver, and bent screwdriver was found at scene: relevant to extreme atrocity/cruelty, deliberate premeditation;

C v Cardarelli **433 M 427 (2001)**—photos of decomposed body (found two months after death, wrapped in plastic in attic crawl space) at autopsy (head with skin & hair cut back) OK, since D claimed not to remember how or why he killed V: severe head trauma, consistent with battery by iron frying pan, relevant to extreme atrocity/cruelty;

C v Meinholz **420 M 633 (95)**—gory photos of murder victim held relevant to extreme atrocity or cruelty **and** deliberate premeditation, **and** consciousness of guilt (body being unearthed from D's cellar);

C v Keohane **444 M 563 (2005)**—gory photos of murder victim held relevant to extreme atrocity/cruelty, premeditation, and those taken at crime scene relevant to prosecution theory of "how the murder occurred"; rejects claim that judge's instructions re: photos were excessive or "overemphasized" the photos; judge informed venire of nature of injuries and that there would be graphic testimony & photos of the injuries (& the 8 people who answered "yes" to question whether difficult/uncomfortable for them to be fair/impartial were excused for cause);

C v Dagenais **437 M 832 (2002)**—gory photos relevant to Commonwealth's theory of case, duct tape with D's fingerprint on it refuting D's story that victim accidentally fell from great height;

C v DeSouza **428 M 667 (99)**—need not exclude grisly videotape (including bodies on floor, blood and tissue on walls) merely because "cumulative," or because D offered to stipulate to facts for which it's offered;

C v Simmons **419 M 426, 430–32 (95)**—trial judges should avoid exposing jury "unnecessarily" to material which would "inflame the jurors' emotions" & deprive D of impartial jury;

C v Hoilett **430 M 369 (99)**—same;

C v Carlino **429 M 692 (99)**—autopsy photos of internal organs shouldn't be admitted here;

C v St. Peter **48 MAC 517, 523 (2000)**—judge abused discretion in allowing introduction of array of 15 photos, arranged on large poster board, taken during and after autopsy and depicting V's open skull and brain, though harmless in circumstances here;

C v Pimental **454 M 475 (2009)**—though D didn't argue on appeal that photos of murder victims body as altered by autopsy shouldn't have been admitted, SJC sua sponte "repeat[ed] and stress[ed] a caution" that photographs showing body as altered during autopsy can be inflammatory/prejudicial and should be admitted only if relevant to resolution of a contested issue;

C v McCray **40 MAC 936 (96)**—because witness had known D for years, witness's selection of D's photo from police files served only to show that police had D's photo; this = error;

C v Prashaw **57 MAC 19 (2003)**—reversal for abuse of discretion in admitting photo whose minimal (or non-existent) probative value was outweighed by prejudicial effect; photo depicted sexually provocative/nude D, and though Commonwealth claimed relevance because photo was in bedroom where drugs were found, D had acknowledged that bedroom was hers (but she'd been away for five days before search & named other person who perhaps had access);

C v Perry **3 MAC 308 (75)**—can show scar if location/dimensions relevant to intent/murder;

C v Storey **378 M 312 (79)**—can admit gun seized D's apartment to show D had means to do crime; jury decides if it's murder weapon;

C v Marangiello **410 M 452 (91)**—2 knives found near D at arrest 10 weeks after stabbing were admissible within judge's discretion;

C v Haney **358 M 304 (70)**—"general rule" = weapons found in D's possession admissible only if they might have been used in commission of crime charged"; otherwise unfair & prejudicial inference of vicious/dangerous propensities;

C v Toro **395 M 354 (85)**—(harmless) error to admit guns that aren't murder weapon because relevance (D's familiarity with weapons) outweighed by prejudice; but see *C v Marquetty* **416 M 445 (93)** knife found in D's car admissible, though not claimed to be the weapon used in fatal stabbing, to show "familiarity with the type of weapon";

C v Richardson **59 MAC 94 (2003)**—error to admit machete when there was no claim that it was weapon (or type of weapon) used by D in assault (with knife); fact that it was in the house and witnesses purportedly feared its accessibility to D was invalid basis for admission;

C v Graham **431 M 282, 287–89 (2000)**—error to admit 5 crossbows (dramatically borne into court by separate officers), but no prejudice because cumulative and D's own case acknowledged archery enthusiast for 45 years;

C v Luna **46 MAC 90 (98)**—gun which was not used in battery was introduced as "similar to" gun used: no error;

C v Monico **396 M 793 (86)**—knife concealed at booking inadmissible, but knife shown before shooting shows state of mind;

C v Weaver **400 M 612 (87)**—D's possession of knife admissible though charge = carrying firearm because relevant to D's intent as participant in altercation;

See Chapter 11-F re: admissibility of guilty pleas; cf, e.g., C v Howard 46 MAC 366 (99) acquittal of person jointly charged but separately tried = not probative of others' innocence;

C v Ortiz **50 MAC 304 (2000)**—co-D's guilty plea had no tendency to exonerate D, being tried as co-venturer in narcotics distribute;

C v Garcia **443 M 824, 835 (2005)**—OK for DA to elicit that prosecution witness had been convicted of being accessory after fact of victim's murder (for which D was being tried) & had received probation, to minimize impact it would have had if instead introduced initially by defense;

C v Best **50 MAC 722 (2001)**—error to allow cop to testify that purported buyer of drugs from D had been arrested before for heroin possession, & was found, in separate trial, guilty of possession heroin based on purported transaction with D;

C v Corsetti **387 M 1, n.3 (82)**—authentication of identification of phone voice;

C v Carpinto **37 MAC 51 (94)**—voice identifier must (1) be familiar with voice, (2) ID voice at time of speech, (3) personally hear conversation **but** answering machine owner for whom tel. messages were left permitted to ID voice as D's (witness had been D's "correctional counselor" at prison): "substantial difference" between voice ID during "ephemeral conversation" & having it on "permanent storage medium such as a tape";

Prop.M.R.Evid. 901—VOICE ID, etc. needs only evidence to support finding (e.g., based on hearing it once);

C v Loach **46 MAC 313 (99)**—even though caller's voice not ID'd, OK to admit testimony about the call because enough confirming circumstances existed to authenticate caller's identity AND evidence of bad acts relevant to intent;

C v Anderson **48 MAC 508, 515–16 (2000)**—no error in excluding testimony by a doctor re: phone call made to doctor by woman ID'ing self as D's wife, BUT if D had noted to trial judge that wife herself had testified earlier to such a call, result maybe different (n.7);

C v Mezzanotti **26 MAC 522 (88)**—voice ID OK if "basic familiarity";

C v Howard **42 MAC 322 (97)**—telephone caller to police ten hours after forcible rape of child identified himself as D & offered to turn self in; cop couldn't ID voice as D, & no other authentication: error to admit;

C v Enos **26 MAC 1006 (88)**—even less familiarity's needed for non-D voice;

C v Sullivan **436 M 799 (2002)**—error to bar D from introducing tape-recorded telephone message with some caller making admission consistent with being murderer (rather than D); neither tentative nature of recipient's identification of the voice nor her subsequent change of mind barred admission of the tape & recipient's grand jury testimony concerning it; FURTHERMORE, "recording was admissible regardless of whose voice it was simply because it suggests that someone—anyone—other than [D] admitted to the killing, & provides a motive unrelated to [D]";

C v Williams **450 M 645 (2008)**—tape recording of telephone conversation among an incarcerated individual, D, and co-D was admissible: co-D told incarcerated man that co-D and D "were kicking his ass nigger", and D re-sponded to co-D's assertion by saying "Yo, chill, chill": D's response could be found not to be a denial, so adoptive admission;

C v Jerome **36 MAC 59 (94)**—tape recording of conversation, if conversation is relevant & not otherwise excludable, is admissible if the tape is "a fair representation of that which it purports to depict"; though not here, **can** be so incomplete as to be untrustworthy/misleading; here, it was fresh complaint to counscling therapist who was available for cross-examination;

C v King **34 MAC 466 (93)**—D's "state of mind" during interrogation = irrelevant, evidence that he terminated questioning by calling cops names = reversal;

C v DiGiacomo **57 MAC 312 (2003)**—error to admit evidence, purportedly to show D's state of mind, that teacher confronted D, told him that students complained to her of D's touching/hugging, and that he requested & was told names of those complaining; "state of mind" may cover statements of an alleged victim if relevant to prove motive or relevant state of mind of D, IF there is evidence it was communicated to D; alleged victim's state of mind at most related to past alleged sexual assaults;

C v Papadinis **402 M 73 (88)**—D's testimony on own state of mind admissible wherever state of mind a "factor" in proof of crime;

C v Lent **46 MAC 705 (99)**—within judge's discretion to admit D's statements about a "master plan" to build shelves/boxes to imprison girls, because relevant to specific intent of kidnapping charge;

C v O'Brien **432 M 578, 590 (2000)**—within discretion of judge to admit newspaper front page found in murder D's bedroom, about unrelated murderers' fascination with movie titled "We're Natural Born Killers" because purportedly relevant to "limited issue as to D's state of mind around the time of this incident" but NOT "offered to show D had a propensity to commit the crime" (note logically inconsistent instructions); *C v Guy* **454 M 440 (2009)**—books on serial killing found in D's apartment four years after murder (plus coworkers' testimony that D often read such books) admissible as relevant to "issue of intent and motive"; see instead *C v LaSota* **29 MAC 15 (90)** ("Logic, experience, and common sense teach that textual underlining may reflect a full range of responses from abhorrence to approval. Less tenable still is a general supposition that opinions, beliefs, or behavioral proclivities may be determined from one's reading materials");

C v Sires **413 M 292 (92)**—D's consumption of drugs or alcohol admissible wherever D's state of mind in issue;

C v Chase **26 MAC 578 (88)**—D's explanation for lying to police admissible with proper offer of proof;

C v Rubin **318 M 587 (45)**—out-of-court "declaration of purpose" = probative of happening/purpose of occurrence;

C v Fortini **44 MAC 562 (98)**—victim's out-of-court declaration ('I will kill them all ... I'm the baddest motherfucker in town') even though not known to D, probative of declarant's purpose in approaching/harassing D (though here exclusion not error because cumulative, etc.);

C v Cyr **424 M 89 (97)**—homicide victim's state of mind (she feared D) not relevant at murder trial; *(See further cases, post, Chapter 11-F);*

C v Magraw **426 M 580 (98)**—homicide victim's state of mind (she feared D would kill her) irrelevant;

C v Arce **426 M 601 (98)**: *C v Wilson* **427 M 336 (98)**—same, but harmless on facts;

C v Jenner **426 M 163 (97)**—same;

C v Emence **47 MAC 299 (99)**—defense witness's explanation for why he vividly remembered repairing complainant's vehicle (he'd stayed four hours past end of shift) wrongly excluded;

C v Ellis **432 M 746 (2000)**—no relief for excluding evidence that ID witness in a murder case was an unreliable identifier of a man allegedly stalking her ("a wholly unrelated matter");

C v Boyarsky **452 M 700 (2008)**—judge not required to allow D to cross-examine cop as to his knowledge of the SJC's DiGiambattista preference that statements be recorded;

C v Montanino (II) **409 M 500 (91)**—cop's testimony that "most" sexual assault victims provide more details as time goes on was inadmissible because it vouched for complainant's credibility;

C v Orton **58 MAC 209 (2003)**—cop who prepared composite sketch with complainant's assistance vouched for her credibility by testifying in essence that she took the right amount of time, neither too little (which would assent to first composite and would be just a guess) nor too much (indicating lack of certainty in what she saw);

C v Roche **44 MAC 372 (98)**—alleged expert's testimony concerning "the profile of a typical" batterer ("abusive male") inadmissible; invited jury to conclude that because D fits profile, he likely committed crimes charged;

C v Poitras **55 MAC 691 (2002)**—reversal for prosecution testimony by psychologist re: sexual abuse of children, which alleged attributes and characteristics of those most likely to abuse children ("profile" testimony), mirroring prosecution's evidence about D (i.e., adult known to child, position of authority, caregiver with access/opportunity, not dating anyone, child often vulnerable because of "disrupted attachment relationship");

C v Day **409 M 719 (91)**—expert testimony that D fit child batterer profile = inadmissible;

Adoption of Keefe **49 MAC 818 (2000)**—diagnosis of child's health problems was "Munchausen Syndrome by Proxy," which meant that a perpetrator caused various many many health problems in another individual as a means of gaining attention, & expert testimony toward this finding was admissible; testimony as to the "typical" perpetrator being the child's mother, often a health care professional, & often w/child's father emotionally/physically absent should NOT have been admitted ("profile"), but here didn't matter;

C v Lonardo **74 MAC 566 (2009)**—expert's testimony that she equated the term "runner" with someone who fraudulently "staged" accidents, when evidence would be that D (an attorney) acknowledged use of "runners" "should not have been allowed," but no objection & no "risk of a miscarriage of justice" found here;

C v Sapoznik **28 MAC 236 (90)**: *C v Ferrara* **31 MAC 648 (91)**—magistrate's finding of probable cause & issuance of search warrant were inadmissible because they vouched for cops' credibility;

C v Garcia **46 MAC 466, 470 (99)**—cop's testimony that he "could have" arrested D at apartment because probable cause, in cop's view, had developed was inadmissible opinion on question of law and belief in D's guilt, "prohibited territory for a witness"; see also *C v Peppicelli* **70 MAC 87 (2007)**—judge had discretion to exclude testimony of expert called by defense to testify generally "about the reasonableness of the use of firearms by civilians for self-defense in various situations"; judge determined that jury didn't need expert assistance in this determination;

C v Rivera **29 MAC 961 (90)**—cops' receipt of medals of honor for incident was inadmissible because it vouched for their credibility;

C v Selby **426 M 168 (97)**—cop's understanding of whether or not SJC opinion approved of deceptive interviewing tactic was irrelevant to issue of whether D's statements were voluntary;

C v Grenier **415 M 680 (93)**—that cop didn't believe D's denial of knowledge = inadmissible & that D became nervous during questioning lacked probative value;

C v Rosario **430 M 505, 508–11 (99)**—"state of police knowledge" rubric "carries a high probability of misuse", and is not to serve as vehicle for introduction of hearsay testimony; purported "knowledge" of police must be relevant to an issue in the case; civilian witness here had no basis to explain police conduct and circumstances of police focus on D were not at issue; "It goes without saying that the testimony may not be used for the truth of the statements that served as the basis for the officer's knowledge";

C v Braley **449 M 316, 323–25 (2007)**—trooper's response to D's question, "How did you get on to me?" ("I told him that his partner wasn't as good as he was in keeping this quiet") SHOULD NOT HAVE BEEN ADMITTED; "state of police knowledge" was irrelevant;

C v Tanner **66 MAC 432 (2006)**—cop's testimony that he asked possessor of drugs where he got them from and, after hearing response, that he went directly and placed D under arrest "was the functional equivalent of telling the jury that [man] had identified [D] as the man who had sold him cocaine" (conviction reversed);

C v Parkes **53 MAC 815 (2002)**—testimony of state troopers referring to several cell phone calls appeared specifically designed to put before jury that truck driver who reported incident in question was not alone in reporting it, & this was inadmissible hearsay, causing prejudice and reversal;

C v Randall **50 MAC 26 (2000)**—perhaps error in any event to permit cop to testify that van fleeing from scene of breaking & entering belonged to D (D argued hearsay because cop said that someone in radio check of license plate told him this), but holding = purported justification that it wasn't for truth, but instead to "explain the state of knowledge possessed by police" was bogus, given DA's substantive use of van ownership during closing argument;

C v Ortega **441 M 170, 180 (2004)**—DA shouldn't have asked question to elicit from cop that D associated with possible drug users;

C v Snow **58 MAC 917 (2003)**—error to admit D's statement that he was a heroin addict, & "limiting" instruction (not to use this to show guilt of breaking & entering and larceny, but as relevant to his knowledge of what principal actor was doing and to his intent that the principal's crime be accomplished) "did not cure but rather perpetuated the impermissible use of [D's] addiction and association with a fellow addict";

See also post, Chapter 11-F, Hearsay, state of mind exception;

C v LaVelle **414 M 146 (93)**—informant's prior false allegations of assault were inadmissible because not within Bohannon exception;

C v Auguste **418 M 643 (94)**—several witnesses testified that their initial police statements were incomplete because of fear, & one witness testified that a man who had been with him at crime scene had recently been shot: SJC held that evidence relevant to explain statement omissions, unwillingness to testify, & to forestall D-request for "missing witness" instruction;

C v Jenkins **34 MAC 135 (93)**—similar; no need to connect D to threats/intimidation; but see *C v Martinez* **431 M 168, 173–74 (2000)** abuse of discretion to conclude that probative value of evidence that D's niece threatened prosecution witness outweighed its unfair prejudicial effect; no suggestion that testimony was changed because of threat;

C v Dunn **407 M 798 (90)**—murder victim's pregnancy was admissible to show D was motivated by belief that someone else was father;

C v Martin **424 M 301 (97)**—rape complainant's direct testimony that she believed D to have AIDS admissible as relevant to/corroborative of her lack of consent;

C v Thevenin **33 MAC 588 (92)**—that D believed sexual assault complainant to have pubic lice relevant to defense of 'no sex occurred';

C v Hunter **427 M 651 (98)**—expert testimony re: D's demeanor during showing of Vietnam video at trial relevant to refute defense of post-traumatic stress disorder;

C v Mandell **29 MAC 504 (90)**—motor vehicle homicide victim's "accident-prone[ness]" was inadmissible;

C v Padgett **44 MAC 359 (98)**—D's "reading on the law" concerning joint venture and felony murder relevant to assess D's credibility when he testified to no knowledge that daytime burglary confederates were armed;

C v Sholley **48 MAC 495: S.C. 432 M 721 (2000)**—in prosecution of D, a "father's rights activist," for threatening prosecutor in the trial of another man for a 209A

violation, no relief for cross-examining D re: his own conviction of A&B and his status as subject of a 209A order issues on behalf of ex-wife and daughter; relevance said to be D's bias against government because of his status as similar to other man AND D's intent in encounter with the "victim"-prosecutor;

C v Hall **50 MAC 208 (2000)**—exclusion of testimony that cops beat D in prolonged violent manner after he'd been handcuffed = reversible error; evidence was probative of bias & bias is never 'collateral';

C v Moure **428 M 313 (98)**—after D's cross of Commonwealth witness, permissible on redirect to show witness's "true" motive, which entailed introduction of D's extraneous bad acts;

C v Williams **428 M 383 (98)**—if D introduced, as "provocation" support, that dead V raped D's sister, Commonwealth could introduce evidence that V was innocent of rape because D's knowledge had bearing on reasonableness of his reaction to claimed provocation (involuntary manslaughter);

C v Lorette **37 MAC 736, 742 (94)**—that alleged child rape victim's mother & father reacted with shock, crying, hysteria, guilt for not "protecting" child = irrelevant; reversal for this and other emotional exhortation;

C v Demars **38 MAC 596 (95)**—child sexual assault convictions reversed because of DA's questioning of victim's father, indicating witness heard extraneous allegations about defendant: witness's "state of mind" was irrelevant to D's guilt;

C v Bonner **33 M 471 (92)**—mother's "reaction" to fresh complaint was irrelevant, for sympathy, but harmless;

C v Montanez **439 M 441 (2003)**—complainant's testimony as to actions taken by guidance counselor after complainant made allegations = improper, served as self-corroboration, indicating that someone believed complainant sufficiently credible; testimony by complainant's mother that she was "totally devastated" by allegations = irrelevant, inadmissible; no reversal chiefly because trial was jury-waived (*but see C v Sugrue* **34 MAC 172 (93)** reversal despite fact of no jury for, inter alia, impermissible "fresh complaint" testimony);

C v McLeod **30 MAC 536, 538–39 (91)**—if issue is whether D committed crime, "ghastliness of the crime and the suffering of" V's family = irrelevant;

C v Smith **58 M 166 (2003)**—victim's injuries, recuperation, and suffering = admissible re: whether assailant intended to kill; evidence re: subsequent treatment and medical complications = error, but not prejudicial here;

C v Degro **432 M 319 (2000)**—direct examination of murder victim's girlfriend = questions about "home life", "work life," including "Do they have some memory of him at [place of employment]?"; while can "humanize" victim, "memory" question "not proper";

See also Chapter 12-J (prosecutorial misconduct in closing argument: improper appeals to sympathy);

C v Johnson **43 MAC 509 (97)**—despite jury's interest, date grand jury returned indictment was irrelevant, and possibly caused jury to explain long time lapse by speculation of earlier conviction and appellate reversal **or** that D had fled from justice; despite instruction that it was not to be considered, reversal of convictions;

C v Fitzgerald **412 M 516 (92)**—error to exclude that experts called by D were actually retained by prosecution;

C v Lara **39 MAC 546 (95)**—repeated references to "Dominicans" as being responsible for cocaine trafficking compelled reversal;

C v Berrio **43 MAC 836 (97)**—references to ethnicity may awaken or exacerbate biases among jurors;

C v Johnson **431 M 535 (2000)**—cross-examination of Commonwealth witness for racial bias properly excluded when only proffer by defense counsel was that witness once asked someone "whether or not she dated black men";

Chipman v Mercer **628 F2d 528 (9th Cir. '80)**—distinguished (better proffer);

C v Moorer **431 M 544, 547 (2000)**—error to exclude cross for racial bias because evidence "created at least a remote possibility that [witness] was racially biased";

C v Donovan **422 M 349 (96)**—spontaneous utterance by dying victim, "they took my wallet" not inadmissible despite ambiguity of "they"; case tried on joint venture theory;

C v Gillette **33 MAC 427 (92)**—8-year-old statement of predisposition was too prejudicial and remote;

C v Magraw **426 M 580 (98)**—D's extramarital affairs irrelevant in his trial for murdering wife when one ended 8 years earlier and other began after D & wife decided to divorce;

See also Chapter 9-C for cases on bias;

11-E. BAD ACTS, OTHER CRIMES, AND UNCHARGED MISCONDUCT

See also 11-D, ante;

See also Chapter 12E, consciousness of guilt evidence;

Liacos, Brodin & Avery, *Massachusetts Evidence,* **§§ 4.4.1, 4.4.6 (7th ed. 1999);**

C v Houston **430 M 616, 626 (2000)**—"Surely, a jury, no matter how much effort the judge may make to purge their mindsets by admonitory instructions, are more likely to conclude that the impeaching [prostitution] convictions show that the complainant should not be believed, not because she is untruthful, but because she has been, and thus continues to be, indiscriminate in sexual relations"; but see *C v Harris* **443 M 714 (2005)**—judge has discretion to allow introduction (for impeachment of rape complainant under G.L. c. 233, § 21B) of prior convictions as common nightwalker;

2 Wigmore, *Evidence,* **§§ 300-07 Chadbourn rev. 1979)**—(overview) §§ 309–65 (various specific crimes);

Prop.M.R.Evid. 403, 405, 609, 803(21) (22);

ABA Standards for Criminal Justice (2d ed. 1986) Discovery 11-2.1(b) (iv)—DA shall warn D if offering such evidence

C v Nassar **351 M 45 (66)**—conversation which only served to inform jury that D previously arrested for murder should not have been admitted;

C v Mendes **75 MAC 390 (2009)**—after cop testified about conducting gunpowder residue test on D's hands, he was asked if he had performed other procedures, & responded, "No. I already had his prints on file"; no objection, no substantial risk of miscarriage of justice found here, "where evidence of guilt is strong and one-sided";

C v Roberts **433 M 45, 51–52 (2000)**—D's giving of a Massachusetts address as well as a NY address when stopped by a NY state trooper admissible because relevant to rebut defense that D didn't live in MA at time of fatal shooting; though "stop"/contact itself purportedly had negative connotation regarding D's character, facts that narcotics were found as result of stop, that D gave false name to trooper, & that he was arrested & convicted of drug possession were all excluded because prejudicial & irrelevant;

C v Valentin **55 MAC 667 (2002)**—despite judicial admonition, cop testified that D's car was stopped initially because of its reported involvement in an armed robbery in Rhode Island; since "why car was stopped" wasn't an issue, only purpose was inadmissible hearsay; "it is expected that a prosecutor who is aware that a police witness might allude to inadmissible prejudicial evidence will take affirmative steps to ensure that such testimony does not come before the jury";

C v Diaz **453 M 266 (2009)**—no error in admitting evidence that homicide victim stated that car being driven by D was stolen: limiting instruction said "not for truth" of accusation, and statements were reason for fatal confrontation (D shot victim after victim accused him of theft and physically attacked him);

C v Colleran **452 M 417 (2008)**—because D's drug use was "important" to defense expert, extent of D's drug use was purportedly relevant to shake foundation of defense expert's opinion and not inadmissible "prior bad act" evidence suggesting criminal propensity;

C v Wilson **52 MAC 411, 415–16 (2001)**—D's testimony on direct that he fled from police because of outstanding warrant for failure to complete drug program did not "open the door" or otherwise allow DA to ask D some 16 questions on cross re: whether there was more than one outstanding warrant, or as many as seven, involving motor vehicle citations, narcotics, some "probation situation," etc.;

C v Holliday **450 M 794 (2008)**—after defense counsel properly tried to discredit witnesses who only recently came forward, suggesting rewards from recent cooperation with prosecution or who did not initially inculpate D, witnesses in redirect permissibly explained their fear of retaliation;

C v Graham **62 MAC 642, 647–48 (2004)**—was within discretion of judge to find that D's testimony on direct (that he attempted to gain entry into apartment building because he was fleeing from police, having suffered serious injury in prior altercation with police a year earlier) opened door to cross-exam re: circumstances surrounding prior incident, "which included his convictions related to the altercation", OR given instructions and lack of mention in closing and strong evidence of guilt, "any error in permitting the inquiry was rendered harmless";

C v Kosior **280 M 418 (32)**—D's admission re: other fires = immaterial/prejudicial & not cured by instruction (not evidence of guilt & take "for what it's worth");

C v Whitlock **39 MAC 514 (95)**—clerk's reading of indictment to jury, charging "second/subsequent" offense = error, prohibited by G.L. c. 278, § 11A;

C v Gonsalves **74 MAC 910 (2009)**—copy of medical subpoena inadvertently included in an exhibit showed D was being charged with "OUI-Liquor . . . 4th offense", and jurors in bifurcated trial sent note to judge asking if this was indeed D's 4th offense: response didn't answer directly, and G verdict came within five minutes; reversal required;

C v Welcome **348 M 68 (64)**—D's prior, distinct crime = inadmissible;

C v Picariello **40 MAC 902 (96)**—in trial for violating protective order, reversible error to introduce evidence of what prompted issuance of the order originally; but see *C v Crimmins* **46 MAC 489, 494 (99)** similar evidence admitted, rationale being that it refuted implied defense that complainant misconstrued or overreacted to "chance encounter"; see also *C v Johnson* **45 MAC 473 (98)** because Commonwealth had to prove complainant "reasonably feared imminent physical harm," prior bad acts evidence admissible;

C v Munafo **45 MAC 597 (98)**—similar;

C v Hall **66 MAC 390 (2006)**—testimony by rape complainant that D had bragged that he had had identified man "take care of" someone who was "causing trouble" was admissible to explain why complainant delayed alleging rape for seven years (until newspaper article saying the identified man had been sentenced to prison); judge must undertake analysis of whether danger of prejudice outweighs probative value of evidence;

C v Eugene **438 M 343 (2003)**—in murder case, OK to introduce fact that victim sought abuse protection order against D, because shows existence of hostile relationship which may be relevant to D's motive to kill; *but see C v Cyr* **424 M 89 (97)**—homicide victim's state of mind (she feared D) not relevant at murder trial; *C v Magraw* **426 M 589 (98)**; *C v Wilson* **427 M 336 (98)** (victim's state of mind = irrelevant); *C v Qualls* **425 M 163 (97)**—murder victim's statement, on night he died, that D would try to kill him that night not admissible; V's state of mind not relevant unless there's proof D was aware of it and would be likely to respond to it; assertion that "state of mind" is hearsay *exception*, allowing its admissibility for *truth*, so

admonition that it is "state of mind" & "not for truth" was nonsensical; [this is contrary to authorities, above; reason suggests that evidence is for the "truth" of what speaker believed, but not whether what speaker believed was in fact true];

C v Lenahan **50 MAC 180 (2000)**—OK to admit, in D's trial for solicitation to murder wife, that he had tried to push her off cliff, "especially" given D's testimony that he was only joking when, from jail on that incident, he contacted a friend and asked him to find a "hit man," and that when he thereafter met with "hit man," he was playing along because frightened of the man;

C v Anderson **448 M 548 (2007)**—D's statements (about ten years after homicide) describing the killing and burying of a woman on Cape Cod and, on another occasion, his boast of skill with a knife, cutting people up "pretty bad", including a woman on the South Shore were relevant, and admissible as admissions (they were not evidence of merely extraneous and prejudicial "bad acts");

C v Guy **454 M 440 (2009)**—books on serial killings, seized from D's apartment four years AFTER murder, held admissible ("issue of intent and motive, and . . . not temporally remote");

C v Montez **450 M 736 (2008)**—at D's murder trial, no error in admitting evidence of D's guilt in three other housebreaks, as showed modus operandi indicative of identity: "interlocking . . . bad act evidence" included I.D. by woman he attacked, saying he had killed before;

C v Francis **432 M 353, 359 (2000)**—error to ask D, on trial for accessory before fact to murder & armed assaults with intent to murder, about incident 5 weeks before murder which resulted in D's indictment for unlawful firearm possession [& subsequent acquittal], but D denied such possession and judge instructed jury both immediately & in final charge that jurors were "required to find that he had, in fact, NOT possessed a gun as alleged", so no prejudice;

C v LeClair **68 MAC 482 (2007)**—regarding issue of whether D knew that alleged joint venturer in robbery (and felony murder) was armed, DA proffered that a few weeks before a witness saw D and joint-venturer together, and when they returned joint venturer possessed jewelry which witness knew to belong to 3rd party, joint venturer then saying to witness "you're not going to worry about [3rd party] anymore"; this evidence was NOT ADMISSIBLE, proffer being insufficient to support finding, by preponderance, that the joint venturer had robbed 3rd party or that D was an actor in such robbery, or that joint venturer had even had a weapon on the earlier occasion;

C v Conway **2 MAC 547 (74)**—D's statement showing arrest history inadmissible;

C v Snow **58 MAC 917 (2003)**—error to admit D's statement that he was a heroin addict, & "limiting" instruction (not to use this to show guilt of breaking & entering and larceny, but as relevant to his knowledge of what principal actor was doing and to his intent that the principal's crime be accomplished) "did not cure but rather perpetuated the impermissible use of [D's] addiction and association with a fellow addict";

C v Hubbard **45 MAC 277 (98)**—even if judge did not abuse discretion in admitting prior assaults upon teenagers allegedly like the one being tried, reversal for DA's argument to use it for propensity;

C v Diaz **49 MAC 587 (2000)**—"plain error" to allow jury to use D's prior convictions of drug distribution and possession with intent to distribute to determine what D's "intent" was concerning drugs for which he was being tried (but harmless since D's testimony conceded guilt);

C v Markvart **437 M 331 (2002)**—in trial re: D's alleged sexual dangerousness, reversal for admitting police report relating to an alleged sexual assault by D which was subject of only a nol-prossed indictment, concerning construction of G.L. c. 123A, § 14(c); *see also C v Given* **59 MAC 390 (2003)** (police report concerning alleged sexual assaults on children which were not subject of any indictment) and *C v Boyer* **58 MAC 662 (2003)**—similar;

C v Wood **380 M 545 (80)**—D's statement to rape complainant re: D's prior rape conviction = admissible;

C v McKinnon **35 MAC 398 (93)**—D's threat (with gun) of child rape complainant's mother years before alleged sexual assault admissible to explain fear & delay in reporting;

C v Lavoie **47 MAC 1 (99)**—fresh enough because though 26 months after last assault, only two weeks after out of D's control, and complainant then only 13 years old, BUT error to instruct jury that they could consider evidence that D allegedly abused complainant's mother in determining freshness: no evidence that complainant ever witnessed such violence;

C v Chalifoux **362 M 811 (73)**—D's statement to complaining witness about having been in jail = relevant to complaining witness's fear, not to prove propensity for crime;

C v Serrano **74 MAC 1 (2009)**—that D had been in prison when girlfriend broke up with him and began dating another provided permissible "context" to D's belated (i.e., upon D's release) harassment, threats, and the eventual homicide of new boyfriend, such that judge didn't abuse discretion in admitting, with limiting instruction;

C v Martin **424 M 301 (97)**—evidence that complainant believed D was HIV+ relevant and admissible since consent was issue in rape trial; AND SEE *C v Thevenin* **33 MAC 588 (92)** evidence that defendant had been told that complainant had "crabs" (pubic lice) admissible not for truth but for defense that he had not, therefore, engaged in natural sex with her;

C v Daggett **416 M 347 (93)**—D's arrest for soliciting a Brockton prostitute during time when D was on duty at water treatment plant in Pembroke ten months before murder of different Brockton prostitute admissible: victim's last work clothes were found partially burned at the water treatment plant, and she disappeared at time when D was sole on-duty employee there;

C v Brown **389 M 382 (83)**—D's confession to unconnected crimes not admissible; probative value did not outweigh prejudice;

C v Gonzalez **47 MAC 255 (99)**—DA shouldn't ask cop whether he knew D before this case;

C v Blaney **387 M 628 (82)**—mugshot and ID testimony should be sanitized to avoid inference of D's prior criminal record *(See Chapter 18-E, re: Identification Issues, including Mugshots)*;

C v Payton **35 MAC 586 (93)**—when ID mugshots were clearly mugshots & D both wanted them admitted & failed to suggest sanitizing, no relief: here, no testimony suggesting photos taken regarding some crime other than one being tried;

C v McCray **40 MAC 936 (96)**—because witness had known D for years, intro of witness's ID of D from photo array served only "to inform the jury that the police had" D's picture: error;

C v Austin **421 M 357 (95)**—OK to introduce videotape of different bank robbery because witnesses ID'd robber in tape as culprit in case being tried (dissent decrying use because of "propensity" prejudice);

C v King **387 M 464 (82)**—common PATTERN/course of conduct (sex with complaining witness's brothers close in time/place/age/manner to trial allegations);

C v Delp **41 MAC 35 (96)**—same;

C v Johnson **35 MAC 211 (93)**—alleged sexual assault occurring 40 months after incidents for which D was on trial, was too remote to be probative;

C v Yetz **37 MAC 90 (95)**—**not** common course of conduct when extraneous sexual relationship, albeit with underage female, was desired & consented to by her, ended 2 years before alleged crimes for which D was on trial, and occurred in place different from site alleged in charges being tried;

C v Barrett **418 M 788 (94)**—"common plan" in sex cases examined;

C v Walker **442 M 185 (2004)**—OK to admit, at trial of D for drugging women & having sex with them (one such woman dying after drugging), testimony from woman that D did this to her, though this incident was not subject of any criminal charges: showed common scheme/pattern, and any unfair prejudice was sufficiently ameliorated by the judge's limiting instruction, given repeatedly;

C v Madyun **17 MAC 965 (83)**—other complaining witness's identification of D OK because strikingly similar modus operandi & highly relevant to identification issue;

C v Pimental **454 M 475 (2009)**—in trial as joint venturer with Silva in murder (kicking/stomping) of stranger in woods, there was evidence of D stating that he had attempted to stop Silva from continuing attack; D proffered evidence that couple of months earlier D saw Silva going after someone with knife and D stopped him; this was NOT '3rd party culprit' evidence, but instead inadmissible prior bad act offered to prove respective characters of Silva and D; EVEN IF '3rd party culprit' rule were applies, non-existent relevant similarity (one with shod foot, one with knife; one in woods, one at D's house; one committed against an acquaintance, one a stranger);

C v Ruiz **51 MAC 346 (2001)**—OK for witness at trial of Ds for attempted home invasion that these Ds had, prior to the incident, approached him & called him "rat," displaying gun, re: witness's pursuing criminal charges against others for robbing him, & that he'd often seen these Ds with the men who had robbed him; probative of identity & motive;

C v Leonard **428 M 782 (99)**—OK to admit evidence of an uncharged arson at home of another woman for whom D had done work; similar modus operandi probative of identity;

C v Mullane **63 MAC 317, further appellate review allowed 444 M 1103 (2005)**—error (abuse of discretion) to admit evidence that D was in control of premises of massage parlor when it had a different name, 20 months earlier, when critical issue at trial was control of the operations at the latter time; **but SJC overrules**, finds no error by trial judge (limiting instructions were given), **445 M 702 (2006)**;

C v Reynolds **429 M 388, 395 (99)**—error to admit D's alleged statement, "in Spain, the drug dealers are easy to rob" (though homicide V here was drug dealer killed during robbery);

C v Conkey **430 M 139 (99)**—OK to allow evidence that D said he liked to break into homes when residents were present ("relevant to . . . D's motive");

C v Emence **47 MAC 299 (99)**—error to allow evidence that, four months after alleged crimes on trial (assault & battery by dangerous weapon, to wit, scalding coffee), D poured boiling hot chocolate on someone;

C v Maldonado **429 M 502 (99)**—D's gang membership relevant to motive for attack;

C v John **442 M 329 (2004)**—gang relevant & necessary background to murder prosecution, and not introduced for criminal propensity; potential jurors were questioned re: this possible unfair influence; limiting charge given;

C v Ragland **72 MAC 815, 818 n.5 (2008)**—phrase "common social thread" = euphemism used to avoid potentially prejudicial effects from info that D and co-D were affiliated with "group known as the 'Made Men'";

C v Smith **450 M 395 (2008)**—gang affiliations relevant to motive and joint venture; though judge gave lengthy limiting instruction, "would have been preferable" to also screen potential jurors re: possible bias about gangs;

C v Rebello **450 M 118 (2007)**—error to admit testimony that D used borrowed gun to shoot named person unrelated to case, and had sold heroin which "killed some people" (unlike other evidence, unrelated to "motive"), but held harmless;

C v Cardarelli **433 M 427 (2001)**—D's post-homicide conduct in wiping out joint bank accounts & gambling in casinos = relevant to motive; D's extensive travels, using false name, living in car relevant to consciousness of guilt, as it pertained to whether he had substantial capacity to understand criminality of his conduct or conform conduct to law;

C v Gaulin **75 MAC 73 (2009)**—D on trial for robbery of elderly neighbor; evidence from other neighbors that she recently, often, & persistently asked for money from them (as she had with robbery victim) = relevant to prosecution theory that D constantly needed money and was incapable of handling the money she had (motive);

C v Grant **71 MAC 205 (2008)**—when D was on trial for both "resisting arrest" and firearms charges (firearm hidden by D in flight from officers seeking to effectuate arrest), testimony re: arrest warrant = admissible; no details regarding warrant were admitted & limiting instruction given twice; that MAC ordered required finding of not guilty on resisting arrest charge didn't change analysis;

C v Jackson **417 M 830 (94)**—when homicide victim, very drunk at death, was purportedly merely "found" by D nude & hogtied (rope binding ankles to wrists connected to another rope around neck) in park, OK to admit evidence that similar victim, not yet dead, was found in D's car, with D standing outside, 2 years earlier, 400 yards from this homicide scene: prior bad act was probative of the identity of the perpetrator, since the 2 acts/crimes had such similarities "as to be meaningfully distinctive";

C v Anderson **439 M 1007 (2003)**—(on Commonwealth's petition under G.L. c. 211, § 3 for relief from ruling on D's motion in limine barring introduction of D's prior bad acts/crimes) at trial of a 1977 murder, no abuse of discretion in judge's ruling barring evidence (purportedly probative of gender-based animus) that in 1977 D tied up and cut around the throat of female hitchhiker but didn't sexually assault her, and that in 1990 (after release from sentence for 1977 attack) he stabbed woman and dragged her to his truck but didn't sexually assault her; murder victim was found with breasts cut off, abdomen sliced open, and internal organs displaced to give appearance of male genitalia, but no indication of rape; "little in common . . . except that all three incidents involve an attack on a woman with a knife," "too remote in time to demonstrate [D]'s state of mind at the time of the murder"; no abuse of discretion in the finding that evidence was more prejudicial than probative; great danger of conviction "simply because he has a history of attacking women";

C v Bonds **445 M 821 (2006)**—testimony by rape complainant's mother that complainant was overly trusting was admissible, because it "gave the jury a clear picture of who the victim was" & served to explain her limited mental capacity (rebuffing argument that it illegitimately played on "sympathy"); criticism that "relevance" objection didn't serve to preserve appellate argument as to impermissible "character" testimony;

C v Adjutant **443 M 649 (2005)**—judge has discretion to admit "specific incidents of violence that the victim is reasonably alleged to have initiated" when D asserts self-defense and identity of first aggressor is in dispute; D needn't have known of such incidents at time of alleged crime;

C v Jewett **442 M 356 (2004)**—vulgar/derogatory remarks about victim, made years after rape and murder, admissible as "hostility . . . relevant to motive";

C v Marrero **427 M 65 (98)**—homicide by knife and beating with a board justified admission of evidence that D had beaten another drug debtor or thief with a board a month earlier; other bad acts by D admissible when cross-examination of Commonwealth witnesses opened door, and they permissibly testified as to WHY they were biased against/afraid of D;

C v Holliday **450 M 794 (2008)**—after defense counsel properly tried to discredit witnesses who only recently came forward, suggesting rewards from recent cooperation with prosecution or who did not initially inculpate D, witnesses in redirect permissibly explained their fear of retaliation;

C v Parreira **72 MAC 308 (2008)**—D's cross-examination of sexual assault complainant suggesting delay in reporting incident included question whether she had told her boyfriend and what his response was opened door to the complained-of "self-corroboration";

C v Torres **437 M 460 (2002)**—in murder case where defense was lack of criminal responsibility and cross-examination of defense expert by DA elicited info about "antisocial personality disorder," D counsel in redirect elicited that expert had not diagnosed D with this disorder, (expert clarifying that he had merely noted some "antisocial tendencies" from this case & "criminal history"); this opened the door to DA in re-cross eliciting D's "long history of trouble with the law";

C v Grissett **66 MAC 454 (2006)**—"grave error for counsel to call [D] to testify and then pose questions on direct . . . which left [D] vulnerable to a predictably devastating cross-examination", i.e., after direct elicited that D had never purchased or used cocaine, prosecutor received permission to impeach D with prior conviction for possession with intent to distribute cocaine;

C v Imbruglia **377 M 682 (79)**—past "fencing" shows modus operandi for receiving stolen securities & counterfeit $;

C v Fidalgo **74 MAC 130 (2009)**—reversal for admitting evidence, in trial for filing false motor vehicle insurance claim, that D had been passenger in three other auto accidents in previous nine years, claiming injuries and seeking damages in each;

C v Brousseau **421 M 647 (95)**—testimony that D asked witness whether someone would be able to match gun shells from murder being tried with shells from another homicide OK because showed D's control over the weapon (in D's possession prior to the shooting) and consciousness of guilt;

C v Triplett **398 M 561 (86)**—D's bad temper & dishonorable discharge inadmissible though D's defense is self-defense;

C v Salone **26 MAC 926 (88)**—(same);

C v McClendon **39 MAC 122 (95)**—murder conviction reversed due to DA's cross of D concerning specific instances of bad temper when drinking, and attempted strangulation of his stepmother once when drunk: no evidence that strangulation of V was "distinctively" similar to attempted stepmother strangulation; "absence of accident" rationale similarly rejected;

C v Sharpe **454 M 135 (2009)**—despicably unprincipled "propensity" evidence allowed: OK to admit evidence that, at least seven years before homicide being tried, D abused a former girlfriend and "look[ed] for money in their apartment": "relevant because it showed a pattern of conduct involving arguments over money with significant women in his life, and the use of a dangerous weapon when the relationship approached the point of disintegration"; error to admit evidence of former wife's obtaining 209A order, but "no prejudice" because "four other" such orders were "properly" admitted concerning victim of homicide being tried (relevant to show existence of hostile relationship/motive);

C v Garuti **454 M 48 (2009)**—even if evidence of 209A order obtained by V against D five years before murder was too remote/error, no prejudice because D himself stated acrimonious relationship for 14 years, until he "lost it" and ran over her with vehicle;

C v Rosenthal **432 M 124 (2000)**—no relief for admission of evidence that D caused victim-wife "black eyes" two years and five years before homicide being tried, in which he used a rock to beat her face beyond recognition, removed her internal organs, and left them impaled on a stake in the backyard, on stated ground that there was "striking similarity between the prior injuries and those inflicted during the murder"; but cf cases in which D sought to have evidence admitted to demonstrate another person's possible culpability: *C v Hunter* **426 M 715 (98)** (act of strangling is a relatively ordinary form of attack);

C v Bregoli **431 M 165, 174–75 (2000)**—act of grabbing person by neck is not similar enough to grabbing person by neck so as to kill her, only common feature being "placement of hands on the neck";

C v King **34 MAC 466 (93)**—that D terminated questioning by calling cops "assholes"= irrelevant/inadmissible: reversal because possible inference = G from silence;

C v Jordan (No. 1) **397 M 489 (86)**—prior beatings of complaining witness & her dog admissible as evidence of intent to murder & hostility towards complaining witness;

C v Fallon **38 MAC 366 (95)**—introduction of evidence that D (money manager) was found in contempt and jailed because he wouldn't account for the money compelled reversal of larceny/securities fraud convictions; contempt was in separate, **civil** action, for failure to provide satisfactory accounting of assets, but likely caused jury to infer D's guilt of larceny (conviction rev'd); BUT ON FURTHER REVIEW, SJC AFF'D CONVICTION, 423 M 92 (96), and found no error here: willingness to go to jail rather than reveal where money was = relevant to prove D's intent to permanently deprive;

C v Fordham **417 M 10 (94)**—prior battery of wife & her supposed lover relevant to D's hostility (murder trial);

C v DeMarco **444 M 678 (2005)**—no error in admitting D's prior emotional and physical abuse of murder victim (D's wife), and D's "earlier extramarital conduct"; "limiting" instruction (admissible only re: "state of mind and his motive and intent");

C v McLeod **39 MAC 461 (95)**—counsel not ineffective in failing to object to evidence of D's horrible acts because reasonable tactical decision to argue that these acts gave sexual assault complainants motive to lie/"get even" with D;

C v Parker **12 MAC 955 (81)**—evidence that D fired from 2 jobs because suspected of stealing not opened up by D's questions re: work history;

C v Maimoni **41 MAC 321 (96)**—murder D's 1st story, that as married man he would not invite other woman to sail alone with him, justified admission of 2 women's testimony that he had so invited them during preceding week (and had made sexual advances); alternatively admissible as 'common plan/pattern' of conduct;

C v Estep **38 MAC 502 (95)**—D's keeping vicious pit bull which prevented EMTs from entering apartment relevant to rebut D's claim that victim's ex-husband entered & killed her (V = D's domestic partner, dead in apartment kitchen);

C v Schoening **379 M 234 (79)**—list of exceptions to "bad acts" rule;

C v Moure **428 M 313 (98)**—after prosecution witness was impeached for one motive, permissible on redirect to show (purportedly) "true motive" which necessitated introduction of D's bad acts;

C v O'Laughlin **446 M 188 (2006)**—evidence of D's smoking crack cocaine and attempts to obtain additional cocaine on night of assault to murder = admissible: D's desperate attempt to obtain more cocaine or money for it permitted inference that robbery was motive for crime, and also relevant because it contradicted D's immediate claims to police as to his recent activities;

C v Walters **12 MAC 389 (81)**—undesirable to include alias unless necessary element or to identify D;

C v Sheline **391 M 279 (84)**—& should delete (hearsay) alias in drug certificate;

US v Grayson **166 F.2d 863, 867 (2d Cir. 48)**—alias "can serve no purpose but to arouse suspicion that the accused is a person who has found it useful or necessary to conceal his identity";

C v Martin **57 MAC 272 (2003)**—motion in limine to prevent reference to D's alias was denied, & D's failure to object thereafter, at trial, to its repeated introduction meant issue wasn't preserved, BUT reversal anyway: alias not relevant to issues, but DA argued "how can you trust somebody who has two names at the outset?"; *on further appellate review,* **442 M 1002 (2004)**, SJC "agree[s] with the reasoning of the Appeals Court";

C v Fetzer **19 MAC 1024, 1025 (85)**—for false name to be admissible as evidence of consciousness of guilt, its use must follow rather than precede the crime;

C v Durango **47 MAC 185 (99)**—alias evidence should not have been admitted; not relevant, and suggested other criminal activity; contrast *C v Manning* **44 MAC 695 (98)** OK to show D's fingerprints were connected by FBI to individual named "Tony Russell" because V ID'd assailant as person known to him as "Tony";

C v Richardson **423 M 180 (96)**—upholding admission of testimony that sexual assault complainant's belated (6 months) allegation was triggered by friend's claim that D raped her (not for "truth", but to explain why made allegation after long silence); but see *C v Montanino* **409 M 500 (91)**;

C v Sapoznik **28 MAC 236 (90)**—D's prior drug arrest 2 weeks earlier to show D's knowledge of drugs' presence was inadmissible because prejudice outweighed probative value;

C v Day **42 MAC 242 (97)**—ineffective assistance of counsel found when, to show that trial witness IDs were tainted, counsel introduced the "wanted" flyer indicating D's suspected guilt of other crimes, that he was likely armed & dangerous, that he was a "Devil's Disciples" gang member, and that the source of his photo was a prison (the witnesses had allegedly seen this flyer before ID'ing D); **also** error to introduce unsanitized "mug" shot;

C v Wolcott **28 MAC 200 (90)**—cop's testimony about D's gang-involvement was inadmissible because conjectural & unduly prejudicial; contrast *C v Philyaw* **55 MAC 730 (2002)**—though D claimed that evidence improperly insinuated "gang" membership, testimony that D "hung out" in area where "kids" had a problem with "kids" in the project and rode in car headed toward that project was OK, relevant to identification;

C v Burns **49 MAC 677, 684 (2000)**—OK to introduce evidence that, 3 years before shooting being tried, a friend of chief Commonwealth witness (who was with victim when V was shot) shot 2 friends of D who were seen with D prior to shooting being tried (motive);

C v Myer **38 MAC 140 (95)**—D's assault of V (his girlfriend) 7 months after alleged assault for which he was on trial admissible re: D's "state of mind";

C v Montanino (II) **409 M 500 (91)**—prosecutor's eliciting, on direct of complainant, D's uncharged but allegedly ongoing abuse of other child[ren] improper as showing complainant's state of mind where complainant had not been impeached;

C v Demars **38 MAC 596 (95)**—child sexual assault convictions reversed because of DA's questioning of victim's father, indicating witness heard extraneous allegations about defendant: witness's "state of mind" was irrelevant to D's guilt;

C v McIntyre **430 M 529, 540 (99)**—witnesses' testimony that they feared D, had "bad vibes", & one knew he should "watch [his] back", INADMISSIBLE; "had no relevance to any contested issue, and served only to implicate the witness's fear of [D], and consequently, [D's] bad character"; alleged "dream" of D that he killed V, recounted by him to 3 witnesses, admissible because it could clarify D's later comment, "I just killed her. . . . I dreamed about it last night";

C v Odell **34 MAC 100 (93)**—at trial of D for plying 4 teenage girls with alcohol or drugs and sexually molesting them while they were semi-conscious, OK to admit evidence that 3 months after his release on bail, he asked his nephew's assistance in having 2 teenage girls visit and indicated his intent to make alcohol & drugs available with plans that they stay the night;

C v Calcagno **31 MAC 25 (91)**—D's prior repeated uncharged sexual abuse of child complainant was admissible to show motive, common scheme, context, etc.;

C v Sosnowski **43 MAC 367 (97)**—same, "to show how the sexual relationship . . . developed";

C v Frank **51 MAC 19 (2001)**—sex assaults on child occurring outside jurisdiction = admissible to show how relationship started/developed;

C v Butler **445 M 568 (2005)**—when alleged victim was called to testify despite Commonwealth's advance knowledge that she would deny that D had hurt her & say she had lied to police when she alleged he had, evidence of D's prior bad acts/restraining orders against him were admissible to show "hostile nature of the relationship between" D and alleged victim, even though such evidence was purportedly inadmissible "to show a pattern or course of conduct by the defendant";

C v Feijoo **419 M 486 (95)**—9 child sex complainants - same modus operandi;

C v Ramos **63 MAC 379 (2005)**—OK to admit evidence of identical uncharged conduct (concerning other patients) at trial of medical doctor for sexual touchings during exams, though "troubling" that evidence of pattern was adequately established already by testimony of the 8 complainants whose charges were being tried; forceful instructions & NG on some charges showed "[in]sufficient prejudice to warrant reversal"; uncharged conduct shouldn't be basis for sentencing;

C v Hanlon **44 MAC 810 (98)**—at trial of D for raping one boy, OK to admit evidence D raped complainant's two younger brothers and two other boys, though some such conduct allegedly occurred as much as nine years after the last act for which D was being tried; "logical consistency and ultimate coherence" of the "doctrinal basis for the allowance of such . . . bad act evidence" might be questioned, id. at 818 n.5; consult *C v Jackson* **132 M 16 (1882)** for what the rule against "propensity" SHOULD mean;

C v Clayton **63 MAC 608 (2005)**—OK to admit evidence that D ordered complainant and D's minor son to engage in sex acts because "demonstrated [D's] willingness to use [complainant] for his own voyeuristic sexual gratification," "probative of a pattern of sexualized conduct with [her] & demonstrative of D's desire for / control over her in sexual matters";

C v Roche **44 MAC 372, 380–81 (98)**—uncharged assaults were subject of more evidence than **charged** crimes and their admissibility should be re-examined at retrial (necessary on another ground);

C v Phoenix **409 M 408 (91)**—murder D's job dissatisfaction was admissible to show motive;

C v Kelleher **42 MAC 911 (97)**—D's sexual assault upon complainant one year after crime charged admissible to show identification;

C v Phinney **416 M 364 (93)**—at trial of D for murder by smashing V's head with camera when she awakened from sleep (after he entered home without permission), OK to introduce evidence that he photographed women sunbathing, etc.;

C v Berry **47 MAC 24, 34 (99)**—when D said cousin did the stabbing, within judge's discretion to admit evidence that D previously identified himself by cousin's name when D was being charged with weapons violations in unrelated case;

C v Goetzendanner **42 MAC 637 (97)**—evidence of witness intimidation admissible in trial for rape/forcible confinement, as consciousness of guilt and to explain complainant's "inconsistent conduct toward" D (e.g., recantation, visiting him in jail); compare/contrast *C v Martinez* **431 M 168 (2000)** abuse of discretion to admit evidence that D's niece threatened chief prosecution witness when witness's testimony hadn't changed;

C v Robertson **408 M 747 (90)**—that D was pimp for murdered prostitutes was admissible to show "whole relationship" & motive to kill;

C v Holloway **44 MAC 469 (98)**—that D showed underage complainant porno movies and purchased alcohol for her consumption before having sex with her was admissible (showed "the relationship," showed D's "state of mind" [Question how it was relevant to the charge] showed "pattern of conduct" [Q how relevant except as propensity toward bad acts];

C v Cyr **425 M 89 (97)**—"showing the relationship between the parties" is not valid basis for admitting hearsay/bad acts of D;

C v Travis **408 M 1 (90)**—murder D's statement to prison official 3 weeks before release that he might rob or kill was admissible to show state of mind;

C v Niemic **427 M 718 (98)**—judge's ruling, at pretrial motion in limine, admitting D's statement that he could hardly wait to put to use a knife (which was used several days later during D's apparent attempt to defuse a situation involving an extremely drunk victim threatening to shoot others) not found erroneous PERHAPS BECAUSE NO OBJECTION WAS LATER LODGED, and evidence would have seemed relevant to deliberate premeditation (this theory was rejected by jury, so there was no apparent prejudice from admission of the statement); cf *Gabbidon* **398 M 1, 7 (86)** though motion in limine was filed and denied, IF D DOESN'T OBJECT WHEN DA INTRODUCES EVIDENCE, D WAIVES right to appellate review;

C v Avellar **416 M 409 (93)**—that D (father) had urged abortion admissible at trial for murder of ensuing infant, age 6 months;

C v Cokonougher **35 MAC 502 (93)**—same (D [mother] considered abortion during 2d month of pregnancy & after birth said she didn't want baby);

C v Cokonougher **32 MAC 54 (92)**—D's prior neglect of other children to show her "deep parental frustration" & intent to kill infant victim was inadmissible because too remote & logically irrelevant; but see *Estelle v McGuire* **502 US 62 (91)** - 7-week-old injuries ok to show battered child syndrome;

C v Anderson **48 MAC 508, 513 (2000)**—no relief for murder D re: callous bad acts to his baby prior to her death, and any error in bad acts toward baby's mother before baby's birth = harmless; but see *C v Almeida* **42 MAC 607 (97)** testimony that D callously and cruelly demanded that then-adult rape complainant abort fetus and threatened to end relationship required reversal of convictions for alleged sexual assaults when complainant was a child, despite lack of objection;

C v Wilson **49 MAC 429 (2000)**—in prosecution of D for A&B on wife, their daughter volunteered during cross that alleged victim returned to marital home out of concern over drug & alcohol abuse by D and their son, & the "weapons in the home and car"; that her children asked why D "was mean to Grammy", that another brother told people that his father was dead (because he wanted no relationship with him), etc.: reversal (in major part because argued basis for admissibility, to corroborate mother's explanation for return to marital home, was inapplicable: it was inconsistent with latter, and no 'personal knowledge' foundation anyway);

C v Nardone **406 M 123 (89)**—D's hostile relationship with spouse was admissible to show motive to kill;

C v Snell **428 M 766 (99)**—V's "spontaneous utterances" to neighbor 18 months before her death admissible to show hostile relationship with D-husband, and motive to kill;

C v Cormier **427 M 446 (98)**—evidence that D previously attacked his wife, threatened her, and expressed to a third party his desire to kill her admissible at his trial for her murder;

C v Ashman **430 M 736, 741 (2000)**—OK evidence of D's prior bad acts against his girlfriend (at trial for her stabbing death); but inadmissible hearsay (implied) found in testimony from V's two friends that they had come to apartment 3 months earlier in response to V's telephone call, and had spoken with her there and called police, and had taken V (with her son and clothing) elsewhere; BUT SEE *C v Seabrooks* **425 M 507 (97)** that homicide V told friend 16 months before death that D inflicted observable injuries was inadmissible hearsay **and** remote; hearsay statements alleging past violence/misconduct **not** admissible to show hostile relationship;

C v Magraw **426 M 589 (98)**—D's extramarital affairs not admissible (too remote) because one ended 8 years before wife's (homicide?) death and another began after their agreement to divorce;

C v Scott **408 M 811 (90)**—D's harassment of other women days before killing was admissible to show sexual frustration;

C v Fortini **44 MAC 562 (98)**—evidence that D was a racist held admissible to show homicide D's state of mind;

C v Jaime **433 M 575, 579–80 (2001)**—that D asked emergency room employee (after shooting his former girlfriend 3 times in head) if she knew what he had done, or what he was capable of doing to her, held "highly probative" of D's state of mind, because it implied that he fully understood what he'd done & wasn't confused or remorseful;

C v Brusgulis **406 M 501 (90)**—prior sexual attacks on strangers in secluded areas were inadmissible to show common scheme or modus operandi because they were not sufficiently similar to crime charged nor sufficiently distinctive;

C v Montez **45 MAC 802, 809–10 (98)**—OK to admit against D items seized from his apartment which were stolen in two apartment burglaries close in time and place to sexual assault being tried, because relevant to question of identity; "distinctiveness" signifying same culprit in all because inferable that culprit on each occasion used a key to enter the apartments (contrast *C v Jackson* **417 M 830, 835–42 (94)**, which applied more stringent criteria for finding "distinctive");

C v Kater **432 M 404 (2000)**—modus operandi so distinctive as to make evidence "highly probative. This is as close as a crime gets to being a 'signature crime'"; apparent abduction, in a car, of 13 & 15 yr old Caucasian girls from rural residential area as they walked with or rode bikes on the road, in the afternoon, after which they were taken to densely wooded area within 20 miles, tied to a tree, bound head to toe & around neck, fully clothed & apparently alive when tied to tree, in area so remote that cries wouldn't be heard; latter girl died of 'positional asphyxia' when her head dropped when she became unconscious/exhausted, but former girl managed to untie herself & escape;

C v Jackson **428 M 455 (98)**—OK to admit that, three days before murder and within two blocks of it, D broke down door of another individual and later pled G to this; also introduced was evidence that, immediately before murder-robbery of drug dealer, he had kicked in door of another apartment in same building because he'd been told, erroneously, that drugs could be obtained there; Court found "a considered mode of operation," relevant to identification;

C v Delong **60 MAC 528 (2004)**—no error in admitting evidence of two prior robberies on issue of identification; BUT dissent convincingly argues that perpetrator's identity in extraneous robberies was not certain, & that jury was required to assess ID of D in the other robberies "is a strange evidentiary construct, given that this other robbery evidence was admitted in the first place for the limited purpose of aiding the jury's determination of whether" D was robber in crime being tried; D "was confronted with extrajudicial and extra-indictment-on-trial identification procedures which were not tested, or testable, in pretrial proceedings" in case being tried:

C v Pinto **45 MAC 790 (99)**—no error in barring D from introducing evidence that his sister's boyfriend was arrested for steroid possession in 1996, when D was being tried for cocaine trafficking and possession of steroids with intent, based on pkg. delivered by U.S. mail to D's residence in 1993 (too remote to warrant holding that judge abused discretion);

C v Mills **47 MAC 500 (99)**—though judge held not to "so far exceed" a reasonable discretion in admitting uncharged ("m.o."/modus operandi) acts/robberies that reversal was required, court reversed for no sua sponte limiting instruction (no request made), i.e., not useable to infer propensity;

C v Perez **47 MAC 605 (99)**—no sua sponte obligation to instruct that gang membership was to be considered solely re motive/state of mind (and not for criminal propensity or bad character);

C v Velasquez **48 MAC 147, 153 (99)**—OK to cross-examine drug D on substance of prior convictions (to rebut claim of mere presence) because priors involved D with same accomplices and same M.O. (drug dealing from apt., drugs stashed in basement);

C v Ortiz-Soto **49 MAC 645 (2000)**—in trial for drug sale to undercover cop in particular apartment four years before trial, ID being likely issue, no error to admit evidence that D had been present during execution of a search warrant for drugs in different apartment ten days before sale in issue (though no drugs were then found);

C v Martinez **47 MAC 839 (99)**—evidence against D in one charged drug deal could be used to defeat required finding of not guilty in other drug deal joined for trial— "presence . . . with same band of sellers and the same customer allows inferences of knowledge and intent to aid" during first transaction;

C v Ruiz **51 MAC 346 (2001)**—Ds' presence/threats to witness as to his reporting extraneous crime relevant to motive/identification;

C v Montez **45 MAC 802 (98)**—bad act not "extraneous": it was joined for trial, and no motion for relief from prejudicial joinder was made;

C v Zagranski **408 M 278 (90)**—prior plan to purchase land from owner & kill him was admissible to show malice & common scheme because sufficiently similar;

C v Roderick **429 M 271 (99)**—D's prior gun possession relevant to rebut his testimony that he wasn't familiar with guns;

C v Oliveira **74 MAC 49 (2009)**—prior convictions used to rebut D's testimony he was peaceful man wishing to avoid conflict, though question "close";

C v Loach **46 MAC 313 (99)**—bad acts relevant to rebut implicit assertion that attempted loan collection was not threatening;

C v Siano **52 MAC 912, 913–14 (2001)**—D should not have been asked, on cross, to "explain" documents seized during search of D's house (blank social security cards, blank NY state driver's license, NJ operator's license, blank NY birth certificate, other documents having "raised seals"); no rational link to cocaine trafficking charge (& merely extraneous criminal/bad conduct), notwithstanding Comm's claim that it impeached D's testimony that he didn't conduct drug sales there;

C v Saunders **45 MAC 340 (98)**—after D presented accountant-witness for testimony that D was so wealthy he had no motive to commit arson for insurance money, OK for DA to cross-examine re debt to IRS of $109,000 and tax lien; no motion in limine had been filed because DA had said he wouldn't use in **direct** case; no relief, BUT D didn't argue he wouldn't have called accountant if he knew of risk;

C v Clark **432 M 1, 20–21 (2000)**—OK to introduce evidence that D was on parole when he was allegedly pulled over by a state trooper and then fatally shot him because relevant to motive; limiting instruction given;

See also Chapters 10–F, Character Witnesses (wide-open cross-examination); 16, Entrapment (same); 9-D, Impeach by Prior Record; 12-E, Consciousness/Guilt; & 5-A, Alias of D (in charging document);

See Chapter 9-C for cases on bias [including pending criminal charges;

See Chapter 11-H for relevant cases on rape;

11-F. HEARSAY (AND CONFRONTATION RIGHTS)

See also Chapter 9, Cross-Examination;

U.S. Constitution, Sixth Amendment—confrontation right;

See Chapter 9-A & 9-C for cases on right to confrontation & bias;

See Chapter 9-F & 9-G for cases on prior inconsistent statements;

See Chapter 7-K - prior recorded testimony;

See Chapter 8, Severance re statements of alleged joint venturers (Bruton problems);

Mass. Declaration of Rights, Article 12—right "to meet the witnesses against him" FACE to FACE" (*See* ***Bergstrom 402 M 534 (88)*** & ***Coy v Iowa 487 US 1012 (88)***, *§ H post, and Chapter 7-K, Prior Testimony);*

Young, Pollets & Poreda, *Evidence,* **§§ 801.1–806 (2d ed. 1998)**—Hearsay rule & exceptions; § 801 (d)(1)(A)(2), prior consistent statements to rebut bias/recent contrivance; BUT SEE qualification to admissibility of prior consistent, e.g., *C v McBrown* 72 MAC 60 (2008);

5 Wigmore, *Evidence*, §§ 1360–1477 (Chadbourn rev. 1974);

6 Wigmore, *Evidence*, §§ 1690, 1714, 1745, 1766 (Chadbourn rev. 1976);

Brodin, M. and Avery, M., *Handbook of Massachusetts Evidence* (8th ed. 2007);

Prop.M.R.Evid. Article 8, Rules 801–6; e.g., *C v Pina* 430 M 66 (99) when D introduced evidence that V's boyfriend confessed to the murder (admission against penal interest exception to hearsay), Commonwealth could introduce for impeachment the boyfriend's denial to cop; Prop.M.R.Evid. 806 adopted, at least for these circumstances; *C v Dajarnette* 75 MAC 88 (2009)—though D wanted admitted another (non-testifying) individual's acknowledgment to cop that he had smoked some of the marijuana and his fingerprints would be on bag of it & perhaps also on cocaine bag, trial counsel agreed that the Commonwealth would be entitled to introduce the rest of the statement, which was clearly self-exculpatory; judge would have been within his discretion to declare defense-proffered material inadmissible because the gist of the statement was NOT really declaration against interest or to allow it with some context to prevent distortion by defense; defense counsel not ineffective for having agreed to ruling;

C v Mahar 430 M 643, 648–50 (2000)—after intro of "spontaneous utterance" of non-testifying witness (D's girlfriend), D entitled to introduce girlfriend's later contradictory statements to impeach the hearsay testimony; Prop. M.R.Evid. 806 adopted;

C v Beatrice 75 MAC 153 (2009), **further review allowed 455 M 1108 (2010)**—but court refused to require introduction of a non-testifying domestic violence "victim's" acknowledgment to police that she had stabbed D four months before incident being tried (D wanted to raise justifiable fear/self-defense in current prosecution); such hearsay statement was not "directly inconsistent with her 911 call";

C v Moses 436 M 598 (2002)—error to deny D opportunity to impeach murder victim's credibility by evidence that would have been admissible if V had testified (prior convictions) when judge admitted as "dying declaration" V's statement ID'ing D as his assailant, but harmless because cumulative and D conceded point by testifying that he had shot V in self-defense;

C v Christian 430 M 552, 559–64 (2000)—error to ask long series of "questions", each answered in the negative, asserting that witness (here, D) "told" 3d party various things; judge should bar additional questions after 1st negative answer, order voir dire of 3d party, or seek assurance from prosecutor that 3d party will testify; "[t]o do otherwise would permit [DA] to smear [D] by extrajudicial statements made by [3d party] while denying [D] opportunity to impeach [3d party's] credibility";

C v Fordham 417 M 10 (94)—error to communicate impressions by innuendo through leading questions with no demonstrated evidentiary or good faith basis;

C v Wynter 55 MAC 337 (2002)—same;

C v Howell 49 MAC 42 (2000)—error for prosecutor to ask defense witness (D's father) whether his and D's brother's purpose in visiting robbery victim was to influence V in his identification ("no"), and then to ask witness for his and D's brother's heights and weights (objection overruled), and then to ask whether witness had asked victim "how much it would take for [the victim] to go away"; judge should have immediately stopped line of questioning and asked DA basis for questions, particularly since Commonwealth had not ever questioned victim (during V's own testimony, completed) about any such confrontation;

C v Alvarado 50 MAC 419 (2000)—prosecutor's attempt to use hearsay to impeach D's alibi testimony = "particularly inappropriate";

C v McIntyre 430 M 529, 538 (99)—deceased's hearsay (that boyfriend didn't stab her) could be impeached with testimony by nurse that deceased at the time was minimally conscious/rational;

C v Bergoli 431 M 265, 273 (2000)—error to exclude evidence of what other person told D, because not offered for truth of matter, but for fact that D had knowledge from source independent of crime scene (Commonwealth argued that D's knowledge was that which only killer would have);

C v Torres 442 M 554 (2004)—D's girlfriend's out-of-court accusations that D was responsible for death of baby held to have legitimate nonhearsay purpose (& judge gave forceful limiting instructions twice), i.e., to refute any inference that D's changed story (neither he nor girlfriend did anything to harm baby) was motivated by sincere desire to help police investigation and stop covering up for the girlfriend;

C v Strahan 30 MAC 947 (91)—statement notifying D to remove himself from premises not hearsay because not offered for truth of matter but to show D received notice he was trespassing; hearsay statements introduced without timely objection allows their admission with "full probative force";

C v Caparella 70 MAC 506 (2007)—statement by D's father (alleged joint venturer) that telemarketing program had ceased wasn't hearsay because not admitted for truth of assertion; further, statement was "an after-action effort to evade discovery," and concealment constituted furtherance of joint venture (so admissible against all venturers); assumed, without deciding, that *Crawford v Washington* 541 US 36 (2004) might consider statement "testimonial" (because he should have expected his answers would develop into info for investigation/prosecution), but no objection & no substantial risk of miscarriage of justice, any error harmless beyond reasonable doubt;

C v Rodriquez 454 M 215 (2009)—witness's testimony that severed co-D had asked him to kill unknown person by putting a wire around his neck was not hearsay, held admissible to establish that co-D was trying to get help to kill victim by the method eventually employed; ignored by SJC = argument that it was not admissible against D because D was obviously NOT a joint venturer at time of statement and it was not probative of D's intent; holding that jury could infer that co-D made same proposal to D as he had to testifying witness;

C v Caillot **454 M 245 (2009)**—purportedly because Commonwealth was not offering most of co-D's out-of-court statements for "truth of" its assertions, but instead for their falsity (and consciousness of guilt), no *Crawford v Washington* violation;

C v Williams **63 MAC 615 (2005)**—DIA Form 110, a document whose completion is required to make claim for worker's compensation, wasn't business/public record, but wasn't being used as hearsay, because not for truth of matter but instead "as proof of the statutorily-required filing itself, and what the filing contained";

C v Mullane **63 MAC 317, 324, further appellate review allowed 444 M 1103 (2005), S.C., 445 M 702 (2006)**—evidence that masseuse at Institute of Massage Therapy "agreed to provide 'extras'" wasn't hearsay (substance of conversation was pertinent evidence of "the character of the house");

C v Jordan **49 MAC 802 (2000)**—at trial of D, evidence that his alleged co-venturer, in D's & V's presence, told D's friend via telephone that they were going to kill V and would come to kill the friend next = admissible; statement was not for truth of matter that they would kill V & friend, but was evidence of existence of conspiracy to murder;

C v Simmarano **50 MAC 312 (2000)**—ineffective assistance of D-counsel found because he failed to rebut prosecutor's "hearsay" objection [& evidence was thus excluded]: what chief prosecution witness had said to D before alleged home invasion was both impeachment of her trial testimony (a prior inconsistent statement) AND made him believe that his entry into and presence in her apartment were permitted ("state of mind" exception to hearsay);

Chambers v Mississippi **410 US 284 (73)**—don't defeat ends of justice with mechanistic rules; [3d party confession = admissible though hearsay];

C v Bohannon **385 M 733 (82)**—[same], but D can't use unavailable witness's hearsay because could've deposed her (*See also Chapter 7-K*);

C v Burnham **451 M 517 (2008)**—rejecting D's belatedly-claimed basis for admission of ex-wife's statements (as against "penal interest"): while SJC acknowledged that declarant was unavailable even though D had not attempted to call her as witness (she'd been indicted for murder along with D, trial severed, tried first, didn't testify, was convicted and appealed), statements did not clearly tend to subject her to criminal liability and were instead at best "consciousness of guilt" equally suggestive of her intent to provide cover for D's criminality, and were not corroborated by circumstances indicating their trustworthiness; a D "has no constitutional right to the admission of unreliable hearsay";

C v Charros **443 M 752, 768 (2005)**—rejects D's claim of error in exclusion of statements by man claimed by D to be owner of drugs (apologizing for leaving D to take the blame, but saying he had to solve his own problems with police): declarant wasn't called to testify & unavailability due to possibility of claim of privilege against self-incrimination won't be presumed; statements didn't qualify as "against penal interest";

C v Semedo **422 M 716 (96)**—MA has no "innominate exception" to hearsay rule for "reliable and trustworthy" hearsay not covered by any other recognized exception;

C v Diaz **426 M 548 (98)**—testimony that someone in large group said that D ordered that eventual murder V be brought out of apartment was inadmissible hearsay; judge's admitting statement "to show the general atmosphere of what was occurring . . . insofar as [the jury] find it has some affect" condemned ("no exception to the hearsay rule such as the court invoked"); but see *C v Rockett* **41 MAC 5 (96)** upholding admission of evidence that unknown person called out "David," & voice came from direction in which burglar was fleeing victim's home; Appeals Court declined to reverse trial judge's purported "exercise of discretion" in finding this a spontaneous utterance (no exciting event was identified); better analysis would be that hearing "David" was circumstantial evidence of someone present by that name;

C v Thissell **74 MAC 773 (2009)**—global positioning system (GPS) records (showing D entered "exclusion zone" covered by stay-away order/condition of probation) not "hearsay", OR, alternatively, are business records; on further review, **457 M 191 (2010)**, SJC discusses "reliability" and holds that evidence supported judge's findings that GPS records were trustworthy; discussion of "computer-generated records" and concern re: "authentication of the generative process";

11-F.1. Failure to Object/Limit Admissibility

C v Atencio **12 MAC 747 (81)**: *C v Adams* **421 M 289 (95)**—failure to object to/move for limited use of hearsay allows its use for all purposes;

C v Semedo **422 M 716 (96)**—D doesn't waive objection to admission of evidence by cooperating on redaction IF he objects to admission of statements after redaction;

C v Whyte **43 MAC 920 (97)**—by lack of objection, inadmissible hearsay sufficed to defeat required finding of not guilty, so ineffective assistance of counsel found (even though counsel claimed it was "trial strategy" not to object);

C v Frisino **21 MAC 551 (86)**—ineffective assistance of counsel in failing to object or seek limit on use of hearsay which, substantively used, defeated required finding of not guilty;

C v White **48 MAC 658, 660 n.5 (2000)**—D-counsel has duty to request limiting instructions; judges ordinarily aren't required to instruct sua sponte "as to the purposes for which evidence is offered at trial"; though appellate counsel argued that failure to limit use of hearsay evidence made it useable substantively and decisively against D, appellate court held counsel used it effectively (no ineffectiveness of counsel);

C v Roberts **433 M 45, 48 (2000)**—request for limiting instruction, made for first time at charge conference, maybe too late (if adversary relied on evidence being admitted for all purposes, & has now rested case);

11-F.1.a. Segregable Portions of Hearsay, Some Admissible and Some Not

C v Cancel **394 M 567 (85)**—part of statement was admissible, part inadmissible hearsay, and they were entirely segregable parts, citing *C v Pleasant* **366 M 100, 103 (74)**—same;

C v Erdely **430 M 149 (99)**—because D sought to show confession involuntary and unreliable due to threat by police to charge his girlfriend, and thus introduced fact that his request to speak to girlfriend was denied, Commonwealth could introduce testimony that she did not want to speak with D; it was neither necessary nor proper to introduce as well her alleged accompanying statement that she believed D responsible for murdering her great aunt (portions of response were entirely segregable);

11-F.1.b. Second Level Hearsay

C v Crawford **417 M 358, 363 (94)**—before admitting hearsay, should require showing of personal knowledge by declarant of info therein;

Prop.M.R.Evid. 805—2d level hearsay exception for each level; 803 - include opinions; e.g., *Julian v Randazzo* **380 M 391 (80)** police report portions with opinions, recommendations, second level hearsay, are inadmissible as "business record";

C v Trowbridge **419 M 750, 760 (95)**—doctor's testimony that child sexual assault complainant's grandmother told him that child said that doctor's examination "felt like when her father touched her," inadmissible;

C v Roman **414 M 235 (93)**—right to produce all favorable proofs under Article 12 did not require admission of extrajudicial statements of nontestifying psychiatrist consulted by testifying psychiatrist;

C v Campbell **37 MAC 960 (94)**—alleged victim's testimony that D's wife told him that D said that he was sorry inadmissible; reversal ordered;

C v Lester **70 MAC 55 (2007)**—cop's testimony that D admitted, to a different cop, making some of the phone calls which were bases for intimidation of witness charges, was inadmissible, and trial counsel was ineffective in failing to object: while "admissions" are an exception to hearsay, no exception permitted a cop to testify to what another cop told him, or reported in writing, that D had said; witness's testimony that he had "reviewed" D's statement didn't establish personal knowledge; record failed to establish that there was a written statement by D as opposed to a written police report summarizing an interview of D;

C v Irving **51 MAC 285 (2001)**—rejecting claim of "totem pole hearsay," because not offered for truth or because merely an "operative" statement, i.e., "affirming the continued existence of a joint venture," or a "verbal act";

11-F.2. Face-to-Face; Confrontation (State and Federal Constitutions)

California v Green **399 US 149, 165 (70)**—hearsay rules and confrontation clause designed to protect similar values; cf., e.g., *C v Rosario* **430 M 505, 508 n.3 (99)** "state of police knowledge" "exception" to hearsay (sic: it's not properly admitted for "truth of" assertions in any event, so isn't hearsay at all) might violate D's confrontation rights under article 12 of Declaration of Rights;

C v Johnson **60 MAC 243 (2003)**—rejects argument that hearsay testimony (that several people told cop that D assaulted V) was admissible to explain how police attention came to be upon D; *see also C v Pleasant* **366 M 100, 103 (74)** & *C v Cancel* **394 M 567 (85)** ("'a lot of people told me you're responsible'" = inadmissible hearsay);

White v Illinois **502 US 346, 353–58 (92)**—confrontation clause not violated by firmly rooted hearsay exceptions; witness unavailability not a constitutional prerequisite for admissibility of statements falling within "firmly rooted" hearsay exceptions; cf. *Ohio v Roberts* **448 US 56, 66 (80)**;

CRAWFORD v WASHINGTON **124 S.Ct. 1354, 1370 (2004) OVERRULED OHIO v ROBERTS:** U.S. Constitution's confrontation clause IS implicated by hearsay;

Davis v Washington **126 S Ct 2266 (2006)**—tape recording of call to "911" was not inadmissible under *Crawford* when statements were not "testimonial": operator's questions and caller's answers had primary purpose of enabling police assistance in ongoing emergency; in other case, however, statements to police officer at asserted crime scene were testimonial (purported domestic violence victim answered officer's questions and executed affidavit at his behest);

Danforth v Minnesota **128 S Ct 1029 (2008)**—*Crawford v Washington* was a "new" rule; federal law doesn't require state courts to apply it to cases which were final when *Crawford* was decided, BUT state courts may give broader effect to such a new rule of criminal procedure than is required under "Teague" rule (*Teague v Lane* **489 US 288**);

C v Beatrice **75 MAC 153 (2009), further review allowed 455 M 1108 (2010)**—D's girlfriend, "out of breath and frantic", called 911 from neighbor's home to report beating by D; dispatcher questioned her as to name of assailant and whether he was still at scene; court rejects D's argument (per *C v Lao* **450 M 215**) that there was no ongoing emergency because girlfriend had escaped, so no immediate danger; statements admissible as excited utterances and no confrontation clause barrier;

C v Nesbitt **452 M 236 (2008)**—stabbing victim's call to 911 naming D as her assailant, was spontaneous utterance, not barred by *Crawford v Washington*; victim's similar statement to neighbor coming to her assistance likewise = spontaneous utterance (victim mortally wounded, pleading for help); even if latter considered testimonial, admission as "dying declaration" not violative of Confrontation Clause, in view of SJC;

C v Gonsalves **445 M 1 (2005)**—"statements made in response to questioning by law enforcement agents are per se testimonial, except when the questioning is meant to secure a volatile scene or to establish the need for or provide medical care . . . out-of-court statements that are not testimonial per se must be examined to determine if they are nonetheless testimonial in fact by evaluating whether a reasonable person in the declarant's position would anticipate his statement being used against the accused in investigating and prosecuting a crime"; "questioning by law enforcement agents, whether police, prosecutors, or others acting directly on their behalf, other than to secure a volatile scene or to establish the need for or provide medical care, is interrogation in the colloquial sense";

C v Burgess **450 M 422 (2008)**—at trial pre-*Crawford*, Commonwealth introduced murder victim's statements to police responding to his 911 calls 2–3 months before his death; though all but one held "testimonial", no objection, no relief; evidence found "cumulative" and/or sufficient without the statements;

C v Robinson **451 M 672 (2008)**—no relief for admission, over Confrontation Clause objection, of unavailable witness's purportedly spontaneous exclamation "That's the two guys", notwithstanding D's persuasive argument, citing *US v Hinton* 423 F3d 355, 360–61 (3d Cir. 2005) & *US v Pugh* 405 F3d 390, 399 (6th Cir. 2005) that witness would have reasonably anticipated that statement would be used in prosecution';

C v Delong **72 MAC 42 (2008)**—in collateral attack D argued that *Crawford v Washington* barred admission of detective's testimony that a store employee who did not testify at trial had ID'd D's photo from array; trial and direct appeal occurred before *Crawford* decision so application not Constitutionally compelled and no objection allowed "substantial risk" standard of review, not found;

C v Burton **450 M 55 (2007)**—statements of joint venturers admitted against D are not excludable on *Crawford v Washington* "confrontation" ground: they're "nontestimonial";

C v Lao **450 M 215 (2007)**—in reversing trial judge's denial of motion for new trial in a first degree murder case after direct appellate review (including G.L. c. 278, § 33E), SJC finds ineffective assistance to have permeated D's direct appeal: appellate counsel didn't make *Crawford v Washington* constitutional claim that victim's hearsay statements to cop and to daughter (admitted as spontaneous utterances) were inadmissible; *Crawford* decision = published 3/8/04, & D's appellate brief was filed on 4/13/04, SJC issuing decision on direct appeal on 3/31/05; court = "unable to conclude, with certainty, that the admission of the statements . . . did not affect the outcome of [D's] trial, thereby resulting in a substantial risk of a mis-

carriage of justice"; without this evidence, jury was left with one witness's testimony that D was seen outside V's home, absence of forensic testimony, and D's alibi evidence;

C v Gonzalez **68 MAC 620 (2007)**—statement that D was driver of Jeep from which shots were fired was NOT admissible as excited utterance, despite fact that speaker had been crying and performing CPR on victim, and its admission was in violation of *Crawford v Washington* 541 US 36 (2004); no relief for D, however (evidence purportedly "cumulative of other evidence");

C v Caillot **454 M 245 (2009)**—purportedly because Commonwealth was not offering most of co-D's out-of-court statements for "truth of" its assertions, but instead for their falsity (and consciousness of guilt), no *Crawford v Washington* violation;

C v Pelletier **71 MAC 67 (2008)**—similar: D's wife's statement that her severe facial injuries were from 'falling down the stairs' admissible (prosecution contending that wife was lying because afraid of nearby D) notwithstanding *Crawford*, which itself said that confrontation clause doesn't bar use of testimonial statements for purposes other than establishing the truth of the matter asserted (541 US 36, 59–60 n.9 [2004]); trial judge's ruling that statement admissible as "setting the context for the police investigation" was acknowledgment that it wasn't "for truth"; see n.6 (rationale of 'context for investigation' is problematic and thorny, citing *US v Maher* 454 F.3d 13, 22 (1st Cir.) cert denied 127 S Ct 568 (2006));

C v Williams **65 MAC 9 (2005)**—statements made by alleged victim of stabbing to police questions were "testimonial," and inadmissible because violative of Confrontation Clause: cops had responded to 911 call re: fight between male and female, had come upon and questioned D in first floor hallway for 5–10 minutes, & only thereafter proceeded upstairs and found alleged victim, who declined medical attention and didn't seem to be in any physical pain, though she had "blotches" on her neck and a little cut on her hand (conviction reversed);

C v Galicia **447 M 737 (2006)**—alleged victim's statements in 911 call during ongoing beating were not testimonial, but her statements to responding police officers in aftermath of beating were testimonial; *Davis v Washington* 126 S Ct 2266 (2006) (concerning two cases concerning 911 calls & initial police investigation) discussed (statements aren't testimonial when made in course of police interrogation under circumstances indicating primary purpose of interrogation is to enable police assistance to meet "ongoing emergency"); content of 911 call was enough, with circumstantial evidence of persons on premises, for conviction (alleged victim didn't testify);

C v Tang **66 MAC 53 (2006)**—statements made by D's five-year-old son in response to police questions focused on "clear[ing] . . . residents" from scene of bloodshed and gun ("who's in the house right now?", "what happened to you?"), and were not "in aid of the investigation or prosecution of a crime", but instead to secure volatile scene in an emergency;

C v Nardi **452 M 379 (2008)**—right of confrontation not violated where medical examiner who did not perform autopsy testified to his own opinion as to cause of death; opinion permissibly based on facts/findings in autopsy report that was not itself admissible, but substitute examiner couldn't testify on direct exam about the facts/findings; but see *C v Avila* 454 M 744 (2009) and *C v Santos* 454 M 770 (2009) and ***Melendez-Diaz v Massachusetts*** **129 S Ct 2527 (2009)** (SJC's interpretation of Confrontation Clause in, e.g., *C v Verde* 444 M 279 (2005) = overruled;

C v Taylor **455 M 372 (2009)**—like *Nardi*, BUT witness should not have been allowed to testify during direct exam about details of autopsy report: no substantial risk of miscarriage of justice, as no dispute re: cause of death; defense was that D was not one of the four assailants;

C v Hensley **454 M 721 (2009)**—medical examiner who did not perform autopsy was permitted to use autopsy report for his expert testimony; limitation upon expert's use of facts or data not in evidence if facts/data are independently admissible held here (fn.7) not to require that such facts/data actually be admitted at trial through percipient witnesses; trial witness's opinion as to cause of death was either not error or, re: specific findings in report made by other examiner which "may not have been admissible at that point in the trial," harmless, re: deliberate premeditation (on which D found guilty, as well as "extreme atrocity/cruelty");

C v Avila **454 M 744 (2009)**—findings in autopsy report = hearsay, & statements made therein = "testimonial" under *Crawford v Washington* 541 US 36 (2004), fn.20; trial witness (who here was not the autopsy report maker) may base opinion on autopsy report because underlying "facts or data" therein = "potentially ... admissible through appropriate witnesses";

C v Santos **454 M 770 (2009)**—medical examiner other than the one who performed autopsy was called as witness, over D's unsuccessful "Crawford" objection; Commonwealth "agreed that [witness] would limit his testimony to the contents of [autopsy doctor's] report", and D then assented, removing the legitimate *Crawford* issue: SJC finds no ineffective assistance because D made much use of this material in arguing self-defense (so legitimate tactical choice to forego objection);

C v Pena **455 M 1 (2009)**—testifying medical examiner could rely on other medical examiner's autopsy report, notwithstanding D's confrontation clause objection; any error in witness's direct testimony about specific findings of autopsy doctor was harmless beyond reasonable doubt because manner/cause of death not contested here;

C v Edwards **444 M 526 (2005)**—SJC adopts "forfeiture by wrongdoing" doctrine, which allowed introduction of "out of court statements" [here, grand jury testimony] of "unavailable" witness against Ds who intimidated, threatened, or murdered witness, or even "colluded" in making the witness unavailable/unwilling to testify at trial; "causal link necessary" may be established when D puts forward

to witness the idea to avoid testifying by threats, coercion, persuasion, or pressure (BUT MERELY INFORMING WITNESS OF RIGHT TO REMAIN SILENT IS NOT SUFFICIENT TO CONSTITUTE FORFEITURE, n.23) or when D actively facilitates the carrying out of witness's independent intent not to testify; Commonwealth must prove by "preponderance of the evidence" that D procured witness's unavailability; parties must be given opportunity to present evidence, including live testimony, at evidentiary hearing outside jury's presence, prior to determination of forfeiture, BUT hearsay evidence, including unavailable witness's out-of-court statements, may be considered;

Giles v California **128 S Ct 2678 (2008)**—at D's trial for murder of ex-girlfriend, prosecution introduced statements of victim to officer weeks earlier concerning domestic abuse by D; trial court rejected D's "confrontation" objection on ground that D had forfeited right to confront because he murdered speaker, making her unavailable to testify; common law doctrine of forfeiture by wrongdoing applied only when D engaged in conduct designed to prevent witness from testifying; "the notion that judges may strip [D] of a right that the Constitution deems essential to a fair trial, on the basis of a prior *judicial* assessment that [D] is guilty as charged, does not sit well with the right to trial by jury"; it's "dispensing with jury trial because [D] is obviously guilty", *Crawford* 541 US at 62;

Melendez-Diaz v Massachusetts **129 S Ct 2527 (2009)**—admission of laboratory certificates without live testimony by analyst violates confrontation clause of 6th Amendment ***overruling, among other cases: C v Verde*** **444 M 279 (2005)** (drug certificate doesn't violate *Crawford v Washington*; it's "akin to a business record & the confrontation clause is not implicated by this type of evidence": that certificate is admissible only as "prima facie evidence of the composition, quality, and weight of the substance" is purportedly ameliorative);

C v Connolly **454 M 808 (2009)**—SJC gives no relief for *Melendez-Diaz* violation: D didn't raise confrontation issue at trial but SJC purports to find any error harmless beyond reasonable doubt (but using what is a "sufficiency-of-other-evidence-to-establish-element" analysis rather than the standard mandated for constitutional error, e.g., "field test" and jurors' claimed ability to "determine that a large, hard ball weighed more than four ounces");

C v DePina **75 MAC 842 (2009)**—D objected to admission of certificates of analysis at trial, and not harmless beyond reasonable doubt on cocaine trafficking charge, "distinguishing" *Connolly* 454 M 808 as to harmlessness on weight issue (here, total weight was but 14.24 grams, according to certificate, but in *Connolly* "large hard ball" purportedly readily adjudged to weigh more than four ounces); re: nature of substance, "closer question," but judge did not make finding that officer's experience permitted him to offer opinion that substance = cocaine;

C v Rodriguez **75 MAC 235 (2009)**—because certificates of drug analysis were admitted in violation of 6th Amendment confrontation requirement and trafficking weight was not proved any other way, trafficking conviction reversed; Appeals Court claims circumstantial evidence enough to sustain other conviction (drug dealing in school zone), and "harmless" beyond reasonable doubt because D admitted drug dealing AND defense was "not so much the nature of the substance," but personal use as opposed to distributive intent; regarding marijuana conviction, detective testified to finding "green herb" with cocaine, scale, and money, but expertise not established "beyond his years of experience as a narcotics officer," so conviction reversed because "too dependent on" the analysis certificates;

C v Harris **75 MAC 696 (2009), further review allowed 455 M 1108 (2010)**—no relief for Melendez-Diaz drug certificate admission: trial objection was to "chain of custody," not Constitutional confrontation right; further, claim that other evidence legitimately established substance = cocaine ("experienced" police officers testified, D signed statement admitting "cocaine," dog made positive hit, "drug paraphernalia, in particular, a scale" = found by police; cop testified that he weighed the drugs), and defense "focus" on chain of custody rather than nature of substance purportedly meant no substantial risk of miscarriage of justice;

C v Vasquez **456 M 350 (2010)**—drug certificates were admitted without objection at trial, in light of binding precedent of SJC's *C v Verde* 444 M 279 (2005) but subsequently US Supreme Court in ***Melendez-Diaz*** held drug certs to be "testimonial"; because objection at trial would have been futile, SJC reviewed error as if properly preserved; admission of certs not harmless beyond reasonable doubt, other evidence not so overwhelming as to nullify any effect the drug certs might have had on establishing element of crimes;

C v Hollister **75 MAC 729 (2009)**—Commonwealth relied on ballistician certificate to meet burden of proof on dimension and operability: that defense theory in closing was D's lack of knowledge that it was in his truck (& not 'inoperability') didn't make error harmless beyond reasonable doubt; that the gun was loaded didn't establish operability; court could not conclude that certificate "did not contribute to the findings";

C v Chery **75 MAC 909 (2009)**—ballisticians' certificates concerning "firearm" and "ammunition" introduced over D's "Crawford" objection = reversal; not harmless beyond reasonable doubt even though gun itself was introduced; even assuming that the ammunition itself (in evidence) could provide inference that it was "designed for use in" firearm and thus be sufficient for conviction, prosecutor relied in argument on its testing by examiner;

C v Ware **76 MAC 53 (2009)**—ballistics certificated admitted over objection = reversal, though handgun was loaded when seized and D's flight was consciousness of guilt, and cop testified without objection that ammunition rounds found in gun had been test fired but not by officers (ADA emphasized expert ballistician's certificate); that D's

defense was didn't "possess", factor not given much weight in light of *Verde* 444 M 279 being controlling then;

C v Rivera **76 MAC 67 (2009)**—drug certs' admission over objection = "Crawford" reversal; evidence that informant "ordered" particular weights of substances didn't make certificates' assertion of weight harmless, "highly unlikely that" lay person would be able to determine weights, particularly to accuracy required in borderline cases; that D "premised his defense" on lack of visual evidence connecting him to drugs rather than nature/weight of substances irrelevant:

C v Nardi **452 M 379, 392 (2008)**—one medical examiner, who did not perform autopsy, should not have been permitted to testify to the findings made by the medical examiner who did the autopsy: latter's findings were inadmissible hearsay and testimonial in nature;

C v Weeks **77 MAC 1 (2010)**—docket sheets admitted to prove prior convictions held not "testimonial," introduction didn't violate Confrontation Clause, distinguishing *Kirby v US* 174 US 47 (1899);

C v Whelton **428 M 24 (98)**—article 12 'face to face' doesn't "involve confrontation rights as applied to hearsay," but instead, when confrontation right under article 12 "has been extended beyond its Federal counterpart," what was involved was "the physical configuration of the courtroom and the defendant's ability literally "to meet" testifying witnesses "face to face" as required by the plain language of article 12"; [but see, e.g. ***Rosario, above 430 M at 508 n.3***] *see also Crawford v Washington* 124 S Ct 1354 (2004);

Idaho v Wright **497 US 805 (90)**—hearsay responses by 2-year-old rape complainant to pediatrician's leading questions were unreliable & violated D's 6th Amendment right of confrontation;

C v DeOliveira **447 M 56 (2006)**—statements made to emergency room pediatrician by six-year-old disclosing anal rape were made for purposes of medical evaluation and treatment and weren't "testimonial" under *Crawford v Washington* (reversing ruling on D's motion in limine pretrial, where child would not testify at trial), despite facts that child was brought to ER by police, contacted by DSS after initial "disclosure," and police were present at hospital; six-year-old wouldn't foresee statements being used in a trial; identity of who had done this WAS excluded as testimonial (at 62–63); leaving open whether and in what circumstances statements made to medical professional may be considered testimonial when made by child re: issue other than sex abuse, or when made by an adult (at 67);

US v Inadi **475 US 387 (86)**—coconspirator hearsay admissible notwithstanding witness's availability;

Maryland v Craig **497 US 836 (90)**—alternatives to face-to-face encounter at trial, such as closed circuit TV, do not violate 6th Amendment if necessary for public policy & reliable; statute here not facially invalid because it requires case-specific finding of extreme trauma to child due to D's presence; *BUT SEE* Article 12 & *C v*

Bergstrom **402 M 534 (88)** (G.L. c. 278, § 16D violates Article 12 "face to face" right);

G.L. c. 233, §§ 81–83—conditions for substantive use of hearsay by children under 10 in sex abuse & some non-criminal proceedings;

C v Joubert **38 MAC 943 (95)**—probation revocation reversed due to improper invocation of G.L. c. 233, § 81 (inadequate foundation); hearsay testimony that D touched daughter's private parts (not "substantially reliable," not spontaneous utterance, not sufficiently corroborated by independent evidence);

Opinion of Justices **406 M 1201 (89)**—child victim's refusal to testify at trial not proper basis for legislative definition of "unavailability" under Article 12;

C v Colin C. **419 M 54 (94)**—Court reserves for future "facial invalidity" challenges to § 81; grafts onto statute extra requirements: (1) must give notice to D of intent to use child hearsay pursuant to § 81; (2) Commonwealth must prove beyond a reasonable doubt that use of hearsay = necessary to avoid "severe & long-lasting emotional trauma to child"; (3) hearing re: reliability of hearsay statements must be on the record & determination of reliability must be supported by specific findings; (4) unless severe emotional trauma would be caused, D & counsel must be permitted to be present at hearing; (5) if "unavailable" finding is based on incompetence, finding of "reliability" likely questionable; (6) independent evidence must corroborate hearsay of child; use of experts' opinion that child was credible as foundational "corroboration" is invalid;

Coy v Iowa **487 US 1012 (88)**—screen between complaining witness & D violates 6th Amendment;

C v Amirault **404 M 221 (89)**—video OK because D's present, need shown, & tape's OK; special trial procedures in courtroom also OK;

C v Johnson **417 M 498 (94)**—"face-to-face" in Article 12 means defendant must be able to **see** witness's face during testimony; accommodations made for child sexual assault complainant here required reversal; in *Souza* **44 MAC 238 (98)** and *Amirault* **424 M 618 (97)** issue held waived;

C v Spear **43 MAC 583 (97)**—record did not support necessity of special seating for child witness;

C v Sanchez **423 M 591 (96)**—that D was seated so as to face his attorney's "back" not shown material to any claim; [see, however, cases recognizing deprivation of right to communicate with counsel when Ds are routinely placed in a courtroom "dock" during trial: *Rae v State* **884 P.2d 163 (Alaska App. 94)**; *Martin v Commonwealth* **11 Va. App. 397 (90)**; *Kennedy v Cardwell* **487 F.2d 101 (6th Cir. '73)**; see also *Illinois v Allen* **397 US 337 (70)**, Brennan, J., concurrence at 347: even if obstreperous D has to be removed from courtroom, court should make reasonable efforts to enable D to communicate with his attorney]

11-F.3. Prior Consistent Statements

ARE HEARSAY, unless offered for limited purpose of rehabilitation, and unless limited strictly to those portions of out-of-court statement which are consistent with trial testimony, and unless they were made BEFORE motive to fabricate arose. See, e.g., *C v Raymond* **424 M 382 (97)** prior consistent statement as inadmissible hearsay;

C v Cruz **53 MAC 393 (2001)**—reversal for introducing dead child's mother's statements to police blaming D, her boyfriend, for the injuries; not admissible as 'prior consistent statements' (1) because no need: mother testified as chief prosecution witness (2) because she lied previously and repeatedly re: injuries, so no guarantee of trustworthiness (3) because no suggestion of "recent" contrivance, but instead of immediate contrivance to protect herself from criminal charges & shift blame elsewhere; "wrong for the Commonwealth to attempt to 'pump up' ... witness's testimony in its direct case, even were the 'prior consistent statement' exception applicable"; hearsay exceeded scope of direct testimony: was more graphic, detailed, & provided ONLY evidence of stomach battery, critical here given medical testimony re: cause of death;

C v Zukoski **370 M 23, 26–27 (76)**—prior consistent statements not admissible merely because witness has been impeached with prior inconsistent statements;

C v Bruce **61 MAC 474 (2004)**—same; no intimation here that some event between shooting and trial gave speaker motive to change testimony such that prior consistent could logically be found to rebut inference of "recent" contrivance; prior consistent not made admissible on rationale that it was spoken at same time as prior inconsistent statements introduced by defense (rule of "completeness" inapplicable); court nonetheless claims here insufficient prejudice for reversal;

C v McBrown **72 MAC 60 (2008)**—when witness testified that D had made admission during interrogation, defense counsel appropriately impeached him by submitting witness's notes of the interrogation, made contemporaneously; THIS DID NOT MAKE ADMISSIB,LE, on redirect examination by Commonwealth, the witness's "subsequently prepared written report" which contained an alleged admission by D during the interrogation; trial judge's reliance on "verbal completeness" illegitimate as report was prepared several days after interrogation, "and accordingly was a different statement from the notes he made during interrogation itself"; alternate ground for admissibility unavailing: mere impeachment of witness does not entitle party "to bolster the in-court testimony of the witness with prior consistent statements" where as here there is no suggestion at trial that witness's trial testimony "was a *recent* fabrication" and "no suggestion that any events between the interrogation and the time of trial might have furnished [witness] with motivation to fabricate his account"; report similarly "not admissible as a past recollection recorded" when witness didn't claim to be unable to recall it;

C v Novo **449 M 84 (2007)**—prior statement consistent with trial testimony usually inadmissible: repetition of statement by witness doesn't make it more trustworthy;

C v Avila **454 M 744 (2009)**—same; crucial prosecution witness gave three statements to police, and cop took notes; doctrine of verbal completeness doesn't permit Commonwealth to ask witness questions about statement that itself would be inadmissible and then get entire "notes" admitted by claiming that cross-examiner chose to ask other equally selective questions about the statement;

C v Jiles **428 M 66 (98)**—ONLY those portions of prior statement which were consistent with witness's trial testimony were properly admissible to rehabilitate him; but counsel failed to object to excess on HEARSAY/ constitutional confrontation ground (admitted here was assertion, in witness's written statement, that "Mack Brown told me that he and [D] did the shooting but that [D] was the one that killed [victim]. [Brown] said that [D] shot [V] in the head"); "beyond the scope of permissible rehabilitation" was not a good enough objection for the SJC here;

C v Rivera **430 M 91 (99)**—witness's prior consistent statement was hearsay, and inadmissible; to come within exception (of refuting claim of "recent" contrivance), must have been made before witness had incentive to lie;

C v Gaudette **441 M 762 (2004)**—since cross-examination didn't suggest that trial testimony was recent contrivance, no pretrial statement of witness, unless inconsistent with witness's trial testimony, was admissible at trial;

C v Foreman **52 MAC 510 (2001)**—alleged victim (AV), a woman who was about to give birth to D's child claimed that he committed assault and battery on her; at trial, AV's neighbor testified that AV had told her some hours before the alleged crime that AV wanted D to go to jail because he wasn't going to take care of her baby and complained as well about his living with another woman; REVERSAL FOR ADMISSION OF "abuse prevention order" (G.L. c. 209A) and documents AV filed to obtain it, two days after the alleged A&B; not admissible as "official record" and not legitimately "prior consistent" statements because made after motive to contrive existed; likely prejudice = extreme, because "judicial imprimatur" on 209A order would convey to jury that judge had already reviewed facts & decided credibility favorably to AV;

C v Almeida **42 MAC 607 (97)**—**non**-fresh complaint not admissible, because it's prior consistent statement & **hearsay;** no indication that judge admitted it, in exercise of discretion, as prior consistent statement to rebut, permissibly, claim of 'recent contrivance'; but see now *C v King* **445 M 217 (2005)**—sexual assault complainant's "first" complaint needn't be "fresh" in order to be admissible;

C v Dargon **74 MAC 330 (2009)**—defense strategy was to stress that complainant's first allegations were only of mugging/purse grabbing, so form titled "sexual assault evidence collection kit, information pertaining to assault"

was largely admissible to rebut what court called "recent contrivance" theory; S.C. *** M *** (7/29/2010);

C v Martinez **425 M 382 (97)**—since "inevitable" that D, on cross, would suggest 'recent contrivance,' no error in allowing introduction of prior consistent statement during direct testimony;

C v Knight **437 M 487 (2002)**—same;

C v Lareau **37 MAC 679 (94)**—introduction of prior consistent statement in rebuttal (after impeachment) = reversible error: motive to lie existed before allegedly "consistent" statement was made;

See Chapter 9-F, re: prior consistent statements;

11-F.4. Prior Inconsistent Statements

See Chapter 9-F, regarding impeachment by prior inconsistent statement or conduct;

C v Ortiz **39 MAC 70 (95)**—convictions reversed because judge's instruction implied that omissions of important info from police officer's report had no evidentiary value & couldn't be considered as impeachment;

C v Clayton **52 MAC 198, 207 (2001)**—at retrial, judge must specifically instruct on omissions as prior "inconsistencies";

ARE INADMISSIBLE HEARSAY IF witness merely denies having any relevant evidence to offer (witness's credibility cannot be at issue, so they are not admissible for "impeachment"); SEE:

C v Benoit **32 MAC 111 (92)**—can't call witness who will say he has no knowledge, simply to put before jury witness's out of court statement (inculpatory of D), purportedly to "impeach";

C v Rosa **412 M 147, 163 (92)**—same;

C v Elliot **430 M 498, 502–3 (99)**—same;

C v McAfee **430 M 483, 489–92 (99)**—same; cf. *C v Costello* **411 M 371 (91)** D's extrajudicial confession (when not substantively corroborated by prosecutor's impeachment of sexual assault complainant's recantation) required entry of not guilty finding;

C v Leonard **401 M 470 (88)**—drunk D's extrajudicial admission that he'd been driving not corroborated by prosecutor's impeaching wife's testimony that she had been driving (wife previously said D drove);

BUT SEE Chapter 9-F, Prior Consistent Statements Used Substantively, e.g.:

C v Noble **417 M 341 (94)**—substantive use of grand jury testimony, called false by the witness at trial, allowed to supply element critical to D's murder conviction, i.e., his knowledge that principal planned to shoot V, SJC adopting *US v Orrico* **599 F2d 113, 118, 119 (6th Cir. '79)**, which, however, supposedly bars such use when grand jury statements "are the only source of support for the central allegations of the charge";

C v Sineiro **432 M 735 (2000)**—similar to & worse than *Noble* **417 M 341 (94)**;

C v Newman **69 MAC 495 (2007)**—rejects *Crawford v Washington* **541 US 36 (2004)** challenge to *Sineiro* policy of allowing previous testimony of witness to be admitted, upon finding by judge that witness is now feigning lack of memory of events; says that since witness is present in court and available for cross-examination (albeit with no memory?), D has no confrontation issue; there "may" be "rare circumstances where a witness's 'total refusal to co-operate' on cross-exam is so prejudicial as to deny" D con-stitutional right to cross;

C v Figueroa **451 M 566 (2008)**—same, re: immu-nized witness; judge found, at voir dire, opportunity for effective cross-exam of witness at trial; grand jury testi-mony permissibly read to jury, SJC rejecting D's *Crawford v Washington* 541 US 36 (2004) challenge;

C v Clements **51 MAC 508 (2001)**—(divided court), further appellate review allowed 434 M 1106 (2001) worst yet conviction by hearsay testimony; **S.C., 436 M 190 (2002)** revises/alters previous "Daye" formulations: for admissibility of prior testimony for its substantive value, (1) the present witness can be effectively cross-examined at trial regarding the accuracy of his prior statement & (2) the prior statement wasn't coerced and was more than a "mere confirmation or denial of an allegation by the inter-rogator," i.e., the statement must be that of the witness and not of the interrogator. IF that evidence "concerns an ele-ment of the crime, there is a separate requirement that the Commonwealth must meet to sustain its burden on the element: there must be other corroborating evidence on the issue" (though the additional evidence "need not be suffi-cient in itself to establish a factual basis for each element of the crime"); SJC disavows prior statements to the con-trary in, e.g., *C v Johnson* **435 M 113, 134 (2001)**; *C v Sineiro* **432 M 735, 741(2000)**; *C v Noble* **417 M 341, 344 (94)**; *C v Berrio* **407 M 37, 45 (90)**;

C v Ragland **72 MAC 815 (2008), further rev. de-nied 452 M 1110 (08) and 453 M 1105 (09)**—first two requirements of *Clements* 436 M 190 were not contested by D; challenge to sufficiency of "corroboration" of re-canted grand jury testimony that witness saw D wield knife during altercation (only evidence of dangerous weapon in D's possession) rejected: "corroboration" con-sisted of [similarly recanted] statements to Boston police detective, recanted statements to Rhode Island police offi-cers (both introduced at trial by the respective police agents), photo ID substantively admissible under *Cong Duc Le* 444 M 431, testimony by different (civilian) wit-ness that she saw blood on D's hand just after the stabbing and D's efforts to wash it off (though this witness at trial also initially recanted, allowing introduction of contrary grand jury testimony and eventual acknowledgment of 'blood' and hand washing), and trial testimony by other percipient witnesses confirming that D was the lead at-tacker on victim; NOTE WELL: D failed to object, on any ground (i.e., hearsay) to detective's testimony as to what witness allegedly said to him, so it "came in for all pur-poses"; as to co-D, court *rejects argument* that witness's incriminating grand jury testimony [and separate photo ID, plus statements to police] as to co-D's role was legally

nullified by witness's trial testimony denying that co-D had anything at all to do with the attack on V (i.e., "evi-dence tending equally to sustain two different proposi-tions", so required finding);

C v Evans **439 M 184 (2003)**—error to admit grand-jury testimony of Commonwealth witness as past recollec-tion recorded where witness had no recollection of what he had told grand jury, and no evidence he adopted his earlier testimony when his memory of events was fresh; further, absent judge's finding that witness was feigning memory loss, grand-jury testimony NOT admissible for substantive purposes under *Sineiro*, 432 M 735 (2000);

C v Cong Duc Le **444 M 431 (2005)**—"*Daye*" rule [**393 M 55, 60–63 (84)**] modified/overruled: now, **Com-monwealth may use pretrial ID evidence SUBSTAN-TIVELY, even if witness testifies that he did NOT make the identification claimed;** *C v Petersen* **67 MAC 49 (2006)**—noting, in response to claimed error in DA's sub-stantive use of "ID" testimony by cop (which should have been limited to impeachment of "ID" witness?), that even if DA argument could be so read, "harmless" given many jury instructions, + (post-trial) holding in *Cong Duc Le* 444 M 431;

C v Raedy **68 MAC 440 (2007)**—though witness at trial denied naming D as assailant, cop's contrary testi-mony was admissible and probative substantively (*Cong Duc Le* cited);

C v Ragland **72 MAC 815, further review denied 452 M 1110 (2008)**—apart from witness's recanted grand jury testimony that D wielded knife during altercation (held to have been substantively admissible), witness's photo ID was substantively admissible under *Cong Duc Le*;

11-F.5. "Indirect"/Implicit Hearsay

C v Cordle **404 M 733 (89)**—not inadmissible hear-say (here) for cop to say arrested D "as a result of" conver-sation;

C v Perez **27 MAC 550 (89)**—cops may explain what they did "as a result of" conversation with others;

C v Soto **45 MAC 109, 113–14 (98)**—despite Com-monwealth argument that evidence was admissible "to establish the state of [cop's] knowledge which led him to the defendant," testimony from cop as to what purported drug buyer had told him WAS INADMISSIBLE HEAR-SAY, i.e., conveyed that buyer must have said that D had just sold drugs to her; also error for cop to testify that he stopped purported buyer because he believed that she had just purchased cocaine from defendant (inadmissible opin-ion as to D's guilt);

C v O'Connell **55 MAC 100, n.4 & n.12 (2002)**—bank employees' testimony that the defendant's father had complained to them that certain checks were not signed by him and were not properly payable, purportedly for the purpose of explaining why bank officials acted as they did thereafter, "implicate hearsay because of necessity they lead by direct inference to statements made by the father";

C v Kirk 39 MAC 225 (95)—woman's 209A affidavit, admitted to establish ID of battering boyfriend, = inadmissible hearsay and required finding of not guilty ordered (woman did not testify, and her statements to passing motorist, while admissible as spontaneous utterances, failed to establish identity of culprit); cop's testimony that he served D = indirect hearsay (i.e., someone had to have told him that D was the culprit), insufficient to establish critical element;

C v Gonzalez 443 M 799 (2005)—trial witness's testimony concerning what coventurers did in "reenacting" fatal fight implicated hearsay concerns despite lack of testimony concerning anything "said" out of court; "conduct can serve as a substitute for words, and to the extent it communicates a message, hearsay considerations apply"; evidence that defendant was present during the reenactment, however, made it admissible as adoptive admission of defendant;

C v Sapoznik 28 MAC 236, 246 (90)—details of search warrant procedure & application (here, accompanied by prosecutor's citation of them in closing argument) are irrelevant at trial, hearsay concerns apparent;

C v Rosario 430 M 505, 508–11 (99)—"state of police knowledge" MUST BE RELEVANT TO AN ISSUE IN THE CASE; evidence may come in only thru testimony of cop, who testifies on basis of own knowledge, must be limited to facts required to establish cop's knowledge (usually just "upon info received" or "as consequence of conversation" = enough); here, civilian witness's testimony re: telephone conversation with deceased shortly before her death inadmissible; state of police knowledge evidence as a whole MAY VIOLATE D'S CONFRONTATION RIGHTS UNDER ARTICLE 12 (id. at 508 n.3);

C v Spencer 53 MAC 45, 51 (2001)—D's motion in limine inadequate to preserve issue of admissibility of what prostitute purportedly said to cops about D being heroin dealer she could "deliver" to them if they would not arrest her for prostitution; on merits, either not hearsay (because not for 'truth', HA!, but just to explain why cops acted) or there was no substantial risk of miscarriage of justice;

C v Ashman 430 M 736, 741 (2000)—inadmissible hearsay found in testimony from V's two friends that they had come to D's apartment 3 months before V's death in response to V's telephone call, and had spoken with her there and called police, and had taken V (with her son and clothing) elsewhere; "equivalent of a statement by the witnesses that the victim had told them that the defendant had abused (or was a threat to abuse) her" & "is no more than the equivalent of repeating statements of the victim"; BUT SEE *C v Rivera* **51 MAC 99, 105–6, further appellate review denied 434 M 1104 (2001)** appellate court fails to acknowledge implicit hearsay (conveyed to jury that co-D was brought to nearby scene to make, and did make, ID of D as cohort; no other relevance possible for contested evidence that co-D was brought to the scene where cops were questioning D);

C v Beaz 69 MAC 500 (2007)—cop permissibly testified that when he arrived on scene, "there were a lot of people in the street all pointing towards two gentlemen," because "not hearsay": prosecution didn't "suggest" that persons pointing were accusing D of robbery, but instead simply directing cop "to the ongoing incident involving" D and person who was holding D down; even if "admitted for hearsay purposes," said to be excited utterance, OK under *Crawford v Washington* because "nontestimonial," i.e., for police assistance to meet ongoing emergency;

C v Eason 427 M 595 (98)—though OK to admit evidence that cops went to home of woman because an individual told cops that woman knew who committed a particular crime, testimony that the individual said that he was not involved in the crime himself was inadmissible; not admissible on "verbal completeness" theory because what woman's boyfriend told individual was entirely segregable from self-serving statements made by individual to cops;

C v Sharpe 454 M 135 (2009)—after Commonwealth introduced four abuse prevention orders obtained by D's dead girlfriend, he wanted affidavits she submitted to obtain them, arguing 'verbal completeness,' showing she provoked D's conduct giving rise to the orders (and thus relevant to whether she provoked him at time of killing): holding = no error, because affidavits "were separate and distinct from the orders"; "not foreclose[ing] possibility" that in a different case such affidavits would be admissible, SJC skittish about violating US Constitutional ban on "mechanistical" application of "hearsay rule" "to defeat the ends of justice";

C v Navarro 39 MAC 161 (95)—cop telephoned apartment and asked for "Ann" & thereafter obtained delivery of drugs, but "Ann" (D's first name) was not admissible against D, found in apartments (no evidence she rented or exercised control over apartment, despite fact that her name was "Ann"); but see

C v Rockett 41 MAC 5 (96)—upholding admission of evidence that unknown person called out "David," voice coming from the direction in which burglar was fleeing victim's home; Appeals Court declined to reverse trial judge's purported "exercise of discretion" in finding this a spontaneous utterance; better analysis would be that shout of "David" was circumstantial evidence that someone by that name was present;

C v Carmenatty 37 MAC 908 (94)—cop testimony that D's personal papers were found in "apartment that is known for selling drugs" = inadmissible hearsay; BUT failure to move to strike = no relief on appeal;

C v Fourteen Thousand Two Hundred Dollars 421 M 1 (95)—in forfeiture action, because Commonwealth's burden was only to show "reasonableness" of cop's action, permissible for cop to testify that tow lot employee told him that plastic bag containing money, cocaine, and marijuana was found under front seat of 1982 Datsun: not for truth but to prove cop's state of mind;

C v Washington 39 MAC 195 (95)—what unidentified 3d parties said after they contacted beeper seized from D was admissible circumstantial evidence of drug dealing;

C v DePina 75 MAC 842, 845 (2009)—seizure of cell phone came within warrant term "implements related to distribution of cocaine" given cop's affidavit; cop could also answer phone (citing *Mendes* 46 MAC 581 [99]); substance of cop's conversation with unidentified caller = admissible (rejecting "hearsay" argument);

C v Mullane 63 MAC 317, 324, **further appellate review allowed** 444 M 1103 (2005)—evidence that masseuse at Institute of Massage Therapy "agreed to provide 'extras'" wasn't hearsay (substance of conversation was pertinent evidence of "the character of the house"); issue not addressed by SJC, 445 M 702 (2006);

C v Miller 361 M 644 (72)—users said D sells drugs = admissible re: undercover cop's good cause (vs. shocking/offensive) because D claims entrapment; But see *C v Urena* 42 MAC 20 (97) D's claim of entrapment **not** permissibly answered by arresting officer's rebuttal testimony that D was approached because named arrestee said D was source of arrestee's 2 kg. cocaine; rejecting argument that it was necessary/admissible to "explain the state of police knowledge which impelled the approach to" D;

Seelig v Harvard Coop 355 M 532 (69)—hearsay admissible re: probable cause to arrest because for state of mind, not truth [not really hearsay];

11-F.6. Spontaneous or Excited Utterances

Be alert to possible "second-level" hearsay issues; demand, as foundation, showing of personal knowledge of event by declarant of spontaneous/excited utterance; see Prop.M.R.Evid. 602 ("A witness may not testify to a matter unless evidence is introduced sufficient to support a finding that he has personal knowledge of the matter. Evidence to prove personal knowledge may, but need not, consist of the testimony of the witness himself . . . ")

*** *C v Hurley* 455 M 53 (2009)—alleged victim's statements to police responding to 911 call held to be testimonial in circumstances here (no ongoing emergency, and given in response to police questioning), governed by *Crawford v Washington* 541 US 36 (2004); these statements were admitted at pretrial detention/"dangerousness" hearing via a police officer who testified after alleged victim, and accordingly there had been no opportunity for cross-exam concerning them (D was not obliged to offer them himself during cross of alleged victim, and was not obliged to call her back to stand after 'excited utterances' had been admitted, see *Melendez Diaz v Massachusetts* 129 S Ct 2527, 2540 [2009]); alleged victim died before trial, and while her testimony was admissible given record here, the alleged excited utterances made to cop were not likewise admissible (but found to be harmless beyond reasonable doubt);

C v Nesbitt 452 M 236 (2008)—statements made by stabbing victim to emergency responder during 911 tele-

phone call identifying D as person who stabbed her admissible as excited utterance, and held not "testimonial," but instead aimed at enabling police assistance for ongoing emergency (victim died shortly after the 911 call, thus unavailable at trial);

C v DePina 456 M 238 (2010)—excited nature of telephone call supports reliability of caller by reasonably negating premeditation or possible fabrication (anonymous call to 911 introduced in suppression hearing, "reliability" analyzed);

C v Simon 456 M 280 (2010)—statements in 911 telephone call by victim suffering from gunshot wound = within spontaneous utterance exception to hearsay rule;

C v Robinson 451 M 672 (2008)—no relief for admission, over Confrontation Clause objection, of unavailable witness's purportedly spontaneous exclamation "That's the two guys", notwithstanding D's persuasive argument, citing *US v Hinton* 423 F3d 355, 360–61 (3d Cir. 2005) & *US v Pugh* 405 F3d 390, 399 (6th Cir. 2005) that witness would have reasonably anticipated that statement would be used in prosecution;

Prop.M.R.Evid. 803 (2)—statement relating to startling event or condition made while declarant was under the stress of the excitement caused by the event or condition; but cf, contra, *C v Middleton* 6 MAC 902 (78) (everyone understands that stress affects [adversely] the reliability of an eyewitness's identification);

C v Thomas 429 M 146, 160 (99)—utterance must "tend . . . to qualify, characterize or explain the underlying event";

C v Santos 402 M 775 (88)—ID 4 hours later not spontaneous utterance;

Brodin, M. and Avery, M., *Handbook of Massachusetts Evidence* **(8th ed. 2007)**—must be still under influence of excitement & explaining without calculation; includes unidentified bystander (citing *C v Harris* 376 M 201 (78));

C v Kirk 39 MAC 225 (95)—woman's 209A affidavit, admitted to establish ID of battering boyfriend, = inadmissible hearsay and required finding of not guilty ordered (woman did not testify, and her statements to passing motorist, while admissible as spontaneous utterances, failed to establish identity of culprit); cop's testimony that he served D = indirect hearsay (i.e., so someone had to have told him that D was the culprit), insufficient to establish critical element;

C v Leavey 60 MAC 249, 251 (2004)—alleged victim of boyfriend's abuse wholly recanted at trial, but her spontaneous utterances to neighbor, in 911 telephone call, and to responding police = sufficient for conviction, citing *C v Moquette* 439 M 697, 702 (2003) ("spontaneous utterance is sufficient, by itself, to support a conviction"); *C v Kelsall* 60 MAC 902 (2003)—same, citing *Moquette*;

C v Negron 441 M 685, 690 (2004)—judge didn't abuse discretion in finding wife's statements to police weren't spontaneous utterances, since cop testified that wife "didn't appear to be upset" despite claimed torching of her apartment and destruction of her car by D;

C v Whitney 63 MAC 351 (2005)—testimony by victim's employer that, when awakened after 11 p.m. by his telephone call to victim's wife, wife responded to his question by saying victim had left home at 9:30 p.m., probably OK as spontaneous utterance, but even if error here, no relief: it was cumulative of inference available from unchallenged evidence;

C v Brown 413 M 693 (92)—responses of 3-year-old scalding victim during questioning at hospital 5 hours after incident admissible as spontaneous utterance because made under stress of exciting event;

C v Gonzalez 68 MAC 620 (2007)—statement that D was driver of Jeep from which shots were fired was NOT admissible as excited utterance, despite fact that speaker had been crying and performing CPR on victim: speaker's caveat that he would deny statement if cop told anyone shows it was product of reflection; its admission was in violation of *Crawford v Washington* 541 US 36 (2004); no relief for D, however (evidence purportedly "cumulative of other evidence" & harmless beyond reasonable doubt);

C v Ivy 55 MAC 851 (2002)—statements by victim at hospital identifying boyfriend as her assailant were admissible as excited utterances (occurred 4½ hours after battery, victim curled in fetal position & whimpering with eye red & swollen, appearing frightened and exhausted from crying [victim didn't appear at trial, & she wasn't shown to be unavailable]); D's argument that admission violated *C v Daye*, 393 M 55 (84) rebuffed, by citation of *C v Medrala* 20 MAC 398 (85), on ground that Daye involved different hearsay exception;

C v Crawford 417 M 358 (94)—passage of 5 hours between exciting event & spontaneous utterance held OK: declarant was young child, in company of father (shooter of mother) for some period thereafter; that later remarks were in response to police questions did not defeat 'spontaneous' quality of the later assertions when child did **not** merely adopt fact suggested in question; reserved question = whether confrontation right of Article 12 requires Commonwealth to show unavailability before using spontaneous utterance;

C v Moquette 439 M 697 (2003), **on further review of 53 MAC 615 (2002)**—OK to admit as spontaneous utterance remarks by two alleged victims, aged nine and eleven, purportedly made forty minutes after the attack, "immediately" after fleeing from D, and fact that one declarant recanted at trial didn't matter: up to jury to decide truth; refusal to add any requirement that spontaneous utterance be corroborated before sufficient for conviction;

C v Whelton 428 M 24 (98)—Article 12 doesn't require witness unavailability before introduction of spontaneous utterance; Commonwealth's sole evidence, in domestic battery prosecution, was "spontaneous utterance" of alleged victim and her daughter, the latter recounting argument between herself and D, during which D allegedly kicked & hit V; error in admitting alleged victim's statements to cop as spontaneous utterance but convictions affirmed;

C v King 436 M 252 (2002)—after foundation requirements for admission of spontaneous utterances were met, judge had no discretion to decide that they were unreliable & thereby exclude them; since witness invoked 5th Amendment at trial, she couldn't be cross-examined re: the utterances, BUT SJC remanded for determination of whether her testimony at voir dire operated to waive the privilege (if so, there was prejudicial error to allow her to invoke the privilege at trial);

C v Tang 66 MAC 53 (2006)—though *C v King* 436 M 252, 255 stated that "as with any other witness, the declarant must have personal knowledge of the event in question, and must be competent," Appeals Court rejected D's argument that spontaneous utterance by five-year-old boy (not called as a witness at trial) could not be admitted without a voir dire examination of the boy to assure his testimonial competency; circumstances must merely indicate that declarant appeared "to have had opportunity to observe personally the matter of which he speaks"; NOTE WELL: only suggestions made by trial counsel were that child was young, and had low verbal skills; footnote 14 gives contrary "cf" law in Ohio and NY (presuming child under ten or twelve, respectively, = incompetent to testify);

C v Evans 438 M 142 (2002)—when police told murder eyewitness that they were bringing suspects for him to view, he refused & said he didn't want to see them, and continued to refuse after being placed in police car, and when they walked by, he gave only cursory look and said they weren't assailants; judge could exclude this on ground that it was not spontaneous utterance, but instead product of reflective thought;

C v Dunn 56 MAC 89 (2002)—allegedly "spontaneous utterances" were, on the evidence, the product of reflective thought; the hearsay exception "is unavailable not only when premeditation or fabrication is actually shown but also when the statement's proponent fails to reasonably negate the presence of either"; statements here were purportedly part of preconceived escape plan & NOT as "essentially spontaneous reaction to the event itself," which occurred over a day earlier;

C v Lawson 46 MAC 627 (99)—avoiding issue whether admission of alleged spontaneous utterance improperly abrogated/defeated spousal privilege of wife not to testify against D;

C v Santiago 52 MAC 667, **further appellate review allowed, 435 M 1105 (2001)**—cop's testimony that when D was being led away in handcuffs, D's girlfriend ran over & yelled in Spanish (purportedly translated for officer by complainant's guidance counselor) that D had told her he went into bedroom & kissed complainant, but "only" put a finger in her vagina & hadn't had "intercourse" = inadmissible; girlfriend's alleged remarks didn't explain or characterize the underlying "exciting" event (i.e., the arrest), but rather the alleged incident occurring the night before; arrest, while unwelcome, shouldn't have been "surprise"; sufficient time had passed so that declarant would have been able to contrive a false story (because she apparently thought this version would be useful to D); *on further appellate review, however, SJC overruled, affirmed conviction: 437 M 620 (2002)*—exciting event allegedly was the arrest, thought to be unjustified because speaker thought D had committed no crime;

C v Reed **444 M 803 (2005)**—D argues that D's denial, when accused by his father, was admissible as spontaneous utterance, but trial judge would have been warranted in concluding, on the record before her, that defense counsel hadn't laid sufficient foundation for concluding both (1) statement being triggered by an "event" sufficiently startling to render inoperative normal reflective thought processes, and (2) statement was spontaneous reaction to the event; [denial of criminal culpability is inadmissible unless hearsay exception applies, but rule doesn't apply when D responds to accusation in "equivocal, evasive or irresponsive way inconsistent with innocence": *C v Cancel* **394 M 567 (85)**, quoted in *C v Dupont* **75 MAC 605 (2009)**—D, after flight from cops, responded to cop's assertion that police had information that he had been involved in a drug transaction and believed there was cocaine in vehicle by saying "there is no cocaine in my vehicle or on me"; this was equivocal, & thus admissible;

C v Alvarado **36 MAC 604 (94)**—despite fact that alleged battery victim testified, in prosecution's case, that D had not bitten her & that marks were inflicted by friend to set up D for false accusation, cop responding to radio call allowed to testify that alleged victim ("hysterical, crying, very emotional, upset") said D hit & bit her (spontaneous utterance); cop observed bite marks;

C v Burnett **417 M 740 (94)**—statement made 1½ hours after fatal car crash, by one driver, that he & V had beers, "hard stuff" & had "smoked shorts" not admissible as spontaneous utterance; Court says "spontaneous" utterances after time lapse are those made by children (*Brown* **413 M 693** and *Crawford* **417 M 358, above**)

C v Cohen **412 M 375 (92)**—statements by victim, 'They shot me, too,' admissible as spontaneous utterances because made under press of exciting event & without time to contrive;

C v Trowbridge **419 M 750 (95)**—child sex assault complainant's response to teacher's question ("why are you crying"), that she didn't want to visit & didn't like her daddy, **not** spontaneous utterance; crying does not equal a startling event (mere purported fact that statement is volunteered doesn't qualify it as spontaneous utterance)

C v Hardy **47 MAC 679 (99)**—statements made by elderly robbery victim during police interview 2½ to 3 hours after incident, not spontaneous utterances despite fact that V was crying, in pain, upset; relevant factors re admissibility = degree of excitement displayed by declarant, whether statement is made at scene of traumatic event or elsewhere, temporal closeness of statement to act it explains, degree of spontaneity;

C v Zagranski **408 M 278 (90)**—statements by murder-D's wife, 'Where's the body, then' (as D being arrested) admissible as spontaneous utterance;

C v Donovan **422 M 349 (96)**—spontaneous utterance by dying V, "they took my wallet," not infirm because "they" was indefinite; Commonwealth proceeded on joint venture theory;

C v Gilbert **423 M 863 (96)**—D, charged with murder of girlfriend, could not have admitted as spontaneous utterance his statement the next day to a nurse that the girlfriend "killed herself last night";

C v Bandy **38 MAC 329 (95)**—D, seriously injured & in hospital, charged with motor vehicle homicide, could not have admitted as spontaneous utterances his statements to nurses that he was not the driver, since he probably knew of the death and he'd been served with citations;

C v McLaughlin **433 M 558 (2001)**—D's statement to police after arrest ("was being robbed . . . bought crack from him . . . it was fake . . . approached . . . tussle[d] . . . He had the knife") not admissible as 'spontaneous utterance' because motive & time to fabricate;

C v Garcia **443 M 824, 834 (2005)**—evidence from cop that he overheard D state in telephone call that victim "flashed his colors" at D (indicating gang membership) = inadmissible hearsay;

C v Twombly **319 M 464 (46)**—if when accusations were made, D denied their truth, statements are incompetent hearsay;

C v Ruffen **399 M 811 (87)**—though both inadmissible, let in D's denial because (post-arrest) accusation got in;

C v Reed **444 M 803 (2005)**—evidence of out-of-court accusation of D made in D's presence shouldn't have been admitted (there was unequivocal denial, so no admission by silence), but no objection/strike motion here; thereafter, judge should have allowed evidence of D's denial (curative admissibility);

C v Cantor **253 M 509 (25)**—exclude D's self-serving post-arrest denial; But see *C v Rowe* **105 M 590 (1870)** D's out-of-court explanation for stolen goods she had should have been admitted (statements to store clerk immediately after D became aware of her possession of allegedly stolen items, before anyone accused her of misdeed; possibly understood as a 'verbal act' or circumstantial evidence supportive of D's innocence);

C v O'Connor **407 M 663 (90)**—complainant's description of battery to mother not admissible as spontaneous utterance: inadequate foundation concerning how promptly statement was made;

Edward E. v Dept of Social Services **42 MAC 478 (97)**—nothing to indicate that alleged spontaneous utterances **were** spontaneous, and substance of assertions was improbable; statements lacking indicia of reliability "do not attain trustworthiness through a process of repetition";

C v Tiexeira **29 MAC 200 (90)**—eyewitness's statement to D, 'Why did you have to hit him with club?,' which were admitted by judge as "res gestae," more properly admissible as spontaneous utterances;

C v Giguere **420 M 226 (95)**—tape recording of telephone call by V's wife to police properly admitted as spontaneous utterance;

C v Brown **46 MAC 279 (99)**—audiotape of telephone calls to 911 admissible as spontaneous utterances, regardless of whether caller available to testify as witness; brush-off of argument that voice to 911 was not person who made the observations being reported (served as "kind of echo"); but see, e.g., *C v. Ennis* **2 MAC 864 (74)** and Prop.M.R.Evid. 805 re: second-level hearsay;

C v Poillucci **46 MAC 300 (99)**—cassette tape of telephone call to police admitted as spontaneous utterance (motorist reporting that adjacent driver was exposing self and masturbating);

C v Rockett **41 MAC 5 (96)**—upholding admission of evidence that unknown person called out "David," voice coming from the direction in which burglar was fleeing victim's home; Appeals Court declined to reverse trial judge's purported "exercise of discretion" in finding this a spontaneous utterance;

C v Capone **39 MAC 606 (96)**—allowing admission of drunken minor's statement to friend that he did not want D near him, but identifying no exciting event as purportedly prompting utterance;

C v DiMonte **427 M 233 (98)**—telecopy (FAX) transmission 8½–11 hours after alleged beating not admissible as spontaneous utterance; writing = suspect as spontaneous utterance, so circumstances indicative of reliability have to be even more persuasive; hospital records (statements made more than 9 hours after alleged beating) not admissible as spontaneous utterance;

11-F.7. State of Mind

SEE CASES IN Chapter 11-D, "state of mind" must have some relevance in the case;

C v Marcotte **18 MAC 391 (84)**—admit details of D's statement to 2d person because relevant to D's state of mind (larceny by faking robbery) [- so not hearsay!];

C v Diaz **426 M 548 (98)**—testimony that someone in large group said that D ordered that eventual murder V be brought out of apartment was inadmissible hearsay; judge's admitting statement "to show the general atmosphere of what was occurring . . . insofar as [the jury] find it has some affect" condemned ("no exception to the hearsay rule such as the court invoked");

C v Fiore **364 M 819 (74)**—prior testimony (recollection refreshed) not hearsay because state of mind, not "truth" [—so not really hearsay];

C v Montanino (II) **409 M 500 (91)**—rape complainant's testimony that he decided to press charges against D 4 years after incident because he heard D's behavior was continuing was inadmissible & required reversal;

C v Santiago **52 MAC 667 (2001): S.C. 437 M 620 (2002)**—(agreeing with Appeals Court re: this issue) within judge's discretion (but must give careful limiting instructions) to admit evidence of more recent sexual assault by D in Connecticut at trial for alleged sexual assaults against same complainant in MA more than 8 years earlier (& which criminal charges purportedly prompted

D's flight from MA): D's alleged statements during recent assault (still in love with her, had been so since 1st time he saw her) purportedly relevant to show "acknowledged & continuing sexual passion", & later act explained why long-delayed prosecution in MA came to be pursued [one could question whether the "why" was relevant];

C v Phoenix **409 M 408 (91)**—witness's statement that he overheard D mention his hostility toward victim 4 months before murder admissible to show D's state of mind; written memo by victim to D's supervisor admissible where there was circumstantial evidence that content communicated to D;

C v Whitman **453 M 331 (2009)**—to support defense of lack of criminal responsibility, D proffered witnesses who would testify that, two weeks or two days before fatal stabbing, D said he "had been hearing voices" and was taking medication because he "hears voices sometimes": exclusion of testimony upheld because statements by D were not of his THEN-present state of mind; (other witnesses did give similar testimony);

C v Porro **74 MAC 676, further rev. allowed 455 M 1106 (2009)**—after hitting motorcyclist with his government-issued car, D took it for repair to out-of-state relative and did not report accident to supervisor as required = consciousness of guilt, but ERROR not to allow introduction of statements made to D by his supervisor regarding previous claim for repair, i.e., tight budget and condemnation of D, probative of D's state of mind (but no relief because cumulative of other evidence);

C v Hall **66 MAC 390 (2006)**—testimony by rape complainant that D had bragged that he had had identified man "take care of" someone who was "causing trouble" was admissible to explain why complainant delayed alleging rape for seven years (until newspaper article saying the identified man had been sentenced to prison); judge must undertake analysis of whether danger of prejudice outweighs probative value of evidence;

C v Zagranski **408 M 278 (90)**—victim's statements to witnesses about sale of land not admissible to show D's state of mind because no evidence ever communicated to D;

C v Simmarano **50 MAC 312 (2000)**—alleged victim's statement to D prior to alleged home invasion & attempted rape admissible to show D's state of mind (i.e., that she wanted him to come to her home at 2 a.m.);

C v Fortini **44 MAC 562 (98)**—victim's declaration of purpose ('I'll kill them all . . . I'm the baddest motherfucker in town"), even though not known to D, was probative: threats admissible to show that person killed was actually attempting to carry out threat (no relief here, though);

C v Rubin **318 M 587 (45)**—same;

C v Travis **408 M 1 (90)**—murder D's statement to prison official 3 weeks before release that he might rob or kill was admissible to show state of mind;

C v Brooks **422 M 574 (96)**—evidence that D said to witness, 2 months before shooting, that if he could not find witness's brother, he has a problem with witness, admissible to show D's state of mind, relevant to his motive in firing upon a group which included witness;

C v Papadinis **402 M 73 (88)**—D's testimony on own state of mind admissible wherever state of mind a "factor" in proof of crime;

C v Carter **39 MAC 439 (95)** aff'd **424 M 409, 412 n.5 (97)**—D's state of mind (telling friend not to use cocaine) held irrelevant to charge of possessing cocaine with intent to distribute: not charged with distribution to friend;

C v Thevenin **33 MAC 588 (92)**—that D had been told by friend that rape complainant had pubic lice was admissible to show D's state of mind (unwillingness to expose himself to lice, so no natural intercourse as alleged);

C v Capone **39 MAC 606, 610 n.2 (96)**—drunken minor sexual assault complainant's statement to friend that he did not want D near him because he was feeling sick admissible in D's trial for sexual assault occurring thereafter;

C v Demars **38 MAC 596 (95)**—D's child sexual assault conviction reversed because DA questioned complainant's father to elicit that he had heard extraneous allegations re: D which caused him concern over daughter: witness's state of mind = irrelevant to D's guilt;

C v Bonner **33 MAC 471 (92)**—because not relevant, fresh complaint witness-mother's testimony about her reaction ("state of mind") upon hearing son tell of abuse by uncle not admissible;

C v Lorette **37 MAC 736 (94)**—similar;

C v Rosario **430 M 505 (99)**—cop's "state of mind" (i.e., circumstances of police focus on D) not at issue, so error to admit testimony by witness who spoke by telephone to deceased shortly before death & who reported conversation to cop;

C v Randall **50 MAC 26 (2000)**—perhaps error in any event to permit cop to testify that van fleeing from scene of breaking & entering belonged to D (D argued hearsay because cop said that someone in radio check of license plate told him this), but holding = purported justification that it wasn't for truth, but instead to "explain the state of knowledge possessed by police" was bogus, given DA's substantive use of van ownership during closing argument;

C v Cyr **425 M 89 (97)**—murder victim's professions of fear of D **not** admissible "to show the relationship," and victim's "state of mind" not relevant at trial; statements of V re: intent to seek child custody, if known to D = relevant to D's motive for killing V;

C v Williams **30 MAC 543 (91)**—statements by murder victim that her relationship with D was on rocks admissible to show D's state of mind where there was circumstantial evidence that her feelings were communicated to D; victim's fear that D would kill her not admissible;

C v Purcell **423 M 880 (96)**—homicide victim's statement to niece, on day of killing, that she had told D to get his things and leave, admissible because jury warranted in inferring that D knew V's state of mind, probative of D's motive to kill;

C v Cyr **433 M 617 (2001)**—V's pleadings in probate/family court filed day before her murder, seeking to gain physical custody of child from D (with only limited supervised visitation by D) admissible, because communicated to D & relevant to motive; pleadings redacted to exclude allegations of domestic violence (as directed in *S.C.* **425 M 89 (97)**);

C v Magraw **426 M 589 (98)**—statement of murder V that she feared her husband and that her death would be made to look like accident inadmissible;

C v Arce **426 M 601 (98)**—evidence that murder V feared her husband should not have been admitted (but here, no relief);

C v Wilson **427 M 336 (98)**—same (victim's state of mind = irrelevant);

C v Jenner **426 M 163 (97)**—same (but here, no relief);

C v Andrade **422 M 236 (96)**—admission of 5 witnesses' testimony that homicide V told them D beat her & threatened to kill her = error (but majority found harmless);

C v Qualls **425 M 163 (97)**—murder victim's statement, on night he died, that D would try to kill him that night not admissible; V's state of mind not relevant unless there's proof D was aware of it and would be likely to respond to it; assertion that "state of mind" is hearsay **exception,** allowing its admissibility for **truth,** so admonition that it is "state of mind" & "not for truth" was nonsensical; [this is contrary to authorities, above; reason suggests that evidence is for the "truth" of what it is that speaker believed, but not whether what speaker believed was in fact true]

C v Seabrooks **425 M 507 (97)**—that homicide victim allegedly told a friend, 16 months before murder, that D had hit her was inadmissible hearsay, notwithstanding trial judge's ruling that it was admitted "not for its truth, but to show the relationship between the parties and their state of mind";

C v Johnson **429 M 745 (99)**—homicide V's assertions, in application for protective order, are inadmissible hearsay (allegations of D being threatening);

C v Lodge **431 M 461, 470 (2000)**—same; evidence of past misconduct to show a hostile relationship is generally not admissible;

C v O'Brien **432 M 578, 588 (2000)**—though D sought to admit murder V's statement that she was afraid of her brother- in-law based on his hostility to her since she threw him out of her house for drug-dealing, & though SJC acknowledged that judge has discretion to admit hearsay "to show that a 3rd party might have committed the crime for which D is being tried, provided the evidence is otherwise relevant . . . and there are other 'substantial connecting links' to the crime," SJC held no error in excluding here because cited "links" were insufficient;

C v Johnson **49 MAC 273, 277–78 (2000)**—error to admit for substantive use an affidavit signed by witness (D's girlfriend) in support of her application for protective order against D when witness "did not recall" various subjects of Commonwealth's questioning (D on trial for firing gun outside witness's hair salon), but purportedly no "abuse of discretion" in admitting affidavit for impeachment purposes (but see, e.g., *C v Benoit* **32 MAC 111, 114–15 (92)** when only purpose of calling witness is to get before jury an alleged statement witness made out-of-court, 'impeachment' is "a mere subterfuge to get before the jury evidence not otherwise admissible");

C v Vinnie **428 M 161 (98)**—homicide V's statements to friends that he wanted to beat up D, would kill D if D abused V's mother again, that he and D had fought, were inadmissible;

C v Erdely **430 M 149 (99)**—because D sought to show confession involuntary and unreliable due to threat by police to charge his girlfriend, and thus introduced fact that his request to speak to girlfriend was denied, Commonwealth could introduce testimony that she did not want to speak with D; it was neither necessary nor proper to introduce as well her alleged accompanying statement that she believed D responsible for murdering her great aunt (portions of response were entirely segregable);

C v Magraw **426 M 589, 595–96 (98)**—murder V's statement that she would not willingly be alone with D admissible to **rebut D's claim** of agreed upon meeting; other 'state of mind' evidence (that she feared/believed he would kill her and make it look like accident) **not** admissible;

C v Silanskas **433 M 678 (2001)**—because D (V's wife's boyfriend) claimed that V was suicidal because his wife ordered him out of house, ok to admit V's statements on day of death that he feared for his life, intended to leave home to find safe place, & never should have married wife, who had come to be under a bad influence;

C v Kilburn **426 M 31 (97)**—noting error in admitting murder V's statements to friend, but finding cure sufficient;

C v Ashley **427 M 620 (98)**—NO OBJECTION to testimony that homicide victim told witness that he had shot two men four days earlier meant that this was argued as motive of D to shoot V, and that D's "mis-ID" defense was greatly impaired;

C v Olszewski **401 M 749 (88)**—dead V's state of mind re: D inadmissible unless D knew;

C v Gilbert **366 M 18 (74)**—V's divorce libel vs. D (alleging brutality) not hearsay because shows her state of mind (she wouldn't have gone with him night she's killed);

C v Van Liew **14 MAC 662 (82)**—statements by murder V to his wife admissible re: D's motive; judge's discretion whether shown that D was aware;

C v Pope **397 M 275 (86)**—state of mind exception applies only to declarant's present intention to act, not to past conduct;

C v McCray **40 MAC 936 (96)**—D's testimony that rape complainant said 'yes' to sex admissible; it's either not 'for truth' but to show consent, or hearsay exception for statement of mental condition, "which includes statements of present intent";

C v Esteves **429 M 636 (99)**—reversal for admission of rape complainant's boyfriend's hearsay assertion that he had not had sex with her (this bolstered complainant's credibility and refuted defense theory of complainant's motive to lie);

C v Mandeville **386 M 393 (82)**—where DA's cross-examination of D put state of mind in issue, D can introduce hearsay statement made to him to explain state of mind;

C v King **34 MAC 466 (93)**—evidence that D was angry during interrogation and terminated it by calling cops "assholes" inadmissible & prejudicial: D's "state of mind" irrelevant except for unconstitutional inference that refusal to cooperate = guilt;

C v Rowe **105 M 590 (1870)**—D's out-of-court explanation for stolen goods he had should've been admitted; [*see post, Chapter 11-G re denials, e.g.,* **Cantor 253 M 509 (25)** *exclude D's self-serving post-arrest denial;* **C v McLaughlin 433 M 558 (2001)** *self-serving post-arrest statement re: self-defense inadmissible*]; but see cases re: admissibility of D's statements contemporaneous with event as relevant to state of mind, e.g., *C v Marcotte* **18 MAC 391 (84)** admit details of D's statement to 2d person because relevant to D's state of mind (larceny by faking robbery);

Declarations of Deceased Person: G.L. c. 233, § 65—declarations of deceased person shall not be inadmissible as hearsay or as private marital conversation; but statute **not** applicable to criminal prosecutions; as opposed to Dying Declarations **Brodin, M. and Avery, M.,** *Handbook of Massachusetts Evidence* **(8th ed. 2007)**: applies only in homicide prosecutions and only when declarant was victim: (a) statement must concern manner in which declarant met death; (b) evidence must show declarant believed he would die immediately; (c) evidence must show declarant did die within very short time;

C v Green **420 M 771, 781–82 (95)**—judge failed to make required "foundation" findings, but evidence would support such findings; jury should be instructed as to foundation requirements and to disregard declaration if requirements not met;

C v Mayne **38 MAC 282 (95)**—"dying declaration" was actually admitted as a prior inconsistent statement by a testifying witness; had jury been instructed as to foundation requirements for 'dying declaration', they would have found declarant believed death imminent (seven gunshot wounds, lying on floor bleeding, saying "dying");

C v Nesbitt **452 M 236 (2008)**—mortally wounded victim's statement to responding neighbor ("Ralph did this to me . . . don't let me die"), even if denominated "testimonial," not violative of Confrontation Clause in opinion of SJC (see *Crawford v Washington* **541 US 36, 56 n.6, leaving issue open**); *C v Slavski* **245 M 405, 413–14 (23)** held no "confrontation" violation in admission of "well recognized exceptions," most prominently dying declarations;

11-F.8. Statements of Coconspirators and Co-venturers

See Chapter 11-G, post, for cases on tacit or adoptive admissions;

See Chapter 8-B for cases in which Bruton rule bans admission of coconspirator & coventurer

C v Prater **431 M 86, 93–94 (2000)**—when witness did not see that to which she testified, but instead formed opinion about it after hearing subsequent conversations by two alleged participants in crime, admitting testimony was error (here harmless); but see Prop.M.R.Evid. 602 ("witness may not testify to a matter unless evidence is introduced sufficient to support a finding that he has personal knowledge of the matter");

C v Babbitt **430 M 700 (2000)**—no Bruton violation because statements by alleged joint venturer to Commonwealth witnesses were made in D's presence and qualified as adoptive admissions (with one exception, but no prejudice, because cumulative);

C v Gonzalez **443 M 799 (2005)**—trial witness's testimony concerning what coventurers did in "reenacting" fatal fight implicated hearsay concerns despite lack of testimony concerning anything "said" out of court; "conduct can serve as a substitute for words, and to the extent it communicates a message, hearsay considerations apply"; evidence that defendant was present during the reenactment, however, made it admissible as adoptive admission of defendant;

C v Francis **432 M 353 (2000)**—statements of alleged principal not admissible at D's trial for accessory before fact: not admissible as "against penal interest," at least as to parts which inculpated D and reported incriminating statements allegedly made by D on night of shooting AND error to allow ADA to cross-examine D concerning such statements: good faith basis to believe D made such statements couldn't be supplied by the principal's statements to police, which had been excluded from evidence (though improperly preserved & SJC held no prejudice in circumstances);

C v Jordan **49 MAC 802 (2000)**—at trial of D, evidence that his alleged co-venturer, in D's & V's presence, told D's friend via telephone that they were going to kill V and would come to kill the friend next was admissible; statement was not for truth of matter that they would kill V & friend, but was evidence of existence of conspiracy to murder: "What counts is the fact that such words were spoken";

C v Caldron **383 M 86, n.5 (81)**—D's statement to co-venturer shortly after alleged robbery admissible re: D's intent during it (though "self-serving");

C v Pleasant **366 M 100 (74)**—joint venturer statement during cooperative effort & in furtherance of it = admissible against D; *(See Chapters 16-B, 17-B, 17-C)*;

C v Treadwell **37 MAC 968 (94)**—because no evidence to show D was engaged in joint venture, other than

hearsay statement of alleged joint venturer beforehand, required finding of NG;

C v Young **10 MAC 410 (80)**—judge must make prima facie finding of joint venture before admitting co-venturer statements against D; joint venture ultimately jury issue;

C v Braley **449 M 316 (2007)**—statements of joint venturer admissible if Commonwealth establishes by "preponderance of the evidence" an "adequate probability of the existence of a common venture, including participation by the given defendant"; evidence to be viewed in light most favorable to Commonwealth;

C v Cruz **430 M 838, 846 (2000)**—even though judge didn't submit to jury issue of D's guilt under theory of joint venture, jury could consider co-D's extrajudicial statement under joint venture exception to hearsay rule;

C v Nascimento **421 M 677 (96)**—jury should be instructed that, before relying on statement of co-venturer, they must find, based on non-hearsay evidence, that joint venture existed;

C v McLaughlin **431 M 241, 249 n.7 (2000)**—though question was not before court, assertion that it's "illogical to require" proof beyond reasonable doubt of D's involvement in conspiracy before coconspirator's statement may be considered against him, "as it renders the admission of such statements totally unnecessary"; evidence of oral agreement between witness and one co-conspirator wasn't "for truth" (so not hearsay) but instead "as proof of an 'operative' statement, i.e., the existence of a conspiracy";

C v White **370 M 703 (76)**—exception ends when joint venture does;

C v Clarke **418 M 207, 218 (94)**—joint venturer's statement about getting rid of guns admissible against D because made at time of active attempts to conceal shooting & avoid detection ("in furtherance of" the joint venture);

C v Angiulo **415 M 502 (93)**—statement of alleged joint venturer to 3d parties, speaking of murder committed sometime in past: judge "within discretion" in ruling there was "an adequate probability of the existence of a continuing common venture" to conceal the crime, so statement admissible against D;

C v Stewart **450 M 25 (2007)**—error to admit statement of 3rd party to co-defendant "shortly after the murder", "tell your friend he's a bad shot", to which co-defendant responded "OK"; doubtful that "OK" was an "adoptive admission," and in any event D was not present and took no part in adopting it; no evidence that statement was made in furtherance of joint enterprise (and jury wasn't instructed as to prerequisites for such use); error, however, held harmless;

C v Mavredakis **430 M 848, 863–64 (2000)**—ample evidence of ongoing attempt to cover up crime, so statements of joint venturers admissible;

C v Hardy **431 M 387, 394 n.3 (2000)**—jury could find continuing joint venture because evidence was that one venturer asked for advice about getting rid of gun and locating a place to go shortly after murder; SJC here upheld introduction of statements at trial despite Comm's acknowledgment prior to trial that severance was required BECAUSE the statements at issue couldn't be admitted at trial of D; if D "presented . . . evidence that" Commonwealth intended its concession "to be binding, or that the defendant understood it to be so," perhaps different result;

C v Brown **9 MAC 609 (80)**—instructions given complaining witness by D's accomplices admissible where judge could find they were acting in concert with D;

C v Tilley **327 M 540 (51)**—principal's guilty plea is inadmissible hearsay at accessory trial;

C v Ortiz **50 MAC 304 (2000)**—no abuse of discretion in barring admission of co-D's guilty plea: no tendency to exonerate allegedly joint-venturing D in narcotics distribution to undercover cop;

US v Dworken **855 F.2d 12 (1st Cir. '88)**—co-D's G plea can't suggest D's guilt;

C v Santiago **425 M 491 (97)**—no abuse of discretion in barring admission at D's trial of G plea of murder D's adversary in exchange of gunfire (to manslaughter of innocent bystander and to armed assault with intent to kill D): no inconsistency in liability for **both** shooters; *S.C.* **(& same holding) 50 MAC 762, 765 (2001)**;

C v Chiappini **72 MAC 188 (2008)**—"victim's" admission in later criminal prosecution was newly discovered evidence supporting D's motion for new trial: D was convicted of assault and battery by dangerous weapon (stabbing V's neck), though at trial had claimed self-defense; his "victim" subsequently admitted to sufficient facts on charge of assault and battery by means of dangerous weapon (pavement), and prosecutor's recitation of facts *then* was that "victim" of D had had D on the pavement and smashed D's head into pavement; "victim" denied during D's trial that D had ever been on ground, allowing prosecution to argue in closing that D easily could have escaped as combatants were only in "stand-up fist-fight"; trial judge's denial of D's motion for new trial = vacated; **S.C., after remand, 76 MAC 1107 (2010)**—order denying motion for new trial = **reversed**;

C v DoVale **57 MAC 657 (2003)**—no error in barring, as evidence of "consciousness of innocence," D's refusal to accept motion judge's proffer of a plea bargain to "time served";

C v Martinez **425 M 382 (97)**—G plea of alleged joint venturer-turned-Commonwealth witness not evidence of D's guilt, and D entitled to jury instruction on request;

C v Powell **40 MAC 430 (96)**—reversal because judge instructed that jury could consider witness's (allegedly a joint venturer with D) conviction of **armed** robbery as circumstantial evidence against D on whether a weapon was used;

C v Haraldstad **16 MAC 565 (83)**—co-D's (severed) NG not relevant, but lack of pending case IS, i.e., to show lack of bias;

C v Best **50 MAC 722 (2001)**—error for cop to testify that purported buyer of drugs from D had been arrested before for heroin possession, & was found, in separate

trial, guilty of possessing heroin based on purported transaction with D;

C v Howard **46 MAC 366 (99)**—acquittal of person jointly charged but separately tried is not probative of others' innocence;

C v Colon-Cruz **408 M 533 (90)**—coventurer's statements made while planning crime & while trying to conceal evidence of crime admissible against D because made during pendency of & in furtherance of joint venture;

C v Fernandes **427 M 90 (98)**—coventurer's threat, made before inception of joint venture and not in D's presence, admissible to show that speaker carried out his intent;

C v Anselmo **33 MAC 602 (92)**—statements of unindicted coconspirators admissible against D if foundational requirements met, even if coconspirator separately acquitted;

C v Cartagena **32 MAC 141 (92)**—once sufficient competent nonhearsay evidence of joint venture admitted, coventurer's statements made during pendency & in furtherance of joint venture admissible, even if made outside D's presence;

C v Collado **426 M 675 (98)**—admissible even **before** sufficient evidence of joint venture exists because if insufficiency remains, D can move to strike;

C v Washington **449 M 476 (2007)**—though jury should be instructed that they may consider against D the hearsay statements of alleged joint venturer only if they determine on basis of independent non-hearsay evidence that joint venture existed, no sua sponte obligation to provide such limiting instruction in absence of objection and/or request for instruction;

C v Vallejo **455 M 72 (2009)**—co-D's counsel stressing co-D's cooperation, full statement to cops, unobjected to by D, did not impinge upon D's right to silence; see also *C v Russo* 49 MAC 579 (2000);

11-F.9. Declarations against Penal or Financial Interest

See Chapter 11-G and Chapter 20A-E for cases on admissions, and Chapter 12-E, re: consciousness of guilt ('admissions' implied by conduct);

Brodin, M. and Avery, M., *Handbook of Massachusetts Evidence* **(8th ed. 2007)**—Declarations Against Interest;

Young, Pollets & Poreda, *Evidence,* **§ 804.4 (2d ed. 1998)**—(same);

5 Wigmore, *Evidence,* **§§ 1455–77 (Chadbourn rev. 1974)**—(same);

Prop.M.R.Evid. 804(b)(3)—(same);

C v Carr **373 M 617 (77)**—statement subjecting declarant to criminal liability that reasonable person wouldn't have made unless believed true = admissible if corroboration clearly indicating trustworthiness;

C v Piper **426 M 8 (97)**—admissibility of declaration against penal interest depends on (1) unavailability of declarant; (2) statement so far tended to subject declarant to criminal liability that speaker would not have said it if untrue; (3) corroboration by circumstances "clearly indicating trustworthiness; in "close" case regarding corroboration factor, judge "should" favor admitting the evidence;

C v Burnham **451 M 517 (2008)**—rejecting D's belatedly-claimed basis for admission of ex-wife's statements (as against "penal interest"): while SJC acknowledged that declarant was unavailable even though D had not attempted to call her as witness (she'd been indicted for murder along with D, trial severed, tried first, didn't testify, was convicted and appealed), statements did not clearly tend to subject her to criminal liability and were instead at best "consciousness of guilt" equally suggestive of her intent to provide cover for D's criminality, and were not corroborated by circumstances indicating their trustworthiness; a D "has no constitutional right to the admission of unreliable hearsay";

C v Ragland **72 MAC 815 (2008)**—after trial in which witnesses recanted their grand jury testimony, jury sent question, "what is the punishment for perjury?", judge with agreement of all parties responded that jurors were not to concern themselves with any punishment for any crime; particularly because D was not entitled to original instruction that recantation was adverse to witnesses' penal interest (because the evidence supporting witness's awareness of such adversity was objected to, and objection was sustained, & evidence thus stricken), no error because no basis for jury to consider what penal consequences might be; even if initial instruction was proper, it required no amplification, no substantial risk of miscarriage of justice;

C v Dupont **75 MAC 605 (2009)**, citing *C v Nawn* **394 M 1 (85)**, *C v Cancel* **394 M 567 (85)**, *C v Machado* **339 M 713 (59)**—D's denial of accusation of guilt isn't admissible unless some other hearsay exception applies, BUT if D responds to accusation in "equivocal, evasive or irresponsive way," D's statement IS admissible; cop's assertion to D that cop "knew he was involved in a drug transaction and believed that there was cocaine in his vehicle" was answered: "there is no cocaine in my vehicle or one me"; D's statement held admissible as "oddly specific" (not unequivocal);

C v Diaz **453 M 266 (2009)**—D's recorded statements denying that he shot anyone, denying he was in Lowell on date of shooting, denying he had been driving Mitsubishi = inadmissible (citing *Nawn* 394 M 1 [85]); argument that they were false and thus admissible as "consciousness of guilt = REJECTED (if such were so, "rule prohibiting evidence of statements of denial would be eviscerated," every denial becoming admissible as 'consciousness of guilt');

C v Clemente **452 M 295 (2008)**—no error in Commonwealth's introduction of a defendant's statements on ground that judge had previously ruled that *defense* could not introduce the conversation; statement was admissible "as the statement of a party opponent," id. at 330 n.48, but "could not be proffered by the defense," citing *Marshall* 434 M 358, 364 (2001);,

C v Dew **443 M 620 (2005)**—no error in barring admission of witness's testimony that D's cousin admitted to

having committed the murder with which D was charged because no "corroboration": witness herself testified that she knew speaker to be a liar, there was no independent evidence that cousin might have done it, and eyewitnesses' identifications were of D, who bore little resemblance to D's cousin;

C v Weichell **446 M 785 (2006)**—evidence held by motion judge to have warranted a new trial would not be admissible as statement against penal interest because motion judge used improper bases to test trustworthiness of declarant's statements, which were written seven months after D's convictions (not "contemporaneous" with D's arrest or conviction);

C v Charros **443 M 752, 768 (2005)**—rejects D's claim of error in exclusion of statements by man claimed by D to be owner of drugs (apologizing for leaving D to take the blame, but saying he had to solve his own problems with police): declarant wasn't called to testify & unavailability due to possibility of claim of privilege against self-incrimination won't be presumed; statements didn't qualify as "against penal interest";

C v Dajarnette **75 MAC 88 (2009)**—though D wanted admitted another (non-testifying, claim of privilege) individual's acknowledgment to cop that he had smoked some of the marijuana and his fingerprints would be on bag of it & perhaps also on cocaine bag, trial counsel agreed that the Commonwealth would be entitled to introduce the rest of the statement, which was clearly self-exculpatory; judge would have been within his discretion to declare defense-proffered material inadmissible (because the gist of the statement was NOT really declaration against interest) or to allow it with limited context to prevent distortion by defense, but defense counsel not ineffective for having agreed to ruling;

C v Morgan **449 M 343 (2007)**—statement by 3rd party, before victim was found, that 3rd party shot him in head and threw him in river (injury and location later discovered to be true), held inadmissible as "against penal interest" exception to hearsay: inadequate "corroboration," says SJC, and wouldn't presume declarant would claim privilege against self-incrimination (so unavailability not shown);

C v Slonka **42 MAC 760 (97)**—written statement (by witness claiming 5th Amendment at trial) did not clearly tend to subject him to criminal liability because "smoked a couple of bowls full" = imprecise, circumstances did not show witness awareness that statement was against his interest;

C v Stewart **422 M 385 (96)**—purported murder confession by another person (now dead) inadmissible because no corroboration;

C v Hearn **31 MAC 707 (91)**—D's statement to police not admissible as declaration against interest because mostly exculpatory & insufficiently trustworthy;

C v Thissell **74 MAC 773 (2009)**—D's statement to global positioning system (GPS) "monitoring staff member" that he was at the beach and going in and out of the water was an admission and not inadmissible as "hearsay", apparently because he had been instructed previously not to submerge transmitter in water, and was responding to the monitor contacting D because of loss of signal; S.C. 457 M 191 (2010);

C v Marrero 60 MAC 225 (2003)—where only discrete references in long narrative statement are self-incriminatory/against declarant's penal interest, entire narrative is not transformed into hearsay-excepted statement (citing *Williamson v US* 512 US 594 [94]);

C v Semedo 422 M 716 (98)—when witnesses claimed 5th Amendment & refused to testify at D's trial, their statements to police were not admissible against him because they were not against **their** penal interest (instead exculpatory of themselves); MA has no "innominate exception" to hearsay rule (making admissible hearsay not within any other exception if it is "reliable and trustworthy");

C v Charles 428 M 672 (99)—corroboration requirement applies not only when statement is offered to exculpate the accused, but also when it inculpates him; here sufficient corroboration found, however; re: confrontation issue, SJC says statement doesn't expressly refer to D; though Commonwealth not particularly diligent in trying to secure declarant's presence, he had failed to appear to answer charges, and "would have" invoked right not to testify if present; but see id. at 679 (it is not to be presumed, generally, that absent witness may invoke right against self-incrimination);

C v McLaughlin 433 M 558 (2001)—D's statement to police after arrest ("was being robbed . . . bought crack from him . . . it was fake . . . approached . . . tussle[d] . . . He had the knife") not admissible as "against penal interest" because such declarations are limited to statements made by witnesses, not parties to the litigation or their privies or representatives; also not admissible as 'spontaneous utterance' because motive & time to have fabricated;

C v Santiago 425 M 491 (97)—G plea of murder D's adversary in exchange of gunfire (to manslaughter of innocent bystander and to armed assault with intent to kill D) inadmissible at D's trial: no inconsistency in liability for **both** shooters;

C v Fernandes 30 MAC 335 (91)—co-D's plea colloquy not admissible as declaration against penal interest because given under press of plea negotiations & not unequivocally exculpatory as to D;

C v Lopera 42 MAC 133 (97)—error to allow introduction of statements of woman, arrested in the act of prostitution, that D was the "keeper" of the apartment and she shared her earnings with him: woman was not "unavailable" since Commonwealth had failed to make diligent search (insufficient to assert merely "can't find"): judge's "finding" that she'd likely claim Fifth Amendment rejected as speculative; **AND** statements in any event not sufficiently against **declarant's** penal interest, because shifting larger blame to D;

Williamson v US 512 US 594 (94)—under Fed.R.Evid., declaration against penal interest exception

does not include statements inculpating others even when included in a statement which is clearly self-inculpatory (MA SJC follows in substance the federal rule on penal interest declarations - see *C v Carr* 373 M 617 (77));

C v Drew 397 M 65 (86)—inadmissible because not clearly corroborated;

C v DiToro 51 MAC 191 (2001)—that D's boyfriend and another guilty party spontaneously and independently told cop that D had nothing to do with the drug deal = inadmissible because no corroboration; boyfriend had motive to lie & other individual maybe had no basis of knowledge on point;

C v Zuluaga 43 MAC 629 (97)—while allowing 5th Amendment claim by witness, court refused to find inference of sufficient "corroboration" to allow intro of hearsay declarations favorable to D;

C v Pope 397 M 275 (86)—suicide note is not against penal interest;

C v Galloway 404 M 204 (89)—abused discretion to find no corroboration; judge "shouldn't be so stringent" or assess credibility of proffered testimony;

See Chapter 20G-4 on informant reliability & declarations against penal interest, e.g.:

C v Melendez 407 M 53 (90)—informant's statement that he bought & used drugs not statement against penal interest because not corroborated by physical evidence & informant not in "reasonable fear of prosecution";

C v Allen 406 M 575 (90)—informant's statement that he bought & used drugs not statement against penal interest because his name was unknown to police;

C v Burgos 36 MAC 903 (94)—not error to exclude testimony of witness who said that, at about the time of the robbery, a man she knew as "Jerry" stated that he had just robbed a white woman: declarant not shown to be unavailable (counsel offering no account of efforts to locate, interview, or produce "Jerry") & statement not corroborated by circumstances indicating its trustworthiness;

C v Parapar 404 M 319 (89)—informant's statements admitting to illegal trafficking immediately after arrest for undercover sale to cop was statement against penal interest because it subjected him to criminal liability;

11-F.10. Hospital and Medical Records

C v Roman 414 M 235 (93)—letter by nontestifying psychiatrist which had been consulted by testifying expert not admissible because notice not given to opposing party as required by G.L. c. 233, § 79G;

C v Dube 413 M 570 (92)—trial judge has discretion to admit hospital record of OUI-D's blood alcohol tests (here, conducted upon D's admission to hospital, "solely because the procedure was good medical practice," after suffering injury from auto accident) even though G.L. c. 233, § 79 bans admission of evidence relating to "question of liability";

C v McCready 50 MAC 521 (2000)—"hospital records of blood tests with a bearing on the patient's degree of intoxication have been admitted routinely in OUI prosecutions", despite § 79's possible applicability re: issue of "liability"; if D truly quibbled over the authenticity of a nurse's note at intake ("strong ETOH on breath") signed "AHunter," should have requested continuance (short) to ascertain his/her identity, but presumption = person having signatory access to the record wasn't outsider; no relief on basis that record went directly to counsel rather than through clerk of court as contemplated by G.L. c. 233, § 79;

C v Francis **450 M 132 (2007)**—"portions" of records produced under G.L. c. 233, § 79 may be offered, though adversary may object on any ground other than authenticity and hearsay; if objection = "completeness," judge should consider and rule whether other portions should be admitted; records ALSO are "always subject to redaction where necessary"; records produced under § 79 are not "an indivisible unit that could be altered only by means of agreed-upon redactions";

C v Lampron **65 MAC 340 (2005)**—G.L. c. 233, § 79 cited to allow hospital records containing notations such as "positive for ETOH", "positive for cocaine", "intoxicated", and "odor of ETOH", notwithstanding D's argument that *Crawford v Washington* 541 US at 50–51, prohibits this "hearsay," as violative of Sixth Amendment confrontation clause (not "testimonial," says Appeals Court); toxicology report labeled "preliminary", should not have been admitted but wasn't prejudicial;

Doyle v Dong **412 M 682 (92)**—personal knowledge of recorder of hospital record that was contained in records of another hospital may be inferred from details;

C v Moran **439 M 482 (2003)**—error to exclude medical record of rape complainant, who testified that she wouldn't have consented to sex because she had had recent laparoscopy, and that she had taken pain killer because of this surgery; record revealed an entirely different medical procedure, involving a different bodily entry point; no privilege applied, & no basis for invoking "Bishop-Fuller" protocol;

Grant v Lewis/Boyle **408 M 269 (90)**—although medical expert may rely on records of nontestifying physician in reaching opinion, such records not admissible under G.L. c. 233, § 79G;

C v Schutte **52 MAC 796 (2001)**—defense counsel took all steps required under G.L. c. 233, § 79G to make admissible at trial a report in letter form from D's physician that he had a balance/equilibrium problem of long standing (to refute alleged failure of field sobriety test); reversible error to exclude it on DA's bogus objection (error compounded by DA exploiting in closing argument the absence of the info he'd succeeded in excluding); fact that a document = inadmissible under G.L. c. 233, § 79 (as prepared in anticipation of litigation) doesn't mean it's inadmissible under § 79G; §79G is NOT limited to civil cases; requirements: signed/subscribed/sworn to under penalties of perjury by examining or treating physician; written notice to opposing party by certified mail, return

receipt requested, at least ten days before report is introduced in court; proponent to file with court clerk affidavit of notice & return receipt;

C v Kirkpatrick **423 M 436 (96)**—expert testimony required to make particular medical records have probative value because they were not "self-explanatory";

C v Bandy **38 MAC 329, 335–36 (95)**—similar;

C v Johnson **59 MAC 164 (2003)**—trial judge has broad discretion in deciding whether a medical record can be read and decoded by jurors and non-expert witness (would "subvert the purpose of the statute [c. 233, § 79]" if medical personnel must always come to court to explain shorthand notes and abbreviations);

C v Russo **30 MAC 923 (91)**—blood tests not related to treatment or diagnosis were admissible because part of routine workup for certain medical problem;

C v Johnson **59 MAC 164 (2003)**—notwithstanding fact that info was in "hospital record," the positive result of a "rapid urine screening test" was noted to be unreliable, and note stressed that "a second method must be used to obtain a confirmed analytical result"; admission of record was an abuse of discretion and error of law;

C v Flaherty **61 MAC 776 (2004)**—though D sought to have hospital records admitted because they failed to note anything about him being intoxicated (& were thus exculpatory), no abuse of discretion in excluding them as possibly misleading: arrest for OUI was at 1:30, and hospital visit occurred after 4:00, with notations being made as much as 90 minutes later, AND focus of visit was "chest pains," not intoxication;

G.L. c. 233, §§ 79, 79G: Hospital Records—if relate to treatment & medical history, NOT to liability; to be admissible as evidence of diagnosis, opinion etc. of physician, party must have given written notice of intention to offer such report or bill as evidence along with copy of same, by certified mail not less than ten days before introduction of same into evidence, and affidavit of notice, along with return receipt, must be filed with clerk of court;

C v Medeiros **456 M 52 (2010)**—defense counsel failed to follow G.L. c. 233, § 79G procedure of notice, but judge in act of discretion allowed hospital records to be admitted; defense counsel's failure to move for redaction was unrelated to procedure, but in circumstances did not cause notable prejudice to D (content consistent with defense theory);

G.L. c. 233, § 78: Business Records—made in good faith, regular course, & prior to beginning of proceeding;

C v Dube **413 M 570, 574 (92)**—"liability" as used in § 79 does not encompass criminal culpability for intoxication;

C v Kirkpatrick **423 M 436 (96)**—rape D permissibly barred from introducing medical records to show that he had sexually transmitted disease at time of alleged crime and that child complainant did not: without expert testimony, records lacked probative value;

C v Franks **359 M 577 (71)**—lab test saying "sperm" OK though no personal knowledge of doctor; confrontation right not violated; contrast *C v Ennis* **2 MAC 864 (74)** exclude diagnosis/opinion because totem-pole hearsay & confusing; prefer doc's testimony;

C v Jaime **433 M 575, 577–78 (2001)**—citing Prop.M.R.Evid. 705—Commonwealth expert testifying to opinion that D had capacity to premeditate should not have been allowed to testify, during direct examination, as to statements made by people he interviewed about D's mood and affect the day before the killing; judge should have precluded admission of hearsay "irrespective of whether they formed the basis of the expert's opinion," though D-counsel could have cross-examined witness about facts underlying opinion; *see also C v Rodriguez* **437 M 554 (2002)**—jury instruction SHOULD be that expert opinion should be disregarded if the assumptions upon which it is based are not true; *C v Hinds* **450 M 1 (2007)**—first degree murder convictions reversed due to erroneous instruction that expert's opinion must be disregarded unless jurors first find that facts assumed by witness in reaching opinion was "proved by Commonwealth beyond a reasonable doubt": expert opinion at issue was that of defense witness, as to D's criminal responsibility; *Superior Court Criminal Practice Jury Instructions* (MCLE 1999) § 4.7.1 = reproduced at n.6, "but this instruction also may have its problems";

C v Atencio **12 MAC 747 (81)**—hospital record's "strong alcohol odor" = OK; if record admitted without objection, all contents considered if relevant;

C v Dube **413 M 570 (92)**—hospital record of blood alcohol level test admissible because ordered by doctor as routine medical practice in course of treating D after motor vehicle accident; but *C v Sheldon* **423 M 373 (96)** though doctor ordered blood alcohol level test, it was not for treating or diagnosing D (instead "only to prove [she] was not intoxicated"); **record** inadmissible as hearsay; test results maybe admissible by testimony of person conducting test (or by attending doctor);

C v Goudreau **422 M 731 (96)**—dictated but unsigned "opinion" letter of Bridgewater doctor not admissible because portions not within medical records statute (G.L. c. 233, § 79) as "relating to treatment and medical history" and "possess[ing] characteristics justifying the presumption of reliability";

C v Pena **455 M 1 (2009)**—testifying medical examiner could rely on other medical examiner's autopsy report, notwithstanding D's confrontation clause objection (*Crawford v Washington* 541 US 36 [2004]);

C v Baldwin **24 MAC 200 (87)**—exclude "diagnosis: molestation" because liability (& from only complaining witness's word, not opinion); illegible writings need stipulation or explanation;

C v DiMonte **427 M 233 (98)**—though records should have been redacted to eliminate "assault" references, "fact-specific references to" reported cause of injuries were admissible because part of medical history & "relevant to treatment" even though "incidental to liability;" hospital records **not** here admissible as spontaneous utterances (made over nine hours after alleged beating);

C v Aviles **58 MAC 459 (2003)**—hospital records contained notation by nurse stating that D "held [complainant] by the shoulders & penetrated her . . . & ejaculated on her abdomen . . . similar assaults repeatedly . . . for the past 1–2 years"; appellate court claimed that this was info for "diagnosis," and that jurors would understand that these were complainant's allegations and not statements of fact by medical personnel;

C v Foley **12 MAC 983 (81)**—"correct practice" = delete "victim," "suspect," "rape" terms from otherwise admissible lab certificate;

G.L. c. 22C, § 41—certificate of state police chemist of result of analysis for sperm cells or seminal fluid is prima facie evidence of presence or absence;

C v Juzba **46 MAC 319 (99)**—D counsel failed to get certificate admitted due to ignorance of statute;

C v Rice **441 M 291, 298 (2004)**—no abuse of discretion in allowing state police chemist to testify to length of time sperm retain their tails in part because of statute (even though quite arguably beyond area of expertise);

See Chapter 7-B, Subpoenas; & Chapter 11-J, post, *Privileges*;

Brodin, M. and Avery, M., *Handbook of Massachusetts Evidence* **(8th ed. 2007)**—re: business records (see G.L. c. 233, § 78, ordinary business records' admissibility, required foundation; G.L. c. 233, § 79J, re use of certified copies of business records); § 8.11.2 re: hospital records (G.L. c. 233, § 79), citing **Bouchie v Murray 376 M 524, 531 (78)** for four-part test determining hospital record material's admissibility; § 8.11.3 - re broad hearsay exceptions under G.L. c. 233, § 79G; § 8.11.4 Prop.M.R.Evid. 803(6)&(7)—would merge into one rule the hospital/business records hearsay exception;

Young, Pollets & Poreda, *Evidence*, **§ 803.6 (2d ed. 1998)**—(business record); § 803.4(a–c) (medical matters, including hospital records & medical reports);

5 Wigmore, *Evidence*, **§§ 1517–61b** (Chadbourn rev. 1974)—(same);

11-F.11. Business Records

C v Duddie Ford, Inc. **28 MAC 426 (90)**—reversed in part on other grounds, 409 M 387 (91) although documents not admissible as business records under G.L. c. 233, § 78 because custodian lacked knowledge of their production, they were admissible to show what bank file contained;

C v Savageau **42 MAC 518 (97)**—in 2d/subsequent cocaine distribution prosecution, probation dept. records admissible to show D represented by or waived counsel on predicate offense because they're "business records" - **but** were they made "before the beginning of the criminal proceeding"? See *Trapp* **396 M 202, 208 (85)**;

C v Purcell **423 M 880 (96)**—worker's time sheet, contradicting D's testimony as to contact with worker, not admissible as business record because it was completed after D's arrest;

Burke v Memorial Hospital **29 MAC 948 (90)**—performance evaluations in personnel files not admissible because opinions contained in business records not admissible;

Prop.M.R.Evid. 803 (4-14)—901-902 - medical/business records, authentication

Bouchie v Murray **376 M 524 (78)**—hospital records exception if (1) relate to diagnosis/treatment, not liability; (2) no 2d level Hearsay (unless 2d exception); (3) [(?)entrant(s) had personal knowledge? - but see *Wingate v Emery* **385 M 402 (82)** preparer needn't have personal knowledge if entry routinely made & entrant(s) have business duty to be accurate];

Kelly v O'Neil **1 MAC 313 (73)**—police reports admissible as business record only as to cop's observations/statements; not for 2d level hearsay conclusions/opinions; accident report by V not regular course of business;

Julian v Randazzo **380 M 391 (80)**—police report portions with opinions, recommendations, 2d level hearsay = inadmissible without other exception(s);

C v Sellon **380 M 220 (80)**—police log of calls = business record; [cf. *C v Neumyer* **432 M 23 (2000)**, on further review of 48 MAC 154 (99) - date, time, and fact of telephone call made by complainant to rape crisis center not privileged under G.L. c. 233, § 20J]

C v Ward W. **47 MAC 208, 212–13 (99)**—transcript and tape of 911 call admissible to establish time period between initial 911 call and response from officer who first saw stolen car;

C v Thissell **74 MAC 773 (2009)**—global positioning system (GPS) records (showing D entered "exclusion zone" covered by stay-away order/condition of probation) not "hearsay", OR, alternatively, are business records;

Wingate v Emery **385 M 402 (82)**—preparer needn't have personal knowledge if entry routinely made & entrant(s) have business duty to be accurate;

C v Hussey **14 MAC 1015 (82)**—Welfare Dept. can't testify re: D's wage records received from D's employers; since Welfare Dept. didn't make record, not business record;

C v Walker **379 M 297 (79)**—caller's statements in police stolen car report not offered for truth of assertion, so not hearsay; business record = OK; [but see cases above questioning relevance of 'state of police knowledge']

C v Wilson **12 MAC 942 (81)**—can exclude complaining witness's school file because had agencies' reports 2d level hearsay & conclusory collective opinions;

C v Trapp **396 M 202 (85)**—jail discipline records made while D awaits trial not business record because made after criminal proceeding began (indictment);

See Chapter 18 re: ID Hearsay; Chapter 7–K, Prior Testimony; & Chapter 21-T, larceny of motor vehicle (special rules);

11-F.12. Official Records

Genova v Genova **28 MAC 647 (90)**—traffic accident report mandated by c. 90, § 26, admissible under official records exception;

Adoption of George **27 MAC 265 (89)**; *Custody of Michel* **28 MAC 260 (90)**—variety of DSS records admissible under official records exception;

C v Martinez **425 M 382 (97)**—trial judge not required to admit foreign documents not strictly authenticated pursuant to Mass.R.Crim.P. 40(a)(2), though had discretion to do so; "double certification" of R.40 requires written document to be attested by person authorized to make attestation "and to be accompanied by certificate which vouches for authenticity by substantiating genuineness of attesting signature and the official position of signer";

K. Smith, *Criminal Practice and Procedure*, **§ 2416 (2d ed. 1983 & Supp.)**—authentication of official Mass. records shown by attested copy by officer having legal custody (or his/her deputy);

11-F.13. Contemporaneous Expressions of Pain or Bodily Sensation

Simmons v Yurchak **28 MAC 371 (90)**—limited common law exception for contemporaneous expressions of pain discussed; cf. Prop.M.R.Evid. 803 (3);

C v Trowbridge **419 M 750, 760 (95)**——doctor's testimony that child sexual assault complainant's grandmother told him that child said that doctor's examination "felt like when her father touched her," inadmissible;

11-F.14. Extrajudicial Statements of Identification or Description

See Chapter 18-E for Daye line of cases relating to statements of identification or description;

C v Berrio **407 M 37 (90)**—Daye rule not limited to identification;

See Chapter 9-F for substantive use of out-of-court statements inconsistent with trial testimony;

C v Morgan **30 MAC 685 (91)**—cop's testimony about eyewitness's extrajudicial description of perpetrator's clothing was inadmissible under Daye rule because eyewitness had not testified about description given to cops;

C v Perez **27 MAC 550 (89)**—same;

C v Martinez **431 M 168, 175–76 (2000)**—**Daye** exception does not serve to make admissible everything which an identifying witness told police, e.g., how many shots fired, color of gun, witness's allegedly good vantage point, or witness's statements as to alleged behavior of D after shooting;

C v Almeida **34 MAC 901 (93)**—prosecutor properly permitted to elicit on redirect that witness identified D's photograph on later occasion where defense had elicited from cop on cross-examination that bank robbery witness identified photo of someone other than D, notwithstanding Daye, because allowed under "rule of completeness";

C v Jones **407 M 168 (90)**—cop's testimony about out-of-court photo identifications by eyewitnesses who denied making them was properly admissible for impeachment purposes, at least where counsel failed to object; but cf *C v Benoit* **32 MAC 111 (92)** can't call witness who will say he has no knowledge, simply to put before jury witness's out of court statement (inculpatory of D), purportedly to "impeach"; BUT NOW cf. *C v Sineiro* **432 M 735 (2000)** if judge finds witness's lack of memory at trial to be "feigned", prior sworn testimony (with opportunity for cross-examination) admissible substantively;

11-F.15. Prior Recorded Testimony

See Chapter 7-K for Daye-type cases on prior recorded testimony (i.e., availability of witness somewhat immaterial); Chapter 7-K for traditional "prior recorded testimony" analysis (witness unavailable at time of trial);

C v Berrio **407 M 37 (90)**—Daye rule not limited to identification);

See Chapter 9-F (evolution of caselaw post-Daye);

C v Donnelly **33 MAC 189 (92)**—diagram used by cop at grand jury substantively admissible under Daye, despite cop's claim that diagram not fair & accurate;

C v Fort **33 MAC 181 (92)**—witness's inconsistent probable cause hearing testimony was substantively admissible under Daye;

C v Sineiro **432 M 735 (2000)**—probable cause hearing testimony admissible substantively despite witness at trial asserting failure of memory, because judge could conclude that failure of memory was feigned (true failure of memory at trial is not "inconsistent" with probable cause testimony/past memory): Daye-contemplated "corroboration" not required prior to substantive use because prior testimony under oath with opportunity for cross-examination is sufficiently trustworthy for presentation for its truth to fact finder in criminal case; "no mythical necessity that the case must be decided only in accordance with the truth of words uttered under oath in court"; SJC reserves judgment whether Prop.M.R.Evid. 804 should be adopted (former testimony of "unavailable" witness); see also *C v Clements* **436 M 190 (2002), S.C., 51 MAC 508 (2001)** (see dissenting opinions therein) - revises/alters previous "Daye" formulations: for admissibility of prior testimony for its substantive value, (1) the present witness can be effectively cross-examined at trial regarding the accuracy of his prior statement & (2) the prior statement wasn't coerced and was more than a "mere confirmation or denial of an allegation by the interrogator," i.e., the statement must be that of the witness and not of the interrogator. IF that evidence "concerns an element of the crime, there is a separate requirement that the Commonwealth must meet to sustain its burden on the element: there must be other corroborating evidence on the issue" (though the additional evidence "need not be sufficient in itself to establish a factual basis for each element of the crime"); SJC disavows prior statements to the contrary in, e.g., *C v*

Johnson **435 M 113, 134 (2001)**; *C v Sineiro* **432 M 735, 741(2000)**; *C v Noble* **417 M 341, 344 (94)**; *C v Berrio* **407 M 37, 45 (90)**;

C v Moquette **439 M 697 (2003), on further review of 53 MAC 615 (2002)**—fact that spontaneous utterance was recanted by declarant at trial didn't negate its admissibility or sufficiency as basis for conviction: up to the jury to decide; refusal to require corroboration of recanted spontaneous utterance before finding evidence sufficient for conviction; Appeals Court's decision lists other jurisdictions' cases holding that admissible hearsay, recanted by declarant, insufficient, when standing alone, for finding of guilt;

C v Carrasquillo **54 MAC 363 (2002)**—admitting at trial substantively witness's testimony before grand jury that D was the shooter when witness testified at trial that he could not ID D as shooter & upholding G because corroborating evidence existed, statement wasn't coerced, & was that of witness rather than interrogator;

C v DiBenedetto **414 M 37 (92)**—witness's probable cause (transfer) hearing testimony not admissible against D at trial where judge had barred counsel from cross-examining witness about areas beyond scope of immunity promised by prosecutor;

C v Childs **413 M 252 (92)**—testimony from 1st trial admissible against D at 2d trial where Commonwealth made diligent search for unavailable witness & where prior counsel's ineffective assistance didn't mar cross-examination of this witness;

C v Tanso **411 M 640 (92)**—district-court-ordered deposition testimony of unavailable prosecution witness not admissible where D didn't validly waive right to cross-examination in District Court;

C v Ross **426 M 555 (98)**—deposition testimony not admissible when Commonwealth failed to make diligent effort to produce witness at trial (she was studying abroad);

C v Florek **48 MAC 414 (2000)**—though court held motive for cross sufficiently similar at hearing on motion to suppress ID to justify admission of witness's hearing testimony at trial, Commonwealth hadn't made diligent enough effort to obtain witness's presence at trial (letters/summonses to a Kentucky address insufficient; should have used Kentucky police, made tel contact with Kentucky relatives, used summons under Uniform Law to Secure Attendance of Witnesses [G.L. c. 13A]);

US v Salerno **505 US 317 (92)**—exculpatory grand jury testimony of unavailable defense witness will be admissible if determined that prosecution had "similar motive" in questioning witness before grand jury as at trial;

C v Arrington **455 M 437 (2009)**—no error in excluding prior recorded testimony of prosecution witness (deceased by time of trial) given at pretrial detention hearing: it was "unreliable" because of her medical condition at time (heavily medicated, in hospice care for terminal cancer, necessitating leading questions by prosecutor), which also meant lack of "reasonable opportunity" for cross-exam earlier;

C v Rivera **37 MAC 244 (94)**—though 2 Commonwealth witnesses invoked 5th Amendment at homicide trial on basis that grand jury testimony was perjurious, they were ordered to testify **and** their grand jury testimony was admitted & given substantive effect;

C v Fisher **433 M 340 (2001)**—after taking stand, prosecution witness belatedly refused to answer questions; not ineffective assistance to fail to proffer witness's probable cause hearing testimony because (1) it wasn't substantially helpful & (2) appellate court might have held that witness wasn't actually unavailable because assertion of privilege was not "valid" (but was instead because witness was now incarcerated & didn't want to be a Commonwealth witness because of feared retribution);

C v Taylor **32 M 570 (92)**—probable cause hearing answers of unavailable witness could be testified to by ADA because ADA was present at hearing & was substantially able to reproduce witness's material testimony;

C v Steven **29 MAC 978 (90)**—co-D's suppression hearing testimony not admissible at trial on D's behalf because prosecution had different motive in cross-examining co-D at hearing;

C v Burbank **27 MAC 97 (89)**—prior trial testimony of unavailable prosecution witness was admissible;

C v Cyr **425 M 89 (97)**—Court allows, as prior recorded testimony, 3 witnesses' recollection of what testimony was given in probate court concerning custody of D's child, borne by homicide victim (more defensible ruling would have been that it was not admitted for truth, but instead because D heard it and it was relevant to his motive/state of mind);

11-F.16. Doctrine of Completeness

C v Hanlon **44 MAC 810 (98)**—Commonwealth's introduction of portion of D's testimony at first trial did not require that all or some unspecified portion of the rest of it be admitted; D failed to proffer what, if any, explained or qualified the admissions which Commonwealth introduced;

C v Carmona **428 M 268 (98)**—after D elicited from cop that cop had received teletype saying that D had turned himself in (consciousness of innocence, purportedly), OK for Commonwealth to introduce qualifier, "because he believed his friend had been charged" with the murder at issue;

C v Richardson **59 MAC 94 (2003)**—after D introduced, in cross-examination, an inconsistent statement of witness given in his two-page statement to police, ERROR to allow witness to read to jury the entire statement, "for rehabilitation," because it neither qualified nor explained the inconsistent statement;

C v Flaherty **61 MAC 776 (2004)**—fact that D used booking report prepared by a nontestifying cop (that D was cooperative & polite) to "impeach" testifying cop who said that D was antagonistic & disruptive at arrest earlier that night (& this was error) DID NOT ENTITLE prosecutor to introduce through questions to the cop the contents

of the nontestifying cop's report concerning his observations of D; latter matter did not clarify, qualify or explain earlier matter, and "if we were to accept the Commonwealth's liberal interpretation of the rule, once a party used one aspect of a police report or grand jury minutes, then theoretically the entire report would be subject to admission in evidence. THIS IS NOT THE STATE OF THE LAW";

C v Almeida **34 MAC 901 (93)**—prosecutor properly permitted to elicit on redirect that witness identified D's photograph on later occasion where defense had elicited from cop on cross-examination that bank robbery witness identified photo of someone other than D, because allowed under "rule of completeness";

C v Hearn **31 MAC 707 (91)**—contents of D's statement to police not admissible even though prosecution evidence included fact that D made statement: unlikely that jury would assume statement was self-incriminating;

C v Santiago **30 MAC 207 (91)**—otherwise inadmissible statements admissible under doctrine of verbal completeness if they explain or qualify portion of statement already admitted;

C v Watson **377 M 814 (79)**—"verbal completeness" lets in only self-serving parts that qualify/explain D's admission that's in evidence;

C v Eugene **438 M 343 (2003)**—after Commonwealth introduced portion of D's statement which said that he'd passed out after drinking and awoke to find victim dead, no error in excluding portion of statement in which D said he'd found V and her new boyfriend in bed ten days earlier; latter not necessary to explain/qualify former;

C v Clark **432 M 1, 14 (2000)**—verbal completeness doctrine allows admission of "other relevant portions of the SAME statement" which serve to clarify context of the admitted portion; no error in excluding D's statements to cops & medical personnel (i.e., that he had picked up hitchhikers) to contradict statement D made to one particular cop at scene (i.e., that he was "alone") because not part of the "same" very limited statement made to single officer, though former apparently were made at roughly the same time and at same roadside scene;

C v Gaynor **443 M 245, 271 (2005)**—portion of crack cocaine dealer's statement admitted on redirect examination did not serve to clarify context of portion admitted during cross-exam by D counsel, nor serve to correct any distortion; involving a different subject, it was inadmissible (but no objection, & no prejudice given other evidence);

C v Avila **454 M 744 (2009)**—crucial prosecution witness gave three statements to police, and cop took notes; doctrine of verbal completeness doesn't permit Commonwealth to ask witness (direct exam) questions about statement that itself would be inadmissible and then get entire "notes" admitted by claiming that cross-examiner chose to ask other equally selective questions about the statement;

C v Slonka **42 MAC 760 (97)**—after Commonwealth introduced portion of (privileged) psych. record of Commonwealth witness, D entitled to introduce another portion refuting desired effect of 1st portion;

11-F.17. Learned Treatises and Hearsay Sources of Expert Opinions

C v Sneed **413 M 387 (92)**—learned treatise exception adopted; see Prop.M.R.Evid. 803 (18);

Simmons v Yurchak **28 MAC 371 (90)**—instructional medical video not admissible as learned treatise;

C v Johnson **59 MAC 164 (2003)**—book purchased at chain pharmacy ("the pill book") was never established as reliable or authoritative and "contained nothing but inadmissible hearsay"; error to allow DA to introduce it by having D read from it (purportedly to describe effects of OxyContin and diazepam) during cross-examination; book also not admissible as exhibit under *C v Sneed* 413 M at 395–96;

C v Reese **438 M 519 (2003)**—learned treatise can only be used in cross-examination after judge has determined it to be a reliable authority; it can't be introduced as an exhibit; error here to allow, at probable cause hearing concerning sexually dangerous person prosecution, introduction by D of articles by researcher;

11-F.18. Ancient Documents

Department of Revenue v Sorrentino **408 M 340 (90)**—passport less than 20 years old not admissible under ancient document exception;

11-F.19. Past Recollection Recorded

See Chapter 9-I for other cases on past recollection recorded;

C v Morgan **449 M 343, 366 (2007)**—"discretionary" admission of past recollection recorded exception to hearsay is only proper if (1) witness has no revivable recollection of the subject, (2) witness had firsthand knowledge of the facts recorded, (3) witness can testify that the statement was truthful when made, and (4) recording was made when events were fresh in witness's memory: because witness at hearing on motion for new trial testified that police did not accurately record his statement (instead he had, even then, been unsure of critical date), #3 not met;

C v Colon **408 M 419 (90)**—memo properly qualified as past recollection recorded admissible in toto or through testimony of declarant;

C v Evans **438 M 142 (2002)**—to be admissible as past recollection recorded, memo must have been made while incident was fresh in witness's mind AND witness must have present failure of memory; if current memory is "refreshed" by the memo, there's no failure of memory;

C v Campbell **60 MAC 215 (2003)**—inadequate proof that car was stolen: testimony that license plate number of stolen rental car matched that of car being driven by D five days later was improperly admitted (over objection), because witness merely read from car rental agreement, and DA failed to elicit foundation for "past recollection recorded"; rejecting Commonwealth argument that opportunity to cross-examine witness rectified erroneous admission;

C v Evans **439 M 184 (2003)**—error to admit grand jury testimony of Commonwealth witness as past recollection recorded where witness had no recollection of what he had told grand jury, and no evidence he adopted his earlier testimony when his memory of events was fresh; further, absent the judge's finding that witness was feigning memory loss, grand jury testimony NOT admissible for substantive purposes under *Sineiro*, 432 M 735 (2000);

11-G. ADMISSIONS OF DEFENDANT—BY CONDUCT, STATEMENT, ADOPTION, SILENCE

See also Chapter 6, Discovery: D's Alleged Statement; Chapter 20, Suppression; Chapter 10, Prepare Defense;

CPCS P/G's 4.4(b), 4.6(g)—& various privileges - R-12(f) plea offer statements, G.L. c. 33, § 23 shrink, etc.];

Young, Pollets & Poreda, *Evidence*, **§ 804.4, § 801.6, §§ 801.12–.21 (2d ed. 1998)**;

4 Wigmore, *Evidence*, **§§ 1048–87 (Chadbourn rev. 1972)**;

K. Smith, *Criminal Practice & Procedure*, **§§ 388–90 (2d. ed. 1983 & Supp.)**—Mass. "humane practice" rule: judge must 1st decide whether [alleged] admission's voluntary beyond reasonable doubt before jury hears & considers anew; "not appropriate" to voir dire re: voluntariness before jury; must submit issue to jury if it's a "live" issue (§ 394);

C v Nassar **351 M 37, 45 (66)**—D's response to cop only "served to inform" jury (of D's prior record) so should've been excluded;

Prop.M.R.Evid. 104(f), 801(d);

U.S. Constitution, 5th Amendment—(self-incrimination); 6th Amendment (right to counsel);

Mass. Declaration of Rights, Article 12—(self-incrimination, right to counsel)

C v Forde **392 M 453 (84)**—no G. unless a confession is corroborated, but need only a corpus delecti (e.g., loss/injury, even without crime); purpose of rule = guard against conviction for imaginary crimes;

C v Smith **33 MAC 947 (92)**—corroboration rule requires only some evidence, besides D's confession, that crime was actually committed;

C v Boothby **64 MAC 582 (2005)**—same: failure to object to admission of hearsay corroborating D's out-of-court admission was ineffective assistance, since without the corroborative evidence that D was driver of car, finding of not guilty was required;

C v Leonard **401 M 470 (88)**—drunk D's extrajudicial admission that he'd been driving not corroborated by prosecutor's impeaching wife's testimony that she had been driving (wife previously said D drove);

C v Hubbard **69 MAC 232 (2007)**—firearm was found underneath female on lawn, & D yelled that "it is not my gun," but D's later statement to police was that he had taken the gun from the house to the yard and fired it: "corroboration" was that there was indeed a gun, and that it was found outside the house from which D said he had taken it, and spent casings were found, corroborating D's having fired it;

C v Villalta-Duarte **55 MAC 821 (2002)**—D's confession to molestation and battery of baby for whom wife provided day care sufficiently "corroborated" by facts that baby cried hysterically when brought to scene when D was there and had diaper rash and facial scratches which disappeared after weeks with new day care provider;

Smith v US **348 US 147 (54)**—"federal test" requires corroboration as well that D was the wrongdoer, when there is "no tangible corpus delecti"; for more cases, see *Chapter 12-G, Required Finding of Not Guilty*]; see particularly *C v DiGiambattista* **442 M 423 (2004)**—SJC declines to require corroboration that D was actual perpetrator of the crime, but counsels attention to "other tools at our disposal to address the issue of alleged false confession, namely strict analysis of the circumstances of the interrogation as they affect the voluntariness of a D's statement" (encouraging, though not requiring electronic recording of interrogations);

C v Parreira **72 MAC 308 (2008)**—tape recording of police interview with D was admitted during trial, but not played to jury, without objection by D; appellate argument that D was thus deprived of right to be present during "evidence-taking part of trial" (because jury could have played and listened to tape during deliberations) = rejected; D knew tape's content and could have had the tape played during trial to effectuate his claimed right to observe jury's reaction to it to make more informed decision on whether to testify;

C v Williams **450 M 879, 892 (2008)**—D's recorded statement was edited, defense wanting omission of references to D's incarceration, drug use, gang membership, & possession of guns, and DA wanting redaction of D's comments re: victim's reputation for violence and intimidation: because self-defense was at issue, victim's reputation was relevant and admissible (and defense counsel was perhaps ineffective in agreeing to this redaction, albeit as a 'quid pro quo' for other redactions: issue of 'tactic'/reasonableness would not be decided without hearing on motion for new trial);

C v Kosior **280 M 418 (32)**—D's admission to other crimes = immaterial/prejudicial;

C v Anderson **448 M 548 (2007)**—D's statements (about ten years after homicide of woman in Plymouth) describing the killing and burying of a woman on Cape Cod and, on another occasion, his boast of skill with a knife, cutting people up "pretty bad", including a woman on the South Shore, were relevant, and admissible as admissions (they were not evidence of merely extraneous and prejudicial "bad acts");

C v Niziolek **380 M 513 (80)**—jury question whether it's "admission" inconsistent with innocence

C v Pike **430 M 317, 324–25 (99)**—psychiatrist-D's statement, while laughing, "I'm sure you've heard of me, I'm the local drug pusher," even though accompanied by statement that he was "only joking," admissible; jury to decide what weight to give statement;

Genova v Genova **28 MAC 647 (90)**—traffic accident report prepared by D was admissible as admission, even though required by statute;

C v Wilson **430 M 440 (99)**—D's statement to arresting detective, while awaiting arraignment, that he wanted to plead guilty, & accompanying incriminating statements = admissible; though M.R.Crim.P. 12(f) makes inadmissible evidence of an OFFER TO PLEAD GUILTY and statements made in connection with same, and SJC held that this is not limited to statements made to a prosecutor or other government attorney, statements must be plea "negotiations" and not merely plea "discussions"; D here didn't condition statements on "quid pro quo," so statements weren't negotiations;

C v Boyarsky **452 M 700 (2008)**—D's recorded telephone comment to friend that he'd be pleased with a 5-year sentence was not an inadmissible "offer to plead" (not made to someone with any authority to negotiate plea;

C v Awad **47 MAC 139, 143–44 (99)**—D's guilt is not properly inferable from D's sister's purported refusal to help police; see also *C v Howell* **49 MAC 42, 46 (2000)** error to allow introduction of evidence that D's father didn't cooperate with police;

C v Martinez **431 M 168 (2000)**—abuse of discretion to admit evidence that D's niece threatened chief prosecution witness when witness's testimony hadn't changed;

C v Johnson **46 MAC 398, 407 (99)**—after D testified that he did not recall what he was doing on day of robbery (but did not commit robbery), improper for DA to argue that if he wasn't guilty, "he damn sure would find out where he was, who he was with, and bring them in here and have them testify to tell you that they were with him";

C v Edgerly **13 MAC 562 (82)**—D's conduct (offer to bribe witness) = admission; & also consciousness of guilt *(See Chapter 12-E)*;

C v Boyer **52 MAC 590, 599 (2001)**—that D, an attorney, failed to speak with a prosecution witness (who claimed he bribed her not to testify in a case in which he represented a criminal defendant) = inadmissible, as was D's acknowledgment that he didn't speak to her because he believed she was wearing a "wire" during the meeting: "there was nothing said by [the witness] to [the attorney] that [attorney] reasonably could have been expected to deny or rebut"; case law expresses "a 'general wariness' of admissions by silence";

Cf C v Lyons **71 MAC 671, 676 n.5 (2008)**—charged with indecent assault and battery (over age 14), D contended that complainant had aggressively attacked him and any contact he made was in self-defense; prosecutor's argument to jury that D's version implausible because he didn't seek criminal charge against complainant for assault was improper, "should not have been made";

C v Guyton **405 M 497 (89)**—retrieval of money for cops at their request was admission by conduct;

LePage v Bumila **407 M 163 (90)**—D's payment of traffic fine & waiver of appeal not admissible as admissions because failure to challenge likely due to its expense;

US v Hubbell **530 US 27 (2000)**—D was granted immunity & forced to turn over documents; "the Independent Counsel" then used the documents' contents to procure indictments of D, & claimed no 5th Amendment violation because didn't intend to use at trial D's "act of production"; Supreme Court held otherwise (government made "derivative use" of the testimonial aspect of the compelled production, because it was 1st step in chain of evidence leading to prosecution, & government had been unable to even describe the documents with reasonable particularity prior to their production);

11-G.1. Conduct as Consciousness of Guilt

C v Fernandes **427 M 90, 93–94 (98)**—D's threats (to kill alleged joint venturer for "shooting off his mouth about" alleged joint venture killing) admissible as admission & consciousness of guilt;

C v Sheriff **425 M 186 (97)**—D's suicide attempt could be seen as consciousness of guilt;

C v Goetzendanner **42 MAC 637 (97)**—witness intimidation as consciousness of guilt;

C v Kruah **47 MAC 341 (99)**—"elders" of community of which D and complainant were part asked D to lift shirt to show absence of scar (to disprove allegation that he sexually assaulted complainant, who stabbed him in self-defense); D's refusal admissible;

C v Boyer **52 MAC 590, 599 (2001)**—that D, an attorney, failed/refused to speak with a prosecution witness (who claimed he bribed her not to testify in a case in which he represented a criminal defendant) because he believed she was wearing "a wire"= inadmissible, despite Commonwealth argument that it showed consciousness of guilt;

C v Burke **414 M 252 (93)**—though D argued that flight from cops was consciousness of guilt not of murder 6 days earlier but of B&E immediately before flight (& shouldn't be admitted) this = issue of fact/weight of evidence rather than question of its admissibility **but** judge can exclude if logical inference is of consciousness of guilt of a different crime;

C v Jackson **419 M 716 (95)**—consciousness of guilt evidence (giving false name) held admissible despite D's argument that the consciousness of guilt in fact concerned different crime; proffer went to weight, not admissibility.

But see Prop.M.R.Evid. 403 (judge may exclude if probative value outweighed by unfair prejudice);

C v Howard **42 MAC 322 (97)**—offer to "turn self in" to police viewed as evidence of consciousness of guilt/ admission that he committed sexual assault;

C v Oeun Lam **420 M 615 (95)**—escape from custody just before trial viewable as consciousness of guilt; though counsel could argue consciousness of innocence from evidence that D initially went voluntarily to police and answered questions & was at home, asleep, when arrested 5 hours later, judge not required to instruct on consciousness of innocence;

C v Stack **49 MAC 227, 239 (2000)**—before jury is allowed to use D's purported "flight" during trial, there must be vigorous effort to find D "and some formality in presenting the evidence about her disappearance"; error here to instruct jury, without any evidence on topic, that they could use it as consciousness of guilt if they found D willfully fled from prosecution;

C v Muckle **59 MAC 631 (2003)—PROTOCOL TO BE FOLLOWED WHEN D FAILS TO APPEAR MIDTRIAL:** judge must determine whether trial should proceed, or mistrial instead, and must first determine whether D's absence is without cause/voluntary; recess for investigation = appropriate; evidence to be produced ON THE RECORD, as to inquiries made, efforts to find D; judge to make finding re: 'without cause/voluntariness of absence'; if judge determine to continue trial in absentia, "neutral instruction" should be given that D may not be present; if there will be no evidence introduced to jury re: consciousness of guilt, judge "may add that the jury should not speculate as to the reasons for D's absence & should not draw adverse inferences"; if ADA seeks to intro evidence to lay foundation for consciousness of guilt instruction, judge should determine whether introduction of such evidence "is warranted"; if so, judge to allow "brief" development, "subject to such discretionary limitations as the judge believes necessary"; if judge determines consciousness of guilt instruction is appropriate, *see C v Toney*, 385 M at 585 (tailored to D's failure to appear at trial) to be given;

C v Pina **430 M 266 (99)**—when ID is the sole issue and no question that culprit ran from the scene, there is no rationale for consciousness of guilt instruction based on such flight; but *C v Rodriguez* **50 MAC 405 (2000)** Pina doesn't mean that there can be no consciousness of guilt evidence in a criminal case when ID is the defense: jury in Rodriguez could have found that D lied to police when he told them he hadn't gotten wet on night in question (but his clothing had wet knees & elbows, & rape had occurred on wet ground) and when he told them he hadn't bought beer when he went to a liquor store but had just used telephone there (rapist had alcohol on breath);

C v Lorenzetti **48 MAC 37 (99)**—evidence that D left house when wife requested he do so (because wife heard allegation of assault complainant) was NOT fairly consciousness of guilt;

C v Mitchell **20 MAC 902 (85)** citing *C v Trefethen* **157 M 180, 199 (1892)**—saying that evidence is admissible as consciousness of guilt may "smack[ ] of circularity": i.e., "reasoning", from evidence of D's guilt, that alibi = false, & then letting jury infer D's guilt in part from fact he gave "false" alibi; here, though, jury could independently determine alibi was improbable;

C v Blaikie **375 M 601 (78)**: *C v Rice* **427 M 203 (98)**: *C v Degro* **432 M 319 (2000)**—flight after a killing not probative of "premeditation," usually;

C v Cardarelli **433 M 427 (2001)**—D's flight, use of false name, etc. after killing not admissible if only question at trial was whether he committed murder or manslaughter, but consciousness of guilt evidence here relevant to whether he lacked substantial capacity to understand criminality of his conduct or to conform it to legal requirements;

C v Cantor **253 M 509 (25)**—exclude D's self-serving post-arrest denial;

See Chapter 11-F (Hearsay), & particularly "statements against penal interest";

C v Rowe **105 M 590 (1870)**—D's out-of-court explanation for stolen goods she had should have been admitted; (statements to store clerk immediately after D became aware of her possession of allegedly stolen items, before anyone accused her of misdeed; possibly understood as a 'verbal act' or circumstantial evidence supportive of D's innocence);

C v Twombly **319 M 464 (46)**—if when accusations were made, D denied their truth, statements are incompetent hearsay;

C v Ruffen **399 M 811 (87)**—though both inadmissible, let in D's denial because (post-arrest) accusation got in;

C v Watson **377 M 814 (79)**—"verbal completeness" lets in only self-serving parts of same statement that qualify/explain D's admission that's in evidence;

C v Fatalo **345 M 85 (62)**—"self-serving" not valid basis for exclusion (evidence proffered by a party is usually "self"-serving); really a hearsay issue; maybe a hearsay exception, e.g., state of mind;

C v Caldron **383 M 86 (81)**—"self-serving" not a valid objection to D's testimony;

11-G.2. Adoptive Admission by Silence

C v Boris **317 M 309 (44)**—D's silence not admission unless accusation heard & understood by D, truth of its facts within D's knowledge, D free to reply, & statement "naturally" called for reply if untrue;

Jenkins v Anderson **447 US 231 (80)**—no (federal) constitutional violation in DA's use of D's pre-arrest silence for impeachment purposes;

C v Babbitt **430 M 700 (2000)**—no Bruton violation because statements by alleged joint venturer to Commonwealth witnesses were made in D's presence and qualified as adoptive admissions (with one exception, but no prejudice, because cumulative);

C v Olszewski **416 M 707 (93)**—friend of D and of murder victim, 2 weeks after murder, asked D "why he did it", D was silent & left house; within judge's discretion to admit as adoptive admission;

C v Reed **397 M 440 (86)**—no adoptive admission where no evidence D heard statement or could reply;

C v Brailey **134 M 527 (1883)**—for jury to consider whether D heard statement &, if untrue, it naturally would've called for a reply;

C v Funai **146 M 570 (1888)**—wife's statement made in presence of husband (not under arrest/duress) = implied admission against husband where he's silent & natural to repudiate if untrue;

C v Williams **450 M 645 (2008)**—tape recording of telephone conversation among an incarcerated individual, D, and co-D was admissible: co-D told incarcerated man that co-D and D "were kicking his ass nigger", and D responded to co-D's assertion by saying "Yo, chill, chill": D's response could be found not a denial, so adoptive admission;

C v Brant **380 M 876 (80)**—D's silence while co-D confesses = inadmissible;

C v MacKenzie **413 M 498 (92)**—D's statement "we didn't mean to hurt her" was admissible as an adoptive admission; questioning by police admissible to place D's responses in context;

C v Ferrara **31 MAC 648 (91)**—drug D's silence in context of incriminatory statements of others admissible as adoptive admission;

C v Ferreira **373 M 116 (77)**—D can explain silence after accusation (which got into evidence);

C v Boyer **52 MAC 590, 599 (2001)**—that D, an attorney, failed to speak with a prosecution witness (who claimed he bribed her not to testify in a case in which he represented a criminal defendant) = inadmissible, as was D's acknowledgment that he didn't speak to her because he believed she was wearing a "wire" during the meeting: "there was nothing said by [the witness] to [the attorney] that [attorney] reasonably could have been expected to deny or rebut"; caselaw expresses "a 'general wariness' of admissions by silence";

11-G.3. Pre-Arrest Silence

See also Chapters 7-H; 10-A.3; 12-E.6

C v Nickerson **386 M 54 (82)**—error (here) to impeach D by PRE-arrest silence because not "natural" for D to have come forward (because D's story would've placed him at crime scene);

C v Irwin **72 MAC 643 (2008)**—reversal (despite no objection) for prosecutor's use in case in chief, in cross-examination, and in closing argument) of D's failure to reach out to police and delay in speaking to police about allegation of sexual assault, citing *Thompson* **431 M 108, 117 (2000)** and *Nickerson* **386 M 54 (82)** (impeachment of D with fact of prearrest silence should be approached with caution, is of "extremely limited probative worth");

C v Gonzalez **68 MAC 620 (2007)**—error (but deemed "nonprejudicial") for DA to impeach D for failure to go to Rhode Island police immediately, or have MA police call RI police, so that they would verify alibi that he was there instead of in MA, when D's wife reported to him that cops believed him guilty of very recent murder;

C v Ferreira **373 M 116 (77)**—D can EXPLAIN silence after accusation (which got into evidence);

C v Aparico **14 MAC 993 (82)**—error to admit D's pre-arrest silence; not "natural" for D to shift blame to husband while cops search house;

C v Barnoski **418 M 523 (94)**—OK for DA to cross-examine D re: failure to call ambulance, police, or someone in victim's family before D's arrest, because D testified that V was good friend & that D saw V's son shoot V in head & threaten to shoot D's wife, prompting their flight from shooting scene;

C v Nickerson **386 M 54 (82)**—(no inference of guilt from pre-arrest silence) distinguished;

11-G.4. Post-Arrest Silence Inadmissible

C v Walker **13 Allen 570 (1866)**—can't admit silence of D in custody at time of accusation because of 5th Amendment;

Doyle v Ohio **426 US 610 (76)**—can't impeach D with post-Miranda silence, unless D testifies he told cops exculpatory version upon arrest;

C v Chase **70 MAC 826 (2007)**—whether or not D is under arrest or in custody, D's invocation of right to silence cannot be used against him; Commonwealth argued that invocation of right *could* be used against D because D was neither under arrest nor in custody and Miranda warnings (given four days earlier) had not been renewed; "Regardless, we still consider the defendant to be exercising a right protected at least by the State Constitution";

C v Johnson **60 MAC 243, 247 (2003)**—introduction & comment upon facts that D said nothing, was "stone faced," to be avoided at retrial;

C v Gaynor **443 M 245, 272 (2005)**—"it would have been preferable to avoid the testimony about the defendant having consulted an attorney (pursuant to a pretrial stipulation, for example)" but because judge here interrupted witness, evidence in context didn't "amount to a comment on his exercise of the right to remain silent" & "there was no suggestion that D should be disparaged" for having retained counsel;

K. Smith, *Criminal Practice and Procedure,* **§ 348 (2d ed. 1983 & Supp.)**—(same);

C v Brum **438 M 103 (2002)**—error to introduce evidence that D twice told cops he didn't want to answer any more questions, but failure to object to cop testimony meant no relief here;

C v Bennett **2 MAC 575 (74)**—error to allow DA to cross-examine D re: failure to tell exculpatory story to police after arrest;

C v Mahdi **388 M 679 (83)**—can't introduce D's post-Miranda silence to infer sanity; even if probative value from exercise of constitutional right, use to infer sanity same as use to infer guilt/impeaching;

C v King **34 MAC 466 (93)**—can't introduce evidence that D terminated interrogation by calling cops assholes; guilty inference invited by invocation of right to silence;

C v Mosby **11 MAC 1, n.3 (80)**—D in "custody" ("deprived of freedom of action in any significant way") has right to silence even if not advised; can't comment on arrested D's failure to deny (after ID by complaining witness);

C v Stevenson **46 MAC 506 (99)**—even if Ds were not yet in custody (questionable), appellate court refused to find foundation (mere presence in vicinity didn't mean they could hear/understand alleged ID; additionally, no affirmative evidence of their silence)

C v Morrison **1 MAC 632 (73)**—bad innuendo to ask if D, after arrest, heard statement about him (though answer = "no," & no evidence of Miranda warning);

C v Freeman **352 M 556 (67)**—can't admit D's silence after stationhouse I.D. where D's attorney was present because natural to let attorney speak, & (though not under arrest) police pressure & D not likely free to leave;

US v Elkins **774 F.2d 530 (1st Cir. '85)**—(same) re: demeanor of D ("arrest didn't phase him");

C v Thurber **383 M 328 (81)**—failure to object to improper DA cross-examination of D re: post-arrest silence opened door to DA rebuttal evidence on subject;

C v Fowler **431 M 30 (2000)**—error to introduce fact that, when detective expressed doubt about D's story, D's eyes teared up, & he said he didn't think he should say anything more; also, ADA exacerbated error by closing argument noting that after D became tearful, he didn't "point out any discrepancies in what [questioning cops] said";

C v Clarke **48 MAC 482, 486 (2000)**—not error to admit cop testimony that, after Miranda rights, D spoke with police for awhile, denying he'd ever seen rape complainant before, but when asked how she knew D's address and could describe home interior, D said he wasn't guilty and had nothing to say about how she could describe house [because useful "not to leave the jury wondering why the interview ended abruptly"], BUT prosecutor committed reversible error in arguing from this that D stopped answering questions because he'd been caught in lie and would have to change his story;

C v Hubbard **69 MAC 232 (2007)**—because defense counsel cross-examined cop to suggest improper questioning procedures during D's interrogation, and asked about questions cop did not ask D, ADA was entitled to elicit explanation & this wasn't improper comment on D's silence;

C v Waite **422 M 792, 799 n.5 (96)**—prosecutors and judges to make efforts "to discern ways to present the questioning as complete, so as to prevent the need to explain a seemingly abrupt end to interrogation";

C v Farley **431 M 306, 310–11 (2000)**—reversal for cross-examination about why D failed to provide certain evidence to police during a statement she made after receiving Miranda warnings; while Commonwealth. may cross-examine "as to the differences between her trial testimony and the statements she gave to the police," Commonwealth can't question "about her postarrest silence," a right apparently invoked by this D after making some statements;

C v Guy **441 M 96 (2004)**—no *Doyle v Ohio* violation to impeach D's trial testimony with content of his post-Miranda conversations with nurse, security guard, and police officer and with answer to booking question re: injuries;

C v Thompson **431 M 108, 118 (2000)**—distinguished (D never invoked right to silence, gave a lengthy statement; Commonwealth could there argue that D didn't ask about his child, an omission logically inconsistent with innocence);

C v Egardo **426 M 48 (97)**—failure to object to evidence of D's post-arrest silence, used to impeach D's testimony at trial concerning duress defense, = ineffective assistance of counsel;

C v Costa **414 M 618, 626 n.5 (93)**—D didn't invoke right to silence by saying he had "no recollection" of his activities at relevant time or by saying he didn't want to be a "canary" or to "squeal" on his friends;

C v Rendon-Alvarez **48 MAC 140 (99)**—error to admit cop testimony that, after Miranda, D answered some questions, but refused to answer questions re: where he had come from, claiming (Spanish language) confusion; ADA highlighted this in closing as consciousness of guilt;

C v Thad T. **59 MAC 497 (2003)**—assumes, without deciding, that principles of *Doyle v Ohio* (can't invite adverse inference from invocation of right to silence) apply to a parent's invocation of juvenile's rights; on merits here says invocation wasn't used "against D," but instead to explain interview ending "abruptly" (citing *C v Habarek* **402 M 105, 110 (88)**);

C v Brown **451 M 200 (2008)**—after D testified on direct, nonresponsively, that he had been "questioned for several hours," prosecutor did not want jury to have impression that D had then told cops "self-defense"; defense counsel, to "clear confusion", asked D if he had given statement to police, and he testified that he had not: DA's concern not well-grounded, clarification not necessary, so "error" implicating right to silence; no objection, no substantial risk of miscarriage of justice;

C v Peixoto **430 M 654, 659 (2000)**—after Miranda rights, D expressed reluctance to speak without attorney, but then stated nothing to hide & gave statement; during cross-examination, ERROR TO ASK D WHETHER 1ST THING HE SAID WAS 'I don't know if I should talk to you or not'; though this wasn't invocation of Miranda and didn't require cops to terminate questioning, inadmissible as matter of state law under due process safeguards of state constitution and article 12; not required for this result that D be under formal arrest, but IS required that D have received Miranda warnings; D entitled to ask about rights, think out loud about them and engage them without being subjected at trial to smearing cross-examination;

C v Beauchamp **424 M 682, 690–91 (97)**: *Doyle v Ohio* **426 US 610 (76)**—protects D's request for attorney because right to counsel = encompassed within Miranda warnings, & claim of right can't carry adverse consequences;

C v Adams **434 M 805 (2001)**—post-arrest silence and requests for counsel may not be used to permit an inference of guilt, or an inference of sanity when criminal responsibility is in issue BUT HERE relief refused, because defense counsel used the evidence "affirmatively at trial . . . on both the issue of sanity and the propriety of police conduct toward [D], as part of an apparent trial strategy"[however misguided];

C v DePace **433 M 379 (2001)**—despite no objection below, reversal for prosecution's display of Miranda form with notation "I want to talk to my attorney" on visual presenter monitor for jury's view, & its admission into evidence; "evidence of the Miranda warnings and a D's exercise of his Miranda rights are not part of a D's statement to police," but are instead only foundation for statement that a D gives while in custody;

C v Connolly **454 M 808 (2009)**—cop's testimony that after D received Miranda warnings he stated that he "did not have anything to say at that time" was error, but D waived objections and accepted judge's curative instructions;

C v Gonsalves **74 MAC 910 (2009)**—**testimony that D refused to answer booking questions until he talked to lawyer = reversal despite "late" objection and no request for curative instruction;** *C v Ayre* **31 MAC 17 (91)**—similar; *C v Wei H. Ye* **52 MAC 390 (2001)**—similar;

C v Isabelle **444 M 416 (2005)**—4:3 decision that DA's eliciting evidence re: D's request for attorney didn't warrant reversal (because purportedly "beyond a reasonable doubt" it didn't contribute to jury's verdict);

C v Somers **44 MAC 920 (98)**—error to introduce signed Miranda rights form claiming right to silence despite Commonwealth claim of relevance to show properly booked and warned (these were not contested issues);

Anderson v Charles **447 US 404 (80)**—can cross-examine D re: post-Miranda statement differing from trial testimony;

C v McClary **33 MAC 678 (92)**—same; can also argue/impeach with "any omission from [D's] post-Miranda statement" which is different from D's trial testimony;

Fletcher v Weir **455 US 603 (82)**—can permit DA's impeachment cross-examination re: D's post-arrest (but no Miranda) silence; not induced to be silent;

C v Thompson **431 M 108, 117 (2000)**—testimony that D, when told of his wife's death, made no response & stared silently at floor for 30 seconds shouldn't have been introduced, although D not in custody and no Miranda warnings had been given (but no objection, and no appellate relief); no error in DA's closing argument urging jury to infer guilt from D's failure to ask questions that an innocent person would ordinarily ask, e.g., what had happened to his wife and whether his daughter was alright (this failure occurred during post-Miranda interrogation during which D made lengthy statement asserting innocence and never invoked right to silence);

C v Senior **433 M 453 (2001)**—not error to admit fact that D failed to answer one question (i.e., where he'd been drinking); if D talks, "what he says or omits is to be judged on its merits or demerits";

11-G.5. Guilty Pleas

C v Lewin **(No. 2) 407 M 629 (90)**—murder D's statement that he was willing to plead guilty to manslaughter was inadmissible because not an admission or confession;

Flood v Southland Corp. **416 M 62 (93)**—guilty plea of civil co-D in related criminal action admissible; Rule 803 (22) of the Proposed Massachusetts Rules of Evidence, substantively identical to the Federal rule of the same number, provides that the hearsay rule does not exclude "evidence of a final judgment, entered . . . upon a plea of guilty . . . adjudging a person guilty of a crime punishable by . . . confinement in excess of one year, to prove any fact essential to sustain the judgment . . .", though such plea would not be conclusive of the issue, or "binding" even as to the person who so pled;

C v Santiago **425 M 491 (97)**—no error in refusal to admit G pleas of D's adversary in street shootout (to manslaughter of innocent bystander and armed assault with intent to kill D) though D's defense to murder charge was self-defense;

11-G.6. Failure to Produce Evidence (as Implicit Acknowledgment of Guilt)

Opinion of Justices **412 M 1201, 1211 (92)**—proposed legislation allowing inference of guilt from failure to take breathalyzer test violated article 12;

C v Zevitas **418 M 677 (94)**—legislatively-mandated jury instruction concerning absence of blood alcohol test ('can only be done with D's consent') violates article 12;

C v D'Agostino **421 M 281 (95) &** *C v Koney* **421 M 295 (95)**—Zevitas error, reversal;

C v Seymour **39 MAC 672 (96)**—reversible error for DA to ask D whether she refused breathalyzer;

C v Quinn **61 MAC 332, 336 n.3 (2004)**—though unremarked by parties, Appeals Court alarmed to see that booking videotape, admitted at trial, depicted D's refusal to take breathalyzer exam;

C v McGrail **419 M 774 (95)**—refusal to perform field sobriety tests inadmissible under Zevitas rationale; [in *C v Ranieri* 65 MAC at 373 n.2, Appeals Court claims that *McGrail* holding was "limited" by *C v Blais* 428 M 294 (98) (while refusal evidence may not be entered into evidence, D has no "right" to refuse to produce real or physical evidence)];

C v Healy **452 M 510 (2008)**—evidence of refusal to undergo field sobriety test harmless beyond reasonable doubt because trial was jury-waived and appellate court assumes trial judge "correctly instructed himself" on law that refusal evidence = inadmissible;

C v Grenier **45 MAC 58 (98)**—error to admit that in refusing to perform the "standing on one leg" test for sobriety, D said that if he did the test and failed that the officer would arrest him and that if he didn't perform the test, the officer would arrest him (cop then agreeing with him); and that D then said "Take me"; appellate court rejected "finding" that D was not refusing, but was conducting "negotiations;

C v Ranieri **65 MAC 366 (2006)**—error to allow police testimony that D refused to recite alphabet, rejecting Commonwealth argument that exchange was "negotiation" rather than "refusal" (after D's refusal, cop questioned whether this was because he didn't know it or because he didn't want to say it, prompting D to recite, with errors); error was NOT harmless beyond reasonable doubt;

C v Vermette **43 MAC 789 (97)**—error to allow police testimony that D refused permission to search car and photograph sneakers;

C v Arruda **73 MAC 901, further appellate rev. allowed 452 M 1110 (2008)**—in interlocutory appeal by Commonwealth, Appeals Court holds that evidence of D's refusal to supply medical personnel with sample of his blood "for medical purposes" was admissible even though D was in custody and police "may have an interest in the results of the tests; "it is "governmental, not private, compulsion that is prohibited by art. 12 of Declaration of Rights;

C v Martinez **34 MAC 131 (93)**—error to allow DA to cross examine D re: failure to volunteer to turn over blood or hair samples, or underwear, or to otherwise "assist police" (reversal despite no objection);

C v Delaney **442 M 604, 616 (2004)**—error for DA to ask D re: failure to produce two items of physical evidence for police (but OK to ask re: D's failure to bring knife to trial, to corroborate his testimonial claim re: its size/condition);

C v Andujar **57 MAC 529 (2003)**—notwithstanding cross-examination of cop seeking to create inference that $375 found in D's pocket could have been from social security check rather than drug sales, ERROR for DA to ask cop on redirect whether D, at arrest offered any explanation of the cash;

C v Grenier **415 M 680 (93)**—can't introduce evidence that, after D denied knowledge of murder, he said "no" when asked if he wanted to give police truthful statement as to what happened that day;

C v Hinckley **422 M 261 (96)**—error under article 12 to admit evidence that D refused police request to turn over sneakers (for police to check for treads matching crime scene prints);

C v Conkey **430 M 139 (99)**—can't introduce evidence that D first agreed to provide fingerprints, but then did not do so (violative of article 12); conduct offered to show D's state of mind is "testimonial" but see *C v Rodriguez* **50 MAC 405 (2000)** no relief for evidence that rape D, when asked to provide sample of pubic hair, first took envelope & comb, but returned with empty envelope, before being asked again and complying; either "unclear that the delay . . . constituted a refusal" or error harmless beyond a reasonable doubt;

C v Jones **75 MAC 38, 46 (2009)**—no abuse of discretion in denying motion for mistrial: D's "single statement that he agreed to take a polygraph exam was inadvertently included on" recorded statement "that was played once for the jury before it was redacted";

C v Bly **448 M 473 (2007)**—evidence at trial was that, though D complied with court order for blood and hair samples, "he had refused to refrain from cutting his hair in order for an adequate hair sample to be taken": no relief, purportedly because choice to produce incriminating evidence or be punished with inference of guilt in refusal "is absent when a D's decision [not] to cooperate is foreclosed by order of a judge"; notes that *South Dakota v Neville* 459 US 553, 564 (83) (evidence of refusal to submit to blood-alcohol test doesn't violate Fifth Amendment) is less protective generally than art. 12, but *C v Delaney* 442 M 604, 608–10 (2004), held that court order changes result;

C v O'Laughlin **446 M 188 (2006)**—"refusal" evidence here admissible because cops' sight of blood stain was admissible & relevant, but SJC cautions that it doesn't "suggest . . . any general validation of refusal evidence": police searching D's apartment with his consent saw reddish stain on closet door & D then revoked consent; when cops returned with warrant, stain had disappeared & D said that he had removed it, thinking it was his own blood; D's statement conveyed same consciousness of guilt inference as the "refusal" testimony, so was only cumulative anyway;

C v Gaynor **443 M 245, 271 (2005)**—after cross-exam established that not all evidence had been sent for examination/analysis (for, inter alia, DNA), ADA was allowed to elicit on redirect that evidence had been preserved and was available for testing by either D or Commonwealth; this is "a sensitive area" because could imply D had burden to test evidence, but no error in circumstances here;

C v Delaney **442 M 604 (2004)**—can introduce evidence that, after D was told of warrant authorizing police to take D to station to be examined by physician, he asked if he was under arrest (no), and then began to walk away

from officers: **evidence of resistance to warrant / court order doesn't violate Article 12**;

C v Johnson **46 MAC 398 (99)**—OK to admit evidence that D had refused initially to participate in voice ID procedure BECAUSE D testified on direct that at voice ID he hadn't disguised his voice (implication that he was cooperative, consciousness of innocence, allowed rebuttal); cf. *C v Mitchell* **12 MAC 354 (81)** in absence of objection, at least, DA can argue D didn't go to cops (& because D testified he was willing to meet cops & explain all); Re: MISSING WITNESS INFERENCE, see *Chapter 12-J* (query: isn't it instructing that D's failure to produce is indicative of his "state of mind", and isn't that just as "testimonial" as the inference found violative of article 12 in Zevitas, Conkey, etc.?)

11-G.7. Admissions During Psychiatric Examination

See *Chapter 7-D&E, Examinations of D for Competency & Responsibility, & Defense of Lack of Criminal Responsibility;*

C v Benoit **410 M 506, 517–20 (91)**—psychiatrist's testimony about court-ordered competency examination to rebut inaccuracies in testimony of D's psychiatrist was admissible, at least where D failed to assert psychiatrist-patient privilege at trial;

C v Williams **30 MAC 543 (91)**—D's statements during court-ordered psychiatric examination were admissible where D waived privilege by testifying about his mental state;

C v Seabrooks **433 M 439 (2001)**—when trial issue was D's criminal responsibility & his experts had used five psych evaluations conducted at jail's behest soonest after his arrest, re: suicide risk, OK for Commonwealth to introduce evaluating psych's testimony, even though exams weren't preceded by *Lamb* **365 M 265, 270 (74)** warnings that his communications might not be kept confidential; G.L. c. 233, § 20B cited, finding 3d statutory exception applied to psychotherapist-patient privilege;

C v Hunter **416 M 831 (94)**—though D had been ordered by court to submit to an examination by Commonwealth psych. expert (pursuant to *Blaisdell* **372 M 753 (77)**, he had 5th Amendment/Article 12 right to refuse to speak when Commonwealth expert wanted a second examination/"follow up": error for Commonwealth expert to testify to D's refusal;

11-H. RAPE, INDECENT ASSAULT AND BATTERY, ETC., CHARGES

See *chapter 11-I re: Experts/Opinions;*

C v Foley **12 MAC 983 (81)**—"correct practice" = delete "victim," "suspect," "rape" terms from otherwise admissible lab certificate; & CPCS P/G's 6.1(c) & (d)—anticipate evidentiary issues & seek advance rulings (e.g., motion in limine);

Brodin, M. and Avery, M., *Handbook of Massachusetts Evidence* **(8th ed. 2007)**—"Rape-Shield" statute;

See *Chapter 13, Privileges & Disqualifications;* § 6.19.2, *"fresh complaint" doctrine;*

Young, Pollets & Poreda, *Evidence* **(2d ed. 1998)**— § 412 (evidence of sexual conduct of sexual assault complainant); §§ 510–12(privileged communications made to social workers, psychotherapists, & "rape crisis counselors");

3A Wigmore, *Evidence,* **§ 924a (Chadbourn rev. 1970)**—(character of rape complainant); § 963 (false allegations by complainant;

Prop.M.R.Evid. 501–3, 510–12;

ABA Standards for Criminal Justice (2d ed. 1986) Trial Judge 6-2.2 (a)—judge should permit full/proper examination & cross-examination, but keep it fair, objective, & due regard for dignity & legitimate privacy;

SJC Rule 3:07, 3.4(c)—can't intentionally violate rules, or 3.4(e) allude to fact without reasonable belief relevant & will be admitted; 4.4 can't use means with no purpose but to embarrass 3d party;

G.L. c. 233, § 81—making admissible out-of-court statements of alleged child abuse victims under age 10, with qualifications *(See Chapter 11-F for cases applying/ disapproving statute)*;

G.L. c. 147, § 4F—admit Public Safety Dept. sperm/ seminal fluid certificate [see § 1]

C v Niels N **73 MAC 689 (2009)**—electronic recording of multidisciplinary teams interview of sexual assault complainants is good practice, but SJC has not required that such recordings be made (citations) and D has not shown "any cognizable harm from the absence of a recording";

C v Erazo **63 MAC 624 (2005)**—inter alia: dates of alleged sexual assaults upon 14-year-old weren't elements, and didn't have to be precisely alleged; error here to have dismissed complaint for failure to specify dates more precisely;

C v Arthur **31 MAC 178 (91)**—sexual assault complainant's reputation for lying & exaggerating in school community was admissible;

C v Adkinson **442 M 410 (2004)**—judge denied D's motion for voir dire re: coercive interviews by prosecutors: children initially accused mother's ex-husband of abuse, & after coercion accused instead D (father); exploration of subject instead at trial here OK (excused?) because trial was jury-waived; "no need for the judge to conduct a separate competency hearing";

C v Cogswell **31 MAC 691 (91)**—rape complainant's diary was admissible as to her credibility even though she disavowed key diary entries;

C v Phillips **162 M 504 (1895)**—complainant can tell age in statutory rape though hearsay;

G.L. c. 265, § 24C—name of [alleged] victim in police/court record withheld from "public" *(See Chapter 6-E, Access to Witnesses);*

11-H.1. Fresh Complaint

6 Wigmore, *Evidence,* **§§ 1760-1 (Chadbourn rev. 1976)**—(fresh complaint);

C v King **445 M 217 (2005), cert. denied 546 US 1216 (2006)—"FRESH" COMPLAINT DOCTRINE AS PREVIOUSLY EXISTED IS ABOLISHED;** new

rules = "first" complaint of sexual assault is presumptively admissible (but not when irrelevant, i.e., when fact of rape and lack of consent aren't in issue); subsequent complaints are NOT admissible; details permitted, both from "first complaint" witness and from complainant, when a complaint witness testifies (overruling *C v Peters*); appropriate instruction must be given preceding "first complaint" witness and in final jury charge (sample instruction set forth);

C v Murungu **450 M 441 (2008)**—Commonwealth may call "second" rather than first complaint witness because first (sister of D) had obvious bias to minimize or distort the complaint or because to "first" witness, victim didn't make outright allegation of rape but instead expressed unhappiness, upset [D is not precluded from calling the "first," for purposes including impeachment];

C v Stuckich **450M 449 (2008)**—though common to rely on counsel's representations in ruling on motion in limine, circumstances here contradicted claim that particular person was "first" person to whom complainant complained; further, though Commonwealth sought to introduce multiple complaints, here a letter was the first complaint and "the further disclosures are not admissible as first complaint evidence"; allowing complainant to testify to multiple complaints is essentially permitting those other witnesses to testify; *C v Kebreau* **454 M 287 (2009)**—holds that *Stuckich* distinguishable because D cross-examined complainant to imply she fabricated abuse allegations to obtain restraining order to have odious father removed from home (so 'opened door'); cop's testimony was purportedly not 'first complaint' but 'in response to' D's cross-examination of complainant re: restraining order;

C v Lyons **71 MAC 671 (2008)**—reversal for introducing, in addition to 911 call recording (the legitimate "first" complaint), the testimony of responding police officer as additional complaint; "first" complaint not required to be via live witness (e.g., also, letter in *Stuckich* 450 M 449);

C v Parreira **72 MAC 308 (2008)**—D's cross-examination of sexual assault complainant suggesting delay in reporting incident included questions whether she had told her boyfriend and what his response was opened door to the complained-of "self-corroboration";

C v Arana **453 M 214 (2009)**—(reversal ordered) complainant's testimony that she told persons other than first complaint witness, "even without the details of the telling," was inadmissible, not necessary to "set the stage" for an admission by D; testimony about complainant's demeanor at police station held admissible "not as first complaint evidence," but as relevant to defense that accusations were fabricated to provide basis for civil lawsuit against D; testimony about complainant's subsequent return to police station admissible not as first complaint, but OK as response to defense that police were biased and "complicitous" in lawsuit; 2d complainant's testimony that she told her parents was inadmissible, not 'first' complaint; if testimony serves no purpose other than to repeat fact of complaint and thus corroborate accusations, it's inadmissible; if, "after careful balancing of" probative vs. prejudicial value, testimony is found relevant and admissible for reasons "independent of first complaint doctrine," admissible within judge's discretion;

C v Monteiro **75 MAC 489 (2009)**—though first complaint witness was complainant's father, prosecution erroneously introduced, in addition, complainant's testimony that he spoke about it next with his mother and the DA's office, and mother's testimony that complainant was interviewed by DSS social worker and by DA's office, and detective's testimony about seeing the taped SAIN interview; Court rejects argument that evidence of additional complaints fell within independent exceptions to hearsay rule: "simply because a separate evidentiary rules applies" (e.g., statement not hearsay or falls within hearsay exception), second or subsequent complaint "is not admissible" so as to defeat restrictions set forth in 'first complaint' law and merely corroborate the allegations;

C v Niels N **73 MAC 689 (2009)**—finding no error in witnesses' testimony that after speaking with complainant, they did certain acts (D argued that this was the equivalent of illegitimately multiple 'first' complaint evidence, court analyzed it, and rejected proposition that it was 'nonverbal conduct . . . intended as an assertion'); nurse's testimony that she examined complainant using sexual assault kit did not violate *Stuckich* 450 M 449 (2008);

C v McGee **75 MAC 499 (2009)**—first complaint witness should have been neighbor who answered complainant's pounding on door and heard her say she had been raped; that responding police officer "heard more details" and spoke with complainant "only a short time after" neighbor did were not valid reasons for substituting him; at retrial, testimony of nurse concerning complainant's "spontaneous utterances" (with "detailed description of the rape") must be "carefully evaluated for probity and prejudice" so as not to "unfairly enhance a complainant's credibility" and evoke emotional response by repeating "horrific details of an alleged crime", using standards set out in *Arana* **453 M 214 (2009)** & *Monteiro* **75 MAC 489 (2009)**;

C v Kebreau **454 M 298 (2009)**—SJC OKs TWO 'first complaint' witnesses: disclosures involved multiple and increasingly more serious assaults during lengthy period (first to mother when complainant was in seventh or eighth grade [genital touching], second to college advisor four to six years later [digital penetrations, intercourse]); caution that any decision re: first complaint testimony is 'fact-specific' requiring 'careful evaluation of circumstances'; if more than one witness is allowed, complaint testimony "must relate to different crimes";

C v Saunders **75 MAC 505 (2009)**—where evidence of long relationship between D and complainant included sex & pregnancy when complainant was 14, though D argued violation of SINGLE "first complaint" rule, the additional witnesses' testimony = proper as fair response to D's cross-examination implying "recent" fabrication that D had been the father of aborted pregnancy (i.e., only

after the couple ended relationship, when complainant was 18); D "opened the door" by questioning complainant about statements she had made (allegedly at D's request at that earlier time) indicating a different male was father; "in anticipation of receiving comparable testimony from" the identified first complaint witness, complainant testified that she had confided in witness that she was pregnant and D was the father; first complaint witness thereafter testified that she was unable to recall any conversations with complainant about relationship with D, but D didn't move to strike prior testimony and did not argue this error in appeal;

C v Dargon **74 MAC 330 (2009)**—defense strategy was to stress that complainant's first allegations were only of mugging/purse grabbing, so form titled "sexual assault evidence collection kit, information pertaining to assault" was largely admissible to rebut what court called "recent contrivance" theory; this was ground independent of "first complaint", which here was the 911 call; S.C. *** M *** (7/29/2010);

C v Licata **412 M 654 (92)**—continuing "need" for fresh complaint doctrine reaffirmed, BUT repetitive testimony from multiple witnesses seen to pose danger of improper bolstering of complainant's credibility; requirement of limiting instructions both when evidence is admitted & during final jury instructions set forth;

C v Montanez **439 M 441 (2003)**—Two justices believe it's time "to revisit antiquated doctrine" of "fresh complaint";

C v Lagacy **23 MAC 622 (87)**—[good fresh complaint overview]; 3½ weeks = fresh; details OK, especially without objections;

C v Lavalley **410 M 641 (91)**—questions about vitality of fresh complaint doctrine later answered by Licata, above; dangers of "piling on" recognized;

C v Peters **429 M 22 (99)**—sexual assault complainant may testify on direct ONLY to fact that complaint was made and to whom, but even then the fresh complaint witness must testify and be available for cross-examination; complainant can't "self-corroborate"; OVERRULED BY *C v King* **445 M 217 (2005)**: NEW law set forth, and previous "fresh complaint" law abolished; if "first complaint" witness testifies at trial, complainant may testify to fact of complaint and details of it;

C v Buelterman **68 MAC 829 (2007)**—case tried prior to *C v King* (new, "first" complaint evidence protocol): no relief from complainant's impermissible "self-corroboration," i.e., her own trial testimony that she had told a friend a couple of years later about the sex assault; Appeals Court asserts that there was no "fresh complaint" violation because no "fresh complaint" witness was called [yes, that's the point; D cited *C v Peters* 429 M 22, 30 (99)], and complainant didn't testify to any details of conversation(s);

C v Montanez **439 M 441 (2003)**—complainant's testimony that she told roughly the same story during taped interview = impermissible self-corroboration;

C v Wentworth **53 MAC 82, 92 (2001)**—defense counsel failed to appreciate strictures of fresh complaint & Peters decision by implicitly agreeing that complainant & her mother could be asked whether she had made complaint sometime (yes); DA had acknowledged beforehand that no complaint allegedly made was remotely "fresh", so hearsay rule should have barred the testimony; appellate court stressed trial counsel's agreement, didn't acknowledge inadmissibility, excused evidence as 'merely' testimony "about the fact that [a complaint had been made]," without any "details";

C v Fales **60 MAC 102 (2003)**—though thirty-nine months was not fresh (& DA agreed), DA sought to admit fact of "conversations" by witnesses with complainant without disclosing substance, "to provide a frame of reference" re: how disclosures occurred, and defense counsel agreed; because defense counsel seemingly made a tactical judgment to use circumstances of disclosure as ground of defense, no relief; BUT trial judge should determine in advance whether defense plans to make reference in opening to circumstances of disclosure and, if not, preclude DA from doing so, and preclude inquiry on disclosure by DA until first addressed during cross-examination by defense; further, limiting instruction should be given;

C v Quincy Q **434 M 859 (2001)**—videotaped interview of child sexual assault complainant's alleged "fresh complaint" to parents & D's mother = inadmissible because "self-corroborating"; complainant's father's "fresh complaint" testimony could not legitimately include (1) that HE had told D's mother to talk to complainant, & "she'll tell you the truth . . . If you can leave the house and not believe her, I'll rethink what I'm thinking,," (2) that during his conversation with the child, "you could see in her eye . . . that she didn't really want to talk"; father's emotional response & state of mind after allegations were inadmissible, irrelevant (he had told a coworker, "who could see that something was wrong," that he was too upset to work);

C v Montgomery **52 MAC 831 (2001)**—Quincy Q distinguished: here, trial defense counsel cross-examined sexual assault complainant about inconsistencies between her trial testimony & her assertions in "SAIN" videotaped interview, & thereafter expressly indicated thereafter that he had no objection to it being played for jury and introduced as an exhibit: NO RELIEF ON APPEAL (despite fact that, e.g., *C v Zukoski* **370 M 23, 26–27 (76)** holds that prior consistent statements aren't admissible just because witness has been impeached with prior inconsistent statements); D "could not complain about corroborative details introduced as a result of his deliberate defense stratagem";

C v Lanning **32 MAC 279, 287 (92)**—fresh complaint witnesses should be voir dired before testifying; written statements may be admissible as fresh complaint evidence (but cf. *C v DiMonte* **427 M 233 (98)** - re: 'spontaneous utterances', a writing [FAX transmission] was "suspect" as spontaneous utterance, some 8½–11 hours

after alleged beating [NOT alleged rape], so circumstances indicative of reliability have to be even more persuasive)

C v LeBeau **42 MAC 945 (97)**—upholding admissibility of fresh "complaint" in case of consensual sex (statutory rape) on facts here (14 year old complainant, 31 year old D, complainant's feelings of self-condemnation, fear, despair), but perhaps basis for exclusion on different facts;

C v Powers **36 MAC 65 (94)**—fresh complaint witnesses' belief that complainant was truthful = inadmissible;

C v Jerome **36 MAC 59 (94)**—OK to admit tape recording of "fresh complaint" conversation between complainant and her counseling therapist; it was only a substitute for his direct testimony as he was in court and cross-examined by defendants; fact that only portions of counseling sessions were taped not fatal unless available tape is "so incomplete as to be untrustworthy" & misleading (Ds here chose not to question counselor about context of unrecorded conversations);

Nolan and Sartorio, *Criminal Law*, **§ 230 (2001)**—fresh complaint;

G.L. c. 233, § 20J—below re: absence of fresh complaint = exculpatory;

See also Chapter 9-F, Prior Inconsistent Statements (& rehabilitation by prior consistent statements;

11-H.1.a. Scope of Fresh Complaint

See C v King **445 M 217 (2005)**—fresh complaint law as previously existing = abolished;

C v Bailey **370 M 388 (76)**—all details of fresh complaint admitted, but instruct jury to consider it only for corroboration; BUT SEE *C v Flebotte* **417 M 348, 351 (94)** acts about which fresh complaint witness testifies must have been testified to by complainant;

C v Gichel **48 MAC 206 (99)**—acts of cunnilingus not testified to by child complainant, so "fresh complaint" about same inadmissible; same re use of dog in abusing child; BUT "tried to penetrate" enough to justify admitting fresh complaint of "did" penetrate her (no objection), and "touched" breasts" enough to justify admitting complaint of "kissing" breasts; fresh complaint admissible only regarding charge of sexual assault, not all "sex crimes", so error to admit fresh complaint re: posing child in the nude or engaged in sexual act (G.L. c. 272, § 29A);

C v Blow **370 M 401 (76)**—if fresh complaint includes other crimes, D gets instruction to consider only re: sex charge;

C v Moreschi **38 MAC 562 (95)**—same;

C v Binienda **20 MAC 756 (85)**—don't extend fresh complaint beyond sex cases;

C v Askins **18 MAC 927 (84)**—fresh complaint OK though more detail than trial testimony; BUT SEE later cases;

C v McCaffrey **36 MAC 583 (94)**—fresh complaint testimony which was sole source of fellatio evidence, including graphic comment (tasted "yucky"), was beyond legitimate "fresh complaint" scope (child complainant testified only to digital penetration) = reversal;

C v Kerr **36 MAC 505 (94)**—fresh complaint testimony which added allegation that D indicated he was going to shoot complainant was beyond scope of complainant's testimony and caused reversal: it buttressed, illegitimately, element of force or threat of bodily injury;

C v King **58 MAC 492 (2003)**—error to admit within fresh complaint testimony by mother that D had threatened child, making him stay in a corner if child didn't comply with sexual advances, because child didn't so testify, but no prejudice because child testified clearly to lack of consent;

C v Almeida **42 MAC 607, 613 n.6 (97)**—fresh complaint doctrine not to be extended "to corroborate testimony concerning uncharged acts" (which here were beyond statute of limitations);

C v Sugrue **34 MAC 172 (93)**—fresh complaint testimony exceeding scope of child complainant's own trial allegations = reversal, even though trial was jury-waived; failure of trial counsel to object = ineffective assistance of counsel;

C v Caracino **33 MAC 787 (93)**—fresh complaint testimony (penile penetration) beyond scope of complainant's testimony ("hand" or "licking"), unobjected to, and used by defense as impeachment by inconsistency = no relief on appeal;

C v Tingley **32 MAC 706 (92)**—fresh complaint testimony which adds details of other similar crimes requires reversal;

C v Lamontagne **42 MAC 213 (97)**—fresh complaints were within scope of events testified to by complainant, OK that they added "details" of the events;

C v Demars **38 MAC 596 (95)**—fresh complaint testimony alleging cunnilingus = beyond scope of complainant's testimony (fellatio, etc.) and therefore harmful error;

11-H.1.b. Number of Fresh Complaint Witnesses/"Piling On"

See C v King **445 M 217 (2005)**—fresh complaint law as previously existing = abolished; henceforth, "first" (not necessarily "fresh") complaint witness may testify, but not any later "complaint" witness (unless extraordinary reason);

C v Lorenzetti **48 MAC 37 (99)**—cataloguing some reversals for too many, but notes additional errors contributed to holdings [*C v Trowbridge* **419 M 750 (95)** four too many; *Powers* **36 MAC 65, 68–71 (94)** four too many; *Swain* **36 MAC 433, 436–42 (94)** six too many]

C v Lamontagne **42 MAC 213 (97)**—5 fresh complaint witnesses not too many here;

C v Swain **36 MAC 433 (94)**—6 fresh complaint witnesses too many (risk that sheer number of witnesses would cause jury to treat testimony as substantive);

C v Morais **431 M 380, 385–86 (2000)**—judge allowed 2 of 4 proffered 'fresh complaint' witnesses to testify; 1 testified to initial complaint, plus 2 more made later to others in witness's presence; 2d witness testified to "4th" such complaint; no error found;

C v Clements **36 MAC 205 (94)**—questioning practice of allowing each of 3 persons who viewed closed circuit TV interview of child complainant to give "fresh complaint" testimony;

C v Lorenzetti **48 MAC 37 (99)**—five fresh complaint witnesses (but none beyond proper scope), flawed initial limiting instruction (failure to explain/define "corroborate"), bad subsequent instruction ("remember my instruction," without specifying which one), standard instruction to "'disregard' if it doesn't corroborate" could illegitimately bar use as inconsistent statement impeaching credibility BUT NO OBJECTIONS, so no relief;

11-H.1.c. Timing: Fresh?

C v King **445 M 217 (2005)**—"fresh" complaint doctrine abolished, in favor of "first" complaint's admissibility regardless of how stale (except when fact of rape and lack of consent aren't in issue);

C v Hall **66 MAC 390 (2006)**—testimony by rape complainant that D had bragged that he had had identified man "take care of" someone who was "causing trouble" was admissible to explain why complainant delayed alleging rape for seven years (until newspaper article saying the identified man had been sentenced to prison); judge must undertake analysis of whether danger of prejudice outweighs probative value of evidence; citing *C v Fales* **60 MAC 102, 107 (2003)**, judge may allow prosecutor, upon request and with proffer, to refer to delay in opening statement and may elicit circumstances of delayed disclosure in direct examination; appropriate to give limiting instruction that evidence admissible only to explain witness's state of mind;

C v Edgerly **13 MAC 562, 569, n.5 (82)**—"fresh" complaint to court clerk day after incident OK though 3 prior complaints;

C v Wilson **12 MAC 942 (81)**—6 fresh complaint witnesses; child complaining witness, so delay OK because still "reasonably prompt"; [see also *Amirault* **404 M 221 (89)** 18 months = OK];

C v Lund **5 MAC 884 (77)**—36 hours not fresh, but harmless;

C v Montanino (II) **409 M 500 (91)**—complaint made after 4-year delay by teenager against scoutmaster was not fresh; testimony that he came forward because he "found out it was still going on" inadmissible allegation of uncharged crimes;

C v Richardson **423 M 180 (96)**—upholding admission of sexual assault complainant's testimony that, after lapse of 6 months before complaint, she asserted rape because her friend told her that D had (also) assaulted her: not for truth, but to explain why came forward after long delay;

C v Errington **390 M 875 (84)**—(similar);

C v Hynes **40 MAC 927 (96)**—nine year delay in reporting alleged rape linked to visit to therapist; no error in testimony that complainant came forward in part because learned that D was seeking custody of ten-year-old daughter;

C v Davids 33 MAC 421 (92)—complaint made 3 months after mother's boyfriend moved out & 8 years after alleged assaults took place was not fresh; date when assailant's control over victim ends merely 1 factor in determining promptness;

C v Costello 36 MAC 689, 697–701 (94)—(dissenting opinion prescribing analysis of "fresh");

C v Fleury 417 M 810 (94)—though "outer limits" of permissible time lapse, complaint made 21 months after last alleged assault fresh: complainant was 8 at time of assaults, D was her father & threatened that no one would like or believe her if she told anyone, complaint was made within 3 days of D's return to MA after 18 month sojourn in Florida;

C v Howell 57 MAC 716 (2003)—15 months lapse before complaint = on borderline of admissibility when complainant = intelligent preteen of considerable self-assurance, no evidence of threats/intimidation, D's control over complainant = minimal at best and altogether absent for the 8 months before complaint, & complaint wasn't spontaneous but instead during harsh questioning of complainant about his own misbehavior; this, with failures to instruct promptly & thoroughly on fresh complaint = reversal;

C v Smith 59 MAC 181 (2003)—first complaint 51 months after alleged assault not "fresh"; "well exceeds the delay countenanced in any of our reported cases"; reversal;

C v Dion 30 MAC 406 (91)—complaint made after 18-month delay by teenage complainant was not fresh because not justified by generalized fear; factors justifying delay in reporting discussed; cases collected in appendix;

C v Swain 36 MAC 433 (94)—10–13 month delay; no threats/intimidation, teenage complainant. "outer limits" of timeliness - convictions reversed due to combination of errors in fresh complaint;

C v Scullin 44 MAC 9 (97)—though court upheld admission of alleged 1987 sexual assault by D upon same complainant alleging 1990 assault for which D was being tried, purported 'fresh complaint' of the 1987 assault (made about 2 years afterward) was inadmissible, counsel ineffective in referring to it before motion in limine was resolved & in failing to object; tactic of having complainant herself testify to alleged fresh complaint noted (criticized?) to be "not typical" [*Peters* 429 M 22 (99) held that sexual assault complainant may testify on direct ONLY to fact that complaint was made and to whom, but even then the fresh complaint witness must testify and be available for cross-examination; complainant can't "self-corroborate]; judge's failure to avoid jury exposure to evidence whose admissibility was not yet settled might have been "alternative basis for reversal";

C v Nurse 50 MAC 36 (2000)—complaint of woman (to cop, after being arrested) that she'd been raped 83 days earlier NOT fresh; rejecting excuse that she wouldn't report crime because, as prostitute, feared police;

C v Gardner 30 MAC 515 (91)—complaint made after 38-month delay by child complainant was not fresh because not justified by amorphous fears of telling mother; instruction that jury could consider child's fears as to state of mind & justification for delay were improper;

C v Traynor 40 MAC 527 (96)—complaint made after at least 2 years not fresh even though D (stepfather) lived in household: no evidence of threats, D wasn't authority to her, she was 14 years old at time of alleged assaults, & not retarded;

C v McKinnon 35 MAC 398 (93)—34-month delay excused because of fear of violent D;

C v Dockham 405 M 618 (89)—complaint made after 11-day delay by 4 year old was fresh in light of familial ties & residence in same household;

C v Allen 40 MAC 458 (96)—complaints made by 8 and 9-year-olds after 3–4 months were fresh inasmuch as D, their father, threatened harm & had access to them;

C v Clements 36 MAC 205 (94)—complaints made 2–3 years after events, but only 14–20 months after D no longer had access, fresh within judge's discretion given death threats;

C v Amirault 404 M 221 (89)—complaint made after 18-month delay by 4 year old against child care providers was fresh;

C v Lavoie 47 MAC 1 (99)—fresh enough because though 26 months after last assault, only two weeks after out of D's control, and complainant then only 13 years old, BUT error to instruct jury that they could consider evidence that D allegedly abused complainant's mother in determining freshness: no evidence that complainant ever witnessed such violence;

C v Perreira 38 MAC 901 (95)—complaint made after 7 years (and 7 years after D last lived in household) not fresh; admission of notebooks written by complainant with graphic details beyond her trial testimony also error;

C v Shiek 42 MAC 209 (97)—complainant of sexual assaults when she was between ages of 8 & 13 did not make 'fresh' complaint when accusation first occurred more than 7 years after 1st alleged assault and 24–32 months after last alleged assault;

C v Foskette 30 MAC 384 (91)—complaint made after 13-hour delay by teenage complainant was fresh;

C v Snow 35 MAC 836 (94)—complaint made six years after alleged sexual assault on 13-year-old not fresh, even though D (mother's boyfriend) lived at house off & on during 5 of the years;

C v Moreschi 38 MAC 562 (95)—rape portion of complaint was not made until lapse of 48 hours, but OK as "fresh" because complaint of vicious assault was immediate and complainant and complaint witness were thereafter "in constant communication"; Court regarded course of contacts as "single event constituting a fresh complaint of rape";

C v Kruah 47 MAC 341 (99)—given strong (immigrant) community mores against bringing such a charge, threats by D, V's vulnerable status, etc., within discretion to find 15 months "fresh";

C v Onouha **46 MAC 904 (98)**—complaint to school counselor 14 months after alleged assault "raised a question of freshness," but testimony cumulative, lacking in color or detail; harmless (and particularly more so because jury-waived; but see *Sugrue* **34 MAC 172, 174 (93)** excessive scope of "fresh complaint" required reversal, even though trial was jury-waived)

C v Spence **38 MAC 88 (95)**—though complaint, by 11-year-old, 15 months after alleged rape was **not** fresh, no appellate relief because D had withdrawn objection because he wanted to, & did, use circumstances of complaint to discredit complainant;

C v Fanara **47 MAC 560 (99)**—no ineffective assistance of counsel in defense attorney's allegedly introducing non-fresh complaint: it was prior inconsistent statement AND furthered defense that witnesses had conspired against him;

C v Taylor **33 MAC 655 (92)**—whether or not complainant's statements to DSS worker made over 11 months after incident was sufficiently fresh, they were admissible as prior consistent statements where D had used some of statements to discredit complainant;

C v D'Entremont **36 MAC 474 (94)**—that complainant had complained to other people before she complained to nurse one hour after incident no bar to nurse's fresh complaint testimony;

C v Almeida **42 MAC 607 (97)**—non-fresh complaints were not admissible to put into "context" the complainant's failure to complain for 9–10 years; Comm's appellate claim that they were admissible as prior consistent statements rejected because trial judge did not exercise discretion with that in mind;

11-H.1.d. Spontaneous v. Coached

C v Lund **5 MAC 884 (77)**—fresh complaint OK though cops used leading questions to elicit because only corroborated info cops had;

C v Allen **40 MAC 458 (96)**—suggestive interviewing techniques may render testimony so tainted as to be unreliable (D argues, unsuccessfully on facts, for *State v Michaels* **136 N.J. 299 (94)** protocol, i.e., a pretrial "competency" hearing to evaluate the effects of repeated child-witness interviews and suggestive techniques employed);

C v Adkinson **442 M 410 (2004)**—judge denied D's motion for voir dire re: coercive interviews by prosecutors: children initially accused mother's ex-husband of abuse, & after coercion accused instead D (father); exploration of subject instead at trial here OK (excused?) because trial was jury-waived; "no need for the judge to conduct a separate competency hearing";

C v Caracino **33 MAC 787 (93)**—rejecting defense argument that fresh complaints were involuntary or coerced by complainant's father or suggested by child interview specialist in DA's office;

11-H.2. Limiting Instructions

C v King **445 M 217 (2005)**—model charge set forth, given new "first" (rather than "fresh") complaint doctrine;

C v McCormick **48 MAC 106 (99)**—failure to request limiting instruction re: fresh complaint not per se ineffective assistance of counsel;

C v McDuffie **16 MAC 1016 (83)**—hospital record fresh complaint went too far; corroborates, not substantive evidence;

C v Mula **19 MAC 993 (85)**—limiting fresh complaint instruction should be given re: hospital records; no limit on # of fresh complaint witnesses (yet?);

C v Almon **30 MAC 721 (91)**—judge's failure to instruct that fresh complaint testimony of 5 witnesses was limited to corroboration posed risk of miscarriage of justice;

C v Trowbridge **419 M 750 (95)**—failure to give limiting instruction **at time** fresh complaint admitted & failure to explain word "corroboration" & too many fresh complaint witnesses (4) = reversal (substantial risk of miscarriage of justice);

C v Scanlon **412 M 664 (92)**—judge's explanation of "corroboration" upon admission of fresh complaint testimony was sufficient;

C v Brouillard **40 MAC 448 (96)**—lack of contemporaneous fresh complaint instruction created substantial risk of miscarriage of justice when there were four such witnesses (danger of substantive use of such testimony);

C v Kachoul **69 MAC 352 (2007)**—refusal to reverse for judge's refusal to instruct that "fresh complaint" could be used to impeach as well as to support complainant's testimony; judge only said for "corroboration," defined as "confirming or supporting," but standard "inconsistent statements" and witness credibility instructions were also given; jury here acquitted D of 7 out of 8 charges (involving inconsistencies between trial testimony and "fresh complaint");

11-H.3. Rape Shield Law

G.L. c. 233, § 21B—("rape shield") alleged victim's sexual conduct inadmissible, except conduct with D or alleged to cause physical feature/condition; requires written motion to admit, offer/proof, & in camera hearing; court weighs relevance/weight vs. prejudice to [complaining witness] & makes written findings; BUT SEE 1A Wigmore, Evidence, § 62 (Tillers rev. 1983) Wigmore "argued strongly to admit chastity or unchastity character in sex offense cases on issue of complaining witness's credibility'";

C v Joyce **382 M 222 (81)**—if relevant to "bias," G.L. c. 233, § 21B does not preclude evidence of prior sexual conduct;

C v McNickles **22 MAC 114 (86)**—promiscuity = motive to lie because complaining witness in child custody fight;

Olden v Kentucky **488 US 227 (88)**—can't exclude complaining witness's cohabitation (re: bias);

C v Houston **430 M 616 (2000)**—SJC split, 3:3, over whether rape shield statute impliedly repeals impeachment by prior conviction statute (G.L. c. 233, § 21) to prohibit rape complainant from being impeached by prior convictions for prostitution (i.e., judge doesn't have discretion to allow such impeachment); though this remains open question, this D received no relief because judge exercised discretion to exclude the prostitution convictions (and allowed use of two other convictions) and D was similarly treated, judge excluding his prior conviction for indecent A&B; **BUT NOW, SEE** *C v Harris* **443 M 714 (2005)**—judge has discretion to allow introduction (for impeachment of rape complainant under G.L. c. 233, § 21B) of prior convictions as common nightwalker;

C v Yelle **390 M 678 (84)**—no interlocutory appeal for DA when D's rape-shield motion granted, and no error in not exercising G.L. c. 211, § 3 relief;

C v McGregor **39 MAC 919 (95)**—male prison inmate alleging rape could be impeached with his statements, found in medical records, showing motive to lie (he was bisexual and traded sex for money or other items, but did not want sexuality known); rape shield statute doesn't bar impeachment use of complainant's prior statements, which here impeached complainant's trial claim that he was "religious" & thus would not consent to homosexual activity;

C v Moran **439 M 482 (2003)**—error to exclude medical record of rape complainant, who testified that she wouldn't have consented to sex because she had had recent laparoscopy, and that she had taken pain killer because of this surgery; record revealed an entirely different medical procedure, involving a different bodily entry point; no privilege applied, & no basis for invoking "Bishop-Fuller" protocol;

C v Fuller **66 MAC 84 (2006)**—Department of Mental Retardation employee testified both as fresh complaint witness and as to mental/emotional characteristics of alleged rape victim; Commonwealth's motion in limine to bar reference to AV's children (because this was "evidence of prior sexual misconduct on her part") was allowed, with defense counsel stating he didn't intend to bring up fact of children; when thereafter he moved to be allowed cross-examination about fact that AV was a mother "and her ability to function as a parent" he argued this was to rebut prosecution's evidence of her mental limitations & was barred from doing so, Appeals Court found no abuse of discretion or error of law, but was apparently angry at counsel's failure to raise issue at motion in limine (see fn.5);

C v Seap Sa **58 MAC 420 (2003)**—no error in barring evidence that very shortly after alleged aggravated rape by D (who said consensual), complainant engaged in sex with boyfriend; D's theory that woman traumatized by rape wouldn't have consensual sex so soon was purportedly unsupported/speculative;

C v Herrick **39 MAC 291 (95)**—though D wanted to intro evidence that complainant's friend told defense investigator that her mother was going to have her examined for virginity (and defense argued this as motive to fabricate rape claim), friend denied this at voir dire, as did complainant: it was thus hearsay & inadmissible;

C v Haynes **45 MAC 192 (98)**—though D wanted to introduce evidence that complainant had said her step-grandfather had inserted carrot into vagina (purportedly basis for explaining physical condition, healed tear on edge of hymen), complainant at voir dire denied memory of any such event; D failed to question doctor on voir dire whether carrot could have caused hymen tear, and made no other offer of proof; alleged statement (purportedly in some DSS document) inadmissible;

C v Elliot **393 M 824 (85)**—D can show complainant's lawsuit against her landlord (D's boss) for the alleged rape because her financial motive to lie = relevant;

C v Mosby **11 MAC 1 (80): G.L. c. 233 § 21B**—only for "sexual" conduct; D can show that complainant knew him on friendly terms without in camera hearing;

C v Fetzer **19 MAC 1024 (85)**—D can show "romantic" relationship between complainant & another (re: motive to lie re: consent with D) without G.L. c. 233, § 21B procedure;

C v Morin **52 MAC 780 (2001)**—reversal for exclusion of cross-examination re: alleged victim's relationship with abusive boyfriend, arguably a motive for her to claim that D's presence in her apartment was nonconsensual;

C v Chretien **383 M 123 (81)**—where complainant denied on voir dire sex activity during time period, D can't question her about this before jury;

C v Pearce **427 M 642 (98)**—unless D produces evidence that twelve-year-old pregnant complainant engaged in sex with some other person, at some particular time, he may not cross-examine her on that topic; though D contended she had accused him (ex-fiancé of her sister) of rape to deflect censure for her own consensual sexual activity with someone else (since some such activity must have occurred in order for her to become pregnant), SJC stated that this "lacked evidentiary support" (pregnant under-age complainant defeats presumption of innocence, and D may not defend, except upon basis of immaculate conception?; burden shift, conclusive and mandatory presumption of guilt?? see *Sandstrom v Montana* **442 US 510 (79)**; *C v Pauley* **368 M 286, 292–99 (75)**)

C v Fitzgerald **412 M 516 (92)**—D (an O-secretor) had right to ask rape complainant (an O-secretor) whether she had sex with anyone other than her boyfriend (an O-secretor) on night of incident to support forensic evidence that attacker was B-secretor; inquiry not designed to attack complainant for her promiscuity & thus not barred by rape shield law;

C v Cameron **69 MAC 741 (2007)**—complainant's underwear had DNA from at least two males, and a "primary sample excluded D as donor," while "secondary sample" neither included nor excluded D; counsel speculated to judge that possible motive to fabricate rape charge against D was that complainant's jailed boyfriend would learn of her consensual activity with someone else; puzzling decision seems to assert that judge allowed D to make this "argument" to jury (id. at 745), but based on less-than-constant/vociferous further proffers, unrevealing voir dire of complainant, and non-final/specific "rulings" no "error" in barring questions regarding complainant's sex prior to date of alleged incident;

C v Elder **389 M 743 (83)**—can exclude complainant's prior sex with boyfriend where D had already shown complainant's bias against him for interfering in relationship with boyfriend; lack of virginity normally not "condition" under G.L. c. 233, § 21B;

C v Kowalski **33 MAC 49 (92)**—rape complainant's fear of boyfriend was admissible to show bias;

C v Grieco **386 M 484 (82)**—"specific instances" of complainant's prior sex with D = admissible; D need not specify exact dates/times;

C v Thayer **20 MAC 234 (85)**—error to instruct jury to disregard complainant's prior sex with co-D where theory of rape was joint venture;

C v Civello **39 MAC 373 (95)**—error to bar cross-examination to show that complainant knew from prior experience, re: another, that accusing D of sexual abuse would result in D's removal from the home: this questioning **not** a violation of rape-shield statute;

C v Thevenin **33 MAC 588 (92)**—evidence that D didn't have sex with rape complainant because he had been told (hearsay) that she had pubic lice admissible to show D's state of mind; (and cf. *C v Martin* **424 M 301 (97)** evidence that complainant believed D was HIV+ was relevant and admissible since consent was issue in rape trial);

C v Barresi **46 MAC 907 (99)**—because D's expert could not provide necessary foundation (i.e., that D's negative test for Chlamydia meant that he could not have raped complainant), no abuse of discretion in excluding fact that complainant had tested positive for this sexually transmitted disease;

C v Whitman **29 MAC 972 (90)**—complainant's prior sex with another 2 weeks before incident was too remote to explain presence of sperm & thus not admissible under rape shield law;

C v Cortez **438 M 123 (2002)**—D must file written motion before cross-examination on evidence of other causes for alleged rape victim's physical condition AND proffered evidence that murder victim had sex with boyfriend two days earlier didn't explain physical injuries (bruises/abrasions on inner thighs, etc.), which were "fresh";

C v Martin **424 M 301 (97)**—bedspread semen stain's non-match with D barred under rape shield statute because insufficient "particularity and showing of recency", **i.e.**, that the stain was left there by her assailant that day; BUT WHY SHOULDN'T THIS GO TO 'WEIGHT' & NOT 'ADMISSIBILITY'? cf. *C v Sheehan* **435 M 183 (2001)**, Sosman, J., concurring (it doesn't "belittle" the privileges at stake to say that D's "right to a fair trial is of greater weight");

C v Stockhammer **409 M 867 (91)**—D had right to cross-examine rape complainant about prior sexual activity with him & boyfriend to show she was motivated to lie to preserve relationship with boyfriend & parents, notwithstanding rape shield law; *(See Chapters 6-D and 11-J for Stockhammer line of cases (discoverability, protocol to obtain in camera review as prerequisite to access, various privileges reviewed))*;

Michigan v Lucas **500 US 145 (91)**—exclusion of exculpatory evidence, because of D's failure to follow state rape-shield procedure, not necessarily a federal constitutional violation;

C v Gauthier **32 MAC 130 (92)**—counsel's failure to file written motion justified excluding his cross-examination to ascertain whether complainant's prior masturbation explained penile abrasion, though otherwise admissible as "physical feature" or "condition" under rape shield law;

C v McGee **42 MAC 740 (97)**—despite rape complainant's infection with sexually transmitted disease, her failure to acknowledge on voir dire her sexual activity with anyone (other than, allegedly, D) prevented D from introducing testimony of witness to whom she had acknowledged intercourse with another because it was not "impeachment" of complainant's testimony before the jury;

C v Gagnon **45 MAC 584 (98)**—if D had argued that rape allegation was made because child complainant feared she was pregnant by someone else, D may have been entitled to introduce evidence that she was found nude in bed with a boyfriend;

C v Fionda **33 MAC 316 (92)**—jury instruction, that jurors to consider evidence of prior sexual conduct between complainant & D only if consensual & not result of intoxication or unconsciousness, was proper;

C v Baxter **36 MAC 45 (94)**—evidence of sexual abuse of complainant by another person relevant because it was inferable that complainant was confused/fabricating: incident alleged against D occurred in similar place and other abuser had same name; complainant suffered from flashbacks and auditory hallucinations; But *C v Hynes* **40 MAC 927 (96)** mere fact of prior abuse not relevant when only "mere speculation" supports a confusion/distortion defense;

C v Syrafos **38 MAC 211 (95)**—**Baxter** distinguished; mere fact of prior rape not relevant to credibility;

11-H.4. Prior Sex Relevant to Knowledge of Terminology and Acts

C v Ruffen **399 M 811 (87)**—admit complaining witness's prior unrelated sex re: knowledge of terminology (if good faith proffer & voir dire);

C v Scheffer **43 MAC 398 (97)**—failure of trial counsel to cite to judge **Ruffen** in support of his attempted cross-examination was ineffective assistance of counsel;

C v Owen **57 MAC 529 (2003)**—D entitled to evidentiary hearing on motion for new trial based on ineffective assistance of trial and appellate counsel for purported failure to show that young sex-assault complainant could have known about sex in some way other than abuse by D: DSS/police reports showed that complainant had seen mother and partner engaged in sex & had thereafter played with dolls in sexual manner, that adolescent cousin had sexually abused her, & that another adolescent had fondled her chest; trial counsel had abandoned the inquiry after judge deferred ruling on D's motion to question complainant about past sex abuse (initially at a voir dire examination); *prior abuse need not be "identical" to the abuse alleged in case being tried, but merely sufficiently similar to account for complainant's knowledge of sex acts now alleged;*

C v Beaudry **445 M 577 (2005)**—*Ruffin* holding (**399 M 811**) does not allow prosecutor to argue that a child wouldn't know about sex or to impose burden on D to explain child's sexual knowledge; reversal here for such a prosecutorial argument; CB Reid, "The Sexual Innocence Inference Theory as a Basis for the Admissibility of a Child Molestation Victim's Prior Sexual Conduct," 91 *Mich. L. Rev.* 827, 852 (1993) (suggesting presumptive ban on use of sexual innocence inference theory of admissibility with children older than twelve at time of trial); *C v Rathburn* **26 MAC 699, 700, 708 (1989)** (rejecting argument that thirteen-year-old witness would be thought to have extraordinary knowledge of sexual matters); *C v Savage* **51 MAC 500, 502, 504 (2001)** (similar re: child who was almost eleven years old when he first alleged sexual abuse);

C v Walker **426 M 301 (97)**—single reference in voluminous DSS records to complaining witness's father's statement that witness's mother had accused him of molesting witness (context of bitter custody fight and drug addicted mother) insufficient to trigger right to Ruffen voir dire or right to cross-examine witness re: prior sexual abuse; in different case, "child's knowledge about sexuality based on information from a secondary source" may be sufficiently relevant to entitle D to cross-examination and/or voir dire; *C v Beaudry* **445 M 577 (2005)**—explicit recognition that sexual knowledge may be acquired other than through personal experience;

11-H.5. Prior False Allegations of Rape

C v Bohannon **376 M 90 (78)**—D can show complaining witness's prior false rape complaints; witness's credibility critical & D made offer/proof re: factual basis;

C v Haynes **45 MAC 192 (98)**—complaining witness denied memory of step-grandfather inserting carrot into her vagina, said on voir dire that she was told this by her mother and D that it happened, and believed it for awhile but now trusted neither, and did not believe that it happened: no Bohannon issue because not shown to be false, and not shown to be witness's statement (rather than D's and witness's mother's);

C v Hrycenko **417 M 309 (94)**—prior claim's falsity not shown by mere failure of complainant to pursue it;

C v Quegan **35 MAC 129 (93)**—no error in refusing admission of fact that child complainant's grandmother (D's ex-mother-in-law), a fresh complaint witness, had accused other family members of sexual abuse of the child: no record basis for inferring falsity;

C v Wise **39 MAC 922 (95)**—evidence of falsity of prior accusation must be "solid" & if not a recantation by complainant herself, must be more than failure/refusal of prosecution authorities to initiate a prosecution;

C v Costa **69 MAC 823 (2007)**—complainant's prior allegations, against a bus driver, not shown to be false: detective had concluded that her statements were "inconsistent," so no charges were filed, and complainant asked if she would be in trouble or go to jail if she were not telling the truth (though after assurances, she denied "making all this up");

C v Pyne **35 MAC 36 (93)**—error in refusing voir dire or continuance to investigate possible prior false rape allegation, but remedy = entertain motion for new trial with evidentiary hearing;

C v Rathburn **26 MAC 699 (88)**—not shown that complainant's prior claims = untrue, or similar enough to explain her knowledge of terms (i.e., *Ruffen* **399 M 811 (87)**) ;

C v Brescia **61 MAC 908 (2004)**—confusing discoverability of nonprivileged info with standard for admissibility under *C v Bohannon* (i.e., proof of falsity of the prior allegations), Appeals Court says no error in denying discovery of complainant's prior allegations of sexual assault;

C v Despres **70 MAC 645 (2007)**—it was learned by defendant after conviction that indecent assault and battery complainant (mentally retarded and having "behavioral issues") had made unreliable reports about being mistreated or having his rights violated at "respite facility"; facility employees' averments about his "significant tendency to misperceive events, exaggerate and fabricate . . . in order to draw attention to himself" = insufficient basis for requiring new trial, so no "abuse of discretion" by trial judge in denying same; "character" evidence being "used to suggest that a mentally impaired witness is inherently untruthful" was "troubling" to Appeals Court; judge was within his discretion in concluding that the witnesses' qualifications were inadequate because they lacked advanced degrees in psychology or psychiatry; fn.1 at 649 says that there's no "Bohannon" issue because complainant's prior allegations weren't re: sexual abuse similar to the complaint at issue in this case;

C v Talbot **444 M 586 (2005)**—asserts that admissibility under Bohannon rule *requires* showing that witness was the victim in the case on trial, her consent was the central issue, she was the only Commonwealth witness on that issue, her testimony was inconsistent and confused, and there was a basis in independent third-party records for concluding that the prior accusations of the same type of crime had been made and were false, BUT the case from 1979 from which quotation was lifted asserted that these were the facts in Bohannon: cases since then (until this nonsense???) have not limited the Bohannon rationale so absurdly;

11-H.6. Privileges

G.L. c. 233, § 20J (84)—counselor can't disclose confidence of sex "assault" [sic] "VICTIM" [sic] without prior written consent; nor discoverable or admissible in court without (same);

See Chapter 11-J, Privileges;

C v Pratt **42 MAC 695 (97)**—D's right to show lack of fresh complaint overrides social-worker–client privilege (G.L. c. 112, § 135A); complainant's specific denial during unrelated G.L. c. 119, §§ 51A–B investigation, that anyone had "touched" her and assertions of safety and happiness, admissible;

8 Wigmore, *Evidence,* **§ 2192** (McNaughton rev. 1961)—trend = expand privileges as if large/basic principles worth pursuing into remote analogies; this attitude = "unwholesome";

C v 2 Juveniles **397 M 261 (86)**—D must show "legitimate need" to see confidential communication under G.L. c. 233, § 20J before judge must review (in camera);

C v Fayerweather **406 M 78 (89)**—psychiatric report that rape complainant heard voices weeks before incident was admissible despite psychotherapist privilege; expert testimony not required;

Pennsylvania v Ritchie **480 US 39 (87)**—due process analysis of right to discover info in youth agency files re: complaining witness; in camera review without counsel;

C v Clancy **402 M 664, 669–71 (88)**—Declaration of Rights may require counsel's participation in in camera review; but no need for any review shown here;

C v Rathbun **26 MAC 699 (88)**—judge could find that psych. records weren't exculpatory;

C v Giacalone **24 MAC 166 (87)**—legitimate need not shown for complainant's psych. records;

C v Jones **404 M 339 (89)**—D gets G.L. c. 112, § 135 (f) records of G.L. c. 119, § 51B report; other § 135 DSS reports not "absolute" privilege (like G.L. c. 233, § 20J), so in camera review without counsel (cf. Lynch/Nolan dissent) sees if "material to defense";

C v Slonka **42 MAC 760 (97)**—after Commonwealth introduced portion of purportedly privileged psychotherapist record, D entitled to introduce a different portion refuting it; "fairness" cited;

See also Chapter 11-J, post, & Chapter 7-L (Informants);

11-H.7. Confrontation Issues

G.L. c. 278, § 16D—alternatives (e.g., video) for complainant under 15 if trauma likely;

G.L. c. 233, §§ 81–83—conditions for substantive use of hearsay by children under 10 in sex abuse & some non-criminal proceedings;

C v Joubert **38 MAC 943 (95)**—reversing for improper invocation of §81;

C v Colin C. **419 M 54 (94)**—Court reserves for future "facial invalidity" challenges to § 81; grafts onto statute extra requirements: (1) must give notice to D of intent to use child hearsay pursuant to § 81; (2) Commonwealth must prove beyond reasonable doubt that use of hearsay = necessary to avoid "severe & long-lasting emotional trauma to child"; (3) hearing re: reliability of hearsay statements must be on the record & determination of reliability must be supported by specific findings; (4) unless severe emotional trauma would be caused, D & counsel must be permitted to be present at hearing; (5) if "unavailable" finding is based on incompetence, finding of "reliability" likely questionable; (6) independent evidence must corroborate hearsay of child; use of experts' opinion that child was credible as foundational "corroboration" is invalid;

C v Bergstrom **402 M 534 (88): G.L. c. 278, § 16D**—violates Article 12 "face to face" right;

Coy v Iowa **487 US 1012 (88)**—screen between complainant & D violates 6th Amendment;

C v Amirault **404 M 221 (89)**—video OK because D's present, need shown, & tape's OK; special trial procedures in courtroom also OK;

M.R.Crim.P. 18(a)—right to be present at all critical stages; see *C v Kater* **409 M 433, 446 (91)** and *C v Conefrey* **410 M 1 (91)**; see also G.L. c. 278, § 16A—closed trials;

11-H.8. Extraneous Bad Acts of Defendant/"Common Scheme"

C v Darby **37 MAC 650 (94)**—reversal because irrelevant photos admitted, one showing D, clothed, but with erect penis exposed and other showing child sexual assault complainant nude in bathtub; that trial was jury-waived did not matter;

C v LaSota **29 MAC 15 (90)**—pamphlet on incest found in D's home was inadmissible to show D's interest in incest because more prejudicial than probative;

C v Jaundoo **64 MAC 56 (2005)**—although evidence that D possessed & showed complainant pornographic materials was relevant to corroborate her testimony, and as evidence of D's "motive or intent to engage complainant in a sexual relationship," admitting substantial quantity of pornography, permitting explicit discussion of it, and permitting jury to view a great deal of the material, "was an abuse of discretion and palpable error";

C v Clary **388 M 583 (83)**—improper to make insinuations about sexual orientation likely to prejudice D;

C v Healy **393 M 367 (84)**—improper to suggest that D's homosexuality made him more likely to commit crime;

C v Gillette **33 MAC 427 (92)**—D's 7-year-old statement, made before daughter's birth, that he would take away her virginity was inadmissible because too remote in time; failure of counsel to file motion in limine to exclude inadmissible evidence of D's predisposition to rape was ineffective assistance;

C v Calcagno **31 MAC 25 (91)**—D's prior repeated uncharged sexual abuse of child complainant admissible to show motive, common scheme, etc., & to put offense in context;

C v Feijoo **419 M 486 (95)**—joinder of alleged sex offenses against 9 different children OK; "modus operandi", same.

See Chapter 8, Joinder; Chapter 11-E, Bad Acts (prohibition against 'propensity' evidence most often "honored in the breach" when allegations concern sexual assault: 'common scheme' [erroneously] invoked as basis for admission of propensity evidence: see, particularly, concerns expressed in C v Hanlon 44 MAC 810 (98) at trial of D for raping one boy, OK to admit evidence D raped complainant's two younger brothers and two other boys, though some such conduct allegedly occurred as much as nine years after the last act for which D was being tried; "logical consistency and ultimate coherence" of the "doctrinal basis for the allowance of such ... bad act evidence" might be questioned, id. at 818 n.5; consult C v Jackson 132 M 16 (1882) for what the rule against "propensity" SHOULD mean;)

11-H.9. Expert Testimony and Scientific Evidence

See Chapter 11-I for cases on DNA profile evidence;

C v Lewandowski **22 MAC 148 (86)**—doctor can say complainant's sex knowledge = high & results of examination by referring to "anatomically-correct" doll; *see C v Beaudry* **445 M 577, 584 (2005)**—where a prosecutor expressly urges in her closing that a child victim's sexual knowledge was derived from identified acts of abuse, there must be an adequate and specific basis in the record for such a claim that excludes other possible sources of such knowledge.

C v Mendrala **20 MAC 398 (85)**—expert can't say if sex was forcible or consented; jury equally capable of decision turning on complaining witness's credibility;

C v Gardner **350 M 664 (66)**—expert can't give opinion whether entry's forcible (i.e., rape); jury equally able to draw conclusion;

C v Guidry **22 MAC 907 (86)**—close, but doctor can say 'consistent' with force; but see *C v Spear* **43 MAC 583 (97)** expert can't say child's "symptoms" were consistent with those of sexually abused child;

C v Baldwin **24 MAC 200 (87)**—medical record "diagnosis = molested" = only from complainant, not doctor's opinion;

C v Ianello **401 M 197 (87)**—exclude (here) (this) (defense) expert re: false sex abuse charges in custody fights; but cf *C v Walker* **426 M 301 (97)** in defeating D's argument on appeal, decision recognizes the likelihood of false charges in custody fight;

C v Hudson **417 M 536 (94)**—while not finding abuse of discretion in admitting expert testimony for "rehabilitation" (**in rebuttal**) about stomachaches and nightmares

being possible features of post-traumatic stress disorder in allegedly sexually abused children, SJC agreed with proposition that such evidence is not admissible to prove that complainant "was in fact sexually abused"; here, NO OBJECTION to insinuation that these "behaviors"/symptoms corroborate credibility;

C v Frangipane **433 M 527 (2001)**—licensed social worker not competent to testify about how trauma victims store and retrieve or dissociate traumatic memories (because it's a scientific/medical matter); at retrial, prior to intro of expert testimony on "dissociative memory loss or recovered memory," **Lanigan** hearing (**419 M 15 (94)**) to occur re: reliability/validity of "recovered memory";

C v Montanino (II) **409 M 500 (91)**—cop's testimony that truthful sexual assault victims commonly provide more details as time goes on was inadmissible because vouching for credibility of another witness; D's prior uncharged sexual abuse of child was inadmissible to show D's state of mind where complainant had not yet been impeached;

C v Federico **425 M 844 (97)**—hypothetical questions of witness, asking witness to "assume" facts consistent with allegations, resulting in opinion that evidence was "consistent with" abuse, could be understood as testimony that sexual abuse occurred; reversal required. See also

C v Brouillard **40 MAC 448 (96)**—child complainants' treating therapist linked his observations of them to several behaviors & syndromes & predictions of further maladies; reversal required;

C v McCaffrey **36 MAC 583 (94)**—child complainant's own treating therapist shouldn't testify to general characteristics of sexually abused children;

C v Spear **43 MAC 583 (97)**—improper to testify that complainant's symptoms are "consistent with those of" sexually abused child;

C v LaCaprucia **41 MAC 496 (96)**—similar re "traumatized children" in "abusive homes" and re profile of "incestuous family" (D and rape complainant daughter allegedly fit); reversal ordered;

C v Poitras **55 MAC 691 (2002)**—reversal for prosecution testimony by psychologist re: sexual abuse of children, which alleged attributes and characteristics of those most likely to abuse children ("profile" testimony), mirroring prosecution's evidence about D (i.e., adult known to child, position of authority, caregiver with access/opportunity, not dating anyone, child often vulnerable because of "disrupted attachment relationship");

C v Perkins **39 MAC 577 (95)**—expert testimony mirroring facts of case, saying not inconsistent with abuse, required reversal; but see *C v Malchionno* **47 MAC 73 (99)** after D elicited from social worker that complainant had specifically denied any sexual assault by D, no relief from admission of social worker's testimony that false denials by children 'not unusual';

C v Colon **49 MAC 289, 290–91 (2000)**—no error found in Commonwealth's expert's testimony (pediatrician with expertise in allegedly sex-abused children), on rebuttal, that only 15–20 percent of girls with confirmed sex-abuse histories showed "physical signs" of vaginal penetration; this was info re: "medical interpretation of an absence of any physical evidence of penetration," a subject "beyond the jury's ken"; [cf. *C v Hrabak* **440 M 650 (2004)**—DA can't assert that no physical evidence could be expected from alleged anal rape, because child's rectum "flexible," because here, no evidence offered; *C v Federico* 425 M 844 (97) commands that expert testimony = necessary to address child complainant's lack of injury;

C v Calderon **65 MAC 590 (2006)**—though doctor's statement that complainant's normal physical exam was "consistent with her disclosure" was improper, error held harmless in circumstances; judge not obliged to hold voir dire before qualifying expert, and judge's finding of expertise is inferable from record;

C v Arana **453 M 214 (2009)**—lengthy presentation of medical testimony concerning examination and collection of "swabs" from complainants' bodies, and concomitant testimony from laboratory chemists, all of which resulted in bottom line of "no physical evidence" showing sexual assaults took place, but with dedicated testimony asserting that such evidence would be nearly impossible to find after five days' time (as here) criticized; suggestion (fn.25) of stipulation to 'no evidence of' assault, and then expert (preferably NOT one who examined subject complainants) testimony concerning general circumstances which could explain absence of physical evidence, countered if desired by defense expert;

C v Ryan **8 MAC 941 (79)**—DA's argument that "sperm does not always occur in ejaculation" not supported by evidence, and "went to the heart of the defense [that the victim's accusation of rape was fabricated]";

C v Colin C. **419 M 54 (94)**—expert's opinion that child sex complainants had been abused required reversal (essentially testimony vouching for credibility);

C v Rather **37 MAC 140 (94)**—therapist testifying on "patterns of disclosure" by child sexual assault victims, in answering "hypothetical" questions, effectively vouched for children's credibility and this was error (harmless here because much corroboration, including eyewitness) - instructions as to how to avoid reversible "vouching" include voir dire and jury instruction that expert testimony **is not** affirmative evidence of abuse and that expert did not assess **this** complainant's veracity;

C v Richardson **423 M 180 (96)**—opinion testimony re: credibility not explicitly linked to particular child witness can nonetheless be impermissible vouching (but here harmless);

C v Mamay **407 M 412 (90)**—expert testimony that complainant suffers from rape trauma syndrome generally admissible;

C v LeFave **407 M 927 (90)**—expert testimony that obtaining pornographic photos is common motive for sexual abuse of children was admissible;

C v LeFave **430 M 169, 177 n.9 (99)**—reserving issue whether expert testimony here proffered (impact of suggestive interviewing techniques on reliability of testimony by child witness) is admissible under *Lanigan* **419 M 15 (94)**;

11-I. OPINIONS OF "EXPERTS" AND LAYPERSONS

G.L. c. 231, § 81—judge shan't charge on matters of fact (*See Chapter 12-K*);

C v Foley **7 MAC 608 (79)**—"some restraint on usual puffery re: expert on polygraph needed to not put on par with more established sciences; statistical reliability invaded jury, = hearsay, & little value;

See Chapter 6, Discovery & Chapter 7-C, Experts for D; & CPCS P/G's 4.4 (g), 4.6 (h), & 6.7 (d), (e);

Brodin, M. and Avery, M., *Handbook of Massachusetts Evidence* **(8th ed. 2007)**—Chapter 7, "Opinion and Expert Evidence";

Young, Pollets & Poreda, *Evidence,* **§§ 701.1 et seq. (2d ed. 1998)**—(opinions by lay witnesses); § 702 (testimony by experts); § 703 (bases of opinion testimony by experts); § 704 (opinion on ultimate issue); § 705 (disclosure of facts or data underlying expert opinion);

7 Wigmore, *Evidence,* **§§ 1917-2093 (Chadbourn rev. 1978);**

Giannelli/Imwinkelreid Scientific Evidence (86);

Moenssens/Inbau Scientific Evidence (86);

Prop.M.R.Evid. 701–6—opinion; Proposed R.703 rejected in *DYS v Juvenile* **398 M 516, 531 (86)** (expert can express opinion based on review of test data not admitted in evidence but which would have been admissible if offered);

C v Rodriguez **437 M 554 (2002)**—jury instruction SHOULD be that expert opinion should be disregarded if the assumptions upon which it is based "are not true," criticizing instruction using, instead, the phrase, "if the assumptions have not been *proven*";

C v Evans **438 M 142 (2002)**—expert may not testify to results obtained by another expert who did not testify (but here, no objection, and no relief, and in circumstances no prejudice because cumulative); police lab criminalist had tested knife and found small amount of human blood, but that criminalist had retired before D's trial, and a fellow criminalist testified to the results;

Frye v US **293 F.Supp 1013 (DC Cir. 1923)**—expert opinion based on scientific technique = inadmissible unless technique = "generally accepted" as reliable in the relevant scientific community;

Daubert v Merrell Dow Pharmaceuticals, Inc. **509 US 579 (93)**—**Frye** standard (**293 F.Supp 1013 (D.C. Cir. 1923)**) reconsidered under federal rules of evidence; test now = Fed.R.Evid. 702, possibly limited by R.703 and R.403; trial judge must make preliminary assessment of whether testimony's underlying reasoning/methodology = scientifically valid and applicable to facts at issue; among relevant considerations = whether theory/technique has been tested, whether it has been subjected to peer review and publication, its known or potential error rate, and the existence and maintenance of standards controlling its operation, and whether it has attracted widespread acceptance within a relevant scientific community; previous "general acceptance" standard under *Frye v US* no longer absolutely necessary prerequisite;

C v Lanigan **419 M 15 (94)**—proponent of scientific opinion evidence may demonstrate reliability by whether community of scientists involved generally accepts theory/process **or** by some other means, though "general acceptance" will continue to be significant, & often only, issue;

Kumho Tire v Carmichael **526 US 137 (99)**—Daubert applies not only to "scientific" evidence, but also to all "expert" testimony, including that based on "technical" and other "specialized" knowledge;

General Electric Co. v Joiner **522 US 136 (97)**—trial court's decision to admit or exclude expert testimony under **Daubert** = reviewable on appeal on standard of only "abuse of discretion";

C v Vao Sok **425 M 787 (97)**—issue of validity of particular scientific methodology is "entitled to the same standard of review as a conclusion of law," **i.e.**, de novo; BUT OVERRULED BY

Canavan's Case **432 M 304 (2000)**—appellate court will review decision to admit/exclude expert testimony on standard of "abuse of discretion," giving trial judge's authority to conduct "the inherently fact-intensive and flexible *Lanigan* **419 M 15 (94)** analysis, while preserving a sufficient degree of appellate review to assure that Lanigan determinations are consistent w/the law and supported by a sufficient factual basis in the particular case"; expert testimony IS NOT EXEMPT from foundational reliability determination under Lanigan on ground that it's "based on personal observations" or "clinical experience"; expert's mere assertion that methodology is reliable isn't sufficient to pass Lanigan test absent any other evidence showing its reliability; *C v Patterson* **445 M 626 (2005)**—while review of judge's Lanigan decision is "for abuse of discretion," and thus "deferential and limited, it is not perfunctory"; judge's findings must apply correct legal standard to facts of case and be supported by examination of the record, and "relevant community" of experts must be sufficiently broad to permit potential for dissent; SJC overturns particular "reliability" determination of judge below; evidence can only be admitted if, in addition to the reliability of the theory and process in general, process is reliable *when applied to the specific issue about which the expert is proposing to testify;* "even reliable procedures can lead to incorrect results";

C v Powell **450 M 229 (2007)**—"bloodstain analysis" based on "scientific principles of physics and mathematics", purporting to establish, e.g. "directionality," ("string method" is one method used to determine origin of blood creating stain) was admitted in judge's discretion, SJC citing other jurisdictions' courts rejecting challenges to it; D's challenge "to the relevant scientific community" rejected;

C v Zimmermann **70 MAC 357 (2007)** judge didn't abuse discretion in admitting, after extensive hearing on reliability, the data from the "event data recorder" (EDR) in vehicle involved in fatal crash;

Ready, petitioner **63 MAC 171 (2005)**—AASI (Abel Assessment for Sexual Interest) test was subjected to a 3-day evidentiary hearing pursuant to *C v Lanigan* (**419 M 19 (94)**), after which judge permissibly ruled that the test had not been accepted in the scientific community and that petitioner had failed to demonstrate test's reliability;

C v Robinson **449 M 1 (2007)**—no error in excluding purported expert witness on subject of "the psychology of police interrogations and confessions" because didn't meet "general acceptance" or "reliability" criteria required by *Lanigan* 419 M 15, 25 (94), and also because it concerned issues within knowledge/experience of laypersons; BUT nonetheless, at 6–7, "the subject of psychological manipulation of a defendant and its relation to false confessions presents a serious issue" and "competent" scientific evidence "may well be useful to a fact finder in this area";

C v Tolan **453 M 634 (2009)**—within judge's discretion to preclude testimony re: alleged relationship between various interrogation techniques and false confessions"; preclusion of testimony about common interrogation methods OK because can be understood by jurors without assistance;

C v Steele **455 M 209 (2009)**—only the lower of the two breath sample/blood alcohol level results could be introduced in accord with statutory and regulatory requirements;

C v Rollins **65 MAC 694 (2006)**—while DA could argue that jury should credit breathalyzer test result of .09% plus police observation of D's demeanor, etc. rather than testimony of D and his relatives, court wasn't "entirely convinced" that DA's more substantive argument (that breathalyzer result was inconsistent with D's claim of having consumed only three beers 2–3 hours before stop) "did not cross the line into territory that required expert testimony";

C v Lonardo **74 MAC 566 (2009)**—expert's testimony that she equated the term "runner" with someone who fraudulently "staged" accidents, when evidence would be that D (an attorney) acknowledged use of "runners" "should not have been allowed," but no objection & no "risk of a miscarriage of justice" found here;

C v Arroyo **442 M 135, 145 (2004)**—to preserve objections to DNA analysis, D must file pretrial motion with grounds, and request hearing pursuant to *Canavan's Case* (**432 M 304**);

C v DelValle **443 M 782 (2005)**—judge had no sua sponte obligation to inquire as to reliability of performing DNA testing on seven-year-old blood stains (D-counsel had retained expert & challenged accuracy of DNA analysis, but didn't present evidence that the samples were of questionable validity);

C v Gaynor **443 M 245 (2005)**—rejecting many arguments to exclude DNA on facts of testing here;

C v Grinkley **75 MAC 798 (2009)**—because "mixed" sample from victim did not contain D's "entire" DNA profile, expert's testimony that only one in 320 billion African-Americans were possible contributors to the mixture found on the sample was "irrelevant" and "misleading"; "[w]hat the Commonwealth submitted here, ostensibly product rule statistics for a mixed sample without an identified primary contributor, was not permissible for reasons which should have been obvious";

C v Ward **14 MAC 37 (82)**—expert (arson) may base opinion on facts outside personal knowledge if those facts are supported by the record;

C v Roman **414 M 235 (93)**—expert may base opinion on facts not in evidence if facts/data = independently admissible & appropriate basis for expert to consider; expert cannot give opinion based on inadmissible evidence;

C v O'Brien **423 M 841 (96)**—same; judge impermissibly barred such cross-examination of court-appointed psychiatrist in juvenile transfer hearing;

C v Hinds **450 M 1 (2007)**—first degree murder convictions reversed due to erroneous instruction that expert's opinion must be disregarded unless jurors first find that facts assumed by witness in reaching opinion were "proved by Commonwealth beyond a reasonable doubt": expert opinion at issue was that of defense witness, as to D's criminal responsibility; *Superior Court Criminal Practice Jury Instructions* (MCLE 1999) § 4.7.1 = reproduced at fn.6, "but this instruction also may have its problems";

C v Jaime **433 M 575, 577–78 (2001)**—citing Prop. M.R.Evid. 705—Commonwealth expert testifying to opinion that D had capacity to premeditate should not have been allowed to testify, during direct examination, as to statements made by people he interviewed about D's mood and affect the day before the killing; judge should have precluded admission of hearsay "irrespective of whether they formed the basis of the expert's opinion," though D-counsel could have cross-examined witness about facts underlying opinion;

Delaware v Fensterer **474 US 15 (85)**—expert testimony OK though he can't say which theory based on; confrontation not violated;

C v Olszewski **401 M 749 (88)**—cop can use shorthand (chrome's from D's car); but no such standard as "reasonable degree of police certainty";

C v Burgess **453 M 422 (2008)**—hypothetical "question" to police detective, requiring him to "assume" pages worth of "facts", was improper, as didn't seek expert opinion but instead asked for his observations, phrased as 'expert' opinion, with invitation for him to evaluate his own testimony as consistent with other testimony and opine on the credibility of prosecution theory of the case; hypothetical questions to medical doctor (e.g., were injuries

'consistent with' attacker coming up from behind, etc.) were OK;

C v Fiore **364 M 819 (74)**—witness can answer "I think," "I believe";

C v Harris **1 MAC 265 [SJC 364 M 236] (73)**—foundation & scope;

C v Sendele **18 MAC 755 (84)**—intent to distribute opinion OK though ultimate issue;

C v Lugo **63 MAC 204 (2005)**—expert testimony that fire was intentionally set = OK despite D's argument that it was "ultimate issue"; cites *C v Cruz* **413 M 686, 689–91 (92)** even though expert's opinion touches on ultimate issue, it's admissible if aids jury in reaching decision;

C v Rucker **358 M 298 (70)**—hypothetical question must be based on case's facts;

C v Federico **425 M 844 (97)**—but such "hypotheticals" examination can be understood, improperly, as expert testimony that sexual abuse complainant is truthful; reversal required;

C v Sneed **413 M 387 (92)**—expert may be cross-examined using learned treatises etc.; see Prop.M.R.Evid. 803 (18);

C v Fitzgerald **412 M 516 (92)**—D had right to show that expert who produced exculpatory test results had been retained by Commonwealth;

C v Pandolfino **33 MAC 96 (92)**—statistical probability evidence & "trial by mathematics" discussed, in context of identification by hair sample;

11-I.1.a. General

C v Watson **430 M 725 (99)**—dog as expert (used for probable cause/search); see also *US v Trayer* **898 F.2d 805 (D.C. Cir. '90)** re: dog reliability factors, suggestibility;

C v Crouse **447 M 558, 570 (2006)**—no error in trooper's testimony that dog "alerted" to corner of D's vehicle, rejecting argument that failure of lab to confirm presence of accelerant meant that "alert" was inadmissible; D had expressly stated he had no objection to dog's qualifications;

C v Almeida **34 MAC 901 (93)**—FBI fabrics/photo analyst can say that jacket found in D's home matched jacket on bank robber in surveillance photo ("wear spots" & a hole matched);

C v Neverson **35 MAC 913 (93)**—OK to exclude opinion of defense expert (professor of physics & biomechanics) that 15-month-old child's fall from 63 inch bunk bed would probably be fatal ("force of 175-200 Gs"): no experience re: **medical** consequences of falls from varying heights;

C v Soares **51 MAC 273, 280–81 (2001)**—Gundjonsson Suggestibility Scale testing by forensic psychologist for D (indicating D highly susceptible to pressure) accorded no weight by motion judge, because D failed to present evidence that it's a "scientifically valid and reliable measure," and because application of test results to custody situation might not be valid;

C v Avellar **416 M 409 (93)**—despite no established expertise in the normal or abnormal psychology of grief, within judge's discretion to allow emergency room doctor to testify that D's concerns about the "physical findings" as to the baby's death was, in his 12 years of practice, unusual behavior for a parent; **Frye** test inapplicable because no "scientific test results" involved; BUT SEE:

Canavan's Case **432 M 304 (2000)**—expert testimony IS NOT EXEMPT from foundational reliability determination under Lanigan on ground that it's "based on personal observations" or "clinical experience"; expert's mere assertion that methodology is reliable isn't sufficient to pass Lanigan test absent any other evidence showing its reliability;

Kumho Tire v Carmichael **526 US 137 (99)**—Daubert test applies not only to "scientific" evidence, but also to all "expert" testimony, including allegedly specialized knowledge;

C v Cifizzari **397 M 560 (86)**—bite mark ID OK without general scientific acceptability;

C v Beliard **443 M 79 (2003)**—motion judge correctly concluded that there's sufficient acceptance of evidence concerning "bunter tool mark" identification on discharged bullet's shell casings to justify admissibility;

C v Lodge **431 M 461, 469 (2000)**—homicide detective shouldn't have been allowed to testify as to "the direction in which blood falls" without appropriate foundation questions, though this wasn't "blood spatter" evidence, and "may well be within the general knowledge" of someone who had investigated 200 homicides in six yrs.;

C v Luna **418 M 749 (94)**—ADA's testimony as expert admissible/appropriate re: "materiality" in perjury prosecution; D charged with perjury concerning false statements in application for search warrant and in police reports;

C v Martin **417 M 187 (94)**—convictions reversed because D's former live-in girlfriend testified to her "instincts" & "suspicion" that D had something sexually to do with female house guest temporarily absent from her bed;

C v Cataldo **326 M 373, 376 (50)**—lay testimony re: type of dust on D OK because comparison = common knowledge fact otherwise hard to describe;

C v Smith **17 MAC 918 (83)**—lay testimony re: grass marks OK if "shorthand" re: facts from common observation & not otherwise describable;

C v Shagoury **6 MAC 584 (78)**—lay testimony re: value (of cables) because familiarity, knowledge, & experience & judge left weight to jury;

C v Paiva **71 MAC 411 (2008)**—witness proffered by D was NOT an expert in use of drugs, but instead a percipient witness to D's own drug habit (including amounts), relevant to dispute "intent to distribute"; error to exclude, as observations not remote in time;

C v LePage **352 M 403 (67)**—cop can say footprints in snow = "fresh";

C v Boyarsky **452 M 700 (2008)**—judge had discretion to admit "expert" testimony by trooper about either of two pairs of shoes creating partial prints, how print was likely created and had been recovered;

C v Atencio **12 MAC 747 (81)**—lay opinion OK re: sobriety (or lack);

C v Sands **424 M 184 (97)**—lay (cop) testimony not OK re "horizontal gaze nystagmus" test (involuntary eyeball movement) for sobriety; necessary to lay foundation that test is generally accepted in scientific community or is otherwise shown to be valid;

C v Santoli **424 M 837 (97)**—expert testimony on capacity of eyewitness to make identification admissible in judge's discretion; guidelines for exercise; on facts here (significant corroboration of ID testimony), no denial of Article 12 or 6th Amendment right to present all favorable proofs. *(For further ID holdings, including experts, See Chapter 18)*;

C v Zimmerman **441 M 146, 154–56 (2004) (concurring opinion)**—"own-race bias" ("performance deficit of one ethnic group in recognizing faces of another ethnic group compared with faces of one's own group") exists, and "the unreliability of cross-racial identification IS a subject 'beyond the ordinary experience and knowledge of the average juror'", and "expert testimony . . . should be admissible";

C v Ellis **373 M 1 (77)**—alleged inconsistencies between test-firing and homicide go to weight of ballistics, not admissibility;

C v Jacobson **19 MAC 666 (85)**—OK expert testimony on arson *(See Chapter 21-Y)*;

11-I.1.b. Photo Images

See Chapter 18, re Identification issues;

C v Devlin **365 M 149 (74)**—bone structure I.D. (OK though opinion = re: ultimate issue);

C v Key **21 MAC 293 (85)**—irrelevant that cop thought D looked like photo of another guy whom V said resembled assailant;

C v Austin **421 M 357, 366 (95)**—witness familiar with D may not give opinion that robber in surveillance videotape is D (here no relief: overwhelming evidence of G);

C v Bourgeois **391 M 869 (84)**—cop can say Ds were people seen in bank photos if knew D's earlier appearance;

C v Pleas **49 MAC 321 (2000)**—citing Prop.M.R. Evid. 701; admissibility of testimony that person in videotape/photo is D depends on several factors; if image is very clear, opinion isn't needed; if it's "hopelessly obscure," witness is no better suited than jury to make identification; witness must be shown to have been very familiar w/person's appearance at time photo was taken; testimony is more likely to be helpful if culprit is disguised in photo or has changed his appearance since time of crime; it would have been preferable here for judge to shield from jurors fact that witness was cop (though he testified to knowing D and D's family socially for 9–10 years, i.e., not "work-related" familiarity);

11-I.1.c.   Voice Identification

C v Lykus **367 M 191 (75)**—voiceprint generally accepted in scientific community;

Corsetti **387 M 1 n.3 (82)**—authentication of identification of phone voice;

See Chapter 18 re: voice ID;

11-I.2.   Psychiatric

C v Vazquez **387 M 96 (82)**—expert can tell opinion re: criminal responsibility but only per McHoul standard; can't just say D "criminally responsible";

C v Westmoreland **388 M 269 (83)**—expert can give opinion that D criminally responsible because question framed under McHoul standard;

C v Pallotta **36 MAC 669 (94)**—judge cannot exclude expert's **McHoul** testimony on ground that **he** believes D to be afflicted only with a personality disorder & drug ingestion; judge cannot "claim superior expertness" and thus "subvert the function of expert testimony as a help to non-experts, including the judge";

C v Schulze **389 M 735 (83)**—licensed DOCTOR (not a shrink) can tell observations, treatment, diagnosis of D seen at time near incident; unless qualified, though, can't give opinion re: responsibility;

C v Callahan **386 M 784 (82)**—expert can tell "all" that's relevant to D's mental illness, e.g., relationship between suicide & homicide;

C v Pike **431 M 212, 223 (2000)**—D's use of expert testimony re: battered woman's syndrome NOT LIMITED to instances where D uses force against her batterer;

C v Nerette **432 M 534 (2000)**—no ineffective assistance in failing to present expert to testify that D's statement had been psychologically coerced, because trial judge asserted, in ruling on post-conviction R.30 motion, that he wouldn't have allowed such evidence to reach jury because "lay people" capable of assessing all factors underlying psychologist's opinion here; SJC found no error;

C v Hunter **427 M 651 (98)**—OK to admit expert testimony that D's conduct at trial is inconsistent with post-traumatic stress disorder (during showing of combat/Vietnam film), citing *C v Smiledge* **419 M 156 (94)** jury may consider D's courtroom demeanor when his sanity is at issue (citing *C v Louraine* **390 M 28, 34 (83)**);

C v Robinson **14 MAC 591 (82)**—if diminished capacity defense, shrink can tell diminished capacity: premeditate, but not diminished capacity: malice (not a defense);

See Chapter 16, Defenses;

See also Chapter 7-G re: opinions as to competence of witness;

C v Reed **417 M 558 (94)**—no error in denying access to murder witness's psychological treatment records given defense claim that examination could have led to psych./expert testimony on the witness's "veracity": no opinion evidence on credibility would have been admissible;

C v Gurney **413 M 97 (92)**—D had right to have expert explain that D's calm trial demeanor was due to antipsychotic medications;

C v Schuchardt **408 M 347 (90)**—expert testimony about emotional harm from threat of nuclear war was not admissible in necessity defense case where it failed to establish that a severe threat was "generally recognized" & "not fairly debatable"; see Liacos dissent;

C v Fayerweather **406 M 78 (89)**—psychiatric report that rape complainant heard voices weeks before incident was admissible without expert testimony to explain its relevance;

C v Day **409 M 719 (91)**—expert testimony that D fit child-batterer profile inadmissible because not relevant;

C v Frangipane **433 M 527 (2001)**—licensed certified social worker not competent to testify to "how a trauma victim stores and retrieves, or dissociates, a traumatic memory", because it's a "scientific"/"medical" matter; furthermore, at retrial, Lanigan hearing to be conducted prior to introduction of expert testimony on "dissociative memory loss or recovered memory," notwithstanding Commonwealth claim that its validity/reliability is "debatable" only in the context of memory recovery techniques in therapy, i.e., not here;

C v Roman **414 M 235 (93)**—letter by nontestifying psychiatrist which had been consulted by testifying expert not admissible because notice not given to opposing party as required by G.L. c. 233, § 79G;

11-I.2.a.   Medical Testimony (and Its Limits)

See also Chapter 11-H, Evidence/Sex Offenses;

C v Gardner **350 M 664 (66)**—expert can't give opinion whether entry's forcible (i.e., rape); jury equally able to draw conclusion;

C v Fayerweather **406 M 78 (89)**—psychiatric report that rape complainant heard voices weeks before incident was admissible without expert testimony to explain its relevance;

C v Kirkpatrick **423 M 436 (96)**—expert testimony required to make particular medical records have probative value because they were "not self-explanatory";

C v Bandy **38 MAC 329, 335–36 (95)**—similar;

C v Barresi **46 MAC 907 (99)**—similar; without such foundation, appellate court refused to hold abuse of discretion in excluding evidence proffered by D;

11-I.2.b.   Cops as "Experts"

C v Woods **419 M 366 (95)**—cop can't testify (over objection) that the exchange he saw was drug deal;

C v Savageau **42 MAC 518 (97)**—same;

C v Griffith **45 MAC 784 (98)**—similar;

C v Tanner **45 MAC 576, 581 (98)**—cop's opinion that possession of specific amount of drugs is more "consistent with" distribution than w/personal use not OK; "there are many potential pitfalls in allowing a percipient witness . . . to provide expert testimony"; in determining whether particular expert testimony is lawful, should "focus the analysis on whether the evidence is explanatory"; but see *C v Martin* **48 MAC 391 (99)** ignoring *Tanner*;

C v Arias **55 MAC 782, 787–88 (2002)**—*Tanner* **45 MAC 576, 581** error, but no objection, no substantial risk of miscarriage of justice here;

C v Delgado **51 MAC 661 (2001)**—"a person who would have that much heroin on him, I would believe would be a distributor of heroin" = opinion as to D's guilt;

C v Dancy **75 MAC 175 (2009)**—"close question" but no relief/harmless: "based upon my training and experience, that would certainly pique my curiosity and it would lead me to believe that there may have been a drug transaction" was testimony of cop/drug "expert";

C v Ortiz **50 MAC 304 (2000)**—cop's opinion that D was "a runner, i.e., someone who brings customers to somebody who is selling" was inadmissible & intrusion into fact-finding function of jury; *see also* **Lonardo 74 MAC 566 (2009)**—expert's testimony that she equated the term "runner" with someone who fraudulently "staged" accidents, when evidence would be that D (an attorney) acknowledged use of "runners" "should not have been allowed," but no objection & no "risk of a miscarriage of justice" found here;

C v Miranda **441 M 783 (2004)**—though concept of "lookout" may be common knowledge, judge had discretion to find that cop's "expert" testimony would assist, i.e., drug dealers often work in pairs, one to conduct the transaction, another to function as the dealer's "eyes and ears" [to contradict evidence that D appeared to be passive bystander];

C v Frias **47 MAC 293 (99)**—OK for cop to testify to modus operandi of generic drug operators, i.e. use of "distribution points" (unfurnished houses or apartments) at "mid-level", i.e., before street sales, but cop should not testify to conformance of present case to model;

C v Harris **47 MAC 481 (99)**—OK for cop to testify that drug dealers use beepers;

C v Labitue **49 MAC 913 (2000)**—though cop shouldn't have testified that it's his "opinion that this is being used for distribution", this wasn't "significantly more prejudicial" than gist of two other cops' testimony that weight/packaging, etc. was "more consistent with intent to distribute than w/intent to purchase sizeable quantity for personal use";

C v Pike **430 M 317, 324–25 (99)**—OK cop testimony re: methods of operations of doctors and drug users in "drug diversion operations"; distinguished from inadmissible "profile" testimony;

C v Munera **31 MAC 380 (91)**—cop's "expert" testimony that dollar bills routinely used by dealers to package cocaine & that chunks consistent with dealing properly admissible;

C v Zavala **52 MAC 770, 775–76 (2001)**—cop opinion that D was "stashing" narcotics in area of a water hose = incompetent testimony (but no objection, no relief here);

C v Cimino **34 MAC 925 (93)**—cop's testimony on basis of "experience" that 17 cars with shot-out windows

sustained damage in same interval of time & by same method as 2 other cars: admissible;

C v Dennis **33 MAC 666 (92): S.C. 416 M 1001 (93)**—cop's "expert" testimony about modus operandi of street level drug dealing admissible;

C v Frias **47 MAC 293 (99)**—OK for cop to testify about modus operandi of "mid-level" drug distribution points (but shouldn't testify about present case conformance to same);

C v Cordero **34 MAC 923 (93)**—cop permissibly testified to ("expert") opinion that drugs were possessed with intent to distribute rather than for personal use;

C v Johnson **410 M 199, 202 (91)**—cop's testimony that 33+g of cocaine not consistent with personal use admissible; BUT SEE *C v Santiago* **41 MAC 916 (96)** opinion that the 13 bags of heroin on D's person were intended for distribution = inadmissible (when specific intent = element of crime, witness's opinion as to what D intended = improper); *C v Desources* **74 MAC 232 (2009)**—(16 "dime" baggies of marijuana, "economic" claim of cheaper in bulk, & **D carried no rolling paper or matches!!!!**) cop both used the "consistent with" terminology AND embellished by stating "this individual possessed these drugs with an intent to distribute them and not just for personal use", but latter = excused as "isolated" error;

C v Grissett **66 MAC 454 (2006)**—whether drugs are for personal use or distribution is not matter of common experience, so expert can opine, but must limit to opinion that hypothetical facts = "consistent with" possession with intent to distribute; witness here, in contrast, repeatedly opined D's guilt ("it's far more than a user would carry" and "it's clearly in my opinion for drug distribution") without cure by judge;

C v Murphy **34 MAC 16 (1993)**—trooper's claim that 7 packets containing total of 2.8 grams of cocaine (plus $355) was inconsistent with personal use because user would have bought single packet for less money was inadmissible "conjecture & surmise";

C v Little **453 M 766 (2009)**—"expert" cops can assert that drugs possessed by D were to be distributed, BUT "economic argument" that mere user would not purchase fifteen individual bags because he could get a better price by buying "bulk" was "likely beyond his expertise"; lack of objection = "substantial risk of miscarriage of justice" analysis, and none found; court found acceptable witness testimony that he hadn't in 20-year career seen "person buying fifteen . . . individual bags for personal use, they'll buy in bulk";

C v Rivera **425 M 633 (97)**—error to allow cop to testify, purportedly based on training & experience, that persons going upstairs to a door, conversing with person inside, & exchanging something were drug buyers, and D was drug seller (harmless here, on evidence, however);

C v Andujar **57 MAC 529, further review denied 439 M 1106 (2003)**—reversal for cop's testimony that he believed that four interactions he witnessed concerning D were street-level drug deliveries: improper intrusion upon jury's fact-finding function;

C v Barbosa **421 M 547 (95)**—error (conceded) for cop to testify (as "expert") that D was involved in drug sales (here harmless);

C v Soto **45 MAC 109, 114 (98)**—error for cop to testify that he stopped particular woman because he believed that she had just purchased cocaine from D: "expert may not . . . offer an opinion as to the defendant's innocence or guilt";

C v Lovejoy **39 MAC 930 (95)**—reversal for cop's "opinion" that exchange concerned drugs and other cop's "opinion" that the driver of a car earlier approached by D "swallowed some crack cocaine" when police approached: these opinions = only speculation;

C v Paniaqua **413 M 796 (92)**—drug lab certification that contents of 3 packets (commingled) contained cocaine did not require finding of not guilty where D seen to throw only 1 aluminum foil ball into trash can where officer claimed to have seen cocaine powder in ball & where officer's expertise not challenged by D at trial;

US v Boissoneault **926 F.2d 230 (2d Cir. '91)**—even if cop's "expert" opinion that totality of evidence suggested "street level distribution of cocaine" was admissible, such opinions are to be given little weight in sufficiency of evidence analysis; cop's opinion that papers were "accounts receivable" of drug transactions was admissible; reversal on sufficiency grounds nonetheless required;

C v Munera **31 MAC 380 (91)**—open question whether profile evidence about drug stash pads etc. is admissible; cop's "expert" testimony that dollar bills routinely used by dealers to package cocaine & that chunks consistent with dealing properly admissible;

C v Woods **36 MAC 950 (94)**—error for cops to testify that they "believed" D was involved in drug transaction; here harmless;

C v Garcia **46 MAC 466 (99)**—cop's testimony that he could have arrested D at apartment because he believed probable cause then existed is inadmissible; cop not legal expert and probable cause is question of law for judge, and this only implied cop's belief in D's guilt, prohibited territory for a witness;

C v Tanner **45 MAC 576 (98)**—cop testifying, "From my experience, I believed a drug transaction had taken place" and, as to another observed action, it "was consistent with a drug deal also": practice of permitting percipient police witness to provide expert testimony should be avoided when possible; "consistent with" locution will not necessarily avoid error; this is same as personal assurance by witness that the crime occurred; focus should be on whether "expert" testimony is explanatory and helps jurors interpret evidence that lies outside common experience; given strength of evidence here, errors harmless;

C v Jackson **45 MAC 666 (98)**—when defense presented testimony of alleged drug buyer that D did not provide the drugs at issue, reversible error for cop to testify that, in his experience of over 300 drug arrests, it was

common for drug buyer to refuse to reveal ID of seller because of fear of retribution; this amounted to "expert" testimony that defense witness was not credible;

C v Dayes **49 MAC 419, 422–23 (2000)**—error (though harmless here) to admit "experienced narcotics officer's" testimony that it was common for out-of-town drug dealer to move in with female and have all bills for the address in female's name, and that "out-of-town" dealer would usually supply female with drugs for her addiction or with money to pay the bills in exchange for his place of operation; other than evidence that female defendant's boyfriend resided out of town, there was no evidence that he was drug dealer or supplied money or drugs to D;

C v Wolcott **28 MAC 200 (90)**—cop's testimony about D's involvement with Jamaican posse inadmissible because witness was not qualified & because testimony conjectural, hearsay-based & prejudicial;

US v Doe **903 F.2d 16 (D.C. Cir. '90)**—cop's "expert" testimony about modus operandi of Jamaican drug dealers inadmissible because irrelevant & prejudicial;

US v Long **917 F.2d 691 (2d Cir. '90)**—FBI agent's "expert" testimony about workings of organized crime families inadmissible;

See also Chapter 21CC re: expert testimony in drug prosecutions;

11-I.2.c. Profile, Syndrome, and Modus Operandi Evidence

C v Federico **425 M 844 (97)**—"hypothetical" questions, based on case's facts, can be understood, improperly, as expert testimony that sexual abuse complainant is truthful; reversal required. See also *C v Spear* **43 MAC 583 (97)**—expert's opinion that child's "symptoms" were "consistent with those of a child who's been sexually abused" was improper endorsement of child's credibility;

C v Swain **36 MAC 433 (94)**—(similar);

C v LaCaprucia **41 MAC 496 (96)**—expert and other testimony was functional equivalent of vouching for child sexual assault complainant's credibility (profile of "incestuous family" and characteristics of "traumatized children" in "abusive homes");

C v Montanino **409 M 500 (91)**—cop's testimony that "most" sexual assault victims provide more details over time inadmissible: improperly vouched for credibility, and **no** witness, whether expert or not may give testimony that another witness's testimony is credible;

C v Trowbridge **419 M 750 (95)**—expert testimony that child complainant's behaviors were "common reaction of sexually abused child", etc. = prohibited endorsement of credibility;

C v McCaffrey **36 MAC 583 (94)**—child sexual assault complainant's own treating therapist should not testify to general behavioral characteristics of abused children: too likely viewed as endorsement of complainant's credibility;

C v Hudson **417 M 536 (94)**—while not finding abuse of discretion in admitting such testimony (in rebuttal, for rehabilitation), SJC asserts that expert testimony as to behaviors associated with "post-traumatic stress disorder" cannot be used to assert/imply that complainant exhibiting those behaviors is truthful, or that sexual abuse occurred;

C v Dockham **405 M 618, 630 (89)**—expert testimony about general behavioral characteristics of sexually abused children held admissible in judge's discretion;

C v Rather **37 MAC 140 (94)**—expert testimony re "hypothetical" child's denial that rape occurred (consistent with abuse): inadmissible vouching (but no relief here);

C v Richardson **423 M 180 (96)**—though harmless here, testimony that it "not unusual for children to not be consistent in terms of times, places" and that it would be "highly unusual" if complainant remembered times/dates, was "probably inadmissible";

C v Deloney **59 MAC 47, 56 (2003)**—permissible = "expert testimony that explains to the jury that child abuse victims may behave in ways that to lay persons may seem illogical"; "expert testimony that describes what a typical victim looks or acts like, and that suggests that child victims in a particular case have acted typically when compared to a 'norm' of child victims, may not be admitted"; concern is "fear that jury's responsibility ultimately to decide . . . whether children are telling the truth will give way to expert opinion that paints the child witness as a victim"; ERROR found in testimony here, but harmless due to D's admissions;

C v Bougas **59 MAC 368 (2003)**—within judge's discretion to admit expert testimony that abused children often delay reporting abuse (such testimony having been admitted for more than 10 years, there's "no basis for [D's] contention that it should have been excluded as unscientific and unreliable"), even as judge excluded testimony proffered by defense that children embroiled in family controversy often fabricate allegations of sexual abuse; latter evidence "essentially brands the class of which the alleged victim is a member as untrustworthy, and directly encourages the jury to disbelieve the specific child witness before them";

C v Colon **49 MAC 289, 290–91 (2000)**—no error found in Commonwealth's expert's testimony (pediatrician with expertise in allegedly sex-abused children), on rebuttal, that only 15–20 percent of girls with confirmed sex-abuse histories showed "physical signs" of vaginal penetration; this was info re: "medical interpretation of an absence of any physical evidence of penetration," a subject "beyond the jury's ken";

C v Day **409 M 719 (91)**—expert's opinion that D fit child-batterer profile inadmissible;

C v Roche **44 MAC 372 (98)**—expert's testimony concerning characteristics of "abusive male"/batterer inadmissible because invited jury to conclude that if D fit profile, likely guilty;

Adoption of Keefe **49 MAC 818 (2000)**—diagnosis of child's health problems was "Munchausen Syndrome by Proxy," which meant that a perpetrator caused various many many health problems in another individual as a means of gaining attention, & expert testimony toward this finding was admissible; testimony as to the "typical" perpetrator being the child's mother, often a health care professional, & often with child's father emotionally/physically absent should NOT have been admitted ("profile" evidence), but here didn't matter;

C v Grimshaw **412 M 505 (92)**—[prior to G.L. c. 233, § 23F,] was open question whether battered women syndrome a valid defense in Massachusetts;

C v Pike **431 M 212 (2000)**—battered woman syndrome evidence has gained acceptance; in appropriate case, may qualify as newly-discovered evidence (because at time of trial the battered woman-D was too enmeshed in such syndrome to realize);

C v Conaghan **433 M 105 (2000)**—SJC orders competency examination under G.L. c. 123, § 15(a), for D on Rule 30 motion to withdraw guilty plea, thereby allowing funds for examination of D to determine whether, at time of G plea, she was "battered woman" and plea was thus involuntary;

C v Rodriquez **418 M 1 (94)**—battered woman evidence admissible to show self-defense,

C v Goetzendanner **42 MAC 637 (97)**—battered woman evidence admissible to explain alleged V's erratic behavior;

C v Crawford **429 M 60 (99)**—battered woman evidence admissible to prove that statements to police = involuntary;

C v Lazarovich **410 M 466 (91)**—expert testimony that D fit battered woman syndrome assumed admissible to show she didn't share specific intent to maim her daughter;

G.L. c. 233, § 23F—admissibility of evidence to establish reasonableness of use of force in particular circumstances (statute promulgated in recognition of "battered woman syndrome");

C v Goetzendanner **42 MAC 637 (97)**—battered woman expert testimony admitted **against** D in aggravated rape, kidnapping, and assaults prosecution, to counter possible impact of victim's erratic conduct vis a vis defendant; advanced degree or clinical training not required for expert status;

C v Mamay **407 M 412 (90)**—expert testimony that complainant fits rape trauma syndrome generally admissible; see Liacos, concurring; But see *C v Montanino* **409 M 500 (91)** cop testimony that most sexual assault victims provide more detail over time requires reversal; improperly vouched for complainant's credibility;

C v Federico **425 M 844 (97)**—similar, use of hypothetical questions;

C v Brouillard **40 MAC 448 (96)**—child sex assault complainants' therapist impermissibly vouched their credibility, both explicitly and by linking his observations of them to general syndromes and predictions of future psychological maladies;

C v Perkins **39 MAC 577 (95)**—experts opining that sexual abuse can occur in a public area, that absence of physical injury was not inconsistent with claimed abuse & neither was willingness to return to abuse scene, required reversal as prohibited endorsement of credibility; but see *C v Malchionno* **43 MAC 73 (94)** after complainant was impeached with prior denials of assault, no relief for "vouching" testimony by social worker (false denials not unusual because complainants are "embarrassed");

C v Colin C. **419 M 54 (94)**—child abuse expert was improperly allowed to testify to her opinion that complainants had been abused (essentially vouching for their credibility);

C v Trowbridge **419 M 750 (95)**—prosecution witness's testimony that child's behavior (clinging to mother, avoiding eye contact during pediatric gynecological visit) was "common reaction" of sexually abused child, and that absence of physical trauma was consistent with digital vaginal penetration and fondling = prohibited endorsement of credibility; defense expert's proffered testimony that child appeared relaxed & affectionate in interaction with D (father) should have been admitted, but testimony that D didn't have personality traits of sex abuser and that child's mother's anger and bitterness caused child to be her ally = inadmissible;

Estelle v McGuire **502 US 62 (91)**—child's prior unrelated injuries to show that victim fit battered child syndrome evidence admissible; federal due process challenge rejected;

C v LeFave **407 M 927 (90)**—expert testimony that obtaining pornographic photos is a common motive for sexual abuse of children was properly admissible;

C v Powers **36 MAC 65 (94)**—4 fresh complaint witnesses (2 "experts") testifying that they believed complainant was truthful = reversal;

C v King **445 M 217 (2005)**—at fn.26: even though "first complaint" witness may testify to complainant's demeanor, witness may not testify to belief in complainant's truthfulness or otherwise supplant fact finder's function in determining credibility;

C v Dennis **33 MAC 666 (92), aff'd, 416 M 1001 (93)**—cop's "expert" testimony about modus operandi of street level drug dealing properly admissible;

C v Wolcott **28 MAC 200 (90)**—cop's testimony about D's involvement with Jamaican posse inadmissible because witness was not qualified & because testimony conjectural, hearsay-based & prejudicial;

US v Long **917 F.2d 691 (2d Cir. '90)**—FBI agent's "expert" testimony about workings of organized crime families inadmissible;

US v Doe **903 F.2d 16 (D.C. Cir. '90)**—cop's "expert" testimony about modus operandi of Jamaican drug dealers inadmissible because irrelevant & prejudicial;

C v Bonds **445 M 821 (2006)**—testimony by rape complainant's mother that complainant was overly trusting was admissible (to excuse her visit to D's residence after telephone conversation in which D asserted interest in sex with her), because it "gave the jury a clear picture of who the victim was" & served to explain her limited mental capacity; criticism that "relevance" objection didn't serve to preserve appellate argument as to impermissible "character" testimony;

11-I.2.d.   Blood, Serology, and DNA

C v Fatalo **346 M 266 (63)**—blood test OK to show no paternity;

C v Beausoleil **397 M 206 (86)**—HLA test proves paternity;

C v Rocha **57 MAC 550 (2003)**—judge didn't abuse discretion in admitting expert evidence (DNA paternity tests) that probability of D's paternity of victim's fetus was 99.7 percent or 98.3 percent, where evidence was relevant to determination of whether D had had intercourse with victim;

C v Smith **35 MAC 655 (93)**—trial judge found testimony re blood alcohol level calculated by "retrograde extrapolation" (i.e., if it was .06 two hours after fatal vehicle crash, was .09 or .10 at relevant time) inadmissible;

C v Senior **433 M 453 (2001)**—judge didn't abuse discretion in finding "retrograde extrapolation" method of calculating blood alcohol level at earlier time admissible given voir dire evidence here, notwithstanding fact that its validity isn't "universally acknowledged";

C v Colturi **448 M 809 (2007)**—expert testimony on "retrograde extrapolation" isn't a prerequisite to admission of breathalyzer test even after 2003 amendment to G.L. c. 90, § 24, "so long as the test is conducted within a reasonable period of time after the driver's last operation of the vehicle", "reasonable time" being defined as up to three hours between testing and operation, with room to argue different period "reasonable" on particular facts and circumstances; statute now makes it illegal, per se, to operate vehicle with blood alcohol level of .08 or more;

C v Gomes **403 M 258 (88)**—electrophoresis blood group test OK; statistical odds (1.2% black males have similar) OK, too, because empirical, not speculative;

C v Cordle **412 M 172 (92)**—cops' failure to conduct blood or gunshot residue on D's hands was valid basis for defense, but judge has discretion not to instruct on it;

C v Yesilciman **406 M 736 (90)**—blood stain evidence admissible even though undetermined whether of human or animal origin;

C v Duguay **430 M 397, 401–2 (99)**—orthotolidine testing, though just "screening test" for presence of blood (& thus gives many false positives), admissible; danger of unfair prejudice doesn't outweigh probative value; test limitations should be revealed on cross-examination;

C v Gordon **422 M 816 (96)**—though D argued on appeal that prosecution witness had testified that orthotolidine test was 'conclusive' for presence of blood & this contrary to **all** scientific opinion, SJC claimed that witness's testimony was that "particular" color changes in the test, in her 8 years of experience, were specific for blood (& that this not necessarily contrary to uniform scientific opinion); **Lanigan** test "inapplicable where witness testimony is based on personal observations rather than dependent on scientific theories or principles";

C v Sims **30 MAC 25 (91)**—blood grouping & phosphoglucomutase evidence tending to exclude D as rapist was not so strong as to require finding of not guilty;

C v Phoenix **409 M 408 (91)**—genetic allotype testing of blood stains was admissible because generally accepted by scientific community; defects in employing test relevant to weight, not admissibility;

C v Russo **30 MAC 923 (91)**—blood tests not related to treatment or diagnosis were admissible because part of routine workup for certain medical problem;

C v Curnin **409 M 218 (91)**—DNA profile evidence inadmissible because lab techniques for determining statistical probability of a "match" not generally accepted in scientific community under Frye test; techniques for determining whether DNA match exists may not be generally accepted either;

C v Lanigan **413 M 154 (92)**—positive DNA match inadmissible because techniques for determining statistical probability not generally accepted; DNA non-match inadmissible because based upon only 1 probe rather than 2 as generally required;

C v Vao Sok **425 M 787 (97)**; *C v Rosier* **425 M 807 (97)**; *C v Fowler* **425 M 819 (97)**—DNA match" testimony admissible on evidence here;

C v Mathews **450 M 858 (2008)**—admissibility of DNA results, even when inconclusive, to be determined on case-by-case basis; when defense was challenge to integrity of police investigation, including adequacy of testing of large number of blood samples, prosecutor could introduce testimony that tests were performed and results (even if inconclusive) were obtained; issue is "primarily one of relevance";

C v Nesbitt **452 M 236 (2008)**—that blood was on handles of a bicycle found ¼ mile away from crime scene, along with testimony that neither victim nor D "could be excluded" as a source of the blood (and in circumstances NO person could be excluded as source) was acknowledged to be "at a minimum, prejudicial"; no substantial likelihood of miscarriage of justice, however, because weight of DNA evidence was effectively challenged on cross, and conceded in DA's closing to have been useless; "for inconclusive DNA evidence to be admissible, it must be probative of an issue of consequence in the case",

C v Grinkley **75 MAC 798 (2009)**—because "mixed" sample from victim did not contain D's "entire" DNA profile, expert's testimony that only one in 320 billion African-Americans were possible contributors to the mixture found on the sample was "irrelevant" and "misleading"; "[w]hat the Commonwealth submitted here, ostensibly product rule statistics for a mixed sample without an identified primary contributor, was not permissible for reasons which should have been obvious"; "product rule" has been held to be valid method for calculating frequency profiles involving NONMIXED DNA samples (and though perhaps victim was the primary contributor, testing did not

use this necessary factor); *C v McNickles* **434 M 839 (2001)**—is distinguished: *McNickles* concerned "use of likelihood ratios, not product rules", former "compar[ing] probability that [D] was a contributor … with the probability that he was not a contributor to the sample," appropriately used for evaluating "test results of mixed samples when the primary and secondary contributors cannot be distinguished" (citing *Gaynor* **443 M 245, 268 (2005)**; **important factor** = whether or not Commonwealth "exaggerate[s] the significance" of given DNA evidence (75 MAC at 805–06); likelihood that D contributed to mixed sample analyzed "was not in any way calculated," and judge abused discretion in allowing Commonwealth to offer statistics based on product rule calculation;

C v Arroyo **442 M 135, 145 (2004)**—to preserve objections to DNA analysis, must file pretrial motion with the specific grounds, and must request hearing under principles in *Canavan's Case* **432 M 304 (2000)**;

C v Sparks **433 M 654 (2001)**—lab director of Cellmark Laboratories could testify though she was not the analyst who had conducted the blood testing and not "the actual staff scientist who had conducted the initial reviews of the analysts' reports," but had instead reviewed all the records; expert may base opinion on facts/data not in evidence if data = independently admissible & a permissible basis for expert to consider in formulating an opinion; *see also C v Duarte* **56 MAC 714 (2002)**;

11-I.2.e. Fingerprints

C v Phoenix **409 M 408 (91)**—photograph of print destroyed during reasonable forensic testing admissible;

C v Drayton **386 M 39 (82)**—fingerprint expert can't say statistical probability of D's prints sharing 12 points; dubious whether stats. ever admissible [maybe to explain opinion (n.10)]; harmless here; [but see *Foley* **7 MAC 608 (79)**];

C v Cintron **438 M 779 (2003)**—"[computerized] automated fingerprint filing & identification system" (AFIS) primer, reliability or lack thereof; D here shows no prejudice from loss of original fingerprint since photo of it formed basis for ID, D's own expert indicated photo of print was "qualitatively excellent," & Commonwealth used only the same evidence;

C v Fazzino **27 MAC 485 (89)**—D's fingerprint at scene sufficient to convict D of B&E only if prosecution evidence reasonably excludes hypothesis that print left at another time; here, additional evidence that D knew how to use torch made fingerprint evidence sufficient;

C v LeClaire **28 MAC 932 (90)**—D's thumb print on window sufficient to convict D of breaking & entering where it formed pattern with other smeared prints, suggesting that D had grasped window through opening, & where D was shown not to have had authorized access to room;

C v Morris **422 M 254 (96)**—D's fingerprint on mask used by an intruder = insufficient to link D to crime;

C v Palmer **59 MAC 415 (2003)**—circumstances were such that D's fingerprint almost certainly was left (inside victim's truck) at time of crime;

C v Baptista **32 MAC 910 (92)**—D's fresh prints near coin box inside broken soda machine sufficient to convict D of breaking & entering;

C v Laguer **448 M 585, 598 (2007)**—assertion that for fingerprints to be "probative," there had to be evidence to establish when they were left on the telephone (as part of rationale used to reject D's claim that four fingerprints on base of telephone whose cord was used to bind rape victim, not matching D, were exculpatory evidence which had to be disclosed pre-trial);

US v Plaza **179 F.Supp 444 (E.D. Pennsylvania 2001)**—reconsideration & vacation of decision 3 months earlier which had barred fingerprint identification testimony as 'unreliable' under *Daubert* **509 US 579 (93)** & *Kumho Tire* **526 US 137 (99)**;

C v Patterson **445 M 626 (2005)**—"most common method of latent fingerprint identification, ACE-V" ("analysis, comparison, evaluation, and verification"), was used to claim that four latent prints were left by D's hand, though no single latent impression on its own could reliably be matched to its allegedly corresponding finger; while ACE-V method is generally sufficiently reliable to be admitted, Commonwealth failed to meet burden of establishing reliability of ID when no single latent print could be individually matched;

11-I.2.f. Hair

C v Pandolfino **33 MAC 96 (92)**—statistical probability that D's hair matched evidence was inadmissible; "trial by mathematics" discussed;

C v Cardozo **29 MAC 645 (90)**—expert testimony that pubic hair sample differed from D's exemplar was admissible on identification issue;

11-I.2.g. Handwriting

C v Camelio **1 MAC 296 n.3 (73)**—discretion whether handwriting expert's qualified; though original's better to compare, copy is discretionary; SEE ALSO *C v Harwood* **432 M 290 (2000)** loss of original letter, without which defendant's expert couldn't evaluate signature [copy inadequate for purpose], justified sanction of preclusion of testimony from prosecution witness saying that the signature wasn't his (Commonwealth contended D forged signature); SJC rejected claim of Commonwealth that action (losing letter) of insurance fraud bureau, funded by insurance companies, but having "close & coordinated relationship" with Attorney General, wasn't imputable to Comm; court reasoned that D had lost opportunity to effectively cross-examine the witness;

C v Murphy **59 MAC 571 (2003)**—D didn't request *Lanigan* hearing [419 M 15, 24–27 (94)] regarding handwriting matching; appellate court says handwriting expert's testimony re: who wrote/signed document is "soft science," "highly dependent on information derived from such sources as personal observations, clinical assessments, and statistical data," and thus defers to trial judge's exercise of discretion; cites to appellate decisions noting (without contest) "handwriting expert" testimony;

C v O'Connell **438 M 658 (2003)**—bank employee with 20 years' experience as teller, customer service representative, & vice-president for security = qualified to opine that signature on checks didn't match account holder's signature even though she had only witnessed his signature once; further, jury could decide whether signatures were made by same person without need of expert testimony;

C v O'Laughlin **446 M 188 (2006)**—no error in exclusion of handwritten note found in victim's bedroom, though D claimed that it implied that V's husband was hostile and motivated to attack V because of her extramarital ongoing affair; V denied that it was in her writing and did not recall writing the note; though expert testimony wasn't required and jurors could have compared this writing to a writing admittedly written by victim, content of note didn't reveal who speaker was and who was subject of speaker's venom, so jury would necessarily only "speculate as to its meaning and genesis";

C v Dubois **451 M 20 (2008)**—prosecution expert testified that specimen of "reverse writing" was "probably" written by the writer of the known samples (D), and acknowledged on cross that she preferred to work with 'original documents when comparing them to known ones,' but had only the "reverse writing" here, could not determine whether the original writing from which reverse writing was created was a fabrication, and that her opinion about author was a "qualified" one; 126-paragraph affidavit submitted by defense expert with motion for new trial, asserting that prosecution witness's testimony was unreliable and inconsistent with accepted body of knowledge and experience in field of document examination = post-conviction criticism by one expert on credibility of another expert not "newly discovered evidence" and not basis for new trial;

11-I.2.h. Drugs and Alcohol

C v Johnson **410 M 199 (91)**—drug lab's calculation of total weight from random sampling of 9 of 71 samples was admissible & survived required finding motion;

Gonzalez v Commissioner of Correction **407 M 448 (90)**—judge's finding that "double-EMIT" urinalysis test did not meet Frye test remanded for determination under lesser standard for DOC disciplinary proceedings;

C v Cruz **413 M 686 (92)**—judge's exclusion of expert opinion that alcohol would have severely affected D's judgment during killing required reversal because relevant to deliberate premeditation & extreme atrocity & cruelty; instruction on blood alcohol level for intoxication in OUI cases not appropriate in homicide cases;

C v Senior **433 M 453 (2001)**—retrograde extrapolation analysis of blood alcohol level admissible here;

11-I.2.i.   Polygraph

[PRIOR LAW, LARGELY IRRELEVANT OR "BAD" AFTER *C v MENDES* **406 M 201 (89)** :

C v Vitello **376 M 426 (78)**—polygraph evidence admissible only for D's credibility, if D testifies at trial;

C v Walker **392 M 152 (84)**—not admissible for witness even if stipulation;

C v Foley **7 MAC 608 (79)**—examiner can't give statistical reliability; caution re: puffery about examiner as expert;

C v Howard **367 M 569 (75)**—reverse jury-waived conviction after trial judge offered D polygraph to resolve case]

C v Mendes **406 M 201 (89)**—all uses of polygraph evidence at trial barred because not "generally accepted by relevant scientific community";

US v Scheffer **523 US 303 (98)**—military rule of evidence barring admission of all polygraph evidence not unconstitutional;

C v Stewart **422 M 385 (96)**—post-trial polygraph results not "newly discovered" for purposes of new trial motion, and SJC makes clear that Lanigan standard for "expert" evidence (413 M 154 ([92]) does not assure admission of polygraph;

C v Kent K. a juvenile **427 M 754, 763 (98)**—SJC faults D for not attempting to meet "the very demanding *Stewart* **422 M 385, 389** standard relating to the reliability of the polygrapher who conducted his test"; no error in denying D hearing on the admissibility of polygraph evidence;

C v Duguay **430 M 397 (99)**—polygraph testimony properly excluded because not established that expert "had in similar circumstances demonstrated, in a statistically valid number of independently verified and controlled tests, the high level of accuracy of the conclusions that [he] reached in those tests"; rejected D's argument that this standard established impossible bar to polygraph evidence;

C v Auclair **444 M 348 (2005)**—police used polygraph on D during his police station interview, & examiner told him that he didn't believe D was being truthful, prompting confession; D hadn't been told prior to going voluntarily to station that polygrapher was waiting, but agreed to take exam, specifically, & examiner recited Miranda warnings: no suppression;

C v Jones **75 MAC 38, 46 (2009)**—no abuse of discretion in denying motion for mistrial: D's "single statement that he agreed to take a polygraph exam was inadvertently included on" recorded statement "that was played once for the jury before it was redacted";

11-J. PRIVILEGES

See Chapter 6-D re records of witness/complainants;
Article 12 and Fifth Amendment—(*See Chapter 7, Preparing for Trial, and Chapter 11-G, Admissions of Defendant; see also Chapter 2, re attorney-client privileges, and Young, Pollets & Poreda, Evidence (2d ed. 1998), Article V, §§501–28*); Rape Counselor, G.L. c. 233, § 20J (*See Chapter 11-H, above*) Rape Victim[sic]'s Name in Police Report, G.L. c. 265, § 24C (86) (*see Chapter 6-E*) Domestic Violence Counselor, G.L. c. 233, § 20K (86) Psychotherapist, G.L. c. 233, § 20B (*See Chapter 11-H above & Chapter 7D, E, F*) Court-Ordered Shrink Examination, G.L. c. 233, § 23B (*See Chapter 7*) DMH records, G.L. c. 123, § 36 [see *O'Brien* **27 MAC 184 (89)**] Social Worker, G.L. c. 112, § 135 (*See Collett* **387 M 424 (82)**, *Chapter 11-H, above, & O'Brien* **27 MAC 184 (89)** *below*] Hospital Record (without consent/court order), G.L. c. 111, § 70 (*See Chapter 7, Subpoenas*) Child of Parent, G.L. c. 233, § 20 (86) Spousal, G.L. c. 233, § 20 [see *C v Maillet* **400 M 572 (87)**] Informants (*See Chapter 6, Discovery*) Priest, G.L. c. 233, § 20A Mediator, G.L. c. 233, §23C (*See Chapter 14E, Mediation*) Fair Info. Practices Act, G.L. c. 66A [see *C v O'Brien* **27 MAC 184 (89)** D gets G.L. c. 119, § 51A investigative reports; [see *Jones* **404 M 339 (89)** D gets G.L. c. 112, § 135 (f) records of G.L. c. 119, § 51B report; other § 135 DSS reports not "absolute" privilege (like G.L. c. 233, § 20J), so in camera review without counsel (cf. Lynch/Nolan dissent) sees if "material to defense";] harm because inconsistencies = exculpatory; in camera review for 233/20B, 123/36, 66A questions re: DMH records]; AIDS test results, G.L. c. 111, § F [see *C v Smith* **58 MAC 381 (2003)**—grand jury could have obtained court order to test D for human immunodeficiency virus after he threatened to kill persons, saying he had AIDS, so counsel's stipulation that D was HIV-positive wasn't ineffective assistance];

C v Vega **449 M 227 (2007)**—G.L. c. 112, § 172, making confidential a communication to an "allied mental health . . . professional," creates an "evidentiary privilege" for such a communication, similar to statutory privileges for psychotherapist, or social worker, or sexual assault or domestic violence counselor, communications;

C v Kane **388 M 128 (83)**—DA can call priest who said he'd keep privilege because reasonable to assume he'd cave in to judge;

In the Matter of a Grand Jury Subpoena **430 M 590 (2000)**—parents of juveniles accused of rape were called before grand jury to testify about what minor children told them; SJC held that G.L. c. 233, § 20 applies only when child is called to testify against parent; subpoenas were stayed pending conclusion of January, 2000 legislative session; further, suggestion that questioning parents about certain communications "would raise serious issues regarding the [juvenile's] privilege against self-incrimination or the right to counsel" (e.g., consultation by the accused with "interested adult" prior to Miranda rights' waiver, or communications between child and parent leading to required written parental consent to juvenile's jury waiver under G.L. c. 119, § 55A) AND particular confidential communications may be privileged under the Fifth Amendment or article 12 (footnotes 1, 15, 17);

Ohio v Reiner **532 US 17 (2001)**—a witness's assertion of innocence doesn't deprive her of 5th Amendment privilege against self-incrimination (context of D's alternate suspect in homicide, i.e., the babysitter, being granted immunity to testify that she had nothing to do with injuries);

Douglas v Alabama **380 US 415 (65)**—denied confrontation to call co-D who took 5th Amendment & then read his confession implicating D;

C v King **436 M 252 (2002)**—after foundation requirements for admission of spontaneous utterances were met, judge had no discretion to decide that they were unreliable & thereby exclude them; since witness invoked 5th Amendment at trial, she couldn't be cross-examined re: the utterances, BUT SJC remanded for determination of whether her testimony at voir dire operated to waive the privilege (if so, there was prejudicial error to allow her to invoke the privilege at trial);

C v Connors **447 M 313 (2006)**—while D had right to refuse to speak to "qualified examiners" in SDP proceedings, he couldn't "selectively invoke this privilege"; no denial of privilege against self-incrimination to require him to submit to exam by Commonwealth's psychiatrist as a condition of the admission of "his" evidence (the result of psych. exam which included interview[s] with D); listing of analogous cases in similar contexts, e.g., *Blaisdell v. Commonwealth* 372 M 753 (77);

C v Hesketh **386 M 153 (82)**—witness taking 5th Amendment shouldn't be before jury, but discretionary where no big harm;

C v Nadile **10 MAC 913 (80)**—(same);

C v Fisher **433 M 340, 349–50 & n.11 (2001)**—witness's invocation of 5th Amendment before jury is prejudicial when witness is accomplice of D, because it implies witness = criminal, & "strongly suggest[s]" D is, also; proper question is whether witness's refusal to testify (whether or not it's based on 5th Amendment) will lead jury to "potentially draw some inference adverse to" D; if it's clear that witness intends to invoke 5th A., witness shouldn't be called before jury; if there's 'some advance warning' that it might occur, judge should conduct voir dire without jury; suggestion that when witness illegitimately invokes 5th A., prior recorded testimony might not be admissible because witness isn't really unavailable;

C v Farley **443 M 740 (2005)**—after trial judge ruled that witness had voluntarily waived 5th Amendment privilege by testifying at first trial, he was compelled to testify at second trial; allowing him to assert 5th Amendment privilege in response to several questions didn't here violate D's right to confrontation; BUT privilege against self-incrimination was held to be waived concerning question about a fact "related to but not necessarily mentioned in" the testimony given at the first trial;

C v DiPietro **373 M 369 (77)**—DA can call wife expecting marital disqualification (i.e., unavailable) before using prior testimony; (ed: circumvention of the rule)

C v Negron **441 M 685 (2004)**—claim of spousal privilege made D's wife "unavailable" at probation revocation hearing, so that cop's testimony re: wife's allegations, if substantial indicia of reliability, admissible;

In the Matter of a Grand Jury Subpoena **447 M 88 (2006)**—spousal privilege (G.L. c. 233, § 20, Second) applies only to "TRIAL", so wife couldn't claim it to avoid testifying before grand jury;

C v Dwyer **10 MAC 707 (80)**—refusal of witness on cross-examination to answer questions re: collateral matters is not ground for striking witness's testimony;

C v Turner **393 M 685 (85)**; *Turner v Fair* **617 F.2d 7 (1st Cir. '80)**—witness taking 5th re: collateral matter (his prior robbery of same store, to show bias) not reason to strike all testimony; [SJC: not only collateral, but inadmissible];

C v Cook **380 M 314 (80)**—ineffective assistance of counsel not to object to co-D taking stand & 5th Amendment;

Namet v US **373 U.S. 179 (63)**—DA can't add to case with witness who avoids cross-examination (by taking 5th re: conspiracy, though had pled G.);

C v Bishop **416 M 169 (93)**—procedure whereby defense attempts to gain access to possibly "privileged" material concerning assault complainant containing relevant and exculpatory information; standard for obtaining in camera review announced here was altered (to D's detriment) in *C v Fuller, post,* **423 M 216 (96)**; BUT NOW SEE *C v Dwyer* **448 M 122 (2006)**—SUMMARIZED, POST;

C v Sheehan **48 MAC 916 (2000)**—reversal for failure to allow defense to use records disclosed after **Bishop** discovery request/allowance; mental health records indicated child complainant had tendency to engage in fantasy, to become dissociated, etc.; judge must resolve any doubt about admissibility in favor of D; decision whether records were more helpful or hurtful to defense was up to defense counsel, NOT trial judge; **S.C.** on further appellate review, **435 M 183 (2001)** records were erroneously withheld (contained info supporting D's claim that complainant had fantasized sexual conduct); Commonwealth's claim that the records were not helpful to D because they attributed complainant's difficulties with reality TO the alleged sexual assault rebuffed: "it was for defense counsel to decide whether their value outweighed their harm"; at least three members of SJC now willing to abandon the convoluted "Bishop-Fuller" procedure for obtaining access to records: it doesn't "belittle" the privileges at stake to say that D's "right to a fair trial is of greater weight" (Sosman, J., concurring opinion); and now see *C v Dwyer* **448 M 122 (2006)**, summarized *post;*

C v Oliveira **431 M 609 (2000)**—perhaps trial counsel was ineffective in failing to seek access to mental health treatment records concerning one of two minors allegedly sexually assaulted by D; remand to determine whether contents of records were such that D was deprived of substantial ground of defense;

C v Neumyer **432 M 23 (2000)**—on further review of 48 MAC 154 (99) - date, time, and fact of telephone call made by complainant to rape crisis center not privileged under G.L. c. 233, § 20J; judge could order production of records under M.R.Crim.P. 14(a)(1) despite fact that prosecutor didn't have custody/control; whether rape center had standing to assert complainant's "due process rights" not reached, though rape center could assert complainant's "statutory right" to privilege; proffer by D held sufficient (recited complainant's probable cause hearing testimony, including her uncertainty, until after telephone call with rape crisis center, that she had been raped, and her apparent fear that D's girlfriend [complainant's best friend] would learn of D's activity with her; fact that she spent night in D's bedroom less than one week after reporting that D raped her);

C v Moran **439 M 482 (2003)**—error to exclude medical record of rape complainant, who testified that she wouldn't have consented to sex because she had had recent laparoscopy, and that she had taken pain killer because of this surgery; record revealed an entirely different medical procedure, involving a different bodily entry point; no privilege applied, & no basis for invoking "Bishop-Fuller" protocol;

C v Fuller **423 M 216 (96)**—rape counselor records (G.L. c. 233, § 20J) subject to in-camera review only if D demonstrates "good faith, specific and reasonable basis for believing that the records will contain exculpatory evidence that is relevant and material to" D's guilt;

C v Dwyer **448 M 122 (2006)**—protocols established by *C v Bishop* and *C v Fuller* are reconsidered, and now changed, as follows: (1) before judge determines whether summons for records may issue to any person or institution, the custodian of records and person who is subject of records shall be given notice and opportunity to be heard re: whether records are relevant or covered by statutory privilege (but privilege will be presumed, and won't be deemed waived even if subject fails to assert statutory privilege, & there's no requirement that judge determine at this stage whether or not the records are in fact privileged); (2) if judge orders issuance of Rule 17(a)(2) summons, all presumptively privileged records so summonsed are retained in court under seal, to be inspected only by counsel of record for D; (3) before inspecting such records, counsel shall sign and file protective order containing stringent nondisclosure provisions [i.e., inter alia, can't copy, disclose, disseminate contents to any person, INCLUDING THE DEFENDANT], and can't disclose to anyone unless and until judge "allows a motion for specific, need-based written modification of the protective order"; this decision is "informed by art. 12 of the Declaration of Rights" but isn't "constitutionally compelled," and thus applies only to cases tried after issuance of rescript in this opinion;

C v Tripolone **425 M 487 (97)**—domestic violence counselor records (G.L. c. 233, § 20K) subject to in-camera view only after D's showing same as **Fuller** re § 20J;

C v Oliveira **431 M 609, 616 (2000)**—Fuller/Tripolone standard for obtaining in camera inspection extended to records of psychotherapist, privileged under G.L. c. 233, § 20B;

C v Maxwell **441 M 773 (2004)**—hospital/medical records containing info regarding infection with HIV (human immunodeficiency virus, "AIDS" status) not "absolutely" privileged (despite G.L c. 111, § 70F); Bishop-Fuller protocol applies;

C v Pare **420 M 216 (95)**—defendant seeking access to privileged records must disclose "Stage 2" **Bishop** submission (relevancy) to Commonwealth or forego seeking access;

US v Nixon **418 US 683, 710 (74)**—don't lightly create, expand privileges because hurt search for truth; [see 8 Wigmore, Evidence, § 2192 (McNaughton rev. 1961) *(Chapter 11-H, above)*]; but see *Pearce v Pearce* **63 Engl.Rep. 950 (1846)** truth, like all good things, "may be loved unwisely . . . & may cost too much.";

C v O'Brien **27 MAC 184 (89)**—D gets G.L. c. 119, § 51A investigative reports.; [see *Jones* **404 M 339 (89)** D gets G.L. c. 112, § 135 (f) records of G.L. c. 119, § 51B rpt.; other § 135 DSS reports not "absolute" privilege (like G.L. c. 233, § 20J), so in camera review w/o counsel (cf. Lynch/Nolan dissent) sees if "material to defense"]; harm because inconsistencies = exculpatory; in camera review for G.I. c. 233, § 20B, G.L. c. 123, §§ 36, 66A questions re: DMH records

C v Clancy **402 M 664, 669–71 (88)**—in camera review may require counsel's input;

C v Lugo **23 MAC 494 (87)**—(same);

See Chapter 6-L, Disclose Informant; [See **Brodin, M. and Avery, M.,** *Handbook of Massachusetts Evidence* **(8th ed. 2007)**): *procedures whereby counsel for criminal defendant may review "privileged" records; Young Pollets & Poreda, Evidence (2d ed. 1998) § 512.1, 513.1; Nolan and Sartorio, Criminal Law (2001) § 156, privileges of witnesses;*

See Chapter 11-C, Evidence, Motions to Strike; Chapter 7B, Summonses; Chapter 9, Cross-Examination.; Chapter 10, Presenting Defense; Chapter 6-D re: Discovery & confidential records;

Purcell v District Atty **424 M 109 (97)**—plaintiff, a legal services attorney, was told by an eviction client that the client intended to burn down the apartment building; attorney notified police; client was later charged with attempted arson and DA tried to make attorney testify: subpoena quashed as "crime fraud" exception to privilege applies only to communications in which lawyer's advice is sought "in furtherance of a crime or to obtain advice or assistance with respect to criminal activity";

In the Matter of a Grand Jury Investigation **453 M 453 (2009)**—client's communications to lawyer threatening harm = privileged UNLESS 'crime-fraud exception'

applies; client, a father in care & protection case in Juvenile Court, left six messages on attorney's answering machine, indicating he knew where judge lived, that she had two children, and that "some people need to be exterminated with prejudice"; attorney disclosed to judge; subsequent subpoenas to attorney for grand jury and District Court detention hearing should have been quashed; though communications were argued not to have been made "in furtherance of the rendition of legal services," & weren't privileged, SJC held that they were expressions of frustration and dissatisfaction with legal system & its participants, & privilege served salutary purposes (dissuading conduct, with option of making limited disclosure to protect likely targets, as done here);

C v Silva **455 M 503 (2009)**—D having alleged that trial counsel was ineffective for telling him he had to testify and for failing to prepare him for direct and cross-examination, D's motion to strike counsel's responsive affidavit was properly denied: attorney-client privilege "must be deemed waived, in part, to permit counsel to disclose only those confidences necessary and relevant to the defense of the charge of ineffective assistance of counsel"; motion judge's review found affidavit disclosed no more than was necessary to the issue;

C v Senior **433 M 453 (2001)**—though defense attorney took client to hospital for blood alcohol testing, with expectation that it might be used in defense, results were incriminating; prosecution could obtain them and introduce them against D, notwithstanding D's argument that hospital/personnel were "agents" of defense counsel (& material thus covered by attorney-client privilege); inter alia, agents have to agree to be agents;

C v Callahan **440 M 436 (2003)**—Commonwealth cannot obtain D's old psychiatric records for use by "qualified examiners to determine alleged sexual dangerousness"; G.L. c. 123A, § 13(b) did not abrogate existing privileges;

Jaffee v Redmond **518 US 1 (96)**—confidential communications between psychotherapist and patient in course of diagnosis or treatment protected from compelled disclosure under Fed.R.Evid. 501; Rule 501 authorizes federal courts to define new privileges by interpreting "the principles of the common law . . . in the light of reason and experience";

C v Brandwein **435 M 623 (2002)**—psychiatric nurse presumably breached confidentiality when she told cops of D's statements to her re: gun & bank robbery, but cops didn't solicit/provoke disclosure by the nurse: no suppression of D's later confession;

G.L. c. 233, § 20B—creates only an "evidentiary privilege" & doesn't prohibit disclosure in settings other than in various court proceedings;

See Chapter 7-H for cases on privilege against self-incrimination and Chapter 11-G for cases on no adverse inference from claim of right to silence or right to counsel;

See Chapter 6-L for cases on informant identity & surveillance location privilege;

See Chapter 11-G for Benoit & Williams on Lamb privileges pertaining to court-ordered psychiatric examinations;

C v Seabrooks **433 M 439 (2001)**—when trial issue was D's criminal responsibility & his experts had used five psych evaluations conducted at jail's behest soonest after his arrest, re suicide risk, OK for Commonwealth to introduce evaluating psych's testimony, even though exams weren't preceded by **Lamb 365 M 265, 270 (74)** warnings that his communications might not be kept confidential;

G.L. c. 233, § 20B—cited, finding 3d statutory exception applied to psychotherapist-patient privilege;

C v Beauchemin **410 M 181 (91)**—school records are nonprivileged, subject to summonsing & admissible if relevant;

C v Souther **31 MAC 219 (91):G.L. c. 119, § 51A**—(mandatory report) overrides G.L. c. 233, § 20B;

Villalta v C **428 M 429 (98)**—privilege of a person not to testify against his/her spouse does not extend to "any proceeding relating to child abuse, including incest (G.L. c. 233, § 20, Clause Second); wife must testify when abuse of ANY child is charged (not limited to offspring of either);

C v Burnham **451 M 517 (2008)**—though D "timely moved, pursuant to G.L. c. 233, § 20, First, to disqualify his former wife from testifying against him," judge correctly ruled disqualification inapplicable to proceedings involving child abuse; SJC rejects D's claim that exception re: child abuse is limited to civil proceedings;

C v Diaz **422 M 269 (96)**—declining to hold here that spousal privilege should be recognized in a "living together" arrangement (no such argument at trial, and privilege was the "wife's," **not** D's, to claim or not);

C v Rosa **412 M 147 (92)**—hearing to see if wife's waiver of spousal privilege was voluntary; use of involuntary testimony "offends fundamental fairness";

C v Rivera **37 MAC 244 (94)**—D held to have no standing to raise issue about abrogation of C witnesses' 5th Amendment privilege (after damaging grand jury testimony, witnesses claimed 5th Amendment at D's trial on ground grand jury testimony was perjurious, but judge ordered them to testify **and** grand jury testimony was admitted substantively); See, however, *C v Rosa* **412 M 147, 160–62 (92)** D permitted to raise issue concerning witness's marital privilege: witness's "decision" to testify had been involuntary, so use of the testimony offended "fundamental fairness" & violated due process;

C v Sylvia **35 MAC 310 (93)**—objection to marital communications evidence (G.L. c. 233, § 20, First) came too late (alleged domestic violence victim testified that D/husband telephoned her the day before trial and asked her to testify that her injuries resulted from drunken fall rather than by D's hand) ; victim's response on redirect, "I plead the 5th on that", **if** an invocation of marital privilege, was not raisable by D (instead personal to witness);

C v Koonce **418 M 367 (94)**—at retrial of murder case, witness who testified for prosecution in 1st trial was called by defendant; after consultation with counsel, witness claimed 5th Amendment (both because of his participation in incident surrounding homicide and because of potential differences between former testimony and what testimony he'd give at 2d trial); judge then held that his 1st trial testimony had been "involuntary" (he was threatened with "accessory" prosecution, not told of rights to appointed counsel & against self-incrimination, had 11th grade education), so it did not act as waiver of 5th Amendment rights: end result was that, at D's request, witness's testimony at 1st trial was read to jury, witness being "unavailable", and though new appellate counsel faulted finding of "involuntariness", court deferred to trial judge's finding of fact;

C v Beauchamp **49 MAC 591 (2000)**—notwithstanding D's argument that waiver of 5th Amendment privilege in giving testimony at his 1st trial was involuntary, such that Commonwealth couldn't introduce it at second trial; Ct deemed testimony admissible as "admission" by party opponent and as prior recorded testimony of now-"unavailable" witness (because Commonwealth couldn't have called him to stand at 2d trial);

Harrison v US **392 US 219, 222 (68)**—distinguished (error to allow government to introduce against D at 2d trial his testimony from 1st trial, because he'd been "virtually coerced" to testify at 1st trial due to government's introduction of illegally obtained confessions, i.e., testimony at 1st trial was tainted by same illegally as the confessions);

C v Wojcik **43 MAC 595 (97)**—based on prosecution's contention that D's statements to social worker were **not** for the purpose of diagnosis or treatment (per G.L. c. 112, §§ 135A-B), but were instead to pad his claim of trauma in a scheme to wreck motor vehicles and defraud insurance companies, privilege defeated (*criminal defendants: lying rape complainant's privilege claim concerning therapist, or rape counselor, or social worker privileges subject to rejection on same basis?);

C v Slonka **42 MAC 760 (97)**—after Commonwealth introduced portion of purportedly privileged psychotherapist record, "considerations of fairness" required that D be allowed to introduce other portion refuting it;

C v Sugrue **34 MAC 172 (93)**—marital communication exclusion (G.L. c. 233, § 20) had to yield to D's constitutional right to confront wife (chief accuser; alleging sexual assault on their son) with her motive to fabricate: he threatened to obtain child custody in upcoming divorce;

C v Perl **50 MAC 445 (2000)**—acknowledged pre-eminence of constitutional right to present evidence over 'evidentiary' marital communications exclusion, but here claiming exclusion of marital communications (probative of D's fear/state of mind in duress defense) harmless because would have been cumulative (BUT court failed to acknowledge prejudice probable because prosecutor's direct examination of D "seeded" a 'missing witness' inference about D's wife on this point.: cf *C v Piedra* **20 MAC 155 (85)** rejecting claim that bias had been sufficiently/

identically aired via evidence other than that which was erroneously excluded;

C v Walker **438 M 246, 254 n.4 (2003)**—noting that "marital communications" exclusion should apply even when husband and wife are engaged together in criminal activity (citing *US v. Rakes* 136 F.3d 1, 4 n.5 (1st Cir. 1998) & *US v Mavroules* 813 F. Supp. 115, 118–20 (D. Mass. 1993), which recognize Federal crime-fraud exception to marital communications disqualification).;

C v Martin **434 M 1016, 1017 (01)**—merely allowing D to point out inconsistencies doesn't justify exclusion of evidence showing bias;

C v Pratt **42 MAC 695 (97)**—complainant's assertions to social worker, inconsistent with later allegation of sexual assault, admissible despite social-worker–client privilege (G.L. c. 112, § 135A);

Bernard v Commonwealth **424 M 32 (96)**—state trooper, though not licensed social worker, was practicing as such in the employee assistance unit (see G.L. c. 112, § 134 exception to licensing requirement) such that D's communications to him were privileged under G.L. c. 112, §§ 135A-B;

C v Marrero **436 M 488 (2002)**—D's statement to manager of Christian rehabilitation center for drug/alcohol addicts not excludable as privileged under G.L. c. 233, § 20A (statements made to "priest, rabbi or ordained or licensed minister of any church or an accredited Christian Science practitioner");

C v Kebreau **454 M 287 (2009)**—statements made by D at "family meeting" held at church (ministers, D's wife, and D's two daughters [sexual assault complainants here]) to confront D admitted over D's objection because D's participation was not "for purpose of seeking spiritual advice or comfort", but to discuss a "family issue"; that D was not member of church and did not regularly attend services not "dispositive" (as, apparently, was fact that pastor assured D that discussion at meeting would remain confidential); SJC brushes aside argument that purpose changed when D specifically questioned pastor about what to do to make it better and was told to follow his conscience (D purportedly "seeking pragmatic advice rather than spiritual guidance");

In the Matter of a John Doe Grand Jury Investigation **418 M 549 (94)**—2 brothers, sole shareholders & directors of a closely-held corporation, could not be compelled to testify but could be ordered to appoint an alternate keeper of **corporate** records, who would then respond to grand jury subpoena duces tecum; cc opinion noted that brothers had no obligation to identify the records for the new "keeper" **and** that new keeper might assert the argument that subpoena was constitutionally inadequate, and that instead search warrant "issued on probable cause to believe that, more likely than not, the records contain[ed] evidence concerning the commission of a crime"; also left open was issue whether brothers would have standing to object to any unlawful seizure of particular "corporate" records;

11-J.1. Waiver of Privilege on Behalf of Dead Person

District Attorney for Norfolk District v Magraw **34 MAC 713 (93)**—DA successfully moved for appointment of executor of murder victim's estate other than husband/ murder suspect, so as to have better chance of obtaining **executor's waiver** of deceased's psychotherapist-patient privilege;

In the Matter of a John Doe Grand Jury Investigation **408 M 480 (90)**—distinguished (executor's refusal to waive attorney-client privilege upheld in context of investigation in which deceased was prime suspect in, rather than victim of, murder);

Swidler & Berlin v US **524 US 399 (98)**—attorney-client privilege survives client's death; Office of Independent Counsel/grand jury barred from obtaining notes taken by attorney during consultation with client nine days before client committed suicide; "testamentary" exception to attorney-client privilege, whereby privileged communications are revealed to further client's intent, not reasonably applicable; Court refuses to hold that attorney-client privilege operates differently in criminal and civil cases; refuses to make exception for "information of substantial importance" in particular criminal cases;

Chapter 12
MISCELLANEOUS TRIAL ISSUES

12-A. IMMEDIATELY PRE-TRIAL

12-A.1. Sequestering Witnesses

CPCS P/G 6.2—shall seek, unless tactically inadvisable, for all witnesses;

Mass. District Court Criminal Defense Manual (MCLE 2000) § 14.4.1(b);

M.R.Crim.P. 21—"discretionary"; judge "may" order anyone but D sequestered;

6 Wigmore, *Evidence*, **§ 1838 (Chadbourn rev. 1976)**—next to cross-examination, one of greatest engines ever invented to detect liars; gets supreme excellence from simplicity & automatism; § 1837: Daniel's biblical judgment (by sequestration) in Susanna's case; § 1839: should "be demandable as of right . . . no contingency can justify its denial"; § 1840 procedure;

K. Smith, *Criminal Practice & Procedure*, **§§ 1754–59 (2d ed. 1983 & Supp.)**—discretionary, but has advantages & is "better practice" for murder (citing *C v Watkins* **373 M 849 (77)**);

Young, Pollets & Poreda, *Evidence*, **§ 615.1 (2d ed. 1998, & Supp.)**;

ABA Standards for Criminal Justice, Trial Judge (2d ed. 1986) 6–3.1—either before trial or at its beginning, judge should make known the "ground rules" for courtroom;

C v Blackburn **354 M 200 (68)**—sequestration = discretionary; appropriate if evidence = involved or conflicting;

C v Sevieri **21 MAC 745 (86)**—denying sequestration without specific reason invites unnecessary appeal problem; encouraging public courtroom not good reason to deny;

C v Clark **432 M 1, 7 (2000)**—trial judge's order barring most recording/broadcasting of trial overturned despite rationale that sequestration order would be made ineffectual without such order;

C v Clark **3 MAC 481 (75)**—discretion to exempt investigating cop because "essential to management of case"; discretion whether to call mistrial if witnesses discuss testimony & violate order;

C v Perez **405 M 339 (89)**—generally undesirable for testifying cop to sit at counsel table, but no risk of miscarriage of justice here;

C v Auguste **414 M 51 (92)**—although trial judge has discretion to allow investigating cop to sit at counsel table, prosecution should be "wary" if cop is essential witness;

US v Anagnos **853 F.2d 1 (1st Cir. '88)**—cop shouldn't sit at counsel table because it implicitly vouches for his/her credibility;

C v Watkins **373 M 849 (77)**—"better practice" in "capital cases" to allow motion; denial based on "usual practice" to deny may be improper; here, no prejudice because Commonwealth's witnesses told different events/ perspectives;

C v Jackson **384 M 572 (81)**—cop & expert exempted; discretion to let witness stay/assist after testimony & recall later; discretion to admit/exclude testimony if witness violates order;

C v Pagan **73 MAC 369 (2008)**—reconsideration of suppression motion may occur when "substantial justice requires," and is not limited to instances of newly discovered evidence, BUT even when judge stated he would "assume" truth of new affidavits, he wasn't required to hold new hearing or reverse suppression order: "allowing 'do-overs' . . . undermines the integrity of the process and threatens the efficacy of the sequestration orders" (initial hearing featured two police witnesses);

C v Pope **392 M 493 (84)**—discretion to make counsel enforce sequestration order; no prejudice from alleged violation;

C v Duncan **71 MAC 150, further rev. allowed 452 M 1110 (2008)**—in the midst of one officer's testimony, prosecutor instructed a different witness-officer to test fire relevant weapons, and that officer called upon testifying witness to do so; court rejected D's claim that contact between the two officers violated sequestration order (officer had testified that they did not discuss their testimony while at firing range together);

C v Crowley **168 M 121 (1897)**—discretion to exclude testimony if order violated; if counsel sees person in room will be witness, should as soon as possible tell to leave;

C v Bianco **388 M 358 (83)**—usually means witness stay outside until testify & shan't discuss testimony with witness yet to testify; remedy = discretionary;

C v Gogan **389 M 255 (83)**—chief purpose = prevent perjury; discretionary to grant & whether admit/exclude testimony of one who violates order;

Geders v US **425 US 80 (76)**—can't bar D-attorney consultation during post-direct overnight recess; other ways to prevent coaching, e.g., delay a recess;

Perry v Leeke **488 US 272 (89)**—BUT can forbid consultation in 15-minute recess;

C v Bonner **33 MAC 471 (92)**—trial judge had discretion to deny D's motion to sequester parents of 14-year-old sexual assault complainant whose supportive presence was requested by Commonwealth even though mother was fresh complaint witness & even though defense witnesses were sequestered;

12-A.2. Witness Seating/Defendant Seating

C v Johnson **417 M 498 (94)**—witnesses cannot be shielded so as to prevent D from seeing their faces during their testimony;

C v Spear **43 MAC 583 (97)**—special seating arrangements for child witness may not occur without "a showing by the Commonwealth, by more than a preponderance of the evidence, of a compelling need for the implementation of such procedure";

C v Sanchez **423 M 591 (96)**—seating counsel at table with child witness, 20 feet from D, did not abridge confrontation right and did not impair attorney-client consultation (usual course = for counsel to stand, away from D, or move around courtroom while questioning witness);

See further cases on this topic in Chapters 9 (Cross-Examination) & 11 (Evidence & Objections);

C v Moyles **45 MAC 350 (98)**—unless, upon specific inquiry, judge finds that "security measures" are necessary, D should be permitted to sit at counsel table; "routine" practice of a judge to the contrary condemned; harmlessness beyond reasonable doubt here found because of finding that access between D and counsel not impaired and seating wouldn't have prejudiced D in jurors' eyes;

12-A.3. Presence of Defendant

See also Chapter 9-A, Cross-Examination, General Principles

Hopt v Utah **110 US 574 (1884)**—D's personal presence = essential at trial; (but see, e.g., *US v Cannatella* **597 F.2d 27 (2d Cir. '79)**—in "unusual" circumstances, for "good cause . . . such as physical endangerment of" D, judge may have a "residue of judicial discretion" to allow a temporary absence);

Snyder v Mass. **291 US 97, 105–6 (34)**—right to be present at every step of proceedings from arraignment to sentence guaranteed by Sixth & Fourteenth Amendments;

C v Bergstrom **402 M 534, 543 (88)**—right to be personally present at every step of proceedings, from arraignment to sentence;

C v Millen **289 M 441, 452 (35)**—it's a common law right; *Snyder v Mass.* **291 US 97, 105–6 (34)** & right of due process under 6th & 14th Amendments to US Constitution; *C v Robichaud* **358 M 300 (70)** right guaranteed by both 6th Amendment and Article 12 of Declaration of Rights;

M.R.Crim.P 18(a)—D entitled to be present at all "critical stages"; need not be present when no evidence is taken; M.R.Crim.P. 18(a)(2) judge may excuse from attendance "person prosecuted for a misdemeanor" if D so requests;

C v Robichaud **358 M 300 (70)**—guaranteed by Mass. Constitution, Declaration of Rights, Article 12;

C v Nwachukwu **65 MAC 112 (2005)**—reversal for D's absence from courtroom for the first 15 minutes of his bench trial: he was outside courtroom because his "inexperienced" attorney believed that D was bound by the order of sequestration of witnesses;

C v Perry **432 M 214, 237–38 (2000)**—issue of whether waiver of D's right to be present at sidebar voir dire of jurors must be made by D personally held waived because D's attorney waived the right in D's absence (so it's not preserved for appellate review!);

C v Campiti **41 MAC 43 (96)**—17 co-Ds were arraigned long before D, and their cases went forward, including 4-day hearing on motions to suppress; when D was later arraigned, D-counsel filed (1) motion to suppress and said he had nothing additional to offer to the judge who had ruled on co-D's identical motions earlier, & (2) motion to preserve rights of D as if he had been party earlier to the motions to suppress; though appellate counsel argued that D was denied his right to be present at the motion to suppress, Court said issue waived by trial counsel's failure to assert, counsel & D "elect(ing)" below "to rely on the evidence and the arguments offered at the earlier hearing";

C v L'Abbe **421 M 262 (95)**—D may waive right to be present, if waiver is knowing and voluntary; one is competent to waive presence if competent to stand trial;

Robinson v Commonwealth **445 M 280 (2005)**—trial judge did NOT have discretion to deem D's unexcused absence from hearing on motion to suppress to be a waiver of the suppression motion, but did have discretion to treat absence as waiver of D's right to be present at the hearing, a critical stage of the case, IF D had adequate notice of time and date of hearing, and judge considers reasons for D's absence, if known, and possible prejudice to Commonwealth or co-Ds or witnesses if hearing doesn't proceed as scheduled; hearing re voluntariness of absence is necessary; waiver of right to be present doesn't constitute waiver of right to the suppression hearing and right to effective assistance of counsel at the hearing;

Geders v US **425 US 80 (76)**—counsel must explain trial events to D (so can't bar D from talking to attorney during recess before DA's cross-examination of D);

Amado v Commonwealth **349 M 716 (65)**—D entitled to be present at voir dire re: voluntariness;

C v Owens **414 M 595 (93)**—D entitled to be present at side bar voir dire of prospective jurors;

C v Barnoski **418 M 523 (94)**—hardship colloquies with potential jurors not 'critical stage' (D & counsel had no right to be present);

C v Thomas **448 M 180 (2007)**—citing trial judge's concern about "security issues and limited court officers assigned to the case" and failure of D to show "prejudice," SJC finds no error in ruling barring D from attending "the view taken by the jury";

C v Morganti **455 M 388 (2009)**—no error in excluding D from jury view of car of type in which victim was shot, with mannequin seated in passenger seat and yellow rod through head to mark bullet's path; judge found "security issues," D having been a fugitive for >10 years; D was offered options of looking from courthouse window (car in parking lot), of private view before jury view, and/or reviewing photos of view (including one of car with mannequin and rod through head);

C v Parreira **72 MAC 308 (2008)**—tape recording of police interview of D was admitted in evidence but not played during trial (D making no objection); appellate court rejected his argument that his right to be present during evidence-taking part of trial was violated by jury's [possible] playing of the tape in jury room; D knew tape content, having been present during its making and having received copy during discovery and could choose to forego playing tape during trial "when he would have been able to observe the jury's reaction" and make purportedly "more informed decision" about testifying;

C v Rios **412 M 208, 214 (92)**—exclusion of Ds from their trial during testimony about surveillance location violated Article 12 confrontation right; even if this error ever could be considered "harmless," Commonwealth must make affirmative showing that error in not allowing D to be present was harmless beyond a reasonable doubt," a burden not met;

Illinois v Allen **397 US 337 (70)**—D's right to be present may be waived by his courtroom misbehavior; see also *C v Chubbuck* **384 M 746 (81)** persistent disruptive behavior in courtroom;

C v White **37 MAC 757 (94)**—D did not waive right to be present by "refusing" to go forward with appointed counsel; reversal because of his banishment during impanelment;

12-A.4. Defaults

Taylor v US **414 US 17, 20 (73)**—right to be present waivable by D's flight from courtroom in midst of trial; see also *C v Flemmi* **360 M 693 (71)** D's voluntary absence from trial is waiver of right to be present;

Crosby v US **506 US 255 (93)**—D not present **at beginning of trial** cannot be tried in absentia (under Fed.R. Crim.P. 43); different if D absents himself thereafter;

C v Elizondo **428 M 322 (98)**—when D defaults after trial "begins," it can proceed; after denial of motion to suppress, D's written waiver of jury & jury waiver colloquy, judge's announcement that would start evidence tomorrow morning, & clerk's telling D he'd been placed at bar for trial, trial had begun (and could continue in D's absence when he defaulted next day);

C v Vickers **60 MAC 24 (2003)**—though D-counsel "chafed at going forward" with trial in absence of D, who left the premises after jury impanelment (& was later found to have voluntarily absented herself), "it was a serious lapse in judgment to refuse to participate for more than a day as the Commonwealth proceeded with its case"; that counsel "deliberately declined to perform any defense functions" resulted in reversal of D's convictions; BUT *"this should not be misunderstood as a reward for deliberately unprofessional behavior"*;

C v Muckle **59 MAC 631 (2003)—PROTOCOL TO BE FOLLOWED WHEN D FAILS TO APPEAR MIDTRIAL:** judge must determine whether trial should proceed, or mistrial instead, and must first determine whether D's absence is without cause/voluntary; recess for investigation = appropriate; evidence to be produced ON THE RECORD, as to inquiries made, efforts to find D; judge to make finding re: 'without cause/voluntariness of absence'; if judge determine to continue trial in absentia, "neutral instruction" should be given that D may not be present; if there will be no evidence introduced to jury re: consciousness of guilt, judge "may add that the jury should not speculate as to the reasons for D's absence & should not draw adverse inferences; IF ADA seeks to introduce evidence to lay foundation for consciousness of guilt instruction, judge should determine whether introduction of such evidence "is warranted"; if so, judge to allow "brief" development, "subject to such discretionary limitations as the judge believes necessary"; if judge determines consciousness of guilt instruction is appropriate, *C v Toney*, 385 M at 585 (tailored to D's failure to appear at trial) to be given;

C v Baro **73 MAC 218 (2008)**—when D fled during lunch recess at beginning of jury deliberations, no error in having jurors in courtroom for response to jury question: D's absence was not mentioned and D's family and courtroom personnel were also absent; "Muckle" protocol prescribed for "mid-trial" absence unnecessary;

The following cases were decided in the context of G.L. c. 278, § 24, imposition of "bench session" sentence upon D's default in jury of six session for proceedings related to then-existing "trial de novo" right (trial de novo abolished by G.L. c. 218, §§ 26A, 27A, amended, effective 1/1/94)

C v Brennick **14 MAC 952 (82)**—hearing re: "solidity" of default (& judge has "discretion), right to counsel (public defenders aren't "fungible");

C v Coughlin **372 M 818 (77)**—shouldn't default when D didn't show up until p.m.; "casual or capricious defaulting of appellants, with the consequences of (G.L. c. 278) § 24, is not in the interests of justice";

C v Bartlett **374 M 744 (78)**—no "solid" default without notice to D (here, notice sent to wrong address); Commonwealth's burden of proof;

C v Faulkner **418 M 352 (94)**—when there's no evidence to show D changed address, and D raises nonreceipt of notice, burden was on probation officer to show notice of probation revocation hearing was properly sent;

12-A.5. Public Trial/Press Issues

See also Chapter 7-S (Miscellaneous Issues in Preparing for Trial, Press Coverage/Open Courtroom);

Richmond Newspapers, Inc. v Virginia **448 US 555 (80)**—press & general public have constitutional right (1st and 14th Amendments) of access to criminal trials;

Globe Newspaper Co. v Superior Court **457 US 596 (82)** holding unconstitutional (violation of 1st Amendment; 6th Amendment issue not reached) **G.L. c. 278, § 16A,** requiring ("mandatory") closure of courtroom during testimony of minors who are allegedly sexual assault victims; any closure requires particularized determinations, case-by-case basis;

Press-Enterprise Co. v Superior Court of California **464 US 501 (84)**—1st Amendment right of press to be present during voir dire of potential jurors/jury empanelment;

Globe Newspaper Co. v Commonwealth **407 M 879, 884 (90)**—"public" guarantee covers voir dire of potential jurors concerning qualifications;

C v Gordon **422 M 816 (96)**—"public" doesn't cover hardship colloquies re excusing from service;

Waller v Georgia **467 US 39 (84)**—if D objects, 6th Amendment bars closure of a suppression hearing unless (1) there is "an overriding interest that is likely to be prejudiced"; (2) closure is no broader than necessary to protect that interest; (3) trial court must consider reasonable alternatives to closing the hearing; and (4) court must make findings adequate to support the closure; general claim here that some persons' privacy would be infringed because such persons' voices were on the wiretaps which were the subject of the suppression motion held insufficient; see also *Gannett Co. v DePasquale* **443 US 368 (79)** (majority of justices believed press & public had a "qualified" constitutional right (1st Amendment) to attend suppression hearings, though question not reached);

George W. Prescott Publishing Co. v Stoughton Division of the District Court Dept **428 M 309 (98)**—judge's order, in contributing to delinquency of minor case, which prohibited newspaper from revealing name/address of any child who testified during proceedings, or any child allegedly engaging in any delinquency in connection with the proceedings, and from photographing any such child, was unlawful prior restraint on press, implicitly rejecting as inadequate the findings of judge (citing legislative interest in affording delinquent children protection from public exposure) to clearly establish and support a compelling state interest to protect against a serious and identified threat of harm; any prior restraint also had to be no greater than is necessary to protect the compelling state interest;

C v Clark **432 M 1, 7 (2000)**—single justice acted appropriately in overturning trial judge's order barring recording or broadcasting of trial except for openings and closings, jury instructions, verdict, and sentencing; SJC Rule 3:09, Canon 3(A)(7)(b) cited; judge's cited reason, i.e., that order of sequestration of witnesses would be ineffectual without prohibition of electronic media during reception of evidence, was insufficient basis on which to limit media access; particular complaints of D (inhibition of attorney-client consultations, and camera placement impeding counsel's view) had been addressed, when they were voiced at trial, by specific directives;

C v Martin **39 MAC 44 (95)**—OK, after prosecution witness claimed intimidation by D's brother & 2 women in courtroom, that further testimony by witness was ordered to occur in absence of all except press, and employees of DA & defense counsel;

C v Marshall **356 M 432 (69)**; *C v Martin* **417 M 187 (94)**—right to public trial extends both to D and to public: First Amendment, U.S. Constitution = public right of access to criminal trials; Sixth Amendment = D's right to public trial;

Globe Newspaper Co. v Superior Ct. **457 US 596, 606-607 (82)**—G.L. c. 278, § 16A, requiring closure of courtroom during trial of, e.g., sex crimes when complainant is under age 18, invalidated on First Amendment grounds: closure prohibited absent compelling interest, and closure narrowly tailored to serve that interest; *Waller v Georgia* **467 US 39, 46–48 (84)**—same result on 6th Amendment grounds, closure order to be accompanied by adequate findings;

C v Adamides **37 MAC 339 (94)**—when judge closed court to public during child sex trial, he obtained D's consent; since 6th Amendment ground was thus waived, D attempted on appeal to assert instead 1st Amendment; decision reserved as to whether a D has standing because this D's failure to assert it at trial held fatal;

C v Edward **75 MAC 162 (2009)**—remanding for hearing on issue of courtroom's alleged closure during testimony by seventeen-year-old sexual assault complainant, issue being raised in motion for new trial filed 13 years after direct appeal: right to public trial is "structural", but can be waived; waiver requires "sound rationale for closure and the defendant's knowing agreement";

C v Young **73 MAC 479 (2009)**—no relief for excluding D's brother from courtroom during testimony of hesitant prosecution witness fearful of that brother;

C v Cohen **456 M 94 (2010)**—blanket closure of courtroom during jury empanelment (as matter of long term practice and policy) = violation of right to public trial (6th and 1st Amendments, US Constitution), structural error not susceptible to harmless error analysis; that some family members and other individuals beyond parties and counsel were present = "partial" rather than full closure, and requires "substantial reason" rather than "overriding interest" to justify;

Presley v Georgia **130 S Ct 721 (2010)**—automatic exclusion of public during jury voir dire (e.g., to prevent interaction/communications between prospective jurors and public) is error; must consider alternatives to closure even when not offered by parties; public's right to be present exists whether or not any party has asserted it; "[t]rial courts are obligated to take every reasonable measure to accommodate public attendance at criminal trials";

C v Jones **71 MAC 568 (2008)**—fn.1: assume without deciding that public trial right extends to pretrial proceedings such as suppression hearing; exclusion of co-D from suppression hearing on D's motion not error; co-D's own suppression hearing and trial had yet to occur, so she "continued to be a potential witness" permissibly subject to sequestration order;

C v Horton **434 M 823, 831–33 (2001)**—individual voir dire should be held in open court, but D here consented to holding it in vacant jury deliberation room (& was himself present) & court found no prejudice TO HIM from this; D didn't "demonstrate( ) that he has standing to press this right of the public";

Foley v Commonwealth **429 M 496 (99)**—jail being used as courtroom for arraignment sessions: to be "public," as required, signs must guide public to courtroom and assure public right of free access; notices must be posted at related District Court houses re: specific arraignments to be held at jail, and what time they will occur; physical layout of jail space and its public accessibility = important (here, decision asserted that courtroom was outside secured housing area, and that courtroom visitors not searched or required to sign in or provide info, and not required to pass thru locked doors; approval here LIMITED to arraignment sessions (evidentiary hearings and trials raise many issues, including re: impartiality of jurors and possible intimidation of witnesses);

C v Patry **48 MAC 470 (2000)**—judge's answering jury question in the deliberation room rather than in open court = reversal; D would have to personally waive right to public trial (not D-counsel); "structural error," never considered harmless;

12-A.6. Judge, Substitution of

C v Carter **423 M 506 (96)**—when, 2 days into trial, judge became ill & hospitalized, no error to have substitute judge, when substitute judge read all pleadings **and** actual transcripts of all proceedings;

M.R.Crim.P. 38(a)—if judge dies, becomes ill, or has other disability during trial, another judge of same court may finish trial after certifying in writing that s/he's familiarized 'self w/trial record; (b) any judge of the court may receive jury's verdict; (c) if presiding judge is unavailable after verdict or G finding, any other judge of the court may fill in, BUT if such judge believes s/he can't perform necessary duties because s/he didn't preside earlier, may order new trial in own discretion or on D's motion;

C v Baro **73 MAC 218 (2008)**—due to trial judge's unavailability (illness), different judge sentenced D; though sentencing judge didn't certify in writing his familiarity with trial record (as required by M.R.Crim.P. 38(c)) he carefully considered counsel's representations re: trial record plus D's criminal history, so no relief;

12-A.7. Swearing Witnesses

C v McCaffrey **36 MAC 583 (94)**—though child witness not formally sworn, Court refused only suggested relief (required finding of NG, argued to result from striking the unsworn testimony);

C v Fleury **417 M 810 (94)**—failure to tell grand jurors viewing videotape of child sex assault complainant

that child had been "sworn" prior to the taped interview did not require dismissal of indictments;

12-B. STIPULATIONS

CPCS P/G 6.6(f)—carefully consider (dis)advantages; **2.1(b)**: don't waive any significant rights at arraignment;

Brodin, M. and Avery, M., *Handbook of Massachusetts Evidence* **(8th ed. 2007).** trial or appellate court can relieve one from stipulation improvidently made or not conducive to justice; stipulations to questions of law "are of no effect," but parties = bound by stipulation that item of evidence is admissible UNLESS court vacates stipulation as improvident or not conducive to justice;

9 Wigmore, *Evidence,* **§ 2593 (Chadbourn rev. 1981)**—unless special circumstances to contrary, stipulation presumed intended by parties to apply to a new trial;

SJC Rule 3:07, 1.2—may accede to "reasonable requests" of opposing counsel which do not prejudice rights of client; (*see Chapter 2, Ethics/Standards*);

M.R.Crim.P. 11—possible fact stipulations to be discussed at pretrial conference (*see Chapter 6, Pretrial Conference, Motions, Discovery;*)

C v Torres **367 M 737 (75)**—can admit photo of assault complainant despite D's concession badly beaten & bled profusely; Commonwealth can 'prove its case';

C v Stirling **351 M 68 (66)**—can admit photos despite offer to stipulate to matters proved thereby; Commonwealth entitled "to prove its case";

C v Nassar **351 M 37, 46 (66)** (same*); (but see Chapter 11-D, Evidence: Relevance/Balancing);*

C v Benoit **389 M 411 (83)**—(same);

C v Roberts **407 M 731 (90)**—Commonwealth cannot be compelled to stipulate to facts to avoid potential for introduction of prejudicial material;

C v Triplett **398 M 561 (86)**—stipulation to "facts" must be accepted by finder; stipulation to "testimony"

leaves facts to finder (see **Brodin, M. and Avery, M.,** *Handbook of Massachusetts Evidence* **§ 2.5 (8th ed. 2007).**);

C v Franklin **358 M 416 (70)**—stipulation normally binding & removable only by judge if clearly unjust; trial stipulation binding on appeal too;

C v Hill **20 MAC 130 (85)**—D's stipulation to facts "conclusive of guilt" requires a colloquy re: waiver of trial rights;

C v Lewis **399 M 761 (87)**—same; cf. *C v McCann* **97 M 580 (1867)**—DA's admission that absent witness would say certain things didn't admit the truth of that testimony;

C v Stevens **379 M 772 (80)**—to preserve appeal rights re: motions, D had jury-waived trial (without cross-examination of DA witness); don't need colloquy re: waive trial rights (except jury) since DA proved case—not like a guilty plea;

C v Garcia **23 MAC 259 (86)**—D suffered convictions in circumstances to preserve right to appellate review of denial of motion to suppress;

C v Shraiar **397 M 16 (86)**—stipulation agreed by D, signed by attorney, solved problem & conflict of attorney as prosecution witness;

C v Garrett **26 MAC 964 (88)**—if important concession/waiver, record must show that D either made concession or acquiesced in lawyer's stipulation; but see *C v Gonzalez* **18 MAC 979 (84)**—no objection to drugs/analysis (defense = alibi/entrapment), so bad instruction (presume drugs = heroin) = harmless;

12-C. OPENING STATEMENTS

CPCS P/G 6.5—consider strategic (dis)advantages re: opening; study law, especially if no defense evidence; familiarize 'self with judge's practice; various objectives; guard against improper DA opening;

M.R.Crim.P. 24(a)—may open after DA's or at close of DA evidence; 15 minute limit, but judge can reasonably reduce/extend (before it begins);

Superior Court Rule 7—15-minute limit, but judge can extend "for cause shown"; (discretion re: D's opening before evidence = overruled by M.R.Crim.P. 24(a) & *Dupree* **16 MAC 600 (83)**);

K. Smith, *Criminal Practice & Procedure,* **§ 1839 (2d ed. 1983 & Supp.)**—if expect DA's opening partly objectionable, alert judge & ask hearing (see motion in limine); § 1835 Mass. rule less broad than 1st Cir. (i.e., *US v Hershenow* **680 F.2d 847 (82)**: D has right to make

opening regardless of whether he intends to call witnesses & may do so immediately after DA's opening, absent good cause shown to the contrary), but opening is OK if reasonably expect to elicit specific evidence on cross-examination;

SJC Rule 3:07, 3.4—shan't allude to any matter that lawyer doesn't reasonably believe is relevant or that will not be supported by admissible evidence;

ABA Standards for Criminal Justice, Prosecution Function & Defense Function (3d ed. 1993) 4-7.4—opening = outline of issues & expected evidence;

C v Lowder **432 M 92 (2000)**—judge has authority to direct verdict of acquittal after prosecutor's opening statement, although shouldn't do so "until it is apparent that (prosecution) cannot supply the evidence necessary to establish ... case"; judge here abused discretion because deprived prosecutor of opportunity to be heard & didn't discuss alternatives to entering findings of not guilty; in future, must do these + state on record reasons for decision to acquit; despite abuse of discretion here, double jeopardy prohibition barred retrial; (compare *C v Brattman* **10 MAC 579 (80)** no right to required finding of not guilty for DA opening; *see Chapter 12-G, Required Findings of Not Guilty*);

C v McJunkin **11 MAC 609 (81)**—may limit D to particularized evidence D expects to adduce; OK to deny D's opening here because D didn't spell it out;

C v Murray **22 MAC 984 (86)**—improper opening; dictum: can't tell if more than counsel's intuition that facts will be smoked out;

C v Medeiros **15 MAC 913 (83)**—discretion to deny opening where only a mere hope of puncturing DA's case somehow through cross-examination; D must have reasonable expectation to elicit specific evidence to have right to open;

C v Mahoney **400 M 524 (87)**—discretion to exclude opening ("pay attention to D's acts on videotape") because not evidence D will offer & because no harm (since opening did raise some issues by discussing D's expected testimony);

C v Dupree **16 MAC 600 (83)**—opening by D OK if contains facts reasonably certain to be elicited on cross-examination;

US v Stanfield **521 F.2d 1122 (9th Cir. '75)**—vital right; judge can't do it for attorneys;

C v French **357 M 356, 404, A-33 (70)**—DA's opening (asking jury to look at Ds "for their physical characteristics," "and with regard to the story that is told about them") OK where judge added a direction to jurors "to look at the judge and all counsel and all parties"; "remarks amount to no more than a suggestion that the jurors carefully watch what was going on as an aid to appraising the evidence";

Leonard v US **277 F.2d 834 (9th Cir. '60)**—DA not to use opening for early argument or to destroy D's character before introducing evidence;

C v Hoilett **430 M 369, 372 (99)**—when prosecutor refers in opening to evidence that is inadmissible or that he doesn't realistically expect to present at trial, mistrial may be appropriate if force of remarks = overwhelmingly prejudicial & likely to leave indelible imprint on jurors' minds (citing *C v Fazio* **375 M 451, 454–55 (78)**);

C v Qualls **440 M 576 (2003)**—absent showing of bad faith "or prejudice," fact that evidence promised by DA in opening statement fails to materialize is not cause for reversal of convictions;

C v Riberio **49 MAC 7, 10–11 (2000)**—DA's opening = diatribe including pointing at D, referring to "his own sick sexual gratification," and "why would (complainant) lie?"; mistrial denied, judge ordered various components struck & cautioned DA in front of jury; though cited statements improper, no further relief ordered; SJC in *Errington* **390 M 875, 883 (84)** said to leave open question "whether an opening statement made in good faith may ever create such prejudice as to entitle a defendant to a mistrial";

C v Lindsey **48 MAC 641, 644–45 (2000)**—DA vouching for informants' credibility in opening statement = error (& judge didn't instruct per *Ciampa* **406 M 257 (89)** on topic, more usually broached by DA in closing argument);

C v Croken **432 M 266 (2000)**—DA exhortation that child sex assault complainant "acted courageously" & "young boys don't keep log books when they're being molested" = error, but no objection, no relief; DA's argument in opening that child hadn't come forward because of fear he would be labeled "homosexual" not shown by D to be without good faith basis (though later evidence did not include such reason for reluctance); compare closing argument found permissible in *C v Ridge* **455 M 307 (2009)**—statement that it took courage for witnesses to testify was reasonable inference from evidence as two witnesses testified that they were afraid of D, and some witnesses did not testify to grand jury until fifteen years after homicides;

C v Samneang Ka **70 MAC 137 (2007)**—DA's opening criticism of D's purported lack of concern for condition of young son said to have been "perhaps of only marginal relevance to the question of her intoxication", but no relief because of strength of Commonwealth's case, and judge's instruction that sympathy shouldn't influence;

C v Dutra **15 MAC 542 (83)**—counsel's statement that he's a "public defender" was "indifferent" & not ineffective counsel;

Lovett v Commonwealth **393 M 444 (84)**—can't say "D won't testify because my advice";

C v DeCicco **44 MAC 111 (98)**—below minimum standard of competence for D-counsel to assert in opening that he believed D would be testifying when counsel had not discussed this with D or prepared D (& D did not later testify);

C v Scott **430 M 351, 357 (99)**—failure to make opening statement wasn't ineffective assistance of counsel but instead reasonable tactical decision because counsel didn't plan to call defense witnesses & intended to put on case through cross-examination of Commonwealth witnesses; also near impossible to show such failure likely influenced jury's verdict;

C v Dupree **16 MAC 600 (83)**—no judicial "discretion" about timing of D's opening; up to D whether after DA's opening or after DA's evidence; D may not know strategy 'til after DA's evidence;

Jones v C **379 M 607, 619 n.23 (80)**—can make tactical use (i.e., argue) of DA's inability to keep his word as outlined in opening (see Performance Guideline 6.5(d));

C v Jackson **384 M 572 (81)**—can deny mistrial for DA's failure to call 2 promised witnesses; no evidence intentional or bad faith;

Anderson v Butler **858 F.2d 16 (1st Cir. '88)**—ineffective for opening promise of witness not called;

C v Carney **34 MAC 922 (93)**—though counsel in opening promised evidence he did not produce, the remarks were "equivocal & undramatic", and it was unlikely jury focused attention on them; trial was hotly-contested & 8 days long, no prejudice found;

Ouber v Guarino **293 F.3d 19 (1st Cir. 2002)**—ineffective assistance of counsel in repeatedly promising that D would testify, & thereafter not calling her: "error attributed to counsel consists of two inextricably intertwined events: the attorney's initial decision to present the petitioner's testimony as the centerpiece of the defense (and his announcement of that fact to the jury in his opening statement) in conjunction with his subsequent decision to advise the petitioner against testifying. Taken alone, each of these decisions may have fallen within the broad universe of acceptable professional judgments. Taken together, however, they are indefensible";

C v Gagliardi **21 MAC 439 (86)**—new trial, in part, because DA ordered to "amend" misleading opening.; then judge finds "tones less ardent than original opening";

K. Smith, *Criminal Practice & Procedure*, **§ 1835 (2d ed. 1983 & Supp.)**—"practice" for co-D with lowest indictment number to open first;

C v Geary **32 MAC 511 (92)**—prosecutor could properly mention testimony of summonsed witness because reasonably expected that witness would appear & not done in bad faith, notwithstanding inability of defense investigators to locate witness;

C v Smith **35 MAC 655 (93)**—no reversible error in prosecutor's opening statement use of "retrograde extrapolation" (saying since breathalyzer was .06 two hours after fatal vehicle wreck, it was .09—.10 at relevant time) since he reasonably expected the evidence to be admitted (judge did not allow its admission later);

C v Sullivan **410 M 521 (91)**—counsel's misplaced reliance in opening statements on pretrial discovery provided by Commonwealth was cured by judge's instruction blaming prosecutor;

12-D. JUDGE QUESTIONS WITNESSES—AND/OR OVERBEARING OR BIASED JUDGE(S)

CPCS P/G 1.3(k)—seek most advantageous forum, e.g., motion to change venue;

See also Chapter 7-M, Recusal; Chapter 2, Contempt, Court Orders; Chapter 1, Court Hierarchy; Chapter 10, Present Defense; & Chapter 19, Mistrials, Double Jeopardy;

Prop.M.R.Evid. 614—judge can call/question witness if necessary for "justice"; objections at next chance without jury;

Young, Pollets & Poreda, *Evidence*, **§ 614.1 (2d ed. 1998 & Supp.)**—while judge may question witnesses, "it is a right that should be carefully exercised," & "cautionary instruction (that jurors shouldn't attach undue weight to inquiry pursued by judge) would seem fairly indicated"; judge shouldn't assume role of advocate or create impression of partisanship/bias; judge's inquiry may disrupt counsel's own timetable for presentation of proof, or reduce effect counsel planned by a more timely inquiry (particularly in cross-examination, in which judge "may do nothing more than forewarn the equivocating witness of the shoals ahead, in time to change course");

3 Wigmore, *Evidence*, **§ 784 (Chadbourn rev. 1970)**—strong defense of judge's right to question witnesses;

C v Urena **417 M 692, 701–2 (94)**—D failed to show prejudice from judge-initiated procedure allowing jurors to question witnesses; in future, should be limited to cases in which "it is particularly appropriate", and (1) jurors must be given specified instructions, including warning that evidentiary rules may forbid certain questions & juror is not to hold this against any party (2) no oral questioning, but instead in writing, after which judge confers with counsel, and (3) parties to be given opportunity for further examination after any juror question is answered;

C v Britto **433 M 596 (2001)**—juror questioning of witnesses upheld, despite bedlam here shown, lack of legislative study/approval; further recommended procedures (after *Urena* **417 M 692 (94)**) set forth (judge should instruct that jurors shouldn't permit 'selves to become aligned with either party & questions should be impartial; jurors can't give answers to their own questions disproportionate weight; jurors should decide independently, without discussion with others, what questions to ask; juror's ID # should be included on question, so that judge will be able "to address problems unique to a juror" without exposing all to potential prejudice; counsel to have opportunity outside hearing of jury to examine questions with judge & make suggestions, register objections, & judge to rule on any objections, including re: particular prejudice from questions; judge to repeat all necessary instructions re: questioning procedure in final charge);

C v Mendez **77 MAC 905 (2010)**—juror questions obliterated well-considered "first complaint" evidentiary law in MA: "permitting jurors to submit questions in criminal cases is not without risk. Suffice it to say that in criminal cases involving subtle evidentiary issues like first complaint, judges should be particularly cautious in exercising discretion to permit jurors to submit questions and, if they are so permitted, in exercising discretion to post particular questions";

C v Hogan **426 M 424 (98)**—judges are not to participate as active negotiators in plea bargaining discussions; but *C v Federico* **40 MAC 616 (96)** then-accurate statement by judge to D, during change-of-plea colloquy, that Commonwealth could move to have D declared sexually dangerous was not an erroneous "interference" with plea bargain;

C v Sweezey **50 MAC 48 (2000)**—no relief for judge's questioning D at sidebar re: right to testify or not (though D argued that jury would have inferred in circumstances that D was invoking right not to testify), though "the clearly preferred practice is to conduct such a colloquy out of the presence of the jury";

C v Dedominicis **42 MAC 76 (97)**—judge (fact-finder on motion to suppress) not to participate in physical demonstration concerning evidence; opposing counsel unable to cross-examine;

C v Zavala **52 MAC 770 (2001)**—instead of ruling on D's motion for required finding of not guilty, judge allowed Commonwealth to reopen case & introduce necessary evidence to defeat the motion: "discretion" does not allow this "reduc(tion of) rule 25(a) to a nullity"; RFNG ordered;

C v O'Brien **423 M 841 (96)**—judge cannot rely on evidence introduced at bail hearing (at which he also presided) in decision on juvenile's amenability to rehabilitation; reliance on extra-record info "implicates fundamental fairness";

C v Zavala **52 MAC 770, 779 (2001)**—instead of ruling on D's motion for required finding of not guilty, judge allowed Commonwealth to reopen case & introduce necessary evidence to defeat the motion: "discretion" does not allow this "reduc(tion of) rule 25(a) to a nullity"; required finding of NG ordered;

ABA Standards for Criminal Justice (2d ed. 1986) Jury Trial, 15-3.8—judge shouldn't express/otherwise indicate to jury personal opinion re: guilt or witness credibility;

C v Krepon **32 MAC 945, 947–48 (92)**—"better practice" is for judge to refer to complaining witness as "alleged" victim, "in spite of the language contained in Model Jury Instructions For Use In The District Court § 4.13 (1988)";

C v Martin **424 M 301 (97)**—though Appeals Court reversed convictions (**39 MAC 658**) because of judge's instruction (which took rape complainant's claim as true that D had HIV), SJC said even **if** bias properly inferable, no substantial risk of miscarriage of justice (no objection at trial);

C v Figueroa **413 M 193, 197–98 (92)**—concern that singling out particular witness's testimony for instruction may intrude on jury's fact-finding function;

C v Lay **63 MAC 27, 32 (2005)**—similar, judge "correctly" declining to give instruction that Commonwealth witness had perjured self at suppression hearing when denying gang membership;

G.L. c. 231, § 81—shan't charge on matters of fact; but can state testimony/law;

C v Sheriff **425 M 186 (97)**—judge's instruction that defendant was at Bridgewater State Hospital voluntarily was both untrue and implied that he was perfectly fine but seeking to pad "insanity" defense: reversal;

C v Belding **42 MAC 435 (97)**—judge's response to jury question invaded "fact-finding" function of jury; stat-

ute was silent as to whether stated facts proved crime, & judiciary cannot fill in;

C v DeLosSantos **37 MAC 526 (94)**—reversal for judge's instruction, in response to jury question, that effectively precluded them from finding recklessness (and thus involuntary manslaughter) if they accepted defense contention that death resulted from dropping baby (slippery because wet) in bathroom;

C v Senbatu **38 MAC 904 (95)**—when defense was that D was consumer rather than dealer of drugs, judge's remark to counsel, in jury's presence, "there's no evidence at all that your client was a user" = error; reversal (with another issue);

Webb v Texas **409 US 95 (72)**—error to scare off D's witness by perjury threat;

C v Long **419 M 798 (95)**—reversal for judge's single-minded "rehabilitation" of potential juror, whose bias was clear, but who was not excused for cause;

C v Lucien **440 M 658 (2004)**—refusal to find error in judge's interruption, after cross-examination question, with "if you don't have a memory, just tell us, please," despite D's claim that this impermissibly "rescued" witness; judge should not have given "folksy send-off" to witness (thanking her, wishing her well in college), but no objection/no substantial likelihood of miscarriage of justice;

C v Sneed **376 M 867 (78)**—judge became biased advocate;

C v Viera **41 MAC 206 (96)**—improper for judge to prosecute/invoke "summary contempt" upon his belief that D lied, prior to trial & not under oath, when he said that person arrested was his cousin rather than self;

C v FitzGerald **380 M 840 (80)**—should use "restraint"; extensive examination by judge not encouraged because possible prejudice; counsel's duty to D may require objection to judge's questions; but see *C v Perez* **390 M 308, 315 (83)** "in light of delicate problem that objections to a judge's actions present to defense counsel, we do not weigh heavily against the D the absence of an objection";

C v Watkins **63 MAC 69 (2005)**—despite fact that trial was to a judge rather than jury, counsel was required to object to judge's questioning of witness in order to preserve issue for appeal;

C v Martelli **38 MAC 669 (95)**—reversal for jury-waived trial judge's refusal to hear closing argument ("don't bury yourself"; "I don't want to hear anything"; "If you want to do it, fine . . . I'm giving you friendly advice");

C v Kirker **362 M 202 (72)**—no objection to judge's questions impugning witness credibility;

C v Hassey **40 MAC 806, 808–9 (96)**—judge's question of defense witness "you didn't go down to the . . . police department and say, 'My friend is wrongfully charged with rape and the woman . . . has said she wants to get even with him?'" was "a too partisan entry on the side of the prosecution," and wasn't harmless;

C v Mosby **11 MAC 1 (80)**—judge's criticism of counsel criticized;

C v Phetsaya **40 MAC 293 (96)**—judge's criticisms of defense counsel, including calling him incompetent & ineffective, were such intimidation as to excuse lack of objection to mistrial declaration: later double jeopardy claim (on basis of no "manifest necessity" for mistrial on alleged ground of counsel's incompetence) successful;

C v Lebon **37 MAC 705 (94)**—lobby conference advice to D that G after jury-waived trial would result in sentence without incarceration, but G after jury trial would result in incarceration yielded involuntary jury waiver and reversal; *C v Hendricks* **452 M 97, 108 n.6 (2008)**—interpreting judge's statements NOT to be a threat that jury would know of his criminal record, but as an attempt to assure D that he would receive a fair trial jury-waived even though judge knew of his criminal history;

Adams v Yellow Cab **12 MAC 931 (81)**—reverse because "repeated jibes" at counsel made counsel ineffective;

C v Anslono **9 MAC 867 (80)**—judge's intimidation throughout trial excuses not objecting to charge;

C v Sylvester **388 M 749 (83)**—judge's comments harassing D's attorney deprived D of fair trial;

C v Ragonesi **22 MAC 320 (86)**—questioning of rape complainant at voir dire was excessive/inexcusable & resulted in thoroughly coerced witness (& new trial);

C v Fiore **364 M 819 (74)**—judge's questions not clearly biased or coercive; cf. *C v Webster* **391 M 271, 274–75 (84)**—judge questioned/intimidated holdout juror, such that she called in "sick" for continuing deliberations next day & was replaced (strident D-counsel objections apparent!);

C v Coleman **390 M 797 (84)**—OK here, but judge shouldn't prejudge case before D's evidence;

C v Grogan **11 MAC 684 (81)**—judge's questions of D's witness OK where showed no bias & clarified matters to D's benefit;

C v Slaney **345 M 135 (62)**—judge can warn witness re: 5th Amendment (while D is cross-examining) (*see Chapter 7-H Fifth Amendment & article 12 issues; but see also Chapter 7-M, Recusal, Misconduct, & Discipline of Judges*);

C v Cohen **27 MAC 1210 (89)**—judge's rebuke of defense counsel in front of jury for his vigorous questioning of impartial witness was improper;

C v Marangiello **410 M 452 (91)**—trial judge's persistent questioning of deaf-mute victim about ability to identify D was proper where done to clarify victim's confusing responses;

C v Conley **34 MAC 50 (93)**—judge's requiring D counsel to inform him of the "area" of each defense witness's expected testimony = STRONGLY disapproved, but no claim that any evidence was barred, & since at sidebar, jury not prejudiced, so no reversal;

C v Sapoznik **28 MAC 236, 241 n.4 (90)**—judge presiding over trial of pro se D should have intervened to prevent improper tactics by prosecutor;

C v Pallotta **36 MAC 669 (94)**—in barring defense psychiatrist's testimony, judge erred: he "could not claim superior expertness" simply because he believed that D merely had a personality disorder & ingested drugs; this was subversion of function of expert testimony as help to non-experts, including judge;

C v Roberio **428 M 278, 281 (98)**—once expert's individual qualifications are ratified and his area of expertise found to be legitimate under *Lanigan* **419 M 15 (94)**, judge cannot deny motion for new trial (on basis of ineffective assistance of counsel in failing to present such testimony at trial) based on judge's assessment of witness's credibility;

C v Green **25 MAC 751 (88)**—pretrial instruction that witnesses don't lie was reversible (with more);

C v Reynolds **429 M 388 (99)**—judge shouldn't make comments which could influence jurors' opinions about a witness;

C v Davis **52 MAC 75 (2001)**—when veracity of "cooperating witness" was sole issue (& though no specific deal had been set for his own pending criminal case, he expected "consideration" in exchange for his testimony against D), reversal because judge responded to jury question wanting to know what "consideration" ('May we please know if there are laws of leniency that may apply here. If so, what are they?'), without consulting counsel & in materially misleading way ("there are no laws of leniency");

C v Ortiz **39 MAC 70 (95)**—reversal for judge's refusal to instruct on impeachment (of cop) by prior inconsistent statement, coupled with statement to jury that "this is not a case on whether or not good police reports are being made" & cop "is not being tried for what he does or doesn't put in his police report";

C v Murchison **418 M 58 (94)**—reversal for judge's instruction that D-counsel's closing argument (that police witnesses were lying) was improper;

C v Caramanica **49 MAC 376 (2000)**—improper incursion into jury's role to instruct that "very few people come into court with an intention to mislead" and credibility means "accuracy more than honesty";

C v Richards **53 MAC 333 (2001)**—judge's repeatedly informing the jury that they were hearing ONLY the best quality of information/"high quality information" (intended to explain/justify bench conferences, excluded evidence, etc.) had effect of improper endorsement of Commonwealth witnesses' testimony, particularly in conjunction with judge's refusal to instruct specifically on possibility of good faith but mistaken identification, & given that pre-trial instructions had included advice that "high quality" evidence was "relevant and reliable and non-prejudicial"; error also specifically equated 'reliability' with 'credibility', & directed that very few witnesses intend to lie;

C v Moorer **431 M 544 (2000)**—reversal for judge's exclusion of cross-examination re: racial bias and his order during defense counsel's closing argument to "get off the racial card. . . . There is no racial card in this case";

C v Wood **37 MAC 917 (94)**—when defense contended police ineptitude & favoritism toward a prosecution witness prevented proper investigation, judge should not have said "effectiveness of police department is not at issue"; error here;

12-E. CONSCIOUSNESS OF GUILT (AND INNOCENCE)

See Chapter 11-G, Evidence: Admissions of D (by Conduct);

See also Argument, Chapter 12-J; Chapters 9-G, 11-G & -J re: inferences from D's silence;

2 Wigmore, *Evidence,* **§§ 273–76 (Chadbourn rev. 1979)**—though consciousness of guilt is highly probative, drawing inference of it from conduct is problematic-inferences differ for same conduct, different persons; assess the evidence as best we can re: particular D; "The wicked flee, even when no man pursueth, but the righteous are bold as a lion"; § 293: judges distrust consciousness of innocence since the conduct's often feigned or artificial, but distrust = "IMPROPER"; let in D's whole conduct;

12-E.1. General

***US v Hernandez-Bermudez* 857 F.2d 50 (1st Cir. '88)** consciousness of guilt often has little probative value; rules questioned by some courts because "innocent sometimes fly";

12-E.2. Flight, Lies, Statements, Particular Actions

***C v Sherick* 23 MAC 338 (87)**—lie to cops = consciousness of guilt;

***C v Fancy* 349 M 196 (65)**—false name at arrest = consciousness of guilt, but (even with mere presence) not enough to support G. finding, especially if outstanding warrants;

***C v Rodriguez* 50 MAC 405, 418 (2000)**—(despite fact that defense in rape case was "mistaken identity") consciousness of guilt evidence is admissible and probative when, e.g., D lied to police about not having gotten wet on night of crime, and not having bought beer;

***C v Travis* 408 M 1 (90)**—D's jailhouse statement that he knew he was going to be indicted for murder & that he could "give" cops a body was admissible to show consciousness of guilt;

***C v Carrion* 407 M 263 (90)**—" wanted" flyer posted for almost one year not admissible to show consciousness of guilt where there was no evidence that D aware of it; D's giving false name & address at booking & his absence from home 20 times police checked was admissible to show consciousness of guilt;

***C v Porro* 74 MAC 676, further rev. allowed 455 M 1106 (2009)**—after hitting motorcyclist with his government-issued car, D took it for repair to out-of-state relative and did not report accident to supervisor as required = consciousness of guilt, but ERROR not to allow introduction of statements made to D by his supervisor regarding previous claim for repair, i.e., tight budget and condemnation of D, probative of D's state of mind (but no relief because cumulative of other evidence);

***C v Roberts* 407 M 731 (90)**—D's attempt to escape on way to court appearance admissible to show consciousness of guilt;

***C v Muckle* 59 MAC 631 (2003)**—definitive protocol for what to do when D fails to appear mid-trial; CAUTION IS NECESSARY; REVERSAL FOR JUDGE'S ACTIONS HERE; no adverse inferences to be invoked so casually;

***C v Spina* 1 MAC 805 (73)**—D's flight from cops = ambiguous, & not enough for G. where other evidence very "slight";

***C v Lorenzetti* 48 MAC 37, 44 (99)**—that D left the house when his wife asked him to (wife having heard allegation that he fondled overnight visitor) was not "flight"/consciousness of guilt;

***C v Haraldstad* 16 MAC 565 (83)**—evidence concerning D's statement to police not what DA said it was, and didn't support consciousness of guilt argument or charge;

***C v Vick* 454 M 418 (2009)**—D had been identified near scene as shooter, by distinctive shirt worn, but in jail cell removed it and gave it to cousin to wear: concurring opinion asserts that this could not be consciousness of guilt BECAUSE D FREELY ACKNOWLEDGED TO police that he had been wearing the shirt and removed it only because his cousin was cold; majority asserts that shirt removal was to avoid witnesses' identifications of him by the shirt (but the ID's had already occurred, at the scene);

***C v Brousseau* 421 M 647 (95)**—testimony that D asked witness whether someone would be able to match gun shells from murder being tried with shells from another homicide OK because showed D's control over the weapon (in D's possession prior to the shooting) and consciousness of guilt;

***C v Tracy* 27 MAC 455 (89)**—D's statements suggesting that he would probably 'end up behind the wall at Concord' for his involvement in supermarket robbery overheard during phone call from police station admissible to show consciousness of guilt, even though it implied that D had prior record;

***C v White* 27 MAC 789 (89)**—false name on D's driver's license & registration assumed to be improper consciousness of guilt evidence; prosecutor's questioning of D about noncooperation with cops not improper where door was opened by defense counsel & where D's testimony that he invoked right to remain silent was not foreseeable;

***C v Carapellucci* 429 M 579, 583 (99)**—D's telephone call to passenger in his car day after accident, saying sorry, he'd never do anything to hurt her, etc., admissible as consciousness of guilt in prosecution for operating after license suspension and leaving scene of accident, despite fact that "expressions of sympathy and regret" are not admissible IN CIVIL CASES as an admission of responsibility or liability;

C v Sheriff **425 M 186 (97)**—OK to instruct that suicide attempt could be considered consciousness of guilt even though "innocent explanation" available, i.e., paranoid schizophrenic is ten times more likely than healthy individual to commit suicide;

C v Person **400 M 136 (87)**—consult attorney after incident not consciousness of guilt;

C v Swafford **441 M 329, 342 (2004)**—fatal gunshots were fired from D's car, but it wasn't consciousness of guilt that the car's formerly clear windows were tinted later, or that D's sister registered the car in her name and he had her retrieve it after it was towed four months after shooting, or that D began to drive a different car two months afterward;

12-E.3. Defaults as Consciousness of Guilt

C v Hightower **400 M 267 (87)**—default not consciousness of guilt (without evidence D knew court date);

C v Kane **19 MAC 129 (84)**—D's disappearance after recess didn't justify DA comment & consciousness of guilt charge because it's speculation that D voluntarily split;

C v Muckle **59 MAC 631 (2003)—PROTOCOL TO BE FOLLOWED WHEN D FAILS TO APPEAR MIDTRIAL:** judge must determine whether trial should proceed, or mistrial instead, and must first determine whether D's absence is without cause/voluntary; recess for investigation = appropriate; evidence to be produced ON THE RECORD, as to inquiries made, efforts to find D; judge to make finding re: 'without cause/voluntariness of absence'; if judge determine to continue trial in absentia, "neutral instruction" should be given that D may not be present; if there will be no evidence introduced to jury re: consciousness of guilt, judge "may add that the jury should not speculate as to the reasons for D's absence & should not draw adverse inferences; IF ADA seeks to introduce evidence to lay foundation for consciousness of guilt instruction, judge should determine whether introduction of such evidence "is warranted"; if so, judge to allow "brief" development, "subject to such discretionary limitations as the judge believes necessary"; if judge determines consciousness of guilt instruction is appropriate, *C v Toney*, 385 M at 585 (tailored to D's failure to appear at trial) to be given;

12-E.4. Not Probative of Malice (Premeditation? Extreme Atrocity or Cruelty?)

C v Riley **433 M 266, 270 n.5 (2001)**—consciousness of guilt evidence (washing off gun, false story to cops) not probative of malice aforethought, i.e., whether murder rather than manslaughter, citing *C v Epsom* **399 M 254, 259 (87)**, though is probative of whether 'criminal homicide' was committed;

C v Blaikie **375 M 601, 605 (78)**—consciousness of guilt evidence (conduct of D after a killing in attempt to avoid detection) is "rarely relevant to the issue of premeditation"; *C v Rice* **427 M 203 (98)**, *C v Degro* **432 M 319 (2000)** similar/related;

C v Auclair **444 M 348, 360–61 (2005)**—"There is no blanket prohibition on use of consciousness of guilt to infer premeditation"; contrary to D's claim here, "lying as evidence of consciousness of guilt has supported conviction based on the theory of extreme atrocity or cruelty" (citing *Torres* **442 M 554, 565–66 & n.9 (2004)**);

12-E.5. Witness Intimidation

C v Goetzendanner **42 MAC 637 (97)**—evidence of witness intimidation admissible in trial for rape/forcible confinement, as consciousness of guilt and to explain complainant's "inconsistent conduct toward" D (e.g., recantation, visiting him in jail); no need to sever trials of (a) witness intimidation and (b) violent assaults, since the witness intimidation was admissible in the latter trial as consciousness of guilt;

C v Scanlon **412 M 664 (92)**—evidence that D swerved car to hit complainant seven months after rape complaint admissible to show consciousness of guilt, even though not necessarily designed to influence or prevent witness's testimony;

12-E.6. Failure/Refusal to Cooperate with Police/Make Statements

See also Chapters 11G, particularly 11-G.1 and -G.4; 7-H; 10-A.3

C v Conkey **430 M 139 (99)**—D's failure to appear at police station for fingerprinting during investigation of housebreak/murder NOT ADMISSIBLE as consciousness of guilt, and use of this evidence VIOLATED ARTICLE 12, Declaration of Rights; while Article 12 doesn't protect person from having to provide "real or physical evidence," it does protect person from being compelled to furnish evidence which has a testimonial aspect; conduct here offered to show D's state of mind was "testimonial"; but see *C v Johnson* **46 MAC 398 (99)** when D testified that he had not disguised his voice during voice ID procedure (thereby making more significant witness's failure to ID him there), OK ("opened the door") for Commonwealth to introduce fact that D refused previously to participate in two scheduled voice ID procedures; D failed to object to DA's closing argument ("would innocent man fail to show up on two separate dates . . . ?") and didn't properly request consciousness of guilt instruction;

C v Irwin **72 MAC 643 (2008)**—reversal (despite no objection) for prosecutor's use in case in chief, in cross-examination, and in closing argument) of D's failure to reach out to police and delay in speaking to police about allegation of sexual assault, citing *Thompson* 431 M 108, 117 (2000) and *Nickerson* 386 M 54 (82) (impeachment of

D with fact of prearrest silence should be approached with caution, is of "extremely limited probative worth");

C v Delaney **442 M 604 (2004)**—can introduce evidence that, after D was told of warrant authorizing police to take D to station to be examined by physician, he asked if he were under arrest (no), and then began to walk away from officers: evidence of resistance to warrant/court order doesn't violate Article 12;

C v Seymour **39 MAC 672 (96)**—no consciousness of guilt from failure to take breathalyzer test: error to cross-examine D on this, compounded by DA's closing argument (see *Opinion of Justices* **412 M 1201 (92)** & *C v Zevitas* **418 M 677 (94)**); see Article 12, Declaration of Rights);

C v Hinckley **422 M 261 (96)**—evidence of D's refusal to allow police to examine his sneakers (for match to prints at crime scene), admitted as consciousness of guilt, violated Article 12: **was** "testimonial" on rationale of *Opinion of Justices* **412 M 1201 (92)**;

C v White **27 MAC 789 (89)**—false name on D's driver's license & registration assumed to be improper consciousness of guilt evidence; prosecutor's questioning of D about noncooperation with cops not improper where door was opened by defense counsel & where D's testimony that he invoked right to remain silent was not foreseeable;

12-E.7. Denial of Guilt Isn't Consciousness of Guilt

C v Mitchell **20 MAC 902 (85)**—DA argued that D's statement of alibi was admissible as evidence of consciousness of guilt, because Commonwealth's proof generally showed D's guilt; argument "smacks of circularity," reasoning from evidence of D's guilt, that his alibi could be found false, and then permitting fact finder to infer the defendant's guilt in part from the fact that he gave a false alibi;

C v Robles **423 M 62 (96)**—though mere denial of guilt not consciousness of guilt, specific statements in D's denial could be found to contain deliberate misstatements intended to "mislead" police, & so viewable as consciousness of guilt; but see *C v Waite* **422 M 792, 801 (96)** use of D's post-charge denials of guilt to infer guilt = clear error, though harmless here;

C v Diaz **453 M 266 (2009)**—D's recorded statements denying that he shot anyone, denying he was in Lowell on date of shooting, denying he had been driving Mitsubishi = inadmissible (citing *Nawn* 394 M 1 [85]); argument that they were false and thus admissible as "consciousness of guilt = REJECTED (if such were so, "rule prohibiting evidence of statements of denial would be eviscerated," every denial becoming admissible as 'consciousness of guilt'); here, however, error=harmless beyond reasonable doubt;

C v Lavalley **410 M 641 (91)**—D's initial "false" statement to cops which substantially differed from his trial testimony was admissible to show consciousness of

guilt so long as purpose was not to suggest D's failure to deny charges;

C v Richotte **59 MAC 524 (2003)**—even if D doesn't testify at trial, his trial "theory" may be "impeached" by its inconsistency with what D stated to cops earlier, citing *Commonwealth v. Donovan*, 58 Mass. App. Ct. 631, 640, 792 N.E.2d 657 (2003), "variance and inconsistency between . . . post-Miranda statements and the defense theory at trial are not off-limits to the prosecution even if the defendant does not testify";

C v Mack **423 M 288 (96)**—though false name at arrest for robbery argued to be consciousness of guilt of robbery, OK to argue consciousness of guilt at trial of unrelated homicide—"weight" not "admissibility";

C v Jackson **419 M 716 (95)**—similar (weight, not admissibility);

C v Burke **414 M 252 (93)**—same;

C v Mortell **42 MAC 947 (97)**—D's hiding in closet admissible as consciousness of guilt even though he argued hiding not because of guilt of crimes charged, but because of feared parole violation arrest for an unrelated crime;

C v Booker **386 M 466 (82)**—D hid from police in closet = consciousness of guilt; motive from unrelated default warrant goes to weight, not admissibility;

C v Prater **431 M 86, 97 (2000)**—though D argued flight was most obviously consciousness of guilt of marijuana possession (found on his person after chase) and shouldn't merit consciousness of guilt instruction re: murder, "for the jury to decide if (D's) actions resulted from consciousness of guilt or some other reason";

C v Hardy **431 M 387, 394–95 (2000)**—similar: D's lie about whereabouts was purportedly because of guilt of drug transaction rather than murder for which he was on trial, but up to jury to determine motivation; see, however, *C v Reveron* **75 MAC 354, 358–59 (2009)**—can't say consciousness was of armed robbery resulting in murder rather than drug deal carrying 15-year mandatory sentence;

12-E.8. Required Finding of Not Guilty if ONLY Evidence = Consciousness of Guilt

C v Mandile **403 M 93 (88)**—intent not shown (though drove car after co-D killed V), so consciousness of guilt (hid co-D's gun) doesn't defeat required finding of not guilty (*Chapter 12-G, Required Finding of NG*);

C v Hunt **50 MAC 565 (2000)**—consciousness of guilt used to defeat required finding of not guilty of receiving stolen vehicle: despite absence of evidence as to when stolen, and thus no otherwise reasonable inference that it was "recently" stolen, implying that D knew it was stolen, D attempted to avoid police, lied about any connection to the car, & parked it so as to hide license plate;

C v Reveron **75 MAC 354 (2009)**—affirming dismissal of indictment for first degree murder as to D, who introduced well-funded drug buyers to major supplier: parties to anticipated drug deal drove away and supplier subsequently shot and killed buyer and fled with money; D's lies to police later insufficient for probable cause to believe D knew of planned robbery, since consciousness of guilt was obvious as to 15-year mandatory minimum drug crime;

12-E.9. Acts/Statements of Another as Probative of Consciousness of Guilt

C v Pringle 22 MAC 746 (86)—co-D's alias not consciousness of guilt re: D (& not part of alleged joint venture);

C v McQuade 46 MAC 827, 829 (99)—alleged joint venturers' false statements of alibi admissible at D's trial; judge within discretion in ruling that there was "adequate probability of the existence of . . . a continuing common venture to conceal the crime" at the time the statements were made so soon after the commission of the crime;

C v Caillot 454 M 245 (2009)—co-defendants' respective statements (purportedly false) admitted at joint trial without limitation, despite no judicial finding that they were made in furtherance of joint venture and judge did not instruct jury of necessity of such finding (n.8): incoherent affirmance of murder conviction nonetheless;

*C v Ciampa 406 M 257 (89)—jury instructions that D's consciousness of guilt may be inferred from testimony of alibi witnesses are improper; consciousness of guilt may only be inferred from D's own conduct or statements;

C v Howell 49 MAC 42 (2000)—error to admit evidence that D's father (trial witness) refused or failed to "cooperate" with police in bringing in D for questioning: witness acknowledged "bias" toward son, and was under no "obligation, legal or otherwise, to honor" police "request";

C v Awad 47 MAC 139, 143–44 (99)—insinuating, in closing argument, D's guilt from D's sister's alleged failure to "help" police, thereby "laugh(ing) off this victim", with other transgressions, = reversal;

C v Jenkins 34 MAC 135 (93) *aff'd* 416 M 736 (94) evidence that someone did "something to (witness's) house," impliedly seeking to discourage her from testifying, admissible even though **no** evidence D played any role; witness's trial testimony was not so inculpatory of D as was her testimony to grand jury and at probable cause hearing;

C v Martinez 431 M 168 (2000)—abuse of discretion to admit evidence that D's niece threatened chief witness (witness's testimony at trial no less adverse than previous statements);

C v Cohen 412 M 375 (92)—cops' testimony that D's father pointed to room where D hiding while simultaneously stating that D wasn't home was admissible to explain cops' approach to D, but not as evidence of third party's consciousness of D's guilt;

C v Mahoney 405 M 326 (89)—acts of a joint venturer amounting to consciousness of guilt may be attributed to another joint venturer if the acts occurred during the course of a joint venture and in furtherance of it; judge either should not have focused on D's husband's conduct (allegedly her joint venturer) in discussing consciousness of guilt or should have explained more fully the limited extent to which the husband's conduct in the vehicle bore on D's guilt, but no reversible error in charge "as a whole";

12-E.10. Flight of the Culprit, Identity in Issue

C v Groce 25 MAC 327 (88)—don't charge consciousness of guilt if culprit fled & issue = identity;

C v Pina 430 M 266 272 (99)—"there is no rationale for a consciousness of guilt instruction where the only contested issue is identification and there is no dispute that the person fleeing the scene of the crime was the same as the assailant";

C v Horsman 47 MAC 262 (99)—although evidence of the assailant's flight "(does) not shed any light on the issue of identification," and an instruction on consciousness of guilt might convey to the jury that the judge believes that it was the defendant himself who fled, court here distinguished *Groce 25 MAC 327*, saying there was consciousness of guilt evidence here connected to this D (e.g., false statements), not just flight by the assailant;

C v Vick 454 M 418, 438 (2009)—concurring opinion (Botsford, J.) believes *Groce* applied (culprit fled, but issue was whether D was the culprit), and instruction based on flight should not have been given; majority opinion had agreed that D's walking away from part of park where police were arresting companions was NOT 'flight', but purported to distinguish earlier conduct ("flight" INTO park) from *Groce*;

C v Rodriguez 50 MAC 405, 418 (2000)—despite fact that defense in rape case was "mistaken identity," consciousness of guilt evidence is admissible and probative when, e.g., D lied to police about not having gotten wet on night of crime, and not having bought beer;

12-E.11. Jury Instructions, Consciousness of Guilt; Consciousness of Innocence

C v Haraldstad 16 MAC 565 (83)—"It is error to instruct a jury on consciousness of guilt based on facts without reasonable support in the record";

C v Porter 384 M 647, 648 n.10 (81)—"fair and well-balanced" consciousness of guilt instructions;

**C v Toney 385 M 575, 585 n.6 (82)—consciousness of guilt instructions must say: (1) don't convict on flight/concealment alone, & (2) MAY, but need not, consider it as 1 factor to prove G.; IF REQUESTED, judge should caution re: dangers in inferring G. from flight—(1) many innocent reasons for flight, & (2) though one feels G., may be innocent; see also *C v Cruz* 416 M 27 (93) strong endorsement of necessity for consciousness of guilt cautionary instructions, though Cruz command to trial judge to

instruct, **sua sponte**, was overturned in *Simmons* **419 M 426 (95)**—judge **not** required to give *Toney* instruction in absence of request;

C v Matos **394 M 563 (85)**—reverse for no Toney charge; "should" give Toney charge **if asked**;

C v Estrada **25 MAC 907 (87)**—reverse because Toney sought & denied;

C v Martin **19 MAC 117 (84)**—OK not to charge on consciousness of innocence; discretion whether to admit consciousness of innocence evidence (n.7);

C v Ouen Lam **420 M 615 (95)**—consciousness of innocence properly left to argument, without jury instructions, even though consciousness of guilt instructions were here requested & given. But see **2 Wigmore, *Evidence*, § 293 (Chadbourn rev. 1979), at 232–33**—since consciousness of guilt is a dubious inference, should not refuse to admit the "scarcely more dubious one" of consciousness of innocence; cf. presumption of innocence, due process, Article 12, 14th Amendment;

C v Pina **430 M 266, 273 (99)**—"judge does not err, or abuse discretion, by refusing to give a consciousness of innocence instruction"; but see Stevens, J., dissenting , in *US v Scheffer* **523 US 303, 331 (98)**;

C v Knap **412 M 712 (92)**—consciousness of innocence instructions not required to counterbalance consciousness of guilt instructions, so long as instructions comply with *Toney* **385 M 575 (82)**; consciousness of innocence best left to D's closing argument;

Superior Court Criminal Practice Jury Instructions, **§ 4.19, Consciousness of Guilt**;

12-F. FAILURE TO TEST—REASONABLE DOUBT FROM WHAT'S MISSING

See also "Missing Witness" inference, Chapter 12-J (Closing Argument); evidence concerning (more) likely suspects, Chapter 18-C (Identification: Right to Show Mistaken Identification);

CPCS P/G's 4.6(h), 6.1(a)(3)—expert help for D; 6.6(d)(7): be alert to omissions/deficiencies in testimony/investigation of DA case; 6.8(c)(1): argue weaknesses in DA case, esp. corroborative stuff missing (& DA burden of proof);

Superior Court Criminal Practice Jury Instructions, **§ 5.6.1 (MCLE)**—absence of investigation or testing;

See also Chapter 7-C & L, Expert for D, Lost Evidence; Chapter 11-I, Evidence: Opinions; & Chapter 9, Cross-Examination;

Mass. Declaration of Rights, Article 12—right to present defense;

U.S. Constitution, Sixth Amendment—(same);

C v Preziosi **399 M 748 (87)**—affirm because counsel didn't object to bad charge re: failure to test for fingerprints;

C v Bowden **379 M 472 (80)**—failure to test or produce evidence (prints on gun) = grounds for reasonable doubt defense; charge to ignore it = error; cf. argument made in *C v Wolinski* **431 M 228, 233 (2000)**—that judge's instruction, in response to jury note saying "questions unanswered; evidence incomplete; cannot decide," that case must be decided on evidence presented and jurors were "not to speculate about any unanswered questions that still remain" should have included admonition about burden being on Commonwealth;

C v Sineiro **432 M 735, 744 (2000), quoting from *DiCarlo v US* 6 F2d 364, 368 (2d Cir. 1925, Learned Hand, J.)**—"If, from all that the jury see of the witness, they conclude that what he says now is not the truth, but what he said before, they are nonetheless deciding from what they see and hear of that person and in court. There is no mythical necessity that the case must be decided only in accordance with the truth of words uttered under oath in court"; jury may conclude from observing a witness that what he says now is not the truth, but what he said before is true: "they are nonetheless deciding from what they see and hear of that person and in court";

C v Gilmore **399 M 741 (87)**—can argue inferences from what's missing—D's booking photo (re: alleged scratches by complaining witness) & his unseized clothing;

C v Benoit **382 M 210 (81)**—inadequacies of tests performed, & existence of more reliable tests, = relevant & admissible;

C v Reynolds **429 M 388 (99)**—error to bar cross-examination and independent testimony concerning tipsters' info pointing to guilt of persons other than D (not for truth, but for fact tips were made and not investigated), though trial judge denied on mere basis that Commonwealth claimed primary police investigator did investigate tips;

C v Silva-Santiago **453 M 782 (2009)**—defense counsel sought to question cop about info received from named person that another named person was the murderer (not D); proffered as "3rd party culprit information" and "to impeach the investigation," i.e., a "Bowden" defense; former basis was infirm, as it was hearsay (offered for truth); same info more likely admissible as part of Bowden defense (and judge erred in ruling that exclusion on former basis required exclusion on latter rationale); voir dire should have occurred, but counsel's proffer defective;

C v Ridge **455 M 307 (2009)**—D was charged with execution-style shooting (in head) of male and female on 6/25, duct tape used over mouth, the male having been a drug dealer; on 6/26 local police received "national broadcast" from Florida police asking for contact from any agency having info on execution-style murder within past week involving two persons, possible male and female, tied to chairs & learned that the head shots and use of silver duct tape was "trademark of Columbians in the Florida drug world"; D didn't appeal trial judge's ruling that this "unknown third-party culprits" evidence was too speculative and remote for admission, but did argue that he should have been allowed to cross-examine police to argue failure to investigate (not hearsay because purportedly not "for truth of matter" that victims were killed by Columbian drug dealers); though there should have been a voir dire, no relief because probative value not shown to have outweighed "risk of unfair prejudice";

C v Raposa **440 M 684 (2004)**—though *C v Bowden* preserves D's right to attack adequacy of police investigation, such attack "is still constrained by" rules of evidence, i.e., no inadmissible hearsay;

C v Young **73 MAC 479 (2009)**—juror voir dire included question, "if Commonwealth presented only testimony of witnesses, and presented no corroborating scientific evidence, would you *automatically* find D not guilty, or would you make an independent assessment of the evidence?"; this was not the equivalent of an instruction, barred by *Bowden* 379 M 472, 485 (80), that 'a lack of scientific evidence is not to be considered in reaching a judgment'; D was not prevented from arguing 'lack of police investigation';

C v Tripolone **57 MAC 901 (2003)**—refusal to instruct or to allow "missing witness" comment on absence of third cop in 3-cop team which visited complainant's home after alleged rape (evidence list, some evidence, and videotape there made, were lost before trial), even though the two testifying cops had different memories; absent witness/testimony said to be "peripheral" (cumulative?);

C v Niels N **73 MAC 689 (2009)**—no error in refusing missing witness instruction when NO investigating police officer was called to testify (D didn't show what testimony of distinct importance they could provide and "does not claim" that witnesses weren't "equally available to him to call at trial" and doesn't explain why he chose not to call them himself);

C v Rodriguez **378 M 296 (79)**—D can show ID suggestiveness & existence of fairer procedures not used;

C v Rivera **424 M 266 (97)**—no right to jury instruction on failure to test D's & other suspects' hands for gunpowder residue; D was permitted to argue inference to jury AND there was testimony that the residue test would have been unreliable due to lapse of time between murder and arrest of D and other suspects and that the test was "unavailable in the Commonwealth";

C v Jackson **23 MAC 975 (87)**—judge can't negate D's argument (re: lack of search for loot) by charging that cops lacked probable cause to search; *compare C v Pena* 455 M 1 (2009)—after defense counsel argued Commonwealth's failure to call its expert witness (examining D for criminal responsibility), judge permissibly instructed sua sponte that jury could not speculate as to evidence not heard, and struck that portion of argument;

C v Baldwin **426 M 105 (97)**—while refusing to require judges to order videotaping of court-ordered psych. evaluation of D by prosecution expert, approving 'impeachment' of expert from his "reluctance to be monitored";

C v Porcher **26 MAC 517 (88)**—D can argue (no prints), but no instruction;

C v Avila **454 M 744 (2009)**—judge repeatedly instructed jury that certain pieces of evidence were being admitted for sole purpose of allowing jury to determine if police investigation was biased or faulty, and refusal to give a "Bowden" instruction in final charge did not serve to remove the issue from consideration;

C v Flanagan **20 MAC 472 (85)**—failure to test goes to cops' bias/credibility; relevance depends on reason why omitted; reason's relevant for both sides; but police opinion re: strength of case not admissible;

C v Lodge **431 M 461, 467 (2000)**—after cross-examination re: alleged deficiencies in the investigation & failure of police to conduct certain tests & pursue other suspects, error for cop to testify on redirect that he hadn't done any of this "because by the physical evidence & D's own words, everything pointed to him" as being G of murder, and to recount all incriminating evidence against D; this was an impermissible "general expression of the officer's opinion of guilt"; though cop "must be allowed to defend" police judgment/actions after defense puts same in issue, method must be "by inquiring . . . the reason for each specific omission or decision"; BEFORE ANY INQUIRY, prosecutor should request sidebar to alert judge to proposed line of questioning, & "if necessary, the specific questions to be asked and their expected responses";

C v Carrion **407 M 263 (90)**—evidence that cops prepared & posted wanted flyer admissible to rebut claim that cops failed to investigate diligently;

C v Avila **454 M 744 (2009)**—if D raises Bowden defense, Commonwealth has right to "rebut it" by testimony defending police judgment and decisions; determination of precisely what evidence is admissible to so rebut = "delicate and difficult decision"; "the more wide-ranging [D's] attack on the police investigation, the broader the Commonwealth's response may be"; here, judge repeatedly gave limiting instructions re: cops' testimony about critical witness's out of court statements;

C v Adams **34 MAC 516 (93)**—though judge is not required to give jury instructions re: failure to test, it's "within (his) discretion" to do so;

C v Cordle **412 M 172 (92)**—cops' failure to conduct blood or gunshot residue on D's hands was valid basis for defense but judge had discretion not to instruct on it;

C v Wolinski **431 M 228, 233 (2000)**—instructions, in response to jury note saying "questions unanswered; evidence incomplete; cannot decide", included thoughtless standard, 'decide case based solely on evidence presented in court & don't speculate about any unanswered questions that remain'; apparent argument on appeal (not here acknowledged or addressed) = violates *Bowden* **379 M 472, 485 (80)** (judge can't remove from jury's consideration the import of perceived evidentiary deficiencies); request "curative" that directs that absence of evidence deemed by jury to be significant should be used in considering whether Commonwealth has met its burden of proving charge beyond reasonable doubt;

C v Remedor 52 MAC 694, 700–701 (2001)—judge's response to jury question, i.e., 'confine consideration to evidence that *was* presented,' negated D's "Bowden" (**379 M 472 (1980)**) defense, creating substantial risk of a miscarriage of justice;

C v Brewster 46 MAC 746 (99)—failure to preserve 911 tape, as ordered by court, relevant to defense (cast doubt on other evidence offered by Commonwealth), but judge permissibly concluded that the particular witness being questioned had no knowledge of the evidence sought;

C v Troy 405 M 253 (89)—instruction that jury could draw adverse inference against Commonwealth from its destruction of blood samples was proper;

C v Pina 430 M 266 (99)—judge instructed jury that they could consider absence of electronic recording as factor in decision whether Commonwealth established voluntariness of D's alleged waiver of silence and ensuing statement, but refused to similarly instruct re: absence of

signed written statement by D: no error; judge did "more than is required";

C v Wood 37 MAC 917 (94)—judge erred in instructing that "effectiveness of police department is not at issue" when defense contended police bias & ineptitude, but here harmless;

C v Reid 29 MAC 537 (90)—although judge has discretion whether or not to give Bowden instruction, "preferable" to instruct that police failure to record names of critical witnesses could create reasonable doubt;

C v Richardson 425 M 765 (97) and *C v Conley* 43 MAC 385, 397 (97)—no reversible error to refuse to instruct jury re: failure of police to test;

C v McIntyre 430 M 529, 544 n.14 (99)—same;

C v Hardy 431 M 387, 395 (2000)—same;

C v Leitzsey 421 M 694 (96)—trial counsel not ineffective in failing to request jury instruction re police failure to conduct certain tests; counsel argued the negative inference to jury & judge would not have been required to instruct anyway;

12-G. MOTION FOR REQUIRED FINDING OF NOT GUILTY

CPCS P/G 6.5(g)—unless clearly frivolous, when DA rests move for required finding of NG on charges &/or aggravating elements & seek immediate ruling; 6.7(l) renew motion after defense;

M.R.Crim.P. 25(a)—judge to enter on D's or own motion if at close of evidence on either side it's insufficient as matter/law to sustain G.; (b)(1) may reserve decision on motion made at close of all evidence (BUT must rule when made at close of DA's case) & decide before or after jury's verdict (or discharge); (b)(2) within 5 days of jury discharge, renew motion &/or for new trial; judge can order new trial, NG, or G of lesser included offense;

C v Brennan 74 MAC 44 (2009)—judge entering required finding of not guilty under R. 25(b)(2) "does not properly exercise discretion concerning the weight or integrity of the evidence," but instead must assess legal sufficiency of evidence pursuant to *Latimore* [378 M 671] standard; MAC here vacated order of trial judge & remanded for sentencing, holding Commonwealth evidence (circumstantial) sufficient to prove beyond reasonable doubt D's identity as gas station B&E culprit;

C v Latimore 378 M 671 (79)—required finding of NG standard: if evidence in light most favorable to DA, could any rational trier of fact find enough "credible" evidence for essential elements beyond a reasonable doubt?; more than "some record evidence";

Jackson v Virginia 443 US 307 (79)—state prisoner is entitled to habeas corpus relief if federal judge finds that upon record evidence at trial no rational trier of fact could have found proof of guilt beyond a reasonable doubt;

McDaniel v Brown 130 S Ct 665 (2010)—in determining whether there should be required finding of not guilty, federal habeas court must consider all of evidence

admitted at trial, even evidence which has been erroneously admitted; if there is reversal for insufficiency of evidence, retrial is barred as double jeopardy violation;

C v Smithson 41 MAC 545, 548 (96)—**M.R.Crim.P. 25(a)** requires judge to **rule** on required finding of NG motion at the time it is made at close of Commonwealth's evidence; "unequivocal" & "mandatory" language does not allow "reservation" of decision for later;

C v Robinson 48 MAC 329, 330 n.2 (99)—same;

C v Stokes 440 M 741 (2004)—if motion for required finding is only "generally phrased," it doesn't preserve for review the denial of motion on specific theory of liability when there WAS sufficient evidence on an alternative theory;

G.L. c. 278, § 11—new trial or NG on renewed motion for required finding of not guilty after jury G. (*see Chapter 15*);

Rule 25(c)—DA appeals required finding of not guilty (or G of only a lesser included) after jury G. (*see Keough 385 M 314 (82) R-25(b)(2)—judge can reduce jury G verdict to lesser included offense even though evidence = sufficient for greater; & Chapter 19, Double Jeopardy); but see Chapter 14, separation of powers (judge cannot reduce charge over Commonwealth objection prior to trial, G plea, admission to sufficient facts*);

K. Smith, *Criminal Practice & Procedure*, § 1905 (2d ed. 1983 & Supp.)—motion for required NG may lie to entire charge or to part of it; § 1921: under 25 (b)(2) after verdict, judge can enter G. lesser included offense though evidence warranted jury's greater G. (& DA can appeal: Rule 25(c)(1));

ABA Standards for Criminal Justice (2d ed. 1986), Jury Trial 15-3.5—can't reserve decision on motion for required finding of NG at close of DA's evidence, but can if motion after all evidence; COMMENT: motion would be futile if D forced to decide on resting without a ruling; (accord, *C v Zavala* **52 MAC 770 (2001)**)

See Chapter 5, Variance; & Chapter 19, Double Jeopardy;

C v Zavala **52 MAC 770 (2001)**—instead of ruling on D's motion for required finding of not guilty, judge allowed Commonwealth to reopen case & introduce necessary evidence to defeat the motion: "discretion" does not allow this "reduc(tion of) rule 25(a) to a nullity"; required finding NG ordered;

C v McGilvery **74 MAC 508 (2009)**—error to allow, after motion for required finding of not guilty of possession of Class A drug, "amendment" of complaint to charge possession of Class B drug; amendment was one of "substance" (new complaint and new trial on Class B not barred);

C v Zuluaga **43 MAC 629, 640–41 (97)**—reversal required when one alternative theory of guilt on which jurors were instructed (constructive possession) **not** supported by evidence and verdict did not specify what theory was found by jury; see also *C v Flynn* **420 M 810 (95)**; *C v Green* **420 M 771 (95)**; *C v Fickett* **403 M 194 (88)**; under federal constitution, US Supreme Court resolved this issue differently (*Griffin v US* **502 US 46 (91)**): affirm conviction if evidence supports any of the alternative theories on which jurors were instructed; but see *C v Stokes* **440 M 741 (2004)**—if motion for required finding is only "generally phrased," it doesn't preserve for review the denial of motion on specific theory of liability when there WAS sufficient evidence on an alternative theory;

****NOW SEE *C v Zanetti* 454 M 449 (2009)—SJC adopts means by which to uphold convictions when evidence is insufficient on one, but not the other option of 'joint venture' vs. 'principal' liability: **judges are to instruct jury that D is guilty if Commonwealth proved beyond reasonable doubt that D "knowingly participated in the commission of the crime charged, alone or with others, with the intent required for that offense";**

C v Rodriguez **58 MAC 610 (2003)**—because no evidence that victim was stabbed by anyone other than D, D couldn't be convicted on joint venture theory (even though D himself requested instruction on joint venture), and this theory couldn't be pursued at retrial necessitated by other error;

Taylor v Commonwealth **447 M 49 (2006)**—after hung jury, D urged that there could be no retrial on joint venture theory because only evidence was that he was the principal (i.e., the shooter); SJC rejected argument, holding that jury could reject witness's testimony that she understood D to have admitted being shooter, while accepting that he was member of group committing home invasion resulting in fatal shooting;

C v MacKedon **60 MAC 901 (2003)**—because the only evidence was that it was D who actually exchanged pills for cash (& he was alone with the buyer/undercover cop then), error to charge jury initially re: joint venture liability; error cured by judge withdrawing that instruction from jury consideration;

C v Hernandez **439 M 688 (2003)**—because evidence insufficient for inference of constructive possession of large quantity of cocaine, required finding of not guilty ordered on theory of principal liability for trafficking (though not on joint venture);

C v Jones **9 MAC 83, 90–91 (80)**—disbelief of evidence is not equivalent of proof to the contrary;

C v Eramo **377 M 912 (79)**—same;

C v Marino **343 M 725, 728 (62)**—same;

Boice-Perrine Co v Kelley **243 M 327, 330 (23)**—similar;

C v Dube **59 MAC 476, 487 (2003)**—can't prove case by producing opinions directly contradicting the conclusion one seeks to have fact-finder reach: disbelief of such opinions furnishes no "basis for finding the other way", quoting *C v Haggerty* **400 M 437, 442 (87)**;

Sturman v Davis **321 M 442, 444 (47)**—while trier of fact could believe parts of Commonwealth evidence and reject other parts, such division must be "reasonable" and "not result in distortion of the evidence";

C v Flynn **420 M 810, 815–18 (95)**—similar, though reasoning fact-specific;

C v Zanetti **454 M 449, 457–59 (2009)**—jury's right to believe/disbelieve parts of testimony doesn't permit distortion or mutilation of any integral portion of testimony to permit them to believe unfounded hypothesis; only by such distortion could there be sufficient evidence of joint venture liability on D's part;

Kater v Commonwealth **421 M 17 (95)**—circumstantial nature of evidence does not require NG finding; "deterioration" of Commonwealth evidence does not occur merely because D presents evidence which contradicts Commonwealth evidence, but instead occurs when necessary Commonwealth evidence is shown to be conclusively incorrect (e.g., *C v Vaughn* **23 MAC 40 (86)** conclusive record evidence of D's incarceration at time crime was committed elsewhere);

G.L. c. 278, § 7—D's burden of production re: license, e.g., firearm *(Chapter 21-BB)*;

C v Nickerson **236 M 281 (20)**—no burden of production on D if lack of authority = element;

D.Ct. Model Instruction 3.10, Note—G.L. c. 278, § 7 inapplicable to elements (e.g., use without authority, drive without insurance)—(*see Chapter 16, Defenses & Burdens of Proof*);

M.R.Crim.P. 14(b)(3)—written license defense notice or exclude it (*see Chapter 5-A, -B, Complaints and Indictments*);

C v Baker **368 M 58 (75)**—no right to required finding of not guilty after DA's opening (*see Chapter 12-C, Opening Statements, but see also *C v Lowder* **432 M 92 (2000)** permitting such required finding NG, with caveats*);

C v Jones **372 M 403 (77)**—can't direct a "guilty" verdict (cf. *Diaz* **19 MAC 29 (84)**, *Chapter 12-K, Jury Instructions*);

Burns v Commonwealth **430 M 444. 450–51 (99)**—prima facie evidence explained;

C v Lovett **374 M 394 (78) (rev'd other ground 610 F.2d 1002)**—motion for required finding of NG limited to "so much as charges nighttime B & E" didn't raise issue of overall guilt;

C v Apalakis **396 M 292 (85)**—trial judge (without objection) "narrowed" indictment by "deleting" 3/4 (alter/ forge/counterfeit) elements (leaving false making);

C v Cote **15 MAC 229 (83)**—DA can reopen (*but see Chapter 12-H, Rebuttal/Reopen*) after motion for required finding NG (to prove no consent to unlawful gas use) because DA mistaken re: burden of production on it; BUT SEE CONTRA *C v Zavala* **52 MAC 770 (2001)** a judge's "discretion" can't be used to so reduce **M.R.Crim.P. 25** "to a nullity";

C v Keough **385 M 314 (82) M.R.Crim.P. 25(b)(2)**—judge can reduce jury G verdict to lesser included offense though evidence sufficient for greater (see R-25(c) re: DA's appeal);

See Chapters 5-D (Complaints/Indictments: Variance & Lesser Included Offenses), 21 (Elements of Common Crimes) & 12-K (Jury Instructions) re: lesser included offenses;

C v Woodward **427 M 659, 666–72 (98)**—judge's reduction of jury verdict upheld (second degree murder reduced to manslaughter); standard of appellate review is "abuse of discretion"; trial judge's power under M.R. Crim.P. 25(b)(2) likened to SJC's power (in convictions of 1st degree murder) under G.L. c. 278, § 33E: "may be used to ameliorate injustice caused by the Commonwealth, defense counsel, the jury, the judge's own error, or, as may have occurred in this case, the interaction of several causes";

C v Therrien **383 M 529 (81)**—trial judge erred in granting post-G required finding of NG under 25(b); D can still ask for new trial under R.30 (fn.8); (*see Chapter 15, Appeals & Postconviction Remedies*);

C v James **424 M 770 (97)**—credibility of witness = solely for jury; no required finding of NG simply because Commonwealth case rested solely on testimony of juvenile witness who admitted lying to police & who received favorable treatment for his testimony;

C v Leavey **60 MAC 249, 251 (2004)**—alleged victim of boyfriend's abuse wholly recanted at trial, but her spontaneous utterances to neighbor, in 911 telephone call, and to responding police = sufficient for conviction, citing *C v Moquette* **439 M 697, 702 (2003)**; recantation goes to weight, but not admissibility or legal sufficiency; *C v Kelsall* **60 MAC 902 (2003)**, citing *Moquette* ("'a spontaneous utterance is sufficient, by itself, to support a conviction'");

C v Robinson **48 MAC 329 (99)**—no D may be convicted solely on testimony of witness testifying under grant of immunity (**G.L. c. 233, § 20I**), but this merely requires that there be some evidence to support testimony of witness on at least one element of proof essential to convict D (citing *Debrosky* **363 M 718, 730 (73)**);

C v Mandile **403 M 93 (88)**—some evidence, however slight, for each element not enough; no G. from piling inference on inference, or conjecture/speculation;

See Chapter 16, Defenses: Circumstantial Evidence;

C v Berry **431 M 326 (2000)**—required finding of not guilty ordered on joint venture theory, because right to such finding vested at close of Commonwealth evidence (& court couldn't deny based on snippets in ensuing defense evidence);

C v Kelley **370 M 147, 150 n.1 (76)**—to send to jury, judge case in light favorable to DA after DA's case notwithstanding D's later evidence; DA case may deteriorate by close of evidence—if so, motion for required finding of NG assesses all evidence;

C v Hastings **22 MAC 930 (86)**—"deterioration" doesn't mean conflict (arising from D's case) which is for jury to decide & not for RFNG;

C v Quinn **61 MAC 332, 334 (2004)**—same; jury could've disbelieved D's claim of "sick" rather than OUI;

C v Pike **430 M 317, 323 (99)**—renewed motion for required finding of NG after D's evidence should be granted (only) if D shows that evidence for Commonwealth necessary to warrant submission of case to jury is "incredible or conclusively incorrect," & standard not here met by evidence of D's good character and some expert testimony contradicting some of Commonwealth's expert evidence;

C v Fickett **403 M 194 (88)**—D's evidence too late to help DA on motion for required finding of NG (fn.2);

C v Amendola **26 MAC 713 (88), further appellate rev. granted, 404 M 1104 (89)**—(same)

C v Berry **431 M 326, 331,-332 & n.6 (2000)**—same, regarding theory of joint venture liability; though there was testimony that a friend of D told him to "put away the knife," and that a shiny object was seen in D's hand (and V died from stab wounds), fact that some witnesses did NOT see a knife in D's hands was not evidence that someone other than D possessed a knife, and could give rise to no inference that someone with whom D was acting in concert wielded knife; D's rights on required finding of NG vested at close of Commonwealth's case, on specific argument then made, i.e., insufficient evidence of joint venture liability; if 'required finding' argument had instead been only "general," no right to required finding of NG; see also *C v Flynn* **420 M 810 (95)**, re: insufficient evidence of individual liability, though sufficient evidence for G on joint venture liability;

C v Torres **442 M 554 (2004)**—vacate conviction (order new trial) because insufficient evidence of principal liability, though sufficient evidence for joint venture, and jury returned only "general" verdict;

C v Suarez **59 MAC 111 (2003)**—insufficient evidence to support instruction on "principal" liability; *C v Green* **420 M 771 (95)** joint venture charge not supported by evidence, though sufficient evidence for G as principal, general verdict of G, reversal required;

***C v Zanetti** 454 M 449 (2009)—required finding of not guilty should have entered on "joint venture" theory of first degree deliberate premeditation murder, but SJC purportedly couldn't infer from record that jury had unanimously acquitted D on "principal" theory, so Commonwealth not precluded from retrying D solely as principal; henceforth, judges are to mask insufficiency of evidence by "general" verdict slips, & convictions will be upheld if there is sufficient evidence to prove D knowingly participated in commission of the crime with intent required to commit the crime;

*C v Hailey** 62 MAC 250 (2004)—rejects D's argument for required finding of NG for homicide on "principal" liability, citing *C v Perry* 432 M 214, 225 (2000), re: when D causes injury which, along with other contributing factors or medical sequella, leads to death, "jurors may determine that the D's acts were the proximate cause of the injury"; D participated in the beating, and no evidence of any particular "discrete" and relatively harmless blow (unlike *Flynn* 420 M 810 (95));

*C v Bouvier** 316 M 489 (44)—D's testimony = only evidence how she shot husband, so can't say not accidental, so required finding of NG;

*C v Salemme** 395 M 594 (85)—conjecture, so required finding of NG where D & another had the same opportunity to kill V, & there was no witness to crime;

*C v Cannon** 449 M 462 (2007)—evidence inadequate to prove D's guilt as principal in shooting drug dealer (witness in another room heard shots fired, insufficient evidence to establish that shots came from more than one gun, and 2–3 assailants fled the scene), and jury verdict didn't specify whether conviction of murder was premised upon theory of principal or joint venture liability; reversal, with remand for new trial solely on joint venture liability; [if evidence sufficient to convict under either theory, general verdict "would have been sound"];

*C v Shellenberger** 64 MAC 70 (2005)—midtrial on charge of motor vehicle homicide by negligent operation, DA switched from "speeding" theory to "under the influence of amphetamines", causing reversal (but not required finding of not guilty): at minimum, there had to be evidence as to amount or concentration of the drug in D's system, and expert testimony indicating that the concentration would impair D's ability to operate a motor vehicle;

*C v Lodge** 431 M 461 (2000)—no required finding of NG for D in murder of live-in girlfriend, though he told tale of four black intruders and his own loss of consciousness after which he was outside apartment circumstantial evidence included deterioration of relationship, fact that D obtained a gun two weeks earlier, & that murder weapon was found well hidden in small opening in wall behind refrigerator in D's apartment, "need not show that no other person could have committed the crime";

*C v Roman** 43 MAC 733 (97), S.C., 427 M 1006, 1008 (98)—no required finding of NG for D on ABDW on baby, though unknown what caused burns on V's body, though Court conceded "case is a close one";

*C v Mandile** 403 M 93 (88)—required finding of NG though motive, means, drove car, had $730, & disposed of co-D's gun; (*see Chapter 16, Joint Venture, Circumstantial Evidence*);

C v Swafford 441 M 329 (2004)—though fatal shots were fired from D's car and D was present along with co-Ds when D's friend/fellow gang member was assaulted earlier, fight occurred at least two hours before shooting: required finding of not guilty (distinguishing *C v Medeiros* 354 M 193 (68) & *C v Evans* 438 M 142 (2002));

*C v Lombard** 419 M 585 (95)—required finding of NG though drove getaway car & were aware of robbery sometime later: no evidence of prior knowledge and intent to assist principal in crime;

Berry v C 393 M 793 (85)—required finding of NG where mother of V had equal opportunity & motive to kill V; double jeopardy bars retrial;

*C v Anderson** 48 MAC 508 (2000)—though D argued that baby's mother had equal opportunity to kill baby, court distinguished **Berry** 393 M 793 (85): here, unlike there, baby's mother testified and her credibility could be weighed by jury, so no required finding of NG;

*C v Torres** 442 M 554 (2004)—though D argues that baby's mother had equal opportunity to kill baby, court distinguishes **Berry** 393 M 793, because D's statement re: how mother killed baby was contradicted by the medical evidence;

*C v Fancy** 349 M 196 (65)—required finding of NG if evidence tends equally to sustain two inconsistent propositions;

*Corson v Commonwealth** 428 M 193 (98)—evidence leading only to speculative guilty inferences when D was charged with insurance fraud/larceny by false pretenses re: theft of her own car meant required finding of NG (context here = hung jury; renewed motion for required finding of NG treated as motion to dismiss for prohibited double jeopardy because RFNG should have been granted; G.L. c. 211, § 3 petition, and resolution by full bench of SJC);

*C v Souza** 34 MAC 436 (93)—no required finding of NG because here **not** "equally" likely that fatal peritonitis was caused by a fall of the victim (for which D was not responsible); 20-minute beating with bat was infinitely more likely cause. See, however, *C v Flynn* 420 M 810 (95)—required finding of NG should have been allowed as to the theory of **individual** liability for homicide (though D kicked V, Commonwealth's proof was that fatal blows, delivered by alleged joint venturer, were on another part of V's body: no act of D himself caused death); see also *C v Cannon* 449 M 462 (2007);

*C v Kalinowski** 360 M 682 (71)—for B&E, DA need only show D broke into building of "another," not named V; (*see Chapter 5, Variance*);

*C v Morrill** 14 MAC 1003 (82)—circumstantial evidence & inferences establish D's ID as rock-thrower; ID testimony not inherently incredible (view from 50 yards); (*see Chapter 18-B, Identification*);

C v Cincotta **379 M 391 (79)**—ID reliability pertinent to motion for required finding of NG;

US v Levi **405 F.2d 380 (4th Cir. '68)**—in one-witness ID case, judge should decide whether total circumstances give very likely mis-ID in deciding motion for required finding of NG;

C v Dineen **70 MAC 1, 10–11 (2007)**—three abuse prevention order convictions upheld, because, inter alia, "matter of common knowledge" that Father's Day falls in mid-June, justifying G on count stating particular day;

C v Forde **392 M 453 (84)**—need some evidence besides D's confession that a loss/injury really happened, i.e., not imaginary;

C v Leonard **401 M 470 (88)**—(same), especially for intoxicated D; drunk D's extrajudicial admission that he had been driving not substantively corroborated by prosecutor's impeachment of his wife's testimony that she'd been driving (i.e., out-of-court, previously, wife stated D was driver);

C v Jackson **428 M 455, 467 (98)**—corroboration of robbery part of deadly assault found: no testimony by a survivor as to stolen items was necessary;

C v Costello **411 M 371 (91)**—D's extrajudicial confession not substantively corroborated by prosecutor's impeachment of sexual assault complainant's recantation: = required finding of not guilty;

C v Landenburg **41 MAC 23 (96)**—D's extrajudicial confession to stealing from store not sufficiently corroborated by evidence that D knew how to evade anti-theft system at store, that he was unemployed at the time he acquired the merchandise, & that the merchandise **could** have come from the store (store could not say that any such particular items were missing from inventory at relevant time);

C v Smith **33 MAC 947 (92)**—corroboration rule requires only some evidence, besides D's confession, that crime was actually committed;

C v Rodriguez **76 MAC 59 (2009)**—same; corroboration of each element of crime not required, nor corroboration that it was D who committed crime;

C v Villalta-Duarte **55 MAC 821 (2002)**—D's confession to molestation and battery of baby for whom wife provided day care sufficiently "corroborated" by facts that baby cried hysterically when brought to scene when D was there and had diaper rash and facial scratches which disappeared after weeks with new day care provider;

Smith v US **348 US 147, 154 (54)**—"federal test" requires corroboration as well that D was the wrongdoer, when there is "no tangible corpus delecti";

C v McNelley **28 MAC 985 (90)**—corroboration requirement for OUI-D's statement of operation discussed;

C v Manning **41 MAC 18 (96)**—smoldering remains of car crashed into toppled traffic signal on a traffic island & odor of alcohol on D & D's knowledge that car was rented & cooperation with field sobriety tests = sufficient corroboration of admissions that he was drunk and had been the driver;

C v Adams **421 M 289 (95)**—sufficient corroboration of D's admission that he was driving car involved in 2-car crash;

C v Morgan **422 M 373 (96)**—only corroboration of D's statement needed in homicide case is evidence that a person is dead; corroboration of statement that robbery was motive here sufficient: victim, a stranger to D, was stabbed after chance encounter as he walked home alone from bar at 12:40 a.m. & witnesses saw D as aggressor as V was backing up;

C v DiGiambattista **442 M 423 (2004)**—SJC declines to expand "corroboration" rule to require corroboration that D was actual perpetrator of the crime; even if it did, says enough here, given D's motive, witness seeing someone resembling D at a relevant time, culprit's use of a key (& D was one of only 3 people to have key), etc.;

C v DeBrosky **363 M 718 (73)**—corroboration necessary re: immunized witness, but only that crime happened; without corroboration, required finding NG (G.L. c. 233, § 20I);

C v Fernandes **425 M 357 (97)**—SJC declines to require that corroboration include evidence of D's participation in crime;

C v Asmeron **70 MAC 667 (2007)**—describing sufficient evidence to corroborate immunized minor's testimony that D derived support from her acts of prostitution;

C v Shaheen **15 MAC 302 (83)**—need no corroboration for fink without immunity; *C v Knowlton* **50 MAC 266, 270 (2000)** similar ("promise" that authorities wouldn't prosecute isn't same as formal immunity for purpose of c. 233, § 20I corroboration requirement);

C v Clark **378 M 392 (79)**—fingerprint at scene not enough for G.;

C v LaCorte **373 M 700 (77)**—(same);

C v Loftis **361 M 545 (72)**—print on table (washed in a.m.) enough for jury;

C v Fazzino **27 MAC 485 (89)**—D's fingerprint, plus his motive, special knowledge of premises, & skill with blowtorch, sufficient evidence;

C v Baptista **32 MAC 910 (92)**—D's fingerprint plus premises' prior inaccessibility to D is sufficient for G;

C v Morris **422 M 254 (96)**—D's thumbprint on clown mask worn by armed assailant not enough for G, despite evidence that print was probably placed on mask "shortly before or during the crime," that D "might have resembled the man who wore" mask, that D was closely associated with two of the culprits, & that D's mother owned car which resembled one seen leaving crime scene: required finding of NG ordered; contrast *C v Palmer* **59 MAC 415 (2003)**—circumstances were such that D's fingerprint almost certainly left (inside victim's truck) at time of crime;

C v Estremera **37 MAC 923 (94)**—D's fingerprint found on car exterior insufficient for G of receiving stolen motor vehicle; suggestion that even if D's prints were found in car interior, still required finding of NG because car owner didn't testify he had closed windows or locked car when he left it;

C v Keaton **36 MAC 81 (94)**—evidence of D's fingerprint at scene, because coupled with evidence reasonably excluding hypothesis it was left at time other than when crime committed, not insufficient;

C v Hoa Sang Duong **52 MAC 861, 866 (2001)**—D's fingerprint on outside of window behind driver's side door of car in which armed robbers were fleeing (+ D being found hiding nearby + 'consciousness of guilt' evidence) = enough for G;

C v McGovern **397 M 863 (86)**—legal insufficiency of evidence is inherently a substantial risk of miscarriage of justice; so appellate review without motion for required finding of NG; (here, uncertain intent to steal (for B&E), vs. to just vandalize);

C v Grandison **433 M 135, 140 n.8 (2001)** similar;

C v Bell **455 M 408 (2009)**—failure to move for required finding when one should have been allowed = substantial risk of miscarriage of justice, so "we need not address this particular ineffective assistance . . . claim";

C v Cormier **41 MAC 76 (96)**—appellate counsel on direct appeal was ineffective for failure to brief required finding of NG issue, so not "waived", & cognizable on appeal of R.30 motion's denial;

C v Haskins **128 M 60 (1880)**—steal AND receive = legally inconsistent; can't be G. of both; *(see Chapter 21-T &-U, Receiving Stolen Property & Chapter 22-F-6, Jury Issues: Inconsistent Verdicts);*

C v Sherry **386 M 682 (82)**—factual inconsistency between two verdicts = OK because maybe compromise/leniency; but 2/3 rape G's for each D = "totally against weight of evidence," so 25(b)(2) required finding of NG;

C v Diaz **19 MAC 29 (84)**—factually inconsistent verdicts OK, but judge can tell jury (without coercing) what verdict(s) IF they find certain facts;

See Chapters 16, 18, & 21 for cases where required findings of not guilty were entered, including Chapter 16-B for joint venture cases & Chapter 18-B for identification cases, & Chapter 21-CC-3 & -5 for cases on possession & possession with intent to distribute;

See Chapter 15 for cases on postconviction motions for required finding pursuant to M.R.Crim.P. 25(b)(2);

C v Oakes **407 M 92 (90)**—motion for required finding of not guilty required to preserve for appeal as-applied challenge to constitutionality of statute;

C v Green **408 M 48 (90)**—required finding entered where Commonwealth failed to prove that cocaine is a "narcotic" under **c. 94C, § 1;**

C v Finegan **45 MAC 921 (98)**—although judge here could have taken judicial notice that heroin is a derivative of opium (because "subject of generalized knowledge readily ascertainable from authoritative sources"), he was not requested to do so, and did not do so implicitly sua sponte, because he would have had to "submit( ) expressly to the jury any factual matters of which he took judicial notice"; required finding of NG entered on charge of operating under influence of narcotic drug because Commonwealth failed to prove heroin = narcotic;

C v Gonzales **33 MAC 728 (92)**—required finding entered on school zone charge where Commonwealth failed to prove that "Worcester Academy" is an "elementary, vocational or secondary school";

C v Lane **27 MAC 527 (89)**—required finding of not guilty entered where victim's identification of another as assailant was equally as strong as her photo & in-court identifications of D;

C v Hall **48 MAC 727 (2000)**—V identified D, but also testified that he had seen intruder several times after the break-in, first in September or October and again in October; though D argued required finding of NG on basis of *Lane* **27 MAC 525** because D had been incarcerated during all of October, Appeals Court found that "the timing of the subsequent sightings . . . was subject to some uncertainty," and all could have occurred in September (no RFNG);

C v Woods **382 M 1 (80)**—new trial in interest/justice where strong documentary proof saying NG; *(see Chapter 15, Appeal);*

C v Vaughn **23 MAC 40 (86)**—required finding of NG ordered because reasonable doubt created as matter of law by evidence of D's incarceration at the crime was committed elsewhere;

C v Maia **429 M 585 (99)**—though there was "documentary evidence" that D was elsewhere at time of crime, Commonwealth in rebuttal presented evidence that the detox program and its inhabitants were not well supervised, and nothing prevented them from leaving the center; *C v Vaughn* distinguished;

C v Crimmins **46 MAC 489, 492 n.5 (99)**—if no motion for required finding of NG was made in trial court, or when such motion was argued on grounds different from those argued on appeal, standard of review is "substantial risk of miscarriage of justice, and ENTIRE RECORD (rather than just Commonwealth evidence) will be used for this analysis, i.e., prosecution's case may be strengthened by D's evidence;

12-H. REBUTTAL (AND/OR REOPEN)

CPCS P/G 6.7 (e)—in developing defense, consider rebuttal implications;

6 Wigmore, *Evidence,* **§ 1873 (Chadbourn rev. 1976)**—generally limited to what's necessary to reply to opponent's case; § 1874: rejoinder—response to rebuttal;

C v Watts **22 MAC 952 (86)**—maybe OK to let DA reopen at time of motion for required finding of not guilty; compare/contrast C v Rodriguez 75 MAC 235 (2009)—carelessness/"oversight" caused ADA to omit from cop's direct examination the requisite "school zone" measurement evidence, but no bar to eliciting on redirect examination of witness;

C v Hurley **455 M 53 (2009)**—although judge "must rule" on motion for required finding of not guilty made at close of Commonwealth's evidence, judge nonetheless has discretion then to allow reopening when D hasn't begun "defense," and won't suffer "unfair, substantial prejudice" and reopening justified by "mere inadvertence; here, D not formally ID'd; case cited gives examples of "establish[ing] venue," ID'g D, "or . . . other technical matters";

C v Cote **15 MAC 229 (83)**—DA can reopen after motion for required finding of not guilty (to prove no consent to unlawful gas use) because DA mistaken re: burden of production on it); but see explicitly contra *C v Zavala* **52 MAC 770 (2001)** instead of ruling on D's motion for required finding of not guilty, judge allowed Commonwealth to reopen case & introduce necessary evidence to defeat the motion: "discretion" does not allow this "re-duc(tion of) rule 25(a) to a nullity"; required finding of not guilty ordered;

C v Guidry **22 MAC 907 (86)**—"nearly unreversible discretion" to let rebuttal respond to opponent's case; new subject = "open to objection" (see *Hurley* **455 M at 69 n.15**);

C v Wood **302 M 265 (39)**—after resting, right to rebut new facts in opponent's case, discretion re: new evidence after resting if not "rebuttal"; **this latter "discretion" is abolished in** *C v Hurley* **455 M 53, 69 n.15 (2009)**—Commonwealth may NOT reopen its case "at any stage of the trial, even in the middle of the defense case";

C v Small **10 MAC 606 (80)**—maybe judge can let (D) reopen after jury deliberations begin;

C v Lawrence **404 M 378 (89)**—OK (here) not to let D reopen after arguments;

C v Yunggebauer **23 MAC 46 (86)**—D reopened for stipulation Monday after both rested Friday;

C v Giontzis **47 MAC 450 (99)**—prosecutorial misconduct: springing expert in rebuttal, after having failed to disclose, in pretrial discovery, his name and credentials, and after having set up D's expert for devastation by the withheld expert; "trial by ambush";

12-I. REQUESTS FOR INSTRUCTIONS/RULINGS AND OBJECTIONS TO CHARGE

See Chapter 12-K

CPCS P/G 6.8(a), 6.9—before argue, must file requests tailored to case; object after judge gives instructions;

Devitt & Blackmar, Federal Jury Practice & Instructions;

District Court Model Jury Instructions—*see Chapter 21-A!!*, i.e., cautioning that so-called "model" instructions are often found to be erroneous, when made the issue of an appeal;

M.R.Crim.P. 24(b)—at close of evidence, or earlier if judge reasonably requires, may file written requests for instruction; judge must inform of proposed response before argument; must object to instructions before deliberations; can't appeal without specific objection & grounds; 26, Request Rulings—in jury-waived case; written & before argument;

C v Porro **74 MAC 676, further app. rev. allowed 455 M 1106 (2009)**—rejecting D's argument that judge's response to jury question during deliberations "broadened basis of criminal liability," and violated M.R.Crim.P. 24(b) (requiring notice to parties of judge's instructions PRIOR TO closing arguments, to enable intelligent argument to jury);

C v Deagle **10 MAC 748 (80)**—can reject requests made after argument;

C v Yunggebauer **23 MAC 46 (86)**—request OK though not 24(b) "timely" because before argument & no harm to DA or judge;

C v Lyons **71 MAC 671 (2008)**—charged with indecent assault and battery on person age 14 or older, D defended on basis that complainant initiated a "scuffle," and any indecent contact occurred as he was pushing her away from him; COMMONWEALTH requested instruction on lesser included offense of assault and battery, and D requested instruction on self-defense, which judge gave without objection by Commonwealth; judge's subsequently withdrawing from jury the self-defense instruction, at Commonwealth's request, was error, undermining defense and D's credibility;

K. Smith, *Criminal Practice & Procedure*, **§ 1845 (2d ed. 1983 & Supp.)**—need not show counsel the planned instructions, § 1879—objection must be precise, before deliberations, & repeated if follow-up instruction not OK;

C v Traylor **43 MAC 239 (97)**—Appeals Court might be flexible about requirement that requests be in writing;

ABA Standards for Criminal Justice (2d ed. 1986) Trial Judge 6-2.4—respect counsel's duty to seek rulings; Jury Trial 15-3.6: counsel & judge must modify/supplement model instructions; let parties tender written instructions; hold charge conference (& tell what instructions will be given) before argument;

C v Finegan **45 MAC 921 (98)**—if judge has taken judicial notice of some fact, jury must be so instructed;

C v Maloney **113 M 21, 213 (1873)**—legally correct instructions are erroneous if given re: state of facts to which they are inappropriate: "tend to mislead the jury either into the supposition that a proper state of facts exists to which the propositions are to be applied by them, or into drawing the suggested inference from facts which do not authorize it";

C v Gilliard **46 MAC 348 (99)**—ineffective assistance of counsel found in failure to request lesser included instruction (either because counsel never considered the possibility, or because considered and decided not to request, i.e., not a reasonable tactical judgment) of A&B in murder case (joint venture, D found by jury not to be fatal stabber, but instead part of punching-beating group, jury could have found D to be participant only in joint venture to beat V with fists);

C v Palmer **59 MAC 415 (2003)**—even if jury instruction failed to convey that D had to know that alleged masked armed robbery joint venturers were armed with dangerous weapon, error HERE did not create substantial risk of miscarriage of justice; *C v Colon* 52 MAC 725 (2001) (generic instruction that Commonwealth had to prove that D shared the mental state required to commit the crime DID NOT suffice to assure jury's knowledge that D had to have known other person was armed) distinguished;

C v Martin **19 MAC 117, 119–20 (84)**—failure to give requested instruction on the use of prior inconsistent statements in assessing the credibility of a witness is error if there is evidence that a witness made prior inconsistent statements;

C v Ortiz **39 MAC 70, 71 (95)**—omission from police report when it would have been natural to include if true = inconsistent statement, & therefore jury should be instructed on such impeachment;

C v Thompson **23 MAC 114 (86)**—D didn't "bring request (re: D off stand (*see Chapter 12-K*)) clearly to judge's attention" because D agreed that the requests were "boilerplate";

C v Pettingel **10 MAC 916 (80)**—error not to rule on requests before argument, but no harm; counsel must request ruling;

C v McJunkin **11 MAC 609 (81)**—no harm by not ruling on requested instructions for ROUTINE matters (e.g., reasonable doubt) & no claim instructions were bad;

C v Thomas **21 MAC 183 (85)**—though 24(b) right to notice of instructions, harmless change (after jury question);

C v Roberts **433 M 45, 48 (2000)**—limiting instruction must be requested AT TIME EVIDENCE IS ADMITTED; charge conference request is too late, because offering party will have relied on evidence being admitted without limitation, and can't be told otherwise when it's too late to offer other evidence on the issue;

C v White **48 MAC 658, 660 n.5 (2000)**—D-counsel has duty to request limiting instructions; judges ordinarily aren't required to instruct sua sponte "as to the purposes for which evidence is offered at trial"; though appellate counsel argued that failure to limit use of hearsay evidence made it useable substantively and decisively against D, appellate court held counsel used it effectively (no ineffectiveness of counsel);

C v Delarosa **50 MAC 623, 631 (2000)**—trial judge responded to cop's gratuitous assertion that D "refused to cooperate," and "wasn't cooperating" by instructing jury curatively that "there's absolutely no requirement on any-body's part who is accused of a crime to cooperate with anyone, including the police," that it is "immaterial whether anyone cooperates or not," and that "the officer knows that and should not have testified to that once, let alone twice. Therefore, I have to strongly give you this instruction so you understand the importance of it and you understand that that is not to be considered by you. It should be disregarded by you. If anything, you should look on it negatively that for some reason the witness felt the need to offer it to you. If there is any negative inference to be drawn, it's to the one stating it, not towards the defendant" (no relief on appeal, despite appellate argument that trial counsel was ineffective in not moving for mistrial);

C v Dreyer **18 MAC 562, 566 n.4 (84)**—let counsel approach bench & object to instructions;

C v Conley **34 MAC 50, 54 n.1 (93)**—judge's abrupt ending of sidebar conference, despite attorney's statement re: further objections to instructions, resulted in review of errors as though preserved;

C v Anslono **9 MAC 867 (80)**—no objection to instructions maybe ineffective, but OK because judge intimidated counsel throughout trial;

C v Brown **392 M 632, 636 n.3 (84)**—though request & denied, must object after instructions to preserve;

C v Engram **43 MAC 804 (97)**—judge's unequivocal rejection during charge conference, of requested instruction, and his giving of instruction inconsistent with D's request, relieved D of burden of objection after charge was given;

C v Williams **54 MAC 236 (2002)**—once D presented his proposal for jury instructions on ID and objected to judge's refusal to instruct on the issue, D discharged his burden; that D asked judge to give specific alternative to the standard ID instruction "did not vitiate the court's obligation to state the applicable law," nor did it suggest that D preferred no instruction at all on the only contested issue at trial when the judge refused to instruct as D requested; if judge "entertained any doubt as to the defense position on this point, moreover, he could easily have cleared it up by making inquiry of counsel";

C v Cutty **47 MAC 671, 677 n.7 (99)**—given judge's "emphatic suppression of any mention of an alibi defense", counsel's failure to request jury instruction on alibi = "understandable";

C v Smiley **431 M 477, 486 (2000)**—D requested instruction (specialized, re: credibility of "cooperating" witness likely to be insulated from criminal penalties) in writing and in conference with trial judge, but judge gave instead only general "credibility" instruction, & D didn't object: issue deemed preserved;

C v Biancardi **421 M 251 (95)**—no waiver of request for instruction (on consequences of NGI verdict) by failure to argue its mandatory nature, failure to ask that "appellate rights be saved", or failure to renew request after charge;

C v Fernandes **46 MAC 455 (92)**—do not say "OK," when judge denies request for instruction (suggestion here that such filler waives the issue);

C v Morgan **422 M 373 (96)**—D **not** required to "specifically object" after judge refused request for additional instruction on drug intoxication: "appellate rights (are) preserved when a specific instruction has been requested and rejected by the judge";

C v Keevan **400 M 557 (87)**—not preserved without explaining reasons & specific objections (before AND after);

C v McDuffee **379 M 353, 357 n.3 (79)**—need specific objection so judge can correct;

C v Franchino **61 MAC 367 (2004)**—although defense counsel made three objections & "had little to show for his trouble" because judge kept missing the point, judge did provide additional instruction in response to each request, so counsel was not excused from objecting again to inadequate charge;

C v Fano **400 M 296 (87)**—D's request not quite accurate & no objection to instruction given (so appellate question = miscarriage of justice?);

C v Matos **394 M 563 (85)**—though no "objection" to instructions given, D asked more instructions (from requests denied), so brought objection to judge's attention & preserved issue—otherwise, "form over substance";

C v Jackson **23 MAC 975 (87)**—objection on multiple grounds "collectively" (though imprecisely) alerted judge & preserved the issue;

*C v Maskell **403 M 111 (88)**—not preserved by blanket reference to numbered requests, but comments after instructions sufficiently alerted judge;

C v Dunton **397 M 101 (86)**—though no post-charge objection, OK because judge said "rights fully protected" (fn.2);

C v Thomas **400 M 676 (87)**—"rights saved" because judge said so (fn.4);

C v Grenier **415 M 680 fn 8 (93)**—same;

12-J. ARGUMENT ON THE MERITS

12-J.1. General Rules

CPCS P/G 6.6(d)—integrate cross-examination, case theory, & argument; 6.8: argue D's theory with DA weaknesses/missing/burden of proof; incorporate testimony, expected charge, & expected DA argument; object to bad DA argument & consider mistrial motion &/or request for curative instructions; follow rules;

M.R.Crim.P. 24(a)(2)—30 minutes for closing argument, but may be extended or shortened in judge's discretion;

C v Johnson **42 MAC 948 (97)**—no abuse of discretion in limiting argument to 20 minutes in 4-witness drug distribution trial;

Herring v NY **422 US 853 (75)**—constitutional right to argue, even jury-waived; though judge can limit duration/scope, can't foreclose arguing inferences from evidence & weakness of opponent's position;

C v Rocheteau **74 MAC 17 (2009)**—requiring defense to argue first does not deprive D of "constitutional right to present an effective closing", citing *C v Seminara* **20 MAC 789 (1985)**;

C v Miranda **22 MAC 10 (86)**—new trial because judge precluded closing argument, saying his mind was made up;

C v Martelli **38 MAC 669 (95)**—reversal for jury-waived trial judge's refusal to hear closing argument ("I don't want to hear anything. Don't bury ... yourself"; then, "if you want to do it, fine with me. I'm giving you friendly advice");

Johns v Smyth **176 FS 949 (E.D.Va. '59)**—fail to argue = ineffective;

C v Street **388 M 281 (83)**—closing "denuded D of a defense," so ineffective assistance of counsel;

C v Sarvela **16 MAC 934 (83)**—ineffective assistance of counsel to shift gears at argument & undermine D's case (& become juror, not advocate);

C v McKie **1 Gray 61 (1854)**—e.g., though no defense evidence, still DA's burden of proof (that touching's unjustified, wrongful);

C v Houston **332 M 687 (55)**—defense, without testimony, gets self-defense instruction from D's hearsay to cops admitted by DA without limitation for all purposes;

C v Bennett **6 MAC 832 (78)**—can argue hypothesis based on admitted hearsay

K. Smith, *Criminal Practice & Procedure*, § 1854 (2d ed. 1983 & Supp.)—may object either during DA argument or after, but before instructions; § 1857—may comment on opponent tactics; demonstrations OK if evidence foundation; § 1858—should seek ruling BEFORE arguing "missing witness"; § 1866—can't refer to excluded evidence, particularly if exclusion was on your successful motion;

C v Boyajian **68 MAC 866 (2007)**—to preserve issue concerning DA's argument, must object BEFORE jury retires to deliberate, though not necessary to interrupt argument of DA with the objection;

C v Kozec **399 M 514, 523 (87)**—once D has objected to some part of DA argument, analysis of whether reversal is required looks to rest of record, including "balance of prosecutor's argument," even if it's unobjected to;

SJC Rule 3:07, 8.4—professional misconduct to engage in conduct involving dishonesty, deceit, or misrepresentation, or which is prejudicial to the administration of justice; 3.4 shan't allude to any matter not supported by evidence, or state personal opinion as to guilt/innocence, or witness credibility, or justness of a cause; see also SJC Rule 3:07, 3.8, Special Responsibilities of a Prosecutor:

shan't assert personal knowledge of facts in issue, except when testifying as witness, or assert personal opinion as to justness of cause, credibility of witness, guilt of D, but only "argue, on analysis of the evidence, for any position or conclusion" re: such matters;

CPCS P/G 1.1—follow all rules; if in doubt seek advice, & interpret good faith ambiguities in favor of client;

C v Earltop **372 M 199, 205 (77)**—(Hennessey conc.) evidence & fair inferences; list of (then) recent cases on DA argument (n.1); DA's often overstep because poor preparation & don't seek advance rulings;

C v Grinkley **75 MAC 798 (2009)**—pointed references to same individual prosecutor being warned previously concerning similar unfair/prejudicial argument in *Deloney* 59 MAC 47 (2003); *cf. C v Smith* 387 M 900, 914 n.3 (83) (Abrams, J., concurring)—whether or not individual is identified in opinion, Board of Bar Overseers may seek sanctions; Berry, J., concurring in *Grinkley* would find such "deep prosecutorial errors in closing" to preclude any harmless error analysis, "structural" sort of governmental error, the excusing of which deprives D of JURY's fair determination;

C v Burts **68 MAC 684 (2007)**—improper for prosecutor to suggest personal belief/opinion and "to blur the boundaries between judge, prosecutor, and jury by placing himself in the jury box as a supplemental or standby juror" ("we need, as people, to get the right person", "we all know he picked out the D", "I think we know that for a fact, based on cross-examination", "I'm going to go you one further. How do we know there wasn't something else? . . . if there was any mistake, I didn't see it" ["troubled by the prosecutor's repeated use of the pronoun 'we'"]);

C v Delacruz **443 M 692 (2005)**—reading verbatim from transcript during closing argument is permissible, so long as counsel gives copy of transcript to opposing counsel beforehand; objections beforehand to be made to judge for resolution;

C v Kozec **399 M 514 (87)**—case law summary re: argument limits; DA can't refer to D's failure to testify, misstate/overstate evidence, argue facts without evidence, state personal belief re: guilt/witness's testimony, play on ethnic/religious prejudice or sympathy/emotion, or comment on verdict consequences; bad D argument doesn't define limits of DA's argument; judge should correct DA's misstatement;

C v Grinkley **75 MAC 798 (2009)**—though prosecutor was responding to inaccurate and/or implausible arguments by defense counsel, prosecutor should have either "objected to [D's] argument or explained its implausibility without trying to exploit it"; "overwrought and inflammatory closing argument" by ADA "which ignored a prior warning from [MAC] about many of the same unacceptable points of argument" = prosecutorial error;

C v Rosa **73 MAC 540 (2009)**—in apparent reliance upon Dept. of Justice guide, defense counsel argued in closing the superior reliability of showing photos one at a time, sequentially (rather than array); prosecutor then argued **IMPROPERLY** that array was necessary because wanted to "move quickly on the investigation," that it was fairer to D (because if his photo had been "first" in a sequential showing, this would have been less "fair", "[t]he reality is . . . that eight picture photo array was more difficult than one at a time"; no evidence introduced re: relative accuracy of the two forms of photo ID, and argument was seen as improper vouching; Commonwealth claimed 'fair response,' but had not "suggest[ed] that defense counsel's argument was improper" and had not objected at trial to it; ALSO: ADA's reference to victim being a firefighter was made 19 times in eight pages of argument, "excessive . . . an improper appeal to sympathy"; judge's reference, during body of instructions, to "injuries [being] terrible" was made precisely because of, and embedded in, instruction NOT to decide based on bias, prejudice, or "sympathy";

C v Rodriguez **57 MAC 368 (2003)**—DA's argument (not objected to) that complainant was simple & sincere person unlikely to have fabricated accusation cited witness's practice of placing a Bible in every window; despite Proposed Mass.R.Evid. 610 (evidence of religious beliefs/opinions not admissible for purpose of showing one's credibility is impaired or enhanced), no relief, court professing that fact was cited to show how "simpleminded" the witness was;

C v Griffith **45 MAC 784 (98)**—many overstatements of evidence, e.g., D "drug dealer" (in case charging only single distribution court of marijuana), exchange of "money" for objects, "two" (rather than single arguable) drug transactions; "as I told you at the beginning of the trial, (D) is a common street level dealer" (language having a "dogmatic 'take it from me' quality that the cases have declared to be impermissible"); and "By no means are these men (cops) not telling the truth" (personal opinion re: credibility);

C v Burke **373 M 569 (77)**—only evidence & fair inferences; not excluded evidence; can "fight fire with fire" to correct opponent's erroneous impression; D's bad character ("want men like D to walk street?") was not opened by D's "D's liberty is in your hands" argument;

US v Flannery **451 F.2d 880 (1st Cir. '71)**—judge should instruct jury that DA argument was IMPROPER (cited *C v Hawley* **380 M 70, 89 n.19 (80)**);

C v Daley **439 M 558 (2003)**—though DA erred in several ways in argument, judge corrected, sua sponte, calling one "completely inappropriate," limiting/eliminating one argued inference by instruction, and interrupting another;

C v DeMars **42 MAC 788 (97), S.C. 426 M 1008 (98)**—reverse for cumulative effect of DA's many transgressions in taunting cross-examination of D and in argument, including assertion without record support;

C v Johnson **441 M 1, 7 & n.9 (2004)**—prosecutor's extra-evidentiary assertion in cross-examination of D ("'would it surprise you to know that the videotape of your booking shows no string on your pants?'") recognized as bad only as to "form," since D's "state of mind" re: videotape = irrelevant; failure to acknowledge damage done by DA's effective testimony as to tape's content, D allotted burden of asserting/showing that DA's representation was false;

C v Collins **386 M 1 (82)**—DA should correct witness's false testimony re: no deal & can't argue false testimony (misleading "aura of credibility");

C v O'Neil **51 MAC 170 (2001)**—prosecutor G of misconduct in failing to correct cooperating witness's falsehood re: promises & in "disingenuous" redirect examination buttressing falsehood, but ground for reversal was defense counsel's failings in bringing falsehood to attention of judge & jury;

C v DeCicco **51 MAC 159, 166 (2001)** (**Brown, J., dissenting**)—any DA should know better than to guarantee that a particular D/cooperating witness will be tried as indicted, because witnesses disappear, weight of evidence shifts, & "11th hour plea agreements are reached," & where prosecutor makes such a promise "trial judge would be well within his or her right to instruct the jury, sua sponte, that no such guarantee can be enforced against the government";

C v Delaney **425 M 587 (97)** (**Lynch, J., dissenting**)—when DA misstates/distorts evidence, unfair to expect jury to shoulder burden of correcting error; lack of objection (and thus lack of attempt to "cure") permits error to have maximum prejudicial effect;

C v Chartier **43 MAC 758 (97)**—error for DA to argue for substantive use of prior convictions admitted to impeach credibility;

C v Bregoli **431 M 265 (2000)**—error for DA to argue substantive use of evidence, contrary to explicit limitation placed on its use by trial judge; (see also *Burns* **49 MAC 677, 683 & n.9 (2000)**, *McIntyre* **430 M 529, 541–43 (99)**);

12-J.2. Putting Facts in Legal Setting

C v Sylvester **13 MAC 360, 368 (82)** (**SJC 388M749 (83)**)—can put facts in context of applicable law;

Leone v Doran **363 M 1, 18 (73)**—analogy, example, hypothesis = OK;

C v Gonzalez **28 MAC 906 (89)**—defense counsel entitled to put facts in legal setting by explaining law to jury; judge's interruptions & admonishments barring counsel from explaining difference between civil & criminal standards were "uncalled for" & contributed to reversal;

C v Rupp **57 MAC 377, 385 (2003)**—DA's argument confounded circumstantial evidence concept with "proof beyond a reasonable doubt," saying that puddles on pavement could/should/would be understood by someone who had been inside all day to prove that it had rained; court

agreed this was improper, effectively trivializing burden of proof (but no relief here);

C v Hubbard **69 MAC 232 (2007)**—DA's closing assertions, "if you look for doubt, you will find doubt and that is not this standard of law that the Commonwealth requires. . . . If you look for doubt, you will find it. That is not what you are supposed to do," should not have been made (but there was no objection, and judge instructed that jurors were to apply law as stated by judge, and gave Webster charge on reasonable doubt); Appeals Court, "while not condoning" prosecutor's role in instructing jury, noted that reference to reasonable doubt as not involving "search for doubt" was "upheld" in *C v Watkins* **425 M 830, 839 (97)**;

C v Ruddock **428 M 288 (98)**—DA can't argue to jury that not guilty by reason of insanity means that D will be released (but no such "direct" argument here, and inference to this effect doubtful);

C v McLaughlin **431 M 506 (2000)**—"egregiously" bad DA argument that "truth" of case wasn't whether or not D's insane, but was whether or not he's guilty;

12-J.3. Dramatic and Rhetorical Techniques

C v Pope **406 M 581 (90)**—imaginary dialogues to dramatize argument not improper if content fairly follows from evidence;

C v Ortiz-Soto **49 MAC 645 (2000)**—similar; contrast

C v Coren **437 M 723 (2002)**—argument that D "yelled," that victim said "don't shoot," etc. NOT supported by evidence; conviction reversed;

C v Dancy **75 MAC 175 (2009)**—argument that D went to NA/AA meeting not because he was sober and clean, but instead to deal drugs there to recovering addicts was improper: evidence was that D sold drugs from car, which was parked near an NA/AA meeting, and then walked to & entered location hosting such meeting (no objection, no relief);

C v Hoppin **387 M 25 (82)**—reverse for DA argument brandishing rawhide strap not in evidence (matching complaining witness's description of "leather thong" binding her); limited value of curative instructions;

C v Masello **428 M 446 (98)**—speculation that D had thought, "You want to leave? You'll leave. But you'll leave on your back" was argument that "should not have been made"; no evidence that D had this vengeful state of mind; strength of Commonwealth case and limiting instruction = no relief;

C v Grimshaw **412 M 505 (92)**—comments on opponent's trial tactics, including reliance on inconsistent alternative theories & evidence promised but not delivered, not improper so long as based on record;

C v Barros **425 M 572 (97)**—error to kick trashcan for theatrical effect, & to argue (in circular fashion) that "you can believe a murderer if you like" (conclude from evidence, including D's testimony, that D was murderer, but disbelieve D's testimony because he was murderer);

C v Rosario **430 M 505, 515–16 (99)**—bad to call D "monster," throw photo and teeth impressions on table in front of him during closing argument;

C v Saunders **75 MAC 505 (2009)**—characterizing D as "swooping down like a vulture" to take advantage of young victim = BAD, & "stronger and more pointed reaction was warranted" than the general admonition about "rhetoric used by counsel" and 'jury not to be swayed by sympathy/emotion' (but no relief given strength of evidence, limited objection by D, etc.);

C v Bregoli **431 M 265, 279 (2000)**—rhetorical questions shouldn't be used "where they could be perceived by the jury as shifting the Commonwealth's burden of proof to the defendant"; here, posing as D-counsel cross-examining Commonwealth witness, DA said "Do you agree with the statement that . . . , as in this book that I am waving in front of the jury because we're not going to call an expert of our own?"; rhetorical flourish disapproved ("the truth of any matters starts in your gut, in your heart, and it works its way to your head, and it lives and resides in your soul");

C v Williams **450 M 879 (2008)**—exhortation, "justice delayed . . . should not mean justice denied" = "crossed the line of proper argument" both because of the rhetoric itself and fact that close to half of 12-year delay attributable to Commonwealth;

12-J.4. Facts Not in Evidence; Misstatement of Evidence; Inferences Unsupported by Evidence

C v Baxter **36 MAC 45 (94)**—improper to argue "D's pattern of lying" gave "insight into his character" even though there was evidence of false statements (admitted as consciousness of guilt);

C v Dowdy **36 MAC 495 (94)**—bad DA argument, misrepresenting D's testimony (by ignoring base testimony that D did not know package contained drugs, making his denial that he intended to use them himself an admission of distribution intent);

C v Pavao **34 MAC 577 (93)**—DA's material misstatement of evidence (going to "get", not "kill") = reversal, despite instruction that judge's memory of the testimony was to the contrary;

C v Moran **75 MAC 513 (2009)**—holding DA's argument (that D was thinking, when he went inside to get knife, that he was going to "kill" victim, i.e., deliberate premeditation) to have been a reasonable inference, and even if not, no prejudice because jury acquitted of deliberate premeditation;

C v Taylor **455 M 372 (2010)**—prosecutor's misstatement as to a critical issue in case (credibility of particular witness) didn't result in substantial risk of miscarriage of justice (no objection, plus boilerplate instructions that arguments aren't evidence and jurors' memories control);

C v Vazquez **65 MAC 305 (2005)**—in prosecution for indecent assault and battery on 12-year-old, DA materially misstated length of kiss by D on mouth of child (evidence = "2 seconds", and DA argued "he lingered there", "stayed on her mouth", "lingered there more than a minute"), and any question of indecency was a very close one: reversal required;

C v Carter **38 MAC 952 (95)**—"plainly improper" for DA to argue, with no basis in evidence, that witness failed to identify D in court because she was afraid, & that jurors should use "common sense" to determine why she was afraid;

C v Ragland **72 MAC 815, further appellate rev. denied 452 M 1110 (2008)**—DA's argument, concerning witnesses' recantation at trial of incriminating grand jury testimony, was "What's different between [grand jury date and trial date]? . . . Grand jury, private proceeding. . . . No one's there. [names of D, co-D]: "ominous import"/ "darker connotation suggesting fear emanating in response to the defendants" disapproved, but here found "ambiguous", witness having given explicit different explanation for change, judge having given [boilerplate] instructions, and jury having acquitted D and co-D of most serious charges;

C v Rosa **73 MAC 540 (2009)**—in apparent reliance upon Dept. of Justice guide, defense counsel argued in closing the superior reliability of showing photos one at a time, sequentially (rather than array); prosecutor then argued **IMPROPERLY** that array was necessary because wanted to "move quickly on the investigation," that it was fairer to D (because if his photo had been "first" in a sequential showing, this would have been less "fair", "[t]he reality is . . . that eight picture photo array was more difficult than one at a time"; no evidence introduced re: relative accuracy of the two forms of photo ID, and argument was seen as improper vouching; Commonwealth claimed 'fair response,' but had not "suggest[ed] that defense counsel's argument was improper" and had not objected at trial to it; no relief because no objection and strong evidence of guilt;

C v Silva-Santiago **453 M 782 (2009)**—33E reversal of first degree murder conviction (without issue having been briefed by counsel) due to DA's arguments that witnesses' failure to ID D as shooter immediately after crime was "maybe [because they were] too scared to identify him" (no evidence of this) and material misstatement of testimony, to place D at site of shooting when it occurred (rather than 10–15 minutes BEFORE occurrence);

C v Auclair **444 M 348, 359 (2005)**—prosecution experts testified to opinions that child's injuries were inconsistent with an accident as described by D, but this evidence did not support DA's argument that the experts testified that the child had been "murdered"; DA's argument was "clearly" improper, but not reversible given corrective instruction, etc.;

C v Rollins **65 MAC 694 (2006)**—while DA could argue that jury should credit breathalyzer test result of .09% plus police observation of D's demeanor, etc. rather than testimony of D and his relatives, court wasn't "entirely convinced" that DA's more substantive argument (that breathalyzer result was inconsistent with D's claim of having consumed only three beers 2–3 hours before stop) "did not cross the line into territory that required expert testimony";

C v Carmona **428 M 268, 272–73 (98)**—no evidence to support DA's implication that one witness's failure to ID D as resident of building where murder occurred and two other witnesses' failure to be "around" for trial was due to fear of D (no objection, no explicit statement, boilerplate charge re arguments not evidence, strong evidence of guilt = no relief);

C v Shellenberger **64 MAC 70 (2005)**—midtrial on charge of motor vehicle homicide by negligent operation, DA switched from "speeding" theory to "under the influence of amphetamines", causing reversal: at minimum, there had to be evidence as to amount or concentration of the drug in D's system, and expert testimony indicating that the concentration would impair D's ability to operate a motor vehicle;

C v Mayne **38 MAC 282 (95)**—" insufficient" evidence to support argument that D's mother was "main mover behind" keeping witnesses quiet; see also *C v West* **44 MAC 150 (98)** no evidence to support claim that D intimidated witnesses;

C v Guy **441 M 96, 111–12 (2004)**—DA's argument that possibly words between V and D were exchanged through open window in D's room was not fairly inferable from evidence (but no likelihood of miscarriage of justice); DA's misstatement, that D (rather than D's sister) had made inconsistent statement to grand jury, was error, but prosecution case was "overwhelming," so no likelihood of a miscarriage of justice;

C v DeMars **42 MAC 788 (97), S.C., 426 M 1008 (98)**—reverse for cumulative effect of DA's many transgressions in taunting cross-examination of D and in argument, including assertion without record support (that D must have known complainant too young because she'd had braces on her teeth at the time of alleged crimes);

C v Murphy **57 MAC 586 (2003)**—cross-examination of D, on trial for rape of seven-year-old son of D's fiancée, included "How did it feel when you were sucking your son's penis?" was improper, sought merely to "degrade"; how D "felt" had no bearing on guilt, & no reasonable DA could have expected this "question" to produce an answer helpful to prosecution; "Trials are a search for truth, not socialized stonings";

C v McCoy **59 MAC 284 (2003)**—error to allow DA to question D about his knowledge (or not) that woman with D at time of arrest (who was neither arrested nor charged) had criminal record for heroin distribution (it was not relevant, and no evidence of purported criminal background was ever introduced); FURTHER, judge's "inexplicable overruling of" D's objection "may have been seen by the jury as judicial endorsement of the improper questioning and innuendo"; further error in DA's closing, which argued, without evidentiary support, that everyone in D's company ("all his friends") were either heroin users or heroin dealers;

C v Rivera **62 MAC 859 (2005)**—error for DA to argue that witness's testimony should be discounted because she did not call police at the time of the confrontation (no evidence introduced as to whether or not witness had called police);

C v Vickers **60 MAC 24 (2003)**—DA misstated evidence as to crucial issue of D's intent (re: larceny from store) when he asserted three times that D "zipped" closed her bag full of merchandise; with other errors = reversal;

C v Hoppin **387 M 25 (82)**—reverse for DA argument displaying rawhide strap not in evidence (matching complaining witness's description of "leather thong" binding her); limited value of curative instructions;

C v Nol **39 MAC 901 (95)**—OK for DA to put a handkerchief in front of his face from nose down to show jury that such limited face-covering as described by robbery victim would not preclude identification (*C v Hoppin* **387 M 25 (82)** distinguished);

See Chapter 19, Double Jeopardy, Mistrial Motions & CPCS P/G 6.8, above;

C v Mosby **11 MAC 1 (80)**—DA can't argue absent evidence excluded by own earlier objection; can't misstate evidence;

C v Haraldstad **16 MAC 565 (83)**—(same); nor that witness was "rehearsed"; or complainant's post-rape behavior inference (without expert);

C v Harris **443 M 714 (2005)**—having obtained a ruling excluding sexual assault complainant's prior convictions for prostitution, and knowing defense to be barred by rape-shield law from presenting evidence that complainant was a prostitute, DA erroneously argued that complainant's demeanor was product of being falsely accused of being a prostitute; "improper for the prosecutor to suggest to the jury that the absence of . . . evidence . . . of prostitution meant that she was not a prostitute";

C v Beaudry **445 M 577 (2005)**—improper for prosecutor to argue that child sexual assault complaint's sexual knowledge could have been acquired only by D raping her, unless there is "adequate and specific basis in record . . . that excludes other possible sources of such knowledge";

C v Schutte **52 MAC 796, 800 n.4 (2001)**—DA argued absence of evidence excluded (wrongly, even) on his own earlier objection; conviction reversed;

C v Padgett **44 MAC 359 (98)**—DA could argue that D's "reading on the law" influenced his testimony as to his role in joint venture resulting in felony murder ;

C v Urrea **443 M 530, 547 (2005)**—DA's argument that D had a "high tolerance for alcohol" held to be permissible inference from the evidence, i.e., discount relevance of .16 blood alcohol level & believe instead witnesses who testified that D was functioning normally;

C v Lyons **71 MAC 671, 676 n.5 (2008)**—in indecent assault and battery (over age 14) trial, D defended on ground that complainant had initiated aggressive physical confrontation and any contact he made was in self-defense:

error ("beyond the scope of the evidence") for prosecutor to argue self-defense not (legally) available to person charged with indecent A&B and that D's version implausible because he did not seek criminal charges against complainant for her assault;

C v Kines **37 MAC 540 (94)**—reversal for injecting racial animosity into case, with no basis in evidence: citing D's statement that he was surprised that he could have been subdued by only three cops, "is that a statement of somebody who has contempt . . . (for) white police officers trying to do their job?";

C v Phoenix **409 M 408 (91)**—statements in both opening and closing suggested "a racial theme" without evidence to support it, with possibility of sweeping jurors beyond fair/calm consideration of the evidence (but no relief here);

C v Pina **430 M 266, 269 (99)**—argument that neighborhood harbored such crime as to make all potential witnesses fearful of cooperating with police either supported by evidence here, or cured by instruction (but otherwise would have been reversible);

C v Thomas **52 MAC 286, 293 (2001)**—reversal for argument that back seat passenger D's guilt of intent to distribute tiny amount of drugs found on sidewalk should be inferred from his presence in a car in which a digital scale & "crack cocaine" were found: no evidence about what drugs were in car & no basis for inference that D (not the driver or owner of car, and not displaying consciousness of guilt) knew of or had access to front-seat scale or drugs; "association is a fundamentally impermissible basis on which to urge an inference of guilt";

See also C v Ortega **441 M 170, 180 (2004)**—DA shouldn't have asked question to elicit from cop that D associated with possible drug users;

C v Lamrini **392 M 427 (84)**—without evidence, DA can't argue robbery = motive;

C v Clary **388 M 583 (83)**—can't argue (lesbian) motive not in evidence;

C v McIntyre **430 M 529, 541–43 (99)**—substantive use of evidence limited to impeachment, asserting with no evidence that V had told D she was going to see her new boyfriend (but no objections and overwhelming evidence of guilt = no relief);

C v Burns **49 MAC 677, 683 (2000)**—improper to argue substantive use of grand jury testimony, with which witness was only impeached; inadequate preservation despite objection, because D failed to object again after judge merely instructed jury (ineffectually, non-curatively) that their memories of evidence controlled;

C v Lodge **431 M 461 (2000)**—without evidence, ADA argued there had been restraining order against D; after judge's interruption, ADA "corrected" remark by citing testimony whose use was limited to something other than that urged by ADA;

C v Santiago **425 M 491 (97)**—can't argue unfounded & inflammatory inference that eight-year-old boy was used as "shield" in gun battle (merely because D fired gun at adversary when boy was two feet away from D);

C v Andrews **427 M 434 (98)**—evidence didn't support argument that D "ambushed" and "executed" V; comments "went beyond mere hyperbole", decidedly improper; no relief, however (no objection);

C v Simmons **419 M 426 (95)**—mere evidence that D had served in Army did not justify argument that "he knows how to kill" and "he knows first aid";

C v. Hrabak **440 M 650 (2004)**—can't assert that no physical evidence could be expected from alleged anal rape, because child's rectum "flexible" (no evidence re: this); *C v Federico* **425 M 844, (97)** commands that expert testimony = necessary to address child complainant's lack of injury;

C v Merry **453 M 653 (2009)**—prosecutor's assertion that "we know" that "person having a seizure does not sit up" = improper because no medical testimony said whether or not person experiencing would be able to remain upright; assertion that "only way" saliva got onto airbag was by D's face hitting airbag at time of crash was improper because of evidence that fluids got on airbag when oxygen mask was placed on D or when D was removed from car, and this assertion went to "centerpiece" of prosecution case;

C v Fredette **56 MAC 253 (2002)**—reversal (despite no objection) for DA's argument, without expert evidence, that victims of sexual abuse commonly delay "disclosure" and maintain relationships with abuser;

C v Vazquez **65 MAC 305 (2005)**—same argument re delayed disclosure as "natural", and asserting that "we know because we see it in the news every single day, . . . the whole church scandal": "church scandal reference" was "serious impropriety", and with other errors required reversal;

C v Ryan **8 MAC 941 (79)**—DA's argument that "sperm does not always occur in ejaculation" not supported by evidence, and "went to the heart of the defense that the victim's accusation of rape was fabricated";

C v Orton **58 MAC 209 (2003)**—DA's misstatements of the evidence in closing argument went to heart of D's case, but harmless here;

C v Hiotes **58 MAC 255 (2003)**—after D's argument that elderly rape complainant (who talked to "space people") was not reliable, DA's argument, that D hadn't produced expert testimony as to her unreliability and was to be condemned because he was merely showing prejudice against the mentally ill, was reversible error;

US v Dworkin **855 F.2d 12 (1st Cir. '88)**—can't argue co-D's G. plea to suggest D's G. by association; *(see also Chapter 11-F, -D, Evidence: Hearsay, Relevance)*

C v Zane Z. **51 MAC 135, 148 (2001)**—in evidence was a stipulation that child sex assault complainant had been indecently assaulted by her grandfather, who had pled G to such assaults; error for DA to argue that such guilty plea proved that this juvenile D was guilty of charged sex offenses also, and that jury should make juvenile "step up to the plate as the grandfather had done";

C v Rivera **52 MAC 321 (2001)**—no evidence to support DA's argument that sex assault complainant's mother could have gotten a ride from 1 of the 15 people in the courtroom to accompany her daughter to counseling (& was therefore evil and to be discredited in her failure to corroborate complainant's story); wholly improper "name calling" to attack defense witness as "a stooge" and a "17-year-old punk";

C v Kater **388 M 519, 533 (83)**—can't suggest facts not in evidence (e.g., that D's long-sleeve trial shirt suggests hairy arms like witness said killer had);

C v Arroyo **442 M 135, 145–46 (2004)**—error to argue that DNA retrieved from jacket was D's, because of purported population demographics in Boston (ethnicity percentages unsupported by any evidence), and to argue that fatal shots were from a 9 millimeter gun (evidence had been excluded), but no objection to one and specific curative instruction as to other;

C v O'Connell **432 M 657 (2000)**—no relief for argument that D "did something" to change appearance of his arm, since Commonwealth argued that arm in photo was D's, and D said it wasn't, and DA's cross-examination of D-expert left open the possibility that difference between photo and D could have resulted from use of a "depilatory like Nair";

C v Wilson **427 M 336 (98)**—bad DA argument that murder weapon was "essentially" found on D (even if shell casing matching murder weapon was found in D's home); argument that surgical gloves were used in murder not supported by evidence;

C v Calcagno **31 MAC 25 (91)**—improper to comment on demeanor of mere onlooker at trial; here, prosecutor's comment that complainant's mother was staring her daughter down & was practically in D's lap was error but not risk of miscarriage of justice;

C v Kelly **417 M 266 (94)**—improper (and reversible) to argue cops were credible because they would not lie & thereby "put their pensions . . . on the line to get these two guys" & because if they were "that kind of cop, after 17 years, there'd be some kind of record of it, & you'd hear about it & you didn't" (LATTER = violation of constitutional dictates re burden of proof/no obligation on part of D to present evidence); no jury instruction "neutralized" impropriety;

C v Riberio **49 MAC 7, 10 (2000)**—"telling the jury that the victims have no reason to lie is over the line of permissible advocacy" (context of DA's opening statement, but quoted re: closing argument issue in *C v Beaudry* **445 M 577, 587 (2005)**), though SJC held that judge's "emphatic instruction" was curative, "particularly" because since D failed to object adequately, such that review was for substantial risk of miscarriage of justice (and D's convictions were reversed on another ground here, anyway);

C v Ramos **73 MAC 824 (2009)**—reversal for argument, 'why would she come in here four years later and say to complete strangers, "I was sexually assaulted. . . .

What does she get from that? . . . What motive to lie . . . does she have?"; rejecting Commonwealth argument that issue was unpreserved (D had moved in limine to preclude comment on complainant's motive to lie, and had objected after the argument; D not obliged to request curative instruction);

C v Helberg **73 MAC 175 (2008)**—finding no error in prosecutor's argument that complainants "had no motive" to lie, which was response to D's argument that there were "many, many reasons why a person would make up charges"; DA's argument made "no suggestion, implicit or explicit," that witnesses "should be afforded greater credibility by reason of their willingness to come into court and testify"; prosecutor's identification and rejection of several possible motives to lie = grounded in evidence;

C v Hiotes **58 MAC 255 (2003)**—DA's argument that D hadn't produced psychiatric evidence showing complainant unreliable = reversible error, particularly when DA opposed D's motion for competency examination of complainant even as DA acknowledged her mental infirmities (she spoke with "space people" regularly);

C v Grimshaw **412 M 505 (92)**—improper for prosecutor to argue matters excluded from evidence, but harmless here;

C v Monson **57 MAC 867 (2003)**—DA's suggestion to jury during argument that police had received tip from someone that D was selling drugs = reversible error (question to jury 'was it a coincidence that when undercover cop entered bar, he went directly to D/confronted D/found cocaine exactly where D was sitting?');

C v Beauchamp **424 M 682 (97)**—prosecutor should not encourage jury to conduct experiments in jury room or to obtain outside information of any sort;

C v Loguidice **420 M 453 (95)**—reversal for arguing "facts" not supported by evidence, i.e., that child rape complainant's neighbors had been at church, and that D committed crimes at that time because he knew that neighbors were away and could not surprise him with the child;

C v Coren **437 M 723 (2002)**—reversal for arguing that victim had said, "don't shoot," that D had been "yelling," and that D had been pushing gun into victim's stomach (none supported by evidence); judge had declined to give particularized instructions re: this, & said only that closing remarks aren't evidence;

C v Lindsey **48 MAC 641 (2000)**—"facts" not in evidence (that D was unemployed in another state & was selling drugs because he needed the money), with other errors = reversal;

C v Hubbard **45 MAC 277 (98)**—no evidence (notwithstanding the smearing content of the DA's own questions, not confirmed by the witness-D) that D had previously assaulted teenagers with a gun and was then the aggressor, "just like" in the case being tried; reversal;

C v Wilson **49 MAC 429 (2000)**—improper to argue (no evidence) that D abused alleged victim, his ex-wife, for the 34 years of their marriage; trial was for single

A&B, complaint as to which was not made until three years after alleged incident, and more than one year after parties' divorce;

C v Gonzalez **28 MAC 906 (89)**—counsel had right to argue that lineups are generally more reliable than 1-on-1 show-ups;

12-J.5. Vouching, Personal Opinion

C v Ianelli **17 MAC 1011 (84)**—"I submit," "contend," "argue" don't improperly suggest personal opinion;

C v Tuit **393 M 801 (85)**—DA can't argue evidence "overwhelming", but no objection, no reversal;

C v Bourgeois **391 M 869 (84)**—DA can't vouch for witnesses' credibility; but affirm because no objection & immediate curative instruction;

C v Sanders **451 M 290 (2008)**—argument that trooper "was absolutely honest when she said, 'I can only tell you where [shell casings] were [when she arrived at the scene]'" was not "vouching,"; instead argument = witness was credible because she limited her testimony and did not seek to provide more info than she actually knew;

C v Burts **68 MAC 684 (2007)**—improper for prosecutor to suggest personal belief/opinion and "to blur the boundaries between judge, prosecutor, and jury by placing himself in the jury box as a supplemental or standby juror" ("we need, as people, to get the right person", "we all know he picked out the D", "I think we know that for a fact, based on cross-examination", "I'm going to go you one further. How do we know there wasn't something else? . . . if there was any mistake, I didn't see it" ["troubled by the prosecutor's repeated use of the pronoun 'we'"]);

C v Meuse **423 M 831 (96)**—reversal for DA's vouching for credibility of accomplice-turned-prosecution witness: 'in order to receive favorable sentence recommendation, witness had to tell truth, and "army of state police" are able to discern "truth" by investigation'; **not cured** by instruction that argument should be disregarded; instead, should have told jury that argument = WRONG, & that government does not know whether witness is telling truth;

C v Villalobos **7 MAC 905 (79)**—DA's "believe me" improperly suggested personal knowledge of facts, opinions of witnesses, & belief in G.;

C v Omonira **59 MAC 200 (2003)**—DA's argument that cop = "the most laid back police officer I ever saw. He's completely honest" = improper vouching;

C v Griffith **45 MAC 784 (98)**—"as I told you at the beginning of the trial, (D) is a common street level dealer" (language having a "dogmatic 'take it from me' quality that the cases have declared to be impermissible"); and "By no means are these men (cops) not telling the truth";

C v Williams **450 M 894 (2008)**—prosecutor's closing argument regaling jury with all steps he had taken, in his "beat up little car" to verify, personally, the account told by prosecution witness (whose murder indictment was subject of nolle prosequi) was not merely "restating what the jury saw on the view", was not cured by instruction (personal beliefs or activities of lawyer, such as personally traveling not relevant, etc.), and resulted in reversal of murder conviction; argument additionally offered prosecutor's personal justifications for indictment and "deal" decisions and was vouching; fn.10 (judge should have interrupted prosecutor immediately upon his "unsworn testimony");

C v Hardy **431 M 387, 399 (2000)**—improper to shore up credibility of immunized witness by argument that witness "only testified at this trial after the Supreme Judicial Court . . . said, 'Mr.(witness), you are going to testify or you're going to be held in contempt and go to jail, and you'd better not lie. . . . You could be prosecuted for perjury" (SJC resented ADA's attempt to use authority of SJC to vouch for witness's credibility) AND improper to suggest personal knowledge, outside record, that Ds had killed before ("This time, they killed one of their own"); only "correct and thorough" instructions specifically targeted to improper remarks prevented reversal;

C v Freeman **430 M 111, 119 (99)**—DA's opinion that his expert's "the best there is," "a premiere forensic psychiatrist in this state, if not the country," and "we want the best and that's who you heard from yesterday" was impermissible vouching (no objection, overwhelming G evidence, no relief);

C v Rosa **73 MAC 540 (2009)**—ADA's improper argument that eight-photo array procedure was better than sequential showing of single photos = "could have been understood by jury to indicate that [ADA] had . . . knowledge about the relative difficulty of the two methods" of ID and police had used the "fairest" one;

C v North **52 MAC 603, 611 (2001)**—DA shouldn't have said that "there are very few cases that a prosecutor presents to a jury in which you really get the feeling that you are representing the Commonwealth in the sense of the definition of Commonwealth"; bad "aroma of personal belief in the case";

C v McCravy **430 M 758 (2000)**—Commonwealth conceded, "prudent(ly)", that DA erred in arguing that it was a "fact" that D was intoxicated and a "fact" that he killed the passenger in his car, and that whole defense was a "sham";

C v DelValle **443 M 782, 795–96 (2005)**—OK to argue for jurors to "think about [87-year-old victim's] life and remember there is nothing in her life history that would prepare her for the kind of violence . . . brutality . . . pain . . . suffering that [defendant] put her through" because "fair comment on consciousness and degree of suffering" of victim = a factor for extreme atrocity/cruelty;

C v McLaughlin **431 M 506, 510 (2000)**—"egregious" error in DA's argument that "case is all about whether or not he's guilty. It's not whether he's insane or not", given that sole issue was D's lack of criminal responsibility, & evidence was such that there was "at minimum a strong argument for" required finding of NG if there were no "presumption" of sanity;

C v Achorn **25 MAC 247 (88)**—DA can argue (here) five-year-old can't lie; (HIGHLY QUESTIONABLE LEGALLY/FACTUALLY)

C v Redmond **370 M 591 (76)**—DA can't promise witness will be prosecuted;

C v Thomas **401 M 109 (87)**—DA shifted burden of proof ("If you find . . . , then NG") & injected own belief ("disbelieve (complaining witness) & I'm a conspirator");

C v Montanino **28 MAC 516, 522 n.4 (90), S.C., 409 M 500 (91)**—use of word "victim" to describe complaining witness disapproved in context of police testimony; cf. *C v Harris* **409 M 461 (91)**—judge should pay "close attention" to behavior & demeanor of victim advocates; visual displays of consolation & support, such as crying, handholding & hugging, are analogous to improper vouching by Commonwealth for complainant's credibility; curative or supplemental instructions may be required;

C v Raymond **424 M 382 (97)**—assertion that "(witness X) told you the truth when he testified" is discouraged (as seeming to be personal belief of prosecutor) though here excused as logical conclusion of permissible argument in favor of witness's credibility;

C v Dumais **60 MAC 70 (2003)**—DA's argument, "I think she was intoxicated," "I think that it was painfully clear that [cops] were being credible," "I think it was painfully obvious how truthful he was" = impermissible;

C v Pagano **47 MAC 55, 62 (99)**—bad to argue that "If I haven't proven this case beyond a reasonable doubt, then let my vote be the thirteenth for not guilty"; bad to refer to personal service as an altar boy, and that "Father Cleary" at the 7-o'clock mass would say "think about it, pray about it, and hopefully you'll do something about it";

C v Lindsey **48 MAC 641 (2000)**—"we have no interest in punishing an innocent person" & "if you are looking for the truth . . . , the Commonwealth is satisfied that you'll find (D) guilty" = BAD;

12-J.6. Inflammatory; Appeal to Sympathy

C v Guy **454 M 440 (2009)**—"appeal to sympathy [is] . . . an obfuscation of 'the clarity with which the jury would look at the evidence and encourage the jury to find guilt even if the evidence [is inadequate]"; Commonwealth should not have argued that "the answer" for V's family and for initial suspect (arrested but released) and for "citizens of the town" was that "we got it right this time" (should not bring "feelings" of V's husband and other community members to jury's attention);

C v West **44 MAC 150 (98)**—DA can't say some testimony came in "too quickly for me to jump up and say . . . that's not (admissible)"; DA, by citing his own attitude against a witness who "sleeps until noon," possibly exacerbated latent racial biases in jurors; suggested without evidence that D had intimidated witnesses; curative instructions ineffectual because errors too numerous; judge can't always "unring the bell";

C v Cobb **26 MAC 283 (88)**—can't urge jury to do "duty" & to justify complaining witness's trust in system; but affirm because no objection by D;

C v Garcia **75 MAC 901 (2009)**—urging return of G verdicts to "acknowledge and affirm" that sex assault complainant's story "will be accepted and understood . . . not scrutinized . . . [or] discounted [or] overlooked", and that she had been "re-victimized" by having to tell her story to police, medical personnel, and jury = reversal; generalized instruction that emotion or sympathy have no place in proceedings didn't cure;

C v Lindsey **48 MAC 641, 646 (2000)**—(in drug prosecution) "as long as (drugs) remain illegal, police officers will risk their lives to fight the war on drugs" = bad;

C v Smith **387 M 900 (83)**—reverse for cumulative effect of DA's inflammatory appeals to sympathy, comment on failure to testify & verdict consequences ("would turn D loose on society");

C v Baran **74 MAC 256 (2009)**—ineffective assistance of defense counsel for failing to object, and ineffective assistance of appellate counsel for failing to brief, improper DA arguments, return G "in the name of justice and decency", and "if ever there was a case where the ends of justice literally cry out for" G, this is it, "truth came literally from the mouths of babes", D "could have raped and sodomized and abused those children whenever he felt the primitive urge to satisfy his sexual appetite", D "like a chocoholic in a candy store"; "I beseech you —I beg you —think of those children and bring back a verdict of guilty on each and every one of these charges"; argument encouraged "sympathy" verdict and that jury would be answerable to the public if NG verdict;

C v Worcester **44 MAC 258, 264 (98)**—reverse for appeal to sympathy (V had "right to life," D deemed V's life worthless, V's family "grieved as much as any of ours would", asking jury "to do something about" killing), and for asserting "facts" unsupported by record (that apartment was crack house, that D had criminal record); "regrettable" that DA called self "government" and otherwise personalized role;

C v Williams **450 M 894 (2008)**—telling jury, "It is your turn to put in work", emphasized phrase used in evidence to signify a revenge killing, and improperly urged something other than "impartial fact finding";

C v Gentile **437 M 569 (2002)**—error to argue that "victim didn't deserve to die this way," that the burden of proof is "the price we pay for living in a free, democratic society," and that defense strategy of accusing three other people was "despicable" (but no objections, no relief);

C v Torres **437 M 460 (2002)**—improper appeal to sympathy to argue "[victims] had a right to sleep in their bed without this man coming in there," "she had rights, she had the right to go to bed at night. She had the right to live. He took those rights. She called out, 'Daddy help me.' But her father was dead. You could answer the call for justice and hold [D] accountable. He's guilty as charged"; last statement = improper personal belief; OK to refer to jury as "conscience of the community" BECAUSE theory was "extreme atrocity/cruelty";

C v Rosa **73 MAC 540 (2009)**—prosecutor's reference to victim's status as firefighter occurred 19 times in eight pages of closing argument, "an improper appeal to sympathy," notwithstanding fact that "public servant" was an element of crime (A&B on public servant);

C v McLaughlin **431 M 506 (2000)**—exhortation to consider rights of victims, in case where sole issue was D's insanity, = bad; ridiculing trial's emphasis on D's mind, asserting that "the truth is that this case is all about whether or not he's guilty. It's not whether he's insane or not" = also "egregious" error;

C v Ingram **14 MAC 999 (82)**—DA can argue public has rights & don't decide on sympathy (see also *Cobb* **26 MAC 283 (88)**)

C v Andrade **422 M 236 (96)**—argument that evidence "cries out for justice" & jurors should "do justice" = improper appeal to emotion and sympathy;

C v LaCorte **373 M 700 (77)**—DA can urge jury to act with "courage";

C v Barros **425 M 572 (97)**—OK to argue 'imagine what V felt like' because relevant to "cruel/atrocious" element; questionable whether evidence supported inference that witness's inability to ID D was result of intimidation (so argument bad, but judge sustained objection & told jury to disregard, so no prejudice);

C v Grinkley **75 MAC 798 (2009)**—"think about what it must have been like for" complainant = improper, as is "invitation to the jury to put themselves in the position of the victim" (citing *C v Jordan* 49 MAC 802 (2000) and *C v Harris* 11 MAC 165, 176 n.9 (81));

C v Esteves **46 MAC 339, rev'd on other grounds 429 M 636 (99)**—error to ask jurors to think about how they'd felt when called up to side bar for individual voir dire and "multiply it times a hundred when (complainant's) up on the stand for hours being cross-examined . . ." (sympathy ploy);

C v Saunders **75 MAC 505 (2009)**—argument suggesting that jurors "enter into the heart and mind of a fourteen year old child" when considering inconsistencies between witness's testimony and prior inconsistent statements (made when she was fourteen) = BAD, but no relief (no objection);

C v Rivera **52 MAC 321, 328 (2001)**—refusal to find error in argument that sex assault complainant "didn't have to subject herself to the humiliation of talking to countless strangers about horribly embarrassing personal experiences in her young life";

C v MacDonald **368 M 395 (75)**—"tell bums/hoodlums of Southie we won't tolerate this" = bad;

C v Marrero **60 MAC 225 (2003)**—argument that gang members, including D, lived by "law of the jungle" = improper (but no relief here);

C v Coyne **44 MAC 1 (97)**—because "traffickers need to know that this system will work," jury should convict = bad, suggesting that verdict concerned drug traffickers in general; in context here, comment about defendants "trying to run & hide" not likely construed as comment on failure to testify (distinguishing *US v Hardy* **37 F3d 753 (1st Cir. '94)**), but if there had been contemporaneous objection, unconstitutional import more likely to be found;

C v Jordan **49 MAC 802 (2000)**—prosecutor shouldn't argue that Commonwealth "expects" convictions, or that jurors MUST return verdict, because it's their "burden" & "duty," no matter how hard/long necessary (since always possible that conscientious jurors can't reach unanimity);

C v Degro **432 M 319, 328–29 (2000)**—closing exhortation to "do your job" not OK, citing *C v Cobb* **26 MAC 283, 286 (88)** (reference to jury's "duty", though without explicit statement that such will result in G verdict, disapproved);

C v Deloney **59 MAC 47, 53 (2003)**—"Now is the time for justice. Find him guilty" = error (but not here prejudicial); *C v Vazquez* **65 MAC 305 (2005)**—"You *need* to find him guilty" conveys that jury has "duty to convict", and with other argument errors (including "This is [D's] case to win or lose," suggesting that it was D's burden to disprove guilt), required reversal;

C v Killelea **370 M 638 (76)**—reverse for arguing that 'not guilty by reason of insanity' puts D back on street;

C v Duguay **430 M 397, 404 (99)**—error to argue to jury the issue of punishment (but here, judge immediately struck the statement);

C v Sevieri **21 MAC 745 (86)**—can't urge women jurors to put 'selves in complaining witness's position or ask jury how they'll explain N.G to their families;

C v Quinn **61 MAC 332 (2004)**—reversal for DA's urging jury to consider how they would explain verdict to "loved one at home or your friend on the phone";

C v Mello **420 M 375 (95)**—bad to argue trial raises question of "what have we become?," & that bad answer may be met by saying to this D & "all others that may even consider similar conduct" that "we're going to do something about it" and "this trial gives you the opportunity";

C v Roberts **433 M 45, 54 (2000)**—disapproving argument that, "in an orderly society governed by law . . . (defendant) is going to be held accountable (for) taking the law into his own hands, that is what we are here for"; equated with asking jury to "send a message"; argument that D and V "lived off of the proceeds of (two witnesses') prostitution" had no relevance to any issue, and "could only have been (made) for unfairly prejudicial purposes";

C v Wallace **45 MAC 930 (98)**—DA asking jury to consider right of people in the neighborhood to feel safe was wrong (but forceful curative instructions prevented reversal);

C v Belton **352 M 263 (67)**—bad appeal to sympathy ("spirit of V hovers over/watching you");

C v Depradine **42 MAC 401 (97)**—bad to say "V is dead, not coming back . . . bleeds like any of us . . . his family grieves like anyone else's family"; also bad to exalt credibility of cops just because they're cops;

C v Drumgold **423 M 230 (96)**—when homicide V was innocent bystander, an 11-year-old girl, prosecutor unfairly invited sympathy by characterizing case as "dispute" between D and the innocent victim;

C v Fruchtman **418 M 8 (94)**—improper appeal to sympathy ("Don't let that threat come true") when child sex assault complainant testified that D told her no one would believe her if she accused him;

C v Sanchez **405 M 369 (89)**—improper for prosecutor to ask jury to "end nightmares" of complainant;

C v Lorette **37 MAC 736 (94)**—same, re: "nightmare" of wife of complainant & her family for "rest of life";

C v Walker **421 M 90 (95)**—bad to argue that victim was robbed not just of money, but security & personal safety & while jury couldn't replace that, it could "do justice" to her "faith in the system, and you, the jurors, the foundation of that system";

C v Ward **28 M AC 292 (90)**—improper for prosecutor to ask jury to confront crime & avenge wrongdoing;

C v Mayne **38 MAC 282 (95)**—bad to argue Commonwealth witness = "hero", "who would probably do anything to keep from being in the position he was put in, being the only person . . . to tell the truth";

C v Ridge **455 M 307 (2009)**—DA's argument that it took "courage" for witnesses to testify = proper, as it was reasonable inference from the evidence, two witnesses testifying they were afraid of D and fourteen years lapsed between homicide and some witnesses' grand jury testimony;

C v McLeod **30 MAC 536 (91)**—improper for prosecutor to ask jury to 'rectify tragedy' of complainant having to humiliate herself by testifying;

C v Woods **414 M 343 (93)**—**BAD** to elicit for jury an identification of victims' parents in courtroom (not "argument" issue);

C v Sanna **424 M 92 (97)**—though "close to" improper, no relief from DA's argument that homicide V's family "should have been able to share more holidays with" V, and that V's photo (a trial exhibit) "should have been displayed on (relative's) mantle" rather than "lying before you next to photo of . . . bludgeoned . . . body";

C v Mathews **31 MAC 564 (91)**—improper for prosecutor to call upon jurors to act as 'conscience of community' & to not tell victim it was 'too bad' you gave incorrect description;

C v Raymond **424 M 382 (97)**—'conscience of community' language & 'imagine her feelings' exhortation OK because relevant to extreme atrocity or cruelty in murder case;

C v Hollie **47 MAC 538 (99)**—disapproving implicit suggestion that V wouldn't subject 'self to ordeal of trial unless it was very important to him to see D brought to justice; D's conduct called "unconscionable," "gutless," "detestable"; repeated references to blind V's vulnerability; Shakespearean exhortation "to thine own self be true" commingled with call for G; implicit reference to jury's moral "duty" to convict;

C v Santiago **425 M 491 (97)**—homicide victim was innocent bystander in gun battle between 2 rival groups: reversible error for DA to assert 12 times in opening & closing that V was only 17 years old and was pregnant, and that argument was occurring "on what would have been her 20th birthday" and for V's sister to be called as witness for only non-material evidence (about V's age, fiancé, pregnancy, schoolwork, employment, recent birthday celebration, & about witness's grief upon learning of death);

C v Kent K **427 M 754 (98)**—"improper" to argue repeatedly that V was very young and it was his birthday, but no relief in part because purportedly relevant to extreme atrocity or cruelty;

C v Burns **49 MAC 677 (2000)**—Commonwealth on appeal conceded improper argument re: "scared, skinny, fifteen-year-old kid running for his life. (three more references to '15 years old') He's not coming home to his mother. . . . He's dead and buried. Fifteen years old. I want you to reflect on that for a minute how young that is. He's just a kid, he's a baby"; also bad = "I'm asking each and every one of you to do something about it. I'm asking you to convict him; no objection, belief that jurors weren't swayed (because only 2d degree murder) = no relief, though "came perilously close to requiring a retrial" and "histrionics seem to have been studied, not careless";

C v Rock **429 M 609 (99)**—witness may not be called for sole purpose of creating sympathy, but instead must testify to something relevant; bad appeal to sympathy to argue "he's dead . . . 21 years old . . . and although (victim) never set foot in this courtroom . . . he spoke to you during this trial";

C v Mitchell **428 M 852 (99)**—DA shouldn't have argued "we're talking about a human being here: (victim) who will be seventeen forever because he was killed," and "(D) has all sorts of rights. But, you know, (victim) didn't have a jury . . . (or) trial . . . didn't have any opportunity for that. No breaks"; no objection, no relief;

C v Lodge **431 M 461 (2000)**—bad argument: victim's "right to live and this man took it";

C v McCravy **430 M 758, 764 (2000)**—"world became a worse place because (passenger in D's car) was killed" = bad (but no relief because no prejudice: D was acquitted of all charges that he was culpable for the death);

See also Chapter 11-D (Evidence, Relevance), e.g., C v Carlino 429 M 692 (99) (gruesome photos not relevant) and C v Johnson 429 M 745, 750 (99) (photo of murder victim's child's crib, empty except for teddy bear: irrelevant, sympathy ploy);

C v Brown **34 MAC 222 (93)**—though "inelegant," not improper sympathy appeal for DA to argue "what they're saying is that the police are lying"; D-counsel had implied , in argument, that police testimony was "implausibly pat;"

C v Kee **449 M 550 (2007)**—finding no error in references to "dangerous" city, cops able to aurally monitor undercover cops "so if the guy's about to die, he can call for help. That little bit they gave him," simply because they were supported by evidence; [object at evidentiary point, if not relevant to any contested issue, since function became solely appeal to passions/sympathy];

C v Hogan **12 MAC 646 (81)**—can't argue D's a "hit man" (inflammatory, beyond evidence) or D's "from lower end of town" (false issue of D against community);

C v Rosario **430 M 505, 515–16 (99)**—bad to call D "monster," throw photo and teeth impressions on table in front of him during closing argument;

C v Stewart **454 M 527 (2009)**—bad to argue D was "unfeeling", "hadn't even acknowledged [son] from birth", such bad character having no connection to the killing of the victim in case being tried;

12-J.7. Ethnic/Racial References

C v Graziano **368 M 325 (75)**—bad appeal to ethnic stereotypes;

C v Montez **450 M 736 (2008)**—argument, "who takes keys: . . . Someone that maybe wants to break into *our* houses, torment *our* women?", in interracial crime of sex and murder (D = dark-skinned Hispanic, victim = white female): phrase "our women" should not have been used;

C v Mahdi **388 M 679 (83)**—bad argument re: D's race & religious (Muslim) beliefs;

C v Kines **37 MAC 540 (94)**—reversal for injecting racial animosity into case, with no basis in evidence: citing D's statement that he was surprised that he could have been subdued by only 3 cops, "is that a statement of somebody who has contempt . . . (for) white police officers trying to do their job?";

Arrieta-Agressot v US **3 F.3d 525 (1st Cir. '93)**—bad to argue, in drug distribution case, "pain & suffering" of many families because of drugs, disruption & corruption of society because of drugs, Ds' lack of concern that people addicted to marijuana, & that Ds were "soldiers in the army of evil . . . whose purpose is to poison, disrupt, corrupt";

C v Westerman **414 M 688 (93)**—bad to argue drug distribution to children (no evidence) & that jury should hold D accountable for his "lifestyle" & effects of his actions on the community: lack of objection & forceful & pointed instructions = no reversal;

C v Gallego **27 MAC 714 (89)**—improper for prosecutor to appeal to jurors' anxiety about 'Columbian drug dealers';

C v Lindsey **48 MAC 641, 646 (2000)**—"Unless we buy the countries of Colombia and Bolivia and other Central American countries and burn them to the ground, drugs are going to keep coming into this country. And as long as they remain illegal, police officers will risk their lives to fight the war on drugs" = reversal, with other over the top rhetoric;

C v Munera **411 M 1103 (91)**—1 or 2 references to D & cohorts as Colombians to show D was part of single nationality trafficking ring not improper; see also *C v Durango* **47 MAC 185 (99)** single question to one defense witness re: where she's from (Colombia), and later question establishing that W had known D "her whole life," not error; no further mention of it, i.e., no suggestion that D guilty merely by virtue of ethnic background;

C v Kines **37 MAC 540 (94)**—reversal for injecting racial animosity into case, with no basis in evidence: citing D's statement that he was surprised that he could have been subdued by only three cops, "is that a statement of somebody who has contempt . . . (for) white police officers trying to do their job?";

12-J.8. Psychologist/Psychiatrist Rhetoric

C v Cosme **410 M 746 (91)**—tasteless & improper for prosecutor to refer to defense experts as 'a dog & pony show' & as 'a little head specialist & wizard';

C v Shelley **374 M 466 (78)**—improper to argue that defense witnesses, psychologists, were "prostitutes" or "mercenary soldiers" (though argument made in "disclaimer form"), or to make emotional allusions to "well meaning ink-blot tests . . . mice . . . goblins";

C v Cruz **424 M 207 (97)**—improper to call defense psychologist "charlatan" (but focused curative instructions here made error harmless);

C v Grimshaw **412 M 505 (92)**—improper for prosecutor to refer to defense experts as 'hired guns';

12-J.9. Missing Witness

District Court Model Jury Instruction ## 4.04 & 4.041, Absent Witness & Announced Witness Does Not Testify and Superior Court Criminal Practice Jury Instructions § 4.9—absent (or missing) witness; (*but see Chapter 21-A's cautions that model jury instructions are often found to be erroneous when subjected to appellate scrutiny*);

C v Bryer **398 M 9 (86)**—DA can argue D's missing witness roommate though he couldn't have fully corroborated D's testimony; D naturally expected to call him because strong DA case, issue's credibility, (& no argument equally available to both);

C v Wilson **38 MAC 680 (95)**—inasmuch as D-counsel shouldn't have argued "missing witness" as to informant, no error in judge instructing that all witnesses are available to all parties & that though D didn't have to call any witnesses, he could have called informant to testify;

Graves v US **150 US 118 (1893)**—presume an unfavorable inference if a peculiarly available missing witness would've elucidated;

McCormick, *Evidence*, § 264 (5th ed. 1999)—"admissions by conduct"—refusal to allow comment or to instruct as to 'missing witness' inference rarely results in reversal, but erroneously instructing jury on the inference or even erroneous argument by counsel "much more frequently requires retrial"; possibility that inference may be drawn invites waste of time in calling unnecessary witnesses or in presenting evidence to explain why they were not called; given "modern discovery," justification & need for the inference is diminished; "courts often require early notice from a party expecting to make a missing witness argument or intending to request such an instruction";

2 Wigmore, *Evidence,* **§§ 285–91 (Chadbourn rev. 1979)**—permissible inferences from missing evidence; **AS TO MISSING "EVIDENCE," SEE SPECIFICALLY, doctrine of "spoliation," and**

C v Kee **449 M 550 (2007)**—Commonwealth failed to preserve or make record of purportedly "marked" bill used to purchase drugs, claimed to have been found on D's person, so D sought (a) exclusion of testimony about it, or (b) jury instruction allowing adverse inference from its absence: SJC asserts that, despite money's materiality, D couldn't show that bill was exculpatory, and accepts explanation that bill had to be used for further "buys"; D at trial focused near-exclusively on absence of bill; **in future, where evidence lost or destroyed, "it may be appropriate to instruct the jury that they may, but need not, draw an inference against the Commonwealth"**, after D's showing that access to the evidence "would have produced evidence favorable to his cause" (query: how to so prove? Presumption of innocence isn't enough? Simple claim by cop that the evidence was inculpatory defeats confrontation and permissible other conclusion?);

C v Franklin **366 M 284 (74)**—factors re: missing witness inference = (1) strong case, so expected to call witness, (2) availability, (3) one's superior knowledge of ID of W (though equally available to both sides); should voir dire D's reason for not calling witness before exercising "cautious discretion" to charge;

C v Ortiz **67 MAC 349 (2006)**—on merits, rejecting D's claim in Rule 30 motion for new trial that prosecutor lied in claiming ignorance of whereabouts of witness, depriving D of a "missing witness" instruction;

C v Johnson **46 MAC 398 (99)**—following D's testimony that he did not know where he was at time of robbery but had not committed it, error for DA to argue that "if he didn't remember what he was doing the night of the robbery and wasn't responsible for that robbery, he damn sure would find out where he was, who he was with, and bring them in here and have them testify to tell you that they were with him"; this was neither "fair nor reasonable comment";

C v Caldwell **36 MAC 570, reversed on other ground, 418 M 777 (94)**—failure to secure judge's permission for missing witness argument risks its interruption and an unfavorable instruction;

C v Evans **42 MAC 618 (97)**—though DA should have obtained permission before arguing missing witness, appellate court assumed, from judge's mere failure to interrupt, that judge found inference justified on evidence;

C v Vasquez **27 MAC 655 (89)**—before arguing adverse inferences from missing witnesses, "proper practice" is to obtain judge's permission;

C v Pena **455 M 1 (2009)**—defense counsel's argument that Commonwealth's expert psych witness wasn't called because couldn't rebut D's witness was made without prior judicial approval, and judge permissibly instructed that jurors were not to speculate re: evidence not heard, and to strike argument from consideration;

C v Johnson **429 M 745 (99)**—(highly questionable holding) though party risks being interrupted by judge, with unfavorable comment, when missing witness argument is made without foundation and permission, "does not ordinarily create a basis for reversal"; (but see post and ante, constitutional rights implicated);

C v Broomhead **67 MAC 547 (2006)**—prosecutor's "missing witness" comments in argument, made without judge's permission, caused reversal despite lack of objection; before allowing prosecutor to make such argument, judge must make ruling "as matter of law, that there is a sufficient foundation for such inference in the record"; absent such ruling, appellate court should be hesitant to conclude that omission of ruling implies foundation in the record; should not "undermine the principle that missing witness arguments should not be made except by express leave of the court"; in 2-witness OUI case (cop vs. D), evidence against D couldn't be said "so strong"; since missing witnesses were said to be D's brother and friend, jury wouldn't have given their testimony much weight [probable bias] AND they were drunk at the time; record didn't show that Commonwealth "was unaware of their whereabouts or was unable to procure their physical presence in court"; while fact that they were "working" at time of trial wasn't a good reason for failing to call them, failure to call could be thought strategic because both had been under influence of alcohol; NB: this conviction followed 2 prior trials with hung juries;

C v Rodriquez **49 MAC 370 (2000)**—after judge told ADA he wouldn't give missing witness instruction against D, error for ADA to argue it anyway; contrary to ADA's assertion ("no way I can be precluded from arguing that"), denial of instruction = ruling that foundation insufficient;

C v Smith **49 MAC 827 (2000)**—judge gave D-counsel permission to argue missing witness against Commonwealth, but thereafter refused to instruct on missing witness, & instead gave standard instruction "don't decide case on basis of any unanswered questions"; same instruction repeated when jury asked question why no other witnesses were presented by Commonwealth = reversal (dicta: no per se reversal for refusal to instruct after permitting argument by D counsel); cf. *C v Remedor* **52 MAC 694, 700–01 (2001)** judge's response to jury question, i.e. 'confine consideration to evidence that *was* presented,' negated D's "Bowden" (**379 M 472 (80)**) defense, creating substantial risk of a miscarriage of justice;

C v Saletino **449 M 657 (2007)**—while agreeing with *Smith* 49 MAC 827 (2000) (after authorizing party to argue "missing witness," jury instruction on issue required), holding that here inference wasn't available because Commonwealth had legitimate tactical reasons for not calling cooperating informant, so no relief for refusing instruction after allowing argument; NOTING THAT nothing said here prevents D from arguing that Commonwealth hasn't produced sufficient evidence, **which may point out that a specific witness or specific evidence has not been produced** (but can't ask jury to draw conclusion about substance of evidence that hasn't been produced, unless foundational prerequisites for adverse "missing witness" are shown); *v Niziolek* 380 M 513 (80)—though witness equally available to both, DA can argue negative inference because strong case against D (so D would've called W if helpful) & foundation = in evidence; (fn.4) should discuss with judge before inviting inference;

C v Hoilett 430 M 369, 373–76 (99)—both Commonwealth and D had phone number for a witness, and no evidence that Commonwealth possessed any advantage in contacting witness: no abuse of discretion to deny D request for missing witness instruction; but see *C v Saletino* 449 M 657 n.17 (2007) and cases cited;

C v Nurse 50 MAC 36 (2000)—individual to whom rape complainant purportedly complained (alleged "roommate") would, according to defense opening, testify didn't even know complainant, but "roommate" didn't appear after defense summons; within judge's discretion to deny 'missing witness' instruction against Commonwealth (though conviction rev'd on another ground);

C v Fulgham 23 MAC 422 (87)—though witness was at court, more available to DA under facts, but judge can deny instruction if DA had reasons (judge let D argue a bit);

C v Niels N 73 MAC 689 (2009)—no error in refusing missing witness instruction when NO investigating police officer was called to testify (D didn't show what testimony of distinct importance they could provide and "does not claim" that witnesses weren't "equally available to him to call at trial" and doesn't explain why he chose not to call them himself);

C v Groce 25 MAC 327 (88)—judge can't charge & DA can't argue missing mother or girlfriend re: alibi because both unlikely to be important or helpful;

C v Ortiz 61 MAC 468 (2004)—judge erred in giving missing witness instruction: missing witness's testimony would have been cumulative of D's girlfriend's testimony; D didn't have superior knowledge of witness's whereabouts, & he wasn't "peculiarly under [D's] influence"; case against D was strong only if Commonwealth's witness was credited over defendant and his girlfriend; witness perhaps absent only because counsel believed that he had summonsed witness, but realized belatedly that he had not done so; nothing in record suggested that witness disavowed prior statements supportive of alibi;

C v Olszewski 416 M 707 (93)—chief witness in murder case testified (a) D confessed to him & said D's father picked D up from a location after D disposed of body & (b) D's sister had quizzed witness on what he had told police: missing witness argument OK; correct instruction should include admonitions that whether such an inference should be drawn depends on strength of case, & jury should **not** draw adverse inference unless persuaded of truth of the inference beyond a reasonable doubt;

C v Alves 50 MAC 796 (2001)—when D's mother became extremely agitated during her direct testimony, & for psych. & cardiac reasons did not testify further, judge should have stricken testimony only, & abused discretion in giving missing witness instruction simply because witness became unavailable to undergo cross-examination;

C v Schatvet 23 MAC 130 (86)—bad DA cross-examination & judge's charge because no foundation (because evidence = cumulative); missing witness needs caution because serious impact & maybe constitutional violation;

C v Tripolone 57 MAC 901 (2003)—refusal to instruct or to allow "missing witness" comment on absence of third cop in 3-cop team which visited complainant's home after alleged rape (evidence list and videotape there made were lost before trial), even though the two testifying cops had different memories;

C v Williams 450 M 894 (2008)—defense counsel had argued in closing "missing witness" inference regarding the victim whose gunshot wounds were not fatal (in murder trial where one of two gunshot victims died), judge ruled thereafter that instruction not warranted because victim didn't want known where he was due to fear and wasn't under control of Commonwealth: no abuse of discretion; fn.5 ("proper practice" = obtain permission before making missing witness argument); judge could have interrupted defense closing with admonition; but D's argument did not justify DA's argument that witness feared testifying against D (DA should have, instead, objected to D's argument, or alternatively, issue should have been discussed BEFORE closing arguments);

C v Matthews 45 MAC 444 (98)—"highly questionable" DA argument on missing witnesses because cross-examination of D showed that the witnesses were not "available" (one in Georgia, one in the Marines, and D only learned of trial date the day before trial began) and also not apparent they would have evidence of distinct importance (D didn't know exactly what he was doing at time of crime, but testified that during that month he was usually working in auto shop, reconstructing a particular car; implicit recognition that neither shop owner nor work colleague in these circumstances had such "distinctly important" evidence); D's failure to offer the witnesses was also thus not "without explanation"; DA should have requested permission for the argument; no objection, "powerful" evidence of G = no reversal;

Opinion of the Justices 412 M 1201, 1211 (92)—Mass. Declaration of Rights, Article 12, forbids instruction allowing adverse inference from D's refusal to take breathalyzer (supporting the argument that Article 12 forbids use of "missing witness" inference against a criminal defendant);

C v Zevitas 418 M 677, 683–84 (94)—following the dictates of G.L. c. 90, § 24(1)(e), the judge gave jury instructions that tended to have the same effect as the admission of refusal evidence, considered in Opinion of the Justices, above, would have had, i.e., strongly implied that the defendant's blood alcohol level had not been tested, and that the reason no test was conducted was that the defendant refused to submit to such a procedure;

C v Hinckley **422 M 261 (96)**—evidence of D's refusal to turn over sneakers for cops to examine belatedly recognized to be "testimonial" and its admission thus violated Article 12;

C v Seymour **39 MAC 672 (96)**—bad DA cross-examination & argument re: D's failure to take breathalyzer;

C v Quinn **61 MAC 332, 336 n.3 (2004)**—though unremarked by parties, Appeals Court alarmed to see that booking videotape, admitted at trial, depicted D's refusal to take breathalyzer exam;

C v Conkey **430 M 139 (99)**—evidence and argument that D failed to appear to give fingerprints at police station violated Article 12: conduct offered to show D's state of mind is testimonial; conduct evidence admitted to show consciousness of guilt is always testimonial because it tends to demonstrate that D knew he was guilty; (suggested improper shift in burden of proof to D); cases to the contrary, e.g., *C v Brown* **24 MAC 979 (87)** OK to argue D's refusal to give blood/hair because purportedly nontestimonial, are no longer good law because of, e.g., *Hinckley* **422 M 261 (96)**);

C v DelValle **443 M 782, 794-795 (2005)**—possible error in DA's asking Boston crime lab director whether "he had an opportunity to sit down with defense counsel and people whom defense counsel had brought with him to the lab, to examine" evidence and "discuss findings" (witness answering "yes"), because presented inference that D elected not to call his experts because he knew their testimony would be damaging; "any error" on evidence here = harmless;

C v Melendez **12 MAC 980 (81)**—DA can comment because not shown why D can't easily call W & no reason why inference unfair; DA followed "sound practice" of first getting permission;

C v Fisher **15 MAC 957 (83)**—DA can argue D's missing car owner in strong case (D found behind wheel; denies operation); (& see *C v Haas* **373 M 545 (77)**);

C v Fatalo **345 M 85 (62)**—D can explain unavailability;

C v Graves **35 MAC 76 (93)** and *C v Luna* **46 MAC 90, 95 n.4 (98)**—D counsel proffers to judge concerning why missing witness argument & instruction should not be made should be by someone under oath and with personal knowledge; but cf., e.g.;

C v Crawford **46 MAC 423 (99)**—reversible error for ADA to argue and judge to instruct on missing witness when the man at issue was involved in selling drugs to undercover cop, was not so "close" to D as to warrant a finding of easy availability (and indeed was perhaps more available to Commonwealth, as he had been arrested at scene), had criminal record ("making him singularly vulnerable on cross-examination"), AND, "(i)f (his) appearance had been compelled, there was the real possibility that (if not yet tried, convicted, and sentenced) he would refuse to testify on the basis of the Fifth Amendment . . . ,

or that he would use the occasion to plea bargain with the prosecutor in return for testimony *against* the defendant"; fact that D here testified did not diminish plausibility of his explanation for not pursuing witness, nor did it increase likelihood that witness's nonappearance was due to defendant willfully withholding or concealing inculpatory evidence; constitutional rights implicated, obvious prejudice to D;

C v Buonopane **9 MAC 651 (80)**—can instruct not to infer from missing witness equally available to both; & DA can argue cop's available to D;

C v Saletino **449 M 657 n.17 (2007)**—refusing to adopt Commonwealth's argument that, since "informant"/ cooperating witness in drug prosecution was present at court, he was "equally available" to D (but ruling that there were "logical tactical reasons" for Commonwealth not to call witness, against whom prior convictions and an arrest [pending case/bias?] would be admissible for impeachment); party "more closely acquainted with" witness would be "naturally expected to call" him;

C v Cobb **397 M 105 (86)**—both argued missing witness; but charge improper without unique availability;

See Chapter 11-G, Evidence: Admissions by D (especially POST-ARREST;

C v Cornish **28 MAC 173 (89)**—improper for prosecutor to refer to co-D as missing witness where co-D's case still pending;

C v Smith **29 MAC 449 (90)**—prosecutor permitted to comment on absence of alibi witnesses when they were mentioned both in D's opening and D's testimony;

C v Boyajian **68 MAC 866 (2007)**—after defense counsel argued to jury that allergies and bad knees, road conditions, traffic, and sunlight could have been responsible for D's allegedly terrible driving and impaired condition, prosecutor could respond that there had been no evidence of these conditions at trial;

C v Sena **29 MAC 463 (90)**—proper for defense to argue Commonwealth's failure to call key witness who was present in courthouse during trial; missing witness instruction that fails to explain that adverse inference may be drawn was meaningless & required reversal; judges have discretion to deny prosecution requests for missing witness instruction even where appropriate foundation laid because of possible conflict with D's constitutional rights;

C v Crawford **417 M 358 (94)**—no error in refusing defense request for missing witness instruction re: D's own daughter, whose "spontaneous utterance" ("Daddy shot Mummy") was admitted; equally available and reason for not calling = spare child "further trauma";

C v Resendes **30 MAC 430 (91)**—improper for prosecutor to pose missing witness questions & make missing witness argument where witness not friendly to D even though related to him;

C v Calcagno **31 MAC 25 (91)**—improper for prosecutor to argue that D should have called sexual assault complainant's mother to stand to corroborate D's claims complainant was discipline problem where prosecutor failed to obtain judge's prior permission & to lay foundation & where mother's testimony would have been cumulative;

C v Smith **49 MAC 827, 833 (2000)**—at retrial, ADA to avoid pointing out that D "failed to present documentary evidence to corroborate the alibi testimony";

C v Anderson **411 M 279 (91)**—missing witness instruction should be given only where "apparent" that witness friendly to opposing side; here, D not entitled to missing witness instruction where not apparent that alleged victim of prison battery, fellow inmate of D's, was friendly to Commonwealth;

C v Santos **440 M 281 (2003)**—rejecting armed robbery D's argument that D was entitled to "missing witness" instruction re: person (in Federal custody) allegedly owing D money & allegedly prompting D to obtain money by force from debtor's household; instruction should be issued "only in clear cases, & with caution";

C v MacKenzie **413 M 498 (92)**—not improper for prosecutor to ask D questions about availability of housemates to testify to D's presence at home on night of murder in (good faith?) attempt to lay foundation;

C v Luna **46 MAC 90 (98)**—D testimony was that, upon arrest, he was happy to learn that time of crime was when he was at a particular club, as a "regular": door opened for vigorous cross about missing witnesses; questioning not unfair "merely because (D's) story (was) badly shaken by it";

C v LeBlanc **30 MAC 1 (91)**—improper for prosecutor to cross-examine D about whereabouts of person to implicitly create missing witness inference where foundation lacking;

C v McQuade **46 MAC 827 (99)**—missing witness instruction OK because witness would have had better evidence than the allegedly cumulative trial testimony of D's grandmother and a friend; furthermore, that D "expressly announced his pretrial intention to call (witness) undercuts present assertion" that evidence unimportant;

C v Thomas **429 M 146 (99)**—similar, and missing witness not impeachable as a relative of D;

C v Bryer **398 M 9 (86)**—that missing witness would not have been able to fully corroborate D's testimony not dispositive; though witness had not been with D during entire relevant period, even partial corroboration would have been expected here given importance of credibility duel;

C v Rollins **441 M 114 (2004)**—missing witness was only partly "cumulative," inasmuch as she alone was with D during period in which he may or may not have consumed alcohol (trial for operating under influence): instruction and argument permissible; *INVITATION?*: at n.1: though appellate counsel belatedly briefed issues about whether missing witness doctrine should be abolished or modified in any respect, this wasn't raised in trial court, and won't be addressed; such an issue would, when appropriately raised, be made available for comment by interested parties;

12-J.10. Comment on Defendant's Exercise of Constitutional Rights

See also Chapter 11-G—Evidence: admissions by silence, conduct, etc.

C v Haas **373 M 545 (77)**—DA's limited right to "fight fire with fire" didn't justify arguing D's post-arrest silence;

C v Williams **450 M 894 (2008)**—defense counsel's argument concerning missing witness inference against one of two shooting victims (the one not fatally wounded) was not license for DA to argue, without foundation, that witness feared testifying against D, even though judge subsequently declined to instruct on adverse 'missing witness' inference; proper response to D's argument would have been an objection or, alternatively, issue should have been discussed/settled before arguments;

C v Rogers **43 MAC 782 (97)**—error for DA to argue that defense counsel had objected (successfully) to particular evidence;

C v Vermette **43 MAC 789 (97)**—error for DA to argue "who asked to go to sidebar more times & who made more objections?" despite D's argument that Commonwealth slanted & suppressed evidence; error harmless given instructions;

C v Burts **68 MAC 684 (2007)**—DA's urging jury to take D's trial counsel "to task" because of his closing argument = improper, impugning "two basic constitutional rights," right to counsel and right to make a defense; also error = urging jurors to be angry at expert testimony presented by defense, urging jurors to trust police witnesses because they were police, urging anger at D and defense attorney "so as to evoke an emotional, rather than a reasoned intellectual response, to the evidence";

C v Person **400 M 136 (87)**—reversal for argument that jury should infer guilt from D's pre-arrest decision to consult attorney;

C v Padgett **44 MAC 359 (98)**—DA could argue that D's "reading on the law" influenced his testimony as to his role in joint venture resulting in felony murder;

C v Olszewski **401 M 749 (88)**—bad "police on trial" argument implying D attacked Commonwealth witnesses' credibility only because no other defense;

C v Simmons **20 MAC 366 (85)**—(same)

C v Murchison **418 M 58 (94)**—defense counsel may argue that police witnesses are lying, if evidence supports inference and if argument not expressed as personal opinion;

C v Grandison **433 M 135, 143 (2001)**—improper for ADA to suggest D counsel shouldn't question veracity of cops ("how dare they?"); such questioning = "the essence of cross-examination"; see also *C v Burts* 68 MAC 684, 688 (2007);

C v McCoy **59 MAC 284 (2003)**—DA improperly suggested that D counsel impermissibly questioned credibility of cops;

Griffin v California **380 US 609 (65)**—argument/ charge re: D failed to testify unconstitutionally allowed negative inference;

C v Vallejo **455 M 72 (2009)**—co-D's counsel stressing co-D's cooperation, full statement to cops, unobjected to by D, did not impinge upon D's right to silence; see also *C v Russo* 49 MAC 579 (2000);

C v Goulet **374 M 404 (78)**—can't suggest that D's shrink testimony was devalued by D's failure to testify;

C v Hawley **380 M 70 (80)**—DA saying facts "uncontested" bad if D's the only one who could contradict;

C v Buzzell **53 MAC 362 (2001)**—repeatedly arguing that evidence was "uncontroverted", that "no explanation" was offered by defense counsel, that "corroboration" was "uncontroverted" = reversal; noting that 1st Circuit, in federal cases, automatically reverses when prosecutor characterizes evidence as uncontradicted, unless judge interrupts immediately & instructs curatively, including that prosecutor was guilty of misconduct; "While that court's approach is not binding on the courts of the Commonwealth, we do not ignore what it teaches with respect to the difficulty of separating permissible from impermissible remarks";

C v Arroyo **49 MAC 672 (2000)**—argument ("Did anybody see the hand to hand sale? No. They didn't or at least nobody that was in this courtroom . . . when you ask . . . well gee is there someone I would have liked to have heard from it was this man right here who said it was the (prosecution witness) who made the sale"—the defense was that Commonwealth witness, rather than D, sold drugs) = error; judge should have intervened on own motion, with immediate instruction on D's right not to testify;

C v Gomes **443 M 502 (2005)**—DA's remark that "the only one in this courtroom that I've heard say that it wasn't this defendant, the only person who took that stand to say that was [defense counsel]" could have been understood as comment on failure of D to take stand or failure to produce witnesses, so was improper; given evidence here, error was harmless beyond reasonable doubt;

C v Pena **455 M 1 (2009)**—after defense argument that killing of D's girlfriend was without motive and thus not "rational," so Commonwealth failed to disprove mental impairment of D, ADA argued 'we don't know why' D did it, since victim died and can't tell and D is only one who knows why he did it; though "close question," SJC says not likely jury would have considered this comment on D's failure to testify (& curative instructions also);

C v Whitman **453 M 331 (2009)**—argument, "he didn't tell us [his motive for the stabbings]" was "unfortunate" but considered in context of full argument and D's statements to police (he heard voice telling him 'to take them out,' and thereafter sat and thought about it), reference was to D's omission in police statement to assert reason for stabbing victims; also, it was permissible response to defense argument that absence of motive showed mental illness/lack of criminal responsibility;

C v Randall **50 MAC 26 (2000)**—ADA used substantively evidence purportedly admitted only for "status of police knowledge," i.e., asserting that culprit was in van which belonged to D, & then arguing "no evidence presented to you that (D) reported van stolen earlier that evening"; reversal;

C v Thomas **44 MAC 521 (98)**—since jury could be assumed to have common experience, OK for DA to argue that D's explanation of only 2 beers did not account for breathalyzer over legal limit quite some time later;

C v Manago **26 MAC 262 (88)**—DA can argue strong points her case & weak points in D's; OK if only passing, indirect, collateral reflection upon what D might've testified;

C v Pullum **22 MAC 485 (86)**—bad DA comment on D's failure to testify & arguing consciousness of guilt from D's not showing teeth/smile because (though complaining witness said gap in burglar's teeth) D not asked to show teeth; contrast *C v O'Connell* **432 M 657 (2000)** cross-examination of D-witness said to provide support for inference that D could have used a "depilatory like Nair" to explain difference between his arm and the arm depicted in incriminating photo;

C v Young **399 M 527 (87)**—bad DA argument urging inference from D sitting impassively (proper behavior) in court; (see also *Kozec* **399 M 514 (87)**, above);

C v Sherick **23 MAC 338 (87)**—(reviews cases & tie between failure to testify, other rules, & 5th Amendment); facts support argument that D's testimony "tailored" to DA case;

C v Person **400 M 136 (87)**—bad argument that D listened & "tailored" testimony (cf. *C v Brookins* **416 M 97 (93)** import of DA's cross-examination of D = suggestion that D tailored story (reversal for judge's failure to allow testimony re: D's prior consistent statement));

C v Kowalski **33 MAC 49 (92)**, citing *C v Person* **400 M 136 (87)**—improper for prosecutor to argue that first time D comes up with reasonable explanation was on witness stand after listening to other testimony;

C v McCray **40 MAC 936 (96)**—same regarding D being "able to conform his story with" rape complainant's testimony;

C v Elberry **38 MAC 912 (95)**—similar;

C v Jones **45 MAC 254 (98)**—reversal for DA's argument conveying that D had had a year to obtain discovery and falsely tailor his testimony to meet the Commonwealth's evidence, and that cop-witness (not having been told D's story earlier) did not anticipate that corroboration of cop testimony would be necessary; violations of D's right to remain silent at arrest, right to be present at trial, right to confront witnesses, right to testify;

C v Ewing **67 MAC 531 (2006), and SJC on FAR agrees, 449 M 1035 (2007)**—reversal for DA's cross-examination and argument "impeaching" D's testimony on grounds that he had advantage of pre-trial discovery to tailor his testimony and had not sought out police between charge and trial to report his exculpatory version of events;

Portuondo v Agard **529 US 61 (2000)**—US Supreme Court refuses habeas relief for prosecutor's argument that D had "big advantage" of listening to all testimony before he testified; terms holding refusal to "extend" rationale of *Griffin v California* **380 US 609 (65)** (involving comment upon D's refusal to testify);

C v Martinez **431 M 168, 176–77 (2000)**—post-*Portuondo v Agard* (though without mention of it), SJC reiterates that "questioning the defendant as to the fact that the defendant sat through the Commonwealth's case" = improper; "(t)o use against (D) his strategy to wait until after the prosecution had made its case before revealing his story would disparage the constitutional rights which allowed him that strategy," citing *C v Beauchamp* **424 M 682, 690–91 (97)**;

C v Gaudette **441 M 762 (2004)**—asserting refusal to adopt rationale and holding of Supreme Court in *Portuondo v Agard* **529 US 61 (2000)**, but here, DA's comment was permissible focus on EVIDENCE elicited, i.e., arguable inconsistencies (omissions by silence) between D's statements to police and his trial testimony, with argument that D's trial testimony was "tailored" to address that which he heard at trial;

C v Kelly **417 M 266 (94)**—improper (and reversible) to argue cops were credible because they would not lie & thereby "put their pensions . . . on the line to get these two guys" & because if they were "that kind of cop, after 17 years, there'd be some kind of record of it, & you'd hear about it & you didn't" (LATTER = violation of constitutional dictates re burden of proof/no obligation on part of D to present evidence); no jury instruction "neutralized" impropriety;

C v Howell **49 MAC 42 (2000)**—error for DA to argue that defense counsel could have shown photos of alternate suspects to the witnesses ("potentially burden-shifting");

C v Stewart **454 M 527 (2009)**—no relief, though argument "close to the line", ADA saying "there may be no trace evidence that places [D] there . . . but there is nothing that excludes him from being there; that proves he wasn't there . . . "; statement was made at end of argument portion reviewing evidence including D's confession to son and testing performed, and was in response to D's closing that emphasized that no evidence at murder scene linked D to crime;

C v Smith **49 MAC 827, 833 (2000)**—ADA at retrial to avoid "pointing out that (D) failed to present documentary evidence to corroborate the alibi testimony"; cf. *C v Martinez* **34 MAC 131, 132 (93)**—cross-examination of D leading jury to believe inference of G warranted from D's failure to come forward voluntarily & provide police/DA with statements, hair samples, blood samples, or underwear worn on evening at issue = reversible error;

C v Person **400 M 136, 138–42 (87)**—similar;

C v Lodge **431 M 461 (2000)**—IMPROPER to ask "question" in argument re: where were sneakers/sweatshirt D wore after purportedly fleeing from assailants in apartment: "Never answered that question, did he . . . ? Why? . . .

Some blood on it?"; these were "comments on the D's right to silence and as such tended to shift the burden";

C v Dargon **74 MAC 330 (2009)**—no error when prosecutor argued that 'there is not a scintilla . . . of evidence that DNA analysis can determine what part of a person's body a suspect has touched" because corrected erroneous impression created by defense counsel; use of term 'red herring' not inappropriate here; S.C. *** M *** (7/29/2010);

C v O'Brien **56 MAC 170 (2002)**—DA's use of specifically excluded evidence in closing argument AND argument that if D had been an employee of garage, as he purportedly stated to a witness, "perhaps there would have been an employee of [the garage] to testify on his behalf" or "he wouldn't have been charged with this crime" resulted in reversal;

C v Egardo **426 M 48 (97)**—improper for DA to argue that D's failure to present his defense (duress) to police upon arrest implied its falsity (& his guilt);

C v Lyons **71 MAC 671, 676 n. 5 (2008)**—in defense of charge of indecent assault and battery on person over age 14, D contended that complainant had initiated "aggressive physical confrontation" and any contact he made with her was thereafter, in self-defense; prosecutor's argument that self-defense was unavailable to D charged with indecent assault and battery and that D was not credible because he did not seek criminal charges against complainant for assault = improper;

C v Waite **422 M 792 (96)**—when prosecutor sought to establish D's lucidity/sobriety & asked arresting cop whether D "fail(ed) to respond to any of your commands," no error for cop to respond, "up to the point he just decided not to talk at all, no", this merely put "abruptly concluded conversation in context";

C v Delarosa **50 MAC 623, 631 (2000)**—trial judge responded to cop's gratuitous assertion that D "refused to cooperate," and "wasn't cooperating" by instructing jury that "there's absolutely no requirement on anybody's part who is accused of a crime to cooperate with anyone, including the police," that it is "immaterial whether anyone cooperates or not," and that "the officer knows that and should not have testified to that once, let alone twice. Therefore, I have to strongly give you this instruction so you understand the importance of it and you understand that that is not to be considered by you. It should be disregarded by you. If anything, you should look on it negatively that for some reason the witness felt the need to offer it to you. If there is any negative inference to be drawn, it's to the one stating it, not towards the defendant" (no relief on appeal, despite appellate argument that trial counsel was ineffective in not moving for mistrial);

C v Beauchamp **424 M 682 (97)**—improper for DA to argue inference of guilt from D's post-arrest silence, request for counsel, and discussions with his attorney (here, that counsel told him 'element' of self-defense & he tailored testimony accordingly);

C v Krepon **32 MAC 945 (92)**—not improper for prosecutor to argue: 'what's D's motive, what's his stake?';

C v Rivera **52 MAC 321, 328 (2001)**—refusal to find error in argument that sex assault complainant "didn't have to subject herself to the humiliation of talking to countless strangers about horribly embarrassing personal experiences in her young life";

C v Pagano **47 MAC 55, 61 (99)**—error for DA to argue that closing was his "favorite time . . . of trial" because the "cloak" of the "presumption of innocence" which previously protected D "now comes off";

C v Awad **47 MAC 139 (99)**—ADA attacks motivations of defense counsel with reference to "some play by Shakespeare" in which a character said "kill all the lawyers" and with assertion that bad reputation of lawyers "comes down to you take a set of facts and see what you can weave . . ."; appeal to sympathy, trivializing comments about the presumption of innocence and burden of proof (convict if the evidence "sounds right"; don't convict if "you can honestly . . . say that this man is innocent of what he did to that woman"; suggestion that "conscience"

should dictate G; jurors enlisted as "members of the community" to protect innocent victims from violent crime); and ERRONEOUS call to hold against D the alleged refusal of D's sister to "help" the police, thereby "laugh(ing) off this victim" (cf. **Howell 49 MAC 42, 46 (2000)** D's father's refusal to "cooperate" with police): reversal;

12-J.11. Preservation of Closing Argument Errors

C v Kelly **417 M 266 (94)**—objection after argument preserves issue; not required to object again after jury instructions; *C v Cancel* **394 M 567 574 (85)** (similar); *but see C v Beaudry* **445 M 577, 587 (2005)**—when argument objection is followed by "particularized", "focused" instructions attempting to cure, counsel must object again (that instructions did not / could not cure argument error); *C v Ramos* **73 MAC 824 (2009)**—D had moved in limine to preclude comment on complainant's motive to lie, and had objected after the argument; D not obliged to request curative instruction;

12-K. CHARGE—AND (JURY-WAIVED) RULINGS OF LAW

12-K.1. In General; Curative and Limiting Instructions

See Chapter 12-I above re: requests, objections, & preservation for appeal;

See Chapter 16, Defenses re: Jury Nullification, Presume Innocent, burden of proof;

See Chapter 7-M, Misconduct of Judges;

Apprendi v New Jersey **530 US 466 (2000)**—OTHER THAN fact of prior conviction, any fact that increases penalty for a crime must be proved TO JURY beyond reasonable doubt (here, "hate crime" statute provided for enhanced sentence if trial judge found, by "preponderance," that D committed the crime in order to intimidate person or group because of, inter alia, race)—it's not merely "sentencing enhancement" issue;

Ring v Arizona **536 US 584 (2002)**—capital sentencing scheme can't allow judge sitting without a jury to find an aggravating circumstance necessary for imposition of death penalty;

Blakely v Washington **124 S.Ct. 2531 (2004)**—reversing enhanced sentence imposed by JUDGE on basis of HIS finding that crime was committed with "deliberate cruelty," a statutory ground for upward departure;

Washington v Recuenco **548 US 212 (2006)**—when, at sentencing for jury conviction of "assault with deadly weapon", judge on basis of his own fact-finding imposed three-year sentence enhancement on ground that firearm was used, this was a violation of Blakely, but S Ct holds that Blakely error can be, and is here, harmless (the only weapon at issue here was a firearm); error not "structural";

US v Booker **125 S.Ct. 738 (2005)**—Sixth Amendment protects D's right to have jury rather than judge find

existence of any particular fact that law makes essential to his punishment;

Cunningham v California **127 S. Ct. 856 (2007)**—because, under California sentencing law, an "upper term sentence" may be imposed only when trial judge finds aggravating circumstance, and because an element of the charged offense doesn't qualify as such a circumstance but instead "aggravating" circumstances depend on facts found solely by judge, and by standard of only a preponderance, *Apprendi*'s bright line rule = violated; except for a prior conviction, any fact that increases penalty for crime beyond prescribed statutory maximum must be submitted to jury and proved beyond a reasonable doubt;

Virginia v Black **123 S.Ct. 1536 (2003)**—model jury instruction that any cross-burning shall be prima facie evidence of an intent to intimidate a person or group = constitutionally overbroad & thus error; "prima facie" instruction skews jury deliberations toward conviction where evidence of intent to intimidate is relatively weak and arguably consistent with a solely ideological reason for burning;

Hedgpeth v Pulido **129 S Ct 530 (2008)**—instructing jury on multiple theories of guilt, one of which is invalid is not "structural error" requiring conviction be set aside without regard to finding of prejudice when a "general" verdict of guilt is returned, and is instead subject to harmless error review in federal habeas corpus case;

See Chapter 21 re: instructions as to elements of specific crimes;

See Chapter 20-B,—D re: instructions as to voluntariness of statements by Defendant, including C v O'Brian **445 M 720 (2006)**—DiGiambattista holding, **442 M 423 (2004)**, that D is entitled to instruction that lack of recording of statement suggests it should be scrutinized with particular care will not be applied retroactively (citing *C v Dagley* 442 M 713, 721 (2004)), cert. denied, 125 S. Ct. 1668 (2005); *C v Zanetti* **454 M 449 (2009)**— DiGiambattista instruction is available to Ds in trials occurring after the date of the decision, regardless of the date of interrogation; *C v Boyarsky* **452 M 700 (2008)**—but judge is not required to allow D to cross-examine cop as to his knowledge of the SJC's DiGiambattista preference that statements be recorded;

District Court Model Jury Instructions (MCLE) & Superior Court Criminal Practice Jury Instructions (MCLE)—CAUTION. When specifically attacked on appeal, many so-called "model" instructions have been found to be erroneous: *see I, above & Chapter 21-A, "Analyzing Elements of Common Crimes"!*

M.R.Crim.P. 26—request rulings in jury-waived case: written, before argument; 24(b): OBJECTIONS must be before jury retires & must specify matters/grounds; upon request, give reasonable TIME to object; objections or requests for additional instructions = out of jury's hearing; *(see Chapter 12-I, above)*;

K. Smith, *Criminal Practice & Procedure*, § 1870 (2d ed. 1983 & Supp.)—IF parties agree, may give jury copies of all/part of charge (but see *C v Baseler* **419 M 500 (95)** judge may give jury audio or video tape recording of jury instructions, even without parties' assent), but (1) judge must tell counsel, (2) tape must be wholly audible & contain entire charge, (3) jury must be instructed how to use, & (4) tape must be marked for identification in record; § 1873: judge can state the testimony, especially her recollection as illustrative of legal rules; § 1874: up to D whether judge instructs on D's not testifying; §§ 1876-7: may not instruct on consequences of verdict, except not guilty "by reason of insanity" (if D assents);

ABA Standards for Criminal Justice (2d ed. 1986) Jury Trial 15-3.6(b)—should have pattern instructions, but modify; 15-3.6(e): may give preliminary instructions before evidence; 15-4.3: additional instructions after jury has begun deliberations;

C v Krepon **32 MAC 945, 947–48 (92)**—"better practice" is for judge to refer to complaining witness as "alleged" victim, "in spite of the language contained in Model Jury Instructions For Use In The District Court § 4.13 (1988)";

C v Maloney **113 M 211, 213 (1873)**—legally correct instructions are erroneous if given re: state of facts to which they are inappropriate: "tend to mislead the jury either into the supposition that a proper state of facts exists to which the propositions are to be applied by them, or into drawing the suggested inference from facts which do not authorize it"; see also *C v Redgate* **25 MAC 965 (88)**;

C v Barros **425 M 572 (97)**—no error in allowing jury to take notes during instructions;

C v Callahan **386 M 784 (82)**—fairness requires fully explaining relevant law, not just DA's side;

C v Kane **19 MAC 129, 138 (84)**—impermissible for judge "to array the facts with a bias (whether or not conscious) and so in effect to 'comment' on the evidence, to convey his own view of where the weight of the evidence lies";

C v Sanchez **70 MAC 699 (2007)**—jury instruction, defining "break" to include entering through an open bedroom window, was argued to require reversal as judge charging on facts (Commonwealth's contention was entry through bedroom window), but only one (dissenting) judge agreed;

C v Porro **74 MAC 676, further app. rev. allowed 455 M 1106 (2009)**—rejecting D's argument that judge's response to jury question "broadened basis of criminal liability," and violated M.R.Crim.P. 24(b) (requiring notice to parties of judge's instructions PRIOR TO closing arguments, to enable intelligent argument to jury); reversing, however, because supplemental instruction on lesser included offense failed to limit jury consideration to the act on which grand jury had returned indictment;

C v Zuluaga **43 MAC 629, 641 (97)**—reversal required when one alternative theory of guilt on which jurors were instructed (constructive possession) **not** supported by evidence and verdict did not specify what theory was found by jury; see also *C v Flynn* **420 M 810 (95)**; *C v Green* **420 M 771 (95)**; *C v Fickett* **403 M 194 (88)**; under federal constitution, US Supreme Court resolved this issue differently (*Griffin v US* **502 US 46 (91)**): affirm conviction if evidence supports any of the alternative theories on which jurors were instructed; see *C v Zanetti* **454 M 449 (2009)**: "specific" verdicts for joint venture vs. 'principal' liability not warranted, unanimity as to one or the other not required;

(*Hedgpeth v Pulido* **129 S Ct 530 (2008)**—instructing jury on multiple theories of guilt, one of which is invalid is not "structural error" requiring conviction be set aside without regard to finding of prejudice when a "general" verdict of guilt is returned, and is instead subject to harmless error review in federal habeas corpus case;)

C v Suarez **59 MAC 111 (2003)**—insufficient evidence to support instruction on "principal" liability;

C v Taylor **50 MAC 901 (2000)**—when Commonwealth based its single charge of indecent A&B on child on each of two incidents, & evidence as to one was insufficient as matter of law, & general verdict didn't specify which incident underlay G, = reversal; contrast *C v Grandison* **432 M 278, 286 (2000)**—SJC framed issue as one in which counsel "failed" to request separate verdict forms and/or a specific unanimity jury instruction (ignoring the legal insufficiency/required finding of not guilty point), and thereby affirmed conviction, sub silentio using rationale of *Griffin v US* rather than Fickett, Green, Flynn, etc.

C v Santos **440 M 281 (2003)**—explanation of types of "specific unanimity"; jury need not be unanimous as to which threat or application of force caused victim to part with her money, distinguishing *C v Accetta* 422 M 642, 647 (96) (specific unanimity as to "theory" of guilt necessary);

C v Black **50 MAC 477 (2000)**—judge should have instructed both that indecent A&B conviction couldn't be based on same act that supported rape conviction ("double" convictions barred) and that jurors had to unanimously agree upon what single penetration rape G was based, but no request, and no objection to absence: here no substantial risk of miscarriage of justice;

C v Gonzalez **47 MAC 255 (99)**—when same jury was trying the issue of whether the just-returned conviction was a "second" one for a like offense, OK (in absence of objection, anyway) to instruct in "abbreviated" fashion, referring to/incorporating instruction given a few hours earlier, i.e., no substantial risk of a miscarriage of justice;

C v Finegan **45 MAC 921 (98)**—although judge here could have taken judicial notice that heroin is a derivative of opium (because it's "subject of generalized knowledge readily ascertainable from authoritative sources"), he was not requested to do so, and did not do so implicitly sua sponte, because he would have had to "submit( ) expressly to the jury any factual matters of which he took judicial notice"; required finding of NG entered on charge of operating under influence of narcotic drug because Commonwealth failed to prove heroin = narcotic;

See Chapter 12-I for cases on requests for instructions & objecting; see Chapter 20-D, Suppression issues, for instructions on voluntariness of statements by D; see Chapter 22-F-5, Jury Issues, concerning specific unanimity;

C v Muckle **59 MAC 631 (2003)**—D not entitled to instruction that all the indictments against him should "stand or fall together";

C v Moyles **45 MAC 350, 351–52 (98)**—failure to explain applicable law is not cured by allowing defense counsel to argue in accord with the applicable law; judge told jury to take the law from him and not the lawyers, and then gave erroneous instruction; cf. *C v Smith* **49 MAC 827 (2000)** (having allowed defense to argue missing witness inference against prosecution, reversible error to refuse instruction on it and, in response to jury question, to say 'decide only on evidence, don't decide on basis of unanswered questions; judge 'removed from jury's consideration precise issue sought to be raised by D');

C v McKay **67 MAC 396 (2006)**—reversal for refusal to instruct on "accident" in violating protective order: D selected from cell phone list of contacts, while driving, "Cindy" rather than "Cindy B"; closing arguments stressing "accident" or not didn't make error harmless;

C v Diaz **426 M 548 (98)**—error in admitting hearsay not cured by purported "limiting" instruction "based on no valid legal principle";

C v Snow **58 MAC 917 (2003)**—error to admit D's statement that he was a heroin addict, & "limiting" instruction (not to use this to show guilt of breaking & entering and larceny, but as relevant to his knowledge of what principal actor was doing and to his intent that the principal's crime be accomplished) "did not cure but rather perpetuated the impermissible use of [D's] addiction and association with a fellow addict";

C v Kosior **280 M 418 (32)**—D's admission re: other fires = immaterial/prejudicial & not cured by instruction (not evidence of guilt & take "for what it's worth");

C v Mills **47 MAC 500 (99)**—failure to instruct, sua sponte, on limited use of extraneous "bad act" evidence required reversal; error "compounded" by supplemental instruction (to jury question) to "give (evidence) whatever degree of weight you deem they are entitled to receive with respect to the fact issues that you have to decide"; see Superior Court Criminal Practice Jury Instructions § 4.20, Defendant's Other Bad Acts (4.20.1, Inadmissible for Any Purpose; 4/20.2, Admissible Only for Limited Purpose);

C v Daley **439 M 558 (2003)**—though DA erred in several ways in argument, judge corrected, sua sponte, calling one "completely inappropriate," limiting/eliminating one argued inference by instruction, and interrupting another;

C v Dilone **385 M 281, 287 n.2 (82)**—endorsing "any reasonable procedure" agreed to by parties by which jury could have written copy of jury instructions;

C v Lavalley **410 M 641 (91)**—complete oral instructions cured omissions in written instructions given to jurors;

C v Martin **424 M 301 (97)**—no error in giving jury written instructions same as oral (parties agreed);

C v DiBenedetto **427 M 414 (98)**—writing elements of murder on blackboard OK;

C v Larkin **429 M 426 (99)**—writing on blackboard instructions only re: greatest offense, i.e., first degree murder, but not for manslaughter, aggravated rape, unarmed robbery: no relief; judge instructed that all instructions important and jury shouldn't consider anything about way she gave instructions as any evidence of her feelings about case, and any questions jury had would be answered;

C v Guy **441 M 96, 108–9 (2004)**—though D objected at trial to judge's providing jury with written instructions ONLY regarding "outline of the elements of the various crimes encompassed by the murder indictment," and not "important concepts of law . . . favorable to the defense, such as . . . self-defense and . . . mitigating factors", no relief;

C v Baseler **419 M 500 (95)**—judge may give jury audio or video tape recording of jury instructions, even without parties' assent, but (1) judge must tell counsel, (2) tape must be wholly audible & contain entire charge, (3) jury must be instructed how to use, & (4) tape must be marked for identification in record;

C v Graham **431 M 282, 284–87 (2000)**—despite *Baseler* **419 M 500 (95)**, no error in sending into jury room, in response to jury request for written definitions of each verdict option (which weren't available), tape recording of oral instruction given in response to this question, with instruction that all instructions, including those given earlier, had to be taken as a whole; *C v Smith* **75 MAC 196 (2009)**—no substantial risk of miscarriage of justice in omitting audio recording of supplemental instructions after providing jury audio recording of original charge;

Superior Court Criminal Practice Jury Instructions § 5.6.19—tape recording of jury charge; § 5.6.20, written copy of jury charge;

C v Riveiro **393 M 224 (84)**—re: directing jurors to disregard foundational testimony of cop about giving Miranda warnings & not to speculate on any statement that may have ensued: "Such an admonition calls to mind the description of a limiting instruction given by Judge Learned Hand in *Nash v US* **54 F.2d 1006, 1007 (2d Cir.), cert. denied, 285 US 556 (32)**, where he calls it a 'recommendation to the jury of a mental gymnastic which is beyond, not only their powers, but anybody's else'";

C v West **44 MAC 150 (98)**—instructions allegedly curing errors in prosecutor's closing arguments not effective when errors are numerous; judge can't un-ring bell;

C v Perkins **39 MAC 577 (95)**—curative instructions inadequate if inadmissible evidence had been repeated/reemphasized;

C v Pavao **34 MAC 577 (93)**—when DA made material misstatement in closing argument, judge instructed that his own memory of the evidence was contrary to DA's statement; conviction reversed nonetheless;

C v Flebotte **34 MAC 676, 680 (93), S.C. 417 M 348 (94)**—"asking the jury to disregard (specified testimony) may be tantamount to asking the jury to ignore that an elephant has walked through the jury box";

C v Houston **430 M 616, 626 (2000)**—limiting instruction ("no matter how much effort the judge may make to purge (jurors') mindsets by admonitory instructions") re: use of prior convictions (prostitution) not likely to be effective, jury "more likely to conclude" that witness shouldn't be believed "not because she is untruthful, but because she has been, and thus continues to be, indiscriminate in sexual relations";

C v McCoy **59 MAC 284 (2003)**—judge refused to acknowledge error in prosecutor's extra-evidentiary assertions in closing argument and then "provided an instruction that was minimally standard and entirely non-curative (being confined to eight words, 'Arguments or statements by lawyers are not evidence'). By his rulings, the judge effectively managed 'to give judicial endorsement to the prosecutor's improper argument'";

C v Rosa **73 MAC 540 (2009)**—ADA's reference to victim being a firefighter was made 19 times in eight pages of argument, "excessive . . . an improper appeal to sympathy"; judge's subsequent reference, during body of instructions, to "injuries [being] terrible" was curative, and not error, as made precisely because of, and embedded in, instruction NOT to decide based on bias, prejudice, or "sympathy";

C v Martin **424 M 301 (97)**—attempted curative/limiting instruction may have effect of "children, don't put beans up your nose" admonition;

C v McCray **40 MAC 936, 937 (96)**—recognizing that counsel's failure to object may have been motivated by a desire NOT to risk a "curative" instruction which would only serve to implant in jurors' minds that which should not have been mentioned;

C v Errington **14 MAC 733 (82), reversed on other grounds 390 M 875 (84)**—limiting instructions "subject to doubt" where evidence is so close to the ultimate issue at hand that there is a greater danger that jury will misuse statement and assume some truth to allegation of past conduct OR where external facts in statement are so inflammatory as to unduly arouse jury's emotions of prejudice or hostility; same is true of delayed curative instructions (citing *C v Crehan* **345 M 609, 614 (63)**; *C v Hoppin* **387 M 25, 31 (82)**);

C v Rodriguez **50 MAC 405 (2000)**—clerk's loss of photo arrays, etc. between first and second trial, addressed by remedial instruction to jury: "if there is a dispute as to the description or any other physical characteristic of that missing physical evidence, and if your collective inability actually to look at that evidence raises in your mind a doubt about the actual description of what it was that the witnesses were talking about or raises in your mind a doubt as to any other physical attribute or characteristic of that evidence, then you must resolve that doubt in favor of the defendant. You must follow that instruction and resolve that doubt . . . in the defendant's favor";

C v Sann Than **59 MAC 410, 414 (2003)**—mixture of correct and incorrect instructions regarding constructive possession = "no way to know which of the two irreconcilable instructions the jurors applied in reaching their verdict," quoting from *C v Ford* **424 M 709, 712 (97)**;

12-K.2. Elements of Offenses (Including "Intent") and Improperly Directing Verdicts

Apprendi v New Jersey **530 US 466 (2000)**—OTHER THAN fact of prior conviction, any fact that increases penalty for a crime must be proved TO JURY beyond reasonable doubt (here, "hate crime" statute provided for enhanced sentence if trial judge found, by "preponderance," that D committed the crime in order to intimidate person or group because of, inter alia, race)—it's not merely "sentencing enhancement" issue;

G.L. c. 231, § 81—shan't charge on matters of FACT; but may state TESTIMONY/law;

C v Belding **42 MAC 435 (97)**—judge's response to jury question invaded fact-finding function of jury; statute was silent as to whether stated facts proved crime and judiciary cannot fill in;

C v Wolinski **431 M 228, 233 (2000)**—in response to jury note, "evidence incomplete; cannot decide," judge instructed that jurors were to 'decide case based solely on evidence that was presented and weren't to speculate about any unanswered questions that still remain'; though SJC excused judge's "decision not to repeat statement (about) Commonwealth's burden" then, what was said should be argued to run afoul of *C v Bowden* **379 M 472, 485 (80)** (judge may not remove from jury consideration perceived evidence deficiencies); SEE ALSO *C v Remedor* **52 MAC 694, 700–701 (2001)** judge's response to jury question, i.e. 'confine consideration to evidence that *was* presented,' negated D's "Bowden" (**379 M 472**) defense, creating substantial risk of a miscarriage of justice;

C v Sineiro **432 M 735, 744 (2000), quoting from Learned Hand, J., in** *DiCarlo v US* **6 F2d 364, 368 (2d Cir 1925)**—"If, from all that the jury see of the witness, they conclude that what he says now is not the truth, but what he said before, they are nonetheless deciding from what they see and hear of that person and in court. There is no mythical necessity that the case must be decided only in accordance with the truth of words uttered under oath in court";

C v DeLosSantos **37 MAC 526 (94)**—judge's response to jury question invaded fact-finding function of jury essentially directing that defense's theory of death was not recklessness (so involuntary manslaughter verdict barred if D's evidence were accepted);

C v Caramanica **49 MAC 376, 379 (2000)**—can't charge that "fact of armed robbery occurred is not in dispute";

C v Sheriff **425 M 186 (97)**—judge's mid-trial instruction, that D had been at Bridgewater State Hospital voluntarily, was both untrue and strongly implied that D was there only to pad his "insanity" defense: reversal;

C v Gunter **427 M 259 (98)**—general intent not correctly defined as "reflex action"; specific intent needs **better** instruction than "thought before action" or "a conscious willingness to do something"; specific intent = acting with purpose or intending certain consequences;

C v Van Winkle **443 M 230, 237 (2005)**—similar (but no substantial risk of miscarriage of justice found);

C v Moore **36 MAC 455 (94)**—general intent is **not** "reflex"; "more or less unconscious" definition should be avoided;

C v Lawson **46 MAC 627 (99)**—simplistic formulations re: "general" and "specific" intent "will not likely assist either judicial analysis or a jury and may be source of confusion for both";

C v Sibinich **33 MAC 246, 249 n.1 (92)**—"The underlying difficulty, in cases in which specific intent is an element of the crime, is the practice of trial judges to explain specific intent by contrasting it to the idea of 'general intent.' Under this practice, 'general intent' is commonly defined as conduct undertaken 'unconsciously . . . a reflex action, such as sitting down in a chair or walking up stairs.' . . . 'general intent,' when defined in this fashion, does not refer to any mental state which is required for the conviction of a crime, and the use of a non-criminal 'general intent' to explain the specific intent required for certain crimes is unnecessary and confusing";

C v Anslono **9 MAC 867 (80)**—inadequate instructions on larceny intent & beyond reasonable doubt; judge took role of advocate, trespassed on fact-finder's role, & commanded result; failure to object maybe ineffective, but judge intimidated;

C v Johnson **45 MAC 473 (98)**—D charged with violating 209A order which barred only "abuse" of complainant, but judge instructed jury (over-broadly) that violation could be established by either "abuse" or "contact" with complainant; despite no objection, reversal (because evidence of over 300 letters from D to complainant would have established contact, but not necessarily abuse);

C v Diaz **19 MAC 29 (84)**—jury can ignore law, give inconsistent verdicts (*see Chapter 22-F-6*); judge can't coerce, but can say what verdict if find certain facts;

C v Cote **5 MAC 365 (77)**—bad instruction to find same on each co-D without same evidence;

C v Borges **2 MAC 869 (74)**—though only general objection, reverse for instruction with judge's opinion re: inference jury should draw;

C v Jones **372 M 403 (77)**—can't direct a G. verdict or compel jury to find an element; but if D offers no evidence of license to carry firearm, judge may withdraw license issue from jury; (*see G.L. c. 278, § 7 (Chapter 12-G, Required Finding of NG) & Chapter 16, Burden of Proof*);

Burns v Commonwealth **430 M 444, 450–51 (99)**—prima facie evidence purportedly explained ("compels the conclusion that the evidence is true," BUT when evidence is introduced that contradicts prima facie evidence, the latter "loses its artificial force and a factual issue arises," AND "burden of persuasion always remains on the party who must prove the point, even though the party is aided by prima facie evidence";

C v Soares **51 MAC 273, 278 n.7 (2001)**—instruction that it's generally reasonable to infer that person intends natural & probable consequences of intentional acts, & that such inference may be drawn "unless there is evidence that convinces you otherwise" upheld; failure to answer last clause's burden shift (no objection at trial here);

C v Munoz **384 M 503 (81)**—DA's burden of proof to prove beyond a reasonable doubt car was "uninsured";

C v Medina **430 M 800, 804 (2000)**—jury instructions regarding "presumption of malice" and necessity of rebutting it = unconstitutional, but harmless beyond reasonable doubt here;

C v Walters **12 MAC 389 (81)**—for malicious destruction of property over $100 must instruct on value;

C v Santiago **425 M 491 (97)**—preferable to instruct **first**, on elements of crime, before instructing on "elements of a defense" (but refusing to require, or find reversible error here);

C v Dyer **389 M 677 (83)**—joint venture instruction OK though no evidence of second assailant, because evidence may have suggested the possible inference; but

C v Ryan **14 MAC 901 (82)**—but not if joint venture evidence too weak;

C v Silanskas **433 M 678 (2001)**—where Commonwealth uses joint venture theory in attempting to convict D of murder, not necessary that Commonwealth prove identity of other joint venturer(s) as long as evidence supports existence of some principal other than D and that D shared the other's intent and was available to help if needed;

C v Gonzalez **443 M 799, 806 (2005)**—Commonwealth needn't prove precise conduct of each individual, & joint venture basis of liability is OK "as long as the evidence supports the existence of some principal other than" D (distinguishing *Green* 420 M 771, 778–81 (92));

C v Stewart **454 M 527 (2009)**—judge's instruction that acts/statements of each joint venturer could be considered against D only if acts/statements were made when joint venture existed or when venturers were acting to conceal the crime and statements/acts "[were] *relevant to the joint venture*"; italicized language = error, statements could be considered only if made "in furtherance of" the joint venture;

See also Chapter 16-B, Defenses: Joint Venture;

C v Kushner **43 MAC 918 (97)**—substantial risk of miscarriage of justice = inherent when elements of a crime are incorrectly stated in charge;

C v Moore **36 MAC 455 (94)**—misdefining basic element of crime required reversal despite no objection;

C v Redmond **53 MAC 1 (2001)**—omission of "an" essential element in jury charge as to crime doesn't require automatic reversal, BUT

C v Petersen **67 MAC 49 (2006)**—even so, reversal here (despite no objection): NO instruction at all given re: "minor in possession of alcohol" & it's not self-evident: alcohol here was at best "constructively" possessed (a "more complex concept" as to which jurors weren't instructed either);

C v Jordan **49 MAC 802, 815 (2000)**—at trial for conspiracy, jury should be instructed on elements of offense which is alleged object of conspiracy IF it is a "technical or unusually complex offense" as to which a juror has no general impression, but not mandatory if offense is "self-defining";

C v Johnson **45 MAC 473 (98)**—when protective order prohibited only "abuse," reversible error (despite no objection) to charge jury to convict for violating the order by abuse "and/or by contacting her";

See Chapter 21 for instructions on elements of particular offenses;

See Chapter 18-B for cases on identification instructions; (but see particularly *C v Cuffie 414 M 632 (93) revised version of "model" Rodriguez instruction which avoids Fitzpatrick error (i.e., time elapsing between crime and "next" opportunity of witness to see D, indicating that witness indeed saw D at crime scene) set forth;

See Chapter 7-E for cases on "insanity" (lack of criminal responsibility) instructions;

C v DiFonzo **31 MAC 921 (91)**—D had right to instruction on possibility of honest but mistaken identification;

C v Caramanica **49 MAC 376 (2000)**—"improper incursion into the jury's role" to instruct that "very few people come into court with an intention to mislead," and credibility means "accuracy more than honesty";

C v Chotain **31 MAC 336 (91)**—error to instruct that crime proven & that only issue was identification, where

crime's occurrence, though not basis of defense, was never explicitly conceded by defense;

C v Conley **34 MAC 50 (93)**—contradictory instructions on elements of crime (1 correct, 1 incorrect) = reversal; can't know which portion jury followed;

C v Allen **430 M 252, 258 (99)**—in felony murder case, instruction that death must be shown to be a "natural and probable consequence" of the underlying felony is required when there is a "legitimate question" whether death was proximately caused by the felony (here no such question);

C v St. Peter **48 MAC 517, 524 (2000)**—no error in refusing instruction that D's conduct had to be shown to be THE proximate cause of death and not merely one of the causes; instruction given said proximate cause was one "which in natural and continuous sequence unbroken by any efficient intervening cause produces the result complained of and without which the result would not have occurred" though could be "assisted or accelerated by other incidental and ancillary matters";

C v Sires **413 M 292 (92)**—suggested instruction on effect of drugs or alcohol on D's mental state set forth;

C v Giguere **420 M 226 (95)**—instruction that "the jury may consider credible evidence of the effects of the defendant's consumption of drugs in deciding whether the Commonwealth has met its burden of proving" D's state of mind beyond a reasonable doubt = all that SJC has required;

C v Wallace **417 M 126, 134 n.11 (94)**—if evidence is "conflicting" re: D's intoxication, he gets instruction;

See also Chapter 16-C: Defenses: Intent, Intoxication

C v James **424 M 770 (97)**—voluntary intoxication instruction not required where evidence does not suggest a condition of debilitating intoxication that could support a reasonable doubt as to whether D capable of forming requisite criminal intent;

C v Rose **47 MAC 168, 177 (99)**—intoxication is NOT "affirmative defense," but instead a "subsidiary factor in the evaluation of whether the Commonwealth has proved a requisite state of mind beyond a reasonable doubt";

C v Spencer **40 MAC 919 (96)**—substantial risk of miscarriage of justice found in failure to explain "intent" element in assault by means of dangerous weapon;

C v Sneed **413 M 387, 394 (92)**—evidence of nonfelonious battery on baby with "high degree of likelihood" of "substantial harm" required instruction on manslaughter; involuntary manslaughter instruction may be required wherever D charged with unintentional killings under 2d & 3d prongs of malice;

12-K.3. Defenses

See Chapter 16, Defense Theories;

C v Guerriero **14 MAC 1012 (82)**—can instruct on self-defense (if evidence warrants) though D relied on ID defense; maybe ineffective assistance of counsel not to ask it;

C v Fickett **403 M 194 (88)**—D gets instruction on withdrawal though said no joint venture;

C v Zaccagnini **383 M 615 (81)**—evidence may need instructions on mutually inconsistent theories (self-defense & accident); (& see *Mathews v US* **485 US 58 (88)**)

C v Houston **332 M 687 (55)**—instruct on self-defense though no defense evidence (because of hearsay admitted without objection);

C v Souza **428 M 478 (98)**—though D requested that there be NO instruction on self-defense, such a claim was made in his statement to police, which had been admitted, and judge did instruct on it; issue of first impression whether such a "defense" instruction may be given over D's objection (and here, Commonwealth didn't request it either), but SJC finds no prejudice from the instruction: "prejudice" to D's cause instead fairly rose from DA's closing argument which asserted that D abandoned self defense claim when forensic evidence gathered after statement and before trial effectively refuted it (so false statement was consciousness of guilt);

C v Rodriguez **370 M 684 (76)**—IF D raises evidence of self-defense, DA's burden of proof beyond a reasonable doubt to negate (because lack of self-defense = element);

C v Carlino **429 M 692 (99)**—instruction that malice is negated by provocation only if provocation is proved beyond a reasonable doubt was wrong (jury should have been instructed that Commonwealth had to prove beyond reasonable doubt that D did not act on reasonable provocation);

C v Beauchamp **424 M 682 (97)**—though D both failed to take direct appeal & had been a fugitive from justice, his late-allowed appeal received benefit of intervening laws re: self-defense jury instructions which shifted burden;

C v Sosnowski **43 MAC 367 (97)**—no error in refusing to instruct on jury nullification;

See Chapter 7-E for cases on criminal responsibility instructions;

See Chapter 12-F for cases on failure to test or investigate (Bowden) instructions;

C v Richardson **425 M 765 (97)**—judge not required to instruct concerning police failure to test (but can't bar defense argument on topic);

C v McIntyre **430 M 529, 544 n.14 (99)**—same;

See Chapter 16-B for cases on joint venture instructions; see, e.g., *C v Melendez* **427 M 214, 216 (98)** (omission of instruction that felony murder D had to know joint venturer was armed **would** require reversal even in absence of objection) (not here);

C v Claudio **418 M 103, 109–17 (94)**—reversing felony murder-one & armed assault in dwelling convictions due to no instruction requiring proof beyond a reasonable doubt that D knew that joint venturer was armed;

See Chapter 16-C for cases on instructions on knowledge & intent, intoxication, mistake, accident & diminished capacity; 16-D for cases on necessity, duress, 'defense of self, others, or property' instructions; 16-E for cases on entrapment instructions;

See Chapter 18-B for cases on identification instructions;

C v Brown **449 M 747, 768 (2007)**—instruction on voluntary intoxication not required absent evidence of "debilitating intoxication" (many cases cited);

C v Garrity **43 MAC 349 (97)**—meaning of unambiguous contract is matter of **law**, not one for jury;

C v Mahoney **405 M 326 (89)**—preferable for judge to instruct that co-venturer's consciousness of guilt not relevant as to D's shared intent;

C v Oeun Lam **420 M 615 (95)**—consciousness of innocence best left to argument, without jury instructions (even though instructions here included consciousness of guilt);

C v Rivera **31 MAC 554 (91)**—Commonwealth limited to proving constructive or actual possession where jury not instructed on joint venture;

C v Ortiz **39 MAC 70 (95)**—error in refusing to instruct on use of prior consistent statements in evaluating (police) credibility was exacerbated by judge's telling jury that "this is not a case on whether or not good police reports are being made" & officer "is not being tried for what he puts or doesn't put in his police report";

C v Robinson **408 M 245 (90)**—"new rule" announced in Henson requiring jury instructions on intoxication where specific intent in issue will not be applied retroactively on collateral review under *C v Bray* **407 M 296 (90)**, banning retroactive application of new rules on collateral review unless "central to an accurate determination of innocence or guilt";

C v Taylor **32 MAC 570 (92)**—discussion of when evidence requires self-defense & manslaughter instructions;

C v Allen **76 MAC 9 (2009)**—while "brandishing" a ten-inch folding knife after opening it not necessarily "deadly" force, uncontroverted testimony = D "tried to hit" V with it; since D wasn't entitled to self-defense instruction, any error in instruction given "could not give rise to" substantial risk of miscarriage of justice;

C v Newhook **34 MAC 960 (93)**—error not to charge jury on defense of reasonable mistake of fact; standard instruction concerning specific intent necessary for robbery didn't adequately tell jury that defense could negate element of intent, or that it was Commonwealth's burden to disprove the defense beyond a reasonable doubt;

C v Power-Koch **69 MAC 735 (2007)**—D's statement to police said "accident" in firing gun, didn't intend to accede to depressed best friend's request that D shoot him, though held gun, not familiar with handguns, didn't know fully loaded, didn't mean to pull trigger; given this evidentiary basis, error found in refusal to instruct on accident, "an unintentional event occurring through inadvertence, mistake, or negligence";

C v Lyons **71 MAC 671 (2008)**—charged with indecent assault and battery on person age 14 or older, D defended on basis that complainant initiated a "scuffle," and any indecent contact occurred as he was pushing her away from him; COMMONWEALTH requested instruction on lesser included offense of assault and battery, and D requested instruction on self-defense, which judge gave without objection by Commonwealth; judge's subsequently withdrawing from jury the self-defense instruction, at Commonwealth's request, was error, undermining defense and D's credibility;

12-K.4. Lesser Included Offenses, Joint Venture Evidence

See Chapters 5-D, Complaints/Indictments & 19-B, Double Jeopardy, for cases on lesser included offenses; see, in particular, Chapter 21 (substantive crimes elements) for specifically available lesser-includeds on given evidence;

C v Lewis **9 MAC 842 (80)**—D gets instruction on lesser offense if rational basis in evidence for it; assault = lesser included offense of assault with intent to rape;

C v Senbatu **38 MAC 904 (95)**—D should have had lesser included offense instruction on both simple possession & possession with intent to distribute when trafficking in >28 grams was charged and 2 amounts of drugs had been aggregated, D acknowledging responsibility for only one amount: only speculation would support thesis that even one amount would still be "trafficking" (albeit in lesser, >14 gram, amount);

C v Blevins **56 MAC 206 (2002)**—conviction for trafficking in over 14 grams of cocaine reversed for failure to instruct on lesser offense of simple possession, because D contended that he and two friends pooled money to buy cocaine, all participated in the negotiation & were present during the exchange of $ for drug, but that immediately afterward D was arrested; simple joint possession is a possible verdict when two or more persons simultaneously and jointly acquire possession of a drug for their own use, intending only to share it together;

C v Santo **375 M 299 (78)**—must instruct on lesser included offense if the evidence provides rational basis for NG on crime charged & G of lesser included offense;

C v Yunggebauer **23 MAC 46 (86)**—(same), but discuss with counsel;

C v Smith **37 MAC 10 (94)**—D gets lesser included offense (only) if there is "tolerable amount of evidence" to support jury finding of lesser crime;

C v Bockman **424 M 757 (2004)**—when D claimed that he wasn't present when wife was killed, and didn't claim that he was provoked in manner so that killing would be mitigated, no right to lesser included instruction on voluntary manslaughter despite prosecutor's closing argument which speculated, on evidence, that killing occurred unexpectedly when wife "said something" / criticized D, causing him to grab some "object of opportunity" and kill her; nothing remotely to suggest what words were spoken or that they could have constituted reasonable provocation;

C v Hall **50 MAC 208, 214 (2000)**—when D simply denies all involvement with drugs seized, no basis for lesser included offense of simple cocaine possession in trafficking prosecution: "judge's duty to charge on lesser included offenses … is not coincident with the jury's unique prerogative as the ultimate fact finder. . . . There must be some evidence on the element differentiating the greater and lesser offenses";

C v Pamplona **58 MAC 239 (2003)**—same, context of assault and battery with dangerous weapon (D denied any assault at all, saying he was victim of excessive force by correction officers);

C v Porro **74 MAC 676, further appellate rev. allowed 455 M 1106 (2009)**—in responding to deliberating jury's question whether D could be convicted on "lesser" offense of assault by means of dangerous weapon on indictment charging assault and battery by means of dangerous weapon, judge said yes, but committed reversible error in failing to limit jury's consideration on the charge to the one act on which grand jury relied; MAC permitted retrial on lesser included offense of assault by means of dangerous weapon under "attempted battery theory" (noting at n.4 that "it is less clear" that "threatened battery theory" of assault by means of dangerous weapon is a lesser included of ABDW);

C v Gonzalez **67 MAC 877 (2006)**—jury could either find D guilty of trafficking in heroin, and in cocaine, in amounts specified by Commonwealth, or it could find him guilty of lesser-included offense of straight possession (on his proffered defense of possession of small amounts for personal use, and the claim that cops planted all the rest of the drugs); there was no basis in evidence for instructing also on "trafficking" in the drugs, but in some amount less than the 28–99 grams charged;

C v Johnson **75 MAC 903 (2009)**—D was convicted of both "trafficking" and possession with intent to distribute, the latter being enhanced for sentencing because it was a "second or subsequent", D receiving 3–5 sentence on trafficking, but 5 to 5 & a day on possession with intent; convictions were duplicative; ordinarily, result would be to dismiss "lesser" offense, but here "lesser" carried the longer sentence (lesser included offense = one with fewer elements, and "having been previously convicted" is NOT an "element" but is instead a sentencing enhancement); HERE, remand for trial judge to decide which to vacate & which judgment to "affirm";

C v Alebord **68 MAC 1 (2006)**—D not entitled to instruction on lesser offense of manslaughter: cited trial evidence was that when co-D shot victim, D believed that co-D was "only" going to fire gun "into the crowd", but scope of risk for this was "plain and strong likelihood of death", consistent only with "malice"/murder culpability; D's attempts (on appeal) to claim thought of firing "near" rather than "into" crowd = unavailing;

C v Tolan **453 M 634 (2009)**—D opposed Commonwealth request for instruction on lesser offense of manslaughter, and it was not given; D's contrary stance on appeal & citation of alleged evidence of "wanton and reckless" conduct rejected, SJC saying insufficient evidence, & defense was premised solely on "accident", & no likelihood of miscarriage of justice;

C v Lyons **71 MAC 671 (2008)**—charged with indecent assault and battery on person age 14 or older, D defended on basis that complainant initiated a "scuffle," and any indecent contact occurred as he was pushing her away from him; COMMONWEALTH requested instruction on lesser included offense of assault and battery, and D requested instruction on self-defense, which judge gave without objection by Commonwealth; judge's subsequently withdrawing from jury the self-defense instruction, at Commonwealth's request, was error, undermining defense and D's credibility;

C v Donovan **422 M 349 (96)**—that D's theory of case is inconsistent with conviction on lesser offense "is not a sound basis for failing to give" lesser included offense supported by the evidence;

C v Gilmore **399 M 741 (87)**—(same), including (dis)believing some/all testimony of complaining witness; but see *C v Egerton* **396 M 499 (86)** enhancing element has to be affirmatively in dispute; possibility of disbelief of portion of Commonwealth evidence not sufficient basis on which to instruct on lesser included offense;

C v Donlan **436 M 329, 337 n.7 (2002)**—SJC "disagree(s)" with Appeals Court's statement in another case that it (the SJC) had "departed from the rule . . . that the possibility of jury disbelief of a portion of the Commonwealth's evidence may in fact provide a basis for an instruction on a lesser included offense";

C v Berry **47 MAC 24 (99)**—judge not bound by D's testimony in the framing of jury instructions AND basis for joint venture charge can come from D's evidence rather than Commonwealth's case in chief, BUT SJC overruled and recognized issue to have been "required finding of not guilty" rather than jury instructions: **431 M 326 (2000)** required finding of not guilty ordered on joint venture theory, because right to such finding vested at close of Commonwealth evidence;

C v Leftwich **430 M 865, 868–69 (2000)**—basis for joint venture charge found in D's statement seeking to limit culpability to after-fact accessorial, plus genetic material on blood which was neither D's nor V's, & unidentified fingerprints;

C v Rosario **13 MAC 920 (82)**—D gets instruction on A & B (lesser included of A&B on police officer) because says he swung at another, missed, & hit cop;

C v Connolly **49 MAC 424 (2000)**—D gets instruction on simple A&B in ABDW, to wit "shod foot", because footwear's status as 'dangerous weapon' is at issue;

C v Campbell **352 M 387 (67)**—need not instruct on hypothesis without evidence; must instruct on manslaughter if murder case evidence would permit finding it; cf. *C v Parker* **420 M 242 (95)**—expert testimony from defense was not prerequisite to obtaining instruction that jury may

consider voluntary intoxication as it affects a defendant's ability to form specific intent required for conviction;

C v Vinnie **428 M 161, 180–81 (98)**—D may not waive right to have jury determine degree of murder; henceforth any murder conviction returned after jury has not been instructed to determine degree of murder, "whether due to a defendant's purported waiver, the Commonwealth's objection or a judge's oversight, shall be subject to reversal";

C v Henry **37 MAC 429 (94)**—OK to instruct on "simple" rape as lesser included offense because cross-examination of complainant had suggested that since no knife was seen, no knife was used; "aggravation" thus questioned, despite D's argument that cross was only general credibility attack;

C v Ortiz **47 MAC 777 (99)**—error to instruct on lesser of indecent assault and battery when testimony as to anal rape was that, although complainant had told cop that D had tried to have anal sex, he was "unsuccessful," what she meant by this was penetration, but no ejaculation; D's conviction for this indecent A&B was reversed, and he couldn't be retried for rape because prior conviction on only the lesser implied acquittal of the greater (double jeopardy);

C v Rodriguez **11 MAC 379 (81)**—even without defense objection, jury can't convict of offense not a lesser included; (being present not lesser included offense of possession);

C v Talbot **35 MAC 766 (94)**—cannot instruct on crime (here, accessory after fact) as requested by D (because it fits his testimony and "theory") when crime is not lesser included offense;

C v Charles **47 MAC 191 (99)**—state of evidence was such that jury should have been instructed on assault and battery by means of dangerous weapon in murder prosecution (jury could believe that fatal wound was from V falling on top of D, who held knife, but could also reject D's story that other stab wounds were in self-defense); assault & battery is a lesser included, and since ABDW is "simply an aggravated form of assault and battery," the circumstances were such that ABDW was a lesser included;

C v Thomas **400 M 676 (87)**—(must instruct that) same act can't be both greater & lesser offense

C v Gilliard **36 MAC 183 (94)**—failure to request lesser included offense may be ineffective assistance of counsel;

C v Chase **433 M 293 (2001)**—but when instruction as to one lesser crime (motor vehicle homicide) was given, not ineffective to request lesser included offense of different comparable crime (involuntary manslaughter); refusal to require trial judge to conduct colloquy with D re: counsel's objection to instruction on lesser included offense, terming question "academic," given judge's duty regardless of D's wishes, to instruct on lesser included offense if evidence supports & Commonwealth requests;

C v Velazquez **61 MAC 667 (2004)**—pursuit of V in car, shooting V, boxing V's car in to shoot again, presented no possible inference that shooting was product of mitigating circumstances, justifiable or excusable, so no instruction on lesser offense of armed assault with intent to kill was warranted (& no ineffective counsel for failing to object to omission/refusal to so charge);

C v Matos **36 MAC 958 (94)**—D does not have absolute right to make "tactical decisions" which determine what theories of liability will be submitted to jury;

C v Pagan **35 MAC 788 (94)**—"judge has no duty to undercut a D's 'all or nothing' strategy"; BUT SEE ***C v Woodward **427 M 659 (98)**—Commonwealth is "entitled" to lesser included offense instruction if evidence so warrants;

C v Vasquez **27 MAC 655 (89)**—Commonwealth not entitled to lesser included instruction over D's objection unless element distinguishing lesser from greater crime charged is in dispute;

Superior Court Criminal Practice Jury Instructions § 5.6.3—"all or nothing" charge;

C v Thayer **418 M 130 (94)**—upholding lesser included offense on "statutory" rape despite fact that defendant was the parent of the six and four-year-old complainants (and "consent" could not thus have been issue): SJC held that disbelief of testimony about threats of slapping/getting "in trouble" could yield lesser included offense verdict;

US v Harary **457 F.2d 471 (2d Cir. '72)**—"Those who have labored in the vineyard of litigation are aware that where the case is a hard one for the government . . . , it will consider its task done if it can secure 'the advantage of offering the jury a choice—a situation which is apt to induce a doubtful jury to find the defendant guilty of the less serious offense rather than to continue the debate'(.)"; unwarranted lesser included offense instruction invites jury compromise when proper verdict is NG;

C v Ford **35 MAC 752 (94)**—can't instruct on lesser included of larceny from person when prosecution claims robbery at gun point of van-load of stereo speakers and D claims he bought speakers for $20,000 in consensual sale;

C v Pagan **35 MAC 788 (94)**—no ineffective assistance of counsel in failure to request lesser included offense instruction on manslaughter when D was charged with arson and murder, and D consistently & strongly denied knowledge of how the fire started; requesting such lesser included offense would "greatly sap the force of" defense made and "might entice . . . jury to compromise on the lesser included offense if they were in doubt about whether the prosecution had proved the greater offense";

C v Walker **426 M 301 (97)**—where there is no dispute that sexual assault complainant is less than 14 years old, indecent A&B on child under 14 is lesser included offense of forcible rape of child under age 16;

C v Sanna **424 M 92 (97)**—when death was by 34 knife wounds and 15 blows to head, no lesser included offense of involuntary manslaughter was available; scope of "risk" = that of 3d prong malice (plain & strong likelihood of death) rather than wanton/reckless conduct consistent with involuntary manslaughter ("high degree of likelihood that substantial harm will result") (*see other cases, Chapter 21-K*);

12-K.5. Presumption of Innocence

C v Drayton **386 M 39 (82)**—D gets 'presumed innocent' if request; (*see also Chapter 16, burden of proof*);

C v Viera **42 MAC 917 (97)**—given failure to instruct that complaint against D did not imply guilt, failure to instruct on presumption of innocence was error; reversal here (additional error in reasonable doubt charge);

C v Huan Lieu **50 MAC 162 (2000)**—presumption of innocence instruction not "constitutionally required," but if requested judge must give; "better practice" is to begin charge with simple statement that indictment is just government's complaint & has no force as evidence, that D is presumed to be innocent, and that prosecution has burden to prove each element of offense; cite to "model instructions" at 1 McIntyre et al., Mass. Superior Court Criminal Practice Jury Instructions § 1.2 (99) and Instruction 2.04 of Model Jury Instructions for Use in District Court;

C v Healy **15 MAC 134 (83)**—anecdote (re: attorney can defend a guilty D) undermined burden of proof & presumption of innocence;

C v Johnson **45 MAC 473, 476 (98)**—pre-impanelment question whether all understood D "is presumed to be guilty" excused even though in correcting 'self, judge referred to the misstatement as "a Freudian slip";

C v Rodriguez **437 M 554 (2002)**—SJC refuses to find error in instruction that "presumption in favor of innocence may begin to disappear" when Commonwealth begins to introduce its evidence, though this is not a "preferred" charge;

C v O'Brien **56 MAC 170 (2002)**—judge "muddied the waters by going on to employ the conceit of the disappearing presumption of innocence," i.e., as evidence accumulates against D, presumption grows less strong & eventually disappears entirely; while technically correct, this instruction should be avoided;

12-K.6. D's Right Not to Testify

C v Buiel **391 M 744 (84)**—D gets instruction re: not testifying if & only if asked;

C v Rivera **441 M 358, 370 (2004)**—SJC will no longer apply *Buiel* rule, which wasn't of "constitutional dimension"; giving instruction (re: D not testifying) over objection isn't prejudicial error;

C v Jackson, **419 M 716 (95)**—error to instruct on right not to testify if D requests instruction not be given;

C v Thomas **400 M 676 (87)**—instruction shouldn't say D "refused" to testify;

C v Jenkins **416 M 736 (94)**—when D requests instruction re not testifying, **preferable to say** "no adverse inference against D may be drawn by you because he did not take the witness stand"; **not** "the fact that D didn't testify is absolutely not to be considered by you" (though latter didn't cause reversal here);

C v Dussault **71 MAC 542 (2008)**—judge failed to give instruction re nontestifying defendant, but D didn't object: no substantial risk of miscarriage of justice here;

C v Delaney **8 MAC 406 (79)**—error to say grand jury hears one side & trial jury hears "both sides" if D didn't testify; aggravated by "D's right not to incriminate himself";

12-K.7. Reasonable Doubt

In re Winship **397 US 358 (70)**—due process means proof beyond reasonable doubt, even for juvenile D;

C v Stellberger **25 MAC 148 (87)**—must define reasonable doubt;

C v James **54 MAC 908 (2002)**—same (reversal for omitting);

C v Cundriff **382 M 137 (80)**—can't equate Commonwealth interests & jury interests;

C v Ferreira **373 M 116 (77)**—examples of jurors' decisions in daily lives "trivializes" "beyond a reasonable doubt";

C v Burnett **428 M 469 (98)**—trivializing examples of jurors' daily decisions in reasonable doubt charge (Ferreira error), but trial occurred 4 years before Ferreira and appellate decision issued 1 year before Ferreira; notwithstanding *Sullivan v Louisiana* (**508 US 275**) holding that reasonable doubt error is not susceptible to harmless error analysis, failure to raise issue on direct appeal waived it (counsel should have realized *Bumpus* **362 M 672 (72)** "foreshadowed" holding in Ferreira);

C v Bonds **424 M 698 (97)**—reversal due to charge equating proof beyond reasonable doubt with proof to "moral certainty", defined as level of certainty required by person in making decisions in "matters of the highest importance concerning his own affairs";

C v Williams **378 M 217 (79)**—"moral certainty" favored to explain reasonable doubt; can't overemphasize consequences of misapplying law (e.g., "lawless reign supreme"); (see also *Sheline* **391 M 279 (84)**);

C v Haley **413 M 770 (92)**—jury instruction defining reasonable doubt as "that type of doubt which would make you pause in making a decision on a grave & important matter in your own personal lives" did not require reversal where no trivializing examples given;

C v Pinckney **419 M 341 (95)**—when "moral certainty" is used, must also have language lending "context" to the phrase & emphasizing high level of certainty required to convict (citing *Victor v Nebraska* **511 US 1 (94)**); judgment reversed for language, "if a reasonable doubt or a mere possibility of innocence were sufficient to prevent a conviction, practically every criminal would be set free to prey upon the community";

C v Webster **5 Cush. 295, 320 (1850)**—the approved reasonable doubt definition: "abiding conviction . . . to moral certainty," not just strong probability;

C v Hurd (No. 1) **65 MAC 788 (2006)**—Federal Judicial Center's Pattern Criminal Jury Instructions, #21, complies with due process (though judge here added a paragraph containing "some" of Webster); D alleged burden shift (must give D benefit of the doubt if "you think there is a real possibility that the Ds are not guilty"); *C v Lebron* **66 MAC 907 (2006)**—"moral certainty" adequately explained by statement saying charge is proved beyond a reasonable doubt "if . . . [jurors] have . . . an abiding conviction to a moral certainty that the charge is true";

Lanigan v Maloney **853 F.2d 40 (1st Cir. '88)**—"to a degree of moral certainty" appeals to emotion & doesn't convey need to approach absolute certainty; moral certainty OK in Webster context, but otherwise confusing;

Victor v Nebraska **511 US 1 (94)**—"moral certainty" may be understood to mean less than the very high level of probability required in criminal cases; if used with rest of **Webster**, not reversible, however; approving additional instruction that jurors should not convict unless they "reach a subjective state of near certitude of the guilt of the accused.";

C v LaBriola **430 M 569 (2000)**—"moral certainty" used 9 times; no reversal here though D argued *Victor v Nebraska*;

C v Byers **62 MAC 148 (2004)**—used language approved in *C v Latimore* **423 M 129, 139 n.9 (96)**, except omitted references to "moral certainty" and instead used "near certitude," a phrase equivalent to beyond reasonable doubt (see *C v Riley* **433 M 266, 272 (2001)**); no objection, but no error overall;

C v Cresta **16 MAC 939 (83)**—"doubt based on a reason" = disfavored reasonable doubt instruction;

C v Anderson **425 M 685 (97)**—"doubt based on reason" = OK, in contrast to "doubt based upon **a** reason", which is perhaps burden-shifting;

Cage v Louisiana **498 US 39 (90)**—bad to say "reasonable doubt" = "grave uncertainty" or "actual substantial doubt";

Contrast? *C v Therrien* **428 M 607, 611 n 6 (98)**—re: "if there is any other reasonable explanation of the evidence of what (you) find happened, if that has caused (you) to have serious unanswered questions about the guilt of the defendant, then he must be given the benefit of the doubt and acquitted", argued to violate Cage, Court claimed that "serious" didn't mean "grave", but instead meant "being in earnest"; note, however, that this was a collateral attack on a first degree murder conviction over twenty years old;

Sullivan v Louisiana **508 US 275 (93)**—constitutionally deficient reasonable doubt charge never harmless;

C v Crawford **12 MAC 776 (81)**—"doubt for which a good reason can be given" = "offending language"; but saved by no objection & other OK language;

C v Robinson **382 M 189 (81)**—Webster is "best source for 'unimpeachable' instructions on reasonable doubt"; "doubt based on reason" = disfavored;

C v Hubbard **69 MAC 232 (2007)**—DA's closing assertions, "if you look for doubt, you will find doubt and that is not this standard of law that the Commonwealth requires. . . . If you look for doubt, you will find it. That is not what you are supposed to do," should not have been made (but there was no objection, and judge instructed that jurors were to apply law as stated by judge, and gave Webster charge on reasonable doubt); Appeals Court, "while not condoning" prosecutor's role in instructing jury, noted that reference to reasonable doubt as not involving "search for doubt" was "upheld" in *C v Watkins* 425 M 830, 839 (97);

C v Riley **433 M 266, 271–73 (2001)**—good defense requests for 'reasonable doubt' charge;

C v Gagliardi **418 M 562 (94)**—*C v Little* **384 M 262 (81)** = OK charge on reasonable doubt **if** judge deletes sentence, "It is not proof beyond all reasonable doubt";

C v Mack **423 M 388, 390 & n.5 (96)**—court refuses to find error in "Commonwealth not required to prove case to 'an absolute or mathematical certainty'";

C v Redmond **53 MAC 1, 9 (2001)**—in attempting to use Mack language in supplemental charge, judge misstated, said Commonwealth not required to prove case to "absolute or moral certainty"; no relief here;

C v Fitzpatrick **16 MAC 99 (83)**—reasonable doubt as being "pretty darn sure" required reversal; "unbroken line of cases . . . all but command that the definition of reasonable doubt be . . . Webster"; (see also *Santos* **402 M 775 (88)**);

C v Souza **34 MAC 436 (93)**—judge's "slip of the tongue" making reasonable doubt "the exact inverse of what it should have been" was corrected sua sponte 90 minutes after deliberations began: no substantial risk of miscarriage of justice;

C v Berth **385 M 784 (82)**—alibi instruction that jury should "believe one side or other" misstated burden of proof;

C v Rodriguez **437 M 554 (2002)**—jury instruction SHOULD be that expert opinion should be disregarded if the assumptions upon which it is based "are not true," criticizing instruction using, instead, the phrase, "if the assumptions have not been *proven*" (because latter phrase prompts confusion about concept of burden of proof);

C v Drumgold **423 M 230 (96)**—instructions making no distinction between prosecution & defense regarding burden of proof and implying that NG verdict requires proof beyond reasonable doubt are WRONG: (1) '4 choices on verdict slip (including NG) must be unanimous beyond a reasonable doubt'; (2) 'you are to determine whether the evidence establishes beyond a reasonable doubt the guilt or innocence of D; (3) you may draw inferences & conclusions only from facts which have been proved to you beyond a reasonable doubt'; (4) 'Alibi. You've heard evidence . . . suggesting that D was at another place . . . you'll have to decide whether or not you believe that evidence';

C v Juvenile **396 M 215(85)**—Model Jury Instruction #2.051 on reasonable doubt saying it's "not proof beyond ALL reasonable doubt" is error (but no harm here);

C v Slonka **42 MAC 760 (97)**—although **Webster** was 1st given, ensuing instruction equated "reasonable" doubt with "fair" doubt, and possibly lowered required burden of proof: reversal despite no objection;

C v Beverly **389 M 866 (83)**—NG on "even balance" improperly suggests slight tilt can mean G.;

C v Saladin **73 MAC 416 (2008)**—though D requested jury instruction that 'when evidence tends equally to sustain either of two inconsistent propositions, either of them can be said to have been established by legitimate proof,' this was a principle applicable to sufficiency of evidence and in instruction context, would diminish required burden of proof;

C v Richardson **425 M 765 (97)**—language "not beyond a 'shadow of a doubt'" should be avoided ("unlikely to be helpful to a jury");

C v Crawford **417 M 358 (94)**—should not, when defining reasonable doubt, contrast it with civil "preponderance of evidence" standard (but no relief here or in *C v Murphy* **415 M 161 (93)**);

C v Allard **429 M 756 (99)**—though judge spoke of "preponderance of evidence" standard in civil case, he did this only to "contrast( ) the heavy burden of proof resting on the Commonwealth" in criminal case, and "stressed the far higher standard required" in criminal case;

C v Santos **402 M 775 (88)**—OTHER CASES' facts will confuse jury & beyond a reasonable doubt standard; use Webster, not 'reasonable doubt' instruction OK'd in *Little* **384 M 262, 266 n.4 (81)**;

C v Sullivan **20 MAC 802 (85)**—beyond a reasonable doubt as "above 50% of civil case" = improper;

C v Viera **42 MAC 917 (97)**—beyond a reasonable doubt as evidence establishing "truth of the facts to a reasonable & moral certainty, a certainty which convinces & directs the understanding, satisfies the reason & judgment of those who are bound to act conscientiously upon it" = too cursory, ambiguous; substantial risk of miscarriage of justice found;

C v Caramanica **49 MAC 376 (2000)**—"firm and settled belief" as synonym for 'beyond reasonable doubt' and phrase "should" (rather than "must") have that degree of certitude not fatal here, but incomprehensible attempt to quantify burden (comparisons with "slight," "mere," "greater," and "strong" probabilities) plus other charge errors caused reversal;

12-K.8. Presumptions and Burden-Shifting

Mullaney v Wilbur **421 US 684 (75)**—can't shift burden of proof to D to prove heat of passion to reduce first degree murder to manslaughter; instead, DA has burden to negate, beyond reasonable doubt, heat of passion;

Sandstrom v Montana **442 US 510 (79)**—can't shift burden of proof by instruction that law "presumes" one intends ordinary consequences of one's voluntary act;

C v Niziolek **380 M 513 (80)**—(same); & no definition of "malice" was given;

C v Nolin **448 M 207 (2007)**—25 years after *Sandstrom*, Commonwealth requested and received jury instruction that "a person is presumed to intend the natural and probable consequences of his acts. So, in considering intent, remember that"; SJC agrees error, but says here harmless beyond reasonable doubt;

C v Giguere **420 M 226 (95)**—instruction that D had burden of proving elements of murder was corrected by judge after counsel told him; language regarding "intentional killing . . . with no extenuating circumstances sufficient to reduce crime to manslaughter" did not mandate a presumption;

C v Carlino **429 M 692 (99)**—instruction that malice is negated by provocation only if provocation is proved beyond a reasonable doubt was wrong (jury should have been instructed that Commonwealth had to prove beyond reasonable doubt that D did not act on reasonable provocation);

C v Richards **384 M 396 (81)**—malice instruction & "if you FIND" language re: self-defense shifted burden of proof to D;

C v Purcell **423 M 880 (96)**—"if you find that D was so drunk he could not entertain malice . . . (then decide whether or not he's G of manslaughter)" = burden-shift; here no prejudice, however;

C v Waite **422 M 792 (96)**—"If you find/are satisfied that D was impaired/intoxicated, you should consider that evidence in deciding whether Commonwealth has demonstrated the requisite mental state" = BAD; no "preliminary finding" by jury is to be made before giving Commonwealth burden of proof beyond reasonable doubt as to requisite mental state;

C v Roberts **423 M 17 (96)**—similar;

C v Rose **47 MAC 168, 177 (99)**—judge should not have charged that instruction that intoxication "must be substantial" before it could negate D's capacity to form intent necessary for murder, and "if you find, not that they were just drunk but if they were so drunk that they could not form an intelligent intent to join" the criminal enterprise, NG; "In truth there is no burden of proof on either side regarding intoxication, rather, intoxication is a subsidiary factor in the evaluation of whether the Commonwealth has proved a requisite state of mind beyond a reasonable doubt"; no objection, no relief;

C v James **424 M 770 (97)**—voluntary intoxication instruction not required where evidence does not suggest a condition of debilitating intoxication that could support a reasonable doubt as to whether D capable of forming requisite criminal intent;

C v Barnette **45 MAC 486 (98)**—same;

C v Callahan **380 M 821 (80)**—"presume" malice from use of dangerous weapon shifted burden of proof;

C v Talkowski **33 MAC 720 (92)**—when verdict could have been voluntary manslaughter, burden-shifting instruction was consequential; legally accurate language re: "inferences" did not cure; see *C v Repoza* **400 M 516 (87)** merely inconsistent language doesn't cure burden shift; must modify and/or explain it;

C v Van Winkle **443 M 230 (2005)**—instruction that jury "may infer, though it is not required to do so, that a person intends the natural and probable consequences of an act that is knowingly done" is correct, in contrast to one that directs that one may presume that person intends natural and probable consequences of act, as in *C v Repoza* **382 M 119, 124 (1980)** (error for judge to equate malice implied with malice presumed);

C v Moreira **385 M 792 (82)**—breathalyzer allows inference (or permissive presumption) under influence, but not conclusive/mandatory presumption;

C v Malcolm **35 MAC 938 (93)**—error to instruct that certificates of analysis were prima facie evidence of nature & weight of substances and had to be accepted as true unless evidence to contrary was introduced;

Francis v Franklin **471 US 307 (85)**—language that merely contradicts & doesn't explain & refute unconstitutional burden-shifting instruction does not "absolve the infirmity";

C v Galford **413 M 364 (92)**—language in abandonment instruction setting forth conditions necessary for D to "escape liability" was "ill-chosen" but negated by charge as a whole;

C v Shelley **411 M 692 (92)**—"finding" language in malice charge was regrettable but negated by instructions taken as whole;

C v Mejia **407 M 493 (90)**—instructions setting forth "preconditions" & "criteria" for self-defense were burden-shifting;

C v Graham **62 MAC 642 (2004)**—D was entitled to instruction on self-defense on charges of resisting arrest and assault and battery on police officer; instruction given below suggested incorrectly that D had burden of establishing that police used excessive force, that D defended 'self with reasonable force," and that he resisted arrest using such reasonable force as was necessary to resist "excessive" force by police; instead, judge must charge that Commonwealth must prove beyond reasonable doubt that police did not engage in excessive force, as well as that D didn't act in self-defense; "gist of" instruction given, *C v Graham* 62 MAC at 654, n.7;

C v Murphy **442 M 485 (2004)**—instruction that "it is alleged that the Commonwealth hasn't proven beyond reasonable doubt that D was present at time/place of crimes. . . . If you believe D's alibi, Commonwealth has failed to prove G beyond a reasonable doubt," said to be taken out of context (!) because judge reiterated Commonwealth's burden of proof, including necessity of proving fact that D "was there at the time"; still, SJC "emphasize[s]" that *McLeod* 367 M 501, 502 n.1 (75) is preferable;

C v Acevedo **427 M 714 (98)**—reversal for instructions which were "exact reverse" of what Commonwealth's burden was; charge was, in order to warrant conviction of voluntary manslaughter, Commonwealth had to prove D inflicted injury causing death, that homicide was committed unlawfully without justification, and that D "injured (V) as a result of sudden combat or in the heat of passion or using excessive force in self-defense"; Commonwealth instead was required to prove, beyond reasonable doubt, that D did NOT act on reasonable provocation;

C v Rodriguez **58 MAC 610 (2003)**—reversal for Acevedo error, which shifted burden of proof in "reasonable provocation" instruction, with effect of saying that malice was negated by provocation only if provocation was proved beyond a reasonable doubt;

C v Hogan **426 M 424 (98)**—finding no burden shift, overall, in instructions concerning withdrawal from joint venture;

C v Skinner **408 M 88 (90)**—instruction that cocking, aiming & firing gun with intent to kill would prove deliberate premeditation created impermissible Sandstrom presumption;

Superior Court Criminal Practice Jury Instructions § 5.6.11—"finding" or "satisfied" language;

12-K.9. Presumption of Sanity

C v Kostka **370 M 516 (76)**—'presumption of sanity' jury instructions, (assailed by dissent in *C v Kappler* **416 M 574 (93)**), here upheld (gist of charge: while prosecution has to prove sanity beyond a reasonable doubt, mere fact that most people are sane provides sufficient basis for jury to conclude that D was also sane);

C v Keita **429 M 843 (99)**—presumption of sanity instruction still OK, though vigorous dissent filed;

C v McLaughlin **431 M 506 (2000)**—presumption of sanity instruction strongly criticized in concurring opinion (signed onto by three SJC justices)

See Chapters 7-E, 16-C below; cf. *C v Jones* **9 MAC 83, 90–91 (80)**; *C v Eramo* **377 M 912 (79)**; *C v Marino* **343 M 725, 728 (62)** (disbelief of testimony is not equivalent of proof to the contrary)

12-K.10. Circumstantial Evidence and Inferences

C v Brooks **422 M 574 (96)**—instructions using examples of inferences or circumstantial evidence "that have numeric or quantifiable implications" likely diminish burden of proof, e.g., picture puzzle having 100 pieces, but you only have 72, draw inference as to what picture is;

C v Rosa, **422 M 18 (96)**—same; "avoid" such examples;

C v Vaughn **32 MAC 435 (92)**—'footprints in snow' analogy in circumstantial evidence instruction was "ill-advised" where case centered on actual evidence of footprints;

C v Dostie **425 M 372 (97)**—every inference drawn need not be based on independently-proven fact, but may instead be based on another inference;

C v Toon **55 MAC 642 (2002)**—instruction that jury may only draw inferences & conclusions from facts proven beyond a reasonable doubt assailed by D on appeal as requiring D to prove facts consistent with innocence beyond a reasonable doubt; appeals court rejected, said instruction clearly applied only to Commonwealth's burden of proof, AND it overstated Commonwealth's burden (not all subsidiary fact, but only elements of offense, need be proven beyond a reasonable doubt);

C v Walker **443 M 213, 222 (2005)**—instruction that jury "may draw inferences or conclusions only from facts which have been proved to you beyond a reasonable doubt" = erroneous, but "unduly burdened the Commonwealth" rather than D;

C v Baez **69 MAC 500 (2007)**—citing *Walker,* calling same claim "meritless," failing to comprehend that DEFENDANT can be burdened when jury refuses to make inferences *he* posits, absent proof of underlying facts beyond a reasonable doubt; subsidiary facts need only be proved by preponderance of evidence (*C v Lawrence* **404 M 378, 394 [89]**);

Superior Court Criminal Practice Jury Instructions § 1.3, Evidence: Direct & Circumstantial;

12-K.11. Consciousness of Guilt, Innocence

See Chapter 12-E for other cases on consciousness of guilt, including *C v Toney* **385 M 474 (82)**, *setting forth model cautionary charge on purported "consciousness of guilt" evidence;*

C v Ciampa **406 M 257 (89)**—jury instructions that D's consciousness of guilt may be inferred from testimony of alibi witnesses are improper; consciousness of guilt may only be inferred from D's own conduct or statements;

C v Knap **412 M 712 (92)**—consciousness of innocence instructions not required to counterbalance consciousness of guilt instructions, so long as instructions comply with *C v Toney* **385 M 575 (82)**; consciousness of innocence best left to D's closing argument;

C v Pina **430 M 266, 273 (99)**—"judge does not err, or abuse discretion, by refusing to give a consciousness of innocence instruction"; but see Stevens, J., dissenting, in ***US v Scheffer* 523 US 303, 331 (98)**;

C v Lavalley **410 M 641 (91)**—D's initial "false" statement to cops which substantially differed from his trial testimony was admissible to show consciousness of guilt where purpose wasn't to suggest D's failure to deny charges; judge's failure to give written supplemental Toney instruction along with other written instructions handed to jurors was cured by its inclusion in oral instructions;

C v Simmons **419 M 426 (95)**—reconsidering and rejecting holding of *C v Cruz* **416 M 27 (93)**: now, unless requested, judge not required to give **Toney** instruction;

C v Mahoney **405 M 326 (89)**—acts of a joint venturer amounting to consciousness of guilt may be attributed to another joint venturer if the acts occurred during the course of a joint venture and in furtherance of it; judge either should not have focused on D's husband's conduct (allegedly her joint venturer) in discussing consciousness of guilt or should have explained more fully the limited extent to which the husband's conduct in the vehicle bore on D's guilt, but no reversible error in charge "as a whole";

C v Pringle **22 MAC 746 (86)**—co-D's alias not consciousness of guilt re: D (& not part of alleged joint venture);

12-K.12. Missing Witnesses

See Chapter 12-J, Closing Argument, for cases on missing witnesses, including foundational deficiencies, constitutional issues;

Superior Court Criminal Practice Jury Instructions § 4.9—(absent or missing witness); District Court Model Jury Instructions ## 4.04, 4.041 ("absent witness," "announced witness does not testify");

C v Rodriquez **49 MAC 370, 373–74 (2000)**—after judge told ADA that he would not give 'missing witness' instruction against defense, ADA COULD NOT ARGUE THE INFERENCE IN CLOSING (& this caused reversal); ADA's thesis (i.e., he couldn't be precluded from arguing inference even though judge refused to endorse it with instruction) = wrong;

C v Graves **35 MAC 76, 80 n.6 (93)**—missing witness charge (if D "did not call a potential witness to testify you are free, not required to, to infer that the witness's testimony would not be favorable to the defendant only if four conditions are satisfied. First, that the Commonwealth's case against D must be strong. Second, that the absent witness or witnesses must be expected to offer important testimony supporting D's innocence. Third, that the absent witness must be available to testify for D. And, fourth, that the witness's absence must not be explained by any of the other circumstances in the case. If all four conditions have . . . been met, you are permitted to draw an inference that the witness's testimony would not be favorable to D, if you find that to be a reasonable conclusion in all the circumstances of this case. If any of the four conditions has not been met, you may not draw such an inference and you should completely disregard the potential witness's testimony as a factor in this case");

C v Olszewski **416 M 707, 724 n.18 (93)**—SJC adds to jury instruction suggested in *Graves* (**35 MAC at 80**) the caution that "the jury should not draw adverse inference from D's failure to call a certain witness unless they were persuaded of the truth of the inference beyond a reasonable doubt");

C v Matthews **49 MAC 365 (2000)**—failure to request, at trial, the *Olszewski* addition to *Graves* charge = no relief on appeal (no "substantial risk of miscarriage of justice");

C v Anderson **411 M 279 (91)**—missing witness instruction should be given only where "apparent" that witness friendly to opposing side; D not entitled to missing witness instruction where not apparent that alleged victim of prison battery, fellow inmate of D's, was friendly to Commonwealth;

C v Spencer **49 MAC 383 (2000)**—reversal for giving missing witness instruction when purportedly missing individual couldn't be found to have testimony of "distinct importance" to D's case; it was speculative to assume that his memory would be better than that of D's and his employer or that of another of D's co-workers, and seemingly he, like witness who was called, was impeachable for friendship with D;

C v Johnson **39 MAC 410 (95)**—missing witness instruction should have directed that no adverse inference against D should be drawn unless jurors "were persuaded of the truth of the inference beyond a reasonable doubt"; if there had been record assertions that witness was (a) equally available to both parties, or (b) not called because he was incarcerated, appellate court might have found inference unavailable;

C v Sena **29 MAC 463 (90)**—missing witness instruction that failed to explain that adverse inferences may be drawn required reversal; judges have discretion to deny prosecution requests for missing witness instruction because of possible conflict with D's constitutional rights, even where appropriate foundation laid; cf. *Opinion of the Justices* **412 M 1201, 1211 (92)**—supporting argument that missing witness instruction against D in criminal case violates Article 12;

12-K.13. Alibi

Superior Court Criminal Practice Jury Instructions § 3.10 (Alibi); District Court Model Jury Instructions #6.01 (Alibi);

C v Berth **385 M 784 (82)**—alibi instruction that jury should "believe one side or other" misstated burden of proof; but see *C v Murphy* **442 M 485 (2004)**—instruction that "it is alleged that the Commonwealth hasn't proven beyond reasonable doubt that D was present at time/place of crimes. . . . If you believe D's alibi, Commonwealth has failed to prove G beyond a reasonable doubt," said to be taken out of context (!) because judge reiterated Commonwealth's burden of proof, including necessity of proving fact that D "was there at the time"; still, SJC "emphasize[s]" that *McLeod* **367 M 501, 502 n.1 (75)** is preferable;

See Chapter 18-C (Identification) for cases on alibi & instructions;

12-K.14. General Credibility

C v Green **25 MAC 751 (88)**—preliminary instructions by judge to venire that witnesses don't intentionally lie required reversal where consent was rape D's defense;

C v Caramanica **49 MAC 376 (2000)**—improper charge: 'very few people come into court with an intention to mislead," & credibility means "accuracy more than honesty";

C v Ragland **72 MAC 815 (2008)**—after trial in which witnesses recanted their grand jury testimony, jury sent question, "what is the punishment for perjury?", judge with agreement of all parties responded that jurors were not to concern themselves with any punishment for any crime; particularly because D was not entitled to original instruction that recantation was adverse to witnesses' penal interest (because the evidence supporting witness's awareness of such adversity was objected to, and objection was sustained, & evidence thus stricken), no error because no basis for jury to consider what penal consequences might be; even if initial instruction was proper, it required no amplification, no substantial risk of miscarriage of justice;

C v Davis **52 MAC 75 (2001)**—when veracity of "cooperating witness" (who expected "consideration" in exchange for his testimony) was sole issue, reversal because judge responded to jury question wanting to know what "consideration" he was receiving ('May we please know if there are laws of leniency that may apply here. If so, what are they?'), without consulting counsel & in materially misleading way ("there are no laws of leniency");

C v Ortiz **39 MAC 70 (95)**—reversal for judge's refusal to instruct on prior inconsistent statement, coupled with his statement to jury that "this is not a case on whether or not good police reports are being made", & cop "is not being tried for what he does or doesn't put in his police report"; *C v Clayton* **52 MAC 198, 207 (2001)**—at retrial, judge must specifically instruct on omissions as prior "inconsistencies";

12-K.15. D's Credibility

US v Dwyer **843 F.2d 60 (1st Cir. '88)**—bad instruction that D has motive to lie; better = judge D like other witnesses (fn.1);

C v Roderick **411 M 817 (92)**—instruction that jury could consider 'the interest or lack of interest of witnesses in outcome of case' was not improper comment on D's credibility even though he was only witness with such interest;

12-K.16. Prior Convictions

C v Riccard **410 M 718, 723–24 (91)**—contradictory instructions on juror's use of witness's prior convictions required reversal;

C v Hurley **32 MAC 620 (92)**—D entitled to instruction limiting use of D's prior convictions to impeachment upon request; failure to request instruction may be deemed "tactical choice";

Superior Court Criminal Practice Jury Instructions § 4.10.2—(proof of conviction of crime, D as wit-

ness); § 4.10.3 (proof of conviction of crime, nondefendant witness);

12-K.17. Testimony of Special Classes of Witnesses: Juvenile, Police, Fresh Complaint, Accomplice, Expert, Immunized and Cooperating Witnesses

C v Avery **14 MAC 137 (82)**—discretion to instruct specially on credibility of child witness; (*see also Chapter 12-J, Closing Argument; C v Achorn* **25 MAC 247 (88)** *DA can argue (here) 5-year-old can't lie; cf. Chapter 11-I, Evidence: Opinions*);

C v Juvenile **21 MAC 121 (85)**—discretion to instruct on classes of witnesses (e.g., kids/cops) provided no imbalance or suggest opinion re: witness;

C v Atkins **386 M 593 (82)**—on scrutiny of accomplice testimony; but see . . . *C v Griffith* **404 M 256 (89)**—but not required;

District Court Model Jury Instruction #4.03—(child witness); # 4.02 (expert witness, but see Comment: avoid term "expert" because may prejudice the jury); Superior Court Criminal Practice Jury Instructions § 4.7 (expert witness); § 4.8 (child witness); § 4.21 (immunized witness); § 4.22 (where plea agreement conditioned on truthfulness);

Higgins v Delta Elevator Service Corp. **45 MAC 643 (98)**—judge instructed jury to assess medical testimony, listing several factors articulated in *Daubert* (**509 US 579 (93)**), but plaintiff argued that the factors were to be used only by judge in deciding admissibility of expert evidence; while "arguably might have been better left unsaid," judge held to have discretion in how to instruct jury on evaluation of evidence, and jury had function of assessing soundness and credibility of the opinion; "not . . . a function of instructions about experts to declare that they are all created equal";

See Chapter 11-H (Evidence: Sex Offenses) for cases on fresh complaint evidence & instructions;

C v King **445 M 217 (2005)**—testimony of witness to whom sexual assault complainant FIRST complained ("first complaint testimony") must be preceded by limiting instruction, which must be repeated in final jury instructions (must convey that "you may not consider this testimony as evidence that the assault in fact occurred");

C v Gagliardi **29 MAC 225 (90)**—instruction on special scrutiny for testimony of immunized witness set forth;

C v Ciampa **406 M 257 (89)**—instruction on special scrutiny for testimony of cooperating accomplice obtained pursuant to plea agreement based on promise of 'truthful' testimony set forth; (*C v Holmes* **46 MAC 550 (99)** *Ciampa* not applied retroactively and no impermissible vouching found in particular plea agreement; "implicit vouching by the Commonwealth will not be readily found");

C v James **424 M 770 (97)**—no need for *Ciampa* instruction because (1) jury not told that agreement to try witness as juvenile was in exchange for "truthful" testimony and (2) witness had already been tried as juvenile & found delinquent, so was not "subject" to the agreement at time of trial;

C v Felder **455 M 359 (2009)**—*Ciampa* instruction not required because witness purportedly did not enter into plea or immunity agreement, but "instead" made agreement "just hours after" murder to tell police what happened on condition that DA protect his safety and dismiss several pending charges (which was done);

C v Fuller **421 M 400 (95)** and *C v Brousseau* **421 M 647 (95)**—no request for *Ciampa* instructions, and either no mention of "truthful testimony" (*Fuller*) or general instruction on credibility sufficient and "truth" not stressed (*Brousseau*);

C v Grenier **415 M 680 (93)**—though no *Ciampa* instruction given, general instruction on credibility, including reference to witnesses' possible interest in outcome of case and bias, = sufficient; here, no bolstering by written plea agreement impliedly vouching "truthful" testimony;

C v Meuse **423 M 831 (96)**—to cure DA's vouching for credibility, only an instruction that argument was WRONG & government could not know whether witness was telling truth would have sufficed;

C v Rolon **438 M 808 (2003)**—[only] because D-counsel in opening statement attacked witness's credibility by purportedly misstating contents of plea agreement, DA could elicit on direct examination that agreement required witness to provide "complete and truthful and accurate testimony";

C v Lindsey **48 MAC 641, 646 (2000)**—DA's vouching, in opening statement, for credibility of co-D rat & informant, not cured/addressed in immediate instruction = part of reason for reversal;

C v Chaleumphong **434 M 70 (2001)**—police witnesses may introduce same prejudice as DAs in vouching for immunized witnesses, but here no relief, because defense counsel's "insistent" questioning said to virtually require cop to answer 'yes' to whether he had "any way of knowing whether the cooperating witnesses were telling the truth," counsel could use answer effectively, & judge gave *Ciampa* instructions; OK (here) for an ADA to testify re: plea agreements with cooperating witnesses;

C v Luna **410 M 131 (91)**—instruction on special scrutiny of testimony of cooperating witness obtained through government offer of prospective rewards set forth;

12-K.18. Sentencing Consequences

C v Gunter **427 M 259 (98)**—instructions should not inform jury of sentencing consequences (invites "result-oriented verdicts" rather than basic G/NG);

C v Ragland **72 MAC 815 (2008)**—after trial in which witnesses recanted their grand jury testimony, jury sent question, "what is the punishment for perjury?", judge

with agreement of all parties responded that jurors were not to concern themselves with any punishment for any crime; particularly because D was not entitled to original instruction that recantation was adverse to witnesses' penal interest (because the evidence supporting witness's awareness of such adversity was objected to, and objection was sustained, & evidence thus stricken), no error because no basis for jury to consider what penal consequences might be; even if initial instruction was proper, it required no amplification, no substantial risk of miscarriage of justice;

C v Ferreira **373 M 116 (77)**—can't instruct on parole/sentencing for murder 1&2;

C v Muckle **59 MAC 631, 643 (2003)**—error to instruct that jury "needed to consider whether the property was worth more than $250 only if you find the defendant guilty, so that I will know the range of sentence the law permits in this case", because it encouraged jury to consider sentences (but error rendered harmless by other instruction);

C v Mutina **366 M 810, 816–23 (75)**—on request, D is entitled to instruction on consequences of NGI verdict;

C v Robbins **422 M 305 (96)**—*Mutina* instruction embellished so as to void its protective effect, i.e., jurors told that in order to obtain D's commitment to mental treatment center, Commonwealth would have to prove beyond reasonable doubt that D was mentally ill **at the time**, & that his discharge would create likelihood of serious harm to self or others: no objection, no relief here;

C v Biancardi **421 M 251 (95)**—reversal due to denial of D's request for specific written instruction on consequences on NGI verdict: judge instead told jury (a) that if they had a question as to consequences of insanity verdict, he would instruct them further, and (b) that if the defendant was insane, "that's the end of the case";

Superior Court Criminal Practice Jury Instructions § 5.6.16—(sentence);

12-K.19. Juror Unanimity

See Chapter 22-F-5, Jury Issues, Specific Unanimity & General Verdicts;

12-K.20. Supplemental Instructions

See Chapter 22-E.3, "Jury Questions, Supplemental Instructions and Readbacks."

C v Johnson **43 MAC 509 (97)**—error in allowing jury to consider/receive info during deliberations about the date grand jury returned indictment not cured by instruction that date was not evidence & should not be considered (inconsistent to give them info & tell them not to consider);

C v Sousa **33 MAC 433 (92)**—counsel's failure to renew objection after supplemental instruction did not waive issue for appeal where supplemental instruction may not have been given in response to counsel's objection to main charge;

C v Conley **34 MAC 50 (93)**—judge should tell jury at beginning & end of supplemental instructions that they are to be considered along with main charge (unless purpose = to correct error in main charge);

C v Wolinski **431 M 228, 233 (2000)**—in response to jury note, "evidence incomplete; cannot decide," judge instructed that jurors were to 'decide case based solely on evidence that was presented and weren't to speculate about any unanswered questions that still remain'; though SJC excused judge's "decision not to repeat statement (about) Commonwealth's burden" then, what **was** said should be argued to run afoul of *C v Bowden* **379 M 472, 485 (80)** (judge may not remove from jury consideration perceived evidentiary deficiencies); but see *C v Tolan* **453 M 634, 652 (2009)**—the two instructions (jurors could consider any deficiencies in investigation and whether they affect quality/reliability of Commonwealth evidence AND jurors not to engage in guesswork about unanswered questions or to "speculate about what the real facts might or might not have been") are correct, conveying recognized principles;

C v Remedor **52 MAC 694, 700–701 (2001)**—judge's response to jury question, i.e., 'confine consideration to evidence that *was* presented,' negated D's "Bowden" (**379 M 472**) defense, creating substantial risk of a miscarriage of justice; cf. *C v Smith* **49 MAC 827 (2000)**—(having allowed defense to argue missing witness inference against prosecution, reversible error to refuse instruction on it and, in response to jury question, to say 'decide only on evidence, don't decide on basis of unanswered questions; judge 'removed from jury's consideration precise issue sought to be raised by D'), contrasting *C v Pratt* **407 M 647, 654, 658 (90)**;

C v Bell **455 M 408 (2009)**—in response to jury question, judge need only consider the question asked, and is not required to instruct on any other matters (despite D's request for additional instruction stressing defense points);

12-K.21. Tuey-Rodriquez "Dynamite" Charge

See Chapter 22-E.5, Jury Issues, Deadlocked Juries & Tuey-Rodriguez Charge;

C v Rodriquez **364 M 87 (73)**—(Tuey-)Rodriquez "dynamite charge";

K. Smith, *Criminal Practice & Procedure*, § 1883 (2d ed. 1983 & supplement)—time when Rodriquez charge should be given;

Superior Court Criminal Practice Jury Instructions § 5.5—(Jury Indecision & Jury Coercion: Deadlocked Jury and the Tuey-Rodriquez Instruction);

C v Webster **391 M 271 (84)**—reverse because judge coerced a juror;

C v Evans **42 MAC 618 (97)**—no coercion found here, but may have been "inappropriate" for judge to comment, before & immediately after empanelment, that case "should" be over & jury finished by noon next day;

C v Martins **38 MAC 636 (95)**—"wrong" for judge to embellish Tuey-Rodriquez charge with admonition that "this case is going to be decided, folks, . . . It's going to be decided by some jury here in Suffolk County," but no relief here;

C v Winbush **14 MAC 680 (82)**—didn't violate c. 234, § 34 (no further deliberations without jury's consent) to twice send back because first time was not after § 34's "due and thorough deliberations"

C v Keane **41 MAC 656 (96)**—same; fact that Tuey-Rodriquez was given only after 2d report of deadlock implied judge's finding only then had deliberations been "due & thorough";

C v Mayne **38 MAC 282 (95)**—similar;

12-L. JURY QUESTIONS

See Chapter 22-E-3, Jury Issues, Jury Questions, Supplemental Instructions & Readbacks, for more complete cases on jury questions;

CPCS P/G 6.9(g)—seek "meaningful" input/hearing on supplementary charge

K. Smith, *Criminal Practice & Procedure*, § 1870 (2d ed. 1983 & Supp.)—OK for procedure agreed to by all to give copy of charge to jury;

C v Baseler **419 M 500 (95)**—judge may allow jury to use audio or video-with-audio tape of jury instructions, even absent parties' consent; tape must be wholly audible & contain entire charge, & judge should instruct jury how to use it, & mark it for identification

C v Patry **48 MAC 470 (2000)**—judge's answering jury questions orally inside the jury deliberating room = violation of 6th Amendment right to public trial, structural error without showing of prejudice; though D can waive right to public trial, D personally must do so (not D counsel); judge shouldn't ever enter jury rooms to conduct the court's business, even with parties' consent or at invitation of jury;

C v Mandeville **386 M 393 (82)**—discretion re: jury getting stenographer's notes after deliberations began because may overemphasize parts of testimony;

C v Webster **391 M 271 (84)**—reverse because judge coerced a juror;

C v Belding **42 MAC 435 (97)**—judge's response ("yes") to jury question (whether "outside residence" was proved if facts were that D was in his own apartment but extended his arm through threshold) was impermissible invasion of jury's province: statute was silent on this point & must be strictly construed (i.e., judge not allowed to "fill-in");

C v Small **10 MAC 606 (80)**—no abuse of discretion not to let D reopen case to answer a jury question because ample chance to offer the evidence earlier;

12-M. PRESERVE APPELLATE RIGHTS

G.L. c. 218, § 27A(h)—invoke, timely, to obtain stenographer for District Court proceedings: request, in writing, addressed to clerk of court, at least 48 hours before stenographer is needed;

District Court Special Rule 211(A)(3)—COUNSEL's responsible for assisting in the creation of an audible record (i.e., speak w/clarity and close to microphones, ask judge to tell others to do so); (A)(4) if case is being appealed, may make motion (can be brought ex parte) to preserve original recording for a longer period; originals of trials, evidentiary hearings G pleas or admissions to sufficient facts, and hearings in care and protection cases, are to be preserved for at least two and one-half years without such motion; (B)(1) covert recordings forbidden;

Hardy v US **375 US 277, 288, 290 (64) (Goldberg, J, concurring)**—"most basic & fundamental tool" of effective appellate advocate is "the complete trial transcript"; availability of a "complete" transcript shouldn't be made to depend on the facts of the case; appointed counsel needs complete transcript to discharge his responsibility; "a lawyer appointed to represent the interests of a defendant should not be required to delegate his responsibility of determining whether error occurred at trial to participants at that trial whose conduct may have formed the very basis for the errors"; the right to notice plain errors or defects "is illusory if no transcript is available at least to one whose lawyer on appeal enters the case after the trial is ended;

Mayer v Chicago **404 US 189, 195 (71)**—where grounds of appeal make out colorable need for complete transcript, burden is on State to show that only a portion of the transcript or an "alternative" will suffice for effective appeal on those grounds;

C v Harris **376 M 74 (78)**—where transcript of criminal case is not available for appeal "through no fault of the parties", new trial not constitutionally required IF trial proceedings can be sufficiently reconstructed;

Parrott v US **314 F.2d 46 (10th Cir. '63)**—unavailability of full transcript made it impossible for appellate court to determine whether errors were harmless, so conviction reversed;

Charpentier v Commonwealth **376 M 80 (78)**—indigent defendant entitled to a complete transcript on appeal;

C v Shea **356 M 358, 361 (69)**—"record" created other than by independent contemporaneous recording opens door to conflicting versions of what occurred at trial, & "the failure to settle these questions satisfactorily might often result in a miscarriage of justice"; "It is conceivable that the defendant in fact suffered no prejudice by the lack of a stenographic record, but as to that we can only speculate. . . . We prefer to resolve any doubts on this score in favor of the defendant(,)" so new trial ordered;

Simmons v State **200 So.2d 619 (Fla. 1967)**—appellants' trial counsel had withdrawn, under circumstances giving little hope for cooperation in obtaining accurate stipulated record; even if cooperative, memories of all parties (incl. trial judge) certainly faded;

C v Harris **371 M 462, 474–76 (76)**—Commonwealth chargeable with unexplained loss of search warrant & supporting affidavit; *C v Marks* Oct 16 1981 MAC disappearance during jury deliberations of exhibits crucial to suggestive ID issue = new trial; Williams, petitioner **378 M 623 (79)** court reporter's neglect = attributable to Commonwealth; delay in preparing transcript may entitle D to stay pending appeal, or even dismissal;

Draper v Washington **372 US 487, 496–97 (63)**—contrasting procedure whereby trial judge recalled and thereafter summarily found what went on at the trial with the "direct scrutiny" afforded by actual trial transcript; prosecutor's affidavit concerning his recollection of trial recognized to be tainted by adversarial interest;

State v Moore **87 N.M. 412 (75)**—absence of transcript of proceedings deprived D of right to appeal where transcript couldn't be prepared due to inaudibility of tape recordings; trial counsel's inability to recall events at trial didn't mean that D should lose appellate claims; conviction reversed;

US v Atilus **425 F2d 816 (5th Cir. '70)**—conviction reversed when, through no fault of D, transcript of trial proceedings was not available; see also *Commonwealth v Norman* **447 Pa. 515 (72)** failure of transcript to contain critical portions of trial may warrant grant of new trial; *Commonwealth v Goldsmith* **452 Pa. 22 (73)** new trial may be required if absence of a record, for whatever reason, makes meaningful appellate review impossible; *State v Robinson* **387 So.2d 1143 (La. 1980)** failure to provide record of trial testimony of two expert witnesses was constitutional and statutory error, & couldn't be found harmless here;

C v Pudder **41 MAC 930 (96)**—trial counsel = responsible for prosecution of D's appeal, **including ordering** cassette tapes of District Court trial, until new attorney files notice of appearance; that counsel's motion to withdraw has been allowed doesn't alter;

C v Woods **419 M 366 (95)**—defense counsel responsible for reconstructing record of inaudible bench conference; mere assertions that objection was there made not accepted by appellate court;

C v Best **50 MAC 722, 729 (2001)**—appellate argument that DA's closing = improper not addressed, since cited argument contained "(inaudible)" notation at critical point;

Foley v Commonwealth **429 M 496 (99)**—appellant SUFFERS THE CONSEQUENCES OF ANY DEFICIENCY IN THE RECORD; counsel must reconstruct record, or file a statement of agreed facts (said to be "most desirable" when a petition under **G.L. c. 211, § 3** "is likely to be brought to the full court"; if no agreed statement can be reached, single justice may transfer case to trial judge for determination;

C v Woody **45 MAC 906 (99)**—appeal will not be dismissed when there's a gap in record through no fault of either party; instead, if gap is material, appellant has burden to "settle the record," but if appellant deems gap not material, he must serve on appellee the available transcript with statement that it's acceptable; if appellee determines that tr. is inadequate and supplemental record is required, burden is on appellee to settle record under App. R 8(c) and (e); if appellate court disagrees with appellant's determination that transcript is sufficient to resolve claims, appellate court may decline to consider claims;

C v Sanchez **74 MAC 31 (2009)**—D's failure to object to order scheduling trial date beyond statutory deadline = waiver of right to trial within statutorily-set period for SDP trial; assertion that "the Commonwealth" has neither "sole responsibility" nor "sole power" to bring D to trial, because "court ultimately sets trial dates";

C v Tanner **417 M 1 (94)**—defense counsel's telling judge that D said juror saw him in shackles = insufficient; counsel had duty to put info "in the form of affidavits"; see also *C v Graves* **35 MAC 76 (93)** and *C v Luna* **46 MAC 90, 95 n.4 (98)** proffers as to why "missing witness" argument & instruction should be barred should be made by one with personal knowledge and under oath (not just counsel proffer);

C v Paiva **71 MAC 411, 415 n.2 (2008)**—when judge barred testimony of defense witness's as sanction for reciprocal discovery violation, counsel should have given reasons for admitting despite absence of notice, and suggested less serious sanction, BUT judge rebuffed counsel's efforts to state grounds for objecting to ruling;

C v Giontzis **47 MAC 450, 455 (99)**—when ADA used a bogus document to devastating effect in cross of D-expert, D-counsel's failure to take further steps after "objection" meant no appellate preservation: counsel should have questioned witness (off stand) to obtain more info to give judge, and told judge of his continuing concern about legitimacy of document/cross-examination (rather than waiting 1–2 days, during which he obtained definitive info about sleaziness);

C v Long **419 M 798, 805 (95)**—if one party makes assertion of fact/present circumstance & adverse party doesn't correct/dispute on record, it will be taken as true on appeal;

C v Charles **57 MAC 595, 598 n.7 (2003)**—when co-D fails to object after another co-D, non-objecting co-D gets review of issue as if preserved: judge was on notice of objection, & facts as to the two Ds weren't different;

C v Mahoney **68 MAC 561, 562 (2007)**—a mistake by counsel that has effect of waiving D's entitlement to a dismissal "would surely constitute a substantial risk of a miscarriage of justice";

Hanlon v Commonwealth **419 M 1005 (95)**—SJC refused to accept in lieu of transcript (or reconstructed record pursuant to App. R. 8(c)) counsel's conclusory assertions that required finding of NG should have been entered for evidentiary insufficiency (and thus that double jeopardy principle barred retrial);

C v Lonardo **74 MAC 566 (2009)**—D's motion in limine to bar "expert" testimony that everyone "on the street" who dealt with "runners" knew that vehicle 'accident' cases they brought to attorneys were "staged"/fraudulent did not preserve issue without "contemporaneous objection to the testimony";

See Chapter 11-B & 11-C, Evidence, for cases on motions in limine, objections, offers of proof, motions to strike & other requirements of record protection; see Chapter 15 for cases on "preservation" requirements for appellate remedies; see also Chapter 20 for requirements of specificity in motions to suppress (e.g., **C v Johnston** 60 MAC 13, 21–22 (2003)—*trial counsel's failure to specify, as precise ground in motion to suppress, that Miranda warnings omitted info that D had right to have attorney present during questioning meant that issue wasn't preserved for appeal: failure might be ineffective assistance of counsel, but Rule 30 motion held necessary to raise here); See Chapter 2–E for cases of ineffective assistance of counsel for failure to raise/preserve meritorious legal arguments;*

C v Whelton **428 M 24 (98)**—motion in limine seeking pretrial evidentiary ruling isn't sufficient to preserve appellate rights, absent a further objection at trial; motion to suppress, however, is reviewable even if no further objection is made at trial;

C v Martin **447 M 274 (2006)**—D's motion to suppress ID, resting on constitutional principles, preserved issue; no need to renew objection after pretrial motion hearing;

C v Oakes **407 M 92 (90)**—motion for required finding of not guilty required to preserve for appeal as-applied challenge to constitutionality of statute;

C v Phetsaya **40 MAC 293 (96)**—failure of counsel to object to declaration of mistrial did not bar double jeopardy claim later: judge had told counsel he was incompetent and ineffective, & such intimidation effectively foreclosed objection;

C v Roberts **433 M 45, 48 (2000)**—limiting instruction must be requested AT TIME EVIDENCE IS ADMITTED; charge conference request is too late, because offering party will have relied on evidence being admitted without limitation, and can't be told otherwise when it's too late to offer other evidence on the issue;

C v Biancardi **421 M 251 (95)**—no waiver of issue concerning requested jury instruction from failure to argue that it was mandatory, from failure to ask that "appellate rights be saved," or from failure to renew request at sidebar after judge's charge to jury;

C v Cutty **47 MAC 671, 677 n.7 (99)**—given judge's "emphatic suppression of any mention of an alibi defense", counsel's failure to request jury instruction on alibi = "understandable";

C v Strahan **39 MAC 928 (95)**—although there is no right of appeal as to a conviction "placed on file" with defendant's consent, this **pro se** D's assent was probably not knowing & intelligent and would not be deemed to have waived appellate rights; but see *C v Stracuzzi* **30 MAC 161, 162 n.1 (91)** if appellate claim applies to the validity of all the convictions (including those placed on file), maybe "appropriate" for appellate court to consider all;

C v Calderon **431 M 21, 28 (2000)**—SJC reversed "filed" conviction as well as others, citing *C v Chappee* **397 M 508, 523 (86)** & *C v O'Brien* **30 MAC 807 n.1 (91)**;

C v Lara **39 MAC 546 (95)**—counsel did not waive objection by failing to persist when initial objections were unsuccessful, or by engaging in damage control necessitated by improper evidence (questioning of witnesses to try to contest whether "irrelevant ethnic label had been properly pinned on" client); **but** *C v Spence* **38 MAC 88 (95)** counsel's withdrawal of objection, in order to obtain benefit from objectionable testimony, forfeits issue on appeal; see also *C v Jordan* **50 MAC 369, 372 (2000)** if failure to object = tactical, enabling some defect to be used to advantage at trial, D won't be allowed to argue on appeal as if objection were made and overruled below;

C v Choice **47 MAC 907 (99)**—when D-counsel pressed for name of individual said by cop-witness to have led cop to D (for buying drugs), and judge said "I'll deny the request," not necessary for counsel to intone "objection" in order to preserve issue for appeal;

C v Roberts **433 M 45, 50 n.6 (2000)**—defense objection purportedly came too late, after witness answered purportedly objectionable question; counsel faulted for not moving to strike answer;

C v Semedo **422 M 716 (98)**—D doesn't waive objection to admission of evidence by cooperating on redaction IF he objects to admission of statements after redaction;

C v Miles **420 M 67, 75 n.6 (95)**—defense counsel's failure to dispute prosecutor's statement at hearing (concerning date on which discovery was given to counsel) caused SJC to accept statements as true; *C v Long* **419 M 798 (95)**—similar, re: defense counsel's unrebutted assertions about "minorities" in jury venire;

C v Fruchtman **418 M 8 (94)**—defense counsel's form response ("defendant is satisfied") at conclusion of jury empanelment was not an abandonment of his earlier stated objections to denial of his peremptory challenges; but see *C v Fernandes* **46 MAC 455 (92)** do not say "OK," when judge denies request for instruction (suggestion here that such filler waives the issue);

C v Beaudry **445 M 577, 587 (2005)**—although objection at close of prosecutor's argument normally preserves argument issue, must object *again*, after jury instruction *if* judge responds to objection with "focused, particularized instructions"; acquiescence or expression of satisfaction with instruction = no preservation of argument issue;

C v Adderley **36 MAC 918 (94)**—judge's refusal to allow counsel to make offer of proof as to testimony which would be given by witness (as to whom judge erroneously refused issuance of a bench warrant) caused appellate court to assume that the witness would recall desired evidence, would have supported D's alibi, and would have been helpful to defense;

C v Frank **433 M 185, 193 (2001)**—offer of proof needed when judge sustains prosecutor's objection to question asked of D on direct;

C v Kelly **417 M 266 (94)**—if D objects properly to DA's closing argument, he's entitled to appellate review "as of right"; not required to object after jury instructions or to renew request for curative instructions; but see *C v Burns* **49 MAC 677, 683 (2000)** improper to argue substantive use of grand jury testimony, with which witness was only impeached; inadequate preservation despite objection, because D failed to object again after judge merely instructed jury (ineffectually, non-curatively) that their memories of evidence controlled;

C v Boyajian **68 MAC 866 (2007)**—to preserve issue concerning DA's argument, must object BEFORE jury retires to deliberate, though not necessary to interrupt argument of DA with the objection;

C v Talbot **35 MAC 766 (94)**—failure to object to DA's closing argument hurts D in 2 ways: (1) standard of review on appeal = relief only if there's substantial risk of miscarriage of justice; (2) absence of objection supports inference that "tone, manner, and substance of" argument were **not** actually harmful;

C v Johnson **46 MAC 398 (99)**—same; cf. *C v Masello* **428 M 446 (98)**—because appellate court might not be able to discern prejudice on "written transcript only," place on record what you observed, e.g., DA waving his arms, speaking extra loudly, or particular reaction to error by one or more jurors;

C v Pagano **47 MAC 55 (99)**—failure to object to first 3 improper questions (next 2 questions received objections, which were sustained) and move to strike answers given meant no relief for D on appeal;

C v Watkins **63 MAC 69 (2005)**—despite fact that trial was to a judge rather than jury, counsel was required to object to judge's questioning of witness in order to preserve issue for appeal;

C v Crimmins **46 MAC 489, 492 n.5 (99)**—if no motion for required finding of NG was made in trial court, or when such motion was argued on grounds different from those argued on appeal, standard of review is "substantial risk of miscarriage of justice", and ENTIRE RECORD (rather than just Commonwealth evidence) will be used for this analysis, i.e. prosecution's case may be strengthened by D's evidence; but *C v Grandison* **43 M 135, 140 n.8 (2001)** findings based on legally insufficient evidence create substantial risk of a miscarriage of justice, so appellate court considers sufficiency even without motion for required finding of NG below;

See Chapter 12-G, Motion for Required Finding of Not Guilty, & Chapter 15, Post-Conviction Remedies (Renew Motion for Required Finding NG, New Trial, Reduce to Lesser Included Offense), & Chapter 14-T re: Revise/Revoke, Stay, (Cedar Junction) sentence appeal;

CPCS P/G 8.1-8.7—ADVISE D about motion to re-voke & revise & appeal); implement client's decision (e.g., seek tape/transcript/stay); counsel's responsible until new attorney's in case;

Pires v Commonwealth **373 M 829 (77)**—counsel must tell D of right to appeal, give professional judgment of merits, & protect rights;

Roe v Flores-Ortega **528 US 470 (2000)**—defense counsel must advise and counsel D about appellate rights; ineffective assistance to fail to so counsel if there is reason to think either (1) that a rational D would want to appeal, or (2) that this particular D reasonably demonstrated to counsel that he was interested in appealing;

Superior Court Rule 65—after G., court advises of appeal right & COUNSEL responsible for perfecting/prosecuting until relieved after hearing on motion to withdraw; 20 days for appeal to Appellate Division (state prison sentence);

M.R.App.P. 4—notice of appeal within 30 days; may file in trial court motion for leave to late-file within 30 days after expiration of the 30-day appeal period, if "excusable neglect"; thereafter, for up to one year after G or sentencing, if sentencing occurs later, may file in appellate court a motion for leave to late-file notice of appeal (and must actually file the notice of appeal thereafter); period of time for filing notice of appeal may not be enlarged beyond one year from date of judgment or order appealed from (**M.R.App.P 4**, and **14(b)**).

C v White **429 M 258 (99)**—MUST FILE NOTICE OF APPEAL WITHIN ONE YEAR AFTER guilty verdict (or sentencing, if it occurs later), or denial of motion for new trial; IF notice is filed within that year, motion for leave to late-file may be allowed, belatedly, after expiration of the year; fact that counsel receives notice of motion denial by mail does not alter deadline (time runs from date of order, not from date of its receipt, and "mailbox rule" doesn't apply to add 3 days);

M.R.App.P. 8—record reconstruction transcription of audiotape record, etc;

C v George **25 MAC 1001 (88)**—Superior Court judge's allowance of late-filing of notice of appeal after 30 days = "nullity"; so D must go to single justice (**M.R. App. P. 14**: within 1 year).

Chapter 13
PLEAS AND PLEA BARGAINING

13-A. PLEA BARGAINING—DEFENSE COUNSEL'S ROLE

See also Chapter 2, Standards, e.g., 2-D, "Control, Direction, & Client's Objectives";

CPCS P/G 5.1-12—should explore alternatives to trial; complete investigation & preparation; complete candor with D; can try persuading D; no plea just because D admits or good disposition; or without fact basis, admission, or Alford;

Padilla v Kentucky **130 S Ct 1473 (2010)—deportation is a "penalty," and a severe one, not simply a "collateral consequence" of criminal proceeding;** Sixth Amendment requires defense counsel to provide *affirmative* (i.e., not just silence) competent advice to a noncitizen D regarding immigration consequences of a guilty plea (& absent such advice, noncitizen may raise claim of ineffective assistance of counsel); there is duty to inquire about citizenship/immigration status initially; *duty to investigate/advise about immigration consequences of plea alternatives and sentencing alternatives;*

Superior Court Standing Order 2-86—DA to make dispositional recommendation in pretrial conference report (to remain "outstanding" for "only" 45 days from date of filing, or 60 days if there was no probable cause hearing; D counsel obligated to confer with client, disclose recommendation; on day of pretrial conference, probation dep't. must tell if D's suitable for probation & must give sentence guideline form to all counsel, "based upon the mate-rials furnished . . . by counsel"; judge must "foster" (constitutional) negotiations;

Aetna v Niziolek **395 M 737 (85)**—G. plea admissible, not conclusive, in later civil suit; but G. finding after trial = conclusive later (cf. M.R.Crim.P. 12, nolo contendere, below);

Wynne v Rosen **391 M 797 (84)**—no false arrest suit unless get equivalent of NG;

Immigration consequences—(*see Chapter 14-A*)

SJC Rule 3:07, 1.2(a)—must seek client's lawful objectives;

ABA Standards for Criminal Justice, Prosecution Function & Defense Function (3d ed. 1993) 4-6.1(b) & Comment—unprofessional to over/understate risks of trial or plea to D; must investigate/advise fully/candidly; 4-6.2, it's D's decision (not counsel's, but counsel must fully consult with D) re: what pleas to enter & whether to accept a plea agreement; 4-6.1 & commentary - duty to explore disposition without trial, & discuss = norm; D's guilt not relevant & counsel doesn't make moral judgments re: guilt; 4-3.8 (b) counsel should explain case to extent necessary to permit client to make informed decisions; 4-4.1—duty to investigate facts relevant to merits of case & the penalty if convicted, e.g., D needs to know probability of conviction if trial, requiring careful evaluation of any problems of proof & possible defenses;

C v Facella **42 MAC 354 (97)**—lawyer's contingent fee agreement, while contrary to (then-existing) SJC Rule 3:08, did not invalidate D's guilty pleas;

C v Indelicato **40 MAC 944 (96)**—attorney erroneously advised that G pleas would not bar future license to carry firearm; little known quirk in interplay of state & federal law barred licensing of D ("a felon") even though plea crimes were misdemeanors per **state** law; no ineffective assistance of counsel, no involuntariness of plea;

McAleney v US **539 F.2d 282 (CA1 '76)**—duty to give accurate & complete info (re: DA's recommendation); otherwise maybe unfit; (*see Chapter 14-V, e.g., Parole*);

C v Ewe **43 MAC 901 (97)**—written plea agreement by which D's mandatory minimum 15 year sentence for trafficking would be reduced because of his "cooperation" failed to bind DA to the degree of reduction believed by D & D counsel to be merited; beware term allotting prosecutor "sole discretion" in this particular;

C v Pelletier **449 M 392 (2007)**—if D is willing to plead guilty to the "underlying offense" part of a complaint, but refuses to accept "subsequent offense portion of the charge," the change of plea colloquy must be followed by trial on existence of prior offenses;

C v Cepulonis **9 MAC 302 (80)**—bad parole advice might invalidate a plea, but probably not unless D relied on it: *see further cases, Chapter 13-E below*, & issue re: counsel's ineffectiveness in misstating parole consequences;

SJC Rule 3:07, 1.14 "Client Under A Disability"—attorney to maintain as normal a lawyer-client relationship as possible with possibly "impaired" client (e.g., youth, mental disability); alert for competency problems, possibly consult others (see 1.6(a) shall not reveal confidential info re: representation of client unless client consents "except for disclosures . . . impliedly authorized in order to carry out the representation," with exceptions in paragraph 1.6(b)); 4.1: no knowingly false statement to 3d party (*see Standards & Ethics, Chapter 2*);

ABA Model Rule of Professional Conduct (83) 1.14—try to maintain normal relationship with impaired client; if can't, ask guardian; 1.6: confidentiality exception for disclosures "impliedly authorized to carry out the representation"; Comment—disclosures facilitating satisfactory negotiations are "impliedly authorized";

C v DelVerde **398 M 288 (86)**—incompetent D can't plead through (guardian &) "substitute judgment" because can't show factual basis (especially responsibility) & no right to plead G.

C v Facella **42 MAC 354 (97)**—fee agreement by which D counsel was paid solely to negotiate plea bargain and in which higher recompense was tied to lower sentence was unethical (but did not invalidate G plea);

DANGER DANGER *C v Luce* **34 MAC 105, 111–12 (93)**—"meetings between the defendant and his counsel and government officers did not constitute plea bargaining that would be inadmissible under M.R.Crim.P. 12(f)"; in context of D's offers of assistance and/or boasts of knowledge which will be helpful to police, GET IT IN WRITING beforehand that no such statements may be admitted against him;

US v Bump **605 F.2d 548 (10th Cir. '79)**—DA can cross-examine D about evidence promised by attorney in plea bargaining because disclosure ended privilege;

C v Lewin (II) **407 M 629 (90)**—murder D's statement that he was willing to plead guilty to manslaughter was inadmissible because not an unequivocal admission or confession & because more prejudicial than probative;

C v DoVale **57 MAC 657 (2003)**—no error in barring, as evidence of "consciousness of innocence," D's refusal to accept motion judge's proffer of a plea bargain to "time served";

C v Chetwynde **31 MAC 8 (91)**—D counsel's lie (that motion to suppress had been filed & denied) made ensuing G plea involuntary; but see *C v DiPietro* **35 MAC 638 (93)**—same lie by D counsel, but refusal to allow G plea withdrawal unless D could establish that lie caused G plea and that counsel provided ineffective assistance in failing to file motion to suppress (i.e. that motion to suppress should have been allowed if filed); *Chetwynde* distinguished as having motion to suppress requiring factual resolutions, so its merit could not be gauged without the suppression hearing; *DiPietro's* motion to suppress = solely questions of law;

C v Walker **443 M 867, 871 (2005)**—if D's plea counsel gives plainly incorrect advice & D relies on it in tendering G plea, it's ineffective assistance & plea is not necessarily "intelligent/knowing"; "constitutional infirmity would create a substantial risk of a miscarriage of justice"; advice here, i.e., that judge's denial of suppression motion presented no appellate issue, wasn't ineffective assistance of counsel because it wasn't "patently wrong" at the time;

C v Moreau **30 MAC 677 (91), cert. denied 502 US 1049 (92)**—counsel's failure to offer mitigating evidence before joint recommendation submitted & to inform D of its terms may have been ineffective assistance;

C v Mahar **442 M 11 (2004)**—a criminal defendant may challenge sentence on ground of ineffective assistance of counsel re: decision to reject plea bargain offer (but no ineffectiveness shown here);

See also *"No Prior Record, Your Honor"* in Chapter 4, Arraignment;

See Chapter 14, Dismissal re: *offer to drop charges for D's civil release;*

13-B. PLEA BARGAINING—D.A.'S ROLE

SJC 3:07, 4.2—lawyer shall not communicate about the subject of the representation with a person the lawyer knows to be represented by another lawyer in the matter, unless the lawyer has the consent of the other lawyer; 4.1

no knowingly false statement of fact or law, & no failure to disclose a material fact; M.R.Crim.P. 12(b): can't promise sentence, only recommendation;

C v Hurst **39 MAC 603 (96)**—DA's plea negotiations with D absent written waiver of counsel = error but no dismissal with prejudice unless factual finding that Ds had not meant to waive counsel, & had suffered prejudice;

See Chapter 6 re: DA's obligation to disclose unavailability of a witness;

ABA Standards for Criminal Justice, Prosecution Function & Defense Function 3-4.1 & Commentary—DA should make known a general policy of willingness to consult with defense re: dispo. by plea, but no obligation to make concessions; 3-4.2 unprofessional to fail to comply with plea bargain absent extenuating circumstances; 3-3.9 DA not obliged to present all charges, e.g., if has reasonable doubt, less harm, punishment's disproportionate, complaining witness's motives improper or is reluctant, D cooperates, D prosecuted elsewhere; should not bring charges greater than reasonably supportable; 3-6.1 fairness, not severity of sentences = index of effectiveness;

K. Smith, *Criminal Practice & Procedure,* **§§ 1203–13 (2d ed. 1983 & Supp.)**—overview;

Superior Court Standing Order 2-86, section III—DA to make dispo recommendation at pretrial conference, recommendation to remain open for at least 45 days (or 60 days if there was no probable cause hearing) see also section V.;

Weatherford v Bursey **429 US 545 (77)**—no constitutional right to plea bargain; (& see *DelVerde* **398 M 288 (86)** that D was incompetent by reason of mental retardation (and would likely never be competent), and couldn't therefore accept a plea-bargained resolution, deprived him of no "right," and court wouldn't approve use of 'substituted judgment' in a criminal action (though here it would enable D's lawyer or guardians to act for him and plead guilty);

US v Benchimol **471 US 453 (85)**—DA need not make plea bargain recommendation "enthusiastically" unless promised;

Correale v US **479 F.2d 944 (1st Cir. '73)**—DA's falsehood not OK though good faith;

C v Tirrell **382 M 502 (81)**—higher sentencing recommendation after trial not vindictive;

Bordenkircher v Hayes **434 US 357 (78)**—unless "vindictive" DA may reindict for "habitual" because D will not plead;

US v Goodwin **457 US 368 (82)**—can indict for felony after plea bargain rejected on misdemeanor (*see Chapter 1-B, Court Hierarchy, & Chapter 19, Double Jeopardy*);

C v Smith **384 M 519 (81)**—DA can usually withdraw offer; (but see Superior Court Standing Rule 2-86: DA's pretrial conference recommendation "shall remain outstanding" for 45 days from report's filing, or 60 days from report's filing if there was no probable cause hearing);

Commonwealth v Johnson **447 M 1018 (2006)**—invoking analogy to contract law, in which "offeror is or-dinarily free to revoke his offer at any time before it is accepted," SJC says there is no intrinsically implied promise to hold plea bargain offer open "for a reasonable time" (& here it was left open, anyway, for two full business days); trial judge erred in enforcing offer when there was no detrimental reliance upon it by D;

Santobello v NY **404 US 257 (71)**—detrimental reliance by D (on DA's promise), so "contract" enforced;

C v Benton **356 M 447 (69)**—reliance; "sovereign held to highest ethics"; so agreement's enforced;

C v O'Brien **35 MAC 827 (94)**—DA's alleged promise (prior to complaint's issuance) to bring sexual assault case only in District Court (indecent assault and battery rather than rape) with D agreeing to waive initial bench trial caused no detrimental reliance: no enforcement therefore unless "required to vindicate principles of fairness encompassed in the notion of due process of law";

C v Eaton **11 MAC 732 (81)**—no showing DA promised dismissal after continuance without a finding, so nothing enforceable;

C v Reddy **74 MAC 304 (2009)**—on 4 District Ct charges, D wanted only cc sentences to run with sentence in unrelated case on which he was being held on parole violation detainer; DA wanted 2½ years H.C.; judge told D he couldn't order "cc" on parole violation case because sentence had not yet been imposed on it; D wanted continuance to accomplish that, and judge scheduled for change of plea, to be "within 30 days", which did not happen; DA indicted D as habitual offender (exposed to mandatory 20-year sentence): appeals court reversed judge's dismissal of indictments: DA had made no promise on which D reasonably could rely (& judge here made factual finding that there was no evidence of "vindictiveness" or "bad faith" of Commonwealth); but see on further review 457 M 1002 (2010);

C v Ewe **43 MAC 901 (97)**—written plea agreement in fact left Commonwealth with "sole discretion" to decide how much of a reduction in charge and sentence D's cooperation merited; that D & his attorney believed strongly that D deserved greater reduction = irrelevant;

Blaikie v DA **375 M 613 (78)**—no reliance by D on offer, so not enforceable;

C v Pelletier **62 MAC 145 (2004)**—plea bargain called for filing some charges without a change in plea, and for D to receive, upon guilty pleas, consecutive sentences totaling six years, with four years of probation from and after that incarceration, and one conviction filed with D's consent; written agreement required D not to request parole until after having been incarcerated for three years, so when she was paroled after two years, OK for judge to enforce agreement by allowing DA to bring forward filed conviction & sentencing D to the extra year on that conviction; rejecting without reasoned analysis D's argument that judge/DA interfered with executive function of parole board (see *Amirault* **415 M 112, 117 (93)**);

US v Papaleo **853 F.2d 16 (1st Cir. '88)**—contract rules apply to plea bargain, but exchange of offers (vs. unilateral contract) not binding until D pleads G.;

C v St. John **173 M 566 (1899)**—no enforcement of police agreement (to drop charge because D confessed & turned state's evidence);

C v Fanelli **412 M 497 (92)**—prosecutor's constantly raising sentence recommendation during plea negotiations condemned as "dishonorable";

Doe v DA for Plymouth District **29 MAC 671 (91)**—D's detrimental reliance on plea bargain sufficient even if guilty plea not yet entered; enforcement of plea bargain is part of criminal proceeding & should not be brought as mandamus or separate civil action;

C v Parzyck **41 MAC 195 (96)**—plea agreement concerned Superior Court & District Court cases & DA agreed to recommend concurrent time in District Court matters after G plea in Superior Court; when judge exceeded DA's recommendation in District Court (by ordering sentences from & after, rather than sentences concurrent with Superior Court case sentences), R.30 motion eventually allowed withdrawal of District Court pleas; so D was put to trial & found G; DA **could not then** recommend consecutive sentence on District Court cases. Remedy was not, however, withdrawal of G pleas in Superior Court cases, but instead resentencing in District Court before different judge with DA recommending sentences to be concurrent with Superior Court cases, i.e., specific performance/enforcement of plea bargain;

C v Mr. M. **409 M 538 (91)**—evidentiary hearing required to determine if D reasonably believed cooperation would result in recommendation of "street time" & whether D relied to his detriment; police role in plea-bargaining discussed;

C v Colon **408 M 419 (90)**—plea agreements with cooperating witnesses should not require conformity with prior statements but rather with truth; safeguards in *C v Ciampa* **406 M 257 (89)** must be followed;

C v Sullivan **410 M 521 (91)**—references in plea agreement to cooperating witness's obligation to testify truthfully should be minimized upon defense request;

13-C. PLEA BARGAINING—JUDGE'S ROLE

M.R.Crim.P. 12, Reporter's Notes (b)(2)—judge may not participate in negotiations; & . . .

K. Smith, *Criminal Practice and Procedure*, § 1212 (2d ed. 1983 & Supp.)—(same) (& see *Damiano* **14 MAC 615 at n.7 (82)**); but see ABA Standards for Criminal Justice (2d ed. 1986), Pleas of Guilty 14-3.3 (82): judge can be "moderator" & tell "acceptable" sentence (reversing prior ABA position); judge to be told of all agreements; judge shan't convey to D or counsel that G plea should be entered or plea agreement should be accepted;

Superior Court Standing Order 2-86—pretrial conference judge shall "foster" (constitutional) plea negotiations;

C v Hogan **426 M 424 (98)**—refusing to find actual bias against juvenile D from transfer judge's discussions with prosecutor and coD's counsel and coD's ensuing testimony for Commonwealth in exchange for remaining in juvenile system; judges nonetheless "remind(ed) not to participate as active negotiators in plea bargaining discussions";

C v Ford **35 MAC 752 (94)**—refusal to vacate convictions (by jury) on ground of purported "presumptive bias" of judge (who apparently attempted to coerce G pleas): no specified trial behavior showed actual bias and sentence after trial was not extreme departure from judge's suggested dispo on plea & far less than DA's recommendation;

C v DelVerde **398 M 288 (86)**—must find "strong factual basis" for plea; & consider interests of society & victims;

Foley v District Court **398 M 800 (86)**—(etc., *see Chapter 14-B*) judge can't suggest dismissal if D agrees not to sue cops (but see *Klein* **400 M 309 (87)** can reopen continuance without a finding because of D's civil suit (because deal was D's suggestion));

C v Colon-Cruz **393 M 150 (84)**—law (or judge) can't threaten more penalty if jury trial;

Longval v Meachum **693 F.2d 236 (1st Cir. '82)**—judge can't coerce plea by threat of longer sentence after trial;

Letters v C **346 M 403 (63)**—mid-trial threat of a consecutive sentence coerced the G plea;

C v Carter **50 MAC 902 (2000)**—judge coerced G plea by promising D "the whole twenty," i.e., the maximum penalty, if jury convicted, but offering six years to six and a day for G plea;

C v Damiano **14 MAC 615 (82)**—no coercion by threat of severity after trial;

C v Bowen **63 MAC 579 (2005)**—although D & attorney's affidavits on motion to withdraw G plea claimed judge agreed to sentence of 8–10 years with consecutive term of probation if D pled G, but threatened 25–30 year sentence if G after trial, judge abused discretion in allowing motion simply for "concern [about] alleged coercion", in an "exercise of caution"; Mass. R. Crim. P. 30(b) has more explicit standards, requiring explicit factual findings; at n.5—circumstances here "emphasize the delicate caution" required of judge re: plea bargaining between DA & defense counsel;

C v Berrios **447 M 701 (2006)**—guilty plea not involuntary simply because D felt that he had no choice but to so plead; consideration of the gravity of charges and possible sentences is "endemic to any system which asks a person to forgo certain rights in order to be spared certain penalties"; that D chose to forgo a "viable defense" did not make situation unique and redressable;

C v Federico **40 MAC 616 (96)**—despite its "derailing" effect, not improper for judge to advise D, during colloquy, that Commonwealth could move to have D declared SDP; this was true at the time, and judge had **obligation** under Crim.R. 12(c)(3)(B) to inform D of this possible consequence of G plea; (prior to R 12(c)(3), see *C v Morrow* **363 M 601 (73)** need factual basis for G; plea OK though no parole & SDP warning;)

NC v Pearce **395 US 711 (69)**—after retrial, judge can't increase sentence only because D appealed; (*see Chapter 19, Double Jeopardy; & Chapter 1-B, Court Hierarchy*);

Blackledge v Perry **417 US 21 (74)**—can't retaliate because D appealed;

Texas v McCollough **475 US 134 (86)**—longer sentence after retrial = OK here;

C v Gordon **410 M 498 (91)**—judges may not accept guilty pleas to lesser included offense (here, murder 2) over Commonwealth objection;

C v Doe **412 M 815 (92)**—trial judge's reduction of multiple trafficking charges to enforce plea bargain vacated where Commonwealth promised only to give D "consideration," but not to recommend reduced charges, where D did receive bail reduction for his cooperation, & where consecutive sentences could have been imposed; cf. *C v Norrell* **423 M 725 (96)** judge cannot order continuance without a finding following bench trial & a finding of sufficient facts if Commonwealth objects; cf. *C v Burr* **33 MAC 637 (92)** after jury conviction of trafficking >100 grams, judge could not reduce (R.25(b)(2)) conviction to a lesser trafficking amount (& thus sentence) when drug weight was not in issue; (*see also Chapter 7-M, Misconduct of Judges*);

C v Pelletier **449 M 392 (2007)**—if D is willing to plead guilty to the "underlying offense" part of a complaint, but refuses to accept "subsequent offense portion of the charge," the change of plea colloquy must be followed by trial on existence of prior offenses; judge cannot play loose and frustrate DA's Executive branch powers to implicitly reduce charge to "first" offender status;

C v Lawrence **404 M 378 (89)**—judges have discretion not to accept *Alford* (**400 US 25 (70)**, i.e., if judge permits, can plead G though deny guilt) pleas;

C v Gendraw **55 MAC 677 (2002)**—no abuse of discretion in either the policy of one judge (to never accept Alford plea) or the policy of a second judge (to accept Alford plea only where D claims lack of memory);

C v Vascovitch **40 MAC 62 (96)**—judge can't dismiss motor vehicle larceny charge over DA's objection, even while ordering restitution to victim: violation of separation of powers and of G.L. c. 266, §§ 28–29 (motor vehicle larceny culprit must pay restitution in addition to punishment **and** such complaint not to be filed or continued without a finding);

13-D. ADMITTING TO SUFFICIENT FACTS—"ASF"

See Chapter 13-A, re: counsel's role & CPCS Performance Guidelines (admission to sufficient facts same as G. plea);

M.R.Crim.P. 12 (a)(3)—may admit to sufficient facts in jury-waived session after NG plea;

C v Crapo **212 M 209 (12)**—no de novo appeal after D Court plea G = historical reason for 'admitting sufficient facts', but de novo appeal procedure eliminated by legislature;

ABA Standards for Criminal Justice, Prosecution Function & Defense Function (3d ed. 1993) 4-5.2—D decides what plea to enter;

C v Hinds **101 M 209 (1869)**—NG not foreclosed after admission to sufficient facts;

C v Norrell **423 M 725 (96)**—judge cannot order continuance without a finding following bench trial & a finding of sufficient facts if Commonwealth objects;

C v Pyles **423 M 717 (96)**—continuance without a finding, over DA's objection, can be allowed after admission to sufficient facts/offer to plead G (rejecting Commonwealth's argument that continuance without a finding violated separation of powers, because judge ordered it after DA did not agree to D's requested disposition);

C v Nydam **21 MAC 66 (85)**—reasonable doubt standard; admission to sufficient facts and guilty finding at jury of six waives appellate review of all non-jurisdictional issues, so colloquy required;

C v Mahadeo **397 M 314 (86)**—without "de novo" appeal, admitting to sufficient facts is equivalent to guilty plea, so need immigration colloquy; (fn. 2: jury waiver = optional!);

C v Brady **59 MAC 784 (2003)**—in "essentially a criminalized civil dispute" about tenants' authority to remove a door which they had installed, judge interrupted trial to propose disposition of restitution which wasn't subsequently paid, prompting judge to enter G finding & sentence of 15 days, suspended with condition that money be paid: absence of "important formalities" required for guilty plea or admission to sufficient facts meant "G" illegitimate; further double jeopardy barred retrial;

US v Nicholas **133 F.3d 133 (1st Cir. '98)**—admission to sufficient facts preceding continuance without a finding, if accompanied by a Duquette waiver (**386 M 834 (82)**) = legitimate basis for enhanced sentence under federal sentencing guidelines;

C v Villalobos **52 MAC 903 (2001), on further review: 437 M 797 (2002)**—continuance without a finding = same as conviction for federal immigration purposes (per 1996 amendment to 8 USC § 1101(a)(48)(A); admission to sufficient facts is functional equivalent of guilty plea for purpose of requiring immigration warnings pursuant to G.L c. 278, § 29D, so judges should warn Ds that continuances without a finding (as well as convictions) can have the immigration consequences identified in G.L. c. 278, § 29D; suggested language for modified warning given;

C v Estrada **69 MAC 514 (2007)**—"That Federal immigration law may work an unfortunate and harsh result is not a basis for vacating admissions or convictions that are otherwise lawful in all respects"; failure to inquire whether D is under influence of alcohol, drugs at time of admission or plea does not alone warrant vacating admission/plea;

C v Mele **20 MAC 958 (85)**—colloquy required (bench session if no de novo jury "appeal" by D);

C v Hoyle **67 MAC 10 (2006)**—D, seeking to withdraw G pleas made 15 years earlier, not entitled to *Mele* holding because his G pleas occurred before *Mele*; no relief, either, on consideration of whether justice "may not have been done" because no evidence pleas not voluntarily & intelligently tendered, and D received very favorable disposition;

M.R.Crim.P. 12(c)(6) and (d)—withdrawal process not (explicitly) for admitting to sufficient facts; but . . .

District Court Standards of Judicial Practice, Sentencing and Other Dispositions (1984) 3:01, Comment—judge should tell D before admission to sufficient facts that judge not bound by agreed recommendation; otherwise permit withdrawal of admission to sufficient facts if will exceed; (*see Chapter 13-E*);

C v Crosby **6 MAC 679 (78)**—jeopardy on admission to sufficient facts (if witness testifies) (*see Chapter 19, Double Jeopardy*);

C v DeFuria **400 M 485 (87)**—no jeopardy if facts are given by ADA, rather than in sworn testimony;

C v Duquette **386 M 834 (82)**—admission to sufficient facts & continuance without a finding in District Court bench session preserves jury right to trial de novo when there is no jury trial waiver and no G-plea colloquy; (NOTE: waiver not mandatory!; can still admit to sufficient facts without it); failure to ensure that (tape) record was preserved doesn't shift to D constitutional burden on voluntariness; but see also . . .

C v Russell **37 MAC 152 (94)**—federal D facing enhanced sentence, in effort to vacate Mass. conviction, argued on R.30 error in failing to conduct *Duquette* colloquy, but Duquette not given "retroactive effect" (and this D knew, from prior experience, what he was giving up);

C v Monteiro **75 MAC 280 (2009)**—though defense counsel wanted to preserve appellate rights on denial of suppression motion by "jury-waived trial on stipulated evidence," and police report was admitted, along with stipulation that firearm worked, colloquy with D failed to establish D knew he was waiving rights to confrontation, cross-examination, testify, against self-incrimination, call witnesses: convictions reversed;

13-E. PLEA OF GUILTY—PROCEDURES

Boykin v Alabama **395 US 238 (69)**—G. plea waives self-incrimination, jury, & confrontation: record must show voluntary & intelligent waiver;

C v Foster **368 M 100 (75)**—same;

C v Hubbard **456 M *** (5/27/2010)**—written jury trial waiver is not required to enter valid guilty plea; absence of written waiver doesn't violate G.L. c. 263, § 6 or M.R.Crim.P. 19(a);

C v Lopez **447 M 625 (2006)**—rejecting D's appellate argument that his multi-day jury trial was essentially a guilty plea requiring plea colloquy, given that he was very adversely impacted at trial by his testimony, his acknowledged confessions to police, and his testimony at codefendants' trials; "it is axiomatic that, if [D] does not plead guilty and . . . waive these rights, the judge need not conduct a plea colloquy"; cite to *US v Escandar* 465 F.2d 438, 442–43 (5th Cir. 1972) (as matter of federal law, no colloquy was required when D inculpated himself at trial);

See cases in Chapter 13-E.3, below

CPCS P/G 5.3—be sure D fully understands, & is prepared for colloquy;

C v Williams **71 MAC 348 (2008)**—in "hindsight," better to state on record basis for permitting resumption of plea colloquy or basis for proceeding without further probing D's change of heart (after D said he was pleading guilty because couldn't get fair trial, because counsel was not prepared, judge said he would not accept plea, but then

permitted counsel to confer with D, and subsequently resume G plea); denial of motion to withdraw G plea affirmed;

Superior Court Standing Order 2-86—after commencement of trial, G plea can be entered in trial session only by leave of assignment judge (§ IV); trial judge may not "accept offers to plead" in trial session without good faith and cause;

M.R.Crim.P. 12(c)—Guilty Plea Procedure; id. (3) "Notice of Consequences of Plea" includes, (B) "where appropriate," the maximum possible sentence on the charge and possibility of community parole supervision for life, any different or additional punishment based upon subsequent offense or sexually dangerous persons provisions, and where applicable that D may be required to register as sex offender, and of mandatory minimum sentence, if any, on the charge;

K. Smith, *Criminal Practice and Procedure*, Chapter 22 (2d ed. 1983 & Supp.)—general discussion, e.g., colloquy (§ 1238);

North Carolina v Alford **400 US 25 (70)**—can plead G though deny guilt (if judge permits);

C v Dilone **385 M 281 (82)**—Alford plea = judge's discretion; (see K. Smith, *Criminal Practice & Procedure*, § 1247 (2d ed. 1983 & Supp.));

C v Gendraw **55 MAC 677 (2002)**—no abuse of discretion in judge's policy never to accept Alford plea, or in different judge's policy to accept Alford plea only when D claims lack of memory of crime;

C v Nikas **431 M 453 (2000)**—13 years after G plea to second degree murder (while maintaining innocence pursuant to *NC v Alford* **400 US 25 (1970)** and saying his attorney told him he didn't "stand a chance in hell" if he went to trial), plea judge allowed R. 30 motion, and SJC aff'd allowance; attorney's record statements in response to 'chance in hell' didn't establish that D knew relevant LAW (only that he'd read police reports, grand jury testimony, etc.), so failure of judge to explain adequately either murder one or murder two elements (and incorrect explanation re: distinction between the two) = involuntary G plea; rejecting Commonwealth argument that "strength of evidence against D" meant that D adequately understood the charge;

See Chapter 13-A, Defense Counsel's Role;

C v Desrosier **56 MAC 348 (2002)**—can plead G if advised of all elements of offense, even if can't remember incident; though judge on Rule 30 motion allowed withdrawal of G plea because plea judge hadn't advised of all elements, appeals court reversed: D's plea counsel testified that he had explained & discussed all possible theories with D;

District/Municipal Court Rules of Crim.P. 4(c)—re: procedure for G or admission to sufficient facts;

CPCS P/G 5.4—advise client of plea consequences, e.g., recidivist sentencing & parole rules (including parole discretion & uncertainty (*see Chapter 14*)); Sex Offender Registration Information & Dissemination (G.L. c. 6, §§ 178C–178P); "Sexually Dangerous Person" status (G.L. c. 123A);

C v Murphy **73 MAC 57 (2008)**—when pleading G to home invasion and armed assaults in dwelling, judge told D of sentencing range applicable to each indictment "if [D] were to receive a committed prison sentence"; D, however, received straight probation, and when he violated its terms found himself serving the mandatory sentence of twenty years to twenty years and one day (and concurrent life terms, the maximum sentence, for each count of armed assault in dwelling); denial of motion to withdraw guilty pleas upheld, even though "risk" that colloquy did not "adequately" convey that the minimum-maximum sentences applied not only if he were to receive "committed" sentence but "remained applicable if he received straight probation" and did not successfully complete it;" noticeably absent" from D's motion was affidavit from plea attorney supporting D's claim of lack of understanding;

C v Glines **40 MAC 95 (96)**—G plea was made knowingly and voluntarily where D knew he would serve five years if he violated probation;

C v McGuirk **376 M 338 (78)**—elements must be explained by judge or by counsel; judge must be satisfied D admits unexplained elements;

C v Jones **60 MAC 88 (2003)**—"facts" were not read in court, and there was no on-record advice re: elements of assault and battery and intimidation of witness: bad plea,

despite Commonwealth's argument that D's and his attorney's signatures on "green sheet"/"waiver of rights" form averred that D was aware of nature and elements of charges to which he was pleading G, and that counsel had explained to D the law regarding jury waiver "and other rights"; signatures inadequate to establish that D had requisite knowledge;

C v Brannon B **66 MAC 97 (2006)**—no error in refusing to allow withdrawal of G plea two months afterward: though D (mid-trial, after robbery victim's testimony) disputed during G plea that he had been the 1 of 3 juveniles who had actually removed victim's purse from her shoulder, the "facts" to which he expressed no disagreement were sufficient for guilt as joint venturer (he pursued victim with the others, taking active part in "commencement of the robbery"); D's "fear that he would be convicted and sentenced as an adult" doesn't make G plea involuntary;

Henderson v Morgan **426 US 637 (76)**—bad plea because D not told an element (intent to murder) & no facts admitted on it;

C v Correa **43 MAC 714 (97)**—bad pleas because D never explicitly admitted facts underlying charges and judge didn't tell charges' nature, elements, or penalties AND no representation that D-counsel had explained elements being acknowledged by plea; but see *C v Duquette* **386 M 834, 842 (82)** (context of "admission to sufficient facts")—D's "failure to ensure that (tape) record was preserved does not shift the constitutional burden on what is alleged to have been a guilty plea by the defendant";

C v Furr **454 M 101 (2009)**—D's admitting to facts establishing each element of the crimes with which he was charged were adequate substitutes in this case for failure to explain "intent" element needed to convict D as principal or joint venturer; D also signed 'waiver of rights' form stating he was aware of nature and elements of charges (though form alone may not substitute for proper colloquy); judge could disbelieve D's belated claim that he did not understand charges (D wasn't novice at the time, and raised claim only after later conviction as armed career criminal which used these G plea cases as predicate);

C v Francis **375 M 211 (78)**—though pled G, D still has 5th Amendment privilege re: co-D's case because D = liable for conspiracy (*see also* **Ianelli 17 MAC 1011 (84)**, **Benson 389 M 473 (83)**, & *Chapter 19, Double Jeopardy*);

C v Nessolini **19 MAC 1016 (85)**—plea to lesser included offense = dismissal of greater, but only if DA agrees (*see Chapters 5 & 19 re: lesser included offenses*);

See also Chapter 19, Double Jeopardy re: reprosecution after pleas, waiver of double jeopardy, etc.;

C v Mazzantini **74 MAC 915, further app. rev. denied 454 M 1111 (2009)**—by pleading guilty to both possession of heroin and being present where same heroin was kept, D waived claim that convictions were duplicative;

13-E.1. "Trial" on Stipulated Facts/Evidence

C v Hill **20 MAC 130 (85)**—trial by stipulation = like G. plea, so must have colloquy;

C v Castillo **66 MAC 34 (2006)**—trial on "stipulated evidence" (here, to preserve right to appeal denial of motion to suppress) "cannot be justified to save court time" when flaws make it anything but time-saving; reversal because judge failed to ask D if he agreed to the procedure & if he was aware of various constitutional rights (confrontation, cross-examination, right to testify, etc.) he was thus waiving; colloquy should be similar to guilty plea (without portion asking D if he is in fact pleading guilty); fn.5: given present posture of case (i.e., invalid conviction after failure to make record of knowing/voluntary waiver of rights), court had no authority to decide what was effectively an "interlocutory appeal" of the suppression motion, since no single justice of SJC had allowed such interlocutory appeal or referred substantive suppression issue to Appeals Court;

C v Babcock **25 MAC 688 (88)**—jury-waived trial on written statements not like plea, but in future suggest colloquy including likelihood of G. finding;

C v Abrams **44 MAC 584 (98)**—proceeding in which 3 co-Ds pled guilty at same time D was ostensibly being tried, jury-waived, with defense counsel stipulating to what Commonwealth evidence would be, was held to be a trial, but "should be avoided";

13-E.2. Judge Exceeding Recommendation

C v Taylor **370 M 141 (76)**—judge may exceed recommendation; no right to withdraw plea (BUT this = PRIOR TO CURRENT RULE 12 (1979))

M.R.Crim.P. 12—tell judge there's "agreement," including agree to disagree, then D can withdraw plea if judge plans to exceed terms which induced G plea (12(c)(2)); colloquy re: rights & waiver; factual basis on record;

G.L. c. 278, § 18—under 1-trial system in District Court, effective 1/1/94, if D & DA cannot agree on joint recommendation, D allowed to tender plea (or admission) plus "dispositional request" which can be withdrawn if court rejects it;

C v Barber **37 MAC 599 (94)**—because judge exceeded DA's recommendation (by a sentence on 1 charge being from & after, albeit suspended, with probation for 2 years, rather than **all** sentences being "committed," but concurrent) & G plea was made with reserved right to withdraw on this basis, appellate court granted relief, but only on that one indictment;

C v Johnson **11 MAC 835 (81)**—must forewarn judge plea is contingent on recommendation, or else no withdrawal of plea under R-12;

C v Parzyck **41 MAC 195 (96)**—noting that M.R. Crim.P. 30 motion had resulted in vacating G plea because District Court plea judge had not given D opportunity to

withdraw pleas when judge exceeded ADA's recommendation (ADA: District Court sentences to be concurrent with Superior Court sentences; District Court judge ordered same length sentences but from and after Superior Court sentence); But see *C v Clerico* **35 MAC 407 (93)** M.R. Crim.P. 30/ineffective assistance of counsel claim unavailing because when D sought to change plea mid-trial, judge **told** D on record that she was **not** likely to adhere to joint recommendation of D & DA & would exceed it **and** D wouldn't be able to withdraw (because jury would have been discharged); further, D did not on record advise judge that plea was contingent upon particular sentence;

US v Dominguex Benitez **542 US 74 (2004)**—D may void G plea on ground that judge didn't warn him (per Fed. R. Crim. P. 11(c)(3)(B)) that plea couldn't be withdrawn if court didn't accept government's recommendation only if D shows reasonable probability that he wouldn't have pleaded G but for the error;

C v Stanton **2 MAC 614 (74)**—plea = OK though judge not told contingent on agreement; OK though confusion re: parole;

13-E.3. Voluntariness/"Intelligence"

See *Boykin v Alabama* **395 US 238 (69)**; *C v Jones* **60 MAC 88 (2003)** *(D's and counsel's signatures on "green sheet" inadequate to establish requisite knowledge), inter alia, at 13-E, above*

C v Hiskin **68 MAC 633, 637 n.5, 639 (2007)**—guilty plea must be made "intelligently," i.e., "with understanding of the nature of the charges . . . and the consequences of his plea" (legal consequences and constitutional rights he foregoes); use of term "knowing" as signifying some additional requirement is wrong ("redundancy in terminology"); D's sworn statements at colloquy "matter greatly" to refute later contrary claims (here, that attorney induced G plea by threats or lack of preparation: no supporting affidavit of attorney was presented) "grounded on extraneous evidence outside the contemporaneous record of the plea proceeding"; "the considered advice of competent counsel does not constitute coercion"; neither state nor federal constitution, nor M.R.Crim.P. 12, mandate that judge made specific findings as to intelligence and voluntariness of guilty plea;

C v Russin **420 M 309 (95)**—plea = OK despite purported suicide attempt day before & despite fact plea was to life without parole (first degree murder): psychiatrist had OKed competency & plea colloquy = very detailed;

C v DeCologero **49 MAC 93 (2000)**—voluntariness inferable from favorable sentencing consequences (amendments to indictments here reduced mandatory minimum sentence by 6 years), despite failure of judge to specifically inquire re: voluntariness; though no explicit info re: elements, cocaine trafficking adequately explained by reference to "marketing" drug, plus lengthy narrative of evidence, encompassing all required elements BUT no explanation re: "conspiracy" to traffic, & no statement that

D-counsel explained elements, & no acknowledgment by D that the recited evidence was accurate made conspiracy G plea involuntary;

C v Furr **454 M 101 (2009)**—though plea colloquy did not raise issue of voluntariness "directly," judge noted that Commonwealth sentence recommendation was "highly favorable" to D, advised of maximum possible sentence (life imprisonment), asked if D satisfied with attorney's representation, noted presence of D's older brothers in court, and gave D opportunity to withdraw plea at end of colloquy: these numerous opportunities for D to tell judge of improper pressure refuted belated 'coercion' claim (following use of convictions as predicate for armed career criminal sentence after later crime); claim that attorney's emphasis on possible life sentence was unfairly coercive (because highly unlikely) rejected;

C v Sullivan **385 M 497 (82)**—plea OK because D was told elements & admitted most;

C v Wiswall **43 MAC 722 (97)**—plea OK because D acknowledged facts & because crime's name (assault with intent to kill) was not vague or ambiguous (by agreeing to plead G to that crime, D acknowledged that he meant to kill cop when he tried to run over him in roadway); but see *C v Jones* **60 MAC 88, 91 (2003) ("assault and battery" and "intimidation of witness" are NOT self-explanatory, so lack of explanation of elements and recitation of "facts" fatal to G plea);**

C v Sherman **68 MAC 797, 800 (2007), and on further appellate rev. 451 M 332 (2008), same result**—affidavit isn't required when motion for new trial/to withdraw G plea relies solely on contemporaneous record of guilty plea proceeding; if D challenges "intelligence" of plea by resting solely on record, question = "wholly a matter of law," and here, while judge didn't explain elements of rape and D's attorney didn't assert that she had explained elements to D, the prosecutor's factual recitation that D "forcibly raped" victim and D's acknowledgment of truth was adequate for "intelligent" (even to layman, "rape" always implies sexual intercourse, though SJC acknowledges that more generally admission to crime "generally will not function as an admission to all of the elements of that crime");

C v Hunt **73 MAC 616 (2009)**—reversing denial of motion for new trial to withdraw guilty plea: unlike "rape," "assault and battery" is not a designation which is "self-explanatory" of its elements, so D's guilty plea not shown to have been "intelligent";

C v Argueta **73 MAC 564 (2009)**—D's appeal from denial of motion for new trial in case which was continued without a finding not moot, as there are serious collateral consequences from the continuance without a finding; under Federal sentencing law, CWOF entered as result of admission to sufficient facts to warrant finding of guilt = "sentence for purposes of calculating criminal history points in sentencing"; error to deny motion for new trial to withdraw admission because colloquy didn't explain ele-

ments of crime ("tagging") and facts necessary to joint venture liability (sharing requisite intent with principal);

C v Bowler **60 MAC 209 (2003)**—withdrawal of G plea to second degree murder NOT allowed: DA proffered detailed facts, & only addition offered by D was that V was "yelling" at him rather than "screaming"; rejection of argument that it was an "Alford" plea; omission of specific warning that D was giving up rights against self-incrimination not fatal in circumstances (*C v Lewis* 399 M 761 [87] distinguished);

C v Pixley **48 MAC 917 (2000)**—withdrawal of G plea allowed because no showing "intelligent," i.e., aware of elements of charge: record here didn't show judge explained, or D counsel's assertion that she'd explained, or that D admitted to facts satisfying elements; court rejected argument that "possession of cocaine with intent to distribute" was self-explanatory (D here aided by fact that during colloquy he'd professed innocence, said he hadn't possessed drugs; though plea judge could still accept plea despite this, prosecution bore burden of showing "strong factual basis for" conviction);

C v Yates **62 MAC 494 (2004)**—because D's recitation of facts (& there was no other at plea colloquy) disclosed issue of provocation (prostitute told D after sex that she was glad to have exposed him to AIDS) possibly mitigating second-degree murder, & nothing showed that it or malice had been explained to D, "G" plea was not made intelligently, & its withdrawal was allowed;

13-E.4. Penal/Collateral Consequences of G Plea (Parole, Recidivist Statutes (e.g., SDP)), Explanations

C v Morrow **363 M 601 (73)**—need factual basis for G.; plea OK though no parole & 'sexually dangerous person' warning (but now see R-12 (c)(3): advise of additional punishment, e.g., SDP, "where appropriate");

C v Mahadeo **397 M 314 (86)**—(same) for admission to sufficient facts if no 'de novo' appeal;

C v Federico **40 MAC 616 (96)**—despite its "derailing" effect, not improper for judge to advise D, during colloquy, that Commonwealth could move to have D declared SDP; this was true at the time, and judge had **obligation** under Crim.R. 12(c)(3)(B) to inform D of this possible consequence of G plea; SEE G.L. c. 123A § 1, definition of "sexually dangerous person";

C v Perry **389 M 464, 470–71 (83)**—G plea not necessarily involuntary because D received inaccurate or incomplete advice from counsel re: penal consequences;

C v Albert A. **49 MAC 269, 270–72 (further review denied 432 M 1104) (2000)**—legislation, passed after guilty plea, required juvenile to register as sex offender and possible dissemination to public of offender info, was "collateral consequence," & didn't invalidate G plea; maybe different if ADA expressly promised that juvenile's records would be treated as confidential;

***C v Cruz* 62 MAC 610 (2004)**—record did not show that DA promised, as part of plea agreement, not to pursue SDP commitment (not surprising since at time of D's plea, no statutory authority for SDP commitments), so motion to "enforce plea agreement" was properly denied; civil commitment not addressed at the plea hearing said to be "collateral consequence" not invalidating G plea;

***C v Shindell* 63 MAC 503 (2005)**—failure to advise D that she could be required to register as a sex offender = collateral consequence (& G.L. c. 6, § 178E(d) explicitly provides that failure to inform "shall not be grounds to vacate or invalidate the plea"), so no withdrawal of G plea is allowed;

***C v Walsh* 376 M 53 (78)**—single bizarre crime can be "compulsive," so sexually dangerous person possibility;

***Cepulonis v Ponte* 699 F.2d 573 (1st Cir. '83)**—parole rules = "key" factor in plea decision by D;

***C v Santiago* 394 M 25 (85)**—plea OK though everyone wrong re: parole rule; (see also ***Stanton* 2 MAC 614 (74)**);

***Hill v Lockhart* 474 US 52 (85)**—erroneous advice by counsel that parole eligibility was at 1/3 of sentence rather than ½ of sentence didn't make G plea involuntary, though not answering question whether erroneous parole advice may ever be ineffective assistance of counsel;

***C v Rodriguez* 52 MAC 572 (2001)**—D should have been told, on record, at time of G plea, that consequences of a probation violation on masked armed robbery conviction (straight probation for two years, to begin upon release from a 'committed' house of correction sentence imposed at same time) would be imposition of minimum mandatory 5 years, & that at least 5 years would have to be SERVED; no relief, however, since record failed to suggest "any weaknesses" in Commonwealth's case on merits, or that he had any defense to the charges;

***C v Murphy* 73 MAC 57 (2008)**—when pleading G to home invasion and armed assaults in dwelling, judge told D of sentencing range applicable to each indictment "if [D] were to receive a committed prison sentence"; D, however, received straight probation, and when he violated its terms found himself serving the mandatory sentence of twenty years to twenty years and one day (and concurrent life terms, the maximum sentence, for each count of armed assault in dwelling); denial of motion to withdraw guilty pleas upheld, even though "risk" that colloquy did not "adequately" convey that the minimum-maximum sentences applied not only if he were to receive "committed" sentence but "remained applicable if he received straight probation" and did not successfully complete it;

***Clark, petitioner* 34 MAC 191 (93)**—written agreement between D counsel & DA at time of G plea that M.R.Crim.P. 29 revoke & revise would be jointly recommended if D not paroled after 3 years void because revoke/revise motion has 60 day filing window; sentence vacated, D given opportunity to withdraw plea; *see also C v McGuinness* **421 M 472 (95)**, *and Chapter 14-T, motions to revoke and revise*;

***C v Indelicato* 40 MAC 944 (96)**—erroneous advice that G pleas would not bar future firearm licensing not ineffective assistance of counsel because quirk in interplay between federal & state law here = little known AND error not "grave and fundamental" failing; plea OK;

13-E.4.a. Immigration Consequences: Required Advice

G.L. c. 278, § 29D—on G plea, judge must advise re: immigration consequences; in absence of record, D shall be presumed NOT to have received required advisement;

***C v Jones* 417 M 661 (94)**—despite more than eleven years between admission to sufficient facts and motion to withdraw same admission, G.L. c. 278, § 29D (specific language of a "general" immigration/deportation warning mandated; permission to withdraw guilty plea to be given if warning not issued; absent a record of warning, presumption is that D did not receive "the required advisement") cited as requiring allowance of motion when recording of proceeding and memories of parties no longer available;

***C v Medeiros* 48 MAC 374 (99)**—though judge's advice that plea to felony drug charges "might" result in deportation was erroneous because deportation was instead mandatory, appellate court held that statutory mandate of c. 278, § 29D was met (though implied that result could be different if a D was seriously misinformed by judge or counsel as to immigration consequences); no constitutional requirement that D be advised of immigration consequences because consequences are "collateral," not "direct";

***C v Pryce* 429 M 556 (99)**—alleged failure to provide immigration warning considered when D tried to vacate conviction which (at least in part) was basis for deportation, and which was used as enhancement to federal sentence for illegal reentry into country: docket entry that "hearing" occurred on change of plea, "usual practice" of giving immigration warning, and fact that D had been given immigration warning at least once during a guilty plea two years before the one at issue meant no relief: FURTHERMORE, signal that Ds may not be able to attack conviction based on no "deportation" warnings if deportation has already occurred, AND holding that if attack after deportation is possible, D must show that this particular conviction caused the deportation (not showable here because there were other convictions); attention invited to "presumption of regularity recently articulated in" *C v Grant* **426 M 667 (98)** and *C v Lopez* **426 M 657 (98)** and its "effect, if any," on statutory presumption of G.L. c. 278, § 29D (but Appeals Court in *Pryce* (**45 MAC 535 (98)**) had cited *Jones* **417 M 661 (94)**, and held that § 29D had priority over *Grant* and *Lopez*, and SJC on further review implicitly held otherwise);

***C v Rzepphiewski* 431 M 48, 51–52 (2000)**—D's attempt to withdraw admission to sufficient facts nine years later upon allegation that he hadn't been advised of deportation/adverse immigration consequences unsuccessful: plea judge cited his own contemporaneously-made notes of the plea hearing & his customary practices, and SJC ruled that judge's "nontestimonial recitation" properly supported reconstruction of plea hearing "record" such that presumption of c. 278, § 29D wouldn't be applied; Commonwealth's motion to expand record to include docket sheets from other cases in which D received statutory deportation advisement (earliest = 9 months after challenged plea) was DENIED; failure of D to assert in motion that he was currently an alien held sufficient ground for denying relief;

C v Diaz **75 MAC 347 (2009)**—12 years after G plea, D alleged G plea invalid for failure to give deportation warning; judge twice denied D's motions without hearing and without input by Commonwealth despite nonexistence of record of warnings required by G.L. c. 278, § 29D: while motion judge's failure to provide explanations/ findings to rebut § 29D presumption of no warnings in absence of written record can result in relief, remand here for prescribed findings (may rely on 'customary' practice at relevant time); criticism of feds for delaying action on deportable conviction;

C v Soto **431 M 340 (2000)**—G plea ordered vacated: judge telling D that conviction could result in being denied citizenship or being deported NOT SUFFICIENT because didn't advise that D could be excluded from admission to US; G.L. c. 278, § 29D has 3 required warnings, put in quotation marks, & "each of them is required to be given";

C v Hilaire **437 M 809 (2002)**—colloquy warned only that conviction could affect D's immigration "status" (so defective under *C v Soto*), & this could not be supplemented by D's signing of "plea tender form" which correctly recited the full required immigration warnings; requirement that "court" give the warnings means "judge";

C v Lamrini **27 MAC 662, 667–68 (89)**—advice only that charge "could result in D being deported," was "barely adequate," but OK because "coupled with the comments of" prosecutor and D-counsel in D's presence, and because consequence, later complained of, was, specifically, deportation;

C v Agbogun **58 MAC 206 (2003)**—similar;

C v Monteiro **56 MAC 913 (2002)**—no withdrawal of G plea allowed despite fact that immigration warnings given didn't advise that one-year suspended sentence would automatically result in deportation (instead, judge said "could" result in deportation);

C v Fraire **55 MAC 916 (2002)**—similar; no ineffective assistance of counsel for failure to advise of adverse immigration consequences; rejection of argument that, as result of changed federal law, adverse consequences were now so "certain" as to be "direct" rather than "collateral" consequences of G plea;

C v Hason **27 MAC 840 (89)**—judge's general immigration warning that guilty plea may have "an effect" on D's alien status was sufficient & did not justify vacating plea;

C v Villalobos **52 MAC 903, 904, further appellate review allowed, 435 M 1104 (2001)**—judge's failure to tell D that a continuance without a finding was equivalent to a conviction for immigration purposes (per 1996 amendment to 8 USC § 1101(1)(48)(A)) & might jeopard-

ize pending application for citizenship = not fatal; any expansion of alien warning statute is for Legislature, not appellate court; *S.C. on further review*, **437 M 797 (2002)**—admission to sufficient facts is functional equivalent of guilty plea for purposes of statute requiring immigration warnings, because admission to sufficient facts "may lead to either an immediate conviction and sentence, or may do so during the continuance period in the event of a violation of the continuance term";

C v Rodriguez **441 M 1002 (2004)**—immigration warnings were not required when Court placed D on pretrial probation without requiring admission to sufficient facts or plea of guilty or nolo contendere, and without entering finding of guilt; fact that U.S. Immigration and Naturalization Service subsequently denied D's application for naturalization based on his "arrest" and "probation" did not mandate different result, so SJC affirmed denial of D's subsequent "motion to strike, expunge or set aside his pretrial probation" due to alleged defect of failure to give immigration warnings; *C v Rodriguez* 441 M at 1004 n.1 (D could ask Commonwealth to affirm to INS that the pretrial probation included neither admission of facts nor guilty findings);

C v Berthold **441 M 183 (2004)**—D not allowed to withdraw G plea on basis that judge gave incomplete warnings required by G.L. c. 278, § 29D, because advice which was given included the adverse consequence which befell this D; in order to withdraw G plea on basis of inadequate warnings, D must show he faces the prospect of an immigration consequence listed in statute;

C v Casimir **68 MAC 257 (2007)**—D not allowed to withdraw G plea simply on claim that he is prevented from becoming lawful permanent resident and is subject to removal from US, given absence of evidence that removal proceedings have been initiated against him or that he has been denied naturalization because of the narcotics G; because D's "claim is not ripe," judge erred in allowing motion;

C v Rodriquez **70 MAC 721 (2007)**—plea withdrawal proper where judge failed to warn D (eleven years ago) that plea might have consequence of exclusion from admission to US because D now faces automatic & permanent denial of readmission following deportation; contrary to Commonwealth's claim, this is not merely "speculative" or a "hypothetical future" consequence; [judge shouldn't have based ruling on "denial of naturalization"];

C v Cartagena **71 MAC 907 (2008)**—when he pled guilty, D was not told he could be denied naturalization, but was later denied opportunity to obtain permanent residency status; denial of permanent residence status is not an immigration consequence cited in G.L. c. 278, § 29D, and the terms 'permanent residency status' and 'naturalization' are not equivalent: no relief;

C v Estrada **69 MAC 514 (2007)**—that federal immigration law may work "unfortunate and harsh result" isn't basis for vacating admissions or convictions; though judge allowed motion to vacate, on ground that D wasn't asked whether he was under influence of alcohol or drugs at time of admission, D has never claimed that he WAS under such influence during the colloquy; judge had no sua sponte obligation to inquire, absent some indication of impairment;

C v Barreiro 67 MAC 25 (2006)—though D was allowed to withdraw G plea to firearm possession because judge failed to advise of possible deportation consequence, withdrawal of plea re: "receiving stolen property" not allowed because it wasn't basis of actual deportation notice (even though firearms were stolen property at issue); that government could have based its deportation notice on "receiving" not relevant;

C v Grannum 457 M 128 (2010)—D waited twelve years to file motion to withdraw guilty plea based on failure to give statutorily required immigration warnings (so no record existed of plea), but **SJC rejected Commonwealth's argument that** the 'presumption of regularity' held applicable to Rule 30(b) motions under *C v Lopez* **426 M 657 (98)** should apply re: G.L. c. 278, § 29D motions to withdraw guilty pleas and thus allot to D burden of proof; D nonetheless lost because he failed to establish more than a hypothetical possibility that he faced immigration consequences on basis of this conviction;

13-E.5. Withdrawal of Guilty Plea

Procedure on Rule 30 motion re: withdrawal of G plea—*C v Conaghan* 48 MAC 304 (99) R.30 is appropriate vehicle for withdrawing allegedly involuntary G plea; in challenging G plea, D can either rely on record of plea colloquy OR extraneous evidence, but if D uses extraneous evidence, Commonwealth may also introduce extraneous evidence; D may proffer materials in addition to the "required" affidavit(s), including medical records, investigative reports, and transcript of other proceedings (here, error to refuse to consider non-affidavit data); though since motion judge here wasn't plea judge, appellate court in "as good a position" to assess strength/effect of materials, appellate court bowed to motion judge's "discredit(ing of) untrustworthy affidavits," after which no evidentiary hearing was required; D not entitled to funds under c. 261, §§ 27A-G because motion wasn't "a prosecution, defense, or appeal" (effective 10-1-2001, M.R.Crim.P. 30(c)(5) provides that, "after notice to the Commonwealth and an opportunity to be heard," a judge considering a Rule 30 motion may exercise discretion to allow the defendant costs associated with the preparation and presentation of the motion); Dreben, J., dissented (given compelling evidence in R.30 papers that D was battered woman, coerced by principal in crime, evidentiary hearing should have been held); SAME CASE (*C v Conaghan*) **on further appellate review, 433 M 105 (2000)** SJC orders use of G.L. c. 123, § 15(a) (psych. evaluation for competency) in remanding case after trial court's denial of R.30 motion to withdraw guilty plea, thereby affording expert assistance/funds; "(n)othing in the statute limits the time within

which" examination for competency may be done, and SJC, a "court of competence jurisdiction" had doubt as to D's competency at time she pled guilty (because may have been involuntary as product of 'battered woman syndrome'); evidence of such syndrome may be considered "newly discovered evidence" warranting a new trial;

See Chapter 15-F regarding Right to Counsel on Rule 30 motion, e.g., *C v Coral* **72 MAC 222, further review denied 452 M 1107 (2008), cert. denied 129 S Ct 1633 (2009)**—avoiding D's claim (citing *Halbert v Michigan* 545 US 605 [2005]) of right to counsel on Rule 30 motion to withdraw guilty plea (is "the only method for challenging a guilty plea a "direct" appeal? a "collateral" attack? a "hybrid"?), by ruling that this D's delay (three years after guilty plea) would "militate against" treating motion as analogous to direct appeal, and instead as a collateral challenge not requiring appointment of counsel;

C v Colon 439 M 519 (2003)—in support of D's claim that G-plea colloquy was inadequate (when no record of it existed), D presented recordings from six colloquies during two years conducted by same judge, which were *randomly selected by an assistant clerk magistrate*; each contained a "woefully deficient colloquy," and this evidence was supplemented by testimony from two attorneys about the judge's regular practice, which had not changed over the years and was consistent with the recordings: SJC held D = entitled to withdraw G plea, on such "overwhelming" evidence of inadequacy [N.B.: D's Rule 30 motion was denied in the trial court, and this ruling was affirmed by the Appeals Court];

C v Sherman **68 MAC 797, 800 (2007), on further review (same result) 451 M 332 (2008)**—affidavit isn't required when motion for new trial/to withdraw G plea relies solely on contemporaneous record of guilty plea proceeding; if D challenges "intelligence" of plea by resting solely on record, question = "wholly a matter of law," and here, while judge didn't explain elements of rape and D's attorney didn't assert that she had explained elements to D, the prosecutor's factual recitation that D "forcibly raped" victim and D's acknowledgment of truth was adequate for "intelligent";

C v DeMarco 387 M 481 (82)—can't withdraw plea unless "justice not done" within Rule 30; (see Chapter 15);

C v Glines 40 MAC 95 (96)—withdrawal of plea on R.30 not allowed here (though judge didn't advise that D could withdraw if sentence exceeded D's recommendation, and consecutive 2½-year suspended sentences did "exceed" concurrent 2½-year suspended sentences); evidentiary hearing on R.30 motion provided evidence that D was aware of what judge was going to do before he did it & that D counsel advised he could take it or go to trial; on R.30, D could instead have "stood on the record made during" plea colloquy & sentencing;

C v McGuinness 421 M 472 (95)—withdrawal of plea not allowed since judge's advice (that he would act favorably in 2 years upon timely filed motion to revoke and revise if D stayed trouble-free during incarceration) came **after** Concord-20 sentence was imposed - it was not a part of the sentence or plea bargain;

C v Walker **443 M 867, 871 (2005)**—if D's plea counsel gives plainly incorrect advice & D relies on it in tendering G plea, it's ineffective assistance, & plea is not necessarily "intelligent/knowing"; "constitutional infirmity would create a substantial risk of a miscarriage of justice"; advice here, i.e., that judge's denial of suppression motion presented no appellate issue, wasn't ineffective assistance of counsel because it wasn't "patently wrong" at the time;

C v Fernandes **390 M 714 (84)**—R.30 new trial because no voluntariness colloquy;

C v Robbins **431 M 442 (2000)**—though D pled G to first degree murder against counsel's advice, denial of motion to withdraw plea affirmed; though D claimed incompetence (depressed, not taking prescribed Prozac) & argued competency hearing necessary upon any offer to plead G to 'life without parole' crime, colloquy/questions answered by D and counsel contained data refuting claimed incompetence; attorney's record statements indicated D was aware of controlling law (i.e., he'd read substantial relevant case law & gone over jury instructions before scheduled trial date);

Bradshaw v Stumpf **125 S Ct 2398 (2005)**—court could rely on defense counsel's assurances to court that counsel has informed D of nature/elements of charged offenses; no G-plea withdrawal simply because state, in obtaining death penalty, said D was triggerman, but in later proceeding re: co-D, produced witness who said co-D was triggerman (because under Ohio law, either aider/abettor was guilty), but remand for new sentencing re: import of prosecutor's tactic;

C v Nikas **431 M 453 (2000)**—13 years after G plea to second degree murder (while maintaining innocence pursuant to *NC v Alford* **400 US 25 (1970)** and saying his attorney told him he didn't "stand a chance in hell" if he went to trial), plea judge allowed R. 30 motion, and SJC aff'd allowance; attorney's record statements in response to 'chance in hell' didn't establish that D knew relevant LAW (only that he'd read police reports, grand jury testimony, etc.), so failure of judge to explain adequately either murder one or murder two elements (and incorrect explanation re: distinction between the two) = involuntary G plea; rejecting Commonwealth argument that "strength of evidence against D" meant that D adequately understood the charge;

C v Andrews **49 MAC 201 (2000)**—withdrawal of G plea allowed when colloquy showed that even judge was uncertain as to whether G plea was to mere possession of drug or possession with intent to distribute, and amount in issue was only 2.73 grams of "rock" cocaine (albeit in 11 bags contained in one larger bag); D and D-counsel averred that D thought he was pleading G to simple possession, as discussed in lobby conference;

G.L. c. 278, § 11A: Standards of Judicial Practice, Trials & Probable Cause Hearings (1981) 2:02—2ND

OFFENSE in complaint = separate plea (or trial) (*see Chapter 5, Complaints, and Chapter 14, recidivist laws*);

C v Chaplin **50 MAC 365 (2000)**—after trial of operating under influence (2d offense) complaint and jury G of operating under, invalid for judge to "move directly to sentencing," with prosecutor asserting then that it was second offense and defense counsel concurring that it was 2d offense within "reach-back" period: D couldn't be sentenced as second offender under the complaint without having been afforded right to trial by jury on that factor; counsel's acquiescence isn't equivalent to G plea; court rejects Commonwealth argument that "conviction" was only for OUI, and sentence properly considered his criminal record as a whole (contrast *C v Fernandes* **430 M 517 (99)** controlled substances repeat-offender statutes are sentence enhancement provisions ONLY, and don't identify "a freestanding crime"; "better practice" = include in indictment the date of prior offense, & date & court of prior conviction);

C v McCready **50 MAC 521 (2000)**—vacating "second offense portion of charge" for defective procedure, whereby after jury G on operating under the influence charge, judge sentenced D as second offender merely upon "counsel's statement that there had been a previous OUI conviction"; *C v Petersen* **67 MAC 49 (2006)**—similar (defense counsel "purported to stipulate that the current charge was a second offense");

C v Hernandez **60 MAC 416 (2004)**—though judge accepted guilty plea to OUI-second offense, there was no factual basis for "second offense" portion, because D had not been convicted of a first offense *as of the time of the crime*; fact that he had been convicted of qualifying "prior" after time of the crime but before time of guilty plea was irrelevant; though this was not "element" of crime charged, D was still entitled to have the fact proven beyond reasonable doubt; motion to withdraw guilty plea to be allowed only as to "second offense" portion, D to be resentenced for OUI as first offense;

C v Orben **53 MAC 700 (2002)**—vacating portion of judgment re: "fourth offense" OUI, because proceeding was "neither a trial nor a plea, but something similar . . . to the procedure repudiated in *C v Zuzick* **45 MAC 71, 74075 (98)**"; without conducting any inquiry of D, judge accepted counsel's representation that counsel had spoken with the 5 police officers waiting in hall to testify re: prior convictions, & that it wouldn't be necessary for prosecution to call them;

13-E.6. Nolo Contendere

M.R.Crim.P. 12—same rules for nolo contendere:

C v Tilton **49 M 232 (1844)**—nolo plea is inadmissible as evidence later;

Olszewski v Goldberg **223 M 27 (16)**—otherwise equivalent to G plea;

13-E.7. Record of Plea Colloquy Missing?

Parke v Raley **506 US 20 (92)**—allowing states to rely on presumption of regularity when old G plea on old crime is challenged in context of enhanced sentence on later conviction;

C v Lopez **426 M 657 (98)**—when motion to withdraw G plea is filed belatedly in context of seeking to avoid enhanced sentence for later crime, and no record of G plea exists, presumption of regularity will suffice to reject challenge to the conviction;

C v Grant **426 M 667 (98)**—same;

C v Pingaro **44 MAC 41 (97)**—R.30 motion asserting, 15 years after fact, that no colloquy preceded D's guilty plea, did not require evidentiary hearing or impose burden of going forward on Commonwealth (stenographer's notes had been destroyed, plea judge died, DA & steno had no memory);

C v Hoyle **67 MAC 10 (2006)**—signed jury trial waiver's absence in file, 15 years after G pleas, didn't entitle D to withdraw pleas; D's self-serving affidavit, with no further evidence or testimony at hearing, insufficient;

C v Gonzales **43 MAC 926 (97)**—R.30 motion brought 10 years after G plea asserting that D was intoxicated & hadn't had assistance of counsel; presumption of regularity sufficient to discount/disbelieve allegations; cf. *C v Wheeler* **52 MAC 631 (2001)** delinquency adjudication occurring 27 years earlier was cause of 17-year-veteran police officer's loss of license to carry a firearm (legislation passed in 1998 mandated this ineligibility) & thus loss of job: presumption of regularity was enough to rebuff D's claim in R.30 motion that his trial attorney had been ineffective and labored under conflict of interest due to representing co-defendants;

C v Correa **43 MAC 714 (97)**—presumption of regularity as to long-closed guilty plea cases does not suffice to refute a contemporaneously-made record showing colloquy deficient for failure to apprise D of crimes' elements;

C v Quinones **414 M 423 (93)**—OK to reconstruct record of G-plea proceedings by testimony from court reporter, defense counsel, and judge's recollection and "customary practice"; plea not involuntary due to failure to explain that appellate review of denial of motions to suppress was being forfeited;

C v Rzepphiewski **431 M 48, 51–52 (2000)**—D's attempt to withdraw admission to sufficient facts nine years later upon allegation that he hadn't been advised of deportation/adverse immigration consequences unsuccessful: plea judge cited his own contemporaneously-made notes of the plea hearing & his customary practices, and SJC ruled that judge's "nontestimonial recitation" properly supported reconstruction of plea hearing "record" such that presumption of c. 278, § 29D wouldn't be applied; Commonwealth's motion to expand record to include docket sheets from other cases in which D received statutory deportation advisement (earliest = 9 months after challenged plea) was DENIED; failure of D to assert in motion that he was currently an alien held sufficient ground for denying relief;

C v Grant **440 M 1001 (2003)**—fact that plea judge has been disciplined for, inter alia, a "pattern of conduct with regard to plea colloquies, whereby he exhibited a willful disregard of the law," perhaps refuted inference of a "usual practice" of assuring to G-plea defendants notice of all rights being relinquished by G plea, such that counsel should be appointed for D to pursue Rule 30 motion;

13-F. EVIDENTIARY MATTERS: USE OF GUILTY PLEAS

See also Chapter 11-F, Evidence, Hearsay concerning effect/relevance of guilty pleas in another proceeding;

C v Michel **367 M 454 (75)**—can cross-examine witness re: plea discussions (& promise), but not advice; no privilege because 3d party (DA) informed;

US v Bump **605 F.2d 548 (10th Cir. '79)**—DA can cross-examine D about evidence promised by attorney in plea bargain because disclosure ended privilege;

C v Luce **34 MAC 105, 111–12 (93)**—"meetings between the defendant and his counsel and government officers did not constitute plea bargaining that would be inadmissible under Mass.R.Crim.P. 12(f)"; in context of D's offers of assistance and/or boasts of knowledge which will be helpful to police, GET IT IN WRITING beforehand that no such statements may be admitted against him;

C v Lewin (II) **407 M 629 (90)**—murder D's statement that he was willing to plead guilty to manslaughter was inadmissible because not an unequivocal admission or confession & because more prejudicial than probative;

C v Fernandes **30 MAC 335 (91)**—co-D's plea colloquy not admissible as declaration against penal interest because given under press of plea negotiations & not unequivocally exculpatory as to D;

LePage v Bumila **407 M 163 (90)**—D's payment of traffic fine & waiver of appeal were not admissible as admissions;

C v Chiappini **72 MAC 188 (2008)**—"victim's" admissions in subsequent criminal prosecution = newly-discovered evidence: D was convicted of assault and battery by dangerous weapon (stabbing V's neck), though at trial had claimed self-defense; his "victim", however, subsequently admitted to sufficient facts on charge of assault and battery by means of dangerous weapon (pavement), and prosecutor's recitation of facts *then* was that "victim" of D had had D on the pavement and smashed D's head into pavement; "victim" denied during D's trial that D had ever been on ground, allowing prosecution to argue in closing that D easily could have escaped as combatants were only in "stand-up fistfight"; trial judge's denial of

D's motion for new trial = vacated; **S.C., after remand, 76 MAC 1107 (2010)**—order denying motion for new trial = **reversed**;

Flood v Southland Corp. **416 M 62 (93)**—civil co-D's guilty plea in related criminal action admissible; Rule 803(22) of the Proposed Massachusetts Rules of Evidence, substantively identical to the F.R.Evid. 803(22), provides that the hearsay rule does not exclude "evidence of a final judgment, entered . . . upon a plea of guilty . . . adjudging a person guilty of a crime punishable by . . . confinement in excess of one year, to prove any fact essential to sustain the judgment . . . ", though such plea would not be conclusive of the issue, or "binding" even as to the person who so pled;

Chapter 14
SENTENCING ADVOCACY, DISPOSITIONS AND PROBATION SURRENDERS

14-A. SENTENCING ADVOCACY, FACTORS, AND HEARING

CPCS P/G 7.5—make sure sentence is accurate;

C v Baro **73 MAC 218 (2008)**—due to trial judge's unavailability (illness), different judge sentenced D; though sentencing judge didn't certify in writing his familiarity with trial record (as required by M.R.Crim.P. 38(c)) he carefully considered counsel's representations re: trial record plus D's criminal history, so no relief;

C v Barriere **46 MAC 286 (99)**—correcting mittimus after sentencing to reflect pretrial credits may be much more problematic than taking the time to get it right at sentencing;

C v Mahar **442 M 11 (2004)**—a criminal defendant may challenge sentence on ground of ineffective assistance of counsel re: decision to reject plea bargain offer (but no ineffectiveness shown here);

Padilla v Kentucky **130 S Ct 1473 (2010)**—6th Amendment requires defense counsel to provide *affirmative* (i.e., not just silence) competent advice to a noncitizen D regarding immigration consequences of a guilty plea (& absent such advice, noncitizen may raise claim of ineffective assistance of counsel); there is duty to inquire about citizenship/immigration status initially; duty to investigate/ advise about immigration consequences of plea alternatives and sentencing alternatives;

BLAKELY v WASHINGTON **124 S Ct 2531 (2004)**—**procedure whereby judge has authority to impose enhanced sentence (beyond the prescribed statu-** **tory maximum) upon finding one or more aggravating facts violates Sixth Amendment under rule of** *Apprendi v New Jersey* **530 US 466, 490 (2000)** & *Ring v Arizona* 536 US 584, 592–93 (2002): such "facts" must instead be determined by a jury (or by D's admission); here, judge could not have imposed the "exceptional" sentence he did solely on the basis of facts admitted in the guilty plea; *McMillan v Pennsylvania* 477 US 79 (86) & *Williams v New York* 337 US 241 (49) distinguished;

C v Saletino **449 M 657 (2007)**—rejects D's argument that *Apprendi* supports "sentencing entrapment" defense (D's position that he was induced to distribute greater amount of drug than he was predisposed to distribute), while purporting to reserve decision on whether "sentencing entrapment" will be recognized as a defense in Massachusetts (not warranted on evidence here, says SJC);

BUT SEE *C v Lawrence* **69 MAC 596 (2007)**—no general entrapment instruction required because D "delivered"/transferred marijuana to undercover cop and acknowledged that he both "shared" marijuana with friends earlier and intended to "share" what he had in his pocket with the cop (who gave D $20 without request or negotiation); **"entrapment" as to school zone charge (i.e., enhanced sentence) = "distinct . . . analytically", but not briefed, so reserved**: "whether the detective's act of leading the defendant into the school zone was government behavior sufficient to entitle the defendant to an entrapment instruction"; fn.5: "if . . . the purpose of the school zone statute is to 'create drug-free zones of safety where children could be . . . free from the potential infection of drugs,' . . . we find it unsettling that a violation of G.L. c. 94C, § 32J, occurred in this case because the defendant followed a police officer into a school zone";

14-A.1. Alternative Dispositions

Drug Courts—exist in many District Courts and some juvenile courts; good alternative if D is serious substance abuser and otherwise facing significant incarceration;

Trial Court Policy for Drug Court Sessions (approved 2001)—contains very good language regarding preservation of D's due process rights in drug courts; CPCS Performance Guidelines, § 9.1—addresses issues relevant to representing Ds in drug court sessions;

Community Corrections Centers—operated by the Office of Community Corrections, an agency within the Probation Department; see enabling statute, G.L. c. 211F (1996); available in District and Superior Courts; good alternative if D otherwise facing significant incarceration;

SJC Standards on Substance Abuse (approved 1998)—see Policy Statement and Standards I, V, and XIII with Commentaries for support when requesting probation with substance abuse treatment in lieu of incarceration

14-A.2. Defense Counsel, Effective Assistance

CPCS P/G 4.12—begin sentencing preparation early; 5.6 . . . & even though plea bargain; 7.1-5 check record/ presentence report; consider judge's practices/expert/ possible treatment?; prepare memo.?; seek best dispo.; call witnesses?; PREPARE; (*see Chapter 2, re: control over case and choice of strategy*);

C v Talbot **444 M 586, 596 (2005)**—if requested by D or D-counsel, probation officers must give D's attorney notice and reasonable opportunity to attend a presentence interview of D; such request here should have been honored (& failure to do so prompted inaccurate representations by parole officer to D, D's signing releases for privileged info (all of which was obtained & affixed to report given to judge, who exceeded prosecution's recommendation for sentence), etc.);

Strickland v Washington **466 US 668 (84)**—6th Amendment right to counsel includes effective sentencing;

C v Brennick **14 MAC 952 (82)**—right to attorney at sentencing (for jury-session default); public defenders aren't fungible & can't make defender #2 handle defender #1's case;

Osborne v C **378 M 104 (79)**—ineffective assistance of counsel because inadequate/misdirected dispositional pitch; mitigating factors almost unlimited, including subsequent good acts;

C v Lykus **406 M135 (89)**—counsel's failure to present mitigating factors, call witnesses & request concurrent sentences was ineffective assistance of counsel;

C v Montanez **410 M 290 (91)**—barebones sentencing pitch with minimal mention of D's background plus failure to request that sentences run concurrently was ineffective assistance;

C v Mamay **407 M 412 (90)**—counsel's failure to argue mitigating factors at sentencing not ineffective assistance where counsel had just argued those factors to judge in support of motions for evaluation in aid of sentencing & "sexually dangerous person"-related motions;

C v Campiti **41 MAC 43, 71 (96)**—because convictions were for 5 crimes with minimum-mandatory sentences & trial evidence was filled with data re D's "activities & lifestyle," it was not ineffective assistance to argue only that sentences be concurrent;

C v Moreau **30 MAC 677 (91), cert. denied, 502 US 1049 (92)**—counsel's joining in recommendation which exceeded sentencing guidelines, failure to offer mitigating evidence until after joint recommendation was submitted, & possible failure to inform D of terms of recommendation may have been ineffective assistance;

C v Cameron **31 MAC 928 (91)**—counsel's failure to make any argument for D at sentencing was ineffective assistance;

C v Leavey **60 MAC 249 (2004)**—because postconviction counsel didn't suggest what mitigating circumstances trial counsel might have argued at sentencing, claim of ineffective assistance failed;

14-A.3. Prosecutor's Responsibilities

ABA Standards for Criminal Justice, Prosecution Function & Defense Function (3d ed. 1993) 3-6.1—DA should seek fairness & not make severity the index of his/ her effectiveness;

SJC Rule 3:07, 3.8(d)—DA's obligation re: sentencing to disclose all known mitigating info;

C v Capparelli **29 MAC 926 (90)**—prosecutor's withholding of evidence material to punishment which might have offset government efforts to tie D to organized crime required remand to determine whether resentencing necessary;

C v Goodwin **414 M 88 (93)**—acquittals can't be considered;

C v Mr. M. **409 M 538 (91)**—prosecutor not bound by cops' promise of sentence recommendation of "street time" for D if he cooperated; remanded for evidentiary hearing to determine if D reasonably believed cooperation would result in recommendation of "street time" & whether D relied to his detriment;

C v Fanelli **412 M 497 (92)**—prosecutor's constantly raising sentence recommendation during plea negotiations condemned as "dishonorable";

C v Ferrara **31 MAC 648 (91)**—judge's reliance on incorrect statement by prosecutor about D's parole eligibility or discharge date required remand for resentencing;

14-A.4. Limitations on Judge's Discretion

C v Burr **33 MAC 637 (92)**—judge could not avoid imposing mandatory sentence after jury conviction of trafficking >100 grams by purporting to act pursuant to M.R. Crim.P. 25(b)(2) to reduce the "degree of guilt" when weight of drugs was not in issue;

C v Gordon **410 M 498 (91)**—G.L. c. 211, § 3 was proper means for prosecutor to challenge judge's erroneous acceptance of guilty plea to lesser charge over Commonwealth objection where there was no "dismissal" from which to appeal under Rule 15(b);

C v Cheney **440 M 568 (2003)**—no (Brandano-type) pretrial probation and dismissal in *Superior Court* (rape of child, G.L. c. 265, § 23) over the objection of prosecutor (violates constitutional separation of powers);

C v Massenburg **442 M 1003 (2004)**—follows *Cheney*, & rejects D's argument that judge needn't accept all conditions that Commonwealth attaches to its consent to dismissal of valid charges prior to verdict, finding, or plea;

C v Tim T. **437 M 592 (2002)**—indictment for rape of child (c. 265, § 23) brought in Juvenile Court can't be disposed of by (Brandano-type) pretrial probation and dismissal if DA objects; CAN accomplish "Brandano" pretrial probation & possible dismissal disposition under c. 278, § 18 (after tender of guilty plea or admission to sufficient facts) IF continuance without a finding isn't "prohibited by law" (but continuance without a finding (CWOF) is prohibited in rape of child case);

C v Powell **453 M 320 (2009)**—distinguishing *Cheney* 440 M 568: disposition of *Superior Court* criminal case AFTER trial or G plea by dismissal contingent on conditions does not infringe on executive branch powers, "at least where the disposition imposed by the judge is one that is recognized by the Legislature"; Legislature has delineated expressly the Superior Court crimes (not all) which may not be continued without finding or dismissed; indictment could not be "filed" without consent of Commonwealth, but this was an inaccurate description of what occurred (which was instead a CWOF pending compliance with conditions, at which time dismissal was anticipated);

C v Quispe **433 M 508 (2001)**—judge's disapproval of immigration consequences of particular charge/disposition didn't allow him to ignore law, violate constitutional separation of powers;

C v Manning **75 MAC 829 (2009)**—after D tendered conditional G plea to two District Court counts (distribution of Class D and school zone violation), requesting reduction of distribution to straight possession and continuance without finding for one year, plus dismissal of school zone charge, Commonwealth requested one day for distribution and two years from and after for school zone, judge could not dismiss school zone charge without trial, G plea

or admission to sufficient facts, simply by stating that he couldn't find sufficient facts (proffer had included school guard testimony that he saw distribution on videotape and D acknowledged to him selling one bag of marijuana); for same 'separation of powers' reason, judge could not accept plea to lesser included offense of simple possession (on distribution count) over Commonwealth objection;

C v Thad T. **59 MAC 497, 510 (2003)**—upon finding of delinquency, judge both committed juvenile to Department of Youth Services and imposed condition that juvenile stay out of town of Groton: G.L. c. 119, § 58 allows judge to EITHER commit juvenile to DYS OR to place juvenile on probation with conditions, but not both dispositions for the same conviction (because term of banishment had expired on 18th birthday, court avoided deciding whether it was constitutional: *see C v Pike* 428 M 393, 402–05 (98);

Lifetime Community Parole: G.L. c. 127, § 133C; G.L. c. 275, § 18; G.L. c. 265, § 45—lifetime parole shouldn't be imposed for offense committed before passage of the Act (i.e., 9/10/99) (because of e.g., *C v Fuller* **421 M 407–08 (95)**—presumption against retroactivity where statute does not specify that its provisions apply retroactively); lifetime parole must be imposed re: rape, rape of child under 16 w/force, rape & abuse of child, assault with intent to rape, kidnapping child under 16, drugging for sex, unnatural & lascivious acts, and any attempt to commit any of the above; BUT if 1st offense of any of these, D may move for hearing to determine whether lifetime parole shall be imposed; lifetime parole may be imposed re: indecent A&B (either under age 14 or 14 & over), indecent A&B of mentally retarded person, and as to any 1st offense of these, prosecutor may request hearing to determine whether lifetime parole should be imposed; D may petition parole board to terminate lifetime parole after 15 years;

C v Pagan **445 M 315 (2005)**—standard and burden of proof ambiguous as to imposition of lifetime community parole in some cases, and so unconstitutional as to those; complaint or indictment must allege that D is repeat offender (if such is essential to imposition of LCP given the crime charged); warning that Supreme Court case law (*Apprendi v NJ*, etc.) dictates that this enhanced sentence cannot be based on factual findings made by judge rather than jury;

C v Boyd **73 MAC 190 (2008)**—no lifetime community parole allowed because indictment did not explicitly assert "repeat offender"; other sentences remanded because judge might have altered them if he knew LCP not available;

See Chapter 13E re attempts to vacate state court guilty pleas/convictions when faced with enhanced punishment later, on basis of prior convictions;

14-A.5. Purposes of Punishment/Treatment, Diversion

C v O'Neal 369 M 242 (75)—purposes of punishment; least restrictive alternative principle (applied to death penalty);

ABA Standards for Criminal Justice, Sentencing (3d ed. 1994) 18-2.1—legislature should consider at least 5 different societal purposes in designing sentencing system: foster respect for law/deter criminal conduct; incapacitate offenders; punish; provide restitution to victims; rehabilitate offenders; 18-2.2 legislature should enact criminal code authorizing imposition of a range of sanctions, from 'compliance programs' to 'economic sanctions' to 'acknowledgment sanctions' to 'intermittent confinement' to total confinement; should also enact community corrections program;

District Court Standards of Judicial Practice, Sentencing & Other Dispositions (1984))—overview of C.J. Zoll's suggestions;

14-A.6. Timing, Procedures at Sentencing, Presentence Report, Probation Department

G.L. c. 279, § 3A—DA must move for sentencing within 7 days of felony G;

G.L. c. 278, § 11A (habitual criminal statute), process for second offense complaint—plea initially only as to current substantive offense; "2d offense" portion of indictment not to be read in court or inquired about; after "G" on substantive, ask for plea on whether prior exists (jury trial right re: this, also) (*see Chapter 5 and Chapter 14-N*);

M.R.Crim.P. 28—reasonably prompt sentence (but may continue); id. (d) presentence investigation shall be made available to counsel, though in "extraordinary" cases, judge may redact portions for listed reasons; records include **no** NG's; id. (b) allocution by D or counsel;

C v Talbot 444 M 586, 596 (2005)—**if requested by D or D-counsel, probation officers must give D's attorney notice and reasonable opportunity to attend a presentence interview of D**; such request here should have been honored (& failure to do so prompted inaccurate representations by probation officer to D, D's signing releases for privileged info (all of which was obtained & affixed to report given to judge, who exceeded prosecution's recommendation for sentence), etc.);

M.R.Crim.P. 29—(motions to revoke/revise), *C v Layne* 386 M 291 (82) motions to revoke and revise may not be based upon factors occurring after the point of sentencing; *C v DeJesus* 440 M 147 (2003)—affidavit with specific support must be filed WITH the motion, not at some later time;

C v McInerney 380 M 59 (80)—assuming right to speedy sentence, 16 months after remand = OK;

C v Vith Ly 450 M 16 (2007)—execution of D's sentences, after unexplained delay of sixteen years on part of Commonwealth to have sentences executed, would violate due process & "principles of fundamental fairness"; sentences had been stayed pending appeal, but after some convictions were affirmed, Commonwealth did not seek execution of those sentences immediately or upon D's subsequent contacts with law enforcement;

K. Smith, *Criminal Practice and Procedure*, **§ 1998 (2d ed. 1983 & Supp.)**—most judges permit D as well as counsel to talk; § 2007 both M.R.Crim.P. 12(e) & 28(d)(3) say both sides get presentence report, 12(e) conditioning access upon written motion;

Gardner v Florida 430 US 349 (77)—no (death) sentence without showing presentence report to D

G.L. c. 276, § 85—probation officer can recommend probation; show "record" to D and attorney; record shall not contain 'not guilty' verdicts;

C v Goodwin 414 M 88 (93)—probation officers can't urge consideration of acquittals & such consideration can't be accomplished "indirectly by a prosecutor through the Commonwealth's sentencing memorandum";

C v Russo 421 M 317 (95)—prior to promulgation of sentencing guidelines (see St. 1993, c. 432), judge has no discretion to downward depart from statutory minimum mandatory sentence; after such promulgation, departure possible upon written statement of mitigating factors;

ABA Standards for Criminal Justice, Prosecution Function & Defense Function (3d ed. 1993) 4-8.1—know sentencing choices/practices of court; 4-4.1, Comment: must investigate mitigating facts & not just rely on facts told by D or broad emotional pitch to court; understand (& explain to D) the significant risks of personal allocution; (*see also Chapter 13, "Pleas"; & Chapter 14-U "seal/expunge records"*);

G.L. c. 123, § 35—cop, doctor, relative, or court official can petition for (max. 30 day) commitment of substance abuser to approved facility (or Bridgewater State Hospital or Framingham);

G.L. c. 123, § 15(e)—shrink/hospital report "in aid of sentencing", evaluation period not to exceed 40 days; § 10 voluntary admission to state hospital;

Ake v Oklahoma 470 US 68 (85)—indigent defendant's right to expert on danger (in death case); (*See "Fees/Costs" in Chapter 7-C*);

14-A.7. Appropriate/Improper Factors

C v Goodwin 414 M 88, 92 (93)—general sentencing goals = punishment, deterrence, protection of the public, & rehabilitation; consider (even hearsay info re:) D's character, behavior, & background, family life, employment, etc.;

C v Healy 452 M 510, 515 and n8 (2008)—that D refused initially to perform field sobriety test (evidence inadmissible as violative of Art. 12) could not be considered "for sentencing purposes," but evidence independent of the refusal held sufficient for belief that D had been drinking, and "alcohol problem" could be considered at sentencing;

C v Jones **71 MAC 568 (2008)**—judge's remark at sentencing (gist = D's expression of remorse "today" not deserving of much credit, i.e., belatedly, after trial) prompting analysis of "fine line" between appropriately considering remorse and punishing a D for exercising rights against self-incrimination and to silence; remorse = factor for lenity, & judge wasn't "bound to credit" its sincerity and thus wasn't bound to use it as "mitigation"; refusal to equate comments with vindictiveness found in *Mills* 435 M at 400–01;

Eddings v Oklahoma **455 US 104 (82)**—youthful age = mitigating;

C v Gould **380 M 672 (80)**—psych. abnormality = less moral turpitude;

G.L. c. 279, § 4B—victim heard or files statement; D can see and rebut; written statement by DA to include documentation of net financial loss; D to have opportunity to rebut if court decides to rely upon V's or DA's statements;

Booth v Maryland **482 US 496 (87)**—bad victim impact statement (death case, with jury) because sympathy/capricious;

C v Lebon **37 MAC 705 (94)**—can't punish D for wanting jury (threat of committed time after jury G, but not after jury-waived G made jury waiver involuntary);

Letters v C **346 M 403 (63)**—can't punish for trying case;

But *C v Ravenell* **415 M 191 (93)**—can find it to be promise of leniency if willing to admit guilt;

C v Banker **21 MAC 976 (86)**—can punish for victim's crime injuries, but not for trauma from testifying;

US v Grayson **438 US 41 (78)**—can consider D's perjury re: rehabilitation potential . . . ; but see *C v Souza* **390 M 813 (84)** . . . can't add to sentence for D's perjury (or for prior dismissed case); *C v Juzba* **46 MAC 319, 325 (99)** can't add to sentence for judge's belief that D perjured self; *C v Monzon* **51 MAC 245, 255–56 (2001)** when judge adopted DA's sentencing recommendation, & DA said recommendation was based in part upon D's alleged perjury during trial testimony, resentencing ordered (avoiding decision on issue that trial defense counsel provided ineffective assistance in failing to request continuance for presentence investigation & report, failing to present mitigating factors, and failing to request sentences be served concurrently);

C v Baldwin **52 MAC 404 (2001)**—judge's comment that D was "a lot less than honest person" in context referred to fact that his affidavit filed with motion to suppress was at odds with his trial testimony and/or said to be ambiguous and not repeated; sentences were less than requested by prosecutor; no relief (perhaps also rationalized as refusal to accept responsibility for actions, & instead blaming victims & D's own cocaine addiction);

C v Coleman **390 M 797 (84)**—(same); discussion of appropriate factors;

C v McFadden **49 MAC 441 (2000)**—resentencing by a different judge ordered when sentence reflected penalty for D's "perjur(ing) himself," for lacking "integrity to stand and take whatever was deserved," for dragging his mother into the case, for insulting integrity of police officers, and for forcing attorney to defend him;

C v White **436 M 340 (2002)**—when case was remanded on appeal for resentencing before a different judge (based on trial judge's error in being influenced by belief that D's prior prison terms on other charges were inadequate), judge could consider D's efforts in prison to rehabilitate himself since being incarcerated on the sentence in this case; judge's stated belief that these were improperly before her was error of law;

C v Sitko **372 M 305, 313 (77)**—when D failed to appear as ordered after 1-week stay of execution of sentence, judge increased sentence because D, inter alia, "took it upon himself to flee the jurisdiction"; even assuming "voluntary" absence (record silent on subject), judge can't summarily punish for failure to appear;

C v D'Amour **428 M 725, 746 (99)**—appellate court "do(es) not review a lawful sentence," but can "review the penalty imposed upon a D who has been sentenced for a crime other than that for which he stands convicted"; SJC claimed, however, that despite DA's improper sentencing pitch (about V being "gunned down in his home," though D was acquitted of homicide), no evidence that judge had been improperly influenced;

C v Henriquez **440 M 1015 (2003)**, affirming **56 MAC 775 (2002)**—judge's comments at sentencing indicated probability that he was sentencing not merely for G verdicts but for uncharged conduct; *resentencing* **BEFORE DIFFERENT JUDGE** *necessary* to restore appearance of justice, distinguishing *C v White* 436 M 340 (2002) (no need for reassignment where judge mistakenly believed she was precluded from considering certain info but otherwise "conducted herself properly and considered only appropriate factors in" sentencing; factors germane to *ISSUE OF REASSIGNMENT TO DIFFERENT JUDGE*;

C v Ramos **63 MAC 379 (2005)**—despite admission of evidence of identical uncharged crimes & ADA's attempt to submit victim impact statements from the "prior bad act" witnesses as well as the actual complainants, judge stated on record that such statements weren't properly considered for sentencing: no relief, citing fact that D could have been sentenced far more harshly than he was;

C v Vega **54 MAC 249 (2002)**—judge sentencing D for being accessory before armed robbery could properly consider that death resulted from the armed robbery;

C v Ruggerio **32 MAC 964 (92)**—where 1 of 2 charges must be dismissed because duplicitous with other, judge may not take that charge into account in fixing length of sentence on other;

C v McCravy **430 M 758, 768 (2000)**—remand for resentencing "solely on the charge of which (D) was convicted" because D was acquitted on 3 indictments charging his culpability for death in car crash but judge stated several times that sentence was based on death involved (thus ruling out otherwise "normal" sentence of probation);

C v Goodwin **414 M 88 (93)**—judge may not consider charges on which D found NG;

US v Watts **519 US 148 (97)**—Supreme Court allows sentencing consideration of conduct/crime as to which D was found NG "so long as the acquitted conduct was proved by a preponderance of the evidence"; Court relied on 18 USC § 3661, and rejected arguments as to double jeopardy & collateral estoppel (different burdens of proof governed criminal conviction (beyond reasonable doubt)) vs. sentencing factor (conduct proved by preponderance));

C v Lewis **41 MAC 910 (96)**—from judge's regaling jurors, after G, with assertions re: D's criminal record, use of aliases & list of courts in which D was "wanted," Court inferred that sentence punished for untried offense: resentencing by a different judge ordered;

C v Leavey **60 MAC 249 (2004)**—though judge had conferred with jurors, and stated during sentencing that jury had been quite close to finding him guilty of a second charge, and though judge showed inordinate interest in a pending charge, no relief; "clear" that judge sentenced D only for single conviction, and inquiry re: pending charge = exploring possibility of disposition for concurrent sentence;

C v White **48 MAC 658, 661–62 (2000)**—resentencing ordered by different judge, despite Superior Court Appellate Division's prior slight reduction of sentences imposed, because trial judge "react(ed) to perceived inadequacies of past sentences in (D's prior) record to increase" present punishment;

C v Le Blanc **370 M 217 (76)**—"consider" pending cases; but can't punish for them or ask D to explain; caution re: inaccuracies;

C v Sitko **372 M 305 (77)**—(same); (see also Rule 28 (judgment, including imposition of sentence, presentence report) and G.L. c. 276, § 85, probation officer's duties);

C v Gill **37 MAC 457 (94)**—can consider school disciplinary records; "reliable" hearsay info about D's character, behavior, and background OK, though info not to be used "to punish . . . for crimes with which (D) had not been charged";

C v Lender **66 MAC 303 (2006)**—rejecting argument that judge improperly examined entire probation record, "including matters that had been dismissed" (unless D can show that sentence punished D for conduct other than that for which D stood convicted in present case, no relief);

C v Junta **62 MAC 120 (2004)**—no error in judge's use of affidavit of D's wife, filed in 209A matter nine years before manslaughter of fellow "hockey dad", alleging that D had earlier "struck another adult in front of minor children"; no indication D was being punished for earlier incident, and if allegations were false "we would expect that he would have tried to rebut them" when they were made by the Commonwealth;

Roberts v US **445 US 552 (80)**—can consider refusal to cooperate (unless 5th Amendment issue (*see Chapter 7-H*));

McKune v Lile **536 U.S. 24 (2002)**—requiring inmates to complete & sign "admission of responsibility" form, accepting responsibility for crimes for which they have been sentenced, & to complete "sexual history form," detailing all prior sex activities, regardless of whether they're criminal (& have or haven't been prosecuted), as condition of participation in Kansas's "Sexual Abuse Treatment Program" doesn't amount to compelled self-incrimination despite loss/reduction of privileges for failure to participate; OBJECT TO ANY SUCH CONDITIONS/PROCEDURE UNDER ARTICLE 12, DECLARATION OF RIGHTS, STATE CONSTITUTION;

C v Delisle **440 M 137 (2003)**—purportedly because letter required by "batterer," treatment program was not required by Commonwealth as a condition of probation (but instead by the program, to assess D's amenability to readmission & treatment), no violation of Fifth Amendment privilege against self-incrimination; **program's policies "prohibited the disclosure of the contents of such letters to anyone outside [program], including probation officers, without the permission of the participant"**; court rejects claim that "compulsion" lay in penalty of probation revocation;

C v Cotter **415 M 183 (93)**—because character & propensity for rehabilitation are appropriate factors in sentencing, D's refusal to agree in open court not to engage in further illegal acts with anti-abortion protesters warranted imposition of full committed sentence rather than the split sentence 1st posited (4 of 7 judges);

C v Damiano **14 MAC 615 (82)**—life sentence not vindictive for D's refusal to cooperate;

Enbinder v C **368 M 214 (75)**—can't condition dismissal on civil release (*see Chapter 14-B*);

C v Howard **42 MAC 322 (97)**—can't punish D for presumed crimes of others or to deter residents of a particular area;

C v Bland **48 MAC 666, 669 (2000)**—but deterrence of others is a permissible consideration in sentencing, so long as it's "general" message and not targeted at particular geographic area based on judge's belief as to its desirability/necessity; reference to "Barnstable County" believed not inappropriate here in circumstances;

C v Johnson **27 MAC 746 (89)**—sentence of 9–15 years after verdict not vindictive even though judge offered 6–9 years for plea at close of evidence; judge may consider D's willingness to admit guilt;

C v O'Connor **407 M 663 (90)**—judge's remark that jury's acquittal on rape 'has nothing to do with sentence I'm about to impose,' did not suggest that judge's imposition of lengthy sentence on simple A&B was vindictive;

C v Derouin **31 MAC 968 (92)**—judge's reliance on OUI-D's foul language to arresting cop not improper because relevant to show D very intoxicated;

C v Ferrara **31 MAC 648 (91)**—judge's reliance on incorrect statement by prosecutor about D's parole eligibility or discharge date required remand for resentencing;

C v Goodwin **414 M 88 (93)**—prosecutors & probation officers not permitted to bring to attention of judge information about D's prior criminal prosecutions on which D acquitted; reversal not required where judge made clear that she didn't rely on this info & where D didn't move for continuance to rebut prosecutor's factual claims; judge may consider hearsay about D's character & prior uncharged conduct, but due process requires resentencing if info inaccurate, unreliable or misleading, or if prior conviction constitutionally invalid;

C v Repoza **28 MAC 321 (90)**—imposition of lengthy sentence to ensure that D would not be released "abruptly" & would have time to "reintegrate" self into society improperly penalized D for time already served;

C v Tart **408 M 249 (90)**—no evidence on record that sentence was vindictive for D's exercise of right to trial or unconstitutionally disproportionate to offense, especially where D didn't object or file motion to revise & revoke; (BUT cf. *C v Perez* **390 M 308, 315 (83)** "in light of the delicate problem that objections to a judge's actions present to defense counsel, we do not weigh heavily against (D) the absence of an objection");

C v Quispe **433 M 508 (2001)**—judge's disapproval of immigration consequences of particular charge/disposition didn't allow him to ignore law, violate constitutional separation of powers;

C v Mills **51 MAC 366 (2001)**—at sentencing, judge alluded to public corruption inuring from a clerk-magistrate's alleged conduct, though there were no charges of this D based on such magistrate's alleged conduct, PLUS unfavorable comment on D's failure to admit wrongdoing, compared to judge's "childhood experience with priests listening to confession in church": "It should go without saying that a judge should not make references to his own personal religious views"; **S.C., 436 M 387, 399–2 (2002)** judge may not punish D "for refusing to confess before sentencing", and agreeing with Appeals Court that judge's "personal feelings" likely "interfered with his sentencing decision";

C v Keon K, **70 MAC 568 (2007)**—that juvenile D had allegedly committed similar offense (nol pross'd before jeopardy attached) was not improper consideration at sentencing; judge's reference to DYS commitment being in interest of "decent people" who wished to pray before the "blessed Virgin Mary without being sexually assaulted" was specific to facts of case (assault in church);

14-A.8. Consequences of Appeal, (Im)propriety of Changes in Sentence

North Carolina v Pearce **395 US 711 (69)**—can't punish for successfully appealing conviction, i.e., by harsher sentence upon 2d conviction, so objective reasons for harsher sentence are to be placed on record (but new information unfavorable to D, including info re: conduct occurring after his original sentencing, may be considered by sentencing judge); but see *Texas v McCullough* **475 US 134 (86)** presumption of vindictiveness upon harsher sentence does not apply if the 2 sentences were assessed by different judges (with inferentially different views of the crime and appropriate punishment);

C v Hyatt **419 M 815 (95)**—per Mass. common law, **McCullough** is not law here; 2d judge may impose harsher second sentence only if reasons are placed on record and only if basis = info which was not before the 1st judge;

C v Gagnon **37 MAC 626, 636–37 (94)**—when one conviction is vacated on appeal and as to another, the appellate court orders entry of lesser degree of guilt, there must be resentencing on affirmed convictions as well when sentencing judge relied upon conduct deemed by higher court **not** legitimately proved; cf. *Ruggerio* **32 MAC 964 (92)** where 1 of 2 charges must be dismissed because duplicitous with other, judge may not take that charge into account in fixing length of sentence on other;

C v Garofalo **46 MAC 191 (99)**—upon reversal of one conviction, Appeals Court invited trial judge to resentence D on affirmed conviction (for which D originally received 5-years probation, to run from & after committed sentence on now-reversed conviction);

C v Martin **425 M 718 (97)**—similar invitation;

C v Boyd **73 MAC 190 (2008)**—no lifetime community parole allowed because indictment did not explicitly assert "repeat offender"; other sentences remanded because judge might have altered them if he knew LCP not available;

C v Clermy **37 MAC 774, S.C., rev'd on another ground, 421 M 325 (95)**—possession of drugs was lesser included offense of poss. of drugs with intent to distribute; former ordered vacated and, because "trial judge may have been influenced in fixing sentence by the fact that the defendant had been convicted upon two complaints, resentencing . . . required";

C v Burden **48 MAC 232 (99), citing Shabazz v C 387 M 292, 295–96 (82)**—"a successful challenge to one sentence imposed at the same time as other sentences . . . opens up all the interdependent, lawful sentences for reconsideration without violating the double jeopardy clause, at least if the aggregate of the original sentences is not increased";

14-A.9. Constitutional Issues (e.g., Sentence Enhancement, Equal Protection)

18 USC § 924(c)(1)—enhanced punishment for use of firearm in drug trafficking; *Smith v US* **508 US 223 (93)**—offering to trade gun for cocaine falls within the enhancing statute; *Bailey v US* **516 US 137 (95)** "use" must connote more than mere possession of a firearm by person who commits drug offense;

Wisconsin v Mitchell **508 US 476 (93)**—sentence enhancement for offense (A&B here) motivated by racial, religious, ethnic, or sexual orientation animosity = OK;

distinguished *R.A.V. v St. Paul* 505 US 377 (92) (striking down statute proscribing offensive **expression**);

Apprendi v New Jersey 530 US 466 (2000)—after D's conviction by jury for shooting into someone's home, prosecutor asked for enhanced sentence because offense was "committed with a biased purpose," as described in applicable statute; D reserved right to challenge any 'hate crime sentence enhancement on the ground that it violates the U.S. Constitution"; though judge held evidentiary hearing on issue of "purpose" in shooting (& D testified), judge found by preponderance of evidence that D did act with racial bias motivation, so applied sentence enhancement; Supreme Court HELD that motivation factor NOT just sentencing issue, but was element of the crime, had to be included in charging document, proved beyond reasonable doubt, and be subject to jury trial unless D waived right; "it is unconstitutional for a legislature to remove from the jury the assessment of facts that increase the prescribed range of penalties to which a criminal defendant is exposed"; fact that state legislature placed its hate crime sentence 'enhancer 'within the sentencing provisions' of the criminal code' does not mean that the finding of a biased purpose to intimidate is not an essential element of the offense; (BUT cf. *C v Bruno, Wilson, Davila* 432 M 489, 500 (2000) placement of SDP provisions "among public welfare chapters of the General Laws" and statute's mouthing of "care, custody, treatment and rehabilitation" (G.L. c. 123A, § 2) cited as supporting holding that potential lifetime commitment isn't punitive);

US v Booker 125 S.Ct. 738 (2005)—U.S. Sentencing Guidelines (18 U.S.C. §§ 3553(b)(1) & 3742(e)) are unconstitutional, violative of the Sixth Amendment right to jury trial: judges are required to "take Guidelines into account," but are not bound to apply them;

Shepard v US 125 US 1254 (2005)—is "prior conviction" exception to Apprendi "eroded by this Court's subsequent Sixth Amendment jurisprudence"?; Thomas, J., says *Almendarez-Torres* 523 US 224 (98) was wrongly decided; possible limitations on prior convictions as enhancers;

C v Parzyck 44 MAC 655 (98)—no constitutional defect in statutorily mandated harsher punishment for failure to return from furlough (maximum 10 years) than for failure to return from work release (maximum 1 year) rational basis because furlough privilege = "more expansive than" work release privilege;

C v Sanchez 405 M 369 (89)—consecutive life sentences not unconstitutionally disproportionate to child rapes; prosecutor's detailed descriptions of D's prior sex offenses did not pose risk of miscarriage of justice;

C v Purdy 408 M 681 (90)—SDP commitment proceeding initiated 2 days before D's parole eligibility from state prison not shown to be presumptively punitive;

C v Allen 73 MAC 862 (2009)—because mittimus failed to include pretrial jail credit, D had been held almost three weeks beyond wrap date: Commonwealth's petition for SDP filed then was properly dismissed as too late;

C v Cory 454 M 559 (2009)—G.L. c. 265, § 47 (requiring person placed on probation after conviction of designated sex offense to wear GPS tracking device) applied to D, BUT because it was punitive and was enacted after date of D's particular sex offense, it violated prohibition against ex post facto provisions of US and MA Constitutions;

Doe v Chairperson of MA Parole Board 454 M 1018 (2009)—same as to statute (G.L. c. 127, § 133D½) requiring GPS device for persons under court-ordered parole supervision or under lifetime community parole;

Rogers v Tennessee 532 US 451 (2001)—application to D of rule abolishing common law "year and a day" rule in homicide prosecutions (death of V had to come within that time after D's action in order to make him criminally liable) NOT violative of ex post facto clause because judicial interpretation of criminal statute was neither unexpected nor indefensible by reference to law as expressed prior to conduct in issue;

14-A.10. Collateral Consequences

D.B. Winslow, et al., *Crime and Consequence: The Collateral Effects of Criminal Conduct*, **Introduction** (MCLE, Inc. 2001)—"punishments imposed in the criminal justice system provide only a starting measure of consequence for criminal conduct";

Padilla v Kentucky 130 S Ct 1473 (2010)— **deportation is a "penalty," and a severe one, not simply a "collateral consequence" of criminal proceeding;** Sixth Amendment requires defense counsel to provide *affirmative* (i.e., not just silence) competent advice to a noncitizen D regarding immigration consequences of a guilty plea (& absent such advice, noncitizen may raise claim of ineffective assistance of counsel); there is duty to inquire about citizenship/immigration status initially; duty to investigate/advise about immigration consequences of plea alternatives and sentencing alternatives;

C v Bauer 455 M 497 (2009)—arrested for OUI after three prior convictions of OUI, D refused breath test, resulting in license suspension for life (G.L. c. 90, § 24(l)(f)(1)); acquitted of OUI after jury trial, D filed motion seeking restoration of license, and trial judge denied motion: appropriate avenue for judicial review of adverse license restoration orders = civil action in nature of certiorari (G.L. c. 249, § 4) to be brought in Superior Court; SJC rejects D's argument that *judicial* decision violated separation of powers (i.e., encroaching on 'executive branch');

Sibron v NY 392 US 40, 50–58 (68)—appeal not moot simply because D has been released from incarceration: collateral consequences noted, e.g., deportation, ineligibility to become citizen, statutory crimes with elements of prior convictions (recidivism statutes), impeachment with conviction if testify in future, sentencing factor in later cases;

Evitts v Lucey 469 US 387, 391 n.4 (85)—collateral consequences include deprivation of civil rights, such as suffrage and right to hold public office; (G.L. c. 50, § 1, & G.L. c. 51, § 1, per amendments in 2001: convicted felons who are confined in correctional facility or jail can't vote);

Carafas v LaVallee **391 US 234, 238 (68)**—collateral consequences of this conviction include bar from engaging in certain businesses, from being labor union official for period of time, from voting in any NY state election, from serving as juror;

Gordon v Registry of Motor Vehicles **75 MAC 47 (2009)**—statute enacted requiring persons with two or more prior convictions of operating under influence who seek new license or reinstatement of license to install ignition interlock device (preventing ignition of engine if D's breath is over preset limit of blood alcohol concentration) upheld against challenge that it's an ex post facto penalty (US Constitution, art. I, § 10; Mass. Constitution, art. 24);

Sex Offender Registration Act, G.L. c. 6, §§ 178C–178P—registration of and publicity about Ds convicted of enumerated offenses, including some you wouldn't find logical/plausible;

Doe v A.G. **426 M 136 (97)**—procedural due process entitled this D (G of indecent A&B on person over age 14) to hearing & determination of whether he had to register & if so whether any info re him would be disseminated on request; ***Doe, SORB No 8725 v SORB*** **450 M 780 (2008)**—Board's determination that Doe had mandatory obligation to register annually solely because of prior conviction (Alford plea twenty-two years earlier to rape charge, two years' probation) violated Doe's due process rights under MA Constitution;

C v Ronald R., a juvenile, **450 M 262 (2007)**—judge denied D's motion for relief from duty to register as sex offender; SJC holds that statutorily mandated hearing re: registration was NOT an extension of sentencing process but was instead a collateral proceeding (even though it involved same participants and same judge); D can't appeal from judge's decision not to waive registration requirement, but D or Commonwealth may petition under G.L. c. 211, § 3 for review of such decision (but standard is "abuse of discretion," i.e., showing that "no conscientious judge, acting intelligently, could honestly have taken the view expressed by him"); D had burden of proof to show no need to register; D may request *evidentiary* hearing and/or written findings and legal conclusions, but judge has discretion to grant or deny; Commonwealth belatedly conceded that D WAS entitled to "consideration of a waiver of registration," given G.L. c. 6, § 178E(f) [so SJC "assume[d] without deciding] that D was "entitled to file his motion for relief from registration", fn.4];

Doe v A.G. **430 M 155 (99)**—sex offender registration statute = unconstitutional as applied to plaintiff whose underlying delinquency adjudication had been for rape of a child, when there was no prior determination (other than that implicit in the statute itself" that plaintiff was in fact likely to reoffend; procedural due process entitled plaintiff to a prior administrative determination whether he was in fact the kind of likely recidivist to whom statutory registra-

tion & notification features were directed; ***C v Miranda*** **54 MAC 502 (2002)** D didn't lose right to assert unconstitutionality as applied simply because he at least partly abided by the registration requirement of the statute;

C v Rosado **450 M 657 (2008)**—homeless defendant listed as his 'permanent' address on required SORB "registration" a homeless shelter, but shelter had daily lottery system for available beds and D actually stayed there only eleven nights in a five-week period: SJC orders required finding of not guilty for "knowingly providing false info and knowingly failing to provide notice of change of address; D had crossed out "temporary" and "mailing" address boxes on form, and registered in person at local police department every 90 days; SORB should amend form to provide practical way to show "homeless";

C v Becker **71 MAC 81 (2008)**—conviction for failure to register (SORB) upheld: that D's offense was almost ten years old, was in NY, and was a misdemeanor did not bar it from being found by rational trier of fact to be a "like offense" to indecent assault and battery on person over age fourteen (D stipulated that he touched woman's buttocks without her consent);

Sexually Dangerous Persons—G.L. c. 123A ("civil" commitment for up to life for "treatment" if conviction is for "sexual offense," defined in c. 123A § 1);

Lifetime Parole—G.L. c. 127, § 133D; G.L. c. 265, § 45;

C v Pagan **445 M 315 (2005)**—standard and burden of proof ambiguous as to imposition of lifetime community parole in some cases, and so unconstitutional as to those; complaint or indictment must allege that D is repeat offender (if such is essential to imposition of LCP given the crime charged); warning that Supreme Court caselaw (*Apprendi v NJ*, etc.) dictates that this enhanced sentence cannot be based on factual findings made by judge rather than jury;

DNA Databank Offenses—G.L. c. 22E, § 3 (murder, manslaughter, indecent A&B, mayhem, assault to murder, attempt to murder by poisoning, armed robbery, armed assault with intent to rob, armed assault in dwelling, use of firearm during commission of felony, home invasion, rape, assault with intent to rape, kidnapping, armed B&E in nighttime with intent to commit felony, unarmed burglary in nighttime, abduction for prostitution, administering drugs with intent to rape, inducing minor to become prostitute, deriving support from child prostitution, open & gross lewdness, incest, dissemination of obscenity, solicitation of child pornography, dissemination of child porno, unnatural & lascivious acts, engaging in sex for fee); see also G.L. c. 106, § 8, requiring inmates to submit DNA sample if they have ever been convicted of a listed offense; requiring persons currently on probation or parole as result of conviction or judicial determination resulting from a charge of any listed offense to submit DNA sample;

Landry v AG **429 M 336 (99)**—creation of DNA database (G.L. c. 22E, §§ 1–15) not barred by Fourth Amendment or Article 14; "minor intrusion of blood test is outweighed by strong state interest in preserving a positive recorded ID of convicted persons";

Murphy v Dept. of Correction **429 M 736 (99)**—even if D is incarcerated for an offense NOT listed in § 3, his DNA can be seized if he has previously been convicted of a listed offense;

C v Smith **444 M 497 (2005)**—requirement of DNA sample applies to persons convicted of any felony, including those stemming from complaint in District Court (& not just on indictments); prerequisite is an "offense . . . punishable by imprisonment in state prison", G.L. c. 22E, § 3 (not whether the particular individual is or can be so sentenced);

Driver's License Suspensions/Revocations for up to five years for drug offenses—(G.L. c. 90, § 22(f); see 540 CMR 20.03); for other offenses (operating under influence, etc.) see G.L. c. 90, §§ 24, 24G, 24I, 24L, 20, 22F (4-year revocation if "habitual traffic offender");

Child Welfare/Child Custody ramifications—see G.L. c. 119, §§ 26, 29A, 29C; G.L. c. 210, § 3, and 110 CMR §§ 7.100 et seq.

Ineligibility for Employment within Executive Office of Health and Human Services—see Human Resource Policy Manual, Procedure No. 001

Loss of Public Housing—see G.L. c. 121B, § 32 & related regulations (760 CMR §§ 5.08 et seq., 6.06); 42 U.S.C. § 1437f (d)(1)(6); 24 CFR §§ 982.552(c), 960.204, 966.4(f)—denial of public housing for criminal activity or drug use; "§ 8" assistance for housing will be denied any applicant for three years after any household member has been evicted from public housing for drug-related activity; § 8 housing may be terminated if tenant is in default, or is violating conditions of probation or parole;

Immigration Consequences—if D is non-citizen, certain convictions make possible deportation, exclusion when seeking re-entry, ineligibility for asylum: see 8 USC § 1101 et seq., Gordon & Mailman's treatise, Immigration Law & Procedure (Clark Boardman, pub.); Blumenson, Fisher, Kanstroom, eds., Massachusetts Criminal Practice (LEXIS 1999) chapter 42, "Immigration Consequences of Criminal Proceedings"—if convicted of "aggravated felony" (INA § 237(a)(2)(A)(iii)) may be detained without bond, & will be deported expeditiously; ineligible for virtually all forms of relief from removal incl. asylum; may be banned from US for life; 'aggravated felony' is relatively new category, but to date has been construed extremely expansively (e.g., 'aggravated driving while under the influence' is a "crime of violence" for which term of imprisonment is at least a year, and thus an aggravated felony); definition of aggravated felony is at 8 USC § 1101(a)(43), also cited as INA § 101(a)(43);—deportable for any firearm violation (including offenses in which possession or use of firearm is essential element of crime) (INA § 237(a)(2)(C)), for crimes of domestic violence (including stalking, child abuse, child neglect & abandonment, certain violations of protective orders) (INA § 237(a)(2)(E)), for controlled substance violations (other

than a single offense of possession for one's own use of 30 grams or less of marijuana) (INA § 237(a)(2)(B)), for being a drug addict or abuser (INA § 237(a)(2)(B)(ii)), for crimes of moral turpitude (under certain circumstances—INA § 237(a)(2)(A)(i–ii));—inadmissible to US if has been convicted of or has admitted committing crime involving moral turpitude (INA § 212(a)(2)(A)(i)(I); convicted or admitted controlled substances law or regulation of a state, US, or a foreign country (INA § 212(a)(2)(A)(i)(II); if has been convicted of 2 or more offenses for which aggregate sentences imposed were 5 years or more (INA § 212(a)(2)(B)); *Padilla v Kentucky* **130 S Ct 1473 (2010)—deportation is a "penalty," and a severe one, not simply a "collateral consequence"** of criminal proceeding; 6th Amendment requires defense counsel to provide *affirmative* (i.e., not just silence) competent advice to a noncitizen D regarding immigration consequences of a guilty plea (& absent such advice, noncitizen may raise claim of ineffective assistance of counsel); there is duty to inquire about citizenship/immigration status initially; duty to investigate/advise about immigration consequences of plea alternatives and sentencing alternatives;

G.L. c. 278, § 29D—judge on plea must warn re: noncitizens & specific possible consequences; (*SEE CHAPTER 13-E herein for specific case law*)

Firearm Licensing St. 1998, c. 180, § 29—severe restrictions/disqualifications from license eligibility for prior criminal convictions: see G.L. c. 14, § 129B; see also federal restrictions, 18 USC §§ 921–22, § 924(e);

Sex Offender Registration—*Doe v AG* **426 M 136, 137 n.3 (97)**—issue whether sex offender registration laws (G.L. c. 6, §§ 178C et seq.) violates constitutional prohibition of ex post facto laws not reached, though opinion lists precedents from other jurisdictions rejecting challenges to similar statutes on ex post facto and double jeopardy grounds;

Roe v Farwell **999 F.Supp 174 (98)**—criticized *Doe v Weld* **954 M 425 (D.Mass '96)**, which held sex offender registration law (G.L. c. 6, §§ 178C et seq.) didn't violate double jeopardy or ex post facto prohibitions;

Doe v AG **426 M 136 (97)**—sex offenders entitled to evidentiary hearings as to classification if threatened classification is level two or three;

Doe v AG **430 M 155 (99)**—sex offender registration statute = unconstitutional as applied to plaintiff whose underlying delinquency adjudication had been for rape of a child, when there was no prior determination (other than that implicit in the statute itself" that plaintiff was in fact likely to re-offend; procedural due process entitled plaintiff to a prior administrative determination whether he was in fact the kind of likely recidivist to whom statutory registration & notification features were directed;

C v Miranda **54 MAC 502 (2002)**—D didn't lose right to assert unconstitutionality as applied simply because he at least partly abided by the registration requirement of the statute, & is entitled to benefit of Doe 430 M 155 (99), decided about two months after D registered;

Doe v Sex Offender Registry Board **428 M 90, 104–5 (98)**—evidentiary hearings may be before SORB rather than in Superior Court; SORB to have burden of proof; appropriateness of risk classification must be proved by preponderance of the evidence; fact-finder to make detailed findings to demonstrate that close attention has been given to the evidence and classification decision; offender may challenge board's decision in Superior Court pursuant to G.L. c. 6, § 178M, but Court may change risk designation only if designation was "arbitrary and capricious, an abuse of discretion, or otherwise not in accordance with law";

Doe, SORB No. 15606 v SORB **452 M 784 (2008)**— as long as there are four sitting Board members, vacancies on Board don't defeat Board's "jurisdiction" to act (though, fn 8, not having two mental health professionals with expertise specified by Legislature "subject[s it] to criticism and places it in violation of a legislative directive"); "penile plethysmograph" admissible as part of plaintiff's probation chronology and SORB in these circumstances wasn't required to allow fees for expert to contest validity;

Doe, SORB No. 89230 v SORB **452 M 764 (2008)**— Board has discretion to grant indigents funds for expert even when Board does not intend to rely on an expert's report or testimony; misconduct underlying a continuance without a finding may be considered re: issue of repetitive/compulsive conduct where actual evidence was not unreliable hearsay (purportedly because D admitted to sufficient facts and because police report reporting victims' observations had level of detail "support[ing] its reliability");

Coe v Sex Offender Registry Board **442 M 250 (2004)**—permissible to post upon internet site info on Level 3 offenders; see also *Smith v Doe* 538 U.S. 84, 105 (2003), concerning Alaska's sex offender registry / notification to public;

C v Bolling **72 MAC 618 (2008)**—in registering as level three sex offender, D listed in space for "permanent address", "streets of Greenfield, Franklin County, MA", and in space for "mailing address," gave a particular address and P.O. Box in Montague, Franklin County (which is adjacent to Greenfield, MA); in prosecution for failure to provide notice of address change/change of residence, that D slept somewhere other than the streets of Greenfield on a wholly transitory basis on occasion was not proof that he had changed his address; proof also failed regarding failure to notify of "secondary address" (statute defining it as four or more nights in any month or fourteen or more nights in a calendar year); "inherently transitory nature of homelessness makes it difficult to apply to homeless sex offenders the same considerations of residence applies to offenders who are not homeless";

Loe v Sex Offender Registry Board **73 MAC 673 (2009)**—while refusing relief on basis of ineffective assistance of counsel in classification before SORB, acknowledgments of counsel's "numerous shortcomings" as listed in fn.6; reserving question of whether *Saferian* (366 M 89,

96 [74]) standard for ineffective assistance controls (but see Sikora, J., cc);

Sexually Dangerous Persons (Need Not Have Multiple Convictions)—G.L. c. 123A—convicted of or adjudicated delinquent or youthful offender by reason of a sexual offense, or charged with a sex offense & found incompetent, or convicted of any "offense, the facts of which, under the totality of the circumstances, manifest a sexual motivation or pattern of conduct or series of acts of sexually-motivated offenses" AND who suffers mental abnormality or personality disorder which makes it likely he will engage in sex offenses if not confined to a secure facility, OR previously adjudicated SDP and . . . (see G.L. c. 123A § 1);

C v Grant **73 MAC 471 (2009)**—judge erred in requiring Commonwealth in SDP trial to prove D (convicted of open and grow lewdness) was likely to cause PHYSICAL harm to others if not confined; this "added" element not in statute; FURTHER REVIEW ALLOWED 453 M 1109, and at 455 M 1022 (2010), appeal dismissed as moot, and reserving for future the issue whether a finding of sexual dangerousness is permissible based on history of noncontact sexual offenses and likelihood of future noncontact offenses;

C v Blake **454 M 267 (2009)**—judge MUST render decision & file written findings in jury-waived SDP trial (G.L. c. 123A, § 14) within thirty days of end of trial "absent extraordinary circumstances" (13-month delay here prompting holding);

C v Dagle **345 M 539 (63)**—no double jeopardy violation found in (G.L. c. 123A) SDP commitment on prison superintendent's petition after sentencing/incarceration for sex offense;

C v Gomes **355 M 479 (69)**—same;

C v Nieves **446 M 583 (2006)**—incompetent individual may be subjected to trial and adjudication as SDP, with only caveat being that he must have an attorney, and that to continue commitment, Commonwealth must seek appointment of court-appointed attorney who "may then exercise the rights of the incompetent person" to periodic reviews of sexual dangerousness;

C v Burgess **450 M 366 (2008)**—even though, because he was incompetent, he was never tried and convicted of the sex offenses (see G.L. c. 123A, § 15); SJC here rejects D's argument that his incompetence prevented fair adjudication re: whether he committed underlying offenses (as prerequisite to SDP); rights granted by GL c.123A may be exercised by counsel when D is incompetent;

C v Purdy **408 M 681 (90)**—SDP commitment proceeding initiated 2 days before D's parole eligibility from state prison not shown to be presumptively punitive;

C v Walsh **376 M 53 (78)**—single bizarre crime can be "compulsive," so SDP;

C v Morrow **363 M 601 (73)**—on G. plea, judge need not warn D; but now see M.R.Crim.P. 12 (c) (3)(B)—SDP warning = part of plea colloquy; (*see Chapter 21, Rape; Chapter 13-E, Plea of Guilty, Procedures*);

(*Solem v Helm* **463 US 277 (83)** & *Rummel v Estelle* **445 US 263 (80)**—re: Cruel & Unusual)

C v Arment **412 M 55 (92)**—statutory amendment's failure to apply new stringent provisions to SDP commitments after certain date was equal protection violation; initiation of SDP examinations/declarations can occur only if a prisoner engages in sexually assaultive behavior while under criminal sentence;

C v Crepeau **427 M 410 (98)**—D ordered released, since under *Arment* (**412 M 55**), his SDP commitment was invalid, having been initiated only because his jailer believed that he appeared to be SDP; SJC rejected implicitly Commonwealth's position that alleged statements by D during psychological evaluations while in custody could constitute "sexually assaultive behavior" (i.e., that he had raped women in addition to the victim in the crime for which he was in custody, that he felt he had to act out aggressive and sexual feelings or kill himself), though invited "new legislation" to create a means by which to detain a person who credibly threatens to assault others if given opportunity;

Sheridan, petitioner **412 M 599 (92)**—legislature cannot condition discharge from SDP confinement on requirement that D submit to psych examination & waive § 20B privilege;

C v Ferreira **67 MAC 109 (2006)**—D had no constitutional right to have counsel attend the "qualified examiner" interviews, or to have them recorded by audiotape; D did have right to refuse to speak to examiners (& he did refuse); D's claim that counsel was ineffective in failing to facilitate the conditions D imposed on interviews (presence of counsel, tape-recording) failed for lack of proof that counsel likely deprived him of substantial ground of defense;

C v Connors **447 M 313 (2006)**—while D had right to refuse to speak to "qualified examiners" in SDP proceedings, he couldn't "selectively invoke this privilege"; no denial of privilege against self-incrimination to require him to submit to exam by Commonwealth's psychiatrist as a condition of the admission of "his" evidence (the result of psych. exam which included interview[s] with D); listing of analogous cases in similar contexts, e.g., *Blaisdell v. Commonwealth* 372 M 753 (77);

C v Callahan **440 M 436 (2003)**—Commonwealth cannot obtain D's old psychiatric records for use by "qualified examiners" to determine alleged sexual dangerousness; G.L. c. 123A, § 13(b) did not abrogate existing privileges;

Mendonza v Commonwealth **423 M 771 (96)**—Declaration of Rights requires that commitment of SDPs be based on proof beyond reasonable doubt, though US Supreme Court has interpreted federal constitution to allow analogous commitment based on clear &convincing evidence;

Wyatt, petitioner **428 M 347, 351 (98)**—double jeopardy not implicated in G.L. c. 123A, § 9 proceedings because statute "does not intend or impose punishment"; Commonwealth's argument that judge shouldn't have instructed that petitioner was presumed NOT sexually dangerous dismissed as "frivolous"; absence of expert evidence from petitioner that he wasn't sexually dangerous did not require finding of dangerousness;

C v Bruno et al. **432 M 489 (2000)**—persons whose offenses occurred long before effective date of newest SDP legislation are nonetheless within its purview because their "mental conditions" are analyzed after Act's effective date; not prohibited as 'ex post facto' anyway because not punitive (because Legislature said Act was for persons' 'care, custody, treatment & rehabilitation,' notwithstanding purpose of 'protect(ing) vulnerable members of our communities from sexual offenders'); prosecutor can't file petition to commit person unless it's "likely" that person has requisite mental condition, & determination must be supported by 'sufficient facts,' not just averred; temporary commitment can't occur merely on filing of petition, but instead must have evidence before a court that person is sexually dangerous & likely to commit future harm; temporary commitment may be sought only when named person is scheduled for release prior to 'probable cause' hearing mandated by the statute (G.L. c. 123A); probable cause standard = the probable cause to arrest standard, i.e., evidence "sufficient to warrant judge in believing that person suffers from mental abnormality or personality defect" & sufficient to warrant judge in believing that person "is likely to engage in sexual offenses" is not confined to secure facility; requires expert testimony; without expert evidence, no temporary commitment may last longer than 24 hours; even with expert evidence, temporary commitment under G.L. c. 123A, § 12(e) may last no longer than 10 business days prior to start of probable cause hearing, "absent unusual circumstances"; at probable cause hearing, Commonwealth's burden of proof is same as for probable cause 'bind-over' hearing., i.e., the "directed verdict" standard, more than probable cause for arrest, but less than would prove D's guilt beyond a reasonable doubt; if probable cause is then shown (& expert evidence is essential for this), person can be committed for not more than 60 days for examination & diagnosis under supervision of 2 qualified examiners; no later than 15 days before expiration of examination period, examiners must file with court written report & recommendation for disposition of the commitment petition; within 14 days of receiving report, DA or AG may petition for a trial to determine whether person is sexually dangerous; rights to jury trial, unanimity of verdict, & burden of proof beyond a reasonable doubt; committed person may petition once every 12 months for examination and discharge;

C v Chapman **444 M 15 (2005)**—fact that D had eventually been declared not SDP under prior law & was returned to DOC custody to serve remainder of sentence didn't preclude Commonwealth from petitioning under new SDP law, prior to D's release from custody, for SDP determination (no "collateral estoppel" because determination pertains to present, not past, status); dissent by Marshall, C.J., joined by Ireland, J., says new petition has no allegation of conduct/thoughts after time of finding of not SDP, & faults as basis mere fact that D didn't undergo treatment/therapy after favorable finding;

C v Reese **438 M 519 (2003)**—ordinary rules of evidence apply in SDP cases & probable cause hearing in such cases; "bindover" standard of probable cause applies (*see Myers v. Commonwealth*, 363 M 843, 850 (73), i.e., a "directed verdict" standard); credibility determinations are left to the TRIAL fact finder EXCEPT in cases where evidence at probable-cause hearing is "so incredible" that no reasonable person could rely on it; SJC rejected hearing judge's finding that expert's claim (that DSM-4 had less value alone than judge believed it did) was "so incredible";

Ready, petitioner **63 MAC 171 (2005)**—AASI test (Abel Assessment for Sexual Interest) was subjected to a 3-day evidentiary hearing pursuant to *C v Lanigan* (419 M 19 (94)), after which judge permissibly ruled that the test had not been accepted in the scientific community and that petitioner had failed to demonstrate test's reliability;

C v Blanchette **54 MAC 165 (2002)**—standard of proof for probable cause in SDP prosecution = same as for such hearing in ordinary criminal cases, i.e., directed verdict standard articulated in *Myers v Commonwealth* 363 M 843 (73);

C v Boucher **438 M 274 (2002)**—"likely" to commit offense, in SDP statute, doesn't mean "more likely than not," & instead it's for trier of fact to decide what "likely" means in assessing the defendant's risk of reoffending, using factors "including the seriousness of the threatened harm, the relative certainty of the anticipated harm, and the possibility of successful intervention to prevent harm";

C v Gagnon **439 M 826 (2003)**—Commonwealth needn't file petition for commitment six months before D's release, nor give D six months' notice of intent to file petition (G.L. c. 123A, § 12(a)&(b)); though Superior Court dismissed SDP petition for failure of qualified examiners to submit reports within 45-day statutory deadline, SJC vacated dismissal because delay didn't result in D's being detained at Treatment Center more than the statutorily-set sixty days before petition for trial, contrasting:

C v Dinguis **74 MAC 901 (2009)**—that Department of Correction didn't give DA 6 months' notice before expiration of D's sentence didn't matter: dismissal not required & though D had right to move for release pending probable cause hearing, judge didn't err in denying: since D was found SDP, there was no loss of liberty which wouldn't have occurred if required notice had been given;

C v Kennedy **435 M 527 (2001)**—dismissal of SDP petition because D was detained for months beyond sixty-day period in which qualified examiners were to report and Commonwealth was to decide whether to petition for trial;

C v Parra **445 M 262 (2005)**—because Commonwealth wasn't notified of judge's determination of "prob-able cause" to believe D was SDP, the statutorily required report of two qualified examiners wasn't ordered and wasn't filed until 69 days after expiration of 60-day evaluation period: dismissal of petition was required;

C v DeBella **442 M 683 (2004)**—G.L. c. 123A, § 14(a) requires trial to be begun within sixty days of Commonwealth filing petition for trial BUT may be continued upon motion by either party "for good cause" shown, or by court on its own motion "if interests of justice so require," unless D is "substantially prejudiced" by continuance; while these are to be "strictly construed," and henceforth findings re: continuances must be on record, D here held to have "acquiesced" in the delay;

C v Gross **447 M 691 (2006)**—when Commonwealth failed to file its "petition for trial" within 14 days **after** the filing of the qualified examiners' reports (& thereby failed to give court the authority to detain D pending outcome of trial), petition for SDP commitment was properly dismissed; petition for trial = mandatory, & "set[s] schedule for remainder of proceedings"; the original § 12(b) petition's form language requesting "trial by jury on the merits" is not equivalent, as it triggers only a probable cause hearing (with examination and qualified examiners' reports to follow);

C v Alvarado **452 M 194 (2008)**—after judge found probable cause to believe D sexually dangerous, D was committed for evaluation and qualified examiners filed reports 43 days later; Commonwealth's petition for trial was filed 16 days after the reports' filing (contrary to statutory directive that petition for trial be filed within 14 days thereafter) BUT because it was within sixty days of the order of commitment, dismissal not required; the "sixty-day time period" limiting confinement is the relevant period re: liberty interest;

C v Dube **59 MAC 476 (2003)**—to meet its burden of proving sexual dangerousness, **Commonwealth must present expert testimony that D is SDP**, citing *C v Bruno* 432 M 489, 513 (2000) & *C v Reese* 438 M 519, 524 (2003) (expert testimony required both to support order of "temporary commitment" and finding of probable cause, a prerequisite to SDP trial); dismissal of petition is appropriate as soon as lack of expert testimony is apparent (here, as to one D, at juncture of probable cause hearing, and as to other D, at point when previously opining expert changed his opinion after access to three other experts' opinions and his own further examination of D);

C v Bradway **62 MAC 280 (2004)**—rejects argument that qualified examiners cannot give testimony without Daubert-Lanigan analysis/test;

C v Boyer **61 MAC 582 (2004)**—Commonwealth's burden not met by expert's "SDP" opinion from an earlier probable cause hearing which had been recanted at trial (although preliminary report was admissible), even as supplemented by other experts' belief that D was pedophile, though not SDP (because not likely to reoffend);

C v Poissant **443 M 558 (2005)**—after examination by two qualified examiners pursuant to G.L. c. 123A,

§ 13(a), neither of whom concluded that D = SDP, D is not obligated to submit to exam by yet another expert selected by Commonwealth; D's refusal to submit is not a ground for excluding expert testimony presented in D's defense at trial; id. at 560 n. 6—RESERVES QUESTIONS WHETHER STATUTE IMPLICITLY REQUIRES AT LEAST ONE "QE" TO BELIEVE SDP IN ORDER FOR COMMONWEALTH TO PROCEED TO TRIAL, & WHETHER CONTINUED DETENTION OF D = UNCONSTITUTIONAL WHEN BOTH QE's SAY D NOT SDP;

*** *Johnstone, petitioner* **453 M 544 (2009)**—at § 9 petition for discharge trial, when both qualified examiners opine that petitioner is no longer sexually dangerous, testimony & report of Community Access Board to the contrary is inadequate to support SDP finding, and "the same reasoning applies to initial commitment proceedings" under G.L. c. 123A, § 12(b);

C v Knapp **441 M 157 (2004)**—allegedly sexually dangerous person must be securely confined after finding of probable cause (G.L. c. 123A, §§ 13(a)&14(a)); *C v Bradway* **62 MAC 280, 291 (2004)**—current SDP statute, unlike former incarnations, neither dictates "less restrictive alternatives to commitment," nor provides for any such options;

C v Shedlock **58 MAC 445 (2003)**—D's sentence for rape was augmented by subsequent from and after sentence for escape; no error in filing petition for SDP commitment toward end of "escape" sentence (instead of before end of prior rape sentence); *McLeod* **437 M 286 (2002)** distinguished (D completed sentences for sex crimes years before);

C v Markvart **437 M 331 (2002)**—in trial re: D's alleged sexual dangerousness, reversal for admitting police report relating to an alleged sexual assault by D which was subject of only a nol prossed indictment, concerning construction of G.L. c. 123A, § 14(c);

McHoul, petitioner **445 M 143 (2005)**—annual treatment reports and "group notes" (records from Treatment Center) = admissible pursuant to statute, despite containing totem-pole hearsay; admissibility of records/reports in SDP proceedings = "radical departure from ordinary evidentiary rules," but this is OK given statutes;

C v Boyer **58 MAC 662 (2003)**—reversal of SDP finding due to substantive use at trial, over objection, of third-party assertions within parole report (that D asked girlfriend's two-year-old daughter if she "was horny"); but see *C v Given* **441 M 741 (2004), on further review of 59 MAC 390 (2003)** (police report concerning a prior sexual offense to which D pled guilty is admissible without redaction, even though it contains statements re: uncharged contemporaneous sexual assault);

See also Chapter 14-N, post, re: Recidivist Sentencing;

14-B. DISMISSAL: MOTIONS TO DISMISS AND ACCORD/SATISFACTION

See also Chapter 14-D;

See "Sealing," Chapter 14-U; specific areas, e.g., Complaints; & Chapter 19, Double Jeopardy & Chapter 1-B, Superceding Indictments;

M.R.Crim.P. 28(d)—dismissal (vs. N.G.) can appear on pre-sentence reports;

M.R.Crim.P. 13—Motion to Dismiss = written, affidavit, memorandum; filing deadlines (*see Chapter 6 & Chapter 14-D*); see Chapter 5 for cases on substantive defects in complaints & indictments;

District Court Standards of Judicial Practice, Arraignment (1977). 6:01—judge's discretion whether to dismiss; if complaining witness & DA ask "drop case" & no dismissal, "clear duty to enter NG" if no evidence;

C v Zannino **17 MAC 73 (83)**—D must file written motion & affidavit; dismissal "with prejudice" no per se bar to reprosecution;

ABA Standards for Criminal Justice, Prosecution Function & Defense Function (3d ed. 1993) 3-3.9(b)—DA not obliged to present all charges (e.g., if has a reasonable doubt, possible improper motives of a complainant, reluctance of victim to testify, disproportion of the authorized punishment in relation to the particular offense/offender, likelihood of prosecution in another jurisdiction, cooperation of the accused in apprehending/convicting others) (*see Chapter 14-C, Nolle Prosequi*);

C v Downs **31 MAC 467 (91)**—motion for reconsideration of final orders of trial judge limited to 30 days; nondispositive order limited to reasonable time during pendency of case; affidavit is desirable but not required; hearing is desirable if motion contains "fresh material" or if judge will "alter substantially" original disposition; explanation of change should be put on record;

C v Avola **28 MAC 988 (90)**—motion to dismiss must generally be raised pretrial to preserve challenge to facial invalidity of complaint;

C v Bell **67 MAC 266 (2006)**—D could be guilty of attempting to rape child and soliciting sex for fee even though, unbeknownst to him, he was negotiating with undercover police officer, so no actual child was at risk; though crime was "factually" impossible, it was not "legally" impossible;

C v Oakes **407 M 92 (90)**—to preserve for appeal an as-applied challenge to constitutionality of statute, pretrial motion to dismiss insufficient; motion for required finding required;

Ventresco v C **409 M 82 (91)**—G.L. c. 211, § 3 petition is proper means for D to challenge denial of motion to dismiss only if single justice finds substantial claim of violation of substantive rights plus irremediable error; judge's denial of D's motion to dismiss based on invalid extension of grand jury sessions upheld;

14-B.1. Dismissals Contingent upon Civil Releases

Enbinder v C **368 M 214 (75)**—judge shouldn't condition dismissal on signing release of store cops from civil liability;

Newton v Rumery **778 F.2d 66 (1st Cir. '85)**—public policy voids D's covenant not to sue (for dropped charges); **480 US 386 (87)** not per se bad, OK if voluntary;

Hall v Ochs **817 F.2d 920 (1st Cir. '87)**—"involuntary" under *Rumery* because D held in jail without attorney unless he signed;

Foley v Lowell District Court **398 M 800 (86)**—condemn judge or DA conditioning dismissal on civil waiver by D;

C v Klein **400 M 309 (87)**—can reopen continuance without a finding because of D's civil suit (because deal was D's suggestion);

14-B.2. Prosecutorial or Judicial Misconduct

See Chapter 6-D for cases on sanctions for discovery violations & Chapter 7-L on sanctions for evidence lost or destroyed by government;

C v Vascovitch **40 MAC 62 (96)**—judge could not dismiss larceny of motor vehicle complaint over DA's objection (albeit while ordering restitution): usurpation of both prosecutorial AND legislative (G.L. c. 266, §§ 28–29) authority;

C v Thurston **419 M 101 (94)**—judge here illegitimately dismissed indictments but SJC recognized a judicial power to dismiss in the interests of justice despite Commonwealth objection; D must file affidavit(s), judge must accord "due process" to Commonwealth;

C v Quispe **433 M 508 (2001)**—judge's personal disapproval of immigration consequences of particular law didn't warrant his override of applicable statute & dismissal of charge;

C v Manning **373 M 438 (77)**—dismissal for interfering with counsel relationship;

C v Teixeira **76 MAC 101 (2010)**—cop's niece was percipient witness in D's case, and cop intentionally approached D to speak of his niece and to be intimidating to D; D and his attorney claimed that cop's conduct made him too fearful to testify in his own defense; IF found that cop threatened to kill D or threatened that D's acquittal would lead to continuing police harassment, "dismissal of the charges might well be appropriate even in the absence of any demonstrated prejudice"; Brown, J., dissenting, says deprivation of right to testify = grave violation of fundamental due process, & that judge's finding re: basis for D's decision to waive right to testify= unreasonable, so would order dismissal with prejudice;

C v King **400 M 283 (87)**—no per se dismissal (no harm here) from eavesdrop on attorney-client talks;

C v Fontaine **402 M 491 (88)**—(same) for jail cell videotaping; harm shown only on one charge;

US v Mastroianni **749 F.2d 900 (1st Cir. '84)**—harmless, unintentional intrusion by informant co-D;

C v Maylott **43 MAC 516 (97)**—no dismissal for denial of telephone call at police station; *But SEE also Chapter 20, suppression issues;*

C v Mason **453 M 873 (2009)**—egregious police misconduct in retaliating against D for his clash with police chief: bail commissioner on call set bail for five times expected amount after phone call from cop, without any opportunity for D's participation, AND thereafter intentional withholding of information led jail officials to believe that D had "no bail" status, depriving him of release between Saturday afternoon and Monday at court; dismissal held to have been too severe a sanction, there having been no "prejudice" affecting right to fair trial; recourse to civil remedies and departmental police discipline available "if appropriate";

C v Lam Hue To **391 M 301 (84)**—dismissal (mistrial) for late disclosure of exculpatory evidence can bar retrial if "irremediable harm" (*see Chapter 19, Double Jeopardy*);

C v Light **394 M 112 (85)**—new trial, not dismissal, for (this) withheld exculpatory evidence, because not intentional or egregious DA misconduct;

C v Baran **74 MAC 256 (2009)**—while affirming allowance of motion for new trial, Court specifically did not "preclude[e] [D] from bringing a motion seeking to dismiss the indictments pursuant to *C v Merry* **453 M 653, 665-666 (2009)"** (dismissal of complaint due to prosecutorial misconduct if it resulted in such irremediable harm that fair trial no longer possible, or where conduct "so egregious that dismissal is warranted to deter similar future misconduct"); in **Merry**, no finding that prosecutor "deliberately" failed to disclose what he understood to be exculpatory evidence or "intentionally misled" jury by knowingly making false statements in closing argument (if otherwise, "might have been grounds for dismissal");

C v Gratereaux **49 MAC 1, 6 (2000)**—dismissal not required because Commonwealth "failed to produce" informant for trial testimony; Commonwealth gave defense informant's last known address, birth date, & social security #, & he wasn't in custody, & no showing Commonwealth "obstruct(ed) . . . access to" him;

C v Barnes-Miller **59 MAC 832 (2003)**—alleged victim of annoying telephone calls was purportedly the "other woman" prompting D's divorce; "victim's" claim of 5th Amendment privilege at deposition in divorce action held legitimate, and judge erred in dismissing, over Commonwealth objection, the criminal case (at which she remained committed to testifying);

C v Tripolone **44 MAC 23 (97)**—failure to give D opportunity to be heard prior to issuance of misdemeanor complaint (G.L. c. 218, § 35A) warranted dismissal (albeit without prejudice); operational policy of particular court to find, automatically, the § 35A exception ("if there is imminent threat of bodily injury, (or) of the commission of a crime") if there was an application for a complaint for a violation of a c. 209A order was contrary to statute;

C v Anderson **402 M 576 (88)**—dismissal "WITH prejudice" won't stand unless "egregious" misconduct or 2d trial can't be fair;

C v Hosmer **49 MAC 188 (2000)**—judge's dismissal of OUI-2d offense complaint with prejudice, when ADA sought (mid-testimony of first witness) to amend, by one day, the date of offense (recognizing belatedly that the stop occurred twenty minutes before the date noted in the complaint), IMPROPER: no prejudice to D; judge's irritation with prosecutor's office ("this has happened before") cannot override "interest of the general public in just disposition of" offense;

C v Connelly **418 M 37 (94)**—no dismissal with prejudice warranted simply because ADA needed continuance due to non-appearance of material police officer witness (no "speedy" issue);

C v Jackson **27 MAC 521 (89)**—no dismissal for cop's nonappearance because cop might not have received summons or might have thought DA would learn of National Guard duty;

C v Lucero **450 M 1032 (2008)**—G.L. c. 211, § 3 relief for Commonwealth after trial court judge's entry of "required finding of not guilty" when case was called for trial, but no opening statements were made or evidence presented: sexual assault complainant had not yet appeared at courtroom & DA said couldn't prove case without her; when DA subsequently learned that she had been present but in wrong courtroom, trial court judge had denied motion for reconsideration;

C v Hrycenko **61 MAC 378 (2004)**—dismissal (without prejudice) for want of prosecution (witness didn't appear; Commonwealth hadn't summonsed her) could be undone by motion to vacate; *C v Steadward* 43 MAC 272 (97) distinguished (dismissal there based on failure to comply with "no-fix" statute, G.L. c. 90C, § 2, re: motor vehicle violations, & Commonwealth didn't seek relief by way of appeal or trial court motion, and instead simply obtained new complaint); if D could show "misconduct" by Commonwealth or prejudice from reinstatement of charges, reinstatement maybe improper);

C v Reddy **74 MAC 304 (2009)**—on 4 District Ct charges, D wanted only cc sentences to run with sentence in unrelated case on which he was being held on parole violation detainer; DA wanted 2½ years H.C.; judge told D he couldn't order "cc" on parole violation case because sentence had not yet been imposed on it; D wanted continuance to accomplish that, and judge scheduled for change of plea, to be "within 30 days", which did not happen; DA indicted D as habitual offender (exposed to mandatory 20-year sentence): appeals court reversed judge's dismissal of indictments: DA had made no promise on which D reasonably could rely (& judge here made factual finding that there was no evidence of "vindictiveness" or "bad faith" of Commonwealth); further review allowed 455 M 1109 (2009) and at 457 M 1002 (2010), same result

as MAC, i.e., order dismissing habitual offender indictment is reversed;

C v Henderson **411 M 309 (91)**—loss of victim's contemporaneous written description of assailant, which was "potentially exculpatory," justified dismissal; neither actual prejudice nor bad faith by government required; federal rule of *Arizona v Youngblood* **488 US 51 (88)**, rejected;

C v Troy **405 M 253 (89)**—judge properly restricted prosecution theories of first degree murder because of government's "careless" destruction of blood sample;

C v Monteagudo **427 M 484 (98)**—"egregious government conduct" is issue of constitutional law and not a jury issue or defense; is not intended to circumvent "predisposition" test in an entrapment defense; should be raised by motion to dismiss or, if misconduct evidence comes to light only at trial, by motion for required finding of not guilty;

C v Hurst **39 MAC 603 (96)**—no dismissal with prejudice for DA's plea negotiations with Ds who had not filed written waiver of counsel unless Ds had not meant to waive counsel and suffered prejudice;

C v Lewin (I) **405 M 566 (89)**—prosecutorial & police misconduct involving either delayed disclosure or fabrication of informant by police didn't justify dismissal where irremediable prejudice to D not established; D entitled to voir dire hearing on potentially exculpatory evidence from putative informant & to elicit at trial government misconduct without rebuttal by prosecutor; motion judge's finding that informant existed was clearly erroneous where there was equally compelling evidence that informant was fabricated;

C v Druce **453 M 686 (2009)**—newspaper obtained videotape (made at prison medical unit of D allegedly reenacting victim's killing as it occurred in prison) and published article in which it was described in detail (videotape never seen by defense counsel during two years postkilling and pre-trial), but SJC held that voir dire of prospective jurors was sufficient to assure no prejudice to D; prison personnel harassed mentally ill D and interfered with counsel right, but no relief;

C v Phillips **413 M 50 (92)**—unlawful Boston Police Department policy authorizing "search on sight" of suspected gang members justified suppression of evidence but not dismissal;

C v Waters **410 M 224 (91)**—misconduct by cops who are members of prosecution team done in pursuit of own unlawful scheme not attributable to Commonwealth; promise of favorable disposition by such cops not binding on Commonwealth;

Doe v DA for Plymouth District **29 MAC 671 (91)**—motion to dismiss or motion for evidentiary hearing under M.R.Crim.P. 12(c)(1) proper means of enforcing prosecution's performance of plea bargain, not mandamus;

C v O'Brien **35 MAC 827 (94)**—no dismissal for alleged promise by DA, prior to complaint's issuance, to bring & keep sexual assault case in District Court because no detrimental reliance by defense and because dismissal not otherwise "required to vindicate principles of fairness encompassed in . . . due process of law";

14-B.3. Grand Jury issues, Lack of Probable Cause to Believe D Guilty of Crime

See Chapter 1-C for cases on motions to dismiss based on deficiencies in presentation before grand jury (e.g., McCarthy & O'Dell motions);

Bank of Nova Scotia v US 487 US 250 (88)—no harm from grand jury abuses;

C v DiBennadetto 436 M 310 (2002)—if application for complaint has been allowed, & complaint has issued after show cause hearing, judge may not conduct new evidentiary hearing to review finding of probable cause to issue process; instead, remedy = motion to dismiss, for failure to present sufficient evidence to clerk-magistrate (or judge), for "violation of the integrity of the proceeding" (e.g., 'unreasonable restrictions' on D's opportunity to present evidence would be denial of right to hearing created by c. 218, § 35A), "or for any other challenge to the validity of the complaint"; though cross-examination of witnesses proffered in support of the complaint goes to credibility of the complainant, there is no "right to cross-examine witnesses at hearing on issuance of process on complaint";

14-B.4. Double Jeopardy

See Chapter 19 for cases on double jeopardy;

Costarelli v C 374 M 677 (78)—"dismissal" after trial (for insufficient evidence) = equivalent to N.G.; no reprosecution though dismissal purported to be "without prejudice"; (see also **Pomerleau 13 MAC 530 (82)**, post);

C v Juvenile 6 MAC 194 (78)—"dismissal" (on motion for required finding of NG) of lesser included offense (lewd & lascivious behavior) bars reprosecution for greater (prostitution);

C v Nessolini 19 MAC 1016 (85)—(plea) G. to lesser included offense = dismissal of greater; but see **C v Johnson 406 M 533 (90)** not unless "lesser" is, strictly construed, on 'elements' test, a lesser INCLUDED offense; D's plea here to B&E in District Court (when prosecution bungled message that case was to be bound over) did not require dismissal of ensuing 'possession of burglarious implements' indictment brought vindictively;

C v Ballou 350 M 751 (66)—no jeopardy from dismissal after motion to suppress allowed; can reprosecute after SJC reversed;

C v Micheli 258 M 89 (27)—D consented to dismissal (not on merits), so retrial OK;

C v Norman 27 MAC 82 (89), affirmed, 406 M 1001 (89)—double jeopardy duplicity claim, because jurisdictional in nature, is not waived by failure to move to dismiss; but see **C v Spear 43 MAC 583 (97)** double jeopardy issue waived for this appeal by pro se D's failure to assert it in motion to dismiss pre-2d trial; convictions reversed on other ground, motion to dismiss OK prior to 3d trial, presumably;

C v Watkins 33 MAC 7 (92)—D not entitled to dismissal of rape conviction simply because he was acquitted on separate identically worded indictment (same date, same victim, several penetrations); see, however, **C v Hrycenko 417 M 309, 317 (94)** separate identically-worded indictments; D acquitted on some, convicted on some, but convictions = reversed on appeal; then, double jeopardy bar prevented retrial because it was impossible to tell which indictments were subject of previous acquittals;

C v Lopez 31 MAC 547 (91)—conviction for duplicitous lesser included cannot be placed on file or given concurrent sentence, & instead must be dismissed;

C v Jarvis 68 MAC 538 (2007)—following D's jury-waived trial on OUI (guilty), D requested new judge for trial re: the existence of three prior OUI convictions; prior to "transferring that part of the case to second judge," first judge sentenced D to two years, one year committed, balance suspended for two years, "on the primary offense of OUI"; though this was procedurally improper (G.L. c. 278, § 11A: sentencing should not occur until bifurcated trial is completed), double jeopardy clause did not bar "resentencing" following the finding of guilt on the subsequent offense charge; D had no legitimate expectation of finality in the prematurely-imposed sentence;

14-B.5. Speedy Trial

See Chapter 7-O for cases on dismissal for speedy trial violations & for want of prosecution; Chapter 1-B for indictment superceding District Court proceedings;

C v Silva 10 MAC 784 (80)—District Court dismissal for speedy (& discovery) violation bars Superior Court reprosecution;

C v Ludwig 370 M 31 (76)—dismissal "with prejudice" on speedy (G.L. c. 276, § 35, as then written, 10-day rule) grounds bars reprosecution;

C v Thomas 353 M 429 (67)—can't nol pros to avoid c. 276, § 35's time requirements (previously no continuance for >10 days if D in custody; now no continuance for >30 days if D in custody & objects);

C v Conant 12 MAC 287 (81)—10-day violation: no presumptive prejudice;

C v Carrunchio 20 MAC 943 (85)—no per se dismissal for "no further continuance" order violation;

C v Borders 73 MAC 911 (2009)—after continuances for several reasons (including unavailability of cop-witness at suppression hearing) Commonwealth's continuance motion on first set trial date (because same cop witness not available) should have been allowed; dismissal with prejudice vacated; separation of powers cited (judge usurped prosecutorial authority);

C v Pomerleau 13 MAC 530 (82)—non-speedy dismissal "without prejudice" = no bar to later prosecution;

C v Joseph **27 MAC 516 (89)**—upholding dismissal for 3 continuances because Commonwealth denied discovery even if no prejudice shown;

14-B.6. Appeal of Dismissal, Preservation of Issue

M.R.Crim.P. 15—DA's right to interlocutory appeal if motion to dismiss allowed (*see Chapter 15*);

See cases, above, Chapter 14-A-4, limitations on judge's discretion: *C v Cheney* **440 M 568 (2003)**, *C v Powell* **453 M 320 (2009)**;

C v Mandile **15 MAC 83 (83)**—judge may take timely motion to reconsider dismissal; but 87 days = untimely without special circumstances;

Monohan v Commonwealth **414 M 1001 (93)**—dismissal with prejudice upon Commonwealth's 2d motion to continue trial date could not be circumvented by refiling the complaints; Commonwealth should have either (a) appealed the dismissal or (b) sought, within 30 days, reconsideration by the judge who ordered dismissal;

C v Borders **73 MAC 911 (2009)**—Commonwealth successfully appealed dismissal with prejudice/denial of continuance of first trial date (though several other continuances had occurred, including one for unavailability of same cop witness [earlier, for suppression hearing]);

C v Turner **71 MAC 665 (2008)**—because, after ordering suppression of evidence, judge dismissed charges "for lack of prosecution" during the time period in which Commonwealth was entitled to seek leave to appeal, dismissal = reversed (as was suppression order);

G.L. c. 111E (formerly G.L. c. 123, §§ 38-55)—"Drug Rehabilitation" = dismissal after drug program success—*see "Drugs" in Common Crimes (Chapter 21) & Chapter 4, Arraignment* ;

14-B.7. Accord and Satisfaction

G.L. c. 276, § 55, accord & satisfaction ("discharges" misdemeanor)—*C v Gonzalez* **388 M 865 (83)** not for rape; private benefit can't defeat public interest;

District Court Standards of Judicial Practice, Arraignment (1977) 6:01, Comment—caution re: dismissal for restitution; voluntary?; using criminal process for civil "collection"?; see *C v Louis Construction* **343 M 600 (60)** (every private wrong not a crime); but see *C v Garrity* **43 MAC 349 (97)** (availability of civil remedy for victims didn't deprive criminal court of jurisdiction); SJC Rule 3:07, 3.4(h) no criminal charge for civil advantage;

SJC Rule 3:07, 3.4(g)—can't offer witness money contingent on testimony or outcome;

G.L. c. 268, § 13B—"endeavors . . . to influence . . . witness" = up to 10 year felony (Chapter 2-H);

C v Rondeau **27 MAC 55 (89)**—unclear if G.L. c. 268, § 13B conflicts with G.L. c. 276, § 55 ("accord & satisfaction" resolution); (*See also Chapter 7, Investigation, and Chapter 21, Crimes: Assault & Battery*);

C v Guzman **446 M 344 (2006)**—accord and satisfaction statute (G.L. c. 276, § 55) upheld against DA's challenge that it violated "separation of powers" clause (Art. 30);

14-C. NOLLE PROSEQUI

M.R.Crim.P. 16—in writing; reasons; any time before sentence; after jeopardy, if nol pros is without D's consent, required entry of N.G.; Reporter's Note: absolute discretion unless "scandalous";

ABA Standards for Criminal Justice, Prosecution Function & Defense Function (3d ed. 1993) 3-3.9(b)—DA not obliged to present all charges, e.g., if has reasonable doubt, less harm, punishment's disproportionate, complaining witness's motives improper or is reluctant, D cooperates, or D prosecuted elsewhere;

C v Dietrich **381 M 458 (80)**—NG if nol pros after jeopardy & without D's consent; (see Chapter 19, Double Jeopardy);

C v Benton **356 M 447 (69)**—plea bargained nol pros of District Court probable cause case bars Superior Court prosecution;

C v Hart **149 M 7 (1889)**—only DA can nol pros; mid-trial nol pros by judge = 'not guilty' for purpose of double jeopardy;

Anderson v Bishop **304 M 396 (39)**—DA immune from suit for nol pros; discretion needed to assure zealous & fearless administration of law;

Carroll, petitioner **453 M 1006 (2009)**—sexual assault complainant applied for criminal complaint, which was issued by magistrate after hearing where neither alleged miscreant or his attorney appeared; alleged miscreant was summonsed for arraignment, but before that date, district attorney nol prossed case; private party had no right to keep criminal case alive, no requirement that nol pros occur only after arraignment;

C v Sitko **372 M 305 (77)**—D not prejudiced (by lack of written reason); can nol pros one element;

C v Harris **75 MAC 696 (2009)**—after D was convicted of cocaine trafficking, prosecutor waived action on "second offender" portion of indictment and moved for sentencing, agreeing that she would be filing nolle prosequi on the second/subsequent offense issue; the nolle prosequi (argued on appeal to have been without the consent of the defendant, though D after conviction of the new substantive offense had moved unsuccessfully to dismiss the second offender charge) did NOT function as an acquittal of the entire indictment; nolle prosequi may be entered as to "any distinct and substantive part" of an indictment; further review allowed 455 M 1108 (2010);

C v Hinterleitner **391 M 679 (84)**—DA can nol pros & indict if no affront to judge's authority;

C v Raposa **386 M 666 (82)**—(same); can't deliberately obstruct process & waste resources;

C v Thomas **353 M 429 (67)**—DA can't threaten nol pros to get improper continuance;

ABA Standards for Criminal Justice (2d ed. 1986) 12-1.3, Comment—continuance restrictions should cover other procedures having same impact, e.g., nol pros & re-charge;

Klopfer v NC **386 US 213 (67)**—nol pros & leave to re-charge violates speedy trial right;

Department of Revenue v Sorrentino **408 M 340 (90)**—civil paternity action not barred by nol pros of criminal non-support charges after appeal of bench trial conviction but before de novo trial; jeopardy lapsed with vacating of bench conviction & had not attached prior to commencement of de novo trial;

C v Miranda **415 M 1 (93)**—revival of nol pros'd indictment on day of trial required reversal where judge didn't have authority to vacate nolle pros as clerical error;

14-D. PRETRIAL MOTION FOR "SUMMARY JUDGMENT"

C v Brandano **359 M 332 (71)**—judge can dismiss in "interest of justice" after continuance without a finding though DA objects—if motion, affidavit, & hearing; DA can then appeal;

C v Edelin **371 M 497, 534 (76) (Hennessey dissents)**—Brandano's essentially "summary judgment";

Rosenberg v Commonwealth **372 M 59 (77)**—motion for pretrial (summary judgment) dismissal for insufficient evidence heard if DA files affidavit/stipulates; DA can then appeal;

C v Cheney **440 M 568 (2003)**—no pretrial probation and dismissal in Superior Court over the objection of prosecutor (violates constitutional separation of powers); but see *C v Powell* 453 M 320 (2009)—Superior Court judge MAY, in certain circumstances, after accepting G plea and imposing conditions, dismiss a valid indictment ('continuance without a finding' procedure);

C v Tim T. **437 M 592 (2002)**—indictment for rape of child (c. 265, § 23) brought in Juvenile Court can't be disposed of by (Brandano-type) pretrial probation and dismissal if DA objects; CAN accomplish "Brandano" pretrial probation & possible dismissal disposition under c. 278, § 18 (after tender of guilty plea or admission to sufficient facts) IF continuance without a finding isn't "prohibited by law" (but CWOF is prohibited in rape of child case);

C v Hare **361 M 263 (72)**—no dismissal for insufficient bill of particulars;

C v Giang **402 M 604 (88)**—pre-trial report of Brandano motion to dismiss for insufficient evidence (based on affidavits/stipulations);

C v Black **403 M 675 (89)**—treat motion to dismiss (bad complaint) as Brandano hearing;

G.L. c. 123, § 17(b)—incompetent D can get dismissal if lack of substantial evidence or if defense other than lack of criminal responsibility (*see Competence, Chapter 7-G*);

14-E. PRETRIAL DIVERSION AND MEDIATION

See also Chapter 4, Arraignment, & Chapter 13, Plea Bargaining;

CPCS P/G 2.1(c)(1)—rarely dispose case at arraignment, except (after investigation) take disposition like diversion (especially if not available later);

ABA Standards for Criminal Justice, Prosecution Function & Defense Function (3d ed. 1993) 4-6.1—defense counsel's duty to explore diversion (if appropriate); 3-3.8: prosecutors "should consider" availability of noncriminal dispo, especially for first offender, & should be familiar with resources of social agencies to assist in evaluating cases for diversion; 3-3.9 prosecutor not obliged to present all charges (e.g., if reasonable doubt, less harm, or disproportionate penalty);

G.L. c. 111E—drug-dependent D gets stay, program, dismissal (*see Chapter 4, Arraign, and Chapter 21-CC, Crimes: Drugs*); drug courts exist in many District Courts and some juvenile courts; good alternative if D is serious substance abuser & otherwise facing significant incarceration;

Trial Court Policy for Drug Court Sessions (approved 2001)—contains good language regarding preservation of D's due process rights in drug court; CPCS Performance Guidelines, § 9.1—issues relevant to representing Ds in drug court sessions; SJC Standards on Substance Abuse (approved 1998)—see Policy Statement and Standards I, V and XIII with Commentaries for support when requesting probation with substance abuse treatment in lieu of incarceration;

G.L. c. 233, § 23C—statements made to mediator = confidential;

C v Raposo **453 M 739 (2009)—D on pretrial probation (G.L. c. 276, § 87) may not be required to wear GPS device;**

G.L. c. 276A—District Court Pretrial Diversion "program" for D aged 17–21 & no priors (except for some traffic violations and matters occurring before age 17); 14 days for evaluation & criminal proceedings to be "stayed" or continued without a finding for 90 days;

District Court Standards of Judicial Practice, Arraignment (1977) 7:02—G.L. c. 276A explained;

District Court Standards of Judicial Practice, Sentencing & Dispositions (1984) 4:01—pretrial probation & dismissal (see below);

Community Corrections Centers—operated by the Office of Community Corrections, an agency within the Probation Department; see enabling statute, G.L. c. 211F

(1996); available in District and Superior Courts; good alternative if D otherwise faces significant incarceration;

C v Melnyk **378 Pa.Super. 42 (88)**—can't deny diversion to poor D just because can't pay restitution; cf. *Bearden v Georgia* **461 US 660 (83)** no (automatic) finding of violation of terms of probation for fine nonpayment, unless no excuse/good faith/alternative (e.g., community service);

14-F. CONTINUANCE WITHOUT A FINDING (WITH OR WITHOUT TRIAL/ADMISSION TO SUFFICIENT FACTS)

See Chapter 14-B re: continuance without a finding in return for D's agreement not to sue cops;

CPCS P/G 6.3—(*see Chapter 14-E, above*); no jury waiver without great caution & full discovery of DA witnesses' availability & likely cross-examination answers;

District Court Standards of Judicial Practice, Sentencing & Dispositions (1984) 3:00–3:04 & Comments—procedures & suggestions re: continuance without a finding, jury-waivers, findings, forms; D gets due process if violation alleged, & (generally) dismissal otherwise; 4:01;

G.L. c. 218, § 38—sittings of District Court may be adjourned; District Court cases may be continued to "any future day";

G.L. c. 276, § 35—may "adjourn" case, but 30-day limit if without D's assent if D in custody;

C v Maloney **145 M 205 (1887)**—no indefinite continuance if D objects;

G.L. c. 276, § 87—pre-trial probation permitted . . . in District Court and juvenile court with D's consent (and might result in eventual disposition not involving incarceration on a sentence, or dismissal: *Rosenberg v C* **372 M 59 (77)**); see also G.L. c. 276, § 42A—pretrial (& post-disposition) conditions permitted upon those accused of domestic violence; see also G.L. c. 276, § 58A ('preventive detention' statute) - pretrial conditions can be imposed on D released on recognizance after a "dangerousness" hearing;

C v Rodriguez **441 M 1002 (2004)**—though D neither pled guilty nor admitted to sufficient facts, pretrial probation resulted in Immigration and Naturalization Service denying naturalization because of "arrest" and "probation" on underlying drug possession charge; suggestion, *C v Rodriguez* 441 M at 1004 n.1, that Commonwealth or judge clarify procedural facts to INS;

C v Argueta **73 MAC 564 (2009)**—D's appeal from denial of motion for new trial in case which was continued without a finding not moot, as there are serious collateral consequences from the continuance without a finding; under federal sentencing law, CWOF entered as result of admission to sufficient facts to warrant finding of guilt = "sentence for purposes of calculating criminal history points in sentencing"; error to deny motion for new trial to withdraw admission because colloquy didn't explain elements of crime ("tagging") and facts necessary to joint venture liability (sharing requisite intent with principal);

Jake J., a juvenile v C **433 M 70, 74 (2000)**—though pretrial conditions CANNOT be imposed with bail release under G.L. c. 276, § 58, SJC inventively upheld validity of pretrial conditions (& revocation of liberty upon juvenile's noncompliance) by holding that the conditions were set pursuant to G.L. c. 276, § 87 (pretrial probation), rejecting argument that § 87 is limited to use as a "dispositional" device (pretrial probation successfully completed leading to charges' dismissal); warning that in future record should be clearer, and consequences of violating "agreed-upon" conditions should be explained;

C v Taylor **428 M 623 (99)**—SJC reversed order of judge continuing case for one year without change of plea, though Commonwealth would then have "every right to ask that the case be tried"; SJC didn't believe that this was "pretrial probation" because no court supervision was ordered (see G.L. c. 276, § 87) concerning conditions imposed by judge; M.R.Crim.P. 10's Reporter's Notes quoted liberally (continuances not to be entered after case is on trial calendar unless "necessary" to insure that the interests of justice are served); G.L. c. 276, § 87 not to be used by judge to continue case over Commonwealth's objection (Mass. Declaration of Rights, Article 30 separation of powers violated); if dismissal is contemplated despite Commonwealth objection, *C v Brandano* **(359 M 332 (71))** hearing + findings of fact required;

C v Sebastian S. **444 M 306 (2005)**—"there is no legally cognizable disposition of 'pretrial probation' after an 'admission to sufficient facts' distinct from a 'continuance without a finding' conditioned on probation, a disposition authorized by G.L. c. 278, § 18"; SJC rejects D's claim that G.L. c. 276, § 87 (probation statute) may be construed with G.L. c. 278, § 18 to obtain "pretrial probation" as a "disposition" under the latter statute; can't avoid legislative prohibition of continuance without a finding disposition re: certain charges by calling the same disposition "pretrial probation" AND the "pretrial probation" terminology can't legitimately be used in attempt to avoid consequences in "other judicial departments and State and Federal law enforcement agencies, and under various regulatory schemes" which have incorporated the "CWOF" disposition into their lexicon;

C v Rezvi **73 MAC 299 (2008)**—sympathy for D's immigration woes drove illegal processes: D first pled G to four counts each of larceny & uttering ($14, 274.57 total restitution), but returned untimely (298 days later) with a motion "to revise and revoke" (which legitimately only can change *sentence*) to get a "continuance without a finding" with the same restitution order; this still not solving his immigration/deportation woes, D filed new trialmotion 18 months later and judge allowed D to be placed on "pretrial probation" for certain period, with condition of the same restitution being paid at rate of $500/month, charges to be dismissed upon full payment; D's defaults on payments on two subsequent occasions resulted in his two *further* signed agreements to make restitution, which D still didn't make, and case was returned to trial list, resulting in NG at jury-waived trial: three years later, D's motion for return of the amounts paid (!) not successful; the payments were result of D's voluntary contractual pretrial agreement ("in exchange for contemplation of dismissal of the charges") & eventual acquittals did not alter agreement's terms;

C v Brandano **359 M 332 (71)**—judge can dismiss in "interest of justice" after continuance without a finding though DA objects—if motion, affidavit, & hearing; DA can then appeal;

Rosenberg v C **372 M 59 (77)**—usually dismissal if D behaves;

US v Nicholas **133 F.3d 133 (1st Cir. '98)**—Mass. disposition of "continuance without a finding", because preceded by admission to sufficient facts, can support enhancement of sentence for later federal crime;

C v Eaton **11 MAC 732 (81)**—not shown DA promised dismissal after continuance without a finding; D should file motion/affidavit & get hearing; question: find G. because D sued cop? de novo cured any error(s) (see *Klein* **400 M 309 (87)** can reopen continuance without a finding because of D's civil suit (because deal was D's suggestion));

C v Brady **59 MAC 784 (2003)**—in "essentially a criminalized civil dispute" about tenants' authority to remove a door which they had installed, judge interrupted trial to propose disposition of restitution which wasn't subsequently paid, prompting judge to enter G finding & sentence of 15 days, suspended with condition that money be paid: absence of "important formalities" required for guilty plea or admission to sufficient facts meant "G" illegitimate; further double jeopardy barred retrial;

C v Duquette **386 M 834 (82)**—continuance without finding = mutually beneficial; D retains de novo right

unless waived (& colloquy) (NOTE: waiver not mandatory! (but see P/G's above));

C v Gomes **419 M 630 (95)**—judge cannot continue without finding after jury-waived "G" finding when DA objects; verdict = alterable only by appeal or motion for new trial; judge had no authority to "withdraw" G finding;

C v LeRoy **376 M 243 (78)**—judge can't continue without finding after jury finds G.;

C v Norrell **423 M 725 (96)**—judge can't continue without finding after finding of sufficient facts following bench trial if DA objects;

C v Cheney **440 M 568 (2003)**—no (Brandano-type) pretrial probation and dismissal in Superior Court (rape of child, G.L. c. .265, § 23) over the objection of prosecutor (violates constitutional separation of powers); but see *C v Powell* **453 M 320 (2009)**—but Superior Court judge CAN accomplish dismissal after continuance without a finding and compliance with conditions, in cases where Legislature has not prohibited 'continuance without a finding' or dismissal;

C v Tim T. **437 M 592 (2002)**—indictment for rape of child (c. 265, § 23) brought in Juvenile Court can't be disposed of by (Brandano-type) pretrial probation and dismissal if DA objects; CAN accomplish "Brandano" pretrial probation & possible dismissal disposition under c. 278, § 18 (after tender of guilty plea or admission to sufficient facts) IF continuance without a finding isn't "prohibited by law" (but CWOF is prohibited in rape of child case);

C v Pyles **423 M 717 (96)**—judge can continue without finding after offer to plead G, even though DA objects;

C v Walsh **43 MAC 924 (97)**—continuance without finding is not an appealable judgment; in criminal case, judgment = sentence; even if D appealed from the final judgment here (dismissal), he was not aggrieved by it & appeal would not be entertained;

In re Rudnicki **421 M 1006 (95)**—similar;

NOTE—some laws forbid continuances without finding, e.g., mandatory sentences

C v Jackson **45 MAC 666 (98)**—when case was continued without finding after offer of a guilty plea, there was no conviction, and thus no recent criminal history which "revived" convictions otherwise too old to be used as impeachment pursuant to G.L. c. 233, § 21;

C v Villalobos **437 M 797 (2002)**—admission to sufficient facts followed by a continuance without a finding is not a "conviction" under Mass. law;

14-G. FILING

G.L. c. 218, § 38—technical rule: unless prohibited, & if jurisdiction, District Court can file (a) any misdemeanor, or (b) felony if no prior felony conviction or filed;

District Court Standards of Judicial Practice, Sentencing & Other Dispositions (1984) 9:02—suggests filing "only after finding G.";

C v Brandano **359 M 332,336 (71)**—unlike dismissal, can bring forward any time;

C v Dowdican's Bail **115 M 133 (1874)**—merely suspends active proceedings;

Marks v Wentworth **199 M 44 (08)**—can't file without D's consent because of speedy trial right;

C v Burden **48 MAC 232 (99)**—because D had already received full appellate review of convictions, no error in later motion judge revising sentences to include placing two convictions on file without D's consent; consent normally required to protect right of appeal (here, judge's order effectively barred any later removal of convictions from "file" for imposition of sentence);

C v Bianco **390 M 254 (83)**—can reopen & sentence D without new misconduct;

C v Simmons **448 M 687 (2007), on further review of 65 MAC 274 (2005)**—after D pled guilty to twelve indictments, receiving concurrent sentences of 8–12 years on six armed robberies, the six other convictions being "placed on file," Commonwealth proceeded to obtain sentence of 18–20 years on one previously "filed" conviction, simply because new robbery charge was brought against D following his release from G-plea sentences; exhaustive history/analysis of "filing" (appellate analysis to date concerns removal from "filing" only when D has successfully appealed from a "parallel conviction" or has violated some "express condition of the filing," but no common law rule so limits the practice); MA "stands alone" on practice of "filing" with consent of D, but continuing the practice is here upheld ("discretion and flexibility afforded to judges, prosecutors, and defendants"); rejects argument re: "right to a speedy sentencing," since by consenting to filing, D consented to delay in sentencing; while rejecting D's argument that D was being illegitimately punished not for the conviction but for untried new criminal charge, acknowledging that sentencing judge's "discretion" had to consider "original sentencing scheme" (six concurrent terms of 8–12 years for SIX convictions of armed robbery), to recognize "discord" in new sentence of 18–20 years "on a single count of armed assault with intent to rob" (resentencing ordered);

Murray v Commonwealth **432 M 1026 (2000)**—D's attempt, via G.L. c. 211, § 3, to have "filed" conviction brought forward and to have counsel appointed for sentencing = unsuccessful, apparently because of flawed assertion that "if Superior Court judge were to deny his request that he be sentenced, he wouldn't have adequate means to appeal" this adverse judgment;

Murray v Commonwealth **442 M 1029 (2004)**—after appeals court refused to address arguments concerning "filed" conviction & D filed motion in Superior Court to "bring forward" the filed conviction and have counsel appointed for sentencing, D should have appealed the denial of that motion (rather than undertake G.L. c. 211, § 3 petitions & appeals from their denial);

C v Lopez **31 MAC 547 (91)**—conviction for duplicitous lesser included cannot be placed on file or given concurrent sentence but must be dismissed;

C v Delgado **367 M 432 (75)**—no right to appeal if consented to filing;

C v Paniaqua **413 M 796 (92)**—filing conviction "suspend(s), for as long as the case remains on file, a D's right to appeal alleged error in the proceeding" leading to that conviction; because here no record of D consenting to filing, Appeals Court would consider appellate arguments; BUT SEE/CONTRAST *C v Stracuzzi* **30 MAC 161 (91)** appellate courts may consider appellate claims which apply equally to convictions placed on file & those on which D was sentenced;

C v Freeman **29 MAC 635 (90)**—same;

C v Connolly **49 MAC 424 (2000)**—after Appeals Court reversed the conviction on which D was sentenced (& barred retrial), court invited Commonwealth on remand to remove the other, previously filed, conviction and get sentence on it, citing *C v Brandano* **359 M 332, 336 (71)** & *C v Bianco* **388 M 358, 364–65, 370 (83)** for similar invitations when Appeals Court reversed one conviction & ordered judgment for D;

G.L. c. 221, § 27A—SJC may by rule or order provide for disposal/destruction of papers/records filed in any court of the commonwealth 20 years after case is "finally disposed of," or 20 years after criminal complaint has "remained on file";

G.L. c. 280, § 6—can give "costs" with filing, but must be "reasonable & actual expenses" of the prosecution; costs not to be imposed as penalty for crime; (see *C v Gomes* **407 M 206 (90)** "Court personnel are not paid on a piecework basis, and defendants may not be charged as if they were");

G.L. c. 277, § 70B—(technically) DA, if seeking to place case on file, must give written reasons, accompanied by D's criminal record;

Check—many statutes bar filing of certain convictions/charges, e.g., G.L. c. 266, § 28 larceny motor vehicle, receiving stolen motor vehicle; G.L. c. 90, § 24 repeat OUI; G.L. c. 269, § 10 carrying firearm; G.L. c. 265, § 18(a) rob elderly; G.L. c. 272, § 6 keep brothel; etc.

14-H. FEES, FINES, FORFEITURE, COSTS, RESTITUTION, AND VICTIM'S COMPENSATION

See Accord & Satisfaction in Chapter 14-B, above;

CPCS P/G 7.5(a)—challenge inappropriate probation condition (e.g., restitution amount);

G.L. c. 280, § 6—costs possible as condition of dismissal, file, probation; costs **not** permissible as penalty for crime; limit = reasonable & actual expense of prosecution;

C v Gomes **407 M 206 (90)**—"Court personnel are not paid on a piecework basis, and defendants may not be charged as if they were"; "costs" must be only those actually calculable as resulting directly from D's willful default; cannot merely assign some amount, without evidence, as "reasonable" for "fair value of the waste of the (court's) time and resources"; M.R.Crim.P. 6(d)(1) and Reporter's Notes cited; judge may not incarcerate indigent D for failure to pay costs or fines without 1st holding due process hearing, determining that failure to pay was willful, & then giving meaningful consideration to reasonable alternatives to incarceration; here, D should have been permitted to work off costs & fines;

G.L. c. 278, § 14—no costs or fees (including charge "for subsistence") if held on bail & not guilty, discharge, etc.;

M.R.Crim.P. 10—costs for continuance without adequate notice;

C v Scagliotti **373 M 626 (77)**—$500 "costs" = bad penalty within G.L. c. 280, § 6;

C v Eaton **11 MAC 732 (81)**—costs ok at dismissal; dubious at continuance without a finding;

In re Scott **377 M 364 (79)**—(#'s 5, 14, 16, 18) improper use of costs & jail for nonpayment fines/restitution;

G.L. c. 127, § 144—incarceration OK for nonpayment of fines (if D able to pay); fine 'worked off' at $30/day; **G.L. c. 127, § 145**—District Court judges "shall discharge from jail persons confined for the nonpayment of fine, or of fine and expenses, if they are of opinion that such persons are not able to pay the same or that it is otherwise expedient"; **G.L. c. 127, § 146**—if prisoner is kept for 30 days for nonpayment of fines, court to inquire re: indigency, discharge D;

Tate v Short **401 US 395 (71)**—equal protection clause of Fourteenth Amendment prohibits state from imposing fine as sentence & then converting it into jail term because D unable to pay fine in full forthwith;

G.L. c. 258B, §§ 3 & 8 victim's rights, inter alia, § 3(o)—DA to assist in seeking restitution; § 8—assessment of $60 (felony)/$35 (misdemeanor) (NOTE: these amounts were those set in St. 1996, c. 151, §§ 485–86); waivable if severe hardship; (see *Booth v Maryland* **482 US 496 (87)** (Chapter 14-A above) re: victim's allocution right);

G.L. c. 258C—Compensation for Victims of Violent Crimes;

Bosworth v Commonwealth **397 M 712 (86)**—(predecessor to G.L. c. 258C, the now-repealed (by St. 1993, c. 478, § 3) G.L. c. 258A) ok to award $ for lost future earnings, though homicide victim was unemployed;

G.L. c. 276, § 87A probation fee—see Chapter 14-I, Straight Probation & Suspended Sentences);

G.L. c. 280, § 6A—25% surfine on fine/forfeiture for adults; can waive if jailed until a fine's paid (if hardship);

G.L. c. 280, § 6B—assessment of $ for drug crimes ($35–100 for misdemeanor, $150–500 for felony); total assessment from single incident not to exceed $500 (these amounts per St. 1989, c. 653, § 107); assessment may be reduced or waived if "undue hardship"; goes to drug analysis fund (§ 6C);

C v Zawatsky **41 MAC 392 (96)**—victim/witness charges aggregated at $1300 held not to be an impermissible charge for "costs" per c. 280, § 6, **BUT** if attributed to convictions reversed on appeal, could not stand (unless trial judge ordered redistribution of the same amount among the convictions which did survive on appeal);

C v Goren **72 MAC 678 (2008)**—D had not paid rent for over a year, and then (toward that antecedent debt) gave landlord two checks which landlord investigated before attempting to cash them (they were drawn on a closed account): Appeals Court held that D's delivery of the bad check was not the means by which he obtained any property or services, so 'larceny by check' conviction was vacated, as was order of restitution because landlord "incurred no loss *as a result of* the bad checks";

G.L. c. 90, § 24D—special probation fee of $250 for alcohol treatment or driver's education program;

G.L. c. 279, § 11—if law gives fine "AND" prison, can remit one if not previously convicted of "a similar crime";

G.L. c. 279, §§ 1 & 1A—can suspend a fine (&/or prison) & order payment to probation; if unable or unwilling to pay, can extend, file, or commit;

G.L. c. 279, § 10—"conditional sentence"—fine by X date or arrested & committed; (see District Court Standards S&D 7:09); § 7 House of Correction for nonpayment of fine;

C v De Pina **10 MAC 929 (80)**—no suspended sentence & jail for violating terms of probation if statute = fine only;

Gallinaro v Commonwealth **362 M 728 (73)**—duplicitous charges, so fine on #1 discharges jail on #2; (*see Chapter 19, Double Jeopardy re: Fines, Forfeitures*);

G.L. c. 276, § 92—restitution condition of (& paid through) Office of Probation;

G.L. c. 231, § 85G—parents' civil liability (for kid aged 8–17) ($5,000 maximum) for kid's injury/damage to property; § 85R1/2 tort liability for shoplifting (up to $500) in addition to any actual damages to merchant for larceny and property damage on premises;

G.L. c. 276, § 92A—mandatory (unless extraordinary/indigency) restitution for motor vehicle theft or insurance fraud; not "pain & suffering"; hearing to decide amount.; (see also G.L. c. 266, § 29);

C v Cromwell **56 MAC 436 (2002)**—judge may order restitution for any injuries caused by D's operating under the influence [here, victim's car was totaled, and judge ordered D to pay the balance of victim's car loan];

C v McIntyre **436 M 829 (2002)**—scope of restitution, while limited to loss/damage which is causally connected to the offense & "bears a significant relationship to the offense," isn't limited to elements of the charged crime; look instead to "underlying facts"; though D wasn't charged with or convicted of malicious destruction of property, his kicking victim's car door and fender as victim retreated to the car to get away from ongoing assault and battery entitled court to assess restitution for car repair;

C v Casanova **65 MAC 750 (2006)**—strict evidentiary rules don't apply at restitution hearing, & reliable hearsay may be admitted; nonetheless, victim's unsubstantiated assertions that he had been diagnosed with mononucleosis and that a doctor told him that D's blows may have triggered a recurrence were inadequate to establish "causation" so as to impose upon D $8,046 in "lost tuition" which V forfeited when he withdrew from college;

C v Caparella **70 MAC 506 (2007)**—Special Olympics employee fraudulently collected "telemarketing" donations, which she secreted in unauthorized bank account for personal use: court rejects D's argument that $200,000 restitution to Special Olympics improper because organization had specific policy against telemarketing; "equitable doctrine of constructive trust conferred recognized property interest upon" the organization;

C v Palmer P. **61 MAC 230 (2004)**—even though D was acquitted of the larceny charge, $1,000 (value of goods taken after break-in), restitution order upheld because, inter alia, D was convicted of breaking & entering, and this bore causal relationship to the larceny (even if D didn't personally take them [he wasn't charged as a joint venturer, and others were involved in the break-in also]);

C v Nawn **394 M 1, 6–9 (85)**—hearing on amount of loss claimed by victim, with opportunity for cross-examination = required on D's request;

C v Chase **70 MAC 826 (2007)**—restitution hearing is to address not only amount of the loss, but **ALSO** "the amount that the defendant is able to pay and how such payment is to be made"; sentencing judge here addressed only amount of loss and cavalierly eschewed the second issue: "at some point, you know, if he can't pay it then some other judge is going to have to make a determination on the ability to pay or what to do about that"; because D made no objection and "did not even suggest an inability to pay," judge's denial of D's M.R.Crim.P. 30(b) motion raising this [motion under Rule 30(a) "would have been more appropriate," fn.10] was not an abuse of discretion; **N.B.:** if revocation is threatened in future for failure to pay restitution, D may assert, at hearing, his inability to pay;

C v Morris M **70 MAC 688 (2007)**—insurance company's estimate of damage to Jeep not excludable on hearsay ground (reliable hearsay admissible in restitution hearing); claim that judge didn't consider D's ability to pay rejected (D didn't raise issue below, and didn't present any evidence as to ability to pay; order merely set amount, without schedule of payment): if probation revocation is threatened for lack of payment, D should raise purported lack of ability;

C v Williams **57 MAC 917 (2003)**—victim not required to submit a claim to any possible insurance company before order of restitution could be made; court could, in determining restitution amount, rely on cost estimates prepared by various vendors rather than actual costs for the repairs;

14-H.1. Constitutional Issues—Indigency, Double Jeopardy, "Excessive Fines" Clause, Forfeiture

Tate v Short **401 US 395 (71)**—US Constitution equal protection violation to jail indigent for nonpayment unless refuses/neglects, & has ability, to pay;

Bearden v Georgia **461 US 660 (83)**—no (automatic) violation of probation for fine nonpayment, unless no excuse/good faith/alternative (e.g., community service);

Williams v Illinois **399 US 235 (70)**—can't jail (for nonpayment) longer than maximum penalty;

G.L. c. 261, §§ 27A-G ("Court Costs of Indigent Persons")—waiver, substitution or state payment of all fees & costs available in any civil, criminal or juvenile proceeding; right to written findings, appeal from District Court to Superior Court & from Superior Court to single justice of Appeals Court;

C v Payne **33 MAC 533 (92)**—incarceration of Medicaid fraud D for failure to pay $40,000 restitution pursuant to deal which gave him time to pay in order to avoid committed sentence did not violate D's due process rights; cf. **Cameron v Justice of Taunton District Court SJC for Suffolk County No. 92-203 (O'Connor, Single J.) (92)** appointed counsel shall not be removed because of D's failure to pay counsel fee;

C v Brown **426 M 475 (98)**—re: forfeiture of $142 found on D's person upon his drug distribution arrest, pursuant to G.L. c. 94C, § 47(a)(5), immediately following D's admission to sufficient facts & continuance without a finding: reading of police report sufficient to show probable cause to believe that the money came from a drug transaction; probable cause in this context = akin to indictment standard, i.e. lesser than probable cause hearing standard & certainly less than 'required finding of not guilty' standard; probable cause standard did not require evidence of link between money seized and a particularized drug transaction; NOTICE required is at least 7 days if by G.L. c. 94C, § 47(i), i.e., motion filed in the related criminal proceeding, or less than or equal to 2 weeks if by G.L. c. 94C, § 47(d), i.e., a Superior Court proceeding **in rem**; BURDEN on D to show not forfeitable because claimant has "considerably more access to proof & opportunity of knowledge re: the source of the money than does the Commonwealth" (e.g., production of pay stub, bank receipt, or "credible testimony" that money = legally obtained);

C v One 2004 Audi Sedan Automobile & others **73 MAC 311 (2008)**—forfeiture complaint only had to "allege facts giving rise to the inference that 'the money was probably derived from illegal drug transactions'"; forfeiture complaint did NOT have to demonstrate "probable cause" (i.e., sufficient nexus between the funds in bank account and the illegal drug activity)at the forfeiture stage, but instead had to do so at the forfeiture trial (where burden would then shift to claimant to prove that property was not forfeitable under the statute); further review allowed 453 M 1104 (2009), and 456

M 434 (2010) superceding opinion of SJC sets forth controlling standards of proof;

***Austin v US* 509 US 602 (93) (93)**—**in rem** forfeiture may be punitive rather than merely remedial and as such may in a given case violate 8th Amendment's "excessive fines" prohibition; Supreme Court declined to establish a test for determining whether a forfeiture is constitutionally "excessive";

***Bennis v Michigan* 516 US 442 (96)**—OK to order forfeiture of car jointly owned by husband & wife when husband used it for sex with prostitute; Court not required to compensate wife, despite her innocence of any wrongdoing;

***C v One 1986 Volkswagen GTI Auto* 417 M 369 (94)**—despite absence of criminal drug prosecution (here due to successful motion to suppress), forfeiture permissible; fact that D's mother = car owner no bar absent proof that mother rather than D exercised dominion & control;

***US v Halper* 490 US 435 (89)**—imposition of large civil fine after D convicted of & punished for criminal charges for false Medicare claims was double jeopardy violation where purpose of fine was punitive, not remedial;

***C v Cory* 454 M 559 (2009)**—G.L. c. 265, § 47 (requiring person placed on probation after conviction of designated sex offense to wear GPS tracking device) applied to D, BUT because it was punitive and was enacted after date of D's particular sex offense, it violated prohibition against ex post facto provisions of US and MA Constitutions; ***Doe v Chairperson of MA Parole Board* 454 M 1018 (2009)**—same as to statute (G.L. c. 127, § 133D½) requiring GPS device for persons under court-ordered parole supervision or under lifetime community parole; ***Alexander v US* 509 US 544 (93)**—8th Amendment "excessive fines" clause limits government's power to extract payments, "whether in cash or in kind (i.e., forfeiture of non-cash assets), as punishment for some offense";

***US v Bajakajian* 524 US 321 (98)**—violation of US Constitution 8th Amendment, excessive fines clause: D attempted to leave US with $357,144, violating statute prohibiting him from leaving with more than $10,000; after punishment of maximum $5,000 fine plus 3 years' probation, prosecution could not demand forfeiture of the $357,144 (grossly disproportional to the gravity of the offense, "solely a reporting offense" involving no loss to the public fisc);

***Kvitka v Board of Registration in Medicine* 407 M 140, cert. denied, 498 US 823 (90)**—medicine board's imposition of fine on physician D after guilty pleas on criminal charges was double jeopardy violation where fine was punitive, not remedial; *See also, for double sentences, Chapter 19-A, 19-B, 19-F (Double Jeopardy)*;

***McKune v Lile* 536 U.S. 24 (2002)**—requiring inmates to complete & sign "admission of responsibility" form, accepting responsibility for crimes for which they have been sentenced, & to complete "sexual history form," detailing all prior sex activities, regardless of whether they're criminal (& have or haven't been prosecuted), as condition of participation in Kansas's "Sexual Abuse Treatment Program" doesn't amount to compelled self-incrimination despite loss/reduction of privileges for failure to participate (5:4 decision); OBJECT TO ANY SUCH CONDITIONS/PROCEDURE UNDER ARTICLE 12, DECLARATION OF RIGHTS, STATE CONSTITUTION;

14-H.2. Restitution

District Court Standards of Judicial Practice, Sentencing & Other Dispositions (1984) 9:04—limit restitution to actual, direct loss; not pain & suffer; includes insurer's loss; documentation & due process re: amount; judge can delegate to probation, but disputes = for judge;

***Novelty Bias Binding Co. v Shevrin* 342 M 714 (61)**—restitution desirable (& here, in embezzlement case, can include covenant not to compete);

***C v Nawn* 394 M 1 (85)**—restitution's appropriate, but reasonable & fair; right to hearing & cross-examination re: amount, ability to pay, D's evidence; DA's burden of proof = preponderance; no jury trial; But see ***C v One 1972 Chevrolet Van* 385 M 198 (82)** jury trial on motor vehicle forfeiture because punishment, not remedial;

***C v Carapellucci* 429 M 579, 584 (99)**—judge's refusal to hold hearing concerning restitution amounts claimed by prosecutor would be independent ground for vacating that portion of sentence (here, convictions rev'd on another issue);

***Roullett v Quincy Court* 395 M 1008 (85)**—if restitution amount is "determined later," D can later take appeal then (see ***C v LaFrance* 402 M 789 (88)** (probation condition giving probation officer blanket search authority = bad without limiting to "reasonable suspicion"; D can appeal condition though not (yet) searched & though 'agreed,' under threat of jail); & CPCS P/G 7.9 above);

***C v Hastings* 53 MAC 41 (2001)**—while victim's loss isn't limited to market value of destroyed property, the replacement vehicle here purchased was perhaps better than the one lost (& thus not a reasonable substitute); remanded for substantiation or not;

***C v McIntyre* 436 M 829 (2002)**—scope of restitution, while limited to loss/damage which is causally connected to the offense & "bears a significant relationship to the offense," isn't limited to elements of the charged crime; look instead to "underlying facts"; though D wasn't charged with or convicted of malicious destruction of property, his kicking victim's car door and fender as victim retreated to the car to get away from ongoing assault and battery entitled court to assess restitution for car repair;

***C v Palmer P.* 61 MAC 230 (2004)**—even though D was acquitted of the larceny charge, $1,000 (value of goods taken after break-in), restitution order upheld because, inter alia, D was convicted of breaking & entering, and this bore causal relationship to the larceny (even if D didn't personally take them [he wasn't charged as a joint venturer, and others were involved in the break-in also]);

14-I. (STRAIGHT) PROBATION AND SUSPENDED SENTENCES

See Chapter 14-J below;

C v Rodriguez 52 MAC 572 (2001)—D should have been told, on record, at time of G plea, that consequences of a probation violation on masked armed robbery conviction (straight probation for two years, to begin upon release from a 'committed' house of correction sentence imposed at same time) would be imposition of minimum mandatory 5 years, & that at least 5 years would have to be SERVED; no relief, however, since record failed to suggest "any weaknesses" in Commonwealth's case on merits, or that he had any defense to the charges;

G.L. c. 276, § 85: probation officer duties—can recommend probation sentence; gives D terms/conditions; § 87 Court can set conditions; G.L. c. 276, § 87A, fee for D on supervised probation = $50/month, but doesn't apply to person accused or convicted of abandon./non-support of spouse or child (G.L. c. 273, §§ 1, 15), where compliance with an order of support for a spouse or minor child is a condition of probation, and fee waivable if restitution is ordered or if undue hardship (but community service); (*see Chapter 14-H, Fees, Fines, Costs, Restitution, & 14-J, Violation of Terms of Probation (Surrender) Hearing*);

Alabama v Shelton 535 U.S. 654 (2002)—if no counsel for guilt adjudication, can't later execute/activate suspended sentence for violating terms of probation; majority suggests no constitutional bar to pre-trial probation, allowing uncounseled defendants to consent to probation before an adjudication of guilt, with a counseled adjudication occurring only if a probation violation occurs; (query: possible speedy trial issues, prejudice from delay)

C v MacDonald 50 MAC 220 (2000), affirmed, 435 M 1005 (2001)—probation revocation premised upon violation of probation officer's direction that D have "no contact" with particular woman vacated, because record of case indicated that judge had ordered less broad "stay away" condition, and "only those probationary terms ordered by the sentencing judge can form the basis for a violation of probation"; rejection of Commonwealth argument that D's signing of probation "contract" with probation officer altered this result;

CPCS P/G's 7.2 seek favorable recommendation from probation officer; 7.3(b) prepare D for presentence interview; 7.3(a) carefully scrutinize presentence report; 7.5(a) challenge inappropriate probation CONDITIONS;

G.L. c. 279, §§ 1, 1A, 1B, 2—authority to suspend & G.L. c. 279, § 3, revoke suspension; G.L. c. 276, § 87 **pretrial** conditions with D's consent;

Aldoupolis v Commonwealth 386 M 260 (82)—can suspend life felony;

Superior Court Rule 56—Standard Probation Terms = (1) comply with all orders of the court, including order for $ payment, (2) report to probation officer as required, (3) notify officer immediately of address change, (4) make effort to obtain & keep employment, (5) make efforts to provide adequate support for dependents, and (6) obey all laws. "Any other condition shall be presumed to be in addition to the foregoing.";

Superior Court Rule 57—"term" of probation, if not specifically stated = 11 months, unless under c. 273 (desertion, non-support), which is for 5 years, 11 months); extension possible;

District Court Standards of Judicial Practice, Sentencing & Other Dispositions (1984) 4:00—supervision = optional; focus = rehabilitation; termination not automatic; 4:01 pretrial probation; 4:03 conditions & form D signs; 4:02 straight probation = full penalty range for violating terms of probation; 6:01 takes "position that" suspended sentence can't be changed if revoked (see § J); accord, *C v Holmgren* 421 M 224, 228 (95) citing G.L. c. 279, § 3—upon finding probation violation and revoking probation, judge **must** order imposition of previously suspended sentence "in its entirety";

C v Powers 73 MAC 186 (2008)—the "threats" statute, G.L. c. 275, § 4, permitting up to six months' imprisonment or "instead of imposing sentence" allowing a "recognizance with sufficient sureties . . . for [a] term, not exceeding six months" did not mean that judge could not order D, convicted of threats, to a five-year-term of probation; G.L. c. 276, § 87 allows probation, and provides more protection of public "than a mere bond requiring a D to keep the peace"; probation statute supplements rather than conflicts with 'threats' statute;

C v LaPointe 435 M 455 (2001)—OK to prohibit D from residing with minor children & limited D's contact with his own minor children, even given probationary period of twenty years, as probation condition after indecent A&B on person over age 14 (here, D's daughter, age15), particularly given prior record;

C v Morales 70 MAC 839 (2007)—D's guilty plea to rape of child resulted in 8–10 years, with probation for 3 years, with special conditions including no contact with children under age of 16; conditions were supplemented thereafter, partly on D's motion, for tactical reasons in anticipation of trial on issue of whether he continued to be sexually dangerous: after jury trial resulted in "no longer SDP", D wasn't entitled to strike probation conditions imposed so belatedly (by judge who wasn't original sentencing judge, because he had retired); restrictive residency condition (any location had to be approved by probation dep't) was imposed after SDP designation, i.e., info not known to judge at time of sentencing, which qualified as material change in circumstances permitting modification in probation conditions, "so long as that change does not constitute punishment"; despite jury verdict on § 9 petition, judge didn't abuse discretion in refusing to modify "nonpunitive" condition "designed to ease [D's] reintroduction into the community, while also protecting the public";

Buckley v Quincy Division of the District Court Department **395 M 815 (85)**—supervisory court sought, illegally, to change probation conditions imposed by sentencing court when there were no material changes in probationer's circumstances; court didn't "outline those situations in which the sentencing court might modify the terms of probation";

Dunbrack v C **398 M 502 (86)**—beyond legitimate period for motion to revoke & revise (M.R.Crim.P. 29), sentencing judge could change conditions of probation when condition originally imposed was inappropriate because probation record had failed to show D's prior OUI offense; D's arguments against this should have been made via M.R.Crim.P. 30 (& appeal from denial of such motion);

King v C **246 M 57 (23)**—can extend probation (& suspended sentence); (see violating terms of probation, below);

Electronically-Monitored Home Confinement (AKA "the bracelet")—used by Dep't of Correction & some county correctional facilities to make probationer spend all or part of day at home: 'house arrest' while awaiting trial, or as condition of probation, or as a classification status during service of part of sentence;

G.L. c. 265, § 47—requires any person placed on probation for certain sex offenses to wear GPS device;

C v Raposo **453 M 739 (2009)**—GPS device requirement does NOT apply to D placed on *pretrial* probation under G.L. c. 276, § 87; *Emelio E, v Commonwealth* **453 M 1024 (2009)**—GPS device requirement doesn't apply to juvenile placed on pretrial supervision either under G.L. c. 276, § 87 or G.L. c. 276, § 58;

C v Cowan **422 M 546, 548 (96)**—firearm carrying statute doesn't allow 'house arrest' with bracelet as substitute for incarceration;

ABA, Principles for Electronically-Monitored Home Confinement (88)—OK if least restrictive alternative for public protection & offense gravity; can't limit to non-indigents; (Comment: caution about "net-widening");

C v Beauchemin **410 M 181, 185–86 (91)**—D, allowed liberty during pendency of appeal (during stay of sentence execution, M.R.Crim.P. 31, M.R.App.P. 6), did not receive credit against sentence despite stay condition that he could not leave home/property;

C v Morasse **446 M 113 (2006)**—though condition of pretrial probation was that D be confined to his home and be monitored there by electronic bracelet, this was not "confinement" for which he received credit on eventual sentence;

C v Maldonado **64 MAC 250 (2005)**—D was entitled to receive credit (19 days) for time in custody when his sentence after conviction had been stayed but his bail had been revoked;

C v Juzba **44 MAC 457 (98)**—sentence of 5–7 years, 18 months to serve, balance suspended with 3 years' probation (on rape), and 3 years' probation concurrent with rape sentence (on A&B): probation began to run on A&B **after** release from commitment on rape sentence, and only

then was concurrent; though judge is not barred from placing a D on probation **during** incarceration, this = uncommon, possibly appropriate where foreseeable that D will cause trouble while jailed (e.g. member of prison "gang");

C v Ruiz **453 M 474 (2009)**—when probation term was to run from and after incarceration sentence and certain noncriminal acts were proscribed during probation term, ERROR to revoke probation based on noncriminal proscribed act committed during incarceration, at least where D was not given adequate notice that 'no contact' condition was in effect during period of incarceration;

Delisle v C **416 M 359 (93)**—sentences = 2½ years, house of correction, 18 months to serve, balance suspended with probation for 4 years AND 5–7 MCI-Cedar Junction, suspended, with probation for 2 years from & after 1st sentence: probation on 2d sentence did not begin until **expiration of probation period** on 1st sentence; G.L. c. 279 § 8A distinguished;

C v Chirillo **53 MAC 75 (2001)**—when judge found D in violation of terms of probation and ordered revocation and execution of sentence, he had to order imposition of all the concurrent sentences; when he instead "unbundled" three 5 to 7 year concurrent sentences from a Concord ten, and ordered service of only the latter with from and after probation (and still the suspended 5 to 7 sentences hanging over D's head), extension of probation resulted in D's incarceration for violation that occurred after original period of probation should have expired; D "cannot be required to serve the sentence in installments"; D did not waive issue by failing to raise it in revoke & revise motion pursuant to M.R.Crim.P. 29; BUT ON FURTHER REVIEW, **437 M 606 (2002)** SJC disagreed with Appeals Court & held that joinder of probationary periods didn't create concurrent sentencing scheme, so judge DID have authority after revocation to impose consecutive sentences;

A.L. v C **402 M 234 (88)**—probation officer liable for not monitoring D's compliance with terms (no contact with children after sexual abuse of children, but D lied to probation officer about employment, & was actually teaching in public school) because it's a nondiscretionary/ administrative function;

14-I.1. Probation Conditions

See Superior Court Rule 56, Standard Probation Terms (listed above)

C v Lally **55 MAC 601 (2002)**—error to revoke probation on ground that D refused to sign probation conditions including random urine screening, because judge had not ordered it; judge's stated probation condition of "treatment as deemed necessary" was ambiguous and improper delegation by judge of authority to impose probationary conditions; probation violation hearing is not the time to add a condition improperly imposed by a probation officer & then to find D in violation of the order;

Griffin v Wisconsin **483 US 868 (87)**—probation officer can search (at home) if "reasonable," (e.g., unauthenticated tip from cop without reliability indicia);

C v LaFrance **402 M 789 (88)**—probation condition giving probation officer blanket search authority − bad without limiting to "reasonable suspicion"; Declaration of Rights Article 14 requires warrant for home; D can appeal condition though not (yet) searched & though agreed (under threat of jail otherwise);

Chandler v Miller **520 US 305, 308 (97)**—collection & testing of urine intrudes upon expectations of privacy, & is a "search" of the person under both 4th A. and Article 14 of Declaration of Rights (*Horsemen's Benevolent & Protective Ass'n v State Racing Comm'n* **403 M 692 (89)**);

C v Gomes **73 MAC 857 (2009)**—after firearms convictions, part of sentence included probation with condition to abstain from drugs and alcohol and undergo random testing: during whole period D would be below legal drinking age, and there was no indication that he had ever used drugs or alcohol; because probation condition was not reasonably related to legitimate probationary goals and involved Constitutional rights against unreasonable search and seizure, substantial risk of miscarriage of justice found;

C v Speight **59 MAC 28 (2003)**—residential treatment for drug/alcohol, a condition of probation, was not incarceration for which D could obtain sentence credit against suspended prison sentence imposed when D subsequently violated terms of probation; *C v Morasse* **446 M 113 (2006)**—though condition of pretrial probation was that D be confined to his home and be monitored there by electronic bracelet, this was not "confinement" for which he received credit on eventual sentence;

C v Powers **420 M 410 (95)**—probation condition of neither D nor her assignees nor representatives acting on D's authority engaging in any profit or benefit generating activity re her criminal acts = OK; not violative of 1st Amendment, & not vague;

C v Kenney **55 MAC 514 (2002)**—OK for judge to order probation condition of surrendering driver's license & not applying for new one during probationary term, after conviction of operating to endanger;

C v Ruiz **453 M 474 (2009)**—judge may certainly order "no contact" with victim beginning immediately, but when 'no contact' has been ordered to be a condition of probation, and probationary term is specifically ordered to begin AFTER sentence of incarceration, D has not received notice that the act is proscribed during the period of incarceration; "violation" of probation and revocation while D is incarcerated and hasn't begun period of probation, to substitute additional period of incarceration for previously-ordered 'from and after' probation = violation of due process;

C v Pike **428 M 393 (98)**—banishment from MA during period of probation infringed on "fundamental right" to interstate travel; while probationers' constitutional rights may be legitimately affected by probationary conditions, they must be "reasonably related to the goals of sentencing and probation"; precedents barring probationers "from certain small geographic areas" distinguished;

C v Cory **454 M 559 (2009)**—G.L. c. 265, § 47 (requiring person placed on probation after conviction of designated sex offense to wear GPS tracking device) applied to D, BUT because it was punitive and was enacted after date of D's particular sex offense, it violated prohibition against ex post facto provisions of US and MA Constitutions; *Doe v Chairperson of MA Parole Board* **454 M 1018 (2009)**—same as to statute (G.L. c. 127, § 133D½) requiring GPS device for persons under court-ordered parole supervision or under lifetime community parole;

C v Woods **427 M 169 (98)**—because conviction reversed, SJC did not reach issue raised re D's rights against compelled self-incrimination: probation condition of psych. treatment & sex offender evaluation even as conviction was being appealed (& was thus not final);

McKune v Lile **536 U.S. 24 (2002)**—requiring inmates to complete & sign "admission of responsibility" form, accepting responsibility for crimes for which they have been sentenced, & to complete "sexual history form," detailing all prior sex activities, regardless of whether they're criminal (& have or haven't been prosecuted), as condition of participation in Kansas's "Sexual Abuse Treatment Program" doesn't amount to compelled self-incrimination despite loss/reduction of privileges for failure to participate (5:4 decision); OBJECT TO ANY SUCH CONDITIONS/PROCEDURE UNDER ARTICLE 12, DECLARATION OF RIGHTS, STATE CONSTITUTION;

C v Cotter **415 M 183 (93)**—as part of sentence for criminal contempt (violation of injunction barring obstruction of abortion clinic), not improper to make as condition of probation the term that D not participate in unlawful activities of anti-abortion groups;

C v Williams **60 MAC 331 (2004)**—though D's crimes were not shown to be alcohol related, they involved "volatile and impulsive" conduct, and ADA and defense counsel agreed that D should enter "anger management program"; no error in/relief from additional condition of probation that D not consume or possess alcohol during probationary term because judge could reasonably conclude that alcohol wouldn't "improve D's chances of dealing successfully with his problems with anger and violence"; judge should, however, give reasons, and here there was no objection;

14-J. PROBATION SURRENDER OR VIOLATE TERMS OF PROBATION ("VTP") HEARING

C v Harrison **429 M 866 (99)**—D has federal constitutional right to be present at surrender hearing; Supreme Court has not yet held that such error may be found harmless (beyond a reasonable doubt); no such finding here possible because D's absence meant no chance to challenge revocation with his own testimony or evidence of mitigating circumstances; Commonwealth's argument that D's guilty plea in federal court constituted voluntary waiver of presence (because he knew that revocation proceeding was pending and that he would be taken into federal custody) REJECTED; federal authorities' refusal to cooperate to allow D's presence criticized;

G.L. c. 279, § 3—probation officer can arrest D with or without warrant (see Chapter 14-I above); Court can then sentence (if none), or continue or revoke a sentence which had been suspended;

Alabama v Shelton **122 S. Ct. 1764 (2002)**—if no counsel for guilt adjudication, can't later execute/activate suspended sentence for violating terms of probation; majority suggests no constitutional bar to pre-trial probation, allowing uncounseled defendants to consent to probation before an adjudication of guilt, with a counseled adjudication occurring only if a probation violation occurs;

Gagnon v Scarpelli **411 US 778 (73)**—due process rights to notice, hearings (preliminary & final); (see *Bearden* **461 US 660 (83)** & *Romano* **471 US 606 (85)**);

C v MacDonald **53 MAC 156 (2001)**—D here due process right to a written statement identifying evidence upon which judge relied in finding probation violation & improper for probation officer to summarize D's criminal record before presenting evidence on alleged violation; no relief because D failed to object to any errors & evidence of violation was overwhelming & since "undoubtedly the judge knew he could not consider" criminal record in reaching decision "on the violation issue";

C v Faulkner **418 M 352 (94)**—D has right to counsel at probation revocation proceeding, and this encompasses right to continuance if counsel has had no opportunity to prepare;

C v Durling **407 M 108 (90)**—unsubstantiated & unreliable hearsay can't be entire basis for probation revocation; if proffered evidence isn't admissible under standard evidentiary rules, must determine "reliability" and whether there's "good cause" for not using witness with personal knowledge;

C v Hector H. **69 MAC 43 (2007)**—an appeal of probation revocation on ground of unreliable hearsay (as to new crimes) will become moot if juvenile thereafter admits to sufficient facts on new charges and is adjudicated "delinquent" on them before the appeal is decided;

C v Wilcox **446 M 61 (2006)**—right of confrontation explicated in *Crawford v Washington* **541 US 36 (2004)** doesn't apply to probation revocation proceeding, though "more flexible right of confrontation described in [Durling]" is a part of "due process" and Article 12; circumstances here allowed revocation on testimony of officer who interviewed witness to D following girls (violating probation condition for no contact with persons under age 16) and testified to D's admissions to him;

C v Nunez **446 M 54 (2006)**—D's calling probation revocation "deferred sentencing", in case in which straight probation had originally been imposed, doesn't mean that *Crawford v Washington* applies, requiring Sixth Amendment "confrontation"; SJC finds hearsay testimony by cop about second attempted robbery nearby & within an hour of first robbery to be reliable (and "must assume" that judge relied on it in decision to revoke probation because of the first robbery, whose victim did testify at revocation hearing); "reliable" finding based on statements being "factually detailed, based on personal knowledge and direct observation and made soon after the events at issue when incident was still fresh in his mind", PLUS corroborated by observations of cop and the testifying victim of other robbery; revocations judge implicitly found the hearsay reliable, but such finding should be stated on record;

C v King **71 MAC 737 (2008)**—probation revocation based on one-page police report = reversed; neither cop nor alleged victim of domestic abuse responded to summons to testify at surrender hearing; claim that broken door frame mentioned in report sufficiently corroborated victim's allegation rejected: victim's affect (as recounted in same report) "fundamentally undermine[d] her credibility";

C v Fallon **53 MAC 473 (2001)**—whatever defect might exist in probation revocation proceeding is considered submerged if revocation was based on new criminal charges and D has [subsequently] been convicted of those;

C v Bartos **57 MAC 751 (2003)**—D's appeal from probation revocation couldn't be dismissed under rationale of Fallon, 53 MAC 473, because new criminal charges were disposed of by admission to sufficient facts and continuance without a finding; admission in this context isn't functional equivalent of guilty plea; [see *C v Villalobos* **437 M 797, 802 (2002)** (admission to sufficient facts followed by a continuance without a finding is not a "conviction" under Mass. law);

C v LaTore **63 MAC 909 (2005)**—when probation surrender hearing was conducted in conjunction with trial on new criminal charges, D was both sentenced on new convictions and committed to sentences imposed after revocation of the prior probation; D's failure to appeal the probation revocation meant that convictions' reversal had no effect on the probation revocation & sentences imposed therein;

C v Dubowski **58 MAC 292 (2003)**—though District Court Rules for Probation Violation Proceedings (2000) mandate a two-stage adjudication, first stage = proving the alleged violation[s], and second stage = what disposition appropriate, judge's finding of violation was implicit on record here though it was formally stated only after testimony directed to disposition (emotional appeal by minor victim's mother regarding his continued suffering)

14-J.1. Counsel, Right To

Williams v C **350 M 732 (66)**—D has right to counsel at parole violation hearing in MA;

C v Faulkner **418 M 352 (94)**—same, at probation revocation hearing, & mere presence of counsel is not effective assistance of counsel; error to deny continuance when attorney had no opportunity to prepare; D's failure to appear at earlier—scheduled hearing is not waiver of right to counsel at subsequent hearing; improper to reject D's protestation of lack of notice of hearing on ground that D failed to notify probation of change of address (an issue to be resolved instead at the hearing itself);

C v Morse **50 MAC 582 (2001)**—counsel, appointed on morning of same-day afternoon probation surrender hearing, failed to request continuance (& made no proffer as to what investigation or evidence would be pursued, **id. at 586)**; further preparation time not automatically required for simple single witness hearing;

14-J.2. Notice

C v Streeter **50 MAC 128 (2000)**—three times as D was on probation, he was charged with new offenses, & each time received "notice of probation surrender and hearing", citing "new offense"; when, finally revocation hearing occurred, six months after 3d notice, judge found violation of new offense, ABDW, & failing to stay away from a particular housing project; ERROR, because notice never alleged violation of "stay away" condition of probation and only "new offense" ever specifically cited by date and docket number in surrender notice was the FIRST "new offense," which was a trespass;

C v Herrera **52 MAC 294 (2001)**—after D was found in violation exclusively for failure to report and using heroin, no error in judge's considering police report & restraining order re: D's allegedly slashing tires of former girlfriend when deciding whether probation should be continued or revoked (i.e., it's like a "sentencing" decision); would be error if, without notice, the allegations were used to find D violated probation terms;

C v Simon **57 MAC 80 (2003)**—no prejudice to D though he was found guilty of a different violation than that alleged in the VTP notice; the violation which was found was one to which D had admitted at time of his arrest, according to police report; even if statement to police was involuntary/in violation of Miranda, it was admissible at probation surrender hearing;

14-J.3. Conduct of Hearing, Disposition Options

C v Milton **427 M 18 (98)**—here not violative of Article 30 Declaration of Rights separation of powers for ADA to address, on behalf of probation department at VTP hearing, legal arguments re D's motion to dismiss and sentence credit;

C v Tate **34 MAC 446 (93)**—Article 30 not violated by coordinated activity of 2 government branches when it's voluntary & 1 doesn't "intrude into the internal function of another" (DA's participation at VTP hearing);

C v Negron **441 M 685 (2004)**—at least when DA participates in revocation proceedings, **Commonwealth may appeal from finding that D hasn't violated probation** (so G.L. c. 211, § 3 can't be used for review of evidentiary issue at revocation hearing);

G.L. c. 276, § 85—probation officer gives written terms & conditions;

Black v Romano **471 US 606 (85)**—D got enough due process; judge need not consider alternatives to jail;

District Court Rules for Probation Violation Proceedings (effective date 1/2000)—at arraignment on any new complaint, D to be served with notice of probation violation & hearing (R.3(b)(i), 3(c)(i), even if D's probation is in different court; judge has discretion to order no further proceedings on the matter (R.3(b)(i), 3(c)(i)); notice may be amended, on D's 1st appearance in the probation court, to include any other bases of violation (R.3(c)(iii); if new offense is IN probation court, original notice to include all probation conditions allegedly violated by D (R.3(b)(ii)), and violation hearing is to be held on date of pretrial hearing on new charge, unless court expressly orders earlier hearing (**id.**); hearing shall be no later than 30 days after service of the notice, and no earlier than 7 days after service of the notice unless D waives notice period (R.3(b)(iii)); if arraignment court is different from probation court, notice issued by arraignment court will order D to appear in probation court on specified date & time for scheduling hearing & appointment of counsel (R.3(c)(ii)); "TRACKING" of violation hearing to resolution of new complaint now prohibited (R.5(e), 7(a), Commentary to Rules 3, 5, & 7), but continuance may be allowed "for good cause shown" (R.5(e)). REQUEST CONTINUANCE TO INVESTIGATE NEW CHARGE WHEN NEW CHARGE IS BASIS OF VIOLATION (must be allowed time to marshal evidence to dispute new allegation); no "bail" for VTP, i.e., either hold or straight release; if held, must afford preliminary probation violation hearing (R.8(a)); preliminary hearing = determine whether probable cause to believe that D has violated condition of probation, AND determine if D should be released or held in custody pending final violation hearing; **if** 'yes' to the latter (but there doesn't have to be "yes" to latter question, even if probable cause is found), D MAY NOT BE RELEASED ON BAIL, & there is no "bail review" in Superior Court, see *C v Puleio* **433 M 39 (2000)**; DA to be served with every notice of violation of terms of probation (R.3(b)(i), 3(c)(iii), 4(b)), & may participate in any probation violation proceeding (R.5(f)(i)), & may make closing statement & dispositional argument (R.(f)(iv)); BUT object if DA's position is different from probation department's position, & argue violation of separation of powers (Article 30, Declaration of Rights; cf. *C v Tate* **34 MAC 446, 447–48 (93)**); HEARSAY admissible at probation violation hearing, BUT if alleged violation is based solely on hearsay evidence, there must be written finding that hearsay is substantially trustworthy and demonstrably reliable; and further, if alleged violation is criminal behavior, must show "good cause" for failure to call a percipient witness (R.6(b)); court must determine whether D violated term of probation (R.7(a)); if failure to prove by preponderance, court must make explicit finding of no violation (id.); written findings of fact required if violation is found (R.7(c)) (though probably explicitly dictated findings on record would suffice); if violation is found, court considers disposition; factors to consider = public safety, seriousness of underlying crime (NOT the new charge), nature of violation & any prior violations, impact on V of underlying crime, any mitigating facts (R.7(d)). NOTE WELL: *C v Holmgren* **421 M 224 (95)** if violation is found & court decides to revoke previously suspended sentence, sentence must be imposed in its entirety (not revision, or imposition of merely portion of same; if several suspended sentences of varying length are involved, however, court may choose to revoke probation & impose sentence on only one of the charges (i.e., of a particular length) & terminate probation on others); (in this regard, see *C v Chirillo* **53 MAC 75 (2001)** when judge found D in violation of terms of probation and ordered revocation and execution of sentence, he had to order imposition of all the concurrent sentences; when he instead "unbundled" three 5 to 7 year concurrent sentences from a Concord ten, and ordered service of only the latter with from and after probation (and still the suspended 5 to 7 sentences hanging over D's head), extension of probation resulted in D's incarceration for violation that occurred after original period of probation should have expired; D "cannot be required to serve the sentence in installments"); BUT ON FURTHER REVIEW, **437 M 606 (2002)** SJC disagreed with Appeals Court & held that joinder of probationary periods didn't create concurrent sentencing scheme, so judge DID have authority after revocation to impose consecutive sentences;

C v Thissell **74 MAC 773 (2009)**—while asserting that evidence not admissible in adversary criminal trial may be admissible at revocation proceedings, and that hearsay is admissible if bearing substantial indicia of reliability and it is substantially trustworthy, court holds that global positioning system (GPS) records (showing D entered "exclusion zone" covered by stay-away order/condition of probation) are not "hearsay", OR, alternatively, are business records; on further review, 457 M 191 (2010), SJC discusses "computer-generated records"; probation revocation's "reliability" concern stems from au-

thentication of the generative process that created the records, but finding record support for finding GPS records untrustworthy and reliable here;

C v Wilcox **63 MAC 131, 140, further appellate review allowed 444 M 1103 (2005)**—judge's failure to make written findings of fact, required by rule 7(c), excused because "judge on the record stated his findings and reasons for revoking probation"; rule requiring written statement "is not an inflexible or invariably mandatory requirement and can be satisfied in other ways" (quoting *C v Morse*, 50 MAC at 592–93); on further review, 446 M 61 (2006), SJC did not address this issue, because order of further review was limited to issue whether Sixth Amendment "confrontation" right of *Crawford v Washington* applies to probation revocation proceedings (it doesn't);

C v Arroyo **70 MAC 228, FURTHER APPELLATE REVIEW ALLOWED 450 M 1104 (2007)—when judge orally articulated reasons for revocation, no relief for failure to issue written findings;**

C v Bruzzese **53 MAC 152 (2001)**—judge could not, at VTP hearing, extend period of probation on one complaint while simultaneously revoking probation & imposing suspended sentences on other three complaints; this improperly increased D's sentence since sentencing scheme imposed previously was for all concurrent sentences; result was to increase D's sentence from 2½ years to 3½ years; **S.C., 437 M 606 (2002)** agreeing with Appeals Court in *Bruzzese*, but disagreeing with resolution of *Chirillo* **53 MAC 75 (2001)**

C v De Pina **10 MAC 929 (80)**—no suspended sentence or committed time after violating terms of probation if law has only fine;

District Court Standards of Judicial Practice, Sentencing & Other Disposition (1984) 3:03: continuance without a finding violation hearing—due process, but suggest less than violating terms of probation hearing; 7:11 "stay" sentence for one last chance to comply (e.g., after VTP) = "inherent power"; 6:01 revoking suspended sentence means impose entire sentence that was suspended (a position later affirmed by *C v Holmgren* **421 M 224 (95)**);

C v Holmgren **421 M 224, 228 (95)**—NG of new crimes is no bar to VTP for such conduct because burden of proof at VTP = preponderance rather than "beyond a reasonable doubt";

Buckley v District Court **395 M 815 (85)**—nonpunitive change terms not "revision" needing R-29 motion; supervising court can't modify terms, unless changed circumstances (e.g., a violation of probationary term) or return to sentencing court (& hearing?); vs. . . .

Dunbrack v Commonwealth **398 M 502 (86)**—sentencing judge can revise illegal (because prior OUI making education program inappropriate not known to judge at time of sentencing); D's arguments against this should have been raised via M.R.Crim.P. 30);

C v Sawicki **369 M 377 (75)**—can extend probationary period, including within a reasonable time after its end, if violation = within original period;

C v McGovern **183 M 238 (03)**—(same) (*see also* **King 246 M 57 (23)** & *Chapter 14-I above*);

C v Ward **15 MAC 388 (83)**—(same) if reasonably prompt;

C v Smith **38 MAC 324 (95)**—5 months before end of probation period, D stopped reporting, and was later convicted of several crimes; extremely belatedly served surrender notice charged 5 crimes all occurring **after** that end point; revocation vacated since they couldn't form basis & since failure to perform community service would not have prompted revocation by itself;

C v Aquino **445 M 446 (2005)**—can't punish by way of revocation proceeding for acts occurring after expiration of D's term of probation; revocation hearing scheduled for before end of term was for "technical" violations, and wouldn't have resulted in state prison sentence here imposed (for criminal conduct); rejects Commonwealth argument that D's request for continuance to retain counsel was waiver of or "estopped" him from asserting his other rights;

C v Arroyo **451 M 1010 (2008), overruling 70 MAC 228 (2007)**—though there were appropriate bases for probation revocation, judge also considered and used violations committed beyond the probationary period; factual question of whether probationer violated condition, and discretionary determination by judge whether violation warrants revocation are separate components, and fair reading of transcript shows judge relied on post-probationary period conduct in decision to impose state prison sentence; Appeals Court had ruled no relief, because judge made clear that substantial weight was given to properly charged and considered violations;

C v Mitchell **46 MAC 921 (99)**—during 3-year probation term (with one-yr suspended sentence) D was to pay restitution of $1200, but had not completed payment, and continued to pay $46.15 weekly; probation officer moved neither to extend or revoke probation; almost 3 years later, surrender hearing was scheduled, and judge ordered further two-year probationary period; INVALID, because not reasonably prompt;

C v Phillips **40 MAC 801 (96)**—criminal conduct occurring after sentencing to probation but before beginning of probation term may be used to revoke probation (probation was to follow committed sentence; D solicited murder while incarcerated);

C v Baillargeon **28 MAC 16 (89)**—surrender proceedings commenced 2 years after expiration of probationary period not unreasonably delayed where warrant was issued during probationary period & where D didn't keep Massachusetts authorities informed of his whereabouts in other states;

C v Collins **31 MAC 679 (91)**—surrender proceedings commenced 4 years after probationary period expired not unreasonably delayed where D surrendered within 3 months of return to Massachusetts & where D suffered no prejudice because incarcerated in another state while pursuing appeal;

14-J.4. Preliminary Hearing

Fay v Commonwealth **379 M 498 (80)**—no preliminary hearing unless held only on probation warrant; written notice not required because judge told D reasons for surrender; (see now District Court Rules for Probation Violation Proceedings, Rule 8(a))

Matter of Scott **377 M 364 (79)**—(stipulations # 6, 7, 14) denials of preliminary hearings & District Court "rough justice" = 3 of many grounds for discipline of judge;

Dist. Ct. R.Prob. Violation Proceedings 5(e), 7(a)—explicitly prohibits "tracking," of VTP matter with disposition of new charge(s) while on probation, though but 5(e) provides opportunity for argument of particularized "good cause" for continuance;

C v Morse **50 MAC 582, 591 (2000)**—any "technical" violation of requirements of preliminary hearing, and notice whether hearing was "preliminary" or "final," here harmless (as well as waived); open (?) issue whether arrest warrant (which must be based upon probable cause) satisfies underlying rationale of preliminary hearing requirement (id. at 591 & n.11);

C v Whooley **419 M 421 (95) though G.L. c. 279, § 3**—calls for disposition of any outstanding warrant within 6 months of a prisoner's application for same, violation of § 3 does not entitle D to dismissal of VTP warrant; D had no "right" to obtain 'concurrent' disposition (VTP term with new sentence), though speedier resolution could have allowed this if VTP judge so ordered;

C v Puleio **433 M 39 (2000)**—after District Court judge found, during preliminary revocation hearing, probable cause to believe D violated terms, & ordered D to be detained pending final revocation hearing, bail review (& release) by Superior Court judge = ERROR, though preliminary probation revocation hearing judge, even after finding probable cause to believe D violated terms of probation, could have chosen not to hold D on VTP, but to set bail & other pretrial release terms ON THE NEW OFFENSE; SJC acknowledged its holding to be contrary to Uniform Magistrate Rules, but embraced instead new District Court Rules for Probation Violation Proceedings;

14-J.5. Sufficiency of Bases for Violation

C v MacDonald **50 MAC 220 (2000), affirmed 435 M 1005 (2001)**—probation revocation premised upon violation of probation officer's direction that D have "no contact" with particular woman vacated, because record of case seemingly indicated that judge had ordered less broad "stay away" condition, and "only those probationary terms ordered by the sentencing judge can form the basis for a violation of probation" (but remand for judge to determine what he had actually ordered because some uncertainty); rejection of Commonwealth argument that D's signing of probation "contract" with probation officer altered this result (no "contract," because no "mutuality of obligation"); (but cf. *Jake J. v Commonwealth* **433 M 70, 75 (2000)** signing of "contract" cited by SJC as indicating D's agreement to be & knowledge of being on G.L. c. 276, § 87 pretrial "probation," rather than (illegitimate under G.L. c. 276, § 58) "bail" with conditions);

C v Odoardi **397 M 28 (86)** cites *Rubera* **371 M 177 (76)**—re: beginning adjudication of whether violated terms of probation after indictment (noting ABA below); can limit cross-examination re: (indisputable) violation, so long as no limits on issue of mitigation; vs. . . .

C v Maggio **414 M 193 (93)**—mere fact of indictment on new charges not sufficient basis for revocation; (but now see District Court R.Prob. Violation Proceedings 5(e), 7(a) explicitly prohibiting postponement of VTP hearing merely to await final adjudication of new criminal charges ("tracking"), though 5(e) provides opportunity for argument of particularized "good cause" for continuance; & cf. *C v Morse* **50 MAC 582 (2000)** implying, though reserving question, that issuance of arrest warrant for new crime, having been predicated on probable cause, satisfies underlying rationale of "preliminary" hearing requirement);

C v Milton **427 M 18 (98)**—neither minor nature of new crime (disorderly person) nor fact of its occurring only 2 months prior to expiration of prob. period prevented VTP finding & imposition of previously suspended 1 year sentence; *C v Tate* **34 MAC 446 (93)** similar = despite minor/explainable/sympathetic rationales for violations of "no contact" order, OK to revoke despite harshness of result;

C v Kendrick **446 M 72 (2006)**—probation condition that D have "no contact" with minors under sixteen years old meant not only that he not touch or speak to such child, but that he refrain from attendance at places where proximity to children was likely, and remove himself from such proximity if encounter arose unexpectedly; this included "car show" to which he took his antique auto and dog (both previously used to "lure" children to him), despite absence of testimony that he touched or spoke to any child there; SJC purports to recognize that since "no contact" is not the equivalent of house arrest, fleeting encounters with children (e.g., post office, grocery store) can't be avoided (but D is to remove self as quickly as reasonably possible);

C v Ruiz **453 M 474 (2009)**—when probation term was expressly said to begin **after** incarceration sentence and certain noncriminal acts were proscribed during probation term, ERROR to revoke probation based on noncriminal proscribed act committed during incarceration, at least where D was not given adequate notice that 'no contact' condition was in effect during period of incarceration;

C v Juzba **44 MAC 457 (98)**—though judge revoked probation (after hearing) saying "there is probable cause to believe D (committed new crimes)", record showed judge found "convincing" evidence, & did not lower burden of proof to less than a preponderance;

Rubera v Commonwealth **371 M 177 (76)**—bench trial G. = enough for VTP though (then-available) de novo appeal to jury session pending; (see also, now, District Court R.Prob. Violation Proceedings 5(e), 7(a), explicitly

rejecting practice of awaiting final adjudication of new criminal charges before proceeding on VTP)

C v Michaels **39 MAC 646 (96)**—neither mere fact of issuance of a restraining order nor evidence of a finding by Court #2 that D was in violation of terms of probation re a Court #2 case is enough for VTP in Court #1; Court #2's records noting a default not enough for VTP because not cited as a ground in notice to D **and** no circumstances of default adduced;

C v Joubert **38 MAC 943 (95)**—alleged victim of a sexual assault by D testified at VTP hearing but never sought criminal complaints: no "separation of powers" or other ground for excluding such evidence (revocation vacated on another (hearsay) ground);

C v Herrera **52 MAC 294 (2001)**—after D was found in violation exclusively for failure to report and using heroin, no error in judge's considering police report & restraining order re D's allegedly slashing tires of former girlfriend when deciding whether probation should be continued or revoked (i.e., it's like a "sentencing" decision); would be error if, without notice, the allegations were used to find D violated probation terms;

Bearden v Georgia **461 US 660 (83)**—fine nonpayment not automatic violation of probationary term;

C v Christian **46 MAC 477, S.C., 429 M 1109 (99) (limiting grant of FAR to App. Ct. dicta)**—no "abuse of discretion" found in revoking probation for D's refusal to sign conditions of probation; D not then "in a position to negotiate the conditions of probation," but "acceptance of conditions . . . does not work a waiver of a probationer's right to move . . . for an amendment" of such conditions; "TO THE EXTENT POSSIBLE, IT IS DESIRABLE THAT PROBATION REVOCATION HEARINGS BE HEARD BY THE JUDGE WHO PLACED THE DEFENDANT ON PROBATION IN THE FIRST INSTANCE"; here, revocation "had some flavor of a (prohibited) resentencing in that the judge heard statements about" D's prior 209A and other convictions, "matter that had been available to the original sentencing judge" (but no relief); on further appellate review: **429 M at 1022–23,** overruling contrary statement by Appeals Court: M.R. Crim.P. 30(a) cannot be used to challenge probation revocation order; it must instead be challenged by direct appeal, with notice of appeal filed within 30 days of imposition of previously suspended sentence; Rule 30(a) may be used to challenge the sentence imposed as a consequence of a probation revocation order; *see also C v LaTore* **63 MAC 909 (2005)**—facts that D's "new" convictions were reversed on appeal & that those convictions were the cause of revocation of probation on prior convictions didn't result in relief from probation revocation or sentences imposed thereon: D hadn't appealed from the probation revocation

C v Lally **55 MAC 601 (2002)**—error to revoke probation on ground that D refused to sign probation conditions including random urine screening, because judge had not ordered it; judge's stated probation condition of "treatment as deemed necessary" was ambiguous and improper delegation by judge of authority to impose probationary conditions; probation violation hearing is not the time to add a condition improperly imposed by a probation officer & then to find D in violation of the order;

C v Delisle **440 M 137 (2003)**—purportedly because letter required by "batterer" treatment program was not required by Commonwealth as a condition of probation (but instead by the program, to assess D's amenability to readmission & treatment), no violation of Fifth Amendment privilege against self-incrimination; **program's policies "prohibited the disclosure of the contents of such letters to anyone outside [program], including probation officers, without the permission of the participant"**; court rejects claim that "compulsion" lay in penalty of probation revocation; court also rejects claim that the requirement that D participate in the specified batterers' program was an improper modification: court had ordered that D "participate in . . . personal counseling or therapy as ordered by the probation department" and the named program was merely "a specific directive predicated on the original condition";

14-J.6. Evidentiary Rules

Prop.M.R.Evid. 1101—rules of evidence don't apply to probation violation hearing (or sentencing);

District Court Rules for Probation Violation Proceedings (eff. date 1/2000)—HEARSAY admissible at probation violation hearing, BUT if alleged violation is based solely on hearsay evidence, there must be written finding that hearsay is substantially trustworthy and demonstrably reliable; if alleged violation is criminal behavior, must show "good cause" for failure to call a percipient witness (R.6 (b));

C v Emmanuel E, a juvenile **52 MAC 451 (2001)**—probation revocation vacated because sole witness was cop who read from his notes; no finding of good cause for not allowing probationer to confront adverse witnesses; hearsay = "fatally devoid of factual detail or corroborating personal observations of the officer sufficient to render it reliable or to establish by a preponderance of the evidence that the juvenile committed the charged crime"; **id. at 455** n.5 notes that new District Court Rules for Probation Violation Proceedings add to Durling requirement that hearsay have "substantial indicia of reliability" the requirement that good cause be shown for not producing percipient witness;

Brown, petitioner **395 M 1006 (85)**—habeas relief for too much/unreliable hearsay at violation hearing;

C v Durling **407 M 108 (90)**—Commonwealth may only rely on "reliable" hearsay to establish probation violation where it can show "good cause" for not presenting live eyewitnesses; hearsay in police report was sufficient basis for surrender where report contained detailed statements of fact eyewitnessed by 2 cops & where new arrests in other counties would place burden on cops to travel to other parts of state; due process requirements discussed; (N.B.: Rule 6 of District Court Rules for Probation Viola-

tion Proceeding, effective 1-3-2000, requires also, if hearsay = sole evidence, that Commonwealth show good cause for not producing percipient witness)

C v Delaney **36 MAC 930 (94)**—reversal of revocation due to use of hearsay when there was (a) no good cause for not allowing confrontation, and (b) witness presentation was possible and hearsay not reliable;

C v Joubert **38 MAC 943 (95)**—hearsay re child sexual assault admitted without necessary determinations re: "good cause" or substantial reliability **and** latter finding could not be made despite allegedly corroborating medical evidence and G.L. c. 233, § 81 (upon particular findings, judge may admit "in any criminal proceeding" hearsay of child under age 10 re: sex assaults); revocation vacated (despite evidence of another basis for revocation) since judge relied in part on the hearsay;

C v Negron **441 M 685 (2004)**—when D's wife claimed spousal privilege & refused to testify at revocation hearing, she was "unavailable"; judge should have decided whether cop's testimony re: her out-of-court allegations had substantial indicia of reliability establishing good cause for eliminating "confrontation" (but mere assertion of spousal privilege didn't make prior alleged statements unreliable); SJC here ruled that statements might be found reliable because factually detailed, based on personal knowledge & direct observation, made close in time to events in question, corroborated by observations of cop BUT because hearing was halted before cross-examination could have altered that supposition, remand necessary; **NOTE: import of *Crawford v Washington* 124 S Ct 1354 (2004) was not briefed by parties here;**

C v Cates **57 MAC 759 (2003)**—no relief [here] from admission of videotape of a "SAIN" [alleged sexual assault] interview, although allegation of sex assault does not by itself constitute good cause to dispense with D's right to cross-examine witness at revocation hearing;

C v Calvo **41 MAC 903 (96)**—hearsay OK (statement by D's mother in law, a percipient witness to the probation violation, written on back of police report & signed under penalties of perjury) despite no showing of witness's unavailability & despite in-court contradiction by D's wife (wife impeached by her like-signed statement, however);

C v Mejias **44 MAC 948 (98)**—police reports sufficient to justify probation revocation: (1) police officers responded to report of breaking glass, and found D and another man, D carrying a hammer and other "burglarious implement," and window pane broken as described in initial complaint, and (2) police officers themselves (in another instance) observed D lighting up pipe of crack cocaine and smoking it; another police report, containing only allegations of D's girlfriend that D had used drugs in her home and that he beat her when she complained about this was NOT used by revocation judge as a basis for action; Court refused to rule that witnesses had to be shown unavailable before intro of the hearsay; fact that charges arising out of police report were later dismissed for lack of prosecution was "immaterial to the validity of the revocation, as would be an acquittal";

C v Simon **57 MAC 80 (2003)**—statement of D recorded in police report could be used at VTP hearing, even if "involuntary" because of no Miranda warnings or intoxication;

C v Harrigan **53 MAC 147 (2001)**—hearsay testimony by cop re: D's girlfriend's statements at scene that D punched her (corroborated by testimony about bruises) not a problem, since D had full right of confrontation, having himself called as a witness the girlfriend, who testified that she had been drunk, didn't remember what she told police, but she had bruised her face when she fell out of auto, not through any act of D; Rule 6(b) of District Court Rules for Probation Violation Proceedings not implicated because probationer had opportunity to confront the witness/test reliability of evidence by cross-examination;

C v Wilcox **63 MAC 131, further appellate review allowed 444 M 1103 (2005)**—Rule 6(B) requirement of written findings concerning good cause for not producing the witnesses (and relying instead on hearsay) & whether hearsay evidence is "substantially trustworthy and demonstrably reliable" not implicated here because revocation wasn't based SOLELY on hearsay evidence (police report); further, corroboration was by D's inculpatory admissions and other evidence; **S.C., 446 M 61 (2006)**—on further review, limited to **question whether Sixth Amendment confrontation right of *Crawford v Washington* 541 US 36 (2004) applies to probation revocation proceedings, SJC holds that it doesn't;**

C v Emmanuel E., a juvenile **52 MAC 451 (2001)**—hearsay testimony of cop here insufficient to prove by a preponderance that D had violated probation by committing a new crime;

C v Ortiz **58 MAC 904 (2003)**—same, cop merely repeating alleged victim's allegations concerning assault and battery and malicious damage to vehicle;

C v Wilson **47 MAC 924 (99)**—police report comprised of hearsay and lacking substantial indicia of reliability: complainant had recently been arrested for extortion of D, and though complainant took stand at revocation hearing, he refused to answer questions on cross; "corroboration" inadequate (though letter from D to complainant confirmed a "close" relationship, it contained no confirmation of a sexual relationship, which would have been the basis for probation revocation);

C v Ivers **56 MAC 444 (2002)**—Chelsea probation officer testified that he had info from East Boston probation officer that latter hadn't seen D for some time and D hadn't complied with terms of the Office of Community Corrections; judge wrote that his finding of violation was based on Chelsea probation officer's testimony: ERROR, because hearsay was too vague to sustain finding of violation; to be "reliable," hearsay must be detailed rather than conclusory;

C v Hector H. **69 MAC 43 (2007)**—an appeal of probation revocation on ground of unreliable hearsay (as to new crimes) will become moot if juvenile thereafter admits to sufficient facts on new charges and is adjudicated "delinquent" on them before the appeal is decided; BUT Appeals Court also claims that cops' hearsay info had "three recognized indicia of reliability," i.e., "factual detail from complainants, complainants' personal knowledge and direct observation of facts reported, and corroborating observations by cops;

C v Podoprigora **48 MAC 136 (99)**—surrender hearing held on allegation that D telephoned home of ex-wife and daughter, in violation of "no contact" order, speaking to daughter to ask telephone number of brother; "sworn statement" by ex-wife and cop's testimony re: interview of daughter in presence of mother/ex-wife were basis for revocation, but Appeals Court reversed, finding "(in)sufficient indicia of reliability to obviate the need for confrontation"; cop's testimony about child's "demeanor" in these circumstances not meaningful, and "sworn statement" was made by someone without personal knowledge of pertinent event; *Calvo* **41 MAC 903 (96)** distinguished on this basis; testimony that D had access to a telephone at time of purported call was insufficient corroboration;

14-J.7. Suppressible Evidence?

Minnesota v Murphy **465 US 420 (84)**—noncustodial statements to probation officer not involuntary & no Miranda rights required (at least under federal law);

C v Olsen **405 M 491 (89)**—evidence obtained in violation of 4th Amendment or Article 14 may be used at surrender hearing to show probation violation, at least where police unaware of defendant's status as probationer;

C v Vincente **405 M 278 (89)**—under federal constitution, statements obtained in violation of Miranda may be used at surrender hearing to show violation of probation, at least where police unaware D on probation;

See also *Commonwealth v Delisle* **440 M 137 (2003)**—regarding claim of violation of guarantee against compelled self-incrimination (D's failure to write self-analysis concerning acts of domestic violence);

C v Wilcox **63 MAC 131, 139, further appellate review allowed 444 M 1103 (2005)**—D's interview at police station was videotaped without his knowledge and consent, and disclosed prior convictions and sexual fantasies, but because tape was recorded in Rhode Island, G.L. c. 272, § 99 didn't prohibit; on further review, **446 M 61 (2006)**, issue limited to whether *Crawford v Washington* 541 US 36 (2004), applies to probation revocation proceedings: SJC held it doesn't;

14-J.8. Closing Argument

C v Marvin **417 M 291 (94)**—no absolute right to "closing argument" at probation revocation hearing, but such argument is the "better practice";

14-K. WEEKEND OR OTHER "SPECIAL" SENTENCE

G.L. c. 279, § 6A—"special" sentence (usually only weekends) for "1st offense of imprisonment"; house of correction or jail sentence of 1 year or less may be served in whole or part on weekends & holidays, or other interval; 6 p.m. Friday to 7 a.m. Monday = 4 days (if Monday = holiday, serve 'til Tuesday 7 a.m.); can rescind on application of D, house of correction, or judge's motion after hearing; if convicted of subsequent crime (other than nonmoving motor vehicle violation) while serving such sentence, terms of 'special' sentence = rescinded & D to complete balance of original sentence non-specially, i.e., consecutively;

C v Swan 38 MAC 539 (95)—dicta = 2 year sentence, split, with committed portion to be served on 10 consecutive weekends, balance suspended = illegal, because weekend sentences must be for less than or equal to one year, and this means **whole** sentence, not just committed portion of a "split";

G.L. c. 90, § 24(1)(a)(3)—weekends/evenings/holiday 'special' sentence OK if D "has not been convicted previously of (operating under influence) or assigned to an alcohol or controlled substance education, treatment or rehabilitation program within ten years preceding the date of the commission of the offense for which he has been convicted";

C v Cowan 422 M 546 (96)—judge could not allow D's mandatory minimum 1 year firearm sentence to be satisfied by 6 months "house arrest" following 6 months in house of correction;

C v Beauchemin 410 M 181, 185–86 (91)—D, allowed liberty during pendency of appeal (by allowance of a stay of sentence execution, M.R.Crim.P. 31, M.R.App.P. 6), did not receive credit against sentence despite stay condition that he could not leave home/property; **C v Morasse 446 M 113 (2006)**—though condition of pretrial probation was that D be confined to his home and be monitored there by electronic bracelet, this was not "confinement" for which he received credit on eventual sentence;

14-L. SPLIT SENTENCES

G.L. c. 279, §§ 1 & 1A—sentence or any part can be suspended with probation; "split" sentence includes both a committed & a suspended term of incarceration, with period of probation; § 1 doesn't permit suspension of the execution of sentence for any crime punishable by death or imprisonment for life; § 1A doesn't permit suspension of the execution of the sentence of any person convicted of a crime "punishable by imprisonment for life or of a crime an element of which is being armed with a dangerous weapon, or of any person convicted of any other felony if it shall appear that he has been previously convicted of any felony"; BUT SEE G.L. c. 127, § 133, portion as amended by St. 1993, c. 432 ("Act to promote the effective management of the criminal justice system through truth-in-sentencing"), § 11, effective 4-12-94: "Sentences of imprisonment in the state prison shall not be suspended in whole or in part"; 120 CMR 200.06 split sentences to state prison are abolished for offenses committed on or after July 1, 1994.

120 CMR 200.06: House of Correction/Reformatory Sentences—Parole eligibility for an individual serving a split house of correction sentence and/or a reformatory sentence is calculated based upon the committed term of the sentence as provided in 120 CMR 200.04(1) and 200.05(2)

C v Holmgren 421 M 224, 228 (95)—if prob. violation is found **and** suspension is revoked, D must be committed on the full suspended portion; when D is serving committed portion of split, parole eligibility = ½ that term; if D is returned on the balance of the split, parole eligibility is ½ of the aggregate of both portions of the split sentence;

See also Chapter 14-V, Parole;

C v Ford 413 M 46 (92)—D's early release pursuant to federal court order to alleviate jail overcrowding did not "wipe out" committed portion of split sentence; unserved committed portion & suspended portions may be imposed on D for probation violation;

C v Cotter 415 M 183 (93)—OK for judge at sentencing to require D to agree to lawful condition of probation (accompanying suspended portion of split sentence) and to order committed sentence instead when D refused;

C v Forkin 413 M 1001 (92)—same;

C v Juzba 44 MAC 457 (98)—concurrent sentence of 3 years probation, anchored to a split sentence, held here to run only upon release from the committed portion of the split sentence; though probation could be ordered to run during incarceration, this would be "unusual";

14-M. EXECUTED SENTENCE—COMMITMENT

See Parole, Chapter 14-V, below; re: eligibility; NOTE: no parole eligibility for sentence UNDER 60 days! (G.L. c. 127, § 128, & 120 CMR 200.04(1)) (see Chapter 13-A, Pleas, Advice to D (Parole, etc.));

120 CMR 200. 04—for "compelling reasons", parole hearing panel may release individual serving house of correction sentence up to 30 days earlier than eligibility date,

& may recommend to full Parole Board that prisoner be released up to 60 days earlier than eligibility date;

Solem v Helm **463 US 277 (83)**—life without parole for uttering checks, without prior violence = grossly disproportionate;

Rummel v Estelle **445 US 263 (80)**—life with parole (12 years) for 3 nonviolent felonies = OK

Wilkinson v Austin **125 S.Ct. 2384 (2005)**—prisoners have liberty interest protected by Due Process Clause in avoiding placement in highly restrictive "supermax" facility in which nearly all human contact is prohibited, placement is of indefinite duration and placement disqualifies inmate for parole (nonetheless, procedures here are upheld);

G.L. c. 218, § 27—District Court can give same sentences as Superior Court, but no "state prison";

G.L. c. 125, § 1—"State Prison" = Cedar Junction (formerly known as MCI-Walpole); "state correctional facility" = any correctional facility owned, operated, administered or subject to the control of the department of correction, owned by Dept. of Correction;

G.L. c. 279, § 5—if statute without penalty, it's "custom & usage"; if misdemeanor G, sentence either to jail or house of correction

G.L. c. 279, § 6—"jail" punishment = either jail or house of correction;

G.L. c. 279, § 23—jail or house of correction maximum = 2½ years;

G.L. c. 279, § 24—"indeterminate" state prison, i.e., maximum (statute) & minimum (1 year); if crime allows for house of correction punishment, minimum state prison term may not be < one year;

G.L. c. 279, § 16—females convicted of crime punishable by jail or house of correction may be sentenced to MCI-Framingham;

District Court Standards of Judicial Practice, Sentencing & Other Dispositions (1984) § 7.01—max. District Court sentence = 2½; id. 7:07–7:08—"indef.," male & female; max.= 2½ years.

G.L. c. 279, § 15—house of correction sentence can be ordered to "any" county;

G.L. c. 123, § 18(a)—jailer may have prisoner examined & then ask court to send prisoner to hospital or Bridgewater if mentally ill (*See Chapter 4, Arraignment re: G.L. c. 123, §§ 15(b), 18 hearings*); court may then order examination, temporary commitments; G.L. c. 123, § 18(b) prisoner may apply for voluntary admission to mental health facility under G.L. c. 123, § 10(a);

Brown v Comm'r **394 M 89 (85)**—state prison sentence only on indictment; can't transfer District Court prisoner to state prison;

Sheriff Middlesex v Comm'r **383 M 631 (81)**—without emergency, Superior Court judge can't order state prison sentence at house of correction;

C v Brown **431 M 772 (2000)**—statutorily-mandated sentence range for home invasion (G.L. c. 265, § 18C), "life or any term not less than twenty years" requires D to be sentenced, at minimum, to 20 years (e.g., 20–25 yrs); rejects D's argument that statute instead directs that upper number has to be at least 20 years (e.g., 3–20 yrs);

103 CMR 420.09 (87)—entitled to meaningful classification reviews every 6 months;

Good v Comm'r of Correction **417 M 329 (94)**—right to meaningful classification reviews even though Mass. sentence was being served in federal prison; Article 26, Dec. of Rights bars cruel & unusual punishment, and a claim under article 26 is stated when plaintiff alleges that the only drinking water available to him in custody poses substantial risk of serious harm to health;

Dougan v Comm'r of Correction **34 MAC 147 (93)**—DOC classification manual, "standard movement chronology," created no **right** to particular placement; classification decision = exercise of administrative discretion;

Turner v Safley **482 US 78 (87)**—"prison walls do not form a barrier separating prison inmates from the protections of the Constitution"; inmate retains rights which are not inconsistent with his status as prisoner or with legitimate "penological objectives of the corrections system";

Langton v Comm'r of Correction **34 MAC 564 (93)**—mandatory tuberculosis testing of inmates, after 3 active cases were diagnosed in one facility, did not violate rights of inmates;

In the Matter of a Grand Jury Subpoena **454 M 685 (2009)**—neither a pretrial jail detainee or a convicted inmate has reasonable expectation of privacy in telephone conversations: all parties have notice that calls are subject to monitoring/recording, and penological interests justify: loss of privacy is an "inherent incident[ ] of confinement"; providing recorded calls to grand jury in response to subpoena = OK;

Pennsylvania Dep't of Corrections v. Yeskey **524 US 206 (98)**—Americans with Disabilities Act, 42 U.S.C. § 12132 (2000) applies to state prisons; *Shedlock v Dep't of Correction* **442 M 844 (2004)**—must make request for accommodation; claim viable even when actions have not resulted in "total" denial of benefits or "complete" exclusion from programs; Federal Rehabilitation Act, 29 U.S.C. § 794 (2000) also applicable to prisons; claim here stated (summary judgment erroneously allowed below) concerned D's request for accommodation for medical problems resulting in limp & use of cane (housing in first-floor cell) and prison "retaliation" for D's "refusing a housing assignment," etc.;

Foucha v Louisiana **504 US 71 (92)**—'not guilty by reason of insanity' Ds who later become sane may not be detained simply because they remain "dangerous";

14-N. RECIDIVIST SENTENCING STATUTES

G.L. c. 279, § 8B—if D is on bail/personal recognizance for pending cases and commits new crimes, sentence for new crimes "shall run consecutively to the earlier sentence for the crime for which he was on release";

C v Hickey **429 M 1027 (99)**—but if D is sentenced FIRST for the later crime, G.L. c. 279, § 8B is no bar to a "forthwith" sentence on the first-occurring crime;

C v Yancey **46 MAC 924 (99)**—no error in denying motion to withdraw G plea on basis that sentence was ordered to run from & after sentence for crime for which D was on bail at time of new crime; Court rejected argument that from & after provision applied only to new crimes committed when D was on "personal recognizance";

Nichols v US **511 US 738 (94)**—use of uncounseled misdemeanor conviction for enhanced sentence on later crime = OK under federal constitution (because D did not receive a committed sentence upon that earlier misdemeanor conviction); federal due process doesn't require misdemeanor D to be warned that conviction might be used for later sentence enhancement (but see M.R.Crim.P. 12(C)(3)(B));

C v Barrett **3 MAC 8 (75)**—barred use of uncounseled misdemeanor conviction to impeach D's credibility, but its construction of federal constitution predated, & is at odds with *Nichols* **511 US 738 (94)** definitive pronouncement re: FEDERAL constitution; *C v Proctor* **403 M 146, 147 (88)** and *Sheridan, petitioner* **422 M 776, 778 (96)** follow *Barrett*; no mention of *Nichols* in latter; cf. *Alabama v Shelton* **122 S. Ct. 1764 (2002)** if no counsel, can't later execute/activate suspended sentence for violating terms of probation; majority suggests no constitutional bar to pre-trial probation, allowing uncounseled defendants to consent to probation before an adjudication of guilt, with a counseled adjudication occurring only if a probation violation occurs;

* **G.L. c. 279, § 25: HABITUAL**—felony G + 2 priors (in which sentenced and committed to prison in this or another state . . . for terms of not less than 3 years each) = MAXIMUM sentence for new felony!;

C v Keane **41 MAC 656 (96)**—statute = "sentencing" statute, and does not create a substantive crime;

C v Burston **35 MAC 355 (93)**—G.L. c. 279, § 25 not barred by double jeopardy principles; fact that prior conviction(s) occurred long ago = irrelevant;

C v Tuitt **393 M 801 (85)**—not cruel & unusual; max. sentence precludes suspended sentence; habitual offender though didn't "serve" 3 years before;

C v Allen **22 MAC 413 (86)**—(same); prior Concord sentence (lenient) = nonetheless "prison"; (unfairness = question for legislature);

C v Cruzado **73 MAC 803 (2009)**—D drove away from gas station an unattended car, but station employee pursued, ripped open door and hung on; 'habitual offender' designation mandated "life" sentence (robbery), not cruel & unusual;

C v Hall **397 M 466 (86)**—enough here; but would prior concurrents suffice?;

C v Keane **41 MAC 656 (96)**—2 prior convictions sufficed, regardless that sentences on them were concurrently run; not error to indict D under habitual offender at same time he was indicted for 3d felony (needn't wait for "G" on 3d felony); conviction of only lesser included offense (rape) did not prevent treatment as habitual offender although indictment specified aggravated rape;

C v Perry **65 MAC 624 (2006)**—rejects D's argument that his four prior predicate offenses didn't qualify because he received sentences of concurrent time;

Deal v US **508 US 129 (93)**—extremely harsh sentence enhancers OK even though six robberies were the subject of a single prosecution & enhancement was applied immediately upon these convictions: D not entitled to "a sentencing windfall" because he for a time evaded prosecution for the 1st 5 so was instead tried for 6 at once; cf. Keane 41 MAC 656 (96);

C v Youngworth **48 MAC 249 (99)**—enough (length of sentence & commitment) for grand jury to make "habitual offender" charge (though perhaps not for actual proof later) = court documents showing D sentenced to 13 yrs MCI-Concord, with mittimus issued for this sentence, and later sentenced in federal court to 9 years' imprisonment, with recommendation that he be "placed in federal correctional institute in New England area"; **BUT SJC, after D filed second motion to dismiss & cited a different ground, granted relief:** *Youngworth v Commonwealth* **436 M 608 (2002)** habitual criminal indictment requires proof of two prior convictions "in this or another state", and had to be dismissed when Commonwealth relied on one conviction in a state court and one conviction in Federal court (though legislature could amend the statute);

C v Parzyck **44 MAC 655 (98)**—predicate convictions = final despite pendency of appeal from denial of R.30 motion to vacate G pleas; assumed, without deciding, that pendency of **direct** appeal would preclude conviction from being used as predicate for "habitual"; R.30 appellate relief as to sentencing issue did not nullify conviction itself;

Lifetime Community Parole: G.L. c. 127, § 133C; G.L. c. 275, § 18; G.L. c. 265, § 45—lifetime parole shouldn't be imposed for offense committed before passage of the Act (i.e., 9/10/99) (because of e.g., *C v Fuller* **421 M 407–8 (95)**—presumption against retroactivity where statute does not specify that its provisions apply retroactively); lifetime parole must be imposed re: rape, rape of child under 16 w/force, rape & abuse of child, assault with intent to rape, kidnapping child under 16, drugging for sex, unnatural & lascivious acts, and any attempt to commit any of the above; BUT if 1st offense of any of these, D may move for hearing to determine whether lifetime parole shall be imposed; lifetime parole may be imposed re: indecent A&B (either under age 14 or 14 & over), indecent A&B of mentally retarded person, and as to any 1st offense of these, prosecutor may request hearing to determine whether lifetime parole should be imposed; D may petition parole board to terminate lifetime parole after 15 years;

C v Pagan **445 M 315 (2005)**—standard and burden of proof ambiguous as to imposition of lifetime community parole in some cases, and so unconstitutional as to those; complaint or indictment must allege that D is repeat offender (if such is essential to imposition of LCP given the crime charged); warning that Supreme Court case law (*Apprendi v NJ*, etc.) dictates that this enhanced sentence cannot be based on factual findings made by judge rather than jury;

See Chapter 13E re attempts to vacate state court guilty pleas/convictions when faced with enhanced punishment later, on basis of prior convictions;

14-N.1. Convictions after Similar Offense

C v Fernandes **430 M 517 (99)**—indictment of two pages, with 1st page "count" charging new drug offense and 2d page "count" simply alleging a prior conviction; "count" 2 not a separate crime, but simply notifies D of sentence enhancement (& sufficient notice given by words "having been previously convicted of a similar offense," though better practice = specify date of prior offense and date and court in which prior conviction was obtained);

C v Durakowski **58 MAC 92 (2003)**—purportedly "like" predicate offense wasn't statutorily the legal equivalent of the Massachusetts crime [but its facts sufficed to show similarity on evidence presented here];

C v Flaherty **61 MAC 776 (2004)**—despite D's arguments that D's guilty plea to OUI in New Hampshire was a "violation" rather than a "conviction" and that it was the registry of motor vehicles rather than the court which required completion of an alcohol intervention program, the NH matter was held to be a qualifying "prior" for conviction of OUI-4th offense;

C v Durakowski **58 MAC 92 (2003)**—a "like" offense in prosecution of one accused of being a four-time violator of firearms law can be a federally proscribed crime, e.g., felon in possession (18 U.S.C. § 922(g)(1)); contrast *Youngworth v Commonwealth* **436 M 608, 611–12 (2002)** (habitual offender statute requiring predicate convictions "in this or another state" precludes use of federal conviction);

Bynum v Commonwealth **429 M 705 (99)**—G.L. c. 94C, § 32A(d) does not create an independent crime (having been convicted of a like drug offense previously), but is instead a sentencing enhancement provision;

C v Harris **75 MAC 696 (2009)**—after D was convicted of cocaine trafficking, prosecutor waived action on "second offender" portion of indictment and moved for sentencing, agreeing that she would be filing nolle prosequi on the second/subsequent offense issue; the nolle prosequi (argued on appeal to have been without the consent of the defendant, though D after conviction of the new substantive offense had moved unsuccessfully to dismiss the second offender charge) did NOT function as an acquittal of the entire indictment; further review allowed **455 M 1108 (2010)**;

C v Miranda **441 M 783 (2004)** cites *Bynum v Commonwealth* **429 M 705 (99)** (repeat-offender components of indictments don't describe independent crimes which may be charged apart from the substantive crimes whose penalties they enhance), "second or subsequent" portion of charge wasn't freestanding crime, so there was no error in "amending" the drug distribution indictment to make the "subsequent" allegation merely a "count" of the indictment itself rather than a separate indictment (no alteration of grand jury's work, because merely combined the first indictment and repeat-offender component of second indictment into a single instrument); G.L. c. 278, § 11A requires that D be tried first on underlying substantive crime & then in separate proceeding on component of charge referring to crime as "second or subsequent";

C v Kulesa **455 M 447 (2009)**—D was entitled to counsel at trial of "subsequent offender" portion of proceedings regarding G.L. c. 278, § 11A (criminal harassment, subsequent offender), and D's waiver of counsel for trial of substantive offense did NOT operate as waiver of counsel for second part of bifurcated proceeding (though judge COULD conduct colloquy prior to trial of substantive offense which clearly covered both portions, this didn't occur here);

G.L. c. 90, § 24—operating motor vehicle under the influence—enhanced penalties

C v Corbett **422 M 391 (96)**—no ex post facto bar to enhanced operating under influence sentence based on OUI offenses 8 years earlier (when "enhancing" penalties were passed in interim, but at time of earlier offense, law was such that use of 8-year-old conviction would have been time-barred);

G.L. c. 266, § 62: COMMON & NOTORIOUS RECEIVER OF STOLEN PROPERTY—"shall" be so adjudged if 1 prior, or 3 at same sitting; = 10 year maximum;

C v McGann **20 MAC 59 (85)**—3 counts of G. = 9–10 MCI Cedar Junction (Walpole);

G.L. c. 266, § 40: COMMON & NOTORIOUS THIEF—"shall" be so adjudged if 2 Superior Court larcenies, or 3 distinct ones at same sitting; = 20 year maximum; *C v Clark* **53 MAC 342 (2001)** consolidated judgment as to "common/notorious thief", on basis of 15 simultaneously-resolved indictments, was recorded on one indictment with offense pre-dating 'truth in sentencing' statute, but OK to make date of 'consolidated judgment' one post-dating 'truth in sentencing,' at least where judge's emphatic advice at plea hearing was consistent with the lengthier incarceration the statute mandated; 'common/ notorious' thief could have been based ONLY on (the 13) crimes post-dating effective date of statute;

Garvey v C **8 Gray 382 (1857)**—normally must allege 2d offense;

C v Crocker **384 M 353 (81)**—unlike 279/25 & 278/11A, can use "common & notorious thief" sentencing designation though no pretrial notice; (*see Chapter 21-R, Larceny*);

G.L. c. 94C, §§ 32, 32A–32D—second/subsequent drug offenses

G.L. c. 269, § 10—illegally carrying firearm

G.L. c. 269, § 10G(a)—armed career criminal;

C v Ware **75 MAC 220 (2009)**—G.L. c. 269, § 10G(a) provides enhanced punishment for person possessing firearm/ammo after having been previously convicted of "violent crime or a serious drug offense" as defined: possession of Class B with intent to distribute was "serious" even though prosecuted in District Court in this instance (because crime itself was punishable by ten years' prison);

C v Furr **58 MAC 155 (2003)**—D's prior adjudication as youthful offender on charges of armed carjacking, armed robbery, ABDW, etc., qualifies as predicate conviction to warrant enhanced sentences in G.L. c. 269, § 10(g);

C v Foreman **63 MAC 801 (2005)**—D, an adult, could be prosecuted as armed career criminal with predicate convictions being juvenile adjudications (*Furr*, above, had still been a juvenile when prosecuted as armed career criminal, and so predicate convictions had necessarily been juvenile adjudications); predicate armed robbery conviction here had knife rather than gun, but still legitimate as "violent crime" in G.L. c. 140, § 121;

C v Connor C **432 M 635 (2000)**—same, for purposes of "repeat offender" provision of G.L. c. 269, § 10(d);

G.L. c. 90, § 24—operating under the influence offenses;

Federal Sentencing Enhancements—U.S. Sentencing Guidelines, §§ 4A1.1, 4A1.2; "Career Offenders" (28 USC § 994(h), USSG § 4B1.1–.2; Federal Firearms Offenses; Domestic Violence convictions, 18 USC §§ 921–22; Armed Career Criminal 18 USC § 924(e);

C v Valiton **432 M 647 (2000)**—second offender conviction of OUI can be sustained on basis of "prior" charge of being delinquent by reason of operating motor vehicle while under influence of intoxicating liquor, with disposition in prior case being license suspension, counseling, & evaluation at a program providing education, treatment, and rehabilitation, & order of probation;

C v Connor C., a juvenile **432 M 635 (2000)**—delinquency adjudication concerning firearm possession sufficed as predicate for enhanced later charge (indictment as a youthful offender for "poss. firearm without license, subsequent offense," G.L. c. 269, § 10(d));

Cf. *C v Flaherty* **61 MAC 776 (2004)**—despite D's arguments that D's (adult) guilty plea to OUI in New Hampshire was a "violation" rather than a "conviction" and that it was the registry of motor vehicles rather than the court which required completion of an alcohol intervention program, the NH matter was held to be a qualifying "prior" for conviction of OUI-4th offense;

14-N.2. Procedure for Determination of "Second/Subsequent"

G.L. c. 278, § 11A: Separate Trial on Issue of Conviction of Prior Offenses (procedure when D is charged with crime for which more severe punishment is provided for 2d/subsequent)—D at arraignment pleads only re crime charged, not to whether it's 2d offense; if NG plea, no mention to jury of prior (except impeachment by prior not necessarily barred if D takes stand), right to trial on whether 'subsequent' (procedure explained); (*see Chapter 5, Contents of Complaint/Indictment*);

C v Murchison **35 MAC 269 (93)**—D had right to jury trial on whether drug charge was a **2d** offense; absence of waiver colloquy caused remand "for appropriate trial of the second offense question"; on further review, **418 M 58 n.5 (94)**, SJC agreed that 2d offender sentence was improper because D hadn't properly waived right to jury on this question;

Apprendi v New Jersey **530 US 466 (2000)**—federal due process/jury trial right to any factor enhancing sentence EXCEPT FOR whether there have been prior convictions;

C v Thompson **427 M 729 (98)**—judge had discretion to deny D's request for **new** jury on "habitual offender" issue (G.L. c. 278, § 11A); discretion either to hold 1st jury for determination of the issue or empanel 2d jury (and D here didn't want 1st jury); following jury trial and conviction, jury waiver as to finding of prior conviction(s) was not invalid because made after the empanelment of the jury trying the case (despite D's argument citing G.L. c. 263, § 6);

C v McCready **50 MAC 647 (2000)**—vacating "second offense portion of charge" for defective procedure, whereby after jury G on operating under the influence charge, judge sentenced D as second offender merely upon "counsel's statement that there had been a previous OUI conviction";

C v Chaplin **50 MAC 365 (2000)**—similar; counsel's acquiescence that D had prior offense wasn't "functional equivalent of" guilty plea; rejecting also Commonwealth argument that D was "convicted" just of OUI & merely sentenced with consideration of his criminal record as a whole; see also *C v Zuzick* **45 MAC 71 (98)** (cited in Chaplin, with refusal to distinguish on basis that Zuzick actually pled NG to 'subsequent' and requested trial on the issue);

C v Orben **53 MAC 700 (2002)**—vacating portion of judgment re: "fourth offense" OUI, because proceeding was "neither a trial nor a plea, but something similar . . . to the procedure repudiated in *C v Zuzick* **45 MAC 71, 74–75 (98)**"; without conducting any inquiry of D, judge accepted counsel's representation that counsel had spoken with the 5 police officers waiting in hall to testify re: prior convictions, & that it wouldn't be necessary for prosecution to call them;

C v Dussault **71 MAC 542 (2008)**—absence of written waiver of D's right to jury trial (bifurcated proceeding, after OUI conviction by jury, on fact of prior convictions to support charge of operating under the influence, 3rd offense) resulted in vacating so much of judgment as found D guilty of OUI 3rd offense; court records admitted would have been sufficient, however, to show identity of prior convictions offender was D, i.e., D's full name, including middle initial and "unusual" last name, with additional biographical information matching D, including date of birth, town of residence, and specific addresses correlating with trial evidence;

C v Zavala **52 MAC 770, 777–79 (2001)**—proof of prior conviction must include proof that D is same person who was arrested & convicted earlier, i.e., not merely same name; reversal here for allowing Commonwealth to re-open evidence, after D's motion for required finding of not guilty; see also *C v Koney* **421 M 295, 301–2 (95)**;

C v Olivo **58 MAC 368 (2003)**—sufficient evidence identifying D as the individual previously convicted, contrasting *C v Koney*;

C v Bowden **447 M 593 (2006)**—even under law prevailing prior to new "Melanie's Law," live testimony by "identifying" witnesses not required to establish D as individual previously convicted; Registry documentation showing identity of current and former addresses, prior court conviction for OUI second offense, Registry document with color photo of D held adequate overall here; *C v Maloney* **447 M 577 (2006)**—re new "Melanie's Law" (G.L. c. 90, § 24(4), inter alia): court record of prior convictions, accompanied by other documentation, may be prima facie evidence of prior convictions; **N.B.:** *C v Koney* [421 M 295, 302] holding must be read into even this new statute (mere identity of name isn't enough to establish even prima facie case);

C v Olivo **58 MAC 368 (2003)**—judge erred in failing to instruct jury that to determine whether there was proof of prior conviction, they were permitted to consider ONLY the evidence introduced during the second trial and not the evidence from the first trial (but error here was harmless);

14-O. CONCURRENT SENTENCES

See "Parole," Chapter 14-V;

G.L. c. 4, § 6, Ninth—statutory penalty shall be for each violation;

G.L. c. 279, § 8—2 or more sentences: serve in order of mittimuses;

Henschel v Comm'r **368 M 130 (75)**—it's concurrent unless explicitly "from & after" (but see G.L. c. 279, § 8B if crime committed while D on bail, sentence for new crime is to be ordered served from and after sentence for charge on which D was on bail (*see Chapter 14-P, Consecutive Sentences*);

"Guide to Parole in Mass." (Chapter 14-V Below)—policy to add time served on #1 before sentence #2 to "avoid harsh result" from interval between 2 dispositions—except if #2 = crime on parole, crime in jail or state prison;

Baranow v Comm'r **1 MAC 831 (73)**—(same);

Carlino v Comm'r **355 M 159 (69)**—a sentence to run from and after concurrent sentences begins after the longest "concurrent";

C v Williams **34 MAC 346 (93)**—following District Court bench trial conviction & sentence of 1 year, D appealed to jury of six, then received 1 year sentence in another court on unrelated charges; when D withdrew jury of six appeal & bench trial sentence of 1 year was ordered to be served from & after, no error: D was not entitled to order of concurrent sentences;

Chalifoux v Comm'r **375 M 424 (78)**—concurrent begins when imposed, not retroactive; credit for California "concurrent" sentence, though fiction, because MA wouldn't rendite;

Abrahams v Commonwealth **57 MAC 861 (2003)**—in absence of statutory prohibition, Superior Court judge could order state prison sentence (3½ to 4 years) to commence "forthwith," and be served concurrently with a federal sentence, even though D was in federal custody, in his 14th month of a 24-month federal sentence;

District Court Standards of Judicial practice, Sentencing & Other Dispositions (1984) 7:03, Comment—District Court can't sentence concurrent with state prison; vs. . . .

In re Kinney, petitioner **5 MAC 457 (77)**—District Court judge could've given concurrent with state prison, but didn't;

Royce, petitioner **28 MAC 397 (90)**—"considerations of fairness" required that sentence for new offense imposed on escapee run concurrently with unexpired portion of 1st sentence where Commonwealth failed to act with reasonable promptness in filing detainer 12 years after D's capture, where sentence not explicitly ordered to run from & after, & where Commonwealth failed to inform D whether he was getting credit while serving earlier intervening sentence of other jurisdiction where detainer lodged;

C v Juzba **44 MAC 457 (98)**—sentence of probation, ordered to run concurrent with a split sentence, held here to have begun only upon D's release from committed portion of split; judge could, however, order probation during incarceration (perhaps appropriate where foreseeable that D could cause trouble in prison, e.g., prison gang member);

C v Barton **74 MAC 912 (2009)**—"concurrent" sentences may be imposed (1) when multiple cc sentences for several different offenses arising from single criminal episode are ordered on and will begin on same date; (2) when multiple cc sentences for several different offenses arising from several different criminal episodes are viewed by later sentencing judge as warranting an order for later-imposed sentences to begin on same date as the first, nunc pro tunc; and (3) when multiple cc sentences are ordered on different dates for different offenses arising from different criminal episodes, but later-imposing judge does not order that they are to begin as of date on which earlier-imposed sentences

commenced, "resulting in the possibility that one or more of the later-imposed sentences will extend beyond the completion date of the sentences imposed earlier"; D here was not entitled to convert instance (3) to instance (2), to get sentencing credit toward sentence two for time between imposition of first sentence and later imposition of second (albeit "concurrent") sentence;

14-P. FROM AND AFTER (F&A) OR CONSECUTIVE SENTENCES

See Parole, Chapter 14-V below;

G.L. c. 279, § 8A—from & after takes effect upon parole or release;

G.L. c. 279, § 8B—if D is on release (bail/personal recognizance) and commits a crime, the sentence imposed for that crime shall run consecutively to the earlier sentence for crime for which he was on release;

C v Hickey **429 M 1027 (99)**—but if D is sentenced FIRST for the later crime, G.L. c. 279, § 8B is no bar to a "forthwith" sentence on the first-occurring crime;

C v Yancey **46 MAC 924 (99)**—no error in denying motion to withdraw G plea on basis that sentence was ordered to run from & after sentence for crime for which D was on bail at time of new crime; rejecting argument that from & after provision applied only to new crimes committed when D was on "personal recognizance";

Kite v Commonwealth **11 Met. 581 (1846)**—from & after takes effect after prior's tipped on appeal;

Wolcott, petitioner **32 MAC 473 (92)**—in construing what effect to give consecutive sentences where "anchor" sentences are vacated, entire sentencing structure more important than judge's literal language in determining intent;

Brown v Comm'r **336 M 718 (58)**—reject "overly legalistic approach"; reversal of 1st case makes "from & after" start on date given;

Henschel **368 M 130 (75)**—aggregate from & after time to get single parole eligibility date; sentence is concurrent unless stated to be from & after;

Crooker v Sup't. **19 MAC 315 (85)**—independently calculate parole eligibility time for each from & after Concord sentence, then add them; don't aggregate the sentences & then figure parole eligibility;

Baranow v Comm'r of Correction **1 MAC 831 (73)**—(same);

Carlino v Comm'r **355 M 159 (69)**—effective date = termination of #1;

Delisle v C **416 M 359 (93)**—sentences = 2½ years house of correction, 18 months to serve, balance suspended with probation for 4 years **and** 5–7 years MCI Cedar Junction, suspended with probation for 2 years, to be served from & after 1st sentence; 2d sentence, i.e. probationary term, did not begin until after probation period in 1st sentence expired; G.L. c. 279 § 8 not violated because it applies only to **committed** sentences (not over solely of "probation");

Lussier v Comm'r **3 MAC 790 (75)**—sentence #1 not wiped out when paroled to #2;

District Court Standards of Judicial Practice, Sentencing & Other Dispositions (1984) 7:04—general discussion;

C v Tart **408 M 249 (90)**—remanded to clarify whether judge intended life sentence for unarmed robbery to run from & after murder 1 sentence;

14-Q. JAIL CREDIT

CPCS P/G 7.5(d)—insure that sentence = accurate re: credit & parole rights;

G.L. c. 279, § 33A—prisoner to be given credit on sentence for days in confinement awaiting & during "such" trial & sentence; (this is matter of right, not discretion (*Manning v Superintendent* **372 M 387, 392 (77)**);

G.L. c. 127, § 129B—(same);

G.L. c. 127, § 129D—deductions from sentence for participation in work, education, and treatment programs while incarcerated, up to 7.5 days per month, BUT can't reduce time served on a mandatory sentence below the mandatory minimum if statute specifically precludes award of 'good conduct credits' (*Lydon v Sheriff of Ply-*

mouth County **393 M 1002 (84)**); credits may be reduced by court upon finding that prisoner abused judicial process;

C v Morasse **446 M 113 (2006)**—though condition of pretrial probation was that D be confined to his home and be monitored there by electronic bracelet, this was not "confinement" for which he received credit on eventual sentence;

McNeil v Comm'r of Correction **417 M 818 (94)**—during pretrial custody, can't "earn" good time (good conduct credits pursuant to G.L. c. 127 § 129D); equal protection argument rejected;

Manning v Superintendent, MCI-Norfolk **372 M 387 (77)**—policy against "dead time"; credit on #2 (from & after) for time on #1 (which is reversed);

Brown v Comm'r of Correction **336 M 718 (58)**—(same); issue is fairness;

Watts v Comm'r of Correction **42 MAC 951 (97)**—D on parole from 5- to 7-year sentence arrested on new charges, held on bail & detainer was lodged; 252 days later, new charges were resolved with a suspended 3–5 year sentence; D not entitled to 252 days credit on the 5–7 year sentence; not "dead time" because could have been a factor in award of only a suspended sentence and would be credited on that if D came to be imprisoned because of a probation violation;

Swain v Superintendent **29 MAC 918 (90)**—sentencing judge properly vacated SDP commitment after initial determination to sentence rather than commit & properly credited D with time served under illegal commitment;

McCormack v C **345 M 514 (63)**—credit on #1 though personal recognizance & though bail was on #2 (got N.G.);

McCormack v C **345 M 514 (63)**, ***C v Grant*** **366 M 272 (74)**—confinement must be related to the proceeding in which credit is to be granted;

C v Aquafresca **11 MAC 975 (81)**—maybe credit for time elsewhere on MA fugitive warrant;

C v Beauchamp **413 M 60 (92)**—D not entitled to credit for out-of-state confinement while challenging rendition, where rendition argument deemed frivolous;

C v Goss **41 MAC 929 (96)**—(same);

C v Frias **53 MAC 488 (2002)**—jail credits begin to accrue for out-of-state prisoner on date D signs extradition waiver (excluding time D was held in other state after arrest on a fugitive warrant during which he "fail(s) to submit to the jurisdiction of Massachusetts");

C v Foley **17 MAC 238 (83)**—credit for unrelated case #1 because D got NG on #2 (because confinement served Commonwealth's interest arising out of proceeding in which credit is sought);

Libby v Comm'r of Correction **353 M 472, 473 (68)**—it's not enough that case was pending during confinement;

C v Boland **43 MAC 451 (97)**—credit for jail in Florida prior to dismissal of Florida charges because fugitive from justice in MA charge was also lodged against D (credit applied on later arson sentence, arson being the MA crime as to which D was fugitive);

Chalifoux v Comm'r of Correction **375 M 424 (78)**—credit for California "concurrent" sentence, though fiction, because MA wouldn't rendite;

NOTE—for concurrent sentences with equal parole ineligibility periods, you need credit on all the sentences to receive any benefit, so credit same pretrial confinement to as many cc sentences as possible; (and sentence is presumed to run concurrent with all other sentences imposed at the same time or previously except those as to which court has specified "consecutive": see ***Henschel v Comm'r of Correction*** **368 M 130, 133 (75)**; ***Baranow v Commissioner*** **1 MAC 831, 832 (73)**; ***West's Case*** **111 M 443, 444**

(1873)) (state & "county" sentences can be served concurrently: ***Henschel*** **368 M 130**)

C v Carter **10 MAC 618 (80)**—credit, but only to one of from & after sentences (i.e., can't credit same pretrial confinement to more than one consecutive sentence); ***C v Harvey*** **66 MAC 297 (2006)**—same;

C v Murphy **63 MAC 753 (2005)**—but can & must give credit for pretrial confinement on both sets of charges on which D failed to make bail set: when D receives lesser sentences concurrent with a greater sentence, "it is incumbent on the sentencing judge to ensure that D receives credit for that time against the higher sentence"; records of the two courts, not those of the sheriff holding D, establish the authority by which D was being held (i.e., here, it was in lieu of posting bail on EACH of the sets of charges); D not entitled to 13 days' credit on Middlesex sentences during period he was being held "solely" on unrelated Suffolk charges and remained free on bail he'd already posted for Middlesex (before the Middlesex bail amount was increased & he did not post it);

Lewis v Commonwealth **329 M 445 (52)**—9 months' credit for robbery reduced on appeal to larceny;

C v Azar **444 M 72 (2005)**—after D's second degree murder conviction was vacated on appeal & he pled G to manslaughter (19–20 year sentence, 4570 days to serve, deemed served, with balance to be suspended during 10 years probation), he was NOT entitled to "statutory good time" credits on the time already served: he had not previously been serving a sentence for a crime to which "good time" credits could inure;

Milton v. Commissioner of Correction **67 MAC 253 (2006)**—even though conviction underlying incarceration was subsequently vacated, D was not entitled to statutory good time against sentences for offense committed during that incarceration; policy behind former G.L. c. 127, § 129 (repealed as to offenses committed on or after 7/1/94) = "encouragement of orderly conduct by prison inmates"; (rejecting rationale that because sentence was result of flawed trial, confinement was unlawful);

Petition of Needel **344 M 260 (62)**—no credit for time serving unrelated sentence; no credit to remedy speedy trial violation (see also ***Strunk v US*** **412 US 434 (73)**), though even sentenced prisoner retains right to speedy trial on outstanding charges (***Smith v Hooey*** **393 US 374 (69)**; M.R.Crim.P. 36(d); G.L. c. 276, App. §§ 1–8);

Harkey v Supt. **356 M 722 (69)**—no credit for #2 for time while returned to #1 sentence on parole violation;

C v Milton **427 M 18 (98)**—"violation of terms of probation" notice (with one year suspended sentence underlying) served on D as he was held for 14 months awaiting robbery trial & **at D's request** VTP hearing continued until robbery dispo; NG on robbery caused withdrawal of surrender notice; later, for disorderly person arrest 2 months before probation period expired D was surrendered: SJC held that D couldn't receive credit for the time awaiting trial on unrelated robbery charge (couldn't "bank" time) and minor nature of new crime didn't bar surrender & sentence imposition; (NOTE: under probation surrender rules, effective 1/2000, can't hold off VTP by "tracking" it with new criminal charge);

Milton v Commissioner of Correction **67 MAC 253 (2006)**—policy of "no dead time" weighed against policy against "banking" time for future offense; D was still serving one sentence when he was convicted of other offenses, & couldn't have anticipated at the time he committed second set of offenses that his conviction subsequently would be reversed, so give credit "from the commencement of his sentence on the erroneous [reversed on appeal] conviction";

C v Maldonado **64 MAC 250 (2005)**—D was entitled to receive credit (19 days) for time in custody when his sentence after conviction had been stayed but his bail had been revoked;

Stearns, petitioner **343 M 53 (61)**—credit for state hospital awaiting-trial time; any "confinement" may be credited, BUT ***C v Beauchemin*** **410 M 181 (91)** D, confined on house arrest as condition of stay of execution of sentence pending appeal, not entitled to jail credit;

C v Speight **59 MAC 28 (2003)**—residential treatment for drug/alcohol, a condition of probation, was not incarceration for which D could obtain sentence credit against suspended prison sentence imposed when D subsequently violated terms of probation;

DuPont v Commissioner of Correction **59 MAC 908 (2003)**—prerelease program in halfway house = correc-tional institution for purpose of withholding good time credits for crime committed while there (G.L. c. 127, § 29);

C v Grant **366 M 272 (74)**—credit for federal time for related charge; bail not a prerequisite (see also ***Stearns*** **343 M 53, 56 (61)** & ***Walters*** **12 MAC 389, 397 (81)**);

C v Barriere **46 MAC 286 (99) AFTER AMEND-MENT**—though originally holding that sentencing credits can no longer be re-calculated/revised by a motion to correct mittimus (and that instead correction should be sought via request to jailer, by "an action against the custodian," or by R.30 (a)), outcry caused revision: "as long as the person sentenced remains in custody . . . as to a statement of the credits to which the prisoner is entitled, the mittimus may be corrected to reflect adjustments required by law";

C v Melo **65 MAC 674 (2006)**—holds it was "error" for judge to allow D's motion to correct mittimus to give D two additional ***days'*** credit, both on procedural ground (D should have sought declaratory judgment to challenge DOC's calculation of sentence) and substantive ground (D couldn't have credit for the extra day in each of two leap years, because sentence was "to a term of years, not to a term of days");

Henderson v Commissioners of Barnstable County **49 MAC 455 (2000)**—though revocation of "statutory good time" credits improper here under governing regulations, not a federal constitutional due process violation;

14-R. FORTHWITH

G.L. c. 279, § 27—if house of correction or jail prisoner gets "forthwith" sentence to state prison, it wipes out house of correction sentence he's currently serving; (say "forthwith, notwithstanding any sentence now being served or to be served," to guard against nonextinguishment of a consecutive house of correction sentence which D has not yet started to serve);

Abrahams v Commonwealth **57 MAC 861 (2003)**—in absence of statutory prohibition, Superior Court judge could order state prison sentence (3½–4 years) to commence "forthwith," and be served concurrently with a federal sentence, even though D was in federal custody, in his 14th month of a 24-month federal sentence;

Dale v Comm'r of Correction **17 MAC 247 (83)**—under G.L. c. 279, § 28 (repealed effective July 1, 1994), prior MCI-Concord survives "house of correction forth-with"; house of correction paroles D & returns D to MCI-Concord; (NOTE: D got credit to MCI Concord for house time); 'forthwith' sentence doesn't wipe out parole/probation warrants; person must be serving sentence at time sentence of 'forthwith' is imposed;

G.L. c. 279, § 8B—if D is on release (bail/personal recognizance) and commits a crime, the sentence imposed for that crime shall run consecutively to the earlier sentence for crime for which he was on release;

C v Hickey **429 M 1027 (99)**—if D happens to be sentenced FIRST for the later crime, however, § 8B is no bar to a 'forthwith' sentence on the first-occurring crime (e.g., here, D on bail & committed assault, and was sentenced first for that assault, sentence thereafter for PRIOR crime was ordered to run "forthwith"; Commonwealth argument that this violated G.L. c. 279, § 8B rejected);

14-S. STAY OF SENTENCE

G.L. c. 279, § 4—sentence to be imposed though appeal;

M.R.App.P. 6(a)—stay motion must, almost always, be made first before trial judge;

M.R.Crim.P. 31—trial judge or appellate single justice discretion to stay prison sentence pending appeal; fine = automatic stay;

CPCS P/G 8.1(c)—if appeal, request a stay;

C v Hodge **(#1) 380 M 851 (80)**—single justices (Appeals Court & SJC) each have discretion, but varying for two issues—(1) security & (2) issue worthy of presenting to Appeals Court; if stay is granted, only question on stay appeal = whether abused discretion;

C v Allen **378 M 489 (79)**—discretion for each judge & full bench(es) on questions of law; no appeal without first presenting to trial judge; clarifies standards; sentence would be served before appeal = factor here;

C v Aviles **422 M 1008 (96)**—given history in this case, SJC acknowledges that it "may be preferable" for SJC single justice to decline to act on stay matter, "leaving . . . the issue in the court where the underlying appeal will be heard"; see **S.C., 40 MAC 440, 441 n.1 (96)** (SJC single justice had, on Commonwealth petition under G.L. c. 211, § 3, greatly increased bail on stay granted by lower court, leaving D imprisoned for years despite greatly-delayed reversal of conviction in Appeals Court);

C v Levin **7 MAC 501 (79)**—likelihood of success; time served isn't reversible; wealthy should get "rights routinely accorded others" (!);

District Court Standards of Judicial Practice, Sentencing & Other Dispositions (1984) 7:11—inherent power to defer or stay; e.g., last chance to comply after violating terms of probation, or tend to personal affairs;

C v Beauchemin **410 M 181 (91)**—D confined on house arrest as condition of stay of execution of sentence pending appeal, not entitled to jail credit;

Stewart v Commonwealth **413 M 664 (92)**—bail pending appeal of R.30 motion is discretionary if appellate result may be a "reversal of the conviction, an order for a new trial or a term of imprisonment less than the time (D) already has served, including the time the appellate process requires"; here SJC said stay issue was ineffective assistance at sentencing for 2d degree murder & armed assault in a dwelling, & since **mandatory** sentence on second degree murder was life, D not eligible for stay;

Hagen v Commonwealth **437 M 374 (2002)**—rape complainant had no standing to move to revoke convicted D's stay of execution of sentence, BUT construes G.L. c. 258B to allow crime victims "to address the court directly when their fundamental right to a prompt disposition is jeopardized" (victim can't be "prohibited from bringing to a judge's attention that there has been a delay in the proceedings");

14-T. MOTION TO REVISE OR REVOKE SENTENCE

See also Chapter 15, Post-Conviction Remedies;

CPCS P/G 8.1—tell D of right to motion to revoke & revise, & file timely if asked;

Jordan v Superior Court **426 M 1019 (98)**—noting that it has never been held that indigent Ds are "automatically entitled to the assistance of counsel or motions to revise or revoke";

M.R.Crim.P. 29 & Reporter's Notes—judge's own motion or D's written motion/affidavit within 60 days of sentence (or losing appeal); judge may rule after 60 days; but see M.R.Crim.P. 42—"clerical mistakes" correctable any time (see Layne 25 MAC 1 (87) - must be actual clerical mistakes, not opportunity for judge to revise on basis of what he purportedly had "intended");

K. Smith, *Criminal Practice & Procedure,* **§§ 2025-36 (2d ed. 1983 & Supp.)**—(general); § 2030—suggests affidavit is required;

C v Layne **386 M 291 (82)**—60 days after dilatory (9 years) appeal = untimely; judge may consider only facts at time of sentencing, **not** post-sentencing events;

C v DeJesus **440 M 147 (2003)**—(on Commonwealth's petition pursuant to G.L. c. 211, § 3) trial judge was **without jurisdiction to revoke and revise sentence, because motion (though filed within a month of sentencing) was filed without any affidavit**; affidavit was not provided until 17 months later; D and judge were motivated to reduce one-year sentence (already served) because of adverse immigration consequences attending a sentence of that length (& SJC reiterates that immigration/deportation consequences are "collateral," and "cannot be basis for judge's decision as to the disposition of . . . any . . . case");

C v Gaumond **53 MAC 912 (2002)**—Rule 29 motion not available for withdrawing guilty plea (pro se D's motion claimed coercion into pleading guilty, & numerous allegations that rights denied prior to plea);

C v Thomas **400 M 676 (87)**—may get motion to revoke & revise opportunity after both sentencing & appellate rescript issuance;

C v Callahan **419 M 306 (95)**—**cannot** file revoke & revise within 60 days of Appellate Division's increase of sentence, and sentencing judge cannot act on previously filed motions after D claims appeal to Appellate Division (sentencing judge = "divested of jurisdiction to act on motions to rehear or to vacate");

DA v Superior Court **342 M 119 (61)**—can revoke & revise after D began serving;

Aldoupolis v C **386 M 260 (82)**—within 60 days, judge can revoke & revise & increase sentence on own motion, but notice & hearing required; (cf. **Dunbrack 398 M 502 (86)**—sentencing judge can revise illegal (because probation record erroneously omitted prior operating under influence conviction, which made 1st-offense education program inappropriate) probationary term, though here accomplished after 60-day window for revoke & revise action on admission to sufficient facts; avenue for stating arguments against this = Rule 30;

C v Layne **25 MAC 1 (87)**—but judge can't change sentence (even to reflect judge's purported intent) after revoke & revise deadline; not a M.R.Crim.P. 42 clerical "mistake" (see Chapter 15, post);

C v Stubbs **15 MAC 955 (83)**—if, after hearing, it's found that counsel promised to file revoke & revise motion but did not (& this is ineffective assistance of counsel), judge should vacate sentence & re-impose it, giving D another 60-day window for timely filing R.29 motion;

C v McNulty **42 MAC 955 (97)**—revoke & revise filed 1 year after sentence = untimely; D's **pro se** motion asserting that he "retained counsel to file" R. 29 motion but heard nothing for 11 months was inadequate **Stubbs (15 MAC 955)** foundation: there was no affidavit from D or successor counsel & no assertion that purportedly "retained" counsel promised to but did not file motion;

C v Fenton F. **442 M 31 (2004)**—no ineffective assistance of counsel shown, so no basis for waiving 60-day window for filing R. 29 motion; not "ineffective" to advise after negotiated G plea & agreed-upon sentence that "as a practical matter" D was "stuck" with bargain, since one can't file motion to revoke & revise without stating grounds on which it's based;

C v Layne **21 MAC 17 (85)**—can't avoid time limit of R. 29 by calling motion "Rule 30 (a)" because mistake re: parole not "unlawful" sentence;

C v Steele **42 MAC 319 (97)**—trial judge having retired, new judge's allowance of revoke & revise was reversed: because he relied on the "same" record used by trial judge, his action was an unwarranted/illegitimate "substitution" of his judgment; if instead new judge considered facts not known to trial judge (but existing at time of sentence), revision possible;

C v Sitko **372 M 305 (77)**—can't consider post-sentence conduct;

District Court Standards of Judicial Practice, Sentencing & Other Dispositions (1984) 8:00—filing time limit absolute, but can rule any time; suggests there's no authority for "vacating Guilty finding"; But see *C v Barclay* **424 M 377 (97)** timely-filed revoke & revise motion could not be considered six years after its filing; motion must be considered within a "reasonable" time after it's filed; But contrast *C v Conaghan* **433 M 105, 111–12 (2000)** (Spina, J., concurring) suggesting use of a revoke & revise motion filed shortly after sentencing, to reopen disposition (though R. 30 motion was filed 5 years after guilty plea and appeal of its denial took additional time); asserting that judge in acting on revoke & revise motion would have discretion to order psychiatric examination to aid in sentencing, pursuant to G.L. c. 123, § 15(e);

C v McCulloch **450 M 483 (2008)**—D pled G to negligent operation of motor vehicle, judge entered G finding and sentenced to one year probation and restitution hearing was scheduled; on that date, D filed R. 29 motion with affidavit saying she had cooperated with probation, remained out of trouble, learned from her experience; SJC holds ERROR in judge's subsequent order "vacating" G finding conditioned on immediate $6,000 restitution payment; consideration under R.29 = limited to facts existing at time of sentencing, AND R. 29 is to revise *sentence*, **not** *finding of guilt*; guilty finding and sentence of probation reinstated;

C v Nessolini **19 MAC 1016 (85)**—can't use R. 29 as motion to withdraw guilty plea; but see . . .

M.R.Crim.P. 25(b)(2)—renew motion for required finding of not guilty within 5 days of G. & can get new trial or not guilty;

M.R.Crim.P. 30(a)—post-conviction relief at any time correcting sentence for unlawful restraint; (*see Chapter 15, Post-Conviction Remedies*);

M.R.Crim.P. 30(b)—(same) for new trial because justice may not be done;

Clark, petitioner **34 MAC 191 (93)**—written agreement between counsel & prosecutor that revise & revoke would be jointly recommended if D not paroled after 3 years so long as he received no "D-reports" was void; 60-day time limit for filing revise & revoke motion under M.R.Crim.P. 29(a) cannot be waived, even by agreement of prosecutor; sentence vacated in interest of justice & case remanded to give D opportunity to decide whether to withdraw guilty plea;

C v Carver **33 MAC 378 (92)**—judge had discretion on own motion to revoke & revise illegal sentence & to impose more severe sentences;

C v Amirault **415 M 112 (93)**—judge may not revoke & revise sentence on ground that Parole Board has denied release of D: violation of (article 30) constitutional separation of powers;

C v Ferrara **31 MAC 648 (91)**—judge's reliance on incorrect statement by prosecutor about D's parole eligibility or discharge date required remand for resentencing;

C v McGuinness **421 M 472 (95)**   after G plea and sentence of Concord-20, judge told D he would act favorably in 2 years upon a timely-filed R&R motion, suspending the balance of the sentence during a probationary term, unless D had any trouble while serving his sentence; though this **was** done, Commonwealth's motion to reconsider (due to D's assaultive behavior in prison) was allowed and the revision was vacated; D's appeal failed: the judge's promise, given its timing **after** plea, did not alter the plea's voluntariness;

McGuinness v Commonwealth **420 M 495 (95)**—denial of motion to revoke & revise may be reviewed by R.30 & appeal from R.30 denial (so G.L. c. 211, § 3 = improper); but see

C v Richards **44 MAC 478 (98)**—while decision on motion to revoke & revise is immediately appealable, review is limited to errors of **law**, **e.g.**, if motion untimely filed per M.R.Crim.P. 29, or if improper factors were considered for sentence;

C v Bland **48 MAC 666 (2000)**—though Court asserted that D's claims would have been raised "more appropriately" by R.30, it considered, on appeal of denial of revoke and revise motion, judge's statements allegedly showing improper factor in sentencing;

14-U. SEALING AND EXPUNGING RECORDS

Rzeznik v Chief **374 M 475 (78)**—seal removes records from public use; (but can use to deny gun license);

G.L. c. 276, § 100A—by right (if asked) 10 years after misdemeanor sentence (or probation), 15 years after felony, if no (non-motor vehicle) G. findings within 10 years; can get public job; can say "no record," & record's inadmissible evidence; police & court told "sealed," but can reopen for later sentencing; others told "no record"; § 100B, juvenile records sealed (if asked) after 3 years if nothing further; § 100C, if NG, no probable cause, or "no bill", automatic seal by Commissioner of Probation unless D asks not to; Court discretion re: nolle prosequi/dismissal, except after "probation"; § 100, probation records not public;

G.L. c. 94C, § 34: poss. of marijuana or Class E substance—automatic probation & then seal for 1st offense, unless D objects or Court files reasons; § 35 (same) for knowing presence of heroin; § 44 shall seal § 34 charge if NG, dismiss, or nol pros, and D can't be guilty of false statement for failing to acknowledge such arrest, indictment, disposition, or sealing;

G.L. c. 6, § 172—CORI law denying public access to criminal records (CPCS = approved access agency);

Bellin v Kelly **435 M 261 (2001)**—(overruling **48 MAC 573 (2000)**) upholding administrative regulation allowing dissemination of criminal record to any member of public if dissemination is connected to ongoing investigation (plaintiff had argued that regulation was contrary to statute);

Globe Newspaper Co. v Pokaski **868 F.2d 497 (89)**—100C's (G.L. c. 276, § 100C-arrest records) all opened unless motion, hearing, & "compelling" need; rarely appropriate; 60 days to comply;

CPCS P/G 8.2—counsel responsible for case until/unless new attorney

Police Comm'r of Boston v Dorchester Court **374 M 640 (78)**—expungement of police records can be ordered, especially for juveniles, so no trace remains;

C v Gavin G., a juvenile **437 M 470 (2002)**—Juvenile Court judge lacked authority to order expungement of probation records (two judges dissented) (involving case dismissed without prejudice over D's objection when prosecution witnesses failed to appear, & defense witnesses were ready to testify that D had been attacked by real perpetrators & was arrested by mistake); rationale = juvenile records are extremely protected in any event by statutes;

C v Keon K **70 MAC 568 (2007)**—even if juvenile's appeal had been successful (issues of alleged improprieties in sentencing to DYS commitment), remedy would have been only resentencing, "not reversal and expungement";

C v Balboni **419 M 42 (94)**—2 years after order of expungement was too late for Dept. of Probation to move to reconsider and vacate; had to have been done within the time allowed for notice of appeal (30 days, with opportunity to enlarge for good cause shown);

District Court Standards of Judicial Practice, Sentencing & Other Dispositions (1984) 9:06—expunge = inherent court power; (suggest can't seal after "pre-trial probation")

C v Vickey **381 M 762 (80)**—no right to seal pardon; but see now . . .

G.L. c. 127, § 152—Pardon = "shall" seal; see also Chapter 15 herein;

C v Doe **420 M 142 (95)**—pursuant to *Pokaski* **868 F.2d 497 (1st Cir. '89)**, 2-stage procedure for hearing petitions to seal under G.L. c. 276, § 100C, 2d paragraph: 1st, informal, at which D must show "prima facie" case in favor of sealing; if D does, 2d hearing, with at least 7 days notice by conspicuous courthouse posting, specific notice to prosecutor (who must advise alleged victim of opportunity to participate) and to Dep't of Probation, and to any other party deemed to have an interest in the case; court must consider all info re: whether "substantial justice" would be served by sealing; a "reasoned" objection by anyone "would pose a very serious obstacle to the petition"; case for confidentiality stronger if dropping of charge = premised on mistake in bringing it (e.g., mis-ID, or if "police acquire credible info exonerating" D); D must show risk of specific harm from existence of unsealed record;

Hawkins v Comm'r of Correction **406 M 898 (90)**—disclosure of prisoner's classification & disciplinary reports for purposes of federal litigation did not violate CORI (G.L. c. 6, §§ 167–78) or FIPA (Fair Information Practices Act, G.L. c. 66A) because not "personal data";

Care & Protection of Frank **409 M 492 (91)**—arrests for marijuana possession which didn't lead to convictions were admissible at care & protection proceeding, notwithstanding G.L. c. 233, § 21;

C v Roberts **39 MAC 355 (95)**—sealing is reserved for "exceptional case" & requires "more than a general interest in reputation and privacy"; sealing more likely when case = "founded on a mistake" than when abandoned merely because of prosecutorial discretion; sealing means only unavailable to **public** & D can respond 'no criminal record' when asked (cf., e.g., G.L. c. 94C, § 44);

C v Boe __ M __ **(3/25/10), overruling 73 MAC 647 (2009)**—although criminal complaint's issuance was premised on a mistake, judge could not order "expungement," but could order sealing under G.L. c. 276, § 100C; sealed record is accessible to fewer people and cannot disqualify individual from "public" employment by Commonwealth or its political subdivisions; Comm'r of Probation must respond to inquiries by anyone OTHER THAN a court or law enforcement agency by saying "no record exists" when record is "sealed"; Appeals Court, more sympathetic to Boe, had upheld "expungement," where complaint never should have been issued (crime was by male, not the female D, and D had been "misdirected" to wrong court session when she appeared for clerk-magistrate's hearing on issuance of complaint so had no opportunity to prevent issuance);

Dempsey v Clerk of Superior Court **454 M 1017 (2009)**—petition in Superior Court to seal certain Superior Court, BMC and District Court criminal records was denied; single justice on 211/3 also denied, because G.L.

c. 276 § 100C doesn't authorize court to seal criminal records where D has been convicted or where charge has been placed on file; though petitioner "may be entitled" to sealing of certain records under G.L. c. 276, § 100A, request must be made to Commissioner of Probation, not court; furthermore, 211/3 inappropriate as could appeal from Superior Court judge's denial of petition to seal records;

14-V. PAROLE AND GOOD TIME

See Executed Sentence, From & After, & Concurrent, all above;

See also specific offenses re: special rules & Chapter 13 re: advice to D in plea bargaining, change of plea;

CPCS P/G 7.5(d)—insure that sentence = accurate re: parole (*see motion to revoke/revise, Chapter 14-T*);

G.L. c. 127, § 128—Parole Bd. authority only if aggregate sentence is 60 days or more;

120 CMR 200. et seq.—parole eligibility now governed by state regulations;

120 CMR 200.05—persons serving **state prison sentences** are eligible for parole after serving the minimum term of sentence minus credits for earned good time. Person serving a total aggregate sentence of 60 days or more to a house of correction is eligible for parole after serving one-half of the total sentence of imprisonment, or after two years, whichever is less, but if "compelling reasons," parole hearing panel may release an individual serving a **house of correction** sentence up to thirty days earlier than the parole eligibility date, and if full Board agrees, individual may be released up to 60 days earlier than that individual's parole eligibility.

120 CMR 200.12—parole eligibility for violation of statute "which expressly provides for a mandatory minimum term of incarceration & which precludes parole release during the mandatory term" = after service of mandatory minimum term of incarceration;

G.L. c. 127, §§ 128-151K—Parole Eligibility statutes, though many §§ repealed by "Truth in Sentencing Act," St. 1993, c. 432, which abolished reformatory ("Concord") sentence and parole eligibility rules previously existing. As to sentences pre-dating change in law (i.e., crimes committed before July 1, 1994), see 120 CMR 200.04 for parole eligibility rules;

G.L. c. 127, 133B—half-time for habitual (G.L. c. 279, § 25; see also 120 CMR 200.17 (eligibility at half of maximum term, & if denied, review every 2 years thereafter);

G.L. c. 127, § 133A—eligibility after 15 years on life sentence, unless conviction is for first degree murder;

G.L. c. 127, §§ 130–46—release/conditions/notice to police etc.

120 CMR 200.04—for offenses committed before 7/1/94, house of correction sentences: parole eligibility after ½ of total sentence of imprisonment, or after two yrs,

whichever is less; "compelling reasons" may obtain slightly earlier release (but see 120 CMR 200.14 & .15 for restrictions); for offenses committed before 7/1/94, parole eligibility for state prison sentences is either 1/3 or 2/3 of the minimum term of sentence, per G.L. c. 127, § 133, as appearing in the General Laws prior to July 1, 1994.

120 CMR 200.16—early parole for pregnant females;

120 CMR 200.05—state prison sentences: parole eligibility after minimum term of sentence minus earned good time credits;

120 CMR 200.06—re: eligibility on split sentences, including when returned to custody after violating terms of probation;

120 CMR 200.07—re: eligibility on concurrent "mixed" sentences;

120 CMR 200.09—if parolee receives sentence of imprisonment while on parole (for a crime committed while on parole), "the parole violation warrant shall not be served until the expiration of the intervening sentence. M.G.L. c. 127, § 149", but if the parole violation warrant is served prior to imposition of the new sentence, the sentence for the new crime may be ordered to be served concurrently with the underlying sentence;

120 CMR 200.10—re: eligibility on consecutive sentences (aggregate parole ineligibility periods of each component sentence);

120 CMR 200.11—re: eligibility on "forthwith sentences";

G.L. c. 127, § 129C—forestry camp: reduce parole eligibility date 2½ days/month, if accepted;

G.L. c. 127, § 129D: educational & work programs—IF placed!; "Good conduct credit earned or to be earned under this section or section 129C" can be reduced by court order if prisoner has filed frivolous lawsuits;

McNeil v Comm'r of Correction **417 M 818 (94)**—can't compile "earned" good time (G.L. c. 127, § 129D) during pretrial custody;

G.L. c. 127, § 83B—forfeit all good time if escape or attempts to escape from forestry camp;

Diafario v Comm'r of Correction **371 M 545 (76)**—aggregate from & after sentences to compute good time;

Barriere v Hubbard **47 MAC 79 (99)**—a drug trafficking sentence of 12–15 years (with a 5-year minimum mandatory) with a 'from & after' sentence of 9–15 was properly aggregated for parole eligibility calculation by recognizing the minimum mandatory five yr sentence, i.e., 5 + 1/3 of 9 (3) = 8 years (rather than D's calculation of 12+9 (21) divided by 3 = 7); this was pre-"Truth in Sentencing";

C v Brown **431 M 772 (2000)**—statutorily-mandated sentence range for home invasion (G.L. c. 265, § 18C), "life or any term not less than twenty years", requires D to be sentenced, at minimum, to 20 years (e.g., 20–25 years); rejects D's argument that statute instead directs that upper number has to be at least 20 years (e.g., 3–20 years);

Sumpter, petitioner **46 MAC 251 (99)**—while D was serving rape sentence, which ran from and after ABDW sentence, he escaped from work release program; though no "good conduct" deductions applied to rape sentence, Dept. of Correction aggregated ABDW and rape sentences in order to effectuate the "statutory good conduct credits" forfeiture provision (G.L. c. 127, § 49); Appeals Court approved;

PAROLE "ELIGIBILITY" DOES NOT MEAN PAROLE WILL BE GRANTED—you may contact the Parole Board for most recent statistics as to percentage released at first eligibility;

G.L. c. 127, § 133E—victims (& parents or guardians of minor victims) of violent crime or sex offense may testify in person at parole board hearing, or may submit written testimony

See Chapter 13, Plea Bargaining: Counsel's Role re: advice to clients;

LIFETIME COMMUNITY PAROLE: G.L. c. 127, § 133C; G.L. c. 275, § 18; G.L. c. 265, § 45—lifetime parole shouldn't be imposed for offense committed before passage of the Act (i.e., 9/10/99)—*cf. C v Fuller* **421 M 400, 407–8 (95)** (presumption against retroactivity where statute does not specify that its provisions apply retroactively); lifetime parole must be imposed re: rape, rape of child under 16 with force, rape & abuse of child, assault with intent to rape, kidnapping child under 16, drugging for sex, unnatural & lascivious acts, and any attempt to commit any of the above; BUT if 1st offense of any of these, D may move for hearing to determine whether lifetime parole shall be imposed; lifetime parole may be imposed re: indecent A&B (either under age 14 or 14 & over), indecent A&B of mentally retarded person, and as to any 1st offense of these, prosecutor may request hearing to determine whether lifetime parole should be imposed; D may petition parole board to terminate lifetime parole after 15 years; *C v Pagan* **445 M 161 (2005)**—some parts of LCP statute held unconstitutionally vague;

C v Renderos **440 M 422 (2003)**—lifetime community parole not just "public protection," but also intended as "enhanced penalty for sex offenders"; G.L. c. 265, § 45, read with G.L. c. 275, § 18, makes clear that upon first-time conviction of certain less serious offenses (here, indecent assault and battery on person aged fourteen or over), there can be no sentence of "lifetime community parole" unless the district attorney makes a motion for such sentence (after which there is a hearing, and appropriate findings, and only then "may" a judge impose, if the decision is supported by "clear and convincing evidence"; judge had no statutory authority to impose sentence sua sponte, without DA motion, and without hearing;

Doe v Chairperson of MA Parole Board **454 M 1018 (2009)**—statute (G.L. c. 127, § 133D½) requiring GPS device for persons under court-ordered parole supervision or under lifetime community parole is unconstitutional ex post facto law as to persons who were already on parole and not subject to GPS monitoring when statute was enacted & became effective;

G.L. c. 127, §§ 148–9—revoke parole & arrest D; credit for time out until revoked (but see details);

Morrissey v Brewer **408 US 471 (72)**—due process for parole revocation; preliminary hearing re: probable cause if D is held in custody; notice, hearing, statement of reasons;

In re Zullo **420 M 872 (95)**—parole revocation warrant served 12 years after its issuance not untimely as matter of law: fact questions whether delay = "unreasonable" in circumstances and whether D was "unfairly" prejudiced by parole board's conduct; if D shows either, by preponderance, denial of revocation OK;

Quegan v Mass. Parole Board **423 M 836 (96)**—CPCS's (limited) statutory authorization to provide counsel for D seeking redress for parole denial;

Pina v Superintendent **376 M 659 (78)**—implements G.L. c. 127 § 149 (arrest for parole violation);

Stefanik v Parole Board **372 M 726 (77)**—no preliminary hearing if probable cause found & bound over to grand jury;

Greenholtz v Inmates **442 US 1 (79)**—no federal constitutional right to parole unless state law creates protected expectation;

C v Hogan **17 MAC 186 (83)**—law of Commonwealth does not create protected expectation of parole;

Lanier v Mass. Parole Board **396 M 1018 (86)**—claim that state constitution affords more protection as to parole rejected as "novel";

Quegan v Mass. Parole Board **423 M 834 (96) citing** *Greenholtz* **(442 US 1 (79))**—holding that parole board policy of denying parole upon refusal to admit guilt does not violate federal due process protections & no different result under Declaration of Rights, Article 12; while saying acknowledgment of G shows rehabilitation, also says lack of acknowledgment of guilt "provides no weight"; reserves question whether due process forbids parole denial **solely** because D did not acknowledge guilt;

Greenman v Mass. Parole Board **405 M 384 (89)**—Board, in denying parole, may consider circumstances of crime charged, even if facts would constitute another uncharged crime, & even if D pled guilty to lesser charge; if parole is denied SOLELY because of circumstances of crime charged, maybe violation of "spirit of G.L. c. 127, § 133A," i.e., gravity of crime was already taken into account by the statutory scheme as to both sentencing and parole (here 2d degree murder parole eligibility after 15 years);

Hamm v Comm'r of Correction **29 MAC 1011 (91)**—aggregation of life & from & after sentences appropriate; refusal to apply to D 1988 policy change withholding aggregation not ex post facto violation;

Connery v Comm'r of Correction **33 MAC 253 (92)**—earned good time under G.L. c. 127, § 129D, must be deducted directly from parole ineligibility period of state prison sentences;

Reynolds v Superintendent **442 M 1007, 1008 (2004)**—when sentence on a charge not qualifying for "good time" is being served concurrently with sentence on separate charge that does qualify, "good time" might be of no practical benefit; it can't be held in reserve for later application & maximum over-all reduction of incarcerated time;

Henderson v Commissioners of Barnstable County **49 MAC 455 (2000)**—though revocation of "statutory good time" credits improper here under regulations, not a federal constitutional due process violation;

Stewart v Chairman, Mass. Parole Board **35 MAC 843 (94)**—at time of imposition of concurrent life sentences with parole eligibility at 15 years, victim notification & right to speak at parole hearing didn't exist; statutory change resulting in deceased's family appearing at hearing. opposing release (resulting in no release) was not prohibited ex post facto law;

14-W. (STATE PRISON) SENTENCE APPEAL TO SUPERIOR COURT APPELLATE DIVISION

G.L. c. 278, §§ 28A-28D—for state prison sentences; must appeal within 10 days (can withdraw later); increase OK, but not without hearing;

C v Alfonso **449 M 738 (2007)**—although G.L. c. 278, § 28A states that appellate division jurisdiction concerning "sentences to the reformatory for women" is for "terms of more than five years," SJC holds that "equal protection jurisprudence mandated by art. 1" (Declaration of Rights) bars any interpretation authorizing men to appeal from state prison sentence of any length but denying same right to women; to determine whether woman's sentence to MCI-Framingham is "state prison," and thus appealable rests on "whether the facts necessary for conviction or the length of the sentence make it evident that the sentence is a state prison sentence"; here, judge explicitly used term "MCI-Cedar Junction" in imposing 3–5 year sentence, so it's "state prison";

Fiscal Year 2000—of 758 cases going to decision, 393 were withdrawn; 365 were heard (9 reduced, 1 increased, 355 "dismissed," i.e., remained the same (452 cases were carried over to Fiscal Year 2001, & some high number likewise had been carried over to Fiscal Year 2000 from Fiscal Year 1999);

Hicks v C **345 M 89 (62)**—can increase without reason; no double jeopardy bar (see Chapter 19, Double Jeopardy);

Walsh v Commonwealth **358 M 193 (70)**—(same); to correct extreme harshness/leniency; (affirmed, *Walsh v Picard* **446 F.2d 1209 (1st Cir. '71)**);

Croteau, petitioner **353 M 736 (68)**—right to counsel re: decision to pursue or not, & to present case;

Superior Court Rule 64—procedures; counsel responsible for perfecting & prosecuting unless withdrawal granted (see also CPCS P/G 8.2);

Superior Court "Guidelines for Appellate Division Proceedings"—adopted 8/5/85, published in Massachusetts Rules of Court (State) (West 2002, & presumably, succeeding years);

C v Grimshaw **31 MAC 917 (91)**—sentences to be reviewed only by Appellate Division, not Appeals Court or SJC, unless sentence based on impermissible sentencing factors, exceeds terms authorized by statute, or is cruel & unusual or otherwise unconstitutional;

Murray v Commonwealth **455 M 1016 (2009)**—if Appellate Division decides that original sentence should stand it shall "dismiss the appeal" (citing G.L. c. 278, § 28B); petitioner's repeated "equity" suits in SJC (seeking "judgment ordering Appellate Division to enter expeditiously a final disposition" of the sentence appeal) failed to comprehend finality of Appellate Division's ruling;

C v Turavani **45 MAC 909 (98)**—lengthy consecutive sentences for 3 counts of assault & battery by means of dangerous weapon, with from & after sentences, suspended and concurrent with each other, for 3 assault & batteries, and stringent probationary conditions for 3 years, were permitted by statute; judge's explicit statement that he was sentencing D only for the crimes of which she was convicted was enough to defeat D's claim that harsh sentence was for mayhem, of which she was acquitted;

Callahan v C **416 M 1010 (94)**—sentencing judge has no authority to modify a sentence properly changed by Appellate Division (attempt here by R.29 revoke & revise motion, proffered with motion for leave to late file (denied without hearing), notice of appeal of its denial (returned to counsel by Superior Court clerk, though clerk had no authority to refuse acceptance of notice of appeal));

C v Callahan **419 M 306 (95)**—when D claims appeal to Appellate Division, original sentencing judge is "divested of jurisdiction to act on motions to rehear or to vacate"; R.30 motion here asserted denial of due process & effective assistance of counsel at Appellate Division, but neither was found; "procedural safeguards" regarding sentencing = notice of right to appeal sentence, aid of counsel in deciding whether to appeal **with its attendant risk**, availability of a record and possible resort to views of trial judge, appearance before the tribunal with assistance of counsel, and "collegial rather than individual judgment".

Chapter 15
APPEALS (INTERLOCUTORY AND POSTCONVICTION) AND OTHER POSTCONVICTION REMEDIES

15-A. MOTIONS TO TRIAL JUDGE

15-A.1. Reconsideration

Monahan v Commonwealth **414 M 1001 (93)**—complaints dismissed with prejudice can only be revived by Commonwealth filing timely motion to reconsider or interlocutory appeal and prevailing; Commonwealth can't merely re-file (despite fact here that judge denied D's motion to dismiss the re-filed complaints, and purported to revoke his earlier order dismissing first complaints);

C v Downs **31 MAC 467 (91)**—motion for reconsideration of final orders of trial judge limited to 30 days; nondispositive order limited to reasonable time during pendency of case; affidavit is desirable but not required; hearing is desirable if motion contains "fresh material" or if judge will "alter substantially" original disposition; explanation of change should be put on record;

C v Cronk **396 M 194, 197 (85)**—availability of appellate review doesn't preclude reconsideration by judge if reconsideration request is made within reasonable time;

C v Lugo **64 MAC 12 (2005)**—reconsideration is "permitted" when "substantial justice requires," and this isn't limited to instances "where there are allegations of new or additional grounds that could not have been reasonably known when the original motion was filed";

C v Rodriguez **443 M 707, 708–09 (2005)**—an issue first raised in a motion for reconsideration may be preserved for appellate review, BUT must file notice of appeal from the denial of the reconsideration motion;

C v Balboni **419 M 42 (94)—motion to reconsider "final"/dispositive order should be filed within 30 days (same as time for filing notice of appeal)**; *but see C v*

Haskell **438 M 790 (2003)**—within judge's discretion to allow reconsideration of denial of suppression motion five years later (D had been on default during that time);

C v Garcia **34 MAC 386, 391–92 (93)**—in reviewing judge's ruling on the suppression motion, appellate court may not rely on facts as developed at trial; see also cases cited; (SO WHEN PRESENTED AT TRIAL WITH MORE FAVORABLE TESTIMONY THAN THAT APPEARING AT MOTION HEARING, MOVE TO RECONSIDER);

15-A.2. M.R.Crim.P. 25(b)(2)

(1st Sentence) if Motion for Required Finding of NG Denied & case given to jury, may "RENEW" within 5 DAYS of jury discharge & may include alternatively motion for new trial; (2d sentence) if jury G., may move (no time limit) to set aside & for new trial, entry of NG, or guilty of lesser included offense;

M.R.Crim.P. 25(a)—motion for required finding of NG at close of DA's or D's case; 25(b)(1) at close of all evidence, judge may reserve decision, submit to jury, & decide before verdict, after verdict, or after jury discharged without verdict;

C v Therrien **383 M 529 (81)**—if required finding of NG = BEFORE jury verdict then no DA appeal because double jeopardy; AFTER jury finds G, DA may appeal (*see Chapter 19, Double Jeopardy*); here, erroneous post-G required finding of NG ((fn.8) but D can still ask R.30 New Trial—see below);

See Chapter 12-G re: motion for required finding of not guilty under 25 (a);

K. Smith, *Criminal Practice & Procedure*, §§ 1918–21 (2d ed. 1983 & Supp.): re: Rule 25(b)(2)—best to file new motion because motion for required finding probably didn't include request for new trial or G of only lesser included offense;

C v Walker **68 MAC 194 (2007)**—judge purported to act under Rule 25(b)(2) and its "statutory predicate, G.L. c. 278, § 11," in magnanimity to misbehaving students on field trip, but rule allowed only three options for relief (new trial, verdict of not guilty, or entry of verdict of a lesser included offense); indecent assault and battery isn't lesser included offense of assault with intent to rape, and as matter of law, there was sufficient evidence for jury's verdicts;

C v Keough **385 M 314 (82)**—no time limit for motion under 2d sentence of 25(b)(2) after G verdict; judge may consider evidence weight & credibility; though DA can appeal judge's decision, reviewed only for abuse of discretion;

C v Gilbert **447 M 161 (2006)**—judge may grant relief of reduction in verdict rather than new trial, though D's motion under M.R.Crim.P. 30 (eleven years after conviction, on basis of jury instruction error) sought relief only in form of new trial; SJC also upheld judge's resolution which gave Commonwealth power to dictate the relief (elect either reduction of first degree murder to second degree, or new trial on first degree);

C v Guy G **53 MAC 271 (2001)**—no time limit for motion under 2d sentence of 25(b)(2), and judge would have been within his discretion in reducing 'open & gross lewdness' delinquency adjudication to indecent exposure, because latter IS lesser included offense (and because judge in these circumstances could properly be motivated to avoid subjecting juvenile to sex offender registration required by the former and to void the basis on which the school system claimed the right to exclude the juvenile (a felony-level delinquency)); remanded to trial judge for the exercise of discretion;

C v Torres **24 MAC 317 (87)**—though under 2d sentence of 25(b)(2), judge may order reduction or new trial based on witness credibility & "interest of justice," for NG to entire offense judge must apply *Latimore* standard (*see Chapter 12-G, Required Finding of NG*)—so reverse D's 25(b)(2) "not guilty" (but trial judge can give new trial);

C v Ghee **414 M 313, 321 (93)**—because trial judge reduced murder one to murder two as more consonant with justice, Commonwealth appeal was meritless; if judge had instead allowed required finding of not guilty, SJC would have been bound to review decision as one of law;

C v Gaulden **383 M 543 (81)**—Rule 25(b)(2) new trial or reduction to lesser included offense can be based on judge's view of witnesses' credibility or weight;

C v Sokphann Chhim **447 M 370 (2006)**—same (reduction of first degree murder, extreme atrocity/cruelty, JOINT VENTURE basis, to involuntary manslaughter—battery); dissent (4:3 decision) says record established that judge used impermissible consideration (i.e., wanted to ameliorate sentence of life without parole);

C v Lyons **444 M 289 (2005)**—holding judge abused discretion in reducing second degree murder to manslaughter (4:3 decision);

C v Auclair **444 M 348 (2005)**—holding judge committed error of law in reducing first degree murder conviction to second degree because reduction was based on erroneous view that there was insufficient evidence to support "extreme atrocity or cruelty";

C v Preston **393 M 318 (84)**—judge can order new trial under R.25(b)(2) though D's motion for new trial was under 30(b); normally 25 = BEFORE appeal, & 30 = AFTER; new trial motion for G against the weight of evidence more closely within scope of 25(b)(2) than 30; (new trial here OK because trial judge evaluated & nuances of conduct, tone, & evidence not apparent in "cold record");

C v Aguiar **400 M 508 (87)**—once appeal's entered, trial judge probably loses 25(b)(2) jurisdiction, but D can try to STAY appeal & press a 25(b)(2) motion (see *Healy* **393 M 367 (84)** no motion for new trial while appealing; but see *Hernandez v Commonwealth* **423 M 1012 (96)** Appeals Court MAY, but is not required to, allow motion to stay proceedings in direct appeal pending filing of and ruling on R.30 motion for new trial; see also *C v Montgomery* **53 MAC 350, 353–54 (2001)** reasons why stay of direct appeal pending ruling on motion for new trial = good idea);

C v Adkinson **442 M 410, 421–22 (2004)**—because no stay of appellate proceedings was granted by single justice of SJC or Appeals Court, trial court was without jurisdiction to act on motion for new trial filed after notice of appeal; SJC refused to consider those issues, though they had been ruled upon and briefed by the parties in conjunction with direct appeal;

C v Greaves **27 MAC 590 (89)**—trial judge's reduction of verdict under Rule 25(b)(2) upheld because not arbitrary or unreasonable, despite procedural errors in hearing;

C v Cornish **28 MAC 173 (89)**—trial judge has discretion to grant new trial under Rule 25(b)(2) where "integrity" of Commonwealth's evidence was suspect, notwithstanding legal sufficiency of evidence; award of costs & attorneys' fees for Commonwealth's appeal upheld, even though Rule 25(b)(2), unlike Rule 30, doesn't make express provision;

C v Burr **33 MAC 637 (92)**—judge's reduction of trafficking over 100grams to possession with intent to distribute not permitted by Rule 25(b)(2) where amount of cocaine not in issue;

C v Doucette **408 M 454 (90)**—same; judge's postconviction entry of required finding of not guilty under Rule 25(b)(2) reversed because evidence met *C v Latimore* standard, notwithstanding judge's concerns about weight of prosecution evidence;

15-A.3. Motion to Dismiss (after Mistrial (Hung Jury)) for Double Jeopardy Violation: Insufficient Evidence at First Trial

Berry v Commonwealth **393 M 793 (85)**—no retrial after hung jury because should've been required finding of NG (better double jeopardy protection under state law than under federal per *US v Richardson* **468 US 317 (84)**);

Aucella v Commonwealth **406 M 415 (90)**—reprosecution after hung jury barred where evidence was legally insufficient; G.L. c. 211, § 3, petition = appropriate vehicle (but G.L. c. 211, § 3 may be pursued only after denial of motion to dismiss in trial court—see *Pena v Commonwealth* **426 M 1015 (98)**);

Koonce v Commonwealth **412 M 71 (92)** reprosecution for murder 1 after hung jury not barred where evidence legally sufficient, notwithstanding D's self-defense claim;

See Chapter 19, Double Jeopardy;

15-A.4. Motion for New Trial under M.R.Crim.P. 30

See Chapter 15- F, post;

15-B. DIRECT APPEAL, POST-CONVICTION

Roe v Flores-Ortega **528 US 470 (2000)**—failure to file notice of appeal after D has instructed counsel to do so = ineffective assistance; there is constitutionally-imposed duty to consult with client re: whether to appeal (1) when a rational D would want to appeal, and (2) when this particular D, regardless of merits, "reasonably demonstrated" to counsel that he was interested in appealing; to show prejudice from ineffective assistance here = demonstrate reasonable probability that D would have timely appealed but for counsel's deficient performance; need not show that appeal would have afforded relief; prejudice is "the forfeiture of a proceeding itself";

C v Kegler **65 MAC 907 (2006)**—appellate counsel's cavalier disregard of briefing deadlines caused dismissal of appeal ("blatant disregard of the rules of appellate procedure is conduct demonstrably below what is to be expected of reasonably competent counsel"); appellate court considered issues presented in months-late brief, after dismissal of appeal, to discern whether counsel's conduct deprived D of "available substantial ground of defense" (it didn't, so order denying motion to reinstate appeal was affirmed);

C v Goewey **452 M 399 (2008)**—on Commonwealth's interlocutory appeal of allowance of D's motion to suppress, defense counsel failed to file any brief, after requesting and receiving extensions of time; MAC should not have held oral argument and decided the case in absence of advocacy on behalf of D; court's "unilateral review of the transcript" was not an adequate substitute for D's right to effective assistance of counsel, and it was not proper for court to determine without benefit of brief or argument from D that D was not prejudiced by absence of counsel; Commonwealth has misinterpreted the significance of *Kegler* 65 MAC 907; *Alvarez* 69 MAC 438, 443 (2007) reiterates *Frank* 425 M 182 (97): due process requires that D who has been denied right to counsel on appeal (actually or constructively) must be placed in same position he would have occupied were he presenting direct appellate claims in ordinary course;

C v Clemmey **447 M 121, 134 (2006)**—appellate court may affirm decision of trial judge on any ground supported by the record;

C v Latour **397 M 1007 (86)**; *C v Barrows* **435 M 1011 (2002)**—if D dies pending his direct appeal, charges are dismissed;

G.L. c. 278, § 28—aggrieved criminal D may appeal to SJC, BUT G.L. c. 211A, § 10—intermediate Appeals Court has concurrent jurisdiction over appeals in criminal cases, and review in the first instance will be undertaken in Appeals Court (unless direct appellate review is ordered under M.R.App.P. 11, or unless conviction is for 1st degree murder, see G.L. c. 278, § 33E);

G.L. c. 278, § 33E—1st degree murder cases receive direct plenary review in SJC; after direct appeal of murder-one conviction, any ruling on subsequent motion in trial court (e.g., M.R.Crim.P. 30, for new trial) may not be appealed absent authorization by SJC single justice ("gatekeeper" role);

C v Doane **428 M 631 (99)**—delinquency adjudications by reason of 1st degree murder are not directly reviewable in SJC (but rationale that such adjudication doesn't have the severe "life" sentence disappeared by legislation later enacted and wasn't applicable to this juvenile, see id. at 634 n.1);

M.R.App.P. 11: Direct Appellate Review—within 20 days after docketing of case in Appeals Court, party may apply in writing to SJC for direct appellate review (no oral argument in support allowed); filing of application doesn't extend time for filing briefs (R.11(e)) (but see exceptions/qualifications to this at R.11(g)); direct review may also occur by SJC justices' vote sua sponte; two SJC judges must vote for direct review, or "majority of justices of the Appeals Court" may transfer case for direct review upon such justices' certification that it's in public interest; required form/content of application prescribed;

M.R.App.P. 27.1: Further Appellate Review—within 20 days of Appeals Court's decision, party may apply in writing to SJC for further appellate review; form/content of application prescribed; three SJC justices must vote favorably to allow further review (or a majority of Appeals Court justices deciding the case can certify that further review is desirable); all issues decided by Appeals Court are before SJC on further appellate review UNLESS the order granting further review states some limitation (see, e.g., *C v Gorassi* **432 M 244 n.1 (2000)**);

C v Garcia **23 MAC 259, 267 (86)** and *C v Hill* **20 MAC 130 (85)**—can't appeal after G plea, or after trial when "facts" (as opposed to "evidence") have been stipulated; to preserve issue of motion to suppress for appellate review, consult these; but see *C v Hogan* **41 MAC 73 (96)** stipulated "facts" may serve to preserve issue of required finding of not guilty (what was possessed by D was not, under applicable statute, a burglarious implement);

Hernandez v Commonwealth **423 M 1012 (96)**—Appeals Court MAY, but is not required to, allow motion to stay proceedings in direct appeal pending filing of and ruling on R.30 motion for new trial; see also *C v Montgomery* **53 MAC 350 (2001)**;

C v Eisen **368 M 813, 814 (75)—if D dies while his conviction is on direct review, SJC's practice is to vacate the judgment and remand the case with a direction to dismiss the complaint or indictment,** thus abating the entire prosecution; *C v Latour* **397 M 1007 (86)** vacating judgment, dismissing indictment; *C v Harris* **379 M 917 (80)** vacating judgment, dismissing indictment;

C v DeLa Zerda **416 M 247 (93)**—policy advanced = "the interests of justice," which "ordinarily require that (a defendant) not stand convicted without resolution of the merits of his appeal, which is an 'integral part of (our) system for finally adjudicating (his) guilt or innocence'"; BUT **if D dies while appeal from denial of his motion for new trial (M.R.Crim.P. 30) is pending, conviction is left in place and appeal is dismissed**;

C v Montalvo **50 MAC 85, 87 (2000)**—though Commonwealth's confession of error "ha(d) heft," appellate court alone had duty to determine error, and so changed substantive law here to affirm conviction;

C v Bennett **414 M 269 (93)**—prevailing party is entitled to argue on appeal that judge was right for the wrong reason, "even relying on a principle of law not argued below"; *C v VaMeng Joe* **425 M 99 (97)**—appellate court is free to affirm ruling on grounds different from those relied on by motion judge if correct/preferred basis for affirmance is supported by record and findings; *C v Hall* **66 MAC 390 (2006)**—same;

C v Lao **450 M 215 (2007)**—in reversing trial judge's denial of motion for new trial in a first degree murder case after direct appellate review (including G.L. c. 278, § 33E), SJC finds ineffective assistance to have permeated D's direct appeal: appellate counsel didn't make *Crawford v Washington* constitutional claim that victim's hearsay statements (admitted as spontaneous utterances) were inadmissible; *Crawford* decision = published 3/8/04, & D's appellate brief was filed on 4/13/04, SJC issuing decision on direct appeal on 3/31/05;

15-B.1. Harmless Error

C v McCravy **430 M 758, 764 (2000)**—even where appellate court finds error, no relief unless error mattered at trial: bad Commonwealth closing argument targeted homicide charges, & D was acquitted on all of those, so no prejudice shown from error; to extent argument mattered to "reckless operation," D's own testimony admitted speeding (& thus, implicitly, recklessness), so also no prejudice;

C v Rosario **430 M 505 (99)**—if constitutional error, can refuse relief only if it's harmless beyond a reasonable doubt;

Chapman v California **386 US 18, 24 (67)**—same; *Yates v Evatt* **500 US 391 (91)** state court used incorrect formulation of 'harmless beyond reasonable doubt' standard;

C v Brazie **66 MAC 315 (2006)**—rejecting Commonwealth argument that this case = exception to principle that reversal is necessary for constitutional confrontation violation;

C v Tyree **455 M 676 (2010)**—when evidence at trial should have been suppressed, determine whether erroneous admission was harmless beyond a reasonable doubt, whether error might have had effect on jury and whether error might have contributed to verdicts; focus is NOT whether jury could have convicted D had tainted evidence been excluded, i.e., test is not "sufficiency" of evidence apart from that erroneously admitted; claim of harmlessness "is most particularly vulnerable where the over-all strength of" prosecution case "radiates from a core of tainted evidence";

C v Perez **411 M 249, 260 n.6 (91)**—nonconstitutional error harmlessness isn't as stringent a test;

C v Peruzzi **15 MAC 437, 445–46 (83) quoting "preeminent" decision on nonconstitutional harmless error,** *Kotteakos v US* **328 US 750, 764–65 (46)**—if sure that error didn't influence jury, or had "but very slight effect," judgment should stand except if error = against specific command of legislature, or violates constitutional norm; inquiry is NOT merely whether there was enough to support result apart from phase affected by the error;

C v Given **59 MAC 390, 395–96 (2003)**—good 'harmless error' discussion, in context of reversing jury finding of sexual dangerousness;

C v Grinkley **75 MAC 798 (2009) (Berry, J., dissenting)**—excellent explanation of how appellate courts' use of "harmless error" analysis deprives D of a JURY's fair determination of case, and mere fact that jury acquitted D of some charges (& though evidence purportedly overwhelming) should not save the convictions in light of "deep prosecutorial errors in the closing"; dissent would find "governmental errors that were so fundamental and so negative as to affect the fair conduct of trial", structural "defect affecting the framework within which the trial proceeds";

C v Paiva **71 MAC 411, 416–17, 419 (2008)**—Commonwealth's argument that error = harmless because of the purported "strength" of prosecution case misses point that error in excluding defense witnesses deprived D of right to JURY determination of material issues;

C v Cancel **394 M 567, 574–76 (85)**; *C v Kines* **37 MAC 540, 543–44 (94)**; *C v Santiago* **425 M 491, 497**

(97); *C v DeMars* **42 MAC 788 (97)**, S.C. **426 M 1008 (98)**; *C v Vickers* **60 MAC 24 (2003)**—several errors less likely to be harmless than would be a single one (even if some or all errors weren't subject of objections at trial, i.e., were "unpreserved);

C v McKay **67 MAC 396 (2006)**—reversal for refusal to instruct on "accident" in violating protective order; closing arguments stressing "accident" or not didn't make error harmless;

C v Douglas **75 MAC 643 (2009)**—because judge withdrew "per se" theory in operating under/motor vehicle homicide case (though complaint had charged both theories), reversal because no expert testimony (contra *Colturi* requirement, 448 M 817–18: though evidence of impairment was strong & trial counsel didn't object, lab supervisor's testimony as to blood alcohol content may have been "the most compelling evidence of intoxication";

15-B.2. Necessity of Transcript of Trial

SJC Rule 1:12—stenographic notes made in any court of the Commonwealth "may be destroyed" after six years from date on which the notes were taken, but this doesn't apply to notes as to which transcripts were ordered but not yet completed, or if court orders otherwise;

Hardy v US **375 US 277, 288, 290 (64) (Goldberg, J, concurring)**—"most basic & fundamental tool" of effective appellate advocate is "the complete trial transcript"; availability of a "complete" transcript shouldn't be made to depend on the facts of the case; appointed counsel needs complete transcript to discharge his responsibility; "a lawyer appointed to represent the interests of a defendant should not be required to delegate his responsibility of determining whether error occurred at trial to participants at that trial whose conduct may have formed the very basis for the errors"; the right to notice plain errors or defects "is illusory if no transcript is available at least to one whose lawyer on appeal enters the case after the trial is ended;

Pixley v Commonwealth **453 M 827 (2009)**—D called witness, who claimed 5th A. and art. 12 privileges, and judge held in camera *Martin* (423 M 496) hearing, finding privilege; on appeal after conviction, D could argue error in privilege determination, but would not be allowed access to "sealed"/impounded transcript of in camera hearing, SJC ruling that appellate judges could review privilege determination without any assistance from the parties, witness's constitutional right against self-incrimination trumping all else;

Mayer v Chicago **404 US 189, 195 (71)**—where grounds of appeal make out colorable need for complete transcript, burden is on State to show that only a portion of the transcript or an "alternative" will suffice for effective appeal on those grounds;

C v Harris **376 M 74 (78)**—where transcript of criminal case is not available for appeal "through no fault of the parties," new trial not constitutionally required IF trial proceedings can be sufficiently reconstructed;

C v Drayton **450 M 1028 (2008)**—passage of time itself (here, 30 years) doesn't make hearing in Superior Court to reconstruct record "inadequate or unavailable", though after hearing evidence judge must determine "in the first instance, "whether a reconstruction is possible and adequate to present on appeal any errors alleged . . . or, if not, the appropriate remedy";

Parrott v US **314 F.2d 46 (10th Cir. '63)**—unavailability of full transcript made it impossible for appellate court to determine whether errors were harmless, so conviction reversed;

Charpentier v Commonwealth **376 M 80 (78)**—indigent defendant entitled to a complete transcript on appeal;

C v Shea **356 M 358, 361 (69)**—"record" created other than by independent contemporaneous recording opens door to conflicting versions of what occurred at trial, & "the failure to settle these questions satisfactorily might often result in a miscarriage of justice"; "It is conceivable that the defendant in fact suffered no prejudice by the lack of a stenographic record, but as to that we can only speculate. . . . We prefer to resolve any doubts on this score in favor of the defendant(,)" so new trial ordered;

C v Mercado **452 M 662, 669 n.11 (2008)**—motion in limine was discussed and ruled upon in an unrecorded conference: "We are impeded in our analysis of the case by the absence of the discussion that occurred in the unrecorded conference, and we emphasize again the importance of recording all conferences";

C v Colon **439 M 519 (2003)**—in support of D's claim (on Rule 30 motion) that G-plea colloquy was inadequate (when no record of it existed), D presented recordings from six colloquies during two years conducted by same judge, which were ***randomly selected by an assistant clerk magistrate***; each contained a "woefully deficient colloquy," and this evidence was supplemented by testimony from two attorneys about the judge's regular practice, which had not changed over the years and was consistent with the recordings: SJC held D = entitled to withdraw G plea, on such "overwhelming" evidence of inadequacy [N.B.: D's Rule 30 motion was denied in the trial court, and this ruling was affirmed by the Appeals Court];

C v Fling **67 MAC 232 (2006)**—judge could grant Commonwealth motion to "correct docket" with evidence from ass't clerk-magistrate and trial prosecutor's file documents & affidavit, thereby defeating D's Rule 36 issue on appeal; "trial judge's correction is essentially conclusive";

C v Sharpe **454 M 147 (2009)**—though court stenographer had not recorded colloquy concerning D's decision to testify, trial judge hearing motion for new trial conducted evidentiary hearing and found (correcting record under M.R.App.P. 8(e)) that he had engaged D in colloquy and that D made decision (to testify) knowingly and voluntarily after consulting with counsel and family, and that trail counsel not ineffective in calling D;

Simmons v State **200 So.2d 619 (Fla. '67)**—appellants' trial counsel had withdrawn, under circumstances giving little hope for cooperation in obtaining accurate stipulated record; even if cooperative, memories of all parties (including trial judge) certainly faded;

C v Harris **371 M 462, 474–76 (76)**—Commonwealth chargeable with unexplained loss of search warrant & supporting affidavit; *C v Marks* **12 MAC 511 (81)** disappearance during jury deliberations of exhibits crucial to suggestive ID issue = new trial (denial of due process); *Williams, petitioner*, **378 M 623 (79)** court reporter's neglect = attributable to Commonwealth; delay in preparing transcript may entitle D to stay pending appeal, or even dismissal;

Draper v Washington **372 US 487, 496–97 (63)**—contrasting procedure whereby trial judge recalled and thereafter summarily found what went on at the trial with the "direct scrutiny" afforded by actual trial transcript; prosecutor's affidavit concerning his recollection of trial recognized to be tainted by adversarial interest;

State v Moore **87 N.M. 412 (75)**—absence of transcript of proceedings deprived D of right to appeal where transcript couldn't be prepared due to inaudibility of tape recordings; trial counsel's inability to recall events at trial didn't mean that D should lose appellate claims; conviction reversed;

U.S. v Atilus **425 F2d 816 (5th Cir. 1970)**—conviction reversed when, through no fault of D, transcript of trial proceedings was not available; see also *C v Norman* **447 Pa. 515 (72)** failure of transcript to contain critical portions of trial may warrant grant of new trial; *Commonwealth v Goldsmith* **452 Pa. 22 (73)** new trial may be required if absence of a record, for whatever reason, makes meaningful appellate review impossible; *State v Robinson* **387 So.2d 1143 (La. 1980)** failure to provide record of trial testimony of two expert witnesses was constitutional and statutory error, & couldn't be found harmless here;

15-B.3. Appellate Delay

C v Libby **411 M 177, 178 (91)**—delay in appeal may rise to level of constitutional error in two circumstances, i.e., "where State agents have deliberately blocked the defendant's appellate rights, or where the delay is 'inordinate and prejudicial'";

Campiti v Commonwealth **417 M 454, 456 (94)**—same;

C v Alvarez **422 M 198, 212–13 (96)**—same (27 months to prepare trial transcript);

Zatsky v Zatsky **36 MAC 7, 12 (94)**—"outer limit for performing the task of assembling a record in the trial court (should) be forty days"; findings of fact "which took eleven months after trial to emerge" should be completed within 30–60 days after close of evidence; when trial judge's decision "seems overdue," litigant should first inquire of judge ("directly, or through . . . clerk's office"), next demand action via chief judge of trial court concerned, next petition SJC under G.L. c. 211, § 3, and last, "a complaint in the nature of mandamus . . . to compel performance of a duty by a judge"; if assembly of the record is cause of delay, could first report problem to Appeals Court clerk before following above steps;

C v Santos **41 MAC 621, 628–29 (96)**—if appeal is long delayed, due merely to bureaucratic inattention or ineptitude in preparing transcripts, and new trial is ordered on the merits of appeal, court MIGHT grant "appropriate" relief if D establishes that the appellate delay has impaired right to fair retrial because of witness unavailability or failure of memory;

Campiti v Commonwealth **426 M 1004 (97)**—G.L. c. 211, § 3 petition seeking relief for appellate delay when merits of appeal were actually under consideration, i.e., almost two years passed after oral argument in Appeals Court with no decision; Appeals Court affirmed D's convictions before full SJC acted on G.L. c. 211, § 3 petition, however, and delay in processing non-meritorious appeal does not require reversal of D's criminal convictions;

Hagen v Commonwealth **437 M 374, 382 (2002)**—record "provides no plausible excuse for a delay of four years in holding the hearing on (D's) motion for a new trial or a delay of almost nine years between the filing of the notice of appeal and the Commonwealth's motion to revoke the stay of (D's) sentence pending appeal";

C v Vith Ly **450 M 16 (2007)**—execution of D's sentences, after unexplained delay of sixteen years on part of Commonwealth to have sentences executed, would violate due process & "principles of fundamental fairness"; sentences had been stayed pending appeal, but after some convictions were affirmed, Commonwealth did not seek execution of those sentences immediately or upon D's subsequent contacts with law enforcement;

15-B.4. Issues on Appeal

C v Holmes **32 MAC 906 (92)**; *C v Paton* **31 MAC 460 (91)** **D bound on appeal by legal theories of defense raised at trial (unless claim ineffective assistance of trial counsel in this regard, & this usually raisable only via M.R.Crim.P. 30)**;

SJC Rule 3:07, 3.1—shan't bring proceeding or assert/controvert issue therein unless non-frivolous basis, but this includes good faith argument for extension, modification, or reversal of existing law; lawyer for criminal D may nonetheless require that every element of case be established;

C v Moffett **383 M 201 (81)**—can't withdraw just because frivolous appeal; if D won't forego claim, present it succinctly & with least harm to D; if ethics absolutely require dissociating, do it in preface (with 30-day notice to D, who may submit additional arguments, pro se, within that time; must certify to court that D has been served with Moffett preface & advice that he may submit additional arguments); contrast *Anders v California* **386 US 738 (67)** if wholly frivolous appeal, may move to withdraw & file brief with anything in record arguably supporting appeal; Court then decides if appeal's wholly frivolous; **ANDERS IS NOT APPLICABLE IN MASS.**; see instead *Moffett* **383 M 201 (81)**;

Jones v Barnes **463 US 745 (83)**—while D has right to make fundamental decisions re: pleading G or NG, waiving jury, testifying in own behalf, or taking an appeal, D has no federal constitutional right to compel appointed appellate counsel to press nonfrivolous points requested by the client; counsel's own professional judgment as to best means of prosecuting appeal;

C v Montalvo **50 MAC 85, 87 (2000)**—though Commonwealth confessed error, appellate court alone had "duty to determine independently whether" error was committed; court then changed substantive law, to affirm conviction;

C v Hawkesworth **405 M 664 (89)**—juvenile court's verbatim adoption of Commonwealth's proposed findings & rulings after remand for new transfer hearing subject to stricter scrutiny, though sufficient here to justify transfer;

C v Garcia **34 MAC 386, 391–92 (93)**—in reviewing judge's ruling on the suppression motion, appellate court may not rely on facts as developed at trial; see also cases cited;

C v Cataldo **69 MAC 465 (2007)**—while appellate court may "supplement" a judge's findings IF evidence is undisputed and judge implicitly or explicitly credited the evidence, fact that witness testified without particular "opposition" or explicit impeachment "should not necessarily be equated with a conclusion that the judge accepted and "credited" the testimony; judicial silence may indeed indicate that the judge did NOT find particular testimony credible;

C v Druce **453 M 686, 699 n.16 (2009)**—appellate court would not consider cited trial testimony in review of decision re: pretrial motion to suppress (even though this was first degree murder case deserving of "33E" review);

15-B.5. Pro Se Representation on Appeal

Martinez v Court of Appeal of California **528 US 152 (2000)**—no federal constitutional right to represent oneself on appeal; 6th Amendment doesn't apply to appellate proceedings;

15-B.6. Effective Assistance of Counsel on Appeal

Pires v C **373 M 829 (77)—must tell D of right to appeal**;

Roe v Flores-Ortega **528 US 470 (2000)—failure to file notice of appeal after D has instructed counsel to do so = ineffective assistance of counsel, & need not show that appeal would have afforded relief**; counsel obligated to advise D about appeal rights; constitutionally-imposed duty to consult with D about appeal when there's reason to think either (1) rational D would want to appeal; or (2) this particular D demonstrated to counsel that he was interested in appealing; should consult anyway about advantages & disadvantages when D has neither directed counsel to file notice nor directed counsel not to pursue appeal;

Douglas v California **372 US 353 (63)—D has constitutional right to effective assistance of counsel on direct appeal**;

C v Kegler **65 MAC 907 (2006)**—appellate counsel's cavalier disregard of briefing deadlines caused dismissal of appeal ("blatant disregard of the rules of appellate procedure is conduct demonstrably below what is to be expected of reasonably competent counsel"); appellate court considered issues presented in months-late brief, after dismissal of appeal, to discern whether counsel's conduct deprived D of "available substantial ground of defense" (it didn't, so order denying motion to reinstate appeal was affirmed);

C v Perry **65 MAC 624 (2006)**—though it's improper to present claims for first time in a "reply" brief, appellate court here addressed them "in order to forestall any future claim that appellate counsel was ineffective";

C v Brown **75 MAC 361 (2009)**—though D did not brief on appeal a claim of 6th Amendment confrontation error pursuant to *Crawford v Washington* and *Melendez-Diaz v Massachusetts* 129 S Ct 25, 27 (2009), D did so by seeking leave to file supplemental brief after oral argument of the appeal: court exercised discretion [M.R.App.P. 16(a)(4)] to consider issue even though not raised in original brief, and reversed conviction (issue was preserved at trial);

C v Jordan **49 MAC 802 (2000)**—fact that D has no right to particular court-appointed attorney doesn't mean that D has no recognizable interest in continued representation (at trial) by appointed attorney with whom he has developed relationship, & who is most familiar with case; court nonetheless had discretion to disqualify attorney because of conflict of interest (court had interest in fair & proper administration of justice);

C v Frank **425 M 182 (97)—failure to file appellate brief is ineffective assistance of counsel**;

C v Alvarez **69 MAC 438 (2007)**—notwithstanding fact that D himself signed affidavit consenting to withdrawal of direct appeal, defense counsel asserting lack of meritorious issues was inadequate by itself to "discharge his constitutional obligations" (*Moffett* [383 M 201 (81)] brief said to be required), citing *Penson v Ohio* 488 US 75 (88); D's attempt to have appeal reinstated asserted that his previous consent was based on misinformation from appellate counsel; if true, consent = involuntary; D's claim of involuntariness is supported by affidavit AND by procedural history of case ("irregularities" noted);

Breese v Commonwealth **415 M 249 (93)— notwithstanding fact that D had no right to appointed counsel on appeal of R.30 denial, such counsel as he did have had to provide effective assistance**;

C v Cardenuto **406 M 450, 453–54 (90)**—appellate counsel provides "ineffective assistance" by failing to argue on direct appeal an issue which, had it been presented to the appellate court, would have required reversal of D's conviction(s); ("if the evidence introduced at trial was insufficient to sustain the conviction, trial counsel's failure to argue this issue on appeal necessarily amounted to ineffective assistance of counsel");

C v Cormier **41 MAC 76, 77 (96)**—same;

C v Baran **74 MAC 256 (2009)**—failure to argue ineffective assistance of trial counsel, argument of only "preserved errors"; appellate counsel, further, had conflict of interest, having represented alleged victim in civil suit against child care center employing D, who was convicted of sexual assaults upon children there; failure to raise issue of D's right to public trial;

Breese v Commonwealth **415 M 249 (93)**—no ineffectiveness by appellate counsel's failure to raise ineffective assistance of trial attorney unless D shows that such claim, if made, would have succeeded;

C v DeCicco **51 MAC 159 (2001)**—Brown, J., dissenting: "It may never be known whether or to what extent the prosecutor had hinted to (witness/co-venturer in murder) . . . that helpful testimony would be rewarded. The temptation for the prosecutor to engage in such conduct with indicted but untried witness is plain: witness has every incentive to 'go all out' in efforts to please prosecutor, while government is permitted to enhance witness's credibility by touting the lack of a plea agreement . . . ultimate disposition of (witness's) case provides sufficient basis to infer secret existence of at least a tacit plea arrangement at time of trial"; 2 of 3 judges believed that prosecutor's misconduct in argument that witness would not "get( ) a deal from this DA's office" & was unimpeachable for interest did not give rise to substantial risk of miscarriage of justice; *all 3 judges faulted D counsel for failing to raise issue on direct appeal rather than in motion for new trial, even though it came to counsel's notice only in Commonwealth's brief on direct appeal that witness had received "deal" some ten months after D's convictions which were the subject of the direct appeal;*

15-B.7. "Retroactivity"/Decisional Law Issued After Trial but Before Appeal

C v Federico **425 M 844, 852 n.14 (97)**—D has benefit of "intervening decisional law" occurring between trial and processing of the direct appeal of the convictions;

C v Beauchamp **424 M 682 (97)**—even if appeal is greatly delayed because D escaped from prison (and appeal couldn't be pursued in the interim); but

C v Adams **421 M 289 (95)**—to receive "retroactive application of a rule of criminal law" (i.e. receive benefit of rule announced after trial and when case is pending on direct appeal), D must have preserved the issue at trial; see, e.g., *C v Pring-Wilson* 448 M 718 (2007)—trial judge permissibly granted new trial motion brought on basis of SJC decision issued after D's notice of appeal but before entry of case in appellate court, D having raised the issue at trial (contrast *C v Peppicelli* 70 MAC 87 [2007] [D never attempted to introduce such evidence at trial]);

C v Blake **49 MAC 134 (2000)**—re: retroactivity of decisional law issued after trial, D gets its benefit IF he preserved issue at trial and case is on DIRECT appeal (not "collateral review") when new rule is announced; if case is

on collateral review, new rule won't be applied retroactively unless within one of two limited exceptions: (1) if new rule places certain primary, private individual conduct beyond the power of the criminal law to proscribe, or (2) if it requires observance of procedures that are implicit in the concept of ordered liberty, "limited, however, to those new procedures of fundamental fairness without which the likelihood of an accurate conviction is seriously diminished" (citations omitted);

C v Lao **450 M 215 (2007)**—in reversing trial judge's denial of motion for new trial in a first degree murder case after direct appellate review (including G.L. c. 278, § 33E), SJC finds ineffective assistance to have permeated D's direct appeal: appellate counsel didn't make *Crawford v Washington* constitutional claim that victim's hearsay statements (admitted as spontaneous utterances) were inadmissible; Crawford decision = published 3/8/04, & D's appellate brief was filed on 4/13/04, SJC issuing decision on direct appeal on 3/31/05;

C v Clemente **452 M 295 (2008)**—"Adjutant" (443 M 649 [2005]) changed law between time of trial and appeal, but was a "new common law rule of evidence to be applied prospectively only"; that the new rule was applied to Adjutant herself was major exception to normal practice: Adjutant at trial had argued the issue and pressed it on appeal, as did *Pring-Wilson* 448 M 718, 735–37 (2007) unlike defendants here (though defendants here first raised issue in motion for new trial, denied by trial judge); further, claimed error in context here caused no prejudice (452 M at 307);

15-B.8. Final Judgment

C v Paniaqua **413 M 796 (92)**—although **"filing" of conviction ordinarily suspends right to appeal errors** underlying a conviction, appellate courts will consider such errors where D didn't consent to filing on record;

C v Grace **43 MAC 905, 907 (97)**—same;

C v Strahan **39 MAC 928 (95)**—though pro se D assented to "filing," he didn't know what that meant, so it didn't act as waiver of right to appellate review;

C v Burden **48 MAC 232 (99)**—in revising sentence, motion judge could place two convictions on file even without D's assent because D had already received full appellate review of the convictions (so usual rule, requiring D's consent to filing to protect right of appeal, = inapplicable);

C v Stracuzzi **30 MAC 161 (91)**—appellate courts may consider claims which apply to validity of convictions placed on file along with those on which sentence(s) were imposed;

C v Freeman **29 MAC 635, 636 n.1 (90)**—same;

C v Prashaw **57 MAC 19 (2003)**—same; *C v Delgado* **367 M 432, 438 (75)**—same; *Murray v Commonwealth* **432 M 1026 (2000)**—same; *C v Spearin* **446 M 599, 606 (2006)**—same;

C v LeBeau **451 M 244, 263 n.20 (2008)**—same; chief conviction = first degree murder; four convictions of larceny held to have been only a single larceny, & relief ordered, even though all had been 'filed' with D's consent;

C v Molligi **70 MAC 108 (2007)**—appellate court will consider "filed" convictions "in cases that present exceptional circumstances, such as where the legal error affects all charges and there is a commonality of effect flowing from the error," citing cases/examples;

C v Rousseau **61 MAC 144 n.6 (2004)**—"filed" conviction supported by no evidence at all was set aside;

C v O'Brien **30 MAC 807 n.1 (91)**—D's claim that search warrant was invalid applied to "filed" conviction as well, and it would be considered despite fact that D consented to filing;

C v Badore **47 MAC 600, 601 n.1 (99)**—same;

C v Chappee **397 M 508, 510, 523 (86)**—though D consented to filing of conviction, SJC vacated it because it was duplicitous (lesser included offense) of another conviction;

C v Calderon **431 M 21, 28 (2000)**—citing *Chappee* and *O'Brien*, SJC reversed filed conviction while reversing others for error in peremptory challenge allowance;

C v Lawson **425 M 528, 529 n.1 (97)**—SJC considered filed convictions, BUT ordered that they be remanded to Superior Court for sentencing unless D consented to their being "placed on file";

Murray v Commonwealth **442 M 1029 (2004)**—after appeals court refused to address arguments concerning "filed" conviction & D filed motion in Superior Court to "bring forward" the filed conviction and have counsel appointed for sentencing, D should have appealed the denial of that motion (rather than undertake G.L. c. 211, § 3 petitions & appeals from their denial);

In the matter of Rudnicki 421 M 1006 (95)—continuance without a finding, which resulted in dismissal of case before denial of D's petition for writ of mandamus and G.L. c. 211, § 3 action (which followed clerk's refusal to accept D's "notice of appeal" of the CWOF), resulted in no appealable final order, and appellate court was without jurisdiction over the criminal matter; *C v Ringuette* **443 M 1003 (2004)**—denial of D's motion to suppress is not a final judgment for collateral estoppel purposes (D isn't obligated to seek leave to file interlocutory appeal); *C v Castillo* **66 MAC 34 (2006)**—trial on "stipulated evidence" (here, to preserve right to appeal denial of motion to suppress) resulted in reversal because judge failed to ask D if he agreed to the procedure & if he was aware of various constitutional rights he was thus waiving; given posture of case (i.e., invalid conviction after failure to make record of knowing/voluntary waiver of rights), court had no authority to decide what was effectively an "interlocutory appeal" of denial of suppression motion, since no SJC single justice had allowed interlocutory appeal;

15-B.9. Claim of Appeal, Timeliness

M.R.App.P. 3(a)—shall take appeal permitted by law by filing notice of appeal with lower court clerk; Rule 4 (b) must file notice of appeal within 30 days of sentence or G. finding; filing a motion for new trial (MRCrim.P.30) within 30 days of guilty verdict or sentencing stops clock, and time for filing notice of appeal will then be computed from date of entry of order denying motion for new trial; 4 (c) **trial court**, if "excusable neglect," can give **NO MORE THAN 30 EXTRA days** for filing notice of appeal; 14(b) **appellate court** or Single Justice **may extend** notice of appeal time **ONLY up to a year from G. verdict or sentencing;**

Callahan v Commonwealth **416 M 1010 (94)**—if court clerk refuses to accept for filing a notice of appeal, remedy lies in request for an order from a Superior Court judge directing the clerk to accept the notice and process the appeal (though in this case D was seeking to file appeal from denial of D's (untimely) motion to revoke and revise a sentence because it had been increased by the Appellate Division, and (on the merits) sentencing judge had no authority to modify the sentence);

Miranda v Commonwealth **392 M 420 (84)**—not even appellate court may enlarge time for filing notice of appeal beyond one year from finding of guilt or imposition of sentence; SJC might, for superintendence (G.L. c. 211, § 3), extend otherwise absolute 1-year time limit of App.R. 14(b);

C v Beauchamp **424 M 682 (97)**—SJC single justice allowed notice of appeal 23 years after conviction (D had escaped from prison after '73 conviction, was returned to MA in '87, and in '96 asked to file notice of appeal); *C v Bonds* **424 M 698 (97)** though appeal was dismissed in '75 (for failure to file brief?), SJC single justice "reinstated" appellate rights in '95;

C v White **429 M 258, 261–62 (99)**—30-day period for filing notice of appeal runs from date of order denying motion for new trial, not date of denial's receipt by counsel; "mailbox rule," adding 3 days to prescribed time period, does NOT apply; **IF notice of appeal has been filed within one year from date of conviction, or sentencing, or the filing of an order which is being appealed, but was not "timely filed" during that year, appellate court may allow, after the passage of the year, leave to have late-filed the notice of appeal;**

C v Pappas **432 M 1025 (2000)**—but no abuse of discretion in Appeals Court dismissal/order refusing to deem timely a notice of appeal filed seven months after subject "final order" (though a District Court judge, without authority in circumstances, purported to allow extension of time) because no demonstration of good cause for needing extension of time;

C v Abreu **66 MAC 795 (2006)**—notwithstanding language of M.R.App.P. 14(b) (re: enlargement of time for filing notice of appeal can't be beyond one year from "date of verdict or finding of guilt or date of imposition of sentence"), appellate court may enlarge time for filing notice of appeal in criminal case from orders concerning "collateral challenges", up to one year after date of such order (and these would rather routinely be past the one year from conviction or sentencing);

C v Butts **21 MAC 972 (86), S.C. sub nom.** *C v Preziosi* **399 M 748 (87)**—Appeals Court held that record failed to disclose any "excusable neglect" to justify trial court's allowance of motion to late-file notice of appeal; because Commonwealth stated appeal was properly before Court, and in interest of judicial economy, SJC considered merits of appeal;

C v Trussell **68 MAC 452 (2007)**—if counsel fails to file timely (within one year of the conviction, or sentence, with permission of appellate court if beyond the 30+30 day period in which trial court may act) the notice of appeal desired by D, finding of excusable neglect or good cause (M.R.App.P. 14(b) and 4(c)) is warranted if judge finds that "lack of timely appeal resulted from act or omission of counsel, whether or not amounting to ineffective assistance, to which the D did not knowingly assent" (rejecting Commonwealth argument that mere omission isn't excusable neglect or good cause, so that D should be relegated to R. 30 for any relief);

C v Barboza **68 MAC 180 (2007)**—ten months after sentencing, counsel filed motion with single justice to late-file notice of appeal, but made no allegations supporting "excusable neglect"; after denial without prejudice, and before one year had elapsed, counsel asserted that trial counsel had prepared and mailed notice of appeal to trial court, but had not checked to verify its receipt there (and it was not ever received there); Appeals Court holds that the "excusable neglect"/"good cause" standard for civil cases may not have same meaning in criminal appeals, and single justice did not abuse discretion in allowing appeal;

C v Boutwell **21 MAC 201 (85)**—trial judge can (and must) deny motion for leave to file late notice of appeal because more than 60 days had passed since G & sentencing, & no error here in denial of motion for new trial; *Evitts v Lucy* **469 US 387 (85)** distinguished because in MA, any possible error may receive appellate review via appeal from denial of R.30 motion for new trial;

C v Burns **43 MAC 263 (97)**—though trial court allowed trial counsel's "Motion to File Notice of Appeal Nunc Pro Tunc", some fourteen months after D was sentenced (based on counsel's affidavit asserting that he prepared notice of appeal and intended that it be timely filed, but just discovered that it must not have been so filed), Appeals Court dismissed appeal; trial judge was without authority to allow such late notice of appeal;

Shaev v Alvord **66 MAC 910 (2006)**—concept of excusable neglect is not meant to apply to "any garden-variety oversight" (though context wasn't criminal case);

C v Guaba **417 M 746, 751 (94)**—time for filing notice of appeal runs from date on which order being appealed (e.g., denial of motion for new trial) is filed, NOT from the date of order's receipt by a party; delay in receiving notice of order should be considered, however, re:

whether "good cause" exists to extend time for filing notice of appeal; filing of notice of appeal in trial court should precede the filing in SJC single justice session of application for leave to appeal;

C v Hartsgrove **407 M 441 (90)**   incarcerated pro se D is deemed to have filed notice of appeal upon placing it in prison mailbox;

C v Cowie **404 M 119 (89)**—no late "direct" appeal via M.R.Crim.P. 30(a) is possible (even if allege late because attorney ineffective) because D has 30 (b) motion for new trial rights (& trial judge must allow if constitutional error); SJC holds that under US Constitution, motion for new trial, and appeal from its denial, is acceptable alternative to direct appeal which was dismissed because of failure to file timely notice of appeal; *Evitts v Lucy* **469 US 387 (85)** (ineffective assistance of counsel found when counsel's (different) action caused forfeiture of direct appeal) therefore inapplicable;

C v Burns **43 MAC 263, 266 (97)**—(despite having done so) trial court was without authority to allow, 14 months after sentencing, a "motion to file notice of appeal nunc pro tunc", filed with affidavit of counsel stating he'd prepared timely notice of appeal, but very belatedly noticed that it hadn't been filed; appeal dismissed, even though parties had already briefed substantive issues;

C v Lopes **21 MAC 11 (85)**—trial judge's allowance of claim of appeal beyond the 60-day period within which he had power to act under M.R.App.P. 4(c) was illegal, a "nullity"; if more than a year has passed without notice of appeal, only "possible" recourse is G.L. c. 211, § 3 (citing *Miranda* **392 M 420 (84)**);

C v Libby **405 M 231 (89)**—deliberate blocking of D's appellate rights by judicial personnel might be violation of right to speedy appeal; retrial might be barred if D unduly prejudiced by lengthy (18-year) delay;

15-B.10. Responsibilities for Assembling Appellate Record

C v Montanez **388 M 603, 604 (83)**—"the defendant bears the burden of producing a satisfactory record";

C v Kater **409 M 433, 448 n.12 (91)**—counsel has responsibility to make certain that those portions of record and transcript relied on by the parties are before the appellate court;

C v Woods **427 M 169, 170 (98)**—"The relatively simple issues underlying this appeal are unnecessarily complicated by an inadequate record, insufficient preservation of the issues below, and the inability or unwillingness of counsel on appeal to recognize and to deal with these inadequacies";

C v Woods **419 M 366, 371 (95)**—"**The burden is on the appellant to ensure that an adequate record exists for an appellate court to evaluate**";

C v Burns **43 MAC 263, 268 n.5 (97)**—"**In order to be entitled to have this court consider and decide an issue, (D) has ... burden of including in a record on**

appeal all of the evidence, facts, or information pertinent to the issue" (after default of D in this regard here, Commonwealth provided transcript containing oral discovery order which D argued had been violated);

C v Robicheau **421 M 176, 184 n.7 (95)—criminal D, as appealing party, has responsibility "to provide an adequate record for review"; appellate court will not assume that D made proper objection when transcript is, at relevant points, "riddled with gaps and inaudible segments"; court treated issue as if unpreserved** (i.e., "substantial risk" analysis);

Cf Donald v Commonwealth **452 M 1029 (2008)**—D moved in Superior Court for free copy of transcript (albeit of Appellate Division proceedings); when motion was denied, he should have filed notice of appeal in Superior Court and judge should/would have made written findings (G.L. c. 261, § 27D), which clerk would forward with other relevant documents to Appeals Court clerk; G.L. c. 211, § 3 was not appropriate avenue for relief;

C v Boyajian **68 MAC 866 (2007)**—in support of appellate claim that he made timely objection to DA's closing argument, appellate counsel pointed to notation of "sidebar conference" following closing argument, but this was not transcribed, and D was obligated to move under M.R.App.P. 8 to reconstruct record in order to establish that he had objected or requested curative instructions (counsel's mere claim was worthless); objection which was on the record came "after the jury retired to deliberate," too late to preserve issue of DA's closing argument;

Hanlon v Commonwealth **419 M 1005 (95)**—though D claimed, in motion to dismiss for double jeopardy violation and in subsequent petition under G.L. c. 211, § 3, that required finding of not guilty should have been allowed at first trial (which resulted in hung jury), and asserted that no trial transcript was available (to support or refute this assertion), Commonwealth furnished SJC single justice with transcript of sex assault complainant's trial testimony, which alone provided sufficient evidence to defeat motion for required finding and to now defeat motion to dismiss;

M.R.App.P. 8(e)—party may move to expand record to correct omission therefrom, but this addition must be something that judge and parties had before them during the proceedings below;

C v Mello **453 M 760, 762 n.1 (2009)**—reprimand for [Commonwealth's] inclusion of 'factual statements' for which no record reference was given, and which SJC "could not locate in the record"; these would not be considered;

M.R.Crim.P. 42—"Clerical Mistakes" from oversight or omission may be corrected by court at any time (sua sponte or on m. of party, after notice to others), but after appeal is docketed in appellate court, corrections can be made by/in lower court only with leave of appellate court; see, e.g.: *C v Tripolone* **44 MAC 23, 26 and nn.5–6 (97)—though Commonwealth sought to "expand" record to include purported fact** that rape indictment was pending against D at time G.L. c. 209A protective order

was lodged against him, and though Appeals Court single justice allowed motion "subject to possible further action by the panel assigned to decide the case," the rape indictment "was not part of the record in this case, and could not have been included in the appendix even if the motion to expand the record had been presented below," i.e., to the trial court judge; **it could not be made part of the "record" because it "was not argued or considered either when the complaint issued or when the motion to dismiss was argued and allowed"**;

C v MacDonald **50 MAC 220, 225 n.12 (2000), affirmed 435 M 1005 (2001) (SJC agreeing with ruling & reasoning of Appeals Court on substantive issue)**—Commonwealth's assertion that judge had actually ordered something different from what docket reflected should have been pursued/settled by a motion to correct record (either M.R.Crim.P. 42 or M.R.App.P. 8(e));

C v Smith **38 MAC 324 (95)**—though probation revocation judge, during pendency of appeal from revocation, allowed Commonwealth's motion to "clarify" the record to include an additional further crime allegedly committed by D during probation period and allegedly before the judge in a copy of D's criminal record, Appeals Court did not accept such "clarification": this (very minor) crime was not actually mentioned during the hearing, though others were;

C v Pavao **423 M 798 (96)**—not accepting Commonwealth's argument for expansion of record, though Appeals Court in same case, **39 MAC 490, 497 n.6**, had allowed it; **policy of requiring sufficient on-record colloquy to assure voluntariness of jury waiver would be frustrated by going beyond record (to include D's jury trial waivers in other cases)**;

C v Rzepphiewski **431 M 48, 56 (2000)**—similar, re guilty plea & immigration/alien warning/advice required by G.L. c. 278, § 29D;

C v Bart B., a juvenile **424 M 911, 916 (97)**—failure of trial counsel to request stenographer at trial (G.L. c. 218, § 27A(h)) argued to be ineffective assistance of counsel, but SJC held that deficient record (produced instead electronically) failed to demonstrate that sidebar conferences (virtually unrecorded) would likely have provided the juvenile with a successful appellate issue; Orwellian, isn't it? analysis instead should be that failure has deprived D of right to any meaningful appeal, & prejudice lies in the forfeiture of that proceeding, regardless of what result there would be: see *Roe v Flores-Ortega* **528 US 470 (2000)** failure to file notice of appeal after D has instructed counsel to do so = ineffective assistance; to show prejudice from ineffective assistance here = demonstrate reasonable probability that D would have timely appealed but for counsel's deficient performance; **need not show that appeal would have afforded relief; prejudice is "the forfeiture of a proceeding itself"**;

M.R.App.P. 8(b)(2)—filing of notice of appeal in Superior Court clerk's office triggers clerk's responsibility to order transcripts from court reporters

M.R.App.P. 8(b)(3)—if trial court proceedings have been tape-recorded rather than stenographically recorded, trial counsel must not only file the notice of appeal, but must also order cassette copies of the recorded proceedings in the trial court, and thereafter designate what portions of the record must be transcribed for the appeal.

C v Pudder 41 MAC 930 (96)—failure of trial counsel to order tape copies of trial at same time he filed notice of appeal resulted in the destruction of the audiotape recording before successor counsel attempted to obtain copy; **THOUGH TRIAL COUNSEL'S MOTION TO WITHDRAW HAD BEEN ALLOWED, HE "REMAINED RESPONSIBLE FOR THE PROSECUTION OF THE DEFENDANT'S APPEAL"** until such time as successor counsel filed a notice of appearance;

C v McCormick 48 MAC 106 (99)—appellate counsel faulted for failing to attempt to reconstruct record of all bench conferences, unrecorded by District Court "taping" system;

C v Kelly 57 MAC 201 (2003)—though D claimed on appeal that he should have new trial because missing portions of trial record made review of certain claims impossible, Court rejected on ground that there was no evidence that D's counsel filed any motion to reconstruct record; when transcript = unavailable, hearing should be held to attempt to reconstruct the proceedings;

C v Dunnington 390 M 472, 479 (83)—"we are not obliged to address the problem in the instant case because (D) has produced a bench trial record that 'is so deficient that we are in no position to rule on the sufficiency of the evidence'";

C v Lopez 426 M 657, 659 n.3 (98) citing G.L. c. 221, § 27A, implemented by SJC Rule 1:12—stenographic notes may be destroyed after six years unless there's order for transcript not yet completed or notes are otherwise subject of a court order;

Morales v Appeals Court 427 M 1009 (98)—pro se litigant's effort, over course of YEARS, to obtain transcript of plea colloquy produced two SJC opinions; this second one held that G.L. c. 261, § 27D provides "detailed and professedly EXCLUSIVE procedure for taking an appeal from the denial of a request for fees and costs made under § 27C" (and D here cited instead G.L. c. 231, § 118); trial court SHOULD HAVE HELD HEARING on D's motion for production of transcript (G.L. c. 261, § 27C(3) and (4)); D must appeal any future denial of such motion within seven days, id., § 27D;

G.L. c. 261, § 27D—(per 2004 amendment) appeals from denial of relief from costs and fees: appeal is to single justice of Appeals Court if denial is in Superior, Land, Probate, or Housing Ct. departments; appeal is to Superior Court if denial is in juvenile court; appeal is to appellate division if denial is in District Court or Boston Municipal Court;

C v Picher 46 MAC 409, 416–17 n.8 (99)—strongly suggests photographing ID photo array before it's returned to police, or at least recording "the numbers of the photos used" in array, so it can be recreated for appellate record;

C v Lawson 425 M 528, 532 n.7 (97)—instead of refusing to do so on ground that request for "marking" was untimely, trial judge should have marked for ID the exhibit he excluded, for appellate record;

C v O'Brien 419 M 470, 477 (95)—though SJC held that it was error to withhold from defense counsel (on purported basis that it was prosecutor's "work product") a document used by prosecutor to refresh witness's recollection on stand, failure to have document made part of record meant that Court could not find that there was "prejudice" from the error; (NOTE: if prosecutor won't make it available voluntarily for record, obtain court order by using M.R.App.P. 8(e), concerning expansion of record to include "something material" omitted from the appellate record by "error"); (but cf. *C v Johnson* 354 M 534, 546 (74) "no requirement that a defendant, denied access to evidence that might prove helpful in his defence, must make a specific showing of just what the evidence would have proved and how far he was prejudiced by the withholding");

but see *Rodriguez v Commonwealth* 449 M 1029 (2007)—G.L. c. 211, § 3 petition to force judge to mark for ID records whose production he had denied D under *Dwyer* [448 M 122] protocol, so that in normal course of appeal if convicted, appellate court could evaluate "prejudice", but SJC denies, saying that later appeal, if successful, would result [only] in order that documents be produced and examined "to determine whether" D entitled to new trial;

C v Fossa 40 MAC 563 (96)—D might have prevailed on motion for new trial due to nondisclosure of lengthy police report recording interview of witnesses and failure to grant short continuance on this basis IF he had explicitly stated the "prejudice" (rather than flat assertions that he could have cross-examined better): making belatedly-disclosed document part of record, **id. at 564 n.2**, and establishing what arguments were made for a continuance, by obtaining tape/transcript or a reconstruction of proceedings before "assignment" judge sending case to trial session, **id. at 565 n.3**, might have helped;

C v Woody 429 M 95, 98–99 (2000)—when there's transcription "gap" through no fault of appellant and appellant believes gap immaterial to appeal, appellant must serve on appellee the available transcript with statement that it's acceptable; if appellee disagrees, it's appellee's burden to settle record pursuant to M.R.App.P. 8(c) and (e); BUT if appellate court later finds that appellant was wrong in appraisal of adequacy of transcript to present claims made, court "may decline to consider" them;

C v Lampron 65 MAC 340 (2005)—though D claimed that he was without (substitute) counsel when jury returned verdict and bail was revoked, this representation was based only upon "the absence of an identifying reference to substitute counsel in the record"; record, however, didn't persuade Appeals Court of the necessary fact of counsel's absence, and it was D's burden to correct the record, by stipulation between parties, or presentation of their differences to judge who heard the case;

***Foley v Commonwealth* 429 M 496, 497 n.2 (99)**— (full bench consideration of G.L. c. 211, § 3 matter) appellant held to "suffer the consequences of any deficiency in the record," so to extent facts in dispute, SJC "adopt(s) the facts asserted by the Commonwealth," which was respondent/appellee here;

***C v Hill* 49 MAC 58, 65 (2000)**—following dismissal after a hearing on D's motion, Commonwealth appealed, & D moved to dismiss appeal because Commonwealth didn't provide transcript of motion hearing, instead relying only on judge's findings, included in appendix to Commonwealth brief: SJC held that transcript here not needed to make the required appellate evaluation BUT Commonwealth should have obtained from D a stipulation as to what parts of proceedings were unnecessary to the appeal (see M.R.App.P. 8(b)(2));

***C v Aboulaz* 44 MAC 144 (98)**—AFTER conviction was reversed on appeal and required finding of NG was ordered to be entered (but before rescript issued to the trial court, because Commonwealth obtained a stay of such issuance), sexual assault complainant came to believe that some of her trial testimony had been omitted from the record; court stenographer was prompted to check and provided two additional pages of testimony, and trial judge granted motion to correct the record; Appeals Court granted rehearing on revised record and affirmed conviction; record correction after issuance of the rescript to the trial court would not have been entertained (id. at 148); D was allowed, after allowance of rehearing, opportunity to consider/brief issues other than the required finding of NG;

***C v Robles* 423 M 62, 72–74 (96)**—SJC allowed obliteration of D's appellate issue upon the trial judge's "correction" of the record on prosecutor's motion (after D filed brief), to reflect oral "affirmation" of verdict by jurors, not recorded in transcript prepared by court reporter (and despite court reporter's affidavit reasserting that transcript as originally prepared was a verbatim record of what reporter had heard that day); see also ***C v Fling* 67 MAC 232 (2006)**—judge could grant Commonwealth motion to "correct docket" with evidence from ass't clerk-magistrate and trial prosecutor's file documents & affidavit, thereby defeating D's Rule 36 issue on appeal; "trial judge's correction is essentially conclusive";

***C v Colleran* 452 M 417, 429–30 & n.9 (2008)**— appellate issue cognizable in transcript as produced was said to be "an obvious stenographic error" in punctuation and separation of paragraphs;

***C v Harris* 376 M 74, 77–78 (78)**—when transcript is unavailable through no fault of parties, new trial should be ordered IF proceedings cannot be reconstructed sufficiently to present D's claims; D is entitled to "meaningful" appeal; ***C v Pudder* 41 MAC 930 (96)** D must make effort to reconstruct the record from sources other than tape/steno record before seeking a new trial based on the absence of a transcript;

***Rodriguez v Commonwealth* 419 M 1006, 1007 (94)**—D's motion for reconstruction of suppression hearing, filed after he learned that stenographer had lost record of suppression hearing, was denied by Superior Court judge, and D attempted to obtain order for such hearing by petitioning under G.L. c. 211, § 3; SJC full bench claimed that D had pending both his appeal in Appeals Court and a motion for new trial in trial court and hadn't show that relief was unavailable "in the normal course of appeal", a prerequisite to relief under G.L. c. 211,§ 3;

***Hardy v US* 375 US 277, 290 (64) (Goldberg, J., concurring)**—lawyer appointed to represent D shouldn't be required to delegate responsibility for determining whether error occurred at trial to trial participants "whose conduct may have formed the very basis for the errors";

***Dobbs v Zant* 506 US 357 (93)**—capital defendant on habeas petition argued that trial counsel provided ineffective assistance at sentencing; Supreme Court held that reliance upon testimony of counsel to refute alleged deficiencies in his own closing argument was not appropriate after actual transcript (earlier said to be unavailable) turned up; review instead of "complete record" necessary; BUT SEE M.R.App.P. 8(e) ("Correction or Modification of the Record. If any difference arises as to whether the record truly discloses what occurred in the lower court, the difference shall be submitted to and settled by that court and the record made to conform to the truth");

***C v Quinones* 414 M 423 (93)**—upholding reconstruction of guilty plea proceedings, in which plea/R.30 judge relied on testimony from court reporter and D's plea attorney AND on his own recollections/customary practices, "particularly . . . when . . . (D) produces no evidence to the contrary"; SJC asserted that judge in circumstances was "not acting as a witness against the defendant in a constitutional sense";

***C v Shea* 46 MAC 196 (99)**—D seeking to withdraw guilty pleas after lapse of 15 years suffered misfortune of news reporter's retention of the transcript copy which he had ordered for use in his reporting; "clarity of the transcript removes any concern" Court might have had about its accuracy (or the validity of the guilty pleas); though M.R.App.P. 8(c) contemplates a hearing for determination of accuracy of statement of the evidence constructed from best available means, D here hadn't requested such hearing;

***C v Long* 419 M 798, 805 (95)—if one party makes assertion of fact/present circumstance & adverse party doesn't correct/dispute on record, it will be taken as true on appeal;**

15-B.11. Stays of Execution of Sentence Pending Appeal

M.R.Crim.P. 31(a)—sentence of imprisonment "may" be stayed; 31(c) **sentence of "fine"/'costs" "SHALL" be stayed** by judge "if there is a diligent perfection of appeal";

M.R.App.P. 6(a)—must ordinarily first seek stay from "lower court"; if motion for stay of sentence is made to appellate court, must show that stay has been sought from and denied by trial court (and what reasons for denial were there given) OR that seeking stay in lower court is not practicable; judge may make order relative to custody of D, or for admitting him to bail; M.R.App.P. 6(c) Commonwealth may move to vacate stay of sentence if D fails to move appeal along;

C v Levin **7 MAC 501 (79)**—to obtain stay, must show "meritorious issue," one worthy of appellate consideration and discussion (needn't show certainty of success); two categories of consideration on stay, security (possibility of flight to avoid punishment, or of further criminal acts during appeal, considering factors such as roots in community, familial status, employment, prior criminal record) and meritorious issue (pure question of law/legal judgment); if trial judge denies stay on basis of security, appellate court judge will not likely hold differently (abuse of discretion standard in "review"), BUT as to "meritorious issue," appellate court judge should make independent determination;

C v Allen **378 M 489 (79) cites G.L. c. 279, § 4 (discretionary power to grant stay lies with sentencing judge, or single justice of Appeals Court or SJC)**—single justice of SJC or Appeals Court won't "ordinarily" act on stay unless it has first been presented to sentencing judge; single justice doesn't "review" decision of sentencing judge, but considers the matter anew, exercising his own judgment and discretion; if stay is denied by Appeals Court single justice, D may seek review of questions of law by panel of Appeals Court AND can ask SJC single justice for relief; while SJC single justice has discretion, he may deny summarily and should review only re: errors of law in prior determinations; same factors specified in G.L. c. 276, § 58 (bail before trial) may properly be considered under G.L. c. 279, § 4 (stays); appeal must have issue worthy of presentation, offering some reasonable possibility of success, and this is pure question of law/legal judgment; full panel may exercise own judgment (no deference to single justice's opinion required), BUT SEE *Christian v Commonwealth* 446 M 1003 (2006)—SJC full bench reviewed SJC single justice's denial of stay only for "errors of law";

C v Hodge **380 M 851 (80)**—(Commonwealth appeal of trial judge's allowance of stay, first to single justice, then to full bench) single justice is not REQUIRED to make independent exercise of discretion after trial judge's action; re: security considerations, trial judge appropriately has discretion, so single justice may properly decline to "substitute his discretion" for that of trial judge; re: meritorious issue, a question of law/legal judgment, single justice also not REQUIRED to make independent discretionary judgment, at least where trial judge has allowed the stay; if, on other hand, "the trial judge has refused to grant a stay, the need for the single justice to exercise his independent dis-

cretion on the defendant's application may be particularly acute," **id. at 855–56**;

C v Cohen **455 M 634 (2010)**—EACH judge or justice has power to consider matter of stay "anew," and may exercise discretion in reviewing a stay request, re: both security and likelihood of success on appeal; SJC disavows any implication in *Hodge* 380 M at 855 that single justice may not exercise own discretion re: security (and must instead defer to trial judge on security);

Christian v Commonwealth **446 M 1003 (2006)**—if judge in trial court and single justice of Appeals Court deny the stay, "presumptive avenue for review is before a panel of the Appeals Court"; here, D next petitioned instead to SJC single justice, so when that judge denied stay, SJC full bench would review only "for errors of law" & found none;

Stewart v Commonwealth **413 M 664 (92)**—bail pending appeal of the allowance of a Rule 30 motion is discretionary BUT here, R.30 relief granted was only resentencing on an armed assault in dwelling conviction, and D had made no claim that additional conviction, for 2d degree murder, was illegitimate, so that sentence remained in place and could not appropriately be "stayed"; bail OK if appellate result can be "a reversal of the conviction, an order for a new trial or a term of imprisonment less than the time he already has served, including the time the appellate process requires";

C v Beauchemin **410 M 181, 185–86 (91)**—though D argued that "stay" condition of house arrest was sufficiently draconian to entitle him to credit for this time against his sentence of imprisonment (after appeal was unsuccessful), SJC held it was legitimate custody condition under M.R.Crim.P. 31(a);

C v Aviles **422 M 1008 (96)**—Commonwealth did have right to petition under G.L. c. 211, § 3 to seek change in conditions of stay of execution of sentence as set by Appeals Court single justice, although increased bail set by SJC single justice on that petition prevented D's release on stay, and Appeals Court later reversed conviction (**40 MAC 440, 441 n.1 (96)**); "(i)t may be preferable (however) for a single justice of (SJC) to decline to act on a request for a stay pending appeal, leaving (or perhaps transferring) the issue in the court where the underlying appeal will be heard," **422 M at 1010**;

C v Senior **429 M 1021, 1022 (99)**—after Appeals Court single justice's allowance of stay motion, Commonwealth petitioned pursuant to G.L. c. 211, § 3 for an order vacating the allowance of the stay; SJC single justice denied petition; on appeal to full bench, SJC stated that SJC single justice could reasonably have concluded that Appeals Court single justice neither abused discretion nor committed error of law in granting stay;

C v Vith Ly **450 M 16 (2007)**—execution of D's sentences, after unexplained delay of sixteen years on part of Commonwealth to have sentences executed, would violate due process & "principles of fundamental fairness"; sentences had been stayed pending appeal, but after some convictions were affirmed, Commonwealth did not seek execution of those sentences immediately or upon D's subsequent contacts with law enforcement;

15-B.12. Preservation of Issues for Appeal

15-B.12.a. General

See also Chapters 12-M, 11-B&C;

C v Long **419 M 798, 805 (95)**—if one party makes assertion of fact/present circumstance & adverse party doesn't correct/dispute on record, it will be taken as true on appeal;

M.R.Crim.P. 22, and Reporter's Notes—OBJECTION at time of ruling & must make known desired action unless had no opportunity; "exceptions", previously required, were abolished by the Rule; while party "MAY" (NOT "MUST," NOT "SHALL") state "precise legal grounds of" objection, party "SHALL NOT" argue or discuss such grounds unless requested by judge;

C v Brown **449 M 747, 760 (2007)**—word "may" "is permissive rather than mandatory" (language NOT in context of Rule 22 or appellate preservation);

C v Bettencourt **447 M 631 (2006)**—after trial court judge ordered suppression of evidence, SJC refused to consider Commonwealth's argument for reversal which was first raised on appeal; "Trial judges cannot be expected to rule, and indeed should not, on theories not presented to them, and defendants cannot respond to arguments not made at the trial level. Our system is premised on appellate review of that which was presented and argued below";

C v Miranda **22 MAC 10 (86)**—without objection at trial, appellate court won't consider, but there are five exceptions: (1) G.L. c. 278, § 33E, SJC review of convictions for first degree murder; (2) "substantial risk of miscarriage of justice" standard enunciated in *C v Freeman* **352 M 556, 563–64 (67)**; (3) "clairvoyance" exception for constitutional errors, basis/analysis for which wasn't sufficiently developed prior to trial; (4) ineffective assistance of counsel; (5) revival by way of motion for new trial, when trial judge considers substantively and rules on issues not raised at trial (**NOTE: #5 NO LONGER "REVIVES"—see *C v Curtis* 417 M 619 (94), unless motion for new trial is filed/ruled upon prior to direct appeal—see *C v Hallet* 427 M 552 (98)**); for application of "substantial risk" standard, there must be (a) genuine question of guilt, (b) plausible that result might have been otherwise but for error & (c) apparent that failure to object not reasonable tactical decision;

C v Hallet **427 M 552, 554 (98)**—when motion for new trial is filed before D's direct appeal proceeds, and when motion judge elects to consider substantively one or more issues which were not preserved for appellate review at the trial itself, those issues are considered on appeal "as if . . . fully preserved at trial for appellate review"; but see *C v Curtis* **417 M 619 (94)** if motion for new trial is instead

acted upon after direct appeal fails, trial judge's substantive consideration of issue will not resurrect it so as to yield a more favorable standard of review; **now see *C v Bly* 444 M 640, 647–51 (2005)**;

C v Stroyny **435 M 635, 640 (2002)**—Rule 30 motion judge approached claims of ineffective assistance of counsel in two ways; re: some evidence D claims erroneously admitted, judge simply rejected claim of ineffectiveness by ruling that counsel's failure to object to the evidence did not show "ineffectiveness", and judge didn't consider whether evidence was properly admitted; as to these issues, SJC applies "substantial likelihood of a miscarriage of justice" standard of review; re: other evidence, judge affirmatively addressed substantive merits of underlying evidentiary issues (and ruled that because evidence was admissible, no ineffectiveness in failing to object; "By reaching the merits of the underlying issues, the judge resurrected the otherwise unpreserved claims of error. We review those claims as if properly preserved by applying the prejudicial error standard of review"; **BUT NOW SEE:**

C v Bly **444 M 640 (2005)**—asserts that "near byzantine requirements to avoid resurrection" have been eliminated; citing *C v Randolph* **438 M 290, 294–96 (2002)**, says "assertions of unpreserved" error offered as the basis of a claim of ineffective assistance of counsel in a motion for new trial are evaluated in first degree murder cases under substantial likelihood of a miscarriage of justice standard and in all other cases under the standard in *C v Saferian* **366 M 89, 96 (74)**; In all cases, "assertions of unpreserved error remains [*sic*] unpreserved"; **"the power of resurrection is no longer viable and will no longer be recognized in criminal cases"** (at 651);

C v Amirault **424 M 618, 640 (97)**—Court wouldn't consider issue on appeal of denial of motion for new trial because D held to have waived the issue by not raising it on direct appeal;

C v Souza **44 MAC 238 (98)**—same;

C v Crawford **430 M 683, 688–89 (2000)**—similar, re failure to raise issue in first motion for new trial; compare/contrast *Bynum v Commonwealth* **429 M 705 (99)** when D won in Appeals Court summary order which contained dicta ("statement of law . . . not essential to that court's conclusion in his favor") that new indictment wouldn't be barred by double jeopardy, D did NOT waive double jeopardy argument by failing to seek further appellate review of the Appeals Court's opinion; (**"It is a curious argument that says that a party who has prevailed on a point in the Appeals Court and does not seek further review is bound by a statement of law in the Appeals Court opinion that is not essential to that court's conclusion in his favor"**); But see **Law of the Case/Collateral Estoppel/Waiver** *C v Williams* **431 M 71 (2000)** though Commonwealth filed a notice of appeal of order suppressing evidence, Commonwealth didn't pursue it by application in SJC for leave to seek interlocutory appeal, and subsequently moved to dismiss indictment because due to suppression order, "no admissible evidence to sustain this indictment"; when, in completely unrelated case, SJC issued decision which would have supported Commonwealth and required denial of motion to suppress, Commonwealth obtained new indictment; HELD: Commonwealth's failure to pursue appeal of suppression order made it law of the case, & Commonwealth = collaterally estopped from 2d indictment; dismissal required; (*see also* "*collateral estoppel*" *section in Chapter 19, "Double Jeopardy*");

C v Shaughessy **455 M 346 (2009)**—Commonwealth did not object to judge's acceptance of ex parte affidavit from D (supporting discovery of informant), BUT because "timely filed" motion to reopen hearing, on which judge held hearing and considered and denied objections on merits, issue = preserved;

C v McGilvery **74 MAC 508 (2009)**—after trial judge erred in allowing Commonwealth to amend complaint substantively after closing arguments at bench trial, Commonwealth agreed before Appeals Court single justice on D's motion for stay of sentence that amendment was one of substance, and took same position in joint motion before trial judge to vacate conviction (trial judge nonetheless denied motion): Commonwealth was therefore estopped from arguing in direct appeal of the conviction that amendment was only one of "form";

C v Douglas **75 MAC 643 (2009)**—because judge withdrew "per se" theory in operating under/motor vehicle homicide case (though complaint had charged both theories), reversal because no expert testimony (contra *Colturi* requirement, 448 M 817–18: though evidence of impairment was strong & trial counsel didn't object, lab supervisor's testimony as to blood alcohol content may have been "the most compelling evidence of intoxication"; substantial risk of miscarriage of justice found, because "may have influenced the verdict of guilt" (75 MAC at 653);

C v Watkins **63 MAC 69 (2005)**—despite fact that trial was to a judge rather than jury, counsel was required to object to judge's questioning of witness in order to preserve issue for appeal;

C v Paiva **71 MAC 411, 415 n.2 (2008)**—when judge barred testimony of defense witness as sanction for reciprocal discovery violation, counsel should have given reasons for admitting despite absence of notice, and suggested less serious sanction, BUT judge rebuffed counsel's efforts to state grounds for objecting to ruling;

15-B.12.b. Failure to Object as Ineffective Assistance of Counsel?

C v Frisino **21 MAC 551, 553–56 (86)**—failure to object was ineffective assistance of counsel;

C v Anslono **9 MAC 867, 868 (80)**—same;

C v Mahoney **68 MAC 561, 562 (2007)**—a mistake by counsel that has effect of waiving D's entitlement to a dismissal "would surely constitute a substantial risk of a miscarriage of justice";

C v Wright **411 M 678 (92)**—G.L. c. 278, § 33E standard (first degree murder convictions) of substantial likelihood of miscarriage of justice is more favorable to D than constitutional ineffective assistance standard (concerning failure to object/preserve issue for appellate review as constituting ineffective assistance of counsel); see also *C v Kater* **432 M 404, 411 (2000)** though appellate court considered issues waived because they hadn't been raised (though available) in prior appeals, SJC nonetheless had to consider them under § 33E;

C v Sowell **34 MAC 229, 231–37, 236 n.4 (93)**—discussion of nonpreservation at trial (or failure to raise issue on direct appeal) as ineffective assistance of counsel;

C v Simmarano **50 MAC 312 (2000)**—failure to object to lack of jury instruction on defense (& instruction wasn't requested by counsel, either) and failure to respond appropriately to prosecutor's illegitimate (but accepted) "hearsay" objection held ineffective assistance of counsel (on direct appeal rather than via M.R.Crim.P. 30 & appeal from denial of motion); see also cases in Chapter 2E herein;

C v Squailia **429 M 101, 110–11 (99)**—D's argument on appeal that trial counsel was ineffective in failing to file motion to suppress statements hampered by D's signature on record document saying "after consultation with counsel no motion to suppress will be filed . . . re: statements" (though merits were addressed, Court finding reasonable tactic/statements useful to defense planned prior to trial);

C v Johnston **60 MAC 13, 21–22 (2003)**—trial counsel's failure to specify, as precise ground in motion to suppress, that Miranda warnings omitted info that D had right to have attorney present during questioning meant that issue wasn't preserved for appeal: failure might be ineffective assistance of counsel, but Rule 30 motion held necessary to raise here; SEE other cases in Chapter 2E, regarding ineffective assistance of counsel, for various failures, including failures to file suppression and other motions;

15-B.12.c. Objection to Disposition

C v Resende **427 M 1005 (98)**—Commonwealth failed to object on record to judge's 'continuance without a finding' disposition;

In the matter of Rudnicki **421 M 1006 (95)**—continuance without a finding, which resulted in dismissal of case before denial of D's petition for writ of mandamus and G.L. c. 211, § 3 action (which followed clerk's refusal to accept D's "notice of appeal" of the CWOF), resulted in no appealable final order, and appellate court had no jurisdiction over the criminal matter;

C v LaFrance **402 M 789 fn 3 (88)**—probation condition that probation officer could search D & premises anytime = "enough to warrant an immediate judicial challenge" even though no action had yet been taken against probationer; "assent"/"voluntary waiver" inapplicable given "coercive quality of the circumstance in which a defendant seeks to avoid incarceration by obtaining probation on certain conditions";

Roullett v Quincy Division of the District Court Dep't **395 M 1008 (85)**—G.L. c. 211, § 3 not necessary to challenge restitution amount which was ordered five months after sentencing (which had included merely generic "restitution to be paid" to victim); though judge refused to allow motion to appeal merely a portion of the sentence, D could have appealed from this ruling, or could have moved to revise or revoke under M.R.Crim.P. 29(a), or for new trial under M.R.Crim.P. 30(b);

15-B.12.d. Continuance

C v Fleenor **39 MAC 25, 28 n.4 (95)**—alleged local practice of merely telling clerk that D objects to continuance not recognized as preserving issue (speedy trial); clerk's minutes, docket entries, and transcripts of available audiotapes instead viewed as official record;

C v Sanchez **74 MAC 31 (2009)**—D's failure to object to order scheduling trial date beyond statutory deadline = waiver of right to trial within statutorily-set period for SDP trial; assertion that "the Commonwealth" has neither "sole responsibility" nor "sole power" to bring D to trial, because "court ultimately sets trial dates";

15-B.12.e. Motions to Suppress

C v Whelton **428 M 24, 25–26 (98)**—"the denial of a motion to suppress evidence on constitutional grounds . . . is reviewable without further objection at trial," laying to rest (albeit without mentioning) contrary assertions in *C v Acosta* **416 M 279 (93)** (even as amended) and *C v Hill* **38 MAC 982 (95)** (concerning failure to object when witness ID'd D in court at trial, though D had previously pressed motion to suppress prospective in-court ID as being fatally tainted by unconstitutionally suggestive earlier ID);

C v Woods **419 M 366, 370 (95), citing** *C v Adams* **389 M 265, 269–70 (83)**—even if D hasn't moved to suppress his statements, burden is still on Commonwealth "upon seasonable objection, to prove affirmatively, prior to the admission of (D's) statements, that the statements were properly obtained and that the defendant waived his rights";

C v Garcia **34 MAC 386, 391–92 (93)**—in reviewing judge's ruling on the suppression motion, appellate court may not rely on facts as developed at trial; see also cases cited; see also *C v Bettencourt* **447 M 631 (2006)**—Commonwealth can't try to overturn on appeal a judge's suppression order on theory never advanced below in testimony or argument;

C v McDuffee **379 M 353, 357 (79)**—**"absent a proper objection at trial, an appellate claim of error 'brings nothing for review to an appellate court'";** notwithstanding, cf., *C v Delaney* **425 M 587, 601–09 (97)** (Lynch, J., dissenting)—where evidence before jury has been distorted, "the failure to object and possibly obtain a curative instruction may be the very thing which permits the remarks to have their maximum prejudicial effect"; (in light of prosecutor's crucial misstatements of evidence) "a jury's verdict can be only as fair as the trial allows";

Redgate, petitioner **417 M 799, 801–02 (94)**—**appellate court has discretion to consider issue not otherwise properly before it when it's presented with argument and a complete record on which to examine issue; failure to present issue at "trial" level not a bar to presentation on appeal if claim is one "whose constitutional significance was not established until after (D's) trial";**

15-B.12.f. Motions in Limine

C v Good **409 M 612 (92)**—to preserve issue for appeal, D must object after admission of evidence, even though motion in limine had been pressed & denied;

C v Gabbidon **398 M 1, 7 (86)**—same;

C v Shea **401 M 731 (88)**—same;

C v Keniston **423 M 304, 308 (96)**—same;

C v Oeun Lam **420 M 615, 617 n.5 (95)**—same;

C v Whelton **428 M 24, 25–26 (98)**—same;

C v Hardy **47 MAC 679, 680, 686 (99)**—same, but court found "substantial risk of a miscarriage of justice" from admission of purported "spontaneous utterance," and reversed conviction despite inadequate preservation;

C v Martin **57 MAC 272 (2003)**—same, but reversing for repeated reference to irrelevant "alias" use by D;

C v Lonardo **74 MAC 566 (2009)**—D's motion in limine to bar "expert" testimony that everyone "on the street" who dealt with "runners" knew that vehicle 'accident' cases they brought to attorneys were "staged"/ fraudulent did not preserve issue without "contemporaneous objection to the testimony";

C v Little **453 M 766 (2009)**—judge's ruling on motion in limine was that priors for drug distribution would be admitted to impeach D (in drug distribution trial), and this caused reversal, despite fact that D failed to preserve issue by objecting at trial;

15-B.12.g. Jury Issues: Impanelment, Extraneous Influences

C v LaFaille **430 M 44, 51 (99)**—defense counsel failed to show trial judge, before the jury selection process, that there was substantial risk that race might influence jury's decision, though trial evidence bore out that risk ("potential" interracial murder with interracial "sexual overtones"; either interracial rape or interracial murder would have REQUIRED individual voir dire on counsel's request); no relief on appeal; judge can't be expected to be clairvoyant and to "anticipate" such trial testimony;

C v Sosnowski **43 MAC 367, 373 (97)**—because D hadn't objected at trial to prosecutor's use of 9 out of 10 peremptories to eliminate men from jury, Commonwealth hadn't been allowed to explain challenges on proper basis; record was thus inadequate to establish that Commonwealth wouldn't have been able to justify challenges, and D couldn't prevail on appeal;

C v Paniacqua **413 M 796, 799–800 (92)**—mid-jury empanelment, D petitioned SJC single justice pursuant to G.L. c. 211, § 3, and justice agreed to reserve and report issue to full bench; because this would have been very lengthy process and D was being held on bail, D instead went forward with trial, announcing that he was not giving up his right to appeal the issue, BUT SJC held that he had waived it by going forward with trial;

C v McCaster **46 MAC 752, 760 (99)**—though Appeals Court was sympathetic to D's claim that trial judge should have made more explicit inquiry as to what extraneous info was given to them by three jurors, issue held waived by D's election to proceed with remaining eleven jurors rather than move for mistrial as repeatedly invited (implicitly, D forfeits either right to trial by first jury impaneled or to an inquiry thorough enough to discern whether that first jury has been tainted: bad rationale);

15-B.12.h. Evidentiary Issues During Trial

C v Hoppin **387 M 25, 29 n.4 (82)**—judge overruled general objection and denied counsel's repeated requests for side bar conference; request for mistrial made thereafter was made at earliest opportunity and preserved appellate rights;

C v Jewett **392 M 558, 561 n.3 (84)**—counsel's offer of proof cut off by judge;

C v Adderley **36 MAC 918, 920 (94)**—judge's refusal to allow counsel to make offer of proof meant that appellate court would assume witness would have supported D's alibi, would be able to recall what time his conversation with D occurred, & that testimony about D's clothing would have been helpful to D;

C v Delrio **22 MAC 712, 721–22 n.12 (86)**—despite fact that trial judge refused to let counsel approach bench and thereafter left courtroom immediately after excusing jury for the day, counsel put his "position on the record" in judge's absence;

C v Parker **12 MAC 955, 956 (81)**—once objected-to evidence has been admitted, appeal rights aren't waived when counsel merely ceases further objection, doesn't move to strike, and/or pursues rehabilitation;

C v Charles **57 MAC 595, 598 n.7 (2003)**—when co-D fails to object after another co-D, non-objecting co-D gets review of issue as if preserved: judge was on notice of objection, & facts as to the two Ds weren't different;

C v Dunton **397 M 101, 102 n.2 (86)**—when judge asserts that D's "rights are protected/saved", counsel is relieved of responsibility for specific/focused objection;

C v Grenier **415 M 680, 686 n.8 (93)**—same, re: jury instruction issue (no need to object at end of jury charge);

C v Stockhammer **409 M 867 (91)**—counsel's repeated efforts to make offer of proof preserved error;

C v Blake **409 M 146 (91)**; *C v Allen* **29 MAC 373 (90)**; *C v Chase* **26 MAC 578 (88)**—counsel's failure to make offer of proof justified exclusion of evidence;

C v Selby **426 M 168, 170 (97)**—because counsel did not object to judge's exclusion of cross-examination question (but see policy of elimination of "exceptions" requirement, Reporter's Notes to M.R.Crim.P. 22) and did not proffer why evidence sought was relevant and admis-

sible, SJC reviewed issue under standard of "substantial risk of a miscarriage of justice," i.e., as if nonpreserved;

C v Navarro **39 MAC 161, 166 (95)**—**after D objection and admission of evidence "de bene," D must later move to strike the evidence when nothing cures the original foundational deficiency** or other objectionable character; without "strike" motion, issue here held not preserved for appeal (so review for "substantial risk" only);

C v Bailey **12 MAC 104, 106 (81)**—error has to be called to judge's attention immediately, or when aggrieved party first learns of it;

C v Foster **411 M 762 (91)**—issue not preserved for appeal where objection made after witness answers objectionable question (& there's no motion to strike);

C v Howell **49 MAC 42, 48 n.7 (2000)**—unfair impeachment evidence introduced first by cop testimony in Commonwealth case, & again later in cross-examination of defense witness; D objected only to latter, but for preservation had to object to former;

C v Martin **417 M 187, 191 (94)**—Court rejects Commonwealth argument that objection was too late, ruling that objection was made precisely when it was "apparent that **any** response would be inadmissible";

C v Cancel **394 M 567, 570–71 (85)**—at time of objection, judge couldn't have known enough of necessary context, and D was obligated to renew his objection and move to strike the earlier testimony "once it became clear"; but see **id. at 573** "unlike previous issue, "the ground for exclusion should have been obvious to the judge and opposing counsel without stating it";

C v Tanner **66 MAC 432 (2006)**—cop's testimony that he asked possessor of drugs where he got them from and, after hearing response, that he went directly and placed D under arrest "was the functional equivalent of telling the jury that [man] had identified [D] as the man who had sold him cocaine"; objection to question concerning substance of cop's statements to drug possessor was sufficient to alert judge to hearsay issue; motion to strike or for curative instruction wasn't necessary to preserve issue;

C v Almeida **34 MAC 901, 902 n.2 (93)**—**need not intone "objection" if it's clear that counsel is conveying to judge what s/he wants the judge to do;**

C v Choice **47 MAC 907, 908 (99)**—counsel wanted cop-witness to reveal identity of man said to have led cop to D, and judge said "I'll deny the request"; D didn't have to intone word "objection" to preserve issue;

C v Gee **36 MAC 154, 158–59 (94)**—though not "a model of clarity," objection was adequate in context to alert judge to potential error so it could be avoided;

C v DeBenedetto **414 M 37 (92)**—counsel's statement, "if you do that judge, the dough might get shot in my face," deemed an objection; use of expressions which don't readily indicate objection cautioned against;

C v MacKenzie **413 M 498 (92)**—**counsel's objection, which conceded admissibility of evidence to which he was objecting, did not preserve issue for appeal;**

C v Huertas **34 MAC 939, 940–41 (93)**—trial counsel's explicit waiver of one theory of relevance (concerning evidence he was trying to introduce) made it unpreserved for appellate review;

C v Spence **38 MAC 88, 89–90 (95)**—when trial counsel has withdrawn objection in order to obtain benefit, issue will not likely be resurrected successfully on appeal;

C v Crimmins **46 MAC 489, 492 n.5 (99)—when no motion for required finding is made, or is made on grounds different from those argued on appeal, standard of review is "substantial risk of a miscarriage of justice," and "entire" record (not just Commonwealth case in chief) is used for this analysis;**

C v Villanueva **47 MAC 905, 907 (99)**—though co-D objected, D didn't; issue not preserved as to D; but see *C v Claudio* **418 M 108, 111–12 n.6 (94)** defense counsel's failure to raise point = excused because prosecutor's identical request had just been denied; *C v Biancardi* **421 M 251, 254 (95)** no reasonable prospect that judge would have repudiated his just-stated position;

15-B.12.i.   Closing Arguments

C v Kelly **417 M 266 (94)**—objection to DA's closing argument, with motion for mistrial, or "at the very least" curative instructions, preserved issue; D not required to renew request for curative instructions at close of charge;

C v Beaudry **445 M 577 (2005)**—if judge responds to closing argument objections with "focused, particularized instructions," counsel must object again after instructions (i.e., that they did not / could not cure argument error);

15-B.12.j.   Jury Instructions

M.R.Crim.P. 24(b)—regarding claimed error in jury instructions: party must object to the giving or failure to give instruction before jury begins deliberations, with specification re: "the matter to which he objects and the grounds of his objection";

C v Drewnowski **44 MAC 687, 691 (98)**—D's request for instruction on lesser included offense during charge conference sufficed to preserve issue despite D's failure to mention it again after jury charge; notwithstanding Commonwealth argument that D had decided to pursue "all or nothing," it was "more reasonable to infer" that D "believed an objection would be futile" because judge had refused the instruction before;

C v Engram **43 MAC 804, 806 n.2 (97)**—when judge responded in pre-instruction charge conference that he would not give requested instruction on interracial ID and would instead give only "standard ID charge," no need for postcharge objection, where the judge had given an instruction that was inconsistent with (D's) request" and there was "no reasonable prospect in the circumstances that, on objection, the judge would have repudiated his stated position";

C v Morgan **422 M 373, 377 (96)**—when D requested specific instruction and judge rejected request, issue pre-

served; D not required to "specifically object" after judge refused request for additional instruction;

C v Franchino **61 MAC 367 (2004)**—although defense counsel made three objections & "had little to show for his trouble" because judge kept missing the point, judge did provide additional instruction in response to each request, so counsel was not excused from objecting again to inadequate charge;

Grenier **415 M 680, 686 n.8 (93)**—when judge tells counsel his "rights are saved" re: jury instruction issue, not required to object at end of jury charge;

C v Horsman **47 MAC 262, 269 and n.9 (99)**—contrary to Commonwealth argument, D adequately preserved issue as to his requested jury instruction by objecting at end of charge to judge's failure to have given it; he was not required to ask for a "corrective" instruction (and had actually said that, at that point, it might do more harm than good);

C v Conley **34 MAC 50, 54 n.1 (93)**—judge failed to give counsel opportunity to object to jury instructions as required by R.24(b), so issue deemed preserved for review;

C v Fernandes **46 MAC 455, 462 and n.5 (99)**—suggestion that defense counsel's response, "OK," (to judge's refusal to give requested jury instruction because "no evidence that D was a purchaser") was waiver of instruction issue;

C v Cutty **47 MAC 671, 677 n.7 (99)**—defense counsel's failure to request alibi instruction forgiven as entirely understandable "in view of the judge's emphatic suppression of any mention of an alibi defense" (the latter causing reversal despite defense failure to give notice of alibi in discovery, since D himself had testified to such alibi);

C v Hooper **42 MAC 730, 734 (97)**—counsel's comment that "I believe there would need to be an instruction in terms of Humane Practice" served to preserve the issue, despite no written request and no objection to its omission from instructions given (but particularly because judge had sua sponte responsibility to instruct regarding this);

See also Chapter 11-B & -C for cases on motions in limine, objections, motions to strike, offers of proof & other requirements of record protection; Chapter 12-M for cases on noticing appeals & preserving appellate rights;

15-B.13.   Possible Adverse Consequences of Appeal

North Carolina v Pearce **395 US 711, 725–26 (69)**—to assure absence of retaliation against Ds who successfully appeal, "whenever a judge imposes a more severe sentence upon a D after a new trial, the reasons for his doing so must affirmatively appear. Those reasons must be based upon objective information concerning identifiable conduct on the part of the D occurring after the time of the original sentencing proceeding";

Texas v McCullough **475 US 134 (86)**—*NC v Pearce* has been limited on many grounds, one being that presumption of vindictiveness is inapplicable when the two sentences were assessed by different judges, who merely took different views of crime and the appropriate level of punishment;

(*McKune v Lile* **536 U.S. 24 (2002)**—requiring inmates to complete & sign "admission of responsibility" form, accepting responsibility for crimes for which they have been sentences, & to complete "sexual history form," detailing all prior sex activities, regardless of whether they're criminal (& have or haven't been prosecuted), as condition of participation in Kansas's "Sexual Abuse Treatment Program" doesn't amount to compelled self-incrimination despite loss/reduction of privileges for failure to participate; **OBJECT TO ANY SUCH CONDITIONS/PROCEDURE UNDER ARTICLE 12, DECLARATION OF RIGHTS, STATE CONSTITUTION**)

C v Hyatt **419 M 815, 819–24 (95)**—though under federal constitution as construed in *McCullough* (**475 US 134**), there would be no error, SJC adopts "as a common law principle a requirement that, when (D) is again convicted of a crime or crimes, the second sentencing judge may impose a harsher sentence or sentences only if the judge's reason or reasons for doing so appear on the record and are based on information that was not before the first sentencing judge";

C v Henriquez **66 MAC 912 (2006)**—sentence after successful appeal (consecutive 15–20 year terms on each of four counts of rape of child, + consecutive 10 years–10 years and a day) was longer than original 45–60 year term, so was prohibited unless supported by additional info; though Commonwealth claimed that continuing/further impact on child victim/family was qualifying additional info, court didn't reach issue of whether this would qualify as fresh info defeating presumption of vindictiveness because the resentencing judge actually placed less reliance on victim impact than did the first sentencing judge: "resentencing judge's reasons for the sentences he imposed accordingly cannot satisfy the *Hyatt* test, 419 Mass. at 823, to rebut the presumption of vindictiveness in a harsher resentencing";

C v Burden **48 MAC 232 (99)**, citing *Shabazz v Commonwealth* **387 M 291, 295–96 (82)**—successful challenge to one sentence imposed at same time as other sentences opens up "all the interdependent, lawful sentences for reconsideration without violating the double jeopardy clause, at least if the aggregate of the original sentences is not increased";

C v Garofalo **46 MAC 191, 195 (99)**—appellate decision invites judge to resentence D (more harshly, apparently) on affirmed conviction(s) when one or more convictions have been reversed on appeal;

C v Boyd **73 MAC 190 (2008)**—no lifetime community parole allowed because indictment did not explicitly assert "repeat offender"; other sentences remanded because judge might have altered them if he knew LCP not available;

C v Martin **425 M 718 (97)**—same; But cf. *C v Kruah* **47 MAC 341, 347–48 (99)** after holding that con-

victions for rape and assault with intent to rape were duplicative and ordering latter conviction vacated, also ordered resentencing on rape conviction because trial judge "may have been influenced in fixing sentence by the fact that the defendant had been convicted upon two indictments" rather than one;

C v Gagnon **419 M 1009 (95) on further appellate review of 37 MAC 626 (94)**—though Appeals Court had reduced the verdict of armed assault with intent to murder to assault with intent to murder, it ordered resentencing only on this revised verdict; because record showed that sentencing judge considered D's alleged shooting behavior when he sentenced on the armed robbery conviction (affirmed on appeal), armed robbery indictment had to be remanded for resentencing; citing "cf." *C v Clermy* **37 MAC 774, 779 (95), S.C. 421 M 325**, conviction of possession of cocaine was duplicative of conviction of possession with intent to distribute, so former ordered vacated and complaint dismissed; although "conviction for possession with intent to distribute cocaine is unaffected by this action," . . . "insofar as the trial judge may have been influenced in fixing sentence by the fact that the defendant had been convicted upon two complaints, resentencing is required";

C v Connolly **49 MAC 424 (2000) after Appeals Court reversed the conviction on which D was sentenced (& barred retrial), court invited Commonwealth on remand to remove the other previously "filed" (i.e., without sentence imposed) conviction and get sentence on it, citing *C v Brandano* 359 M 332, 336 (71) & *C v Bianco* 388 M 358, 364-65, 370 (83) for similar invitations when appellate court reversed one conviction & ordered judgment for D;**

C v Beauchamp **49 MAC 591 (2000)**—D unpleasantly surprised to learn that, after obtaining new trial via M.R.Crim.P. 30, his testimony given at trial #1 could be introduced in trial #2; case argued by D (*Harrison v U.S.* **392 US 219 (68)**) provides only **limited** exception;

C v Urkiel **63 MAC 445, 454 (2005)**—"commonly at retrial the slate is clear: changes of position are matter of course" (citations in original);

C v Zanetti **454 M 449 (2009)**—although SJC ruled required finding of not guilty should have been allowed on "joint venture" liability, Commonwealth wasn't precluded from retrying D solely as principal, where it couldn't be inferred from record that jury had unanimously acquitted D on "principal" liability theory; henceforth, judges "permitted" to use general verdict slip even when there is differing evidence as to principal or accomplice status of D; convictions to be upheld on appeal if there is sufficient evidence to prove D knowingly participated in commission of the crime with intent required to commit the crime (shift from 'joint venture' language to that of 'aiding and abetting');

15-B.14.   Dismissal of Appeals

Voluntary Dismissal of Appeal: M.R.App.P. 29—(a) if appeal isn't docketed yet in appellate court, appeal may be dismissed in lower court by parties signing and filing stipulation for dismissal OR upon motion/notice by appellant; (b) appeal may be dismissed on motion of appellant in appellate court upon such terms as may be agreed upon by the parties or fixed by the court; (c) if case is settled/disposed of while appeal is pending, counsel for appellant shall notify clerk of appellate court "forthwith";

Doe v Sex Offender Registry Bd. **429 M 654 (99)**—voluntary dismissal motion should ordinarily be granted, because "a litigant is entitled to win if he is in the right; he is not entitled to litigate and obtain an appellate opinion to his liking if his adversary has no desire to oppose the relief he seeks"; motion should be denied, however, if party is seeking dismissal to evade judicial review and frustrate court order, or if party claims the appeal is moot merely because the party is voluntarily refraining from the objected-to conduct; here, Bd. had been enjoined from the particular conduct, and was not merely refraining voluntarily;

Involuntary Dismissal of Appeal for Failure to File Brief: Appeals Court's "Standing Order Concerning Dismissals of Appeals ... for Lack of Prosecution"—whenever Appeals Court clerk hasn't received brief of appellant when it's due, clerk shall send notice, to attorney of record and to criminal appellant at his last known address and to all other parties or counsel of record, that the appeal of such appellant or the report, as the case may be, will be dismissed as to him for lack of prosecution unless, within thirty days of the date of such notice in a criminal case, the clerk shall receive a motion by such appellant to enlarge to a date certain set forth therein the time for serving and filing such brief and appendix, AND an affidavit of such appellant (or his attorney) which shall set forth all the facts which such appellant wishes to have considered by the single justice of this court, who will act on such motion. If no motion and affidavit are received, clerk shall forthwith dismiss appeal;

Evitts v Lucey **469 US 387 (85)**—counsel's incompetency caused dismissal of state appeal, so D gets it reinstated, retrial, or release via federal habeas corpus petition, 28 USC §§ 2241–54;

15-B.15.   "Mootness"

NOTE: appeal is not moot simply because D may have completed sentence prior to appellate resolution, as there may be extremely harsh collateral consequences of the conviction quite apart from imprisonment or probationary or parole conditions:

Sibron v NY **392 US 40, 50–58 (68)**—appeal not moot simply because D has been released from incarceration: collateral consequences noted, e.g., deportation, ineligibility to become citizen, statutory crimes with elements of prior convictions (recidivism statutes),

impeachment with conviction if testify in future, sentencing factor in later cases;

Evitts v Lucey **469 US 387, 391 n.4 (85)**—not "moot" because collateral consequences include deprivation of civil rights, such as suffrage and right to hold public office;

Carafas v LaVallee **391 US 234, 238 (68)**—not "moot" because collateral consequences of this conviction include bar from engaging in certain businesses, from being labor union official for period of time, from voting in any NY state election, from serving as juror;

C v Streeter **50 MAC 128 (2000)**—full service of sentence didn't make moot D's appeal from judgment revoking probation: collateral consequences include decisions about bail, sentencing & parole in future proceedings;

C v Johnson **75 MAC 903 (2009)**—R.30 motion properly heard despite D having served maximum sentence on each conviction, because of collateral consequences of conviction itself;

C v McCulloch **450 M 483 (2008)**—SJC has discretion to review case regardless of its mootness, and did so, meaning of M.R.Crim.P. 29 being of significant public importance & there being apparent uncertainty about it;

C v Argueta **73 MAC 564 (2009)**—D's appeal from denial of motion for new trial in case which was continued without a finding not moot, as there are serious collateral consequences from the continuance without a finding (federal courts count as conviction a CWOF following D's admission to sufficient facts, so "criminal history points" accrue for sentencing);

See also Chapter 14A, Sentencing, Collateral Consequences, for Mass. examples;

C v Resende **427 M 1005 (98)**—though Commonwealth filed notice of appeal of judge's order continuing cases without findings, Commonwealth failed to file a motion to stay the "sentences" pending appeal (i.e., six months' continuance with court costs and victim-witness fees to be paid), and cases had thus been dismissed (after the six months, as promised) before appeal was reached: issues were moot, appeal was dismissed (and furthermore, no record cite to support Commonwealth's claim of objecting to "continuance without a finding" disposition when it occurred, so not preserved for appeal);

Lenardis v Commonwealth **452 M 1001 (2008)**—though petitioner sought review by way of G.L. c. 211, § 3 of order to provide "buccal swab", single justice denied relief and before consideration by SJC full bench, petitioner complied with order: issue = moot;

15-B.16.   What Happens after Appellate Decision?

M.R.App.P. 27.1: further appellate review petition—file within twenty days after Appeals Court's decision: serve opposing counsel AND clerk, Appeals Court;

M.R.App.P. 27: petition for reconsideration/re-hearing—file within fourteen days after either Appeals Court's or SJC's decision;

M.R.App.P. 28—twenty-eight days after appellate court releases its decision, it will be "issued"/sent formally to lower court ("issuance of the rescript"); time may be shortened or enlarged by order; timely filing of petition for rehearing or further appellate review will stay issuance;

C v Vith Ly **450 M 16 (2007)**—execution of D's sentences, after unexplained delay of sixteen years on part of Commonwealth to have sentences executed, would violate due process & "principles of fundamental fairness"; sentences had been stayed pending appeal, but after some convictions were affirmed, Commonwealth did not seek execution of those sentences immediately or upon D's subsequent contacts with law enforcement;

C v Keon K **70 MAC 568 (2007)**—even if juvenile's appeal had been successful (issues of alleged improprieties in sentencing to DYS commitment), remedy would have been only resentencing, "not reversal and expungement";

15-B.17. Particular Results

C v Thibeau **384 M 762, 765 (81)**—because clear that evidence = insufficient after suppression (ordered on appeal), order entry of required finding of not guilty;

C v Straw **422 M 756, 763 (96)**—after suppression, no evidence to support conviction, required finding of not guilty must be allowed;

C v Pierre P. **53 MAC 215, 219 (2001)**—same;

C v Silva **366 M 402, 410–11 (74)**—same;

C v DuBois **44 MAC 294, 298 (98)**—after ordering suppression, judgment reversed, finding of guilt set aside, "judgment is to enter for the defendant";

C v Damian D **434 M 725, 731 (2001)**—required finding of not guilty ordered after suppression of critical evidence;

C v Holley **52 MAC 659, 666 (2001)**—same;

C v Rosenthal **52 MAC 707, 716 (2001)**—same;

C v Rodriguez **74 MAC 314 (2009)**—required finding of not guilty ordered on one charge (drug "possession") after suppression of one amount of cocaine, but ALSO reversal of other conviction because use of this evidence strengthened Commonwealth case on other charge, distribution of a different quantity of cocaine; superseded by S.C. on further review, 456 M 578 (2010);

C v Tyree **455 M 676 (2010)**—principle of 'harmless beyond a reasonable doubt' to be applied "with restraint"; claim of harmlessness "is most particularly vulnerable where the over-all strength of the Commonwealth's case radiates from a core of tainted evidence"; DA repeatedly tied D to crimes by referring to tainted evidence (which should have been suppressed);

15-C. INTERLOCUTORY APPEALS

15-C.1. M.R.Crim.P. 15; G.L. c. 278, § 28E

M.R.Crim.P. 15, INTERLOCUTORY Appeal—"absolute" right of interlocutory appeal is only for prosecution upon either allowance of defense motion to dismiss or denial of motion to transfer juvenile for trial as adult; must still be claimed, by timely notice of appeal (within 30 days of order); either D or Commonwealth may seek permission to appeal interlocutorily a ruling on a motion to suppress, BUT Standing Order of SJC, effective 2/1/97, requires party seeking interlocutory appeal of ruling on motion to suppress to file, **WITHIN SEVEN DAYS OF ISSUANCE OF NOTICE OF THE ORDER BEING APPEALED, OR SUCH ADDITIONAL TIME AS THE TRIAL JUDGE OR THE SINGLE JUSTICE SHALL ORDER**" (1) notice of appeal in trial court clerk's office, and (2) application to SJC single justice for leave to appeal (**"notwithstanding the ten day provision of M.R. Crim.P. 15(b)(1)"** there set forth as governing application for leave to appeal ruling on motion to suppress);

SJC Rule 2:21 as amended 434 M 1301 (2001) (appeal from single justice denial of relief on interlocutory ruling)—must give reasons why review of trial court decision can't be obtained on appeal from any final adverse judgment in trial court, or by other available means;

C v Wermers **61 MAC 182, 185–86 (2004)**—under Rule 15, Commonwealth may appeal dismissal, even though it's "without prejudice";

C v Turner **71 MAC 665 (2008)**—because, after ordering suppression of evidence, judge dismissed charges "for lack of prosecution" during the time period in which Commonwealth was entitled to seek leave to appeal, dismissal = reversed (as was suppression order);

C v Casimir **442 M 1031 (2004)**—D's motion to vacate guilty plea = essentially motion for new trial, so Commonwealth had right to appeal from order allowing it (& thus, G.L. c. 211, § 3 relief unavailable);

C v Guaba **417 M 746 (94)**—notice of appeal, for interlocutory appeal, must be filed within 30 days of day order is filed, NOT day order is delivered to party; delay in delivery MIGHT be deemed "good cause" to extend time for filing notice of appeal by appropriate motion and supporting affidavit under M.R.App.P. 4(c) or 14(b);

G.L. c. 278, § 28E ("Appeals by Commonwealth or D of Questions of Law in Criminal Cases Prior to Trial, etc.")—Commonwealth may appeal allowance of motions to dismiss and to suppress evidence, and denials of motions to transfer; Commonwealth may appeal orders "allowing a motion for appropriate relief under" M.R.Crim.P. (e.g., allowances of motions pursuant to M.R.Crim.P. 25 or 30: *C v Therrien* **383 M 529 (1981)**, or allowance of R.29 revoke and revise motion: *C v Amirault* **415 M 112 (93)**, or allowance of motion to continue (M.R.Crim.P. 10) complaint for one year, though Commonwealth appeal route for this = also G.L. c. 211, § 3: *C v Taylor* **428 M**

623 (99); but NOT motion to admit evidence under rape-shield statute: *C v Yelle* **390 M 678 (84)**); application for leave to appeal decision on suppression motion may be filed in the SJC by Commonwealth or D (but if denied, or if granted and interlocutory appeal is heard by single justice, the suppression issue is open to review by full court after trial "to the same extent as determinations of such motions not appealed under" this interlocutory procedure;

C v Yelle **390 M 678 (84)**—neither Rule 15 nor G.L. c. 211, § 3 for DA's interlocutory appeal of evidentiary ruling (even rape-shield); almost never G.L. c. 211, § 3 for DA;

C v Ringuette **443 M 1003 (2004)**—denial of D's motion to suppress is not a final judgment for collateral estoppel purposes (D isn't obligated to seek leave to file interlocutory appeal);

C v Rivera **424 M 1007 (97)**—no appeal lies from denial by a single justice of a petition for leave to appeal; petition pursuant to G.L. c. 211, § 3 is sole remedy remaining once a single justice has denied the Commonwealth leave to appeal, but such remedy is "exceptional" and different from "appeal"; see SJC Rule 2:21(3); rule concerning appeal from single justice denial of relief on interlocutory ruling does NOT apply to matters governed by M.R.Crim.P. 15;

C v Boncore **412 M 1013 (92)**—no right to appeal from single justice's denial of application for leave to appeal suppression ruling (so here, because Commonwealth claimed to have been "misdirected" by a clerk, Commonwealth's pleadings were treated as petition under G.L. c. 211, § 3);

C v Lopez **430 M 244 (99)**—Rule 15 **"requires"** Commonwealth to pay defendant "his or her costs of appeal together with reasonable attorney's fees after unsuccessful interlocutory appeal by Commonwealth; Court rejects Commonwealth's argument that order for payment lies in discretion of appellate court, for instance on ground that Commonwealth believed the appeal was "meritorious"; (defense attorneys here were privately retained at trial and on appeal, **id. at 245 and n.1**);

C v Gonsalves **432 M 613 (2000), and 437 M 1022 (2002)**—SJC first upheld allowance of attorney fees against the Commonwealth over a constitutional challenge from DA's office; single justice's award of $17,000 was reduced to $11,000 upon DA's motion to reconsider; full bench held that single justice had authority to reconsider & reduce, but remand for explanation of reduction (& D counsel might get further fees for litigation concerning the reduction);

C v Ennis **441 M 718 (2004)**—defendant must file Rule 15(d) request for fees within 30 days of either denial of Commonwealth's application for leave to file interlocutory appeal or the issuance of rescript from court which decides the appeal, unless D on motion shows good cause for enlargement of time; counsel failed to show that $200/hour was reasonable here or that 64 hours was rea-

sonable, exacerbated by failure to respond to Commonwealth's assertions in opposition;

15-C.2. M.R.Crim.P. 34—"Report"

M.R.Crim.P. 34—REPORT of law question so important/doubtful that needs Appeals Court answer; either PRE-trial or, if D consents, AFTER G;

G.L. c. 211A, § 10—reported case is within the concurrent jurisdiction of Appeals Court and SJC (though case is to be sent "in the first instance" to Appeals Court);

C v Vaden **373 M 397 (77)**—if judge allows interlocutory report, should say why; interlocutory reports aren't to "become additional causes of the delays . . . which are already too prevalent";

Rosenberg v Commonwealth **372 M 59 (77)**—can report pre-trial dismissal (*see Chapter 14-D*);

C v Fitta **391 M 394 (84)**—judge should have decided issues rather than report them to SJC, since Commonwealth had right to appeal if judge granted motion to dismiss, and appellate review was available to D if conviction ensued after denial of motion to dismiss; if trial = short, issues clear-cut, and D agrees to facts ONLY for purposes of report, questions shouldn't have been reported;

C v Paasche **391 M 18 (84)**—if, after trial judge reports question, Commonwealth fails to file brief, appellate court will deem inaction to be election not to prosecute criminal charge (& constitutional questions won't be answered unless they have to be);

M.R.App.P. 5—report of a case for determination by appellate court = "equivalent of a notice of appeal," and aggrieved party will be treated as appellant; if criminal case is reported without "decision or verdict," criminal defendant is treated as appellant;

15-C.3. Appeal to Full Bench, SJC, from Single Justice Ruling

SJC Rule 2:21, 421 M 1303 (95), "Appeal From Single Justice Denial of Relief on Interlocutory Ruling," applicable to civil and criminal cases—"(1) When a single justice denies relief from a challenged interlocutory ruling in the trial court and does not report the denial of relief to the full court, the party denied relief may appeal the single justice's ruling to the full court. Unless the court otherwise orders, the notice of appeal shall be filed with the clerk of the Supreme Judicial Court for Suffolk County within seven days of the entry of the judgment appealed from. Unless the single justice or the full court order otherwise, **neither the trial nor the interlocutory ruling in the trial court shall be stayed.** (2) The appeal shall be presented to the full court on the papers filed in the single justice session, including any memorandum of decision. Nine copies of the record appendix must be filed in the office of the Clerk of the Supreme Judicial Court for the Commonwealth within fourteen days of the filing of the notice of appeal. The record appendix shall be accompanied by eight copies of a **memorandum of not more than ten pages, double-spaced, in which the appellant must set forth the reasons why review of the trial court decision cannot adequately be obtained on appeal from any final adverse judgment in the trial court or by other available means**. No response from the prevailing party shall be filed, unless requested by the court. (3) This rule shall not apply to interlocutory appeals governed by Rule 15 of the Massachusetts Rules of Criminal Procedure. (4) The full court will consider the appeal on the papers submitted pursuant to this rule, unless it otherwise orders.

Carrasquillo v Commonwealth **422 M 1014, 1015 (96)**—single justice's denial of a petition legitimately brought under G.L. c. 211, § 3 may be appealed to full bench; appellate relief in full bench pursuant to SJC Rule 2:21, in contrast, is available only where single justice denies relief from an interlocutory ruling and doesn't report ruling to full bench;

King v Commonwealth **430 M 1002 (99)**—Rule 2:21 isn't satisfied by assertion that party is correct on the merits; Court refused to accept for review appeal from single justice's denial of G.L. c. 211, § 3 petition after original complaint had been dismissed for lack of prosecution but dismissal was "without prejudice," and new complaint was brought, and motion to dismiss on speedy trial ground was denied in trial court;

C v Rivera **424 M 1007 (97)**—no appeal lies from denial by a single justice of a petition for leave to appeal; petition pursuant to G.L. c. 211, § 3 is sole remedy remaining once a single justice has denied the Commonwealth leave to appeal, but such remedy is "exceptional" and different from "appeal"; see SJC Rule 2:21 (3); rule concerning appeal from single justice denial of relief on interlocutory ruling does NOT apply to matters governed by M.R.Crim.P. 15;

Dantas v Commonwealth **429 M 1006 (99)**—appeal from single justice's G.L. c. 211, § 3 denial of relief to D concerning discovery motion: conclusory assertions that the discovery was "exculpatory and dispositive" and that D couldn't obtain adequate review on appeal (with citation to opinion which mentioned "avoidance of participating in an unnecessary trial and the saving of unnecessary expense") = insufficient "reasons" under Rule 2:21;

Palmer v Commonwealth **428 M 1013 (98)**—full bench affirmed denial by single justice of G.L. c. 211, § 3 petition which sought a continuance of D's criminal trials until civil actions for the same causes pending against him were tried or otherwise disposed of; D's assertion that a professional insurance policy would cover him in the civil suits ONLY if he hadn't been convicted of the criminal charges beforehand "d(id) not constitute the requisite explanation why review on appeal, or by other available means, would be inadequate";

15-C.4. G.L. c. 211, § 3

G.L. c. 211, § 3—(1) SJC's GENERAL SUPERINTENDENCE of inferior courts to correct or prevent errors/abuses "**if no other remedy is expressly provided**"; SJC issues "all writs/processes" to courts or individuals to further justice & execute laws; (2) general superintendence of "ADMINISTRATION" of all courts (including prompt dispo of their pending cases); issues writs, processes, orders, directions, & rules "necessary or desirable; SJC prohibited from exercising superintendence power "superced(ing)" any statute except where, under its original or appellate jurisdiction, statute is found to be unconstitutional in a case or controversy; SJC further prohibited from exercising or superseding powers & duties delegated to chief justice for administration & management unless majority makes written finding stating "extraordinary circumstances leading to a severe, adverse impact on the administration of justice"; (Does this violate Article 30, separation of powers clause of state constitution?);

K. Smith, *Criminal Practice & Procedure,* **§§ 1492–95 (2d ed. 1983 & Supp.)**—G.L. c. 211, § 3 overview;

Costarelli v Commonwealth **374 M 677 (78)**—for 211/3, need (1) substantial claim of important substantive violation, AND (2) error's irreversible—new trial, normal appeal not enough; substantial double jeopardy claim needs 211/3;

Crimmins v Commonwealth **391 M 1004(84)**—211/3 used sparingly to prevent irreparable loss of significant rights if normal trial/appeal won't be adequate or for pressing, recurrent questions of proper administration of justice;

Cohen v Commonwealth **448 M 1005 (2007)**—SJC denied G.L. c. 211, § 3 relief from trial court's refusal to sever co-Ds (review can adequately be obtained on appeal from any eventual conviction);

C v Richardson **454 M 1005 (2009)**—after D's motion post-trial seeking investigation of possible extraneous influence on jury, judge ordered cautious inquiry including showing photos of jurors to affiant who overheard conversation suggesting such influence; Commonwealth's 211/3 petition (maintain 'integrity of the jury trial process'! protect jurors from risk to their safety!) rejected: **"[n]o party, including the Commonwealth, should expect this court to exercise its extraordinary power of general superintendence lightly"**;

C v Feliciano **442 M 728 (2004)**—single justice is empowered to act on 211/3 petition alleging foul play/abuse by an interlocutory order of a panel of the Appeals Court considering a direct appeal from D's conviction; subject order merely directed delivery to appeals court of records held in Superior Court after finding/ruling by trial court judge that they contained nothing discoverable under Bishop-Fuller protocol, a matter as to which D sought review in direct appeal (SJC holds that if D's original proffer made plausible showing of relevance, the judge's in camera decision that records provide nothing or relevance IS

SUBJECT TO APPELLATE REVIEW, and court must have access to the records;

***C v Bell* 442 M 118 (2004)**—SJC, on Commonwealth's G.L. c. 211, § 3 petition, bars D in "school zone" drug prosecution from using Department of Education regulation defining "secondary school," because this was underinclusive in context of criminal statute's purpose; 211/3 appropriate (even though no actual ruling yet & "evidentiary" rulings normally not subject to 211/3 review), because judge refused to report to Appeals Court how jury should be charged re: essential element of offense;

***C v Negron* 441 M 685, 688 (2004)**—because Commonwealth may appeal finding of no probation violation, review under 211/3 inappropriate for claimed evidentiary error at revocation hearing;

***C v Clark* 454 M 1001 (2009)**—even though trial judge denied Commonwealth's motion to continue and then dismissed indictments "without prejudice" due to victim's unavailability on trial date, so that there were at least two remedies other than 211/3 review (i.e., re-indicting, and M.R.Crim.P. 15(a)(1), G.L. c. 278, § 28E), full bench upheld single justice's conclusion that trial judge abused her discretion: "there was no abuse of discretion on the part of the single justice" in vacating dismissal;

***C v O'Brien* 432 M 578 (2000)**—on G.L. c. 211, § 3 petition by Commonwealth, case was considered by full bench, and ordered reassigned from a judge who refused to recuse himself; this order was not reviewable on subsequent direct appeal from ensuing conviction, and Court had authority to act/intervene "in the interest of justice";

***C v Kerns* 449 M 641 (2007)**—Commonwealth's 211, 3 petition (denied by single justice) acted upon to prevent jury-waived trial judge from misinstructing himself as to applicable law (at "required finding of not guilty" stage); single justice had not had actual record of trial judge's rumination/action, and "[w]hen similar situations occur, deference by the single justice to the action of the trial judge will likely be the norm and not the exception";

***Matter of Desaulnier* 360 M 757 (71)**—SJC's inherent common law & constitutional power to protect/preserve system's integrity & supervise administration of justice;

***Fadden v Commonwealth* 376 M 604 (78)**—(same) re: double jeopardy; SJC single justice may decide petition, report to full bench, or transfer to Appeals Court under G.L. c. 211, § 4A;

***Donald v Commonwealth* 452 M 1029 (2008)**—D moved in Superior Court for free copy of transcript (albeit of Appellate Division proceedings); when motion was denied, he should have filed notice of appeal in Superior Court and judge should/would have made written findings (G.L. c. 261, § 27D), which clerk would forward with other relevant documents to Appeals Court clerk; G.L. c. 211, § 3 was not appropriate avenue for relief;

***Leaster v Commonwealth* 385 M 547 (82)**—no G.L. c. 211, § 3 if legislature expressly limited appeal;

***Taylor v Newton Division of District Court Department* 416 M 1006 (93)**—single justice not required to grant hearing or make findings on G.L. c. 211, § 3 petition (citing SJC Rule 2:11 as appearing in **382 M 1006 (93)**);

***Foley v Commonwealth* 429 M 496, 497 n.2 (99)**—statement of agreed facts desirable on G.L. c. 211, § 3 petition, and if such agreement can't be reached, single justice "might well conclude that the case should be transferred to a trial court for determination"; appellant held to "suffer the consequences of any deficiency in the record," so to extent facts in dispute, Court "adopt(s) the facts asserted by the Commonwealth";

***County of Barnstable v Commonwealth* 410 M 326 (91)**—single justice may deny relief under G.L. c. 211, § 3, & transfer case to Superior Court for further fact-finding;

15-C.5. Appeal from Single Justice's Ruling on c. 211, § 3 Petition

***Carrasquillo v Commonwealth* 422 M 1014, 1015 (96)**—single justice's denial of a petition legitimately brought under G.L. c. 211, § 3 may be appealed to full bench in accord with statute itself; appellate relief pursuant to SJC Rule 2:21, in contrast, is available only where single justice denies relief from an interlocutory ruling and doesn't report ruling to full bench (but R.2:21, by its terms, id. at (3), doesn't apply to cases governed by M.R. Crim.P. 15);

***Locks v Commonwealth* 421 M 1003 (95)**—single justice denied G.L. c. 211, § 3 relief on ground that D's rights could be protected in normal appellate process, and full bench afforded no relief, quoting prior case, that denial of motion to dismiss pursuant to M.R.Crim.P. 13(c)(1) "may not be appealed until after trial, and relief under G.L. c. 211, § 3 is not available as a matter of right"; BUT IF motion to dismiss is on ground of double jeopardy, there is 211/3 right because trial itself ("second" jeopardy) is the harm sought to be avoided (see, e.g., ***Creighton v Commonwealth* 423 M 1001 (96)**);

***Dempsey v Clerk of Superior Court* 454 M 1017 (2009)**—petition in Superior Court to seal certain Superior Court, BMC and District Court criminal records was denied; single justice on 211/3 also denied, because G.L. c. 276, § 100C doesn't authorize court to seal criminal records where D has been convicted or where charge has been placed on file; though petitioner "may be entitled" to sealing of certain records under G.L. c. 276, § 100A, request must be made to Commissioner of Probation, not court; furthermore, 211/3 inappropriate as could appeal from Superior Court judge's denial of petition to seal records;

***Lenardis v Commonwealth* 452 M 1001 (2008)**—nonparty directed to provide evidence (buccal swab) can challenge order by refusing to comply and appealing from any order of contempt that results; this petitioner instead sought relief from SJC single justice ("county court") via G.L. c. 211, § 3 petition, which was denied without hearing; appeal to full bench = moot because petitioner complied with order AND single justice's ruling would not be disturbed because party should have suffered contempt and appealed from contempt order;

Hines v Commonwealth **425 M 1013 (97)**—SJC full bench found no error of law or abuse of discretion in single justice's denial of G.L. c. 211, § 3 petition alleging various errors in the handling of a sentence appeal by the Appellate Division of Superior Court; petition was supported by no documentation supporting claims of error;

Schipani v C **382 M 685 (80)**—single justice's 211/3 ruling reviewed by full bench only for abuse discretion or clear error;

C v Boncore **412 M 1013 (92)**—although Commonwealth not entitled to appeal single justice's denial of leave for interlocutory appeal of allowed suppression motion, it may bring G.L. c. 211, § 3, petition because no other remedy available;

Carrasquillo v Commonwealth **422 M 1014, 1015 (96)**—single justice's denial of a petition legitimately brought under G.L. c. 211, § 3 may be appealed to full bench; appellate relief in full bench pursuant to SJC Rule 2:21, in contrast, is available only where single justice denies relief from an interlocutory ruling and doesn't report ruling to full bench;

15-C.6. Issues Appropriately Raised (or Not) via c. 211, § 3 Petitions

15-C.6.a. Pretrial

Hadfield v C **387 M 252 (82)**—**probable cause hearing & grand jury procedures (& DA misconduct)** can be raised in normal appeal, not 211/3; see also *C v Frado* **372 M 866 (77)**;

Corey v Commonwealth **364 M 137 (73)**—211/3 re: **cross-examination rights at probable cause hearing**;

Lataille v District Court. **366 M 525 (74)**—211/3: no **right to finish probable cause hearing** if indicted;

Sinath Im v Commonwealth **432 M 1018 (2000)**—no 211/3 relief when trial court judge denies **motion for funds** and single justice thereafter affirms such denial under appellate avenue prescribed by G.L. c. 261, § 27D;

G.L. c. 261, § 27D—(per 2004 amendment) appeals from denial of relief from costs and fees: appeal is to single justice of Appeals Court if denial is in Superior, Land, Probate, or Housing Ct. departments; appeal is to Superior Court if denial is in juvenile court; appeal is to appellate division if denial is in District Court or Boston Municipal Court;

Barry v Commonwealth **390 M 285(83)**—211/3 re: denial of motion to dismiss, to solve **confusing M.R. Crim.P. 36 speedy trial issues**;

Pentlarge v Commonwealth **445 M 1012 (2005)**—no 211/3 to force speedier trial of petition for discharge of sexually dangerous person: "can be remedied on appeal from any adverse judgment" (SJC says, furthermore, that during pendency of this litigation, D received prospective trial date, albeit three months after date of SJC's decision);

Chubbuck v Commonwealth **453 M 1018 (2009)**—D being held, incompetent, on two complaints lodged six months apart though arising out of same incident, and wanted dismissal of first on basis of G.L. c. 123, § 16(f) [and D didn't claim entitlement to dismissal of second]: no G.L. c. 211, § 3 relief as D wasn't being held unlawfully and could not show 'no remedy' (direct appeal) if later found competent, tried, & convicted on first complaint;

Abbott A v Commonwealth **455 M 1005 (2009)**—juvenile found incompetent for trial was to be subjected to § 58A hearing, but counsel argued juvenile to be incompetent to assist attorney in § 58A hearing and petitioned pursuant to G.L. c. 211, § 3; SJC held petition untimely, and would be entertained only upon adverse ruling after 58A hearing (review then would include issue of whether it was appropriate to have held 58A hearing at all);

Brunson v Commonwealth **369 M 106 (75)**—maybe 211/3 to **challenge grand/petit juror selection for gender discrimination**;

Murrell v Commonwealth **454 M 1020 (2009)**—SJC refuses G.L. c. 211, § 3 relief to defendant who wanted order compelling all city and town clerks in the county to respond to survey re: how resident lists used to develop lists of potential jurors are compiled; SJC says if convicted he can raise on appeal, including claim as part of his underrepresentation challenge his claim that he was unfairly deprived of the data needed to make such a challenge;

Pena v Commonwealth **426 M 1015, 1016 n.2 (98)**—SJC will not entertain, in the future, 211/3 petitions for **double jeopardy relief** unless petitioner has first presented in trial court a motion to dismiss based on double jeopardy protections, and it has been denied; here, petitioner contended that required finding of not guilty should have been granted at close of first trial (but full bench held that there was sufficient evidence to withstand motion for required finding of NG);

Nettis v Commonwealth **415 M 1001 (93)**—denial of D's **motion to dismiss**, premised upon statute of limitations, wouldn't be considered on G.L. c. 211, § 3; *Ackerman v Commonwealth* **445 M 1025 (2006)**—same, notwithstanding D's argument that right not to be tried at all was like "double jeopardy," which IS appropriately considered on petition pursuant to G.L. c. 211, § 3;

Ventresco v Commonwealth **409 M 82 (91)**—G.L. c. 211, § 3 petition is proper means for D to challenge denial of **motion to dismiss** only if single justice finds substantial claim of violation of substantive rights plus irremediable error; judge's denial of D's motion to dismiss based on invalid extension of grand jury sessions upheld;

Doe v Commonwealth **435 M 1001 (2001)**—denial of D's **motion to dismiss** not reviewable under G.L. c. 211, § 3; fact that D would lose benefit of extremely favorable plea bargain disposition if he went to trial, so that issue could be presented later on direct appeal = inadequate reason for relief;

C v Lucero **450 M 1032 (2008)**—211/3 for relief for Commonwealth after trial court judge's entry of "required finding of not guilty" when case was called for trial, but no opening statements were made or evidence presented: sexual assault complainant had not yet appeared at courtroom & DA said couldn't prove case without her; when DA subsequently learned that she had been present but in wrong courtroom, trial court judge had denied motion for reconsideration;

Duggan v Commonwealth **455 M 1001 (2009)**—claim that probation surrender proceeding was too tardily initiated (so should be dismissed) not reviewable on 211/3;

C v Moran **453 M 880, 883 n.6 (2009)**—Commonwealth should have sought review of dismissal of indictment under G.L. c. 278, § 28E and M.R.Crim.P. 15(a)(1) rather than 211/3, but single justice had reported case to SJC and it was briefed, so SJC addressed merits;

Foley v District Court **398 M 800 (86)**—though appeal de novo wiped out bench errors & made 211/3 inappropriate, SJC uses "broader inherent common law & constitutional power to supervise administration of justice" to condemn bench **judge's offer to dismiss if D signs liability release** for cops: SJC dismisses case before jury of six trial;

Juvenile v Commonwealth **380 M 552 (80)**—**juvenile transfer challenge** = G.L. c. 211 § 3 because "working relation" between two departments & needs supervision;

C v A Juvenile **409 M 49 (91)**—G.L. c. 211, § 3 petition is proper means for prosecutor to **challenge no probable cause finding at juvenile Part A transfer hearing**; prosecutor not entitled to relief where D not transferred after Part B hearing;

Fitzpatrick v Commonwealth **453 M 1014 (2009)**—G.L. c. 211, § 3 can't be used to "circumvent" SJC Rule 2:21, and isn't available for review of attempt to overturn juvenile court judge's finding probable cause and public interest in juvenile being charged as adult, leading to indictments (offenses allegedly committed < age 17, but arrest > age 18);

C v O'Brien **432 M 578 (2000)**—211/3 by Commonwealth obtained overruling of **judge's refusal to recuse himself** following SJC's reversal of judge's refusal to order transfer of juvenile; but see *Ewing v Commonwealth* **451 M 1005 (2008)**—if *D* seeks review of judge's refusal to recuse, no 211/3 because he didn't establish that review could not be adequately obtained on appeal from possible conviction;

Cousins v Commonwealth **442 M 1046 (2004)**—no relief under G.L. c. 211, § 3 for D demanding **severance** from co-D because co-D's change of counsel caused delay and D wanted a speedier trial (issue = denial of speedy trial urged by D to be irremediable years later, on direct appeal);

Marrero v Commonwealth **447 M 1013 (2006)**—211/3 petition rejected because D could obtain relief for speedy trial claim on direct appeal if necessary (D argued that no remedy adequate because delay had allowed prosecution to obtain evidence it wouldn't have had otherwise);

Lombard v Commonwealth **427 M 1001 (98)**—**discovery denial** not usually addressed by 211/3 petition/power; here, SJC suggested motion for reconsideration in trial court, with citation to recent SJC opinion; EDITOR'S NOTE: **meaningful appellate review of discovery orders possible (i.e., to show prejudice from withholding discovery) only if withheld material is available to appellate judges** (i.e. identified, marked, impounded if necessary; cf. *C v O'Brien* **419 M 470, 477 (95)** though SJC held that it was error to withhold from defense counsel a document used to refresh witness's recollection on stand (on purported basis that it was prosecutor's "work product"), failure to have document made part of record meant that Court could not find that there was "prejudice" from the error; *Pixley v Commonwealth* **453 M 827 (2009)**—D called witness, who claimed 5th A. and art. 12 privileges, and judge held in camera *Martin* (423 M 496) hearing, finding privilege; on appeal after conviction, D could argue error in privilege determination, but would not be allowed access to "sealed"/impounded transcript of in camera hearing; single justice's denial of D's 211/3 petition thus affirmed;

Reddy v Commonwealth **422 M 1002 (96)**—**denial of access to records** of complainant could be reviewed on direct appeal of conviction (so no error in denying 211/3);

C v Pare **420 M 216 (95)**—though single justice addressed on merits 211/3 **claim that D was entitled to ex parte hearing on his stage 2 proffer under *Bishop* (416 M 169 (93))**, a discovery matter, and D appealed to full bench, SJC held that normal process of appeal would protect any rights D had (?so single justice should have said that, instead of ruling substantively?);

C v McCoy **443 M 1015 (2005)**—no relief for the Commonwealth pursuant to G.L. c. 211, § 3, although trial court judge "has not adhered to the precise steps and sequence of the **Bishop-Fuller protocol**," because these "technical errors do not amount here to a substantial claim of violation of substantive rights";

Clairmont v Commonwealth **425 M 1025 (97)**—**denial of discovery of confidential informant** (even though same was alleged to have exculpatory info) not entertained on 211/3 because D could obtain review/relief in normal course of appeal after any conviction; but *C v Dias* **451 M 463 (2008)**—discovery order requiring Commonwealth to disclose informant was considered on 211/3, single justice reserving and reporting it to full court;

Ayala v Commonwealth **454 M 1015 (2009)**—no 211/3 for relief from judge's allowing US Attorney's motion to quash summonses to law enforcement agencies regarding paid Federal informant who allegedly had stated that D was innocent of murder charge (issue may be raised on appeal from conviction);

C v Mello **453 M 760 (2009)**—SJC on 211/3 overturned judge's discovery order that Commonwealth reveal whether or not named person was acting as agent of Commonwealth when person introduced D to undercover cop against whom D made allegations sufficient to raise entrapment;

C v Narea **454 M 1003 (2009)**—SJC on Commonwealth's 211/3 vacated trial judge's sanction for destroying purported "buy money" (i.e., precluding testimony at trial concerning it), saying D had to have "concrete evidence" that evidence was exculpatory/would have created reasonable doubt;

Ray v Commonwealth **447 M 1008 (2006)**—no 211/3 relief for defense counsel pre-trial from order barring him from disclosing to D the identities of "civilian" witnesses against him, revealed in discovery materials given to counsel;

Gilday v Commonwealth **360 M 170 (71)**—211/3 to review 5th Amendment rights **re: order giving prosecutor D's alibi witness list** because rights would be irretrievably lost (because interlocutory review not available & trial judge wouldn't report);

Lenardis v Commonwealth **452 M 1001 (2008)**—nonparty directed to provide evidence (buccal swab) can challenge order by refusing to comply and appealing from any order of contempt that results; this petitioner instead sought relief from SJC single justice ("county court") via G.L. c. 211, § 3 petition, which was denied without hearing; appeal to full bench = moot because petitioner complied with order AND single justice's ruling would not be disturbed because party should have suffered contempt and appealed from contempt order;

Sliech-Brodeur v Commonwealth **447 M 1004 (2006)**—though D resisted discovery orders by 211/3, her requests for stays were denied by both SJC single justice & full bench, and when she complied with the orders & was quickly tried and convicted, her appeal from single justice's ruling on the "interlocutory" matter = moot; direct appeal now available from conviction;

Cargill v Commonwealth **430 M 1006 (99)**—ruling that D is **competent to stand trial** not subject to interlocutory review; any error reviewable through usual appellate process;

Murphy v Commonwealth **455 M 1002 (2009)**—denial of D's motion to represent himself with aid of standby counsel not reviewable on 211/3;

Womack, petitioner **444 M 1015 (2005)**—judge's **finding that petitioner had waived his privilege against self-incrimination** and could be forced to testify at hearing on motion for new trial wasn't reviewable under 211/3, because he could appeal from contempt order which would enter if he continued to refuse to testify;

Blazo v Superior Court **366 M 141 (74)**—211/3 fixes rights to stenographer & summons;

Blaisdell v Commonwealth **372 M 753 (77)**—211/3 for matters of "great import" to D & DA; available ANY TIME necessary (e.g., 5th Amendment & insanity defense);

Heang v Commonwealth **454 M 1011 (2009)**—principal (A) was charged with murder of a police officer, and several associates of A were present at the scene of the shooting, including this D's brother; D's brother was not charged in connection with the shooting, but D was

charged as accessory after fact to murder and for carrying firearm without license; by motion in limine D sought to raise defense based on G.L. c. 274, § 4, but judge denied on basis that D's brother had not been charged, and D instead assisted A, with whom D had no familial relation: no 211/3 relief, rejecting D's claim that he'd be required to take stand to make record for appeal after trial: SJC directed steps to be taken to preserve without such testimony;

15-C.6.b. Evidentiary

C v Beausoleil **397 M 206 (86)**—some **pre-trial motions, e.g., motion in limine**, MAY merit interlocutory relief by R.15 or 211/3 (fn.2) * for justice, regular execution of laws, improving court administration & efficiency; but *Kater v Commonwealth* **421 M 1008 (95)** no 211/3 to review allowance of Commonwealth's **motion to introduce D's prior bad acts**;

C v Steele **455 M 209, 210 n.3 (2009)**—though SJC not "required to exercise" 211/3 superintendence powers, it did so to review (& affirm) trial judge's denial of Commonwealth's motion in limine seeking to introduce TWO breath sample/ blood alcohol level results (only the lower of the two could be introduced in accord with statutory and regulatory requirements);

Smith v Commonwealth **386 M 345 (82)**—no 211/3 to challenge witness's immunity here;

Villalta v Commonwealth **428 M 429 (98)**—Commonwealth successfully petitioned under G.L. c. 211, § 3 for result different from trial judge's **ruling that wife did not have to testify** in trial of her husband for rape of child in day care of wife; full bench held that relief in these circumstances was an "appropriate" discretionary exercise of the power of general superintendency, but was not "required"; SJC "le(ft) open the question whether the Commonwealth ever is entitled as a matter of right to G.L. c. 211, § 3 relief";

C v Yelle **390 M 678 (84)**—neither Rule 15 nor 211/3 for DA's interlocutory appeal of **EVIDENTIARY RULING (even rape-shield)**; almost never 211/3 for DA;

15-C.6.c. Post-Conviction

C v Miranda **22 MAC 10 (86)**—G.L. c. 211 § 3 possible for postconviction, **obtaining direct appeal though notice of appeal is time-barred**;

Roullett v Quincy District Court **395 M 1008 (85)**—could've appealed **order of restitution** (or could have moved to revise or revoke under M.R.Crim.P. 29(a), or for new trial under M.R.Crim.P. 30(b)) when set in too-high amount 6 months after G. finding, so no 211/3;

C v McCulloch **450 M 483 (2008)**—211/3 for Commonwealth to redress judge's illegitimate allowance of motion to revoke and revise, based on improper factors and improperly used to vacate G finding on condition of immediate restitution payment;

Dunbrack v C **398 M 502 (86)**—R.30, not 211/3, appeals **changed probation condition**;

C v Gordon **410 M 498 (91)**—G.L. c. 211, § 3, was proper means for prosecutor to challenge judge's erroneous **acceptance of guilty plea to lesser charge** over Commonwealth objection where there was no "dismissal" from which to appeal under Rule 15(b);

C v Dery **452 M 823 (2008)**—due to disqualifications and peremptory challenges, jury venire was reduced to only five people; after consultation with counsel, D agreed to trial by five (full colloquy under oath, oral waiver) and was acquitted: Commonwealth petitioned under G.L. c. 211, § 3, saying jury of five not legitimate, and D hadn't signed required written waiver (M.R.Crim.P. 19(b)); Commonwealth had failed to object, no relief;

McGuinness v Commonwealth **420 M 495 (95)**—no 211/3 for denial of M.R.Crim.P. 29 **motion to revoke and revise**;

C v Cowan **422 M 546 (96)**—**illegal sentence** (not the mandatory one) imposed by District Court judge vacated in 211/3, but if it had been illegal sentence in Superior Court, Commonwealth remedy instead would have been by G.L. c. 278, § 28E;

Semedo v Commonwealth **429 M 1006 (99)**—no 211, § 3 to review **denial of motion to withdraw guilty plea** (instead, file notice of appeal from what was essentially a motion under M.R.Crim.P. 30, and direct appeal would then go to Appeals Court); *C v Casimir* **442 M 1031 (2004)**—D's **motion to vacate guilty plea** = essentially motion for new trial, so Commonwealth had right to interlocutory review of order, which **allowed** it (& thus, G.L. c. 211, § 3 relief unavailable);

Murray v Commonwealth **442 M 1029 (2004)**—after Appeals Court refused to address arguments concerning "filed" conviction & D filed motion in Superior Court to **"bring forward" filed conviction** and have counsel appointed for sentencing, D should have appealed the denial of that motion (rather than undertake G.L. c. 211, § 3 petitions & appeals from their denial);

15-D. MOTIONS TO REVOKE AND REVISE—M.R.CRIM.P. 29

M.R.Crim.P. 29—within 60 days of sentencing, or of withdrawal of appeal, or of order having effect of making convictions final, motion in trial court to REVISE/REVOKE SENTENCE if justice not done; motion to be decided by sentencing judge;

See Chapter 14-T, below, for essential cases;

C v Layne **386 M 291 (82)**—M.R.Crim.P. 29 establishes strict jurisdictional time limits for the filing of motions to revise or revoke a sentence;

C v DeJesus **440 M 147 (2003)**—(on Commonwealth's petition pursuant to G.L. c. 211, § 3) trial judge was **without jurisdiction to revoke and revise sentence, because motion (though filed within a month of sentencing) was filed without any affidavit**; affidavit was not provided until 17 months later; D and judge were motivated to reduce one-year sentence (already served) because of adverse immigration consequences attending a sentence of that length (& SJC reiterates that immigration/deportation consequences are "collateral," and "cannot be basis for judge's decision as to the disposition of . . . any . . . case");

C v Callahan **419 M 306 (95)**—60-day revoke/revise period does NOT run ("again") from time Appellate Division of Superior Court revised sentence (here, increasing it); once D claimed appeal to Appellate Division, original sentencing judge was "divested of jurisdiction to act on motions to rehear or to vacate";

Callahan v Commonwealth **416 M 1010 (94)**—(remedy for trial court clerk's refusal to accept for filing D's notice of appeal from the denial of motion to revoke/revise would have been request for order from trial court judge directing clerk to accept the notice and process the appeal);

C v Layne **21 MAC 17 (85)**—claim for relief on basis that trial judge was mistaken re: parole eligibility under sentence given should be raised by motion under R.29 (& here too late); not R.30 (a) "illegal";

C v Layne **25 MAC 1 (87)**—stenographic records & clerk's minutes of judge's sentence control over judge's "intention"; judge can't "correct" sentence 4 years later;

C v Richards **44 MAC 478 (98)**—overview of appealability of R.29 rulings: denial of motion to revoke and revise is "immediately appealable," BUT appellate review of sentencing issues is "usually limited to errors of law" (examples given); "(b)eyond these outer limits, sentencing decisions and consequences are matters with which an appellate court has no concern";

McGuinness v Commonwealth **420 M 495 (95)**—no G.L. c. 211, § 3 for denial of M.R.Crim.P. 29 motion to revoke and revise; instead, file motion pursuant to M.R. Crim.P. 30 (alleging that judge, in vacating his previous allowance of motion to revoke and revise, improperly considered D's conduct after the initial sentencing) and appeal its denial;

15-E. SENTENCE APPEALS

G.L. c. 278, §§ 28A–C—appellate division of Superior Court established for review of sentences to state prison, and, for women, "reformatory" sentences of more than five years; appellate division to consist of three Superior rior Court justices to be designated by chief justice of Superior Court; two such justices shall constitute quorum; upon imposition of sentence which may be reviewed under § 28A, clerk must notify D of right to appeal for review of sentence; notice of appeal of sentence must be filed with clerk of sentencing court within ten days of sentencing; decision of appellate division as to sentence = FINAL;

See Superior Court Rules, Appellate Division—sittings commencing first Mondays of May and November; prob. dep't to provide specified info in writing to each justice; district attorney to provide each justice with specified info, including victim impact statement, and DA papers to be made available to defense counsel "seasonably before the hearing"; counsel's representation of a defendant at trial court is construed to continue for sentence appeal, which is merely a continuation of "disposition" aspect of representation; motion to withdraw appearance by D-counsel to be filed with appellate division clerk (NOT clerk in county where sentencing occurred); if appearing counsel didn't represent D at original sentencing, counsel to consult with prior attorneys; appellate division "expect(s)" an official transcript of (original) sentencing proceedings" where "feasible"; defense counsel "encouraged to submit sentencing memoranda for the assistance of the Division"; motions for continuance to another session to be in writing, & "normally" entertained "only upon personal appearance of the attorney so moving, and oral argument";

Hicks v Commonwealth **345 M 89 (63)**—appellate division has power to increase sentence as well as decrease; no double jeopardy bar to increased sentence; D assumes risk of unfavorable result because he alone initiates sentence appeal;

Walsh v Commonwealth **358 M 193 (70)**—same; and no due process violation for "vindictiveness" in increased sentence unless D alleges and proves such motivation;

C v Callahan **419 M 306 (95)**—procedural "safeguards" concerning sentence are: notice of right to appeal sentence, aid of counsel in deciding whether to appeal sentence (with attendant risk), availability of a record and possible resort to view of trial judge, appearance before tribunal with assistance of counsel, and "collegial rather than individual judgment"; 60-day revoke/revise period does NOT run ("again") from time Appellate Division of

Superior Court revised sentence (here, increasing it); once D claimed appeal to Appellate Division, original sentencing judge was "divested of jurisdiction to act on motions to rehear or to vacate"; D's claim in R.30 motion that he had received ineffective assistance of counsel at Appellate Division rejected (counsel can't predict how appellate division would rule, and D was told on record sentence could be increased);

Hines v Commonwealth **425 M 1013 (97)**—SJC full bench found no error of law or abuse of discretion in single justice's denial of G.L. c. 211, § 3 petition alleging various errors in the handling of a sentence appeal by the Appellate Division of Superior Court; petition was supported by no documentation supporting claims of error;

C v Richards **44 MAC 478 (98)**—on appellate review of conviction (NOT "Superior Court Appellate Division review") review of sentencing issues is "usually limited to errors of law" (examples given); "(b)eyond these outer limits, sentencing decisions and consequences are matters with which an appellate court has no concern";

C v D'Amour **428 M 725, 746 (99)**—though D argued on direct appeal in SJC that two sentences of ten to twelve years, concurrent, for perjury convictions were invalid because D was being punished instead, really, for the related homicide, of which D was acquitted, Court noted it doesn't review "lawful sentences"; while issue of D being "sentenced for a crime other than that for which he stands convicted" is a legitimate appellate issue, Court claimed no evidence here that judge was influenced by ADA's improper sentencing pitch re: victim "gunned down in his home";

C v Turavani **45 MAC 909, 910 (98)**—Court rejects similar argument that D's incredibly lengthy sentences for 3 counts of ABDW and 3 counts A&B were really sentences for mayhem, of which she was acquitted; Court noted D had failed to appeal to Appellate Division of Superior Court, and that D's timely-filed motion to revoke and revise (M.R.Crim.P. 29) was denied;.

15-F. M.R.CRIM.P. 30

C v Conceicao **388 M 255 (83)**—no constitutional right to assistance of appointed counsel in preparing/presenting post-conviction motion for new trial; decision to appoint counsel in these circumstances = discretionary with judge;

Parker v Commonwealth **448 M 1021 (2007)**—single justice did not order CPCS to appoint counsel for D's post-conviction motion for new trial, but instead referred the case to CPCS "for evaluation only, that is, so that CPCS could determine whether [D's] case warranted an assignment of counsel"; subsequent decision not to assign counsel was not basis for CPCS to be held in contempt of court order;

C v Coral **72 MAC 222, further rev. denied 452 M 1107 (2008), cert. denied 129 S Ct 1633 (2009)**—avoiding D's claim (citing *Halbert v Michigan* 545 US 605 [2005]) of right to counsel on R.30 motion to withdraw guilty plea (is "the only method for challenging a guilty plea a "direct" appeal? a "collateral" attack? a "hybrid"?), by ruling that this D's delay (three years after guilty plea) would "militate against" treating motion as analogous to direct appeal, and instead as a collateral challenge not requiring appointment of counsel;

C v Morgan **453 M 54 (2009)**—to get discovery under motion for new trial based on newly discovered evidence, D must make specific (not speculative or conclusory) allegations that the newly discovered evidence would have materially aided defense against pending charges and that this evidence if further explored through discovery, could yield evidence which might have "played an important role in jury's deliberations and conclusions, even though it is not certain that evidence would have produced" NG verdict; mere speculation that different lab's testing might result in different conclusion = insufficient to support request for post-conviction expert;

***Montefusco v Commonwealth* 452 M 1015 (2008)**— D's petition for "mandamus" relief to force DA's office to produce file and discovery from his previously-concluded criminal case (presumably preparatory to filing motion for new trial) rejected: M.R.Crim.P. 30(c)(4) allows judge to authorize such discovery by specified procedure, and mandamus relief inappropriate when alternative means exist to obtain documents requested (including, presumably, obtaining documents from prior counsel); DA has no "clear cut duty to produce case file or other discovery" in these circumstances;

***District Attorney's Office v Osborne* 129 S Ct 2308 (2009)**—D's federal court suit brought under 42 USC § 1983 sought access to DNA for more sophisticated testing; left open = whether suit instead should have been under 28 USC § 2254; questionable whether there is a federal constitutional right to be released upon proof of "actual innocence" (but this would be a § 2254 claim in any event); there is no "freestanding right to access DNA evidence for testing" under the Due Process clause; after conviction following fair trial, D does not have presumption of innocence or the "same liberty interests as a free man";

See Chapter 13-E, Plea of Guilty—Procedures, for cases allowing withdrawal of guilty pleas by way of Rule 30, e.g., *C v Carter* **50 MAC 902 (2000)** guilty plea involuntary because coerced by judge's threat of 20 years after trial, but only 6 years on G plea; *C v Berrios* **447 M 701 (2006)**—guilty plea not involuntary simply because D felt that he had no choice but to so plead; consideration of the gravity of charges and possible sentences is "endemic to any system which asks a person to forgo certain rights in order to be spared certain penalties"; that D chose to forgo a "viable defense" did not make situation unique;

C v Colon **439 M 519 (2003)**—evidence submitted to support claim of inadequate G plea colloquy when recording was unavailable;

C v Casimir **442 M 1031 (2004)**—D's motion to vacate guilty plea = essentially motion for new trial, so Commonwealth had right to interlocutory review of order allowing it (& thus, G.L. c. 211, § 3 relief unavailable);

M.R.Crim.P. 30—(a) "Unlawful Restraint"—if imprisoned/restrained of liberty pursuant to criminal conviction, right ANY TIME to file motion for trial judge to release or correct sentence because violative of Constitution or laws of US or MA; (b) "New Trial"—new trial motion anytime & allowable "if it appears JUSTICE may not have been done"; 30(c)(1) serve office of prosecutor who represented Commonwealth in trial court; 30(c)(2) all grounds for relief shall be raised by D in "original or amended mo-

tion"; any ground not so raised = waived unless judge in discretion permits subsequent raising, or unless grounds couldn't reasonably have been raised in original or amended motion; 30(c)(3) moving party SHALL FILE & serve affidavits supporting position, & judge can rule on papers (without hearing) "if no substantial issue is raised by the motion or affidavits; 30(c)(4) judge on motion may authorize discovery, but only after notice to adverse party & opportunity to be heard; 30(c)(5) judge, in discretion, may appoint counsel to represent D in preparation & presentation of R.30 motions, and (as of 10-2001), after notice to Commonwealth & opportunity to be heard, judge may allow D "costs associated with preparation & presentation of" R.30 motion, e.g., DNA testing; 30(c)(6) judge may hear motion without D's presence; 30(c)(7) trial judge may hear the motion wherever s/he is then sitting, but only after at least 30 days' notice unless judge finds good cause to order hearing sooner; 30(c)(8) either party may appeal the judge's decision on the motion; though D can be admitted to bail pending decision in the appeal, D can't be "discharged from custody" pending final decision in the appeal; D might get costs/attorney fees if Commonwealth appeals & loses; **CAVEAT:** if there has already been direct appeal of conviction, appeal from R.30 decision in first degree murder cases may occur only if SJC single justice grants leave to appeal ("on the ground that it presents a new and substantial question which ought to be determined by the full court"): see G.L. c. 278, § 33E); *C v Azar* **444 M 72, 77 (2005)**—NEED NOT BE "INCARCERATED" to pursue remedy under Rule 30(a), so long as issue is not merely "hypothetical"; issue here concerned whether D, on probation & not in custody, could (when probation was revoked) legally be committed to prison on a suspended sentence "the legality of which he challenges"; SJC disavows any contrary inference from *C v Lupo* 394 M 544, 546 (85);

C v Simmons **448 M 687 (2007)**—Rule 30(a) = appropriate to raise D's argument that removing conviction from "file" and sentencing on it was improper, and remedy sought was to vacate the sentence; even if D wasn't currently incarcerated on this sentence, SJC could properly consider his motion under Rule 30(a), because vacated sentence could be applied as credit against whatever sentence D WAS currently serving;

C v Johnson **75 MAC 903 (2009)**—D failed to object when he was convicted of & sentenced for both "trafficking" in cocaine and possession with intent to distribute, having been convicted of like offense previously: principle of "waiver" did not operate to bar Rule 30 motion raising duplicative convictions issue; Rule 30 motion may be brought any time, as of right; that D had already served maximum sentence on each conviction did not make issue moot, as there were collateral consequences to the conviction[s] themselves;

C v Daniels **445 M 392 (2005)**—trial judge abused her discretion in denying D's motion for post-trial discovery, on newly discovered information casting doubt on credibility of ID made by sole eyewitness: Commonwealth allegedly withheld exculpatory evidence which he had specifically requested before trial; if the discovery supports, D may file renewed motion for new trial and for hearing, AND a motion for costs;

C v Kobrin **72 MAC 589 (2008)**—Appeals Court rejects Commonwealth argument that D had to show "it would not have been impossible for counsel to have uncovered the new evidence before trial": D "need not jump quite so high a hurdle," and instead had only to show "that reasonable diligence would not have led his trial counsel to the material"; judge's memo underscored appellate counsel's extensive discovery efforts; Appeals Court find that new evidence "would probably have been a real factor in the jury's deliberations";

C v Cronk **396 M 194 (85)**—once party enters an appeal, lower court is divested of jurisdiction to act on motions to rehear or vacate; *C v Adkinson* **442 M 410, 422 (2004)**—same; SJC refused to consider issues in motion for new trial filed and ruled upon by trial judge after direct appeal was pending in Appeals Court (even though they had been briefed by parties);

C v Montgomery **53 MAC 350 (2001)**—trial court may not act upon a Rule 30 "or any related motion" while D's direct appeal is pending (without obtaining leave of appellate court, and stay of appellate proceedings for this purpose);

C v Rodriguez **443 M 707 (2005)**—D's claim made in Rule 30 motion was rejected on ground of "direct estoppel", inasmuch as the validity of the no-knock warrant had been raised in pretrial motion to suppress and was addressed in her direct appeal, and was an essential issue in her case;

C v Goodreau **442 M 341 (2004)**—hearsay in affidavits supporting Rule 30 motion may be ignored by motion judge; appellate counsel's affidavit re: what trial counsel said wasn't confirmed by trial counsel's own affidavit; "judge may take into account the suspicious failure to provide pertinent information from an expected and available source"; *C v Rebello* **450 M 118 (2007)**—judge was entitled "to ignore the hearsay statement of trial counsel contained in appellate counsel's affidavit";

Napolitano v Attorney General **432 M 240 (2000)**—single justice's decision in "gatekeeper" capacity (after G.L. c. 278, § 33E review, when party tries to appeal decision of trial judge on R.30 motion) "is final and unreviewable," can't be appealed to full court, and can't be collaterally attacked on merits via complaint for declaratory relief; single justice should grant leave to appeal only if case "presents a new & substantial question which ought to be determined by the full court"; rejects claim that this D was treated differently from similarly-situated Ds with same issue ("any similarities (are) only general in nature");

Dickerson v AG **396 M 740 (86)**—because 1st degree murder D gets "plenary" SJC review (G.L. c. 278, § 33E), no equal protection violation to deny appeal by right from denial of motion for new trial;

C v Lanoue (III) **409 M 1 (90)**—although murder D not ordinarily entitled to appellate review of new trial motions raising claims not previously raised on appeal receiving G.L. c. 278, § 33E review, D's ineffective assistance claims merited review because trial counsel could not have been expected to have raised such claims against himself on appeal;

C v Francis **411 M 579 (92)**—Commonwealth must obtain leave of single justice to appeal allowance of new trial motion for murder 1 pursuant to G.L. c. 278, § 33E; 20-year "delay" between affirmance & filing of new trial motion not a waiver of issue by D;

C v Preston **393 M 318 (84)**—judge can order new trial under R.25(b)(2) though D's new trial motion was under 30 (b); normally 25 = BEFORE appeal, & 30 = AFTER; new trial motion for G. against the weight of evidence more closely within scope of 25(b)(2) than 30; (new trial here = OK because trial judge evaluated & nuances of conduct, tone, & evidence not apparent in "cold record");

C v Gilbert **447 M 161 (2006)**—seven years after first degree murder conviction was affirmed by SJC on direct appeal, D filed R. 30 motion seeking new trial on ground that erroneous jury instructions created substantial risk of miscarriage of justice because jury may have convicted of first degree while only finding what correctly "was second degree murder or even manslaughter": motion judge's reduction of verdict to second degree murder (after he asked **Commonwealth** to elect either this result or new trial on first degree murder) was upheld by SJC, which also held that the order was appropriately subject to G.L. c. 278, § 33E "gatekeeper" provision (here allowed) and review by SJC;

C v Gordon **13 MAC 1085 (82)**—OK new trial for trial judge's "grave misgivings" re: ID of D; reversal for abuse of discretion = "extremely rare";

C v Masonoff **70 MAC 162 (2007)**—reversing allowance of motion for new trial (20 years later, by judge who wasn't trial judge): requirement of showing "that justice may not have been done" wasn't met by motion judge's belief that trial counsel should have filed a motion to sever trial from co-D (motion judge's "ineffective assistance" ruling also reversed);

C v Woods **382 M 1 (80)**—denial of motion for new trial = abuse of discretion because documentary evidence put SJC in equal position to trial judge to weigh the evidence;

C v Sperrazza **399 M 1001 (87)**—trial judge discretion to give new trial for wrong standard he says he used to admit D's statement;

C v Roberio **428 M 278 (98)**—improper for trial judge, having found ineffective assistance for failure to raise mental impairment defense, to then remove the issue of credibility of the defense from the jury; "judge's inquiry should have ended when he concluded that the defendant was deprived of a substantial available defense";

C v Hensley **454 M 721 (2009)**—unlike in *Roberio*, judge did not decide trial counsel was ineffective and then deny motion based on adverse determination of expert's credibility; here, judge found good reasons for trial counsel not to have presented expert and documentary evidence, & so rejected "ineffective assistance" claim;

C v Pike **431 M 212 (2000)**—judge on motion for new trial, even if she wasn't trial judge, may deny new trial simply because judge, unlike expert, doesn't believe that D suffered from battered woman syndrome; judge could find that expert's opinions were dependent on accuracy/reliability of facts presented to expert by D, AND that D was conning the experts;

C v Gagliardi **21 MAC 439 (86)**—late discovery, overcharging, & bad opening = new trial;

C v Merry **453 M 653 (2009)**—opinion of Commonwealth expert about cause of damage to vehicle windshield and that there was no evidence that D was sitting up at time of vehicle crash (D theory = suffered seizure, collapsed, body rigid, foot stuck on accelerator) not disclosed until after conviction: material and exculpatory, new trial required;

Dunbrack v C **398 M 502 (86)**—R.30, not G.L. c. 211, § 3, appeals changed probation condition;

C v Christian **429 M 1022 (99)**—Rule 30(a) may not be used to challenge validity of a probation revocation order (must instead pursue direct appeal), but R.30(a) may be used to challenge a sentence imposed in consequence of a probation revocation order;

C v Cook **380 M 314 (80)**—R.30(b) standard same as old G.L. c. 278, § 29; new trial necessary if prejudicial constitutional error (e.g., ineffective counsel permitted cross-examination of co-D re: 5th Amendment) & optional for miscarriage of justice; (& see *C v Cowie* **404 M 119, fn. 9 (89)**);

Teague v Lane **489 US 288 (89)**—new constitutional rules should not be applied "retroactively" to criminal cases or collateral review, with two limited exceptions: (1) if "primary, private" conduct has been held beyond the power of legislature to proscribe, or (2) if new law mandates "procedures that ... are implicit in the concept of ordered liberty"; latter exception means rule/holding is "central to accurate determination of innocence or guilt" in "basic due process sense";

C v Bray **407 M 296 (90)** applies *Teague v Lane* **489 US 288 (89)**;

15-F.1. Procedures

Rule 30, Reporter's Notes—"recusal of trial judge should be exercised liberally" for motion for new trial; R.30 consolidates state habeas & writs of error; since 1964, new trial motion may be filed anytime; but see K. Smith, *Criminal Practice & Procedure*, § 2080 (2d ed. 1983 & Supp.)—"respectfully disagrees with Reporter" re: recusal of trial judge;

Sheriff of Suffolk County v Pires **438 M 96 (2002)**—habeas corpus petition can only be used when person is entitled to immediate release; it isn't substitute for appeal where appellate remedies exist; habeas isn't correct way to contest bail revocation order (G.L. c. 211, § 3 was instead the proper method of appealing revocation of bail, and "immediate release" wasn't in the cards, as D was held on $25,000 bail on new charges, bail having been revoked on prior charges due to new arrest/probable cause);

C v Huenefeld **34 MAC 315, 322 (93)**—rejecting D's claim that trial judge should have recused self from R.30 motion because it urged that trial judge had erred in evidentiary rulings at trial;

Hernandez v Commonwealth **423 M 1012 (96)**—appellate court MAY, but is not required to, allow motion to stay proceedings in direct appeal pending filing of and ruling on R.30 motion for new trial;

C v Montgomery **53 MAC 350, 354 n.9 (2001)**—when appeal from denial of motion for new trial is entered in Appeals Court in conjunction with direct appeal from criminal conviction, "matter of practice" = consolidation of the appeals on "court's own motion or on application of a party";

C v Montgomery **53 MAC 350, 354 (2001)**—while trial court generally has no jurisdiction to act on new trial motion while a docketed appeal is pending, "commonly applied exception" is when appellate court "stays" the direct appeal to permit consideration of/ruling on R.30 motion; to be considered re: stay of appeal = possibility that motion for new trial will be allowed, economy of consolidating appeal from denial of motion for new trial with direct appeal, advantages to D of such consolidated review (see *C v Curtis* **417 M 619, 623–27 (94)** re less favorable standard of review when new trial motion is decided "post-appeal"; *C v Azar* **435 M 675, 676 (2002)** similar), benefit of speedier re-trial when motion for new trial is allowed;

C v Montanez **410 M 290 (91)**—motion for reconsideration or notice of appeal must be filed within 30 days of denial of new trial motion; motion for reconsideration stops appeal period from running only if timely filed & only until motion denied;

Stewart v Commonwealth **413 M 664 (92)**—bail pending appeal of the allowance of a Rule 30 motion is discretionary BUT here, R.30 relief granted was only re-sentencing on an armed assault in dwelling conviction, and D had made no claim that additional conviction, for 2d degree murder, was illegitimate, so that sentence remained in place and could not appropriately be "stayed"; bail OK if appellate result can be "a reversal of the conviction, an order for a new trial or a term of imprisonment less than the time he already has served, including the time the appellate process requires";

C v Gagnon **37 MAC 626, 634–35 (94)**—not error to have denied D's motion for appointment of counsel for motion for new trial pursuant to M.R.Crim.P. 30, despite fact that D (eventually, long after) prevailed in claim for substantive relief, with able counsel on appeal of the denial of motion for new trial; rationale was that R.30 issues related either to court's sentencing jurisdiction or judge's charge to jury and "involved no factual issues," and were "not legally complex"; though SJC allowed application for further review, counsel appointment issue was not addressed, **419 M 1009 (95)**;

C v Davis **410 M 680 (91)**—(pre-alteration of R.30(c)(5)) indigent moving for new trial after SJC affirmed his murder-one conviction not entitled to funds for scientific testing; **BUT**, effective 10/2001, M.R.Crim.P. 30(c)(5) gives judge discretion to allow "costs associated" with preparation & presentation of" R.30 motion;

C v Dubois **451 M 20 (2008)**—G.L. c. 261, § 27C does not cover costs associated with motion for new trial, and though judge under M.R.Crim.P. 30(c)(5) has discretion to allow D costs associated with preparation of motion for new trial, no abuse of discretion in denying funds when judge "found that there was no basis to conclude that justice may not have been done";

C v Henlsey **454 M 721 (2009)**—no abuse of discretion in judge's allowing motion for funds to retain expert for motion for new trial in amount of $3,000 rather than the $6,000 requested; SJC "decline[s]" request to approve larger amount;

C v Denis **442 M 617, 633 (2004)**—in affidavit supporting motion for new trial, D claimed that audiotaped Miranda warnings were erased and rerecorded twice, until D gave up request for counsel; before refusing to hold hearing on motion, judge allowed D's motion for funds for expert to examine original tape for evidence of such rerecording (no confirmation of rerecording was produced),

C v Bray **407 M 296 (90)**—new rules will not be retroactively applied on collateral review unless "central to an accurate determination of innocence or guilt";

C v Robinson **408 M 245 (90)**—"new rule" announced in Henson requiring jury instructions on intoxication where specific intent in issue will not be applied retroactively on collateral review under Bray;

C v Peppicelli **70 MAC 87 (2007)**—refusing to apply retroactively the *Adjutant* holding (443 M 649 [2005]) that trial judge has discretion to admit evidence of specific acts of prior violent conduct by victim where identity of first aggressor is in dispute; extensive discussion of retroactivity and of "clairvoyance" exception to waiver doctrine;

15-F.2. Hearings

C v Epsom **442 M 1002 (96)**—evidentiary hearing ordered on first degree murder D's claim in motion for new trial that trial counsel failed to call witness re: self-defense, and appellate counsel had failed to raise this in appeal or in first motion for new trial;

C v Companonio **420 M 1003 (95)**—though trial judge allowed motion for new trial on basis of affidavits and legal arguments concerning ineffective assistance of counsel in failing to investigate fully murder D's possible mental impairment, SJC on Commonwealth appeal vacated allowance and ordered evidentiary hearing, including testimony from trial defense counsel re: nature and extent of D's instructions concerning trial strategy;

C v Stewart **383 M 253 (81)**—judge can deny new trial motion based on affidavits if they raise no substantial issue;

C v Dubois **451 M 20, 30, 32 (2008)**—one expert's opinion of "credibility" of prosecution expert's trial testimony did not raise substantial issue requiring a hearing;

C v Licata **412 M 654 (92)**—evidentiary hearings on new trial motions should be held where "serious issues" are raised, assuming affidavits true;

C v Delacruz **61 MAC 445 (2004), overruled on other ground, 443 M 692 (2005)**—hearing on motion for new trial should have been held, because maybe ineffective assistance to have failed to call one of perhaps three (but maybe only two) culprits in armed robbery, who had pled G, because he proffered that D was not involved; second culprit had plea-bargained and was chief witness against D; fact that uncalled witness was impeachable as felon not dispositive;

C v Edward **75 MAC 162 (2009)**—as to all but one claim in D's motion for new trial filed 13 years after direct appeal, failure to focus on alleging or showing impact of claimed errors "has direct bearing on D's entitlement to a hearing" (i.e., failure to raise "substantial issue"); remanding for hearing only on issue of courtroom's alleged closure during testimony by seventeen-year-old sexual assault complainant;

C v Candelario **446 M 847 (2006)**—no evidentiary hearing on new trial motion required when hearing wouldn't appreciably add to written material, which didn't cast doubt on counsel's competence or tactical decisions;

C v Denis **442 M 617, 633 (2004)**—in affidavit supporting motion for new trial, D claimed that audiotaped Miranda warnings were erased and rerecorded twice, until D gave up request for counsel; before refusing to hold hearing on motion, judge allowed D's motion for funds for expert to examine original tape for evidence of such rerecording; no confirmation of rerecording was produced, & unsubstantiated allegation of wrongdoing by police didn't raise substantial issue;

C v Wheeler **52 MAC 631 (2001)—delinquency adjudication occurring 27 years earlier was cause of 17-year-veteran police officer's loss of license to carry a firearm (legislation passed in 1998 mandated this ineligibility) & thus loss of job: presumption of regularity was enough to rebuff D's claim in R.30 motion that his trial attorney had been ineffective and labored under conflict of interest due to representing co-defendants;** motion counsel had specifically eschewed evidentiary hearing, and while issue raised = serious, D's factual showing was seriously deficient (e.g., failure to proffer docket sheets concerning co-defendants, disposition of their cases);

C v Meggs **30 MAC 111 (91)**—judge's denial of new trial motion on affidavits was error where defense expert raised "substantial issue" requiring evidentiary hearing on newly available blood grouping evidence; blood grouping of semen donors not available at time of trial deemed newly discovered evidence;

C v Chiappini **72 MAC 188 (2008)**—D was convicted of assault and battery by dangerous weapon (stabbing neck), though at trial had claimed self-defense; his "victim", however, subsequently admitted to sufficient facts on charge of assault and battery by means of dangerous weapon (pavement), and prosecutor's recitation of facts *then* was that "victim" of D had had D on the pavement and smashed D's head into pavement; "victim" denied during D's trial that D had ever been on ground, allowing prosecution to argue in closing that D easily could have escaped as combatants were only in "stand-up fistfight"; trial judge's denial of D's motion for new trial = vacated: "victim's admissions held to be newly discovered evidence and motion/trial judge's findings to contrary = error of law; **S.C., after remand, 76 MAC 1107 (2010)**—order denying motion for new trial = **reversed**;

C v Buck **64 MAC 760 (2005)**—rejects Commonwealth's argument that trial counsel should have been more diligent, such that purportedly "newly discovered evidence" was available to counsel pretrial (upholding trial court judge's grant of motion for new trial); that the evidence could not have conclusively proved D's innocence/alibi was not required; **determination of "whether justice was done" "is not dependent on the actual guilt or innocence of the defendant"**, though is "informed by the strength of the evidence as it may have influenced the jury's verdict";

C v Conaghan **433 M 105, 109 (2000)**—evidence of battered woman syndrome may be considered newly discovered evidence warranting a new trial, "even if there were some knowledge of the abuse at trial" (or, as here, at time of G plea); remanded for G.L. c. 123, § 15(a) competency hearing (re: competence of D at time of plea, relevant to voluntariness of plea and (in)competence to rationally assist counsel in defense at that earlier time);

C v Fappiano **69 MAC 727 (2007)**—though this trial predated *Pike* and *Conaghan* decisions, significance of this D's abuse history were, or should have been, well known to both D and trial defense counsel; not "newly discovered," so no error in denying motion for new trial; fn.13 notes that appellate counsel had not claimed ineffective assistance of trial counsel (but perhaps only because [fn.8] motion for funds for battered woman diagnosis was denied?);

C v Weichell **446 M 785 (2006)**—though *C v Pike* [431 M 212, 222 (2000)] might be thought to have carved out a "coercion" or "fear" exception to reasonable diligence requirement of newly-discovered evidence in the context of a "battered woman" who did not perceive her condition at the earlier time, judge on motion for new trial committed error of law when he held that letter was "newly discovered" because D reasonably feared violence would befall his family if he was duly diligent at the appropriate time; duty to uncover evidence through reasonable diligence before trial or before motion for new trial lies not only with defense counsel, but also with D himself;

C v Trung Chi Truong **34 MAC 668 (93)**—evidentiary hearing required on previously-denied without-hearing R.30 motion, "to ascertain the true probative value of the newly discovered evidence";

C v Delong **60 MAC 122, 137 (2003)**—though decision not to hold evidentiary hearing gets "substantial deference," here, there should have been evidentiary hearing concerning newly discovered evidence of surveillance tape which purportedly showed robber "casing" store three days before robbery; different county claimed, however, that at the time D was robbing a different store;

C v Haley **413 M 770 (92)**—appellate courts will not defer to rulings on new trial motions where judge other than trial judge made ruling without evidentiary hearing, especially where judge's memorandum taken "virtually verbatim" from papers of one of parties;

C v Brookins **33 MAC 626 (92)**—allegations in new trial motion that trial counsel failed to secure testimony of exculpatory neutral eyewitness raised a "substantial issue" that merited hearing, and appellate court ordered new trial on basis of ineffective assistance; BUT SJC on further appellate review (**416 M 97 (93)**) held that, without evidentiary hearing or stipulation as to facts, appellate court couldn't determine whether or not there had been ineffective assistance (SJC nonetheless reversed convictions on another ground)

Hagen v Commonwealth **437 M 374, 382 (2002)**—record "provides no plausible excuse for a delay of four years in holding the hearing on (D's) motion for a new trial";

15-F.3. Waiver of Issues Not Raised at First Opportunity

C v Crawford **430 M 683 (2000)**—when motion judge didn't exercise discretion to consider argument, they were deemed waived because they could have been raised in first motion for new trial;

C v Hallet **427 M 552, 554 (98)**—when motion for new trial is filed before D's direct appeal proceeds, and when motion judge elects to consider substantively one or more issues which were not preserved for appellate review at the trial itself, those issues are considered on appeal "as if . . . fully preserved at trial for appellate review"; BUT SEE *C v Curtis* **417 M 619 (94)**; *C v Amirault* **424 M 618, 640 (97)** if motion for new trial is instead acted upon after direct appeal fails, trial judge's substantive consideration of issue will not resurrect it so as to yield a more favorable standard of review;

C v Curtis **417 M 619 (94)**—if issue was preserved at trial but appellate counsel fails to argue it on direct appeal, issue will be considered on subsequent "post-conviction" review only on standard of whether there's substantial risk of miscarriage of justice; failure to raise "constitutional issue" at "earliest reasonable opportunity" may mean it's waived; trial judge's discretionary power to consider, in R.30 motion, issues not raised at trial or on direct appeal, "should be exercised only in those extraordinary cases where . . . miscarriage of justice might otherwise result"; if there has been appellate review of a conviction or a prior motion for new trial, judge should say that s/he is exercising discretion to consider substantively; even if judge below considers substantively, appellate court will not apply a more favorable standard of review than "substantial risk of a miscarriage of justice" (previously, substantive consideration on R.30 would resurrect issue not preserved by objection at trial; this is no longer true);

C v Randolph **438 M 290 (2002)**—claim of error is normally considered waived if not raised at first available opportunity; exceptions include "clairvoyance" and "resurrection" (see Curtis & Hallet, above); in post-appeal motion for new trial, standard of review is whether there's "substantial risk of a miscarriage of justice," i.e., whether there is "a serious doubt whether the result of the trial might have been different had the error not been made"; here, instruction on provocation impermissibly shifted burden of proof to D, BUT no substantial risk of miscarriage found;

C v Bly **444 M 640 (2005)**—asserts that "near byzantine requirements to avoid resurrection" have been eliminated; citing *C v Randolph* 438 M 290, 294–96 (2002), says assertions of unpreserved error offered as the basis of a claim of ineffective assistance of counsel in a motion for new trial are evaluated in first degree murder cases under "substantial likelihood of a miscarriage of justice" standard and in all other cases under the standard in *C v Saferian* 366 M 89, 96 (74); "In all cases, assertions of unpreserved error remain[ ] unpreserved"; "the power of resurrection is no longer viable and will no longer be recognized in criminal cases";

C v Edward **75 MAC 162 (2009)**—finding of waiver doesn't end analysis, but waived claims = reviewed under "substantial risk of a miscarriage of justice standard," with four "related questions" to be considered: (1) was there error; (2) was D prejudiced by error; (3) considering error in context of entire trial, "would it be reasonable to conclude that the error materially influenced the verdict?"; (4) is it inferable that counsel's failure to object or raise claim at earlier date was a reasonable tactical decision?;

C v Martinez **420 M 622, 624 (95)**—if D has failed to raise issue at trial or on appeal, and it's raised 1st in motion for new trial, "simple denial" of motion won't "breathe vitality into" such issue, but trial judge's consideration of such issue on its merits means appellate court (on appeal of denial of m. new trial) will consider it "to determine if there has been a substantial risk of a miscarriage of justice";

C v Kater **432 M 404, 411 (2000)**—though appellate court considered issues waived because they hadn't been raised (though available) in prior appeals, SJC nonetheless had to consider them under G.L. c. 278, § 33E in direct appeal of first degree murder conviction;

C v Gagliardi **418 M 562 (94)**—motion for new trial "may not be used as a vehicle to compel . . . review and consideration of questions of law, on which" D has either had his day in appellate court or "forgone that opportunity"; judge nonetheless has "discretion" to grant new trial despite his opportunity to infer waiver as a matter of law (and D should show that otherwise "miscarriage of justice might . . . result); on appeal of denial of motion for new trial when judge has deemed issues waived by failure to raise on appeal, appellate court must consider "only those issues that have some constitutional basis, or which were not open to the defendant on direct appeal" if the case is a "non-capital" one; hearing should be held if motion for new trial raises "substantial issue" (shown by "seriousness" of issue, and its presence in the case, and prejudice resulting from it);

C v Alicea **27 MAC 1147 (89)**—constitutional error raised for first time in new trial motion subject to "harmless beyond reasonable doubt" standard of review, at least where law was undeveloped at time of trial;

C v Colon-Cruz **408 M 533 (90)**—issues not properly preserved at trial can be raised in new trial motion only in extraordinary cases where miscarriage of justice would result;

C v Sibinich **33 MAC 246 (92)**—trial judge's substantive consideration in postconviction proceedings of issue which D failed to preserve at trial resurrected it for appellate consideration;

C v Egardo **426 M 48, 49–50 (97)**—no waiver of ineffective assistance of counsel issue from failure to raise it in direct appeal (though it was apparent on record), because trial counsel was member of "same firm" (CPCS Public Defender Division) as counsel on direct appeal;

C v Williams (No. 1), **68 MAC 287 (2007)**—same when motion for new trial is by CPCS Public Defender division and trial was by CPCS Public Defender Division: new, non-Public Defender attorney-counseled, direct appeal can raise trial counsel's alleged failures and shortcomings, and won't be charged with having waived the issues for failure to raise them in earlier motion for new trial; notwithstanding favorable ruling on waiver, however, the issues of ineffective assistance had to be raised by Rule 30 motion (fn.4);

C v Lanoue (III) **409 M 1 (90)**—although murder D not ordinarily entitled to appellate review of new trial motions raising claims not previously raised on appeal receiving G.L. c. 278, § 33E review, D's ineffective assistance claims merited review because trial counsel could not have been expected to have raised such claims against himself on appeal; see also *C v Egardo* 426 M 48 (97); *C v Williams (No. 1)* 68 MAC 287 (2007);

Habarek v Commonwealth **421 M 1005 (95)**—1st degree murder D didn't waive ineffective assistance of counsel claim because same attorney represented D at trial and on appeal; SJC ordered evidentiary hearing on D's motion for new trial based on ineffective assistance of counsel;

C v Gilliard **36 MAC 183, 191–92 (94)**—appeals court, sua sponte, directed that new counsel be appointed to raise in R.30 motion the issue of possible ineffective assistance of counsel (in failing to request instruction on lesser offense), when trial counsel continued to represent D on appeal;

C v Hallet **427 M 552, 555 (98)**—if judge considers substantively, on motion for new trial filed before direct appeal, an issue which could have been but wasn't preserved at trial, issue is revived for purposes of appellate review;

C v Lewis **48 MAC 343 (99)**—brief discussion by judge and assertion that, "had she been asked, she would have given (specific unanimity) instruction," didn't revive the issue of her failure to give such instruction;

C v Deeran **397 M 136 (86)**—discretion to deny review of constitutional error raised for first time on 2d motion for new trial;

C v Valliere **437 M 366 (2002)**—claim that armed robbery convictions merged with first degree murder convictions, so that former should have been vacated, was waived because not brought in either of two prior motions to correct sentences (& was a recognizable issue at least by time of second motion);

15-F.4. Ineffective Assistance of Counsel Claims

See cases above, in "Waiver,"—concerning failure to raise ineffective assistance of counsel on direct appeal when same attorney represented D at trial and on direct appeal (no waiver imputed); see also Chapter 2-E (Competent and Effective Counsel);

C v Adamides **37 MAC 339 (94)**—claim of ineffective assistance of counsel can be raised on DIRECT APPEAL (rather than R.30 motion) only "when the factual basis of the claim appears indisputably on the trial record"; record of trial here insufficient to resolve/present claim that trial counsel should have called certain witnesses, or should have filed motion to suppress;

C v Zinser **446 M 807 (2006)**—failure to argue ineffective assistance of counsel in direct appeal WAS NOT A WAIVER OF ISSUE, & judge's contrary holding in refusing to hear motion for new trial was error; "our courts strongly disfavor raising claims of ineffective assistance on direct appeal" & "[*Adamides* 37 MAC 339,344] exception", i.e., when factual basis appears indisputably on trial record, "is narrow"; here, failure to investigate & proffer mental impairment defense obviously required affidavits/more evidence;

C v Cortez **438 M 123 (2002)**—alleged ineffectiveness of trial counsel (who merely tried to impeach fingerprint testimony by state trooper with report signed by state police technician, and was told by trial judge that he'd have to call the technician, and thereafter did not so call) wouldn't be resolved on direct appeal, as evidence re: why counsel didn't call (strategic reasons possible) needed to be taken;

C v Garuti **454 M 48 (2009)**—SJC declines D's demand that trial counsel be required to provide affidavit regarding ineffective assistance claim raised on R.30 mo-

tion: in circumstances here, trial counsel responded to affidavit prepared for him by counsel by saying "sorry ... cannot help ... contents ... inaccurate", and made no response to follow-up request to just write an accurate affidavit: trial counsel's "refusal to be more specific (and thus contradict [D]) reasonably can be seen as fulfilling a duty to [D]";

C v Crespo **59 MAC 926 (2003)**—record of trial allowed appellate court to reject claim of ineffective assistance in failure to move for suppression (without need for motion for new trial);

C v Grissett **66 MAC 454, 459 n.11 (2006)**—ineffective assistance found on trial record when defense counsel opened the door to predictable and devastating impeachment of D;

C v Ye **52 MAC 390 (2001)**—no ineffective assistance in failure to file motion to suppress, because evidence at trial showed D had no expectation of privacy as to some evidence; as to others, record on direct appeal inadequate to establish whether or not D had any reasonable expectation of privacy (so motion for new trial would be necessary to press the claim);

C v McCormick **48 MAC 106 (99)**—appellate counsel faulted for "not having followed the recommended course of making a motion for a new trial," and instead raising argument on direct appeal that trial counsel provided ineffective assistance; but see *C v Simmarano* **50 MAC 312 (2000)** trial counsel's failure to request jury instruction re: defense, & failure to offer justification for evidence critical to that defense held to be ineffective assistance on direct appeal rather than via R.30 motion; "ineffective" analysis used instead of more usual "substantial risk of miscarriage of justice" analysis (because trial counsel failed to object/preserve for appeal these same issues);

C v Smith **49 MAC 127 (2000)**—by affidavit, trial counsel recounted his reasoning behind failing to call particular witness; no error in refusing hearing on motion for new trial;

C v Companonio **420 M 1003 (95)**—though trial judge allowed motion for new trial on basis of affidavits and legal arguments concerning ineffective assistance of counsel in failing to investigate fully murder D's possible mental impairment, SJC on Commonwealth appeal vacated allowance and ordered evidentiary hearing, including testimony from trial defense counsel re: nature and extent of D's instructions concerning trial strategy;

C v DiRusso **60 MAC 235 (2003)**—claim on appeal of ineffective assistance for trial counsel's failure to request individual voir dire on possible extraneous influence based on subject allegations of childhood sexual abuse rejected: could be tactical judgment that inquiry itself would activate latent prejudice: need affidavit (?) asserting not tactical reasoning;

C v Ortiz **67 MAC 349 (2006)**—though trial counsel supplied affidavit in support of D's motion for new trial, appellate court noticed that affidavit was silent as to reasons for not presenting witness (claimed by successor counsel to have been so important that ineffective assistance should be found);

C v McKinnon **35 MAC 398, 406 (93)—appellate court refused to "pass on the performance of trial counsel without the benefit of the judgment of the trial judge, including his findings of fact, that M.R.Crim.P. 30(b), 378 M 900 (1979), was designed to secure"**;

C v Plouffe **52 MAC 543, 545 (2001)**—claim of ineffectiveness of counsel in failing to use sexual assault complainant's counseling records needed to be made via Rule 30 rather than direct appeal; on present record, failure to introduce records wasn't "manifestly unreasonable";

C v Brookins **416 M 97 (93)**—though Appeals Court in same case had found ineffective assistance of counsel (**33 MAC 626 (92)**), because D's R.30 motion was denied without hearing and there was no stipulation of facts, SJC held itself not in position to know whether there had been behavior of counsel falling measurably below that expected of ordinary fallible lawyer and whether it likely deprived D of otherwise available substantial ground of defense;

C v Collins **36 MAC 25, 30 (94)**—when R.30 motion alleged ineffective assistance of counsel from failure to call two witnesses, fatal to omit affidavits from these two people re: what testimony would have been;

C v Alvarez **62 MAC 866 (2005)**—refusal to find ineffective assistance of counsel (per se) simply because trial of first degree murder charge occurred just ten days after counsel's first appearance in the case: postconviction counsel (fatally) failed to file affidavits of trial counsel or of any potential witnesses setting forth testimony they would have given if interviewed; court disparaged value of D's own affidavit ("self-serving statements regarding trial counsel's strategy");

C v Caban **48 MAC 179 (99)**—when R.30 motion alleged ineffective assistance of counsel, with affidavit from D and from his employer (including business records) substantiating alibi and asserting that D had told counsel to contact employer, abuse of discretion to deny motion without evidentiary hearing;

C v Baker **440 M 519 (2003)**—after judge allowed motion for funds for expert concerning hair embedded and indentation made in wall, judge revoked allowance upon DA's assertion that prosecution would not claim that baby's head was smashed against wall; when prosecution at trial made exactly this claim, defense counsel ineffective in failing to renew request for funds and move for continuance; SJC reversed order denying motion for new trial (accompanied by expert affidavits that hair was not from dead baby and indentation not made by baby's head);

C v Aviles **40 MAC 440, 445–46 (96)**—evidence which trial counsel failed to offer/introduce was basis for successful R.30 motion on ground of ineffective assistance of counsel; trial judge denying the R.30 motion "misperceived" value of evidence: it was not required that omitted evidence "prove" that D "could not have committed the assault";

C v Roberio **428 M 278 (98)**—improper for trial judge, having found ineffective assistance for failure to

raise mental impairment defense, to then remove the issue of credibility of the defense from the jury; "judge's inquiry should have ended when he concluded that the defendant was deprived of a substantial available defense"; but see *C v Pike* **431 M 212 (2000)** judge on motion for new trial, even if she wasn't trial judge, may deny new trial simply because judge, unlike expert, doesn't believe that D suffered from battered woman syndrome; judge could find that expert's opinions were dependent on accuracy/reliability of facts presented to expert by D, AND that D was conning the experts;

C v Lykus **406 M 135 (89)**—new trial motion based on counsel's ineffective assistance in failing to file suppression motion properly denied because suppression motion wouldn't have been successful; contrast *C v Pena* **31 MAC 201 (91)** suppression motion, if filed, probably would have been successful, so probably ineffective counsel, but remand for suppression hearing to allow Commonwealth opportunity to prove otherwise; SEE also cases in Chapter 2-E.7, inter alia;

15-F.5. Newly Discovered Evidence

C v Grace **397 M 303 (86)**—new trial motion for "Newly Discovered Evid." must show: (1) it was unknown at trial time, (2) not discoverable by due diligence, AND (3) "substantial risk" jury might've said NG with it; new trial motion hearing can admit AFFIDAVITS if from personal knowledge (**id. at 313**);

C v Bennett **43 MAC 154 (97)**—court should rule upon R.30 motion based on evidence withheld prior to trial (and allegedly exculpatory) in manner respectful of role of jury; issue is not what, if any, impact the late disclosed evidence has on judge's personal assessment of trial record, but whether it would have played an important role in jury's deliberations and conclusions; *C v Tucceri* **412 M 410, 413–14 (92)** cited/quoted;

C v Schand **420 M 783, 787–88 (95)**—in R.30 claim that Commonwealth failed despite specific request to turn over exculpatory info re: out-of-court ID, D had to prove that evidence existed, that it tended to exculpate him, that Commonwealth failed to deliver it to D in discovery, AND that there was "a substantial basis for claiming prejudice from the nondisclosure" (latter requirement said to be definition of "materiality," and apparently imposing higher degree of proof on D than merely "exculpatory");

C v Merry **453 M 653 (2009)**—Commonwealth turned over, post-conviction, material and exculpatory info previously withheld: new trial required; *C v Dubois* **451 M 20 (2008)**—while affirming conviction and denial of motion for new trial, SJC explicitly "permit[ted]" D to file motion to obtain info re: tape recording of his conversation with police soon after the murder with which he was charged six years later;

C v Duest **30 MAC 623 (91)**—evidence not introduced at trial because forgotten by D until after trial was not "newly discovered";

C v Dubois **451 M 20 (2008)**—prosecution expert testified that specimen of "reverse writing" was "probably" written by the writer of the known samples (D), and acknowledged on cross that she preferred to work with 'original documents when comparing them to known ones,' but had only the "reverse writing" here, could not determine whether the original writing from which reverse writing was created was a fabrication, and that her opinion about author was a "qualified" one; 126-paragraph affidavit submitted by defense expert with motion for new trial, asserting that prosecution witness's testimony was unreliable and inconsistent with accepted body of knowledge and experience in field of document examination = postconviction criticism by one expert on credibility of another expert, & not "newly discovered evidence," not basis for new trial; affiant was consulted by defense during trial;

C v Whitlock **74 MAC 320 (2009)**—that a different individual resembling D in appearance (very tall, thin, black male) and actually called "Woody," the name of the crack dealer from whom cop bought, lived next to location of sale would purportedly not have been a factor in verdict without actual evidence that he, rather than D, sold drug to cop; further, no showing that evidence was not reasonably discoverable by time of trial (trial counsel asked cop question about "Woodrow", and D's former girlfriend's affidavit revealed that she had known the info belatedly claimed to be 'newly discovered'; Appeals Court's decision fails to connect D's claim of ineffective assistance of trial counsel with this issue;

C v Moore **408 M 117 (90)**—new trial motion properly denied because newly discovered evidence wouldn't have been factor in jury's deliberations;

C v Lykus **451 M 310 (2008)**—newly discovered evidence not basis for allowing new trial because it was cumulative of evidence admitted at trial;

C v Holmes **46 MAC 550 (99)**—as to R.30 claim that prosecutor had intimidated prosecution witness to prevent his intended trial testimony recanting his grand jury testimony, Court noted that witness's own affidavit failed to claim that he had lied or testified inaccurately at trial; as to claim that Commonwealth failed to disclose exculpatory evidence, i.e., that a different witness expected to, and did, receive favorable treatment on a pending charge, Court asserted that "fact that (witness) expected to, and did, receive favorable treatment after the defendant's trial does not amount to a deal";

C v LaFave **430 M 169, 181 (99)**—expert testimony not to be considered "newly discovered" for purpose of new trial motion "simply because recent studies may lend more credibility to expert testimony that was or could have been presented at trial";

C v Pike **431 M 212 (2000)**—judge on motion for new trial, even if she wasn't trial judge, may deny new trial simply because judge, unlike expert, doesn't believe that D suffered from battered woman syndrome; judge could find that expert's opinions were dependent on accuracy/reliability of facts presented to expert by D, AND that D was conning the experts;

C v Despres **70 MAC 645 (2007)**—it was learned by defendant after conviction that indecent assault and battery complainant (mentally retarded and having "behavioral issues") had made unreliable reports about being mistreated or having his rights violated at "respite facility"; facility employees' averments about his "significant tendency to misperceive events, exaggerate and fabricate . . . in order to draw attention to himself" = insufficient basis for requiring new trial, so no "abuse of discretion" by trial judge in denying same; "character" evidence being "used to suggest that a mentally impaired witness is inherently untruthful" was "troubling" to Appeals Court; judge was within his discretion in concluding that the witnesses' qualifications were inadequate because they lacked advanced degrees in psychology or psychiatry;

15-G. PARDONS/COMMUTATIONS

See Chapter 14-T, Sentencing: Revise/Revoke and Chapter 14-U Seal;

Mass. Constitution, Pt. 2, C.2, Article 8—pardon power for Governor with advice/consent of Governor's Council;

G.L. c. 127, § 154—Parole Board = Advisory Board of Pardons; § 152 Governor gives pardons with advice/consent of Council, with or without conditions; records then sealed, not admissible, no disqualification, & D can say "no conviction"

Comm'r MDC v Dir.Civ.Serv. **348 M 184 (64)**—if pardon's not because NG, criminal acts can be considered re: character; but G. alone can't be a disqualification;

C v Childs **23 MAC 33 (86)**—can't impeach with a pardoned prior conviction (because G.L. c. 127, § 152);

C v Lindsey **396 M 840 (86)**—though D maybe alive only because gun violation, relief only from another branch of government;

Hicks v Commissioner of Correction **425 M 1014 (97)**—petitioner claimed in G.L. c. 211, § 3 petition that the commutation of his sentence was illegal: having been convicted of second degree murder, he received commutation in the form of a reduction of his sentence from "life" (with parole eligibility after 15 years) to "a term of 21 yrs. and 3 mos. to life", making him parole eligible six months from the time of commutation; when he was not paroled, he argued that the purported commutation was illegal (given the mandatory nature of the sentence for second degree murder), and instead should have reduced the verdict to manslaughter; though Court didn't reach merits (because avenue of relief could have been an appeal from the denial of a habeas corpus petition), dicta expressed rejection of petitioner's substantive argument;

Chapter 16
DEFENSE THEORIES—
COMMON AND UNCOMMON

(See Chapter 10, Prepare/Present Defense (e.g., Character Witnesses), Chapter 7, Insanity & Speedy Trial, Chapter 11, Evidence (e.g., Motives), Chapter 12, Required Finding of Not Guilty/Instructions (e.g., burden of proof, beyond reasonable doubt), Chapter 14B, Dismissal (e.g., Prosecutorial Misconduct), Chapter 17 (i.e. accessory after fact, defense of close relative), Chapter 18, Identification (including right to present evidence of another's motive, opportu-nity, physical resemblance, etc.); Chapter 21, Common Crimes; etc.) Chapter 22 F-1 for Jury Nullification;

Robinson, P.H., *Criminal Law Defenses* (1984 & pocket parts);

LaFave, W.R. and Scott, A.W., Jr., *Substantive Criminal Law*, Chapters 3–5 (1986 & pocket parts);

16-A. IN GENERAL—PRESUME INNOCENT, JURY (NULLIFICATION), SPIRIT OF LAW, STRICT CONSTRUCTION, CIRCUMSTANTIAL CASE, "AFFIRMATIVE DEFENSE," SELECTIVE PROSECUTION

Mass. Superior Court Criminal Practice Jury Instructions (99)—§ 1.1, reasonable doubt; § 1.2, presumption of innocence; § 1.3, Evidence, Direct & Circumstantial; § 1.4 inferences. See also § 5.1, Crafting a Proposed Jury Charge; § 5.2.4, Formulating Proposed Instructions: Relating Factual Theory to Legal Standards; § 5.6.8 Defense Theory of the Case; § 5.6.13, Jury Nullification;

See Chapter 12-K, Instructions re: presume innocent, reasonable doubt, etc.;

Apprendi v New Jersey **530 US 466 (2000)**—OTHER THAN fact of prior conviction, any fact that increases penalty for a crime must be proved TO JURY beyond reasonable doubt (here, "hate crime" statute provided for enhanced sentence if trial judge found, by "preponderance," that D committed the crime in order to intimidate person or group because of, inter alia, race)—it's not merely "sentencing enhancement" issue;

Coffin v US **156 US 432, 454f (1895)**—presumption of innocence = axiomatic foundation of criminal law; Sparta, Athens, Rome, & canon law; Emperor Julian: "If it suffices to accuse, what will become of the innocent?"; Blackstone, etc.: "better that 10 guilty persons escape punishment than that 1 innocent suffer"; (see Chapter 2);

C v Anthes **5 Gray 185, 230 (1855, CJ. Shaw)**—(same, 9 guilty persons)—rule of law & humanity, related to Mass. Declaration of Rights, Article 12 jury right, double jeopardy, & reasonable doubt; jury has no right to decide law, but verdict's incidentally judgment on it;

C v Moyles **45 MAC 350 (98)**—instruction that taking had to be against the will of three-year-old alleged victim was reversible error; letting counsel argue that taking was NOT against the will of the child's mother was no excuse for failure to state correct law (taking had to be against will of mother, child "incapable of having" a will recognizable at law);

16-A.1. Jury Nullification

Sparf v US **156 US 51 (1895)**—(same) re: jury ("nullification")—jury's "duty" to apply law & can't instruct otherwise;

Duncan v Louisiana **391 US 145 (68)**—when jury differs from judge, it's usually because they're serving their role, safeguard against compliant/biased judge;

Jackson v Virginia **443 US 307 (79)**—jury can err on side of mercy with unreasonable NG;

McCann v Adams **126 F.2d 774 (2d Cir. '42, Hand, J.)**—only unaccountable/anonymous who melt into community can take away liberty;

US v Dougherty **473 F.2d 1113 (DC Cir. '72)**—jury nullification = prerogative-in-fact throughout history; but risks anarchy, so no jury instruction OK'ing it; But see id., Bazelon's dissent from this "lack of candor";

C v Leno **415 M 835, 842 (93)**—(Liacos, J. dissenting) (similar to Bazelon's dissent in Dougherty);

C v Fernette **398 M 658, 670–71 (86)**—("We do not accept the premise that jurors have a right to nullify the law");

C v Kirwan **448 M 304 (2007)**—regarding "Model Jury Instructions on Homicide 19 (1999)", which states ". . . if the evidence allows you to find the defendant guilty of murder in the first degree, you may return a verdict of guilty of murder in the second degree," SJC asserts (a) the instruction was about "felony murder" (not here relevant), and (b) "we have consistently declined to recognize jury nullification instructions such as this," "inconsistent with a jury's duty to return a guilty verdict of the highest crime proved beyond a reasonable doubt";

C v Lopez **447 M 625 (2006)**—in refusing relief to D upon his argument that his jury trial, at which he testified, amounted to a lengthy guilty plea (& thus required a colloquy concerning waiver of rights), SJC acknowledges/ accepts premise that trial testimony was used to diminish D's "apparent moral (if not legal) culpability, and thereby

sway the consciences of the jurors," and that jurors could have voted "conscience" and returned acquittals;

Re jury nullification, see also Chapter 22-F-1;

16-A.2. Proof Beyond Reasonable Doubt, Due Process, Strict Construction of Penal Statutes, Civil Wrongs

Thompson v Louisville **362 US 199 (60)**—constitutionally "due" process voids conviction without evidence;

C v Latimore **378 M 671 (79)**, *Jackson v Virginia* **443 US 307 (79)**—must be enough evidence to satisfy rational trier of fact of each essential element beyond reasonable doubt;

C v Louis Construction **343 M 600 (60)**—every private (civil) wrong not a crime; But see *C v Garrity* **43 MAC 349 (97)** availability of civil remedy does not 'deprive Superior Court of jurisdiction' over criminal charge;

Church Holy Trinity v US **143 US 457 (1892)**—law's letter, but not spirit reaches these facts—no legislative intent for alien hiring law to cover church rector because "alien" obviously didn't include professionals; But see *C v Donovan* **395 M 20 (85)** legislative intent unclear, so D gets benefit of doubt (7 V's = only 1 larceny) (*See Chapter 19-B, Double Jeopardy, unit of prosecution*);

C v Hughes **364 M 426, 433 (73) (Hennessey dissents)**—"strict construction" of penal laws;

C v Devlin **366 M 132 (74)**—(same);

C v Strauss **188 M 229 (05)**—(same);

Aldoupolis v Commonwealth **386 M 260 (82)**—(same);

C v Black **403 M 675 (89)**—(same); *C v Conway* **2 MAC 547 (74)**—(same) re: law governing misdemeanor arrest;

C v Clinton **374 M 719 (78)**—(same) re: G.L. c. 90C, § 2 dismissal for no citation; *C v Moulton* **56 MAC 682 (2002)**—failure to give citation at accident scene didn't result in dismissal because officer hadn't completed investigation until he interviewed D at hospital;

C v Richards **426 M 689 (98)**—(same) statute penalizing harassing telephone calls not construed to cover telecopies transmitted via phone lines;

C v Carter **61 MAC 205 (2004),** *further app. review allowed by* **442 M 1103 (2004)**—strict construction (re: "infernal machine"), plus rule of lenity in construing "ambiguous" statute; *S.C.* **442 M 822 (2004)**—agreeing with Appeals Court that possessing components which could be used to construct infernal machine isn't enough for G of possession of infernal machine;

C v Clay **65 MAC 215 (2005)**—strict construction re: attempted "escape from 'penal institution'", so that attempt to escape from police station cell block was not within the statutory crime;

C v Thompson **45 MAC 523 (98)**—conviction of D for violating abuse prevention order prohibiting contact, "either in person, by telephone, in writing or otherwise" with named woman did not violate First Amendment; the harm created by contact in these circumstances is "distinct from and unrelated to any message the abuser might be seeking to send";

C v Triplett **426 M 26 (97)**—interfering with testimony of witness in an "investigation" is not interfering . . . in a judicial proceeding", required for proof of common law obstruction of justice; **ALSO** SJC leaves open the argument that common law obstruction of justice was "superseded by . . . enactment of" G.L. c. 268, § 13B;

C v Steadward **43 MAC 271 (97)**—G.L. c. 90C, § 2 dismissal for no motor vehicle citation even when prosecution begun by citizen's complaint;

C v Crosscup **369 M 228 (75)**—ambiguity in criminal law resolved in favor of lenity; mailing of license suspension notice = prima facie evidence of notice; D's burden of production to rebut, then DA burden of proof beyond a reasonable doubt;

C v Miller **22 MAC 694 (86)**—dictionary "dirk" not enough for law's "weapon"; but see *C v Krasner* **358 M 727 (71)** burglarious tool intent can be trespass; (contra dissent by Spaulding: violates strict construction rule)

C v Fancy **349 M 196 (65)**—required finding of not guilty on circumstantial evidence if it tends equally to sustain 2 inconsistent theories because neither is proven, so conjecture & surmise; (presence at theft scene & later at loot = NG, even with alias);

C v Lodge **431 M 461 (2000)**—circumstantial evidence sufficient to show D = murderer; implausibility of story of black men coming into apartment & D losing consciousness and finding 'self outside; deterioration of relationship between D and V; D buying gun 2 weeks earlier; murder gun found hidden in small opening in wall behind refrigerator in D's apartment (the murder scene); Commonwealth "need not show that no other person could have committed the crime";

C v Maldonado **429 M 502 (99)**—can't assault and batter dead person, but Court claimed sufficient evidence for jury to find that first gunshot not fatal (basis for ABDW), so second shot was basis for murder;

C v Kartell **58 MAC 428 (2003)**—D fired two shots (second one to back of head) at mutual combatant, & argued that first shot was in self-defense, and would have been fatal, so second shot shouldn't be considered/wasn't causative/& it wouldn't be homicide to shoot a dead body; BUT victim, though mortally wounded, was alive when D fired second shot, which also inflicted mortal wound; "there may be more than one proximate cause of a victim's death"; justification for first shot didn't prevent consideration of [lack of] justification for second shot;

C v Croft **345 M 143 (62)**—circumstantial evidence must exclude all reasonable hypotheses to moral certainty; ($80 heroin maybe for D's use to see if really kicked habit);

C v O'Laughlin **466 M 188 (2006)**—finding sufficient evidence for conviction of D, reversing/overruling Appeals Court's finding to the contrary (see **63 MAC 805 (2005)**—substantial "third party culprit evidence" led to required finding of not guilty even though prosecution's evidence against D included motive, means, and opportu-

nity, as well as consciousness of guilt evidence;) *C v Phinney* **446 M 155 (2006)**—failure to present third-party culprit evidence was ineffective assistance of counsel (trial court judge's allowance of motion for new trial in murder case upheld by SJC after allowance of Commonwealth's "gatekeeper" petition);

C v Gonzalez **47 MAC 255 (99)**—evidence sufficient to prove D = seller rather than buyer; opinion catalogs cases in which required finding of NG was/was not ordered in this context;

C v Tanner **66 MAC 432 (2006)**—evidence sufficient to show that D = seller, because other guy had drugs (though was buying "more" afterward?) and D was found to have no drugs, but was "surreptitiously" counting $130;

C v Clark **446 M 620 (2006)**—evidence sufficient to show D = seller rather than buyer (D received money in the transaction, and other guy threw down packet of heroin while fleeing);

C v Ward W. **47 MAC 208 (99)**—despite D's presence in robbed car within 7 blocks and about 2 minutes, and despite enough evidence to show joint venture guilt of persons other than driver, required finding of NG ordered;

Corson v C **428 M 193 (98)**—entirely too many inferences/too much speculation required to convict D of boyfriend's larceny, so required finding of NG;

C v Merrill **14 Gray 415 (1860)**—equivocal acts equally consistent with no intent to rape;

C v Eramo **377 M 912 (79)**—no more compelling to infer D prescribed drugs without medical purpose;

Berry v C **393 M 793 (85)**—required finding of NG because equally likely D or V's mom killed V;

C v Santiago **425 M 491 (97)**—when D engages in gun battle with another with intent to kill or do grievous bodily harm, D responsible for fatal shooting of 3d person even if fatal shot was fired by D's opponent and even if D did not fire first shot (though Commonwealth is required to prove beyond a reasonable doubt not "self defense");

C v Constantino **443 M 521, 528 (2005)**—jury was charged properly in motor vehicle homicide case that D guilty if he was in some way a partial cause of the accident, and not guilty if some other person was the direct or substantial cause of death;

C v Shellenberger **64 MAC 70 (2005)**—midtrial on charge of motor vehicle homicide by negligent operation, DA switched from "speeding" theory to "under the influence of amphetamines", causing reversal: at minimum, there had to be evidence as to amount or concentration of the drug in D's system, and expert testimony indicating that the concentration would impair D's ability to operate a motor vehicle;

C v Wade **428 M 147, 151 n.4 (98)**—D's actions must not only be proximate cause of death, but death must be shown to be natural and probable consequence;

C v St. Peter **48 MAC 517, 524 (2000)**—no error in refusal to instruct specifically that D's conduct had to be "THE proximate cause of death and not merely one of the causes of death"; instruction was that proximate cause =

any cause which in natural & continuous sequence unbroken by any efficient intervening cause produces the result complained of and without which the result wouldn't have occurred; "may be assisted or accelerated by other incidental or ancillary matters," but "if it continues as an operative & potent factor, chain of causation is not broken";

C v Baker 67 MAC 760 (2006)—though D's beating of V "in and of itself" did not cause V's death, but instead acted more severely upon her physical condition as it was compromised by both acute alcohol intoxication and the effects of chronic alcoholism, D's manslaughter conviction was appropriate; *C v Rhoades* 379 M 810, 825 (80) & subsequent cases establish that a "contributing" cause of death may also be a "proximate" cause of death (though can't just be any "link" no matter how remote in chain of events leading to death); furthermore, medical evidence concerning "preexisting condition/injuries" and head trauma included circumstantial evidence that D had inflicted THOSE batteries, & was relevant to show hostile nature of the relationship, including an abuse prevention order;

C v Carlson 447 M 79 (2006)—when D failed to yield right of way/stop at intersection and hit car broadside, victim suffered multiple chest wall fractures, which exacerbated preexisting chronic obstructive pulmonary disease; though victim might have improved to her preexisting (impaired) condition, she did not want to continue attachment to mechanical breathing machine and died shortly after her decision to be removed from life support; court rejected D's argument that, as matter of law, decision was independent occurrence breaking chain of causation; jury is to decide whether intervening act was reasonably foreseeable and thus followed naturally from D's conduct or was instead "unforeseeable," breaking chain of causation; tort concept of taking V as one finds him applies to criminal law;

C v Chongarlides 62 MAC 709 (2004)—D not entitled to NG on basis that he had supplied victim only with heroin, and medical examiner testified that blood contained potentially lethal quantities of heroin and cocaine and that either one could have caused death; there can be more than one proximate cause of a victim's death;

C v Casanova 429 M 293 (99)—though death (allegedly from shooting by D) did not occur until six years after the shooting, D was prosecuted for murder and moved to dismiss for violation of right to speedy trial and due process; no relief: no statute of limitations for murder (and thus no deprivation of "substantive due process"), and prior case (*C v Lewis* 381 M 411 (80), cert denied 450 US 929) abolished common law "year and a day" rule limiting murder prosecutions to those in which death occurred within that period of time after infliction of injury; SJC won't replace it with different period re: limitation concerning causation, though legislature can;

Rogers v Tennessee 532 US 451 (2001)—application to D of rule abolishing common law "year and a day" rule in homicide prosecutions (death of V had to come within that time after D's action in order to make him criminally liable) NOT violative of ex post facto clause because judicial interpretation of criminal statute was neither unexpected nor indefensible by reference to law as expressed prior to conduct in issue;

C v Niemic 427 M 718, 727 (98)—intervening conduct of a 3d party will relieve D of culpability IF such an intervening response was not reasonably foreseeable and case law "do(es) not foreclose the conclusion that reckless medical care is not reasonably foreseeable"; such a defense is viable (1st degree murder prosecution);

C v Angelo Todesca Corporation 446 M 128 (2006), overruling/reversing 62 MAC 599 (2004)—company truck lacked an alarm to signal it was backing up, & SJC holds that reasonable jury could find that truck's collision with victim was foreseeable result of absence of alarm on truck backing up, and that other trucks' frantic air horns would not have conveyed the same message as the distinctive beeping sound of a vehicle operating in reverse; even if victim were contributorily negligent, this "does not excuse a defendant whose conduct also causes the death", and jurors here were properly instructed and listened to extensive argument by lawyers on this point;

C v Salemme 395 M 594 (85)—D with V & H 10 minutes before V killed, then fled: equal chance H did it; BUT compare/contrast *C v DiBenedetto* 427 M 414 (98) when sufficient evidence of joint venture exists, Commonwealth need not prove which venturer fired fatal shots;

C v Echavarria 428 M 593 (98)—same;

C v Brown 50 MAC 253 (2000)—reversal of multiple convictions of each of 3 D's, though 3 Ds were seen running together after gunshots: "logical inference that 2 of the 3 Ds may each have possessed a gun is not a substitute for proof beyond a reasonable doubt that an identified D possessed a specific gun";

C v Duncan 71 MAC 150, further review allowed 452 M 1110 (2008)—three defendants were nearby two hot dry guns in trash can which otherwise held wet refuse, and MAC says finding of not guilty not required; fn.5 purports to distinguish *Brown* 50 MAC 253, perhaps illegitimately;

C v Cannon 449 M 462 (2007)—evidence inadequate to prove D's guilt as principal in shooting drug dealer (witness in another room heard shots fired, insufficient evidence to establish that shots came from more than one gun, and 2–3 assailants fled the scene), and jury verdict didn't specify whether conviction of murder was premised upon theory of principal or joint venture liability; reversal, with remand for new trial solely on joint venture liability; [if evidence sufficient to convict under either theory, general verdict "would have been sound"];

C v Mazza 399 M 395 (87)—saying V deserved death, proximity to where body's found, & flight = required finding of NG; But see *C v Jacobson* 19 MAC 666 (85) motive, presence at fire with key, impede investigation enough for G. of arson;

C v Souza 34 MAC 436 (93)—D argued unsuccessfully that it was "equally" likely that V's death proximately caused by his drunken fall from truck (rather than 20-minute beating inflicted by D ½ hour later); but see *C v Flynn* **420 M 810, 815 (95)** though there was evidence that D kicked V, evidence was insufficient to prove any **individual** act of D caused death, so error to allow individual liability theory for homicide to go to jury (evidence sufficient for G as joint venturer);

C v Suarez **59 MAC 111 (2003)**—insufficient evidence to support instruction on "principal" liability;

See also K. Smith, Criminal Practice and Procedure (2d ed. 1983 & Supp.) § 1912 re: circumstantial inferences to defeat required finding of NG;

See also Joint Venture (e.g., Mandile, Intent, etc., below; Chapter 18, Identification; etc.;

C v Sokorelis **254 M 454 (26)**—D's burden of production on affirmative defense; if some evidence, DA's burden of proof beyond reasonable doubt to disprove (accessory consanguinity);

C v Kappler **416 M 574, 591 (93)**—(O'Connor, J., **dissenting**, and cases cited) when Commonwealth had burden of proof on issue & only evidence on that issue is favorable to D, mere disbelief is not proof to the contrary, and Commonwealth cannot prevail;

C v Lowe **391 M 97 (84)**—DA's case may raise defense (accident) & DA's burden (beyond reasonable doubt) to disprove (see also self-defense, etc.);

C v Power-Koch **69 MAC 735 (2007)**—D's police statement said "accident" in firing gun, didn't intend to accede to depressed best friend's request that D shoot him, though held gun, not familiar with handguns, didn't know fully loaded, didn't mean to pull trigger; error found in refusal to instruct on accident, "an unintentional event occurring through inadvertence, mistake, or negligence";

C v Burbank **388 M 789 (83)**—D's hearsay (admitted without objection) raised self-defense issue;

G.L. c. 278, § 7—D's burden of production re: LICENSE, e.g., firearm (*see Chapter 12-G, Required Finding of NG*);

C v Robbins **422 M 305 (96)**—no "burglary" (breaking & entering) unless D had no right of occupancy in wife's apartment and knowledge he had no such right (D had key);

G.L. c. 277, § 37—exception must be negatived in indictment only if in enacting clause or if necessary for a complete definition;

Sullivan v Ward **304 M 614 (39)**—(same) re: burden of proof (but see modern cases forbidding shifting burden of proof to D (Chapter 12-K));

C v Crawford **18 MAC 911 (84)**—bad instruction that certificates' (drug/gun (G.L. c. 111, § 13; G.L. c. 140, § 121A)) "prima facie" means "compelling" (*cf. Chapter 12G, K (motion for required finding of not guilty, charge & jury-waived rulings of law)*); *see Chapter 5, Complaints;* K. Smith, *Criminal Practice and Procedure*, § 726 (2d ed. 1983 & Supp.), re "negativing excuses, exceptions" in statutory description of offense;

C v Palladino **358 M 28 (70)**—elements include judicially-required ones;

C v David **365 M 47 (74)**—D's burden of producing exemption from (unlicensed broker) law; no help from G.L. c. 277, § 37 though exemption's in law;

C v Adelson **40 MAC 585 (96)**—territorial jurisdiction not a defense for jury here because evidence didn't raise; *C v Gilbert* **366 M 18, 28 (74)** distinguished;

C v Hood **389 M 581 (83)**—best not to exclude entire defense on DA's motion in limine; *see further cases in Chapter 11-B;*

[see *Heang v Commonwealth* **454 M 1011 (2009)**— D sought pretrial ruling on viability of defense (that under G.L. c. 274, § 4, as brother of offender, he could not be guilty of being accessory after fact), but it was denied because brother himself had not been charged, though had been present during murder and was friend of alleged murderer: SJC refuses G.L. c. 211, § 3 relief, advising D to make record at trial;

See specific defenses, e.g., Crosscup, above, 369 M 228 (75); Coercion, Necessity, Mistake, Entrapment, Self-Defense, all below; Insanity (Chapter 7); & specific crimes (Chapter 21);

See Chapter 6 re: Reciprocal Discovery & Rule 14 duty to notify re: defenses of insanity, alibi, & license or claim authority/ownership;

C v Garrity **43 MAC 349 (97)**—defense of "reliance on advice of counsel";

C v Luna **418 M 749 (94)**—defense of reasonable reliance on superior authority rejected (as matter of law) in circumstances of perjury prosecution;

C v O'Neil **418 M 760 (94)**—defense of 'judicial immunity' not available to court clerk who assaulted & battered court officers ordered by judges to bring clerk to judge; clerks **may** be entitled to judicial immunity for conduct directed by a judge;

16-A.3. Selective Prosecution

Yick Wo v Hopkins **118 US 356 (1886)**—selective/discriminatory prosecution barred by equal protection clause;

C v Palacios **66 MAC 13 (2006)**—racial profiling isn't a substantive defense at trial, but is instead "properly addressed in a pretrial motion to dismiss because of selective enforcement based on race"; to obtain dismissal, D must offer evidence permitting inference of unlawful discrimination by showing that a broader group of persons than those prosecuted has violated the law, that failure to prosecute others was either consistent or deliberate, and that decision not to prosecute others was based on impermissible classification factor such as race, religion, or sex; if D satisfies initial burden, Commonwealth must then rebut inference of selective enforcement, or case should be dismissed; "Denial of the motion to dismiss does not by itself eliminate the right . . . to challenge at trial the testimony of a witness on the ground of racial bias", but judge may reasonably limit scope, & without plausible showing of racial bias, judge may prohibit reference to witness's alleged bias "altogether";

Epps v C **419 M 97 (94)**—allegedly discriminatory practice by which DA nol pros'd 77% of mandatory "school zone" cases against white Ds, but nol pros'd only 45% of such cases against black or Hispanic Ds not addressed on G.L. c. 211, § 3 petition;

C v Franklin **376 M 885 (78)**—if reasonable inference of selective prosecution (e.g., racial), DA must rebut or dismissal merited;

C v King **374 M 5 (77)**—violate equal protection IF discrimination between prostitutes & customers;

C v Unnamed D **22 MAC 230 (86)**—under Mass. Equal Rights Amendment (Am. 106), dismissal for discriminating between prostitutes & customers;

C v Lafaso **49 MAC 179 (2000)**—dismissal for prosecuting prostitutes & not customers;

C v Archer **49 MAC 185 (2000)**—D probably didn't establish reasonable inference of selective prosecution re: prostitute, and if she did, Commonwealth rebutted it;

C v Bernardo B **453 M 158 (2009)**—upholding pre-trial discovery order that Commonwealth provide information to allow investigation of and support for D's claim that he was being selectively prosecuted because of his gender: D was 14-year-old boy charged with statutory rape of 12-year-old girls, and his attempts to have those girls charged with raping *him* "in connection with the same alleged incidents" had been unsuccessful;

C v Lora **451 M 425 (2008)**—evidence of racial profiling = relevant to determine whether traffic stop was product of selective enforcement; statistical evidence demonstrating disparate treatment based on race may be offered to meet D's burden to present sufficient evidence to shift burden to Commonwealth to provide race-neutral explanation for such stop;

C v Betances **451 M 457 (2008)**—categorical unsupported request for all of an arresting officer's police reports, even for six month period cannot justify automatic production order under M.R.Crim.P. 14(a)(1)(A);

C v Thomas **451 M 451 (2008)**—appropriate means by which to obtain statistical evidence to demonstrate traffic stop was made on basis of race/ethnicity (info is not within possession, custody, control of prosecutor or persons under his direction/control);

Wayte v US **470 US 598 (85)**—OK military draft enforcement only against those reported by 'self or others';

C v Smith **40 MAC 770 (96)**—D must show, among other facts, that decision not to prosecute was based on "an impermissible classification such as race, religion or sex";

C v Latimore **423 M 129 (96)**—not impermissible for DA to give weight to homicide V's family's wishes in rejecting offer of G to manslaughter (despite "unequal" treatment of Ds charged with murder as a consequence);

C v Ellis **429 M 362 (99)**—re: conflict of interest on part of prosecutors: self-proclaimed insurance fraud vic-

tims' financial leverage over prosecutorial decisions held to be no problem? or found not to exist?;

C v Murchison **418 M 58 (94)**—D can argue that police witness has reason to want to convict a D who was arrested by witness or who was target of witness's evidence-gathering;

See Chapter 7-E for cases on defense of lack of criminal responsibility;

See Chapter 7-O for cases on statutes of limitations;

See Chapter 10-A for cases on right to present a defense;

See Chapter 12-F for cases on failure to test or investigate (C v Bowden) as basis for defense; but generally, rule is C v Cordle 412 M 172 (92) defects in government's forensic testing is valid defense, but judge has discretion not to instruct on it; see also *C v Wolinski* **431 M 228, 233 (2000)** instructions, in response to jury note saying "questions unanswered; evidence incomplete; cannot decide", included thoughtless standard instruction, 'decide case based solely on evidence presented in court & don't speculate about any unanswered questions that remain'; apparent argument on appeal (not here acknowledged or addressed) was that this instruction violates *Bowden* **379 M 472, 485 (80)** (judge can't remove from jury's consideration the import of perceived evidentiary deficiencies); request "curative" that directs that absence of evidence deemed by jury to be significant should be used in considering whether Commonwealth has met its burden of proving charge beyond reasonable doubt; in response to Bowden defense, cop can't respond/defend investigation with "general expression of the officer's opinion of guilt" such as recounting all incriminating evidence against D (*C v Lodge* **431 M 461, 467 (2000)**), but, e.g., *C v Avila* **454 M 744 (2009)**—CAN otherwise defend, in rebuttal, his investigation/judgment after it has been questioned under *Bowden*;

C v Remedor **52 MAC 694, 700–01 (2001)**—judge's response to jury question, i.e. 'confine consideration to evidence that *was* presented,' negated D's "Bowden" (**379 M 472**) defense, creating substantial risk of a miscarriage of justice;

See Chapter 18 for cases on mistaken identification & alibi defenses, including "somebody else did it"; see in particular *C v Cutty* **47 MAC 671 (99)** D himself cannot be precluded from testifying as sanction for failure to give notice of alibi (M.R.Crim.P. 14(b)(1)(D)) AND judge cannot bar counsel from using D's testimony in closing argument;

16-A.4. Religious Beliefs

C v Nissenbaum **404 M 575 (89)**—religious use is not a defense to drug possession;

C v Twitchell **416 M 114 (93)**—"spiritual treatment" by Christian Science practitioners, despite G.L. c. 273, § 1, did not bar conviction for involuntary manslaughter, **but** retrial for presentation of "entrapment by estoppel" defense;

16-A.5. Entrapment, Estoppel, Good Faith Belief that Conduct = Lawful

C v Twitchell **416 M 114 (93)**—Christian Science practitioner believed (reasonably?) government had authorized defense of religious healing here;

C v LeBlanc **30 MAC 1 (90)**—good faith belief that D, in buying drugs, was acting as agent for government is a valid defense; contrast *C v Murillo* **32 MAC 379 (92)** that D was acting as a "procuring agent" for a buyer is not a defense to drug charges (defense discussed in *C v Harvard* **356 M 452 (69)** = eliminated);

C v Bell **67 MAC 266 (2006)**—D could be guilty of attempting to rape child and soliciting sex for fee even though, unbeknownst to him, he was negotiating with undercover police officer, so no actual child was at risk; though crime was "factually" impossible, it was not "legally" impossible;

C v Wilkinson **415 M 402 (93)**—bail bondsman's agent defending kidnap & assault charges: "lawful authority" defense (right to seize principal within MA for surrender in another state was abrogated by Uniform Criminal Extradition Act); *See C v Cabral* **443 M 171 (2005)**—bail surety & his agents have lawful authority to apprehend, detain, and deliver a principal to a court house, and a defendant surety bears only burden of raising defense of "lawful authority," after which burden is on Commonwealth to prove beyond reasonable doubt that he wasn't a surety; jury instructions re: agency relationship & D's actions as possibly outside scope of agency;

C v Colon **431 M 188 (2000)**—"consent" of minor child no defense to kidnapping of such child;

C v Disler **451 M 216 (2008)** & *C v Filopoulos* **451 M 234 (2008)**—"enticement" statute, G.L. c. 265, § 26C requires, in addition to enticing words/gestures, that person who entices does so with intent to violate 1 or more enumerated statutes, e.g., statutory rape (G.L. c. 265, § 23) or indecent A&B on child under age 14 (G.L. c. 265, § 13B); Commonwealth must prove that D INTENDED that object of sexual advances be an underage individual;

Disler 451 M at 221–22 - merely "sending words" IS sufficient evidence for "enticement" (additional "overt act" not required) if other element (intent to violate specific criminal statutes) is satisfied; that "victim" was not "real" irrelevant (cop was pretending online to be 14 year old girl); "factual impossibility" not a defense to crime; not unconstitutionally vague, and merely sending sex messages over computer not criminalized (additional "intent" element necessary); 1st Amendment challenge also rejected;

C v Robinson **74 MAC 752 (2009)**—convicted of wantonly and recklessly permitting substantial bodily injury to 13-year-old child in her custody (G.L. c. 265, § 13J(b)), D on appeal argued judge should have instructed jury to consider D's and her daughter's "constitutional right to refuse medical treatment"; not raised below, no evidence or arguments made suggesting that inaction was due to such "right," and even if so, state may intervene to protect child's well-being (here, child was emaciated, near death due to perforated intestine); court rejects argument that child herself chose to forgo medical care and was "mature" enough to make such decision (which in any event was not "informed");

C v Landry **438 M 206 (2002)**—person in needle exchange program (extant in Cambridge) could possess the needle throughout the Commonwealth (including places where there was no such program);

C v Coleman **64 MAC 558 (2005)**—D's conduct was not a suppressible "fruit" of police action ("whatever one may think about the wisdom of [such action]"): after police responded to highway altercation and spoke first with other driver, D said he couldn't wait longer, and was leaving, but was ordered by police to remain (cop attempted to break D's car window to stop/arrest him [G.L. c. 90, §§ 25, 21], causing D to flee and lead cops on high speed chase); court's "decision is limited to the application of the exclusionary rule," allowing evidence obtained after D's failure to comply with order to stop; viability of any defense based upon actions of police "necessarily will depend upon the evidence adduced at trial";

16-B. JOINT VENTURE

Superior Court Criminal Practice Jury Instructions § 4.4, Joint Venture;

See also Chapter 6, Discovery (of alleged statements of D & co-D), Chapter 8, Sever, Chapter 2, Ethics (re: Attorney-D Privilege, Interviewing co-D, etc.), Chapter 17, Parties;

Nolan & Sartorio, *Criminal Law*, §§ 631–35 (3d ed. 2001)—("Parties to a Crime");

District Court Model Instruction (*See Chapter 21A below*) 5.05—must be present at scene of crime; note, id., citing *C v Lafayette* **40 MAC 534 (96)** (liability as joint venturer requires presence at scene of crime, while liability as accessory before fact does not, citing *C v Green* **420 M 771, 779 (95)**; no broad complicity like felony murder,

"fundamentally wrong" to convey that when there's a joint enterprise, each is responsible for any 'secondary' crime committed by cohorts which flows naturally and probably from the enterprise, regardless of participation/intent re: secondary crime, citing *C v McMaster* **21 MAC 722, 731–32 (86)**; WITHDRAWAL; hearsay exception "humane practice," etc.;

C v Ortiz **424 M 853 (97)**—2 theories for joint venture in felony: 1 requires (a) presence at scene (b) knowledge that another intends to commit crime (c) agreement of willingness and availability to help if necessary. Other is by aiding in commission of felony or being accessory before fact by counseling, hiring or otherwise procuring felony to be committed. Presence not required for latter joint venture culpability;

C v Harris **74 MAC 105 (2009)**—D drove friend and female to motel and paid for a room for friend & female, picking them up later (on D's evidence) or actually stayed and watched sexual activity between female and three men (on Commonwealth's evidence), charged as joint venturer in statutory rape (female was 13 years old): on either version, D was "present" enough to make judgment about female's age and could be convicted as joint venturer in statutory rape on a "presence" theory without proof of "specific intent" to commit crime; if case presents "joint venture" only on "aiding" theory, due process (maybe) requires instruction and proof beyond reasonable doubt of D's knowledge of crime, i.e., complainant's age [D noted that vendors of contraception could become rapists if products they distribute "aided" someone in sex with minor];

C v Parreira **72 MAC 308 (2008)**—two slightly older male teenagers and two female teenagers in a vacant apartment paired off in two separate bedrooms: required finding of not guilty for D ordered on theory of joint venture liability for co-D's rape of co-D's partner: D's intent to have sex with D's partner was not the requisite "common intent"; for joint venture liability in sex crimes, precedents reveal a common victim, physical presence at immediate scene, and/or physical participation in the act;

C v Braley **449 M 316 (2007)**—statements of joint venturer admissible if Commonwealth establishes by "preponderance of the evidence" an "adequate probability of the existence of a common venture, including participation by the given defendant"; evidence to be viewed in light most favorable to Commonwealth;

C v Stewart **454 M 527 (2009)**—judge's instruction was that acts/statements of each joint venturer could be considered against D only if acts/statements were made when joint venture existed or when venturers were acting to conceal the crime and statements/acts "[were] *relevant to the joint venture*"; italicized language = error, statements could be considered only if made "in furtherance of" the joint venture;

C v Lepper **60 MAC 36 (2003)**—D's criminal culpability (larceny by false pretenses) could be founded upon false statements he caused another individual to make, regardless of whether the other individual knew statements were false (and thus whether the latter was a joint venturer);

Separate instruction re intoxication & effect on specific joint venture intent?—See *Ferreira* **417 M 592, 595 (94)**;

K. Smith, *Criminal Practice and Procedure,* **§ 1835 (2d ed. 1983 & Supp.)**—"practice" for co-D with lowest indictment # to go 1st in opening statements, etc.;

C v Charles **428 M 682 n.6 (99)**—alleged joint venturer in motor vehicle insurance fraud did not have to be present at time of co-D's submission of false claim to be convicted;

C v DiBenedetto **427 M 414 (98)**, *C v Andrews* **427 M 434 (98)**, *C v Nolan* **427 M 541 (98)**—when there's

enough for joint venture beyond reasonable doubt, Commonwealth need not prove which person fired fatal shot; *Nolan* **427 M at 544**, rejects argument that jurors were required unanimously to agree either (1) that D was principal or (2) that he was joint-venturer;

****VERY IMPORTANT:* **C v Zanetti** **454 M 449 (2009)**—when there's evidence that more than 1 person participated in crime, judges must instruct jury that D may be found guilty "if the Commonwealth has proved beyond reasonable doubt that D knowingly participated in the commission of the crime charged, alone or with others, with the intent required for that offense"; judges should charge jury in this way, rather than by separate narration of (a) required elements of charged offense and (b) the "three familiar elements" of "joint venture liability"; trial judge may give jury "general" verdict slip even when there's differing evidence that D was principal or accomplice; required finding of not guilty to be denied if evidence sufficient to show D "knowingly participated" in the commission "of the crime charged, with the intent required to commit th[at] crime";

C v Perry **432 M 214 (2000)**—where multiple assailants participate in joint venture to commit murder, Commonwealth not required to prove the precise conduct of each individual;

C v Brown **50 MAC 253 (2000)**—reversal of multiple convictions of each of 3 D's, though 3 Ds were seen running together after gunshots: "logical inference that 2 of the 3 Ds may each have possessed a gun is not a substitute for proof beyond a reasonable doubt that an identified D possessed a specific gun";

C v Leftwich **430 M 865, 869 (2000)**—joint venture instruction warranted because of D's statement attempting to limit himself to "after-the-fact" knowledge/accessorial culpability ("I did not kill (V); I only helped dump his body"), plus presence of unidentified fingerprints and "genetic material" on blood inside D's van (D argued no evidence of two culprits, so no possible joint venture liability);

C v Pike **431 M 212, 215 (2000)**—though D argued no basis for joint venture because jury should believe either co-D's testimony that D shot V, OR D's testimony that D didn't shoot V and wasn't joint venturer in co-D's shooting of V, SJC held joint venture option permissible: jury could believe co-D lied to protect himself (and that co-D shot V), but that co-D was otherwise credible, making D joint-venturer;

C v Berry **47 MAC 24, 29–30 (99)**—evidence to support joint venture theory/jury instruction need not have come in Commonwealth's case in chief; rejects D's argument that required finding of NG should have been entered, since there was basis other than joint venture in Commonwealth's case in chief on which case could have been submitted to jury; OVERRULED/REVERSED: **S.C., 431 M 326 (2000)** because D's argument for required finding of NG at close of Commonwealth's case was specific as to insufficiency of evidence of joint venture, required finding of NG should have been entered on that theory;

though jurors were given option of joint venture or individual liability, G verdict didn't specify which, so conviction had to be reversed; Commonwealth evidence that shiny object was seen in D's hand, that someone told D to "put away the knife," and that V died from stab wounds, even when coupled with other testimony that some witnesses did NOT see knife in D's hands, was insufficient basis for joint venture instruction; disbelief of evidence that D was principal was not the equivalent of joint venture evidence;

C v Melton **50 MAC 637 (2001), S.C. 436 M 291, 300 (2002)**—though even DA's closing acknowledged that it was most likely that individual other than D fired the single shot, appellate court held evidence sufficient for individual liability beyond reasonable doubt as well as joint venture, avoiding reversal of convictions (because jury's verdict did not specify which theory: see *C v Flynn* **420 M 810, 815 (95)**);

C v MacKedon **60 MAC 901 (2003)**—though another man was present and participating at initial meeting for sale of drugs to undercover cop, D alone responded to subsequent pager contact and exchanged pills for cash: "where, as here, [D] is the sole principal actor, he cannot be found guilty as a joint venturer"; error in charging jury initially on joint venture cured by judge's subsequent withdrawal of that instruction;

C v Fancy **349 M 196 (65)**—insufficient evidence of joint venture; no guilt by association;

C v McCoy **59 MAC 284 (2003)**—error to allow DA to question D about his knowledge (or not) that woman with D at time of arrest (who was neither arrested nor charged) had criminal record for heroin distribution; FURTHER, judge's "inexplicable overruling of" D's objection "may have been seen by the jury as judicial endorsement of the improper questioning and innuendo"; further error in DA's closing, which argued, without evidentiary support, that everyone in D's company ("all his friends") were either heroin users or heroin dealers;

C v Swafford **441 M 329, 339 (2004)**—required finding of not guilty, though fatal shots were fired from D's car and D was present along with co-Ds when D's friend/fellow gang member was assaulted earlier, fight occurred at least two hours before shooting (distinguishing *C v Medeiros* 354 M 193 (68) & *C v Evans* 438 M 142 (2002));*C v Benders* **361 M 704 (72)**—presence & fail to prevent not joint venture; charge overemphasized lack of disengagement, rather than participation criterion; joint venturer for larceny doesn't mean joint venturer for ABDW in aftermath of larceny; BUT *C v Lynch* **428 M 617 (99)** D's interpretation of the complete segregability of crimes of rape and murder was not the only reasonable inference from the evidence;

C v Namey **67 MAC 94 (2006)**—though D was only a passenger in car driven by another, evidence suggesting D's culpability in impending crimes (i.e., two disguises in plain view on back seat, along with dent puller and "other tools", and "a map of the local area"), with visible damage to car showing it stolen (ignition "popped", door lock either "out or damaged"), plus flight and concealment from police, held sufficient for guilt of receiving stolen property (the car);

C v Netto **438 M 686 (2003)**—see supplemental instructions given on joint venture felony-murder, including, inter alia, killing had to be "incidental to and the natural and probable consequence of the armed robbery," and this meant that killing "must have taken place during a single logically related continuing criminal transaction at a time when the nonstabber was actively involved as a participant in the armed robbery"; if killing took place after the nonstabber was no longer actively involved in committing a crime, then the nonstabber is NG of armed robbery felony murder; consider whether there was break in logical chain of events between the robbery & the killing/separation of an appreciable amount of time; whether killing "occurred at a place that was different and separate from the nonstabber";

C v Murphy **1 MAC 71 (73)**—presence not enough (passenger before driver's act, driver 30 minutes later, & evasive answers);

C v Ward W. **47 MAC 208 (99)**—despite D's presence in robbed car within 7 blocks and about 2 minutes, and despite enough evidence to show joint venture guilt of persons other than driver, required finding of NG;

C v Ahart **37 MAC 565 (94)**—though 45 minutes after purse snatch D was stopped while driving car into which snatcher had entered to escape his pursuers (& 2 men were already in the car), & front seat passenger at time of stop was snatcher, required finding of NG for D—driver, despite necessity of few blocks' pursuit (allegedly consciousness of guilt);

C v Perry **357 M 149 (70)**—know, agree, conspire not joint venture, even with concealment later; must participate, or be in position to aid, co-D's robbery;

C v Caramanica **49 MAC 376, 380–82 (2000)**—noting trial judge's confusion re: "presence" requirement for criminal liability under joint venture theory, questioning why prosecutors rarely use as basis for indictment the available "statutory accessory crimes" instead of joint venture "aiding/abetting"; positing that "conspiracy" crimes are also "generally" pursued by prosecutors via "common law joint venture" because of, inter alia, difficulty of "affirmative proof of a prior agreement, separate and distinct from the shared intent that may be reflected in the actions of joint venturers at the time the substantive offense is committed";

C v Fuentes **45 MAC 934 (98)**—Commonwealth need not prove that D plotted with others far in advance of crime, but merely that, at climactic moment, D consciously acted with others to commit crime;

C v Springer **49 MAC 469 (2000)**—though D argued that alleged joint venturer's intoxication meant D couldn't be convicted based on agreement/shared intent (because alleged joint venturer didn't have capacity to agree and share intent), Appeals Court said this confused crime of "conspiracy" with proof necessary for joint venture; careless statement that no "meeting of the minds is required" for joint venture liability; (SEE INSTEAD *C v Richards* **363 M 299 (73)**, post);

C v Spina **1 MAC 805 (73)**—presence, even with flight, not joint venture, especially if sudden act by co-D (threw rock during rally);

C v Henderson **47 MAC 612 (99)**—D-driver was person who had argued with V in past and on this day; enough for joint venture that his passenger crossed street to shoot V 2 minutes after argument, as D waited in car, and D drove speedily away with gunman after shooting (inconsistent with any inference of sudden anger or impulse by passenger, who was unknown to V);

C v Funches **379 M 283 (79)**—presence & association with robbers not enough;

C v Brown **50 MAC 253 (2000)**—reversal of multiple convictions of each of 3 Ds because only speculation as to which one of them had actually possessed any of firearms; joint venture/constructive possession likewise conjectural; "logical inference that 2 of the 3 Ds may each have possessed a gun isn't substitute for proof beyond a reasonable doubt that an identified D possessed a specific gun";

C v Alves **70 MAC 908 (2007)**—it's enough to indict D that in a "crate" in trunk of car belonging to D's mother (D alone, as driver) there was small gray nylon bag with cocaine and a duffel bag containing men's clothing (though not enough for constructive possession/guilt under *C v Garcia* **409 M 675, 680 [91]**);

C v McCarthy **385 M 160 (82)**—mere presence at rape;

C v Avery **44 MAC 781 (98)**—mere presence of D (albeit in tiny space of barroom's bathroom) when other man committed armed robbery and battered V = required finding of NG;

C v Lafayette **40 MAC 534 (96)**—though D not present at B&E's entry of joint venturers into building for larceny, his selection of rock to be used previously to break window and disable security system, with intent of later break & entry, warranted G;

C v Saez **21 MAC 408 (86)**—not "lookout" from looking around at drug sale;

C v DeJesus **48 MAC 911 (99)**—D's looking up & down street from window at drug-selling apartment for 15 minutes prior to search, during which there was "visiting pattern . . . indicative of drug traffic," plus D's presence with 3 others in small bedroom containing lots of heroin, cash, and drug packaging materials = enough for joint venture possession; "(p)eople do not ordinarily engage in repetitive crimes in the presence of someone who is not a collaborator" (contra, inter alia, *Funches* **379 M 283 (79)** mere knowledge of others' crimes insufficient for joint venture);

C v Burrell **389 M 804 (83)**—though joint venture to rob, murder here not a natural/probable consequence, & D not in concert with killer (5 surround V, 1 shoots); in MOB each D judged separately by own intent (fn. 6);

C v Lendon **35 MAC 926 (93)**—but joint venturer in 2d degree murder need only know there's substantial likelihood of V's being killed (D drove car in pursuit of rival gang members providing gunman opportunity to shoot V at "point-blank range");

C v Richards **363 M 299 (73)**—joint venturer must SHARE INTENT, at least CONDITIONAL, of substantive crime; natural/probable consequence not enough; (joint venture to kill by giving robbery partner a loaded gun);

C v Padgett **44 MAC 359 (98)**—though D may not have wanted assaults or armed robbery to occur, his participation in B&E's, knowing cohorts armed, warranted inference of conditional intent that actions be taken to effectuate B&E plan, or to escape;

C v Washington **15 MAC 378 (83)**—though joint venture shown for A&B, not for ABDW without knowing of or intending co-D's dangerous weapon use; *C v Charles* **57 MAC 595 (2003)**—in armed assault with intent to murder on theory of joint venture, error in failure to instruct jury that they had to find that each D knew **before** the shooting that an apparent accomplice had a gun;

C v Cook **419 M 192 (94)**—joint venture only for unarmed robbery (no evidence D know cohort armed), but nature of robbery nonetheless provided basis for proper felony murder conviction; *C v Gilliard* **36 MAC 183, 192 (94)** ineffective assistance of counsel not to request instruction re: lesser included offense for joint venturer, convicted of 2d degree murder, but perhaps properly G only of A&B (no knowledge of weapon);

C v Newman **437 M 599 (2002)**—sufficient evidence to find D knew co-D had gun: "an accomplice so closely associated with the venture could not fail to know what would be the central question in any robbery: how the robbers were to force the . . . employees to part with the money"; *C v Savoy* **21 MAC 519 (86)**—joint venture to obtain sexual favors (NG of rape, after jury trial) doesn't extend to co-D's malicious destruction of property;

C v Flowers **1 MAC 415 (73)**—joint venture: kidnap, assault, terrorize, not joint venture for robbery by co-D in another room without evidence D knew/intended it;

C v Lashway **36 MAC 677 (94)**—no proof of shared intent to rob;

C v Echavarria **428 M 593 (98)**—given proof of joint venture in case involving robbery and execution of drug dealer, not necessary to prove that D was present in room where it occurred (prove only knowledge, and assist in planning, and share purpose it be committed);

C v Watson **388 M 536 (83)**—no joint venture to felony murder unless know robbery partner's armed (i.e., conditional intent);

C v Claudio **418 M 103 (94)**—no joint venture to felony murder unless know cohort(s) in B&E felony assaulting person therein are armed;

C v LeClair **68 MAC 482 (2007)**—D's knowledge that perpetrator is armed with dangerous weapon "can be inferred where the robbery transpires 'in a public place under circumstances where it can be anticipated that a means must be found to persuade the victim to surrender his property quickly and without resistance'" (location was Burger King parking lot at inferably busy time in evening);

C v Cruz **430 M 182, 195 (99)**—though D bound no one during robbery (acting primarily as lookout), G as joint venturer because he knew duct tape would be used to bind at least one building occupant's hands, feet, and mouth: homicide when tape on 7-year-old covered both her mouth and nose (asphyxiation);

C v Melendez **427 M 214, 216 (98)**—reversible error, **despite no objection**, if jury instructions omitted knowledge element;

C v Harris **9 MAC 708 (80)**—joint venture to rob, but not ABDW by co-D (hooker D lured V back to hotel room & fled after robbery);

C v Pimental **25 MAC 971 (88)**—joint venture = lure V away & steal car (larceny), but not robbery or ABDW;

C v Walsh **407 M 740 (90)**—evidence that D was beating up one person while co-D was fatally stabbing another established shared intent to jointly attack, but not to murder;

C v Mandile **403 M 93 (88)**—no murder intent though D KNEW co-D armed (prior joint venture stole gun), drove for B&E, hid gun, & had $730 (but robbery unproven);

C v Tracy **27 MAC 455 (89)**—evidence that D, getaway driver, knew co-D was about to rob store, plus other circumstantial evidence, was enough to infer he knew co-D had a gun;

C v Patterson **432 M 767, 773 (2000)** & *C v Ellis* **432 M 746, 762–63 (2000)**—circumstantial evidence of knowledge of gun: jury could reasonably conclude that D wouldn't undertake to rob armed man (police officer on private "detail") unless he was armed himself or knew joint venturer was armed;

C v Palmer **59 MAC 415 (2003)**—even if jury instruction failed to convey that D had to know that alleged masked armed-robbery joint venturers were armed with dangerous weapon, error HERE did not create substantial risk of miscarriage of justice; *C v Colon* **52 MAC 725 (2001)** (generic instruction that Commonwealth had to prove that D shared the mental state required to commit the crime DID NOT suffice to assure jury's knowledge that D had to have known other person was armed) distinguished;

C v Hogan **379 M 190 (79)**—D sitting in car G. of co-D's ABDW in V's house, but no intent to maim (for mayhem);

C v Knapp **26 M 496 (1830)**—need only be in position to render aid, even without being within sight/hearing of crime, if ready & (tacit) agreement/knowledge because encouraging/emboldening = aid;

C v Powell **40 MAC 430 (96)**—D drove car away from robbery; G despite testimony of D & principal that D = NG (i.e., didn't know robbery occurred); insufficient evidence D knew armed, however, so only G of unarmed robbery;

C v Drew **4 MAC 30 (76)**—lookout sat in getaway car few blocks from stores being robbed (with D's KNOWLEDGE) (but see *Saez* **21 MAC 408 (86)** not "lookout" from looking around at drug sale);

C v Pope **15 MAC 505 (83)**—infer D was intentionally in place as lookout, decoy, or for other possible aid to co-D;

C v McKay **50 MAC 604 (2000)**—though D purportedly in position to serve as lookout, lacking was proof that he agreed to participate or took any meaningful action to assist principal: required finding of NG;

C v Barry **397 M 718 (86)**—enough evidence D knowingly assisted armed robbery;

C v Noble **34 MAC 415 (93)**—no evidence D aware of killer's intent to shoot victim: NG;

C v Scott **355 M 471 (69)**—trot with co-D who snaps purse, then fled together & get some of the loot = joint venture;

C v Fortes **47 MAC 214 (99)**—not required that D personally know that danger of serious harm existed in contemplated purse snatch (leading to V's fall, dislocated kneecap, blood clots, death by coronary embolism six days later) if he had knowledge of facts that would cause reasonably prudent person to know such danger existed; here evidence from which jury could infer that D (joint venturer) and principal knew V was elderly before she was knocked down, & elderly are less sure-footed and hardy; D can't "escape responsibility merely because he hoped (V wouldn't resist purse snatch)";

C v Lombard **419 M 585 (95)**—though D assisted purse snatcher in escaping from pursuer, and though D know afterward that snatch occurred, NG: no proof of shared intent to complete robbery at time of assistance;

C v Griffin **19 MAC 174 (85)**—passenger aided/encouraged murder by driver;

C v Soares **377 M 461 (79)**—presence, knowledge, & intent to render aid in Combat Zone stabbing (see especially thin case vs. co-D Allen (at 471–72));

C v Longo **402 M 482 (88)**—presence, ill will, knew co-D had knife, & agreement to help + intent = inferable; (but see **23 MAC 518 (87)**—Appeals Court disagreed);

C v Mangula **2 MAC 785 (75)**—D in car knowing co-D takes gun into B&E = joint venture to rob because conditional intent to rob (& position to render aid);

C v Gendraw **55 MAC 677 (2002)**—instruction that Commonwealth must prove beyond reasonable doubt that there was "a substantial likelihood that [D] had knowledge that another would commit a crime" is WRONG; correct = Commonwealth must prove beyond a reasonable doubt that D knew that there was substantial likelihood that his accomplice would commit the crime;

C v Knight **16 MAC 622 (83)**—joint venture to rob & know of gun & mask = joint venture for masked armed robbery;

C v Christian **430 M 552, 556–57 (2000)**—joint venture armed robbery (1) must know principal = armed; (2) must possess mental state required for armed robbery; (3)

must intentionally assist in robbery; instruction that "any type of assistance" satisfies element (3) bad because would cover acts of mere accessory after fact; here, however, added words were "as long as it was for purpose of helping accomplish an armed robbery," plus examples conveying correct "assistance";

C v Amaral **13 MAC 238 (82)**—overview (participate & seek to make succeed);

C v Green **302 M 547 (39)**—joint venture not abandoned/withdrawn unless both appreciable interval BEFORE crime's probable & NOTICE to co-D's;

C v Branch **42 MAC 181 (97)**—upholding judge's refusal to charge on abandonment because at best D's detachment came too late;

C v Sokphann Chhim **447 M 370 (2006)**—though D argued for required finding on basis of abandonment of joint venture, evidence most favorable to prosecution included testimony that D did not drive away prior to vicious beating (though he remained inside car), & so was available to help; dissent claims that D's separation into car was actually means of assisting principals, since he moved one car so they could flee in other car;

C v Elliot **430 M 498 (99)**—given D's prior acts, even though D ignored co-D's order to shoot victims and it was co-D who fired shots, no required finding of NG on joint venture armed assault to kill and 2d degree murder, AND dicta that judge erred in even giving "withdrawal" instruction, because purported withdrawal came too late;

C v Cook **419 M 192 (94)**—(same);

C v Allen **430 M 252, 257 n.5 (99)**—D's presence at scene "did not negate abandonment" necessarily;

C v Fickett **403 M 194 (88)**—DA must prove no withdrawal appreciably before crime; no joint venture to commit armed robbery (for felony murder) unless know co-D's armed;

C v Serrano **74 MAC 1 (2009)**—D was armed with gun when he arrived to harass/fight ex-girlfriend's paramour, but upon entreaties by bystanders, he disarmed, giving gun to a friend, and began fist fight with paramour; victim broke away from D, and D's friend shot V in head: though Appeals Court holds "no error" in refusing to instruct on "withdrawal", SJC allowed further appellate review, 454 M 1106 (2009);

C v Hogan **426 M 424 (98)**—(as practical matter,) joint venturer in felony likely liable for felony murder because not easy/possible to withdraw sufficiently "appreciably before" homicide;

Nolan & Sartorio, *Criminal Law*, **§ 688 & Model Penal Code §§ 2:06(b), 5:01(4) (3d ed. 2001)**—withdrawal/abandonment;

C v Lafayette **40 MAC 534 (96)**—though D told principals that it was not a good idea to return to "break" scene to enter, his simultaneous offer to buy proceeds from entry warranted jury finding of no withdrawal;

C v Joyce **18 MAC 417 (84)**—jury question on withdrawal by D;

C v Galford **413 M 364 (92)**—jury instruction on abandonment setting forth conditions necessary for D to "escape liability" was "ill-chosen" & burden-shifting;

Superior Court Criminal Practice Jury Instructions § 4.4—4.4.1(a), withdrawal; 4.4.1(b), knowledge of weapon; 4.4.2, hearsay statement of co-venturers; § 3.14, withdrawal or abandonment;

District Court Model Jury Instruction #5.05, Joint Venture;

C v Szemetum **3 MAC 651 (75)**—irrelevant evidence amounts to G. by association;

C v Tilley & US v Dworkin—(Chapter 11, Evidence) co-D's G. plea inadmissible re: D;

C v Powell **40 MAC 430 (96)**—principal's G plea to armed robbery inadmissible re: D's guilt though admissible to impeach principal's testimony;

C v Haraldstad **16 MAC 565 (83)**—co-D's (severed) NG not probative, BUT lack of pending case is, to show no bias; *C v Howard* **46 MAC 366, 370 (99)** evidence of NG of alleged joint venturer, separately tried, not probative of D's innocence;

C v Ryan **14 MAC 901 (82)**—no joint venture instruction because not asked or merited (passenger in getaway car & lied to cops); question was who went in & robbed;

C v Jones **403 M 279 (88)**—fact that co-D (alleged j-venturer) was found NG (at separate trial) doesn't bar D's joint-venturer conviction ("nothing inconsistent" about this);

C v Williams **450 M 645 (2008)**—co-D's acquittal at SAME trial didn't require finding of NG for D as joint venture because evidence supported existence of some actor with D and shared intent: evidence sufficient to show other person[s] was involved in fatal shooting and binding victim; jury's question which could be understood as asking whether "joint venture" referred only to the two charged Ds, implausibly found to be "confusing," so permissibly answered "unable to answer question because I do not understand it";

C v Rivera **31 MAC 554 (91)**—Commonwealth limited to proving constructive or actual possession where jury not instructed on joint venture;

C v Robinson **43 MAC 257 (97)**—joint venture and constructive possession are "alternative theories" to connect D to crime; evidence that D was with principal in same area ten times in prior month relevant to show it unlikely that D was "accidentally or unknowingly associated with" drug dealer;

C v Sanchez **40 MAC 411 (96)**—though evidence sufficient to establish D-passenger's constructive possession of drugs in trunk, evidence insufficient to show any meeting of the minds of D & driver necessary for joint venture guilt;

See post, at Chapter 16-F, "Possession," as well as Chapter 21-CC-5 for cases on constructive possession;

C v Meehan **33 MAC 262 (92)**—evidence that D had several private conversations with co-D bartender & had large amount of cash & list of names in different handwriting from that found on bartender was not sufficient to establish nexus between D & coke in co-D's purse;

***US v Swiderski* 548 F2d 445 (2d Cir. 1977)**—one cannot be both purchaser of drugs and joint venturer in sale of the drugs;

***C v Fernandes* 46 MAC 455 (99)**—no Swiderski instruction for D, who hopped in undercover cop's car and pointed him toward drug seller, and told seller "we want a twenty," though D testified cop had told her he would give her some; a "hope" on D's part for a share didn't make her a co-purchaser; joint venture responsibility can be found without showing actual or constructive possession;

***C v Smith* 413 M 275 (92)**—evidence that D shared goal of killing victim with deliberately premeditated malice aforethought insufficient;

***C v Cardenuto* 406 M 450 (90)**—evidence insufficient to show that D left restaurant open for associate to set it afire;

***C v Flynn* 420 M 810, 815 (95)**—evidence that D joined in attack, by kicking body of V, warranted G on joint venture homicide but required finding of NG on individual liability since death caused instead by blow(s) to head (reversal because jury was given individual liability option, and G verdict was non-specific); see also ***C v Green* 420 M 771 (95)** evidence insufficient for joint venture liability, but sufficient for individual liability; ***C v Leftwich* 430 M 865 (2000)** parsing evidence to justify instruction on joint venture as well as individual liability;

***C v Armand* 411 M 167 (91)**—evidence that D knew what alleged joint venturer was going to do before he did it & that he shared malicious intent to destroy property was speculative;

***C v Mahoney* 405 M 326 (89)**—judge should have explained that co-D's consciousness of guilt was not relevant as to D's shared intent, although relevant for other purposes;

16-C. INTENT—AND INTOXICATION, MISTAKE, ACCIDENT, AND DIMINISHED CAPACITY

See also Chapter 7, Lack of Criminal Responsibility ("Insanity"), Joint Venture, above (shared/conditional intents, withdrawal/abandonment), Chapter 17, Attempts, Chapter 21, Crimes, and Chapter 12K, Jury Instructions;

Model Penal Code § 2.02—re mental states required for criminal culpability ("purposefully," "knowingly," "recklessly," "negligently," and strict liability);

District Court Model Jury Instructions 3.04—general vs. specific intent; 6.06 Intoxication—(may also create reasonable doubt as to knowledge); 6.031 mental impairment less than insane; 3.051 knowledge;

Superior Court Criminal Practice Jury Instructions 1.9—Intent: General & Specific; § 3.3, effect of mental impairment or intoxication on state of mind (diminished capacity);

Nolan & Sartorio, *Criminal Law*, § 102 (3d ed. 2001)—"culpability is the foundation for criminal liability"—generally act & intent (general or specific); §§ 102–3 SCIENTER Holmes: even a dog can distinguish being stumbled over from being kicked; general vs. specific; may "infer" but not "presume" D intends natural & probable consequences (see ***Sandstrom v Montana* 442 US 510 (79)**); motive relevant, but not necessary or sufficient; § 675 intoxication; § 686 mistake or ignorance (ignorance of the law is no defense to a crime, but mistake might be);

***Arthur Andersen LLP v US* 125 S.Ct. 2129 (2005)**—federal crime's element of "knowingly corruptly persuade" required prosecution to prove that D was conscious of wrongdoing; conviction reversed due to jury instruction that conviction permissible even if D believed its conduct was lawful;

***C v Ramirez* 69 MAC 9 (2007)**—in prosecution for "knowingly failing to register" as sex offender, Commonwealth can't meet burden merely by establishing that

knowledge was available to D (e.g., if he had happened to look in newspapers); *Lambert v California* 355 US 225 (57) cited re: constitutional due process requirements; if Commonwealth had relied on theory that after receiving notice (by arrest) that he was required to register, result could have been different IF complaint listed a range of dates instead, as here, one date prior to arrest;

***C v Kenney* 449 M 840 (2007)**—rejecting First Amendment challenge to G.L. c. 272, § 29C (possession of child pornography) as overbroad, distinguishing *Ashcroft v Free Speech Coalition* 535 US 234 (2002); as to "scienter" requirement (D knows or should know person is underage), Commonwealth "must prove that no reasonable person would not have known that the child subject was under the age of eighteen";

***C v Disler* 451 M 216 (2008) & *C v Filopoulos* 451 M 234 (2008)**—"enticement" statute, G.L. c. 265, § 26C requires, in addition to enticing words/gestures, that person who entices does so with intent to violate 1 or more enumerated statutes, e.g., statutory rape (G.L. c. 265, § 23) or indecent A&B on child under age 14 (G.L. c. 265, § 13B); Commonwealth must prove that D INTENDED that object of sexual advances be an underage individual; *Disler* 451 M at 221–22 - merely "sending words" IS sufficient evidence for "enticement" (additional "overt act" not required) if other element (intent to violate specific criminal statutes) is satisfied; that "victim" was not "real" irrelevant (cop was pretending on-line to be 14-year-old girl); "factual impossibility" not a defense to crime; not unconstitutionally vague, and merely sending sex messages over computer not criminalized (additional "intent" element necessary); First Amendment challenge also rejected;

C v Gould **380 M 672 (80)**—to keep the community's respect, the law must grade condemnation according to the D's moral turpitude;

C v Gaboriault **439 M 84 (2003)**—though SJC repeatedly states that there is no "diminished capacity" defense in Massachusetts, *C v Gould* 380 M 672 (80) stands for proposition that D may produce psych evidence to allow jury to consider whether D lacked mental capacity required for crime charged; tactical decision to withdraw defense of lack of criminal responsibility in favor of diminished capacity claim wasn't ineffective assistance of counsel, because experts would support latter but not former; see also *C v LaCava* **438 M 708 (2003)** (similar);

C v Murphy **442 M 485 (2004)**—while there is no "diminished capacity" defense in Massachusetts, mental impairment may be relevant to deliberate premeditation, extreme atrocity or cruelty, & intent and knowledge; voluntary intoxication may preclude D from forming "malice," and may thus be a mitigating factor;

C v Ogden O., a juvenile, **448 M 798 (2007)**—rejecting argument that ten-year-old did not have capacity to form specific intent necessary to commit mayhem: juvenile sprayed victim with dry gas, then threw lighted piece of paper on him, and laughed as victim tried to extinguish fire; underpinnings of juvenile justice system are already based on principle that juveniles frequently lack capacity to appreciate consequences of actions and should be afforded greater protections than adults;

C v Robidoux **450 M 144 (2007)**—can't blame trial counsel for not pursuing more avidly "diminished capacity" defense, as competent D wanted nothing to do with psych. issues; counsel did convey to jury that D's beliefs "were different from the norm" and stressed D's father and sister's substantial influence over D, and unsuccessfully requested jury instruction to highlight D's unique state of mind and susceptibility re: his religious group, including in analysis of third prong malice;

C v Mixer **207 M 141 (10)**—STRICT LIABILITY for "police power" (e.g., transporting booze)—see also *Miller* **385 M 521 (82)** strict liability for sex with underage partner;

C v Brien **67 MAC 309 (2006)**—statute described both administrative sanctions and criminal prosecutions, the latter referring to G.L. c. 142A, § 19: required finding of not guilty ordered inasmuch as prosecutor and judge erroneously believed that crime could be established without scienter (willful & knowing); context = contractor who took deposits & payments but later declared bankruptcy and didn't perform work;

Nolan & Sartorio, *Criminal Law,* **§ 103 (3d ed. 2001)**—PUBLIC WELFARE offenses & SCIENTER; BUT SEE *C v Kraatz* **2 MAC 196 (74)** (making "false statements" in application for driver's license implies scienter: knowledge is essential element of the offense; word "false" is ambiguous, could mean only incorrectness, or it may import intentional incorrectness, & ambiguity must be resolved in favor of the defendant; *Wallace* **14 MAC 358 (82)** (re: operating vehicle under the influence of

drugs (G.L. c. 90, § 24(1)(a) n.2) and operating vehicle negligently so that the lives or safety of the public might be endangered" (G.L. c. 90, § 24(2)(a)), D was barred from introducing evidence that he had no prior warnings or knowledge of the effects of doctor-prescribed medication, & judge refused to instruct that Commonwealth was required to prove that he knew or should have known that the drug might affect his ability to drive safely: convictions reversed), *Crosscup* **369 M 228 (75)** (operating after suspension needs knowledge because no clear legislative intent for strict liability); *Buckley* **354 M 508 (68)** ('being present with drugs needs' knowledge (no strict liability)); *Smith v California* **361 US 147 (59)** (pornography seller must know it's obscene);

C v Erickson **74 MAC 172 (2009)**—G.L. c. 272, § 77 portion punishing person having custody of animal and failing to provide it with proper food, drink, sanitary environment doesn't require proof that D specifically intended to cause harm, instead requiring proof D acted "intentionally" rather than "accidentally" in leaving animals dehydrated, unfed, lying in their own excrement in apartment;

C v Reynolds **67 MAC 215 (2006)**—D's conviction for felony motor vehicle homicide (operating vehicle to endanger, under influence of intoxicants) upheld despite total absence of evidence she ingested prescription drugs in any manner other than as prescribed; appellate court's rationale was that written warnings accompanying prescriptions cautioned that perceptions and skills could be impaired (ignoring likelihood of concomitant impairment of one's ability to sense one's impaired state);

C v Tofanelli **67 MAC 61 (2006)**—finding sufficient evidence for inference that D knew that pills (being sold by co-D to undercover cop) were "counterfeit";

C v Wolf **34 MAC 949 (93)**—upholding exclusion of minister's testimony re D's religious beliefs (trespass at abortion clinic);

C v Spencer **40 MAC 919 (96)**—alleged victim's being "scared" is not substitute for requirement of proof beyond reasonable doubt that D intended to cause fear (by alleged "threatened battery" assault);

C v Musgrave **38 MAC 519, S.C., 421 M 610 (95)**—same; without "criminal" intent, there is no crime;

Holmes, *The Common Law* **(1881)**—"a spasm is not an act";

C v Nickerson **388 M 246 (83)**—specific intent = conscious act with determination of mind to do an act; contemplation, not reflection; must precede act;

C v Blow **370 M 401 (76)**—specific intent = "purpose/objective";

US v Bailey **444 US 394 (80)**—need some culpability for each element of crime; "specific intent" = similar to Model Penal Code's "purpose"; "general" intent's like "knowing";

C v Paiva **71 MAC 411 (2008)**—witness proffered by D was NOT an expert in use of drugs, but instead a percipient witness to D's own drug habit (including amounts), relevant to dispute "intent to distribute"; error to exclude, as observations not remote in time;

C v Fuller **22 MAC 152 (86)**—general intent = intend act (vs. accident);

C v Moore **36 MAC 455 (94)**—general intent is **not** merely "reflex"; "more or less unconscious" definition should be avoided;

C v Lawson **46 MAC 627 (99)**—simplistic formulations re: "general" and "specific" intent "will not likely assist either judicial analysis or a jury and may be source of confusion for both";

C v Ware **375 M 118 (78)**—though kidnap may (not) need specific intent, attempt to kidnap surely does;

C v Wallace **14 MAC 358 (82)**—mistake or accident means NG unless strict liability;

C v Zezima **387 M 748 (82)**—due process: DA must disprove shot was ACCIDENTAL;

C v Lowe **391 M 97 (84)**—DA's case raised accident issue re: shooting;

C v Power-Koch **69 MAC 735 (2007)**—D said "accident" in firing gun, didn't intend to accede to depressed best friend's request that D shoot him, though held gun, not familiar with handguns, didn't know fully loaded, didn't mean to pull trigger; error found in refusal to instruct on accident, "an unintentional event occurring through inadvertence, mistake, or negligence," evidentiary basis in D's statements to police;

C v Bouvier **316 M 489 (44)**—required finding of NG because D's testimony re: accident = only version (disbelief is not proof to the contrary);

C v NYCent. & Hudson River RR **202 M 394 (09)**—accident = defense unless strict liability (as here);

C v McKay **67 MAC 396 (2006)**—reversal for refusal to instruct on "accident" in violating protective order: D selected from cell phone list of contacts, while driving, "Cindy" rather than "Cindy B"; court rejected Commonwealth argument that D should have used more care in pressing buttons or by removing former fiancee's entry from stored numbers; criminal intent had to encompass more than pushing the [incorrect] button; attorneys' closing arguments stressing "accident" or not didn't make error harmless;

C v Hutchinson **395 M 568 (85)**—"accident" differs from "X did it";

C v Fuller **22 MAC 152 (86)**—indecent assault and battery needs intentional, not accidental, touch;

District Court Model Jury Instruction # 6.09—(*see Chapter 21, Analyzing Elements of Crimes*) accident definition; DA burden of proof for act, not result;

Superior Court Criminal Practice Jury Instructions § 3.13—Accident;

C v Ferguson **30 MAC 580, 583 (91)**—conviction for assault and battery reversed for failure of judge to instruct that if D kicked in an effort to right himself from his position of being backward over a fence, contact with cop was accidental (so not guilty);

C v Oliver **60 MAC 770, affirmed by decision at 443 M 1005 (2005)**—required finding of not guilty for D, because insufficient evidence to show, beyond a reasonable doubt, that when D took complainants' money for services to be rendered sometime in future, he did so under false pretenses, with intention of never providing the paid-for services;

C v Puleio **394 M 101 (85)**—transferred intent (to harm X) covers harm to V (i.e., not "accident");

C v Raymond **54 MAC 488 (2002)**—D couldn't be guilty of violating "no contact" order re: ex-wife if the contact was either incidental to a permitted activity or an accidental or unknowing violation: he testified that he went to a house owned by his mother and himself and in which his mother lived, in order to get some clothes and begin removing property, as necessitated by an order condemning the house, and did not know that the ex-wife was present;

16-C.1. Knowingly

Morissette v US **342 US 246 (52)**—need criminal intent though not in statute; not larceny if reasonable belief it's abandoned property;

Smith v California **361 US 147 (59)**—pornography seller must know it's obscene;

C v Crosscup **369 M 228 (75)**—operating after suspension needs knowledge because no clear legislative intent for strict liability;

C v Dellamano **393 M 132 (84)**—receiving stolen motor vehicle (or stolen property) requires actual knowledge, not just "reason to know" (though statute appears only to require latter);

C v Sampson **383 M 750 (81)**—must have general knowledge (flare) gun = "firearm";

C v Buckley **354 M 508 (68)**—'being present with drugs needs' knowledge (no strict liability);

C v Kraatz **2 MAC 196 (74)**—false license application law must be broken knowingly though statute not explicit;

C v Miller **385 M 521 (82)**—not if strict liability (statutory rape mistake re: age of sex partner); see also *C v Knap* **412 M 712 (92)** reasonable mistake of fact as to identity of under-age sex partner = no defense;

C v Wright **60 MAC 108 (2003)**—posing child in state of nudity (G.L. c. 272, § 29A) requires proof D knew alleged victim was under age eighteen; disbelief of D's testimony as to lack of knowledge does not establish the contrary proposition: required finding of not guilty;

C v Dellamano **393 M 132 (84)**—receiving stolen property needs ACTUAL knowledge (see also *Boris* **317 M 309 (1944)**);

C v Crosscup **369 M 228 (75)**—operating after suspension required proof D received notice of suspension;

See also Attempt, Chapter 17; & Nolan & Sartorio, Criminal Law (3d ed. 2001) §§ 651–52 re: attempt;

C v Lee **331 M 166 (54)**—DA need not prove D knew package had marijuana; But see *C v Antobenedetto* **366 M 51 (74)**—may need scienter for possess marijuana; & . . .

C v Aguiar **370 M 490 (76)**—D must KNOW mystery mail contains marijuana;

C v Sabetti **411 M 770 (92)**—Commonwealth not required to prove that D knew weight of drugs in his possession because weight is not an element of trafficking;

C v Podgurski **44 MAC 931 (98)**—weight of drugs D intentionally possessed was altered without his knowledge (by wife's addition of a cutting agent); Appeals Court implicitly recognized merit of defense (claiming that jury instructions adequately set it forth);

C v Tata **28 MAC 23 (89)**—D's intent to use portion of drugs personally does not reduce amount for purposes of trafficking thresholds;

SEE CHAPTER 12-K, JURY INSTRUCTIONS, particularly:

C v Lawson **46 MAC 627 (99)**—simplistic formulations re: "general" and "specific" intent "will not likely assist either judicial analysis or a jury and may be source of confusion for both";

C v Sibinich **33 MAC 246, 249 n.1 (92)**—"The underlying difficulty, in cases in which specific intent is an element of the crime, is the practice of trial judges to explain specific intent by contrasting it to the idea of 'general intent.' Under this practice, 'general intent' is commonly defined as conduct undertaken 'unconsciously . . . a reflex action, such as sitting down in a chair or walking up stairs.' . . . 'general intent,' when defined in this fashion, does not refer to any mental state which is required for the conviction of a crime, and the use of a noncriminal 'general intent' to explain the specific intent required for certain crimes is unnecessary and confusing";

See Chapter 21-CC, Re: intent, drug possession/ distribution/trafficking;

C v Broderick **16 MAC 941 (83)**—willful, wanton, reckless conduct may substitute for (or allow inference of) intentional conduct for A&B (pointed cocked gun during argument);

C v Fortes **47 MAC 214 (99)**—not required that D personally know that danger of serious harm existed in contemplated purse snatch (leading to V's fall, dislocated kneecap, blood clots, death by coronary embolism six days later) if he had knowledge of facts that would cause reasonably prudent person to know such danger existed; here evidence from which jury could infer that D (joint venturer) and principal knew V was elderly before she was knocked down, & elderly are less sure-footed and hardy; D can't "escape responsibility merely because he hoped (V wouldn't resist purse snatch)";

C v Domingue **18 MAC 987 (84)**—1 act (shoot) = 2 intents (A&B, malicious destruction of property); BUT cf. *C v Redmond* **53 MAC 1 (2001)** in this crime (G.L. c. 266, § 127), willful doing of the unlawful act doesn't suffice to prove malice; required state of mind = cruelty, hostility, or revenge, in addition to intent to inflict injury to property; breaking window, dismantling alarm, & forcing doors = merely the means to computer theft after B&E, so required finding of NG of malicious destruction; here, more akin to "wanton" destruction of property, with which D wasn't charged (& it's not lesser included); *C v O'Neil* **67 MAC 284 (2006)**—for "harassment" (G.L. c. 265, § 43A(a)), needn't prove that D intended harmful consequences of intentional acts [letter-writing after being served with "no trespass"/contact order] or that he was motivated by cruelty, hostility, or revenge; "[a]s usually applied, the willful doing of an unlawful act suffices to prove malice", but ?need also to show, e.g. that "reasonably prudent person would have foreseen the actual harm that resulted";

16-C.2. Inferences Re: Mental State

Sandstrom v Montana **442 US 510 (79)**—permissive inference, not presumption, that one intends natural & probable consequences of his/her voluntary acts;

C v Perron **11 MAC 915 (81)**—infer intent was B&E with intent to commit felony (A&B by DW)—intent to beat complainant with coat rack or anything handy was inferable;

C v Holiday **349 M 126 (65)**—infer accessory D knew (escapee's) felony;

C v MacKenzie **376 M 148 (78)**—D's prior acts suggest intent (malicious);

C v Wygrzywalski **362 M 790 (73)**—sleeping drunk had B&E 'specific' intent to commit felony;

C v McGovern **397 M 863 (86)**—infer B&E only to vandalize, not for larceny;

C v Ferguson **384 M 13 (81)**—unnatural lascivious act wasn't intended to be public;

C v Fafone **416 M 329 (93)**—Florida drug supplier, D, shipped drugs to Connecticut and was never in Massachusetts: lack of evidence that D knew or intended his acts to have effect in MA meant required NG because "failure of proof of territorial jurisdiction";

C v Portnoy **318 M 274 (45)**—not D's burden of proof to negate specific intent; but . . .

C v Huffman **11 MAC 185 (81)**—must let D testify re: intent (own drug use); [*C v Paiva* **71 MAC 411 (2008)**—witness proffered by D was NOT an expert in use of drugs, but instead a percipient witness to D's own drug habit (including amounts), relevant to dispute "intent to distribute"; error to exclude, as observations not remote in time];

C v Caldron **383 M 86 (81)**—(same) re: helping, not robbing V; "self-serving" no problem; D's statement post-incident admissible re: state of mind;

C v Papadinis **402 M 73 (88)**—must let D tell his state of mind (drove off, killing cop, because scared from prior run-in with cop);

C v Contos **435 M 19, 22 (2001)**—though D placed before the jury D's out-of-court statements to psychiatrist because he wanted them used to discern D's state of mind when he killed girlfriend & two children, judge properly instructed that statements were not admitted for probative value & couldn't be used as evidence of the truth of their contents (& this meant that there was no evidence to support voluntary manslaughter instructions, since "provocation" inference available only from such statements);

See also Chapter 10-A, right to present defense;

16-C.3. Intoxication, Bearing on Intent and/or Criminal Responsibility

Superior Court Criminal Practice Jury Instructions § 3.3;

Model Jury Instructions for Use in the District Court #6.06;

C v Brown **449 M 747, 768 (2007)**—citing cases, "instruction on voluntary intoxication is not required absent evidence of 'debilitating intoxication'";

C v Grey **399 M 469 (87)**—experts saying retarded D had no specific intent to kill or do great harm merited jury charge re: malice capacity; not "excuse," rather negating the specific intent necessary here AND IN OTHER crimes (e.g., robbery); (Hennessey: fear (Pandora's Box); culpability gradations should be addressed by legislative penalties);

C v Perry **385 M 639 (82)**—intoxication admissible re: deliberate premeditation & extreme atrocity;

C v Tevenal **401 M 225 (87)**—intoxication & specific intent re: underlying armed robbery, but not re: felony murder because assault with intent to rob is inherently dangerous (so malice aforethought (*see Chapter 21, Homicide*);

C v Sama **411 M 293 (91)**—intoxication relevant re: "circumstances known to D" when jury deliberates re: malice (and extreme atrocity/cruelty); "Without more, we hold that evidence of a defendant's voluntary intoxication is a factor for the jury to consider whenever the Commonwealth bears the burden of establishing the knowledge of the defendant beyond a reasonable doubt";

C v Militello **66 MAC 325 (2006)**—intoxication instruction required concerning furnishing alcohol to minors: "furnish" is defined as knowingly or intentionally supplying, and is construed here as requiring proof of a "specific" intent, so "debilitating intoxication may affect [D's] ability to form such intent"; if "knowledge" element is instead only a "more general kind", intoxication said to be not relevant; contributing to delinquency of minor held NOT to require specific intent, so no intoxication instruction required;

C v Ferreira **417 M 592 (94)**—still "open" = question whether separate intoxication instruction on ability to form joint venture shared intent is required (issue reserved 1st in *C v Parker* **402 M 333 (88)**)

C v Fickett **403 M 194 (88)**—D gets intoxication instruction re: specific intent for robbery, larceny, & joint venture;

Robinson v California **370 US 660 (62)**—cruel & unusual to punish just addiction;

Powell v Texas **392 US 514 (68)**—can punish alcoholic for public drunkenness; (no longer a sufficient formulation of law = *C v Sheehan* **376 M 765 (78)** voluntary alcohol intoxication doesn't negate specific intent; (insufficient offer/proof to merit Majority Rule & give such instruction); addict = "voluntary," & not "disease" = for not guilty by reason of "insanity", i.e., not criminally responsible);

C v Brennan **399 M 358 (87)**—involuntary/unforeseeable intoxication = defense;

C v Wallace **14 MAC 358 (82)**—involuntary intoxication = OUI defense; e.g., unaware prescribed drug will impair; no legislative intent to impose strict liability;

C v Reynolds **67 MAC 215 (2006)**—D's conviction for felony motor vehicle homicide (operating vehicle to endanger, under influence of intoxicants) upheld despite total absence of evidence she ingested prescription drugs in any manner other than as prescribed; appellate court's rationale was that written warnings accompanying prescriptions cautioned that perceptions and skills could be impaired (ignoring fact of concomitant impairment of one's ability to sense one's impaired state);

C v Henson **394 M 584 (85)**—voluntary intoxication can cause reasonable doubt re proof of any specific intent crime (e.g., assault with intent to murder, but not ABDW); Mass. joining majority rule; maybe due process mandates it; BUT SEE *C v Lawson* **46 MAC 627 (99)**—simplistic formulations about specific vs. general intent not helpful: judge erroneously instructed that intoxication couldn't be considered re: resisting arrest; Commonwealth was required to prove D "knowingly" attempted to prevent cop acting under color of official authority from arresting;

C v McDowell **62 MAC 15 (2004)**—conviction under G.L. c. 266, § 126A requires only "wanton" conduct (willful and malicious not needed), so D's extreme intoxication didn't call into doubt proof of this "general intent" crime;

C v Sanna **424 M 92 (97)**—where only evidence re D's state of mind when he killed V was that he had voluntarily ingested crack cocaine, no right to instruction on lack of criminal responsibility;

C v Hagenlock **140 M 125 (1885)**—jury question: too drunk for assault intent (to harm/injure)?;

C v Shelley **381 M 340 (80)**—no insanity by voluntary use of alcohol, but qualified by:

C v Herd **413 M 834 (92)**—mental disease or defect caused solely by consumption of drug does qualify for application of **McHoul** test (**352 M 544 (67)**): D's cocaine-induced paranoid psychosis included hallucinations and delusions; in deciding what D had reason to know about the consequences of his drug consumption, jury to consider the question solely from D's point of view, including his mental capacity; Court "unwilling, in order to justify a homicide conviction, to permit the moral fault inherent in the unlawful consumption of drugs to substitute for the moral fault that is absent in one who lacks criminal responsibility";

C v Angelone **413 M 82 (92)**—judge must instruct that voluntary alcohol consumption is factor in determining criminal responsibility where D has latent mental disease or defect which might have been triggered by alcohol;

C v Ruddock **428 M 288, 291 (98)**—when jurors were instructed that D would be criminally responsible if he had consumed drugs "knowing or having reason to know" that he would lose substantial capacity to appreciate his conduct's criminality or the capacity to conform his conduct to the requirements of law, D argued that this violated *Herd* **413 M 834 (92)** calling for "objective" rather than "subjective" standard; given evidence here, from D's own witness, that D knew of drug use's adverse consequences on his mental condition, defect not harmful;

C v Whitman **453 M 331 (2009)**—failure to give *Herd* (413 M 834) instruction not error as no evidence to support premise that alcohol consumption could have "triggered" D's mental illness; hearsay testimony admitted only to demonstrate basis for doctor's opinion (friend of D's sister said D reported to her that he heard voices when intoxicated); instruction using "reason to know" (rather than actual knowledge) was not warranted by the evidence (because no evidence that D knew alcohol would exacerbate mental condition) but held merely "superfluous", causing no prejudice;

C v Baldwin **426 M 105, 106 n.1 (97)**—"no 'diminished capacity' defense in this Commonwealth," but mental impairment = relevant to whether crime was committed at all, given elements of intent & knowledge to be proved in many prosecutions;

C v Parker **420 M 242, 245 n.3 (95)**—same;

C v Gould **380 M 672 (80)**—(de facto) diminished capacity from drugs re: first degree murder deliberate premeditation & extreme atrocity;

[*see C v Blache* **450 M 583 (2008)**—regarding sexual assault complainant's capacity to consent despite intoxication]

C v Cutts **444 M 821 (2005)**—trial counsel not ineffective for failing to present insanity defense (i.e., that D's conduct was result of unanticipated cocaine-induced psychotic episode), despite postconviction counsel's presentation of affidavits from two addiction experts; trial counsel had retained expert who concluded that D wasn't suffering from any psychosis, and trial counsel pursued "diminished capacity" defense, based on "homosexual panic" in conjunction with paranoia heightened by cocaine use;

C v Boateng **438 M 498 (2003)**—mental illness can reduce assault with intent to murder to assault with intent to kill;

C v Yancy **440 M 234 (2003)**—asserting that "the jury was properly instructed that it could consider 'diminished capacity' both as to deliberate premeditation and malice aforethought, conformably with *C v Grey* 399 M 469 (87), and *C v Gould* 380 M 672, 680–83 (80)";

C v Benjamin **430 M 673 (2000)**—refusal to take into account effect of words on D due to drug/alcohol impairment or "hypervigilance" (expert psych. diagnosis) in context of provocation negating malice;

C v Contos **435 M 19, 22 (2001)**—though D placed before the jury D's out-of-court statements to psychiatrist because he wanted them used to discern D's state of mind when he killed girlfriend & two children, judge properly instructed that statements were not admitted for probative value & couldn't be used as evidence of the truth of their contents (& this meant that there was no evidence to support voluntary manslaughter instructions, since "provocation" inference available only from such statements);

C v Robinson **14 MAC 591 (82)**—expert couldn't say no malice aforethought because of diminished capacity (so no reduction to manslaughter);

C v Loretta **386 M 794 (82)**—23 drinks not diminished capacity without expert re: capacity; but see/contra:

C v Mello **420 M 375, 394 (95)**—rejecting argument that trial counsel ineffective in failing to use expert to "develop" intoxication issue;

C v Parker **420 M 242 (95)**—(same); counsel elicited evidence in cross re D's intoxication;

C v Frank **433 M 185, 193, n.6 (2001), citing *C v Cruz*** **413 M 686, 691 (92)**—SJC has NOT held that expert testimony is required in order to raise issue of mental impairment due to intoxication;

C v Scott **430 M 351, 356–57 (99)**—counsel not ineffective in failing to request insanity instruction & instead asking 2d degree based on diminished capacity due to substance abuse; D's attempts at suicide during ten days before murder not enough to support insanity instruction;

C v Milton **49 MAC 552 (2000)**—counsel ineffective in failing to request psych evaluation;

C v Wallace **417 M 126 (94)**—when evidence = "conflicting" re: intoxication, D entitled to jury instruction;

C v Herbert **421 M 307 (95)**—no right to intoxication instruction regarding intent element (of murder 1 by extreme atrocity or cruelty) when only evidence = several hours earlier, D had "couple of beers";

C v James **424 M 770, 789 (97)**—voluntary intoxication instruction not required where evidence doesn't suggest condition of debilitating intoxication "that could support a reasonable doubt as to whether (D) was capable of forming the requisite criminal intent";

C v Barnette **45 MAC 486, 493 (98)**—same; *C v Anderson* **58 MAC 117 (2003)**—same;

C v Purcell **423 M 880 (96)**—unconstitutional shift of burden of proof to instruct "if you find that D was so drunk he could not entertain malice aforethought . . . you would decide . . . whether or not he is guilty of manslaughter"; Commonwealth bears burden of proof on malice;

C v Rose **47 MAC 168, 177 (99)**—no burden of proof on either side regarding intoxication; intoxication is a subsidiary factor in evaluation of whether Commonwealth has proved required state of mind beyond a reasonable doubt;

C v Delaney **418 M 658 (94)**—3d prong malice instruction requires specification that judgment is to be re "circumstances known to D" (not merely 'reasonable person') & whether in those circumstances reasonable person would know plain & strong likelihood of death;

C v Flynn **37 MAC 550 (95) S.C. 420 M 810, 815 (95)**—intoxication relevant in manslaughter defense re: circumstances known to D at time he acted (& whether reasonable person with such knowledge would recognize high degree of likelihood of substantial harm to another);

C v Ward **426 M 290 (97)**—extreme intoxication & expert testimony re resulting mental impairment & judge's refusal to instruct on relevance of impairment to ability to deliberately premeditate = SJC's reduction of conviction from 1st to 2d degree murder;

C v Traylor **43 MAC 239 (97)**—omission of intoxication instruction caused no prejudice when counsel's argument to jury said sole issue = ID and only evidence of impairment was V's testimony that assailants appeared drunk and accomplice's testimony that D drank vodka before;

C v Sires **413 M 292 (92)**—wherever D's state of mind is in issue, jury should be instructed to consider all credible evidence concerning D's consumption of drugs or alcohol;

C v Smith **449 M 12 (2007)**—though "model" instruction on intoxication is recommended, failure to give it isn't error; "[a]ll that we have ever required . . . would be satisfied by a simple instruction that the jury may consider credible evidence of the effects of the [D]'s consumption of drugs [or alcohol, or both] in deciding whether the Commonwealth had met its burden of proving the [D]'s state of mind beyond a reasonable doubt"; trial counsel's decision to forego defense relying on impaired mental state due to alcohol's exacerbation of Tourette's Syndrome was reasonable because DA told counsel of rebuttal evidence and because D had boasted after killing that he would "get off" because of Tourette's;

C v Barros **425 M 572 (97)**—intoxication's effect on perceptions = irrelevant to self-defense if belief as to imminent danger objectively unreasonable;

C v Benjamin **430 M 673 (2000)**—refusal to take into account effect of words on D due to drug/alcohol impairment or "hypervigilance" (expert psych. diagnosis) in context of provocation negating malice;

C v Troy **405 M 253 (89)**—intoxication & its effect on specific intent not admissible as to rape or felony murder (but cf., contra, *C v Sires* **413 M 292 (92)** whenever D's state of mind is in issue, jury should be instructed to consider all credible evidence concerning D's consumption of drugs or alcohol);

C v Robinson **408 M 245 (90)**—"new rule" announced in Henson requiring jury instructions on intoxication where specific intent in issue will not be applied retroactively on collateral review under *C v Bray* **407 M 296 (1990)**, banning retroactive application of new rules on collateral review unless "central to an accurate determination of innocence or guilt";

C v Seabrooks **425 M 507 (97)**—testimony that D had attempted suicide immediately after killing girlfriend, that he was not making any sense, "looked very incoherent" and said that he had "freaked out" and "lost control" = insufficient "to implicate a lack of criminal responsibility," so no instruction required;

C v Vazquez **419 M 350 (95)**—rejects argument that evidence of prodigious alcohol consumption entitled D, as matter of law, to NG of murder: whether D possessed requisite intent was issue of fact;

C v DelValle **443 M 782, 793–94 (2005)**—no error in excluding testimony of D's wife that D "had a serious problem with drugs at the time the murder was committed", because not specific to night at issue (& thus irrelevant); even if admitted, wouldn't have "warranted" instruction on voluntary intoxication (required only where evidence suggests "condition of debilitating intoxication that could support a reasonable doubt as to whether a D was capable of forming the requisite criminal intent");

C v Presby **14 Gray 65 (1859)**—MISTAKE of FACT = defense . . . (but . . .

C v Miller **385 M 521 (82)**—. . . not if STRICT LIABILITY (statutory rape mistake re: age of sex partner); *C v Knap* **412 M 712 (92)** (statutory rape mistake re: identity of sex partner); cf. *C v Colon* **431 M 188 (2000)** "consent" of minor child no defense to kidnapping of such child; and, according to the Appeals Court, if not the SJC, not if it's a 'sexual assault' case of any sort, it seems: *C v McCrae* **54 MAC 27 (2002)** "honest mistake of fact about willingness of complainant to engage in sexual foreplay" is "a defense not available . . . as a matter of law"; BUT SEE

C v Lopez **433 M 722 (2001)**—in this case & probably most cases, requirement that Commonwealth prove "force" "should negate any possible mistake as to consent," but holding only that "this case does not persuade us that we should recognize mistake of fact as to consent as a defense to rape in *all* cases"; *C v Urban* **67 MAC 301 (2006)**—reversal for judge's failure/refusal to charge that inability to consent to sex could be shown only by finding complainant to be "wholly insensible" (or "utterly senseless"), not simply drunk/affected by intoxicants; in contrast = sleep, stupefaction, unconsciousness, & helplessness—states which "ordinarily" preclude voluntary consent; jury must be aware of "the high degree of intoxication required to negate the capacity to consent";

C v LeBlanc **30 MAC 1 (90)**—good faith belief that D, in buying drugs, was acting as agent for government is a valid defense;

C v White **5 MAC 483 (77)**—honest/reasonable belief complaining witness owed D the money = defense to robbery/larceny, but not assault by dangerous weapon; (but see *Marcotte* **18 MAC 391 (84)** re D's belief negating assault);

C v Larmey **14 MAC 281 (82)**—(same) to recover stolen $ & return to owner;

C v Newhook **34 MAC 960 (93)**—honest/reasonable belief complainant owed D the money;

C v Vives **447 M 537 (2006)**—D's belief that he was collecting a debt due him = "affirmative defense" (peculiarly within knowledge of D, particularly since here, victim

= dead), but Commonwealth still has burden of proof because the defense goes to an element of the crime, i.e., intent to steal; D has "burden of production," but thereafter Commonwealth must disprove the defense, & jury must be instructed re: honest/reasonable belief; if Commonwealth claims that debt = result of illegal transaction, must prove this to jury beyond reasonable doubt (& this would defeat the defense);

C v Marcotte 18 MAC 391 (84)—honest belief clerk's staging D's robbery & consenting would mean it's only larceny;

C v Gelpi 416 M 729 (94)—ineffective assistance of counsel found in failing to request instruction that prosecution had to prove beyond reasonable doubt that D did not have honest/reasonable belief that alleged victim's jewelry was his (given as collateral for (drug?) deal);

C v Francis 24 MAC 576 (87)—though no knowledge element, assault & battery on correctional officer D has defense if honest/reasonable belief complaining witness not a correctional officer (& self-defense);

C v Simmarano 50 MAC 312 (2000)—D's belief that his entry into dwelling was authorized by "cumulative practice"/permission = defense; ineffective assistance of counsel in failing to request jury instruction & in failing to justify admission of evidence of dweller's consent;

16-C.4. Lawful Authority Defenses

C v Swan 38 MAC 539 (95)—larceny (unpaid bill) defense: Attorney General's regulations. re: unfair & deceptive practices by auto repair shop required written records authorizing repairs; since shop had none, bill was unlawful;

C v Bell 442 M 118 (2004)—SJC, on Commonwealth's G.L. c. 211, § 3 petition, bars D in "school zone" drug prosecution from using Department of Education regulation defining "secondary school";

C v Wilkinson 415 M 402 (93)—though this D, an agent for Oklahoma bail bondsman, was permitted to use 'lawful authority' defense to kidnapping and assault by means of dangerous weapon charges, SJC held that Uniform Criminal Extradition Act implicitly abrogated common law right of bondsman to seize principal within MA for surrender in another state; *See C v Cabral* 443 M 171 (2005)—bail surety & his agents have lawful authority to apprehend, detain, and deliver a principal to a court house, and a defendant surety bears only burden of raising defense of "lawful authority," after which burden is on Commonwealth to prove beyond reasonable doubt that he wasn't a surety; jury instructions re: agency relationship & D's actions as possibly outside scope of agency;

C v Twitchell 416 M 114 (93)—Christian Science practitioner believed (reasonably for non-lawyer? citing G.L. c. 273, § 1 & AG's opinion) government would not prosecute person pursuing spiritual treatment for son (who died from bowel obstruction/perforation correctable by surgery);

C v Landry 438 M 206 (2002)—person in needle exchange program extant in Cambridge may possess needle anywhere in Commonwealth (i.e., including where there are no such programs);

C v Garrity 43 MAC 349 (97)—defense of "reliance on advice of counsel" (good faith reasonable mistake of law) D (1) acting in good faith & not seeking an opinion to shelter himself, (2) gives full disclosure of facts, (3) is doubtful of his legal rights, (4) has reason to know counsel is competent, (5) complied with advice, (6) counsel has sufficient training & experience to exercise prudent judgment;

C v Luna 418 M 749 (94)—cop-D's defense in perjury—reliance on superiors' authority—rejected as matter of law: not reasonable;

16-D. SELF-DEFENSE (PROPERTY/OTHER), NECESSITY, DURESS, COERCION (INVOLUNTARINESS)

See Chapter 11, Evidence re: "victim" being an inappropriate description of complaining witness;

District Court Model Jury Instructions (*see Chapter 21-A, Analyzing Elements of Common Crimes*) 6.02—Necessity & Duress;

Superior Court Criminal Practice Jury Instructions §§ 3.6—3.9, self-defense, defense of another, defense of property; § 3.11, necessity; § 3.12, duress;

C v Janvrin 44 MAC 917 (98)—self-defense is invoked re crimes committed against person while defending self; "necessity" applies to other crimes committed in defending self, *e.g.*, possession of firearms;

C v Garuti 23 MAC 561 (87)—necessity = circumstances forced act; duress/coerced = human being(s) forced it;

US v Bailey 444 US 394 (80)—(same); modern cases blur distinction; (can deny jury instruction re: escape because continuing offense & alternative existed if D never surrendered);

Dixon v US 548 US 1 (2006)—Supreme Court presumes that Congress intended D to bear burden of proving duress by preponderance of evidence in charges of receiving firearm while under indictment (18 USC 922(n)) and another; S Ct holds no due process violation in this burden; (D had argued error in refusing to instruct that prosecution had to disprove duress beyond reasonable doubt); opinion notes that "**Government recognized at oral argument that there may be crimes where the nature of the mens rea would require the Government to disprove the existence of duress beyond a reasonable doubt**";

C v Allen 430 M 252 (99)—reserves question whether duress defense may apply to murder; even if applicable, judge here could have rejected because D "placed himself recklessly in a situation where coercion will probably be applied"; *C v Rebello* **450 M 118, 124 n.5 (2007)**—still not decided whether duress is defense to murder;

C v Perl **50 MAC 445 (2000)**—re: charge that duress requires that: D must have received present & immediate threat which caused him to have a well-founded fear of imminent death or serious bodily injury if he didn't do criminal act; threat had to be imminent and present throughout the commission of crime; D must have had no reasonable opportunity to escape, & D "or any other person of reasonable firmness" must have had no other choice, unable to do otherwise in circumstances; "duress" can include threat to another person; appellate court rejects D's arguments, however, that duress defense doesn't require, after *Egardo* **42 MAC 41, 44 n.2 (97)**, fear of "imminent" death or serious bodily injury AND that the standard was not that of "reasonable person" but instead whether D himself acted under compulsion rather than free will (a "pure inquiry into voluntariness" of act);

C v Schuchardt **408 M 347 (90)**—trespass & wanton destruction at nuclear missile components' manufacturing plant: evidence insufficient to raise necessity defense; defense limited to when: (1) D faced with "clear & imminent," not "debatable/speculative" danger; (2) D can reasonably expect that D's action will be effective as direct cause of abating danger; (3) no legal alternative effective to abate danger; (4) legislature has not acted to preclude the defense "by clear & deliberate choice regarding the values at issue";

C v Lora **43 MAC 136 (97)**—(D operating after license suspension because very ill and on way to pharmacy for medications) since factor (4) of Schuchardt is beyond jury's competence, charge should either omit it or judge should tell jury legislature has not acted;

C v Egardo **42 MAC 41, 44–45 (S.C. 426 M 48) (97)**—instruction on duress **shouldn't** include language, "a threat of future harm is not enough"; but SEE *C v Perl* **50 MAC 445, 451 & n.10 (2000)** holding in Egardo did not do away with the "duress" requirement that threat be "imminent" and "present throughout the commission of the crime";

C v Pike **428 M 393 (98)**—no right to "necessity" instruction in trial for unauthorized use of motor vehicle because no "imminent" danger, and no showing there was no lawful alternative to abate the danger;

C v Morris M **70 MAC 688 (2007)**—court believes that alternatives of calling police on cell phones or running short distance home were alternatives to using vehicle without authority, so D not entitled to required finding of not delinquent (D's formulation of issue on appeal, id. at 696; trial was jury-waived);

C v Kendall **451 M 10 (2008)**—no right to "necessity" instruction for operating under the influence to drive seriously injured girlfriend to hospital (bleeding head wound) because neighbor with car was 40 feet away and fire station was 100 yards away; SJC rejects D's argument that judge/court should not usurp power of jury to decide

whether "necessity" lay: "judge need not instruct on a hypothesis that is not supported by evidence in the first instance"; *three justices dissented*, id. at 16–19, citing countervailing facts/evidence relevant to jury determination;

C v Livington **70 MAC 745 (2007)**—necessity instruction should have been requested (& given) when D briefly drove on wrong side of road (reckless operation) trying to get to assistance for his own gunshot wound;

C v Kiss **59 MAC 247 (2003)**—D, asleep or passed out in car with motor running in mall parking lot, argued without success for "shelter defense," to avoid criminal penalty when he removed vehicle from roadway because he believed himself to be under the influence;

C v Leno **415 M 835 (93)**—SJC upheld refusal to instruct on necessity defense (D distributing clean needles to addicts, stemming spread of HIV);

C v Hutchins **410 M 726 (91)**—medical necessity is not a defense to drug possession;

US v Oakland Cannabis Buyers' Cooperative **532 US 483 (2001)**—when legislature has made determination of purportedly competing values, i.e., that marijuana had no medical benefits worthy of exception to federal drug laws other than government-approved research, defense of 'legal necessity' can't succeed;

C v Manning **41 MAC 696 (96)**—appellate court upheld refusal to charge on necessity defense in prosecution for violating injunction prohibiting obstruction of abortion clinic access **and** says judge properly precluded D from explaining his actions based on religious beliefs, because evidence "irrelevant to the charge of contempt";

C v Brogan **415 M 169 (93)**—upholding exclusion of necessity defense in prosecution for obstruction of abortion facilities;

C v Wolf **34 MAC 949 (93)**—upholding exclusion of minister's testimony re D's religious beliefs (trespass at abortion clinic);

C v McCambridge **44 MAC 285 (98)**—jury should have been instructed re necessity concerning firearm possession, so that conviction (but not homicide) was reversed;

Nolan & Sartorio, *Criminal Law*, § 677 (3d ed. 2001)—coercion/compulsion: criminal liability only for voluntary acts; § 678 necessity = same basic problem; starving D maybe can steal food

C v Hood **389 M 581 (83)**—best not to exclude entire defense on DA's motion in limine;

C v Lora **43 MAC 136 (97)**—error to exclude, on DA's motion in limine, medical records substantiating long-term illness, relevant to defense of necessity;

C v Brooks **99 M 434 (1868)**—NG if didn't voluntarily block street with wagon (because D himself was V of a traffic jam);

C v Rider **8 MAC 775 (79)**—NG of carry gun in car because involuntary presence (necessary element) in cruiser for D under arrest;

C v Robinson **382 M 189 (81)**—duress = not free will, voluntary, criminal intent (which DA must prove); even for serious felony if serious threat;

C v Barnes **369 M 462 (76)**—DA must disprove beyond reasonable doubt compulsion/force of other(s); (wife no longer presumed coerced by nearby husband);

C v Luna **418 M 749 (94)**—cop-D in perjury case could not use defense of reasonable reliance on (superiors') authority because not reasonable/lawful to file illegal affidavit in court; "doubtful" that defense would lie in any serious criminal case;

C v Melzer **14 MAC 174 (82)**—defense if reasonably fear another's serious injury (better to give instruction, but can deny if retreat was possible);

Q v Dudley **14 QBD 273 (1884)**—lifeboaters can't cannibalize though starving; . . .

US v Holmes **26 Fed.Cas. 360 (3d Cir. 1842)**— . . . nor ditch anyone though overloaded;

C v Thurber **383 M 328 (81)**—DA must disprove necessity for escape, but no defense unless D immediately surrendered (see also *Bailey* **444 US 394 (80) & *Robinson* 382 M 189 (81)**);

C v O'Malley **14 MAC 314 (82)**—necessity = defense to escape because immediate threat & futile complaint; no time for court, used no force, & immediately surrendered;

C v Coleman **64 MAC 558 (2005)**—D's conduct was not a suppressible "fruit" of police action ("whatever one may think about the wisdom of [such action]"): after police responded to highway altercation and spoke first with other driver, D said he couldn't wait longer, and was leaving, but was ordered by police to remain (cop attempted to **break D's car window with the handle of his gun,** to stop/arrest him [G.L. c. 90, §§ 25, 21], causing D to flee and lead cops on high speed chase); court's "decision is limited to the application of the exclusionary rule," allowing evidence obtained after D's failure to comply with order to stop; viability of any defense based upon actions of police "necessarily will depend upon the evidence adduced at trial";

C v Averill **12 MAC 260 (81)**—no necessity instruction for trespass because no immediate threat from nuke plant & D's acts won't solve problem;

C v Brugmann **13 MAC 373 (82)**—(same), even if D's acts would stop immediate danger, no defense unless no non-futile alternatives existed; "justice" values may supercede law's values;

C v Lindsey **396 M 840 (86)**—maybe necessity/self-defense for carry gun, but no instruction warranted if threat not immediate, serious, & continuous;

C v Ben B **59 MAC 919 (2003)**—finding no error in refusal to instruct re: necessity in gun-carrying case; "evidence of imminent danger was incomplete"; even if D needed to remove gun from stroller, "he was not entitled to walk around with it . . . for fifteen minutes in a public place";

C v Iglesia **403 M 132 (88)**—DA must disprove necessity for carry gun where D says disarmed X & taking gun to police; jury decides if it's right choice;

C v Foster **48 MAC 671 (2000)**—D not entitled to instruction on "necessity" defense (so couldn't be harmed by flaws in instruction given), because he didn't testify "that there was any clear and imminent danger for which no legal alternative was available" & there was no evidence that anyone "expressed an intention to use the gun" which D found on ground and purportedly picked up to prevent someone from being hurt;

C v Adjutant **443 M 649 (2005)**—judge has discretion to admit "specific incidents of violence that the victim is reasonably alleged to have initiated" when D asserts self-defense and identity of first aggressor is in dispute; **D needn't have known of such incidents at time of alleged crime;**

C v Pring-Wilson **448 M 718 (2007)**—affirming trial judge's allowance of new trial based on *Adjutant*, because at trial, D repeatedly and aggressively sought to introduce evidence of V's (and his cohorts') violent histories and before direct appeal, D renewed request for relief, citing *Adjutant* (decided after D's trial);

C v Peppicelli **70 MAC 87 (2007)**—refusing relief to D on *Adjutant* issue, because D didn't attempt to introduce any such evidence at trial, and instead raised issue only by post-conviction motion; no "retroactive" application of *Adjutant*;

C v Benoit **452 M 212 (2008)**—although "self-defense" instruction was legitimately refused (because D could have retreated), judge did instruct on voluntary manslaughter: D argued logical extension of Adjutant, i.e., prior violent acts by deceased argued to be admissible in context of whether he initiated sudden and violent combat which would cause reasonable person to be provoked to heat of passion; because of newness of Adjutant rule and lack of opportunity to examine its impact, SJC "not prepared to extend the rule *at this time*", but reversed conviction on different ground; Ireland, J., believed "court should have undertaken a full analysis of the merits of extending the *Adjutant* rule to this case, instead of dismissing it as premature":

C v Gaynor **73 MAC 71, further review allowed 452 M 1110 (2008)**—no error in excluding prior violent behavior by victim when identity of first aggressor was not in dispute (it was victim), and no live issue whether D was precluded from asserting self-defense on ground that it was he who had started fight; even if "Adjutant" evidence theoretically admissible, judge could exercise discretion to exclude proffered evidence as different in nature (domestic violence) from "street fight" being tried and as remote (4 years earlier); DA's closing argument did not exploit absence of Adjutant evidence, instead arguing that fight was over, D didn't fear imminent harm, and had opportunity to retreat;

C v Kendrick **351 M 203, 211 (66)**—self-defense for armed D if reasonable fear of "great bodily harm"; "infirmity of human impulses" = considered;

C v Harrington **379 M 446 (80)**—(same);

C v Santos **454 M 770 (2009)**—reversal of first degree murder conviction (despite no objection below) because erroneous jury instructions told jurors that excessive force in self-defense negated the defense entirely, to the end of conviction of murder; instead, imperfect self-defense would result in manslaughter conviction; abundant language that appellate court should not parse evidence and make its own appraisal of credibility/viability of defense;

C v Silva **455 M 503 (2009)**—an "element" of self-defense = reasonableness of force used to defend oneself; if Commonwealth "fails to disprove all the elements of self-defense except the element of reasonableness of the force used, i.e., that D used excessive force in self-defense, . . . self-defense does not lie, but excessive force in self-defense will mitigate murder to voluntary manslaughter"; particular clause to be omitted from instruction in future, as it contradicts prior assertion re: self-defense;

C v Diaz **453 M 266 (2009)**—self-defense instruction unwarranted: after victim punched D, D walked to and entered car to retrieve weapon, didn't attempt to leave scene, got gun, shot V, then shot V twice more as he lay on ground; no evidence D reasonably believed himself in danger of serious bodily harm/death; no error, therefore, in refusal to instruct on 'excessive force in self-defense';

C v Espada **450 M 687 (2008)**—same result, variant facts;

C v Haith **452 M 409 (2008)**—though D argued entitlement to instruction on "imperfect defense of another" (his two children) to give jury option of voluntary manslaughter, even if he acted under coercion or fear that his children would be hurt, brutal and purposeful murder of V was here "obvious[ly]" [as matter of law?] unreasonable and inappropriate;

C v Pimental **5 MAC 463 (77)**—D's weakness & physical condition = factor;

C v Jardine **143 M 567 (1887)**—D's injuries = factor;

C v Moreira **388 M 596 (83)**—if know police officer is performing duty, no right to resist unless police use excessive force; "disposition of the case depends on the application of the rules pertaining to self-defense"; see *C v Miranda* **77 MAC 76 (2010);**

C v Urkiel **63 MAC 445 (2005)**—while warrantless entry of D's home was unconstitutional (because it was for misdemeanor not committed in presence of police and/or because no exigent circumstances) & arrest was thus "bad," and *Gomes* 59 MAC 332 (2003) establishes that such unlawful entry isn't a defense to charge of resisting arrest, D had legitimate **self-defense** claim on facts here, & judge erred in assuming it inapplicable;

C v Williams **53 MAC 719, 723 (2002)**—concepts of excessive force & self-defense are closely related;

C v Graham **62 MAC 642 (2004)**—D was entitled to instruction on self-defense on charges of resisting arrest and assault and battery on police officer; instruction given below suggested incorrectly that D had burden of establishing that police used excessive force, that D defended self with reasonable force, and that he resisted arrest using such reasonable force as was necessary to resist "excessive" force by police; instead, judge must charge that Commonwealth must prove beyond reasonable doubt that

police did not engage in excessive force, as well as that D didn't act in self-defense;

Daniels v Commonwealth **455 M 1009 (2009)**—reprosecution not barred: while evidence entitled D to self-defense instruction, Commonwealth evidence sufficient to disprove self-defense beyond reasonable doubt;

C v Barros **425 M 572 (97)**—determination whether D's belief re: his exposure to danger was "reasonable" may not take into account his intoxication;

C v Ramirez **44 MAC 779 (98)**—same;

C v Alebord **49 MAC 915 (2000)**—no error in refusing self-defense instruction because no reasonable apprehension of imminent physical harm (D had "highly active imagination" due to V's beating of D 5 years earlier, but no one approached D or made hostile remark; perception that they looked at a hammer & giggled insufficient);

C v Alves **50 MAC 796 (2001)**—any error in self-defense instruction given not ground for reversal because D not entitled to self-defense instruction: he had adequate means of escape on public street;

C v Pike **428 M 393 (98)**—no error in refusing self defense instruction because D could have avoided further combat and because evidence didn't support reasonable fear of imminent serious bodily harm or death "avoidable only by throwing a heavy metal object at (V's) head";

C v Moran **75 MAC 513 (2009)**—D's statement to police admitted he was able to leave fight to go back inside building, but there he got knife and returned to stab victim: any error in unobjected-to instruction regarding jury's obligation to consider first and second degree murder before considering voluntary & involuntary manslaughter didn't create substantial risk of miscarriage of justice;

C v Fortini **68 MAC 701 (2007)**—despite fact that D armed self and waited on front porch in dark following loud threats from strangers in car, jury entitled to consider both self-defense (see S.C., 44 MAC 562 (98)) and provocation on sudden combat (because the strangers came onto porch and "lunged" for the gun held by D); motion for new trial should have been allowed due to error in manslaughter instruction, i.e., saying Commonwealth must prove D acted with reasonable provocation for verdict of manslaughter (should have been instruction that Commonwealth must prove beyond a reasonable doubt that D didn't act on reasonable provocation);

C v Peloquin **437 M 204 (2002)**—"castle law," G.L. c. 278, § 8A (no duty to retreat if victim is in D's dwelling unlawfully & D used reasonable means to defend self or others) doesn't eliminate duty to retreat if other person is lawfully on premises, i.e., an invited guest, even when guest launches life-threatening assault on D;

C v McKinnon **446 M 263 (2006)**—"castle law" doesn't apply if victims were on exterior stairs leading to house's porch or when they were on the porch itself; G.L. c. 278, § 8A limits the defense to an occupant who injures someone unlawfully IN the dwelling;

C v Vives **447 M 537 (2006)**—even though incident occurred inside D's apartment building, he had duty to retreat because common stairway outside apartment wasn't part of his "dwelling" within meaning of castle law;

C v Carlino **449 M 71 (2007)**—evidence, even in light most favorable to D, was that he and victim were in the driveway, not in D's dwelling, so G.L. c. 278, § 8A ("castle law") did not apply;

C v Monico **373 M 298 (77)**—the less fear, the less force is O.K.;

C v Bastarache **382 M 86 (80)**—D not armed, self defense with nondeadly force OK if reasonable "concern for personal safety" (lesser standard);

C v Baseler **419 M 500 (95)**—(same) right to use nondeadly force in self defense arises at lower level of danger;

C v Noble **429 M 44 (99)**—same; reversal for failure to instruct on nondeadly force; fact that force of fists, hands, arms results in death does not ALONE make it "deadly" force, which is force intended or likely to cause death or serious bodily harm; jury question whether headlock here was deadly force;

C v Mann **116 M 58 (1874)**—discharge gun maybe OK to scare in self defense; (see Necessity, above, ***Lindsey*** **396 M 840 (86)** & ***Iglesia*** **403 M 132 (88)**)

C v Cataldo **423 M 318 (96)**—brandishing gun without firing is "deadly force" **if** D intends to shoot gun (jury question); D is protected in his actions if he creates apprehension he will resort to deadly force, if necessary, when he is threatened with harm that cannot be repelled except by threat of deadly force;

C v Allen **76 MAC 9 (2009)**—while "brandishing" a 10-inch folding knife after opening it not necessarily "deadly" force, uncontroverted testimony = D "tried to hit" V with it; since D wasn't entitled to self-defense instruction, any error in instruction given "could not give rise to" substantial risk of miscarriage of justice;

C v Hubbard **45 MAC 277, 278 n.1 (98)**—instructions should have focused on "crucial question," i.e., "whether the defendant, in holding the unloaded rifle at 'port arms,' intended to use that weapon in a deadly manner"; Commonwealth's burden of proof to negate self defense (if raised);

C v Santiago **425 M 491 (97)**—instruction re "elements of a defense" should occur **after** instruction re elements of crime & judge should "remind jury at end of instructions that self-defense negate(s) culpability" & Commonwealth bears burden of proving lack of self defense;

C v Williams **450 M 879 (2008)**—rejecting argument that self-defense instructions (based on Model Jury Instructions on Homicide [1999]) were burden-shifting, despite their use of conditions like "the person must have" and there "must be": outline of "what the law recognizes as self-defense" necessary so that jury "could understand what the Commonwealth has an obligation to disprove";

C v Carlino **429 M 692 (99)**—despite no objection, reversal because instructions conveyed, possibly, that self defense was not a complete defense and that excessive force in self-defense would be murder rather than manslaughter;

C v Johnson **412 M 368, 371 (92)**—valid defense of another does not reduce murder to manslaughter but relieves D of all liability; excessive use of force reduces murder to manslaughter;

C v Walker **443 M 213 (2005)**—*rejects* argument that if D responds with deadly force after being put in fear of physical harm (i.e., by mere "push"), culpability is for voluntary manslaughter rather than murder (rationale of "excessive force" in legitimate self-defense); (*C v Toon* **55 MAC 642, 654 (2002)**—same); threshold for use of deadly force is if person has reasonable apprehension of great bodily harm and reasonable belief that no other means would suffice to prevent such harm; "once the level of force used by a person is ascertained, that level of force will determine whether the deadly or nondeadly force standard will apply"; "the two standards are distinct, self-contained definitions of self-defense. . . [,] mutually exclusive";

C v Tirado **65 MAC 571 (2006)**—holds that on facts, instruction as to self-defense "not warranted" because evidence didn't support reasonable doubt as to presence of prerequisites for either "non-deadly" or "deadly" force, and "did not support a finding that [D] availed himself of reasonably available means of retreat"; for purposes of determining whether self-defense instruction was required, "whether the amount of force used was reasonably necessary is not a consideration";

C v Pichardo **45 MAC 296 (98)**—(gunshot) excessive force in defense of another not viable defense because V had begun to walk away from adversary AND no weapon was visible during encounter (though V stabbed someone earlier this night);

C v Fluker **377 M 123 (79)**—no required finding of NG (here) on Commonwealth case;

C v Richards **384 M 396 (81)**—"if you find self-defense, then NG" shifted burden of proof;

C v Mejia **407 M 493 (90)**—instructions setting forth "preconditions" & "criteria" for self-defense were burden-shifting;

C v Williams **450 M 879 (2008)**—rejecting claim of burden-shifting self-defense instructions;

C v Bertrand **385 M 356 (82)**—self-defense not raised;

C v Hogue **6 MAC 901 (78)**—issue raised; error not to instruct;

C v Kivlehan **57 MAC 793 (2003)**—evidence sufficient to raise defense of another; substantial risk of miscarriage of justice not to so instruct;

C v Gill **37 MAC 457 (94)**—even without D request, judge has sua sponte duty to instruct on self-defense *if* there is evidence supporting it;

C v Souza **428 M 478 (98)**—though D requested that there be NO instruction on self-defense, such a claim was made in his statement to police, which had been admitted, and judge did instruct on it; issue of first impression whether such a "defense" instruction may be given over D's objection (and here, Commonwealth didn't request it either), but Court finds no prejudice from the instruction: "prejudice" to D's cause instead fairly rose from DA's closing argument which asserted that D abandoned self defense claim when forensic evidence gathered after statement and before trial effectively refuted it (so false statement was consciousness of guilt);

C v Deagle **10 MAC 748 (80)**—issue raised, so error to refuse instruction; JURY's function to decide, even if judge thinks evidence raising self-defense is incredible; cf. *Apprendi v New Jersey* **530 US 466 (2000)** OTHER THAN fact of prior conviction, any fact that increases penalty for a crime must be proved TO JURY beyond reasonable doubt;

C v Burbank **388 M 789 (83)**—raised by D's admissions (in without objection);

C v Beatrice **75 MAC 153 (2009), further review allowed 455 M 1108 (2010)**—judge wouldn't permit introduction of D's statement to cop, alleging prior incident in which girlfriend had stabbed him with knife, so D was obliged to testify to raise issue of self defense in present prosecution of him for assault and battery months later; judge was "well within his discretion" to require testimony from someone who observed the stabbing; "logistics of raising the self-defense claim" were left to D and his attorney;

C v Galvin **56 MAC 698 (2002)**—failure to instruct on self-defense when it's raised by evidence = substantial risk of miscarriage of justice; instruction that property owner may use reasonable force to remove trespasser if trespasser has been told to leave property but refused = error because it assumed that D was trespasser (this is for jury to decide, on proper instruction; D testified that she had come to drop off mail for husband, from whom she was separated);

C v Miranda **77 MAC 76 (2010)**—even though D's version of events denied she touched/hit officer, "defense of another" instruction was required because test = "any view of the evidence" rather than limiting right to instruction to D's version of events;

C v Houston **332 M 687 (55)**—instruct on self defense though no direct evidence (*see Chapter 12-K, Jury Charge*); (cf. *C v Dyer* **389 M 677 (83)** can instruct (on joint venture) without direct evidence (because injuries suggest two assailants));

C v Acevedo **446 M 435 (2006)**—where evidence supports it, D is entitled to correct instructions on both provocation and self-defense; jury must have opportunity to consider voluntary manslaughter on both theories; correct instruction on self-defense doesn't cure erroneous instruction on provocation or eliminate prejudice from failure to instruct at all on provocation as theory of voluntary manslaughter; trial counsel's failure to request "provocation" instruction deprived D of an available defense;

C v Haddock **46 MAC 246 (99)**—mere introduction of evidence supporting defense of property, self-defense, and a personal history of domestic abuse victimhood did not entitle D to required finding of NG; status of having been victim "does not provide blanket justification" for use of force in resolving disputes;

C v McDermott **393 M 451 (84)**—unclear how much force OK to resist rape, but instruction here was OK because self-defense covered such scenario;

C v Montes **49 MAC 789 (2000)**—no right to resist even unlawful arrest, unless cops using excessive force (and thus no right to 'defend' person being arrested, with same qualification);

C v Martin **369 M 640 (76)**—DEFEND ANOTHER (fellow prisoner);

C v Montes **49 MAC 789 (2000)**—defense of someone being arrested OK only if there's "excessive force" by police;

C v Monico **373 M 298 (77)**—availability not limited to threat of great harm; but threat here had ended before D's acts;

C v Sullivan **17 MAC 981 (84)**—given D's version (deceased was chasing D's brother with a baseball bat), jury would not have grafted upon to "defense of another" the "retreat rule" for self defense, on which judge had earlier instructed;

C v Lynn **123 M 218 (1877)**—force OK to recover PROPERTY (dictum);

C v Hakkila **42 MAC 129 (97)**—judge instructed re defense of expensive equipment, at D's request; Appeals Court rejected D's appellate argument of error in failure to give unrequested self-defense charge ("indulgently read," D's trial testimony contained "only the germ of concern about his person");

C v Dougherty **107 M 243 (1871)**—sexton removes undertaker;

C v Goodwin **3 Cush 154 (1849)**—homeowner removes lewd trespasser;

C v Kuyamjian **18 MAC 680 (84)**—deputy sheriff (alleged victim) was in the right;

C v Klein **372 M 823 at fn. 8 (77) citing Model Penal Code 3:06(3)(d)**—dangerous weapon OK if unlawful "dispossession" of D's dwelling is occurring, or to prevent arson, burglary, or other act of felonious theft or property destruction; HERE, though, burglars of nearby drugstore had already accomplished burglary/theft, and were in process of flight from scene;

C v Klein **372 M 823 (77)**—force to ARREST (see Chapter 3): in this context (citizen's arrest) adopts Model Penal Code § 3:07 deadly force not permitted in arrest for property crime only (if perpetrators aren't using or threatening deadly force);

C v Marler **11 MAC 1014 (81)**—reasonable force for protective custody;

Tennessee v Garner **471 US 1 (85)**—cop's deadly force only to arrest violent D;

Nolan & Sartorio, *Criminal Law,* **§§ 679–85 (3d ed. 2001)**—Self-Defense, Defend Others/Property, Force in Making Arrest, Prevent Crime, "Domestic Authority (parents)" and Teachers;

District Court Model Jury Instructions (*see Chapter 21-A, Elements of Crimes*) 6.07—(same); (*see Chapter 21-D, Resist Arrest*); Superior Court Criminal Practice Jury Instructions §§ 3.6—3.9;

C v Bray **19 MAC 751, 761 (85)**—self-defense available to aggressor, but limited;

C v Cataldo **37 MAC 957 (94), S.C. 423 M 318 (96)**—Commonwealth's view that D = aggressor is not controlling; right to instruction on self-defense depends on evidence in light most favorable to D; **LaFave & Scott, *Substantive Criminal Law*, § 5.7(e) (West 1986, w/updated supplements)**—even if initial aggressor, D has right to self-defense if he has withdrawn & announced such or, if adversary responds with deadly force (to initiator's non-deadly), D has right to deadly force in self-defense;

C v Doucette **430 M 461, 469–70 (99)**—self-defense not available to charge of armed home invasion (armed person unlawfully entering dwelling can't argue self-defense D when occupant uses force);

C v Evans **390 M 144 (83)**—no defense for armed robber (unless withdrew);

C v Shaffer **367 M 508 (75)**—duty to retreat, generally—pre-G.L. c. 278, § 8A;

C v Vives **447 M 537 (2006)**—no instruction on self-defense warranted because D didn't use all proper means to avoid combat, even if accept D's statement that V was first to brandish weapon; right to claim self-defense "is forfeited by one who commits armed robbery";

C v Hart **429 M 614 (99)**—former robbery cohorts fought D over proceeds and yelled threat of killing D; D left, ostensibly to retrieve proceeds, returned with proceeds, and shot adversaries; unquestionably didn't use reasonable means to avoid;

G.L. c. 278, § 8A—no duty to retreat in own dwelling if reasonable;

C v Jefferson **36 MAC 684 (94)**—statute no defense for a D taking gun from his apartment into common hallway (*i.e.*, not D's "dwelling") to shoot obnoxious visitor;

C v Painten **429 M 536 (99)**—G.L. c. 278, § 8A is not applicable when victim was invited guest/lawfully on premises; allegation that V then threatened D with knife did not make his presence unlawful;

C v Gregory **17 MAC 651 (84)**—then-current "retreat" rule;

C v Noble **429 M 44 (99)**—D had no duty to retreat because in his basement apartment, even though adversary owned the building and had a business in basement; "law of trespass" should guide jury (G.L. c. 266, § 120);

C v Rubin **318 M 587 (45)**—complaining witness's violent reputation admissible if known to D; & threats by witness, even if unknown to D, admissible for inference witness tried to carry them out; (but see *C v Alebord* **49 MAC 915 (2000)** D had "highly active imagination" due to V's beating of D 5 years earlier, but no one approached D or made hostile remark; perception that they looked at a hammer & giggled insufficient for reasonable apprehension of imminent physical harm);

C v Fortini **44 MAC 562 (98)**—excluded evidence of V's aggressive acts and threats to others was somewhat cumulative of other evidence;

C v Fontes **396 M 733 (86)**—complaining witness's violent past known to homicide D (without "reputation");

C v Edmonds **365 M 496 (74)**—complaining witness's reputation testimony by another witness;

C v Pidge **400 M 350 (87)**—(same);

C v Williams **892 (2008)**—D's recorded statement was edited, defense wanting omission of references to D's incarceration, drug use, gang membership, & possession of guns, and DA wanting redaction of D's comments re: victim's reputation for violence and intimidation: because self-defense was at issue, victim's reputation was relevant and admissible (and defense counsel was perhaps ineffective in agreeing to this redaction, albeit as a 'quid pro quo' for other redactions: issue of 'tactic'/reasonableness would not be decided without hearing on motion for new trial);

C v Dilone **385 M 281 (82)**—complaining witness's reputation (violent) & D's (peaceful);

C v Devico **207 M 251 (11)**—D's peaceful reputation;

C v Papadinis **402 M 73 (88)**—D's fear of cop from prior brutality gets in to show why D drove off (& killed cop);

C v Stirk **16 MAC 280 (83)**—old sex assault on D not relevant because no expert saying connected to self defense claim;

C v Benjamin **430 M 673, 677–79 (2000)**—murder V's violent character, known to D, NOT ADMISSIBLE re: D's state of mind in "extreme atrocity or cruelty" first degree murder case;

C v Rodriguez **418 M 1 (94)**—judge abused discretion in excluding as too remote victim's violence toward D occurring more than 2 weeks before killing;

C v Grimshaw **412 M 505 (92)**—open question whether battered woman syndrome a valid defense in Massachusetts (but see G.L. c. 233, § 23F, subsequently enacted);

C v Lazarovich **410 M 466 (91)**—battered woman syndrome assumed to be admissible to show that D didn't share with co-D specific intent to maim her daughter;

G.L. c. 233, § 23F—making admissible evidence that D had suffered past harm/abuse & expert testimony regarding pattern of abusive relationships, the effects of such relationships, & whether D displayed characteristics common to abuse victims;

C v Conaghan **48 MAC 304 (99)**—(context of denial of R.30 motion to vacate guilty plea, & appeal therefrom) must show 3-stage "cycle of abuse"?; discussion of whether syndrome is "mental disease/defect" negating criminal responsibility; dissent suggested expert testimony admissible re: syndrome as part of defense of coercion when crime V is someone other than batterer; S.C., overruling Appeals Court affirmance of denial of motion for new trial, **433 M 105 (2000)** incompetence to rationally assist defense counsel and involuntariness of guilty plea may be result of battered woman syndrome (& SJC remands for competency examination under G.L. c. 123, § 15(a)); failure to raise syndrome until years after guilty plea may be excused as consistent with its "learned helplessness which manifests itself in the inability to perceive (one)self as abused and to communicate the abuse to others";

C v Pike **431 M 212, 223 (2000)**—REJECTING Commonwealth argument that "use of (battered woman) expert testimony is limited to instances where (D) uses force against her batterer, or that such testimony is limited to general characteristics of the syndrome"; defense NOT held waived for failure to present it at trial (instead of on R.30 motion), because "failure to recognize (or be able to communicate to one's attorney or others) that she is a battered woman is itself a specific characteristic of the syndrome"; (accord with former point implicitly and latter point explicitly, *C v Conaghan* **433 M 105, 109–10 (2000)**);

16-E. ENTRAPMENT

Genesis 3:13—"And the Lord said unto the woman, 'What is this thou hast done?' And she replied, 'The serpent beguiled me & I did eat'";

Superior Court Criminal Practice Jury Instructions § 3.5—District Court Model Jury Instructions # 6.04;

Nolan & Sartorio, *Criminal Law*, § 689 (3d ed. 2001)—overview, including evidence issues & various policy reasons;

C v Tracey **416 M 528 (93)**—D can both deny crime & claim entrapment;

Sorrells v US **287 US 435 (32)**—ESTOPPEL if act's product of cop's creation;

C v Miller **361 M 644 (72)**—if any evidence of inducement (more than solicited) DA must disprove beyond reasonable doubt D's predisposition & offensive/shocking cops; (fn.3) both issues permit Hearsay, Reputation, Bad Acts;

C v Madigan **449 M 702 (2007)**—D entitled to learn, in discovery, promises and rewards given to informant, asserted by D to have been agent of entrapment; entrapment issue to be heard and decided by jury, not foreclosed or frustrated by prosecution prior to trial;

C v Vargas **471 M 792 (94)**—crime of narcotics possession not similar to narcotics distribution for purpose of proving predisposition;

Sherman v US **356 US 369 (& Frankfurter concurrence) (58)**—rationale; questions about evidentiary rules;

See Chapters 10-F (Character Evidence), 11E (Bad Acts, Hearsay, Motions in Limine);

C v Thompson **382 M 379 (81)**—solicit/request is not inducement without plead/argue, persist, coerce, play on emotion; error to exclude issue, but no jury question raised; (sample instruction);

C v Shuman **391 M 345 (84)**—close case, but a bit more than 1 solicitation's needed to raise issue, e.g., pleaded/argued;

C v Tracey **416 M 528, 537 n.10 (93)**—attributes to **Shuman** holding that defense may be raised by evidence of inducement "by government agent or one acting at his direction," but ostensibly reserves issue whether the middleman must know he is being used by government;

C v Silva **21 MAC 536 (86)**—private (co-D) inducement not entrapment unless cops recruited him, or he passed on cops' inducement;

C v Coyne **44 MAC 1 (97)**—no entrapment if government agent induces middleman to commit crime & middleman "takes it upon himself" to induce another person (D) to participate; AND citing federal case holding that when "agent" status of snitch is acknowledged, it is error to put that issue to jury as one of fact;

C v Doyle **67 MAC 846 (2006)**—facts indicate that rewards to informant for setting up D with undercover officer were admitted, relevant and material (though court refused to find error in exclusion of "cumulative" but over-ridingly prejudicial hearsay evidence that informant began working for police after a gun he had owned was implicated in a murder, an allegation "vigorously disputed" by prosecutor (id. at 863 n.22));

C v Curcio **26 MAC 738 (89)**—simple greed, unwary criminal, not entrapment;

C v Lacend **33 MAC 495 (92)**—entrapment = trial issue, **not** a motion to dismiss; cop's posing as drug seller alone is not inducement, D's initiation of request for drugs = proof of predisposition to possess;

C v Gratereaux **49 MAC 1 (2000)**—no required finding of NG on basis of entrapment defense; evidence of D's predisposition was introduced, & jury didn't have to believe D's version of events;

C v Quirk **27 MAC 258 (89)**—instructions were generous re: addiction & entrapment;

C v Remedor **52 MAC 694, 699 (2001)**—appellate court agreed that no jury instructions on entrapment were warranted (much predisposition, no prodding by government agent), BUT was troubled by response to jury question ("does the law allow us to consider a legal defense which has not been presented, specifically: entrapment or encouragement to commit a crime?"); trial judge's answer was that while the law does allow consideration of a defense not presented, law required jurors to decide the case based on the evidence, & jurors "are precluded from considering something that is not raised by the evidence at all" & must limit themselves to "the evidence that you have heard and seen"; this could be viewed as dictating what inferences were available from the evidence (in violation of G.L. c. 231, § 81 (shall not charge on matters of fact; but may state testimony/law));

Mathews v US **485 US 58 (88)**—instruct on entrapment if evidence supports it, even if D's also denying the act/intent (*see Chapter 7-E re: BIFURCATED trial when NGI = defense*);

C v Lawrence **69 MAC 596 (2007)**—no entrapment instruction required because D "delivered"/transferred marijuana to undercover cop and acknowledged that he both "shared" marijuana with friends earlier and intended to "share" what he had in his pocket with the cop (who gave D $20 without request or negotiation); "entrapment" as to school zone charge = "distinct . . . analytically", but not briefed, so reserved: "whether the detective's act of leading the defendant into the school zone was government behavior sufficient to entitle the defendant to an entrapment instruction";

C v McMiller **29 MAC 392 (90)**—Commonwealth's threat to prosecute government agent if she supported D's claim of entrapment was improper & required reversal;

C v LeBlanc **30 MAC 1 (90)**—entrapment distinguished from government agent defense;

C v Hardy **31 MAC 909 (91)**—undercover cop's repeated requests to buy drugs plus D's initial refusal required entrapment instruction; trial judge's disbelief in D's credibility irrelevant;

Jacobson v US **503 US 540 (92)**—deceptive mailing campaign by postal agents to induce D to purchase child porno went "too far"; any predisposition by D was not proven to be "independent & not product of" mail campaign;

C v Monteagudo **427 M 484 (98)**—predisposition may be established by circumstantial evidence;

C v Dingle **73 MAC 274 (2008)**—D's prior criminal acts may be admitted to show predisposition, but must be similar to the charged conduct; charges here = distributing child pornography, and D admitted to witness that he had had sex with and indecently assaulted little boys; ERROR to admit record of 1976 Arizona conviction for "felony child abuse" and related police report, 1986 police report re allegations of raping two boys in Lynn, and a 1987 District Court docket sheet showing count of indecent exposure which was dismissed (D having pled NG) but held cumulative of D's admissions;

C v Garcia **421 M 686 (96)**—"sentencing entrapment" defense rejected as matter of law (concerning undercover cop's insistence upon buying larger quantities of drug than D had ever before sold, so as to obtain trafficking conviction rather than lesser crime); but see *US v Barth* **990 F.2d 422 (93)** entrapment as to quantity of drugs warrants "downward departure" under federal sentencing guidelines; consider also import of *Apprendi v New Jersey* **530 US 466 (2000)** to this scenario;

C v Saletino **449 M 657 (2007)**—reserves question of whether sentencing entrapment defense will be recognized in Massachusetts (claiming it wasn't warranted on evidence here), but holding that *Apprendi* doesn't change case law relative to sentencing entrapment, as "fact" of quantity of cocaine distributed was submitted to jury; opines that sentencing entrapment focuses on D's predisposition, but defense of "sentencing factor manipulation" is based instead on behavior of government/outrageous conduct solely for purpose of increasing D's sentence (contrary authority [1st Cir.] cited); fact that undercover cop could have arrested D after first transaction but didn't wasn't improper, and doesn't "demonstrate inducement";

C v Twitchell **416 M 114 (93)**—"entrapment by estoppel" defense: statute (G.L. c. 273, § 1) plus AG's opinion could have led person untrained in law to believe that no criminal prosecution (involuntary manslaughter) could be brought against Christian Scientists pursuing spiritual treatment for son (who died from bowel obstruction/perforation correctable by surgery);

16-E.1. Dismissal?

C v Lacend **33 MAC 495 (92)**—entrapment is issue for trial only, not a valid ground for dismissal;

C v Shuman **391 M 345, 353 (84)**—outrageous government conduct, like entrapment, should be presented at trial rather than by a pretrial motion to dismiss; rationale of judicial economy (also proffered in *Gratereaux* **49 MAC 1, 5 n.2 (2000)**); BUT SEE *US v Santana* **6 F.3d 1, 3 (1st Cir. '93)** (defendants alleged outrageous government conduct in a pretrial motion to dismiss);

US v Ayyub **998 F.Supp 81, 82 (D.Mass '98)**—(same), and *C v Monteagudo* **427 M 484 (98)** "egregious government conduct" is NOT JURY ISSUE, but issue of **law**, raisable by motion to dismiss or, if evidence known only at trial, by required finding of NG; "the focus . . . is not on the propensities and predisposition of (D), but on 'whether the police conduct revealed in the particular case falls below standards, to which common feelings respond, for the proper use of governmental power,'" BUT it's not mere device to circumvent predisposition test in entrapment defense;

C v Gratereaux **49 MAC 1 (2000)**—"defense" of outrageous government conduct presented by pretrial motion to dismiss, and properly failed because (1) no evidence of informant's "pressuring" was presented at motion hearing; (2) even if "pressure" evidence believed (informant allegedly promised to get desperately-needed green card for D), and even though informant was paid $6000 for engineering arrest (precise amount was determined after-fact by drug task force), this not enough to "support dismissal," didn't "rise( ) to the high level of outrageousness necessary," though D cited Florida case granting relief where informant stood to gain contingent fee;

16-F. POSSESS (DOMINION/CONTROL AND KNOW), JOINT AND CONSTRUCTIVE

See also Chapter 21-BB & CC, Analyzing Elements, Firearms & Drugs; & Intent, re: knowledge;

District Court Model Jury Instructions (*see Chapter 21-A, Analyzing Elements, in General*) 3.11—possession & joint possession;

Superior Court Criminal Practice Jury Instructions § 4.12, knowledge—§ 2.49.4, possession of controlled substance;

C v Lee **331 M 166 (54)**—possession = control + intent to exercise control; mystery mail recipient need not KNOW contents (under old drug law); cf. *C v Antobenedetto* **366 M 51 (74)** knowledge not needed (under old drug law) & instruction not asked; may need knowledge in future;

C v Szemetum **3 MAC 651 (75)**—no possession without KNOWING what it is;

C v Aguiar **370 M 490 (76)**—(now) G.L. c. 94C needs KNOWING possession; usually infer from dominion & control, but not for mystery mail without more (e.g., open & keep package);

C v Sheline **391 M 279 (84)**—(same); infer knowledge from statements/acts;

C v Sabetti **411 M 770 (92)**—Commonwealth not required to prove D knew weight of drugs in his possession;

C v Sampson **383 M 750 (81)**—must have general knowledge (flare) gun = "firearm".

C v Harvard **356 M 452 (69)**—momentary "passing" = possession;

C v Tivnon **8 Gray 375 (1857)**—joint possession & constructive possession of burglar's tool because 1 D held for 2d D—mutual agreement & access inferred;

C v Johnson **7 MAC 191 (79)**—(same) for passenger & tools in car trunk;

C v Blevins **56 MAC 206 (2002)**—conviction for trafficking in over 14 grams of cocaine reversed for failure to instruct on lesser offense of simple possession, because D contended that he and two friend pooled money to buy cocaine, all participated in the negotiation & were present during the exchange of $ for drug, but that immediately afterward D was arrested; simple joint possession is a possible verdict when two or more persons simultaneously and jointly acquire possession of a drug for their own use, intending only to share it together;

C v Nichols **4 MAC 606 (76)**—dope in D's apartment = constructive possession if know & intentional dominion and control; BUT SEE *C v Brown* **50 MAC 253 (2000)** reversal of multiple convictions of each of three Ds because only speculation as to which one of them had actually possessed any of firearms; joint venture/constructive possession likewise conjectural; "logical inference that 2 of the 3 Ds may each have possessed a gun isn't substitute for proof beyond a reasonable doubt that an identified D possessed a specific gun"; as to gun under sofa where 2 Ds were sitting, inference that they had no knowledge was at least as reasonable an inference as that one or more Ds recently possessed it;

C v Funcy **349 M 196 (65)**—NG of receiving stolen property for loot in co-D's apartment; knowledge not enough;

C v Rabb **70 MAC 194 (2007)**—D's own statement cited as sufficient proof of constructive possession of drug stash he said belonged to co-D: while claiming personal possession of one stash in motel room, he acknowledged awareness of other stash, and jury didn't have to believe his denial of possession, particularly when D displayed awareness of consequences for possession of aggregate amount; D had paid for room and drugs were stored in "common portions" of it (heater and kitchen cabinet);

Chandanais v Commonwealth **448 M 1013 (2007)**—SJC found sufficient to show D's knowing possession: 47 marijuana plants in residence's backyard and areas around and behind its garage, one of which was four feet tall and growing directly under bathroom window of house, cop testified that he knew D lived there because he had found D's name (along with other family members' names) on voter list for that address, and knew D owned the land "because of previous 'other incidents at that property'"; photos indicated mowing pattern to promote weeds to hide marijuana plants; possession can be "joint" rather than exclusive;

C v Darnell D. **445 M 670 (2005)**—even if D plausibly was identified as front seat passenger in car, evidence insufficient to establish his possession of car (for conviction of receiving stolen motor vehicle), notwithstanding Commonwealth arguments as to "consciousness of guilt" and claim that D must have "directed" driver to convey him to "his aunt's house";

C v Curry **341 M 50 (60)**—though conspiracy, no joint possession of drugs in co-D's room (though next door to D's);

C v Hernandez **439 M 688 (2003)**—because evidence insufficient for inference of constructive possession of large quantity of cocaine, required finding of not guilty ordered on theory of principal liability for trafficking (though not on joint venture, given sufficient evidence that D knowingly assisted in delivering drug to customers);

C v Minor **47 MAC 928 (99)**—involuntary manslaughter and drug distribution D (victim died of overdose) could not argue "joint possession" with V rather than D's own distribution simply because V contributed money to fund with which D bought the drugs; IF V were actively involved in buy, negotiating with supplier, paying that supplier $, sampling, instruction on lesser offense of mere possession required;

C v Robinson **43 MAC 257 (97)**—constructive possession and joint venture = alternative theories by which to connect D to crime;

C v Campiti **41 MAC 43 (96)**—constructive possession found: large scale drug dealer who sought never to physically possess cocaine, using underlings both to transport it from Florida & to sell it here, could not lessen his criminal culpability: Court deemed scheme a principal—agent relationship;

C v Flaherty **358 M 817 (71)**—can't exclude beyond a reasonable doubt that D = casual visitor to apartment, despite fact that "valise" bearing D's name was in apartment (five Ds charged with drug possession, drugs found in one of four bedrooms, & in an unidentified coat; no evidence as to who rented or lived in apartment);

C v Vasquez **75 MAC 446 (2009)**—though 5 men were in house at time of search warrant execution (1 of whom attempted to escape and could be inferred to have attempted to flush $274), it was D's residence and he had $493 on his person, and he had sold to undercover cop there twice before: evidence sufficient to show D's constructive possession of cocaine (with sandwich bags, and scale) found in kitchen cabinet; [S.C. on other single issue reported to SJC by MAC is at 456 M 350 (2010)];

C v Shmieder **58 MAC 300 (2003)**—constructive possession of drugs by D not shown, though she answered door to condo, because no evidence connecting her to bedroom and bathroom in which drugs were found; that she had in her purse a pager, two "wads" of money, a cigarette box containing $331, and two sheets of paper with names and numbers = not enough;

C v Clarke **44 MAC 502 (98)**—NG of shotgun under mattress in 1 bedroom which also contained drug distribution paraphernalia, though evidence sufficient to establish D's possession of cocaine with intent to distribute given drugs and money and handguns in 2d bedroom in which his clothing and ID were located;

C v Delarosa **50 MAC 623 (2000)**—D-driver's key ring contained key to apartment where secret compartment in closet contained cocaine and McDonald's bags identical to one for which D was reaching in car; D had paid rent for apartment more than once (though rent receipts and utility bills were in names of other identified persons); in plain view in kitchen were scales and packaging materials; D previously observed to twice make delivery of some "small item" for currency after departing from apartment in car; sufficient evidence for constructive possession of cocaine in closet, BUT NOT FOR gun found in same space;

C v Frongillo **66 MAC 677 (2006)**—though evidence was sufficient to show that D had knowledge of and ability to control guns & ammunition found in closets of apartment rented by his girlfriend (her husband had moved out two months earlier, D was seen at the apt. at all hours, including when girlfriend wasn't there, and "unidentified" male clothing was found in closets), insufficient proof of D's **"intent** to exercise dominion and control" means required finding of NG, despite evidence of D's involvement in shooting (with no proven connection to the particular guns in closets);

C v Ramos **51 MAC 901 (2001)**—NG for D on constructive possession of handgun & shotgun, though he was seated in bedroom so as to be aware of shotgun protruding from underneath compatriot/co-D, and on shelf in room was an envelope addressed to male D, albeit at different address, containing two letters to "Faith"; D's knowledge of shotgun didn't support inference he had intention/ability to exercise dominion & control over it; no personal belongings of D found at apartment, & no evidence he possessed keys to apartment or bedroom;

C v Sann Than **442 M 748 (2004)**—constructive possession requires proof of knowledge coupled with ability and intention to exercise dominion and control; overall, instructions here conveyed this, though part suggested just "ability" sufficed;

Jordan v Superintendent, MCI-Cedar Junction **53 MAC 584 (2002)**—insufficient evidence of knowledge & control necessary for "possession" at prison disciplinary proceeding: inmate X, about to be caught with contraband weapon, placed newspaper on floor of plaintiff's cell through a slot in door intended for food trays, & inside folded newspaper was the weapon; guard immediately entered cell & removed item;

C v Duffy **4 MAC 655 (76)**—no evidence of D's control of trailer he leased;

C v Pursley **2 MAC 910 (75)**—NG though drugs in male suit with D's papers in it because females occupied site, papers were five months old & without address, & D not seen there;

C v Amparo **43 MAC 922 (97)**—NG though D possessed beeper and with 2 others attempted to flee from apartment being searched; no papers, etc. seized contained D's name;

C v Williams **3 MAC 370 (75)**—NG for drugs/guns in kitchen for D in bed & seen coming/going few times; not owner or dominion/control;

C v Sespedes **442 M 95 (2004)**—NG for D re: possession of drugs hidden in dropped ceiling of vacant apartment being renovated, though he had key to apartment and had been seen leaving that apartment once; ability to exercise control over premises and brief presence inside not enough to imply possession of hidden contraband;

US v Holland **445 F.2d 701 (DC Cir. '71)**—can't lightly infer constructive possession for visitor without frequency, special relationship, etc. (male under bed, male clothes in female's closet, drugs on dresser);

C v Cormier **41 MAC 76 (96)**—NG for back seat passenger in car from which driver fled carrying shoes containing cocaine, though shoes taken from car floor closest to D;

C v Cruz **34 MAC 619 (93)**—D NG though lived in 2-bedroom apartment & attempted to flee; other man's papers were in bedroom with drugs & that man had on person drugs, cash, & apartment key;

C v Prentice P. **57 MAC 766 (2003)**—that D was kneeling beside stolen vehicle which had been "jacked up," with doors and trunk open and tire and crowbar nearby, even when supplemented by flight ("consciousness of guilt"), was insufficient for conviction of larceny of motor vehicle; evidence = inadequate to show any actual or constructive possession of vehicle;

C v Blevins **56 MAC 206 (2002)**—though D had been sitting in front passenger seat and gun was found in plain view "in front of the back seat" where co-D had sat, sufficient to establish actual or constructive possession of gun by D because (1) ease of access & control, and (2) D had just participated in assault using gun [evidence was that both Ds used firearms during assault preceding arrest];

C v Cotto **69 MAC 589 (2007)**—back seat passenger's conduct (striking placement of his feet shoving something underneath front seat, plus purportedly "alarming" eye contact with trooper) held sufficient to establish requisite connection to firearm found under front seat; "interpretation" (i.e., credibility) of troopers' testimony re: D's conduct = matter for jury;

C v Bienvenu **63 MAC 632 (2005)**—front seat passenger could be found G of cocaine tightly wrapped in duct tape ball found between driver's seat & gear shift in console area because she owned the vehicle, and it was inferably her personal effects found in back seat close to electronic scale and box of baggies;

C v Brown **34 MAC 222 (93)**—presence and awareness of drug dealing insufficient to show D's possession;

C v Boria **440 M 416 (2003)**—that D lived in apartment and was girlfriend of a man who lived there (& was arrested) = insufficient to prove joint or constructive possession of nine small bags of cocaine inside a videocassette recorder, even though items in plain view in kitchen were purportedly used in processing cocaine for distribution;

US v Bonham **477 F.2d 1137 (3d Cir. '73)**—though some drugs in plain view, no joint possession of hidden drugs by joint occupant of bedroom;

C v Minor **47 MAC 928 (99)**—involuntary manslaughter and drug distribution D (victim died of overdose) could not argue "joint possession" with V rather than D's own distribution simply because V contributed money to fund with which D bought the drugs; IF V were actively involved in buy, negotiating with supplier, paying that supplier $, sampling, instruction on lesser offense of mere possession required;

C v Carmenatty **37 MAC 908 (94)**—male D G of drugs found on female by either joint venture or joint/constructive possession because his personal papers were mingled with hers in drawer, and in another drawer with men's & women's clothes was a scale with drug residue; D's possession of $100 even though on welfare "significant";

C v Lee **2 MAC 700 (74)**—infer possession from frequency of male-D's visits to female occupant's apartment & by D's personal papers in drug room;

C v Watson **36 MAC 252 (94)**—though D argued that other man was G because his papers were in apartment and

he did most talking during undercover buys, possession need not be exclusive & may be proved circumstantially;

C v Gill **2 MAC 653(74)**—D's G of drugs in man's coat because it's her apartment, her papers there, & she admits co-ownership of $700 cash with boyfriend;

C v Xiarhos **2 MAC 225 (74)**—female D living with mom & sister G of drugs in closet with male clothes;

C v Araujo **38 MAC 960 (95)**—male D asleep in bed, reaching for handgun, G of that gun & one under mattress but NG of shotgun in closet with "male" clothing not otherwise linked to D;

C v Johnson **42 MAC 948 (97)**—D seen to distribute black bag of marijuana retrieved from vacant lot G of possession with intent to distribute smaller reddish zip lock bags of marijuana found in same lot;

C v Rarick **23 MAC 912 (86)**—drug in purse with D's papers in his bedroom = G;

C v Gray **5 MAC 296 (77)**—though car driver can possess guns on back seat, can't instruct jury to infer dominion and control from knowledge—both are jury questions;

C v Deagle **10 MAC 563 (80)**—though knowledge, no control by rear passenger over drugs on seat, & being smoked, in front;

C v Whitlock **39 MAC 514 (95)**—erroneous instruction invited jury, on basis of D's "proximity", to infer not only knowledge of drugs but constructive possession of them;

C v Almeida **381 M 420 (80)**—no knowledge/control by D-driver for console gun because borrowed car & no evidence how big console is (though D's wallet in it);

C v Santana **420 M 205 (95)**—D-driver-owner G of cocaine in bag under front seat passenger's seat: failure to pull over immediately and presence of scale in bag on back seat cited;

C v Manzanillo **37 MAC 24 (94)**—D driver NG of drugs in paper bag in "hip bag" under shopping bag behind driver's seat when 2 others were in the van;

C v Movilis **46 MAC 574 (99)**—though D was car driver and had beeper and $232 on person, and was arrested at café table on which there was small packet of .06 gram white powder, NG of 25.3 grams found in hidden compartment built into rear-facing part of front passenger seat; car was registered to someone else; tipster had said 2 people matching D's and other's appearance would transact drug business at café that night;

C v Boone **356 M 85 (69)**—no (hot car) passenger knowledge of gun under driver;

C v Bennefield **373 M 452 (77)**—front passenger NG of shotgun rear passenger shoving under seat; no knowledge shown without more (e.g., ownership, time present);

C v Hill **15 MAC 93 (83)**—front passenger NG of gun under his seat; knowledge not shown without ownership, operation, or plain view;

C v Brown **401 M 745 (88)**—rented car driver NG of 2 shotguns hidden under front passenger seat, though both D's bent forward as cops approached;

C v Bean **15 MAC 168 (83)**—infer passenger knew/possessed seat/trunk guns/ammunition;

C v Albano **373 M 132 (77)**—infer knowledge for driver because Dad's car, plain view (protrudes under seat), 4:30 a.m., nervous, & plate's covered;

C v Horton **63 MAC 571, 578 (2005)**—can infer possession by back seat passenger who was observed to make furtive gestures and kick at something below seat in front of him, where gun was found partly protruding from under driver's seat onto floor area directly in front of D;

C v Donovan **17 MAC 83 (83)**—borrowed car driver G of gun under his seat with pills he admitted owning;

C v Rosa **17 MAC 495 (84)**—rear passenger G of drugs in driver door (he rented car & made statement suggesting some knowledge);

C v Miller **4 MAC 379 (76)**—rear passenger G of drug bag beside him because $500 in pocket & he said, "Cops. Let's go.";

See also Chapter 21-CC-5, Analyzing Elements, Specific Crimes (Controlled Substances), for cases on actual & constructive possession.

Chapter 17
PARTIES—ATTEMPT, CONSPIRACY, ACCESSORY

See also Chapter 16-B, Defenses, re: joint venture;

17-A. ATTEMPT—(INTENT, AND OVERT ACT REASONABLY CLOSE TO SUCCESS, AND FAIL)

G.L. c. 274, § 6—attempt to commit crime with max. sentence of 5 years or more max. crime = punishable by 5 years max.; others = punishable by 1 year max.; attempted larceny = 2½ years max.; (see also Chapter 21, specific crimes, e.g., G.L. c. 265, § 16 attempted murder; G.L. c. 265, § 25 attempted extortion; G.L. c. 266, § 5A attempted arson; & assault with intent . . .);

G.L. c. 277, § 79—Complaint/Indictment forms (see Chapter 5, Contents of Complaints & Indictments);

Nolan & Sartorio, *Criminal Law,* **§§ 651–52 (3d ed. 2001)**—elements: act(s) plus intent—(1) act must be directed toward "present preparation of the crime"; initial act not enough if further acts over period of time are required; (2) act must at least be apparently adapted to completion of the crime; (3) act must come somewhat near actual accomplishment of the crime; (4) act must not result in the completed crime; must prove failure; but see District Court Model Instruction 5.02 (*see Chapter 21-A, post (Elements of Common Crimes) re: Model Jury Instructions*); Notes: may not need to prove failure;

Model Penal Code § 5.01—7 examples of a "substantial step" in a course of conduct planned to culminate in commission of the crime;

Perkins & Boyce, *Criminal Law,* **Chapter 6, § 3, at 611–42 (3d ed. 1982)**;

C v Banner **13 MAC 1065 (82)**—OK if attempt (arson of motor vehicle) law's penalty exceeds completed crime's maximum sentence (at least here, where D got less than the latter);

C v Peaslee **177 M 267 (01)**—"mere preparation" (to pile combustibles & try hire torch) because alleged overt act (piling, not soliciting) not D's last act or present intent to set;

C v Ali **7 MAC 120 (79)**—G.L. c. 266, § 5A overruled Peaslee & criminalized placing combustibles with intent "eventually" to set/procure fire;

C v Hamel **52 MAC 250, 258 (2001)**—contra Model Penal Code, Appeals Court holds that overt act must be one which is "dangerously close to the consummation of the object crime," focusing on what had yet to be done, rather than on what actor did toward attaining the substantive crime; here, in "attempt to commit murder" prosecution, supplying "hit men" (undercover police officers) with sketches of victims' house, with marking to show which rooms were likely to be unoccupied for window access, and with written descriptions of the intended victims = not enough; evidence sufficient for solicitation to commit a felony (irrelevant that the crime wasn't committed);

C v Bell **455 M 408 (2009)**—though D met by pre-arrangement with undercover cop, negotiated price for intercourse with unseen child, and began to drive car toward park where child was said by cop to be, not enough "overt act" for attempted rape (though enough for G of solicitation); D could have decided not to commit the crime and no evidence as to exactly where or when he would commit crime; failure to move for required finding = substantial risk of miscarriage of justice;

C v Senior **454 M 12 (2009)**—"attempted subornation of perjury" in violation of G.L. c. 268, § 3 "is type of attempt crime where the crime itself and the overt act are one and the same"; if D wanted more info, should have moved for bill of particulars;

C v Bell **67 MAC 266 (2006)**—D could be guilty of attempting to rape child and soliciting sex for fee even though, unbeknownst to him, he was negotiating with undercover police officer, so no actual child was at risk; though crime was "factually" impossible, it was not "legally" impossible;

C v Kennedy **170 M 18 (1897)**—put poison in complaining witness's cup with intent to kill = attempt though nonlethal dose because grave crime, uncertain result, & D had non-absurd expectation he'd done enough; shoot post thinking it's person = OK, but shoot at person with bad aim = criminal attempt;

C v McDonald **59 M 365 (1850)**—pick empty pocket = attempt; factual impossibility no defense;

C v Parenti **14 MAC 696 (82)**—can't attempt involuntary manslaughter because it has no intent;

C v Musgrave **421 M 610 (96), S.C. 38 MAC 519, 521–25 (95)**—attempted battery = assault, requiring proof of D's intent to cause apprehension/fear;

C v Ware **375 M 118 (78)**—reverse attempted. kidnap because no instructions on need for specific intent to commit completed crime;

C v Gosselin **365 M 116 (74)**—attempt's a lesser-included of a completed crime (escape), but can't convict of it here because no overt act alleged;

C v Foley **24 MAC 114 (87)**—(same); (see Chapter 5, Contents of Complaints & Indictments);

C v Burns **8 MAC 194 (79)**—(same); attempted larceny motor vehicle complaint dismissed without overt act, & particulars can't cure;

C v Banfill **413 M 1002 (92)**—asking 13-year-old girl for directions & telling her to get into truck was not attempted kidnapping; open question whether mere statement enough for overt act;

C v Ortiz **408 M 463 (90)**—driving around & unsuccessfully searching for complainant in order to commit ABDW upon him was not overt act;

C v Beattie **29 MAC 355 (90)**—strangulation is overt act sufficient for attempted murder;

C v Anolik **27 MAC 701 (89)**—overt act must be alleged, even under specific attempt statutes;

17-B. CONSPIRACY, STATEMENTS OF CO-CONSPIRATORS AND JOINT VENTURERS

G.L. c. 274, § 7—if underlying substantive crime = 20–life, conspiracy max. = 20 years; if 10+, conspiracy max. = 10; if felony under 10, conspiracy max. = 5; or else conspiracy max. = 2½;

G.L. c. 94C, § 40—DRUG conspiracy—max. penalty = same as substantive crime;

M.R.Crim.P. 9(e)—must SEVER conspiracy from substantive unless D moves joinder; Reporter's Notes purpose of 9(e), vs. former G.L. c. 278, § 2A (mandatory without optional joinder); but see

Campagna v Commonwealth **454 M 1006 (2009)**—before trial, counsel urged severance of substantive offense from trial of 7 conspiracy indictments, but judge refused; after evidence closed, judge acknowledged that the substantive offense was within the scope of the alleged conspiracy indictments and D was entitled to severance, and "offered [D] a choice of submitting substantive offense to jury (and "withdrawing" severance motion) or standing on the motion (resulting in mistrial on the substantive indictment); D stood on motion, which SJC considered to be a consent to mistrial, and retrial was not barred;

GL. c. 277, § 79—form complaint/indictment (*see Chapter 5, ante*);

Nolan & Sartorio, *Criminal Law*, **§§ 441–52 (3d ed. 2001)**—§ 443 "Dyer" rule (**243 M 472 (22)**, i.e., that conspiracy may be found even though neither its object nor the means of the conspiracy = crime) has been criticized; § 446 most states/fed. require OVERT ACT, but, § 450, not MA; § 448 trial issues (co-D statements, evolving conspiracies, imputed liability, etc.); § 688 WITHDRAWAL defense (purportedly e.g., Model Penal Code) criticized as valueless to completed crime of conspiracy, i.e., the agreement itself, BUT text misapprehends requirement of MPC 5.03, which recognizes affirmative defense only when actor, after agreeing, THWARTS the success of the conspiracy under circumstances showing complete & voluntary renunciation of criminal purpose;

Model Penal Code § 5.03—object of conspiracy must be crime; affirmative defense if thwart success of conspiracy, in circs showing voluntary renunciation of crime;

District Court Model Instruction 5.06 & Notes—(*see Chapter 21-A (Elements of Common Crimes) re: model jury instructions*);

Mass. Superior Court Criminal Jury Instructions, §§ 4.5–4.6 (1999);

C v Stack **49 MAC 227, 235 (2000)**—jury instructions re: conspiracy need not include specific explanation, by elements, of the "object" offense unless such crime is "some technical or unusually complex offense of which the trier of fact has no general impression";

C v Beckett **373 M 329 (77)**—co-D acts/statement not admissible vs. D until judge infers conspiracy, then becomes jury issue whether there's imputed liability;

C v Fernandes **427 M 90 (98)**—threat by alleged joint venturer prior to inception of joint venture admissible in D's trial because offered to prove declarant's state of mind & that he carried out intent;

Nolan & Sartorio, *Criminal Law*, **§ 448 (3d ed. 2001)**—imputed liability only for co-D acts during/furthering conspiracy;

C v Stasiun **349 M 38 (65)**—D's NG of co-D's substantive crime unless joint venture—though D's a co-conspirator;

C v Parreira **72 MAC 308 (2008)**—2 slightly older male teenagers and 2 female teenagers in a vacant apartment paired off in 2 separate bedrooms: required finding of not guilty for D ordered on theory of joint venture liability for co-D's rape of co-D's partner: D's intent to have sex with D's partner was not the requisite "common intent"; for joint venture liability in sex crimes, precedents reveal a common victim, physical presence at immediate scene, and/or physical participation in the act;

C v Caramanica **49 MAC 376, 381 (2000)**—noting that prosecutors "generally" pursue conspiracy crimes via "common-law joint venture" because of, inter alia, the difficulty of "affirmative proof of a prior agreement, separate and distinct from the shared intent that may be reflected in the actions of joint venturers at the time the substantive offense is committed";

Blumenthal v US **332 US 539 (47)**—conspiracy is not born full grown; equally G though join later than others;

C v McLaughlin **431 M 241 (2000)**—despite lack of evidence to show that, at time co-conspirator made statement about a "contract of a husband on a wife," the co-conspirator had had any contact at all with D (a husband) or D's wife or any other alleged co-conspirator in THIS crime, no relief; citation to cases holding that statements of co-conspirators pre-dating conspiracy may be admissible; holding that statement wasn't hearsay testimony because not offered for the truth of the matters asserted, but as proof of an 'operative' statement, i.e., existence of a conspiracy";

C v Stewart **454 M 527 (2009)**—D argued that man's solicitation of his friends to murder wife not admissible because statements were made months before any alleged joint venture with D was formed, but SJC rejects argument: statement probative of man's intent to kill wife and inferentially of later action, and wasn't hearsay because not offered to prove any fact contained in statement but only to prove he was seeking contract killer; as to another statement, however, no additional evidence that speaker was joint venture participant, so statement was inadmissible hearsay; statement by killer, "I offed that bitch," made less than a year after murder was not made in furtherance of joint venture and obviously not in effort to conceal crime, so should not have been admitted;

C v Vazquez **69 MAC 622 (2007)**—statement of co-conspirator may not be admitted if made after criminal enterprise ended, but conspiracy here was continuing because parties were trying to conceal evidence of the crime;

C v Brum **438 M 103 (2002)**—co-D's statement admissible to show continuing conspiracy because D and co-D gave identically false statements to police;

C v Stewart **454 M 527 (2009)**—judge's instruction was that acts/statements of each joint venturer could be considered against D only if acts/statements were made when joint venture existed or when venturers were acting to conceal the crime and statements/acts "[were] *relevant to the joint venture*"; italicized language = error, statements could be considered only if made "in furtherance of" the joint venture;

C v Rodriquez **454 M 215 (2009)**—witness's testimony that severed co-D had asked him to kill unknown person by putting a wire around his neck was not hearsay, held admissible to establish that co-D was trying to get help to kill victim by the method eventually employed; ignored by SJC = argument that it was not admissible against D because *D* was obviously NOT a joint venturer at time of statement and it was not probative of *D's* intent; SJC held jury could infer that co-D made same proposal to D as he had to testifying witness;

C v Themelis **22 MAC 754 (86)**—NG because no "bilateral" conspiracy (because co-D deigned agreement);

C v Nighelli **13 MAC 590 (82)**—Massachusetts requires no overt act; co-D NG means D, too, only if tried together; withdrawal no defense (but see here fn. 5);

C v Wilson **38 MAC 680, 686, 687 (95)**—overt act not necessary, but must establish more than D's knowledge of others' agreement; proof must allow inference of participation in furtherance of enterprise;

C v Shea **323 M 406 (48)**—G/NG on substantive crime permits conspiracy case; not double jeopardy (*see Chapter 19, post, Double Jeopardy*);

Carrasquillo v Commonwealth **422 M 1014 (96)**—(same);

C v Cerveny **387 M 280 (82)**—G though co-D NG in other trial; multiple (7 false forms) acts = at most 3 agreements, so duplicitous; (*see Ch. 19*); compare *C v Nighelli* **13 MAC 590, 595 (82)** if jointly tried, NG for 1 of (only) 2 alleged conspirators = NG for other; but see *C v Dyer* **243 M 472 (23)** 1 or more alleged co-conspirators need not be indicted/tried;

Campagna v Commonwealth **454 M 1006 (2009)**—though Commonwealth obtained 7 indictments for conspiracy, judge at "required finding" stage ruled that evidence established only one overarching conspiracy extending through period alleged in the indictments (not 7 distinct conspiracies), and entered NG on 6; 8th indictment, for theft, was found to be a substantive offense within the conspiracy, so D was entitled to severance under Rule 9(e) (and at D's election, mistrial on that charge was declared before submitting case to jury); D was NOT entitled to bar retrial on the substantive indictment (theft) nor on the one conspiracy indictment (on which jury could not reach verdict);

C v Winter **9 MAC 512 (80)**—can't split conspiracy into 2 acts;

C v Royce **20 MAC 221 (85)**—can try conspiracy after substantive NG, but can't relitigate issue D won (e.g., robbed); robbery NG inadmissible at conspiracy trial;

US v Felix **503 US 378, 388 (92)**—prior conviction on underlying offense does not preclude subsequent prosecution for conspiracy; *Grady v Corbin* **495 US 508, 521 (90)** limited & distinguished on ground that charges there were functional equivalent of lesser included offenses;

SEE Chapter 19, Double Jeopardy, re lesser included's/'same' offense;

C v Fancy **349 M 196 (65)**—no G by association, even if consciousness of guilt;

C v David **335 M 686 (57)**—not shown druggist D knew what co-D would do with 20,000 empty drug capsules (later used for heroin);

C v Nelson **370 M 192 (76)**—infer D knew conspiracy object; need not know specific means (drugging horses) after paying co-D $1,000;

C v Shapiro **10 MAC 678 (80)**—wife-D didn't have participation/shared intent/agreement with husband, though knew & concealed evidence;

C v Deagle **10 MAC 563 (80)**—rear passenger NG without agreement; though knowledge, no evidence of even joint possession of front-seat (smoking) joint;

C v Amparo **43 MAC 922 (97)**—though D possessed beeper and attempted with 2 others to flee apartment in which drugs & money & drug paraphernalia found, NG of both conspiracy & possession;

C v Cook **10 MAC 668 (80)**—complaining witness falls, co-D assaults, & D threatens; no agreement shown to spontaneous act, though maybe joint venture (*see Chapter 16-B, Joint Venture*);

C v Costa **55 MAC 901 (2002)**—returning to site where cohort was maliciously breaking glass, & throwing rocks at building, not conspiracy, but instead 'classic paradigm of accomplice adding encouragement to a crime in progress'; rejecting Commonwealth request to allot to participation in commission of substantive offense enough inferential value for conspiracy conviction as well;

C v Assimakopoulous **12 MAC 978 (81)**—discussing point spread not agreement;

C v Camerano **42 MAC 363 (97)**—D, homeowner, allowed P. to keep a "utility trailer" on his property, and P. introduced D to H., who thereafter paid D $200/month for space on the property for his house trailer; roofless "garden structure" with 18 foot tall plywood sides, adjacent to the trailers, was found to contain marijuana plants; required finding of NG for D on charge of conspiracy to possession with intent to distribute marijuana; though maybe enough evidence to infer D's knowledge, this was not enough "affirmative acquiescence" to establish G of conspiracy;

US v Jensen **462 F.2d 763 (8th Cir. '72)**—nexus to robbery target-bank not shown (3 Ds in hot car with guns & masks);

C v Dellinger **10 MAC 549 (80)**, ***reversed on other ground*** **383 M 780 (81)**—object need not be imminent; intent to steal shown, but not rob/burglarize (Ds with criminal records, masks, & tools were following a UPS-jewel truck);

C v Dyer **243 M 472 (22)**—agree to "unlawful" end or means = conspiracy (though neither is a crime) if injury to public interest; cf. *C v Bessette* **351 M 148 (66)** dismiss conspiracy to break DPW contract rules because non-crime unlawfulness maybe never enough, but at least must be big harm & clear wrong (see Nolan & Sartorio/Model Penal Code, above);

In re Enforcement of a Subpoena **435 M 1 (2001)**—crime of conspiracy is "not restricted to arrangements having (a) criminal objective or contemplating (the) use of criminal means to accomplish (a) lawful objective," citing

C v Gill **5 MAC 337, 340 (77)**; but to establish criminal conspiracy apart from those situations, there must be "prejudice to the general welfare or oppression of the individual of sufficient gravity to be injurious to the public interest";

C v Engleman **336 M 66 (57)**—no conspiracy to commit larceny because no agreement re: tools (co-D stole), & trade secrets not "property" for larceny;

C v Chagnon **330 M 278 (53)**—(conspiracy to) place bets no crime unless keep/occupy place with apparatus;

Gebardi v US **287 US 112 (32)**—NG if overt act is crime requiring agreement between D & co-D (e.g., Mann Act)—"Wharton Rule" (see Nolan and Sartorio, Criminal Law, §§ 442, 452 (3d ed. 2001), noting "Wharton" = 2 F. Wharton, Criminal Law, § 16-4 (12th ed. 1932): agreement by 2 persons to commit a particular crime can't be prosecuted as a conspiracy when nature of the crime necessarily requires participation of 2 persons for its commission);

C v Schoening **379 M 234 (79)**—Wharton adoption = open Mass. question; here, there was 3d participant;

Iannelli v US **420 US 770 (75)**—Congress didn't intend to merge § 1955 gambling & § 371 conspiracy, so no Wharton's;

C v Cantres **405 M 238 (89)**—Wharton's Rule barring conspiracy prosecution for offenses which necessarily require 2 or more participants, even if adopted, would not apply to conspiracy to distribute drugs;

C v Dellinger **383 M 780 (81)**—conspiracy to commit larceny over dubious lesser included offense to conspiracy to commit robbery because latter doesn't allege value of $100;

C v Kelly **24 MAC 181 (87)**—conspiracy to commit larceny = lesser included offense of conspiracy to rob, because value = element of punishment, not offense;

C v Saia **18 MAC 762 (84)**—conspiracy to commit unarmed robbery = lesser included to conspiracy to commit armed robbery;

C v Frazier **410 M 235 (91)**—possession of cocaine is not element of conspiracy, so D didn't have automatic standing to challenge search of co-D's purse;

C v Pratt **407 M 647 (90)**—evidence that husband & wife conspired to possess drugs with intent to distribute was sufficient; open question whether husband & wife can be coconspirators under common law (not raised below, and no substantial risk of a miscarriage of justice); "issue whether a husband and wife may be coconspirators is not a question of the sufficiency of the evidence, but a question of law";

C v Gagnon **408 M 185 (90)**—evidence that D conspired with another to burn car to conceal involvement in a murder was sufficient;

17-C. ACCESSORY BEFORE FELONY

G.L. c. 274, § 2—(aider or) accessory before by counseling, hiring, or otherwise procuring a felony = punished as principal; § 3 can try with principal or after his G., or try for the felony though principal = NG; venue rules; no 'accessory before misdemeanors'—*C v Sherman* **191 M 439 (06)**;

Mass. Superior Court Criminal Jury Instructions (1999), § 4.4 n.1—discussing *C v Ortiz* 424 M 853, 856 (97);

See also Chapter 16 re: Joint Venture (principals);

C v Zanetti **454 M 449 (2009)**—when there's evidence that more than one person participated in crime, judges must instruct jury that D may be found guilty "if the Commonwealth has proved beyond reasonable doubt that D knowingly participated in the commission of the crime charged, alone or with others, with the intent required for that offense";

C v Ortiz **424 M 853 (97)**—presence at crime not required for joint venture culpability when "accessory before fact" proved; discussion of legislative background and interrelationship between G.L. c. 274, §§ 2 (whoever aids in commission of felony or is accessory before fact by counseling, hiring, or otherwise procuring, shall be punished like principal felon) and 3 (whoever counsels, hires, or procures commission of felony may be indicted/convicted as accessory before fact OR be indicted/convicted of substantive felony (emphasis added); query whether G.L. c. 273, § 3 vitiates holdings of *C v Merrick* **255 M 510 (26)** can charge as both accessory before & principal, and *C v DiStasio* **297 M 347 (37)** can be G. as accessory before after NG as principal; *(see Chapter 19, Double Jeopardy & duplicity)*; But see *C v Fafone* **416 M 329 (93)** D, Florida drug supplier, shipped drugs to CT and was never in MA: lack of evidence that D knew or intended his acts to have effect in MA = required finding of NG ("failure of territorial jurisdiction");

C v Caramanica **49 MAC 376, 381 (2000)**—prosecutors "apparently rarely use( ) as a basis for indictment" the available "statutory accessory crimes" and instead pursue conviction on "joint venture" theory of "aiding of abetting" in the commission of a crime;

C v Tavares **61 MAC 385 (2004)**—presence is NOT required where D actually aids or abets in commission of crime, but presence IS required where G is sought on basis of sharing principal's criminal intent even if merely standing by ready to assist if necessary; Commonwealth isn't required to prove identity of actual perpetrator (here, child abuse by married couple having exclusive physical custody of child, all living in small motel room);

C v Moure **428 M 313, 317 (98)**—when one is accused of being accessory before fact of particular crime, indictment may be under G.L. c. 274, § 2, OR under G.L. c. 274, § 3 (stating when and how an access. before fact of any substantive crime may be tried); rejecting D's argument that, since alleged principal had been acquitted (of murder), indictment against D had to be brought under § 3 because that section specifically states that it's irrelevant whether principal felon has or hasn't been convicted;

C v Barsell **424 M 737 (97)**—crime of "solicitation of a felony" (even though felony = murder) is common law misdemeanor (only house of correction sentence);

G.L. c. 277, § 79—form complaint (*see Chapter 5, Contents of Complaints & Indictments*), "charge principal felony & proceed . . . ";

Nolan & Sartorio, *Criminal Law*, **§ 633 (3d ed. 2001)**—accessory before maybe brains with more malice than underlying principal; accessory can be tried before principal; no accessory before to manslaughter;

C v Lepper **60 MAC 36 (2003)**—D's criminal culpability (larceny by false pretenses) could be founded upon false statements he caused another individual to make, regardless of whether the other individual knew statements were false (and thus whether the latter was a joint venturer);

District Court Model Jury Instructions 5.01 (*see Chapter 21, post*)—elements = counsel/hire/arrange someone else to do felony, & have accessorial intent; join & significant role; encourage or there to help; if try together, NG if principal = NG;

C v Smith **49 MAC 127 (2000)**—evidence sufficient to show D procured principal to commit armed robbery of persons seeking to buy drugs; D telephoned principal to come, spoke in private with principal immediately before crime, left scene with principal afterwards, shared in proceeds;

C v Morrow **363 M 601 (73)**—significant participation—more than acquiesce & less than physical;

C v French **357 M 356, 391 (70)**—(same); approval enough because co-D wouldn't kill without it; conspiracy not enough;

C v Reynolds **338 M 130 (58)**—must prove principal's guilt beyond reasonable doubt;

C v Alicia **6 MAC 904 (78)**—(same), & not just by principal's G. plea/record;

C v Valentin **420 M 263 (95)**—in proving D's guilt as joint venturer in murder, no error in introducing evidence of principal's drug-dealing, as a drug debt was motive for the murder;

C v Richards **363 M 299 (73)**—accessory before robbery & felony murder because conditional intent if gave gun to co-D;

C v Serrano **74 MAC 1 (2009)**—D was armed with gun when he arrived to harass/fight ex-girlfriend's paramour, but upon entreaties by bystanders, he disarmed, giving gun to a friend, and began fist fight with paramour; victim broke away from D, and D's friend shot V in head: though Appeals Court holds "no error" in refusing to instruct on "withdrawal", SJC allowed further appellate review, 454 M 1106 (2009);

C v Padgett **44 MAC 359 (98)**—joint venture culpability for assaults, armed robbery, and felony murder could be inferred by conditional intent from D's participation with armed cohorts in daytime breaking and entering;

C v Perry **357 M 149 (70)**—conspire/acquiesce with co-D's robbery not accessory before; can be G. of accessory before on principal indictment (fn.1) (but see G.L. c. 274, §§ 2–3, 1973 amendment as opposed to *DiStasio* **297 M 347**);

C v Sitko **372 M 305 (77)**—D counseled/assisted B & E, not just larceny from safe;

C v Lafayette **40 MAC 534 (96)**—D was present as lookout at "break," and thus could be joint venturer even though not present at subsequent entry;

C v MacKedon **60 MAC 901 (2003)**—though another man was present and participating at initial meeting for sale of drugs to undercover cop, D alone responded to subsequent pager contact and exchanged pills for cash: "where, as here, [D] is the sole principal actor, he cannot be found guilty as a joint venturer"; error in charging jury initially on joint venture cured by judge's subsequent withdrawal of that instruction;

C v Raposa **413 M 182, 185 (92)**—mother's knowing failure to protect retarded daughter from boyfriend's sexual advances did not make her liable as accessory before, even if failure was wanton or reckless;

C v James **30 MAC 490 (91)**—D guilty as accessory for drug possession even though identities of principals never established; D equally liable on joint venture theory;

C v Sanchez **40 MAC 411 (96)**—though evidence sufficient to establish D-passenger's constructive possession of drugs in trunk, evidence insufficient to show any "meeting of the minds" of D and driver necessary for G as joint venturer; conviction reversed because jury instructed on this theory and no specification by jury as to G theory;

17-D. ACCESSORY AFTER FELONY

See also Chapter 2, Ethics re: obstruction of justice;

G.L. c. 268, § 36—compound/conceal felony—take reward & agree to compound, conceal, not prosecute, or not give evidence of, known felony (see District Court Model Jury Instruction 5.04);

G.L. c. 274, § 4—after felony, harbor/conceal/assist/aid principal or accessory before felony knowing he committed a felony, with intent he'll avoid detention/punishment = 7 year maximum; (certain close relatives exempt (husband/wife, "or by consanguinity, affinity, or adoption," the parent, grandparent, child, grandchild, brother, or sister of D), even from open cross-examination); § 5 triable without principal, & venue's flexible;

Heang v Commonwealth **454 M 1011(2009)**—principal (A) was charged with murder of a police officer, and several associates of A were present at the scene of the shooting, including this D's brother; D's brother was not charged in connection with the shooting, but D was charged as accessory after fact to murder and for carrying firearm without license; by motion in limine D sought to raise defense based on G.L. c. 274, § 4, but judge denied on basis that D's brother had not been charged, and D instead assisted A, with whom D had no familial relation: SJC denied relief prior to trial on G.L. c. 211, § 3, saying D would not be required to take stand to make record for appeal, and should renew his request at trial to present the defense, with a proffer of evidence, and then object to any denial of renewed request (OR at trial lodge objection to denial of his original motion);

G.L. c. 277, § 79—form indictment (*see Chapter 5, Contents of Complaints & Indictments*), "charge principal felony & proceed . . . ";

Nolan & Sartorio, *Criminal Law,* **§ 634 (3d ed. 2001)**—elements = (1) completed felony, (2) then harbor/conceal/assist principal or accessory before felony, (3) knowing his ID, (4) & that he did it, (5) with intent he'll avoid arrest/punishment; can be principal, accessory before, and/or accessory after—no double jeopardy, see *C v DiStasio* **297 M 347, 354–58, cert. denied, 302 US 683 (37)** (BUT SEE G.L. c. 274, § 3: basis for urging that accessory before fact & substantive crime prosecutions/convictions are duplicative);

C v Gajka **425 M 751 (97)**—can't be G of both substantive crime **and** being accessory after same;

C v Eagan **357 M 585 (70)**—principal's G. must be proven beyond reasonable doubt, & G. plea not enough; but she need not be convicted;

C v Devlin **366 M 132 (74) (& *C v Corcione* 366 M 139)**—must know ID of felon & what it was, at least its substantial facts; wipe/hide knife = NG;

C v Sims **41 MAC 902 (96)**—can be G even if voluntarily turned self in (along with principal): justice obstruction need not continue long nor be successful;

C v Tilley **327 M 540 (51)**—aided (e.g., to avoid arrest) by arranging return of stolen property by paying thief $400; accessory to larceny = lesser included offense to accessory to B & E/larceny;

C v Talbot **35 MAC 766 (94)**—though joint venturer murder-D testified he'd only helped dispose of body & had not known of crime & was not present before or when committed, no right to jury instruction on "accessory after fact"—not a lesser included offense & could have misled/confused;

C v Kelly **1 MAC 441 (73)**—intent maybe to save 'self, not shield co-D (after co-D arrest, & 7 weeks after robbery, D had gun & planned to dispose);

C v Sokorelis **254 M 454 (26)**—IF D produces consanguinity evidence, DA's burden to disprove it beyond reasonable doubt;

C v Mahoney **405 M 326 (89)**—consanguinity is an affirmative defense to accessory after felony under G.L. c. 274, § 4.

Chapter 18
IDENTIFICATION ISSUES

18-A. OVERALL STRATEGY, E.G., CHOOSING IN-COURT ID OPTIONS

M.R.Crim.P. 14(a)(1)(A)(viii) (effective 9-7-2004)—automatic, mandatory discovery includes "a summary of ID procedures, and all statements made in the presence of or by an ID witness that are relevant to issue of ID or to fairness or accuracy of the ID procedures";

CPCS P/G 2.2(b)—prevent ID opportunities at arraignment; 4.5(a) discover details of ID procedures & examine photos; 4.7(a) consider motion for nonsuggestive option(s) if appropriate & D wants; (*see, herein, Chapter 6-K, Discovery of ID Procedure, & 6-B, Pre-Trial Conference, e.g., preserve/obtain turret tape (911 call)*—see *C v Allen* **22 MAC 413 (86)** omissions in complainant's statements there impeached ID of D (reversal for exclusion of tape, although tape was incomplete);

K. Smith, *Criminal Practice & Procedure*, Chapter 7, Identification (2d ed. 1983 & Supp.)—discovery & voir dire rights; lineup & counsel's role; suppress; evidence; instructions;

US Department of Justice, Eyewitness Evidence: A Guide for Law Enforcement (1999)—cited and relied upon by SJC in, e.g., *Silva-Santiago* **453 M 782, 797–98 (2009)**, and purportedly supported by Massachusetts District Attorneys Association and incorporated into Boston Police Dept. procedures, as cited in *C v Watson* **455 M 246, 251–52 (2009)**;

C v Dougan **377 M 303 (79)**—due process right to ID procedures meeting basic standard of fairness "would mean little if it did not carry with it the right to be informed of the details of any out-of-court identification, even if it were not used at trial; before any retrial here, should be "voir dire hearing at which all the circumstances surrounding the pretrial identification . . . can be developed";

C v Tucceri **412 M 401 (92)**—Commonwealth's failure to produce exculpatory booking photos showing D with mustache required reversal despite D's failure to make specific request;

C v Daniels **445 M 392 (2005)**—trial judge abused discretion in denying post-trial discovery, given motion alleging newly discovered info that Commonwealth had withheld exculpatory info which had been specifically requested, and which cast doubt on credibility of ID made by sole eyewitness;

C v Naylor **73 MAC 518 (2009)**—judge abused discretion in denying evidentiary hearing on R.30 motion alleging ineffective assistance of trial counsel in failing to support misidentification defense with photo of D taken close in time to shooting, showing he had shoulder-length braids and mustache and beard; trial counsel elicited testimony that shooter had no facial hair but nothing about hairstyle, and failed to direct jury's attention to dramatic difference between D's appearance at trial and photo selected from array (affidavit submitted with new trial motion asserted D wore long braids and facial hair on date of offense as well as at trial);

Loftus & Doyle, *Eyewitness Testimony, Civil and Criminal* (3d ed. 1997, w/2000 cumulative supplement)—for full discussion of strategies for trying identification cases, excellent analysis of psychological issues; § 6.13: potential harm of positive lineup ID mandates "extreme caution" in asking one; alternative: defense investigator shows witness photo array, etc. (but see *C v Drumgold* **423 M 230 (96)** defense counsel, pretrial, showed prosecution witness single photo of D, creating out of court ID where it did not previously exist);

M.R.Crim.P. 18—D's right to be present at all "critical stages"; can "waive" right in misdemeanor cases (Reporter's Notes: D can forfeit right by failing to appear or by obstreperous conduct); 13: motions, requirements for (affidavit, etc.)

C v Jones **375 M 349 (78)**—counsel's role at probable cause hearing includes asking for lineup or that D be seated in court audience;

C v Ceria **13 MAC 230 (82)**—discretion re: motion for nonsuggestive ID at probable cause hearing, but must be written, with affidavit, & timely filed before probable cause hearing;

C v Rodriquez **378 M 296 (79)**—1-on-1 confrontation (at probable cause hearing) = great risk of mistaken ID; counsel may reduce suggestiveness by asking lineup or D in audience, or witness be sequestered during taking of evidence;

C v Dougan **377 M 303 (79)**—for motion for nonsuggestive ID, counsel must provide all relevant facts (*see Chapter 6-K, Discovery*);

US v Thoreen **653 F.2d 1332 (9th Cir. '81), cert. denied 455 US 938 (82)**—D's look-alike at counsel table delayed case & violated ABA DF-4.9 (candor/truth), custom, & sequestration;

In re Gross **435 M 445 (2001)**—with similar intent, defense counsel orchestrated "impersonation" scheme, having D's friend come forward, sign continuance notice (impersonating D); to evade responsibility, counsel thereafter coached pertinent parties to lie and say "confusion"; suspended from practice for 18 months;

C v Napolitano **378 M 599 (79)**—court must reduce suggestiveness of in-court ID;

C v Moore **379 M 106 (79)**—"ordinarily" let D sit at counsel table, unless security requires otherwise;

Young v Callahan **700 F.2d 32 (1st Cir. '83)**—reverse for having D in dock;

Moore v Illinois **434 US 220 (77)**—after "adversary proceedings" (e.g., when arraignment or probable cause hearing), right to counsel at "corporeal" ID procedure involving D, so counsel can object to suggestiveness;

Kirby v Illinois **406 US 682 (72)**—(same), after charge, probable cause hearing, indictment, arraignment;

C v Donovan **392 M 647 (84)**—cop asked probable cause hearing witness for ID in courtroom without notice to counsel = per se excluded for 6th Amendment violation;

C v Key **19 MAC 234 (85)**—witness can ID D awaiting arraignment because unaware dock's for D's & no counsel right yet; (see P/G 2.2(b), & *Cincotta* **379 M 391(79)** witnesses called to hearing will, understandably & reasonably, expect to see the culprit, & defense counsel is charged with knowing this; if counsel wants precautionary measures, s/he should seek them; this isn't situation in which prosecution contrived to renew and bolster an identification in a setting which couldn't be anticipated by defense counsel;

Martin v Donnelly **391 F.Supp 1241 (D.Mass '74)**—suppress suggestive arraignment ID because counsel unaware;

C v Perry **15 MAC 932 (83)**—accidental encounter in court hallway & ID = OK; **but see**

C v Jones **423 M 99 (96)**—**ID, product of suggestive confrontation and without independent source, suppressed as *unreliable*; irrelevant that government agents weren't responsible for confrontation;** but see *Odware* 429 M 231 (due process doesn't require exclusion of ID testimony if "suggestive circumstances do not arise from police activity), and, e.g. *C v Powell* 72 MAC 22, 27 (2008) (citing *Jones* for proposition that encounters not orchestrated by police "have been held not to raise due process considerations even if the encounter occurs in a suggestive setting"); See post, 18-F.9.

C v Bly **448 M 473 (2007)**—D argued unreliable ID because occurred through TV report of D's indictment, ID didn't occur until 2½ years after crime, ID occurred while witness was driving, dealing with recent bereavement, work problems, and unspecified "medical condition", and ID was cross-racial (no suppression; all issues aired on cross-examination);

C v Charles **397 M 1 (86)**—(probably) no right to be present at post-lineup witness interview;

C v Tanso **411 M 640 (92)**—open question whether counsel has right to be present at post-lineup interview;

C v Doe **408 M 764 (90)**—grand jury may not order suspect to appear in lineup without articulable justification under *Terry v Ohio* **392 US 1 (1968)**;

C v Colon-Cruz **408 M 533 (90)**—discovery was sufficient to notify counsel that victim could & probably would identify D at probable cause hearing;

C v Kater (III) **409 M 433 (91)**—witness is not required by confrontation clause to look at D, unless ability to make identification in issue;

C v Drumgold **423 M 230 (96)**—defense counsel, pretrial, showed prosecution witness single photo of D, creating out of court ID where it did not previously exist; similarly, allowing D to go on view produced another out-of-court ID by same witness (who lived in area); SJC held (unconvincingly?) that this was not ineffective assistance of counsel;

18-B. REQUIRED FINDINGS OF NOT GUILTY, INSTRUCTIONS AND (JURY-WAIVED) RULINGS

See Chapter 12-G (motions for required findings), -I (requests for instructions), & -K (instructions);

C v Woods **382 M 1 (80)**—new trial because strong (documentary) proof D's NG;

C v Vaughn **23 MAC 40 (86)**—reasonable doubt re: ID when security video cameras captured likenesses of seemingly robbers on two occasions, the latter of which being a time when D was incarcerated; if strong evidence of NG, judge maybe equally able as jury to evaluate & prevent injustice, & here, unlike Woods, court ordered RFNG rather than retrial opportunity; see **id. at 44** ("We are not unmindful of the fact that eyewitness testimony, however sincere, is occasionally wrong. 'The vagaries of eyewitness identification are well-known; the annals of criminal law are rife with instances of mistaken identification.' *United States v. Wade*, **388 US 218, 228 (1967)**");

C v Lane **27 MAC 527 (89)**—required finding of not guilty entered where victim's identification of another as her assailant was equally as strong as her photo & in-court identifications of D;

C v Hall **48 MAC 727 (2000)**—**Lane**, above, distinguished: though victim saw culprit later, it was uncertain when the sightings occurred, and so it was possible that D was the person later sighted;

C v Cincotta **379 M 391, 397 (79)**—ID reliability pertinent to motion for required finding of NG;

C v Morrill **14 MAC 1003 (82)**—evidence & inferences enough to ID D (as rock-thrower); seeing D from 50 yards not inherently incredible;

C v Brennan **74 MAC 44 (2009)**—circumstantial evidence of D's identity as gas station B&E culprit = enough for proof beyond reasonable doubt, MAC vacating order of required finding of not guilty made by trial judge;

C v Price **72 MAC 280 (2008)**—though only one of three victims ID'd D in court, another had ID'd him in photo array, D had made admissions and there was abundant circumstantial evidence of his guilt;

US v Levi **405 F.2d 380 (4th Cir. '68)**—in 1-witness ID case, judge should decide whether total circumstances gives very likely mis-ID in deciding motion for required finding of not guilty;

C v Snow **80 M 385 (1860)**—"looked like D; I won't hardly say it's D" = required not guilty;

C v Amado **387 M 179 (82)**—out-of-court photo ID & in-court "not D" = required not guilty (*see Chapter 18-E*);

C v Marsh **26 MAC 933 (88)**—witness #2's ID (with better observation) overcomes required finding of not guilty, though witness #1 says it's not D; Commonwealth can argue (non-IDing) witness "paralyzed by fear"—& jury can so find;

18-B.1. Fingerprints, Sufficiency

C v Clark 378 M 392 (79)—fingerprint at scene not enough for G;

C v LaCorte 373 M 700 (77)—same;

C v Morris 422 M 254 (96)—fingerprint on mask used in armed assault insufficient, even with other evidence: required finding of not guilty;

C v Fazzino 27 MAC 485 (89)—D's fingerprint at scene sufficient to convict D of B&E only if prosecution evidence reasonably excludes hypothesis that print was left at another time; here, additional evidence that D knew how to use torch made fingerprint evidence sufficient;

C v Loftis 361 M 545 (72)—print sufficient for G because table washed in a.m.;

C v Ye 52 MAC 390, 391–94 (2001)—evidence reasonably excluded possibility that fingerprints inside a cabinet in home of B&E victims were left at any other time;

C v LeClaire 28 MAC 932 (90)—where D was shown not to have had authorized access to room, his thumbprint on window sufficient to convict of breaking & entering where it formed pattern with other smeared (& thus unidentifiable) fingerprints, suggesting that D had grasped window through opening;

C v Baptista 32 MAC 910 (92)—D's fresh prints near coin box inside broken soda machine sufficient to convict D of breaking & entering;

18-B.2. Instructions, Right to; Model(s)

US v Telfaire 469 F.2d 552 (DC Cir. '72)—(then) "model" ID instruction; Bazelon concurs & urges instruction that cross-racial ID's less reliable; (*S v Long* 721 P.2d.483, n.8 (Ut '86) model instruction replacing Telfaire & highlighting stress, post-event info., & cross-racial problem);

C v Rodriguez 378 M 296 (79)—adopt Telfaire ID instruction;

**C v Fitzpatrick* 18 MAC 106 (84)—should modify Rodriguez re: witness's "NEXT" opportunity to see D AFTER CRIME because suggests guilt; instead, 'consider the time lapse after crime until see & ID the D as the offender';

***C v Pires* 453 M 66 (2009)—*include henceforth in model Rodriguez instruction* the **Pressley** (390 M 617 [83]) language (though witness may be sincere and honest in belief that D committed offense, jury must still return NG unless convinced beyond a reasonable doubt that ID is accurate); [*C v Delong* 72 MAC 42, 47–48 (2008) had questioned whether Pressley charge is required inasmuch as subsequent cases mandating particular ID charge had omitted Pressley's particular concept, but "le[ft the precise answer to another day (or another court)"];

C v Cuffie 414 M 632 (93)—*Fitzpatrick* modification included in model instruction;

C v Walker 421 M 90 (95)—failure to object to *Fitzpatrick* flaw means no reversal; *C v Melo* 67 MAC 71 (2006)—use of "next opportunity" language doesn't by itself create substantial risk of miscarriage of justice, & charge here had only similar flaw;

District Court Model Instructions 6:05—Rodriguez etc.; 6.01 alibi;

C v Hoilett 430 M 369, 374 (99)—improper for prosecutor during direct of non-ID witness to refer to masked robber as "the defendant," because it implies that the witness has made such ID; here, clear that witness didn't claim to ID D as robber, and judge gave curative instructions;

C v Bowden 379 M 472 (80)—if ID issue's fairly raised, right to ID instruction;

C v Delrio 22 MAC 712 (86)—reverse for no instruction re: COPS'S ID (implicitly no different from any other witness, i.e., as human, subject to same ID factors);

C v Hallett 427 M 552 (98)—judge's failure to bring to jury's attention three considerations important to weighing ID = reversal;

C v Brewster 46 MAC 746, 751 n.4 (99)—"There is nothing iniquitous about adhering to pattern texts suggested in the opinions"; irritation at trial judge's gutting from model the points germane to defense (here, failure to instruct that IDs from group of similar individuals are more reliable than 1:1 ID);

C v Francis 390 M 89 (83)—assumes: (1) memories fade with time, (2) stress impairs information acquisition, & (3) memories & post-event facts get mixed;

C v Santoli 424 M 837 (97)—remove from model charge factor re: "strength of witness's certainty";

C v Pina 430 M 266 (99)—when ID is contested issue at trial, no rationale for consciousness of guilt instruction based on the guilty party's running from scene (no dispute that assailant was the person so running);

C v Watson 455 M 246 (2009)—SJC "decline[s] . . . to mandate" "cautionary" jury instructions when Commonwealth has not strictly followed Dep't of Justice guidelines for ID procedures;

18-B.3. Cross-Racial

C v Charles 397 M 1 (86)—instruction not (yet?) required on cross-racial ID (because no supporting evidence?; see *Francis* 390 M 89 (83); *US v Telfaire*, above, **469 F.2d 552 (DC Cir. '72)** Bazelon concurrence urges instruction that cross-racial ID's less reliable;

C v Hyatt 419 M 815, 818–19 n.1 (95)—judge, in discretion, may give cross—racial ID instruction; cf. **id.**—instruction perhaps required if "relevant empirical study" is proffered in support;

C v Engram 43 MAC 804 (97)—no abuse of discretion in refusing cross-racial instruction, given evidence;

C v Jean-Jacques **47 MAC 909 (99)**—judges should consider request for cross-racial ID instruction "with a measure of favorable inclination to grant it";

C v Zimmerman **441 M 146, 154–56 (2004) (concurring opinion)**—"own-race bias" ("performance deficit of one ethnic group in recognizing faces of another ethnic group compared with faces of one's own group") exists, and "the unreliability of cross-racial identification IS a subject 'beyond the ordinary experience and knowledge of the average juror'", and "expert testimony . . . should be admissible";

18-B.4. Degree of Self-Confidence in ID

C v Santoli **424 M 837 (97)**—henceforth, ID instruction should omit any suggestion that the confidence a witness has in his identification is a valid indicator of its accuracy; issue left to cross and argument; doubt of witness in accuracy, on other hand, understood to be significant;

C v Orton **58 MAC 209 (2003)**—instruction including "strength" of witness's identification was requested by D and given, but in combination with other errors = substantial risk of miscarriage of justice & reversal;

C v Cowans **52 MAC 811, 814 (2001)**—declining to "extend" *Santoli* to bar witness from testifying on direct examination to his level of confidence in his ID of defendant; *C v Watkins* **63 MAC 69, 74 (2005)**—SJC has neither barred witness testimony regarding ID certainty, nor prevented counsel from probing/arguing subject;

C v Cruz **445 M 589 (2005)**—refusing to find error in judge's refusal to give instruction that confidence of identifying witness did not correlate to accuracy of ID, and (despite *Santoli*) claiming that, "after conducting our own review of the research cited by [D], it is not at all clear that there is 'no proven relationship' between confidence and accuracy"; defendants invited to call expert witnesses (at 597, though judge has "discretion" to exclude them!);

C v Jones **423 M 99, 110 n.9 (96)**—1st case noting possible unsound premise remedied in *Santoli*;

C v Horsman **47 MAC 262 (99)**—though *Santoli* issue preserved/raised by trial counsel, no appellate relief because trial was pre-*Santoli*;

C v Silva-Santiago **453 M 782, 798 (2009)**—at time of ID procedure, witness should be asked about degree of certainty, because "certainty" may be pegged higher at time of trial simply because law enforcement agents have 'confirmed' witness's ID;

C v Watson **455 M 246, 254 (2009)**—witness's expression of 95% certainty at time of photo array = a factor which judge could use in deciding whether cop's actions may have been unduly suggestive; certainty here "was not being considered in the context of a secondary analysis following a judicial determination that [ID] was impermissibly suggestive";

18-B.5. Good Faith, but Mistaken

C v Pressley **390 M 617 (83)**—if facts allow possibility, right to instruction re: "possible honest, but mistaken ID";

C v Williams **58 MAC 139 (2003)**—error to refuse Pressley instruction in case in which cops were the ID witnesses; alibi defense isn't prerequisite to giving the instruction;

C v Caramanica **49 MAC 376 (2000)**—when, in 'good faith/mistaken ID' charge, judge instructed that "very few people come into court with an intention to mislead" and credibility thus means "accuracy more than honesty," this was "improper incursion into the jury's role";

C v Delrio **22 MAC 712 (86)**—reverse for no instruction re: COPS'S ID (implicitly no different from any other witness, i.e., as human, subject to same ID factors); "heart" of *Rodriquez* **378 M 296 (79)** = "forceful warning" that misidentification maybe mistake, not venality; see also *C v Williams* **54 MAC 236 (2002)** (similar);

C v Rosado **428 M 76 (98)**—error to refuse instruction re: witness's "clothes of culprit" ID (honest but mistaken), but here no prejudice;

C v DiFonzo **31 MAC 921 (91)**—D had right to instruction on possibility of honest but mistaken identification;

C v Pires **453 M 66 (2009)**—D requested instruction re: possibility of honest but mistaken ID, but judge said only "in analyzing identification testimony, you may consider whether or not the witness might simply be mistaken"; SJC said no "prejudicial error" to this D, **BUT in future, include in ID instruction the language in Pressley** (even if witness is sincere and honest in belief that D committed offense, you must still return NG unless you're convinced beyond reasonable doubt that ID is accurate); [MAC had questioned in *C v Delong* 72 MAC 42, 47–48 (2008) whether *Pressley* was still required];

C v Crowley **29 MAC 1 (90)**—judge's failure to instruct on possibility of honest but mistaken identification not error because not requested by defense;

C v Burns **49 MAC 677, 685 (2000)**—no substantial risk of miscarriage of justice in failure to charge on good faith mistaken ID, because (a) at trial defense was that ID witness was biased and lied that D was culprit, and (b) evidence didn't warrant such instruction because witness had known D for years, shooting occurred during daylight, and witness was only 20 feet away from culprit;

C v Elam **412 M 583 (92)**—judge's failure to give instruction on honest but mistaken identification did not require reversal where D did not request it & where Rodriguez instruction given;

C v Traylor **43 MAC 239 (97)**—(same);

C v Evans **42 MAC 618 (97)**—(same); failure to request honest/mistaken ID possibility and ID from 'group' more reliable than one on one was not ineffective assistance of counsel;

C v Velazquez **61 MAC 667 (2004)**—failure to request honest/mistaken ID instruction not ineffective assistance because D "was entitled to no more" than model ID and alibi instructions: challenge to IDs was based on witnesses' veracity & evidence didn't "raise the possibility that they were mistaken";

C v Spencer **45 MAC 33 (98)**—refusal to give 'honest but mistaken ID' instruction required reversal where accuracy of ID could reasonably be questioned, and independent evidence linking D to crime "not overwhelming";

C v Odware **429 M 23 (99)**—error (here harmless) to refuse to instruct on honest but mistaken ID;

C v Williams **54 MAC 236 (2002)**—reversal for refusal to instruct on honest but mistaken ID when there was only one (cop) eyewitness (despite his allegedly observing culprit for up to 90 minutes and from as close as 10 feet), no corroborating evidence, & contrary defense testimony; "(o)nce (D) presented his proposal for jury instructions on identification & objected to the judge's refusal to instruct on the issue, (D) fully discharged his burden to raise the issue";

C v DeJesus **71 MAC 799 (2008)**—judge's instruction covered, at length, the *Pressley* concept, even if not in exact wording requested by D;

18-B.6. One-to-One IDs

C v Gonzalez **28 MAC 906 (89)**—counsel had right to argue that lineups are generally more reliable than 1-on-1 showups;

C v Cuffie **414 M 632 (93)**—in case involving 1:1 showup, error to omit from ID charge the standard caution

that ID from group of similar individuals is more reliable than presentation of D alone to witness;

C v Ye **52 MAC 850, 856 (2001)**—no objection to judge's omitting instruction re: picking person out of group of similar individuals = more reliable than 1:1; while including it would have been "preferable," no substantial risk of miscarriage of justice;

C v Brewster **46 MAC 746, 751 n.4 (99)**—irritation at trial judge's gutting from model the points germane to defense (here, failure to instruct that IDs from group of similar individuals are more reliable than 1:1 ID);

18-B.7. Alibi

C v McLeod **367 M 500 (75)**—don't call alibi a "defense," single it out "rigid scrutiny," or suggest it's "easily contrived"; if do so, right to balancing instruction re: "the only refuge of the innocent"; (see also Model Jury Instructions);

C v Murphy **442 M 485 (2004)**—instruction that "it is alleged that the Commonwealth hasn't proven beyond reasonable doubt that D was present at time/place of crimes. . . . If you believe D's alibi, Commonwealth has failed to prove G beyond a reasonable doubt," said to be taken out of context (!) because judge reiterated Commonwealth's burden of proof, including necessity of proving fact that D "was there at the time"; still, SJC "emphasize[s]" that *McLeod* **367 M 501, 502 n.1 (75)** is preferable;

18-C. RIGHT TO SHOW MISTAKEN ID, INCLUDING BY EXPERT AND ALIBI

C v Poggi **53 MAC 685 (2002)**—judge erred in excluding D's attempt to display to jury tattoos on his forearm as means of rebutting eyewitness IDs, where display was demonstrative rather than testimonial, and where there was sufficient evidence that D had tattoos at time of crime to require at least voir dire as to adequacy of foundation for admitting the evidence;

C v Naylor **73 MAC 518 (2009)**—judge abused discretion in denying evidentiary hearing on R.30 motion alleging ineffective assistance of trial counsel in failing to support misidentification defense with photo of D taken close in time to shooting, showing he had shoulder-length braids and mustache and beard; trial counsel elicited testimony that shooter had no facial hair but nothing about hairstyle, and failed to direct jury's attention to dramatic difference between D's appearance at trial and photo selected from array (affidavit submitted with new trial motion asserted D wore long braids and facial hair on date of offense as well as at trial);

C v Evans **438 M 142 (2002)**—when police told murder eyewitness that they were bringing suspects for him to view, he refused & said he didn't want to see them, and continued to refuse after being placed in police car, and when they walked by, he gave only cursory look and said

they weren't assailants; judge could exclude this on ground that it was not spontaneous utterance, but instead product of reflective thought;

18-C.1. Expert Witnesses

See Chapter 18-A, ante; Loftus/Doyle (at Chapter 11) re: possible expert testimony; see also Chapter 7-C, ante, Fees for Indigents, Experts/Expenses; & P/G 4.7 (h); Chapter 11-I, ante, Experts;

C v Francis **390 M 89 (83)**—discretion re: admit expert on ID reliability; not (yet) shown expert can help, & (then) only 1 court had admitted;

C v Hyatt **419 M 815 (95)**—judge has discretion to admit expert testimony re ID; *C v Bly* **448 M 473 (2007)**—same, no abuse of discretion in excluding, citing "substantial corroboration" of sole eyewitness ID (from witnesses helping D beforehand and hearing D's admissions after murder);

C v Santoli **424 M 837 (97)**—in case with **significant corroboration of witness's ID** by physical evidence, still discretionary whether to admit expert re: ID; factors to guide exercise of discretion listed; upon request, remove from jury instructions the factor of "strength of witness's certainty" as indicator of worth of ID (reliability and confidence aren't necessarily correlated);

C v Ashley **427 M 620 (98)**—same; evidence corroborating IDs cited;

C v Watson **455 M 246 (2009)**—expert testimony concerning reliability of eyewitness ID is not admissible as of right, but is left to judge's "discretion", indigent D may request funds for expert witness on eyewitness ID (citing *Zimmerman* 441 M 146, 152–53 [2004]); SJC declines to find ineffective assistance in defense counsel's failure to have moved for funds (D had retained counsel & until last moment told counsel he would have $ for expert also, & decision to forego attempt to retain & offer expert was not manifestly unreasonable when made; ID challenge made forcefully in cross, etc.); SJC "decline[s] . . . to mandate" admission of expert testimony and "cautionary" jury instructions when Commonwealth has not strictly followed DOJ guidelines for ID procedures;

C v Walker **421 M 90 (95)**—discretionary whether to admit expert testimony re cross-racial ID's; but see *C v Jean-Jacques* **47 MAC 909 (99)** trial judges should consider request for cross-racial ID instruction "with a measure of favorable inclination to grant it";

C v Silva-Santiago **453 M 782 (2009)**—extensive discussion of defense expert's testimony re: flawed ID procedures, lengthy explication of possible doubt as to D's guilt, culminating in 33E reversal of first degree murder conviction on issue not briefed by appellate counsel;

C v Bly **448 M 473, 496 (2007)**—declines to hold that jury instruction on topic is required when cross-racial ID is at issue, while acknowledging "significant body of scientific literature on the problems inherent in" same: particular instruction here requested might have been responsible? ("instruction requested . . . is expressed in broad language that ostensibly replaces the common understanding of the juror");

C v Zimmerman **441 M 146, 154–56 (2004) (concurring opinion)**—"own-race bias" ("performance deficit of one ethnic group in recognizing faces of another ethnic group compared with faces of one's own group") exists, and "the unreliability of cross-racial identification IS a subject 'beyond the ordinary experience and knowledge of the average juror'", and "expert testimony . . . should be admissible"; *C v Kent K.* **427 M 754 (98)**—no abuse of discretion in excluding expert testimony re ID;

C v Pagano **47 MAC 55 (99)**—discretionary whether to admit expert testimony re voice ID;

People v Lee **NY Ct. App. 5/8/2001**—expert testimony in ID cases isn't per se inadmissible; courts shouldn't exclude merely because it purportedly "invades the jury's province"; here, however, no abuse of discretion found in excluding;

State v Gunter **554 A.2d 1356 (N.J.App.Div. 1989)**—expert ID evidence may be admissible; case remanded;

People v McDonald **690 P.2d 709 (Calif. '84)**—expert ID testimony should have been admitted;

Campbell v People **814 P2d 1 (Col. '91)**—expert ID testimony should have been admitted;

State v Chapple **660 P.2d 1208 (Ariz. '83)**—expert ID testimony should have been admitted;

State v Hamm **430 NW2d 584 (Wis. Ct. Appls '98)**—expert ID testimony should have been admitted, but here harmless error;

Echavarria v State **839 P2d 589 (Nev. '92)**—same;

C v Cardozo **29 MAC 645 (90)**—expert testimony that pubic hair sample differed from D's exemplar was admissible to show identification;

US v Moore **786 F.2d 1308 (5th Cir. '86)**—expert testimony about counterintuitive facts may be admissible;

18-C.2. Suggestiveness: Failure to Use Less Suggestive ID Procedures

C v Rodriguez **378 M 296 (79)**—D can show suggestiveness, & existence of fairer procedures not used;

C v DiBenedetto **427 M 414 (98)**—not error to exclude question to ID witness whether anyone in lineup other than D looked in any way like murderer; such opinion not admissible and jury saw video of lineup to make its own determination;

C v Jones **362 M 497, 500 (72)**—counsel must cross-examine to bring out any facts casting doubt on ID;

"Eyewitness Evidence: A Guide for Law Enforcement" (US Department of Justice, 2001)—recommendations for how police should handle interviews, line-ups, photo arrays; essential for cross-examination;

C v Rosa **73 MAC 540 (2009)**—in apparent reliance upon Dept. of Justice guide, defense counsel argued in closing the superior reliability of showing photos one at a time, sequentially (rather than array); prosecutor then argued **IMPROPERLY** that array was necessary because wanted to "move quickly on the investigation," that it was fairer to D (because if his photo had been "first" in a sequential showing, this would have been less "fair", "[t]he reality is . . . that eight picture photo array was more difficult than one at a time"; no evidence introduced re: relative accuracy of the two forms of photo ID, and argument was seen as improper vouching; Commonwealth claimed 'fair response,' but had not "suggest[ed] that defense counsel's argument was improper" and had not objected at trial to it;

Showing Witness's Limited Opportunity to Observe, Unreliability of ID of Defendant

C v Montez **45 MAC 802 (98)**—not error to bar counsel from covering array faces except for nose and eyes for jury exhibit, or to bar counsel from requiring witness to select D's photo from altered array because altered array was not accurate description of her observations;

C v Bourgeois **404 M 61 (89)**—judge's exclusion of victim's failure to identify D's photo was proper where victim had no opportunity to view 1 of 2 assailants, made photo identification of other assailant, & where both Ds were apprehended almost immediately;

Pettijohn v Hall **599 F.2d 476 (1st Cir. '79)**—D can call witness whose ID D got suppressed to show he'd ID'd another; suppressed ID is then admissible;

C v Odware **429 M 231 (99)**—when one ID witness asserted 5th Amendment and D elicited from cop that witness had ID'd person other than D, no error in subsequent examination eliciting that the ID witness, on another occasion, ID'd "someone" other than the person mentioned during D's examination;

C v Franklin **366 M 284 (74)**—D can show mis-ID of former co-D, because relevant to reliability of ID of D;

C v Ellis **432 M 746 (2000)**—no relief for excluding cross-examination of witness concerning her unreliable/problematic ID of culprit IN AN UNRELATED MATTER (descriptions, selection of photo unlike description) despite D's arguments that it would have shown witness unreliable in capacity to perceive/remember people & would have refuted Commonwealth claim that witness's "misidentification" of culprit in case at bar was deliberate, from fear;

C v Allen **22 MAC 413 (86)**—D can show inconsistencies in ID witness's 911 call (even if part of tape's inaudible);

18-C.3. Alibi Issues

C v Berth **385 M 784 (82)**—co-D's alibi casts doubt on ID of D, so (though D had none) D gets reversal for bad alibi instruction;

CPCS P/G 6.7—carefully prepare witnesses for cross-examination & anticipate rebuttal; (*For preparing alibi witness, see Chapter 10, Prepare Defense; Chapters 11-G & 9-G, re: impeachment by no report to police*);

SJC RULE 3:07, 3.4(f)—don't request person (not client) not give another party relevant info (unless relative or other person's interests not adversely affected; BUT cf. G.L. c. 258B, § 3(m) (victims/witnesses have "right" to be informed of "right" to submit to or decline interview by defense, "except when responding to lawful process," and if submit, "right" to impose reasonable conditions on conduct of interview);

C v Aviles **31 MAC 244 (91)**—counsel's failure to request alibi instruction & to present objective evidence of D's medical incapacity to commit crime may have been ineffective assistance;

C v Smith **29 MAC 449 (90)**—prosecutor permitted to comment on absence of D's alibi witnesses where they had been mentioned in defense opening & D's testimony;

C v Emence **47 MAC 299 (99)**—even before DA sought to cast doubt on defense witness's memory, defense was entitled (on direct) to elicit that witness remembered event because he had been required to stay at work four hours after shift ended in order to finish repairs to alleged victim's vehicle (and "victim" was there, in company of D, before and long after alleged time of rape/robbery); though admissibility wasn't dependent upon DA attacking witness's credibility, such attack on cross subsequently was "funda-

mentally unfair" as a manipulation of the absence of evidence the DA had succeeded in excluding during direct; evidence was all the more relevant and "independently admissible" for purpose of rehabilitation during redirect;

M.R.Crim.P. 14—reciprocal discovery re: alibi—*see Chapter 6-M;*

C v Cutty **47 MAC 671 (99)**—D himself cannot be precluded from testifying as sanction for failure to give notice of alibi (M.R.Crim.P. 14(b)(1)(D)) AND judge cannot bar counsel from using D's testimony in closing argument; (*See also Chapter 18-B ante, re: "alibi" instructions*);

18-C.4. Some Other Dude Did It

C v Scott **408 M 811 (90)**—police report of similar attack at nearly same time & place might have been discoverable had it been requested by D;

C v Keizer **377 M 264 (79)**—can't exclude evidence of similar robbery while D in custody, but need close connection in time/method;

C v Jewett **392 M 558 (84)**—D needs lesser degree of similarity than DA to introduce evidence of other crimes; only "normal rules of relevancy" preclude mis-ID evidence;

C v Miles **420 M 67 (95)**—error in judge's exclusion (on DA's motion in limine) of questioning about another suspect, but here harmless;

C v O'Laughlin **446 M 188 (2006), overruling 63 MAC 805 (2005)**—despite substantial "third party culprit evidence" and while acknowledging that the question was "close," SJC held circumstantial evidence of D's culpability (ID, i.e., "who did it") sufficient for conviction (motive, opportunity, means, and consciousness of guilt);

C v Phinney **446 M 155 (2006)**—failure to present third-party culprit evidence was ineffective assistance of counsel (trial court judge's allowance of motion for new trial in murder case upheld by SJC after allowance of Commonwealth's "gatekeeper" petition);

C v Caillot **454 M 245 (2009)**—failure to 'investigate other suspect' not ineffective assistance as there was only "speculation regarding the possibility" that another man killed victim; "substantially more" info linking him to shooting would have been needed to put before jury;

C v Conkey **430 M 139, 147 (99)**—no error in excluding evidence that V's landlord had previously raped and taken sexually explicit photos of a woman; here, crime wasn't similar; "primary motive appear(ing) to be burglary and larceny"; that landlord refused to submit to DNA or polygraph testing "was collateral to (his) motive or opportunity to commit the crime";

But see *C v Conkey* **443 M 60 (2004)**—reversal of murder conviction for exclusion of third-party culprit's pattern of sexually aggressive acts against women (he was victim's landlord, & victim had declined his requests to date);

C v Sullivan **436 M 799 (2002)**—error to bar D from introducing tape-recorded telephone message with some caller making admission consistent with being murderer (rather than D); neither tentative nature of recipient's identification of the voice nor her subsequent change of mind barred admission of the tape & recipient's grand jury testimony concerning it; FURTHERMORE, "recording was admissible regardless of whose voice it was simply because it suggests that someone—anyone—other than (D) admitted to the killing, & provides a motive unrelated to (D)";

Jansen, petitioner **444 M 112 (2005)**—upheld judge's allowing D's pretrial motion for order for "buccal swab" of a third party for DNA sample (D had made very substantial showing that such a sample with pristine chain of custody would show third party rather than D to be source of sperm);

C v Rosario **444 M 550 (2005)**—after D summonsed person counsel believed to be true culprit in sale of drugs (for which D was on trial instead) & witness invoked privilege against self-incrimination, D had right to display the individual and his physical features before the jury; SJC rejects rationale that this was impermissibly "parading" witness to communicate to jury that he was invoking privilege; for appellate preservation, D-counsel adequately expressed to judge that middleman in sale to undercover cop would ID the witness as middleman's supplier (at 558 n.2);

C v Charros **443 M 752, 768 (2005)**—rejects D's claim of error in exclusion of statements by man claimed by D to be owner of drugs (apologizing for leaving D to take the blame, but saying he had to solve his own problems with police): declarant wasn't called to testify & unavailability (due to possibility of claim of privilege against self-incrimination) won't be presumed; statements didn't qualify as "against penal interest";

C v O'Brien **432 M 578, 588 (2000)**—evidence that murder victim was afraid of her brother-in-law (not D), based on his anger at her for throwing him out of her house for drug-dealing, excluded, & no "abuse of discretion" found by SJC (though trial judge has discretion to admit hearsay "to show that a 3rd party might have committed the crime for which (D) is being tried," there must be other 'substantial connecting links' to the crime);

C v Pimental **454 M 475 (2009)**—in trial as joint venturer with Silva in murder (kicking/stomping) of stranger in woods, there was evidence of D stating that he had attempted to stop Silva from continuing attack; D proffered evidence that couple of months earlier D saw Silva going after someone with knife and D stopped him; this was NOT '3rd party culprit' evidence, but instead inadmissible prior bad act offered to prove respective characters of Silva and D; EVEN IF '3rd party culprit' rule were applies, nonexistent relevant similarity (one with shod foot, one with knife; one in woods, one at D's house; one committed against an acquaintance, one a stranger);

C v Keohane **444 M 563 (2005)**—no showing that racial animus was a motive for any third party suspect to kill V, so this component of D's claim was properly excluded;

C v Alammani **439 M 605 (2003)**—D (father) sought to blame mother of shaken baby for the death, but no error in exclusion of her statements that she hadn't "bonded" with victim, and, to D, that she was "sorry": statements were too ambiguous to be probative of alleged consciousness of guilt;

C v Torres **442 M 554 (2004)**—If D had evidence that his girlfriend, four years earlier, had broken the arm of the older brother of fatally battered baby, it would have been relevant/admissible; medical records, however, "affirmatively indicate[d]" that the girlfriend wasn't responsible;

C v Evans **438 M 142 (2002)**—when police told murder eyewitness that they were bringing suspects for him to view, he refused & said he didn't want to see them, and continued to refuse after being placed in police car, and when they walked by, he gave only cursory look and said they weren't assailants; judge could exclude this on ground that it was not spontaneous utterance, but instead product of reflective thought;

C v Key **19 MAC 234 (85)**—D's evidence that 2 others did the robbery not similar enough crimes/methods;

C v Ridge **455 M 307 (2009)**—D was charged with execution-style shooting (in head) of male and female on 6/25, duct tape used over mouth, the male having been a drug dealer; on 6/26 local police received "national broadcast" from Florida police asking for contact from any agency having info on execution-style murder within past week involving two persons, possible male and female, tied to chairs & learned that the head shots and use of silver duct tape was "trademark of Columbians in the Florida drug world"; D didn't appeal trial judge's ruling that this "unknown third-party culprits" evidence was too speculative and remote for admission, but did argue that he should have been allowed to cross-examine police to argue failure to investigate (not hearsay because purportedly not "for truth of matter" that victims were killed by Columbian drug dealers); though there should have been a voir dire, no relief because probative value not shown to have outweighed "risk of unfair prejudice";

C v Hunter **426 M 715 (98)**—other available suspect's aggressive act toward murder D's girlfriend (who was not murder victim) not distinctive enough to require admission as probative of ID of killer ("the act of strangling is a relatively ordinary form of attack");

C v Bregoli **431 M 265, 274–75 (2000)**—act of grabbing a person by neck is not sufficiently similar to the lethal "crab strike" that jury could infer killed victim, only common feature being "placement of hands on the neck";

C v Rosa **422 M 18 (96)**—D's evidence re look-alike not "relevant" since "substantial connecting links" not shown; no abuse of discretion in excluding;

C v Pina **430 M 66, 77 & nn.20–21 (99)**—though D was allowed to intro fact that V's boyfriend had assaulted her three months before her murder, within judge's discretion to exclude incidents 8 months earlier and three years earlier; D's right to introduce is "limited by the fundamental principle that evidence must be relevant . . . evidence cannot be too remote or speculative";

C v Murphy **282 M 593 (33)**—similar larceny while D in custody, plus mis-ID of D; jury considers other crimes unless too remote or too weak;

C v Clarke **44 MAC 502 (98)**—not error to exclude criminal record of man police let leave apartment containing drugs with whose possession D was charged, since constructive possession need not be exclusive; man's prior crimes "were not unique or sufficiently unusual to compel inference that he, alone, was the likely perpetrator";

C v Perito **417 M 675 (94)**—similar crimes evidence D sought to introduce was correctly barred: some robberies (after D's jailing) were not "significantly comparable" as to method or description of culprit and another robbery occurred before D's arrest: he did not show he was not its perpetrator;

C v Dew **443 M 620 (2005)**—D had no right to introduce evidence of murder two days earlier in same building, also involving crack cocaine, because he didn't "provide a basis for a conclusion that he was not the perpetrator of that crime" as well; judge didn't err in limiting D's access to grand jury minutes re: that crime;

C v Graziano **368 M 325 (75)**—can cross-examine DA's witness re: his own motive/opportunity to do D's crime;

C v Rise **50 MAC 836, 844 (2001)**—that others had motive to kill V not admissible absent evidence suggesting that one or more of them actually did so;

C v Mandeville **386 M 393 (82)**—D can show someone else did it, but only by relevant, admissible evidence, not conjecture; see also *C v Silva-Santiago* **453 M 782, 799-805 (2009)**—similar; can't be just hearsay/rumor (though SJC notes that same evidence may be proffered as probative of police failure to investigate all leads);

C v Pinto **45 MAC 790 (98)**—discretion not abused in refusing to allow evidence that D's sister's boyfriend had been arrested for steroid possession 2–3 years after D's being charged with possession of steroids delivered to D's residence by postal service: evidence too remote;

See Chapter 11-I, Opinions of Experts, for relevant cases on forensics;

18-D. HYPNOTIZED WITNESSES—(HYPNOTICALLY AIDED TESTIMONY)

C v Kater (Kater I) **388 M 519 (83)**—hypnotically-aided testimony not reliable; if not recalled before hypnosis, not admissible; prospective rules for pre-hypnotic memory evidence; if admitted, D gets instruction re: hypnosis effects;

C v Brouillet **389 M 605 (83)**—witness's post-hypnosis ID = reversible error;

C v Dodge **391 M 636 (84)**—hypnotically-aided testimony re: events not recalled without hypnosis = inadmissible;

C v Kater (Kater II) **394 M 531 (85)**—pretrial judge should not have terminated evidentiary hearing on D's motion to suppress: he was obligated to conduct it & to suppress anything not shown to have been a pre-hypnotic memory;

C v Kater (Kater III) **409 M 433 (91)**—trial judge misapplied *Kater (I)* & *(II)* by failing to exclude identifications & descriptive details which exceeded witness's

pre-hypnotic memory; absolute ban not adopted; procedures clarified; dicta: hypnotized Ds have constitutional right to testify to posthypnotic facts;

C v Juvenile **381 M 727 (80)**—overview of treatment elsewhere of hypnotically-aided testimony; fn. 8: Kater guidelines; but see *C v Watson* **388 M 536 (83)** (pre-Kater) though hypnosis increased witness's certainty, ID testimony OK;

C v Stetson **384 M 545 & n.10 (81)**—(pre-Kater) hypnotically-aided testimony = cumulative & no harm;

C v Burke **20 MAC 489 (85)**—(pre-Kater) DA's burden of proof that witness's memory & testimony not influenced by hypnosis;

Liacos, Brodin & Avery, *Handbook of Massachusetts Evidence*, § 10.1.3 (7th ed. 1999)—re: IDs following hypnosis;

18-E. HEARSAY, PHOTOS, MUG SHOTS, AND EVIDENCE ISSUES

See Chapter 11-F, hearsay evidence;

18-E.1. Extrajudicial IDs: Admissibility Limits, Who May Testify Concerning

C v Daye **393 M 55 (84)**—to admit extrajudicial ID substantively, witness must acknowledge it (though now says it's mistaken); D can then cross-examine on circumstances of ID for confrontation; ID at grand jury maybe substantive evidence IF: (1) transcribed or witness recalls testimony, (2) not merely yes/no answers to leading questions, (3) testimony not coerced, (4) witness was percipi-

ent, & (5) there's additional ID evidence; **BUT SEE, NOW:**

C v Cong Duc Le **444 M 431 (2005)**—**eliminates requirement that witness must acknowledge having made the ID;** witness who purportedly observed the extrajudicial ID may testify to it, and it is substantive proof of ID;

C v Raedy **68 MAC 440 (2007)**—even though witness denied making ID of perpetrator to cop, "a reasonable jury could credit [cop's] contrary testimony", and because witness was present in court, there was no "confrontation" issue; extrajudicial identifications are admissible as probative evidence "even when they were made by the declarant in the form of a conclusory statement or accusation" (i.e., when they aren't from lineup or photo array or showup);

C v Cash **64 MAC 812 (2005)**—at trial pre-*Cong Duc Le*, D objected to testimony of cop re: 3rd person's alleged ID of D, objection was only on basis that DA was purportedly seeking to impeach cop with prior inconsistent statement (& this was incorrect, as what was happening was refreshing cop's recollection by reference to his earlier testimony at probation surrender hearing); court held even if error, no substantial risk of miscarriage of justice;

C v Kirk **39 MAC 225 (95)**—while judge didn't abuse discretion in allowing, as spontaneous utterance, evidence that victim said that her boyfriend beat her, reversal & required finding of not guilty because prosecution couldn't prove identity of boyfriend by use of pleadings & order in G.L. c. 209A domestic violence case; assertions in those documents = inadmissible hearsay; decision cites *C v Weichell* **390 M 62 (83)** (under Proposed M. R. Evid. 901[d][1][C] and case law, statement of prior identification isn't hearsay if made by witness who testifies at trial and is subject to cross-examination concerning it), *C v Kater* **409 M 433, 447 (91)** (where witness doesn't acknowledge a prior extrajudicial identification, such identification can't be proved by testimony of person who observed the identification, and can't be admitted for its probative value), and *C v Daye* **393 M 55 (84)**;

But now see *C v Cong Duc Le* **444 M 431 (2005)**—"*Daye*" rule [**393 M 55, 60–63 (84)**] modified: **now, Commonwealth may use pretrial ID evidence SUBSTANTIVELY, even if witness testifies that he or she did NOT make the identification claimed** (so long as witness is available at trial to be examined) confrontation concerns rejected by Supreme Court in *US v Owens* **484 US 554, 559–63 (88)**;

C v Robinson **451 M 672 (2008)**—no relief for admission, over Confrontation Clause objection, of unavailable witness's purportedly spontaneous exclamation "That's the two guys", notwithstanding D's persuasive argument, citing *US v Hinton* 423 F3d 355, 360–61 (3d Cir. 2005) & *US v Pugh* 405 F3d 390, 399 (6th Cir. 2005) that witness would have reasonably anticipated that statement would be used in prosecution, and was thus "testimonial";

C v Delong **72 MAC 42 (2008)**—detective testified that he showed photo array to four store employees and that each ID'd D as robber: this testimony as to the one employee who did NOT appear as a trial witness was inadmissible "irrespective of *Crawford v Washington* 541 US 36 (2004)" Confrontation clause ground (not Constitutionally required to be applied here because Crawford decided after direct appeal here) but no substantial risk of miscarriage of justice;

C v Ragland **72 MAC 815, further rev. denied 452 M 1110 (2008)**—apart from witness's recanted grand jury testimony that D wielded knife during altercation (held to have been substantively admissible), witness's photo ID was substantively admissible under *Cong Duc Le*;

C v Ivy **55 MAC 851 (2002)**—Appeals Court rejects D's argument under *C v Daye* that purported "spontaneous utterance" of victim identifying D as her assailant was inadmissible because victim did not testify at trial & wasn't shown to be unavailable; decision cites *C v Medrala*, 20 MAC 398 (85), saying "different hearsay exception" is involved in *C v Daye*;

C v Martin **417 M 187 (94)**—witness "not sure" that probable cause hearing transcript was her testimony: description of assailant's clothing there given thus not admissible as substantive evidence; court again reserves question whether prior testimony admissible to impeach present claimed lack of memory (when circumstances indicate that witness is "falsifying a lack of memory");

C v Sineiro **432 M 735 (2000)**—if judge concludes trial witness is falsifying lack of memory, probable cause hearing admissible substantively despite lack of corroborative testimony, citing *Daye* **393 M 55 (84)** and purporting to reserve judgment on whether Prop.M.R.Evid. 804 should be adopted;

C v Fitzgerald **376 M 402 (78)**—non-ID (e.g., cop) witness's testimony = substantive re: W#2's extrajudicial ID though no trial ID by W#2, but only if W#2 acknowledges making the prior ID;

C v Bassett **21 MAC 713 (86)**—cop can't tell of witness's ID (especially by unsanitized mug shots) because witness didn't so testify;

C v Muse **35 MAC 466 (93)**—(same);

C v Rivera **51 MAC 99, 105–6, further appellate review denied 434 M 1104 (2001)**—Appeals Court fails to acknowledge implicit hearsay (conveyed to jury that co-D was brought to nearby scene to make, and did make, ID of D as cohort; no other relevance possible for contested evidence that co-D had been brought to the scene where cops were questioning D); for recognition of implicit hearsay of this type in non-identification context, see *C v Ashman* **430 M 736, 741 (2000)**;

C v McAfee **430 M 483, 493 (99)**—after witness ID's D at trial, evidence that witness made prior extrajudicial ID of D = admissible both to corroborate in-court ID and as substantive evidence of D's guilt; mug shots used in extrajudicial ID may be admitted IF Commonwealth shows some need for their introduction, they are offered in form that doesn't imply prior record, and manner of intro doesn't "call attention to their source";

C v Martinez **431 M 168, 175–76 (2000)**—neither "verbal completeness" doctrine nor *C v Daye* is authority for introducing every prior consistent statement made by identification witness out of court to police (e.g., witness's version of how many shots were fired, color of gun, witness's allegedly good vantage point, witness's out-of-court statements as to assailant's alleged behavior after the shooting); prior consistent statements are inadmissible hearsay (*see Chapter 11-F, Hearsay*);

C v Britto **433 M 596, 609 (2001)**—after admitting videotape of witness identifying defendant in lineup as man that "could be" assailant, error to allow introduction of statements by witness in cruiser later that he was sure because he knew what it's like "to be locked up" and didn't "want to identify someone who didn't do it; can't use for "corroborative" value in witness's direct examination "matters outside the extrajudicial identification procedure" (& cf. *C v Santoli* **424 M 837 (97)** upon request, remove from "model" jury instructions the factor of "strength of witness's certainty" as indicator of worth of ID (reliability and confidence aren't necessarily correlated));

C v Day **42 MAC 242 (97)**—failure to object to cop's telling of witness's ID (witness did not so testify) = ineffective assistance of counsel;

C v Warren **430 M 137, 141 (88)**—witness other than ID'g witness can't testify to out-of-court ID until after ID witness has testified to the out-of-court ID;

C v Dinkins **415 M 715 (93)**—cop's testifying to a timely ID by witness (denied by witness at trial) should have been limited to impeachment, but failure to object & other circumstances = no relief;

See Chapter 7-K (Prior Reported Testimony as Substantive Evidence), and Chapter 11-F (Evidence, Hearsay) for cases on Daye rule, i.e., C v Berrio **407 M 37 (90)** *Daye rule not limited to identification;*

C v Riccard **410 M 718 (91)**—cop's testimony about eyewitness's photo identification should have been suppressed where eyewitness's in-court identification was stricken as product of suggestive showing of single photo of D by prosecutor 1 or 2 days before trial;

C v Morgan **30 MAC 685 (91)**—cop's testimony about eyewitness's out-of-court description was inadmissible where eyewitness did not testify about prior description;

C v Perez **27 MAC 550 (89)**—same; BUT SEE NOW

C v Machorro (no. 1) **72 MAC 377 (2008)**—*Cong Duc Le* **444 M 431 (2005)** effectively overruled *Morgan*; here, 2 women followed their assailant on street, obtained police assistance for his arrest, and (according to cops) ID'd him on street at his arrest; neither could ID D at trial, but one affirmed that she had ID'd assailant on street, and other was not asked if she had made such ID; cop's testimony as to latter's on-street ID = admissible, D being free to cross-examine the woman re: her trial testimony that she was "pretty sure" man arrested was assailant;

C v Almeida **34 MAC 901 (92)**—where defense elicited from cop on cross-examination that witness to bank robbery identified photo of someone other than D, prosecutor did not violate *Daye* rule when on redirect prosecutor elicited that witness identified D's photograph on later occasion because allowed under "rule of completeness";

C v Furtick **386 M 477 (82)**—cop can't substantively prove extrajudicial ID by witness who denies making it; but can tell it to impeach the witness; BUT SEE *C v Benoit* **32 MAC 111 (92)** though DA asserted that D's brother had previously told others that D confessed to him, DA also advised that the brother would testify now that he never had any conversation with D; ERROR to introduce this testimony (in effect, that witness had no evidence to offer) for sole purpose of "impeaching" it (with info that

would undoubtedly be used substantively, despite "limiting" instruction that there was thus no testimony before jury); and *C v McAfee* **430 M 483 (99)** embracing logic and holding of *Benoit* **32 MAC 111 (92)**;

C v Rivera **397 M 244 (86)**—witness #1 can tell about witness #2's ID, including "I never forget face," because #2 corroborated it; BUT see *C v Santoli* **424 M 837 (97)** degree of confidence isn't indicator of accuracy (so irrelevant) and *C v Britto* **433 M 596 (2001)** witness's self-corroboration re: ID = disapproved;

C v Vitello **376 M 426 (78)**—extrajudicial ID may "in appropriate case" suffice for G. without more; ID near event generally more reliable;

C v Odware **429 M 231 (99)**—in case where ID witness took 5th Amendment, and D introduced, in direct examination of cop-witness, that non-testifying witness ID'd someone other than D, cop could testify to fact that witness, on different occasion, ID'd "another person";

C v Jones **407 M 168 (90)**—cop's testimony about out-of-court photo identifications by eyewitnesses who denied making them was properly admissible for impeachment purposes, at least where counsel failed to object; but see *C v Benoit* **32 MAC 111, 114–15 (92)** (non-ID issue) when a witness has no positive evidence to offer, "impeachment by prior inconsistent statement may not be permitted where employed as a mere subterfuge to get before the jury evidence not otherwise admissible" (citations omitted);

C v Evans **438 M 142 (2002)**—when police told murder eyewitness that they were bringing suspects for him to view, he refused & said he didn't want to see them, and continued to refuse after being placed in police car, and when they walked by, he gave only cursory look and said they weren't assailants; judge could exclude this on ground that it was not spontaneous utterance, but instead product of reflective thought;

C v Amado **387 M 179 (82)**—without proof of positive extrajudicial ID by witness now saying D not the assailant, required finding of not guilty; see *C v Ivy* **55 MAC 851 (2002)**—Appeals Court rejects D's argument under *C v Daye* that purported "spontaneous utterance" of victim identifying D as her assailant was inadmissible because victim did not testify at trial & wasn't shown to be unavailable; decision cites *C v Medrala*, **20 MAC 398 (85)**, saying "different hearsay exception" is involved in *C v Daye*;

18-E.2. Bite Mark

C v Cifizzari **397 M 560 (86)**—ID by bite mark admissible;

18-E.3. Voice ID

C v Perez **411 M 249, 262 (91)**—telephone voice identification admissible if 3-part foundation laid (witness must be familiar with caller's voice, & must have identified voice at time of call & personally heard the conversation), citing *Chartrand v Registrar of Motor Vehicles* **345 M 321 (63)**;

C v Cruz **445 M 589, 596 (2005)**—model ID instruction (*Rodriguez* 378 M at 310–11) is adequate, "applicable to assessing 'earwitness' testimony as well"; judge purportedly "made clear to jurors that a witness may use different senses to make [ID]";

C v Carpinto **37 MAC 51 (94)**—woman to whom call was made, tape-recorded the call; though she made no ID at time of call, she later made voice ID (after hearing D whisper to her in court "I didn't do it") out of & in court: OK because tape was "permanent storage medium" unlike "ephemeral conversation that cannot be recreated for the witness (or the jury)";

C v Lykus **367 M 191 (75)**—voiceprint = scientifically accepted (see *Marini* **375 M 510 (78)** voice = "grave dangers," so should avoid 1-to-1 auditions & witness seeing participants; don't use words from incident; but no per se exclusion of 1:1 voice ID; & Chapter 11-I, Opinions (voice ID))

C v Saunders **50 MAC 865 (2001)**—after witness made no ID at police station showup & witness was leaving area, he heard D speak & immediately ID'd voice as that of robber; police hadn't prompted D, & words weren't those spoken at robbery: no suppression;

18-E.4. Mug Shots (and Other Evidence of Prior Criminality), Limitations on Use, Sanitize, Cautionary Instructions

K. Smith, *Criminal Practice & Procedure*, §§ 466–68 (2d ed. 1983 & Supp.)—mug shots, sanitizing photos, source, etc.

C v Smith **21 MAC 619 (86) (aff'd 400 M 1002)**—mug shot bad if no ID issue;

C v Barrett **386 M 649 (82)**—(same), but harmless here;

C v McCray **40 MAC 936 (96)**—when ID not in issue, bar intro of mug shot array: irrelevant & prejudicial;

C v Blaney **387 M 628 (82)**—mug shot introduced (& testimony) should be "sanitized" to avoid inference D has prior record;

C v McAfee **430 M 483 (99)**—mug shots may be admitted where (1) prosecution shows need for introduction (2) they are offered in form that does not imply prior criminal record (3) manner of introduction doesn't call attention to source;

C v DeJesus **71 MAC 799 (2008)**—police testimony accompanying admission of array pointed out compilation from database of those with arrest history, and made clear that D was not available to be photographed contemporaneously with THIS crime (so police already had his photo prior to this shooting) and should not have been elicited; judge immediately offered curative instruction which defense counsel declined in favor of inclusion in final general jury charge, whose curative power SJC found insufficient ("stronger instruction was required directing the jury to ignore the testimony insofar as it indicated that [D] had a prior arrest record"); SJC finds lacking second prong of ineffective assistance claim (counsel's omission did not deprive D of otherwise available substantial ground of defense);

C v Day **42 MAC 242, 246–48 (97)**—sanitizing essential;

C v Gee **36 MAC 154 (94)**—conviction reversed for failure to sanitize D's mug shot or any others in array (each holding police department placard, witness calling pictures "criminals", evidence making clear that photo existed before D's current arrest);

C v Taylor **455 M 372 (2009)**—cautionary instruction that police have individuals' photos for numerous reasons, when repeated, gave as one reason "applications for gun permits"; this = "unfortunate," because prosecution contended D had a gun used in murder (defense being D had no part in crime, witness lying): no objection, no relief;

C v Martin **447 M 274 (2006)**—no error in admitting mugshot of D which victim failed to select, to indicate that failure was because D's appearance at time of crime differed from photo;

C v Naylor **73 MAC 518 (2009)**—asserting ineffective assistance of counsel in failing to utilize a booking photo of D (for different charges) taken 5 weeks before date of offense being tried, showing distinctive hairstyle and facial hair not said to characterize culprit; n.11: re: any reluctance to introduce out of concern for prejudicial effect of separate arrest, redaction to eliminate circumstances "may well have been possible by stipulation or otherwise";

C v Smith **29 MAC 449 (90)**—prosecution was entitled to introduce sanitized photo array to show how D came to be identified;

C v Kachoul **69 MAC 352 (2007)**—rejects D's argument that ID lineup and selection shouldn't have been admitted since ID was conceded by D: credibility of complainant (who used antipsychotic medications) was at issue, and her ability to ID D months later in fair lineup = relevant to her memory, powers of observation, & recollection, AND, unlike mugshots, lineup didn't signal that D had history of criminal involvement (because it was only because of current accusations); because here there was some "probative value" to the lineup ID, judge had discretion to admit it;

C v Hrycenko **61 MAC 378 (2004)**—given 16 months between crime/identification & trial, & witnesses' inability to ID D in court (known before trial because lineup on morning of trial resulted in ID of cop rather than D), OK to introduce police photo (front & profile) as ground for jury inference that failure to ID D on day of trial resulted from change in his appearance;

C v Day **42 MAC 242 (97)**—D counsel's intro of unsanitized flyer (D's photo with text asserting criminal record, gang membership, and 'armed & dangerous'), albeit to show tainted IDs by witnesses, was ineffective assistance of counsel;

C v Vardinski **438 M 444 (2003)**—D counsel was entitled to cross-examine ID witness, and to introduce fact that witness signed a photo of D on which there was recorded info that D had been previously convicted of gun possession (to imply that witness's ID was thus bolstered in witness's mind); judge's redaction of photo under these circumstances was reversible error;

C v Thayer **39 MAC 396 (95)**—unsanitized mug shot with notation "armed robbery" = reversal;

C v Austin **421 M 357 (95)**—videotape of bank robbery (not one being tried) was used by witnesses for ID; no error in its introduction because "not amenable to" sanitization and curative instructions given;

C v Cruz **445 M 589 (2005)**—no error in allowing introduction of 5 different photos of D, all selected by sole witness from police file of 1,344 photos: ID/alibi was defense and witness recognized the voice of masked & hatted robber as convenience store customer;

C v Richardson **425 M 765 (97)**—"better" to both sanitize mug shots and sever the 2 views (front/side), but within judge's discretion not to crop the views;

C v Payton **35 MAC 586 (93)**—same; not ineffective assistance of counsel to urge admission, given trial strategy of demonstrating that IDs were suggested by array's composition (only D was heavy-set);

C v Key **21 MAC 293 (85)**—cop's reasons for including D's photo (unrelated crime & "resembled" suspect) = irrelevant/prejudicial;

C v Delong **72 MAC 42, 50 (2008)**—detective's testimony ID'ing D as man in photo taken from surveillance video not relevant or admissible, though given in course of explanation why D was arrested: "[w]hether the photographs were of [D] was for the jury, not for a conclusion by a witness";

18-E.5. Opinions as to Identity

C v Key **21 MAC 293 (85)**—error to admit evidence re: circumstances in which photograph had been taken, including testimony that, after D had been arrested on unrelated charge, cop thought D looked like photo selected earlier by V as resembling her assailant;

C v Austin **421 M 357 (95)**—witness's testimony that D was person depicted in bank's surveillance videotape was inadmissible "opinion" evidence (here harmless);

C v Delong **72 MAC 42, 50 (2008)**—detective's testimony that D was person depicted in surveillance video inadmissible, but no objection, no relief here;

C v Pleas **49 MAC 321 (2000)**—it was within trial judge's discretion to allow witness who had known D & his family socially for 9 years to testify that robber in ATM surveillance videotape was D; admissibility dependent on several factors, but shouldn't allow such opinion testimony if image is "unmistakably clear" (no need) or "hopelessly obscure" (witness is no better able than jury to decide);

witness must be shown to be quite familiar with person's appearance at time photo was taken; such testimony more likely to be helpful if culprit disguised 'self in photo or changed appearance since time of crime; this witness happened to be cop, & it would have been preferable for him not to reveal such occupation (cop's knowledge of D was social, not professional);

C v DiBenedetto **427 M 414 (98)**—witness's opinion as to whether anyone in lineup other than D looked in any way like culprit (sought by D counsel) properly excluded as opinion; jury viewed video of lineup and could make own determination of possible infirmities;

18-E.6. Composite Sketches

C v Weichell **390 M 62 (83)**—composite sketches = substantive evidence of ID as long as not prepared under suggestive circumstances;

C v Thornley **400 M 355 (87)**—composite sketch created jointly by two witnesses & not overly suggestive procedure = admissible;

K. Smith, *Criminal Practice & Procedure,* **§ 471 (2d ed. 1983 & Supp.)**—composites;

18-E.7. Lost/Missing Evidence Re: Identification

See Chapter 7-L (Evidence Lost by Police/DA), Chapter 6-D (Sanctions for Discovery Violations);

C v Rodriguez **50 MAC 405 (2000)**—when exhibits at rape trial were lost while in possession of clerk of Superior Court between 1st trial and 2d trial, & defense was identification, jurors were instructed that "if there is a dispute as to the description or any other physical characteristic of that missing physical evidence, and if your collective inability actually to look at that evidence raises in your mind a doubt about the actual description . . . or . . . a doubt as to any other physical attribute or characteristic of that evidence, then you must resolve that doubt in favor of the defendant"; dismissal of charges not required (because evidence had been available to D previously, & was analyzed, with opportunity for D to engage own experts & cross-examine Commonwealth experts at 1st trial);

C v Walker **14 MAC 544 (82)**—if D asks, DA should preserve; if lost, weigh government culpability, materiality, & prejudice; none shown from failure to take prints & losing beer can, nor in commingling (i.e., losing) the photo witness said "resembled" culprit;

C v Perito **417 M 674 (94)**—"fuzzy" videotape of convenience store robber, returned to store before D became a suspect, and later destroyed by store: no culpability, useless, no prejudice;

C v Cameron **25 MAC 538 (88)**—no dismissal, but D can cross-examine re: lost videotape, & DA can't say defective because that explanation's too late & speculative;

C v Harwood **432 M 290 (2000)**—loss of original letter, without which defendant's expert couldn't evaluate signature (copy inadequate for purpose), justified sanction of preclusion of testimony from prosecution witness saying that the signature wasn't his (Commonwealth contended D

forged signature); court reasoned that D had lost opportunity to effectively cross-examine the witness;

18-F. SUPPRESSION

See also Chapters 6–7, Pretrial Conference & Discovery (of ID & Photos), Motions, Continuances;

C v Powell **72 MAC 22 (2008)**—though defense counsel made no objection to judge's decision not to hold evidentiary hearing on motion to suppress ID apart from jury-waived trial and thus no relief for this D, "seamless integration of a hearing on a motion to suppress with a trial on the merits should be avoided"; "distinct hearing, even if in voir dire, is preferable to what occurred here";

Loftus/Doyle (Chapter 18-A, ante) at § 6.17—suggestive ID's; (*See also 18-A, ante, re: right to counsel for in-court ID's*);

C v Simmons **383 M 46 (81)**—unless extreme case, ID of inanimate thing isn't under same due process rules;

C v Spann **383 M 142 (81)**—(same) for ID of dead V (but voir dire was OK);

***C v Silva-Santiago* 453 M 782 (2009)**—extensive citation of defense expert's testimony re: suggestive vs. recommended ID procedures; recognition that "double blind" procedure (administered by officer who does NOT know identity of suspect) is "the better practice because it eliminates the risk of conscious or unconscious suggestion"; assertion that it is "practicable in nearly all circumstances" before photo array is shown to make clear that wrongdoer may or may not be in the array, that regardless of whether ID is made, investigation will continue, that officer should "ask the witness to state, in own words, how certain he is of any identification, that persons in array may not appear exactly as on date of incident because of changeable features (hair, weight), etc.; recognition that "simultaneous" rather than 'sequential' display of photos may lead to false positive (as judgment/ID may be only a "relative" one), though assertion that there is ongoing "debate among scholars" re: this;

C v Watson **455 M 246 (2009)**—noting that *Silva-Santiago* 453 M 782 "declined to hold" that absence of ID protocol or prescribed warnings (just as important to "clear" innocent person as to ID guilty; culprit might not be in array; police would continue investigation regardless of whether witness made ID) = reversal, and again declining to do so "but reiterat[ing] our expectation that the [ID] protocol set forth in [Silva-Santiago] will be employed in the regular course of administering [arrays]"; no suppression here despite facts that cop told witness that suspect's photo WAS in array;

18-F.1. Discover Pertinent Facts

CPCS P/G 4.5(a)—discover ID details; 4.7(g): consider motion to suppress ID;

C v Dougan **377 M 303 (79)**—right to be informed of the details of any out-of-court identification, even if it were not used at trial;

Utility of motion to suppress, though don't expect to win, for—(1) discovery, (2) counsel, D, DA, & judge evaluate DA's case & witnesses, & (3) create inconsistent statements; drawbacks = (1) DA & witness rehearse, & (2) hurts plea bargain if witnesses do well; schedule hearing well before trial to get transcript;

Kimmelman v Morrison **477 US 365 (86)**—ineffective assistance of counsel in not filing motion to suppress (statement) because got no discovery (because relied on DA's "practice" of volunteering info);

K. Smith, *Criminal Practice & Procedure*, **§ 1342 (2d ed. 1983 & Supp.)**—discretion to hear from expert re: motion to suppress ID (*see Chapter 18-A*);

18-F.2. Motion to Suppress, Form

Loftus/Doyle (Chapter 18-A, ante) §§ 6.19–6.28—motions, memos, & strategy;

M.R.Crim.P. 13—Pretrial Motions = written, timely, state grounds, have affidavit "detailing all facts relied upon . . . & signed . . . with personal knowledge"; motion to suppress must have memorandum of law when filed;

Superior Court Rule 61—motion to suppress must be filed within 7 days after date for filing pretrial conference report, or at such other time as court may allow;

C v Chase **14 MAC 1032 (82)**—insufficient motion to suppress affidavit ("information & belief" ID's "suggestive & unreliable");

C v Martin **63 MAC 587, 591 (2005), reversed on other ground [merits], 447 M 274 (2006)**—D's motion to suppress ID, resting on constitutional principles, preserved issue; "no need . . . to renew his objection after the pretrial motion hearing";

18-F.3. Unnecessarily Suggestive ID, Due Process Violation; Burdens of Proof

C v Botelho **369 M 860 (76)**—due process: suppress unnecessarily suggestive procedure conducive to irreparably mistaken ID; then DA's burden of proof "clear & convincing" that in-court ID has independent source; factors: (1) opportunity to observe culprit, (2) witness's attentiveness at time, (3) prior descriptions, ID'd another, or failed to ID D, (4) witness's certainty at ID (no longer legitimate factor—see *Santoli* 424 M 837 (97); but see *Silva-Santiago* 453 M 782, 798 (2009)—at time of ID procedure, witness should be asked about this, as "certainty" may be pegged higher at time of trial simply because law enforcement agents have 'confirmed' witness's ID)), (5) time gap from incident;

C v Watson **455 M 246, 254 (2009)**—witness's expression of 95% certainty = a factor which judge could use in deciding whether cop's actions may have been unduly suggestive; certainty here "was not being considered in the context of a secondary analysis following a judicial determination that [ID] was impermissibly suggestive";

Manson v Brathwaite **432 US 98 (77)**—"reliability" = "linchpin" suppression issue; though suggestive out-of-court ID, admit in-court if "reliable"; factors (p. 114 & *Botelho* above) especially opportunity to observe; [but SJC rejects "reliability" test in *Johnson* 420 M 458 (95)]

C v Venios **378 M 24 (79)**—SJC undecided between *Manson* "reliability" & *Botelho* "independent source" tests, so trial judges are asked to use both; here, showing 1 photo after showing arrays—OK

C v Thornley (II) **406 M 96 (89)**—array in which D's photo was only one with glasses was unduly suggestive & required suppression where witness relied on glasses in making identification; open question whether *Manson v Braithwaite* will be adopted in Massachusetts; see fn. 3 at 98 for proper application of *Botelho*;

C v Johnson **420 M 458 (95)**—SJC rejects *Manson v Braithwaite*, (unnecessarily suggestive IDs admissible if judge believes they're reliable), instead adopts under Article 12 per se rule that unnecessarily suggestive IDs = inadmissible and subsequent IDs inadmissible unless shown ("clear & convincing" evidence) to have independent source (factors = opportunity to observe offender, time lapse between event & ID, any prior errors in description, any ID of another person, and failure to ID D, receipt of suggestions);

C v Martin **447 M 274 (2006)**, 4:3 decision, reversing Appeals Court's order of suppression (63 MAC 587), and holding that D didn't meet burden of proving showup so unnecessarily suggestive & conducive to irreparable mistaken identification as to deny him due process of law; fact that V's father was present at showup independently, inferably because HE had selected D as the culprit by description, not controlling given motion judge's findings as to V's independence & credibility; DISSENT charges that majority opinion "eviscerates" holding in *Austin* 421 M 357 (95) that there should be a GOOD REASON to conduct inherently suggestive showup; "recharacterizes" a showup as instead a "continuous nonsuggestive line up"; & essentially calls into question the holding in *Johnson* (420 M 458 (95)) which specifically rejected the "reliability" test of *Manson v Brathwaite*;

C v Hill **64 MAC 131 (2005)**—showup conducted 24 hours after crime OK: car & its driver stopped for running a red light matched description of car (with unique features) & culprit in housebreak < mile away on the preceding morning; driver was detained an extra 15 minutes for ID by victim; traffic-stop cop was same cop who interviewed victim & neighbor who described car;

Loftus/Doyle (Chapter 18-A, above) §§ 6.17(d), 6.18, 9.5(b)—problem is showing that in-court ID is "fruit," i.e., no independent source;

C v Viriyahiranpaiboon **412 M 224 (92)**—witness permitted to describe features of person he saw even though identification itself suppressed;

C v Watson **455 M 246 (2009)**—D didn't establish that first ID from array was impermissibly suggestive, so Commonwealth not required to show subsequent ID had "independent source"; second ID wasn't unnecessarily suggestive either (witness's first photo array ID was at hospital, and he was medicated and just awakened, though wanted to go forward; second photo array ID [same photos, but different placement of D in sequential showings of individual pictures] occurred next day when witness wasn't so impaired); fn.7: IF first ID was impermissibly suggestive, second one couldn't be used "to bolster first" ID so as to make it admissible;

18-F.4. Showups, One-on-One Identifications

Stovall v Denno **388 US 293 (67)**—1:1 showup OK if exigency makes speed imperative; showup at witness's hospital room (for major surgery) = OK ID;

C v Moon **380 M 751 (80)**—no exigency justified showing 1 photo (D's license) & saying D's a suspect;

Contrast: *C v Whitlock* **74 MAC 320 (2009)**—1 cop showing undercover cop-drug buyer a single photo after stating his belief that he knew identity of seller "may have been suggestive," but MAC excuses on blanket assertion that "experienced" cop was "obviously alert and using every opportunity he had to observe"; context here = claim of ineffective assistance of counsel for failing to file motion to suppress ID, and holding = suppression motion "had no realistic chance of success"; but cf. *Williams* 54 MAC 236, 242–43 (2002) (refusal to instruct on ID by cop = reversal); *Williams* 58 MAC 139, 142 (2003) (refusal to instruct on possibility of undercover cop's good-faith mistake in ID = reversal); *Martinez* 67 MAC 788, 800 n.4 (2006) (Berry, J., dissenting) ("that it was [cop], rather than a lay person, who was shown an unnecessarily suggestive photograph does not . . . trump overarching constitutional protections"); *Brathwaite* 432 U.S. at 130 (Marshall, J., dissenting) (mere fact that police officer has been "trained" to be "observant" does not guarantee that he is correct in a specific case and his ID testimony should be scrutinized just as carefully as that of lay witness); see also *Kelly* 417 M 266, 271–72 (94); *McCoy* 59 MAC 284, 296–97 (2009) (improper to urge jury to trust cop witnesses simply because they are cops);

C v Coy **10 MAC 367 (80)**—showups "promptly" after crime = OK for; "efficient investigation" immediately after crime; exigency not required; fresh memory preferable; if negative, cops can keep looking;

C v Bumpus **354 M 494 (68)**—OK to bring D fitting description to witness 30 minutes after B&E;

C v Martinez **67 MAC 788 (2006)**—OK to bring single "surveillance" photo of D to undercover cop who purchased drugs 20 minutes earlier;

C v Walker **421 M 90 (95)**—OK to bring D to witness 2 weeks after robbery when witness alerted police that she had just seen culprit again;

C v Johnson **420 M 458 (95)**—not OK to bring witness to 2 Ds day after crime;

C v Martin **447 M 274 (2006):** in 4:3 decision, SJC overruled Appeals Court's holding that showup was unnecessarily suggestive (see **63 MAC 587 [2005]**—showup ID made four days after assault suppressed by App. Ct. as unnecessarily suggestive ["this case falls completely outside the realm of those approved in the past . . . no exigent circumstances . . . [not] within the immediate aftermath of the crime"]; victim's father had assiduously assisted in dragnet search for culprit & was the person who initiated the detention of D); dissent is appalled at use by majority of term "continuous nonsuggestive lineup" as substitute for "showup" ("before today, this court has on no occasion concluded that a showup was not inherently suggestive because it had been preceded by other showups . . . it is unclear how, after this decision, we can continue to declare that showups are");

C v Santos **402 M 775 (88)**—1:1 at police station too suggestive where witness retarded, suggestible, & off in descriptions;

C v Levasseur **32 MAC 629 (92), cert. denied, 506 US 1053 (93)**—1-on-1 confrontation after victim had looked at thousands of mug shots & after selecting D's photo from array of 60 not unduly suggestive;

K. Smith, *Criminal Practice & Procedure*, §§ 445–52 (2d ed. 1983 & Supp.)—showups, one-on-one identifications, & accidental encounters;

C v Drumgold **423 M 230 (96)**—DEFENSE COUNSEL CREATED 1:1 photo ID (where no ID by witness previously existed) by showing D's photo to prosecution witness during trial preparation; SJC (unconvincingly) held no ineffective assistance of counsel; allowing D to attend jury view created another out-of-court ID by same witness;

C v Storey **378 M 312 (79)**—1:1, photo or person, = serious danger & "disfavored"; but no per se exclusion rule;

C v Sylvia **57 MAC 66 (2003)**—no relief for showing only two photos to undercover cop after his purchase of drugs; cop observed D for five minutes, ID was made 30–40 minutes later; *C v Martinez* **67 MAC 788 (2006)**—OK to show single "surveillance" photo of alleged drug seller to undercover cop within twenty minutes of drug buy; cop had clear view of seller as he leaned into car window for hand to hand exchange; *C v Vasquez* **75 MAC 446 (2009)**—appellate counsel argued ineffective assistance in trial counsel's failure to move to suppress 1:1 photo ID made by undercover cop one day after drug buy: while procedure "may not have been favored, it was permissible"; that it would have been possible to use a larger array did not make this procedure impermissibly suggestive;

[S.C. on other single issue reported to SJC by MAC is at 456 M 350 (2010)];

18-F.5. One-on-One Voice ID

C v Marini **375 M 510 (78)**—voice ID = "grave dangers," so should avoid 1-to-1 auditions & witness seeing participants; don't use words from incident; but no per se exclusion of 1:1 voice ID; see also *White* **11 MAC 953 (81)**;

C v Miles **420 M 67 (95)**—voice ID properly admitted;

C v Powell **10 MAC 57, n.4 (80)**—1:1 voice ID repeating assailant's words = unnecessarily suggestive;

See K. Smith, *Criminal Practice & Procedure*, § 444 (2d ed. 1983 & Supp.)—voice ID during lineup;

C v Saunders **50 MAC 865 (2001)**—after witness made no ID at police station showup & witness was leaving area, he heard D speak & immediately ID'd voice as that of robber; police hadn't prompted D, & words weren't those spoken at robbery: no suppression;

C v Pagano **47 MAC 55 (99)**—within discretion to exclude defense expert on high potential for inaccurate voice ID when based on contact of short duration;

C v Enos **26 MAC 1006 (88)**—more leeway for non-D voice ID; (*cf. Chapter 11-D, "Relevance & Materiality"*);

18-F.6. Photo Arrays

Loftus/Doyle (§ A, above) at §§ 4.5–4.6—Photos;

K. Smith, *Criminal Practice & Procedure*, §§ 435–40 (2d ed. 1983 & Supp.)—suggestive photo ID's;

C v Gordon **6 MAC 230 (78)** though photo array unfair (only D's hair braided), irreparable mis-ID unlikely, so OK within Manson; cf. *C v Moon* **380 M 751 (80)** in response to witness's very general description of culprit, cop said "sounds like (D)," cop entered nearby car surmised by witness to be connected to culprit (after learning by radio it belonged to D), cop took from car a photo of D & showed it, alone, to witness, who ID'd D as culprit: suppression of ID, and of wallet & photo; SJC left open issue of whether manner in which police obtained photo itself required suppression of identification as the fruit of illegal search and seizure;

C v Napolitano **378 M 599 (79)**—all array photos need not match culprit's description, especially changeable characteristics;

C v Mobley **369 M 892 (76)**—OK though 6 photos & only D had hat (like robber);

C v Silva-Santiago **453 M 782, 795 (2009)**—OK though purportedly only D had "fade" haircut;

C v Avery **12 MAC 97 (81)**—OK though 3 photos of D in array of 18; where opportunity to observe = several hours, it's reliable;

C v LaFaille **430 M 44 (99)**—OK though array included two photos of D (different hairstyles);

C v Thornley **400 M 355 (87)**—13 photos & only D with glasses (like suspect) = suggestive; remand re: conducive to mistake & violate due process;

C v Melvin **399 M 201, n.10 (87)**—though we "disapprove" if array distinguishes 1 suspect from others on a physical characteristic, we've sustained many where clearly not picked on that basis;

C v Downey **407 M 472 (90)**—cop's deliberate inclusion of D's photo in array improper only where array too small (here 9 was ample); cop's removal of look-alike photo previously identified by witness was not miscarriage of justice (i.e., OBJECT, and there may be a different result!);

C v Scott **408 M 811 (90)**—successive arrays with D's photos not unduly suggestive where D's photos varied substantially & photos of others also repeated;

C v Paszko **391 M 164 (84)**—though *Simmons v US* **390 US 37, 383 (68)** notes that danger of mis-ID increases if police show witness "pictures of several persons among which the photograph of a single such individual recurs or is in some way emphasized," duplication of D's photo in one or more arrays doesn't compel exclusion of resulting ID; see also *C v Kostka* **370 M 516, 523–24 (76)** (witness shown 12 photos including 2 of D); *C v Mobley* **369 M 892, 896–97 (76)** (witness shown six photographs including 1 of D, then shown second array including photo of D committing unrelated robbery);

C v Santos **41 MAC 621 (96)**—fact that only D's photo appeared in 2 successive arrays of about 13 photos did not compel suppression of resulting ID;

C v Martin **447 M 274 (2006): SJC (4:3 decision) overrules** Appeals Court's finding [63 MAC 587] of unnecessary suggestiveness in showup ID made 4 days after assault where victim's father had assiduously assisted in dragnet search for culprit & was the person who initiated the detention of D, & photo ID later on same day was by photo of D wearing same clothes as at showup;

C v Smith **414 M 437 (93)**—not unduly suggestive to show witness more than 300 photos (no ID) and then show an array of 8, in which D's photo was only one not shown previously;

18-F.7. Lineups

See Chapter 18-A re: lineup requests & counsel's role at them;

K. Smith, *Criminal Practice & Procedure,* **§§ 441–44 (2d ed. 1983 & Supp.)**—suggestive lineups;

Kirby v Illinois **406 US 682 (72)**—due process forbids lineup if unnecessarily suggestive & conducive to irreparable mistaken ID;

US v Wade **388 US 218 (67)**—post-indictment lineup = critical stage with right to counsel; suggested lineup procedure (n.26), e.g., prior written description by witness;

C v Simmonds **386 M 234 (82)**—no counsel right at lineup before charged; lineup OK though some with uniforms, mustaches (& culprit's clean-shaven);

US v Ash **413 US 300 (73)**—no counsel right when photo array shown to witness;

Foster v California **394 US 440 (69)**—where no ID in 1st lineup & tentative ID at later 1:1, 2d lineup denied due process;

C v Correia **381 M 65 (80)**—lineup ID OK though cops repeatedly showed D's photo before lineup & D had lightest hair;

C v Crowe **21 MAC 456 (86)**—12 people, none resembling D, = OK lineup;

18-F.8. Influence by Another Person (Joint Viewing, "Confirmations" by Police)

C v Moynihan **376 M 468 (78)**—though "obvious pitfalls" if 2 witnesses view photos together, not ipso facto suppressed;

C v Wen Chao Ye **52 MAC 850 (2001)**—refusal to find suggestiveness in 2 witnesses' simultaneous viewing of suspects, on purported ground that a police officer was present "to ensure [HOW?] that one did not influence the other";

C v Worlds **9 MAC 162 (80)**—too suggestive if 2 witnesses jointly view D (only black) at station; in-court ID of 1 suppressed because no clear/convincing proof of independent source;

C v Martin **447 M 274 (2006):** SJC in 4:3 decision overrules Appeals Court's holding (63 MAC 587) that suppression was required in part because victim's father had assiduously assisted in dragnet search for culprit & was the person who initiated the detention of D; father & several uniformed police officers were standing nearby during showup;

C v Bonnoyer **25 MAC 444 (88)**—after picking D's photo, witness expressed doubt, & cop said co-D confessed/fingered D—suppress both out-of-court AND in-court ID because D can't fairly cross-examine re: doubts without showing co-D confessed;

C v Vardinski **53 MAC 307 (2001)**—judge's barring D-counsel from cross-examining ID witness as to suggestiveness inherent in mug shot's revealing that D had been previously arrested on a firearm charge (confirmatory of witness's identification) & from introducing it in evidence as it was shown to the witness = reversal; judge had redacted from the mug shot this 'prejudicial' info & had barred mention of it before the jury; *on further appellate review, 438 M 444 (2003), SJC agrees:* judge unconstitutionally restricted D's right to cross-examine re: fairness of ID procedure;

C v Juvenile **402 M 275 (88)**—OK to suppress out-of-court & in-court ID's where cops showed 1 photo & told witness it's person charged, & where DA didn't call witness to meet burden of proof for in-court ID;

C v Martinez **67 MAC 788 (2006)**—OK to bring single "surveillance" photo of D to undercover cop who purchased drugs 20 minutes earlier; photo was used "to confirm accuracy of their investigatory information";

C v Riley **26 MAC 550 (88)**—can't tell witness #2 that #1 picked D or about D's record—even after pick, because it confirms; but reliable; judges can relieve dilemma re: cross-examination about suggestion (from D's other crimes) if asked;

C v Jackson **419 M 716 (95)**—after witness picked D's photo "immediately" from array, cop assured witness that D was guilty because of past crimes & was already in custody on unrelated charge: no taint of initial ID and, implicitly, no need thus to show subsequent IDs free of taint; (failure to acknowledge "confirmatory" value of cop's assertions)

C v Huan Lieu **50 MAC 162 (2000)**—in courthouse crowd victim pointed out, to a friend, one assailant, & friend said he knew the man as "Go"; previously, in hospital, victim had been told that one of the assailants was named "Go"; suppression not required just because witness "later learned confirmatory facts";

C v Howell **49 MAC 42, 50–51 (2000)**—after defense, during trial, elicited testimony pointing to two other men as the robbers and introduced photos of these two men, police detective showed these photos to the 3 robbery victims and detective thereafter was allowed to testify (in rebuttal) that "none of the victims recognized the two men"; appellate court asserted, disingenuously, that it was unaware of why any identification procedure which produced no identification could be found suggestive and thus unreliable and inadmissible (BUT CF, e.g., *C v Riccard* **410 M 718, 722–23 (91)** display of D's photo to witness during meeting with prosecutor days before trial unnecessarily suggestive; *C v Botelho* **369 M 860, 865–70 (76)** ID of D tainted by suggestive confrontation at courthouse; see, generally, Liacos, Brodin & Avery, *Handbook of Massachusetts Evidence*, § 4.2.3, Negative Evidence (7th ed. 1999); § 8.1, hearsay defined (testimony at issue constituted hearsay, i.e., victims said, outside court, that the photos did not depict the culprits));

C v Florek **48 MAC 414, 419 (2000)**—showup ID of D not unnecessarily suggestive on account of his being surrounded by cops and being asked to remove his shirt for ID, though appellate court relied on ID witness's testimony that he would have ID'd D even if he was wearing a shirt;

C v Austin **421 M 357 (95)**—ID of D from videotape of bank robbery **not** the one being investigated was suggestive but not "unnecessarily" so;

C v Day **42 MAC 242 (97)**—suppress photo IDs by 2 witnesses who saw police flyer on wall, bearing same photo of D and identifying D as responsible for the crime; that viewing was 'accidental' not relevant; when ID = subject of unnecessarily suggestive procedure, not admissible despite claimed reliability; but in-court ID allowed here (Commonwealth carried its burden of 'clear & convincing' on independent source);

18-F.9. Taint of Suggestiveness without Government Misconduct

C v Day **42 MAC 242 (97)**—suppression of IDs after witnesses accidentally saw police flyer identifying D as responsible for crime;

C v Otsuki **411 M 218 (91)**—witness's "accidental" confrontation with wanted poster of D not unduly suggestive;

C v Jones **423 M 99 (96)**—ID, product of suggestive confrontation & without independent source, suppressed as unreliable; irrelevant that government agents not responsible for confrontation;

US v Bouthot **878 F.2d 1506 (1st Cir. '89)**—due process may require suppression of testimony resulting from series of unduly suggestive identification procedures, even where some of procedures not orchestrated by government;

C v Colon-Cruz **408 M 533 (90)**—complainant's exposure to newspaper photo did not require suppression where cops didn't contrive its publication;

C v Odware **429 M 231 (99)**—*C v Jones* **423 M 99 (96)** distinguished; IDs in suggestive circumstances for which government not responsible admitted because not so tainted as to be unreliable, given ample other evidence (admissions, consciousness of guilt evidence, and untainted IDs); suggestiveness went to weight, not admissibility;

18-F.10. Suppression of Identification as Fruit of Illegal Search or Seizure

See also Chapter 20, post, Suppression of Physical Evidence & Statements; IDs may be 'fruit' of unconstitutional police action, e.g., C v Bodden 11 MAC 964 (81) remand to see if ID of D was "exploitation" of the illegal arrest;

US v Crews **445 US 463 (80)**—illegal arrest doesn't bar in-court ID where complaining witness described culprit before D's arrest & ID'd from observations at crime; ID not fruit of arrest because D was suspect before arrest;

C v Crowe **21 MAC 456 (86)**—discussion of Crews & independent source test;

C v Ceria **13 MAC 230 (82)**—bad arrest would require suppress later ID;

C v Moon **380 M 751, 761 (80)**—"strong possibility" that ID of D's license photo inadmissible "fruit" of illegally seized wallet, but issue wasn't raised;

C v White **11 MAC 953 (81)**—ID suppressed because unlawful arrest of D & suggestive 1:1 voice ID; in-court ID not independent or reliable;

C v Ramos **430 M 545 (2000)**—without probable cause, cops seized D by threats of having door broken down if she didn't emerge; photo of D which was then taken, and undercover cop's ID of it, ordered suppressed as fruits of illegal seizure;

18-F.11. Appellate Preservation

C v Picher **46 MAC 409, 416–17 n.8 (99)**—protect appellate rights/preserve record by photographing the array for scrutiny by appellate court (here photos were returned to police department); recording photo "numbers" so array can be recreated = seemingly acceptable alternative;

C v Hill **38 MAC 982 (95)**—after ID suppression is denied pretrial, for appellate preservation must object at trial when ID is elicited (but see *C v Whelton* **428 M 24, 25–26 (98)** denial of motion to suppress evidence on constitutional grounds "is reviewable without further objection at trial");

18-F.12. Suppression Hearing Testimony Admitted at Trial

C v Florek **48 MAC 414 (2000)**—prosecution introduced at trial the identifying witness's testimony at the hearing on D's pretrial motion to suppress ID (instead of any live testimony from this witness); appellate court found testimony "reliable," i.e. issues at both proceedings essentially same, BUT here held error only because Commonwealth not shown to have made diligent enough efforts to produce the witness at trial; BUT if motion judge limited cross-examination of witness, e.g., to bar cross on witness's capacity to have observed, should be inadmissible (cf. *C v DiBenedetto* **414 M 37, 42–44 (92)** prior judge's limitation of cross-examination (at deposition) rendered testimony inadmissible at trial).

Chapter 19
DOUBLE JEOPARDY

19-A. GENERAL PRINCIPLES AND PROCEDURES

U.S. Constitution, Fifth Amendment—no person shall be subject for the same offense to be twice put in jeopardy of life or limb;

Berry v Commonwealth **393 M 793 (85)**—Mass. double jeopardy = common law, but protections maybe (& are here (see below)) greater than state/federal constitutions; but see *Powers v Commonwealth* **426 M 534, 540 n.13 (98)** in context of driver's license revocation followed by prosecution for, **inter alia**, operating under the influence & causing serious bodily injury, Massachusetts double jeopardy protection would not be broader than Supreme Court's interpretation of 5th Amendment;

Mass. Constitution, Declaration of Rights, Article 12—no arrest, imprisonment but by "law of the land";

G.L. c. 263, § 7—prior acquittal on facts & merits bars later prosecution for same crime, notwithstanding any defect in form or substance of indictment or complaint on which he was acquitted; § 8, but no bar if acquittal was for variance or defective complaint (*see* ***ante*** *Chapter 5-D, Contents of Complaint/Indictment: Variances*); § 8A can't try D in District Court or Housing Court on 2d complaint for offense already tried on merits in such a court;

K. Smith, *Criminal Practice and Procedure,* **§§ 1303–20 (2d ed. 1983 & Supp.)**—OVERVIEW; 5th Amendment double jeopardy bar applies to states; if "same offense," bars multiple punishment or reprosecution after acquit/convict; bars increased sentence after serving;

"attaching" of jeopardy; mistrials; appeals; "same offense" rules; collateral estoppel; etc.;

LaFave, Israel, & King, *Crim. Procedure*, §§ 25.1–25.5 (2d ed. 1999)—(overview);

***Green v US* 355 US 184 (57)**—deeply ingrained idea that powerful state shouldn't have repeated chances & subject D to embarrassment, ordeal, continuing anxiety; can't discontinue trial & disband jury without D's consent; but D's appeal either waives double jeopardy bar or is continuing jeopardy; BUT guilty of lesser included offense (*see Chapter 19-B, below*) implies not guilty of greater, so can only retry for lesser included offense after appellate reversal; NOW SEE, HERE, ***C v Zanetti* 454 M 449 (2009)**—judge charged jury that if found D guilty of murder, had to specify EITHER 'principal' or 'joint venturer'; conviction as joint venturer could not stand/insufficient evidence, so required finding of not guilty ordered BUT SJC held D could be re-tried because would not infer acquittal from silence on verdict slip ("unless a conviction of one crime logically excludes guilt of another crime") and claimed evidence was sufficient to convict D as principal; change in law of joint venture liability (D = guilty if Commonwealth proves beyond reasonable doubt that D knowingly participated in crime charged, alone or with others, with intent required for the offense), rejection of special verdict slips in this context;

***C v Anthes* 5 Gray 185, 230 (1855)**—jury verdict = final & related to Mass. Constitution, Declaration of Rights, Article 12 (*see Chapter 16-A, Jury Nullification*);

***Illinois v Vitale* 447 US 410 (80)**—double jeopardy bars multiple punishment or reprosecution after acquittal or conviction IF "same offense" (including lesser/greater);

***US v DiFrancesco* 449 US 117 (80)**—if jeopardy & same offense, double jeopardy exceptions = mistrial at D's request or when there is manifest necessity for mistrial, or new trial after appeal & reversal;

19-A.1. When Jeopardy "Attaches" (Trial, Guilty Plea)

***Serfass v US* 420 US 377 (75)**—jeopardy attaches when "put to trial" jury-waived; = when 1st witness sworn;

***C v DeFuria* 400 M 485 (87)**—(same, re: jury-waived);

***C v Lucero* 450 M 1032 (2008)**—judge committed clear error of law in purporting to enter required finding of not guilty when necessary Commonwealth witness had not yet appeared on trial day, but no opening statements had been made and no testimony had been given: jeopardy doesn't attach until jury-waived trial judge "begins to hear evidence"; G.L. c. 211, § 3 petition's allowance by single justice = affirmed by full SJC;

***C v Love* 452 M 498 (2008)**—combined suppression hearing and jury-waived trial began in District Court, but before completed D was indicted: jeopardy had attached in District Court proceeding, and indictments had to be dismissed (though case could be completed in District Court);

practice of combining suppression hearing and trial must be eliminated, & decision on motion should be issued before trial begins (trial may take place before expiration of ten-day period permitted for interlocutory review only if both parties have waived their rights to seek such review on the record);

***C v Ludwig* 370 M 31 (76)**—(same); BUT ***Crist v Bretz* 437 US 28 (75)**—jeopardy attaches at swearing of jury (because D's interest in keeping chosen jury);

***Lupi v Commonwealth* 434 M 1018 (2001)**—after individual voir dire of 18 prospective jurors, continuance due to discovery dispute, & termination of empanelment process: no attachment of jeopardy;

***C v Johnson* 426 M 617 (98)**—after swearing of jury & reading of indictments, judge excused 2 and impaneled 3 more jurors (because belatedly recognized 'protracted' trial): no termination of 1st jeopardy, so no "double" jeopardy infraction;

***C v Dale D.* 431 M 757 (2000)**—grand jury refused to indict D, a juvenile, on charges of forcible rape of child and indecent A&B on person fourteen or older, but this did not bar prosecution of D in juvenile court on complaints for same actions; grand jury's refusal to indict meant only that Commonwealth could not impose harsher penalty upon juvenile;

***C v Therrien* 359 M 500 (71)**—accept G PLEA = jeopardy; but retract plea to lesser included offense waives double jeopardy re: greater; can reprosecute (because no implied NG on greater); but cf. ***C v Johnson* 406 M 533 (90)** guilty plea in District Court to breaking & entering (which frustrated Commonwealth's bungled intent to instead prosecute in Superior Court) = no bar to subsequent Superior Court prosecution on indictment charging "possessing burglarious implements," because latter not strictly (on "elements" test) a lesser included offense, so not "same" offense (under ***C v Arriaga* (44 MAC 382 (98)**) analysis, Johnson holding now questionable, i.e., "same offense" maybe defined differently from strict elements test if successive prosecutions/trials occur);

***Ricketts v Adamson* 483 US 1(87)**—can reprosecute for greater after D pled G to lesser included offense because breached plea agreement (re: testifying against co-D);

***C v Gonzalez* 388 M 865 (83)**—indict rape OK when District Court continued without a finding the lesser included offense of A&B, but later bound over to grand jury because D didn't pay 'accord & satisfaction' on which continuance without a finding was predicated; (alternate rationale of 'no jurisdiction' in District Court over the greater offense, so no double jeopardy bar = illegitimate under ***Waller v Florida* 397 US 387 (70)** & ***Brown v Ohio* 432 US 161 (77)**, as recognized in ***C v Norman* 27 MAC 82 (89)**, aff'd, **406 M 1001 (89)**));

***Burke v Commonwealth* 373 M 157 (77)**—2d probable cause hearing or indictment OK after District Court "no probable cause" because no jurisdiction & no 'trial' (so no jeopardy);

C v DeFuria **400 M 485 (87)**—no witness or jeopardy, so can bind over to grand jury after DA read facts on offered admission to sufficient facts & agreed recommendation;

C v Crosby **6 MAC 679 (78)** if no announcement by judge, admission to sufficient facts in District Court on concurrent felony (& witness testifies) = "jeopardy," so can't bind over to grand jury/indict; (*See also Chapter 1 re District Court Declining Jurisdiction & Indictment Superceding District Court proceedings*);

19-A.2. Retrial after Dismissal?

US v Scott **437 US 82, 94 (78)**—judge's mid-trial "dismissal" (for prejudice from pre-indictment delay) intended finality (vs. "mistrial", which denotes intent to re-try); government can appeal & re-try (like mistrial) if it's dismissed at D's request, unless it was for "insufficient evidence" (overruling *US v Jenkins* **420 US 358 (75)** no government appeal after any post-jeopardy "dismissal" UNLESS remand won't require new trial (e.g., required finding of not guilty AFTER jury's G.) because double jeopardy harm = 2d trial);

C v Micheli **258 M 89 (27)**—if Ds consent, generally can reprosecute after (non-NG) dismissal because D "loses right to argue it's in effect an NG";

C v Dias **12 MAC 282, 285 (81)**—dismissal of illegitimate charge (after evidence) because lack of (Mass.) jurisdiction (i.e., "begetting" may have occurred in Rhode Island) = no bar to reprosecution for non-support because not on merits; D's consent (motion) to dismissal bars later objection on double jeopardy ground;

C v Juvenile (#2) **6 MAC 194 (78)**—"dismissal" after motion for required finding of NG bars retrial;

C v Brusgulis **398 M 325 (86)**—dismissal "with prejudice" was not on merits;

19-A.3. Retrial after Allowance of Motion for Required Finding?

Fong Foo v US **369 US 141 (62)**—double jeopardy bars retrial after mid-trial "required finding of not guilty" (for prosecutorial misconduct AND incredible witness) though rulings were "egregiously erroneous";

C v Lowder **432 M 92 (2000)**—after judge, in jury trial, directed verdict for D upon prosecutor's opening statement, retrial was barred EVEN THOUGH judge's action was, in circumstances here, an abuse of discretion (rejecting Commonwealth argument that judge's order directing "NG" was "nullity" without double jeopardy consequences);

C v Smith **58 MAC 166 (2003)**—judge first allowed D's motion for required finding of not guilty, but prior to closing arguments changed decision and sent case to jury; no double jeopardy because judge's "correction" did not require a second proceeding, and judge's power to reconsider own decisions during pendency of case is well estab-

lished; **overruled by U.S. Supreme Court,** *Smith v Massachusetts* **125 S.Ct. 1129 (2005)**—Commonwealth failed to show that "required finding of not guilty" ruling was automatically or presumptively nonfinal, so "NG" was treated as final for double jeopardy purposes;

C v Therrien **383 M 529 (81)**—double jeopardy bars appeal of required finding of not guilty before jury verdict, but not AFTER jury finds G.; (*see also Chapter 12, Trial Issues, Required Finding of Not Guilty*);

M.R.Crim.P. 25(c)—DA can appeal required finding of not guilty (or judge-order of guilty of only lesser-included) if required finding = entered AFTER jury's G or judge's order of G on lesser included offense;

C v Costarelli **374 M 677 (78)**—judge's "dismissal" after evidence for larceny of motor vehicle (& telling DA to charge use without authority) equivalent to required finding of not guilty & bars reprosecution for use without authority;

US v Martin Linen **430 US 564 (77)**—judge's label (mistrial, NG, dismissal) inconclusive for double jeopardy purposes; "dismissal" AFTER jury's G = appealable because reversal restores conviction, & isn't 2d trial; but required finding of not guilty after hung jury bars reprosecution;

McDaniel v Brown **130 S Ct 665 (2010)**—in determining whether there should be required finding of not guilty, federal habeas court must consider all of evidence admitted at trial, even evidence which has been erroneously admitted; if there is reversal for insufficiency of evidence, retrial is barred as double jeopardy violation;

C v Lam Hue To **391 M 301 (84)**—no double jeopardy bar to retrial after mistrial & dismissal (as discovery sanction) for late exculpatory evidence disclosure because no (*Oregon v Kennedy* **456 US 667 (82)**) intent to prompt mistrial motion; BUT retrial maybe barred if judge finds "irremediable harm" to fair trial;

C v Gaulden **383 M 543 (81)**—judge's entry of lesser included offense after jury's G = appealable;

C v Hart **149 M 7 (1889)**—judge's mid-trial (unconsented by D) "nol pros" unauthorized & tantamount to 'not guilty', so bars reprosecution;

C v Babb **389 M 275 (83)**—appealable & reverse 'not guilty' (given because no citation issued for motor vehicle homicide) because erroneous ruling & not based on innocence;

C v Azer **308 M 153 (41)**—no double jeopardy because 1st 'not guilty' was for material variance (booze's buyer), so not same offense;

C v Johnson **426 M 617 (98)**—can empanel 3 more jurors & excuse 2 already empanelled, following swearing of jury & reading of indictment (belated recognition that trial would be protracted), because no termination of "**1st**" jeopardy;

19-A.4. Retrial after Hung-Jury Mistrial?

US v Richardson **468 US 317 (84)**—can retry after hung jury (even if evidence was insufficient);

Burks v US **437 US 1 (78)**—BUT can't retry after appellate reversal for insufficient evidence because double jeopardy purpose = bar "2d bite" for DA; but see . . .

Lockhart v Nelson **488 US 33 285 (88)**—can retry if (appellate-ruled) inadmissible evidence was what defeated required finding of not guilty; BUT SEE, in MA, e.g., *C v Funches* **379 M 283 (79)** no re-trial after appeal because without evidence which shouldn't have been admitted, should be required finding of not guilty;

Berry v Commonwealth **393 M 793 (85)**—no retrial after hung jury because should've been required finding of not guilty (better protection under state law than under federal per *US v Richardson* **468 US 317 (84)**); (See K. Smith, *Criminal Practice & Procedure*, §§ 1309 & 1318 (2d ed. 1983 & Supp.); *and see Chapter 19-E, below* (*Therrien* **359 M 500 (71)** etc.));

Aucella v Commonwealth **406 M 415 (90)**—reprosecution after hung jury barred where evidence was legally insufficient;

Koonce v Commonwealth **412 M 71 (92)**—reprosecution for murder 1 after hung jury not barred where evidence legally sufficient, notwithstanding D's self-defense claim;

Daniels v Commonwealth **455 M 1009 (2009)**—reprosecution not barred: while evidence entitled D to self-defense instruction, Commonwealth evidence = sufficient to disprove self-defense beyond reasonable doubt;

Taylor v Commonwealth **447 M 49 (2006)**—after hung jury, D urged that there could be no retrial on joint venture theory because only evidence was that he was the principal (i.e., the shooter); SJC rejected argument, holding that jury could reject witness's testimony that she understood D to have admitted being shooter, while accepting that he was member of group committing home invasion resulting in fatal shooting;

C v Mayfield **398 M 615 (86)**—can retry for first degree murder after jury's hung 11-1 for 2d degree because no "verdict" unless announced;

Gelmette v Commonwealth **426 M 1003 (97)**—can retry for 1st degree murder after hung jury (11 for manslaughter, 1 for NG)

US v Perez **9 Wheat. 579 (1824)**—hung jury = manifest necessity, can re-try;

US v Martin Linen **430 US 564 (77), etc.**—(judge gives required finding of not guilty after hung jury);

Thames v Commonwealth **365 M 477 (74)**—judge's discretion when to mis-try for hung jury, & can re-try; DISTINGUISH *Berry v Commonwealth* **393 M 793 (85)** . . . but not if motion for required finding of not guilty should have been granted;

Fuentes v Commonwealth **448 M 1017 (2007)**—after trial lasting about a day and deliberations for a total of about seven hours, judge gave instructions per *Tuey-Rodriquez* (with D's assent), but "shortly thereafter," jury sent note (not shared with counsel before judge responded to it in open court) prompting judge to declare hung jury and mistrial; though D was given no opportunity to be heard prior to this (and that would have been "the more prudent course"), judge didn't abuse discretion, and retrial would not be barred;

Daniels v Commonwealth **441 M 1017 (2004)**—judge is not required to accept partial verdict, and didn't do so on first day of deliberations; jurors, next day, apparently reconsidered and had no verdict on ANY of the charges; when utter deadlock on all charges on fourth day prompted mistrial with D counsel's agreement, no basis for dismissal, on double-jeopardy ground, of indictment on which there had purportedly been initial agreement;

Cramer v Commonwealth **419 M 106 (94) and *Hanlon v Commonwealth* **419 M 1005 (95)**—because evidence was sufficient for G, hung jury did not bar retrial; retrial not violative of double jeopardy bar;

US v Hotz **620 F.2d 5 (1st Cir. '80)**—4 hours = too soon (without hearing) though reported deadlock 11-1 after 2 hours; can't ask split, but can consider it if revealed; (See also Kent Smith, *Criminal Practice & Procedure*, § 1314 (2d ed. 1983 & Supp.) (mistrial because of long jury deliberations);

19-A.5. Retrial after Other Mistrial?

US v Scott **437 US 82 (78)**—double jeopardy may bar re-trial after mistrial, but OK to reprosecute after mid-trial dismissal at D's request unless it's for insufficient evidence;

K. Smith, *Criminal Practice & Procedure*, §§ 1310-15 (2d ed. 1983)—must OBJECT; no meaningful formula for "manifest necessity"; question: other ALTERNATIVES?; even if consent, no retrial if evidence was insufficient;

Wade v Hunter **336 US 684 (49)**—D's right to completed trial before particular tribunal sometimes subordinate to public interest in justice;

US v Jorn **400 US 470 (71)**—no retrial after mistrial unless "manifest necessity" or D's request (unless DA or judge overreaches); double jeopardy where judge called mistrial for witness to consult lawyer (see *Illinois v Somerville* **410 US 458, 469 (73)**) because alternatives existed;

C v Brusgulis **398 M 325 (86)**—can re-try because D consented to dismissal (even with prejudice), same as to mistrial; dismissal "with prejudice" (& denial of required finding of not guilty) didn't resolve facts, & judge applied wrong standard re: witness competency;

Campagna v Commonwealth **454 M 1006 (2009)**—before trial, counsel urged severance of substantive offense from trial of 7 conspiracy indictments, but judge refused; after evidence closed, judge acknowledged that the substantive offense was within the scope of the alleged conspiracy indictments and D was entitled to severance, and "offered [D] a choice of submitting substantive offense to jury" (and "withdrawing" severance motion) or standing on the motion (resulting in mistrial on the substantive indictment); D stood on motion, which SJC considered to be a consent to mistrial, and retrial was not barred;

Jones v Commonwealth **379 M 607 (80)**—bad mistrial over objection because judge didn't explore alternatives, e.g., severance (where co-D's counsel fought judge);

Barton v Commonwealth **385 M 517 (82)**—same; juror feared co-D, so judge called mistrial over D's objection without voir dire of jurors, severance, etc.;

C v Nicoll **452 M 816 (2008)**—after empanelling & swearing only six jurors, a juror knew first witness, and raised possible partiality: judge excused juror after questioning, and declared mistrial after stating erroneously that criminal trial could not proceed with five jurors: because trial could have proceeded with D's consent (and D objected to mistrial), no "manifest necessity" justified mistrial and double jeopardy barred second trial;

Chandanais v Commonwealth **448 M 1013 (2007)**—juror's report that D had contacted and intimidated her during lunch recess prompted mistrial, with D's consent;

Illinois v Somerville **410 US 458 (73)**—no formula/meaningful categorization for "manifest necessity" & "ends of justice"; but they justify mistrial for incurably defective indictment (so trial would have been futile because no jurisdiction (*see Chapter 5-E, Jurisdictional Defects*));

Arizona v Washington **434 US 497 (78)**—DA met heavy burden & showed manifest necessity for mistrial for D's bad opening which made jury biased; judge fully heard parties & considered alternatives; (fn.24: not manifest necessity for DA missing a witness);

C v Pyburn **17 MAC 927 (83)**—bad mistrial for counsel's opening because alternatives (e.g., instructions) not explored; but see *Lovett v Commonwealth* **393 M 444 (84)** manifest necessity for mistrial on counsel's opening; D suggested no curative instructions & they probably wouldn't have helped anyway;

C v Steward **396 M 76 (85)**—bad mistrial on 2d day (because 3/14 jurors absent) because judge didn't consider alternatives (e.g., continue or use 11) & D objected;

Picard v Commonwealth **400 M 115 (87)**—bad mistrial (for D's cross-examination) because no hearing re: alternatives;

Cuoto v Commonwealth **18 MAC 913 (84)**—no manifest necessity (for V visiting D's counsel re: civil suit) because alternatives (e.g., instruction) existed;

Oregon v Kennedy **456 US 667 (82)**—double jeopardy if D requests mistrial only if DA (or judge: cf. *C v Ellis* **432 M 746 (2000)**) must have "intentionally provoked"; harass/overreaching acts not enough; (but see Stevens + 3: concur in result, but subjective standard for overreaching = useless);

State v Kennedy **295 Or. 260 (83)**—on remand, reject Supreme Court mens rea standard (under state constitution) & require only intentional misconduct + "indifference" re: mistrial;

Pool v Superior Court **677 P.2d.261 (Ariz. S. Ct. 84)**—(same);

LaFave, Israel, & King (*Chapter 19-A, above*) § 25.2—agree with Stevens, J., et al. in *Oregon v Kennedy*;

C v Lam Hue To **391 M 301 (84)**—no double jeopardy bar to retrial after mistrial & dismissal (as discovery sanction) for late exculpatory disclosure because no *Oregon v Kennedy* intent; BUT retrial maybe barred if judge finds "irremediable harm" to fair trial;

C v Murchison **392 M 273 (84)**—judge can reserve mistrial ruling (for DA's questions) until after verdict; remand re: dismissal's finality under Kennedy or Lam Hue To;

C v Smith **404 M 1 (89)**—Mass. standard = same as federal *Oregon v Kennedy*; no overreaching shown here;

Donovan v Commonwealth **426 M 13 (97)**—double jeopardy bar only if "intentional prosecutorial misconduct calculated to provoke a D into moving for a mistrial";

C v Cousin **449 M 809 (2007)**—no bar to retrial after mistrial prompted by prosecutor's running criminal record check of deliberating jurors, disclosing criminal histories by several who did not reveal same on juror questionnaire, and when they were discharged, insufficient number to deliberate; "trial judge was warranted in finding" that DA didn't act with intent to cause mistrial, and warranted in dismissing the jurors;

C v Ellis **432 M 746 (2000)**—implicit acknowledgment that judicial misconduct causing mistrial (hung jury) can bar retrial but here finding that D failed to make "the requisite showing of bad faith";

Elder v Commonwealth **385 M 128 (82)**—mistrial at D's request (because of DA's press comments) during jury-waived trial, no manifest necessity because judge says unbiased, so remand; (fn.1: if jury trial, D's mistrial request would trigger (*Oregon v Kennedy*) inquiry; (see subsequent *C v Elder appeal* **389 M 743 (83)** remand & find G = OK);

C v McCormick **130 M 61 (1881)**—manifest necessity because biased juror = "physical or moral necessity" without fault on part of prosecution;

C v Murray **22 MAC 984 (86)**—discretionary manifest necessity because of D's improper opening; D didn't suggest curative instruction (& judge found none would work);

C v Reinstein **381 M 555 (80)**—OK mistrial (for newspaper ad (by D's friends) saying frame-up) because no alternative (e.g., voir dire of jury might aggravate);

C v Denson **16 MAC 678 (83)**—OK mistrial (for D's mother's outburst) because no alternative;

C v Clemmons **370 M 288 (76)**—(if D objects) no manifest necessity to suspend District Court trial to fix DA error (& amend to intent to distribute, then bind over); double jeopardy mandates NG;

Pellegrine v Commonwealth **446 M 1004 (2006)**—surprise evidence (not provided by Commonwealth in discovery) resulted in mistrial; D's silence = consent, so no need to consider whether there was manifest necessity (counsel here "plainly had the opportunity to object");

Chandanais v Commonwealth **448 M 1013 (2007)**—though D consented to mistrial during deliberations (upon report by juror that D had contacted and intimidated her), this did not bar him from raising double jeopardy bar on ground that evidence was insufficient as a matter of law (SJC found evidence sufficient, however);

C v Phillips **12 MAC 486 (81)**—no manifest necessity (without hearing/consent) just because judge scheduled elsewhere next day;

Downum v US **372 US 734 (63)**—no manifest necessity for absent DA witness (2 hours after empanel 100 witness case) because DA had reason to know no summons served (5-4 decision);

Poretta v Commonwealth **409 M 763 (91)**—personal assent by D to mistrial motion not required as matter of state law which follows federal rule of *US v Dinitz* **424 US 600 (76)**; *Daniels v Commonwealth* **441 M 1017, 1018 n.2 (2004)**—same;

C v Sanchez **405 M 369 (89)**—failure of counsel & judge to fully inform D of options, including striking of unavailable witness's direct examination by prosecutor, not a bar to reprosecution, where D acquiesced in counsel's motion for mistrial;

C v Stracuzzi **30 MAC 161 (91)**—trial judge's erroneous directing of guilty verdicts not a bar to reprosecution because not functionally equivalent to a declaration of mistrial without manifest necessity;

Collins v Commonwealth **412 M 349 (92)**—DA's mid-trial unavailability due to death in family didn't warrant mistrial where judge refused to consider alternatives (e.g., polling jurors re: continuance);

C v Horrigan **41 MAC 337 (96)**—judge's mid-trial unavailability due to family medical emergency did not warrant mistrial where no inquiry as to how long judge would be unavailable, no alternatives were explored, and counsel given no opportunity to be heard;

C v Cassidy **410 M 174 (91)**—jury note that deliberations were being influenced by a juror's prior sexual abuse was manifest necessity justifying mistrial over D's objection;

C v Troila **410 M 203 (91)**—juror's unauthorized view of murder scene was manifest necessity justifying mistrial;

C v Phetsaya **40 MAC 293 (96)**—double jeopardy barred 2d trial after judge declared mistrial because **he** thought case should not have been tried and D-counsel had neither "presence before the jury" nor strategy appreciated by the judge: no manifest necessity;

C v Carver **33 MAC 378 (92)**—prosecutor's late mid-trial disclosure of key evidence not a bar to reprosecution where D not provoked to move for mistrial;

Mercedes v Commonwealth **405 M 693 (89)**—drug cop's improper testimony elicited by defense counsel not a bar to reprosecution where D not provoked to move for mistrial;

19-A.6. Immediate Retrial?

C v Avery **14 MAC 137 (82)**—can re-try with same jury pool after manifest necessity mistrial;

19-A.7. Retrial after Appellate Reversal?

C v Funches **379 M 283 (79)**—no re-trial after appeal because without bad evidence (i.e., which should have been struck upon D's motion), there would have been required finding of not guilty;

C v Dellinger **383 M 780 (81)**—(same); remand to enter not guilty;

McDaniel v Brown **130 S Ct 665 (2010)**—in determining whether there should be required finding of not guilty, federal habeas court must consider all of evidence admitted at trial, even evidence which has been erroneously admitted; if there is reversal for insufficiency of evidence, retrial is barred as double jeopardy violation;

C v Zanetti **454 M 449 (2009)**—judge charged jury that if found D guilty of murder, had to specify EITHER 'principal' or 'joint venturer'; conviction as joint venturer could not stand/insufficient evidence, so required finding of not guilty ordered BUT SJC held D could be re-tried because would not infer acquittal from silence on verdict slip and claimed evidence was sufficient to convict D as principal; change in law of joint venture liability (D = guilty if Commonwealth proves beyond reasonable doubt that D knowingly participated in crime charged, alone or with others, with intent required for the offense), rejection of special verdict slips in this context;

C v Kirouac **405 M 557 (89)**—erroneous admission of key evidence which deprives prosecution of legally sufficient evidence requires entry after appellate reversal of required finding of not guilty; remanded here to determine whether prosecution has "reasonable prospect for filling the gap in its proof";

C v DiBenedetto **414 M 37 (92)**—appellate reversal for erroneously admitted evidence (here, prior recorded testimony) did not require dismissal of murder 1 conviction where prosecution had "reasonable prospect" of filling gap in proof if witness could be found & persuaded to testify;

C v Lester **70 MAC 55 (2007)**—quotes from *Kater*, 421 M at 18: "If the evidence admitted at trial was sufficient to send case to jury, but is insufficient to send case to jury if all improperly admitted evidence is disregarded, double jeopardy principles nevertheless do not bar a retrial" (i.e., Commonwealth might be able to fill gap, but hadn't been aware below that further/different evidence was necessary); here, however, even counting D's inadmissible statement in "the evidentiary calculus," 12 indictments should have been required finding of NG;

C v Straw **422 M 756, 762–63 (96)**—Supreme Judicial Court orders required finding of not guilty (no retrial) after holding that drugs and admissions should have been suppressed;

US v Ball **163 US 662 (1896)**—usually can retry after D's appeal & reversal;

Green v US **355 US 184 (57)**—when D has been found G of 2d degree murder on a 1st degree murder indictment, and when appeal results in retrial, he may be put to trial only for 2d degree murder: "this case can be treated no differently, for purposes of former jeopardy, than if the jury had returned a verdict which expressly read: "We find the defendant not guilty of murder in the first degree but guilty of murder in the second degree";

BUT: C v Carlino **449 M 71, 76–80 (2007)**—at retrial of D for first degree murder, double jeopardy didn't bar resubmission to jury on felony-murder because mere failure of first jury to check verdict slip "box" for felony murder didn't operate as acquittal on that theory (boxes for deliberate premeditation and extreme atrocity/cruelty had been checked); see, however, *Crawford* 429 M 60, 70 n.18 (99), *Almonte* 444 M 511, 512 n.1 (2005), and *DePace* 433 M 379, 386 n.5 (2001), whose import was disputed by SJC here; "a true acquittal requires a verdict on the facts and merits";

Bullington v Missouri **451 US 430 (81)**—death penalty case D sentenced to life in prison cannot be sentenced to death after 2d trial necessitated by appellate reversal of 1st conviction;

19-A.8. New Facts after First Jeopardy

Jeffers v US **432 US 137 (77)**—OK to reprosecute for greater if new facts arise;

C v Vanetzian **350 M 491 (66)**—can reprosecute for murder for V's delayed death (after D had been tried & convicted of assault and battery by means of dangerous weapon);

C v Cabrera **449 M 825 (2007)**—items in D's car found after a stop led to charge of receiving stolen property, to which D pled guilty; four years later, investigation revealed that D, with others, had broken into store from which the property was obtained and stole it, thereafter hiding it in a residence, from which D retrieved items days later; SJC rules subsequent trial for breaking and entering with intent to steal was not barred;

Cf. *C v Jarvis* **68 MAC 538 (2007)**—following D's jury-waived trial on OUI (guilty), D requested new judge for trial re: the existence of three prior OUI convictions; prior to "transferring that part of the case to second judge," first judge sentenced D to two years, one year committed, balance suspended for two years, "on the primary offense of OUI"; though this was procedurally improper (G.L. c. 278, § 11A: sentencing should not occur until bifurcated trial is completed), double jeopardy clause did not bar "resentencing" following the finding of guilt on the subsequent offense charge; D had no legitimate expectation of finality in the prematurely-imposed sentence;

19-A.9. Alleged First Jeopardy as a "Nullity"

G.L. c. 263, § 7—can plead "former NG" though 1st complaint was defective (unless, see G.L. c. 263, § 8, acquittal was because of such defect/'variance');

See US v Ball **163 US 662 (1896)**—double jeopardy after not guilty on facts, even though indictment = defective;

C v Lowder **432 M 92 (2000)**—after judge, in jury trial, directed verdict for D upon prosecutor's opening statement, retrial was barred even though judge's action was, in circumstances here, an abuse of discretion (rejecting Commonwealth argument that judge's required finding of not guilty order was "nullity" without double jeopardy consequences);

C v Arriaga **44 MAC 382, further appellate review denied 427 M 1105 (98)**—double jeopardy bar checks courts and prosecutors, but not legislature; "same offense" in MA (**BUT NOT PER SUPREME COURT/ FEDERAL CONSTITUTION** (see *US v Dixon* **509 US 688, 704 (93)**)) = defined differently depending on whether issue is successive prosecutions or merely multiple convictions/punishments at single trial. Re: multiple punishments/single trial, "same offense" determined by strict 'elements' test; re: successive prosecutions, 'conduct-based' definition of same offense, i.e., if, to establish an essential element of an offense charged in 2d prosecution, government will prove conduct that constitutes an offense for which D has already been prosecuted, 2d trial is barred; (but see *Petite v US* **361 US 529 (60)** federal "policy" against multiple (federal) prosecutions for 1 transaction (for fairness & efficiency));

C v Katsirubis **45 MAC 132 (98)**—reiterated *C v Arriaga* re: different meanings of 'same offense'; but see

C v Cabrera **449 M 825 (2007)**—items in D's car found after a stop led to charge of receiving stolen property, to which D pled guilty; four years later, investigation revealed that D, with others, had broken into store from which the property was obtained and stole it, thereafter hiding it in a residence, from which D retrieved items days later; SJC rules subsequent trial for breaking and entering with intent to steal was not barred; see also *Solomon v Commonwealth* **453 M 1020 (2009)**—similar; D pled guilty in BMC to receiving stolen property, operating after suspension, possession of burglarious tools, violating a municipal ordinance, then argued double jeopardy re: Woburn District Court charges of breaking and entering with intent to commit felony and larceny from building; former charges arose only hours after the latter house break; SJC hews to "elements" test, ignoring fact of separate prosecutions; see, in particular, *Brown v Ohio* **432 US 161 (77)** & *Waller v Florida* **397 US 387 (70)** ; SEE ALSO *C v Norman* **27 MAC 82, 87–88, affirmed 406 M 1001 (89)**—involving successive prosecutions in separate state courts, recognizing import of *Brown* and *Waller*;

19-A.10. Impossible to Discern What Incidents Resulted in Acquittals at First Jeopardy (Too-Vague Indictments)?

C v Hrycenko **417 M 309 (94)**—on 6 **identically worded indictments** charging aggravated rapes, D found NG on 4, and remaining 2 were reversed on appeal; prior to retrial, motion to dismiss on ground that it was unknowable whether D had been found NG on these already by jury: SJC agreed, retrial barred;

C v Riberio **49 MAC 7, 11–12 (2000)**—re: 3 identically-worded rape indictments, judge submitted only one to jury because of *Hrycenko* issue/concern; error in not submitting all 3 to jury because D had opportunity to obtain (via bill of particulars) sufficient info to understand charges/prepare defense, BUT retrial now barred because it was impossible to discern which specific act formed the basis of D's (single) rape conviction (& new jury might be considering an alleged act for which D had already been convicted and sentenced);

19-A.11. How To Present Double Jeopardy Claim; Waiver of Double Jeopardy Bar

G.L. c. 277, § 47A—defects in institution of prosecution . . . shall only be raised pre-trial & by motion under M.R.Crim.P.;

C v Medina **64 MAC 708, 713 n.8 (2005)**—double jeopardy claim may be waived by failure to raise it prior to the proceeding that would offend the protected rights;

C v Mazzantini **74 MAC 915, further app. rev. denied 454 M 1111 (2009)**—by pleading guilty to both possession of heroin and being present where same heroin was kept, D waived claim that convictions were duplicative (and conceded they aren't 'same' under elements-based analysis); fn.2 asserts not 'same,' neither is lesser included offense of other;

Pena v Commonwealth **426 M 1015, 1016 n.2 (98)**—double jeopardy issue will **not** henceforth be entertained under G.L. c. 211, § 3 until after trial court filing of, and denial of, motion to dismiss;

Aucella v Commonwealth **406 M 415 (90)**—reprosecution after hung jury barred where evidence was legally insufficient; G.L. c. 211, § 3, petition = appropriate vehicle;

C v Cardenuto **406 M 450 (90)**—same; trial counsel's failure to raise issue on first appeal did not waive D's claim on second appeal;

K. Smith, *Criminal Practice & Procedure*, **§ 1303 (2d ed. 1983 & Supp.)**—double jeopardy = appropriately (and necessarily, see *Pena* **426 M 1015 (98)**) raised in G.L. c. 211, § 3 petition;

Creighton v Commonwealth **423 M 1001 (96)**—appropriate steps = motion to dismiss; then G.L. c. 211, § 3 to single justice, then appeal to full bench; here, after single justice's denial, D was put to trial, convicted, & then sought "reconsideration" of prior § 1303211, § 3 decision; normal appeal route was just as good now, given that 2d trial had already occurred, so 211/3 would not be entertained;

C v Chatfield-Taylor **399 M 1 (87)**—appropriate steps = motion to dismiss new case, then G.L. c. 211, § 3 to SJC single justice; SJC reviews here though premature (motion for "stay" of retrial allowed in Superior Court & D took "appeal" on denial of motion for required finding of not guilty);

Abney v US **431 US 651 (77)**—double jeopardy is in small class of cases reviewable before final judgment because rights would be otherwise undermined;

C v Thomas **401 M 109 (87)**—can first raise duplicity on appeal;

C v Norman **27 MAC 82, 87–88, affirmed 406 M 1001 (89)**—involving successive prosecutions in separate state courts, double jeopardy bar "touches on the 'very power of the State to bring the defendant into court to answer the charge brought against him,'" so is "similar to that of jurisdiction, (which) may be raised at any stage of the proceedings" & isn't lost by failure to raise it below by way of motion to dismiss; But *C v Spear* **43 MAC 583, further appellate review denied 426 M 1105 (97)** double jeopardy issue waived for this appeal by pro se D's failure to assert it prior to 2d trial, despite *Thomas*, *Gallinaro*, & *Norman*, **above** (convictions in Spear = reversed on another ground, & motion to dismiss prior to any 3d trial not barred in this opinion) (but, CPCS query: failure to pursue legitimate double jeopardy bar = ineffective assistance of counsel, & right to relief on that basis?);

C v Bennett **52 MAC 905, 906 (2001)**—failing to file motion to dismiss assault & battery by dangerous weapon indictment (when D filed motion to dismiss reckless operation of vehicle charge, prompting Commonwealth to dismiss that charge) waived double jeopardy claim;

Costarelli v Commonwealth **374 M 677 (78)**—double jeopardy not waived (for de novo jury of six session) by bench court silence; G.L. c. 211, § 3 relief necessary to prevent double jeopardy's harm;

Menna v NY **423 US 61 (75)**—double jeopardy not waived by guilty plea to second case, BUT *C v Johnson* **406 M 533 (90)** District Court prosecution for breaking & entering (D's guilty plea there, when prosecutor neglected to know/advise court that case was being indicted) does not bar subsequent prosecution in Superior Court for possession of burglar's tools; "same transaction" test rejected;

Ricketts v Adamson **483 US 1 (87)**—reneging on plea bargain waived double jeopardy protection;

19-B. "SAME OFFENSE": DUPLICITY, MERGER, LESSER INCLUDED OFFENSES, GREATERS, AND REMEDIES

19-B.1. Defining "Same Offense"

Morey v Commonwealth **108 M 433 (1871)**—adultery & lewd cohabit not double jeopardy though same acts because each statute requires proof of additional fact; multiple punishments for same act = issue for grand jurors, prosecutor, judge at sentencing, & governor re: pardon—not SJC;

Blockburger v US **284 US 299 (32)**—adopt *Morey* (108 M 433) test; no double jeopardy for sell drugs without prescription & sell without original package; consecutive sentences = OK;

Austin v US **509 US 602 (93)**—statutory **in rem** forfeiture, though denominated "civil," = punishment, & is subject to 8th Amendment's "excessive fines" prohibition; civil sanction that can't fairly be said SOLELY to serve remedial purpose (but also either deterrent or retributive purposes) is punishment (citing *US v Halper* **490 US 435, 448 (1989)**);

US v Dixon **509 US 688 (93)**—D on bail, condition being commit no criminal offense or bail would be revoked & D punished for contempt of court; D arrested for cocaine possession with intent, & prosecuted for **contempt** at a show cause hearing (4 cops testifying to facts of alleged drug offense, court finding beyond a reasonable doubt that D committed drug offense, & D sentenced to 180 days): subsequent prosecution for drug offense barred on double jeopardy basics; underlying substantive criminal offense = "a species of lesser included offense";

C v Smith **44 MAC 394 (98)**—**specifically rejecting standard** of sameness defined as consideration of the "realities of the offenses and the circumstances within which they occurred" (as per *Costarelli v Commonwealth* **374 M 677 (78)**; *C v St. Pierre* **377 M 650 (79)**; *C v Jones* **382 M 387 (81)**; *C v Sullivan* **20 MAC 802 (85)**); carjacking & kidnap not duplicative; carjacking & unarmed robbery not duplicative; from & after sentence for kidnap OK;

C v Pileeki **62 MAC 505, 512 (2004)**—burning a dwelling not duplicative of involuntary manslaughter (reckless/wanton conduct theory); but see CONCURRING OPINION for overview/history of "duplicative convictions" case law;

C v Vick **454 M 418 (2009)**—armed assault with intent to murder not duplicative of assault and battery by means of dangerous weapon, causing serious bodily injury, despite fact that single swift act of raising gun and firing was the entire criminal event; "elements" analysis = neither is a lesser included offense of the other, so not 'same'; acknowledges that *Cabrera* 449 M 825, *Keohane* 444 M 563, *Jones* 441 M 73, *Wolinski* 431 M 228, *Morin* 52 MAC 780 use amalgamation of 'elements' test and actual conduct, but says latter's test of "closely related in fact as to constitute in substance but a single crime" is pertinent (if all charges are tried in a single proceeding) ONLY to

preclude convictions (and consecutive sentences) in which one is a lesser included offense of the other;

C v Healy **452 M 510, 512 n.5 (2008)**—SJC doesn't "necessarily agree" that "failure to stop (a civil infraction) is a lesser included offense of "operating to endanger", but issue was not before the Court;

C v Kulesa **455 M 447 (2009)**—"criminal harassment" not duplicative of violating 209A order (here) because conduct forming basis of harassment charge predated service of the 209A order; SJC distinguished;

Edge v Commonwealth **451 M 74 (2008)**—D could not be prosecuted for "stalking" in violation of 209A Order when the violations of the 209A order that served as basis of stalking charge had already been subject of D's convictions and sentences;

C v Keohane **444 M 563 (2005)**—first degree murder and armed assault in dwelling aren't duplicative;

C v Gallant **65 MAC 409 (2006)**—attempted kidnapping (G.L. c. 274, § 6) and assault with intent to commit felony (G.L. c. 265, § 29) aren't duplicative, rejecting argument that *Keohane* imposed test (i.e., "so closely related in fact as to constitute in substance but one crime") other than "elements" test of *Morey*;

C v Smith **75 MAC 196 (2009), further rev. granted 456 M 1101 (2010)**—armed home invasion and armed assault with intent to murder not duplicative because differing elements (even though based on "same conduct");

C v Putnam **75 MAC 472 (2009)**—armed assault in dwelling (G.L. c. 265, § 18A, requiring entry while armed, assault on someone inside, and specific intent accompanying the assault to commit a felony) not duplicative of armed home invasion (G.L. c. 265, § 18C, requiring knowingly entering dwelling of another, knowing or having reason to know that someone is present within or entering without such knowledge but remaining after acquiring or having reason to acquire it, being armed, and using force or threatening force upon person within or intentionally causing injury to person within): despite the crimes here arising from a "single course of conduct", they have "mutually exclusive elements";

*C v Arriaga **44 MAC 382, further appellate review denied 427 M 1105 (98)**—double jeopardy bar checks courts and prosecutors, but not legislature; "same offense" in MA (**BUT NOT PER SUPREME COURT/FEDERAL CONSTITUTION** (see *US v Dixon* **509 US 688, 704 (93)**) = defined differently depending on whether issue is successive prosecutions or merely multiple convictions/punishments at single trial. Re multiple punishments/single trial, "same offense" determined by strict 'elements' test; re successive prosecutions, 'conduct-based' definition of same offense, i.e., if, to establish an essential element of an offense charged in 2d prosecution, government will prove conduct that constitutes an offense for which D has

already been prosecuted, 2d trial is barred; (but see *Petite v US* **361 US 529 (60)** federal "policy" against multiple (federal) prosecutions for 1 transaction (for fairness & efficiency));

C v Katsirubis **45 MAC 132 (98)**—reiterated *C v Arriaga* re different meanings of 'same offense'; but see *C v Bennett* **52 MAC 905, 906–07 (2001)**—result-oriented here, refusing to apply *Arriaga*, calls for SJC to give explicit direction if "successive prosecutions" scenario requires different definition of "same" offense; no relief for successive prosecutions for negligent operation of vehicle so as to endanger & assault & battery by dangerous weapon, court applying only "elements" test, and finding crimes not "same";

C v Mazzantini **74 MAC 915 (2009)**—at n.2: same conduct analysis "applies, if at all, only to instances of successive prosecution, not multiple charges tried in a single proceeding"; but see *C v Niels N* **73 MAC 689 (2009)**—where no "separate and distinct act" instruction was given and actions underlying offenses here were "so closely related in fact as to constitute a single crime," substantial risk of miscarriage of justice found (vacate 2 of 3 convictions);

Edge v Commonwealth **451 M 74 (2008)**—after D pled guilty to violating abuse prevention order issued pursuant to G.L. c. 209A (id. § 7),and was sentenced, indictment later for crime of stalking "in violation of the same 209A order (G.L. c. 265, § 43(b)) was ordered dismissed; reported question, "whether a prosecution under § 43(b) implicates double jeopardy concerns if the Commonwealth relies on conduct previously the subject of [D]'s convictions of violating the 209A order," is answered "yes";

Glawson v Commonwealth **445 M 1019 (2005)**—D engaged in various criminal activities in a spree over course of several days, resulting in indictments in three different counties for specific acts allegedly committed in each county; D pleaded guilty to many indictments in one county, and then sought G.L. c. 211, § 3 relief to bar prosecution in other counties, claiming they would be based on "same conduct, episode, occurrence and arrest"; held, NO double jeopardy bar, though court should be alert for "harassment in multiple and successive prosecutions"; D didn't move to consolidate various counties' charges pursuant to M.R.Crim.P. 9(a) and M.R.Crim.P. 37(b)(2);

C v Medina **64 MAC 708 (2005)**—acquittal of D on indictments charging sexual assaults on child in one county did not bar trial on indictments charging sexual assaults on same child in different county;

19-B.2. Occasionally Cited Different Standards, Some Subsequently Condemned

*cf. K. Smith, *Criminal Practice & Procedure*, § 1316 (2d ed. 1983 & Supp.)—"same evidence," not "same transaction," test; but can't HARASS/OPPRESS; (cf. *Jones* **382 M 387 (81)** etc., re: legislative overrides);

Cepulonis v Commonwealth **374 M 487 (78)**—"same transaction" test especially bad for dual sovereigns (*see* Chapter 19-G); state gun without license differs from federal "unregistered" gun;

Grady v Corbin **495 US 508 (90) (OVERRULED BY US v DIXON 509 US 688 (93))**—double jeopardy clause bars subsequent prosecution where government, to prove an essential element, must rely on conduct that constitutes an offense for which D already prosecuted; prior conviction for motor vehicle assault barred subsequent prosecution for homicide;

US v Felix **503 US 378 (92)**—conspiracy prosecution not barred even where D has been convicted of substantive offenses based on some of same overt acts; *Grady v Corbin* distinguished as involving "species" of lesser included offenses; (*See Therrien* **359 M 500 (71)**/*Ricketts* **483 US 1 (87)**, *Chapter 19-A above*, re: reprosecuting greater after G plea to lesser included offense); cf. *Ashe v Swenson* **397 US 436 (70)** (Brennan, J., concurrence urges "same transaction" test);

C v Cerveny **373 M 345 (77)**—duplicity for larceny by false pretenses & perjury (because latter's purpose = enrichment, & materiality = inducement), and *C v Catania* **377 M 186 (79)** uttering = lesser included offense of larceny because it was the false pretense, so no consecutive sentence; BUT *C v Crocker* **384 M 353 (81)** overrule Cerveny/Catania's relaxing the Morey rule by looking at "evidence"; utter larceny not duplicitous because (Morey test shows) LEGISLATURE INTENDS 2 crimes (vs. *Jones* **382 M 387 (81)**); (fn. 7: maybe look at FACTS re: successive prosecutions, e.g., *Costarelli*, *Brown*; accord, *C v Arriaga* **44 MAC 382 (98)**); 3 checks on 3 dates = 3 crimes (+ common notorious thief);

C v Jones **382 M 387 (81)**—though motor vehicle homicide not lesser included offense of manslaughter, close enough that no legislative intent for from & after sentences; remedy = vacate the G on lesser, i.e., inadequate to just have concurrent sentences;

C v Mazzantini **74 MAC 915 (2009)**—'unit of prosecution' intended by legislature shown by disjunctive "or", prohibiting possession of either large capacity weapon *or* large capacity feeding device designed for it;

C v Lopes **455 M 147, 148 n.1 (2009)**—first degree felony murder and armed robbery duplicative, and "filing" latter conviction was inadequate remedy: must vacate and dismiss armed robbery conviction;

C v Juvenile **6 MAC 194 (78)**—barring prosecution for prostitution after previous prosecution on same evidence for being a lewd, wanton, and lascivious person in speech and behavior;

C v Mahoney **68 MAC 561 (2007)**—"simple" embezzlement held to be lesser included offense of embezzlement by a city, town, or county officer (G.L. c. 266, § 51), so no error in instructing jury and obtaining conviction on lesser offense, BUT on evidence here this conviction was duplicative of separate conviction for larceny ("nothing turns on the allegation that D's theft exceeded

$250, a factor of significance in determining the level of larceny, but of no relevance with respect to embezzlement"), which had to be dismissed;

C v Gallarelli **372 M 573 (77)**—no "same transaction" test unless harassed; can prosecute conspiracy (to bribe juror) after trial & sentence for contempt (by same bribe) because Morey test; (concurrence by Kaplan/Liacos, JJ: "same evidence" test = "arid & inadequate," but improved by court's recognition of "harassment" limit; urge Model Penal Code test);

C v Ianelli **17 MAC 1011 (84)** & *C v Benson* **389 M 473 (83)**—conspiracy & underlying crime not "same";

C v DiStasio **297 M 347 (37)**—can charge as principal after NG as accessory before; test = legally/factually the same (or lesser/greater), not "same act"; (*see Chapter 17-C, Accessory*);

Missouri v Hunter **459 US 359 (83)**—no multiple punishment for same (under Blockburger test) offense—UNLESS clear legislative intent;

C v Nardone **406 M 123 (89)**—although conviction of lesser included offense generally bars reprosecution for greater, not so here because improper finding of guilt on assault to kill did not logically imply not guilty to assault to murder;

19-B.3. Lesser-Included Offenses (Strict Elements Test under Blockburger/Morey)

C v Juvenile (#2) **6 MAC 194 (78)**—dismissal (on motion for required finding) of lesser included offense (lewd/lascivious) bars prosecution for 'greater' (prostitution);

Price v Georgia **398 US 323 (70)**—G on lesser included offense implies NG on, & bars prosecution for, greater (see also *Green v US* **355 US 184 (57)**);

Brown v Ohio **432 US 161 (77)**—(same); double jeopardy bars both greater (larceny of motor vehicle) & lesser (use without authority for same car because "same" regardless of sequence; test = Blockburger, though 9 days' "continuation" of possessing/using car, state can't divide crime into series of temporal units (by days) or spatial units (by different counties in which car was driven);

C v McCan **277 M 199 (31)**—Superior Court rape prosecution OK after District Court conviction of lesser included offense (A&B) because no District Court rape jurisdiction, BUT OVERRULED: *C v Norman* **27 MAC 82 (89)** aff'd, **406 M 1001 (89)** can't indict armed robbery after District Court G-plea to larceny of motor vehicle (because it's lesser included offense), notwithstanding fact that greater offense "couldn't" have been prosecuted in court of "inferior" jurisdiction lacking final authority over felony, first recognition that *Brown v Ohio* **432 US 161 (77)** & *Waller v Florida* **397 US 387 (70)** invalidate *McCan* **277 M 199 (31)** & *Mahoney* **331 M 510 (54)** rationale (i.e., inferior state courts' legislatively-mandated

incompetence over certain crimes doesn't trump/override constitutional prohibition against repeated jeopardy);

Waller v Florida **397 US 387 (70)**—successive "municipal" & "state" prosecutions—double jeopardy bar to larceny prosecution after disorderly/destroy property, when latter is lesser included offense of former; state's argument that there was no jurisdiction in lower court over greater offense REJECTED: state statutes delineating various courts' subject matter jurisdiction can't defeat constitutional protection against double jeopardy (*C v Norman* **27 MAC 82, aff'd, 406 M 1001 (89)** recognizes that *Waller v Florida* and *Brown v Ohio* invalidate *C v Mahoney* **331 M 510 (54)** (can indict greater (robbery) offense after District Court found "no P/C" & G of lesser included offenses because no District Court jurisdiction) and *C v McCan* **277 M 199 (31)** (Superior Court rape prosecution OK after District Court conviction of lesser-included A&B, because rape couldn't be tried in lower court);

Kuklis v Commonwealth **361 M 302 (72)**—though D pled G to all 3, 2 were duplicitous (& remedy = dismissal) because possession = identical in law & fact to possession with intent to distribute (under Morey test) & legislature intends only 1 punishment for being present, too, where evidence was identical; but see *C v Rodriguez* **11 MAC 379 (81)** being present where heroin is kept not lesser included offense to possess "no matter how nearly related in fact";

C v Fernandez **48 MAC 530, 535 n.7 (2000)**—same;

C v Johnson **75 MAC 903 (2009)**—D was convicted of both "trafficking" and possession with intent to distribute, the latter being enhanced for sentencing because it was a "second or subsequent", D receiving 3–5 sentence on trafficking, but 5 to 5 & a day on possession with intent; convictions were duplicative; ordinarily, result would be to dismiss "lesser" offense, but here "lesser" carried the longer sentence (lesser included offense = one with fewer elements, and "having been previously convicted" is NOT an "element" but is instead a sentencing enhancement); HERE, remand for trial judge to decide which to vacate & which judgment to "affirm";

C v Fitzpatrick **14 MAC 1001 (82)**—indecent A&B not lesser included offense of rape here, because different acts, so crimes factually differ; vs. . . .

C v Thomas **401 M 109 (87)**—rape duplicative of indecent A & B because same (factual) offense;

C v Zane Z **51 MAC 135 (2001)**—failure to instruct that rape and indecent A&B charges had to be based on different facts meant that conviction of both may well have been duplicative; usual remedy = vacate G on lesser offense, but here, there were two separate incidents, & no way of knowing basis for indecent A&B G, so here reverse it; failure to give specific unanimity instruction = additional basis for reversal of both rape and indecent A&B convictions;

C v Howze **58 MAC 147 (2003)**—act of removing complainant's clothing (alleged indecent A&B) was sufficiently bound up with and necessary to act of penetration (rape of child) that due process forbids separating the conduct into discrete units for prosecution;

C v Berrios **71 MAC 750 (2008)**—given DA's closing argument and judge's instructions (failing to make clear that charge of A&B had to be based on acts separate from those supporting rape), the "choking" cited as force for rape charge was possibly the basis for assault and battery conviction: A&B conviction vacated; that sentences were concurrent "does not prevent a substantial risk of a miscarriage of justice";

C v Niels N. **73 MAC 689 (2009)**—juvenile was convicted of assault with intent to rape, assault and battery (as lesser included offense of charged "rape"), and indecent assault and battery, but jurors not told by prosecution or trial judge what conduct could form predicate for which offense "and which offense needed to be predicated on separate and distinct acts"; acts were so closely related in fact as to constitute single crime (juvenile pushed child onto bed, pulled down her pants, and got on top of her); latter two convictions here vacated;

C v Miller **361 M 644 (72)**—duplicity remedy = required finding of not guilty on 1/2 charges;

C v Dutney **4 MAC 363 (76)**—if lesser included offenses, either allow motion for election, or required finding on one, or instruct jury not to convict on both; but see *Fadden v C* **376 M 604 (78)** no duplicity anyway, but DA need not elect unless "substantial rights" prejudiced otherwise; can charge motor vehicle homicide by both negligence and operating under influence, so long as no consecutive sentence;

C v Jones **382 M 387 (81)**—if duplicitous convictions, remedy is not concurrent sentences, but instead vacating less serious conviction;

C v Clermy **421 M 325 (95)**—same, re possession of cocaine and possession of same cocaine with intent to distribute; but see post, re: "unit of prosecution" (e.g., *C v Richardson* **37 MAC 482 (94)** sale to cop (distribution of cocaine) immediately followed by search & seizure of large amount of cocaine (trafficking) involved distinct portions of drug: no duplicity in 2 convictions);

C v Gaskins **49 MAC 903 (2000)**—no double jeopardy bar to 2 convictions for one loaded firearm, i.e., possessing firearm (G.L. c. 269, § 10(a)) & possessing ammunition, albeit only inside gun (G.L. c. 269, § 10(h));

C v Costa **65 MAC 227 (2005)**—conviction of unlawful possession of firearm is duplicative of unlawful possession of large capacity weapon (conviction on lesser = vacated);

C v Hammond **50 MAC 171 (2000)**—no relief for conviction of both G.L. c. 266, § 101 (intentionally damaging property or injuring person by explosion of gunpowder or any other explosion) and G.L. c. 266, § 102 (placing OR throwing explosive with intent to damage property or injure person); footnote noted D's argument that one can't cause explosion without at least placing an explosion, but didn't "confront (its) logical conundrum";

C v Van Winkle **443 M 230, 243–44 (2005)**—armed robbery not duplicative of first degree murder because D was found guilty on not only "felony murder" theory, but also on theory of deliberate premeditation; see also *C v Felder* **455 M 359 (2009)** (same); *C v Lopes* **455 M 147, 148 n.1 (2009)**—first degree felony murder and armed robbery duplicative, and "filing" latter conviction was inadequate remedy: must vacate and dismiss armed robbery conviction;

Illinois v Vitale **447 US 410 (80)**—can't prosecute greater after G of lesser included offense; but remand for Blockburger question: was manslaughter "reckless" provable by other than the lesser included offense (failing to stop car)?;

Edge v Commonwealth **451 M 74 (2008)**—after D pled guilty to violating abuse prevention order issued pursuant to G.L. c. 209A (id. § 7),and was sentenced, indictment later for crime of stalking "in violation of the same 209A order (G.L. c. 265, § 43(b)) was ordered dismissed; reported question, "whether a prosecution under § 43(b) implicates double jeopardy concerns if the Commonwealth relies on conduct previously the subject of [D]'s convictions of violating the 209A order," is answered "yes";

C v Rodriguez **11 MAC 379 (81)**—being present not lesser included offense to possess (at least here) "no matter how nearly related in fact"; *C v Fernandez* **48 MAC 530, 535 n.7 (2000)** being present where heroin is kept not lesser included offense to possession of heroin;

C v Owens **414 M 595 (93)**—possession of heroin with intent to distribute = lesser included offense of heroin trafficking (same, indistinct, quantity of drug);

C v Gosselin **365 M 116 (74)**—though attempt = lesser included offense to completed crime, attempted escape factually different unless overt act = both attempt & complete; so can try for attempt after NG escape (*see also Chapter 5, Complaints*);

C v Gagnon **37 MAC 626 (94), aff'd 419 M 1009 (95)**—attempted murder = lesser included offense of armed assault with intent to murder; former conviction vacated (concurrent sentences didn't solve/remedy double jeopardy violation);

C v Shuman **17 MAC 441 (84)**—arson's "included" in burn building to defraud (because latter involves malice) though former has higher maximum penalty; *C v Ploude* **44 MAC 137 (98)** burning building (G.L. c. 266, § 2) is lesser included offense of burning building with intent to defraud insurer (G.L. c. 266, § 10); remedy = vacate former conviction (not just sentences);

C v Jones **441 M 73 (2004)—says *C v Anolik* 27 MAC 701, 712 (89) correctly overruled *Shuman* 17 MAC 441**, because "same evidence" test is not to be used; use "elements" test instead: burning motor vehicle (c. 266, § 5) and burning insured property with intent to defraud insurer (c. 266, § 10) not duplicative on "elements" test; former protects personal property and embodies public safety component also; latter punishes "an economic crime";

C v Santos **440 M 281 (2003)**—though assault by means of dangerous weapon is not lesser included offense of armed robbery, given the theory of "assault" here used, "elements" test met, so that convictions of armed robbery and assault by means of dangerous weapon were duplicative;

C v St. Pierre **377 M 650 (79)**—A&B by dangerous weapon/mayhem not "same evidence" & no harassment because concurrent sentences; (D's motion "artlessly" asked election);

C v Page **42 MAC 943 (97)**—A&B by dangerous weapon/mayhem based on "separate acts" (albeit during one attack with claw hammer), so not duplicative in fact/ on evidence here; *C v Drew* **67 MAC 261 (2006)**—same re: ABDW, "bat", but duplicative re: ABDW "space heater"; (but *C v Martin* **425 M 718 (97)** A&B by dangerous weapon **is** lesser included offense of 2d branch of mayhem statute, G.L. c. 265, § 14);

C v Ogden O., a juvenile, **448 M 798 (2007)**— ABDW by dry gas/fire was lesser included offense of mayhem (second theory); remedy = vacate both the conviction and sentence on lesser included and affirm conviction on more serious offense;

C v Wooden **70 MAC 185 (2007)**—armed robbery and armed assault with intent to rob not duplicative here, because based on separate and distinct acts (taking money and jewelry at gunpoint separate from unsuccessful later attempt to steal car at gunpoint); other possible basis for "attempt" was frustrated goal of obtaining large sum of money D believed V to have for car payment;

C v Anderson **58 MAC 117 (2003)**—sua sponte, Appeals Court vacates conviction of assault and battery by means of dangerous weapon, because duplicative of conviction for mayhem, second theory;

C v Baldwin **52 MAC 404 (2001)**—separate armed robbery & larceny convictions upheld: sequence = knife-point robbery of wallet, money, and ATM card in deserted location, followed by coerced revelation of personal ID#, & withdrawal of money from V's bank account;

C v Gardner **67 MAC 744 (2006)**—indictment for robbery (knocking 70-year-old to ground & taking purse) properly dismissed following D's conviction in District Court for, inter alia, receiving stolen property (the purse), though Appeals Court "resolved [issue] without resort to principles of double jeopardy", on ground that the convictions were inconsistent as matter of law & constitutional issue need not/should not be reached if nonconstitutional basis for disposition exists; "judicial estoppel" invoked, preventing party from asserting position in one legal proceeding that is contrary to position it had previously asserted in another proceeding;

C v Kopsala **58 MAC 387 (2003)**—in jury-waived trial, D made no argument that indecent assault and battery was subsumed within rape, and when argument was made first in appeal, court would presume that judge correctly instructed himself that the crimes would have had to be based on separate acts (pulling up shirt to expose breasts, pulling off jeans, removing underpants = separate from penetration); but see *C v Howze* **58 MAC 147 (2003)**—act of removing complainant's clothing incidental/necessary to penetration (continuous stream of conduct within short time frame, governed by single criminal design); due process forbids separating conduct into discrete units for prosecution; indecent A&B conviction vacated (statutory rape conviction affirmed);

Salemme v Commonwealth **370 M 421 (76)**—A&B by dangerous weapon & armed assault with intent to murder not duplicative; from & after sentence OK;

C v Sullivan **20 MAC 802, 809–10 (85)**—A&B by dangerous weapon (hand stabbed) held duplicative of homicide (back stabbed): "sequence of blows was so close that as a matter of fact & sense the acts involved were so intertwined as to be one";

C v Morin **52 MAC 780, 786 (2001)**—court willing to bar multiple punishments "for convictions arising out of the same act"; wrist grab & breast touching found NOT to be so closely related as to be single course of conduct, so A&B conviction and indecent A&B conviction both OK; but here, D couldn't be sentenced for both indecent A&B and "assault with intent to rape", since those were duplicative in fact on evidence here;

C v Niels N. **73 MAC 689 (2009)**—juvenile was convicted of assault with intent to rape, assault and battery (as lesser included offense of charged "rape"), and indecent assault and battery, but jurors not told by prosecution or trial judge what conduct could form predicate for which offense "and which offense needed to be predicated on separate and distinct acts"; acts were so closely related in fact as to constitute single crime (juvenile pushed child onto bed, pulled down her pants, and got on top of her); latter two convictions here vacated;

C v Pillal **445 M 175 (2005)**—touching breast and squeezing nipple can't support TWO convictions of indecent A&B: no evidence that these "were in any way separate events";

C v Johnston **60 MAC 13, 22 (2003)**—pulling complainant's hair was conduct separate from rape (for separate A&B conviction), but "assume without deciding" that act of wrapping legs around her legs & bruising her could be NOT separate from rape;

C v Hogan **379 M 190 (79)**—though A&B dangerous weapon & mayhem not duplicative, no from and after sentences if same evidence (BUT NOW SEE *C v Martin* **425 M 718 (97)** A&B dangerous weapon **is** lesser included offense of 2d branch of mayhem statute, G.L. c. 265, § 14);

C v Simpson **44 MAC 154 (98)**—hammer blow to head followed by knife stabbing in neck and then knife slashing from ear to mouth: separate convictions for assault to murder & mayhem OK and consecutive sentences OK;

C v Smith **44 MAC 394 (98)**—carjacking & kidnap not duplicative; carjacking & unarmed robbery not duplicative; from & after sentence for kidnap OK (court rejects 'circumstances' of occurrence test, uses only 'elements' in context of a single prosecution/trial);

C v Cabrera **449 M 825 (2007)**—items in D's car found after a stop led to charge of receiving stolen property, to which D pled guilty; four years later, investigation revealed that D, with others, had broken into store from which the property was obtained and stole it, thereafter hiding it in a residence, from which D retrieved items days later; SJC rules subsequent trial for breaking and entering with intent to steal was not barred: strict elements test, and no acknowledgment of any differing test applicable for successive prosecutions (as opposed to several convictions at a single trial);

C v Williams **46 MAC 700 (99)**—A&B dangerous weapon not lesser included offense of assault with intent to kill;

C v Gaskins **49 MAC 903 (2000)**—no double jeopardy in G on both possession of (loaded) firearm & possession of ammunition;

C v Katsirubis **45 MAC 132 (98)**—no double jeopardy in forgery of official record (G.L. c. 267, § 1), uttering (G.L. c. 267, § 5), & false making of a certificate of nomination (G.L. c. 56, § 11);

C v Bachir **45 MAC 204 (98)**—no double jeopardy in violating restraining order (G.L. c. 209A, i.e., no contact with son or wife) & parental kidnapping (G.L. c. 265, § 26A);

C v Garcia **48 MAC 201 (99)**—after acquittal of receiving stolen property, prosecution in juvenile court for contributing to delinquency of minor (on basis of such receiving) barred;

C v Johnson **45 MAC 473 (98)**—multiple punishments (successive sentences) OK for violation of G.L. c. 209A order and for crimes of threatening to commit A&B, murder, & malicious destruction;

19-B.4. One Crime Enhancing Another (Greater) Crime: Convictions/ Sentences on Each?

Shabazz v Commonwealth **387 M 291 (82)**—maybe legislature can impose multiple punishment for same (Morey) offense; but no such legislative intent for murder & underlying felony; vacate from & after sentence for robbery because maybe it's the "felony" murder basis;

Bynum v Commonwealth **429 M 705 (99)**—"3 charges"/counts of indictment: (1) distributing cocaine, (2) that this was repeat offense, and (3) distribution occurred in school zone: repeat offender "count" is not a separate "crime" but is instead a sentencing enhancement provision; prior offense is not an element of crime for which D is charged, but concerns only the punishment to be imposed is he's convicted of current distribution, and prior offense is proved; double jeopardy not applicable "in the sentencing context";

C v Miranda **441 M 783 (2004)**—similar, citing *Bynum v Commonwealth* **429 M 705 (99)**; *see also C v Owen* **61 MAC 711 (2004)**—applying *Miranda* **441 M 783** to "habitual offender" sentencing after conviction of

robbery, rejecting D's argument of being "twice punished" for armed robbery conviction (though docket should be corrected to dismiss free-standing indictment for "unarmed robbery habitual offender" because there were not two **separate** convictions and life sentences);

C v Padgett **44 MAC 359 (98)**—armed robbery = lesser included offense of felony murder; *C v DeCicco* **44 MAC 111 (98)** arson lesser included offense of felony murder;

C v Gunter **427 M 259, 275–276 (98)**—armed assault in dwelling = lesser included offense of felony murder; *C v Anderson* **425 M 685 (97)** first degree murder could have been felony murder or deliberate premeditation; failure to specify = vacating armed robbery conviction because **possibly** duplicitous;

C v Robinson **449 M 1 (2007)**—SJC vacates underlying conviction for armed robbery as it affirms first degree murder on felony murder theory with armed robbery as predicate felony;

C v Marrero **436 M 488 (2002)**—general verdict of "G" on first degree felony murder, when predicate felonies of both armed home invasion and armed robbery were presented: only one of the two felonies held to be "duplicative," and, because Commonwealth was "entitled to verdicts on the highest crimes charged," armed robbery conviction was vacated;

C v Bennett **424 M 64 (97)**—same re armed burglary & felony murder; *C v Mello* **420 M 375 (95)** 2d degree murder might have been felony murder based on arson: arson conviction vacated;

C v Rasmusen **444 M 657 (2005)**—convictions of home invasion and armed burglary, along with felony murder, resulted in vacating conviction of armed burglary, SJC believing that this conviction "was better suited to serve as the predicate felony" on the facts here;

C v Martins **38 MAC 636 (95)**—"aggravation" in aggravated rape G could have been kidnapping or because joint venturers involved; failure to specify = only concurrent sentence on kidnap (not from & after) because possibly duplicitous (but see *C v Jones* **382 M 387 (81)** requiring different remedy, i.e., vacate conviction); cf. *C v Connolly* **49 MAC 424 (2000)** failure to instruct jury on A&B as lesser included offense of ABDW-shod foot = reversal, AND because jury possibly convicted D at 1st trial of both A&B and A&B dangerous weapon on basis of same act (because judge refused to charge that conviction on both charges had to be based on discrete acts), no retrial on A&B by dangerous weapon permitted now (though Commonwealth can bring forward for sentencing, on remand, the previously "filed" A&B conviction);

C v Moran **439 M 482 (2003)**—vacate conviction for assault and battery because judge failed to instruct that convictions on indecent assault and battery and simple assault and battery had to be predicated on separate acts (or otherwise two convictions for "same," i.e., greater and lesser included offense);

C v Berry **420 M 95 (95)**—burglary with actual assault (G.L. c. 266, § 14) = lesser included offense of 1st degree felony murder: vacate former conviction;

C v Doucette **430 M 461, 471 (99)**—felony murder and count of armed home invasion indictment re: same victim = duplicative; latter conviction vacated; *C v Hoilett* **430 M 369, 376 (99)** felony murder, masked armed robbery; latter vacated; *C v Robinson* **48 MAC 329, 341–42 (99)** second degree felony murder, kidnapping; latter vacated;

C v Vives **447 M 537 (2006)**—felony murder and armed robbery convictions: latter conviction & sentence vacated, since it was the only predicate felony for the murder conviction;

C v Wolinski **431 M 228, 238–39 (2000)**—though armed robbery was duplicative of felony murder, SJC rejected additional argument that A&B by dangerous weapon should be vacated as "lesser" crime of armed robbery (former requires proof of battery and latter doesn't; latter requires proof of larceny and former doesn't); But see *C v Payne* **425 M 692 (98)** when murder 1 conviction premised on **both** felony murder and extreme atrocity or cruelty (special verdict) not necessary to vacate for "duplicity" underlying felony of armed robbery;

C v Williams **23 MAC 716 (87)**—armed robbery & aggravated rape by armed robbery = duplicitous;

C v Petrillo **50 MAC 104, 110–11 (2000)**—because aggravation of "aggravated" rape may have been kidnapping, vacate kidnapping conviction (no jury instruction required finding separate events, despite fact that evidence provided basis for finding kidnapping on date different from rape);

C v Jarvis **68 MAC 538 (2007)**—following D's jury-waived trial on OUI (guilty), D requested new judge for trial re: the existence of three prior OUI convictions; prior to "transferring that part of the case to second judge," first judge sentenced D to two years, one year committed, balance suspended for two years, "on the primary offense of OUI"; though this was procedurally improper (G.L. c. 278, § 11A: sentencing should not occur until bifurcated trial is completed), double jeopardy clause did not bar "resentencing" following the finding of guilt on the subsequent offense charge; D had no legitimate expectation of finality in the prematurely-imposed sentence;

19-B.5. "Unit of Prosecution"

C v Hawkins **21 MAC 766 (86)**—don't make 1 transaction multiple crimes (armed robbery & use gun (G.L. c. 265, § 18B, on which this holding relied, was rewritten in 1998, and wouldn't now support));

C v Richardson **37 MAC 482 (94)**—sale to cop (distribution of cocaine) immediately followed by search & seizure of large amount of cocaine (trafficking) involved distinct portions of drug: no duplicity in 2 convictions;

C v Rabb **431 M 123 (2000)**—no duplicity in separate convictions for possessing cocaine with intent and cocaine trafficking when charges involved separate bulks of cocaine in different locations; active sales at one location, and separate stash held for future sales (though court might not tolerate separate charges re: multiple amounts "hidden separately at one location"); BUT COMPARE *C v Ortiz* **431 M 134 (2000)** allowing aggregation of heroin on D's person and heroin he constructively possessed at another location (to impose harsher minimum mandatory sentence); but cf. ***Brown v Ohio* 432 US 161 (77)** state can't divide crime into temporal/spatial units, i.e., larceny of motor vehicle followed by use without authority in different county on later date;

C v Tracy **50 MAC 435 (2000)**—5 shots fired within 30 seconds (2, then changed position of gun, and paused between each of next 3 shots, last 2 when V called D name, & repeated it) OK basis for separate convictions and consecutive sentences for assault with intent to murder V (at least 2 shots into V's body) & assault with intent to maim same V (shot to arm);

C v Levia **385 M 345 (82)**—2 V's, same place = 2 robberies; *C v Flanagan* **76 MAC 456 (2010)**—when 2 V's seriously injured, 2 convictions of causing serious bodily injury while operating vehicle negligently and under influence of alcohol appropriate (legislature in G.L. c. 90, § 24L(l) intended to adopt judicial construction of G.L. c. 90, § 24G);

C v Antonmarchi **70 MAC 463 (2007)**—though only one "entry" of dwelling place, two convictions OK under G.L. c. 265, § 18C (armed home invasion, using force upon any person within such dwelling) when both resident and her male friend were battered by ex-boyfriend; cite to *C v Doucette* 430 M 461 (99);

C v DeCicco **44 MAC 111 (98)**—1 molotov cocktail but 2 homes burned = 2 arsons;

C v Lester **70 MAC 55 (2007)**—hypothetically, one telephone call (or letter, or personal encounter) could support several counts of witness intimidation under G.L. c. 268, § 13B, because "unit" = discrete/independent threat or "varied offering of things of value," e.g., threat to physically harm witness, threat to kill family member, offer of money, offer of drugs;

C v Buzzell **49 MAC 902 (99)**—one order that D remove nuisance (i.e., barking dogs) can't support 16 convictions/violations of dog removal order (16 dogs? 16 occasions of barking?); violation of a nuisance statute (G.L. c. 140, § 157) over a period of time is continuing offense, not multiple offenses; when Legislature intends that each day = separate offense, it expressly provides ("e.g., G.L. c. 131, § 40, ¶ 32");

C v Vega **36 MAC 635 (94)**—1 sexual attack on 1 victim, but OK to split into 2 rapes (anal & vaginal) and impose lengthy consecutive sentences;

C v Murray **401 M 771 (88)**—5 years, 180 checks, $4 million = 180 larcenies;

C v North **52 MAC 603, 606 (2001)**—20 larceny by false pretenses indictments OK for "multitude of separate acts on different dates by differing artifices," though D argued only 4 victims;

C v Gurney **13 MAC 391 (82)**—each statement at grand jury = separate perjury unless substantially identical;

C v Crawford **430 M 683 (2000)**—one gunshot = two homicides (pregnant woman + unborn (but "viable") fetus deprived of oxygen);

C v Melton **50 MAC 637 (2001)**—one gunshot = 4 assaults by means of dangerous weapon (4 occupants of car into which shot was fired; shooting "endangered lives of all four");

C v Constantino **443 M 521 (2005)**—driver who causes single accident and leaves scene = one G of "operating so as to endanger" and one G of "leaving scene of accident resulting in death", although two people were killed; SJC vacates one conviction of each charge as duplicative; unit of prosecution for "motor vehicle homicide" = number of persons killed, but D wasn't convicted on these indictments, but instead of lesser included offenses of operating so as to endanger;

C v Stasiun **349 M 38 (65)**—successive takings = single larceny scheme;

C v LeBeau **451 M 2444 (2008)**—D, convicted of first degree murder (deliberate premeditation and extreme atrocity/cruelty) had three of four accompanying larceny indictment convictions vacated: though four items of property were taken (2 rings, cash, lottery tickets), it was a single larceny;

C v Winter **9 MAC 512 (80)**—can't split conspiracy into 2 parts (*see Chapter 17-B, Conspiracy*); *Campagna v Commonwealth* **454 M 1006 (2009)**—though Commonwealth indicted for 7 conspiracies, judge ruled that there was only "a single overarching conspiracy extending through the time period alleged in the indictments, not seven distinct conspiracies", and at D's urging entered required findings of not guilty on 6; SJC rejected D's subsequent attempt to bar retrial (when jury couldn't reach verdict) for altering work of grand jury (*Barbosa* 421 M 547 [95]), holding that there was no change in substance to grand jury's work;

C v Donovan **395 M 20 (85)**—7 victims, but 1 night & 1 phony deposit-box, so 1 continuing intent/scheme; legislative intent unclear, so D gets benefit of doubt;

C v Beacon **14 MAC 570 (82)**—20 obscene films, 1 day = 1 crime; (See also *C v Crocker* **384 M 353 (81)**, & *Missouri v Hunter* **459 US 359 (83)** above);

C v Piersall **67 MAC 246 (2006)**—re: statute criminalizing unauthorized access to computer system (G.L. c. 266, § 120F), unit of prosecution = each unauthorized "log-in"; prosecution failed to introduce any evidence (expert or otherwise) to support fifteen such crimes (14 convictions were reversed & set aside);

C v Mazzantini **74 MAC 915 (2009)**—re: statute (G.L. c. 269, § 10(m)) punishing possession of "large capacity weapon *or* large capacity feeding device therefor", unit of prosecution = EACH, so conviction & sentence for weapon and separate conviction & sentence for feeding device;

19-B.6. "Merger" of Offenses

(*Robinson v US* **388 A.2d.1210 (DC '78)**—63-pace kidnap merges into rape);

(*P v Cassidy* **40 NY2d 763 (76)**—kidnap = incidental means to rape, so "merged");

C v Sumner **18 MAC 349 (84)**—2 hour kidnap not incidental; even if duplicative, give jury both & dismiss one later (see *Miller* **361 M 644 (72)** duplicity remedy = required finding of not guilty on 1/2 charges; *C v Dutney* **4 MAC 363 (76)** if lesser included offenses, either allow motion for election, or required finding on one, or instruct jury not to convict on both);

C v Vasquez **11 MAC 261 (81)**—kidnap not incidental (bus station to house);

C v Talbot **5 MAC 857 (77)**—kidnap not incidental (rob, cops arrive, then kidnap);

C v Boyd **73 MAC 190 (2008)**—confinement or restraint exceeding that necessary for commission of other charged offenses = "independent, not incidental, conduct," and not a basis for finding merger/duplication;

C v Rivera **397 M 244 (86)**—reject *Cassidy* (**40 NY2d 763 (76)**) rule (so far?) "this case"; though *Jones* **382 M 387 (81)** recognized different Morey charges maybe "so closely related as to preclude punishing both," drag V across street & behind house not "same act" as rape; (even if so, remedy = give jury both & dismiss one later);

C v Harvey **397 M 803 (86)**—no merger of kidnap if "pulled V towards woods";

C v Rivera **397 M 244, 254 (2000)**—no merger of kidnap and 1st degree murder by extreme atrocity or cruelty (SJC "unwilling to adopt a rule that requires treatment of confinement or asportation used as a means to facilitate the commission of such crimes (assaults) as merged in the substantive crime");

C v Sullivan **20 MAC 802 (85)**—assault and battery with dangerous weapon (hand stabbing) merged with homicide (back stabbing)—"sequence of blows so close . . . intertwined as to be one";

C v Ford **397 M 298 (86)**—no discussion, but no merger of breaking & entering, larceny, & malicious destruction of property;

C v Padgett **44 MAC 359 (98)**—breaking & enterings and larcenies don't merge;

C v Quigley **391 M 461 (84)**—in felony murder, predicate felony must be 'separate from the acts of personal violence which constitutes a necessary part of the homicide itself';

C v Niels N. **73 MAC 689 (2009)**—juvenile was convicted of assault with intent to rape, assault and battery (as lesser included offense of rape), and indecent assault and battery, but jurors not told by prosecution or trial judge what conduct could form predicate for which offense "and which offense needed to be predicated on separate and distinct acts" (latter two convictions here vacated);

C v Claudio **418 M 103, 109 (94)**—breaking & entering dwelling, nighttime, with intent to commit felony and being armed or making assault on person therein (G.L. c. 266, § 14) did not merge with homicide so as to prevent culpability for 1st degree felony murder; But *C v Gunter* **427 M 259, 271–275 (98)** armed entry of dwelling & assault on person therein with intent to commit felony (G.L. c. 265, § 18A), **if** only victim was subsequently killed, could not serve as predicate felony for felony murder because armed assault would merge with (& be lesser included offense within) felony murder; here, **id.** at 274, proof of armed assaults on 3 others as well as homicide V, provided adequate (non-lesser included offense) predicate; in future, indictment must specify non-merging felony or no **felony** murder conviction will lie;

C v Garner **59 MAC 350 (2003)**—joint venture possession of firearm did not merge so as to bar conviction for second degree felony murder in circumstances here;

C v Kilburn **438 M 356 (2003)**—no merger where there was evidence of assault by means of brandishing gun in addition to assault of shooting that caused V's death; *C v Murphy* **442 M 485 (2004)**—purportedly no merger because entering dwelling while armed with knife with intent to rob Vs, stabbing each several times and inflicting NONFATAL wounds was separate from the stabbings that resulted in death; convictions under G.L. c. 265, § 18A upheld in addition to first degree murders on each of three bases;

C v Brown **66 MAC 237 (2006)**—though it's not "kidnapping" by which rape can be "aggravated" if there is only the degree of "confinement" which is a necessary incident to rape, confinement isn't merged within rape if jury could reasonably find that D's action exceeded the restraint which was merely incidental to rape's commission;

SEE CHAPTER 21-K (ELEMENTS OF COMMON CRIMES: HOMICIDE) FOR "MERGER" CASES RE: FELONY MURDER, POST—GUNTER

19-B.7. "Civil" Infractions (If Truly "Civil") Don't Implicate Double Jeopardy

US v Halper **490 US 435, 448 (89)**—imposition of large civil fine after D convicted of & punished for criminal charges for false Medicare claims was double jeopardy violation where purpose of fine was punitive, not remedial; but see

Hudson v US **522 US 93 (97)**—Supreme Court disavows analysis it used in 1989 in **Halper**, approving instead *US v Ward* **448 US 242, 248–249 (80)**: if legislature denominated statutory scheme civil/remedial, only "the clearest proof" that it is "so punitive either in purpose or effect" will make court call it "criminal", with double jeopardy implications; **Hudson** allowed "statutes re violation of fed. banking administratively-imposed penalties" & "occupational debarment" followed by indictment for same conduct;

C v Cory **454 M 559 (2009)**—in context other than double jeopardy, SJC analyzes range of federal case law in determining whether statute (G.L. c. 265, § 47, requiring probationer convicted of specified sex crimes to wear GPS monitor) is civil or criminal (and finding pronounced punitive effect) to hold it's prohibited ex post facto law as applied to D;

Kvitka v Board of Registration **407 M 140, cert. denied 498 US 823 (90)**—medicine board's imposition of fine on physician D after guilty pleas on criminal charges was double jeopardy violation where fine was punitive, not remedial;

Powers v Commonwealth **426 M 534 (98)**—motor vehicle crash prompted D's "indefinite" driver's license suspension, but this did not bar prosecution subsequently on indictments charging, inter alia, operating under the influence and causing serious bodily injury; license suspension = protection of public, not punitive & thus civil;

Luk v Commonwealth **421 M 415 (95)**—(similar);

Leduc v Commonwealth **421 M 433 (95)**—(similar);

C v Dias **12 MAC 282 (81)**—double jeopardy not applicable to non-support proceeding under G.L. c. 273, § 15 because it's remedial rather than punitive;

Cepulonis v Commonwealth **426 M 1010 (98)**—D "sanctioned" administratively for escaping from penal institution ("restitution" of $10,774), but this no bar to criminal prosecution for escape; though time served both remedial & deterrence goals, this didn't make it "criminal"

C v Forte **423 M 672 (96)**—assault & battery on correctional officer followed by special confinement in prison's "disciplinary unit" (remedial & deterrent purposes as well as punitive) = no double jeopardy bar to criminal prosecution;

US v Ursery **518 US 267 (96)**—civil forfeiture not additional penalty for criminal act but instead "remedial" civil sanction unless so punitive in fact as not to be legitimately civil in nature;

C v Penta **423 M 546 (96)**—civil forfeiture not punishment for double jeopardy purposes under 5th Amendment; no argument re greater protection under state law/constitution made (cocaine trafficking, forfeiture of D's vehicle used to facilitate the trafficking);

C v Vieira **41 MAC 927 (96)**—civil forfeiture of cash and 2 vehicles did not require dismissal of indictments for drug crimes; forfeitures = "compensatory and remedial" because proceeds used to defray costs of criminal investigations/prosecutions; state law argument will be reached only in a case with a disparity between "remedial costs and the value of the forfeiture" since only then would forfeiture be solely "punishment";

Albano v Commonwealth **423 M 1005 (96)**—forfeiture of items used in drug distribution no bar to criminal prosecution for drug distribution;

Montana Dept. of Revenue v Kurth Ranch **511 US 767 (94)**—"tax" conditioned on commission of crime, extracted only after D's arrest = second punishment which must be imposed during first prosecution or not at all;

Austin v US **509 US 602 (93)**—"civil" forfeiture of property used in drug offense is punishment, & is subject to 8th Amendment's "excessive fines" prohibition, even if forfeiture serves some remedial purpose;

Department of Revenue v Sorrentino **408 M 340 (90)**—civil paternity action not barred by nol pros of criminal non-support charges after appeal of bench trial conviction but before de novo trial; jeopardy lapsed with vacating of bench conviction & had not attached prior to commencement of de novo trial;

Mahoney v Commonwealth **415 M 278 (93)**—30-day incarceration for civil contempt of G.L. c. 209A orders did not bar criminal prosecution on 2 criminal complaints (1 for violating the protective order and 1 for A&B);

See Chapter 5-D, Complaints & Indictments: Variance & Lesser Included Offenses, & Chapter 21, Analyzing Elements of Common Crimes, for cases on lesser included offenses;

19-C. MULTIPLE PUNISHMENT OR INCREASE OF SENTENCE

See also Chapter 19-B, above, for whether a sanction is punishment (criminal) or "remedial" (civil);

US v Ball **163 US 662 (1896)**—(& others, from Chapter 19-A) can retry after appellate reversal;

Mann v C **359 M 661 (71)**—can increase sentence after de novo appeal;

Colten v Kentucky **407 US 104 (72)**—(same);

Wasman v US **468 US 559 (84)**—can also increase sentence on retrial because of D's conduct since 1st sentence (if judge so explains)

North Carolina v Pearce **395 US 711 (69)**—no double jeopardy violation, but due process says heavier sentence on retrial (after D gets reversal & new trial) OK only if judge shows reasons why it's not vindictive; i.e., presume vindictive;

Blackledge v Perry **417 US 21 (74)**—not double jeopardy, but due process presumption of vindictiveness for indictment after D's "de novo" appeal; BUT *US v Goodwin* **457 US 368 (82)** OK to indict pre-trial, while District Court case pending, because of D's refusal to plead; (*See also Chapter 13, Plea Bargains*);

Thigpen v Roberts **468 US 27 (84)**—reaffirm *Blackledge* **417 US 21 (74)**;

Lovett v Butterworth **610 F.2d 1002 (1st Cir. '79)**—Blackledge bars burglary indictment (& 10-20 state prison) after conviction & appeal for breaking & entering (+ 2½ years house of correction);

Texas v McCullough **475 US 134 (86)**—trial judge can increase sentence (from 20 to 50) because he himself granted new trial (& had reasons), so no vindictiveness;

C v Hyatt **419 M 815, 819, 824 (95)**—though under federal constitution as construed in *McCullough* (**475 US 134**), there would be no error, SJC adopts "as a common law principle a requirement that, when (D) is again convicted of a crime or crimes, the second sentencing judge may impose a harsher sentence or sentences only if the judge's reason or reasons for doing so appear on the record and are based on information that was not before the first sentencing judge";

Bullington v Missouri **451 US 430 (81)**—D initially sentenced to life imprisonment (in death penalty case) = protected by double jeopardy clause from death penalty upon any retrial of case following reversal of conviction;

C v Henriquez **66 MAC 912 (2006)**—sentence after successful appeal (consecutive 15–20 year terms on each of four counts of rape of child, + consecutive 10 years–10 years and a day) was longer than original 45–60 year term, so was prohibited unless supported by additional info; though Commonwealth claimed that continuing/further impact on child victim/family was qualifying additional info, court didn't reach issue of whether this would qualify as fresh info defeating presumption of vindictiveness because the resentencing judge actually placed less reliance on victim impact than did the first sentencing judge: "resentencing judge's reasons for the sentences he imposed accordingly cannot satisfy the *Hyatt* test, 419 Mass. at 823, to rebut the presumption of vindictiveness in a harsher resentencing";

US v DiFrancesco **449 US 117 (80)**—sentence not final (& increase OK) until after right of government to appeal it; cf. M.R.Crim.P. 29—motion to revoke & revise by judge sua sponte or by D within 60 days;

Aldoupolis v Commonwealth **386 M 260 (82)**—sentence, though begun serving, not "final" until after Rule 29's 60 days for motion to revoke and revise; can be increased in public interest & no double jeopardy because *DiFrancesco* (**449 US 117 (80)**); (fn. 16 SJC bound by US Supreme Court's interpretation of double jeopardy, BUT can, see, e.g., *Berry v Commonwealth* **393 M 793 (85)**, hold differently (& give **more** protection) under Mass. "common law"); *see also C v Hyart* **419 M 815 (95)**;

C v Layne **25 MAC 1 (87)**—judge can't change sentence (to reflect his "intent") after deadline for M.R. Crim. P. 29 revoke & revise motion (*See Chapter 14-T, Sentencing Advocacy, Dispositions: Motions to Revoke & Revise*);

US v Bynoe **562 F.2d 126 (1st Cir. '77)**—can't increase (probation to fine) sentence 1 week after began serving; query whether sentencing falsehood justifies surrender;

Gavin v Commonwealth **367 M 331 (75)**—Superior Court Appellate Division can increase sentence because no real chance it's vindictive;

Walsh v Picard **446 F.2d 1209 (1st Cir. '71)**—(same); no need for reasons;

C v Jarvis **68 MAC 538 (2007)**—following D's jury-waived trial on OUI (guilty), D requested new judge for trial re: the existence of three prior OUI convictions; prior to "transferring that part of the case to second judge," first judge sentenced D to two years, one year committed, balance suspended for two years, "on the primary offense of OUI"; though this was procedurally improper (G.L. c. 278, § 11A: sentencing should not occur until bifurcated trial is completed), double jeopardy clause did not bar "resentencing" following the finding of guilt on the subsequent offense charge; D had no legitimate expectation of finality in the prematurely-imposed sentence;

C v Burden **48 MAC 232 (99), citing** *Shabazz v Commonwealth* **387 M 291, 295–296 (82)**—"a successful challenge to one sentence imposed at the same time as other sentences . . . , opens up all the interdependent, lawful sentences for reconsideration without violating the double jeopardy clause, at least if the aggregate of the original sentences is not increased"; see also, e.g., *C v Connolly* **49 MAC 424 (2000)** reversal & no retrial on charge on which sentence was imposed, so appellate court invites Commonwealth to bring forward previously "filed" conviction from same trial;

C v Sneed **3 MAC 33 (75)**—not double jeopardy to charge escape (and get sentence for that crime) & deduct good time credits as well on previous sentence;

19-D. COLLATERAL ESTOPPEL (ISSUE PRECLUSION)

K. Smith, *Criminal Practice & Procedure,* **§ 1317 (2d ed. 1983 & Supp.)**—collateral estoppel = alternative to Morey standard for double jeopardy's "same offense"; D's burden to show no other rational basis for prior ruling;

Ashe v Swenson **397 US 436 (70)**—collateral estoppel is within 5th Amendment's double jeopardy bar& is binding on states; can't relitigate ultimate fact's final judgment between same parties; same incident, different victim, still collateral estoppel because issue was identification;

Bobby v Bies **129 S Ct 2145 (2009)**—issue preclusion doctrine bars relitigation of issues actually determined *and necessary to the ultimate outcome* of a prior proceeding; it was not clear that issue of mental retardation was actually determined in earlier proceedings, and even if it was, courts' statement regarding D's mental capacity were not necessary to the judgments affirming his sentence (death); S Ct holds that lower courts wrongly applied *Ashe v Swenson*;

Yeager v US **129 S Ct 2360 (2009)**—D's trial resulted in acquittals on some counts, and hung jury on other counts; prosecution "refined" its case in new indictments and lower court held that because of hung jury counts, D could not establish that jury had decided favorably to him on dispositive "issue preclusion" factors; Supreme Court holds that consideration of hung counts has no place in issue preclusion analysis; District Court and Circuit Court came to different conclusions regarding what issues of ultimate fact jury had "necessarily resolved in his favor" in acquitting him;

C v Ringuette **60 MAC 351 (2004)**—"**offensive use" of collateral estoppel:** barring D from relitigating, in second set of indictments, suppression motion heard and denied when filed in first set of indictments; D's argument that principle doesn't apply to issue which is not "a final judgment on the merits" rejected, on ground that 'right to seek interlocutory review was sufficient to cloak judge's order with finality sufficient to permit its preclusive use';

C v Cabrera **449 M 825 (2007)**—D litigated suppression motion concerning car stop leading to charges of receiving stolen property, but after motion was denied, D pled guilty; four years later, further charge (breaking and entering the store from which the property was stolen) was brought, & SJC holds D was collaterally estopped from relitigating the suppression issue (having had opportunity to appeal before but foregoing it to plead guilty, the judgment was final);

C v Rabb **70 MAC 194 (2007)**—fact that co-D's motion to suppress was denied doesn't preclude D from suppression motion; suppression hearing is "critical stage" at which D has right to effective assistance of counsel & meaningful opportunity to participate;

C v Stephens **451 M 370 (2008)**—alleged drug buyer's case stayed in District Court, and his motion to suppress was allowed; alleged drug seller's case (this D's) was in Superior Court, and (after the co-D's motion's success, of which he was unaware), his motion to suppress was denied; motion for reconsideration in light of co-D's result was also denied: SJC holds Commonwealth was not collaterally stopped on issue of legality of seizures because mutuality of parties was required for estoppel;

C v Micheli **258 M 89, 91 (27)**—acquittal of crime of begetting child would bar prosecution for neglecting to support same child (but mere dismissal of begetting not same as acquittal);

C v Scala **380 M 500 (80)**—collateral estoppel doesn't bar felonies for drugs D had at arrest on day after other drugs seized at apartment, though NG in District Court for apartment drugs: not same offense, but maybe due process basis for collateral estoppel if inefficiency/ harassment; but not here re: motion to suppress allowed in District Court because , even if "ultimate fact" (fn.4), no record or right of appeal for DA after District Court motion to suppress was allowed (NOTE: this was pre-Rule 15(a)(2));

C v Gardner **67 MAC 744 (2006)**—since one cannot be both the thief and the "receiver" of the stolen goods, Commonwealth was judicially estopped from prosecuting D for unarmed robbery after his conviction in District Court on complaint charging receiving stolen property (the same purse he allegedly "robbed" from elderly woman);

C v Allain **36 MAC 595 (94)**—"no probable cause" order resulting from successful motion to suppress at probable cause hearing did not bar indictment, and "collateral estoppel" did not bar Superior Court hearing on, & denial of, motion to suppress; habeas corpus denied sub nom. *Allain v Mass.* **998 F.Supp 57 (D.Mass '98)**;

C v Royce **20 MAC 221 (85)**—collateral estoppel no bar to try conspiracy after NG on substantive (robbery; bar to using evidence of participation because 1st jury found NG (but harmless!); no bar to using evidence of planning & fruits;

C v Pero **402 M 476 (88)**—can charge conspiracy (essence = agreement) after NG possession with intent to distribute, but can't re-litigate latter;

C v Benson **389 M 473 (83)**—collateral estoppel no bar to conspire: arson after arson NG; D's participation/ assistance admissible because not clear why 1st jury found NG;

Carasquillo v Commonwealth **422 M 1014 (96)**— collateral estoppel no bar to conspiracy to commit murder after NG on murder;

C v DeCillis **41 MAC 312 (96)**—collateral estoppel did not bar trial of substantive offenses after NG on conspiracy indictments, even though substantive offense proof would be (only) D as joint-venturer; result could have been different if D argued more specifically, e.g., re "instructions on which the conspiracy charges were sent to the jury";

C v Lopez **383 M 497 (81)**—can indict/convict of armed assault to murder after District Court's 'probable cause' & bindover to grand jury though District Court found NG on related firearm, because latter had unrelated elements & lacked proof unnecessary to assault to murder;

C v Conkey **452 M 1022 (2009)**—acquittal of armed robbery did not bar trial (re-trial after appellate reversals of convictions) of armed assault in dwelling and armed burglary because D could not establish that "factual issue whether he committed a larceny was determined in his favor" (e.g., jury could have found lacking proof that property was taken from victim's "person or her immediate control" or accomplished by actual/constructive force); also, actual commission of intended felony is not element of either crime to be re-tried, which are instead complete when D has felonious *intent* & commits requisite underlying acts; acquittal of armed robbery did not bar retrial on first degree felony murder (verdicts based on armed burglary and armed assault in dwelling felonies) or on other theories of first degree murder (armed robbery acquittal NOT a finding of misidentification/'some other dude did it');

C v Williams **431 M 71 (2000)**—following allowance of suppression motion, Commonwealth notice of appeal but withdrawal of same, and dismissal of indictment, SJC decided suppression issue (in wholly unrelated case) favorably to Commonwealth's position in withdrawn appeal, but Commonwealth could not re-indict; allowance of motion to dismiss new indictment affirmed; "need not decide whether constitutionally based issue preclusion principles may be applied outside of a situation where jeopardy does not attach because this case can be resolved by application of common-law issue preclusion principles . . . (i.e.,) order allowing (D's) motion to suppress had become 'the law of the case'";

C v Garcia **48 MAC 201 (99)**—D was charged with contributing to delinquency of minor and receiving stolen property, and the latter was tried in District Court (not guilty) prior to trial of the "contributing" charge in juvenile court (which has exclusive jurisdiction: see G.L. c. 119, § 63): though, given the evidence, required finding of not guilty was ordered on appeal of the conviction, conviction might be barred under collateral estoppel aspect of double jeopardy clause;

C v Fickett **403 M 194 (88)**—murder retrial maybe barred by NG on carrying gun;

C v Shagoury **6 MAC 584 (78)**—other rational basis for 1st NG in other county;

C v Nardone **406 M 123 (89)**—although conviction of lesser included offense generally bars re-prosecution for greater, not so here because improper finding of guilt on assault to kill did not logically imply not guilty to assault to murder; BUT SEE *Fuller v Commonwealth* **394 M 1014 (85)** double jeopardy bars non-support for period AFTER D found NG for same because NG possibly based only on nonpaternity (no mention of collateral estoppel); but compare *C v Teixera* **396 M 746 (86)** reverse & order required finding of not guilty on non-support (G.L. c. 273, § 15) because no evidence D could pay; but no double jeopardy bar to G.L. c. 273, § 12 (civil) or § 15 (again) for period subsequent to 1st complaint;

C v Evans **101 M 25 (1869)**—D's G of A&B = conclusive evidence (of lack of justification) in later manslaughter trial (after V died); (no mention of collateral estoppel);

C v Cerveny **387 M 280 (82)**—no nonmutual collateral estoppel, so can prosecute D though co-conspirators acquitted—(but can't convict only one at same trial);

C v Diaz **19 MAC 29 (84)**—inconsistent verdicts OK because maybe just a break;

Dunn v US **284 US 390 (32)**—(same); compromise or mistake OK;

C v Jones **403 M 279 (88)**—OK G. though co-venturer found NG;

C v Nazzaro **7 MAC 859 (79)**—no collateral estoppel after District Court "reduction" & sentence because no jurisdiction (NO LONGER VALID as rationale, per *Waller v Florida* **397 US 387 (70)** and *C v Norman* **27 MAC 82, aff'd 406 M 1001 (89)**, above: state statutes delineating various courts' subject matter jurisdiction can't defeat constitutional protection against double jeopardy;

Aetna v Niziolek **395 M 737 (85)**—in civil suit, D's prior "guilty" finding conclusive (though no mutuality); but guilty plea is only admissible, not conclusive;

Dowling v US **1493 US 342 (90)**—admission at subsequent unrelated trial of evidence of crime for which D had been acquitted not prohibited by either double jeopardy or collateral estoppel principles;

US v Felix **503 US 378 (92)**—intro of relevant evidence of particular misconduct is not same as "prosecution" for that conduct;

C v Francis **432 M 353 (2000)**—issue of whether collateral estoppel principles under Mass. Constitution barred Commonwealth from introducing evidence of alleged prior misconduct (of which D had been acquitted in earlier trial) not reached because D won here on "evidentiary" law; court noted no such bar under federal constitu**Kion**; *Krochta v Commonwealth* **429 M 711, 716–717 (99)**—again (after *C v Scala* **380 M 500, 505 (80)**) considering, without deciding, whether collateral estoppel protection is part of constitutional right to due process, independent of double jeopardy clause; cites *Allain v Massachusetts* **998 F.Supp 57, 60–61 (D.Mass '98)** for "discussion of the 'legal landscape' concerning federal and state decisions regarding whether the due process clause, independent of the double jeopardy clause, requires application of collateral estoppel principles in criminal proceedings");

Krochta v Commonwealth **429 M 711 (99)**—"collateral estoppel" doesn't bar criminal prosecution of D for offenses following a finding in his favor at a probation revocation hearing triggered by the alleged commission of the same offenses;

C v Woods **414 M 343 (90)**—at bench trial in District Court, D acquitted of operating under the influence but G of 2 counts vehicular homicide by negligent operation & operating after suspension: double jeopardy did not bar introduction of alcohol evidence at jury-6 trial de novo on latter charges;

C v DiRenzo **44 MAC 85 (97)**—admission at murder trial of evidence of violent assaults committed on same night in other towns by group of which D was part not barred by collat. estoppel simply because grand jury did not indict D for the assaults: "collateral estoppel applies to factual issues, not evidence";

Gelmette v Commonwealth **426 M 1003 (97)**—1st degree murder jury hung 11 for manslaughter & 1 for NG did not bar retrial of 1st degree murder (no **verdict**/final judgment rejecting malice)

19-E. DUAL SOVEREIGNS—FEDERAL, STATE, AND LOCAL

Bartkus v Ill **359 US 121 (59)**—subsequent state prosecution = OK (5-4);

Abbate v US **359 US 187 (59)**—subsequent federal prosecution = OK (6-3);

Petite v US **361 US 529 (60)**—federal policy (4/6/59 memo by Attorney General) against duplicating state prosecutions, unless "compelling" reasons;

Waller v Florida **397 US 387 (70)**—municipal court & "state" court not 2 sovereigns; can't prosecute state court felony (larceny) after municipal court trial/sentence (for concededly lesser included offenses of disorderly & destroying property)

ABA Standards for Criminal Justice, Prosecution Function & Defense Function (3d ed. 1993) 3-3.9—DA not obliged to present all charges, e.g., if D being prosecuted elsewhere; Comment: "overcharging" line is subjective one;

K. Smith, *Criminal Practice & Procedure*, § 1305 (2d ed. 1983 & Supp.)—proceedings to which double jeopardy prohibition doesn't apply;

C v Cepulonis **374 M 487 (78)**—state can prosecute for related but different (under "duplicity" analysis) crimes after federal government does; though no constitutional problem (because Bartkus-Abbate, above), SJC might be more generous in "common sense" (especially because of Petite Policy)—but not here;

Angiulo v Commonwealth **401 M 71 (87)**—federal G on same elements bars later Mass. prosecution unless federal maximum punishment much less (applying *Cepulonis* dictum); so dismiss conspiracy/murder, but approve accessory/murder after federal RICO/murder;

Chapter 20
SUPPRESSION—OF PHYSICAL EVIDENCE OR ALLEGED STATEMENTS

20-A. IN GENERAL; MOTIONS, FILING, ETC.

See Chapter 3, Defendant's Entry into Criminal Justice System and Chapter 20-M, Investigative Stops of People & Cars; & K. Smith, Criminal Practice & Procedure, §§ 61–131 (2d ed. 1983 & Supp.)—re: Arrest; *See also Chapter 4-A, "presentment" delay/arraignment/bail delay*;

CPCS P/G 2.3—be alert for discovery at arraignment; 4.3 scrutinize/amend pretrial conference form; 4.4 discover physical evidence & D's alleged written/oral statements; 4.6 (g): should consider filing motion to suppress seized evidence, alleged statements of D; 4.2 file only motions strategically appropriate & only after investigation; **caution re: adverse impact of motions & re: affidavits**; 4.10 consider interlocutory appeal;

C v Healy **452 M 510 (2008)**—conducting suppression hearing and (jury-waived) trial simultaneously causes problems, and is a practice "discouraged" by appellate courts; procedure has "potential to cause confusion or misapplication of the respective rules of evidence governing suppression hearings and trials, and the respective burdens of proof," and also may "giv[e] the appearance that the challenged evidence has been accepted on the merits"; denies parties rights to apply for leave to pursue interlocutory appeal before jeopardy attaches; **"the practice should be eliminated"**; see also, in context of motion to suppress *identification*, *C v Powell* **72 MAC 22 (2008)**—though defense counsel made no objection to judge's decision not to hold evidentiary hearing on motion to suppress ID apart from jury-waived trial and thus no relief for this D, "seam-less integration of a hearing on a motion to suppress with a trial on the merits should be avoided"; "distinct hearing, even if in voir dire, is preferable to what occurred here";

C v Love **452 M 498 (2008)**—combined suppression hearing and trial began in District Court, but before completed D was indicted: jeopardy had attached in District Court proceeding, and indictments had to be dismissed (though case could be completed in District Court); practice of combining suppression hearing and trial must be eliminated, & decision on motion should be issued before trial begins; trial may take place before expiration of ten-day period permitted for interlocutory review only if both parties have waived their rights to seek such review on the record;

C v Monteiro **75 MAC 280 (2009)**—though D intended to preserve right to appeal denial of suppression motion, his jury waiver and "stipulate[ion] to the truth of the narrative in the police report and as to if the firearm was operable" were incapable of supporting a conviction because D not informed on record that he was surrendering rights to confrontation, cross-examination, right to testify, right not to incriminate self;

C v Rodriguez **74 MAC 314 (2009)**—seller of drugs had no standing to challenge search of buyer; as to different seizure) court "emphasize[d]" that D's affidavit sufficed to raise constitutional issues, but "that affidavit is not evidence at the suppression hearing" [still: caution is mandatory; see cited cases]; BUT <u>ON FURTHER REVIEW, 456 M 578 (2010)</u>, SJC orders required finding of not guilty on distribution counts, and new suppression hearing;

C v Mubdi **456 M 385 (2010)**—suppression motion and accompanying affidavit must accomplish 2 purposes: (1) must be sufficient for judge to determine whether evidentiary hearing is necessary (i.e., allege facts to establish that evidence was obtained through search/seizure for which Commonwealth must prove probable cause, reasonable suspicion, or consent to search, and that D has standing to challenge constitutionality of search/seizure) and (2) affidavit must be sufficiently detailed to give notice to prosecution of what particular search[es] or seizure[s] D is challenging so prosecution may determine what witnesses to call and what evidence to offer to meet burden of proving probable cause, reasonable suspicion, or consent; IF crime charged is one alleging possession of (e.g. drugs) at the time of search, standing is automatic, but affidavit must make clear here that D was contesting both search of vehicle and search of his person; UNLESS COMMONWEALTH RAISES ISSUES OF motion/affidavit deficiencies on these points at trial court level, they are waived; either prosecution or judge may move/order more particularized affidavit or prosecution may move that motion be denied without hearing for failure to give Commonwealth fair notice as to search being challenged; **insistence on strict requirements which deprives D of hearing on constitutional claim "may be an abuse of discretion" ("[t]he rules were not intended to be administered inflexibly")**; under art. 14 (unlike 4th Amendment) question of standing is separate from question of reasonable expectation of privacy: where D has automatic standing (because he's charged with a possessory offense and search is of a private place where object he is alleged to possess was found), he need not show reasonable expectation of privacy in place searched; automatic standing is *not limited to joint possession cases* (i.e., in which a co-D purportedly has the reasonable expectation of privacy); MA standing rule is that of *Jones v US* 362 US 257 (abandoned by US S Ct in *Salvucci* 448 US 83); exception to automatic standing is when D had no right to be in the house or auto where evidence was found; D must still show that there was a "search" in constitutional sense, i.e., that someone had reasonable expectation of privacy in the place searched (because only then would justification be needed); affidavit accompanying motion may not be offered in evidence by D at hearing and isn't substitute for D's testimony; at trial prosecution may use D's affidavit only to cross-examine as to prior inconsistent statements;

C v Castillo **66 MAC 34 (2006)**—trial on "stipulated evidence" (here, to preserve right to appeal denial of motion to suppress) "cannot be justified to save court time" when flaws make it anything but time-saving; reversal because judge failed to ask D if he agreed to the procedure & if he was aware of various constitutional rights he was thus waiving; fn.5: given present posture of case (i.e., invalid conviction after failure to make record of know-ing/voluntary waiver of rights), court had no authority to decide what was effectively an "interlocutory appeal" of the suppression motion, since no single justice of SJC had allowed such interlocutory appeal or referred substantive suppression issue to Appeals Court;

C v Ferrer **68 MAC 544, 546 n.3 (2007)**—though D captioned motion as "motion in limine", court looked "to substance rather than nomenclature" to discern that it was "a motion to suppress evidence on constitutional grounds" (so that no further objection at trial was required for preservation);

C v Cataldo **69 MAC 465 (2007)**—though appellate court has [too] often "supplemented" motion judge's findings, opinion here notes that mere fact that witness testifies without express impeachment to a fact "should not necessarily be equated with a conclusion that the judge accepted his or her testimony"; judicial silence, as reflected in absence of a finding supportive of witness, may "suggest [ ] that the judge rejected the testimony"; litigants looking to appeal should assess record, consider motion to clarify and or reconsider, for ambiguous record/findings;

C v Ramos **72 MAC 773 (2008), citing** *C v Isaiah I* **448 M 334, 337 (2007)**—appellate court recites facts from "findings of motion judge and from *uncontested evidence necessarily credited by him*";

C v Pagan **73 MAC 369 (2008)**—suppression hearing judge is "entitled to believe all of what the witnesses told him, some of it, or none of it," and here clear that judge's ruling "essentially rested on his fundamental disbelief" of police witnesses' account of sale arrangements, arrest, and discovery of the drugs;

C v Espada **450 M 687, 702 n.17 (2008)**—noting lack of authority for proposition that unless judge specifically discredits statement, it should be/is being credited;

Kimmelman v Morrison **477 US 365 (86)**—ineffective assistance for no motion to suppress (because got no discovery, because relied on DA to turn over evidence & complaining witness to drop case); *see Mass. cases in Chapter 2E*—Ineffective Assistance of Counsel (e.g., *C v Pena* **31 MAC 201 (91)** failure to file motion to suppress was ineffective assistance);

C v Clemente **452 M 295 (2008)**—not ineffective assistance to fail to file motions having minimal chance of success: statements would not have been suppressed because, according to SJC, D not in custody when questioned so no need of Miranda warnings (D was questioned in "neutral location, a room in a court house" and "voluntarily agreed" to speak with detective, and was allowed to leave to attend son's arraignment, not arrested until after that arraignment), and SJC believed no question of voluntariness either;

See also *C v Berrios* **64 MAC 541 (2005)**—ineffective assistance claim for failure to litigate viable motion to suppress **here** did NOT depend on whether motion would have succeeded, because issue was whether withdrawal of G plea (allegedly involuntary) should be allowed on basis of ineffective assistance of counsel: D said his "confession" was product of beating by cop, and D's mother and girlfriend could provide corroboration, i.e., testimony about D's physical appearance;

C v Rabb **70 MAC 194 (2007)**—fact that co-D's motion to suppress was denied doesn't preclude D from suppression motion; suppression hearing is "critical stage" at which D has right to effective assistance of counsel & meaningful opportunity to participate;

Liacos, Brodin & Avery, *Handbook of Massachusetts Evidence*, Chapter 9, "Confessions & Incriminating Statements" (7th ed. 1999)—suppression issues, e.g., Miranda, voluntariness, Sixth Amendment violations, Fourth Amendment/fruit of poisonous tree; delayed arraignment; right to use telephone; right to interpreters; statements during court-ordered psych. exams; statements during plea negotiations, counsel-assignment proceedings, or pretrial diversion assessment;

K. Smith, *Criminal Practice & Procedure*, Chapters 4–6, Search & Seizure, Stop & Frisk, & Interrogation (2d ed. 1983 & Supp.);

LaFave, W.R., *Search & Seizure: A Treatise on the Fourth Amendment* (3d ed. 1996)—excellent & authoritative;

U.S. Constitution, Fourth, Fifth, Sixth, and Fourteenth Amendments—*see below*;

Mapp v Ohio **367 US 643 (61)**—exclusionary rule for state courts;

C v Gomes **59 MAC 332 (2003)**—D cannot invoke exclusionary rule to suppress evidence of his own unlawful conduct in response to police actions in violation of constitutional protections against unlawful search and seizure; even if cop made unlawful entry, cop's use of force to prevent D from closing door on him did not result in seizure of contraband or lead to police observations of contraband or unlawful activity;

Pettijohn v Hall **599 F.2d 476 (1st Cir. '79)**—D can call witness whose ID D got suppressed to show he'd ID'd another; suppressed ID is then admissible (judge had ruled that after obtaining suppression, D couldn't use evidence);

Pennsylvania Board of Probation v Scott **524 US 357 (98)**—evidence seized in violation of Fourth Amendment not excluded from use at parole revocation hearing;

Mass. Constitution, Declaration of Rights, Articles 12 & 14;

See Declaration of Rights foundations in holdings in, inter alia, *Upton* **394 M 365 (85)**—*Sheppard* **394 M 381 (85)**; *Ford* **394 M 421 (85)**; *Blood* **400 M 61 (87)**; *Framingham* **373 M 783 (77)**; but see *C v Eagleton* **402 M 199 (88)**—D made "no Declaration of Rights Article 14 argument worthy of the name";

Chin, G.J. & Wells, S.C., "The 'Blue Wall of Silence' as Evidence of Bias and Motive to Lie: A New Approach to Police Perjury," **59 U Pittsburgh Law Review 233 (Winter 1998)**, and Fisher, S.Z., "'Just the Facts, Ma'am': Lying and the Omission of Exculpatory Evidence in Police Reports," **28 New England Law Review 1 (1993)**;

C v Diaz **422 M 269 (96)**—while refusing to require contemporaneous electronic recording of D's interrogation/statement, SJC encourages defense to call for adverse inferences (including actual nonexistence of any statement) from this omission; *C v LeBlanc* **433 M 549, 553 n.5 (2001)** failure to record statement electronically doesn't mean suppression (citing *Fernandes* **427 M 90, 98 (98)** & *Ardon* **428 M 496, 498 (98)**); *C v DiGiambattista* **442 M 423 (2004)—if prosecution introduces D's statement which is product of custodial interrogation or interrogation conducted at a place of detention, and there is "not at least an audiotape recording of the COMPLETE INTERROGATION," D entitled on request to jury instruction that highest court prefers such full recording and its absence means that alleged statement should be weighed with great caution and care, AND that absence of recording permits (but doesn't compel) jury to conclude failure of proof of voluntariness beyond reasonable doubt;**

C v Pimental **454 M 475 (2009)**—refusal to hold unrecorded statements to police "per se inadmissible";

C v Jones **75 MAC 38 (2009)**—D wasn't in custody or place of detention so adverse instruction not required; even if it should have been given, "no error" because judge did tell jurors they should weigh unrecorded statement with great care;

M.R.Crim.P. 13, Pretrial Motions—written, signed, time limits (D); state with particularity all (separately numbered) reasons, defenses, & objections then available; otherwise waived unless judge gives relief; detailed factual affidavit signed with personal knowledge; law memo maybe required for motions, must be for motion to suppress evidence (except warrantless search & seizure); can renew a motion previously heard/denied; 15(c) must decide motion to suppress before jeopardy; may move that trial judge reconsider other judge's ruling on pretrial motion to suppress (see *C v Ortiz* **431 M 134, 142 n.7 (2000)**, context of motion to suppress statements);

C v Balboni **419 M 42 (94)—motion to reconsider "final"/dispositive order should be filed within 30 days (same as time for filing notice of appeal)**; but see *C v Haskell* **438 M 790 (2003)**—within judge's discretion to allow reconsideration of denial of suppression motion five years later (D had been on default during that time);

C v Turner **71 MAC 665 (2008)**—because, after ordering suppression of evidence, judge dismissed charges "for lack of prosecution" during the time period in which Commonwealth was entitled to seek leave to appeal, dismissal = reversed (as was suppression order);

C v Silva **440 M 772 (2004)**—failure to assert "knock and announce" issue in motion to suppress = waiver, despite D's claim (rejected by court) that testimony at hearing "specifically identified" the issue;

C v Johnston **60 MAC 13 (2003)**—motion's claim that D not advised of Miranda rights held not to include particular claim that rights given failed to convey that D had right to attorney's presence during questioning; rule requiring particularity is to let judge determine whether moving party can meet initial burden of establishing necessary facts and to provide reliable notice to opposing party of facts supporting motion; precedents cited;

Superior Court Rule 61, motions to suppress, return property—written, specific facts, affidavit, & R.13; (*See also Chapter 6, Motions, Pretrial Conference, Discovery and Chapter 7-N, Continuance*);

C v Lewin (II) **407 M 629 (90)**—"ambiguous" statement suppressed because more prejudicial than probative;

C v Gillette **33 MAC 427 (92)**—failure to file motion in limine to exclude inadmissible evidence of D's predisposition to rape was ineffective assistance;

C v Donahue **430 M 710, 715–16 (2000)**—counsel not ineffective in introducing psych expert testimony concerning D's statements to him, even though they bolstered proof of premeditation and extreme atrocity/cruelty; counsel had little with which to work, and pursued insanity/lack of specific intent with this evidence;

C v Whelton **428 M 24, 25–26 (98)**—denial of motion to suppress evidence on constitutional grounds is reviewable **without further objection at trial**, in accord with *C v Sherman* **389 M 287, 290 n.2 (83)**; lays to rest contrary language of *C v Acosta* **416 M 279 (93)**;

C v Lay **63 MAC 27 (2005)**—that two civilian witnesses denied, at suppression hearing, gang membership, while DA acknowledged, at trial, that they were gang members did not by itself establish that DA knew at the time that earlier testimony was false; judge correctly declined to charge jury that witnesses had lied previously;

C v Scott **52 MAC 486 (2001)**—appellate court will accept as true 'uncontradicted' testimony only if there's not only a lack of "contradiction," but also a belief that motion judge either explicitly or implicitly credited the witness's testimony; see, however, **S.C. after remand, further appeal [57 MAC 36 (2003)], and further appellate review: 440 M 642 (2004);**

C v Bryant **447 M 494 (2006)**—appellate court affirmed denial of motion to dismiss by holding D had no standing, avoiding merits of issue;

C v Gonsalves **441 M 1007 (2004)**, citing *C v Murphy* **423 M 1010 (1996)** and *C v. Gonsalves* **432 M 613, 615–22 (2000)**—district attorney, pursuant to M.R.Crim.P. 15(d), required to pay fees and costs of D in Commonwealth's appeal of suppression order;

20-A.1. Suppression Motion, Timeliness; Burden of Showing Voluntariness

C v DeArmas **397 M 167 (86)**—no motion to suppress physical evidence because not filed **pre**-trial;

Robinson v Commonwealth **445 M 280 (2005)**—trial judge did NOT have discretion to deem D's unexcused absence from hearing on motion to suppress to be a waiver of the suppression motion, but did have discretion to treat absence as waiver of D's right to be present at the hearing, a critical stage of the case, IF D had adequate notice of time and date of hearing, and judge considers reasons for D's absence, if known, and possible prejudice to Commonwealth or co-Ds or witnesses if hearing doesn't proceed as scheduled; hearing re voluntariness of absence is necessary; waiver of right to be present doesn't constitute waiver of right to the suppression hearing and right to effective assistance of counsel at the hearing;

C v Riveiro **393 M 224 (84)**—D gets Miranda voir dire though no motion to suppress because DA didn't give timely discovery of statement; though statement was excluded, still error because jury heard it;

C v Harris **371 M 462 (76)**—right to voir dire re: coerced statement though no motion to suppress;

C v Iglesias **426 M 574, 579 (98)**—request for voir dire = a "proper method of challenging the admissibility of a defendant's statement";

C v Van Melkebeke **48 MAC 364 (99)**—reversal because judge refused request for voir dire on voluntariness of statement, on ground that it had already been decided at suppression hearing, but only Miranda waiver had been addressed at such hearing, and the two are discrete questions; judge also refused here to instruct jurors on their independent duty under humane practice rule (decide voluntariness of statement beyond a reasonable doubt before considering it as evidence);

C v Brown **449 M 747 (2007)**—when D didn't raise voluntariness prior to trial or when statements were admitted, judge didn't err in granting DA's subsequent request for "ruling" that they were voluntarily made, though D asked deferral until defense evidence of lack of criminal responsibility was admitted: D's strategy was to question whether the statements had been made at all, AND voluntariness of all D's statements doesn't automatically become live issue when D raises insanity defense;

C v Adams **389 M 265 (83)**—can object without motion to suppress, and burden is on Commonwealth "to prove affirmatively, prior to the admission of (D's) statement, that the statements were properly obtained and that the defendant waived his rights";

C v Woods **419 M 366 (95)**—same;

C v Woods **427 M 169 (98)**—same; *C v Samneang Ka* **70 MAC 137 (2007)**—same, but disregard of rule here found harmless beyond a reasonable doubt "even if we were to assume they should have been suppressed";

C v Davis **58 MAC 412 (2003)**—D should have filed pretrial motion to suppress or requested voir dire re: Miranda rights given; cop's testimony omitted "statement may be used as evidence against you" warning, and though ADA proffered document to cop and cop said he gave "those rights in their entirety," failure to mark document means that burden not met BUT here harmless beyond reasonable doubt;

C v Rubio **27 MAC 506 (89)**—where D objects at trial to admissibility of statement on Miranda or voluntariness grounds, judge should stop trial & hold hearing, even if D had failed to move to suppress or exclude in limine before trial;

C v Florek **48 MAC 414 (2000)**—trial judge erred in overruling D's objection on voluntariness and Miranda grounds when DA asked cop-witness at trial what D said; motion to suppress had been filed pre-trial, but counsel hadn't pressed for hearing; trial judge should have stopped trial and held hearing;

C v Bongarzone **390 M 326 (83)**—extend motion to suppress time limit if D needs info; but once obtained, limit = reasonableness (trial day too late);

C v White **44 MAC 168 (98)**—upholding denial of hearing on late-filed motion to suppress (day before trial) but addressing motion to suppress substantively anyway because of ineffective assistance of counsel claim;

20-A.2. Motions, Affidavit

C v Luce **34 MAC 105 (93)**—failure to file affidavit supporting motion to suppress statements may be "dispositive of the . . . motion";

C v Prater **431 M 86, 91 (2000)**—submitting "copy" rather than original of signed affidavit fatal; info said to be "not properly before" judge;

C v Smallwood **379 M 878 (80)**—affidavit needs personal knowledge;

C v Parker **412 M 353 (92)**—counsel's affidavit citing conclusions of expert did not meet Rule 13 requirement that affiant have personal knowledge;

C v Zavala **52 MAC 770 (2001)**—late-filed affidavit contained only general "laundry list" of possible grounds of suppression, in violation of M.R.Crim.P. 13(a)(2) and requirement of affiant with personal knowledge, justifying judge in refusing to hear motion;

C v Clegg **61 MAC 197 (2004)**—counsel's failure to file any affidavit with motion to suppress would have warranted DENIAL of motion without any hearing or, "at the very least," insistence upon affidavit before scheduling hearing; absent affidavit setting forth factual basis for expectation of privacy in seized bag, there was no legal basis for finding "search in the constitutional sense";

C v Colon **449 M 207 (2007)**—D has burden of demonstrating reasonable expectation of privacy in place searched (here, D's girlfriend's apartment, & SJC upholds motion judge's ruling of no such expectation);

C v Costa **65 MAC 227 (2005)**—D's motion and supporting affidavit didn't raise expectation of D's privacy in vehicle searched, and such failure "would have warranted the denial of his motion without a hearing or, at the very least, insistence on a proper affidavit" (but because judge/Commonwealth didn't flag this below, court addresses consent issue there litigated); D can't raise on appeal grounds not raised in suppression motion or hearing;

C v Fudge **20 MAC 382 (85)**—affidavit gets hearing re: search warrant because apprised court of grounds & enough for D's burden of production; don't need memo if not D's burden of proof (*see below*), e.g., search & seizure = beyond search warrant's scope;

C v Rodriguez **74 MAC 314 (2009)**—D's affidavit asserted that on 9/25/06 "in area of Franklin Square park", police stopped, searched, and arrested him and seized evidence in violation of federal and state constitutions and G.L. c. 276, § 1, and Commonwealth knew claims were based upon warrantless search; while Commonwealth offered evidence to establish that some drugs were taken from D's buyer (so D had no standing to contest), Commonwealth offered no evidence at all concerning another amount of cocaine, ADA merely asserting (without personal knowledge, unsworn) that drug had been found on ground (i.e., abandoned by D): "the mere assertion of a prosecutor that police found items of evidence and did not search for or seize them turns suppression jurisprudence on its head"; **ON FURTHER REVIEW, 456 M 578 (2010)**, SJC orders required finding of not guilty on distribution counts, and new suppression hearing;

C v Santosuosso **23 MAC 310 (86)**—affidavit must have facts satisfying D's burden; District Court transcript would suffice, & if unavailable, counsel's affidavit (re: testimony) OK because unlikely cop will sign for D;

C v Chase **14 MAC 1032 (82)**—affidavit "information & belief ID's suggestive & maybe unreliable" = inadequate & may not merit hearing;

C v Ramirez **416 M 41 (93)**—absence of affidavit excused because allegations didn't lend themselves to presentation by affidavits; instead, copious other material & "extensive written analysis of" same sufficed;

C v Trigones **397 M 633 (86)**—(DA) affidavit OK to force blood test because NO OBJECTION;

C v Rodwell **394 M 694 (85)**—no hearing because affidavit showed no state action;

C v Roy **349 M 224 (65)**—motion to suppress needs particularity re: evidence to be suppressed;

C v Slaney **350 M 400 (66)**—must state all grounds;

C v Lewin (III) **408 M 147 (90)**—defense questioning at evidentiary hearing gave prosecutor sufficient notice of items sought to be suppressed, even though items not mentioned in suppression motion;

C v Santiago **30 MAC 207 (91)**—**judge's denial of suppression motion without hearing because of technical defects in motion was abuse of discretion where affidavits gave prosecution sufficient notice**;

C v Robles **48 MAC 490 (2000)**—grounds for suppression must be stated with "particularity", and motion must be accompanied by affidavit "detailing all facts relied upon in support of the motion and signed by a person with personal knowledge of the factual basis of the motion";

C v Zavala **52 MAC 770 (2001)**—no error in refusing to hold suppression hearing: motion itself asserted "a veritable laundry list of possibly grounds for suppression," lacking any particularity AND no affidavit was initially filed with it; affidavit eventually filed was signed by D, but **contained no factual assertions about search of D's person which would support suppression** (further, excuse that D wasn't present during other challenged searches, of purported drug customer of D and area around a garden hose, availed D nothing here) (try affidavit by counsel asserting personal knowledge of what cops claim occurred at time of searches/seizures); **docket entries HERE didn't support D's understanding/argument that some prior judge had ordered suppression hearing to occur immediately prior to trial;**

C v Griffin **45 MAC 396 (98)**—finding probable cause for "all persons present" in circumstances; motion ground of "application for warrant failed to provide probable cause" held to encompass attack on "all persons present" feature of warrant;

C v Rotolo **45 MAC 927 (98)**—failure to include particular ground in motion to suppress "probably fatal to the appeal," which pressed the point (previously made only "at the close of the evidentiary portion of the motion hearing");

C v Accaputo **380 M 435 (80)**—can't argue on appeal ground not argued below;

Langton v Commissioner of Correction **404 M 165 (89)**—theory underlying motion to suppress cannot be changed on appeal; but see *C v DuBois* **44 MAC 294, 297 and n.3 (98)** Commonwealth, as **the "prevailing party" on motion to suppress below, allowed to abandon theory argued below** to justify warrantless search and seizure; "entitled to argue on appeal that the judge was right for the wrong reason, even relying on a principle of law not argued below";

C v Scala **380 M 500 (80)**—can't argue on appeal ground not argued below; (pre-Rule 15 (DA right to interlocutory appeal)) no collateral estoppel bar to DA relitigating motion to suppress D won in District Court (*see Chapter 19*);

C v Stephens **451 M 370 (2008)**—alleged drug buyer's case stayed in District Court, and his motion to suppress was allowed; alleged drug seller's case (this D's) was in Superior Court, and (after the co-D's motion's success, of which he was unaware), his motion to suppress was denied; motion for reconsideration in light of co-D's result was also denied: SJC holds Commonwealth was not collaterally stopped on issue of legality of seizures because mutuality of parties was required for estoppel;

C v Ballou **350 M 751 (66)**—can dismiss after motion to suppress granted & suppression isn't binding because never jeopardy; BUT cf. *C v Williams* **431 M 71, 74–76 (2000)** because Commonwealth could have pursued interlocutory appeal, its failure to do so made allowance of suppression the "law of the case", despite subsequent appellate decision in unrelated case resolving suppression issue of law in Commonwealth's favor; Commonwealth's subsequent new indictment properly dismissed;

C v Mesrobian **10 MAC 355 (80)**—District Court judge heard suppression motion & merits together, ordered suppression, & dismissed = trial, so double jeopardy prohibition bars re-trial at Superior Court (*see Chapters 19; 1-B*): BUT SEE *C v Allain* **36 MAC 595 (94)** motion to suppress allowed by District Court judge in conjunction with probable cause hearing did not bar subsequent in-

dictment & further proceedings (even though suppression of drugs would require NG);

20-A.3. Interlocutory Appeal

C v Boncore **412 M 1013 (92)**—single justice's denial of leave for interlocutory appeal of allowance of suppression motion cannot be appealed by Commonwealth, but G.L. c. 211, § 3, petition is available;

C v Gonsalves **432 M 613 (2000)**—when Commonwealth appeal of suppression is unsuccessful, defense counsel may obtain court order for payment of defense costs & attorney fees under M.R.Crim.P. 15(d); if budget of "the Administrative Office of the Trial Court" has no funds for same, DA's budget must provide (rejecting DA's constitutional arguments against such order);

M.R.Crim.P. 15(a)(2)—interlocutory appeal: either D or Commonwealth may apply to SJC single justice for leave to appeal decision on motion to suppress evidence; justice may grant leave & hear the appeal, or may report it to full bench of SJC or to Appeals Court; (a)(4) "No interlocutory appeal or report may be taken of matters arising out of a probable cause hearing"; R. 15(b)(1): application for leave to appeal suppression order must be made by filing, within 10 days of "issuance of notice of the order being appealed, or such additional time" as trial judge or SJC single justice, both notice of appeal (in the trial court) and application for leave to appeal (to SJC single justice); **BUT, notwithstanding Rule 15's more liberal time limit, Standing Order of SJC**, effective 2/1/97, requires party seeking interlocutory appeal of ruling on motion to suppress to file, **WITHIN SEVEN DAYS OF ISSUANCE OF NOTICE OF THE ORDER BEING APPEALED, OR SUCH ADDITIONAL TIME AS THE TRIAL JUDGE OR THE SINGLE JUSTICE SHALL ORDER** (1) notice of appeal in trial court clerk's office, and (2) application to SJC single justice for leave to appeal ("notwithstanding the ten day provision of M.R.Crim.P. 15(b)(1)" there set forth as governing application for leave to appeal ruling on motion to suppress);

C v Ringuette **443 M 1003 (2004)**—denial of D's motion to suppress is not a final judgment for collateral estoppel purposes (D isn't obligated to seek leave to file interlocutory appeal);

C v Cabrera **449 M 825 (2007)**—D litigated suppression motion concerning car stop leading to charges of receiving stolen property, but after motion was denied, D pled guilty; four years later, further charge (breaking and entering the store from which the property was stolen) was brought, & SJC holds D was collaterally estopped from relitigating the suppression issue (having had opportunity to appeal before but foregoing it to plead guilty, the judgment was final);

C v Mark M. **65 MAC 703 (2006)**—though appellate court remanded case for findings of fact, motion judge wasn't required by the order to hold further evidentiary hearing, notwithstanding Commonwealth's claim to this effect;

C v Castillo **66 MAC 34 (2006)**—trial on "stipulated evidence" (here, to preserve right to appeal denial of motion to suppress) resulted in reversal because judge failed to ask D if he agreed to the procedure & if he was aware of various constitutional rights he was thus waiving; fn.5: given present posture of case (i.e., invalid conviction after failure to make record of knowing/voluntary waiver of rights), court had no authority to decide what was effectively an "interlocutory appeal" of the suppression motion, since no single justice of SJC had allowed such interlocutory appeal or referred substantive suppression issue to Appeals Court;

20-A.4. Rehearing of Motions?

M.R.Crim.P. 13(a)(5)—upon showing that "substantial justice requires," judge may permit previously denied pretrial motion to be renewed;

C v Pagan **73 MAC 369 (2008)**—reconsideration of suppression motion may occur when "substantial justice requires," and is not limited to instances of newly discovered evidence, BUT even when judge stated he would "assume" truth of new affidavits, he wasn't required to hold new hearing or reverse suppression order: "allowing 'do-overs' . . . undermines the integrity of the process and threatens the efficacy of the sequestration orders"; "clear" that initial ruling rested on judge's "fundamental disbelief of" police witnesses' account of how sale arrangements, arrest, and discovery of drugs occurred";

K. Smith, *Criminal Practice & Procedure*, **§ 1282 (2d ed. 1983 & Supp.)**—judge sua sponte can rehear motion to suppress mid-trial if new evidence;

District Court Standards of Judicial Practice, Trials & Probable Cause Hearings (1981), 1:04—suggests don't rehear a motion without new facts;

C v Ortiz **431 M 134, 142 n.7 (2000)**—trial judges may reconsider other judges' ruling on pretrial motions to suppress, though should "inform counsel and allow counsel opportunity to be heard" (re: motion to suppress statements);

C v Griffin **19 MAC 174 (85)**—no new facts on voluntariness for voir dire after motion to suppress denied; (but see *Valdez* **402 M 65 (88)**);

C v McCauley **391 M 697 (84)**—though there was new favorable evidence at trial (re: coerced statement) after motion to suppress was denied, judge could deny renewed "motion to suppress"; no sua sponte obligation to hold "voluntariness" voir dire at trial on this basis (here, counsel didn't request it);

C v Garcia **34 MAC 386, 391–92 (93)**—in reviewing judge's ruling on the suppression motion, appellate court may not rely on facts as developed at trial; *see also* cases cited;

C v Lay **63 MAC 27 (2005)**—that two civilian witnesses denied, at suppression hearing, gang membership, while DA acknowledged, at trial, that they were gang

members did not by itself establish that DA knew at the time that earlier testimony was false; judge correctly declined to charge jury that witnesses had lied previously;

C v Cryer **426 M 562 (98)**—no error in denying rehearing of suppression motion because judge heard it 1st time & could find D's affidavit assertions not credible (that D was coerced into confessing and that "confusion" caused D not to testify at earlier hearing) and cop credible (despite assertions of inconsistent trial testimony);

Robinson v Commonwealth **445 M 280 (2005)**—D's failure to appear for suppression motion (if, after hearing, absence is found to be voluntary, & other considerations) may be deemed, in judge's discretion, a waiver of his right to be present at such suppression hearing, BUT judge has no discretion to deem such absence a waiver of the motion itself or the right to effective assistance of counsel at such motion;

20-A.5. Effect of Suppression Motion/ Evidence upon Trial Evidence

Taylor v C **369 M 183 (75)**—talk to cops doesn't waive Fifth Amendment for trial (*see Chapter 7-H*);

Simmons v US **390 US 377 (68)**—D's testimony on motion to suppress inadmissible re: guilt;

C v Rivera **425 M 633 (97)**—purportedly inconsistent "omissions" in D's affidavit supporting motion to suppress may be used to impeach D's trial testimony (after voir dire, if D requests voir dire);

Prop.M.R.Evid. 104(d)—D's testimony on preliminary matter doesn't open up DA's cross-examination on other issues;

C v Rivera **425 M 633, 637–39 (97)**—though on request of D there should be a voir dire beforehand re: use of affidavit, DA may use affidavit of D on suppression motion & testimony of D at suppression hearing to impeach D at trial; jury should be instructed re: factors germane to finding 'inconsistency' or not; see also *C v Amendola* **406 M 592, 598 (90)**;

C v Judge **420 M 444 (95)**—scope of cross-examination of D on motion to suppress OK: all were "proper matters to test the credibility of" D's testimony on direct; rejecting arguments that failure to limit cross to voluntariness issues "chilled" right to testify at trial and compelled self-incrimination; apparently D could refuse to answer, but would direct be struck?; D had recess to consult with counsel here; (*see also Chapter 20-B & 20-F below re: impeach D by suppressed evidence*);

Pettijohn v Hall **599 F.2d 476 (1st Cir. '79)**—D can call witness whose ID D got suppressed to show he'd ID'd another; suppressed ID is then admissible (judge had ruled that after obtaining suppression, D couldn't use evidence);

C v Wallace **70 MAC 757 (2007)**—even if items were legally seized, they can be found inadmissible if probative value lacking, or outweighed by potential for unfair prejudice;

C v Rodriguez **74 MAC 314 (2009)**—2 separate drug items were introduced, and one should have been suppressed (for required finding of NG on that "possession" charge); while evidence was sufficient to defeat RFNG as to other ("distribution")charge, the drug which should have been suppressed made D's guilt on distribution charge "immeasurably more plausible," such that Court reversed conviction on it; **ON FURTHER REVIEW, 456 M 578 (2010)**, SJC orders required finding of not guilty on distribution counts, and new suppression hearing;

20-A.6. Hearing, Suppression Motion

US v Matlock **415 US 164 (74)**—evidentiary rules (maybe) relaxed at motion hearing;

K. Smith, *Criminal Practice & Procedure*, **§ 1341 (2d ed. 1983 & Supp.)**—evidentiary rules ordinarily normal, but some relaxation at suppression hearing;

C v Rodriguez **74 MAC 314 (2009)**—"relaxation" doesn't mean that prosecutor can merely assert that drugs were found without search or seizure of D: this "turns suppression jurisprudence on its head" since D's motion and affidavit asserted warrantless search and seizure; because Commonwealth presented no evidence, suppression ordered; see further appellate review decision at **456 M 578 (2010)**;

C v Clegg **61 MAC 197 (2004)**—judge abused discretion in denying Commonwealth request for continuance when sole witness (cop) on motion to suppress failed to appear and thereby allowing suppression and, effectively, dismissal;

C v Pagan **73 MAC 369 (2008)**—reconsideration of suppression motion may occur when "substantial justice requires," and is not limited to instances of newly discovered evidence, BUT even when judge stated he would "assume" truth of new affidavits, he wasn't required to hold new hearing or reverse suppression order: "allowing 'do-overs' . . . undermines the integrity of the process and threatens the efficacy of the sequestration orders";

C v Dedominicis **42 MAC 76 (97)**—judge at suppression hearing can't participate in courtroom demonstration here (feeling "bulge" to conclude no reasonable belief it was weapon, for **Terry** frisk);

Prop.M.R.Evid. 101—evidentiary rules apply to all courts, all proceedings, except fact questions on preliminary hearings re: admissibility under R.104; R.104 (a): not bound by evidence rules EXCEPT hearings on motions to suppress;

C v Rushin **56 MAC 515 (2002)**—judge can't take judicial notice of a city ordinance in the trial of a case, but can do so at hearing of motion to suppress, so that witness's testimony about it (purportedly city ordinance against public drinking) sufficed in lieu of introduction of actual ordinance itself;

C v Brazeau **64 MAC 65 (2005)**—that three tiny objects were suspended from the rear-view mirror of a vehicle did not provide "reasonable suspicion" for stop, despite claim that it suggested violation of G.L. c. 90, § 13 (prohibiting operation of vehicle with "anything which may interfere with or impede the proper operation of the vehicle"): "finding" of motion judge that cop observed reflection of the plastic "prism" (& so had basis for believing such "reflection" could distract driver) was not supported by the evidence;

20-A.7. Harmless Error Re: Confession/ Admission

Arizona v Fulminante **499 US 279 (91)**—erroneous admission of coerced confession subject to harmless error analysis; factors why not harmless here set forth;

C v Caze **426 M 309, 312 (97)**—no harm from D's confession, **possibly** obtained after intentional deprivation of right to telephone call (G.L. c. 276, § 33A), because of overwhelming evidence including D's statements to numerous individuals inculpating self & co-defendant;

C v Samneang Ka **70 MAC 137 (2007)**—even assuming D's admission of drinking "some Heinekens" should have been suppressed for failure to give Miranda warnings before cop's question whether D had consumed any alcohol (judge erred in failing to hear & rule on suppression motion before trial, but unlikely motion would have been granted), evidence was cumulative of cops' testimony that D smelled of alcohol, was unsteady, incomprehensibly recited alphabet without prompting, and had glassy bloodshot eyes;

20-B. SUPPRESS ALLEGED STATEMENTS STATE ACTION, BURDEN OF PROOF, "FRUIT," STATION PHONE CALL, AND OVERVIEW

See also Chapter 11-G, Admissions (by Silence, Statement, etc.) & K. Smith, *Criminal Practice & Procedure*, § 335 (2d ed. 1983 & Supp.) *and Chapter 4-A Station House/Delay in Arraignment*;

Regarding delay in arraignment, see:

C v Rosario **422 M 48 (96)**—**otherwise admissible statement not to be excluded on basis of arraignment delay if statement is made within six hours of arrest**; though right to prompt arraignment (no longer than six-hour delay) may be waived, waiver "form" should include

notice to arrestee of right to probable cause determination by neutral magistrate and notice of "the time at which the defendant could next be taken to court";

McNabb v US **318 US 332 (43) and** *Mallory v US* **354 US 449 (57)**—arrested person's confession is inadmissible if given after unreasonable delay in bringing him before a judge;

Corley v US **129 S Ct 1558 (2009)**—holding that 18 USC § 3501 (enacted in response to *Miranda v Arizona* 384 US 436 and to the application of *McNabb/Mallory* in some courts) did not eliminate *McNabb/Mallory* rule; suppression judge must find whether D confessed within six hours of arrest (unless longer delay was reasonable considering means of transportation and distance to nearest available magistrate) and if it did and was voluntary, it's admissible; if confession occurred beyond 6 hours and before presentment, judge must decide whether delay was unreasonable or unnecessary under *McNabb/Mallory* cases, and if so, must suppress;

See Chapter 20-F re: physical evidence—fruits, state action, etc.;

C v Miller **68 MAC 835, 844 n.5 (2007)**—the "motion to suppress" filed below was inartfully framed and confused, "in the main" addressing Miranda, but also "referenc[ing]" *Tavares*, 385 M at 145 (i.e., voluntariness); as result no pretrial evidentiary hearing on voluntariness occurred (while Miranda argument was rejected on basis of no state action, interrogation having been conducted by private investigators) (conviction reversed);

C v Robinson **449 M 1 (2007)**—no error in excluding this purported expert witness on subject of "the psychology of police interrogations and confessions" because didn't meet "general acceptance" or "reliability" criteria required by *Lanigan* 419 M 15, 25 (94), and also because it concerned issues within knowledge/experience of laypersons; BUT nonetheless, at 6–7, "the subject of psychological manipulation of a defendant and its relation to false confessions presents a serious issue" and "competent" scientific evidence "may well be useful to a fact finder in this area";

20-B.1. Corroboration Rule

C v Forde **392 M 453 (84)**—no G. solely from confession (*see Chapter 12, Required Finding, for other cases, and (in)sufficiency of particular "corroborating" evidence*);

20-B.2. Is Statement an Admission of Guilt?

C v Niziolek **380 M 513 (80)**—jury question whether it's "admission" inconsistent with N.G. plea;

C v Diaz **453 M 266 (2009)**—D's recorded statements denying that he shot anyone, denying he was in Lowell on date of shooting, denying he had been driving Mitsubishi = inadmissible (citing *Nawn* 394 M 1 [85]); argument that they were false and thus admissible as "consciousness of guilt = REJECTED (if such were so, "rule prohibiting evidence of statements of denial would be eviscerated," every denial becoming admissible as 'consciousness of guilt');

C v Lewin (II) **407 M 629 (90)**—murder D's statement that he was willing to plead guilty to manslaughter was inadmissible because not an unambiguous admission & because more prejudicial than probative;

C v MacKenzie **413 M 498 (92)**—D's statement "we didn't mean to hurt her" was admissible as adoptive admission; prosecutor allowed to introduce police questioning to place D's responses in context;

C v Ferrara **31 MAC 648 (91)**—drug D's silences in context of incriminatory statements of others admissible as adoptive admissions;

C v Guyton **405 M 497 (89)**—D's retrieval of money for police at their request was admission by conduct;

See Chapter 11-G for full line of cases on adoptive admissions & admissions by conduct;

20-B.3. Complete Statement Admissible?

C v Watson **377 M 814 (79)**—"verbal completeness" lets in **only** such "self-serving" parts that qualify/explain D's admission that's in evidence; (*see Chapter 11-G*);

C v Fernette **398 M 658 (86)**—if record conversation, best to record all of it;

20-B.4. "Confessions" Distinct from "Admissions"?

C v Garcia **379 M 422 (80)**—Miranda applies to 'admissions', too (not just "confessions");

C v Collins **11 MAC 126 (81)**—"humane practice" re: involuntariness for admissions, too;

20-B.5. Prerequisite to Admissibility: Voluntariness; "State Action" Issues

C v Tavares **385 M 140 (82)**—voir dire mandatory & DA's burden of proof beyond a reasonable doubt it's voluntary (regardless of whether state action) if some evidence it's involuntary; *C v Adams* **389 M 265 (83)** (and (if custody & questioning) without Miranda, it's involuntary as matter of law);

C v Adams **389 M 265 (83)**—DA's burden of proof that all rights given; suppress, even mid-trial, if not shown;

C v Rubio **27 MAC 506 (89)**—similar;

C v Iglesias **426 M 574, 579 (98)**—request for voir dire was a "proper method of challenging the admissibility of a defendant's statement" (D argued ineffective counsel in failing to file motion to suppress);

C v Woods **427 M 169 (98)**—despite fact that defense counsel failed to file either motion to suppress or motion for voir dire ("the proper methods for challenging the admissibility of statements allegedly obtained in violation of" Miranda), conviction rev'd for failure to require prosecutor to lay foundation (raised by motion in limine);

C v Davis **58 MAC 412 (2003)**—D should have filed pretrial motion to suppress or requested voir dire re: Miranda rights given; cop's testimony omitted "statement may be used as evidence against you" warning, and though ADA proffered document to cop and cop said he gave "those rights in their entirety," failure to mark document means that burden not met, BUT here harmless beyond reasonable doubt;

C v Day **387 M 915 (83)**—"Mass. Practice" = DA's burden of proof beyond a reasonable doubt: Miranda waiver's knowing/intelligent; but see *Colorado v Connolly* **479 US 157 (86)** DA's (fed.) burden of proof = preponderance (not even "clear & convincing"); (See also *C v Vasquez* **387 M 196**; *C v Allen* **395 M 448 (85)**; *C v Dyke* **394 M 32**; & *Riveiro* **393 M 224 (84)**; *Harris* **371 M 462 (76)**; *McCauley* **391 M 697 (84)**);

K. Smith, *Criminal Practice & Procedure*, § 322 (2d ed. 1983 & Supp.)—voluntariness & voluntary Miranda waiver = separate questions; § 1288 no discretion but to stop trial, even sua sponte, for voir dire (though no motion to suppress) re: D's statement (not limited to "involuntariness"); §§ 369–70 burden of proof

C v Murphy **426 M 395 (98)**—no sua sponte obligation to have voir dire re: voluntariness of statement to lifelong friend when D appeared normal & coherent & not intoxicated, though spoke of suicide;

C v Libran **405 M 634 (89)**—mentally retarded, schizophrenic, manic depressive D can make voluntary statement; *C v Rivera* **441 M 358 (2004)**—mentally ill D can make voluntary statement and voluntarily waive Miranda rights; "totality of circumstances" test appropriate to determine validity of waiver; *C v Boyarsky* **452 M 700 (2008)**—specific factual finding/conclusion of voluntariness was supported on evidence notwithstanding D's claim that panic attacks precluded such conclusion;

C v Tolan **453 M 634 (2009)**—duration of interview = "merely one factor in overall voluntariness assessment"; minimal intake of food/water, and failure to use restroom are relevant, but not necessarily "of great significance" re: voluntariness;

K. Smith, *Criminal Practice & Procedure*, §§ 342 & 384 (2d ed. 1983 & Supp.)—(alleged) statements to private citizens OK under Miranda, but not if involuntary;

C v Allen **395 M 448 (85)**—no state action (for Miranda, Sixth Amendment) by nurse's questions, with cops present holding D (& no question of voluntariness, which needs no state action);

Harrison v US **392 US 219 (68)**—when trial error "virtually coerces" D to testify, that testimony can't be introduced at trial #2, necessitated by the error at trial #1;

C v Silanskas **433 M 678, 696–97 (2001)**—reporter's jailhouse interview with D not suppressible as violating right to counsel (reporter knew counsel wouldn't permit; reporter gained access to D by telling jailers he was friend of D); no state action;

C v Fallon **38 MAC 366 (95)**—overruled in results, but aff'd **in pertinent part**, **423 M 92 (96)**—testimonial & documentary evidence obtained from D under court order in a civil case (discovery & deposition testimony) can be admitted in later criminal trial, when judge in civil matter advised D of privilege against self-incrimination & D did not invoke it or raise "voluntariness" "in either the civil or criminal proceedings";

C v Luna **418 M 749 (94)**—cop-D argued, unsuccessfully, that affidavit acknowledging perjury in a particular search warrant application/affidavit was involuntary because Superior Court judge ordered him to file affidavits about his search for informant referred to in application;

C v Rodwell **394 M 694 (85)**—cellmate not state agent/action re: Sixth Amendment violation;

C v Rancourt **399 M 269 (87)**—(same), because inmate not asked/promised by cops;

C v Harmon **410 M 425 (91)**—jailhouse informant told by cops to "keep his ears open" not a state agent for Sixth Amendment right to counsel purposes, where no inducements had been offered to informant;

C v Gajka **425 M 751 (97)**—though prisoner asked to be D's cellmate in hope of getting admissions & trading them for leniency in his own case, government had not sought his assistance or encouraged his actions: no suppression (despite **fact** of later favorable treatment);

C v Tevlin **433 M 305, 321 (2001)**—fact that prisoner sought to obtain change in housing in trade for providing info D told him earlier didn't make prisoner state agent at relevant time; even if he were deemed "agent" after he made 1st contact with state police, info obtained thereafter was relatively insignificant, and only probative of 'consciousness of guilt';

C v Murphy **448 M 452 (2007)**—where government has entered into an "articulated agreement containing a specific benefit or promise thereof", recipient inmate is government agent (here, with [federal] US attorney's office) for purposes of Sixth Amendment and art. 12, "even if the inmate is not directed to target a specific individual"; state prosecutor's assertion that she had no deal with informant-witness and was in no position to reward him: this was "incorrect" as prosecutor subsequently informed US Attorney of informant's cooperation, and US Attorney then filed motion to reduce informant's sentence by 50%; the federal agency relationship should have been charged to the Commonwealth as prosecutor here; even IF federal courts would disagree with interpretation of D's rights under *Massiah*, art. 12 protects D's right to counsel here; SJC overrides motion judge's conclusion that agent didn't deliberately elicit D's statements; "[t]hrough his conduct, he created an environment that lured the D into a false sense of trust . . ."; after informant obtained incriminating statements from D, informant contacted informant's attorney for deal negotiation;

C v Reynolds **429 M 388 (99)**—error to have denied motion to suppress without hearing when jailhouse informant's lawyer set up reward for him during his access to conversations with D; agency relationship probable;

US v LaBare **191 F.3d 60 (1st Cir. 99)**—if government asks inmate to report incriminating statements by anyone but hasn't focused attention on individual D, the inmate's inquiries maybe aren't government "interrogation" (rejecting 3rd and 5th Cir.'s approach which uses targeting of individual D as "merely one factor" re: whether *Massiah v US* **377 US 201 (64)** is triggered); informant's testimony here = harmless, given other evidence;

US v Henry **447 US 264 (80)**—cellmate was paid informant, so state action;

Maine v Moulton **474 US 159 (85)**—questions by co-D instructed by cops = state action;

C v Tynes **400 M 369 (87)**—questions by off-duty cop outside jurisdiction not state action;

C v Jordan **439 M 47 (2003)**—though D was working as a drug informant for Federal authorities and had a letter of immunity from them (saying that if D told truth nothing he said could be used against him directly), state detectives (who didn't sign letter & had no authority to make such agreement) questioned him re: murder, telling him he was a suspect & that they could make no inducements or promises; D's statement (admitting presence & being armed, but saying another person shot V) wasn't product of deception, wasn't involuntary;

Illinois v Perkins **496 US 292 (90)**—undercover cop posing as cellmate not required to give Miranda warnings where D held on unrelated charge;

C v Conkey **443 M 60 (2004)**—judge on motion for new trial was warranted in concluding that police officer who purportedly elicited info from D's girlfriend in flirtatious manner, gave her false inculpatory info about D, and "tacitly gave her the 'go ahead' to elicit statements from" D, did not make girlfriend a state agent; cop didn't ask her to visit or obtain info from D;

C v Moran **75 MAC 513 (2009)**—no evidence that cops intentionally placed D's sister in room to "deliberately monitor [D's] statements to her", or that she was acting as police agent; cop "accidentally" overheard D's admissions to her, & case doesn't present question re: police practice of placing friend/relative in room with D to surreptitiously monitor or evoke inculpatory info;

C v Juvenile **402 M 275 (88)**—DYS worker questioning D was state action;

C v Snyder **413 M 521 (92)**—school officials not required to give Miranda warnings, at least where no evidence of routine cooperation with police; open question under Article 12; *C v Ira I.* **439 M 805 (2003)**—written statements taken by school's assistant principal (re: after-school beating) were in his possession, and he wasn't acting as agent of police: no Miranda warnings required, and there wasn't "custody" [holding here = error in dismissing charges on ground that DA failed to comply with discovery orders because he didn't provide these statements]; *C v Monteiro* **75 MAC 280 (2009)**—though frisk was performed at school, it was by police officer, so reasonable suspicion required; *Safford Unified School Dist. No. 1 v Redding* **129 S Ct 2633 (2009)**—search by school officials of 13-year-old student's bra and underpants violated Fourth Amendment even though reasonable suspicion student had brought forbidden prescription and over-the-counter drugs to school;

C v Carp **47 MAC 229 (99)**—DSS investigator, at D's home, specifically told D it wasn't a criminal investigation & he didn't need to give Miranda rights, asked questions re alleged sexual assaults, and when D asked whether he should have attorney present, was told it wasn't "necessarily necessary" = involuntary. See also 110 C.M.R. § 4.27(5)

(1993) (requiring written notice to parents/caretakers about G.L. c. 199, § 51A report, possible consequences of investigation, and that info can be used in court);

C v Morais **431 M 380 (2000)**—incriminating statements made by D to DSS social worker investigating report of abuse (G.L. c. 119, § 51A) of D's cousin; social worker told D what she was investigating, & D agreed to meet with her; SJC rejects argument that social worker in such circumstances is required to give a "minimal cautionary warning" that statements made are not privileged & may be disclosed to others (like in *Lamb* **365 M 265 (74)**, when psychotherapist conducts a court-ordered interview); given no violation of rights re: social worker, D's statements to police later, after Miranda warnings, weren't suppressible as 'cat out of bag' or 'fruit' of any prior illegality; (*See also Chapter 20-G re: state action for search and seizure of physical evidence*);

C v Hunt **392 M 28 (84)**—statement inadmissible if coerced by private person(s);

C v Mahnke **368 M 662 (75)**—coerced (& involuntary & inadmissible) by private citizens, but later statement OK—not tainted "cat-out-of-bag"; but see *Colorado v Connolly* **497 US 157 (86)** Supreme Court admits involuntary statement unless BOTH coerced & state action;

20-B.6. Ineffective Assistance of Counsel Resulting in Suppressible Statement

US v Frappier **615 F.Supp 51 (D.Mass '85)**—attorney's advice to D to give testimony at preliminary hearing, was ineffective assistance of counsel; testimony suppressed from use in later proceedings; see also *C v Moreau* **30 MAC 677 (91), cert denied, 502 US 1049 (92)** record didn't support judge's conclusion that attorney's advice to confess didn't constitute ineffective assistance of counsel; "circumstances favoring a confession to police are rare, and such advice may constitute ineffective assistance of counsel," citing *Frappier*, above, *People v Wilson* **133 A. D. 2d 179, 180–81 (N.Y. 1987)**, & *Escobedo v Illinois* **378 US 478, 488 (64)**, quoting from *Watts v Indiana* **338 US 49, 59 (49)** (Jackson, J., concurring in part and dissenting in part) (**"(A)ny lawyer worth his salt will tell the suspect in no uncertain terms to make no statement to police under any circumstances"**);

C v Smiley **431 M 477, 480 (2000)**—motion judge made factual finding that attorney didn't tell D to make statement, but instead told him NOT to, & D nonetheless wanted to make statement (despite counsel's contrary advice + advice that D could be guilty even if he didn't pull trigger himself), so *Moreau* (**30 MAC 677 (91)**) inapposite;

C v Segovia **53 MAC 184 (2001)**—ineffective assistance of counsel found in failure to file motion to suppress D's videotaped custodial interrogation where D had viable claim that cop ignored D's request for translator & paralegal before continuing the questioning, and where fruit of the interrogation was prosecution's discovery of a witness who provided damaging trial testimony;

20-B.7. Permissible Uses of Otherwise Suppressed Evidence

Harris v NY **401 US 222 (71)**—(federal) **suppressed statement can impeach D**; . . . .

C v Harris **364 M 236 (73)**—(same); but . . . *C v Kleciak* **350 M 679 (66)**— . . . but NOT if involuntary (see *Mahnke* **368 M 662 at n.40**);

Mincey v Arizona **437 US 385 (78)**—(same); (*see Chapter 20-D*); & . . . *C v Ferrer* **47 MAC 645 (99)**— statement of juvenile suppressed because of failure to accord meaningful conversation with interested adult prior to Miranda waiver **could** be used for impeachment if D testified, judge having found, permissibly, that it was "voluntary" (youth = 1 relevant factor re: voluntariness, but not conclusive);

Kansas v Ventris **129 S Ct 1841 (2009)**—statements obtained in violation of right to counsel (informant planted in D's cell) may be used to impeach D's testimony;

James v Illinois **493 US 307 (90)**—suppressed statements obtained in violation of Fourth Amendment may not be used to impeach defense witnesses other than D;

C v Ly **454 M 223 (2009)**—without having filed motion to suppress, defense counsel objected to cop testifying about D's admission (ground = counsel had not received a signed Miranda form in discovery provided) and after voir dire, judge suppressed statement, holding failure to prove Miranda and voluntariness; Commonwealth's 211/3 petition mid-trial produced single justice ruling allowing use of statement to impeach D's testimony, justice overruling the 'involuntariness' finding;

C v Vincente **405 M 278 (89)**—**under federal constitution**, statements obtained in violation of Miranda may be used at **surrender hearing to show violation of probation**, at least where police unaware D on probation;

C v Olsen **405 M 491 (89)**—evidence obtained in violation of Fourth Amendment **or Article 14** may be used at surrender hearing to show probation violation, at least **where police unaware of defendant's status as probationer**;

C v Fini **403 M 567 (88)**—to deter cops, **can't use bad wiretap evidence even to impeach D**;

Michigan v Harvey **494 US 344 (90)**—suppressed statements obtained in violation of (Sixth Amendment) right to counsel may be used to impeach D;

20-B.8. Fruit of Poisonous Tree

Harrison v US **392 US 219 (68)**—when trial error "virtually coerces" D to testify, this testimony can't be introduced at trial #2, necessitated by the error at trial #1;

C v Charros **443 M 752, 766 (2005)**—D's testimony at trial explaining illegally admitted evidence was considered "tainted", citing, inter alia, *Fahy v Connecticut* **375 US 85, 91 (63)** & *C v McCleery* **345 M 151 (62)**;

Wong Sun v US **371 US 471 (63)**—not fruit of poisonous tree if attenuated connection & purged of taint;

though it's both from illegal arrest & confession of co-D cross-examination, can use D's statement though illegal arrest because D made it after returning voluntarily to station; & can use drugs from co-D because D has no standing to contest their seizure;

Brown v Illinois **422 US 590 (75)**—Miranda warnings help, but don't per se cure, illegal arrest; FACTORS = time lapse, intervening facts, cops' purpose & flagrancy (see K. Smith, above, § 1334, statements as fruit of illegal arrest);

C v Chongarlides **52 MAC 366, 375–77 (2001)**—police entry into residence to find & question D = illegal, but D's inculpatory statements, made later at station after two sets of Miranda warnings & signed waiver not tainted by illegality;

C v Martinez **74 MAC 240 (2009)**—D's postarrest statements were fruit of unjustified stop and frisk;

C v Brandwein **435 M 623 (2002)**—psychiatric nurse presumably breached confidentiality when she told cops of D's statements to her re: gun & bank robbery, but cops didn't solicit/provoke disclosure by the nurse: no suppression of D's later confession; G.L. c. 233, § 20B creates only an "evidentiary privilege" & doesn't prohibit disclosure in settings other than in various court proceedings;

US v Brignoni-Ponce **422 US 873 (75)**—suppress statement after bad car-stop;

C v Sylvia **380 M 180 (80)**—confession OK though arrest warrant maybe without probable cause, because cops' good faith & D's "free will," so no deterrence;

Oregon v Elstad **470 US 298 (85)**—2d statement OK (for US Supreme Court) though "fruit";

C v Smith **412 M 823 (92)**—**2d (Mirandized) statement made by D after 1st statement was obtained in violation of Miranda is presumed tainted as matter of state common law rule of evidence; federal rule of *Oregon v Elstad* 470 US 298, 314 (85), rejected;**

Missouri v Seibert **542 US 600 (2004)**—divided majority of justices condemned two-step interrogation technique where police deliberately withheld Miranda warnings while they questioned in-custody suspect in hope that unwarned statements would loosen her tongue in later interview after warnings had been given;

Michigan v Tucker **417 US 433 (74)**—OK witness though ID'd by D's (Miranda) suppressed statement;

C v Segovia **53 MAC 184 (2001)**—ineffective assistance of counsel found in failure to file motion to suppress D's videotaped custodial interrogation where D had viable claim that cop ignored D's request for translator & paralegal before continuing the questioning, and where **fruit of the interrogation was prosecution's discovery of a witness who provided damaging trial testimony;**

C v Lyles **453 M 811 (2009)**—knowledge that D had outstanding warrant was fruit of seizure without reasonable suspicion: drugs and cash taken from D during booking procedure = suppressed;

NY v Harris **495 US 14 (90)**—warrantless search of D's home in absence of exigency or consent, in violation of *Payton v NY* **445 US 573 (80)**, did not require suppression of D's later stationhouse confession because police did not exploit bad search to obtain it;

C v Marquez **434 M 370 (2001)**—SJC adopts reasoning of *NY v Harris* **495 US 14 (90)** (statement given at police station after Miranda warnings, but following an illegal arrest, needn't be suppressed); *C v Street* **56 MAC 301 (2002)** (same);

C v Cruz **442 M 299 (2004)**—illegal entry of D's home didn't require suppression of stationhouse statements, because Miranda warnings, manner of interrogation, D's knowledge of co-D's implicating D, lapse of 4 hours, etc. "combined to attenuate the illegality" of entry;

C v Waters **420 M 276, 278 n.2 (95)**—seemingly accepts that fruits of search warrant must be suppressed **if** warrant was issued on reliance upon involuntary statement of D (but SJC finds statement voluntary);

C v Dimarzio **436 M 1012 (2002)**—suppress marijuana found in desk drawer because fruit of D's statement that it was there; statement itself was obtained in violation of *Miranda v Arizona* **384 US 436 (66)**;

C v Lahti **398 M 829 (86)**—suppress witnesses ID'd first through D's coerced statement because flagrant abuse;

K. Smith, above, § 1335—identification of witness as 'fruit'; § 1328—'fruit' doctrine overview; (*see also Chapter 20-F, below re: "fruit" of bad search or seizure*; & *Mahnke* **368 M 662 (75)**);

C v Sarourt Nam **426 M 152 (97)**—though first statement = suppressed, it did not incriminate D (did not place him at crime scene, or link him with victim close to time of shooting), so "cat was not out of the bag"; subsequent, **post**-Miranda, statements not suppressible;

C v Garner **59 MAC 350 (2003)**—first statement was suppressed, and placed D at crime scene, but judge permissibly determined that there was sufficient intervening break so as to remove taint from later statements at police station (D hadn't been arrested, and voluntarily went to station next day, and wasn't then restrained, etc.);

C v Benoit **410 M 506 (91)**—although tape of murder D's voluntary phone statements properly suppressed because unconsented-to, testimony of phone operator about statements was admissible;

C v Straw **422 M 756, 762–63 (96)**—suppress admissions which were product of unlawful search & seizure of drugs, resulting in required finding of not guilty;

C v Muckle **61 MAC 678 (2004)**—required finding of not guilty after suppression of marijuana;

C v Coleman **64 MAC 558 (2005)**—D's conduct was not a suppressible "fruit" of police action ("whatever one may think about the wisdom of [such action]"): after police responded to highway altercation and spoke first with other driver, D said he couldn't wait longer, and was leaving, but was ordered by police to remain (cop attempted to break D's car window to stop/arrest him [G.L. c. 90, §§ 25, 21], causing D to flee and lead cops on high speed chase); court's "decision is limited to the application of the exclusionary rule," allowing evidence obtained after D's failure to comply with order to stop; viability of any defense based upon actions of police "necessarily will depend upon the evidence adduced at trial";

20-B.9. G.L. c. 276, § 33A: Right to Phone Call at Station after Arrest (Inform Forthwith, Permit within One Hour);

C v Jones **362 M 601 (75)**—suppress ID because G.L. c. 276, § 33A violated;

C v Alicea **55 MAC 505 (2002)**—suppression of D's incriminatory statement made shortly after intentional violation of D's right to telephone (G.L. c. 276, § 33A) AND later incriminatory statement, because latter was fruit of poisonous tree;

C v Carey **26 MAC 339 (88)**—can tell of right, then video D before let call, *if within 1 hour*, & especially to family (not attorney);

C v Caze **426 M 309 (97)**—while evidence obtained after intentional deprivation of telephone call should be suppressed, rule "has not been extended" to unintentional failures to inform of telephone call right; no need here to determine intentional or not, because D made many & unrelated admissions/confessions to others (so no prejudice from confession);

C v Haith **452 M 409 (2008)**—D was arrested in North Carolina, and Federal authorities notified MA state police that D would be held by US marshals there; MA troopers arrived after D in Federal custody for six hours and read to D his Miranda rights from a Federal form which did not include MA statutory right to make telephone call; D made statement after signing waiver; EVEN IF telephone call right applies to MA authorities when arrestee is held in Federal custody in another state, suppression would be appropriate remedy only upon showing intentional withholding of telephone right in order to gain advantage/coerce statement & this not shown here (D has burden); *Pixley v Commonwealth* **453 M 827 (2009)**—D called witness, who claimed 5th A. and article 12 privileges, and judge held in camera *Martin* (**423 M 496**) hearing, finding privilege; on appeal after conviction, D could argue error in privilege determination, but would not be allowed access to "sealed"/impounded transcript of in camera hearing, SJC ruling that appellate judges could review privilege determination without any assistance from the parties, witness's constitutional right against self-incrimination trumping all else;

C v Harris **75 MAC 696 (2009)**, **further review allowed 455 M 1108 (2010)**—that D's use of telephone was delayed because there was no telephone in or near interview room was no cause for relief: D didn't establish "intentional deprivation" (D was informed of telephone right on form signed at 12:21 a.m., and booking occurred at 12:55 a.m., D then using telephone); concurring justice would grant relief on this ground (because detective admitted that he told D that he could not make telephone call until booking, and so after D provided new "untainted" confession, he was booked & allowed telephone) if not bound by *Carey* 26 MAC 339 (88) (so long as telephone call is within one hour of advice of right, no relief [unless judge finds as fact "intentional deprivation" for advantage);

C v LeBeau **451 M 244 (2008)**—not deciding whether telephone right statute required person NOT IN CUSTODY but at police station must be advised of telephone rights within one hour of time police have probable cause to arrest or "merely within one hour of the time his formal arrest takes place": holding that statute does not impose obligation to interrupt a voluntary interview, once probable cause is established but before interview has ended, to notify D of statutory telephone rights;

C v Perry **432 M 214, 232 (2000)**—G.L. c. 276, § 33A (right to telephone call) = "plainly inapplicable where D already is incarcerated on another matter" when police arrive to question him;

C v Rivera **441 M 358, 374–75 (2004)**—citing *C v Caputo* **439 M 153, 162 n.11 (2003)**—police not required to inform D that he's entitled to telephone call until D is arrested; argument that "in custody" occurred earlier & triggered telephone call right = rejected;

C v Novo **442 M 262 (2004)**—D wasn't "formally arrested" until after interview, so there wasn't any violation of § 33A that would affect admissibility of statements;

C v Dagley **442 M 713 (2004)**—same;

C v Pileeki **62 MAC 505, 512 (2004)**—same, saying SJC recently rejected argument that statute "should be interpreted broadly to extend to persons in custody as well as under arrest";

C v Alicea **428 M 711 (99)**—re: claim of no advice of telephone right, motion judge ruled (erroneously?) that D not in custody at time of statement, but SJC said no reason to suppress because, in his own **trial** testimony, D said he'd been informed of telephone call right before making any statement;

C v Johnson **422 M 420 (96)**—though D was left handcuffed to police station wall for two hours before booking, "factual" finding controls (that delay in allowing telephone call was not "designed to gain inculpatory information but to allow the officers involved to be present at booking");

K. Smith, *Criminal Practice & Procedure,* **§§ 396–97 (2d ed. 1983 & Supp.)**—telephone right; (*see also Chapter 3, Defendant's Entry Into Criminal Justice System, & Chapter 21-DD, Operating Under the Influence*);

C v White **422 M 487 (96)**—record of the telephone number which D called could be introduced against him at trial ("policy" of G.L. c. 276, § 33A not frustrated, & Miranda not required (not fruit of custodial interrogation));

C v Silanskas **433 M 678, 684 n.7 (2001)**—noting that trial court suppressed statements D made to counsel during telephone conversation from police station, overheard by zealous cop;

In the Matter of a Grand Jury Subpoena **454 M 685 (2009)**—neither a pretrial jail detainee or a convicted inmate has reasonable expectation of privacy in telephone conversations: all parties have notice that calls are subject to monitoring/recording, and penological interests justify: loss of privacy is an "inherent incident[ ] of confinement"; providing recorded calls to grand jury in response to subpoena = OK;

20-B.10. Article 36, Vienna Convention on Consular Relations

C v Diemer **57 MAC 677 (2003)**—D, a German national, argued for suppression because he wasn't advised of right to have consulate notified, without delay, of his detention, and of right to communicate with consulate; appellate court declined to order suppression as remedy; D cited *Breard v Greene* 523 US 371 (98) (does article 36 of Vienna Convention confer individual rights which are privately enforceable?);

Sanchez-Llamas v Oregon **548 US 331 (2006)**—even assuming, without deciding, that the Convention creates judicially enforceable rights, suppression isn't "an appropriate remedy for a violation"; Convention leaves Article 36's implementation to domestic law, and "[i]t is beyond dispute that [US Supreme Court does] not hold a supervisory power over [state] courts" (citation omitted);

Medellin v Texas **128 S Ct 1346 (2008)**—though International Court of Justice had held (in *Case Concerning Avena and Other Mexican Nationals*) that US had violated Article 36(1)(b) of Vienna Convention on Consular Relations by failing to inform 51 named Mexican citizens of their Vienna Convention rights, US S Ct had held that Convention didn't preclude application of state "default" rules, and then Presidential Memorandum sought to have State courts give effect to decision of International Court; holding in Medellin = neither the ICJ decision nor the Presidential Memorandum is directly enforceable as domestic law in state court;

20-C. FIFTH AMENDMENT—MIRANDA

Miranda v Arizona **384 US 436 (66)**—no statement from custodial interrogation without knowing/intelligent waiver of rights (silent, used against, lawyer before questioning, court-appointed); stop if D wants, or wants attorney;

Berghuis v Thompkins **** US ** (6/1/2010)**—after receiving Miranda warnings, D was largely silent during 3-hour interrogation but near end said "yes" when asked if he prayed to God to forgive him for the shooting; silence during interrogation did not operate to invoke right to remain silent; cites analogous holding in *Davis v US* 512 US 452 regarding Miranda right to counsel;

US v Patane **124 S Ct 2620 (2004)**—physical evidence derived from an unwarned statement made by D in response to police interrogation need not be suppressed, so long as the statements were not the product of improper coercion, i.e., were "voluntary";

C v Martin **444 M 213, 215 (2005)**—SJC REJECTS *US v Patane*, adopts a "common-law rule" as a matter under Article 12 that physical evidence derived from unwarned statements where Miranda warnings would have been required by Federal law in order for them to be admissible, "is presumptively excludable from evidence at trial as 'fruit' of the improper failure to provide such warnings";

C v Costa **65 MAC 227 (2005)**—because D didn't raise issue below, Appeals Court wouldn't address argument that, following arrest, cop's question of whether D had gun & request for consent to search & for keys to vehicle (without any prior Miranda warnings) violated Fifth Amendment rights, or argument that Miranda warnings are required prior to request for consent to search from person already in custody, or whether act of production of keys to vehicle is a testimonial statement protected by Miranda;

C v Cruz **442 M 299 (2004)**—illegal entry of D's home didn't require suppression of stationhouse statements, because Miranda warnings, manner of interrogation, D's knowledge of co-D's implicating D, lapse of 4 hours, etc. "combined to attenuate the illegality" of entry (following holdings in *NY v Harris* **495 U.S. 14 (90)** & *C v Marquez* **434 M 370 (2001)**);

Brown v Texas **443 US 47 (79)**—talk to man in high-drug alley not reasonable suspicion; detain to ask ID = seizure;

Hiibel v Sixth Judicial Court **542 US 177 (2004)**—"stop & identify" statute not invalid here; doesn't require production of driver's license or other document; request for name doesn't "ordinarily" violate Fourth Amendment; no Fifth Amendment violation because disclosure of name/identity presented no reasonable danger of incrimination;

See Chapter 11-G.4, Post-Arrest Silence Inadmissible, and Chapter 9-G, Silence as Prior Inconsistent Statement, for more cases and distinctions, e.g.,

Doyle v Ohio **426 US 619 (76)** **D's post-Miranda silence may not be used against him at trial (either for inference of guilt or, if D testifies, to impeach his testimony); but compare/contrast**

C v Guy **441 M 96 (2004)**—**no *Doyle v Ohio* violation to impeach D's trial testimony with content of his post-Miranda conversations with nurse, security guard, and police officer and with answer to booking question re: injuries;**

C v Chase **70 MAC 826 (2007)**—whether or not D is under arrest or in custody, D's invocation of right to silence cannot be used against him; Commonwealth argued that invocation of right *could* be used against D because D was neither under arrest nor in custody and Miranda warnings (given four days earlier) had not been renewed; "Regardless, we still consider the defendant to be exercising a right protected at least by the State Constitution"; on view

that error was harmless beyond a reasonable doubt, this was "exceptional case" in which Court refused relief;

C v Rodriguez **67 MAC 636 (2006), and on further appellate review, 450 M 302, 304 & n.7 (2007), SJC "agree[s] with the reasoning and holding of the Appeals Court"**—Spanish-speaking cop came into cell, making small talk about D's Puerto Rican heritage after giving Miranda rights: D's response of "if you think I am going to cooperate, don't waste your time. You chose to be a . . . cop, that is your job. I chose my job, I will do my time" was not inadmissible as a post-Miranda silence to impeach exculpatory story advanced at trial by D; even if first part was invocation of silence, later statement = spontaneous inculpatory remarks;

Dickerson v US **530 US 428 (2000)**—**Miranda rule IS A "constitutional decision," and legislation passed by US Congress CANNOT OVERRIDE IT**; 18 USC § 3501, passed two years after Miranda and purporting to make admissible any statement of D if it were "voluntary" notwithstanding fact that statement was made without benefit of Miranda warnings, **is invalid/unconstitutional**; prior cases suggesting that Miranda rule wasn't "constitutional" are now disavowed;

K. Smith, *Criminal Practice & Procedure*, §§ 331–82 (2d ed. 1983 & Supp.)—overview; Miranda includes both exculpatory (§ 333) & "admissions" (§ 334);

Escobedo v Illinois **378 US 478 (64)**—any lawyer worth his salt will tell client not to talk to police;

C v Moreau **30 MAC 677 (91), cert. denied 502 US 1049 (92)**—even before Sixth Amendment right to counsel attaches, the Miranda right to counsel to effectuate Fifth Amendment would be meaningless if it didn't entitle D to competent/effective assistance of counsel; record here didn't support judge's conclusion that attorney's advice to D to confess was not ineffective assistance of counsel; see also *US v Frappier* **615 F.Supp 51 (D.Mass '85)** D's statements suppressible as fruit of ineffective assistance of counsel;

Withrow v Williams **507 US 680 (93)**—rejects government attempt to exclude Miranda issues from federal habeas corpus relief if there has been a "full & fair review" in state court (i.e., like *Stone v Powell* **428 US 465 (76)**, for Fourth Amendment claims);

See Chapter 7-H, Fifth Amendment & Article 12 privilege against self-incrimination, and see also Chapter 11-G, EVIDENCE—re: Silence of D or Request for Counsel = inadmissible as admission, e.g., C v DePace **433 M 379 (2001)** reversal for Commonwealth's display of D's Miranda card invoking right to counsel & its introduction into evidence; "evidence of the Miranda warnings and a D's exercise of his Miranda rights are not part of a D's statement to police . . . admissible only as the foundation for a statement the D actually gives while in custody . . . (in circumstances here,) they 'are not competent testimony against' him";

C v Isabelle **444 M 416 (2005)**—4:3 decision that DA's eliciting evidence re: D's request for attorney didn't warrant reversal (because purportedly "beyond a reasonable doubt" it didn't contribute to jury's verdict);

C v Peixoto **430 M 654 (2000)—cross-examination of D about his post-Miranda musings whether to get an attorney, and whether to remain silent impermissible** under due process and Article 12, despite fact that the musings were NOT an invocation of Miranda rights/right to silence)

C v Alves **35 MAC 935 (93)**—appellate court accepts finding of fact that Portuguese text of Miranda was "close enough" to accurate; no suppression of statements on ground that bilingual cop was used as interpreter at station;

C v Vuthy Seng **436 M 537 (2002)**—two sets of Miranda warnings were given to D, and though English version was correct, Khmer version was fatally flawed, requiring reversal of murder convictions;

C v Mitchell **47 MAC 178 (99)**—when rights were read to D from a card, suppression not required because cop couldn't recall, on stand, exact rights he recited;

C v Adams **389 M 265 (83)**—omission of 1 warning in cop's recounting of warnings given (cop testified that he advised D orally, without reliance on a card/writing) = suppression;

C v Miranda **37 MAC 939 (94)**—similar; omission of right to have attorney present during questioning = suppression; *C v Johnston* **60 MAC 13, 21–22 (2003)**—trial counsel's failure to specify, as precise ground in motion to suppress, that Miranda warnings omitted info that D had right to have attorney present during questioning meant that issue wasn't preserved for appeal: failure might be ineffective assistance of counsel, but Rule 30 motion held necessary to raise here;

C v Dagraca **447 M 546 (2006)**—omission of warning that whatever D said could be used against him (cop didn't read from card) required suppression & given real defense here presented, failure to suppress was NOT harmless beyond a reasonable doubt (required standard because "constitutional");

C v Coplin **34 MAC 478 (93)**—suppression required: omission of advice that anything D said could be used against him shown here not merely by testing witness's memory on stand (because evidence = warning was omitted from arrest booking sheet form) **and** no "carry over" of full warnings, given earlier as D was face-down on floor, because D didn't manifest understanding;

C v Ayala **29 MAC 592 (90)**—cop testified that he'd recited Miranda rights to D from memory (rather than reading from card), and that he'd told D that he could make a statement if he wished, but that he was entitled to an attorney; failure to advise that any statement made could & would be used against D in court = involuntary, inadmissible;

C v Alcala **54 MAC 49 (2002)**—when cop said he'd read rights to D from Miranda card & judge "found" that full warnings were given, it wasn't fatal that prosecutor failed to introduce the card into evidence, though introduc-

ing the card is 'good practice,' citing *C v Lewis* **374 M 203 (78)**;

C v Ghee **414 M 313 (93)**—D had been charged with motor vehicle offenses and warning given was: "you are not obligated to say anything, in regard to this offense you are charged with"; inadequate, because it implied that while D didn't have to talk about vehicular crimes, he **did** have to speak about his girlfriend's dead body in the trunk, not having been "charged" with murder (yet); **harmless beyond reasonable doubt here (statements did not include a confession)**; *C v Dagraca* **447 M 546 (2006)**—even though statement didn't include confession, erroneous admission of statement made without full Miranda warnings = NOT harmless beyond reasonable doubt; that statement was consistent with prosecution's circumstantial evidence did not mean that the evidence was merely "cumulative";

C v Souza **428 M 478 (98), citing *Raymond* 424 M 382 (97) and *Meehan* 377 M 552 (79)**—after Miranda warnings, not involuntary when cop tells D it's in his "best interest" to "tell . . . what happened that day," **but there may be** no assurance, express or implied, that statement will aid the defense or result in a lesser sentence;

C v Tolan **453 M 634 (2009)**—[only] if police "assure" D that confession will aid defense or result in lesser sentence may involuntariness be inferred; 'you can do yourself a lot of good if you tell us what happened', 'now it's time to help yourself out', 'we'll help you because that's why we're here, to find the truth,' and 'you need to help yourself by telling the truth' held not to have been forbidden "assurance";

C v O'Brian **445 M 720 (2006)**—not involuntary for cop to tell D's father (passed along to D by father) that if D cooperated and told truth, cop would communicate this to DA, and D "may see the light of day down the road" (murder during course of armed robbery); whether there was, further, an assurance of leniency, i.e., a promise of a manslaughter charge if D confessed, was question of fact, resolved against D by motion judge; not raised below was fact of cop's minimization of the crime (cop's statement to father that he thought that the shooting was an "accident"), which implied leniency (but other facts contradicted this);

C v Jackson **377 M 319 (79)**—lie that D's girlfriend gave statement impermissibly trenched on D's prior invocation of silence;

C v DiGiambattista **442 M 423 (2004)**—officers' display to D of falsely labeled videotape and empty file, with questions intended to convey, falsely, that police had proof of D's guilt, accompanied by expressions of sympathy for his actions & opinions that he needed alcoholism counseling, & that crime wasn't particularly serious ("minimization" technique of interrogation), meant that Commonwealth failed to show beyond reasonable doubt that confession was voluntary;

C v O'Brian **445 M 720 (2006)**—*DiGiambattista* holding that D is entitled to instruction that lack of recording of statement suggests it should be scrutinized with particular care will not be applied retroactively (citing *C v Dagley* 442 M 713, 721 (2004), cert. denied, 125 S Ct 1668 (2005));

C v Boyarsky **452 M 700 (2008)**—but judge is not required to allow D to cross-examine cop as to his knowledge of the SJC's DiGiambattista preference that statements be recorded;

C v Felice **44 MAC 709 (98)**—because **Miranda** given (repeatedly) at outset, court turns blind eye to vitiation of those rights by "sympathetic" cops who assured D they'd get him "help" and didn't want him to go to jail; *Magee* **423 M 381 (96)** purportedly distinguished (before getting the promised mental/emotional "help," Magee was repeatedly told she had to answer questions first, and that she had to "wait" for next law enforcement official);

C v Novo **442 M 262 (2004)**—statements induced by police lies re: evidence, accompanied by assertions that D was guilty and had to tell his story "now or never" ("if you don't give us a reason right now why you did this, a jury's never going to hear a reason" (latter being "misrepresentation of ... right to defend 'self at trial, ... particularly egregious intrusion on rights that art. 12 declares to be fundamental") = suppression, but statements (denying guilt but providing info re: V's "care") made before cop said jury would never hear held admissible/voluntary; purported Miranda compliance by assertion that D could terminate questioning "for the purpose of consulting an attorney" was inadequate because conveyed that this was the ONLY reason D could terminate questioning, but this didn't affect initial Miranda waiver;

C v Gaboriault **439 M 84 (2003)**—cop, whom D knew, gave Miranda warnings before D's confession, saying that they were "just a formality"; "any use of words that characterize or minimize a suspect's Miranda rights should be avoided," but here, given all circumstances (including warnings given three times), confession = admissible;

Duckworth v Eagan **492 US 195 (89)**—cop's warning that D would have to wait for court to appoint attorney did not invalidate Miranda warnings;

Florida v Powell **130 S Ct 1195 (2010)**—the "Miranda" warnings given D said that he had right to talk to lawyer "before answering any ... questions," and that he could invoke this right "at any time ... during the interview" were held sufficient to convey that D could have access to attorney during questioning (and not just before answering the first question);

C v Colby **422 M 414, 418 (96)**—adequacy of warning that if D couldn't afford attorney, Commonwealth would **attempt** to provide one not really reached (despite cite to *Duckworth v Eagan*) because any violation harmless here, **but**, specifically noting that Court was not here "asked to apply any state law principles to this issue, such as adopting the views of the dissent" in *Duckworth*;

C v Ortiz **53 MAC 168 (2001)**—D, arrested in Stoughton for shooting in Boston, was given Miranda warnings at arrest & again at Stoughton police station, & signed acknowledgment of understanding; Boston police took custody of D after booking & drove him to Boston & weren't required to again give Miranda in the car before asking "what had happened," within ninety minutes of the Miranda warnings given in Stoughton;

C v Sirois **437 M 845 (2002)**—Miranda rights given at 6 p.m. (D said he wanted to help police), at 9 p.m. (D gave statement after he voluntarily came to police station), and at 2 a.m. (D gave clothing & hair sample); failure to give warnings again at 4:45 a.m. when, during a second interview, D broke down & confessed, doesn't result in suppression: lapse of time not so significant, and cops reminded D of previous warnings/confirmed D's understanding of them immediately before interview at issue;

C v Cruz **373 M 676 (77)**—Miranda warnings, once given, aren't to be accorded "unlimited efficacy or perpetuity";

C v Smith **426 M 76 (97)**—no requirement that **Miranda** be given in writing, and no requirement of a "fifth" warning, i.e., that D could stop the questioning at any time;

C v Groome **435 M 201 (2001)**—no requirement that D sign Miranda card in order to waive rights;

C v Silanskas **433 M 678 (2001)**—advice as to right to terminate questioning at any time ("5th warning") not required;

20-C.1. "Public Safety" Excuse for Omitting Warnings

NY v Quarles **467 US 649 (84)**—reasonable concern for "public safety" excuses no Miranda warnings/waiver (*see Chapter 20-A & Chapter 20-F re: Mass. Constitution*);

C v Waite **422 M 792 (96)**—public safety excused question to D, 'where's the gun?'; *C v Kitchings* **40 MAC 591 (96)** public safety excused question re: gun's location; *C v Alan A* **47 MAC 271 (99)** cop's fear for safety = question of fact for motion judge's determination;

C v Dillon D., a juvenile **448 M 793 (2007)**—notwithstanding Commonwealth's failure to prove Miranda warnings were given to juvenile in presence of an adult, and failure to allow private consultation between parent and 13-year-old juvenile, SJC refuses to suppress, saying "public safety" exception: D was showing bag of fifty bullets to other students, "enough to support the inference that a gun was in close proximity" to middle school and residents of the neighborhood;

C v Clark **432 M 1 (2000)**—public safety exception applied to cop questioning D, discovered lying shot in head and arm on roadside embankment nearby state trooper, also lying shot on ground, but with gun in hand; cop asked D if there was anyone else with him (no) and cop asked again, telling D not to "lie" (still no); SJC didn't decide issue left open previously, i.e., whether public safety exception is limited to cases in which there's "grave threat to public safety, and not just speculative threat to an individual police officer," because here, "dark," & "not known whether there was an armed assailant in the vicinity of a residential neighborhood or perhaps nearby on the adjacent major highway";

C v White **74 MAC 342 (2009)**—female driver in car "stop" was ordered out of seat and to place hands on car roof; while waiting for female cop to pat frisk; weapon had already been taken from a passenger, and cop said, "you better tell us if you have anything because we're going to find it": ensuing admission that gun was in her waistband not suppressed (public safety exception to any Miranda requirement);

20-C.2. Fifth Amendment Right to Counsel (Miranda Waiver Covers) vs. Sixth Amendment Right to Counsel (Doesn't Attach Until Formally Charged)

Moran v Burbine **475 US 412 (86)**—Miranda's Fifth Amendment, not Sixth, so statement admissible if Miranda waiver obtained (though attorney asked cops not to question D—because no right to counsel before arraignment—see § E below); *C v Cryer* **426 M 562, 568 (98)—reserved issue whether Article 12 mandates result different from** *Moran v Burbine*;

C v Mavredakis **430 M 848 (2000)**—police can't bar attorney from contact with suspect being interrogated; duty to inform suspect of attorney's efforts to render assistance is necessary to "actualize the abstract rights listed in *Miranda v Arizona*"; **Article 12 mandates broader protection from self-incrimination than does Fourth Amendment under** *Moran v Burbine* **475 US 412 (86)**;

C v Anderson **448 M 548 (2007)**—D, even if he is represented by counsel, can still choose to initiate contact with police and validly waive Sixth Amendment right to counsel during postindictment interview; different case under article 12 would exist if cop hadn't told D of attorney's entry into case and attorney's request that D not be interviewed (waiver then would not be knowing and intelligent); D here was serving 25-year sentence on unrelated case, out of state; SJC declines to follow *People v Hobson* 39 NY2d 479 (76) (once a lawyer has entered criminal proceeding representing D in connection with criminal charges under investigation, D in custody may not waive right to counsel in absence of the lawyer);

C v Ghee **414 M 313 (93)**—D had been charged with motor vehicle offenses and warning given was: "you are not obligated to say anything, in regard to this offense you are charged with"; inadequate, because it implied that while D didn't have to talk about vehicular crimes, he **did** have to speak about his girlfriend's dead body in the trunk, not having been "charged" with murder (yet); harmless beyond reasonable doubt here (statements did not include a confession);

C v Rainwater **425 M 540 (97)**—no relief from police interrogation of D, who had invoked right to counsel at arraignment, because Miranda said to be validly waived, & fruits of interrogation were used against D for crimes with

which he had not yet been charged (though such crimes were arguably overwhelmingly "related" to crime on which Sixth Amendment right to counsel had been invoked);

C v Gaynor **443 M 245 (2005)**—though defense counsel directed police to have no contact with D re: investigation concerning "fourth victim," police visited D at work, told him of test results re: fourth victim and that they would not question him about that case; no suppression of conversation thereafter in which D asked "spontaneously" about investigation of other murders and thereafter said he did not know victims depicted in photos; D wasn't in custody, and Sixth Amendment right to counsel hadn't attached because no criminal proceeding had begun against him;

Texas v Cobb **532 US 162 (2001)**—Sixth Amendment invocation at arraignment doesn't bar police interrogation, without notice to counsel, about any crime which is not, on the "elements" test of *Blockburger v US* **284 US 229 (32)**, the "same" crime for which D has invoked counsel;

C v Sherman **389 M 287 (83)**—Miranda violation for interfering with counsel consulting D PRE-arraignment; but see *C v Currie* **388 M 776 (83)** attorney tells D not to talk, rights given again, & D talks = admissible;

C v Mandeville **386 M 393 (82)**—counsel's request (6 days before) not to talk to D wasn't a request to be at arrest & didn't vitiate waiver;

C v Mahnke **368 M 662 (75)**—(*Chapter 20-B, 20-D*) suppress if cops thwart efforts of D & attorney to consult;

MacNeil v Wisconsin **501 US 171 (91)**—attachment of Sixth Amendment right to counsel at arraignment does not bar police from obtaining Miranda waivers on unrelated offenses; invocation of Fifth Amendment right to counsel distinguished; but see *Arizona v Roberson* **486 US 675 (88)**;

Texas v Cobb **532 US 162, 177–88 (2001)**—only DISSENTING justices assert that D's invocation of right to counsel on one charge means that he is entitled to counsel's assistance in deciding whether to waive Miranda rights as to charge(s) on which he has not yet been arraigned; *Mavredakis* supports possible contrary holding under Article 12, Declaration of Rights, despite travesty that was:

C v Rainwater **425 M 540 (97)**—SJC, in violation of *McNeil* and *Michigan v Jackson* (**475 US 625, 633 (86)**), refuses suppression of statements made upon police-initiated interrogation (with **Miranda** waiver) after appointment of counsel in one case, though interrogation concerned **both** recently-arraigned case and those not yet charged against D (statements allowed to be used in cases on which D had not yet been charged); BUT *Jackson* should have precluded initiation of the interviews since one of its subjects was case on which D had already requested counsel (at arraignment); purportedly, even SJC majority would have ordered suppression if uncharged cases were found to be "inextricably intertwined" or "closely related" to those in which D claimed counsel;

C v St. Peter **48 MAC 517 (2000)**—D got counsel at arraignment on outstanding OUI charge, but OK next day to get Miranda waiver and question him about unrelated homicide;

See Chapter 20-E, post (Massiah/counsel right) & G.L. c. 276, § 33A, telephone call (Chapter 20-B, ante);

20-C.3. Custody

C v Bryant **390 M 729 (84)**—questions at D's home not custody; factors = place, focus on D, probable cause yet, aggressive or informal, free to leave?;

C v Gendraw **55 MAC 677 (2002)**—no custody, here, in D's home; 4 factors to consider = place of interrogation inherently coercive?, did police convey that D was suspect?, was interrogation accusatory/aggressive?, was D free to end the interview?;

C v Smith **35 MAC 655 (93)**—stop of van matching description of hit & run culprit & cop opening driver's side door not custody **and** driver "spontaneously volunteered" "why did you stop us? We didn't hit anything"; further statements, after **Miranda**, not suppressible despite D's argument that arrest was without probable cause ("ample" probable cause, said court);

Berkemer v McCarthy **468 US 420 (84)**—(traffic) stop not custody (*cf. Chapter 3 & 20-M, post*), unless reasonable D would think "arrest"; Miranda includes minor crimes;

C v D'Agostino **38 MAC 206, S.C. 421 M 281 (95)**—during traffic stop, question by police 'where are you coming from?' didn't make setting custodial (despite response "I had a couple drinks");

C v Becla **74 MAC 142 (2009)**—cop having probable cause to arrest intoxicated motorist asked questions and successfully evaded Miranda requirement by not "arresting" D until after D refused to do third sobriety test (MAC holding no "custody" and reversing suppression);

C v DePeiza **449 M 367 (2007)**—cop's question of D whether he had firearm didn't make the on-street interaction "custodial"; motion judge found that cops' "tone" was "conversational" and interaction didn't become "aggressive"; *C v Gomes* **453 M 506 (2009)**—although approach by cops to D standing in doorway wasn't seizure, D was seized when cop immediately frisked D after asking him what he was doing;

C v Ware **76 MAC 53 (2009)**—seizure occurred only after D fled and cop began pursuit, cop then having reasonable suspicion that D had gun, and cop knew D too young to lawfully possess;

C v Haskell **438 M 790 (2003)**—"Terry" stop of defendant in car after 911 report of man with gun was nonetheless "custodial" such that Miranda warnings were required prior to question whether he had license to carry firearm (though an "order" to produce or exhibit license would have been OK, because production of physical evidence isn't testimonial; but cf. *C v Zevitas* **418 M 677 (94)** line of cases, including *C v Conkey* **430 M 139 (99)**—

can't introduce evidence that D first agreed to provide fingerprints, but then did not do so [violative of article 12]; conduct offered to show D's state of mind is "testimonial"); justifiable safety precautions during Terry stop (handcuffing suspect, drawn weapons) may create level of coercion equivalent to formal custody;

C v Irwin **72 MAC 643 (2008)**—reversal (despite no objection) for prosecutor's use in case in chief, in cross-examination, and in closing argument) of D's failure to reach out to police and delay in speaking to police about allegation of sexual assault, citing *Thompson* **431 M 108, 117 (2000)** and *Nickerson* **386 M 54 (82)** (impeachment of D with fact of prearrest silence should be approached with caution, is of "extremely limited probative worth");

C v Arruda **73 MAC 901, further appellate rev. allowed 452 M 1110 (2008)**—in interlocutory appeal by Commonwealth, Appeals Court holds that evidence of D's refusal to supply medical personnel with sample of his blood "for medical purposes" was admissible even though D was in custody and police "may have an interest in the results of the tests"; it is "governmental, not private, compulsion" that is prohibited by art. 12 of Declaration of Rights;

C v White **74 MAC 342 (2009)**—female driver in car "stop" was ordered out of seat and to place hands on car roof; while waiting for female cop to pat frisk; weapon had already been taken from a passenger, and cop said, "you better tell us if you have anything because we're going to find it": ensuing admission that gun was in her waistband not suppressed (public safety exception to any Miranda requirement);

C v Cameron **44 MAC 912 (98)**—at roadside, custody did not occur when cop formed belief that D was intoxicated;

C v Ayre **31 MAC 17 (91)**—questioning of motorist temporarily detained at side of road for traffic stop not "custodial"; Miranda warnings not required before field sobriety tests; open questions apparently remain under Article 12;

C v LaFleur **58 MAC 546 (2003)**—in response to emergency medical technician's inquiry regarding what had happened (D in driver's seat in one of two cars involved in accident), D said "I had too much to drink"; no "custody" when EMT passed info to cop, and cop at scene asked D what he had drunk, and at hospital asked similar questions; D's restraint on stretcher by EMTs wasn't inherently coercive;

C v Sauer **50 MAC 299 (2000)**—stop of D on roadside after vehicle swerved repeatedly not custodial despite D's self-incriminating response to question "what are you doing?";

C v Downs **31 MAC 467 (91)**—parking lot questioning of intoxicated D not "custodial";

C v Jones **42 MAC 378 (97)**—custody: D seated in back of cruiser with door open & officer standing at the door; counsel ineffective in failing to move for suppression

but overwhelming evidence of guilt, so no relief— HARMLESS;

C v Claiborne 423 M 275 (96)—in vehicles, stop of D on probable cause that he'd very recently robbed, frisk & cop statement that D matched description of recent robber & less-recent robbers—no custody;

C v Gordon 47 MAC 825 (99)—**even "Terry" stop can be custodial, & was here; even "preliminary" questions must be preceded by warnings;** what amounted to a confession was not harmless beyond reasonable doubt (despite significant other proof);

C v Costa 65 MAC 227 (2005)—because D didn't raise issue below, Appeals Court wouldn't address argument that, following arrest, cop's question of whether D had gun & request for consent to search & for keys to vehicle (without any prior Miranda warnings) violated Fifth Amendment rights, or argument that Miranda warnings are required prior to request for consent to search from person already in custody, or whether act of production of keys to vehicle is a testimonial statement protected by Miranda;

US v Hensley 469 US 221 (85)—officer may ask suspect to ID himself during Terry stop;

Brown v Texas 443 US 47 (79)—talk to man in high-drug alley not reasonable suspicion; detain to ask ID = seizure;

Hiibel v Sixth Judicial Court 542 US 177 (2004)— "stop & identify" statute not invalid here (contrast *Kolender v Lawson* 461 US 352, unconstitutionally vague statute requiring production of "credible & reliable identification" upon request); doesn't require production of driver's license or other document; request for name doesn't "ordinarily" violate Fourth or Fifth Amendment; dissent notes that statute imposes duty to speak upon specific class of individuals, i.e., those detained under circumstances that reasonably indicate that the person has committed, is committing, or is about to commit a crime;

C v Alvarado 427 M 277, 285 (98)—remand for inquiry re "arrest or at least custody," after car was stopped by 3 cops, occupants ordered out at gunpoint, search revealed handgun hidden in D's seat (& D was asked "you got a gun?");

C v Gallati 40 MAC 111 (96)—questions in office of D's superior correctional officer = custodial (**despite fact he** wasn't threatened with job loss and **was allowed to leave after questioning**);

C v Barros 56 MAC 675 (2002)—custody in D's home found; police arrived, said they had warrant for his arrest (default warrant for disturbing the peace, but cops testified later that they didn't intend to "execute" the warrant unless interview re: murder was fruitful), & this was used to gain entry to question D; questioning in small room began without Miranda warnings; D was 17 years old, dressed in underclothes, appeared to have been sleeping; question whether D owned paintball gun was interrogation because evidence of such gun's use was found at crime scene; D's leading cops to paintball gun's box gave cops view of bloody sneakers; ALL SUPPRESSED, as

was later statement at police station, after finding of *Edwards v Arizona* (451 US 477 (81)) violation;

C v O'Brien 432 M 578, 581 (2000)—interview of D at hospital (as self-proclaimed victim of recent crime) not custodial;

C v Coleman 49 MAC 150 (2000)—custody in D's aunt's home, when D (19-years old, black, 11th grade education) sat on bed, one white 6-foot tall cop sitting next to him and two other large white male cops blocking closed door of 11 ft by 12 ft room, cop propounding his "theory" of what happened and claiming (falsely) that D's fingerprint was found on gun clip; **that cop three times told D he could leave room was "meaningless mouthing";**

C v Sneed 440 M 216 (2003)—two investigators' two-hour interview of D in her home (though she was stressed, sick, asthmatic, and required emergency treatment 3 hours later, and though she was accused of larceny from her employer) held not custodial and, further, statements not involuntary; "objective" standard purportedly applied;

C v Groome 435 M 201 (2001)—trooper's assertion to D that he wasn't under arrest (+ unaccompanied trips to the bathroom) enough here for "no custody" finding;

C v Shine 398 M 641 (86)—**objective test re: custody, not cop's intent;**

C v Sparks 433 M 654, 657 (2001)—same; **fact that cops had "heightened suspicions" about D & placed him under surveillance after interview didn't make questioning "custodial";**

C v Bly 448 M 473 (2007)—D had burden of showing "custody," and here failed; D was "asked" to accompany detectives to station, he agreed, and was interviewed by detectives for 45 minutes in office with door open, D agreeing to have interview taped ("cordial and conversational, not aggressive or coercive"), and acknowledging on tape that his presence was voluntary/willing; after opportunity to make corrections, cops gave him ride back [home];

C v Trombley 72 MAC 183 (2008)—D appeared at police station with his mother and her boyfriend, saying he'd heard there was arrest warrant for him; this was not true and after eventually obtaining D's confession, police allowed him to leave; that D had not known previously that he was free to leave did not make his Miranda waiver invalid;

C v Conkey 430 M 139 (99)—questions in D's room at rooming house not custodial;

C v Clemente 452 M 295 (2008)—not ineffective assistance to fail to file motions having minimal chance of success: statements would not have been suppressed because, according to SJC, D not in custody when questioned so no need of Miranda warnings (D was questioned in "neutral location, a room in a court house" and "voluntarily agreed" to speak with detective, and was allowed to leave to attend son's arraignment, not arrested until after that arraignment);

C v Morse 427 M 117 (98)—*Bryant* 390 M 729 (84) **factors re: custody no longer controlling, given** *Stansbury v California* 511 US 318, 323–24 (94): **cop's subjec-**

tive beliefs irrelevant, except to extent they influence "objective conditions surrounding" interrogation; no "custody" here despite fact D was at station & was confronted by cops repeatedly, with friend's contrary recollections, and was told that it was "imperative" that he be truthful, given crime at issue (murder);

Yarborough v Alvarado **541 US 652 (2004)**—state court's failure to consider suspect's status as a juvenile inexperienced with police interrogations when court determined that during questioning juvenile was not "in custody" wasn't an "unreasonable application of federal law" (so federal habeas relief not necessary);

C v Juvenile **402 M 275 (88)**—DYS detention = custody; (*see also Chapter 20-B re: state action*); but see *Escobedo v Illinois* **378 US 478 (64)**, etc. re: "focus" on D triggering counsel right;

C v Sarourt Nam **426 M 152 (97)**—**though D "agreed to accompany" cops to police station (after his wife was found fatally shot in his car), custody found;**

C v Duguay **430 M 397 (99)**—no custody found after D agreed to accompany police to station in cruiser; officer's response ("just tell (us) what happened") to D's asking what police wanted to know "did not amount to questioning";

C v Murphy **424 M 485 (2004)**—no custody found at police station, to which D went voluntarily, with a group, to provide background info re: neighbors who were murdered, and he had been free to end interview and leave;

C v Hilton **443 M 597 (2005)**—though D didn't grasp meaning of Miranda warnings, and motion judge suppressed on this basis, SJC says no custody (so no suppression) when D was at police station voluntarily and would reasonably have believed free to leave until after the point at which she "initially" confessed; she had been free to leave 2 days earlier, and cops didn't convey to her any change in status (from their further investigation); fact that D was escorted to the bathroom by female trooper after 50 minutes of questioning wasn't point of "custody" here ("escort" being for purpose of direction and privacy rather than preventing D from leaving); suppression of statements made to trooper who thereafter questioned D as to particulars of fire-setting; **same case, second interlocutory appeal by Commonwealth, 450 M 173 (2007)**—on issue of "voluntariness," not considered in first appeal, motion judge incorrectly believed that D had been found "incompetent" around time of her statement, and a finding that D = unable to make voluntary intelligent waiver of Miranda rights "is not enough, standing alone, to support the finding that her statements were involuntary";

K. Smith, *Criminal Practice & Procedure*, §§ 336–40 (2d ed. 1983 & Supp.)—"custody," (including "focus" as a factor);

C v Larkin **429 M 426 (99)**—D in custody on one case, was brought to an office to speak with troopers; no Miranda for 10 minutes; Orwellian or "Alice in Wonderland" "no custody"; D has burden of proving "custodial";

C v Koumaris **440 M 405, 409 (2003)**—D, serving sentence, wanted to "get something off his conscience," but thereafter was handcuffed during the time he gave confession to long-ago murder; though D argued that handcuffs meant "custodial" (citing *C v Larkin* 429 M 426, 434 (99)), dispositive here = no "interrogation";

C v John **442 M 329 (2004)**—D, serving sentence, wasn't "in custody" for Miranda purposes when visited by FBI agent concerning his prospective testimony against former criminal cohorts; his confession to murder, in an attempt to avoid being forced to testify, was admissible against him despite the absence of Miranda warnings;

Illinois v Perkins **496 US 292 (90)**—undercover cop posing as cellmate not required to give Miranda warnings where D held on unrelated charge;

C v Magee **423 M 381 (96)**—***custody*, despite facts that D came to station on her own, was not explicitly told she couldn't leave, and eventually did leave**, though was then followed by police, directly to mental health center; before getting mental/emotional "help" she was repeatedly told she had to answer questions first, and that she had to "wait" for next law enforcement official;

C v Almonte **444 M 511 (2005)**—when D, having obtained religion, came to NY police station to confess involvement in a shooting in MA ten years earlier (about which NY cop knew absolutely nothing), cop's request for more specific info didn't transform encounter into custodial interrogation;

C v Damiano **422 M 10 (96)**—***custody*, even though allegedly "protective" in nature**; rejecting Commonwealth arguments that physical evidence should not be suppressed because it would have been found anyway (not **"inevitable"/harmless**);

C v Azar **32 MAC 290 (92)**—questioning of D not "custodial" where cops invited D to stationhouse to continue conversation without interruptions & allowed him to leave afterwards; Miranda rights given in abundance of caution;

C v Sparks **433 M 654, 657 (2001)**—that D was allowed to leave station, despite being under surveillance, meant no "custody"; *C v Trombley* 72 MAC 183 (2008)—similar;

C v Doe **37 MAC 30 (94)**—questioning of snitch, in his home, not custodial, when snitch approached local police to tell of robbery in adjacent town and local police passed along info to investigating officers, who met with snitch (though had prior info that snitch's own car was used in the crime);

C v Osachuk **418 M 229 (94)**—D who took drug overdose victim to hospital (dead on arrival), was "asked" by cop to come to station to make statement; 1st statement (no Miranda) was admissible (no custody), but cop called D "liar" and aggressively confronted D with fact that another witness said otherwise, prompting 2d statement, & then **Miranda** before 3d statement = both 2d & 3d statements should have been suppressed: **use of inconsistencies** to "leverage a further statement" would convey, to reasonable person, *not* free to leave;

C v Kirwan **448 M 304 (2007)**—though cop told D that D was the only person who had contact with dead victim and that victim had stab wound in his chest, and "asked", "you don't know how it got there?", D wasn't in custody in the apartment in which he lived with his father; "possibility that an incriminating response might be forthcoming does not necessarily elevate the nature of questioning to a custodial level";

C v Ferrara **31 MAC 648 (91)**—questioning of D during execution of search warrant at place of business not "custodial" where D unaware of any intent by cops to arrest him;

C v Burbine **74 MAC 148 (2009)**—after D' girlfriend had D removed from home, she gave to cop a bag of D's possessions which she wanted out of house: bag held guns, & cop called D to station "to retrieve some of his property," without ID'ing it; though cop acknowledged D wouldn't likely be able to leave if he acknowledged owning bag contents, uncommunicated thoughts didn't make cop's questions to D "custodial";

20-C.4. Interrogation

Rhode Island v Innis **446 US 291 (80)**—interrogation = words/acts reasonably likely to elicit answer;

C v Chadwick **40 MAC 425 (96)**—cop saying that 'this isn't a question' but 'rape is not always what people think it is . . .' **was** a question about the crime;

C v Clark C. **59 MAC 542 (2003)**—motion judge "found" that cop's statement to juvenile, "you said you were going to turn yourself in yesterday when I spoke to you," was attempt to verify voice he heard, but didn't recognize, on telephone the previous day, so was functional equivalent of interrogation; appeals court holds that this was a finding of fact rather than conclusion of law;

C v Torres **424 M 792 (97)**—even though cop intended kind gestures to produce statement, "interrogation" occurs only when reasonable person in suspect's position would perceive statements or conduct to be interrogation; furthermore, Miranda warnings were given after the kind gestures & before statements;

C v Rodriguez **75 MAC 235 (2009)**—cop, neighbor of D, asked on behalf of D's girlfriend if he had any extra money for his children; D "apologized to [cop] for conducting business across the street from him and said he meant no disrespect," and gave cop money to give to girlfriend: D's nonresponsive apology was not result of interrogation;

C v King **17 MAC 602 (84)**—after booked, D volunteered "I raped her";

C v Ferrer **68 MAC 544 (2007)**—D's remark to cop (who drove D in wagon to station for booking on trespassing) "your boys are dumb. They could have me for seven or eight years instead of this trespassing bullshit" was volunteered, was what prompted cop's response that they

were pretty smart and good at what they do; latter was not interrogation; D's further incriminating remarks, inter alia, "they'll never find it," not suppressed;

C v Diaz **422 M 269 (96)**—after arrest & **Miranda**, some incriminating statements, but next day, when about to be printed, volunteered, "This is really going to fuck me up," cop's "why?" is not equal to questioning, but mere 'natural reflex action' to D's statement;

Arizona v Mauro **481 US 520 (87)**—cop can use D's conversation (in cop's presence) with D's wife because cops didn't elicit;

C v Chipman **418 M 262 (94)**—after D claimed rights to silence & counsel, he asked what initial proceedings would be; booking & arraignment were explained; D next asked why he was being portrayed on TV as armed & dangerous & was told that "the gun is still missing" prompting reply "I don't have any rifle. Those guys were supposed to have buried that gun"- no "interrogation";

C v Figueroa **56 MAC 641 (2002)**—during drive to Massachusetts after D's arrest, D asked police about named gang, said members had been harassing him, asked if co-D had been caught, and when police said that he had, D said, "That night [co-D] did this thing and fucked up my life"; no "interrogation," no suppression;

C v Braley **449 M 316, 323–25 (2007)**—though D was in custody of police when he was in Florida airport being returned to MA, their "light conversation and banter" with him didn't concern the crime, and D's question, "How did you get on to me?" wasn't result of "interrogation"; trooper's response, "I told him that his partner wasn't as good as he was in keeping this quiet" SHOULD NOT HAVE BEEN ADMITTED; "state of police knowledge" was irrelevant;

C v Caputo **439 M 153 (2003)**—cop's use of telephone in D's presence, with D thus hearing conversation that tended to implicate him, did elicit D's statements (after he had previously declined to make statements), but no "interrogation";

C v Delrio **22 MAC 712 (86)**—if questions = by cops' interpreter, it's interrogation;

Blackburn v Alabama **361 US 199 (60)**—though volunteered, statement scrutinized re: mental capacity; (*see* K. Smith, *Criminal Practice & Procedure*, § 344 (2d ed. 1983 & Supp.); & *Chapter 20-D, below*);

C v St. Peter **48 MAC 517 (2000)**—after booking officer gave Miranda, D volunteered "That's a bad one. I might have just killed someone": no interrogation found;

C v Harkess **35 MAC 626 (93)**—finding that D volunteered that gun was not his, but he knew whose it was;

C v Clark C. **59 MAC 542 (2003)**—when cop was admitted to juvenile's bedroom to arrest him, and told him that he had a warrant for arrest and to get up and get dressed and come with him, juvenile's response, "Did my grandmother turn me in?" was not product of interrogation; telephone call to cop (purportedly by D in response to cop's previous conversation with D's grandmother) in which caller said, "I didn't do all that lady said I did, I just hit her," also not product of interrogation;

C v Mitchell **35 MAC 909 (93)**—after D's booking for minor crime, police conversed with each other re: whether D fit the description, & D "volunteered" what he was wearing the day before; Appeals Court contrasted:

*C v Brant **380 M 876 (80)**—cops elicited by saying co-D had confessed & letting D talk to co-D (& retract his desire for silence & attorney);

C v Harvey **390 M 203 (83)**—cop's bringing D to station with warrant, but without booking him and putting him in room with co-D, was "elicitation;"

C v Jackson **377 M 319 (79)—lie by cops violated silence invocation**;

C v Cameron **44 MAC 912 (98)**—field sobriety tests not interrogation (because do not elicit "testimonial or communicative evidence" and so do not trigger Article 12 or Fifth Amendment protections); BUT refusal to perform such test IS testimonial (*C v McGrail* **419 M 74 (95)** evidence of refusal to perform field sobriety tests violates Article 12; *C v Grenier* **45 MAC 58 (98)** similar);

C v Haskell **438 M 790 (2003)**—question during "Terry" stop (coercive enough to require Miranda warnings, though not "arrest"), 'do you have license to carry firearm' = questioning (invitation to 'relate a factual assertion or disclose information') though a mere order to produce/exhibit license would not have violated prohibition against forced self-incrimination ("subtle . . . distinction");

K. Smith, *Criminal Practice & Procedure*, **§ 341 (2d ed. 1983 & Supp.)**—"interrogation"

C v Mitchell **47 MAC 178 (99)**—1 cop's comment, as 2 were driving D to station after arrest & Miranda, "tough luck getting locked up this close to Christmas," not interrogation;

C v Duguay **430 M 397 (99)**—no custody found after D agreed to accompany police to station in cruiser; plus officer's response ("just tell (us) what happened") to D's asking what police wanted to know "did not amount to questioning";

C v Chadwick **40 MAC 425 (96)**—after request for attorney, & awaiting transport to house of correction, D's statement ("that he knew he did not rape his daughter") did not allow cop to elicit further statement by comment "I will tell you one thing, but this is not meant to be a question. Rape is not always what people think and things like oral sex are rape";

C v Clark **432 M 1 (2000)**—after Miranda rights given, & D asked for lawyer, cops asked D to sign Miranda form they had read to him at outset; he responded that "he would except he was left handed & couldn't sign due to condition of his left arm"; admission of "left-handedness" was material and introduced at trial; SJC held that statement wasn't made in response to "interrogation";

20-C.5. Booking/"Preliminary" Questions

C v Mahoney **400 M 524 (87)**—booking questions not necessarily interrogation;

Pennsylvania v Muniz **496 US 582 (90)**—un-Mirandized OUI-D's statements at booking desk in response to police questioning calling upon him to calculate date of sixth birthday was suppressed because designed to elicit not "biographical data necessary to complete booking or pretrial services," but rather information for "investigatory purposes";

C v Sheriff **425 M 186, 198–99 (97)**—cop's "preliminary" questions to hospitalized D re: whether he remembered officers being there 2 days earlier sought possibly incriminating evidence because goal = refute possible claim of insanity, prove time/place/person orientation; hearing should be held;

C v Gonsalves **74 MAC 910 (2009)—testimony that D refused to answer booking questions until he talked to lawyer = reversal despite "late" objection and no request for curative instruction;**

C v Gordon **47 MAC 825 (99)**—even "Terry" stop can be custodial, & was here; **even "preliminary" questions must be preceded by warnings**; what amounted to a confession was not harmless beyond reasonable doubt (despite significant other proof);

C v DiMarzio **52 MAC 746 (2001)**—though "combustible combination of a gun, intoxication, and conflict" along with observation of circumstances at D's office (haphazard car parking and door left open suggested D was "in a rush") was exigency making it reasonable for cops to enter premises through open door peaceably in broad daylight, suppression of marijuana from inside desk drawer ordered: D had been handcuffed and was asked, without Miranda warnings, 'where's marijuana?' (smelled by cops, rolling papers observed); rejecting Commonwealth claims of legitimate desk search because exigent circumstances, "search incident to arrest" or "inevitable discovery"; **on further appellate review, 436 M 1012 (2002),** SJC agrees re: suppression, but instead simply because discovery was fruit of Miranda violation & no inevitable discovery;

C v Woods **419 M 366 (95)**—where arrestee's employment status may prove incriminatory, police must give Miranda before asking questions about employment (& equally applicable to any question whose answer may prove incriminatory);

C v Guerrero **32 MAC 263 (92)**—although questions about employment status should be "scrubbed" from booking procedure, failure to give Miranda warnings did not require suppression where D never moved to suppress or strike; but see *C v Kacavich* **28 MAC 941 (90)** routine booking questions not interrogation; incriminating answers re: address & employment admissible;

C v Guy **441 M 96 (2004)—can impeach D's trial testimony concerning alleged attack by victim with D's statements to booking question concerning whether he** had any injuries (D had said then only that he had been hit on side of head);

C v Carey **26 MAC 339, 341–42 (88)**—had D not received Miranda, questions & answers at booking re where & how long drinking should have been deleted;

C v Acosta **416 M 279 (93)**—booking response as to **address** used against D (trial issue = dominion/custody/control of drugs in apartment); make explicit argument/motion to suppress/motion in limine;

C v Carey **26 MAC 339 (88)**—booking video OK if nontestimonial, & 2 admissions OK because D said he understood Miranda;

C v Dayes **49 MAC 419, 421 (2000)**—because D was given Miranda rights at arrest & was immediately transported to police station, Appeals Court refused to suppress D's statement (in response to booking question) that she was unemployed; claimed that, in cases cited by D, Ds hadn't been given Miranda rights previously; **NOTE**: obvious point is that D wouldn't think s/he had right to refuse to answer 'administrative' questions like booking, see *Kacavich* **28 MAC 941 (90)**, above; cf. *Maylott* **43 MAC 516 (97)** refusal to condemn police for withholding bail consideration for arrestees who fail to cooperate with booking (so does claim of right to silence/right to consult with attorney/invocation of Miranda justify withholding bail?); cf. *Edwards v Arizona* **451 US 477 (81)** after desire for lawyer, questioning must cease & can't resume again even with rights/waiver; (query: if D had been advised of Miranda rights at arrest and invoked rights to silence and counsel, aren't police required to forego any subsequent questions, even "booking" ones, on rationale of Dayes?);

20-C.6. Video/Record Interview

C v DeSouza **428 M 667, 669 (99)**—SJC commends police for videotaping interview, so as to prove voluntariness, Miranda waiver and absence of intoxication/exhaustion;

C v Diaz **422 M 269, 273 (96)**—declining, for 2d time (see *C v Fryar* **414 M 732, 742 n.8 (93)**), to require contemporaneous electronic recording of D's statements/interrogation BUT defense invited to argue stringently to judge and jury that failure to record should be considered in deciding voluntariness & whether D was properly advised of rights, & whether any statement attributed to D was actually made;

C v Ardon **428 M 496 (98)** and *C v Pina* **430 M 66 (99)**—similar;

C v St. Peter **48 MAC 517 (2000)**—judge not REQUIRED to **instruct jury that failure to record alleged confession could be considered re: voluntariness, though such instruction may be given** (and wouldn't be "error"); D may argue this inference to jury;

C v DiGiambattista **442 M 423 (2004)**—**if prosecution introduces D's statement which is product of custodial interrogation or interrogation conducted at a place of detention, and there is "not at least an audiotape recording of the COMPLETE INTERROGATION," D entitled on request to jury instruction that highest court prefers such full recording and its absence means that alleged statement should be weighed with great caution and care, AND that absence of recording permits (but doesn't compel) jury to conclude failure of proof of voluntariness beyond reasonable doubt;**

C v Diaz **453 M 266, 277–79 (2009)**—cops' statements during interrogation of D concerning fact that "people" had ID'd him as shooter were plainly hearsay and "contrary to the judge's conclusion that [they] were offered 'to show their effect on the hearer,'" jury could have considered for their truth, no limiting instruction having been given; no 'substantial risk of miscarriage of justice' for hearsay violation as ID'ing witnesses testified at trial; no relief on Constitutional *Crawford v Washington* ground as harmless beyond reasonable doubt; at 281–82, questions and answers during interrogation concerning extraneous bad acts "should have been excluded on the basis of their lack of relevance," and "[c]ounsel should have sought to exclude them"; **"[t]he fact that the questions were asked during a police interview in which the defendant voluntarily participated does not render the responses admissible at trial";**

C v Dagley **442 M 713, 720 (2004)**—DiGiambattista's holding re: jury instruction = exercise of power of superintendence over courts, not a new constitutional rule, so won't be applied "retroactively" to entitle this D to new trial with benefit of the instruction;

C v Burton **450 M 55 (2007)**—SJC refuses again to make electronic recording a prerequisite to statement's admissibility;

K. Smith, *Criminal Practice & Procedure*, §§ 345–54 (2d ed. 1983 & Supp.)—manner, frequency, specifics of warnings; cf. *C v Gordon* **422 M 816, 833 (96)** tape recording of D's booking admitted at trial (relevant to sobriety at time of crimes) upheld, though technically G.L. c. 272, § 99P mandates suppression;

C v Morganti **455 M 388 (2009)**—arrested in CA on fugitive from justice MA warrant, D was video/audiotaped in interview room as he was alone, making telephone call to female: no suppression, as D was told police intended to record what was said in interview room, and [additional] telephone recording similarly OK as D was aware that he was subject to monitoring/recording, AND D repeated the only materially incriminating statement after cop was in room, listening, & D was still on phone;

C v Trombley **72 MAC 183, 187 (2008)**—concerning suppression motion judge's stated belief that officers' failure to record D's statements required him to view Miranda waiver with skepticism (D purportedly said no when asked if he wanted interview to be recorded): absent 'overbearing or coercive tactics by the police,' failure to record "should not be made the dominant factor in determining" confession to be involuntary;

20-C.7. Waiver of Miranda (Factors) vs. Invocation of Right to Silence

North Carolina v Butler **441 US 369 (79)**—infer waiver from acts/words—silence not enough, but explicit not necessary;

C v Luce **34 MAC 105 (93)**—immediately after police found cocaine on his person & gave him Miranda rights, D sought to learn what benefits he could gain from "cooperation" with police; these statements not inadmissible as **statements made in connection with plea bargaining** (M.R.Crim.P. 12(f)); furthermore, later D-statements, during meetings between D **and his** attorney & government officers held admissible despite M.R.Crim.P. 12(f);

C v Grenier **415 M 680 (93)**—after Miranda, cop asserted that reason D had blood on himself was he'd assisted in murder; D "dropped his head," & cop said, "did you know when you set up the old guy for the robbery that they were going to murder him?"; D dropped head, said "no," shook his head, hesitated, then denied he had been at murder scene, "done" murder, or that he knew anything about a murder: entire sequence admissible as "equivocal response to an accusation of guilt";

C v Mandeville **386 M 393 (82)**—**no response (when asked if want to talk) not unequivocal exercise of right; then taking Fifth Amendment on only some questions showed OK waiver on others;**

C v Robidoux **450 M 144 (2007)**—D's willingness to "share stories and discuss his guiding principles" was "interspersed with refusals to talk about his family": where D has not asserted right to remain silent, "he cannot pick and choose which questions to answer, because '[i]f he talks, what he says or omits is to be judged on its merits or demerits, and not on some artificial standard that only the part that helps him can be later referred to'"; contrast in topics about which D was willing to talk "was relevant evidence of his state of mind"; D does "retain[] the right to cut off the interrogation by [ ]asserting his right to silence", but this must be by "either an expressed unwillingness to continue or an affirmative request for an attorney";

C v Raymond **424 M 382 (97)**—denial of involvement, plus silent head shaking in response to questions not invocation of silence: could have been continuing denial of involvement & nervousness or desire to think before answering;

C v Hussey **410 M 664 (91)**—**D's statement that he had "nothing else (to) say" plus thinking aloud about remaining silent didn't amount to invocation of right to silence;**

C v Brown **449 M 747 (2007)**—D's response of "no, I don't," to cop question of whether D "had anything further to add to his statement" was simply indication that statement was complete, and wasn't assertion of right to silence;

C v Todd **408 M 724 (90)**—wondering aloud about advisability of having attorney was resolved, after equivocation, by D's signing Miranda waiver, i.e., was not assertion of right to counsel;

C v Scoggins **439 M 571 (2003)**—mere inquiry regarding need for an attorney doesn't require police to cease interrogation;

C v Hartford **425 M 378 (97)**—that D had IQ of 73 & other disabilities did not make him, as a matter of law, incapable of waiving Miranda and making voluntary statements; motion judge's finding of fact upheld;

C v Dingle **73 MAC 274 (2008)**—no ineffective assistance of counsel in failure to file motion to suppress statements on ground of D's low IQ (plus: D's "ability to offer" exculpatory explanation for pornography, i.e., believed children were over age 18 = "significant evidence" that statements were voluntary);

C v O'Brien **432 M 578, 586 (2000)**—judge's finding of waiver not reversed despite D's argument that judge should have given more weight to D's age, physical condition, lack of experience with criminal justice system, D's reliance on father, father's weakened emotional condition after seeing murder victim's body;

C v Jackson **432 M 82, 86–87 (2000)**—evidence of IQ of 65 could be discounted by judge (particularly?) given other evidence that D attended public schools (including "in the regular classroom"), had never been diagnosed as being retarded, held down several jobs during life & hadn't been fired for failure to perform appropriately;

C v Ewing **30 MAC 285 (91)**—D's selective refusal to answer some questions not invocation of right to silence where D answered others & signed written waiver;

C v James **427 M 312 (98)**—D's response "nope" to question whether he wanted to make a statement did not bar cop's further question whether he "wanted to talk about what happened"; "finding of fact," not clearly erroneous, was that "nope" does not equal silence, but just no "formal statement";

Davis v US **512 US 452 (94)**—"maybe I should talk to a lawyer" was not a clear request for lawyer, when D subsequently said he didn't want a lawyer (in response to police statement that questioning would end if he was requesting attorney);

Berghuis v Thompkins **** US ** (6/1/2010)**—after receiving Miranda warnings, D was largely silent during 3-hour interrogation but near end said "yes" when asked if he prayed to God to forgive him for the shooting; silence during interrogation did not operate to invoke right to remain silent; cites analogous holding in *Davis v US* regarding Miranda right to counsel;

C v Contos **435 M 19, 29–30 (2001)**—**"I think I'm going to get a lawyer" = unambiguous invocation of D's right** to counsel; even if it were ambiguous, **court didn't agree that "clarification of the request for counsel would have been constitutional";**

C v Jones **439 M 249 (2003)**—D's statement that he was "going to need a lawyer sometime" wasn't affirmative request for an attorney;

C v Morganti **455 M 388 (2009)**—when D, in jail, said that he was "thinking I might need a lawyer and want to talk with him before talking to you," this wasn't unequivocal invocation of right to counsel (instead "musing about" possibility of stopping" questioning); D next said discussing charges would be easier if in less-air conditioned room with something to eat;

C v Denis **442 M 617, 631 (2004)**—D's request that police contact his former high school guidance counselor wasn't a clear and unambiguous request for counsel, despite D's claim that this request was for someone who would help him find counsel (citing *Fare v Michael C.* **442 US 707, 719 (79)**, regarding D's request to contact probation officer after arrest);

C v Segovia **53 MAC 184 (2001)**—ineffective assistance of counsel found in failure to file motion to suppress D's videotaped custodial interrogation where D had viable claim that cop ignored D's request for translator & paralegal before continuing the questioning, and where fruit of the interrogation was prosecution's discovery of a witness who provided damaging trial testimony;

C v Magee **423 M 381 (96)**—no waiver when cops merely pointed to telephone after D professed ignorance re: how to obtain attorney at 5 a.m. on July 4 holiday, particularly given D's physical & emotional condition; **also** involuntary because medical/psychiatric treatment withheld until D provided statement;

C v Silanskas **433 M 678, 683 (2001)**—fact that D "mentioned the name of his attorney and recited the attorney's telephone number" wasn't invocation of counsel, because cop purportedly asked D if he wanted to telephone attorney, & D said "no";

C v Pennellatore **392 M 382 (84)**—comment about needing attorney (20 minutes before rights) not invocation of right to silence/counsel;

C v Dubois **451 M 20 (2008)**—after Miranda warnings, troopers told D they were there to discuss D's ex-wife who was killed > six years earlier; D's comment "this sounds serious. Maybe I better get a lawyer" and his silence when asked then if he did want a lawyer held not invocation of right to silence/counsel (even though D did not respond to particular further questions, ,i.e., whether he bought guns and whether he had killed victim, and said 'you can't make me look at [proffered photo of victim] . . . I want a lawyer"; only latter explicit assertion held to be invocation of [silence]/counsel right;

C v Peixoto **430 M 654 (2000)**—after receipt of Miranda warnings, D's musings that he didn't know if he should talk or not and that maybe he should have attorney present were NOT invocation of Miranda rights BUT cross-examination of D about such musings (no doubt for inference of guilt) was impermissible as matter of state law under due process and Article 12; that D not formally arrested didn't matter, but necessary to holding was that Miranda rights had been given already;

C v Costa **414 M 618 (93)**—D's statements (1) that he had no recollection of his activities at relevant time & (2) that he didn't want to be a "canary" or "squeal" on friends not invocation of right to silence;

C v Daniels **366 M 601 (75)**—diminished capacity a factor re: waiver, e.g., retarded; expert can help;

C v Cameron **385 M 660 (82)**—(same); (see also *Blackburn v Alabama* **361 US 199 (60)** though volunteered, statement scrutinized re: mental capacity; & *Chapter 20-D below*);

C v Stone **70 MAC 800 (2007)**—citing *C v Prater* 420 M 569 (95), despite low IQ (low to mid-70s) and history of special education classes, can voluntarily waive Miranda rights: D worked at Dunkin' Donuts for ten years, and has "conduct[ed] regular financial transactions," such as renting apartment and "mak[ing] regular payments on electronic equipment" (experts were presented); because D put in issue D's ability to understand Miranda warnings, Commonwealth could introduce fact that D had received Miranda warnings in the past (though without any details, or why);

C v Cain **361 M 224 (72)**—"yes, I didn't do it" not a waiver by agitated 15-year-old denied access to parent;

20-C.8. Juveniles—Special Rules (Interested Adult)

C v Juvenile **389 M 128 (83)**—special waiver rules for juveniles;

C v MacNeill **399 M 71 (87)**—juvenile waiver OK because opportunity to consult adult;

C v McCra **427 M 564 (98)**—SJC rejected juvenile D's argument that his aunt could not act as the consulting adult since the murder victims included her sibling (D's parent); no **per se** rule that a relative's presence is inherently coercive;

C v Robinson **449 M 1, 4 n.6 (2007)**—Massachusetts doesn't require consent of parent or guardian prior to interview when juvenile is seventeen years old;

C v Trombley **72 MAC 183 (2008)**—though D appeared at station with his mother, D was seventeen years old, and one cop's asking to speak with the mother (who was led away from interview room), while inferably aimed at weakening D's resistance to confessing, was not fatal to voluntariness of Miranda waiver and confession; appellate court rejected motion judge's view that waiver was contingent upon mother's continued presence, or at least advice that D could stop answering until mother returned;

C v Philip S. **414 M 804 (93)**—juvenile's Miranda waiver valid where mother reasonably appeared to interrogating officers to be "interested adult" who was not antagonistic, had capacity to appreciate situation & give advice, & had actual opportunity to consult, even though she counseled him to waive his rights & tell the truth;

C v Escalera **70 MAC 729 (2007)**—foster parent of juvenile may be "interested adult" despite having contractual relationship with the State (DSS), if has "relationship with juvenile" and "is sufficiently interested in the juvenile's welfare to afford the juvenile appropriate protection";

C v Ward **412 M 395 (92)**—although cops not required to inform juvenile & adult of right to confer privately before Miranda waiver, **they may not refuse requests to do so**;

C v Ferrer **47 MAC 645 (99)**—statement of juvenile suppressed because of failure to allow meaningful conversation with interested adult prior to Miranda waiver **could** be used for impeachment if D testified, judge having found, permissibly, that it was "voluntary" (youth = 1 relevant factor re: voluntariness, but not conclusive);

C v Alan A. **47 MAC 271 (99)**—parents of juvenile, while asserting that on advice of counsel, there would be no statements or answers to questions, were willing to allow juvenile to show cops where gun was hidden, & juvenile's volunteered statements during search for gun were admissible; no argument here that 'public safety' exception to Miranda (covering initial police question to D) not applicable to juveniles (argument rejected in other jurisdictions);

C v Dillon D., a juvenile **448 M 793 (2007)**—notwithstanding Commonwealth's failure to prove Miranda warnings were given to juvenile in presence of an adult, and failure to allow private consultation between parent and 13-year-old juvenile, SJC refuses to suppress, saying "public safety" exception: D was showing bag of fifty bullets to other students, "enough to support the inference that a gun was in close proximity" to middle school and residents of the neighborhood;

C v Guthrie G **66 MAC 414, and S.C. on further appellate review, 449 M 1028 (2007), "agree[s] with Appeals Court's result for essentially the reasons articulated**—despite fact that cops' info was that "gun" was BB gun, court holds "exigency"/public safety justified police in going to juvenile's home and asking for gun ("inculpatory evidence," as recognized by App. Ct. dissent), and following him into his bedroom as he retrieved it (all without benefit of adult, since juvenile was home alone); juvenile (age 14) held to have been appropriately questioned at police station, as cops gave Miranda to juvenile and father, and waited for arrival of father at station, explaining to father "why he was there" (albeit giving no opportunity for consultation in private, because not requested sua sponte);

C v Guyton **405 M 497 (89)**—minor may not act as "interested adult";

C v Leon L **52 MAC 823 (2001)**—Appeals Court reverses judge's suppression order: from perspective of interrogating cops, juveniles' mothers comprehended events, asked questions, signed Miranda forms, notwithstanding judge's view that they didn't "sufficiently understand situation" to provide "meaningful consultation"; **suppression anyway on alternative ground of involuntariness due to cops' pressure, slamming table, etc.**;

C v Alfonso A **53 MAC 279 (2001), S.C. on further appellate review 438 M 372 (2003)**—suppression ordered because cops didn't ever inform adult of juvenile's constitutional rights, or even of the fact of her son's interrogation, though she was at home; juvenile was held in a different apartment for 2½ hours before interrogation began, while cops awaited arrival of search warrant, & facts that juvenile himself said that he knew his rights, had been arrested twice before, & didn't want his mother present were not controlling; SJC says police "offers to get" juvenile's mother did not provide the requisite protection (mother should have been immediately available for consultation for juvenile's purported waiver to be legitimate);

C v Mark M. **59 MAC 86, 91 (2003)**—fact that police questioning began immediately after D and grandmother received Miranda warnings was improper, but admissions came later, after arguable break in stream; there is no absolute requirement that police inform of the right to consult, though SJC has stated this is advisable (*C v Philip S.* **414 M 804, 811 n.5 (93)**); for there to be "actual opportunity" to consult, adult must "at least understand that there is an opportunity to consult and his or her own role in that consultation"; remand for findings necessary (did adult understand rights? Did adult understand role as potential source of advice? Did juvenile get opportunity for consultation? Was there break in chain of events?); after remand for further findings, *C v Mark M.* **65 MAC 703 (2006)**—motion judge found that initial statement was incriminating, that "several minutes" wasn't enough time to insulate later statements from taint, and that there was no evidence that 13-year-old juvenile's grandmother understood Miranda warnings or her role as advisor; further, there was no opportunity for juvenile and grandmother to consult; motion judge on remand was not required by remand order to take further evidence;

C v Berry **410 M 31 (91)**—although parental "disability" at time of stationhouse consultation with juvenile a factor to be considered, not enough here to invalidate juvenile's Miranda waiver;

C v Snyder **413 M 521 (92)**—school officials not required to give Miranda warnings where cooperation with police not routine; open questions under Article 12 remain;

C v Hosey **368 M 571 (75)**—no waiver because D's drunk/incoherent;

K. Smith, *Criminal Practice & Procedure,* **§§ 365–82 (2d ed. 1983 & Supp.)**—"voluntary" waiver—age, mental state, etc.

Yarborough v Alvarado **541 US 652 (2004)**—state court's failure to consider suspect's status as a juvenile inexperienced with police interrogations when court determined that during questioning juvenile was not "in custody" wasn't an "unreasonable application of federal law" (so federal habeas relief not necessary);

20-C.9. Subsequent Statements Tainted?

C v Smith **412 M 823 (92)**—presumption is that any statement made after violation of Miranda is tainted; presumption may be overcome (1) after illegally-obtained statement, break in stream of events insulating post-Miranda statement from the tainted one, or (2) illegally-obtained statement did not incriminate D (i.e., did not "let the cat out of the bag");

C v Larkin **429 M 426 (99)**—taint of earlier Miranda violation may be removed if EITHER (1) sufficient time has elapsed and sufficient break in course of events allows conclusion that taint has dissipated, OR (2) pre-Miranda interview led to no inculpatory statement;

C v Garner **59 MAC 350 (2003)**—first statement was suppressed, and placed D at crime scene, but judge permissibly determined that there was sufficient intervening break so as to remove taint from later statements at police station (D hadn't been arrested, and voluntarily went to station next day, and wasn't then restrained, etc.);

C v Harris **75 MAC 696 (2009)**—judge properly allowed motion to suppress D's first statement, made without Miranda warnings at scene of drug sale; second statement was made at police station almost two hours later with "involvement of different police personnel" and was a sufficient break to insulate second statement from taint of first; further, D appeared to have been motivated to exonerate his cousin with whom he shared apartment; that D's use of telephone was delayed because there was no telephone in or near interview room was no cause for relief: D didn't establish "intentional deprivation" (D was informed of telephone right on form signed at 12:21 a.m., and booking occurred at 12:55 a.m., D then using telephone);

C v Damiano **422 M 10 (96)**—rejecting Commonwealth arguments both that there was break in chain of events and that pre-Miranda statements were not incriminating (placed D at scene & were factually implausible);

C v Osachuk **418 M 229 (94)**—2d statement was in violation of Miranda & 3d was tainted by it ("cat out of bag," no break in events);

C v Prater **420 M 569, 580–81 n.10 (95)**—unclear whether **both** factors from, e.g., *Smith* (**412 M 823 (92)**—presumption is that any statement made after violation of Miranda is tainted; presumption may be overcome (1) after illegally-obtained statement, break in stream of events insulating post-Miranda statement from the tainted one, or (2) illegally-obtained statement did not incriminate D (i.e., did not "let the cat out of the bag")) must exist, to defeat presumption, but here, "break" found (90-minute lapse and D no longer intoxicated);

C v Pileeki **62 MAC 505 (2004)**—cat-out-of-bag-suppression rejected on basis that "break in stream of events" consisted of fact that D was very intoxicated at first statement but wasn't intoxicated at second (equating "coercive circumstances" with "intoxication") AND purportedly because "evidence [doesn't] suggest that . . . 2d statement was motivated by a feeling she had let the cat out of the bag"; refusal to redact from second statement references to first, suppressed, statement held harmless here;

See also Chapter 11-G re: Inadmissibility of D's SILENCE or invoking rights;

C v King **34 MAC 466 (93)**—D's invocation of right to silence is **inadmissible** at trial, though Commonwealth claimed relevance re: D's "state of mind"; *C v Grenier* **415 M 680 (93)** error for cop to testify (a) that he told D he didn't believe D's denial, (b) that D then became "nerv-

ous", and (c) that D declined when asked to give a truthful statement; *C v Rendon-Alvarez* **48 MAC 140 (99)** error to admit testimony that D refused to answer further questions;

C v McClary **33 MAC 678 (92)**—when D was **not** silent after Miranda ("I don't want to say too much," "you found all the drugs that I've got here," & explanation of "cooker" device he purchased 8 years earlier for extracting THC from marijuana), proper to cross-examine D at trial re: inconsistency between trial testimony & those statements;

C v Egardo **426 M 48 (97)**—**can't use** post-arrest silence to impeach trial testimony as to duress; *C v Jones* **45 MAC 254 (98)** can't use D's silence until testimony to argue lying/false testimony; *C v Nickerson* **386 M 54, 62 (82) before trying to use pre-arrest silence to impeach trial testimony, prosecutor should seek voir dire**; *C v Rivera* **425 M 633 (97)** upon D request, judge should conduct similar voir dire before prosecutor attempts to impeach D's trial testimony with alleged inconsistencies in D's affidavit supporting motion to suppress;

C v Fowler **431 M 30 (2000)**—unconstitutional testimony that, after Miranda warnings and statements to cops, D "reflect(ed)," "teared up", and "said he didn't think he should say anything more" after cop told D nobody would believe his story; also unconstitutional testimony that since D didn't speak further, "we didn't have an opportunity to clear up a lot of the details and get more specifics";

C v DePace **433 M 379 (2001)**—invocation of right to counsel inadmissible: adverse inference was only possible "relevance"; prosecutor displayed Miranda card on overhead projector; see also *C v Peixoto* **430 M 654 (2000)**, summarized above;

20-C.10. "Scrupulously Honor" Request for Silence, Attorney

Edwards v Arizona **451 US 477 (81)**—after desire for lawyer, questioning must cease & can't resume again even with rights/waiver;

Arizona v Roberson **486 US 675 (88)**—(same), even though 2d cop unaware of D's request;

Maryland v Shatzer **130 S Ct 1213 (2010)**—when detective sought to question D about newly alleged crime, D was incarcerated on different conviction and declined to speak with the detective without an attorney, ending the interview; 2½ years later different detective received "more specific allegations" about the same incident and went to different correctional facility to which D had been transferred, interviewing him in a "maintenance room," after reading Miranda rights and obtaining a written waiver: "Edwards" rule = re-written; after D asserts right to counsel/silence, police may re-approach him after fourteen days' break in Miranda custody, to again "ask his permission to be interrogated", again giving Miranda warnings; a suspect who has been incarcerated throughout, serving different sentence after conviction, is not 'in custody' with regard to questioning on the offense being investigated; D's "release back into the general prison population" after cop's attempt to question him and his invocation of counsel right, was 2½ year "break in Miranda custody";

Montejo v Louisiana **129 S Ct 2019 (2010)**—D may waive right to counsel whether or not he is already represented by counsel, and the decision to waive need not itself be counseled (citing *Michigan v Harvey* 494 US 344, 352–53); holding here is that courts need not presume "invalid" such waiver after counsel is appointed; if D has never himself asked for counsel, police may approach and ask for consent to interrogation; BUT 5th Amendment cases of *Miranda-Edwards* (451 US at 484), *Minnick* (498 US at 153) case law requires D, when he is first approached and given Miranda warnings, to invoke right to silence without counsel present; that Miranda et al are designed to protect 5th Amendment. rather than 6th Amendment rights doesn't matter;

C v Galford **413 M 364 (92)**—federal rule of *Edwards v Arizona* **451 US 477 (81)**, did not require suppression of Mirandized statements made 3 days after request for lawyer where D had been released from custody during interval; open question under state constitution;

C v Lopes **455 M 147 (2009)**—while D was in custody, he invoked right to silence, but subsequently his handcuffs were removed and he was told that he was not under arrest, but was "asked" if he would stay and wait to speak to other city's police, and then "asked" if he would go to station for interview: no obligation to refrain from further questioning because of "release" from custody (& this D was given Miranda and waived them at station anyway);

Minnick v Mississippi **498 US 146 (90)**—once arrestee asserts (Fifth Amendment right to counsel, interrogation forbidden unless: 1. counsel present or 2. D initiates further conversation & clearly waives counsel;

C v Perez **411 M 249 (91)**—bright-line rule of *Minnick* **498 US 146 (90)** assumed to require suppression of Mirandized statements made in response to police-initiated questioning after 6-month break in questioning, where D remained in custody, BUT any error was harmless;

C v Sarourt Nam **426 M 152 (97)**—cop's question why D wanted attorney, excused as attempt to clarify request for presence of attorney in light of D's "subsequent initiation of conversation with" cop; but see dissent (**it should never matter "why" D wants attorney**); even majority said usually **no** proper basis for this question;

C v Contos **435 M 19, 29–30 (2001)**—"**I think I'm going to get a lawyer**" = **unambiguous invocation of D's right** to counsel; even if it were ambiguous, **court didn't agree that "clarification of the request for counsel would have been constitutional**";

C v Barros **56 MAC 675 (2002)**—suppression upheld when, after Miranda warnings, D said, "I don't think I want to talk to you anymore without a lawyer," but cops came back into room after few minutes and told D he was being charged with murder; when D became upset, cops asked if he wanted to talk [i.e., initiated questioning] & he said he did;

C v Auclair **444 M 348 (2005)**—(citing *Todd* **408 M 724, 726 (90)** & *Corriveau* **396 M 319, 331–32 (85)**) when police responded to D's statement by saying that victim's injuries couldn't have been caused by the accident D described, his response wasn't invocation of right to counsel making further questioning impermissible ("well, that's the way I'm telling you and if you don't believe that, you can do whatever you want and go proceed with it. . . . It's hard on me as it is. That's my story. I'll get a lawyer. That's my story"); motion judge listened to recordings of D's statements;

C v Sicari **434 M 732, 749 (2001)**—SJC reserves issue of whether it will adopt "clear articulation rule" of *Davis v US* **512 US 452 (94)** (if suspect's statement is not an unambiguous or unequivocal request for counsel, officers have no obligation either to stop questioning him or to ask clarifying questions); SJC doesn't "disturb the judge's finding" here that, after 2 written waivers of silence & during lengthy interview, 30 to 40 minute period of silence was neither an invocation of right to silence or an "ambiguous" circumstance requiring cops to ask "clarifying" questions as to meaning of the silence; *C v Dubois* **451 M 20, 26 (2008)**—silences during total of ten to fifteen minutes of questioning not interpreted as "*expressed* unwillingness to continue questioning";

C v Scoggins **439 M 571 (2003)**—mere inquiry regarding need for an attorney doesn't require police to cease interrogation;

C v DiMuro **28 MAC 223 (90)**—even ambiguous assertion by D of right to counsel precludes further police questioning; but not, after *Davis v US* **512 US 452 (94)** on basis of federal law (cite Article 12 instead);

Oregon v Bradshaw **462 US 1039 (83)**—OK because cops stopped when D asked for counsel, but then D resumed talking;

C v LeClair **445 M 734 (2006)**—D invoked right to counsel at station but thereafter twice asked one officer whether he needed counsel and once whether he was "most likely in big trouble"; these remarks were held to indicate a desire for more conversation about the killing;

C v Avellar **70 MAC 608 (2007)**—after cops broke down door without warrant and arrested D, giving Miranda warnings, D stated he did not wish to speak to officers; after D was held, guarded, on sofa for two hours police obtained and showed him search warrant, and THEN "asked general question along lines of whether he wanted to say anything about the events of the day": appellate court holds that this question wasn't "interrogation," citing *Brant* 380 M 876 and *D'Entremont* 36 MAC 474;

Connecticut v Barrett **479 US 523 (87)**—oral statement OK after asking for attorney (to help with written statement);

C v Chadwick **40 MAC 425 (96)**—after request for attorney, & awaiting transport to house of correction, D's statement ("that he knew he did not rape his daughter") did not allow cop to elicit further statement by comment "I will tell you one thing, but this is not meant to be a question.

Rape is not always what people think and things like oral sex are rape";

C v Wallace **70 MAC 757 (2007)**—D was at station, had received Miranda warnings, and wanted attorney, but subsequent consent to search upheld because he wasn't in custody!; instead D's presence = voluntary, and D's written consent included "understanding" that he did not have to consent;

K. Smith, *Criminal Practice & Procedure,* **§§ 350–60 (2d ed. 1983 & Supp.)**—Miranda's right to counsel; PER SE rule if D asks counsel, UNLESS D initiates further talk;

Arizona v Mauro **481 US 520 (87)**—OK because later questions = by D's wife;

C v D'Entrement **36 MAC 474 (94)**—though D invoked rights to both silence & counsel, OK for cop to say, "if you change your mind, I'll be willing to talk to you"; this does not equal interrogation and D initiated further communication (saying he wanted to tell his side of story), so there was no right-to-counsel (*Edwards*) violation;

C v Gore **20 MAC 960 (85)**—when D took Fifth Amendment, cops can't repeat Miranda, tell D about other witnesses, & offer chance to explain;

Michigan v Mosley **423 US 96 (75)**—cops scrupulously honored D's desired silence because stopped questions & resumed few hours later only after more warnings;

C v Brum **438 M 103 (2002)**—IF D in custody exercises right to silence, police must scrupulously honor, but here, no "custody," because only "voluntarily" at police station when claimed silence; thereafter, at his home, D was arrested and brought to station, given Miranda rights, and made statement, so no suppression;

C v Jackson **377 M 319 (79)**—more questions 30 minutes after D desired silence (**& lie** that D's girlfriend confessed) ruined waiver;

C v Doe **37 MAC 30 (94)**—following Miranda on Friday, D wanted weekend period to think about "cooperating"; Miranda should have been given again on Monday, when D responded that he needed more time and cop said "we would at least like to get the gun back"—Miranda warnings "are not to be accorded unlimited efficacy or perpetuity"; here harmless;

C v Williams **388 M 846 (83)**—after asking silence, D placed with co-D & then confessed—no use, eliciting, or violation; (but see *Brant* **380 M 876 (80)** cops elicited by saying co-D had confessed & letting D talk to co-D (& retract his desire for silence & attorney));

C v Almonte **444 M 511 (2005)**—after D came to NY police station to confess spontaneously to involvement in a MA shooting ten years earlier, describing it, its location, and naming some participants, he was read Miranda rights as he looked at a copy of the same printed form: after the final question, which asked if he would answer questions, D stated, "I believe I've said what I have to say," but this was not an invocation of silence, since he immediately agreed when asked if he would answer some additional questions;

20-C.11. Advice Re: What's the Charge

Colorado v Spring **479 US 564 (87)**—need not tell D what charge is; waiver re: guns covered murder, too;

C v Hooks **38 MAC 301 (95)**—Miranda waiver not involuntary under Article 12 for failure to inform D of crime charged (though may be a factor re: "total circumstances");

C v Wills **398 M 768 (86)**—need not tell (hospitalized) D crime suspected;

C v Raymond **424 M 382 (97)**—rejecting argument that Miranda warnings were given "too soon," **i.e.**, waiver obtained before D knew he was suspect in murder & that co-D had implicated him;

C v Medeiros **395 M 336 (85)**—waiver OK, at least if questions = about related crime;

K. Smith, *Criminal Practice & Procedure,* **§ 380 (2d ed. 1983 & Supp.)**—lack of knowledge = factor re: voluntary waiver; § 376—lies = a factor re: waiver

20-C.12. Police Lies/Trickery

C v Forde **392 M 453 (84)**—tricks/lies = 1 factor re: waiver, but not conclusive;

C v Nero **14 MAC 714 (82)**—(same);

C v Dustin **373 M 612 (77)**—but misadvice re: rights ruined waiver;

C v Auclair **444 M 348 (2005)**—police used polygraph on D during his police station interview, & examiner told him that he didn't believe D was being truthful, prompting confession; D hadn't been told prior to going voluntarily to station that polygrapher was waiting, but agreed to take exam, specifically, & examiner recited Miranda warnings: no suppression; D's low intelligence, borderline personality disorder, & emotional reaction to being told of polygraph "failure" didn't make statements involuntary;

C v Colby **422 M 414 (96)**—lies concerning infallibility of polygraph did not require "involuntariness" finding, and new **Miranda** not required after D failed polygraph (no break, said SJC, in interrogation process);

C v Selby **420 M 656 (95)**—similar; after Miranda wavier and statements, lies that D's prints were at scene/on shell casing;

C v Jones **75 MAC 38 (2009)**—cops placed in interview room in "office building" a clear plastic bag containing a bra and white sweater, file folder containing crime scene photographs, and a file with the letters "DNA" written on the front (clothes had no connection to case, and no DNA evidence had been recovered); false suggestions of inculpatory evidence "did not render [D's] statements involuntary"; that D maintained innocence, gave exculpatory explanation for possibility of DNA, indicates rational intellect/voluntariness; D wasn't in custody here;

But see *C v Jackson* **377 M 319 (79)** lie that D's girlfriend gave statement impermissibly trenched on D's prior invocation of silence;

C v Novo **442 M 262 (2004)**—statements induced by police lies that D's girlfriend was currently implicating D in abuse of child, that medical examiner had taken fingerprints from bruises on child & "done the measurements" to match to D, accompanied by repeated assertions that D was guilty and had to tell his story "now or never" ("if you don't give us a reason right now why you did this, a jury's never going to hear a reason" (latter being "misrepresentation of . . . right to defend 'self at trial, . . . particularly egregious intrusion on rights that art. 12 declares to be fundamental") = suppression, but statements (denying guilt but providing info re: V's "care") made before cop said jury would never hear held admissible/voluntary;

Moran v Burbine **475 US 412 (86)**—hiding attorney calls from D not fatal trickery; but see *C v Mavredakis* **430 M 848 (2000)** Article 12 mandates broader protection from self-incrimination than does Fourth Amendment under *Moran v Burbine* **475 US 412 (86)**; suppression required when cop policy prevented D from knowledge that attorney was present at station to advise him (and attorney was refused admission/consultation) despite Miranda and purported waiver;

C v Trombley **72 MAC 183 (2008)**—though it was inferable that police hoped, by asking to speak to D's mother away from interview room, to weaken D's resistance to confessing, tactic was neither surreptitious nor trickery; confession not involuntary (D was 17);

See also Chapter 20-D post re: involuntariness of statement (vs. waiver);

20-D. VOLUNTARINESS (PRODUCT OF RATIONAL MIND)— AND "HUMANE" PRACTICE

See Chapter 7, Preparation re: Competence, Responsibility, & Experts for D; See also Chapter 4A—Delay in Arraignment;

C v Hunter **416 M 831 (94)**—competency & ability to make voluntary statement "share common attributes"; humane practice requires, upon request, voir dire as to voluntariness of statements to private citizens (as well as to government agents);

C v Miller **68 MAC 835 (2007)**—at least "where there is squarely framed a substantial question concerning the voluntariness" of a confession, trial judge must conduct <u>evidentiary</u> hearing and make a preliminary (i.e., BEFORE introduction of the statements at trial, outside presence of jury) determination that confession was voluntary; this is "constitutionally required" even when, as here, confession was obtained by private investigators (Home Depot in-house investigators) rather than government agents; judge here improperly reasoned (perhaps precisely because defense counsel and ADA gave widely conflicting descriptions of interrogation, fn.3) that the issues were to be left for jury's deliberations; rejects Commonwealth argument that failure to hold evidentiary voir dire or pretrial hearing is "cured" by submitting voluntariness issue to jury;

C v Louraine **390 M 28 (83)**—inadmissible because not product of rational mind because mental illness— though no custody, no coercion, & volunteered;

C v Brown **449 M 747 (2007)**—when D didn't raise voluntariness prior to trial or when statements were admitted, judge didn't err in granting DA's subsequent request for "ruling" that they were voluntarily made, though D asked deferral until defense evidence of lack of criminal responsibility was admitted: D's strategy was to question whether the statements had been made at all, AND voluntariness of all D's statements doesn't automatically become live issue when D raises insanity defense; while humane practice rule covers statements made by D to private parties in aftermath of criminal conduct, "we have never applied it to statements made by a D during the commission of his crime";

C v Hensley **454 M 721 (2009)**—motion for new trial alleged ineffective assistance of trial counsel concerning suppression motion: no relief, though with expert and medical records, new counsel argued involuntariness & inability to waive Miranda due to combined effects of carbon monoxide poisoning (attempted suicide), ingestion of sleeping pills, cognitive impairments due to depression, and stress of interrogation, plus major depression; decision not to call particular expert at trial was not manifestly unreasonable for specified reasons, including probable admission of expert's opinion that D did not lack criminal responsibility;

C v Smith **426 M 76, 83 (97)**—though admissions/ confessions to civilians have to be voluntary, the issue/ question must be raised by D; no substantial risk of miscarriage of justice from admission of D's statements to his siblings;

C v Ferrer **47 MAC 645 (99)**—**statement of juvenile could be found "voluntary," so that it would be admissible for impeachment if D testified (though inadmissible otherwise for failure to accord "interested adult" consultation prior to Miranda waiver)**; youth/immaturity not "conclusive" as to involuntariness;

C v Murphy **426 M 395 (98)**—D's (non-custodial) statement to life-long friend (no indicia of incoherence, intoxication, or coercion), despite mention of suicide, did not require sua sponte voluntariness voir dire;

C v Anderson **425 M 685 (97)**—voluntariness not live issue at trial, since only evidence suggesting involuntariness was at voir dire, **i.e.**, not before jury;

C v Ardon **428 M 496 (98)**—rejecting D's argument that inculpatory statements could not be found voluntary in the absence of contemporaneous electronic recording; also, non-English-speaking Ds need not be afforded a non-police interpreter during police interrogations (an "impossible burden");

K. Smith, *Criminal Practice & Procedure,* §§ 365–82 (2d ed. 1983 & Supp.)—"voluntariness"—factors: age, mental capability, etc.; Miranda vs. overall voluntariness;

C v Soares **51 MAC 273, 280–81 (2001)**—Gundjonsson Suggestibility Scale testing by forensic psychologist for D (indicating D highly susceptible to pressure) accorded no weight by motion judge, because D failed to present evidence that it's a "scientifically valid and reliable measure," and because application of test results to custody situation might not be valid;

C v St. Peter **48 MAC 517 (2000)**—neither low IQ nor consumption of alcohol "necessarily mandate(s)" finding that confession was involuntary;

C v Allen **395 M 448 (85)**—OK here, but must be product of rational mind, not insanity, intoxication, drugs, head injury—even though to private person & without coercion;

C v Hilton **450 M 173 (2007)**—on issue of "voluntariness," motion judge incorrectly believed that D had been found incompetent around time of her statements, and erroneous finding of incompetency to stand trial couldn't support ultimate finding of involuntariness; a finding that D = unable to make voluntary intelligent waiver of Miranda rights "is not enough, standing alone, to support the finding that her statements were involuntary"; remand held necessary (despite fact that judge also credited numerous experts' testimony that D was mildly retarded, functionally illiterate, suffered from schizophrenia and schizotypal personality disorder with psychotic episodes, had tenuous connection to reality, auditory hallucinations, and fixed delusions); statement is voluntary only if it is product of "a rational intellect and a free will"; a finding of voluntariness "must appear from the record with unmistakable clarity";

C v LeBlanc **433 M 549 (2001)**—though suppression judge found that D was intending suicide from ingestion of bullet prior to his confession, OK also to find significance lay not in his inability intelligently to waive (Miranda) or to make voluntary confession, but in fact that it made it easier for him to confess because it "allowed him to rationalize that he wouldn't be around to face legal consequences of his actions"; *C v Lopes* **455 M 147 (2009)**—suicidal ideation does "not necessarily negate the voluntariness of" confession";

C v Carp **47 MAC 229 (99)**—DSS investigator, at D's home, specifically told D it wasn't a criminal investigation & he didn't need to give Miranda rights, asked questions re alleged sexual assaults, and when D asked whether he should have attorney present, was told it wasn't "necessarily necessary" = involuntary. See also 110 C.M.R. § 4.27(5) (1993) (requiring written notice to parents/caretakers about § 51A report, possible consequences of investigation, and that info can be used in court);

C v Morais **431 M 380 (2000)**—incriminating statements made by D to DSS social worker investigating re-

port of abuse (G.L. c. 119, § 51A) of D's cousin; social worker told D what she was investigating, & D agreed to meet w/her; SJC rejects argument that social worker in such circumstances is required to give a "minimal cautionary warning" that statements made are not privileged & may be disclosed to others (like in *Lamb* **365 M 265 (74)**, when psychotherapist conducts a court-ordered interview);

C v Seabrooks **433 M 439 (2001)**—when trial issue was D's criminal responsibility & his experts had used five psych evaluations conducted at jail's behest soonest after his arrest, re suicide risk, OK for Commonwealth to introduce evaluating psych's testimony, even though exams weren't preceded by *Lamb* (**365 M 265, 270 (74)**) warnings that his communications might not be kept confidential; G.L. c. 233, § 20B cited, finding 3d statutory exception applied to psychotherapist-patient privilege;

C v Paszko **391 M 164 (84)**—statement to cellmate OK because no threats or promises, & drug withdrawal didn't impair reliability;

Colorado v Connelly **479 US 157 (86)—federal standard = not 'involuntary' unless coerced by state agent;**

Mincey v Arizona **437 US 385 (78)**—statement not product of rational mind & can't even use to impeach (D in pain & intensive care; questioned for 4 hours after asking to stop); (*see Chapter 20-B*);

C v Tavares **385 M 140 (82)**—can be involuntary though OK under Miranda and when in issue, judge must find beyond a reasonable doubt, before statement is introduced, that it's voluntary; finding "must appear from the record with unmistakable clarity" (*see Chapter 20-B re: burden of proof & Chapter 20-A re: voir dire*);

C v Ortiz **431 M 134, 140 (2000)**—motion judge's assertion that incriminating statements are "prima facie voluntary" and burden is on D to establish legal basis for their exclusion said to be "awkward" formulation probably intended to refer to **D's "initial burden of production with respect to a motion to suppress statements"**; no harm here because jury-waived trial judge independently considered voluntariness and enunciated correct legal standard for admissibility; trial judges may reconsider other judges' rulings on pretrial motions to suppress, but should "inform counsel and allow counsel an opportunity to be heard," **id. at 142 n.7**;

C v Van Melkebeke **48 MAC 364 (99)**—reversal because judge refused request for voir dire on voluntariness of statement, on ground that it had already been decided at suppression hearing, but only Miranda waiver had been addressed at such hearing, and the two are discrete questions; judge also refused here to instruct jurors on their independent duty under humane practice rule (decide voluntariness of statement beyond a reasonable doubt before considering it as evidence);

C v Selby **420 M 656 (95)**—detectives' intentional use of false information to obtain statements from D (claims to have found prints inside house & on shell casings) was a factor re: voluntariness, but not controlling/dispositive (no suppression);

C v Edwards **420 M 666 (95)**—same, **but** if D's invocation of silence is thwarted by such tactics, suppression: *C v Jackson* **377 M 319 (79)**;

C v Knapp **26 M 495 (1830)**—inadmissible confession extorted by threat/promise;

C v John **442 M 329 (2004)**—finding of fact, that federal "immunity" notice promised immunity ONLY if D testified against former gang cohorts, wouldn't be overturned; D's goal was to avoid testifying, & when threatened that he could/would be made to testify by filing of immunity notice (eliminating Fifth Amendment privilege), he attained his goal by confessing murder (knowing that prosecutor would not use confessed murderer as witness);

C v Magee **423 M 381 (96)**—involuntary confession because medical/psych. treatment withheld for 7 hours until statements made; *C v Felice* **44 MAC 709 (98)** *Magee* distinguished, not persuasively;

C v LeBlanc **433 M 549, 553 (2001)**—fact finding that D's requests for "help" referred to need for emotional help, not requesting counsel, but there wasn't promise of psych help in exchange for confession or waiver of silence;

Brown v Mississippi **297 US 278 (36)**—coerced confession inadmissible under due process;

C v Mahnke **368 M 662 (75)**—coercion by private citizens who kidnapped & threatened D for 6 hours; but statement 2 hours later to police = OK;

C v Lopes **455 M 147 (2009)**—D's father didn't coerce confession by advising that it was right thing to do;

Harrison v US **392 US 219 (68)**—introduction of confession at D's trial effectively coerced him to testify; when conviction reversed because confession was erroneously introduced, government could not introduce at trial D's testimony from the 1st trial;

C v Brusgulis **41 MAC 386 (96)**—distinguishing *Harrison* (392 US 219), with rationale that erroneous introduction of prior bad acts did **not** here "virtually coerce" D's testimony;

C v Beauchamp **49 MAC 591 (2000)**—no error in introducing, at 2d trial, D's testimony from 1st trial; *Harrison* (392 US 219) inapposite; rationale for admissibility = either "admission" by party opponent or "prior recorded testimony" by now-unavailable witness (because Commonwealth couldn't call D to the stand, D was "unavailable" to the Commonwealth); eminently "reliable," and same parties & issues were involved;

C v Meehan **377 M 552 (79)**—cop can urge telling truth & it would be made known; but involuntary if say it'll help case (though without promise);

C v Shine **398 M 641 (86)**—(same);

C v Raymond **424 M 382 (97)**—similar;

C v Souza **428 M 298 (98)**—similar; *Meehan* **377 M 552 (79)** says there may be **no** "express **or implied**" assurance that statement will aid defense or result in lesser sentence;

C v Luce **34 MAC 105 (93)**—D's statements during meetings between government agents, D-counsel & D (cooperation/plea bargain talks) held admissible. But see

M.R.Crim.P. 12(f): **get it in writing** that no statement will be used, or have D say **nothing**;

C v Raymond **424 M 382 (97)**—though cops said D's mother was accessory after fact (for lying on D's behalf) and urged D not to let co-D's statement (largely blaming D) stand as the only version, not involuntary;

C v Berg **37 MAC 200 (94)**—cop's statement that both D & D's mother (present in D's apartment) would be charged unless drug ownership was known did not make D's statement involuntary; "false" statements may not be made to induce confession—but see *Selby* **470 M 656 (95)** and *Edwards* **420 M 666 (95)**; inducements not coercive where cops only promised to discuss leniency if D told gun's location;

C v Leahy **445 M 481 (2005)**—cop's statement, in response to D's statement 20 minutes earlier that he didn't want to talk right then because he "need[ed] to figure some things out," was "when you need to figure things out, it's good to talk to somebody else about them"; this wasn't a false promise of police aid overriding ability to voluntarily waive rights; that D's initial refusal to talk was not "scrupulously honored" (*Michigan v Mosley* 423 US 97) when cop returned was an argument not made below and thus waived (so only reviewed for substantial likelihood of miscarriage of justice);

C v Doe **37 MAC 30 (94)**—statements of snitch re: participants in robbery and how it had been carried out not 'involuntary' as matter of law despite facts (1) he was not told that he was a target & cops already had info **his** car was involved and (2) his previous snitchings had led him to believe he would not be targeted/prosecuted;

Garrity v NJ **385 US 493 (67)**—statements by cops under investigation & threatened with firing = coerced;

C v Luna **418 M 749 (94)**—cop-D argued, unsuccessfully, that affidavit acknowledging perjury in a particular search warrant application/affidavit was involuntary because Superior Court judge ordered him to file affidavits about his search for informant referred to in application; (but see *C v Gallati* **40 MAC 111 (96)** questions in office of D's superior correctional officer were custodial (despite no threat of job loss));

C v Hunt **12 MAC 841 (81)**—threat to prosecute D's wife;

Brogan v US **522 US 398 (98)**—simple denial of guilt to federal agents = legitimate basis for conviction for making false statement under 18 USC § 1001; Fifth Amendment does not "confer ( ) a privilege to lie"; better reasoning in Ginsburg, J. concurrence, cited by 2 dissenters; cf. *Harrison v US* **392 US 219 (68)** is D "virtually coerced" to say something?

C v Vazquez **387 M 96 (82)**—suppress statement only if D's psychosis was proximate cause of giving it; voluntariness = live issue for jury;

C v Zagrodny **443 M 93 (2004)**—admission to a private citizen = admissible unless coerced, even "if not the result of a meaningful act of volition";

C v Allen **395 M 448 (85)**—"humane practice": motion to suppress denied & jury instructed to decide voluntariness beyond a reasonable doubt;

C v Watkins **425 M 830 (97)**—jurors' decisions to use arguably involuntary statement need not be unanimous, but each juror who does use it must conclude, beyond a reasonable doubt, that it's voluntary;

C v Adams **416 M 55 (93)**—error to exclude, before jury, evidence relevant to voluntariness (i.e., presence of D's mother "psychologically coerced" him to confess because of their past relationship);

C v Crawford **429 M 60 (99)**—error to exclude expert testimony on battered woman syndrome at voluntariness voir dire and before jury, on subject of voluntariness of statements (which were the sole evidence of D's guilt of murder);

C v Nerette **432 M534 (2000)**—SJC upholds trial judge's rejection of 'ineffective assistance of counsel' claim for failure to present expert on (in)voluntariness: lay people capable of assessing all factors here (and trial judge claimed, after fact, that he wouldn't have permitted expert testimony to reach jury even if it had been offered);

Crane v Kentucky **476 US 683 (86)**—though motion to suppress denied, unreliability = jury question;

C v Alicea **376 M 506 (78)**—no instruction unless it's a "live issue";

C v Pavao **46 MAC 271 (99)**—& no sua sponte voir dire when no voluntariness issue;

C v Sheriff **425 M 186, 192–96 (97)**—**despite absence of D request, error to omit voir dire and jury instructions on voluntariness of statement** made by hospitalized D 2 days after suicide attempt; irrelevant that statements were not "confessions"; they were used by Commonwealth as evidence of "sanity"/criminal responsibility;

See Chapter 20-A re: right to hearing/voir dire (inter alia, C v Riveiro **393 M 224 (84)** D gets Miranda voir dire though no motion to suppress because DA didn't give timely discovery of statement; though statement was excluded, still error because jury heard it);

C v Sands **424 M 184 (97)**—when there was no mention of breathalyzer or D's refusal to take it, Commonwealth could introduce D's statement made while refusing test, "I'm not drunk, but I'm over";

C v Pina **430 M 66 (99)**—police not required to administer sobriety tests to assure voluntariness/not impaired;

C v Gallagher **408 M 510 (90)**—D's averments in affidavit that he was impaired by drugs & alcohol when he made statements to private parties entitled him to voir dire on voluntariness;

C v Duffy **36 MAC 937 (94)**—neither low level of intelligence nor consumption of alcohol made statements involuntary; *C v Simmons* **417 M 60 (94)** "intoxication alone is not sufficient to negate otherwise voluntary act" (BURDEN SHIFTING HERE?);

C v Wolinski **431 M 228, 233 (2000)**—voluntariness may be found despite belief of drug and alcohol use; great "motor control" in signing waivers cited, as was "rational effort at self-preservation" in first false statement; accurate and precise description of where item could be found; stated decision that he'd make his telephone call only after learning what amount bail would be strongly implied rational thought; alleged police "coercion in the form of disdain" toward D is "not the type of unfair conduct that requires suppression"; but cf. *C v Mahdi* **388 M 679 (83)** "May a prosecutor use evidence of a defendant's exercise of his or her Miranda rights, not to infer guilt nor to impeach an exculpatory story, but rather, to infer sanity? We question the probative value of the exercise of one's Miranda rights to indicate sanity. Insanity is not the equivalent of stupidity"; *C v Brown* **449 M 747, 764 (2007)**—says that unlike in *Mahdi*, testimony was to show that D apparently understood what cop said to D, "and as such was relevant to the question of his sanity. *Mahdi* protects the exercise of rights, not the understanding of their content";

C v Libran **405 M 634 (89)**—mental impairment requires suppression only if D would not have made statement "but for" mental impairment;

C v Hartford **425 M 378 (97)**—IQ of 73 doesn't make D incapable, as a matter of law, of waiving Miranda & making voluntary statement;

C v Rivera **425 M 633 (97)**—D's affidavit supporting motion to suppress is not "involuntary" merely because M.R.Crim.P. 13(a)(2) requires that affidavit be filed (no error in allowing prosecutor to impeach D's trial testimony with alleged inconsistencies in affidavit);

C v Bandy **38 MAC 329 (95)**—re: D's statement to EMT after his body was rolled to put out fire engulfing him & with evidence of some alcohol consumption, that he wanted his mommy & 'it's all my fault . . . it was on fire before I hit him'—no sua sponte obligation on part of judge to have voir dire;

C v Benoit **410 M 506 (91)**—although intoxicated D had psychotic episode around time of incident, voluntariness was not "live issue" where expert testified that statement was made during lucid interval;

C v Hooper **42 MAC 730 (97)**—hospitalized D, intubated & restrained, said to orderly: "I know you're taking me to jail"; error to admit as consciousness of guilt without "voluntariness" instruction to jury (& prejudicial because defense was ID);

C v Todd **408 M 724 (90)**—cops' compliance with Miranda & validity of D's waiver are matters of law for judge, not for jury; cf. *C v Rosa* **412 M 147 (92)** hearing required to determine whether D's wife's waiver of spousal privilege was voluntary in light of police coercion;

20-E. VIOLATION OF RIGHT TO COUNSEL

See Chapter 14-B, dismissal for police misconduct, attorney-client disruption; See also Chapter 4A, Delay in Arraignment (see also Chapter 20-C, above re: Miranda's right to counsel; Chapter 20-B, above re: G.L. c. 276, § 33A right to telephone call at station);

C v Rosario **422 M 48 (96)**—otherwise admissible statement will not be excluded for unreasonable delay in arraignment, if statement is made within six hours of arrest or if D makes voluntary written or recorded waiver of right to be arraigned without unreasonable delay: self-induced disability (drug/alcohol intoxication) prevents beginning of 6 hour period;

Rothgery v Gillespie County, Texas **128 S Ct 2578 (2008)**—right to counsel attaches at first appearance before judicial officer at which D is told of formal accusation against him and restrictions are imposed on liberty; that public prosecutor (as opposed to police officer) be aware of initial proceeding or involved in its conduct is NOT required; D's arrest without warrant as purported "felon" in possession of firearm was followed by appearance before a "magistrate judge" for proceeding which combined a finding of probable cause with setting of bail; D's oral and written requests for counsel were unheeded until indictment and further delay more than six months later (and counsel promptly learned that arrest as "felon" was premised on an erroneous record);

C v Moran **75 MAC 513 (2009)**—D was apprehended in a different county, and "courtesy booking" occurred there before he was transported to department seeking arrest, allegedly delaying his arraignment and appointment of counsel; only three hours elapsed between arrest and D's overheard conversation with his sister; no unreasonable delay found;

C v Obershaw **435 M 794 (2002)**—six-hour rule not violated because court finds that actual "arrest" of D occurred more than seven hours after police first "encountered" D, who offered to 'voluntarily stay & cooperate'; response ("can I talk to a lawyer first?") made to question whether he would take police to victim's body wasn't invocation of right to counsel: D was told to use the telephone, but declined & said he wanted to go outside and spend time with his dogs; after doing so, he initiated conversation with cop, who told him that if he wanted a lawyer, he could use the telephone & further conversation wasn't permissible if he wanted counsel (D declined again);

C v Morganti **455 M 388 (2009)**—"safe harbor" rule of Rosario applies only to persons arrested in MA who could be arraigned in MA; this D was arrested in California as fugitive from justice; further, "circumstances of this interrogation" didn't violate "spirit" of rule (MA cop left for CA day after learning D's identity and interviewed D later that day);

Massiah v US **377 US 201 (64)**—questions to co-D (post-indict, pre-arraign, non-custody) violated Sixth Amendment;

Kansas v Ventris **129 S Ct 1841 (2009)**—statements obtained in violation of right to counsel (informant planted in D's cell) may be used to impeach D's testimony;

C v Young **73 MAC 479 (2009)**—eventual prosecution witness to whom D talked in holding cell had repudiated cooperation agreement, so was not Commonwealth agent; even if 'agent', no evidence Commonwealth intentionally placed witness in cell with D, AND D's "volunteered" statements were not product of questioning;

C v Torres **442 M 554 (2004)**—troopers, serving D at the house of correction with indictment and arrest warrant, proceeded to read the indictments to D purportedly because they knew he could not read English; D interrupted with statements, was told twice to stop, and was then given Miranda warnings plus particular advice that he shouldn't speak because trooper knew he already had a lawyer, but D nonetheless "insisted" that he wanted to speak to troopers; motion judge found as fact that troopers hadn't deliberately elicited statements by (decidedly unusual?) procedure of visiting D to read the indictment to him (so perhaps they believed that D's attorney couldn't read?), so no suppression;

Escobedo v Illinois **378 US 478 (64)**—suppress pre-indictment statement because cops interfered with talk with known, retained attorney; adversary system begins when investigation = accusatory, then must permit consultation (at 492);

Kirby v Illinois **406 US 682 (72)**—Escobedo is Fifth Amendment (silence), not Sixth Amendment (counsel);

Fellers v US **540 US 519 (2004)**—Sixth Amendment right to counsel is violated when D's statements are obtained by law enforcement officials "deliberately elicit[ing]" them after he has been indicted and in the absence of counsel (*Massiah v US* **377 US 201**), but D is "interrogated" for purposes of Miranda & Fifth Amendment privilege against self-incrimination when agent makes statements that reasonable officer would know are likely to elicit an incriminating response; opinion here expressly notes the distinction, says circuit court erred in employing Fifth Amendment standard in this Sixth Amendment case; S. Ct. reserved question whether "fruit of poisonous tree" analysis (inapplicable in Fifth Amendment context under *Oregon v Elstad* **470 US 298**) applies in context of Sixth Amendment violations;

C v Mavredakis **430 M 848 (2000)**—police can't bar attorney from contact with suspect being interrogated; duty to inform suspect of attorney's efforts to render assistance is necessary to "actualize the abstract rights listed in *Miranda v Arizona*"; Article 12 mandates broader protection from self-incrimination than does Sixth Amendment under *Moran v Burbine* **475 US 412 (86)**;

C v Vao Sok **435 M 743 (2002)**—canny avoidance of *Mavredakis* holding for indigent non-English speaking culprit in highly publicized rape/murder of child: "fact" finding that D chose to continue with polygraph examination and police interrogation despite having been informed of his attorney's efforts to reach him; disingenuous claim that police/DA failure to immediately inform D of attorney's attempts to render assistance didn't produce anything incriminating;

C v Nelson **55 MAC 911 (2002)**—cops don't have to tell D that a third party intends to retain legal counsel for D; *C v Mavredakis* applies ONLY when attorney who has identified himself or herself as D's counsel is attempting to render assistance [AND claim that Mavredakis didn't announce new constitutional right, so failure to assert issue on direct appeal & first motion for new trial = waiver];

C v Collins **440 M 475 (2003)**—no suppression despite fact that counsel, retained by D before D's arrest, told police beforehand that he wanted to be present during any interview of D; subsequently-arrested D's own "waiver" of Miranda rights prior to interrogation controlled, since he spoke of his attorney and thus was certainly aware of his right to consult; this isn't case of lawyer being denied access to client in custody/under interrogation;

K Smith, *Criminal Practice & Procedure*, §§ 323–30 (2d ed. 1983 & Supp.)—Sixth Amendment issues;

Michigan v Jackson **475 US 625 (86)**—Sixth Amendment rights begin at arraignment; Miranda waiver after asking counsel = invalid; Michigan v Jackson = overruled by Montejo 129 S Ct. 2019 (2010)

Montejo v Louisiana **129 S Ct 2019 (2010)**—D may waive right to counsel whether or not he is already represented by counsel, and the decision to waive need not itself be counseled (citing *Michigan v Harvey* 494 US 344, 352–53); holding here is that courts need not presume "invalid" such waiver after counsel is appointed; if D has never himself asked for counsel, police may approach and ask for consent to interrogation; BUT 5th Amendment cases of *Miranda-Edwards* (451 US at 484), *Minnick* (498 US at 153) case law requires D, when is first approached and given Miranda warnings, to invoke right to silence without counsel present; that Miranda et al are designed to protect 5th Amendment. rather than 6th Amendment rights doesn't matter;

Patterson v Illinois **487 US 285 (88)**—valid Miranda waiver though indicted because not yet arraigned, i.e., Miranda covers Sixth Amendment right to counsel as well as Fifth Amendment right to silence, **so long as D has not yet retained or accepted appointment of attorney** ("Once an accused has a lawyer, a distinct set of constitutional safeguards aimed at preserving the sanctity of the attorney-client relationship takes effect. See *Maine v. Moulton*, 474 U.S. 159, 176 (1985)."); NOW SEE *Montejo v Louisiana* **129 S Ct 2079 (2009)—even when D has accepted appointment of counsel, police may approach, seek interrogation consent;**

C v Smallwood **379 M 878 (80)**—complaint & warrant don't trigger Massiah;

C v Lepore **349 M 121 (65)**—police station not yet "accusatory";

C v Mahoney **400 M 524 (87)**—no counsel right before booking; but see *C v Gonsalves* **74 MAC 910 (2009)—testimony that D refused to answer booking questions until he talked to lawyer = reversal despite "late" objection and no request for curative instruction;**

C v Torres **442 M 554 (2004)**—Sixth Amendment right to counsel attached as of time of indictment, not arraignment; person is entitled to counsel once government has committed itself to prosecute; D can waive, however, and Miranda warnings are sufficient to convey Sixth Amendment rights (though devised to inform Ds of Fifth Amendment rights);

Brewer v Williams **430 US 387 (77)—Massiah violation after arrest, before arraignment, because D (former mental patient) told by attorney not to talk**, but cajoled by cops to show them grave's location;

C v Bandy **38 MAC 329 (95)**—probation officer interviewing D for indigency determination (after he had counsel) asked him what he was charged with, & replied "these are real serious charges" did not "deliberately elicit" D's self-incriminating remarks;

C v Hilton **443 M 597 (2005)**—as court officer escorted D to cell after arraignment, D spontaneously remarked with regard to her son, "I hope he forgives me," prompting response of "Excuse me?" which led to assertion, "I could have killed my grandchildren"; these statements were not suppressed, but those made in response to court officer's subsequent questions (did D light the fire? Why had she done it?, etc.) were suppressed; for purposes of Sixth Amendment analysis (Massiah), **court officer = law enforcement agent; same case, on second interlocutory appeal: 450 M 173 (2007)**—on issue of "voluntariness," not considered in first appeal, motion judge incorrectly believed that D had been found "incompetent" around time of her statement, and a finding that D = unable to make voluntary intelligent waiver of Miranda rights "is not enough, standing alone, to support the finding that her statements were involuntary";

C v Howard **446 M 563 (2006)**—incriminating statements made by D to DSS investigator who initiated interview of D at jail in the absence of his attorney should have been suppressed;

Maine v Moulton **474 US 159 (85)**—post-arraignment talk to co-D (police agent, but no questions or custody) violated Sixth Amendment; (See also *Rodwell* **394 M 694 (85)** cellmate not state agent/action re: Sixth Amendment violation; *US v Henry* **447 US 264 (80)** cellmate was paid informant, so state action; *Chapter 20-B, above*);

Moran v Burbine **475 US 412 (86)**—can question D though attorney asked not to, because no counsel right before arraignment; Miranda's Fifth Amendment only; but see *C v Sherman* **389 M 287 (83)** under Miranda, violation to question D without saying attorney called & wants to talk to D; (see also *C v McKenna* 355 M 313 (69));

*****C v Mavredakis* 430 M 848 (2000)—Miranda waiver illegitimate because police failed to inform D that attorney was attempting to contact him, waiting to speak with him; Article 12 provides greater protection than Fifth and Sixth Amendments (*Moran v Burbine* 475 US 412 (86)); "the duty to inform a suspect of an attorney's efforts to render assistance is necessary to actualize the abstract rights listed in Miranda . . . (T)he day is long past . . . where attorneys must shout legal advice to their clients, held in custody, through the jailhouse door" (citation omitted);

C v Beland 436 M 273 (2002)—no ineffective assistance found in counsel's failure to telephone police station to direct police not to talk to D before he could speak with counsel; right to assistance of counsel didn't attach before criminal proceedings began;

C v Vao Sok 435 M 743 (2002)—canny avoidance of *Mavredakis* holding for indigent non-English speaking culprit in highly publicized rape/murder of child: "fact" finding that D chose to continue with polygraph examination and police interrogation despite having been informed of his attorney's efforts to reach him; disingenuous claim that police/DA failure to immediately inform D of attorney's attempts to render assistance didn't produce anything incriminating;

C v Menconi 28 MAC 504 (90)—cops' refusal to allow D to privately confer with attorney at stationhouse about taking breathalyzer was improper, but didn't require dismissal;

C v Drumgold 423 M 230 (96)—D, in custody on drug charges, was at court & learned about to be charged with murder; murder attorney was on way to courthouse; judge allowed D to be taken from court only for photo & printing, with order **not** to interrogate; subsequent interrogation statements suppressed;

C v Barnes 40 MAC 666 (96)—though CPCS-assigned counsel was looking for D (who was giving statements, following **Miranda** waivers), no evidence that police knew that CPCS had arranged for counsel or that they interfered with D's access to counsel: no suppression; *Rosario* (422 M 48 (96) also cited re: safe harbor of 6 hours for questioning before arraignment);

C v Cryer 426 M 562, 564 (98)—while Mass. police were questioning D (who was in New Hampshire custody on NH charges) re: Mass. murder, D's attorney telephoned NH jailers & instructed "no interview without counsel's permission"; NH jailers did not inform Mass. police or stop the interview; no relief per federal constitution (*Moran v Burbine* cited); Article 12 not reached and specifically reserved (NH officials not bound by Article 12 in any event);

C v Mahnke 368 M 662 (75)—(*Chapter 20-B, 20-D, above*) suppress if cops thwart D & attorney consulting;

C v Rodriguez 425 M 361 (97)—D, held in Florida on a Mass. homicide case, was questioned by Florida police (at request of Mass. police); *Miranda* waived; too-tardy

appellate assertion that (possible) presence of right to counsel at the prior "fugitive bond hearing" was basis for suppressing confession (no record evidence re: this);

MacNeil v Wisconsin 501 US 171 (91)—attachment of Sixth Amendment right to counsel at arraignment does not bar police from obtaining Miranda waivers on unrelated offenses.

C v Chase 42 MAC 749 (97)—D's **request for counsel on armed robbery charge (counsel then appointed for bail only) did not operate to bar questioning of D for unrelated larceny and homicide; if D had ever invoked "Miranda right to counsel for interrogation regarding one offense, he (could) not be reapproached regarding any offense" in the absence of counsel;**

Minnick v Mississippi 498 US 146 (90)—once arrestee asserts (Fifth Amendment) right to counsel, interrogation forbidden unless: 1. counsel present or 2. D initiates further conversation & clearly waives counsel;

C v Rainwater 425 M 540 (97)—SJC, in violation of *McNeil v Wisconsin* and *Michigan v Jackson*, refuses suppression of statements made upon police-initiated interrogation (w/*Miranda* waiver) after appointment of counsel in one case, though interrogation concerned **both** recently-arraigned case and those not yet charged against D (statements allowed to be used in cases on which D had not yet been charged); BUT *Jackson* should have precluded initiation of the interviews since one of its subjects was case on which D had already requested counsel (at arraignment); purportedly, even SJC majority would have ordered suppression if uncharged cases were found to be "inextricably intertwined" or "closely related" to those in which D claimed counsel;

Michigan v Harvey 494 US 344 (90)—suppressed statements obtained in violation of (Sixth Amendment) right to counsel may be used to impeach D;

Kansas v Ventris 129 S Ct 1841 (2009)—statements obtained in violation of right to counsel (informant planted in D's cell) may be used to impeach D's testimony;

C v Brazelton 404 M 783 (89)—D has no right to counsel before deciding whether to take breathalyzer under either state or federal constitution;

C v DiMuro 28 MAC 223 (90)—ambiguous assertion by D of (Fifth Amendment) right to counsel bars further police questioning;

C v Harmon 410 M 425 (91)—jailhouse informant told by cops to "keep his ears open" not a state agent for Sixth Amendment right to counsel purposes, where no inducements offered; *C v Gajka* 425 M 751 (97) though prisoner asked to be D's cellmate in hope of getting admissions & trading them for leniency in his own case, government had not sought his assistance or encouraged his actions: no suppression (despite fact of **later** favorable treatment); *C v Reynolds* 429 M 388 (99) error to have denied motion to suppress without hearing when jailhouse informant's lawyer set up reward for him during his access to conversations with D; agency relationship probable;

C v Lenahan **50 MAC 180 (2000)**—preservation lapses and harmlessness of any possible error (violation of right to counsel) in using D's statements to snitch and police undercover agent ("hit man");

20-F. PHYSICAL EVIDENCE: MASS. CONSTITUTION, BURDEN OF PROOF, STATE ACTION, "FRUITS," AND OVERVIEW

See also Chapter 20-A: CPCS Performance Guidelines, Mass. Constitution, motions to suppress, generally, filing, hearing, etc.;

20-F.1. In General

Mass. Declaration of Rights, Articles 12 & 14—law of land; security from unreasonable searches & seizures; warrants need oath/affirmation, designation of persons/objects, & formalities of law; See, e.g., *Framingham* **373 M 783 (77)**, *Bottari* **395 M 777 (85)**, *Upton* **394 M 363 (85)**, *Ford* **394 M 421 (85)**, *Toole* **389 M 159 (83)** (*Chapter 20-H*), *Sheppard* **394 M 381 (85)** (*Chapter 20-J*);

Davis v Mississippi **394 US 721 (69)**—"to argue that the Fourth Amendment does not apply to the investigatory stage is fundamentally to misconceive the purposes of the Fourth Amendment"; dragnet seizures of "Negro youths" for fingerprinting at the police station (to match up prints left on window sill by rapist) unconstitutional, finger and palm prints suppressed;

Landry v Attorney General **429 M 336 (99)**—collection of convicted persons' blood for DNA database held "reasonable" under Article 14 & Fourth Amendment, given convicts' purportedly "low expectation of privacy in their identity" and the "minimal" nature of a "pin prick" intrusion;

C v Rice **441 M 291 (2004)**—D, serving a sentence, had no reasonable expectation of privacy in his bed sheets and prison uniform when he passed them out of cell in ordinary course for laundering (DNA samples were subsequently obtained from these items);

G.L. c. 276, § 1—judge may issue warrant for seizing/searching person/property, for crime (fruits/instruments/weapons); if "incident to arrest," seizure only of "fruits, instruments, contraband & other evidence of crime **for which arrest made**, to prevent destruction/concealment, & removing any weapons that arrestee might use to resist . . . or escape"; otherwise inadmissible; search warrant a must, & not without probable cause evidence will be destroyed, for documentary evidence possessed by lawyer, shrink, priest who would have testimonial privilege (but this doesn't apply when there's probable cause to believe lawyer/shrink/priest himself has committed/is committing crime); §§ 2–2A—form of search warrant (day/night); § 2B—affidavit with facts relied upon including reliability of source; § 3 seize the property/articles described & (disposition);

C v D'Amour **428 M 725 (99)**—though G.L. c. 276, § 1 did not authorize warrant for "writings containing names of persons known to the deceased," and Commonwealth conceded this, SJC **avoided decision whether**

"common law" continues to allow warrant authorization to search for "mere evidence";

C v Rufo **429 M 380 (99)**—why to consider fairly immediately filing a **motion for return of non-contraband property** (feds were given $38,000 wrongfully seized from D, and D couldn't get it back);

Ornelas v US **59 517 US 690 (96)**—in analyzing legality of police conduct undertaken without warrant, appellate court to perform **de novo** review of ultimate "mixed" question of law and fact whether there was "reasonable suspicion" or "probable cause"; findings as to what occurred (historical facts) are to be given due deference, re: community's "distinctive features & events," and experience & expertise of local police;

C v Antobenedetto **366 M 51 (74)**—**arrest or search & seizure without warrant: DA has burden of proof to show constitutional;**

C v Taylor **10 MAC 452 (80)**—(same); if there's a warrant, it's D's burden of proof it's illegally executed—unless facially invalid (DA's burden of proof);

C v LePage **352 M 403 (67)**—D's burden of proof that arrest is bad; but see K. Smith, *Criminal Practice & Procedure*, §§ 1343–45 (2d ed. 1983 & Supp.)—moving party's burden of proof, except warrantless search & seizure = "presumed unreasonable"; if warrant, D's burden of persuasion & "going forward," but may shift mid-hearing; DA's burden of proof if "D challenges warrant as intrinsically invalid"; D's burden of proof that arrest = bad, but see *C v Hason* **387 M 169 (82)** implying DA's burden of proof;

C v Gomes **75 MAC 791 (2009)**—rejecting Commonwealth argument that D "waived" argument presented on appeal by not making specific challenges to exit order or reliability of call to 911/police: clear from motion papers that lawfulness of warrantless search was placed in issue, and it was Commonwealth's burden to prove lawful and based on reasonable suspicion;

C v Mubdi **456 M 385 (2010)**—D's motion and affidavit must give info sufficient to enable judge to determine whether to conduct evidentiary hearing (i.e., that there was a search/seizure for which Commonwealth must prove probable cause, reasonable suspicion, or consent) and to give notice as to what particular search[es] and seizure[s] D challenges (e.g., say BOTH search of place and search of person), to enable prosecution to determine what witnesses to call and what evidence to offer to meet its burden; if motion/affidavit fail in this regard, Commonwealth should move before hearing for more particularized affidavit, or to deny motion for failure to give fair notice to Commonwealth as to search being challenged; Commonwealth waives any objection to particularity if not made before appellate level; may be abuse of discretion to deprive D of fair hearing on motion raising constitutional claim by "insistence on strict requirements"; in MA, automatic standing when D is charged with possessory offense and search is of private place in which object he is alleged to possess was found (D need not show that he has reasonable expectation of privacy in place searched UNLESS D had no right to be in the place where evidence was found); "automatic standing" doesn't require that there be a co-D and 'constructive' possession issue; here, D was, at minimum, passenger in parked auto, and had standing to challenge search of auto even without automatic standing;

C v McCambridge **44 MAC 285 (98)**—though DA has burden of proof for warrantless search, D must 1st show that a search/seizure "in the constitutional sense has occurred" (& here no search when gun dropped from D's clothes as he was placed into an ambulance by EMT, who then gave gun to police);

C v Colon **449 M 207 (2007)**—D has burden of showing reasonable expectation of privacy (here, not shown in D's girlfriend's apartment, though D sometimes babysat his own children there, had last stayed overnight there six days earlier, and "engage[d] in intimate relationship with" girlfriend there; motion judge not required to believe D's girlfriend's testimony as to D having much more involvement with, and keys to, the apartment);

C v Porter P **456 M 254 (2010)**—D had legitimate expectation of privacy in room he shared with his mother at "transitional family shelter", though staff members had master key and could enter room;

C v Grandison **433 M 135 (2001)**—"(f)ollowing someone for the purposes of surveillance is not pursuit" despite fact that cops here clearly communicated that D was not free to "leave" the company of shadowing police officers who followed him twice as he changed course, once with "high beams" activated on cruiser, & then with even brighter "alley lights" trailing him into an alley; prior case *C v Williams* **422 M 111 (96)** "**following or observing someone without more, such as using a siren or lights, attempting to block or control an individual's path, direction, or speed, or commanding the individual to halt, is not pursuit**"; notwithstanding Grandison result (finding 'stop' only when cop commanded D to stop, & this occurred after D spit something out of mouth, which provided reasonable suspicion), law remains that if reasonable person wouldn't have believed himself free to leave, there is 'stop' requiring constitutional justification;

C v Nestor N **67 MAC 225 (2006)**—unmarked but recognizable van's circling block to approach dispersing youths from the front, + cop's approach, "hang on a second; Boston Police, can I talk to you?" wasn't a stop requiring justification; stop did occur under art. 14 when cop grabbed D's hands as D reached toward/into waistband, but was justified by reasonable suspicion that D was going for weapon; D had walked "funny," favoring one side (which hadn't been enough, without "reach", in *DePeiza*

66 MAC 398, further appellate review allowed 447 M 1105 [06]); Brown, J., concurring, in DePeiza = "amazed how a peculiar gait automatically triggers a stop and an inquiry"; "I think I have finally discerned an underlying rationale for 'stops' of persons of color within the scope of *Terry v Ohio* . . . It is *motion*. . . . I can only hope that these practices will not degenerate into stops based upon 'breathing while black'" [emphasis and sarcasm in original]); **on further appellate review, 449 M 367 (2007)**—SJC holds that announcement of intention to frisk required justification by reasonable suspicion + reasonable belief "armed," a standard which was met by "straight arm" manner of walking, nervousness, and furtive movements, plus character of neighborhood;

C v Ware **76 MAC 53 (2009)**—D, known to police to be too young to legally possess firearm, fled upon eye contact with police and grabbed at something above his waist under shirt; pursuit and seizure upheld on reasonable suspicion;

C v Phillips **413 M 50 (92)**—unlawful Boston Police Department policy authorizing "search on sight" of suspected gang members justified suppression of evidence but not dismissal; evidence of other unconstitutional searches was properly admissible to show existence of policy;

Matter of Lavigne **418 M 831 (94)**—**adversary hearing before any order for blood extraction (from non-indicted subject)**; must be probable cause to believe subject committed crime & probable cause to believe that source of blood at crime scene would aid in investigation of crime **AND** judge must weigh seriousness of crime, importance of the evidence to the investigation and less intrusive options against right to be free from bodily intrusion;

C v Miles **420 M 67 (95)**—pre-Lavigne, ex parte order compelling D to submit to visual inspection of his body (because rape had occurred in bed of poison ivy); exigency—"time was of the essence in order to preserve the evidence";

C v Powell **450 M 229 (2007)**—rejects D's argument that grand jury petition for blood sample from D was erroneously allowed: D argued that knowing D's own blood was on, e.g., hammer (purportedly used to kill V) was useless, but "overlook[ed] the utility in the investigation of excluding him as the source of blood found on his person and clothing"; D waived, by failing to object to, requirements that petition be signed by foreperson under oath and/or having supporting affidavit from DA or grand juror; judge's failure to include in order the findings mandated by *Williams* 439 M 678 (2003), immaterial because order was preceded by adversary hearing and record supported order authorizing extraction of D's blood;

C v Straw **422 M 756 (96)**—**when, as result of suppression of evidence, there is nothing to support conviction, result is NOT GUILTY (not just dismissal)**;

C v Holley **52 MAC 659 (2001)**—ordering judgments of NG when suppression was ordered;

C v Pierre P **53 MAC 215 (2001)**—same;

(the following cases are from Chapter 19, Double Jeopardy—*C v Funches* 379 M 283 (79) no re-trial after

appeal because without bad evidence (i.e., which should have been struck upon D's motion), there would have been required finding of not guilty;

C v Dellinger 383 M 780 (81)—(same); remand to enter not guilty;

C v Kirouac 405 M 557 (89)—erroneous admission of key evidence which deprives prosecution of legally sufficient evidence requires entry after appellate reversal of required finding of not guilty; remanded here to determine whether prosecution has "reasonable prospect for filling the gap in its proof"; *C v DeBenedetto* 414 M 37 (92) appellate reversal for erroneously admitted evidence (here, prior recorded testimony) did not require dismissal of murder 1 conviction where prosecution had "reasonable prospect" of filling gap in proof if witness could be found & persuaded to testify);

US v Havens 446 US 620 (80)—can impeach D by suppressed physical evidence (*see Chapter 20-B, Harris*);

C v DiPietro 35 MAC 638 (93)—**federal** magistrate issued search warrant for drugs, which were subject of eventual **state** prosecution, & appellate court strained to find Aguilar-Spinelli/Article 14 standards were met, in order to avoid decision as to whether state (Article 14) or fed (Fourth Amendment/*Illinois v Gates*) was applicable: resolution of this issue would depend on whether court viewed exclusionary rule's principal interest as deterrence of illegal police conduct (federal standard would suffice) or "judicial integrity" & protection of privacy (application of stricter rule required);

C v Gonzalez 426 M 313 (97)—**federal investigation's results not suppressed despite tactics violative of Article 14 and state wiretap law (G.L. c. 272, § 99),** because investigation **not** "a combined enterprise between Federal and State authorities" (notwithstanding aid of local police by surveillance and shared info); see also *C v Cryer* **426 M 562 (98)** (N.H. police not bound by Article 12 of Mass. Declaration of Rights);

C v Angiulo 415 M 502 (93)—**because wire recordings were authorized by federal court and made by federal agents, state discovery provision (G.L. c. 272, § 99 O I) not applicable**;

C v Pinto 45 MAC 790 (98)—federal postal authorities obtained warrants from federal magistrate, and Massachusetts had no involvement in search/seizure, so federal law applied;

See below re: searches made as incident to arrest & inventory searches & seizures, probable cause, search warrants, etc.;

20-F.2. State Action

DA v Coffey 386 M 218 (82)—phone company's cross frame (*Chapter 20-N*) not state action required by both U.S. Amendment 4 & Mass. Declaration of Rights, Article 14;

C v Robinson 34 MAC 610 (93)—D's wife went through D's files and found proof, provided to police, that D's alibi for arson was false: no state action;

C v Crowley 43 MAC 919 (97)—no state action in boarder's tape recording her landlords' beatings of 7-year-old daughter (& no suppression)

C v Gonzalez 68 MAC 620 (2007)—witness recorded his telephone conversation with D, not at direction of police and, according to motion judge, "not made secretly": court "agree[s] with judge's legal conclusion that the exclusionary rule ought not to be applied";

C v Leone 386 M 329 (82)—no state action by private guard unless deputy/special police officer **AND** not acting in purely private role (e.g., protecting employer's property);

C v Carr **76 MAC 41 (2009), further review allowed 456 M 1103 (2010)**—Boston College campus police could enter dorm room without warrant to address violation of BC policy prohibiting weapons in dorm, whether lawful or unlawful; policy (contract signed by students) permitting seizure by campus police of items in plain view was legitimately extended by students' written consent for more widespread search (court rejecting motion judge's ruling that initial entry and discovery of weapons was unlawful and subsequent 'consent' was fruit); failure of police to advise that students could refuse consent held not to "vitiate the consent given";

US v Jacobsen 466 US 109 (84)—though express company can open parcel & give bags to Drug Enforcement Agency, **state action for DEA to open/test bags**; but reasonable, like plain view;

Walter v US 447 US 649 (80)—bad FBI view (after private opening of) film;

C v Nielson 423 M 75 (96)—though by contract student consented to search of his dorm room by college residence staff, residence staff could not enlarge consent scope to cover campus police called in to photograph & seize growing marijuana;

C v Russo 30 MAC 923 (91)—drawing & testing of D's blood by hospital staff was not search or seizure under Fourth Amendment where not done at cops' request or direction;

C v St. Hilaire 43 MAC 743 (97)—despite fact that cops held D down as it was done (D in "protective custody" irrational, refused all treatment, spat at personnel);

C v St. Hilaire 43 MAC 743 (97)—blood drawing at physician's order not state action, though D had been placed in protective custody;

Ferguson v City of Charleston 532 US 67 (2001)—policy formed in consultation with police whereby hospital maintained "chain of custody" & reported to police re: pregnant patients' urine samples, to facilitate prosecution for drug offenses and/or child neglect = unconstitutional;

C v Ames 410 M 603 (91)—taking D to hospital where police offered blood alcohol test by "neutral" health care provider satisfied statutory requirements, despite subsequent failure to notify D of rights under G.L. c. 263, § 5A;

Doe v Senechal **431 M 78 (2000)**—former mental patient filed civil suit against residential treatment facility for allegedly tortious sexual contact by employee resulting in patient's pregnancy and childbirth; plaintiff obtained discovery order requiring alleged father to undergo "buccal swab paternity test," for DNA match to child; SJC didn't believe Fourth Amendment applied to "private" litigants' civil actions, but said test here ordered met "standard of reasonableness";

Vernonia School District v Acton **515 US 646 (95)**—suspicionless random drug testing of public secondary school athletes, positive test having consequence of either giving up sports or participating in 'anti-drug program' = no Fourth Amendment violation;

C v Damian D. **434 M 725 (2001)**—(marijuana ordered suppressed) though **Supreme Court has exempted school searches from Fourth Amendment's warrant and probable cause requirements, searches of students by school administrators must still be "reasonable," and a search is not "reasonable" simply because a student has disobeyed school rules**, i.e., here, being out of class for a period of time during the day; further, search was for evidence of contraband, not "truancy"; **left open = question whether Declaration of Rights Article 14 imposes a standard stricter than reasonableness on student searches**;

C v Monteiro **75 MAC 280 (2009)**—though student was frisked at school, police officer performed it, so reasonable suspicion required;

Safford Unified School Dist. No. 1 v Redding **129 S Ct 2633 (2009)**—search by school officials of 13-year-old student's bra and underpants violated Fourth Amendment even though reasonable suspicion student had brought forbidden prescription and over-the-counter drugs to school: no reason to suspect drugs presented a danger or were concealed in underwear;

C v Considine **448 M 295 (2007)**—chaperones' search of private school students' hotel room, etc., during field trip was not state action (citing *Rendell-Baker v Kohn* 457 US 830, 837–43 [82]), and holding also that search not unlawful under Declaration of Rights, art. 14; concurrence points out that private school officials "may conduct searches of their students for no articulable reason";

Jansen, petitioner **444 M 112 (2005)**—upheld judge's allowing a criminal D's pretrial motion for order for "buccal swab" of a third party for DNA sample (D had made very substantial showing that such a sample with pristine chain of custody would show third party rather than D to be source of sperm); order doesn't "implicate . . . rights under" Fourth Amendment or Article 14, because no government involvement & Commonwealth has advocated vigorously AGAINST the criminal D's attempts to get the sample, BUT, at 120 n.13, leaves open issue re: state action if D later turns over to Commonwealth the swab for use in a future criminal prosecution;

20-F.3. Extraterritorial/Citizens' Actions?, Civil Offenses

See Chapter 3-C for cases on arrests beyond police jurisdiction;

C v Morrissey **422 M 1 (96)**—cop from town B in town A at request of A's police to assist, stopped motorist in town A at direction of police A = valid; failure or refusal by **anyone** to help a cop when directed to do so "in the name of the Commonwealth" = crime (G.L. c. 268, § 24);

C v LeBlanc **407 M 70 (90)**—unauthorized pursuit & stop for nonarrestable offense outside police jurisdiction required suppression of evidence;

C v Zorrilla **38 MAC 77 (95)**—pursuit and stop, outside jurisdiction, for broken taillight required suppression of evidence (nonarrestable civil offense);

C v Riedel **456 M 1103 (2010)**—extraterritorial pursuit/stop justified by "objective," rather than officer's subjective, analysis of whether D committed arrestable offense, court here finding evidence implied driving under influence;

C v Coburn **62 MAC 314 (2004)**—D drove too fast in Concord & was pursued, stopping & failing sobriety test just short of sign indicating border of Lincoln; that defense counsel later discovered a stone marker 30 feet before the town line sign showing a letter "L" on southern face and "C" on northern face, indicating that D's vehicle came to stop in Lincoln, didn't result in suppression despite court's "assum[ption] without deci[sion] that the stop & arrest were extraterritorial";

C v Twombly **435 M 440 (2001)**—D drove too fast & passed improperly at time of 'moderate' traffic; G.L. c. 37, § 13 authorized extraterritorial stop to preserve the peace, protect public; police in town into which cop followed D authorized cop to make the stop, & statute allows such request/authorization for, inter alia, aid in preserving the peace (keeping safe from injury, harm, or destruction) here applicable; **OVERRULING/VACATING** *C v Twombly* **50 MAC 667 (2001)** pursuit and stop outside police jurisdiction for speeding and illegal passing required suppression (civil offenses); though cop radioed 2d town and was told to make the stop, mere mention of existing "mutual aid agreement" pursuant to G.L. c. 40, § 8G insufficient to justify (i.e., no evidence as to relevant terms of agreement, particularly what is required from personnel of one town in order to authorize action by the other); refusal also to justify stop under G.L. c. 37, § 13 (authorizing officer to request aid in criminal case, in preservation of the peace, or in apprehending/securing person for breach of peace): speeding and improper passing in manner here described not a breach of peace;

C v Nicholson **56 MAC 921 (2002)**—police officer who had been sworn in as special police officer in adjoining town had authority to stop D in that adjoining town; cop here had been so sworn, pursuant to G.L. c. 41, § 99 (town's authority to specially designate police officers from other cities/towns & give them same immunities and privileges as they have in their own cities/towns);

C v Zirpolo **37 MAC 307 (94)**—arrestable offense committed in presence of broadcasting officer justified other officer's extraterritorial pursuit and stop ("collective knowledge" doctrine);

C v Dise **31 MAC 701 (91)**—extraterritorial arrest by cop valid as private citizen arrest because he had probable cause to believe D had committed felony;

C v Claiborne **423 M 275 (96)**—extraterritorial arrest by cop valid because probable cause to believe D committed felony; mere citizen could arrest lawfully only if person in fact committed the felony;

C v Callahan **428 M 335 (98)**—Hollis, N.H. cop had been appointed "special police officer" for Pepperell, MA pursuant to G.L. c. 41, § 99 and could pursue speeding motorist into Pepperell and make stop there;

C v Mullen **40 MAC 404 (96)**—"special state police officer" (college campus) had no authority even to stop motorist for nonarrestable civil offense (failure to yield at intersection; see G.L. c. 90C, §§ 1–3);

C v Hernandez **456 M 528 (2010)**—B.U. campus police = special State police officers", but they arrested D on outstanding warrant for misdemeanor motor vehicle offense which was not committed in/on B.U. property, and execution of warrant occurred when D was not present on B.U. property; there was no common law/"citizen" right to execute arrest warrant; drugs found in inventory search of vehicle = suppressed;

C v Gray **423 M 293 (96)**—pursuit initially for speeding (civil, nonarrestable) became pursuit for arrestable offense of failure to stop for police officer, justifying extraterritorial pursuit; despite fact that "failure to stop" charge was dismissed;

Scott v Harris **127 S. Ct. 1769 (2007)**—cop "terminated" suspect's flight by forcing chased car off the road: though result was that suspect became quadriplegic, cop was entitled to summary judgment in later civil action because reckless high speed flight jeopardized lives of citizenry;

C v Owens **414 M 595 (93)**—cop, after observing suspicious behavior involving 2 cars, radioed for stolen vehicle and warrants check, and received info that owner of one car had outstanding warrants for serious felony: ok to follow/arrest driver outside jurisdiction; fact that driver was not car owner/subject of warrant didn't matter (pat down revealed gun and nonmatched ammunition, leading to seizure of shotgun in trunk);

C v O'Hara **30 MAC 608 (91)**—car's crossing lines & wavering speed warranted belief that driver committing OUI or other "arrestable offense" justified fresh pursuit to make extraterritorial arrest under G.L. c. 41, § 98A;

G.L. c. 276, § 28 (amended)—authorizes arrest upon probable cause that misdemeanor was committed in violation of restraining or no-contact order; authorizes arrest for larceny committed in his presence, regardless of value of goods stolen; authorizes arrest for misdemeanor, without having a warrant for such arrest in his possession, if the officer making such arrest has actual knowledge that there is in fact an outstanding arrest warrant for the person;

C v Gagnon **16 MAC 110 (83)**—search & seizure by foreign cops valid unless shock conscience or US cops participated: **(aff'd 391 M 869 (1984) sub nom *C v Bourgeois*)**;

C v Gagnon **16 MAC 110 (83)**—OK search & seizure by foreign cops unless shock conscience & US cops participate; OK here (Canadians in Quebec);

See also Chapter 20-B, above, state action re: alleged statements & K. Smith, *Criminal Practice & Procedure*, §§ 155–56 (2d ed. 1983 & Supp.);

20-F.4. Fruits

C v Ferguson **410 M 611 (91)**—D's statement suppressed as fruit of bad search;

C v Pandolfino **33 MAC 96 (92)**—showup identification of D not product of possibly unlawful arrest but rather of his presence in area;

C v Gomes **59 MAC 332 (2003)**—D cannot invoke exclusionary rule to suppress evidence of his own unlawful conduct in response to police actions in violation of constitutional protections against unlawful search and seizure; even if cop made unlawful entry, cop's use of force to prevent D from closing door on him did not result in seizure of contraband or lead to police observations of contraband or unlawful activity;

C v Vanya V **75 MAC 370 (2009)**—juvenile argued (a) initial patfrisk = bad, (b) search of backpack at scene thereafter = bad, and (c) stationhouse opening of locked bank bag found inside backpack = bad, but majority said needn't consider first two events "because neither yielded anything that juvenile sought to suppress or that . . . supports the drug charges against him"; concurring opinion (Berry, J.) recognizes that bad patfrisk cast "continuing taint over the seizure of the locked bank bag" which required suppression "*unless* there existed an intervening event in the police encounter that provided independent, constitutionally acceptable grounds for the opening of the locked container"; majority had suppressed for bad "inventory" justification;

Boston Housing Authority v Guirola **410 M 820 (90)**—observation of drugs by exterminators was independent source, so suppression not required because drugs not fruit of subsequent bad search;

C v Balicki **436 M 1 (2002)**—cops executing warrant in 1996 illegally expanded the authorized search by taking still and video photos of entire house, & Commonwealth didn't meet burden of showing that items photographed would have been discovered & properly seized later without such photos; cops had obtained 1997 search warrant in probable reliance upon the 1996 photos;

NY v Harris **495 US 14 (90)**—warrantless search of D's home in absence of exigency or consent, in violation of *Payton* (v NY 445 US 573 (80)), did not require suppression of D's later stationhouse confession because police did not exploit bad search to obtain it;

C v Wilson **38 MAC 680 (95)**—though seized drugs were suppressed for failure to get a warrant in the available three hours (in a prior case), undercover cop's observations came before any illegitimate search/seizure (and were enough for G of conspiracy to distribute over 100 grams cocaine);

C v Manning **44 MAC 695 (98)**—though D's booking photo was obtained when he was arrested without probable cause for a particular crime (and that charge was dismissed), Court refused to "suppress" from use that booking photo, i.e., when the victim of a shooting 2 weeks before the photo was taken ID'd it as depicting his assailant; also refused to dismiss indictment, though testimony about D's possession of firearm in dismissed case was given to grand jury in shooting case; BUT if purpose of 'bad' arrest had been to obtain the evidence for use in prosecuting the earlier charge, result would be different;

C v Loughlin **385 M 60 (82)**—D's consent was fruit of bad detention/frisk; not given right to decline, no time lapse from bad stop, & no break in chain;

Florida v Royer **460 US 491 (83)**—(same) (*see also Chapter 20-G,–K, -M*);

C v Mateo-German **453 M 838 (2009)**—cop engaged in "community caretaking" asked D's consent for dog sniff of car's exterior: this was not a seizure requiring probable cause; D's consent was not product of unlawful detention, consent for dog sniff not required as exterior sniff not a "search";

Framingham v BMC **373 M 783 (77)**—for deterrence under Declaration of Rights, Article 14 (though probably OK for U.S. Supreme Court), illegal evidence suppressed from Civil Service hearing;

C v Borges **395 M 788 (85)**—D's flight & hiding dope = fruit of illegal detention (*see Chapter 20-G,–K, & -M below*), not intervening/independent acts;

C v Straw **422 M 756, 762–63 (96)**—D's admissions = fruit of illegal seizure of briefcase;

C v Chongarlides **52 MAC 366 (2001)**—though entry into house where D was found = illegal, D's eventual statement at police station hours later, following Miranda waiver, not suppressed;

US v Crews **445 US 463 (80)**—photo ID & later lineup = bad fruits of illegal arrest (but in-court ID not tainted);

C v Crowe **21 MAC 456 (86)**—(same); Cf. *C v Thinh Vao Cao* **419 M 383 (95)** photo taken during encounter (& ID from it) would have been suppressed if there had been a "seizure" beforehand, SJC deferring to motion judge's finding of its absence;

C v White **11 MAC 953 (81)**—showup ID 2 days post-event = bad fruit of bad arrest, & in-court ID suppressed because independent source not shown;

C v Villar **40 MAC 742 (96)**—though D argued that search warrant was fruit of illegal ploy (placing arrested man in front of door & knocking, so occupants would open door, thinking it was that man who wanted admission), no relief;

C v Peters **453 M 818 (2009)**—gun and drugs found during illegitimate second "protective sweep" infected search warrant subsequently obtained, such that evidence seized during execution of warrant was suppressed;

C v Webster **75 MAC 247 (2009)**—because cops illegitimately entered apartment (and stayed there for 7 hours, "securing" it) with only arrest warrant for D, their seizure of him after he entered and fled produced gun and statement, which were suppressed; no suppression of gun found inside after search warrant was obtained;

C v King **389 M 233 (83)**—though illegal stop and frisk, co-D's pulling/shooting gun = intervening cause so can arrest & seize and search;

C v Kolodziej **69 MAC 199 (2007)**—although trooper's pursuit of D perhaps not justified because car inspection sticker's color was not alone enough to support conclusion that it had expired, driver-D's violent struggle with passenger and movement into back seat as car was still moving at 25 mph = intervening cause justifying seizure (operating to endanger, even though D was never cited for this offense, prosecution instead predicated upon abundant alcoholic beverage containers/intoxication);

C v Saia **372 M 53 (77)**—D's willful act intervened after bad entry;

C v Gallant **381 M 465 (80)**—(same);

C v Mock **54 MAC 276 (2002)**—after report that 'heavy set black male' had attempted (without success) to break into apartment, no reasonable suspicion to stop black male (perhaps heavy set, perhaps 'medium' build) about ten minutes later who was walking on the street in the direction of the named apartment, holding something bulky, & who just walked faster when hailed by the police in residential neighborhood "populated by African-Americans" (stopping only when cop alighted from car & told him to "stop," which amounted to pursuit & seizure); judge may or may not have credited cop's assertion that it was "high crime" area; BUT APPEALS COURT nonetheless reverses suppression order on ground that D's throwing of a VCR at the cops (striking one on the leg) broke the causal chain & justified arrest;

Hayes v Florida **470 US 811 (85)**—**suppress fingerprints from bad arrest**;

C v Fredette **396 M 455 (85)**—suppress fingerprints from bad arrest, but allow fingerprint motion now because grand jury indictment (& probable cause thus found) = intervening cause;

US v Ceccolini **435 US 268 (78)**—**witness's testimony = voluntary act, not fruit of bad search** (of envelopes with betting slips discovered while talking to witness, D's employee, at D's shop);

C v Caso **377 M 236 (79)**—purely voluntary testimony of witness = OK though he's located through illegal tap on D;

C v Waters **420 M 276 (95)**—though D contended that purpose of search of an apartment (not his) was to obtain statements against him from a person in the apartment at time of search, and that no probable cause for warrant existed, (1) witness's eventual testimony at trial held not to be a "fruit", and (2) D had no expectation of privacy in apartment

C v Cataldo **69 MAC 465 (2007)**—after illegal entry into apartment, must strike from subsequent search warrant application all information obtained from entry, & remainder must show probable cause to believe that items sought are related to crime under investigation and that they may reasonably be expected to be located in the place to be searched at the time of warrant's issuance; affidavit here refers only to crimes in which apartment resident was NOT involved, and gave no info supporting nexus to apartment;

20-F.5. Inevitable Discovery

Nix v Williams **467 US 431 (84)**—"inevitable discovery" exception to exclusionary rule;

C v Somers **44 MAC 920 (98)**—though search of car occurred before arrest & was thus bad, gun would have been discovered in inventory search (because D would have been arrested for OUI and/or operating to endanger); *C v Baptiste* **65 MAC 511 (2006)**—subjective "investigative" interest didn't render inventory search impermissible;

C v Benoit **382 M 210 (81)**—"inevitability" of warrant doesn't cure bad search & seizure;

See also Chapter 20-B, above & **K. Smith, *Criminal Practice & Procedure*, §§ 1328 et seq. (2d ed. 1983 & Supp.) re: fruits**—e.g., Wong Sun, etc.;

C v Damiano **422 M 10 (96)**—when judge made factual findings that physical evidence was found "based on statements unlawfully obtained" from D, Commonwealth's mere assertion of "inevitable discovery" was unavailing; suppression upheld;

C v O'Connor **406 M 112 (89)**—"inevitable discovery" under Article 14 limited: "discovery by lawful means must be certain as a practical matter"; Commonwealth has burden of proving facts by preponderance of evidence; factors include: severity of constitutional violation by cops; whether cops' violation done to accelerate discovery of evidence; here, any defects in protective custody search cured by inevitable discovery at booking inventory;

C v Perrot **407 M 539 (90)**—discovery of stolen pocketbook as product of right to counsel violation not cured by inevitable discovery doctrine where its discovery otherwise wasn't "virtually certain";

C v Damiano **422 M 10 (96)**—when judge made factual findings that physical evidence was found "based on statements unlawfully obtained" from D, Commonwealth's mere assertion of "inevitable discovery" was unavailing; suppression upheld;

C v Gomes **408 M 43 (90)**—inevitable discovery doctrine applied only where "clear" cops didn't act in bad faith to accelerate discovery of evidence; here, cop should have known case law made no knock warrant invalid;

C v Ferguson **410 M 611 (91)**—search of bag taken from jacket of fleeing D not justified by inevitable discovery doctrine where D not in custody & custody not inevitable;

C v DiMarzio **52 MAC 746 (2001)**—"inevitable discovery" doesn't authorize admission of evidence from warrantless seizure "even if it was inevitable that, if sought, a search warrant would have been issued & the evidence would have been found"; here, D was purportedly arrested for recent marijuana usage (odor apparent, & rolling papers) and was handcuffed when, without Miranda warnings, he was asked where marijuana was (A: in desk drawer); **on further appellate review, 436 M 1012 (2002),** SJC agrees re: suppression (but not because of 'exigent circumstances' or search incident to arrest, and instead merely, flatly, because discovery was fruit of Miranda violation) & no inevitable discovery; *C v Garden* **451 M 43 (2008)**—odor of burnt marijuana allowed search of car's occupants and passenger compartment, but not warrantless search of trunk;

C v McAfee **63 MAC 467 (2005)**—although D's statement (as to presence & location of handgun within dwelling) was fruit of illegal entry into home (after "exigency" created by cops, in going to D's door and alerting him to their interest, rather than obtaining a warrant for which probable cause had existed for at least four days), cops did obtain warrant after conducting a "sweep" to "impound" premises while warrant was sought, and gun would have been discovered during search for drugs & related items under the warrant, "inevitable" discovery principle supporting denial of suppression of gun;

20-F.6. What Is to Be Suppressed?

See Chapter 20-I, post, for cases on standing;

C v Hill **49 MAC 58, 61 (2000)**—because D had no standing to contest search/seizure of drugs from another, she pressed same constitutional issue in motion to dismiss, arguing that her own seizure (resulting from the prior search/seizure) was unconstitutional, and since there were no "fruits" of that transgression, dismissal should be remedy: appellate court rejected argument (**"illegal arrest, without more, has never been viewed as a bar to subsequent prosecution"**);

C v Gomes **59 MAC 332 (2003)**—D cannot invoke exclusionary rule to suppress evidence of his own unlawful conduct in response to police actions in violation of constitutional protections against unlawful search and seizure; even if cop made unlawful entry, cop's use of force to prevent D from closing door on him did not result in seizure of contraband or lead to police observations of contraband or unlawful activity; reserved = question whether circumstances under which an entry occurs might be so outrageous as to preclude imposition of a criminal penalty for resistance (citing *US v Russell* 411 US 423, 431–32 (1973));

James v Illinois **493 US 307 (90)—suppressed statements** obtained in violation of Fourth Amendment **may not be used to impeach defense witnesses other than D;**

C v Olsen **405 M 491 (89)**—evidence obtained in violation of Fourth Amendment or Article 14 may be used at

surrender hearing to show probation violation, at least where police unaware of defendant's status as probationer;

20-G. PROBABLE CAUSE, INCLUDING HEARSAY AND INFORMANTS

See also Chapter 20-F & -M;

See also Chapter 3-B, ante, & K. Smith, *Criminal Practice & Procedure,* Chapter 3-E (2d ed. 1983 & Supp.) re: probable cause for arrest;

20-G.1. In General; "Anticipatory"; "Collective" Knowledge of Cops

K. Smith, *Criminal Practice & Procedure,* **§ 103 (2d ed. 1983 & Supp.)**—probable cause; §§ 105 & 118 search & seizure probable cause same as arrest, except search & seizure not indefinite, can get stale; § 114 no probable cause by trespass (see plain view); §§ 115–31; hearsay/informants rules (same with & without warrant)—"victim"(sic) has no motive to falsify (§ 120); §§ 193–216 probable cause for search warrants; but cf. *US v Ventresca* **380 US 102 (65)** search warrant may save a marginal case (*see Chapter 20-J*);

Brinegar v US **338 US 160 (49)**—facts that would lead man of reasonable caution to believe past/present crime by D; more than suspicion, less than beyond reasonable doubt;

Wong Sun v US **371 US 471 (63)**—(same); no probable cause from flight from narcotic officer at door; evidence discovered after illegal search and seizure can't justify it;

C v Sweezey **50 MAC 48 (2000)**—reasonable suspicion to stop motorist-D: surveillance of parking lot known for frequent drug transactions, one car signaling D's car with flashing lights, D following & obtaining paper bag from other driver; D's attempted getaway, in car, from cops approaching him at stop light in traffic gave probable cause for 'drugs';

C v Takvorian **75 MAC 836 (2009)**—after stop of car for expired license plate and D's statement that he was a chemist running business and lab out of his house selling performance products (to explain "vials" in plain view inside plastic tote container in back seat), D also stated he had needles and drugs in the containers and prescriptions for them; cop saw bottles labeled in manner consistent with steroids; simultaneous inventory search revealed Oxycontin pills and hypodermic needles in front seat area: held: sufficient probable cause for warrant to search D's residence because G.L. c. 112, § 30 says no one but pharmacist may dispense ANY substance intended for hypodermic use; "vial" denotes liquid, supporting inference of hypodermics' necessity; SJC rejected Commonwealth claim that illegal nature of performance-enhancing steroids is matter of common knowledge (many substances banned in sports are not illegal);

C v Vazquez **74 MAC 920 (2009)**—police responding to call re: man being "jumped" & severely beaten were

told by witness at scene on cell phone, "that's him," referring to man in sports jersey walking away; officers stopped that man (D), who said that he had witnessed fight; during questions, officer became concerned for safety & D became argumentative, resulting in being cuffed and returned to scene; witness there reported further that different man had been kicking victim in head and that when witness approached D looked at witness and then whistled to assailant and told him to stop: though suppression motion judge had ruled that this report eliminated probable cause (inferring that crime was committed by only the kicking assailant), App. Ct. held that D's actions were consistent with "lookout," and thus joint venturer, as to whom there was probable cause to arrest (suspicion ripening to probable cause after witness's further statement);

C v Fernandez **57 MAC 562 (2003)**—probable cause to arrest D, a passenger sitting in parked car from which drug sales were solicited by third person moving back and forth from the car; police could reasonably think that someone engaged in drug transactions wouldn't tolerate presence of someone unconnected to the transactions; appellate court purported to distinguish *U.S. v DiRe* 332 U.S. 581 (48) & *C v Sampson* 20 MAC 970 (85), regarding "mere presence";

C v Eckert **431 M 591 (2000)**—trooper approached D's car stopped at rest area, to check on well-being of occupant, aroused D from "resting" condition, & detected bloodshot eyes & odor of alcoholic beverage; only "reasonable suspicion" rather than probable cause was required prior to asking D to get out and perform field sobriety tests, & case was remanded for determination whether reasonable suspicion existed; critical to determination whether questioning D about 'drinking' & sobriety tests OK = whether engine was running, because if so, "operation," and probable cause for arrest for OUI existed; NO constitutional justification was required for trooper's approach & inquiry whether D 'alright';

C v Garden **451 M 43 (2008)**—marijuana odor = sufficiently distinctive that it alone can supply probable cause; odor of burnt marijuana coming from vehicle occupant's clothes = probable cause to search vehicle; cite to Johnson v US 333 US 10 (48) (odors alone may be enough for probable cause under Fourth Amendment); *C v Laskoski* **74 MAC 858 (2009)**—same;

C v Pinto **45 MAC 790 (98)**—trained narcotics-sniffing dog's "alert" gave probable cause for warrant, and probable cause not "invalidated" when package was later found to contain substance other than ones for which dog was trained;

C v Watson **430 M 725 (99)**—discussing **use of dogs for probable cause**; *US v Taylor* **898 F.2d 805 (D.C. Cir.**

'90) factors re: dog (un)reliability, including (even unintended) suggestion of handler;

C v Mateo-German **453 M 838 (2009)**—cop engaged in "community caretaking" asked D's consent for dog sniff of car's exterior: this was not a seizure requiring probable cause, and D's consent wasn't needed anyway, as dog sniff of exterior not a "search under art. 14;

C v Donahue **430 M 710, 714 n.1 (2000)**—affidavit filed in support of search warrant application asserted that polygraph test of D indicated "extreme deception" in answers about his wife's disappearance; SJC didn't decide **whether polygraph results may be used for probable cause** because there was probable cause without this data; (*See also Chapter 20-F, ante, & -M, post, re: stops & flight as fruit*);

C v Murphy **63 MAC 11, 19 n.9 (2005)**—D's possession of a false identification did not constitute a crime establishing "independent and objectively reasonable grounds for arrest, *see Devenpeck v Alford* **125 S. Ct. 588, 595 (2004)**, and for a search of his person incident to that arrest"; that "warrant check," while negative, provided allegation that D's driver's license had been suspended, was not basis for detention where no indication D was driving any vehicle;

C v Zimmerman **70 MAC 357 (2007)**—warrant application to search car's "event data recorder (EDR)" provided probable cause, despite (affidavit's?) acknowledgment that D's loss of control of vehicle was "for reasons not conclusively determined": affiant state trooper assigned to collision analysis section ("training and experience" cited) affirmed "probable cause to believe" D drove "at a rate of speed that was greater than reasonable and prudent" resulting in "motor vehicle homicide via negligent operation so as to endanger the lives & safety of the public"; belief as to speed implicitly based upon affiant's observations re: road conditions, "rotation, sliding, and violent crash", and severe fatal trauma to passenger;

C v Gauthier **425 M 37 (97)**—**anticipatory warrant-triggering event need not be on warrant's face nor attached to it (affidavit), but suppression ordered here because triggering event hadn't occurred and no probable cause existed without it;**

US v Grubbs **126 S Ct 1494 (2006)**—anticipatory warrant valid when there is probable cause to believe items will be present upon occurrence of triggering event; suppression not required on basis that triggering event wasn't on warrant's face and affidavit wasn't attached; dissent would require that affidavit, or at least triggering event, be shown to homeowner to explain/justify authority for search;

C v Staines **441 M 521 (2004)**—info in affidavit proffered for "anticipatory" warrant provided probable cause that cocaine would be found in D's car when warrant was executed; requirement that item will arrive at search locus at specified time, i.e., "sure and irreversible course" doctrine discussed; search/seizure not limited to the cocaine being bought by undercover officer, and authorization to seize included any additional cocaine in the vehicle;

C v Celestino **47 MAC 916 (99)**—rejecting argument that anticipatory warrant was required since police on Wednesday had probable cause to believe D would have drugs on Friday: "warrantless arrest in public place is permissible if arresting officer has probable cause";

C v DiToro **51 MAC 191 (2001)**—absence of warrant excused since probable cause existed only when D's boyfriend actually emerged from a car with black bag containing cocaine; earlier, go-betweens seemed unable to consummate drug deal; *C v Wigfall* **32 MAC 582 (92)** distinguished, where probable cause existed at far earlier point, so "exigency" couldn't justify failure to obtain warrant;

C v Cruz **430 M 838 (2000)**—though D argued that warrant application failed to show probable cause for apartment unless executed after routine delivery of drugs there by specific vehicle, or probable cause for vehicle unless executed during transport of drugs to apartment, SJC seemingly ignored latter argument, and held probable cause existed in apartment apart from vehicle's deliveries, albeit for lesser quantities of drugs;

C v Chaisson **358 M 587 (71)**—**probable cause by collective knowledge of cooperating cops;**

C v Quinn **68 MAC 476 (2007)**—reasonable suspicion for investigative stop of car based on collective knowledge of other officers (who knew that footsteps in snow from site of break-in led to automobile going in a particular direction, and D's car was the only car in vicinity);

C v King **67 MAC 823 (2006)**—"collective knowledge" doctrine doesn't allow officer to offer hearsay testimony as to what a different officer allegedly observed (D's *Crawford v Washington* (541 US 36 [2004]) argument not reached); sight of "green leafy vegetable matter" failed to provide probable cause for search of car because (1) record did not establish that nontestifying cop saw this from OUTSIDE the car (and he didn't have right beforehand to be inside the car) and (2) nothing in record established that the "matter" (which vanished before suppression hearing & could have been "a remnant of lettuce") was recognizable as contraband;

C v Kotlyarevskiy **59 MAC 240 (2003)**—though D appeared for pre-arranged marijuana sale to undercover cop, D aborted deal after conversing: there was probable cause to arrest after D entered his car nearby because, in circumstances, there was reasonable belief he possessed marijuana; D had argued no probable cause for "conspiracy" because can't conspire with undercover cop & none for "attempt" to sell marijuana because no overt act (court probably disagreed with latter assertion [n.2]);

C v Gullick **386 M 278 (82)**—radio call OK—if collective probable cause;

C v Zirpolo **37 MAC 307 (94)**—same, validating extraterritorial stop after pursuit (arrestable offense having been committed in presence of radioing officer, whose knowledge was imputed to stopping officer);

C v Twombly **435 M 440 (2001)**—D drove too fast & passed improperly at time of 'moderate' traffic; G.L. c. 37, § 13 authorized extraterritorial stop to preserve the peace, protect public; police in town into which cop followed D authorized cop to make the stop, & statute allows such request/authorization for, inter alia, aid in preserving the peace (keeping safe from injury, harm, or destruction) here applicable;

***Whiteley v Warden* 401 US 560 (71)—BUT radio call from cop must be supported by probable cause & basis;**

C v Antobenedetto **366 M 51 (74)**—radio dispatch needs probable cause; (& see *C v Wainio* **7 MAC 863 (79)**);

C v Riggieri **438 M 613 (2003)**—police may stop car for motor vehicle violation based on dispatcher's report even if they don't observe violation: dispatcher recognized caller as off-duty police officer (& thus a reliable informant), who advised dispatcher of erratic operation & gave regular updates as to vehicle's activity;

C v Lopes **455 M 147 (2009)**—Boston cop hearing radio broadcast telephoned Brockton police detective, telling him of shooting involving big brown van with tinted windows and Cape Verdean flag, van operated by black male; van stop OK, on information source of victim's cousin, who had ID'd self to police and had seen van before but not minutes after victim was shot and left in vehicle with motor running; upholding speculation that van was used to block victim's vehicle and that Cape Verdeans might go to Brockton;

C v Davis **63 MAC 88 (2005)**—cop on detail who heard radio dispatch, based on anonymous phone call re: drunk female getting into white SUV with specific license plate number, tossing out beer cans, etc., could stop the car; "that report of an apparently drunk driver was anonymous did not require the police to ignore it" (*C v Fortune* **47 MAC 923 (2003)**); after stop, sufficient evidence for arrest found;

C v Costa **448 M 510 (2007)**—anonymous telephone tipster's reliability purportedly OK because she placed herself at risk by telephoning police to report D's possession of handgun as she stood near D; this provided objectively reasonable suspicion for frisk;

C v Rodriquez **70 MAC 904 (2007)**—though 911 caller did not give name, he ID'd self as driver for "Community Taxi," and said someone had just backed up and hit his car at named intersection, providing make, model, color and plate number of other car; second 911 call from same man said car had driven away and he was in pursuit on named road and direction; citing *Costa* **448 M 510 (2007)**, holds reliability should be accorded greater weight than anonymous tipster because identifiable from employer;

C v Berment **39 MAC 522 (95)**—lack of evidence to establish reliability of broadcast re: man with gun (stop and frisk case);

C v Gomes **75 MAC 791 (2009)**—no evidence that 911 caller placed self at risk or was otherwise reliable; level of detail of info (black male wearing gray shirt and yellow pants, standing outside green Honda, holding gun in air on named street) standing alone = insufficient to establish call's reliability re: illegality; that police came

and saw person matching description sitting in green car with female not sufficient corroboration to establish 'reasonable suspicion';

C v Lelos **61 MAC 626 (2004)**—identified citizen reported auto "casing" her neighborhood & gave info re: car description and plate number, and "baseball hat" occupant; cop found evidence of attempted break-in area, confirmed with other citizens the car's continuing suspicious presence, and located car: stop was justified, cop drew gun only upon suspicious movement of car occupants' feet: probable cause found, & immediate post-Miranda agreement to identify sites of burglaries made OK the search of car for proceeds of burglary, "security" concerns being "minimal at best" because Ds were handcuffed and under arrest; fact that D was purportedly arrested only for "disorderly conduct" after attempted flight didn't matter;

C v Riggieri **53 MAC 373 (2001)**—on basis of radio dispatch from cop in adjacent town re two cars driving erratically, cop stationed himself near town border and followed the two cars for a mile, observing no infractions, but stopping one of them & thereafter finding support for OUI charge; because Commonwealth didn't present testimony from anyone who had observed any infraction to justify the stop, suppression of observations ordered;

C v Wilkerson **436 M 137 (2002)**—refusing to suppress evidence seized as result of warrantless arrest for whose "probable cause" cops relied on street scene computer check yielding erroneous info provided by Registry of Motor Vehicles re: status of D's license; there was "no unlawful conduct to be deterred by exclusion of the evidence";

C v White **422 M 487 (96)**—though info went from witnesses to Malden police to Boston police roll call, Commonwealth presented sufficient evidence at hearing that broadcast was based on police interviews with witnesses at crime scene; see *C v Harmon* **63 MAC 456, 461 n.4 (2005)** (citation omitted) ("persons who supply information only after being interviewed by police officers, or who give info as witnesses during the course of an investigation, are not informers");

C v Heughan **40 MAC 102 (96)**—even throwing out broadcast, there was legitimate stop for speeding and driving without license justified warrantless arrest;

C v Willis **415 M 814 (93)**—Flint, Michigan police teletype to Boston detailed that D would be on Greyhound bus arriving at 6:50 p.m., carrying no luggage but instead blue & white striped pillowcase, and armed with handgun; **reliability of message found by police corroboration** (D known to Boston police and ID'd at bus station); but see *Oliveira* **35 MAC 645 (93)**;

C v Hawkins **361 M 384 (72)**—if no cooperation, no imputation/collective probable cause (for bonds seized while executing drug search warrant); different name = no probable cause;

20-G.2. Staleness

C v Reddington **395 M 315 (85)**—Jan. reliable tip = stale; Jan.-Aug. = no reliability/basis; Aug. tip reliable, but no basis, loading trunk after fink told D to clear out = too innocent for corroboration;

C v Luce **34 MAC 105 (93)**—two informants were reliable, but their info about D was 6 and 8 months old; untested informant had detailed and fresh info re: D, and his info about others involved was verified by other narcotics investigators: probable cause found;

C v Matias **440 M 787 (2004)**—informant info in March, but evidence found in D's trash in October indicated continuing drug activity, so probable cause for warrant;

C v Morton **26 MAC 949 (88)**—no present probable cause because affidavit doesn't tell when fink made (alleged) observations;

C v Contos **435 M 19, 36 (2001)**—court "troubled" by staleness of info that, two months before search, D was improperly storing ammunition in military base locker (but this defect immaterial here because D had no reasonable expectation of privacy);

C v James **424 M 770 (97)**—warrant to search residences of defendants 18 days after murder for knives, sneakers, dark clothing, and masks: not stale here because items were of "durable" nature, not inherently incriminating to possess, and Ds were unaware they'd been ID'd as culprits;

C v Beliard **443 M 79 (2004)**—though most recent info in affidavit supporting application for warrant was about six weeks old, the two guns sought would not likely have been destroyed because there was no evidence they had been used in any other crime or that anyone knew that they had been identified to the police;

C v Malone **24 MAC 70 (87)**—led to 1 prior arrest maybe not probable cause; stale anyway because **drugs = disposable so must observe recently;**

C v Javier **32 MAC 988 (92)**—present tense verbs & reference to ongoing investigation in affidavit sufficient to suggest that information was fresh, despite absence of dates & times;

C v Mantinez **44 MAC 513 (98)**—warrantless "stop" of D on reasonable suspicion, which ripened to probable cause, despite fact that info on which suspicion was founded was 2 months old: **"time is of less significance" in drug distribution which is, allegedly, "ongoing";**

C v Rodriguez **49 MAC 664 (2000)**—informant's assertion that D was dealing heroin, and that he saw heroin in apartment 3 days earlier not stale (despite D's argument that there was no 'basis of knowledge' for claim of "dealing," & failure to specify that large amount was seen left it equally likely that D had consumed the amount personally in interim);

C v Cruz **430 M 838, 843 (2000)**—passage of two weeks between last controlled purchase and issuance of search warrant didn't matter given "ongoing criminal activity to distribute cocaine";

C v Rice **47 MAC 586 (99)**—despite fact that info in affidavit supporting warrant application only alleged drug activity at least six weeks before warrant issued, probable cause found because interlocking tips & police corroboration indicated consistent drug sales at same location for 15 months (so likely to continue 1½ months later);

C v Alvarez **422 M 198 (96)**—info from arrestee that he bought drugs from apartment 1½ weeks earlier & 2 times before that not fatally stale because he said that 648 vials of crack cocaine seized from his person the day before warrant issued came from same apartment **and** time is of less significance when affidavit recites activity indicating "protracted or continuous conduct";

20-G.3. Nexus to Items or Crime

C v Couture **407 M 178 (90)**—civilian report that D seen with handgun in back pocket did not amount to probable cause that D had committed any crime;

C v Frazier **410 M 235 (91)**—corroborated innocent details from informant, suspicion that female D was involved in male co-D's drug dealing, D's association with co-D, & her denial of it, along with propinquity to D, did not amount to probable cause to justify search of her pocketbook;

C v Allard **37 MAC 676 (94)**—state trooper saw, from public road in front of D's house, garden containing marijuana plants; no need to establish reliability or basis of knowledge of citizen who "tipped" trooper; re: "scope", reasonable to infer that items relating to cultivation & distribution would be found in D's house & shed, D having prior drug convictions;

C v Monterosso **33 MAC 765 (92)**—landlord's report of odor of marijuana & volume of visitors making brief visits, D's prior drug convictions, plus police corroboration of odor trail was "marginal(ly)" sufficient to make out probable cause, at least where trouble taken to obtain warrant; informant "not an informant in the usual sense" because he had merely made controlled buys at behest of police; *C v Garden* **451 M 43 (2008)**—odor of burnt marijuana allowed search of car's occupants and passenger compartment, but not warrantless search of car trunk;

C v Watson **430 M 725 (2000)**—drug courier profile data critical to stop (upheld here) of car driven by man after he retrieved heavy suitcases from motel room of possible "courier"; additional factor was subject's driving in manner consistent with interest in detecting surveillance; implausible responses of the two men re: suitcases = "reasonable . . . to seize" the suitcases; men were not "seized" upon detention of the suitcases or during roadside questioning; search warrant was obtained, and SJC excused affidavit's assertion that dog named Maxie, well-trained in narcotics-sniffing, alerted to the luggage (different dog, "Roxy," was used, and this was taken to be merely a mistake of name, not a fatal omission about the relevant dog's qualifications); but cf. *C v Hooker* **52 MAC 683 (2001) fact that D looked back at car (unmarked vehicle with**

plainclothes cops) following taxi in which he was riding wasn't remarkable, particularly in high crime area; D shouldn't have been ordered out of car because police had no reasonable apprehension of danger;

C v Halsey **41 MAC 200 (96)**—during execution of search warrant for D's house and auto (D accused of child sexual assault), police permissibly seized pornographic videotapes, scrapbook with pornographic pictures, and photos/poster of nude persons: though not specified in warrant, they were "inadvertently discovered" and were seizable on test for "mere evidence" (1) plausibly related to proof of criminal activity of which officer was already aware and (2) useful to apprehend or convict culprit (cop testified to opinion that such pornography is often used "to initiate children into sexual activity");

C v Kaupp **453 M 102 (2009)**—OK to seize/"secure" D's computer pending issuance of search warrant given "ease with which computer files may be accessed and deleted" but warrant was necessary prior to forensic analysis of contents; suppression ordered as no probable cause to believe it contained child pornography: facts that it could have accessed some on a networked computer's open share and that D "could not guarantee" that there were no child porn images "stored in electronic format within his computer" did not provide "substantial basis" for believing them present; fn.18: SJC did not address whether child porn found in private files would have been in plain view while searching same files for copyrighted material for which there was probable cause;

C v Hawkins **361 M 384 (72)**—though OK search warrant for drugs, no probable cause to seize bonds;

C v Pierre **71 MAC 58 (2008)**—warrant to search apartment, the subject's car, and the subject's person, for drugs, drug paraphernalia, and documentation establishing control/custody of apartment provided authority to search locked storage locker in basement identified as "belonging to" specified apartment; OK to open boxes in locker and incriminating/unlawful nature of bootleg/copied compact discs found there was apparent (so plain view);

C v McDermott **448 M 750 (2007)**—warrant that authorizes a search for records "permits the seizure of computers and disks that electronically may hide and store such records"; "container" analogy used; after seizure of computers, a second warrant was obtained for search of the computers and disks, and SJC rejects claim that the search of such computers was overbroad (search of internet activity limited to "specific subject matters"); "[a]dvance approval for the particular methods to be used in the forensic examination of the computers and disks is not necessary"; here, "keyword search method resulted in a cursory inspection of only approximately 750 files out of the 100,000 files contained in the defendant's computer media";

C v Wedderburn **36 MAC 558 (94)**—no probable cause merely from dropping what appeared to be plastic bag (so immediate arrest and search of person bad, even though dropped/abandoned bag subsequently found to contain drugs packaged for sale);

C v Alabarces **12 MAC 958 (81)**—no probable cause from exchange "something" for $;

C v Santaliz **413 M 238 (92)**—observations by experienced cop of D-2 taking something from waistband, handing it to D-1, who walked over to taxicab which had just pulled over, & exchanged object for money which he then passed to D-2, was sufficient to make out probable cause; *C v Kennedy* **426 M 703 (98)** in "high crime/high drug" area, probable cause when man previously arrested for narcotics sales spoke with driver, left, returned with something, exchanged through car window for something;

C v Gant **51 MAC 314 (2001)**—exchange of "something" with woman in high crime area upheld as probable cause, though barely; at sight of police, woman dropped folded papers to ground, & D went inside bar; *C v Gomes* **453 M 506 (2009)**—D's displaying something in flat-open hand to another, and swallowing it upon seeing police = reasonable suspicion (but frisk not justified);

C v Albert **51 MAC 377 (2001)**—exchange of something through driver's side window = probable cause;

C v Kennedy **426 M 703 (98)**—probable cause from motorist stopping, man approaching/conversing/running away & returning, possible exchange through car window, all in "high crime area": stop of motorist and search OK, though SJC would "prefer more extended testimony on an officer's 'inferential process'";

C v Coronel **70 MAC 906 (2007)**—probable cause sufficient under *Kennedy* 426 M 703: call by female from pay phone, female and male in car followed white Toyota subsequently passing by slowly, both cars stopping after turning a corner, male going into Toyota for ten to fifteen seconds and emerging with something which he put into his coat pocket; Toyota known by officer to have been used identically in previous cocaine trafficking;

C v Dellinger **383 M 780 (81)**—criminal records, following UPS driver, & evasive answers not probable cause to search car;

C v Sampson **20 MAC 970 (85)**—talk to working bookie not probable cause;

C v Chavis **41 MAC 912 (96)**—within ½ hour of break, two men matching description of those fleeing by car the recent B&E scene, ID'd by car owner as having been using the car until ten minutes earlier = probable cause to arrest; square-type object in pocket seizable in "search incident to arrest," preventing destruction/concealing of evidence of the crime for which there is probable cause to arrest (i.e., search didn't have to be justified here as "weapons" search);

C v Sanna **424 M 92 (97)**—D's fingerprint at murder scene and cuts & scratches on hands & forehead = probable cause;

C v McCleery **345 M 151 (62)**—can't order D out of car after license/registration check (*see Chapter 20-M*);

Re: "all persons present" search authorization— *see Chapter 20-J*;

C v O'Connor **21 MAC 404 (86)**—sit in park lot & bend under dash not probable cause;

C v Benitez **37 MAC 722 (94)**—plastic baggie and placing it down pants front = probable cause;

C v Calderon **43 MAC 228 (97)**—probable cause to seize jewelry discovered in course of arrest of female and frisk of two companions (though housebreak in which items were stolen had not yet been reported), plus "strong likelihood" it "would be lost if not immediately seized";

C v Clermy **421 M 325 (95)**—probable cause to arrest/search D for narcotics violation after his arrest on default warrant and frisk yielded 3-inch brown prescription bottle from "genital area";

C v Garcia **34 MAC 645 (93)**—sighting of 1" by 1½ "baggie on car floor (seized to reveal "some sort of powder residue inside") is NOT probable cause to search vehicle, despite cop's testimony that baggies are often used for distribution of controlled substances;

C v Dolby **50 MAC 545 (2000)**—without 1st smelling, experienced trooper assessed, from outside of a car, that "residue" inside clear plastic "bong" on the car's rear passenger floor was marijuana, & therefore established probable cause; **Appeals Court asserted that there had been no challenge to the cop's "credibility" re: this;**

C v Skea **18 MAC 685 (84)**—without smell, trained cop can seize hand-rolled cigarette (with pinched end) from beside co-D in D's car; when asked, D asks for "a break," = probable cause to arrest D;

C v Henley **63 MAC 1 (2005)**—after legitimate determination to impound car & its trunk was opened for valid inventory search, odor of marijuana provided probable cause to believe contraband within, to arrest occupants, and to conduct investigatory search of car and contents;

C v Garden **451 M 43 (2008)**—odor of burnt marijuana on passengers' clothes allowed search of car's occupants and passenger compartment BUT NOT CAR TRUNK;

C v Lites **67 MAC 815 (2006)**—fresh odor of burnt marijuana from opened door of stopped car, PLUS passenger's furtive gestures at his waist area provided probable cause to arrest passenger;

C v Allain **36 MAC 595 (94)**—sight of four marijuana cigarettes in car ashtray = probable cause to arrest and search for marijuana and other controlled substances;

C v Crespo **59 MAC 927 (2003)**—**sight of substantial amount of white powder in plastic baggie on ground at vehicle crash scene gave probable cause to search nearby dark plastic bag and the rest of the vehicle; field of debris appearing to come from car may be regarded as part of the car for purposes of search;**

C v Paredes **35 MAC 666 (93)**—further info, acquired after obtaining warrants to search particular place and the persons of D and another, gave probable cause and exigency to stop D's car and seize/search her then;

20-G.4. Nexus to Place

C v Cefalo **381 M 319 (80)**—search warrant (vs. arrest warrant) probable cause must show items related to investigation are likely to be in the location;

C v Anthony **451 M 59 (2008)**—"expert" cop re: pedophiles/child pornographers asserted in search warrant affidavit that such persons keep and hide their pornography, so SJC holds sufficient nexus/probable cause for warrant to search storage locker rented by homeless D (under false name and invalid address), said by D's friend to own up to five laptop computers, and confirmed by computer repair company to own two which were being repaired there;

C v Cinelli **389 M 197 (83)**—arrest probable cause not necessarily home-search & seizure probable cause, but probable cause for warrant to search home re: armed robbery = probable cause for bullets, too;

C v McDermott **448 M 750 (2007)**—after D shot and killed seven people at workplace, probable cause existed to search residence for will (ostentatiously witnessed at work recently) and further firearms/ammunition; additionally, observations during permissible "sweep" of residence (justified by exigency) of firearms manual and ammunition supplied probable cause; seizure of documents related to mental state/functioning justified by D's conduct in aftermath of the shootings;

C v Chongarlides **52 MAC 366 (2001)**—affidavit supporting warrant to search a residence did not even properly allow inference it was D's residence (though D was found by police there on day after homicide); even if it did, no nexus between place at which V suffered fatal heroin overdose and this residence (person's guilt of a crime doesn't automatically = probable cause to search his residence); that D allegedly brought heroin to fatality site provided no reason to believe that, after 2 days of drug use by 3 persons, D still possessed drugs almost 3 days later;

C v Matias **440 M 787 (2004)**—informant info, supplemented by cop's investigation re: D's residence, plus info gained in search of trash, gave probable cause for the particular third floor apartment at address;

C v Rabb **70 MAC 194 (2007)**—info that D was seller's supplier and contacted D for additional drugs when supply ran out, plus walkie-talkie radio contact between the two, plus "contextual underpinning suggesting that" motel room was "likely" base for D's operations, established probable cause to search room;

C v Lodge **431 M 461 (2000)**—probable cause (& warrant) to search D's apartment for evidence of crime, including guns, ammo, expended bullets & casings, after D's girlfriend's dead body was found in apartment kitchen allowed search inside slight gap between circuit breaker box and wall surface behind apartment's refrigerator (gun found there), because within apartment's "curtilage," and not accessible/open to anyone other than tenant of this apartment; alternate ground = if not within curtilage, D didn't have standing to contest search of "common" area;

C v Pierre **71 MAC 58 (2008)**—relationship between apartment and its identified locked storage locker in basement to which access was not restricted met the cartilage test set out in *US v Dunn* 480 US 294 (1987); warrant to search D's brother's apartment, car, and person held to encompass storage locker and boxes within it;

C v Perez **76 MAC 439 (2010)**—search warrant for first-floor apartment of two-family dwelling held to cover freshly disturbed earth near side entrance to house, next to foundation and beneath first-floor window; cops dug and found cocaine packages;

C v Jean-Charles **398 M 752 (86)**—no probable cause for search warrant for doctor's office for records of patients (in phony accident-insurance scam);

C v Harmon **63 MAC 456, 461 (2005)**—probable cause to search apartment for gun, ammo, specifically-described clothing, blood, body fluids, hair, fibers, "and items containing traces of the above mentioned articles" found on the simple basis that witness said that she had dropped D and shooter near apartment building about 3 hours after shooting, & apartment resident acknowledged that the two had been inside apartment at that time: "probable" cause doesn't demand certainty, & fact that the two demonstrated trust in resident by seeking his help in getting transportation for purchase of tools of disguise, etc. was significant in finding "nexus"; probable cause buttressed by fact that "trace evidence" was likely on culprits as victim's head had been blown apart, likely dispersing much blood on those nearby;

C v Olivares **30 MAC 596 (91)**—**probable cause to search D's place of business based on controlled buy by informant didn't make out probable cause to search D's home,** even though D had been at home minutes before sale, because D had not been seen carrying anything from home to business;

C v Takvorian **75 MAC 836 (2009)**—after stop of car for expired license plate and D's statement that he was a chemist running business and lab out of his house selling performance products (to explain "vials and vial tops" in plain view inside plastic tote container in back seat), D also stated he had needles and drugs in the containers and prescriptions for them; told to remove them as cop did not want car towed with needles and drugs inside, D did so and cop observed bottles labeled in manner consistent with steroids and piece of mail with specific address; simultaneous inventory search revealed Oxycontin pills and hypodermic needles in front seat area: held: sufficient probable cause for warrant to search D's residence because G.L. c. 112, § 30 says illegal for anyone except pharmacist to dispense . . . ANY substance intended for hypodermic use; both the piece of mail and D's license specified residence location;

C v Stegemann **68 MAC 292 (2007)**—warrant application did not establish probable cause to believe that drugs were at D's residence, even as it established abundant cause to arrest D; fact that D stopped at home "—once, and then only *after* making a sale" failed to do so, as did assertion that once upon a time D "cook[ed] a large quantity of cocaine" (basis of knowledge, as well as date, utterly absent);

C v O'Day **440 M 296 (2003)**—although controlled buys and apparent drug sales were made only at bar where D worked, other facts gave probable cause to search his home as well (pattern of short visits at home, fact that drug supply seemed to be conveyed in truck from home to bar, etc.);

C v Smith **57 MAC 907 (2003)**—affidavit didn't supply probable cause to search D's home even though D was seen driving to his home after one controlled buy, and from his home directly to another controlled buy;

C v Pina **453 M 438 (2009)**—that D drove from apartment to site of sale of cocaine to informant, on one occasion did not provide basis for probable cause three days later for search warrant for apartment;

C v Medina **453 M 1011 (2009)**—that D drove from apartment to prearranged location where he sold cocaine and then drove back to apartment did not establish probable cause to search apartment;

C v Rodriguez **75 MAC 290 (2009)**—on one occasion D was observed going from apartment directly to sale and on another occasion, observed going from sale directly to apartment; purports to distinguish *Pina* and *Smith*, AND says there was probable cause to search D's apartment for items listed on warrant application other than cocaine, e.g., telephone records tying D to telephone number used by informant; magistrate "could infer that [D] kept business records" and most likely storage was in residence;

C v Turner **71 MAC 665 (2008)**—even if affidavit didn't supply probable cause to believe drugs were kept in D's residence, there was probable cause to search for "monies derived from the sale of illegal drugs," because controlled buys had used money whose serial numbers had been recorded and after each of three buys D went directly to his residence, "the last time within 72 hours of the affidavit"; if warrant to be considered invalid re: drugs ("a question we do not address"), Court opines that drugs were in plain view during permissible search for money, and if D disagrees, should on remand seek hearing on this issue (id. at 670);;*C v Luthy* **69 MAC 102 (2007)**—Appeals Court finds probable cause that D's home contained drugs, despite observation only once that D drove from there to prearranged sale; AFTER other controlled buy, D was observed to return to the home (but no observations as to where he had been before that first controlled buy);

C v Wade **64 MAC 648 (2005)**—that D twice drove from a residence in a green car to deliver drugs to informant did not give probable cause to search the green car on basis of warrant issued the day after the second delivery, and executed four days after issuance; warrant contained no basis to infer that drugs would be present at time of issuance of warrant or at time of execution; *C v Burt* 393 M 703 (85) distinguished;

C v Hardy **63 MAC 210 (2005)**—unlike in *Smith* **57 MAC 907**, here, D was observed at two controlled buys and over a month-long period of surveillance driving directly from home to drug transactions & then back home; his method was to deliver the drugs away from apartment, but inference was that he kept the drugs within residence;

C v Gallagher **68 MAC 56 (2007)**—similar to *Hardy*;

C v Cruz **430 M 838 (2000)**—though D argued that warrant application failed to show probable cause for apartment unless executed after routine delivery of drugs there by specific vehicle, or probable cause for vehicle unless executed during transport of drugs to apartment, SJC seemingly ignored latter argument, and held probable cause existed in apartment apart from vehicle's deliveries, albeit for lesser quantities of drugs;

C v Baldasaro **62 MAC 925 (2004)**—Appeals Court asserts that SJC in *Cruz* **430 M 842 n.2** and *O'Day* **440 M at 302** laid to rest argument that controlled buy isn't adequate to establish probable cause, but acknowledges that here, it served to corroborate info previously supplied by informants;

C v White **374 M 132 (77)**—OUI & marijuana cigarette not probable cause to search car trunk (*see Chapter 20-L*); see also *C v Garden* **451 M 43 (2008)**—odor of burnt marijuana on passengers allowed search of passengers and passenger compartment, but not car trunk;

C v Toole **389 M 159 (83)**—(*Chapter 20-H*) no probable cause there's contraband/weapon in car after D's arrest;

C v Peterson **61 MAC 632 (2004)**—probable cause (supporting warrant) there are weapons in D's residence after he wielded gun in unsuccessful attempt (at other location) to evade arrest as fugitive from justice, given info from law enforcement officer (D's brother-in-law) that D always talked about having guns, & info from D's sister and mother that he "always" had guns;

C v Amendola **26 MAC 713 (88)**—no probable cause re: car #2 after arrest/search/seizure at car #1;

C v Rodriguez **49 MAC 664 (2000)**—**warrant to search particular apartment included cellar storage area "associated with" apartment;** that cellar couldn't be entered via street address of apartment, but was instead reachable only via a different address, didn't matter because cellar underlay the single building which comprised both street addresses; "no reasonable probability that another premises might be mistakenly searched";

20-G.5. Informant's Tip: Reliability Prong

Aguilar v Texas **378 US 108 (64)**—two-prong test re: informant probable cause—his/her credibility & the basis of his/her knowledge; (*See also Spinelli v US* **393 US 410 (69)** & *US v Harris* **403 US 573 (71)**); this construction of **federal constitution** requirements was **overruled by**

Illinois v Gates **462 US 213 (83)**—"total circumstances," rather than the "2 prongs"; **BUT in Massachusetts, still, SEE . . .** *C v Upton* **394 M 363 (85)** Mass. Declaration of Rights, Article 14 still uses Aguilar tests;

here, no probable cause under G.L. c. 276, § 2B (*See Chapter 20-F*);

C v DiPietro **35 MAC 683 (93)**—thorny issue when state prosecution is based on drugs seized pursuant to federal warrant (issued under federal *Illinois v Gates* standard rather than *Aguilar-Spinelli/Rojas* **403 M 483 (88)** standard);

C v Vazquez **426 M 99 (97)**—several citizens on street pointed to D, said "gun" and "armed assault", D next standing by open window of car, which pulled away, and no gun found on D = probable cause to stop and search car for gun;

Florida v J.L. **529 US 266 (2000)**—anonymous telephone tip reporting that gun was being carried by young black male wearing plaid shirt and standing at particular bus stop: no reasonable suspicion for frisk, and Supreme Court explicitly **declines to adopt** *Terry v Ohio* **"firearm exception"**;

C v Atchue **393 M 343 (84)**—named fink more reliable, but not conclusive (even if participant); probable cause here, especially with corroboration;

C v Saleh **396 M 406 (85)**—unnamed fink & conclusory reliability not probable cause (fn.6); but led to 3 prior arrests is;

C v Bowden **379 M 472 (80)**—ordinary citizen/witness more reliable *than "informant"; (see K. Smith, Criminal* Practice & Procedure, § 120 (2d ed. 1983 & Supp.)); (but see *Rojas* **403 M 483 (88)** below);

C v Billups **13 MAC 963 (82)**—(same) for (alleged) victim;

C v Zorn **66 MAC 228 (2006)**—though D complained that affiant for search warrant application used only "totem pole hearsay," the source in each of two "chains" of information (one via family therapist, one via child's mother to DSS intake) was "the victim" herself, i.e., eight-year-old complaining of sexual abuse by her grandfather: probable cause found;

C v Rabb **70 MAC 194 (2007)**—**may infer basis of knowledge from affidavit assertions;**

C v Mubdi **456 M 385 (2010)**—though could infer from level of particularity that anonymous 911 caller had directly seen individuals in particular car at particular location within previous 15 minutes, veracity of caller's allegation of possible firearm was not shown or inferable; police confirmed only innocent facts of presence of car and two black males; "high crime" nature of area "did not materially bolster the reliability of the caller's information";

C v Alvarado **427 M 277 (98)**—source of info re what seemed to be sawed-off shotgun was an "identified and disinterested" paramedic on duty;

C v Butterfield **44 MAC 926 (98)**—named resident's report of mailboxes struck by black Ford Bronco, corroborated by cop's timely sighting of such car on street named = reasonable suspicion to support stop;

C v Love **56 MAC 229 (2002)**—tipster presenting self at state police barracks reporting dangerous operation of identified car wasn't asked his identity, but desk officer wrote down his license plate number as he left: tipster

NOT treated as anonymous, subject to greater scrutiny (though he would have been if refused to ID self or if didn't present self in person); *C v Costa* **448 M 510 (2007)**—informant placed her anonymity at risk (call was being recorded and number she was calling from had been identified) even though she was anxious to terminate call and didn't leave her name: SJC believes she was concerned about D, not the police, knowing her identity if she were to be observed on cell phone;

C v Campbell **69 MAC 212 (2007)**—although there was no evidence to support inference that callers were known or identifiable to police by means of caller ID, voice recording, or other method, Commonwealth compensated for this by corroborating details of broadcast ("immediate danger to public safety," man in bar with gun, gunshots heard, quick arrival of police who saw vehicle "similar in type" and matching color and plate number supplied: investigatory stop upheld;

C v Harmon **63 MAC 456, 461 n.4 (2005)** (citation omitted)—"persons who supply information only after being interviewed by police officers, or who give information as witnesses during the course of an investigation, are not informers";

C v Rojas **403 M 483 (88)**—**anonymous "concerned CITIZEN" = like informant (not an ID'd citizen/victim)** (fn.2); fink whose info had "led to 1 (named) **arrest**" not shown reliable without prior arrest/info details (e.g., ensuing conviction, or particular contraband seized during arrest); (& Mass. precedents re: prior arrests were all **corroborated** tips (fn.5)); 2 tips not detailed enough corroboration to replace veracity, nor for mutual corroboration; **"arrests," without assertion of "convictions"/drugs seized, as result of informant's info, insufficient to establish reliability;**

C v Soto **35 MAC 340 (93)**—in contrast to Rojas information re: mere "arrest," this cited info resulted in some formal probable cause determination because target was "awaiting trial," but really police corroboration made up for deficiency in "reliability" prong;

C v Ilges **64 MAC 503 (2005)**—two confidential informants held to have provided info with sufficiently "interlocking detail" to make up for lack of "veracity" in either alone; for each case of "interlocking detail", "analysis reduces to the standard of 'I know it when I see it'" (id. at 511); police investigation here corroborated details as possible;

C v Motta **34 MAC 921 (93)**—that informant gave info for prior arrests not enough, and insufficient corroboration because all info could be obtained by "uninformed bystander";

C v Santana **411 M 661 (92)**—information that prior tips by informant lead to 2 **arrests** not enough to make out reliability, even though current tip corroborated by 2 anonymous tips over police hotline;

C v Mejia **411 M 108 (91)**—same; information that prior tips by informant lead to 3 arrests not enough;

C v Perez-Baez **410 M 43 (91)**—information that prior tip by informant lead to arrest **& seizure of drugs** established informant's reliability;

C v Lapine **410 M 38 (91)**—information that prior tip by informant resulted in arrests & that details about presence & amount of drugs & description of house "proved reliable" established informant's reliability;

C v Willis **415 M 814 (93)**—unnamed informant's info, passed along to Boston police via teletype from Flint, Michigan police, held **sufficient because so detailed** & Boston police "corroborated" by merely saying D was as described;

C v Oliveira **35 MAC 645 (93)**—rejecting claim that veracity was "self-proved" because of amount of detail provided, quoting Pooh-Bah in "The Mikado ("detail, intended to give artistic verisimilitude to an otherwise bald & unconvincing narrative"); **fabrication "in fine detail" is as easy "as with rough brush strokes";**

See Chapter 20-J and Chapter 6 re: Discovery of Informant's ID & Franks hearings;

C v Grinkley **44 MAC 62 (97)**—**telephone tipster's giving of her alleged name, even with specified police corroboration not enough for reliability:** no telephone # left, and alleged street address did not exist, plus significant details of the tip proved unreliable;

C v Rosenthal **52 MAC 707 (2001)**—**fact that trooper knew informant's identity did not make him reliable;**

C v Alfonso A **438 M 372 (2003)**—police knowledge of informant's identity and whereabouts not alone enough to establish reliability, but is "factor" weighing in that direction; further, police corroborated significant "details";

C v Rodriguez **75 MAC 290 (2009)**—that police know who informant is distinguishes such informant from anonymous one, factor toward reliability; that cop/affiant did not provide info as to case name and docket number allegedly founded upon informant's past efforts permitted "subtraction" from supportive info; better practice is to include identification of prior prosecution, unless circumstances threaten exposure of informant, which should be asserted as explanation for omission;

C v Barros **49 MAC 613 (2000)**—"white, well-dressed, middle-aged man" in pickup truck (who didn't want to ID self) motioned cop to stop & told cop he'd just seen someone (described by height, skin, & clothes, at location of two streets) pull gun from waistband & show it to friends before returning it to waist; 8 minutes later, cop yelled to D, said he wanted to speak, but D kept walking & stopped only at 2d command, after arrival of backup cops & 1st cop's exit from cruiser; seizure here occurred prior to D's moving hands toward waistband area, so suppression of gun was ordered because **"report that someone is carrying a gun does not by itself constitute reasonable suspicion to conduct a stop & frisk of that individual";** if seizure occurred instead after hand movement, no suppression because 'frisk' would have been warranted, at gunpoint (as occurred) if necessary to ensure cop's safety; cc opinion suggested that if suspect looked younger than

21 years old, reasonable suspicion existed (G.L. c. 140, § 131 prohibits person under 21 from being licensed to carry firearm); no recognition of any issue re: deficiency in tipster's reliability/veracity; **S.C. 435 M 171, 176–77 (2001) face-to-face anonymous informants are to be treated no differently from unnamed anonymous telephone callers (5 of 7 justices agree); must still analyze reliability and basis of knowledge,** for probable cause finding; **"corroboration" that informant had indeed described a nearby person didn't make tip reliable;** even if info = reliable, D's possession of handgun didn't give cop reasonable suspicion of illegality; suggestions that Commonwealth argue that D looked to be under-age for firearm licensing (now, minimum age 21) and/or that cop approach and demand either showing of gun license or forfeiture of gun (as per G.L. c. 140, § 129C); BUT SEE

C v Costa **448 M 510 (2007)**—by providing info to police after knowing that her call was being recorded and that the number she was calling from was identified, caller placed anonymity sufficiently at risk that her reliability should have been accorded greater weight than that of anonymous informant; caller was principally concerned about D, not police, knowing her identity "if she were to be observed on the cell phone"; purports to distinguish *Florida v J.L.* 529 US 266, 274 (2000); reasonable suspicion for frisk found (basis of knowledge appeared within tip, i.e., personal observation of handgun when standing near D);

C v Monteiro **75 MAC 280 (2009)**—(reasonable suspicion case, for frisk, based on tip) high school student told teacher that he'd seen particularly described student with gun this day; student's identity was known, favoring his veracity (D did not contest veracity/reliability here, id. n.2); 'reasonable suspicion' of crime because D was 17, not old enough to be licensed for possessing firearm;

C v Grinkley **44 MAC 62, 69 (97)**—**"It does not follow that if the name of the person providing the information is disclosed, then he is by virtue of that fact alone properly characterized as a citizen-informer, entitled to the presumption of reliability,"** though is a "factor" to consider;

C v Va Meng Jo **425 M 99 (97)**—tipster was reachable by INS agent and this, with corroboration and specificity of tip, = enough for reliability;

C v Bottari **395 M 777 (85)**—led to 1 prior G. = reliable, but no basis for tip (that D with gun, specific place & car) & no corroboration except (less helpful) innocent details;

C v Borges **395 M 788 (85)**—pedestrian-stranger says D in bar dealing, not probable cause without reliability; corroboration (though infer personal knowledge) from clothes-match not enough;

C v Distefano **22 MAC 535 (86)**—unnamed/untested fink, but reliability OK because cops' stakeout corroborated;

C v Saleh **396 M 406 (85)**—reliable fink who'd negotiated drug sale, but no basis for belief drugs in D's apartment; but cops corroborated;

C v Crawford **410 M 75 (91)**—where credibility of cop's assertion that informant's prior tip led to arrests & drug seizure was necessary to justify warrantless search, D entitled to in camera hearing for names of arrestees; remanded for hearing at which counsel may not be excluded; **S.C., 417 M 40 (94)** but SJC later rewarded prosecutor's obstinance upon motion judge's finding that **cop** was "credible" in claiming, without specifics, that informant was reliable; **dissent (Liacos, C.J.) understands that issue is not veracity of officer, but veracity of informant, & "bald assertion" of cop is not sufficient;**

20-G.6. Statements Against "Penal Interest" as Reliable (or Not)

C v Allen **406 M 575 (90)**—anonymous informant's statement that he bought & used drugs doesn't contribute to his reliability as statement against penal interest because his name was unknown to police; nor did D's 4-year-old marijuana conviction contribute to reliability of informant's information;

C v Watson **36 MAC 252 (94)**—informant's assertion that he has bought drugs from target is not "reliable" as statement against penal interest because "no reason to believe that this anonymous informant would realistically have feared prosecution for the offense";

C v Melendez **407 M 53 (90)**—informant's statement that he bought & used drugs did not contribute to his reliability as statement against penal interest because it was not corroborated by physical evidence & informant not in "reasonable fear of prosecution"; D's prior conviction for possession didn't contribute to reliability;

C v Muse **45 MAC 813 (98)**—grandmother immediately told police her grandson (informant) had stolen her jewelry, police arrested/interrogated him within a day & he gave very specific descriptive info of where he'd bought drugs with theft proceeds & from whom; his veracity OK because against penal interest in larceny crime despite D's argument that grandson—informant's statement was not against penal interest re: **narcotics** offense (uncorroborated confession);

C v Parapar **404 M 319 (89)**—informant's statements admitting to illegal trafficking immediately after arrest for undercover sale to cop did contribute to reliability of information as statement against penal interest;

C v Simpson **442 M 1009 (2004)**—after woman outside bar volunteered to obtain cocaine for undercover officer, and told him she'd get it from black male playing pool inside bar, and thereafter delivered the cocaine, her further statement with more detailed description, made after immediate questioning by identifiable cops, held to be statement against penal interest, sufficient for "reasonable suspicion";

C v Alvarez **422 M 198 (96)**—similar, while noting that arrestee was a **named** informant;

20-G.7. Informant's Tip: Basis of Knowledge Prong

C v Spence 403 M 179 (88)—reliable fink without basis not corroborated enough; But see *C v Robinson, Santana, Gonzalez, Farrow*, 403 M 163, 167, 172, 176 (88)

C v Ruiz 51 MAC 346 (2001)—**rejecting Aguilar-Spinelli applicability, because callers "appear to have been eyewitnesses," making "citizen reports of ongoing suspicious activity and criminality"**;

C v Cox 56 MAC 907 (2002)—cop may stop car for motor vehicle violation based solely on report from motorist IF motorist is reliable informant with personal knowledge; radio dispatch, followed by cop locating target car, and seeing driver following behind, gesturing to cop by pointing at the car and continually flashing lights on and off; not "faceless" informant, but willing to identify herself;

C v Bakoian 412 M 295 (92)—informant tip giving specific, non-obvious & predictive information established reliability & basis of knowledge sufficient to make out probable cause that car contained heroin; *Lyons* 409 M 16 (90) distinguished (Aguilar-Spinelli test used to determine whether informant tips amount to reasonable suspicion under Article 14; **here, tip by anonymous informant about males traveling in described car did not give sufficiently specific, non-obvious & predictive information to make out basis of knowledge**;

C v Avalo 37 MAC 904 (94)—reliable informant's tip that blonde "Dominican" female, 5'5"–5'8" tall, would arrive at location in 20 minutes to deliver cocaine, which would be carried in a false-bottomed container, lacked sufficient corroboration to make up for absence of basis of knowledge (despite arrival of blonde 5'5"–5'8" woman, with Hispanic male, in 15 minutes, of whom cop "requested" ID & then "plain-viewed" in woman's purse a metal aerosol spray container of window cleaner, seized to reveal a false bottom: **CORROBORATION OF INNOCUOUS DETAILS IN UNSUSPICIOUS CIRCUMSTANCES** were insufficient to support probable cause;

C v Lubiejewski 49 MAC 212, 214 (2000)—same, re "reasonable suspicion" for vehicle stop; **"anyone can telephone the police for any reason"; police corroboration was re: only easily obtainable obvious details** re particular vehicle;

C v Mubdi 456 M 385 (2010)—police radio dispatch referred to info conveyed by anonymous 911 caller: two black males in blue Dodge Charger, specific license plate numbers, observed 15 minutes earlier at particular address, observed money and object being passed, "believed to be a firearm"; patrol car found the car and individuals near cited location, with a third individual leaning into door and speaking, but leaving when saw cops; though 'personal knowledge'/viewing by caller could be inferred, veracity could not be established re: firearm (notwithstanding "high crime" area, or that shots fired in area night before); suppression of marijuana found in car search AFTER individuals were hauled out of car with drawn gun, frisked, cuffed, and placed in cruiser (no weapons or drugs found in frisks);

C v Davis 63 MAC 88, 91 (2005)—has different result BECAUSE info alleged intoxication, "present[ing] a grave danger to the public";

C v Byfield 413 M 426, **reversing** 32 MAC 912 (92)—informant tip about personally observing purchase of a "forty" at drug house sufficient to establish basis of knowledge;

C v Rodriguez 49 MAC 664 (2000)—though D argued that informant's assertion that he had seen, once, unspecified amount of heroin in D's apartment didn't establish basis of knowledge for claim that D was presently and previously "dealing" heroin, court ignored distinction, said 'personal knowledge';

C v Brown 31 MAC 574 (91)—informant's tip as to D's name, physical appearance, age, mode of travel, & time & place of arrival, **despite corroboration of most details, was not sufficient to establish basis of knowledge**;

C v Washington 39 MAC 195 (95)—corroboration of tip made up for absence of basis of knowledge prong;

C v Powers 39 MAC 911 (95)—same; *C v O'Brien* 30 MAC 807 (91)—informant's conclusory tip didn't establish basis of knowledge;

C v Fleming 37 MAC 927 (94)—"first-hand," direct knowledge of drug transaction was implicit in informant's claim that he was the intended recipient of drug delivery at specific time & place, via specifically described individual;

20-G.8. Informant's Tip: Independent Corroboration

C v Filippidakis 29 MAC 679 (91)—independent police corroboration of information about informant's prior tips leading to arrests for matters under investigation which were not generally known was sufficient to cure defects in reliability prong;

C v Campbell 69 MAC 212 (2007)—police corroboration of identified car in vicinity made up for lack of reliability showing concerning anonymous phone tipsters (gun in bar, shots fired);

C v Tshudy 34 MAC 955 (93)—"2d-hand" basis of knowledge excused (informant said he placed order with street dealer & paid cash, & that street dealer went to D's residence for drugs & delivered to informant) because cops corroborated this sequence via informant's controlled buy; *Kuszewski* 385 M 802 (82) & *Allen* 406 M 575 (90) distinguished (no controlled buys there);

C v Hall 50 MAC 208 (2000)—basis of knowledge lacking (because informant was present and heard only street-level dealer's side of telephone conversation, purportedly with D, concerning delivery of drugs, & dealer then told informant), but police corroboration of D's arrival in described vehicle at time & place predicted = reasonable suspicion, elevated to probable cause by D's flight and throwing of object (66 g. cocaine);

C v Dasilva **66 MAC 556 (2006)**—seizure occurred when cop began chasing D and ordered D to stop, but court found reasonable suspicion (corroboration of appearance of two men at place noted by 3rd hand anonymous source, plus D's evasion and placing hand at waistband, "indicative of the presence of a gun", plus pending gun and assault charges against D);

C v Gates **31 MAC 328 (91)**—independent police corroboration that D associated with known drug dealers was sufficient to cure defects in informant's tip that, 3 days earlier, associate of D had offered to sell him cocaine;

C v Villela **39 MAC 426 (95)**—informant of no established reliability arranged for another person to make controlled buy: despite no search of that person prior to buy, OK, because he was "under police surveillance during the buy";

C v Luna **410 M 131 (91)**—controlled buy provides probable cause for warrant, but not "standing alone"?—but see *C v Carrasquiello* **45 MAC 772, 777 n.7 (98)** controlled buy, in MA, has been treated as "corroboration of the informant's reliability";

C v Desper **419 M 163 (94)**—controlled buy, by informant whose reliability/veracity was not established, was sufficient for probable cause despite no mention of police search/pat down beforehand & despite no cop supervision after informant entered multi-unit apartment building; nonetheless, **at *minimum*, controlled buy should entail police search of informant & close physical supervision to ensure informant's veracity;**

C v Warren **418 M 86 (94)**—inadequate monitoring of controlled buy (i.e., close supervision/verification of **which** apartment entered) excused on ground that "police may consider the safety of the officers & the informant";

C v Figueroa **74 MAC 784 (2009)**—reliability of first-time informant lacking, but two controlled buys compensated for this; that police did not see which apartment inside multi-unit building informant entered to make buys was excused; that building contained "only a small number of units" = material to this holding, plus info was corroborated by neighbors' complaints of heavy traffic to and from 3rd floor, consistent with drug activity;

C v Richardson **37 MAC 482 (94)**—though prior information led only to "arrests" ("convictions"/drug seizures not noted: see *Rojas* **403 M 483 (88)**), controlled buy made up for deficiency (though reservations expressed about (lack of) police supervision re: controlled buy);

C v Brown **31 MAC 574 (91)**—although cops independently corroborated accuracy of informant's tip as to D's name, physical appearance, age, mode of travel, & time & place of arrival, informant failed to describe particulars of D's clothing or that he'd be carrying maroon shoulder bag; corroboration here insufficient to cure defects in basis of knowledge prong; details all "innocuous"; level of particularity failed to meet *Draper v US* **358 US 307 (1959)**;

C v Ramon **31 MAC 963 (92)**—independent corroboration of arrival of 3 in car of given description & license

number as predicted, coupled with "highly suspicious activity" involving exchange of money in parking lot, was sufficient to overcome defects in other 2 prongs;

C v Welch **420 M 646 (95)**—corroboration of arrival of named & described D in car as described at a Cambridge corner (car registered to the named D) made up for defects in both prongs; level of detail cited as basis for inferring "direct knowledge" & fact that police knew name & address or telephone # of informant said to "bolster" reliability; but see *C v Lubiejewski* **49 MAC 212 (2000)** unknown motorist's tip didn't give rise to reasonable suspicion for stop because police corroborated only existence of described car at location given; corroboration of only obvious details, easily obtainable by anyone, and "anyone can telephone the police for any reason";

C v Redd **50 MAC 904 (2000)**—anonymous telephone caller, purportedly worker at hospital, told police dispatcher that silver Chevrolet with specified plate # was stolen from hospital site by Hispanic male in his 20s wearing white bandana, blue jeans, & jacket; responding detectives who had also heard radio that car was abandoned 2 blocks from hospital had reasonable suspicion (enough corroboration) for stopping 2 "dark skinned males" in mid- to late 20s, one wearing white bandana & maybe blue jeans, walking on street less than block away from abandoned car & getting into cab, & moving to put something onto cab floor;

C v Butterfield **44 MAC 926 (98)**—police corroboration helpful for reasonable suspicion supporting "stop";

Florida v J.L. **529 US 266 (2000)**—anonymous telephone tip reporting that gun was being carried by young black male wearing plaid shirt and standing at particular bus stop: though police corroborated described male's presence there, no reasonable suspicion for frisk, and Supreme Court explicitly declines to adopt *Terry v Ohio* "firearm exception"; see above, *C v Barros* **435 M 171, 176–77 (2001)**;

C v Va Meng Jo **425 M 99 (97)**—police corroboration of D's arrival, as predicted, alone & in specified auto, & purportedly suspicious conduct consistent with drug delivery as planned, enough for probable cause given specificity of tip (& fact that tipster was "known" to/reachable by INS agent);

C v Alfonzo A. **438 M 372 (2003)**—affidavit provided probable cause: informant's identity & whereabouts were known to police, police corroborated much info, informant had personal knowledge & gave extensive detail;

C v Mebane **33 MAC 941 (92)**—independent police corroboration of descriptive details of man arriving at train station at specified time coupled with D's statement that he was heading to site of recent drug raid, & strange comment that "all he knew" was that box he was carrying contained cellular telephone, was sufficient to overcome defects in basis of knowledge prong;

C v Russell **46 MAC 513 (99)—though not one of the 5 unnamed informants' bases of knowledge and veracity was established, court found probable cause**

from their "mutual" corroboration and some independent police corroboration;

C v Triantafillakos **33 MAC 949 (92)**—independent police corroboration of descriptive details of man arriving with bag at 1 of 2 specified locations at specified time in taxi with registration number 677 was sufficient to make up deficiencies in other prongs;

C v Rosario **37 MAC 920 (94)**—though one informant was previously reliable, the **other** informant (no record of reliability) was the one giving info about particular transaction expected to occur "at any minute" (& his basis of knowledge was a **3d** person of unstated veracity): probable cause found because of wealth of specific detail and police corroboration;

C v Spano **414 M 178 (93)**—independent police investigation including controlled buy, record check confirming that D had history of drug dealing & observations of known drug users visiting premises sufficient to confirm informant's reliability;

C v Reyes **423 M 568 (96)**—veracity of informant not shown and purported police corroboration (reference to "information received in the past" from unspecified persons, claimed personal knowledge that apartment lessor had made cocaine sales in the past, insufficient; and that D had attempted to retrieve from police the car of a drug arrestee in the past) insufficient;

C v Bottari **395 M 777 (85)**—led to 1 prior G. = reliable, but no basis for tip (that D with gun, specific place & car) & no corroboration except (less helpful) innocent details;

C v Borges **395 M 788 (85)**—pedestrian-stranger says D in bar dealing, not probable cause without reliability; corroboration (though infer personal knowledge) from clothes-match not enough;

C v Distefano **22 MAC 535 (86)**—unnamed/untested fink, but reliability OK because cops' stakeout corroborated;

C v Saleh **396 M 406 (85)**—reliable fink who'd negotiated drug sale, but no basis for belief drugs in D's apartment; but cops corroborated;

20-H. ARREST, SEARCH INCIDENT, BOOKING, INVENTORY, AND BODY SEARCHES

20-H.1. Arrest

Re: authority to arrest (citizen, extraterritorial, etc.), see also Chapter 3;

Atwater v City of Lago Vista **532 US 318 (2001)**—officer may arrest even for most minor of offenses without violating Fourth Amendment as long as there is probable cause to believe that person committed such criminal offense in officer's presence; only if arrest is made "in an extraordinary manner, unusually harmful to (individual's) privacy or even physical interests" is arrest unreasonable and thus actionable under civil rights statute, 42 USC § 1983; arrest, separation from children, handcuffing, mug shots, removal of shoes, eyeglasses, etc., placed in cell, for driving without seat belt and not securing children in seatbelts not extraordinary, just normal "humiliation," embarrassment, & inconvenience(!);

Virginia v Moore **128 S Ct 1598 (2008)**—rather than issuing summons required by state law, police arrested D for misdemeanor of driving on suspended license, and search incident to arrest yielded crack cocaine: S Ct refuses to "incorporate" state law arrest limitations into Constitution, holding that warrantless arrests for crimes committed in presence of arresting officer are reasonable under Fourth Amendment, and search incident to safeguard evidence and assure safety = permissible;

C v Swanson **56 MAC 459 (2002)**—when police passed D's room (on their way to arrest person in different room in rooming house), they observed razor blade and plate on bed and that room was smoky; order to D not to leave room was a seizure without even reasonable suspicion of crime; subsequent police observation of D throwing something into closet was product of illegal seizure and couldn't justify entry and search;

Brendlin v California **127 S. Ct. 2400 (2007)**—when cops stopped car for no good reason, passenger would not have felt free to leave, either, so has Fourth Amendment right to challenge; traffic stop is constitutional seizure of all occupants of car;

C v Knight **75 MAC 735 (2009)**—citing *C v Ocasio* 71 MAC 304, 306, 311 (2008) & *C v Katykhin* 59 MAC 262 (2003), "arrest" wasn't "complete" when D was ordered out of car or even when he was handcuffed (so that "resisting arrest" conviction was upheld on basis of behavior occurring until he was placed in cruiser);

C v Molina **439 M 206 (2003)**—though complainant's accusations of rape gave probable cause, warrantless entry into dwelling to arrest D (who opened door in response to police knock, but police immediately stepped inside threshold and subsequently made observations and seizures which D sought to suppress) could be justified only upon proof of exigent circumstances; here, "[b]ecause the very entry itself was unlawful, we need not address the propriety of the subsequent march from room to room as it pertains to admissibility of observations and statements"; contrast *C v Duarte* 56 MAC 714 (2002) (probable cause with exigent circumstances justified entry of dwelling to arrest D, who had raped complainant at knifepoint 45 minutes earlier and, because she knew him, there was danger he would flee);

C v Morrissey **422 M 1 (96)**—cop from neighboring town assisting in town A, at request of police in town A, stopping motorist in town A = OK; G.L. c. 268, § 24 decrees that **anyone** may be directed/required "in the name of the Commonwealth" to assist police officer in the performance of his duties (& failure/refusal to do so = crime);

C v Savage **430 M 341 (99)**—Vermont state trooper receiving info from civilian that car with Mass. plates was being driven "all over the road" at great speed southbound on I-91 could not stop that car in MA (he'd radioed Mass. police, but was told no Mass. troopers were in immediate area); G.L. c. 276, § 10A empowers officer of another state to arrest suspected felon in MA only if in "fresh pursuit," but this condition not here met because Vermont trooper didn't personally observe any illegal conduct of D in Vermont; further, OUI = misdemeanor, not felony (so no "citizen's arrest" OK either);

C v Magazu **48 MAC 466 (2000)**—Whitman police officer in E. Bridgewater observed erratic driving suggesting OUI, and followed D into Whitman, and then onto a private driveway which was across a town line, into Hanson; G.L. c. 41, § 98A authorized pursuit from Whitman into Hanson for arrestable offense; fact that cop didn't activate siren or lights didn't negate "pursuit"; (*re: "Arrest" (vs. Investigatory "Stop"), see Chapter 20-M below*);

K. Smith, *Criminal Practice & Procedure*, **§§ 238– 48 (2d ed. 1983 & Supp.)**—search incident to arrest: arrest must be lawful, not pretext (e.g., long delayed arrest, lie in wait for minor motor vehicle case); broader (e.g., home) search than normal; G.L. c. 276, § 1 limiting searches incident to arrest probably a result of Robinson; "plain view" (vs. Chimel) search/seizure must be "inadvertent" unless per se illegal/dangerous; scope; must be contemporaneous in time/place; car inventory scope (§ 273)— containers depend on circumstances;

See Chapter 20-I below re: plain view, including during/after search incident to arrest;

C v Baez **42 MAC 565 (97)**—deputy sheriff can arrest only for crimes involving breach of peace (G.L. c. 90, § 21); bad arrest here for operating after revocation (discovered after stop for defective headlight);

C v Vaidulas **433 M 247 (2001)**—fact that cop had not undergone the training required by G.L. c. 41, § 96B "prior to exercising police powers" was not a ground for suppressing fruits of a civil infraction car stop (i.e., evidence of operating under influence), but can use to impeach;

C v St. Hilaire **43 MAC 743 (97)—fact that D was handcuffed did not negate "protective custody"**; evidence supported implicit finding that D was "incapacitated" (G.L. c. 111B, § 3), overriding his right to refuse all treatment; while protective custody is a "seizure in the constitutional sense, it was not an arrest", medical dr., not police, ordered blood test "only for medical reasons," & cops holding D down did not alter this conclusion;

G.L. c. 111 B, § 8, Protective Custody—& right to frisk (*see Chapter 3-C*);

C v O'Connor **406 M 112 (89)**—invalid protective custody search cured by inevitable discovery during booking inventory;

20-H.2. Search Incident to Arrest

G.L. c. 276, § 1 (*see Chapter 20-F*)—Mass. search incident to arrest limited to evidence of the arrest crime, or weapons D might use;

C v Desources **74 MAC 232 (2009)**—but G.L. c. 276, § 1 doesn't prohibit additional seizure of items which "are plainly contraband or evidence of other criminality for which . . . police have probable cause to arrest or search";

C v Laskoski **74 MAC 858 (2009)**—though D claimed 'patfrisk without reasonable suspicion that he had weapon,' Appeals Court found instead "probable cause to search" because of strong odor of burnt marijuana coming from D's clothes: that officer himself justified frisk (illegitimately) on subjective belief that D might have weapon on his person "because a domestic dispute had taken place" was not controlling;

Chimel v California **395 US 752 (69)**—search incident to arrest of person & area of immediate control for evidence/weapons, but not whole house;

C v Washington **449 M 476 (2007)**—despite having had probable cause to arrest Ds, police did not arrest them: unless search and arrest are "roughly contemporaneous," search can't be upheld as "incident to arrest," because this would "create a wholly new exception for a 'search incident to probable cause to arrest'"; search here upheld on rationale that evidence would otherwise be "lost" (evidence was bundled money with which drugs had recently been purchased);

C v Stephens **451 M 370 (2008)**—undercover troopers conducting surveillance of parking lot known as drug sales rendezvous point followed two vehicles from there, approached the vehicle in which both men were meeting, reasonably feared for their safety because of black object in D's hand, opened door, and saw much money and clear plastic bags with corners cut: given probable cause to arrest, search of car OK as incident to arrest even though "arrest" occurred after search;

C v Pierre **453 M 1010 (2009)**—when ordered to show his hands, D dropped plastic bag, which cop placed inside vehicle that D was about to enter when arrested; later search of bag, after vehicle was towed to police station and searched, was not a search incident to arrest, as too far removed physically and temporally from arrest; distinguishes *Nattoo* 452 M 826 (2009) (no expectation of privacy in bags left at side of public road at time and scene of arrest; no issue there of "contemporaneity requirement" here considered);

US v Robinson **414 US 218 (73)**—seize contraband unrelated to arrest crime;

C v Toole **389 M 159 (83)**—G.L. c. 276, § 1 = Robinson dissent; can't search D's car while D in custody at cruiser because no "control" (& no probable cause there was contraband/weapon);

C v Brown **354 M 337 (68)**;

C v Cassidy **32 MAC 160 (92)**—warrantless search of knapsack in D's car after D arrested & seated in cruiser was not proper search incident to arrest under G.L. c. 276, § 1, because cops had no reason to believe knapsack contained weapons to help D escape or evidence related to arrest for kidnapping;

C v Kegler **65 MAC 907 (2006)**—at arrest of D, there was probable cause to believe that cash had been stolen from victim, so D's wallet could be searched as incident to arrest, and since cash could be hidden in folded paper inside wallet, it could be opened (though it revealed drugs instead);

C v Lelos **61 MAC 626 (2004)**—identified citizen reported auto "casing" her neighborhood & gave info re: car description and plate number, and "baseball hat" occupant; cop found evidence of attempted break-in area, confirmed with other citizens the car's continuing suspicious presence, and located car: stop was justified, cop drew gun only upon suspicious movement of car occupants' feet: probable cause found, & immediate post-Miranda agreement to identify sites of burglaries made OK the search of car for proceeds of burglary, "security" concerns being "minimal at best" because Ds were handcuffed and under arrest; fact that D was purportedly arrested only for "disorderly conduct" after attempted flight didn't matter;

C v DiMarzio **52 MAC 746 (2001)**—though D was arrested for obvious recent smoking of marijuana, G.L. c. 276, § 1 didn't authorize search of desk drawer after D had been handcuffed and was on opposite side of desk from drawer; further, Commonwealth "gloss(ed) over" factual issue of whether drawer search would have occurred absent improper (without Miranda warnings) questioning of D re: where it was; **on further appellate review, 436 M 1012 (2002),** SJC agrees re: suppression, but instead of on grounds rejecting Commonwealth arguments of 'search incident to arrest' or 'exigent circumstances' simply because discovery was fruit of Miranda violation & no inevitable discovery;

C v Garden **451 M 43 (2008)**—odor of burnt marijuana allowed search of passengers and passenger compartment, but not car's trunk;

C v Johnson **49 MAC 273 (2000)**—cop's 4 a.m. interview of named individual reporting shots fired, probably from described car, + another named individual's info that alarm in street-level business establishment had gone off around same time gave rise to reasonable suspicion to stop car, 45 minutes later and 1½ miles from shooting; car's flight from cop and tossing gun from car window = probable cause to arrest for discharging gun within 500 ft. of dwelling (& search incident for that crime, turning up ammo in car); that cop said arrest (when car crashed into cruiser which was part of roadblock) was for failure to stop for cop wasn't controlling (search incident to arrest for that crime wouldn't have allowed search of car);

C v Sweezey **50 MAC 48 (2000)**—reasonable suspicion to stop motorist-D: surveillance of parking lot known for frequent drug transactions, one car signaling D's car with flashing lights, D following & obtaining paper bag from other driver; D's attempted getaway, in car, from cops approaching him at stop light in traffic gave probable cause; fact that cops testified that arrest was for assault & battery on police officer rather than drugs didn't prevent court from finding drug probable cause instead, so that

G.L. c. 276, § 1 didn't bar seizure of bag with 304 grams cocaine;

C v McCambridge **44 MAC 285 (98)**—dicta: D's clothes not seizable in search incident to arrest because no nexus to arrest offenses of OUI, negligent operation, and operating after license suspension;

C v Blevines **54 MAC 89 (2002), overruled on further review, 438 M 604 (2003)**—[Appeals Court decision: cops questioned D as to name/age, & believed that D was lying, so arrested him for public drinking, & took keys from pocket in ensuing pat frisk; warrant checks as to names of D, obtained from D & a cohort, revealed no matches; cops still believed correct identity withheld, so tried the car keys in a car parked about 15 feet away, & eventually saw plastic bag with rock cocaine underneath car's front seat; keys not seizable under G.L. c. 276, § 1 because not connected to public drinking & no evidence supported any finding that keys presented danger to cops/public; even IF seizure of keys were proper, no justification for subsequent search, i.e., use of keys to connect D to the car, and thereafter observing contraband; nothing warranted belief that car contained evidence of criminal activity; **"to uphold a search for identification in the circumstances . . . here would be to 'sanction a principle having no apparent stopping place'",** quoting from *C v Pacheco* 51 MAC 736, 742 (2001)]; *SJC decision*: seizure of keys permissible as search incident to arrest where the hard object could have been used as a weapon, but police were entitled to remove keys only for safety reasons and not for investigative purposes;

C v Cullen **62 MAC 390 (2004)**—following late night urban car stop on reasonable suspicion that its two occupants were culpable in same-night burglary & severe beating of resident, cops' reach into pocket to discern contents (mass of heavy metallic sounding items falsely said by D to be "keys") upheld as "integrated part of a safety-based weapons patfrisk", and court refuses relief for cops' removing the coins after determining no threat ("plain feel" argument, i.e., that incriminatory nature of the coins wasn't immediately apparent, rejected, on circumstantial evidence/inferences); SEE *Minnesota v Dickerson* **508 US 366 (93),** *Bond v US* **529 US 334 (2000);**

C v Chavis **41 MAC 912 (96)**—given probable cause to arrest for **very** recent B&E (and proceeds not in car used), "search incident" justified pat-down and seizure of jewelry, despite no reasonable belief Ds were armed; that "formal arrest" didn't occur until later didn't matter;

C v Brown **57 MAC 326 (2003)**—because tip (with corroboration) provided probable cause, seizure of bag found at D's feet was justified as "search incident to lawful arrest," even though search preceded formal arrest; compare and contrast

Smith v Ohio **494 US 541 (90)**—search of paper bag tossed by D who sought to prevent search after having been stopped & questioned about bag's contents without probable cause was not incident to lawful arrest; 'justifying arrest by the search & search by the arrest will not do';

C v Maylott **43 MAC 516 (97)**—videotape of D at booking desk (showing lack of cooperation suggestive of alcohol consumption) not violative of right against compulsory self-incrimination; *see also Chapter 20-L for cases on protective sweeps*;

C v Peters **48 MAC 15 (99)**—though D was first arrested only for operating after license suspension, inventory search provided probable cause to arrest for possession of drugs, so further search of D's person OK on this basis;

***Rodriques v Furtado* 410 M 878 (91)—manual body cavity searches may be undertaken only "with a strong showing of particularized need supported by a high degree of probable cause"**;

Vale v Louisiana **399 US 30 (70)**—search & seizure in house not search incident to arrest of D on front steps;

C v Lopez **38 MAC 748 (95)**—immediately after D sold drugs to undercover cop in D's apartment, waiting cops' entry to arrest D & seize marked bills from wallet = OK (untested informant had taken cop to apartment, so warrant wasn't possible);

C v Elizondo **428 M 322 (98)**—immediately after D sold drugs to undercover cop & seemed to have procured them from bathroom, four waiting cops entered & cuffed D, but could thereafter search bathroom and open false-bottomed can there;

C v Netto **438 M 686 (2003)**—after arrest of Ds in motel room (& noticing items then), cops could seize the items after Ds were removed from room, i.e., still valid as "search incident to arrest"; cites *C v Madera* 402 M 156, 160–71 (88) (even absent exigent circumstances, cops can seize immediate personal possessions of suspects arrested on warrant, where possessions were near where arrests occurred & there was probable cause to believe that items contained evidence of crimes for which arrests were made);

C v Cohen **359 M 140 (71)**—cubes in refrigerator not within control of arrested D;

C v Walker **370 M 548 (76)**—post-arrest safety check of other rooms = OK; BUT SEE CONTRA *C v DuBois* **44 MAC 294 (98)** (entry to arrest fleeing individual didn't justify further search of building);

See **K. Smith,** *Criminal Practice & Procedure,* **§§ 245–46 (2d ed. 1983 & Supp.)** *& Plain View (Chapter 20-I below)*;

C v Forde **367 M 798 (75)**—during search incident to arrest can seize items in plain view;

C v Raedy **24 MAC 648 (87)**—standard operating procedure to take out ignition key after arrest, then gun was in plain view;

C v Clermy **421 M 325 (95)**—D, observed to be sitting on front steps of "crack house", was arrested on outstanding "motor vehicle default warrant," & 1st frisk yielded beeper & $60; 2d frisk after cuffing yielded, from genital area, 3-inch brown prescription bottle; SJC rationalizes that this was probable cause for a second "arrest," & search incident, so bottle could be opened without warrant (also claim that hard object in genital area could have been

weapon, and test. that even cuffed Ds had gained access to weapons);

C v Madera **402 M 156 (88)**—can seize & search D's bag at lawful arrest, even under Declaration of Rights, Article 14 & G.L. c. 276, § 1, because probable cause it had arrest-drug;

C v Pagan **440 M 62 (2003)**—while opening bag to search for weapons ("Terry" stop) not justified if police presence = substantial & risk of D repossessing bag = minimal, circumstances here distinguished ("threat" not yet neutralized, so bag search OK); furthermore, cops not obligated to hand bag back to D (for him to retrieve identification from it) prior to assuring that no weapon was in bag;

C v Skea **18 MAC 685 (84)**—1 marijuana cigarette = probable cause & "exigent" (to see if more), so can check pockets though policy not to arrest for 1 joint; then can seize diamond;

C v Garden **451 M 43 (2008)**—odor of burnt marijuana allowed search of car passengers and passenger compartment, but not car's trunk;

C v Washington **449 M 476 (2007)**—SJC embraces *Skea*, to uphold search of Ds' persons for money recently used to purchase drugs; probable cause existed for such search, but undercover operation didn't want to reveal itself and had stopped Ds on unrelated ground (speeding); money said to be "fungible," and thus "evanescent" ("search now or never"); SJC acknowledges that *Cupp v Murphy* 412 US 291 (73) may not actually support this result;

C v Prophete **443 M 548 (2005)**—D, observed smoking marijuana and acknowledging same, prevented search of his "groin" area, while search of his clothing (pat-down plus search of pockets) turned up no drugs; police, acknowledging undertaking "strip search", ordered D to remove clothing one article at a time, and with removal of pants, plastic bag of drugs fell to floor; SJC holds that this wasn't a strip search because underwear wasn't removed; search of D's person was permissible as incident to lawful arrest on probable cause, even though "arrest" occurred after search; [see *Washington* 449 M 476 (2007): to be legitimate "search incident to arrest," however, arrest **must** be "roughly contemporaneous" with search];

C v Desources **74 MAC 232 (2009)**—in "patfrisk" "incident to [D's] imminent [though subsequent] arrest" for public drinking cop felt "some hard objects" which were small plastic bags of marijuana; cop's subjective motivations and ludicrous notion of "hard" irrelevant & search upheld, as was later 'inventory' search at station producing more marijuana inside undershorts' pockets;

C v Togo **356 M 60 (69)**—car search 1 hour after arrest not search incident to arrest;

US v Chadwick **433 US 1 (77)**—bad container (locker) search, though probable cause it had contraband, because 1 hour after arrest not search incident to arrest & cops had exclusive control;

C v Straw **422 M 756 (96)**—need warrant to search briefcase thrown out window as cops arrived to execute arrest warrant;

Illinois v Lafayette **462 US 640 (83)**—standard operating procedure to inspect D's bag after disturbing peace arrest;

NY v Belton **453 US 454 (81)**—arrested car occupant's control = entire passenger area (& glove box) & containers—though D's outside;

Arizona v Gant **129 S Ct 1710 (2009)**—police may search passenger compartment of vehicle incident to a recent occupant's arrest only if it is reasonable to believe (per *Chimel v California* 395 US 752) that arrestee might access the vehicle at time of search or (per *Thornton v US* 541 US 615, 632) that vehicle contains evidence of the arrest offense; neither rationale permitted search here as five cops cuffed and secured D and two other suspects in separate patrol cars before search began AND D was arrested for driving after license suspension (evidence of which could not be reasonably expected inside vehicle); *NY v Belton* not to be read "expansively";

C v Cavanaugh **366 M 277 (74)**—doubt car's within reach if D held on sidewalk;

Thornton v US **541 US 615 (2004)**—under Fourth Amendment, cop can conduct warrantless search of passenger compartment of vehicle even though cop's first contact with arrestee is after arrestee has stepped out of vehicle; *NY v Belton* rule for search of vehicle's passenger compartment includes both occupants and "recent occupants" lawfully arrested;

C v Beasley **13 MAC 62 (82)**—passenger section & closed container in glove box = OK; not trunk;

C v Woodman **11 MAC 965 (81)**—can't search van (D was driving when lawful rape arrest) 2 days later because no exigency, so search warrant needed;

C v Brillante **399 M 152 (87)**—3 arrested D's outside car, 2 cops can seize & search bag in car for weapon/contraband;

C v Alvarado **420 M 542 (95)**—2 arrested Ds (for drugs, found on person of passenger/car owner), illegal "search incident" of a boxed coffee maker inside car, though driver was seen to "remove hand" from area of car in which it was found; *C v Pena* **69 MAC 713 (2007)**—marijuana found on person of car passenger didn't give probable cause to search under rear seat cushion for more drugs, distinguishing cases holding probable cause when drugs previously discovered in locations having "some connection to the vehicle searched, rather than to a particular individual who happened to arrive at location in vehicle" (but allowing search as "protective");

C v Rose **25 MAC 905 (87)**—bad G.L. c. 276, § 1 seizure & search of D's bag in car after D removed for OUI arrest; booze not likely in personal luggage;

C v Somers **44 MAC 920 (98)**—stop of D for wrong-way on exit ramp, smell alcohol, through window see unopened beer bottle, open door to reach "for the bottle & any further signs of alcohol use"—gun seen, then D ac-

knowledged prior false name operating after license revocation: gun would have been discovered during lawful inventory search so inevitable discovery;

C v Bongarzone **390 M 326 n.18 (83)**—can seize & search car containers though D outside, if probable cause of G.L. c. 276, § 1 evidence related to arrest;

C v King **389 M 233 (83)**—after shootout, can open car-trunk's duffel-bag; but see *C v Podgurski* **386 M 385 (82)** expect privacy in car (closed van)'s interior; (*see also Chapter 20-L & -M, below re: car seizure & search & its scope*; & K. Smith, *Criminal Practice & Procedure*, § 243, Containers (2d ed. 1983 & Supp.));

20-H.3. Inventory Searches

South Dakota v Opperman **428 US 364 (76)**—inventory (car) search to protect D's property & cops against claims/danger;

Colorado v Bertine **479 US 367 (87)**—good faith justifies inventory car search of closed knapsack after OUI arrest because standard operating procedure;

C v Dunn **34 MAC 702 (93)**—when pulled over for speeding, D stopped in parking lot of closed business (& was subsequently arrested for OUI); though motion judge suppressed fruits of inventory search on basis that impoundment of truck was not necessary, Appeals Court upheld impoundment (cops could be reasonably concerned for potential liability in leaving truck exposed to theft/vandalism in unattended lot and re: burden to property owner); remanded for determining propriety of ensuing inventory search & police policy for same;

C v Delong **60 MAC 528 (2004)**—no ineffective assistance in failing to move for suppression on ground that car was illegitimately impounded: D wasn't accompanied by anyone who could have taken custody of the car, which was parked in private lot limiting parking to customers of nearby businesses, and thus that "private towing was a real possibility if the police did not impound the car";

G.L. c. 127, § 3 sheriff & assistants must keep record of all prisoners' property;

C v Wilson **389 M 115 (83)**—LSD in wallet taken under G.L. c. 127, § 3, not G.L. c. 276, § 1;

C v Pigaga **12 MAC 960 (81)**—license from wallet at station not fruit of the arrest-crime under G.L. c. 276, § 1 & not inventory;

C v Ford **394 M 421 (85)**—inventory opening of trunk after impounding car bad under Mass. Declaration of Rights because not standard operating procedure;

C v Bishop **402 M 449 (88)**—inventory search must have OK written standard operating procedures; closed container maybe out of bounds under Declaration of Rights, Article 14 (fn.1);

C v Silva **61 MAC 28 (2004)**—given failure to proffer extant writing justifying "inventory" search, court rejects claim that it was OK to search for info re: ownership in cases in which car is to be towed following stop ("inventory light"); since cops had no right to be searching for ownership documents potentially within the car, "plain view doctrine does not save seizure of drugs from constitutional infirmity";

C v Goncalves **62 MAC 153 (2004)**—distinguishes *Silva* because car door was left open & motor was left running in a no-parking area, when D alighted during legitimate stop & subsequent arrest; officer awaiting tow truck leaned in to turn off ignition, saw gun in plain view;

C v Sullo **26 MAC 766 (89)**—bad inventory search of papers in business card holder because no procedures & because inventory search isn't close scrutiny, reading documents;

C v Muckle **61 MAC 678 (2004)**—opening of crumpled Dunkin' Donuts bag inside vehicle wasn't justifiable under written inventory policy requiring that passenger area of vehicle be "thoroughly examined" and that all personal property be removed and secured at police station; "bag of refuse that must be opened for its contents to be visible is like any other unlocked closed container"; *but see*

C v Bienvenu **63 MAC 632 (2005)**—in "inventory" search, police took a "softball sized" gray duct-taped ball found between driver's seat and gear shift, peeled back layer of duct tape, some plastic, and newspaper, and uncovered cocaine: opinion asserts that cop's action = consistent with particular inventory policy's requirement of searching closed "containers";

C v Rostad **410 M 618 (91)**—inventory search of closed containers in D's possession are invalid unless written policy makes specific provision for closed containers;

C v Vanya V **75 MAC 370 (2009)**—written inventory policy provided that any container/article found on arrestee's person or carried by him shall be opened and its contents inventoried, but inside D's bag was a locked zippered bank bag: cutting open the bank bag (after keys on D's person didn't open it) = impermissible because written policy did not say what to do with "locked" as opposed to merely "closed" containers, and did not say what to do when didn't have key as opposed to having key; "permitting . . . officer to destroy or break into a locked container runs counter to the very purpose of the inventory exception";

C v Allen **76 MAC 21 (2009)**—written inventory policy was admitted at hearing, and provided that "All unlocked containers shall be opened" and their contents inventoried separately; opening of a closed container the size of a shoe box, found inside a closed book bag inside the trunk, was upheld;

C v Difalco **73 MAC 401 (2008)**—locked safe inside car trunk could not be opened, because written inventory procedure omitted authorization for this;

C v Garcia **409 M 675, 684 (91)**—inventory search of trunk pursuant to policy authorizing search of car was valid even though policy didn't explicitly mention trunks;

C v Caceres **413 M 749 (92)**—inventory search of unlocked closed container visible in trunk of car pursuant to valid written policy was valid under Article 14; impoundment OK where only available person to drive car off was

off was passenger with probably expired out-of-state driver's license; [see *C v Bettencourt* **447 M 631 (2006)**: after proper stop, driver was arrested; cop asked passenger whether he had license, and he said no; further questioning of passenger for name and date of birth resulted in knowledge of outstanding warrants, passenger's arrest, and discovery of cocaine on his person: SJC orders suppression, since no ground for questioning D/believing D involved in crime; Commonwealth's belated argument that it was "community caretaking" to find a driver to take charge of car rather than tow/impound it was rebuffed, because not raised at trial court by testimony or argument;

C v Henley **63 MAC 1 (2005)**—after driver was arrested for outstanding warrants, and Avis car rental agreement listed only one authorized driver (who was neither the arrested driver nor either of the two passengers), police could impound car (& weren't obligated to call Avis, or to have called the renter/authorized driver for her instructions); after trunk was opened, odor of marijuana provided probable cause to believe contraband within, to arrest occupants, and to conduct investigatory search of car and contents;

C v Baptiste **65 MAC 511 (2006)**—car was legitimately stopped for speeding, and license check revealed that neither driver nor passenger had valid license, so state police policy required towing and inventory prior to towing; that cop observed suspicious (but not probable cause) white powder earlier did not invalidate inventory search revealing drugs in "console" arm rest (a repository akin to glove compartment); subjective "investigative" interest didn't render inventory search impermissible; that cop used flashlight to determine what was impeding release of "cup holder" in console was OK, because probable cause existed at point white powder spilled onto seat and floor when cop lifted arm rest;

C v Lites **67 MAC 815 (2006)**—fresh odor of burnt marijuana from opened door of stopped car, PLUS passenger's furtive gestures at his waist area provided probable cause to arrest passenger;

C v Bienvenu **63 MAC 632 (2005)**—after driver was arrested on outstanding warrant, cops weren't obligated to give owner/passenger (who had no valid license) opportunity to make arrangements as alternative to having car towed from night-time stop alongside two-lane road;

C v Ellerbe **430 M 769 (2000)**—under police policy re: cars of arrested drivers, only option open to police which didn't involve inventory of car was "leav(ing) it with person having apparent authority to assume control over it," and only person immediately available here was passenger who didn't have driver's license with her (driver must have license to operate on person or in vehicle, G.L. c. 90, § 11); inventory search upheld (search of black leather coin bag thus valid);

Florida v Wells **495 US 1 (90)**—inventory search of locked suitcase in OUI-D's impounded car was invalid where Florida highway patrol had no standard policy on closed containers;

C v Peters **48 MAC 15 (99)**—contrary to D's belief , Commonwealth not **required** to introduce written inventory policy, but motion judge erred in placing burden on D to show that warrantless search was unreasonable; written policy = best proof of its content, & mere testimony about it might not establish that it's explicit enough to guard against 'discretionary' opening of closed wallets or handbags, or that it meets *Sullo* requirements (**26 MAC 766, 768 (79)**) including that it "not become a cover or pretext for an investigative search";

C v Horton **63 MAC 571 (2005)**—record permits Appeals Court to find impoundment was contemplated from beginning of traffic stop & wasn't pretext, despite failure of motion judge to make findings: car didn't have valid plates, registration, or insurance, & impoundment of such auto is "typically proper" (n.4);

C v Brinson **440 M 609, 611–12 & n.2 (2003)—D must object to "hearsay testimony regarding the written [inventory] procedure"; if D objects, evidence concerning the written procedure may be excluded "on best evidence or hearsay grounds";**

C v Figueroa **412 M 745 (92)**—inventory search of closed container on wall panel behind driver's seat which was open to view was valid where state police policy authorized search of "all open areas";

C v DeVlaminck **32 MAC 980 (92)**—inventory search of closed container in OUI-D's car was valid even though cop technically violated policy by initially recording contents on scrap paper & by failing to list items other than contraband; testimony of 6 other D's to show pattern of noncompliance made no difference;

C v Alvarado **420 M 542 (95)**—search of car was investigatory, **not** inventory, as drug-sniffing canine unit was called to barracks even before arresting trooper arrived there; *C v Murphy* **63 MAC 11 (2005)**—suppression ordered where police transformed 'inventory' search of D's person at police station after arrest to investigatory, taking keys from him, removing them from station, matching them (by info on key-ring) to illegally parked car, and only then ordering impoundment, enabling 'inventory' search of car (which produced gun);

C v O'Connor **406 M 112 (89)**—invalid protective custody search cured by inevitable discovery during booking inventory;

C v Evans **50 MAC 846 (2001)**—searching inside D's shoes at booking for operating without license (cocaine and marijuana found) OK: both inventory & "removal of any items that may be used by the arrested person to injure himself"; SJC on further appellate review didn't speak to this issue, **436 M 365 (2002)**;

C v Murphy **63 MAC 11 (2005)**—cops illegitimately converted "inventory" of D's possessions at booking (car keys) into an investigatory search for the car itself to impound and search it;

20-H.4. Body Searches

Rodriques v Furtado **410 M 878 (91)**—*manual* body cavity searches may be undertaken only "with a strong showing of particularized need supported by a high degree of probable cause";

C v Thomas **429 M 403 (99)**—probable cause needed for "strip" and *visual* body cavity searches, which should occur in private; probable cause here to believe that arrested D (for particular reasons) had more drugs on his person (& plastic bags of crack cocaine were found between D's buttocks);

C v Ramirez **56 MAC 317 (2002)**—D, arrested for being minor in possession of alcohol, was pat frisked, yielding knife and bottle of cognac; second (thorough) search at squad car yielded nothing additional; unconstitutional to conduct strip search at station (though it produced cocaine): no probable cause to believe that strip search would reveal weapon, contraband, or fruits or instrumentalities of criminal activity; "bulky" pants didn't constitute adequate reason for strip search; STRIP SEARCH MAY NOT BE PERFORMED AS INCIDENT TO JUST ANY LAWFUL ARREST;

C v Prophete **443 M 548 (2005)**—D, observed smoking marijuana and acknowledging same, prevented search of his "groin" area, while search of his clothing (pat-down plus search of pockets) turned up no drugs; police, acknowledging undertaking "strip search", ordered D to remove clothing one article at a time, and with removal of pants, plastic bag of drugs fell to floor; SJC holds that this **wasn't a strip search because underwear wasn't removed**; search of D's person was permissible as incident to lawful arrest on probable cause, even though "arrest" occurred after search; D & cohort had twice sought to evade police & knew police aware of marijuana, drugs had been discovered on cohort's person already, D had prior drug arrests, D gave false name and ID & prevented search of groin area, and had cash, cell phone, and pager on person, combined to legitimate intention to conduct strip search; here, there was a written policy about "strip" searches; SJC "emphasize[s]" existence of probable cause to justify police belief that D had drugs secreted on his person;

C v Angivoni **383 M 30 (81)**—bad blood test because bad consent (because drunk, dazed, & not told of right to refuse) & not exigent;

C v Carson **72 MAC 368 (2008)**—though D has no "constitutional right to refuse a blood test or breathalyzer test, *C v Davidson* 27 MAC 846, 848 (1989)," G.L. c. 90, § 24(1)(e–f) requires D's actual consent to breath or blood testing as condition of admissibility of results in evidence; "consent" needn't be 'knowing/voluntary/intelligent, but suppression order based on motion judge's findings of fact = affirmed (MAC's language = "robotic manifestations of acquiescence by one no longer possessed of the ability to choose"; "consent form", a "cryptic writing" drawn by police lieutenant = "[date, time] [D] advised of consent to Blood Test");

Schmerber v California **384 US 757 (66)**—body specimen = Fourth Amendment seizure & search (not Fifth); must be reasonable & strongly necessary; OUI blood test OK;

Rochin v California **342 US 165 (52)**—stomach pump shocks conscience & violates due process;

Winston v Lee **470 US 753 (85)**—court-ordered bullet removal not compelling enough need (because some risk; & other evidence against D);

Chandler v Miller **520 US 305, 308 (97)**—collection & testing of urine intrudes upon expectations of privacy, & is thus a 'search' of the person;

Horsemen v Racing Comm'n **403 M 692 (89)**—urine drug-test needs search warrant & probable cause;

C v Trigones **397 M 633 (86)**—court-ordered blood test OK after hearing & probable cause;

Matter of Lavigne **418 M 831 (94)**—adversary hearing required prior to compelling non-indicted subject to submit to blood extraction: must be probable cause to believe him guilty and probable cause to believe that source of blood at crime scene would aid in investigation; balancing test also required;

C v Miles **420 M 67 (95)**—pre-Lavigne ex parte order compelling D to submit to visual "nonintrusive" inspection of his body (rape occurred in poison ivy bed)—"exigent circumstances" because rash would be temporary; "time . . . of the essence . . . to preserve the evidence";

C v Downey **407 M 472 (90)**—grand jury may compel detention for blood tests on unindicted D so long as there is probable cause to indict or arrest; D must be given opportunity to oppose order;

In the Matter of a Grand Jury Investigation **427 M 221 (98)**—because prosecution "reasonably believed" that autistic and profoundly retarded woman's pregnancy was caused by either her father or brother, grand jury could obtain from a judge an order compelling each to submit to blood sampling (when grand jury is involved, "reasonable" search & seizure here did not require proof that it was more probable than not that one or the other of the men committed the crime);

C v Miller **42 MAC 703 (97)**—similar, but precharge; grand jury investigation controlling case;

C v Maxwell **441 M 773, 777–78 (2004)**—summarizing requirements for warrants and orders for physical testing of suspects at different stages of investigation and prosecution;

C v Beausoleil **397 M 206 (86)**—paternity D sought blood test, so useable;

C v Draheim **447 M 113 (2006)**—Commonwealth wanted "buccal swabs" from female D's two children and from rape complainants because prosecution alleged that the children were products of D's statutory rapes of teenaged boys; notwithstanding quashing judge's rationale protective of the relationship between child and D's ex-husband (held irrelevant by SJC), burden was only to establish that the DNA evidence will probably provide evidence relevant to D's guilt; judge should consider seriousness of crime, importance of evidence, and [un]availability of less intrusive means of obtaining the evidence, factors relevant re: prosecution attempts to obtain physical samples from person's body; source of authority to compel nonparty to provide swab = M.R.Crim.P. 17(a)(2);

Lenardis v Commonwealth **452 M 1001 (2008)**—nonparty directed to provide evidence (buccal swab) can challenge order by refusing to comply and appealing from any order of contempt that results; this petitioner instead sought relief from SJC single justice ("county court") via G.L. c. 211, § 3 petition, which was denied without hearing; appeal to full bench = moot because petitioner complied with order AND single justice's ruling would not be disturbed because party should have suffered contempt and appealed from contempt order;

C v Powell **450 M 229 (2007)**—rejects D's argument that grand jury petition for blood sample from D was erroneously allowed: D argued that knowing D's own blood was on, e.g., hammer (purportedly used to kill V) was useless, but "overlook[ed] the utility in the investigation of excluding him as the source of blood found on his person and clothing"; D waived, by failing to object to, requirements that petition be signed by foreperson under oath and/or having supporting affidavit from DA or grand juror; judge's failure to include in order the findings mandated by *Williams* 439 M 678 (2003), immaterial because order was preceded by adversary hearing and record supported order authorizing extraction of D's blood;

C v Brown **24 MAC 979 (87)**—DA can comment on D's refusal to give blood/hair because nontestimonial, but **no longer good law**: see *C v Zevitas* **418 M 677 (94)** & *Opinion of the Justices* **412 M 1201, 1211 (92)** (D's refusal = equivalent of D's statement "I know this evidence will be very damaging"); *C v Vermette* **43 MAC 789 (97)** error to introduce testimony that D refused police permission to search car & photo sneakers (harmless here, given D's testimony);

C v Lydon **413 M 309 (92)**—similar, re gunpowder residue test, refusal to submit;

C v Arruda **73 MAC 901, further appellate review allowed 452 M 1110 (2008)**—in interlocutory appeal by Commonwealth, Appeals Court holds that evidence of D's refusal to supply medical personnel with sample of his blood "for medical purposes" was admissible even though D was in custody and police "may have an interest in the results of the tests; it is "governmental, not private, compulsion that is prohibited by art. 12 of Declaration of Rights;

C v Healy **452 M 510 (2008)**—evidence of refusal to undergo field sobriety test harmless beyond reasonable doubt because trial was jury-waived and appellate court assumes trial judge "correctly instructed himself" on law that refusal evidence = inadmissible;

C v Marini **375 M 510 (78)**—bad voice ID by witness because 1-on-1, crime words used, & saw D while heard (*see Chapter 18*);

Landry v Attorney General **429 M 336 (99)**—collection of convicted persons' blood for DNA database held reasonable under Article 14 & Fourth Amendment;

Cupp v Murphy **412 US 291 (73)**—fingernail scrapings;

US v Mura **410 US 19 (73)**—handwriting exemplar;

US v Dionisio **410 US 1 (73)**—voice exemplar;

US v Wade **388 US 218 (67)**—lineup;

C v Burgess **426 M 206 (97)**—compelled production of IRS tax returns to Commonwealth not "testimonial" evidence, so no "self-incrimination" constitutional violation BUT implicit statements incidental to performance of the act of production may not be used, and "refusal" evidence (D fought against production) can't be used;

Langton v Commissioner of Correction **404 M 165 (89)**—strip searches of prison inmates not violative of Fourth Amendment where not unreasonable or abusive;

Doe v Senechal **431 M 78 (2000)**—former mental patient filed civil suit against residential treatment facility for allegedly tortious sexual contact by employee resulting in patient's pregnancy and childbirth; plaintiff obtained discovery order requiring alleged father to undergo "buccal swab paternity test," for DNA match to child; SJC didn't believe Fourth Amendment applied to "private" litigants'

civil actions, but said test here ordered met "standard of reasonableness";

C v Russo **30 MAC 923 (91)**—drawing & testing of D's blood by hospital staff was not search or seizure under Fourth Amendment where not done at cops' request or direction;

C v Senior **433 M 453 (2001)**—Commonwealth could summons hospital records of D's blood alcohol test after fatal car collision and introduce them into evidence, despite D's arguments re: "confidentiality of medical records" (G.L. c. 111, §§ 70, 70E), and "attorney-client privilege" (test was done at behest of defense counsel, but "agency" relationship not thereby created);

C v Beldotti **409 M 553 (91)**—testing for occult (invisible) blood on D's hands upheld even though pursuant to defective warrant under unusual circumstances of case;

20-H.5. Arrest/Booking; "Compelled" Statements

See cases in Chapter 20-C, above (e.g., C v Guerrero 32 MAC 263 (92));

C v Gordon **422 M 816 (96)**—surreptitious taping of booking not suppressed though "literal reading" of G.L. c. 272, § 99P supports suppression;

See Chapter 7, Preparation: Fifth Amendment & Lost Evidence; & Chapter 21-DD, OUI;

20-I. STANDING; "REASONABLE EXPECTATION OF PRIVACY"; "SEARCH/SEIZE?" (VS. PLAIN VIEW)

See Chapter 20-M re: seizure of person;

20-I.1. Reasonable Expectation of Privacy

K. Smith, *Criminal Practice & Procedure*, §§ 1337–39 (2d ed. 1983 & Supp.), standing—US Supreme Court abolished automatic standing; test = "legitimate expectation of privacy"; §§ 157–63, areas protected; § 246, Plain View & search incident to arrest; § 227, plain view after search warrant;

C v Ford **394 M 421 (85)**—intrusion = search though not so intended;

C v Billings **42 MAC 261 (97)**—no reasonable expectation of privacy in soles of sneakers (cop could testify to their appearance, having asked D to lift foot & display, during non-custodial interview); Article 14 ground not decided;

C v Sparks **433 M 654, 658 (2001)**—looking at soles of shoes not a search; thereafter D consented to remove them and allow them to be photographed as part of interview process;

C v Cabral **69 MAC 67 (2007)**—D had no reasonable expectation of privacy in his expectorated spittle (spat onto a public sidewalk and retrieved by a private investigator) or in the DNA derived therefrom (fn.9: due to collection technique, results weren't admissible "in a court of law,"

but results apparently were basis for obtaining a court order requiring D to submit DNA sample);

C v Bly **448 M 473 (2007)**—D had no reasonable expectation of privacy in cigarette butts and water bottle he had abandoned, even though police secretly intended he provide DNA by drinking the water and smoking the cigarettes left available to him in interview room; D had previously declined to provide blood sample; though institution rules prohibited D from taking the items with him when he left area, Court says D didn't try to take them, or protest rule, or try to return to retrieve;

C v Ewing **67 MAC 540, further appellate review allowed 447 M 1113 (2006), but SJC agrees with Appeals Court on all issues, including this one, 449 M 1035, fn.1 (2007)**—even if police gave D beverage and cigarette with intention of obtaining DNA evidence from them, D had no expectation of privacy in cigarette butts and straw when he left them as trash in interview room;

C v Connolly **454 M 808 (2009)**—installation of global positioning system device (GPS) on D's vehicle was "seizure" under article 14;

C v Pina **406 M 540 (90)**—intrusion into wallet left behind by D at halfway house when he was transferred to another facility not a "search" under Fourth Amendment;

C v Carter **424 M 409 (97)**—D had no reasonable expectation of privacy in stranger's exterior porch through which he fled from police (and in which he left a wallet & cocaine); BUT D and confederate are to be treated as one for purpose of determining reasonable expectation of privacy, because otherwise person who carried contraband might go free while confederate would not;

C v Williams **453 M 203 (2009)**—no reasonable expectation of privacy in unfinished basement accessible by police through unlocked rear door after building's owner (D's mother, who did not live in the multi-family building) gave full permission for police search and seizure; that D without permission deposited some possessions and perhaps was sleeping on a mattress there (as "squatter") did not make any subjective privacy expectation reasonable, though squatter "may develop rights", e.g., by owner's acquiescence to presence (brief "passive sufferance" distinguished); that a seized letter was in a "sealed" envelope doesn't alter conclusion;

C v Herring **66 MAC 360 (2006)**—though apartment entered was leased to D's uncle, both uncle and D were charged with possession of cocaine with intent to distribute; D wasn't required to show "reasonable expectation of privacy" in area searched;

C v Colon **449 M 207 (2007)**—D has burden of showing reasonable expectation of privacy (here, not shown in D's girlfriend's apartment, though D sometimes babysat his own children there, had last stayed overnight there six days earlier, and "engage[d] in intimate relationship with" girlfriend there; motion judge not required to believe D's girlfriend's testimony as to D having much more involvement with, and keys to, the apartment);

C v Murphy **63 MAC 11, 12 n.2 (2005)**—to the extent that D is co-D of person on whose person drugs were found, D may assert an expectation of privacy in the items seized from co-D so long as possession is an element of the crime with which D is charged;

C v Contos **435 M 1936–37 (2001)**—D had no expectation of privacy in his 'gear locker' at Air National Guard base building "used strictly for Guard members' performance of their official duties" (despite fact he'd placed lock on it);

C v Nattoo **70 MAC 625 (2007), FURTHER APPELLATE REVIEW ALLOWED (Feb. 2008)**—D, being evicted from trailer by its new owner, asked for time to remove his belongings, and carried most of them in large plastic trash bags, with tv set, to edge of property, next to road, calling girlfriend to pick him up with belongings; before she arrived, police arrested D on outstanding warrant; Appeals Court denies suppression, contra motion judge: while D did NOT "intend" to abandon, court says no reasonable expectation of privacy in the plastic bags left at roadside; **on further review, 452 M 826 (2009)**—same result, cop went to scene at D's request to retrieve bags for D, and could search them to ensure safety before transporting them; *C v Pierre* **453 M 1010 (2009)**—distinguishes *Natoo*, as plastic bag dropped by D when

told to show his hands could not be searched as "incident to arrest" when search occurred much later, after bag was placed inside vehicle, which was towed to station; *Nattoo* didn't involve "contemporaneity" argument;

C v Duncan **71 MAC 150, further appellate review allowed 452 M 1110 (2008)**—defendants, seeing cops, moved behind a fence and then emerged, walking toward officers again; Ds had no expectation of privacy in trash can behind that fence (guns found there);

C v Rice **441 M 291 (2004)**—D, serving a sentence, had no reasonable expectation of privacy in his bed sheets and prison uniform when he passed them out of cell in ordinary course for laundering (DNA samples were subsequently obtained from these items); any interest he may have had in his own worn-out T-shirt was abandoned when he surrendered it for replacement;

In the Matter of a Grand Jury Subpoena **454 M 685 (2009)**—neither a pretrial jail detainee or a convicted inmate has reasonable expectation of privacy in telephone conversations: all parties have notice that calls are subject to monitoring/recording (this is essential), and penological interests justify: loss of privacy is an "inherent incident[ ] of confinement"; jail's providing recorded calls in response to grand jury subpoena = OK; *C v Hart* **455 M 230 (2009)**—though jail telephone records should have been procured via M.R.Crim.P. 17(a)(2) and *C v Lampron* **441 M 265 (2004)** procedure, and not by subpoena directing delivery of records to DA's office, suppression not warranted on this ground absent prejudice (citing *C v Odgren* **455 M 171 [2009]**);

C v Aviles **58 MAC 459 (2003)**—D conceded that his wife had authority to consent to search of the home and could relinquish to police D's soiled clothing and towels; if police lawfully obtain evidence, it may be subjected to testing (D's personal consent unnecessary prior to DNA testing of clothing);

C v Porter P **456 M 254 (2010)**—legitimate expectation of privacy in room shared by D and his mother at transitional family shelter, to which they had key and in which they lived, even though staff had master key; director had no actual authority to consent to search, and allegedly "apparent" authority would have been refuted if cops had diligently inquired, as necessary;

Soldal v Cook County **506 US 56 (92)**—Fourth Amendment protections apply to D's possessory interests in property, even where privacy interests are not implicated;

Samson v California **547 US 843 (2006)**—state statute requires all parolees to agree in writing to be subject to suspicionless search or seizure, and this = upheld against Fourth Amendment challenge: parole = variant of imprisonment, so no reasonable expectation of privacy under "totality of circumstances" analysis;

C v Feodoroff **43 MAC 725 (97)**—D had no reasonable expectation of privacy in her telephone billing records (G.L. c. 271, § 17B gave DA right to obtain records) as against AG or ADAs; "taps", used to record conversations, & "pen registers," used to record #s dialed from a particular line, & "cross frame traps," recording #s of incoming calls, distinguished: **may** be different result if requesting authority has no reasonable grounds for belief telephone is being used for illegal purpose; **may** be argument that First Amendment is violated; see also *C v Vinnie* **428 M 161 (98)** albeit "thin" as a "ground", belief that D used telephone to fabricate alibi;

C v McCambridge **44 MAC 285 (98)—gun fell out of D's clothing as he was being placed in ambulance: not product of any search by person acting at behest of police** (though EMT gave it to police thereafter);

C v Sergienko **399 M 291 (87)**—flashlight into car not intrusion (*see Chapter 20-M re: seizure of person*);

C v Doulette **414 M 653 (93)**—no reasonable expectation of privacy/no "search" when item seen inside car parked in commuter lot (albeit seen with aid of flashlight);

C v Podgurski **386 M 385 (82)**—stick head inside van = intrusion; in car, also, can have legitimate expectation of privacy;

Minnesota v Olson **495 US 91 (90)—overnight guest has expectation of privacy in home of host;** BUT SEE *C v Morrison* **429 M 511 (99)** invited guest has no expectation of privacy when willing host has outstanding protective order against guest;

C v Mallory **56 MAC 153 (2002)**—friend of family who lived in a bedroom in their home had no expectation of privacy in bedroom after he beat and raped family daughter & fled out the window when pursued by her father;

C v Garcia **34 MAC 386 (93)—D had reasonable expectation of privacy in locked mailbox in building's entryway because he had box key & "mail" is recognized by society as deserving of privacy** (even though D was not a building tenant and box held drug stash);

C v PorterP **456 M 254 (2010)**—legitimate expectation of privacy in family's "room" in transitional shelter (mother had key) even though staff had master key;

C v Rodriguez **74 MAC 314 (2009)**—D had no standing re: search/seizure of person to whom he allegedly sold drugs (proof of distribution charges against D); see decision on further appellate review, **456 M 578 (2010)**, SJC orders required finding of not guilty on distribution counts, and new suppression hearing;*C v Harmon* **63 MAC 456, 457 n.3 (2005)**—though search warrant was for apartment occupied by another person, parties agreed that D had standing/expectation of privacy because D's personal papers were seized from bedroom of the apartment;

C v Panetti **406 M 230 (89)**—under Article 14, D has **expectation of privacy in conversations in his apartment that could be heard from basement crawl space, where no others had access**; conversations suppressed because cops had no right to be eavesdropping from crawl space;

C v Santoro **406 M 421 (90)—D has no standing to challenge search of 3d party's home in which he has no expectation of privacy, even though evidence seized therefrom was used to obtain search warrant for D's home;**

C v Manning **406 M 425 (90)**—D has no standing to challenge unlawful arrest of 3d party even though evidence obtained from him was used to obtain search warrant for D's home;

C v Waters **420 M 276 (95)**—D has no standing to challenge search of 3d party's apartment in which he had no expectation of privacy, though he contended its purpose was to obtain statement against D from a person there present (that person's eventual trial testimony ruled not suppressible, anyway);

C v Midi **46 MAC 591 (99)—because D was charged with possession of gun & ammo in bedroom of apartment leased to another person, he had standing to litigate legality of police entry into apartment** (to arrest still another person without any warrant): D "had standing to contest the legality of the search leading to the seizure of" the evidence;

C v Cote **407 M 827 (90)**—D has no expectation of privacy in messages left with 3d party's answering service;

C v Pellegrini **414 M 402 (93)**—D had no reasonable expectation of privacy in her infant's medical records (which indicated D's use of cocaine when infant was **in utero**);

Compare/contrast *Ferguson v City of Charleston* **532 US 67 (2001)**—policy of hospital to test pregnant patients suspected of drug abuse & maintain chain of custody for ensuing urine samples & report to police = unconstitutional in absence of informed consent;

C v Mamacos **409 M 635 (91)**—D has no expectation of privacy in truck's brakes, even after fatal accident;

C v Garcia **409 M 675 (91)**—D has no expectation of privacy in stationhouse phone conversation while cops are standing nearby; unless telephone call is to counsel? see *C v Silanskas* **433 M 678, 684 n.7 (2001)** cops didn't respect "sanctity of the attorney-client privilege" by lurking to overhear telephone conversation; suppression by trial court judge noted, issue not presented on appeal;

C v Welch **420 M 646 (95)**—D, a firefighter, had no expectation of privacy in fire station's "lieutenants' room," despite his claim that a cot in room made it "living quarters"; D's superior could consent to police presence there (and narcotic-trained dog "alerted" at lockers there, for which search warrant was then obtained);

C v Porter P **456 M 254 (2010)**—D had expectation of privacy in his family's room at transitional shelter even though staff had "master" key and could enter room for business purposes (including checks for drugs or weapons and for compliance with daily housekeeping rules); majority rejects dissent's assertion that *Welch* 420 M 646 controls (firefighter had no reasonable expectation of privacy in station room in which he slept while on duty because area freely accessible to others);

C v Bryant **447 M 494 (2006)**—D (attorney) had no expectation of privacy in computer files of his law firm, which were open & accessible to any employee of firm who needed such file; D didn't own premises, computers, or files, & nature of charge (conspiracy to commit larceny) was not such as to confer automatic standing;

C v Montanez **410 M 290 (91)**—D has no expectation of privacy in ceiling of common hallway where he doesn't own or control access to area frequently used by others;

C v Lodge **431 M 461 (2000)**—probable cause (& warrant) to search D's apartment for evidence of crime, including guns, ammo, expended bullets & casings, after D's girlfriend's dead body was found in apartment kitchen allowed search inside slight gap between circuit breaker box and wall surface behind apartment's refrigerator (gun found there), because within apartment's "curtilage," and not accessible/open to anyone other than tenant of this apartment; alternate ground = if not within curtilage, D didn't have standing to contest search of "common" area;

C v Rise **50 MAC 836 (2001)**—either D did have access to entire premises (2 apartments), so his "lack of particularity" argument re: search warrant failed, or he didn't have access to 1st floor apartment & so had no reasonable expectation of privacy in those premises & thus no standing to argue for suppression of gun found there;

C v A Juvenile (II) **411 M 157 (91)**—warrantless search of exterior of car suspected of involvement in vehicular homicide in private residential driveway didn't disturb any legitimate expectations of privacy where car visible from public view; *Coolidge v New Hampshire* **403 US 443 (71)** distinguished;

C v Butterfield **44 MAC 926 (98)**—driveway, and walkway from it to back door of home—no legitimate expectation of privacy (in absence of shrubs, trees, fence or other obstruction), so cop could walk onto driveway & observe D on walkway;

C v Knowles **451 M 91 (2008)**—radio dispatch relaying anonymous caller info that man at particular intersection was swinging a baseball bat; officer went there, saw described man leaning into an open vehicle trunk, the bat propped against an adjacent telephone pole, & upon seeing officer get out of cruiser, man reached into pocket and threw something into trunk; when officer ordered man to stop, step away from car and come towards him with hands out of pockets (man complied), man was seized without reasonable suspicion of crime; subsequent inspection of open trunk yielded view of small packages of drugs; suppression ordered; no legitimate "plain view" (*C v Helme* 399 M 298 cited);

C v Yehudi Y **56 MAC 812 (2002)**—undercover police buying of drugs at D's home didn't impinge upon expectation of privacy, since persons generally were invitees to buy drugs; second entry of home, however, was into portion not used by invited buyers; "consent" to search thereafter, from D's parents, after 90 minutes' discussion, was product of illegal entry;

US v Dunn **480 US 294 (87)**—though trespass, D's open field/curtilage OK unless expectation of privacy (e.g., inside fence around home, but not all 198 acres);

C v Hurd **51 MAC 12 (2001)**—not OK to go onto premises to view what was inside cage when yard = enclosed partially by 8-foot high stockade fence;

California v Ciraolo **476 US 207 (86)**—aerial search = OK though in curtilage;

Florida v Riley **488 US 44 (89)**—helicopter passes at 400 feet altitude not illegal "search" under Fourth Amendment;

C v One 1985 Ford Thunderbird Automobile **416 M 603 (93)**—while **not** suggesting that person has no legitimate expectation of privacy from government's intrusion in his backyard, or that aerial surveillance without warrant can never amount to a "search" for purposes of Article 14, 3 flights here (at 1500 feet, 800 feet & 700 feet) based on detailed tip & not violating applicable laws held not to intrude on justifiable expectation of privacy;

O'Connor v Ortega **480 US 709 (87)**—while on leave (because investigation), doctor's files/desk have reasonable expectation of privacy;

C v Bloom **18 MAC 951 (84)**—no privacy right in public area of bathroom, e.g., through wall in open urinal area;

C v D'Onofrio **396 M 711 (86)**—doorman never checks, so not search to enter private club by pretending to be guest of member;

C v Cadoret **388 M 148 (83)**—club = private if enforce rules & exclude cop;

C v Page **42 MAC 943 (97)**—D had no standing to contest search of victim's car in which D had driven victim to hospital before handing keys to police & saying car belonged to victim (no reasonable expectation of privacy in auto of another, "where there is no evidence he had a right to be");

C v Hooker **52 MAC 683 (2001)**—reversing trial court's judgment that D had no expectation of privacy in taxi: D did reasonably expect that police wouldn't arbitrarily order him from taxi and look beneath a jacket he'd placed on the seat, notwithstanding diminished expectation of privacy inherent in interior of vehicle visible to others during travel on public way;

C v Morrison **429 M 511 (99)**—invited guest has no expectation of privacy when willing host has outstanding protective order against guest;

C v Hall **366 M 790 (75)**—D had standing in 3-decker hallway because owned building & had buzzers to exclude public;

C v Dora **57 MAC 141 (2003)**—police could enter locked hallway to D's apartment, because it was open to other 120 tenants & their invitees; police entry was by keys found in housebreak victim's room, & trying key in D's apartment door OK because reasonable suspicion D committed break-in; "technical trespass" said to be of no constitutional consequence, analysis instead being 'expectation of privacy';

C v Martinez **74 MAC 240 (2009)**—Commonwealth waived C v Dora argument below, but MAC panel here discomfited by its rationale in circumstances where police gained entry to building's locked common area by threatening violence;

C v Bui **419 M 392 (95)**—gun which could have been used in the murders was found at D's parents' apartment & D had burden of showing his own objectively reasonable expectancy of privacy in the place where it was found (possession of gun not element of murder);

C v Serbagi **123 MAC 57 (86)**—though trespass by cops' observations from condo hall, no standing for D with only 2% interest in hall, because no reasonable expectation of privacy;

Katz v US **389 US 347 (67)**—eavesdrop invades legitimate expectation of privacy;

Kyllo v US **533 US 27 (2001)**—obtaining by sense-enhancing technology any info re: home's interior which could not otherwise have been obtained without physical intrusion into constitutionally-protected area = search, at least where technology in question (here, thermal imaging device suggesting "grow lights" for marijuana cultivation) is not in general public use;

C v Feyenord **445 M 72 (2005), on further review of 62 MAC 200 (2004)**—dog sniffing exterior of stopped car didn't intrude upon reasonable expectation of privacy (cites *US v Morales-Zamora* **914 F.2d 200, 205 (10th Cir. 1990)**); sniff of person or odors from private homes MIGHT have different result (at 83 n.12: "would have to be evaluated based on whether the privacy expectation in each of those settings is one society is willing to deem reasonable");

US v Knotts **460 US 276 (83)**—beeper to follow car in public = OK;

US v Karo **468 US 705 (84)**—beeper in ether can in D's house invaded privacy, so "search," because it's home & cops used it to learn when can's moved;

20-I.2. Intrusion Requiring Constitutional Justification?

C v Dowdy **36 MAC 495 (94)—2 cops' approach to 2 men & 'casual conversation' (re: whether they had "heard any shots") not a "stop"**; view, of white powder in partially opened package in D's hand, was "plain": no suppression;

C v Caldwell, **36 MAC 570, 578–79 (94), S.C., 418 M 777**—similar approach/conversation, and no basis for suppression in use of "ruse" to learn what cigarette brand D smoked;

C v Thomas **38 MAC 928 (95)**—engaging D in "casual conversation" on street does not equal a stop, or seizure, & when cop observed plastic packets of white powder in D's mouth in plain view, there was probable cause to "seize", i.e., order to spit it out; contrast *C v Houle* **35 MAC 474 (93)**—contraband not seen prior to 'spit' order;

C v DePeiza **449 M 367 (2007)**—around midnight, cops on patrol drove past walking D, but reversed and returned, driving to D again and calling out to him: SJC says no seizure of D when cops first stepped out of car (following

"short conversation during which D continually shielded his right side from" cops), and position of cops on either side of D didn't block him or restrict freedom of movement; seizure did occur when cops announced intention to frisk (but by then, SJC says, although "close" question, there was reasonable suspicion);

C v Lopez **451 M 608 (2008)**—one uniformed cop in marked cruiser at 2 a.m. followed D, who was on bike, and another uniformed cop also arrived as first was stopping and motioning D to come to him, saying, "Can I speak with you?"; despite D's assertion and motion judge's ruling that D did not feel free to continue riding, SJC says there was no "stop" for which justification was needed, a "question" being "an inquiry" rather than a "command"; cites to *Rock* **429 M 609 (99)** & *Gunther G* **45 MAC 116 (98)**; drugs dropped to ground as D approached cop held admissible;

C v Ware **76 MAC 53 (2009)**—seizure occurred only after D fled and cop began pursuit, cop then having reasonable suspicion that D had gun, and cop knew D too young to lawfully possess;

C v Eckert **431 M 591 (2000)**—trooper approached D's car stopped at rest area, to check on well-being of occupant, aroused D from "resting" condition, & detected bloodshot eyes & odor of alcoholic beverage; only "reasonable suspicion" rather than probable cause was required prior to asking D to get out and perform field sobriety tests, & case was remanded for determination whether reasonable suspicion existed; critical to determination whether questioning D about 'drinking' & sobriety tests OK = whether engine was running, because if so, "operation," and probable cause for arrest for OUI existed; **NO constitutional justification was required for trooper's approach & inquiry whether D 'alright';**

C v Gomes **453 M 506 (2009)**—although approach by cops to D standing in doorway wasn't seizure, D was seized when cop immediately frisked D after asking him what he was doing;

C v Murphy **63 MAC 11 (2005)**—directing D to stand aside while police dispersed crowd isn't seizure since D was seemingly free to leave; label for subsequent interaction ("field interrogation observation") didn't "insulate it from constitutional scrutiny"; that D approached police & advised that he had a gold chain belonging to arrestee, and that he offered his observations of recent melee didn't provide ground for pat-frisk or detention; demand for ID wasn't request for voluntary cooperation, but instead was seizure;

C v Watson **430 M 725 (2000)**—drug courier profile data critical to stop (upheld here) of car driven by man after he retrieved heavy suitcases from motel room of possible "courier"; additional factor was subject's driving in manner consistent with interest in detecting surveillance; implausible responses of the two men re: suitcases = "reasonable . . . to seize" the suitcases; men were not "seized" upon detention of the suitcases or during roadside questioning;

***Bond v US* 529 US 334 (2000)**—border patrol agent on bus at standard checkpoint in Texas **"squeezed" soft-sided luggage** in overhead storage space above seats; while passenger should expect that such bag would be handled by other passengers or bus employees, **"exploratory" manner of handling here violated Fourth Amendment**;

***US v Place* 462 US 696 (83)**—dog "sniff" not a (Fourth Amendment) "search";

***C v Feyenord* 445 M 72 (2005)**—SJC holds that dog's sniff and "alert" isn't, under Article 14, a search of properly stopped vehicle: D didn't have reasonable expectation of privacy in the odor of cocaine emanating from his car (agreeing with Appeals Court, 62 MAC 200 (2004), and *Illinois v. Caballes* 125 S Ct 834, 838 (2005) ("dog sniff conducted during a concededly lawful traffic stop that reveals no information other than the location of a substance that no individual has a right to possess does not violate the Fourth Amendment") and *Indianapolis v. Edmond* 531 US 32, 40 (2000) (while vehicle stop effectuates Fourth Amendment seizure, use of narcotics-detection dog around vehicle's exterior does not transform seizure into search); Greaney, J., concurrence, is uncomfortable, noting (a) traffic stops of black and Hispanic motorists disproportionately; & (b) addition of dog to scene is "more than a de minimis intrusion into the detained individual's privacy interests";

***C v Mateo-German* 453 M 838 (2009)**—trooper conversing with out-of-gas motorist on roadside asked for permission to have dog sniff vehicle's exterior; 4 out of 7 justices say this didn't make encounter "seizure," and that consent wasn't required to have dog sniff (per *Feyenord* 445 M 72 (2005);

***C v O'Connor* 21 MAC 404 (86)**—**open car door = "search"**;

***C v Summerlin* 393 M 127 (84)**—same;

***C v Podgurski* 386 M 385 (82)**—(same)

***C v Tompert* 27 MAC 804 (89)**—same. **But see *C v Leonard* 422 M 504, 508 (96)** ignoring all the prior holdings—"not clear" that trooper's actions, "including opening the automobile door," constituted an "intrusion" requiring justification; dissent = stinging and compelling; Leonard = followed in later cases (see "community caretaking" section, post);

***C v Briand* 71 MAC 160 and, S.C., sub nom *C v Clark* 452 M 1022 (2008), agreeing with MAC reasoning**—officer at night came upon car parked in cul de sac in a boat ramp/parking area with male and female inside, and activated white "take down lights" before getting out and approaching, and smelling marijuana before ordering occupants to put hands on dashboard: no suppression of marijuana and pistol viewed in truck, as using light for illumination is not a seizure (cites *C v Oreto* 20 MAC 581 [85], *C v Grandison* 433 M 135 [2001], *C v Evans* 436 M 369 [2002]); blocking truck, use of 'blue lights, flashers, or sirens', or display of weapon or threatening words/tone

would have been indication of seizure; order of hands on dash occurred after probable cause to arrest for marijuana;

***US v Jacobsen* 466 US 109 (84)**—(*Chapter 20-F, above*) though private express company opened bag, DEA then "seized"; but OK because had probable cause & already opened, so amounts to plain view; **"field test" = seizure, but OK because privacy not invaded;** but cf. *Soldal v Cook County* **506 US 56 (92)** Fourth Amendment protections apply to plain view seizures, not simply to seizures flowing from prior search; plaintiff's mobile home was "seized"/evicted from a trailer park, & Fourth Amendment applied to possessory interest in **property**, even where "privacy" interests not implicated;

***C v Villar* 40 MAC 742 (96)**—no suppression of observations (supporting later search warrant) gained by placing arrested man (drugs) in front of door of suspect apartment and knocking on door, so that occupants would open door upon belief that this man, their colleague, was the one seeking entry/response;

***C v Acosta* 416 M 279 (93)**—no search when cops, with arrest warrant for D, knocked on apartment door & it was opened by D (who dropped bags of cocaine in attempted flight); anyone can knock on a door;

***C v Lopez* 74 MAC 815, further review allowed 455 M 1103 (2009)**—cop's knocking on motel room door wasn't seizure; because purpose was to retrieve needle in manager's room in response to manager's request, entry "not a search in the constitutional sense"; female who answered door had apparent authority to consent to entry; (re: apparent authority, see *C v Porter P* 456 M 254 (2010)—director of "transitional family shelter", though she possessed master key, did not have actual authority to consent to search of family's room); cops' belief in apparent authority to consent must be based on their diligent inquiry;

***Brendlin v California* 127 S Ct 2400 (2007)**—when cops stopped car, passenger would not have felt free to leave, either, so has Fourth Amendment right to challenge;

***C v Laureano* 411 M 708 (92)**—cops following, but not "pursuing," D into restroom of bar not a "seizure"; *C v Thibeau* 384 M 762 (81) ("stop starts when pursuit begins"), distinguished;

***C v Perry* 62 MAC 500 (2004)**—though cop ran after D when D fled after making eye contact with cop, no "seizure" "in the constitutional sense" until after cops saw D throw gun into bushes;

***C v Dasilva* 66 MAC 556 (2006)**—seizure occurred when cop began chasing D and ordered D to stop, but court found reasonable suspicion (corroboration of appearance of two men at place noted by 3rd hand anonymous source, plus D's evasion and placing hand at waistband, "indicative of the presence of a gun", plus pending gun and assault charges against D);

***C v Sykes* 449 M 308 (2007)**—when cops approached in unmarked Crown Victoria, D pedaled bike away, continuing & speeding up when cops asked to speak with him; cops also sped up and followed, first in car and then on foot after D abandoned bike and fled, "grabbing at his waistband"; D discarded object before being tackled by cops; SJC holds that seizure occurred at point of foot chase of D, but that there was then "reasonable suspicion," so no suppression of gun; "We acknowledge that this is a close case" and neither presence in high crime area nor flight from cops "is sufficient to justify a stop";

C v Franklin **456 M 818 (2010)**—D fled upon seeing unmarked Crown Victoria recognizable as cop car, and held hand to waist as he fled; though cops alighted and chased him, no seizure until they grabbed him as he climbed fence, but then, "reasonable suspicion" existed;

C v Monteiro **71 MAC 477 (2008)**—similar, (cops talking to four males "known for gun-related incidents" saw one make hand gesture to D, nearby on bike, and D pedaled away, followed by cops in unmarked car without siren or lights; when asked "can we talk to you?", D sped up , dropped bike, and ran, pursued on foot by cops; D threw gun onto roof as he ran; see two judges dissenting (*Sykes* was acknowledged to be "close case" & had "considerably more compelling facts"; see now, also *C v Narcisse* 457 M 1 (2010), disapproving police "escalation" of encounter lacking reasonable suspicion of crime;

C v Hernandez **448 M 711 (2007)**—reasonable suspicion (D pacing in area of high incidence of drug trafficking, giving other man item hidden in his shoe, but no "exchange") apparently became probable cause simply because D fled from plainclothes cop who approached him, identifying himself as cop: holding as to probable cause eliminates resolution of D's expectation of privacy in area around parked vehicle where he allegedly dumped glassine bags of heroin; this disposition allows SJC to reject D's claim of ineffective counsel in failing to file motion to suppress;

C v Alvarez **422 M 198 (96)**—taking key ring from search warrant site to apartment nearby said by anonymous tipster to be storage site for drugs (a) insertion of key & turning to see if it fit = reasonable, because minimal expectation of privacy in "lock tumbler" and (b) walkthrough to secure premises prior to warrant issuance "not unreasonable" (and no info from this use); *SEE ALSO Chapter 20-M, post, "Investigative Stops"* (i.e., what is a stop requiring only 'reasonable suspicion,', what is a seizure requiring probable cause, whether police action is either a stop or a seizure)

20-I.3. Abandonment

C v Chappee **397 M 508 (86)**—trash = abandoned, not "search";

C v Straw **422 M 756 (96)**—briefcase thrown out window as cops arrived to arrest D—**not** abandoned because action was intended to deprive police of access without precluding D's own reclamation (warrantless seizure & search required suppression);

C v Augello **71 MAC 105, S.C. 452 M 1021 (agreeing with MAC analysis) (2008)**—police investigating theft of liquor from bar went to two Ds' shared home and

were invited inside; they asked D about large overstuffed black suitcase in view, but he denied ownership, suggesting it might belong to coD/co-resident; when co-D arrived home, he also denied ownership: opening suitcase immediately on theory that it was "abandoned property" − suppression because placing suitcase in home = strong expectation of privacy not overcome by disavowal of ownership; fn.8: outcome = consistent with policy re: automatic standing (i.e., standing even if D disclaims ownership interest in place searched, *Amendola* 406 M 592, 600 [90]) fn.4: "recursory argument" that there was consent = rejected because allowing police entry to speak is not the same as permission to search apartment and items therein;

C v Krisco Corp **421 M 37 (95)**—there **was** reasonable expectation of privacy in a dumpster, located for sole use of D and access was intentionally made difficult by dumpster's placement in alley with closed gates at both ends; warrantless search unjustified;

C v Paszko **391 M 164 (84)**—abandonment's a question of intent;

C v Wedderburn **36 MAC 558 (94)**—dropping bag & walking away = abandonment (though triggered by knowledge of stealthy plainclothes cops in unmarked cruiser approaching), BUT seizure of D & search of his person, **before** retrieving bag & checking its contents, was without probable cause (& bag on person had to be suppressed);

C v Wooden **13 MAC 417 (82)**—overbearing cops caused abandonment, so bad search & seizure;

C v Mulero **38 MAC 963 (95)**—D relinquished control of bag before any "seizure", and stop was justified;

C v Garcia **34 MAC 386 (93)**—cops stopped & searched man believed to have bought drugs from D (& thereafter pursued D, with probable cause); court held D lacked standing to challenge seizure/search of buyer: "once possession or a claim of right to possession of the contraband ends, so does standing to contest the search"; cf. *C v Hill* **49 MAC 58, 61 (2000)** in similar circumstances, D argued remedy was dismissal of prosecution was appropriate, since her own seizure/stop was fruit of unconstitutional search of purported buyer (and there were not other "fruits" of her own arrest): "illegal arrest, without more, has never been viewed as a bar to subsequent prosecution";

See also consent; & fruits, probable cause, & stop/frisk re: flight from illegal cops;

C v Chappee **397 M 508 (86): abandoned property**—no reasonable expectation of privacy;

C v Rice **441 M 291 (2004)**—D, serving a sentence, abandoned his worn-out T-shirt when he surrendered it for replacement by prison administrators; no reasonable expectation of privacy in it, though DNA samples were subsequently obtained from it;

C v Ewing **67 MAC 540, further appellate review allowed 447 M 1113 (2006), but SJC agrees with Appeals Court on all issues, including this one, 449 M 1035, fn.1 (2007)**—even if police gave D beverage and cigarette with intention of obtaining DNA evidence from them, D had no expectation of privacy in cigarette butts and straw when he left them as trash in interview room;

C v Bly **448 M 473 (2007)**—D had no reasonable expectation of privacy in cigarette butts and water bottle he had abandoned, even though police secretly intended he provide DNA by drinking the water and smoking the cigarettes left available to him in interview room; D had previously declined to give blood sample;

C v Duarte **56 MAC 714 (2002)**—D, arrested, for a rape at knifepoint, left knife in police cruiser; because he abandoned it, no expectation of privacy/standing to object to seizure of it;

C v Paszko **391 M 164 (84)**—no standing after D abandoned his motel room;

C v Brass **42 MAC 88 (97)**—no reasonable expectation of privacy in hotel room occupied after check-out time (unless D shows re-registration, or has been billed for further occupancy); reserved question whether holding = same for "holdover tenant in more permanent quarters";

C v Netto **438 M 686 (2003)**—Ds were arrested in motel room; they no longer had reasonable expectation of privacy when motel personnel called police next day to retrieve items from the room;

C v Mallory **56 MAC 153 (2002)**—friend of family who lived in a bedroom in their home had no expectation of privacy in bedroom after he beat and raped family daughter & fled out the window when pursued by her father; BUT cf.

C v Ferguson **410 M 611 (91)**—D did not relinquish expectation of privacy in contents of jacket which he left behind during chase by cops; **(for cases considering when/whether D is "seized"**, *see Chapter 20-M, Investigative Stops*, **post** (e.g. *Williams* **422 M 111 (96)**);

C v Nattoo **70 MAC 625 (2007), further appellate review allowed (Feb. 2008)**—D, being evicted from trailer by its new owner, asked for time to remove his belongings, and carried most of them in large plastic trash bags, with tv set, to edge of property, next to road, calling girlfriend to pick him up with belongings; before she arrived, police arrested D on outstanding warrant; Appeals Court denies suppression, contra motion judge: while D did NOT intend to abandon, court says no reasonable expectation of privacy in the plastic bags left at roadside; *on further review*, **452 M 826 (2009)**—search/seizure "reasonable" on these "unique facts" because cop knew D had just been arrested on outstanding warrant involving firearm, and search before transporting D's belongings (left at roadside) to station where D was being held served to ensure cop's safety;

C v Small **28 MAC 533 (90)**—D, a ticketed airline passenger, didn't abandon suitcases by leaving them unclaimed at airport baggage carousel for 3 hours; 'abandonment' not established by D dropping bags and disclaiming ownership because search preceded alleged abandonment; "verbal disclaimer" standing alone isn't abandonment;

Smith v Ohio **494 US 541 (90)**—D didn't relinquish expectation of privacy in paper bag he tossed onto hood of his car when cops approached & questioned him about bag without probable cause;

C v Watson **430 M 725, 726 n.4 (2000)**—two men stopped by cops disclaimed ownership of the two suitcases which they had taken from hotel room of suspected drug courier and were transporting in their car, but this did not, contrary to Commonwealth claim, operate as a waiver of standing;

C v Pratt **407 M 647 (90)**—D had no expectation of privacy under Article 14 in garbage bags left in street near his driveway;

C v Perkins **450 M 834 (2008)**—cops interviewing D at prison brought cigarettes and soda cans with them, and D smoked and drank, leaving behind can and butts (subsequently used for DNA tests): no expectation of privacy in can because D knew prison policy prohibited him from taking it with him when leaving visit room, and abandonment of butts found as fact; *Groome* **435 M 201, 218–19** (invalidity of wavier of right based on ruse) unsuccessfully) deemed inapplicable, cops promised D nothing in exchange for abandonment;

C v Nutile **31 MAC 614 (91)**—D had no expectation of privacy in items tossed from car during chase by police;

C v Murphy **63 MAC 11 (2005)**—no suppression of drugs discarded by D as he attempted to flee from police who had observed him commit assault and battery;

20-I.4. Plain View Seizure, Scope of Justification

Coolidge v New Hampshire **403 US 443 (71)**—plain view = lawful intrusion, inadvertence, **& immediately apparent it's contraband/evidence**;

Horton v California **496 US 128, 130 (90)**—warrantless seizure of evidence in plain view doesn't require suppression under Fourth Amendment even if discovery not "inadvertent";

C v Sabetti **411 M 770 (92)**—"inadvertent" plain view sighting of drugs & common paraphernalia in car & in co-D's pocket gave cop probable cause to search car; drugs in car established probable cause to search D; dicta suggests that "inadvertence" requirement survives *Horton*, above, under Article 14;

C v Santana **420 M 205 (95)**—reserved question whether Article 14 retains "inadvertence" requirement; here, inadvertence found (fact);

C v Balicki **436 M 1 (2002)**—**SJC DECLINES COMMONWEALTH REQUEST TO ELIMINATE "inadvertence" requirement**; "inadvertence requirement" means only that police lacked probable cause to believe, prior to the search, that specific items would be discovered during search; HERE, limited search authorized by warrant was converted into "general" search of home for potential evidence, & ordering suppression of still photos & videotape recordings of entire home + testimony of cops re: same;

C v Pierre **71 MAC 58 (2008)**—warrant to search apartment, the subject's car, and the subject's person, for drugs, drug paraphernalia, and documentation establishing control/custody of apartment provided authority to search locked storage locker in basement identified as "belonging to" specified apartment; OK to open boxes in locker and incriminating/unlawful nature of bootleg/copied compact discs found there was apparent to searching cop (so plain view); days later, recording industry consultant merely confirmed (and did not 'create') cop's belief ;

C v D'Amour **428 M 725, 731 n.9 (99)**—SJC has not yet decided whether to retain the requirement that police show that they only inadvertently came upon a seized item not listed in search warrant; here, warrant for search for writings concerning firearm ownership entitled police to check the "paper" at issue (love letter from D (who was V's wife) to another man); but now see *C v Balicki* 436 M 1 (2002) (under Article 14, inadvertence requirement retained);

C v Hason **387 M 169 (82)**—without inadvertence, plain view permits seizure of contraband/hot goods/weapons;

C v LaPlante **416 M 433 (93)**—similar, plus OK to seize, during warrant execution, clothes only then ID'd by D's brother as having been worn by D on day of murder (could not have been listed in warrant authorization);

C v Kaupp **453 M 102 (2009)**—warrant application failed to establish probable cause to believe D's computer contained child pornography; fn 18: not decided = whether child porn would have been in plain view while searching for "copyrighted material" for which there was probable cause to search;

C v Tyree **455 M 676 (2010)**—refusing to hold "exigency" justifying warrantless search of home simply because "violent crime" or "involving a firearm"; no evidence that police or others were in danger, no evidence that home occupants were aware of police presence and interest; that money was taken in robbery was not ground of exigency based on feared destruction or loss of evidence; no evidence of impracticability of obtaining warrant; testimony from officers at scene did not suggest exigency existed (this instead the suggestion of motion judge); later search, with warrant upheld, after eliminating from warrant application info obtained during warrantless search; excising from application the descriptions of drug paraphernalia seen at home would defeat probable cause to search for such items, BUT SJC says 'plain view' since seen/found during search whose scope & intensity were consistent with valid portions of the warrant;

C v Cruz **53 MAC 24, 28–29 (2001)**—search warrant for drugs didn't allow officer with specialized expertise in cell phone cloning to test object(s) and then assert propriety of their seizure as being contraband in plain view; incriminating character of objects wasn't immediately apparent to 'protective sweep' cop (who triggered use of an extra search team with specialized "cell phone fraud" training in execution of warrant to search for drugs): **"use**

of the concept of a protective sweep search and of the plain view doctrine can present a potentially far-reaching encroachment on the rights protected by Article 14 and the Fourth Amendment. . . . This case graphically illustrates how police, by clever resort to these doctrines, can entirely circumvent the warrant requirement" (**id. at 36**);

C v Vesna San **63 MAC 189 (2005)**—in immediate investigation of 911 call at 1:00 am alleging burglars in kitchen, police learned description of individual male fleeing scene, and description of black van said to have been circling the area; sighting of the man standing outside the van, two miles away, gave reasonable suspicion to block the van from exiting a driveway & to detain the man, to order van occupants to exit, & to make a protective sweep of the van; sighting of item believed to have been taken in the burglary prompted victims' arrival to identify it (all actions said to be proportional to circumstances);

C v Lopes **455 M 147 (2009)**—protective sweep of stopped van would have been OK though two known occupants had already been removed and cuffed: van was large, had four rows of seats, and unclear whether more than two people were involved in homicide;

C v Straw **422 M 756 (96)**—**"plain view" applicable only when a closed container's *contents* were in plain view & seen to be contraband** (inapplicable to justify opening of briefcase thrown out window as cops entered house);

C v King **67 MAC 823 (2006)**—sight of "green leafy vegetable matter" failed to provide probable cause for search of car because (1) record did not establish that cop saw this from OUTSIDE the car (and he didn't have right beforehand to be inside the car) and (2) nothing in record established that the "matter" (which vanished before suppression hearing & could have been "a remnant of lettuce") was recognizable as contraband; "collective knowledge" doctrine doesn't allow officer to offer hearsay testimony as to what a different officer allegedly observed (D's *Crawford v Washington* (541 US 36 [2004]) argument not reached);

Bond v US **529 US 334 (2000)**—border patrol agent on bus at checkpoint in Texas **"squeezed" soft-sided luggage** in overhead storage space above seats; while passenger should expect that such bag would be handled by other passengers or bus employees, **"exploratory" manner of handling here violated Fourth Amendment**; passenger's "agreement" that bag be opened was not argued to be a voluntary consent;

C v Forde **367 M 798 (75)**—not plain view because not lawfully on premises;

C v Swanson **56 MAC 459 (2002)**—when police passed D's room (on their way to arrest person in different room in rooming house), they observed razor blade and plate on bed and that room was smoky; order to D not to leave room was a seizure without even reasonable suspicion of crime, & cop was posted at D's door; subsequent police observation of D throwing something into closet was product of illegal seizure and couldn't justify entry and search;

C v Ramos **430 M 545 (2000)**—police telling D they'd wait outside until she came out of apartment and threatening they'd have fire dept break down door if she didn't come out was not a mere "ruse" making her appearance voluntary; there was a "seizure," and photo of D (and ID by witness from it) ordered suppressed as fruits of illegal seizure;

Arizona v Hicks **480 US 321 (87)**—during exigent search (bullet fired through apartment's floor into apartment underneath, striking occupant), police moved stereo (= a search) to see (and write down) serial # on its back = suppression; **though lawfully there, scope of search exceeded its justification;**

C v Cruz **53 MAC 24, 28–29 (2001)**—search warrant for drugs didn't allow officer with specialized expertise in cell phone cloning to test object(s) and then assert propriety of their seizure as being contraband in plain view;

C v Bass **24 MAC 972 (87)**—OK entry for armed robbery suspect after ½ hour, but gun found behind dry bar exceeded exigency;

C v Hawkins **361 M 384 (72)**—though OK **search warrant for drugs, no probable cause to seize bonds;**

C v Neilson **423 M 75 (96)**—plain view doesn't justify search/seizure by campus police in dorm room, since campus police were not lawfully present in room (though they were called there by residence staff, who were lawfully in room);

C v Midi **46 MAC 591 (99)**—not plain view because not lawfully on premises and D, who was not the "owner" of the apartment or the subject police were seeking to arrest when they entered, **did** have standing;

C v Accaputo **380 M 435 (80)**—though not in search warrant, can seize weapons/contraband/loot (e.g., gun, drugs in bag), but not drugs on shelves or ledgers;

Texas v Brown **460 US 730 (83)**—can seize "mere evidence" (marijuana) seen after OK car stop—if probable cause;

C v Irwin **391 M 765 (84)**—(same);

C v Halsey **41 MAC 200 (96)**—"mere evidence" seizable during warrant execution (for other, specified, items) if plausibly related to crime of which officer is already aware, and is useful to convict or apprehend the culprit;

C v Sondrini **48 MAC 704 (2000)**—police at scene to remedy water leaking from 2d floor apartment into 1st floor apartment **not justified in search of apartment closet for evidence of crime** after sighting a pipe-like apparatus used to smoke marijuana (warrant required);

Soldal v Cook County **506 US 56 (92)**—Fourth Amendment protections apply to plain view seizures, not simply to seizures flowing from prior search; plaintiff's mobile home was "seized"/evicted from a trailer park, & **Fourth Amendment applied to possessory interest in *property*, even where "privacy" interests not implicated**; Fourth Amendment applies to "noncriminal" en-

counters, and improper state action outside "law enforcement" setting;

C v Franco **419 M 635 (95)**—because "reason to believe" arrest warrant subject was present, cops could enter apartment & then had **plain view/smell of acetone in sink, used in narcotics trafficking** (& probable cause to arrest D); motion judge found, as fact, that cops took D into other part of apartment because he was suffering adverse reaction to acetone exposure (rather than to search for other contraband), so gun & drugs were in legitimate plain view;

C v Thomas **38 MAC 928 (95)**—engaging D in "casual conversation" on street does not equal a stop, or seizure, & when cop observed plastic packets of white powder in D's mouth in plain view, there was probable cause to "seize", i.e., order to spit it out; contrast *C v Houle* **35 MAC 474 (93)**—contraband not seen prior to 'spit' order;

C v Ye **52 MAC 390 (2001)**—D's claim on direct appeal that trial attorney was ineffective in failing to move to suppress items from D's toolbox at work could not be resolved: unknown from record whether D controlled the toolbox, and whether it was closed or open when officer was shown around by D's employer;

C v Rand **363 M 554 (73)**—**"plain view" not properly invoked to take car to station and search within its front grille**, etc. (because not inadvertent); here, however, cops had probable cause to believe car had "hit and run" 3 hours before it wrecked with another car; SJC refuses to disapprove of search of car at the station after towing, since there was probable cause to search it at the scene of the latter collision;

C v Lett **393 M 141 (84)**—**though not inadvertent, can seize drugs (if probable cause) during search under search warrant having probable cause for diamond, but not drugs;**

C v Pigaga **12 MAC 960 (81)**—**license from wallet at station not "inadvertent";**

US v Jacobsen **466 US 109 (84)**—(*Chapter 20-F, above*) **though private express company opened bag, DEA then "seized"; but OK because had probable cause & already opened, so amounts to plain view;** "field test" = seizure, but OK because privacy not invaded;

US v Dunn **480 US 294 (87)**—though trespass, D's open field/curtilage OK unless expectation of privacy (e.g., inside home-fence, not all 198 acres);

C v Hurd **51 MAC 12 (2001)**—NOT OK to go onto premises to view what was inside a cage when yard = enclosed partially by 8-foot high stockade fence;

20-I.5. Automatic Standing

Wong Sun v US **371 US 471 (63)**—(*Chapter 20-B & -G above*) no standing re: drugs taken from co-D;

Jones v US **362 US 257 (60)**—standing if legitimately present or possessory crime; BUT . . . ; *US v Salvucci* **448 US 83 (80)** no more automatic standing for federal constitutional claims; must have reasonable expectation of (own) privacy; **possessory crime or legitimately on premises not enough under Fourth Amendment**; (*see also Rakas v Illinois* **439 US 128 (78)**, *Rawlings v Kentucky* **448 US 98 (80)** no Fourth Amendment standing for drugs in another's purse or for car's passenger);

U.S. v Padilla **508 US 77 (93)**—Supreme Court extinguishes rule by which all alleged coconspirators have standing; instead, each D seeking to suppress must establish legitimate expectation of privacy in place searched or property seized;

C v Albert **51 MAC 377 (2001)**—no standing for D re: search of coconspirator's shirt, because possession of cocaine not essential element of "conspiracy to traffic in cocaine";

C v Podgurski **386 M 385 (82)**—maybe still automatic standing under Declaration of Rights, Article 14; passenger had reasonable expectation of privacy in van (& glove box, etc.); (& *see also King* **389 M 233 (83)**);

C v Mora **402 M 262 (88)**—no Fourth Amendment standing even under Jones because no presence/possession/ownership at time/place of search & seizure;

C v Amendola **406 M 592 (90)—D has automatic standing under Article 14 where possession of seized evidence at time of search is essential element of crime charged**; but D has no automatic standing to challenge possession of non-contraband (e.g., scale); **federal rule of *US v Salvucci* 448 US 83 (80) rejected**;

C v Colon **449 M 207 (2007)**—motion judge held that D had no reasonable expectation of privacy/standing to challenge search of girlfriend's apartment, but D argued automatic standing because gun found there was basis of his possession charge (concerning point at which V was killed): SJC doesn't "decide" whether D had automatic standing, because rules that warrant was supported by probable cause in any event;

C v Price **408 M 668 (90)**—D has no automatic standing to challenge videotapes recording drug deal because their possession not element of crime;

C v Bui **419 M 392 (95)**—gun which could have been used in the murders was found at D's parents' apartment & D had burden of showing his own objectively reasonable expectancy of privacy in the place where it was found (possession of gun not element of murder);

C v Frazier **410 M 235 (91)—automatic standing rule of *Amendola* (406 M 592 (90)) extended to places or things in addition to cars & homes (e.g., friend's pocketbook) so long as D would be required to forfeit right against self-incrimination as to possession of con-**traband in order to make Article 14 challenge**; automatic standing not available to challenge evidence of conspiracy because possession not an element;

C v Ware **75 MAC 220 (2009)**—in order to trigger art. 14 suppression analysis, must be governmental action, standing, and expectation of privacy, but where there are codefendants and constructive possession triggers automatic standing, there is limited exception to requirement that each D have expectation of privacy in place searched; here, D could challenge search of confederate's home because charges "can be viewed as [alleging]" actual or constructive possession of firearm located there;

C v Garcia **34 MAC 386, 390–91 nn.4–5 (93)**—catalog of cases re: "automatic standing";

C v Montes **49 MAC 789, 793–94 (2000)**—because D had no standing to contest unlawful arrest of another, D couldn't use it to excuse/defend against charge of assault and battery on cops;

Barbara F. v Bristol Division of Juvenile Court **432 M 1024 (2000)**—pregnant woman sought emergency relief/review of judge's order that an unrelated pregnant woman be taken into custody of court and to some medical facility to determine her general health & anticipated delivery date & "furnish the court with a recommended prenatal treatment plan as deemed necessary by the examining physician", but plaintiff had no standing (despite allegation of fear that, because she was frequently in Bristol County, she would be similarly restrained); **"representative" standing unavailable, as "generally limited to cases in which it is difficult or impossible for the actual right holders to assert their claims"**;

20-I.6. Target Standing

C v Waters **420 M 276 (95)—if target standing is to be recognized, it will be in a case in which police (mis)conduct is "serious" and "distinctly egregious"**; D has no standing to challenge search of 3d party's apartment in which he had no expectation of privacy, though he contended its purpose was to obtain statement against D from a person there present (that person's eventual trial testimony ruled not suppressible, anyway); see also *C v Kirschner* **67 MAC 836 (2006)**;

C v Scardamaglia **410 M 375 (91)**—open question whether "target standing" available under Article 14; not available here because evidence seized from 3d party used only to obtain warrant, but was not introduced against D at trial; see also *C v Manning* **406 M 425 (90)**;

20-J. WARRANTS, ARREST OR SEARCH

Johnson v United States **333 US 10 (1948)**—point of Fourth Amendment, "which is not grasped by zealous officers, is not that it denies law enforcement the support of the usual inferences which reasonable men draw from evi-dence. Its protection consists in requiring that those inferences be drawn by a neutral and detached magistrate";

C v Blood **400 M 61, 72-73 (87)**—purpose of warrant requirement in article 14 is to subject police suspicions to scrutiny of neutral and detached magistrate instead of leaving them to be judged by the officer;

C v Moran **353 M 166 (67)**—"inferences leading to the issuance of a warrant should be drawn by a neutral magistrate rather than by a police officer";

See Chapter 20-G re: "probable cause"; & -I re: plain view after search warrant;

See Chapter 20-L for incursion into homes for service of arrest warrants, e.g. **Steagald v US 451 US 204 (81)**—can't enter D's home with arrest warrant for X, without search warrant; *but see C v Silva* **440 M 772 (2004)—no suppression of evidence against D, gained when police entered X's apartment upon a valid arrest warrant for X; under Article 14, need only reasonable belief that warrant subject both lived in and was present at the residence;**

C v Webster **75 MAC 247 (2009)**—though police had reasonable belief that D lived in targeted apartment, nothing supported judge's conclusion that they reasonably believed D was in apartment when they entered it without search warrant (though with arrest warrant); illegal to then "secure" it from inside, where they remained for seven hours;

20-J.1. General

G.L. c. 276, §§ 1–8 (*see Chapter 20-F*)—search warrant identifying person/property, for crime (fruits/instruments/weapons); form; affidavit; execution (within 7 days);

C v Kaupp **453 M 102 (2009)**—regarding whether failure to complete "forensic examination of [D's] computer within seven days constitutes a violation of GL c.276, §3A," SJC said 'no,' because written return listing devices to be examined (painstakingly, over time, after seizure) was filed within seven days after warrant issued;

G.L. c. 276, § 3—items seized, if obtained by theft or otherwise in commission of crime, shall be returned to rightful owners; other property shall be disposed of as the court orders, & may be forfeited & either sold or destroyed;

M.R.Crim.P. 6 arrest warrant—prefer summons; form; service;

C v Connolly **454 M 808 (2009)**—use of GPS (global positioning system) device was "not for tangible property," provisions of G.L. c. 276 re: search warrants = inapplicable; instead, GPS tracking warrants are issued under common law authority of courts; monitoring period must be no longer than fifteen days from date of warrant's issuance;

C v Guaba **417 M 746 (94)—Article 14 requires that officers executing search warrant have it *in hand*, unless exigent circumstances permit a warrantless search**; *C v Blake* **49 MAC 134 (2000)** D, convicted in 1990, couldn't get benefit of *Guaba* rule in postconviction motion (M.R.Crim.P. 30) for "new trial";

C v Forish **61 MAC 554 (2004)**—warrant provided no description of objects of search, and affidavit supporting warrant application (which specified objects) wasn't attached to it: suppression required;

Groh v Ramirez **124 S.Ct. 1284 (2004)**—search warrant failed to describe objects of search and failed to incorporate by reference the objects listed in both the warrant application & supporting affidavit;

C v Brown **68 MAC 261 (2007)**—though warrant identified items to be seized, and D's residence as place to be searched, it did not specifically ID D as person to be searched, other than authorizing "any person present"; because application failed to provide probable cause for "any person present", search of D = illegal; *C v DePina* **75 MAC 842, 845 (2009)**—warrant authorized not only search of D's 3rd floor apartment but also search of D's person (& seizure of cell phone from his person came within "implements related to distribution of cocaine" given cop's affidavit; valid alternative basis was 'search incident to arrest');

C v Celestino **47 MAC 916 (99)**—warrantless arrest in a public place is permissible if arresting officer has probable cause; no requirement that police obtain anticipatory warrant;

Zurcher v Stanford Daily **436 US 547 (78)**—search warrant of non-suspect if probable cause that there is evidence, fruits, or instrumentalities of crime there;

US v Ventresca **380 US 102 (65)**—may sustain marginal search and seizure only with search warrant;

Beldotti v Commonwealth **41 MAC 185 (96)**—D's motion for return of "sexually explicit" materials properly denied;

20-J.2. Securing Premises

C v Blake **413 M 823 (92)**—under Fourth Amendment and Article 14, police may "secure" area to be searched before warrant is procured as long as the search doesn't begin until warrant is obtained;

C v Voris **38 MAC 377 (95)**—knock on door, entry, explanation that cops were "impounding" premises while awaiting search warrant but were not "arresting" anyone—OK;

C v Swanson **56 MAC 459 (2002)**—when police passed D's room (on their way to arrest person in different room in rooming house), they observed razor blade and plate on bed and that room was smoky; order to D not to leave room was a seizure without even reasonable suspicion of crime; subsequent police observation of D throwing something into closet was product of illegal seizure and couldn't justify entry and search;

C v Taylor **426 M 189 (97)**—OK "detention" of D until search warrant for his clothes & shoes could be obtained (presence of fire accelerant suspected);

C v Powers **39 MAC 911 (95)**—police (about to be?) armed with search warrants for D & D's car and other named individuals & a residence could lawfully search D as he left the named residence (police not required to ignore possibility that D was about to drive off with the evidence);

C v Feyenord **62 MAC 200 (2004), & on further appellate review, SJC also upholds search 445 M 72**

(2005)—upholds 30-minute detention of motorist (after stop for broken headlight during daytime hours) for **sniff by drug-detecting dog**, by holding there was probable cause for arrest (though no actual arrest) for lack of license on person; "Feyenord's Fourth Amendment argument is foreclosed by decisions of the Supreme Court, including Illinois v. Caballes, 125 S.Ct. 834, 838 (2005) ('dog sniff conducted during a concededly lawful traffic stop that reveals no information other than the location of a substance that no individual has a right to possess does not violate the Fourth Amendment') and *Indianapolis v. Edmond*, 531 U.S. 32, 40 (2000) (while vehicle stop effectuates Fourth Amendment seizure, use of narcotics-detection dog around vehicle's exterior does not transform seizure into search)";

C v Phillips **452 M 617 (2008)**—detention of D, matching description of one of three men running from bloody (homicide) crime scene twenty minutes earlier = permissible under "Terry", even though D was handcuffed and placed in police wagon until witness arrived to make show-up ID;

C v Watkins **425 M 830 (97)**—seven-hour stay at D's residence (grandmother's apartment) pending arrival of warrant OK: question of illegal entry not reached because nothing then seized & no info from entry was used in warrant application;

C v Navarro **39 MAC 161 (95)**—after arrest of drug dealer who confessed that more drugs plus a sleeping individual were at apartment, OK for police to go, advise formerly sleeping occupant that warrant was coming and she could stay or go (but anything she took with her would be searched); OK to seize/look inside open purse to which she lunged (reasonable fear for safety);

C v Kaupp **453 M 102 (2009)**—OK to seize/"secure" D's computer pending issuance of search warrant given "ease with which computer files may be accessed and deleted"; 9-day delay in seeking warrant held not to have rendered seizure unreasonable;

K. Smith, *Criminal Practice & Procedure*, 167–92 & 217–37 (2d ed. 1983 & Supp.);

20-J.3. "Technical" Defects in Application, Affidavit, Warrant or Return

C v Torres **45 MAC 915 (98)**—though G.L. c. 276, § 3A requires that warrant be returned to Court not later than 7 days from issuance date (with relevant info), omission from return of info that 2 ounces of cocaine were allegedly seized did not result in suppression of the cocaine, though different result possible if D showed prejudice or "evidence of police misconduct";

C v Bryant **447 M 494 (2006)**—D argued for suppression on ground that return was not timely made on computer files seized (Commonwealth claimed more time was required to analyze the "electronically stored files"), but SJC reserved for later this issue of first impression;

US v Leon **468 US 897 (84)**—OK to rely in good faith on search warrant (lacking probable cause);

Massachusetts v Sheppard **468 US 981 (84)**—(same), though search warrant lacked particularity (drug warrant application form used for murder search/seizure);

Herring v US **129 S Ct 695 (2009)**—after D's arrest on warrant listed in adjacent county's database, search incident to arrest yielded gun and drugs; warrant, however, had been recalled months earlier though this info hadn't been entered into database: NO SUPPRESSION when police mistakes leading to search = result of isolated negligence attenuated from the search rather than systemic error or reckless disregard of constitutional requirements;

Illinois v Krull **480 US 340 (87)**—evidence not suppressed when seized in good faith under authority of statute later found unconstitutional; BUT SEE *C v Sheppard* **394 M 381 (85) no Mass. good-faith exception**; G.L. c. 276 = tougher than Mass./U.S. constitutions, & probable cause must be in affidavit.; suppress if substantial violation of Declaration of Rights Article 14 or G.L. c. 276, § 2B, e.g., lack of probable cause; here = insubstantial; *C v Valerio* **449 M 562, 569 (2007)**—Mass. still doesn't adopt "good faith" exception, but SJC says here, technically defective warrant met substantive requirements of particularity, so search wasn't "general" and unlawful (in portion of standard search warrant application calling for description of property to be seized, cop erroneously described instead the place to be searched, BUT 8-page affidavit plus "extensive supporting documentation" were attached "by paperclip" to warrant application, which incorporated by reference the info in affidavit; attachments were likewise affixed to warrant itself);

C v Censullo **40 MAC 65 (96)**—though cop stopped D because he believed D going wrong way on one way street, street here had been 2-ways for 5 years; "good faith" exception is applied by U.S. Supreme Court when the police good faith action is flawed because of fatal error by some **other** entity, not cop's own failure/mistake;

C v Coburn **62 MAC 314 (2004)**—distinguishes Censullo, because cop's lack of knowledge of imaginary line between Concord and Lincoln contradicting roadside sign designating town line wasn't unreasonable or based on misconduct attributable to police;

C v Wilkerson **436 M 137 (2002)**—refusing to suppress evidence seized as result of warrantless arrest for whose "probable cause" cops relied on erroneous info provided by Registry of Motor Vehicles re: status of D's license; there was "no unlawful conduct to be deterred by exclusion of the evidence";

C v Bass **24 MAC 972 (87)**, citing *C v Truax* **397 M 174 (86)**—(form) affidavit OK despite fact that it incorporated attached, but unsworn, document & facts;

C v Jordan **397 M 494 (86)**—(same) for 2 search warrants & affidavits on same day;

C v Hecox **35 MAC 277 (93)**—police show of force/ arrest of D **not** excused on ground that cop believed that D had not yet been arraigned on charges & that there was outstanding arrest warrant; **police were at fault for not informing themselves**; *US v Leon* excuses, under **federal** constitution, police reliance on erroneous finding by magistrate; Hecox made no separate state constitutional claim;

C v Curcio **26 MAC 738 (89)—oral clerk's permission (papers later) = NO search warrant**;

C v Fredette **396 M 455 (85)—no oral arrest warrant**;

C v Rotolo **45 MAC 927 (98)**—warrant issued at 2 p.m., but affidavit purportedly supporting application for it was not sworn until 2:20 p.m.: failure to include this as ground in written motion to suppress "probably fatal," but appellate court also willing to believe (without record inquiry as to why) it was merely a "clerical error";

C v Ocasio **434 M 1 (2001)**—loss of original warrant not necessarily fatal: if judge finds that original became unavailable otherwise than through the serious fault of Commonwealth & that reasonable search had been made for it, "secondary" evidence = admissible to establish its contents;

C v Byfield **413 M 426, reversing 32 MAC 912 (92)**—information in affidavit about transaction was sufficient where magistrate could draw on common knowledge & common sense in community & common sense inferences that "a forty" means $40 worth of drugs;

C v Pellagrini **405 M 86 (89)**—judge's failure to sign search warrant didn't invalidate it;

C v McRae **31 MAC 559 (91)**—information contained in wanted poster attached to affidavit was properly incorporated by reference;

C v Forish **61 MAC 554 (2004)**—warrant provided no description of objects of search, and affidavit supporting warrant application (which specified objects) wasn't attached to it: suppression required; *Groh v Ramirez* **124 S Ct 1284 (2004)**—search warrant failed to describe objects of search and failed to incorporate by reference the objects listed in both the warrant application & supporting affidavit;

C v Donahue **430 M 710, 714 n.1 (2000)**—affidavit filed in support of search warrant application asserted that polygraph test of D indicated "extreme deception" in answers about his wife's disappearance; SJC didn't decide whether polygraph results may be so used because there was probable cause without this data (and here no claim that test results were falsified or stated with reckless disregard as to accuracy);

C v Watson **430 M 725 (2000)**—SJC excused search warrant application affidavit's assertion that dog named Maxie, well-trained in narcotics-sniffing, alerted to the subject luggage (different dog, "Roxy," was used, and this was taken to be merely a mistake of name, not a fatal omission about the relevant dog's qualifications);

C v Villela **39 MAC 426 (95)**—magistrate should specify in warrant that search is authorized only after triggering event (here, a controlled buy), but not fatal because affidavit supporting warrant application "informed magistrate of the circumstances . . . to occur prior to the search";

C v Gauthier **425 M 37 (97)**—"triggering event" for execution/approval of search need not be on warrant's face

or attached to it (in affidavit) (overruling **S.C., 41 MAC 765 (96)** and *C v Callahan* **41 MAC 420 (96)**); suppression ordered nonetheless because correct "triggering event" hadn't occurred **and** SJC held no probable cause here absent that event; reserved question = whether triggering event necessary "even if . . . no triggering event was necessary to establish probable cause";

C v Sbordone **424 M 802 (97)**—though it was a **"constitutional violation" for civilian (albeit "investigator") to participate in execution of search warrant**, suppression not required (because all important tasks were performed by others);

C v Douglas **399 M 141 (87)**—violates **particularity rules** of Declaration of Rights Article 14, G.L. c. 276, §§ 1 & 2, & Fourth Amendment for search warrant to let cop determine area; even under *US v Leon*, **cop's "good faith" can't cure general search warrant**;

C v Forish **61 MAC 554 (2004)**—warrant provided no description of objects of search, and affidavit supporting warrant application (which specified objects) wasn't attached to it: suppression required;

20-J.4. False Affidavits and Franks Hearings

C v Reynolds **374 M 142 (77)**—hearing if preliminary showing (affidavit) "worthy of hearing"; suppress if intentional & material, not inadvertent & without negligence;

Franks v Delaware **438 US 154 (78)**—if preliminary showing (by affidavit) that affidavit's intentionally/recklessly false, D gets hearing & suppress if D proves it & if remainder isn't probable cause;

Kalina v Fletcher **522 US 118 (97)**—when prosecutor signs arrest warrant affidavit, asserting "facts" under pains of perjury, prosecutor is merely acting as a witness & has no absolute prosecutorial immunity from damages suit under 42 USC § 1983;

C v Long **454 M 542 (2009)**—intentionally or recklessly OMITTED material may form basis for mounting *Franks v Delaware* challenge (citations); where omission forms basis for challenge, judge considers whether the affidavit, supplemented by the omitted info, furnishes probable cause; **where D seeks suppression of wiretap evidence based on use of "truncated excerpts" of oral recordings to establish probable cause, motion judge shall conduct de novo review of affidavit and omitted evidence pursuant to GL c. 272, §99E-F, and "ordinarily need not be concerned with the *Franks* requirements"**;

C v Carpenter **22 MAC 911 (86)**—cop's drug indictment doesn't compel Franks hearing or informant disclosure; but could give "preliminary evidentiary hearing";

C v John **36 MAC 702 (94)**—refusing to enforce discovery order allowing defendant particulars as to alleged controlled buys by informant, because viewed as fishing expedition toward a Franks motion; presumption of validity of affidavits supporting search warrant application cited;

C v Nine Hundred Ninety Two Dollars **383 M 764 (81)**—"reckless" = (at minimum) reason to disbelieve; affiant responsible for 2d cop's lie, maybe paid informant too; reserves issue whether Article 14 requires suppression of all evidence following deliberate (rather than reckless) misrepresentation in affidavit supporting warrant application, even if misrepresentation was not necessary to probable cause;

C v Valdez **402 M 65 (88)**—**no suppression for negligence, even under Declaration of Rights article 14**; discretion to give Franks hearing though criteria unmet & though judge #1 denied;

C v Bennett **414 M 269 (93)**—cites Article 14 as **possibly** providing greater sanctions (cite to *Nine Hundred and Ninety Two Dollars* **383 M 764, 768**), i.e., maybe suppression even if probable cause existed without the "deliberate misrepresentation";

C v Bennett **39 MAC 531 (95)**—notes possibility alluded to in $992 and *Bennett* **414 M 269**; but doesn't answer the question;

C v Ramos **402 M 209 (88)**—can deny (but COULD give) hearing because no substantial showing that it was intentional/reckless; (Declaration of Rights, Article 14 may not need materiality if intentional);

C v Watson **430 M 725 (2000)**—SJC excused affidavit's false assertion that dog named Maxie, well trained in narcotic sniffing, alerted to the luggage (different dog, "Roxy," was used, and this was taken to be merely a mistake of name, not a fatal omission about the relevant dog's qualifications);

C v Ramos **72 MAC 773 (2008)**—affiant ("affirmatively misstated) overstated sniff-dog's expertise and accuracy, and without the inflated figure and omitted evidence that handler had specifically warned against false indications and acknowledged recent false positives, there was no probable cause for warrant issuance; hearing judge's findings supporting suppression were "well supported";

C v Lewin (I) **405 M 566 (89)**—prosecutorial & police misconduct involving either delayed disclosure or fabrication of informant by police didn't justify dismissal where irremediable prejudice to D not established; D entitled to voir dire hearing on potentially exculpatory evidence from putative informant & to elicit at trial government misconduct without rebuttal by prosecutor; motion judge's finding that informant existed was clearly erroneous where there was equally compelling evidence that informant was fabricated;

C v Amral **407 M 511 (90)**—**in camera hearing must be held where defense affidavits make "substantial preliminary showing"** that affiant intentionally or recklessly made false statements; counsel not entitled to be present but may submit questions; judge may allow prosecutor to be present & may question informant as well as affiant; detailed procedures discussed;

C v Crawford **410 M 75 (91)**—where credibility of cop's assertion that informant's prior tip led to arrests & drug seizure necessary to justify warrantless search, D

entitled to in camera hearing to demand names of arrestees; **counsel may not be excluded at hearing to determine sufficiency of tip;**

C v Pignato **31 MAC 907 (91)**—D had right to in camera hearing where D provided new affidavit of person claiming to be anonymous informant & where information "substantially refuted in material ways" statements by cop contained in search warrant affidavit;

C v Padilla **42 MAC 67, 71 (97)**—counsel's failure to request action on *Franks* motion resulted in waiver (investigation disclosed that affiant had, in cited cases, attributed info/assistance to someone **else**, and this was enough for a hearing, in a motion judge's discretion);

C v Corriveau **396 M 319(85)**—omissions weren't significant/misleading;

C v Luce **34 MAC 105 (93)**—so long as affiant makes out probable cause with correct info, affiant "not bound to recite investigative efforts that didn't pan out", though D argued there was duty to include such "exculpatory" info;

C v Assad **393 M 418 (84)**—fact that D's prior case was NG, not G (as search warrant said) = reckless, but the rest = probable cause;

C v Douzanis **384 M 434 (81)**—informant disclosure not required, but judge has discretion to give D some discovery or even a hearing (e.g., in camera);

K. Smith, *Criminal Practice & Procedure*, §§ 186–92 & 202–07 (2d ed. 1983 & Supp.)—Franks hearings & "informant's privilege"; (*See also Chapter 6, Discovery of Informants & Chapter 20-G, informant probable cause*);

C v Ramirez **416 M 41 (93)**—prior to trial, & after judge's interview of detective, D's motion to compel disclosure of informant's identity was denied, BUT post-conviction, as result of intense labor and revelations concerning Boston Police fabrication of informants in other cases, **Franks** hearing ordered (and suppression, rather than a new trial, would be appropriate remedy if informant shown to be fictitious entity); **since defense allegations didn't lend themselves to affidavit form, OK to have made showing by voluminous other material & "extensive written analysis"** of same; here, *C v Singer* **29 MAC 708 (91)** is overruled, to extent it implied or held that no *Franks* hearing necessary unless D had "direct evidence of perjury" ("too high a burden on a criminal defendant presenting a legitimate grievance");

C v Ramirez (II) **49 MAC 257 (2000)**—because D has burden of proving falsity, motion judge's rejection of informant's testimony (informant denied the 'personal knowledge' attributed to informant in cop's affidavit supporting search warrant) in favor of cop's version (that informant did tell cop he had personal knowledge) = no relief for D; **refusal to find error in exclusion of D from courtroom while informant and detective testified, barring counsel from discussing testimony with D, & impounding judge's decision after the 'Franks' hearing** (only one small question was to be explored at hearing, D failed to show prejudice);

C v Martino **412 M 267 (92)**—D not entitled to Franks hearing where cop's reasonable, though mistaken, 'surmise' that videotape had been erased was not shown to have been intentionally, knowingly, or recklessly made;

C v Russell **46 MAC 513, 521 (99)**—though D presented affidavits from himself & another swearing that conversations allegedly reported by informants did not occur, nothing to show cop affiant knew or should have known that they did or did not occur, so no abuse of discretion to deny *Franks* hearing;

C v Blake **413 M 823 (92)**—D not entitled to Franks hearing where affiant's statement that D proceeded "directly" to certain location was not misleading;

C v Mebane **33 MAC 941 (92)**—D not entitled to Franks hearing simply because affiant stated that D's train would be arriving 9:30 when in fact it was scheduled to arrive at 9:00;

C v Dion **31 MAC 168 (91)**—D not entitled to Franks hearing where he failed to establish that false statement was necessary to probable cause determination;

C v Donahue **430 M 710, 714 n.1 (2000)**—affidavit filed in support of search warrant application asserted that polygraph test of D indicated "extreme deception" in answers about his wife's disappearance; SJC didn't decide whether polygraph results may be so used because there was probable cause without this data (and here no claim that test results were falsified or stated with reckless disregard as to accuracy);

20-J.5. Nighttime Searches

C v Garcia **23 MAC 259 (86)**—search warrant must specify nighttime, but need not show reason; & D must show both harm & lack of reason;

C v Grimshaw **413 M 73 (92)**—unauthorized nighttime search does not automatically require suppression because merely a statutory violation of G.L. c. 276, § 2, not a state or federal constitutional violation; **"nighttime" search defined for future as between 10 p.m. & 6 a.m.;**

C v Yazbeck **31 MAC 769 (92)**—forcible nighttime entry allowed only if "reasonable" under Article 14, even where nighttime search properly authorized & knock & announce requirements met; factors include: lateness of hour, D in nightclothes, single family residence, police conduct, etc.; cops' entry here didn't cross line;

C v Siano **52 MAC 912 (2001)**—presumption = that magistrate had cause for issuing "nighttime" warrant; no requirement that magistrate state or identify cause for issuance, no apparent constraints (statutory or other) on authorization of nighttime execution of warrants;

20-J.6. Knock and Announce Requirement

US v Ramirez **523 US 65 (98)**—common law principle of announcement before entry is element of "reasonableness" inquiry under Fourth Amendment; no-knock OK if police have reasonable suspicion that knock and announce,

under the particular circumstances, would be dangerous or futile, or would "inhibit effective investigation of crime," e.g., allowing destruction of evidence;

Hudson v Michigan **126 S. Ct. 2159 (2006)**—5:4 decision: under Fourth Amendment, suppression is not required as remedy for failure to knock and announce; "reasonable wait time standard" is necessarily vague;

C v Silva **440 M 772 (2004)**—must specifically assert, in written motion to suppress, issue of failure to knock & announce, or it's waived; in absence of 'no knock' warrant, can justify failure to knock & announce upon appraisal of circumstances at threshold of search/arrest; here, failure to announce purpose = justified by concern about imminent destruction of evidence;

C v Scalise **387 M 413 (82)**—no-knock search warrant OK if affidavit with particularity supports premise that there's danger or evidence that will be destroyed);

C v. Ortega **441 M 170 (2004)**—no-knock warrant probably OK because affidavit detailed occupants' "assaultive history" and info from informant (D didn't allow customers into his apartment, used several different vehicles), plus assertion that apartment was on third floor, making it more likely that occupants would have advance knowledge of police present (and ability to dispose of evidence); failure to file motion to suppress wasn't ineffective assistance of counsel;

C v Manni **398 M 741 (86)**—bad no-knock entry because alleged fear known at time of search warrant application without a no knock authorization request;

C v Cundriff **382 M 137 (80)**—can enter apartment without knock if reasonable fear;

C v Gomes **408 M 43 (90)**—cops may make no-knock entry only where there is "special need" & where safety, privacy, & property interests plus deterrent function of rule are served; unjustified no-knock warrant doesn't automatically require suppression; battering door with sledgehammer required suppression;

C v Allen **28 MAC 589 (90)**—no-knock entry justified by officer's reasonable fears;

C v Carrasco **405 M 316 (89)**—knock & announce requirement met where cops made presence known before forcibly entering apartment;

C v Siano **52 MAC 912 (2001)**—though 'knock & announce' rule was violated by police entering enclosed porch (furnished as family room) by police opening its unlocked door from the exterior and proceeding to kitchen door (purportedly ajar), facts that cop then knocked on kitchen door, and twice addressed occupant by name, saying 'it's the . . . police,' and "we have a search warrant for your house," and that D invited them in meant that "objectives" of rule were substantially achieved; no constraints announced on authorization of nighttime execution of warrants; if magistrate issues "nighttime" warrant, "he is presumed to have had cause for doing so";

C v Brisson **31 MAC 418 (91)**—D has burden of proving unauthorized no-knock violation because rule not constitutionally based; BUT SEE, contra, *US v Ramirez*

523 US 65 (98) (knock and announce **is** a legitimate inquiry re: "reasonableness" requirement of Fourth Amendment, though not always reasonable to require it);

C v Rodriguez **415 M 447 (93)**—cops armed with no-knock warrant **not** required to reappraise situation at threshold and knock if "there was no need not to"; 'no-knock' upheld simply because large quantities of drugs indicated target was unusually "sophisticated" & affiant claimed that handguns were danger to officers in drug searches; **LATTER JUSTIFICATION NO LONGER SUFFICES: INFO MUST BE PARTICULARIZED TO SEARCH TO BE UNDERTAKEN PRESENTLY—see** *C v Jiminez* **438 M 213, 220 n.5 (2002), citing** *Richards v Wisconsin* **520 US 385 (97)**; nonetheless, Rodriguez doesn't get any relief: *see C v Rodriguez* **443 M 707 (2005)**;

C v Macias **429 M 698 (99)**—no-knock warrant BAD; **MA (unlike U.S.) requires probable cause to believe that in the particular circumstances, evidence will be destroyed; fact that subject is drugs is not enough**, & here, drugs' storage in several locations around apartment made quick disposal unlikely; likelihood that D could spot cops coming = not enough to establish probable cause; that undercover cop "might" be used is not enough (when here, one was not so used inside the apartment);

C v Santiago **70 MAC 519, FAR allowed, 450 M 1104 (2007)**—Commonwealth claimed "no knock" warrant valid because warrant was for, inter alia, a BB pistol, but no claim that it was a safety concern or that D had it for use against intruders; list of D's criminal history, including arraignments for firearms violations and assault and battery/abuse prevention order, didn't suggest that D might use force against executing officers; fact that D owned pit bull and "mutt" didn't indicate their likely use as weapons: no-knock warrant affidavit failed to establish threat to officer safety, so suppression ordered; **ON FURTHER REVIEW, 452 M 573 (2008)**—suppression order reversed, warrant application not to be read in hypertechnical fashion; majority holds that, by itself, presence of a dog, even one of a breed which is considered aggressive, = not enough for no-knock, but in combination with other factors here, no-knock permissible (Cowin, J., wrote separately to disagree with the "dog" point); *US v Gonzalez* **164 F.Supp.2d 119, 125 (D. Mass. 2001)** (presence of Rottweiler alone without evidence that D himself was violent did not constitute sufficient safety risk to justify no-knock entry);

C v Jimenez **438 M 213 (2002), supplanting/overruling in part 53 MAC 902 (2001)**—while mere assertion that Ds were drug dealers and drug dealers often possess guns wasn't sufficient even to satisfy "reasonable suspicion" prerequisite to 'no-knock' warrant under Federal constitution, SJC found probable cause to believe that evidence would be destroyed if police first knocked (front door to building was three floors below apartment to be searched, & its windows overlooked route police would be taking, & drug operation had been conducted in extreme secrecy); BUT at time of search, no probable cause for no-

knock existed because it was dark out, front door was unlocked, and no one was at windows or watching for police; use of battering ram to knock down apartment door, instead of knock & announce, means suppression;

Richards v Wisconsin **520 US 385 (97)**—affidavit for no-knock can't merely state that in affiant's experience handguns are danger to cops during drug searches; must have SPECIFIC INFO RE: SEARCH TO BE UNDERTAKEN; any contrary intimation in *C v Rodriguez* **415 M 447, 448–51 (93)** is thus no longer good law;

C v Sepulveda **406 M 180 (90)—peaceful ruse by police may circumvent knock and announce requirement**;

C v Watson **36 MAC 252 (94)**—undercover officer's pretending to be drug buyer was permissible method of enticing D to open door;

C v Goggin **412 M 200 (92)**—cops' use of private party known to D (former little league coach) to knock & announce did not make forcible entry a no-knock violation even though D tried to shut door after voluntarily opening it;

C v Chausse **30 MAC 956 (91)**—although there is no "blanket exception" for drug cases, information in warrant about "very recent" cutting of drugs by D with pending drug cases excused failure to knock;

C v Prunier **33 MAC 944 (92)**—recent drug arrest of D in same apartment nine weeks earlier justified issuance of no-knock because D may have been prepared for quick disposal;

C v Antwine **417 M 637 (94)**—police knocked & stated "police" shortly before midnight & then forced way into apartment without announcing "their purpose", but SJC said that would be "useless gesture," since D "would already know" what police wanted in the middle of the night (3 arrest warrants due to defaults);

C v Herring **66 MAC 360 (2006)**—citation to *Antwine*, applying "useless gesture" exception to knock and announce requirement if D "would know why the police were present or where the occupants were asleep and would not have heard the announcement"; basis for application seems simply to be that occupants did not hear police knocking/announcing [meaning that police actually did knock and announce, a finding of fact?];

C v Bush **71 MAC 130 (2008)**—after no response within five seconds to knock/announce, forcible entry upheld on particular facts (but not always);

C v Lopez **31 MAC 547 (91)**—cops' announcing presence as they entered wide open front door excused unjustified no-knock warrant;

C v Wornum **421 M 220 (95)**—no-knock entry excused when officer had told resident of warrant and this resident accompanied officer to apartment building, **where resident's key was used (without consent) to enter; not necessary that "every" resident have the info; objectives of the knock and announce rule (decreasing potential for violence, protecting privacy, preventing unnecessary damage to homes) were "substantially achieved"**;

C v Rivera **429 M 620 (99)**—extremely aggressive and incessant knocking on door, ultimately opened by D, is not "forcible entry"; absent forcible entry, knock & announcement requirement not violated;

20-J.7. Particularity of Place/Persons to Be Searched, Items to Be Seized (Including "Any Persons Present")

See also "Plain View: . . . . scope," above;

C v Clarke **44 MAC 502 (98)**—cop supervised informant's controlled buy at premises, then sought warrant for #6 Hiawatha Rd, & cop was one of several executing warrant; D's claim that the building was #2 (per city assessor's lot map) unavailing with finder of fact (& Appeals Court), given cop's testimony that he **saw** #6 on door of correct building; no reasonable possibility that place other than intended one would be searched;

C v Gonzalez **39 MAC 472 (95)**—site: apartment in building at corner of Tyler & Eastern Avenue, & warrant specified a particular first floor apartment, but gave address of Tyler, (which instead was the address for all 2d floor, while "Eastern" address was for 1st) no relief: affiant was the officer who actually executed the warrant, after entry through window of D's bedroom, & there wasn't reasonable probability that wrong premises would be searched;

C v Treadwell **402 M 355 (88)**—description of D's apartment = close, but off;

C v Toledo **66 MAC 688 (2006)**—lengthy search warrant affidavit had informant saying West *Newton* Street, rather than West *Dedham* Street, though abundant further efforts by affiant-cop spoke exclusively of West Dedham Street: despite fact that warrant application and warrant itself repeated the erroneous West *Newton* Street address, no suppression because affiant led the party executing the warrant, had described distinctive feature of correct building; N.B. the affidavit supporting the warrant application would not have been possessed by the police executing the warrant, because the clerk-magistrate was required to retain possession of it (id. at 694–95 n.12);

C v Erickson **14 MAC 501 (82)**—**bad search warrant for multifamily building** because no probable cause for ALL units or reason to think it's 1-family;

C v Dominguez **57 MAC 606 (2003)**—suppression properly denied when officers who applied for and executed search warrant had no reason to know that building was not single-family dwelling;

C v Rise **50 MAC 836 (2001)**—OK to search "entire" building, i.e., each of two apartments, because affiant in warrant application knew that "members of the family" occupied entire premises, and that both D and his cousin (also charged in homicide) ran toward structure after gunshots, & lived at the address; plus, D at booking said lived at "second floor," & gun was found on first floor in couch, so could also say "no standing"; if he instead had expectation of privacy in whole premises, then "particularity" argument would fail, because "multi-unit character of premises evaporates in a constitutional sense";

C v LaPlante **416 M 433 (93)**—because police couldn't have known it was 2-unit building and because D had access to both units, lack of particularity excused;

C v Dew **443 M 620 (2005)**—search warrant affidavit detailed investigation sufficiently showing that D had enough access/control over the entire structure so as to warrant finding of probable cause to search entire building, even though it had three units (occupied by D's relatives);

C v Douglas **399 M 141 (87)**—violates particularity rules of Declaration of Rights, Article 14, G.L. c. 276, §§ 1 & 2, & Fourth Amendment for search warrant to let cop determine area even under *US v Leon*; cop's good faith can't cure general search warrant;

C v Laughlin **40 MAC 926 (96)**—though probable cause to believe D was supplying drug dealers at a particular address, no probable cause to believe drugs would be found at D's **residence**, contrasting *C v Blake* **413 M 823 (92)** observations of D leaving residence en route to drug sales repeatedly;

C v Carrasco **405 M 316 (89)**—warrant to search 2d floor authorized search of 1 of 2 upstairs apartments where there was no evidence that cops should have known there were 2 apartments; particularity requirement of G.L. c. 276 & Article 14 not different from Fourth Amendment's;

C v Walsh **409 M 642 (91)**—warrant to search entire house authorized search of upstairs apartment; description was sufficient to allow cops to "locate & identify" place "with reasonable effort," despite absence of street address;

C v Luna **410 M 131 (91)**—warrant to search house authorized search of both apartments in it where there was no evidence that cops knew there were 2 separate apartments; D entitled, upon request, to hearing on whether cops reasonably should have known there were more than one apartment;

C v Scala **380 M 500 (80)**—though Fourth Amendment says warrants aren't to be read with "poetic license", they are to be read with "common sense"; designation of 2d floor apartment included 3d floor attic when no other apartments shared attic and it had no apparent connection with 1st floor business establishment either;

C v Wallace **67 MAC 901 (2006)**—attic (with padlocked door) was part of second floor apartment even though access to it was outside rear door of apartment: "landing" there accessed stairs going down, & only second floor apartment had relevant key (to lock on rear door of apt., which also fit lock on door at street-level stair bottom); warrant could be read to include attic & cop not required to apply for additional warrant after seeing configuration of space;

Maryland v Garrison **480 US 79 (87)**—can search D's apartment though search warrant was for X's apartment because no reason to know 2 are on floor or that they were not in X's apartment;

C v Powers **39 MAC 911 (95)**—police (about to be?) armed with search warrants for D & D's car and other named individuals & a residence could lawfully search D as he left the named residence (police not required to ignore possibility that D was about to drive off with the evidence);

***Ybarra v Illinois* 444 US 85 (79)**—bad seizure & search (under state law) of **all persons present** at bar because probable cause of dope sales not probable cause re: everyone there;

***C v Wing Ng* 420 M 236 (95)**—**Article 14 forbids** *automatic* **right to frisk anyone in the company of an individual being arrested lawfully** (must be particularized fear of "armed"/danger to cops);

***C v Smith* 370 M 335 (76)**—though here, can search all present under "all persons present" search warrant because probable cause that they're all involved in the criminal activity (drugs), strict scrutiny of such requested authorization (& usually violative of 'particularity' requirement); factors delineated;

***C v Perez* 68 MAC 282 (2007)**—affidavit established probable cause for "all persons present" (premises = private single-family dwelling and curtilage, controlled buys of marijuana there from occupant & another male, observations of many individuals [some known to have drug conviction] entering and leaving in less than five minutes, marijuana [item sought] easily concealed on persons present); this D arrived during search, knocked on door & attempted to enter, but tried to leave when he saw police: cops' stop and search of him (cocaine found) = upheld;

***C v Perez* 76 MAC 439 (2010)**—search warrant for first-floor apartment of two-family dwelling held to cover freshly disturbed earth near side entrance to house, next to foundation and beneath first-floor window; cops dug and found cocaine packages;

***C v Brown* 68 MAC 261 (2007)**—though D was sole target of drug investigation, warrant authorized search of the apartment in which he lived with his mother, and "any person present," omitting to specify D; because application didn't establish probable cause to search "any person present", search of D = illegal; here, investigation showed that D did not want transactions in apartment because of mother, and controlled buys were transacted entirely outside the apartment; court refused to go beyond authorization in warrant itself to discern whether probable cause to search D could be understood (neither at warrant issuance nor at warrant execution was affidavit attached to specify D as object of search);

***C v Catanzaro* 441 M 46 (2004)**—on basis of warrant to search apartment and "all persons present," seizure of D and his girlfriend, after they had stood on porch and then walked some distance away, upheld (strongly divided Court, dissenting opinions);

***C v Charros* 443 M 752 (2005)**—under Fourth Amendment, police had no authority, under warrant to search home, to seize subject & his wife one mile from their home, or to return & detain them in the home while search took place; reserving question whether Article 14 affords greater protection than Fourth Amendment re: off-premises seizures of occupants incident to execution of search warrant; informant's info in warrant application,

however, gave probable cause for warrantless arrest of subject (for committing felony of selling cocaine to informant);

***C v Ilges* 65 MAC 503 (2005)**—police who followed D as he drove away from home could not have compelled D to return to home simply because they had a search warrant for there; stop & search (purportedly "frisk," but not for safety/weapons: $3,400 instead seized) upheld on basis of probable cause to arrest D;

***C v Griffin* 45 MAC 396 (98)**—finding probable cause for all persons present in circumstances; motion ground of "application for warrant failed to provide probable cause" held to encompass attack on "all persons present" feature of warrant;

***C v Baharoian* 25 MAC 35 (87)**—no gaming probable cause for anyone present at store;

***C v Souza* 42 MAC 186 (97)**—"all persons present" search not supported by probable cause **and** refusal to uphold lesser pat frisk: nothing to suggest that D was armed/dangerous;

***C v DePina* 75 MAC 842, 845 (2009)**—warrant specifically authorized not only search of D's 3rd floor apartment but also "search of [D's] person"; seizure of cell phone came within warrant term "implements related to distribution of cocaine" given cop's affidavit;

***C v Taylor* 383 M 272 (81)**—bad general search warrant because jewelry store items not described; list was submitted, but not attached or taken by cops;

***US v Klein* 565 F.2d 183 (1st Cir. '77)**—"pirate" tapes not particular enough;

***C v Kenneally* 383 M 269 (81)**—best to describe documents, but OK here;

***Stanford v Texas* 379 US 476 (65)**—search warrant for written materials concerning "Communist Party"= too general;

***C v Rutkowski* 406 M 673 (90)**—warrant to search for 'stolen handguns & jewelry with description to be supplied in affidavit' failed to meet particularity requirement where affidavit not attached & no evidence cops had it with them or ever showed it to D; *See also "Scope of Search", below*;

20-J.8. Scope of Search

See also Chapter 20-I, Plain View re: Scope, Inadvertence, etc.;

***C v Willis* 398 M 768 (86)**—search scope (album) OK for target item (knife);

***C v Signorini* 404 M 400 (89)**—search warrant reaches containers/car without special probable cause; cf. ***US v Ross* 456 US 798 (82)** can open any container if car probable cause covers it (warrantless search);

***C v Bui* 419 M 392 (95)**—with no-knock warrant to search apartment for D (for whom there was also an arrest warrant for brutal murders), cop could kick over a mattress on floor (in a room where there were 2 women and a man); cops could act for their own safety; apartment had not yet been "secured";

C v Pacheco **21 MAC 565 (86)**—OK search warrant for common area if probable cause for an apartment;

C v Hall **366 M 790 (75)**—search warrant for 2d-floor (D's) apartment no authority to search vacant 3d-floor unit (though D owned building);

C v Rodriguez **49 MAC 664 (2000)**—search warrant for D's apartment = authority to search cellar storage associated with apartment even though access to cellar was via different street address (single building comprised each of 2 street addresses, & cellar underlay single building);

C v Pierre **71 MAC 58 (2008)**—relationship between apartment and its identified locked storage locker in basement to which access was not restricted met the cartilage test set out in *US v Dunn* 480 US 294 (1987); warrant to search D's brother's apartment, car, and person held to encompass storage locker and boxes within it;

C v Santiago **410 M 737 (91)**—warrant to search apartment doesn't extend to car parked on public street; car parked on private property within curtilage distinguished;

C v McCarthy **428 M 871 (99)**—warrant to search apartment doesn't extend to the parking spot in apartment complex's lot used by the apartment tenant on day of search: no "roaming zone of curtilage" to reach his car, without warrant;

C v Perez **76 MAC 439 (2010)**—search warrant for first-floor apartment of two-family dwelling held to cover freshly disturbed earth near side entrance to house, next to foundation and beneath first-floor window; cops dug and found cocaine packages;

C v Catanzaro **441 M 46 (2004)—(divided Court)** upholding seizure of drugs from D's girlfriend's purse, despite fact that there was only a search warrant for apartment and "all persons present", and D and girlfriend, unaware of surveillance prior to execution of search warrant, had stood on porch and walked quite some distance from apartment before being stopped, and taken back to apartment; refusal to afford greater protection under Article 14 than Supreme Court's construction in *Michigan v Summers* 452 US 692 (81); **see dissent, for reasons why even Summers should not uphold seizure/search scenario here;**

Michigan v Summers **452 US 692 (81)**—OK to detain, on doorstep of private home, occupant of premises which were being searched pursuant to warrant;

C v Luna **410 M 131 (91)**—warrant to search house authorized search of both apartments in it where there was no evidence that cops knew there were 2 separate apartments; D entitled, upon request, to hearing on whether cops reasonably should have known there were more than one apartment;

C v Halsey **41 MAC 200 (96)**—though not specified in search warrants, police could seize pornographic pictures and videos; **"mere evidence" is seizable if inadvertently discovered & has "nexus with the crime under investigation"** (here, child sexual assault), & cop testified to opinion that pornography is used to "initiate children into sexual activity");

C v Cruz **53 MAC 24, 28–29 (2001)**—search warrant for drugs didn't allow officer with specialized expertise in cell phone cloning to test object(s) and then assert propriety of their seizure as being contraband in plain view; when 'mere evidence' of criminal activity is in plain view, it may be seized without a warrant only if cops recognize it as "plausibly related to criminal activity of which they were already aware";

C v DePina **75 MAC 842, 845 (2009)**—warrant specifically authorized not only search of D's 3rd floor apartment but also "search of [D's] person"; seizure of cell phone came within warrant term "implements related to distribution of cocaine" given cop's affidavit; cop could also answer phone (citing *Mendes*, 46 MAC 581 [99]); substance of cop's conversation with unidentified caller also admissible (rejecting "hearsay" argument);

C v Balicki **436 M 1 (2002)**—limited search authorized by warrant was converted into "general" search of home for potential evidence; suppression of still photos & videotape recordings of entire home + testimony of cops re: same;

C v Feijoo **419 M 486 (95)**—when warrant application alleged that D had used nightsticks or clubs and dirty movies in committing homosexual assaults on students, OK to seize 'gay oriented magazines,' Playgirl magazines, and four phallic-shaped plaster molds, because probable cause to believe they "bore a nexus to crimes under investigation";

20-K. CONSENT

See also Chapter 20-I above, "Search" vs. Plain View;

See Chapter 20-F re: consent as fruit of cops' illegality; See also Chapter 20-D, ante, re: Voluntariness of Statements;

K. Smith, *Criminal Practice & Procedure,* **§§ 249–58 (2d ed. 1983 & Supp.)**—can infer it; DA's burden of proof on consent issue; factors; fraud; etc.;

Vernonia School District v Acton **515 US 646 (95)**—random suspicionless drug testing for all public secondary school athletes (consequence of positive = retest; 2d positive = give up sports or participate in "anti-drug program"); (i.e., 'consent' to search from knowingly participating in sports program);

Schneckloth v Bustamonte **412 US 218 (73)**—consent must be voluntary, but no need to inform of rights, e.g., to refuse;

Ohio v Robinette **519 US 33 (96)**—voluntariness of consent to be determined by totality of circumstances and failure of cop to tell speeding driver he was free to go was but one factor; contrast *C v Torres* **424 M 153 (97)** evidence seized after "consent" suppressed because continued detention, after D produced license & registration following traffic stop, was illegal;

C v Mateo-German **453 M 838 (2009)**—cop engaged in "community caretaking" asked D's consent for dog sniff of car's exterior: asking for consent didn't convey that D wasn't free to leave (and wasn't a seizure), and D's consent wasn't required anyway, as dog sniff of car exterior isn't a search under art. 14; 3 justices dissented from holding that D wasn't seized at point of "question" seeking permission for dog sniff;

C v McGrath **365 M 631 (74)**—"I'm clean" & spread hands not consent;

C v Cantalupo **380 M 173 (80)**—"Search me" & opening of jacket gave cops reasonable belief D consented to search/seize whole body;

C v Rousseau **61 MAC 144, 154 (2004)**—D either showed officer hidden compartment or told her about it, so consent could be inferred;

C v Hamilton **24 MAC 290 (87)**—not consent to open door for cops; but cf.

C v Villar **40 MAC 742 (96)**—cops' obtaining opening of door by placing arrested man in front of door & knocking, so occupants would think it was arrested man seeking contact—no relief;

C v Watson **36 MAC 252, 258 (94)**—officer's trickery (pretending to be drug purchaser) was a permissible method of enticing D to open door (for execution of drug search warrant);

C v Rogers **444 M 234 (2005)**—strictly scrutinizing purported "consent" to enter residence, i.e., the gesture of woman who answered door and, in response to police question of "where is [D]?", pointed toward rear of apartment: evidence warranted finding of NO consent; Commonwealth "failed to demonstrate that [cop's] question concerning [D's] whereabouts was not a demand for entry, and that [woman's] response thereto was anything other than 'mere acquiescence' to a claim of authority"; distinguishes *Voisine* **414 M 772 (93)** because woman (there, actually lessee of apartment.) testified that she was aware of her right not to admit police; at 245, **"it is not incumbent on the defendant to refute all possible theories that might justify legal entry into the home. On the contrary, it is the Commonwealth's obligation to establish its theory of entry and prove lawful entry based on that theory"**;

C v Costa **69 MAC 823 (2007)**—finding of consent upheld: cop asked D's mother if D at home, non-English speaking mother nodded and pointed down hall, cop asked if he could "go and see him", and in response mother walked further into house and pointed into bedroom; motion judge's finding that mother understood English (while not speaking it) based on her beginning to answer questions on stand before interpreter translated them (fn.5);

C v Buchanan **384 M 103 (81)**—voluntary though cops said they'd stand guard, get search warrant, & charge D if suspect found inside;

C v Rosenthal **52 MAC 707 (2001)**—D's emptying of pocket NOT voluntary after trooper, claiming "administrative" inspection, told D he'd have to use force to obtain by himself if D wouldn't reveal (trooper also announced he was in fear);

C v Ramos **430 M 545 (2000)**—police telling D they'd wait outside until she came out of apartment and threatening they'd have fire dept break down door if she didn't come out was not a mere "ruse" making her appearance voluntary; there was a "seizure," and photo of D (and ID by witness from it) ordered suppressed as fruits of illegal seizure; "ruses must be designed to elicit consensual entry," but here there were instead "threats of intimidation or violence";

Bumper v North Carolina **391 US 543 (68)**—mother acquiesced to authority, not consent, because cops said they had search warrant;

US v Matlock **415 US 164 (74)**—when D has cotenant/co-inhabitant, he assumes risk that other person may give valid consent to search/enter;

Illinois v Rodriguez **497 US 177 (90)**—burden of establishing authority to consent to search rests on state, but consent legitimates search if police reasonably believe person consenting to search has common authority over the premises;

C v Porter P **456 M 254 (2010)**—though director of "transitional family shelter" had master key to all rooms, she had no actual authority to consent to search and officer's alleged belief in her "apparent" authority was based on mistake of law, not fact: suppression required (fruits = gun in room and inculpatory statement by D after seizure of gun); good faith belief in apparent authority must be reasonable, after cops' diligent inquiry of consenting individual's common authority over home;

C v Dejarnette **75 MAC 88 (2009)**—with good info that arrest warrant fugitive was inside apartment, police forcibly entered and arrested him; thereafter, obtained voluntary consent from lawful tenant for unlimited search therein (so extending to closed containers within her control); tenant, mother of child, had apparent authority to consent to search of "Dr. Seuss" child's backpack (which had an INTERIOR label showing instead D's ownership, & contained drugs and ammunition); though tenant told cops that D had put his backpack in kitchen, court says this info was given in tenant's statement to cops AFTER the search, & D didn't show cops were told beforehand;

Georgia v Randolph **547 US 103 (2006)**—when D is present and expressly refuses consent to search, police can't use consent of D's estranged wife to override D's refusal;

C v Ware **75 MAC 220 (2009)**—distinguishes *Randolph*, 547 US 103 on ground that absence of consent would not be inferred: to counteract wife's consent, he should have expressed refusal to consent affirmatively and unequivocally (not just by apparent refusal to answer knocks);

C v Ocasio **71 MAC 304, further review denied 451 M 1106, cert. denied 129 SCt 314 (2008)**—D's mother = apartment tenant, but permitted D to stay there; while D was held under arrest outside apartment door, mother was in management office of building and eventually consented to apartment search: *Georgia v Randolph* distinguished, because D did not raise protest or objection during searches occurring as he stood at the door;

C v Krisco Corp **421 M 37 (95)**—acquiescence, not consent, to search by Dept. of Environmental Protection agent purporting to make an "administrative" search;

C v Roland R. **448 M 278 (2007)**—past signs stating that all bags = "subject to manual search", juvenile entered courthouse, but when informed by court officer that bag was going to be searched, juvenile declined, picked up bag and left building; he ran when told to "come here"; SJC says judge erred in ordering suppression of marijuana inside bag; citing *C v Harris* 383 M 655 (81), "area-entry inspections at court house entrances, for safety and security purposes" = OK without warrant or individualized suspicion of wrongdoing or danger; D "implicitly demonstrated consent" by passing signs, placing bag on table and going through metal detector, and "was not entitled to withdraw his consent after the inspection had commenced"; fn.4: "Nothing that we have said . . . should be read to suggest that" D would not have been free to turn back and leave building before placing bag on table near x-ray device and stepping through electronic metal detector;

C v Hurd **51 MAC 12 (2001)**—home owner's "Do what you have to do," in response to animal control officer & cop who had entered into owner's back yard to see dead & dying dogs = fruit of prior illegal entry; suppression ordered;

C v Yehudi Y **56 MAC 812 (2002)**—undercover police buying of drugs at D's home didn't impinge upon expectation of privacy, since persons generally were invitees to buy drugs; second entry of home, however, was into portion not used by invited buyers; "consent" to search thereafter, from D's parents, after 90 minutes' discussion, was product of illegal entry;

Bond v US **529 US 334 (2000)**—border patrol agent on bus at standard checkpoint in Texas "squeezed" soft-sided luggage in overhead storage space above seats; passenger's "agreement" that bag be opened was not argued to be a voluntary consent (and Fourth Amendment violation found);

C v Harmond **376 M 557 (78)**—**must be no express/ implied coercion or mere acquiescence, e.g., D drunk & cops say they'll get search warrant;**

C v Kipp **57 MAC 629 (2003)**—taint of prior unlawful entry dissipated before "consent" to search; "consent" finding of fact here upheld despite police threats to destroy home/possessions during search if forced to obtain warrant and to charge D's wife; but see *U.S. v Kampbell* 574 F.2d 962 (8th Cir. '87) ("[i]t was not only, in effect, that we're telling you if we have to get a search warrant, we can tear

your place apart, but the implication that was intended to be conveyed, I think was 'By God, we will'"); *U.S. v Taft* 769 F.Supp. 1295, 1302 (D. Vt. '91) (similar); *Waldron v U.S.* 219 F.2d 37 (D.C. Cir. '55) (similar); *U.S. v Wilcox* 357 F.Supp. 514 (E.D. Pa. '73) (similar); see also *C v Ramos* 430 M 545 (2000) (police telling D that they would wait outside until she came outside, and threatening that they would have fire department break down door if she didn't emerge made her subsequent appearance "involuntary", & fruits [photo, ID] had to be suppressed);

Rogers v Richmond **365 U.S. 534 (61)**—confession coerced by police interrogator indicating that he was "about to have petitioner's wife taken into custody" for questioning; *C v Hunt* 12 MAC 841 (81)—implicit threat or promise that D's wife would not be released unless D both confessed and affirmed that wife was not involved; taunt that he should be "man enough" to do this; "concern for one's family may be as significant in inducing an involuntary confession as a concern for oneself";

C v Heath **12 MAC 677 (81)**—young (23) D, smoked marijuana, cuffed, alone, 2 cops, = not consent (overruling trial judge);

Hayes v Florida **470 US 811 (85)**—not consent to go to station under threat of arrest, so suppress fingerprints;

C v Haas **373 M 545 (77)**—bar D from home, hand on D, & motion to cruiser—not consent;

C v Corriveau **396 M 319 (85)**—several cops, gun drawn, touching, & tone—but no threat, & consent by educated D;

C v Walker **370 M 548 (76)**—lessee opened door on demand because fear D, not cops;

C v Angivoni **383 M 30 (81)**—no blood test consent if D drunk & not told can refuse;

C v Carson **72 MAC 368 (2008)**—no blood test consent when D sobbing and crying, rocking on her knees, calling out for her "mommy", screaming of her fear, but an hour later acquiescing to blood test, phlebotomist subsequently delaying blood drawing due to D's extreme emotional agitation, + vomiting and dry-heaving;

C v Welch **420 M 646 (95)**—**superior officer of D, a city firefighter, could consent** to police search of fire station's "lieutenants' room";

C v Sanna **424 M 92 (97)**—consent to enter D's parents' home validly given by D's father in response to request to speak to D re: homicide; not vitiated by failure to "disclose everything they might have had in mind in seeking" entry; arrest of D not held to exceed scope of consent (probable cause to arrest ripened upon seeing D's hands & forehead cut & scratched);

C v Thomas **67 MAC 738 (2006)**—after D was arrested at his apartment (& had allowed cops to look around to see if anyone else was in apartment), he asked cops to lock the door; cop discovered key was necessary to do so, & one cop went to ask D where key was (on hook in a closet), but other cop rummaged throughout, including drawer of bedroom nightstand, where gun was found: scope of consent was exceeded = suppression;

C v Wallace 70 MAC 757 (2007)—because D acceded to police request to come to station without asking to move his car from the handicapped space in which he was sitting illegally, towing of car to station was OK, and was not an illegality vitiating D's written consent at the station for it to be searched;

C v Gaynor 443 M 245 (2005)—rejects claim that consent was involuntary because he was "misled" to believe that blood sample given would be used only for specific comparison and not for any other person; there was no express representation, & cops had no obligation to inform D of all purposes for which blood test would be used; D placed no condition or limit, express or implied, on consent (finding of fact);

C v Aviles 58 MAC 459 (2003)—D conceded that his wife had authority to consent to search of the home and could relinquish to police D's soiled clothing and towels; if police lawfully obtain evidence, it may be subjected to testing (D's personal consent unnecessary prior to DNA testing of clothing);

C v Maloney 399 M 785 (87)—**consent by lawful occupant** (boyfriend);

C v Lopez 74 MAC 815, further review allowed 455 M 1103 (2009)—cop, believing he was at door of motel manager's room, was there to retrieve hypodermic needle at manager's request: woman who answered door had apparent authority to consent to his entry (subsequent sighting of marijuana and finding gun not suppressed); dissent by Lenk, J.(do not lightly presume authority to consent to entry of 'home': in determining actual authority to consent, focus on relationship between consenter and property searched, not on relationship between consenter and D; cop should have asked who woman was/authority over room; majority misconceives burden of showing facts affirmatively known to cop to permit reasonable belief in consenter's authority; majority places undue weight on benign purpose / "good faith" of cop's entry);

C v Porter P 456 M 254 (2010)— director of transitional family shelter had master key to rooms, but lacked actual authority to consent to search; cops' belief in her "apparent" authority was based on mistake of law, requiring suppression because no diligent inquiry by cops as to consenting individual's "common authority" over home (no warrant, no exigency);

C v Noonan 48 MAC 356 (99)—**estranged girlfriend of D, who returned to their shared apartment** to retrieve her possessions, found earrings in a pocket of D's jacket slung over chair; no ineffective assistance in failure to move to suppress these and other evidence found in apartment; she had lawful access to apartment and **authority to consent** to search by police; focus is upon relationship between consenting party and property searched, not relationship between consenting party and D;

C v Podgurski 44 MAC 929 (98)—police entry of closed residence door excused because of (implied?) consent of D's wife who would have known police would go there to serve on D notice of a G.L. c. 209A protective order concerning wife;

Florida v Jimeno 500 US 248 (91)—under Fourth Amendment, D's **general consent to search car for drugs included consent to search closed containers in which drugs could be found; locked suitcase distinguished**;

C v Gaynor 443 M 245 (2005)—cops weren't required to get additional consent to use blood sample given by D for testing re: murders other than the specific one mentioned to D; though D would have been entitled to limit the scope of his consent, he did not;

Illinois v Rodriguez 497 US 177 (90)—warrantless entry of home valid under Fourth Amendment where cops obtain consent by 3d party whom they reasonably if mistakenly believe to have common authority over premises (not yet decided under Article 14); (cf. *US v Leon*'s 'good faith' excuses);

C v Ploude 44 MAC 137 (98)—**though owner does not generally have authority to consent to search of building leased to another,** this owner retained an office in the building, had keys, had to go through D's space to get to office, & "had free reign of the building"; owner's consent to search = valid;

C v Martino 412 M 267 (92)—D's consent to search van & turn over clothing not invalid despite his exhaustion & emotional turmoil over death of girlfriend day before, his belief he had to consent, & coercive setting of DA's office; cf. *C v Eldridge* 28 MAC 936 (90) adults with mental capacity of 4 to 9 year old cannot consent to sex;

20-L. EXIGENT, HOME, CAR, AND ADMINISTRATIVE SEARCHES AND SEIZURES

See Chapter 20-H re: Scope of Search Incident to Arrest; & Chapter 20-I re: plain view; See also Chapter 20-B re: no-knock entry;

C v Blake 413 M 823 (92)—may "secure" area to be searched before warrant is procured as long as search does not begin until after warrant is obtained;

C v Guaba 417 M 746 (94)—Article 14 requires that officers executing search warrant have it **in hand**, unless exigent circumstances permit warrantless search; *C v Blake* 49 MAC 134 (2000) D, convicted in 1990, couldn't get benefit of *Guaba* rule in postconviction motion (M.R.Crim.P. 30) for "new trial";

C v Valerio 449 M 562 (2007)—because of arising exigency, D was handcuffed and Miranda-ized in apartment kitchen and informed that police were there to execute search for drugs, while actual warrant and attachments remained outside in police vehicle; even when warrant was brought inside, its attachment (which set forth particularized objects of search) was not shown to D, but D didn't ask to see it and didn't protest against search, instead nodding in direction of bedroom when responding to question whether there were drugs present; warrant here had authorized both "no knock" and search of any persons present;

20-L.1. Searches of Homes

K. Smith, *Criminal Practice & Procedure*, §§ 171–74, 262–64, Homes (2d ed. 1983 & Supp.)—175, Administrative; 265–300, Cars—rationale = less privacy, not exigency (265) vs. (268) no per se car exemption & need exigency after probable cause;

Payton v NY **445 US 573 (80)**—**home entry per se bad** without exigency (though probable cause to arrest for murder) or warrant; but if arrest warrant could search home;

C v Rogers **444 M 234 (2005)**—strictly scrutinizing purported "consent" to enter residence, i.e., the gesture of woman who answered door and, in response to police question of "where is [D]?", pointed toward rear of apartment: evidence warranted finding of NO consent; at 245, **"it is not incumbent on the defendant to refute all possible theories that might justify legal entry into the home. On the contrary, it is the Commonwealth's obligation to establish its theory of entry and prove lawful entry based on that theory"**; lengthy refutation of points made in dissent by Greaney, J. = great reading!;

C v Marquez **434 M 370 (2001)**—cops' warrantless arrest of D at threshold of his apartment bad; SJC declines to follow/distinguishes *US v Santana* 427 US 38 (76); in *Santana*, D was, of her own accord, at threshold of open exterior door, exposed to public, & was there seen by cops, who had not instigated the door opening; here, D answered apartment door inside building, at cops' knock; FURTHERMORE, analysis shouldn't turn on where D is standing when s/he opens door, & warrant should be required even if cops are standing in common hallway & D is at/on threshold of apartment;

C v Tyree **455 M 676 (2010)**—after warrantless arrest of D in warrantless search of his home, SJC ordered suppression of his shoes, worn by him to police station and there seized; unlike speech issue in Marquez, physical items in arrestee's possession that are seized following illegal warrantless search are the fruit of the arrest in the home rather than someplace else; "cannot assume [D] would have been wearing the same shoes had the police proceeded by summons or waited to arrest him lawfully at another time or place";

C v Cruz **442 M 299 (2004)**—police went to D's home intending to "determine his willingness to talk about" crimes: when no one answered door and note left on door indicating D went to hospital was investigated and believed to be falsehood, police obtained assistance of maintenance worker to enter apartment and therein opened closed door to find D sleeping; NO EXIGENCY, but no suppression of later stationhouse statement because Miranda warnings, etc. held to have dissipated taint;

C v Duarte **56 MAC 523 (2002)**—exigent circumstances found to justify warrantless entry of home to arrest D who had raped victim at knifepoint 45 minutes earlier and, because victim knew him, there was danger he might flee;

C v McDermott **448 M 750 (2007)**—after D shot and killed seven people at place of work, using at least two weapons, police permissibly entered D's apartment for five minutes, not touching or moving any items, "to check . . . for additional victims" who might have been unconscious or unable to seek help, citing cop's "knowledge of past cases and personal experience with a former case" in which victims were found both at a suspect's residence and workplace;

C v Ocasio **71 MAC 304, further review denied 451 M 1106, cert. denied 129 S Ct 314 (2008)**—with witness complaining of having just been threatened by D with a gun, cops went to apartment, D emerged and was arrested; though D said no one else in apartment, cops obtained entry to apartment (rented by D's mother) via building manager and verified no one else present, but left door ajar as they remained in building hallway; cop entry then to answer ringing phone WAS improper; caller was D's mother, who verified D was allowed to stay there; no suppression as mother arrived and signed consent to search; Court distinguished *Georgia v Randolph* 547 US 103 (2006) (an objecting co-tenant cannot be overridden by consent of co-tenant), saying D never objected to searches as they were occurring in his immediate presence;

Kirk v Louisiana **536 US 635, 71 Cr L 2094 (2002)**—(per curiam) cops with info re: drug sales stopped buyer outside D's home, then knocked on door, entered, & arrested D; frisk yielded cocaine: Supreme Court reversed state court's "conclusion that the officers' actions were lawful, absent exigent circumstances" (but make no findings/holding about exigent circumstances); (Louisiana court had upheld conviction on ground that cocaine was found on D's person rather than in home);

Steagald v US **451 US 204 (81)**—can't enter D's home with arrest warrant for X without search warrant;

US v Curzi **867 F.2d 36 (1st Cir. '89)**—(same) even if probable cause that X is there & dangerous;

C v Derosia **402 M 284 (88)**—(same) for D at mom's house;

C v Jackmon **63 MAC 47 (2005)**—North Carolina authorities obtained SEARCH warrant for the person of D at particular residence (arrest warrant / fugitive from justice already existed), and N.C. law was applied re: adequacy of affidavit / probable cause showing; informant's info had only to establish probable cause that D was at the address, not probable cause that D was a fugitive or had committed crimes;

NY v Harris **495 US 14 (90)**—warrantless search of D's home in absence of exigency or consent, in violation of Payton, did not require suppression of D's later stationhouse confession because police did not exploit bad search to obtain it;

Minnesota v Olson **495 US 91 (90)**—overnight guest has expectation of privacy in home of host, so arrest there required warrant, consent or exigent circumstances; D's subsequent confession suppressed;

C v Porter P **456 M 254 (2010)**—room shared by juvenile and his mother at shelter was their home, and mother had key to room; that shelter staff had master key and could enter for "professional business purposes" did not diminish legitimacy of privacy interest;

C v Chongarlides **52 MAC 366, 375–77 (2001)**—police entry into residence to find & question D = illegal, but D's inculpatory statements, made later at station after two sets of Miranda warnings & signed waiver not tainted by illegality;

C v DeJesus **439 M 616 (2003)**—pursuant to Article 14, cops who secure dwelling (to prevent destruction or removal of evidence) while warrant is being sought may NOT enter dwelling absent specific info supporting objectively reasonable belief that evidence will be removed or destroyed unless preventative measures are taken; at minimum, must believe someone is inside; no suppression, however, of evidence seized pursuant to warrant even though warrant application used info from initial illegal entry (because probable cause remained even after striking from the affidavit the illegally-gained info), citing *Murray v US* **487 US 533, 537–38 (88)**;

C v Streeter **71 MAC 430 (2008)**—expert smelling cop (fresh! Not burned! Marijuana detected inside apartment from building's hallway), plus D reluctantly emerging and after evasion acknowledging presence of friend inside allowed "securing" from within prior to seeking search warrant, citing DeJesus;

C v Webster **75 MAC 247 (2009)**—because cops lacked reasonable belief that D was in the apartment, their entry with only 'arrest' warrant was illegal, as was "securing" apartment for six hours (by staying inside it); these illegalities tainted cops' recovery of gun from D's waistband, & his statements, following chase of him when he entered apartment, but fled on seeing cops;

C v McAfee **63 MAC 467 (2005)**—after detaining a drug buyer away from site of seller & preventing him from contacting his seller, cops didn't have justification to create their own exigency by returning to seller's door and asking to speak to him (so that when he refused and went away from door they forcibly entered and swept the premises); cops had probable cause for four days beforehand & didn't seek warrant;

C v Cataldo **69 MAC 465 (2007)**—after staking out a multi-unit building, and chasing and arresting two suspects in violent crime after they departed in vehicle, no exigency justified cops' forcible entry of apartment thereafter, notwithstanding no response to knock/announce, and hearing running footsteps; the items at issue (gun, ammunition) weren't susceptible to destruction/removal and no evidence that apartment occupant knew of off-site arrest; re: "running footsteps," cops can't "deliberately create the exigency" by alerting occupant of law enforcement interest prematurely; cops could have secured outer perimeter of apartment building while awaiting warrant;

Welsh v Wisconsin **466 US 740 (84)**—bad home arrest to check blood alcohol for minor (noncriminal operating under influence) motor vehicle offense;

C v Kiser **48 MAC 647 (2000)**—complaint of loud party prompted cops to knock on apartment door, but after D opened door and responded "yeah, OK" to request to turn down music, cops couldn't push on through (because they knew him to be a gang member, because an un-ID'd person ran across the room behind him, and because D pushed them back when they tried to lean into room for better view); D entitled to use reasonable force against intrusion if cop is attempting illegal entry; *Welsh v Wisconsin*, above (**466 US 740 (84)**), cited as **constitutional limitation upon reach of G.L. c. 41, § 98 (home entry to quell "riot" or breach of peace**; cases upholding this statute as basis for warrantless home entry have involved "violent fighting, with the attendant fear that someone inside was in physical danger"); (as to right to resist, see, however, *C v Montes* **49 MAC 789, 792 (2000), citing *C v Moreira* 388 M 596, 601 (83)** common law right to resist unlawful arrest was abolished);

C v Gomes **59 MAC 332 (2003)**—absent use of excessive/unnecessary force *upon an individual's person,* he may not forcibly resist even an unlawful entry into his residence by one he knows or has good reason to believe is a police officer engaged in the performance of his duties;

US v Cardona **903 F.2d 60 (1st Cir. '90)**—good faith warrantless arrest of parolee in home upheld where done at request of parole officer who had reasonable belief that D in violation of parole;

Samson v California **547 US 843 (2006)**—state statute requires all parolees to agree in writing to be subject to suspicionless search or seizure, and this = upheld against Fourth Amendment challenge: parole = variant of imprisonment, so no reasonable expectation of privacy under "totality of circumstances" analysis;

C v Blake **413 M 823 (92)**—neither Article 14 nor Fourth Amendment prohibit cops from securing residence to be searched before warrant is procured **as long as search doesn't commence before issuance of warrant**; here, D was validly arrested before residence secured;

C v Midi **46 MAC 591 (99)**—police not free to enter a home without arrest warrant to make "routine felony arrest," even though Commonwealth claimed exigency because allegation was domestic abuse (alleged V was not present & no evidence that harm was imminent);

C v Franco **419 M 635 (95)**—arrest warrant for one "Melendez," plus "reason to believe" he was at a particular apartment allowed cops to direct D back into apartment (when he failed to answer knocks & tried to leave via backdoor), and to enter front door (when he finally answered it), saying they were going to search apartment for Melendez; thereafter, plain "smell"/plain view of narcotics—related substance = probable cause to arrest D;

C v DiBenedetto **427 M 414 (98)**—D argues that Article 14 requires police to have probable cause to believe D is actually present at dwelling in order to enter to execute arrest warrant; SJC reserves decision, saying here cops had info "satisfy(ing) even the higher probable cause standard"; see:

C v Silva **440 M 772 (2004)**—**no suppression of evidence against D, gained when police entered X's apartment upon a valid arrest warrant for X; under Article 14, need only reasonable belief that warrant subject both lived in and was present at the residence;**

C v Rivera **429 M 620 (99)**—muddled decision obscuring issue of dragnet search, before 7:30 a.m., of multi-unit 4-story apartment building by which to serve arrest warrant on D; after knocking on windows & doors of many apartments, suspicion focused on one & aggressive incessant knocking & yelling eventually caused D to open the door, so there was "actual knowledge" he was present, legitimizing the arrest;

C v Acosta **416 M 279 (93)**—with arrest warrant for D & tip as to his residence, cops went there & knocked on door, answered by D: no "search" because any citizen can knock on door;

20-L.2. Exigent Circumstances

Warden v Hayden **387 US 294 (67)**—enter/search to avoid serious injury; e.g., hot pursuit of armed robber can search washing machine in cellar;

C v Franklin **376 M 885 (78)**—(same) for ominous bulge in mattress;

C v Moore **54 MAC 334 (2002)**—exigency justified police entry of building with drawn guns upon multiple reports of shots fired & advice from person in front of building that "they have" a particular semiautomatic handgun & "have been shooting out the window of the second floor", and thereafter, person who answered door knock at 2d floor apartment (& said he rented/controlled the apartment) let police enter after telling that some friends were in the back bedroom; there, scent of gunpowder, & one gun in plain view, warranted opening of adjacent duffle bag after 'frisk' revealed 'hard object' maybe weapon (another gun);

C v Dejarnette **75 MAC 88 (2009)**—forcible warrantless entry of home excused, "exigency" said to be knowledge that individual was inside for whom there was arrest warrant for (joint venture) shooting; before obtaining consent for search of apartment from its lawful tenant, cops "searched for nothing other than [arrest fugitive] and stopped after they apprehended him;

C v Kirschner **67 MAC 836 (2006)**—no emergency exception applied to justify police (investigatory) entry into backyard for persons who might have set off fireworks earlier (misdemeanor, G.L. c. 148, § 39), prompting call from neighbor; premises were dark and quiet when police arrived;

C v Williams **76 MAC 489(2010)**—no exigency justified police taking D's clothes from nurse at hospital after D entered for treatment of stab wounds, though police said necessary to best preserve/prevent degradation of evidence (place in paper bag rather than plastic bag) and D didn't forfeit possessory interest in his clothing; generic testimony that "sooner is better" = insufficient to show exigency, and failed to proffer time it would take to get warrant; but compare/contrast *C v McCarthy* **71 MAC 591 (2008)**—officer dispatched to restaurant on report of unconscious woman, who was 'thrashing about' on floor, unable to communicate effectively; responding EMTs told officer believed woman suffered drug overdose, and asked if he knew what she had taken; officer saw open handbag near woman, searched it for drugs to assist EMTs in treatment: no suppression of drugs found therein;

Mincey v Arizona **437 US 385 (78)**—no per se exception for serious crime, e.g., murder scene once D & V are gone;

C v Beauchamp **424 M 682 (97)**—**no "murder scene" general exigency: after D was removed from area & need for protective sweep evaporated, warrant required;**

C v Tyree **455 M 676 (2010)**—refusing to hold "exigency" justifying warrantless search of home simply because "violent crime" or "involving a firearm"; no evidence that police or others were in danger, no evidence that home occupants were aware of police presence and interest; that money was taken in robbery was not ground of exigency based on feared destruction or loss of evidence; no evidence of impracticability of obtaining warrant; testimony from officers at scene did not suggest exigency existed (this instead the suggestion of motion judge); later search, with warrant upheld, after eliminating from warrant application info obtained during warrantless search; excising from application the descriptions of drug paraphernalia seen at home, would defeat probable cause to search for such items, but SJC says 'plain view' since scope and intensity of search were consistent with valid portions of the warrant;

C v Ortiz **435 M 569 (2002)**—exigency found for forceful warrantless entry of D's fruit store because unruly crowd of missing woman's friends/relatives were about to break into the locked store & there were objectively reasonable grounds to believe that V was either injured or dead, & had been last seen going into the store with D;

C v Townsend **453 M 413 (2009)**—emergency exigency found for breaking into apartment due to reasonable grounds to believe victim was inside and in distress, whether injured by D's abuse (there was history or same) or by reason of cocaine binge: victim was missing > 3 days, last heard from via telephone call from apartment, V's car was present and not moved for days, V had missed appointments, repeated attempts to contact V unsuccessful, no one answered repeated knocks, landlord had no key; fn 12 asserts that obtaining fire department's help logical as more immediate assistance to V than getting warrant;

Brigham City v Stuart **547 US 398 (2006)**—["an odd flyspeck of a case," according to Stevens, J., concurring] cops investigating complaint of loud party at 3 a.m. saw juveniles drinking beer in yard, and, through window, four adults restraining juvenile with such force as to cause refrigerator to move, and juvenile's punch causing victim to spit blood into sink; warrantless entry into home excused on "emergency aid" rationale, and it was irrelevant whether cops' actual motivation was instead to arrest and gather evidence; *Welsh v Wisconsin* 466 US 740 (not tumultuous/emergency) distinguished; no violation of "knock and announce" because cops announced and weren't heard or observed over tumult;

Michigan v Fisher **130 S Ct 546 (2009)**—police responding to complaint of "disturbance" saw smashed-front truck, damaged fenceposts, three broken house windows, with glass on ground, blood on hood of truck and on clothes inside it, as well as on one door to house, occupant inside screaming and throwing things, but refusing to answer knocks; furniture was placed to block front door, and back door was locked; occupant profanely refused officers' offer of medical attention and demanded that they get warrant; officer pushed front door open and went inside, where occupant pointed gun at him: in per curiam opinion, S. Court says "emergency" exception, and not to be replaced with "hindsight determination that there was in fact no emergency";

Michigan v Tyler **436 US 499 (78)**—though firemen need (administrative (see below)) warrant to investigate, can enter to fight fire & stay reasonable time to investigate;

Michigan v Clifford **464 US 287 (84)**—unless exigent, firemen need search warrant to gather evidence, administrative warrant to investigate;

C v Ringgard **71 MAC 197 (2008)**—police responded to passerby's "predawn" report of audible alarm and possible break-in at residence; further dispatch report of possible fire in progress, confirmed by billowing black smoke from broken window in front door, view inside was of flames coming out from around stove in kitchen beyond inner door; man inside did not respond to yells to get out of house and inquiry re: presence of anyone else; police forced open door to remove man, who screamed 'get out of my house'; handgun on floor in plain view during police struggle to re-remove man (after he entered following initial removal) was not suppressed; that fire was subsequently extinguished with only kitchen tap water was not justifiable cause to second guess apparent emergency/danger to life; even if cops could be confident D was owner, they weren't required to permit him to endanger himself and responding officers and firefighters;

Thompson v Louisiana **469 US 17 (84)**—2 hour crime scene search after D & V gone = bad, even after phone call for medical assistance;

Welsh v Wisconsin **466 US 740 (84)**—bad home arrest to check blood alcohol for minor (noncriminal operating under influence) motor vehicle offense;

C v DiGeronimo **38 MAC 714 (95)**—though probable cause to believe other driver in rear-end collision was drunk & left scene, he had telephoned police from home to report accident (with slurred speech & profanity): no exigency justified cop's use of security guard's passkey to enter D's apartment when D didn't respond to knocks & yells (though cop claimed need to check on D's "welfare"); **"destruction of evidence" exigency (proof of intoxication dissipating over time) rejected;** warrant could have been obtained during cop's 50-minute stay at accident scene—**"no exigency is created simply because there is probable cause to believe that a serious crime has been committed";**

Vale v Louisiana **399 US 30 (70)**—bad entry after arrest of D, though family still had access to house;

C v Peitrass **392 M 892 (84)**—bad entry/arrest 13 hours after rape (of complaining witness 2 doors away) without evidence D armed or will flee; strict DA burden of proof;

C v Huffman **385 M 122 (82)**—smell marijuana & see Ds bagging it = not exigent;

C v Hamilton **24 MAC 290 (87)**—no exigency to enter & search for drugs;

C v Lopez **38 MAC 748 (95)**—untested informant took undercover cop to D's apartment, where cop bought drugs, left, & immediately signaled waiting cops to enter & arrest D (& seize marked bills from wallet): since cop could have arrested immediately, there was "no significant additional intrusion on" D's privacy, seizure/arrest OK (N.B. there was no **further** search or seizure here);

Framingham v BMC **373 M 783 (77)**—bad entry in cop's house after he's outside & shot by X outside;

C v DiMarzio **52 MAC 746 (2001)**—though "combustible combination of a gun, intoxication, and conflict" along with observation of circumstances at D's office (haphazard car parking and door left open suggested D was "in a rush") was exigency making it reasonable for cops to enter premises through open door peaceably in broad daylight, suppression of marijuana from inside desk drawer ordered: D had been handcuffed and was asked, without Miranda warnings, where was marijuana (smelled by cops, rolling papers observed); rejecting Commonwealth claims of legitimate search OF DESK as "search incident to arrest" and "inevitable discovery"; **on further appellate review, 436 M 1012 (2002),** SJC agrees re: suppression, but instead merely, flatly, because discovery was fruit of Miranda violation & no inevitable discovery;

C v Rosenthal **52 MAC 707 (2001)**—trooper used pretext of administrative search powers to investigate D for drug possession, & won't be allowed to claim "fear" when D resisted showing contents of pocket to trooper; "(t)o the extent there was any actual exigency here, it was created by (trooper's) own unlawful conduct, actions the Commonwealth cannot be permitted to exploit at trial";

C v Bradshaw **385 M 244 (82)**—**ruse to get D out needs exigency**; OK if reasonable belief D armed/dangerous & weekend warrant difficulty;

C v Ford **35 MAC 752 (94)**—speedy investigation/ exigency of finding armed robbers at van rental agency justified lack of warrant;

C v Bass **24 MAC 972 (87)—OK entry for armed robbery suspect after ½ hour, but gun found behind dry bar exceeded exigency in scope;**

C v Saunders **50 MAC 865 (2001)**—though "reasonably close" question, OK for cops to gain entry to apartment via maintenance man's pass key after armed robbery "several hours" before; factors to be considered re: 'exigency' = whether crime is violent, or suspect armed/dangerous; whether there's probable cause to believe suspect has committed felony & "strong reason" to believe he's in dwelling; whether entry is made peaceably, preferably in daytime; whether there's risk of escape; whether there's reasonable basis for believing delay would subject officers or others to physical harm;

C v Bui **419 M 392 (95)**—in executing murder arrest warrant via no-knock warrant for particular apartment, cop could act for his safety in kicking over a mattress on floor, in room where there are 3 people, when apartment was "not yet secured";

C v Donoghue **23 MAC 103 (86)**—D might destroy evidence/harm someone because probable cause he just slashed complaining witness with knife;

C v Rotolo **45 MAC 927 (98)**—D was overheard on telephone from police station, asking his father to remove items from his room before police arrived with search warrant; exigency justified warrantless search;

C v Amaral **16 MAC 230 (83)**—reasonable belief D will destroy drugs = exigency;

C v Sondrini **48 MAC 704 (2000)**—though officials came onto property to assist first-floor tenant re: water leak into apartment from second floor apartment, their sighting (through 2d floor window) of a pipe-like apparatus for marijuana-smoking triggered criminal investigative search, and warrant should have been obtained;

C v Taylor **426 M 189, 195 (97)**—OK to "detain" D until police could obtain warrant to seize his clothing & sneakers because they might have traces of fire accelerant;

C v Skea **18 MAC 685 (84)**—though not arresting D for 1 joint, exigency search/seizure = OK to check for more (& seize diamond);

C v Garcia **34 MAC 386 (93)**—even assuming probable cause to arrest D for drug sale, search of locked nearby mailbox (key on D's person) not justifiable on "exigent circumstances" rationale (or as search incident to arrest);

C v Sawyer **389 M 686 (83)**—rendition law OK's motel entry for (indicted) D

Arizona v Hicks **480 US 321 (87)**—exigent entry but scope too far (*see Chapter 20-I*); see also *C v Dubois* **44 MAC 294 (98) entry to arrest fleeing individual didn't justify further search of building**;

C v Viriyahiranpaiboon **412 M 224 (92)**—violent double stabbing, likelihood D present & armed, & possibility of escape created exigency justifying warrantless peaceable entry & search of D's home;

C v Martino **412 M 267 (92)**—potential loss or destruction of evidence created exigency justifying warrantless seizure of evidence from D's attorney as he was removing items from D's home immediately after murder;

C v Kaupp **453 M 102, 106 n.7 (2009)**—OK to seize/ "secure" D's computer pending issuance of search warrant given "ease with which computer files may be accessed and deleted"; exigency = potential destruction of evidence, but warrant was required before "forensic analysis of" computer's contents;

C v Krisco Corp. **421 M 37 (95)**—when surveillance revealed pattern of disposal of illegal waste in dumpster immediately before regular garbage pick-up time, there was probable cause to believe it would occur then, & warrant should have been obtained;

C v Paniaqua **413 M 796 (92)**—radio call of gunshots plus woman pointing to apartment, stating, "They ran in there," created exigency justifying warrantless entry, even though man inside told cops he knew nothing of shots;

C v Figueroa **412 M 745 (92)**—D's flight from car upon cop's discovery of brown bag created exigency justifying warrantless seizure & opening of bag;

C v Wigfall **32 MAC 582 (92)—warrantless seizure 3 hours after exigency developed not justified as cops had time to get warrant;**

C v DiToro **51 MAC 191 (2001)**—absence of warrant excused since probable cause existed only when D's boyfriend actually emerged from a car with black bag containing cocaine; earlier, go-betweens seemed unable to consummate drug deal;

C v Lee **32 MAC 85 (92)—likelihood that marked money used in drug buy would be lost** plus impracticability of obtaining warrant created exigency justifying warrantless search of supermarket basement;

C v Washington **449 M 476 (2007)**—SJC upholds (pretextual) frisk for weapons on ground that fungible money from drug deal wouldn't be verified unless search occurred immediately; there was probable cause to arrest D as supplier to drug seller targeted by undercover operation, but cops didn't want to alert/reveal such operation yet, and instead stopped car for speeding, but had to justify exit order and pat-search which revealed the money; SJC refuses to adopt "blanket rule that all persons suspected of drug activity are to be presumed armed and dangerous for constitutional purposes," so exit order simply because probable cause to believe guilty of drug distribution = invalid;

C v Collazo **34 MAC 79 (93)**—undercover agent/ "drug buyer" wearing wire during pre-arranged deal, but warrant impracticable because prior to point when 2 Ds took drugs from inside their pants, it was uncertain where the transaction would take place, and there would have been no probable cause for a search warrant for the apartment;

C v Martinez **47 MAC 839 (99)—undercover agent did not know scene of drug transaction beforehand, so no warrant possible;** surveillance officers' entry into motel room/arrests/seizures OK because of exigent circumstances ("safe to assume . . . participants would disperse" speedily after drug sale);

C v Rodriguez **450 M 302 (2007)—**exigent circumstances and probable cause justified warrantless interception of conversation: when police discovered cocaine in a package being sent from Colombia, they obtained anticipatory search warrant for address to which box was being delivered, but after delivery of box and execution of warrant, the arrested recipient named D as person to whom he was to deliver the box, and at cops' behest, called D to retrieve it; while awaiting D's arrival, cop placed electronic monitoring and recording device inside recipient's shirt pocket, enabling verification of recipient's tale when D arrived: "given the unexpected turn of events," police had no opportunity to obtain warrant, and could reasonably seek to substantiate recipient's story "promptly," not being required to delay D's pickup of the package;

20-L.3. Community Caretaking

See cases, post, Chapter 20-M, e.g., *C v Lubiejewski* **49 MAC 212 (2000)—**unidentified motorist telephoned state police to report pickup truck with specific plate # was traveling on wrong side of Rt. 195 in vicinity of Rt. 140, but called back again to say truck crossed grassy median & proceeded on right side of road before turning south on Rt. 240 in Fairhaven; dispatcher also conveyed Fairhaven address to which truck was registered; trooper stopped the truck, not for any observed violation, but for tipster's report; odor of alcohol & failure of sobriety tests followed, but evidence ordered suppressed; no corroboration of anything but obvious details = insufficient to compensate for unknown reliability of informant; *C v Hurd* **29 MAC 929 (90)** distinguished ("emergency" there because tip concerned allegedly drunk man getting into & driving specific car containing 3 small children; police corroborated vehicle's presence & its approach to high-speed highway; no emergency here because no report of "drunk" & once driver went to correct side of road, "emergency . . . ended"); community caretaking function (advanced only on appeal) must be "totally divorced from the detection, investigation, or acquisition of evidence relating to the violation of a criminal statute," & this wasn't (trooper was investigating for evidence of the crime of driving wrong way on highway);

C v Davis **63 MAC 88 (2005)—**cop on detail who heard radio dispatch, based on anonymous phone call re: drunk female getting into white SUV with specific license plate number, tossing out beer cans, etc., could stop the car; "that report of an apparently drunk driver was anonymous did not require the police to ignore it" (*C v Fortune* **47 MAC 923, (2003)**);

C v Love **56 MAC 229 (2002)—**though upholding stop on other grounds, refusal to uphold "emergency" ground for car stop after citizen told of it chasing a truck at 80 miles per hour on single-lane road during rush hour;

C v McDevitt **57 MAC 733 (2003)—**cop could conduct "well-being" check of car stopped in breakdown lane despite having received tips that same car was driving erratically & cop had searched for the car: "community caretaking" includes concern for safety of public using roadway, not just that of car's occupant[s];

C v Gaylardo **68 MAC 906 (2007)—**cop could approach D, sitting in car in parking lot in winter at 2:38 a.m., car headlights and interior lights on, driver's door open; this wasn't a "stop," and approach was justified for "community caretaking"; observations then led to arrest for operating under influence of alcohol; questioning during "well-being check" isn't "interrogation"; that cop referred to his approach as "stop" was irrelevant;

C v Mateo-German **453 M 838 (2009)—**trooper on routine patrol on 4-lane highway saw D's car abruptly slow, activate hazard lights, and pull into breakdown lane: inquiry revealed out of gas, D using cell phone to call friend to bring gas; trooper stayed, conversing, suspicious of tinted windows, strong air freshener scent from car, & D's nervousness; 4 of 7 justices say trooper's request for permission to have dog sniff exterior was OK, wasn't detention/"seizure" requiring constitutional justification and consent wasn't involuntary as fruit; dog's alert (with other facts?) = probable cause; *dissent cites,* inter alia, C v Eckert 431 M 591, 595-596 (2000), noting community caretaking encounter can "ripen" into "seizure" requiring constitutional justification; stranded nervous motorist "should not be subjected to a persistent and unlimited line of inquiry" by cop "merely because . . . had misfortune to run out of gasoline or to break down" on side of road (**Ireland, J., dissenting**);

C v McCarthy **71 MAC 591 (2008)—**officer dispatched to restaurant on report of unconscious woman, who was 'thrashing about' on floor, unable to communicate effectively; responding EMTs told officer believed woman suffered drug overdose, and asked if he knew what she had taken; officer saw open handbag near woman, searched it for drugs to assist EMTs in treatment: no suppression of drugs found therein;

C v Kirschner **67 MAC 836 (2006)—**rejects Commonwealth argument that cops were entitled to go inside dark house to rid it of invited guests and lock up, simply because adult resident was being arrested and his parents were away for the weekend: "no reasonable basis to believe there was any imminent and serious danger to persons or property requiring immediate action";

20-L.4. Emergency Search for Missing Persons

C v Bates **28 MAC 217 (90)—**although standard for "emergency" search for missing persons "less stringent" than "exigent" search for evidence, three-hour delay by police suggested there was no emergency;

C v Snell **428 M 766 (99)**—wife-victim's family members had been unable to contact her for 2 days, after husband had posted bail on charges of threatening to murder V; warrantless entry of the marital home OK (emergency exception); dead body and evidence found;

C v Erickson **74 MAC 172 (2009)**—building resident said dog in rear apartment had been barking for over fourteen hours, that an odor was emanating from apartment, & that he had not seen apartment tenant for quite some time; officer saw, through window, emaciated dog, & stench led to concern that decaying body might be inside, no response to yelling and banging on door; removal of window grate & finding 50 animal carcasses in refrigerator and/or kitchen cabinets upheld despite absence of warrant;

20-L.5. Protective Sweeps

Maryland v Buie **494 US 325 (90)**—limited "protective sweep" of premises allowed under Fourth Amendment if entry lawful & reasonable belief dangerous persons present;

C v Lewin (II) **407 M 617 (90)**—once exigency justifying "protective sweep" ends, authority to search ends & warrant required; items subsequently seized as result of warrantless search of murder scene suppressed;

C v Peters **453 M 818 (2009)**—after 911 call and evidence that gun had been fired into one house from neighboring house and car was seen to speedily leave the latter house after sounds of argument within, there was reasonable belief that shooter or victim in need of assistance could be inside: protective sweep/warrantless entry legitimate BUT second sweep 15–20 minutes later, simply to be more thorough, was unlawful; gun and drugs found then infected search warrant subsequently obtained;

C v DuBois **44 MAC 294 (98)**—when officers don't reasonably believe themselves or others to be in danger, protective sweep improper; mere presence of a person elsewhere in building doesn't justify;

C v Nova **50 MAC 633 (2000)**—after breaking down door to chase & arrest D after his flight out rear door, preparatory to awaiting arrival of landlord to repair door, cops not allowed to walk back through apartment, announcing "police": no justifiable inference here that anyone was in the apartment;

C v DeJesus **70 MAC 114, further app. review denied 450 M 1101 (2007)**—reversing allowance of suppression, claiming that arrest subject's history of violent felonies alone made protective sweep of entire premises permissible, notwithstanding fact that D answered door, submitted to arrest, and was handcuffed before police questioned two women and, merely upon their acknowledgment that a person was in the basement where music was playing, "protectively" "swept" basement, finding in plain view a gun belonging to D; opinion's "distinction" of *DuBois* unpersuasive; standard "policy" of "violent fugitive

apprehension section" implicitly approved; see, however, *Buie*, 494 US 325, and progeny;

C v Ware **75 MAC 220 (2009)**—'protective sweep' used to justify search of home after D was arrested, simply because cops "had not located the firearm allegedly used by him" and could "insure their own safety by ascertaining that there were no other individuals at the dwelling who could potentially pose danger"; but see DuBois and Nova, supra, and Cruz, 53 MAC at 28–29; further, assertion that "exclusion of the evidence was not required as long as the subsequent search warrant was properly obtained";

C v Mejia **64 MAC 238 (2005)**—police traced ransom call to residence, culprits fled as they approached, police entered with drawn guns and found victim bound and hooded: flipping mattress off box springs "to make certain that no one was hiding beneath the bed" OK'd as protective sweep, court ignoring defense point that no person "could hide between a mattress and a box spring"; alternative basis for rejecting suppression of gun said to be no expectation of privacy because D didn't live or work there & "no personal papers or belongings" of D were found there (though D was charged/convicted of gun possession);

C v Cruz **53 MAC 24, 28–29 (2001)**—search warrant for drugs didn't allow officer with specialized expertise in cell phone cloning to test object(s) and then assert propriety of their seizure as being contraband in plain view; incriminating character of objects wasn't immediately apparent to 'protective sweep' cop (who triggered use of an extra search team with specialized "cell phone fraud" training in execution of warrant to search for drugs): **"use of the concept of a protective sweep search and of the plain view doctrine can present a potentially far-reaching encroachment on the rights protected by Article 14 and the Fourth Amendment . . . .** This case graphically illustrates how police, by clever resort to these doctrines, can entirely circumvent the warrant requirement" (**id. at 36**);

C v Vesna San **63 MAC 189 (2005)**—in immediate investigation of 911 call at 1:00 a.m. alleging burglars in kitchen, police learned description of individual male fleeing scene, and description of black van said to have been circling the area; sighting of the man standing outside the van, two miles away, gave reasonable suspicion to block the van from exiting a driveway & to detain the man, to order van occupants to exit, & to make a protective sweep of the van; sighting of item believed to have been taken in the burglary prompted victims' arrival to identify it (all actions said to be proportional to circumstances);

C v Lopes **455 M 147 (2009)**—after van's occupants were removed and handcuffed upon reasonable vasis to believe armed and dangerous, cop could go inside van to retrieve ID's when driver told cop his ID was inside; "limited" search for ID yielded incriminating cash; ALSO, "protective sweep" would have been OK (van had four rows of seats, cops weren't sure that only two individuals had been involved in shooting homicide);

20-L.6. "Accomplice Sweep"

C v DuBois **44 MAC 294, 297 n.4 (98)**—dicta, noting a "parallel" to protective sweep, rationale enabling police to investigate possible presence of accomplices to crime for which an arrest has been made on the premises: not here adopted; record lacked support for reasonable belief that original arrestee had an accomplice there (fact that person is present doesn't establish that he's "accomplice");

20-L.7. Automobiles

Carroll v US **267 US 132 (25)**—seizure/search of car OK if probable cause to arrest, or for fruits/contraband/weapons;

Chambers v Maroney **399 US 42 (70)**—(same) even at station after arrest;

C v Lara **39 MAC 546 (95)**—warrantless search of car taken to police station (after its driver/passenger delivered drugs to customer) OK;

Pennsylvania v Labron **518 US 938 (96)**—government need not have exigent circumstances to justify warrantless search of auto stopped in transit or seized in public place, on probable cause;

Arizona v Gant **129 S Ct 1710 (2009)**—police may search passenger compartment of vehicle incident to a recent occupant's arrest only if it is reasonable to believe (per *Chimel v California* 395 US 752) that arrestee might access the vehicle at time of search or (per *Thornton v US* 541 US 615, 632) that vehicle contains evidence of the arrest offense; neither rationale permitted search here as five cops cuffed and secured D and two other suspects in separate patrol cars before search began AND D was arrested for driving after license suspension (evidence of which could not be reasonably expected inside vehicle); *NY v Belton* not to be read "expansively";

C v Street **56 MAC 301 (2002)**—since there was probable cause to believe car contained evidence of crimes, there was no requirement of exigent circumstances for warrantless search; "inherent mobility" of car = enough;

C v Vazquez **426 M 99 (97)**—search of car, stopped in public place, OK without warrant, given probable cause to believe gun inside used in armed assault;

C v Watson **430 M 725 (2000)**—drug courier profile data critical to stop (upheld here) of car driven by man after he retrieved heavy suitcases from motel room of possible "courier"; additional factor was subject's driving in manner consistent with interest in detecting surveillance; implausible responses of the two men re: suitcases = "reasonable . . . to seize" the suitcases; men were not "seized" upon detention of the suitcases or during roadside questioning; search warrant was obtained for suitcases (but SJC believed warrant unnecessary in circumstances);

C v Gajka **425 M 751 (97)**—OK to seize van parked in public place because witness ID'd it as having left area of homicide near in time to crime; but see *Coolidge v New Hampshire* **403 US 443 (71)** bad seizure/search of D's car

after home arrest because could've gotten search warrant beforehand;

C v Cast **407 M 891 (90)**—lawful warrantless search of vehicle generally extends to all containers (open or closed) found within;

C v Bostock **450M 616 (2008)**—speedy response to report of described suspect breaking into vehicles and stealing resulted in finding matching suspect within minutes and in vicinity of described path; sighting of two described items (stolen phone, duffel bag used for transport) inside truck (+ D's denial of ownership) = probable cause to search, so vehicle search including containers OK under automobile exception to warrant requirement;

C v Upton **394 M 363 (85)**—Declaration of Rights, Article 14 needs exigency to **search mobile home** (–contrast *California v Carney* **471 US 386 (85)**, probable cause enough for mobile home for US Supreme Court under Fourth Amendment); (*see Chapter 20-M below re: 'stop & frisk' of cars*);

C v Rand **363 M 554 (73)**—after accident, can tow car to station & search there, so long as had probable cause at the scene;

C v Lugo **64 MAC 12 (2005)**—cops had warrant to search van, and towing the inoperable van to police station to perform search was within authority of the police pursuant to the search warrant; D had no right to require search in front of apartment rather than at station; distinguishes *Emery v Holmes* 824 F.2d 143 (1st Cir 1987), where vehicle was POSSIBLY not covered by warrant for premises, and where police waited six days after towing vehicle to search it; case "does not stand for the proposition that the car should have been searched before it was towed," but instead questioned legality of the seizure of the car under the warrant in question;

C v White **422 M 487 (96)**—police need not stand guard over car stopped on public way while warrant is obtained;

C v Crespo **59 MAC 927 (2003)**—**sight of substantial amount of white powder in plastic baggie on ground at vehicle crash scene gave probable cause to search nearby dark plastic bag and the rest of the vehicle; "field of debris" appearing to come from car may be regarded as part of the car for purposes of search, and police action further approved because accident scene needed to be made passable for general public on roadway;**

C v Motta **424 M 117 (97)**—under Article 14, upon probable cause, can search vehicle parked in public place & apparently capable of being moved (& can do it at station instead of on street); **but** unreasonable delay in conducting search will render it invalid;

C v Eggleston **453 M 554 (2009)**—though D argued too much delay between "probable cause" and warrantless search of automobile, SJC indicated delay "reasonable" or "permissible" to corroborate info received, and since expected additional evidence would subsequently be located in auto, and/or that suspect or another would commit additional criminal acts; "plain & ample opportunity to obtain warrant" doesn't by itself require obtaining warrant when "readily mobile" vehicle involved; two dissenting justices decry complete elimination of warrant requirement for auto in public place by ignoring "plain and ample opportunity" principle;

C v Markou **391 M 27 (84)—police station search OK only if reasonably immediate**; if probable cause, don't need search warrant for car because moveable = exigent;

C v Woodman **11 MAC 965 (81)**—car search at station after D bailed, 48 hours after arrest, = bad without search warrant;

C v Agosto **428 M 31 (98)**—requirement of warrant is **not** "indefinitely suspended by an ongoing automobile exception"; car here was searched at least 10 times between June 21 seizure & July 12 drug discovery; rejecting "incident to forfeiture" exception to warrant requirement either from time property possibly subject to forfeiture is seized or from point Commonwealth agents form intent to seek forfeiture; SJC reserves question whether Article 14 protects against warrantless searches of property subject to forfeiture;

C v King **35 MAC 221 (93)**—though reliable informant & controlled buy & corroboration gave probable cause and warrant could have been obtained, lack of warrant for suspects' car as it returned to MA after drug-buying in NY excused; car's mobility and "diminished feeling of privacy" re: cars cited;

C v Sergienko **399 M 291 (87)**—though probable cause to search car, need search warrant or exigency;

C v Stephens **451 M 370 (2008)**—undercover troopers conducting surveillance of parking lot known as drug sales rendezvous point followed two vehicles from there, approached the vehicle in which both men were meeting, reasonably feared for their safety because of black object in D's hand, opened door, and saw much money and clear plastic bags with corners cut: given probable cause to arrest, search of car OK as incident to arrest even though "arrest" occurred after search;

C v Ngo **14 MAC 339 (82)**—exigency for D in car, probable cause, & no time for search warrant;

C v Powers **39 MAC 911 (95)**—with probable cause to search D (who sold/supplied drugs) at the "target residence" of warrant, police could search him as he left the premises "in the face of the oncoming search team";

C v Paredes **35 MAC 666 (93)**—later-breaking info from informant gave probable cause & exigent circumstances to stop & search D as she traveled in her car (in addition to the residence & persons of D & another there for which warrant had been obtained, based on info from same informant);

C v King **389 M 233 (83)**—after shootout & arrest of 1/2 guys, can search whole car, even glove box & inside duffel bag under *Ross* **456 US 798 (82)** (below);

C v Myers **16 MAC 554 (83)**—exigency for drugs seen through car window while home-arrest by warrant; but contrast non-car (home) scene: *C v Sondrini* **48 MAC**

704 (2000) though officials came onto property to assist first-floor tenant re: water leak into apartment from second floor apartment, their sighting (through 2d floor window) of a pipe-like apparatus for marijuana-smoking triggered criminal investigative search, and warrant should have been obtained;

C v Alvarado **420 M 542 (95)—despite drugs** in passenger's pants, & probable cause to arrest driver as well, bad warrantless search of car;

C v Dunn **34 MAC 702 (93)**—when stopped for speeding (& then arrested for OUI), D had pulled into parking lot of closed business, and motion judge had ruled car impoundment improper (& suppressed fruit of purported inventory search); Appeals Court said impoundment OK (spare property owner trouble of dealing with vehicle & possible police liability for vandalism or theft if vehicle left in unattended lot) but remanded for "inventory" propriety; but Cf. *C v Caceres* **413 M 749 (92) (analysis of (un)availability of other driver)**;

C v Ellerbe **430 M 769 (2000)**—in similar circumstances, after **analysis of Boston police compliance with impoundment and inventory policy, search upheld**;

C v Wallace **70 MAC 757 (2007)**—because D acceded to police request to come to station without asking to move his car from the handicapped space in which he was sitting illegally, towing of car to station was OK, and was not an illegality vitiating D's written consent at the station for it to be searched; cop's testimony that towing was consistent with department's written protocol apparently shifted burden to D to offer the policy in evidence (D's presentation of "a memorandum in which he offered his understanding of the policy" not adequate, id. at 760–61 & n.1);

C v Goncalves **62 MAC 153 (2004)**—when D alighted from car during legitimate stop (in no-parking area) & subsequent arrest for operating after suspension, officer awaiting tow truck leaned into car to turn off ignition, saw gun in plain view; "once public safety or security concerns exist to justify decision to impound vehicle, officer is empowered to carry out any physical act minimally necessary to accomplish that purpose"; this wasn't "inventory" case (distinguishing *C v Silva* **61 MAC at 33** (even brief foray into vehicle = inventory search));

C v Nicholson **58 MAC 601 (2003)**—after arrest of D for operating under influence, impoundment and inventory of car = lawful, AND since there was probable cause to believe some items = evidence of crime (liquor bottles), warrantless seizure of them permissible; acknowledgment that *C v Alvarado* **420 M 542 (95)** probably suggests that immobilization of the car extinguishes any general "automobile" exception to warrant requirement;

C v Sanchez **40 MAC 411 (96)**—following stop of car for no rear lights, driver had no license & had outstanding warrants, and registration showed owner was neither driver nor any of the 3 passengers, only one of whom had license (and that person stated merely that she was getting a ride),

OK to impound car & inventory it; police not required to suggest instead that licensed passenger drive car from scene;

C v Bettencourt **447 M 631 (2006)**—after proper stop, driver was arrested; cop asked passenger whether he had license, and he said no; further questioning of passenger for name and date of birth resulted in knowledge of outstanding warrants, passenger's arrest, and discovery of cocaine on his person: SJC orders suppression, since no ground for questioning D/believing D involved in crime; Commonwealth's belated argument that it was "community caretaking" to find a driver to take charge of car rather than tow/impound it was rebuffed, because not raised at trial court by testimony or argument;

C v Brinson **440 M 609 (2003)**—lawful inventory search was dependent upon propriety of impoundment of car; impoundment improper because car was legally parked in a commercial parking lot and arrest of its owner occurred elsewhere; no "community caretaking" justification because car posed no threat to public safety and was not itself imperiled; G.L. c. 266, § 120D is NOT "grant of discretionary authority for police to tow a car from private property";

C v Murphy **63 MAC 11 (2005)**—police improperly transformed an inventory search of D's person at booking into an investigatory search, examining car keys to determine they belonged to rental car with particular plate number, and taking keys to street to find car match, after which (ticketed) car was impounded for "inventory" search; contrasts situation where police prepare to impound and tow illegally parked vehicle without regard to info obtained elsewhere (*C v Henley* 63 MAC 1 (2005)); gun in car = suppressed;

C v Pacheco **51 MAC 736 (2001)**—after valid stop for expired inspection sticker, driver presented facially valid license and registration in a different name, & said car belonged to father of passenger; passenger had no identification, but gave name whose last name matched that of registered car owner: OK to request passenger to leave car, & OK to arrest & cuff & secure him in cruiser after warrant check revealed default warrants for shoplifting, trespass, A&B; NOT OK to search car, including under floor mat, on purported rationale of search for identification pursuant to G.L. c. 276, § 1 (for fruits, instrumentalities, contraband, & evidence of crime for which arrest has been made (failure to appear in court, G.L. c. 276, § 82A?) to prevent destruction/concealment); claim that search for evidence of identification was OK because not "certain" that D correctly identified himself SOUNDLY REJECTED ("would be to sanction a principle having no apparent stopping place & could risk the possibility of a general exploratory search for evidence of criminal activity");

C v Saint Louis **59 MAC 928 (2003)**—IF cop has seen liquor in car, knows that car owner is underage, and all car occupants appear to be under age twenty-one, there is reasonable suspicion to stop car;

C v Bakoian **412 M 295 (92)—police not required to immobilize car & obtain warrant unless they have "plain & ample" opportunity to obtain warrant;**

C v Harris **47 MAC 481 (99)**—even when car is inoperable & parked in private driveway, when surveilling police have just watched its use as retail outlet for drug purchases, and D is sitting in car smoking marijuana;

C v Killackey **410 M 371 (91)**—warrantless search of car which cops had probable cause to believe contained drugs justified by danger that drugs would be removed if they waited for warrant;

C v Cast **407 M 891 (90)**; *C v Moses* **408 M 136 (90)**—automobile exception discussed;

Whren v US **517 US 806 (96)**—stop of motorist for traffic law violation OK even though reasonable officer would not have stopped car absent some additional law enforcement motive (here, hunch re drugs);

C v A Juvenile (II) **411 M 157 (91)**—warrantless search of exterior of car suspected of involvement in vehicular homicide in private residential driveway didn't disturb any legitimate expectations of privacy where car visible from public view; once incriminating damage revealed, warrantless seizure justified by exigency of automobile exception; *Coolidge v New Hampshire* **403 US 443 (71)**, distinguished;

20-L.8. Closed Containers in Automobiles

Cf. *C v Straw* **422 M 756 (96)**—need search warrant to search briefcase thrown out of window into yard as cops entered to execute arrest warrant (**not** abandoned); any exigency ceased to exist when briefcase was seized; **"plain view" applicable only when container's contents are in plain view and are seen to be contraband;**

C v Muckle **61 MAC 678 (2004)**—opening of crumpled Dunkin' Donuts bag inside vehicle wasn't justifiable under written inventory policy requiring that passenger area of vehicle be "thoroughly examined" and that all personal property be removed and secured at police station; "bag of refuse that must be opened for its contents to be visible is like any other unlocked closed container"; "What is important is whether the item constitutes a closed container capable of holding personal property of value";

Walter v US **447 US 649 (80)**—need search warrant to open film box though legal seizure;

Arkansas v Sanders **442 US 753 (79)**—need search warrant for car, luggage though probable cause to seize;

Robbins v California **453 US 420 (81)**—(same) for container lawfully seized;

US v Ross **456 US 798 (82)—can open any container if car probable cause covers it;**

California v Acevedo **500 US 565 (91)—warrantless search of closed containers in motor vehicles may be made under Fourth Amendment if there is probable cause that vehicle contains evidence or contraband; Chadwick & Sanders overruled;**

US v Johns **469 US 478 (85)**—OK to search car containers 3 days after arrest;

C v White **374 M 132 (77)**—driving under & 1 joint not probable cause to search trunk;

C v Irwin **391 M 765 (84)**—Declaration of Rights Article 14 may bar seizure & search of container without search warrant, but marijuana visible from outside car, so not a search;

C v Cast **407 M 891 (90)**—**warrantless search of open or closed containers in motor vehicles may be made under Article 14 if there is probable cause to search vehicle; automobile exception discussed;**

C v Wunder **407 M 909 (90)**; *C v Moses* **408 M 136 (90)**—same; *C v Crespo* **59 MAC 926 (2003)**—same; seeing clear baggie with lots of white powder justified search of other containers in "debris field" surrounding roll-over car accident;

C v Watson **430 M 725 (2000)**—drug courier profile data critical to stop (upheld here) of car driven by man after he retrieved heavy suitcases from motel room of possible "courier"; additional factor was subject's driving in manner consistent with interest in detecting surveillance; implausible responses of the two men re: suitcases = "reasonable . . . to seize" the suitcases; men were not "seized" upon detention of the suitcases or during roadside questioning; search warrant was obtained for suitcases (but SJC believed warrant unnecessary in circumstances;

Florida v Wells **495 US 1 (90)**—warrantless search of locked suitcase in operating-under-the-influence D's impounded car was **improper inventory search where Florida highway patrol had no standard policy on closed containers;**

Florida v Jimeno **500 US 248 (91)**—D's general consent to search car for drugs included consent to search closed containers in which drugs could be found under Fourth Amendment; locked suitcase distinguished;

Bond v US **529 US 334 (2000)**—border patrol agent on bus at standard checkpoint in Texas "squeezed" soft-sided luggage in overhead storage space above seats; while passenger should expect that such bag would be handled by other passengers or bus employees, "exploratory" manner of handling here violated Fourth Amendment; passenger's "agreement" that bag be opened was not argued to be a voluntary consent;

See also Chapter 20-H—inventory; 20-I- Plain View; 20- M- "Investigative Stop" (& roadblock);

20-L.9. Administrative Searches

Camara v Municipal Court **387 US 523 (67)**—regulatory or administrative inspection (building code) OK without probable cause if reasonable standards, but usually needs search warrant;

C v Accaputo **380 M 435 (80)**—(same); administrative warrant on less probable cause if reasonable standards, purpose, & scope; here, some drugs OK, but others & gun = beyond scope;

C v Roland R. **448 M 278 (2007)**—past signs stating that all bags = "subject to manual search", juvenile entered courthouse, but when informed by court officer that bag was going to be searched, juvenile declined, picked up bag and left building; he ran when told to "come here"; SJC says judge erred in ordering suppression of marijuana inside bag; citing *C v Harris* **383 M 655 (81)**, "area-entry inspections at court house entrances, for safety and security purposes" = OK without warrant or individualized suspicion of wrongdoing or danger; D "implicitly demonstrated consent" by passing signs, placing bag on table and going through metal detector, and "was not entitled to withdraw his consent after the inspection had commenced";

C v Jung **420 M 675 (95)**—"administrative" search exceeded proper scope/lacked "particularity"; fire officials' assistance to private investigator (employed by insurance company) **might** call for suppression of fruits of investigator's search (unless insurance contact gave prospective consent to such private investigator);

C v Carkhuff **441 M 122 (2004)**—2 a.m. suspicionless stop of car traveling on rural road adjacent to water supply reservoir (due to fear of terrorists) not legitimate as roadblock because no plan; not legitimate as administrative "screening" search because no steps to minimize intrusiveness, i.e., prior notice that motorists = subject to stop/search;

C v Krisco Corp **421 M 37 (95)**—"administrative" justification was a "subterfuge" for a criminal investigative search;

C v Rosenthal **52 MAC 707 (2001)**—suppression required: trooper used pretext of administrative search (State Racing Commission at Suffolk Downs) of tack room to perform investigative search of D's person for drugs (on basis of snitch's unreliable tip);

C v Tremblay **48 MAC 454 (2000)**—OK for "administrative" inspection (under G.L. c. 140, § 66) to be triggered by allegation that 3 stolen cars were on D's auto salvage lot; important to halt "inspection" and seek search warrant immediately after confirmation that some car in lot was stolen, to "respect( ) a dividing line between administrative procedure and pursuit of evidence of motor vehicle crime";

C v Hurd **51 MAC 12 (2001)**—animal control officer's entry onto private premises in response to report of dead (mistreated) dog, followed by unsuccessful attempts to locate home owner, & then returning to premises with cop, & 2d entry into largely enclosed yard area meant "consent" to "go ahead, do what you have to do" was involuntary, obtained through exploitation of prior illegal entry; "plain view" argument rejected, as was "exigency" (belied by delay in seeking home owner at place of employment, trip to police, etc.), & G.L. c. 129, § 7 (right of animal inspector to enter, created by statute, doesn't override constitution);

C v Lipomi **385 M 370 (82)**—G.L. c. 90, § 30 drug search & seizure needs warrant; warrant here too broad;

C v Frodyma **386 M 434 (82)**—administrative warrant must show some need/specificity;

New York v Burger **482 US 691 (87)**—reasonable law can permit warrantless searches/seizures necessary for pervasively regulated business;

C v Eagleton **402 M 199 (88)**—(same) under G.L. c. 140, § 67; (no Article 14, Declaration of Rights argument);

C v Cadoret **15 MAC 654 (83)**—though bars are closely regulated, laws don't permit forced entry to private club;

Horsemen's Benevolent & Protective Ass'n v State Racing Commission **403 M 692 (89)**—no urine tests without probable cause even though closely regulated area;

Vernonia School District v Acton **515 US 646 (95)**—suspicionless random drug testing of public **school athletes** OK under Fourth Amendment (consent rationale);

C v Damian D. **434 M 725 (2001)**—(marijuana ordered suppressed) though Supreme Court has exempted school searches from Fourth Amendment's warrant and probable cause requirements, searches of students by school administrators must still be "reasonable," and a **search is not "reasonable" simply because a student has disobeyed school rules**, i.e., here, being out of class for a period of time during the day; further, search was for evidence of contraband, not "truancy"; left open = question whether Declaration of Rights Article 14 imposes a standard stricter than reasonableness on student searches;

C v Smith **72 MAC 175 (2008)**—students wishing to enter Brighton High School were on notice of and had to consent to entry though specified entrance at specified times, requiring passage through metal detector used to prevent by deterrence or confiscation importation of weapons into building; search of D was reasonable because D had entered by some other means, avoiding metal detection, had foregone usual practice of leaving belongings in assistant headmaster's office, was found in unauthorized area, and was on the premises in violation of previous day's directive that he could not return without parent; search by assistant headmaster was only of D's jacket, whose heaviness prompted him to find gun in pocket;

C v Considine **448 M 295 (2007)**—but if chaperones of private school's field trip search students' hotel room, etc., there is no state action, and chaperones had authority to summon hotel "security" head (also not a state actor), and subsequent action of state trooper was by consent of school authorities (who were in control of the room);

C v Lawrence L **439 M 817 (2003)**—procedure comported with *New Jersey v T.L.O., 469 US 325 (85)*: principal could search student on reasonable basis for believing student to be concealing illegally possessed controlled substance; memo of understanding between schools and police did not dictate when to search (and so school NOT agent of police), but instead just had guide for reporting detected criminal behavior to police, & for turning over any contraband; "school" search must merely be "reason-

able," justified at inception and limited in scope (contrast: warrant requirement & probable cause);

Safford Unified School Dist. No. 1 v Redding **129 S Ct 2633 (2009)**—search by school officials of 13-year-old student's bra and underpants violated Fourth Amendment even though reasonable suspicion student had brought forbidden prescription and over-the-counter drugs to school: no reason to suspect drugs presented a danger or were concealed in underwear;

Michigan v Tyler **436 US 499 (78)**—though **firemen** need (administrative (see below)) warrant to investigate, can enter to fight fire & stay reasonable time to investigate;

Michigan v Clifford **464 US 287 (84)**—unless exigent, firemen need search warrant to gather evidence, administrative warrant to investigate;

C v Bizarria **31 MAC 370 (91)**—"administrative inspection" by Registry's auto theft unit under G.L. c. 90, § 32 (regulating garage owners & repairmen), violated Article 14 because statute permits unlimited "general search," & because Registry had no standard procedures for administrative searches;

C v Tart **408 M 249 (90)**—warrantless administrative inspection under c. 130, § 80, to determine whether fishing vessel has valid permit to land raw fish upheld under Fourth Amendment & Article 14;

Griffin v Wisconsin **483 US 868 (87)—probation officer can search (at home) if "reasonable" (e.g., unauthenticated tip from cop without reliability indicia);**

US v Knights **534 US 112 (2001)—Fourth Amendment allows cops to make warrantless search of probationer's home upon "reasonable suspicion" when probationer is subject to a probation condition authorizing warrantless searches;**

C v LaFrance **402 M 789 (88)—probation condition giving probation officer blanket search authority = bad without limiting to "reasonable suspicion"; Declaration of Rights, Article 14 requires warrant for home; D can appeal condition though not (yet) searched & though agreed (under threat of jail otherwise); (*see Chapter 14-I*);**

US v Flores-Montano **541 US 149, 152–53 (2004)**—routine border searches are not subject to warrant requirement of Fourth Amendment; perhaps particularly destructive search of property is not "routine" (*US v Cortez-Rocha* 394 F3d 1115, 1119 (9th Cir), cert. denied 546 US 849 (2005) (cutting open spare tire during border search not so destructive as to be unreasonable);

C v McBrown **72 MAC 60 (2008)**—Logan Airport customers inspector's search of computer bag, including small incision made by knife to inner fabric lining of bag (to discern reason for heavy weight absent computer itself) didn't require warrant (Fourth Amendment holding);

20-L.10. Random Drug Testing and Other Special Needs Searches

Guiney v Police Commissioner of Boston **411 M 328 (91)**—Police Department rule authorizing random urinalysis of cops violates Article 14 because compelling interest for policy not shown & cannot be presumed; federal analysis of *National Treasury Employees Union v Von Raab* **489 US 656 (1989)**, distinguished; 'constitutional rights should not be sacrificed to war on drugs';

O'Connor v Police Commissioner **408 M 324 (90)**—random urinalysis of police cadets upheld as "reasonable" under Article 14 because necessary & because "agreed" to as condition of employment;

Vernonia School District v Acton **515 US 646 (95)**—random drug testing of all public secondary school athletes OK (consequence of positive = give up sports or participate in "anti-drug program");

Horsemen's Benevolent & Protective Ass'n v State Racing Commission **403 M 692 (89)**—no urine tests without probable cause even though closely regulated area;

20-M. INVESTIGATIVE "STOPS," OF PEOPLE AND CARS (AND ROADBLOCKS)

See also Chapter 20-G, Probable Cause;

K. Smith, *Criminal Practice & Procedure*, §§ 301–8, Stop & Frisk (2d ed. 1983 & Supp.)—276–79, Cars; 282, Roadblock; & *Chapter 3, above, Arrest*;

20-M.1. Investigative Stops and Protective Frisks

Terry v Ohio **392 US 1 (68)**—don't need probable cause if, from objective facts, reasonably suspect crime, & if limited (pat/frisk) intrusion;

C v Alverado **423 M 266 (96)—under Article 14 Declaration of Rights, existence of reasonable suspicion *not* determined by "imprecise" federal "totality of circumstances" test, but instead *Upton*/Aguilar, if tip (i.e., informant's basis of knowledge and reliability/veracity);**

See *C v Narcisse* **457 M 1 (2010) and** *C v Martin* **457 M 14 (2010), post (separate prongs of *Terry* may not be conflated; seizure occurred when cop announced intention to frisk, and reasonable suspicion of crime AND that D was armed/dangerous had to precede such frisk; overly permissive tolerance of police escalating street encounters ('field interrogation observations') seemingly abandoned;** *C v Perachio* **61 MAC 591 (2004)—** when cop had to brake heavily to avoid accident with driver who pulled in front of him, and thereafter observed that driver was D, known by cop to have been intoxicated 72 minutes earlier (and having been told then not to drive), there was reasonable suspicion supporting request to perform field sobriety tests;

20-M.2. "Stop" (Needs Only "Reasonable Suspicion") vs. "Arrest" (Requires Probable Cause)

Florida v Royer **460 US 491 (83)**—"stop" if reasonable belief not free to leave (vs. reasonable belief arrest); stop = temporary/limited; here, became arrest without probable cause;

Dunaway v NY **442 US 200 (79)**—take D to station for questioning = unconstitutional arrest without probable cause;

US v Brignoni-Ponce **422 US 873 (75)**—accost & restrain freedom = seize within Fourth Amendment;

US v Mendenhall **446 US 544 (80)**—not objectively a seizure for non-uniformed agents to ID 'selves & request ID/ticket (without saying D can decline); seizure occurs when reasonable person, "in view of all of the circumstances surrounding the incident," believes self not free to leave;

US v Drayton **536 US 194 (2002)**—cops conducting "consensual interviews" & searches of interstate bus passengers don't have to tell passengers of their right not to cooperate;

Michigan v Chesternut **486 US 567 (88)**—cops' pursuit in marked cruiser of D who fled on spotting police not a "seizure" because it didn't communicate that reasonable persons not free to ignore cops' presence;

Whren v US **517 US 806 (96)—ulterior motives/beliefs of police officers irrelevant; objective standard for probable cause/reasonable suspicion controls;**

C v Edwards **71 MAC 716, further review denied 452 M 1103 (2008), cert. denied 120 S Ct 1673 (2009)—** police had adequate grounds to conduct investigatory stop of D in identified car eighteen hours after report of "shots fired" and immediate investigation corroborated ID of shooter by name, address, and car; sighting of firearm under front seat occurred during stop; D had argued impropriety of warrantless arrest for 'completed misdemeanor', but court found *US v Hensley* 469 US 221 (85) unsupportive of D's claim; unlike *Couture* 407 M 178 (90) (unadorned fact of firearm possession not 'probable cause'), here there was firing of gun, combined with flight from scene;

C v Grandison **433 M 135 (2001)**—cruiser's **following D**, simply because he did immediate about-face upon seeing cops in area of frequent drug crimes, & again following him, with "high beams" activated, when he changed direction, & shining even brighter "alley lights" after him when he walked into an alley held not to be a "stop" requiring justification (though maybe different result if evidence showed effectively that D was trapped in dead-end alley); D's spitting something out of mouth gave reasonable suspicion (cop 'expert' testimony that illegal drugs often hidden in mouths), so "stop" command justified; "(f)ollowing someone for the purposes of surveillance is not pursuit";

C v Sykes **449 M 308 (2007)**—when cops approached in unmarked Crown Victoria, D pedaled bike away, continuing & speeding up when cops asked to speak with him; cops also sped up and followed, first in car and then on foot after D abandoned bike and fled, "grabbing at his waistband"; D discarded object before being tackled by cops; SJC holds that seizure occurred at point of foot chase of D, but that there was then "reasonable suspicion," so no suppression of gun; "We acknowledge that this is a close case" and neither presence in high crime area nor flight from cops "is sufficient to justify a stop";

C v Gomes **453 M 506 (2009)**—high crime area, 4 a.m., D swallowing that which he had been displaying to another man, after seeing cops, = reasonable suspicion, but no "fear" justifying immediate patfrisk, so suppression ordered;

Florida v Bostick **501 US 429 (91)**—cop's boarding of buses & requesting permission of passengers to search luggage without individualized suspicion not a "seizure" if reasonable passenger would feel free to decline request or terminate encounter;

California v Hodari D. **499 US 621 (91)**—**"seizure" doesn't occur under Fourth Amendment until D submits to application of physical force or to assertion of authority by cops**; mere "show of authority" doesn't constitute a "seizure"; open question whether Mendenhall reasonable person standard survives;

Brendlin v California **127 S Ct 2400 (2007)**—when cops stopped car for no good reason, passenger would not have felt free to leave, either, so has Fourth Amendment right to challenge;

Arizona v Johnson **129 S Ct 781 (2009)**—in traffic stop setting, first "Terry v Ohio" condition is met whenever it's lawful to detain auto and occupants pending inquiry into vehicular violation; under Fourth Amendment, police need not have in addition cause to believe any auto occupant is involved in criminal activity; patdown is OK when there is reasonable suspicion that the person being frisked is armed and dangerous; see/compare *C v Gonsalves* **429 M 658 (99)**—under Article 14 **cannot order driver out of auto for routine traffic stop unless reasonable belief that safety of officer or others is in danger, with** *Pennsylvania v Mimms* **434 US 106 (77) (once vehicle has been lawfully detained for traffic violation, police may order driver to get out of vehicle without violating Fourth Amendment;**

C v Harkess **35 MAC 626 (93)**—seizure of D in accord with Hodari D & D didn't ask Article 14 analysis; nonetheless, 3 a.m. high crime, subject of info from state police (drugs & gun involvement), & flight upon mere eye contact with police = reasonable suspicion justifying pursuit with drawn gun;

C v Stoute **422 M 782 (96)**—**under Article 14, Declaration of Rights officer must have reasonable suspicion of criminal activity in order to justify pursuit designed to effect a "stop"; pursuit which, objectively considered, indicates to a person that he would not be free to leave area or remain there without first responding to cop's inquiry, is equivalent of "seizure";** person is "plainly the object of an official assertion of authority"; failure to stop can contribute to "reasonable suspicion", but here reasonable suspicion was 1st had when identifiable on-street person called out to police that the individual had a gun;

C v Lopez **451 M 608 (2008)**—one uniformed cop in marked cruiser at 2 a.m. followed D, who was on bike, and another uniformed cop also arrived as first was stopping and motioning D to come to him, saying, "Can I speak with you?"; despite D's assertion and motion judge's ruling that D did not feel free to continue riding, SJC says there was no "stop" for which justification was needed, a "question" being "an inquiry" rather than a "command";

C v Jeudy **75 MAC 579 (2009)**—court assumed without deciding that "stop" occurred when pursuit of D & another began (when they saw unmarked though identifiable cop car & fled, after cops were responding to "shots fired" and had learned from neighbors that shots were attributed to particular gang, of which cop knew D to be a member), but held there to have been reasonable suspicion for "stop" at time pursuit was begun (motion judge had held no "stop" until cop found D crouching by trash barrel and there frisked him, and gun found in trash barrel had thus been "abandoned");

C v Franklin **456 M 818 (2010)**—defendant fled upon seeing unmarked Crown Victoria recognized as police vehicle, and though cops alighted and chased D, SJC says no "seizure" until they grabbed D as he was climbing a fence; at that point, there was reasonable suspicion of crime, D having held hand to waist as he ran, and cops by "experience and training," believed contraband, probably weapon, was in waistband;

C v Murphy **63 MAC 11 (2005)**—directing D to stand aside while police dispersed crowd isn't seizure since D was seemingly free to leave; label for subsequent interaction ("field interrogation observation") didn't "insulate it from constitutional scrutiny"; that D approached police & advised that he had a gold chain belonging to arrestee, and that he offered his observations of recent melee didn't provide ground for pat-frisk or detention; demand for ID wasn't request for voluntary cooperation, but instead was seizure;

C v Marrero **33 MAC 440 (92)**—cop's appropriate approach for threshold inquiry & pursuit not a "seizure" where D fled prior to "show of authority"; D's abrupt flight in response to threshold inquiry added to reasonable suspicion; open question whether Thibeau holding & Mendenhall reasonable person standard survives Hodari D., & whether Article 14 is more protective re: Terry-stops than Fourth Amendment;

C v Jeudy **75 MAC 579 (2009)**—assuming without deciding that "stop" occurred at time of pursuit, there was reasonable suspicion based on shots fired, conversation with neighbors saying members of particular gang were culprits, sighting gang members sitting three blocks away, and D's (& one other's) flight upon seeing unmarked Crown Victoria with multiple antennae, D known to have been previously involved in firearm-related offenses; gun discarded during pursuit was not fruit of poisonous tree;

C v Perry **62 MAC 500 (2004)**—though cop ran after D when D fled after making eye contact with cop, no "seizure" "in the constitutional sense" until after cops saw D throw gun into bushes;

C v Dowdy **36 MAC 495 (94)**—cops' approach & casual conversation not a "stop";

C v Johnson **454 M 159, 162 n.4 (2009)**—telling D to take his hands out of pockets not "seizure";

C v DeJesus **72 MAC 117 (2008)**—order to exit van occurred before D's "suspicious behavior" (refusal to get out, nervousness, telling police they needed a warrant); police cannot turn hunch into reasonable suspicion by inducing conduct justifying suspicion;

C v DaSilva **56 MAC 220 (2002)**—D (stabbing victim who refused to cooperate with police two days earlier) was riding a bicycle with his hand inside his pants and failed to stop even though ordered to do so three times; when cop next alighted to confront D, D feigned stop and then sped away; seizure occurred at the latest upon the second order to stop, and there was then no reasonable suspicion; flight "cannot be used to supply the requisite reasonable suspicion to justify the PRIOR police action"; suspicion that D had a gun wasn't adequate because this can be legal for adult (& D appeared to be adult); both gun and inculpatory statements suppressed;

C v Smith **55 MAC 569 (2002)**—cop's observation of three individuals speaking, D gesturing, and all three proceeding to an alleyway before one male reached into pocket prompted him to believe drug sale was about to occur; none responded to cop's question what they were doing, and he ordered them to stop; two did stop, but D didn't & rode bike toward cop, not stopping after three orders to do so; cop blocked D's path, causing D to fall, & spit up cocaine; suppression ordered, because no reasonable suspicion when D was initially ordered to stop; "high crime" area, D's directing people to alleyway, & the hand placed in pocket weren't enough;

C v Caldwell **36 MAC 570 (94) S.C. 418 M 777**—cops' conversation with D, who matched description of rapist, does not equal stop; no basis, either, for suppression of knowledge of D's brand of cigarettes, though obtained by "ruse";

C v Evans **436 M 369 (2002)**—OK to approach, with blue lights activated, car parked in breakdown lane with right blinker flashing & to inquire, after rousing a sleeping & subsequently somewhat disoriented driver, "what are you doing?"; though driver responded, "nothing," **OK thereafter to demand license & registration, & this was a "minimal intrusion" rather than a "seizure"**;

C v Campbell **69 MAC 212 (2007)**—though car was already stopped in traffic at a stop light, Appeals Court acknowledges that stop occurred: cruiser first passed D's car, then circled back and stopped next to it so closely that adjacent car doors could not be opened; after repositioning, cops got out of cruiser, one placing himself behind suspect car, accompanied by arrival of additional, marked, cruiser with lights and siren (reasonable person would not believe self free to leave); seizure of gun dropped out of car door upheld on rationale of corroborated tip providing reasonable suspicion;

C v Werner **73 MAC 97 (2008)**—cruiser with flashing blue lights pulled up outside bar inside which were about 25 patrons; flashing lights did not make cops' "exploratory questioning" of D or others present a "stop" (subsequent signals by bartender and patrons gave basis for cop's question to D, and his subsequent gesture prompted cop's removal of gun from D's waistband);

C v Scott **52 MAC 486 (2001)**—when cop turned cruiser around & followed D, turned cruiser spotlight on D, & yelled that he wanted D to come back some 40 feet and talk to him, Appeals Court held there was no seizure; cop's order to D thereafter to "stop and stay" when he reached point 20 feet away from cop = seizure; critical issue = whether cop was able to see, as he claimed, from 20 feet in poor light, particular facial characteristics matching those of rapist in area six weeks and three months earlier; without such match, no reasonable suspicion to stop D; appellate court will accept as true such testimony only if there's not only a lack of "contradiction," but also a belief that motion judge either explicitly or implicitly credited the witness's testimony; S. C., 440 M 642 (2004), after remand, further Commonwealth appeal (57 MAC 36 (2003)), and further appellate review, **SJC affirms allowance of suppression: because "stop" at 20 feet not on reasonable suspicion,** based upon judge's findings of fact (as to what cop could see then), SJC did not decide whether seizure occurred when D was "called" by cop from distance of 30–40 feet; 'tall, muscular, black male' at night, in place where nighttime attacks occurred 2 months earlier not reasonable suspicion;

C v Laureano **411 M 708 (92)**—cops following, but not "pursuing," D into restroom of bar not a "seizure"; *C v Thibeau* **384 M 762 (81)** ("stop starts when pursuit begins"), distinguished;

C v Wedderburn **36 MAC 558 (94)**—no pursuit when officer drove unmarked cruiser across opposing traffic lane at 45 degree angle at normal pace;

C v Rock **429 M 609 (99)**—cruiser following men for 150 feet, including the wrong way on one-way street "does not necessitate" conclusion that reasonable person would feel he was not free to leave;

C v Grandison **433 M 135 (2001)**—cops following D as he twice reversed direction to evade cops, + following D into alley not 'pursuit' (unless siren, lights, attempt to block/control D's path, direction, speed, or order to stop);

C v Wallace **45 MAC 930 (98)**—unmarked cruiser's backing up, cops alighting & walking to within 12 feet of D before saying "police," not a stop; D's flight & effort to conceal justified "response" of pursuit & cop could seize abandoned item;

C v Lopez **55 MAC 741 (2002)**—tip, deficient on "basis of knowledge," was adequately corroborated when D appeared in specified car at place described; reasonable suspicion justified approach and inquiry, including precaution of ordering D to put hands on steering wheel; when D instead kept one had down, with clenched fist, there was both probable cause to believe he was concealing illegality and reasonable concern for safety justifying police opening the fist;

C v Rupp **57 MAC 377 (2003)**—cops made no "show of authority" before D began to flee; flight, combined with cops' confirming details of citizen's report of gun transaction, gave reasonable suspicion of criminal activity;

C v McHugh **41 MAC 906 (96)**—to check on car stopped on road, cop approached in car from opposite direction, so that both drivers were opposite each other, & when driver didn't respond to inquiry, cop got out & spoke to driver from closer position (intoxication observed)—no "stop"/seizure;

C v Doulette **414 M 653 (93)**—no 'stop' when cop approached parked car in which D & passenger were sitting in a commuter parking lot, though car interior was first illuminated by cruiser's spotlight & then by cop's flashlight (no "specific articulable facts" supporting belief in criminal activity necessary);

C v Stephens **451 M 370 (2008)**—no "stop" when cop approached vehicle, but opening of vehicle door = stop, reasonable because then officer reasonably feared black object in D's hand; reasonable suspicion of drug sale given cars' rendezvous in restaurant parking lot and movement to more remote location to complete transaction;

C v Knowles **451 M 91 (2008)**—officer on cruiser patrol received radio dispatch at 6:40 p.m. that a man at particular intersection, in described clothing, was swinging a baseball bat; officer went there, saw described man leaning into an open vehicle trunk, the bat propped against an adjacent telephone pole, & upon seeing officer get out of cruiser, man reached into pocket and threw something into trunk; when officer ordered man to stop, step away from car and come towards him with hands out of pockets (man complied), man was seized without reasonable suspicion of crime; subsequent inspection of open trunk yielded view of small packages of drugs; suppression ordered; no objective basis for believing D's well-being or public safety = immediately endangered, and "objective view of" officer's actions = "he was in fact conducting a criminal investigation"; officer could legitimately 'inquire,' and could "ask" rather than "order" D to step away from area to speak about radio report; if D refused, maybe basis for "the type of protective seizure employed here", citing Fraser 410 M 541, 545-546;

C v Thinh Van Cao **419 M 383 (95)**—while leaving intact purported finding of fact (that there was no "seizure") in the "Asian gang"—inspired "field interrogation observation" (FIO), **"better practice" = *tell* individuals approached that they're free to leave;** here, subject allegedly consented to being photographed (& photo was ID'd as robber);

C v Moore **32 MAC 924 (92)**—officer's approach & request for identification of D who matched drug courier profile not a "seizure" until bulge discovered during consensual frisk & cop began to struggle with D;

*** *C v Lyles* **453 M 811 (2009)**—officers (plain clothes, though armed) approached D on sidewalk at 1:30 p.m. only because there had been complaints about drug activity in area; after displaying badges they asked D's name and for ID, which they retained (without consent) as they ran warrant check; retention of ID = seizure without reasonable suspicion; drugs and cash found on D at booking for outstanding warrant = suppressed;

C v Thomas **429 M 403 (99)**—officer's approach of D & request for name & address & question whether D "had any money on him" was not a seizure, & only when D produced marked money from undercover drug buy was there a seizure, on probable cause; but see *C v Bettencourt* **447 M 631 (2006)**—after proper stop, driver was arrested; cop asked passenger whether he had license, and he said no; further questioning of passenger for name and date of birth resulted in knowledge of outstanding warrants, passenger's arrest, and discovery of cocaine on his person: SJC orders suppression, since no ground for questioning D/believing D involved in crime; Commonwealth's belated argument that it was "community caretaking" to find a driver to take charge of car rather than tow/impound it was rebuffed, because not raised at trial court by testimony or argument;

C v Pimental **27 MAC 557 (89)**—approach by 3 cops leading D to drop bag of cocaine not a "seizure" where cops didn't make "show of authority" which would make reasonable person feel he wasn't free to leave;

C v Martinez **74 MAC 240 (2009)**—court didn't decide whether D was seized on porch after following him and demanding ID, though such conclusion = "reasonable"; at latest D was seized when cops ordered companion to open exterior door (after she and D had gone inside, but she stayed nearby while D went upstairs), threatening to kick it in, and subsequently grabbed D on interior stairway;

C v Grandison **433 M 135 (2001)**—cops following D, even as he reversed direction twice, and went into an alley not a pursuit until cop ordered D to stop (after he spit projectile out of mouth); purportedly if siren or lights were used, or if attempt "to block or control . . . path, direction, or speed," there would be 'pursuit' requiring constitutional justification;

C v Watson **430 M 725 (2000)**—drug courier profile data critical to stop (upheld here) of car driven by man after he and another retrieved heavy suitcases from motel room of possible "courier"; additional factor was subject's driving in manner consistent with interest in detecting surveillance; implausible responses of the two men re: suitcases = "reasonable . . . to seize" the suitcases; men were not "seized" upon detention of the suitcases or during roadside questioning;

C v Fraser **410 M 541 (91)—cop's approaching D & asking him to remove hands from pocket not a "seizure"**; radio call of 'man with gun' plus D's bending over & then keeping hands in pockets in high-crime area justified frisk; *Fraser* claim that its circumstances were "anomalous" because pat-down was not preceded by forcible stop reconsidered in:

C v Narcisse **457 M 1 (2010)**—although cops' alighting from car and conversing with D was consensual field interrogation observation, "seizure" occurred when cops told D they intended to pat frisk him; "exigencies of real life police-citizen encounters often blur the tidiness of the two-pronged Terry analysis"; "**police officers may not escalate a consensual encounter into a protective frisk absent a reasonable suspicion that an individual has committed, is committing, or is about to commit a criminal offense _and_ is armed and dangerous**"; such suspicions may occur simultaneously, e.g., if D appears ready to commit violence (i.e., has weapon and appears inclined to use it), he is about to commit "crime"; HERE, D and companion behaved in no way indicating criminal activity or that he was armed and dangerous; facts that area was "hot spot" feared to be a site of prospective violence in retaliation for an incident in Randolph and D was from Randolph = insufficient to justify escalation of encounter to seizure/frisk;

C v Martin **457 M 14 (2010)**—that frisk may be justified even when not preceded by forcible stop does not mean that the two-prong Terry analysis may be abandoned; cops' approach of D in high crime area to discern whether he was individual for whom they were looking to execute arrest warrant was OK, but cops immediately discerned that D didn't match arrest subject's appearance; D's hesitation in giving his name, lying about either his date of birth or age, nervousness, lack of response to inquiry concerning weapons, and pushing aside cop's hands when cop stated he was going to frisk D = NOT enough to justify "escalation" to "seizure", which itself occurred at point of attempting frisk; "nervousness is a common and entirely natural reaction to police presence" (citation omitted); D had right to ignore questions asked by cops, so refusal to answer question re: whether he had gun "cannot provide reasonable suspicion for his seizure"; "[n]either prong of Terry [was] satisfied"; pushing away cop's hands was NOT the reason for the frisk, which had already been initiated (was not "intervening" act dissipating taint of original unlawful seizure);

C v Stephens **451 M 370 (2008)**—no "stop" when cop approached vehicle, but opening of vehicle door = stop, reasonable because then officer reasonably feared black object in D's hand (SJC citing *Fraser* 410 M 541); reasonable suspicion of drug sale given cars' rendezvous in restaurant parking lot and movement to more remote location to complete transaction;

C v Isaiah, I., a juvenile **450 M 818 (2008), after remand in 448 M 334 (2007)**—in neighborhood plagued by armed robberies committed by black or Hispanic males between age fourteen and twenty, police saw D peering through front window of store, "manipulating something in his right front pants pocket"; at officers' approach D went quickly into the store and cop followed, observing D bend toward right foot and place something in right sock: SJC holds no "seizure" until D was ordered not to move upon standing up again, & frisk then upheld;

C v Pena **31 MAC 201 (91)**—parking in D's driveway was "seizure" of D (on foot);

C v Hart **45 MAC 81 (98)**—rejecting standard of "reasonable African-American" as to belief that he was under arrest/not free to leave; finding cop made no intrusion by asking to speak to 2 men, "that cop thereafter acted reasonably in ordering one suspect to place his hands on head, because of concern for personal safety; no intrusion/stop by following other suspect into unlocked foyer of rooming house, where suspect placed cocaine inside an open mailbox (plain view);

C v Sanderson **398 M 761 (86)—reasonable belief arrest (without probable cause) if 40-minute detention, cruisers block car, dogs brought to smell**;

C v Feyenord **62 MAC 200 (2004), and S.C. on further appellate review, 445 M 72 (2005)**—upholds 30-minute detention of motorist (after stop for broken headlight during daytime hours) for sniff by drug-detecting dog, by holding there was probable cause for arrest (though no actual arrest) for lack of license on person; dissent says detention not reasonably related in scope to justification for stop, cites cases re: suppression for drug-sniffing dogs after simple traffic stops;

C v Taylor **426 M 189, 195 (97)**—reasonable to "detain" D (at police station, after questioning) "at least until (police) obtained & executed the search warrant to seize his clothing & sneakers";

C v Borges **395 M 788 (85)—though OK stop, order to remove shoes = arrest (without probable cause), so suppress D's flight/dropsy of dope**, (fn.3: holding = Declaration of Rights, Article 14); (contrast *C v Billings* **42 MAC 261 (97)** during non-custodial interview of D, cop could ask to see sneaker bottoms—no reasonable expectation of privacy);

C v Starr **55 MAC 590 (2002)**—cop following car could run license plate number (& learn that it didn't match car to which it was affixed); observation of license plate wasn't search, & merely following car wasn't pursuit; BUT if evidence of racial/ethnic profiling, would be "at the very least," cause for concern;

US v Place **462 US 696 (83)—briefly hold bag for dog sniff not seizure/search, so OK if reasonable suspicion; 90 minutes too long,** because had prior info & weren't prepared;

C v Dora **57 MAC 141 (2003)**—trying a key in the lock of a door only requires reasonable suspicion;

C v Bottari **395 M 777 (85)**—without fear, block D's car, order out at gunpoint = arrest;

C v Willis **415 M 814 (93)—3 cops with drawn guns stopping D = "Terry stop"** because Michigan police said

D would be on particular Greyhound bus, carrying only an blue & white striped pillowcase, but **armed with handgun** and Boston cop had arrested D previously for an armed robbery (though robbery charge was dismissed);

C v Santiago **53 MAC 567 (2002)** given reasonable suspicion that driver of car which committed traffic offenses was serial rapist who had very recently used dangerous weapons, single cop making stop was justified in approaching with drawn gun & handcuffing D ("reasonable efforts to ensure the officer's safety do not transform a stop into an arrest"); Appeals Court upholds further search of car purportedly because driver might actually have been released subsequently and would have been able to attack cop "upon the suspect's reentry into the vehicle";

C v Jackson **73 MAC 411 (2008)**—2 a.m. 'high crime area' sighting of parolee recently released for firearms offense + weighty object in jacket pocket = sufficient for frisk; not necessary that cop believe his *own* safety is in jeopardy; "safety of the public" or reasonable belief that D is armed/dangerous is adequate basis for frisk;

C v Preshaw **57 MAC 19 (2003)**—D was identified by neighbor as being involved in a breaking and entering, & this provided reasonable suspicion; appellate court claims it wasn't an arrest, despite use of handcuffs on D;

C v Blake **23 MAC 456 (87)**—block car with cruisers = just stop, not arrest;

C v Hecox **35 MAC 277 (93)**—not deciding whether 3 cruisers' blocking of D's car & officer's pointing gun at D with order to put hands on steering wheel was "arrest";

C v Stawarz **32 MAC 211 (92)**—surrounding parked car by 4–5 cruisers & 8–10 uniformed cops turned stop into "arrest" which wasn't justified by probable cause;

C v Torres **433 M 669 (2001)**—following stop of car for failure to stop at stop sign, all 4 doors of car opened & 1 passenger fled, leaving 5 car occupants; because cop suspected, from 3 rear seat passengers' being "bent over," that they were hiding gun, he ordered them to put hands on heads, which they did after cop drew weapon; subsequent frisk, after arrival of more cops, producing gun from a waistband, = OK, said SJC: once officer reasonably concluded risk to safety & ordered occupants out, proper to conduct frisk for weapons; standard for frisk is same as standard required to justify an "exit" order; detention of occupants while awaiting backup didn't "transform the stop into an arrest"; Appeals Court (**49 MAC 348**) and District Court judge had held suspicion of gun "unfounded";

C v Vazquez **74 MAC 920 (2009)**—police responding to call re: man being "jumped" & severely beaten were told by witness at scene on cell phone, "that's him," referring to man in sports jersey walking away; officers stopped that man (D), who said that he had witnessed fight; during questions, officer became concerned for safety & D became argumentative, resulting in being cuffed and returned to scene; witness there reported further that different man had been kicking victim in head and that when witness approached D looked at witness and then whistled to assailant and told him to stop: though suppression motion judge had ruled that this report eliminated probable cause (inferring that crime was committed by only the kicking assailant), App. Ct. held that D's actions were consistent with "lookout," and thus joint venturer, as to whom there was probable cause to arrest (suspicion ripening to probable cause after witness's further statement);

C v Barros **425 M 572 (97), citing *Salerno*** **356 M 642 (70)**—at gunpoint, "frisk" of suspects in shooting & "request" that they go to shooting scene (for ID) = reasonable part of investigative stop;

C v Ruiz **51 MAC 346 (2001)**—**"precautions" taken by police prior to any "inquiry" (blocking suspects' car, drawing guns) didn't "convert" "stop" into "arrest"**;

C v Hall **50 MAC 208 (2000)**—**attempting to block car with two police vehicles** (after it arrived, as predicted by informant, purportedly to deliver drugs to street-level dealer) **held to be only investigative stop**, reasonable "because of the chance that the suspect may flee upon the approach of police with resulting danger to the public as well as to the officers involved"; implication that blocking with more than 2 cars might have been "arrest," but testimony by cops that they were converging to "arrest" (subjective intent) irrelevant;

C v Williams **422 M 111 (96)**—cruiser following running men without activating lights or siren not "pursuit", but only "surveillance" (& no justification was needed) (N.B.—here, men had not seen cruiser, & would not have felt constrained by it); pursuit began when officers began to chase on foot; **detention of D as he attempted to scale fence was OK threshold inquiry (even though accomplished with drawn gun & handcuffs),** given that D was covered with blood & radio broadcast about nearby shooting OK to take D to scene for ID by witnesses;

20-M.3. Reasonable Suspicion

US v Sharpe **470 US 675 (85)**—reasonable suspicion to stop truck & hold 20 minutes (after check papers) for DEA (who smelled marijuana);

C v Lites **67 MAC 815 (2006)**—fresh odor of burnt marijuana from opened door of stopped car, PLUS passenger's furtive gestures at his waist area provided probable cause to arrest passenger;

C v Avellar **70 MAC 608 (2007)**—that stop of car was pretextual, to troll for evidence of drug trafficking didn't matter, so long as one officer testified that driver "failed to signal a turn off the road servicing moderate traffic"; "reasonable suspicion" that traffic violation concerned allowed stop and succeeding events held justifiable upon cops' smelling marijuana and viewing plastic bag of same;

C v Pinto **45 MAC 790 (98)**—investigative detention of express mail package, on reasonable suspicion by federal authorities (heavily duct-taped, sent from airport "known to be used by drug couriers," fictitious return address & no named sender, etc.) OK; dog-sniff "alert" gave probable cause for anticipatory federal warrant; that package was found later to contain steroids, for which dog was not trained, did not invalidate probable cause finding;

G.L. c. 41, § 98—cop can examine D if reasonable suspicion of unlawful design, demand business, & arrest if not satisfied; reasonably suspect danger & may search & seize dangerous weapon or anything illegal; (*see also* G.L. c. 111b, § 8 *Protective Custody, Chapter 20-H above*);

C v Badore **47 MAC 600 (99)**—despite police testimony that resident had twice called, complaining of "disturbance," no reasonable suspicion of criminal activity when nothing was observed during 1st response and merely an idling car was observed on 2d response (when 2 cruisers parked so as to block car);

C v Martinez **74 MAC 240 (2009)**—911 report of attempted B&E, by white male in gray T-shirt with orange stripe and some kind of writing on front, and blue jean shorts, did not provide reasonable suspicion to stop light-skinned Hispanic D, walking with female on perpendicular street, D wearing long pants and a long-sleeved button-down multi-colored (with blue, gray, and orange) shirt with a cast on his arm; further fact that D abandoned ID card after giving it, by retreating behind locked door, did not add enough for reasonable suspicion, either;

C v Murphy **63 MAC 11 (2005)**—directing D to stand aside while police dispersed crowd isn't seizure since D was seemingly free to leave, but label for subsequent interaction ("field interrogation observation") didn't "insulate it from constitutional scrutiny"; that D approached police & advised that he had a gold chain belonging to arrestee, and that he offered his observations of recent melee didn't provide ground for pat-frisk or detention;

Sibron v NY **392 US 40 (68)**—talk to addicts over 8 hours not reasonable suspicion;

C v Knowles **451 M 91 (2008)**—officer on cruiser patrol received radio dispatch at 6:40 p.m. that a man at particular intersection, in described clothing, was swinging a baseball bat; officer went there, saw described man leaning into an open vehicle trunk, the bat propped against an adjacent telephone pole, & upon seeing officer get out of cruiser, man reached into pocket and threw something into trunk; when officer ordered man to stop, step away from car and come towards him with hands out of pockets (man complied), man was seized without reasonable suspicion of crime; subsequent inspection of open trunk yielded view of small packages of drugs; suppression ordered; no objective basis for believing D's well-being or public safety = immediately endangered, and "objective view of" officer's actions = "he was in fact conducting a criminal investigation"; officer could legitimately 'inquire,' and could "ask" rather than "order" D to step away from area to speak about radio report; if D refused, maybe basis for "the type of protective seizure employed here", citing *Fraser* 410 M 541, 545-546;

C v Pierre P. **53 MAC 215 (2001)**—no 'reasonable suspicion' for pat frisk intrusion, despite claimed violation of city's "loitering" ordinance, because no evidence that

youths were obstructing, hindering, or preventing others from passing by, as required by the ordinance;

C v Souza **42 MAC 186 (97)**—D, arriving during execution of search warrant, illegitimately searched under "all persons present" language, and no frisk was justified otherwise;

Brown v Texas **443 US 47 (79)**—talk to man in high-drug alley not reasonable suspicion; detain to ask ID = seizure;

Hiibel v Sixth Judicial Court **542 US 177 (2004)**—"stop & identify" statute not invalid here; doesn't require production of driver's license or other document; request for name doesn't "ordinarily" violate Fourth Amendment;

C v Crowley **13 MAC 915 (82)**—furtive move after OK stop not reasonable suspicion to frisk;

C v Davis **41 MAC 793 (96)**—bizarre jittery behavior of motorist stopped for speeding, did not warrant reasonable belief of danger: pat-down is a "serious intrusion upon the sanctity of the person";

C v Goewey **69 MAC 429 (2007)**—fact that D (back seat passenger in car stopped for invalid inspection sticker and then seen to have no occupants wearing seatbelts) didn't look like the proffered driver's license (which had expired and would have been many years old) caused cop to question him further (ID necessary for writing seatbelt citation); that he was nervous and subsequently seemed to reach into coat, or down below seat = enough here for exit order/frisk; motion judge had suppressed because cop's next contact after "furtive" showed that D had been getting cigarette; justification for exit order not dependent on presence of immediate threat at precise moment of order, but instead on safety concerns in entire circumstances; **on further appellate review, 452 M 399 (2008)**—exit order upheld: while inability to produce some form of ID "may not, by itself, be suspicious," false ID is, and furtive movements could be considered not merely obtaining cigarette but also weapon; SJC disapproved of MAC deciding case without benefit of brief or oral argument on behalf of D (D-counsel having defaulted in obligations without explanation); Commonwealth's appeal was "devoid of any advocacy on behalf of" D, "not, as it should have been, an adversary process," MAC's "unilateral review not an adequate substitute for D's right to effective assistance of counsel;

C v Brown **75 MAC 528 (2009)**—cab passenger not wearing seatbelt lacked ID; facts that he & other passenger looked nervous, that cop was "outnumbered," & that it was high crime area insufficient for exit order and frisk;

C v O'Laughlin **25 MAC 998 (88)**—walk fast, then run as cops pursue not reasonable suspicion to pursue/stop, so flight/dropsy = bad fruit (*see Chapter 20-F*);

C v Thibeau **384 M 762 (81)**—sudden bike turn when see cop not stop reason;

C v Gunther G **45 MAC 116 (98)**—cop's observations, matching radio reports re: 3 males, dog, shots fired, coupled with D's "unprovoked flight" = "reasonable suspicion and a right to pursue"; gun was tossed to ground during pursuit;

C v DePeiza **66 MAC 398, further appellate review allowed 447 M 1105 (2006)**—that D was walking and talking on cell phone, but holding his right arm rigid and pressed to his side "as if he were holding something" & after police stop, that he avoided eye contact and "shifted his weight from side to side" did not justify police grabbing/searching his pocket when he turned away upon cops' announcement of frisk intention; see Brown, J., concurring: ". . . I think I have finally discerned an underlying rationale for 'stops' of persons of color within the scope of *Terry v Ohio* . . . It is *motion*. . . . I can only hope that these practices will not degenerate into stops based upon 'breathing while black'"; **on further review, however, SJC, 449 M 367 (2007)** holds there was reasonable suspicion that D was carrying concealed unlicensed firearm, justifying frisk;

C v Monteiro **75 MAC 280 (2009)**—high school student told teacher that he had seen a particularly described student possessing gun this day; teacher told on-site cop; personnel located only individual meeting that description in 200–300 students in cafeteria; basis of knowledge found to be personal observation by student, whose identity was known, favoring his veracity (D did not contest veracity/reliability here, id. n.2); 'reasonable suspicion' of crime because D was 17, not old enough to be licensed for possessing firearm; circumstances required protection of vulnerable population;

C v Doocey **56 MAC 550 (2002)**—at 3:24 a.m., dispatcher received info from identified citizen-witness re: shots fired, two males in black clothing leaving park; second identified informant gave report 2 minutes later; stop of D, in dark navy jacket & jeans, 12 minutes later and ½ mile away, upheld: D was the only person in area, & at cop's approach, D seemed intoxicated & uneasy, & frisk produced gun;

C v Ancrum **65 MAC 647 (2006)**—despite no evidence as to source of information relayed in radio broadcast and no suggestion that source was a named person, court found it "reasonable to infer that the source of the information was a firsthand witness to the event", there having been police "confirmation" of a recent shooting from which described persons/car were inferably fleeing; that car's colors didn't match description, and that there were four occupants in car rather than two was claimed by court to be "not significant"; patfrisk of Ds & "protective sweep" of car for weapons held OK;

C v White **74 MAC 342 (2009)**—victim reported armed home invasion by four black men, one wearing white headcloth, all departing in red car: < 5 minutes after hearing radio broadcast, officer stopped red car with 3–4 occupants and two wore white head cloths; fact that driver was female not significant as she wore bulky hooded jacket concealing features and the headcloth hid hair length; exit order, taking keys from driver, handcuffing of passenger as "safety precaution" during frisk (gun discovered in waistband) all upheld: though motion judge said "hunch," Appeals Court said reasonable suspicion;

C v Pagan **63 MAC 780 (2005)**—plain clothes cops in unmarked vehicle alighted by double-parked car in front of pizza joint in gang/guns area (& this wasn't any intrusion requiring Constitutional justification): one man's throwing something inside car and other man's "look of panic," followed by his turning and walking away, & reaching toward his waist = reasonable suspicion for pat-frisk;

C v Wren **391 M 705 (84)**—flight from cops not reasonable suspicion, but enough if more (e.g., parked late, residential area tip by special police officer that car was casing neighborhood);

C v Ware **76 MAC 53 (2009)**—seizure occurred only after D fled and cop began pursuit, cop then having reasonable suspicion that D had gun, and cop knew D too young to lawfully possess;

C v Quezada **67 MAC 693 (2006)**—D was, at 1:10 p.m., with person known to have been recently released from prison, D's manner suggested possible influence of narcotics, it was high crime area, & D fled from plain clothes cop alighting from unmarked vehicle; flight can't be considered in "reasonable suspicion" calculation because there was no basis for initiating stop; it's only "speculation" by Commonwealth that D "appeared to be intoxicated by 'angel dust'"; D's flight was nonverbal response that D was NOT in need of assistance; *on further appellate review,* **450 M 1030 (2008)**—SJC holds that motion judge's order of suppression (of firearm) should be affirmed for reasons given by Appeals Court;

C v Wilson **52 MAC 411 (2001)**—flight is relevant factor in "reasonable suspicion," if it has not been triggered by inappropriate police action; police, with "emergency lights" on, pursued car after it drove by at high speed; it then rolled through stop sign & stopped in middle of intersection, and D then fled from car, discarding bag of drugs;

C v Harkess **35 MAC 626 (93)**—seizure of D in accord with Hodari D & D didn't ask Article 14 analysis; nonetheless, 3 a.m. high crime, subject of info from state police (drugs & gun involvement), & flight upon mere eye contact with police = reasonable suspicion justifying pursuit with drawn gun;

C v Fisher **54 MAC 41 (2002)**—immediate pat-down upheld given aggregated circumstances: evasive reaction of D & cohorts to police, late night, high crime area known for presence of illegal guns, D's quick motion toward his waist;

C v Wright **48 MAC 912 (99)**—D's eye contact with cops, placing hand in his pocket, and walking quickly away from group of black teenagers in high crime area, and ignoring cops' order to stop NOT reasonable suspicion; action of D in ignoring stop order "cannot be treated as affecting the analysis without empowering the police to create articulable suspicion where none existed before"; court distinguished *C v Williams* **422 M 111 (96)** (fleeing D discarded shirt, ran through backyards, scaled chain link fences, dropped beeper);

Illinois v Wardlow **528 US 119 (2000)**—in area known for drug dealing, D ran when he saw cops; Supreme Court says reasonable suspicion; 5 judges say individual's **presence in high crime area not alone enough to support reasonable particularized suspicion; flight alone is neither "always" enough or "never" enough to give reasonable suspicion**; Stevens, J., opinion noted that innocent persons do in fact flee at sight of police, especially in high crime areas most likely to be poor minority neighborhoods; see also *C v Cheek* **413 M 492 (92)** ("The problems that may face the Grove Hall section of Roxbury or any other similar 'high crime area" will not be resolved any more readily by excluding the individuals who live there from the protections afforded by our Constitution.");

C v DeJesus **72 MAC 117 (2008)**—citizens in "high crime" area have same right as other citizens to be free from unlawful seizures;

C v Mock **54 MAC 276 (2002)**—after report that 'heavy set black male' had attempted (without success) to break into apartment, no reasonable suspicion to stop black male (perhaps heavy set, perhaps 'medium' build) about ten minutes later who was walking on the street in the direction of the named apartment, holding something bulky, & who just walked faster when hailed by the police in residential neighborhood "populated by African-Americans" (stopping only when cop alighted from car & told him to "stop," which amounted to pursuit & seizure); judge may or may not have credited cop's assertion that it was "high crime" area; BUT APPEALS COURT nonetheless reverses suppression order on ground that D's throwing of a VCR at the cops (striking one on the leg) broke the causal chain & justified arrest;

C v Medeiros **45 MAC 240 (98)**—no reasonable suspicion to stop driver because he knocked on door of house & asked resident whether he wanted him to shovel snow;

C v Gomes **59 MAC 332 (2003)**—resident's observations prompting call to police, with investigations disclosing apparent unlawful entry, hushed voices outside, and a shadowy motion followed by a door closing = reasonable suspicion that crime had occurred and that culprits might have fled to nearby location; BUT while further inquiry was necessary, cop's repeated demand that person answering neighboring door provide identification, and cop's refusal to allow individual to close the door "exceeded what was constitutionally permissible"; no probable cause to believe that culprit had fled to this address nor exigency justifying warrantless entry;

C v Wren **391 M 705 (84)** flight from cops not reasonable suspicion, but enough if more (e.g., parked late, residential area tip by special police officer that car was casing neighborhood)) distinguished, & even **it** was "close" case against suppression;

C v Hooker **52 MAC 683 (2001)—fact that D looked back at car (unmarked vehicle with plainclothes cops)** following taxi in which he was riding wasn't remarkable, particularly in high crime area: D shouldn't have been ordered out of taxi;

C v Holmes **34 MAC 916 (93)**—police stopped car to return to driver the registration mistakenly kept earlier;

sight of gun-shaped bulge in passenger's pocket justified request that he step out; passenger's slamming door into cop & fleeing = probable cause to arrest (for battery) & seize gun in pat-down; if stop was pretext, taint held to have been attenuated;

C v Bettencourt **447 M 631 (2006)**—after proper stop, driver was arrested; cop asked passenger whether he had license, and he said no; further questioning of passenger for name and date of birth resulted in knowledge of outstanding warrants, passenger's arrest, and discovery of cocaine on his person: SJC orders suppression, since no ground for questioning D/believing D involved in crime; Commonwealth's belated argument that it was "community caretaking" to find a driver to take charge of car rather than tow/impound it was rebuffed, because not raised at trial court by testimony or argument;

C v Groves **25 MAC 933 (87)**—car-flight (from cops, without signal/obstruct) & facts (e.g., drove over curb) = reasonable suspicion;

C v Sanchez **403 M 640 (88)**—flight after consent (& no show of authority) = reasonable suspicion;

C v Roland R. **448 M 278 (2007)**—past signs stating that all bags = "subject to manual search", juvenile entered courthouse, but when informed by court officer that bag was going to be searched, juvenile declined, picked up bag and left building; he ran when told to "come here"; SJC says judge erred in ordering suppression of marijuana inside bag; citing *C v Harris* **383 M 655 (81)**, "area-entry inspections at court house entrances, for safety and security purposes" = OK without warrant or individualized suspicion of wrongdoing or danger; D "implicitly demonstrated consent" by passing signs, placing bag on table and going through metal detector, and "was not entitled to withdraw his consent after the inspection had commenced";

C v Watson **430 M 725 (2000)**—drug courier profile data critical to stop (upheld here) of car driven by man after he retrieved heavy suitcases from motel room of possible "courier"; additional factor was subject's driving in manner consistent with interest in detecting surveillance, and this could be taken into account because no "pursuit" in a constitutional sense (no communication of attempt to capture or intrude upon freedom of movement) occurred prior to actual stop of car;

C v Mercado **422 M 367 (96)**—evasive action by Ds & frantic activity by shirtless D to make purchase in sporting attire store & nearby shooting and witness' info that men went in direction where Ds (matching description) were located = reasonable suspicion and justified pat-down though neither evasive behavior, proximity to crime scene, nor matching general description, is **alone** sufficient for reasonable suspicion;

C v Barbosa **49 MAC 344 (2000)**—after radio dispatch re: convenience store armed robbery at 4 a.m. on Rt. 27 by three 18-yr-old Cape Verdean youths, 1 in green sweatshirt & 1 in black hooded sweatshirt, with culprits in car headed toward Brockton, reasonable suspicion to stop car seen in convenience store parking lot one block from

Rt. 27 in Brockton containing Cape Verdean youths with matching clothes; illumination by white lights prior to stop wasn't a search; shutting of car door and driving away after spotting cops enhanced the suspicion; given reasonable suspicion that suspects were armed, OK to approach with drawn guns, order occupants to put hands on car ceiling, &, after backup arrived, to emerge 1 by 1& be frisked;

C v Emuakpor **57 MAC 192 (2003)**—similar, re matching suspects with dispatch concerning armed robbery, direction of flight of described car, description of robbers (though two extra men were in car), time elapsed and physical proximity of crime scene to place of stop; approach with drawn guns didn't convert "stop" to arrest requiring probable cause, and cops' guns = reasonably necessary because robbery with gun was reported;

C v Lopes **455 M 147 (2009)**—"big brown van with tinted windows & Cape Verdean flag in the back" was close enough to maroon/ "reddish brown" van with tinted windows and such flag hanging from rear view mirror observed in Brockton, even before cop obtained confirmation from driver that he'd just come from Boston (site of homicide);

C v Grinkley **44 MAC 62, 72 (97)**—group members' walking quickly away did not elevate circumstances to reasonable suspicion even though firearm allegedly involved;

C v Ellis **12 MAC 476 (81)**—man gives $ to driver for? not car-stop reason; but see *C v Kennedy* **426 M 703 (98)** probable cause found (high crime area; man conversed with driver, then ran away & returned before possible exchange);

C v Clark **65 MAC 39 (2005)**—no reasonable suspicion for car stop from cop's observation of D standing by his car at 11:20 p.m. in high drug area outside bar, handing "item" to a man coming out of bar (who went back into bar), and counting money; because stop was impermissible, court won't reach arguments that D's conduct after the stop gave rise to probable cause or consent to search;

C v Gomes **453 M 506 (2009)**—in high crime/drug area at 4 a.m., seeing D holding out flat hand to another as though displaying something, and swallowing it after seeing approaching cops = enough for reasonable suspicion, but immediate frisk not justified (no reasonable inference that D was armed and presented danger to cops or others);

C v Bacon **381 M 642 (80)**—youths, fancy car, early a.m., hide face—no reasonable suspicion;

C v Deramo **436 M 40 (2002)**—OK to stop D-motorist because cop knew that D's license had, as of two months earlier, still been subject to two lengthy periods of revocation; cop could reasonably conclude that vehicle was being driven by its registered owner if he did not actually ID D as driver before the stop;

C v Rodriguez **75 MAC 235 (2009)**—while waiting to execute search warrant at D's residence, cops saw him drive away, and in lobby of address to which he was expected to go, cops approached and arrested him when he

attempted to swallow bags of cocaine: court finds reasonable suspicion for approach, and probable cause to arrest;

C v Saint Louis **59 MAC 928 (2003)**—IF cop has seen liquor in car, knows that car owner is underage, and all car occupants appear to be under age twenty-one, there is reasonable suspicion to stop car;

C v Thompson **427 M 729 (98)**—1:15 a.m., high crime area, car parked with motor running, in front of townhouse which was subject of narcotics investigation = reasonable suspicion, cruisers could stop so as to block; probable cause when radio check revealed car was stolen;

C v McGrath **365 M 631 (74)**—D's prior record not itself reasonable suspicion for stop and frisk;

C v Wooden **13 MAC 417 (82)**—stuff something in pocket not itself reasonable suspicion;

C v Lehan **347 M 197 (64)**—G.L. c. 41, § 98 threshold questions OK on reasonable suspicion, but not search;

C v Mulero **38 MAC 963 (95)**—reasonable suspicion that D defaulted on court case for which questioning cop had arrested him 6 months earlier (because no "court action" on case), & D's behavior during stop = disorderly conduct leading to arrest;

C v Helme **399 M 298 (87)**—Cadillac parked in bar lot (drug area) not reasonable suspicion for stop (by block car with cruiser);

C v Censullo **40 MAC 65 (96)**—though cop believed street was one-way & stopped D for wrong-way, cop was wrong; no alleged "good faith" mistake saved stop;

C v Feyenord **62 MAC 200 (2004), and S.C. on further appellate review, 445 M 72 (2005)**—court OKs traffic stop, during daylight hours, for one nonfunctioning headlight ("not properly equipped for travel");

C v Whitehead **49 MAC 905 (2000)**—no reasonable suspicion supported stop of car: it idled in parking lot at 9:30 p.m. in January ("warming up") with lights off & loud exhaust system, & started to back out of parking space; belief that commission of civil motor vehicle infractions was imminent (operating vehicle on public way without lights on, too-loud exhaust) = insufficient basis;

C v Brazeau **64 MAC 65 (2005)**—that three tiny objects were suspended from the rear-view mirror of a vehicle did not provide "reasonable suspicion" for stop, despite claim that it suggested violation of G.L. c. 90, § 13 (prohibiting operation of vehicle with "anything which may interfere with or impede the proper operation of the vehicle"): "finding" of motion judge that cop observed reflection of the plastic "prism" (& so had basis for believing such "reflection" could distract driver) was not supported by the evidence, and there was no other "particularized and objective basis for suspecting a traffic violation";

Reid v Georgia **448 US 438 (80)**—drug courier profile (early a.m. from Florida, only with carry-on) & looking back—not reasonable suspicion; but see

US v Sokolow **490 US 1 (89)**—facts support airport stop with or without drug courier profile;

C v Bartlett **41 MAC 468 (96)**—after citation for speeding, D should have been allowed to leave; that rental cars and beepers are used by drug couriers, that a Cambridge resident was driving a rental car from Logan Airport "a point of entry for drugs", & that drugs had been seized previously on "the Lowell Connector" **not** a "reasonable stimulus for investigation"; cc opinion at 473 ("interrogated on suspicion of being Hispanic"; "ethnicity plus a beeper does not equal probable cause");

C v Lyons 409 M 16 (90)—Aguilar-Spinelli test used to determine whether informant tips amount to reasonable suspicion under Article 14; here, tip by anonymous informant about males traveling in described car did not give sufficiently specific, nonobvious & predictive information to make out basis of knowledge; contrast *Alabama v White* 496 US 325 (90) "totality of circumstances" test used to determine whether anonymous tips as corroborated by police observation amount to reasonable suspicion under Fourth Amendment;

C v Carrasquillo 30 MAC 783 (91)—independent police corroboration was insufficient to cure defects in reliability & basis of knowledge of anonymous tip that on certain day D would be transporting cocaine from New York in car with Hispanic male;

C v Lubiejewski 49 MAC 212 (2000)—un-ID'd motorist telephoned state police to report pickup truck with specific plate # was traveling on wrong side of Rt. 195 in vicinity of Rt. 140, but called back again to say truck crossed grassy median & proceeded on right side of road before turning south on Rt. 240 in Fairhaven; dispatcher also conveyed Fairhaven address to which truck was registered; trooper stopped the truck, not for any observed violation, but for tipster's report; odor of alcohol & failure of sobriety tests followed, but evidence ordered suppressed; no corroboration of anything but obvious details = insufficient to compensate for unknown reliability of informant; *C v Hurd* 29 MAC 929 (90) distinguished ("emergency" there because tip concerned allegedly drunk man getting into & driving specific car containing 3 small children; police corroboration vehicle's presence & its approach to high-speed highway; no emergency here because no report of "drunk" & once driver went to correct side of road, "emergency . . . ended"); community caretaking function (advanced only on appeal) must be "totally divorced from the detection, investigation, or acquisition of evidence relating to the violation of a criminal statute," & this wasn't (trooper was investigating for evidence of the crime of driving wrong way on highway);

C v Cox 56 MAC 907 (2002)—cop may stop car for motor vehicle violation based solely on report from motorist IF motorist is reliable informant with personal knowledge; radio dispatch, followed by cop locating target car, and seeing driver following behind, gesturing to cop by pointing at the car and continually flashing lights on and off; not "faceless" informant, but willing to identify herself;

C v Love 56 MAC 229 (2002)—tipster who presented self at state police barracks to tell of dangerous driver wasn't "anonymous," though desk officer didn't ask for his name (officer wrote down his plate number as he left);

C v Cheek 413 M 492 (92)—**where police rely on radio call to make investigatory stop, Article 14 requires Commonwealth to present evidence of specific & articulable facts to establish reliability of radio call & that D committed a crime**; stopping & frisking D, black male wearing "¾ length goose" matching description in radio call of stabber, mile from scene near midnight, not justified where description fit many in area & where source of radio call never revealed; D's constitutional protections not reduced by presence in "high crime area"; law enforcement officials may not conduct a "broad sweep," stopping individuals who happen to be about, hoping to nail suspect;

C v Berment 39 MAC 522 (95)—same principles;

C v Acevedo 73 MAC 453 (2009)—police didn't "stop" defendants when they approached and said they were investigating armed robbery and "asked them whether they would agree to a patfrisk" (this was "field encounter" instead); "stop" occurred at frisk (though allegedly consented-to) and continued during detention for show-up ID; denial of suppression upheld for two black males stopped 3 minutes later 3 blocks from robbery, one wearing white Converse sneakers but neither's clothing otherwise matching description; *Cheek* 413 M 492 implausibly distinguished; **on further review, 455 M 1013 (2009)**—SJC holds that "totality of circumstances" found by motion judge provided reasonable suspicion justifying stop; S.C., 455 M 1013 (2009), affirming MAC decision;

C v Ferguson 410 M 611 (91)—**although frisk of D's jacket seized from D during chase was justified by information that D was armed with gun, cops weren't justified in opening black bag with drugs once they realized it didn't contain gun;**

C v Alvarado 427 M 277 (98)—paramedic's report of seeing item believed to be a sawed-off shotgun in car justified 3 cops stopping car & ordering occupants out at gunpoint, though what was seen was a steering wheel locking device; tiny handgun found hidden in car not suppressed; contrast *C v Alvarado* 423 M 266 (96) tip about handgun in car "did not disclose any imminent threat to public safety" & SJC "reluctant to relax (its) established rule that the report of the carrying of a firearm is not, standing alone, a basis for having a reasonable suspicion of criminal activity"; reliability of tipster lacking anyway; cf. *C v Couture* 407 M 178 (90) sighting of gun protruding from D's right rear pocket does not equal probable cause, without any additional information;

C v DeJesus 72 MAC 117 (2008)—911 caller said he had seen on particular street a white van with a few kids, a few handguns; responding officers > 30 minutes later found white van, frisked every Hispanic male in or near it (4–5 youths outside, then driver, and finally ordered front seat passenger (D) out of van); D asked why, seemed nervous, and told officers they needed a warrant; they told him he'd be arrested if he didn't emerge: suppression of handgun ordered because no grounds to believe D had committed or was about to commit crime (3:30 p.m., though 'high crime' area; officers saw that D was not a minor); "suspicious behavior" didn't occur until after exit order;

C v Edwards **71 MAC 716, further review denied 452 M 1103 (2008), cert. denied 120 S Ct 1673 (2009)**—police had adequate grounds to conduct investigatory stop of D in identified car eighteen hours after report of "shots fired" and immediate investigation corroborated ID of shooter by name, address, and car; sighting of firearm under front seat occurred during stop; D had argued impropriety of warrantless arrest for 'completed misdemeanor', but court found *US v Hensley* 469 US 221 (85) unsupportive of D's claim; unlike *Couture* 407 M 178 (90) (unadorned fact of firearm possession not 'probable cause'), here there was firing of gun, combined with flight from scene; while firing gun within 500 feet of dwelling = misdemeanor, it involves threat to public safety;

C v DePeiza **449 M 367 (2007)**—cops here had reasonable suspicion of not only "concealed firearm", but illegally-possessed concealed firearm (midnight, D walking with "straight-arm" gait, D attempting to hide pocket from cops' view, high crime area); "It is the concealment of his pocket from police that supplies the reasonable suspicion that the firearm was illegal";

C v Fitzgibbons **23 MAC 301 (86)**—informant call describing car of man pointing gun enough reasonable suspicion for Terry car stop/order out;

C v Berment **39 MAC 522 (95)**—radio call about man waving gun at particular address did not justify frisk of 2 men standing & talking with woman and with another man in car, in parking lot next to address;

C v Johnson **36 MAC 336 (94)**—person known to cop telling cop that specific woman on street had gun on person enough reasonable suspicion for frisk of purse;

Florida v J.L. **529 US 266 (2000)**—specifically refuses to adopt "firearm exception" under *Terry v Ohio* to hold that stop and frisk is OK upon any tip at all, despite failure of tip to meet reliability test (here, anonymous telephone tipster saying black male in plaid shirt at particular bus stop was carrying gun); but see contra?: *C v Costa* **448 M 510 (2007)**—anonymous telephone tipster's reliability purportedly OK because she placed herself at risk by telephoning police to report D's possession of handgun as she stood near D; this provided objectively reasonable suspicion for frisk;

C v Foster **48 MAC 671 (2000)**—tip re person "displaying" gun (believed to mean "flaunting ostentatiously"), in conjunction with 5:30 a.m. time and gunfire from "after hours" parties in this particular neighborhood on past occasions allowed stop and frisk; but cf. *C v Alvarado* **423 M 266 (96)** tip about handgun in car "did not disclose any imminent threat to public safety" & court "reluctant to relax (its) established rule that the report of the carrying of a firearm is not, standing alone, a basis for having a reasonable suspicion of criminal activity"; reliability of tipster lacking anyway; *C v Couture* **407 M 178 (90)** sighting of gun protruding from D's right rear pocket

does not equal probable cause, without any additional information;

C v Barros **49 MAC 613 (2000)**—"white, well-dressed, middle-aged man" in pickup truck (who didn't want to ID self) motioned cop to stop & told cop he'd just seen someone (described by height, skin, & clothes, at location of two streets) pull gun from waistband & show it to friends before returning it to waist; 8 minutes later, cop yelled to D, said he wanted to speak, but D kept walking & stopped only at 2d command, after arrival of backup cops & 1st cop's exit from cruiser; seizure here occurred prior to D's moving hands toward waistband area, so suppression of gun was ordered because "report that someone is carrying a gun does not by itself constitute reasonable suspicion to conduct a stop & frisk of that individual"; if seizure occurred instead after movement, no suppression because 'frisk' would have been warranted, at gunpoint (as occurred) if necessary to ensure cop's safety; cc opinion suggested that if suspect looked younger than 21 years old, reasonable suspicion existed (G.L. c. 140, § 131 prohibits person under 21 from being licensed to carry firearm); **S.C., 435 M 171 (2001)** similar, plus *face-to-face anonymous informants are to be treated no differently from unnamed anonymous telephone callers;*

C v Heughan **40 MAC 102 (96)**—OK stop for speeding ripened to probable cause for arrest (no license) & **car equivalent of "frisk" OK given furtive gesture and report of gunfire;**

C v Avellar **70 MAC 608 (2007)**—that stop of car was pretextual, to troll for evidence of drug trafficking didn't matter, so long as one officer testified that driver "failed to signal a turn off the road servicing moderate traffic"; "reasonable suspicion" that traffic violation concerned allowed stop and succeeding events held justifiable upon cops' smelling marijuana and viewing plastic bag of same;

C v Reed **23 MAC 294 (86)**—anonymous tip (re: van, 3 black males, steal hubcaps in lot) = reasonable suspicion when confirmed;

C v Moscat **49 MAC 622 (2000)**—report of youths drinking and causing "ruckus" prompted cops to approach 5–6 kids & see at their feet bottles, some with beer still inside; though kids left at cop's order, one was doing so on bike, with difficulty, because holding one hand close to body as if to conceal something; cop ordered 'stop,' asked what was there, and began to reach to frisk: gun dropped to ground; appellate court didn't reach whether valid basis for Terry stop/frisk, holding probable cause to arrest for being minor in possession of alcohol (& "not important" that search preceded formal arrest);

C v Mantinez **44 MAC 513 (98)**—informant info & later observed activity believed to be drug deal = reasonable suspicion; probable cause found when money found at frisk and reasonable belief that D produced false license;

C v Sweezey **50 MAC 48 (2000)**—**reasonable suspicion to stop motorist-D: surveillance of parking lot known for frequent drug transactions, one car signaling D's car with flashing lights, D following & obtaining** paper bag from other driver; **D's attempted getaway, in car, from cops approaching him at stop light in traffic gave probable cause;** fact that cops testified that arrest was for A&B on cop rather than drugs didn't prevent court from finding drug probable cause instead, justifying seizure of brown bag on front seat;

C v Montgomery **23 MAC 909 (86)**—Mercedes cruises high-crime mall 2 a.m. = reasonable suspicion;

C v Smigliano **427 M 490 (98)**—report by motorist of erratic driving & cop's observations of D almost striking parked cars justified cop's approach of D's stopped vehicle (& would have supported stop) & questioning of D (slumped, with head on steering wheel); analysis of info (reliability/basis of knowledge) purportedly less rigorous because 'stop' rather than 'arrest'; BUT cf. *Florida v. J.L.* **529 US 266 (2000)**, ante (no "firearm exception" justifies stop/frisk when tip can't be found reliable); see also *C v Barros* **435 M 171 (2001)** (but see also suggestions that reasonable suspicion exists if D looks to be underage (21) for firearm licensing, and that cops can request verification of license under G.L. c. 140, § 129C;

C v Alvarado **420 M 542 (95)**—reasonable suspicion for stop of car going very slowly & moving "peculiarly" on Rt. 495, & OK to question passenger about furtive gesture, & "clear plastic" placed down front of pants— probable cause to pat down for drugs & to arrest & then probable cause to arrest driver, after passenger's statements; suppression ordered as to contents of coffee maker in car, though (laughable) claim of "inventory" justification made;

C v Quinn **68 MAC 476 (2007)**—reasonable suspicion for investigative stop of car based on collective knowledge of other officers (who knew that footsteps in snow from site of break-in led to automobile going in a particular direction, and D's car was the only car in vicinity);

C v Roland R **448 M 278 (2007)**—police officer saw other officers chasing juvenile, and joined in, eventually catching him: "fact that [officers] were not personally aware of the circumstances leading to the chase is irrelevant";

C v Houle **35 MAC 474 (93)**—sound/appearance of D having something in his mouth, in high crime area, not reasonable suspicion for intrusion/order to spit it out, despite claim that cop had previously arrested 10–12 people with drugs in mouth;

C v Grandison **433 M 135 (2001)**—high crime area for drug activity + attempt to evade police + spitting 'small projectile' out of mouth (+ testimony that crack cocaine commonly hidden in mouths and spit out or swallowed to avoid detection) = reasonable suspicion for "stop" command;

C v Hill **49 MAC 58 (2000)**—use of public telephone at MBTA station, then drive to parking lot of McDonald's made surveillance cop believe drug buy imminent; car parked next to 1st car; 1st driver got out and opened passenger door of 2d car and reached inside with right hand extended before going back to 1st car, where cops saw plastic bag with white substance in his right hand; stop of

2d car (after it left) held OK (reasonable suspicion); driver's "spontaneous statement" of driver that she'd obtained $10 from "friend" in parking lot plus presence of $10 bill gave probable cause;

C v Varnum **39 MAC 571 (95)**—info from 3 witnesses, broadcast: 3 males in particular car (make, model, license plate) may have broken & entered home, taking TV, VCR & shotgun: OK to follow car and, when it stopped, approach with drawn gun & order occupants out; single officer made the stop, in isolated area at night & feared for safety;

C v Cullen **62 MAC 390 (2004)**—burglary & battery victim's immediate 911 call, connected by disinterested motorist's report of particular car and described occupants' reckless flight from point "only 900 feet" from crime scene, plus purported consciousness of guilt behavior upon sighting police, gave reasonable suspicion; large volume of coins subsequently found in pockets corroborated suspicion; subsequent show-up OK also, court finding, by that point, probable cause for arrest;

C v Doulette **414 M 653 (93), affirming 32 MAC 506 (92)**—cars parked at night in remote area of commuter parking lot, scene of prior unlawful activity, plus flickering light & D's bending over as if to conceal something was reasonable suspicion justifying cop's approach with flashlight;

C v Crowley **29 MAC 1 (90)**—contradictory responses by D justified 20 minute detention & transportation to scene for show-up identification procedure;

C v Kitchings **40 MAC 591 (96)**—contradictory responses of men in stopped car to explain name of different man on car rental contract & recently—burned marijuana smell & frisk revealing large amount of cash prompted enough suspicion to justify placing 2 men in backseat of cruiser and, after sighting of loaded gun clip, the other 2 men as well; actions "involved a degree of intrusion which was proportional to the degree of suspicion that prompted the intrusion and did not exceed the scope of an investigative stop";

C v Correia **66 MAC 174 (2006)**—odor of burnt marijuana coming from already-stopped car gave probable cause to search for evidence of marijuana use/possession "whether or not [police] had probable cause to arrest any particular occupant"; ordering occupants out of vehicle to conduct the search = permissible;

C v Lites **67 MAC 815 (2006)**—fresh odor of burnt marijuana from opened door of stopped car, PLUS passenger's furtive gestures at his waist area provided probable cause to arrest passenger;

C v Garden **451 M 43 (2008)**—odor of burnt marijuana on clothes of car occupants here allowed search of occupants and passenger compartment, but did not permit warrantless search of car trunk;

C v Feyenord **62 MAC 200 (2004), and S.C. on further appellate review, 445 M 72 (2005)**—upholds 30-minute detention of motorist (after stop for broken headlight during daytime hours) for sniff by drug-detecting dog, by holding there was probable cause for arrest (though no actual arrest) for lack of license on person; dissent says detention not reasonably related in scope to justification for stop, cites cases re: suppression for drug-sniffing dogs after simple traffic stops;

C v Lopes **455 M 147 (2009)**—after van's occupants were removed and handcuffed upon reasonable vasis to believe armed and dangerous, cop could go inside van to retrieve ID's when driver told cop his ID was inside; "limited" search for ID yielded incriminating cash; ALSO, "protective sweep" would have been OK (van had four rows of seats, cops weren't sure that only two individuals were involved in homicide);

C v Prevost **44 MAC 398 (98)**—driver struggling as cop approached to put on overcoat after OK car stop (wrong way on one-way street)—**OK, after no explanation, for cop to open car door & order to remove coat & expose waist area**;

C v George **35 MAC 551 (93)**—sudden grab of bag & transfer to passenger = reasonable suspicion to frisk after stop for speeding, no license, & false statements;

C v Calderon **43 MAC 228 (97)**—OK to frisk and remove hard object from D's pocket and to look inside it (a sock containing screwdriver, pliers & knife) after D & another male became "agitated" at the arrest of female companion—all known to have criminal histories "be-speak(ing) disregard of risk of physical harm to others" (burglary & robbery), nighttime, area of criminal/drug activity, & arrests "often escalate to violence";

C v Kimball **37 MAC 604 (94)**—"dilapidated" condition of car (missing side windows, hole where trunk lock should be) isn't reasonable suspicion; "looking straight ahead" instead of at cops not reason for suspicion; even if stop OK, should have been permitted to leave; registration was in same surname, but different first name & this was illegitimate basis for suspicion of larceny;

C v Butterfield **44 MAC 926 (98)**—OK stop of D as he was walking toward his back door: reasonable suspicion of specified property damage by person driving black Ford Bronco, given info by identified resident (though info wasn't later substantiated): presence of described car in location corroborated by police;

C v Andrews **34 MAC 324 (93)**—D's **activity consistent with "casing" jewelry store** provided reasonable suspicion of his involvement in different nearby jewelry store robbery the next day; gunpoint "stop" of D & 3 cohorts (by one cop) held OK & within 15 minutes probable cause from victim's IDs;

C v Tosi **14 MAC 1029 (82)**—if robbery reasonable suspicion & evasiveness, can hold 20 minutes for victim to come ID visible goods;

C v Johnson **49 MAC 273 (2000)**—cop's 4 a.m. interview of named individual reporting shots fired, probably from described car, + another named individual's info that alarm in street-level business establishment had gone off around same time gave rise to reasonable suspicion to stop car, 45 minutes later and 1½ miles from shooting; car's

flight from cop and tossing gun from car window = probable cause to arrest for discharging gun within 500 feet of dwelling (& search incident for that crime, turning up ammunition in car); that cop said arrest (when car crashed into cruiser which was part of roadblock) was for failure to stop for cop wasn't controlling (search incident to arrest for that crime wouldn't have allowed search of car);

C v Hooker **52 MAC 683 (2001)**—reversing trial court's judgment that D had no expectation of privacy in taxi: D did reasonably expect that police wouldn't arbitrarily order him from taxi and look beneath a jacket he'd placed on the seat, notwithstanding diminished expectation of privacy inherent in interior of vehicle visible to others during travel on public way; D shouldn't have been ordered out of car because police had no reasonable apprehension of danger; **fact that D looked back at car (unmarked vehicle with plainclothes cops)** following taxi in which he was riding wasn't remarkable, particularly in high crime area;

C v Starr **55 MAC 590 (2002)**—cop following car could run license plate number (& learn that it didn't match car to which it was affixed); observation of license plate wasn't search, & merely following car wasn't pursuit; BUT if evidence of racial/ethnic profiling, would be "at the very least," cause for concern;

C v Kimball **37 MAC 604 (94)**—"dilapidated" condition of car (missing side windows, hole where trunk lock should be) isn't reasonable suspicion; **"looking straight ahead" instead of at cops not reason for suspicion**; even if stop OK, should have been permitted to leave; registration was in same surname, but different first name & this was illegitimate basis for suspicion of larceny;

C v Redd **50 MAC 904 (2000)**—anonymous telephone caller, purportedly worker at hospital, told police dispatcher that silver Chevrolet with specified plate # was stolen from hospital site by Hispanic male in his 20s wearing white bandana, blue jeans, & jacket; responding detectives who had also heard radio that car was abandoned 2 blocks from hospital had reasonable suspicion (enough corroboration) for stopping 2 "dark skinned males" in mid- to late 20s, one wearing white bandana & maybe blue jeans, walking on street less than block away from abandoned car & getting into cab, & moving to put something onto cab floor;

20-M.4. "Terry" Frisk/Car Exit Orders, Field Searches of Vehicle; Necessity of Reasonable Belief That Safety of Officer or Others Is in Danger

C v Cantalupo **380 M 173 (80)**—OK stop, but no reason to frisk/search;

C v Gutierrez **26 MAC 42 (88)**—(same); 5–10 minutes = too long to detain without more reason than stop's; judge could find cops lied about bulge; they didn't become aware of "bulge" until they "delved into" pockets;

C v Martinez **74 MAC 240 (2009)**—911 report of attempted B&E at 5 a.m.: stop of D (significantly differing from description of culprit) not supported by reasonable suspicion AND frisk not supported by reasonable belief D was armed/dangerous, despite fact that cops were suspicious of D's abandonment of his ID card after request, by retreating behind locked door;

C v Feyenord **62 MAC 200 (2004), and S.C. on further appellate review, 445 M 72 (2005)**—upholds 30-minute detention of motorist (after stop for broken headlight during daytime hours) for sniff by drug-detecting dog, by holding there was probable cause for arrest (though no actual arrest) for lack of license on person; dissent says detention not reasonably related in scope to justification for stop, cites cases re: suppression for drug-sniffing dogs after simple traffic stops;

C v Wing Ng **420 M 236 (95)—Article 14 forbids automatic frisk of anyone in the company of person being lawfully arrested; there must be articulable facts warranting reasonable suspicion that the particular person might be armed & a threat to safety;**

C v Calderon **43 MAC 228 (97)**—OK to frisk and remove hard object from D's pocket and to look inside it (a sock containing screwdriver, pliers & knife) after D & another male became "agitated" at the arrest of female companion—all known to have criminal histories "bespeak(ing) disregard of risk of physical harm to others" (burglary & robbery), nighttime, area of criminal/drug activity, & arrests "often escalate to violence";

C v Wilson **441 M 390 (2004)**—"plain feel" doctrine, authorizing cop to seize nonthreatening contraband discovered when lawfully pat frisking suspect's outer clothing and feeling object which makes its identity as contraband immediately apparent, doesn't violate article 14 or Fourth Amendment; admissible here = bundles of marijuana at D's waistband ;

C v Osborne **62 MAC 445 (2004), further appellate review allowed as to unrelated issue 443 M 1104 (2005)**—after tip re: D selling cocaine, threshold inquiry / pat-frisk turned up "747 folding knife," but record didn't establish what this was & whether possession = unlawful; nonetheless, continued pat frisk OK, and "plain feel" located hard object between buttocks, justifiably seizable because apparently drugs;

C v Cullen **62 MAC 390 (2004)**—following late night urban car stop on reasonable suspicion that its two occupants were culpable in same-night burglary & severe beating of resident, cops' reach into pocket to discern contents (mass of heavy metallic sounding items falsely said by D to be "keys") upheld as "integrated part of a safety-based weapons patfrisk", and court refuses relief for cops' removing the coins after determining no threat, holding "probable cause" to seize as proceeds of crime ("plain feel" argument, i.e., that incriminatory nature of the coins wasn't immediately apparent, rejected, on circumstantial evidence/inferences);

C v Pigaga **12 MAC 960 (81)**—evidence suppressed because **seized in a "direct" "immediate" search of D's pockets rather than in course of pat-down for weapons;**

C v Laskoski **74 MAC 858 (2009)**—though D claimed 'patfrisk without reasonable suspicion that he had weapon,' Appeals Court found instead "probable cause to search" because of strong odor of burnt marijuana coming from D's clothes: that officer himself justified frisk (illegitimately) on subjective belief that D might have weapon on his person "because a domestic dispute had taken place" was not controlling;

C v Vanya V **75 MAC 370, 377 (2009), Berry, J, concurring:** majority ordered suppression on other ground, but concurrence asserted that patfrisk of juvenile simply because it was cop's "standard procedure" when driving any juvenile home to parents was inadequate justification under Terry (requiring, before frisk, specific facts that juvenile was armed and dangerous);

C v Fisher **54 MAC 41 (2002)**—immediate pat-down upheld given aggregated circumstances: evasive reaction of D & cohorts to police, late night, high crime area known for presence of illegal guns, D's quick motion toward his waist;

C v VaMengJo **425 M 99, 107 n.10 (97)**—reserving issue whether external pat-down is "invariably necessary first step in every protective search";

C v Davis **41 MAC 793 (96)**—bizarre jittery behavior of motorist stopped for speeding, did not warrant reasonable belief of danger: **pat-down is a "serious intrusion upon the sanctity of the person";**

C v Cardoso **46 MAC 901 (98)**—that front seat passenger was fidgeting & cop felt he was hiding something not reasonable suspicion for frisk after car's driver produced valid license (stop was for lack of inspection sticker); "no legal basis for (trooper's) apprehension to result in a search "even if trooper was "genuinely apprehensive";

C v Bettencourt **447 M 631 (2006)**—after proper stop, driver was arrested; cop asked passenger whether he had license, and he said no; further questioning of passenger for name and date of birth resulted in knowledge of outstanding warrants, passenger's arrest, and discovery of cocaine on his person: SJC orders suppression, since no ground for questioning D/believing D involved in crime; Commonwealth's belated argument that it was "community caretaking" to find a driver to take charge of car rather than tow/impound it was rebuffed, because not raised at trial court by testimony or argument;

C v Patti **31 MAC 440 (91)**—D's placing of hands in pocket as cop approached justified frisk where D had been standing in front of car with hood up & engine running in early morning in parking lot where car thefts had been occurring;

C v Johnson **454 M 159 (2009)**—that D kept rummaging in pockets after being told not to justified frisk, despite facts that it was broad daylight, there had been no recent report of criminal activity, and group of young people not "collectively" engaged in suspicious/threatening activity; one in group was arrested as being in violation of a 'no trespass' order, and it was "high crime area" ("itself a general and conclusory term that should not be used to justify a stop or a frisk, or both, without requiring the articulation of specific facts demonstrating the reasonableness of the intrusion");

C v Rosenthal **52 MAC 707 (2001)**—despite trooper's claim of fear, no objective basis; purported awareness that "horse trainers often carry, on their person, tools of the trade such as knives and scissors" = inadequate justification; didn't "pat-down" outer clothing before reaching in, & if he had, he wouldn't have felt anything like a weapon;

C v Ferguson **410 M 611 (91)**—although frisk of D's jacket left behind by D during chase was justified by information that D had gun, cops not justified in opening black bag once they realized it didn't contain gun;

C v Dedominicis **42 MAC 76 (97)**—when cop said bulge felt hard and motion judge was unwilling/unable to say cop was lying, judge could not feel the bulge himself to come to contrary conclusion (& reject basis for seizure of money wad);

20-M.5. Vehicle Stop Exit Orders

Pennsylvania v Mimms **434 US 106 (77)**—if OK vehicle stop, even traffic, can order D out (under Fourth Amendment); Mass. law differs);

NY v Class **475 US 106 (86)**—can order D out of car after OK motor vehicle stop, & can look at VIN #;

Maryland v Wilson **519 US 408 (97)**—*Mimms* (if OK car stop, can order driver out) extended to car **passengers**;

Knowles v Iowa **525 US 113 (98)**—routine traffic stop resulting in speeding citation cannot support "full field-type search" of the car stopped;

Delaware v Prouse **440 US 648 (79)**—bad random car stop to check license/registration, but OK if less intrusive, less discretion (*see Roadblocks, below & Chapter 20-L, above, Cars*);

Ohio v Robinette **519 US 33 (96)**—**need not inform D he was free to leave, after license production & valid traffic stop, before getting consent to search**; compare/contrast

C v McCleery **345 M 151 (62)**—**if papers ok, no reasonable suspicion for more questions or order to exit**;

C v Torres **424 M 153 (97)**—same, so **"consent" to search obtained after continued detention = invalid under Article 14** (despite fact that driver was from Medellin, Columbia, and lived in area known for "drug activity") and passenger did not immediately respond to cop's presence at window);

C v Ellsworth **41 MAC 554 (96)**—similar- no basis for ordering car owner & "furtive gesture" passenger out of car; "consent" bogus;

C v Pacheco **51 MAC 736 (2001)**—after valid stop for expired inspection sticker, driver presented facially valid license and registration in a different name, & said car belonged to father of passenger; passenger had no identification, but gave name whose last name matched that of registered car owner: OK to request passenger to leave car, & OK to arrest & cuff & secure him in cruiser after warrant check revealed default warrants for shoplifting, trespass, A&B; NOT OK to search car, including under floor mat, on purported rationale of search for identification pursuant to G.L. c. 276, § 1 (for fruits, instrumentalities, contraband, & evidence of crime for which arrest has been made to prevent destruction/concealment); claim that search was OK because not "certain" that D correctly identified himself SOUNDLY REJECTED see also *C v Bettencourt* **447 M 631 (2006)** (after valid arrest of driver, no permissible ground for investigatory questioning of D, a passenger);

C v Feyenord **62 MAC 200 (2004), and S.C. on further appellate review, 445 M 72 (2005)**—court OKs traffic stop, during daylight hours, for one nonfunctioning headlight ("not properly equipped for travel"); exit order justified because driver couldn't produce license, registration certificate was in another person's name, cop was "outnumbered", and D was nervous;

C v Brown **75 MAC 528 (2009)**—at time of exit order, two cops present, and two cab passengers: officers "not outnumbered";

C v Watts **74 MAC 514 (2009)**—after car failed to stop at intersection "stop" sign, legitimate to pull it over; though judge suppressed drugs on ground that further detention was illegitimate after production of valid driver's license, cop simultaneously learned that rental agreement for the car had expired, which justified telephone call to rental company, which said D-driver's use was no longer authorized; presence of "laundry dryer sheets" and Dutch Masters cigars in car, plus finding that same car had been "queried" in Barnstable County within past 30 days, with cop's knowledge of "narcotics being transferred between Springfield and Barnstable through the use of rental cars" warranted calling canine unit: suppression order reversed; though police could have impounded car after learning D's use was no longer authorized, immediate impoundment wasn't required; detention of car was for no longer than one hour;

C v Nunez **70 MAC 752 (2007)**—exit order and frisk upheld: valid stop for peeling out from stop light, front seat passenger-D, told to take hands out of pocket, did so but put them back in, necessitating second order to do so, and was breathing heavily ("nervous"): marijuana roach observed on car floor as D was exiting, frisk revealed gun;

C v Holley **52 MAC 659, 662 (2001)**—**standard for a pat frisk = same as standard required to justify an exit order** when vehicle is stopped for traffic violations; despite motion judge's **buzzword of "furtive gesture,"** testimony that D leaned dramatically to his right with arm toward passenger's side visor didn't support finding of reaching toward floor, or finding that cop frisked right pocket because he thought D placed something there;

"ambiguous gesture which, at best, could not be deemed to be either furtive or threatening"; similar re buzzword of "high crime area"; *C v Brown* **75 MAC 528 (2009)**—law-abiding citizens live and work in high crime areas; this not enough for car exit order or frisk;

C v Loughlin **385 M 60 (82)**—if papers OK, no reasonable suspicion for more questions/exit order;

C v Santana **420 M 205 (95)**—**before compelling driver to step out of vehicle, there must be basis for finding that reasonable person would be warranted in believing his or others' safety is in danger;**

C v Williams **46 MAC 181 (99)**—same, suppressing when **driver acted nervous** & ignored 1st request to step out, and grabbed her jacket pocket as she was stepping out, on 2d request;

C v Knight **75 MAC 735 (2009)**—citing *C v Ocasio* 71 MAC 304, 306, 311 (2008) & C v *Katykhin* 59 MAC 262 (2003), "arrest" wasn't "complete" when D was ordered out of car or even when he was handcuffed (so that "resisting arrest" conviction was upheld on basis of behavior occurring until he was placed in cruiser);

C v King **389 M 233 (83)**—can stop (block) by policy all stopped cars in winter & check license & registration, but when confirmed, no reason to order out/frisk;

C v Gonsalves **429 M 658 (99)**—*under Article 14* **cannot order driver out for routine traffic stop unless reasonable belief that safety of officer or others is in danger;** see also *C v Bettencourt* **447 M 631 (2006)**—notwithstanding valid arrest of driver, no permissible basis here for suspecting passenger of criminal activity, so questions as to identity, etc., NOT PERMITTED (& arrest for outstanding warrants, plus search incident to arrest = bad);

C v Bostock **450 M 616 (2008)**—officers responding speedily to report of breaking/entering of vehicle obtained equally speedy further info as to another like vehicle break/entry/theft and description and path of walking suspect, and found D (matching descriptions) inside a parked truck; after exit order and questions, officer saw inside truck items matching description of property stolen from vehicles; *C v Gonsalves* holding (requiring safety fear before exit order = limited to routine traffic stops; here, reasonable suspicion of recent criminal activity made exit order reasonable to prevent escape by or assault with vehicle;

C v Santos **65 MAC 122 (2005)**—stop for traffic offense was valid, but arrest for failure to produce Mass. license was not (driving without having license in possession is an offense [G.L. c. 90, § 11], but if one is an "in-state" driver, it's not an arrestable offense (G.L. c. 90, § 21)) [D had told officer his date of birth and that he had an "active" Mass. driver's license]: cuffing D and securing him in cruiser was "arrest," despite cop's disclaimer of same, as cop searched car for indicia of ownership ("investigative" rather than "protective"), & found gun; that stop occurred in "high crime" area and that D sat up from a reclined position & leaned forward weren't enough; "citizen is not required to sit absolutely motionless in stopped vehicle"; ordinary checks of identity and vehicle owner-

ship should have been completed before exit order & cuffing D & searching car;

C v Horton **63 MAC 571 (2005)**—back seat passenger's kicking something under front seat = reasonable concern for safety, & basis for exit order, citing *Stampley* 437 M 323 (2002), *Vanderlinde* 27 MAC 1103 (89), *Prevost* 44 MAC 398 (88), etc.; that stop occurred during night in high crime area (not enough alone) buttressed justification;

C v Robles **48 MAC 490 (2000)**—before cop had opportunity to check driver's license and registration after he ran stop sign, cop could order car passengers out when they failed to obey cop's direction to keep hands in sight and instead "appeared nervous" and leaned forward with hands between legs on the floor, and spoke in a language he didn't understand to crowd which had gathered; frisk revealing an empty shoulder holster justified search of car for gun;

C v Rivera **67 MAC 362 (2006)**—after stop for unlit headlamp, driver's extreme nervousness + sighting of police baton protruding from space between bucket seats = enough for exit order and patfrisk, though "close" question ("high crime" area a factor here);

C v Brown **75 MAC 528 (2009)**—that passengers in cab (stopped for traffic violation) didn't have seat belts buckled & didn't have license or other ID to enable accurate citation (purportedly "overreacting" by looking tense & nervous and saying they were just being driven in taxi) was insufficient basis for exit order and frisk (no reasonable inference that individuals were armed and dangerous); "high crime area", cop being "outnumbered", & nervousness, even combined, don't suffice; "adding up . . . innocuous observations . . . does not produce a sum of suspicion";

C v Bartlett **41 MAC 468 (96)**—after citation for speeding, D should have been allowed to leave; that rental cars and beepers are used by drug couriers, that a Cambridge resident was driving a rental car from Logan Airport, "a point of entry for drugs", & that drugs had been seized previously on "the Lowell Connector" **not** a "reasonable stimulus for investigation"; cc opinion at 473 (**"interrogated on suspicion of being Hispanic"; "ethnicity plus a beeper does not equal probable cause"**);

C v Starr **55 MAC 590 (2002)**—cop following car could run license plate number (& learn that it didn't match car to which it was affixed); observation of license plate wasn't search, & merely following car wasn't pursuit; BUT if evidence of racial/ethnic profiling, would be "at the very least," cause for concern;

C v Alvarez **44 MAC 531 (98)**—under Article 14, can't interrogate/demand IDs of passengers in car after legitimate stop of driver for speeding; G.L. c. 85, § 16 (permitting nighttime demands for names & addresses of drivers and passengers) probably unconstitutional but not here reached (cop did more than that);

C v Santana **420 M 205 (95)**—cops pulled out to follow car "in disrepair" and observed broken taillight, but car didn't stop after blue lights, for > one mile—OK to order occupants out, **prior** to license/registration check because of failure to stop & fact that driver didn't turn off motor & observation of popped ignition; when passenger handed cop a gallon of milk inexplicably, cop could place it back inside car (& then "plain view");

C v Blais **428 M 294 (98)**—after approaching motorist (who had driven into restaurant parking lot) to tell of speeding & broken headlight, cop came to have probable cause for OUI arrest, even if cop didn't understand/believe this, **though subsequently requiring driver to perform field sobriety tests was a search or seizure, only reasonable suspicion need be shown for same; cop need not tell motorist he can refuse, and while motorist purportedly has no right to refuse, his refusal can't be introduced against him & he cannot be "forced" to comply**;

C v Johnson **413 M 598 (92)**—D's placing something in waistband when cops stopped his speeding car justified frisk because "swift measures" necessary, even if cops didn't believe waistband bulge was weapon;

C v Robbins **407 M 147 (90)**—cop making lawful stop may make protective Terry-frisk of limited portions of car for weapons;

C v Cruz-Rivera **76 MAC 14 (2009)**—after D drove in unsafe manner almost striking police cruiser and leaned toward center console and bent down after stopping, cop ordered exit and conducted frisk; upon finding no weapons and intending to release D, further search inside car was probably impermissible, and certainly impermissible to open small pill bottle found in car's center console (notwithstanding cops' testimony about existence of "very small weapons, such as single-shot pen-sized guns, knives, or razors"); unreasonable to believe that D, upon release, would open a pill bottle and obtain weapon < 4½ inches by 1¾ inches, in effort to harm "two nearby, fully armed [cops] who had just released him";

C v Moses **408 M 136 (90)**—**cop making lawful stop for drug activity entitled under Article 14 to make "protective search" of D & area in car from which he might obtain weapon**; cop directing stopped motorist to turn off ignition & hand over key not an "arrest" but a "reasonably prudent protective measure";

C v Santiago **53 MAC 567 (2002)**—given reasonable suspicion that driver of car which committed traffic offenses was serial rapist who had very recently used dangerous weapons, single cop making stop was justified in approaching with drawn gun & handcuffing D ("reasonable efforts to ensure the officer's safety do not transform a stop into an arrest"); Appeals Court **upholds further search of car purportedly because driver might actually have been released subsequently and would have been able to attack cop "upon the suspect's reentry into the vehicle"**;

C v Lantigua **38 MAC 526 (95)**—though police were following D because of his contact with a man known to him, stop was for stop sign violation and D, outside car, said had to get registration from glove compartment; cop's

concern for his safety allowed cop either to get registration himself or "frisk" car interior before letting D get it (D observed to lean down & to right before getting out of car); *C v Santos* **65 MAC 122, 127–28 (2005)**—distinguished from *Lantigua*, because D couldn't locate registration in glove compartment & only then did cop cuff and "secure" D in cruiser, thereafter searching car himself for registration or other identifying papers; that D couldn't produce his assertedly active Mass. driver's license (though computer check with date of birth & name revealed he had one) or car registration (car belonged to his mother, and wasn't reported "stolen") were insufficient factors to warrant investigatory search, notwithstanding "high crime" area;

C v Pagan **440 M 62 (2003)**—in circumstances, cops not obligated to hand bag back to D (for him to retrieve identification from it) prior to assuring that no weapon was in bag; whether pat frisk of bag is necessary before immediate opening depends on whether such frisk can establish whether a weapon is present or not; though bag here was soft/pliable, it held hard heavy objects, so that frisk couldn't "dispel the suspicion" of objects *useable as* weapons;

C v Lucido **18 MAC 941 (84)**—**can check car for weapons after arresting D because his friends (alleged gang) were taking car;**

C v Pena **69 MAC 713 (2007)**—two of three vehicle occupants were not under arrest, though all had been removed from vehicle (marijuana discovered on person of one passenger [arrested], driver probably to be issued only m.v. citation for driving offense, other passenger behaving erratically, refusing to sit still): "protective" search extending to area underneath rear seat cushion upheld (guns);

C v Heon **44 MAC 254 (98)**—motorcyclist stopped for speeding could be frisked because he was wearing "Hells Angels" jacket, cop knew of ongoing violent feud between that group & another, & cyclist was not locating registration without difficulty—"totality of circumstances" cited, including suspicion of vehicle theft or other crimes;

C v Riche **50 MAC 830 (2001)**—combination of circumstances after driver was stopped for speeding and unilluminated license plate, & had no valid license (early a.m., high crime area, mention of prior drug offense, purportedly "implicat(ing) the possibility of guns," etc.) made exit orders to passengers OK;

C v Washington **449 M 476 (2007)**—SJC refuses to adopt "blanket rule that all persons suspected of drug activity are to be presumed armed and dangerous for constitutional purposes," so exit order simply because probable cause to believe guilty of drug distribution = invalid (search by means of frisk upheld, nonetheless, on ground that [fungible] money from drug deal wouldn't be verified unless search occurred immediately);

C v Gomes **453 M 506 (2009)**—in high crime/drug area at 4 a.m., seeing D holding out flat hand to another as though displaying something, and swallowing it after seeing approaching cops = enough for reasonable suspicion, but immediate frisk not justified (no reasonable inference that D was armed and presented danger to cops or others);

that there had been "numerous" firearm incidents and four police officer-involved shootings in area inadequate to particularize suspicion as to this D;

C v Grant **57 MAC 334 (2003)**—emergency road-block aimed at catching fleeing dangerous suspect = reasonable, & didn't require individualized suspicion; separate, sequential exit orders for driver and passengers OK because cop fearful for safety; view of firearm occurred during exit process;

C v Dellinger **383 M 780 (81)**—OK stop for tailing UPS truck; but can't check for weapons (because criminal records, evasive answers) if license/registration/ID = OK;

Michigan v Long **463 US 1032 (83)**—car "stop & frisk" of D outside can extend inside to areas that could hide weapon; (*see Chapter 20-H & 20-L above re: Scope*);

C v Hooker **52 MAC 683 (2001)**—D shouldn't have been ordered out of taxi because police had no reasonable apprehension of danger; fact that D looked back at car (unmarked vehicle with plainclothes cops) following taxi in which he was riding wasn't remarkable, particularly in high crime area; see also *C v Brown* **75 MAC 528 (2009)** (cab passengers shouldn't have been frisked);

C v Robles **48 MAC 490 (2000)**—before cop had opportunity to check driver's license and registration after he ran stop sign, cop could order car passengers out when they failed to obey cop's direction to keep hands in sight and instead "appeared nervous" and leaned forward with hands between legs on the floor, and spoke in a language he didn't understand to crowd which had gathered; frisk revealing an empty shoulder holster justified search of car for gun;

C v Torres **433 M 669 (2001)**—following stop of car for failure to stop at stop sign, all 4 doors of car opened & 1 passenger fled, leaving 5 car occupants; because cop suspected, from 3 rear seat passengers' being "bent over," that they were hiding gun, he ordered them to put hands on heads, which they did after cop drew weapon; subsequent frisk, after arrival of more cops, producing gun from a waistband, = OK, said SJC: once officer reasonably concluded risk to safety & ordered occupants out, proper to conduct frisk for weapons; detention of occupants while awaiting backup didn't "transform the stop into an arrest"; Appeals Court (**49 MAC 348**) and District Court judge had held suspicion of gun "unfounded";

C v Vesna San **63 MAC 189 (2005)**—in immediate investigation of 911 call at 1:00 a.m. alleging burglars in kitchen, police learned description of individual male fleeing scene, and description of black van said to have been circling the area; sighting of the man standing outside the van, two miles away, gave reasonable suspicion to block the van from exiting a driveway & to detain the man, to order van occupants to exit, & to make a protective sweep of the van; sighting of item believed to have been taken in the burglary prompted victims' arrival to identify it (all actions said to be proportional to circumstances);

C v Lopes **455 M 147 (2009)**—after van's occupants were removed and handcuffed upon reasonable vasis to

believe armed and dangerous, cop could go inside van to retrieve ID's when driver told cop his ID was inside; "limited" search for ID yielded incriminating cash; ALSO, "protective sweep" would have been OK (van had four rows of seats, cops weren't sure that only two individuals were involved in homicide);

20-M.6. Scope of Stop/Frisk

C v Silva **366 M 402 (74)**—OK to stop & frisk, but not to open packet too small for weapon;

C v Desources **74 MAC 232 (2009)**—in "patfrisk" (albeit here a search incident to subsequent/'imminent' arrest for observed "open container" violation), "tightly wrapped plastic bags of marijuana" were "hard objects . . . merit[ing] further scrutiny";

C v Flemming **76 MAC 632 (2010)**—permissible scope of Terry frisk = confined to what was minimally necessary to learn whether D was armed and dangerous; rather than lifting D's shirt to see cause of bulge beneath D's T-shirt, officer should have pat-frisked exterior clothing; only after pat-down gives indication that weapon is present do police have privilege to search further; more immediate search beneath clothing permissible upon particularized info suggesting weapon is in location searched, or where D's actions suggest reaching for weapon;

C v Ilges **64 MAC 503 (2005)**—police, who had search warrant for D's home and tip that he would leave home to sell drugs in bar at particular time, stopped D after he drove away from home: patfrisk disclosing $3,400 cash was improper because not based on fear for safety; rejects motion judge's conclusion of "inevitable discovery," but upholds search/seizure on ground of probable cause to arrest D, so concomitant right to search him;

Minnesota v Dickerson **508 US 366 (93)**—**after D was stopped for seeking to evade police when coming out of "crack"/drug house, scope of permissible pat-down was exceeded when cop felt small lump, slid it about, felt it was crack in cellophane, took it out of pocket; if during pat-down item's character as contraband is apparent,** *can* **take it out;** cf. *Bond v US* **529 US 334 (2000)** border patrol agent's physical manipulation of carry-on luggage in overhead storage space on bus was a search (and D had reasonable expectation that it wouldn't be so manipulated even though the opaque canvas bag itself was exposed to the public); "brick like" object found to be drugs (ordered suppressed);

C v Crowley **13 MAC 915 (82)**—roll call advice, plus location of D, gave reasonable suspicion of drug activity, but immediate search of D's companion's paper bag, followed by frisk of companion, followed by telling D "you're next" were actions unsupported by belief 'armed/dangerous'; "so called furtive or evasive movement made by (D) occurred after the officer had begun to frisk (D) and, as a result, cannot be used to validate an otherwise illegal intrusion";

C v Gomes **59 MAC 332 (2003)**—resident's observations prompting call to police, with investigations disclosing apparent unlawful entry, hushed voices outside, and a shadowy motion followed by a door closing = reasonable suspicion that crime had occurred and that culprits might have fled to nearby location; BUT while further inquiry was necessary, cop's repeated demand that person answering neighboring door provide identification, and cop's refusal to allow individual to close the door "exceeded what was constitutionally permissible"; no probable cause to believe that culprit had fled to this address nor exigency justifying warrantless entry;

20-M.7. Community Caretaking

Cady v Dombrowski **413 US 433 (73)**—police "community caretaking functions" may intrude on privacy, permissibly;

C v Sondrini **48 MAC 704 (2000)**—though officials came onto property to assist first-floor tenant re: water leak into apartment from second floor apartment, their sighting (through 2d floor window) of a pipe-like apparatus for marijuana-smoking triggered criminal investigative search, and warrant should have been obtained;

C v Canavan **40 MAC 642 (96)**—stopping vehicles with lights & siren, because cop observed driver/car motionless for 3 minutes as driver seemed lost, before driver proceeded at slow speed, with no traffic violations, at 1 a.m., was seizure without reasonable suspicion (despite ostensible benign purpose of help); contrast *C v Leonard* **422 M 504 (96)** driver already stopped & cop could not get her attention to inquire if OK/ill—OK to open car door;

C v Smigliano **427 M 490 (98)**—though cc opinion would allow any intrusion in name of "community caretaking" deemed "reasonable" after the fact by a court, majority unwilling to approve such "essentially standardless" "discretion";

C v Evans **436 M 369 (2002)**—OK to approach, with blue lights activated, car parked in breakdown lane with right blinker flashing & to inquire, after rousing a sleeping & subsequently somewhat disoriented driver, "what are you doing?"; though driver responded, "nothing," **OK thereafter to demand license & registration, & this was a "minimal intrusion" rather than a "seizure"**; when driver had no license & cop learned it had been revoked, OK to arrest, & inventory search yielded drugs;

C v Gaylardo **68 MAC 906 (2007)**—cop could approach D, sitting in car in parking lot in winter at 2:38 a.m., car headlights and interior lights on, driver's door open; this wasn't a "stop," and approach was justified for "community caretaking"; observations then led to arrest for operating under influence of alcohol; questioning during "well-being check" isn't "interrogation"; that cop referred to his approach as "stop" was irrelevant;

C v Murdough **428 M 760 (99)**—OK for cops to order D out of car as it was parked in rest area on interstate after he was incoherent & fell asleep while responding to their inquiries (drugs were in plain view after D got out of car);

C v Knowles **451 M 91 (2008)**—because cop did not have reasonable suspicion of crime (based merely on anonymous call and subsequent radio dispatch that a man at a particular intersection at 6:40 p.m. was 'swinging a bat'), order that man step away from car (into whose trunk he was leaning, back to officer) and come toward officer with hands out of pockets was unconstitutional seizure such that subsequent peering into trunk and observation of drugs was not permissible "plain view";

C v Evans **50 MAC 846 (2001), S.C. 436 M 365 (2002)**—OK "community caretaking" for cruiser to activate blue lights & park behind car parked in breakdown lane of "desolate section of Route 20" at 11:35 p.m.; appellate court rejected D argument that lights indicated "seizure", requiring justification; appellate court rejected D argument that caretaking justification ended when D said "nothing" when cop asked what he was doing (resting in isolated section of desolate road "calls for an inquiry," e.g., requesting license & registration); HERE, at least, trooper's request for the defendant's license & registration not a seizure;

See K. Smith, *Criminal Practice & Procedure*, **Chapter 3, Arrest (2d ed. 1983 & Supp.)**; & *Brown v Texas* **443 US 47 (79)**;

C v Trompert **27 MAC 804 (89)**—investigatory checks of all vehicles in highway rest area at nighttime to determine if aid needed pursuant to state police policy upheld as reasonable under Fourth Amendment; lone cop's opening door & ordering out passengers justified by D's furtive gestures plus turning off light upon cop's approach;

C v Eckert **431 M 591 (2000)**—trooper approached D's car stopped at rest area, to check on well-being of occupant, aroused D from 'resting' condition, & detected bloodshot eyes & odor of alcoholic beverage; only "reasonable suspicion" rather than probable cause was required prior to asking D to get out and perform field sobriety tests, & case was remanded for determination whether reasonable suspicion existed; critical to determination whether questioning D about 'drinking' & sobriety tests OK = whether engine was running, because if so, "operation," and probable cause for arrest for OUI existed; NO constitutional justification was required for trooper's approach & inquiry whether D 'alright';

C v McCaffery **49 MAC 713 (2000)**—upon reasonable belief that D was incapacitated within the meaning of G.L. c. 111B, § 3 (protective custody), cop could ask D to perform field sobriety test; that D was walking in middle of road at 3 a.m., apparently intoxicated, provided reasonable belief that he was "likely to suffer . . . physical harm" as covered by statute; during test, wallet from burglary was seen, & that cops' motive may have been desire to unearth evidence of burglary rather than protect D = irrelevant; but see *C v Lubiejewski* **49 MAC 212 (2000)** unidentified motorist telephoned state police to report pickup truck with specific plate # was traveling on wrong side of Rt.

195 in vicinity of Rt. 140, but called back again to say truck crossed grassy median & proceeded on right side of road before turning south on Rt. 240 in Fairhaven; trooper stopped the truck, not for any observed violation, but for tipster's report; odor of alcohol & failure of sobriety tests = suppressed; no corroboration of anything but obvious details = insufficient to compensate for unknown reliability of informant; community caretaking function must be "totally divorced from the detection, investigation, or acquisition of evidence relating to the violation of a criminal statute," & this wasn't (trooper was investigating for evidence of the crime of driving wrong way on highway);

C v Davis **63 MAC 88 (2005)**—cop on detail who heard radio dispatch, based on anonymous phone call re: drunk female getting into white SUV with specific license plate number, tossing out beer cans, etc, could stop the car; "that report of an apparently drunk driver was anonymous did not require the police to ignore it" (**C v Fortune 47 MAC 923, (2003)**);

C v Quezada **67 MAC 693 (2006)**—D was, at 1:10 p.m., with person known to have been recently released from prison, who was assisting "staggering" and head-bandaged D in crossing street; plainclothes cop alighted from unmarked car & (not identifying self) "asked" to speak to them and D fled; cop chased & tackled D; appeals court held not "community caretaking" because D was being assisted by another (& flight was "nonverbal response" that D wasn't in need of assistance), & wasn't operating car; protective custody (G.L. c. 111B, § 8) refers to incapacitation by alcohol, which wasn't suspected; expansion of statute to include incapacitation due to suspected drugs or other reasons would be matter for legislature, not court; gun obtained from D = suppressed;

20-M.8. Roadblocks and Checkpoints

Michigan Dept. of State Police v Sitz **496 US 444 (90)**—drunk driving checkpoint OK under Fourth Amendment, given balance between State's interest in preventing drunken driving, the extent to which this system can reasonably be said to advance that interest, and the degree of intrusion upon individual motorists who are "briefly stopped";

C v Rodriguez **430 M 577 (2000)**—temporary roadblock in Holyoke to confiscate illegal narcotics, apprehend persons transporting illegal narcotics in vehicles and deter narcotic trafficking = UNCONSTITUTIONAL under Article 14, Declaration of Rights; purpose was not ensuring public safety (like "operating under influence" roadblocks), but instead discovery of evidence of crime; concurring opinion by Lynch, J., said sobriety checkpoint and drug interdiction roadblocks are indistinguishable, and that both should be held to violate Article 14;

C v Swartz **454 M 330 (2009)**—that written policy controlling roadblock to deter drunk driving also directed diversion of vehicles to secondary screening when observations provided reasonable suspicion of commission of

felony or violation of narcotics law did not make it unconstitutional under *Rodriguez* 430 M 577: officers needn't turn blind eye to evidence in plain view providing reasonable suspicion that crime has been or is being committed;

Indianapolis v Edmond **531 US 32 (2001)**—drug checkpoint unconstitutional; since primary purpose was "to advance 'the generalized interest in crime control,'" individualized suspicion was required (though different result possible if roadblock were appropriately tailored to "thwart an imminent terrorist attack or to catch a dangerous criminal who is likely to flee by way of a particular route"; finding re: "primary purpose" is to be made "at the programmatic level and is not an invitation to probe the minds of individual officers acting at the scene";

C v Grant **57 MAC 334 (2003)**—emergency roadblock aimed at catching fleeing dangerous suspect = reasonable, & didn't require individualized suspicion; separate, sequential exit orders for driver and passengers OK because cop fearful for safety; view of firearm occurred during exit process;

C v Anderson **406 M 343 (90)**—extending OUI roadblock 15 minutes beyond plan required suppression under Article 14 & Fourth Amendment;

C v Donnelly **34 MAC 953 (93)**—roadblock not justified by 2-year-old letter stating that 77 OUI arrests had been made on the six-mile-long street where roadblock was set; site selection was too wholly discretionary & Commonwealth had not adhered to its own guidelines;

C v Trompert **27 MAC 804 (89)**—investigatory checks of all vehicles in highway rest area at nighttime to determine if aid needed pursuant to state police policy upheld as reasonable under Fourth Amendment; lone cop's opening door & ordering out passengers justified by D's furtive gestures plus turning off light upon cop's approach;

C v McGeoghegan **389 M 137 (83)**—roadblock for drunks must be by supervised plan, minimal inconvenience, maximum safety, some notice, & not arbitrary;

C v Murphy **454 M 318 (2009)**—roadblock conducted pursuant to "state police general order "TRF-15" did not allow "impermissible discretion" in officer to divert cars stopped to an area for further checking simply by use of word "may" rather than "must/shall" (though order has been revised to eliminate apparent grant of discretion, and now reads, "shall", fn.3); constitutional issues re: roadblocks has focused on reasonableness of *initial* stop of vehicle, which is seizure without individualized suspicion; "secondary screening" under plan here had to be based on articulable facts/reasonable suspicion, so no error; that TRF-15 did not specifically forbid questioning as to driver's intoxication was here remedied by a supplemental "operations plan" governing particular roadblock, allowing such inquiry only at the "secondary screening", possible only after reasonable articulable suspicion based on observations of the initial screening officer";

C v Swartz **454 M 330 (2009)**—same, re: import of "may" in TRF-15;

C v Amaral **398 M 98 (86)**—bad roadblock though captain set up, because no plan;

C v Trumble **396 M 81 (85)**—OK roadblock because careful plan & followed;

C v Shields **402 M 162 (88)**—roadblock OK without proof of absolute necessity;

C v Carkhuff **441 M 122 (2004)**—2 a.m. suspicionless stop of car traveling on rural road adjacent to water supply reservoir (due to fear of terrorists) not legitimate as roadblock because no plan; not legitimate as administrative "screening" search because no steps to minimize intrusiveness, i.e., prior notice that motorists = subject to stop/search;

20-N. WIRETAPS AND ELECTRONIC EAVESDROPPING

See also Chapter 20-E, above, Violations of Counsel Right;

Katz v US **389 US 347 (67)**—eavesdropping invades legitimate expectation of privacy;

18 USC §§ 2510–20, Title III—Omnibus Crime Control & Safe Streets Act ('68);

C v Damiano **444 M 444 (2005)**—18 USC § 2515 prohibits admission into evidence of any unlawfully intercepted wire or oral communications & any evidence derived therefrom; it applies to both cell phone and cordless phone conversations, and doesn't allow for a "clean hands" exception (when citizen intercepted phone conversation over police "scanner" and alerted police to possible drug deal); taint of illegality dissipated as to some evidence here;

C v Gonzalez **68 MAC 620 (2007)**—witness recorded his telephone conversation with D, not at direction of police and "not made secretly": court "agree[s] with judge's legal conclusion that the exclusionary rule ought not to be applied";

G.L. c. 272, § 99—Interception of Wire & Oral Communications;

C v Long **454 M 542 (2009)**—intentionally or recklessly OMITTED material may form basis for mounting *Franks v Delaware* challenge (citations); where omission forms basis for challenge, judge considers whether the affidavit, supplemented by the omitted info, furnishes probable cause; **where D seeks suppression of wiretap evidence based on use of "truncated excerpts" of oral recordings to establish probable cause, motion judge shall conduct de novo review of affidavit and omitted evidence pursuant to G.L. c. 272, § 99E–F, and "ordinarily need not be concerned with the *Franks* requirements";**

C v Connolly **454 M 808 (2009)**—GPS (global positioning system) installed on D's vehicle was an electronic surveillance device allowed government's use of vehicle to track movements and interfered with D's interest (including right to exclude others) notwithstanding his continued possession of it;

C v Crowley **43 MAC 919 (97)**—no suppression of tape recording made by private citizen (non-wire) of Ds beating their daughter: **G.L. c. 272, § 99P alone does not provide mechanism for suppression;**

C v Ricci **57 MAC 155 (2003)**—though state wiretap statute (G.L. c. 272, § 99) requires return to the warrant to be filed within 7 days after termination of warrant, no sup-

pression as remedy for slight delay if good faith, no tactical advantage, and no evidence that tapes have been compromised; court rejected claim of "particularity" defects in warrant (because didn't describe all persons whose communications might be intercepted), and of "minimization" requirement violation (federal wiretap statute requires wiretap seizures to be conducted so as to minimize interception of communications not targeted appropriately);

C v Ennis **439 M 64 (2003)**—audiotape recording by Department of Correction of three-way telephone conversation among house of correction inmate, criminal D and his co-D not suppressed (no willful/secret recording, no culpability, no "deterrent" purpose to be served): co-D had managed to override systems in place to prevent additional party being added to two-party conversation, and there was DOC announcement that conversation would be recorded;

C v Boyarsky **452 M 700 (2008)**—a recording made with actual knowledge of all parties is not an interception even if party has not "affirmatively authorized or consented to it"; when D made calls from jail, automated system informed party called by D that call was subject to monitoring and recording, but message did not replay if party called by D passed telephone to third person; assuming 'interception' and that D has standing, still no relief, because no willful/culpable/negligent conduct by jail; jailer's dissemination of calls to police violated no reasonable expectation of privacy;

In the Matter of a Grand Jury Subpoena **454 M 685 (2009)**—neither a pretrial jail detainee nor a convicted inmate has reasonable expectation of privacy in telephone conversations: all parties have notice that calls are subject to monitoring/recording, and penological interests justify: loss of privacy is an "inherent incident[ ] of confinement"; providing recorded calls to grand jury in response to subpoena = OK; but for monitoring/recording of conversations using "telephones in the visitation booths at the jail" (where it wasn't policy to record, and there was no warning to prisoners and visitors that conversations would be recorded) wiretap warrant was obtained, and suppression ordered on particular facts in *C v Long* **454 M 542 (2009)**;

C v Barboza **54 MAC 99 (2002)**—no suppression of tape recordings of telephone conversations between D & rape V when recordings were made by V's father without consent of either D or V; recordings didn't violate Federal wiretap statute, 18 USC §§ 2510 et seq., since parent was acting to protect his minor child from sexual exploitation by D;

C v Penta **423 M 546 (96)**—informant wearing "wire" to transmit to police his conversations with D; police obtained warrant to receive & record but authorization/request was not pursuant to G.L. c. 272, § 99F; held: § 99B4 exemption applied (1 party consent **and** purportedly involving "organized crime") AND "wired party" situation can be authorized under G.L. c. 276, no violation of Article 14;

C v Abdul-Kareem **56 MAC 78 (2002)**—cops obtained "regular" warrant under G.L. c. 276, rather than electronic surveillance warrant (under G.L. c. 272, §§ 99F–M), but electronic surveillance evidence OK under § 99B4, because one party (police informant) consented, and investigation was for one or more "designated offenses" in § 99B4, and organized crime connection was "adequately suggested" by informant's description of D's desire to kill one target and shoot another in the knees, D's plan to supply informant with gun, silencer, car, and airline ticket, etc., "suggesting that [D] was not acting alone but was drawing on other resources," supplying inference of "discipline and organization";

C v Vitello **367 M 224 (75)**—purposes of Title III, e.g., MINIMUM, not maximum standards; though not in G.L. c. 272, state must execute warrant forthwith & minimize innocent talk intercepted (like Title III);

C v Rodriguez **450 M 302 (2007)**—exigent circumstances excused absence of wiretap warrant when cops placed electronic monitoring and recording device in arrested person's pocket to substantiate his story that D was to come and retrieve package containing cocaine which police had just "control-delivered" to arrested person's address (cops **had** obtained an anticipatory search warrant for the address beforehand);

G.L. c. 271, § 17B—upon reasonable grounds to believe telephone is being used for unlawful purpose, AG or DA may demand from telephone company records relating to service;

C v Feodoroff **43 MAC 725 (97)**—D had no reasonable expectation of privacy in her telephone billing records obtained by prosecutor under G.L. c. 271, § 17B; **might** be different result (suppression) if prosecutor lacked "reasonable grounds" under § 17B; Court might be receptive to more thorough 1st Amendment argument;

C v Vinnie **428 M 161 (98)**—telephone's use "for the unlawful purpose of fabricating an alibi" ("thin" ground, but accepted as justification for obtaining records under G.L. c. 271, § 17B);

C v Jarabek **384 M 293 (81)**—joint federal-state investigation governed by c. 272, so suppress because no warrant, no consent, & not shown "organized crime"; (but live testimony of party = OK);

C v D'Amour **428 M 725 (99)**—wiretap warrant obtainable only on probable cause that "organized crime" was involved, but flimsy showing here didn't matter to

SJC (murder V's wife & her paramour suspected with perhaps 3d party);

C v Long **454 M 542 (2009)**—at the very least, must be an organized plan from which one reasonably may infer existence of ongoing criminal operation to "supply illegal goods and services"; prosecution's theory here was merely that D committed murder, unmotivated by pecuniary interest, and that D was purportedly trying to get friends to help cover up evidence of his involvement: "entire alleged conspiracy revolved around a single, albeit heinous, crime motivated by revenge", because no nexus to "organized crime" as defined, suppression proper;

C v Terzian **61 MAC 739 (2004)**—one-party consent OK (with G.L. c. 276, § 1 warrant: see G.L. c. 272, § 99 B 4) to conversations party had with attorney who was purportedly attempting to solicit perjury regarding party's testimony concerning criminal culpability of third person: "organized crime" nexus findable "where the nature of the crime involved lends itself to the inference of organization and discipline involving more than two parties"; distinguishes *Jarabek* **384 M 293 (81)**, in which police were certain that kickback scheme involved only two municipal officers;

C v Gonzalez **426 M 313 (97)**—federal agents, in **federal** investigation (though local police assisted with info & surveillance) acted in violation of G.L. c. 272, § 99, but turned over to state the evidence because drug amounts too low to warrant federal prosecution—federal officer exemption to § 99 applied: no suppression and Article 14 didn't apply to these federal agents' action either;

C v Wilcox **63 MAC 131, 139, further appellate review allowed 444 M 1103 (2005)**—D's interview at police station was videotaped without his knowledge and consent, and disclosed prior convictions and sexual fantasies, but because tape was recorded in Rhode Island, GL c. 272, § 99 didn't prohibit; tape was introduced in probation revocation hearing; **on further review**, SJC did not mention or address issue of videotape, but affirmed revocation of probation, **446 M 61 (2006);**

C v Look **379 M 893, cert. denied 449 US 827 (80)**—D's incriminating statements to police officer in interrogation room at police station were overheard by other officers through intercom system, & were reported to state police officers who questioned D and testified at trial: SJC rejected D's argument that evidence derived from the overheard statements should have been suppressed because of "unlawful interception" through intercom system;

C v Pierce **66 MAC 283 (2006)**—D's conversations with his confederates as they were in separate but nearby cells at police station were overheard by officer at front desk via audio-visual intercom system in place for "security"/safety of both prisoners and police; no error in admitting D's overheard admissions; court assumed without deciding that this was "interception" (but maybe not because it wouldn't have been "secret" that there was surveillance), but this was an office intercommunication system which was an exception to illegality under G.L.

c. 272, § 99D(1), particularly in light of G.L. c. 40, § 36B (which mandated that at least one cell within any lockup facility shall have installed within it an electronic audio system "whereby a police officer . . . is brought within audible range of such cell");

C v Morganti **455 M 388 (2009)**—arrested in CA on fugitive from justice MA warrant, D was video/audio-taped in interview room as he was alone, making telephone call to female: no suppression, as D was told police *intended* to record what was said in interview room (though had not told D that recorder was actually operatin), and [additional] telephone recording similarly OK as D was aware that he was subject to monitoring/recording, AND D repeated the only materially incriminating statement after cop was in room, listening, & D was still on phone;

C v Thorpe **384 M 271 (81)**—warrantless, but DA shows "reasonable suspicion" they'd find "organized crime";

C v Mejia **64 MAC 238 (2005)**—similar, with one-party consent; wiretap statute is not solely a "Mafia busting tool"; kidnapping and extortion crimes adequately imply possibility of "organized" crime; activation of caller ID function thus lawfully obtained;

Dalia v US **441 US 238 (79)**—covert entry OK; but see G.L. c. 272, § 99F: application must specify;

C v Blood **400 M 61 (87)**—**no ONE-PARTY consent in MA** (but see *US v Caceres* **440 US 741 (79)** "Neither the Constitution nor any Act of Congress requires that official approval be secured before conversations are overheard or recorded by Government agents with the consent of one of the conversants.");

DA v Coffey **386 M 218 (82)**—cross-frame unit to trace annoying calls was phone company, not state action; but could violate G.L. c. 272 (but didn't);

US v NYTEL **434 US 159 (77)**—penregister tracing #'s not an interception;

Smith v Maryland **442 US 735 (79)**—penregister not a search within Fourth Amendment;

DA v NET **379 M 586 (80)**—cross-frame unit tracing #'s not interception within federal law, but installation governed by G.L. c. 272; (maybe search under Declaration of Rights, Article 14)

C v Westerman **414 M 688 (93)**—valid warrant authorizing wiretap of a telephone line permits installation of **cross-frame unit trap (to record telephone #s of incoming calls to the telephone line under surveillance**); cc. opinion of Liacos, J, asserts privacy rights of the incoming caller & **standing** if necessary;

Crosland v Horgan **401 M 271 (87)**—hospital secretary listening to extension phone (at cop's request) for bomb threatener = G.L. c. 272, § 99 ordinary business, no eavesdrop;

C v Vieux **41 MAC 526 (96)**—rape complainant's sister listening on extension phone, hearing D's comment after he believed line was hung up, = ordinary business; no

suppression/no violation (if recording device had been used by sister, possibly different);

C v Eason **427 M 595 (98)**—at police behest, D's friend telephoned D and elicited from him statements about a crime, as cops listened to the conversation on an extension telephone & recorded it: D held to have had no reasonable expectation that no one would be listening on an extension; **recording**, however, not admissible, & possible further relief if cop "relied on a recording in presenting his testimony";

C v Picardi **401 M 1008 (88)**—though no timely motion to suppress, G.L. c. 272, § 99 bars eavesdrop evidence because no service on D of documents and copies of intercepted conversations at least 30 days before trial;

C v Rodriguez **67 MAC 636 (2006)**—but without motion to suppress, D "nonetheless must direct the judge to the provision in some manner", and **S.C. on further appellate review, 450 M 302, 309 (2007)**—D must object on some specific ground in order to "put to test" the Commonwealth on particular provision of the wiretap act, e.g., here, although prosecutor was required to provide D with transcript of intercepted conversation or sworn statement as to conversation overheard, in accord with G.L. c. 272, § 99 O2, trooper testified to his recollection of it in rebuttal without complying with mandated procedure (and SJC says no substantial risk of miscarriage of justice);

C v Fini **403 M 567 (88)**—to deter cops, can't use bad eavesdrop evidence to impeach D on stand, BUT fink can tell it live; (*see Chapter 20-B, Fruits*);

C v Fenderson **410 M 82 (91)**—informant's refusal to introduce agents to D for fear of reprisals, impossibility of undetected visual surveillance, & unsuccessful searches of D's telephone records & garbage, properly established that "normal investigative procedures" would fail;

C v Gordon **422 M 816 (96)**—taping of Ds at booking was, technically, electronic surveillance conducted without Ds' knowledge (and G.L. c. 272, § 99P, technically, mandates suppression), but no relief when tape admitted at trial, relevant to sobriety at time of crimes; SJC believed legislature intended Act to cover "surreptitious eavesdropping as an investigative tool";

C v Santoro **406 M 421 (90)**—suppression of unconsented-to tapes of D's telephone conversations by private party in violation of G.L. c. 272, § 99, not required;

C v Barboza **54 MAC 99 (2002)**—recordings of two telephone conversations between child under sixteen and D, made by child's father without the consent of either party, with purpose of protecting child from sexual exploitation by D, didn't have to be suppressed: no state action was involved in the recording so no deterrent purpose would be served by suppression;

C v Cote **407 M 827 (90)**—D has no expectation of privacy in messages left with 3d party's answering service; *C v Blood* **400 M 61 (87)** distinguished;

C v Rodriguez **67 MAC 636, further appellate review allowed (2006)**—though in *C v Blood*, 400 M 61, SJC held that one-party-consent to recording in private home didn't defeat expectation of privacy by close associate/friend that what was said would not become more widely known (such that warrant = required), present case held different because D engaged in arm's length business transaction with home resident (& "consenter") he had hired to sign for/receive package containing drug, so no reasonable expectation of privacy, citing *Price* 408 M 668, 672–73 & *Collado* 42 MAC 464, 469; <u>on further review, SJC at 450 M 302, 308 (2007) does NOT adopt this holding</u>, **but "assume[s], without deciding, that [D] had a reasonable expectation of privacy in the private home in which [witness] was staying. See *C v Blood*, [400 M at 68]"**;

C v Benoit **410 M 506 (91)**—although tape of murder D's voluntary phone statements properly suppressed because unconsented-to, testimony of phone operator about statements was admissible.

C v Anguilo **415 M 502 (93)**—under G.L. c. 272, § 99(O)(I), when prosecution intends to offer in evidence any **portion** of wire interceptions, D must be served with copy of **all** recordings made; because this interception was authorized/made by **federal** court/government, discovery provision was inapplicable (though D did receive copies of all the tapes which Commonwealth intended to use in evidence);

C v Collazo **34 MAC 79 (93)**—undercover cop/drug "buyer" wearing wire, which transmitted to backup officers & provided probable cause to seize drugs & defendants; though warrantless "wire" was improper, only remedy = exclusion of testimony of officers who listened to it;

C v Alves **414 M 1006 (93)**—wiretap intercepted private marital conversations between D and wife, then these were used in obtaining a second wiretap warrant; SJC held that probable cause for 2d warrant existed without considering the marital conversations;

Chapter 21
ANALYZING ELEMENTS OF COMMON CRIMES

21-A. IN GENERAL

G.L. c. 277, § 79—form complaints & indictments *(See Chapter 6, Contents of Complaints & Indictments)*; **CPCS P/G 6.6 (a)**—research elements of each charge for (defenses);

Nolan and Sartorio, *Criminal Law* **(3d ed. 2001)**— cf. encyclopedias, e.g., Wharton's Criminal Law; C.J.S.; LaFave & Scott, Substantive Criminal Law (1986 & pocket parts); Perkins & Boyce, Criminal Law, etc; cf.

District Court "Model Jury Instructions" (updated '97) CAUTION: **MODEL JURY INSTRUCTIONS ARE NOT NECESSARILY CORRECT, BEYOND REPROACH, GOOD LAW, OR LOGICAL! DON'T FOLLOW THEM UNTHINKINGLY!** SEE, e.g. . . .

C v Juvenile **396 M 215 (85)**—criticizes Model Jury Instruction on reasonable doubt;

C v Connolly **394 M 169 (85)**—tips Model Jury Instruction on operating under the influence;

C v Munoz **384 M 503 (81)**—Model Jury Instruction on uninsured motor vehicle = "improper";

C v Peruzzi **15 MAC 437 (83)**—Model Jury Instruction on malicious destruction of property = "flawed";

C v Teixera **396 M 746 (86)**—Model Jury Instruction on non-support flawed; (but D asked for it);

C v Juvenile **27 MAC 78 (89)**—Model Jury Instruction requiring prove D's age is unnecessary;

C v Cavallaro **25 MAC 605 (88)**—Model Jury Instruction OK, but didn't explain case's issue;

C v Collier **427 M 385 (98)**—Model Jury Instruction re violating protective order didn't allow resolution of critical issue (intent): reversal despite no objection;

C v Kushner **43 MAC 918 (97)**—noting that model jury instruction on assault by dangerous weapon (immedi-

ately - threatened battery - type) was held erroneous in *Musgrave* **38 MAC 519, S.C., 421 M 610 (96)**;

C v Hinds **450 M 1 (2007)**—first degree murder convictions reversed due to erroneous instruction that expert's opinion must be disregarded unless jurors first find that facts assumed by witness in reaching opinion were "proved by Commonwealth beyond a reasonable doubt": expert opinion at issue was that of defense witness, as to D's criminal responsibility; *Superior Court Criminal Practice Jury Instructions* (MCLE 1999) § 4.7.1 = reproduced at fn.6, "but this instruction also may have its problems";

See also Chapter 16, Defenses, e.g., strict construction; (e.g. C v Clay **65 MAC 215 (2005)**) *Chapter 2 re: Perjury, Intimidate Witness, Obstruct Justice;*

See Chapter 5 for cases on complaints & indictments, variances, lesser included offenses, jurisdictional defects & statutes of limitations;

See Chapter 12-G for cases on required findings;

See Chapter 16 for cases on common defenses;

C v A Juvenile **27 MAC 78 (89)**—Commonwealth not required to prove age unless D introduces evidence D not a juvenile because age not an element of delinquency;

Model Penal Code (copy reproduced in LaFave and Scott, Substantive Criminal Law (1986), Appendix A;

21-B. ASSAULTS AND BATTERIES

G.L. c. 265, § 13A, etc.; & G.L. c. 277, § 79—form complaints); See also affray (G.L. c. 277, §§ 39, 79; G.L. c. 279, § 5); see Nolan and Sartorio, Criminal Law (3d ed. 2001), Chapter 14 (including simple and aggravated assaults);

District Court Model Jury Instructions 5.40–402 (See Chapter 21-A);

Superior Court Criminal Practice Jury Instructions §§ 2.21 et seq.;

G.L. c. 265, § 13C—assault and battery for purposes of collecting a loan: *C v Thompson* **56 MAC 710 (2002)**—G gave victim drugs with understanding that victim would sell drugs & give part of proceeds to G; when victim used drugs but didn't give G money, D and G confronted V about the money owed, & D beat up victim; evidence sufficient for G, because advancing person property on understanding that it will be paid for at later date = loan;

21-B.1. "Battery": Two theories— Intentional OR Wanton/Reckless; (N.B.—Confusion Re: "Intent" Needed and Touchings Not "Assaultive")

C v McCan **277 M 199 (31)**—"intentional & unjustified use of force, however slight," upon person of another;

C v Welch **16 MAC 271 (83)**— . . . OR, intentional act (general intent) willful, wanton, & reckless in nature, AND causes "personal INJURY";

C v Garofalo **46 MAC 191, 193 (99)**—error in instruction that it wasn't necessary that D intended to touch V, but only necessary that he intentionally did the act which resulted in the touching, as opposed to having done it accidentally: "intentional and unjustified use of force" type of battery DOES require proof of specific intent to touch; Commonwealth need not prove that D intended to use purportedly dangerous weapon "in a dangerous fashion" (here D allegedly hit V in face with candleholder); *C v Mitchell* **67 MAC 556 (2006)**—same error, but no objection & on evidence here, no substantial risk of miscarriage of justice;

C v Burno **396 M 622 (86)**—(same); "injury" must interfere with health or comfort, not be transient/trifling; if hit complaining witness's car, it may be extension of person & battery on complaining witness;

C v Medina **43 MAC 534 (97)**—reversal for failure of jury instructions to require that unintentional was wanton/reckless and caused injury (assault & battery on police officer case);

C v Moore **36 MAC 455 (94)**—same;

C v Broderick **16 MAC 941 (83)**—reckless shooting injury;

C v LeBlanc **3 MAC 780 (75)**—hit by car door; was "intentional";

C v McIntosh **56 MAC 827 (2002)**—D who punched and broke window pane, causing physical injury to two people on other side who were cut by flying glass was guilty of assault & battery by means of dangerous weapon regardless of whether act was intentional or reckless;

C v Appleby **380 M 296 (80)**—no injury needed for ABDW; also discusses A & B, ADW; ABDW = general intent only (see E, below);

C v Malone **114 M 295 (1873)**—intoxication no defense *(cf. Chapter 16, Defenses: Intent)*;

C v Ordway **12 Cush 270 (1853)**—need intent to injure, or at least touch, when snatch (bank-note) - see Richards, etc. below;

C v Ruggles **6 Allen 588 (1863)**—need intent to injure (cited in Appleby, above); accident & inadvertence also defenses; *(See Chapter 16)*;

C v Hagenlock **140 M 125 (1885)**—intent to injure = proven (but necessary?);

C v De La Cruz **15 MAC 52 (82)**—"force & violence" not necessary (citing Appleby) where unconsented fondling by doctor;

C v Burke **390 M 480 (83)**—touching must be either "harmful" (or likely), or "offensive" because unconsented; *(See Chapter 21-C, below)*; 6A C.J.S., A & B § 71: intent to injure "ordinarily is essential"; vs. . . .

Wharton Crim.L. (14th) § 178—"immaterial if D didn't intend to harm"; See also Nolan and Sartorio, Criminal Law (3d ed. 2001) § 322; (Series of blows = single event? see *C v Hogan* **7 MAC 236 (79)**; (aff'd, but SJC casts doubt, 379 M 190 (79))

21-B.2. "Assault"

Either: (a) attempted battery ("bodily harm"); or (b) (objectively) put in fear of battery by conduct; not words alone—

C v Gorassi **432 M 244 (2000)**—under attempted battery form of assault, "attempt to inflict psychological harm" is NOT assault, and V's apprehension of, or fear created by, attempt is immaterial to whether assault occurred;

C v Slaney **345 M 135 (62)**—complaining witness's fear (or awareness) irrelevant to (a); inability irrelevant to (b);

C v Chambers **57 MAC 47 (2003)**—required findings of not guilty on two of four indictments for assault by means of dangerous weapon, where jury didn't specify whether attempted battery or threatened battery was involved: two of the four occupants of car into which D drove his car were not aware of the impending hit before it occurred;

C v Werner **73 MAC 97 (2008)**—"assault" readily inferable when D entered 15-year-old victim's apartment against her pleas (at 10 p.m. when she was home alone with infant) and threatened to kill all in house as result of victim's father's debt, saying that he knew sleeping places of all household members, and implying prior violence against other victims; additional "assault" in dwelling presented when D stood on porch but his hand or arm crossed into threshold of dwelling to touch victim's face with handgun as she stood just inside screen door (these hold-

ings = context of G.L. c. 265, § 18A, armed assault in dwelling); see also *C v Doucette* **430 M 461 (99)**—dwelling house includes secured common hallways;

C v Kushner **43 MAC 918 (97)**—omission of intent element in assault by means of dangerous weapon/ "immediately threatened battery type" = reversal (D must have intended to cause V fear or apprehension of immediate harm);

C v Spencer **40 MAC 919 (96)**—same; failure to **answer** jury question re whether it necessary that D intend to put person in fear or "simply the person's scared";

C v Cowans **52 MAC 811, 819 (2001)**—reversal for charge that 'mere entry of house with weapon in hand is sufficient to trigger the assault aspect of' armed home invasion (G.L. c. 265, § 18C); Commonwealth must instead prove that D engaged in 'objectively menacing conduct with intent to put the victim in fear of immediate bodily harm";

C v White **110 M 407 (1872)**—conditional threat vs. present assault;

C v Richards **363 M 299, 303 (73)**—robbery = different: victim must be aware of attempted battery ("Slaney . . . has dubious bearing on robbery"); *(See Nolan and Sartorio, Criminal Law (3d ed. 2001) § 286 & Chapter 21-H)*;

C v Delgado **367 M 432 (75)**—"informational words" (threat to shoot) took place of acts for assault (re: robbery);

C v Ramos **6 MAC 955 (78)**—tug-of-war over money is "assault" for assault with intent to rob;

C v Appleby **380 M 296 (80)**—assault by dangerous weapon & A&B by dangerous weapon maybe lesser intent than assault (See also "Threats," § HH below);

C v Porro **74 MAC 676, further app. review allowed 455 M 1106 (2009)**—in responding to deliberating jury's question whether D could be convicted on "lesser" offense of assault by means of dangerous weapon on indictment charging assault and battery by means of dangerous weapon, judge said yes, but committed reversible error in failing to limit jury's consideration on the charge to the one act on which grand jury relied; MAC permitted retrial on lesser included offense of assault by means of dangerous weapon under "attempted battery theory" (noting at n.4 that "it is less clear" that "threatened battery theory" of assault by means of dangerous weapon is a lesser included of ABDW);

21-B.3. Acknowledgement of Satisfaction (Accord and Satisfaction)

G.L. c. 276, § 55—A&B & other misdemeanors (not A&B on police officer); complaining witness files, judge "can" discharge;

C v Dowdican's Bail **115 M 133 (1874)**—judge's discretion re: accord & satisfaction;

C v Gonzalez **388 M 865, 867, n.4 (83)**—private benefit can't defeat public interest; improper for serious felony (reduce rape to A & B);

C v Guzman **446 M 344 (2006)**—accord and satisfaction statute (G.L. c. 276, § 55) upheld against DA's challenge that it violated "separation of powers" clause (Art. 30) (context = "domestic" A&B);

Nolan and Sartorio, *Criminal Law* **(3d ed. 2001) § 618, n.5;**

G.L. c. 268, § 13B—intimidate witness: offer something to "influence"; as of 3/3/2006, includes conduct that "threatens, or attempts or causes . . . emotional injury";

See Chapter 2-H, Standards/Ethics for Defense Counsel: obstruction of justice/influencing witness & Chapter 14-B, Dispositions: Dismissal re: accord & satisfaction ethical issues, influencing witnesses, etc.;

C v Ferguson **30 MAC 580 (91)**—should have instructed on disproving accident because int. to touch had to be proven;

21-C. JUSTIFICATIONS, E.G., CONSENT

See Chapter 16, Defenses, re: Accident, Self-Defense, Necessity, Defense of Property, Defense of Another, & Making Lawful Arrest;

Nolan and Sartorio, *Criminal Law* **(3d ed. 2001) § 322**—urban & suburban life involve jostling, pushing, & shouting; somewhat "offensive" but justified if not excessive (quoted in *Appleby* **380 M 296 (80)** instructions to jury (n.4));

C v Burke **390 M 480 (83)**—(maybe) consent defense if touching not harmful;

C v Simmons **8 MAC 713 (79)**—patient implies consent to normal treatment;

In re Spring **8 MAC 831 (79)**—(rev'd other ground 380 M 629) without consent or emergency, medical treatment's a battery;

C v Coffey **121 M 66 (1876)**—dad went too far in moving ill child;

C v Appleby **380 M 296, 310–11**—consent irrelevant to ABDW;

C v Blache **450 M 583 (2008)**—context of sexual assault, jury instruction regarding complainant's capacity to consent despite intoxication;

21-D. ASSAULT AND BATTERY ON POLICE AND OTHER PUBLIC OFFICERS

Assault & Battery On Police & Other Public Officers —engaged in performance of duty (G.L. c. 265, § 13D & § 13I)):

C v McCrohan **34 MAC 277 (93)**—cop was performing his duty when he accompanied adjacent town's cop to interview suspect in adjacent town: there was a "mutual aid" agreement between the two towns' police departments invoked by request in this case;

21-D.1. Knowledge by D that Complaining Witness Is Officer, Otherwise A&B

C v Sawyer **142 M 530 (1886)**; *C v Kirby* **2 Cush 577 (1849)**; *C v Moore* **36 MAC 455 (94)**—must prove D knew V to be cop engaged in performance of his duties; intoxication is factor to be considered re: whether prosecution has proved intent/knowledge beyond a reasonable doubt;

21-D.2. Intend to Strike Cop, Otherwise A&B

C v Rosario **13 MAC 920 (82)**—but see *C v Correia* **50 MAC 455, 456 (2000)** "recklessness" theory of A&B held OK in prosecution for A&B on public employee here: D, a prisoner, kicked and flailed arms while struggling against being placed into cell;

21-D.3. Resistance If "Mere Trespasser" (Unlawful Arrest)?

C v Moreira **388 M 596 (83)**—if know police officer is performing duty, no right to resist unless police use excessive force; "disposition of the case depends on the application of the rules pertaining to self-defense";

C v Urkiel **63 MAC 445 (2005)**—while warrantless entry of D's home was unconstitutional (because it was for misdemeanor not committed in presence of police and/or because no exigent circumstances) & arrest was thus "bad," and *Gomes* **59 MAC 332 (2003)** establishes that such unlawful entry isn't a defense to charge of resisting arrest, D had legitimate **self-defense** claim on facts here, & judge erred in assuming it inapplicable;

C v Williams **53 MAC 719, 723 (2002)**—concepts of excessive force & self-defense are closely related;

C v Graham **62 MAC 642 (2004)**—D was entitled to instruction on self-defense on charges of resisting arrest and assault and battery on police officer; instruction given below suggested incorrectly that D had burden of establishing that police used excessive force, that D defended 'self with reasonable force," and that he resisted arrest using such reasonable force as was necessary to resist "excessive" force by police; instead, judge must charge that Commonwealth must prove beyond reasonable doubt that police did not engage in excessive force, as well as that D didn't act in self-defense; "gist of" instruction given, id. at 654, n.7;

C v Montes **49 MAC 789 (2000)**—right to resist arrest was abolished in Moreira, w/exception for situation in which excessive force is used in making arrest; further, "there is little evidence that a common-law right ever inhered in third parties to assist another in resisting an unlawful arrest"; even if there was unlawful arrest ongoing, third parties had no "standing" to vicariously assert violation of the arrestee's 4th Amendment rights; "defense of others" defense not available here because no right to resist even an unlawful arrest (unless evidence demonstrated 'excessive force,' and appellate court claimed that here, it did not);

C v Kuyamjian **18 MAC 680 (84)**—no wrongdoing by complaining witness (deputy sheriff)

C v Kiser **48 MAC 647 (2000)**—complaint of loud party prompted cops to knock on apartment door, but after D opened door and responded "yeah, OK" to request to turn down music, cops couldn't push on through (because they knew him to be a gang member, because an unidentified person ran across the room behind him, and because D pushed them back when they tried to lean into room for better view); D entitled to use reasonable force against intrusion if cop is attempting illegal entry;

21-D.4. G.L. c. 276, § 33 Police Duty to Examine D for Injuries

See Chapter 3, Police Station; Chapter 6, Discovery;

G.L. c. 233, § 79—hospital records exception to hearsay rule; *(See Chapter 11-F);*

Eldredge v Mitchell **214 M 480 (13)**—(booking) photo (of injured D) authenticated w/o photographer if fair & accurate

21-D.5. 21-D.5. RESISTING ARREST (G.L. c. 268, § 32b)

C v Grandison **433 M 135, 146 (2001)**—since D was arrested out on street, obstreperous behavior at station during booking could not be basis for "resisting arrest" conviction; *C v Katykhin* **59 MAC 261 (2003)**—D's standing rigidly, refusing to bend to enter police cruiser after arrest = legitimate basis for 'resisting arrest' conviction; though "purely passive conduct not involving the use or threat of force or violence, such as that characteristic of nonviolent protestors" was distinguished; *C v Smith* **55 MAC 569 (2002)**—D's flight from cops' attempt at investigative stop pursuant to *Terry v. Ohio* (which included refusing four orders to stop, & D's riding of bike toward cop, & D's being knocked off bike & pepper-sprayed) is NOT basis for "resisting arrest"; *C v Pagan* **63 MAC 780 (2005)**—required finding of not guilty of resisting arrest when plainclothes cop was "in the process of restraining [D] in order to conduct a protective patfrisk," rather than of arresting D;

C v Lender **66 MAC 303 (2006)**—distinguishing *Pagan* [63 MAC 780] and *Smith* [55 MAC 569] on ground

that here, D resisted not only cop's initial attempt to pat frisk him but also cop's efforts to cuff him and place him in cruiser;

C v Grant **71 MAC 205 (2008)**—D fled at sight of police cruiser & though cops had arrest warrant and intended to effect arrest, this was not communicated to D by words or actions as he fled (notwithstanding fact that several cops were chasing and following D in lengthy chase over 8-foot tall fences): required finding of not guilty on resisting arrest;

C v Vanya V **75 MAC 370 (2009)**—distinguishing Smith, above: cop told juvenile, at first struggle, that he was under arrest (though he had not initially intended to arrest juvenile for trespassing at high school and had intended only to drive juvenile home to parents, after 'policy' pat-frisk before letting juvenile ride in cruiser;

C v Knight **75 MAC 735 (2009)**—citing *C v Ocasio* 71 MAC 304, 306, 311 (2008) & *C v Katykhin* 59 MAC 262 (2003), "arrest" wasn't "complete" when D was ordered out of car or even when he was handcuffed (so that "resisting arrest" conviction was upheld on basis of behavior occurring until he was placed in cruiser);

C v Quintos Q, a juvenile **73 MAC 828 (2009) & 457 MAC 107 (2010)**—though D was passenger in car pursued by police with lights and sirens, and fled on foot after car crashed, cop then chasing on foot yelling "stop, police", Appeals Court holds no evidence of "objective communication . . . that officers were attempting to" arrest (rather than traffic stop) & no evidence D understood such intent (D 'was simply running away'); further, circumstances of flight didn't expose pursuers to substantial risk of bodily injury;

C v Montoya **73 MAC 125 (2008) & 457 MAC 102 (2010)**—"arrest" was, at latest, when (after pursuing D for some time following observation of him firing gun) officers confronted D and ordered him to raise arms: D's subsequent flight and jumping into canal 25 feet below = sufficient for resisting arrest, circumstances of *this* flight exposing cops to substantial risk of bodily injury (even though they did not follow him into canal);

C v Maylott **65 MAC 466 (2006)**—D's "stiffening his arms" and refusing to place his hands behind his back to be handcuffed held sufficient as element (G.L. c. 268, § 32B) of "using . . . physical force or violence against the police officer or . . . using any other means which creates a substantial risk of causing bodily injury to such police officer": "it took four officers to handcuff [D]";

21-D.6. Cross-Complaint

See Chapter 3;

See also Chapter 14, Dispositions: Dismissal, re: coercing D to sign a civil release;

21-D.7. Police Officer's Liability for "Excessive Force"

Kiser **48 MAC 647 (2000)**—complaint of loud party prompted cops to knock on apartment door, but after D opened door and responded "yeah, OK" to request to turn down music, cops couldn't push on through (because they knew him to be a gang member, because an unidentified person ran across the room behind him, and because D pushed them back when they tried to lean into room for better view); D entitled to use reasonable force against intrusion if cop is attempting illegal entry; above

G.L. c. 263, § 3—assisting police officers liable only for excessive force;

Eldredge v Mitchell **214 M 480 (13)**—(booking) photo (of injured D) authenticated without photographer if fair & accurate;

Powers v Sturtevant **199 M 265 (08)**; *C v Klein* **372 M 823 (77)**—force to arrest;

C v Martin **369 M 640 (76)**; *Human Rts. Comm'n v Assad* **370 M 482 (76)**—police officer's G. though D also G.;

Delaney v Dias **415 FS 1351 (D.Ma. '76)**—42 U.S.C. § 1983 action;

Aetma v Niziolek **395 M 737 (85)**—G finding conclusive vs. D in later civil suit; G plea's later admissible, not conclusive

C v Montes **49 MAC 789 (2000)**—no right to resist even unlawful arrest, unless cops using excessive force (and thus no right to 'defend' person being arrested, with same qualification);

C v Moore **28 MAC 979 (90)**—G.L. c. 127, § 38B (A&B on correctional officer, with sentence of up to ten years, to run from & after other sentences being served) applies to pretrial detainees as well as to sentenced "prisoners"; cf. Superior Court Criminal Jury Instructions § 3.6.3(k) & (l)

21-E. ASSAULT AND BATTERY BY MEANS OF DANGEROUS WEAPON (G.L. C. 265, § 15A)—"ABDW"

District Court Model Jury Instruction #5.401;

Superior Court Criminal Practice Jury Instructions § 2.22;

See Chapter 21-B, "assault" case law, including requisite intent, ante.;

G.L. c. 265, § 15A(d)—ABDW causing "serious bodily injury" defined as bodily injury which results in permanent disfigurement, loss or impairment of a bodily function, limb or organ, or a substantial risk of death;

C v Baro **73 MAC 218 (2008)**—permanent "impairment" not required (permanent modifies only "disfigurement" in § 15A(d)); *C v Jean-Pierre* **65 MAC 162 (2005)**—"serious" injury needn't be "permanent under G.L. c. 265, §§ 13A(c) and 15A(d);

C v Manning **6 MAC 430 (78)**—must be "BY USE OF a dangerous weapon";

C v Washington **15 MAC 378 (83)**—no joint venture without knowledge of co-D's dangerous weapon & shared intent to use;

C v Davis **10 MAC 190 (80)**—human teeth (& body parts) not "dangerous weapon";

C v Appleby **380 M 296 (80)**—(a) "riding crop" = dangerous weapon because intentionally used for, & capable of causing, serious bodily harm (case-by-case question); (b) if dangerous weapon, need only general intent to touch (not to injure); (c) no consent to ABDW;

C v Delaney **442 M 604 (2004)**—small "utility" or "pocket" knife isn't dangerous weapon per se, as it isn't designed for purpose of bodily assault or defense (so instruction that "knife" was dangerous weapon = error, but no objection means no relief here);

C v Ford **424 M 709 (97)**—where judge gave only the "intentional" touching theory to jury, error to instruct that Commonwealth need prove only that D intentionally did the act which resulted in touching, Commonwealth had to prove beyond a reasonable doubt that D "intended to commit ABDW, and having intended to commit the assault did touch V with dangerous weapon";

C v Garofalo **46 MAC 191, 193 (99)**—same, plus holding that Commonwealth need not prove that D intended to use purportedly dangerous weapon "in a dangerous fashion" (here D allegedly hit V in face with candleholder);

C v Porro **74 MAC 676, further app. review allowed 455 M 1106 (2009)**—in responding to deliberating jury's question whether D could be convicted on "lesser" offense of assault by means of dangerous weapon on indictment charging assault and battery by means of dangerous weapon, judge said yes, but committed reversible error in failing to limit jury's consideration on the charge to the one act on which grand jury relied; MAC permitted retrial on lesser included offense of assault by means of dangerous weapon under "attempted battery theory" (noting at n.4 that "it is less clear" that "threatened battery theory" of assault by means of dangerous weapon is a lesser included of ABDW);

C v Dreyer **18 MAC 562 (84)**—any "force"; no "specific" intent required for the A&B; but need intent USE item as dangerous weapon; but see *C v Kushner* **43 MAC 918 (97)** if A&B in ABDW is the "immediately-threatened battery type," Commonwealth must prove D's intent to cause V fear/apprehension of immediate harm;

C v Musgrave **421 M 610 (95)**—approving *S.C.* **38 MAC 519, 524–25 (95)**—"menacing conduct" type of assault = action "intended or calculated to make (alleged victim) fearful or apprehensive of bodily harm or as conscious & voluntary action reasonably supporting an inference of such intention" (D here said he was trying to get rid of inoperable pellet pistol by pushing it down his pants leg);

C v Tarrant **367 M 411 (75)**—dog as dangerous weapon; *C v Fettes* **64 MAC 917 (2005)**—rejecting D's argument for required finding of not guilty on purported basis that evidence failed to establish that D deliberately provoked dog to attack victim or acted recklessly by intentionally releasing grip on leash: these were questions of fact for jury;

C v Farrell **322 M 606, 615 (48)**—lighted cigarette as dangerous weapon;

C v Lednum **75 MAC 722 (2009)**—natural gas line inside house uncapped and turned on by D, D knowing people asleep inside house = dangerous weapon; D's actions fit within either definition of "assault" (attempted battery or threatened battery);

C v Barrett **12 MAC 1001 (81): SJC 386 M 649** (82)—aerosol-type spray was jury question (complaining witness driving a car);

C v Cruzado **73 MAC 803 (2009)**— gas station employee saw fellow employee's car being driven away and pursued it, ripping open driver's door, hanging onto door and inside of the car's roof as D accelerated and tried with hands to push employee off, victim eventually jumping off: sufficient for ABDW, rejecting argument that victim brought himself into contact with car;

C v Lord **55 MAC 265 (2002)**—mace, sprayed from can, = "dangerous per se" because "designed for the sole purpose of bodily assault or defense & . . . constructed to inflict serious bodily harm through incapacitation" (& D here used it in such manner);

C v Davis **10 MAC 190 (80)**—shoe, not foot, is the dangerous weapon for "shod foot";

C v Rumkin **55 MAC 635 (2002)**—testimony only that D was "kicking" driver's side door of car where driver was seated, "booting" the car = insufficient evidence of dangerous weapon, because no evidence about type of footwear or whether it was used in dangerous fashion;

Appleby **380 M 296 (80)**—definition (& instructions) re: dangerous weapon;

C v Turner **59 MAC 825 (2003)**—straight knives are generally dangerous per se, but folding knives, "at least those without a locking device," typically are not; required finding of not guilty on c. 269, § 10(b) charge (re: possession of dangerous weapon when being arrested on warrant), because knife was folded in D's back pocket entire time (object, "as used by" D was not "capable of producing serious bodily harm"); *C v Molligi* **70 MAC 108** **(2007)**—"nine-inch steak knife with a four-inch straight blade" held sufficient for "dangerous weapon"; even if not "per se" dangerous weapon, D's openly carrying it on public street at 2:30 a.m. around pedestrians + flight from cop supported inference of no "innocent purpose";

C v Sexton **425 M 146 (97)**—concrete pavement (onto which V's head was "banged") is dangerous weapon, reversing **41 MAC 676 (96)** (pavement, as "stationary part of surroundings," can't be dangerous weapon) and **criticiz**-

ing reasoning of *C v Shea* **38 MAC 7 (95)** (ocean can't be dangerous weapon because it can't be possessed or controlled); instead, **Shea** result was OK because harm to V lay not in V's contact with ocean, but with D's **abandoning** V at sea; if D dropped V in vat of acid, acid could be dangerous weapon;

C v Lefebvre **60 MAC 912 (2004)**—throwing victim from overpass into concrete flood control chute forty feet below = basis for assault & battery by means of dangerous weapon; intent to murder also inferable from facts;

C v Marrero **19 MAC 921 (84)**—jury question: footwear = capable of serious injury? (stomped, karate skills, serious injuries (& maybe boots));

C v Spencer **49 MAC 383, 392 (2000)**—judge erred in instructing that 'there's a statute . . . that makes a shod foot a dangerous weapon'; whether shod foot has been used as dangerous weapon is instead question of fact for jury to determine in the circumstances;

C v Zawatsky **41 MAC 392 (96)**—lack of evidence as to shoe type worn does not equal required finding of NG; vicious kicks in head & head injury enough to show dangerous as used; contrast *C v Turner* **59 MAC 825 (2003)** **(folded knife, kept in D's pocket as he was arrested on** **warrant [G.L. c. 269, § 10(b), second provision], was not** **being "used" by him as dangerous weapon, so required** **finding of NG)**

C v Connolly **49 MAC 424 (2000)**—no error in refusing to instruct that Commonwealth required to prove D "intended" to use his sneaker as dangerous weapon; dangerousness of object which isn't inherently dangerous turns on manner in which it's used (objective test), not intention of actor when using it (subjective test);

C v Durham **358 M 808 (70)**—shod foot instructions (not cited) were OK;

C v Mercado **24 MAC 391 (87)**—"sort of kick . . . like nudge" not A&B dangerous weapon;

C v Fernandez **43 MAC 313 (97)**—sneaker-shod D "wildly & continuously kicked" 2 cops, 1 in "midsection & upper chest" and 1 in "midsection & groin area"; kick to groin area held by Court to be "capable of causing severe injury without regard to the manner and force of the kick";

C v Tevlin **433 M 305 (2001)**—sneaker on foot, used to stomp elderly victim's stomach to cause her to let go of her purse after she fell to the ground, held to make out "armed" robbery, and thus felony murder, intent to commit felony serving as malice necessary for murder (force crushed aorta, which remained crushed because calcified w/cholesterol plaque, impairing blood flow to spinal cord & lower extremities: gangrene, complications, death); "weapon used during the course of criminal conduct may be deemed dangerous on the basis of factors concerning the victim that are unknown to the defendant";

Nolan and Sartorio, *Criminal Law* **(3d ed. 2001)** § 324—"perfectly legitimate" object may be dangerous weapon by manner in which it's used;

P v Graham **455 P.2d.153 (Cal. '69)**—good discussion;

Ransom v S **460 P.2d.170 (Alas. '69)**—body part not a dangerous weapon; NG unless a foot "implement"; vs. . . .

Berfield v S **458 P.2d.1008 (Alas. '69)**—same brawl, but "dangerous weapon" by this D;

Smith v S **152 P.2d.279 (Okla.Crim.App. '44)**—shod foot = dangerous weapon;

P v Buford **244 NW2d.351 (Mich.Ct.App. '76)**—same).

C v Roman **427 M 1006 (98)**—despite lack of proof as to what caused the burns upon 17-month-old child, and acknowledgment that case was "close," no required finding of NG for D;

21-F. OTHER AGGRAVATED ASSAULTS

See Chapter 16, Defenses: Intent, etc.;

21-F.1. Mayhem (G.L. c. 265, § 14)

G.L. c. 265, § 14—(a) "malicious intent to maim or disfigure" & enumerated injuries; or

G.L. c. 265, § 14—(b) (similar) intent, use of dangerous weapon, & "serious or permanent injury":

C v Martin **425 M 718 (97)**—A&B dangerous weapon is lesser included offense of **2d** branch of mayhem statute, but **not** lesser included offense of 1st branch of mayhem statute (*C v Hogan* **379 M 190 (79)**);

C v McPherson **74 MAC 125 (2009)**—ABDW = lesser included offense of mayhem when D swung bat to head of victim, causing, inter alia, severe injury to eye;

C v Sparks **42 MAC 915 (97)**—intent to maim/disfigure inferable from prolonged nature of attack and nature of injury (bone fracture setting eye back 3 mm into socket), despite fact that D was initially victim of robbery by V;

C v Drew **67 MAC 261 (2006)**—requisite intent inferable from vicious beating of victim with bat, which moved unconscious victim ever closer to hot surface of space heater (burning skin so that it "dripp[ed] from his face"); A&B dangerous weapon (bat) conviction not duplicative of mayhem because there was break between initial ABDW (bat) when victim was knocked unconscious, and later bat attack; duplicative of mayhem, however, was the ABDW ("space heater");

C v McPherson **74 MAC 125 (2009)**—specific intent inferable from "preplanned . . . use of a bat to smash, without warning, a defenseless person's head"; distinguishing case in which action = "spur of the moment";

C v Farrel **322 M 606 (48)**—permanent injury by cigarette lighter;

C v Tavares **61 MAC 385 (2004)**—"serious" (if not "permanent") injury to child's fingers caused by sharp needle-like object being stuck under fingernails; corneal abrasion and ulceration in both eyes sufficient for "first branch" mayhem, even though scarring did not permanently impair victim's vision;

C v Hogan **379 M 190 (79)**—need specific intent by each D; ABDW not lesser included offense;

C v Cleary **41 MAC 214 (96)**—required finding of NG since requisite intent could not be inferred from one blow with ax handle (despite poor prognosis for any vision in eye struck);

C v Johnson **60 MAC 243 (2003)**—required finding of not guilty of mayhem because requisite intent not inferable from single strike with beer bottle which was intact before it struck V's head; retrial (necessitated by evidentiary error) only on indictment charging assault & battery by means of dangerous weapon;

C v Lazarovich **410 M 466 (91)**—battered woman syndrome assumed admissible to show D didn't share specific intent to maim her daughter; see Superior Court Criminal Practice Jury Instructions § 2.18, Mayhem

21-F.2. "Assault by Means of Dangerous Weapon" (G.L. c. 265, § 15B)

See also Appleby, etc., Chapter 21-B, above;

Superior Court Criminal Practice Jury Instructions § 2.20;

C v Foley **17 MAC 238 (83)**— no dangerous weapon shown, but infer from threat/opportunity to dispose;

C v White **110 M 407 (1872)**—unloaded gun = assault by dangerous weapon;

C v Henson **357 M 686 (70)**—(same)—"apparent ability";

C v Burkett **5 MAC 901 (77)**—assault by means of dangerous weapon must USE dangerous weapon, not lesser included offense within armed assault to murder;

C v Delgado **367 M 432 (75)**—verbal assertion ("informational" words) as "act" re: robbery - vs. mere threat;

C v Howard **386 M 607 (82)**—"armed with" (armed robbery) vs. "by means of" (ABDW); but cf. *C v Turner* **59 MAC 825, 830 (2003)**—for conviction of being in possession of dangerous weapon when arrested on warrant, D must actually "use" in dangerous manner instrument which isn't per se dangerous (here, folding knife);

C v Domingue **18 MAC 987 (84)**—specific intent

21-F.3. "Assault with Intent . . ." (G.L. c. 265, § 24 (Rape) § 18 (Rob or Murder))

Nolan and Sartorio, *Criminal Law* **(3d ed. 2001)** § 289—assault with intent to rob needs less intent than attempt to rob;

See Chapter 16, Defenses: Intent & Chapter 21-H, 21-K, 21-L, post: robbery, homicide, rape;

G.L. c. 265, § 29—FELONY; § 15, murder/main; § 18, armed, murder/rob; § 20, rob; (see also G.L. c. 265,

§ 16—attempted murder" (attempting "to commit murder by poisoning, drowning or strangling . . . , or by any means not constituting an assault w/intent to commit murder");

Superior Court Criminal Practice Jury Instructions § 2.23;

C v Dixon **34 MAC 653 (93)**—though A&B is **not** lesser included offense of "attempted murder by strangulation," simple assault is lesser included offense);

C v Henson **394 M 584 (85)**—assault with intent to murder or kill = specific intent (for malice);

C v Grey **399 M 469 (87)**—(same) for intent crimes; *(see Chapter 16, Defenses);*

C v Ennis **20 MAC 263 (85)**—(same), fleeing felon;

C v Hebert **373 M 535 (77)**—assault to kill (i.e., § 29) = lesser included offense if intent would be voluntary manslaughter; no attempted involuntary manslaughter; (Quirico concurs: assault with intent must be closer to success than attempt (see Nolan and Sartorio, Criminal Law (3d ed. 2001) § 289));

C v Parenti **14 MAC 696 (82)**—same re: assault with intent to kill & voluntary manslaughter;

C v Burkett **396 M 509 (86)**—use of dangerous weapon not enough;

C v Lefebvre **60 MAC 912, 914 (2004)**—intent to murder inferable from fact that D threw V from overpass into concrete flood control chute forty feet below, even though mere one-foot depth of water in chute may not have been known;

C v Benoit **389 M 411 (83)**—"Now I'm going to have to kill somebody." = too general;

C v Smith **58 MAC 381 (2003)**—evidence sufficient to sustain assault with intent to murder indictment when D was combative to correction officers, threatened that he was going to hurt/kill them, said he was HIV positive, and bit officer, and cop testified that a named doctor told him it would be possible to transmit virus to another by biting if skin broke and D's "gums contained blood"; grand jury could have obtained court order to test D for human immunodeficiency virus, so counsel's stipulation that D was HIV positive wasn't ineffective assistance;

C v Boateng **438 M 498 (2003)**—"malice" in context of assault with intent to murder does NOT have same meaning as malice in murder charge & instruction created substantial risk of miscarriage of justice; malice in assault to murder means lack of justification, excuse, or mitigation, & extensive evidence of mental illness (a mitigating factor) was introduced; but see

C v Johnston **446 M 555 (2006)**—malice as element of assault with intent to murder "means only the absence of justification, excuse, and mitigation"; instruction on malice isn't required unless/until evidence of justification, excuse, or mitigation is introduced; evidence of D's depressed state could not be "mitigation", SJC disavowing any "confusion" or implication to the contrary in *C v Boateng* **438 M 498, 517 (2003);**

C v Williams **312 M 553 (42)**—robbery intent from beating/groping, though no words & money not found

G.L. c. 265, § 24—assault with intent to rape; § 24B assault on child under age 16 with intent to rape—*(see Chapter 21-L below);*

C v Lefkowitz **20 MAC 513, n.15 (85)**—assault with intent to rape = more intent than rape;

C v Derby **263 M 39 (28)**—assault with intent to rape;

C v Merrill **14 Gray 415 (1860)**—(touch/straddle/ask sex) = "equivocal";

C v Brusgulis **41 MAC 386 (96)**—grabbing of jogger in dark, throwing her down & straddling her, attempting to drag her toward more secluded area = enough for intent to rape;

C v Brattman **10 MAC 579 (80)**—jury question re: intent;

C v Sevieri **21 MAC 745 (86)**—infer intent to rape from prior lewd gesture & lack of other motive;

C v Martin **447 M 274 (2006)**—though there was no apparent sexual touching or language used during attack, notes by D found nearby suggested rape intent (plus no evidence of attempt to take purse);

C v Lewis **9 MAC 842 (80)**—assault as lesser included offense;

C v Nardone **406 M 123 (89)**—instruction on assault to kill in assault to murder trial was error where there was no evidence of mitigation;

C v Vick **454 M 418 (2009)**—though altercation was not apparently begun by D or his group, it initially consisted of pushing, shoving, yelling, and arguing, and V was not armed when he approached D: because D "deliberately prepared himself for possibility of fatal confrontation by carrying a loaded firearm," SJC refused to find possible any "mitigation" and there was no error in refusing to instruct on lesser included offense of "armed assault with intent to kill";

C v Sires **413 M 292 (92)**—wherever D's state of mind is in issue, jury should be instructed to consider all credible evidence concerning D's consumption of drugs or alcohol;

C v Robinson **408 M 245 (90)**—Henson rule not to be applied retroactively on collateral review;

21-F.4. Crimes Against Elderly or Child

G.L. c. 265, § 15A (ABDW)—§ 15B (ADW), § 18 (Armed Assault with intent to Rob), § 19 (robbery); **G.L. c. 266, § 25** (larceny from the person))—Mandatory Sentences for repeat D's;

C v Pittman **25 MAC 25 (87)**—complaining witness not asked & no proof her age under 65; BUT age & infirmities enter into sentencing for lesser included offense of regular robbery;

G.L. c. 265, § 13L—reckless endangerment of child (wantonly or recklessly engaging in conduct creating substantial risk of serious injury or sexual abuse to child or wantonly or recklessly failing to take reasonable steps to alleviate such risk when there is duty to act; risk must be of such nature and degree that disregard of risk = "gross deviation from the standard of conduct that a reasonable person would observe in the situation");

C v Hendricks **452 M 97 (2008)**—G.L. c. 265, § 13L encompassed D's nighttime conduct of high-speeding away from cop seeking to stop him for driving after license revocation, driving fast down unpaved rutted road, abandoning car after driving it over an embankment, fleeing into woods pursued by cop, all while D's three-year-old daughter was with him; rejecting argument that statute is void for vagueness or that it would encompass any driver speeding with child passenger;

21-F.5. Indecent A&Bs

G.L. c. 265, § 13B—(complaining witness UNDER 14, strict liability, i.e., need not prove D knew complainant is underage); § 13H (complaining witness 14+))

G.L. c. 218, § 26—District Court jurisdiction (1981 amendment);

G.L. c. 265, § 13F—indecent A&B (knowingly) on retarded person; (see *Thomas* **401 M 109 (87)**; [*C v Portonova* 69 MAC 905 (2007): unobjected-to failure to instruct jury on element of lack of consent in indecent assault and battery on retarded person held here to result in substantial risk of miscarriage of justice, conviction reversed];

District Court Model Jury Instruction #5.403–5.404;

Superior Court Criminal Practice Jury Instructions §§ 2.16–2.17;

C v Eaton **2 MAC 113 (74)**—lesser included offenses = A&B or assault ("indecent or lascivious liberties"); fn.2: open question re: touch complaining witness's clothing (see *Burno* **396 M 622 (86)**);

C v Taylor **50 MAC 901 (2000)**—conviction couldn't be premised on evidence that child (D's daughter) "reached for (D's) penis" when D had been naked in front of her;

C v Burke **390 M 480 (83)**—CONSENT defense (if complaining witness capable), sexual touching; BUT . . .

G.L. c. 265, § 13B—(as of 10/6/86) complaining witness under 14 = incapable of consent;

C v Disler **451 M 216 (2008)** & *C v Filopoulos* **451 M 234 (2008)**—"enticement" statute, G.L. c. 265, § 26C requires, in addition to enticing words/gestures, that person who entices does so with intent to violate one or more enumerated statutes, e.g., "statutory rape (c. 265, § 23) or indecent A&B on child under age fourteen (c. 265, § 13B); Commonwealth must prove that D INTENDED that object of sexual advances be an underage individual; *Disler* 451 M at 221–22—merely "sending words" IS sufficient evidence for "enticement" (additional "overt act" not required) if other element (intent to violate specific criminal statutes) is satisfied; that "victim" was not "real" irrelevant (cop was pretending on-line to be 14-year-old girl); "factual impossibility" not a defense to crime; not unconstitutionally vague, and merely sending sex messages over

computer not criminalized (additional "intent" element necessary); First Amendment challenge also rejected;

C v Feijoo **419 M 486 (95)**—re: alleged indecent A&B under 14 occurring before statutory amendment abolishing consent as defense **and** alleged indecent A&B on person over 14: required finding of NG where consent obtained by false representations/promises of social or economic benefits, but rejecting consent claim when, e.g., "without warning & therefore without . . . opportunity to consent or object," D forced club into child's rectum;

C v Shore **65 MAC 430 (2006)**—when 47-year-old employer grabbed breast of 15-year-old employee (after massaging her back in response to her complaint of pain from "cheerleading" and after she told D it felt good), her failure to rebuke him or pull away (he stopped when customer came into store) did not require a finding of not guilty (on element of "lack of consent"): "acceptance of a massage for a sore back is a far cry from consent to grab a breast";

C v Brenner **18 MAC 930 (84)**—capacity to consent;

C v Portonova **69 MAC 905 (2007)**—D failed to object to judge's failure to charge as to lack of consent as to indecent assault and battery, but consent was the focus of the case, and D was acquitted on rape charges as to which "consent" instructions were given: substantial risk of miscarriage of justice found, conviction reversed;

C v Traynor **40 MAC 527 (96)**—neither A&B nor indecent A&B of complainant 14 or over is lesser included offense of indecent A&B on child under 14: lack of consent = element of both these crimes (but not of indecent A&B < 14); required finding of NG because evidence failed to establish complaining witness was less than 14;

C v De La Cruz **15 MAC 52 (82)**—not "vague" re: M.D. fondling patient;

C v Miozza **67 MAC 567 (2006)**—statute not vague re: D holding girl (age 8–10 and age 6–8) on top of him as he lay on bed & kissed her on lips & placed his hands on her back or buttocks or back of her head; "improper sexual overtones . . . can explain physical contact that may otherwise be ambiguous"; here, fondling/kissing was surreptitious, and open-mouth kisses were requested [though not given];

C v Thayer **20 MAC 234 (85)**—touch areas "commonly thought private";

C v Lavigne **42 MAC 313 (97)**—D's touching inner thigh of hitchhiking V, within 3 inches of genitals, sufficient for G (D first asking if V wanted to "make some money");

C v Lawrence **68 MAC 103 (2007)**—though D was the complainant's mother (complainant age ten at trial), "indecency" inferable beyond reasonable doubt by arrangement of clothing so as to expose; photography of same, allegedly seen by complainant on D's computer screen; protests by complainant that she stop; and complainant's feelings of sadness and shame;

C v Rosa **62 MAC 622 (2004)**—inserting finger or thumb into mouth of 11-year-old girl, with question, "Do you know how to suck on it?", held sufficient for G, with other evidence, including D's admission to police that he was referring to penis, and intended to continue to molest child if he had succeeded in getting her into garage; "intimate" parts, not necessarily "sexual" parts, may suffice; jury could consider D's statements to girl & police in deciding indecency; girl's subjective understanding of comments admissible on issue of whether touching was "objectively indecent";

C v Perretti **20 MAC 36 (85)**—instruction ("immodest, immoral . . . ") OK; cf. *Rushia v Ashburnham* **582 FS 900 (D.Mass. 83)** lewd, lascivious, or indecent is overbroad under First Amendment;

C v Conefrey **37 MAC 290 (94):** *S.C.* **420 M 508 at n.3 (95)**—(though reversing on different ground, SJC "content with" Appeals Court holding re: indecent assault & battery)—D's state of mind not relevant (despite D's argument that Commonwealth be required to show touching for purpose of D's sexual arousal/gratification); crime proved if conduct, viewed in light of "contemporary moral values," is "indecent" under "common understanding and practices";

C v Portonova **69 MAC 905 (2007)**—D's forcing female to "play with herself" was indecent assault and battery on mentally retarded person (G.L. c. 265, § 13F); retardation factor not essential to holding (*C v Nuby* **32 MAC 360** [92]: essence of crime of forcible rape is "the outrage of compelled sex");

C v Davidson **68 MAC 72 (2007)**—D himself needn't perform the touching (D induced child to touch D's penis);

C v Castillo **55 MAC 563 (2002)**—D's nonconsensual kissing & forcing tongue into mouth of 14-year-old friend of D's stepdaughter = within "indecent," given age & authority disparity, surreptitious nature of act & subsequent conversation, & use of force ("grabbing"); [NOTE WELL: this is departure from/exception to 'private parts' element usually extant];

C v Vazquez **65 MAC 305 (2005)**—partially-opened mouth kiss on 12-year-old's mouth, even WITHOUT tongue use, held sufficient for "indecent" in circumstances here, in which "additional context" was provided by D's sexually aggressive behavior toward 15-year-old sister of 12-year-old and fact that D's actions were surreptitious; but see fn.3: D should have moved for severance? or should have insisted upon limiting instruction concerning seepage of proof between charges?, however probable it was that evidence of one would have been admitted at even a "severed" trial, as "pattern"/bad act evidence;

C v Thomas **401 M 109 (87)**—rape/indecent A&B = duplicitous unless separate acts; § 13F D must know that complaining witness = retarded;

C v Aitahmedlamara **63 MAC 76 (2005)**—expert psychiatric testimony not required to establish retardation; evidence here that complainant received services from DMR & that only those with IQ below 76 were eligible, AND D was employed at group home in which all residents were retarded;

G.L. c. 119, § 51A—child abuse reporting rule, DSS investigation, etc.;

C v Farrell **31 MAC 267 (91)**—A&B not lesser included of indecent A&B of child following 1986 legislation;

See also Chapter 21-L, Rape; Chapter 11-H, Evidence: Sexual Assault Cases;

21-F.6. Armed Assault in Dwelling, Armed Home Invasion (G.L. c. 265, §§ 18A, 18C) (vs. G.L. c. 266, § 14, Armed Burglary)

Superior Court Criminal Practice Jury Instructions § 2.30;

C v Liakos **12 MAC 57 (81)**—must be armed at entry;

C v Ricardo **26 MAC 345 (88)**—must be dwelling "of another;"

C v Mitchell **67 MAC 556 (2006)**—(in armed burglary, G.L. c. 266, § 14) "person lawfully therein" can be someone who came home after D had broken and entered and was still inside;

C v Smith **42 MAC 906 (97)**—reversal because jury instructions allowed G even if only felony intended was assault on occupant to gain entry into dwelling;

C v Fleming **46 MAC 394 (99)**—D's "frequent and arguably unobjected-to-visits entitled" D to have jury consider whether he had permission or privilege to enter OR "reasonably would have thought he had a right to enter"; reversal for refusal to so instruct;

C v Putnam **75 MAC 472 (2009)**—while "entry" into dwelling isn't unlawful if it's consensual, in response to invitation, or privileged, "purported consent to entry" isn't "legally significant unless the occupant has been made aware that" person about to enter is armed with dangerous weapon and is about to commit assault once inside; evidence here permitted finding that victim let D into house out of fear, AND that D pulled out knife, dragged victim about, and raped her "warranted" determination that entry was unlawful; for "consent" to enter to be "valid," person giving consent must be aware that D is armed AND that he has intent to commit crime while inside (D unsuccessfully argued for "or" rather than "and"); "absence of either element will negate consent";

C v Marshall **65 MAC 710 (2006)**—while entitled to jury instruction (here given), D not entitled to required finding on element that dwelling house be "of another" (i.e., not his own dwelling), despite his argument that after girlfriend's break-up with him he continued to have frequent contact with her & her son, contributed to household expenses, etc.;

C v Simmarano **50 MAC 312 (2000)**—re: "home invasion" (G.L. c. 265, § 18C) conviction, ineffective assistance of counsel found because failed to request jury instruction on cumulative practice of authorized entry into home of long-time girlfriend & because failed to proffer evidence crucial to this defense;

cf. *C v Mahar* **430 M 643 (2000)** (re: G.L. c. 265, § 18C—armed home invasion) though D argued that he entered with consent of occupant, SJC found sufficient evidence of unlawful entry: D was neither occupant nor accustomed to enter it without permission, and testimony was that he "barged" in; though statute doesn't include "situations where an invited guest in a home suddenly turns violent," consent seems ineffective if guest enters with unlawful intent and is armed; *C v Marshall* **65 MAC 710 (2006)**—jury had sufficient evidence to find D didn't have right of habitation or occupancy of the apartment at the time of the charged home invasion (despite specified evidence, including his contributions to household expenses and child care);

C v Morris **64 MAC 51 (2005)**—no relief for alleged "Fleming" error (omitting instruction on consensual entry, *which was not requested by trial counsel*, because instruction requiring proof that D "unlawfully made his way into" dwelling "by themselves carry the implication of an entry without permission"; but "[t]his is not to say that a judge would err by giving such an instruction" because "it could be helpful to the jury to supply the elaboration . . . rather than leave it to be implied by the word "lawful";

C v Flanagan **17 MAC 366 (84)**—assault by means of dangerous weapon not lesser included offense;

C v Powell **10 MAC 57 (80)**—only B&E (lesser included offense to G.L. c. 266 § 14) unless dangerous weapon in house Home Invasion (G.L. c. 265, § 18C) penalty = life or ≥ 20 years - armed at time of entry into dwelling; knew/should have known at time of entry that person(s) present within **OR** remained after such knowledge; used force or threatened imminent use of force or intentionally caused injury to person within;

C v Werner **73 MAC 97 (2008)**—"assault" readily inferable when D entered 15-year-old victim's apartment against her pleas (at 10 p.m. when she was home alone with infant) and threatened to kill all in house as result of victim's father's debt, saying that he knew sleeping places of all household members, and implying prior violence against other victims; additional "assault" in dwelling presented when D stood on porch but his hand or arm crossed into threshold of dwelling to touch victim's face with handgun as she stood just inside screen door;

C v Ruiz **426 M 391 (98)**—arming self with V's crutch after entry not sufficient for G;

C v Smith **75 MAC 196 (2009)**—G.L. c. 265, § 18C doesn't set out two "separate offenses," but instead contains "an element with alternative scienter clauses" ("knowing or having reason to know that one or more persons present therein" OR "having entered without such knowledge, remains in dwelling after acquiring or having reason to have acquired such knowledge"; fact that indictment's language "merged the two into one" did not limit the Commonwealth to what D claimed was one version of the "offense"; "entry" shown by foot crossing threshold of the door and when gun was inserted into apartment;

C v Dunn **43 MAC 58 (97)**: G.L. c. 265, § 18C—is not unconstitutionally vague and prescribed punishment is not cruel and unusual;

C v Zapata **455 M 530 (2009)**—language of current G.L. c. 265, § 18C omits language prohibiting probationary sentence (while stating punishment as "life" or any term not less than twenty years), and when read in context of amendments, rendered ambiguous proposition that sentence of "probation" was illegal (sentence of five years' probation upheld against Commonwealth challenge);

21-F.7. Civil Rights Act

G.L. c. 265, § 37—force interfering with exercise of a right = 1 year; but "bodily injury" = 10 years;

District Court Model Jury Instructions #5.69— = (including some secured rights);

Superior Court Criminal Practice Jury Instructions §§ 2.44 et seq.;

US v Ehrlichman **546 F.2d 910 (DC '76)**—must affect complaining witness's rights;

C v Stephens **25 MAC 117 (87)**—"willful" = purpose to deprive of right, or reckless disregard of legal right;

Redgrave v BSO **399 M 93 (87)**—civil (vs. criminal) civil rights suit (G.L. c. 12, § 11I) requires no intent to deprive of rights;

G.L. c. 265, § 39—A&B, damage property to intimidate because of race/religion (2.5 years);

C v Anderson **38 MAC 707 (95)**—dismissal of complaint under G.L. c. 265, § 39 for racist graffiti painted on stone wall once supporting an end of a railroad trestle;

C v Barnette **45 MAC 486 (98)**—unprovoked tirade by D against neighbors as "Mexicans" ("don't fit here," "get the hell out," "damn Mexicans") argued insufficient to convict because no proof that allegedly assaultive behavior was to 'compel' or 'deter' victim's conduct in any manner (meaning of "intimidation" in G.L. c. 12, § 11H), but court held "intimidate" means, here, only "to make timid or fearful"; Commonwealth must prove that D had specific intent to put V in fear because of V's membership in protected class;

Apprendi v New Jersey **530 US 466 (2000)**—sentence enhancement for offense "committed with a biased purpose" (like "hate crime") held to be not just sentencing issue, but instead an element of the crime which had to be included in the charging document, proved beyond a reasonable doubt, and be decided by jury unless D waived jury trial right;

G.L. c. 266, § 127B—complaining witness's civil action for civil rights action damages/injunction;

C v Guilfoyle **402 M 130 (88)**—for Juvenile (& contempt in Superior Court)

R.A.V. v St. Paul **505 US 377 (92)**—ordinance criminalizing placing burning crosses, swastikas, & other symbols on another's property in order to arouse anger, alarm, or resentment on basis of race, religion or gender, violates First Amendment because content-based;

C v Pike **52 MAC 650 (2001)**—rejecting First Amendment challenge to conviction: considering content of D's statements in circumstances in which she made them, words constituted threats of force against homosexual neighbors;

Screws v US **325 US 91 (45)**—"willful" means purpose is to deprive of enjoyment of right or reckless disregard; see Probate Court P/O's: 208, 218, 208/34B, 208/34C, 209/32, 209C/20;

C v Gordon **407 M 340 (90)**—"abuse" includes threat/assault; "vacate" includes stay away;

21-F.8. Abuse Prevention

See Chapter 21-PP, post;
G.L. c. 209A—(police protection & restraining orders);
G.L. c. 208, § 34C—(misdemeanor for violations);
District Court Model Jury Instructions #5.61;
G.L. c. 151A—(amendments approved 8/2001)—persons who 'lose their jobs' due to domestic violence against themselves or their dependent child(ren) are eligible for unemployment benefits (motive/bias inquiry?);

21-F.9. Carjacking

G.L. c. 265, § 21—punishes anyone who assaults, confines, maims or puts another in fear for purpose of & with intent to steal motor vehicle, whether or not theft successful; greater punishment if done while armed with dangerous weapon;

See Chapter 21-K, Kidnapping; Carjacking;

21-F.10. Stalking and Criminal Harassment

G.L. c. 265, § 43—(stalking) punishes anyone who willfully, maliciously & repeatedly follows or harasses & who makes threat with intent to put another in fear of serious bodily harm; purports to make stalking in violation of restraining or other designated court order subject to mandatory one year; mandatory two years for repeat offenders; § 43(a), stalking by harassment and stalking by following are lesser included offenses of stalking by harassment or stalking by following *in violation of a court order* (set forth in § 43(b)): *C v Alphas* **430 M 8, 12 n.4 (99);**

Edge v Commonwealth **451 M 74 (2008)**—after D pled guilty to violating abuse prevention order issued pursuant to G.L. c. 209A (id. § 7),and was sentenced, indictment later for crime of stalking "in violation of the same 209A order (G.L. c. 265, § 43(b)) was ordered dismissed; reported question, "whether a prosecution under § 43(b) implicates double jeopardy concerns if the Commonwealth relies on conduct previously the subject of [D]'s convictions of violating the 209A order," is answered "yes";

G.L. c. 265, § 43A—(harassment) tracks stalking statute but omits element of threat, requires proof of behavior such as to cause reasonable person substantial emotional distress;

C v Braica **68 MAC 244 (2007)**—that D made many complaints to government officials about neighbor (digging in wetlands, unleashed dog, smoke from furnace, debris on premises) (several complaints leading to enforcement actions) could not support conviction for criminal harassment; only other evidence, yelling/cursing from second floor window, not shown to seriously alarm complainant, so required finding of not guilty; complaints to government officials "directly implicate constitutionally protected speech";

C v Welch **444 M 80 (2005)**—at least three incidents are required to prove criminal harassment's element of "pattern" of conduct or "series" of actions; required finding of NG here because evidence established only two qualifying incidents after statute's effective date; "harassing" speech is within criminal harassment statute; statute not violative of First Amendment because intended to reach primarily what would be considered "fighting words", but challenges may be made on an "as applied" basis, & SJC will "ensure its application only to speech that is accorded no constitutional protection";

Superior Court Criminal Practice Jury Instructions § 2.24, disapproved in *C v Robinson* 444 M 102, 107 (2005) with regard to definition of "substantial emotional distress";
District Court Model Jury Instructions # 5.62;
C v Kwiatkowski **418 M 543 (94)**—two modes of proof: (1) maliciously & repeatedly "following" or (2) maliciously & repeatedly "harassing"; plus, with either, threat with intent to place V in imminent fear of death or serious bodily injury; stalking by following must be charged separately from stalking by harassing; proof of stalking requires evidence of one pattern of conduct or series of acts, but three separate incidents; Commonwealth must prove that D engaged in such conduct "knowingly" and "over a period of time" and that the conduct seriously alarmed or annoyed a person and would cause a "reasonable person to suffer substantial emotional distress";

C v Bibbo **50 MAC 648, 653 n.5 (2001)**—noting that, after *Kwiatkowski* **418 M 543 (94)**, Legislature amended G.L. c. 265, § 43 to "eliminate the distinction made between stalking by harassment and stalking by following";

C v Martinez **43 MAC 408 (97)**—"repeatedly" means more than two times; Commonwealth's concession that charge here concerned "following" (& not "harassing") meant required finding of NG since only two followings were proved;

C v Clemens **61 MAC 915 (2004)**—on four occasions, D attempted social contact with complainant (who declined, e.g., to step out for a cup of lemonade), but only after the 4th encounter would D have been aware that his attentions were decidedly unwanted; the 5th encounter was thus the only one "willful/malicious," so not guilty;

C v Matsos **421 M 391 (96)**—evidence sufficient to show intent to place V "in imminent fear of death or serious bodily injury" (40 letters to V, with references to guns & silencers, dangerous friends, illegal activities, & specific events making clear to her that she was being followed constantly, with assertion that when she finally wanted to come & see him "your eyes will always be closed"; letters filled with sexual references, detailed sexual fantasies about V, expressions of anger toward V, sometimes couched in racial terms);

C v Jenkins **47 MAC 286 (99)**—that separate incidents of harassment and following occurred within one day didn't make them "one" incident for purposes of minimum number of charged acts;

HARASSMENT STATUTE, G.L. c. 265, § 43A(a) "tracks" stalking statute, but stalking statute contained additional element of making a threat to induce fear of death or bodily injury; *C v Paton* **63 MAC 215 (2005)**— meaning of "malice" in § 43(a) is willful doing of injurious act without lawful excuse; that D appeared over 20 times at bar where complainant worked, and repeatedly at other places where she was could be found not accidental; arguments that complainant's alarm wasn't reasonable or "substantial" were rejected;

C v Robinson **444 M 102 (2005)**—acts must be such as to cause reasonable person "substantial emotional distress", & instruction erred in defining "substantial" as simply "more than trifling or passing emotional distress"; quoting, among other definitions, "serious invasion of the victim's mental tranquility"; **"MODEL" jury instruction (Superior Court Criminal Practice: Jury Instructions § 2.24 re: stalking statute has comparably erroneous definition)**;

C v O'Neil **67 MAC 284 (2006)**—inmate-D's many letters to female who didn't know him caused her to obtain "no trespass" order, served upon him; his subsequent letters were "willful," because intentional; not necessary to prove that he intended "harmful consequences" (i.e., her fear & distress), or that he was motivated by "cruelty, hostility, or revenge"; proof sufficient here that victim was seriously alarmed and that any reasonable person would be greatly alarmed in similar circumstances;

21-F.11. A&B upon Child, Causing Substantial Injury; Wantonly/ Recklessly Permitting Substantial Bodily Injury to Child by A&B (G.L. c. 265, § 13J)

C v Tavares **61 MAC 385 (2004)**—error in including wanton/reckless theory on verdict slip, when judge hadn't instructed on this theory as to two indictments, but no risk of miscarriage of justice;

C v Macey **47 MAC 42 (99)**—rejects claim, in "shaken baby" scenario, that statute was unconstitutional because lacking "scienter" requirement; common law defenses of A&B apply (i.e., either intentional and unjustified use of force upon the person of another, however slight OR willful, wanton and reckless act which results in personal injury to another; latter form of A&B allows "inference" of intentional conduct); Commonwealth need not prove that D knew that she was causing substantial bodily injury at time;

C v Garcia **47 MAC 419 (99)**—both mother and father of infant were charged with A&B upon child causing substantial injury AND with recklessly permitting substantial bodily injury to child by A&B; convicted of the latter ("permitting another" in inflict such injury), convictions upheld: injuries were apparently inflicted on more than one occasion and were such that ordinary person having care/custody would recognize child was suffering inflicted injuries; persons "may be reckless within the meaning of the law although they themselves thought they were careful";

C v Panagopoulos **60 MAC 327 (2004)**—"persons having care and custody" not limited to legal guardians/ parents, and includes "any persons . . . who have assumed either permanent or temporary responsibility for a child's care"; statute not impermissibly vague;

C v Torres **442 M 554 (2004)**—D, as live-in boyfriend of children's mother, assisted the mother with their care, children called him "Daddy," etc.; whether caregiver role has been imposed by law or by "less formal arrangements," G.L. c. 265, § 13J imposes obligations;

C v Chapman **433 M 481 (2001)**—prosecution and conviction under G.L. c. 265, § 13J proper even though child actually died & D could have been prosecuted instead for involuntary manslaughter; though D claimed that only "injuries" were small pinpoint hemorrhages on baby's eyelids, a symptom of oxygen deprivation, "injuries" not limited to those visible; internal impairments causing death by drowning (baby left unattended in bathtub) sufficed;

C v Robinson **74 MAC 752 (2009)**—D failed to seek medical attention when 13-year-old daughter, six months after piercing her own navel, became very sick, emaciated and weak with swollen abdomen (perforated intestine): wanton/reckless conduct by act OR omission when there is duty to act= sufficient for conviction; appellate claim that there was constitutional right to refuse treatment was not raised below (e.g., by request for instruction); instruction given (objective and subjective components of wanton and reckless conduct) held proper;

21-F.12. Placing, Hurling Explosive Devices (G.L. c. 266, § 102), Intentional Damage or Destruction of Property or Injury to Person by Explosion of Gunpowder or Other Material (G.L. c. 266, § 101)

C v Hammond **50 MAC 171, 176 (2000)**—statutory element of intent to injure includes "significant emotional injury"; § 102 is not a lesser offense of § 101, but inadequate explication of why this is so when merely "placing" warrants a conviction under § 102 (opinion continually referred to § 102 as the "throwing" offense, and justified it as a separate offense because of "special element of terror in hurling an explosive at a person or into property"); but cf. id. at 175 n.3 (acknowledgment that merely "placing" can be basis of § 102 conviction);

21-G. LARCENY FROM THE PERSON

G.L. c. 266, § 25 & § 25a—(elderly victim) *(cf. Chapter 21-R, Larceny)*;

Nolan and Sartorio, *Criminal Law* (3d ed. 2001) § 291;

District Court Model Jury Instruction #5.414;

Superior Court Criminal Practice Jury Instructions § 2.42;

C v Nolan **5 Cush. 288 (1850)**—value immaterial;

C v Luckis **99 M 431 (1868)**—"asportation" without removal from pocket;

C v Knapp **61 MAC 514 (2004)**—though D failed to remove money from cash drawer successfully, dropping it because he had a sock on his hand, "exertion of control over V's property was itself sufficient to supply" element of 'taking';

C v Bradley **2 MAC 804 (74)**—"fish through" pocket *(See also Chapter 21-K, Flowers)*;

C v Dimond **3 Cush. 235 (1849)**—stealth irrelevant;

C v Jones **362 M 83 (72)**—"from person" = complaining witness's presence & area of control;

C v Homer **235 M 526 (20)**—(same), including another room;

C v Davis **7 MAC 9 (79)**—inartful pickpocket;

C v Drewnowski **44 MAC 687 (98)**—seemingly, larceny from person is always lesser included offense of armed robbery, distinguished from greater offense only by latter's enhancing element "that the taking was accomplished by force or fear," plainly in issue here;

C v Fortune **105 M 592 (1870)**—classic joint venture;

C v Cline **213 M 225 (13)**—"unknown" V boarding trolley - need not allege value, nor allege (or prove) any property;

C v Sherman **105 M 169 (1870)**—empty pocket;

C v Crawford **12 MAC 883 (81)**—conjecture whether wallet taken (overt act);

21-H. ROBBERY

G.L. c. 265, § 19—(unarmed robbery) & 17 (armed robbery: if armed with firearm, prison for not less than 5 years, or if 2d offense, not less than 15 years))

Superior Court Criminal Practice Jury Instructions § 2.27;

District Court Model Jury Instruction 5.633, Robbery By Juvenile;

G.L. c. 277, § 39—definition;

Nolan and Sartorio, *Criminal Law* (3d ed. 2001), Chapter 12; (see also G.L. c. 265, § 21—punishing one who, with intent to commit larceny or any other felony, confines . . . or puts in fear for purpose of stealing from a building, bank, safe, vault, or other depository, of money, bonds, or other valuables . . .);

C v Richards **363 M 299 (73) (1)**—"assault" by (a) force (battery) OR (b) fear; AND (2) INTENT to steal (-but . . . (see § B, above re: "assault"—different for robbery? (Nolan, § 286)); .

C v Mahoney **331 M 510 (54)**—assault = lesser included offense; (see also *C v Eaton* **2 MAC 113, 118 (74)**)

C v Smith **44 MAC 394 (98)**—jury instruction that "indifference whether the victim recovered his property automatically constituted proof of an intent to deprive permanently" compelled reversal of robbery & carjacking convictions;

C v Olieveira **48 MAC 907 (99)**—no substantial risk of miscarriage of justice in failure to instruct on use without authority in armed robbery prosecution (car = proceeds), because lesser included offense was here "inapposite to the condition of the case": "element of violence takes unauthorized use . . . out of the picture" and "joy riding assumes returning" the car or abandonment in place "where it might be recovered"; NOTE WELL: defendant

didn't request at trial any instruction on lesser offense *(See Chapter 5-D, Complaints & Indictments: Lesser Included Offenses and Chapter 12-K, Trial Issues: Jury Instructions, on standards for giving of instructions on lesser included offenses)*

C v Jones **362 M 83 (72)**—purse snatch "force" (awareness);

C v Tevlin **433 M 305 (2001)**—purse snatch from unyielding elderly victim, who fell to pavement and was stomped upon by D, = "armed" robbery (shod foot), and thus felony murder;

C v Jones **12 MAC 489 (81)**—can amend force/fear (after closing arguments);

C v Brown **2 MAC 883 (74)**—purse snatch without complaining witness's awareness?;

C v Ahart **37 MAC 565 (94)**—no error in refusing lesser included offense instruction of larceny from person (handbag snatch) when defense was mis-ID, but (DICTUM?) "the snatching of a purse necessarily involves the use of force";

C v Ramos **6 MAC 955 (78)**—grab at money in complaining witness's hand;

C v Novicki **324 M 461 (49)**—need force or fear at least simultaneous with taking, vs. fear afterwards; larceny is lesser included offense;

C v Davis **70 MAC 314 (2007)**—bank teller's testimony that he wasn't afraid, because of bulletproof partition, but was concerned for safety of customer next to robber doesn't result in required finding of not guilty for D: "assault" doesn't require that "fear" be for teller himself; despite NG of "armed" element, jury could find that D's mask, conduct, and gesture of patting his sweatshirt sufficed to prove teller's fear (& thus assault);

C v Santo **375 M 299 (78)**—larceny = lesser included offense, but not here;

C v Drewnowski **44 MAC 687 (98)**—seemingly, larceny from person is always lesser included offense of armed robbery, distinguished from greater offense only by latter's enhancing element "that the taking was accomplished by force or fear," plainly in issue here; no required finding of NG for robbery because force need only be "connected to the objective of stealing property," here satisfied by alleged victim's testimony that D threw a wrench at him to facilitate escape;

Carter v US **530 US 255 (2000)**—under applicable federal statutes & a strict "elements" test, D charged with bank robbery not entitled to jury instruction on larceny from bank, because latter not a lesser included crime;

C v Davis **7 MAC 9 (79)**—classic pickpocket isn't robbery, but infer fear here;

C v Smith **21 MAC 619 (86)**—rolling a decoy-cop "drunk" was force/fear;

C v Blow **370 M 401 (76)**—intent to rob at taking?;

C v Moran **387 M 644 (82)**—larceny from person if intent/rob = afterthought to assault;

C v Rajotte **23 MAC 93 (86)**—robbery if force to escape (though after took money);

C v Cruzado **73 MAC 803 (2009)**—gas station employee saw fellow employee's car being driven away by D (two blocks away) and pursued it, ripping open driver's door and hanging onto door and inside of the car's roof as D accelerated and tried to push employee off: sufficient for robbery; employee had "a protective concern for" the car; sufficient also for assault and battery by dangerous weapon (rejecting D's argument for required finding, that "victim" brought himself into contact with car);

C v Marcotte **18 MAC 391 (84)**—complaining witness's fear must be D's intent (D, believing that gas station clerk was "in" on the scheme of robbery, didn't believe he would be in fear);

C v Sheehan **376 M 765 (78)**—need intent to steal; but drugs don't negate, at least in this case; *(See Chapter 16, Defenses)*;

C v Borden **5 MAC 847 (77)**—when intent to rob?;

C v Henson **394 M 584 (85)**—(Hennessey, concurs, but asserts (erroneously) that robbery = "general" intent;

C v Grey **399 M 469 (87)**—DICTUM: need specific intent for rob;

C v Tevenal **401 M 225 (87)**—(same), & intoxication affects specific intent *(See Chapter 16, Defenses)*;

C v Flowers **1 MAC 415 (73)**—robbery complete when D's control (see larceny from person, above);

C v Homer **235 M 526 (20)**—"from person" = "area of control," e.g., next room;

Jones **362 M. 83, 87 (72)**—(same);

C v Lashway **36 MAC 677 (94)**—same; jacket taken from ground, where it fell as victim pulled self away from assailant, who taunted him, holding jacket ("is this what you want? You're not going to get it."); required finding of NG for passenger in van driven by robber, though passenger was wearing jacket half hour later;

C v Glanden **49 MAC 250 (2000)**—taking of auto & its contents (including purse) was "from the person of" owner when she was using pay telephone three feet away; element of force and violence ("even if not intended at the start of the theft") fulfilled when the taking, "still unaccomplished, was pursued over the victim's personal resistance," i.e., she ran to driver's side, reached into half-open window to unlock door, and was dragged along by D's closing the window, trapping her arm, & accelerating;

C v Weiner **255 M 506 (26)**—title immaterial; question is custody (if not D's);

C v Grassa **42 MAC 204 (97)**—robbery of car can be from 'presence of' cop who was seeking to prevent the theft (of then-unknown person's car);

C v Stewart **365 M 99 (74)**—"victim" = employees & customers, though store money;

C v Levia **385 M 345 (82)**—2 employees = 2 crimes & consecutive sentences (though one cash register) *(See Chapter 19, Double Jeopardy)*;

C v Nickologines **322 M 274 (48)**—"armed," though without V's awareness;

C v Boiselle **16 MAC 393 (83)**—armed at some time during robbery;

C v Ferguson **365 M 1 (74)**—co-D armed *(See Chapter 16, Defenses, re: joint venture & intent)*;

C v Powell **40 MAC 430 (96)**—evidence sufficient for D's guilt as joint venturer (driver of getaway car, poised w/door open, which made illegal left turn out of parking lot) despite robber's immediate protestation of D's innocence when stopped 20 minutes later, but insufficient to show D's knowledge of any weapon (so G of only unarmed robbery);

C v Christian **430 M 552, 566–67 (2000)**—jury instruction requirements re: "armed robbery" joint venturer's culpability;

C v Tarrant **367 M 411 (75)**—dangerous weapon = a fact question: "apparent" danger?;

C v Delgado **367 M 432 (75)**—"verbal" dangerous weapon: complaining witness's reasonable belief;

C v Howard **386 M 607 (82)**—"apparently" dangerous OK to infer dangerous weapon, but D must be "actually armed" (NG if clearly wasn't);

C v King **69 MAC 113 (2007)**—OK to infer actually armed because D threatened to "shoot" V, and had opportunity to dispose of weapon prior to arrest, but stating that burden isn't satisfied "merely by evidence that robber said he was armed"; says O'Connor, J.'s concurring analysis in *Howard*, 386 M at 615 (i.e., that simple passage of time and that at arrest D didn't have gun, isn't sufficient), "has not been adopted";

C v Powell **433 M 399 (2001)**—"armed", even though indicated concealed "weapon" was really a wooden replica of sawed off shotgun, with clothes pin replicating the "hammer"; jurors were properly instructed that for fake weapon to be considered "dangerous," it would have to be reasonable for victim to believe that the weapon was real or capable of inflicting death or serious bodily injury; *C v Howard* means only that where robber has no instrumentality at all, conviction of armed robbery not warranted;

C v Powell **16 MAC 1016 (83)**—infer "armed"; (see J. O'Connor's qualms);

C v Jackson **419 M 716 (95)**—infer "armed", taking D at word & available evidence not refuting (likened to **Delgado** rather than **Howard**);

C v Simpson **54 MAC 477 (2002)**—sufficient basis for grand jury to find probable cause for "armed" robbery: D told V she was armed and held one hand out of the line of V's sight;

C v Harris **9 MAC 708 (80)**—specific dangerous weapon in indictment = not essential;

C v Novicki **324 M 461 (49)**—armed, but no force or fear, is larceny from person

C v Flynn **362 M 455, 477–8 (72)**—"masked" (= 5 year minimum);

C v Cincotta **6 MAC 812 (79)**— . . . or "disguised"

C v Santos **41 MAC 621 (96)**—required finding of NG on "masked" element = D wore baseball hat, sunglasses, and 3-inch Band-Aid on one cheek (remand for resentencing on simple armed robbery);

C v White **5 MAC 483 (77)**—must be larceny (felonious taking, etc.), not honest belief it's D's property;

C v Donahue **148 M 529 (1889)**—(same); (see larceny, 14 MAC 281 (82)); (re: intent to permanently deprive, see larceny of motor vehicle, larceny, & Nolan and Sartorio, Criminal Law (3d ed. 2001) § 287, "With Intent to Steal");

C v Gelpi **416 M 729 (94)**—same

C v Larmey **14 MAC 281 (82)**—*(Chapter 21-H)* (same) for property of 3d person; (but force may be A&B);

C v Ross **339 M 428 (59)**—infer robbery from possess recently taken proceeds (but see NG as to passenger in *C v Lashway* **36 MAC 677 (94)**);

C v Dedrick **33 MAC 161 (92)**—D's using gun to assist his escape after stealing gun from cop was armed robbery because D became armed "at a point directly related to the commission & completion of the robbery";

21-I. (ATTEMPTED) EXTORTION

G.L. c. 265, § 25—(1) malicious threat, (2) to named person, (3) of injury (or accuse crime), (4) with intent to extort money or compel an act (= 15 year maximum):

Nolan and Sartorio, *Criminal Law* (3d ed. 2001) § 333;

Superior Court Criminal Practice Jury Instructions § 2.26;

C v DeVincent **358 M 592 (71)**—elements; includes recovery of a just debt;

C v Miller **385 M 521 (82)**—includes injury to reputation;

C v Matchett **386 M 492 (82)**—elements; not basis for felony-murder unless conscious disregard of human life;

C v Downey **12 MAC 754 (81)**—"intangible business interest";

C v Corcoran **252 M 465 (25)**—"threat" measured by objective standard;

C v Saylor **27 MAC 117 (89)**—beat up complaining witness, ask how much money he has, grab $20, = extortion;

C v Schafer **32 MAC 682 (92)**—extortion by threatening economic injury under G.L. c. 265, § 39(b), discussed;

21-J. KIDNAP; CARJACK

G.L. c. 265, § 26—kidnap - (10 year maximum): (without authority, forcibly or secretly, confine, against will) (. . . OR . . .):

Nolan and Sartorio, *Criminal Law* (3d ed. 2001) § 334;

Superior Court Criminal Practice Jury Instructions § 2.25.1—(kidnapping); §§ 2.28 & 2.29 (carjacking without dangerous weapon, & while armed with dangerous weapon;

G.L. c. 265, § 21A—carjacking;

C v Cabral **443 M 171 (2005)**—bail surety & his agents have lawful authority to apprehend, detain, and deliver a principal to a court house, but no more force than necessary in circumstances, and no more force than would be proper to execute an arrest;

C v Campbell **352 M 387 (67)**—not (yet) restraint in car without moving;

C v Ware **375 M 118 (78)**—specific intent? *(See also Chapter 16, Defenses);*

C v Saylor **27 MAC 117 (89)**—don't need specific intent to confine;

C v Lent **46 MAC 705 (99)**—confinement shown by "any restraint of a person's movement; "asportation" accomplished here when girl was "forced to walk at gunpoint to the truck";

C v Burkett **5 MAC 901 (77)**—100 feet = completed, not attempt; *(MERGER into robbery or rape? See Chapter 19, Double Jeopardy);*

G.L. c. 265, § 26A—kidnap by relative

District Court Model Jury Instruction #5.405, Custodial Interference by Relative (§ 26A)

C v Banfill **413 M 1002 (92)**—stopping truck, asking 13-year-old girl for directions & telling her to "get in," not sufficient evidence for attempted kidnapping;

C v Beals **405 M 550 (89)**—parent's taking child from Commonwealth for prolonged period is not parental kidnapping under G.L. c. 265, § 26A, unless custody order violated;

C v Moyles **45 MAC 350 (98)**—instruction that taking had to be against the will of three-year-old alleged victim was reversible error; letting counsel argue that taking was NOT against the will of the child's mother was no excuse for failure to state correct law (taking had to be against will of mother, child "incapable of having" a will recognizable at law);

C v Colon **431 M 188 (2000)**—"consent" of twelve-year-old girl not a defense to kidnapping ("tender years" doctrine precludes her consent to leaving custody of parents or legal guardians); carjacking: G.L. c. 265, § 21A (whoever, with intent to steal a motor vehicle, assaults, confines, maims or puts in fear for the purpose of stealing a motor vehicle shall, whether he succeeds or fails in the perpetration of stealing the motor vehicle, shall be punished);

C v Pena **39 MAC 332 (95)**—evidence sufficient to show D intended to drive car away (before woman snatched key & left);

21-K. HOMICIDE CRIMES

Superior Court Criminal Practice Jury Instructions § 2.1 through § 2.8—(elements of murder, first degree murder, second degree murder, elements of manslaughter, voluntary manslaughter, involuntary manslaughter, vehicular homicide); see also Instructions §§ 2.9–2.10 (lack of criminal responsibility, self-defense), and § 2.11 (supplemental instructions, concerning cause of death, definition of death, object of killing must be a human, killing as a result of accident, self-defense, or defense of another, use of dangerous weapon, mental impairment/intoxication as it applies to proof of knowledge or intent, consequences of not guilty by reason of lack of criminal responsibility, joint venture & knowledge of weapon, unanimity, questions from jury, jurors' obligation on guilty or innocence)

C v Fleury **64 MAC 282 (2005)**—rejects D's claim that "second degree murder" is merely an occasion for mitigation of punishment, and not a crime to which D can offer G plea;

21-K.1. Generally

Nolan and Sartorio, *Criminal Law* (3d ed. 2001), Chapter 8;

Wharton's *Criminal Law* (14th ed.), Chapters 7–9;

C v Raymond **424 M 382 (97)**—jury should be told to decide if D = G of murder and, if so, whether G of first degree;

C v DePace **442 M 739 (2004)**—indictment for "murder" charges first, rather than second, degree murder, and needn't allege each theory of murder which the grand jury determined to be supported by probable cause; no relief, either, on argument that first trial jury's G was only under extreme atrocity or cruelty (and not deliberate premeditation), and no way of knowing whether this was a ground found by grand jury beforehand;

C v Pimental **454 M 475 (2009)**—jury instruction "you have obligation to return verdict of highest degree of murder that Commonwealth has proved beyond a reasonable doubt" = proper, rejecting argument that G.L. c. 265, § 1 (degree of murder shall be found by jury) gives jury full discretion to find degree or murder lower than that proved by Commonwealth;

C v Perry P. **418 M 808 (94)**—unless juvenile waives right to indictment, Commonwealth must proceed by indictment against a juvenile charged with murder;

C v Golston **373 M 249 (77)**—brain death;

C v Cass **392 M 799 (84)**—fetus is "person" (for motor vehicle homicide); but see *C v Edelin* **371 M 497, 517 (76)** manslaughter "assumes that the victim was a live and independent person"—very doubtful that manslaughter statute "spoke to prenatal conduct" (v Reardon/Quirico, concurring, 527–29);

C v Crawford **430 M 683 (2000)**—denying R.30 motions for new trial: involuntary manslaughter of pregnant girlfriend and fetus (two convictions); OK instruction for guilt if fetus was "viable"/"potentially able to live outside the mother's womb, notwithstanding artificial aid," but better instruction would be "reasonable likelihood of . . . sustained survival outside womb, with or without artificial support"; conviction OK even if D unaware of existence of fetus or that it was viable;

C v Bianco **388 M 358 (83)**—(D's A & B not CAUSE of death of V who jumped into (pushed) car & drowned), & *C v Rhoades* **379 M 810 (80)** "CAUSATION" (vs. torts);

C v DePace **442 M 739 (2004)**—indictment for "murder" charges first, rather than second, degree murder, and needn't allege each theory of murder which the grand jury determined to be supported by probable cause; no relief, either, on argument that first trial jury's G was only under extreme atrocity or cruelty (and not deliberate premeditation), and no way of knowing whether this was a ground found by grand jury beforehand;

C v Perry **432 M 214 (2000)**—though medical examiner believed "pneumonia" = cause of death, this was "direct consequence of" stresses/injuries inflicted upon V by multiple assailants & not an intervening cause negating D's actions as proximate cause of death; D's acts needn't be sole or exclusive cause of death; Commonwealth not required to prove specific acts of multiple assailants acting in joint venture to commit murder, or that a particular beating caused the death and D was present at such beating (because the multiple beatings and abuses weren't "independent crimes or ventures");

C v Casanova **429 M 293 (99)**—common law "year and a day" rule (i.e., D can't be prosecuted for murder unless V dies within a year and a day of act inflicting injury) was abolished by SJC in a 1980 case, and SJC declines to replace it with some other period of limitation arguably relevant to "causation"; proof of causation beyond reasonable doubt is all D may claim as matter of right;

C v Santiago **425 M 491 (97)**—when D engaged in gun battle during which innocent bystander was fatally shot, D may be held liable even if it was D's opponent who fired fatal shot, "no inconsistency in finding both shooters criminally responsible for" V's death;

C v Santiago (II) **428 M 39, 42–44 (98)**—Santiago (I) was not a "new" rule, so D must be subject to it; court has "grave doubt as to the continuing validity of the principle set forth in Campbell," 7 Allen 541 (1863), but also distinguished *Campbell and Balliro* **349 M 505, 515 (65)** on facts;

C v Santiago **50 MAC 762, 764 (2001)**—intermediate appellate court not free to disregard SJC's earlier pronouncement that D may be held liable for death of bystander because D engaged in shootout with another party; Commonwealth need not prove that D's bullet caused V's death;

C v Angelo Todesca Corporation **446 M 128 (2006), overruling/reversing 62 MAC 599 (2004)**—company truck lacked an alarm to signal it was backing up, & SJC holds that reasonable jury could find that truck's collision with victim was foreseeable result of absence of alarm on truck backing up, and that other trucks' frantic air horns would not have conveyed the same message as the distinctive beeping sound of a vehicle operating in reverse; even if victim were contributorily negligent, this "does not excuse a defendant whose conduct also causes the death", and jurors here were properly instructed and listened to extensive argument by lawyers on this point;

C v Shine **25 MAC 613 (88)**—must be THE proximate cause;

C v Tevlin **433 M 305 (2001)**—no relief for failure to instruct that death must have been 'natural & probable consequence of D's actions'; ok instead: 'action of D was the proximate cause of V's death . . . a cause, which, in natural continuous sequence, produces a death, & without which . . . death would not have occurred'; D's 'stomp' upon stomach of elderly V, to induce her to relinquish purse after she fell to pavement, crushed aorta, which remained crushed because of cholesterol plaque, impairing blood flow to spinal cord & extremities, leading to gangrene;

C v Niemic **427 M 718 (98)**—may defend against homicide charge on basis of intervening conduct of a third party as causing the death (e.g., reckless medical care made fatal the stab wounds which wouldn't ordinarily have been fatal) IF the intervening cause was not reasonably foreseeable; reckless medical care might not be reasonably foreseeable (case law "do(es) not foreclose (such a) conclusion"), so trial counsel not ineffective in pursuing this defense;

C v Osachuk **43 MAC 71 (97)**—D gave V methadone, loaned her money to buy cocaine, gave her heroin which she used to inject "speedball," & injected her later with cocaine in effort to rouse her to consciousness: that V voluntarily consumed all but final dose of cocaine did not "relieve D of liability" for death;

Cramer v Commonwealth **419 M 106 (94)**—re: scalding death of eleven-month old baby, not necessary for Commonwealth to show that "it was not in the power of any . . . person other than D to commit the crime";

C v Paulding **438 M 1 (2002), overrules C v Brown 392 M 632 (84)** (which said judge must always instruct on second degree if indictment is first degree); NOW, if only theory presented by evidence is first degree felony murder (and there is no evidence of malice which would support conviction of murder on theory of deliberate premeditation or extreme atrocity or cruelty), instruction on second degree murder isn't required;

C v Vinnie **428 M 161, 180–81 (98)**—D may not waive statutory right (G.L. c. 265, § 1) to have jury determine degree of murder; "Guilty verdicts returned in those cases in which the jury have been prevented from determining the degree of murder, whether due to a defendant's purported waiver, the Commonwealth's objection or a judge's oversight, shall be subject to reversal" after date of this case;

C v Troy **405 M 253 (89)**—judge properly restricted prosecution theories of 1st degree murder because of government's "careless" destruction of D's blood sample which might have supported drug/alcohol intoxication theory; dismissal re: felony murder theory not required as felony (aggravated rape) was general intent crime; D found NG on deliberate premeditation theory;

C v Barsell **424 M 737 (97)**—solicitation of felony, to wit: murder = common law **misdemeanor**; legislature is invited to codify crime, as it did with "attempts" & "conspiracy";

C v Talbot **35 MAC 766 (94)**—notwithstanding D's story that he had merely helped a murderer bury body, no error in refusing to instruct on "accessory after the fact": it's not lesser included offense, & instruction on crime not charged "might serve only to mislead & confuse jury";

C v Ghee **414 M 313 (93)**—Commonwealth's appeal of trial judge's reduction of murder-1 conviction to murder-2, pursuant to Crim.R.25 (b) was meritless; judge had discretion to act if he concluded lesser verdict = more consonant with justice; if, instead judge ruled "required finding of NG" on murder-1, appeal would lie; see also *C v Woodward* **427 M 659 (98)** judge could reduce murder 2 conviction to manslaughter under R.25(b)(2) as more consonant with justice;

21-K.2. (Second Degree) Murder (G.L. c. 265, § 1)

21-K.2.a. Kill with "Malice Aforethought"

G.L. c. 277, § 39—(definition)

C v Gendraw **55 MAC 677 (2002)**—jurors needn't be unanimous as to which of the three prongs of malice had been proved;

C v Pierce **138 M 165 (1884)**—If no intent to kill (or grievous harm), question =

C v Chance **174 M 245 (1899)**— . . . plain & strong likelihood of death?

Virginia v Black **538 U.S. 343 (2003)**—model jury instruction that any cross burning shall be prima facie evidence of an intent to intimidate a person or group = constitutionally overbroad & thus error; PERTINENT TO INSTRUCTION THAT MALICE MAY BE INFERRED FROM THE INTENTIONAL USE OF A DANGEROUS WEAPON;

C v DiRenzo **44 MAC 95 (97)**—third prong malice definition including not only acts creating "plain and strong likelihood that **death**" but also of "serious bodily injury" = reversal here;

C v Williams **428 M 383, 386–87 (98)**—same, plus "frame of mind" definition of malice "ought . . . to be omitted";

C v Pov Hour **446 M 35 (2006)**—not necessary for conviction of D as joint venturer in first degree murder by deliberate premeditation or extreme atrocity/cruelty to prove that he knew that principal was using a knife (citations omitted);

C v Starling **382 M 423 (81)**—& foreseeable to reasonably prudent D?; less force on child V = malice aforethought;

C v Grey **399 M 469, n.4 (87)**—reasonable prudence (objective) test applied to facts known (SUBJECTIVE) to D; mental impairment (& drugs/booze) re: malice *(See Chapter 16, Defenses: Intent)*;

C v Swift **382 M 78 (80)**;

C v Lowe **391 M 97, 107–8 (84)**;

C v Griffin **19 MAC 174, 189 (85)**;

C v Lendon **35 MAC 926 (93)**—enough for joint venturer guilt of second degree: intent that V be killed, or assisting, knowing that there's substantial likelihood of V's being killed;

C v Fox **7 Gray 585, 588 (1856)**—not normally from minor blow;

C v Eagles **419 M 825, 836 (95)**—should **NOT** define malice as "frame of mind which includes not only anger, hatred, and revenge, but also any other unlawful or unjustifiable motive";

C v Johnson **422 M 420 (96)**—same;

C v Burke **414 M 252 (93)**—'frame of mind' language first condemned;

C v Niland **45 MAC 526, 529 (98)**—"frame of mind" language wasn't objected to, and correct third prong malice instruction was also given, so no reversal; consciousness of guilt is relevant to whether unlawful killing was committed but "is not evidence of malice aforethought";

C v Dagenais **437 M 832 (2002)**—D fled after V's death, & judge refused to instruct that consciousness of guilt can't be used to infer premeditation; while SJC agreed that consciousness of guilt isn't normally relevant to deliberate premeditation because it comes after the killing, it would be if there were evidence of pre-planning for flight, concealment, or destruction of evidence;

C v Pierce **419 M 28 (94)**—error to define malice as "all intention to inflict injury"

C v Sama **411 M 293 (91)**—third prong malice requires proof that in circumstances known to D, a reasonable person would know that his conduct is likely to cause death; jury allowed to consider whether D's intoxication prevented him from knowing he was stabbing victim & that death might follow;

C v McLean **32 MAC 978 (92)**—same;

C v Mello **420 M 375 (95)**—re: third prong malice, jury should be told to consider (1) nature & extent of D's knowledge at time he acted (subjective component) and (2) whether, in the circumstances known by D, a reasonably prudent person would recognize that Ds' conduct would create plain & strong likelihood of death (objective component); D intoxicated, so Commonwealth had to prove D knew he was setting fire to occupied apartment building;

C v Delaney **418 M 658 (94)**—error to refuse to instruct, as D requested, re: third prong malice with overlay of possible post-traumatic stress-induced flashback to Vietnam (here harmless, though);

C v Morgan **422 M 373, 381 n.7 (96)**—third prong malice does **not** include plain & strong likelihood of mere 'grievous bodily harm' from intentional act;

C v Sneed **413 M 387, 394 (92)**—instruction that second prong malice involves intent to do less than serious or grievous bodily injury is erroneous;

C v Caines **41 MAC 812 (96)**—error to charge that third prong malice = intent to do act creating plain & strong likelihood of death **or grievous bodily harm**;

C v Pichardo **45 MAC 296 (98)**—same, reversal;

C v Vizcarrondo **427 M 392 (98)**—same, reversal; specifically listing cases in which reviewed charges have included this (erroneous) language but whose convictions have been affirmed without comment about/correction of this language, either because correct instructions were included or third prong malice wasn't directly at issue; these cases "are not to be read to suggest that something less than a plain and strong likelihood of death is sufficient for proof of the third prong of malice";

C v Riley **433 M 266, 273 (2001)**—SJC declines invitation to abolish third prong malice; firing point blank at someone's head left no room for error, & second degree murder conviction not inconsistent with "moral culpability" present in circumstances; consciousness of guilt evidence NOT evidence of 'malice aforethought'; but see *C v Dagenais*, 437 M 832 (2002) (if there were evidence of PRE-planning for flight, concealment, or destruction of evidence, this would be relevant to premeditation);

C v Dahl **430 M 813 (2000)**—error to charge that malice is any bad "frame of mind" like "anger, hatred, and revenge," and also error to define 3d prong malice as doing act "creating plain and strong likelihood that death OR GRIEVOUS BODILY HARM would follow", but here no prejudice because evidence didn't "warrant a finding of a risk of harm less than a strong likelihood of death" (striking V on back of head with golf club, and using broken club as spear, impaling V as he lay on ground); contrast *C v Cherubin* **55 MAC 834 (2002)** (here, malice couldn't be "ineluctably inferred," so error harmed D);

C v Azar **50 MAC 767 (2001), affirmed 435 M 675 (2002)**—Rule 30 allowed based on 3d prong malice instruction error (doing of an act creating plain likelihood that death OR GRIEVOUS BODILY HARM would result), despite no objection at trial & failure to raise issue on direct appeal of conviction six years before filing of motion for new trial;

C v Reed **427 M 100, 105 n.4 (98)**—rejecting D's request that "grievous bodily injury" should be defined as one that reasonable person would see to pose plain & strong likelihood of death: "impermissibly intermingles" second and third prong malice concepts; rejecting argument that third prong malice should apply subjective standard (e.g., 16-year-old's comprehension rather than that of "reasonably prudent person");

C v Johnson **426 M 617, 622 (98)**—clear error to omit, in third prong malice definition, direction to consider "nature & extent of D's knowledge of the circumstances at the time he acted" (here, however, no prejudice);

C v Sires **413 M 292 (92)**—wherever D's state of mind in issue, jury should be instructed to consider all credible evidence concerning D's consumption of drugs or alcohol; "risk" for purposes of third prong malice = plain & strong likelihood of **death** (not just 'grievous bodily injury'); killing without malice "does not automatically become involuntary manslaughter"; scope of risk here = malice, so no right to instruction on manslaughter;

C v Moran **75 MAC 191 (2009)**—D's statement that he "slammed" seven-week old baby into her crib and her head hit crib railing (cracking skull) = enough for plain and strong likelihood of death; no error in refusing to reduce verdict to manslaughter;

C v Repoza **28 MAC 321 (90)**—A&B is not lesser included of second degree murder;

C v Smith **37 MAC 10 (94)**—nothing in testimony "matched" mere A&B; no one said D, convicted of second degree murder, merely punched or pushed V & D himself said he'd "shot" in direction of V (so either NG or self-defense or G of manslaughter);

C v Gilliard **36 MAC 183 (94)**—sua sponte, Appeals Court suggests motion for new trial for ineffective assistance of counsel (failure to request lesser included offense instruction re: A&B in homicide case; D was mere joint venturer, and could have been found to intend only fist-beating, not attack with weapon); but cf. *C v Pov Hour* **446 M 35 (2006)**—not necessary for conviction of D as joint venturer in first degree murder by deliberate premeditation or extreme atrocity/cruelty to prove that he knew that principal was using a knife (citations omitted);

C v Blake **409 M 146, 155 (91)**—(1) intend get plaintiff (2) objectively: in circumstances known to D, reasonable person would know likely to cause death; but ok (here) to instruct intoxication irrelevant;

C v Rivera **50 MAC 532 (2000)**—instruction that jurors may infer that person intends natural & probable consequences of act knowingly & voluntarily done isn't forbidden "presumption" of malice language;

21-K.2.b. (Second Degree) Felony-Murder (Non-Life Felony)

C v Chase **42 MAC 749 (97)**—mere "crime against property" **can** be basis for 2d degree felony murder: if felony is not "inherently dangerous," must be committed in manner demonstrating conscious disregard of risk to human life; here, as D was driving away the truck he had just stolen, he drove it directly at a man pursuing him, running him down;

C v Brum **458 M 103 (2002)**—felony must be causally related to homicide, not afterthought, e.g., if D stole V's wallet as afterthought after assaulting & killing V, not felony murder;

C v Matchett **386 M 492 (82)**—extortion: "conscious disregard of the risk to human life";

C v Rego **360 M 385 (71)**—(See Moran & Watson, below)

C v Gruning **46 MAC 842 (99): G.L. c. 265, § 18C**—(entering dwelling while armed and using force therein) = inherently dangerous (& thus OK predicate);

C v Burton **450 M 55 (2007)**—armed (firearm) home invasion wasn't felony punishable by life imprisonment at time of this offense (10-24-99, because of 1998 amendment to G.L. c. 265, § 18C), so first degree felony murder conviction reduced to second degree murder;

C v Scott **428 M 362 (98)**—unarmed robbery NOT, as matter of law, inherently dangerous (citing precedents) and jury instruction that it was up to jury to decide whether it was = error; no relief because D's conduct evinced conscious disregard of risk to life;

C v Pike **431 M 212, 216 (2000)**—breaking and entering with intent to steal and larceny of car = OK predicate felonies because committed with conscious disregard of risk to human life (despite argument that these = "mere property crimes");

21-K.3. First Degree (G.L. c. 265, § 1)

C v Charles **47 MAC 191 (99)**—in circumstances here, jury in first degree murder trial should have been instructed on "lesser included offense" of ABDW (jury could disbelieve claim of self-defense, and believe that D stabbed V, but believe that only the chest wound was cause of V's death and that it occurred when V fell onto knife);

21-K.3.a. Deliberate Premeditation: Conscious, Fixed Purpose to Kill for a Length of Time

C v Jenks **426 M 582 (98)**—only 1st prong malice supports deliberate premeditation conviction;

C v Diaz **426 M 548 (98)**—same;

C v Stockwell **426 M 17 (97)**—rejecting Commonwealth's argument that *Judge* **420 M 433 (95)**, should be reconsidered, such that third prong malice can support finding of deliberate premeditated murder;

C v Jiles **428 M 66 (98)**—though first degree murder portion of instructions included description of all three prongs of malice and failed to include "precise words that the defendant 'specifically intended to kill the victim,'" no miscarriage of justice found;

C v Plunkett **422 M 634 (96)**—though first degree murder was presented to jury with options of deliberate premeditation and felony murder, evidence insufficient to prove any intent to kill, necessary for deliberate premeditation theory; not knowable whether jury convicted on theory for which evidence was sufficient, so new trial ordered; rationale of *Griffin v US* **502 US 46, 54–56 (91)** rejected; (**Griffin** holds that jury verdict will be considered to have been on the theory for which there was adequate evidence);

C v Lanoue **392 M 583, 590 (84)**;

C v McInerney **373 M 136, 153–54 (77)**;

C v Tucker **189 M 457, 486–96 (05)**—plan formed within a few seconds;

C v LeClair **429 M 313, 318 n.6 (99)**—OK charge: "1st the deliberation and premeditation, then the decision to kill, and lastly the killing in furtherance of the decision";

C v Jackson **432 M 82, 88 (2000)**—killing by manual strangulation in course of struggle = adequate evidence of premeditation;

C v Stewart **398 M 535, 540–41 (86)**: *C v Blaikie* **375 M 601, 605 (79)**—deliberate premeditation requires proof of "cool reflection";

C v Degro **432 M 319, 329 (2000)**: *C v Rice* **427 M 203, 209–10 (98)**—cited for 'action taken after homicide which is purportedly probative of a consciousness of guilt isn't probative of premeditation (unless consciousness of impending guilt could be inferred by action taken before homicide)'; *C v Dagenais* **437 M 832 (2002)**—same; but if there's evidence of PRE-planning for flight, concealment, or destruction of evidence, it's relevant to deliberate premeditation;

C v Riley **433 M 266, 270 n.5 (2001)**—consciousness of guilt evidence is NOT evidence of malice aforethought; cf. *C v Epsom* **399 M 254, 259 (87)** consciousness of guilt evidence can't be used to prove 'murder' rather than 'manslaughter,' but is admissible re: whether criminal homicide has been committed;

C v Phinney **416 M 364 (93)**—DICTA, but strongly suggests that, notwithstanding D's version of events (striking V out of 'panic'), medical evidence of six "distinct, violent blows to the head" could support verdict of deliberate premeditation;

C v Puleio **394 M 101 (85)**—first vs. second degree;

C v Farley **431 M 306, 312 (2000)**—sufficient evidence of deliberate premeditation: 11 stab wounds, location of wounds, duration of attack, inference that D carried knife from kitchen to upstairs bedroom; *C v Townsend* **453 M 413 (2009)**—similar;

C v Bregoli **431 M 265, 270 (2000)**—deliberate premeditation = "sustained pressure to" V's neck, though here also evidence of D's statements that he wanted to kill V (ex-wife);

C v Podlaski **377 M 339 (79)**—"I had to do him in" & V's injuries = deliberate premeditation;

C v Rivera **50 MAC 532 (2000)**—condition of deceased's body relevant to deliberate premeditation AND extreme atrocity/cruelty;

C v Basch **386 M 620 (82)**—D's acts afterwards didn't suggest deliberate premeditation;

C v Blaikie **375 M 601 (78)**—D's conduct afterwards, in attempt to avoid detection, "rarely relevant to the issue of premeditation"; cf. *C v Niland* **45 MAC 526, 529 (98)** consciousness of guilt is relevant to whether unlawful killing was committed but "is not evidence of malice aforethought";

C v Costa **360 M 177 (71)**—drugs may bar premeditation *(See Chapter 16, Defenses: Intent)*; no error in refusing to instruction on manslaughter, where there was evidence of D's diminished mental capacity not amounting to legal insanity;

C v Gould **380 M 672 (80)**—mental impairment ("diminished capacity") *(Chapter 16, Defenses: Intent)*;

C v Ward **426 M 290 (97)**—error not to charge re D's mental impairment (history of Attention Deficit Disorder with hyperactivity, affecting capacity to weigh pros & cons, etc.), relevant to deliberate premeditation;

C v Skinner **408 M 88 (90)**—instruction that cocking, aiming & firing gun with intent to kill would prove deliberate premeditation created impermissible Sandstrom presumption;

C v Chipman **418 M 262 (94)**—deliberate premeditation sufficiently shown by evidence that two men amused themselves by shooting M-1 carbine w/telescopic sight from woods at vehicles traveling on Route 25; identity of fatal shooter didn't matter as joint venture shown (contrast *Salemme* **395 M 594 (85)**);

C v Judge **420 M 433, 441–42 (95)**—only 1st prong malice is applicable to deliberate premeditated 1st degree murder;

21-K.3.b. Cruel or Atrocious—Usually Inferable from Injuries

C v Benjamin **430 M 673, 677 (2000)**—term "extreme atrocity or cruelty" not unconstitutionally vague;

C v Golston **373 M 249, 259 (77)**—single blow can be extreme cruelty or atrocity;

C v Podlaski **377 M 339 (79)**—need not "intend" extreme cruelty or atrocity - if malice; V need not suffer;

C v Chaleumphong **434 M 70 (2001)**—D's knowledge that acts = extremely atrocious/cruel isn't element of murder by extreme atrocity or cruelty, & Commonwealth likewise has no burden to prove such knowledge where D acts in joint venture; *C v Sokphann Chhim* **447 M 370 (2006)**—same;

C v Avellar **416 M 409 (93)**—number & severity of injuries to six-month-old victim enough for extreme atrocity or cruelty;

C v Townsend **453 M 413 (2009)**—58 stab wounds, some defensive, plus blood evidence indicating that stabbing occurred in both kitchen and living room = sufficient time for D's reflection and to form requisite malice (conviction of extreme atrocity or cruelty);

C v Auclair **444 M 348, 363–65 (2005)**—notwithstanding lack of evidence of repeated blows, severity of force intentionally brought to bear upon head of three-month-old victim = enough for extreme atrocity or cruelty, making judge's reduction of verdict to second degree murder (as a matter of law) ERROR;

C v Gould **380 M 672 (80)**—mental impairment mitigates;

C v Judge **420 M 433 (95)**—third prong malice is relevant to only extreme atrocity or cruelty of first degree murder options;

C v Cunneen **389 M 216 (83)**—impairment = one factor; no specific intent; extreme-atrocity-or-cruelty factors = indifference to or taking pleasure in V's suffering, consciousness & degree of suffering of V, extent of physical injuries, number of blows, manner & force with which delivered, instrument employed, disproportion between means needed to cause death & those employed;

C v Williams **428 M 383, 390 (98)**—at least one *Cunneen* factor must be proved beyond a reasonable doubt for extreme-atrocity-or-cruelty verdict;

C v Hunter **427 M 651 (98)**—jurors not required to agree unanimously re: which *Cunneen* factor(s) applied; factors merely "evidentiary considerations" to guide jury rather than "separate theories of culpability" or "discrete acts or incidents, each of which, independently, constitutes a crime" (as contemplated in "specific unanimity" case precedents); no required finding of NG on extreme atrocity or cruelty here (V was shot repeatedly at close range, in head after falling to floor from body wounds, and prior to being shot had pleaded for her life and tried to defend self from attack);

C v Raposa **440 M 684 (2004)**, citing *C v Obershaw* **435 M 794 (2002)**—even in light of *Richardson v US* 526 US 813 (99) and *Apprendi v New Jersey* 530 US 466 (2000), D is not entitled to a "*Cunneen*" unanimity instruction; *C v Perez* **444 M 143, 154 (2005)**—same, even after *Ring v Arizona* 536 US 584 (2002), *Blakely v Washington* 124 S.Ct. 2531 (2004), & *US v Booker* 125 S.Ct. 738 (2005); *C v Almonte* **444 M 511, 523 (2005)**—same; jury need not be unanimous on the "evidentiary considerations"

that guide a jury in determining whether murder was committed with extreme atrocity or cruelty; *C v Morganti* **455 M 388 (2009)**—same;

C v Benjamin **430 M 673, 677 (2000)**—jury needn't be unanimous as to which *Cunneen* factor underlies verdict of first degree murder based on extreme atrocity or cruelty; *C v McDermott* 448 M 750, 778 (2007)—same;

C v Hunter **416 M 831 (94)**—instruction that extreme atrocity or cruelty "is not limited to such cases of such evidence" as *Cunneen* factors = error;

C v Johnson **426 M 617 (98)**—same;

C v Sarmanian **426 M 405 (98)**—**Hunter** not "retroactive";

C v Ellis **432 M 746, 763–64 (2000)**—though jury charge violated **Hunter** 416 M 831 (94) re *Cunneen* factors not required for extreme atrocity or cruelty, no relief: jury also returned 'G' on felony murder, & no substantial risk of miscarriage of justice (no objection below) because verdict could, given evidence, "readily depend" on a *Cunneen* factor;

C v Blackwell **422 M 294 (96)**—questionable whether instruction that extreme atrocity or cruelty can be based on "single gunshot" is reversible error;

C v Jenner **426 M 163 (97)**—noting issue, but here irrelevant because death was by 12 stab wounds to stomach & chest;

C v Perry **385 M 639 (82)**—intoxication a factor;

C v Barros **425 M 572 (97)**—if D requests, entitled to instruction re: being overcome by intoxicating substances as to be incapable of committing murder with extreme atrocity or cruelty—2d degree murder if all other elements are present;

C v Cadwell **374 M 308 (78)**: *C v Mandile* **403 M 93 (88)**—(below)

C v Friedberg **405 M 282 (89)**—factors which jurors may consider; proof of intent to inflict extraordinary pain or suffering not required;

C v Murphy **426 M 395 (98)**—that killing occurred in presence of V's young son = relevant to V's suffering (knowing this) and to D's indifference to V's suffering, extreme-atrocity-or-cruelty factors;

C v Rivera **50 MAC 532, 537 (2000)**—didn't need to decide whether single gunshot could support conviction of extreme atrocity/cruelty, because G here also on deliberate premeditation ground;

C v Patterson **432 M 767, 774 (2000)**—five gunshots to head fired from within two feet (any one would have been fatal) enough for extreme atrocity/cruelty: both 'significant # of extensive wounds' and 'significant disproportion between means necessary to cause death & those employed' were *Cunneen* factors which could have been found; that V was probably asleep & didn't consciously suffer didn't matter ("suffering has never been an indispensable element of the crime of murder with extreme *atrocity or cruelty*");

C v Cruz **413 M 686 (92)**—judge's exclusion of expert opinion that alcohol would have severely affected D's judgment during killing required reversal because relevant to deliberate premeditation & extreme atrocity & cruelty; instruction on blood alcohol level for intoxication in OUI cases not appropriate in homicide cases;

21-K.3.c. (First Degree Felony-Murder) (if LIFE felony—G.L. c. 265, § 1)

C v Jackson **432 M 82 (2000)**—crime may be predicate offense for first degree felony murder if it's punishable by death or life imprisonment; if predicate offense isn't inherently dangerous to human life, Commonwealth must prove that circumstances were such that D consciously disregarded risk to human life; "unarmed" assaultive burglary (G.L. c. 266, § 14) here held to be inherently dangerous to human life for purposes of 1st degree felony murder;

C v Brum **458 M 103 (2002)**—felony must be causally related to homicide, not afterthought, e.g., if D stole V's wallet as afterthought after assaulting & killing V, not felony murder;

C v Quigley **391 M 461 (84)**—must have separate felony from killing;

C v Gunter **427 M 259 (98)**—if only felony committed apart from the murder itself is the assault upon the V which results in death of V, assault merges w/the killing & cannot be relied upon as ingredient of 'felony' murder;

C v Kilburn **438 M 356 (2003)**—when V opened door, D pointed gun at him & pushed him backward AND a second armed assault in dwelling occurred later when D shot V in head & killed him; jury should have been instructed that felony murder G OK only if G of the FIRST armed assault (because second merged into the homicide);

C v Murphy **442 M 485 (2004)**—purportedly no merger because entering dwelling while armed with knife with intent to rob Vs, stabbing each several times and inflicting NONFATAL wounds, was separate from the stabbings that resulted in death; convictions under G.L. c.265, § 18A upheld in addition to first degree murders on each of three bases;

C v Wade **428 M 147 (98)**—rejecting D's argument that doctrine of merger precluded felony murder conviction when underlying felony was "aggravated" rape (aggravation possibly/likely being serious bodily injury, which resulted in death);

C v Roberio **428 M 278 (98)**—armed robbery assault didn't merge with assault necessary to the murder because there were numerous assaults on V after the initial robbery assault;

C v Tevlin **433 M 305 (2001)**—sneaker on foot, used to stomp elderly victim's stomach to cause her to let go of her purse after she fell to the ground, held to make out "armed" robbery, and thus felony murder, intent to commit felony serving as malice necessary for murder (force crushed aorta, which remained crushed because calcified with cholesterol plaque, impairing blood flow to spinal cord & lower extremities: gangrene, complications, death); no merger because intent to steal, NOT 'dangerous

weapon' or 'assault' factor, serves as substitute for malice requirement;

C v Gruning **46 MAC 842 (99)**—no merger of "entering dwelling while armed and using force therein (G.L. c. 265, § 18C) with second degree felony murder because there were two additional and separate felonious assaults (i.e., two additional victims of assaults, one fatal (manslaughter) and one not);

C v Robinson **48 MAC 329 (99)**—"virtually" always the question whether felony is independent of the homicide is issue of law to be decided by judge, subject to appellate review (but cf. *C v Ramos* **47 MAC 792, 797 (99)**;

C v Travis **408 M 1, 7–10 (90)**—though felony here was kidnapping, it was accomplished by wrapping rope around V's neck and knocking him unconscious with gun; court held no "merger" of kidnapping and felony murder because the FURTHER means of restraint (i.e., gag in mouth, pillowcase tied over head) were not essential to the kidnapping ("separate and distinct acts of physical violence"), and one or the other of these was cause of death by asphyxiation;

C v Christian **430 M 552, 556 (2000)**—armed robbery will always support conviction of felony murder; rejecting argument that armed robbery "merged" (Gunter) with murder since the fatal shots were the force used to make the theft a robbery; D who heightens the possibility of the victim's death by shooting the victim first cannot escape application of the felony murder rule; rejecting also necessity of instruction on 2d degree felony murder (on theory that theft was mere afterthought to killing, but this inappropriate since there wouldn't be requisite causal connection between the felony and the homicide);

C v Claudio **418 M 103 (94)**—(pre-Gunter) though reversing on other ground, upholding felony murder conviction (against "merger" argument) when underlying felony = G.L. c. 266, § 14 (B&E nighttime felony, to wit, armed assault in dwelling, & thereafter assaulting person therein); "the elements of a breaking and entering in a residence in the night time sufficiently distinguish a violation of G.L. c. 266, § 14, from armed assault in other circumstances, so as to justify treating a violation of that statute as predicating a charge of murder in the first degree by reason of felony-murder";

C v Prater **431 M 86, 95–97 (2000)**—despite argument that Gunter, above, decreed otherwise, SJC held that armed assault with intent to rob V is OK predicate felony for felony murder of same V; underlying felony "is equivalent to the malice aforethought required for murder"; "focus of analysis" is "on the substitution of the intent, not on the number of assaults";

C v Moran **387 M 644, 647–51 (82)**—conscious disregard for life;

C v Matchett **386 M 492 (82)**—(same);

C v Currie **388 M 776 (83)**—but inherent in use of gun;

C v Doucette **430 M 461, 468 n.6 (99)**—armed home invasion, G.L. c. 265, § 18C, is "inherently dangerous felony" for purpose of 1st degree felony murder;

C v Baez **427 M 630 (98)**—forcible rape of child is inherently dangerous to human life; when this is the predicate for felony murder, jury needn't be instructed as well on "conscious disregard for the risk to human life";

C v Eagles **419 M 825 (95)**—rejecting argument for abolition of felony-murder doctrine, plus holding that underlying home invasion was nothing but 'life' felony (so no lesser included offense of 2d degree felony murder possible);

C v Wojcik **65 MAC 758 (2006)**—second degree felony murder was properly predicated upon "[attempted] larceny over $250", because it arose from an insurance fraud scheme whereby D intentionally caused vehicle accident; in order to convict, jury must find that circumstances of the not-inherently-dangerous crime demonstrated D's conscious disregard of the risk to human life (citing *C v Matchett* 386 M at 507); that the larceny over $250 wasn't completed because insurer refused to pay wasn't dispositive;

C v Gordon **422 M 816 (96)**—need not prove, for felony murder, that felony still in progress at time of homicide; enough if at substantially same time & place (here 1 V killed after D robbed him of jacket, & other V killed because he witnessed robbery & first killing);

C v Nichypor **419 M 209 (94)**—similar, plus holding irrelevant alleged fact that separate/independent plan to kill was hatched by 2 co-D's;

C v Netto **438 M 686 (2003)**—see supplemental instructions given on joint venture felony-murder, including, inter alia, killing had to be "incidental to and the natural and probable consequence of the armed robbery," and this meant that killing "must have taken place during a single logically related continuing criminal transaction at a time when the nonstabber was actively involved as a participant in the armed robbery"; if killing took place after the nonstabber was no longer actively involved in committing a crime, then the nonstabber is NG of armed robbery felony murder; consider whether there was break in logical chain of events between the robbery & the killing/separation of an appreciable amount of time; whether killing "occurred at a place that was different and separate from the nonstabber";

C v Mavredakis **430 M 848, 855 (2000)**—rejecting argument that shooting occurred during breaking and entering, not a robbery: larceny as contemplated may be converted into robbery because assault was committed (with gun) on someone who had protective concern for goods taken and who interfered with theft; rejecting argument that armed robbery of V "merged" and didn't support felony murder conviction;

C v Watson **388 M 536 (83)**—robber N.G. unless knows co-D (killer) = armed;

C v Carter **396 M 234 (85)**—& has willingness to see shooting happen;

C v Simmons **417 M 60 (94)**—same;

C v Fickett **403 M 194 (88)**—(same); & D's testimony = too late for motion for required finding of not guilty;

C v Gilliard **36 MAC 183 (94)**—possible ineffective counsel for failure to request lesser included offense of simple A&B on behalf of joint venturer in attack which culminated in death (D could be found not to know of weapon);

C v Donovan **422 M 349 (96)**—though D charged with felony murder & armed robbery, there was basis in evidence for lesser included offense of involuntary manslaughter: D himself only punched V, & jury could have found he did not know co-D had knife & neither knew of nor participated in robbery, and acted without malice but in reckless or wanton disregard of consequences of his actions; even though defense was that D played **no** role in assault, this does not relieve judge of responsibility to instruct on lesser included offense;

C v Padgett **44 MAC 359 (98)**—D knew co-D had guns during daytime house breaks; armed robbery of persons for a truck to facilitate getaway later = OK predicate for D's guilt of 2d degree felony murder; **DICTA**: "judge may have been correct in determining that the daytime (armed) breaks into a dwelling house were inherently dangerous";

C v Walker **17 MAC 194 (83)**—felony murder if know co-D has unloaded gun because "inherent danger"; *(See Chapter 16, Defenses: Intent)*;

C v Dias **419 M 698 (95)**—suggesting instruction: no person can be G of homicide or felony murder theory unless act is either actually or constructively his, & it can't be his act unless committed by own hand or someone acting in concert with him in furtherance of common object/purpose;

C v Tevenal **401 M 225 (87)**—intoxication admissible re: specific intent for underlying armed robbery, but not re: felony murder because armed robbery = inherent danger (so malice aforethought);

C v Blackwell **422 M 294 (96)**—jury can properly convict of underlying felony & acquit of felony murder, **e.g.,** when felony & murder aren't "sufficiently related";

C v Miller **435 M 274 (2001)**—felony murder (aggravated rape) conviction upheld; presence of semen not required for proof of penetration in rape; rejecting D's argument that mere disbelief of his statement that intercourse was consensual not proof to the contrary; evidence included testimony from murder V's neighbor that she heard woman crying out "Don't, don't, no", followed by a loud bang & silence;

C v Wade **428 M 147 (98)**—aggravated rape of 83-yr-old woman, following D's dragging her from her residence to his, and involving fractures of her hip and wrist, was followed 20 days later by respiratory failure "associated with a pulmonary condition that is the major cause of the high mortality rate for elderly persons who break a hip"; jury was charged only that jurors were required to find that the injuries were the proximate cause of V's death, and D argued that charge should also say must prove that death was "a natural and probable consequence of" D's action; no prejudice here given evidence, but element "should be included in cases in which the facts raise an issue in this regard" (id. at 151 n.4) (cf. *C v Fortes* **47 MAC 214 (99)** purse snatch from elderly victim, including her fall to pavement, led to embolism and death, and involuntary manslaughter conviction upheld); (see also *C v Niemic* **427 M 718 (98)** valid defense of lack of causation if intervening conduct of a third party (allegedly reckless medical care) caused death AND was not reasonably foreseeable);

C v Allen **430 M 252, 258 (99)**—instruction that V's death was a "natural and probable consequence of" the underlying felony (here, armed robbery) is necessary ONLY where evidence raises "legitimate question that V's death was proximately caused by the felony underlying," and no such question here;

C v Mandile **403 M 93 (88)**—NG for wheelman because robbery not shown (though D had $730), nor INTENT (for premeditation.) though presence, means, & hid gun';

21-K.3.d. G.L. c. 278, § 33E—Broad Appellate Review; Facts, Too

C v Almon **387 M 599(82)**: *C v Tavares* **385 M 140 (82)**—*(See Chapter 15, Postconviction Remedies);*

21-K.4. Manslaughter (G.L. c. 265, § 13): Unlawful Kill without Malice Aforethought

Nolan and Sartorio, *Criminal Law* **(3d ed. 2001) §§ 201–6;**

Wharton's Criminal Law (14th ed.), Chapter 9;
G.L. c. 277, § 79—form indictment;

C v Ware **438 M 1014 (2003)**—provocation is not an element of voluntary manslaughter but is instead a defense to murder; malice & adequate provocation or mitigation = mutually exclusive;

C v Baker **67 MAC 760 (2006)**—when only manslaughter is charged, malice isn't factor in analysis because it isn't element of crime; manslaughter, standing alone, simply requires proof that D intentionally inflicted injury likely to cause death & which did cause death, & that D acted unlawfully; there is no extra element of required proof that D killed V in heat of passion;

C v Medeiros **395 M 336 (85)**—"voluntary" vs. "involuntary";

C v Accetta **422 M 642 (96)**—when evidence supports charge on both voluntary & involuntary manslaughter, verdict slip should list the alternative options (insures unanimity);

C v Jones **75 MAC 38 (2009)**—rejecting D's argument that voluntary manslaughter was not a lesser included option within first degree murder;

C v Pimental **454 M 475 (2009)**—judge in first degree murder trial instructed jury on lesser included crimes of voluntary manslaughter (reasonable provocation and excessive force in self defense) and involuntary manslaughter (assault and battery resulting in unlawful kill-

ing), but properly rejected request for lesser offense of assault and battery by dangerous weapon (shod foot) because ABDW is not a lesser included offense of murder;

C v Berry **47 MAC 24 (99)**—evidence sufficient to support voluntary manslaughter on both excessive force in self-defense AND "provocation deemed adequate in law to cause the accused to lose his self-control in the heat of passion", so jury properly was instructed on both; judge not bound by D's trial testimony in framing of instructions; support for joint venture instruction may be found in defense case (not limited to Commonwealth's case in chief);

C v Walker **443 M 213, 221 (2005)**—when jurors were instructed on all three theories of voluntary manslaughter (heat of passion on reasonable provocation, heat of passion induced by sudden combat, and excessive use of force in self-defense), they should NOT have been instructed that they had to be unanimous as to which theory applied, but no substantial likelihood of miscarriage of justice here;

C v Campbell **352 M 387 (67)**—battery (without malice);

21-K.4.a. Voluntary—Intentionally Kill, but Heat of Passion and Reasonable Provocation

C v Webster **5 Cush 295, 307–08 (1850)**;

C v DelVerde **398 M 288 (86)**—act, not death, must be intentional;

C v Squailia **429 M 101 (99)**—voluntary manslaughter instruction not warranted because D's version/testimony was "accident"; but cf., e.g., *C v Thayer* **418 M 130, 132–33 (94)** (sex assault case) lesser included offense matched neither Commonwealth theory nor D's defense, but SJC rejected D's argument that judge erred in instructing jury on lesser offense;

C v Spear **2 MAC 687 (74)**—provocation not element of manslaughter, but murder defense;

Ariel A., a juvenile v Commonwealth **420 M 281 (95)**—voluntary manslaughter not lesser included offense of murder because not **necessarily** included within murder; evidence must establish "additional element not present in murder", i.e., reasonable provocation sufficient in law to mitigate but not excuse unlawful killing;

C v Berry **431 M 326 (2000)**—even absent Commonwealth request, judge may/should charge on lesser included offenses over D's objection, if evidence warrants conviction of lesser crime; D has no right to employ 'all or nothing' strategy re: charged crime (here, 2d degree murder); evidence here supported voluntary manslaughter on theory of heat of passion on reasonable provocation; after reversal on other ground, D could only be retried for voluntary manslaughter on this theory (& not for murder);

C v Acevedo **446 M 435 (2006)**—where evidence supports it, D is entitled to correct instructions on both provocation and self-defense; jury must have opportunity to consider voluntary manslaughter on both theories; correct instruction on self-defense doesn't cure erroneous instruction on provocation or eliminate prejudice from failure to instruct at all on provocation as theory of voluntary manslaughter; trial counsel's failure to request "provocation" instruction deprived D of an available defense;

C v Fortini **68 MAC 701 (2007)**—despite fact that D armed self and waited on front porch in dark following loud threats from strangers in car, jury entitled to consider both self-defense (see S.C., 44 MAC 562 (98)) and provocation on sudden combat (because the strangers came onto porch and "lunged" for the gun held by D); motion for new trial should have been allowed due to error in manslaughter instruction, i.e., saying Commonwealth must prove D acted with reasonable provocation for verdict of manslaughter (should have been instruction that Commonwealth must prove beyond a reasonable doubt that D didn't act on reasonable provocation);

C v Benoit **452 M 212 (2008)**—although "self-defense" instruction was legitimately refused (because D could have retreated), judge did instruct on voluntary manslaughter: D argued logical extension of *Adjutant* 443 M 649 (2005) (prior violent acts of victim admissible when issue of "first aggressor" is in dispute in context of self-defense), i.e., prior violent acts by deceased argued to be admissible in context of whether he initiated sudden and violent combat which would cause reasonable person to be provoked to heat of passion; because of newness of Adjutant rule and lack of opportunity to examine its impact, SJC "not prepared to extend the rule *at this time*", but reversed conviction on different ground; Ireland, J., believed "court should have undertaken a full analysis of the merits of extending the *Adjutant* rule to this case, instead of dismissing it as premature":

C v Yates **62 MAC 494, 498 n.3 (2004)**—issue is whether D had time to cool off between the incident of provocation and the striking of the blow; his conduct FOLLOWING the blow = irrelevant to issue of provocation, despite Commonwealth claim that D's failure to summon help after the blow, as V lay dying, refuted 'heat of passion';

C v Zagrodny **443 M 93 (2004)**—D's wife's statement that she was leaving and taking the kids held inadequate as "provocation sufficient to warrant a voluntary manslaughter instruction", and even if it were sufficient, the wounds D inflicted upon her immediately weren't fatal; fatal wounds occurred during second attack, after more than sufficient time for D to "cool off";

C v Keohane **444 M 563 (2005)**—minimum of 3½ hours between V's attack on D & time of murder, and reasonable person would have cooled off, so no basis for manslaughter instruction; furthermore, when D leaves scene of provocation & then returns to attack victim, "D is considered to have had adequate opportunity for his anger to subside"; enunciating plans for attack after leaving scene, and preparing for revenge attack isn't consistent with heat of passion;

C v Benson **453 M 90 (2009)**—last overt act of "stalking" of D by victim was several days before killing,

and this D's actions were deliberate, not passionate; no manslaughter instruction warranted; that stalking victims experience distress and fear both during and after 'stalking' might in some other case justify a change in the "cooling off clock['s]" start time;

C v Garcia **443 M 824, 835 (2005)**—no basis for "heat of passion" since "the color of clothing worn by a complete stranger" on the street wouldn't produce homicidal passion "even if it suggests the possibility of gang membership", and also D undertook planning of shooting which occurred 12 hours after the stabbing of his friend;

C v Burgess **450 M 422 (2008)**—evidence did not warrant finding reasonable provocation as insults and arguments = insufficient; alleged "push" of D against refrigerator also inadequate; D didn't testify, & police statement didn't explain how knife became involved, etc., leaving jury only impermissible speculation;

C v LeClair **445 M 734 (2006)**—rejects Model Penal Code principle that "heat of passion" may be based on conduct of a third party and needn't be caused by the victim; "evidence of provocation by a third party, rather than the victim of a homicide, is insufficient to warrant a voluntary manslaughter instruction";

C v Emerson **430 M 378 (99)**—no abuse of discretion in refusal to instruct on voluntary manslaughter because no evidence that killing arose from sudden combat, reasonable provocation, or heat of passion (and also no evidence as to how/why killing occurred at all, there being no witnesses and no statements by D, but this didn't bar conviction for deliberate premeditation 1st degree murder);

C v Gaouette **66 MAC 633 (2006)**—when D came to site intending to fight to settle grudge, arming himself and loading gun beforehand (purportedly for "possibility" that his adversaries might have weapons), he wasn't entitled to "provocation/sudden combat/heat of passion" instructions despite facts that adversaries thereafter approached D's car quickly, smashed car window with bat, etc.;

C v Bockman **424 M 757 (2004)**—when D claimed that he wasn't present when wife was killed, and didn't claim that he was provoked in manner so that killing would be mitigated, no right to lesser included instruction on voluntary manslaughter despite **prosecutor's closing argument** which speculated, on evidence, that killing occurred unexpectedly when wife "said something" / criticized D, causing him to grab some "object of opportunity" and kill her; nothing remotely to suggest what words were spoken or that they could have constituted reasonable provocation;

C v Gruning **46 MAC 842 (99)**—provocation must come FROM THE DECEASED to warrant voluntary manslaughter instruction;

C v McLeod **394 727 (85)**—distinguished (D mistakenly believed that V was his adversary, so voluntary manslaughter charge warranted);

C v Ruiz **442 M 826, 838–40 (2004)**—provocation / sudden combat must come from deceased; no error in failure to instruct, sua sponte, on "sufficient provocation" from mere statement when statement conveys, e.g., sexual infidelity: words here used were "mere insults," conveying no new information as D had known of affair for months;

C v Amaral **389 M 184 (83)**—for a jury to find that a "defendant formed an intent to kill in a transport of passion or in the heat of blood, . . . (t)here must be evidence that would warrant a reasonable doubt that something happened which would have been likely to produce in an ordinary person such a state of passion, anger, fear, fright, or nervous excitement as would eclipse his capacity for reflection or restraint, and that what happened actually did produce such a state of mind in the defendant"; no such evidence here;

C v Boucher **403 M 659 (89)**—if Commonwealth doesn't prove absence of provocation beyond reasonable doubt, there can be no finding of malice; "(m)alice and adequate provocation are mutually exclusive";

C v Hicks **356 M 442 (69)**—heat of passion, upon reasonable provocation;

C v Acevedo **427 M 714 (98)**—instruction that, for G of voluntary manslaughter, Commonwealth had to prove D caused the death, that it was without justification, and that D "injured (V) as a result of sudden combat or in the heat of passion or using excessive force in self-defense"; this last was exact reverse of Commonwealth's burden: Commonwealth must prove beyond reasonable doubt that D didn't act on reasonable provocation;

C v Dempsey **49 MAC 247 (2000)**—same; reversal for Acevedo error;

C v McLaughlin **433 M 558 (2001)**—reversal for Acevedo error, distinguishing cases in which no reversal was ordered;

C v Lapage **435 M 480 (2001)**—reversing for Acevedo error;

C v Whitman **430 M 746 (2000)**—jury should have been instructed that killing "would be reduced to voluntary manslaughter if the Commonwealth fails to prove absence of provocation beyond a reasonable doubt"; WRONG to say "in order for a killing which would otherwise be murder to be reduced . . . , there must be proof of adequate provocation";

C v Gonzalez **443 M 799, 808 (2005)**—"Commonwealth has burden of disproving elements of voluntary, not involuntary manslaughter";

C v Vives **447 M 537 (2006), citing** *C v Pov Hour* **446 M 35 (2006)**—Model Jury Instructions on Homicide (1999) adequately instruct that Commonwealth bore burden of proving beyond reasonable doubt the absence of mitigating factors;

C v Carlino **429 M 692 (99)**—instruction that malice is negated by provocation only if provocation is proved beyond a reasonable doubt = reversal; correct = because evidence raised possibility that D acted on reasonable provocation. Commonwealth must prove beyond a reasonable doubt that D didn't act on reasonable provocation;

C v Williams **428 M 383, 389 (98)**—Commonwealth doesn't bear burden of proving existence of provocation in order to sustain manslaughter conviction, but must prove absence of provocation;

C v Zukoski **370 M 23, 28 (76)**—insults not reasonable provocation;

C v Seabrooks **425 M 507 (97)**—estranged girlfriend's accusing D of being intoxicated and attempting to telephone police not reasonable provocation;

C v Vatcher **438 M 584 (2003)**—that D's son (who had physical and mental disorders) kicked D, got into wrestling match with D, kicked planter, & tried to destroy mother's birthday cards, wasn't adequate provocation;

C v Baker **346 M 107 (63)**—sudden combat;

C v Mahnke **368 M 662, 702 (75)**—slap in face;

C v Masello **428 M 446, 450 (98)**—though claim that V threw punches at D, this occurred hours before killing; there was "more than sufficient time" for D to "cool off"; no basis for voluntary manslaughter as lesser offense;

C v Bermudez **370 M 438, 440–2 (76)**—words, but not PAST adultery, maybe reasonable provocation;

C v Schnopps **383 M 178 (81)**—estranged wife's verbal admission to PRESENT adultery maybe reasonable provocation;

C v LeClair **429 M 313 (99)**—words alone maybe sufficient provocation if "sudden oral revelation of infidelity," BUT revelation here not surprise because D told police and jury that he suspected it for several weeks; court didn't reach whether infidelity words as provocation legitimate even when parties aren't married, id. at n.4, though D said yes, citing *Jefferson* **416 M 258, 264 (93)**;

C v Yates **62 MAC 494 (2004)**—because D's recitation of facts (& there was no other at plea colloquy) disclosed issue of provocation (**prostitute told D after sex that she was glad to have exposed him to AIDS**) possibly mitigating second-degree murder, & nothing showed that it or malice had been explained to D, "G" plea was not made intelligently, & its withdrawal was allowed;

C v Zanetti **454 M 449, 469 (2009)**—prosecutor's closing argument "arguably suggested" evidence supportive of manslaughter instruction (reasonable provocation, D's actual belief at time);

C v Jefferson **416 M 258 (93)**—D got more than he was "entitled" to instruction re: reasonable provocation as learning from words something constituting immediate & intense offense to lover's sensitivities ("just face it, the relationship is over" & "I don't want you no more");

C v Griffin **19 MAC 188 (85)**—obscene gestures not reasonable provocation;

C v Pierce **419 M 28 (94)**—invitation to homosexual activity, even if accompanied by a "perhaps offensive" gesture (grabbing D's testicles) not reasonable provocation;

C v Morales **70 MAC 526 (2007)**—jury instruction that physical contact was required for heat of passion upon reasonable provocation = ERROR; reversal here despite no objection;

C v Correia **18 MAC 178 (84)**—no provocation; (overview);

C v Thomas **429 M 146, 154–55 (99)**—despite D argument that unrecognized vehicle was "bearing down on" him in street, no reasonable provocation from V's driving car down road toward D because no evidence this was "in a menacing fashion", or that vehicle "came on him suddenly"; D stood in street, watched vehicle approach, could have stepped onto sidewalk, but instead shot driver;

C v Boucher **403 M 659 (89)**—deceased's initiation of combat was reasonable provocation;

C v Halbert **410 M 534 (91)**—"salacious invitation" to sex by deceased was not reasonable provocation;

C v Azar **32 MAC 290 (92)**—baby's crying was not reasonable provocation;

C v Benjamin **430 M 673 (2000)**—words of unarmed victim that he was going to come back and kill D not reasonable provocation, despite D's claim (with expert testimony) that this particular D "suffered" from "a heightened level of vigilance"; exception to general rule that words alone are not reasonable provocation is "very limited"; declined to expand exception to take into account particular D's sensitivities, be they from drug or alcohol impairment or, as here, "heightened vigilance";

C v Rivera **441 M 358 (2004)**—no error in refusing to instruct, with respect to "provocation," about D's subjective beliefs (delusional schizophrenic); rejecting again "the proposition that a middle ground exists between insanity and criminal responsibility that would not exonerate a defendant but would reduce the degree of the crime from murder to manslaughter, i.e., a defense of 'diminished responsibility' or 'diminished capacity'";

21-K.4.b. Excessive Force in Self-Defense

See Chapter 16, Defenses;

Superior Court Criminal Practice Jury Instructions § 2.10, 3.6–3.7—§ 3.8 re: defense of another, § 3.9 re: defense of property'

C v Young **35 MAC 427 (93)**—rejecting claim that evidence of provocation, as matter of law, entitled D to required finding of not guilty on malice issue; though V swung 'stick' at one D, there was evidence that the two Ds had prepared earlier for gun assault upon V;

C v Kendrick **351 M 203 (66)**: *C v Stokes* **374 M 583 (78)**;

C v Alfonso **19 MAC 599 (85)**:*C v Medeiros, above*, **395 M 336, 341 (85)**;

C v Cyr **425 M 89 (97)**—if V used excessive force in repelling D from dwelling, manslaughter instruction appropriate;

C v Burbank **388 M 789 (83)**—must instruct on excessive force (manslaughter), not just self defense as all-or-nothing (see also **Boucher** above);

C v Santos **454 M 770 (2009)**—reversal of first degree murder conviction (despite no objection below) because erroneous jury instructions told jurors that excessive force in self-defense negated the defense entirely, to the end of conviction of murder; instead, imperfect self-defense would result in manslaughter conviction; abundant

language that appellate court should not parse evidence and make its own appraisal of credibility/viability of defense;

C v Barros **425 M 572 (97)**—determination re: whether D's belief concerning his exposure to danger was reasonable may not take into account his intoxication;

C v Johnson **412 M 368 (92)**—valid defense of another does not reduce murder to manslaughter but relieves D of all liability; excessive use of force does reduce murder to manslaughter;

C v Carlino **429 M 692 (99)**—jury could have believed from instructions (erroneously) that excessive force in self-defense or defense of another justified murder verdict (rather than lesser, manslaughter);

C v Taylor **32 MAC 570 (92)**—D who claims to act in self-defense because in imminent fear of serious bodily harm but who did not abide by duty to retreat entitled to instruction on voluntary manslaughter;

C v Niemic **427 M 718, 722 n.2 (98)**—if D purports to act in self-defense but fails to retreat when has opportunity, manslaughter is NOT appropriate (contra dicta in *Gagne* **367 M 519, 526 (75)**); only "imperfect" self-defense which can result in manslaughter verdict is use of excessive force when some lesser degree of force is justified;

C v Walker **443 M 213 (2005)**—**rejects** argument that if D responds with deadly force after being put in fear of physical harm (i.e., by mere "push"), culpability is for voluntary manslaughter rather than murder (rationale of "excessive force" in legitimate self-defense); (*C v Toon* **55 MAC 642, 654 (2002)**—same); threshold for use of deadly force is if person has reasonable apprehension of great bodily harm and reasonable belief that no other means would suffice to prevent such harm; "once the level of force used by a person is ascertained, that level of force will determine whether the deadly or nondeadly force standard will apply"; "the two standards are distinct, self-contained definitions of self-defense . . . [,] mutually exclusive";

C v Casavant **426 M 368 (98)**—no manslaughter instruction warranted when D choked prostitute in his car until she passed out & then stabbed her in chest 4 times: no view of evidence "warranted a reasonable doubt as to whether D took all proper means to avoid physical combat before attacking his smaller, unarmed victim with a knife";

21-K.4.c. Involuntary—UNINTENTIONAL Kill, but Wanton or Reckless Disregard; OR (Non Life-Endangering) Misdemeanor

District Court Model Jury Instruction #5.636, Involuntary Manslaughter (by Juvenile)

Wharton's Criminal Law § 167—Modern trend = abandon misdemeanor-manslaughter rule;

C v Campbell **352 M 387 (67)**—intentional act & accidental death;

C v Sneed **413 M 387, 394 (92)**—evidence of non-felonious battery on baby with "high degree of likelihood" of "substantial harm" required instruction on manslaughter; involuntary manslaughter instruction may be required where D charged with unintentional killings under 2d & 3d prong malice;

C v Williams **428 M 383, 390 (98)**—for battery manslaughter, there must have been "battery not amounting to a felony," when (D) knew or should have known that the battery he was committing endangered human life and knew or should have known that conduct created a high degree of likelihood that substantial harm would result to another (not merely "conduct that could lead to substantial harm or death");

C v Pimental **454 M 475 (2009)**—judge in first degree murder trial instructed jury on lesser included crimes of voluntary manslaughter (reasonable provocation and excessive force in self defense) and involuntary manslaughter (assault and battery resulting in unlawful killing), but properly rejected request for lesser offense of assault and battery by dangerous weapon (shod foot) because ABDW is not a lesser included offense of murder;

C v Pease **49 MAC 539 (2000)**—D's two-handed hard "push" of V's chest, causing backwards fall and V's head to split open on sidewalk (skull fracture of 10–12 inches) enough for involuntary manslaughter; alleged internal inconsistency in jury verdict (NG of "battery" manslaughter, but G of involuntary manslaughter by wanton and reckless conduct) no ground for relief;

C v Power-Koch **69 MAC 735 (2007)**—D said "accident" in firing gun, didn't intend to accede to depressed best friend's request that D shoot him, though held gun, not familiar with handguns, didn't know fully loaded, didn't mean to pull trigger; error found in refusal to instruct on accident, "an unintentional event occurring through inadvertence, mistake, or negligence," evidentiary basis in D's statements to police;

C v Depradine **42 MAC 401 (97)**—that gun was fired when only inches from V's chest, that D acknowledged playing with the gun, which was likely to have been loaded, that V said "do you want to kill me?" = sufficient to establish "high degree of likelihood that substantial harm" would result to another;

C v Braley **449 M 316, 331–32 (2007)**—no basis in evidence for manslaughter when (best) evidence was that D "shot into the crowd": intentionally discharging firearm in direction of another person creates plain and strong likelihood of death;

C v Levesque **436 M 443 (2002)**—failure to take adequate steps either to control a fire accidentally started, or to report it to proper authorities was sufficient basis on which to ground involuntary manslaughter indictments (warehouse fire which killed six firefighters was begun by homeless couple's knocking over a candle during a physical altercation); "omission when there is a duty to act can constitute manslaughter if the omission is wanton or reckless";

C v Dagenais **437 M 832 (2002)**—no error in failure to instruct on involuntary manslaughter given D's testimony that victim had been sitting on ledge of bridge over river as they discussed whether she would testify for him in upcoming trial; when she refused, he approached her, she backed up, yelled to D to stay away, & fell into river; on D's version, said SJC, it was just an accident, with no conduct on his part leading to death;

C v Fortes **47 MAC 214 (99)**—purse snatch (and any robbery from a person, "with the possible exception of pickpocketing") held to involve "high degree of likelihood that substantial harm will result to another," justifying involuntary manslaughter conviction (elderly victim died from coronary embolism from blood clots which developed after surgery to repair kneecap dislocated during the snatch, which she resisted); "immaterial" that joint venturers might not have anticipated the danger; standard = "reasonably prudent person";

C v Matos **36 MAC 958 (94)**—basis for lesser included offense of involuntary manslaughter found in D's statements to police (D gave loaded gun to very drunk V, who shot himself); D not entitled to bar jury consideration of lesser included offense (see also *Woodward* **427 M 659 (98)**)

C v Sheppard **404 M 774 (89)**—involuntary manslaughter by battery = death where "harm was likely";

C v Reed **427 M 100 (98)**—knife-stabbing death: no lesser included offense of involuntary manslaughter (unintentional killing from "battery not amounting to felony) because knife = deadly weapon, & knife attack = "felony in this Commonwealth";

C v Sullivan **29 MAC 93 (90)**—evidence that D waved knife to get attackers off him, accidentally stabbing v, required instruction on manslaughter;

C v Pierce **419 M 28 (94)**—no involuntary manslaughter lesser included offense warranted where scope of risk = clearly, death likely (throat slit, severe choking, & two knives stuck in head, one up to handle);

C v Robinson **48 MAC 329 (99)**—similar; scope of risk consistent with 3d prong malice, not merely "high degree of likelihood that substantial harm will result"; D knocked V unconscious and placed rope around neck, gag in mouth, pillowcase over head; further, D was convicted of felony murder (and where it "applies," "generally (D) is not entitled to an instruction on manslaughter";

C v Hall **45 MAC 146 (98)**—no involuntary manslaughter warranted (14 stabbings, 8 "major" wounds, including lethal one to heart = 3d prong malice (plain and strong likelihood of death), not merely "high degree of likelihood that substantial harm will result"); rejecting argument that D, suffering "battered woman's syndrome" and intoxicated, entitled to involuntary manslaughter instruction on some "diminished capacity" theory (no such "defense in this Commonwealth," id. at 154);

C v DeLosSantos **37 MAC 526 (94)**—judge's instruction improperly precluded jury from finding recklessness (holding slippery baby over sink while splashing water on her): degree of risk of physical harm created by particular conduct was issue for jury, and was only differentiation between 3d prong malice (murder) and involuntary manslaughter;

C v Kinney **361 M 709, 712 (72)**—reckless shooting;

C v Atencio **345 M 627 (63)**—Russian roulette;

C v Ward **426 M 290 (97)**—rejecting argument that Russian roulette fatalities should be only involuntary manslaughter as matter of law;

C v Tatro **4 MAC 295 (76)**—armed robbery = wanton act, so heart attack = manslaughter;

C v Starling **382 M 423 (81)**—beat infant;

C v Bianco **388 M 358 (83)**—D's A & B not cause of death of V who jumped into (pushed) car & drowned;

C v Joyce **18 MAC 417 (84)**—D caused death of V killed by train;

C v Juvenile **17 MAC 988 (84)**—intent to fend off, not stab = involuntary;

C v Welansky **316 M 383, 396–401 (44)**—wanton or reckless, not just grossly negligent; breach of duty;

C v Grey **399 M 469, n.4 (87)**—wanton/reckless = both objective & subjective (facts known to D);

C v Flynn **37 MAC 556 (94)**—reversed on other ground, 420 M 810 (95)—error to instruct that intoxication has no bearing on crime of manslaughter;

C v Bouvier **316 M 489 (44)**—D's testimony (tripped, grabbed gun, it discharged) = accident, maybe negligent, not wanton and reckless (assume foreseeable risk);

C v Figueroa **56 MAC 641 (2002)**—D not entitled to instruction on accident because evidence didn't support both unintentional and not wanton/reckless: joint venture co-D pulled loaded revolver out, and while holding finger on trigger, threw punch at victim;

C v Gallison **383 M 659 (81)**—reckless omission to care for child;

C v Michaud **389 M 491 (83)**—no reckless failure to feed/care;

C v McCauley **355 M 554 (69)**—shooting may be unintended;

C v Jackmon **63 MAC 47 (2005)**—accident is not a defense to felony murder; on causation instruction here, jury must have found that joint venturer was shot by D, disposing of D's argument that correct "accident" instruction failed to convey defense theory that joint venturer had accidentally fallen on his gun and shot himself;

C v Papadinis **402 M 73 (88)**—D's fear admissible to explain why he drove off (& killed cop);

C v Hebert **373 M 535 (77)**—no such thing as "attempted involuntary" manslaughter;

C v Parenti **14 MAC 696 (82)**—no assault with intent to commit involuntary manslaughter;

C v Sanna **424 M 92 (97)**—killing without malice does not automatically constitute involuntary manslaughter;

C v Catalina **407 M 779 (90)**—"unlawful act" (misdemeanor) manslaughter abolished except where battery causes death; evidence of D's selling heroin to known addict sufficient to support manslaughter indictment on theory of wanton or reckless conduct;

C v Perry **416 M 1003 (93)**—procuring heroin for person known by D to be addict who dies as result of overdose sufficient to support indictment for involuntary manslaughter; "all heroin of unknown strength is inherently dangerous & (use) carries with it a high probability that death will occur";

C v Walker **442 M 185 (2004)**—despite fact that drug prescribed for D's insomnia had legitimate uses, D's use of it (in an amount 4–6 times the recommended dosage for a person of victim's age) in alcoholic drinks to drug woman = sufficient for involuntary manslaughter conviction; drug was a controlled substance, with labels warning not to give it to anyone else and not to drink any alcohol when taking it; further conviction for mingling "poison" with drink (G.L. c. 265, § 28) also valid because, despite fact that drug was not, per se, poison, it was a controlled substance not prescribed for V, AND D gave V four to six times the "therapeutic dose", and there were warnings not to ingest alcohol when taking it;

C v Vaughn **43 MAC 818 (97)**—injecting heroin, albeit ½ normal "dose", into vein of another = sufficient for G of involuntary manslaughter; Court refuses to distinguish **Catalina**, etc. re sufficiency of evidence for indictment; no expert testimony required re danger of heroin;

Marshall v Commonwealth **413 M 593 (92)**—evidence that overdose victim died as result of another's wanton or reckless conduct in giving or selling her drugs was insufficient;

C v Selby **426 M 168 (97)**—killing occurred during armed assault in dwelling (G.L. c. 265, § 18A) as D intended to commit robbery & gun fired when D "reflexively" pulled trigger after V grabbed gun: convicted of deliberate premeditation & felony murder, no error in refusing instruction on involuntary manslaughter: "accidental" discharge of gun is of no consequence when killing is during commission of felony inherently dangerous to human life"; as matter of law, 3d prong malice shown if "uncontradicted evidence" = believed;

C v Gould **413 M 707 (92)**—counsel's failure to request involuntary manslaughter instruction not ineffective assistance where evidence was that victim sustained massive injuries from numerous blows, notwithstanding D's claim that victim fell;

C v Clark **432 M 1, 21 (2000)**—at trial for fatal shooting of a state trooper, no error in failing to instruct on manslaughter despite appellate counsel's suggestion that jurors could have believed that D fired accidentally, or that D didn't intend to kill because would have known trooper was wearing bullet-proof vest: no evidence presented to support either of these theories;

C v Jenks **426 M 582 (98)**—firing pistol seven times in crowded room is more than "wanton & reckless conduct" and is instead "malicious conduct in the plainest sense"; no right to instruction on involuntary manslaughter;

C v Ferreira **417 M 592 (94)**—evidence of binding V's hands behind back & tying V's feet with cables attached to metal tool box before throwing him into Cape Cod Canal did not entitle D to lesser included offense of involuntary manslaughter; scope of risk of harm = only consistent with malice;

C v Alebord **68 MAC 1 (2006)**—D not entitled to instruction on lesser offense of manslaughter: cited trial evidence was that when co-D shot victim, D believed that co-D was "only" going to fire gun "into the crowd", but scope of risk for this was "plain and strong likelihood of death", consistent only with "malice"/murder culpability; D's attempts (on appeal) to claim thought of firing "near" rather than "into" crowd = unavailing;

C v DeMarco **444 M 678 (2005)**—D not entitled to instruction on involuntary manslaughter, because he testified that he "could have stopped wrestling with" victim (wife), and admitted that he choked and strangled her after having slammed her into steel locker, etc. (only plain and strong likelihood of death);

C v Knight **37 MAC 92 (94)**—evidence sufficient for manslaughter conviction: V's body concealed by D, D lied about her whereabouts & attempted to cash V's welfare check, and allegedly said that he and V had been fighting and he thought he might have killed her;

C v Holmes **32 MAC 906 (92)**—wanton & reckless conduct & 3d prong manslaughter distinguished; evidence of stabbing from behind, without other mitigating factors, did not require instruction on manslaughter;

C v Sanna **424 M 92 (97)**—risk of harm from 34 knife wounds and 15 blows to head = plain & strong likelihood of death (3d prong malice) rather than wanton and reckless conduct amounting to invol. manslaughter ("high degree of likelihood that substantial harm will result"), so no lesser included offense involuntary manslaughter instruction warranted; see also *C v Sires* **413 M 292 (92)** - similar;

21-K.5. Motor Vehicle Homicide (G.L. c. 90, § 24G)

G.L. c. 90, § 24G—(operating under influence, operating after revocation, reckless or negligent, + endanger lives & safety (= misdemeanor, but felony if both):

G.L. c. 218, § 26—District Court jurisdiction;

C v Campbell **394 M 77 (85)**—general discussion;

C v Burke **6 MAC 697 (78)**—ordinary negligence;

C v Diaz **19 MAC 29 (84)**—motor vehicle homicide has looser causation standard (cf. *Bianco* **above, 388 M 358 (83)** D's A&B not cause of death of V who jumped into (pushed) car & drowned;);

C v Williams **73 MAC 833 (2009)**—following jury-waived trial (one complaint for misdemeanor motor vehicle homicide by operating while under the influence, and separate complaint for operating to endanger [not including element of death], judge said NG of motor vehicle homicide by operating under influence and G of operating to endanger but also "guilty of vehicular homicide by negligent operation"; later, the judge ordered that—instead of recording *a new count of the complaint* after trial—the homicide crime was to be recorded as an amendment "of

form" to operating to endanger complaint: error, as it was amendment of substance AND could not have been found within vehicle homicide complaint as written; though same statute set forth both homicide by OUI and homicide by negligent operation, text of complaint charged ONLY the OUI form; bill of particulars could not expand essential elements not charged in complaint, allegation of 'no prejudice' rejected;

C v Carlson **447 M 79 (2006)**—legislature intended statute to provide middle ground between felony of manslaughter and misdemeanor of driving to endanger; finding of ordinary negligence = sufficient to establish violation; that D's driving broadside into car would have caused only minor injuries to healthy person irrelevant; take victim as find her (preexisting chronic pulmonary disease was hugely exacerbated and victim chose not to be on ventilator, so died; jury could find this reasonably foreseeable result of D's failure to yield at intersection);

C v Doyle **73 MAC 304 (2008)**—D argued error in judge's failure to charge on "accident," but requested instruction (determine "whether D intentionally committed an act that was a criminal offense, or whether what occurred was a pure and simple accident") was not the law: relevant element is reckless or negligent operation of vehicle so as to endanger human life or safety; operating at excessive speed, knowing that children in cargo area of sport utility vehicle were not secured "did not provide a rational basis for" accident instruction; refusal to instruct on lesser included offense of 'operating to endanger' not error as distinguishing element (deaths caused by the operation) not rationally in issue;

C v Angelo Todesca Corporation **446 M 128 (2006)**—corporation may be held criminally liable for motor vehicle homicide arising out of the negligent operation of vehicle by its agent while he was engaged in authorized corporate business; despite fact that truck driver told victim he was about to back up, rolled down his window, checked his mirrors, turned off his radios, and operated truck very slowly, sufficient proof that he did not exercise reasonable care for detail officer's safety could be found from his knowledge that a functioning back-up alarm was mandated by company's written safety policy and knowledge that it was missing; company held responsible for employee's negligence;

C v Jones **382 M 387 (81)**—not lesser included offense to manslaughter; but no from & after sentence *(See Chapter 19, Double Jeopardy)*;

Fadden v C **376 M 604 (78)**—can charge negligent operation & OUI, but no from & after sentence;

C v Meehan **14 MAC 1028 (82)**—2 victims = 2 crimes *(See Chapter 19, Double Jeopardy)*;

C v Drew **11 MAC 517 (81)**—need CITATION (G.L. c. 90C, § 2)—(see § DD below)

21-L. RAPE

Superior Court Criminal Practice Jury Instructions §§ 2.12–2.15—(rape, assault with intent to rape, rape of a child with force, rape of child)

District Court Model Jury Instruction #5.632, Rape by Juvenile, Aggravated Rape by Juvenile;

Nolan and Sartorio, *Criminal Law* (3d ed. 2001) §§ 221–31;

See also Assault above, including indecent assault & battery Chapter 21-F, Other Aggravated Assaults);

Stephanie Page, et al., *Trying Sex Offense Cases in Massachusetts* (MCLE 1997 with 2001 Supp.);

C v Walter R. **414 M 714 (93)**—though common law presumed that person under age 14 is incapable of rape, this is not the law in Massachusetts now (no legal or medical basis for such presumption);

C v Smith **431 M 417 (2000)**—"INCEST" (G.L. c. 272, § 17) not accomplished except by "natural intercourse"; inserting finger into daughter's vagina and having her perform fellatio = dismissal; (NOTE WELL: statute subsequently rewritten by Legislature, & now includes acts alleged here); *C v Rahim* **441 M 273 (2004)**—current incest statute (G.L. c. 272, § 17) makes criminal only relationships between persons related by blood or adoption (i.e., not stepdaughter here);

C v Parreira **72 MAC 308 (2008)**—two slightly older male teenagers and two female teenagers in a vacant apartment paired off in two separate bedrooms: required finding of not guilty for D ordered on theory of joint venture liability for co-D's rape of co-D's partner: D's intent to have sex with D's partner was not the requisite "common intent"; for joint venture liability in sex crimes, precedents reveal a common victim, physical presence at immediate scene, and/or physical participation in the act;

G.L. c. 272, § 3—drugging person for purpose of unlawful sexual intercourse; *C v LeBlanc* **456 M 135 (2010)**—requires proof of "administering" or "causing to be taken", which is not merely giving or providing cocaine to sex partner (though here, partner's subsequent incapacity to consent led to rape conviction);

21-L.1. Forcible (G.L. c. 265, §§ 22 & 22A (Child))

G.L. c. 277, § 39—intercourse (including unnatural), by force/threat, & against will;

C v Brattman **10 MAC 579 (80)**—penetration = genital or anal;

C v Gichel **48 MAC 206 (99)**—"touching" of vulva or labia is sufficient; testimony that D "would touch me down below," in area called "vagina," enough here;

C v Kirkpatrick **423 M 436, 444–45 (96)**—D "ma(d)e me put his penis in my mouth. . . . But I wouldn't let him" and "touched (me) in my rear end" with his penis, though she 'wouldn't let him put it inside' "arguably described penetration";

C v Baldwin **24 MAC 200, 204–5 (87)**—"(i)ntrusion into the vagina itself is not required to make out the wrongful penetration. Touching by the male of the vulva or labia, as may surely be inferred from spreading Vaseline and ten minutes or so of attempted penile penetration, is intrusion enough";

C v Nylander **26 MAC 784 (89)**—child complainant, dolls, doctors show penetration; & defined OK re: 'natural' rape, but vague re: 'unnatural' because included anal "area";

C v Miller **435 M 274 (2001)**—felony murder (aggravated rape) conviction upheld; presence of semen not required for proof of penetration in rape; rejecting D's argument that mere disbelief of his statement that intercourse was consensual is not proof beyond a reasonable doubt of no consent; evidence included testimony from murder V's neighbor that she heard woman crying out "Don't, don't, no", followed by a loud bang & silence;

C v McDonald **110 M 405 (1872)**—consent considered during any part of act; degree of resistance = an important factor;

C v Goldenberg **338 M 377, 382–4 (59)**—need force, not just fraud;

C v Caracciola **409 M 648 (91)**—in context of sufficient evidence on which to return indictment, impersonating cop & threatening to arrest complainant was constructive force & thus rape;

Suliveres v Commonwealth **449 M 112 (2007)**—no rape where consent was achieved by fraud rather than force: in darkness, D impersonated complainant's boyfriend (D's brother); SJC says legislature has not acted to "overrule our decision in *Goldenberg* [338 M 377 (1959)]", despite amending the rape statute in other ways three times since 1959; "fraud in the factum" must mean, in context of rape, that complainant was defrauded as to the nature of the act performed rather than reason for doing it; here, as in *Goldenberg*, fraud was "in the inducement";

C v Moniz **43 MAC 913 (97)**—proof of 'force' sufficient re: 6-year-old complainant (testimony that she didn't want D to touch her as he did, was frightened by it, didn't tell because didn't want him to hurt her again); instruction OK that "physical" force not necessary & could instead be "constructive force"; *C v Armstrong* **73 MAC 245 (2008)**—actual physical force shown when child V was asleep, and "without opportunity [therefore] to resist", and also when she was awake and D pulled apart her legs for oral sex; convictions also sustainable under theory of constructive force (V was in care of D and wife, D was authority figure, D much older and larger); that V stated she was neither threatened nor scared by D didn't matter ("resignation" = "reflective of the very nature of . . . constructive force . . . [re:] rape of a young person";

C V Parreira **72 MAC 308 (2008)**—that complainant was "nudged" onto floor of closet, that D removed three layers of her clothing without her assistance, that she told him "no" and he did not stop when she first asked, and that she made crying sounds during intercourse = sufficient proof of force;

C v Fuller **66 MAC 84 (2006)**—though D argued error in judge's instructing jury on the "Massachusetts law of mental retardation" because it wasn't element of any indictments before jury & instruction was inconsistent with more professional definitions of retardation, court held it relevant to "consent" (trial judge had said relevant to "constructive or circumstantial force");

C v Urban **450 M 608 (2008),** *C v Blache* **450 M 583 (2008)**—jury instructions on sexual assault complainant's capacity to consent may not convey that mere intoxication/drunkenness equals incapacity to consent; intoxication must be extreme before it renders complainant incapable of consent; *C v Rodriguez* **76 MAC 59 (2009)**—same;

C v Frank **51 MAC 19, 24 (2001)**—proof of force sufficient: testimony by complainant that D "forced" her leg's apart and performed cunnilingus upon her after she refused to submit; additional assertion that "force" shown by threat that complainant (D's stepdaughter) would "lose her place in the family and cause harm to her mother and brothers" if she did not submit (citing *Caracciola* **409 M 648 (91)**);

C v Martin **47 MAC 240 (99)**—no error found in judge's answer to jury question that a threat to harm complainant's mother constituted a threat of bodily injury sufficient to prove force (citing *Caracciola* **409 M 648, 651–52 (91)**);

C v Haynes **45 MAC 192, 201 (98)**—telling twelve-year-old daughter of D's female companion that it's part of American Indian tradition for a father to be the first to have sex with daughter = constructive force (?!) because she "wanted to be his daughter" although she was afraid; *Caracciola* **409 M 648 (91)** cited; "force needed for rape may, depending on the circumstances, be constructive force, as well as physical force, violence, or the threat of bodily harm";

C v D'Ambrosio **318 M 779 (45)**—D got complainant drunk & incapable of consent;

C v Molle **56 MAC 621 (2002)**—instruction that sex complainant wouldn't have been capable of consent to sex if drunk SHOULD NOT HAVE BEEN GIVEN, because appropriate only when complainant is "wholly insensible" (& not here, where only 2–3 drinks, and testimony that she's not affected/intoxicated); instruction here was wrong in saying that there could be no consent if complainant was 'restrained from exercising her will because of the use of alcohol'; no objection, so no relief here (though dissents disagree);

C v Urban **67 MAC 301 (2006)**—Appeals Court reverses for judge's failure/refusal to charge that inability to consent could be shown only by finding complainant to be "wholly insensible" (or "utterly senseless"), not simply drunk/affected by intoxicants; in contrast = sleep, stupefaction, unconsciousness, & helplessness—states which "ordinarily" preclude voluntary consent; jury must be

aware of "the high degree of intoxication required to negate the capacity to consent"; **on further appellate review, 450 M 608 (2008)**—SJC reaches same result: Commonwealth must prove beyond reasonable doubt that because of consumption of drugs or alcohol, or some other reason (e.g., sleep, unconsciousness, mental retardation, or helplessness), complainant "was so impaired as to be incapable of consenting to intercourse"; see also *C v Blache* **450 M 583 (2008), decided same day** (if jury finds Commonwealth has proved beyond reasonable doubt complainant's incapacity according to this standard, this finding satisfies element of lack of consent, so Commonwealth need further prove, for rape conviction, only the amount of force "necessary to accomplish intercourse");

C v Rodriguez **76 MAC 59 (2009)**—same;

C v Sherry **386 M 682, 696 (82)**—open question: good faith MISTAKE by D re: complainant's consent?; *(See Chapter 16, Specific Intent)*;

C v Grant **391 M 645 (84)**—no "good faith" defense (here); i.e., no "specific intent" re: complaining witness's lack of consent;

C v Lefkowitz **20 MAC 513, 520, n.16 (85)**—(same ruling) but "in appropriate circumstances, a reasonable good faith mistake in assuming consent might be a defense";

C v Cordeiro **401 M 843 (88)**—judge went beyond what's required by instructing D must KNOW no consent by complainant & must have specific intent;

C v Simcock **31 MAC 184 (91)**—reasonable & good faith mistake that complainant consented is not valid defense to general intent crime of rape; preferable for judge not to instruct jury on this; cf. *C v Ascolillo* **405 M 456 (89)**;

C v Lopez **433 M 722 (2001)**—in this case & probably most cases, requirement that Commonwealth prove "force" "should negate any possible mistake as to consent," but holding only that "this case does not persuade us that we should recognize mistake of fact as to consent as a defense to rape in *all* cases";

C v McCrae **54 MAC 27 (2002)**—asserting flatly that there is no "honest mistake of fact" defense for alleged sexual assault, thus overstating SJC's view of the law (*C v Lopez* **433 M 722 (2001)**), though in accord with Appeals Court pronouncement in *Simcock* **31 MAC 184 (91)**;

C v Blache **450 M 583 (2008)**—declines to overrule *Lopez* **433 M 722 (2001)**, still will not recognize 'mistake of fact defense' (G.L. c. 265, § 22 doesn't require proof of D's knowledge of victim's lack of consent or intent to engage in nonconsensual intercourse as a material element of the offense);

C v Blair **21 MAC 625 (86)**—no intoxication defense (here?) to aggravated rape by joint venture; *(See Chapter 16, Defenses: Intent)*;

C v Sumner **18 MAC 349 (84)**—kidnap & "serious bodily injury" = aggravated;

C v Moreschi **38 MAC 562 (95)**—ABDW and batteries were completed crimes before rape occurred but sufficient for conviction of aggravated rape ("one continuous episode and course of conduct"; underlying crime need not occur at "precise moment of vaginal penetration");

C v Gallant **373 M 577, 584 (77)**—"unnatural" - fellatio or anal opening;

C v Hackett **383 M 888 (81)**—(same); (see *Nylander* **26 MAC 784 (89)** (vague re: unnatural because included anal "area");

C v Whitehead **379 M 640 (80)**—female D joint venture OR penetration;

C v McCan **277 M 199, 203 (31)**—A&B and assault are lesser included offenses;

C v Egerton **396 M 499 (86)**—(fn.3) assumes indecent A & B = lesser included offense;

C v Gilmore **399 M 741 (87)**—rational basis for G of lesser included offense of A&B rather than rape: defense wasn't alibi (contrast *Egerton* **396 M 499, 504 (86)**), & D's testimony admitted being with complainant, and that she resisted his advances, even to the point of biting his arm & drawing blood; jury could have believed portions of testimony of both complainant and D, finding that A&B occurred but that D didn't penetrate complainant;

C v Mamay **407 M 412 (90)**—rape & indecent A&B not duplicitous where there was evidence of sexual intercourse & French kiss;

C v Zane Z **51 MAC 135 (2001)**—failure to instruct that rape and indecent A&B convictions had to be based on different facts meant that G on both may well have been duplicative (even though Commonwealth introduced evidence of two separate incidents); though usual remedy = vacating the lesser offense, here had to reverse, because of additional failure to instruct as to specific unanimity as to any verdict;

C v Ortiz **47 MAC 777 (99)**—indecent A&B conviction can't stand since jury shouldn't have been instructed on the lesser included offense: on facts here, there was no basis for such finding (i.e., not in cross-examination question, re: whether complainant told cop that D "tried to have anal intercourse but had been unsuccessful," explained then by complainant to mean that D hadn't ejaculated during anal penetration);

C v Walker **426 M 301 (97)**—indecent A&B on child less than 14 = lesser included offense of forcible rape of child under 16 when complainant's age = undisputed and young enough to satisfy either age element; in future, indictment should state age of child to avoid this "technical flaw";

C v Gonzalez **388 M 865, n.4 (83)**—improper to arrange "Accord & Satisfaction" for A&B (reducing from rape)—*(See Chapter 14-B, Dispositions/Sentencing: Dismissal);*

C v Eldridge **28 MAC 936 (90)**—general verdict required new trial where evidence was legally sufficient on rape by force but not by threat of force; adults with mental capacity of 4 to 9 year old cannot consent to sex;

C v Ewing **67 MAC 531, further appellate review allowed 447 M 1113 (2006), but SJC thereafter (449 M 1035 [2007]) agrees with Appeals Court**—rapist's con-

duct of physically overpowering complainant in her own bedroom implied threat of bodily harm (no "express" threat required);

C v Nuby **32 MAC 360 (92)**—D's forcing girlfriend's son to engage in unnatural sexual intercourse with his girlfriend was forcible rape of child; *C v Portonova* **69 MAC 905 (2007)**—D's forcing mentally retarded female to "play with herself" was indecent assault and battery on mentally retarded person (G.L. c. 265, § 13F);

C v Watkins **33 MAC 7 (92)**—D not entitled to rape dismissal simply because acquitted on other identically worded indictment (same date, same victim, several penetrations);

21-L.1.a. Aggravated

C v Scott **408 M 811 (90)**—gag tied around complainant's face was dangerous weapon sufficient for attempted aggravated rape;

C v McCourt **438 M 486 (2003)**—because rape and aggravating factor were a continuous episode, it's aggravated rape even though beating of & injury to victim occurred after the rape; overruling as to this point *C v Kickery* **31 MAC 720 (91)** (evidence that complainant was "overpowered" during rape & tied to tree afterwards not enough for kidnapping to make out aggravated rape);

C v Martins **38 MAC 636 (95)**—"aggravation" element could have been found by jury to be kidnapping or joint venture; consecutive sentence for conviction on kidnapping indictment violative of double jeopardy prohibition;

C v Brown **66 MAC 237 (2006)**—though it's not "kidnapping" by which rape can be "aggravated" if there is only the degree of "confinement" which is a necessary incident to rape, confinement isn't "merged" within rape if jury could reasonably find that D's action exceeded the restraint which was merely incidental to rape's commission;

21-L.2. Statutory Rape (G.L. c. 265, § 23)

C v Thayer **418 M 130 (94)**—even though consent not actually in issue, can instruct on lesser included offense of statutory rape in prosecution for rape of child with force, purportedly on disbelief of children's claims that rapes by parents were preceded by threats of spanking/slapping/"getting in trouble";

C v Miller **385 M 521 (82)**—strict liability; knowledge of complainant's age not element; no mistake of fact defense; *(See Chapter 16, Defenses);*

C v Dunne **394 M 10 (85)**—same, re: assault with intent to commit statutory rape;

C v Harris **74 MAC 105 (2009)**—D drove friend and female to motel and paid for a room for friend & female, picking them up later (on D's evidence) or actually stayed and watched sexual activity between female and three men (on Commonwealth's evidence), charged as joint venturer in statutory rape (female was thirteen years old): on either version, D was "present" enough to make judgment about female's age and could be convicted as joint venturer in statutory rape ("presence" theory) without proof of "specific intent" to commit crime; if case presents "joint venture" only on "aiding" theory, due process (maybe) requires instruction and proof beyond reasonable doubt of D's knowledge of crime, i.e., complainant's age [D noted that vendors of contraception could become rapists if products they distribute "aided" someone in sex with minor];

C v Rowe **18 MAC 926 (84)**—indecent A&B is not lesser included offense of statutory rape;

C v O'Connell **432 M 657 (2000)**—concerning G.L. c. 272, § 29A, posing child in state of nudity: cited *C v Pittman* **25 MAC 25, 27 (87)**: fact finder can't rely entirely on physical appearance to judge age except in cases involving "marked extremes of old age and youth," since "judging age on physical appearance is a guess and a guess is not a basis for sending someone to jail";

See Chapter 5-C, Complaints & Indictments for cases on bills of particulars;

See Chapter 7-O, Preparing for Trial for cases on statutes of limitations;

See Chapter 9-A, Cross-Examination for cases on right of face to face confrontation of child complainants;

C v Knap **412 M 712 (92)**—reasonable mistake as to identity (& thus age) of sexual partner is no defense to strict liability crimes of statutory rape & indecent A&B of child;

Compare/contrast C v Disler **451 M 216 (2008)** & *C v Filopoulos* **451 M 234 (2008)**—"enticement" statute, G.L. c. 265, § 26C requires, in addition to enticing words/gestures, that person who entices does so with intent to violate one or more enumerated statutes, e.g., "statutory rape (c. 265, § 23) or indecent A&B on child under age fourteen (c. 265, § 13B); Commonwealth must prove that D INTENDED that object of sexual advances be an underage individual;

C v LeFave **407 M 927 (90)**—indecent A&B on child (before 1986 change in G.L. c. 265, § 13B) not lesser of child rape;

C v Foskette **30 MAC 384 (90)**—indecent A&B of person over 14 is lesser included of aggravated rape, but not child rape;

21-L.3. G.L. c. 272, § 3 (Stupefy by Drug)

Superior Court Criminal Practice Jury Instructions § 2.12.1(b) Complainant Unconscious or in a Stupor

21-L.4. Evidentiary Issues

See Chapter 11, Evidence & Chapter 9, Cross-Examination;

21-L.5. Semen Test

Egerton **396 M 499 (86)**;

Chapter 11-H, 11-I, Evidence: Sex, Experts; Chapter 6-D & 6-E, Discovery; Chapter 6-M, Reciprocal Discovery (D's expert); Chapter 7-C, Money for Experts & Other Expenses for Indigent Defendants;

21-L.6. G.L. c. 278, § 16A Closed Courtroom for Sex Charge if Complaining Witness under 18

Globe v Superior Court **457 U.S. 596 (82)**—case-by-case question;

C v Hobbs **385 M 863 (82)**—& cases cited: 2d witness (not complainant), too;

C v Marshall **356 M 432 (69)**—can't exclude if "direct interest," e.g., D's "friend"

21-L.7. Sexually Dangerous Person (G.L. c. 123A)

See Chapter 14-N, Disposition: Recidivist Sentencing Statutes;

C v Bruno **432 M 489 (2000)**—clarifying issues re: procedure & proof;

K. Smith, *Criminal Practice & Procedure*, Chapter 60 (2d ed. 1983 & Supp.);

C v Jarvis **2 MAC 8 (74)**—one case not "repetitive" & not bizarre enough for compulsive;

C v Walsh **376 M 53 (78)**—this (murder) "bizarre" enough for "compulsive"; future danger also shown; can't use past misconduct alone, but don't need prison misconduct;

Page v C **13 MAC 384 (82)**—release because past (20 years ago) misconduct alone not enough for beyond reasonable doubt SDP;

Poulin, petit'r **22 MAC 988 (86)**—tough to show past crimes & current condition make current danger, but OK here;

Swanson, petitioner **403 M 1004 (88)**—review & uphold judge's finding of not SDP (without deciding double jeopardy question) though expert disagreed;

Hosie, petitioner **54 MAC 624 (2002)**—that one Treatment Center psychiatrist concluded that D wasn't sexually dangerous and one concluded that he was didn't mean that judge couldn't find D to be SDP;

C v Hall **6 MAC 918 (78)**—distinguished;

C v Proctor **403 M 146 (88)**—DA must show prior convictions had counsel;

M.R.Crim.P.12 (c)(3)—warning re: sexually dangerous person possible categorization now part of G-plea advice/warnings;

G.L. c. 123A, § 1—subject to possible lifetime commitment if convicted of or adjudicated delinquent or youthful offender by reason of 'sexual offense'; also so subject if incompetent to stand trial for sexual offense (see G.L. c. 123A, § 15);

C v Ferreira **67 MAC 109 (2006)**—D had no constitutional right to have counsel attend the "qualified examiner" interviews, or to have them recorded by audiotape; D did have right to refuse to speak to examiners (& he did refuse); D's claim that counsel was ineffective in failing to facilitate the conditions D imposed on interviews (presence of counsel, tape-recording) failed for lack of proof that counsel likely deprived him of substantial ground of defense;

See Chapter 6-D for cases on discovery, including Stockhammer line of cases;

See Chapter 9-B & 9-C, Cross-Examination for cases on right to cross-examine complainant on mental impairment, bias & motive to fabricate;

See Chapter 11-H & 11-I, Evidence: Sex Offenses & Opinions of Experts for cases on rape shield requirements, as well as fresh complaint, syndrome, profile & forensic evidence;

21-M. "UNNATURAL ACTS"

G.L. c. 272, §§ 35 & 35A—(alleged victim under 16)); See also Rape, above

District Court Model Jury Instruction #5.421;

C v Mamay **5 MAC 708 (77)**—same meaning as G.L. c. 265 rape;

C v Gallant **373 M 577 (77)**—per os;

C v Gonzales **5 MAC 705 (77)**—per anus; (cf. *C v Nylander* **26 MAC 784 (89)** child complainant, dolls, doctors show penetration; & defined OK re: 'natural' rape, but vague re: 'unnatural' because included anal "area"; etc.,) *(Chapter 21-L above)*;

C v Brattman **10 MAC 579 (80)**—more than "fondling";

C v Zeitler **7 MAC 543 (79)**—not "fondling"; consent at 16 or 18?;

C v Smith **46 MAC 822 (99), aff'd by 431 M 417 (2000)**—"INCEST" (G.L. c. 272, § 17) not accomplished except by "natural intercourse"; inserting finger into daughter's vagina and having her perform fellatio = dismissal; call for Legislature to change statute to include "unnatural" penetrations; *** effective 5-1-02, G.L. c. 272, § 17 is amended: definition of incest adds the following language: "oral or anal intercourse, fellatio, cunnilingus, or other penetration of a part of a person's body, or insertion of an object into the genital or anal opening of another person's body, or the manual manipulation of the genitalia of another person's body";

C v Balthazar **366 M 298 (74)**—not private, consensual adults;

Balthazar v M **573 F.2d 698 (1st Cir. '78)**—differs from 'crime against nature'; not vague;

C v Benoit **26 MAC 641 (88)**—consent/private no defense to 35A; cunnilingus without penetration's enough (cf. *Nylander* **26 MAC 784 (89)** etc.);

C v Scagliotti **373 M 626 (77)**—public place;

C v Ferguson **384 M 13 (81)**—"public";

C v Bloom **18 MAC 951 (84)**—public restroom = public;

C v Reilly **5 MAC 435 (77)**—jury question whether consent/public;

C v Nicholas **40 MAC 255 (96)**—required finding of not guilty because evidence insufficient to prove D recklessly disregarded substantial risk of exposure to one or more persons (consensual homosexual activity occurring 100 feet into woods via path from interstate truck "weigh" station, which a sign indicated to be closed; neither parking lot nor highway was visible from the spot, & no other person was in vicinity (except intruding trooper));

C v Morrill **68 MAC 812 (2007)**—second floor holding cell of courthouse (actually monitored by video camera) and courthouse basement hallway were both "public places," and evidence sufficient to show D recklessly disregarded substantial risk of disclosure to others when he (court officer) accepted female prisoner's offer to do "just about anything" for a cigarette; Commonwealth had burden of demonstrating that D failed to take reasonable measures to secure privacy; fact that no one observed the basement incident wasn't dispositive;

C v Appleby **380 M 296 (80)**—sadism/masochism CONSENT?

21-N. OPEN/GROSS LEWD/LASCIVIOUS (G.L. C. 272, § 16 FELONY) AND INDECENT EXPOSURE (§ 53 MISDEMEANOR)

District Court .Model Jury Instructions #5.42 & 5.423;

G.L. c. 277, § 79—form complaint

C v Broadland **315 M 20 (43)**—"INDECENT" = offensive to one person;

C v Bishop **296 M 459 (37)**—indecent exposure would also be open & gross/lewd & lascivious;

C v Fitta **391 M 394 (84)**—open & gross lewdness: produce alarm or shock;

C v Sefranka **382 M 108 (80)**—same; to avoid unconstitutionality, § 53 construed to prohibit **only** commission of conduct in public place, or public solicitation of conduct to be performed in public place;

C v Ora **451 M 125 (2008)**—D, having danced nude at "anti-Christmas" protest in Harvard Square, argued statute to be blanket prohibition against public nudity and thus unconstitutional restriction on "expressive conduct protected by the First Amendment": precedents have limited reach of statute, e.g., can't be applied where lewdness/

nudity occurred before willing audience (go-go dancers); rejects challenge, holding statute = "legitimate conduct neutral restriction on expressive activity" under *US v O'Brien* 391 US 367, 377 (68);

C v Roy **420 M 1 (95)**—D drove by 14 year old girl repeatedly, then told her he had something 'big, hard & juicy' for her, but drove away when interrupted by another motorist: required finding of not guilty on § 53 complaint (no basis for finding D soliciting conduct to be performed in public place; Court declined to make different statutory construction when solicitation is of a minor (legislature could address));

C v Swan **73 MAC 258 (2008)**—no required finding of not guilty of open/gross or indecent exposure: evidence was that elementary school janitor used boys' lavatory urinals inferably with intent "to expose himself beyond the degree necessary for urination," staring at one boy, and talking so as to encourage attention from another boy (including sexually explicit comments); evidence insufficient, however, for disorderly conduct under "peeping Tom"/ voyeurism theory;

C v Bell **455 M 408 (2009)**—G.L. c. 272, § 53A (offering/agreeing to engage in sex for fee) held to include, despite D's claim it was limited to solicitation for sex between customer and prostitute for fee, negotiations for sex between D and "child" offered by undercover cop; D's argued limitation would preclude G for negotiation with pimp for sexual conduct with third party;

C v Adams **389 M 265 (83)**—drive & masturbate need only offend one person;

C v Gray **40 MAC 901 (96)**—D performing fellatio on another man in shopping mall's restroom prompted disgust of mall maintenance man: "alarm" inferable from his immediate call to police; D was joint venturer with man whose genitals were exposed; children need not be the victims of such exposure;

C v Kessler **442 M 770 (2004)**—required finding of not guilty for D because the observers of alleged (felony) open & gross lewdness, boys aged approximately 10 and 13, were not shown to have been actually "alarmed or shocked," instead giggling, nervous, excited; "serious negative emotional experience" = required by statute; indecent exposure conviction (misdemeanor) requires instead only that exposure be "offensive to one or more persons"; supplementary "tender years" instruction, from *C v Wardell* 128 M 52 (1880), maybe relevant re: possibly different subjective reaction of "alarm/shock," but cannot operate to eliminate requirement of proving all elements;

C v Dickinson **348 M 767 (64)**—"open" in car (vs. "public");

C v Cummings **273 M 229 (30)**—open & gross lewdness: (same); offensive to ONE person;

C v Quinn **439 M 492 (2003)**—pulling down pants to expose thong-clad buttocks to four 13-year-old girls sufficient for open/gross lewdness (G.L. c. 272, § 16), but unconstitutionally vague as to this D, not previously on notice;

Revere v Aucella **369 M 138 (75)**—(consent) defense;

PBIC, Inc. v Byrne **313 F.Supp 757 (D.Mass. '70)**—consenting audience

C v Arthur **420 M 535 (95)**—D pulled down one side of bathing suit to knee, causing other side to be jerked down to midthigh; although movement revealed "crotch area", woman and 9-year-old daughter turned away: exposure of "genital area" or pubic hair is not indecent exposure (G.L. c. 272, § 53), though exposure of genitalia **is**;

21-O. LEWD AND LASCIVIOUS PERSON IN SPEECH/BEHAVIOR (G.L. C. 272, § 53)

C v Templeman **376 M 533 (78)**—not private or expressive conduct;

C v Kelley **25 MAC 180 (87)**—"reckless disregard" re: public = enough;

C v Kessler **442 M 770 (2004)**—recklessness requires more than negligence or showing that someone "might" see D;

C v Nicholas **40 MAC 255 (96)**—required finding of not guilty because no such reckless disregard shown (D was engaged in sex act, but was observed by cop who walked about 100 feet into woods along a path from a closed truck weigh station);

C v Nebel **59 MAC 316 (2003)**—though D argued required finding of not guilty because no reckless disregard when located down a path into woods from a highway rest area, court says no bathrooms at this rest stop, and path was well worn & without vegetation, "a sure sign of use" [AND D was actually observed by four unrelated individuals];

C v Sefranka **382 M 108 (80)**—lesser included offense of prostitution; new definition, not vague; need conduct, not just "person"/status, need non-private aspect for constitutionality;

C v Juvenile **6 MAC 194 (78)**—(same);

District Court Model Jury Instruction #5.422;

C v Beauchemin **410 M 181, 184 (91)**—sex acts in parking lot during snowstorm & in empty faculty lounge during weekend school event not likely to be observed by casual passerby so not guilty finding required;

21-P. PROSTITUTION

G.L. c. 272, § 53A—(1983 amendments: includes prostitution customers, "Johns")

C v King **374 M 5 (77)**—pre-'83 elements = indiscriminate sex for hire; no sex discrimination shown—*(See Chapter 16-A, Defenses: Selective Prosecution);*

District Court Model Jury Instruction #5.57;

C v Unnamed D 22 M AC 230 (86)—dismissal for discrimination between prostitutes/customers; *(See Chapter 16-A, Defenses: Selective Prosecution)*;

C v Walter 388 M 460 (83)—genital "massage" for one dollar;

C v Lavigne 42 MAC 313 (97)—sufficient for G: D asking hitchhiker if he wanted to make some money and, in response to "how?", placing hand on V's inner thigh, within 3 inches of genitals before asking whether V had ever tried or thought about "it";

Sefranka 382 M 108 (80): & *Juvenile* 6 MAC 194 (78)—above: lewd & lascivious = lesser included offense;

C v Blavackas 11 MAC 746 (81)—on these facts, prostitute wasn't disorderly person; *(See Chapter 21-EE, post)*;

G.L. c. 272, §§ 4B & 7—deriving support from prostitution (see Model Jury Instruction #5.58);

G.L. c. 277, § 79—form complaint (under old law)

C v Thetonia 27 MAC 783 (89)—giving ride to prostitute in return for gas money & drugs not within intended ambit of "deriving support" statute;

21-Q. COMMON NIGHTWALKER (G.L. C. 272, § 53)

Thomes v C 355 M 203 (69)—must actually "solicit";

G.L. c. 277, § 79—form complaint (. . . "habitual" . . .);

District Court Model Jury Instruction #5.59—see notes re whether 'continuing offense'; cf. *C v Wetherell* 340 M 422 (60) "common" = substantial time (re: gaming);

C v King 374 M 5 (77)—"common" = time/place/frequency; not necessarily repeater;

C v Proctor 22 MAC 935 (86)—enough to infer time, place, frequency; selective prosecution not claimed *(See Chapter 16 & 21-P, above)*;

21-R. LARCENY (G.L. C. 266, § 30, ETC.)

District Court Model Jury Instruction ##5.41–5.418
Superior Court Criminal Practice Jury Instructions §§ 2.38–2.43—(larceny by stealing, by false pretenses, embezzlement, from a building, from the person, of a motor vehicle);

21-R.1. Elements (Includes Embezzlement and False Pretenses)

G.L. c. 277, § 39—DEFINITION: (1) criminal, (2) take, obtain, or convert, (3) personal property, (4) intent to defraud or deprive owner permanently of use;

G.L. c. 277, § 41—complaint can just say "stole";

Swift v American Universal 349 M 637 (65)—elements;

Nolan and Sartorio, *Criminal Law* (3d ed. 2001) §§ 341–55;

C v Corcoran 348 M 437 (65)—D can have bill of particulars re: manner

C v Nadal-Ginard 42 MAC 1 (97)—jury properly instructed on both embezzlement (if jury found D had fiduciary custody of the funds) and false pretenses (if he did not, but obtained them by false pretenses); D had not argued required finding of not guilty on false pretenses theory below, and did not object to the two theories being put to jury, and jurors were properly instructed on unanimity;

C v Mills 51 MAC 366 (2001)—D received pension moneys, but was required to refund pension payments dollar for dollar if his income exceeded annually-set income limitation; lying on his yearly earnings report (under penalties of perjury) and failing to return any moneys did not make the crime "embezzlement," since D was not in a position of trust or confidence with the Retirement Board, and "mere debtor-creditor relationship does not permit a

finding of" either embezzlement or larceny; (Commonwealth claimed D fraudulently converted money, because only "conditionally entitled" to the pension amount received); **S.C. on further appellate review 436 M 387 (2002)** jurors were instructed only re: traditional larceny, and D's alleged act wasn't this, but instead only larceny by false pretenses, so new trial ordered; no required finding of not guilty, because of G.L. c. 277, § 41 (allegation that D stole property shall be sufficient, & may be supported by proof of larceny, embezzlement, or obtaining by false pretenses);

C v Williams 63 MAC 615 (2005)—though D faked an injury and obtained an order from the Department of Industrial Accidents that his employer pay him money, employer had consistently contested D's claim, and payment was not in reliance upon D's misstatements but instead upon judicial reliance upon them, "resulting in a compelled transfer of the defrauded party's property": required finding of not guilty on charge of larceny by false pretenses;

C v Cheromcka 66 MAC 771 (2006)—larceny by false pretenses convictions largely upheld: D, bus drivers' supervisor, added extra hours to time sheet of drivers & initialed them (approving payment) when drivers performed personal errands for D rather than work for employer; that D obtained "services" rather than "property" not dispositive (what D stole, "albeit indirectly," was employer's money, paid to drivers for services to D rather than employer); though D's signing of credit card slips (for personal items rather than items for employer) wasn't a misrepresentation to employer, D's "approval" of the credit card bills, which were then submitted to employer for payment, was an implied misrepresentation that items purchased were intended for employer use; employer's payment of bill meant it parted with money to discharge D's personal debt; when D was given $1,400 cash advance to pay for her own and other employees' expenses at employer-related out-of-state conference, she did not obtain the money by false pretenses: mere failure to fulfill a promise isn't a misrepresentation; D's appropriation of petty cash funds was larceny by false pretenses because jury could have found that D had obtained the money by misrepresenting in "vouchers" the amounts that had been expended for school-related purchases;

21-R.2. Personal Property—See G.L. c. 266, § 30(2)

C v Yourawski **384 M 386 (81)**—copy of movie on tape not "property";

C v Baker **368 M 58 (75)**—bail bonds not "money"; (see G.L. c. 277, § 23); (re: specific items (some separate offenses), see Nolan and Sartorio, Criminal Law (3d ed. 2001) § 344))

C v Rivers **31 MAC 669 (91)**—use of landfill without sufficient payment not a theft of "property";

C v Catalano **74 MAC 580 (2009)**—electricity and gas are "property" subject to larceny; may be stored and conveyed, consumption is measurable, and value of either may be subject of testimony and exhibits;

C v Geane **51 MAC 149 (2001)**—that D induced subcontractors to provide services by calculated false promises was NOT theft of "property"; "equipment rental services" larceny not possible because larceny requires intent to deprive of property "permanently";

C v Gall **58 MAC 278 (2003)**—insurance policy is property, allegedly obtained for reduced premium by false statements;

C v DiJohnson **63 MAC 855 (2005)**—D, hired by medical professional to perform billing services, was entitled to required finding of not guilty, though she was convicted of larceny of "database" (information concerning alleged victim's patients, stored in electronic format on D's computer): while such electronically stored data is indeed "property" which can be stolen, evidence failed to establish that the parties' business relationship was violated by what occurred, "nor was it made to appear that D had been retained to create a computerized record-keeping system for [alleged victim], as opposed to being hired to perform billing services using tools and methods of her choice"; if it was the latter, the database "was merely the means by which the work for [alleged victim] was to be accomplished and not property belonging to [her]";

21-R.3. Criminal Taking (vs. Honest Mistake)

C v White **5 MAC 483 (77)**—D's honest belief complaining witness owed D = defense;

C v Larmey **14 MAC 281 (82)**—D's honest belief complaining witness had stolen from X, & D intends to return it, = defense;

C v Stebbins **8 Gray 492 (1857)**—honest belief it's D's = defense;

C v Donahue **148 M 529 (1889)** (same) *(See Chapter 16, Defenses)*;

C v Vives **447 M 537 (2006)**—D's belief that he was collecting a debt due him = "affirmative defense" (peculiarly within knowledge of D, particularly since here, victim = dead), but Commonwealth still has burden of proof because the defense goes to an element of the crime, i.e., intent to steal; D has "burden of production," but thereafter Commonwealth must disprove the defense, & jury must be instructed re: honest/reasonable belief; if Commonwealth claims that debt = result of illegal transaction, must prove this to jury beyond reasonable doubt (& this would defeat the defense);

C v Swan **38 MAC 539 (95)**—ineffective assistance of counsel found in abandonment of defense of auto repair shop's violation of AG's regulations on unfair/deceptive practices (D stopped payment on check for auto repairs he said he had not authorized);

C v Titus **116 M 42 (1874)**—vs. lost goods if reason to know owner;

Morissette v US **342 US 246 (52)**—criminal intent re: abandoned property?;

C v Dimond **3 Cush 235 (1849)**—question = intent when took $ (to go buy tickets);

C v Moreton **48 MAC 215 (99)**—re: larceny by check: insufficient funds in bank for payment for a fish: majority says "mere failure to make good on a commercial transaction, . . . particularly in context of bankruptcy, does not establish" criminal intent required; no evidence here of false pretenses in obtaining the blue fin tuna; unmentioned is G.L. c. 266, § 37 (writing check returned for insufficient funds is prima facie evidence of intent to defraud and larceny, unless check-writer makes it good within two days of receiving notice of its return);

C v Catalano **74 MAC 580 (2009)**—over course of eleven years, home resident obtained utility accounts in five different names (identity fraud) after account in own name was terminated for failure to pay: "fact that a few small payments were made" does not "undermine" permissible inference that D never intended to repay outstanding debt;

C v Oliver **443 M 1005 (2005), on further review of, but agreeing with, 60 MAC 770 (2004)**—required finding of not guilty for D on both theories, embezzlement and larceny by false pretenses, because insufficient evidence to show, beyond a reasonable doubt, that when D took complainants' money for services to be rendered sometime in future, he did so under false pretenses, with intention of never providing the paid-for services (larceny) and D's relationship with alleged victims was not "confidential or fiduciary" such that "conversion" of funds made out embezzlement;

C v Brien **67 MAC 309 (2006)**—statute described both administrative sanctions and criminal prosecutions, the latter referring to G.L. c. 142A, § 19: required finding of not guilty ordered inasmuch as prosecutor and judge erroneously believed that crime could be established without scienter (willful & knowing); context = contractor who took deposits & payments but later declared bankruptcy and didn't perform work;

C v Lent **46 MAC 705 (99)**—intent to permanently deprive needn't occur at "exact moment of taking," in these circumstances (D, attempting to kidnap girl, held onto her backpack as he walked her to vehicle, but she slipped out of it and fled, leaving him holding backpack, later found in D's car);

C v Patti **10 MAC 857 (80)**—proof by circumstances & admissions, without owner;

Nolan and Sartorio, *Criminal Law* **(3d ed. 2001) § 678**—possible necessity defense *(Chapter 16, Defenses)* for starving food-thief; See Receiving Stolen Property, below—can't be G of both larceny (taking) & "receiving" stolen property;

C v Prentice P. **57 MAC 766 (2003)**—that D was kneeling beside stolen vehicle which had been "jacked up," with doors and trunk open and tire and crowbar nearby, even when supplemented by flight ("consciousness of guilt") was insufficient for conviction of larceny of motor vehicle; appellate court held evidence inadequate to show any actual or constructive possession of vehicle;

21-R.4. Of Another: Ownership and Trespassory Taking

G.L. c. 277, § 25—owner's name need not be alleged

C v Delgado **367 M 432, 439 (75)**—need non-hearsay proof that D not the owner (v *C v Patti* **10 MAC 857 (80)** proof by circumstances & admissions, without owner);

C v Souza **397 M 236 (86)**—infer D's not the radio's owner;

C v Coffee **9 Gray 139 (1857)**—theft of contraband;

C v Finn **108 M 466 (1871)**—theft from a thief

C v Bundza **54 MAC 76 (2002)**—required finding of NG for D, the tenant of the alleged larceny victim: no inference, merely from photos showing that removed items left hanging wires, holes, & exposed pipes, that personal property that has been affixed to real estate belongs to landlord rather than tenant, and no direct testimony that landlord owned such property;

C v DiJohnson **63 MAC 855 (2005)**—D, hired by medical professional to perform billing services, was entitled to required finding of not guilty, though she was convicted of larceny of "database" (information concerning alleged victim's patients, stored in electronic format on D's computer): it was not shown that D "had been retained to create a computerized record-keeping system for [alleged victim], as opposed to being hired to perform billing services using tools and methods of her choice"; if it was the latter, the database "was merely the means by which

the work for [alleged victim] was to be accomplished and not property belonging to [her]";

C v Mahoney **68 MAC 561 (2007)**—property owner needn't be a person; owner here was city of Lowell, property being money from parking fines & excise taxes;

21-R.5. Asportation: Momentary Transfer of Control

C v Davis **41 MAC 901 (96)**—that D had not left store's premises not controlling; he removed magnetic security sticker from merchandise & hid it before going through security stanchions and had no credit cards or sufficient money to purchase item;

C v Vickers **60 MAC 24 (2003)**—D stealthily placed store merchandise into beach bag, but tipped over bag & emptied it onto floor when approached by store security: "element of asportation may be satisfied if [D's] behavior establishes that he or she removed the goods from store's control to his/her own"; larceny provable even when there's abandonment of effort to remove merchandise from premises;

C v Luckis **99 M 431 (1868)**—"control for an instant" without removing from complaining witness's pocket; *(see larceny from the person, Chapter 21-G above)*;

C v Bradley **2 MAC 804 (74)**—"fish through" pocket

21-R.6. Intent to Permanently Deprive vs. Mere "Conversion to Use"

Nolan and Sartorio, *Criminal Law* **(3d ed. 2001) § 346;**

C v Mason **105 M 163 (1870)**—need only deprive of part of value;

C v Salerno **356 M 642 (70)**—larceny of motor vehicle after 24 hours & used twice: "indifferent" if owner recovers can support finding of intent to permanently deprive (here, required finding of NG issue, **not** jury instruction); (but see *Stovall* **22 MAC 737 (86)** below); *(see use without authority and larceny of motor vehicle, Chapter 21, below specifically C v Smith 44 MAC 394 (98))*;

C v Moore **36 MAC 455 (94)**—larceny requires proof of intent to permanently deprive, **not** just 'indifference' to whether owner recovers property later, though "indifference" is factor which may be considered; jury instructions substituting/equating 'indifference' with the intent to permanently deprive = reversible error;

21-R.7. Civil "Conversion"

Reni v Courtney **4 MAC 235 (76)**—complete though return not demanded

21-R.8. One Taking, Property of Several Persons

C v Sullivan **104 M 552 (1870)**—extra V's = extra counts *(See Chapter 19, Double Jeopardy, re: unit of prosecution)*;

C v Donovan **395 M 20 (85)**—1 larceny ,though 7 Vs, because 1 night deposit box;

21-R.9. "Relationship of Debt" as Defense

C v Leland **311 M 447 (42)**—was fraud, not "loan"; see also *C v Greenberg* **339 M 557 (59)**; *C v Stovall* **22 MAC 737 (86)**;

G.L. c. 224, § 19—fraud with loans;

21-R.10. "Subsequent Inability to Deliver" = Insufficient

C v Hull **296 M 327, 335 (37)**—stockbroker's use of stocks wasn't larceny;

21-R.11. "Recently" Stolen Goods— Inference from Possession of Them

C v Wilbur **353 M 376, 384–5 (67)**;

C v Torrealba **316 M 24, 29 (44)**; *(See also C v Porter* **15 MAC 331 (83)**; *Barnes v US* **412 US 837 (73)**; *C v Burns* **388 M 178 (83)**; *etc., in Receiving Stolen Property, Chapter 21-U, post)*;

C v Rousseau **61 MAC 144 (2004)**—time lapse of "ten days, at most" satisfies "recently" stolen;

C v McCaffery **49 MAC 713 (2000)**—D can't be G of both larceny and receiving stolen property; vacate G on latter and dismiss = remedy;

21-R.12. Value (< or > $250)

See also Malicious Destruction, Chapter 21-Z below;

21-R.12.a. Thing Stolen Must Have Some Value

C v Weston **241 M 131 (22)**;
C v Lavery **101 M 207 (1869)**

21-R.12.b. Allegation of Value Sustained by Proof of Any Value

G.L. c. 277, § 24—must allege only "(not) more than $X";

C v Riggs **14 Gray 376 (1860)**;

21-R.12.c. Over-Under: DA's Burden of Proof as to Value

C v Walters **12 MAC 389 (81)**—but can infer;

C v Hosman **257 M 379 (26)**—infer from common knowledge;

C v Shagoury **6 MAC 584 (78)**—lay opinion OK;

C v Kelly **24 MAC 181 (87)**—value = element of punishment; up to jury;

District Court Model Jury Instruction 5.41—value

21-R.12.d. Larceny Is "Over" for Successive Takings, Single Scheme

C v Pina **1 MAC 411, 412, n.2 (73)**;
See Chapter 19, Double Jeopardy: unit of prosecution;

21-R.13. Lack of Motive—D's Income Admissible

C v Ellison **376 M 1, 27, n.17 (78)**—(see also Nolan and Sartorio, Criminal Law (3d ed. 2001) § 107 re: DA's right to show motive)

21-R.14. SJC Rule 3:07, #3.4(h)

SJC Rule 3:07, #3.4(h)—lawyer shall not "present, participate in presenting, or threaten to present criminal or disciplinary charges solely to obtain an advantage in a private civil matter":

District Court Arraignment Standard 6:01—civil claims vs. crimes;

C v Drew **19 Pick. 179 (1837)**—leave private wrongs to civil remedies;

C v Louis Construction **343 M 600 (60)**—every private wrong not a crime; but see *C v Garrity* **43 MAC 349 (97)**—availability of civil remedy in probate court for victims of fiduciary embezzlement did not deprive criminal court of jurisdiction;

C v Gonzalez **388 M 865, 867 n.4 (83)**—private benefit can't defeat public interest; "accord & satisfaction" improper for serious felony;

21-R.15. Shoplift (266/30A) = Take/ Conceal, Switch Tags, etc. (No House of Correction until 3d Time)

C v Sollivan **40 MAC 284 (96)**—shoplifting may be prosecuted under G.L. c. 266, § 30A or under general larceny statute (G.L. c. 266, § 30(1)), but **not** under "larceny in a building" statute (G.L. c. 266, § 20), a felony regardless of value of merchandise

District Court .Model Jury Instruction #5.68;

Sutherland Statutory Construction (4th ed.) §§ 51.03—in pari materia: (special law supercedes if enacted after general law & overlaps); but see *US v Batchelder* **442 US 114 (79)** not too vague (by federal standard) to have 2 laws, 2 penalties, & DA discretion;

C v Hudson **404 M 282 (89)**—30A didn't implicitly repeal 30 in stores; DA can choose which *(See also Cedeno, Chapter 21-CC)*;

C v Balboni **26 MAC 750 (89)**—conceal = acts to hinder discovery; shown (& also intend to steal) here by furtiveness, put in bag, & have no money;

G.L. c. 231, § 94B—store can detain on "suspicion";

C v Torrealba **316 M 24 (44)**—joint venture, though co-D had goods; lack of sales slips & register record shows G.;

21-R.16. Embezzlement—Convert without Consent

Superior Court Criminal Practice Jury Instructions § 2.40;

District Court Model Jury Instruction #5.415;

C v Ryan **155 M 523 (1892)**—(v common-law larceny); (definition);

Seelig v Harvard Coop. **355 M 532 (69)**—D forms intent to keep;

C v Hays **14 Gray 62 (1859)**—N.G. because bank's error, not D's;

C v Cooper **130 M 285 (1881)**—entrusted for illegal purpose = no excuse;

C v O'Connell **274 M 315, 322 (31)**—intent to repay later = no excuse;

C v Mahoney **68 MAC 561 (2007)**—"simple" embezzlement held to be lesser included offense of embezzlement by a city, town, or county officer (G.L. c. 266, § 51), so no error in instructing jury and obtaining conviction on lesser offense, BUT on evidence here this conviction was duplicative of separate conviction for larceny ("nothing turns on the allegation that D's theft exceeded $250, a factor of significance in determining the level of larceny, but of no relevance with respect to embezzlement"), which had to be dismissed; owner of property needn't be a person (here, = city of Lowell);

21-R.17. False Pretenses

(See specific statutes; & Nolan and Sartorio, Criminal Law (3d ed. 2001) § 347);

G.L. c. 277, § 39—definition: false representations such that, with intent to influence another, are "punishable";

District Court Model Jury Instruction #5.413;

Superior Court Criminal Practice Jury Instructions § 2.39;

C v Louis Construction Co. **343 M 600 (60)**—every private (civil) wrong not crime; but see *C v Garrity* **43 MAC 349 (97)** rejecting argument that estate beneficiaries' right to sue him in probate court for alleged embezzlement as executor deprived criminal court of jurisdiction;

C v Leonard **352 M 636 (67)**—elements;

C v Green **326 M 344, 348 (50)**—(same);

C v Hildreth **30 MAC 963 (91)**—that D intended to (& occasionally did) repay victims not a defense; intent to permanently deprive not an element;

C v Reske **43 MAC 522 (97)**—case with mentally retarded victim of repeated truck sales in which salesman both inflated sticker price and grossly understated value of vehicle traded in; 2 of 3 justices say there is such a thing as "false statement" re: value of item; false pretense "may consist of an act, symbol, or token calculated to deceive, such as grossly off-market prices or credits stated on forms of an established automobile agency";

C v Schnackenberg **356 M 65 (69)**—sufficient for G: D, officer of Turnpike Authority, at whose home work was done by a corporate co-defendant upon his request to its president, named as coconspirator, knew that the corporation would furnish false information to the Authority to the effect that the work had been done for the Authority, and Authority relied on such information and paid the corporation for the work;

C v McDuffy **126 M 467 (1879)**—no intent to defraud if purpose to secure duty owed by complaining witness;

C v Burton **183 M 461, 466 (03)**—(same);

C v True **16 MAC 709 (83)**—subsequent nonperformance vs. intent to defraud;

C v Ancillo **350 M 427 (66)**—representation as to future performance must be false when made;

C v Drew **19 Pick. 179 (1837)**—(same); scienter;

C v Catania **377 M 186 (79)**—guilty knowledge when statement made;

C v Quinn **222 M 504 (16)**—"seller's talk" vs. assertion of fact;

C v Norton **11 Allen 266 (1865)**—need actual & reasonable reliance by complaining witness on false statement;

C v Jacobson **260 M 311 (27)**—complaining witness is corporation;

C v Stovall **22 MAC 737 (86)**—G. though D says intended to repay "loan"; (but see, e.g., *C v Moreton* **48 MAC 215 (99)** re: larceny by check: insufficient funds in bank for payment for a fish: majority says "mere failure to make good on a commercial transaction, . . . particularly in context of bankruptcy, does not establish" criminal intent required; no evidence here of false pretenses in obtaining the blue fin tuna);

C v Greenberg **339 M 557 (59)**—larceny by false pretenses may be based upon obtaining loan: "bank was defrauded when it advanced the moneys relying on false representations as to the validity of the collateral";

C v Lewis **48 MAC 343 (99)**—subject of larceny was a "loan," i.e., use of complainant's money, so D could be convicted even without intent to permanently deprive (and even if he actually repaid the money as promised); elements = (1) false statement of fact; (2) knowledge or belief that statement false at time made; (3) intent that V rely on the statement; (4) actual reliance and consequent parting of V and property; venue = any county where false reps were made OR where property was rec'd (G.L. c. 277, § 59);

C v Iannello **344 M 723 (62)**—need actual & personal knowledge by D of falsity of statement;

C v Lougee **8 MAC 353 (79)**—husband NG of wife's acts

21-R.18. Larceny by Check (G.L. c. 266, § 37): Prima Facie Evidence of Intent if Don't Pay within 48 Hours after Notice

District Court Model Jury Instruction 5.412;

C v Ohanian **373 M 839 (77)**—notice; intent; "drawer";

C v Solari **12 MAC 993 (81)**—infer intent from facts;

C v Dunnington **390 M 472 (83)**—(same);

C v Klein **400 M 309 (87)**—(same); law's not too vague

C v Green **66 MAC 901 (2006)**—though evidence was sufficient to establish D's guilt of attempted larceny, the subject document was a single check bearing name of Ritz Carlton Hotel, for $320,000, payable to D's business; the check was not a document which would support conviction under G.L. c. 267, § 10 or § 12 (for uttering or possessing false/forged/counterfeit "note", "certificate", or "bill");

C v Goren **72 MAC 678 (2008)**—D's delivery of two bad checks to landlord in December 2004 was for "antecedent debt," i.e., nonpayment of rent for over a year before tender of checks; because D did not obtain property or services in exchange for the checks, "larceny" proof insufficient, conviction reduced to attempted larceny (in which insufficient funds or actually closed checking account is prima facie evidence of intent to defraud); N.B., id. at 682: D here did not challenge any element of "attempted larceny: further, landlord incurred no loss "as a result of the bad checks," so restitution order vacated;

21-R.19. Credit Card Fraud; Identity Fraud

G.L. c. 266, § 37A—D (27 offenses, e.g., receiving stolen credit card (§ U below));

G.L. c. 266, § 37E(B), identity fraud;

C v Liotti **49 MAC 641 (2000)**—required finding of not guilty for D on charge of fraudulent use of credit card, on evidence that he used a Sears credit card in the name of someone else, but said that it was his name; failure of Commonwealth to produce any evidence that D's use of the card was unauthorized or that D stole the card was fatal to prosecution; falsehood as to his identity didn't support inference that D obtained the card without cardholder's consent;

C v Catalano **74 MAC 580 (2009)**—D, whose utilities had been cut off for failure to pay, thereafter used name of 18-year-old nephew: though nephew was not expressly asked if he had authorized D to use his personal info, this was permissible inference; nephew was high school senior, living with his family (NOT with D), who received bill from collection agency, and contacted police, saying "somebody" had used his info to obtain utility services;

C v Giavazzi **60 MAC 374 (2004)**—though D represented himself to be person to whom checks were made,

required finding because Commonwealth failed to prove that that person did not expressly authorize D to assume his identity when giving D the checks to cash for him;

21-R.20. Larceny in Building—G.L. c. 266, § 20

Superior Court Criminal Practice Jury Instructions § 2.41;

District Court Model Jury Instruction #5.411;

McDermott v W. T. Grant **313 M 736 (43)**—not larceny in building because the property was protected by the employees, not the building;

C v Thomson **14 MAC 902 (82)**—larceny in building = felony though no value alleged (for gold);

C v Barklow **52 MAC 765 (2001)**—elements: D (1) took property (2) which belonged to another (3) from a building (4) with intent to deprive person of property permanently; re element (3), must prove that property was "under the protection of the building," and not under personal care of someone in the building, but needn't prove that no one was in the building at time of theft; no basis here for lesser-included instruction on simple larceny (theft from store at 3 a.m., after it was closed at 10 p.m.);

C v Rudenko **74 MAC 396 (2009)**—"delivery hall" of Home Depot store shared wall with roofed portion of store, but had no roof itself, but was enclosed on its other three sides by gated and locked fence and used for storage of valuable merchandise; here held to be "building"

21-R.21. Venue—Where Property Possessed as Well as Taken (G.L. c. 277, § 58)

21-R.22. Common and Notorious Thief

G.L. c. 266, § 40—"shall" be adjudged 'common & notorious thief' if 2 Superior Court larcenies or 3 at same sitting (20 year max.);

Nolan and Sartorio, *Criminal Law* (3d ed. 2001) § 353—*(See also Chapter 14-N, Sentencing: Recidivist Laws & Chapter 19, Double Jeopardy);*

C v Collins **315 M 167 (43)**—includes larcenies "under" (though misdemeanors);

C v Crocker **384 M 353 (81)**—need no special warning before plead G to larceny;

21-S. FORGE AND UTTER (G.L. C. 267, §§ 1 & 5)

G.L. c. 277, § 39—definition;

Nolan and Sartorio, *Criminal Law* (3d ed. 2001) §§ 381–85;

District Court Model Jury Instruction ##5.331–5.332;

C v Apalakis **396 M 292 (85)**—after judge narrowed indictment by deleting "alter or forge," "false making" means execution, maker's ID—not just false facts;

C v O'Connell **438 M 658 (2003)**—evidence that D forged his father's signature on five checks he made payable to himself, and endorsed and cashed them = sufficient for uttering and forgery, despite no testimony from the father; dissent sided with Appeals Court's contrary decision (55 MAC 100 (2002)); bank employee's with 20 years of experience was qualified to opine that signatures on checks didn't match the father's; D's signatures on the 5

checks in evidence could be used by jury to compare with the disputed signatures to decide authorship even without expert testimony;

21-T. LARCENY OF MOTOR VEHICLE, RECEIVING STOLEN MOTOR VEHICLE, AND USE WITHOUT AUTHORITY

G.L. c. 266, § 28—larceny of motor vehicle, receiving stolen motor vehicle (& steal parts; conceal thief): (a) "reason to know" stolen; (b) altered I.D. # is evidence of knowledge;

G.L. c. 90, § 24—use without authority; see also G.L. c. 265, § 21A (carjacking: whoever, with intent to steal motor vehicle, assaults, confines, maims or puts in fear any person for the purpose of stealing a motor vehicle, whether or not he succeeds in stealing motor vehicle, shall be punished)

District Court Model Jury Instructions #5.18—(use without authority) & 5.321 (larceny of motor vehicle, receiving stolen motor vehicle);

Superior Court Criminal Practice Jury Instructions § 2.43—larceny of a motor vehicle;

G.L. c. 276, § 92A—restitution = mandatory (unless extraordinary, indigency); procedures, e.g., hearing *(See Chapter 14-H, Dispositions: Fees, Fines, Costs, Restitution)*;

G.L. c. 266, § 29—restitution & restitution default procedures;

G.L. c. 278, § 6A—testimony of owner/witness taken at arraignment or continuance if DA shows "need" (& after "time for counsel to consult with D"); no continuance without preserving testimony & costs;

G.L. c. 147, § 4G—title certificate admissible & presume unauthorized; D rebuts & continuance for owner;

C v Guerro 357 M 741 (70)—each G.L. c. 266, § 28 clause is separate crime;

C v Dellamano 393 M 132 (84)—can charge receiving stolen motor vehicle & larceny of motor vehicle, but not G. on both; "reason to know" not enough, but can be evidence of actual knowledge; *C v McArthur* 55 MAC 596 (2002)—though D argued for required finding of not guilty on "receiving" because it was clear that he actually stole the vehicle, court held that one who has stolen a vehicle may be guilty of possessing it (i.e., just can't be CONVICTED of both);

C v Woody 45 MAC 906 (98)—very thin evidence held enough to find that D "either knew or believed (car) was stolen";

C v Smith 3 MAC 144 (75)—infer knowledge from # of hot cars; *(re: receiving stolen motor vehicle; see also Receiving Stolen Goods, Chapter 21-U, post)*;

C v Bynoe 49 MAC 687 (2000)—use without authority is not lesser included offense of receiving stolen motor vehicle;

Costarelli v C 374 M 677 (78)—use without authority = lesser included offense of larceny of motor vehicle;

C v Linder 17 MAC 967 (83)—"use" is "take . . . away"; use without authority is lesser included of larceny of motor vehicle;

C v Olieveira 48 MAC 907 (99)—no substantial risk of miscarriage of justice in failure to instruct on use without authority in armed robbery prosecution (car = proceeds), because lesser included offense was here "inapposite to the condition of the case": "element of violence takes unauthorized use . . . out of the picture" and "joy riding assumes returning" the car or abandonment in place "where it might be recovered"; NOTE WELL: defendant didn't request at trial any instruction on lesser offense *(See Chapter 5-D, Contents of Complaints & Indictments, Variances and Chapter 12-K, Jury Instructions, on standards for giving of instructions on lesser included offenses)*;

C v Coleman 252 M 241 (25)—"authority"; "use";

C v Subilosky 352 M 153 (67)—larceny motor vehicle: intent to deprive owner permanently;

C v Garcia 46 MAC 466 (99)—receiving stolen motor vehicle requires proof of intent to deprive owner of it;

C v Hunt 50 MAC 565 (2000)—circumstantial evidence (including false statements indicative of consciousness of guilt) sufficient for G of receiving stolen motor vehicle, despite absence of proof of how recently motor vehicle had been stolen;

C v Salerno 356 M 642 (70)—"indifference" re: owner's recovery (keep car 24 hours & use twice) = enough for larceny of motor vehicle;

C v Mahnke 13 MAC 1057 (82)—(same); but see *C v Smith* 44 MAC 394 (98) jury instruction that indifference whether the victim recovered his property automatically constituted proof of an intent to deprive permanently = reversible error in robbery & carjacking prosecution; indifference is factor to consider, but is not itself the requisite element;

C v Moore 36 MAC 455 (94)—reversing for instruction that larceny of motor vehicle required proof of **either** intent to permanently deprive or indifference whether owner recovered property;

C v Souza 428 M 478, 491 n.26 (98)—reconciling **Moore** with **Salerno** 356 M 642 (70): in **Moore**, judge said **must** find G if find indifference (wrong: mandatory and conclusive inference) & in **Salerno**, judge said **may** find/infer G if indifference (OK permissible inference);

C v Hogg 365 M 290 (74)—larceny motor vehicle vs. mere "skylarking" (joyriding)

C v Delgado **367 M 432 (75)**—need (non-hearsay) proof of owner;

C v Patti **10 MAC 857 (80)**—prove owner by circumstances & admission;

C v Campbell **60 MAC 215 (2003)**—inadequate proof that car was stolen: testimony that license plate number of stolen rental car matched that of car being driven by D five days later was improperly admitted (over objection), because witness merely read from car rental agreement, and DA failed to elicit foundation for "past recollection recorded";

C v Boone **356 M 85 (69)**—passenger: infer less knowledge;

C v Conway **2 MAC 547 (74)**—NG for passenger;

C v Johnson **6 MAC 956 (78)**—(same); flight & alias don't help;

C v Butler **7 MAC 918 (79)**—flight, but D's role speculative;

C v Darnell D. **445 M 670 (2005)**—even if D plausibly was identified as front seat passenger in car, evidence insufficient to establish his possession of (exercise and dominion over) car (for conviction of receiving stolen motor vehicle), notwithstanding Commonwealth arguments as to "consciousness of guilt" and claim that D must have "directed" driver to convey him to "his aunt's house";

C v Campbell **60 MAC 215 (2003)**—NG for passengers; flight didn't help; but see *C v Namey* **67 MAC 94** **(2006)**—though D was only a passenger in car driven by another, evidence suggesting D's culpability in impending crimes (i.e., two disguises in plain view on back seat, along with dent puller and "other tools", and "a map of the local area"), with visible damage to car showing it stolen (ignition "popped", door lock either "out or damaged"), plus flight and concealment from police, held sufficient for guilt of receiving stolen property (the car); Commonwealth not required to prove when the car was stolen (D argued no proof that D was "present at the scene of the crime of receipt");

21-T.1. Must Use Be on "Public Way"?

G.L. c. 233, § 79F—proof by certificate or testimony re: appearance;

C v Clancy **261 M 345 (27)**—yes;

C v Armenia **4 MAC 33 (76)**—yes (see annotations to MGLA for G.L. c. 266, § 28);

C v Giannino **371 M 700 (77)**—maybe;

Costarelli v C **374 M 677, 684 n.4 (78)**—maybe not; but see . . . .

Model Jury Instruction #5.18—see Note 4, re whether proof of "public way" use is necessary or not;

C v Morris M **70 MAC 688 (2007)**—"public way" is NOT an element of use without authority (cases implicitly contrary, above, were dicta);

21-U. RECEIVE STOLEN GOODS

G.L. c. 266, § 60—(1) buy, receive, or aid in concealment, (2) of stolen property, (3) knowing stolen, ((4) over $250 = felony)

District Court Model Jury Instruction #5.32

Nolan and Sartorio, *Criminal Law* **(3d ed. 2001) §§ 361–68;**

G.L. c. 277, § 79—form complaint;

G.L. c. 277, § 42—thief need not be convicted (or apprehended or identified); venue includes place where stolen (G.L. c. 277, § 58A)

C v Budreau **372 M 641 (77)**—not "stolen," because owner can't identify;

C v Rossi **15 MAC 950 (83)**—jury question. re: identification of property; but see *C v Campbell* **60 MAC 215 (2003)**—required finding of NG on element of whether property (car) was what was stolen; valid hearsay objection;

C v Santucci **13 MAC 933 (82)**—D's admission ("hot"), etc., suggests both stolen & knowledge (see *Rowe* **105 M 590 (1870)** admit D's out-of-court explanation);

C v Weston **241 M 131 (22)**—may not need intent to permanently deprive (at least with these unusual and complicated facts); but cf. *C v Garcia* **46 MAC 466 (99)** do need intent to deprive owner (judge so charged in receiving stolen property, but not re: receiving stolen motor vehicle, causing reversal of latter (after jury NG on former);

P v Jaffe **185 NY 497, 78 NE 169 (06)**—not "stolen" after recovered;

C v Colella **2 MAC 706 (74)**—can allege all 3 (buy/receive/conceal) without election; (see *Dellamano* **393 M 132 (84)** & *Haskins* **128 M 60 (1880)** etc., below);

C v Matheson **328 M 371 (52)**—"conceal" = make harder for owner to recover;

C v Ciesla **380 M 346 (80)**—"conceal"; continuing crime re: statute of limitations;

C v Haskins **128 M 60 (1880)**—can't both steal AND receive;

C v Janvrin **44 MAC 917 (98)**—same;

C v Dellamano **393 M 132 (84)**—(same) legally inconsistent;

C v McCaffery **49 MAC 713 (2000)**—same; vacate conviction on receiving & dismiss indictment;

C v Pettingel **10 MAC 916 (80)**—can try both, but not guilty on one;

C v McCann **16 MAC 990 (83)**—D gets charge to jury re: not guilty if the thief; but contrast *C v McArthur* **55 MAC 596 (2002)**, concerning G.L. c. 266, § 28(a) (receiving stolen motor vehicle): though evidence may have been "overwhelming" that D was thief and not merely recipient of stolen vehicle, court held that one may "possess" stolen vehicle even though he's the one who stole it; prohibit only conviction of both;

C v Corcoran **69 MAC 123 (2007)**—though D stole jewelry in Rhode Island, facts did not bar his conviction in MA of receiving stolen property (D left goods for sale in MA consignment store, where victim found them); record doesn't reveal whether or not D was ever charged in RI with larceny;

C v Gardner **67 MAC 744 (2006)**—indictment for robbery (knocking 70-year-old to ground & taking purse) properly dismissed following D's conviction in District Court for, inter alia, receiving stolen property (the purse); Appeals Court "resolved [issue] without resort to principles of double jeopardy" on ground that the convictions were inconsistent as matter of law;

C v Carson **349 M 430 (65)**—can't steal both stock & sale proceeds;

C v Boris **317 M 309 (44)**—need actual knowledge (not "reason to know", negligence);

C v Dellamano **393 M 132 (84)**—(same);

See Chapter 16, Defenses, Intent;

C v Garcia **48 MAC 201 (99)**—evidence insufficient to show knowledge that property was stolen (such conclusion here based at best "on tendentious winks and nudges";

C v Bethel **13 MAC 955 (82)**—knowledge = issue; not imputed (here);

C v Porter **15 MAC 331 (83)**—infer knowledge if "recently" stolen . . .

Barnes v US **412 US 837 (73)**— . . . "infer" OK (due process & 5th Amendment.)

C v Wilbur **353 M 376 (67)**— . . . "recent" rule doesn't chill 5th Amendment;

C v Burns **388 M 178 (83)**— . . . But, make D explain = bad burden-shift!;

US v Redd **438 F.2d 335 (9th Cir. '71)**—no formula for "recent"; rule's constitutional;

C v Sandler **368 M 729 (75)**—2–8 months = is a fact issue;

C v Kelly **1 MAC 441 (73)**—7 weeks not "recent" (re: "accessory" case);

C v Kelley **333 M 191 (55)**—54 days, etc. = "recent" (old rule: D's burden of proof);

C v Rousseau **61 MAC 144, 146 n.3 (2004)**—"ten days, at most" = "recent";

C v Kirkpatrick **26 MAC 595 (88)**—"recent" = inference of knowing & up to jury; "cautious vigilance," but instruction OK though 18 months (because of other facts);

C v Rowe **105 M 590 (1870)**—admit D's out-of-court explanation; *(See Chapter 11-F, 11-G, Evidence, Hearsay & Admissions by D)*;

C v Smith **3 MAC 144 (75)**—if not recent, number of hot cars suggests knowledge;

C v Kronick **196 M 286 (07)**—conceal after learning stolen;

C v Fancy **349 M 196 (65)**—no inference if D didn't really possess;

C v Chinn **6 MAC 714 (78)**—joint liability though co-D possessed;

C v Scarborough **5 MAC 302 (77)**—NG for passenger with goods in trunk;

C v Johnson **6 MAC 956 (78)**—passenger *(See Chapter 16, Defenses)*;

G.L. c. 266, § 37B—receive stolen credit card *(See also credit card fraud, Chapter 21-R, above)*;

G.L. c. 266, § 62—common & notorious receiver of stolen property—1 prior, or 3 at same sitting;

C v McGann **20 MAC 59 (85)**—9-10 MCI Cedar Junction for 3 counts of G.;

See Disposition: Recidivists, Chapter 14-N; Double Jeopardy, Chapter 19; & Indictments, Chapter 5;

See also Chapter 21-T, Receiving Stolen Motor Vehicle, & Chapter 21-R, Larceny, re Value; & Chapter 16, Defenses: Possession;

21-V. BREAK AND ENTER—(G.L. C. 266, §§ 14–19)

See also G.L. c. 265, § 18A—(armed assault in a dwelling)); (see also G.L. c. 265, § 18C (armed home invasion));

G.L. c. 266, § 20—larceny in a building = felony (5 year max.);

G.L. c. 266, § 16A—breaking & entering with intent to commit misdemeanor in a building, car (6 month max.);

C v Scott **71 MAC 596 (2008)**—conviction of B&E with intent to commit misdemeanor of "trespass" upheld, rejecting D's argument that trespass is inherent in B&E so merges,(& can't be separate 'intent' element);

Wharton's Criminal Law, Ch. 20; § 329—consent defense? (yes, see, e.g., *C v Simmarano* **50 MAC 312 (2000)**);

C v Dunn **43 MAC 58 (97)**—"entry" means unlawful entry; *C v Mahar* **430 M 643 (2000)**—though D argued that he entered with consent of occupant, SJC found suffi-

cient evidence of unlawful entry: D was neither occupant nor accustomed to enter it without permission, and testimony was that he "barged" in; though statute (G.L. c. 265, § 18C—armed home invasion) doesn't include "situations where an invited guest in a home suddenly turns violent," consent seems ineffective if guest enters with unlawful intent and is armed; even occupant might be charged with criminally entering his own home???? id. at 652 n.5;

C v Perry **65 MAC 624 (2006)**—though D had been a guest at cookout hosted by V earlier in evening, circumstances of D's leaving (including physical fight/wrestling with home-owner [V] & D's threat to kill V) refuted D's argument that he didn't know he didn't have permission to return to the home & enter it;

C v Cowans **52 MAC 811, 819 (2001)**—reversal for charge that 'mere entry of house with weapon in hand is sufficient to trigger the assault aspect of' armed home invasion (G.L. c. 265, § 18C); Commonwealth must instead prove that D engaged in 'objectively menacing conduct w/intent to put the victim in fear of immediate bodily harm";

C v Mitchell **67 MAC 556 (2006)**—(in armed burglary, G.L. c. 266, § 14) "person lawfully therein" can be someone who came home after D had broken and entered and was still inside;

C v Robbins **422 M 305 (96)**—reversing conviction for armed burglary (& felony murder): D had a key, given to him by wife's daughter, had lived in apartment with wife off & on since marriage, no restraining order in effect; had spent previous night in apartment, though wife told him before this that relationship "was over";

C v Marshall **65 MAC 710 (2006)**—D NOT entitled to required finding of not guilty on *Robbins*-like basis, but did get a jury instruction; circumstances attending D's entry (prying open lock on back door) glaringly inconsistent with consensual entry into apartment of erstwhile girlfriend;

C v Doucette **430 M 461 (99)**—(armed home invasion case, G.L. c. 265, § 18C) though D argued error in judge's refusal to instruct that if D only entered unlocked outer door of building and walked up common interior stairway, but never entered subject apartment, = NG of entering "dwelling house of another", SJC asserted merely that it was "fact question" for jury (without defining what "dwelling" is); but cf. *C v Goldoff* **24 MAC 458 (87)** area in question was common hallway, but it was protected by locked door to which only building occupants had keys;

C v Scott **71 MAC 596 (2008)**—that D was seen emerging from building interior via front door leading to steps connecting to second floor apartment was sufficient for guilt of B&E: that door had been secured against public access by lock, even if hallway/stairs were denominated "common", proof that D entered the apartment itself not necessary;

District Court Model Jury Instruction #5.31;

C v Poff **56 MAC 201 (2002)**—District Court model jury instruction 5.31, which instructs that some particular crime is a felony ("if you concluded that D intended to commit [offense] after entering . . . , I instruct . . . as a matter of law that [offense] is a felony"), fails to make clear that the D's intent to commit felony has to be proven to have been present at the time of the break; substantial risk of miscarriage of justice found (no objection below);

Superior Court Criminal Practice Jury Instructions § 2.34–2.35.1—(burglary; B&E daytime; dwelling house, entry at night; B&E; supplemental instructions re: constructive breaking, breaking & entering in daytime as lesser included offense)

C v Lewis **346 M 373 (63)**—break = open unlocked door; entry = arm opens it;

C v Burke **392 M 688 (84)**—window smashed = "break"; bloody hand = "entry";

C v Smith **75 MAC 196 (2009)**—"entry" shown by foot crossing threshold of the door and when gun was inserted into apartment (GL c. 265, § 18C [armed assault in dwelling] case);

C v Tilley **355 M 507 (69)**—"break" = open a window; *C v Porter* **70 MAC 901 (2007)**—window had been opened, screws removed from lock, and blinds were knocked off window sill AND D was standing between previously locked storm door and front door: "break" supported on either basis;

C v Hall **48 MAC 727 (2000)**—entry through open window not intended for use as an entrance = break, but going in through unobstructed entrance such as open door is not a break;

C v Cextary (No. 1), **68 MAC 752 (2007)**—"break" = scrambling onto car roof & entry through open sunroof;

C v Chotain **31 MAC 336 (91)**—"breaking" requires evidence that D "moved to a material degree something that barred his way";

C v Lafayette **40 MAC 534 (96)**—there may be time lapse between breaking & entering, so long as initial breaking was done with intent to enter (rock thrown through store's glass door, with intent to make entry sometime later, i.e., after police responded & door was boarded up & alarm system was thus disabled);

C v Stokes **440 M 741 (2004)**—"entry" = when any part of the culprit's body is within any part of the house; could infer that D "had broken the plane of the door with his arm" when he stood at threshold and waved gun, pointing it at occupant on other side of threshold;

C v Labare **11 MAC 370 (81)**—"constructive" break by fraud;

C v Randall **50 MAC 26, 29 (2000)**—error to imply that felonious intention could be formed after entering building;

C v Perron **11 MAC 915 (81)**—D intended to assault & batter by means of dangerous weapon;

C v Ronchetti **333 M 78 (55)**—though A&B, infer intent to steal;

C v Lewis **346 M 373 (63)**—infer intent to steal over $100;

C v Lattimore **6 MAC 873 (78)**—larceny in building (G.L. c. 266, § 20) is felony regardless of value of items intended to be stolen; *C v Graham* **62 MAC 642, 647 (2004)**—same;

C v Noonan **48 MAC 356, 361–62 (99)**—bad instruction that it's ordinary & fair inference in absence of contrary evidence that person breaking and entering in daytime intends to steal, but here no substantial risk of miscarriage of justice (no objection);

C v Maia **429 M 585 (99)**—B&E during daytime (when most people are away from home), entry by breaking through window screen, and subsequent threats by D of V warranted inference of intent to commit larceny (despite facts that, when immediately confronted by V, D said that he thought he was in his girlfriend's house, and D left premises when directed to do so by V);

Wharton's Crim. Law § 326—further from completion than "attempt";

C v Wainio **1 MAC 866 (74)**—seek bill of particulars if unspecified felony;

C v Wygrzywalski **362 M 790 (73)**—sleeping drunk's specific intent to commit felony - vs. G.L. c. 266, § 16A (intent: misdemeanor);

C v Hobbs **385 M 863 (82)**—specific felony is surplusage (if no prejudice to defense);

C v Walter **40 MAC 907 (96)**—failure of jury instructions to define "felony" plus judge's answer to jury question ("yes, breaking and entering is itself a felony") = reversal;

C v McGovern **397 M 863 (86)**—infer malicious destruction of property, not intent to commit larceny;

See Chapter 5-D, Complaints & Indictments: Variances;

Mirich v State **593 P.2d.590 (Wyo. '79)**—trespass as lesser included offense;

Wharton's Criminal Law § 343—(same);

C v Vinnicombe **28 MAC 934 (90)**—improper for judge to charge on & jury to convict of simple "breaking & entering" because no such crime exists; proof of intent to commit a felony or misdemeanor required; trespass not a lesser included;

C v Bibbo **50 MAC 648 (2001)**—appellate court rejects argument that possible intended felony in 'B&E with intent to commit felony' could not be "stalking" (because stalking requires repetitive acts which couldn't be accomplished upon the single entry); record here was replete with many prior incidents on which 'stalking' continuation could be based; further, 'stalking' didn't "merge" with B&E: unlike homicide, where every death is accompanied by some kind of assaultive act, not every burglary includes act of stalking;

C v Tuck **20 Pick. 356 (1838)**—larceny as lesser included offense;

C v Hope **22 Pick.1 (1839)**—(same)

C v Powell **10 MAC 57 (80)**—armed vs. unarmed (G.L. c. 266, §§ 14 & 15);

C v Liakos **12 MAC 57 (81)**—armed entry for G.L. c. 265, § 18A.

C v Lowrey **158 M 18 (1893)**—joint venturer lets D in;

C v McGorty **114 M 299 (1873)**—inference from possess recently stolen goods; *(See C v Burns 388 Mass. 178 (83), C v Porter 15 Mass. App. Ct. 331 (83) & Barnes v US 412 US 837 (73), in Receiving Stolen Property, Chapter 21-U, above);*

C v Murphy **353 M 433 (68)**—dwelling defined;

C v Swahn **5 MAC 642 (77)**—G.L. c. 266, § 17 (put in fear); building = dwelling;

C v Kingsbury **378 M 751 (79)**—rented, but not yet occupied;

C v Correia **17 MAC 233 (83)**—motel;

C v Goldoff **24 MAC 458 (87)**—secured common areas of multifamily building = dwelling;

C v Ricardo **26 MAC 345 (88)**—though D was separated from his wife, he was habitually there, had keys, spent the night, etc.: Commonwealth was required to prove beyond a reasonable doubt that the "dwelling"/apartment in question wasn't D's, i.e., that he had no right of habitation or occupancy in the apartment at the time;

C v Perris **108 M 1 (1871)**—must be property "of another";

C v Kalinowski **360 M 682 (71)**—alleged owner = irrelevant; issue = not D's;

C v DeRome **6 MAC 900 (78)**—but wrong apartment alleged = fatal variance;

G.L. c. 277, § 25—owner need not be alleged if property's described;

G.L. c. 278, § 10—"nighttime" (sunset plus 1 hour., to sunrise minus 1 hour):

C v Kingsbury **378 M 751 (79)**—circumstances & common knowledge prove nighttime;

C v Bennett **424 M 64 (97)**—Court found enough for nighttime: D's statement that he went to rob V "one night"; medical examiner's opinion that death occurred between 2 & 5 a.m., all exterior & interior lights were on when body was discovered, and V's wife had been unable to reach him by telephone after 6:30 p.m. & jury's general knowledge of sunrise/sunset at particular time of year;

C v Sitko **372 M 305 (77)**—"daytime" is lesser included offense within "nighttime"; Double Jeopardy for both B & E AND underlying felony? see Wharton's § 338; vs. *C v Ford* **20 MAC 575 (85) (Rev'd by 397 M 298, 490 N.E.2d 1166 (Mass. Apr 14, 1986))** no "merger" B&E/Larceny *(See Chapter 19, Double Jeopardy);*

C v Fazzino **27 MAC 485 (89)**—D's fingerprint at scene sufficient to convict D of B&E only if prosecution evidence reasonably excludes hypothesis that print left at another time; here, additional evidence that D knew how to use torch made fingerprint evidence sufficient;

C v LeClaire **28 MAC 932 (90)**—D's thumbprint on window sufficient to convict D of breaking & entering where it formed pattern with other smeared suggesting that D had grasped window through opening & where D was shown not to have had authorized access to room;

C v Baptista **32 MAC 910 (92)**—D's fresh prints near coin box inside broken soda machine sufficient to convict D of breaking & entering;

21-W. BURGLARY TOOLS (G.L. C. 266, § 49)

Nolan and Sartorio, *Criminal Law* **(3d ed. 2001) § 409;**
District Court Model Jury Instruction #5.54;
Superior Court Criminal Practice Jury Instructions § 2.36;

C v Redmond **53 MAC 1, 6 (2001)**—Superior Court standard instruction WRONG, because it omits requirement that D must have intended to use tool to effectuate B&E, & "compounds" error by emphasizing that required intent = to steal rather than to use tool to accomplish the break;

G.L. c. 277, § 79—form complaint;

C v Collardo **13 MAC 1013 (82)**—"master keys" must be alleged;

C v Jones **355 M 170 (69)**—"innocent" tool, but D's G.; (see *Tivnon* **8 Gray 375 (1857)** "If they are suitable for the purpose, so that they can be used to break and enter burglariously, it is wholly immaterial that they were also designed and adapted for honest and lawful uses.");

C v Porter **70 MAC 901 (2007)**—intent to use wire cutters as burglarious tool shown;

C v Purcell **19 MAC 1031 (85)**—not guilty for gloves;

C v Krasner **358 M 727 (71)**—trespass = "other crime"; "battering ram" = burglarious implement;

C v Sneed **6 MAC 855 (78)**—insufficient intent; *(See Chapter 16, Defenses, Intent)*;

C v Dellinger **10 MAC 549 (80)**—(rev'd other grounds 383 M 780) just "casing" the place = NG;

C v Armenia **4 MAC 33 (76)**—IF alleged, must prove intend steal therefrom; car theft equally likely by dentpuller, so NG;

C v Graud **8 MAC 915 (79)**—(same); *(See Chapters 16, Defenses, Intent & 5, Complaints & Indictments, Variance)*;

C v Walter **40 MAC 907 (96)**—crime's intent is to steal **or** "to commit any other crime", & D here admitted "trespass" intent;

C v Tivnon **8 Gray 375 (1857)**—can have joint possession; need not allege building/owner *(See also Chapter 16, Defenses, Possession)*;

C v Tilley **306 M 412 (40)**—"depository" includes car's trunk;

C v Hogan **41 MAC 73 (96)**—"depository" is not parking meter with bike lock (though parking meter = depository for fees it holds); "depository" = **enclosed** area;

C v Aleo **18 MAC 916 (84)**—car (windows smashed in);

C v Dreyer **18 MAC 562 (84)**—"locked" passenger area of car;

C v Schultz **17 MAC 958 (83)**—not a partially open fence (boat storage area fenced on two sides, open to sky above); "expert" opinion: *(See Chapter 11, Evidence; Chapter 6, Pretrial Conference/Discovery (CPCS P/G 4.4 (g)); & Chapter 7, Preparation for Trial: Expert for D)*;

C v Rudenko **74 MAC 396 (2009)**—though lacking a roof, "locked, fenced-in delivery hall" shared a wall with Home Depot's "roofed" portion, and protected valuable stored merchandise, and was held to be "building";

C v Garreffi **355 M 428 (69)**—cop says "safe-cracker's tools";

C v Johnson **199 M 55 (08)**—chisel & cartridges = burglarious implements;

21-X. TRESPASS (G.L. C. 266, § 120)

(enter, remain; on property of another; without right; it posted or notified by someone authorized (or Chs. 209A; 208/34B));

District Court Model Jury Instruction #5.34

Nolan and Sartorio, *Criminal Law* **(3d ed. 2001) § 410;**

Wharton's Criminal Law § 343—with Model Penal Code defenses;

C v Juvenile **6 MAC 106 (78)**—fence & lock = "notice" entry's forbidden;

Fitzgerald v Lewis **164 M 495 (1895)**—"reasonable" (posted) notice; D's actual knowledge = unnecessary (mistake = no defense); *(See Chapter 16, Defenses, Intent)*;

C v Einarson **6 MAC 835 (78)**—no authority for signs closing park, so NG;

C v Richardson **313 M 632 (43)**—implied license from (tenants') doorbells;

C v Egleson **355 M 259 (69)**—includes public building;

C v Nelson **74 MAC 629 (2009)**—Boston Housing Authority's 'no trespass' order to D could not override BHA residential tenant's invitation to and permission for D to enter; *Richardson* 313 M 632, involved private landlord, but distinction doesn't defeat reasoning as to nature of residential tenancy; lease acknowledges residents' right to have guests in apartments, which necessitates transit through common areas; no evidence that D lingered/loitered in common area; landlord DOES have lawful control of common areas; "not guilty" ordered; constitutional argument re: freedom of association not reached;

Hurley v Hinckley **304 FS 704 (D.Mass. 69)**—"public" property & 1st Amendment rights;

G.L. c. 266, § 123—trespass on certain state & governmental properties;

C v Gangemi **19 MAC 585 (85)**—Camp Edwards = Commonwealth property (for G.L. c. 131, § 59 trespass) necessity or competing harm defense? *(See Chapter 16, Defenses)*:

C v Averill **12 MAC 260 (81)**—not here . . .

C v Brugmann **13 MAC 373 (82)**—or here . . .

C v Hood **389 M 581 (83)**—or here; Draper Lab not "public" re: 1st Amendment.; license to enter, not to remain;

C v Santos **58 MAC 701 (2003)**—crane operator invading only "airspace" (momentarily conveying object through airspace over property without causing any harm to, interference with, or danger to anyone's use of property) is not a trespass;

21-Y. ARSON

G.L. c. 266, § 1—(dwelling), § 2 (building), § 5A (attempt)

Nolan and Sartorio, *Criminal Law* (3d ed. 2001) §§ 421–26;

Superior Court Criminal Practice Jury Instructions § 2.32;

District Court Model Jury Instruction #5.634 (arson by juvenile);

G.L. c. 266, § 8—set fire on another's land & injure property (= misdemeanor);

G.L. c. 266, § 7—wanton or reckless set fire & injure;

G.L. c. 277, § 79—form complaints & indictments *(See Chapter 5, Contents of Complaints & Indictments);*

C v DiGiambattista **59 MAC 190, further appellate review allowed 440 M 1106 (2003) S.C. 442 M 423 (2004)**—burning a building (G.L. c. 266, § 2) is not a lesser included offense of burning a dwelling house (G.L. c. 266, § 1); rejecting also, on evidence, argument that house wasn't "dwelling" because it was too dilapidated to be habitable;

C v Black **4 MAC 512 (76)**—must burn part of building;

C v McIntosh **10 MAC 924 (80)**—charring floor = enough;

C v Goodwin **122 M 19 (1877)**—regular "malice" = willful & unlawful act without excuse (vs. "malicious mischief," e.g., malicious destruction of property, below);

C v Niziolek **380 M 513 (80)**—"willful & malicious";

C v Lamothe **343 M 417 (61)**—"malice";

C v Mezzanotti **26 MAC 522 (88)**—best use *Niziolek* **380 M 513,** but malice instruction OK;

C v McLaughlin **431 M 506, 512–13 (2000)**—1995 judges' "chargebook" contains erroneous understanding of *C v Ely* **388 M 69, 74 ((83),** as does *C v DeCicco* **44 MAC 111, 117 (98)**; should use *Niziolek* **380 M 513 (80)**; confusing & erroneous here to say malice = "ordinary meaning," "improper, selfish motive", "inferable . . . from the willful act of burning without legal justification"; 'act done with evil disposition, a wrong and unlawful motive or purpose,' is synonymous (at least in arson cases) with the willful doing of an injurious act without lawful excuse;

C v Glenn **23 MAC 440 (87)**—instructions didn't adequately rule out negligent;

C v Rhoades **379 M 810 (80)**—G by circumstantial evidence;

C v DeStefano **16 MAC 208 (83)**—"dwelling" = "habitable" (but not occupied);

C v Shuman **17 MAC 441 (84)**—arson's "included" in burning building to defraud;

C v Ianelli **17 MAC 1011 (84)**—D's financial motive; cf. *C v Chery* **36 MAC 913 (94)**—re: burning motor vehicle, motor vehicle insurance fraud (circumstantial evidence sufficient);

C v Harris **1 MAC 265, aff'd 364 M 236 (73)**—EXPERT foundation/scope;

C v Ward **14 MAC 37 (82)**—(same);

C v Jacobson **19 MAC 666 (85)**—(same);

See Chapter 11, Evidence; Chapter 6, Discovery; Chapter 7, Experts for D; & CPCS P/G's 4.4 (9), 4.6 (h);

21-Z. MALICIOUS DESTRUCTION OF PROPERTY (G.L. C. 266, § 127, ETC.)

G.L. c. 218, § 26—District Court jurisdiction for § 127 (at least for "personal" property);

District Court Model Jury Instructions #5.301—(willful & malicious destruction of property) & 5.30 (wanton destruction of property);

Wharton's Criminal Law § 488—Defenses, e.g., mistake, accident, intoxication;

C v Savoy **21 MAC 519 (86)**—most damage not proven, & no joint venture evidence re: co-D's = required finding of not guilty;

C v Peruzzi **15 MAC 437 (83)**—"malice"; pipe twice through bus window could be "wanton"; (then-existing District Court Model Jury Instruction #5.301 was "flawed");

C v Hosman **257 M 379 (26)**—"malice" = hostility, etc.; but maybe not personal; SEE *McLaughlin* **431 M 506, 512 (2001)** INSTEAD, and see especially *Redmond* **53 MAC 1 (2001),** post;

C v Williams **110 M 401 (1872)**—"hostility";

C v Byard **200 M 175 (08)**—"wanton" = willful act & reckless disregard;

C v Welansky **316 M 383, 397–8 (44)**—"wanton" (re: manslaughter);

C v Domingue **18 MAC 987 (84)**—both malice & assault by means of dangerous weapon by same activity;

C v Ford **20 MAC 575 (1985) rev'd by 397 Mass. 298, 490 N.E.2d 1166 (Mass. Apr. 14, 1986) (1985) rev'd by 397 Mass. 298, 490 N.E.2d 1166 (Mass. Apr 14, 1986)**—no "merger" with B&E *(See Chapter 19, Double Jeopardy);*

C v Aleo **18 MAC 916 (84)**—could find broken window = not malice, but B & E;

C v Wynn **42 MAC 452 (97)**—smashing glass in locked door before reaching in to unlock it & enter apartment to rob and terrorize occupants = sufficient for malicious destruction (but see *Redmond* **53 MAC 1 (2001), post);**

C v Cimino **34 MAC 925 (93)**—riding around & shooting out parked cars' windows with BB gun sufficient for 'willful & malicious'; D need not know property owner to act "maliciously" (i.e., out of "hostility, cruelty, or revenge");

C v Morris M **70 MAC 688 (2007)**—required finding of not guilty on "malicious" because D's acts of injuring car, fence and turf, while willful, were done to escape adversary (albeit heedlessly and in reckless disregard of rights of others) rather than out of hostility to owners [wanton destruction was not charged, & isn't a lesser included offense];

C v Armand **411 M 167, 170–71 (91)**—evidence that D shared malicious intent of co-D to break steering column during fight with others was insufficient, because damage to car by joint venturer was only incidental to common narrow goal of attacking two victims;

C v Redmond **53 MAC 1 (2001)**—in this crime (G.L. c. 266, § 127), willful doing of the unlawful act doesn't suffice to prove malice; required state of mind = cruelty, hostility, or revenge, in addition to intent to inflict injury to property; breaking window, dismantling alarm, & forcing doors = merely the means to computer theft after B&E, so required finding of NG of malicious destruction; here, more akin to "wanton" destruction of property, with which D wasn't charged (& it's not lesser included);

C v Smith **17 MAC 918 (83)**—malicious vs. "willful";

C v Ruddock **25 MAC 508 (88)**—if no likelihood of substantial injury, conduct is neither wanton nor reckless; enough for 'G' here because D risked enough harm to a compact car by jumping over its hood while carrying megaphone; on complaint for "malicious" (G.L. c. 266, § 127), D guilty of "lesser included" (sic: see *Schuchardt*, post) of "wanton";

C v Schuchardt **408 M 347 (90)**—wanton destruction not a lesser included of malicious destruction; wanton conduct involves an intentional act with a high likelihood of substantial harm, even though actor may be indifferent to consequences; willful & malicious conduct involves intentional infliction of harm motivated by "cruelty, hostility or revenge," but does not require that intended harm be substantial;

C v Wynn **42 MAC 452 (97)**—line distinguishing 'wanton' from 'malicious' destruction of property = "imprecise";

C v McDowell **62 MAC 15 (2004)**—conviction under G.L. c. 266, § 126A requires only "wanton" conduct (wilful and malicious not needed), so D's extreme intoxication didn't call into doubt proof of this "general intent" crime;

Rich v United Mut. **328 M 133 (51)**—"vandalism" vs. "child play";

C v Faherty **57 MAC 150 (2003)**—jamming parking meter (which only took quarters) by using two pennies wrapped in paper caused meter to register "out of order"; though police were able to repair meter, taking "several minutes" to do so, there was substantial harm sufficient for guilt of wanton destruction; fact that injury was short-lived was mere "matter of luck";

C v Walters **12 MAC 389 (81)**—must allege (& prove) value for over (now $250); fn.4—question: value of property or value of damage? if not $250, it's max.3

months HC (i.e., misdemeanor? *Peruzzi* **15 MAC 437 at n.1 (83)** vs. Modern Penal Code definition (in Wharton § 492): not felony unless $500 damage);

C v Lauzier **53 MAC 626 (2002)**—not reaching issue how the $250 threshold is to be measured since not raised below, & all on notice of expanded valuation measure;

C v Pyburn **26 MAC 967 (88)** citing G.L. c. 266, § 127—it's value of "property so destroyed or injured", not amount of **damage** to such property/how much it costs to repair; **overruled by** *C v Deberry* **441 M 211 (2004)— correct standard = "the pecuniary loss," i.e., "the reasonable cost of the repairs necessitated by the malicious conduct"** (D punched hole the size of a light switch plate in a house's kitchen wall, and Commonwealth claimed that market value of the whole house = relevant value); **see also** *C v Kirker* **441 M 226 (2004)— proper measure of value = replacement cost of two tires on car, NOT the value of the car itself**;

C v Beale **434 M 1024, 1025 n.2 (2001)** citing *Apprendi v New Jersey* **530 US 466 (2000)**—overrules *Pyburn* holding, **26 MAC 967, 969 (88)**, that value of property isn't essential element of crime, but is instead mere sentencing enhancement factor; it's element, for jury determination beyond reasonable doubt;

C v Cimino **34 MAC 925 (93)**—failure to prove property's value required vacating 'greater' & sentence thereon; but cf. *C v Kelly* **24 MAC 181, & n.4 (87)** jury-waived trial on robbery indictment succeeded in G on only lesser-included of larceny; appellate court rejected argument that larceny (over) wasn't lesser included offense because robbery had no "element" re: value; fact-finder to decide value for larceny;

C v Cox **7 Allen 577 (1863)**—need not allege value for "under";

C v Hosman **257 M 379 (26)**—infer value (of car) = over $100;

C v Dougherty **6 Gray 349 (1856)**—realty? (§ 127 now includes dwelling/building);

C v Anderson **38 MAC 707 (95)**—a stone wall that had once supported one end of a railroad trestle was neither a building nor personal property, so D not guilty under G.L. c. 266, § 127 for spray painting graffiti on it; prosecution would lie under G.L. c. 266, § 126 (defacing public or private objects);

C v Rudenko **74 MAC 396 (2009)**—though lacking a roof, fenced-in and locked "delivery hall" sharing wall with roofed Home Depot store = building;

G.L. c. 266, § 104—willful injury to dwelling or building;

G.L. c. 266, § 114—breaking glass - (TITLE = "trees & fences"); lesser included offense within malicious destruction?;

G.L. c. 266, § 126A—anti-graffiti statute - defacement of real or personal property, including wall, fence, building, sign, rock, monument, gravestone, or tablet (state prison for ≤ 3 years, fine of $1500. or 3 times the value of property, pay for cleanup, suspension of drivers license for one year or add one year before eligible for license (if D = under age 16);

G.L. c. 266, § 126B—"tagging" - applying paint or a sticker to building, wall fence, sign, etc.;

G.L. c. 266, §§ 96, 98, 113, 129—etc. - specific kinds of property;

G.L. c. 266, § 127 & G.L. c. 265, § 39—Civil Rights provisions—*(See Chapter 21F-7, above)*;

Superior Court Criminal Practice Jury Instructions § 2.45.2—property damage for the purpose of intimidation;

G.L. c. 266, § 127A—willful/intentional or wanton/without cause destroying, defacing, or marring church, synagogue, etc.;

C v Dipietro **33 MAC 776 (92)**—"egging" Hindu temple = sufficient evidence of defacing/marring, even though eggs could be washed off;

21-AA. CARRY (NON-FIREARM) DANGEROUS WEAPONS (G.L. C. 269, § 10(B))

21-AA.1. Specified

(E.G., Switch-Blade, Metallic Knuckles, Blackjack) = Dangerous Weapon Per Se;

C v Perry **455 M 1010 (2009)**—"expandable baton" was NOT a "blackjack", and statute did not say 'blackjack or "similar weapon" or one "which can be put to similar use"; those phrases *were* used regarding other weapons, so rules of statutory construction barred such expansion here: "not guilty" ordered;

21-AA.2. Other Dangerous Weapon's Illegal IF Carried when Arrested Either: (A) on Warrant, or (B) while Committing "Breach of Peace"

G.L. c. 277, § 79—form complaint *(See Chapter 5, Contents of Complaints & Indictments)*;

District Court Model Jury Instruction #5.602–5.603;

C v Blavackas **11 MAC 746 (81)**—not this knife;

C v Thompson **15 MAC 974 (83)**—knife = dangerous weapon here;

C v Miller **22 MAC 694 (86)**—required finding of NG because dictionary definition "dirk knife" doesn't satisfy § 10 "stabbing weapon";

C v O'Connor **7 Allen 583 (1863)**—must allege & prove lawful arrest; (Confusing) PENALTY: 5 year (state prison) maximum unless no prior felony; (felony? must allege prior? *(See Chapter 5 (G.L. c. 278, § 11A "2nd/subsequent" complaint))*; cf. *Bynum v Commonwealth* **429 M 705 (99)**, G.L. c. 94C, § 32A(d) does not create an independent crime (having been convicted of a like drug offense previously), but is instead a sentencing enhancement provision;

C v Fernandes **430 M 517 (99)**—indictment of two pages, with 1st page "count" charging new drug offense and 2d page "count" simply alleging a prior conviction; "count" 2 not a separate crime, but simply notifies D of sentence enhancement (& sufficient notice given by words "having been previously convicted of a similar offense," though better practice = specify date of prior offense and date and court in which prior conviction was obtained);

21-BB. CARRY FIREARM, RIFLE, SHOTGUN

G.L. c. 269, § 10(a) & § 10(c)—Sawed Shotgun); G.L. c. 140, § 131N possession of covert weapon, i.e., anything constructed in shape not resembling handgun, rifle or shot gun OR not detectable as weapon by X-ray machine or metal detector;

District of Columbia v Heller **128 S Ct 2783 (2008)**—Second Amendment to US Constitution protects an individual right to possess firearm unconnected with service in militia, and to use firearm for lawful purposes such as self-defense within the home; BUT right is not unlimited, and isn't a right to keep and carry any weapon whatsoever in any manner whatsoever and for whatever purpose; total ban on handgun possession within home, and trigger lock requirement (as applied to self-defense) violates Second Amendment; D here had conceded that DC licensing law was permissible if not enforced arbitrarily, so remedy = permitting D to register handgun and issuing him license to carry it in home;

McDonald v City of Chicago ***** US *** (6/28/2010)**—Second Amendment applies to states via

Fourteenth Amendment, and ordinance acting as total handgun ban = unconstitutional;

21-BB.1. General

Nolan and Sartorio, *Criminal Law* (3d ed. 2001), Chapter 13, "Weapons & Explosives";

District Court Model Jury Instructions #5.60–5.601

G.L. c. 269, § 12D—carry loaded rifle or shotgun without G.L. c. 131 license ;

G.L. c. 269, § 12E—discharge firearm, etc. near dwelling;

G.L. c. 269, § 10(a)—(as amended) mandatory one year minimum for simple possession of unlicensed firearm outside residence or place of business; see paragraph (h);

G.L. c. 269, § 10(j)—(as amended) penalizes carrying of firearm in any school or college without authorization of school authorities even if firearm is licensed;

C v Connor C. **432 M 635 (2000)**—delinquency adjudication under G.L. c. 269, § 10(a) constitutes a prior conviction, such that juvenile could be indicted for "2d offense gun charge" under G.L. c. 269, § 10(d);

C v Furr **58 MAC 155 (2003)**—D's prior adjudication as youthful offender on charges of armed carjacking, armed robbery, ABDW, etc., qualifies as predicate conviction to warrant enhanced sentences in G.L. c. 269, § 10(g);

G.L. c. 265, § 18B (1998)—whoever, "while in the commission or attempted commission of" offense punishable by state prison, "has in his possession or under his control" a firearm, rifle or shotgun shall be punished by at least five years' imprisonment in addition to penalty for such offense: *C v Hines* **449 M 183 (2007)**—that there was a gun in a locked safe in bedroom of D's apartment and in bedroom (but not safe) also was found enough cocaine to infer distributive intent was sufficient for the extra § 18B punishment; five years' *probation* was not a legitimate sentence under § 18B;

21-BB.2. "Firearm": Less Than 16" and Capable of Discharging Shot/Bullet

G.L. c. 140, § 121—definition;

C v Sampson **383 M 750 (81)**—not flare gun;

C v Rhodes **389 M 641 (83)**—not air rifle, BB gun; contrast *C v Sayers* **438 M 238 (2002)**—adult carrying BB gun on school/university grounds guilty under c. 269, § 10(j), because § 10(j) defines firearm as rifle or pistol from which a "shot, bullet, or pellet" can be discharged, a broader definition than c. 269, § 10(a); even person with license can't carry on school/university property without written authorization of board or officer in charge;

C v Fenton **395 M 92 (85)**—not C02 revolver;

C v Sperrazza **372 M 667 (77)**—infer less than 16 inches;

C v Gonzalez **68 MAC 91 (2007)**—CANNOT infer less than 16 inches on this evidence;

C v Smith **58 MAC 166 (2003)**—judge first allowed D's motion for required finding of not guilty because no proof of barrel length, but prior to closing arguments changed decision; appellate court said no required finding necessary, element inferable from mere testimony that gun was a "pistol," and that it was a ".32 or .38";

C v Watts **22 MAC 952 (86)**—though "more likely," no proof barrel's under 16;

G.L. c. 140, § 121A—ballistician's certificate admissible & prima facie evidence (if from Dep't. Public Safety & qualified "expert") [but admission without ballistician violates D's Sixth Amendment confrontation right, *Melendez-Diaz v MA* 129 S Ct 2527 (2009)];

C v Crawford **18 MAC 911 (84)**—not a "presumption";

Melendez-Diaz v Massachusetts **129 S Ct 2527 (2009)**—admission of laboratory certificates without live testimony by analyst violates confrontation clause of Sixth Amendment;

C v Chery **75 MAC 909 (2009)**—ballisticians' certificates concerning "firearm" and "ammunition" introduced over D's "Crawford"/6th Amendment objection = reversal; not harmless beyond reasonable doubt even though gun itself was introduced; even assuming that the ammunition itself (in evidence) could provide inference that it was "designed for use in" firearm and thus be sufficient for conviction, prosecutor relied in argument on its testing by examiner;

Virginia v Black **123 S Ct 1536 (2003)**—model jury instruction that any cross burning shall be prima facie evidence of an intent to intimidate a person or group = constitutionally overbroad & thus error;

C v Nieves **43 MAC 1 (97)**—required finding of NG because ballistics certificate excluded on D's objection, and no other evidence of gun's capacity to discharge bullet (e.g., testimony that it was fired, or used, or had ammo. inside, or testimony by someone who handled it or was familiar with it); *C v Brown* **75 MAC 361 (2009)**—when ballistics certificate should have been excluded under *Crawford v Washington* 541 US 36 (2004) (denial of 6th Amendment confrontation right), & there was no other evidence of operability (no shots fired, no bullets in gun), constitutional error wasn't harmless beyond reasonable doubt;

C v Bartholomew **326 M 218 (50)**—expert: needs only slight repair to be operable = sufficient (absence of easily replaceable firing pin didn't destroy "character" of "machine gun");

C v Prevost **44 MAC 398 (98)**—despite fact that handgun had broken firing pin, no required finding of NG: testimony was that its replacement = simple 10-minute task; operability established unless weapon "so defective or damaged that it has lost its initial character as a firearm";

C v Fancy **349 M 196, 204 (65)**—don't need expert; proof by appearance;

C v Stallions **9 MAC 23 (80)**—(same);

C v Tuitt **393 M 801 (85)**—(same);

C v Rhodes **21 MAC 968 (86)**— . . . but not if only experts could fix;

C v Sylvester **35 MAC 906 (93)**—don't need expert , or **gun itself**, after V described "hand-held weapon which he thought was a .25 caliber Baretta automatic";

C v DeJesus **44 MAC 349 (98)**—required finding of not guilty because no proof of barrel length of "shotgun";

See Chapter 6, Discovery: Expert; Chapter 7: Preparation: Expert for D; Chapter 11-I, Evidence: Opinions; & P/G's 4.4 (g), 4.6 (h);

21-BB.3. "General" Knowledge Item Is a Firearm

C v Sampson **383 M 750 (81)**—must have general knowledge it's firearm;

C v Jackson **369 M 904 (76)**—(same); need not prove knew it's unregistered;

C v Papa **17 MAC 987 (84)**—need only know it's "conventional firearm," not "exact capabilities";

C v Bacon **374 M 358 (78)**—complaint need not allege knowledge *(See Chapter 5, Contents of Complaints & Indictments)*;

C v O'Connell **432 M 657 (2000)**—D's ignorance of gun's length not a valid defense (shotgun = ¼ inch shorter than legal limit);

21-BB.4. G.L. c. 269, § 10(a)

G.L. c. 269, § 10(a)—possessing or having under control in vehicle, firearm, loaded or unloaded, without being present in residence or place of business, or without having license to carry (G.L. c. 140, §§ 131, 131F, or 129C & 131G) (v § 10 (h) "possession" without firearm identification card (G.L. c. 140, § 129C) (misdemeanor): previous DISTINCTION between § 10(a) ("carrying") & 10(h) ("possession"), of 'movement' NO LONGER SIGNIFICANT, AFTER LEGISLATIVE REVISION IN 1990;

C v Atencio **345 M 627 (63)**—Russian roulette = possession;

C v Morrissey **351 M 505 (67)**—temporary "possession" during shooting;

C v Osborne **5 MAC 657 (77)**—(same) on D's bed;

C v Ashley **16 MAC 983 (83)**—infer "carry" because not home;

C v Seay **376 M 735 (78)**—"carrying" defined - "movement";

C v Cullinane **9 MAC 895 (80)**—sneak attack suggests "carried";

C v Stallions **9 MAC 23 (80)**—30 to 40 feet = "movement"

C v Williams **422 M 111 (96)**—sufficient evidence despite finding no gun: shots fired, D fled building & had V's blood on his white shirt (V died from gunshot wounds), D was within 200–400 yards from scene, and could be found to have been in flight continuously after shots;

21-BB.5. Under Control in vehicle

See Chapter 16, Defenses: Possession, and Chapter 21-CC, Controlled Substances, post, for sufficiency of evidence of "possession";

C v Boone **356 M 85 (69)**—no knowledge by passenger, though in car 40 minutes;

C v Bennefield **373 M 452 (77)**—front passenger N.G. of rear floor shotgun;

C v Hill **15 MAC 93 (83)**—no knowledge of gun under seat;

C v Almeida **381 M 420 (80)**—no knowledge (in console of friend's car);

C v Gray **5 MAC 296 (77)**—(& id. 300 (Brown, J.)) control not inferred from knowledge—need both;

C v Sann Than **442 M 748 (2004)**—instructions, taken as whole, adequately conveyed that constructive possession requires not only knowledge & ability to control, but also "intention" to control (Appeals Court had held (59 MAC 410, 414 (2003)) that instructions inadequately conveyed "intention");

C v Rider **8 MAC 775 (79)**—NG if D's presence in (cruiser) is involuntary; maybe "possession";

C v Diaz **15 MAC 469 (83)**—passenger can control;

C v Albano **4 MAC 843 (76); SJC 373 M 132 (77)**—Appeals Court = NG; SJC = G;

C v Donovan **17 MAC 83 (83)**—borrowed car, but lots to infer G;

C v Araujo **38 MAC 960 (95)**—despite sufficient evidence for possession of hand guns by bed and between mattress & box spring on bed where he had been asleep, required finding of NG re: sawed off shotgun in bedroom closet (no proof D lived in apartment, or even knew of shotgun);

21-BB.6. "Possession" (Including Ammunition) Needs FID; Statute, Since 1990, Generally Requires [for gun] License, Not Just FID, Except in Home or Place of Business

C v Bachman **41 MAC 757 (96)**—exemption in G.L. c. 140, § 129C(m) for temporary holding, handling, or firing of firearm for examination, trial, or instruction in presence of license-holder here inapplicable;

G.L. c. 140, § 129C—(with exceptions) firearm identification card for rifle or regular shotgun;

C v Mendes **44 MAC 903 (97)**—need not prove current "functionality" of ammo for possession of ammo (G.L. c. 269, § 10(h)); need only prove "designed for use in" some firearm;

C v Grasso **375 M 138 (78)**—(under then-existing statute,) possession as lesser included offense of "carry"; can carry rifle or (non-sawed) shotgun with F.I.D.;

C v DiMatteo **12 MAC 547 (81)**—(same);

C v Landry **6 MAC 404 (78)**—F.I.D. vs. license to carry;

C v Lee **10 MAC 518 (80)**—129C EXEMPTION for nonresident, unloaded, in a "case"

21-BB.7. Home or Business

C v Brass **42 MAC 88 (97)**—once D remained beyond his rental period in hotel, his room was not residence;

C v Dunphy **377 M 453 (79)**—backyard = "common area"; see also *C v Statham* **38 MAC 582 (95)**—unless D had 'exclusive control' over background of multi-unit building, it was not his 'residence';

C v Seay **376 M 735 (78)**—foyer = common area;

C v Belding **42 MAC 435 (97)**—rejecting D-landlord's argument that entire 3-unit building was his property such that he was exempted from license requirement; argument that whole building was D's place of business called "dubious"; exemption for residence did not cover common areas of building;

C v Morales **14 MAC 1034 (82)**—firearm. I.D. permits gun at home;

C v Samaras **10 MAC 910 (80)**—sidewalk not D's exclusive control;

C v Coren **437 M 723 (2002)**—required finding of not guilty because evidence showed only that D possessed gun on walkway to his home and in backyard, both of which are within boundaries of "residence" under statute;

C v Moore **54 MAC 334 (2002)**—reversal because judge's instruction in response to jury question focused on 'exclusive' control, & this D could have been found to share his residence with roommates & still been within his residence even if he possessed the firearm in a roommate's bedroom; "in a dwelling with multiple units, a residence may be the entire unit if the person dwelling therein is not excluded from any part thereof and has access to all the rooms; a common area is an area outside the residence to which all of the tenants in a building have access and the landlord maintains control"; issue was one of fact for jury;

21-BB.8. License (D's Burden of Production)

G.L. c. 140, § 131—license to carry if show "proper purpose & suitable";

G.L. c. 278, § 7—D must "prove" license; until then "presume" unauthorized;

C v Gonzalez **68 MAC 91 (2007)**—rejecting D's arguments that D could not be required to bear burden of proving purported co-D's license or firearm identification card (D never having himself possessed weapon allegedly used in attempted robbery); rejecting also argument that crimes of "unlicensed" possession of firearm, or ammunition, can't be predicated on joint venture liability (since statute doesn't speak to WHO must be licensed: all alleged joint venturers? The one in actual possession of gun/ammo?);

C v Parzick **64 MAC 846 (2005)**—D's conviction affirmed, despite argument that he had previously had FID, which had expired, but before expiration he had applied for renewal and submitted fee, and was not informed that application had been denied; ?better argument?, raised too late, = G.L. c. 140, § 129B(12) (affirmative defense to those found in possession of firearm "whose FID card . . . is invalid for the sole reason that it has expired");

C v Farley **64 MAC 854 (2005)**—charged with carrying firearm in vehicle, D moved to dismiss, on basis that he was disqualified from carrying [only] because his license had expired, and he wasn't disqualified from renewing it; statute (G.L. c. 140, § 131(m)) provides in some such circumstances (limited, "innocent") that D might be guilty of only a civil infraction rather than crime; the circumstance is also an affirmative defense which should be put to jury with appropriate instructions (after D has satisfied his burden to present evidence to contest presumed

fact that he had no justification for lack of license); denial of license application is not "ineffective" for not having been put in writing; but it was jury issue whether evidence of oral notice of denial was credible/sufficient to meet "beyond reasonable doubt" standard of proof;

M.R.Crim.P.14 (b)(3)—written notice of license defense within pretrial motion time limit (or at time judge directs) or excluded; *(See Chapter 6, Pretrial Conference, Motions, & Discovery)*;

C v Jones **372 M 403 (77)**—any evidence & burden of proof shifts to Commonwealth.;

C v Munoz **384 M 503 (81)**—(same); *(See Chapter 16, Defenses & Chapter 12-G, Required Finding of Not Guilty)*;

C v Cowan **40 MAC 939 (96)**—rejecting D's argument that he was entitled to jury instruction on lesser included offense of possession within home (non-mandatory sentence) on theory that while he was not entitled to have gun in home (no FID), necessity justified his possession of it outside home due to aggression by another;

C v Lydon **413 M 309 (92)**—where D presents no evidence of license to carry, better practice is for judge to instruct that jury is not to consider whether D had license;

21-BB.9. "Justification," e.g., Self-Defense, etc.?

See Chapter 16, Defenses;

C v Brown **10 MAC 935 (80)**—bad "justification" charge (D said seized gun to give to police);

C v Franklin **376 M 885, 888 n.2 (78)**—D didn't raise issue of self-defense;

US v Gant **691 F.2d 1159 (5th Cir. '82)**—defenses (duress, necessity, self-defense) available, but not here;

C v Mann **116 M 58 (1874)**—self-defense for shooting;

C v Lindsey **396 M 840 (86)**—no self defense instruction merited though threat., because not imminent enough; but assume some temporary possession could be necessary/lawful; *(See Chapter 16, Defenses & Chapter 15, Pardon)*;

C v Iglesia **403 M 132 (88)**—DA must disprove necessity for carry gun where D says disarmed X & taking it to police; jury decides if right choice;

21-BB.10.   Sawed-off Shotgun (G.L. c. 269, § 10(c)) (possess = life max.)

C v Brimley **19 MAC 978 (85)**—must show "capable of firing"?

C v O'Connell **432 M 657 (2000)**—D's ignorance of gun's length not a valid defense (shotgun = ¼ inch shorter than legal limit);

21-BB.11. G.L. c. 265, § 18B

G.L. c. 265, § 18B—possession of firearm while committing a felony = at least five years' imprisonment, but if firearm = "large capacity" weapon, = at least ten years' imprisonment; for 2d or subsequent such offense,

minimum mandatory sentences = 20 years and 25 years ("large capacity" weapon);

21-CC. CONTROLLED SUBSTANCES (G.L. C. 94C)

21-CC.1. General

Nolan and Sartorio, *Criminal Law* (3d ed. 2001)—Chapter 22, "Narcotic Drugs—Control and Offenses";

G.L. c. 90, § 22—(G.L. c. 241, 1989 Acts): Registry of Motor Vehicles shall suspend, without hearing, license of D found G. of G.L. c. 94C law (max. 5 years; D under 18, at judge's discretion, not licensed up to 21);

District Court Model Jury Instructions #5.52–5.532;

Superior Court Criminal Practice Jury Instructions §§ 2.49 et seq.—Controlled Substance Violations;

C v Hutchins **410 M 726 (91)**—medical necessity is not a defense to drug possession;

US v Oakland Cannabis Buyers' Cooperative **532 US 483 (2001)**—defense of legal necessity can't succeed when legislature itself has made a determination of values; here US Congress determined that marijuana had no medical benefits worthy of an exception other than government-approved research;

C v Nissenbaum **404 M 575 (89)**—religious use is not a defense to drug possession;

C v Sapoznik **28 MAC 236 (90)**—magistrate's finding of probable cause to issue warrant not admissible at trial because it vouches for cops; but see *C v Ferrara* **31 MAC 648 (91)** Sapoznik-type error claimed, but no objection for this reason below, and no mention at trial of magistrate's specifically finding "probable cause"; this meant only slight tendency to bolster/vouch, and no substantial risk of miscarriage of justice;

C v Green **408 M 48 (90)**—required finding entered where Commonwealth failed to prove that cocaine is a "narcotic" under G.L. c. 94C, § 1;

C v LaPerle **19 MAC 424 (85)**—though residue, paraphernalia suggests distribution;

Marcoux v AG **375 M 63 (78)**—can penalize marijuana for personal use;

C v Rise **7 MAC 106 (79)**—must hold hearing, because addiction = substantial question re: competency;

C v Fafone **416 M 329 (93)**—Florida resident sold drugs to Mass. man by conveying them via train to Conn.; convictions for being accessory before fact of trafficking reversed due to failure of proof that Floridian intended his acts to have effect within the Commonwealth (lack of territorial jurisdiction);

C v Berth **385 M 784 (82)**—chain of custody (I.D.) of drugs goes to weight, not admissibility;

G.L. c. 277, § 38—distribution complaint need not allege to whom; "presume" no authority;

G.L. c. 277, § 79—form complaint;

C v Whitlock **39 MAC 514 (95)**—in reading complaint to sworn jury, must **omit** allegation of "second or subsequent";

Bynum v Commonwealth **429 M 705 (99)**—"repeat offense" (G.L. c. 94C, § 32(d)) is not a separate "crime"; instead, it's a sentencing enhancement provision";

C v Fernandes **430 M 517 (99)**—repeat-offender statutes are sentence enhancement provisions ONLY, and don't identify "a freestanding crime"; "better practice" = include in indictment the date of prior offense, & date & court of prior conviction;

C v Sepulveda **6 MAC 868 (78)**—need not allege "knowledge" *(See Chapter 5, contents of Complaints & Indictments)*;

C v Lee **331 M 166 (54)**—don't need knowledge package has marijuana;

C v Antobenedetto **366 M 51 (74)**—possession may need scienter (see Nolan and Sartorio, Criminal Law (3d ed. 2001) § 103);

C v Aguiar **370 M 490 (76)**—under G.L. c. 94C, § 34, knowing possession must be proven;

C v DePalma **41 MAC 798 (96)**—evidence sufficient to infer D knew package given to him (in exchange for box containing $28,000) contained controlled substance; not necessary to prove knowledge that it contained cocaine (see *C v Rodriguez* **415 M 447, 454 (93)**);

21-CC.2. Chemist's Certificate

G.L. c. 111, § 13—D.P.H. or D.E.A.—("net weight, when appropriate")

G.L. c. 147, § 4D—Dept. Public Safety, too;

C v Verde **444 M 279 (2005)**—drug certificate doesn't violate *Crawford v Washington*; it's "akin to a business record & the confrontation clause is not implicated by this type of evidence": that certificate is admissible only as "prima facie evidence of the composition, quality, and weight of the substance" is purportedly ameliorative, BUT Commonwealth's analyst wasn't required to testify simply because D offered evidence to rebut the certificate; Verde was overruled by U.S. Supreme Court in:

Melendez-Diaz v Massachusetts **129 S Ct 2527 (2009)**—admission of laboratory certificates without live testimony by analyst violates confrontation clause of Sixth Amendment;

C v Chappee **397 M 508 (86)**—prima facie, plus facts = deny motion for required finding of not guilty;

C v Sheline **391 M 279 (84)**—must sanitize the report;

C v Fernandes **46 MAC 455, 460–61 (99)**—presence of D's name on certificate of drug analyst (no objection at trial) not prejudicial, did "not lend itself to an inference about what the defendant had to do with the drugs analyzed" since jury already knew that D was a suspect;

C v Claudio **26 MAC 218 (88)**—instruction ("prima facie . . . presumption") may've shifted burden of persuasion (but no objection & harmless);

C v Crawford **18 MAC 911 (84)**—(same), but reversible (with other) error;

Burns v Commonwealth **430 M 444, 450–51 (99)**—"prima facie" evidence explained (without due regard to burden-shifting problem?);

C v Reynolds **36 MAC 963 (94)**—absence of impressed "seal" on jurat of notary public who attested signature on certificate of analysis does not invalidate D's conviction;

C v Johnson **32 MAC 355 (92)**—stamping of notary's signature does not invalidate certificate;

C v Johnson **410 M 199 (91)**—net weight should not have been noted on certificate as it had not been "requested" pursuant to G.L. c. 111, § 13; D must make timely objection;

C v Cordero **34 MAC 923 (93)**—because ascertainment of drugs' weight is implicit in official request for chemical analysis, prosecution's alleged failure to make specific request did not invalidate the weight calculation made or deprive certificate of **prima facie** value;

C v Villella **39 MAC 426 (95)**—that chemist performing analysis had been found, previously, to have tampered w/analysis or given false evidence was not basis for striking the certificates;

See Chapter 6-E, Discovery of Expert(s); Chapters 6-M & 7-C, Experts for D; Chapter 11-I, Evidence: Experts; & CPCS P/G's 4.4 (g), 4.6 (h);

C v Dawson **399 M 465 (87)**—it would be a "rare case" in which it's sufficient proof of substance to have mere witness opinion that substance "looks like" particular drug;

C v Alisha **56 MAC 311 (2002)**—despite failure to introduce pills or certificate of analysis, circumstantial evidence sufficient to support inference that pills were Klonopin (D's statements, fact that D's mother discovered such pills missing, description of subject pills by color and appearance of letter "K," physician's testimony describing Klonopin likewise);

21-CC.3. Distribution and Possession/ Intent to Distribute—G.L. c. 94C, §§ 32–32D

G.L. c. 94C, § 1—"DISTRIBUTE" = "transfer," etc.;

G.L. c. 218, § 26—(7/14/88)—District Court jurisdiction for District A (§ 32(a)) or B (§ 32A(a));

Cedeno v Commonwealth **404 M 190 (89)**—DA's choice; (can charge under § 32A(a) or § 32A(c); latter has mandatory minimum sentence); *Gagnon* **387 M 567 (82)** distinguished;

C v Zwickert **37 MAC 364 (94)**—more stringent recidivist sentence properly applied to D (§ 32A(c) rather than § 32A(a));

C v Bradley **35 MAC 525 (93)**—prosecutorial discretion regarding whether to proceed against a repeat cocaine distributor under G.L. c. 94C, § 32A(d) or § 32A(b), the former being much harsher (minimum mandatory 5 years & not more than 15 years, v 3 to 10 year range in § 32A(b)); failure of indictment to specify (d) did not prevent D from being punished under (d), query whether a G **plea** would have been voluntary without knowledge of sentencing range (this D went to trial);

C v Lovejoy **39 MAC 930 (95)**—observed hand-to-hand exchanges with cars' drivers, plus claim by cop that one driver swallowed crack cocaine when cop approached plus D's refusal to open door for 5–10 minutes for identified police = sufficient evidence for drug distribution, **BUT** reversal because "opinions" of cop that D was engaged in drug transactions and that driver swallowed cocaine = only speculation;

C v Harvard **356 M 452 (69)**—not "sale" if agent of buyer; but see *C v White* **38 MAC 987 (95)** no required finding of not guilty for D, who directed buyer to sellers & accompanied buyer to seller's apt., expecting to be paid for her role in the transaction; D charged with "distribution," not "sale";

C v Fernandes **46 MAC 455, 462 (99)**—similar to White, above; D testified that undercover cop-buyer told her that he would give her some if she took him to a seller, but "hope" for a cut didn't show "she was intended to be a copurchaser"; no "abuse of discretion" in judge's refusal to instruct that D couldn't be both purchaser and in joint venture with seller;

US v Swiderski **548 F.2d 445 (2d Cir. '77)**—"sharing" vs. distribution;

C v Johnson **413 M 598 (92)**—where 2 persons simultaneously & jointly acquire possession of drugs for their own use intending only to share it together, "their only crime is simple joint possession";

C v DePalma **41 MAC 798 (96)**—no instruction on joint possession warranted (no evidence of "simultaneous" acquisition);

C v Croft **345 M 143 (62)**—heroin worth $80 = consistent with personal use; but see *C v Monterosso* **33 MAC 765 (93)** no required finding of not guilty for D simply because amounts of drugs consistent with personal use as well as distribution: additional evidence = scale, records of drug transactions, and admission of intent to use drugs **with friends** at party;

C v LaPerle **19 MAC 424 (85)**—though residue, paraphernalia suggests distribution;

C v Thibeau **384 M 762 (81)**—9 packs PCP = "doubtful" intent/distribute;

C v Tripp **14 MAC 997 (82)**—not intent to distribute (8 x $80 bags plus 2 x $40 bags of heroin, plus 2 packets of cocaine in socks);

C v Ellis **356 M 574 (70)**—distributed 1 drug, but only possessed 2d;

C v Wilson **52 MAC 411 (2001)**—despite possession of 244.41 grams of cocaine (street value $25,000) & holding that D not entitled to instruction on simple possession of that drug, required finding of not guilty on charge of intent to distribute marijuana found in D's pants pocket: no testimony as to how much marijuana there was, except that it fit in pants pocket; that D obviously possessed different drug with intent to distribute didn't have sufficient "inferential value" to prove intent to distribute marijuana; But see *C v Rivera* **44 MAC 452 (98)** though quantity of cocaine seized from D was small, intent to distribute it could be inferred from D's observed distribution of marijuana and possession of marijuana in packages consistent with distribution intent;

C v Burke **44 MAC 76 (97)**—similar (only .21 gram heroin);

C v Griffin **45 MAC 396 (98)**—on D's person, searched by warrant as an "any person present at" site of ongoing drug activity, were 9 small packets of marijuana and $400 in tens and twenties; despite fact he didn't live at apartment and that no other drug amounts and paraphernalia found at apartment were connected to him, enough for G of possession with intent to distribute; cop testimony that packets would sell for $20 each and were "consistent with distribution" cited;

C v Huffman **11 MAC 185 (81)**—D can say intent = to use; *(See Chapter 16, Defenses, Intent)*;

C v Wooden **13 MAC 417 (82)**—$660 "street value," packaging = consistent with buyer;

C v Pena **40 MAC 905 (96)**—intent to distribute inferable from six $10 bags of marijuana inside larger bag (& beeper & $61.11 & D in area known for drug dealing);

C v Martin **48 MAC 391 (99)**—though no drug transaction was observed and quantity of crack cocaine was small (2.04 grams, in 18 separately-wrapped "dime bags"), intent to distribute inferable from packaging, high incidence of drug activity in area, "expert police testimony," and the "vigor" of flight by which D attempted to avoid cops; (but see *C v Dennis* **33 MAC 666, 672 (92), S.C. 416 M 1001 (93)** walking away from companions and ignoring officer's order to stop = "as suggestive of the defendant's awareness that he was in possession of cocaine as it is of" any intent to distribute it);

C v Fiore **9 MAC 618 (80)**—"street value" admissible; cop as expert;

C v Cordero **34 MAC 923 (93)**—cop expert's opinion re distribution intent OK; BUT SEE *C v Tanner* **45 MAC 576, 581 (98)** re: whether amount of drugs or other circumstances is "consistent with" distribution rather than personal use; use of percipient witness as "expert" should be avoided when possible;

C v Dennis **33 MAC 666 (92)**: *C v Dennis* **416 M 1001 (93)**—OK for cop-expert to testify re: "different roles played by individuals jointly engaged in the distribution of drugs on the streets";

C v Zavala **52 MAC 770, 775–76 (2001)**—not OK for cop to opine that D was "stashing" narcotics in area of water hose;

C v Tucker **2 MAC 328 (74)**—cop expert says paraphernalia = seller's;

C v Murphy **34 MAC 16 (93)**—required finding of not guilty on distribution intent (seven paper packets containing 2.8 grams of cocaine) because cop testimony was mere conjecture & surmise (i.e., if D intended to **use** could have bought merely one larger packet for less money than unknown price actually paid);

C v Sendele **18 MAC 755 (84)**—amount, facts, & expert suggest distribution; (see also *Nichols* **4 MAC 606 (76)**);

C v McShan **15 MAC 921 (83)**—12 joints, $100, etc. = distribution; but can cross-examine cop re: amount suggesting use instead;

See Chapter 6-E, *Discovery, DA's Expert;* Chapter 7-C, *Preparation, D's Expert;* Chapter 11-I, *Evidence: Opinion;* & CPCS P/G's 4.4 (g), 4.6 (h);

C v Scala **380 M 500 (80)**—jury question from quantity/value;

C v Miller **4 MAC 379 (76)**—quantities (drugs & $) suggest distribution;

C v Santiago **41 MAC 916 (96)**—error for cop to testify that **this** heroin was intended for distribution, but harmless given D's testimony admitting intent to give some to girlfriend;

C v Davis **376 M 777, 788 (78)**—evidence of packaging is admissible;

C v LaPerle **19 MAC 424 (85)**—paraphernalia suggests distributing;

C v Sauer **50 MAC 299 (2000)**—intent evidence sufficient (one pill in a bank envelope, envelopes known by cop to be used to package drugs, 24 bank envelopes in car, pills in D's pocket and fist);

C v Roman **414 M 642 (93)**—upholding trafficking indictment against challenge to sufficiency of evidence presented to the **grand** jury, simply because amount was > 25 grams cocaine; dissent collects cases re: sufficiency of evidence of intent to distribute;

C v Ahart **63 MAC 413 (2005)**—sufficient evidence of intent to distribute crack cocaine, despite total weight of only 1.87 grams because it was in ten individually wrapped bags, D had a razor blade (& dealers used this to cut rocks into smaller sizes), worth of drugs was $200-$400 & D was 17-year-old high school student arrested 30 minutes before lunch (when sales often occur);

C v Senati **3 MAC 304 (75)**—something passed, but who's the seller?;

C v Reid **29 MAC 537 (90)**—required finding entered where equally likely D was purchaser as seller on scanty evidence of drug sale;

C v Gonzalez **47 MAC 255 (99)**—evidence here sufficient to establish that D was seller rather than purchaser; lists (at 258) prior cases on this subject, going both ways (required finding of not guilty and not);

C v Soto **45 MAC 109, 112 (98)**—evidence sufficient to establish D was seller rather than buyer;

C v Szemetum **3 MAC 651 (75)**—drug "area," but knowledge by D not shown;

C v DeJesus **48 MAC 911 (99)**—no required finding of not guilty for D as joint venturer in possession of heroin with intent to distribute, in part because "People do not ordinarily engage in repetitive crimes in the presence of someone who is not a collaborator";

C v Hernandez **439 M 688 (2003)**—because evidence insufficient for inference of constructive possession of large quantity of cocaine, required finding of not guilty ordered on theory of principal liability for trafficking (though not on joint venture, given sufficient evidence that D knowingly assisted in delivering drug to customers);

C v Rabb **70 MAC 194 (2007)**—D's own statement cited as sufficient proof of constructive possession of drug stash he said belonged to co-D: while claiming personal possession of one stash in motel room, he acknowledged awareness of other stash, and jury didn't have to believe his denial of possession, particularly when D displayed awareness of consequences for possession of aggregate amount; D had paid for room and drugs were stored in "common portions" of it (heater and kitchen cabinet);

C v Thomas **52 MAC 286, 293 (2001)**—reversal for prosecutorial argument that back seat passenger D's guilt of intent to distribute tiny amount of drugs (found on sidewalk next to where he was placed by cops) should be inferred from his presence in a car in which a digital scale & "crack cocaine" were found: no evidence about what drugs were in car & no basis for inference that D (not the driver or owner of car, and not displaying consciousness of guilt) knew of or had access to front-seat scale or drugs; "association is a fundamentally impermissible basis on which to urge an inference of guilt";

Kuklis v Commonwealth **361 M 302 (72)**—distribution duplicitous with possess (lesser included offense)—*(See Chapter 19, Double Jeopardy)*;

See Chapter 11-1, 11-2 & 11-3 for cases on cops as experts & on profile & modus operandi evidence;

C v LeBlanc **30 MAC 1 (91)**—good faith belief that D was acting as agent for government in purchasing drugs is a valid defense;

C v Murillo **32 MAC 379 (92)**—participation as a "procuring agent" of a buyer is not a defense to drug charges, eliminating defense of *C v Harvard* **356 M 452 (69)**; See also *C v Johnson* **413 M 598 (92)** - being a "joint purchaser" no defense to distribution unless alleged joint purchaser was present at acquisition as well: only if the 2 "simultaneously acquired" would there be simple joint possession by middleman;

C v Blevins **56 MAC 206 (2002)**—conviction for trafficking in over 14 grams of cocaine reversed for failure to instruct on lesser offense of simple possession, because D contended that he and two friend pooled money to buy cocaine, all participated in the negotiation & were present during the exchange of $ for drug, but that immediately afterward D was arrested; simple joint possession is a possible verdict when two or more persons simultaneously and jointly acquire possession of a drug for their own use, intending only to share it together;

C v Diaz **49 MAC 587 (2000)**—D's testimony = he had gotten high with informant for eight years and that he thought this was opportunity to do so again when she asked if he "had anything"; he took her to place where he bought 2 rocks of cocaine for $, handed informant cocaine, & received $ from her; this full confession of G of possession with intent made otherwise reversible ("plain") error harmless;

C v Minor **47 MAC 928 (99)**—evidence that drug overdose victim contributed to pool of money with which D bought drugs did not make D mere "joint possessor" rather than distributor; if V here had been "actively involved in the buy itself," by negotiating with supplier, or paying him $, or examining/sampling drugs, maybe D would have been entitled to lesser included offense instruction (merely "possession" rather than distribution);

C v Ridge **37 MAC 943 (94)**—no required finding of NG for D: not only did jury not have to believe claim that D was only holding cocaine for true owner out of concern that police were "closing in on" true owner, D's own story (that he planned to give drugs **back** to true owner) would make him guilty of intending to "distribute";

C v Labitue **49 MAC 913 (2000)**—no required finding of NG; jury didn't have to believe that source of more than $5000 in D's possession was wedding present from mother and proceeds from personal injury lawsuit;

C v Ruggiero **32 MAC 964 (92)**—D not entitled to charge on lesser included of simple drug possession where indicted only for separate sale; possession with intent dismissed because duplicitous with distribution;

C v Munera **31 MAC 380 (91)**—open question whether profile evidence about drug stash pads admissible; cop "expert" could testify that dollar bills routinely used by dealers to package cocaine & that chunks consistent with dealing;

C v Pike **430 M 317, 324 (99)**—OK expert cop testimony about methods of operation of doctors and drug users in "drug diversion operations"; distinguished from impermissible "profile" testimony (*C v Day* **409 M 719, 723 (91)**), which relates "to the typical attributes or characteristics 'which are common to some or most individuals who commit particular crimes'";

C v Frias **47 MAC 293 (99)**—not "profile" testimony, but "modus operandi" testimony re: distribution chain for narcotics and "midlevel drug distribution points"; would be improper for these cops to express opinion "about the conformance of the present case to a model";

C v Dayes **49 MAC 419 (2000)**—error to admit cop testimony that it's common for 'out of town' drug dealer to 'hook up' with female & have bills for place of operation in female's name so no evidence of drug dealer's control, & that dealer would give female drugs for her addiction, or $ for bills in exchange for place of operation; D here was female & had out-of-town boyfriend (but no evidence he was drug dealer or supplied $ or drugs to D);

C v Harris **47 MAC 481 (99)**—OK cop testimony that "beepers" = "predominant tools of the (drug) trade";

C v Johnson **410 M 199, 202 (91)**—cop's testimony that 33+ grams of cocaine not consistent with personal use admissible;

C v Gonzales **33 MAC 728 (92)**—although possession of only 10 glassine packets of heroin a "close" case, bundling together of packets with dealer's scorpion trademark plus $167 found in pocket of unemployed D made evidence sufficient;

C v Murphy **34 MAC 16 (93)**—trooper's claim that 7 packets containing total of 2.8 grams of cocaine (plus $355) was inconsistent with personal use because user would have bought single packet for less money was improper "conjecture & surmise"; evidence of intent to distribute was thus insufficient;

C v Wolcott **28 MAC 200 (90)**—cop's testimony about D's involvement with Jamaican posse inadmissible because witness was not qualified & because testimony conjectural, hearsay-based & prejudicial;

US v Doe **903 F.2d 16 (D.C. Cir. '90)**—"expert" police testimony on modus operandi of Jamaican drug dealers inadmissible because irrelevant & prejudicial;

US v Long **917 F.2d 691 (2d Cir. '90)**—"expert" FBI agent's testimony on working of organized crime families inadmissible; Cf. *C v Day* **409 M 719 (91)** expert opinion that D fit child abuser profile inadmissible;

See Chapter 11-I, Evidence: Opinions of Experts;

C v Johnson **410 M 199 (91)**—not improper for drug lab to calculate weight from average weight of random sample of 9 of 71 specimens;

C v Coplin **34 MAC 478 (93)**—same, re: weighing 20 specimens out of 174;

21-CC.3.a. School-Zone Statute

G.L. c. 94C, § 32J—mandatory minimum 2 year on & after sentence for manufacturing, distributing or possessing with intent to distribute controlled substance within 1,000 feet of public or private accredited preschool, accredited Head Start facility, elementary, vocational, or secondary school whether or not in session (as amended through St. 1998, c. 194, §§ 146, 443); lack of knowledge of boundaries is not a defense;

C v Manning **75 MAC 829 (2009)**—after D tendered conditional G plea to two District Court counts (distribution of Class D and school zone violation), requesting reduction of distribution to straight possession and continuance without finding for one year, plus dismissal of school zone charge, Commonwealth requested one day for distribution and two years from and after for school zone, judge could not dismiss school zone charge simply by stating that he couldn't find sufficient facts (proffer had included school guard testimony that he saw distribution on videotape and D acknowledged to him selling one bag of marijuana): violation of separation of powers, judge effectively

'nol prossing,' an act reserved to executive branch; judge also could not accept plea to lesser included offense (simple possession on count charging distribution) over Commonwealth objection;

C v Gonzales **33 MAC 728 (92)**—Commonwealth must prove that structure is "elementary, vocational or secondary school"; "Worcester Academy" not enough;

C v Burke **44 MAC 76 (97)**—"Calvary Temple Preschool", for children aged 3–5½, not enough: required finding of NG;

C v Vasquez **33 MAC 950 (92)**—"Woodland Street/ Community School" not enough;

C v Ellerbe **430 M 769, 772 (2000)**—similar;

C v Laro **68 MAC 556 (2007)**—"circumstantial" evidence sufficient to show "Immaculate Conception School" was an elementary school (crossing guards, children arriving on school buses or being conveyed by parents, one witness saying grandchildren attended it for several years);

C v Thomas **71 MAC 323, further review denied 451 M 1102 (2008)**—language in G.L. c. 94C, § 32J concerning necessity of proof that school is "accredited," held to apply only to "private" facilities; failure of proof of accreditation (testimony = accredited? "I believe it is. I'm not positive though") of "public prekindergarten and kindergarten" held immaterial;

C v Bell **442 M 118 (2004)**—SJC, on Commonwealth's G.L. c. 211, § 3 petition, bars D in "school zone" drug prosecution from using Department of Education regulation defining "secondary school," because this was underinclusive in context of criminal statute's purpose;

C v Roucoulet **413 M 647 (92)**—undercover officer waited at seller's home as seller went to obtain drugs from supplier-D, such transaction being conducted in D's van, at & around convenience store where seller met D; store = 325 feet from elementary school; liability;

C v Williams **54 MAC 236 (2002)**—reconstructed record (from inaudible tapes) revealed that Commonwealth evidence was that D's arrest was 680 feet from school & that this was in "same area" as alleged drug transaction, so required finding of NG, because arrest didn't occur at same location as the drug transaction (notwithstanding Commonwealth arguments that "680 feet" reference was implicitly testimony as to where transaction occurred, and that DA's closing argument to this effect, unobjected to by defense counsel, meant that there was such evidence);

C v Cavanaugh **63 MAC 111 (2005)**—D obtained 50 bags of heroin at particular point, but its distance from school was calculated by mathematical theorem (Pythagorean); judge excluded calculation because no evidence that theorem should apply (i.e., only to a "right" triangle); App. Ct. notes that D's vehicle containing the heroin came within 600 feet of school as it passed particular intersection, and this was sufficient for conviction (he possessed it within 1000 feet, with intention to distribute it somewhere);

C v Tanner **66 MAC 432 (2006)**—that defense cross-examination raised questions about accuracy of measurement (which relied on Pythagorean theory) didn't make evidence insufficient as matter of law;

***US v Soler* 275 F.3d 146 (1st Cir., 1-4-02)**—under federal school zone prosecution (21 U.S.C. § 860(a)), must prove distance from school to actual transaction site, not merely to the curtilage or exterior wall of structure where sale occurs; videotape introduced (for other purpose) was insufficient basis on which to establish missing distance;

***C v Cintron* 59 MAC 905 (2003)**—OK to measure as here measured, from fifteen feet from the front door of building in which apartment is located, to the "curbstone located at the outside perimeter of a grassy area surrounding the [school]," though says that here, even adding some horizontal distance to back of building would not yield "not guilty"; declines to follow *US v Soler*, 275 F.3d 146 (02), applying 21 USC § 860(a), a statute analogous to G.L. c. 94C, § 32J;

***C v Spano* 414 M 178 (93)**—straight line measurement of distance from school = OK; statute not "vague" in this regard, & not necessary to require that measurement be on 'most direct automobile route on public roads'; but see *US v Coates* **739 F. Supp. 146 (SDNY '90)** simply because D possessed drugs for distribution and happened to be riding on a subway near a school should not make him liable for enhanced 'school zone' penalty;

***C v Labitue* 49 MAC 913 (2000)**—police observed D engaged in suspicious activity (enter building briefly, emerge, look up & down street, reenter car, drive away), but stopped him at a point 3 blocks later, which was close enough to a school for 'zone' prosecution; court rejected D's argument that appropriate site of measurement had to be point of 'suspicious activity'; court said prior cases rejected this "sentencing enhancement theory"—defense;

BUT SEE *C v Lawrence* **69 MAC 596 (2007)**—no general entrapment instruction required because D "delivered"/transferred marijuana to undercover cop and acknowledged that he both "shared" marijuana with friends earlier and intended to "share" what he had in his pocket with the cop (who gave D $20 without request or negotiation); **"entrapment" as to school zone charge = "distinct . . . analytically", but not briefed, so reserved**: "whether the detective's act of leading the defendant into the school zone was government behavior sufficient to entitle the defendant to an entrapment instruction"; fn.5: "if . . . the purpose of the school zone statute is to 'create drug-free zones of safety where children could be . . . free from the potential infection of drugs,' . . . we find it unsettling that a violation of G.L. c. 94C, § 32J, occurred in this case because the defendant followed a police officer into a school zone";

***C v Alvarez* 413 M 224 (91)**: ***C v Taylor* 413 M 243 (92)**—rejecting variety of constitutional challenges to school zone statute;

***C v Santaliz* 413 M 238 (92)**—same as *Alvarez* **413 M 224 (91)**;

***C v Davie* 46 MAC 25 (98)**—"park" includes parks without playgrounds; statute requires proof of EITHER ("or"), not both ("and");

21-CC.4 Trafficking—G.L. c. 94C, § 32(E)

***C v Beverly* 389 M 866 (83)**—quantity counts dilutants (mixers);

***C v Bongarzone* 390 M 326 (83)**—(old) penalty was vague; possession with intent = lesser included offense;

***C v Chappee* 397 M 508 (86)**—possession with intent to distribute is lesser included offense within trafficking;

***C v Johnson* 75 MAC 903 (2009)**—D was convicted of both "trafficking" and possession with intent to distribute, the latter being enhanced for sentencing because it was a "second or subsequent", D receiving 3–5 sentence on trafficking, but 5 to 5 & a day on possession with intent; convictions were duplicative; ordinarily, result would be to dismiss "lesser" offense, but here "lesser" carried the longer sentence (lesser included offense = one with fewer elements, and "having been previously convicted" is NOT an "element" but is instead a sentencing enhancement); HERE, remand for trial judge to decide which to vacate & which conviction to "affirm";

***US v Acosta* 963 F.2d 551 (2d Cir. 92)**—improper to include weight of liqueur solvent in net weight of cocaine "mixture";

***US v Machecha-Onofre* 933 F.2d 623 (936 F.2d 623) (1st Cir. '91)**—proper to include weight of suitcase chemically bonded to cocaine;

***Chapman v US* 500 US 453 (91)**—proper to include blotter paper in net weight of LSD because drug need not be extracted before capable of ingestion;

***C v Sabetti* 411 M 770 (92)**—weight is not element of trafficking so Commonwealth not required to prove that D knew weight of drugs in his possession;

***C v Rodriguez* 415 M 447 (93)**—same, plus need not prove D knew "exact nature of the controlled substance"; but see *Apprendi v New Jersey* **530 US 466 (2000)** OTHER THAN fact of prior conviction, any fact that increases penalty for a crime must be proved TO JURY beyond reasonable doubt (here, "hate crime" statute provided for enhanced sentence if trial judge found, by "preponderance," that D committed the crime in order to intimidate person or group because of, inter alia, race)—it's not merely "sentencing enhancement" issue; Cf. *C v Podgurski* **44 MAC 929 (98)** implicit recognition of viability of defense that D knowingly & intentionally possessed only X amount, the quantity existing before his wife added an unknown amount of inositol, unbeknownst to him;

***C v Tata* 28 MAC 23 (89)**: *Tata v. Carver* **917 F.2d 670 (1st Cir. '90)**—D's intent to use some portion of drugs personally does not reduce amount for purposes of trafficking thresholds;

***C v Manrique* 31 MAC 597 (91)**—evidence of D's bringing drugs into Commonwealth was sufficient even though no direct evidence of border crossing;

C v Burr **33 MAC 637 (92)**—trial judge can't reduce trafficking verdicts pursuant to Crim.R.25(b)(2) solely to defeat mandatory minimum sentences;

C v Garcia **421 M 686 (96)**—rejecting argument that jury should be instructed on "sentencing entrapment" in case of arguable government overreaching in inducing D to sell larger quantities of the drug than he was accustomed to selling (but inviting Mass. Sentencing Commission to consider allowing judge sentencing discretion in such a circumstance);

21-CC.5. POSSESS: Dominion/Control, "Constructive" Possession, and Knowledge

See also Chapter 16, Defenses: Possession & Intent;

C v Campiti **41 MAC 43 (96)**—D (Mr. Big) constructively possessed drugs in hands of his agents/underlings; failure to instruct on joint venture not only did not prejudice D, but was not error;

C v Fernandez **48 MAC 530, 532 (2000)**—constructive poss. and actual poss. NOT "different theories," but instead "simply two possible ways of defining the same legal principle"; essential elements of either are knowledge plus ability and intention to control;

C v Harvard **356 M 452 (69)**—momentary passing = "possession";

C v Pellegrini **414 M 402 (93)**—indictment for cocaine possession OK solely on evidence that D's just-born infant's urine was found to contain cocaine metabolites; Commonwealth did not appeal dismissal of indictment for unlawful distribution to person under age 18 based on same evidence;

C v Flaherty **358 M 817 (71)**—D may be just casual visitor, so NG;

C v Williams **3 MAC 370 (75)**—D in bed, but control not shown;

C v Gonzalez **42 MAC 235 (97)**—though cocaine was on porch, to which 5 apartments in addition to the one in which D was found had access, sufficient evidence given $1,269, lactose, scale, & pager found in apartment with D's papers, plus consciousness of guilt evidence (lengthy default);

C v Velasquez **48 MAC 147 (99)**—sufficient evidence for guilt of drugs in basement, though five other apartments' occupants had access there as well;

C v Vasquez **75 MAC 446 (2009)**—though five men were in house at time of search warrant execution (one of whom attempted to escape and could be inferred to have attempted to flush $274), it was D's residence and he had $493 on his person, and he had sold to undercover cop there twice before: evidence sufficient to show D's constructive possession of cocaine (with sandwich bags, and scale) found in kitchen cabinet; ***BUT SEE, on further review*, 456 M 350 (2010)**: reversal of convictions for Confrontation Clause violation, "drug certifications", in light of *Melendez-Diaz v MA* 129 S Ct 2527 (2009);

C v Figueroa **74 MAC 784 (2009)**—after info that three Hispanic males were dealing cocaine from specific apartment, two controlled buys were made, and warrant was obtained: D, the only person present, refused to admit executing officers, who broke down door; constructive possession evidence sufficient for 100 individual packages of cocaine found in kitchen wastebasket: D had ten such packages in his pocket, trafficking paraphernalia in plain view, and mail addressed to D was found in apartment (plus inference of consciousness of guilt in failure to admit police);

C v Duffy **4 MAC 655 (76)**—control not shown because (maybe) absent 6 days;

C v Deagle **10 MAC 563 (80)**—knowledge (in car) but no control;

C v Manzanillo **37 MAC 24 (94)**—required finding of NG for D, driver of van in which 123.4 grams of cocaine found in "hip bag" under paper shopping bag behind driver's seat; D's comment ("not mine") insufficient to show even knowledge, because cop told him earlier that arrest (with 2 passengers) was for "drugs";

C v Movilis **46 MAC 574 (99)**—required finding of NG for D, driver of car in which cocaine found in hidden compartment built into rear-facing portion of front passenger seat; man to whom car was registered not shown to have any connection to D, despite D's presence near .06 gram of powder cocaine on table inside café at which D parked car and despite D's possession of beeper and $232 in cash; no similarity in quality or packaging shown between car cocaine and table cocaine;

C v Cormier **41 MAC 76 (96)**—insufficient proof of D's possession of sneakers containing cocaine, despite fact they were in rear floor of car, closest to where D was seated as passenger; car driver (& owner) grabbed sneakers before attempting flight; counsel ineffective on direct appeal for waiving this argument;

C v Fernandez **48 MAC 530 (2000)**—sufficient proof that D (front seat passenger) possessed drugs discarded by driver; failure of judge to instruct on joint venture "not a precondition for a finding of joint possession";

C v Bienvenu **63 MAC 632 (2005)**—front seat passenger could be found G of cocaine tightly wrapped in duct tape ball found between driver's seat & gear shift in console area because she owned the vehicle, and it was inferably her personal effects found in back seat close to electronic scale and box of baggies;

C v Mott **2 MAC 47 (74)**—sufficient control over apartment for constructive possession;

C v Nichols **4 MAC 606 (76)**—(same); expert: (empty) package = large amount;

C v Sespedes **442 M 95 (2004)**—NG for D re: possession of drugs hidden in dropped ceiling of vacant apartment being renovated, though he had key to apartment and had been seen leaving that apartment once; ability to exercise control over premises and brief presence inside not enough to imply possession of hidden contraband;

C v DeJesus **48 MAC 911 (99)**—no required finding of NG for D as joint venturer in possession of heroin with intent to distribute, in part because "People do not ordinarily engage in repetitive crimes in the presence of someone who is not a collaborator";

C v Brown **34 MAC 222 (93)**—though D lived in apartment, insufficient evidence to prove her ability/ intention to exercise control over drugs;

C v Camerano **42 MAC 363 (97)**—though evidence maybe sufficient to show D-property owner's knowledge that garden structure (maintained by individual paying him monthly rent to pitch house trailer on property) contained marijuana, required finding of NG on conspiracy to possess with intent to distribute;

C v Lee **2 MAC 700 (74)**—D's papers & visits = constructive possession;

C v Pichardo **38 MAC 416 (95)**—stash from which D obtained cocaine to sell to cop found to contain heroin also: constructive possession found;

C v Amparo **43 MAC 922 (97)**—D's attempted flight & possession of beeper insufficient for constructive possession of drugs in apt. (no papers there contained his name); two other men also arrested in attempted flight;

C v Sanchez **40 MAC 411 (96)**—evidence (barely?) sufficient for car passenger D's constructive possession of cocaine in trunk, but insufficient to establish D as joint venturer with driver; reversal because jury instructed on both theories, and G-theory was not specified;

C v Robinson **43 MAC 257 (97)**—theories of constructive possession and joint venture are **alternative** means by which to connect D to possession with intent; here, sufficient evidence to establish joint venture;

C v Antonio **45 MAC 937 (98)**—Commonwealth didn't attempt to prove "constructive" possession, but instead "joint venture" theory, held sufficiently shown because D attempted both to bar entry to, and to flee from, search warrant's subject apartment, because he acted nervous when police approached hidden drugs, and because D's personal belongings were found in "close proximity" to drugs hidden inside coffee mug; *C v Sespedes* **442 M 95, n.8 (2004)**—distinguished (apartment not "fortified", inadequate additional evidence connecting D to drugs);

C v Beverly **389 M 866 (83)**—joint possession;

C v Watson **36 MAC 252 (94)**—"possession need not be exclusive"; joint possession may be proved circumstantially; evidence here showed both D & other man could produce drugs from hidden stash on demand;

C v Aguiar **370 M 490 (76)**—infer knowledge of mystery mail (here);

C v Sheline **391 M 279 (84)**—(same)

C v Rivera **40 MAC 308 (96)**—evidence sufficient to establish joint venture to traffic in cocaine (wiretaps yielding evidence that D directed others **not** to sell to undercover cop in large amounts, D's possession of safety deposit box key, box yielding the money used in buys);

C v Dennis **33 MAC 666 (92):** *C v Dennis* **416 M 1001 (93)**—D's proximity to place where drugs found, his

possession of 5 matching packets & lots of cash, plus head gesture, not enough to establish joint constructive possession of drugs sold by another, or possession of stash found in nearby "abandoned vehicle";

C v Santana **420 M 205 (95)**—though drugs were under car's front seat, passenger side, & passenger was seated there, no required finding of NG for D, owner & driver of car, who failed to pull over for > one mile, and who repeatedly looked back at car during license/registration check; electronic scale was in bag on back seat;

C v Caraballo **33 MAC 616 (92)**—D's presence in hallway by a chair underneath ceiling panel where drugs hidden & statement of his residing in apartment near panel not enough to show constructive possession;

C v Johnson **42 MAC 948 (97)**—testimony that dealers commonly work from more than one stash & observed distribution by D of black opaque bag of marijuana inferably retrieved from vacant lot enough to establish G of his possession of 5 smaller reddish plastic bags of marijuana found in same lot;

C v Meehan **33 MAC 262 (92)**—evidence that D was dealing,& that he had frequent private conversations with co-D bartender not sufficient to establish he knew of & had ability & intention to exercise dominion & control over cocaine in co-D's purse;

C v Carmenatty **37 MAC 908 (94)**—when search warrant was executed, woman's person yielded 6 bags of cocaine & D (a welfare recipient) had 2 $50 bills; dresser contained papers of D & woman commingled, plus men's & women's clothing covering a precision scale: though "possible" that woman alone was selling drugs, no required finding of NG for D (prosecuted on two theories, constructive/joint possession and joint venture);

C v Caterino **31 MAC 685 (91)**—D's knowledge that cocaine was present in apartment not enough to establish dominion & control over apartment or its rooms;

C v Cruz **34 MAC 619 (93)**—though D's attempted flight during search warrant execution showed his knowledge of presence of drugs, flight & presence insufficient to show he had joint control, with bedroom occupant, of cocaine found in bedroom; listing of cases with insufficient evidence of joint possession;

C v Adames **41 MAC 14 (96)**—evidence sufficient to establish D as joint venturer in trafficking of cocaine found in 3d floor unit, as D was one found with money in heavily barricaded 1st floor unit from which sales were made (after retrieval of drug from 3d floor)

C v Rivera **31 MAC 554 (91)**—D linked to drugs in one bedroom but not another;

C v Clarke **44 MAC 502 (98)**—evidence sufficient to show D's possession of drugs in one bedroom but not possession of gun in another; that another man (let go by police) had prior conviction for drug dealing did not exonerate D: constructive possession need not be exclusive;

C v Booker **31 MAC 435 (91)**—drugs found in common area of D's apartment after D seen chasing an armed gunmen into it not enough to establish D's possession because drugs could have belonged to gunman or D's roommates;

C v Handy **30 MAC 776 (91)**—D's presence plus his possession of drugs in different packaging not enough to establish possession of drugs in drug house;

C v Whitlock **39 MAC 514 (95)**—reversal because jury instruction allowed proximity to and knowledge of drug dealing to be sufficient evidence of D's constructive possession of drugs without other indicia permitting inference of his control over them; argument concerning whether there were two or one "rocks" of cocaine & certificate of analysis went to weight, but not admissibility;

C v Ahart **63 MAC 413, 416 n.3 (2005)**—though trial evidence was that D possessed packets of "rock" cocaine, drug certificate indicated "powder"; presumably because the rock could have broken down to powder, no error found, citing *Whitlock* 39 MAC 514, 520–21 (95) (argument went to weight of evidence, not admissibility);

C v Paniaqua **413 M 796 (92)**—drug lab certification that commingled contents of **3** packets contained cocaine did not require finding of not guilty where D seen to possess/throw only 1 aluminum foil ball into trash can where officer claimed to have seen cocaine powder in ball & where officer's expertise not challenged by D at trial;

C v Senbatu **38 MAC 904 (95)**—when three packets of cocaine weighed just over 28 grams, and defense contended that D possessed only two of the packets (3d being put into his jacket on chair by another person), error to refuse lesser included offense instruction re: possession with intent to distribute; lesser included offense of trafficking between 14 & 28 grams **not** available as based on only speculation (no evidence as to weight of contested packet); see also *C v Bonilla* **32 MAC 942 (92)** sufficient evidence for knowledge and constructive possession: D was employee/manager of gas station, drugs were in filing cabinet under perfume D claimed was for his girlfriend;

C v Yazbeck **31 MAC 769 (92)**—sufficient evidence to show D in possession of marijuana (giving off noticeable odor) in locked closet in residence basement, when jury could infer that D was at least one of residence's regular occupants and D acknowledged ownership of briefcase elsewhere, containing 43 grams of cocaine;

Alicea v Commonwealth **410 M 384 (91)**—finding insufficient evidence that D, driver and sole occupant of a car owned by "friend," knew of concealed heroin from (1) the fact that the defendant was traveling on Route 495 in the middle of the night, (2) his consent to the search, or (3) his reaction when the first trooper showed the package to him, BUT these facts plus D's "obvious agitation" (in marked contrast to previously calm demeanor) when searching cop came close to discovering drugs was enough to deny required finding of NG;

C v Montanez **410 M 290 (91)**—drugs above "dropped ceiling" in common hallway outside D's apartment;

C v James **30 MAC 490 (91)**—enough to show D's possession of drugs in 3d floor apartment: admission that he was presently staying at the address (though not specifically

3d floor), D's papers inside 3d floor apartment, D's flight toward that apartment, upon arrival of police ('defensive behavior exhibited collectively by D and his group'), bags which D discarded in flight were indistinguishable in appearance from those found in apt.;

21-CC.6. Presence of Heroin— G.L. c. 94C, § 35

C v Buckley **354 M 508 (68)**—KNOWLEDGE = element;

C v Tirella **356 M 271 (69)**—justification if not "acquiescent"; (cf. Spaulding, J. at 276: constitutional?);

Kuklis v C **361 M 302 (72)**—duplicitous with possession of same drug

C v Rodriguez **11 MAC 379 (81)**—(but) not lesser included offense of possession

C v Fernandez **48 MAC 530, 535 n.7 (2000)**—not duplicitous of poss. with intent to distribute and not lesser included offense of possession with intent "even if the jury might have used the same evidence to establish possession under § 32 and knowledge under § 35";

21-CC.6.a. Exploitation of Minors

G.L. c. 94C, § 32K—using child under 18 for drug distribution; purports to establish 5 year mandatory minimum sentence;

C v Kirkpatrick **44 MAC 355 (98)**—no required finding of NG although two other adults were also involved (and perhaps more so) in sale to undercover cop: inferable that both child & D knew that the mission was to deliver six bags of heroin;

C v Montalvo **50 MAC 85 (2000)**—notwithstanding contrary assertion in *C v Kirkpatrick* **44 MAC 355, 357 (98)**, Commonwealth not required to prove that D knew person was under age 18;

21-CC.7. Miscellaneous Provisions

G.L. c. 277, § 38—allegations & proof ("presumes" unauthorized);

G.L. c. 94C, § 1—DEFINITIONS, including "PRESCRIPTION drug" (Class E);

G.L. c. 94C, § 32G—distributing "COUNTERFEIT" substance (defined in § 1);

G.L. c. 94C, § 32I—sell "drug PARAPHERNALIA";

G.L. c. 94C, § 44—mandatory SEAL of records, including dismissals (*See Chapter 14-U, Dispositions: Sealing & Expunging Records*);

C v Chavis **415 M 703 (93)**—'second or subsequent' element satisfied if conviction concerns any controlled substance listed in G.L. c. 94C, § 31, and may be from out of state;

C v Lisasuain **44 MAC 933 (98)**—same (current = heroin; prior = NY, cocaine);

C v Koney **421 M 295, 301–2 (95)**—mere identity of named D not enough to prove prior conviction;

C v Olivo **58 MAC 368 (2003)**—sufficient evidence identifying D as the individual previously convicted, contrasting *C v Koney*;

C v Bowden **447 M 593 (2006)**—even under law prevailing prior to new "Melanie's Law," live testimony by "identifying" witnesses not required to establish D as individual previously convicted; Registry documentation showing identity of current and former addresses, prior court conviction for OUI second offense, Registry document with color photo of D held adequate overall here; *C v Maloney* **447 M 577 (2006)**—re new "Melanie's Law" (G.L. c. 90, § 24(4), inter alia): court record of prior convictions, accompanied by other documentation, may be prima facie evidence of prior convictions; **N.B.:** *C v Koney* [421 M 295, 302] holding must be read into even this new statute (mere identity of name isn't enough to establish even prima facie case); *C v Dussault* **71 MAC 542 (2008)**—conviction records sufficient, matching D's full name and middle initial (and D's last name was "unusual"), containing additional biographical info correlating with D's identity (date of birth, town of residence, specific addresses also matching D);

C v Garcia **421 M 686 (96)**—rejecting argument that jury should be instructed on "sentencing entrapment" in case of arguable government overreaching in inducing D to sell larger quantities of the drug than he was accustomed to selling (but inviting Mass. Sentencing Commission to consider allowing judge sentencing discretion in such a circumstance);

G.L. c. 94C, § 32H catch-all sentencing provision

21-CC.8. Forfeiture G.L. c. 94C, § 47

See Chapter 14-H;

C v Goldman **398 M 201 (86)**—D gets hearing on timing (speedy delay?) & merits (money or property used in, or proceeds of, crime?);

C v 1972 Chevrolet **385 M 198 (82)**—jury right for forfeiture of car;

C v $7246 **404 M 763 (89)**—not shown that the money was marijuana proceeds;

C v One 1987 Mercury Cougar **413 M 534 (92)**—knowingly conveying participant to scene of drug transaction `facilitates' drug distribution, making car subject to forfeiture;

C v One 1987 Ford Econoline Van **413 M 407 (92)**—Commonwealth held in contempt for failure to return van;

C v One 69 Mercedes Auto **375 M 663 (78)**—mere possession of a controlled substance not enough;

21-DD. MOTOR VEHICLE OFFENSES (G.L. C. 90–90D)

See also Use Without Authority, Larceny of Motor Vehicle, Motor Vehicle Homicide, above;

21-DD.1. Generally

Nolan and Sartorio, *Criminal Law* **(3d ed. 2001), Chapters 26–27;**

G.L. c. 90, § 20—penalties for miscellaneous offenses;

District Court Model Jury Instruction ## 5.10–5.28—(various offenses)

G.L. c. 233, § 76—copies of registry records can't be admitted unless bearing original attestation of registrar or agent;

C v Deramo **436 M 40, 48 (2002)**—photocopy of attested document doesn't serve purpose of attestation requirement; error here unpreserved, no prejudice;

C v Crosscup **369 M 228 (75)**—operating after suspension: must prove notice of suspension;

C v Lora **43 MAC 136 (97)**—though notice of license suspension was sent to "Box 312, Line St, Boston", notation in Registry record listed D's "residential" address as "20 East Brookline St, Boston"; Appeals Court held sufficient to infer notice sent to correct address (because G.L. c. 90, §§ 8 & 26A, require D to provide Registry w/correct address);

C v Blake **52 MAC 526 (2001)**—though notice of revocation was sent to address other than one on license, appellate court claimed that it was OK, since 3 weeks LATER, D told cop he was living at address to which the notice had been sent; notices of revocation admissible at trial because revocation for prior OUI offense was element of crime being charged, G.L. c. 90, § 23, 2d paragraph, operating after license revocation due to conviction for operating under the influence of liquor; judge SHOULD HAVE REDACTED EXTRANEOUS INFO on the notices; prior OUI conviction was element of the offense being tried, & not merely a sentencing enhancement factor, so no right to bifurcated trial (i.e., second trial only for purpose of proving prior conviction, see G.L. c. 278, § 11A);

C v Munoz **384 M 503 (81)**—insured: not D's burden of proof (& not G.L. c. 278, § 7);

***Brach v Chief Justice of District Court Department* 386 M 528 (82)**—can't take license, but surrender can be condition/probation; District Court Admin. Reg. = invalid; (see *Mackey v Mackey v Montrym* **443 US 1 (79)** below);

C v Whynaught **377 M 14 (79)**—speeding; radar OK, if foundation; *(See Chapter 20, suppression re: Roadblocks);*

C v Shea **324 M 710 (49)**—speculative that D operated; (See *Hilton* **398 M 63 (86)**);

C v Woods **414 M 343 (93)**—that D was operator at time of crash = inferable from facts that his legs were in driver's side foot well, with foot wedged under brake pedal, that his chest injuries were consistent with impact against steering wheel & that car was owned by his father;

C v Congdon **68 MAC 782 (2007)**—refusal to find ineffective assistance of counsel by trial counsel's question to cop that he'd never seen D in the vehicle (answer being he saw her in it only when she got her purse from it); inferences/circumstances were sufficient to show operation even without this testimony (no one else in area, D was walking toward car from woods [only ten feet away], D's statement that she was coming from friend's house in town at least three miles away, and going to her home);

C v Clarke **254 M 566 (26)**—"operation" = set car in motion;

C v Uski **263 M 22 (28)**—"set machinery in motion";

C v Plowman **28 MAC 230 (90)**—instruction that sitting in driver's seat of parked car with motor running sufficient to make out "operation" is erroneous;

C v Sudderth **37 MAC 317 (94)**—"operation" = intentionally doing any act or making use of any mechanical or electrical agency which alone or in sequence will set in motion the motive power of the vehicle; here, sufficient evidence for OUI when D = asleep or passed out in car, & motor was running;

C v Towers **35 MAC 557 (93)**—evidence sufficient to show operation on public street (D standing beside car, engine running, stopped off road on sidewalk area, with front-end damage, near parked car with rear-end damage; D said she had driven car);

Nolan and Sartorio, *Criminal Law* **(3d ed. 2001)** § 552—insert key = enough for operation;

C v Adams **421 M 289 (95)**—evidence sufficient to corroborate D's admission of 'operation';

C v O'Connor **420 M 630 (95)**—same;

C v Cavallaro **25 MAC 605 (88)**—Model Instruction didn't go far enough to explain difference between "permanent" (vs. temporary) stop;

C v Donohue **41 MAC 91 (96)**—required finding of NG denied for leaving scene of personal injury without making self known: though only unconscious/dead V was present, it was for jury to determine whether call to police 30–40 minutes later (from payphone 2–3 miles away) was reasonable under statute; D had 'panicked' & gone home first, & passed at least 5 pay telephones on way, at least 2 of which were operable;

C v Porro **74 MAC 676, further app. review allowed, 455 M 1106 (2009)**—D collided with motorcyclist during road rage incident, but thought noise was instead gunshot and only stopped ½ mile away, there finding that hole in window was inconsistent with gunshot; deliberating on indictment charging leaving scene of accident after causing personal injury, jury asked if 'knowledge of colliding with a person' had to be contemporaneous with incident; judge answered that if Commonwealth proved D knew he had collided with or caused injury, he was obligated to stop and provide info (to victim or some public officer at or near place and time of injury) as soon as he knew; court rejected D's argument that this expanded criminal liability and violated his right to know prior to closing argument what instructions would be given (M.R. Crim.P. 24(b));

C v Robbins **414 M 444 (93)**—alleged fact that victim sustained injury by jumping out of D's car, through no fault of D, did not relieve D of responsibility for leaving scene after injury to person (G.L. c. 90, § 24(2)(a)); statute applies to any "actor" involved in a person's injury concerning motor vehicle even if actor is not at fault;

C v Dowler **414 M 212 (93)**—Commonwealth's failure to give notice that operating after license suspended due to OUI conviction carried 60-day minimum mandatory sentence plus fine mandated by G.L. c. 90, § 23O, did not violate D's statutory or constitutional rights (and was not a defense to operating after suspension);

C v LeBlanc **407 M 70 (90)**—police can't arrest out of jurisdiction for civil traffic violation outside jurisdiction;

C v Valchuis **40 MAC 556 (96)**—motor vehicle citation which indicated that criminal complaint would be sough did not toll statute of limitations; complaint issued > 6 years after alleged leaving scene of accident causing personal injury & property damage was time-barred; these **not** "continuing offenses" (though agreed by Commonwealth to be such, so as to defeat **any** limitations claim);

C v Ferreira **70 MAC 32 (2007)**—negligently operating to endanger proof sufficient even though it lasted but an instant: cop testified that in mid-day, busy shopping center parking lot with "moderate to heavy" vehicle and pedestrian traffic, on surface recently subject to much snow, D backed out of parking space and accelerated forward, causing "screech," and wheels to spin and back end to fishtail;

21-DD.2. G.L. c. 90C, § 3: Decriminalized Minor Ones

G.L. c. 90C, §§ 1–2;

C v Sasu **404 M 596 (89)**—appeal of civil violation (magistrate, judge, appellate division);

C v Santos **65 MAC 122, 123 n.2 (2005)**—driving without having one's Mass. license in one's *possession* is an offense (G.L. c. 90, § 11), but isn't "arrestable" offense if one is an in-state driver (G.L. c. 90, § 21); cop should have checked via radio/computer whether D did have active license he claimed, providing date of birth, (and/or whether car was stolen) before "securing" D in cruiser and searching car for indicia of ownership;

C v Healy **452 M 510, 512 n.5 (2008)**—SJC doesn't "necessarily agree" that "failure to stop" (a civil infraction) is a lesser included offense of "operating to endanger", but issue was not before the Court;

21-DD.3. G.L. c. 90C, § 2—Timely CITATION for "Motor Vehicle Offense" (or DISMISS):

Nolan and Sartorio, *Criminal Law* **(3d ed. 2001),** § 572—citation procedure;

C v Riley **41 MAC 234 (96)**—can't circumvent G.L. c. 90C, § 2 by having citizen apply for complaint pursuant to G.L. c. 90C, § 4;

C v Gorman **356 M 355 (69)**—no citation if D's = arrested, otherwise   ;

C v Clinton **374 M 719 (78)**—dismissal if no timely citation (& no excuse);

C v Kenney **55 MAC 514 (2002)**—no dismissal because D fled scene, & thereafter Commonwealth needed time to determine nature of violation/identity of violator (statutory exceptions thus applied); though Commonwealth had no excuse for subsequent time, dismissal not warranted because record showed that D was explicitly on notice that charges were probable: pedestrian in a crosswalk was hit by D & "catapulted" 40 feet forward; D "hit and ran"; D promptly (within two days after incident) engaged counsel to defend against probable charges;

C v Marchand **18 MAC 932 (84)**—dismissal; "strictly construed";

C v Mullins **367 M 733 (75)**—(same);

C v Drew **11 MAC 517 (81)**—motor vehicle homicide = "motor vehicle offense" (as opposed to use without authority, larceny of motor vehicle); but "filed";

C v Perry **15 MAC 281 (83)**—excusable delay for motor vehicle homicide;

C v Babb **389 M 275 (83)**—excusable delay;

C v Roviaro **32 MAC 956 (92)**—54-day delay in issuing citation required dismissal;

C v Cameron **34 MAC 44 (93)**—cop's delay in issuing operating to endanger citation 2 days after investigation of auto accident completed because cop was off duty did not fall within statutory exception to immediate citation rule allowing additional time "reasonably necessary to determine the nature of the violation or the identity of the violator"; dismissal justified; **OVERRULED** in *C v Cameron* **416 M 314 (93)** purposes of statute (G.L. c. 90C, § 2) not frustrated by delay because D was aware of seriousness (cyclist almost died) and, given near-death, "'fix' is virtually excluded" by the circumstances;

C v Moulton **56 MAC 682 (2002)**—failure to give citation at accident scene didn't result in dismissal because officer hadn't completed investigation until he interviewed D at hospital;

C v Carapellucci **429 M 579 (99)**—even though D fled scene, and even though locating address of D took as long as a week thereafter, dismissal ordered: police failed to mail or deliver the citation to D "as soon as possible" (G.L. c. 90C, § 2) because they didn't mail or deliver it at all;

C v Hrycenko **61 MAC 378 (2004)**—dismissal (without prejudice) for want of prosecution (witness didn't appear; Commonwealth hadn't summonsed her) could be undone by motion to vacate; D did not base motion to dismiss on "no fix" statute, so it's waived, and even if it weren't, D acted unlawfully to evade detection, justifying 5-day delay in citation; *C v Steadward* **43 MAC 272 (97)** distinguished (dismissal there based on failure to comply

with "no-fix" statute, G.L. c. 90C, § 2, re: motor vehicle violations, & Commonwealth didn't seek relief by way of appeal or trial court motion, and instead simply obtained new complaint);

21-DD.4. "Public Way"

G.L. c. 233, § 79F—proof by certificate; otherwise . . . ;

C v Hayden **354 M 727 (68)**—insufficient circumstantial evidence;

C v Smithson **41 MAC 545 (96)**—insufficient evidence that road on private business property was public way on national holiday, on which business was closed (and public did not necessarily have access as invitees/licensees), "objective appearance of the way" controls, rather than "subjective intent of property owner";

C v George **406 M 635 (90)**—public school baseball field not a "public way";

C v Stoddard **74 MAC 179 (2009)**—roads in privately-owned seasonal campground barred to those without gate card issued to registered campers not public ways;

C v Belliveau **76 MAC 830 (2010)**—exhaustive analysis of "public way," context of pier in Charlestown Navy Yard; notwithstanding "close" question, inference = D drove on public way to get there;

C v Mara **257 M 198 (26)**—sufficient circumstantial evidence;

C v Hart **26 MAC 235 (88)**—could reasonably conclude private way = "public";

C v Kiss **59 MAC 247 (2003)**—shopping mall parking lot, even when mall shops are closed, = public way;

21-DD.5. Operate Under Influence (G.L. c. 90, § 24)

G.L. c. 90, § 24—license suspension 1 year; 45–90 days if § 24D program; 120 if no test; 90 if fail;

C v Ferola **72 MAC 170 (2008)**—G.L. c. 90, § 24(l)(a)(1) criminalizes operation under influence of only those narcotics, stimulants, or depressants defined in § 1 of G.L. c. 94C; evidence that D was under influence of depressants Klonopin and amitriptyline was insufficient absent some evidence that these were drugs which "contain[ed] any quantity of a substance which the US Attorney General has by regulation designated as having a potential for abuse because of its depressant . . . effect on the central nervous system or its hallucinogenic effect", given plain language of statute; fn.4: required proof may be expert testimony, introduction of pertinent regulations in evidence or judicial notice "(subject to jury evaluation)";

C v Palacios **66 MAC 13 (2006)**—at trial of D for operating after license suspension for alcohol-related reason, judge and prosecutor erroneously spoke of D having been "convicted" of operating under influence (such that license was suspended), but he had actually avoided such conviction by admission to sufficient facts, while having had penalty of license suspension for 45 days imposed; no objection, no substantial risk of miscarriage of justice; "erroneous labeling of the disposition of prior proceeding" was immaterial;

Nolan and Sartorio, *Criminal Law* **(3d ed. 2001), Chapter 26;** "Scientific Evidence," Moenssens & Inbau (3d ed.) - blood alcohol, etc.;

District Court Model Jury Instruction ##5.10, 5.101, 5.102—operating under influence of intoxicating liquor, or of drug, operating under the influence & causing serious bodily injury;

C v Lampron **65 MAC 340 (2005)**—while jury instruction permitted conviction of D even if alcohol was "only one contributing cause of [D's] diminished capacity or if the effect of the alcohol was magnified by some other cause" (i.e., drug ingestion), this didn't mean that there were "separate theories of culpability" such that one (drugs) lacked evidentiary support;

C v Hernandez **60 MAC 416 (2004)**—though judge accepted guilty plea to OUI-second offense, there was no factual basis for "second offense" portion, because D had not been convicted of a first offense *as of the time of the crime*; fact that he had been convicted of qualifying "prior" after time of the crime but before time of guilty plea was irrelevant; though this was not "element" of crime charged, D was still entitled to have the fact proven beyond reasonable doubt; motion to withdraw guilty plea to be allowed only as to "second offense" portion, D to be resentenced for OUI as first offense;

C v Zuzick **45 MAC 71 (98)**—neither prosecuting office's "practice" of not specifying, e.g., "third offense" OUI in a complaint (but simply demanding at sentencing that D be sentenced for that crime) nor policy of judge simply to rely on records of probation office to establish prior OUI convictions, could override legislature's command that D is "entitled to a trial by jury on the issue of conviction of a prior offense, subject to all provisions of law governing criminal trials," G.L. c. 278, § 11A;

C v Chaplin **50 MAC 365 (2000)**—trial judge (in OUI 2d prosecution) moved directly from jury "G" to sentencing, & counsel's acquiescence then that D was a prior offender wasn't functional equivalent to "G" plea; FURTHER, rejects Commonwealth argument that D "convicted" only of substantive offense but sentenced with consideration of criminal record as whole (for enhanced punishment as 2d offender); D entitled to jury trial on prior, and Zuzick holding not distinguishable on ground that he "asked" for jury trial or pled "NG" to that specific portion;

C v McCready **50 MAC 521 (2000)**—sentencing as 2d offender merely upon counsel's statement that there had been a previous OUI conviction (this isn't equivalent to D pleading G) required vacating judgment; G.L. c. 278, § 11A procedure is to be followed;

C v Dussault **71 MAC 542 (2008)**—absence of written waiver of D's right to jury trial (bifurcated proceeding, after OUI conviction by jury, on fact of prior convictions to support charge of operating under the influence, 3rd offense) resulted in vacating so much of judgment as found D guilty of OUI 3rd offense;

C v Valiton **432 M 647 (2000)**—"previous offense" of OUI can be made out by charge of delinquency by reason of OUI, which was disposed of by license suspension & probation, with evaluation & counseling at a treatment program;

C v Flaherty **61 MAC 776 (2004)**—despite D's arguments that D's guilty plea to OUI in New Hampshire was a "violation" rather than a "conviction" and that it was the registry of motor vehicles rather than the court which required completion of an alcohol intervention program, the NH matter was held to be a qualifying "prior" for conviction of OUI-4th offense;

C v Finegan **45 MAC 921 (98)**—required finding of NG because Commonwealth failed to introduce evidence that heroin is "narcotic drug" and failed to ask judge to take judicial notice of this point (which would have required judge to expressly tell jurors));

Mackey v Montrym **443 US 1 (79)**—can suspend license for test refusal & give hearing later (but see *Brach* **386 M 528 (82)**) ;

C v Bauer **455 M 497 (2009)**—arrested for OUI after three prior convictions of OUI, D refused breath test, resulting in license suspension for life (G.L. c. 90, § 24(l)(f)(1)); acquitted of OUI after jury trial, D filed motion seeking restoration of license, and trial judge denied motion: appropriate avenue for judicial review of adverse license restoration orders = civil action in nature of certiorari (G.L. c. 249, § 4) to be brought in Superior Court; SJC rejects D's argument that judicial decision violated separation of powers (i.e., encroaching on 'executive branch');

C v Crowell **403 M 381 (88)**—§ 24N PER SE = OK due process (even PRE-trial) because Registry of Motor Vehicles hearing (& prompt blood test could rebut) & ASSUME 24N lets D rebut;

C v Connolly **394 M 169 (85)**—must show impaired driving ability; District Court Model Jury Instructions = "improper";

C v Sudderth **37 MAC 317 (94)**—evidence sufficient to show under influence (empty beer cans, strong odor of alcohol from breath & person, D's belligerence & unsteadiness) despite no observed **driving** impairment; (see also *C v Tynes* **400 M 369 (87)**);

C v Riley **48 MAC 463 (2000)**—no error found: Model Jury Instruction 5.10 given jury, including reference to "consum(ing) enough alcohol to reduce (one's) mental clarity, self-control, and reflexes and thereby le(aving one) with a reduced ability to drive safely", but upon jury question, jurors were told that Commonwealth had to prove beyond reasonable doubt "impairment", but had to prove beyond reasonable doubt only one of the "mental clarity, self-control, and reflexes" "factors";

C v Lindner **395 M 144 (85)**—D's rights = blood test & phone call;

C v Andrade **389 M 874 (83)**—dismissal because not given independent test option;

C v Scott **359 M 407 (71)**—dismissal because D's test refusal admitted;

C v Alano **388 M 871 (83)**—no right to police breathalyzer;

C v Atencio **12 MAC 747 (81)**—lay opinion re: sobriety = OK;

C v Bowden **379 M 472 (80)**—defense from investigation weaknesses;

C v Williams **19 MAC 915 (84)**—not "shall" infer; exclude D's prior;

C v Moreira **385 M 792 (82)**—.10 breathalyzer = "infer," not "presume";

C v Angivoni **383 M 30 (81)**—can't extract blood without D's consent;

California v Trombetta **467 US 479 (84)**—(same);

C v Neal **392 M 1 (84)**—Smith & Wesson Model 900A breathalyzer = OK; can destroy ampules because not shown RE-TEST = generally accepted & because D could've had independent test;

C v Cochran **25 MAC 260 (88)**—breathalyzer must PASS a simulator TEST;

C v Steele **455 M 209 (2009)**—only the lower of the two breath sample/blood alcohol level results could be introduced in accord with statutory and regulatory requirements; Secretary of Public Safety promulgated requirement that when two breath samples differ "within +/- 0.02 blood alcohol content units", the lower of the two samples shall be taken as D's blood alcohol level (501 CMR § 2.57), and regulation valid notwithstanding Commonwealth's criticisms;

C v Carson **72 MAC 368 (2008)**—though D has no constitutional right to refuse breath or blood test when there is probable cause to believe she has operated vehicle while impaired, G.L. c. 90, § 24(1)(e–f) requires D's actual consent to such testing as condition of admissibility of the results in evidence; Here, even "the minimal criteria satisfying the consent requirement of the statute" (i.e., NOT that required for waiver of constitutional rights) = lacking ("cryptic writing" drawn by cop served as "consent form" and D so distraught [rocking, vomiting, dry-heaving] that phlebotomist delayed drawing blood);

C v Smythe **23 MAC 348 (89)**—can't exclude D's breathalyzer EXPERT if qualified;

See Chapter 6-B, 6-D & 6-E, Pretrial Conference/ Discovery; Chapter 7-C, Money for D's Expert; & Chapter 11-I, Evidence, Opinions of Experts, & CPCS P/G's 4.4 (g), 6 (h);

C v Wallace **14 MAC 358 (82)**—need mens rea (KNOW) medicine's effect;

C v Hilton **398 M 63 (86)**—infer OUI from asleep at wheel (see above)

C v Plowman **28 MAC 230 (90)**—instruction that sitting in driver's seat of parked car with motor running sufficient to make out "operation" is erroneous;

C v Sudderth **37 MAC 317 (94)**—sufficient evidence for OUI when D = asleep or passed out in car, & motor is running;

C v Kiss **59 MAC 247 (2003)**—D, asleep or passed out in car with motor running in mall parking lot, argued without success for "shelter defense," to avoid criminal penalty when he removed vehicle from roadway because he believed self to be under the influence;

C v LeRoy **376 M 243 (78)**—no continuance without a finding after jury's G. verdict;

C v Murphy **389 M 316 (83)**—prior continuance without a finding = 1st "offense" re: subsequent case;

Dunbrack v Commonwealth **398 M 502 (86)**—no § 24D alternative disposition if it's 2d offense, even though not charged;

G.L. c. 278, § 11A—trial of "prior" *(See Chapter 5); (re: proof of prior, see Chapter 14-N, Sentencing: Recidivist Sentencing Statutes);*

G.L. c. 90, § 23—mandatory 60-day minimum for OUI after revocation (see *Groden* **26 MAC 1024**);

G.L. c. 90, § 24(L)—OUI causing "serious INJURY" (District Court jurisdiction);

C v Carey **26 MAC 339 (88)**—can tell D of phone right *(Chapter 3-E, Defendant's Entry Into Criminal Justice System: Police Station; see also Chapter 20-B, Suppression Issues, Station Telephone Call)* but video D before letting use phone;

C v Cameron **25 MAC 538 (88)**—video shows sobriety & doubt re: cop's testimony;

C v Brazelton **404 M 783 (89)**—no right to call attorney before deciding whether to take breathalyzer;

C v Mencoboni **28 MAC 504 (90)**—cops' refusal to allow D to confer privately with attorney at stationhouse about taking breathalyzer was due process denial of counsel, but didn't require dismissal where prejudice not shown;

C v Barbeau **411 M 782, 786 (92)**—breathalyzer evidence admissible only upon showing by Commonwealth that police complied with periodic testing program required by G.L. c. 90, § 24K;

C v Livers **420 M 556 (95)**—mere failure of state to promulgate regulations for breathalyzer testing prior to D's arrest and breathalyzer test did not warrant suppression of test result;

Morris v Commonwealth **412 M 861 (92)**—upheld DPS Guidelines, 501 C.M.R. 2.41, for testing program for breathalyzers;

C v Kelley **39 MAC 448 (95)**—rejecting D's many arguments for excluding breathalyzer test results;

C v Smith **35 MAC 566 (93)**—though blood alcohol level estimate by "retrograde extrapolation" excluded here, DA was not unreasonable to include it in opening; such evidence was noted in *C v Cruz* **413 M 686 (93)** without adverse comment;

C v Senior **433 M 453 (2001)**—judge didn't abuse discretion in finding "retrograde extrapolation" method of calculating blood alcohol level at earlier time admissible given voir dire evidence here, notwithstanding fact that its validity isn't "universally acknowledged";

C v Colturi **448 M 809 (2007)**—expert testimony on "retrograde extrapolation" isn't a prerequisite to admission of breathalyzer test even after 2003 amendment to G.L. c. 90, § 24, "so long as the test is conducted within a reasonable period of time after the driver's last operation of the vehicle", "reasonable time" being defined as up to three hours between testing and operation, with room to argue different period "reasonable" on particular facts and circumstances; statute now makes it illegal, per se, to operate vehicle with blood alcohol level of .08 or more; if prosecution is *only* on "impaired ability theory" and breathalyzer result of .08 or above is to be offered, expert testimony on significance of level "as it pertains to impairment" must be offered; IF Commonwealth relies on both "impaired operation" theory AND "per se" theory, no prejudice in admitting breathalyzer test results without expert testimony concerning significance of test level to degree of intoxication/impairment;

C v Douglas **75 MAC 643 (2009)**—because judge withdrew "per se" theory in operating under/motor vehicle homicide case (though complaint had charged both theories), reversal because no expert testimony (contra Colturi requirement, 448 M 817–18: though evidence of impairment was strong & trial counsel didn't object, lab supervisor's testimony as to blood alcohol content may have been "the most compelling evidence of intoxication";

C v Hubert **453 M 1009 (2009) on further review of 71 MAC 661 (2008)**—indictment charged violation of G.L. c. 90, § 24(l)(a)(1) by driving while under the influence of intoxicating liquor, and no mention made in indictment of driving with blood alcohol of .08 or greater, so error to allow introduction of breathalyzer evidence and instruct jury they could infer violation on this basis without accompanying expert testimony; absence of expert testimony was also inconsistent with judge's admonition that only "impairment" theory could be presented; rejects 'harmless error' argument;

C v McNelley **28 MAC 985 (90)**—D's statement of operation requires corroboration; *(cf. cases in Chapter 12-G, Trial Issues: Required Finding of Not Guilty: no conviction on D's confession alone, e.g.,* **C v Boothby** *64 MAC 582 (2005)*—failure to object to admission of hearsay corroborating D's out-of-court admission was ineffective assistance, since without the corroborative evidence that D was driver of car, finding of not guilty was required);

Pennsylvania v Muniz **496 US 582 (90)**—police booking questions calling upon OUI-D to calculate date of 6th birthday were improperly designed to elicit information for "investigatory purposes," not "biographical data necessary to complete booking or pretrial services"; cf. *C v Guerrero* **32 MAC 263 (92)** questions about employment status should be "scrubbed" from booking procedure in absence of Miranda warnings;

Daley v Board of Appeal on Motor Vehicle Liability Policies & Bonds **406 M 857 (90)**—registrar must suspend for 2 years license of those twice convicted of OUI within six years, regardless of court disposition;

C v Corbett **422 M 391 (96)**—enhanced punishment for OUI - third offense did not violate ex post facto prohibition, and neither did legislation increasing the "reach back" period in which prior convictions can be used for mandatory sentence enhancers;

C v Koney **421 M 295 (95)**—required finding of NG on 'subsequent' nature of offense: "mere identity of name is not sufficient to indicate an identity of person"; identification card which was relevant to this proof had not been introduced during the **separate** trial required (G.L. c. 278, § 11A) for 'subsequent' nature of offense;

C v Ames **410 M 603 (91)**—taking D to hospital where police offered blood alcohol test by "neutral" health care provider satisfied statutory requirements, despite subsequent failure to notify D of rights under G.L. c. 263, § 5A;

C v Russo **30 MAC 923 (91)**—drawing & testing of D's blood by hospital staff was not search or seizure under 4th Amendment where not done at cops' request or direction; blood tests on injured OUI-D were admissible because standard procedure for D's medical problem;

C v Senior **433 M 453 (2001)**—when drawing & testing of D's blood at hospital was sought by D's attorney shortly after fatal car crash, hospital didn't become "agent" of counsel so as to protect results from Commonwealth subpoena on basis of attorney-client privilege (purported agent didn't manifest consent to such agency, & record didn't show that attorney "expressly communicated" expectation of 'agency' to hospital; judge didn't abuse discretion in finding sufficiently reliable for introduction "retrograde extrapolation" method of determining blood alcohol levels at points prior to the testing;

C v Hampe **419 M 514 (95)**—arrested for OUI & "failing" police breathalyzer tests twice, D wanted independent test and quick bail; when police instead held him to "sleep off" alleged effects, D's motion to dismiss OUI complaint allowed by trial court; SJC held possible remedy instead = suppression of police breathalyzer & jury instructions re: police viol. of statutory right, **IF** there is "overwhelming evidence of guilt apart from" breathalyzer and police testimony concerning events after denial of D's right;

C v Priestley **419 M 678 (95)**—police are not required to telephone bail commissioner and apparently need not tell D of his right to do so, since here, D telephoned attorney, among others; **Hampe** distinguished (police there made deliberate choice to keep D in custody);

C v Whitcomb **37 MAC 929 (94)**—no right to bail (and concomitant opportunity for independent medical examination) until booking complete (uncooperative D, refusing to answer questions or sign form);

C v King **429 M 169 (99)**—"policy" of bail magistrate for OUI arrestees who refused to take breathalyzer was not to hold bail hearings and instead direct police to hold D until next a.m., preventing D from obtaining independent medical examination, justified dismissal; if D is left to telephone bail magistrate on his own, D must tell magistrate that he wants G.L. c. 263, § 5A independent medical examination; Commonwealth may overcome presumption of prejudice to D "by overwhelming evidence of intoxication" or by other evidence indicating that the omission wasn't prejudicial in the circumstances;

C v Rosewarne **410 M 53 (91)**—cops may not deprive D of reasonable opportunity to obtain independent blood alcohol test but need not "assist" him by driving him to hospital;

C v McIntyre **36 MAC 193 (94)**—same; hospital's refusal later to test in absence of cop was a "policy" not arranged or dictated by police; police failure to advise D of rt. to independent test inconsequential as D's father, present, cited it to cops;

C v Mandell **61 MAC 526 (2004)**—neither Article 12 of Declaration of Rights nor Sixth Amendment to U.S. Constitution requires that one arrested for operating under the influence of DRUGS be advised by police that he can arrange for independent medical exam; G.L. c. 263, § 5A, concerning such right when arrested for OUI alcohol, doesn't provide basis for "equal protection" / due process constitutional claim;

C v Sabourin **48 MAC 505 (2000)**—no suppression of breathalyzer results: D consented in writing to the test, but machine malfunctioned, so D was taken to another place where he gave another sample; consent was never withdrawn and "impliedly contemplates the taking of a VALID test," so "carried over to taking the second test";

C v Dube **413 M 570 (92)**—trial judge has discretion to admit hospital record of OUI—D's blood alcohol tests (here, conducted upon D's admission to hospital after suffering injury from auto accident) even though G.L. c. 233, § 79 bans admission of evidence relating to "question of liability";

Opinion of Justices **412 M 1201 (92)**—proposed statute making refusal to take breathalyzer test admissible violates Article 12, Mass. Declaration of Rights;

C v Zevitas **418 M 677, 683–84 (94)**—following the dictates of G.L. c. 90, § 24(1)(e), the judge gave jury instructions that tended to have the same effect as the admission of refusal evidence, considered in Opinion of the Justices, above, would have had, i.e., strongly implied that the defendant's blood alcohol level had not been tested, and that the reason no test was conducted was that the defendant refused to submit to such a procedure; conviction reversed—(violation of Article 12);

C v Quinn **61 MAC 332, 336 n.3 (2004)**—though unremarked by parties, Appeals Court alarmed to see that booking videotape, admitted at trial, depicted D's refusal to take breathalyzer exam;

C v Downs **53 MAC 195 (2001)**—finding no error in judge's instruction that they weren't to think about or consider fact that no evidence was offered concerning a breathalyzer test (because didn't advise that test can be informed only if D consents, & thus didn't imply that absence of test was because D believed he'd fail);

C v Lively **30 MAC 970 (91)**—directing D's attention to posted rights plus access to telephone was sufficient;

C v Green **408 M 48 (90)**—required finding entered where Commonwealth failed to prove that cocaine is a "narcotic" under G.L. c. 94C, § 1;

C v O'Hara **30 MAC 608 (91)**—car's crossing lines & wavering speed warranted belief that driver committing OUI or other "arrestable offense" justified fresh pursuit to make extraterritorial arrest under G.L. c. 41, § 98A;

C v Anderson **406 M 343 (90)** extending OUI roadblock 15 minutes beyond plan required suppression under Article 14 & 4th Amendment;

C v Avola **28 MAC 988 (90)**—non-eyewitness cops may be designated under G.L. c. 90C, § 3(B), to sign OUI complaint as "complainants"; pretrial motion to dismiss generally required to preserve challenge to facial invalidity of complaint; 1986 Safe Roads Act (S.R.A.): (lic. susp. 1 yr.; 45–90 (or 180 if under 21 yrs) day if 40-hour if § 24d program (license to probation at disposition); 120 days if "refuse" test; 90 from arraignment if fail); 24D fees (most waivable with affidavit) = $250 assess. + $100 (head injury fund) + $500 (program) + $30/mo. (prob) + $30–50 (V-witness) + $200 (reinstate license)

Blood Alcohol Approximations(fn*)	Drinks (per hr).	Weight
.25	5	100
.21	5	120
.18	5	140
.15	5	160
.13	5	180
.12	5	200
.20	4	100
.16	4	120
.14	4	140
.12	4	160
.10	4	180
.09	4	200
.15	3	100
.12	3	120
.10	3	140
.09	3	160
.08	3	180
.07	3	200
.09	2	100
.08	2	120
.06	2	140
.05	2	160
.05	2	180
.04	2	200
.04	1	100
.03	1	120
.02	1	140
.02	1	160
.02	1	180
.01	1	200

(subtract .01 per 40-minutes drinking)

(fn*) (SOURCES: 12/29/88 N.Y. Times & Erwin, above, § 15) See also *C v Senior* **433 M 453 (2001)** re "retrograde extrapolation" method of calculating blood alcohol level at earlier time;

21-EE. DISORDERLY PERSON (G.L. C. 272, § 53)

Alegata v C **353 M 287 (67)**—(surviving) Model Penal Code ELEMENTS: (1) intend public inconvenience, annoyance, or alarm; & (2) (a) create hazard without legitimate purpose, or (b) violent/tumultuous;

C v Juvenile **368 M 580 (75)**—Alegata elements, minus 1st Amendment activities; "physically offensive"; "tumultuous"; "public";

C v Marcavage **76 MAC 34 (2009)**—D, disobeying police order to stop using megaphone (being used within a foot of people's faces on Halloween night in Salem), attracted crowd, resisted arrest, and "engendered hostility toward police and disrespect for their authority among" large and raucous crowd, sufficient for conviction; that underlying conduct (dissemination of religious message) enjoyed First Amendment protection did not allow disregard of police commands "reasonably calculated at ensuring public safety";

C v Harrington **74 MAC 14 (2009)**—Appeals Court rejects "report" of District Court judge seeking ruling that Alegata decision violated "separation of powers" by using Model Penal Code; legislature has twice amended statute since Alegata & hasn't rejected Alegata construction;

C v Collins **36 MAC 25 (94)**—Court rejects argument (factual?) that police station corridor not a "public" place; tumultuous behavior there punishable as disorderly;

C v Mulvey **57 MAC 579 (2003)**—required finding of not guilty because conduct occurred on purely private property with no showing that the disturbance had or was likely to have impact upon persons in an area accessible to the public; cops came to driveway of D's mother's house to serve him with an out-of-state restraining order, and he became distraught, shouting to police to leave; **police presence alone doesn't convert purely private outburst into disorderly conduct;**

C v LePore **40 MAC 543 (96)**—"peeping Tom" behavior punishable under G.L. c. 272, § 53; fact that object of voyeurism was not aware of it = irrelevant;

C v Swan **73 MAC 258 (2008)**—no required finding of not guilty of open/gross (G.L. c. 272, § 16) or indecent exposure (G.L. c. 272, § 53): evidence was that elementary school janitor used boys' lavatory urinals inferably with intent "to expose himself beyond the degree necessary for urination," staring at one boy, and talking so as to encourage attention from another boy (including sexually explicit comments); evidence insufficient, however, for "peeping Tom"/voyeurism theory of disorderly conduct, which is "designed to protect legitimate and widely shared expectations of privacy possessed by those who have purposely closed themselves off from public view in an enclosed space or area" (i.e., not "open" character of five urinals placed side by side);

C v Blavackas **11 MAC 746 (81)**—not for prostitution (on these facts); cf. G.L. c. 277, § 79: form COMPLAINT (3 months neglect lawful business & frequent houses of ill fame, tippling shops, etc.) - (see *C v Lombard* **321 M 294 (47)**: this was old language);

C v Richards **369 M 443 (76)**—G. for conduct, though speech too;

C v Carson **10 MAC 920 (80)**—(same); "tumultuous";

C v Feigenbaum **404 M 471 (89)**—political protest not hazardous because not "without legitimate purpose";

C v Zettel **46 MAC 471 (99)**—woman who was trying to pick up child from elementary school insufficiently obedient to police officer who ordered her, first, to move her car, and then to move it from a private driveway instead of remaining to pick up the child: required finding of NG because not "tumultuous" and because the purportedly hazardous or offensive condition wasn't created by an "act which serves no legitimate purpose of the actor"; refusal to restrict "legitimate purpose" clause to instances of "political expression";

C v Molligi **70 MAC 108 (2007)**—D's merely standing on public street at 2:30 a.m. ("well-traveled" purportedly because pedestrians were emerging from bars & eateries) holding a knife in his hand had frightened at least one person (who reported it to cop) + fleeing from cop's "stop" order sufficient for G of "disorderly";

C v Lopiano **60 MAC 723 (2004)**—required finding of not guilty because D's yelling at cop and flailing arms in agitation ("you're violating my civil rights") wasn't violent or tumultuous behavior;

Lewis v New Orleans **415 US 130 (74)**—foul speech = protected;

C v Sholley **48 MAC 495 (2000)**—"father's rights activist" couldn't be convicted of disorderly person based on loud words about judge ("that . . . bitch sent him back to jail?") or for "clarion call for 'war against the judicial system'," made loudly in hallway outside courtroom; First Amendment barred this (and D also couldn't be convicted of "disrupting court proceeding," G.L. c. 268, § 13C, because no evidence that any proceeding had been disrupted; G, however, for threatening prosecutor ("intention to bully" inferable from D's past history, his presence in courtroom, his menacing gesture; words alone ("watch out counselor") insufficient as "threat to commit" particular crime; OVERRULED AS TO DISORDERLY CONVICTION: 432 M 721, 728 (2000) D's conduct could be found both "threatening" and "tumultuous"; same result as Appeals Court re: disrupting court proceeding & threat to prosecutor;

C v Manzelli **68 MAC 691 (2007)**—news reporting activities/constitutionally protected acts can't provide basis for disorderly conduct conviction, BUT evidence here supported conviction for disorderly conduct under theory of fighting or violent behavior, "as to which First Amendment considerations are inapplicable"; discussion of impermissible shift of burden of proof;

C v Chou **433 M 229 (2001)**—disorderly person conviction upheld for D's apparent "sneaking into" school of former girlfriend overnight, and posting flyers containing photo of ex-girlfriend with word "MISSING" printed across top; flyers contained sexually explicit & derogatory comments; threats may serve as basis for conviction under "accosting"/"annoying" provision of G.L. c. 272, § 53; equal protection argument (concerning statute's reach only to 'persons of the opposite sex') not addressed because deemed "facial challenge," which has to be made by pretrial motion to dismiss under M.R.Crim.P. 13 (c);

C v Cahill **446 M 778 (2006)**—upholding conviction under G.L. c. 272, § 53 for repeated requests by fellow cashier for dates/invasion of physical space/touching complainant's back /aggressive question why she didn't return his call;

C v Ramirez **69 MAC 9 (2007)**—that D stared at complainant at swimming pool and asked why she was leaving, and that the next day he offered to buy her candy and sang a song about falling in love with a little girl couldn't establish guilt of accosting or annoying person of opposite sex (G.L. c. 272, § 53): there was no physical contact or attempt at such, and that D's acts were "unwelcome and unsettling" to complainant was insufficient for G; court rejects argument that acts were "inherently threatening . . . given the alleged 'sexual overtones' implicit in his words and actions"; "not all noxious and disturbing remarks are criminal threats";

C v Whiting **58 MAC 918 (2003)**—D's telling 13-year-old girls that he was drunk, gay, "looking for dick," etc., caused them to flee indoors and testify that they were scared, confused, uncomfortable, afraid that D would hurt them, and was enough for G of c. 272, § 53 (offensive/disorderly toward someone of the opposite sex);

Hill v Colorado **530 US 703 (2000)**—1st Amendment rights of speaker not here abridged by protection which statute provides for unwilling listener, i.e., person within 100 feet of health care facility entrance may not be approached closer than eight feet by person displaying a sign, or engaged in oral protest, education, counseling or passing leaflets; fact that enactment of statute was motivated by conduct of partisans on one side of abortion debate did not make it violative of 1st Amendment;

Nolan and Sartorio, *Criminal Law* **(3d ed. 2001) § 266;**

District Court Model Jury Instruction #5.43;

21-FF. DISTURB PEACE (G.L. C. 272, § 53)

C v Jarrett **359 M 491 (71)**—old "definition";

C v Orlando **371 M 732 (77)**—redefined - need (victim(s));

C v Piscopo **11 MAC 905 (81)**—tended to, & did, "annoy" good citizens; cf. G.L. c. 272, §§ 38–42A—disturb schools, meetings, etc.;

C v Federico **70 MAC 711 (2007)**—sufficient for guilt: inference that D awakened and disturbed residents when, at midnight in residential neighborhood, he tripped motion sensors and failed to stop when ordered to do so by pursuing homeowner (who lay in wait for D, a peeping Tom and enticer of adolescent inside home);

C v Hokanson **74 MAC 403 (2009)**—though Federico (70 MAC at 715, n.5) refused to uphold conviction on basis of D's conduct at time of arrest, THIS D's behavior at arrest = disturbing peace (shouting, flailing, agitated; group of people gathered, appeared "alarmed");

District Court Model Jury Instruction #5.44;

21-GG. OBSCENITY DISSEMINATION

G.L. c. 272, § 29—punishing anyone disseminating or possessing with intent to disseminate any matter which is obscene, knowing it to be obscene;

Ferrari v Commonwealth **448 M 163 (2007)**—rejecting D's argument that failure to introduce actual videotapes D allegedly showed to minor required a finding of not guilty (since jury could not then decide whether as a whole tapes lacked literary, artistic, political, or scientific value): minor's testimony "as to the entire contents of the 'porn' videotapes she personally observed was sufficient";

C v Rollins **60 MAC 153 (2003)**—**evidence that on four occasions D littered the ground with "pornographic" material (videocassette box, pages torn from sexually explicit magazines) was sufficient in circumstances to show conscious effort to display it to persons; required finding of not guilty, however, on charge of disseminating to minor (G.L. c. 272, § 28), because** no evidence that minor saw it, and insufficient evidence of D's intent that minor view it;

C v Belcher **446 M 693 (2006)**—seventeen-year-old mentally retarded female (D's niece) claimed he had shown her adult videotapes depicting sex acts, and several photos of D and women engaged in sex acts; D & wife testified that niece had viewed such items without their permission and had been reprimanded; to argument that jury instruction should have charged that D wasn't guilty absent "purposeful or intentional dissemination," there was no objection to charge that Commonwealth must prove that D "exhibited or displayed" the material "to a person" under age 18, and no substantial likelihood of any misunderstanding that "purposeful" conduct was essential, given evidence, dictionary meanings of "exhibit"/"display" and closing arguments;

C v Militello **66 MAC 325 (2006)**—dissemination of matter harmful to minors (G.L. c. 272, § 28) not here proved by boys' testimony regarding D showing them *Playboy* magazine with pictures of naked women (magazine itself not introduced); D's lewd comments accompanying showing not considered, given statutory definition of "matter" (G.L. c. 272, § 31);

G.L. c. 272, § 29A—(a) person knowing that a person is under 18 years old, or "in possession of such facts that he should have reason to know that such person is a child under" 18 years old, "with lascivious intent," causes or permits child to pose in state of nudity for the purpose of representation or reproduction in any visual material" - not less than ten nor more than twenty years' imprisonment, plus fine; (b) same, re: causing/permitting child to participate or engage in any act that depicts, describes, or represents sexual conduct for the purpose of representation or reproduction in any visual material, or to engage in any live performance involving sexual conduct;

C v Bean 435 M 708 (2002)—required finding of not guilty ordered on "lascivious intent" by aspiring photographer who was exceptionally above-board & open, asking minor's mother for permission & at minor's request, picking up her boyfriend to accompany them to photo-shoot; listing of "factors" relevant to D's state of mind, citing *US v Dost* **636 F.Supp 828, 832 (S.D. Cal. '86)**; these photos alone don't show sufficient evidence of required intent;

G.L. c. 272, § 29B—dissemination of material depicting sexual conduct by children (a) with lascivious intent, disseminates or possesses with intent to disseminate any visual material that contains a representation or reproduction of any posture or exhibition in a state of nudity involving the use of a child who is under eighteen years of age; (b) same, re depiction or description or representation of sexual conduct participated or engaged in by a child who is under eighteen years of age;

C v Perry 438 M 282 (2002)—"visual material" in child pornography statute, G.L. c. 272, § 31) encompasses computer images IF actual children were used in underlying photograph/digital image; if instead images were "virtual" children, & not pictures of real people, state can't prohibit unless "obscene" (*Attorney General v Free Speech Coalition* 535 U.S. 234 (2002));

District Court .Model Jury Instruction #5.64;

Miller v California **413 US 15 (73)**—(1) appeal to prurient interest; (2) patently offensive; (3) no serious literary, artistic, political, scientific value . . .

Pope v Illinois **481 US 497 (87)**—community standards to judge #1, 2, but not #3;

C v Sullivan **55 MAC 775 (2002)**—facts that judge at bench trial didn't live in Hampden County and that no evidence of Hampden County standards was introduced didn't matter: "beneath county variations . . . lies a baseline", and appellate court claimed "no reasonable & disinterested observer anywhere in the Commonwealth would think [the material] suitable for display to children";

C v Lotten Books **12 MAC 625 (81)**—"possession" & "dissemination";

C v Thureson **371 M 387 (76)**—no knowledge;

C v Kocinski **11 MAC 120 (81)**—knowledge of obscene dancers;

C v Rosenberg **379 M 334 (79)**—no knowledge; *(See Chapter 16, Defenses: Intent)*;

C v United Books **389 M 888 (83)**—not vague; knowledge = items, not "obscene";

C v Oakes **401 M 602 (88)**—kiddy porn law's too broad; see '88 amendment);

C v O'Keefe **48 MAC 566 (2000)**—dissemination of "printed material" harmful to minors (G.L. c. 272, § 28) doesn't include hand-written sexually explicit notes left inside a book in classroom desk of 5th grade student;

C v Dane #2 **389 M 917 (83)**—expert/non-expert evidence *(See Chapter 11-I, Evidence, Opinions of Experts & Laypersons)*;

C v Dane #1 **397 M 197 (86)**—"context" pertinent re: patently offensive;

C v Dane #2 **397 M 201 (86)**—D's witness not "expert" on community standards;

Reno v ACLU **521 US 844 (97)**—"Communications Decency Act of 1996," seeking to protect minors from "harmful" internet material, held facially overbroad and violative of First Amendment in part; other part saved by striking words "or indecent" from provision prohibiting knowing transmissions of 'obscene or indecent' messages to any recipient under age 18;

21-HH. THREATS

G.L. c. 275, §§ 1–6—"Proceedings to Prevent Crime";

G.L. c. 275, §§ 2–3—no complaint for threats to commit crime is to issue without examination of complainant under oath;

C v Powers 73 MAC 186 (2008)—the "threats" statute, G.L. c. 275, § 4, permitting up to six months' imprisonment or, "instead of imposing sentence" allowing a "recognizance with sufficient sureties . . . for [a] term, not exceeding six months," did not mean that judge could not order D, convicted of threats, to a five-year term of probation; G.L. c. 276, § 87 allows probation, and provides

more protection of public "than a mere bond requiring a D to keep the peace"; probation statute supplements rather than conflicts with 'threats' statute;

C v Jacobsen 419 M 269 (95)—violation of G.L. c. 275, §§ 2–3 (warrantless arrest of D & no record evidence that complainant was placed in fear of imminent serious physical harm) did not warrant dismissal, but instead suppression of any evidence gained as fruit of seizure of D;

C v Chalifoux **362 M 811 (73)**—need apparent ability by D & justified fear by complaining witness (citing *Robinson v Bradley* **300 F.Supp 665 (D.Mass. 69)**);

C v Haggins **38 MAC 976 (95)**—same;

C v Elliffe **47 MAC 580 (99)**—enough for G of threat despite NG of assault and battery; even if verdicts were inconsistent factually, D not entitled to relief from a conviction;

C v Gillis **358 M 215 (70)**—spousal threat not privileged by G.L. c. 233, § 20;

C v Ditsch **19 MAC 1005 (85)**—prisoner's letter conveyed apparent ability;

C v Strahan **39 MAC 928 (95)**—environmental activist with history of picketing & protesting at Aquarium told ship worker that he was "assessing the enemy" and was "looking for . . . a place to put a hole in the boat" and D wearing knapsack & worker knew hull was only 1/8–1/16 inches thick below water line = sufficient for G of G.L. c. 275, § 2;

C v Meier **56 MAC 278 (2002)**—essential to prove that D intended threat to be communicated to victim; purportedly "conditional" nature of threat doesn't matter here;

C v Furst **56 MAC 283 (2002)**—since it couldn't reasonably be inferred that D intended info to be conveyed to victim, her communication with person whose help she sought in killing victim wasn't legitimate basis for "threats" conviction; *C v James* **73 MAC 383 (2008)**—similar; inmate's letter to fellow inmate soliciting him to kill inmate's allegedly unfaithful girlfriend, rejecting prosecution argument that D must have intended killer to inform victim that killing was retribution on behalf of D;

C v Troy T. **54 MAC 520 (2002)**—if a "threat" may be communicated by a third party to D's intended victim, Commonwealth must prove that D "intended to communicate the threat to the third party who acts as an intermediary," but "burden will be an onerous one where the third party intermediary is also an eavesdropper"; comment that "the dumb blondes have to go, too" insufficient in these circumstances as an expression of intent to inflict injury;

C v Maiden **61 MAC 433 (2004)**—instruction in *Troy T.* could've misled jury given evidence that D intended that victim herself hear the threat by D; not necessary to prove that D intended that nearby detective tell victim, who though nearby, hadn't heard; actual receipt of threat directly from D to V isn't necessary element;

C v Simmons **69 MAC 348 (2007)**—during "therapy" session ordered as part of probation (following committed sentence for domestic abuse of former girlfriend) D stated he was going to "kill" victim and her present boyfriend, and therapist could "write that down"; therapist had told D at outset that there was no confidentiality if D gave info about harming himself or wanting to harm or kill anyone else; probation revocation for "threats" upheld; evidence warranted finding by "preponderance" that D intended his threats to reach the targeted persons;

C v Hokanson **74 MAC 403 (2009)**—witness sitting inside police station testified that D entered, sat next to him, and made reference to things "having been different" under a former police chief, subsequently becoming "volcanic", and "terribly angry about something", and then whispering to witness while simulating pointing a gun, "next time I come in here, boom, boom, boom. . . . Nobody will be standing": sufficient for G of 'threat' because D "should reasonably have expected that a stranger who saw him [pantomime and speak as he did] would communicate that threat to the officers," i.e., D had "no expectation of silence on [witness's] part"; lack of attempt at concealment refutes suggestion that D was just "confiding" in witness;

C v Hughes **59 MAC 280 (2003)**—threat by speech conducted by mail or use of a telephone while subject to a domestic abuse restraining order (G.L. c. 265, § 43(a)): citing *Troy T.* **54 MAC 520**, element is that D must have intended that the threat be conveyed to the person protected by restraining order, whether or not it was so conveyed; D may be criminally responsible for threat which fails to reach intended victim;

C v Kerns **449 M 641 (2007)**—construing G.L. c. 269, § 14(b)(1) (criminalizing communication of any threat that a deadly device, substance or item is or will be present or used at specified place/location) and holding that communication of the threat to an intended victim is NOT required for conviction; judge's intent to instruct himself according to general "threat" statute, G.L. c. 275, § 2 = error; but REJECTS invitation to read "communication" element to include even words exchanged between coconspirators or coventurers, as to do so would render required element of communication "essentially meaningless"; as joint venturers allegedly conveyed the plan to at least two people outside the core group, evidence sufficient to withstand motion for required finding of not guilty;

C v Milo M. **433 M 149 (2001)**—12-year-old child's drawing depicting person labeled as the child holding gun to head of figure labeled as teacher, who was saying 'please don't kill me,' with 3d figure whose head wasn't attached to body in background, and 'blood' noted under feet = enough for G of threat under G.L. c. 275, § 2; apparent inability to carry out threat immediately (child was at desk in hallway awaiting arrival of principal) brushed off with assertion that child was later loitering around teacher's car;

C v Sholley **432 M 721 (2000)**—affirming "threats" portion of *C v Sholley* **48 MAC 495 (2000)** G for threatening prosecutor ("intention to bully" inferable from D's past history, his presence in courtroom, his menacing gesture; words alone ("watch out counselor") insufficient as "threat to commit" particular crime; proof requires expression of intent to inflict evil, injury, or damage, made in circumstances "that would reasonably justify apprehension on the part of an ordinary person";

C v Daly **12 MAC 338 (81)**—complaining witness need not sign complaint;

District Court Model Jury Instruction #5.03—reasonable fear D had intention/ability; supplemental instruction that it's not required that alleged victim actually became apprehensive, BUT it's probative of whether D made alleged threat under circumstances which could reasonably have cause a victim to fear that D had intention & ability to carry out threat; cf. G.L. c. 269, § 14A - annoying telephone calls (see District Court Model Jury Instruction #5.70);

21-II. NON-SUPPORT (G.L. C. 273, §§ 1–10, 15A)

See also Illegitimacy, post, at JJ

See Chapter 14, Probation, Suspended Sentence, & Hearing on Violating Terms of Probation, Dispositions;

G.L. c. 273, § 12A—BLOOD TEST to exclude PATERNITY;

State v Akers **287 S.W.2d. 370 (Mo.App. 1956)**—theoretical underpinnings;

C v Zarrilli **5 MAC 518 (77)**—reasonable" support to wife & minors;

C v Hall **322 M 523 (48)**—capacity and means;

C v Whiston **306 M 65 (40)**—withdrawal = unreasonable;

C v Hussey **14 MAC 1015 (82)**—evidence;

Silvia v Silvia **9 MAC 339 (80)**—both parties obligated;

C v Teixera **396 M 746 (86)**—no evidence on willfulness; Model Jury Instruction flawed; must have ability to support;

21-JJ. ILLEGITIMACY (G.L. C. 272, §§ 11–18)

C v Kennedy **389 M 308 (83)**—§ 12 civil; § 15 criminal; inherited features & characteristics, & offer money for abortion, to infer paternity;

C v MacKenzie **368 M 613 (75)**—non-criminal approach;

C v Fanciullo **11 MAC 64 (80)**—need paternity conviction for § 15; § 12 has effectively replaced § 11;

C v Lobo **385 M 436 (82)**—§ 12 proceeding = civil, "quasi-criminal";

C v Dias **385 M 455 (82)**—no double jeopardy re: § 12;

C v Chase **385 M 461 (82)**—need reason to know of fatherhood;

C v Teixera **396 M 746 (86)**—must have ability to support;

C v Gruttner **385 M 474 (82)**—no statute of limitations as to paternity finding; six years for non-support;

C v Galvin **388 M 326 (83)**—paternity = non-criminal; not lesser included offense of non-support;

C v Blazo **10 MAC 324 (80)**—blood tests for all (see G.L. c. 273, § 12A);

C v Stappen **336 M 174 (57)**—blood test to exclude D;

C v Possehl **355 M 575 (69)**—blood test for indigent; *(See Chapter 7-C, Money for Expert & Other Expenses)*;

C v Beausoleil **397 M 206 (86)**—HLA = tissue, not blood, test; maybe admissible re: paternity *(See Chapter 11-I, Opinions)*;

C v D'Avella **339 M 642 (59)**—blood test;

Sullivan v C **383 M 410 (81)**—no jeopardy under §·11;

Fuller v C **394 M 1014 (85)**—§ 15 (non-paternity) finding = double jeopardy;

C v Juvenile **387 M 678 (82)**—juvenile defendant;

21-KK. MUNICIPAL ORDINANCES—PUBLIC DRINKING; LOITERING; ETC.

G.L. c. 40, § 21—enabling law for local ordinances & bylaws;

Powell v Tex **392 US 514 (68)**—can punish alcoholic for drunk in public;

C v Lammi **386 M 299 (82)**—"open container" laws = constitutional;

C v Casey **42 MAC 512 (97)**—sufficient for G of open container: ½ - empty bottle of Sambuca, **capped**, inside insulated bag found between front bucket seats of car;

C v Williams **395 M 302 (85)**—loitering = unconstitutionally vague;

C v Weston W. **455 M 24 (2009)**—Declaration of Rights protects "a fundamental right of free movement,"

and criminal processes and punishments in Lowell's "Youth Protection Curfew for Minors" held not to be least restrictive means of accomplishing ordinance's purposes, and not sufficiently tailored to survive "strict scrutiny" standard; civil enforcement provisions held OK;

G.L. c. 272, § 59—can arrest without warrant;

G.L. c. 233, § 75—PROOF = by attested copy of ordinance . . .

C v Einarson **6 MAC 835 (78)**— . . . not judicially-noticeable;

C v Perretti **20 MAC 36 (85)**—(same); must put it into evidence;

21-LL. PERJURY

Superior Court Criminal Practice Jury Instructions § 2.48;

District Court Model Jury Instruction #5.65

C v Kelley **33 MAC 934 (92)**—D's false grand jury testimony that he paid $15,000 for a car instead of $20,000 was not material & thus not perjury;

C v D'Amour **428 M 725, 743–44 (99)**—materiality shown because false statement had a "reasonable and natural tendency to" influence the pertinent determination; fact that prosecutor was not misled because he knew D was lying (because he had proof of it in undisclosed telephone wiretap) = irrelevant;

C v White **70 MAC 71 (2007)**—at trial for rape, D assailed complainant-wife's credibility, saying that she fabricated charges to avoid repayment of $20,000 loan, proffering a copy of the check which had "loan" written in memo line; after acquittal, wife obtained from her bank copies of the check and showed DA that the "loan" notation had been written by D AFTER wife had received check and after its processing by bank, contrary to D's testimony; subsequent perjury conviction upheld, appellate court finding that the false testimony about the "loan" notation was material, as it bore on the wife's credibility, "central to a rape trial devoid of physical evidence of the crimes"; Appeals Court rejects argument that "materiality" element of crime of perjury "should be withdrawn from the jury", distinguishing *C v Mitchell* 15 MAC at 581;

C v Silva **401 M 318 (87)**—alters rule that perjury must be proved by either direct testimony of two witnesses or one witness plus independent evidence of strong corroborating circumstances: conviction OK with "highly reliable" evidence of "direct or clear & compelling character" & "objectively inconsistent with innocence of" D; policy = prevent conviction of perjury when there's only word of one witness against D;

C v Knowlton **50 MAC 266 (2000)**—testimony of two witnesses plus telephone records and circumstantial evidence satisfied Silva standard;

C v Kelly **69 MAC 751 (2007)**—prosecution for making false written report under penalty of perjury to police officer about theft of vehicle (G.L. c. 268, § 39): D signed blank form when cop told her he'd complete it later in accord with her oral statement, and thereafter argued unsuccessfully that her signature alone wasn't "false written report": evidence was that D repeatedly orally pursued the false charges of motor vehicle theft (she had given permission for its use) despite opportunities to withdraw them, and her signature was immediately below notice that statements made were punishable under penalty of perjury; alternate statute (G.L. c. 269, § 13A) criminalizes knowingly making false report of crime, but its penalty is much less;

21-MM. GAMBLING (G.L. C. 271, § 5A)

C v Frate **405 M 52 (89)**—gambling device must have drum or reel;

21-NN. ANNOYING TELEPHONE CALLS (G.L. C. 269, § 14A)

District Court Model Jury Instruction #5.70;

C v Wotan **422 M 740 (96)**—"repeatedly" means at least three times; when complaint specified two particular traceable calls, additional alleged calls could not be used "to prove an element of the crime charged"

C v Strahan **30 MAC 947 (91)**—required finding entered because D's harassment of "ex" not "sole" purpose for his 11 phone calls in 7 minutes;

C v Roberts **442 M 1034 (2004)**—that some statements during calls were "at least superficially phrased as concern for the daughter and her children" didn't make it impermissible for jury to infer that actual sole purpose of calls was to annoy/harass [so failure to move for required finding of NG wasn't ineffective assistance of counsel];

C v Richards **426 M 689 (98)**—statute doesn't cover FAX transmissions;

21-OO. INTIMIDATING A WITNESS OR JUROR OR JUDGE (G.L. C. 268, § 13B)

District Court Model Jury Instruction #5.66; as of 3/3/2006, statute G.L. c. 268, § 13B, specifically addresses conduct that "threatens, or attempts or causes . . . emotional injury";

C v Potter **39 MAC 924 (95)**—after stalking prosecution is brought, further similar behavior can support complaint for witness intimidation;

C v Conley **34 MAC 50 (93)**—reversal because intimidation defined as "attempt to influence," and definition **should** have required proof also of intimidation, force, or threat of force in such attempt;

C V Gallant **453 M 535 (2009)**—concerning threats toward and intimidation of judge with intent to impede, etc. "with a criminal investigation, grand jury proceeding, trial or other criminal proceeding of any type," statute did not apply when judge was in Juvenile Court conducting care and protection proceeding, CIVIL in nature: dismissal of complaint upheld;

C v King **69 MAC 113 (2007)**—D's statement to store clerk after robbery that "if he saw [victim] on 22 News he was going to come back" & kill V and V's family = sufficient for conviction, notwithstanding D's arguments that threat only concerned V's going to "news media," rather than police, and that V wasn't, at the time, "presently" engaged in furnishing info to criminal investigator;

C v Cruz **442 M 299 (2004)**—rejecting defendant's argument that plea agreement with D's alleged coventurer is an "interference" with a witness (in violation of G.L. c. 268, § 13B), which makes coventurer's testimony "irretrievably unreliable" and thus excludable;

C v Burt **40 MAC 275 (96)**—only need be shown that target possibly will be called to testify at any "official proceeding"; target need not have 'direct knowledge' of charges against D (here, target was mother of D's dissatisfied customer);

C v Wiencis **48 MAC 688 (2000)**—irrelevant that D was found NG of criminal charge for which witnesses were present to testify at time of intimidation;

C v Gordon **44 MAC 233 (98)**—juror intimidation does not require that V fearful of actual harm, but instead is making person fearful, for purpose of compelling or deterring conduct; sufficient that D stood "inches" from juror, commented on her youth & that she was juror in his son's murder trial, asked her place of residence & whether she had boyfriend, & suggested she see a particular (very violent) film; "reasonable woman in her situation would have been intimidated";

C v Casiano **70 MAC 705 (2007)**—D's pointing cellular telephone camera at undercover cop waiting to testify against D, accompanied by statement implying that he would disseminate cop's likeness over internet = sufficient for G of witness intimidation (despite fact that no photos were found, and no verification that phone was capable of connecting to internet); attempt at intimidation needn't be successful;

C v Belle Isle **44 MAC 226 (98)**—witness intimidation covers D's conduct in severing phone cord when V's wife was attempting to telephone police to report D's beating of her husband: not necessary that criminal proceeding be "ongoing" at time of intimidation;

C v Drumgoole **49 MAC 87, 92 (2000)**—required finding of NG when witness was not present for language (outside restaurant, to friend of witness) which would have connected a physical act (bumping in a crowded restaurant) with witness's role as a potential witness; no required

finding of NG just because alleged intimidations occurred two months before trial, didn't occur at courthouse, and were arguably just ventings of "angry man, apparently goaded by two seeming taunters" (one of whom was ex-husband of D's wife) without intent to influence taunters in their role as witnesses;

C v McCreary **45 MAC 797 (98)**—no required finding of NG despite fact that D's speech and conduct not so "obviously related to (cop-alleged victim's) functioning as a witness"; place, time, and circumstances made it possible for jury to find that purpose was to influence cop's conduct as witness;

C v Cathy C. **64 MAC 471 (2005)**—intimidation of witness (G.L. c. 268, § 13B) established by D's threats to victim/witness at trial, in court after verdict had been announced but before any postconviction motions had been heard and before conviction had been reduced to final judgment, despite D's argument that evidence showed conduct only AFTER the criminal proceeding: trial doesn't end when verdict is announced; element of "intent to influence" witness doesn't mean only attempting to influence substance of testimony; any "acts of intimidation" "directly related to a victim's role as juror or witness" are within statute's purpose of preventing interference with administration of justice;

C v Robinson **444 M 102, 109 (2005)**—D's acting aggressively and glaring at victim at show cause hearing, & asking him "in a bloodcurdling way, 'are you sure you want to go on with this?' = enough for G; D's photographing V's family later that day = sufficient for finding intimidation with intent to influence testimony;

C v Triplett **426 M 26, 29 n.6 (97)**—leaving open the argument that passage of § 13B eliminated common law crime of obstruction of justice; requiring, for proof of the latter, existence of judicial proceeding;

C v Belete **37 MAC 424 (94)**—D's requests to (including attempted bribes of) a court appointed interpreter for D's Ethiopian dialect, that interpreter **not** appear at court on continuance dates did not constitute intimidation of/interference with "witness": required finding of NG should have been entered;

21-PP. VIOLATION OF PROTECTIVE ORDER (G.L. C. 209A, § 5)

District Court Model Jury Instruction #5.61;

G.L. c. 151A—(amendments approved 8/2001)—persons who 'lose their jobs' due to domestic violence against themselves or their dependent child(ren) are eligible for unemployment benefits;

Sorgman v Sorgman **49 MAC 416 (2000)**—209A order could be obtained by D's ex-stepdaughter (parsing G.L. c. 209A, § 3's definition of "family or household members", i.e., "are or were residing together in same household," "are or were related by blood or marriage"),

though D's marriage to woman's mother ended over twenty years earlier;

C v Delaney **425 M 587 (97)**—failure of service of order no bar to conviction because service of temporary order constituted constructive notice that it would be extended at designated hearing if D failed to appear (G.L. c. 209A, § 4); *C v Kulesa* **455 M 447 (2009)**—same; no error in judge's refusal to instruct that Commonwealth had to prove D had knowledge that 209A order had been extended and had knowledge of terms of extended order: D cannot escape being charged with knowledge that order was extended and its terms "merely because he failed to attend the hearing on the extension of the order";

C v Mendonca **50 MAC 684 (2001)**—return of service = "strong evidence" of D's knowledge of order, but even if no service, ample other evidence of D's knowledge of order; prosecution for violating terms relied on 'no contact' portion of order, and lack of abuse or fear irrelevant (D telephoned frequently from Bridgewater State Hospital, where confined);

C v Welch **58 MAC 408 (2003)**—conviction under c. 209A reversed: no evidence that the ex parte order was ever served on D in any manner (so no proof of notice, opportunity to be heard, or knowledge of the proscribed conduct);

C v Molloy **44 MAC 306 (98)**—**Delaney** distinguished: actual notice of **annual** extension required for conviction, but need not prove service of extension order if D's knowledge of its terms may be otherwise shown;

C v Munafo **45 MAC 597 (98)**—though G.L. c. 209A, § 7 requires that copy of underlying complaint be served upon D along with the temporary restraining order BUT no relief because no prejudice (but see *Zullo v Goguen* **423 M 679 (96)**);

C v Crimmins **46 MAC 489 (99)**—upholding inference that annual extension was served upon D despite absence on "service" form of a check mark in any of the available boxes describing permissible service (albeit with an officer's written assertion on form that she made service of the order on particular date at particular time); cogent dissent by Warner, C.J.;

Crenshaw v Macklin **430 M 633 (2000)**—though initial G.L. c. 209A order can't be entered for period longer than one year, after expiration of initial order, judge has discretion (under G.L. c. 209A, § 3) to make order permanent and needn't limit to specific period;

C v Delaney **425 M 587 (97)**—listing what violations of G.L. c. 209A order may be punished pursuant to id., § 7, & what punishable instead as criminal contempt; to prove criminal contempt, must show, beyond a reasonable doubt, (1) there is clear, outstanding order of court, (2) D knew of order, & (3) D clearly & intentionally disobeyed order in circumstances in which he was able to obey it; to prove "statutory offense", **i.e.** criminal violation of c. 209A, Commonwealth need prove "no more knowledge than that D knew of order";

Edge v Commonwealth **451 M 74 (2008)**—after D pled guilty to violating abuse prevention order issued pursuant to G.L. c. 209A (id. § 7),and was sentenced, indictment later for crime of stalking "in violation of the same 209A order (G.L. c. 265, § 43(b)) was ordered dismissed; reported question, "whether a prosecution under § 43(b) implicates double jeopardy concerns if the Commonwealth relies on conduct previously the subject of [D]'s convictions of violating the 209A order," is answered "yes";

C v Finase **435 M 310 (2001)**—violation of "stay at least 100 yards away" provision of abuse prevention order could be prosecuted under G.L. c. 209A, § 7 because it is a violation of 'no contact,' enumerated in § 7; "no contact" order includes a "stay away" order; see also *C v Kendrick* **446 M 72 (2006)** (condition of probation was to stay away from children under age 16, but D placed himself in parking lot of candy store "by deliberate design," participating in "car show" with his dog);

C v Stoltz **73 MAC 642 (2009)**—woman went to restaurant, seated 'self and ordered food, and subsequently saw D (seated at bar, staring at her): parties agreed that their simultaneous presence was completely coincidental; nonetheless, sufficient for conviction of violating "you are ordered not to contact . . . and to stay at least 50 yards from" plaintiff even if the plaintiff seems to allow or request contact" if D either failed to remove himself reasonably promptly or if he followed her outside restaurant (after she was outside, in car, awaiting police, she saw D outside smoking cigarette); reversal because jury not properly instructed that Commonwealth was required to prove beyond reasonable doubt that D failed to make reasonable efforts to terminate accidental encounter; cite to *Kendrick* 446 M at 76.

C v O'Shea **41 MAC 115 (96)**—required finding of NG for D re: violating terms of protective order by which he was to stay at least 100 yards away from woman and stay away from her workplace (within 100 yards); she was not at work at the time and D would have been able to see that her car was not in lot; being in "vicinity" of workplace not a violation of order;

C v Basile **47 MAC 918 (99)**—not reaching argument that order to "stay away from" ex-girlfriend's stated address violated due process/was insufficiently precise, because special verdict also found that D violated "no contact" provision (jury didn't have to believe, and did not believe, D's version of events);

C v Picariello **40 MAC 902 (96)**—admission of evidence of D's misdeeds which caused issuance of protective order required reversal (sole issue at trial was whether D came to complainant's house at time D claimed to have been elsewhere);

C v Kirk **39 MAC 225 (95)**—woman's 209A affidavit, admitted to establish ID of battering boyfriend, = inadmissible hearsay and required finding of not guilty ordered (woman did not testify, and her statements to passing motorist, while admissible as spontaneous utterances, failed to establish identity of culprit); cop's testimony that he served D = indirect hearsay (i.e., so someone had to have told him that D was the culprit), insufficient to establish critical element;

C v Johnson **45 MAC 473 (98)**—amended 209A order, obtained after alleged violation of 209A order for which D was on trial, wasn't relevant & shouldn't have been admitted; jury instructions including all three definitions of "abuse" within statute shouldn't have been given because two weren't relevant to case; jury instruction that D could be convicted upon proof of "abusing" the complainant "and/or by contacting her" caused reversal because the relevant 209A order did not prohibit contact;

C v Rauseo **50 MAC 699 (2001)**—when protective orders (& modifications thereto) against D were issued or addressed in both a "209A action" and the docketed divorce case in probate/family court, the orders entered in the 209A case control over inconsistent orders for custody or visitation entered in the other proceeding; restraining orders & amendments thereto MUST BE MADE IN WRITING (& oral modifications are illegitimate) because they must be transmitted in written form to law enforcement agencies and to D; "to supersede the protective provisions of another court's 209A order, the Probate Court must modify that other court's abuse prevention order by entering the modification on the 209A form of order";

C v Robicheau **421 M 176 (95)**—rejecting D's argument that First Amendment prohibited his liability for violating protective order by placing V "in reasonable apprehension of imminent serious physical harm";

C v Thompson **45 MAC 523 (98)**—D's argument that abuse prevention order violated his First Amendment rights rejected, citing *Roberts v US Jaycees* **468 US 609, 628 (84)**; D had sent three letters to the 209A complainant on 3 successive days;

Mahoney v Commonwealth **415 M 278 (93)**—when D, against whom were lodged protective orders concerning both his wife and girlfriend, was charged with violating protective order & making threats vs. girlfriend and with A&B on wife, judge at arraignment held D in "civil contempt" re: protective orders & jailed him for 30 days; SJC rejected argument that double jeopardy barred subsequent criminal prosecutions;

See also Chapter 19, Double Jeopardy;

C v Collier **427 M 385 (98)**—D was in car being driven by his son at time victim was nearly run down; Commonwealth had to prove beyond reasonable doubt that the violation of the protective order "was an intentional act by the defendant";

C v McKay **67 MAC 396 (2006)**—reversal for refusal to instruct on "accident" in violating protective order: selected from cell phone list of contacts, while driving, "Cindy" rather than "Cindy B";

C v Kendrick **63 MAC 142 and** *C v Wilcox* **63 MAC 131, FURTHER APPELLATE REVIEW ALLOWED 444 M 1103 (2005)**—special condition of probation, that D have "no unsupervised contact with anyone under the age of 16," was violated if D, "by deliberate design, intentionally and inconsistently with the probationary restriction, positions and interposes himself in a place wherein [he] knew or reasonably should have known that a protected person would be present, and nonetheless proceeds intentionally to position himself in that critical space in close proximity to a protected class. . . ."; Wilcox purportedly drove car very close to girls walking home from school or a store, "with a persistence that bordered on stalking," & Kendrick placed himself at "car show" held in local candy store parking lot and remained in close proximity to children present there; that D doesn't speak to or have physical interaction with any child doesn't matter;

Kendrick **446 M 72 (2006): SJC agrees, affirming revocations; as to** *Wilcox***, 446 M 61 (2006), SJC finds evidence sufficient for revocation, AND holds that** *Crawford v Washington* **confrontation right doesn't apply to probation revocation proceedings;**

C v Habenstreit **57 MAC 785 (2003)**—that D's ex-girlfriend was home, sick, when D came by her workplace and, from his vehicle, and shouted obscenities and threats to new boyfriend, didn't matter; stay-away-from-workplace order wasn't conditioned on ex's presence there;

C v Raymond **54 MAC 488 (2002)**—if D didn't know that his wife was in a condemned house which he owned with his mother and in which his mother resided, he should not have been convicted of violating a 'no contact' order when he went there to get clean clothes and begin emptying the house of its contents as necessitated by the condemnation order; if contact = either incidental to permitted activity or an accidental or unknowing violation, NG; jury instructions failed to convey this, so reversal;

C v Silva **431 M 194 (2000)**—though D entitled under terms of order to telephone residence to speak with kids and thus "inevitably" would have contact with wife-subject of protective order (& no "G" possible if he spoke only briefly & nonabusively), SJC rejected required finding of NG argument: D was "verbally abusive" to the wife and shouldn't have been (despite her alleged refusal to let him speak with daughter); Commonwealth not required to prove that D had "unlawful purpose" when placing the calls;

C v Leger **52 MAC 232 (2001)**—even if contact is initiated by a D subject to a c. 209A order, NG if not threatening or uncivil & it's incidental to D's right to speak to his children;

C v Consoli **58 MAC 734 (2003)**—while polite response to son's unsolicited greeting wouldn't have violated 209A "no contact" order, additional profanity-laden comment heard by wife was enough for violation, regardless of D's testimony that this comment about wife was made not to wife but to D's passenger;

C v Stewart **52 MAC 755 (2001)**—no required finding of NG for "technical violation" of 209A order when D escorted six-year-old son into building foyer after permissible visitation with son; order said D was to remain in his vehicle at all times during visitation pick up and drop off, but older child hadn't accompanied younger one, as normally occurred, because of illness this day;

C v Silva **431 M 401 (2000)**—to establish violation of G.L. c. 209A, § 7, Commonwealth must prove (1) valid order was in effect on date of alleged violation, (2) D violated the order, & (3) D had knowledge of the order; though element (3) would have failed without hearsay evidence (cop testified that he served temporary order, etc. by leaving them with woman who said she'd give them to D & that D was already aware of the order), SJC refused to find ineffective assistance of counsel in counsel's failure to object or to have such evidence excluded or limited; alternative trial "strategy" held reasonable (but see dissent by Lynch, J.); defense was that complainant, not D, caused violation of the 209A order by seeking contact with D (but order "plainly state(d) that . . . complainant's allowance of or request for contact does not relieve" D of obligation to comply with 'no contact' provision, id. at 408); majority said that defense was recognized/accepted in jury instructions, although creatively used italics to make such implication;

C v Fortier **56 MAC 116 (200)**—though c. 209A, § 1(a) definition of "abuse" includes "attempting to cause . . . physical harm," ERROR in defining such attempt as "to make an effort to do something"; though D asked schoolmate to beat up the 209A complainant, "attempt" proof must include overt act towards the commission of the physical harm, and overt act had to be some undertaking that could reasonably be expected to cause physical harm; D's statement, even when coupled with go-between's telling complainant of it, was insufficient to satisfy "proximate execution" requirement for legal attempt (particularly because schoolmate refused D's request);

C v Hughes **59 MAC 280 (2003)**—threat by speech conducted by mail or use of a telephone while subject to a domestic abuse restraining order (G.L. c. 265, § 43(a)): citing *Troy T.* 54 MAC 520, element is that D must have intended that the threat be conveyed to the person protected by restraining order, whether or not it was so conveyed;

Chapter 22
JURIES: SELECTION, DELIBERATIONS, DISCHARGE, VERDICTS

22-A. RIGHT TO JURY TRIAL

U.S. Constitution, Sixth & Fourteenth Amendments & Article 3, § 2, cl. 3—federal constitutional right to trial by impartial jury;

***Duncan v Louisiana* 391 US 145 (68)**—Sixth & Fourteenth Amendment right to jury trial for all "serious" crimes applicable to states; history & purposes of jury trials discussed;

Mass. Constitution, Declaration of Rights, Article 12—right to judgment of peers & to jury trial;

***Opinion of Justices* 375 M 795 (78)**—Article 12 guarantees right to jury trial in all criminal cases; offenses with "petty" civil penalty of less than $1000 don't require trial by jury; but see ***Baldwin v NY* 399 US 66 (70)**—federal constitutional right to jury trial applies to all non-"petty" crimes subjecting D to over 6 months' incarceration;

***Opinion of Justices* 360 M 877 (71)**—6-person juries in District Court meet state constitutional requirements;

***C v Nicoll* 452 M 816 (2008)**—surveys US Supreme Court's decisions re: jury size and Constitution (six jurors OK; statute requiring misdemeanor criminal cases be tried by jury of only five not OK; conviction by five out of six not OK); SJC rejects Commonwealth argument that 5-person jury trial would be a "nullity" (D could have waived right to six, so mistrial was not manifestly necessary); ***C v Dery* 452 M 823 (2008)**—trial before five jurors after D's informed waiver of right to six (resulting in NG verdict) was not a nullity, despite Commonwealth's post-verdict claim;

***C v Francis* 450 M 132 (2007)**—there is no constitutional right NOT to be tried by jury; G.L. c. 263, § 6 legitimately bars D from waiving jury trial in "capital" case (first degree murder is capital case, even without death penalty here);

***C v Dresser* 71 MAC 454 (2008)**—"sexually dangerous persons" trials = civil, not criminal, so right to jury trial is by statute, not required by Constitution; though better practice would be to have both a recorded waiver colloquy with D and a written waiver, record indicated D was aware trial would be jury-waived (and court didn't require more);

See Chapter 12-D, Judge Questions Witnesses, Overbearing Judge;

G.L. c. 231, § 81—judge shall not charge on matters of fact (usurpation of jury function);

***C v Senbatu* 38 MAC 904 (95)**—in drug trafficking case judge told D-counsel, in jury's presence, that no evidence D was user; this was "close to . . . interference with jury's fact-finding function";

***Apprendi v New Jersey* 530 US 466 (2000)**—any fact other than a prior conviction which is necessary to support a sentence exceeding the maximum authorized by facts established by a guilty plea or a jury verdict must be admitted by D OR PROVED TO A JURY BEYOND A REASONABLE DOUBT; ***US v Booker* 125 S.Ct. 738 (2005)**—6th Amendment protects D's right to have jury rather than judge find existence of any particular fact that law makes essential to his punishment;

***US v Booker* 125 S.Ct. 738 (2005)**—US Sentencing Guidelines (18 U.S.C. §§ 3553(b)(1) & 3742(e)) are unconstitutional, violative of the Sixth Amendment right to jury trial: judges are required to "take Guidelines into account," but are not bound to apply them;

***Shepard v US* 125 US 1254 (2005)**—**is "prior conviction" exception to Apprendi "eroded by this Court's subsequent Sixth Amendment jurisprudence"?; Thomas, J., says Almendarez-Torres 523 US 224 (98) was wrongly decided; possible limitations on prior convictions as enhancers;**

***Blakely v Washington* 124 S. Ct. 2531 (2004)**—reversing enhanced sentence imposed by JUDGE on basis of HIS finding that crime was committed with "deliberate cruelty," a statutory ground for upward departure;

***Oregon v Ice* 129 S Ct 711 (2009)**—Sixth Amendment doesn't prevent states from assigning to judges rather than juries the fact finding necessary to imposition of consecutive rather than concurrent sentences for multiple offenses, Court refusing to "extend" Apprendi/Blakely;

***Washington v Recuenco* 548 US 212 (2006)**—when, at sentencing for jury conviction of "assault with deadly weapon", judge on basis of his own fact-finding imposed three-year sentence enhancement on ground that firearm was used, this was a violation of *Blakely*, but S. Ct. holds that *Blakely* error can be, and is here, harmless (the only weapon at issue here was a firearm); error not "structural";

***Cunningham v California* 127 S. Ct. 856 (2007)**—because, under California sentencing law, an "upper term sentence" may be imposed only when trial judge finds aggravating circumstance, and because an element of the charged offense doesn't qualify as such a circumstance but instead "aggravating" circumstances depend on facts found solely by judge, and by standard of only a preponderance, *Apprendi*'s bright line rule = violated;

***C v Pagan* 445 M 161 (2005)**—standard and burden of proof ambiguous as to imposition of lifetime community parole in some cases, and so unconstitutional as to those; complaint or indictment must allege that D is repeat offender (if such is essential to imposition of LCP given the crime charged); warning that Supreme Court case law (*Apprendi v NJ*, etc.) dictates that this enhanced sentence cannot be based on factual findings made by judge rather than jury;

M.R.Crim.P. 19—waiver of right to jury trial by D must be in writing; all co-D's must waive, unless judge severs; judge may refuse on record to allow D to waive jury;

C v Osborne **62 MAC 445 (2004)**—absence of signed written jury waiver couldn't be remedied by incomplete transcript of waiver colloquy supplemented by affidavit of judge re: "usual practice"; "Adequacy of the colloquy is . . . academic where no signed written waiver has been obtained"; <u>S.C.</u> **on further review, 445 M 776 (2006)**— "where the Legislature has clearly indicated that a defendant can waive his right to a jury trial only by signing a written waiver, and our prior decisions have recognized a 'bright line' rule regarding the requirements for an effective waiver, [D's] conviction must be reversed";

C v Mendonca **50 MAC 684, 689 (2001)**—particular omissions in jury waiver colloquy excused, given D's signing waiver form & counsel's affirmation that (s)he'd explained "paper work" 4 times to D (despite appellate counsel's claim (rejected given other facts here) that D's waiver invalid due to D's illiteracy, lack of education, psych. history, & poor English);

C v Kopsala **58 MAC 387 (2003)**—rejecting argument that jury waiver, because purportedly made in reliance upon allegedly exculpatory info in crime lab report [which, upon better scrutiny, would have been understood as a typographical error], was involuntary; purpose of mandated colloquy isn't to probe reasons why D made tactical decision to waive jury;

C v Berte **57 MAC 29 (2003)**—misadvice as to sentence, during jury waiver colloquy, doesn't invalidate D's jury waiver;

C v Eddington **71 MAC 138 (2008)**—jury waiver not illegitimately "induced" simply because D told judge that he wanted trial by judge because jurors would be prejudicially inflamed by photographs of victims' injuries; judge told D that he himself had seen photo evidence re: one victim (when presided at co-D's guilty plea) and would likely himself consider photos if D waived jury for trial; judge neither initiated nor encouraged D's jury waiver;

G.L. c. 263, § 6—waiver of jury trial must occur before jurors are empanelled & jury may not be waived unless all co-Ds agree;

C v Collado **426 M 675, 677 (98)**—simultaneous trial of 1 D by jury and 1 D jury-waived violated G.L. c. 263, § 6, but court found no prejudice to D and refused "remedy" of reversal;

C v Thomas **44 MAC 521, 527–28 (98)**—after close of evidence at jury trial, judge responded to D's offer of G plea on some charges by suggesting jury-waiver as to those counts; while this conversion to jury-waived trial violated G.L. c. 263, § 6, Court refused to redress/remedy by reversing conviction;

C v Lebon **37 MAC 705 (94)**—jury waiver involuntary when judge pledges committed sentence upon jury conviction but no commitment if G after jury-waived trial;

C v Towers **35 MAC 557 (93)**—waiver colloquy inadequate, despite affirmation that D discussed it with attorney, when only advice is that there's constitutional right to jury, jury would determine if G or NG & judge's only function, if G, would be to sentence;

Singer v US **380 US 24 (1965)**—no federal constitutional right to jury-waived trial;

C v Pavao **423 M 798 (96)**—absence of jury waiver colloquy (see *Ciummei v Commonwealth* 378 M 504, 509 [1979]) compelled reversal, despite D's signed waiver here & previous jury waivers: "bright line" rule, not subject to harmless error analysis; solemnity of written waiver and formality of colloquy further purpose of assuring that ultimate decision regarding jury waiver be left to D himself, not his attorney;

C v Dussault **71 MAC 542 (2008)**—absence of written waiver of D's right to jury trial (bifurcated proceeding, after OUI conviction by jury, on fact of prior convictions to support charge of operating under the influence, 3rd offense) resulted in vacating so much of judgment as found D guilty of OUI 3rd offense;

C v Hendricks **452 M 97 (2008)**—D executed written jury trial waiver form, which was also signed by D's attorney, who certified by the form that he had informed Hendricks of very specific incidents of the jury trial right and its difference from judge as trier of fact; judge's colloquy with D next occurred, but omitted in particular requirement of unanimity in jury trial: no relief, SJC holding that Ciummei did not prescribe "rigid list of questions" by judge for determination of wavier as "intelligent and voluntary";

C v Hardy **427 M 379, 384 (98)**—(reversing Appeals Court's finding of absence of showing of knowing/ intelligent jury waiver) despite deficiencies, jury-waiver colloquy adequate because D-counsel, as well as D, "signed a written waiver of jury trial," allowing judge to infer "that counsel and the defendant had discussed the waiver";

C v Onouha **46 MAC 904 (98)**—upholding jury waiver despite absence of inquiry re: any pressure to waive jury, whether under influence of intoxicants, and whether D understood difference between jury trial and bench trial; D signed printed waiver, judge able to judge D's demeanor (re: pressure or intoxicants "in the picture"), D-counsel "endorsed" printed waiver signed by D, per G.L. c. 218, § 26A (D-counsel to sign certificate indicating s/he "has made all the necessary explanations and determinations regarding such waiver");

C v Adkinson **442 M 410 (2004)**—colloquy in jury-waiver did not use word, "recusal," but inferentially referred to issue; fact that jury-waived trial judge had heard & denied pretrial suppression based on adverse finding of D's credibility didn't require reversal;

C v Taylor **69 MAC 526 (2007)**—judge had no sua sponte obligation to inform D of right to revoke jury waiver or proceed to trial before different judge, after this judge heard change of plea colloquy, including D's affirmative response to whether prosecutor's recitation of evidence was what had happened, before D "balked" in response to question whether she wanted to enter admission to sion to sufficient facts; no relief from immediately succeeding conviction after trial by same judge;

C v Hernandez **42 MAC 780 (97)**—to reject D's claim of involuntary jury waiver, court cited form purportedly mandated by G.L. c. 218, § 26A, by which D-counsel asserted that s/he explained to D all rights involved in jury-waiver & that, **in counsel's opinion**, D's jury waiver was made voluntarily, knowingly & intelligently, & in which D himself asserted that he understood his right to jury & waived it; form version no longer in use & has grave problems per Article 12 & Sixth Amendment; Cf. *In re Grand Jury Investigation* **407 M 916, 917–19 & n.4 (90)** (concerning subpoenas by which a prosecutor attempts to compel attorney to provide evidence concerning a person who is represented by the attorney: ethical concerns include "the chilling of the attorney-client relationship, the implication of Sixth Amendment concerns, the creation of conflicting interests between an attorney and his or her client, and the possibility for adversarial abuse"; threatened is "the keystone of the attorney-client relationship, most notably the trust placed by clients in their attorneys"); and *US v Klubock* **832 F2d 649, 653 (1st Cir. '87)** (ethical issues raised by the serving of a subpoena on actual or prospective defense counsel; immediate conflict of interests created between the attorney/witness and his client; "(a)s a witness, the attorney/witness has separate legal and practical interests apart from those of his client"; "mere possibility of such a conflict is sufficient to create a problem");

C v Dresser **71 MAC 454 (2008)**—"sexually dangerous persons" trials = civil, not criminal, so right to jury trial is by statute, not required by Constitution; though better practice would be to have recorded waiver colloquy with D and a written waiver, record indicated D was aware trial would be jury-waived (and court didn't require more);

See Chapter 12-K for cases on jury instructions;

See Chapter 19-D for cases on mistrials & double jeopardy;

See E. Blumenson, S. Fisher, D. Kanstroom, *Mass. Criminal Practice* **(1998)**—Chapters 30 (Juror Examination & Selection) and 36 (The Jury: Contamination, Instructions, Deliberation, and Verdict);

22-B. JURY SELECTION

22-B.1. In General

M.R.Crim.P. 20—rules governing challenges to array, peremptory challenges, challenges for cause, voir dire, alternates, replacing disabled jurors, & sequestration & separation of deliberating jurors, set forth;

Superior Court Rule 6—rules governing peremptory challenges in noncapital cases set forth;

G.L. c. 234A—provisions governing qualification, summoning, excusing, selecting jurors & establishment of jury commissioner set forth; see: § 3—non-discrimination provision; § 4—qualifications; §§ 22–23, 32—contents of questionnaire, use during voir dire, misrepresentations by jurors; § 40—excusing jurors for hardship or inconvenience for trials over 3 days; § 69—translation assistance for deaf jurors; § 70—right of parties to instruction that no juror is better qualified to determine facts or deliberate solely because of occupation or reputation; § 71—jury tampering penalized; § 73—challenges to jury pool; see also § 74, below; NB: G.L. c. 234A has been extended by SJC to cover all counties in Commonwealth & supersedes cognate provisions in G.L. c. 234;

C v Brown **449 M 747 (2007)**—judge prompted all college students in venire to request hardship exemption if they didn't do so on own, and they eventually did so; no objection = no relief, but SJC agreed that this exclusion, "insofar as it was systematic, was improper"; "hardship" excuse of any kind is to be based on individualized finding rather than blanket rule;

C v Cousin **449 M 809 (2007)**—prosecutor has authority pursuant to G.L. c.6, § 172 to conduct criminal offender record information checks of jurors; info must be shared immediately (or at start of empanelment, if info is obtained by DA earlier than that) with defense counsel; concurrence expresses concern over timing of CORI check, i.e., when jurors were deliberating, proffering that check (absent special reason) should occur if at all before Commonwealth declares satisfaction with empanelled jury;

C v Angiulo **415 M 502 (93)** citing **G.L. c. 277, § 66 (1990 ed.)**—("prisoner indicted for a crime punishable with death or imprisonment for life, upon demand by him or his counsel upon the clerk, shall have a list of the jurors who have been returned) and holding that D, charged as an accessory before the fact to murder in the first degree and punishable with life imprisonment without the possibility of parole, is a member of the class to whom the subject statute is addressed; error to have impaneled "anonymous jury" (though jurors were not told of anonymity);

C v Robichaud **358 M 300 (70)**—D has right to be present when jurors are examined re their qualifications;

C v Owens **414 M 595 (93)**—exclusion of D from individual voir dire at side bar error, but here harmless beyond a reasonable doubt;

C v Skinner **34 MAC 490 (93)**—D entitled to be present during side bar questioning of jurors who have reservations about serving as jurors, but harmless here;

C v Perry **432 M 214, 237–38 (2000)**—issue of whether D alone has right to waive presence at side-bar jury voir dire not reached because counsel acted on his own to waive presence, & SJC thus says "not preserved"! (D's counsel had replied that "for this *I* would rather have him sit back there"); but see *C v White* **37 MAC 757, 761 (94)** citing federal authority, doubtful that attorney can waive D's right to be present during jury selection;

C v Johnson **426 M 617, 624 (98)**—no appellate relief when, after jury sworn, 2 jurors were discharged & 3 others empaneled: judge belatedly realized trial could be protracted; no "double jeopardy" right implicated (because "continuing" jeopardy);

C v Burnoski **418 M 523 (94)**—large # of persons excused by judge after his examination into their unwillingness/inability to be transported from Hampden to Middlesex County & be sequestered for 4 weeks; on appeal D argued error in failure of judge to have him (or his attorney) present during this, but court held no error because "purely administrative" matter;

G.L. c. 234A § 74—verdicts will not be vacated nor mistrials declared on basis of irregularities or defects in qualifying, selecting, excusing, impaneling, or instructing jurors, unless objection made as soon as possible after defect discovered or should have been discovered, & special prejudice shown;

C v Pena **455 M 1 (2009)**—nine seated jurors mingled with rest of venire during short break during empanelment: D's motions for mistrial, voir dire, etc., permissibly denied because no evidence they were exposed to extraneous info, and no prejudice shown;

C v Sheehy **412 M 235 (92)**—G.L. c. 234A, § 74 requirement of prejudice & timely objection not applicable to judge's failure to keep alternates apart from deliberating jurors under G.L. c. 234A, § 68, because violative of Article 12 right to fair jury & Article 30 separation of powers doctrine;

G.L. c. 234—for provisions on qualifying, summoning, selecting jurors, including: § 1—exemptions from jury service; § 1A—excusing juror for undue hardship, unusual inconvenience, or for possible embarrassment by facts of rape or sexual assault charges; §§ 26 & 26B—impanelment, selecting alternates, discharging jurors; § 28—voir dire; § 33—right to new trial if opponent makes threat or offers gratuity to juror; § 34—restriction on sending deadlocked jury out more than twice without their consent; § 35—view of crime scene;

C v Benjamin **430 M 673, 676–77 (2000)**—no error in refusing defense request to have sole jury pool member sharing D's race seated out of order to ensure minority presence on jury; can't "ignore procedural requirements governing jury selection in an attempt to include members of a particular race on the jury";

C v Campbell **394 M 77 (85)**—although judge's delegation to jurors of authority to choose foreperson, over objection, was improper, reversal not required because prejudice not shown;

C v Allen **379 M 564 (80)**—in order to intelligently exercise for-cause & peremptory challenges, D entitled to conduct pretrial investigation of prospective jurors, including interviews of neighbors, but may not contact jurors or their families; precautions to minimize risks of improper investigations set forth;

C v Angiulo **415 M 502 (93)**—henceforth, **no anonymous** jury is to be impaneled **unless** judge has determined, on adequate evidence, that anonymity is truly necessary; at n.19: OK if names & addresses are given only to counsel & not D;

G.L. c. 277 § 66—"capital" defendant is entitled to list of jurors;

C v Fruchtman **418 M 8 (94)**—specifically object to disallowance of peremptories, and use language to counter expected argument that "express(ing) satisfaction" with jury you eventually get abandons your objection;

22-B.2. Statutory Questioning of Group

G.L. c. 234 § 28, paragraph 1—judge must ask "statutory questions": whether any juror is related to either party; has interest in case; has expressed or formed opinion; is sensible of bias or prejudice; & understands that D presumed innocent, that Commonwealth has burden of proving guilt beyond reasonable doubt, & that D not required to present evidence;

C v Tatro **42 MAC 918 (97)**—judge did not ask questions required by G.L. c. 234, § 28 & R.20(b)(1), but instead told jurors that it was important to be impartial, & that there is presumption of innocence, & that G must be proved beyond a reasonable doubt; while questioning was preferable, no relief ordered: legislature's objectives were satisfied & D could show no prejudice;

C v Figueroa **451 M 566 (2008)**—omission of specific statement that D is presumed innocent, but no injury shown, no relief; even if error, no substantial likelihood of miscarriage of justice because presumption = "closely tied to . . . burden of proof beyond a reasonable doubt," as to which judge did advise/ask questions;

M.R.Crim.P. 20(b)(1)—judge must question jurors upon request as to whether any juror is related to either party; has interest in case; has expressed or formed opinion; is sensible of bias or prejudice; judge may allow objecting party to introduce competent evidence to support challenge;

C v Sheline **391 M 279 (84)**—judge required to ask statutory questions; advisability of questions regarding jurors' inclination to give greater credence to police testimony; *C v Silva* **455 M 503 (2009)**—no abuse of discretion in judge's refusal to ask police credibility question; maybe general questions covered it, and case did not turn on officer credibility (D didn't "materially dispute" any cop's testimony at trial);

C v Soares **51 MAC 273 (2001)**—no harm from late addition of daughter in household, in addition to mom (owner of ransacked jewelry boxes) & son (who discovered D in home), because cumulative, though D also argued that jurors hadn't been questioned at impanelment whether they knew such daughter; question to venire had been whether they knew named witnesses or 'any member of their immediate family';

C v Horton **376 M 380 (78), cert. denied sub nom.** *Widemon v Massachusetts* **440 US 923 (1979)**—judge has discretion whether or not to ask questions not mandated by G.L. c. 234, § 28 or case law;

C v Lopes **440 M 731 (2004)**—no right to individual voir dire re: jurors' (& family members') experiences with violent crime, BUT "it would have been preferable" for judge to collectively question venire; "We would expect judges to ask the question in cases of violent crime"; *C v Silva* **455 M 503 (2009)**—no reversal for judge's refusal to ask this question; juror questionnaire asked for past or present involvement as party to civil or criminal litigation and relationship to police or law enforcement officer, and judge asked venire questions re: any reason why would not be completely impartial;

C v Yameen **401 M 331 (87)**—judge not required to ask jurors in operating under influence case about opinions towards alcohol consumption; nor is judge required to give full explanation of presumption of innocence & reasonable doubt;

C v Young **73 MAC 479 (2009)**—juror voir dire included question, "if Commonwealth presented only testimony of witnesses, and presented no corroborating scientific evidence, would you ***automatically*** find D not guilty, or would you make an independent assessment of the evidence?"; this was not the equivalent of an instruction, barred by *Bowden* 379 M 472, 485 (80), that 'a lack of scientific evidence is not to be considered in reaching a judgment'; D was not prevented from arguing 'lack of police investigation';

C v Kudish **362 M 627 (72)**—judge had discretion under G.L. c. 234, § 28, not to collectively question jurors about religious prejudices where D charged with performing unlawful abortion;

C v Stack **49 MAC 227, 240 (2000)**—no error in refusal to ask 2 special questions of venire as whole re prejudice/bias as to "people of color" (Latin Kings/Queens gang affiliates);

C v Cross **33 MAC 761 (92)**—judge not required to conduct voir dire as to any effect television cameras might have on jurors' capacity to impartially judge the evidence, though might be "advisable" to instruct jurors to inform judge if presence of TV cameras interferes with their ability to concentrate & render fair verdict;

C v Bodden **24 MAC 135 (87)**—although judges should individually question at sidebar jurors who respond affirmatively to statutory questions, failure to do so requires reversal only if prejudice shown;

C v Foley **402 M 703 (88)**—judge should not segregate jurors who respond affirmatively to statutory questions; judge is obligated instead to inquire into affirmative response and determine whether juror impartial;

22-B.3. Individual Voir Dire: In General

G.L. c. 234 § 28, paragraph 2—if juror appears not indifferent because might base decision on extraneous issues (e.g., community attitudes, possible exposure to prejudicial material or preconceived opinions about credibility of classes of persons), court shall specifically examine juror; judge has discretion to allow parties to examine jurors; examination may include brief statement of facts & shall be conducted individually outside presence of other venire members;

M.R.Crim.P. 20(b)(2)—same;

C v Kater **432 M 404 (2000)**—no error in refusal to question prospective jurors about D's commission of near-identical crime ten years earlier: because evidence of it was admissible, it wasn't an "extraneous issue";

C v Ashman **430 M 736, 738 (2000)**—implicit acknowledgment that procedure used was NOT "individual voir dire" (venire as a group was asked whether any one had "any opinions about mental illness . . . that you think might interfere with your ability . . . to be . . . impartial," and only those jurors who responded affirmatively to this question were questioned individually);

C v King **391 M 691 (84)**—judge has discretion, upon showing of "special circumstances" justifying departure from regular practice, to allow attorneys to conduct voir dire, but is rarely, if ever, required to do so;

C v Auguste **414 M 51 (92)**—judge has duty to make "meaningful inquiry" where juror makes affirmative response to statutory question or appears not indifferent; error for judge to suggest/coerce, by ridicule and badgering, facially satisfactory assertions of impartiality;

Morgan v Illinois **504 US 719 (92)**—general "can-you-be-fair" & "can-you-follow-the-law" questions don't meaningfully probe into extraneous influences; particular holding here = refusal to inquire whether potential jurors would automatically impose the death penalty upon convicting D violates Fourteenth Amendment due process, and such a juror should be struck for cause;

C v Horton **376 M 380 (18), cert. denied sub nom.** *Widemon v Massachusetts* **440 US 923 (79)**—questioning jurors about extraneous influences under paragraph 2 must be conducted individually;

C v Shelley **381 M 340 (80)**—"preferable" to conduct individual questioning outside presence of other jurors, not at sidebar;

C v Owens **414 M 595 (93)**—error to exclude D from individual voir dire;

C v DiRusso **60 MAC 235 (2003)**—absent trial counsel—request for individual voir dire, failure to inquire individually [here, as to child sexual abuse] not an issue for appeal: absence of request may be tactical judgment that inquiry may be counter-productive;

22-B.4. Individual Voir Dire: Racial Prejudice

Ham v South Carolina **409 US 524 (73)**—federal due process requires that prospective jurors be questioned about racial prejudice whenever "charges & defenses (in case) explicitly implicate racial issues";

Ristaino v Ross **424 US 544 (75)**—even where federal constitution does not require specific questioning about racial prejudice, "wiser course" is to do so wherever D requests it;

C v Lumley **367 M 213, 216–17 (75)**—"as a practical matter, when a motion that prospective jurors be interrogated as to possible racial prejudice is presented . . . trial judge should grant that motion";

C v Sanders **383 M 637 (81)**—in cases of interracial rape, judge, at defense request, must individually examine prospective jurors about racial prejudice;

C v Young **401 M 390 (88)**—mandatory individual voir dire, on request, in cases of interracial murder;

C v Hobbs **385 M 863 (82)**—mandatory individual voir dire, on request, in cases of interracial sexual offenses against children;

C v Stephens **15 MAC 461 (83)**—maybe right to individual voir dire in all cases of interracial sex & violence;

C v Grice **410 M 586 (91)**—no right to individual voir dire in interracial armed robberies unless D can show substantial risk of extraneous influence by racial prejudice; judge retains discretion to allow individual voir dire;

C v Hooper **42 MAC 730, 731 (97)**—white D, charged with kidnapping & assaults with intent to rape 2 black children, entitled on request to individual voir dire; combination of race, sex, and violence means "race is an unavoidable extraneous issue";

C v Ramos **31 MAC 362 (91)**—"wiser" for judge to conduct individual racial voir dire in case of unprovoked attack by "dark skinned" group on whites; but judge's failure to question individually not error where race of attackers not specified, "gangs" not mentioned & trial as whole "racially neutral"; *C v Stack* **49 MAC 227, 240 (2000)** no error in refusal to ask 2 special questions of venire as whole re: prejudice/bias as to "people of color" (Latin Kings/Queens gang affiliates);

C v Ramirez **407 M 553 (90)**—requirement that judge hold colloquy with D personally on individual race-related voir dire abolished, overruling *C v A Juvenile (II)*, **396 M 215 (85)**;

C v Koonce **418 M 367 (94)**—not ineffective assistance of counsel to fail to request individual voir dire on racial bias, since there is potential that prejudices may be inflamed but not eradicated in eventually-seated jurors;

C v Crowder **49 MAC 720 (2000)**—dodging issue whether attorney must advise D of right to individual voir dire (& whether it's D's or counsel's decision to insist upon or forego) because motion judge rejected claim that attorney failed to inform D of right;

C v De La Cruz **405 M 269 (89)**—"Hispanic" D not entitled to individual voir dire on race where victim was "white" because "Hispanic" refers to national origin, not race; but cf. *C v Otsuki* **411 M 218 (91)** possibly acknowledging that "Japanese"/white (criminal D/victim) = interracial;

C v Rivera **50 MAC 532, 536 n.10 (2000)**—parties erroneously assumed that "Hispanic" victim was black; his death certificate listed "white" as race;

C v Ortiz **47 MAC 777, 781 (99)**—individual voir dire not required in sexual assault case when D's "Hispanic" and complainant was "white"; within judge's discretion to decide whether "ethnic considerations had sufficient potential for unfair prejudice so that individual voir dire of the jurors on the ethnic issue was warranted";

C v Pina **430 M 66 (99)**—no error in refusing individual voir dire in murder case where V was white, of Portuguese descent, and D was of "Cape Verdean"(rather than assertedly specifically "black") "ethnicity"; counsel failed to specify to trial judge that the case presented conflict between persons of different skin colors or other dominant "RACIAL" (rather than "ethnic") features;

C v Hunter **427 M 651, 654 (98)**—Caucasian male D charged with murder of estranged wife, native of the Philippines; though there was request for individual voir dire re: bias/prejudice based on "ethnicity," counsel didn't proffer evidence that V and D were members of "different races in the traditional sense," so no error in refusing individual voir dire (PLUS counsel perhaps conceded that potential bias wasn't "a live issue");

C v Bodden **24 MAC 135 (87)**—black D not entitled to individual voir dire on race where victim described only as "light-skinned" & "Puerto Rican," because former refers to skin complexion & latter to place of origin, but neither refer to race;

C v Otsuki **411 M 218 (91)**—although Japanese murder D may have been entitled to individual voir dire on race (where victim was white) to determine whether jurors were biased against "Asians," reversal not required because request was not adequately raised before judge & no prejudice was shown; *C v Young* **401 M 390 (87)**, mandated individual voir dire on request in "interracial" murder);

Hernandez v NY **500 US 352 (91)**—(plurality) membership in distinct language community may be equivalent to membership in racial group; prosecutor's use of peremptory challenges to exclude Latino jurors found "race-neutral" where prosecutor explained that during voir-dire challenged jurors seemed reluctant to accept interpreter's translation of Spanish-speaking witnesses;

C v LaFaille **430 M 44, 51 (99), reversing 46 MAC 144 (99)**—though trial turned out to involve "potential" interracial murder (assault & battery by dangerous weapon and firearm offenses), with "sexual overtones" (black D purportedly "flirting"/harassing group of white girls), SJC held that counsel failed to make this showing to the judge, on record, prior to impanelment ("judge cannot be expected to be clairvoyant" and to anticipate that testimony, or other events at trial, might give rise to an extraneous issue (which could influence jurors)), so judge did not err in denying individual voir dire; Marshall, J., believed that trial judge should have conducted individual voir dire after two prospective jurors, in side bar colloquies, "told the judge that they could not be objective in this case for reasons relating explicitly to racial bias";

22-B.5. Individual Voir Dire: Other Prejudice or Bias

See Chapter 22-H for cases on extraneous influences generally;

C v Flebotte **417 M 348, 355 (94)**—as matter of 'general superintendence', SJC orders that when D is charged with sexual assault upon a minor, D entitled to individual voir dire re: whether prospective juror was a V of childhood sexual offense;

C v Holloway **44 MAC 469, 472 (98)**—reversing for refusal to voir dire per **Flebotte**;

C v Whiting **59 MAC 104 (2003)**—*C v Holloway* 44 MAC 469 (98) did not "expand" *C v Flebotte* to impose **requirement** of individual voir dire re: sexual abuse of family members or close personal friends (though during individual voir dire conducted here pursuant to *Flebotte*, four prospective jurors volunteered that their impartiality would be affected by fact of family members having been sexually assaulted, and though there is discretion to inquire individually);

C v Sanchez **423 M 591 (96)**—D tried prior to **Flebotte** decision not entitled to reversal for refusal to conduct individual voir dire at trial alleging sexual offenses against minors; *C v DiRusso* **60 MAC 235 (2003)**—absent trial counsel—request for individual voir dire, failure to inquire individually as to child sexual abuse not an issue for appeal: absence of request may be tactical judgment that inquiry may be counter-productive;

C v Proulx **34 MAC 494 (93)**—though court refused to require individual voir dire in homosexual rape case in which defense is consent, potential for prejudice was called "obvious" & trial judges were encouraged "to respond generously" to motions for individual voir dire about possible prejudice;

C v Sheline **391 M 279 (84)**—although judge should ordinarily ask jurors about bias toward police credibility, individual questioning required only if D can show substantial risk of extraneous influence; prejudice in favor of police not as "indurated & pervasive" as racial bias; ordinarily left to judge's discretion;

C v Robinson **24 MAC 680 (87)**—where jurors acknowledge having relatives in law enforcement, better practice is for judge to conduct individual voir dire; but reversal not required unless prejudice shown;

US v Anagnos **853 F.2d 1 (1st Cir. '88)**—judge's refusal to question juror's (collectively) about bias toward police officers or agents required reversal where police testimony was central to case;

C v Torres **453 M 722 (2009)**—mere fact that juror is related to police officer does not disqualify juror or show bias; failure of counsel to peremptorily strike not 'ineffective assistance';

C v Boyer **400 M 52 (87)**—individual questioning about bias against homosexuals required only if D can show substantial risk of extraneous influence;

C v Plunkett **422 M 634, 640–41 (96)**—individual voir dire invited by SJC but not **required** in "circumstances of this case" given that 100% of venire had responded to collective question whether the V's possible homosexuality or bisexuality would interfere with ability to be impartial (conviction reversed on other grounds);

C v Estremera **383 M 382 (81)**—individual questioning about bias against psychiatrists required only if D can show substantial risk of extraneous influence;

C v Seguin **421 M 243, 249 (95)**—henceforth, whenever criminal D indicates that criminal responsibility "may be placed in issue," individual voir dire required re: whether juror has any opinion which would prevent returning NGI verdict; also "may be desirable" to give entire venire brief description of facts "in form agreed to by" parties;

C v Ashman **430 M 736, 738 (2000)**—SJC won't "expand" *Seguin* requirement (**421 M at 249**) to cases in which evidence of mental illness/impairment is presented; if there were basis in particular record to require judge to determine there was substantial risk of extraneous influence on jury (G.L. c. 234, § 28; M.R.Crim.P. 20(b)(2)), result should be different; question used by judge here held "sufficient to ensure that no juror was biased . . . because of (D's) reliance on" evidence of mental impairment;

C v Campbell **378 M 680 (79)**—assumed that individual questioning about bias against prisoners as witnesses required if D can show substantial risk of extraneous influence;

C v Stack **49 MAC 227, 231, further appellate review denied, 432 M 1104 (2000)**—no error in refusing individual voir dire re: bias against "gangs," though this question was put to venire as a whole, resulting in excluding 17 potential jurors for anti-gang bias; to be entitled to individual voir dire, Ds had to demonstrate "substantial risk that the case would be decided in whole or in part on the basis of extraneous issues," and Ds failed to do so;

C v Lao **443 M 770 (2005)**—(on facts here, anyway) no requirement that jurors be questioned individually "as to the issue of domestic violence";

Leonard v US **378 US 544 (64)**—improper to select jurors for 2d trial from jury which had just convicted D at 1st trial on separate charges;

C v Hicks **377 M 1 (79)**—meaningful questioning of jurors about exposure to "scuttlebutt" in jury room required along with appropriate admonition;

C v Jones **9 MAC 103 (80), S.C., 382 M 387 (81)**—affidavit with "hard facts" on type of bias useful to show substantial risk of extraneous influence;

C v Keohane **444 M 563 (2005)**—judge wasn't required to conduct individual voir dire concerning specific photos (including of autopsy), & displaying them to venire could have unduly emphasized them; judge did inform venire of nature of injuries and that there would be graphic testimony & photos of the injuries (& the 8 people who answered "yes" to question whether difficult/uncomfortable for them to be fair/impartial were excused for cause);

22-B.6. Individual Voir Dire: Pretrial Publicity

C v Kendrick **404 M 298 (89), reversing 26 MAC 48 (88)**—judge's denial of individual voir dire on pretrial publicity or alternative relief did not create substantial risk of extraneous influence, even though numerous articles about D & family ("worst family in Lynn") recently appeared in local press;

C v Burden **15 MAC 666 (83)**—individual questioning about pretrial publicity required only if D can show substantial risk of extraneous influence;

C v James **424 M 770 (97)**—despite massive pretrial publicity and candlelight march & vigil protesting violence (both specific to this case and in general) held two days before murder trial, individual voir dire established that seated jurors were impartial (though some had prior knowledge of case): SJC would not reverse due to denial of venue-change and/or continuance of trial date;

C v Clark **432 M 1 (2000)**—fact that 35% of prospective jurors were excused at least in part because prejudiced by exposure to publicity about case didn't mean that those who didn't acknowledge bias were biased; no error in denial of motion for change of venue;

C v Leahy **445 M 481 (2005)**—though D cited *Irvin v Dowd* 366 US 717 (1961) to argue exclusion for cause of all potential jurors exposed to any publicity re: present case, jurors' assertions of impartiality are to be accepted unless "extraordinary circumstances" give reason to question them;

C v Druce **453 M 686 (2009)**—newspaper obtained videotape (made at prison medical unit of D allegedly re-enacting victim's killing as it occurred in prison) and published article in which it was described in detail (videotape never seen by defense counsel during two years post-killing and pre-trial), but SJC held that voir dire of prospective jurors was sufficient to assure no prejudice to D;

22-B.7. Challenges for Cause

M.R.Crim.P. 20(b)—juror may be challenged for cause before juror sworn; juror may be challenged after being sworn but before evidence presented only with permission of court; grounds for challenge must be stated & judge must make ruling; grounds may be stated at bench;

Superior Court Rule 6—examination & challenges for cause made first; after judge finds all jurors indifferent, peremptories then exercised, Commonwealth first; party may not challenge juror not previously challenged when given opportunity;

C v Bryant **447 M 494 (2006)**—though clerk announced that counsel should make "cause" objections after jurors were called but before they were sworn, judge excused all but 28 of venire after individual voir dire; when counsel didn't challenge "judge's implicit decision concerning juror impartiality" until after judge seated the first 14 potential jurors & declared to them that he and counsel

found them indifferent, and after Commonwealth exercised peremptory challenges, SJC held that D had waived right to challenge for cause; "even if [D didn't so waive,] there was no abuse of discretion" here (D didn't request additional peremptory challenges);

C v Dupont **75 MAC 605 (2009)**—after full jury was empaneled *but before being sworn*, prosecutor noticed that juror's questionnaire revealed that juror had actively supported DA's opponent in last election, opponent's chief issue being disagreement with "draconian adherence" to drug laws; judge further questioned juror, who "could not state that he would be impartial"; no error in belatedly striking for cause;

C v Susi **394 M 784 (85)**—where judge fails to excuse juror for cause, D must exhaust all peremptories **& request additional peremptory** to preserve error for appeal; judge's refusal to excuse blind juror for cause required reversal where defense was mistaken identification; cf. G.L. c. 234A, § 69 translation assistance for deaf jurors to be provided;

US v Martinez-Salazar **528 US 304 (2000)**—when judge erroneously refuses to dismiss potential juror "for cause," and D uses a peremptory to get rid of juror, D has no Sixth Amendment issue on appeal because no "biased" juror sat; fact that number of peremptory challenges was thereby diminished is not ground for relief under fed. rules or constitution; SO as you use a peremptory and request an extra peremptory to make up for one wasted on "cause" challenge, CITE DECLARATION OF RIGHTS, ARTICLE 12, M.R.Crim.P. 20(c)(1), and *C v Auguste* **414 M 51, 58–59 (92)**;

C v Long **419 M 798 (95)**—juror could say only that he'd "do (his) best" to be impartial to Cambodian D, though that ethnicity affected his ability to be impartial, **and** said "emphatically" that he "would lean to the police officer" (Caucasian) over the Cambodian civilian witness; cause challenge denied and peremptories had been exhausted; murder & other convictions rev'd; **either** (n.6) bias would require that juror be struck for cause;

C v Jaime J. **56 MAC 268 (2002)**—in spite of jurors' alarming statements, no relief from denial of "cause" challenges, citing judge's "discretion" in determining whether juror = impartial; apparently not all "equivocal language," like "probably" shows partiality (see *Beaz* 69 MAC at 509);

C v Chongarlides **62 MAC 709 (2004)**—that juror "knew" homicide victim from living in same town and attending same high school did not require her to be struck "for cause"; judge's determination of impartiality wasn't abuse of discretion;

C v Clark **446 M 620 (2006)**—potential juror believed that African Americans as a group were more likely to commit crimes because of their economic status than people of other racial/ethnic groups (though said she could be impartial, and ["ambiguously"] that "it would depend on the person's circumstances") should have been excused for cause; though she didn't sit because D peremptorily challenged her, D would have challenged a specific other juror peremptorily if he had not exhausted those challenges (& court listed D's reasons supporting peremptory challenge of the juror who was seated); diminution of peremptory challenges is per se prejudicial (citing Article 12 & *C v Susi* 394 M 784, 789 [85]);

C v Beaz **69 MAC 500 (2007)**—despite responses strongly suggesting partiality, D failed to request removal for cause and didn't use peremptory challenge: court refused to resolve claim of ineffective assistance of counsel on direct appeal, and likewise refuses to find error in judge's failure to strike sua sponte for juror's use of "equivocal language," citing *C v Jaime J* 56 MAC 268, 274 (2002);

Irwin v Dowd **366 US 717 (61)**—8 of 12 jurors' statements during voir dire that they had preconceived belief in D's guilt in high-profile murder case violated D's constitutional right to impartial jury even though jurors subsequently claimed they could be fair & impartial;

C v Auguste **414 M 51 (92)**—error for judge to suggest/coerce, by ridicule and badgering, facially satisfactory assertions of impartiality; judge should instead conduct meaningful inquiry into acknowledged biases and should not suggest or "require" what jurors' answers must be;

C v Mangum **357 M 76 (70)**—judge must excuse for cause jurors unable or unwilling to say they will judge case on merits;

C v Bryant **447 M 494 (2006)**—jurors responding "I think I could do that" or "I feel I could. I hope I would" (hold prosecution to burden of proof, listen to the evidence/be impartial, despite having connection with insurance companies involved in case as "victims") = good enough; "This court does not revisit credibility determinations absent a compelling reason";

C v Melo **67 MAC 71 (2006)**—juror stated that he might know police officers involved in case & that he was involved in civil lawsuit that "may tend to skew my view of the system," & that he was "not certain" that he could be impartial, but trial counsel didn't challenge for cause or peremptorily: no relief on appeal ("it was not an abuse of the judge's broad discretion to conclude that the juror was indifferent");

C v Somers **44 MAC 920 (98)**—error not to excuse for cause juror expressing doubt about his ability to be impartial, whose fiancée was an assistant district attorney in adjacent county, who had "really strong opinions about gun control" in part because a friend was shot, who "would not want me on a jury" if he were defendant and who "d(id not) know" whether he could make decision solely on evidence;

C v Emerson **430 M 378, 384 (99)**—no error in refusing to excuse for cause 2 jurors who had "family experience with domestic violence" in case in which D was charged with murder of woman who had once obtained protective order against him; jurors weren't themselves victims of domestic violence;

C v Monahan **349 M 139 (65)**—although jurors should be excused for cause & substitute jurors seated before jury is sworn, doing so after jury sworn but before trial commenced did not require reversal where no prejudice shown;

C v Ascolillo **405 M 456 (89)**—cops need not automatically be removed for cause; *C v Ortiz* **50 MAC 304 (2000)** not ineffective assistance to fail to save peremptory challenge for cop seated after peremptories were exhausted (& cop found by judge to be impartial);

22-B.8. Peremptory Challenges

M.R.Crim.P. 20(c)—peremptory challenges: life felony: 12 (but not more than 16) + 1 for each alternate; non-life Superior Court felony: 4 + (by practice) 1 for each alternate; jury-of-6: 2 + (by practice) 1 for every 2 alternates; for multiple defendants, each gets full number, prosecutor gets total number; peremptories made after court determines jurors indifferent but before jurors sworn;

Superior Court Rule 6—struck system": jurors called until "full number" obtained (= # jurors + # alternates + # peremptories of D & prosecutor); examination & challenges for cause made first; then after all jurors found indifferent, peremptories exercised, (D & Commonwealth alternating), with Commonwealth 1st, until parties stop or exhaust peremptories; party may not challenge juror not previously challenged when given opportunity;

C v Ouellette **58 MAC 711 (2003)**—D's challenge for cause rejected when potential juror said only that she knew names of police officer—witnesses ("because she lived in a very small town"), but ADA's later advice (before jurors were sworn) was that juror's in-laws employed cop's wife and had been cop's landlord: denial of D's peremptory challenge then was reversible error (only question was whether challenge was "timely," and it was, needing only be made "prior to the time the jury was sworn" [citing *C v Johnson* 426 M 617, 627 (98)];

C v Burden **15 MAC 666 (83)**—assuming that judge has authority to grant request for additional peremptory challenges, though Rule 20(c)(1) doesn't specifically mention;

C v Walker **379 M 297 (79)**—summary reveals that trial judge allowed extra peremptories (& no adverse comment re: this by SJC);

C v Hyatt **409 M 689 (91)**—judge's allowing D to exercise only 1 of 2 valid peremptories required reversal;

C v Wood **389 M 552 (83)**—judge's refusal to allow D exercise of valid peremptory to which D entitled requires reversal without showing prejudice; **BUT SEE *US v Martinez-Salazar* 528 US 304 (2000)** "unlike the right to an impartial jury guaranteed by the Sixth Amendment, *peremptory challenges are not of federal constitutional dimension*" (so having to use one to be rid of a juror who should have been removed for cause yields no federal issue on appeal, so long as no biased juror sat in judgment); fn. questions "oft-quoted language" of *Swain v Alabama* **380 US 202, 219 (65)** that denial or impairment of right to exercise peremptory challenges is reversible error without showing of prejudice; footnote foreshadows:

***Rivera v Illinois* 129 S Ct 1446 (2009)**—just as state law controls existence and exercise of peremptory challenges, state law determines consequences of erroneous denial of such challenge; S Ct will not disturb Illinois court's holding that although D's peremptory challenge should have been allowed, error did not warrant reversal of D's conviction; holding = erroneous denial of peremptory challenge does not require automatic reversal of D's conviction as matter of federal law;

***C v Bockman* 442 M 757 (2004)**—judge's refusal to allow D's peremptory challenge of juror held to have caused no prejudice when the juror was dismissed the following day for cause, having become very emotional about the content of the trial (rejects D's argument that prejudice existed because if he had been able to exercise his challenge, a different juror would have been seated); BUT says it's still the rule that D need not show prejudice when exercise of peremptory challenge is erroneously denied & the challenged juror participates in deciding case;

***C v Lattimore* 396 M 446 (85)**—assumed that judges have discretion to grant additional peremptory challenges;

See E. Blumenson, *Mass. Criminal Practice*, § 30.3A & n.69 ('98 ed.)—judge should grant additional peremptories to correct for pretrial publicity & other unfairness;

***C v Barrows* 391 M 781 (84)**—Rule 6 has force of law & must be followed except in capital cases or if judge expressly orders to contrary;

***C v Brown* 395 M 604 (85)**—judge's failure to follow Rule 6 by requiring D to exercise peremptories after individual voir dire, but before full number of jurors obtained, required reversal;

***C v Ptomey* 26 MAC 491 (81)**—judge's failure to follow rule 6 by requiring D to exercise peremptory after individual voir dire required reversal, even though D did not exhaust all peremptories; judge's effort to "specially order" alternative procedure under Rule 6 not valid because not justified by special circumstances; purpose of Rule 6 is to enhance comparative choice;

***C v Jean-Louis* 70 MAC 740 (2007)**—after amendment of Rule 6 in 1989, trial judge may allow judge to compel party to exercise peremptory challenge to juror immediately after individual voir dire, i.e., before "box" is full; "juror by juror" method may "help streamline process; *C v Sires*, 413 M 292, 308 n.19 (92) controls: judge has discretion to require exercise of peremptories as occurred here;

***C v Bartie* 401 M 1009 (88), S.C., 23 MAC 479 (87)**—although it was violation of Rule 6 for judge to permit Commonwealth to exercise peremptory of juror it had failed to challenge when it had opportunity, reversal not required because D failed to make timely objection & show special prejudice under G.L. c. 234A, § 74;

***C v Freiberg* 405 M 282 (89)**—judges may require capital D to exercise peremptories as each juror seated;

***C v Mello* 420 M 375 (95)**—court refused to require that D's consent to counsel's failure to exercise peremptories be placed on record; not ineffective assistance to fail to peremptorily challenge relatives of law enforcement or fire-fighting officers;

***C v Ortiz* 50 MAC 304 (2000)**—no ineffective assistance found in failure to save a peremptory to challenge cop, who was seated after counsel had exhausted peremptories; one judge dissented, finding absence of challenge "manifestly unreasonable" in trial at which sole evidence was undercover cop's testimony re: drug buy;

22-B.9. Improper Peremptory Challenges Based on Group Affiliation

***C v Soares* 377 M 461 (79)**—peremptory challenges based on juror's affiliation with "cognizable group" such as sex, race, color, creed or national origin, violate Article 12 due process; presumption that peremptories valid = rebuttable by prima facie showing that jurors challenged because of group membership; burden shifts to party exercising peremptory to give group-neutral explanation; if peremptory improper, jurors already seated & possibly remainder of venire may be dismissed;

***Batson v Kentucky* 476 US 79 (86)**—prosecution's purposeful discrimination in jury selection by use of peremptory challenges on basis of race violates D's right to equal protection under Fourteenth Amendment; once D makes prima facie showing that peremptory used to exclude members of particular race, burden shifts to prosecutor to articulate "race-neutral" explanation;

***Snyder v Louisiana* 128 S Ct 1203 (2008)**—*Batson* has 3-step process for trial court to use: D must make prima facie showing that peremptory was exercised on basis of race; if showing made, prosecution must offer race-neutral basis for strike; trial judge must determine whether D has shown purposeful discrimination, and this involves evaluation of prosecutor's credibility, often tied to demeanor, to be sustained unless clearly erroneous; if prosecutor says juror's demeanor = cause for peremptory, judge to evaluate whether juror's demeanor exhibited what's claimed by prosecutor; HERE, prosecutor's proffered reasons did not withstand scrutiny by appellate court (e.g. white jurors with conflicting obligations at least as serious were not challenged);

***C v Suarez* 59 MAC 111 (2003)**—it's D's burden to establish prima facie case of impropriety in exercise of peremptory challenge, and mere citation to surname, "Lugo," insufficient ("Hispanic or Italian"): D should have asked judge to ASK JUROR; even if Hispanic, DA's single challenge not obviously "pattern," because didn't challenge, previously, surnames of "Demaina" and "Clemente"; another possible reason for challenge apparent on record;

***Johnson v California* 125 S.Ct. 2410 (2005)**—*Batson* requires, as first step, only that party raising claim of improper peremptory challenges produce evidence sufficient to permit trial judge to draw an inference that discrimination has occurred; California's more onerous standard, i.e., requiring showing that it was "more likely than not that the other party's peremptory challenges, if unexplained, were based on impermissible group bias", is REJECTED;

Miller El v Dretke **125 S.Ct. 2317 (2005)**—Supreme Court makes searching factual inquiry about peremptory challenges, "ferreting out discrimination in selections discretionary by natures and choices subject to myriad legitimate influences," and orders habeas corpus relief;

Duncan v Louisiana **391 US 145 (68)**—D's right to impartial jury under Sixth & Fourteenth Amendments;

Georgia v McCollum **505 US 42 (92)**—D not entitled to exercise peremptories on racially discriminatory grounds under Fourteenth Amendment equal protection clause;

Powers v Ohio **499 US 400 (91)**—D entitled to raise 3d party equal protection challenge under Fourteenth Amendment to prosecutor's discriminatory use of peremptories, even though D (white) not member of same race as excluded jurors (black);

C v Cavotta **48 MAC 636, 637 n.1 (2000)**—judge and prosecutor speculation about skin tone and national heritage of D unnecessary: D may object to race-based exclusions of jurors "whether or not (D) and the excluded jurors share the same race"; see also *C v Calderon* **431 M 21, 23–24 (2000)**;

J.E.B. v Alabama ex rel. T.B. **511 US 127 (94)**—equal protection clause bars exercise of peremptory on basis of gender (context here = civil paternity action, on complaint pursued by state of Alabama);

C v Rivera **50 MAC 532 (2000)**—"youth" not protected class in context of peremptory challenges;

C v Evans **438 M 142 (2002)**—college students aren't a distinctive group for Sixth Amendment purposes;

C v Jordan **439 M 47 (2003)**—protections against discriminatory peremptory challenges extended under article 12 of Declaration of Rights to "combined" race-gender groups, e.g., "white males" (an issue not previously reached by U.S. Supreme Court);

Holland v Illinois **493 US 474 (90)**—D not entitled to make Sixth Amendment (right to impartial jury) challenge to prosecutor's discriminatory use of peremptories, where D (white) not member of same group as excluded jurors (black);

C v Little **384 M 262 (81)**—D entitled to *Soares* claim even if not member of same group as challenged jurors;

C v Burnett **418 M 769 (94)**—prosecutor challenged 4 out of 5 black jurors, and judge stated only that prosecutor's asserted reasons were "not related to race", allowing the challenges; reversed because judge should have made finding as to whether the non-race-related reasons were a sham, **and** should not have foreclosed rebuttal by D-counsel;

C v Cavotta **48 MAC 636, 638 (2000)**—because judge didn't follow Burnett procedure (explicitly find whether or not there was prima facie showing of discriminatory intent, and if so, further find, explicitly, whether

challenging party has satisfied burden of rebuttal (by giving bona fide reasons rather than sham excuses)), Appeals Court gave no "substantial deference" to judge's allowance of peremptories; DA's proffering of reasons implicitly acknowledged that prima facie showing had been made; reference to juror's questionnaire "eluded appellate review" because not preserved in record; claim as to "demeanor" deemed bogus because no voir dire inquiry occurred during which DA could have formed legitimate opinion; DA's reference to juror's "accent" charitably termed "oblique";

C v Smith **58 MAC 166 (2003)**—mere failure to follow *Burnett* procedure didn't create substantial risk of miscarriage of justice; DA's challenges of female jurors didn't mandate finding of discriminatory intent, particularly since two of the three were replaced with females and five females were on the deliberating jury;

C v Roche **44 MAC 372, 375 (98)**—judge's disallowance of D's challenge to black nurse in assault case in which medical records would be offered & doctors would testify required reversal of conviction; judge's seeming attempt to construct demographically representative jury by accepting some peremptories but not others was error; right to jury representative of cross section of community cannot require that each jury include constituency of every group in the population; judge saying D's reason "not a good one" because it struck only black juror violated procedure whereby judge was to find whether the offered reason was "bona fide or a sham";

C v Benjamin **430 M 673, 676–77 (2000)**—no error in refusing defense request to have sole jury pool member sharing D's race seated out of order to ensure minority presence on jury; can't "ignore procedural requirements governing jury selection in an attempt to include members of a particular race on the jury";

C v Carleton **418 M 773 (94)**—error to have allowed Commonwealth challenge of 3 Catholic Irish-heritage persons, given bogus reason that 1 was widower and 2 were of "limited" education: they were high school graduates and, given issues at trial, education level was not important;

C v Garrey **436 M 422 (2002)**—DA's challenge of sole black juror upheld, given proffered reason that juror was a guidance counselor & thus likely to be 'overly sympathetic' to defendants (distinguishing *C v Burnett* **36 MAC 1, S.C., 418 M 769 (94)**); though judge failed to specify that there had been "pattern" of improper exclusion, judge could treat as pattern early use of challenges when there's only few members of group;

C v Caldwell **418 M 777 (94)**—prosecutor's challenges to all 4 black persons in venire upheld, SJC deferring to trial judge's evaluation of good faith in reasons (a) 5th grade education, (b) possible acquaintance of DA with juror's children & juror resided close to D, & (c) reluctance of juror to serve, citing planned trip;

C v Reid **384 M 247 (81)**—judge may grant request of party making successful *Soares* objection that jurors improperly stricken be seated along with others already selected & that remainder of venire not be dismissed; D's refusal to explain challenge to all 6 males (& no females) on panel was *Soares* violation;

C v Harris **409 M 461 (91)**—peremptory challenge of even 1 juror for improper reasons violates *Soares*; prosecutor's challenge of sole black in venire was *Soares* violation, even though "pattern" not shown, where prosecutor's explanation that excluded juror reminded him of D's mother (also a black female) didn't withstand scrutiny;

C v DiMatteo **12 MAC 547, 553 (81)**—same;

C v Fryar **414 M 732 (93)**—challenge of single black juror enough to constitute prohibited pattern; error for judge to **suggest** bogus reason for ADA to parrot, i.e., that juror came to side bar inappropriately (notwithstanding the side bar visits, judge had twice ruled juror qualified to serve);

C v Serrano **48 MAC 163 (99)**—though D-counsel objected to DA's challenge of sole black juror and asked judge to obtain a race-neutral reason for the challenge, DA retorted that she didn't have to, because no "pattern"; judge merely told her that if she challenged any more "minority" jurors, he would require race-neutral reason: no relief, judge implicitly found no "pattern," and "there was adequate record support for the judge's decision," apparently because there were still 3 "minority" (Hispanic) jurors remaining; if the challenge had left the jury with no "minority" jurors, "a prima facie case of discrimination would have been established," & would have required that DA provide good faith race-neutral reason or suffer disallowance of the challenge; here, also factors: (1) trial not for type of offense naturally exciting racial biases, and (2) Ds were all members of a different group than challenged juror;

C v Curtis **424 M 78, 80–83 (97)**—judge's disallowance of D's peremptory challenge of sole black prospective juror not error: SJC held that, despite judge's noting that he was **not** accusing D-counsel of doing anything "improper," and was (instead) sensitive to the need for there to be a racial balance," judge was implicitly finding that reason was "sham" (reason, in interracial rape case, was that the juror's wife was DSS caseworker, & counsel believed that such employment "gives people a particular point of view");

C v Calderone **46 MAC 1118 (99), aff'd 431 M 21 (2000)**—DA's challenge of sole black juror, on basis that her husband was cop, should not have been allowed; appellate court won't give deference to judge's conclusions unless judge specifically determines whether proffered explanation for challenge is bona fide or sham; here, judge failed to do so AND failed to allow D-counsel to offer rebuttal to Commonwealth's explanation; Appeals Court found it "remarkable . . . to put it mildly," that DA was objecting to police officer relationship; regarding the additional reason cited, i.e., that juror allegedly smiled at D-counsel: "the so-called smirk or smile objection has long been discounted by this court"; SJC stated (**431 M at 27**) that "common sense" would call into question a DA's ob-

jection on basis "that (juror) might be prejudiced in favor of the police";

C v Maldonado **439 M 460 (2003)**—reversal for Commonwealth's peremptory of last remaining African American juror: **"the ultimate issue is not whether there is a 'pattern' of excluding a discrete group, but whether the challenge made to any member of the panel is impermissibly based on the juror's membership in one of the discrete groups protected under *C v Soares*";** demand that record contain judge's separate findings as to both adequacy and genuineness and, if necessary, an explanation of those findings"; **challenges based on "subjective data such as a juror's looks or gestures, or a party's 'gut' feeling should rarely be accepted as adequate,"** because easily used as pretext for discrimination; perfectly reasonable explanation in abstract "must be rejected" if judge doesn't believe it's real reason;** SJC rejects *Purkett v Elem* 514 US 765, 768 (95) (silly reason = adequate to overcome prima facie case of discrimination); "marginally adequate" reason here (juror was single and childless) to be discounted because other like jurors weren't challenged; *three justices in concurring opinion bemoan impossible task allotted trial judges re: divining reasons, believe peremptories should be abolished or substantially restricted;*

C v Smith **450 M 395 (2008)**—unclear whether in fact potential juror was homosexual, or transgendered; single challenge not asserted at trial to have been a "pattern," so no obligation on judge's part to make finding whether presumption of propriety was rebutted;

C v Benoit **452 M 212 (2008)**—reason given for peremptory challenge must be not only "genuine" but "adequate": where necessary findings ("independent evaluation and determination of adequacy and genuineness of reasons) by judge are absent, appellate court considers directly the stated reasons, here finding them inadequate (black juror's occupation, and lack of familiarity with criminal law terms, i.e., saying she would discuss case with fellow jurors and consider with them whether they should "prosecute," when she meant "convict"; prospective juror affirmed, to 3 separate questions, that "stress" of service would not interfere with her ability to serve);

C v Douglas **75 MAC 643 (2009)**—*C v Maldonado* requires judge to find peremptory challenger's explanation to be both "adequate" and "genuine," and judge may not supply the reasons to justify the challenge; judge did not address stated reason that juror was "staring" at prosecutor, and rejected claim of juror's being "slow"; findings must be made contemporaneously (here not made until after overnight recess and case law consultation); "adequate" reason = personal to juror and not based on group affiliation, and related to particular case being tried (reason may be inadequate even if genuine);

C v Van Winkle **443 M 230, 236 (2005)**—judge had discretion to disallow D's challenge of sole black juror; that D himself requested the challenge didn't matter; that D felt juror would not look at him as she passed & gave him a "negative" look from jury box were not reasons conveyed contemporaneously to judge, and if they had been, needn't have been accepted (citing *Maldonado* 439 M at 465);

C v Hamilton **411 M 313 (91)**—prosecutor's challenge of 2 out of 3 of blacks on venire (67%) & only 14% of whites was prima facie case of *Soares* violation; prosecutor, however, offered race-neutral justifications such as demeanor & inconsistent responses of jurors;

C v Brown **11 MAC 288 (81)**—prosecutor's challenge of all 3 blacks in venire was prima facia *Soares* violation; prosecutor's explanation that D had similarly challenged white jurors not adequate race-neutral explanation;

C v Burns **43 MAC 263, 269 (97)**—Commonwealth's 5th peremptory prompted objection by co-D: it was 2d one of "Jewish-surnamed" person: initial burden of showing impropriety not met here;

C v Sosnowski **43 MAC 367, 373 (97)**—D's failure to object at trial to Commonwealth's use of 9 out of its 10 peremptories to strike men in statutory rape trial meant no record adequate to raise *Soares*: challenging party had no opportunity to explain;

C v Santos **41 MAC 621 (96)**—same+ unclear that struck person was only black person in panel;

C v LeClair **429 M 313, 319–21 (99)**—though D objected to DA challenging 8 men as a block, without challenging any women, judge's response (that he'd wait until Commonwealth finally content to rule) meant that judge found that presumption of proper use of peremptories had not been rebutted; furthermore, panel for trial consisted of 12 men and 4 women, and deliberating jury was 11 men, 1 woman;

C v Green **420 M 771 (95)**—D's challenge to 2 of 4 black jurors prompted DA's objection & judge's questioning; reasons were one of jurors had close relative who was a shooting victim and perhaps was related to victim in another homicide case in which he was defense counsel, and other juror's father & uncle were Boston cops; SJC said judge shouldn't have disallowed peremptory challenges on basis that jurors said they could be impartial (that standard prevails to reject only challenges for cause) AND should not even have questioned D-counsel without actually finding an impropriety;

C v Mathews **31 MAC 564 (91)**—prosecutor's challenge of 1 of 2 blacks in venire & white woman with black ex-boyfriend was prima facie *Soares* violation; prosecutor's explanation that 1 was "flaky" & that other approached bench for reasons unrelated to questions not adequate race-neutral explanation;

C v Long **419 M 798 (95)**—prosecutor's challenge of 2 out of 2 Hispanic jurors was prima facie *Soares* violation;

C v Young **401 M 390 (87)**—prosecutor's challenge of 3 of 7 blacks on venire was not prima facie Soares violation where prosecutor left 2 blacks on jury;

C v Herbert **421 M 307 (95)**—upholding trial judge's allowance of prosecutor's challenge of 3d black juror (out of 6) because trial judge in better position than appellate

court to assess validity of challenge to juror "based on demeanor & hesitancy " answering crucial questions;

C v Hyatt **409 M 689 (91)**—D's challenge of 2 young white women but not black woman of same age group not *Soares* violation where D didn't challenge other whites & where D gave plausible race-neutral explanation; judge's allowing D to exercise only 1 of these 2 peremptories required reversal;

C v Wood **389 M 552 (83)**—judge's refusal to permit D's peremptories based on age of jurors required reversal because age not cognizable group;

C v Samuel **398 M 93 (86)**—prosecutor's challenges to young women not *Soares* violation because "young persons" not a cognizable group & because women jurors not systematically excluded;

C v Rivera **50 MAC 532 (2000)**—though prosecutor peremptorily challenged 2 young black males, said by trial defense counsel to be only young black males in venire, this wasn't necessarily 'pattern' of challenges to members of constitutionally protected group: at least one older black woman sat on jury, & record was unclear whether there were any older black males, or black females of any age in venire; 'youth' not proper basis for objection to peremptory challenges; though judge failed to follow *Burnett* procedure (**418 M 769 (94)**), & Appeals Court thus examined challenges' validity on de novo basis, no relief; though parties assumed homicide V was "black," he was "Hispanic," & death certificate listed race as "white" (Commonwealth argued that it had no racial incentive to strike black jurors since both D & V were black);

C v Matthews **406 M 380 (90)**—suburban parents not cognizable group;

C v Gagnon **16 MAC 110 (83), reversed sub nom. *C v Bourgeois* 391 M 869 (84)**—party exercising peremptories which have been challenged on *Soares* grounds entitled to opportunity to give race (group)-neutral justification; although prosecutor's challenge to 19 of 23 jurors with French-Canadian names was possible *Soares* violation, reversal not required because prosecutor was denied opportunity to explain;

C v Hutchinson **395 M 568 (85)**—D's explanation that challenges to women jurors were based on their "responses" was vague & pretextual;

C v Odell **34 MAC 100 (93)**—D's challenges to 7 of 8 women explained by claim that women with young children would be "dangerous" to D in child sexual assault case: by allowing 1 of 2 challenges to women over age 60, judge let D have peremptory to which he was not entitled;

C v Fruchtman **418 M 8 (94)**—child sexual assault D's challenges to women **not** uniformly allowed; "D alone cannot claim the right to a representative jury," Court "categorically reject(s)" suggestion that females are more likely to harbor bias against D so charged;

C v Legendre **25 MAC 948 (88)**—D's explanation that challenged woman juror was relative of cops was pretextual;

C v Valentin **420 M 263 (95)**—DA's explanation that peremptorily challenged Hispanic surnamed juror had himself come forward to say he had trouble understanding English was not pretextual;

22-B.10. Motion to Dismiss Venire, Array, or Jury Pool

G.L. c. 234A, § 73—challenge to composition of jury pool requires written motion before voir dire begins, unless judge orders otherwise; affidavit must specify facts & demographic data; judge may decide challenge on papers or after testimony; remedy is discharge of entire juror pool; form motion to quash panel or array appended to statute;

M.R.Crim.P. 20(a)—written motion to dismiss array supported by affidavit must be filed before impanelment; challenges to array shall be tried by court, including taking of testimony at adversarial hearing;

Smith v Commonwealth **420 M 291, 298 (95)**—D (non-white) charged in Suffolk County was to be subjected to trial in Middlesex County because the Chelsea District Courthouse was closed because crumbling; D moved for change of venue back to Suffolk because non-white population in Suffolk = 34% and in Middlesex = 8%; motion should have been allowed;

C v Siciliano **420 M 303 (95)**—another Chelsea D argued for dismissal of charges because of "improper transfer from Suffolk County to Middlesex County" & claimed right to jurors from Chelsea or Revere: such geographical groups are not cognizable as Sixth Amendment claim;

C v Rankins **429 M 470 (99)**—D successfully moved for change of venue to escape pretrial publicity, but 10 days later (week before trial), D moved for reconsideration, claiming that the new county had a smaller minority population than did the original county; when D moved for venue change, he should have considered the possible consequences of his action, AND COULD HAVE SOUGHT TO LIMIT THE COUNTIES TO WHICH CASE WOULD BE TRANSFERRED; no relief here (though 1st county had 7.5% minority population, and 2d county had only 2.6%);

C v Gaynor **443 M 245 (2005)**—when D moved for change of venue from Springfield (Hampden) due to publicity, he had no state constitutional right to move only to county having a minority population at least as great as Hampden County, and no abuse of discretion to hold trial in Berkshire; *Smith v Commonwealth* 420 M 291 distinguished: D there had not sought a change of venue;

C v Bastarache **382 M 86 (80)**—prima facie showing of fair cross-section violation under Article 12, Sixth Amendment, & G.L. c. 234, § 1, requires proving: 1. "distinctive group"; 2. group not fairly & reasonably represented; & 3. underrepresentation due to systematic exclusion in selection process; burden shifts to Commonwealth to rebut; prima facie showing of equal protection violation requires: proof 1. "identifiable group"; 2. disproportionate treatment over time; 3. statistical underrepresentation; bur-den shifts to Commonwealth; D's challenge to pool based on underrepresentation of persons 18–34 years old failed to meet first prong of both claims;

C v Aponte **391 M 494 (84)**—systematic, if unintentional, underrepresentation of Hispanics in Essex county grand juries based on "key man" system for 5 year period required dismissal of indictments under Article 12; prima facie showing of underrepresentation by appropriate statistical methods not rebutted by Commonwealth; random selection methods required;

C v Arriaga **438 M 556 (2003)**—SJC adopts "absolute disparity" test for whether there has been discrimination in jury selection: D must show that group is (1) distinctive, and (2) is not fairly represented in the venire in relation to its proportion of the population, and (3) that underrepresentation is due to systematic exclusion; "absolute disparity" test means subtracting the percentage of the group's population in the jury venire (in this case, 1.46% of venire were Hispanic) from the percentage of the group's population in the community (here, 5.5%), and if number is less than 10%, D fails to meet his burden **[RESULT: NO MINORITY GROUP WITH LESS THAN 10% OF POPULATION WILL BE ABLE TO SHOW UNDERREPRESENTATION, EVEN IF NO MEMBER OF THE MINORITY IS EVER CALLED FOR JURY DUTY; SJC CLAIMS THAT IT WON'T APPLY TEST RIGIDLY, WILL REDRESS IF D PROVES SYSTEMATIC EXCLUSION, ALBEIT WITH LESS THAN 10% DISPARITY]; jury commissioner should require disclosure of racial and ethnic background on juror confirmation form** ;

C v Pope **392 M 493 (84)**—challenges to composition of grand juries must be raised by pretrial motion to dismiss & cannot be raised on appeal or by new trial motion by claim of ineffective assistance of counsel; judge had discretion to deny D's challenge to composition of grand jury & to grant evidentiary hearing where D failed to file affidavit or memorandum of law; But see *C v Iglesias* **426 M 574, 579 (98)** implying that belated claim could be made, asserting ineffective assistance of counsel, but failing here to establish since appellate attorney made no showing that pretrial motion to dismiss would have been successful;—attaching to brief document entitled 'Results of Racial & Ethnic Survey for the Hampden Judicial District' did not suffice;

C v Colon **408 M 419 (90)**—D failed to prove systematic underrepresentation of minorities in Worcester County venires where 1-day, 1-trial system based on census lists sufficiently random;

Murrell v Commonwealth **454 M 1020 (2009)**—SJC refuses G.L. c. 211, § 3 relief to defendant who wanted order compelling all city and town clerks in the county to respond to survey re: how resident lists used to develop lists of potential jurors are compiled; SJC says if convicted he can raise on appeal, as part of his underrepresentation challenge his claim that he was unfairly deprived of the data needed to make such a challenge;

C v Fryar **425 M 237 (97)**—grand & petit jurors compiled from names from annual census, supplemented by recent additions to registered voters; neither visual observation nor surname analysis is reliable guide to racial or ethnic identification; D failed to meet burden of showing that any alleged underrepresentation was due to systematic exclusion; court used "absolute disparity test" to determine whether there was "substantial underrepresentation" (subtract percentage number of group in jury venire from percentage number of group in population, and if number is less than ten, disparity will never be deemed "substantial");

C v Leitzsey **421 M 694 (96)**—to challenge, must present pretrial motion, with affidavit & memo, establishing (a, b & c in *Tolentino*, below)

C v Tolentino **422 M 515 (96)**—to make out prima facie case of unconst. jury selection under Sixth Amendment, D had to show (a) 'distinctive' group (b) group not fairly & reasonably represented in venires in relation to proportion in community (c) underrepresentation = due to systematic exclusion in jury selection process; Court willing to allow use of '90 census in '95 motion, **but** census included some undetermined percentage of population which would be ineligible for jury service for age or other reasons, so D didn't establish what % of Essex County population eligible for jury service was Hispanic; visual observation not good basis for saying "no Hispanics"; anecdotal/subjective data in counsel's affidavit re Essex County jury venires' compositions won't do; even unintentional discrimination against minority group would raise constitutional question;

C v Prater **431 M 86, 90–91 (2000)**—court ignored 2 affidavits (because not "originals") and termed other exhibits in support of motion to dismiss jury venire (newspaper article and excerpt from 1994 report to SJC) not "competent evidence"; judge held to have discretion to deny motion to introduce testimony of jury commissioner and city clerks for Lynn and Lawrence because moving papers had failed to make out prima facie case of underrepresentation or systematic exclusion;

C v Serrano **48 MAC 163 (99)**—motion to dismiss venire for alleged systematic exclusion of racial and ethnic minorities, but no record of what the venire composition was, and no evidence that available venire did not contain a representative no. of minority members; affidavits from defense lawyers re: recollections about venire compositions in other trials was "anecdotal"/"inadequate";

C v Gaskins **419 M 809 (95)**—allegation of ineffective assistance of counsel on appeal because venire contained no black or "minority" jurors failed for utter lack of record; no R.30 motion had ever attempted to meet burden on the claim of unconstitutional underrepresentation;

C v Duteau **384 M 321 (81)**—Athol residents not an "identifiable group" for equal protection purposes;

C v Stone **366 M 506 (74)**—evidence insufficient to show that "paupers" an "identifiable group";

Taylor v Louisiana **419 US 522 (75)**—state laws operating to exclude women as jurors violate right to fair & impartial jury under Sixth & Fourteenth Amendments;

Duren v Missouri **439 US 357 (79)**—state law disproportionately exempting from jury service women who request exemption due to domestic responsibilities violates Sixth Amendment "fair cross-section" requirement;

C v Manning **41 MAC 696 (96)**—statutory right of persons over age 70 (G.L. c. 234A, § 4) to exempt selves from jury service not violative of Sixth Amendment 'fair cross section' right, & not "irrational";

Holland v Illinois **493 US 474 (90)**—Sixth Amend. cross-section requirement applies only to entire array, not to jury panel;

Castenada v Partida **430 US 482 (77)**—equal protection challenge requirement of proof of purposeful discrimination discussed; prima facie case made out by showing substantial underrepresentation of identifiable group; Mexican-Americans members of identifiable group;

22-C. SEQUESTRATION AND SEPARATION

M.R.Crim.P. 20(e)—sequestration of jury within judge's discretion; separation of deliberating jury authorized;

C v Sperazza **379 M 166 (79)**—judge's refusal to sequester juror in murder 1 trial not abuse of discretion;

C v Clark **432 M 1 (2000)**—fact that 3 jurors reported exposure to extraneous influences (2 were dismissed and other not affected) did not mean that decision not to sequester jury was abuse of discretion or error of law;

C v Benjamin **369 M 770 (76)**—although preferable for trial judge to ask daily whether nonsequestered jurors followed instructions not to read about or discuss case, reversal required only if prejudice shown;

C v Allen **379 M 166 (79)**—judge's separation of deliberating jurors (here, to allow jurors to go to polls to vote) not abuse of discretion requiring reversal unless prejudicial extraneous influence shown;

C v Marshall **373 M 65 (77)**—same in murder 1 trial;

22-D. ALTERNATES, AND DISCHARGING AND REPLACING JURORS

G.L. c. 234A § 68—at least 2 alternates impaneled for juries of 12; at least 1 alternate for juries of 6; alternates chosen by lot (except for foreperson) & kept apart from jurors while deliberating but subject to same rules; juror who dies, or becomes ill or unable to perform duties for good cause shown may be discharged & replaced by alternate drawn by lot; jury must "renew" deliberations; parties may stipulate to other procedures or to verdict by less than full jury;

G.L. c. 234A § 39—prior to deliberations, juror may be discharged for "extreme hardship"; during deliberations, juror may be discharged only after hearing & finding of "emergency" or "other compelling reason"; judge has discretion at any other time to "in best interest of justice"; jurors should be prepared to serve 3 days;

G.L. c. 234 § 26B—same;

M.R.Crim.P. 20(d)(2) & (3)—same as G.L. c. 234A § 68; not more than 16 jurors; at "final submission," if more than 12 jurors still available, names except foreperson's placed in box & jury reduced to 12; alternates to be kept separate from other jurors but subject to same rules; if, after submission, juror dies, becomes ill, or unable to perform duties for any other cause, judge may discharge & replace with alternate; jury shall renew deliberations;

C v Young **73 MAC 479 (2009)**—judge permissibly discharged seated, but unsworn, juror upon finding her body odor to be extremely strong and discomfiting to other jurors;

C v Alvarado **50 MAC 419 (2000)**—no relief for judge's non-random designation of particular juror as alternate (prior to any deliberations), because juror failed to disclose on questionnaire that he'd been tried for A&B 3 weeks earlier; though "irregular," such irregularity not ground for setting aside verdict without showing prejudice (see G.L. c. 234A, § 68);

M.R.Crim.P. 19—D's waiver of right to verdict by full jury must be signed & in writing; all co-D's must agree;

C v Nicoll **452 M 816 (2008)**—after empanelling & swearing only six jurors, a juror knew first witness, and raised possible partiality: judge excused juror after questioning, and declared mistrial after stating erroneously that criminal trial could not proceed with only five jurors: because trial could have proceeded with D's consent (and D objected to mistrial), no "manifest necessity" justified mistrial and double jeopardy barred second trial;

C v Dery **452 M 823 (2008)**—due to disqualifications and peremptory challenges, jury venire was reduced to only five people; after consultation with counsel, D agreed to trial by five (full colloquy under oath, oral waiver) and was acquitted: Commonwealth petitioned under G.L. c. 211, § 3, saying jury of five not legitimate, and D hadn't signed required written waiver (M.R.Crim.P. 19(b)); Commonwealth had failed to object, no relief;

C v Haywood **377 M 755 (79)**—before deliberating juror discharged, judge should hold hearing at which presence of juror or others with relevant information required; if discharge & replacement found necessary, judge must instruct jurors to disregard all prior deliberations & to begin deliberations anew & must explain that discharge was for reasons entirely personal to juror; statutory procedure upheld as constitutional;

C v Connor **392 M 838 (84)**—judge's failure to hold hearing & make findings of "good cause" for discharge required reversal; suspicions that juror was mentally ill & his asserted inability to abide by oath didn't establish

"good cause"; expressions of alarm by deliberating jurors should be treated as sign of deadlock; judge should tell remaining jurors that any dismissal was entirely personal to juror and not related to juror's views or relationship with remainder of jury;

C v Olavarria **71 MAC 612 (2008)**—after report, twice, of impasse in deliberations, the second note including "deadlocked at 11 to one", judge instructed pursuant to Tuey-Rodriquez, and received further note of continuing deadlock and that holdout juror had brought into deliberations law dictionaries' definition of 'reasonable doubt' & 'moral certainty'; D's mistrial motion was denied; examination of juror resulted in her assurance that she would make "every effort" to disregard her retrieved definitions (substance of which included disapproved concepts relating to personal decisions of "great importance", but judge refused juror's request to identify what in those definitions was wrong) but did not "honestly" know that she could guarantee this: no error in discharging juror, there being no indication that discharge was because of hold-out status;

C v Peppicelli **70 MAC 87 (2007)**—judge's statement to jurors that he "[had] had to excuse one of your deliberating colleagues", and "ask[ed] them 'not to speculate about the reason'" which had "nothing to do with your deliberations" held sufficient, given that D didn't offer different suggested instruction and didn't object; a week earlier, judge had explained that a deliberating juror could only be removed for "personal emergency" and not for any positions he might be taking in deliberations;

C v Garrey **436 M 422 (2002)**—upholding discharge of juror whose son, arrested the prior night, was held in lieu of bail at the same house of correction as D, despite juror's assertion that she could remain impartial, & her lack of knowledge that D was so held (G.L. c. 234, § 26B requires "compelling reason" for such discharge);

C v Daughtry **417 M 136 (94)**—hearing not required prior to discharge of deliberating juror who had informed all, during selection process, of scheduled extensive medical treatment in hospital for "very serious condition";

C v Sanders **451 M 290 (2008)**—two jurors had informed all during empanelment that they could not serve past a certain date (one having nonrefundable international vacation plane tickets, the other having long-planned business trip), but deliberations continued up until that date and jurors' note reminded judge of preexisting plans: after separate colloquies with the jurors, judge legitimately found good cause for discharge of "plane tickets" juror; "business trip" juror indicated that trip could possibly be postponed if judge thought juror should stay, but judge permitted juror "to choose whether to remain" on deliberating jury; SJC held no "abuse of discretion" in discharge (if pressured to remain, juror might have rushed jury to verdict);

C v Francis **432 M 353 (2000)**—juror not to be discharged for reasons related to issues of the case, juror's views on case, or relationship with fellow jurors; though discharged juror's fear here was product of her own residential surroundings coupled with "the nature of this case" (i.e., belief that gang members were in her neighborhood), SJC upheld discharge: juror had twice failed to appear during trial (had to be escorted by police) & trial judge found her to be extremely "upset";

C v Arana 453 M 214 (2009)—(not-yet-deliberating) juror's observation of witness on stand seeming to respond to spectator led her to believe that witness was being coached; this was NOT an "extraneous" influence: juror was entitled to observe and consider "all aspects of the witness's testimony in order to assess . . . credibility", and judge should not have dismissed juror on ground that she was no longer 'impartial';

C v Keaton 36 MAC 81 (94)—in order to obtain hearing/relief, counsel should have supplied affidavits re juror allegedly sleeping through testimony; judge's finding of no problem, purportedly based on his own observation, was here accepted in absence of such affidavits, though judge must ensure all jurors hear evidence & sleeping juror jeopardizes D's right to fair trial; *C v Hernandez* 63 MAC 426 (2005)—though judge sua sponte questioned juror who seemed to be "nodding off," judge was satisfied with juror's denial and explanation; no ineffective assistance of counsel in failing to move for mistrial or replacement of juror;

C v Morales 453 M 40 (2009)—though D's affidavit in motion for new trial stated he alerted trial counsel to sleeping juror (but counsel replied that he had not seen this, but if it occurred it was during direct exam of prosecution witness and so would not harm D), no relief where trial judge stated that he had watched jury carefully and if one had slept, he would have done something about it at the time (special deference to motion judge's factual findings where he also was trial judge);

C v Braun 74 MAC 904 (2009)—after "contemporaneous observations" of apparently sleeping juror by court officer, defense counsel, and judge himself, judge abused discretion by failing to conduct voir dire simply because he wasn't "certain" juror was asleep; judge failed to have info necessary for proper exercise of discretion;

C v Dancy 75 MAC 175 (2009)—judge observed at bench conference at half-way point of trial transcript that juror "keeps falling asleep"; record raised "distinct possibility" that juror slept through significant portion of trial, a structural error infringing on D's right to basic component of fair trial, never harmless: new trial motion invited;

C v Stokes 440 M 741 (2004)—no error in dismissing without voir dire juror who repeatedly "dozed off"; G.L. c. 234A, § 39 cited (Court's discretionary authority to dismiss juror at any time "in the best interests of justice");

C v Johnson 426 M 617, 624–25 (98)—after swearing of jury & before evidence, discharge of 2 and empanelment of 3 others due to judge's belated recognition that trial could be protracted; D counsel had agreed; no remedy on appeal;

C v Hamilton 411 M 313 (91)—judge's removal of black juror's card along with foreperson's from box from which alternates chosen did not require reversal where

judge did so to enhance diversity of jury & where no objection made or prejudice shown; BUT SEE *C v Roche* 44 MAC 372 (98) judge cannot attempt to "construct demographically representative jury" by accepting some peremptory challenges & rejecting others;

C v Martins 38 MAC 636, 639 (95)—during deliberations, report that foreman had introduced 'self and said he had "lapses of memory" followed 3 requests for reinstruction on "kidnapping"; after foreman denied problem with memory, no abuse of discretion in refusing to discharge him or question other jurors;

C v Rock 429 M 609 (99)—on 5th day of murder trial, judge permissibly discharged juror after questioning both the juror and the sister of murder V, who claimed to have overheard juror saying that he smoked marijuana in order to stay awake during the trial proceedings; appraisal of credibility was for judge (who apparently disbelieved juror's denial of such statement/practice);

C v Young 401 M 390 (87)—judge's refusal to discharge deliberating juror who was concerned he had seen D before not an abuse of discretion where judge properly questioned juror in presence of counsel before finding insufficient cause for discharge;

C v Perez 30 MAC 934 (91)—judge's discharge & replacement of "missing juror" in midst of deliberations required reversal because done in absence of D & counsel & because no facts on record show juror unable to perform functions;

C v Swafford 441 M 329 (2004)—judge permissibly discharged deliberating juror who said she could not be fair/impartial after hostility and name calling between herself and another juror; appellate court deferred to trial judge's finding of fact that juror's "reclusive and abdicatory behavior" was problem "personal to her"; [but see *C v Connor* 392 M 838, 844–45 (84)—discharge OK only for reasons having nothing to do with issues of case or with juror's relationship with fellow jurors];

C v Rodriguez 63 MAC 660 (2005)—reversal for judge's discharge of deliberating juror, since it was apparently "inextricably connected to her relations to her fellow jurors, the deadlock, and her apparent hold-out status"; jury instruction re: the discharge = additional basis for reversal, since it didn't say that reason for discharge was "entirely personal and has nothing to do with the discharged juror's views on the case or relationship with fellow jurors" (per *C v Connor* 392 M 844); further, some juror accessed on internet G.L. c. 234, § 26B, re: impaneling, sequestering, & discharging juror, an extraneous matter (& this "reinforce[d] conclusion" that convictions be reversed;

C v Peppicelli 70 MAC 87 (2007)—despite discharge of juror who held view of NG/self-defense, court holds that remaining jurors here would not have inferred that his removal was because of his viewpoint;

C v Dosanjos 52 MAC 531, 535 (2001)—"serious error" for judge to exclude D from individual voir dire of jurors remaining after discharge of one juror who belatedly recognized, during deliberations, that she recognized D &

defense witnesses from workplace, but no relief because D didn't show prejudice;

C v Zimmerman **441 M 146 (2004)**—judge didn't abuse discretion in dismissing deliberating juror (who belatedly revealed that she recognized D's mother as a neighbor, and had seen one D in neighborhood during trial), but remaining jurors should have been instructed so as to "quell any inappropriate speculation regarding juror 2's dismissal"; to preserve issue, D must request instruction BEFORE new jury retires to deliberate, but here, substantial risk of miscarriage of justice found [objection was not timely];

C v Tennison **440 M 553 (2003)**—judge properly dismissed deliberating juror after D-counsel revealed that D had communicated with juror throughout trial; appellate argument that jury should have conducted "second" voir dire to determine extent of jury contamination due to juror's removal was not made to trial judge, & no 'substantial risk of miscarriage of justice' found; first voir dire had resulted in no juror acknowledging contact with any party;

C v Kalinowski **12 MAC 827 (81)**—judge's unobjected-to replacement of ill juror during deliberations, instructions that jury begin deliberations anew, & provision of new verdict slips not a double jeopardy violation, even though jurors had previously reached verdicts on 2 of 4 charges before ill juror was replaced;

C v Robinson **449 M 1 (2007)**—no relief for replacement of deliberating juror who first reported that she wasn't coming in because her child's caretaker was ill, then that the caretaker was better (but that nonetheless juror was "not happy about having to come in"), and thereafter that she was still ill and juror wasn't coming to court; while G.L. c. 234A, § 39 contemplates "hearing," juror wasn't available for such hearing; juror concerned about child's welfare "would be distracted and unable to concentrate . . . or deliberate fairly";

C v McCarthy **37 MAC 113 (94)**—though jury had returned verdict on 1 of 3 indictments, no hearing was required prior to replacing non-appearing ill juror; jurors were instructed to begin deliberations anew as to remaining charges;

C v Gonzalez **28 MAC 10 (89)**—judge's discharge of mentally ill juror & replacement with alternate, after other 11 individually complained that juror was causing deadlock & after judge conducted private investigation, required new trial where D objected & moved for mistrial, because jury might have viewed judge's action as endorsement of their positions;

C v Morales **440 M 536 (2003)**—though three jurors complained to court officer about "distracting" behavior of one juror, judge after consideration did nothing, and parties concurred; no relief on appeal;

C v Torres **453 M 722 (2009)**—after foreman sent note saying one juror was unable to deliberate in coherent/logical manner and seeking guidance, judge questioned foreperson, reinstructed jury about deliberating, took subsequent notes from foreperson and from the juror, & with

parties' assent interviewed foreperson [again] and juror, stressing not to disclose details of deliberations, juror implicitly expressing impartiality: decision not to discharge juror = "sound";

C v Leftwich **430 M 865, 872–73 (2000)**—judge's discharge of juror who was shaking "head to toe," very emotionally distraught, and claiming difficulty with "stress," upheld despite absence of examination by a medical professional, though SJC repeated that jurors shouldn't be excused for reasons related to "issues of the case"; no suggestion here that jurors were at impasse or that juror's statements were euphemisms for fact that juror was asserting a minority position during deliberations; in contrast to:

C v Webster **391 M 271 (84)**—judge's questioning of holdout juror in view of other jurors after receiving note from jury was coercive & required new trial where juror called in sick following day & was replaced;

C v Freeman **442 M 779 (2004)**—judge's discharge of juror who arrived late for second day of deliberations and continued apologizing in incoherent and lengthy manner about her spouse's neurological disorder was accompanied by judge's on-record comment that "I don't know whether she was enormously upset because of this case or she was enormously upset because of her own personal situation"; no error acknowledged, though D noted discharge illegitimate if it's related to issues in the case (*see* **Leftwich 430 M at 872–73**);

C v Martino **412 M 267 (92)**—judge's discharge of juror in D's absence not error where discharge was agreed to by D & counsel, & juror was discharged in counsel's presence;

C v Caldwell **45 MAC 42 (98)**—deliberating juror discharged after colloquy (requested by D-counsel) after DA and cops recognized him as previously convicted of drug offenses, which he had not disclosed on juror questionnaire, as "required"; despite absence of D, and his consternation on record later, and though record of hearing was missing (and it was D's burden to reconstruct, which he didn't do), and though judge might not have asked juror why he failed to disclose criminal record and whether prior convictions affected ability to perform duty as juror ("both desirable lines of inquiry under the circumstances"), no relief: harmless beyond reasonable doubt despite fact that D's right to be present at trial is "basic right( ) that an attorney cannot waive without the fully informed and publicly acknowledged consent of the D";

C v Jiminez **22 MAC 286 (86)**—discharge of juror just before deliberations was not abuse of discretion where juror's opportunity for job interview was "good cause";

C v McCaster **46 MAC 752 (99)**—two jurors who undertook independent investigation during deliberations were discharged, as well as one juror who said she couldn't be impartial after hearing of the investigation's results, and D elected to proceed with only 11 jurors (see M.R.Crim.P. 19(b)); in doing so, rather than moving for mistrial (after 5 invitations to do so), he waived issues regarding the adequacy of the judge's inquiry of the remaining jurors;

C v Peppicelli **70 MAC 87 (2007)**—deliberating juror's conversation with police officer in store check-out line was extraneous influence necessitating discharge of the juror (officer expressed opinion that "victim" group as well as Ds were "all pieces of crap", juror opining NG, self-defense); judge disbelieved juror's contrary account of contact;

C v Santiago **50 MAC 762, 766 (2001)**—one juror became aware that D had been convicted previously (that conviction was reversed on appeal), & stated in response to whether could continue to be impartial, "I don't feel like I heard anything different than what I've already heard"; no error in denying mistrial motion (& D didn't ask for lesser remedy of removing this juror);

See Chapter 22-H for cases on extraneous influences;

22-E. DELIBERATIONS, QUESTIONS, DEADLOCKS AND MISTRIALS

22-E.1. Privacy of Deliberations

G.L. c. 234A § 68—alternates to be kept apart from deliberating jurors but subject to same rules;

M.R.Crim.P. 20(d)—same;

C v Smith **403 M 489 (88)**—allowing alternates in jury room during deliberations required new trial, even though counsel & prosecutor consented; no remand for evidentiary hearing because prejudice presumed; open question whether D has right to personally waive issue for appeal;

C v Jones **405 M 661 (89)**—Smith, above, applied to cases where direct appeal pending;

C v Sheehy **412 M 235 (92)**—jury deliberations are to be conducted privately & without extraneous influence; presence of alternates in jury room during deliberations requires new trial under G.L. c. 234A, § 68; G.L. c. 234A, § 74 requirement of prejudice & timely objection would violate Article 12 right to fair jury & Article 30 separation of powers doctrine endowing courts with function of judicial review;

C v Casey (no. 1) **442 M 1 (2004)**—that alternate juror walked into jury room and stayed for two minutes after deliberations began, and asked a question before leaving wasn't ground for allowing new trial;

US v Olano **507 US 725 (93)**—under Fed.R.Crim.P. 24(c), presence of alternates during deliberations not reversible error, they being presumed to follow instructions not to participate so no prejudice shown (contra Mass. Declaration of Rights, Article 12, construed in *Sheehy* **412 M 235 (92)**);

22-E.2. What Goes into Jury Room: Including Sanitized Exhibits, Chalks, Jurors' Notes, Written Instructions

C v Lockley **381 M 156 (80)**—mug shots should be sanitized before being sent into jury room;

C v Sheline **391 M 279 (84)**—D's alias on drug certificate should have been stricken;

C v Lappas **39 MAC 285 (95)**—failure to redact the penalty provisions from copy of statute available to deliberating jury was subject of corrective instructions to the jurors: no relief on appeal for D;

C v Walter **10 MAC 255 (80)**—judge has discretion to send chalks into jury room;

C v Guy **454 M 440 (2009)**—"notebooks" (copy marked for identification) provided to jurors during testimony of DNA analyst helped them follow complex testimony and "visually comprehend its import"; error to allow jurors' use of the "DNA notebooks" during deliberations, but not prejudicial ("did not expose them to extrinsic material outside the record");

C v Hrycenko **31 MAC 425 (91)**—judge's sending deliberating jury photographs which had been identified but not admitted into evidence required reversal because it belatedly expanded record without giving D opportunity to defuse impact;

C v Federici **427 M 740 (98)**—during deliberations, jury foreperson opened box of exhibits and saw folder of photos not admitted as exhibits: judge replaced foreperson with alternate and found that none of other jurors had seen, denying individual voir dire of them re: this issue; before they began deliberations anew, judge instructed that she understood that no one else had seen the contents, but that "if that is not correct, if there is anybody else who did," person(s) should tell court officer immediately; no error, "sound discretion of the trial judge";

C v Pixley **42 MAC 927 (97)**—binoculars used by cop when he allegedly observed D selling cocaine were admitted without objection & without request for limiting instruction that jurors were not to experiment with them; no substantial risk of miscarriage of justice found;

C v Beauchamp **424 M 682, 691 (97)**—disapproving prosecutor's invitation to jurors to try to make an abrasion on a knee by making deep indentation in wall with it, so as to disprove D's story: jury should not be encouraged to conduct experiments or obtain outside info of any sort;

C v Marks **12 MAC 511 (81)**—jury's inability to review key photos which had been admitted into evidence & which were lost in middle of trial required reversal;

Superior Court Rule 8A—judge has discretion to allow jurors to take notes during evidence, summation or instructions; guidelines must be announced; notes to be destroyed after verdict;

C v St. Germain **381 M 256 (80)**—note-taking left to judge's discretion; judge should instruct that jurors should limit note-taking to key points to allow them to observe witnesses, & that deliberating jurors should not argue that note-taking jurors' memories = superior;

C v Barros **425 M 572, 585 (97)**—no error in allowing note-taking during jury instructions;

C v Dykens **438 M 827 (2003)**—no abuse of discretion in judge's allowing jurors to take notes during second portion of the charge (re: elements of offenses), but not during first part (principles such as presumption of innocence, proof beyond reasonable doubt, & inferences); jurors were told not to consider any instruction more or less important than another, etc.'

C v Baseler **419 M 500 (95)**—judge may allow jury to use audio or video-with-audio tape of jury instructions, even absent parties' consent; tape must be wholly audible & contain entire charge, & judge should instruct jury how to use it, & mark it for identification; *C v Graham* **431 M 500 (2000)**—no error when judge gave jury tape of only supplemental instructions; *C v Smith* **75 MAC 196 (2009), further review allowed on other grounds 456 M 1101 (2010)**—no substantial risk of miscarriage of justice in providing jury complete recording of original charge, but not of supplemental instructions;

C v Lavalley **410 M 641 (91)**—endorses written jury instruction if parties agree, & complete oral instructions cured omissions in written instructions;

C v Walker **68 MAC 194 (2007)**—written instructions OK even when D doesn't consent; "content *and* manner of delivery of jury instructions is ultimately a matter that must be left to the discretion of the trial judge"; even if D's reading of *Lavalley* is correct, D couldn't show prejudice from distribution of written instruction without D's express consent; Court criticized judge for giving "abbreviated" reasonable doubt instruction in the "written" version of charge, judge should have given Webster or approved modern equivalent;

C v Martin **424 M 301 (97)**—reiterating approval of written jury instructions;

C v Patry **48 MAC 470 (2000)**—judge shouldn't ever enter jury room to conduct the court's business, even with parties' consent or at invitation of jury; judge's answering jury questions orally inside the jury deliberating room = violation of Sixth Amendment right to public trial, structural error without showing of prejudice; though D can waive right to public trial, D personally must do so (not D counsel);

22-E.3. Jury Questions, Supplemental Instructions and Readbacks

See Chapter 12-L for other cases on jury questions;
See Chapter 12-K for cases on jury instructions;

C v Lyons **71 MAC 671 (2008)**—charged with indecent assault and battery on person age 14 or older, D defended on basis that complainant initiated a "scuffle," and any indecent contact occurred as he was pushing her away from him; COMMONWEALTH requested instruction on lesser included offense of assault and battery, and D re-

quested instruction on self-defense, which judge gave without objection by Commonwealth; judge's subsequently withdrawing from jury the self-defense instruction, at Commonwealth's request, before deliberations began, was error, undermining defense and D's credibility;

C v Robinson **449 M 1, 8 n.11 (2007)**—while it's "tempting" just to repeat the closest original instruction in response to a jury question, the jury has heard those original instructions and has nonetheless submitted question; a "direct answer to the question presented" is the way to provide the additional guidance requested; here the judge should have just answered, "yes, a statement may be both coerced and true";

C v Dilone **385 M 281, 287 n.2 (82)**—endorsing "any reasonable procedure" agreed to by parties by which jury could have written copy of jury instructions;

C v Lavalley **410 M 641 (91)**—complete oral instructions cured omissions in written instructions given to jurors;

C v Martin **424 M 301 (97)**—no error in giving jury written instructions same as oral (parties agreed);

***Thames v Commonwealth* 365 M 477 (74)**—messages or questions from jurors should be in writing, shown to counsel & placed on record; judge's replies should be put on record in presence of counsel;

C v Patry **48 MAC 470 (2000)**—judge's answering jury questions orally inside the jury deliberating room = violation of Sixth Amendment right to public trial, structural error without showing of prejudice; though D can waive right to public trial, D personally must do so (not D counsel); judge shouldn't ever enter jury rooms to conduct the court's business, even with parties' consent or at invitation of jury;

C v Urena **417 M 692 (94)**—finding no prejudice here, SJC failed to outlaw judge-initiated procedure of jurors putting questions to witnesses, **but** procedure should be used infrequently & with great caution & is "fraught with potential for error": questions only in writing (and judge will discuss with attorneys), specific instructions that rules of evidence may forbid particular questions, & parties should be given opportunity to examine witness further after any jury questions;

C v Britto **433 M 596 (2001)**—juror questioning of witnesses upheld, despite complete bedlam here shown & lack of legislative study/approval (see concurrence by Cowin, J); recommended procedures set forth;

C v Mendez **77 MAC 905 (2010)**—juror questions obliterated well-considered "first complaint" evidentiary law in MA: "permitting jurors to submit questions in criminal cases is not without risk. Suffice it to say that in criminal cases involving subtle evidentiary issues like first complaint, judges should be particularly cautious in exercising discretion to permit jurors to submit questions and, if they are so permitted, in exercising discretion to post particular questions"; "satisfying the jury's desire for more information ordinarily should not trump a party's deliberate choice as to how most effectively to present its case while avoiding the possibility of error";

C v Donovan **15 MAC 269 (83)**—jurors have right & duty to ask for reinstruction on legal matters they don't understand;

C v Hicks **22 MAC 139 (86)**—judge should respond to jury questions only after consulting with counsel & prosecutor;

C v Porro **74 MAC 676, further app. review allowed 455 M 1106 (2009)**—rejecting D's argument that judge's response to deliberating jury's question "broadened basis of criminal liability," and violated M.R.Crim.P. 24(b) (requiring notice to parties of judge's instructions PRIOR TO closing arguments, to enable intelligent argument to jury);

C v Williams **450 M 645 (2008)**—co-D's acquittal at SAME trial didn't require finding of NG for D as joint venturer because evidence supported existence of some actor with D and shared intent: evidence sufficient to show other person[s] was involved in fatal shooting and binding victim; jury's question which could be understood as asking whether "joint venture" referred *only* to the two charged Ds, implausibly found to be "confusing," so permissibly answered "unable to answer question because I do not understand it" (despite D's request for answer that confined G/NG to joint venture by the two charged co-Ds);

C v DeJesus **44 MAC 349 (98)**—error, but no prejudice shown, for judge to have responded to jury question without notice to counsel (Q: did D plead NG to all indictments? A: yes); *C v Baro* **73 MAC 218 (2008)**—when D fled during lunch recess at beginning of jury deliberations, no error in having jurors in courtroom for response to jury question: D's absence was not mentioned and D's family and courtroom personnel were also absent; "Muckle" protocol (59 MAC 631, 639 [2003]) prescribed for "mid-trial" absence unnecessary;

C v Bell **455 M 408 (2009)**—in response to jury question, judge need only consider question asked, and is not required to instruct on any other matters (despite D's request for additional instruction stressing defense points);

C v Bacigalupo **49 MAC 629 (2000)**—given absence of counsel and failure to consult counsel, it was error for judge to respond to jury note ('could we have a copy of (Commonwealth witness's) testimony?') with note that they could have the testimony read back, but no relief because clear here that judge would have exercised her discretion in same manner; procedure violated D's right to assistance of counsel at important juncture & D's right to be present at all critical stages; better practice would be to instruct that jury should consider the read-back testimony along with other evidence (but no such instruction was here requested, & here both cross-examination and direct of witness was read back, & 'reasonable doubt' instruction was repeated at this point also at jury's request);

C v Floyd P. **415 M 826 (93)**—note from jury (that verdicts had been reached on 2 charges, but 2 jurors would change votes if aggravated rape verdict required conviction as well as first degree murder) should have been shown to counsel, who should have been given opportunity to help frame response & to lodge any objections;

C v Thomas **21 MAC 183 (85)**—"necessity, extent, & character" of supplemental instructions within judge's discretion; supplemental joint venture instruction proper where it would have been appropriate as initial instruction;

C v Ragland **72 MAC 815 (2008)**—after trial in which witnesses recanted their grand jury testimony, jury sent question, "what is the punishment for perjury?", judge with agreement of all parties responded that jurors were not to concern themselves with any punishment for any crime; particularly because D was not entitled to original instruction that recantation was adverse to witnesses' penal interest (because the evidence supporting witness's awareness of such adversity was objected to, and objection was sustained, & evidence thus stricken), no error because no basis for jury to consider what penal consequences might be; even if initial instruction was proper, it required no amplification, no substantial risk of miscarriage of justice;

C v Davis **52 MAC 75 (2001)**—when veracity of "cooperating witness" was sole issue (& though no specific deal had been set for his own pending criminal case, he expected "consideration" in exchange for his testimony against D), reversal because judge responded to jury question wanting to know what "consideration" ('May we please know if there are laws of leniency that may apply here. If so, what are they?'), without consulting counsel & in materially misleading way (answer was "there are no laws of leniency");

C v Hakkila **42 MAC 129, 131 (97)**—on second day of deliberations, substitute (non-trial) judge decided not to answer jury's question, awaiting trial judge's return to duty next day, but jury then convicted without requested supplemental instruction: "judge has discretion in determining whether to suspend jury deliberations while considering their questions";

C v Collins **36 MAC 25 (94)**—prior to receiving answer from judge to a jury question, jury said it had reached verdicts: no error in taking verdicts; within judge's discretion to bar or allow continued deliberation during preparation to answer jury question;

C v Skinner **408 M 88 (90)**—judge's erroneous supplemental instruction on malice & deliberate premeditation required reversal under G.L. c. 278, § 33E, even though main instructions were proper;

C v Belding **42 MAC 435 (97)**—judge answered 'yes' to jury question whether "outside residence" included situation in which D's arm, when he fired gun, extended into common area from apartment door's threshold; finding the statute to be silent on this issue, Appeals Court said it was question of **fact** for jury: conviction reversed;

C v Pares-Ramires **400 M 604 (87)**—judge not required to give supplemental instruction on self-defense where already given in main instructions & not responsive to jury request for explanation of "3 degrees of murder";

C v Gonzalez **47 MAC 255 (99)**—jury convicted D of possessing heroin with intent to distribute; same jury deliberated issue of whether D had previously been convicted of like offense, and judge's instructions prior to 2d deliberations were abbreviated, "referring to and incorporating" what jurors were told about 3 hours earlier; no objection, and no substantial risk of miscarriage of justice found;

C v Mandeville **386 M 393 (82)**—judge has discretion not to grant jury request for readback of stenographer's notes of trial testimony because it may "overemphasize certain aspects of the case";

C v Phong Thu Ly **19 MAC 901 (84)**—no abuse of discretion in allowing jury to hear tapes of two witnesses' testimony, when tapes were played only once, in entirety (both direct & cross-examination), & judge instructed jury not to place undue emphasis on testimony;

C v Richenburg **401 M 663 (88)**—same; 'entirely appropriate that resolution of ambiguities regarding a witness's testimony be left to recollection of jury';

C v McColgan **31 MAC 932 (91)**—judge had discretion to grant, over D's objection, jury's request to listen to tapes of testimony of rape complainant & fresh complaint witness, where other witnesses did not testify to contrary;

C v Johnson **43 MAC 509 (97)**—judge should not have provided answer to jury question, when question demonstrated that jury was considering and wanted more info on pt. they had been instructed (properly) not to consider; "inconsistent" to simultaneously grant request for info & tell jury not to consider it;

C v Small **10 MAC 606 (80)**—although judge may allow D to reopen evidence after deliberations commenced to answer specific jury question, not abuse of discretion to deny request where D had earlier opportunity; judge not required to answer factual question whether D was left- or right-handed;

C v Webster **391 M 271 (84)**—judge's questioning of/instruction to holdout juror in view of other jurors after receiving note from jury was coercive & required new trial where juror called in sick following day & was replaced;

22-E.4. Preverdict Inquiries into Extraneous Influences

See Chapter 22-A-3 for cases on determining extraneous influences during voir dire;

See Chapter 22-G for cases on determining extraneous influences in post-verdict proceedings;

See Chapter 22-H for cases on variety of extraneous influences;

C v Tavares **385 M 140 (82)**—although *Fidler* **377 M 192 (79)** (*below at Chapter 22-G-1*) ban on probing of jurors' subjective or deliberative processes generally applicable to pre-verdict inquiries, "plainest principles of justice" require more probing inquiry under certain circumstances, as where racial slurs uttered during deliberations; judge's finding after hearing that verdict unaffected by racial prejudice was proper;

C v Maldonado **429 M 502 (99)**—mid-trial, juror reported fear for his safety after being approached by a coworker while picking up his paycheck (D on trial for gang-related murder), and was dismissed; judge individually questioned other jurors re: any possible contamination by either the dismissed juror or news reports, and one juror admitted hearing news describing D as 'hit man'; though this juror was not dismissed (judge implicitly finding he remained impartial), he did not deliberate (was alternate); no relief;

C v John **442 M 329 (2004)**—juror's note to judge at close of first day of trial: "Guns, drugs, gangs, murder. Should I have any reason to be worried about my own safety as a juror?"; following reassurance by judge and statement that she had not mentioned concerns to fellow jurors, no errors in allowing juror to remain and refusing to question other jurors;

C v Delp **41 MAC 435 (96)**—juror, on Monday after Friday "G", came forward to acknowledge bias against D because of belief that D was homosexual, but ADA elicited at hearing on motion for new trial that juror tried not to be biased, didn't hate any group, and when he left courtroom after verdict believed he had done his duty; judge implicitly found merely "2d thoughts" which commonly exist in conscientious juror; Appeals Court **faulted** D for not insisting upon answers to questions re other jurors' possible bias when juror stated that he did not "want to implicate any other juror," but alluded to other jurors' remarks about D's homosexuality;

C v Jackson **376 M 790 (78)**—where potentially extraneous influence (here, mid-trial media coverage) is reliably brought to judge's attention, judge should determine whether material goes beyond record & raises serious question of possible prejudice; if so, voir dire should be held to determine if any jurors saw or heard material; if any juror responds affirmatively, judge should individually examine jurors outside presence of others to determine extent of exposure & its effects on juror's ability to give impartial verdict; standards for determining extraneous influence in jury selection to be applied;

C v Clemente **452 M 295 (2008)**—while court officer left post momentarily, a newspaper article about the case was slipped under door of jury room on third day of deliberations; judge questioned two jurors individually who might have come into contact with material and determined no taint, and satisfied himself that remaining jurors, questioned en masse, had not been exposed to material and fact of incident itself had not affected them;

C v Stewart **450 M 25 (2007)**—when defense counsel told judge that two jurors might have seen D in lockup cell, court officers could only say that door had been open (but didn't know if jurors saw); judge asked jury, collectively, if anyone had seen anything while "coming into court or leaving court" which affected their impartiality (no responses); judge's "delicate attempt" to determine whether any juror saw D was enough; individual voir dire not required;

C v McCaster **46 MAC 752 (99)**—various individuals in temporarily deadlocked jury (a) accessed the Internet to learn about cocaine, (b) asked police officers about quantities involved in "trafficking," and (c) asked a friend about the street cost of cocaine; all other jurors were questioned, & one who could no longer be impartial was dismissed, as were the two who spoke with others about cocaine, but neither party objected to the "Internet" juror remaining on the panel; D elected to proceed with only 11 jurors, and did not move for mistrial despite 5 invitations to do so, so was held to have waived any issue about the adequacy of the inquiry; court nonetheless expressed skepticism that the information gleaned was so insignificant and stated that "asking each of the nonoffending jurors to state what the three intermeddlers had actually said about their illicit investigations, without delving further," would **not** have been a prohibited intrusion into jury deliberations;

C v Peppicelli **70 MAC 87 (2007)**—deliberating juror's conversation with police officer in store check-out line was extraneous influence necessitating discharge of the juror (officer expressed opinion that "victim" group as well as Ds were "all pieces of crap", juror opining NG, self-defense); judge disbelieved juror's contrary account of contact;

C v Cormier **427 M 446, 453 (98)**—though on 2d day of deliberations, jury discussed case before "official start of deliberations that morning," there was no extraneous influence, and no need for new trial;

22-E.5. Deadlocked Juries and Tuey-Rodriquez Charge

G.L. c. 234, § 34—if jury "returns to court" without verdict "after due & thorough consideration," court may restate evidence, re-explain law, &/or send out for further deliberations; if jury returns to court second time without agreeing on verdict, judge may not send out again without jury consent, unless they request further explanation of law;

C v Jenkins **416 M 736 (94)**—after reported deadlock & Tuey-Rodriquez charge, jurors sent note reporting eight votes by jurors & no one willing to change, and requesting that the judge suggest a further course of action"; SJC held that this was not a "second return" because jury **asked** for further "suggestion(s)"; Liacos, J., dissented;

C v Rodriquez **364 M 87 (73)**—modified Tuey "dynamite" charge instructing jurors that no future jury better equipped to decide case & urging reexamination of positions without ceding personal convictions;

Allen v US **164 US 492 (1896)**—approving stronger language in original Tuey dynamite charge for federal system;

Superior Court Criminal Practice Jury Instructions § 5.5—(Jury Indecision and Jury Coercion: Deadlocked Jury & Tuey-Rodriquez Instruction);

US v Angiulo **485 F2d 37, 39 (1st Cir. '73)**—when judge conveys to jury that there WILL be a verdict, this causes jury "to agree when they might otherwise never have come to agreement, thereby losing for the defendant whatever safeguard he might have had in a hung jury, a declaration of mistrial, and either a new trial or a subsequent decision by the prosecutor not to retry the case";

US v Fioravanti **412 F.2d 407, 416 (3d Cir.), cert denied sub nom.** *Panaccione v US* **396 US 837 (69)**—"it is a cardinal principle of the law that a trial judge may not coerce a jury to the extent of demanding that they return a verdict";

C v Lugo **64 MAC 12 (2005)**—trial judge's denial of deliberating jury's request for permission for a break outside court house to smoke was not an abuse of discretion resulting in a compelled verdict;

C v Jordan **49 MAC 802, 816–17 nn.16–17 (2000)**—prosecutor's closing argument that jury had "burden" and "duty" to decide case, no matter how hard or long jurors had to work to reach unanimous verdict, "because that is what we are here for," = improper (but no objection, no relief: "overwhelming" evidence of guilt);

C v Brown **367 M 224 (75)**—instructions that (only) minority jurors were to re-examine their positions & references to costs of 2d trial required new trial because unduly coercive of verdict;

Jenkins v US **380 US 445 (1965)**—"You've got to reach verdict in this case" required new trial because unduly coercive;

C v Sosnowski **43 MAC 367, 374–75 (97)**—on second day of deliberations *Rodriquez* embellished with judge's personal knowledge that some juries deliberate 4&5 days before verdict: no reversal, though acknowledgment that charge must be used with caution & may be coercive: urged **just** *Rodriquez*;

C v Mayne **38 MAC 282 (95)**—"gratuitous" but not coercive to tell jury that initial deadlock happens "probably" 85% of the time;

C v Whitney **63 MAC 351 (2005)**—court rejects D's claim that judge's instruction about "common sense", made at beginning of fourth day of deliberations, had coercive effect on jury ("person could have twenty Ph.D.s . . . and not have an ounce of it," D implying without basis that one such degreed juror was a "hold out" for acquittal);

C v Brazie **66 MAC 315 (2006)**—trial judge's telling jury at 6:01 p.m. on the day before Thanksgiving that, if they didn't reach verdict by 6:20 p.m., they would return on Monday morning to complete deliberations, wasn't coercive (despite fact that G verdicts were returned at 6:19 p.m.); instructions were "simply part of the common everyday administration of the courtroom";

C v O'Brien **65 MAC 291 (2005)**—when jury, only shortly after beginning deliberations, sent note saying "impasse", all agreed it was too soon for *Tuey-Rodriguez* charge & judge should (& did) only "review" options on verdict slip, again requiring unanimity: no objection, no error, BUT judge should have acknowledged in some fashion jury's perception of "impasse," and pointed to *Rodriguez* 364 M at 102 (Appendix B), as the appropriate instructions to be given (unanimity, duty to consult with one another, each to decide case for himself after impartial consideration with fellow jurors; shouldn't hesitate to re-examine own views, while shouldn't surrender honest conviction for mere purpose of returning verdict);

C v Rollins **354 M 630 (68)**—Tuey charge should not be given prematurely, judge had discretion to give charge after only 4 hours of deliberations; D not prejudiced by omissions;

C v Wilson **443 M 122, 143 (2004)**— notification that jurors are deadlocked is not prerequisite for Tuey-Rodriquez charge, though judge's giving charge sua sponte "runs a risk of acting prematurely; no coercion evident here, because verdict was not returned until a full day after the charge;

C v Valliere **366 M 479 (78)**—returns by jury to court to receive answers to questions don't qualify as "returns" under G.L. c. 234, § 34; returns to court not made "after due & thorough consideration" don't qualify as "returns"; judge had discretion to decide that 13 hours of deliberations not "due & thorough consideration"; note by foreperson ("I do not feel any more progress can be made") deemed to express personal view of foreperson & not collective opinion of jury; judge's sending jury out after 4th courtroom appearance of jury thus did not violate § 34;

C v Keane **41 MAC 656 (96)**—judge could decide that deliberation from Tuesday a.m. until Wednesday at 3 or 4 p.m. was not due & thorough, so sending them for more deliberations after 2d report of deadlock (at 9:50 a.m. Thursday) was not violative of § 34;

C v Mayne **38 MAC 282 (95)**—judge could decide that 4 hours of deliberations after 5-day trial with complex issues was not due & thorough; judge has discretion to determine whether deliberations "due & thorough" based on complexity of case, extent of evidentiary conflict, & length of time; 2 hours, including lunch, not "due & thorough;" Tuey-Rodriquez instruction approximately 8 or 9 hours into deliberations not premature;

C v Scanlon **412 M 664 (92)**—Tuey-Rodriquez instruction not premature where jury, after deliberating for 10 hours over 2 days, sent note to judge that they were deadlocked without progress since yesterday;

C v Haley **413 M 770 (92)**—Tuey-Rodriquez instruction given after 4 hours of deliberations not premature where issues simple & evidence brief;

C v Bacigalupo **49 MAC 629 (2000)**—no error found in judge's giving of "the ABA charge" (recommended in *C v Rodriquez*, and now called "Tuey-Rodriquez" in this Commonwealth, see **id. at 637, fn 8**) on the morning after jury deliberated a full day and had taken several votes, but merely requested to adjourn for the day; following "supplemental" "ABA charge," jury deliberated six more hrs & reported deadlock; Tuey-Rodriquez instruction then given, and verdict followed < 1 hour later; note at end of 1st day

wasn't a "return without verdict," and "ABA charge" wasn't the coercive "Tuey-Rodriquez", but "is intended for use either as part of the original instructions to the jury or as a supplemental instruction when the jurors appear to be running into difficulty reaching a verdict";

C v Gonzalez **28 MAC 10 (89)**—improper for judge to invite jurors to write individual communications explaining reasons for deadlock;

C v Webster **391 M 271 (84)**—judge's questioning of holdout juror in view of others jurors was coercive & required new trial even though juror was replaced after calling in sick following day;

C v Clark **292 M 409 (35)**—19-minute guilty verdict in murder case did not require reversal on ground that jurors didn't give evidence adequate consideration;

22-E.6. Hung Juries and Mistrials

M.R.Crim.P. 27(b)—judge has discretion to declare mistrial as to verdicts on which jurors cannot agree; if mistrial declared on some charges, judge may require return of verdicts, if any, on other charges;

See Chapter 19 for cases on double jeopardy—i.e., whether there was "manifest necessity" justifying mistrial (because if not, and D objected, retrial is barred by double jeopardy prohibition);

US v Perez **22 US (9 Wheat.) 579) (1824)**—hung jury is manifest necessity justifying mistrial;

Logan v US **144 US263 (1892)**—same; judge had discretion to declare mistrial after jury was unable to reach verdict after 40 hours of deliberations;

Thames v Commonwealth **365 M 477 (74)**—judge has discretion to declare mistrial where there is no reasonable hope of unanimous verdict; not abuse of discretion for judge to declare mistrial after 2 jury messages suggested deadlock, even though jury out for only 4½ hours;

C v Andrews **10 MAC 866 (74)**—judge had discretion to declare mistrial where jury deliberated for 8 hours & sent note suggesting they were genuinely deadlocked & wished to be excused;

C v Torres **453 M 722 (2009)**—rejecting D's argument that there was hung jury necessitating mistrial when jury returned to court, ostensibly with G verdict, but one juror, when polled, said 'not guilty'; sending jury back out for deliberations = proper;

Gelmette v Commonwealth **426 M 1003 (97)**—hung jury in first degree murder trial, split 11 for manslaughter and 1 for NG was **not** a verdict; retrial and conviction of first degree murder not barred;

22-F. VERDICTS

22-F.1. In General; Unanimity, Jury Nullification

See also Chapter 16-A, Defenses;
M.R.Crim.P. 27(a)—jury verdicts must be unanimous;

McHoul, petitioner **445 M 143, 155 (2005)**—at trial, parties agreed that all 13 jurors would deliberate, and SDP petitioner raised no objection to instruction that verdict could be returned by 11 of the 13 jurors: under prior version of § 9 "discharge" law, verdict could be by 5/6 jurors, & D didn't object, so issue = waived;

***Gelmette v Commonwealth* 426 M 1003 (97)**—hung jury in murder one, 11 for manslaughter and 1 for NG, was not "verdict"; no double jeopardy prohibition against re-trial and conviction for murder one;

***C v Tennison* 440 M 553, 560 n.11 (2003)**—sealed verdict that is later nullified should be destroyed without being opened; here, partial verdict was returned, but jurors requested to reconsider it after deliberations began anew with one replacement juror;

G.L. c. 234A, § 68—parties may stipulate to verdict by less than full number of jurors;

See Chapter 15-C, Post-Conviction Remedies, for cases on motions to set aside verdict;

***Horning v DC* 254 US 135 (1920)**—(Holmes, J.) "the jury has the power to bring in a verdict in the teeth of the law & facts";

***C v Hebert* 379 M 752 (80)**—"it is improper for a ju-ror to disregard the law as given by the judge, (but) it re-mains within the power of a juror to vote his or her con-science";

***C v Fernette* 398 M 658 (86)**—judge not required to instruct jurors they have power of nullification;

***C v Sosnowski* 43 MAC 367 (97)**—(same);

***C v Leno* 415 M 835 (93)**—snarl that though there may **be** jury nullification, SJC majority would not accept that jurors have a **right** to nullify law and D doesn't have right to have jury informed of this power; in dissent, Li-acos, CJ, lauded social worth of nullification: "common sense judgment . . . standing as a check on arbitrary en-forcement of the law ";

***C v Kirwan* 448 M 304 (2007)**—regarding "Model Jury Instructions on Homicide 19 (1999)", which states ". . . if the evidence allows you to find the defendant guilty of murder in the first degree, you may return a verdict of guilty of murder in the second degree," SJC asserts (a) the instruction was about "felony murder" (not here relevant), and (b) "we have consistently declined to recognize jury nullification instructions such as this," "inconsistent with a jury's duty to return a guilty verdict of the highest crime proved beyond a reasonable doubt";

***C v Lopez* 447 M 625 (2006)**—in refusing relief to D upon his argument that his jury trial, at which he testified, amounted to a lengthy guilty plea (& thus required a col-loquy concerning waiver of rights), SJC acknowledges/ accepts premise that trial testimony was used to diminish D's "apparent moral (if not legal) culpability, and thereby sway the consciences of the jurors," and that jurors could have voted "conscience" and returned acquittals;

***C v Hakkila* 42 MAC 129 (97)**—verdict returned be-fore judge answered jury's question valid, when judge did not instruct that deliberations should be suspended;

***C v Dickerson* 372 M 783 (77)**—approving instruc-tion that if it found D guilty, jury should return verdict on highest crime proven;

***C v Evans* 42 MAC 618, 626 (97)**—omission from verdict slip of words "with intent to commit felony" did not invalidate conviction of B&E daytime, with felonious intent; indictment was attached to slip and charge to jury had been complete;

***C v McCarthy* 37 MAC 113, 116–17 (94)**—that nei-ther signed verdict slip nor verdict read in open court con-tained weight of cocaine involved in trafficking did not invalidate conviction for > 200 grams: weight of cocaine was not a live issue at trial, and both counsel highlighted weight requirement in argument, as did judge's instructions;

***C v Zekirias* 443 M 27 (2004)**—when jurors returned verdict of "negligent" A&B, after having been charged explicitly that only "intentional" or "reckless" A&B are crimes (& NOT "negligent"), judge should not have re-sponded to foreperson's response to his question ("reck-less" was intended verdict) with leading question to each juror, asking each to affirm "reckless" rather than what was plainly written on verdict slips and announced in open court; judge should have simply declined to accept the written verdict, called attention to apparent misunderstand-ing of instructions, reinstructed, sent jury out for further deliberations;

***C v Woodward* 427 M 659, 666–72 (98)**—judge's re-duction of jury verdict upheld (2d degree murder reduced to manslaughter); standard of appellate review is "abuse of discretion"; trial judge's power under M.R.Crim.P. 25 lik-ened to SJC's power (in convictions of first degree murder) under G.L. c. 278, § 33E: "may be used to ameliorate in-justice caused by the Commonwealth, defense counsel, the jury, the judge's own error, or, as may have occurred in his case, the interaction of several causes";

22-F.2. Affirmance of Verdict and Polling of Jurors

M.R.Crim.P. 27(a)—verdict must be returned by jury to judge in open court; verdict slips to be filed with clerk;

M.R.Crim.P. 27(d)—judge has discretion to poll ju-rors before verdict recorded; if concurrence not unani-mous, judge may send jury out for further deliberations or may discharge;

***Lawrence v Stearns* 28 M (11 Pick.) 501 (1831)**—verdict not valid until announced, affirmed in open court as unanimous act, & recorded; dissent by even 1 juror in open court invalidates verdict even where verdict slips had been signed by all 12 jurors & sealed night before;

***C v Clements* 36 MAC 205 (94)**—foreperson need not orally announce verdict, but may hand verdict slip to clerk (who here announced verdict, and received en masse oral affirmation by jurors);

***Rich v Finley* 325 M 99 (49)**—verdict affirmed by 11 jurors after juror had died night before, not valid even though deceased juror had signed verdict slips, because not affirmed by unanimous jury in open court;

C v Kalinowski **12 MAC 827 (81)**—verdict not effective until announced by foreperson in open court, recorded by clerk, foreperson confirms it & clerk proclaims it;

C v Gagnon **37 MAC 626 (94), S.C., 419 M 1009 (95)**—though Indictment charged armed assault with intent to murder, "caption," read by clerk omitted "armed"; though foreman replied "guilty as charged," conviction could be only for **unarmed**;

C v McCarthy **37 MAC 113 (94)**—clerk's failure to add phrase, "with intent to commit felony" when asking jury for its verdict on indictment charging B&E daytime with felonious intent, did not render conviction void;

C v Andino **34 MAC 423 (93)**—clerk's slip of tongue in announcing verdict of guilty of receiving stolen "property" rather than receiving stolen "motor vehicle" did not invalidate conviction of latter crime;

C v Hebert **379 M 752 (80)**—judge's statement to juror (who expressed reservations during polling) that evidence of D's guilt was clear required new trial, especially where notes from jury had indicated juror's inability to convict as "matter of conscience";

C v Lawson **425 M 528, 532 (97)**—though transcript revealed no affirmation by response from entire jury, foreperson's announcement & clerk's proclamation of verdicts in open court in presence of all jurors & without public indication of any dissention was sufficient evidence of unanimity;

C v Fowler **431 M 30, 34 (2000)**—history of "colloquy" ritual recounted ("so you all say, members of the jury?"), said not to be required by rule or statute; after performing colloquy for first two convictions, clerk "neglected to add, 'so say you all,'" after the third conviction: no substantial likelihood of miscarriage of justice found; simple objection would allow immediate remedy;

C v Robles **423 M 62, 72–74 (96)**—transcript did not record oral affirmation by **all** jurors but trial judge, on ADA's motion after filing of D's appellate brief, "corrected" record to reflect trial DA's memory and "usual practice" of courtroom clerk; SJC upheld correction order, obliterating appellate issue;

C v Wilson **427 M 336, 356 (98)**—though "better practice" is to obtain a clear sign of each juror's assent, by polling or otherwise, judge not required to poll jurors unless there's specific evidence that verdicts aren't unanimous;

C v Zekirias **443 M 27 (2004)**—when jurors returned verdict of "negligent" A&B, after having been charged explicitly that only "intentional" or "reckless" A&B are crimes (& NOT "negligent"), judge should not have responded to foreperson's response to his question ("reckless" was intended verdict) with leading question to each juror, asking each to affirm "reckless" rather than what was plainly written on verdict slips and announced in open court (this was subtle but not insubstantial coercion); judge should have simply declined to accept the written verdict, called attention to apparent misunderstanding of instructions, reinstructed, sent jury out for further deliberations;

C v Dias **419 M 698, 703 (95)**—whispered 'no' by juror, unheard by any person in courtroom, could not qualify as public disagreement with verdict; subsequent disclosure of subjective disagreement with her apparent vote not basis for vacating judgment;

C v Nettis **418 M 715 (94)**—though judge refused request to poll jury, D attorney provided affidavit asserting that one juror was shaking her head no & mouthing "no" as other jurors as a group were affirming verdict; polling was then allowed, & juror stated she was saying NG though had voted G in jury room; judge did not err in declaring mistrial;

C v Torres **453 M 722 (2009)**—rejecting D's argument that there was hung jury necessitating mistrial when jury returned to court, ostensibly with G verdict, but one juror, when polled, said 'not guilty'; sending jury back out for deliberations = proper;

C v Brown **367 M 24 (75)**—jury may correct "formal & clerical" errors in recording verdicts;

C v Diaz **19 MAC 29 (84)**—judge had discretion to send jury back to continue deliberations on 3d charge where verdicts on other 2, which had been revealed but not yet affirmed, logically required finding on 3d; *C v Zekirias* **443 M 27, 34 n.3 (2004)**—distinguishing *Diaz*, etc., because judge's questioning wasn't "neutral attempt to obtain clarity";

C v Fernandes **30 MAC 335 (91)**—D's motion to poll jury after verdict recorded was untimely;

C v Hardy **431 M 387, 399 (2000)**—though there's discretion re: whether or not to poll jury before verdict is recorded, jury shouldn't be polled AFTER verdict's recorded "unless one or more of the jurors indicate(s) a 'public disagreement' with the verdict as it (is) being received"; though D counsel said one juror shook head, 'no,' as verdicts were read, 2 were crying, & 1 collapsed in hallway, trial judge purported to find as fact that the juror had NOT shaken her head (& judge said she'd been focused on this juror), & SJC said judge "was entitled to rely on her own observations" re: whether any 'public disagreement';

C v Jenkins **416 M 736 (94)**—in polling, better course is to poll each juror individually, or at least show of hands, but no "abuse of discretion" here to "collective oral response" called for;

C v Chandler **29 MAC 571 (90)**—would have been better practice to have put 'not guilty by reason of insanity' on all verdict slips;

C v Gomes **419 M 630 (95)**—once judge (in jury-waived trial) announced "guilty" in open court, verdict was final & cannot be converted into continuance without a finding;

22-F.3. Partial Verdicts

M.R.Crim.P. 27(b)—judge has discretion to take partial verdicts on some but not all charges & to send jury back for deliberations on other charges on which they cannot agree;

C v Roth **437 M 777 (2002)**—when a jury deadlocks, judges MAY NOT TAKE PARTIAL VERDICTS on lesser included offenses contained within a single complaint or indictment; M.R.Crim.P. 27(b) provides for taking verdicts on less than all the indictments or complaints being tried, but doesn't permit taking verdict on anything less than the entirety of a single complaint or indictment;

Daniels v Commonwealth **441 M 1017 (2004)**—judge is not required to accept partial verdict, and didn't do so on first day of deliberations; jurors, next day, apparently reconsidered and had no verdict on ANY of the charges; when utter deadlock on all charges on fourth day prompted mistrial with D counsel's agreement, no basis for dismissal, on double-jeopardy ground, of indictment on which there had purportedly been initial agreement;

C v Floyd P. **415 M 826 (93)**—error for judge to have demanded return of verdicts when note sent indicated that they were "tentative or conditional," **i.e.**, that 2 votes would change if aggravated rape conviction dictated return of G on first degree murder;

C v Foster **411 M 762 (92), reversing 30 MAC 588 (91)**—judge had discretion to take partial verdicts on 2 of 4 charges, & sending jurors out to complete deliberations on others, even though judge had promised to wait for jury to complete deliberations on all charges;

C v LaFontaine **32 MAC 529 (92)**—judge's taking of partial verdicts before responding to jury questions on remaining charges not improper;

C v Tennison **440 M 553, 560 n.11 (2003)**—sealed verdict that is later nullified should be destroyed without being opened; here, partial verdict was returned, but jurors requested to reconsider it after deliberations began anew with one replacement juror;

C v Diaz **19 MAC 29 (84)**—judge had discretion to send jury back to continue deliberations on 3d charge where verdicts on other 2, which had been revealed but not yet affirmed, logically required finding on 3d;

C v McCarthy **37 MAC 113, 116–17 (94)**—that neither signed verdict slip nor verdict read in open court contained weight of cocaine involved in trafficking did not invalidate conviction for > 200 grams: weight of cocaine was not a live issue at trial, and both counsel highlighted wt. requirement in argument, as did judge's instructions;

22-F.4. Special Questions and Special Verdicts

M.R.Crim.P. 27(a)—verdicts must be unanimous & general; But see *C v Accetta* **422 M 642 (95)** (to effectuate unanimity requirement, alternate theories (involuntary and voluntary manslaughter) should be listed on verdict slip);

SEE NOW, HOWEVER: *C v Zanetti* **454 M 449, 465 n.18 (2009)**—it would be an "artificial" restriction to require jury to be unanimous in deeming D to be principal, or unanimous instead as to "joint venturer" status;

C v Flynn **420 M 810 (95)**; *C v Green* **420 M 771 (95)**; *C v Plunkett* **422 M 634 (96)**; *C v Fickett* **403 M 194 (88)**; *C v Sanchez* **40 MAC 411 (96)**; *C v Taylor* **50 MAC 901 (2000)**—when jury is instructed on a theory of G not supported by evidence and G verdict is not identified by theory, convictions will be reversed even though G warranted on some theory (contra U.S. Supreme Court's *Griffin v US*, **502 US 46 (91)**); but see *C v Grandison* **432 M 278, 286 (2000)** SJC characterized issue as one of D's failure to request either specific unanimity jury instruction or separate verdict forms, & D lost (but 1 "theory" of 'resisting arrest' was legally unsupportable);

****NOW SEE *C v Zanetti* **454 M 449 (2009)**—SJC adopts means by which to uphold convictions when evidence is insufficient on one, but not the other option of 'joint venture' vs. 'principal' liability: judges are to instruct jury that D is guilty if Commonwealth proved beyond reasonable doubt that D "knowingly participated in the commission of the crime charged, alone or with others, with the intent required for that offense"; discouraging use of "specific" verdict slip (first degree murder case);

C v Rodriguez **67 MAC 636, further appellate review allowed (2006), but SJC doesn't address this issue 450 M 302 (2007)**—evidence sufficient to sustain guilty verdict under both theories submitted to jury, so general verdict slip not ground for reversal (jurors were instructed that they had to be unanimous as to either or both theories);

M.R.Crim.P. 27(c)—special questions may be submitted to jury in discretion of trial judge;

C v Beneficial Finance Co. **360 M 188 (71)**—special questions may not be used to 'lead jurors down guilty trail';

Heald v Mullaney **505 F.2d 1241 (1st Cir. '74), cert. denied, 420 US 955 (75)**—special questions should be used "sparingly" because of danger of leading juror toward "logical" conviction;

C v Licciardi **387 M 670 (82)**—although judge has discretion to submit special questions asking jurors to decide issues of fact essential to verdict, judge may not usurp jury function by deciding special verdict based on facts found by jurors; instruction requiring jury to specify theory of murder & whether rape statutory or forcible within judge's discretion; due process limitations discussed;

C v Trung Chi **34 MAC 668 (93)**—refusing to find error in judge's refusing D's requested instructions, tailored to Commonwealth's theory and proof re: conspiracy indictment ('if you doubt D was present at time/place of offenses, you must acquit', and 'if you aren't satisfied beyond reasonable doubt that D drove car, must find NG'); assertion that judge instructed on conspiracy elements, and that while crime must be proved beyond a reasonable doubt, no particular piece of evidence must be so proved (effectively ignoring circumstances of case and proof);

22-F.5. Specific Unanimity and General Verdicts

In re Sheridan, petitioner **422 M 776, 777 (96)**—verdict of jury requires only 5/6 of jurors rather than unanimity at G.L. c. 123A, § 9 sexually dangerous person hearing;

C v Comtois **399 M 668 (87)**—although unanimity required as to 'each incident which is basis of jury's finding,' judge's refusal, without objection, to give instruction that specific unanimity required as to which of several incidents allegedly occurring "on divers dates" that verdict was based on, was not substantial risk of miscarriage of justice given overwhelming evidence;

C v Lemar **22 MAC 170 (86)**—same;

C v Keevan **400 M 557 (87)**—judge's failure to give instruction that specific unanimity required as to which act of intercourse rape verdict based on not substantial risk of miscarriage of justice;

Contra C v Conefrey **420 M 508, 514 (95) = C v Kirkpatrick 423 M 436, 443–44 (96)**—failure to instruct on specific unanimity re multiple indictments for sexual assaults of child not error because jury will either believe or doubt that repetitive pattern of sexual abuse occurred; evidence didn't create risk of nonunanimous verdict; due process doesn't require Commonwealth to "attempt the artificial task of identifying a specific instance of abuse as a basis for indictment";

C v Sanchez **423 M 591, 598–600 (96)**—same;

C v Erazo **63 MAC 624, 630-631 (2005)**—noting and contrasting *Conefrey & Kirkpatrick/Sanchez*, & ruling tentatively, in advance of trial, that specific unanimity instruction would not be required since complainant can't separate alleged criminal episodes by specific dates & they are so closely connected as to amount to a single criminal episode; *C v Medina* **64 MAC 708 (2005)**—specific unanimity instruction not required "[i]n cases involving a resident child molester . . . where [complainant] testifies to pattern of repetitive and abusive conduct by [D]"; *id.* at 718: different result if crimes arose "from discrete episodes or incidents of particular acts";

C v Federico **70 MAC 711 (2007)**—no substantial risk of miscarriage of justice in failure to give "specific unanimity" instruction because critical issue was credibility of complainant (who testified to four incidents, though only two complaints were brought/tried);

C v Ramos **47 MAC 792, 798–99 (99)**—no request for specific unanimity instruction, though 5 alleged sex assaults were subject of testimony; defense was only "allegations were false," & court held error, if any, didn't matter;

C v Black **50 MAC 477 (2000)**—though jurors should have been required to unanimously agree what one penetration (out of 5 in evidence) was basis for single rape conviction, no request for such instruction nor objection to its absence; same re fact that indecent A&B conviction couldn't be based on same act that supported rape conviction; no substantial risk of miscarriage of justice found;

C v Lewis **48 MAC 343, 349–50 (99)**—no substantial risk of miscarriage of justice in judge's failure to give specific unanimity instruction (which trial counsel hadn't requested), though there were allegedly numerous false statements/transfers of money as part of single scheme to defraud complainant;

C v Conefrey **420 M 508 (95)**—specific unanimity required as to "particular set of facts" when there was only one indictment re: indecent A&B, but testimony concerned eight incidents;

C v Thatch **39 MAC 904 (95)**—similar;

Chambers v Commonwealth **421 M 49, 52 (95)**—(concerning indictment charging rape of child "on diverse dates between 9/5/92 & 4/30/93") warning that if there is testimony concerning multiple rapes & one conviction results, verdict will be set aside unless there is adequate reason to conclude that the jury agreed unanimously on at least one incident;

C v Zane Z **51 MAC 135 (2001)**—when evidence of two sexual assaults admitted, lack of specific unanimity charge resulted in reversal of convictions;

C v Berry **420 M 95 (95)**—judge on request must give specific unanimity charge re what theory of first degree murder is found;

C v Accetta **422 M 642, 643 (96)**—in future, to effect unanimity, verdict slip should list, in case where evidence supports each theory, "voluntary" and "involuntary" manslaughter;

C v Santos **440 M 281 (2003)**—explanation of types of "specific unanimity"; jury need not be unanimous as to which threat or application of force caused victim to part with her money (*C v Accetta* 422 M 642 (96) distinguished);

C v Lonardo **74 MAC 566 (2009)**—no "specific unanimity" required re: identifying party[ies] with whom D allegedly conspired; only one conspiracy (to commit insurance fraud) was charged; that two of three alleged co-conspirators obtained RFNG not controlling "because entire fraudulent scheme depended on [that third person]";

C v Viera **42 MAC 916 (97)**—specific unanimity instruction necessary only when G finding can be based on alternative set of facts or theories; omission of general unanimity instruction didn't result in substantial risk of miscarriage of justice because jurors "affirmed" the G verdict unanimously (apparent refusal to acknowledge worthlessness of such "general" affirmation);

C v Cyr **433 M 617, 621–22 (2001)**—SJC refused to require specific unanimity re: cause of death, i.e., either stabbing, or subsequent arson of dwelling/burning of victim;

C v Benjamin **430 M 673, 677 (2000)**—jury needn't be unanimous as to which *Cunneen* factor(s) (**389 M 216, 227 (83)**) underlie verdict of 1st degree murder based on extreme atrocity or cruelty; *C v Almonte* **444 M 511, cert denied, 126 S. Ct. 750 (2005)**—same; *C v Pov Hour* **446 M 35 (2006)**—same;

C v Gendraw **55 MAC 677 (2002)**—jurors needn't be unanimous as to which of the three prongs of malice had been proved;

Schad v Arizona **501 US 624 (91)**—instruction that jurors unanimously agree on 1 of 2 alternative theories, felony murder or deliberate premeditation, for 1st degree murder conviction, not required under federal due process clause;

C v Ramos **31 MAC 362 (91)**—"specific unanimity" instruction that jurors unanimously agree on whether D was principal or accomplice not required because proof of shared mental state made both equally culpable;

C v Nolan **427 M 541, 544 (98)**—failure of D-counsel to seek separate jury determinations on two alternative bases for determining guilt of deliberately premeditated murder not ineffective assistance, since "jury did not have to be unanimous in concluding that the defendant was either the principal or the joint venturer";

C v Andrews **427 M 434, 441 (98)**—similar;

C v Ellis **432 M 746, 761 (2000)**—similar;

C v Plunkett **422 M 634 (96)**—when case was submitted to jury on theories of both deliberate premeditation and felony-murder and no specific verdict was given, insufficiency of evidence to warrant G of deliberate premeditation required that conviction be reversed;

C v Anderson **425 M 685 (97)**—general verdict of 1st degree murder could have been based on felony murder, so conviction of underlying felony of armed robbery was vacated as duplicative;

C v Fickett **403 M 194 (88)**—general verdict requires new trial where evidence of 1 of 2 alternative theories of guilt submitted to jury was legally insufficient; evidence legally sufficient for deliberately premeditated murder with D as principal but not of joint venture felony murder by armed robbery where evidence insufficient that D knew co-D had gun;

C v Kickery **31 MAC 720 (91)**—same; general verdict required new trial where evidence was legally sufficient for aggravated rape by joint venture but not by kidnapping;

C v Zuluaga **43 MAC 629 (97)**—same; general verdict required new trial where evidence legally insufficient to establish constructive possession of certain drugs found in co-D's basement, though sufficient to establish D's actual possession earlier in the day at different location;

C v Eldridge **28 MAC 936 (90)**—general verdict required new trial where evidence was legally sufficient on rape by force but not by threat of force;

C v Flynn **420 M 810 (95)**—general verdict required new trial where evidence was legally sufficient for joint venture manslaughter culpability but insufficient for conviction of D on an individual liability theory;

C v Prater **431 M 86, 100 (2000)**—armed assault with intent to rob charge based on either of 2 ways of assault (force/violence OR placing V in fear of immediate bodily injury), and jurors were instructed they must be unanimous as to theory; SJC affirmed, rejecting argument that evidence insufficient as to latter theory;

Griffin v US **502 US 46 (91)**—under federal law, less protection for D than under *Fickett*, *Plunkett*, *Flynn*, above (inter alia): although preferable for judge to not leave unsupported theories to jury for (general) verdict, reversal not required here because verdict could rest on a factual theory which was supported by sufficient evidence;

Hedgpeth v Pulido **129 S Ct 530 (2008)**—instructing jury on multiple theories of guilt, one of which is invalid is not "structural error" requiring conviction be set aside without regard to finding of prejudice when a "general verdict" of guilt is returned,, and is instead subject to harmless error review in federal habeas corpus case;

Superior Court Criminal Practice Jury Instructions § 4.23—(multiple incidents or theories in one count);

22-F.6. Inconsistent Verdicts

C v Hamilton **411 M 313 (91)**—factual inconsistency of verdicts (guilty of murder & armed robbery, not guilty of possession of shotgun) not ground for relief because finding of not guilty can result from compromise, compassion, or other factors unrelated to guilt or innocence; required finding analysis supported convictions;

C v Elliffe **47 MAC 580 (99)**—same; "legally" inconsistent verdicts distinguished (e.g., can't be G of both larceny and receiving stolen goods);

C v Brown **66 MAC 237 (2006)**—same;

C v Carson **349 M 430 (65)**—legal inconsistency of verdicts may require reversal where legally impossible to be guilty of both (e.g., guilt as to receiving & larceny);

C v Nascimento **421 M 677, 683 (96)**—guilty verdicts of both larceny and receiving stolen property required vacating & dismissing the receiving conviction & indictment;

C v McCaffery **49 MAC 713 (2000)**—same;

C v Gajka **425 M 751, 754 (97)**—D found G of (joint venture) armed robbery & murder, & also of being accessory after fact of murder & armed robbery: latter = improper convictions: verdicts properly "corrected" by vacating accessory convictions;

C v Chandler **29 MAC 571 (90)**—'not guilty by reason of insanity' on murder & guilty on carrying firearm not inconsistent & impossible as matter of law;

C v Graves **35 MAC 76 (93)**—G on aggravated rape and NG on ABDW-knife not necessarily inconsistent on evidence, since aggravation could have been seen as ABDW by choking with V's gold neck chain: thus, error for judge to have reduced aggravated rape to simple rape;

C v Medeiros **456 M 52 (2010)**—D's conviction of aggravated rape by reason of joint enterprise vacated because jury simultaneously (same trial) acquitted sole other member of alleged joint enterprise rape (though found him guilty of assault and battery, a charge concerning different acts, i.e., not lesser included offense within aggravated rape); discussion of 'inconsistent verdicts' case law (a thicket);

C v McLaughlin **431 M 506 (2000)**—holding that NGI as to two homicides but G of involuntary manslaughter as to third homicide, occurring almost immediately there-after not necessarily inconsistent, and no basis for relief;

C v Lowe **21 MAC 934 (85)**—guilty on B&E in dwelling in nighttime with intent to commit felony & as-sault therein plus NG on armed house invasion did not require reversal;

C v Simcock **31 MAC184 (91)**—factual inconsistency between verdicts of guilt on indecent A&B but acquittal on rape did not require reversal even though only evidence of touching was intercourse;

C v Pease **49 MAC 539, 542–43 (2000)**—purportedly inconsistent verdicts of G of manslaughter by wanton/reckless conduct and NG of assault and battery no ground for relief and perhaps weren't even inconsistent, because judge gave erroneous (& too favorable to D) instruction on A&B;

C v Chery **36 MAC 913 (94)**—G of fraudulent motor vehicle insurance claim, and NG of unlawful burning of motor vehicle, burning insured property with intent to de-fraud insurer, and false statements on stolen motor vehicle report did not require relief, though "inconsistent";

C v Mortell **42 MAC 947 (97)**—B&E daytime with intent to commit felony conviction upheld despite simulta-neous NG of assault with intent to rape;

C v Robicheau **421 M 176, 184 (95)**—NG of threat-ening to commit crime, G of violating protective order by "abusing" victim was factual inconsistency entitling D to no relief even though it indicated possibility of jury com-promise;

C v Sherry **386 M 682 (82)**—although NG on kid-napping & (joint venture) aggravated rape, but guilty on 3 counts simple rape not legally impossible or inconsistent, 2 counts set aside as contrary to weight of evidence;

C v Scott **355 M 471 (69)**—NG on murder but guilty on robbery not legally inconsistent even though based on same evidence;

C v Cerveny **387 M 280 (82)**—prior NG for cocon-spirator does not bar guilty for D on conspiracy charge based on same agreement even though logically inconsistent;

22-G. IMPEACHMENT OF VERDICTS

Patterson v Colorado **205 US 454 (1907)**—(Holmes, J.) "the conclusions to be reached in a case will be induced only by evidence & arguments in open court, & not by any outside influence, whether of private talk or public print";

C v Fidler **377 M 192 (79)**—although jurors may be examined to determine whether exposed to extraneous matter, juror may not be probed about subjective or delib-erative processes; once D has made prima facie showing that extraneous material has made its way into delibera-tions, Commonwealth has burden to show absence of prejudice on hypothetical average jury beyond reasonable doubt; exposure of single juror to prejudicial extraneous material may require reversal;

See Prop.M.R.Evid. 606(b)—same;

C v Tavares **385 M 140 (82)**—*Fidler* ban on probing of jurors' subjective or deliberative processes not applica-ble where "plainest principles of justice" require more probing inquiry (as where racial slurs uttered by juror dur-ing deliberations); see also *C v McCaster* **46 MAC 752 (99)** "asking each of the nonoffending jurors to state what the three intermeddlers (who consulted the internet, an acquaintance, and a cop about trial evidence) had actually said about their illicit investigations, without delving fur-ther," would **not** have been a prohibited intrusion into jury deliberations;

*C v Amirault **399 M 617 (87)**—judge's post-verdict examination into juror bias properly focused on juror's memory & state of mind; where D makes reasonable post-verdict claim of juror bias or misconduct, D entitled to hearing to show juror actually biased because juror dis-honestly answered material question on voir dire; here, child-rape-D failed to prove by preponderance of evidence that juror who failed to disclose that she had been raped as child was actually biased against him;

C v DiPietro **373 M 369 (77)**—party learning of juror exposure to extraneous material must notify judge imme-diately to preserve issue;

C v Mahoney **406 M 843 (90)**—D entitled to have counsel present at post-verdict hearing into extraneous influences;

C v Solis **407 M 398 (90)**—although counsel should not initiate post-verdict contact with jurors, information learned from juror about extraneous influences will not be subject to exclusionary rule; court officer's improper re-sponse to jury request for readback that jurors must rely on collective memories usurped judge's authority required new trial where Commonwealth failed to prove absence of prejudice beyond reasonable doubt;

SJC Rule 3:07, 3.5(d)—after jury discharged, lawyer may not initiate communication w/juror without leave of court for good cause shown; if juror initiates, lawyer may respond but may not ask questions or make comments intended only to harass, embarrass or influence future jury service & may not inquire into deliberation process;

C v Dixon **395 M 149 (85)**—counsel has right to probe details of juror exposure to extraneous matters where juror makes unsolicited contact; improper to ques-tion jurors about deliberations; private communication or contact with juror about pending case during trial pre-sumptively prejudicial; But see *C v Allen* **379 M 564 (80)** D entitled to conduct pretrial investigation of prospective jurors, including interviews of neighbors, but may not con-tact jurors or their families;

See Chapter 22-H for cases on extraneous influences generally;

22-H. EXTRANEOUS INFLUENCES: JURY SELECTION, TRIAL, DELIBERATIONS AND POST-VERDICT

C v Angiulo **415 M 502 (93)**—error to conduct questioning in absence of parties;

C v Arana **453 M 214 (2009)**—juror's observation of witness on stand seeming to respond to spectator led her to believe that witness was being coached; this was NOT an "extraneous" influence: juror was entitled to observe and consider "all aspects of the witness's testimony in order to assess ... credibility", and judge should not have dismissed juror on ground that she was no longer 'impartial';

22-H.1. Racial and Other Prejudices; False Answers in Voir Dire

See Chapter 22-B-3 & 4 for cases on inquiries during voir dire into racial & other forms of prejudice & other extraneous influences during jury selection;

C v Laguer **410 M 89 (91)**—evidentiary hearing on new trial motion required to determine whether ethnic bias deprived D of right to fair trial by impartial jurors; if ethnic bias found, new trial required without further inquiry into deliberations; **S.C.** after remand: **36 MAC 310 (94)** Appeals Court deferred to hearing judge's determination that bias accusations were not true;

C v Tavares **385 M 140 (82)**—judge's finding after hearing that verdict unaffected by racial prejudice was not abuse of discretion;

C v Delp **41 MAC 435 (96)**—though juror came forward on first work day after G to confess to bias against D, because of belief homosexual, judge obtained assent to characterizing sequence as juror's satisfaction with G at verdict, but merely had second thoughts about it over the weekend and implicitly found this, rather than real bias; juror also said he didn't hate any group & tried not to be biased, & had listened to all evidence, believing when he left courtroom that he had done his duty;

C v Howard **46 MAC 366 (99)**—though jurors on Sixth day of trial expressed concern that D had access to juror questionnaire which listed their addresses and telephone numbers, and D moved for mistrial, appellate court said response was adequate (judge addressed jurors as group in closed courtroom, saying that questionnaire was available only briefly and that all were kept secret thereafter and "shredded" after 30 days; then individual questioning as to whether any further questions and whether could be fair/impartial);

C v Perez **44 MAC 911 (98)**—during trial, juror questioned court officer how juror questionnaires were used, **i.e.**, whether there would be "repercussions"; all jurors interviewed, judge found them impartial; Appeals Court rejected D's argument that question implied premature disposition to convict; But cf. *C v Angiulo* **415 M 502 (93)** citing G.L. c. 277, § 66 (1990 ed.) ("prisoner indicted for a crime punishable with death or imprisonment for life, upon demand by him or his counsel upon the clerk, shall have a list of the jurors who have been returned) and holding that D, charged as an accessory before the fact to murder in the first degree and punishable with life imprisonment without the possibility of parole, is a member of the class to whom the subject statute is addressed; error to have impaneled "anonymous jury" (though jurors were not told this, and as consequence several were distressed during trial about possible "repercussions", prompting judge to speak to jurors in absence of parties (error));

C v Cassidy **410 M 174 (91)**—jury note that deliberations were being influenced by a juror's prior sexual abuse was manifest necessity justifying mistrial over D's objection;

C v Hynes **40 MAC 927, 928–29 (96)**—D, convicted of sexual assaults on child, claimed on appeal that judge erred in refusing to conduct post-verdict inquiry of juror(s) as to whether any had been childhood sexual assault V, one of whom had 'struggled with an illness similar to that of D" according to a note the juror sent the judge; appellate court said note merely concerned a "subjective opinion" or "attitudinal exposition";

C v Yameen **401 M 331 (87)**—judge not required to ask jurors in OUI case about opinions towards alcohol consumption; nor is judge required to give full explanation of presumption of innocence & reasonable doubt;

C v Luna **418 M 749 (94)**—juror's statement during deliberations that he was prejudiced against police & thought police officers should never lie, in trial of cop for perjury, held to have been merely "an expression of the individual's personal philosophy";

C v Kudish **362 M 627 (72)**—judge had discretion under G.L. c. 234, § 28, not to collectively question jurors about religious prejudices where D charged with performing unlawful abortion;

C v Coleman **389 M 667 (83)**—D's midtrial revelation that juror may have given false voir dire answer to question whether he had ever been witness in criminal case did not require reversal where judge conducted appropriate inquiry & found juror impartial;

C v Torres **437 M 460 (2002)**—posttrial discovery that juror had lied when, on questionnaire, she denied being a party in a criminal proceeding; judge found not intentional lie, & that juror would have testified that it wouldn't have affected impartiality (& if anything, her status as criminal D in drug case would have been of concern to Commonwealth rather than to D);

22-H.2. Prejudicial Media Exposure

C v Jackson **376 M 790 (78)**—where potentially extraneous influence (here, mid-trial media coverage) is reliably brought to judge's attention, judge should determine whether material goes beyond record & raises serious question of possible prejudice; if so, voir dire should be held to determine if any jurors saw or heard material; if any juror responds affirmatively, judge should individually examine jurors outside presence of others to determine extent of exposure & its effects on juror's ability to give impartial verdict; standards for determining extraneous influence in jury selection to be applied;

C v Fredette **56 MAC 253 (2002)**—deadlocked jury sent judge note during deliberations advising that one juror had watched television interview with sex assault complainant's mother, but that juror felt that it was not influencing him; judge's response, without consulting counsel, was merely to instruct jury to decide case solely on evidence; after verdict, during poll of jurors at D's request, each juror denied being influenced, but acknowledged discussing the mother's interview allegations; REVERSAL: (1) judge should have consulted counsel before responding, (2) inquiry into actual deliberations was erroneous/forbidden, and (3) judge failed to follow *Jackson* 376 M 790 & *Fidler* 377 M 192;

Irwin v Dowd **366 US 717 (61)**—widespread prejudicial pretrial publicity violated D's constitutional right to impartial jury even though jurors who originally expressed preconceived opinion in D's guilt subsequently claimed they could be fair & impartial;

C v Sinnott **399 M 863 (87)**—jurors' exposure to media reports of jury tampering & speculation about possible plea bargaining in case & didn't violate D's right to impartial jury where judge adhered to procedures in Jackson;

C v Hanscomb **367 M 726 (75)**—juror exposure to press headline that judge in unrelated consent-rape case chastised jurors for acquittal didn't violate D's right to impartial jury where judge conducted appropriate inquiry;

C v James **424 M 770 (97)**—marchers against violence, carrying murder V's photo & name, publicized 2 days before D's trial began; appropriate voir dire was conducted—no error in refusing change of venue or continuance;

C v Morales **440 M 536 (2003)—despite judge's order that media not photograph jurors during view, newspaper photo showed at least one juror, whose family recognized him and told him of photo: no relief despite argument that juror so identified would have felt pressure to convict;**

22-H.3. Improper Contact Amongst Jurors

C v Hicks **377 M 1 (79)**—juror's assertion that she overheard "scuttlebutt" about case in jury room required meaningful questioning & admonition; but see *C v McQuade* **46 MAC 827 (99)** re: similarly vague assertion by mail 3 weeks after verdict (no evidentiary hearing required);

C v Maltais **387 M 79 (82)**—although pre-deliberation conversation between juror & foreperson about weight to be accorded expert witness was 'close to line,' reversal not required where judge properly examined jurors about their exposure to conversation;

C v Royster **15 MAC 970 (83)**—juror's post-verdict assertion that she was "bullied" into voting guilty fell within *Fidler* ban on inquiry into deliberative process;

See Chapter 22-E-1 for cases on privacy for deliberating juries;

22-H.4. Improper Contact with Judges and Court Personnel

Sargent v Roberts **18 M 337 (1823)**—improper for judge to make unilateral contact with deliberating jury;

C v Buckley **17 MAC 373 (84)**—"unwise," "regrettable," for judge to conduct unrelated arraignment & jocular welcoming ceremony for new judge in presence of jurors;

C v Gonzalez **28 MAC 10 (89)**—improper for judge to invite jurors to write individual communications explaining reasons for deadlock;

Parker v Gladden **385 US 363 (66)**—court officer's comments to jurors that D was "wicked" & "guilty" & that any error in convicting D would be corrected by Supreme Court violated D's right to impartial jury & to confrontation & required reversal;

C v Solis **407 M 398 (90)**—court officer's improper response to jury request for readback that jurors must rely on collective memories usurped judge's authority and required new trial where Commonwealth failed to prove absence of prejudice beyond reasonable doubt;

C v Donovan **15 MAC 269 (83)**—court officer's refusal to pass on jury question to judge & response to jury that, because their question raised matter of evidence not law, it was their memory which governed, required reversal; prejudice presumed;

C v Drumgold **423 M 230, 261 (96)**—court officer told juror that he hoped another juror, reportedly wishing for mistrial before deliberations began, would not be on jury because it would "drag" trial on & it was "already costing the state too much money", that jurors would be limited to voting G or NG & only judge could declare mistrial; "mistrial" remark repeated by officer to another juror—SJC upheld denial of relief, saying that while remarks shouldn't have been made, they weren't "extraneous influence";

22-H.5. Prior Knowledge of, or Improper Contact with, Parties or Witnesses

C v Bolduc **383 M 744 (81)**—jurors should not be friends, antagonists or relatives of witnesses; judge should disclose names of all potential witnesses to jurors, should inform jurors that some witnesses might not be called, & should not reveal which side intends to call them or addresses of any defense witnesses currently incarcerated; judge's requiring defense counsel to read list of potential defense witnesses to jury prior to empanelment required reversal;

C v Richardson **454 M 1005 (2009)**—after D's motion post-trial seeking investigation of possible extraneous influence on jury, judge ordered cautious inquiry including showing photos of jurors to affiant who overheard conversation suggesting such influence; Commonwealth's 211/3 petition attacking judge's order (maintain 'integrity of the jury trial process'! protect jurors from risk to their safety!) rejected: **"[n]o party, *including the Commonwealth*, should expect this court to exercise its extraordinary power of general superintendence lightly"**;

C v Johnson **426 M 617, 626–27 (98)**—judge should have made **specific** inquiry of seated juror concerning info that juror's husband attended murder V's wake, instead of questioning whether she knew V or his family; on remand, juror's response that she did not know whether or not her husband had attended wake gave D no ground for relief: **juror's own** bias was the only concern, & her husband's relationship to V was relevant "only as it bears on that question";

C v Theberge **330 M 520 (53)**—conversation between prosecution witnesses & spectators about key matters relating to trial in presence of juror required new trial, even though juror insisted he had not overheard conversation & that he remained impartial;

C v Costa **414 M 618 (93)**—deliberating jury foreman received telephone call from unknown "Frank," suspected by foreman to be D's alleged joint venturer; foreman questioned if others had received call, then reported to judge; foreman preferred to be excused but no error in denying mistrial when others claimed continued impartiality;

C v John **442 M 329 (2004)**—juror's note to judge at close of first day of trial: "Guns, drugs, gangs, murder. Should I have any reason to be worried about my own safety as a juror?"; following reassurance by judge and statement that she had not mentioned concerns to fellow jurors, no errors in allowing juror to remain and refusing to question other jurors;

C v McQuade **46 MAC 827 (99)**—letter from juror to judge 3 weeks after convictions spoke of "rumor that (co-D not tried with D) had fingered (D)", not "court evidence," "could have added a tint of guilt", and that the juror who conveyed this "rumor" "might have known something more than said"; though D filed m. new trial on basis of letter, no error in judge's hearing of arguments without any evidentiary hearing: D had not shown that jury exposed "to specific facts reflecting a significant extraneous influence";

C v Kincaid **444 M 381 (2005)**—SJC affirms trial judge's order of new trial after his finding that jurors were exposed to info about flight of D's coventurer (SJC overruling **61 MAC 657 (2004)**, which opined that probably jurors didn't have "extraneous" info but instead made inference from record evidence); SJC says that finding of fact by trial judge won't be deemed clearly erroneous unless appellate court is "left with the firm conviction that a mistake has been committed"; case law doesn't require identification of source of juror's knowledge of the extraneous matter; judge may not inquire into deliberative process of jury; jurors can be told to respond about any info

that wasn't mentioned during trial, but NOT to describe how jurors used that info or effect of that info on the thinking of any juror; "As soon as the judge determines that D has satisfied his burden of establishing the existence of an extraneous influence, the questioning of all jurors should cease"; if "inappropriate" info is learned during the inquiry, it can't be ignored, so new trial is required when judge learns that juror has in fact been influenced by extraneous info;

C v Murphy **59 MAC 571 (2003)**—sitting juror disclosed, at party, that he was juror at trial of D, and other party attendee replied that D had another pending criminal case; attendee was D's attorney in the other case; appellate court claimed that trial judge's factual finding that juror remained impartial was not clearly erroneous (as it was based on credibility determination);

Smith v Phillips **455 US 209 (82)**—juror's job application, during trial, for position as investigator with DA's office & DA's withholding of information about it, did not require new trial where judge conducted proper post-verdict inquiry & found no prejudice to D;

C v Harris **409 M 461 (91)**—judge should pay "close attention" to behavior & demeanor of victim advocates; visual displays of consolation & support, such as crying, handholding & hugging, are analogous to improper vouching by Commonwealth for complainant's credibility; curative or supplemental instructions may be required;

C v Daughtry **417 M 136 (94)**—encounter by deliberating jurors in elevator with 3 persons possibly believed to be D's friends prompted individual questioning of jurors & discharge of 2 who could no longer be impartial; neither mistrial nor discharge of the many who acknowledged they were "bothered" by it was necessary after their assurance they could decide on evidence & law; judge "in best position" to evaluate jurors' credibility;

C v Koumaris **440 M 405 (2003)**—no abuse of discretion in trial judge's failure to question jurors about their possibly overhearing conversation between defense counsel and another attorney re: how trial was going (only 35 minutes of testimony had occurred, and evidence to that point not "key to outcome");

C v Gregory **401 M 437 (88)**—juror contact with victim's widow who introduced self to juror did not require reversal where juror claimed continued impartiality;

C v Lovett **374 M 394 (78), reversed on other grounds sub nom.** *Lovett v Butterworth* **610 F.2d 1002 (1st Cir. '79), cert. denied, 447 US 935 (80)**—juror's remark to government witness applauding him for his "good composure," did not require reversal where remark was casual, unrelated to issues in case & did not suggest pro-Commonwealth bias;

C v Patten **401 M 20 (87)**—judge had discretion not to discharge juror (US postal cop) who was acquainted with prosecution witness (security officer at a post office);

C v Roberts **433 M 45, 58 (2000)**—post-verdict inquiry not required upon affidavit of defense witness asserting that a juror had been a volunteer at a "sober house" at which witness had stayed, & thus knew the witness; nothing "extraneous," said SJC, because witness's "drug problem" was already before jurors through his own testimony;

22-H.6. Extraneous Information about D: Prior Convictions, Currently in Custody

C v Kamara **422 M 614, 620 (96)**—deliberating juror told other jurors she knew D as friend of niece's boyfriend, that he was gang member, that she thought D guilty; judge dismissed her & found, after interviewing others, that they could remain impartial; SJC affirmed, rejecting argument that review should focus on 'hypothetical average juror' rather than jurors in actual case, and refusing to substitute its opinion for the factual finding of trial judge;

C v Hunt **392 M 28 (84)**—even a single juror's uncommunicated knowledge of extraneous matters might require reversal; juror's awareness of D's prior record did not require reversal where evidence overwhelming & where not communicated to other jurors until after unanimous verdict reached;

C v Santiago **50 MAC 762, 766 (2001)**—one juror became aware that D had been convicted previously (that conviction reversed on appeal), & stated in response to whether could continue to be impartial, "I don't feel like I heard anything different than what I've already heard"; no error in denying mistrial motion (& D didn't ask for lesser remedy of removing this juror);

C v Murphy **59 MAC 571 (2003)**—sitting juror disclosed, at party, that he was juror at trial of D, and other party attendee replied that D had another pending criminal case; attendee was D's attorney in the other case; appellate court claimed that trial judge's factual finding that juror remained impartial was not clearly erroneous (as it was based on credibility determination);

Leonard v US **378 US 544 (64)**—improper to select jurors for 2d trial from jury which had just convicted D at 1st trial on separate charges;

Estelle v Williams **425 US 501 (76)**—requiring D to wear prison garb before jury violates presumption of innocence; but see *C v Thomas* **448 M 180, 185–86 (2007)**—"reasonable strategic decision" agreed to by D, to have D wear prison clothing at trial (purportedly allaying jurors' fears that NG by reason of insanity would mean release into community);

C v Moore **379 M 106 (79)**—D should not be required to sit in dock unless judge rules on record that extraordinary security measures required;

Walker v Butterworth **599 F.2d 1074 (1st Cir. '79)**—seating D in prisoner's dock before jury dilutes presumption of innocence;

C v Brown **364 M 471 (73)**—procedures to be followed where D presents unusual security risk;

C v MacDonald (II) **368 M 403 (75)**—'great care should be taken to avoid any encounter between D & juror outside courtroom'; if it occurs, cautionary instruction

often preferable, if no objection by D; judge's failure to poll other jurors after 1 observed D in handcuffs did not require reversal;

C v Edgerly **390 M 103 (83)**—judge's denial of D's motion for mistrial & failure to poll jury not abuse of discretion where single, brief, accidental observation by some jurors of D in custody found not prejudicial to D;

C v Tanner **417 M 1 (94)**—it is counsel's responsibility to press for voir dire upon report that juror(s) saw D in shackles; mere report to judge establishes neither an objection nor prejudice;

US v Garcia-Rosa **876 F.2d 209 (1st Cir. '89)**—fleeting observation by deliberating juror of D in handcuffs did not require reversal where D failed to move for post-verdict inquiry & where no prejudice shown;

Deck v Missouri **125 S.Ct. 2007 (2005)**—"The Constitution forbids the use of visible shackles during the penalty phase, as it forbids their use during the guilt phase, unless that use is justified by an essential state interest—such as the interest in courtroom security—specific to the defendant on trial";

22-H.7. Unauthorized View of Scene and Exposure to Nonevidentiary Materials

C v Coles **44 MAC 463 (98)**—upholding trial judge's allowance of motion for new trial because of long-deliberating jurors' visits to crime scene, making of maps for jury's use, when defense in shooting was misidentification, involving questions of vantage points, directions & distances;

C v McCaster **46 MAC 752 (99)**—various individuals in temporarily deadlocked jury (a) accessed the Internet to learn about cocaine, (b) asked police officers about quantities involved in "trafficking," and (c) asked a friend about the street cost of cocaine; one juror exposed to some or all of this info from her fellows could no longer be impartial and was dismissed, as were the two who spoke with others about cocaine, but neither party objected to the "internet" juror remaining on the panel; D elected to proceed with only 11 jurors, and did not move for mistrial despite 5 invitations to do so, so was held to have waived any issue about the adequacy of the inquiry; court nonetheless expressed skepticism that the information gleaned was so insignificant and stated that "asking each of the nonoffending jurors to state what the three intermeddlers had actually said about their illicit investigations, without delving further," would **not** have been a prohibited intrusion into jury deliberations;

C v Peppicelli **70 MAC 87 (2007)**—deliberating juror's conversation with police officer in store check-out line was extraneous influence necessitating discharge of the juror (officer expressed opinion that "victim" group as well as Ds were "all pieces of crap", juror opining NG, self-defense); judge disbelieved juror's contrary account of contact;

C v Guisti **434 M 245 (2001)**—trial judge erred in denying D's motion for voir dire of juror who, during juror service, sent and received e-mails about her service/the case, but eventually, at **449 M 1018 (2007)**, SJC upheld trial judge's decision, after hearings and findings, that neither new trial nor further proceedings was necessary;

C v Federici **427 M 740 (98)**—during deliberations, jury foreperson opened box of exhibits and saw folder of photos not admitted as exhibits: judge replaced foreperson with alternate and found that none of other jurors had seen, denying individual voir dire of them re: this issue; before they began deliberations anew, judge instructed that she understood that no one else had seen the contents, but that "if that is not correct, if there is anybody else who did," person(s) should tell court officer immediately; no error, "sound discretion of the trial judge";

C v Cuffie **414 M 632 (93)**—judge's refusal to conduct post-verdict inquiry into juror's unauthorized view of crime scene required reversal, even though another juror claimed that deliberations unaffected, where layout of street potentially relevant to identification issue;

C v Troila **410 M 203 (91)**—juror's unauthorized view of murder scene created manifest necessity justifying mistrial;

C v Philyaw **55 MAC 730 (2002)**—judge should have held hearing on issue of jurors delegating one to view the scene and report back over whether or not the D could climb fence, as culprit did (D's defense of misidentification supported by physical disability making climb impossible); judge couldn't ignore issue on ground that first affidavit was from person to whom friend of juror revealed this, and that second affidavit was from the friend of the juror in whom the juror confided; **there's no requirement that there be a direct communication from juror before inquiry is permitted;**

C v Jones **15 MAC 692 (83)**—jurors' unauthorized view of crime scene, a "much used" public facility, did not require reversal where judge conducted proper inquiry, & where evidence established beyond reasonable doubt no prejudice to D;

Fitzpatrick v Allen **410 M 791 (91)**—jurors' unauthorized consultation of home medical reference during deliberations in medical malpractice case required reversal;

C v Lappas **39 MAC 285, 289–90 (95)**—no relief for jury's exposure to copy of unredacted statute, containing penalty provisions: mid-deliberations, judge gave corrective instructions;

C v Rodriguez **63 MAC 660 (2005)**—some juror accessed on internet G.L. c. 234, § 26B, re: impaneling, sequestering, & discharging juror, an extraneous matter (& this "reinforce[d] conclusion," already announced on ground of erroneous discharge of deliberating juror, that convictions be reversed;

INDEX

All references are to section numbers.

A

Abandonment, 16-B, 20-I.3

ABDW, 21-E, 21-F.2, 21-F.4

Aborted fetus, destroyed, 7-L.3

Abuse
Defined, 3-C
Homicide victim, 11-E
Joinder of offenses, 8-A
Prevention, 21-F.8
Warrantless arrest, 3-C

Accessory after felony, 9-D, 11-D, 17-D

Accessory before felony, 17-C

Accident, defense of, 12-K.3, 16-C, 21-K.4.C

Accomplice
Instruction regarding, 12-K.17
Sweep, 20-L.6
Witness, 12-K.17

Accord-and-satisfaction defense, 2-H, 5-G, 7-A, 14-B.7, 21-B.3, 21-L.1

Adjutant rule, 11-D, 16-d

Administrative search, 20-L.9, 20-M.3

Admission, harmless error, 20-A.7

Admission of guilt, 11-D, 11-E, 20-B.2

Admission of responsibility form, 14-I.1

Admissions by defendant
Conduct as consciousness of guilt, 11-G.1, 11-G.6
Evidence, failure to produce, 11-G.6
Flight, 11-G.1
Generally, 11-D, 11-E
Guilty plea, 11-G.5
Harmless error, 20-A.7
Newly discovered evidence, as, 11-F.8
Post-arrest silence, 11-G.4
Pre-arrest silence, 11-G.3
Private citizen, to, 20-D
Psychiatric examination and, 11-G.7
Silence, adoptive admission by, 11-G.2

Admitting to sufficient facts, 13-D

Adoptive admissions, 6-I

Advisory opinions, ABA, 2-B

Affidavit requirements, 6-C.2, 6-D, 14-A.6, 14-A.7, 15-F, 20-A, 20-A.2, 20-J.1, 20-J.3, 20-J.6, 20-J.7

Affidavits, false, 20-J.4

Affirmative defenses, 6-C.1, 16-A.2, 16-C.3

Aggravated assault
Abuse prevention, 21-F.8
Burglary, armed, 21-F.6
Carjacking, 21-F.9
Child victim, 21-F.4, 21-F.11
Civil Rights Act, 21-F.7
Dangerous weapon, 21-F.2
Dwelling, armed assault in, 21-F.6
Elderly, crimes against, 21-F.4
Explosive devices, placing or hurling, 21-F.12
Indecent, 21-F.5
Intent to commit other crime, 21-F.3
Mayhem, 21-F.1
Stalking, 21-F.10

Aggravated rape, 8-A, 19-B.6, 21-L.1.A

Aggravating circumstances, 12-K.1, 22-A

AIDS, 4-I.10

Alcohol, 4-I.2, 4-I.3, 5-G, 12-J.4, 16-C.3

Alcoholism, 7-E.4, 7-G, 9-B, 16-C.3

Alford plea, 13-E, 14-A.10

Alias, 11-E, 12-E.9

Alibi
Closing argument comment on, 12-J.10
Consciousness of guilt, 12-E.7
Generally, 6-M
Identification and, 18-B.7, 18-C.4
Instruction on, 12-K.8, 12-K.13, 18-B.7
Notice of, 6-F

Alien warning statute, 13-E.4.A

Aliens, advice to, 2-E, 13-A, 14-A, 14-A.10

Allied mental health professional privilege, 11-J

Ambiguity in law, 16-A.2

Americans With Disabilities Act, 14-M

Ammunition, 11-F.2, 21-BB.2

Amnesia, 7-D

Ancient documents, 11-F.18

Animals, cruelty to, 16-C

Annoying telephone calls, 21-nn

Antisocial Personality Disorder, 7-E.4

Appeal
Access to record on appeal, 6-D, 15-C.4
Adverse consequences of, 15-B.13
Briefs, 15-B.6

Claim of, 15-B.9
Closing argument, 15-B.12.i
Delay in, 15-B.3
Direct, post-conviction, 15-B
Dismissal from, 15-C.1
Dismissal of, 2-E.17, 15-B, 15-B.14
Effective assistance of counsel, 15-B.6
Ethics and, 2-D, 2-E.7, 2-E.16
Evidentiary trial issues, 15-B.12.h
Filed convictions, consideration, 15-B.8
Final judgment, 15-B.8
Further review, petition for, 15-B.16
Generally, 12-L
Grounds for affirmation of trial judge's decision, 15-B
Harmless error, 15-B.1
Interlocutory
    See interlocutory appeal
Involuntary dismissal of, 15-B.14
Issues on, 15-B.4
Jury instruction, 15-B.12.j
Jury issues, 15-B.12.g
Late, 15-B.9
Mootness, 15-B.15
Motion to dismiss, 14-B.6
Murder conviction, 21-K.3.d
Preservation of issues for
    Closing argument, 12-J.11, 15-B.10, 15-B.12.i
    Continuance, 15-B.12.d
    Disposition, objection to, 15-B.12.c
    Generally, 15-B.12.a
    Hearsay, 15-B.12.h
    Identification, suppression of, 18-F.2
    In limine, motions, 12-M, 15-B.12.f
    Ineffective counsel, failure to object to, 15-B.12.b
    Judge questioning witness, 12-M, 15-B.12.a
    Jury instruction, following, 12-M
    Questioning by judge, objection to, 12-D
    Reconsideration, 15-A.1
    Suppress, motion to, 12-M, 15-B.12.e, 20-A.2, 20-C, 20-C.3
Pro se representation, 15-B.5
Probation violation, 14-J.3, 15-C.4
Reconsideration, 15-A.1, 15-B.16
Record, assembly of, 15-B.10
Reply brief, 15-B.6
Results, 15-B.17
Retrial after, 15-B.13
Retroactivity of decisional law, 15-B.7
Revise sentence, motion to, 15-D
Revoke sentence, motion to, 15-D
Rule 30
    Evidence, newly discovered, 15-F.2, 15-F.5
    Hearings, 15-F.2

Juveniles *(cont'd)*
Sexual innocence inference theory,
11-H.4, 12-J.4, 21-F.5
Stenographer, 7-C
Transfer probable cause hearing, 1-B.3
Witness, instruction regarding, 12-K.17
Youthful offender, 1-D.2

K

Kiddie porn law, 5-G, 16-C, 20-G.4,
20-I.4

Kidnapping
Electronic eavesdropping and wiretaps,
20-N
Elements of, 21-J
Forcible foreign, 3-A
Venue, 1-E

Knock and announce requirement,
20-J.6

Knowingly, 16-C, 16-C.1, 16-F

L

Lamb **warning**, 7-D

Larceny
Asportation, 21-R.5
Automobile, 21-T
Building, larceny in, 21-R.20
Check, 14-H, 21-R.18
Civil conversion, 21-R.7
Conversion to use, 21-R.3, 21-R.6
Credit card fraud, 21-R.19
Criminal taking, 21-G, 21-R.3
Debt as defense, 21-R.9
Delivery, subsequent inability to,
21-R.10
Double jeopardy, 1-B.5
Electronic database, 21-R.2, 21-R.4
Embezzlement, 21-R.1, 21-R.3,
21-R.16
False pretenses, 21-R.1, 21-R.3,
21-R.17
From person, 21-G
Generally, 21-R
Identity theft, 21-R.19
Motive, 21-R.13
Motor vehicle, 7-O
Multiple owners, 21-R.8
Ownership, 21-R.4
Permanently deprive, intent to, 21-R.6
Personal property, 21-R.2
Possession of recently stolen goods,
inference, 21-R.11
Recently stolen, 21-R.11
Shoplifting, 21-R.15
Thief, common and notorious, 21-R.22
Third-party culprit evidence, 18-C.5
Trespassory taking, 21-R.4
Value, 21-R.12, 21-V
Venue, 1-E
Venue of property, 21-R.21
Workers' compensation, 21-R.1

Lawful authority, 16-A.5, 16-C.4

Layperson's opinion, 11-I

Leading questions
Generally, 10-B.2
Grand jury witness, 1-C, 11-A
Recollection revived, 9-I

Learned treatises, 11-F.17

**Legal authority, failure to cite
correct**, 2-E.9

Legitimate expectation of privacy,
6-C.2, 20-A.2, 20-B.9, 20-F.1, 20-I.1,
20-I.2, 20-I.3, 20-i.5

Lesser included offense
Armed assault, 12-K.4
Assault and battery, 5-D, 21-B.2, 21-E
Controlled substances, 21-CC.4
Double jeopardy, 19-A.11, 19-B.2,
19-B.3
Embezzlement, 19-B.2
Instructions, 12-I, 12-K.4, 22-E.3
Manslaughter, 12-K.4, 21-K.4
Plea bargain, 13-C
Rape, 5-D

Lewd and lascivious, 21-N, 21-O

Liberty interest, 14-M

License, 6-M

Lie detectors, 7-C, 11-G.6, 11-I.2.I,
20-C.12

Lies or trickery by police officers,
20-C.12

Lies to client, 2-E.17

Life felony, 7-B

Lifetime parole, 14-A.10, 14-V

Limine
See motion in limine

Limiting jury instruction
Failure to request, 2-E.13, 11-H.2
Generally, 12-K.1
Hearsay evidence, 11-F
Nature of, 11-C

Lineups, 18-F.6

Loitering, 21-KK

Lost or destroyed evidence
Defense neglect, 7-L.1
Identification, 18-E.7
Prejudice, 7-L.2
Remedies, 7-L.4
Third-party control, 7-L.3

M

Malice, 12-E.4, 12-K.2, 21-F.3,
21-F.10, 21-K.4

Malice aforethought, 21-K.2.A

Malicious destruction of property,
5-D, 21-Z

Malpractice, 2-B

Mandamus, 6-D, 15-E

Manslaughter, 10-F, 12-K.4, 16-A.2,
16-D, 19-B.1, 21-K.4, 21-K.4.A,
21-K.4.C

Marital communication exclusion,
11-J

Marital disqualification, 11-J

**Material misrepresentation by
counsel**, 2-E.17

Materiality of evidence, 11-D

Maximum sentence, 1-B.2

Mayhem, 5-D, 16-C, 19-B.3, 21-F.1

McHoul **standard**, 7-E.4

Media comments, 2-K

Media exposure, jury, 22-H.2

Mediation, 4-I.6, 14-E

Medical examiners, 11-F.2, 11-F.10

Medical records, 6-D, 7-B, 11-F.10,
11-H.9, 11-J, 19-C.5

Medical test, right to independent,
3-E.4

Medical testimony, 11-D, 11-H.9,
11-I.2.A, 12-J.4

Medical treatment, right to refuse,
16-A.5

**Medication, right to be tried
without**, 7-E.8

Melanie's law, 5-G, 11-A, 14-n.2,
21-CC.7

Mental disease or defect, 7-E.4, 9-B

Mental health legal advisors, 7-D,
7-F

Mental health of defendant
See Competency

**Mental health professional
privilege**, 11-J

Mental state, inferences regarding,
16-C.2

Mentally retarded defendant, 7-D,
13-B, 21-F.5

Merger, 19-B.6, 21-K.3.c

Metal detectors, 20-L.9

Ministerial acts, 1-B.1, 3-A, 3-C, 3-F

**Minor, contributing to delinquency
of**, 1-D.1

Miranda **rights**
Application, 20-C.10
Audiotaped interview, 15-F.1, 15-F.2
Booking, 20-C.5
Charge, disclosure of, 20-C.11
Commitment, defendant under, 20-C.3
Common law rule, 20-C
Custody, defined, 20-C.3
Generally, 20-C
Interrogation, defined, 20-C.4
Juveniles, 20-C.1, 20-C.8